Price on
Contemporary
Estate Planning

PRICE ON CONTEMPORARY ESTATE PLANNING 2012 EDITION

Chapters 1-12

John R. Price

Dean Emeritus, School of Law
University Of Washington
Of Counsel (Retired), Perkins Coie LLP
Seattle, Washington

and

Samuel A. Donaldson

Associate Dean and Professor of Law
School Of Law, University Of Washington
Of Counsel, Perkins Coie LLP
Seattle, Washington

Chapter 13: Estate Planning for Retirement Plans and IRAs by Gair Bennett Petrie, Esq.

Randall Danskin
Spokane, Washington

.CCH

a Wolters Kluwer business

CCH, a Wolters Kluwer business
4025 W. Peterson Ave.
Chicago, IL 60646-6085
1 800 248 3248
http://CCHGroup.com

ISBN: 978-0-8080-2712-6

To my wife, Suzanne,
our sons, John and Steven,
and family members no longer with us
JRP

In loving memory of my mother, Myrtle C. Donaldson,
and my father, Harold H. Donaldson
SAD

To Gair and Linda's parents:
Alec and Alice, Bella and Leon
GBP

Summary of Contents

CONTENTS

CHAPTER 4
WILLS AND RELATED DOCUMENTS
A. Introduction

CHAPTER 5
THE GIFT AND ESTATE TAX MARITAL DEDUCTIONS
A. Introduction

CHAPTER 6
LIFE INSURANCE
A. Introduction

Contents

CHAPTER 7
PLANNING LIFETIME NONCHARITABLE GIFTS
A. Introduction

CHAPTER 8

GIFTS TO CHARITABLE ORGANIZATIONS

A. Introduction

CHAPTER 9
LIMITING ESTATE SIZE THROUGH INTRAFAMILY TRANSACTIONS
A. Introduction

CHAPTER 10
TRUSTS
A. Introduction

CHAPTER 12
POST-MORTEM PLANNING
A. Introduction

CHAPTER 13
ESTATE PLANNING FOR RETIREMENT PLANS AND IRAs
Summary

APPENDICES

Table of Forms and Tables

PREFACE

May you live in interesting times." Unfortunately for estate planners, today is a most interesting time. Against everyone's expectations, the scheduled one-year repeal of the federal estate and generation-skipping transfer (GST) taxes in 2010 under the Economic Growth and Tax Relief Reconciliation Act of 2001 actually came to pass, though by the end of the year the taxes had been restored with all-time-high exemptions of $5 million and a flat tax rate of 35 percent. The temporary repeal of the estate tax was accompanied by the emergence of the carryover basis regime, an administrative nightmare that many planners hoped would never come to pass. As it turned out, the carryover basis regime was limited to those estates of decedents dying in 2010 that elected out of the application of the "new-and-improved" estate tax with its $5 million exemption and 35-percent rate. Even then, the Tax Relief, Unemployment Insurance Reauthorization and Job Creation Act of 2010 reintroduced uncertainty, as it effectively postponed the sunset of the 2001 Act until the end of 2012. Planning in these interesting and utterly unpredictable times is frustrating, as is writing a treatise that hopes to remain useful once (if?) Congress finally enacts permanent legislation. Given that Congress has demonstrated a prolonged pattern of inaction mixed with hasty, last-minute legislation, we determined that the appropriate approach for this edition was to assume that federal estate, gift, and GST taxes will, on January 1, 2013, actually reset to the exemptions and tax rates in effect in 2001. While we suspect a $1 million exemption and a 55-percent maximum rate may not last long (if at all) in 2013, we have learned not to be surprised if Congress lets us all down once more. Most of the discussion of the taxes themselves and the planning considerations for ameliorating the resulting tax liabilities they impose will remain relevant regardless of the size of the applicable exemption amount and the rate of tax.

The examples, forms, checklists and worksheets in this book are included for purposes of illustration only. Accordingly, they should, of course, not be used without the assistance of competent counsel. Neither the authors nor the publisher makes any representation regarding their sufficiency or suitability for use in connection with the legal affairs of any person.

October 2011

John R. Price

Samuel A. Donaldson

ACKNOWLEDGMENTS

The original author of the first editions of this book, John Price, is pleased and proud to welcome Professor Samuel A. Donaldson as co-author of the 2007 and future editions. John also gratefully acknowledges the support and encouragement that all his endeavors have received from his wife Suzanne and their two sons, John and Steven, and the guidance and inspiration provided by his late brother, Professor H. Douglas Price of the Department of Government, Harvard University. John and his brother's colleagues and students were all influenced by Doug's high ideals, integrity, and dedication to teaching and intellectual rigor.

Sam Donaldson is thrilled to have the opportunity to collaborate with Professor Price, a man who manages simultaneously to be a patient mentor, a persistently pleasant colleague, and a good friend. As John has been inspired by his late brother, Sam has been and remains inspired by the loyalty, character and love of his brother, Bruce Jay Donaldson.

The authors gratefully acknowledge the direct and indirect contributions made to the book by their colleagues, friends, research assistants and students. They are particularly grateful to Gair B. Petrie, Esq., of Randall Danskin, Spokane, Washington, who generously continues as the author of Chapter 13 of the book, which provides a comprehensive review of income tax and estate planning for retirement plans and IRAs..

Prior editions of this book were assisted mightily by members of the staff of Little, Brown & Company—particularly by the Executive Editor Monte Van Norden. Editions of the book published by Aspen Publishers and CCH, a Wolters Kluwer business, were helpfully nurtured and facilitated by several able editors and staff, including particularly Susan Chazin and Susan Frayman.

Cartoons from The New Yorker appear in Chapters 1 and 10 with the permission of The New Yorker Magazine, Inc. A cartoon from Momma appears in Chapter 4 with the permission of Mell Lazarus. An excerpt in Chapter 5 from Professor Sheldon Kurtz's article, Allocation of Increases and Decreases to Fractional Share Marital Deduction Bequest, 8 Real Prop., Prob. & Tr. J. 450, 460 (1973), is reprinted by permission of the Real Property, Probate and Trust Section of the American Bar Association.

Because of the emphasis the authors place on the ethical dimensions of estate planning, the text of various rules of professional conduct and the comments to the rules are quoted and referred to throughout the book. The ethical rules in effect in most states are largely verbatim copies of the Model Rules of Professional Conduct (MRPC) and the Comments to the Rules promulgated and published by the American Bar Association (ABA). With the permission of the ABA the discussion of ethics in prior editions of this book was based on selected provisions of the MRPC and related Comments. While the ABA was willing to grant permission to publish portions of the MRPC and Comments in exchange for the payment of a fee, it refused to grant permission to reprint them in electronic form. The ABA's refusal severely restricted the online availability of the text. Accordingly, this edition quotes and refers to versions of the rules and comments adopted by two states, Washington and Delaware, that are based on the MRPC and Comments. The Washington and Delaware rules and comments have the same numbering system as the MRPC and related Comments, but are in the public domain. Unless otherwise noted, the rules and comments quoted or referred to in this edition are taken from the Washington Rules of Professional Conduct and related Comments. As noted, in some instances they are based on the Delaware Rules of Professional Conduct. References to the "RPC" or "the Rules" are thus to the Washington or Delaware rules as appropriate to the text.

CITATION FORM AND REFERENCES

Citation Form. Most citations follow widely used and perfectly orthodox forms. However, for the sake of brevity some short forms are used to refer to commonly used materials. Thus, sections of the Internal Revenue Code of 1986 are referred to by citing the section number alone (*e.g.,* § 1361(d)). Similarly, references to sections of the Treasury Regulations are made by citing "Reg." Followed by the numbers of the sections. Private Letter Rulings and Technical Advice Memoranda (TAM) are cited "LR" followed by the number of the LR or TAM. The numbers of LRs and TAMs issued prior to 1999 consist of seven numbers, the first two of which indicate the year, the next two the week of the year in which the LR or TAM was published, and the last three the numerical sequence of the LR or TAM in the weekly pamphlet in which it was published, (*e.g.,* 9845033). Beginning in 1999 LRs and TAMs are identified by nine numbers, the first four of which indicate the year of publication (*e.g.,* LR 200019011). Major tax acts are cited simply by reference to the year of their enactment. Thus, the Tax Reform Act of 1976 is the "1976 Act," and the Taxpayer Relief Act of 1997 is the "1997 Act." Citations to the "RPC" or "the Rules" are to the Washington Rules of Professional Conduct or, where indicated, the Delaware Rules of Professional Conduct, as explained in the Acknowledgments. References to the Code of Professional Responsibility are noted as the Model Code (or MCPR).

Books, Periodicals, Looseleaf Services and Websites. Each chapter includes a bibliography that cites relevant books, articles, and other resource materials. Nonetheless, at this point it may be helpful to mention some of the books, periodicals and services that are particularly valuable to estate planners. Special mention should also be made of the outstanding estate planning materials that are published by the California Continuing Education of the Bar.

Several treatises and texts deal with various tax and nontax aspects of estate planning. They include the following, many of which are supplemented annually or more frequently:

American College of Trust & Estate Counsel, ACTEC Commentaries on Model Rules of Professional Conduct (4th ed. 2006)

B. Abbin, Income Taxation of Fiduciaries and Beneficiaries (2011)

B. Bittker & L. Lokken, Federal Taxation of Income, Estates and Gifts (1-4 vols. 3d ed. 1999, vols. 4A and 5 2d ed. 1989)

A. J. Casner & J. N. Pennell, Estate Planning (6th ed. 2003)

M. Ferguson, J. Freeland & M. Ascher, Federal Income Taxation of Estates and Beneficiaries (3d ed. 1999)

C. Harrington, L. Paine & H. Zaritsky, Generation-Skipping Transfer Tax (2d ed. 2001)

M. Jordan, Durable Powers of Attorney and Health Care Directives (4th ed. 2004)

J. Price, Tax Management 801-2d, Conflicts, Confidentiality and Other Ethical Considerations in Estate Planning (2007)

A. Scott, Trusts (vols. 1 & 2, 5th, M. Ascher ed. 2006, vols. 3-6A, 4th, W. Fratcher ed. 1987)

R. Stephens, G. Maxfield, S. Lind, D. Calfee and R. Smith, Federal Estate and Gift Taxation (8th ed. 2002)

C. Teitel, Deferred Giving (2 vols. 1999)

>   Outright Charitable Gifts (1990)

>   Charitable Lead Trusts (1983)

>   Planned Giving (1986)

H. Zaritsky, Tax Planning for Family Wealth Transfers (4th ed. 2002)

H. Zaritsky, N. Lane & R. Danforth, Federal Income Taxation of Estates and Trusts (3d ed. 2001)

Papers presented at various tax institutes are also very helpful in research and planning. Fortunately, the papers from several major institutes are reprinted each year, including those from the University of Miami's Philip E. Heckerling Institute on Estate Planning, New York University's Institute on Federal Taxation, and the University of Southern California's Tax Institute. Papers presented at some institutes are available through various electronic retrieval sources such as Lexis and Westlaw.

Current developments are discussed and articles of interest are published in a number of periodicals including Estate Planning, Journal of Taxation, Journal of Taxation of Estates and Trusts, Probate and Property, Real Property, Probate and Trust Journal, Tax Lawyer, Tax Advisor, Tax Law Review and Trusts and Estates. In addition, the BNA Tax Management Portfolio series, which is available on the Web, includes a number that are very useful to estate planners. They include ones on Estate Planning, the Estate Tax Marital Deduction, and Personal Life Insurance Trusts. Helpful ethics and estate planning materials are also available at a number of other Web sites, including ones maintained by the American Bar Association and various commercial and noncommercial sources. The Web site of the American College of Trust and Estate Counsel is also useful—particularly the portions that are accessible to members. The basic ABA Web sites for estate planning are: Donald Kelley's article, *Using the Internet and Software for Tax Research and Planning* (available at http://www.actec.org/Documents/Misc/GreatPlains2002.pdf) contains a comprehensive and very helpful list of free Internet reference sources.

ABA Network, *http://www.americanbar.org/aba.html*

ABA Real Property, Probate and Trust Law Section, *http://www.americanbar.org/groups/real_property_trust_estate.html*

ABA Taxation Section, *http://www.americanbar.org/groups/taxation.html*

Finally, statutes, regulations, rulings and cases relating to estate planning are available in electronic form from a variety of sources, including Lexis and Westlaw. They are also available from some government Web sites. Finally, they continue to be compiled in looseleaf services by CCH and RIA.

1

Professional Responsibility and Estate Planning

A. OVERVIEW

§1.1. INTRODUCTION

AN ESTATE PLANNING LAWYER SHOULD STRIVE TO PROVIDE
CLIENTS WITH HIGH QUALITY PERSONAL SERVICES AND COM-
PREHENSIVE, FULLY INTEGRATED ESTATE PLANS (WHAT MIGHT
BE CALLED "HOLISTIC ESTATE PLANNING").

The lawyer's principal role in estate planning consists of advising clients regarding the effective and economical organization and disposition of their wealth, which
usually involves much more than the preparation of a will or trust. A comprehensive
estate plan may include a will, one or more trusts, a durable power of attorney and a
health care directive. In addition, the plan may also involve making inter vivos gifts,
forming a family limited partnership (FLP) or a limited liability company (LLC),
changing beneficiary designations in employee benefit plans or life insurance policies, acquiring new life insurance policies or transferring existing ones, and changing
investments or the form of a business enterprise. Accordingly, a lawyer must be
competent in a number of important areas of substantive and tax law. In addition, a
lawyer must be sensitive to the ethical rules applicable to an estate planning practice
and alert to avoid acts of professional malpractice. Fortunately, an estate planner can

avoid most malpractice risks by fulfilling three basic ethical requirements—to be competent, to maintain the confidences of clients, and to avoid conflicts.

A lawyer must also recognize and deal sensitively with the human dimension of an estate planning practice, which may require the lawyer to learn and deal with a client's innermost feelings. For many clients these include a fear of death, anxiety about seeing a lawyer, ambivalent feelings about some relatives, and uncertainty and concern about future events. Above all, the lawyer must provide personal services that are tailored to meet the needs of the whole client. Each client must be recognized and respected as an individual. The lawyer may literally have hundreds of clients, but the client probably has only one lawyer, who may be the only lawyer the client has ever consulted professionally.

Professional responsibility involves two related but distinct sets of rules—the ethical rules applicable to the legal profession and the standards of care by which a lawyer's civil liability is determined. The violation of an ethical rule may subject the lawyer to disciplinary action while the violation of a standard of care may result in malpractice action against the lawyer. As explained below, the same act may violate both sets of rules. Malpractice issues are discussed at appropriate points throughout the text. However, this chapter focuses primarily on the ethical rules that apply to lawyers in the estate planning and estate administration contexts. The following discussion also refers briefly to the special rules that apply to lawyers in government service, including the Internal Revenue Service (IRS) Rules of Conduct.

The ethical rules represent serious efforts at self-regulation by the legal profession in each state for the purpose of protecting the public, the profession and the legal system as a whole. Notably, the violation of an ethical rule may result in a disciplinary action against the lawyer, which could cause the lawyer to be censured, suspended from practice, or disbarred. The same conduct could also have serious civil consequences, including invalidation of documents prepared by the lawyer, the recovery of fees paid to the lawyer, *Eriks v. Denver*, 118 Wash. 2d 451, 824 P.2d 1207 (1992), and the imposition of liability on the lawyer for damages suffered as a result of the lawyer's actions. Restatement, Third, Law Governing Lawyers ("Restatement") §6. If a lawyer engages in a serious conflict of interest or the lawyer otherwise breaches duties owed to a client, the fees paid to the lawyer are subject to partial or total forfeiture. *See, e.g., Crawford & Lewis v. Boatmen's Trust Co.*, 1 S.W.3d 417 (Ark. 1999) (regardless of whether the trust was harmed, the court denied fees to law firm that represented the residuary beneficiary of a trust who was also one of the co-trustees, whose interests conflicted with those of the trust); *Burrow v. Arce*, 997 S.W.2d 229 (Tex. 1999) (partial or total forfeiture of fee is appropriate if the lawyers engaged in a serious violation of duty to a client); and Restatement §49.

"And please protect me from the appearance of wrongdoing."
Drawing by Lorenz; ©1982 The New Yorker Magazine, Inc.

Estate Planning Malpractice. Examples of estate planning malpractice range from failing to assure that a will is properly executed (as a result of which the will is not admitted to probate); or failing to protect the bequests in a will from invalidation by the testator's planned marriage, *e.g., Heyer v. Flaig*, 70 Cal.2d 223, 499 P.2d 161 (1969), to not filing an estate tax return within the time allowed. In many states the scrivener of a will is liable to the testator's intended beneficiaries who are negligently omitted from the will. *E.g., Ogle v. Fuiten*, 466 N.E.2d 224 (Ill. 1984). However, as noted below, in a minority of states actions cannot be brought by disappointed beneficiaries unless the claimants and the lawyer were in privity (*i.e.*, a contractual relationship existed between them). In other states, actions are allowed under variations of a third party beneficiary theory—but some limit actions to cases in which the intent to benefit the beneficiary is evident from the will itself. *See* § 1.6.1.

Malpractice actions against the lawyer for a fiduciary ordinarily must be brought by the fiduciary—not the beneficiaries. However, an action may be brought by the beneficiaries if the trustee was implicated in the misconduct. *E.g., Wolf v. Mitchell, Silberberg & Knupp,* 90 Cal. Rptr. 2d 792 (Cal. App. 1999).

Tax Related Practice. The discussion deals primarily with the duties of lawyers, although certified public accountants (CPAs) and other persons enrolled to practice before the IRS can prepare tax returns and represent clients before the IRS as provided in Treasury Circular 230, 31 C.F.R. Part 10 ("Circular 230"). Lawyers and CPAs in good standing in any state can practice before the IRS. 31 C.F.R. § 10.3.

Federal preemption protects nonlawyers who represent clients in tax matters within the limits allowed by Circular 230 against a charge that they also engaged in the unauthorized practice of law. *See* §1.6.21. The conclusion derives from the United States Supreme Court decision in *Sperry v. Florida,* 373 U.S. 379, 83 S. Ct. 1322 (1965), which held that a patent agent registered before the Patent Office was not subject to the State of Florida's licensing requirements with respect to the preparation and prosecution of patent applications. The same result should be reached with respect to the representation of taxpayers before the IRS by nonlawyers who are enrolled to practice before the IRS. *See* Restatement §3. Several cases have reached that result including *Grace v. Allen,* 407 S.W.2d 321 (Tex. Civ. App. 1966), which held that *Sperry v. Florida,* mandated such a result. *See also Waugh v. Kelley,* 555 N.E.2d 857 (Ind. App. 1990). In *Grace v. Allen,* the court stated that, "[t]he rights conferred by the admission to practice before the Treasury Department are federal rights which cannot be impinged upon by the states in their praiseworthy efforts to protect their citizens from unskilled and unethical practitioners of the law." 407 S.W.2d at 324. However, §10.32 of Circular 230 provides that, "Nothing in the regulations in this part shall be construed as authorizing persons not members of the bar to practice law."

Ethical Rules and Malpractice Standards Distinguished. As indicated above, the ethical rules are related to, but distinct from, the standards of care by which a lawyer's civil liability (malpractice) is determined. A comprehensive article in the Emory Law Journal provides a helpful analysis of the areas in which malpractice may occur in a tax or estate planning practice. Todres, Malpractice and the Tax Practitioner: An Analysis of the Areas in Which Malpractice Occurs, 49 Emory L. J. 547 (1999). Malpractice issues are mentioned at appropriate places throughout this part because of the interrelationship between ethical and malpractice standards. However, the ethics rules are not rules of civil liability. The following passage from the Scope of the Washington Rules of Professional Conduct ("RPC") is typical of that in most states:

> Violation of a Rule should not itself give rise to a cause of action against a lawyer nor should it create any presumption in such a case that a legal duty has been breached. In addition, violation of a Rule does not necessarily warrant any other nondisciplinary remedy, such as disqualification of a lawyer in pending litigation. The Rules are designed to provide guidance to lawyers and to provide a structure for regulating conduct through disciplinary agencies. They are not designed to be a basis for civil liability.
> . . .

As explained in the Acknowledgements, the quotations of the rules of professional conduct and related comments in this book are from the versions of the rules and comments adopted by two states, Washington and Delaware that are, except as otherwise noted, the same as the Model Rules of Professional Conduct and Comments, but are in the public domain.

Although the ethics rules do not establish an independent basis for civil liability, the rules are admissible in some states as evidence in malpractice actions; *e.g., Allen v. Lefkoff, Duncan, Grimes & Dermer, P.C.,* 453 S.E.2d 719 (Ga. 1995); *Two Thirty Nine Joint Venture v. Joe,* 60 S.W.3d 896 (Tex. Civ. App. 2001); *Waldman v. Levine,* 544 A.2d 683 (D.C. App. 1992). However, a narrower view is taken by some courts. For example, in

Hizey v. Carpenter, 830 P.2d 646 (Wash. 1992), the court held that an expert may quote from the rules if relevant to the witness's opinion, but may not identify the source of the language.

   Ethical Guidelines Issued by Other Professional Groups. Ethical guidelines adopted by other professional groups, such as the American Institute of Certified Public Accountants (AICPA), are important to estate planners in those professions. The guidelines include the AICPA's Code of Professional Conduct, which consists of the mandatory Rules and the aspirational Principles, and the AICPA, Statements on Responsibilities in Tax Practice, issued by the AICPA Federal Taxation Executive Committee. The Statements provide useful guidance regarding the responsibilities of CPAs in various areas. They are not mandatory standards of practice. *See* Crawford & Loyd, CPA's Multistate Guide to Ethics and Professional Conduct (CCH 2009). However, the ethical rules applicable to lawyers are generally more extensive and well defined than those adopted by other groups. Ethical guidelines have also been issued by the Institute of Certified Financial Planners.

§1.2. Sources of Ethical Rules Applicable to Lawyers

   The next few pages describe the sources of the ethical rules and their interaction and the various roles of lawyers in estate planning. At the outset it is important to note that the conduct of lawyers in a tax or estate planning practice is often subject to multiple sets of rules. Not only are lawyers subject to the ethical rules of the jurisdictions in which they are licensed to practice, they are subject to the provisions of the Internal Revenue Code of 1986 (the "Code") and the rules promulgated by the Treasury, primarily in Circular 230 (cited throughout with appropriate identification of the specific section or sections to which reference is made). In some instances rules are imposed by specific judicial bodies. For example, the Tax Court has adopted the Model Rules. Unhappily, the rules prescribed by the several authorities are not entirely consistent. The conduct of lawyers employed by the government is subject to some special regulations and provisions of the Code and some criminal statutes.

§1.2.1. Model Rules of Professional Conduct ("Model Rules")

   A majority of states adopted ethical rules based upon the Model Rules of Professional Conduct ("Model Rules"), which were approved by the American Bar Association (ABA) in 1983. The Model Rules contain black letter rules with explanatory Comments that are intended to provide guidance for practicing in compliance with the rules. The Comments, of course, also assist in the interpretation and application of the rules. The version of the Model Rules adopted by most states varies to some extent from the Model Rules, particularly in connection with Model Rule 1.6 (Confidentiality). As noted above, a rule adopted by the Tax Court provides that the Model Rules apply to proceedings before it. Tax Ct. Rule 201.

   Ethics 2000. Concerned that the existing text of the Model Rules might not adequately meet the current needs of the public and the profession, in 1997 the ABA appointed a Commission on Evaluation of the Rules of Professional Conduct (the "Ethics 2000 Commission"). Reports made by the Commission in 1999 and 2000 resulted in a series of amendments to the Model Rules that were adopted in 2002 and

2003. In some cases the changes, in effect, made previously issued ethics opinions obsolete. The extent to which the changes will be adopted by the states remains to be seen.

The changes adopted in 2002 and 2003 made significant amendments to several model rules, including ones made to Rules 1.2, 1.6, 1.7, 1.8, 1.9, and 1.14. New Rules were also added including Rules 1.0 (Terminology) and 1.18 (prospective clients), and one rule was deleted—Rule 2.2 (Intermediary). The latest versions of the rules are discussed at appropriate points below. Note that earlier forms of those rules remain in effect in many states. Two of the terms defined in RPC 1.0 (Terminology) are particularly important to understanding the revised form of the rules. They are:

> (b) "Confirmed in writing" when used in reference to the informed consent of a person, denotes informed consent that is given in writing by the person or a writing that a lawyer promptly transmits to the person confirming an oral informed consent . . . .If it is not feasible to obtain or transmit the writing at the time the person gives informed consent, then the lawyer must obtain or transmit it within a reasonable time thereafter.
> (e) "Informed consent" denotes the agreement by a person to a proposed course of conduct after the lawyer has communicated adequate information and explanation about the material risks of and reasonably available alternatives to the proposed course of conduct.

Furthermore, under Rule 1.0(n), a writing includes a tangible or electronic record, including e-mail, and a "signed" writing includes one that is "attached to or logically associated with a writing and executed or adopted by a person with the intent to sign the writing."

Meaning and Construction of Rules. The manner in which the rules should be construed and applied is indicated in the Scope section of the Rules. It states, in part, that,

> The Rules of Professional Conduct are rules of reason. They should be interpreted with reference to the purposes of legal representation and of the law itself. Some of the Rules are imperative, cast in the terms "shall" or "shall not." These define proper conduct for purposes of professional discipline. Others, generally cast in the term "may" are permissive and define areas under the Rules in which the lawyer has professional discretion to exercise professional judgment. No disciplinary action should be taken when the lawyer chooses not to act or acts within the bounds of discretion. Other Rules define the nature of relationships between the lawyer and others. The Rules are thus partly obligatory and disciplinary and partly constitutive and descriptive in that they define a lawyer's professional role. Many of the Comments use the term "should." Comments do not add obligations to the Rules but provide guidance for practicing in compliance with the rules.

Ethics Opinions. Guidance regarding the application of the rules of a state that are based on the Model Rules to a tax and estate planning practice is also provided by the formal and informal ethics opinions issued by the ABA Committee on Ethics and Professional Responsibility (the "Committee"). Opinions issued by the ABA are classified "formal" (*i.e.,* ones that deal in detail with more important issues or "informal" (*i.e.,* ones that respond to a specific or narrow question). Wolfram, Modern Legal Ethics (1986) §2.6.6, n. 11. While opinions issued by the ABA are not binding, they may be considered authoritative and entitled to respect by state ethics committees and the courts. ABA Formal Op. 85-352, is an example of the type of opinions issued by the ABA Committee. It expresses the ethical rules that apply to a lawyer advising a client regarding positions that might be taken by the client in a tax return. *See* §1.2.2. (The rules regarding tax return preparation, valuation and disclosure were subsequently changed by Congress and the IRS.) Ethics questions may be researched for a fee with the assistance of the ABA Center for Professional Responsibility— ETHIC Search (1-800-285-2221 or e-mail to ethicsearch@staff.abanet.org).

Although opinions issued by state and local ethics committees are not binding on courts, they too provide useful guidance regarding the local version of the ethical rules. Ethics committees in some states also issue formal and informal opinions. The significance of the distinction varies. In Washington State, "Formal opinions are issued by the RPC Committee (or one of its predecessor committees) and have been formally approved and adopted by the Association's Board of Governors. Formal opinions generally address matters of wide concern and interest and, once adopted by the Board of Governors, are routinely published in the Washington State Bar News. Informal ethics opinions are not individually approved by the Board and do not reflect any official position of the Association . . . . Informal opinions reflect only the opinion of the Rules of Professional Conduct Committee." Wash. St. Bar. Assn., Resources 2006-2007, 431.

A state's ethics rules govern virtually all aspects of a lawyer's professional life including the lawyer's conduct in relation to clients, other lawyers, nonclients, the courts and administrative agencies such as the IRS, the profession and the public. As noted above, a violation of an ethical rule can result in a disciplinary action against the lawyer. In addition, a violation of the rules may cause the lawyer to suffer a reduction in the amount, or complete loss, of fees. If the violation gives rise to a malpractice action, damages may also be assessed against the lawyer.

§1.2.2. Internal Revenue Code Requirements and Treasury Circular 230

As previously indicated, lawyers must also comply with the provisions of the Code, including ones that subject them and their clients to penalties in various circumstances. The Code imposes penalties on taxpayers for fraud, §6663, and for underpayment of taxes due to negligence, understatement of tax, and over- and under-valuations. §6662. *See* §8.7-8.7.4. In addition, accuracy related penalties are imposed on understatements with respect to reportable transactions (*i.e.,* ones identified as having a potential for tax avoidance or tax evasion as defined in §6707A). §6662A. A taxpayer who fails to file the notices or returns required by §6048 regarding foreign trusts is subject to the penalties imposed by §6677. Persons who prepare income tax returns are subject to special return preparer penalties described in §6994. The penalties apply to the underpayment of tax caused by willful or reckless actions or by taking a filing position for which there was not a realistic possibility of success. Penalties are also imposed on anyone who willfully aids or assists another person in understating any federal tax liability. §6701. Persons who participate in the organization or marketing of tax shelters are subject to the penalties described in § 6700. The preparation of opinion letters is within the scope of activities subject to § 6700.

Treasury Circular 230. Lawyers and other practicing before the IRS are also subject to the rules set forth in Circular 230, which was significantly amended in 2005. 31 C.F.R. Part 10. The provisions apply to lawyers, accountants, enrolled agents, enrolled actuaries and other persons authorized to practice before the IRS. Circular 230 was issued by the Secretary of the Treasury pursuant to authority granted by 31 U.S.C. § 330. Lawyers and CPAs who are licensed to practice in any state are automatically admitted to practice before the IRS. Violation of the rules prescribed in Circular 230 can lead to suspension or disbarment from practice before the IRS.

Unfortunately, state ethics rules and Circular 230 are not entirely compatible. For example, under ABA Formal Op. 85-352, a lawyer may take a position on a return "most favorable to the client" if the lawyer has a good faith belief that the position is warranted by existing law or can be supported by a good faith argument for an extension, modification or reversal of existing law. The formulation need not involve any quantification of the possibility that the position would be upheld by the courts. In contrast, Circular 230 requires that a positions taken on a return have a realistic possibility of success, which means that the position have a one-in-three or greater probability of being upheld on the merits. § 10.34(a), (d)(1).

Final Form of Changes in Circular 230. Significant changes to Circular 230 were proposed in December, 2003. A revised, final version of the regulations was issued on December 20, 2004, with an effective date of June 20, 2005. Regulations issued in May 2005 provided some clarification of the new rules and relaxed some of their requirements.

Best Practices. The changes to Circular 230 include the addition of the following list of "best practices" to § 10.33:

> (1) Communicating clearly with the client regarding the terms of the engagement and the form and scope of the advice or assistance to be rendered; (2) establishing the relevant facts, including evaluating the reasonableness of any assumptions or representations; (3) relating applicable law, including potentially applicable judicial doctrines, to the relevant facts; (4) arriving at a conclusion supported by the law and the facts; (5) advising the client regarding the import of the conclusions reached; and (6) acting fairly and with integrity in practice before the IRS.

Although the best practices are aspirational in nature, they are accompanied by an admonition that tax advisors with the responsibility for overseeing a firm's practice of providing tax advice "should take reasonable steps to ensure that the firm's procedures for all members, associates, and employees are consistent with the best practices set forth in paragraph (a) of § 10.33." The intended effect of the promulgation of the best practices is described in the "Explanation of Provisions" of T.D. 9165:

> These best practices are aspirational. A practitioner who fails to comply with best practices will not be subject to discipline under these regulations. Similarly, the provision relating to steps to ensure that a firm's procedures are consistent with best practices, now set forth in § 10.33(b), is aspirational. Although best practices are solely aspirational, tax profes-

sionals are expected to observe these practices to preserve public confidence in the tax system.

Mandatory Requirements. Most important, the final version of § 10.35 extends the application of the mandatory requirements to a much broader range of tax advice than the tax shelter opinions that were the primary focus of the proposed regulations. In particular, the final regulations extend the mandatory requirements to apply to "covered opinions" as defined in § 10.35(b)(2). Also, § 10.37 imposes some mandatory requirements with respect to written tax advice that is not a covered opinion.

Covered Opinions. According to the Explanation of Provisions, mandatory requirements apply to "covered opinions," which are defined in § 10.35(b) as any form of written advice, including electronic communications, that concerns one or more federal tax issues arising from:

> (1) a listed tax shelter transaction; (2) any plan or arrangement, the principal purpose of which is tax avoidance or evasion of any tax; (3) any plan or arrangement a significant purpose of which is the avoidance or evasion of tax advice if the written advice (A) is a reliance opinion, (B) is a marketed opinion, (C) is subject to conditions of confidentiality, or (D) is subject to contractual protection. A reliance opinion is written advice that concludes at a confidence level of at least more likely than not that one or more significant Federal tax issues would be resolved in the taxpayer's favor.

The Explanation continues to say that, "the final regulations provide that a practitioner providing a covered opinion, including a marketed opinion, must not assume that a transaction has a business purpose or is potentially profitable apart from tax benefits, or make an assumption with respect to a material valuation issue."

The Explanation notes that written advice will not be treated as a reliance opinion if it includes a prominent statement that it was not written and cannot be used for the purpose of avoiding penalties. Because of this provision some lawyers include a "nonreliance" statement in virtually all of their written communications other than formal opinions, including letters, form letters, e-mails, memos, and publications. A statement might read along these lines: "Important Tax Notice: This communication is not written to be used, and cannot be used, by a taxpayer for the purpose of avoiding penalties that may be asserted against the taxpayer under the Internal Revenue Code of 1986, as amended." Similarly, under § 10.35(b)(5), written advice will not be treated as a marketed opinion if it prominently states that the advice was not intended and cannot be used to avoid any penalties, it was written to support the promotion or marketing of the transactions described in the advice, and the taxpayer should seek independent advice based on the taxpayer's individual circumstances. One of the May 2005 changes requires that the statement regarding penalties must be (1) located in a separate section that is not a footnote and (2) printed in the same or larger size type face than the remainder of the document.

The May 2005 regulations also provide some helpful guidance regarding the identification of transactions the "principal purpose" of which is tax avoidance or evasion. Specifically, the principal purpose of a transaction is tax avoidance or evasion "if that purpose exceeds any other purpose." The regulation helpfully continues to provide that the principal purpose of a transaction is not tax avoidance or evasion if the transaction has as its purpose the claiming of tax benefits in a manner consistent with the statute and Congressional purpose. Under that test presumably the principal purpose of written advice regarding transactions that are expressly authorized by the Code (*e.g.,* CRTs, QTIPs, QDOTs, QPRTs, and GRATs) would not be tax avoidance or evasion.

The May 2005 regulations also provide that three specific types of advice will not be considered to be covered opinions. The excluded types are: (1) written advice given after a tax return is filed; (2) advice by an in house lawyer regarding the tax liabilities of his or her employer; and (3) advice that does not reach any favorable tax conclusion even at a low confidence level.

Requirements for Covered Opinions. If written tax advice is a covered opinion, it must meet the requirements set forth in § 10.35(c) and summarized below. In addition, § 10.35(d) requires that the author of a covered opinion must be competent to issue the opinion and "must be satisfied that the combined analysis of the opinions, taken as a whole, and the overall conclusion, if any, satisfy the requirements of this section." Finally, a covered opinion must contain the disclosures enumerated in § 10.35(e).

A covered opinion must comply with the following requirements:

1. *Factual Matters.* § 10.35(c)(1). The practitioner must use reasonable efforts to ascertain the facts, and determine which facts are relevant. The opinion must identify and consider all facts that the practitioner determines to be relevant. The opinion cannot be based on unreasonable factual assumptions or unreasonable factual representations, statements or findings of the taxpayer or any other person.

2. *Relate Law to Facts.* § 10.35(c)(2). The opinion must relate the applicable law (including potentially applicable judicial doctrines) to the relevant facts and may not assume the favorable resolution of any significant federal tax issue except in the case of a limited scope opinion. The opinion must not contain internally inconsistent legal analyses or conclusions.

3. *Evaluation of Significant Federal Tax Issues.* The opinion must consider all significant Federal tax issues and must state the practitioner's conclusion as to the likelihood that the taxpayer will prevail on the merits of each issue considered in the opinion. If the practitioner cannot reach a conclusion with respect to an issue, the opinion must state that fact. The opinion must describe the conclusions, including the facts and analysis supporting the conclusions or describing why the practitioner is unable to reach a conclusion as to one or more issues. If the opinion fails to reach a conclusion at a level of at least more likely than not with respect to a significant issue, the opinion must include the disclosures required by § 10.35(e), including a boldface banner stating that the opinion does not reach a "more likely than not" conclusion on all issues.

The opinion may not base the conclusion on the possibility that the tax return will not be audited, that an issue will not be raised on audit, or that an issue will be resolved through settlement if raised. § 10.35(c)(3)(iv).

Requirements Applicable to Tax Advice Other than Covered Opinions. The Explanation of Provisions includes the following summary of the requirements of

§ 10.37 that apply to tax advice that is not a covered opinion. According to the Explanation,

> [A] practitioner may not give written advice if the practitioner: (1) bases the advice on unreasonable factual or legal assumptions; (2) unreasonably relies upon representations, statements, finding or agreements of the taxpayer or any other person; (3) fails to consider all relevant facts; or (4) takes into account the possibility that a tax return will not be audited, that an issue will not be raised on audit, or that an issue will be settled . . . .The scope of the engagement and the type and specificity of the advice sought by the client, in addition to all other facts and circumstances, will be considered in determining whether a practitioner has failed to comply with the requirements of § 10.37.

Conclusion. The final regulations should be amended to narrow and clarify their scope and application. As written the regulations are ambiguous and overly broad. The over breadth of the regulations arguably supports imposing their requirements on a wide range of innocent written communications between estate planners and their clients. Estate planners and their clients should not be forced to bear the substantial additional costs of complying with mandatory rules in the case of most straightforward communications.

The regulations' lack of clarity is easily illustrated. For example, are simple letters to a client regarding annual exclusion gift planning or dealing with the availability of the marital deduction for gifts to a spouse covered opinions that must comply with the requirements of § 10.35(c)? Are periodic form letters or newsletters that are sent to clients regarding federal tax issues covered opinions? The requirements should most certainly not apply to simple letters to clients, to periodic form communications to clients, or to outlines, articles or books written by a tax practitioner. Further, how can one reliably differentiate between tax advice, "the principal purpose" of which is the avoidance of a federal tax, and tax advice, "a significant purpose" of which was the avoidance of a federal tax?

§ 1.2.3. Model Code of Professional Responsibility ("Model Code")

The Model Code, which was adopted by the ABA in 1969, was the precursor of the Model Rules. Most states adopted the Model Code soon after it was approved by the ABA. The Model Code consists of three related parts: Nine Canons, which are very general "statements of axiomatic norms" (*e.g.,* Canon 4, which simply states that, "A lawyer should preserve the confidences and secrets of a client."); Disciplinary Rules (DRs), which contain more explicit, mandatory rules of conduct; and Ethical Considerations (EC), which are aspirational in nature. According to the Preamble to the Model Code, the DRs "state the minimum level of conduct below which no lawyer can fall without being subject to disciplinary action." The Model Code has some continuing significance in a small minority of states.

§1.2.4. Model Rules and Areas of Legal Specialization

The Model Rules represent a significant improvement over the Model Code in terms of organization and content, but do not deal adequately with the ethical issues that arise in specialized areas of practice, including estate planning and taxation. The need to address the specific ethical issues that arise in specialized areas of practice led Judge Stanley Sporkin and others to suggest that particularized rules be adopted with respect to various areas of legal specialization. Sporkin, The Need for Separate Codes of Professional Conduct for the Various Specialties, 7 Geo. J. Legal Ethics 149 (1993). Some professional groups responded to the perceived need by publishing statements of the rules that their members should observe. Among the first was the pamphlet, Bounds of Advocacy, issued by the American Academy of Matrimonial Lawyers. More recently, the National Academy of Elder Law Attorneys (NAELA) promulgated Aspirational Standards for the Practice of Elder Law with Commentaries (Nov. 21, 2005).

Perhaps the most comprehensive and helpful guidance for estate planners is provided by the ACTEC Commentaries on the Model Rules of Professional Responsibility ("ACTEC Commentaries"), the initial version of which was adopted in 1993 by the Board of Regents of the American College of Trust and Estate Counsel (ACTEC) (formerly the American College of Probate Counsel). Updated editions of the ACTEC Commentaries were adopted and published in 1995, 1999, and 2006, respectively. One of your authors was the Reporter for the 1993 and 1995 editions of the ACTEC Commentaries, upon which portions of this chapter are loosely based. Copies of the ACTEC Commentaries may be purchased from the ACTEC Foundation, 901 15th Street, N.W., Suite 525, Washington, D.C. 20005, Tel. (202) 684-8460. The Preface to the ACTEC Commentaries states that "ACTEC has developed the following Commentaries on selected rules to provide some particularized guidance to ACTEC Fellows and others regarding their professional responsibilities."

Useful guidance to estate planners is also provided by the Restatement, which was adopted by the American Law Institute in 1998. The views regarding estate planning expressed in the Restatement are generally consistent with those of the ACTEC Commentaries and in this chapter.

B. ROLES OF ESTATE PLANNERS AND STAGES OF ESTATE PLANNING

§1.3. VARIOUS ROLES OF ESTATE PLANNERS

The role of the lawyer in estate planning can range from counseling a client regarding prospective actions, such as gifts of property, to advocating on behalf of a client regarding the consequences of past actions. The Rules that relate primarily to those roles are discussed below. As a counselor, the primary duty of the lawyer is to provide competent, timely advice as required by Rules 1.1 and 1.2. In addition, the lawyer is bound to maintain confidences, Rules 1.6 and 1.18 (duties to prospective client), and avoid conflicts of interest. Rules 1.7 and 1.8 deal with conflicts of interest regarding present clients, while Rule 1.9 deals with conflicts of interest involving former clients.

The lawyer's most important duties, such as the duty of confidentiality, run almost exclusively to the client. However, some other duties, such as the duty of competence, are sometimes held to extend to client's intended beneficiaries, who may be characterized as third party beneficiaries of the engagement between the lawyer and client or are otherwise entitled to protection. The lawyer's duties apply most extensively and forcefully during the active period of a representation (*i.e.*, while the lawyer is preparing estate planning documents, supervising transfers and otherwise implementing an estate plan and assisting in the preparation and filing of appropriate tax returns).

§1.4. STAGES OF THE INTER VIVOS ESTATE PLANNING PROCESS

An inter vivos estate planning representation usually moves through several more-or-less discrete stages, during each of which several Rules are usually involved. A table listing the rules that are applicable at various stages appears at the end of this section. The relevant rules are reviewed, and their application in the estate planning context is discussed, in § 1.6.1-1.6.22.

Promptly after making an appointment with a prospective client it is helpful to send an introductory letter or e-mail to the client. The length of the letter or e-mail depends on the purpose of the meeting, but it would typically confirm the time and place of the scheduled meeting, include directions, and enclose a questionnaire or data collection form. If appropriate it might recommend that the prospective client consider who should serve in various fiduciary capacities (personal representative, trustee, and guardian of any minor children). A sample form letter to prospective clients who are married and have minor children appears below, Form 1-1, along with a sample questionnaire form, Form 1-2. In appropriate cases the estate planner may also include a summary of the existing state and federal transfer tax systems.

Form 1-1. Introductory Letter to Prospective Client

[Address]

Re: Our meeting, xx:xx [A.M./P.M.], [date]

Dear Mr. & Mrs. _____:

This confirms the appointment we have to meet in my office at _____ [A.M./P.M.] next [day of week], [month and day]. My office is on the _____ floor of the _____ Building at [street and number]. Parking is available in an underground garage in our building.

Enclosed is a copy of a Confidential Estate Planning Questionnaire that I would like you to complete and bring along to our conference. Although the questionnaire may look daunting, most of the questions call for information such as birth dates, Social Security numbers, etc, that are probably readily available. Also, if they are handy, please also bring to our meeting copies of your existing wills, living wills or health care directives, powers of attorney, deeds to any real estate you own, any trusts in which you have an interest, and any agreements between you regarding the ownership of your property. For completeness we may later need to review additional documents such as insurance policies on your lives.

Who might serve as your executors, guardians and trustees. Prior to our meeting please give some thought to the persons you might want to appoint to serve as a fiduciary (e.g., executors, guardians, trustees and agents under powers of attorney). Each will should designate an executor (the person who will be in charge of administering your property and carrying out the terms of your will). As you might expect, husbands and wives often appoint each other to serve as executor. Although the need may not arise, your wills should designate an alternate to serve as executor if needed. They should also name one or more individuals to serve as guardian(s) and successor guardian(s) of your minor children should neither of you be able to act. A guardian would be responsible for making decisions regarding a child's health care, education and general welfare that are normally made by a parent. Because of the personal nature of the position a corporation may not serve as a guardian of the person of a minor. The wills should also name an individual or corporate trustee to serve as guardian of the estate (property) of a minor and be responsible for the management of the minor's property.

Protecting your children. In the unlikely event that you both die leaving minor children, you will probably want to leave your property in trust for their benefit. If your wills do not include contingent trusts for your children, any property that becomes distributable to a minor child would be received and managed for the child by a guardian of the child's estate. A trust is preferred to a guardianship, which is generally more cumbersome and expensive to administer. If you go the trust route, your wills should name one or more trustees to invest and manage the trust property and make distributions to, or for the benefit of your children. If you wish, the person you nominate to serve as guardian of a child could be appointed to serve as trustee of a trust for the child.

About trusts. Trusts are attractive because of the degree of flexibility and discretion that can be given trustees over the investment and management of the trust funds. For example, the power to invest and manage the assets of a trust can be virtually unlimited or tightly restricted by the terms of a trust. Likewise a trust may give a trustee broad, or very limited, authority to make distributions to the beneficiaries of the trust.

If more than one child survives, many parents choose to place their property in a single trust until all of the educational expenses of the youngest child are met, which may consume a disproportionate part of the income and principal of the trust. When the youngest child's education is completed, or when the youngest living child attains a specified age the trust fund may be divided into separate shares and distributed to the children, or retained in one or more trusts for an additional period.

Gifts to other relatives, friends and charities? You might also give some thought to whether you might want to make any gifts to relatives, special friends, or charities. Please also consider how you would like your property distributed if neither you nor any of your children or grandchildren survive the two of you.

Looking forward to seeing you next week, I am,

Sincerely yours,

Form 1-2. Confidential Estate Planning Questionnaire

	General	
	Husband	Wife
Name		
Home Address		
Preferred phone		

	Husband	Wife
Fax		
E-mail		
Employer or business		
Business address		
Business phone		
Fax		

Personal

	Husband	Wife
Citizenship		
Soc. Sec. No.		
Age		
Date & place of marriage		
List any other states lived in during marriage		
Prior marriages (if any)		

Children, Grandchildren & Parents

Children and Grandchildren, list names, ages, addresses and Social Security numbers (indicate if children of prior marriage):

1.
2.
3.
4.
5.

[continue on additional pages as required]

	Husband	Wife
Parents' (name, age/year of death, address)		

Assets (estimated net values) and Liabilities

	Husband	Wife
Residence		
Recreational or Other Real property		
List brokerage accounts		
Publicly traded securities,		
Common stocks		
Preferred stocks		
Bonds		
Other		
Closely held stock and partnership interests		
Cash (bank accounts & other; location)		
Jewelry		
Furniture		
Antiques		
Art		
Cars		
Boats or planes		
Other valuables		
Safe deposit boxes (location)		
ERISA benefit plans (plan description, value & named beneficiary		

	Husband	Wife
IRAs (type, value and beneficiary designation)		
Life insurance (term or cash owner, value, face amount, loans, beneficiary)		
Debts		
Mortgages		
Life insurance loans		
Other		

Other advisors (list names, addresses & contact info)		
	Husband	Wife
Other lawyers		
Accountants		
Stock brokers		
Investment advisors		
Life Insurance		
Real estate advisors		
Physicians		
Religious advisors		
Other advisors		

Overall objectives, comments and concerns

Initial Stage—Client Intake. The initial stage, client intake, naturally involves checking for conflicts that might affect the representation (Rules 1.7, 1.8, and 1.9), determining the lawyer's competence to handle the matter (Rule 1.1), defining the work to be performed (the scope of the representation) (Rule 1.2), assessing the capacity of the prospective client (Rule 1.14), considering the issues posed by multiple and entity clients (Rules 1.6, 1.7, and 1.9, respectively), and assuring the client of confidentiality (Rules 1.6 and 1.18). At an early point, the lawyer should meet personally with a prospective client, which can be critical if his or her capacity is, or may become, an issue. A lawyer's duties to a client with diminished capacity are discussed at §1.6.11. Note that under the substituted judgment law in effect in some states, the court may approve an estate plan that is created by a conservator for a conservatee. In those states, a court order approving a plan may bind all parties who had notice and an opportunity to participate in the substituted judgment proceeding. *See* Baer & Johnson, Wake-Up Call, 147 Tr. & Est. 59 (Aug. 2008).

During the initial stage the lawyer should obtain from the client relevant information about the client's family, finances, and personal goals and objectives. The necessary information can be obtained through personal interviews, questionnaires (printed or electronic), or a combination of methods. The information ordinarily includes dates of birth, Social Security numbers, tax data, and information about a client's other personal advisors (*e.g.,* accountants, financial and insurance advisors, physicians, and religious advisors). Data should also be obtained from a client regarding the client's online accounts, passwords and other relevant information. The list may be electronic and managed by an internet based service. Lamm, To my Son, I Leave All my Passwords, 148 Tr. & Est. 22 (July 2009).

At or before the end of the initial stage, the lawyer should provide the client with an engagement letter that details the work to be performed and describes the manner in which fees will be determined and how issues of confidentiality and conflicts will be handled. ACTEC has also published a very useful model set of engagement letters, copies of which are available from the ACTEC Foundation. Engagement Letters: A Guide for Practitioners (1999, 2d. Ed. 2007). If a prospective client is not accepted, the lawyer should consider sending a declination letter. Engagement and declination letters are discussed in connection with Rule 1.2 at §1.6.2.

Second Stage—Counseling and Educating the Client. The second stage, counseling and educating the client, involves rules that require competence (Rule 1.1), diligence (Rule 1.3), communication (Rule 1.4), and confidentiality (Rule 1.6). During this stage the lawyer assists the client in formulating a plan that meets the client's needs. In order to assist the client in deciding upon a plan the lawyer may provide the client with estimates of the tax implications of various approaches. Software programs that are available allow tax projections based on varying assumptions to be made efficiently and economically. In this stage, or at an earlier point, it may be helpful to provide an estate planning client with some background information about federal transfer taxes and relevant estate planning techniques.

Third Stage—Document Preparation and Execution. The third stage, document preparation, execution and implementation, also requires competence, diligence, communication with the client, confidentiality, and supervision of nonlawyer staff members (Rules 1.1, 1.3, 1.4, 1.6, and 5.3, respectively). In this stage the lawyer may also be responsible for coordinating activities with a client's other professional advisors, including financial and insurance advisors, accountants, and trust officers. The lawyer is also often responsible for follow-up matters, which might include, retaining original documents, preparing and filing any tax returns that are required, and periodically reminding the client to review the sufficiency of the client's estate planning documents.

Tax Return Advice. Providing advice about, or preparing, tax returns implicates additional Model Rules and specific provisions of the Code and of Circular 230. As stated in ABA Formal Op. 314 (1965) (which was promulgated while the Canons of Professional Ethics were in effect and was modified by ABA Formal Op. 85-352), "In all cases, with regard both to the preparation of returns and negotiating administrative settlements, the lawyer is under a duty not to mislead the Internal Revenue Service deliberately and affirmatively, either by misstatements or by silence or by permitting his client to mislead." The statement is consistent with the provisions of Rule 4.1, which prohibits a lawyer from misleading nonclients.

In all events a lawyer, of course, owes the IRS at least the duties that are owed to other nonclients. In particular, Rule 4.1 prohibits a lawyer from knowingly making a false statement of fact or law "to a third party" or failing to disclose material facts to a third person where disclosure is required in order to prevent assisting a criminal or fraudulent act by a client. However, the IRS is generally regarded as an adversary and not as a court or tribunal. ABA Formal Op. 314 states that the IRS "is neither a true tribunal, nor even a quasi-judicial institution." Instead, it is "the representative of one of the parties." Accordingly, Opinion 314 holds that the lawyer for a taxpayer is not bound to disclose to the IRS weaknesses in the taxpayer's case.

Under §10.21 of Treasury Circular 230, a lawyer is required to inform a client of any error or omission that the lawyer discovers in a client's return and the client's duty to correct the error. However, a lawyer is not required to disclose to the IRS weaknesses in a client's case or legal authority that is contrary to the client's position.

Table 1-1
Rules Involved in Various Stages of Inter Vivos Estate Planning Process

Stage			*Subjects*	*Rules Implicated*
I.	Client Intake			
	A.		Initial Conference	
			Lawyer's ability to handle (competence)— involve or consult others	1.1
			Scope of the representation	1.2
			Client of uncertain capacity	1.14
			Conflicts with other clients (waivable, nonwaivable?)	1.7, 1.9, former 2.2
			Conflicts of interests of lawyer (waivable, nonwaivable?)	1.7(a)(2), 1.8
			Conflicts with prior clients (waivable, nonwaivable)	1.9
			Fees	1.5
			Confidentiality	1.6, 1.18
	B.		Acceptance	
			Diligence	1.3
			Communication	1.4
		1.	Engagement letter	

§1.4.1. Termination of Lawyer-Client Relationship; Completion of Work; Passage of Time; Hiring New Counsel; Retention of Original Documents

After the current work for a client is completed, the lawyer-client relationship may terminate or continue for an extended period, unless the lawyer or the client takes some action to end it at an earlier point. Termination is discussed in connection with Rule 1.16 (*See* §1.6.12). *Heathcoat v. Santa Fe International Corp.*, 532 F. Supp. 961 (E.D. Ark. 1982) (lawyer-client relationship terminated when estate planning documents were executed). In contrast, the lawyer-client relationship continued in a case in which estate planning documents had been executed in 1976, the law firm advised the client regarding employment contract matters in 1983 and 1984 and the client was sent estate planning reminder letters in 1983 and 1984. In addition, the firm had retained the originals of the executed estate planning documents. *Manoir-Electroalloys Corp. v. Amalloy Corp.*, 711 F. Supp. 188 (D.N.J. 1989).

The lawyer-client relationship also generally terminates if the client employs new counsel in the same matter. *Artromick Intern Inc. v. Drustar, Inc.*, 134 F.R.D. 226 (S.D. Ohio 1991).

Among other things, a lawyer's engagement letter might briefly describe the nature of the relationship following the completion of the current work. *See* Form 1-1, §1.6.2. ("The execution of documents and implementation of your plan will conclude our active role as your estate planners. However, as a service to you, we will periodically send reminder letters to you, reminding you to review your estate plan and consider whether any changes should be made.") If the lawyer-client relationship is not terminated by either party, it may continue, albeit on an inactive, "stand-by," or "dormant" basis. Until the representation is activated, the lawyer's duties to the client are diminished.

Retention of Original Documents. The lawyer's retention and safekeeping of a client's original estate planning documents can be helpful to the client and is good client relations. Before undertaking to retain a client's original documents, the lawyer should consider whether doing so may result in the indefinite continuation of the lawyer-client relationship for purposes of conflicts and disqualification issues. In ruling on a motion to disqualify plaintiff's counsel, one court apparently gave no weight to the fact that the law firm had retained the original of a will they had prepared for the defendant 23 years before. *Pishka v. Welsh*, 2010 Conn. Super. Lexis 1970 (Windham Dist. 2010).

§1.4.2. Former Clients; Deceased Clients; Conflicts and Confidentiality

Without the consent of a former client, a lawyer cannot represent another person in the same or a substantially related matter whose interests are materially adverse to the interests of the former client (Rule 1.9.) The duty of confidentiality also extends to former clients and protects the confidences and secrets of a deceased client from disclosure. *Swidler & Berlin and Hamilton v. U.S.*, 118 S. Ct. 2081 (1998), which deals with the corresponding evidentiary privilege, is discussed below in connection with Rule 1.6, §1.6.6. However, the evidentiary privilege generally does not prohibit disclosures from being made with the consent of the decedent's personal representative or that were impliedly authorized by the decedent. §1.6.6.

C. GOVERNMENT LAWYERS

§1.5. DUTIES OF LAWYERS EMPLOYED BY THE GOVERNMENT

A lawyer who has served or is currently serving as a public officer or employee is personally subject to the Rules of Professional Conduct, including the prohibition against concurrent conflicts of interest stated in Rule 1.7. Comment [1] to Rule 1.11.

As indicated by the quotation above from Comment [1] to Rule 1.11, lawyers employed by the government are generally subject to the ethical rules of the jurisdiction in which they practice. They are also subject to rules imposed by statute or by regulations of the agency (*e.g.*, Circular 230.) Thus, the lawyer for an agency is generally subject to the same duties of confidentiality and conduct toward nonclients. Moreover, the lawyer for an agency should not communicate directly with an individual whom the lawyer knows is represented by counsel. Direct contact would violate Rule 4.2, which is assumed to apply equally to lawyers for a governmental agency. *See* Mulroney, Report on the Invitational Conference on Professionalism in Tax Practice, 11 Am. J. Tax. Pol. 369, 382 (1994).

Importantly, the Code provides that returns and return information are confidential and, except as otherwise authorized, may not be disclosed by any officer or employee of the United States. § 6103(a). The restriction extends to "a former officer or employee."

The Rules, Circular 230, and federal criminal statutes impose special restrictions on lawyers who move into or out of government service. The Rules, principally Rules 1.11 and 1.13, are largely concerned with conflicts of interest, as are some of the provisions of Circular 230, § 10.25, and of the statutes. Federal criminal law is particularly concerned with instances in which an employee solicits future employment or engages in other conflicts of interest. 18 U.S.C. § 207.

D. APPLICABLE RULES REVIEWED AND ANALYZED

§ 1.6. RULES OF PROFESSIONAL CONDUCT

The Rules provide the most comprehensive set of rules applicable to estate planning and tax lawyers. The rules discussed below are the most relevant and important for estate planners and tax practitioners. The basic obligations of a lawyer are summarized in the Preamble to the Rules:

> In all professional functions a lawyer should be competent, prompt and diligent. A lawyer should maintain communication with a client concerning the representation. A lawyer should keep in confidence information relating to representation of a client except so far as disclosure is required or permitted by the Rules of Professional Conduct. [In the Preamble to the Model Rules this passage concludes with the words "or other law".]

Under the Rules, the determination of which rules apply in a particular case depends primarily upon the nature of the relationship between the lawyer and the other party or parties. The rules, which are largely client-centered, deal most extensively with the lawyer's duty to clients. However, not infrequently lawyers are subject to malpractice actions against them by nonclients—often the disappointed beneficiaries of a failed or flawed estate plan.

Fewer rules deal with the lawyer's duties toward nonclients, including represented and unrepresented third parties. However, as noted previously, under Rule 4.1 a lawyer cannot knowingly make a false statement of material fact or law to a third person or fail to disclose a material fact when disclosure is necessary to avoid assisting in a criminal or fraudulent act by a client, unless disclosure is prohibited by the rules of confidentiality (Rule 1.6). As discussed later, a lawyer also owes some strict duties to courts and court personnel. Rules 3.1 through 3.9 deal with the lawyer's duties as advocate, which include duties of candor and truthfulness to the court (Rule 3.3) and to preserve the impartiality and decorum of the tribunal (Rule 3.5). A lawyer appearing before a legislative or administrative body in a nonadjudicative proceeding must disclose that the appearance is in a representative capacity and observe some of the rules applicable to court proceedings.

Individual and Multiple Clients. The Rules focus almost entirely on the client as an isolated individual. Consistently, a lawyer who represents one family member does not thereby necessarily assume any duties to anyone else in the family. In such a case the other members of the family are treated simply as nonclient third parties, to whom the lawyer owes only very limited duties, such as the duty to be truthful and not knowingly to mislead them (Rule 4.1). However, if there is no disabling conflict, a lawyer may appropriately represent multiple clients in the same matter. Common examples are husband and wife or parent and child. As developed below, representing multiple clients can involve difficult issues of confidentiality and conflicts. *See* §1.6.6 and 1.6.7.

Fiduciary Clients. A lawyer who represents a fiduciary with respect to an estate, trust or guardianship estate is usually considered to represent only the fiduciary and not the "fiduciary estate" or its beneficiaries. However, Comment [27] to Rule 1.7 states that, "In estate administration the identity of the client may be unclear under the law of a particular jurisdiction. Under one view, the client is the fiduciary; under another view the client is the estate or trust, including its beneficiaries. In order to comply with conflict of interest rules, the lawyer should make clear the relationship to the parties involved." Despite the language of the Comment, an estate or trust is seldom considered to be the client of the lawyer for the fiduciary. Although the beneficiaries are generally not considered to be clients, in some circumstances they have, along with the fiduciary, been considered to be joint clients of the lawyer.

If the interests of a fiduciary (and the fiduciary estate) do not conflict with the interests of a beneficiary, the lawyer is generally free to represent both the fiduciary and the beneficiary. On the other hand, if the interests of the fiduciary and a beneficiary conflict, the lawyer may be unable to represent both. The same lawyer can represent a fiduciary in both a representative and a personal capacity if there are no conflicts. However, a lawyer should not do so if the fiduciary's personal interests conflict with his or her duties as fiduciary. Thus, a lawyer who represents a fiduciary generally should not assist the fiduciary in pursuing a claim against the estate or otherwise taking a position adverse to the interests of the beneficiaries of the estate.

As discussed later, in connection with Rule 4.3, §1.6.19, the lawyer for a fiduciary should inform the beneficiaries of the lawyer's role and, in most cases, that the lawyer does not represent them. The same information should be given the creditors and any other parties who communicate with the lawyer and might otherwise assume that the lawyer represents them or will protect their interests.

The beneficiaries of a fiduciary estate may assert a claim against the lawyers for the fiduciary if the lawyers assist the fiduciary in committing a breach of fiduciary duty. *Wolf v. Mitchell, Silberberg & Knupp,* 90 Cal. Rptr. 2d 792 (Cal. App. 1999). The decision in *Wolf* follows similar rulings in *Atascadero v. Merrill Lynch, Pierce, Fenner & Smith, Inc.,* 68 Cal. App. 4th 445 (Cal. App. 1998) and *Pierce v. Lyman,* 1 Cal. App. 4th 1093 (Cal. App. 1991). The *Wolf* opinion states that, *"Pierce v. Lyman* held that an attorney may be liable to a trust beneficiary for the attorney's active participation in a trustee's breach of duty if the attorney acted in furtherance of his or her own financial gain, or committed actual fraud by making express misrepresentations to the beneficiary." 90 Cal. Rptr. 2d at 798.

§1.6.1. Rule 1.1: Competence; Malpractice

> A lawyer shall provide competent representation to a client. Competent representation requires the legal knowledge, skill, thoroughness and preparation reasonably necessary for the representation.

The duty to provide competent representation required by Rule 1.1 applies to all of the contexts in which a lawyer may represent a client—as planner and counselor, return preparer, and as advocate and litigator. A similar requirement was imposed by DR 6-101(a) under the Model Code, which provides that a lawyer shall not, "(1) Handle a legal matter which he knows or should know that he is not competent to handle, without associating with him a lawyer who is competent to handle it. (2) Handle a legal matter without preparation adequate in the circumstances. (3) Neglect a legal matter entrusted to him." Malpractice cases against a tax or estate planning lawyer are generally based upon the lawyer's alleged negligence or breach of contract, both of which usually make an issue of the lawyer's competence. One of the options open to a lawyer who lacks the competence to handle a matter is to decline the representation: "[I]n light of Morse's [the lawyer's] thirty-year membership in the Florida Bar, Morse should have declined the representation or become sufficiently competent in the probate matter." *Florida Bar v. Morse*, 784 So. 2d 414, 416 (Fla. 2001).

The ethical duty of competence exists independent of the right of an affected party to maintain a malpractice action against the lawyer for inadequate representation (*e.g.*, negligence). Despite the freedom of a lawyer and client to define the scope of the representation, by analogy to Rule 1.8(h) it is doubtful that the duty of competence can be waived—certainly not unless the client is independently represented. Rule 1.8(h) provides, in part, that, "A lawyer shall not: (1) make an agreement prospectively limiting the lawyer's liability to a client for malpractice unless the client is independently represented in making the agreement . . . ." Rule 1.8 is discussed at §1.6.8.

Standards of Competency. Comment [1] to Rule 1.1 describes the factors that are relevant to determining whether a lawyer employs the requisite knowledge and skill in a particular matter:

> [R]elevant factors include the relative complexity and specialized nature of the matter, the lawyer's general experience, the lawyer's training and experience in the field in question, the preparation and study the lawyer is able to give to the matter and whether it is feasible to refer the matter to, or associate or consult with, a lawyer of established competence in the field in question.

The conclusion of the comment suggests that in some cases a lawyer must meet a higher standard: "In many instances, the required proficiency is that of a general practitioner. Expertise in a particular field of law may be required in some circumstances."

There are no established criteria by which to measure competency in particular estate planning matters. The lack was noted in *Bucquet v. Livingston*, 57 Cal. App. 3d 914, 129 Cal. Rptr. 514 (1976), in which the court stated,

> [W]e are not aware of any cases or guidelines establishing in a civil case a standard for the reasonable, diligent and competent assistance of an attorney engaged in estate planning and preparing a trust with a marital deduction provision. We merely hold that the potential tax problem of general powers of appointment in *inter vivos* or testamentary marital deduction trusts were within the ambit of a reasonably competent and diligent practitioner from 1961 to the present. 129 Cal. Rptr. at 521.

Higher Standards Applicable to Specialists. A lawyer who is a specialist or holds himself or herself out as having special skills, may be subject to a higher standard of performance than a nonspecialist. *E.g., Neel v. Magana, Olney, Levy, Cathcart & Gelfand*, 98 Cal. Rptr. 837, 844 (1971). (If an attorney "specializes within the profession, he must meet the standards of knowledge and skill of such specialists.") Restatement Comment *d* to §52. ("A lawyer must 'exercise any special skill he has.'") Accordingly, courts will probably require lawyers who are certificated specialists or hold themselves out to be specialists or to possess special skills, to perform at a higher level than nonspecialists. The testimony of an expert witness may establish the standard of care applicable to a tax specialist. *Streber v. Hunter*, 221 F.3d 701 (5th Cir. 2000).

Model Rules; Malpractice and Privity. Because of the distinction between the disciplinary rules and the limitations on malpractice actions, a lawyer may be subject to discipline for not handling a matter competently although a malpractice action could not be brought against the lawyer under the local law. For example, some states bar suits from being brought by a decedent's beneficiaries against the decedent's estate planner, because the beneficiaries were not "in privity" with the estate planner. As explained below, the requirement of privity is enforced in a minority of states. Other states recognize a third-party beneficiary exception to the privity requirement, while still others allow an action by beneficiaries who are named in a will or trust, but do not receive the intended benefits. Note also that some of the privity states allow a decedent's personal representative to bring an action against the decedent's estate planners for malpractice that caused monetary damage to the decedent or the decedent's estate. Most important, the largest number of states do not require privity—they instead apply a multi-factor test in determining whether an intended beneficiary may bring an action against a lawyer who drew a decedent's will or trust.

With some variations, malpractice actions sound either in tort (the defendant breached a duty of care to the plaintiff) or contract (the defendant breached a duty owed to the third party beneficiaries of the contract between the client and the lawyer). Some states bar a tort action unless the plaintiff and the defendant were "in privity" (*i.e.*, that there was a direct contractual relationship between them).

Malpractice: Privity States.

> [I]n Texas, a legal malpractice claim in the estate-planning context may be maintained only by the estate planner's client. This is the minority rule in

the United States—only eight other states require strict privity in estate-planning malpractice suits. In the majority of states, a beneficiary harmed by a lawyer's negligence in drafting a will or trust may bring a malpractice claim against the attorney, even though the beneficiary was not the attorney's client. *Belt v. Oppenheimer, et al.*, 192 S.W.3d 780 (Tex. 2006)

As noted below, courts in some privity states draw a distinction between actions brought by a decedent's intended beneficiaries for their losses and actions brought by a decedent's personal representative for damages suffered by the decedent or the decedent's estate.

With varying degrees of intensity, the privity rule bars suits by beneficiaries in a minority of states, including Alabama, Maryland, Nebraska, New York, Ohio, Texas, and Virginia. For example, the privity defense prevailed in an Alabama suit brought by a beneficiary against a deceased client's lawyer for failure to follow the decedent's directions. *Robinson v. Benton*, 842 So. 2d 631 (Ala. 2002). Likewise, the Ohio Appellate Courts have given a negative answer to the following: "Whether a decedent's attorney may be sued by the decedent's intended beneficiaries and the court-appointed administrator for the attorney's negligence in failing to obtain the statutorily required signature of an attesting witness, which results in the probate court denying admission of decedent's will to probate." *Dykes v. Gayton*, 744 N.E.2d 199 (Oh. App. 2000), appeal dismissed, 743 N.E.2d 921 (Ohio 2001). The decision follows *Simon v. Zipperstein*, 512 N.E.2d 636 (Ohio 1987), which held that the intended beneficiary of a will did not have standing to sue the lawyer who drew the will, because the beneficiary was not in privity with the testator who was the attorney's client. *See also In re Lombardo*, 343 B.R. 115 (Bankruptcy App. Panel for 6th Cir. 2006).

The leading Texas decision, *Barcelo v. Elliott*, 923 S.W.2d 575 (Tex. 1996), barred an action by the intended beneficiaries against the lawyer-draftsman ("an attorney retained by a testator or settlor to draft a will or trust owes no professional duty of care to persons named as beneficiaries under the will or trust").

Malpractice; Privity States; Actions by Personal Representatives. Importantly, some privity states, including New York, Ohio and Texas allow a decedent's personal representative to bring a malpractice action against an estate planning lawyer for losses suffered by the decedent's estate. For example, an Ohio case holds that an action may be brought for failing to advise the decedent sufficiently regarding the steps she might take to minimize the estate tax that would be payable by her estate. *Hosfelt v. Miller*, 2000 Ohio 2619 (2000). In *Belt v. Oppenheimer, et al*, 192 S.W.3d 780 (Tex. 2006), the court held that a personal representative may maintain a legal malpractice claim on behalf of the decedent's estate against the decedent's estate planners. Citing approvingly the Texas decision in the *Belt* case, a unanimous New York Court of Appeals held that "privity, or a relationship sufficiently approaching privity, exists between the personal representative of an estate and the estate planning attorney." *Estate of Schneider v. Finmann*, 15 N.Y.3d 306 (2010). A later New York State Ethics Opinion, Opinion 865, held that a lawyer who prepared a decedent's estate plan may represent the decedent's personal representative if the lawyer does not perceive a colorable claim of legal malpractice arising out of the estate planning. *See §§* 1.6.7, 1.6.12 (Rule 1.16).

In privity states, perhaps the lawyer for an estate planning client should be required to disclose the existence and effect of the privity rule to the client (*i.e.*, that the client's intended beneficiaries would be unable to bring an action against the lawyer if the work performed by the lawyer is deficient and fails to effectuate the client's intentions). Going a step further, perhaps the lawyer should also be required to assist the client by devising a way that would allow the client's intended beneficiary to overcome the privity rule—which might be done if the intended beneficiaries also became clients in the matter.

Malpractice: Third Party Beneficiary States. At least some privity states allow beneficiaries who are not in privity with the lawyer to bring an action against the lawyer on a third party beneficiary rationale. For example, in *Simpson v. Calvas*, 650 A.2d 318 (N.H. 1994), the court relied on the third party beneficiary exception to the privity rule: "We hold that where, as here, a client has contracted with an attorney to draft a will and the client has identified to whom he wishes his estate to pass, that identified beneficiary may enforce the terms of the contract as a third-party beneficiary." In these states, the critical question is what is required to be considered to be a third party beneficiary of the contract between the client (testator or trustor) and the lawyer. A curious Virginia opinion holds that the intended beneficiaries of the deceased client's estate were not clearly enough identified as the intended third party beneficiaries of the contract for services between the lawyer and the testator to allow them to bring an action against the lawyer. *Copenhaver v. Rogers*, 384 S.E.2d 593 (Va. 1989).

Duty to Beneficiaries Named in Will, Trust or Other Estate Planning Document. Despite lack of privity, some states allow an action by "the direct, intended, and specifically identifiable beneficiaries of the testator as expressed in the will." *E.g., Meirs v. DeBona*, 550 N.W.2d 202 (Mich. 1996) (a beneficiary may not "use extrinsic evidence to prove that the testator's intent is other than set forth in the will"); *Bullis v. Downes*, 612 N.W.2d 435 (Mich. App. 2000) (will, revocable trust and deeds); *Espinosa v. Sparber, Shevin, Shapo, Rosen & Heilbronner*, 612 So.2d 1378 (Fla. 1993) (an action is allowed in Florida "if the intent shown by the will or trust itself is defeated by the lawyer's negligence"). Citing *Miers v. DeBona*, the Michigan Supreme Court upheld a summary judgment in favor lawyers who were charged with malpractice by failing to advise the deceased trustors regarding the consequences of not including a *Crummey* clause in the trust they prepared. *Sorkowitz v. Lakritz, Wissbrun & Associates, P.C.*, 706 N.W.2d 9 (Mich. 2005). A Florida appellate decision concluded that the lawyer who drew a will that disinherited a client's daughter did not owe a duty to the daughter although she was also a client and had been a beneficiary under the client's prior will. *Chase v. Bowen*, 771 So. 2d 1181 (Fla. App. 2000).

In some states, estate planning malpractice claims may be brought by a decedent's personal representative, but not by the beneficiaries of the decedent's estate. For example, *Nevin v. Union Trust Co.*, 726 A.2d 694 (Me. 1999), the court concluded "that individual beneficiaries do not have standing to sue estate planning attorneys for malpractice when they are not the client who retained the attorney and when the estate is represented by a personal representative who stands in the shoes of the client." 726 at p. 701.

Duty to Intended Beneficiaries. Courts in some other states have held that the lawyer who prepares a will or trust for a client owes a duty of care to the client's intended beneficiaries. Thus, in *Blair v. Ing*, 21 P.3d 452 (Haw. 2001), the court concluded that, "where the relationship between an attorney and a non-client is such that we would recognize a duty of care, the non-client may proceed under either negligence or contract theories of recovery." In that case the plaintiffs alleged that the lawyer drafted a defective trust for their father, as a result of which substantial additional death taxes were paid to the federal and state governments. Although the trust referred to a bypass trust, the document failed to include a mechanism for funding it. In determining that the scrivener owed a duty to his client's intended beneficiaries the court held that the intended beneficiaries could assert their claim whether or not they were named as beneficiaries in the will or trust. In doing so it stated that, "To limit a malpractice cause of action by a non-client to the face of the testamentary document that does not reflect the testator's true intent would render the recognition of a cause of action meaningless." *Id.* at 467. The court continued to state that, "the only obligation owed by the attorney to named beneficiaries is to exercise the requisite standard of care in fulfilling the intent of the testator as expressed in the will." *Id.* at 467. According to the court the facts alleged by the plaintiffs were sufficient to sustain causes of action for negligence and for breach of a third-party beneficiary contract.

Duties to Wards of Guardianships and Others Similarly Situated. In some states the attorney for a guardian is treated as having a lawyer-client relationship with the ward of the guardianship. *Branham v. Stewart*, 307 S.W.3d 94 (Ky. 2010). *See* § 1.6.11. Other states extend protection in other ways to those who lack legal capacity. Thus, in 2010 the Nebraska Supreme Court relaxed the privity rule in the case of minor children who were the statutory beneficiaries of a wrongful death action that a lawyer failed to commence within the time allowed. *Perez v. Stern*, 777 N.W.2d 545 (Neb. 2010). In *Perez* the court stated that where "a third party is a direct beneficiary of an attorney's retention, such that the end and aim of the attorney's representation is to affect the third party, then the interests favoring privity are not threatened by recognizing an attorney's duty to a third party whose interests he or she was actually hired to represent." (The court held that minor children were allowed to bring a malpractice claim against a lawyer who had been retained by the personal representative of their father's estate to bring a wrongful death action on their behalf, but who had failed to do so within the time allowed). While the Nebraska court stated that "it is entirely in keeping with the fiduciary and ethical duties attorneys owe their clients to require an attorney, who has been informed of the client's intent to benefit a third party, to exercise reasonable care and skill in that regard" it expressed approval of a prior decision that held "an attorney who prepared a decedent's will owed no duty to any particular alleged beneficiary of the will." One would think the outcome should be the same in both cases. That is, it would seem clear that a client's "end and aim" of retaining a lawyer to prepare a will is to assure that the persons designated by the client receive the benefits the client wishes them to receive.

Malpractice: Multifactor States. A large and growing number of states allow an action to be maintained by an intended beneficiary under the so-called multi-factor test that was first applied to lawyers by the California Supreme Court. *Biakanja v. Irving*, 320 P.2d 16 (Cal. 1958). In that case the court stated that whether, in the absence of privity, a lawyer would be held liable to a third party "is a matter of policy and involves the balancing of various factors, among which are the extent to which the transaction was intended to affect the plaintiff, the foreseeability of the harm to him, the degree of certainty that the plaintiff suffered injury, the closeness of the connection between the defendant's conduct and the injury suffered, the moral blame attached to the defendant's conduct and the injury suffered, and the policy of preventing future harm." 320 P.2d at 19 (Cal. 1958). *See also, e.g., Lucas v. Hamm*, 364 P.2d 685 (1961), *cert. denied*, 368 U.S. 987 (1962). In *Johnson v. Wiegers*, 46 P.3d 563 (Kan. App. 2002), the court considered the duty of the lawyer for a daughter, who obtained the services of the lawyer to change the beneficiary of her mother's IRA from her stepfather to herself and her siblings and, ultimately, to herself alone. The stepfather had already prevailed in an action to set aside the beneficiary designations because the decedent lacked capacity and was subject to undue influence. The Kansas Court of Appeals upheld dismissal of the action against the lawyer who represented the daughter and assisted her mother in changing the beneficiary designations of the IRA. According to the court, the lawyer represented the daughter and owed no duty to her stepfather, whose interests were adverse to her. According to the court, "if the client of the attorney and the third party are adversaries, no duty arises under *Nelson*." 46 P.3d at 468. *See* the discussion of *Haynes v. First National Bank*, 432 N.E.2d 890 (N.J. 1981), and ABA Formal Op. 02-428 at § 1.6.7.

A California Court of Appeal has held that under the multifactor test a lawyer owes a duty of care to an intended beneficiary who provides custodial care to a testator. The duty requires a lawyer to advise a client regarding the steps that must be taken to overcome the presumption of disqualification that otherwise applies to a beneficiary who is a custodial caregiver. *Osornio v. Weingarten*, 21 Cal. Rptr.3d 246 (6th Dist. 2004). According to the court, it was readily apparent that the intended beneficiary, Osornio, "*could have alleged* that Weingarten breached a duty of care owed to her: Weingarten negligently failed to advise Ellis [the testator] that the intended beneficiary under her 2001 will, Osornio, would be presumptively disqualified because of her relationship as Ellis's care custodian. Under this theory, Weingarten was negligent not only by failing to advise Ellis of the consequences of section 21350(a), he was also negligent in failing to address Osornio's presumptive disqualification by making arrangements to refer Ellis to independent counsel to advise her and to provide a Certificate of Independent Review required by section 21351(b)." 21 Cal. Rptr.3d at 262.

Self Improvement. A lawyer who lacks the knowledge or skills necessary to handle a particular matter may overcome the deficiency further study and effort. Thus, in some instances a lawyer can gain the necessary competence through preparation, research and study. Comment [2] to Rule 1.1 states that, "A lawyer can provide adequate representation in a wholly novel field through necessary study." Comment [4] continues to say that, "A lawyer may accept representation where the requisite level of competence can be achieved by reasonable preparation." There are, naturally, limits on the amount that a client can be billed for the lawyer's self-education.

Referral, Association or Consultation. A lawyer who lacks the competence to handle a matter may be under a duty to involve an expert, by referral, association, or consultation. Before involving an expert, the lawyer should first obtain the client's consent. An Ethical Consideration issued under the Model Code, E.C. 2-22, expresses the same view: "Without the consent of his client, a lawyer should not associate in a particular matter another client outside his firm."

In *Horne v. Peckham*, 158 Cal. Rptr. 714 (Cal. App. 1979), the court held that the lawyer who lacked the requisite skill was negligent for failing to involve an expert in preparing a short-term trust that did not achieve the intended income tax goal. In that case, the court approved a jury instruction stating that the lawyer was obligated to involve an expert:

> It is the duty of an attorney who is a general practitioner to refer his client to a specialist or recommend the assistance of a specialist if under the circumstances a reasonably careful and skillful practitioner would do so.
>
> If he fails to perform that duty and undertakes to perform professional services without the aid of a specialist, it is his further duty to have the knowledge and skill ordinarily possessed, and exercise the care and skill ordinarily used by specialists in good standing in the same or similar locality and under the same circumstances. A failure to perform any such duty is negligence. 158 Cal. Rptr. at 720.

An expert must, of course, be selected with care and adequately supervised by the lawyer. In *Estate of Lohm*, 440 Pa. 268, 269 A.2d 451 (1970), the court denied fees to the lawyer who was also a co-executor and to the expert retained by the co-executors for losses suffered by the estate, because of the executors' failure to file a federal estate tax return on time.

As suggested by the Court in *Horne*, a lawyer who lacks the skill to handle a particular matter could refer a client to an expert. Doing so may, of course, result in the client forming a permanent relationship with the expert and dropping the referring lawyer. Alternatively, the lawyer can seek the client's approval of associating an expert. The client's approval is required because the association will almost certainly involve the disclosure of confidential information to the expert. It is also necessary to reach an agreement with the client and the expert regarding the payment of the expert's fees.

Finally, the lawyer could, at his or her own expense, retain an expert as a consultant. However, "When one lawyer consults about a client matter with another lawyer who is not associated with him in the matter, both the consulting lawyer and the consulted lawyer must take care to fulfill their ethical obligations to their respective clients." ABA Formal Op. 1998-411. In particular, the consulted lawyer would be required to maintain the confidences of the consulting lawyer's client. Even so, in such a case, it is best to delete identifying information from documents provided to the expert. Such an approach also runs the risk that the expert will not receive all of the relevant information and does not have an opportunity personally to meet with the client.

While Opinion 1998-411 notes the value of "hypothetical or anonymous consultations" and states that the consulting lawyer may be impliedly authorized to disclose certain information, it cautions that both the consulting lawyer and the consulted lawyer must be careful to assure that their ethical duties are fulfilled. The opinion recommends steps that might be taken by both lawyers to minimize the potential risks to clients.

EXAMPLE 1-1

Lawyer, *L*, whose general practice includes some estate administration work, was retained by Client, *C*, who was named as executor of the will of her deceased uncle *U*. The primary asset of *U*'s estate of about $10 million was a 2,500 acre ranch that he had operated. *L*, who recognized that the federal estate tax return should be prepared by a more experienced person, recommended that *C* engage a recognized expert, *E*, to do so. In due course *C* retained *E*, who assumed all responsibility for preparing and filing the estate tax return, prepared and filed the return in a timely manner. Unfortunately, the return failed to elect the benefits of §§ 2032A and 6166 which injured the estate.

L, who is subject to the standard of care applicable to nonspecialists, probably fulfilled her responsibilities with respect to the federal estate tax returning by recommending that it be prepared by an expert, who assumed all responsibility for it. *E*, who is subject to a higher standard, is most likely liable for any loss caused by his negligent preparation of the return.

Drafting Error: Ambiguous Documents. A lawyer who prepares a will, trust or other estate planning document that is ambiguous may be subject to a malpractice action because of his or her failure of competence. Thus, an action may be brought by an incompletely or incorrectly described beneficiary. In some circumstances courts have held that the scrivener of a will or trust is not liable for costs that were incurred because the document was ambiguous; *e.g., Ventura County Humane Society v. Holloway*, 40 Cal.App.3d 897, 115 Cal. Rptr. 464 (1974) (ambiguous description of charitable beneficiary). In other instances, litigation may arise over an ambiguous direction regarding the payment of death taxes. In *Creighton University v. Kleinfeld*, 919 F. Supp. 1421 (E.D.Cal. 1995), the court denied the defendant-lawyers' motion for summary judgment dismissing a malpractice action that was based on failure to express clearly testator's intention regarding payment of death taxes and held that extrinsic evidence would be admissible to determine testator's intent.

Malpractice in Tax Matters. Malpractice claims in tax matters extend from ones based on the negligent loss of the marital deduction or the alternative valuation option, to the failure properly to plan or draft a life insurance trust or a disclaimer, and to the improper preparation or filing of tax returns. Feinschreiber and Kent, Estate Tax Malpractice, 84 Tax Notes 909 (May 9, 1999).

Clients may recover damages from lawyers who improperly advise them regarding tax matters. *See* § 1.6.3. Lawyers are generally "not required to exercise perfect judgment in every instance," *Ramp v. St. Paul Fire & Marine Ins. Co.*, 269 So. 2d 239, 244 (La. 1972). A lawyer may be liable, however, for having incorrectly advised a client regarding a tax matter even though no penalties are imposed on the client in litigation over the amount of taxes that were due, because there was "substantial authority" for the client's factual position. *Streber v. Hunter*, 221 F.3d 7001 (5th Cir. 2000). The outcome turns on the difference between the technical meaning of having "substantial authority" for a reporting position and whether advising a client to take such a position breached the duty of care.

Typographical Error. Lawyers may also be responsible for damages that result from typographical or other clerical errors in documents prepared by them. In the leading case, *Prudential Insurance Co. v. Dewey, Ballantine, Bushby, Palmer & Wood*, 573 N.Y.S.2d 981 (App.Div. 1991), the court rejected a motion to dismiss a claim based upon damages allegedly suffered because of the law firm's mistaken insertion of the sum $92,855 instead of $92,855,000. Liability might similarly be imposed on a lawyer who makes mistaken entries on tax returns, wills or trusts, and other documents.

Other Evidence of Incompetence. Preparation of seriously deficient tax returns is strong evidence of incompetence. On the document preparation side, a Los Angeles ethics opinion "seriously questions whether an attorney is performing competently if he or she drafts or amends a will in which he or she receives a gift under circumstances reasonably suggestive of undue influence." L.A. County Formal Op. 462 (1991). Drafting a document for an unrelated client that includes a substantial gift to the lawyer is barred by Rule 1.8(c). *See* § 1.6.8.

Duties of Fiduciaries. An executor or trustee is generally not required to review a document to determine whether it will achieve a desired tax saving. *Hatleberg v. Norwest Bank Wisconsin*, 700 N.W.2d 15 (Wis. 2005), (Court declines "to impose a general duty to review a trust document drafted by another and draw legal conclusions as to its effectiveness.") However, a trustee that negligently encouraged a trustor to continue making gifts to a trust that did not qualify for annual gift tax exclusions is liable for the additional estate taxes on the grantor's estate. *Id.*

§ 1.6.2. Rule 1.2: Scope of Representation and Allocation of Authority Between Client and Lawyer

> (a) Subject to paragraphs (c) and (d), a lawyer shall abide by a client's decisions concerning the objectives of the representation and, as required by Rule 1.4, shall consult with the client as to the means by which they are to be pursued. A lawyer may take such action on behalf of the client as is impliedly authorized to carry out the representation. A lawyer shall abide by a client's decision whether to settle a matter. In a criminal case, the lawyer shall abide by the client's decision, after consultation with the lawyer, as to a plea to be entered, whether to waive jury trial and whether the client will testify.
>
> (b) A lawyer's representation of a client, including representation by appointment, does not constitute an endorsement of the client's political, economic, social, or moral views or activities.
>
> (c) A lawyer may limit the scope of the representation if the limitation is reasonable under the circumstances and the client gives informed consent.
>
> (d) A lawyer shall not counsel a client to engage, or assist a client, in conduct that the lawyer knows is criminal or fraudulent, but a lawyer may discuss the legal consequences of any proposed course of conduct with a client and may counsel or assist a client to make a good faith effort to determine the validity, scope, meaning, or application of the law.

Rule 1.2(a) appropriately recognizes that a lawyer may take actions that are impliedly authorized by the representation. Although paragraph (c) allows a lawyer to limit the scope of a representation if the limitation is reasonable and the client gives informed consent, it is unclear how the requirement of informed consent will be applied in the estate planning field. Rule 1.0(e) defines informed consent as "the agreement by a person to a proposed course of conduct after the lawyer has communicated adequate information and explanation about the material risks of and reasonably available alternatives to the proposed course of conduct." In light of the definition of informed consent, if a client asks a lawyer to assist the client only with respect to one or two specific matters, must the lawyer advise the client of all of the risks, etc., of not engaging the lawyer more fully? Thus, if a lawyer wishes to accept a representation that is limited to helping a client collect the proceeds of life insurance polices on the life of a decedent, must the lawyer inform the client fully regarding tax matters, possibilities of disclaimers, and the like? One would hope not.

Acceptance of Representation: Engagement Letters. A lawyer must initially determine whether to accept a proffered representation. If the representation is accepted, the lawyer should send the client an engagement letter that defines the scope of the representation, including a description of the specific work to be performed, summarizes the basis upon which the lawyer's fee will be determined and describes how conflict and confidentiality issues will be handled. It is perhaps best to go over a draft of the engagement letter at the initial conference and for the final version to be signed by the lawyer and the client. A form of engagement letter, Form 1-1, is included at the end of this subsection. Even in jurisdictions that do not require lawyers to use engagement letters, it is desirable to provide a client with a written statement that covers these basic matters.

With regard to fees, Rule 1.5(b) provides: "The scope of the representation and the basis or rate of the fee and expenses for which the client will be responsible shall be communicated to the client, preferably in writing, before or within a reasonable time after commencing the representation, except when the lawyer will charge a regularly represented client on the same basis or rate." Rules in some jurisdictions require information regarding fees to be disclosed in a writing. *See, e.g.,* D.C. Rule 1.5(b) (2005). Also, California requires a written contract for services if the lawyer's fee will exceed $1,000. Cal. Bus. & Prof. Code § 6148 (2011).

Quoting a fixed fee to a client can lead to a dispute between the lawyer and the client if the work proves to be more complicated than anticipated, the documents require repeated revisions, or the client requires an unusual amount of consultations. Accordingly, a lawyer who quotes a fixed fee to a client should qualify the fee quote in an appropriate way. Providing a client with an estimate can cause a client to be very unhappy if the lawyer's actual billings exceed the amount of the estimate. See the discussion of the basis for determining fees and the use of an hourly or fixed rate fee approach in § 1.6.5.

An engagement letter is particularly important if the lawyer will represent multiple clients, such as co-fiduciaries or the beneficiaries of a fiduciary estate. In such a case the letter should specify what rule of confidentiality will apply consistent with Rule 1.6 and what action the lawyer will take if a conflict between the clients develops, Rule 1.7. A 1999 decision by the New Jersey Supreme Court illustrates the importance of clearly specifying whether the lawyer may, or must, disclose the confidences of one co-client to another. *A. v. B. v. Hill Wallack,* 726 A.2d 924 (N.J. 1999). Although there is an actual or potential conflict of interest between prospective clients, it may be possible for the lawyer to represent them. Doing so normally requires the full disclosure of the conflict, its consequences and informed consent by the clients, confirmed in writing. Rule 1.7; ABA Formal Op. 05-436. *See* § 1.6.7.

Engagement letters can provide clients with a better understanding of the scope of the representation, the time within which the services will be performed, and their cost. Otherwise, some clients, or their successors, may expect the lawyer to perform other, additional, or less expensive services. Failing to define the scope of the representation in an engagement letter creates a risk that the client may complain that the lawyer did not perform all of the services that the client expected. Thus, if the scope of the representation is not clearly defined, a decedent's children may claim that they were damaged when the lawyer who was hired to assist in the administration of a parent's estate failed to advise the surviving parent that she could disclaim some assets she was entitled to receive by reason of her husband's death. *Linck v. Barokas & Martin*, 667 P.2d 171 (Alaska 1983) (complaint states a cause of action); *Leipham v. Adams*, 77 Wash. App. 827 (1995) (claim denied, lawyer was retained to perform only specific services that did not include estate planning for surviving spouse); *Estate of Fitzgerald v. Linnus*, 765 A.2d 251 (N.J. Super. App. Div. 2001) ("The suggestion that an attorney retained to represent an estate has an affirmative obligation to engage an executrix-wife in post-mortem estate planning fails to recognize the realities of the retention and that of a limited attorney-client relationship." *Id.* at 259.)

Existing Clients, New Matters and Engagement Letters. In order to avoid misunderstandings, if there is any significant change in the scope of a representation, the lawyer should send the client a supplemental engagement letter. For example, if a lawyer agrees to assist an existing estate planning client in a new matter (*e.g.*, purchasing real estate or an interest in a business), the scope of the representation should be defined in a supplemental engagement letter. Similarly, as noted in §1.6.7, a lawyer who agrees to represent additional members of a client's family "must be sure that all parties understand who the lawyer represents and the role that the lawyer will play, including the limitations within which the lawyer must operate." The formality of a supplemental engagement letter depends on the circumstances and the relationship of the parties; in some cases, it may be appropriate to confirm the new or changed, representation in a short, informal note.

Reliance Upon Factual Representations by Clients; Duty to Inquire Further. As a matter of routine, a lawyer should point out to new clients the necessity that the client disclose all relevant facts to the lawyer. Some lawyers seek to obtain the required information by asking clients to complete rather comprehensive data collection forms while others rely primarily on personal interviews with the client. In either case, the client may be more forthcoming if the lawyer emphasizes that the information provided by the client will remain confidential.

In most instances a lawyer can accept factual statements made by a client without further inquiry. Thus, Circular 230 provides that a practitioner "generally may rely in good faith without verification upon information furnished by the client." §10.34(c).

For clarification and confirmation of important facts, a lawyer may send a client a follow-up letter that recounts the most important factual information provided by the client. If the client's circumstances are unusual, the lawyer should consider asking the client to confirm specific items of information. Verification can be particularly important if the client's objectives include asset protection. Some commentators suggest that, "If a client is already insolvent, faced with an impoverishing claim, or only *threatened* with an impoverishing claim, the attorney should undoubtedly decline any work in connection with transferring assets offshore." Duncan Osborne,

New Age Estate Planning, Offshore Trusts, U. Miami, 27th Inst. Est. Plan.,¶1701.4 (1993).

In some circumstances a lawyer who is consulted by a prospective client has a duty to make a factual inquiry prior to accepting the representation. In *Butler v. State Bar*, 228 Cal. Rptr. 499, 502 (Cal. 1986), the court stated that, "While an attorney may often rely upon statements made by the client without further investigation, circumstances known to the attorney may require investigation."

Declination Letter. If a representation is declined by either the lawyer or a prospective client, the lawyer should consider sending a "nonengagement" letter to the nonclient. Unless the lawyer sends such a letter, the declined prospective client may think that the lawyer-client relationship had been created between them. *Togstad v. Vesely, Otto, Miller & Keefe*, 291 N.W.2d 686 (Minn. 1980). *See* Pamela Blake, The Nonengagement Letter and the Disengagement Letter, 46 Wash. St. B. News 44 (1992). If the interests or claims of the declined client are, or may be, subject to time limitations, the declination letter should urge the declined client to consult other counsel promptly and warn that it might be necessary to take action promptly in order to avoid having possible claims barred by a statute of limitations. Such a warning is appropriate in the tax context if, for example, the time within which to file a return or a refund claim will soon expire. A sample form of declination letter, Form 1-2, appears at the end of this section.

If appropriate, a declination letter should also state that the person who consulted the lawyer did not communicate any confidential information to the lawyer. *See* Rule 1.18, §1.6.13. In that way the lawyer can reduce the risk that the lawyer will later be disqualified from representing a client whose interests are adverse to the person whose representation was declined.

Subsection (d) Prohibits Counseling or Assisting in Fraudulent Conduct. According to Comment [9], the rule prohibits "a lawyer from knowingly counseling or assisting a client to commit a crime or fraud." Importantly, the Comment distinguishes between "presenting an analysis of legal aspects of questionable conduct and recommending the means by which a crime or fraud might be committed with impunity." While a lawyer may not counsel or assist a client to engage in criminal or fraudulent conduct, he or she may discuss the legal consequences of any proposed course of conduct. In doing so, a lawyer may make a good faith effort to determine the validity, scope, meaning or application of the law.

As stated in Comment [12], "Paragraph (d) applies whether or not the defrauded party is a party to the transaction." Accordingly, a lawyer should not participate in a transaction "to effectuate criminal or fraudulent avoidance of tax liability."

Duties to Beneficiaries of Fiduciary Estate. Comment [11] also notes that "Where the client is a fiduciary, the lawyer may be charged with special obligations in dealing with a beneficiary."

Errors and Omissions in Tax Returns. Under §10.21 of Circular 230, a practitioner who is retained to assist a client with respect to a matter before the IRS and "knows that the client has not complied with the revenue laws of the United States or has made an error in or omission from any return, document, affidavit or other paper filed with the IRS," is required to advise the client of the noncompliance, error or omission. Accordingly, a lawyer who learns that a client has not filed gift tax returns with respect to gifts made in prior years, must advise the client of the omission. The lawyer should also advise the client to remedy the matter by reporting the gifts on appropriately prepared returns. If the required returns are not filed, the lawyer would be barred by Rule 1.2(d) from assisting the client in preparing and filing gift tax returns for subsequent years: If the earlier gifts are not properly reported, the later returns would be misleading or fraudulent. There is, however, generally no duty to file an amended tax return.

Clarify Limits on Lawyer Conduct. If a lawyer knows that a client expects the lawyer to assist the client in ways not permitted by the Rules or other laws, the lawyer must clarify the matter for the client. Thus, a lawyer who knows that a client expects the lawyer to assist the client in preparing a gift tax return that does not properly reflect prior unreported gifts, must inform that client that the lawyer cannot do so.

Form 1-1
Sample Engagement Letter

Mr. & Mrs. John Q. Client
1001 Washington Street
Our Town, XX 00000-0000
    Estate Planning
Dear Mr. & Mrs. Client:

Thank you for asking me to help you with your estate planning, which I will be pleased to do. As promised at our initial meeting, this letter describes the main aspects of my role. At the outset I should emphasize that I and all of our employees are obligated to hold confidential any information you provide to us.

Services to be Performed. We will perform such of the following services as we believe are reasonably necessary to assist you in designing, preparing and implementing a comprehensive estate plan:

1. Review your existing wills and other dispositive instruments (trusts, life insurance policies, etc.);
2. Review your property holdings, including how the property was acquired, the way in which title to the property is held, and tax bases;
3. Help you identify your estate planning goals and the ways by which those goals might be achieved, including how you wish to dispose of the property over which you have any power of disposition (including life insurance and employee benefits);
4. Prepare estimates of the federal tax consequences of the various ways in which your estate planning goals might be achieved;
5. Prepare the estate planning documents necessary to implement the plan you select, including drafting wills, trusts, property status agreements, health care directives and durable powers of attorney;
6. Supervise the execution of documents, changes of beneficiary, transfer of property, and other steps required to implement your plans, and
7. Prepare any tax returns that may be required because of the implementation of your plans

The execution of documents and implementation of your plan will conclude the active phase of our engagement. However, as a service to you, we will periodically send you letters suggesting that you review your estate plan and consider whether any changes should be made. We usually send the first reminder letter on the third anniversary of the date of execution of your documents.

Fee for Services. You will be billed for our estate planning services monthly [quarterly; when our work is completed]. As I explained when we met, the fee for our work will be based upon the time actually required to prepare and implement your plans. As supervising attorney I will be responsible for seeing that the work is carried out economically and efficiently, in which I may be assisted by other attorneys and legal assistants in our firm. My time will be billed at an hourly rate of $xxx. The hourly rates of my associates range between $xxx and $xxx and my legal assistants between $xxx and $xxx. (Our rates are usually adjusted upward slightly each year, effective xxxxxx.) While the total amount of our fee will be affected by the number and length of our meetings, the complexity of the plans you adopt and the number of drafts we prepare of various documents, based upon the information I now have, I estimate that the cost of formulating and implementing your estate plans will be between $xxxx and $xxxx.

[Alternate Text 1: Fee for Services. The fee for our estate planning services consists of two components: a document preparation fee and an hourly services fee. You will be billed a fixed documentation preparation fee for each document we prepare in connection with your estate plan according to the following schedule: [list fee for each document]. In addition, you will be billed for our services monthly [quarterly; when our work is completed] based upon the time actually spent in conferences, analysis, research, and related activities apart from preparing an initial draft of the documents in accordance with your instructions. As supervising attorney I will be responsible for seeing that the work is carried out economically and efficiently, in connection with which I may be assisted by other attorneys and legal assistants. My time for the hourly services will be billed at an hourly rate of $xxx. The hourly rates of my associates range between $xxx and $xxx and my legal assistants between $xxx and $xxx. (Our rates are usually adjusted upward slightly each year, effective xxxxxxx.) While the total amount of our hourly services fee will be affected by the number and length of our meetings and the complexity of the plans you adopt, I estimate that the total cost of formulating and implementing your estate plans will be between $xxxx and $xxxx.]

[Alternate Text 2: Fee for Services. Based on my understanding of your personal circumstances and your estate planning objectives, we will prepare a comprehensive estate plan for you, including reciprocal wills, durable powers of attorney, health care directives and an irrevocable life insurance trust for a fixed fee of $4,500. You will be billed for our services when our work is completed, which we anticipate can be done by [insert date]. The preparation of your estate plan will include the services described above other than step 7, the preparation of tax returns. The services include an allowance for having some additional meetings and consultations, making a reasonable number of changes and revisions in draft estate planning documents and assisting you in the implementation of your plan. We will consult with you before undertaking any additional work that would increase the amount of our fee, such as the preparation of tax returns, extensive revisions of estate planning documents, or, preparation of an unexpected number of additional estate planning documents.]

Confidentiality. Any information that we receive from either or both of you may be shared with others in our office in order to carry out our engagement. The information will not be communicated to others, particularly persons outside our office except to the extent we believe it is reasonably appropriate to review it with your financial advisors. As between yourselves, you have agreed that there will be complete and full disclosure and exchange of all information we receive from either of you that is relevant and material to our engagement. Accordingly, we will be free to share information with one of you that we receive from the other regardless of the time or manner in which it is communicated to us.

Conflicts. Each of you is free to develop an independent plan for the disposition of your property. Some couples establish plans that are mirror images of each other, but others do not. It is entirely possible that there may be some differences between your plans and the manner in which you each choose to dispose of your property. Such differences would not prevent us from assisting both of you. However, as I explained, we may not be able to represent both of you if it becomes necessary to negotiate and define your respective property interests in a property status agreement or if other conflicts of interest develop. Should a conflict arise, we may be required to withdraw from representing one or both of you.

If the foregoing accurately expresses our agreement, please sign and return the enclosed copy of this letter in the envelope provided.

Yours very truly,

Lawrence L. Lawyer

We confirm the engagement of your firm on the foregoing terms:

_____   _____

John Q. Client   Mary T. Client

Date: _____   Date: _____

Form 1-2
Declination Letter

Mr. John Q. Nonclient
1001 Washington Street
Our Town, XX 00000-0000
     Estate of Mrs. Nonclient
Dear Mr. Nonclient:

Thank you for visiting with me yesterday regarding the possibility that our firm would represent you in connection with a matter related to your late wife's estate. This confirms my oral advice to you that we will not be able to represent you.

From our brief conversation I understand that you may wish to pursue an estate tax refund claim on behalf of Mrs. Nonclient's estate. We have not seen a copy of Mrs. Nonclient's estate tax return and did not discuss with you the details of the claim you propose to make. However, because refund claims must be filed within a fixed period time after the estate tax return was filed, you should promptly pursue the possibility of filing a refund claim. Accordingly, I urge you to engage other counsel as soon as possible.

We regret that we were unable to assist you in this matter.

Yours very truly,

Lawrence L. Lawyer

§1.6.3. Rule 1.3: Diligence

A lawyer shall act with reasonable diligence and promptness in representing a client.

The subjects of this rule, diligence, and Rule 1.4, communication, are closely related. Procrastination, which is proscribed by this rule, is a common failing that can cause serious economic and emotional harm to clients.

Lack of diligence can result in particularly serious problems in the estate planning and tax areas. In particular, the failure promptly to prepare a dispositive document may have adverse tax consequences or prevent the client's intended beneficiaries from receiving their bequests.

Failure to Prepare or Obtain Execution of Documents. A client's intended beneficiaries may be without recourse against a dilatory lawyer particularly in states that require privity in order to maintain a malpractice action. Relevant cases include, *Victor v. Goldman*, 344 N.Y.S.2d 672 (N.Y. Sup.Ct. 1973) ("absent privity of contract, the simple omission by an attorney to prepare a new will or codicil naming a new beneficiary of some part of the decedent's estate does not, by itself, render the attorney liable to the alleged beneficiary"), *aff'd mem.*, 43 A.D.2d 1021, 351 N.Y.S.2d 956 (1974); *Krawczyk v. Stingle*, 543 A.2d 733 (Conn. 1988) (in reversing a decision for the disappointed beneficiaries, the court stated, "that the imposition of liability to third parties for negligent delay in the execution of estate planning documents would not comport with a lawyer's duty of undivided loyalty to the client"); *Gregg v. Lindsay*, 649 A.2d 935 (Pa. Super. 1994); *Radovich v. Locke-Paddon*, 35 Cal. App.4th 946, 41 Cal. Rptr. 2d 573 (1995) (the court held the lawyer owed no duty to intended beneficiary where lawyer met with terminally ill client in June, delivered draft will to her in October and made no follow up and client died in December without having executed the will). The *Radovich* case was followed in *Chang v. Lederman*, 172 Cal. App.4th 67 (2009) and *Hall v. Kalfayan*, 190 Cal. App.4th 927 (2010). Note, however, that in some circumstances an attorney may owe a duty of care to an intended beneficiary. For example, the same court that decided *Radovich* later held that the testator's lawyer owed a duty of care to a beneficiary named in her will, whose gift was presumptively subject to disqualification because the beneficiary provided custodial care to the testator. *Osornio v. Wingarten*, 21 Cal. Rptr.3d 246 (2004), *see* §1.6.3. In any case, a lawyer who delays in the preparation of estate planning documents for a client takes serious risks.

Unreasonable delay by a lawyer in assisting a client may cause a client unnecessary anxiety and emotional distress. In an extreme case, *People v. James*, 502 P.2d 1105 (Colo. 1972), a Colorado lawyer who had been censured on two prior occasions was disbarred for failing, for eight months, to prepare a will for an anguished elderly client. In another Colorado case, *People v. Van Nocker*, 490 P.2d 698 (1971), a Colorado lawyer was indefinitely suspended for repeatedly failing to respond to her clients, for apparently failing to file her clients' income tax returns and to return their wills to them.

Delay in Tax Matters. On the tax side, the failure to file a timely tax return or refund claim may result in disciplinary action against the lawyer. In *Matter of*

Robertson, 612 A.2d 1236 (D.C. App. 1992), the lawyer was suspended for 90 days for failure, for several years, to file income tax returns for a client. A New York lawyer was censured for several violations, including the failure to file an estate inventory and the New York state estate tax return within the time required. *In re Frank T. D'Onofrio*, 205 A.D.2d 115, 618 N.Y.S.2d 829 (1994). (The same lawyer was later suspended for two years for other violations. *In re Frank T. D'Onofrio*, 242 A.D.2d 311, 672 N.Y.S.2d 889 (1998).) In particularly egregious cases, the IRS Director of Practice may take action against the lawyer. In addition, the injured parties may recover damages from the lawyer in a malpractice action. *E.g., Cameron v. Montgomery*, 225 N.W.2d 154 (Iowa 1975). However, unless the injured parties promptly bring a malpractice action, doing so may be barred by the relevant statute of limitations. *U.S. v. Gutterman*, 701 F.2d 104 (9th Cir. 1983) (holding that under California law the statute of limitations for negligent tax services would begin to run no later than the date of the resulting tax assessment).

If a tax return is not filed on time, penalties may be imposed unless the failure was due to reasonable cause. The failure to file an estate tax return on time is not excused by the personal representative's reliance on an attorney's advice, which does not constitute "reasonable cause" that would avoid the imposition of a late-filing penalty. *U.S. v. Boyle*, 469 U.S. 241 (1985). A personal representative or trustee may, however, pursue a malpractice action against a lawyer or accountant whose negligence was responsible for the imposition of a penalty. *E.g., Pair v. Queen*, 2 A.3d 1063 (D.C. App. 2010) (action by two of the co-personal representatives against a lawyer who was also the third personal representative for his negligence in the preparation and filing of the estate tax return).

Due Diligence under Circular 230. Section 10.23 of Circular 230 touches on promptness by prohibiting practitioners from unreasonably delaying the disposition of any matter before the IRS. Also, a lawyer was reprimanded for canceling five appointments with IRS appeals officers without cause, which constituted a violation of § 10.23. Scenarios of Disciplinary Action Taken by the Director of Practice, 1995-2 C.B. 510.

Rule 1.3 and the Comments to it appear to impose a duty of diligence only in terms of promptness. In contrast, § 10.22 of Circular 230 requires that practitioners obtain adequate information regarding tax matters. Specifically, § 10.22 requires persons admitted to practice before the IRS to exercise due diligence in (1) preparing, approving and filing returns and other documents, (2) determining the correctness of representations made by him or her to the Department of the Treasury, and (3) determining the correctness of representations made by his or her clients regarding any matter before the IRS.

Section 10.34(a) also imposes duties upon practitioners in preparing returns and in advising clients to take a position on returns. In brief, a practitioner may not sign a return if the practitioner determines that the return contains a position that does not have a realistic possibility of being sustained on the merits unless the position is not frivolous and is adequately disclosed on the return. As described in § 10.34(d)(1), a position has a realistic possibility of being upheld if a reasonable inquiry by a knowledgeable person indicates that it has at least a one-in-three likelihood of being upheld. Consistently, a practitioner may not advise a client to take a position on a return unless the position has a realistic possibility of being upheld on the merits or the position is not frivolous and the practitioner advises the client of the opportunity to avoid penalties by adequately disclosing the position.

Further, under § 10.51 a practitioner may be disciplined for a variety of offenses, including knowingly giving, or participating in any way in the giving, of false or misleading information to the Treasury or the IRS.

Section 10.34(c) provides that a practitioner "generally may rely in good faith without verification upon information furnished by the client." Despite the language of § 10.34(c), the Scenarios of Disciplinary Action issued by the Office of the Director of Practice (1997-1 C.B. 827), indicate that a tax return preparer cannot safely rely on a client's characterization of certain matters, such as the business use of an automobile or the business purpose of travel. According to the Scenarios, the failure to inquire further in such cases constitutes a lack of diligence in preparing returns required by § 10.22, which the Director of Practice may consider to be a violation of § 10.51.

§ 1.6.4. Rule 1.4: Communication

 (a) A lawyer shall:

   (1) promptly inform the client of any decision or circumstance with respect to which the client's informed consent, as defined in Rule 1.0(e), is required by these Rules;

   (2) reasonably consult with the client about the means by which the client's objectives are to be accomplished;

   (3) keep the client reasonably informed about the status of the matter;

   (4) promptly comply with reasonable requests for information; and

   (5) consult with the client about any relevant limitation on the lawyer's conduct when the lawyer knows that the client expects assistance not permitted by the Rules of Professional Conduct or other law.

 (b) A lawyer shall explain a matter to the extent reasonably necessary to permit the client to make informed decisions regarding the representation.

Effective communication between a lawyer and client is essential to the establishment and continuation of a satisfactory professional relationship—particularly in the tax and estate planning context. First, the lawyer must provide the client with sufficient information to allow the client to make informed choices regarding the scope of the representation. Ethical Consideration 7-8 agrees: "A lawyer should exert his best efforts to insure that decisions of his client are made only after the client has been informed of relevant considerations. A lawyer ought to initiate this decision making process if the client does not do so." Second, the lawyer must keep the client informed regarding the progress of the representation. Finally, the lawyer must respond promptly to a client's requests for information.

The extent to which a client must be provided with information naturally depends upon the nature of the representation and the terms upon which the lawyer accepted the engagement. These matters should be set out in an engagement letter, together with a tentative time table. As stated in Comment [5] to Model Rule 1.4, "The guiding principle is that the lawyer should fulfill reasonable client expectations for information consistent with the duty to act in the client's best interests, and the client's overall requirements as to the character of [the] representation."

A client can be informed about estate planning options in a variety of ways. Some lawyers do so primarily through discussions at early client conferences, perhaps supplemented by computer generated tax estimates. Others provide clients by with memos that deal with the basics of the federal transfer tax system and describe estate planning techniques (*e.g.*, ones concerning the advantages of inter vivos gifts (*see* Chapters 2 and 7); the use of irrevocable life insurance trusts (*see* Chapter 6); qualified personal residence trusts (*see* Chapter 9); and family limited partnerships or limited liability companies (*see* Chapter 11). Some firms provide clients with descriptive audio or video tapes on selected topics.

Note that the duty properly to inform a client of all relevant information may qualify a lawyer's duty not to disclose confidences of a co-client. *See A. v. B. v. Hill Wallack*, 726 A.2d 924 (N.J. 1999), § 1.6.6.

Unless a lawyer and client otherwise agree, subsections (a)(3) and (4) of this rule require a lawyer to keep a client reasonably informed regarding the status of a matter and to comply with reasonable requests for information. The degree of communication that is required will, of course, vary according to the nature of the representation, the circumstances of the client and the lawyer, and the reasonable expectations of each. Restatement § 20 also requires that a lawyer keep a client reasonably informed, consult with a client to a reasonable extent regarding decisions to be made regarding the representation, and promptly comply with a client's reasonable requests for information.

The Model Code does not contain a requirement similar to this rule. However, under DR 6-101(A)(3) a lawyer may not "neglect a legal matter entrusted to him." In addition, some E.C.s indicate that lawyers should keep their clients informed as the representation progresses. (Ethical Consideration 9-2 states that, "a lawyer should fully and promptly inform his client of material developments in the matters being handled for the client.")

Informed Decisions; Educating the Client. Rule 1.4(b) requires a lawyer to explain a matter to the extent necessary to allow the client "to make informed decisions regarding the representation." In some cases lawyers have been disciplined for failing to keep clients informed or failing to respond to client inquiries. A client who is injured by a lawyer's failure to communicate may also bring a malpractice action against the lawyer. In *Matter of Winter,* 187 Wis.2d 308, 522 N.W.2d 504 (1994), a lawyer was suspended for 60 days for failure to keep clients reasonably informed and to respond to their reasonable requests for information as required by Rule 1.4 and for failure to act with reasonable diligence in the probate of an estate in violation of Rule 1.3. As indicated by ABA Formal Op. 02-426, in order to inform an estate planning client adequately, a lawyer may disclose that the lawyer would be willing to serve as a fiduciary: "The lawyer is required by Rule 1.4(b) to discuss frankly with the client her options in selecting an individual to serve as fiduciary . . . .When exploring the options with his client, the lawyer may disclose his own availability to serve as a fiduciary." *See* §1.6.7.

§1.6.5. Rule 1.5: Fees

(a) A lawyer shall not make an agreement for, charge, or collect an unreasonable fee or an unreasonable amount for expenses. The factors to be considered in determining the reasonableness of a fee include the following:

  (1) the time and labor required, the novelty and difficulty of the questions involved, and the skill requisite to perform the legal service properly;

  (2) the likelihood, if apparent to the client, that the acceptance of the particular employment will preclude other employment by the lawyer;

  (3) the fee customarily charged in the locality for similar legal services;

  (4) the amount involved and the results obtained;

  (5) the time limitations imposed by the client or by the circumstances;

  (6) the nature and length of the professional relationship with the client;

  (7) the experience, reputation, and ability of the lawyer or lawyers performing the services; and

  (8) whether the fee is fixed or contingent.

(b) The scope of the representation and the basis or rate of the fee and expenses for which the client will be responsible shall be communicated to the client, preferably in writing, before or within a reasonable time after commencing the representation, except when the lawyer will charge a regularly represented client on the same basis or rate. Any changes in the basis or rate of the fee or expenses shall also be communicated in writing.

(c) , (d) [The rules regarding contingent fees and division of fees, which were changed in several respects in 2002, are omitted.] (Text of Rule 1.5 quoted from the Delaware Rules of Professional Conduct.)

Both Rule 1.5(a) and Restatement §34 ban charging fees that are unreasonable under the circumstances. Note that under paragraph (b) at the outset of a representation the lawyer must, in most instances, communicate with the client about the scope of the representation and the fee, preferably in writing. A client should be informed at the outset of any practices the lawyer has regarding changes in the basis of determining the fee or charging expenses. Without such a disclosure, a lawyer may not unilaterally increase his or her rates once a representation has begun. Note that the last sentence of paragraph (b) requires that any change in the basis or rate of the fee or expenses must be communicated in writing.

Basis of Fee. The basis upon which a lawyer's fee is to be determined is one of the subjects that is appropriately discussed at the initial meeting with a client and covered in an engagement letter. Unless the lawyer will charge a regularly represented client on the same basis or rate, subsection (b) requires the lawyer to communicate the basis or rate of the fee to the client, "preferably in writing, before or within a reasonable time after commencing the representation." Model Code E.C. 2-19 is to the same effect, fees should be discussed "as soon as possible after a lawyer has been employed." As noted in Comment [2] to Rule 1.5, "A written statement concerning the terms of the engagement reduces the possibility of misunderstanding."

Under Restatement § 38(1), "Unless the communication is unnecessary for the client because the lawyer has previously represented that client on the same basis or at the same rate, a lawyer must inform a client of the basis or rate of the fee before or within a reasonable time after beginning to represent a client. The information should be given "in writing when applicable rules so provide."

If it is reasonably foreseeable that the lawyer's fee will exceed $1,000, California requires a written contract for services, which specifies the hourly rates, statutory fees or flat fees, and other standard rates, fees and other charges, the nature of the services to be performed, and the respective responsibilities of the lawyer and the client. Cal. Bus. & Prof. Code. § 6148(a) (2011). If the requirements of § 6148 are not complied with, the agreement is voidable at the option of the client, in which case the lawyer is entitled to recover a reasonable fee. § 6148(c).

Hourly or Fixed Rate Fee: Percentage Schedules. The most common fee arrangements for estate planning services are based either on an hourly rate or on a flat, or fixed, fee for certain services. For example, a lawyer and client may agree that the fee for a lawyer's services will be based upon an agreed hourly rate (*e.g.,* $xxx per hour) or for a fixed dollar amount (*e.g.,* $3,500). Some thoughtful commentators believe that a fixed fee (project or value) approach billing for estate planning services is generally more acceptable to clients than hourly billing. Harrison & Kuo, Fees: How to Charge, Collect and Defend Them, 148 Tr. & Est. 50 (Mar. 2009). According to the authors, "The hourly rate concept is often from the outset perceived as unfair by consumers, independent of the actual amount of the rate or its relation to the marketplace. That's why we and others suggest that practitioners get away from hourly billing and, as much as possible, engage in project/value billing for estate planning."

Until the last quarter of the 20th century, the fees of lawyers for estate administration services were usually determined by applying a percentage schedule to the value of the estate subject to administration. In some states the fee of the lawyer for a personal representative is still largely determined in that manner. *E.g.,* Cal. Prob. Code § 10810 (2010). However, in *Goldfarb v. Virginia State Bar,* 421 U.S. 773 (1975), the U.S. Supreme Court held that fee schedules prescribed by bar associations violated federal anti-trust laws. The Court did not pass on the legality of fee schedules prescribed by states, which are presumably within the "state action" exception to the Sherman Antitrust Act. Courts in some states condemn the use of percentage schedules. *E.g., Estate of Presont,* 560 A.2d 160 (Pa. Super. 1989).

In any case, Rule 1.5 requires a lawyer's fee to be reasonable in light of the relevant facts. A lawyer may be disciplined for charging an excessive fee in a probate matter. *In re Tuley,* 907 P.2d 844 (Kan. 1995) (lawyer publicly censured for charging fee of $97,500 where the estate was under $1.2 million).

§ 1.6.5

According to Comment [4] a fee paid in property instead of money may be subject to the stringent requirements of Rule 1.8. Consistently, Comment [1] to Rule 1.8 advises that the requirements of Rule 1.8 must be met if "the lawyer accepts an interest in a client's business or other nonmonetary property as payment of all or part of a fee."

Document Preparation Fees. Some practitioners use a combination approach that includes a fixed "base fee" or "document preparation fee" for each document drafted as part of the estate plan, plus an hourly fee for conferences, analysis, research, and the like. The document preparation fees are often billed at the time the client receives the draft documents for review, while the hourly fees are normally billed after the client executes the documents. Practitioners using this hybrid billing approach should be careful to explain it carefully in an engagement letter. Suggested language explaining this arrangement is provided in the alternate text in the sample engagement letter at §1.6.2.

Premium Rates: Discounts. In some cases the circumstances may justify charging an hourly or fixed rate that is higher than normal. For example, higher rates are justified when clients impose short deadlines or a client's plan involves an unusually high degree of expertise or risk due to the amounts involved or its complexity. Charging a higher rate in such cases is justified and authorized by the factors listed in Rule 1.5(a). The factors include: "the time and labor required, the novelty and difficulty of the questions involved, and the skill requisite to perform the legal service properly," "the amount involved and the results obtained," and "the time limitations imposed by the client or by the circumstances."

Executive Estate Planning; Discounts. Some lawyers offer discounts to estate planning clients in some circumstances. For example, a "volume discount" might be offered to a business that pays the cost of providing estate planning services to its executives. Likewise, a lawyer may discount the cost of providing services to members of a group who participate in the same, or similar, insurance and employee benefit plans. On the same theory some lawyers discount the fee for services provided to multiple members of the same family.

Tax Deductibility; Lifetime Estate Planning Services. A portion of the lawyer's fee for estate planning services may be deductible by a client under §212. However, the deduction is subject to the 2 percent floor on the deductibility of miscellaneous itemized deductions imposed by §67. In the case of an individual, §212 allows a deduction for ordinary and necessary expenses incurred during the taxable year,

(1) for the management, conservation, or maintenance of property held for the production of income; or

(2) in connection with the determination, collection, or refund of any tax.

In Rev. Rul. 72-545, 1972-2 C.B. 179, the IRS held that a deduction was allowable under §212(3) for the portion of a lawyer's fee attributable to advice regarding the income, gift, and estate tax consequences of a divorce. Some part of the lawyer's fee incurred in connection with the creation and administration of a revocable trust composed of income producing property may be deductible under §212(3). However, the creation of the trust may be for personal reasons and not for the management of income producing property. *See Arthur K. Wong*, 58 T.C.M. 3519 (1989). In *Wong* the court allowed a deduction for the portion of the lawyer's fee that related to tax advice regarding the creation and administration of the trust.

Statements sent to a client for estate planning services should identify the amount that is deductible under § 212, subject to the limit of § 67. In order to support such an allocation the lawyer should keep adequate records of the time spent on various work for a client. It is not enough that the lawyer performed work that had some tax consequences.

Nondeductible Personal Expenses. Note, however, that § 262 disallows deductions for "personal, living, or family expenses" not otherwise allowed. The preparation of a will and related documents is considered to be personal in nature and not deductible under § 212. *Estate of Helen S. Pennell*, 4 B.T.A. 1039 (1926). Health care directives, durable powers of attorney and other similar documents should be treated in the same way. Expenses incurred in connection with the defense or perfection of title to property are generally not deductible. § 263 (capital expenditures) and Reg. § 1.212-1(k).

Tax Deductibility; Post Mortem Services. The fees of the personal representative and the lawyer for the personal representative are deductible for income or estate tax purposes, but not for both. *See* § 12.13. Under the regulations, a portion of a deduction may be claimed for income tax purposes and the balance for estate tax purposes. Reg. § 1.642(g)-2. Under § 2053 the fees are deductible whether they are incurred with respect to property subject to claims or not subject to claims. Reg. § § 20.2053-3; 20.2053-8. However, fees incurred by beneficiaries are generally not deductible by the estate (they are not administration expenses) or by the beneficiaries (they are personal in nature).

Charges for Nonlegal Services and Disbursements. ABA Formal Op. 93-379 states that "A lawyer may not charge a client for overhead expenses generally associated with properly maintaining, staffing and equipping an office; however, the lawyer may recoup expenses reasonably incurred in connection with the client's matter for services performed in-house, such as photocopying, long distance telephone calls, computer research, special deliveries, secretarial overtime, and other similar services, so long as the charge reasonably reflects the lawyer's actual cost for the services rendered. A lawyer may not charge a client more than her disbursement for services provided by third parties like court-reporters, travel agents or expert witnesses except to the extent that the lawyer incurs costs additional to the direct cost of the third party services."

Change in Basis of Fee. At the initial conference a lawyer and client should discuss and agree on the way in which the lawyer's fee will be determined and the agreement should be confirmed in writing such as an engagement letter. If the lawyer's time will be billed at an hourly rate, the agreement should indicate whether the rate is subject to periodic adjustment—otherwise the lawyer's hourly rate may not be increased without the client's informed consent. *See* Form 1-1, § 1.6.2; Fucile, *Changing Horses in Midstream—Modifying Fee Agreements*, 64 Wash. St. Bar J. 33 (Dec. 2010).

Overbilling. ABA Ethics Opinions state the obvious regarding some fee matters: A lawyer who has agreed to be compensated on an hourly basis may not, (1) bill for more than the number of hours actually worked on a client's matter; (2) charge the same hours to more than one client; and (3) may not charge a second client for research already performed and charged to another. ABA Formal Op. 93-379. The opinion states that "A lawyer who flies for six hours for one client, while working for five hours on behalf of another, has not earned eleven billable hours."

"My fees are quite high, and yet you say you have little money. I think I'm seeing a conflict of interest here."

(Drawing by Leo Cullum; © 1989 The New Yorker Magazine, Inc.)

Time entries should be made on a current basis and should describe the work performed with reasonable detail. The following passage from a disciplinary case points out the unreliability of reconstructed records and billings based on estimates of the lawyer's time:

> Guidance from two federal appellate courts is relevant here. The Tenth Circuit has written that "we believe that reconstructed records generally represent an overstatement or understatement of time actual expended." *Ramos v. Lamm*, 713 F.2d 546, 553 n. 2 (10th Cir. 1983). The Second Circuit has noted that "[t]here is no excuse for an established law firm to rely on estimates made on the eve of payment and almost entirely unsupported by daily records." *In re Hudson & Manhattan R.R. Co.*, 339 F.2d 114, 115 (2d Cir. 1964). *Matter of Dann*, 136 Wash. 2d 67 (1998).

The opinion reinforces the necessity of maintaining accurate, contemporaneous time records.

Contingent Fees. Rule 1.5 does not itself bar the use of a contingent fee in a tax or estate planning matter. Circular 230 indicates that it is permissible to have a contingent fee agreement relating to various estate planning matters including, for example, an estate or gift tax refund claim. ABA Formal Op. 94-389 states that, "It is ethical to charge contingent fees so long as the fee is appropriate and reasonable and the client has been fully informed of the availability of alternative billing arrangements." Another ABA opinion, Formal Opinion 93-373, discusses "reverse" contingent fee agreements, in which the fee is determined by the amount saved for a client. A 1963 decision by the New York Court of Appeals allowed fees to be recovered under a single contingent fee contract entered into by a taxpayer on the one hand and by a lawyer and an accountant on the other. *Blumenberg v. Neubecker*, 12 N.Y.2d 456, 191 N.E.2d 269 (1963). However, some states more extensively regulate the use of contingent fee contracts. *E.g.*, Cal. Bus. & Prof. Code § 6147 (2011). An earlier version of Circular 230 required a practitioner who had entered into a contract to represent a client before the Treasury Department on a wholly or partially contingent fee to file a written statement "containing the terms of the contract as they relate to compensation." Former Circular 230, § 10.2, quoted in *Muldoon v. West End Chevrolet, Inc.*, 338 Mass. 91, 153 N.E.2d 887 (1958).

Subsection 10.27(a) of Circular 230 prohibits practitioners from charging an unconscionable fee for representing a client before the IRS. Subsection (b) prohibits contingent fees for preparing an original return or for any advice rendered in connection with a position taken on an original tax return. Standing alone, Rule 1.5 does not prohibit a contingent fee arrangement in connection with the preparation of an original return. However, such an arrangement is barred by subsection (c), which prohibits contingent fees that are prohibited by "other law." Subsection (b)(3) of Circular 230 allows a contingent fee to "be charged for preparation of or advice in connection with an amended tax return or a claim for refund (other than a claim for refund made on an original return) if the practitioner reasonably anticipates at the time the fee arrangement is entered into that the amended return or claim will receive substantive review by the Internal Revenue Service."

Expert Witness. The Model Code and the Model Rules both prohibit lawyers from paying a witness a fee that is contingent on the outcome of the case. Model Rule 3.4(b); Model Code DR 7-109(C). Section 302 of the Ethics Rulings of AICPA bans the use of contingent fees for accounting services. However, it provides, "Fees are not regarded as being contingent if fixed by courts or other public authorities or, in tax matters, if determined based on the results of judicial proceedings or the findings of governmental agencies." *See Shore v. Parklane Hosiery Co., Inc.*, 1978 U.S. Dist. LEXIS 14211 (S.D.N.Y. 1978). The Model Code provides in DR 7-109(C) that a lawyer, "shall not pay, offer to pay, or acquiesce in the payment of compensation to a witness contingent upon the content of his testimony or the outcome of the case." Rule 3.4(b) which provides that a lawyer shall not, "falsify evidence, counsel or assist a witness to testify falsely, or offer an inducement to a witness that is prohibited by law," is also considered to bar the fee of a witness from being tied to the outcome of a case. Comment [3] to Rule 3.4 states that, "The common law rule in most jurisdictions is that it is improper to pay an occurrence witness any fee for testifying and that it is improper to pay an expert witness a contingent fee."

Fee Splitting With Nonlawyers. Rule 5.4(a), and its counterpart in the Model Code, DR 3-102(A), prohibit lawyers from splitting fees with nonlawyers. The prohibition is intended to preserve the independence of lawyers in representing a client. Comment [1], Rule 5.4. A similar concern prevents lawyers from being engaged by an intermediary, whose interests and directions may be contrary to the interests of the client. The concern was raised in *Joffe v. Wilson*, 381 Mass. 47, 407 N.E.2d 342 (1980), in which an accountant retained a lawyer to bring an income tax refund claim on behalf of a plaintiff who had engaged the accountant on a contingent fee basis. Although the arrangement constituted intermediation, the court upheld allowing the accountant a reasonable fee for his services—in an amount equal to the contingent fee provided for in his contract with the taxpayer. The New York Court of Appeals has held that the rule does not prevent a lawyer and an accountant from entering into a single contingent fee contract to render services to in their respective fields to a client in a tax matter. *Blumenberg v. Neubecker*, 12 N.Y.2d 456, 191 N.E.2d 269 (1963). The opinion in *Blumenberg* states that, "It is of no consequence that their retainer was effected by a single agreement or that their compensation was to be equal or that it was specified in a lump sum contingency percentage, as long as the fee provided for the accountant was to be for accounting services rendered by him, and the fee for the lawyer for legal services which he was to perform." 191 N.E.2d at 271.

In the ordinary case making gifts to persons who refer business to a lawyer is permissible. The same is true of hosting luncheons, dinners or parties for them. A lawyer should, however, be wary of making substantial gifts to sources of business—at least ones that might be considered to involve a disguised form of fee-sharing.

The extent to which lawyers may engage in a mixed practice with nonlawyers, such as accountants, financial advisors and insurance professionals varies somewhat from jurisdiction to jurisdiction. The drive to authorize greater interdisciplinary practice was, in effect, derailed by the financial scandals that involved Enron and many other businesses in the early years of the 21st century.

No Rebates, Kickbacks or Secret Benefits. A lawyer may not obtain and retain undisclosed economic benefits in connection with a representation. ABA Formal Op. 93-379 reflects the proper approach: "if a lawyer receives a discounted rate from a third party provider, it would be improper if she did not pass along the benefit of the discount to her client rather than charge the client the full rate and reserve the profit to herself." Similarly, a lawyer cannot accept payments from other professionals to whom the lawyer refers clients for services. L.A. County Op. 443 (1987) (physician). Most opinions conclude that the prohibition is not lifted by disclosing the benefit to the client and obtaining the client's apparent consent. San Diego Op. 89-2, "Disclosure and consent by the client (per Rule 3-300) does not cure the abuse."

Commissions for Nonlegal Services. Some earlier ethics opinions allowed lawyers to retain commissions paid by nonclients. For example, N.Y. Formal Op. 107(a) (1970) held that with full disclosure and client consent, a lawyer could retain a commission paid by a financial company with respect to amounts deposited by the lawyer's clients. However, note that the opinion is inconsistent with a subsequent opinion, N.Y. Op. 619 (1991), which held that a lawyer could not offer life insurance products to estate planning clients if the lawyer had a financial interest in the particular products recommended. South Carolina Op. 90-16 (1990) concludes that with full disclosure lawyer's may refer estate planning clients to an insurance agency which is 50-percent owned by the law firm. Virginia reached essentially the same result in Opinion 1754 (2001), which concludes that an estate planning lawyer who is also a licensed insurance agent may, with full disclosure and consent, collaborate with an insurance agent in designing a comprehensive insurance plan and receive one-half of the commissions payable with respect to insurance policies purchased by the client. The opinion notes that, "since the transaction will create a business relationship between the attorney and the client, Rule 1.8(a) requires that the transaction must be fair and reasonable and the terms fully disclosed to the client, in writing. In addition, the client must be 'advised in writing of the desirability of seeking, and is given a reasonable opportunity to seek the advice of independent counsel on the transaction,' and the client gives informed consent in a signed writing that includes the essential terms of the transaction and the lawyer's role in it."

Referral Fees. Ethics opinions differ as to whether a lawyer may accept a referral fee from a third party who provides services to the lawyer's client. Some states, including North Carolina, prohibit lawyers from accepting referral fees. For example, North Carolina Formal Op. 99-1 concluded that a lawyer may not receive a referral fee from a third party, an investment advisory firm, even with full disclosure to the client:

> If a lawyer will receive a referral fee from the third party, the lawyer's professional judgment in making the referral is or may be impaired. Written disclosure to the client will not neutralize the potential for the lawyer's self-interest to impair his or her judgment.

In contrast, ethics opinions from some other states hold that Rules 1.7 and 1.8 do not absolutely prohibit the acceptance of a referral fee. For example, Joint Formal Op. 2000-100 of the Pennsylvania Bar Association Legal Ethics and Professional Responsibility Committee and the Philadelphia Bar Association Professional Guidance Committee states that:

> A lawyer should exercise extreme caution when offered a referral fee by a service provider. Before accepting a referral fee, the lawyer must reasonably believe that accepting the fee will not interfere with the lawyer's exercise of independent professional judgment and duty of loyalty, and the client must consent to payment of the fee only after full disclosure and consultation. In many cases, the above analysis will lead the lawyer to conclude that the lawyer may not accept the fee or should rebate the fee to the client.

An opinion by the State Bar of Utah, Op. 99-07 (1999), is to the same general effect: "It is not per se unethical for a lawyer to refer a client to an investment advisor and take a referral fee from the commission paid to that advisor, although the lawyer has a heavy burden to insure compliance with the applicable ethical rules."

The Supreme Court of Ohio has ruled that a lawyer may provide financial planning services through a law firm if the services are related to the provision of legal services. Ethics Op. 2000-4. However, the opinion cautions that the fee for the services should not be based upon the total value of the fund, which might subject the lawyer and the lawyer's records to state inspection. Instead, the opinion suggests the lawyer should charge a fixed, flat, or hourly fee. A subsequent opinion from Utah concluded that "charging clients an annual fee for estate planning and asset protection legal services based on a percentage of the value of the assets involved is likely to be ethical only in extraordinary circumstances."

Incidental Benefits. Minor incidental benefits, such as frequent flier miles accrued on trips made for clients, should not present a problem. Mass. Op. 94-1. However, free tickets or other significant benefits that accrue as a result of frequent trips taken on behalf of a single client should be utilized for the benefit of that client. Utah Op. 01-04 (2001).

§1.6.6. Rule 1.6: Confidentiality of Information

(a) A lawyer shall not reveal information relating to representation of a client unless the client gives informed consent, the disclosure is impliedly authorized in order to carry out the representation, or the disclosure is permitted by paragraph (b).

(b) A lawyer may reveal information relating to the representation of a client to the extent the lawyer reasonably believes necessary:

> (1) to prevent reasonably certain death or substantial bodily harm;
>
> (2) to prevent the client from committing a crime or fraud that is reasonably certain to result in substantial injury to the financial interests or property of another and in furtherance of which the client has used or is using the lawyer's services.
>
> (3) to prevent, mitigate, or rectify substantial injury to the financial interests or property of another that is reasonably certain to result or has resulted from the client's commission of a crime or fraud in furtherance of which the client has used the lawyer's services.
>
> (4) to secure legal advice about the lawyer's compliance with these Rules;
>
> (5) to establish a claim or defense on behalf of the lawyer in a controversy between the lawyer and the client, to establish a defense to a criminal charge or a civil claim against the lawyer based upon conduct in which the client was involved, or to respond to allegations in any proceeding concerning the lawyer's representation of the client; or,
>
> (6) to comply with other law or a court order. (Text of Rule 1.6 quoted from the Delaware Rules of Professional Responsibility.)

Rule 1.6 was changed in 2002 and 2003, most notably by the addition of subsections (b)(2) and (b)(3). Neither the prior nor the present version of the rule deals expressly with the duty of confidentiality in the context of the representation of multiple clients such as family members in the same matter. As stated in the ACTEC Commentaries, such a joint representation has been thought, impliedly, to authorize the lawyer to communicate freely between, or among, the clients regarding the subject of the representation. Restatement §60, Comment *l*, notes that, "Sharing of information among the co-clients with respect to the matter involved in the representation is normal and typically expected. As between the co-clients, in many such relationships each co-client is under a fiduciary duty to share all information material to the co-client's joint enterprise." Note, also, that ABA Formal Op. 02-428 concludes that assisting various family members does not necessarily involve a conflict and that, "Considerable efficiency is gained through having one lawyer or firm manage the legal affairs of all family members. The firm learns about family businesses, assets, documents and personalities and thus is able to provide quality representation requiring less time. [Citing ACTEC Commentaries]"

Rule 1.14 was amended in 2002 to permit disclosures of confidential information regarding a client with diminished capacity to the extent required to protect his or her interests: "(c) Information relating to the representation of a client with diminished capacity is protected by Rule 1.6. When taking protective action pursuant to paragraph (b), the lawyer is impliedly authorized under Rule 1.6(a) to reveal information about the client, but only to the extent reasonably necessary to protect the client's interests." *See* § 1.6.11.

Disclosures to Prevent Crimes or Fraud and to Prevent, Mitigate or Rectify Injuries. The Report of the Ethics 2000 Commission recommended changes in Rule 1.6, including the addition of subsections (b)(2) and (b)(3). According to the Commission, disclosure is permitted "when necessary to prevent or rectify substantial injury to the financial or property interests of another but only when the lawyer's services have been or are being used to further a crime or fraud by the client. In both instances, use of the lawyer's services for such improper ends constitutes a serious abuse of the client-lawyer relationship by the client, thereby forfeiting the protection of the Rule." According to the Report a significant number of states allowed or required that disclosures of client misconduct be made in some cases: "Eight jurisdictions permit and three require disclosure when clients threaten crimes or frauds likely to result in substantial injury to the financial or property interests of another. Twenty-five jurisdictions permit and one requires a lawyer to reveal the intention of a client to commit a crime without regard to the amount or nature of the injury caused. Thirteen jurisdictions permit disclosure to rectify the consequences of a crime or fraud in which the lawyer's services were used."

In August 2003, the ABA added subsections (b)(2) and (b)(3) to Rule 1.6. Note that the text of the subsections allow, but do not require, a lawyer to disclose of information relating to the representation of a client. The Restatement provides that a lawyer's discretionary decision to disclose or not to disclose confidential information to prevent reasonably certain death or serious bodily harm, § 66, or to prevent or mitigate a crime or fraud that threatens substantial financial loss, § 67, is not itself, subject to discipline or liable for damages. *See also* Restatement § 66, Comment *g* and § 67, Comment *h*. Whether the courts will adopt that view is open to question. That is, a lawyer may incur some liability if a client is injured by a failure to make a disclosure in a case within the scope of one of the subsections.

Prevention of Crimes and Frauds, (b)(2). The current version of Rule 1.6 allows a lawyer to disclose information in order to prevent a client from committing a crime or fraud that is reasonably certain to result in substantial injury to the financial or property interests of another in which the lawyer's services are implicated. However, note that the rule limits disclosures to instances in which a "substantial" injury is "reasonably certain" to follow. In most instances the limitation will require a lawyer to speculate about the future conduct of a client. The requirement that an injury be "substantial" should be satisfied if an injury is substantial in light of the circumstances of either the miscreant (the client) or of the victim or victims collectively.

§ 1.6.6

Prevent, Ameliorate or Rectify, (b)(3). Before 2003, several states, including New Jersey, had adopted a rule similar to (b)(3) which allowed disclosures to be made to rectify a client's "criminal, illegal or fraudulent act in furtherance of which the lawyer's services have been used." In *A. v. B. v. Hill Wallack*, 726 A.2d 924 (N.J. 1999), the court relied upon the rule to allow a lawyer who had assisted a husband and wife in estate planning to disclose to the wife that the firm had learned that the husband was the defendant in a paternity action. The theory was that disclosure was necessary to protect the wife from the husband's fraud in concealing the paternity claim from his wife when their wills were prepared and executed.

Fiduciary Clients. Identifying the client is a necessary first step in analyzing the duties of a lawyer who represents a fiduciary. Ethics opinions and court decisions generally treat the lawyer for a fiduciary as representing the fiduciary and not the fiduciary estate or its beneficiaries. For example, Michigan Probate Court Rule 5.117A was amended effective April 1, 1992 to state that: "An attorney filing an appearance on behalf of a fiduciary or trustee shall represent the fiduciary or trustee." The comment by the Probate Rules Committee stated that the amendment clarifies that the lawyer "represents the fiduciary or trustee and not the estate." Oregon Op. 2005-62 (2005) also holds that the lawyer for a personal representative represents the personal representative and not the estate or the beneficiaries as such.

Some commentators suggest that under Rule 1.13: Organization as Client, the fiduciary estate should be treated as the client. *E.g.*, Pennell, Representations Involving Fiduciary Entities: Who Is the Client?, 62 Fordham L. Rev. 1319 (1994).

Unfortunately, neither Rule 1.6 nor the other provisions of the Model Rules distinguish between the duties a lawyer owes to a fiduciary client in its representative capacity and the duties that are owed to a fiduciary client that is represented in an individual capacity. The distinction is important although the addition of subsections (b)(2) and (3) allow more disclosures than before to be made by a lawyer who represents a fiduciary in either capacity. A fiduciary that a lawyer represents in its representative capacity is generally treated as the client of the lawyer—not the fiduciary "estate" or its beneficiaries. It is only realistic, however, to recognize that the "estate" or, derivatively, its beneficiaries, are the affected parties—not the fiduciary. The personal interests of the beneficiaries of a fiduciary estate, and not those of the fiduciary, are involved when a lawyer represents a fiduciary client in the fiduciary's representative capacity.

The difference between representing a fiduciary in a fiduciary capacity and representing it in an individual capacity is recognized by many courts in the discovery context—when the fiduciary seeks to bar a beneficiary from discovering communications between the fiduciary and counsel for the fiduciary. For example, in *Hoopes v. Carota*, 531 N.Y.S.2d 407 (App. Div. 1988), *aff'd mem.*, 543 N.E.2d 73 (N.Y. 1989), the court allowed discovery of communications between the fiduciary and his counsel, stating that the evidentiary privilege does not attach in such cases. "Several courts have held that the privilege does not attach at all when a trustee solicits and obtains legal advice concerning matters impacting on the interests of the beneficiaries seeking disclosure, on the ground that the fiduciary has a duty to the beneficiaries whom he is obligated to serve in all his actions, and cannot subordinate the interests of the individual beneficiaries, directly affected by the advice sought, to his own private interests under the guise of the privilege." The court continued:

Plaintiffs may have been directly affected by any decision defendant made on his attorney's advice. The information sought is highly relevant to and may be the only evidence available on whether defendant's actions respecting the relevant transactions were in furtherance of the interests of the beneficiaries of the trust or primarily for his own interests in preserving and promoting the . . . rewards and security of his position as a corporate officer. The communications apparently related to prospective actions by defendant, not past actions. Plaintiffs' claims of defendant's self-dealing and conflict of interests are at least colorable, and the information they seek is not only relevant, but specific. On the other hand, defendant made no showing, either at the EBT or in his opposition to the motion to compel disclosure before the Supreme Court, of any factors that would militate in favor of applying the privilege to the information sought. For example, defendant might have shown that he solicited advice from counsel solely in an individual capacity and at his own expense, as a defensive measure regarding potential litigation over his disputes with the trust beneficiaries.

Some authorities indicate that the duty of confidentiality under the pre-2003 version of Rule 1.6 is paramount to the other duties of a lawyer. For example, ABA Formal Op. 94-380 held that the former version of Rule 1.6 prohibited the lawyer for a fiduciary from disclosing acts of misconduct by the fiduciary. In effect, Op. 94-380 ruled that the duty of confidentiality trumps the duty of loyalty. Note that in such a case disclosure might now be permitted by subsection (b)(3). Given the adoption of subsection (b)(3), the continued validity of Op. 94-380 is doubtful. *Huie v. deShazo*, 922 S.W.2d 920 (Tex. 1996), and *Wells Fargo Bank v. Boltwood*, 990 P.2d 591 (Cal. 2000), ignore the distinction and hold that a fiduciary client is no different than any other client and the duty of confidentiality trumps all of the lawyer's other duties.

Confidentiality and Evidentiary Privilege. The duty of confidentiality imposed by this rule prohibits a lawyer from disclosing information in a nonevidentiary context. A related, but narrower, evidentiary rule, the lawyer-client privilege, generally protects confidential information from involuntary disclosure in a judicial or quasi-judicial setting. The distinction between the ethical obligation and the evidentiary privilege is explained in E.C. 4-4: "The attorney-client privilege is more limited than the ethical obligation of a lawyer to guard the confidences and secrets of his client. This ethical precept, unlike the evidentiary privilege, exists without regard to the nature or source of information or the fact that others share the knowledge . . . . A lawyer owes an obligation to advise the client of the attorney-client privilege and timely to assert the privilege unless it is waived by the client." In both instances the objective is the same: To allow clients to disclose confidential information to their lawyers without fear that the information will be disclosed by the lawyer.

Unless co-clients have otherwise agreed, Restatement §75(2) provides that a communication by one client regarding matters within the scope of the representation is not within the scope of the attorney-client privilege in a subsequent action between them.

§1.6.6

EXAMPLE 1-2

Lawyer, *L*, assisted Parent, *P*, and Son, *S*, in-estate planning matters—including the creation of a plan under which *P*'s interest in the family business will pass outright to *S* when *P* dies. Subsequently *S* asked *L* for help in enrolling in a drug rehab program and in holding *S*'s creditors at bay.

    L urged *S* to inform *P* of the circumstances, which would almost certainly cause *P* to change his estate plan. *S* refused to do so. If there is no agreement between *L, P* and *S* regarding confidentiality, the manner in which *L* should proceed is unclear. Under the prior provisions of Rule 1.6 (*i.e.*, in the absence of subsections (b)(2) and (3)), if *S* will not consent to *L* disclosing the information to *P*, the most common approach has been for *L* to resign from representing *S* or *P*. The underlying theory is that *L* cannot breach *S*'s confidence, which trumps *L*'s duty of loyalty to *P*. However, the content of *L*'s resignation letter might alert *P* to the need to investigate the situation. (Restatement §60, Comment *l*, states that in such a case, "In the course of withdrawal, the lawyer has discretion to warn the affected client that a matter seriously and adversely affecting that person's interests has come to light, which the other co-client refuses to permit the lawyer to disclose.") Unless *P* is somehow made aware of the situation, the family's financial interests might be seriously damaged when *P* dies. Perhaps, subsection (b)(2) or (3) would permit *L* to disclose *S*'s circumstances—substantial economic injury might result from the failure to disclose *S*'s problems—in connection with which *L* has provided services. An approach that emphasizes loyalty, would require *L* to disclose the information to *P*. The same result might be reached on the theory that the authority to make such a disclosure was an implied term of *L*'s engagement.

    Duration of Duty. The duty of confidentiality begins with an initial consultation and persists after a representation has been concluded. The continuation of the duty is noted in E.C. 4-6: "The obligation of a lawyer to preserve the confidences and secrets of his client continues after the termination of his employment." Restatement §15, Comment *c* recognizes the duty of confidentiality with respect to confidential information imparted by a prospective client. *See* Model Rule 1.18, discussed in §1.6.13.

    Post Mortem Disclosures. The evidentiary privilege and the duty of confidentiality continue, subject to limited exceptions, even after the death of a client. A 1998 decision by the United States Supreme Court, *Swidler & Berlin v. United States*, 118 S. Ct. 2081 (1998), affirmed that the evidentiary privilege survives a client's death. In that case the Court noted that about half of the states allow the privilege to be waived by the personal representative of a decedent. 118 S. Ct. at n. 2. Comment (*e*) to Restatement §60 also recognizes that the duty "extends beyond the end of the representation and beyond the death of the client."

    A client may expressly or impliedly authorize a lawyer to disclose confidences in order to effectuate the client's intent. Otherwise, unless the will contest exception applies or the decedent's personal representative consents to disclosure, a lawyer is generally required to preserve a deceased client's confidences. *See Hitt v. Stephens*, 675 N.E.2d 275 (Ill. App. 1996). In *Hitt* the court stated that the contest exception is grounded in the assumption that a decedent "would (if one could ask him) waive the privilege in order that the distribution scheme he actually intended be put into effect."

With the consent of the personal representative of a deceased client, the lawyer is free to disclose the content of documents, including wills, that reflect the deceased client's intent. The lawyer should also be free to do so in order to deter a will contest or other litigation that might defeat the client's intentions or put the estate to undue expense.

> It has long been recognized that the privilege of nondisclosure of confidential information between a client and his or her attorney survives the client's death. [Citations omitted.]Further, we have acknowledged that an executor or administrator of a deceased client may exercise in favor of the client's estate the right to waive the privilege, and call upon the attorney to disclose as a witness communications made to him by the client. *District Attorney for Norfolk District v. Magraw*, 628 N.E. 24 (Mass. 1994).

Consistent with the Magraw decision, by statute or judicial decision a majority of states allow the personal representative of a decedent to waive the decedent's right to assert the attorney-client privilege. E.g., Mayorga v. Tate, 302 App. Div.2d 11 (2002). In the absence of a statute, some courts have held that a personal representative may not waive the privilege with respect to protected communications between a decedent and his or her counsel. *In re Miller*, 584 S.E.2d 772 (N.C. 2003) (the decedent was a suspect in a murder investigation). In such cases, the trial court may conduct an *in camera* examination to determine whether parts of the communications are not within the privilege and are, as a result, subject to disclosure.

Implied Authorization to Disclose. In some circumstances a lawyer is impliedly authorized to make disclosures on behalf of a client. The authority is recognized in Restatement § 61, "A lawyer may use or disclose confidential client information when the lawyer reasonably believes that doing so will advance the interests of the client in the representation." For example, a lawyer generally has implied authorization to consult with a client's accountants and other financial advisors regarding taxes, insurance and other relevant matters. Also, under Rule 1.14, § 1.6.11, if a lawyer reasonably believes that a client has diminished capacity, is at risk of substantial physical, financial or other harm unless action is taken, and the client cannot himself or herself take adequate action, the lawyer "may take reasonably necessary protective action. The action may include consulting with individuals or entities that have ability to take action to protect the client and, in appropriate cases, seeking the appointment of a guardian ad litem, conservator or guardian." Note that, under an earlier version of Rule 1.14, ABA Informal Op. 89-1350 recognized that, "the disclosure by the lawyer of information relating to the representation to the extent necessary to serve the best interests of the client reasonably believed to be disabled is impliedly authorized within the meaning of Model Rule 1.6. Thus, the inquirer may consult a physician concerning the suspected disability."

As discussed in connection with Rule 1.14, lawyers should assist clients in planning for possible disability, including authorizing the lawyer to take reasonable action to protect the client's interests. For example, clients could authorize the lawyer, agents under durable powers of attorney, family members, health care providers and physicians to confer and disclose relevant confidential information to each other. Connecticut Informal Op. 00-5 concludes that the earlier version of Rule 1.14 allowed an estate planning lawyer, without a client's consent, to disclose the client's intent to commit suicide.

Also, a lawyer who retained the original of a client's will is, after the client's death, impliedly authorized to disclose its existence. N.Y. Op. 724 (1999).

Multiple Simultaneous (Joint or Common) Representations. A lawyer who is asked to represent multiple clients regarding the same matter should consider giving each prospective client the opportunity to meet with the lawyer alone. In *Lovett v. Estate of Lovett*, 593 A.2d 382 (N.J. Super. 1991), the court said, with respect to the representation of a husband and wife that, "In most circumstances meeting with a client alone would be well advised." By meeting separately with the clients, the lawyer may be better able to determine whether their interests conflict to a degree that would preclude a joint representation. Doing so may also encourage more open communication, which might otherwise be inhibited. Note, in this connection, that Rule 1.18, added in 2002, explicitly recognizes that the duty of confidentiality extends to communications made by prospective clients to a lawyer. § 1.6.13.

Agreement Allowing Relevant Information to be Shared by Joint Clients. An engagement letter should indicate the extent to which joint clients have agreed that the lawyer may communicate information to one client that was provided by the other client. *See* Form 1-1, § 1.6.2. In the estate planning setting, it should be possible for joint clients to give advance consent to a policy of full disclosure by the lawyer. However, the validity of such an agreement is less certain in the other contexts, including ones involving litigation. For example, "[w]hether any agreement made before the lawyer understands the facts giving rise to the conflict may satisfy 'informed consent' (which presumes appreciation of 'adequate information' about those facts) is highly doubtful." Formal Op. 08-450 (lawyer retained by an insurance company to represent an insured employer and an employee whose conduct is at issue may be unable to enter into information sharing agreement with the clients).

Co-Clients and Confidentiality. In most jurisdictions if co-clients have not made an agreement regarding disclosure, the extent to which the duty of confidentiality bars a lawyer from disclosing material information to one co-client that was communicated in confidence to the lawyer by the other (or another) co-client is unclear. According to Restatement § 60, Comment *l*, co-clients typically expect that information will be shared among them. The conflict between the lawyer's duty of confidentiality to the communicating client and of loyalty and competence to the noncommunicating client can be intense. The lawyer's duty of loyalty and the duty to explain a matter sufficiently, Rule 1.4(b), are also implicated. In *A. v. B. v. Hill Wallack*, 726 A.2d 924 (N.J. 1999), the court stated that "A lawyer's obligation to communicate to one client all information needed to make an informed decision qualifies the firm's duty to maintain the confidentiality of a co-client's information." According to some earlier opinions the lawyer in such a case may not disclose the information to the noncommunicating client. N.Y. Op. 555 (1984) (confidential disclosure by one co-client that he was breaching terms of partnership agreement could not be disclosed to the lawyer's other co-client).

As suggested in the ACTEC Commentaries, if a lawyer learns confidential information from a joint client (the communicating client), who directs the lawyer not to disclose the information to the other joint client, the lawyer should attempt to persuade the communicating client to disclose the relevant information to the other client, or allow the lawyer to do so. If those efforts are not successful, some authorities suggest that the only option is for the lawyer to withdraw from representing one or both clients. Florida Op. 95-4 (lawyer who prepared wills for husband and wife cannot disclose husband's confidence that he has executed codicil that makes substantial provision for his mistress). Other states would require the lawyer to withdraw, which might be sufficiently "noisy" to alert the noncommunicating client of the reason for the lawyer's withdrawal (*i.e.*, the refusal of the communicating client to share material information with the noncommunicating client). The ACTEC Commentaries suggest that the lawyer confronted with such a problem should weigh all of the relevant factors, including the potential harm to the noncommunicating client, and act accordingly.

The default rule stated in the Restatement adopts a similar approach—one that gives the lawyer discretion to inform the noncommunicating client of the confidence if, "in the lawyer's reasonable judgment, the immediacy and magnitude of the risk to the affected co-client outweigh the interest of the communicating client in continued secrecy." § 60, Comment *l*.

Because of the unsettled state of the law, the issue of confidentiality should be carefully reviewed with prospective co-clients, such as a husband and wife, who may ask the same lawyer to represent them jointly. If their interests conflict, such a review is required by Rule 1.7(b), discussed in § 1.6.7. The review should include an explanation of the lawyer's duty of confidentiality, which would shield confidences from disclosure to third parties, and that the clients could authorize the lawyer to communicate all material information to each client, including disclosures made by the other client. Without such authority a lawyer may not be able to protect the interests of the noncommunicating client. In order to be able to advise each client adequately, the lawyer should have the ability to disclose all relevant considerations to each.

Some ethics opinions hold that a lawyer undertaking a joint representation is not required to discuss issues involving confidentiality at the outset of the representation. Fla. Op. 95-4. The opinion is described as follows in an article by Hollis F. Russell and Peter A. Bicks, Joint Representation of Spouses in Estate Planning: The Saga of Advisory Opinion 95-4, Fla. Bar J. 39 (Mar. 1998):

> In a joint representation between husband and wife in estate planning, an attorney is not required to discuss issues of confidentiality at the outset of representation. The attorney may not reveal confidential information to the wife when the husband tells the attorney that he wishes to provide for a beneficiary that is unknown to the wife. The attorney must withdraw from the representation of both husband and wife because of the conflict presented when the attorney must maintain the husband's separate confidences regarding the joint representation.

Can Multiple Clients be Represented in the Same Matter Separately—Without Sharing Material Confidences? Dicta in the *Hill Wallack* case suggests that it is possible for a lawyer to represent a husband and wife, or two or more other co-clients, as entirely separate clients, whose unilateral confidences are not to be revealed to each other. In *A. v. B. v. Hill Wallack*, the court indicated that "[C]o-clients can agree that unilateral confidences or other confidential information will be kept confidential by the attorney." The conclusion is supported by Comment *l* of the Restatement §60 which states, "Co-clients . . . may explicitly agree to share information" and "can also explicitly agree that the lawyer is not to share certain information . . . with one or more other co-clients. A lawyer must honor such agreements."

A so-called separate representation is fraught with risk for the clients and the lawyer. In such a case, how could the lawyer possibly fulfill his or her duties of competency and loyalty to each client? The ACTEC Commentaries (4th ed. 2006), states, in part, that, "There does not appear to be any authority that expressly authorizes a lawyer to represent multiple clients separately with respect to related legal matters. However, with full disclosure and the consent of the clients, some experienced estate planners regularly undertake to represent husbands and wives as separate clients." Such an arrangement is inconsistent with the lawyer's primary duty of loyalty: How could a lawyer adequately represent both spouses if he or she has agreed that the confidences of each would not be disclosed to the other? The risks inherent in the simultaneous, separate representation of clients are pointed out in the Reporter's Note to Restatement §130.

Drafting Options and Agreements to Disclose. In light of the uncertain ability of the lawyer for a fiduciary to disclose any breaches of duty by the fiduciary, an estate planner should work with an estate planning client to produce a plan, and documents, that most effectively carries out a client's intention. Such a plan should include protecting the client's intended beneficiaries against misconduct by the fiduciary. Thus, a client might wish to condition the appointment of a fiduciary upon the fiduciary's agreement to allow disclosure to the court of any misconduct by the fiduciary. Of course, some fiduciaries might not accept an appointment subject to such a condition. Under another approach, the lawyer retained by the fiduciary might accept appointment only if the fiduciary agrees to disclosure by the lawyer.

Planning for Death or Disability of Lawyer: Implied and Express Authorization to Disclose. A single practitioner or member of a small firm should take steps to protect clients against the neglect of their matters that might otherwise take place if the lawyer becomes disabled or dies. The duty was recognized in ABA Formal Ethics Op. 92-369, which states that lawyers should "make arrangements for their client files to be maintained in the event of their death." Restatement §60, Comment *e*, takes the same position: "A lawyer must also take reasonably appropriate steps to provide for return, destruction, or continued safekeeping of client files in the event of the lawyer's retirement, ill health, death, discipline, or other interruption of the lawyer's practice." Allowing another lawyer to examine the files under such circumstances may have been impliedly authorized by the client. Otherwise, Rule 1.6 might limit the extent to which another lawyer might be permitted to examine the files of a disabled or deceased lawyer. The potential problem can be discussed in advance with a client, who could expressly authorize another lawyer to review the client's file if the client's present lawyer becomes disabled or dies.

Evidentiary Privilege and Third Party Communications.

> There is no common law accountant's or tax preparer's privilege . . . and a taxpayer must not be allowed, by hiring a lawyer to do the work that an accountant, or other tax preparer, or the taxpayer himself or herself, normally would do, to obtain greater protection from government investi-

gators, than a taxpayer who did not use a lawyer as his tax preparer. *U.S. v. Frederick*, 182 F.3d 496, 500 (7th Cir. 1999).

In broad terms the IRS Restructuring and Reform Act of 1998 extended the lawyer-client evidentiary privilege in noncriminal federal tax proceedings, to nonlawyers authorized to practice before the IRS. The privilege protects communications between such a nonlawyer and a taxpayer "to the extent the communication would be considered a privileged communication between a taxpayer and an attorney." § 7525(a)(1). However, the privilege does not apply to written communications between a federally authorized tax practitioner and a director, officer, shareholder, employee, agent or representative of a corporation in connection with the promotion of a tax shelter as defined in § 6662(d)(2)(C)(iii). § 7525(b). Although the new statute did not apply, it was briefly discussed in *U.S. v. Frederick*. In *Frederick*, the court held that the drafts of returns, workpapers and correspondence of a lawyer-accountant regarding the preparation of taxpayers under audit were discoverable by the IRS. According to the court, engaging a lawyer to prepare the returns did not cloak the communications and workpapers with the lawyer-client privilege.

E-Mail Communications. ABA Formal Op. 99-413 states that "A lawyer may transmit information relating to the representation of a client by unencrypted e-mail sent over the Internet without violating the Model Rules of Professional Conduct (1998) because the mode of transmission affords a reasonable expectation of privacy from a technological and legal standpoint." The opinion continues to state that, "The same privacy accorded U.S. and commercial mail, land-line telephonic transmissions, and facsimiles applies to Internet e-mail. A lawyer should consult with the client and follow her instructions, however, as to the mode of transmitting highly sensitive information relating to the client's representation." State ethics opinions usually also allow lawyers to communicate with clients via the Internet.

§ 1.6.7. Rule 1.7: Conflict of Interest: Current Clients

    (a) Except as provided in paragraph (b), a lawyer shall not represent a client if the representation involves a concurrent conflict of interest. A concurrent conflict of interest exists if:

        (1) the representation of one client will be directly adverse to another client; or

        (2) there is a significant risk that the representation of one or more clients will be materially limited by the lawyer's responsibilities to another client, a former client or a third person or by a personal interest of the lawyer.

    (b) Notwithstanding the existence of a concurrent conflict of interest under paragraph (a), a lawyer may represent a client if:

        (1) the lawyer reasonably believes that the lawyer will be able to provide competent and diligent representation to each affected client;

        (2) the representation is not prohibited by law; and

> (3) the representation does not involve the assertion by
> one client of a claim against another client repre-
> sented by the lawyer in the same litigation or other
> proceeding before a tribunal; and
>
> (4) each affected client gives informed consent, con-
> firmed in writing. (Text of Rule 1.7 quoted from the
> Delaware Rules of Professional Responsibility.)

Comment [27] to Rule 1.7 provides a helpful introduction to the application of Rule 1.7 in estate planning:

> [C]onflict questions may arise in estate planning and administration. A
> lawyer may be called upon to prepare wills for several family members,
> such as husband and wife, and, depending upon the circumstances a
> conflict of interest may be present. In estate administration the identity of
> the client may be unclear under the law of a particular jurisdiction. Under
> one view, the client is the fiduciary, under another view the client is the
> estate or trust, including its beneficiaries. In order to comply with the
> conflict of interest rules, the lawyer should make clear the lawyer's
> relationship to the parties involved.

Rule 1.7, as rewritten in 2002, appears to significantly relax the prohibitions against representations that involve conflicts of interest. The analytic starting point is now whether there is a current conflict of interest as defined in subsection (a). A current conflict exists if either (1) the representation of one client will be directly adverse to another client; or (2) there is a significant risk that the representation of one or more clients will be materially limited by the lawyer's responsibilities to another client, a former client, a third person, or by a personal interest of the lawyer. Note that under the revised form of Rule 1.7(b), a concurrent conflict can be waived if the lawyer reasonably believes that the lawyer will be able to provide competent and diligent representation to each affected client, and, each affected client gives informed consent, confirmed in writing. However, conflicts cannot be waived if the representation is prohibited by law or if the representation involves the assertion of a claim by one client against another client in the same litigation or proceeding.

According to Comment [8], "even where there is no direct adverseness, a conflict of interest exists if there is a significant risk that a lawyer's ability to consider, recommend or carry out an appropriate course of action for the client will be materially limited as a result of the lawyer's other responsibilities or interests." As an example, the Comment states that, "a lawyer asked to represent several individuals seeking to form a joint venture is likely to be materially limited in the lawyer's ability to recommend or advocate all possible positions because of the lawyer's duty of loyalty to the others." However, unless the interests of a husband and wife actually conflict, the concurrent representation of a husband and wife in estate planning is generally permissible without their informed consent. In contrast, a lawyer should not represent the specific and residuary beneficiaries of a decedent's will, if their economic interests seriously conflict. On the other hand, it is generally possible for a lawyer to represent more than one member of a class of beneficiaries, whose interests are consistent—such as the residuary beneficiaries of a decedent's estate.

As explained in more detail below, a lawyer may represent an individual as personal representative and individually as a beneficiary of the estate so long as there is no conflict. *Matter of Birnbaum*, 460 N.Y.S.2d 706 (N.Y. Sur. Ct. Monroe Co. 1983) ("where the attorney represents his client in both capacities, he may not act to advance the personal interests of a fiduciary in such a way as to harm his other client, the estate"). A questionable Oregon ethics opinion holds that a lawyer may properly represent an individual in multiple, conflicting, capacities, because the lawyer only has one client. Oregon Formal Op. 2005-119. ("representing one person who acts in several different capacities is not the same as representing several different people.") According to the Oregon opinion, a lawyer may represent a personal representative individually and as personal representative although the client's "personal interests may conflict with her obligations as a fiduciary" because the lawyer "has only one client."

Referral Fees. Whether a lawyer may accept a referral fee for referring a properly informed client to a third party varies from state to state. As explained at § 1.6.5, some jurisdictions prohibit lawyers from accepting a referral fee from nonlawyers in any case, while other jurisdictions permit the acceptance of a referral fee if the client gives informed consent.

Rule 1.7 Allows Lawyer to Represent a Client who Disinherits Another Client. According to ABA Formal Op. 05-434, Rule 1.7 does not prevent a lawyer from representing a testator who wishes to disinherit a person whom the lawyer represents in an unrelated matter:

> [O]rdinarily there is no conflict of interest when a lawyer undertakes an engagement by a testator to disinherit a beneficiary whom the lawyer represents on unrelated matters. However, this may not be the case if the testator is restricted by a contractual or quasi-contractual legal obligation from disinheriting the beneficiary, or if there is a significant risk that the lawyer's responsibilities to the testator will be materially limited by the lawyer's responsibilities to the beneficiary, as may be the case if the lawyer finds herself advising the testator whether to proceed with the disinheritance.

Opinion 05-434 is consistent with a Florida appellate decision which concluded that the lawyer who drew a will for a client that disinherited the client's daughter did not owe a duty to the daughter although she was also a client and a beneficiary under the client's prior will. *Chase v. Bowen*, 771 So. 2d 1181 (Fla. App. 2000). The majority opinion states that, "a lawyer who prepares a will owes no duty to any previous beneficiary, even a beneficiary he may be representing in another matter, to oppose the testator or testatrix in changing his or her will and, therefore, that assisting in that change is not a conflict of interest."

Conflicts and Confidentiality Agreements. An Illinois ethics opinion deals with the ethical concerns that arise when an accounting firm proposes to a client a "package of ideas that can significantly reduce Client A's taxes if: (1) Client A pays Accounting Firm a fee for the information and (2) Client A and Client A's Lawyer each enter into a confidentiality agreement pursuant to which Client A and Lawyer A agree to never divulge the ideas in the package." Ill. Op. 00-01. The opinion concludes that if Lawyer were to sign the agreement it would create a conflict of interest within the meaning of MRPC 1.7(b) with regard to subsequent clients who might benefit from the information learned in connection with the representation of the original client. "In the case at hand, the Lawyer's own interests in honoring the Confidentiality Agreement would 'materially limit' her responsibilities to Clients B, C, and D [subsequent clients] because lawyer would be prohibited from providing beneficial tax information to Clients B, C, and D." In addition, entering into such an agreement may violate the spirit of MRPC 5.6, which prohibits a lawyer from agreeing to limit his or her practice. Rule 1.7 also prohibits a lawyer from representing a client if the representation will be adversely affected by the lawyer's own interests. For example, a conflict may arise if the lawyer will receive payments from third parties with respect to services provided to the client. This point is elaborated in the discussion of Rule 1.5 in §1.6.5 and of Rule 1.8 in §1.6.8. Accordingly, lawyers generally should not enter into confidentiality agreements that would bar the lawyer and one or more of the lawyer's clients from disclosing to others the details of estate planning techniques that are communicated to the lawyer by a third party for use by the client(s).

Estate Planning for Multiple Parties: Husbands and Wives and Intergenerational Planning. Comment [27] to Rule 1.7, quoted above, notes that in preparing wills for several family members depending upon the circumstances, "a conflict of interest may be present." Despite the possibility of conflict between joint (or common) clients, there may be none. In fact, the interests of multiple family members may be entirely harmonious and free of conflict. Thus, the representation of a parent and child, or of siblings, does not involve any inherent conflict. In this connection, note that according to ABA Formal Op. 02-428, assisting various family members does not necessarily involve a conflict and that, "Considerable efficiency is gained through having one lawyer or firm manage the legal affairs of all family members. The firm learns about family businesses, assets, documents and personalities and thus is able to provide quality representation requiring less time. [Citing ACTEC Commentaries]."

As recognized by Comment [29] to Rule 1.7, a lawyer who undertakes a joint representation is required to "be impartial between commonly represented clients." The Comment continues, noting that "representation of multiple clients is improper when it is unlikely that impartiality can be maintained." In general, each client is, of course, free to formulate his or her own estate plan and to dispose of his property as he or she wishes. Of course, the law may give a spouse or others a right to claim an interest in a decedent's estate, contrary to the provisions of the decedent's estate plan.

Representing Husband and Wife. The reasoning of a 1996 Montana ethics opinion takes what may be the most practical and reasonable position regarding the representation of a husband and wife:

> The marital relationship itself is not in most cases adversarial in nature and no conflict inherently exists in representing both parties. Generally speaking, the fact that the clients are married does not materially limit the responsibilities to either client. Therefore, it is not necessary to advise a couple of the possibility of a potential conflict unless there is evidence suggesting such advisement is appropriate. Montana Op. 960731.

The first paragraph of Montana Op. 960731 states that Rule 1.7 does not apply if there is no evidence of conflict between the spouses in the estate planning process. The status of marriage alone is not sufficient to create a substantial potential for a material limitation upon the lawyer's representation of either spouse. If Rule 1.7(b) were applicable merely because the two clients were married to each other, no lawyer could accept representation of the couple without a waiver.

California Bar Rule 3-310(c) (2011) provides that a lawyer"shall not without the informed written consent of each client, (1) accept representation of more than one client in a matter in which the interests of the clients potentially conflict, or (2) accept or continue representation of more than one client in a matter in which the interests of the client actually conflict. . . . " Because of the requirement, many California lawyers obtain consent letters from husbands and wives they are asked to represent. Obtaining consent letters provide a degree of protection although they may not strictly be required in many cases.

In some instances, the conflict of interests are so intense that the same lawyer would usually be barred from representing both parties. For example, the same lawyer should almost never represent both parties to a prenuptial agreement. Not uncommonly, both parties, on their own, have themselves worked out the terms of a prenuptial agreement, which is then drafted by the lawyer for one of them and submitted for review to the lawyer for the other. The same approach should be taken if a husband and wife wish to enter into a post-nuptial agreement regarding the characterization of the property they own. With consent the same lawyer might be able to represent multiple family members with regard to some economic matters. However, although the parties may have agreed upon the basic terms of a family transaction such as an installment sale or private annuity, it may be unwise for the same lawyer to represent all of the parties.

EXAMPLE 1-3

Lawyer, *L*, has represented Husband, *H*, and Wife, *W*, for many years. *H* has asked *L* to assist him in financial matters relating to his retirement, including whether to roll over funds from a qualified pension plan to an IRA. *H* has also asked *L* about the extent to which *H* could leave property to persons other than *W*. As *L* has represented both *H* and *W* in the past, *L* should exercise great care in discussing either subject with *H* alone. The interests of *W* could be adversely affected if *H* rolls over funds from his pension plan to an IRA. (ERISA protects the interests of a participant's spouse in a qualified plan, but not in an IRA.) Both subjects could, however, be discussed with *H* and *W* together. Of course, a serious issue can arise if either *H* or *W* asks *L* *confidentially* to assist in a transaction that would disadvantage the other.

Intergenerational Planning. Lawyers often provide effective assistance to members of multiple generations of a family in formulating an estate plans for the senior generation and, perhaps, for some members of younger generations. Doing so obviously requires a heightened sensitivity to ethical issues, including ones of confidentiality and conflicts. In some cases, the lawyer only represents the senior generation, with or without providing younger generation members with information regarding estate planning. Conducting periodic family meetings can facilitate communications among family members, provide a forum for sharing information and assist in planning for the effective intergenerational transfer of wealth.

A lawyer who is asked to undertake a representation that involves multiple family members must be sure that all parties understand who the lawyer represents and the role that the lawyer will play, including the limitations within which the lawyer must operate. Lawyers who undertake such a representation often preside over periodic meetings that review the continuing sufficiency of an estate plan in light of changes in the business, the family, or the law. Other specialists, including accountants and family planning consultants, can make valuable contributions to family understanding and planning. An article by three authors who are all associated with "BMC Associates, a multidisciplinary mediation and consulting company in Arlington, Virginia" encourages the use of "mediation techniques and family dynamics specialists to facilitate the pre-estate planning process" within families. Gage, Gromala & Kopf, Holistic Estate Planning and Integrating Mediation in the Estate Planning Process, 39 Real Prop., Prob. & Tr. J. 509 (2004).

Designating Scrivener as Fiduciary.

> In the Committee's opinion, a lawyer may accept appointment as fiduciary under a will or trust that the lawyer is preparing for a client, so long as the lawyer discusses with the client information reasonably necessary to enable the client to make an informed decision in selecting the fiduciary. If there is significant risk that the lawyer's interest in being named a fiduciary will materially limit his independent professional judgment in advising the client in her choice of a fiduciary, the lawyer also must obtain the client's informed consent, confirmed in writing. Although a lawyer serving as a fiduciary of an estate or trust may appoint himself or other lawyers in his firm to represent him as fiduciary, his compensation received in both capacities must be considered in determining what is reasonable compensation for his services as lawyer. Finally, a lawyer who is serving as a fiduciary ordinarily must not represent a beneficiary or creditor of an estate or trust in a matter adverse to the estate or trust. When representing a beneficiary in a matter unrelated to the estate or trust, the lawyer must satisfy the requirements of Rule 1.7. ABA Formal Op. 02-426.

The Model Rules do not deal directly with the propriety of a lawyer drafting an instrument that appoints the lawyer to a fiduciary office. However, as indicated by the conclusion of ABA Formal Op. 02-426 quoted above, "a lawyer may accept appointment as a personal representative or trustee named in a will or trust the lawyer is preparing for a client subject to complying with Rule. 1.4(b) and, in some circumstances with Rule 1.7(b)." Opinion 02-426 also points out that, in order to comply with Rule 1.7, "The lawyer must not, however, allow his potential self-interest to interfere with his exercise of independent professional judgment in recommending to the client the best choice of fiduciaries." Importantly, the Opinion holds that, because the appointment of a lawyer to a fiduciary office "is not a 'business transaction with a client,' Rule 1.8(a) does not apply . . . ." Note that in some locales, notably Boston and Philadelphia, law firms are commonly appointed to fiduciary offices.

Ethical Consideration 5-6, issued under the Model Code (*i.e.*, pre-1983), discusses the propriety of appointing the scrivener to a fiduciary office. E.C. 5-6 states that a lawyer should not consciously influence a client to appoint him to a fiduciary office. It continues to provide that, "In those cases where a client wishes to name his lawyer as such, care should be taken by the lawyer to avoid even the appearance of impropriety." While the Model Rules do not include an "appearance of impropriety" standard, the admonition of the E.C. should be followed.

Most jurisdictions permit a client who has received proper cautionary counsel to appoint whomever the client wishes to serve in a fiduciary capacity. *E.g.*, Va. Op. 1358 (1990); S.C. Op. 91-07 (1991; Ga. Op. 91-1 (1991). Wash. Informal Op. 86-1. New York Op. 487 (1981) allows a lawyer to prepare a will that appoints the lawyer to a fiduciary office if the testator is competent, there has been a longstanding relationship between the lawyer and client and the suggestion that the lawyer serve originates with the client. Some Surrogate courts impose more stringent rules. *See* N.Y. Op. 610 (1990), which quotes the Surrogate's Court Rules in Suffolk County. Indeed, some courts have, in effect, banned the practice for all except clients related to the lawyer. *See State v. Gulbankian*, 196 N.W.2d 733 (Wis. 1972).

Some opinions, such as Connecticut Informal Op. 00-08, conclude that the lawyer who draws a will may be named as executor, may act as such, and may also serve as lawyer for the "estate." The Connecticut ruling continues to conclude, generally, that the lawyer may also act as the trustee of the deceased client's revocable trust.

A California statute limits the circumstances under which the scrivener of a will or trust can be appointed to a fiduciary office and limits the compensation a lawyer can receive for serving both as fiduciary and counsel. Some other states also limit the compensation that can be paid to a lawyer for acting both as fiduciary and as counsel. California prohibits lawyers from collecting dual compensation unless it is specifically authorized by the court in a guardianship, conservatorship, or estate matter or, in the case of an inter vivos trust, is not objected to by any beneficiary. Cal. Prob. Code § § 2645 (guardian or conservator), 10804 (estates), 15687 (trusts) (2011). The prohibition does not apply if the lawyer is related by blood or marriage to, or is, or was, a cohabitant with, the ward, conservatee, decedent or trustor.

If a client wishes to appoint the scrivener to a fiduciary office, the lawyer should consider the request seriously and critically. Some authorities suggest that lawyers should accept such appointments reluctantly, if at all, because of the duties and risks they involve. Laurino, The Duties and Responsibilities of the Attorney/Fiduciary, U. Miami, 19th Inst. Est. Plan., Ch. 16 (1985). The lawyer for an unrelated client who wishes to appoint the lawyer to a fiduciary office, should explain to the client the implications of such an appointment. The explanation should include the other persons who might serve, alternative costs, and the possibility, in most jurisdictions, that the lawyer would elect also to serve as the lawyer for the fiduciary.

Helping Client Select a Fiduciary. As indicated above under Rules 1.4(b) and 1.7(b), a lawyer should counsel a client completely and candidly regarding the selection of a fiduciary and not allow his potential self interest to interfere with the exercise of independent judgment in recommending to the client the best choices for fiduciaries. In particular, a lawyer should not influence a client to appoint to a fiduciary office a person who is a business associate or a client of the lawyer. *See* Rule

1.7, Comment [10]. A corporate fiduciary should be recommended by a lawyer only if it is in the best interests of the client to do so. If a client is considering the appointment of a corporate fiduciary, the lawyer should tell the client if the corporate fiduciary has a practice of retaining as its counsel in the matter the lawyer who drew the instrument that names it as fiduciary. The client is entitled to know about such practices before a fiduciary is chosen.

Transactions With Another Client. If a lawyer is asked to represent a client in connection with a negotiation or other dealing with another client, the lawyer may be able to do so if the conflict is waivable. Also, under former Rule 2.2, (*see* §1.6.15), the lawyer may be able to represent both clients as an intermediary. In addition, if the lawyer is not representing either client in connection with the same matter (*e.g.*, a lease negotiation), the lawyer should be free to represent either or both in unrelated, nonadversarial matters such as estate planning. Thus, if a lawyer represents Client *A* in the negotiation of a lease with Client *B,* with the informed consent of Clients *A* and *B,* the lawyer should be free to represent Client *B* in an unrelated matter such as estate planning or a tax matter. *See* Rule 1.7, Comment [6].

Membership on Board of Charity; Lectures. Lawyers who are on the board of a charitable organization should exercise care in representing clients who may make a gift to the charity or name it as a beneficiary under a will or trust. Consistently, a lawyer who is on the board of a charity should not represent the charity and another client in connection with a gift annuity, charitable trust, or similar transaction. Oregon Op. 2005-116 (formerly 1989-525) (charitable unitrust). Interestingly, the opinion states that in such a case the lawyer could draft an individual client's will which contains a gift to the charity if the lawyer discloses his representation of the charity.

Lectures and Seminars. A lawyer is generally free to conduct seminars open to the public on legal subjects so long as the publicity of the event and his conduct at the seminar do not offend rules regarding advertising and solicitation. *E.g.*, Ohio Op. 94-13. A lawyer may participate in a seminar or lecture organized by a church or other charitable organization. If a lawyer does so, the lawyer can agree to represent individuals who attended the event. In doing so, however, the lawyer must represent the interests of the client faithfully, uninfluenced by the interests of the church, charity, or other sponsor of the event. In contrast, a lawyer should not undertake to prepare documents for laymen who attended a seminar conducted by a nonlawyer, on the basis of instructions given by the nonlawyer. *Butler Co. Bar. Assn. v. Bradley,* 665 N.E.2d 1089 (Ohio 1996).

Do Not Direct Fiduciary to Retain Scrivener. A lawyer should not draft an instrument that directs the fiduciary to retain the draftsman as counsel. There is usually no justification for such a designation. Moreover, as a technical matter, such a designation generally does not bind the personal representative, who is free to employ the lawyer of his or her own choice. However, an Illinois ethics opinion concludes that if the client consents after full disclosure regarding the conflict of interest inherent in such situations, a lawyer may prepare a trust that provides that the trustee is to retain the lawyer to provide legal services to the trust. Ill. Op. 99-08. The Opinion also notes that "full disclosure is required and should be documented in writing."

Was a Lawyer-Client Relationship Established? In some cases it is not clear whether a lawyer-client relationship was established as a result of a meeting between a lawyer and a prospective client. If not, and no confidential information was disclosed to the lawyer, it should be possible for the lawyer to represent another party whose interests are adverse to the person who met with the lawyer, but did not become a client. *See* Rule 1.18 and §1.6.13 regarding the lawyer's duties to a prospective client. A lawyer-client relationship should not be created by a single meeting between a lawyer and a prospective estate planning client during which no confidences were disclosed and the prospective client indicated a lack of interest in retaining the lawyer. Accordingly, such a meeting should not prevent the lawyer from representing persons who contest the will executed by the prospective client. *State ex rel. Defrances v. Befell*, 446 S.E.2d 906 (W.Va. 1994).

Client's Estate Planner May be Prevented from Acting as Attorney for Deceased Client's Executor; Disclosure of Colorable Claims. In sum, if the lawyer who prepared the estate plan knows at the outset or anytime after the representation of the executor commences that the quality of the plan is subject to a colorable challenge (or where the plan has in fact been challenged) on grounds that it was incompetently prepared, the lawyer cannot represent the executor and, furthermore, must disclose to the executor any facts that would permit the executor to evaluate the apparent malpractice. If not, the lawyer may represent the executor in the administration of the estate. N.Y. Op. 865 (2011).

In the absence of a conflict of interest the lawyer who prepared a client's estate plan may act as the lawyer for the decedent's personal representative. However, as indicated in N.Y. Op. 865, if the lawyer knows of a potential claim against him or her for legal malpractice, the conflict is not consentable "and the lawyer (and all lawyers associated with his firm) must decline or withdraw from the representation and the lawyer must inform the executor of the facts giving rise to the claim." If the lawyer becomes aware of a potential estate planning malpractice claim after undertaking to represent a deceased client's personal representative, Rule 1.16 requires the lawyer to withdraw, and to "take steps, to the extent reasonably practicable, to avoid unforeseeable prejudice to the right of the client."

Client Asks Lawyer to Prepare Documents for Another Person. Lawyers who are asked by a client to prepare estate planning documents for another person may be faced with a serious conflict of interest. However, as indicated in ABA Formal Op. 02-428, there may not be a conflict if the lawyer represents each party independently. The matter is, of course, more complicated if the existing client offers to pay part or all of the lawyer's fee for representing the other party. The conclusion of ABA Formal Op. 02-428 is instructive:

> A lawyer who is recommended by a potential beneficiary to draft a will for a relative may represent the testator as long as the lawyer does not permit the person who recommends him to direct or regulate the lawyer's professional judgment pursuant to Rule 5.4(c). If the potential beneficiary agrees to pay or assure the lawyer's fee, the testator's informed consent to the arrangement must be obtained, and the other requirements of Rule 1.8(f) must be satisfied. If the person recommending the lawyer also is a client of the lawyer, the lawyer must obtain clear guidance from her as to the extent to which he may use or reveal that person's protected information in representing the testator. The lawyer should advise the testator that he also is concurrently performing estate planning services for the

other person. Ordinarily there is no significant risk that the lawyer's representation of either client will be materially limited by his representation of the other client; therefore, no conflict of interest arises under Rule 1.7.

Opinion 02-428 does not deal with the problems that may arise if the existing client is unwilling to have information about her estate plan disclosed to the other party (the testator). In some cases, it would be important for the testator to have information regarding the existing client's estate plan. For example, the nature of the testator's plan might depend upon knowledge of the other party's existing plans and intentions. According to some ethics opinions, a lawyer who is asked by a son or daughter to prepare a new will for a parent may be considered to represent both the child and the parent—which, at a minimum, would require an explanation of potential conflicts of interest. San Diego Op. 1990-3. The lawyer usually represents the person for whom a document is prepared for execution. In many instances it would be inappropriate for the lawyer also to represent a child or other potential beneficiary with regard to the same matter. Indeed, Rule 1.8(f), discussed in §1.6.8, provides that if another person pays the lawyer's fee, the client for whom the services are performed must give informed consent, the arrangement must not interfere with the lawyer-client relationship and lawyer's independence of professional judgment and, the information relating to the representation must be protected as required by Rule 1.6. Similarly, Restatement §134 allows a lawyer to accept compensation from a person other than the client if the client gives informed consent as provided in §122.

The facts of *Estate of Gillespie*, 903 P.2d 590 (Ariz. 1995), illustrate the problems that can arise when the lawyer retained by an adult child draws dispositive instruments for a parent, who had been represented by another lawyer. It involved a deathbed will prepared by the lawyer for the testator, Grace, who was hired by her son James. The will changed the disposition of the testator's estate and named James as executor. The opinion notes that, "The lawyers who drafted these documents prepared them for James, and not for Grace [the testator]. They represented James and billed him for their services. Indeed, they never communicated with Grace." The opinion continues, to say that, "The 1992 Will was the will of James, not Grace. Grace did not ask anyone to draw up a new will for her. She already had a Will and a lawyer. James took it upon himself to substitute his judgment for hers. He asked his lawyer to draft a Will and a trust agreement that expressed his will. He then presented one of them to his mother on her deathbed and failed to disclose its contents to her . . . .On these undisputed facts we conclude as a matter of law that the 1992 Will is invalid because Grace lacked any understanding of its contents and indeed was misled as to its true nature."

A lawyer should not prepare a will, trust, durable power of attorney or any other document for a person without personally meeting with him or her, preferably in private. The possibility of a conflict of interest was not discussed by the court in some cases in which it appears to have been present. For example, in *Persinger v. Holst*, 639 N.W.2d 594 (Mich. App. 2001), *appeal denied*, 649 N.W.2d 74 (Mich. 2002), the court held that a lawyer who prepared a durable power of attorney for an elderly client was not required to attempt to prevent the client from appointing an unsuitable person as her agent. No consideration was apparently given to the fact that the agent had been a client of the lawyer and that the client had formerly been represented by another lawyer.

Haynes v. First National Bank, 432 A.2d 890 (N.J. 1981), is another case involving a will favoring the child who procured its preparation and execution. In it the court found the circumstances gave rise to a presumption of undue influence: "There must be imposed a significant burden of proof upon the advocates of will where a presumption of undue influence has arisen because the testator's attorney has placed himself in a conflict of interest and professional loyalty between the testator and the beneficiary." 432 A.2d at 900.

Lawyer for Fiduciary. The lawyer for a fiduciary may also represent the fiduciary in an individual capacity if doing so does not involve a conflict between the interests of the fiduciary estate and of the fiduciary. However, the lawyer should not represent the fiduciary individually with respect to a claim against the fiduciary estate or in connection with any other matter in which the individual's interests conflict with the duties of a fiduciary to be impartial.

According to some opinions, a lawyer who reasonably believes a fiduciary client is acting contrary to the interests of the estate must call upon the fiduciary to act properly, must refrain from assisting in any misconduct, and may be forced to withdraw. N.Y. Op. 649 (1993). Other cases and opinions would require the lawyer to disclose the misconduct to the court. *E.g., Estate of Minsky*, 376 N.E.2d 647 (Ill. App. 1978); Ill. Op. 91-24. An unusual Oregon Ethics Opinion, 2005-119, concludes that a lawyer may represent a decedent's widow individually and as personal representative because the lawyer would have "only one client". The opinion fails to note the distinction between the individual's actions as personal representative and ones taken in her personal capacity.

The application of Rule 1.7 to a personal representative is discussed in the following passage from *Estate of Gory*, 570 So.2d 1381 (Fla. App. 1990),

> In Florida, the personal representative is the client rather than the estate or the beneficiaries. Rule 4-1.7, Rules Regulating the Florida Bar (Comment). It follows that counsel does not generate a conflict of interest in representing the personal representative in a matter simply because one or more of the beneficiaries takes a position adverse to that of the personal representative. A contrary result would raise havoc with the orderly administration of decedent's estates, not to mention the additional attorney's fees that would be generated.

Because of a concern that a lawyer who represents a fiduciary might inadvertently assume a responsibility to a person to whom the fiduciary owes fiduciary obligations, Ohio enacted Ohio Rev. Code § 5815.16 (formerly § 1339.18), which provides:

> § 5815.16. Attorney for Fiduciary Not Liable to Third Parties.
>
> (A) Absent an express agreement to the contrary, an attorney who performs legal services for a fiduciary, by reason of the attorney performing those legal services for the fiduciary, has no duty or obligation in contract, tort, or otherwise to any third party to whom the fiduciary owes fiduciary obligations.

§ 1.6.7

(B) As used in this section, "fiduciary" means a trustee under an express trust or an executor or administrator of a decedent's estate.

Express and Implied Waiver of Conflicts. If the will or trust authorizes the fiduciary to engage in a specified conflict of interest, it should be possible for the lawyer to represent the fiduciary in the matter in both capacities. For example, if a trust authorizes the trustee to vote the stock of a closely held corporation in ways that might directly or indirectly benefit the trustee, the lawyer should be free to represent the trustee in both capacities regarding such matters. In most circumstances a lawyer should not represent both the residuary legatee of a decedent's estate and a party against whom the personal representative is asserting a claim on behalf of the estate.

If a decedent's will authorizes or directs the personal representative to take a position that conflicts with the interests of one or more of the beneficiaries, the personal representative may do so although it affects his or her personal interests. Such authorization may even be implied: For example, a co-personal representative to whom the testator gave an option to purchase stock in a closely held company at the finally determined federal estate tax value of the stock, may be impliedly authorized to file a petition in Tax Court to oppose a higher valuation of the stock proposed by the IRS. *Estate of Vance,* 11 Wash. App. 375, 522 P.2d 1172 (1974). Whether Rule 1.7 would preclude the lawyer for the personal representative from assisting the personal representative in connection with the petition is not clear. The safer course would be to recommend that the personal representative be represented by other counsel in connection with the petition and other matters which involve a conflict of interest.

Partners, Partnerships, and Similar Entities. The representation of one or more partners or a partnership in tax or other matters may cause the lawyer to undertake duties to others. With proper disclosures a lawyer can represent multiples clients in the formation of a partnership and, later, the partnership. In *Griva v. Davison,* 637 A.2d 830 (D.C. App. 1994), the court stated that after obtaining the informed consent of multiple parties, it was proper for a law firm to represent them in forming a partnership and in representing, on a continuing basis the partnership and some of the partners. However, the representation could not continue if an actual conflict arose. The issue is often highly fact specific. "The relationship a partnership attorney has with the individual partners will vary from case to case. A rule which may seem appropriate for an attorney representing a two-person general partnership may be entirely inappropriate for an attorney representing a limited partnership with scores or even hundreds of partners." *Responsible Citizens v. Superior Court,* 20 Cal. Rptr. 2d 756, 765 (Cal.App. 1993).

A lawyer who has represented a general partner generally should not undertake to represent the limited partners if their interests are, or may be, adverse to the general partner. Thus, a lawyer who has represented the general partner in connection with the formation and marketing of limited partnership interests should not represent the limited partners if, as the result of the loss of the expected tax benefits, their interests do, or may, conflict with those of the general partner. *Eriks v. Denver,* 118 Wash.2d 451, 824 P.2d 1207 (1992) (because of conflicts, the lawyer was required to disgorge all fees).

Waiver of Existing and Future Conflicts. A lawyer who represents a fiduciary as executor, trustee, guardian or in another representative capacity may be disqualified from representing another party whose interests are adverse to the personal interests of the fiduciary. The rule is generally followed although, logically, the fiduciary acting in a representative capacity should be treated as a client distinct and apart from the fiduciary acting on its own behalf. The problem naturally arises most often in connection with corporate fiduciaries. Thus, if Lawyer, *L*, represents Bank A as executor of the will of John Q. Smith, Bank A might be able to disqualify *L* from representing any other person in a matter adverse to Bank A. The greater ability to waive future conflicts under the revised version of Rule 1.7 was recognized in ABA Formal Op. 05-436, which withdrew the more restrictive Formal Op. 93-372.

EXAMPLE 1-4

> A Lawyer (*L*) in the Miami office of a firm is retained by Bank of America to represent it as personal representative of the estate of a decedent who resided in Florida. Subsequently a client of the San Francisco office of the same firm asked Lawyer 2 (*L-2*) to represent her in negotiating a loan from the San Francisco office of Bank of America. Under the traditional view *L-2* would be barred from representing the client in negotiating the loan unless Bank of America gave its informed consent. The same would be true if the client sought assistance in connection with any matter that was adverse to Bank of America. The representation of Bank of America in connection with the Florida estate did not involve the personal interests of the bank—it was simply acting in a representative capacity. Why should that representation prevent another lawyer in the same firm from representing another client, in another matter, whose interests are adverse to those of the bank?

Note that the problem may be avoided if the fiduciary signs a sufficient waiver of the conflict that might arise if the lawyer representing it as the fiduciary of an estate or trust wishes to represent a party whose interests are adverse to the fiduciary in an unrelated matter. *See* ABA Formal Op. 05-436, which withdraws ABA Formal Op. 93-372 and allows waivers in a broader range of circumstances. Comment [22] to Rule 1.7 expressly recognizes waivers of future conflicts.

Circular 230. Section 10.29 of Circular 230, which is similar to Rule 1.7, prohibits practitioners from representing persons before the IRS whose interests conflict (*i.e.*, their interests are directly adverse or if there is a significant risk that the representation of one or more clients will be materially limited by the practitioner's responsibilities to another client or to a third party or by a personal interest of the practitioner). However, even if a conflict exists, the practitioner may represent a client if the representation is not prohibited by law, and the practitioner reasonably believes that the practitioner will be able to provide competent and diligent legal representation to each client and each affected client gives informed consent, confirmed in writing.

§1.6.8. Rule 1.8: Conflict of Interest: Current Clients: Specific Rules

(a) A lawyer shall not enter into a business transaction with a client or knowingly acquire an ownership, possessory, security or other pecuniary interest adverse to a client unless:

> (1) the transaction and terms on which the lawyer acquires the interest are fair and reasonable to the client and are fully disclosed and transmitted in writing to the client in a manner which can reasonably be understood by the client;
>
> (2) the client is advised in writing of the desirability of seeking and is given a reasonable opportunity to seek the advice of independent legal counsel on the transaction; and
>
> (3) the client gives informed consent, in a writing signed by the client, to the essential terms of the transaction and the lawyer's role in the transaction, including whether the lawyer is representing the client in the transaction.

* * *

(c) A lawyer shall not solicit any substantial gift from a client, including a testamentary gift, or prepare on behalf of a client an instrument giving the lawyer or a person related to the lawyer any substantial gift, unless the lawyer or other recipient of the gift is related to the client. For purposes of this paragraph, related persons include a spouse, child, grandchild, parent, grandparent or other relative or individual with whom the lawyer or the client maintains a close, familial relationship.

* * *

(h) A lawyer shall not:

> (1) make an agreement prospectively limiting the lawyer's liability to a client for malpractice unless the client is independently represented in making the agreement; or
>
> (2) settle a claim or potential claim for such liability with an unrepresented client or former client unless that person is advised in writing of the desirability of seeking and is given a reasonable opportunity to seek the advice of independent legal counsel in connection therewith.

* * *

    (j) A lawyer shall not have sexual relations with a client unless a consensual sexual relationship existed between them when the lawyer-client relationship commenced.

    (k) While lawyers are associated in a firm, a prohibition in the foregoing paragraphs (a) through (i) that applies to any one of them shall apply to all of them. (Text of Rule 1.8 quoted from the Delaware Rules of Professional Conduct.)

Changes made to Rule 1.8 in 2002, extend the scope of the rule and tighten the requirements with respect to some transactions. Note that under Rule 1.8(k), any of the prohibitions in supbparagraphs (a)-(i) that apply to a lawyer in a firm apply to all lawyers in the firm.

    Rule 1.8(a) requires that business transactions between a lawyer and client meet stringent requirements of disclosure, fairness, and opportunity for the client to obtain independent advice. In addition, the client must give informed consent to the transaction in a writing signed by the client that discloses the essential terms of the transaction, and the lawyer's role in the transaction, including whether the lawyer was representing the client. Comment [1] points out that the rule applies to the sale of goods or services related to the practice of law, such as the sale of title insurance or investment services to existing clients and that it applies to "lawyers purchasing property from estates they represent." However, the rule does not apply to standard business transactions between the lawyer and client with respect to goods or services that the client normally markets to others (*e.g.*, banking services, office products, medical services, etc.). As noted in the Comment, in those transactions the lawyer has no advantage in dealing with the client. A lawyer clearly should not borrow from a client. *Giovanazzi v. State Bar of California*, 619 P.2d 1005 (Cal. 1980); *In re Hendricks*, 580 P.2d 188 (Or. 1978) ("[I]t is axiomatic that attorneys should not borrow or accept gifts from their clients unless the client has had advice from independent counsel or a knowledgeable person." 580 P.2d at 190). A lawyer who represents the co-executors of a decedent's will engages in a conflict of interest when she also undertakes to act as a broker for them in selling real property owned by the estate. In *Matter of Lake*, 702 N.E.2d 1145 (Mass. 1998), the Supreme Judicial Court upheld admonishing the lawyer, who acted "as counsel and as a broker" without full disclosure of the differing interests.

    As stated in ABA Formal Op. 02-426, the appointment of a lawyer to a fiduciary office is not a gift to the lawyer (or to his or her firm) and is not a business transaction that is subject to Rule 1.8. However, such an appointment is subject to Rule 1.7.

    Virginia Op. 1754 (2001) concludes that an estate planning lawyer who is also a licensed insurance agent may, with full written disclosure and the client's written consent, collaborate with an insurance agent in designing a comprehensive insurance plan and receive one-half of the commissions payable with respect to insurance policies purchased by the client. The opinion notes that, "since the transaction will create a business relationship between the attorney and the client, Rule 1.8(a) requires that the transaction must be fair and reasonable and the terms fully disclosed to the client, in writing. In addition, the client must be given a reasonable opportunity to

seek the advice of independent counsel, and consent in writing to the transaction."
See also § 1.6.5.

Gifts to a Lawyer or a Person Related to the Lawyer. The prior version of Rule
1.8(c) simply stated that, "A lawyer shall not prepare an instrument giving the lawyer
or a person related to the lawyer as parent, child, sibling, or spouse any substantial
gift from a client, including a testamentary gift, except where the client is related to
the donee." Thus, on its face, the prior version only barred preparing "an instrument"—by its terms, the Rule 1.8(c) did not prohibit a lawyer from accepting a gift
from an unrelated client. In contrast, the present version of Rule 1.8(c) specifically
bars lawyers from soliciting a substantial inter vivos or testamentary gift to the
lawyer or a member of the lawyer's family unless the lawyer or other recipient is
related to the client. As before, the present version prohibits a lawyer from drafting a
document that gives the lawyer or a person related to the lawyer any substantial gift
unless they are related. Statutes in some states ban testamentary gifts to lawyers who
are not related to the client. For example, Tex. Prob. Code § 58b voids testamentary
gifts that are made to (1) the lawyer who prepared, or supervised the preparation of,
the will, or (2) such a lawyer's parent, descendant of a parent, or employee of the
lawyer (or to the spouse of any of them) unless the beneficiary is the testator's
spouse, or a person related within the third degree of sanguinity or affinity. Tex. Prob.
Code § 58b (2011). The exception to the prior rule for gifts "where the client is related
to the donee" did not define who was "related" to the client, an ambiguity exemplified by Cooner v. State Bar, 59 So.3d 29 (Ala. 2010). Cooner held that the term related
included persons related by blood or marriage--specifically that the husband of the
lawyer's aunt was a relative for purposes of Rule 1.8(c).

Under the present version of Rule 1.8(c), the term "related" applies to a broader
class of persons than before. The term now includes, "a spouse, child, grandchild,
parent, grandparent or other relative or individual with whom the lawyer or the
client maintains a close, familial relationship." Importantly, the term now extends to
persons with whom a lawyer maintains a close familial relationship. That expansion
is consistent with prior decisions that allowed lawyers to draft wills that benefited
persons who had been their close friends for many years. The bar of Restatement
§ 127 by its terms only applies to lawyers. However, Comment *c* to § 127 states that,
"A client's gift to a member of the lawyer's family, or to a person or institution
designated by the lawyer, is treated as a gift to the lawyer if it was made under
circumstances manifesting an intent to evade the rule of this Section."

Unfortunately, paragraph (c) still does not attempt to define what constitutes a
"substantial" gift. A gift should be considered substantial if it is substantial in
relation to the size of either the client's or the lawyer's estate. Wash. Informal Op.
86-1 states that, "In determining whether the subject of a particular gift is 'substantial'
the Committee believes the lawyer should focus on the economic nature of the
proposed gift when viewed from the perspective of both the client and the lawyer at
the time the will is prepared." Thus, although a gift that is small in relation to the size
of a client's estate might be substantial in relation to the size of the lawyer's estate,
and vice versa. The ACTEC Commentaries and the Restatement both adopt this
approach. ACTEC Commentaries (4th ed. 2006) 112; Restatement § 127, Comment *f*.

Comment [6] to Rule 1.8 provides that "A lawyer may accept a gift from a client,
if the transaction meets general standards of fairness. For example, a simple gift such
as a present given at a holiday or as a token of appreciation is permitted." One might

reasonably infer that the Rule prohibits a lawyer from accepting a substantial inter vivos gift from an unrelated client. However, Comment [6] provides that, "If a client offers the lawyer a more substantial gift, paragraph (c) does not prohibit the lawyer from accepting it, although such a gift may be voidable by the client under the doctrine of undue influence, which treats client gifts as presumptively fraudulent." The Comment concludes by stating that a lawyer may not suggest that an unrelated client make a substantial gift to or for the benefit of the lawyer.

As indicated by Rule 1.8(c), the taint extends to gifts by a client to the lawyer's spouse or children. *See, e.g., Matter of Peeples*, 374 S.E.2d 674 (S.C. 1988) (lawyer reprimanded for drawing will for client that made gifts to lawyer's daughters); *Estate of Maples*, 738 S.W.2d 853 (Mo. 1987) (joint accounts between client and his grand-nephews, one of whom was his lawyer, but neither was a beneficiary under his will); *In re Gillingham*, 896 P.2d 656 (Wash. 1995) (lawyer who drew will making gift to himself and naming himself executor was disciplined, no exception for informed consent by client). The courts may permit a lawyer to retain a substantial gift made by an unrelated client who was a "close personal friend." *In re* Tonkon, 642 P.2d 660 (Or. 1982) (gift to the lawyer of $75,000 of a $6 million estate; lawyer managed client's financial affairs under a power of attorney.)

Sanctions. A lawyer who prepares a will for an unrelated client that makes a substantial gift to the lawyer may be disciplined. In addition, as a matter of public policy the will may be set aside. *Estate of Marie Haneberg*, 14 P.3d 1088, 1098 (Kan. 2000), However, the *Haneberg* opinion points out that "the better policy is to void that particular gift [to the lawyer] instead of voiding the entire will."

Life Insurance Beneficiary Designations, Joint Tenancies and Other Beneficial Arrangements. Rule 1.8(c) should be viewed as prohibiting a lawyer from assisting an unrelated client in naming the lawyer or a person related to the lawyer as the beneficiary of a substantial amount under a life insurance policy or employee benefit plan. The bar should also extend to giving the lawyer or a member of the lawyer's family a substantial interest in a joint tenancy or any other survivorship arrangement. *See Estate of Maples*, 738 S.W.2d 853 (Mo. 1987). Drawing an instrument that gives the lawyer an option to purchase property at a preferential price or otherwise gives the scrivener substantial economic benefits should also be barred by the rule. *Matter of Rentiers*, 374 S.E.2d 672 (S.C. 1988) (public reprimand upheld where lawyer exercised option but later reconveyed the property).

Exoneration from Liability. Rule 1.8(h)(1) limits the circumstances under which a lawyer may enter into an agreement that either settles an existing or potential claim with an unrepresented client or former client or prospectively limits the lawyer's malpractice liability to a client unless the person is first advised in writing that independent representation is appropriate. Comment [15] to Rule 1.8(h) states that, although a lawyer may enter into an agreement with a present or former client that settles a claim or potential claim for malpractice, "the lawyer must first advise such a person in writing of the appropriateness of independent representation in connection with such a settlement."

Rule 1.8(h) should also be read to prohibit a lawyer from preparing an instrument that exonerates the lawyer from liability for serving as a fiduciary or in some other capacity. A Washington decision holds that "the attorney engaged to write the decedent's will [defendant] is precluded from reliance on the clause to limit his own liability when the testator did not receive independent advice as to its meaning and effect." *Fred Hutchinson Cancer Research Center v. Holman*, 732 P.2d 974, 980 (1987). The law regarding the enforceability of exoneration clauses varies widely among the states. *See* R. Whitman, Exoneration Clauses in Wills and Trust Instruments, 4 Hofstra Prop. L.J. 123 (1992).

Nonclient Pays Lawyer's Fee or Procures Document. One person may pay the cost of a lawyer providing legal services to another if the requirements of Rule 1.8(f) are satisfied. The rule requires that the client give informed consent, that there be no interference with the lawyer's independence of professional judgment and that confidentiality be maintained as required by Rule 1.6.

No matter who initially asks the lawyer to provide the legal services and agrees to pay for them, the person who will execute a legally significant document is usually considered to be the client. In contrast, in such a representation, the payor of the lawyer's fee is generally not a client of the lawyer. As stated in San Diego Op. 1990-3: "[I]n our view the person who will be signing the document is clearly a client of the attorney, and must be treated as such." The payor may, of course, also be a client, which may create a more serious problem, particularly if the payor is preferred by the estate planning documents.

In an extreme case a will or trust that benefits the payor or other person who procured the preparation of the document disproportionately in relation to other equally related persons may be set aside because of the presumed undue influence. *Haynes v. First National Bank*, 432 A.2d 890 (N.J. 1980). However, as stated by the Kansas Court of Appeals:

> The scrivener's representation of clients who may become beneficiaries of a will does not by itself result in a conflict of interest in the preparation of the will. Legal services must be available to the public in an economical, practical way, and looking for conflicts where none exist is not of benefit to the public or the bar. *Estate of Koch*, 849 P.2d 977, 998 (Kan. App. 1993).

Blissard v. White, 515 So.2d 1196 (Miss. 1987) is consistent with the *Koch* opinion.

Undue influence may be inferred although the person who benefits disproportionately under the document did not pay for its preparation—the inference can arise from simply procuring the lawyer's services.

Sexual Relations With Client. The basic reasons for prohibiting sexual relations between a lawyer and client are described in Comment [17] to Rule 1.8. They include, the potential for unfair exploitation of the lawyer's role, the risk that the lawyer's emotional involvement might disable the lawyer from representing the client with independent professional judgment and the risk of loss of the attorney-client evidentiary privilege. The same bar does not apply to the continuation of sexual relations that predate the lawyer-client relationship. However, "the existence of an ongoing sexual relationship between Lawyer and Client could present a substantial risk that Lawyer's representation of Client will be materially limited within the meaning of Oregon RPC 1.7(a)(2)." Oregon Formal Op. 2005-140 (which notes that "Such a conflict could be waived only if the requirements of Oregon RPC 1.7(b) are met.").

Imputed Disqualification. Under Rule 1.8(k), the prohibitions on individual conduct expressed in 1.8(a) through (i) apply to "all lawyers associated in a firm with the personally prohibited lawyer." Comment [20] to Rule 1.8. Thus, if Rule 1.8(c) prohibits a lawyer from drawing a will for a client, the will cannot be drawn by one of the lawyers who are associated with the prohibited lawyer.

§1.6.9. Rule 1.9: Duties to Former Clients

(a) A lawyer who has formerly represented a client in a matter shall not thereafter represent another person in the same or a substantially related matter in which that person's interests are materially adverse to the interests of the former client unless the former client gives informed consent, confirmed in writing.

(b) A lawyer shall not knowingly represent a person in the same or a substantially related matter in which a firm with which the lawyer formerly was associated had previously represented a client

   (1) whose interests are materially adverse to that person; and

   (2) about whom the lawyer had acquired information protected by Rules 1.6 and 1.9(c) that is material to the matter, unless the former client gives informed consent, confirmed in writing.

(c) A lawyer who has formerly represented a client in a matter or whose present or former firm has formerly represented a client in a matter shall not thereafter:

   (1) use information relating to the representation to the disadvantage of the former client except as these Rules would permit or require with respect to a client, or when the information has become generally known; or

   (2) reveal information relating to the representation except as these Rules would permit or require with respect to a client.

Comment [1] to Rule 1.9 properly notes that, "After termination of a client-lawyer relationship, a lawyer has certain continuing duties with respect to confidentiality and conflicts of interest and thus may not represent another client except in conformity with this Rule." At base, the Rule simply requires lawyers to observe some basic continuing duties to former clients.

A lawyer's duties to a present client are, naturally, greater than those owed to a former client. Because of the difference, it is important for lawyers to clarify the status of persons with whom the lawyer has had a professional relationship. Clarification is important because the existence of a lawyer-client relationship is typically determined by the "reasonable" subjective belief of a nonlawyer.

As stated in the ACTEC Commentary on Rule 1.9, "The completion of the specific representation undertaken by a lawyer often results in the termination of the lawyer-client relationship." Whether the relationship terminates upon completion depends upon the nature of the representation and the action, or inaction, of the lawyer and client. Thus, the completion of the administration of an estate may terminate the lawyer's representation of the personal representative. In contrast, as noted in the ACTEC Commentary, "The execution of estate planning documents and implementation of the client's estate plan may, or may not, terminate the lawyer's representation of the client with respect to estate planning matters. In such a case, unless otherwise indicated by the lawyer or client, the client typically remains an estate planning client of the lawyer, albeit the representation is dormant or inactive." Of course, by giving notice a lawyer or client is generally free to terminate a representation.

Some relatively minor changes were made to Rule 1.9 in 2002. First, the title was changed from "Conflict of Interest: Former Client" to "Duties to Former Clients". Second, the consent requirements of paragraphs (a) and (c) were strengthened. Specifically, in paragraphs (a) and (c) the words "gives informed consent, confirmed in writing" were substituted for "consents after consultation." Finally, in addition, in (c)(1) and (2) the words "these Rules" were substituted for "Rule 1.6 or Rule 3.3."

Rule 1.9 permits lawyers to undertake representations that involve conflicts with former clients that would generally not be permitted with respect to current clients. The difference makes it important for lawyers to determine whether a person is a present or former client.

Exit Letters. If neither the lawyer nor the client has acted to terminate a lawyer-client relationship, it may persist for years—even though there was no further direct contact between the lawyer and the client. The uncertainty leads some lawyers to use "exit" letters at the conclusion of a significant matter for a client. However, writing such a letter without offending a client is a daunting challenge. As a formula, the letter should discuss the termination of the present matter and the present relationship, thank the client for having selected the lawyer, invite the client to consult the lawyer with regard to future matters, enclose a final billing, and arrange for the return of any original documents in the lawyer's possession. Note that a court might conclude that a lawyer-client relationship has continued if the lawyer retains custody of the client's original documents.

Completion Letters. Lawyers who do not attempt to sever the relationship may choose to send the client a letter that mentions the completion of the current matter and the "stand-by," or dormant, nature of their continuing relationship. The concept of a dormant representation is discussed at length in ACTEC Commentaries (4th ed. 2006). Among other things the letter might say that in two (or three) years the lawyer would send the client a reminder to review his or her estate planning documents and let the lawyer know if the client wishes to confer about them or make any changes in them. Apart from that, the letter could say, "In the meantime I remain available, should you need assistance, but do not plan to make any other contact with you regarding legal matters."

Periodic Reminders. Sending periodic reminders has been approved by various authorities. For example, ABA Formal Op. 210 (1941) states that, "Periodic notices might be sent to the client for whom a lawyer has drawn a will suggesting that it might be wise for the client to reexamine his will to determine whether or not there has been any change in his situation requiring a modification of his will." *See also* N.Y. Op. 188 (1971).

Rule 1.9 prohibits a lawyer from using information gained in a prior representation to the disadvantage of the former client. However, in many cases the ban can be lifted if the former client gives informed consent. The rule can come into play in the estate planning context in a variety of ways. For example, in most cases this rule would bar a lawyer who had represented a husband or wife in estate planning matters from representing the other of them in a domestic relations dispute. *E.g., Mathias v. Mathias*, 525 N.W.2d 81 (Wis. App. 1994). The same result would follow if the lawyer had initially represented both spouses in estate planning matters. Representation of one of them might be possible if the domestic relations matter were not substantially related to the former matter or if the confidential information obtained in the prior representation could not be used to the disadvantage of one of the parties. However, neither of those conditions is likely to exist.

Under Rule 1.9, a firm that has represented an individual and his companion may be barred from subsequently representing the individual's estate in a paternity action brought by the companion against his estate. *See Santacroce v. Neff*, 134 F. Supp. 2d 368 (D.N.J. 2001). In *Santacroce* the court found that RPCs 1.7 and 1.9 barred the firm from representing the decedent's executors in the suit brought by the companion. The information that the firm had learned during the course of representing her could be used to her disadvantage in the pending action.

§1.6.10. Rule 1.10: Imputation of Conflicts of Interest: General Rule

(a) Except as provided in paragraph (e), while lawyers are associated in a firm, none of them shall knowingly represent a client when any one of them practicing alone would be prohibited from doing so by Rules 1.7 or 1.9, unless the prohibition is based on a personal interest of the prohibited lawyer and does not present a significant risk of materially limiting the representation of the client by the remaining lawyers in the firm.

(b) When a lawyer has terminated an association with a firm, the firm is not prohibited from thereafter representing a person with interests materially adverse to those of a client represented by the formerly associated lawyer and not currently represented by the firm, unless;

    (1) the matter is the same or substantially related to that in which the formerly associated lawyer represented the client; and

    (2) any lawyer remaining in the firm has information protected by Rules 1.6 and 1.9(c) that is material to the matter.

(c) A disqualification prescribed by this rule may be waived by the affected client under the conditions stated in Rule 1.7.

* * *

(Model Rule 1.10 does not include the first clause of paragraph (a) or a paragraph (e).)

In effect this rule assures clients that the duty of loyalty that an individual lawyer owes to a client will not be breached by the conduct of another member of the lawyer's firm. The underlying premise is that "each lawyer is vicariously bound by the obligation of loyalty owed by each lawyer with whom the lawyer is associated." Comment [2] to Rule 1.10. For purposes of the Rules, the "term 'firm' denotes lawyers in a law partnership, professional corporation, sole proprietorship or other association authorized to practice law; or lawyers employed in a legal services organization or the legal department of a corporation or other organization." Comment [1] to Rule 1.10. As explained in Comment [20] to Rule 1.8, a prohibition that applies under Rule 1.8(a)-(i) to one lawyer in a firm also applies to other lawyers who are associated in the firm with the prohibited lawyer. *See also,* Comment [8] to Rule 1.10.

§1.6.11. Rule 1.14: Client With Diminished Capacity

(a) When a client's capacity to make adequately considered decisions in connection with a representation is diminished, whether because of minority, mental impairment or for some other reason, the lawyer shall, as far as reasonably possible, maintain a normal client-lawyer relationship with the client.

(b) When the lawyer reasonably believes the client has diminished capacity, is at risk of substantial physical, financial, or other harm unless action is taken and cannot adequately act in the client's own interest, the lawyer may take reasonably necessary protective action, including consulting with individuals or entities that have the ability to take action to protect the client and, in appropriate cases, seeking the appointment of a guardian ad litem, conservator or guardian.

(c) Information relating to the representation of a client with diminished capacity is protected by Rule 1.6. When taking protective action pursuant to paragraph (b), the lawyer is implied authorized under Rule 1.6(a) to reveal information about the client, but only the extent reasonably necessary to protect the client's interests.

Summary. Paragraph (a) requires a lawyer to maintain, so far as possible, a normal lawyer-client relationship with a client whose capacity to make adequately reasoned decisions is diminished. The same requirement is imposed by Restatement §24(1). In any case, Comment [2] to Rule 1.14 points out that, "the fact a client is disabled does not diminish the lawyer's obligation to treat the client with attention and respect." Indeed, if a client's capacity is diminished, the lawyer may have a special obligation to communicate with the client clearly and effectively. Comment [2] continues to suggest that, "Even if the person has a legal representative, the lawyer should as far as possible accord the represented person the status of client, particularly in maintaining communication."

Under certain circumstances, paragraph (b) allows a lawyer to take protective action on behalf of a client, including seeking the appointment of a guardian. However, the lawyer may only do so if: the lawyer reasonably believes that the client, (1) has diminished capacity; (2) is at risk of substantial physical, financial, or other harm; and (3) cannot adequately act in his or her own interests. The first condition was certainly implied in the former version; the second was similarly implied, and the third was express. Comment [5] to Rule 1.14 appropriately suggests that, "In taking any protective action, the lawyer should be guided by such factors as the wishes and values of the client to the extent known, the client's best interests and the goals of intruding into the client's decision making to the least extent feasible, maximizing client capacities and respecting the client's family and social connections."

Paragraph 1.14(c) first states the obvious—that information regarding a client with diminished capacity is protected by Rule 1.6. Importantly, the rule continues to say that a lawyer is impliedly authorized to reveal information about the client to the extent reasonably necessary to protect the client's interests. The extent to which a lawyer may make disclosures about a client's capacity is discussed below.

If the capacity of a client or prospective client appears to be diminished, the lawyer should attempt to determine the extent of the disability. In determining the extent to which an individual's capacity may be diminished, Comment [6] to Rule 1.14 provides the following advice:

> [T]he lawyer should consider and balance such factors as: the client's ability to articulate reasoning leading to a decision, variability of state of mind and ability to appreciate consequences of a decision; the substantive fairness of a decision and the consistency of a decision with the known long term commitments and values of the client. In appropriate circumstances, the lawyer may seek guidance from an appropriate diagnostician.

Section E of the Aspirational Standards for the Practice of Elder Law With Commentaries (2005), 17-24 includes a helpful discussion of issues regarding client capacity.

Varying Degrees of Diminished Capacity. Lawyers need to keep in mind that a person may be incapable of performing some legal acts, but fully competent to perform others. Thus, courts not infrequently conclude that a person who is subject to a conservatorship or guardianship nonetheless has the capacity necessary to execute a valid will. In *Estate of Mann*, 184 Cal. App .3d 593, 229 Cal. Rptr. 225 (1986), the court stated that, "The express basis of the conservatorship was decedent's inability to manage her person and property. Inability to transact ordinary business does not establish testamentary incapacity." That clients may have differing degrees of capacity underlies the statement in Comment [1] to Rule 1.14 that, "a client with diminished capacity often has the ability to understand, deliberate upon, and reach conclusions about matters affecting the client's own well-being."

What if a Client May Lack Testamentary Capacity? The lawyer is faced with a challenging situation if a person appears to lack testamentary capacity. Lawyers have traditionally, and most commonly, been advised that they should not prepare a will for a person whose testamentary capacity is in doubt. *E.g.,* H. Drinker, Legal Ethics 93 (1953). Consistently, San Diego Op. 1990-3 concludes that, "If the lawyer is not satisfied that the client has sufficient capacity and is free of undue influence and fraud, no will should be prepared. The lawyer may simply decline to act and permit the client to seek other counsel or may recommend the immediate initiation of a conservatorship." However, the Florida Supreme Court held otherwise in *Vignes v. Weiskopf*, 42 So.2d 84 (Fla. 1949). In that case, the court held it was proper for a lawyer to prepare and supervise the execution of a will for a client who was terminally ill and sedated to the point of incapacity. According to the court, "the lawyer should have complied as nearly as he could with the testator's request, should have exposed the true situation to the court, which he did, and should have then left the matter to that tribunal to decide whether in view of all facts surrounding execution of the codicil it should be admitted to probate." In the court's view it would have been improper for the lawyer to arrogate to himself the power and responsibility for deciding the capacity of the testator.

Some decisions suggest that a lawyer is not legally obligated to determine the testamentary capacity of a client. For example, *Moore v. Anderson, et al.*, 135 Cal. Rptr. 2d 888, 895 (Cal. App. 2003), states that the imposition of such a duty on a lawyer would "place an intolerable burden on attorneys. Not only would the attorney be subject to potentially conflicting duties to the client and to potential beneficiaries, but counsel also could be subject to conflicting duties to different sets of beneficiaries." 135 Cal. Rptr. 2d at 896. The court was concerned that, if such a duty were imposed, "Any doubts as to capacity might be resolved by counsel by refusing to draft the will as desired by testator, turning the presumption of testamentary capacity on its head and requiring the testator represented by a cautious attorney to prove his competency." In addition to an analysis of existing California decisions, the opinion relies upon the Restatement and decisions from several other states, including *Logotheti v. Gordon*, 607 N.E.2d 1015 (Mass. 1993), *Morgan v. Roller*, 704 P.2d 1313 (Wash. App. 1990) and *Francis v. Piper*, 597 N.W.2d 922 (Minn. App. 1999).

Under the approach taken by a Michigan decision, a lawyer who makes a reasonable inquiry into a client's understanding of the nature and legal effect of a document cannot be charged with malpractice for failing to determine that the client was incompetent. *Persinger v. Holst*, 639 N.W.2d 594 (Mich. App. 2001), *appeal denied*, 649 N.W.2d 74 (Mich. 2002). According to the opinion, "Although Fuite [the client] was subsequently adjudicated incompetent, at the time she executed the power of attorney defendant exercised reasonable professional judgment with regard to its execution. Further, even if defendant was mistaken, 'mere errors in judgment by a lawyer are generally not grounds for a malpractice action.' "

Capacity to Make Nontestamentary Transfers. Some courts have applied the testamentary capacity test to determine the capacity of a client to designate life insurance beneficiaries, *e.g., McPeak v. McPeak*, 593 N.W.2d 180 (Mich. App. 1999), make gifts or engage in other estate planning. In passing on an individual's capacity to execute an assignment of property and her will, the Oklahoma Supreme Court stated that, the decedent cannot be "found to have capacity to execute one and found to have lacked capacity to execute the other." *Estate of Maggie Carano*, 868 P.2d 699 (Okla. 1994) ("Where capacity' is discussed in this opinion, whether termed testamentary capacity,' mental capacity' or capacity' its meaning will be the same."). The capacity required to make a gift of real property is established if the donor "has an intelligent perception and understanding of the dispositions made of property and the persons and objects he desires to be the objects of his bounty." *Horner v. Horner*, 719 A.2d 1101, 1102 (Pa.Super. 1998). However, the *Horner* case notes that in *Null's Estate*, 153 A. 137 (Pa. 1931), the Pennsylvania Supreme Court stated that, "generally speaking, it requires more business judgment to make a gift than to make a will, as the former is immediately effective, while the latter is prospective."

Preserving Evidence of Capacity. If a client's capacity to execute a will or create a trust may be questioned, the lawyer should consider taking appropriate steps to preserve evidence regarding the client's capacity. The lawyer might give extra attention to planning and conducting the execution ceremony, including the careful selection of credible witnesses. In addition, the lawyer might interview the testator at some length regarding matters that relate to the issue of testamentary capacity. Finally, in some cases, a lawyer may arrange for the execution ceremony to be videotaped. Doing so might deter a will contest or other controversy.

Client's Instructions. A client's disability may, of course, affect the extent to which the lawyer should follow the client's subsequent directions. As noted in the Comment [4] to Rule 1.2, if "the client appears to be suffering diminished capacity, the lawyer's duty to abide by the client's decisions is to be guided by reference to Rule 1.14." Restatement § 24(2) provides that if no guardian or other representative has been appointed to act for a client whose capacity is diminished, the lawyer should, with respect to a matter within the scope of the representation, "pursue the lawyer's reasonable view of the client's objectives or interests as the client would define them if able to make adequately considered decisions on the matter, even if the client expresses no wishes or gives contrary instructions."

Disclosure of Confidential Information on Behalf of Client. A lawyer should be allowed to take reasonable actions on behalf of a client whose capacity appears to be diminished. In particular, a lawyer should be allowed to communicate relevant information regarding a client to persons who might be in a position to assist the client, including family members, health care providers, diagnosticians and persons who are acting in a fiduciary capacity on behalf of the client. Comment [6] to Rule 1.14 advises that when the client's disability is an issue, the lawyer "may seek guidance from an appropriate diagnostician." The recommendation is consistent with the holding of an earlier informal opinion that if the lawyer is concerned about the competency of a client, the lawyer is impliedly authorized to consult with a diagnostician regarding the client's condition. ABA Informal Op. 89-1530.

Anticipating and Planning for Incapacity; Authorizing Disclosure of Confidences. A lawyer should encourage competent clients to plan for the possibility that as a result of injury, illness or advanced age they might become incapable of managing their property. Common precautionary options include transferring property to revocable trusts, executing durable powers of attorney and health care directives, and expressly authorizing the lawyer and other professionals to share information regarding the client's mental and physical condition and estate planning considerations. The client should consider giving the agent under the durable power of authority explicit authority to deal with federal tax matters. The requirements of a power of attorney for tax matters are set out in Reg. § 601.503(a). A properly completed Form 2848 will satisfy the requirements. However, the IRS will recognize a power of attorney in another form, provided it meets the requirements of Reg. § 601.503(a). Under another approach, the IRS will recognize a Form 2848 that is signed by an agent acting under a durable power of attorney that authorizes the agent to handle federal tax matters. The agent must submit a copy of the durable power of attorney and a declaration signed under penalty of perjury that the durable power of attorney is valid under the laws of the governing state.

Advance authorization to disclose information can allow the professionals who assist a client ethically to confer among themselves and with family members regarding the best way in which to protect the client's person and property.

§ 1.6.11

Involvement of Family Members; Protective Action. Cases in which the lawyer is contacted by members of the family of an elderly, ill or disabled person can raise difficult issues involving the identity of the client, the extent of the duty of confidentiality, and of actual or potential conflicts of interest. Comment [3] to Rule 1.14 notes that a client may wish to have family members or others participate in discussions with the lawyer. In any case, the Comment states that, "the lawyer must keep the client's interests foremost and, except for protective action authorized under paragraph (b), must look to the client, and not the family members to make decisions on the client's behalf." Under Rule 1.14(b), "When a lawyer reasonably believes that the client has diminished capacity, is at risk of substantial physical, financial or other harm unless action is taken and cannot act in the client's own interest, the lawyer may take reasonably necessary protective action, including . . . in appropriate cases, seeking the appointment of a guardian ad litem, conservator or guardian."

Effect of Diminished Capacity on Formation of Lawyer-Client Relationship. Rule 1.14 suggests that a pre-existing lawyer-client relationship will survive the client's incapacity. However, Opinion 96-404 indicates that the contrary may be the case—at least in some instances. If a lawyer-client relationship did not previously exist, an incapacitated person may lack the requisite contractual ability to establish a new lawyer-client relationship. Of course, the nature and extent of the client's lack of capacity may affect the issue. A client might, for example, lack capacity to make decisions regarding financial matters, but be able to make decisions regarding other issues—such as health care.

Duties of Lawyer for Guardian or Conservator; Protecting the Ward; Disclosures and Malpractice. A lawyer-client relationship, of course, exists between a guardian (or conservator) and the lawyer engaged to represent the fiduciary. As provided in Comment [4] to Rule 1.14, "If a legal representative has already been appointed for the client, the lawyer should ordinarily look to the representative for decisions on behalf of the client." The Comment continues to state that, "If the lawyer represents the guardian as distinct from the ward, and is aware that the guardian is acting adversely to the ward's interest, the lawyer may have an obligation to prevent or rectify the guardian's misconduct." *See* Rule. 1.2(d). Restatement § 24(3) is generally to the same effect.. In some states the lawyer for a guardian is considered to have a lawyer-client relationship with the ward. *Branham v. Stewart*, 307 S.W.3d 94 (Ky. 2010) ("[T]he attorney retained by an individual in the capacity as a minor's next friend or guardian establishes an attorney-client relationship with the minor and owes the same professional duties to the minor that the attorney would owe to any other client"). As discussed below the courts in other states have invoked other theories to protect the interests of persons who lacked full capacity.

The prevailing view is that a lawyer-client relationship exists between a guardian or conservator and the lawyer who has been engaged to advise the guardian or conservator with respect to the ward or conservatee. However, the relationship between a guardian (or conservator) and the lawyer who represents the guardian is viewed differently in some states. For example, an Illinois opinion holds that because a guardian is required to act for the primary benefit of the ward, the lawyer for the guardian should be treated as representing the ward. *Schwartz v. Cortelloni*, 685 N.E.2d 871 (Ill. 1997). An Illinois ethics opinion states that "the guardian is not represented personally by the attorney but is represented only in his capacity as guardian for closing out the guardianship estate." Ill. Op. 91-24 (1992). The opinion continues to say that the lawyer's duty to the guardianship estate requires the lawyer to protect the estate from possibly fraudulent actions by the guardian. A later Illinois opinion concluded that the law firm that represented a guardian "has a duty to insist that the guardian rectify the fraud committed upon the court using the firm's services. If the guardian refuses to take or authorize remedial action, the Committee believes that the firm would be required to make limited, but sufficient disclosure to the court to the extent necessary to rectify the guardian's misconduct." Il. Op. 98-07.

Cases and opinions from other jurisdictions also indicate that the lawyer for a guardian (or conservator) is obligated to act to protect the interests of the ward. Thus, in *Matter of Fraser*, 523 P.2d 921 (Wash. 1974), a disciplinary action against a lawyer, the court concluded that the lawyer for a guardian should not be "faulted for refusing to abandon the ward at the guardian's request." The court continued to say that the lawyer owed a duty to the ward as well as to the guardian. 523 P.2d at 928. Some courts have imposed liability on lawyers who represented guardians and failed to act to protect the interests of the ward. Thus, in *Fickett v. Superior Court*, 558 P.2d 988 (Ariz. App. 1976), the court stated, "In fact, we conceive that the ward's interests overshadow those of the guardian."

Powers of Attorney. A lawyer who represents the attorney-in-fact under a durable power of attorney may also have a lawyer-client relationship with the principal. In *Keatinge v. Biddle*, 789 A.2d 1271 (Me. 2002), the court stated that, "The mere fact that the person holding the power of attorney retains counsel does not create an attorney-client relationship between the attorney and the grantor. However . . . facts may develop in particular cases that could support a finding that such an attorney-client relationship between attorney and grantor has been created." 789 A.2d at p. 1276. *See also Simon v. Wilson*, 684 N.E.2d 791 (Ill. App. 1997); *Albright v. Burns*, 503 A.2d 386 (N.J. Sup., App. Div. 1986).

An attorney-in-fact may have authority to discharge a client's lawyer and engage another one. Thus, a Connecticut ethics opinion advises that a law firm which holds the original of a client's will should, at the request of the client's attorney-in-fact, transfer the original will to the client's new lawyer. Conn. Op. 03-06 (2003).

Client's Selection of Agent. In *Persinger v. Holst*, 639 N.W.2d 594 (Mich. App. 2001), *appeal denied*, 649 N.W.2d 74 (Mich. 2002), the lawyer was charged with failing to dissuade an elderly client from appointing an agent who the lawyer allegedly knew was "an illiterate, financially incompetent." The court refused to impose such "an extraordinary duty on the defendant." According to the court, "as a matter of law, defendant did not have a legal duty to prevent Fuite [the client] from designating the agent of her choice and the trial court properly dismissed this claim." The outcome of this case is surprising in light of allegations that, (1) the person who was appointed as agent had been represented by the defendant (*i.e.*, he was either the lawyer's present or former client); (2) the agent procured the lawyer's services; and (3) the principal had previously been represented by a different lawyer. In light of those facts, the lawyer may have had a serious conflict of interest and should have done more to protect the aged client.

Emergency Legal Action. According to Comment [9], "a lawyer may take legal action" on behalf of a person with seriously diminished capacity if the person's health, safety or financial interest is threatened with imminent irreparable harm, "even though the person is unable to establish a client-lawyer relationship or to make or express considered judgments about the matter, when the person or another acting in good faith on that person's behalf has consulted with the lawyer." Note that the Comment does not require the lawyer to act; instead, it permits the lawyer to take action. Also note that, according to the Comment, a lawyer is only allowed to take action if the lawyer has been consulted by the person whose capacity is seriously diminished or by a by another acting in good faith on that person's behalf. The qualification imposed by the last clause of the sentence suggests that if a lawyer merely observes the circumstances of a person whose capacity is serious diminished, the lawyer may not be authorized to take emergency action on behalf of that person. According to the Comment, in such a case the lawyer may only take action to the extent necessary "to maintain the status quo or otherwise avoid imminent and irreparable harm." A lawyer who undertakes to act in such an emergency is, of course, subject to the duties imposed by the Rules with respect to clients, including limitations on the disclosures that may be made.

§1.6.12. Rule 1.16: Declining or Terminating Representation

(a) Except as stated in paragraph (c), a lawyer shall not represent a client or, where representation has commenced, shall withdraw from the representation of a client if:

    (1) the representation will result in violation of the rules of professional conduct or other law;

    (2) the lawyer's physical or mental condition materially impairs the lawyer's ability to represent the client, or

    (3) the lawyer is discharged.

(b) Except as stated in paragraph (c), a lawyer may withdraw from representing a client if:

    (1) withdrawal can be accomplished without material adverse effect on the interests of the client,

    (2) the client persists in a course of action involving the lawyer's services that the lawyer reasonably believes is criminal or fraudulent;

    (3) the client has used the lawyer's services to perpetrate a crime or fraud;

    (4) a client insists upon pursuing an objective that the lawyer considers repugnant or with which the lawyer has a fundamental disagreement;

    (5) the client fails substantially to fulfill an obligation to the lawyer regarding the lawyer's services and has been given reasonable warning that the lawyer will withdraw unless the obligation is fulfilled;

    (6) the representation will result in an unreasonable financial burden or has been rendered unreasonably difficult by the client; or

    (7) other good cause for withdrawal exists.

(c) A lawyer must comply with applicable law requiring notice to or permission of a tribunal when termination a representation. When ordered to do so by a tribunal, a lawyer shall continue representation notwithstanding good cause for terminating the representation.

(d) Upon termination of representation, a lawyer shall take steps to the extent reasonably practicable to protect a client's interests, such as giving reasonable notice to the client, allowing time for employment of other counsel, surrendering papers and property to which the client is entitled and refunding any advance payment of fee or expense that has not been earned or incurred. The lawyer may retain papers relating to the client to the extent permitted by other law. (Text of Rule 1.16 quoted from the Delaware Rules of Professional Conduct.)

Mandatory Withdrawal. Withdrawal is mandatory in the circumstances described in paragraph (a). Restatement § 32(1) is to the same effect. An attorney-in-fact may have the power to discharge a client's lawyer and engage a new one. *See* Conn. Op. 03-06 (2003). A lawyer who is discharged by a client, is ordinarily required to withdraw. However, some exceptions exist. For example, in *Matter of Fraser*, 523 P.2d 921 (Wash. 1974), the court held that because of the lawyer's duty to the ward, it was proper for the lawyer to continue to serve as counsel to the guardian until he was replaced by another lawyer although he had been discharged by the ward's guardian. See § 1.6.11, Duties of Lawyer for Guardian or Conservator; Protecting the Ward; Disclosures and Malpractice.

A lawyer may be required to withdraw if he or she learns of a nonconsentable conflict after a representation began. For example, N.Y. Op. 865 held that if the lawyer becomes aware of a potential estate planning malpractice claim after undertaking to represent a deceased client's personal representative, Rule 1.16 requires the lawyer to withdraw, and to "take steps, to the extent reasonably practicable, to avoid unforeseeable prejudice to the right of the client." See § § 1.6.1, 1.6.7.

Discharge by Client. Comment [4] notes that a client normally has the right to discharge a lawyer at any time "with or without cause, subject to liability for payment for the lawyer's services." However, Comment [6] points out that a client whose capacity is seriously diminished may lack the legal capacity to discharge the lawyer. According to Comment [6], in such a case, "the lawyer should make special effort to help the client consider the consequences and may take reasonably necessary protective action as provided in Rule 1.14" Generally speaking, a lawyer who represents multiple parties such as co-fiduciaries may be discharged by either.

Voluntary Withdrawal. Under the circumstances described in Rule 1.16(b) a lawyer may, optionally, withdraw from a representation. Restatement § 32(3) is generally to the same effect. A withdrawing lawyer must, however, take reasonable steps to protect a client's interests. In the estate planning context there is usually no need to take special action to protect the interests of a client. All that is usually required is for the lawyer to return original documents to the former client and provide him or her with copies of relevant file documents. The former client should, of course, be cautioned regarding steps to be taken in pending matters, particularly if action is required within a specific time frame (*e.g.*, filing a tax refund claim within the time allowed).

Completion of Representation. A lawyer-client relationship may end when a representation is completed. For example, the completion of an estate administration proceeding normally ends the lawyer-client relationship between the lawyer and the decedent's personal representative. On the other hand, a lawyer-client relationship between a lawyer and a living estate planning client may continue for some period following the completion of the estate plan unless the relationship is expressly terminated by the lawyer or the client. Termination and the concept of a dormant representation are discussed in § 1.4.1.

§ 1.6.13. Rule 1.18: Duties to Prospective Client

    (a) A person who discusses with a lawyer the possibility of forming a client-lawyer relationship with respect to a matter is a prospective client.

    (b) Even when no lawyer-client relationship ensues, a lawyer who has had discussions with a prospective client shall not use or reveal information learned in the consultation, except as Rule 1.9 would permit with respect to information of a former client.

    (c) A lawyer subject to paragraph (b) shall not represent a client with interests materially adverse to those of a prospective client in the same or a substantially related matter if the lawyer received information from the prospective client that could be significantly harmful to that person in the matter, except as provided in paragraph (d). If a lawyer is disqualified from representation under this paragraph, no lawyer in a firm with which that lawyer is associated may knowingly undertake or continue representation in such a matter, except as provided in paragraph (d).

    (d) When the lawyer has received disqualifying information as defined in paragraph (c), representation is permissible if:

        (1) both the affected client and the prospective client have given informed consent, confirmed in writing, or;

        (2) the lawyer who received the information took reasonable measures to avoid exposure to more disqualifying information than was reasonably necessary to determine whether to represent the prospective client; and

            (i) the disqualified lawyer is timely screened from any participation in the matter and is apportioned no part of the fee therefrom; and

            (ii) written notice is promptly given to the prospective client. (Text of Rule 1.18 quoted from the Delaware Rules of Professional Conduct.)

Rule 1.18, added to the Model Rules in 2002, describes the duties that a lawyer owes to a prospective client (a term that is defined in paragraph (a) as "a person who discusses with a lawyer the possibility of forming a client-lawyer relationship with respect to a matter"). Although lawyers previously owed some to duties to prospective clients, it is helpful to have the clarification provided by Rule 1.18.

A person is usually a prospective client for a brief period at the conclusion of which the lawyer and prospective client will either create, or not create, a lawyer-client relationship. If a lawyer-client relationship is created, the lawyer will owe the client the full panoply of duties that are owed to clients. If a lawyer-client relationship is not created, the prospective client becomes a former prospective client, to whom the lawyer owes duties analogous to those owed to a former client under Rule 1.9. In particular, as provided in paragraph (b), if no lawyer-client relationship is created, the lawyer 'shall not use or reveal information learned in the consultation,' except as Rule 1.9 would permit with respect to information of a former client. Under paragraph (c), a lawyer may be disqualified from representing a person "with interests materially adverse to those of a prospective client in the same or a related matter if the lawyer received information from the prospective client that could be significantly harmful to that person in the matter..." The provisions of Restatement § 15 are generally consistent with those of Rule 1.18.

In addition to providing clarification and guidance, the new rule may also help lawyers avoid "planned disqualifications"—brief communications, sometimes from another lawyer, that are intended to disqualify the recipient from later undertaking an adverse role in a matter. The scenario typically begins with a telephone call from another lawyer or a person who poses as a prospective client, during which little, if any, confidential information is communicated to the recipient. The recipient is not retained by, and has no further contact with, the caller. If the lawyer later wishes to represent a party whose interests are adverse to the caller, the caller may argue that the recipient is disqualified from representing anyone else in the matter. However, under the rule disqualification occurs only 'if the lawyer received information from the prospective client that could be significantly harmful to that person in the matter.' Even if disqualifying information was communicated to the lawyer, representation of another party is permissible with the informed consent of all parties as provided in paragraph (d).

Limit Information Communicated by Persons Making Initial Communications to Lawyer. Lawyers should consider taking steps to limit the information that is communicated in cold calls to them regarding a possible representation. For example, a lawyer might state at the outset that the person should not communicate any confidential information to the lawyer until the lawyer has explored whether any conflicts might prevent the representation and the lawyer has decided to accept it. Comment [4] recognizes that, "In order to avoid acquiring disqualifying information from a prospective client, a lawyer considering whether or not to undertake a new matter should limit the initial interview to only such information as reasonably appears necessary for that purpose."

Not all persons who communicate information to a lawyer qualify as prospective clients. Thus, as provided in Comment [2], "A person who communicated information unilaterally to a lawyer, without any reasonable expectation that the lawyer is willing to discuss the possibility of forming a client-lawyer relationship, is not a 'prospective client' within the meaning of paragraph (a)."

Declination Letters. If a lawyer declines to represent a person who has made initial contact with the lawyer, the lawyer should consider sending that person a declination letter. For a form of declination letter, see Form 1-2, § 1.6.2. The letter should recite that the communications between them were limited, that the lawyer had declined the representation and that the person should take prompt steps to consult another lawyer, particularly if a limitations period might be involved.

§ 1.6.14. Rule 2.1: Advisor

> In representing a client, a lawyer shall exercise independent professional judgment and render candid advice. In rendering advice, a lawyer may refer not only to law, but also to other considerations such as moral, economic, social and political factors, that may be relevant to the client's situation.

This rule emphasizes the necessity of providing clients with the lawyer's best advice and judgment. Doing so is even more necessary if the client's judgment of a matter appears to be unrealistic. Indeed, the requirement of candor that is imposed by this rule might be viewed as required by the duty of Rule 1.1 to provide clients with competent legal representation. Some clients may initially complain if a lawyer delivers an unwelcome legal evaluation. However, with adequate counseling they will often come to appreciate the importance of receiving candid and truthful advice.

As noted in the second sentence of Rule 2.1, a lawyer may counsel a client regarding nonlegal considerations that may be relevant to the client's legal affairs. Thus, a lawyer might counsel a client in a tax matter regarding the frustration, disruption, and stress that might occur if the client takes an overly aggressive tax stance that results in a tax audit or litigation. Similarly, a lawyer might counsel a client who plans to make unequal gifts to his children regarding the possibly adverse impact that doing so might have on the children and their relationship to each other. A lawyer might also caution clients about other actions that may be unwise or have adverse family consequences. For example, providing in a trust that a beneficiary's right to receive distributions will terminate if the beneficiary marries (or divorces), may be unwise: If the benefits of a trust will terminate if the beneficiary marries, the beneficiary may choose to live with another person without entering into a formal marriage.

Consistent with this rule, in appropriate circumstances, a lawyer may suggest that a client consult other professionals, such as a health care provider, a financial advisor or a counselor in the client's religion. The advice of other professionals can be helpful in dealing with a wide range of issues, including family business succession planning. Lawyers should be cautious about giving specific advice regarding matters beyond their ken, particularly with regard to investments. While it is entirely proper to point out the desirability of diversifying a client's investment portfolio, it is questionable whether a lawyer should recommend any particular investment. Making specific recommendations regarding investments can expose the lawyer to unnecessary risks. Also, lawyers who undertake to provide advice regarding investments may unwittingly violate federal and state laws that regulate investment advisors.

§1.6.15. Rule 2.2: Intermediary (Deleted from Model Rules in 2002)

(a) A lawyer may act as intermediary between clients if:

  (1) the lawyer consults with each client concerning the implications of the common representation, including the advantages and risks involved, and the effect on the attorney-client privileges, and obtains each client's consent to the common representation;

  (2) the lawyer reasonably believes that the matter can be resolved on terms compatible with the clients' best interests, that each client will be able to make adequately informed decisions in the matter and that there is little risk of material prejudice to the interests of any of the clients if the contemplated resolution is unsuccessful; and

  (3) the lawyer reasonably believes that the common representation can be undertaken impartially and without improper effect on other responsibilities the lawyer has to any of the clients.

(b) While acting as intermediary, the lawyer shall consult with each client concerning the decisions to be made and the considerations relevant in making them, so that each client can make adequately informed decisions.

(c) A lawyer shall withdraw as intermediary if any of the clients so requests, or if any of the conditions stated in paragraph (a) is no longer satisfied. Upon withdrawal, the lawyer shall not continue to represent any of the clients in the matter that was the subject of the intermediation.

Rule 2.2 was deleted from the Rules on the theory that representation of multiple parties was more appropriately subject to the provisions of Rule 1.7. Former Rule 2.2 is discussed here because it remains in effect in some states. Under Former Rule 2.2, a lawyer who consults with multiple parties about implications of a common representation and receives their consent may act as intermediary in assisting them to achieve their common goals. Acting as intermediary does not diminish the lawyer's duty to provide loyal and diligent representation to each party. The text of the rule assumes that all relevant information will be shared between the clients. Otherwise it would be impossible to comply with the requirements of the rule, particularly paragraph (b).

Preconditions, Rule 2.2(a). A lawyer can proceed with an intermediation if the three preconditions of Rule 2.2(a) are satisfied. First, that each party is aware of the advantages and disadvantages of the intermediation and each consents. Second, that the lawyer reasonably believes the matter can be resolved in a manner consistent with the clients' best interests, that each client will be able to make informed decisions, and the failure of the intermediation would not materially prejudice the interests of any of the clients. Third, the lawyer reasonably believes he or she can act impartially without improper effect on other responsibilities the lawyer may have to any party. As a point of comparison, recall that under Rule 1.7 one of the preconditions to undertaking a representation if there is a concurrent conflict of interest is that the lawyer "reasonably believes that the lawyer will be able to provide competent and diligent representation to each affected client." *See* § 1.6.7.

Relationship to Rule 1.7. A lawyer who satisfies the requirements to act as an intermediary in the manner authorized by Former Rule 2.2 could, almost certainly, pass the conflicts tests of Rule 1.7. The Former Rule 2.2 enables a lawyer to act primarily as a scrivener in a matter, in effect, translating the agreement of multiple parties into a legally effective document.

Impartiality. As indicated by subparagraph (a)(3), a lawyer who acts as intermediary is required to be impartial in representing the common clients. Intermediation is improper if the lawyer cannot act fairly and impartially on behalf of all parties.

Organization of Business Entity or other Joint Representation. A lawyer can act as an intermediary in a variety of tax and family planning contexts. A common example is in the organization of a family business as a partnership, corporation or LLC. Such a representation calls for a specially crafted engagement letter that informs all parties of the nature and limitations of the lawyer's role, the risks involved in multiple representations (particularly the need to be free to communicate all facts to each party), and the requirement that the lawyer withdraw if a conflict develops or if any party asks the lawyer to withdraw. In a business formation intermediation, if the clients are unable to reach agreement regarding the terms upon which the entity will be formed, the intermediation has failed and each party should obtain independent representation.

Termination, Rule 2.2(c). Paragraph (c) requires the lawyer to withdraw if either party asks the lawyer to withdraw or if any of the three preconditions is no longer satisfied. The rule continues to provide, "Upon withdrawal, the lawyer shall not continue to represent any of the clients in the matter that was the subject of the intermediation." Note, however, that Rule 2.2(c) does not prohibit a withdrawing lawyer from representing one of the parties in an unrelated matter. Thus, a lawyer who has participated in a failed business formation intermediation could continue to represent one of the parties in unrelated tax or estate planning matters.

A lawyer should be permitted to continue to represent one of the parties in the present matter if the other party does not object. Thus, a lawyer who initially represented a husband and wife an estate planning matter should, so long as their interests are not adverse, be allowed to continue to represent one of them, despite being discharged by the other. Allowing the lawyer to do so is logically consistent with other relevant rules, particularly Rule 1.9. In such a case the lawyer should obtain a written waiver from the consenting party.

§ 1.6.16. Rule 3.3: Candor Toward the Tribunal

   (a) A lawyer shall not knowingly:

   (1) make a false statement of material fact or law to a tribunal or fail to correct a false statement of material fact or law previously made to the tribunal by the lawyer;

      (2) fail to disclose to the tribunal legal authority in the controlling jurisdiction known to the lawyer to be directly adverse to the position of the client and not disclosed by opposing counsel; or

      (3) offer evidence that the lawyer knows to be false. If a lawyer, the lawyer's client, or a witness called by the lawyer, has offered material evidence and comes to know of its falsity, the lawyer shall take reasonable remedial measures, including, if necessary, disclosure to the tribunal. A lawyer may refuse to offer evidence, other than the testimony of a defendant in a criminal matter, that the lawyer reasonably believes is false.

   (b) A lawyer who represents a client in an adjudicative proceeding and who knows that a person intends to engage, is engaging, or has engaged in criminal or fraudulent conduct related to the proceeding shall take reasonable remedial measures, including, if necessary, disclosure to the tribunal.

   (c) The duties stated in paragraph (a) and (b) continue to the conclusion of the proceeding, and apply even if compliance requires disclosure of information otherwise protected by Rule 1.6.

   (d) In an ex parte proceeding, a lawyer shall inform the tribunal of all material facts known to the lawyer that will enable the tribunal to make an informed decision, whether or not the facts are adverse. (Text of Rule 3.3 quoted from the Delaware Rules of Professional Conduct.)

A lawyer acting as an advocate before a court, legislative committee, or administrative tribunal is obligated to be truthful and not to withhold material facts when disclosure is required in order to avoid assisting in a criminal or fraudulent act. According to Rule 3.9, the duties of Rule 3(a)-(c) apply to lawyers who appear as advocates in nonadjudicative proceedings. Thus, a lawyer who offers a will for probate may not fail to disclose that the testator left a will later than the one offered by the lawyer. *In re Hedrick*, 822 P.2d 1187 (Or. 1991) (until 2002 Oregon was a Model Code state); *Reynolds v. Givens*, 588 P.2d 113 (Or. App. 1978), (fees of the personal representative and lawyer disallowed because the petition prepared by the lawyer that resulted in the appointment of personal representative falsely stated that decedent died intestate). Similarly, a lawyer's attempt to mislead the court about his fraudulent conveyance of real estate to his father in order to avoid payment of a judgment against him can result in disbarment. *Florida Bar v. Rood*, 620 So.2d 1252 (Fla. 1993) (serious prior disciplinary history). On the other hand, an ABA opinion holds that a lawyer may properly file a civil action although the lawyer knows that it is barred by the statute of limitations. ABA Formal Op. 94-387.

    The requirement of truthfulness extends to documents prepared by the lawyer. Thus, a lawyer cannot present the court with an accounting or other document the lawyer knows to be false or misleading. A lawyer should decline a request to prepare a false or misleading document. If the client insists, the lawyer may have no alternative but to withdraw from the representation.

The IRS is generally considered to be an adversary and not a "tribunal" for purposes of this and other rules. *See* ABA Formal Op. 314 (1965) (applying the Model Code; reconsidered in ABA Formal Op. 85-352). In this connection, note that Rule 4.1 prohibits a lawyer from misleading the IRS or permitting a client to do so.

Ex Parte Proceedings. As indicated in paragraph (d) of the rule, ex parte proceedings are subject to a strict requirement of disclosure and fairness. Comment [14] to this rule states that, "The judge has an affirmative responsibility to accord the absent party just consideration. The lawyer for the represented party has the correlative duty to make disclosures of material facts known to the lawyer and that the lawyer reasonably believes are necessary to an informed decision." Thus, in submitting an ex parte matter to the court, a lawyer must inform the court of important facts relating to the matter. For example, a lawyer must inform the court if a decedent left a later will or that another party had initiated a prior estate administration proceeding.

§ 1.6.17. Rule 4.1: Truthfulness in Statements to Others

In the course of representing a client a lawyer shall not knowingly:

>   (a) make a false statement of material fact or law to a third person; or
>   (b) fail to disclose a material fact to a third person when the disclosure is necessary to avoid assisting a criminal or fraudulent act by a client, unless disclosure is prohibited by Rule 1.6.

This rule requires a lawyer to be truthful in making statement of fact or law to third parties. As noted in Comment [2], "Under generally accepted conventions in negotiations, certain types of statements ordinarily are not taken as statements of material fact. Estimates of price or value placed on the subject of a transaction and a party's intentions as to acceptable settlement of a claim are in this category and so is the existence of an undisclosed principal except where nondisclosure of the principal would constitute fraud." The rule also does not prohibit "puffing" or exaggeration in negotiations. Finally, the rule does not require the lawyer to disclose confidential information that is protected from disclosure by Rule 1.6. ABA Formal Op. 93-375 (examination of bank that is lawyer's client).

The application of the rule is difficult—and the line between misleading statements and "honest" puffing can be hard to draw. The difficulty of the lawyer's task is referred to in the Preamble to the Model Rules: "[a]s negotiator, a lawyer seeks a result advantageous to the client but consistent with the requirements of honest dealing with others."

Application to Tax Matters. Circular 230 and Rule 4.1 prohibit a lawyer from preparing a false tax return. ABA Formal Op. 85-352 makes it clear that the rule applies to the preparation of tax returns and negotiations with the IRS.

If a lawyer or other tax practitioner discovers that a client has made an error in a tax return, Circular 230 requires that the lawyer advise the client of the error and of the possible consequences under the Code and Regulations. § 10.21. However, under Rule 1.6, the lawyer could not disclose the error to the IRS or others without the client's consent. Essentially the same action is required of CPAs by AICPA Statements of Responsibilities in Tax Practice, No. 7. If the taxpayer refuses to remedy the error, the lawyer may be obligated to withdraw from the representation. In any case, the lawyer could not prepare subsequent documents, such as gift tax returns, that are based on the accuracy of previously filed returns. As pointed out in a leading text, it is not clear whether a practitioner is obligated to disclose a favorable mathematical error to the IRS. B. Wolfman, J. Holden & K. Harris, Standards of Tax Practice § 403.2.1 (3d ed. 1995). Under ABA Informal Op. 86-1518, a lawyer should inform opposing counsel that the adversary had inadvertently omitted an important clause in a contract that would be of advantage to the adversary.

A decedent's personal representative is required to report all of a decedent's property on the decedent's estate tax return. Property that is discovered after the return is filed and before the three-year limitations period has run should be reported on a supplemental return. It is not clear whether a personal representative who made a good faith effort to locate and report all of a decedent's property is obligated to report property that is discovered after the end of the three-year period. However, Circular 230 does not draw any distinction. Under it, a lawyer who knows of "an omission from any return" is required to "advise the client promptly of the fact of such . . . omission." As a practical matter, if the personal representative has made a good faith effort to locate and report all of a decedent's property, it may be unnecessary to report property that is discovered after the limitations period has expired. In such cases, the IRS typically advises lawyers who file supplemental returns that the collection of any additional tax is time barred.

§ 1.6.18. Rule 4.2: Communication with Person Represented by Counsel

> In representing a client, a lawyer shall not communicate about the subject of the representation with a person the lawyer knows to be represented by another lawyer in the matter, unless the lawyer has the consent of the other lawyer or is authorized to do so by law or a court order.

This rule protects a party who is represented by a lawyer in a matter from being overreached or otherwise being disadvantaged by lawyers who represent other parties in the matter. Parties can generally communicate directly without the presence of counsel. However, the rule bars some direct communications between clients. For example, direct communication between parties is impermissible if the communications by one of the parties is "scripted" by his counsel, or is otherwise directed by counsel. *See* Cal. Formal Op. 1993-131 (discussing Cal. Bar Rule 2-100). For purposes of this rule a lawyer proceeding pro se is not permitted to communicate directly with the opposing party who is represented by counsel. D.C. Op. No. 258 (1995).

The scope of the rule is clarified by Comment [8] under which the prohibition only applies in "circumstances where the lawyer knows that the person is in fact represented in the matter to be discussed." Communications with a person who is not known to be represented by counsel must comply with the requirements of Rule

4.3—the lawyer may not state or imply that he is disinterested and if the lawyer knows or reasonably should know the unrepresented person misunderstands the lawyer's role, the lawyer must make reasonable efforts to correct the misunderstanding.

Without the consent of the lawyer for a nonclient, a lawyer should not discuss a pending matter with the nonclient, even one who initiates the communication. When confronted with such a problem, the lawyer should courteously inform the nonclient of the substance of this rule and the lawyer's consequent inability to communicate directly with the nonclient. Accordingly, the lawyer for a personal representative should not communicate with a represented party who has filed a creditor's claim or is otherwise interested in the decedent's estate.

Review of Another Lawyer's Work. Rule 4.2 does not prohibit a lawyer from rendering a "second opinion" regarding a legal matter. *In re Mettler*, 748 P.2d 1010 (Or. 1988) (prior version of Rule 4.2 under the Model Code). In the words of a Utah ethics opinion, "The purposes of Rule 4.2 are not served by restricting an individual's ability to discuss his or her case with an attorney who is not connected with the matter." Utah Op. 110 (1993). In such a case the lawyer is not acting on behalf of another client in communicating with the person requesting the review.

§1.6.19. Rule 4.3: Dealing with Unrepresented Person

> In dealing on behalf of a client with a person who is not represented by counsel, a lawyer shall not state or imply that the lawyer is disinterested. When the lawyer knows or reasonably should know that the unrepresented person misunderstands the lawyer's role in the matter, the lawyer shall make reasonable efforts to correct the misunderstanding. The lawyer shall not give legal advice to an unrepresented person, other than the advice to secure counsel, if the lawyer knows or reasonably should know that the interests of such a person are or have a reasonable possibility of being in conflict with the interests of the client.

A lawyer who must have contact with unrepresented third parties in connection with a representation should ensure that those parties understand the role of the lawyer in the matter. Thus, in connection with the representation of a fiduciary, the lawyer should make it clear to the beneficiaries of the fiduciary estate that the lawyer does not represent them. Of course, in some cases the same lawyer may appropriately represent the fiduciary and a beneficiary. The clearest case is when the fiduciary is also the only beneficiary of the fiduciary estate. In appropriate cases the lawyer should suggest that the beneficiaries, or other third parties, such as creditors, obtain their own counsel. In some instances it is appropriate for the lawyer to inform a creditor that the lawyer does not represent the creditor and suggest that the creditor obtain independent representation. In *Heutel v. Stumpf*, 783 S.W.2d 421 (Mo.App. 1989), the court held that the lawyer for the personal representative properly informed a creditor that he represented the personal representative and that she should obtain her own counsel.

§ 1.6.20. Rule 5.3: Responsibilities Regarding Nonlawyer Assistants

With respect to a nonlawyer employed or retained by or associated with a lawyer:

(a) a partner, and a lawyer who individually or together with other lawyers possesses comparable managerial authority in a law firm shall make reasonable efforts to ensure that the firm has in effect measures giving reasonable assurance that the person's conduct is compatible with the professional obligations of the lawyer;

(b) a lawyer having direct supervisory authority over the nonlawyer shall make reasonable efforts to ensure that the person's conduct is compatible with the professional obligations of the lawyer; and

(c) a lawyer shall be responsible for conduct of such a person that would be a violation of the Rules of Professional Conduct if engaged in by a lawyer if:

    (1) the lawyer orders or, with the knowledge of the specific conduct, ratifies the conduct involved, or

    (2) the lawyer is a partner or has comparable managerial authority in the law firm in which the person is employed, or has direct supervisory authority over the person, and knows of the conduct at a time when its consequences can be avoided or mitigated but fails to take reasonable remedial action.

* * *

[A]s our cases have made plain, an attorney must supervise work done by lay personnel and a lawyer stands ultimately responsible for work done by his non-lawyer employees . . . .We have stated:

While delegation of a task entrusted to a lawyer is not improper, it is the lawyer who must maintain a direct relationship with his client, supervise the work that is delegated and exercise complete, though indirect, professional control over the work product. The work of lay personnel is done by them as agents of the lawyer employing them. *Oklahoma Bar Ass'n v. Mayes*, 977 P.2d 1073, 1082 (Okla. 1999).

Under this rule a lawyer who employs the services of paraprofessionals or other legal assistants may delegate functions to them, so long as the lawyer supervised and is responsible for their work. In fact, lawyers may be required to use staff for those purposes in order to provide clients with efficient and economical legal services. For example, if the lawyer's fee in an estate administration proceeding is challenged, the court may bar the lawyer from being compensated at professional legal rates for routine tasks that could have been performed by nonlawyers. *E.g.*, *Estate of Larson*, 694 P.2d 1051 (Wash. 1985). In inter vivos estate planning, a lawyer may use properly supervised legal assistants to draft wills, trusts, or other documents. In such cases, the lawyer is, of course, ultimately responsible for the work product. A lawyer who fails to supervise nonlawyers who are "retained by or associated with the lawyer" may be subject to discipline. For example, a lawyer may be disciplined for failing to supervise nonlawyer client service representatives of a group of companies that prepare estate planning documents. *In re Flack*, 33 P.2d 1281 (Ks. 2001).

Although a lawyer may properly use nonlawyers to perform routine nonlegal tasks and some preparatory legal tasks, strictly legal tasks cannot be delegated to a nonlawyer. Thus, a legal assistant or other nonlawyer should not be allowed to supervise the execution of a will. Courts in some jurisdictions have properly concluded that a nonlawyer who supervises the execution of a will has engaged in the unauthorized practice of law, which could subject his or her lawyer-supervisor to disciplinary action.

A lawyer must give nonlawyers appropriate instructions and supervision regarding the ethical responsibilities of lawyers and their employees. As noted in Comment [1] to Rule 5.3, a lawyer "must give such assistants appropriate instruction and supervision concerning the ethical aspects of their employment, particularly regarding the obligation not to disclose information relating to representation of the client, and should be responsible for their work product."

Many firms provide nonlawyer staff members with written materials that describe their ethical responsibilities. Office manuals or memoranda can provide a firm's staff with accessible and reliable reference sources. Comment *f* to Restatement §11 notes that all lawyers in a firm must take reasonable steps to ensure that the conduct of all nonlawyers in the firm is compatible with the professional obligations of the lawyer. In addition, each lawyer "must make reasonable supervisory efforts with respect to the particular nonlawyers over whom the lawyer has direct supervisory authority." As suggested in an article by the Nevada State Bar Counsel, "It pays to take time out and meet with your staff in a serious mode from time to time to ensure that they conduct themselves in a manner compatible with your professional obligations." Rob W. Bare, 10 Most Common Bar Complaints—and How to Avoid Them, 5 Nev. Lawyer 15 (1997).

In serious cases, lawyers who fail adequately to supervise staff members or other nonlawyers who are associated with them, may be reprimanded or suspended from practice. For example, an Ohio lawyer was suspended from practice for six months for failing utterly to supervise a secretary who embezzled over $200,000 from estates, trusts, and guardianships of which the lawyer was serving as a fiduciary or as counsel. *Office of Disciplinary Counsel v. Ball*, 618 N.E.2d 159 (Ohio 1993). Courts in other states have imposed similar sanctions; *e.g., In re Flack*, 33 P.3d 1281 (Ks. 2001) (lawyer given two years supervised probation and public censure); *In re Fortson*, 606 S.E.2d 461 (S.C. 2004) (suspension for two months for failure to supervise handling of money and performance of other services of two firms he engaged to assist in real estate matters).

§1.6.21. Rule 5.5: Unauthorized Practice of Law

(a) A lawyer shall not practice law in a jurisdiction in violation of the regulation of the legal profession in that jurisdiction, or assist another in doing so.

(b) A lawyer who is not admitted to practice in this jurisdiction shall not

　　(1) except as authorized by these Rules or other law, establish an office or other systematic and continuous presence in this jurisdiction for the practice of law; or

　　(2) hold out to the public or otherwise represent that the lawyer is admitted to practice in this jurisdiction.

(c) A lawyer admitted in another United States jurisdiction, and not disbarred or suspended from practice in any jurisdiction may provide legal services on a temporary basis in this jurisdiction that:

　　(1) are undertaken in association with a lawyer who is admitted to practice in this jurisdiction and who actively participates in the matter;

　　(2) are in or reasonably related to a pending or potential proceeding before a tribunal in this or another jurisdiction if the lawyer, or a person the lawyer is assisting, is authorized by law or order to appear in such proceeding or reasonably expects to be so authorized;

　　(3) are in or reasonably related to a pending or potential arbitration, mediation, or other alternative dispute resolution proceeding in this or another jurisdiction, if the services arise out of or are reasonably related to the lawyer's practice in a jurisdiction in which the lawyer is admitted to practice and are not services for which the forum request pro hac vice admission; or

　　(4) are not within paragraphs (c)(2) or (c)(3) and arise out of or are reasonably related to the lawyer's practice in a jurisdiction in which the lawyer is admitted to practice.

(d) A lawyer admitted in another United States jurisdiction, and not disbarred or suspended from practice in any jurisdiction, may provide legal services in this jurisdiction that:

　　(1) are provided to the lawyer's employer or its organizational affiliates and are not services for which the forum requires pro hac vice admission; or

　　(2) are services that the lawyer is authorized to provide by federal law or other law of this jurisdiction. (Text of Rule 5.5 quoted from the Delaware Rules of Professional Conduct.)

Rule 5.5 allows lawyers to engage, at least temporarily, in an expanded range of multijurisdictional services in states where they are not admitted to practice. Changes and additions to the rule made in 2002 were most welcome because of the prior lack of guidance regarding the extent to which a lawyer admitted to practice in one state might advise clients regarding matters involving the law of other states.

Rule 5.5(a) prohibits lawyers from practicing law in a jurisdiction in violation of the regulation of the legal profession in that jurisdiction. The critical questions are: "what constitutes practicing law in a jurisdiction," and "what limits do the rules of the jurisdiction impose on the practice of law." As indicated in Comment [2], "The definition of the practice of law is established by law and varies from one jurisdiction to another." Paragraph (b)(1) properly provides that a lawyer who is not admitted to practice in State A cannot open a law office or have a systematic and continuous presence in that state and engage in the general practice of law there. Similarly, a lawyer not admitted to practice in State A cannot regularly travel to State A and advise residents of State A regarding matters subject to the law of State A. In a pre-2002 case a lawyer was disciplined by his "home" jurisdiction for appearing in a number of cases before a federal district court in another jurisdiction in which he was not admitted to practice. *Office of Disciplinary Counsel v. Scuro*, 522 N.E.2d 572 (Ohio 1988).

Paragraph (c) allows a lawyer who is admitted to practice in one state to provide legal services on a "temporary basis" in another state if the requirements of one of the four subparagraphs are met. In considering the applicability of this rule, note that, as stated in Comment [6], "[t]here is no single test to determine whether a lawyer's services are provided on a 'temporary basis' . . . "

Involving Lawyer in Foreign State. Turning to the subparagraphs, (c)(1) allows a lawyer admitted in State A to provide legal services in State B, provided they are undertaken in association with a lawyer who is authorized to practice in State B and participates actively in the representation. This paragraph would allow a lawyer who is only admitted to practice in State A, to draft a will, deed, or other document that affects property located in State B in association with a lawyer admitted to practice in State B. As before, it should be sufficient if the State B lawyer reviews the documents. The safest course is, generally, for a lawyer to associate or consult with a qualified lawyer in another state regarding matters of its law. Doing so better protects both the client and the lawyer in the "home" jurisdiction. Given the wide variety of laws regarding the rights of surviving family members to claim homesteads and family allowances and to elect against a will, a client who is domiciled in a foreign jurisdiction or owns property there, would be ill served by a lawyer who, unassisted, draws a will for him or her.

A lawyer admitted to practice in State A does not assist in the unauthorized practice of law by providing legal advice on matters subject to the law of State A to a State B lawyer (not licensed to practice in State A) who, in turn, uses that advice in drafting opinions and documents or otherwise advising his or her own clients. As explained by a representative of the Florida Bar:

> There are many situations where a Florida attorney may communicate with a member of another state bar on Florida matters. For example, out-of-state attorneys may consult with a Florida attorney on Florida law as it relates to a real estate transaction for the purpose of giving that informa-

tion to their client or incorporating that information into an opinion for their client. Such communication is not prohibited . . . .[A]ttorneys are often asked to review estate planning documents drafted by out-of-state attorneys. This review is not improper and is in fact encouraged. Bateman, Letter to Action Line, Vol. XXVI, No. 1, Fall 2004.

Pending or Potential Litigation. Subparagraph (c)(2) allows lawyers to participate in a pending or potential proceeding before a tribunal if the lawyer or a person the lawyer is assisting is authorized by law to participate or reasonably expects to be authorized to participate. As pointed out in the ACTEC Commentaries (4th ed. 2006) 162-163: "Thus, a lawyer asked to assist or handle estate litigation could investigate the underlying facts, meet and counsel clients, and provide related services, provided the lawyer reasonably expected to be admitted *pro hac vice.*"

Pending or Potential Alternative Dispute Resolution (ADR) Proceeding. Under subparagraph (c)(3) a lawyer may participate in a "pending or potential arbitration, mediation or other alternative dispute resolution proceeding", if the services "arise out of or are reasonably related to the lawyer's practice in a jurisdiction in which the lawyer is admitted to practice and are not services for which the forum requires pro hac vice admission." As pointed out in the ACTEC Commentaries this exception should allow a State A lawyer to engage in settlement discussions in State B that are reasonably related to the lawyer's practice in State A: "logically a lawyer should be able to assist a client with settlement negotiations in a non-admitted jurisdiction if the lawyer could assist the client with ADR."

Services Related to Practice in Home State. Importantly, subparagraph (c)(4) "permits a lawyer admitted to practice law in another jurisdiction to perform certain legal services on a temporary basis in this jurisdiction that arise out of or are reasonably related to the lawyer's practice in a jurisdiction in which the lawyer is admitted but are not within subparagraphs (c)(2) or (c)(3) [litigation or ADR]". Accordingly, a lawyer admitted to practice in State A should be allowed to advise an estate planning client who resides in State A regarding estate planning implications of the ownership of property in other states. Indeed, such a lawyer should be allowed to prepare documents relating to property in other states and its disposition, including wills, deeds and trusts. However, particularly because of differences in state law, the safest course is to have such documents prepared, or reviewed, by lawyers who are admitted to practice in the other states.

Federal Tax Practice, etc. Paragraph (d)(2) recognizes that a lawyer who is legally entitled to practice in a jurisdiction in the United States may practice law in another jurisdiction to the extent allowed by federal law or the law of the other jurisdiction. This exception is, in effect, mandated by the federal preemption doctrine, which allows a lawyer who is admitted to practice before the IRS to advise clients regarding federal tax matters in jurisdictions in which the lawyer is not admitted to practice. In *Grace v. Allen*, 407 S.W.2d 321 (Tex. Civ. App. 1966), a Texas appellate court stated that, "The rights conferred by the admission to practice before the Treasury Department are federal rights which cannot be impinged on by the states in their praiseworthy efforts to protect their citizens from the unskilled and unethical practitioners of the law." 407 S.W.2d at 327.

Accordingly, a lawyer admitted in State A may advise residents of State A regarding federal tax matters that affect property located in other jurisdictions.

Likewise, a State A lawyer should be able to meet in another state with clients who are domiciled in State A regarding federal tax issues and matters subject to the law of State A. As indicated above, subparagraph (c)(4) would allow the lawyer to give advice with respect to a broader range of issues that are reasonably related to an existing representation in State A.

Using Properly Supervised Paralegals and Legal Assistants is Permissible. Rule 5.5(b) prohibits lawyers from assisting others to engage in the unauthorized practice of law. However, Comment [2] points out that the rule does not prohibit a lawyer from delegating work to paralegals or other office assistants so long as the lawyer supervises the work and is responsible for it. Comment *g* to Restatement §4 also recognizes the propriety of using properly supervised nonlawyers to conduct activities that, if conducted without supervision, would constitute the unauthorized practice of law. Thus, paralegal assistants may, with the supervision of a lawyer, interview clients, draft and file documents, and perform other nondiscretionary tasks. Paralegals should not supervise the execution of wills or other documents, attempt to provide legal advice, or appear in court.

§1.6.22. Rule 8.3: Reporting Professional Misconduct

> (a) A lawyer who knows that another lawyer has committed a violation of the Rules of Professional Conduct that raises a substantial question as to that lawyer's honesty, trustworthiness or fitness as a lawyer in other respects, shall inform the appropriate professional authority.
>
> (b) A lawyer who knows that a judge has committed a violation of the applicable rules of judicial conduct that raises a substantial question as to the judge's fitness for office shall inform the appropriate authority.
>
> (c) [The text of this paragraph varies from jurisdiction to jurisdiction: in some it "does not require" a lawyer to disclose of information about the misconduct of another lawyer or a judge that would otherwise be protected from disclosure by Rule 1.6; in others it "does not permit" a lawyer to disclose such information.] (Text of paragraphs (a) and (b) of Rule 8.3 quoted from the Delaware Rules of Professional Conduct.)

The Rule is an incident of the self-regulation of the legal profession. It does not apply to minor violations by a lawyer or judge. Under the very text of the Rule, it only applies to "substantial" questions of the honesty, trustworthiness, or fitness of a lawyer or judge. The rule obviously does not require disclosure by a lawyer who is retained to represent a lawyer whose professional conduct is in question. Comment [4].

An estate planning lawyer who learns that another lawyer charged clearly excessive fees in an estate matter is obligated to report the misconduct. Ariz. Op. 94-09. However, if the lawyer learned of the excessive charge from a client, "it would appear that he must obtain the consent of the client before he discloses information to the state bar." *Ibid.*

A lawyer who learns through unprivileged communications of serious misconduct by a client's former attorney is obligated to report the misconduct although the client does not wish the misconduct to be reported. Ill. Op. 91-7. However, a lawyer who represents a client in a malpractice action against the client's prior lawyer, may not report the misconduct of the prior lawyer without the client's informed consent. D.C. Op. No. 246 (revised Oct. 1994). ABA Formal Op. 94-383 states that a lawyer may not threaten to file disciplinary complaints against another lawyer in order to induce a settlement or gain an advantage in a civil case. Similarly, a New York opinion condemns filing a report of misconduct in order to gain an advantage. N.Y. Op. 635 (1992). Courts may discipline a lawyer who fails to report the serious misconduct of a client's former lawyer and negotiates a settlement with the prior lawyer in which the client agrees not to initiate any criminal, civil or attorney disciplinary action against him. *In re Himmel*, 533 N.E.2d 790 (1988) (lawyer suspended for one year).

E. CONCLUSION

§1.7. CONCLUSION

Lawyers who are engaged in an estate planning practice must be thoroughly familiar with the ethical rules applicable to their practices. A sufficient understanding of the rules benefits the lawyers and their clients. For example, with appropriate disclosures and the informed consent of the client, a lawyer may be able to represent multiple clients, such as family members or business associates. Similarly, with the consent of a former client, Rule 1.9 permits a lawyer, in a related matter, to represent another party whose interests are adverse to the former client. A lawyer who fails to comply with the rules puts too much at risk—in terms of the lawyer's interests and those of the client.

BIBLIOGRAPHY

ABA, Annotated Model Rules of Professional Conduct (5th ed. 2003)

ACTEC, ACTEC Commentaries on the Model Rules of Professional Conduct (4th ed. 2006)

Allen, Power to Contractually Appoint "Attorney for the Estate," a Non-Existent Right of a Decedent, 21 J. Legal Prof. 145 (1997)

American Law Institute, Restatement (Third), Law Governing Lawyers (2000)

Basson, M., A View from Inside the IRS Estate and Gift Tax Program—Sometimes You Really Do Have a Friend at the IRS!, U. Miami, 28th Inst. Est. Plan., Ch. 16 (1994)

Berall, Engagement Letters Clarify a Lawyer's Representation, 30 Est. Plan. 315 (July 2003)

Blattmachr, Gans & Rios, The Circular 230 Deskbook (2006)

Collett, T., And the Two Shall Become One . . . Until the Lawyers Are Done, 7 Notre Dame J. Law, Ethics & Pub. Pol. 101 (1993)

Corneel, F., Ethical Guidelines for Tax Practice, 28 Tax L. Rev. 1 (1972)

Crawford & Loyd, CPA's Multistate Guide to Ethics and Professional Conduct (2009)

Durst, T., The Tax lawyer's Professional Responsibility, 39 U. Fla. L. Rev. 1027 (1987)

English, The Uniform Health-Care Decisions Act, 15 Prob. & Prop. 19 (May/June 2001)

The Ethics of Intergenerational Representation, 62 Fordham L. Rev. 1453 (1994)

Feinschreiber & Kent, Estate Tax Malpractice, 84 Tax Notes 909 (Aug. 9, 1999)

Fogel, Estate Planning Malpractice, Special Issues in Need of Special Care, 17 Prob. & Prop. 20 (Jul/Aug. 2003)

Frolik, Old Age With Fears and Ills: Planning for the Very Old Client, U. Miami, 38th Inst. Est. Plan., Ch. 17 (2004)

Fox, The Top Ten Ethical Challenges Facing Estate Planning Practitioners Today and the Best Practices for Addressing Them, U. Miami, 42nd Inst. Est. Plan. Ch. 16 (2008)

Gage, Gromala & Kopf, Holistic Estate Planning and Integrating Mediation in the Estate Planning Process, 39 Real Prop., Prob. & Tr. J. 509 (2004)

Harris, K., On Requiring the Correction of Error Under the Federal Tax Law, 42 Tax Law. 515 (Spring 1989)

Harrison & Kuo, Fees: How to Charge, Collect and Defend Them, 148 Tr. & Est. 50 (Mar. 2009)

Hazard, G., Triangular Lawyer Relationships: An Exploratory Analysis, 1 Geo. J. Legal Ethics 15 (1987)

Hazard, Geoffrey C., Jr. and Hodes, William, The Law of Lawyering (2d ed. 1996) (looseleaf)

Johns, Older Clients with Diminishing Capacity and their Advance Directives, 39 Real Prop., Prob. & Tr. J. 107 (2004)

Lamm, To my Son, I Leave All my Passwords, 148 Tr. & Est. 22 (July 2009)

Lischer, Professional Responsibility Issues Associated With Asset Protection Trusts, 39 Real Prop. Prob. & Tr. J. 561 (Fall 2004)

Mancini, The Impact of Ethics and Circular 230 on the Attorney Engaged in Tax Planning, U. Miami, 41st Inst. Est. Plan., Ch. 15 (2007)

Mulroney, M., Report on the Invitational Conference on Professionalism in Tax Practice, Washington, D.C., October, 1993, 11 Am. J. Tax Policy 369 (Fall 1994)

National Academy of Elder Law Attorneys, Aspirational Standards for the Practice of Elder Law with Commentaries (2005)

Price, J., Duties of Estate Planners to Nonclients: Identifying, Anticipating and Avoiding the Problems, 37 So. Tex. L. Rev. 1063 (1996)

Professional Responsibility in Federal Tax Practice (B. Bittker ed. 1970)

Rogers, Avoiding Malpractice Claims in Planning and Administration, 22 Est. Plan. 359 (1995)

Ross, Picking Up the Pieces When Law and Ethics Collide, U. Miami, 34th Inst. Est. Plan., Ch. 8 (2000)

Timbie, R., The Hazards of Return Preparation: Preparer Penalties, Aiding and Abetting Penalties, Substantial Understatement Penalties, and Worse, N.Y.U. 46th Inst. Fed. Tax. Ch. 47 (1988)

Tuttle, R., The Fiduciary's Fiduciary: Legal Ethics in Fiduciary Representation, 1994 U. Ill. L. Rev. 889

Volkmer, Malpractice Liability of Fiduciaries and Estate Planning Attorneys, 33 Est. Plan. 51 (Sept. 2006)

Watson, C., Tax Lawyers, Ethical Obligations, and the Duty to the System, 47 Kan. L. Rev. 847 (1999)

Weinstein, Tax Shelters—The Ethical Dilemma, U. Miami, 38th Inst. Est. Plan., Ch. 15 (2004)

Wolfman, Bernard, Standards of Tax Practice (2004 ed.)

Wolfman, Bernard, Holden, James P. and Schenk, Deborah, Ethical Problems in Federal Tax Practice (3rd ed. 1995)

2

Basic Transfer Tax Laws and Estate Planning Strategies

A. INTRODUCTION

§2.1. SCOPE

This chapter opens with an historical review and summary of the main features of the federal gift and estate taxes. Next, a longer look is given to the present version of the generation-skipping transfer tax (GSTT) and the recent tax imposed on recipients of gifts from so-called covered expatriates. The chapter concludes with a discussion and classification of the most important basic estate planning tax strategies. Depending upon the reader's background, the chapter may serve either as an initial orientation to the federal transfer taxes or as a refresher. In either case, the chapter introduces the remainder of the book. Later chapters explore the federal taxes in more detail and examine the various devices that can be used to carry out the basic planning strategies. The income taxation of trusts and estates is summarized in Chapters 10 and 12, respectively, and relevant income tax considerations are discussed throughout the book. Later materials also consider the major nontax considerations that bear on the selection and implementation of various estate planning techniques.

That this chapter's scope is limited to federal wealth transfer taxes is not to suggest that state and local estate and gift taxes are insignificant. Prior to the enactment of the Economic Growth and Tax Relief Reconciliation Act of 2001, most states imposed an estate tax equal to the credit for state and local estate taxes under former §2011. *See* §2.16. When the 2001 Act limited and ultimately repealed the credit, these states were left to decide whether to impose a stand-alone estate tax in lieu of the "pick-up" tax under the federal credit. State and local transfer taxes are now imposed in about half the states, so planners should be careful to consider state transfer tax implications of their recommendations to clients. For a summary of the basic planning issues at play, *see* Breed & Civitella, The State Matters, Priv. Wealth 49 (Apr.-May 2008).

B. UNIFIED TRANSFER TAX SYSTEM

§2.2. HISTORICAL NOTE

Federal inheritance taxes were imposed for three short periods between 1797 and 1902 in order to meet temporary fiscal emergencies. The federal estate tax was adopted in 1916, largely to finance the cost of military preparations for participation in World War I. *See* Eisenstein, The Rise and Decline of the Estate Tax, 11 Tax L. Rev. 223, 230-231 (1956). It has remained essentially the same, although refinements have been made over the years to meet new challenges and to deal with changed circumstances. For example, important changes have been made in the taxation of powers of appointment, §2041, and of life insurance, §2042. The adoption of a limited marital deduction in 1948, §2056, was perhaps the single most important change made between 1916 and 1976. The most sweeping changes in the federal transfer tax laws were made by the 1976 Act, which unified the gift and estate tax structure, the 1981 Act, which removed the quantitative limits on the amount of the marital deduction, and the 1986 Act, which imposed a new form of GSTT, and the 2001 Act, which introduced a temporary repeal of the federal estate tax and GSTT through gradually increasing exemption amounts and gradually decreasing tax rates.

The first federal gift tax was adopted in 1924 and repealed two years later. That short-lived tax was seriously flawed by the fact that it was calculated annually on a noncumulative basis. It was also weakened by a large annual exemption. In 1932, the existing graduated, cumulative gift tax was adopted in more or less its present form. It was intended to help bolster federal tax revenues, which had sagged with the onset of the Great Depression, and to supplement the income and estate taxes. A gift tax provides valuable protection for income and estate taxes by imposing a tax on transfers that would deplete the amount of a donor's income and the size of his or her estate. Perhaps because it was adopted at a later time, the gift and estate taxes were largely independent of each other until their unification in 1976.

Unification was spurred by the extraordinary preferences the dual system accorded to inter vivos gifts, which resulted from three of its basic features. First, although the gift and estate tax rate schedules had identical brackets, at each interval the gift tax was only 75 percent of the estate tax rate. Second, the gift tax was based upon only the net value of the property transferred (*i.e.,* the gift tax on a transfer was not "grossed up" and included in the tax base). In contrast, the estate tax was based upon the total amount of the decedent's gross estate (*i.e.,* the amount of the estate tax itself was included in the tax base). Third, inter vivos gifts were usually not included in the donor's gross estate or otherwise included in the estate tax base.

Although the gift tax was calculated on the cumulative total of gifts made by the donor after June 6, 1932, gifts completed more than three years prior to death were generally not included in the donor's estate tax base. When an inter vivos gift was included in the donor's gross estate, the donor's estate was allowed a credit for any gift tax paid (or due) on the gift. Despite the allowance of the credit, the amount of the gift tax was not included in the estate tax base. In fact, a deduction was allowed for any gift tax that was due but unpaid at the time of death. Deathbed gifts were strongly encouraged by the availability of the credit and the failure to include the amount of the gift tax in the donor's estate tax base.

The operation of the dual transfer tax system under the pre-1977 law is illustrated by Example 2-1.

EXAMPLE 2-1.

X and *Y* each owned property worth $2 million. *X* made no gifts during his lifetime. Accordingly, when he died, his entire estate was subject to the old estate tax. Under the old rates an estate tax of $726,200 would have been due from *X*'s executor, leaving his family $1,273,800. *Y* made a lifetime gift of $1 million to her family, which would have been subject to a gift tax of $227,625. The remaining $772,375 would have been subject to an estate tax of $220,035 when she died. Thus, taxes of $447,660 would have been paid with respect to *Y*'s transfers, leaving $1,552,340 for her family. By giving half of her estate away during her lifetime *Y* could pass almost $280,000 more to her family than *X*, who made no inter vivos gifts.

Commentators frequently charged that the preference shown for inter vivos gifts was unjustified and discriminatory and proposed various remedial steps, including the adoption of a unified transfer tax system. A form of unified transfer tax was advanced in the 1969 tax reform proposals that were published by the Treasury Department. Tax Reform Studies and Proposals, 91st Cong., 1st Sess. (Comm. Print 1969).

In 1976 Congress concluded that the dual transfer tax system was inequitable and undesirable, and sought to remedy the situation by unifying the existing gift and estate tax systems. Staff of Joint Comm. on Taxn., General Explanation of the Tax Reform Act of 1976, 94th Cong., 2d Sess., 526 (1976). The unification largely eliminated the features of the dual system that preferred inter vivos gifts. However, the changes do not require the gift tax paid on a transfer made more than three years prior to death to be grossed up and included in the tax base. The 1976 Act also left intact the gift tax annual exclusion, which sheltered annual gifts of $3,000 or less per donee from both the gift and the estate tax.

The 1981 Act increased the amount of the gift tax annual exclusion to $10,000 per donee. The 1997 Act indexed the amount of the annual exclusion for gifts made in calendar years after 1998 based on the increase in the cost of living after 1997. However, if the amount of the adjustment is not a multiple of $1,000, the amount of the exclusion is rounded down to the next lowest multiple of $1,000. The annual exclusion increased to $11,000 in 2002 and to $12,000 in 2006, and to $13,000 in 2009. By regularly making gifts within the amount of the exclusion an individual can transfer a substantial amount of property to the donees completely free of tax. The remaining tax incentives for making lifetime gifts are discussed in detail in Chapter 7.

§2.3. UNIFICATION UNDER THE TAX REFORM ACT OF 1976 AND SUBSEQUENT CHANGES

The transfer tax system was unified by adopting a single progressive rate schedule that applies to the cumulative total of lifetime and deathtime taxable transfers. As a result, the tax on lifetime gifts more closely approximates the tax cost of equivalent transfers at death. However, making lifetime gifts remains attractive because the tax paid on lifetime gifts is only "grossed up" and included in the transfer tax base if the donor dies within three years of making the gift. *See* § 2035(b). Thus, the tax exclusive feature of the gift tax strongly encourages wealthy individuals to make lifetime gifts. The change to a unified system does substantially reduce the large disparity in the tax imposed on the two taxpayers described in Example 2-1, above. Any retroactive effect of unification was avoided by cumulating only the amount of post-1976 gifts. § 2001(b)(2).

The unified rate schedule adopted in 1976, § 2001(c), opens at a higher rate than the prior one but the rates increase more slowly and end at a lower rate than before. Also, the 1976 Act substituted a single unified credit for the former separate lifetime $30,000 gift tax and $60,000 estate tax exemptions. The unified credit, which applies to lifetime or deathtime transfers, increased in roughly equal annual increments from $30,000 in 1977 to $47,000 in 1981, the latter of which was equal to the tax imposed on a taxable transfer of $175,625. The adoption of the unified credit eliminated the estate tax on about two-thirds of the estates that would otherwise have been required to file estate tax returns.

The effect of the unification is most evident when it comes to calculating the estate tax due from the estate of a person who made taxable gifts after December 31, 1976. First, a "tentative tax" is determined by applying the unified rate schedule to the sum of the post-1976 taxable gifts and the taxable estate. § 2001(c). Then the estate tax is determined by subtracting the amount of gift tax on post-1976 gifts. (Pre-1977 gifts are not included in the tax base at death and no credit is allowed for any gift tax paid with respect to them.) The amount of the estate tax thus calculated is then reduced by the unified credit allowable for the year of the decedent's death. § 2010(a). The unified credit is always allowed in the full amount, because all post-1976 taxable gifts are included in the base upon which the estate tax is calculated, either as an adjusted taxable gift or as an item included in the donor's gross estate. Credits are also allowed against the estate tax for taxes paid on prior transfers, § 2013, and for foreign death taxes, § 2014.

EXAMPLE 2-2.

T made taxable gifts of $150,000 prior to 1977 and taxable gifts of $1,600,000 in 2008. *T* paid a gift tax of $283,700 on the 2008 gifts, which is the amount by which the tax on the gifts ($629,500) exceeded the amount of *T*'s unified credit ($345,800) allowable at the time. *T*'s gift tax was calculated as follows:

Taxable gifts prior to 1977	$150,000
Plus Taxable gifts in 2008	1,600,000
Lifetime total of taxable gifts	$1,750,000
Tentative tax on total taxable gifts	$668,300
Less: Tax on pre-1977 gifts	38,800
Gift tax on 2008 gifts	$629,500

Less: Unified credit	345,800
Gift tax payable for 2008	$283,700

T died in 2009 leaving a taxable estate of $3,900,000 including the gift tax of $283,700 that was paid within 3 years of death. *See* §2035(b). In 2009, the applicable exclusion amount was $3.5 million, the tax on which $1,455,800.

An estate tax of $616,300 is due from *T*'s estate, calculated as follows:

Post-1976 taxable gifts	$1,600,000
Plus Taxable estate	3,900,000
Tax base	5,500,000
Tentative tax	2,355,800
Less: Gift tax paid on post-1976 gifts	283,700
Estate tax	$2,072,100
Less: Unified credit	1,455,800
Estate tax payable	$616,300

The Omnibus Budget Reconciliation Act of 1981 increased the unified credit in unequal annual stages from $47,000 (the tax on $175,625) in 1981 to $192,800 (the tax on $600,000) in 1987 and thereafter, which further diminished the number of estates required to file estate tax returns.

Under the 1981 Act, the maximum gift and estate tax rates would decrease 5 percent annually in each of the following four years. Between 1981 and 1984, the maximum rate decreased from 70 percent to 55 percent. Practically speaking, the fourth reduction never took place. In an attempt to help control the size of the federal deficit, the scheduled reduction in the maximum rate to 50 percent was deferred in 1984 and again in 1987. The Revenue Reconciliation Act of 1993 eliminated the reduction to 50 percent that was scheduled to take effect in 1993. The retroactive change in the federal estate tax rate was upheld in *National Taxpayer's Union, Inc. v. United States*, 68 F.3d 1428 (D.C. App. 1995). The result was anticipated in light of the unanimous decision in *United States v. Carlton*, 512 U.S. 26 (1994), which upheld the retroactive amendment of §2057. In *Nationsbank of Texas v. United States*, 269 F.3d 1332 (Fed. Cir. 2001), *cert. denied*, 537 U.S. 813 (2002), the court upheld the constitutionality of the reinstatement of the 55-percent rate by the 1993 Act.

Between 1981 and 1987, the "spread" between the lowest and the highest marginal rates at which the estate tax is payable shrank from 38 percent (70 percent – – 32 percent) to only 18 percent (55 percent — 37 percent), or 23 percent, taking account of the 5 percent surtax applicable to taxable estates in excess of $10 million. The shrinkage increased the advantages of deferring the payment of any estate tax and decreased the advantages of equalizing the sizes of the spouses' estates. A consideration of the relative advantages of deferral and equalization must take other factors into account, including the effect of inflation on the amount of property subject to tax and the yield that can be earned on the amount of any taxes that are deferred.

Impact of Unification and Other Changes. The unification of the gift and estate tax and the adoption of the GSTT (See §§2.24-2.42) improved the overall equity of the transfer tax system. Changes made since 1976 also sealed some important loopholes. At the same time the increases in the unified credit relieved the vast majority of estates of the obligation to file an estate tax return and to pay any federal transfer tax. Unfortunately, changes made since 1976 have increased the complexity of the transfer tax laws, which inevitably increases the compliance costs and the potential for estate planning malpractice. Alas, neither simplicity nor stability is a hallmark of the federal transfer tax system.

Income Tax Rates Applicable to Individuals and Fiduciary Estates. Changes made in the 1980s and 1990s compressed the income tax rates applicable to individuals and fiduciary estates—of which the latter was by far the most severe. The extreme compression of the rates applicable to fiduciary estates largely eliminated the income splitting advantages that once flowed from the creation and maintenance of separate fiduciary estates. A table showing the income tax rates applicable to various classes of taxpayers appears below, Table 2-4, at § 2.46. The 2001 Act reduced most income tax rates applicable to individuals and trusts and estates. However, the 10-percent rate bracket only applies to individual taxpayers—not to trusts and estates. See § 2.46.

Taxpayer Relief Act of 1997. The 1997 Act introduced scheduled increases in the unified credit. Under the 1997 Act, the credit was scheduled to reach $345,800 (the tax on $1 million) in 2006. The 1997 Act changed the terminology of the credit provisions, replacing "unified credit" with "applicable credit amount." In turn, § 2010 was amended to provide that the "applicable credit amount" in a particular year was the amount of the tentative tax imposed on a stated "applicable exclusion amount."

The 1997 Act amended § 6034A to require that beneficiaries report items in a manner consistent with the positions taken by trusts and estates or disclose the inconsistencies in their returns. The change applies with respect to returns filed after the effective date of the Act, August 7, 1997.

Economic Growth and Tax Relief Reconciliation Act of 2001. The 2001 Act made sweeping cuts in the income tax, reduced the estate tax and generation-skipping transfer (GSTT) tax, and provided that the latter taxes would not apply after December 31, 2009. The 2001 Act contained a "sunset" provision, however, meaning that the pre-existing law would be restored on January 1, 2011.

The 2001 Act is to blame for much of the present uncertainty regarding the federal wealth transfer tax system. The 2001 Act initially fixed the gift tax credit equivalent amount at $1 million and provided for a number of increases in the estate tax credit equivalent. For 2006, 2007, and 2008, the estate tax credit equivalent and the GSTT exemption amount was $2 million; for 2009, these amounts increased to $3.5 million. The 2001 Act called for repeal of both the estate tax and GSTT in 2010, but only for that year. Come 2011, the 2001 Act would sunset, meaning that the estate tax and GSTT exemption amounts would return to $1 million at that time

The changes partially reversed the unification of the estate and gift tax rates that came into effect in 1976. The "decoupling" of the estate tax and gift tax exclusion amounts in some cases had an adverse effect. For example, a donor who made a taxable gift of $1.5 million in 2008 had to pay a gift tax of $210,000. If the donor died in 2009 with a taxable estate of $2 million, the tentative tax would be computed on a tax base of $3.5 million, on which no tax would be due by reason of the $3.5 million estate tax credit equivalent. However, the donor's estate would not be entitled to any refund of the gift tax that was paid.

The 2001 Act also reduced the maximum estate and gift tax rates by 5 percent, from 55 percent to 50 percent, followed by a series of additional 1 percent decreases, bottoming out at 45 percent as of January 1, 2007. For 2010, the maximum gift tax rate was cut to 35 percent.

The 2001 Act did not repeal the gift tax, which remained in effect for 2010 even after the purported repeal of the estate tax and GSTT, albeit with a significantly lower maximum rate (35 percent). The gift tax was retained in an effort to preserve the integrity of the income tax. Legislators feared that if the gift tax were also repealed, the unlimited tax-free transfer of property among family members might substantially erode the impact of the income tax.

The 2001 Act also phased out the former estate tax credit allowed for state death taxes. The credit was converted to a deduction. The deduction is, of course, of no benefit to the states that imposed a soak-up tax equal to the maximum amount of the former state death tax credit.

Surtax. Former § 2001(c)(2), added by the Revenue Act of 1987, imposed a 5-percent surtax on estates in excess of $10 million. It applied to the extent necessary to phase out the benefits of the unified credit and of the lower rates that apply to the first $3 million. From 1987 to 1998 the maximum addition to tax, which applied to taxable amounts between $10 million and $21,040,000, was $552,000. (The amount equal to the maximum $192,800 unified credit formerly allowable, plus the $359,200 benefit of the lower rates that apply to the first $3 million of a taxable estate.) The 1997 Act inadvertently eliminated the surtax on the unified credit; it was later restored. As amended former § 2001(c)(2) increased the tentative tax by an amount equal to "5 percent of so much of the amount (with respect to which the tentative tax is to be computed) as exceeds $10,000,000 but does not exceed the amount at which the average tax rate under this section is 55 percent." In effect the addition to tax applied to taxable amounts between $10,000,000 and $17,184,000. The 2001 Act repealed the surtax altogether, though this provision too was subject to the sunset of the 2001 Act in 2011.

Tax Relief, Unemployment Insurance Reauthorization, and Job Creation Act of 2010. The 2010 Act restored the federal estate tax retroactively to January 1, 2010, but with a $5 million applicable exclusion amount and a flat tax rate of 35 percent on all amounts in excess of this exclusion. Perhaps because the legislation was conceived and passed very late that year, the 2010 Act gave personal representatives of decedents dying in 2010 the ability to elect out of the application of the federal estate tax. The election comes at a cost, however, as beneficiaries of those estates electing out of the estate tax must grapple with the carryover basis rules of § 1022.

The 2010 Act retained both the 35-percent flat tax rate and the $1 million applicable exemption amount for the federal gift tax, applicable to gifts made in 2010. The 2010 Act restored the GSTT retroactively to January 1, 2010, with a $5 million exemption similar to that in effect for the federal estate tax. The GSTT rate, however, was set a zero percent for 2010 only, meaning that some transfers in 2010 that would otherwise be subject to the GSTT would be exempt from the tax.

For 2011 and 2012, the 2010 Act reunified the applicable exclusion amount for federal estate and gift taxes. Both taxes now have a $5 million exclusion and feature a flat tax rate of 35 percent. Similarly, the GSTT has a $5 million exemption and a flat tax rate of 35 percent in effect for those years. For decedents dying in 2011 and 2012, the 2010 Act offers a new "portability" election whereby the decedent's personal representative can elect to transfer any unused applicable exclusion amount to the decedent's surviving spouse.

The 2010 Act formally extended the "sunset" of the 2001 Act for two years. Accordingly, on January 1, 2013, the aforementioned changes made by the 2001 Act and the 2010 Act will expire. As a result, the applicable exclusion amount for the federal estate and gift taxes will revert to $1 million (as will the exemption amount for the GSTT, though this exemption amount is subject to an inflation adjustment indexed from 1997), and the applicable tax rates will again be progressive, reaching a maximum of 55 percent.

Table 2-1 summarizes the increases to the applicable exclusion amount made by the 2001 Act and the 2010 Act.

Table 2-1
Estate Tax Applicable Exclusion Amount Under 2001 Act and the 2010 Act

Decedents Dying in:	Applicable Exclusion Amount
2002-2003	$1 million
2004-2005	1.5 million
2006-2008	2 million
2009	3.5 million
2010	5 million*
2011	5 million
2012	5 million**
2013***	1 million

* Personal representatives of decedents dying in 2010 can elect out of the application of the federal estate tax, though there may be income tax consequences to those acquiring property from the decedent arising from the election.
** The $5 million exclusion in 2012 is subject to an inflation adjustment.
*** Under the sunset provisions of the 2001 Act and the 2010 Act the pre-existing law is restored on January 1, 2013.

The credit equivalents and maximum rates under the prior law and the combination of the 2001 Act and the 2010 Act are compared in Table 2-2.

Table 2-2
Credit Equivalents and Maximum Tax Rates Under Prior Law and the 2001 and 2010 Acts

Calendar Year	Estate, Gift, and GSTT Credit Equivalents under Prior Law	Estate and GSTT Deathtime Credit Equivalents under 2001 and 2010 Acts	Gift Tax Credit Equivalent under 2001 and 2010 Acts	Prior Law	Maximum Estate and Gift Tax Rate under 2001 and 2010 Acts
2002	$700,000	$1 million	$1 million	55%	50%
2003	700,000	1 million	$1 million	55%	49%
2004	850,000	1.5 million	$1 million	55%	48%
2005	950,000	1.5 million	$1 million	55%	47%
2006	1,000,000	2 million	$1 million	55%	46%
2007	1,000,000	2 million	$1 million	55%	45%
2008	1,000,000	2 million	$1 million	55%	45%
2009	1,000,000	3.5 million	$1 million	55%	45%
2010	1,000,000	$5 million	$1 million	55%	35%
2011	1,000,000	$5 million	$5 million	55%	35%
2012	1,000,000	$5 million	$5 million	55%	35%
2013	Sunset provisions of 2001 Act and 2010 Act restore prior provisions of all taxes.				

* Until January 1, 2004, the GSTT exemption was fixed at $1 million, adjusted for post-1997 inflation (*i.e.*, $1,060,000 in 2001). Since 2004, the GSTT exemption and the estate tax credit equivalent have been unified (*i.e.*, $2 million in 2006-2008, etc.).

Portability of Unused Exclusion Amounts Between Spouses. The 2010 Act changed the definition of the applicable exclusion amount from a fixed dollar figure to the sum of two other amounts: the "basic exclusion amount" ($5 million) and, in the case of a surviving spouse, the "deceased spousal unused exclusion amount"(DSUEA). § 2010(c)(2)-(3). The DSUEA is generally equal to the amount by which the basic exclusion amount of the surviving spouse's "last deceased spouse" at the time of such deceased spouse's death exceeded such deceased spouse's taxable estate. In no event, however, can the DSUEA exceed the basic exclusion amount in effect at the time of the surviving spouse's death. § 2010(c)(4).

EXAMPLE 2-3.

H died in 2011 with a taxable estate of $2 million. *H* was survived by his spouse, *W*. *H*'s executor timely filed an estate tax return computing a DSUEA of $3 million and elected to allow *W* to use the DSUEA. At *W*'s death in 2012, the "applicable exclusion amount" for her estate is $8 million, the sum of her basic exclusion amount ($5 million) and the DSUEA ($3 million).

EXAMPLE 2-4.

Assume the same facts from Example 2-3, except that *W* marries *H2* in late 2011. *H2* dies in early 2012, survived by *W*, with a taxable estate of $4 million. *H2's* executor timely filed an estate tax return computing a DSUEA of $1 million and elected to allow *W* to use the DSUEA. At *W's* death later in 2012, the "applicable exclusion amount" for her estate is only $6 million, the sum of her basic exclusion amount ($5 million) and the DSUEA from *H2* ($3 million). *W's* estate may not claim the DSUEA from *H* because it is limited to the DSUEA of the "last deceased spouse", which in this case is *H2*.

In order to claim the DSUEA, the executor of the last deceased spouse's estate must file an estate tax return that computes the DSUEA and elects to allow the surviving spouse to claim the DSUEA. The election must be made on a timely-filed return (including extensions). § 2010(c)(5)(A). Since it will be impossible to know at the death of the first spouse whether the surviving spouse will need the first spouse's DSUEA, most planners will probably err on the side of caution and advise modestly-sized estates to file a return and make the election.

The DSUEA election makes the leftover exclusion amount from a deceased spouse's estate "portable" to the surviving spouse. Practitioners have taken to calling the DSUEA election (an ugly acronym, to be sure) the "portability election" or, even more simply, "portability".

The portability election is only available to decedents dying after 2010. § 2010(c)(4). Thus, for example, if a surviving spouse's last deceased spouse died in 2008, the surviving spouse cannot claim a DSUEA. Because of the 2010 Act's sunset at the end of 2012, the portability election is scheduled to be available for only 2011 and 2012. Because of what would appear to be bipartisan support for portability, however, it is reasonable to expect that Congress will eventually extend the availability of the election.

The DSUEA is also available for purposes of the gift tax. The unified credit for gift tax purposes is generally defined as the tax on the applicable exclusion amount "under section 2010(c) which would apply if the donor died as of the end of the calendar year." § 2505(a)(1). Because the applicable exclusion amount for estate tax purposes would include the DSUEA, it is therefore available for purposes of the gift tax, too. This can give a surviving spouse a substantial exclusion to use for inter vivos gifts.

EXAMPLE 2-5.

Assume the same facts from Example 2-3. Following *H's* death, *W* makes a $7 million gift. Because *W's* applicable exclusion amount for gift tax purposes is $8 million (had she died in the year of the gift, her applicable exclusion amount would have been her $5 million basic exclusion amount plus the $3 million DSUEA from *H's* estate), she will pay no federal gift tax on this transfer.

EXAMPLE 2-6.

Assume the same facts from Example 2-4. Following *H2's* death, *W* makes a $7 million gift. Because *W's* applicable exclusion amount for gift tax purposes is $6 million (had she died in the year of the gift, her applicable exclusion amount would have been her $5 million basic exclusion amount plus the $1 million DSUEA from *H's* estate), she will have to pay $350,000 in federal gift tax (35% x $1 million) on this transfer.

A potential trap awaits a surviving spouse who fully utilizes the DSUEA of a deceased spouse for gift tax purposes but then remarries a wealthier spouse who also predeceases. If the wealthier spouse makes better use of the applicable exclusion amount, the DSUEA will likely be reduced below the amount already utilized through inter vivos gifting, ensuring not only that the surviving spouse's taxable estate at death will be fully subject to estate tax but also the risk that the surviving spouse's estate would have to pay estate tax on the amount previously gifted. The Joint Committee on Taxation opines that it does not matter whether the executor of the wealthier spouse's estate makes a portability election. JCX-55-10 (Dec. 10, 2010).

EXAMPLE 2-7.

Assume the same facts from Example 2-5 (*W* makes a $7 million gift after *H's* death but pays no tax because her applicable exclusion amount for gift tax purposes is $8 million). After the gift, *W* marries *H2*. *H2* then dies with a taxable estate of $4 million, and *H2's* executor makes a timely DSUEA election for the remaining $1 million of H2's exemption. At *W's* death, her applicable exclusion amount will be only $6 million (her $5 million basic exclusion amount plus the $1 million DSUEA from *H2's* estate). Because of the prior $7 million gift, any amount in *W's* taxable estate will be subject to federal estate tax. Furthermore, her estate may be required to pay estate tax on the $1 million by which her adjusted taxable gifts ($7 million) exceeds her applicable exclusion amount ($6 million). To the extent *W* got to make a $7 million gift and did not have to pay gift tax until her death, this is not necessarily a bad result.

C. FEDERAL GIFT TAX HIGHLIGHTS

§2.4. BASIC NATURE OF THE FEDERAL GIFT TAX

This section presents a basic overview of the main features of the federal gift tax law. The tax and other considerations involved in making noncharitable gifts are reviewed in Chapter 7 and those concerning charitable gifts are explored in Chapter 8.

The federal gift tax is an excise tax imposed on the transfer of property by gift during any calendar year. §2501(a)(1). It applies although the identity of the donee may not be known or ascertainable at the time of the gift. The donor is primarily liable for payment of the tax. §2502(d).

Neither the Code nor the Regulations attempt to define the term "gift"; however, the latter explains that the term includes "all transactions whereby property or property rights or interests are gratuitously passed or conferred upon another, regardless of the means or device employed." Reg. §25.2511-1(c). The tax applies to all gratuitous transfers, whether direct or indirect, whether outright or in trust, and whether the property transferred is real or personal, tangible or intangible. §2511(a); Reg. §25.2511-1(a). However, as indicated in §2.4.1, the gift tax does not apply to transfers made by a nonresident alien of property that does not have a United States situs. LR 9527025. Under Reg. §25.2511-3(b)(3), shares in a United States corporation constitute property within the United States and shares in a foreign corporation constitute property situated outside the United States. The situs of property may be affected by the terms of a treaty. An indirect gift can result from a variety of circumstances. For example, a gift results if a surviving spouse allows a pecuniary marital deduction trust for her benefit to be underfunded. Rev. Rul. 84-105, 1984-2 C.B. 197. Indirect gifts may also result from the inaction of a shareholder. *See* §2.5.6.

EXAMPLE 2-8.

Father, *F*, sold 1,000 shares of XYZ, Inc. common stock to his daughter, *D*, for $10 per share on a day when the mean price of the stock on an established exchange was $25 per share. *F* made a gift to *D* of $15 per share—the difference between the mean price of $25 per share and the price he received. The transaction was part sale, part gift, and not a bona fide business transaction. *D*'s carryover basis in the stock is determined under §1015. No income tax deduction is allowable when there is a "loss" on the sale or exchange of property between related taxpayers. §267.

Net Gifts. The amount of a gift may be reduced by the donee's obligation to pay any gift tax that is due with respect to the gift. *See* §7.26. The same is true with respect to a donee's agreement to pay any estate tax that might be due because of the gift tax inclusion if the donor dies within three years of making the gift. *See* §7.26 and *McCord v. Commissioner*, 461 F.3d 614 (5th Cir. 2006).

Temporary Decoupling of Unified Taxes. The 2001 Act partially reversed the unification of the gift tax, the estate tax, and the GSTT. As explained above, from 2004 through 2010, the gift tax credit exemption equivalent was fixed at $1 million while the estate tax credit equivalent and the GSTT exemption increased at irregular intervals until reaching $3.5 million in 2009 and $5 million in 2010. The 2010 Act largely restored the unification of the gift tax, estate tax, and GSTT exemption equivalents for 2011 and 2012, with all three exemptions initially set at $5 million.

Making taxable gifts in excess of the gift tax credit equivalent may result in a nonrefundable overpayment of tax. The point is illustrated by the following example:

EXAMPLE 2-9.

Prior to 2002, Donor, D, had made no taxable gifts. In 2002, D made taxable gifts of $1.5 million. In April 2003, D reported the gifts and paid a gift tax of $210,000. D died in 2009 leaving a taxable estate of $2 million. The tentative tax on D's estate is computed on a base of $3.5 million (a taxable estate of $2 million, plus adjusted taxable gifts of $1.5 million). The $3.5 million estate tax credit equivalent offsets the entire amount of the tentative tax. The gift tax paid by D is nonrefundable and is not needed to offset the estate tax. Of course, had D not made the gifts his estate would have included the gift tax paid ($210,000) and the value of the donative property at the time of his death. Also, had D died within 3 years of making the gifts the amount of gift tax would have been includible in his gross estate under § 2035(b).) Finally, to the extent the assets gifted in 2002 appreciated in value from the date of the gift until D's death, such appreciation was not subject to gift or estate tax; had D held on to these assets until death, such appreciation would have been part of D's taxable estate.

§ 2.4.1. Scope of Tax

The gift tax applies essentially to all gifts that are subject to United States jurisdiction for purposes of taxation and, except as otherwise provided by treaty, to all gifts made by citizens or residents and to gifts by nonresident aliens of property that has a situs in the United States. For more on the application of United States gift tax to transfers by nonresident aliens, *see* § 2.43.2.

§ 2.4.2. Gift Tax Exemption Replaced by Credit

As indicated above, the unification of the gift and estate tax laws in 1976 replaced the separate lifetime $30,000 gift tax exemption with the unified credit. The use of the unified credit is mandatory—it must be applied by the donor as a credit against the tax on taxable gifts as they are made. Rev. Rul. 79-398, 1979-2 C.B. 338; LR 9250004. Rev. Rul. 81-223, 1981-2 C.B. 189. Otherwise, by paying the gift tax and preserving the unified credit a donor might be able to eliminate from his or her gross estate the amount of the gift tax paid and preserve the full value of the unified credit. This rule has particular significance in planning "net" gifts. *See* § 7.26.

§2.4.3. Completed Gifts

The gift tax applies only to completed gifts. A gift is complete as to any property over which the donor has so parted with dominion and control as to leave the donor with no power to change its disposition. *See* Reg. §25.2511-2. Thus, a gift is incomplete if the transferor retains a lifetime or testamentary general or special power to appoint the property. In such a case the gift is completed if the transferor releases the retained power. *See Estate of Sanford v. Commissioner*, 308 U.S. 39 (1939). In some circumstances a client may wish to transfer property to an irrevocable trust over which he or she retains sufficient powers to make the transfer incomplete for gift tax purposes. *See* LR 8940008 (trustor retained power to revoke the trust with the consent of an independent trustee); §10.33. Of course, retention of such a power would require inclusion of the property in the trustor's estate. The retention of only a power to change the manner or time of enjoyment, such as a power to accelerate the time of distribution to a trust beneficiary, does not make the gift incomplete. Reg. §25.2511-2(d).

Relation Back Doctrine. A gift of a check or note is not completed by its mere delivery: the gift of a note is complete when it is paid or transferred for value and the gift of a check is complete when it is paid, certified, accepted by drawee, or is negotiated for value to a third person. Rev. Rul. 67-396, 1967-2 C.B. 351. Under the relation back doctrine a gift of a check to a charity which subsequently negotiates the check may be treated as a completed transfer at the time it was delivered to the charity. *See* §8.6.

The relation back doctrine has generally not been applied to noncharitable gifts. *E.g., Estate of Elizabeth C. Dillingham*, 88 T.C. 1569 (1987), *aff'd*, 903 F.2d 760 (10th Cir. 1990). However, the doctrine was applied in *Estate of Albert F. Metzger*, 100 T.C. 204 (1993), *aff'd*, 38 F.3d 118 (4th Cir. 1994), to uphold the allowance of annual gift tax exclusions in 1985 for checks drawn by the donor's attorney-in-fact to his wife and himself that were deposited in their bank account on December 31, 1985. In *Metzger* the majority opinion stated that,

> [W]e are presented with a very limited situation in which there is no uncertainty as to the donor's intent and unconditional delivery of the gifts, and no danger of a scheme to avoid estate taxes. In such limited circumstance, where noncharitable gifts are deposited at the end of December and presented for payment shortly after their delivery but are not honored by the drawee bank until after the New Year's holiday, we agree with the Tax Court that the gifts should relate back to the date of deposit. 38 F.3d at 123.

Estate of Metzger was followed in *Estate of Rosano v. United States*, 245 F.212 (2d Cir. 2001), and *Frank M. DiSanto*, 78 T.C.M. (CCH) 1220 (1999).In 1996 the IRS changed its position with respect to the application of the relation back doctrine to checks delivered to noncharitable donees. Delivery of a check to a noncharitable donee will be considered a completed gift when the check is deposited, cashed against available funds, or presented for payment in the calendar year for which completed gift treatment is sought if certain conditions are met. Rev. Rul. 96-56, 1996-2 C.B. 161.

Gifts in Trust. A transfer in trust does not constitute a completed gift if the property of the trust can be reached by the creditors of the transferor. LR 9639056 (Illinois law). Transfers made by a husband and wife to an irrevocable trust are incomplete where each transferor holds lifetime and testamentary special powers of appointment, which permit the property to be appointed only to family members. LR 9535008 (TAM). The TAM holds that the gifts will become complete when the powers are exercised, released, or terminated by action of the trustees.

Gifts by Attorney-in-Fact. Gifts made by an attorney-in-fact acting under a durable power of attorney may be revocable by the principal and thus incomplete unless the attorney-in-fact is expressly authorized to make the gifts. *See* §4.35.4. Revocable gifts made by the attorney-in-fact are includible in the gross estate of the deceased principal. *E.g., Estate of Casey v. Commissioner*, 948 F.2d 895 (4th Cir. 1991) (Virginia).

Stock Options. In Revenue Ruling 98-21, 1998-1 C.B. 975, the IRS ruled that the transfer of a compensatory nonstatutory stock option is completed on the later of: (1) the transfer, or (2) when the donee's right to exercise the option is no longer conditioned on the performance of services by the optionee-donor. Until the donee's right to exercise the option is perfected, the donor could negate the effect of the gift by failing to perform the required services. Revenue Procedure 98-34, 1998-1 C.B. 993 describes valuation models that will be accepted by the IRS in valuing gifts of compensatory stock options that relate to publicly traded stock. *See* §2.13. A nonqualified stock option, the exercise of which is no longer subject to restrictions, can be gifted. LR 199927002. The same ruling also concludes that the transfer of a stock option to a family member or to a trust for a family member is not a disposition for purposes of §83. Planning for gifts of stock options is thoughtfully discussed in Daniel H. Markstein III in Giving Well Is the Best Revenge: Planning Opportunities with Stock Options, U. Miami, 34th Inst. Est. Plan., Ch. 13 (2000).

§2.4.4. Valuation of Retained Interests, §§2702-2704

In general the gift tax applies to the extent of the value of interests transferred by a donor. *See* §2512(b). If the gift consists of a "split" interest, such as a life estate, term of years, annuity, or remainder interest, it is valued by reference to actuarial tables prescribed by the IRS. *See* Reg. §25.2512-5(d)(1). However, in some instances the value of a split interest is calculated by subtracting from the net value of the property the value of the interest retained by the donor, which may be zero under the special valuation rules of Chapter 14, §§2701-2704. *See* §§9.1, 9.40-9.44. If those rules apply to a particular transfer, the value of the donor's retained interest is decreased or disregarded entirely unless it meets certain requirements.

§2.4.5. Basis of Property Transferred by Gift, §1015

Under §1015(a) the donor's basis in property generally carries over to the donee. However, for the purpose of determining loss, the donee's basis is limited to the lesser of the donor's basis or the fair market value of the property at the time of the gift. As explained in §7.12, the donee's basis is increased by a portion of the gift tax paid with respect to a gift of appreciated property. *See* §1015(d)(6).

§ 2.5. ANNUAL GIFT TAX EXCLUSION, § 2503(b)

The continuing availability of the gift tax annual exclusion is a major reason for the popularity of inter vivos gifts. Under § 2503(b) the first $13,000 of property or interests in property, other than future interests, given to each person is excluded in computing the donor's taxable gifts for the year. (The exclusion is $10,000 per donee, adjusted for post-1997 inflation. Prior to 1982 the exclusion was $3,000 per donee.) The exclusion extends to gifts of interests to a minor in a trust that meets the requirements of § 2503(c), but not to "future interests." *See* § § 2.5.1, 2.5.4. A donor is not required to file a gift tax return with respect to gifts that (1) are within the exclusion of § 2503(b), (2) qualify for the marital deduction under § 2523, or (3) are outright charitable gifts or gifts of easements in real property described in § 2522(d). *See* § 6019; § 2.10. In most other cases the donor must file a return. A return must also be filed for a donor to split gifts with his or her spouse under § 2513 or to claim a gift tax marital deduction for qualified terminable interest property or a charitable deduction for gifts that are not entirely charitable.

The annual exclusion only applies to donative transfers to the actual donee. That is, annual exclusion is not available with respect to transfers made to nominal donees, who merely act as conduits to pass the property along to members of the donor's family. *E.g., Heyen v. United States*, 945 F.2d 359 (10th Cir. 1991):

> The evidence at trial indicated decedent intended to transfer the stock to her family rather than to the intermediate recipients. The intermediary recipients only received the stock certificates and signed them in blank so that the stock could be reissued to a member of decedent's family. Decedent merely used those recipients to create gift tax exclusions to avoid paying gift tax on indirect gifts to the actual family member beneficiaries. 945 F.2d at 363.

In *Heyen* the appellate court upheld a civil fraud penalty of $28,836. Gifts to nominal donees were also disregarded in *Estate of Marie Bies*, 80 T.C.M. (CCH) 628 (2000). In *Bies* the court stated that, "[w]e conclude that the inter vivos transfers of MBI shares to Gayle, Loretta, and Cheryl were, in fact, indirect transfers of additional shares to decedent's sons and grandson."

Annual exclusions are not allowed for equivalent gifts of stock made by each parent-sibling and his wife to trusts for their children and for the children of other parent-siblings. The transfers were related and resulted in each transferor being in an essentially unchanged position. *Sather v. Commissioner*, 251 F.3d 1168 (8th Cir. 2001) (reciprocal trust doctrine applied). *See* § § 7.35.1 (gifts to custodians) and 10.32 (gifts to trusts). The Eighth Circuit later applied the reciprocal gift doctrine in *Estate of Schuler v. Commissioner*, 282 F.3d 575 (8th Cir. 2002).

No Annual Exclusion for Unborn Persons. Professor Paul Caron has pointed out the shortcomings of the tax law affecting unborn children. When Does Life Begin for Tax Purposes?, 68 Tax Notes 320 (1995). As he observed, according to the IRS no annual exclusion is allowed for a gift to an unborn person. Rev. Rul. 67-384, 1967-2 C.B. 348 (gift made in trust in December for child born in the subsequent year). In contrast, in *Mary DuPont Faulkner*, 41 B.T.A. 875 (1940), the Board of Tax Appeals allowed an annual exclusion for gifts made in December 1935 in trust for a child that was born three months later. According to the Board, "The gift here was wholly for the benefit of the unborn child. We think that it was a valid gift of a present interest as distinct from a future interest. The statutory deduction of $5,000 in respect thereof is allowed." *Id.* at 880. Curiously, *Faulkner* was not cited in Rev. Rul. 67-384.

The unqualified forgiveness of an intrafamily loan may be treated as a gift; where that is the case, it should qualify for the annual exclusion. §7.25.

Annual Exclusion Indexed. Under the 1997 Act, the amount of the annual exclusion is indexed for gifts made in calendar years after 1998 based upon changes in the cost of living after 1997. If the amount of the increase is not a multiple of $1,000, the amount is rounded to the next lower $1,000. That is, no change will be made until the increases equal in the aggregate $1,000 or more. The exclusion increased to $11,000 in 2002, Rev. Proc. 2001-59, 2001-2 C.B. 623, to $12,000 in 2006, Rev. Proc. 2005-70, 2005-2 C.B. 979, and to $13,000 in 2009, Rev. Proc. 2008-66, 2008-45 I.R.B. 1.

Prospective increases in the annual exclusion may require that changes be made in existing wills and trusts. If a provision such as a *Crummey* withdrawal clause needs to be limited to the amount of the exclusion allowable under §2503(b), the limits should be expressed in that manner rather than by using a specific dollar amount. *See* §7.36.

Gifts to Tax Exempt Organizations. A gift to a tax exempt organization qualifies for a single gift tax exclusion under Reg. §25.2511-1(h)(1) (gifts to a charitable, public, political, or similar organization). LR 9818042.

§2.5.1. Present and Future Interests

For the purposes of §2503(b), the term future interest "includes reversions, remainders, and other interests or estates, whether vested or contingent, and whether or not supported by a particular interest or estate, which are limited to commence in use, possession or enjoyment at some future date or time." Reg. §25.2503-3(a). Thus, if X transfers Blackacre to A for life, remainder to B, the life interest transferred to A is a present interest, but the remainder transferred to B is a future interest. No annual exclusion is available with respect to the future interest given to B although it is indefeasibly vested, may be of great value, and is freely alienable by B.

The question of whether a particular interest constitutes a present or a future interest is primarily determined by the nature and extent of the transferee's interest and not by the character of the property. As the Regulations explain:

> The term has no reference to such contractual rights as exist in a bond, note (though bearing no interest until maturity), or in a policy of life insurance, the obligations of which are to be discharged by payments in the future. But a future interest or interests in such contractual obligations may be created by the limitations contained in a trust or other instrument of transfer used in effecting a gift. Reg. §25.2503-3(a).

Thus, an outright gift of a note on which payments are due in the future is a gift of a present interest. In contrast, a gift of such a note to a trust, the beneficiaries of which have no present right to receive distribution from the trust, is a future interest. *See* §2.5.2.

The annual exclusion for gifts to each donee is renewable, but not cumulative. A single exclusion is available annually to each donor with respect to gifts to a particular donee, whether or not gifts were made to the donee in any preceding years. Thus, gifts of present interests having a value less than the annual exclusion amount are generally not subject to the gift or the estate tax.

Bogus Withdrawal Powers Held by Charities. Annual exclusions are not allowed for the powers of withdrawal held by charities over assets the donor transfers to an irrevocable trust of which the charities are also partial remainder beneficiaries. LR 200341002 (TAM). (In addition, no charitable deductions were allowable for the transfers to the split-interest trust, which did not meet the requirements of §2522(c).) In the TAM, the donor's two children and the spouse of one of his children were also beneficiaries of the trust, to whom the trustee (one of his children) could distribute as much of the income and principal of the trust as the trustee decided, "for the education, health, maintenance and support of the beneficiaries." Under the circumstances, the TAM holds that annual exclusions are not available because "we do not believe that the charities' withdrawal powers were viable." Even if the powers were valid, the TAM reasoned that once the withdrawal period passed and "the transfers remained in Trust subject to invasion for the benefit of the individual beneficiaries," the situation was analogous to a transfer subject to a condition under Reg. §25.2522(c)-3(b)(2).

§2.5.2. Gifts in Trust

The present interest-future interest dichotomy is most difficult to resolve in the case of transfers in trust. For gift tax purposes a transfer in trust is treated as made to the beneficiaries and not to the trust or the trustee. *Helvering v. Hutchings*, 312 U.S. 393 (1941). A transfer in trust qualifies for annual exclusions to the extent the beneficiaries have the unrestricted right to the immediate use, possession, or enjoyment of the property or the income from it. Reg. §25.2503-3(b). The donee of an income interest in a trust that requires its income to be distributed currently has a present interest in the income. The value of such an income interest, or a remainder or other limited interest in a trust, is ordinarily determined under actuarial tables issued by the Internal Revenue Service in accordance with §7520. However, use of the tables is "not appropriate in the case of nonincome yielding investment . . . ." *Berzon v. Commissioner*, 534 F.2d 528, 532 (2d Cir. 1976). The IRS has consistently ruled that no annual exclusion is allowable with respect to the income beneficiary's interest in a trust funded with a gift of nonincome producing stock. LR 83200007 (TAM). Also, no annual exclusion is allowable with respect to the income interest in a trust if the trust reflects an intention that the trustee invest for future growth rather than current income. Rev. Rul. 69-345, 1969-1 C.B. 225. As noted below, the use of the actuarial tables to value the life interest of a beneficiary is not appropriate if the beneficiary is terminally ill. Also, a donor's retained term interest in a trust may be valued at zero under the rules of §2702.

Regulations adopted in 1995 provide that the actuarial tables may not be used in connection with the valuation of an annuity, interests for life or for a term of years, or a remainder or reversion of a person who "is known to have an incurable disease or other deteriorating physical condition... [and] there is at least a 50 percent probability that the individual will die within 1 year." Reg. §20.7520-3(b)(3).

The interest of the beneficiary of a completely discretionary trust is not a present interest, as any distribution to the beneficiary is dependent upon the trustee's subsequent exercise of discretion.

§2.5.3. Gifts in Trust: *Crummey* Powers of Withdrawal

The present interest requirement is satisfied to the extent the beneficiary has a presently exercisable power to withdraw property transferred to the trust. This power, sometimes called a *Crummey* power, is discussed at §7.38. Giving a *Crummey* power to the beneficiaries of an irrevocable life insurance trust is particularly useful. *See* §6.24.4. Depending upon the terms of the trust, the lapse of a *Crummey* power may constitute a completed gift by the power holder of a future interest in the property subject to the power. However, if the holder of the power which lapses continues to hold a power to direct the disposition of the property, such as a special testamentary power of appointment, any gift resulting from the lapse is incomplete and not then subject to the gift tax. *See* §2.4.3.

EXAMPLE 2-10.

> T transferred $10,000 to a trust for the benefit of *B*. The trust required the trustee to notify *B* of the transfer. Under the terms of the trust *B* has, until 30 days following notification of a transfer of property to the trust, the noncumulative right to withdraw the transferred property. The income and principal are distributable to *B* in the discretion of the trustee. Upon *B*'s death the trust property will be distributed to whomever *B* appoints by will. The $10,000 transferred by *T* to the trust qualifies for the annual gift tax exclusion because of *B*'s *Crummey* power. The lapse of the power does not involve any gift by *B* because the trust property is subject to B's testamentary power of appointment. Reg. §25.2511-2(b).

An annual exclusion gift made to a *Crummey* trust is not subject to the GSTT if the beneficiary is the only person to whom income or principal may be distributed during the beneficiary's lifetime and the portion of the trust attributable to the gift will be included in the beneficiary's estate if the beneficiary dies before receiving distribution of the trust property. §2642(c)(2). *See* §2.42.3.

§2.5.4. Gifts in Trust: §2503(c) Trusts (Trusts for Minors)

A transfer of property to a trust for the benefit of a minor also qualifies for the annual exclusion if the requirements of §2503(c) are met. *See* §7.37. In brief, a trust meets the requirements of §2503(c) if the trustee is empowered to distribute the income or principal of the trust to the minor without the imposition of any substantial restriction and the property is distributable to the minor at age 21. A Technical Advice Memorandum holds that a gift of nonincome producing stock to a §2503(c) trust qualifies for the annual gift tax exclusion because of the trustee's power to use all of the property for the benefit of the minor and to distribute the balance to the beneficiary at age 21. LR 8320007 (TAM).

§2.5.5. Gifts to Corporations

A gift to a corporation is considered to be made to its shareholders. Reg. §25.2511-1(h)(1). Such a gift is not a present interest unless the shareholders have a power similar to a *Crummey* power to withdraw the property or an immediate right to use the property. *See* LR 9104024. Otherwise, shareholders do not have a direct right or interest in property that is transferred to the corporation. *See, e.g., Heringer v. Commissioner*, 235 F.2d 149 (9th Cir.), *cert. denied*, 352 U.S. 927 (1956); *CTUW Georgia Ketteman Hollingsworth*, 86 T.C. 91 (1986); LR 7935115.

EXAMPLE 2-11.

T transferred real property worth $750,000 to a closely-held corporation in exchange for a $500,000 note. *T* has made a gift of $250,000 to the shareholders: Each gift is in proportion to the shareholder's ownership of the corporation's stock. The gifts are future interests. *CTUW Georgia Ketteman Hollingsworth,* 86 T.C. 91 (1986).

A gift of property by the members of a partnership to a nonstock tax exempt club for construction of a new clubhouse constitutes a gift from the members of the partnership to the noncontributing members of the club. LR 9323020.

Forgiveness of a debt owed by a corporation is a gift of a future interest for which no annual exclusions are allowable. *Estate of Lavonna J. Stinson v. United States,* 1998 U.S. Dist. Lexis 16894 (N.D.Ind. 1998), *aff'd,* 214 F.3d 846 (7th Cir. 2000).

§2.5.6. Indirect Gifts by Controlling Shareholder

A gift to other shareholders may result from the action or inaction of the controlling shareholder. A gift of stock by the controlling shareholder to key employees is a pro rata gift to other shareholders. LR 9114023. Indirect gifts to other shareholders may arise in a variety of settings. For example, in LR 89403010 the controlling shareholder made a gift to the other common shareholders by permitting the corporation to fail to pay the required dividends on his noncumulative preferred stock in order to pay dividends on the common stock.

In LR 9420001 (TAM), the IRS held that the owner of all of the voting stock of a corporation made an indirect gift to her children when she failed to use a portion of the corporation's unneeded cash to redeem the convertible preferred shares owned by her children. The gift was completed when the children converted their preferred shares into common stock. The controlling shareholder's failure to cause the corporation to pay dividends on their noncumulative preferred stock did not result in a gift where there were valid business reasons for using the corporation's funds for other corporate purposes—expanding its inventory and opening new stores. *Joseph M. Daniels,* 68 T.C.M. (CCH) 1310 (1994).

There are ways of making gifts to the shareholders of a closely-held corporation that do qualify for the annual exclusion. A donor might transfer the property to the corporation in exchange for additional stock and give those shares of stock to the donees. Another approach would be to give the property to the donees, who then transfer their interests to the corporation in exchange for shares of stock. Either of these approaches might have been used to good effect in Example 2-6, above.

§2.5.7. Gifts to Partnerships

A gift of an ownership interest in a partnership or a limited liability company (LLC) is analogous to a gift of shares of stock in a corporation and qualifies for the annual exclusion under the same rules. For example, outright gifts and gifts to *Crummey* trusts of interests in limited partnerships qualify for the annual gift tax exclusion. The annual exclusion is allowable for gifts of limited partnership interest although the donor was the general partner and, as such, held extensive powers of management. LRs 9131006 (TAM); 9415007. Under state law, the general partner is bound by strict fiduciary duties in exercising those powers. LR 8445004 (TAM); LR 8611004 (TAM). The transferred interests may not be includible in the donor's estate under §§2036 or 2038 because the donor's powers were exercisable in a fiduciary capacity. *See United States v. Byrum*, 408 U.S. 125 (1972); LR 9131006 (TAM) and §§ 2.19-2.20.

Transfers of partnership units do not qualify for the annual exclusion if the interests of the donee are dependent upon the exercise of discretion by the donor-general partner. *See* §§11.5.1, 11.5.4. Thus, in LR 9751003 (TAM) the IRS disallowed annual exclusions with respect to gifts of partnership units that could not be sold or transferred by the donees and carried no right to receive distributions. In effect, the donor-general partner retained too much power under the partnership agreement, and the agreement relieved the general partner of the fiduciary duty that normally applies to a general partner with respect to distributions.

Similarly, annual exclusions may not be allowed for gifts of limited partnership or LLC interests that do not confer substantial economic benefits upon the donees. For example, in *Catherine M. Hackl*, 118 T.C. 279 (2002), the Tax Court upheld disallowance of annual exclusions for gifts of LLC units where the operating agreement "foreclosed the ability of the donees presently to access any substantial economic or financial benefit that might be represented by the ownership units." In particular, a donee could not unilaterally withdraw his or her capital account and could not "transfer, assign, convey, sell, encumber or in any way alienate all or any part of the Member's Interest except with the prior written consent of the Manager" which was subject to "the Manager's sole discretion." Moreover, under the operating agreement the members did not have any right to receive distributions of income—which were to be made in the manager's discretion. Perhaps the *Hackl* problem with respect to gifts to trusts could be avoided if the trust agreements were to include *Crummey* withdrawal provisions and the trusts are first "seeded" with cash or other liquid assets sufficient to satisfy the exercise of all withdrawal rights in a single year. The *Hackl* decision was affirmed by the Seventh Circuit. 335 F.3d 664 (7th Cir. 2003). The appellate opinion rejected the taxpayer's arguments, noting that the taxpayers did not establish that their transfers qualified for the annual gift tax exclusion and that, "exclusions are matters of legislative grace that must be narrowly construed."

Gifts to the capital account of a partner are superficially analogous to gifts to a corporation. The annual exclusion is available for gifts to a partner's capital account if the partner has the unrestricted right to withdraw amounts from his or her capital, which a partner has under the Uniform Partnership Act. *Wooley v. United States*, 736

F. Supp. 1506 (S.D. Ind. 1990). The existence of such a right of withdrawal, analogous to a *Crummey* power of withdrawal, supported the allowance of the annual exclusion in *Wooley*. *See* LR 9104024. In order to avoid any questions regarding the availability of annual exclusions, gifts of interests in a partnership should be made before any significant restrictions on the transfer or disposition of interests are imposed. Problems are also minimized if the donor first gives property directly to the donees, who then join to form the partnership.

In some circumstances the transfer of property to a partnership results in an indirect gift to other partners—in other cases it does not. In *Estate of W.W. Jones, II*, 116 T.C. 121 (2001), the court held that the transfer of property to a limited partnership in exchange for partnership interests did not constitute a gift where the contributed property was allocated to the transferor's capital account. Essentially the same result was reached earlier in *Estate of Albert Strangi*, 115 T.C.478 (2000), *revd on other grounds*, *Gulig v. Commissioner*, 293 F.3d 279 (5th Cir. 2002). In contrast, an undiscounted, indirect gift may result to the extent a partner's contribution of property is allocated on a pro rata basis to all partners. *J. C. Shepherd*, 115 T.C. 376 (2000) *aff'd*, 283 F.3d 1258 (11th Cir. 2002) (Tax Court treated the donor's gift of land to partnership as indirect gifts of fractional interests in the land to his sons and not as gifts of partnership units). The result is the same in the case of contributions to a corporation. *See* §2.5.5.

Language in some state court decisions support the allowance of a substantial discount in valuing partnership interests. For example, in *Estate of Cooper*, 913 P.2d 393 (Wash. App. 1996), the court referred to the discounted valuation of partnership interests made by a special master appointed by the Superior Court that were accepted by the Superior Court. According to the Court of Appeals, "These values reflected a 60-percent discount because Mr. Cooper's interest was a minority interest and therefore not easily marketable." The court continued to say that the trial court "agreed with Mr. Cummin's valuation of the Eight-0-One and Hillside partnerships." Although the appellate opinion does not deal directly with valuation, the recited acceptance by the trial court of the deep discount is a helpful illustration of the practice in nontax cases. Consistently, in LR 200212006 (TAM) the IRS ruled that a contribution of publicly traded municipal bonds to a family limited partnership was an indirect gift of the bonds to her children. Because the bonds were readily marketable, the TAM concluded that "no discount is allowable in valuing the interest in these bonds."

In general, charitable contributions by a partnership are treated as pro rata gifts by each partner. Reg. §1.702-1(a)(4). Thus, each partner is entitled to deduct a portion of the value of a conservation easement granted by the partnership. LR 200208019.

§2.5.8. Gifts to a Noncitizen Spouse, §2523(i)

The marital deduction is not allowed with respect to gifts made after July 13, 1988 to a spouse who is not a citizen of the United States. Instead, the annual gift tax exclusion allowed under §2503(b) is increased to $100,000 for transfers to a noncitizen spouse. §2523(i). This exclusion, adjusted for post-1997 inflation, was $136,000 in 2011. Rev. Proc. 2010-40, 2010-2 C.B. 663. Of course, the donative property may or may not be included in the donee spouse's gross estate depending on the circumstances that exist at the time of his or her death. For example, if the noncitizen spouse is a resident of the United States at the time of death, all of his or her property is subject to the federal estate tax. On the other hand, if the noncitizen spouse dies a nonresident, only the property that has a situs in the United States is subject to the federal estate tax. *See* § 2.43.3. Marital deduction planning considerations relevant for persons married to citizens and noncitizen spouses are discussed in Chapter 5.

§ 2.6. EXCLUSION FOR PAYMENT OF TUITION AND MEDICAL EXPENSES, § 2503(e)

Section 2503(e), which was added by the 1981 Act, allows gift tax exclusions for tuition payments made directly to educational institutions described in § 170(b)(1)(A)(ii) and payments of medical expenses (including medical insurance) made directly to the individuals or organizations providing the services. Rev. Rul. 82-98, 1982-1 C.B. 141. The exclusions are allowable regardless of the relationship or absence of relationship between the donors and the donees. They are particularly helpful because most taxpayers were probably unaware that payments of educational or medical expenses constituted a gift under the prior law (except to the extent the payor was legally obligated to make the payments).

Unfortunately, only direct payments are excluded: A reimbursement of such expenses made to the donee as intermediary does not qualify. Reg. § 25.2503-6(c), Example 4.

Insofar as educational expenses are concerned, the exclusion extends only to tuition payments, although a strong argument can be made for broadening it to cover other associated costs (e.g., books, supplies, and room and board). In LR 199941013 (TAM) the IRS ruled that prepaid, nonrefundable tuition payments made by a grandparent to a private school on behalf of two grandchildren met the requirements of § 2503(e). As a result the tuition payments would not be subject to the GSTT. § 2642(c) (direct skips that are not taxable gifts by reason of § 2503(e) have an inclusion ratio of zero). Note also that the GSTT does not apply to transfers that qualify for this exclusion if made by an individual. § 2611(b)(1). The subject is reviewed in Handler, *Tax-Free Gifts of Prepaid Tuition*, 142 Tr. & Est. 20 (Feb. 2003).

The exclusion for medical expenses extends to those described in § 213. However, medical expense payments are excludable regardless of the percentage limitation of § 213.

Qualified Tuition Programs, § 529. For gift tax purposes, contributions made to a qualified tuition plan are not treated as future interests or as a qualified transfer under § 2503(e). § 529(c)(2). Instead, such transfers qualify for even more beneficial treatment.

Importantly, if a donor contributes more than the amount of the annual exclusion, the donor can elect to treat the gift as being made ratably over five years. § 529(c)(2)(B). In effect, a donor who contributes $60,000 to a qualified tuition plan in 2008 may elect not to treat any portion of the contribution as a taxable gift. If the donor dies before the end of the five-year period, the donor's estate must include the portion of the contribution allocable to the years following the donor's death. § 529(c)(4)(C), *see* § 2.13. Distributions from a qualified state tuition plan are not treated as gifts. § 529(c)(5)(A). Moreover, distributions made from a plan for qualified higher educational expenses are not includible in the beneficiary's income.

§ 529(c)(3)(B). However, the exclusion does not apply to distributions made in tax years beginning before January 1, 2004. § 529(c)(3)(B)(iii).

The 2001 Act expanded the section, effective with respect to tax years beginning after 2001, to apply not only to contributions made to state plans, but also to contributions made to plans established by eligible educational institutions, including privately operated ones. Previously, the section only applied to plans established by states or their instrumentalities. Planning with existing qualified state tuition programs is reviewed by Beverly R. Budin in *Section 529 Plans: What They Are and Who Should Use Them,* U. Miami, 35th Inst. Est. Plan., Ch. 8 (2001).

Under the Pension Protection Act of 2006, § 529 was spared from the pending Sunset of the 2001 Act, so Qualified Tuition Programs are now a permanent feature of the Code and an important component of education planning. Qualified Tuition Programs and Coverdell Education Savings Accounts (formerly Education IRAs) are discussed in detail in Chapter 7.

§ 2.7. Gift Splitting, § 2513

In order to equalize the gift tax on gifts of community and noncommunity property, § 2513 permits married persons to elect to treat all gifts made to third parties during a calendar year as made one-half by each. However, the option to split gifts is only available if both spouses are citizens or residents of the United States at the time of the gift. § 2513(a)(1). For estate tax purposes the actual donor and not the consenting spouse is regarded as the transferor. *English v. United States,* 284 F. Supp. 256 (W.D. Fla. 1968) (§ 2035). For purposes of finality in the valuation of gifts, § 2504(c) and § 2.10.3, the requirement of adequate disclosure is satisfied if the gift is adequately disclosed in the return of one of the spouses. Reg. § 301.6501(c)-1(f)(6).

The privilege of splitting gifts does not apply to community property because it is naturally "split" between the spouses from the outset: When a gift of community property is made to a person outside the community, each spouse is necessarily the donor of one-half of the property. Each spouse is considered to be the donor of one-half of the total value of community property gifts even in states that permit one spouse alone to make gifts of community property. Rev. Rul. 56-408, 1956-2 C.B. 600. However, as a matter of practice both spouses should join in making gifts of community property in order to avoid any uncertainty regarding the effectiveness of the gift.

Gift splitting is also recognized for GSTT purposes. In particular, § 2652(a)(2) provides that if a gift is split under § 2513, each spouse will be treated as a transferor of one-half of the property for GSTT purposes. This opportunity makes it easier to use each spouse's GSTT exemption. *See* § 2.27.

In effect, § 2513 doubles the exclusions available for gifts of noncommunity property made by a husband and wife to third parties. Gift splitting also allows the spouses to equalize the unified transfer tax rates that are applicable to each of them. Prior to the adoption of the unlimited marital deduction, which allows free interspousal gifts, gift splitting was more important.

In order to split gifts, both spouses must signify their consent to split gifts for the period in question. If only one spouse is required to file a return, the consent of both spouses must be signified on that return. If gifts made to each third party do not exceed $20,000 and none is of a future interest, only the donor spouse must file a return. Reg. § 25.2513-1(c). The regulation specifically refers to $20,000, although it should be interpreted to mean twice the gift tax annual exclusion amount in effect for the taxable year. The same result can be achieved by making a tax-free gift from one spouse to the other, after which each makes equal gifts to third parties.

EXAMPLE 2-12.

H transferred $24,000 of his separate property to his son, *S*, on December 30. Neither *H* nor *W* made any other gifts during that year. The gift to *S* must be reported on *H*'s gift tax return for the calendar year. The short form of the gift tax return, Form 709A, may be filed in such a case. If *W* signifies her consent on *H*'s gift tax return the amount of the gift will be completely offset by the annual exclusions available to *H* and *W* and no gift tax will be due. *W* is not required to file a return because she did not make any gifts during the year, and the gift she is considered to have made to *S* did not exceed her annual exclusion and was not a future interest. *See* Reg. § 25.2513-1(c).

When both spouses are required to file gift tax returns, the consent of each spouse to split gifts may be signified on either return, or both. Reg. § 25.2513-2(a)(1)(i). A decedent's personal representative may consent to split gifts made prior to the decedent's death. *See* § 12.25.

None of the property actually transferred by the donor spouse is includible in the gross estate of the consenting spouse. For estate tax purposes, the consenting spouse is not treated as the transferor of property that was actually transferred by the other spouse. Thus, property held by a consenting spouse as custodian under the Uniform Transfers to Minors or the Uniform Gifts to Minors Act at the time of death is not includible in his or her gross estate when the custodial property was actually transferred to the minor by the other spouse and the consenting spouse was only treated as the donor for gift tax purposes. Rev. Rul. 74-556, 1974-2 C.B. 300 (involving § 2038). However, the amount of taxable gifts, including split gifts, is taken into account in computing the consenting spouse's gift and estate tax liability.

Where the state gift tax law also permits gift splitting, the state and federal elections can be made independent of each other (*i.e.*, gifts made by a couple may be split for federal, but not for state, tax purposes). In states that determine the gift tax in part according to the relationship between the donor and donee, the state gift tax may be lower in some cases if the gift is not split. Such a result may occur, for example, where the donor spouse is closely related to the donee, but the consenting spouse is unrelated to the donee. Thus, if a donor makes a gift to his or her parents, the state gift tax may be lower if the gift is not split with the donor's spouse, who probably would be considered to be unrelated to the donor's parents. Elements of gift-splitting are reviewed in Handler & Chen, *Fresh Thinking About Gift-Splitting*, 141 Tr. & Est. 36 (2002).

§2.8. CHARITABLE DEDUCTIONS, §2522

The income, gift, and estate tax rules applicable to charitable gifts are reviewed in detail in Chapter 8. In brief, §2522 allows an unlimited deduction for the value of gifts made by a citizen or resident of the United States to charities described in §2522(a). With slight variations the same organizations are qualified donees under the income, gift, and estate tax laws. *See* §8.2.

Planning outright gifts to charitable organizations is usually simple enough, although the valuation of some assets can present a problem. However, that problem is eased considerably and the risk that a penalty might be imposed for overvaluation of the property is virtually eliminated if the donor obtains a contemporaneous appraisal of the property by a qualified expert. Planning becomes much more complex when the charitable gift consists of less than the donor's entire interest in the property. A deduction is generally allowed for gifts of split interests only if it takes the form of, (1) a charitable remainder trust or pooled income fund (*See* §§8.20-8.30), (2) a guaranteed annuity interest or unitrust interest (*See* §8.32), (3) a nontrust remainder interest in a personal residence or a farm (*See* §8.15), or (4) an undivided portion of the donor's entire interest (*See* §8.16). Special care is required if the gift is to be made to a private foundation. *See* §170(e)(5).

EXAMPLE 2-13.

D transferred marketable securities to the trustee of an irrevocable trust, the income of which is payable to her daughter, *X*, for life, with the remainder to a charity described in §2522(a). The gift of the remainder interest to the charity is not deductible for income, gift, or estate tax purposes because it is not in one of the approved forms. Prior to 1969, federal tax deductions would have been allowed for the value of the charitable remainder interest. If *X* made a qualified disclaimer of her income interest, the charitable remainder would accelerate and the donor would be entitled to a gift tax charitable deduction for the full value of the property transferred to the trust. Likewise, a charitable deduction will be allowed if the trust is reformed to conform to the requirements of §2522. §2522(c)(4); *see also* §8.35.

Because of the complexity of the income, gift, and estate tax rules, gifts of split interests to charities must be planned very carefully.

§2.9. MARITAL DEDUCTION, §2523

Section 2523 allows an unlimited marital deduction for qualifying gifts made by a citizen or resident of the United States to a spouse who is a citizen of the United States. As indicated in §2.5.8, the marital deduction for gifts made on or after July 14, 1988 is limited to gifts made to citizens of the United States. §2523(i). However, an annual exclusion of $100,000 is allowable for gifts made to a spouse who is not a citizen of the United States. §2523(i)(2). This exemption, adjusted for post-1997 inflation, is $136,000 in 2011. *See* §2.42.2.

The marital deduction provisions were more complicated in the period between 1977 and 1982: A marital deduction was fully allowable for the first $100,000 of noncommunity property given to a spouse. No deduction was allowable for the next $100,000. Thereafter a 50-percent deduction was allowable. The amount of the allowable estate tax deduction was reduced if the marital deduction for post-1976 inter vivos gifts exceeded 50 percent.

Under changes made by the 1981 Act, an unlimited marital deduction is allowed for gifts made after 1981, provided the donee spouse receives a sufficient interest in the property. The deduction is available on an elective basis for gifts of qualified terminable interest property (QTIP). See § 5.23. Again, however, no marital deduction is allowable with respect to gifts made to a noncitizen spouse after July 13, 1988.

No gift tax marital deduction was allowable for gifts of community property made prior to January 1, 1982, § 2523(f), nor for gifts of nonqualifying terminable interests, § 2523(b).

Estimates of the overall gift and estate tax consequences of various interspousal gift programs should be prepared and given to the client for consideration before any substantial gifts are made. The estimates should indicate the tax consequences of making gifts of various amounts assuming, alternatively, that the donor predeceases the donee and vice versa. Although the effect of the gifts may seem obvious, estimates provide a valuable check that may lead to a beneficial refinement of the plan.

Where the federal transfer tax features progressive rates, the overall gift and estate tax burden may be minimized if the sizes of the spouses' estate are equalized. See § § 5.28-5.31. A plan can easily provide for equalization if the wealthier spouse happens to die first. Lifetime interspousal gifts provide a hedge against the possibility that the poorer spouse will die first. These gifts may be in the form of a QTIP trust in which the donee spouse receives only a life estate. § 2523(f). Several letter rulings allow the donor spouse to retain a successive life estate in an inter vivos QTIP trust without requiring the trust to be included in the donor's estate unless the donee spouse (or his or her estate) claims a marital deduction in connection with a later disposition of the property. See § 5.23.6. Thus, the sizes of the estates can be equalized for estate tax purposes although the donor spouse "hedges" the gift by retaining a successive life estate. Of course, if the gift tax marital deduction is claimed with respect to the gift, the property is includible in the donee spouse's estate under § 2044.

Equalization is of little value unless the estate of one spouse is much larger than the estate of the other and the applicable rates are progressive. Between the 2001 Act's increase in the estate tax exemption amount, its reduction in the maximum estate tax rate, and the 2010 Act's continuation of a flat rate of tax, equalization may have even less value. In 2011, for instance, the estate tax was not imposed unless the taxable estate exceeded $5 million. The first dollar in excess of this exemption was taxed at 35 percent, the maximum tax rate under § 2001(c) for that year. Accordingly, there is no more "spread" between the marginal rate applicable to the first dollar over the exemption amount and the maximum tax rate.

The significant increases in the unified credit made by the 1981, 1997, 2001 and 2010 Acts generally enhanced the advantages of deferral and decreased the importance of equalization. If gifts are made for purposes of equalization, the donee's estate should be planned so as to dispose of the donative property in a way that will not cause the property to be included in the donor's estate if the donee dies before the donor. For example, the donee might leave the donor spouse a limited interest in the property or leave the property to their children or to a bypass trust for the benefit of the donor.

Substantial interspousal gifts are sometimes made to the poorer spouse so that the donee's estate can use the full amount of the unified credit and the GSTT exemption should the donee predecease the donor. As indicated above, the gifts might be made to a QTIP trust of which the poorer spouse is given only a life income interest. Unless such gifts are made, the unified credit of the donee spouse may be wasted if he or she predeceases the wealthier spouse. The estate of a poorer spouse can be built up without federal transfer tax cost by making gifts to him or her. A program of outright gifts might be undesirable, however, for other reasons, such as the possibility of marital dissolution.

General Planning Comments. Gifts to a spouse are usually made in order to, (1) equalize the sizes of the spouses' estates and (2) create an estate for the "poorer" spouse as a hedge against the donee's earlier death and consequent loss of the marital deduction to the donor. *See* §§5.28-5.31. As noted above, gifts to the poorer spouse may be made to preserve the benefit of the donee's unified credit and GSTT exemption. When the spouses' estates are entirely community, an interspousal life-time gift program is seldom indicated. In that case their estates are equalized naturally, which eliminates most of the tax advantages of making interspousal gifts. Of course, in any case the tax on the death of the first spouse can be completely deferred under the unlimited marital deduction.

Inter vivos gifts to a spouse are not generally made for income tax purposes because the advantages of income splitting are already available by filing joint income tax returns. However, couples sometimes convert separate property into community property so the whole of the property will receive a stepped-up basis on the death of either spouse. *See* §1014(b)(6) and §3.35.4. Also, during periods that capital gains are taxed at a substantially lower rate than ordinary income, gifts may be helpful. For example, a sale at the more favorable capital gains rates may be facilitated by transferring the property from one spouse, in whose hands the property is not a capital asset, to the other spouse, in whose hands it will be. *See* §7.9.2. The general tax factors discussed in §§7.12-7.17 should also be considered in selecting property to transfer to a spouse.

§2.10. Gift Tax Returns

A federal gift tax return (Form 709) is filed individually and not jointly or collectively with other taxpayers. §6019. However, no return is required for gifts that are not included in total gifts for the year by reason of §2503(b) (annual gift tax exclusion) and §2503(e) (qualified transfers to an educational institution or health care provider), gifts that qualify for the marital deduction under §2523 and outright charitable gifts and charitable gifts of easements in real property described in §2522(d). §6019. A short form (Form 709A) can be used where a return is required only to split gifts between the spouses and the resulting gifts are within the amount of the allowable annual exclusions. As noted in §2.7, it is necessary to file gift tax returns in order to take advantage of gift splitting under §2513.

A return must be filed on or before April 15 of the year following the close of the calendar year in which the gifts were made. However, a return for the year that includes the death of the donor must be filed no later than the time for filing the donor's estate tax return (*i.e.*, nine months after death). § 6075(b)(3).

EXAMPLE 2-14.

T made a gift of $50,000 to *X* on January 1 and died on January 15. A gift tax return reporting the gift to *X* is due at the same time as *T*'s estate tax return, that is, October 15.

Since 1996, the gift tax return, Form 709, has required taxpayers to disclose if the value of any of the gifted property has been discounted. If any discount is claimed, the instructions require the taxpayer to attach an explanation that states the amounts and bases for taking them. *See* § 2.45.1.

In 2003, several changes were made to Form 709. Perhaps the most important is the addition of a requirement, Part 3, that a donor identify any gifts that are subject to the gift tax and may later be subject to the generation-skipping transfer tax. The requirement would apply to the creation of trusts that have some nonskip person beneficiaries, but might later be the subject of a taxable termination or make taxable distributions. See § 2.32.

§ 2.10.1. Community Property Gifts

A gift of community property to a person outside the marital community is considered to be two gifts—each spouse is treated as having made a gift of one half of the whole value of the community property. Accordingly, where community property is given to a third party, each spouse may be required to file a gift tax return. However, neither spouse is required to file a gift tax return for a gift of a present interest in community property that does not exceed double the amount of the gift tax annual exclusion. *See* § 2.7.

EXAMPLE 2-15.

H and *W* gave their daughter, *D*, community property cash last year in an amount equal to twice the gift tax annual exclusion in effect last year. Because each of them is considered to have made a gift of one-half of the community property to *D*, neither *H* nor *W* is required to file any gift tax return respecting the gift. *H* and *W* would be required to file returns on or before April 15, however, if they had made any other gifts to *D* during the year. In January of this year, *H* and *W* gave *D* community property worth $50,000. *H* and *W* are each required to file a return reporting a gift of $25,000 on or before April 15 of next year.

§ 2.10.2. Manner and Time of Filing

The donor should file a gift tax return with the Internal Revenue Service Center with which the donor's federal income tax return is, or would be, filed. Instructions for Form 709. Otherwise, the return may be hand carried to the office of the district director for the district in which the donor resides. *See* § 6091(b)(4).

Under § 7503, if the last day prescribed for filing is a Saturday, Sunday, or legal holiday, the time is extended to the next succeeding day that is not a Saturday, Sunday, or legal holiday. A return is considered timely filed if it is mailed within the time allowed. The pertinent regulations provide generally that a document is deemed filed on the date of the postmark stamped on the cover in which it was mailed. Reg. § 301.7502-1(a). If the date of mailing or receipt is important, returns and other documents mailed to the IRS should be sent by certified or registered mail, return receipt requested.

An addition to tax of five percent per month for each month a gift tax return is delinquent, up to a maximum of 25 percent, will also be imposed under § 6651(a)(1) unless the failure to file the return was for reasonable cause. Because the penalty for a late return is a function of the gift tax due, there is effectively no penalty for the late filing of a gift tax return where no tax is due (*e.g.,* where cumulative taxable gifts do not exceed the $1 million gift tax exemption amount).

A negligence penalty is often not imposed where the donors report gifts that were not disclosed on their initial gift tax returns prior to the commencement of an audit of the returns. *E.g.,* LR 9244004 (TAM).

§ 2.10.3. Changes in Valuation, § § 2504(c); 6501(c)(9)

Gifts Made After August 5, 1997. The 1997 Act amended the provisions of § 2504 that precluded the IRS from revaluing gifts after the gift tax had been paid and the limitations period had run. Once the limitations period of § 6501 expires, § 2504(c) was amended to bar changes in the gift tax value of gifts that are adequately disclosed in a return. A companion change amended § 6501(c)(9) to provide that the usual three year limitations period applies to "an item which is disclosed in such return, or in a statement attached to the return, in a manner adequate to apprise the Secretary of the nature of such item." These provisions apply to gifts made after August 5, 1997. Similarly, the disclosure of a completed transfer made for an adequate and full consideration in money or money's worth starts the statute of limitations running even though the transaction is not a gift and no gift tax return is required. Reg. § § 301.6501-1(f)(4) and 301.6501-1(f)(7), Ex. (2).

Once the valuation of a post-August 5, 1997 gift is finally determined, the determination "applies to adjustments involving all issues relating to the gift, including valuation issues and legal issues involving the interpretation of the gift tax law." Reg. § § 20.2001-1(b); 25.2504-2(b). Under the cited regulation the amount of a taxable gift as "finally determined" for gift tax purposes is: "The amount of the taxable gift as shown on a gift tax return, or a statement attached to the return, if the Internal Revenue Service does not contest such amount before the time has expired under section 6501 within which gift taxes may be assessed."

In order to constitute adequate disclosure, the regulations require that a return (or a statement attached to the return) provide: (1) a description of the property transferred and any consideration received by the transferor; (2) the identity of the transferee and the relationship between the transferor and transferee, if any; (3) if the transferee is a trust, the TIN of the trust and a description of the terms of the trust or a copy of the trust instrument, and, (4) a detailed description of the method by which the fair market value of the property was determined, including information regarding any discount that is claimed. Reg. § 301.6501(c)-1(f)(2). The regulations describe in detail the information that must be provided in order to satisfy the last requirement. A valuation based on an appraisal by an unrelated qualified appraiser may be adequately disclosed by providing a copy of the appraisal and information about the appraiser. Reg. § 301.6501(c)-1(f)(3). Transfers made to members of the transferor's family in the ordinary course of business, such as salary payments, need not be disclosed if they are "properly reported by all parties for income tax purposes." § 301.6501(c)-1(f)(4). In the case of split gifts, adequate disclosure by one spouse satisfies the requirement with respect to both spouses. Reg. § 301.6501(c)-1(f)(6).

Gifts Prior to August 6, 1997. The prior provisions of § 2504(c) barred the IRS from revaluing gifts for gift tax purposes after the tax has been paid and the statute of limitations has run. The bar only applied, however, when a tax "was assessed or paid." Thus, it did not bar revaluation where the donor's unified credit was used to offset the tax. The IRS sought to avoid the bar of § 2504(c) by arguing that it does not prohibit a revaluation of the amount of taxable gifts in connection with the determination of a deceased donor's estate tax liability. The argument was rejected in *Boatmen's First National Bank v. United States,* 705 F. Supp. 1407 (W.D.Mo. 1988), which noted that the IRS was attempting to do indirectly what it could not do directly. "This approach, in practice, would extend the statutory limitations period on gift valuation indefinitely, limited only by how long the donor survived after giving a gift. Congress could not have intended this, in light of its clearly established three-year limitation." 705 F. Supp. at 1413.

The Tax Court proved to be a somewhat more hospitable forum for the IRS. In *Estate of Frederick R. Smith,* 94 T.C. 872 (1990), the Tax Court held that § 2504(c) did not bar revaluation of gifts for estate tax purposes. In doing so the Tax Court recognized that a revaluation of a decedent's gifts "requires the subtraction for gift taxes be adjusted to take into account any increase in the value of the previous gifts." 94 T.C. at 879. If such an adjustment were not made, the IRS would be permitted "to collect the barred gift taxes through the imposition of a higher estate tax without an offsetting adjustment." 94 T.C. at 880.

The approach taken by the Tax Court in *Estate of Frederick R. Smith* was followed in *Estate of Stalcup v. United States,* 91-2 U.S.T.C. ¶ 60,086 (W.D. Okla. 1991). In *Estate of Inez Robinson,* 101 T.C. 499 (1993), the Tax Court held that the excess amount of annual gift tax exclusions claimed by the decedent could properly be included by the IRS in the amount of adjusted taxable gifts made by the decedent. That decision is consistent with *Levin v. Commissioner,* 986 F.2d 91 (4th Cir.), *cert. denied,* 114 S. Ct. 66 (1993), which held that although the gift tax statute of limitations had run, the estate tax imposed on a decedent's estate could be determined by increasing the amount of adjusted taxable gifts by the amount of project notes of which she had made gifts but had not treated as taxable. Levin was followed by the Eighth Circuit in *Evanson v. United States,* 30 F.3d 960 (1994).

In LR 9718004 (TAM) the IRS recognized that if the donor only claimed the unified credit with respect to prior gifts, § 2504(c) does not prevent the donor from discounting in a current gift tax return the value of the previously reported gifts. In particular, the donor may claim discounts resulting from gifts of fractional interests in real property. If the adjustments are not made during the donor's lifetime, it should be possible to make them in connection with the determination of the donor's estate tax. This possibility is consistent with the approach taken in *Estate of Smith* and related cases.

A Chief Counsel's Advice, LR 200221010, holds that the limitations period with respect to a pre-August 6, 1997 gift does not begin to run unless the nature of the gift is reasonably disclosed. It concludes that the statement that the gift consists of "Class B units in ABC LLC. Units acquired on 4/6/97 for $200,000 cash" does not reasonably disclose the nature of the gift. According to the CCA, the gift tax return should have disclosed the number of units in the LLC, the class or type of the units, and the percentage ownership that the gift represented. Interestingly, the IRS asserted that the units, which were acquired on April 6, 1997 and were transferred to the donees on April 7, 1997, were worth $14 million. What a difference a day makes!

§ 2.10.4. Payment and Penalties

Under § 6151(a), the gift tax must be paid at the time the return is due, though an extension may be allowed under § 6161 in cases of "undue hardship." *See* § 6161(b)(1); Reg. § 25.6161-1(b). However, the donor's unified credit is available to offset the gift tax and must be used for that purpose to the full extent it remains available to the donor. Unlike the case of the $30,000 lifetime gift tax exemption that was available under § 2521 prior to 1977, the donor has no option regarding the use of the unified credit.

Checks or money orders in payment of the tax should be drawn to the order of "Internal Revenue Service" and carry the donor's social security number.

Any tax that is not paid when due is subject to an interest charge at the floating annual rate established under § 6621 until it is paid. § 6601(a). The interest rate applicable to deficiencies is the Federal short-term rate plus three percent. § 6621(a)(2). The interest rate for tax overpayments, naturally, is the federal short-term rate plus 2 percent. § 6621(a)(1). A penalty is imposed by § 6662 with respect to an estate or gift tax underpayment of $5,000 or more that is due to the valuation of property on the return at 65 percent or less of its correct valuation. § 6662(g). The penalty is an addition to tax of an amount equal to 20 percent of the underpayment attributable to the undervaluation. Under § 6664(c) no penalty may be imposed if the underpayment was due to reasonable cause. Presumably no penalty would be imposed if the donor's valuation of the property was based on a written appraisal by a qualified expert.

D. FEDERAL ESTATE TAX HIGHLIGHTS

Death taxes are ancient taxes. They were known to the Egyptians, as well as the Romans and Greeks. Even the complaints against them have a venerable pedigree. Pliny the Younger provides as good an example as any. He is among the earliest critics who have left summaries of their complaints. Pliny eloquently argued that a tax on the shares of direct heirs "was an 'unnatural' tax, augmenting the grief and sorrow of the bereaved." Almost two thousand years later the same argument was still being heard. For in 1898 Senator Allen forcefully inquired whether it was right "to stand with the widow and children at the grave side of a dead father to collect a tax," and then he sympathetically referred to the widow "in weeds" and the children "in tears." Eisenstein, The Rise and Decline of the Estate Tax, 11 Tax L. Rev. 223 (1956).

§ 2.11. NATURE AND COMPUTATION OF THE TAX

The federal estate tax is "neither a property tax nor an inheritance tax." Reg. § 20.0-2(a). Instead, it is an excise tax imposed on the transfer of the entire taxable estate of the decedent. § 2001(a). A decedent's taxable estate is determined by subtracting the deductions allowable under § § 2053-2058 from the decedent's gross estate. As explained at § 2.3, the tentative amount of the estate tax is calculated by applying the unified rate schedule, § 2001(c), to the sum of a decedent's taxable estate plus the amount of post-1976 taxable gifts made by the decedent. However, in order to avoid taxing the same property twice, gifts that are includible in a decedent's gross estate are not counted as post-1976 taxable gifts. *See* § 2001(b). The gross amount of the estate tax is determined by subtracting the gift tax on a decedent's post-1976 taxable gifts from the amount of the tentative tax. The gross tax is then reduced by the unified credit allowable in the year of the decedent's death and any of the other credits that are allowable under § § 2011-2014. Most estates utilize only the unified credit.

The taxable estate, together with a decedent's post-1976 taxable gifts, is the base on which the decedent's tax liability is determined. It is calculated by subtracting deductions, § § 2053-2058, from the gross estate, § § 2033-2044.

The federal estate tax return is due nine months after the date of a decedent's death. Extensions of time within which to file the federal estate tax return and to pay the estate tax are reviewed at § § 12.42 and 12.43, respectively. The IRS has recognized that delivery to certain private delivery services satisfies the "timely mailing as timely filing/timely paying" rule of § 7502.

§ 2.12. ESTATES OF QUALIFIED DECEDENTS, § 2201

Under § 2201(a), the executor of a "qualified decedent" may elect to determine the decedent's estate tax liability according to the rates set forth in § 2201(c) rather than those of § 2001(c). A qualified decedent is either, (1) a citizen or resident of the United States who dies while on active service in a combat zone or as a result of wounds, injuries, or disease suffered in the line of duty while serving in a combat zone, or (2) a person (other than a participant or conspirator) who dies as a result of wounds or injuries suffered in the Oklahoma City terrorist attack of April 19, 1995 or the terrorist attacks of September 11, 2001 or who dies as a result of an anthrax attack occurring on or after September 11, 2001 and before January 1, 2002.

The rate schedule of § 2201(c) fixes the estate tax at a rate equal to 125 percent of the amount of the maximum state death tax credit specified in former § 2011(b). After the tax is calculated, it is offset by the unified credit. Revenue Ruling 2002-86, 2002-2 C.B. 993, illustrates how the estate tax is determined for the estates of qualified decedents dying in 2005. It states:

> If § 2001 applies, the estate tax (including the aggregate amount of gift tax payable on any adjusted taxable gifts under § 2001(b)(2)) is computed in the same manner as provided in § 2001(b), except that the rate schedule in § 2201(c) is used to compute that tax instead of the rate schedule in § 2001(c). The rate schedule contained in § 2001(c) continues to be used to determine the applicable credit amount (the unified credit) available to the estate under § 2010(c).

§ 2.13. GROSS ESTATE

The property and interests described in §§ 2033-2044 are included in the gross estate and valued in accordance with §§ 2031-2032A. Although the gross estate includes the property subject to administration in a decedent's estate under state law, the gross estate is a much broader and more inclusive concept. As explained below, it may include property that the decedent no longer owned at death.

General Composition of the Gross Estate. The scope of §§ 2033-2044 and § 2046 is described in the following paragraphs, which are largely adapted from Reg. § 20.2031-1(a).

1. **Owned Property, § 2033.** Property owned by a decedent at death is includible in the decedent's gross estate under § 2033. The section extends to future interests as well as present possessory interests. Section 2034 merely provides that the property is includible in the decedent's estate even though the decedent's surviving spouse has an interest in the property, such as dower or curtesy. The estate of a donor is required to include a portion of the donor's contribution to a qualified tuition plan that exceeded the annual exclusion amount if the donor elected to treat the contribution as a gift made ratably over a five-year period and dies prior to the expiration of that period. § 529(c)(4)(C). *See* § 2.6. The estate is required to include the portion properly allocable to periods after the date of the donor's death. *Ibid.*

2. **Property Transferred During Lifetime, §§ 2035-2038.** Property transferred within three years of death is generally not includible in the gross estate of a transferor who dies after December 31, 1981. A contrary rule applied to the estates of persons dying prior to 1982.

   Other lifetime transfers are includible under §§ 2036-2038 unless the transferor received full and adequate consideration for the transfer in money or money's worth. In general, § 2036 requires the inclusion of property with respect to which the decedent retained either the use or income from the property or the power to designate who would receive its use or income. Property transferred by the decedent is includible under § 2037 if it could be enjoyed by others only if they survive the decedent and the decedent retained a reversionary interest, the value of which immediately before the decedent's death exceeded five percent of the value of the property. The scope of § 2038 is essentially the same as that of § 2036 although § 2038 speaks specifically of a power, retained by the decedent, to alter, amend, revoke, or terminate the transfer.

3. **Annuities; Joint Interests; Powers of Appointment and Life Insurance, §§ 2039-2042.** Sections 2039 through 2042 deal with special types of property and powers of appointment held by the decedent. Section 2039 requires the inclusion of certain interests in annuities and other payments made pursuant to a contract or other agreement under which the decedent had a right to receive payments for life or for a period not ascertainable without reference to his or her death. Section 2040 governs the inclusion of interests in joint tenancies and tenancies by the entirety. Property subject to certain powers of appointment is includible in the power-holder's estate under § 2041. Finally, § 2042 requires the inclusion of insurance receivable by the insured's executor or over which the insured retained any incident of ownership.

4. **Consideration offset § 2043.** Under § 2043. the amount includible in a decedent's estate under §§ 2035-2038 and 2041 is reduced by the amount of consideration in money or money's worth that the decedent received in exchange for the transfer of the property or the release or exercise of the power. This section deals with cases in which the decedent received insufficient consideration in money or money's worth for the transfer, release, or exercise. The amount of consideration received by the decedent is "frozen" at the time of the transfer, while the value of the property transferred by the decedent is determined on the appropriate valuation date, (*i.e.,* the value of the property included in the transferor's estate may increase or decrease after the date of the transfer, but the amount of the consideration is fixed on that date). *See* § 9.41.

5. **QTIP, § 2044.** Under § 2044 a decedent's gross estate includes any property that was transferred to the decedent and for which a marital deduction was allowed as qualified terminable interest property (QTIP) under § 2523(f) (gift tax) or § 2056(b)(7) (estate tax). *See* § 5.23.

6. **Qualified Disclaimers, § 2046.** The estate tax recognizes that a qualified disclaimer under § 2518 does not constitute a transfer for purposes of the estate tax. § 2046.

7. **Time of Creation, § 2045.** Section 2045 merely directs that unless otherwise provided the rules of §§ 2034-2042 apply to transfers, interests, and powers whenever made, created, exercised, or relinquished.

8. **Encumbered Real Property.** Under Reg. § 20.2053-7, the full unpaid amount of an encumbrance is deductible if the full value of the underlying property is included in the decedent's estate—which is required if the decedent was personally liable on the debt (*i.e.,* the debt was "recourse"). If the decedent was not personally liable on the debt (*i.e.,* the debt was "nonrecourse"), only the net value of the property is includible. The difference in treatment is most important for the estates of nonresident aliens which, in the case of a recourse indebtedness is deductible only in the proportion that the value of property included in the gross estate bears to the total value of the decedent's estate. § 2106(a)(1). For a case illustrating the operation of the limita-

tion see *Estate of Hon Hing Fung*, 117 T.C. 247 (2001), *aff'd by unpub. opinion*, 91 A.F.T.R.2d 1228 (9th Cir. 2003).

The scope and application of §§ 2035, 2036, and 2038-2041 are examined in more detail in §§ 2.18-2.22. Particular attention is given to some of the traps created by those sections and how to avoid them. Some other provisions explored at greater length are the life insurance section, § 2042, in Chapter 6, and the marital deduction sections, §§ 2044, 2056 and others, in Chapter 5.

§ 2.14. VALUATION

For estate and gift tax purposes, property is generally valued at its fair market value, which is the "price at which the property would change hands between a willing buyer and a willing seller, neither being under any compulsion to buy or sell and both having reasonable knowledge of the relevant facts." Reg. §§ 20.2031-1(b), 25.2512-1. The possible revaluation of taxable gifts made by a decedent is discussed at § 2.10.3. A client should be fully informed about the ways in which the client's assets might be arranged so as to control or depress their value. Shrinking or freezing the value of the estate is one of the most important estate planning strategies. *See* § 2.46-2.47.

§ 2.14.1. Discounts and Premiums

The fair market value of property necessarily reflects the peculiar characteristics of that property. It is not enough, for example, to value shares of stock in a corporation solely with reference to their liquidation value (*i.e.*, the amount the shareholder would receive upon liquidation of the corporation), for stock carries other property interests like the right to vote on certain corporate matters. Accordingly, all assets are subject to various discounts and premiums in computing their fair market values. Note that difficulties can arise if a decedent's estate includes a controlling interest in a business, which will cause it to be valued at a premium, and lesser (*i.e.*, noncontrolling) interests pass to the surviving spouse or to charity, or both. *See* § 5.5.2.

Minority Interest Discount and Lack of Marketability Discount. Where the subject property represents a minority interest in an asset or a business entity, it is proper to discount the property's value to reflect the holder's lack of control. Similarly, where the subject property cannot be sold readily in the open market, whether because of applicable laws, contractual restrictions, or both, the value of the subject property is discounted to reflect its lack of marketability. Substantial discounts are frequently allowed in valuing minority interests in a business enterprise or undivided interests in real property. The same interests may also qualify for a discount for lack of marketability. Thus, in *Harwood Investment Co.*, 82 T.C. 239 (1984), *aff'd without opinion*, 786 F.2d 1174 (9th Cir.), *cert. denied*, 479 U.S. 1007 (1986), a discount of 50 percent was allowed in valuing gifts of interest in a family limited partnership.

Aggregation. If a donor transfers shares in a corporation to each of the donor's children, the factor of corporate control in the family is not considered in valuing each transferred interest for purposes of section 2512 of the Code. For estate and gift tax valuation purposes, the Service will follow *Bright, Propstra, Andrews* and *Lee* in not assuming that all voting power held by family members may be aggregated for purposes of determining whether the transferred shares should be valued as part of a controlling interest. Consequently, a minority discount will not be disallowed solely because a transferred interest, when aggregated with interests held by family members, would be part of a controlling interest. This would be the case whether the donor held 100 percent or some lesser percentage of the stock immediately before the gift. Rev. Rul. 93-12, 1993-1 C.B. 202

Revenue Ruling 93-12 was issued after the IRS lost a succession of valuation cases in which it had argued that the property in question should be valued by aggregating the interests owned by non-hostile family members. Accordingly, a valuation discount will ordinarily be allowable in valuing community property; in which each spouse owns a half interest and neither spouse has control. Similarly, a discount should be allowable if the owner of 100 percent of an asset transfers a half interest to a donee in one year and the other half the following year. Under the existing law the transfers are valued independent of each other.

Control Premium. Conversely, in some cases an interest that carries control of a business may be valued at a premium. For example, a premium was attached to the 51 percent of a business that qualified for the marital deduction in *Estate of Dean E. Chenoweth*, 88 T.C. 1577 (1987).

Fractional Interest Discount. It is no secret that co-ownership of property introduces cumbersome hassles. The owner of a tenancy in common interest, for example, may be required to partition the property to realize its liquidation value. Even where the owner does not wish to divide the property, the owner must tolerate the actions of the co-tenant. Accordingly, courts have approved discounts, usually in the range of 10 – 15 percent, to undivided interests in property. *See* § 2.45.1 Some experienced practitioners have reported settling disputes with the IRS agreeing to fractional interest discounts as high as 25 – 30 percent. As regards real property, the IRS has argued that fair market value should be based upon the fractional value of the whole, reduced by the same proportion of the cost of partitioning the property. LR 199943003 (TAM). A similar approach was used by the Tax Court in *Andrew K. Ludwick*, 99 T.C.M. 1424 (2010), where the court ultimately applied a 17-percent fractional interest discount in valuing the contribution of one-half interest in a Hawaii vacation home to each of two qualified personal residence trusts created by the taxpayers.

In one case, the court denied a fractional interest discount in valuing the decedent's undivided one-half interest in 19 paintings. *Stone v. United States*, 2007-1 U.S.T.C. (CCH) ¶ 60,545 (N.D. Cal. 2007), *aff'd*, 2009-1 U.S.T.C. (CCH) ¶ 60,572 (9th Cir. 2009). The court gave significant weight to the fact the estate's expert could not cite a single example of a fractional interest discount applying to a sale of art. It rejected the expert's attempts to analogize co-ownership of a painting to the co-ownership of land and interests in closely-held businesses. The court concluded, however, that a discount to reflect the costs to partition and sell the art collection at auction would be proper, and ultimately this amount was set at 5 percent.

Built-in Gains Discount. Until 1999 the IRS, supported by the Tax Court, disallowed any discount for the built-in capital gain of a C corporation. *Estate of Pauline Welch*, 75 T.C.M. (CCH) 2252 (1998), *rev'd in unpub. op.*, 85 A.F.T.R.2d (RIA) 1200 (6th Cir. 2000). However, the appellate courts properly allowed appropriate discounts. *Eisenberg v. Commissioner*, 155 F.3d 50 (2d Cir. 1998); *Estate of Davis*, 153 F.3d 726 (10th Cir. 1998). The IRS acquiesced in the *Eisenberg* decision "to the extent that [the court] holds that there is no legal prohibition against such a discount." AOD 1999-01, 1999-1 C.B. 332. The availability of the discount and its amount will be treated as factual matters, subject to expert testimony.

Estate of Beatrice Dunn v. Commissioner, 301 F.3d 339 (5th Cir. 2002), holds that "under the court's asset-based approach—determination of the value of Dunn Equipment must include a reduction equal to 34% of the taxable gain inherent in those assets as of the valuation date." Thus, in the Fifth Circuit, the asset-based value of stock in a C corporation must be reduced, dollar-for-dollar, for all built-in gain.

In valuing S corporation stock under the discounted future cash flow approach, the Tax Court and, by a divided court, the Sixth Circuit held that it is not proper to deduct hypothetical corporate income taxes. *Gross v. Commissioner*, 272 F.3d 333 (6th Cir. 2001).

In LR 200303010 (TAM), the IRS ruled that the value of U.S. savings bonds could not be discounted for lack of marketability or for built-in income tax liability.

In *Estate of Jelke v. Commissioner*, 507 F.3d 1317 (11th Cir. 2007), the decedent's gross estate included a relatively small interest in a closely held corporation that mostly owned marketable securities. The net asset value of the corporation was about $188 million, but the company would incur a $51 million capital gains tax if it were to liquidate all of its holdings. In determining the value of the decedent's stock, the estate first reduced the corporation's net asset value by the entire $51 million built-in capital gains tax liability and then applied discounts for lack of marketability and control. The IRS claimed that the amount of the discount should be adjusted to $21 million, its present value. The Tax Court held that the Service's approach was correct, reasoning that a willing seller of the company's stock would not reduce the stock price for all potential built-in capital gains tax, because the company had a track record of little turnover in its holdings. It thus approved the Service's approach of adjusting the net asset value by the present value of the anticipated built-in capital gains tax liability. On appeal, the estate argued that the value of the stock should be discounted by the full amount of the built-in capital gains tax liability; and the Eleventh Circuit agreed, holding that a full discount is proper, because it assumes the corporation liquidates on the date of death "without resort to present value or prophecies." The court preferred this more objective approach, because judges lack training in valuation and should not have to spend precious time wading through expert testimony. It also found that the full discount approach better reflects the depressing effect taxes have on market selling prices.

Another taxpayer victory occurred in *Estate of Marie J. Jensen*, 100 T.C.M. 138 (2010). At the decedent's death in 2005, her revocable trust held 164 shares of stock in a closely held C corporation that operated a summer camp for girls on a 94-acre waterfront parcel in New Hampshire. The corporation owned the land, and its improvements included state-of-the-art playing fields, an indoor gym, a horse stable, a dining hall, cottages, and bunkhouses. An appraisal determined that the net asset value of the company was about $4.2 million. From that, the appraisal subtracted an estimated built-in long-term capital gain tax of $965,000 even though neither a sale nor a liquidation of the company nor a sale of its assets was imminent or even contemplated. The Service determined a deficiency after reducing the built-in gains discount to about $250,000. Before the Tax Court, the Service's expert concluded that the discount for built-in gains should be limited to about 45 percent of the company's estimated tax liability (here, about $425,000), because that was consistent with discounts taken in valuing various closed-end mutual funds. The court agreed with the estate that reference to closed-end funds was inappropriate, because closed-end funds tend to invest in various economic sectors, whereas the corporation here operated a single business activity (the camp) with a single principal asset (the land). After computing a range of potential values for the corporation's assets and estimating the present value of the potential capital gains tax liabilities, the court ultimately determined that the estate's claimed built-in gain discount was proper, because it was within the range of acceptable values.

Blockage and Absorption Discounts. The value of property may qualify for a blockage discount if the market could not absorb the quantity involved in the transfer. The concept applies to publicly traded stock and other property. *Estate of McClatchy*, 147 F.3d 1089 (9th Cir. 1998) (IRS conceded blockage discount of 15 percent). In LR 9719001 (TAM), the IRS held that the donor's transfer of shares in a publicly traded corporation to a trustee, to be allocated equally to three separate trusts, each of which was held for the benefit of a grandchild of the donor, could not be aggregated. Instead, "[f]or federal gift tax purposes, the Donor is treated as having made nine separate gifts, each consisting of a block of shares of stock in Company M."

Blockage discounts are also allowable with respect to art objects. *Estate of David Smith*, 57 T.C. 650, *aff'd*, 510 F.2d 479 (2d Cir. 1975), *cert. denied*, 423 U.S. 827 (1976); *Louisa J. Calder*, 85 T.C. 713 (1985); *Estate of Georgia O'Keefe*, 1992 RIA T.C.M. ¶92,210. In *O'Keefe*, the Tax Court held that one-half of the decedent's works were subject to a 75-percent discount and the other half was subject to a 25-percent discount. In *Calder*, the Tax Court held that for gift tax valuation purposes, the donor cannot claim a blockage discount based on aggregating the gifts. Thus, the regulations and court decisions continue to require that the discount be applied separately to each gift for purposes of valuation. Blockage discounts are appropriate in valuing art objects for nontax purposes as well. *Estate of Andy Warhol* (unpublished), 1994 N.Y. Misc. 687 (Surr. Ct. 1994) (lawyer's fee based on value of estate). In *Estate of Emanuel Trompeter*, 75 T.C.M. (CCH) 1653 (1998), the court held that a blockage discount does not apply to an outstanding collection of rare gold coins.

In *Estate of Eldon I. Auker*, 75 T.C.M. (CCH) 2321 (1998), the court allowed a market absorption discount of 6.189 percent against the valuation of three apartment complexes that were held in a revocable trust created by the decedent. The apartments in the complexes constituted 20 percent of the total comparable apartment units in the county in which they were located. The court assumed that it would take 18 months to sell one complex at its undiscounted value; 24 months to sell the second; and 42 months to sell the third. Using a present value analysis, it determined that an average discount of 6.189 percent was appropriate. No discount was allowed for real estate held indirectly through corporations.

§2.14.2. Valuation of Particular Assets

Certain assets require their own valuation methods, usually because the traditional approach of determining liquidation value and then applying applicable discounts and premiums is not suitable given some unique characteristic of the asset.

IRAs and Other IRD Items. For estate tax purposes, a discount is not allowable in valuing items of income in respect of a decedent (IRD), although they carry a built-in income tax liability. Instead, under § 691(c) the recipient is entitled to a deduction for the portion of the estate tax attributable to the IRD. Consistently, a discount would not be allowable in valuing an IRA includible in an estate. Under the "willing seller-willing buyer" test, an IRA would be valued at its face amount: a willing buyer would pay the estate the full face an IRA because the estate would be responsible for paying the income tax liability attached to the IRA. As seller, the estate, which has the income tax liability, would want to maximize the amount it received for the IRA.

In LR 200247001 (TAM), the IRS ruled that the estate tax value of IRAs was not subject to a discount because of the built-in income tax liability or because of any delay in their distribution or payment. The TAM relies upon *Estate of Robinson,* 69 T.C. 222 (1977) (no discount allowed for income tax due on remaining installment payments due on promissory note) and the remedial effect of the deduction allowable under § 691(c). According to the TAM, "section 691(c) specifically addresses the income tax inherent in assets that are also subject to estate tax and provides a statutory remedy, a reduction in income tax, to alleviate the situation. This income tax reduction operates in lieu of an estate tax reduction in the form of a valuation discount."

Illegal Items. A decedent's estate may be required to include the fair market value of property that was in the decedent's possession at the time of death but was later confiscated by the government or recovered by owners from whom it was stolen. Thus, in LR 9207004 (TAM), the decedent's estate included the street value of marijuana being transported by the decedent at the time of his death in an airplane crash, although it was later confiscated by the state of Florida. In addition, the TAM held that public policy against drug trafficking prohibited allowance of any deduction for the confiscation of the contraband. Likewise, in LR 9152005 (TAM), the decedent's estate was required to include the value of art objects the decedent had stolen while on duty in Europe with the United States military following World War II. No deduction was allowed the estate for the recovery of the art objects, claims to which were asserted against the decedent's beneficiaries only after a reasonable time within which to complete the administration of the estate had passed.

Funds withdrawn from a trust in breach of the fiduciary's duties and deposited into his individual brokerage account were required to be included in the fiduciary's gross estate in *Estate of Hester v. United States,* 2007-1 U.S.T.C. (CCH) ¶ 60,537 (W.D. Va. 2007), because the decedent exercised dominion and control over the assets. The court also disallowed an offsetting deduction under § 2053, reasoning that any claim for reimbursement from a beneficiary of the trust would now be precluded by the statute of limitations and that § 2053 does not permit a deduction for theoretical liabilities of the estate.

Initial Public Offering. The valuation of the stock of a closely held company should take into account the possibility that there might be a public offering of the stock. In *Estate of Ross N. Freeman,* 72 T.C.M. (CCH) 373 (1996), the Tax Court criticized the petitioner's expert witness for failing "to take any account of a public offering, which actually occurred within 8 months of decedent's death, and the possibility of which was discussed before his death." The Tax Court assumed "that a potential purchaser would be interested in such plans and might pay a premium depending on her judgment of the likelihood of such an offering." *See also, Morris M.*

Messing, 48 T.C. 502 (1967) ("[A] publicly traded stock and a privately traded stock are not, as respondent would have us assume, the same animal distinguished only by the size, frequency, or color of its spots. The essential nature of the beast is different." *Id.* at 509.)

Contingent Claims. The fair market value of a contingent claim is established according to expert testimony and the court's own judgment. For example, the decedent's one-half interest in a personal injury judgment of $7,750,000 ($3,875,000) that was the subject of an appeal at the time of the decedent's death was determined to be $1,750,000 in *Estate of Ann Marie Lennon*, 60 T.C.M. 92,360 (1991). The valuation reflected a discount of roughly 53 percent from the amount of a one-half interest in the amount of the judgment subject to the appeal or a discount of about 26 percent from the amount actually received. After the decedent's death the estate accepted a settlement in the total amount of $5,250,000, of which the estate was entitled to receive a net of $2,456,131.

Life Estates, Annuities, Remainders. The valuation of life estates, annuities, remainders, and other split interests must be made in accordance with the rules of §7520. The regulations, adopted on December 13, 1995, reflect the pre-existing position of the IRS with respect to the use of the actuarial tables to value the interests of persons who are terminally ill:

> [T]he mortality component prescribed under section 7520 may not be used to determine the present value of an annuity, income interest, remainder interest, or reversionary interest if an individual who is a measuring life dies or is terminally ill at the time the gift is completed. An individual who is known to have an incurable illness or other deteriorating physical condition is considered terminally ill if there is at least a 50 percent probability that the individual will die within 1 year. However, if the individual survives for eighteen months or longer after the date the gift is completed, that individual shall be presumed to have not been terminally ill at the date the gift was completed unless the contrary is established by clear and convincing evidence. Reg. § 25.7520-3(b)(3)(i); *see also* Regs. § § 1.7520-3(b)(3), 20.7520-3(b)(3).

Restricted Beneficial Interests. The regulations provide that a restricted beneficial interest, one "subject to any contingency, power, or other restriction, whether the restriction is provided for by the terms of the trust, will, or other governing instrument or is caused by other circumstances," should be valued according to its fair market value and without regard to the §7520 annuity tables. Reg. § 20.7520-3(b)(1)(ii). Thus, for example, the value of an interest subject to the exercise of a discretionary invasion power or a discretionary withdrawal power would not be determined under the §7520 tables. In *Anthony v. United States*, 520 F.3d 374 (5th Cir. 2008), the court held that the decedent's interest in three unassignable annuity contracts were not restricted beneficial interests and thus were valued using the §7520 tables. The estate argued that the §7520 tables did not apply and that a marketability discount for the unassignable annuities was proper, but the court concluded that the exception for restricted beneficial interests should be read narrowly to mean restrictions which, like contingencies and powers, "threaten to end an annuitant's right to receive any future payments." The non-assignability feature of the decedent's annuities did not affect *whether* payments would be made—it only affected *to whom* the payments would be made.

Lottery Payments. According to the Tax Court the nonassignable future payments due to the winner of a lottery are valued as an annuity under §7520. Accordingly, no discount is allowed on account of the inalienability of future payments. *Estate of Paul Gribauskas,* 116 T.C. 142 (2001); *Estate of Gladys Cook,* 82 T.C.M. (CCH) 154 (2001) (a discount was allowed in valuing the decedent's interest in the limited partnership which held the lottery ticket and had the right to receive future payments), *aff'd,* 349 F.3d 850 (5th Cir. 2003). The Ninth Circuit has ruled to the contrary, concluding that the nonassignability feature made valuation under §7520 "unrealistic and unreasonable." It held that the value of the future payments should be made according to the "willing buyer-willing seller" approach—although the payments were in fact nontransferrable. As a result, the value of the payments was reduced by half—from slightly more than $4 million to slightly more than $2 million. *Estate of Shackleford v. United States,* 262 F.3d 1028 (9th Cir. 2001).

In 2003, the Second Circuit reversed the Tax Court decision in *Estate of Paul Gribauskas* on the ground that the estate had met the burden of proving that a valuation of the right to future payments based on the actuarial tables would produce an unrealistic and unreasonable result. 342 F.3d 85 (2d Cir. 2003).

The results reached by the Second and Ninth Circuits conflict with the contrary result reached by the Fifth Circuit in *Gladys Cook,* 349 F.3d 850 (5th Cir. 2003), which upheld the application of the §7520 tables to the valuation of the annuity payable to the lottery winner (the partnership). The *Gladys Cook* holding is based upon the court's decision that a lottery prize is properly valued as a private annuity. The Sixth Circuit joined the Fifth Circuit in holding that the §7520 tables are the proper method to value the right to future payments of a lottery jackpot prize. *Negron v. United States,* 553 F.3d 1013 (6th Cir. 2009). The taxpayer in that case, a personal representative bringing a refund claim on behalf of an estate, argued that the §7520 tables produced an unreasonable result in that it caused the estate to include an amount greater than what the estate actually received. But the Sixth Circuit ruled that "equity arguments are insufficient to invalidate properly enacted Treasury Regulations, such as those requiring the use of the IRS annuity tables." Further, the court observed that the nonmarketability aspect of annuities like lottery jackpots is already an underlying assumption of the §7520 tables, so an additional marketability discount is not required.

§2.14.3. Other Valuation Issues

Valuation issues have proven to be fertile ground for disputes between taxpayers and the IRS. Consequently, a number of fact-intensive principles have emerged in recent years.

Interim Transfers Ignored. Applying the substance over form doctrine, the IRS and courts may ignore interim transfers and deny minority and nonmarketability discounts. *Griffin v. United States,* 42 F. Supp. 2d 700 (W.D. Tex. 1998). In this case, the husband transferred 45 percent of the stock in a closely held corporation to his wife. One month later, the wife and husband each transferred 45 percent of the stock to an irrevocable trust. The husband was treated as having transferred the entire 90 percent of the stock.

Indirect Gifts on Formation of a Family Limited Partnership. In *Estate of W.W. Jones, II,* 116 T.C. 121 (2001), the court held that the transfer of property to a limited partnership in exchange for partnership interests did not constitute a gift where the contributed property was allocated to the decedent's capital account. Essentially the same result was reached earlier in *Estate of Albert Strangi,* 115 T.C. 478 (2000), *rev'd on other grounds, Gulig v. Commissioner,* 293 F.3d 279 (5th Cir. 2002). In contrast, an indirect gift may result to the extent a partner's contribution of property is allocated on a pro rata basis to all partners. *J. C. Shepherd,* 115 T.C. 376 (2000), *aff'd,* 283 F.3d 1258, 89 A.F.T.R.2d (RIA) 1251 (11th Cir. 2002) (Tax Court treated the donor's gift of land to partnership as indirect gifts of fractional interests in the land to his sons and not as gifts of partnership units). The result is the same in the case of contributions to a corporation. *See* § 2.5.5.

Duty of Consistency. The IRS may appropriately insist that gifts of minority or fractional interests to charity, or in satisfaction of marital deduction bequests, also be valued subject to the same discounts. Thus, a discount may be applied if a portion of the shares that do not carry control is distributed in satisfaction of a marital deduction bequest. LR 9403005. *See* § 5.5.2. The risk is, of course, that a decedent's estate will include an interest that is valued at a premium, but the charitable or marital deduction would be based on a fractional or minority interest, the value of which would be discounted.

Formula Clauses. Some gift plans include a formula clause designed to discourage the IRS from challenging a valuation by providing for a gift over to charity to the extent the value of the donative property exceeds a specified amount. Advocates of the plan believe the IRS would have little incentive to challenge the valuation of a gift if the excess value would pass in a way that is not subject to the gift or estate taxes. For example, a plan may give the donor's children units in an LLC, provided that if the units are finally determined to have a value in excess of a specified amount, units equal in value to the excess will pass to a designated charity. Applying the reasoning of *Commissioner v. Procter,* 142 F.2d 824 (4th Cir. 1944), the IRS refused to give effect to such a clause. FSA 200122011. Formula clauses are, of course, widely recognized as effective in defining the amount of marital deduction gifts, QTIP elections, etc. Whether the courts will respect them in the present context is less certain.

In LR 200245053, the IRS refused to recognize a formula clause that would change the terms of the sale of a family partnership to an irrevocable trust if the value of the interests were changed. The ruling distinguishes the use of formulas for legitimate purposes, such as in marital deduction elections, from uses that are designed to discourage challenges to a taxpayer's valuation of assets:

> We believe the legitimate and accepted uses of formula clauses as a practical way to implement Congressionally sanctioned tax benefits are in stark contrast to the situation presented in the instant case. The creation of a partnership and the use of the valuation formula clause in the sale of the partnership interests are all part of an integrated transaction the primary purpose of which is to transfer assets to the natural objects of Taxpayer's bounty at a discounted value, while foreclosing any realistic opportunity to challenge the transaction. The Taxpayer created and funded the limited partnership primarily, if not solely, to generate valuation discounts, with the goal of enabling her irrevocable trust to acquire the interests at a

reduced purchase price. Taxpayer employed the formula clause as part of the transaction in an attempt to ameliorate any adverse consequences if the Service challenged the transaction and thereby to discourage any such challenge. The clause does not serve a legitimate purpose, such as ensuring that the purchase price accurately reflects the fair market value. Rather, the clause recharacterizes the nature of the transaction in the event of a future adjustment to the value of the partnership interests by the Service. Under these circumstances the adjustment clause should not be effective for gift tax purposes.

In *Charles T. McCord*, 120 T.C. 358 (2003), *rev'd* 461 F.3d 614 (5th Cir. 2006), the Tax Court declined to give effect to a formula clause that was included in an assignment agreement entered into among members of a family limited partnership. Under the formula clause, the donor's children, trusts for the children, and a charitable organization received partnership interests of a total stated value and another charitable organization was to receive any value in excess of the stated amount. As the majority opinion explained:

> The assignment agreement provides a formula to determine not only CFT's [the second charity] fraction of the gifted interest but also the symphony's [the first charity] and the children's (including their trusts') fractions. Each of the assignees had the right to a fraction of the gifts' interest based on the value of that interest as determined under Federal gift tax valuation principles. If the assignees did not agree on that value, then such value would be determined (again based on Federal gift tax valuation principles) by an arbitrator pursuant to the binding arbitration procedure set forth in the partnership agreement. There is simply no provision in the assignment agreement that contemplates the allocation of the gifted interests based on some fixed value that might not be determined for several years. Rather, the assignment agreement contemplates the allocation of the gifted interest based on the assignee's best estimation of that value. Moreover, each of the assignees' percentage interests was determined exactly as contemplated in the assignment agreement (without recourse to arbitration), and none can complain that they got any less or more than petitioners intended them to get. Had petitioners provided that each donee had an enforceable right to a fraction of the gifted interest determined with reference to the fair market value of the gifted interest as finally determined for federal gift tax purposes, we might have reached a different result. However, that is not what the agreement provides.

The Tax Court thus refused to reply on the formula clause in computing the value of the gifts. Instead, it looked to a "confirmation agreement" signed by the donees following the gifts. In that agreement, the donees set forth the percentage interests received by each donee based on their estimates of value. For the Tax Court, this was better evidence of what was transferred than what the assignment agreement provided.

Although the Tax Court majority might have enforced a formula clause that adjusted for the values as finally determined for federal gift tax purposes, the IRS has been less willing to do so. As noted above, the IRS has denied effect to formula clauses that provided for adjustments based upon finally determined values for gift tax purposes. LRs 200245053 (TAM); 200337012 (TAM).

The Fifth Circuit reversed the Tax Court's decision in *McCord*. 461 F.3d 614 (5th Cir. 2006). The appellate court was more forgiving as to the precise wording of the formula clause in the assignment agreement. Where the Tax Court found the donees' post-transfer collective agreement to be more persuasive evidence as to the amounts actually gifted, the Fifth Circuit concluded that the assignment agreement was the only official source as to what the donors conveyed:

> The Majority's key legal error was its confecting sua sponte its own methodology for determining the taxable or deductible values of each donee's gift valuing for tax purposes here. This core flaw in the Majority's inventive methodology was its violation of the long-prohibited practice of relying on post-gift events. Specifically, the Majority used the after-the-fact Confirmation Agreement to mutate the Assignment Agreement's dollar-value gifts into percentage interests in [the partnership]. It is clear beyond cavil that the Majority should have stopped with the Assignment Agreement's plain wording. By not doing so, however, and instead continuing on to the post-gift Confirmation Agreement's intra-donee concurrence on the equivalency of dollars to percentage of interests in [the partnership], the Majority violated the firmly-established maxim that a gift is valued as of the date that it is complete; the flip side of that maxim is that subsequent occurrences are off limits.

Post-Death Events. The valuation of an asset at the time of the owner's death may be determined or affected by subsequent events. For example, in *Estate of Alice Kaufman v. Commissioner*, 243 F.3d 1145 (9th Cir. 2001), the court reversed a Tax Court valuation of the decedent's 19.86 percent interest in a closely held company. The appellate court held that the value of the shares at death was controlled by the sale of two smaller blocks of the company's stock made two months after the decedent's death at a price determined by an appraisal made by a securities firm. In *Estate of Helen M. Noble*, 89 T.C.M. (CCH) 649 (2005), the Tax Court held that the sale of two small blocks of closely-held stock (ten and seven shares, respectively) in the 15 months prior to the decedent's death did not control the value of the 116 shares held by the decedent at death. Rather, their value was established by the price at which the shares were actually sold 14 months after death. "In determining the value of unlisted stocks, actual sales made in reasonable amounts at arm's length, in the normal course of business, within a reasonable time before or after the basic date, are the best criterion of market value." Post-death events generally do not affect the valuation of contingent claims or liabilities. The valuation of claims against an estate is subject to the same rule. *See* Chapter 12.

Aggregation of Assets Includible in Decedent's Estate. The IRS has contended that for purposes of valuation, interests owned outright could be aggregated with interests otherwise includible in a decedent's estate (*e.g.,* under § 2044). The position has been rejected by the courts. *Estate of Bonner v. United States*, 84 F.3d 196 (5th Cir. 1996); *Estate of Harriet R. Mellinger*, 112 T.C. 25 (1999). The *Bonner* approach tracks earlier cases in which family attribution was rejected by the courts. *Propstra v. United States*, 680 F.2d 1248 (9th Cir. 1982); *Estate of Bright v. United States*, 658 F.2d 999 (5th Cir. 1981) (*en banc*).

Field Service Advice 20011901 accepts the outcome of *Estate of Bonner, Estate of Mellinger,* and similar cases which did not allow stock held in a QTIP trust, and includible in the surviving spouse's estate under § 2044, to be aggregated with stock owned outright. However, it upheld aggregation of a surviving spouse's owned stock with stock held in a § 2056(b)(5) trust, over which she held a general power of appointment and was includible in her estate under § 2041. Subsequently the Tax Court upheld aggregation of stock held by a § 2056(b)(5) trust, over which the decedent held a general power of appointment with owned stock. *Estate of Aldo H. Fontana,* 118 T.C. 318 (2002).

In LR 200648028 (TAM), the IRS ruled that shares of stock in a closely-held corporation held outright by a decedent could, for purposes of applying a control premium, be combined with shares held by a trust whose assets are included in the decedent's gross estate. The decedent in the ruling created a living trust that required distributions of net income to the decedent for life. The trust held some voting stock in a closely-held corporation, and the decedent owned voting and nonvoting shares of the same corporation outright. The trust gave the decedent a limited testamentary power of appointment over the shares, which she exercised in favor of a charity. The IRS ruled that the shares held outright should be combined with the shares owned by the trust but includible in the decedent's gross estate so that the stock would be valued "as a single controlling block of stock." According to the IRS, the facts at issue were more like those in *Fontana* instead of those in *Bonner* and *Mellinger.* The IRS concluded that the facts here were "clearly distinguishable" from those presented in the marital deduction cases to which it ultimately acquiesced. In those cases, the decedents did not create the marital trusts and had no control over their administration. Here, however, the decedent retained full control over all the shares and, importantly, all such shares would have been subject to the decedent's creditors.

More recently, in *Estate of Adler,* 101 T.C.M. 1118 (2011), the Tax Court agreed with the IRS's position that real property conveyed in equal shares to the decedent's five children in which the decedent retained a life estate should be valued as a single parcel and not, as the estate argued, as five separate 20-percent interests, each entitled to a fractional interest discount. The estate argued that *Mellinger* applied here too, but the court rejected this argument. "One reason the interests were valued separately [in *Mellinger*] was that at no time did the wife 'possess, control, or have any power of disposition' over the interest held in the trust. Unlike the wife in *Estate of Mellinger,* [the decedent] controlled the [subject] property. He transferred remainder interests in the property in 1965, and he retained a life estate in the property from 1965 until his death in 2004." Accordingly, the IRS's determination that the property must be valued without any fractional interest discount was proper.

Statement of Value. In Rev. Proc. 96-15, 1996-1 C.B. 627, the IRS described the procedure for obtaining a Statement of Value that would determine the value of an object for income and transfer tax purposes. At least one of the objects must have a value of $50,000 or more in order to make use of the service. Apparently the statement can only be obtained after a transfer is made, which diminishes its utility considerably. Use of the procedure is deterred by the $2,500 minimum fee and that the statement might not be issued for six months or more.

Alternate Valuation Date and Special Use Valuation. Under § 2031(a), property included in a decedent's gross estate is valued on the date of the decedent's death. Extensive regulations issued under § 2031 describe the manner in which various types of property are to be valued, including annuities, life estates, terms for years, and remainders. *See* Reg. § 20.2031-10. The valuations are made utilizing the actuarial tables issued pursuant to § 7520. However, § 2032 allows the executor to elect to value a decedent's gross estate on an alternate valuation date (specifically, the date six months after the decedent's death) if the election will result in a decrease in the value of the gross estate and in the total amount of the estate and GST taxes. § 2032(c). If the election is made, any assets that are distributed, sold, exchanged, or otherwise disposed of within six months following death must be valued on the date of distribution, sale or exchange. Any assets that are not distributed, sold, or exchanged within six months following death must be valued as of the date six months following the decedent's death. Changes in value due to the mere lapse of time are not taken into account for purposes of the alternate valuation. Section 2032A allows certain closely-held farm and business real property to be valued specially according to the property's actual use and not its fair market value. Alternate valuation and special use valuation under § 2032A are described more fully in §§ 12.15-12.19.

Special Valuation Rules. The 1987 Act added an extraordinarily complex provision, § 2036(c), that was intended to prevent the use of preferred stock recapitalizations, multi-tiered partnerships, and other estate tax freezing techniques to reduce or to eliminate value from a transferor's estate at little or no gift tax cost. The 1990 Act replaced § 2036(c) with Chapter 14, §§ 2701-2704, which is designed to prevent the depressed valuation of interests that are transferred inter vivos to family members. Chapter 14, which is considered in more detail in Chapters 9 and 11, prescribes special gift tax rules for the valuation of retained interests in family corporations and partnerships, § 2701; options and buy-sell agreements, § 2703; and the effect of lapses of voting and liquidation rights, § 2704. The special rules of § 2702 apply to the valuation of retained interests in trusts.

Compounded Discounts Through Tiered Partnership Arrangements. The Tax Court has held that applicable valuation discounts can apply at multiple levels in tiered partnership arrangements. In *Jane Z. Astleford*, 95 T.C.M. (CCH) 1497 (2008), the taxpayer contributed her interest in a real estate general partnership and 14 other properties to a family limited partnership. She then made gift transfers of limited partnership interests to her children, claiming applicable valuation discounts. The IRS challenged the valuation of the underlying real properties and the minority and marketability discounts claimed on the returns. The court first had to grapple with the valuations of the underlying properties that were still in dispute, most notably the general partnership interest. The taxpayer argued that the general partnership interest should be valued as an assignee interest, because she transferred the interest to the family limited partnership without the consent of the other general partner, but the court agreed with the IRS that, in substance, the taxpayer transferred a general partnership interest. As the court observed, the taxpayer continued to have all rights associated with the general partnership interest even after its transfer to the family limited partnership. Having concluded that the interest held by the family limited partnership was a general partnership interest, the court then considered the appropriate valuation discount to apply. The taxpayer's expert claimed a 40 percent blended minority and marketability discount based on comparable transactions involving real estate limited partnerships; the expert for the IRS said it would be redundant to apply discounts to this interest if the family limited partnership interests themselves would be subject to discounts. The court did not like either

§ 2.14.3

approach—it did not like some of the comparables used by the taxpayer's expert and it noted that "two layers" of discounts have been used in several prior cases, including *Estate of Piper*, 72 T.C. 1062 (1979) and *Robert and Kay Gow*, 79 T.C.M. (CCH) 1680 (2000), *aff'd*, 2001-2 U.S.T.C. (CCH) ¶ 50646 (4th Cir. 2001). So, on its own, the court concluded that a 30 percent blended discount was appropriate.

The analysis in *Astleford* thus indicates that tiered partnership arrangements may be effective in multiplying the applicable valuation discounts. Still, there is precedent to suggest that multiple layers of discounts will not apply where the interest in the "subsidiary" entity is a significant portion of the "parent" entity's assets. *Roy O. Martin, Jr.*, 50 T.C.M. (CCH) 768 (1985) (interest in lower-tier entity was 75 percent of upper-tier entity's assets, so tiered discounts did not apply).

§2.15. BASIS OF PROPERTY ACQUIRED FROM DECEDENT, § 1014

Under § 1014 the basis of property acquired from a decedent is usually the federal estate tax value of the property in the decedent's estate. The survivor's interest in community property takes the same basis if at least one-half of the community property was included in the decedent's gross estate. § 1014(b)(6).

In the case of nonresident aliens, the basis of property acquired by bequest, devise, or inheritance, but which is not included in the decedent's gross estate, is the property's fair market value on the date of the decedent's death. Rev. Rul. 84-139, 1984-2 C.B. 168.

Duty of Consistency. Where the discounted value of an asset included in the decedent's gross estate for federal estate tax purposes is accepted by the IRS, the common law duty of consistency prevents the estate or the beneficiaries from claiming a higher, undiscounted value in the property as its basis for federal income tax purposes. The duty was applied in two cases involving the estate of Sidney Janis. *Janis v. Commissioner*, 469 F.3d 256 (2d Cir. 2007); *Janis v. Commissioner*, 461 F.3d 1080 (9th Cir. 2006). At his death in 1989, Sidney Janis's living trust owned several pieces from his sole proprietorship art gallery. The undiscounted value of these works totaled $36.6 million. For estate tax purposes, the estate reported the value of the art at $12.4 million after applying a blockage discount. The IRS determined that the value was $14.5 million. The estate stipulated to the $14.5 million value and agreed to the resulting adjustments computed by the IRS.

The artwork remained in the trust following the conclusion of the valuation dispute. Fiduciary income tax returns for later years valued the artwork at $36.6 million for basis purposes, resulting in significant losses when the artwork sold. With the statute of limitations on the estate tax return closed, the IRS computed deficiencies on the fiduciary income tax returns on the grounds that the basis should have been set at $14.5 million. The fiduciaries contested the deficiencies, but the Tax Court upheld them, holding that the duty of consistency prevented the fiduciaries from claiming the higher, undiscounted value as the tax basis of the collection on the income tax returns.

Each fiduciary appealed the decision, one to the Ninth Circuit and one to the Second Circuit. Both courts affirmed. The Ninth Circuit explained that the duty of consistency applies if the taxpayer made a representation or report on which the IRS relied and, after the applicable statute of limitations ran out, attempted to change the previous representation or to recharacterize the situation in a way that harmed the IRS. Where, as here, these three elements are present, the IRS may act as if the taxpayer's previous representation remains true, even if it is not, and the taxpayer is estopped from asserting to the contrary. The Second Circuit rejected the fiduciary's claim that the blockage discount applies only for estate tax purposes, concluding that the discount is relevant in determining "fair market value," a standard used not only for estate tax purposes but also for purposes of § 1014.

Carryover Basis Rules in Play for 2010. The rules for determining a recipient's basis in property acquired from a decedent may be different in the case of decedents dying in 2010. As discussed in § 2.3 above, the 2010 Act allows estates of decedents dying in 2010 to elect out of the application of the estate tax. Obviously, estates with assets far in excess of the $5 million applicable exclusion amount available in 2010 would generally be eager to make this election. Yet the election comes at a cost: where the estate of a decedent dying in 2010 elects out of the application of the federal estate tax, a recipient's basis in property acquired from such decedent is determined under the modified carryover basis rules of § 1022. Under this regime, the basis of each asset acquired from a decedent is generally the lesser of (1) the decedent's adjusted basis, or (2) its fair market value on the date of the decedent's death. § 1022(a). Each estate may allocate among a decedent's assets up to $1.3 million in aggregate basis plus the amount of unused built-in losses and unused loss carryovers, provided that the total basis assigned to any one asset does not exceed its fair market value as of the date of the decedent's death. § 1022(b)(2). An additional $3 million in aggregate basis can be allocated among "qualified spousal property" that is acquired by a surviving spouse outright or as qualified terminable interest property (essentially through a QTIP trust, *See* § 5.23). § 1022(c).

Under § 1022(d)(1)(B)(III)(iv), a surviving spouse's half interest in community property is treated as having been acquired from the decedent. A rule similar to the present § 1014(e) would prevent an allocation of basis to assets acquired by the decedent by gift within three years of death. § 1022(d)(1)(C).

§ 2.16. DEDUCTIONS

Sections 2053 to 2058 describe the deductions that are allowed against the gross estate in calculating a decedent's taxable estate. In brief, the sections provide as follows:

1. **Funeral and Administration Expenses, § 2053.** Deductions are allowed for funeral and administration expenses and claims against the estate, including certain taxes and charitable pledges. Essentially the same deductions are allowable whether or not there is an estate administration. The personal representative may elect to deduct administration expenses either on the estate tax return or on the estate's income tax return. This and other important post-mortem elections, are described in Chapter 12.

2. **Losses, § 2054.** A deduction is allowed for the amount of uncompensated losses suffered during administration of the estate on account of fires, storms, shipwrecks or other casualties, or from theft.

3. **Charitable Transfers, § 2055.** Section 2055(a) allows a deduction for the value of charitable transfers of property included in the decedent's estate.

However, if a transfer is made for both a charitable and a noncharitable purpose, a deduction is allowed for the value of the charitable interest only if the transfer takes one of the forms described in §2055(e)(2). The allowance of charitable deductions for such "split interests" is explored in more detail in Chapter 8.

No deduction is allowable under §2055 unless the value of the amount passing to charity is definitely ascertainable at the time of the decedent's death. Thus, no deduction was allowed in *Estate of David N. Marine*, 97 T.C. 368 (1991), *aff'd*, 990 F.2d 136 (4th Cir. 1993), for a residuary gift to charity that might be reduced by the executor's exercise of discretion to appoint up to one percent of the value of the decedent's gross estate to an unlimited number of noncharitable beneficiaries.

4. **Marital Deduction, §§2056, 2056A.** Section 2056 allows a decedent's estate an unlimited marital deduction for property or qualifying interests in property that are transferred to a surviving spouse who is a United States citizen. All of the property of a married person may be passed, free of tax, to or for the benefit of his or her surviving spouse. Also, the deduction is available on an elective basis for part or all of the value of property in which the surviving spouse is given a qualifying income interest for life. §2056(b)(7). §5.23. Likewise, a marital deduction is available for the current interest in a qualifying charitable remainder trust given to a surviving spouse. §2056(b)(8). §5.24.

   If a decedent's surviving spouse is not a United States citizen, the marital deduction is allowable only to the extent the decedent's property passes to a qualified domestic trust for the benefit of the surviving spouse. §§2056(d), 2056A. *See* §5.25.

   Under paragraph 3 of Article XXIX-B of the 1980 United States – Canada Tax Convention as modified in 1995, a special "marital credit" is allowable against the United States estate tax with respect to certain transfers made to a surviving spouse. The paragraph imposes five conditions on the allowance of the credit. First the property must be qualifying property; second, the decedent must have been either a resident of Canada or the United States or a citizen of the United States; third, the surviving spouse must have been, at the time of the decedent's death, a resident of Canada or the United States; fourth, if both the decedent and the surviving spouse were residents of the United States at the time of the decedent's death, at least one of them must have been a citizen of Canada; and fifth, the executor of the decedent's estate must elect to claim the credit and waive benefits of any estate tax marital deduction that would otherwise be allowed.

5. **State Death Taxes, §2058.** The estates of persons dying after 2004 may deduct the amount of state death taxes ("estate, inheritance, legacy, or succession taxes actually paid to any State or the District of Columbia"). §2058(a). In contrast, estates of persons who died prior to 2005 could claim a credit for state death taxes paid, limited as provided in §2011, but not a deduction. The credit disappeared in 2005, replaced instead by the §2058 deduction.

   The deduction for state death taxes is unlimited. Under the old §2011 credit, there was a limitation on the maximum amount of state death taxes creditablc against the federal estate tax otherwise due. §2011(b). While there is no such limitation on the §2058 deduction, the deduction is likely not as valuable to estates as the old §2011 credit, for while the credit reduced federal estate tax liability dollar for dollar (a $100 credit would offset $100 in estate tax), a deduction only saves tax at the marginal tax rate applicable to the estate, which in no event can exceed the maximum estate tax rate (a $100 deduction saves, at most, about $35 in estate tax). As was the case under the old §2011 credit, the state death taxes must actually be paid, generally within four years of filing the federal estate tax return. §2058(b)(1). Certain exceptions to this deadline apply in cases where the estate has received a notice of deficiency, where the estate has made a claim for refund, and where the estate has received extension of time to pay federal estate tax under §§6161 or 6166. *See* §2058(b)(2).

A planner must have a good grasp of the rules regarding the deductions, particularly charitable and marital deductions, in order to advise clients competently regarding the formulation of estate plans. A comprehensive understanding of the deductions is also necessary in order to do an effective job of post-mortem planning. Of course, in some cases the inter vivos or post-mortem planning may require the assistance of an expert on the particular subject.

§2.17. CREDITS

Sections 2010 through 2016 describe the credits that are allowable against the federal estate tax. The most important is the unified credit that is allowed by §2010 to the estate of each citizen or resident. §2.3. In addition to the unified credit, credits are allowed for:

1. **Credit for Gift Tax on Pre-1977 Gifts, §2012.** A credit is allowed for gift taxes paid on gifts made prior to January 1, 1977, when the same property is included in the donor's gross estate. In determining the amount of the estate tax the amount of gift tax attributable to post-1976 gifts is deducted from the tentative tax. *See* §2001(b).

2. **Previously Taxed Property Credit, §2013.** Section 2013 allows a credit for the estate tax paid with respect to the transfer of property to the decedent by or from a person who died within ten years before or two years after the death of the decedent. The transferred property is not required to be identified in the estate of the later decedent, nor must it be in existence at the time of his or her death. The amount of the credit is limited to the lesser of (1) the amount of the tax attributable to the interest in the estate of the transferor and (2) the amount of the tax attributable to the interest in the estate of the present decedent. §2013(b)–(c). The full amount of the credit is allowable if the later decedent died within two years of the time the property was transferred to him or her. Thereafter the amount of the credit diminishes by 20 percent every two years, so that no credit is allowable if the transferor died more than ten years preceding the death of the later decedent.
   Note that a substantial credit may be allowed with respect to the value of a life income interest, such as the surviving spouse's interest in a QTIP trust that the decedent received from the estate of a prior decedent. Such an

interest is valued under §7520 as of the date of the death of the transferor (the prior decedent). The credit is allowable although the life estate or other transferred property is not included in the estate of the transferee (the later decedent). Rev. Rul. 59-9, 1959-1 C.B. 232. Of course, no credit is allowable to the extent the marital deduction was claimed by the estate of the prior decedent in connection with the transfer. §2013(d)(3); *United States v. Denison*, 318 F.2d 819 (5th Cir. 1963). No credit is allowable for a purely discretionary income interest, which permits distributions to be made to other beneficiaries as well. LR 8944005 (TAM).

3. **Foreign Death Tax Credit, §2014.** A credit may be allowed for the amount of death taxes actually paid to any foreign country with respect to property situated in that country and included in the decedent's gross estate. The allowance of the credit may be affected by the terms of a gift and estate tax treaty between the United States and the foreign country imposing the tax. Under the protocol to the 1980 United States – Canada Tax Convention, a credit is allowable against the United States estate tax on a proportional basis. Under paragraph 2 of Article XXIX-B, a pro rata credit is allowed to a Canadian resident decedent for purposes of computing the federal estate tax. A credit of between $13,000 and $192,800 is allowable based on the proportion of the decedent's estate that is situated in the United States. Thus, if half of the gross estate of a citizen and resident of Canada was located in the United States, the decedent's estate would be entitled to a credit of $96,400. (Presumably the amount of the allowable credit will be increased to levels now allowed under §2010.)

4. **Credit for Deferred State and Foreign Death Taxes, §2015.** This section concerns the allowance of the credits for state and foreign death taxes attributable to remainder or reversionary interests with respect to which the payment of the estate tax has been deferred under §6163(a). In essence, the section allows credits for the state and foreign death taxes if they are paid within the time for payment of the deferred portion of the estate tax. Note that the provisions of this section do not apply to deferrals under §6166.

5. **Notification of State and Foreign Death Tax Credits, §2016.** A person who receives a refund of any state or foreign death tax that was claimed as a credit under §2014 must notify the district director of the refund within 30 days of its receipt. The amount of the estate tax is then redetermined and the amount of any additional tax due by reason of the redetermination must be paid by the executor.

The unified credit is particularly important in planning relatively small estates. However, in some instances the other credits offer important planning opportunities. The previously taxed property credit that is allowed for a portion of the tax paid with respect to a life estate, §2013, can be particularly valuable. Planning for possible use of the credit may include the creation of a QTIP trust for the surviving spouse.

§2.18. TRANSFERS WITHIN THREE YEARS OF DEATH, §2035

Beginning in 1982, property transferred within three years of death is generally not includible in the estate of the transferor. §2035. However, the value of such property may be included for the purpose of determining the qualification of the deceased transferor's estate for special treatment under §§ 303, 2032A, and 6166. § 2035(c)(1)-(3). Thus, a donor cannot make large deathbed gifts of nonbusiness property in order to qualify his estate for the benefits of §§ 303, 2032A and 6166. Insurance on the life of the transferor and certain other property transferred within three years of death are includible under the provisions of § 2035(a).

Section 2035(b) requires the inclusion of the amount of any gift tax paid by the decedent or the decedent's estate on any gift made by the decedent or the decedent's spouse within three years of the decedent's death. Accordingly, in *Estate of Frank Armstrong, Jr.*, 119 T.C. 220 (2002), the Tax Court upheld the inclusion of more than $4.6 million in gift taxes that were paid by the decedent within three years prior to his death. The IRS takes the position that the date of death itself counts in determining whether a gift is made within three years of death. LR 200432016 (TAM). Thus, for example, if a decedent made a taxable gift on April 1, Year One, paid federal gift tax on that transfer in Year Two, and then died on April 1, Year Four, the gift was made three years and one day prior to death. Accordingly, the federal gift tax paid in Year Two is not included in the decedent's gross estate.

In LR 9214027, the IRS ruled that the nondonor spouse's estate must include the full amount of gift tax paid by her on gifts made by her husband that are split between them for gift tax purposes. Conversely, it stated that "no part of the paid gift tax will be includible in the decedent's [donor's] gross estate under section 2035(c) of the Code if the decedent should die within three years of making the gifts." Prior to 1977, the law strongly encouraged deathbed gifts because it did not require such a "gross up." The application of § 2035 is illustrated by the following example:

EXAMPLE 2-16.

In 2009, *X* gave stock worth $10,000 to her daughter, *D*. She also gave a $250,000 policy of insurance on her life that had a present value of $2,500 to her son, *S*. *X* died in 2011 when the stock was worth $50,000. *S* received the insurance proceeds of $250,000. None of the value of the stock is includible in *X*'s gross estate. The entire proceeds of the life insurance policy are includible by reason of § 2035(a)(2) because the proceeds would have been includible in the estate of the insured under § 2042 had the policy not been transferred.

§ 2.19. RETAINED INTERESTS AND POWERS, §§ 2036, 2038

Property transferred during lifetime is includible in the transferor's estate under § 2036(a) to the extent the decedent retained "for his life or for any period not ascertainable without reference to his death or for any period which does not in fact end before his death—(1) the possession or enjoyment of, or the right to the income from, the property, or (2) the right, either alone or in conjunction with any person, to designate the persons who shall possess or enjoy the property or the income there-from." Thus, this section extends to transfers, in trust or otherwise, under which the transferor retains the use or enjoyment of property or the right to designate the persons who could possess or enjoy the property or the income from it. Similarly, property transferred during lifetime is includible in the transferor's gross estate under §2038(a)(1) to the extent "the enjoyment thereof was subject at the date of his death to any change through the exercise of a power (in whatever capacity exercisable) by the decedent alone or by the decedent in conjunction with any other person . . . to alter, amend, revoke, or terminate . . . ." Together, §§2036(a) and 2038(a)(1) target lifetime transfers where the decedent's retained interest in or control over the transferred property is sufficient to warrant inclusion of the transferred property in the decedent's gross estate.

§2.19.1. Retained Income or Enjoyment, §2036(a)(1)

Where the decedent retains either or both the right to income from transferred property or the right to possess or enjoy the transferred property, the date-of-death value of the transferred property will generally be included in the decedent's gross estate under §2036(a)(1) if the decedent retained such interests for life, for a period not ascertainable without reference to the decedent's death, or for a term of years that does not in fact end before the decedent's death. Consequently, inclusion under § 2036(a)(1) results where the decedent transfers property to a beneficiary, retains a life estate for a 50-year term, and then dies before expiration of the term. Likewise, inclusion results where the decedent retains the right to income from the transferred property for a term ending three months prior to the decedent's death, for the term of the retained income interest cannot be determined without reference to the date of the decedent's death.

In *Estate of Margot Stewart*, 92 T.C.M. 357 (2006), the decedent conveyed a 49 percent tenancy-in-common interest in New York City property to her son. The decedent and her son resided on the first two floors of the property, and the remaining three floors were leased to an unrelated business that paid rent of $9,000 per month. The decedent kept all of these rents. The federal estate tax return included only the decedent's 51 percent interest in the property, but the IRS determined that the entire value of the property was includible in the decedent's gross estate under §2036(a)(1), because she continued to reside at the property and received all of the rental income from the commercial tenant. The Tax Court agreed, holding that the decedent's receipt of the rental income was sufficient to trigger inclusion in her gross estate of the full value of the property.

On appeal, however, a divided Second Circuit vacated the Tax Court's decision and remanded the case for further findings of fact. 617 F.3d 148 (2d Cir. 2010). The appellate court was unconvinced that the decedent's retained interest related to all of the property. Certainly there was no evidence of any implied agreement that the decedent would retain enjoyment of "the *residential* portion" of the son's 49-percent interest. As the majority explained:

> Decedent did not have exclusive possession of, nor did she exclude [her son] from, [his] 49% interest in the Manhattan property—or, for that matter, the entire property. [W]here, as here, the Tax Court has made no specific findings relating to enjoyment of the residential portion of the property, and the Commissioner points to nothing besides the mere co-

occupancy between the donor and the donee, a conclusion based on an implied agreement concerning the residential portion cannot stand.

But the Second Circuit held that the Tax Court was not erroneous in finding "an implied agreement that Decedent would enjoy for her life the substantial *economic* benefit of some part—indeed, perhaps all—of the rental portion of the Manhattan Property." Still, it needed to remand the case to determine "the extent to which Decedent enjoyed the substantial economic benefit of [the son's] 49% interest during her life. And, because the Tax Court did not consider 'all facts and circumstances surrounding the transfer and subsequent use of the property,' it is appropriate to vacate and remand so that the Tax Court may do so."

Writing in dissent, Judge Livingston observed that the majority:

> does not—and cannot—explain how the Tax Court clearly erred as a factual matter in concluding that [the decedent] retained all these benefits, given that her relationship to the property changed in *not one significant respect* from the period preceding transfer to the period after. Instead, the majority, misreading a body of case law that primarily involves transfers of 100% of a family member's interest in a property to another family member, concludes that post-transfer co-occupancy is near-conclusive evidence that the transferor can no longer enjoy the substantial economic benefits of residence to the extent of the transferred interest. Indeed, the majority finds such co-occupancy dispositive even here, where the transfer concerned only a fraction of the transferor's interest, created a tenancy in common that guaranteed the transferor continued access to the entirety of her property, and involved a transferor and transferee who the majority agrees were found *correctly* by a court of law to have reached an agreement undercutting the economic substance of the very transfer under consideration. This turns the proper—and longstanding—construction of section 2036 on its head. It also opens up a loophole that will vitiate to a considerable degree the efficacy of this section. . . .

The amount included in the gross estate under §2036(a)(1) is limited "to the extent of any interest therein" held by the decedent at the time of death. Thus, where the decedent retains the right to one-half of the income from transferred property for life, only one-half of the value of the transferred property will be included in the decedent's gross estate. Reg. §20.2036-1(a).

"Understanding or Agreement." In some instances, the assets of a family limited partnership (FLP) or family LLC are includible in a decedent's estate under §2036(a)(1), because the facts indicate that there was an understanding or agreement that the decedent would continue to enjoy the property or its income. *E.g., Estate of Ida Abraham*, 87 T.C.M. (CCH) 975 (2004). However, there must be a factual basis for finding, or implying, that there was such an agreement. As the judge in *Estate of Ida Abraham, supra*, pointed out:

> Whether there exists an implied agreement is a question of fact to be determined with reference to the facts and circumstances of the transfer and the subsequent use of the property. *Estate of Reichardt v. Commissioner, supra*. And, the taxpayer 'bears the burden (which is especially onerous

for transactions involving family members) of proving that an implied agreement or understanding between decedent and his children did not exist when he transferred the property at issue to the trust and to the partnership.' *Id*. at 151-152. *See also Estate of Hendry v. Commissioner*, 62 T.C. 861 (2000).

In *Estate of Ida Abraham, supra*, the court concluded that the documentary evidence and the understanding of the decedent's children and legal representatives was "that decedent was entitled to any and all funds generated from the partnerships for her support first. Only after this could any excess be distributed in proportion of the partners supposed ownership interests . . . .Accordingly, we sustain respondent's determination that decedent retained the enjoyment of the FLP interests transferred within the meaning of section 2036."

Another example of an implied understanding of continued enjoyment by the decedent is found in *Estate of Thompson v. Commissioner*, 382 F.3d 367 (3d. Cir. 2004). In *Thompson*, the decedent (through his two children pursuant to a durable power of attorney) created two family limited partnerships, one for each child's family. The decedent transferred over $1.4 million in marketable securities to the partnerships, along with notes receivable from the children. Each partnership was managed by a corporate general partner, which the decedent controlled. Although the decedent made inter-vivos gifts of partnership interests for the next few years, the decedent still owned controlling interests in both partnerships (as well as the corporate general partners) at his death. The estate tax return included those controlling interests, but applied a combined 40-percent marketability/minority interest discount. The IRS argued that the entire value of both partnerships should be included in the decedent's estate under § 2036, because the decedent retained "the economic benefit and control of the transferred assets." The Tax Court noted that at the time of the transfers to the partnerships, "there was an implied agreement or understanding that decedent would retain the enjoyment and economic benefit of the property he had transferred." For instance, the decedent's daughter insisted on assurances that the decedent would be able to access money from the partnerships to make annual exclusion gifts. The Tax Court also noted that the decedent transferred essentially all of his assets to the partnerships, leaving enough in his name only to meet living expenses for two years. That suggested to the court that there was at least an implied understanding that the decedent would be able to access funds from the partnerships if needed for basic support. That was enough to warrant inclusion of the underlying assets under § 2036(a).

On appeal, the estate argued that these facts did not establish an implied understanding of retained benefits, because the decedent had a *de jure* lack of control over the transferred property (the decedent had to get permission from the general partners to withdraw any amounts from the partnership). The Third Circuit rejected this argument, finding that the general partners in this partnership would not have refused such a request. The court thus affirmed the Tax Court's decision to include the undiscounted value of the partnership's assets in the decedent's gross estate. Importantly, the court concluded that the decedent's transfers were not within the bona fide sale exception to § 2036, because neither partnership engaged in any legitimate business activity and the decedent did not receive any potential nontax benefit from the transfers. While the dissipation of estate tax value that results from the transfer of marketable securities to a family limited partnership may not itself require a court to conclude that the transfer was not made for adequate consideration, it "should trigger heightened scrutiny into the actual substance of the transaction."

In *Estate of Virginia A. Bigelow*, 89 T.C.M. 954 (2005), the Tax Court held that the decedent's estate included the full value of the assets of a family limited partnership created by the decedent's revocable living trust. The court found an implied arrangement for the decedent to retain the income from and enjoyment of the assets contributed to the partnership, principally a parcel of rental property. The partnership had made payments on a $350,000 loan owed by the revocable trust, not the partnership. In addition, the partnership made regular cash distributions to the revocable trust to compensate the decedent's monthly cash flow shortage from living expenses. No other partners received any distributions from the partnership during this time. As the court concluded, "Decedent's use of partnership income to replace the income lost because of the transfer of the [rental property] to the partnership shows that there was an implied agreement between decedent and [the other partners] that she would retain the right to the income from the [rental property]." The court rejected the estate's argument that § 2036 should not apply because of the bona fide sale exception, because "[t]he transfer of the [rental property] to the partnership left decedent unable to meet her financial obligations." Moreover, "[t]he parties' failure to respect the provisions of the agreement governing their transaction tends to show that the transaction was not entered into in good faith." The court observed that the partners failed to follow the capital account maintenance rules required by their partnership agreement and improperly reflected the $350,000 loan as a liability of the partnership.

On appeal, the Ninth Circuit affirmed. 503 F.3d 955 (2007). That the partnership paid the loan owed by the revocable trust was "evidence itself of an implied agreement that the [decedent's] children would supplement decedent's financial needs because decedent's transfer of her main asset, while retaining the indebtedness secured by it, would have left her unable to meet her monthly expenses without resort to partnership funds." The fact that the formalities of the partnership form were not observed "buttresses the conclusion that there was an implied agreement." As to the applicability of the bona fide sale exception, the court announced that "[t]o avoid the reach of § 2036(a), the Estate must also show the 'genuine' pooling of assets . . . and a 'potential (for) intangibles stemming from pooling for joint enterprise.'" *See* § 2.19.3. The court held that no such pooling occurred here, so the exception did not apply. The morals of *Bigelow* are clear: avoid using a partnership to pay the founder's personal expenses, do not transfer substantially all of the founder's assets to the partnership such that the founder must rely upon distributions from the partnership to meet basic needs, and follow the formalities of the partnership agreement.

For proof that the morals from *Bigelow* should be taken seriously, consider *Estate of Erma V. Jorgensen*, 97 T.C.M. 1328 (2009). In that case, the Tax Court held that § 2036(a)(1) applied to include the undiscounted value of assets contributed to two family limited partnerships in the decedent's gross estate, because no books or records were ever kept for the entity, the decedent continued to make personal use of partnership funds by writing checks from the partnership to cover personal gifts and expenses (as a limited partner, no less), and the partnership paid estate taxes attributable to the decedent's estate.

Also consider *Estate of Valeria M. Miller*, 97 T.C.M. 1602 (2009), where the IRS challenged a family limited partnership created by the decedent in the year before her death. She transferred various securities to the partnership, because she wanted to continue her husband's long-term investment strategies that had proved so successful. The decedent named her son as the general partner at formation. The decedent then gave some limited partnership interests to her children (including the same son). The decedent's living trust held the remaining limited partnership interests. In 2003, as her health declined, the decedent transferred additional securities to the partnership. Following these transfers, the decedent did not have sufficient assets outside of the partnership to pay her expected state and federal estate tax liabilities. The IRS argued that the undiscounted value of the securities was includible in the decedent's gross estate under §2036(a)(1). The Tax Court held that the discount claimed by the estate was proper as to the securities the decedent transferred to the partnership in 2002, for this transfer was a bona fide sale for adequate and full consideration and the decedent had substantial nontax reasons for the transfer. But the claimed discount with respect to the 2003 transfers was rejected by the court, since the transfers were made only for tax reasons in contemplation of decedent's declining health and because the decedent effectively retained the economic benefit of the transferred securities since it was expected that they would be used to help pay the resulting state and federal estate taxes.

Retained enjoyment of partnership property was also involved in *Estate of Hilde Erickson*, 93 T.C.M. 1175 (2007). The decedent held a general power of appointment over the assets in a credit shelter trust established under her husband's will. The decedent gave one of her two daughters a power of attorney shortly before being diagnosed with Alzheimer's disease. In 2001, the decedent's health began to fade, so the daughters met with counsel and signed the documents to form a family limited partnership. The agreement provided that the daughters would be general and limited partners, while the decedent, her son-in-law, and the credit shelter trust would be limited partners. The partnership remained unfunded for two months, and then the daughter with power of attorney instructed the decedent's broker to transfer the decedent's entire account to the partnership. No other transfers occurred for a few more months until the decedent was placed in hospice care. Then the flurry began: the next day, two condominiums were conveyed to the partnership, and the decedent (through her daughter as attorney-in-fact) gave limited partnership interests to three trusts for the benefit of the decedent's grandchildren. Two days later, the decedent died. Later, when the personal representative needed some cash to pay federal estate tax, the estate sold the decedent's home to the partnership for $123,500. The partnership then transferred $104,000 to the estate as a "redemption" of some of the decedent's partnership interest. The Service took the position that §2036(a)(1) applied, because the decedent retained possession or enjoyment of the assets transferred to the partnership and that such transfers were not bona fide sales for adequate and full consideration.

The Tax Court agreed, noting that the delay in transferring assets to the partnership suggested that the parties did not respect the formalities of the partnership. The court also had trouble with the partnership's payments to the decedent's estate:

This fact is telling in two respects. First, disbursing funds to the estate is tantamount to making funds available to [the decedent] (or the estate) if needed. Second, although the estate designated the funds disbursed to the estate as a purchase of [the decedent's] home and a redemption of units rather than a distribution, the estate received disbursements at a time that no other partners did.

The court was also bothered by the fact that the partnership was not fully funded until days before the decedent's death.

A similar result occurred in *Estate of Concetta H. Rector*, 94 T.C.M. (CCH) 567 (2007). Here, the decedent's revocable trust (of which the decedent's two sons were co-trustees) transferred substantially all of its assets to a partnership. In exchange, the decedent became the 2-percent general partner and her revocable trust became the 98-percent limited partner. The decedent and her sons did not negotiate the terms of the entity's formation and the sons did not obtain independent legal advice in the matter. Besides the revocable trust, the only other means of support for the decedent was a credit shelter trust set up by her husband's will, but her expenses substantially exceeded the income distributions that she received from the credit shelter trust. Consequently, the partnership paid some of the decedent's expenses directly and made large distributions to her. During the two-year period prior to her death, almost 90 percent of the partnership's distributions were made to the decedent even though at that time she held less than 90 percent of the partnership interests because of gifts made in 1999, 2001, and 2002. Following the decedent's death, the partnership borrowed money to help the estate pay the federal and state estate tax liability of the decedent.

The estate tax return valued the decedent's total partnership interest at about $4.7 million after applying a 19-percent marketability and minority interest discount. The return reported the partnership's total net asset value at about $8 million, and this figure was the amount the IRS determined should have been included in the gross estate. The estate challenged the deficiency before the Tax Court, but the court held that all of the facts recited above indicated there was an implied agreement that the decedent would retain enjoyment of the transferred assets for a period that did not end before her death. It thus sustained the Service's assessed deficiency.

In *Estate of Thelma G,. Hurford*, 97 T.C.M. (CCH) 422 (2008), the court held that §2036(a)(1) applied and required inclusion in the decedent's gross estate of the undiscounted value of the assets contributed to two family limited partnerships, interests in which were subsequently sold to the decedent's beneficiaries through a private annuity transaction. The court found sufficient evidence of an implied agreement that the decedent would continue to enjoy benefits of the contributed assets. The court observed that the decedent transferred nearly all that she owned into the partnerships, that the decedent remained sole signatory on many accounts supposedly contributed to the partnerships, and that, on at least two occasions, funds from one of the partnerships were transferred to the decedent's bank account without any adjustment to her capital account.

The foregoing analysis of the decisions in *Estate of Thompson*, *Estate of Bigelow*, *Estate of Erickson*, *Estate of Rector*, and *Estate of Hurford* should not be read to mean that the IRS prevails in all family limited partnership cases. In *Estate of Anna Mirowski*, 95 T.C.M. (CCH) 1277 (2008), for example, the Tax Court held there was no implied arrangement equivalent to retained enjoyment of the assets transferred by the decedent to the partnership, largely because the decedent retained assets outside of the partnership of sufficient size to meet the decedent's living expenses, including the payment of federal gift taxes resulting from gifts of partnership interests. It no doubt helped the estate that the formalities of the partnership arrangement, including maintenance of capital accounts, were observed and that the decedent died unexpectedly shortly after the formation of the entity and her gifts of partnership interests to her daughters. *Estate of Mirowski* thus offers hope: where formalities are carefully observed and the decedent is careful not to transfer substantially all assets to the partnership, it may be difficult for the IRS to prove an implied arrangement that the decedent retained the income from or enjoyment of the property transferred to the partnership.

Escaping §2036. Letter Ruling 9815023 suggests a technique to reduce the amount includible in a grantor's estate under §2036. The ruling concerned the gift and estate tax consequences of terminating an irrevocable trust created by *A* in 1941 in which *A* had retained a life-income interest. The ruling holds that the termination and distribution of the assets of the trust to the beneficiaries in accordance with the actuarial valuation of their interests under §7520 would not involve a gift or be subject to §2702. Importantly, the ruling holds that if *A* survives the termination of the trust by three years, no portion of the trust would be includible in *A*'s gross estate under §2036(a). The IRS specifically stated that it was not ruling on "whether all or any portion of the value of the Trust corpus will be subject to inclusion in *A*'s gross estate under section 2035(a), if *A* dies within three years of the termination of the Trust. *See United States v. Allen*, 293 F.2d 916 (10th Cir.), *cert. denied*, 368 U.S. 944 (1961)." Of course, any amount distributed to *A* that remains in her possession at death would be includible in her gross estate under §2033.

EXAMPLE 2-17.

A transferred $1 million to an irrevocable trust in 1990 reserving a life-income interest. The gift of the remainder interests in the trust was subject to the federal gift tax. Under LR 9815023, if *A* and the remainder beneficiaries terminate the trust and distribute its assets, now valued at $3 million, in accordance with the actuarial values of their respective interests, the distributions will not generate any gift tax liability. If *A* survives the termination of the trust by three years or more, none of the trust is includible in his gross estate under §2036(a). His estate would, of course, include the value of any assets distributed to him that he owned at the time of his death.

The current beneficiary of a trust, who consents to its termination and distribution to the remainder beneficiary, makes a present gift to them. LR 9802031. The ruling holds that a gift results even though his right to receive distributions was discretionary with the trustee. The same result was reached in LR 9811044.

§ 2.19.2. Retained Power to Control Enjoyment, § § 2036(a)(2), 2038

Where a donor retains the power to revoke or materially change the wealth transfer, then the donor still has ownership-like control over the transferred property that justifies inclusion in the gross estate. This is the concept behind both § § 2036(a)(2) and 2038(a)(1). Section 2036(a)(2) requires inclusion of transferred property where the decedent retained the right "to designate the persons who shall possess or enjoy the property or the income therefrom" for one of the prescribed periods (for life, for a period not ascertainable without reference to the decedent's death, or for a period that does not in fact end before the decedent's death) even though the decedent does not directly retain any rights to income, use, or enjoyment with respect to the transferred property. Likewise, § 2038(a)(1) requires inclusion of property previously transferred by the decedent as a gift if, at the decedent's death, enjoyment of that interest was subject to a power held by the decedent to alter, amend, revoke, or terminate.

Although § § 2036(a)(2) and 2038(a)(1) overlap, there is a distinction between the two inclusion provisions. Section 2036(a)(2) only applies to the extent the decedent's retained interest affects the right to income from the transferred property. Reg. § 20.2036-1(b)(3). Section 2038(a)(1) is not so limited.

EXAMPLE 2-18.

T transferred property to a trust that pays income to *P* or *P*'s estate for *T*'s life. At *T*'s death, the trust will terminate and the remainder will be paid to *R* or *R*'s estate. *T* retained the power to substitute *B* as the remainder beneficiary of the trust. This power was exercisable by *T* at any time while *T* was alive. *T* died never having exercised the power. Under § 2038(a)(1), the value of the remainder interest (which equals the value of the entire trust principal, because *P*'s income interest expires at *T*'s death) will be included in *T*'s gross estate, because *T* held a power to alter the enjoyment of the remainder interest at T's death. But § 2036(a)(2) would not apply, because *T*'s power did not affect enjoyment of the income received by *P* or *P*'s estate during *T*'s lifetime. Although § § 2036(a)(2) and 2038 reach different results, the value of the remainder interest is included in *T*'s gross estate, for inclusion is required if any one Code provision supports it.

Relinquishment of a Power or Interest. Inclusion under § § 2036(a)(2) or 2038(a)(1) may be required if a decedent voluntarily relinquishes an interest or power that would otherwise require inclusion. However, the termination of an interest or power by reason of an event beyond the decedent's control does not constitute a relinquishment. Dodge, *Transfers With Retained Interests and Powers,* Tax Management Portfolio 50-5 A-78, 80; Stephens, Maxfield, Lind, Calfee and Smith, *Federal Estate and Gift Taxation* (8th ed.), 4-194–195.

The scope of § 2038(a)(1) is essentially the same as that of § 2036(a)(2) and specifically extends to any interest in property transferred by the decedent, in trust or otherwise, if the enjoyment of the property was subject at the date of the decedent's death to change through the exercise of a power by the decedent to alter, amend, revoke, or terminate the interest. Inclusion is also required if the decedent relinquished the power within the three-year period ending on the date of the decedent's death. *See* §2038(a)(1); Reg. §20.2035-1(b). Section 2038 requires inclusion if a transferor may alter, amend, revoke or terminate a trust—alone or in conjunction with any other person. Thus, inclusion is required if the transferor and an independent trustee have the power to terminate a trust by accelerating distributions to the beneficiary. *Lober v. United States*, 346 U.S. 335 (1953).

EXAMPLE 2-19.

T purchased securities that were registered in *T*'s name as custodian under the Uniform Transfers to Minors Act for *T*'s 10-year-old nephew, *N*. The registration of the securities constituted an irrevocable gift subject to the gift tax. If *T* dies while acting as custodian, the securities are includible in *T*'s gross estate under §2038 because of *T*'s power under the Uniform Act to distribute the securities to *N* prior to the time when custodianship would otherwise terminate. *See* §7.35.2.

Section 2036(a)(2) and General Partners. Through most of the 1990s, the IRS consistently ruled that under the principles of *United States v. Byrum*, 408 U.S. 125 (1972), the fiduciary duties of the general partner of an FLP would prevent the assets of a properly created and operated FLP from being included in the estate of the transferor-general partner. *E.g.*, LRs 9026021, 9131006 (TAM), 9415007 and 9710021. The IRS subsequently took a contrary position. As indicated in *Estate of Albert Strangi*, 85 T.C.M. (CCH) 1331 (2003), the courts may choose to ignore the prior position of the IRS: "[W]e are unpersuaded that any different result should obtain on account of the Commissioner having taken a contrary position in certain previous administrative rulings." In addition, rulings have no precedential effect and may be ignored by the courts.

The initial position of the IRS regarding the impact of *Byrum* is described in the passage below, taken from LR 9131006 (TAM). The TAM involved an FLP, which the decedent created on December 28, 1986, for the stated purpose of owning, developing and operating real estate and other property. The day after the FLP was created the decedent transferred a one-half interest in 110 acres of unimproved real property. After transferring the land to the FLP, the decedent assigned units to her four children and 15 grandchildren. A few months prior to her death in 1988, the decedent transferred additional units to the same donees. The TAM concluded that the gifts were of present interests for which annual gift tax exclusions were properly allowable and that the gifts were includible in her estate under §2036.

In the present situation, the decedent was (after the initial transfers) the controlling general partner who held management authority over the partnership including the express authority to control partnership distributions. However, similar to the decedent in *Byrum*, the decedent in the instant case occupied a fiduciary position with respect to the other partners and could not distribute or withhold distributions, or otherwise manage the partnership for purposes unrelated to the conduct of the partnership business. Therefore, as was the case in *Byrum*, the value of the transferred units is not includible in the transferor's estate under section 2036 of the Code. *See also Estate of Gilman v. Commissioner*, 65 T.C. 296, 316 (1975).

The IRS was willing to reach the same result with respect to FLPs that were entirely funded with liquid assets (cash). LR 9415007. The transferor was the "general partner of the Partnership and as such has management authority over the Partnership, including the authority to control partnership distributions." Because of the transferor's fiduciary duties, however, the ruling concluded that, "the value of the partnership interests proposed to be transferred by the Transferor will not be includible in his gross estate under sections 2036 or 2038 by reason of his status as general partner."

More recently, the IRS has argued, and some courts have agreed, that inclusion under § 2036(a)(1) is required if the transferor, in effect, retained the income or use of the property. *Estate of Albert Strangi*, 85 T.C.M. (CCH) 1331 (2003), *aff'd*, 417 F.3d 468 (5th Cir. 2005) (decedent transferred 98 percent of his assets, including his residence, to an FLP in which he owned a 99 percent interest). That is, inclusion under § 2036(a)(1) is not precluded by any fiduciary duties the decedent may have had to other members of an FLP or LLC. In addition, the IRS has argued, and at least one court has agreed, that a court should not presume that the fiduciary constraints that were found to exist in *Byrum* exist with respect to all FLPs and LLCs. In particular, in the *Strangi* case, Judge Cohen concluded that

> [T]he estate's averment that decedent's 'rights' . . . were severely limited by the fiduciary duties of other people who (according to *Byrum*) presumably could be counted on . . . [to] observe those restraints' rests upon a faulty legal premise and ignores factual realities. First, the Supreme Court's opinion in *United States v. Byrum, supra*, provides no basis for 'presuming' that fiduciary obligations will be enforced in circumstances divorced from the safeguards of business operations and meaningful independent interests or oversight. Second, the facts of this case belie the existence of any genuine fiduciary impediments to decedent's rights.

The approach of the IRS to the applicability of the *Byrum* principles is somewhat reminiscent of its subsequently abandoned argument that the shares of closely related family members should be aggregated for the purpose of determining whether a decedent's interests carried control. *See* Rev. Rul. 93-12, 1993-1 C.B. 202.

In arguing for inclusion under § § 2036 or 2038, the IRS is, of course, seeking to include the full value of the assets that a decedent transferred to an FLP or LLC. Under the facts of some cases, inclusion under those provisions would be contrary to their very text. In others, the application of the provisions is at least somewhat dubious. The issues require a close review of the statutes and the facts of a particular case. Helpful recent articles include, Grove, Taming the Tiger: Designing, Implementing and Operating an FLP to Avoid a Section 2036 Attack, U. Miami, 38th Inst. Est. Plan., Ch. 7 (2004), and Porter, Bulletproofing the Family Limited Partnership— Current Issues, U. Miami, 38th Inst. Est. Plan., Ch. 6 (2004).

Section 2036(a)(2) applies only if, *at the time of the decedent's death,* the decedent held the power to designate who would possess or enjoy the property. (As indicated above, whether the principles of the *Bryrum* case preclude inclusion is not clear.) Inclusion under § 2036(a)(2) is improper if the decedent neither possessed such a power at death nor relinquished such a power within three years of death. Inclusion should not be required if the power terminated prior to the decedent's death by an event that was beyond his or her control. Thus, the automatic switch of a general partner to a limited partner or the automatic removal of the manager of an LLC, upon disability as provided in an FLP or LLC agreement, should not be considered to involve the "relinquishment" of the powers of the general partner.

§ 2.19.3. Exception for Bona Fide Sales for Adequate and Full Consideration

The general rule of §§ 2036(a) and 2038(a)(1) do not apply "in case of a bona fide sale for an adequate and full consideration in money or money's worth." This exception applies only if the transfer is (1) a bona fide sale, and, (2) the transferor receives full and adequate consideration in money or money's worth. Unfortunately, just what is required to satisfy the two elements is far from clear. Qualifying for the exception has become especially important since the IRS has seized upon § 2036(a) as the weapon of choice to use against FLPs and family LLCs that exploit the substantial valuation discounts applicable to business entities.

Insofar as the exception is concerned the regulations tell us that, "To constitute a bona fide sale for an adequate and full consideration in money or money's worth, the transfer must have been made in good faith and the price must have been an adequate and full equivalent reducible to a money value." Reg. § 20.2043-1(a).

The opinion in *Estate of Ida Abraham,* 87 T.C.M. (CCH) 975 (2004), states, "In construing bona fide sale, the word sale means an exchange resulting from a bargain. *Estate of Harper v. Commissioner,* T.C. Memo. 2002-121 (quoting *Mollenberg's Estate v. Commissioner,* 173 F.2d 698, 701 (2d Cir. 1949))." Thus, if property is transferred to a family partnership or LLC without any bargaining, negotiation, or contribution of property by other investors some courts have held that the transfer is not within the bona fide sale exception. *E.g., Estate of Concetta H. Rector,* 94 T.C.M. (CCH) 567 (2007); *Estate of Albert Strangi,* 85 T.C.M. (CCH) 1331 (2003), aff'd, 417 F.3d 468 (5th Cir. 2005); *Estate of Morton B. Harper,* 83 T.C.M. (CCH) 1641 (2002).

According to the court in *Kimbell v. United States,* 371 F.3d 257 (5th Cir. 2004), the transfer of property to an FLP was bona fide although the FLP was formed by family members, the transfer did not involve negotiations and the FLP was created, at least in part, for tax purposes. According to the court the estate satisfied the bona fide sale requirement by submitting evidence "in support of the estate's position that the transaction was entered into for substantial business and other non-tax reasons." Because the formation of family limited partnerships and family LLCs are almost always motivated by tax and nontax objectives, the *Kimbell* interpretation of the bona fide sale requirement is relatively easy to meet.

The *Kimbell* court also held that a transfer is for full and adequate consideration if each of the following questions is answered affirmatively:

> (1) whether the interests credited to each of the partners was proportion-
> ate to the fair market value of the assets each partner contributed to the

partnership, (2) whether the assets contributed by each partner to the partnership were properly credited to the respective capital accounts of the partners, and (3) whether on termination or dissolution of the partnership the partners were entitled to distributions in amounts equal to their respective capital accounts.

Curiously this approach totally ignores the monetary value of the interests received by the transferor, which is required by the regulations. In addition, the *Kimbell* opinion concludes that the investment by others in an FLP or LLC need not meet any minimum standard. ("[W]e know of no principle of partnership law that would require the minority partner to own a minimum percentage interest in the partnership for the entity to be legitimate and its transfers bona fide.")

The *Kimbell* opinion rejected the IRS contention that a transfer in exchange for FLP or LLC units is not made for adequate and full consideration if the value of the units received is less than the value of the transferred property. According to the court:

> The government is attempting to equate the venerable 'willing buyer-willing seller' test of fair market value (which applies when calculating gift or estate tax) with the proper test for adequate and full consideration under § 2036(a). This conflation misses the mark: The business decision to exchange cash or other assets for a transfer-restricted, non-managerial interest in a limited partnership involves financial considerations other than the purchaser's ability to turn right around and sell the newly acquired limited partnership interest for 100 cents on the dollar. Investors who acquire such interests do so with the expectation of realizing benefits such as management expertise, security and preservation of assets, capital appreciation and avoidance of personal liability.

The court concludes that such an exchange is "a classic informed trade-off."

The way the *Kimbell* court dealt with the adequate and full consideration issue appears to be based upon a questionable premise: That the unsubstantiated value of the "financial considerations" that a transferor receives in "a classic informed trade-off" constitutes consideration in money or money's worth and that its value equals the amount of the discount that was claimed in valuing the FLP units received by the transferor. The Kimbell estate does not appear to have established the monetary value of the financial considerations that are part of the equation—presumably the considerations were the management expertise, security and preservation of assets, capital appreciation and avoidance of personal liability identified by the court. Even if it were possible to value the items, it is questionable whether it would be appropriate to consider the value of benefits that the transferor was already receiving (*i.e.*, the management expertise of her son and the potential for capital appreciation). The court's approach appears to be contrary to the requirements of Reg. § 20.2043-1(a).

The bona fide sale exception may apply if the transaction is at arm's length and all partners make contributions to a partnership in exchange for a pro rata share of partnership units. For example, the transfers to five family partnerships involved in *Estate of Eugene E. Stone*, 86 T.C.M. (CCH) 551 (2003), were found to have been within the exception: "Based upon our examination of the entire record before us, we find that the respective transfers of assets by Mr. Stone and Ms. Stone to each of the Five Partnerships were bona fide sales for adequate and full consideration in money or money's worth under section 2036(a)." In *Stone,* the court held that the contributions to the partnerships made by the children would be taken into account although the contributed property was traceable to gifts made by the decedent: "Mr. Stone gave certain property to each of the children, which they then transferred to one or more of the Five Partnerships in return for partnership interests. Mr. Stone reported the gifts that he made to the children in his 1997 gift tax return. The children owned the assets that he gave them when they respectively transferred such assets to one or more of such partnerships."

The Bona Fide Sale Exception Requires a Nontax Motive for the Transaction. Estate of Wayne C. Bongard, 124 T.C. 95 (2005), also holds that units of a holding company that the decedent transferred to a family limited partnership were included in his estate under § 2036. Inclusion was required because the decedent's 99-percent ownership interest in the partnership allowed him to retain control over the interest in the holding company. The bona fide sale exception did not apply because "(e)state tax savings did play an important role in motivating the transfer to BFLP [the family limited partnership]. The record does not support that the nontax reasons for BFLP's existence were significant motivating factors."

If the existence of a family limited partnership or LLC is scrupulously respected, personal use property, such as a residence, is not transferred to the partnership, books and records are properly maintained, appropriate proportional distributions are made to the owners, and accounts and other information are provided to the owners, it is much less likely that the transfers will be found to be subject to an understanding or agreement that the decedent retained an interest in the transferred property. The mere fact that a decedent transferred limited partnership or LLC interests to family members does not support a conclusion that the decedent retained an interest in the underlying property. Basically, inclusion should not result simply because a decedent transferred some assets to a family limited partnership or LLC from which they reasonably expect to receive regular distributions. In contrast, the cases make it clear that transferring one's residence and all, or virtually all, of one's liquid assets to a partnership or LLC is risky for § 2036 purposes.

In *Estate of Virginia A. Bigelow,* 503 F.3d 955 (9th Cir. 2007), the Ninth Circuit announced that in order for a family limited partnership arrangement to meet the bona fide sale exception, there must be a "'genuine' pooling of assets . . . and a 'potential (for) intangibles stemming from pooling for joint enterprise.' . . . The validity of the adequate and full consideration prong cannot be gauged independently of the non-tax-related business purposes involved in making the bona fide transfer inquiry." Although this language suggests the Ninth Circuit would want evidence of some synergy created by the pooling of a partnership's assets, the court actually used this language as a bridge to examine the alleged nontax reasons for the formation of the partnership, citing *Bongard* with approval.

In *Estate of Concetta H. Rector,* 94 T.C.M. (CCH) 567 (2007), the Tax Court, citing *Bongard,* held that the bona fide sale exception does not apply to the formation of an FLP if there is "no change in the underlying pool of assets or the likelihood of profit." It appears, then, that the court wants to see evidence that the formation of the partnership is motivated by the desire to establish a different investment plan and not to simply "recycle" the value of the property transferred to the entity.

The Tax Court found there were significant, nontax reasons for the formation of the family limited partnership in *Estate of Anna Mirowski*, 95 T.C.M. (CCH) 1277 (2008). There, the court found credible the testimony of the decedent's two daughters who confirmed that the entity was formed for joint management of family assets, for consolidating assets to provide better investment opportunities, and for providing for the daughters on an equal basis.

§ 2.19.4. Retained Voting Rights, § 2036(b)

Section 2036 was broadened in 1976 and 1978 to require inclusion of stock in a "controlled corporation" that was transferred during lifetime if the transferor retained, directly or indirectly, the right to vote the stock alone or in conjunction with any person. The provision was adopted in order to overcome the effect of *United States v. Byrum*, 408 U.S. 125 (1972), which held that the power to control a corporation through a retained power to vote its stock did not require inclusion of the stock under § 2036. Section 2036(b) does not apply to the transfer of nonvoting stock. Thus, the IRS has ruled that, § 2036(b) does not require the inclusion of nonvoting Class B common stock transferred by the decedent prior to death although the decedent retained all of the Class A voting common stock. LR 9004009. Inclusion is required if the decedent, as a general partner, held the right to vote stock in a controlled corporation that he had transferred to a family limited partnership. LR 199938005 (TAM). *See* § § 10.39.3 and 11.5.1.

A controlled corporation is one in which the transferor at any time after the transfer of the property, and within three years of death, owned or had the right to vote stock that represented at least 20 percent of the combined voting power of all classes of stock. § 2036(b)(2). The attribution rules of § 318 apply for the purpose of determining whether the transferor owned the requisite interest in the stock. Thus, the stock owned by the transferor's spouse and children are taken into account in determining the percentage of stock owned by the transferor.

For purposes of applying § 2035, the relinquishment or cessation of voting rights is treated as a transfer of property made by the decedent. § 2036(b)(3). Consistently, The IRS has ruled that if the transferor relinquishes the right to vote the transferred stock more than three years prior to her death, the stock is not includible under § 2036(b). LR 199903025 (trusts to which control stock was transferred was amended to bar transferor from voting the stock).

Closely held stock may be includible in the estate of a donor who retained indirect control over the manner in which it will be voted. Rev. Rul. 80-346, 1980-2 C.B. 271 (agreement by trustee to consult with donor and obtain donor's consent regarding voting stock). However, the IRS has recognized that the mere fact that the trustee is a relative does not require the stock to be included in the donor's estate under § 2036(b). LR 8936032.

In LR 9527025 the IRS held that nonvoting stock in a controlled corporation that was transferred by the donor during his lifetime would not be included in his estate under § 2036(b) although he retained voting stock. The ruling followed Rev. Rul. 81-15, 1981-1 C.B. 487. The same result was reached in LR 9543050, which involved nonvoting shares in an S Corporation in which the donor retained voting shares. In contrast, in LR 9518002 (TAM), the decedent's estate was required by § 2036(b) to include the remainder interest in shares in a controlled corporation that were indirectly transferred to his children and were subject to the decedent's right to vote the shares under a voting trust.

In LR 9515003 (TAM), the IRS rejected the estate's argument that the control stock that decedent had given to an irrevocable trust in 1989 should be included in his estate by reason of an alleged oral agreement that his daughter, as trustee of the trust, would vote the stock as he directed. The unusual action of the estate was motivated by the fact that the stock was worth considerably more when the gift was made than it was when the donor died. Under § 2001(b), the value of an adjusted gift is not included in the estate tax base if the same property is included in his gross estate.

In LR 9509027, the IRS held that stock given to the children of X and Y would not be included in the estate of X or Y under former § 2035(d)(2) if the existing shareholder agreement were amended to provide that any of the shares of stock that had been transferred to the children during the lifetime of a parent would be redeemed by the corporation upon the parent's death. According to the ruling,

> Assuming that the price at which the children's [sic] shares are to be redeemed does in fact represent the fair market value of the shares (determined without regard to the agreement) we conclude that the proposed agreement to the shareholder's [sic] agreement will not cause X and Y to be deemed to have retained any powers or rights with respect to the transferred stock that would cause the stock to be includible in the estate of either X or Y under § 2035(d)(2).

The provisions of § 2036(b) create a trap for the unwary and raise a host of complex issues that will require litigation to resolve. *See* McCord, The 1978 Anti-Byrum Amendment: A Cruel Hoax, U. Miami, 14th Inst. Est. Plan., Ch. 12 (1980). A serious trap exists because § 2036(b) requires inclusion of stock in a controlled corporation with respect to which the decedent retained the right to vote in any capacity. For example, the section extends to stock over which the transferor held the right to vote solely in a fiduciary capacity, such as the trustee of a trust, as custodian under the Uniform Transfers to Minors Act, or as general partner of a partnership.

§ 2.19.5. Anti-Freeze Provision, Former § 2036(c)

Former § 2036(c), added by the 1987 Act and repealed by the 1990 Act, was designed to eliminate the estate tax advantages of most "estate freezes" entered into after December 17, 1987. In brief, the provision required inclusion in the donor's estate of an interest in an enterprise that was transferred to a family member during the donor's lifetime if the transferred interest carried a disproportionately large share of the potential appreciation and the donor retained an interest in the income or other rights of the enterprise. The provision was aimed at techniques such as the preferred stock recapitalization or the multi-tiered partnership by which the members of a senior generation transfer the future growth in the equity of a family enterprise to the younger generations at little or no transfer tax cost. *See* Chapter 11. However, the broad scope of the subsection threatened some gifts and other relatively innocent transactions that were not related to any objectionable attempt to shift future appreciation to others. In short, § 2036(c) was objectionably overbroad. Some clarifying amendments were made by the 1988 Act, which also added some important safe harbor provisions. As noted in §2.14, *supra*, §2036(c) was repealed in 1990 and a different approach was taken by its replacement, §§2701-2704. *See* Chapter 9.

§2.20. ANNUITIES AND OTHER DEATH BENEFITS, §2039

Section 2039 requires the inclusion of an annuity or other payment receivable by any beneficiary by reason of surviving the decedent under the terms of certain contracts or agreements to the extent that the annuity is attributable to contributions made by the decedent or the decedent's employer. The estate tax consequences of the inclusion of an annuity are offset in many cases by the availability of the marital deduction. Under §2056(b)(7)(C) the marital deduction is available with respect to an annuity under which only the decedent's surviving spouse has the right to receive payments. *See* §5.23.5.

§2.21. JOINT TENANCIES, §2040

Joint tenancies and tenancies by the entirety are widely used (particularly by married persons) to hold title to property because each of the tenancies carries a right of survivorship. That is, upon the death of one tenant the decedent's rights in the property terminate and all rights in the property are owned by the survivor. The estate tax disadvantage of spouses holding property in joint tenancy form was largely eliminated by the adoption of the unlimited marital deduction. Joint tenancies, tenancies by the entirety and other co-tenancies are discussed in Chapter 3.

§2.21.1. Joint Tenants Other Than Husband and Wife

The two basic rules that govern the taxation of joint tenancies are stated in §2040(a). First, where the joint tenancy was acquired by the decedent and the other joint owner by gift, devise, or inheritance, the decedent's fractional interest in the property is included in the decedent's gross estate. This rule is simple and logical in its application, at least in states that permit a joint tenant to sever the joint tenancy and convert it into a tenancy in common with no right of survivorship. The second rule includes the entire value of the property in the decedent's gross estate except to the extent it is attributable to the contributions in money or money's worth made by the other tenant. For this purpose, the contributions of the other tenant are not taken into account to the extent they are attributable to money or other property acquired from the decedent for less than full and adequate consideration.

EXAMPLE 2-20.

T's will left Blackacre to her children, *A* and *B*, as joint tenants with right of survivorship. *T* also left a cash gift of $100,000 to *A*, which *A* used to purchase Whiteacre in the name of *A* and *B* as joint tenants. The purchase of Whiteacre involved a gift from *A* to *B* of $50,000 (half of its total value). If *A* dies survived by *B*, a half interest in Blackacre and the whole interest in Whiteacre are includible in A's estate under §2040(a). Because the value of Whiteacre is included in A's gross estate, the amount of the prior taxable gift is not taken into account in computing the estate tax on A's estate. *See* §2001(b). Otherwise, the same property would be taxed twice.

§2.21.2. Husband and Wife as Joint Tenants; Qualified Joint Interests, §2040(b)

In 1976, Congress added §2040(b), under which only half of the value of a qualified joint interest is includible in a deceased spouse's gross estate. A qualified joint interest is an interest in property held by the decedent and the decedent's spouse as tenants by the entirety or as joint tenants with right of survivorship, but only if they are the sole tenants. Only half of a qualified joint interest is includible in the decedent's gross estate regardless of which spouse provided the consideration for the acquisition of the property. A marital deduction is allowable under §2056 for the amount included in the decedent's estate as a qualified joint interest. Again, the benefits of §2040(b) are not available unless decedent's surviving spouse is a citizen of the United States. §2056(d)(1)(B). Under §2523(i)(3) the rules of former §§2515 and 2515A apply to the transfer of property into joint tenancy with a spouse who is not a citizen. According to former §2515, the creation of a joint tenancy in real property does not involve a gift, but under §2515A each spouse was considered to have an equal interest in a joint tenancy in personal property.

The partial inclusion rule of §2040(b) is fair, simple to understand, and easy to administer. It is also consistent with the adoption of the unified transfer tax system that substantially reduced the advantages of making lifetime gifts. However, §2040(b) originally applied only to a joint tenancy created after 1976 by one or both spouses that was treated as a gift. In addition, only the spouses could be parties to the tenancy. The 1978 Act added provisions that allowed conversion of pre-1976 joint tenancies into qualified joint interests. *See* former §§2040(d)-(e). The 1981 Act repealed §§2040(c)-(e), and made the qualified joint interest rule applicable to all joint tenancies between a husband and wife in which there was no other joint tenant.

The estate of the spouse first to die includes only half of the total value of qualified joint interests, including post-gift appreciation. However, under *Gallenstein v. United States*, 975 F.2d 286 (6th Cir. 1992), and cases that have followed it, if the joint tenancy was created prior to 1977 and the surviving spouse made no contribution towards its acquisition, the full value of the property is includible in the decedent's estate. *See* §3.15. In cases subject to this rule the surviving spouse would have a new basis in the whole of the property. In any case, the entire value of the property is includible in the estate of the surviving joint tenant.

§2.22. Powers of Appointment, §2041

The flexibility of an estate plan is increased substantially by giving powers of appointment to survivors that can be used to alter the distribution of income and principal in light of changed future circumstances. However, arrangements involving powers of appointment must be carefully planned because of their important tax consequences, particularly for estate tax purposes. Section 2041 defines the extent to which the property subject to a power of appointment is includible in the estate of the power holder, but it does not apply to powers that a transferor retains over property that he or she transfers to others. *See* Reg. §20.2041-1(b)(2). In such a case the property is subject to inclusion in the transferor's estate under §§2036 and 2038.

Under §2041, property over which a decedent possessed, exercised, or released a general power of appointment is usually includible in the decedent's gross estate. A general power of appointment is one that is exercisable in favor of "the decedent, his estate, his creditors, or creditors of his estate." §2041(b)(1).

Property subject to a nongeneral power of appointment is not includible in the gross estate of the holder of the power under §2041. In light of that rule, wills and trusts are frequently drafted to give a surviving family member the power to appoint the property to and among a limited class or a class that includes everyone other than the holder of the power, his creditors, his estate, and the creditors of his estate. Unfortunately, powers are often created that are too restrictive. For example, a power may exclude the spouses of descendants from the class of persons to whom appointments might be made. Of course, such a restricted power does prevent the property from being appointed out of the family line.

§2.22.1. Exceptions

There are some important exceptions to the basic rules regarding the taxation of powers under §2041. To begin with, property subject to a general power of appointment created before October 22, 1942 is not includible in the decedent's gross estate unless the power is exercised. §2041(a)(1). The release of a pre-October 22, 1942, general power of appointment may be combined with disclaimers by children of the disclaimant in way that preserve the exemption of the trust from the GSTT under the effective date rules. *See* LR 9245011 and §2.42.5. Also, a power is not considered to be a general power of appointment if the power is exercisable only with the consent or joinder of, (1) the creator of the power, or (2) a person having a substantial adverse interest. §2041(b)(1)(C). Finally, a power limited by an ascertainable standard relating to the health, education, support, or maintenance of the power-holder is not a general power of appointment. §2041(b)(1)(A). These exceptions are explained further in Chapter 10.

§2.22.2. Release of Post-1942 General Powers

Property subject to a post-October 21, 1942 general power of appointment is also includible in a power holder's estate if the power is exercised or released in such a way that the property would have been includible in his or her estate under §§2035-2038 had it been a transfer of property owned by the decedent. §2041(a)(2). Thus, property that had been subject to a general power of appointment is includible in the power-holder's estate if the power-holder releases the power but retains the income, use, or control of the property.

EXAMPLE 2-21.

After October 21, 1942, G transferred property in trust to pay the income to X for life, then to distribute the principal to Y. The trust gave X a power to withdraw the trust principal whenever X chose to do so. X irrevocably released the power. The property of the trust is includible in X's gross estate under § 2041(a)(2) and is treated as if X had transferred property to the trust and reserved the income in the property for life. Of course, the release also involved a gift to Y. § 2514(b). If § 2702 applies, the gift would be determined without regard to the value of X's retained life estate. *See* § 7.38.2; LR 9804047.

§ 2.22.3. Lapses of General Powers; "5 or 5" Powers

The lapse of a general power created after October 21, 1942 is treated in the same way as a release. § 2041(b)(2). Thus, property subject to a general power that lapses is includible in the power-holder's estate if the power-holder retains an interest or power in the property described in § § 2036-2038. However, lapses of powers during any calendar year are treated as releases only to the extent that the property subject to the power exceeds the greater of $5,000 or 5 percent of the value of the property out of which the exercise of the power could have been satisfied. Thus, a person can be given a "5 or 5 power," the noncumulative annual right to withdraw the greater of $5,000 or 5 percent of the value of a trust without causing the property to be included in the power holder's gross estate (other than for the property subject to withdrawal under the power at the time of the power holder's death). This rule, together with the exception for powers limited by ascertainable standards, allows an individual to hold important powers of withdrawal without requiring any substantial part of the trust principal to be included in his or her gross estate. These rules are explored in more detail in Chapter 10. Note, however, that for income tax purposes the powerholder may be treated as the owner of the portion of the trust with respect to which the power of withdrawal lapsed. *See* § 678 and § 10.24.1.

§ 2.23.   Life Insurance, § 2042

Insurance proceeds "receivable" by the insured's executor are includible in the estate of the insured under § 2042(1). This rule applies although the insured never owned or had any interest in the underlying insurance policy. It extends also to proceeds that are "receivable by another beneficiary but are subject to an obligation, legally binding upon the other beneficiary, to pay taxes, debts, or other charges enforceable against the insured's estate." Reg. § 20.2042-1(b). The rule would apply, for example, to the proceeds of a policy owned by a trust that required the trustee to apply to proceeds in satisfaction of the insured's debts or the taxes imposed on his or her estate.

Insurance proceeds are includible in the insured's estate under § 2042(2) if, at the time of death, the insured possessed any incident of ownership in the policy, exercisable alone or in conjunction with any other person. The term "incidents of ownership" is not defined in the Code. However, the Regulations indicate that it refers generally to "the right of the insured or his estate to the economic benefits of the policy. Thus, it includes the power to change the beneficiary, to surrender or cancel the policy, to assign the policy, to revoke an assignment, to pledge the policy for a loan, or to obtain from the insurer a loan against the surrender value of the policy." Reg. § 20.2042-1(c)(2). The mysteries of incidents of ownership are examined in more detail in § 6.28.

Life insurance often plays a major part in estate planning. Irrevocable life insurance trusts, which are discussed at §§ 6.24-6.25, can be particularly advantageous from a tax perspective.

E. GENERATION-SKIPPING TRANSFER TAX (GSTT)

§ 2.24. BACKGROUND

The need for a GSTT arises from the fact that by transferring property in trust the transferor may insulate the property from the reach of the estate and gift taxes for several generations. (As a general rule, neither the estate tax nor the gift tax applies to the distribution of property from a trust to a beneficiary.) The opportunity to pass property through successive generations free of federal transfer taxes arose largely because the estate tax only applies to property that was owned or transferred by a decedent or with respect to which the decedent had a significant power or incident of ownership: The estate tax does not require a decedent's estate to include any interest in property in which the decedent held a life interest created by others. The difference in tax cost between leaving property to a child outright or to a generation-skipping trust for the benefit of a child and successive generations of beneficiaries is illustrated by the following example:

EXAMPLE 2-22.

T died in 1950, leaving a will that transferred $1,000,000 to a testamentary trust. The income of the trust was payable at the discretion of the trustee to *T*'s son, *S*, for life and thereafter for successive generations of the descendants of *S*. Twenty-one years after the death of the last of *T*'s descendants who were living at the time of *T*'s death the trust will terminate and the principal will be distributed by right of representation among those of *S*'s descendants who are then living. The property that *T* transferred to the trust was subject to the estate taxation when *T* died. When *S* died in 2002 the trust had a value of $20,000,000. None of the trust, which now benefits *S*'s children, was included in his gross estate. Indeed, the trust property will not again be subject to a federal transfer tax until after the trust terminates and the property has been distributed to *T*'s descendants. Had the trust terminated in 2002 the beneficiaries would have received $20,000,000. The termination of life interests and the shifting of beneficial interests from generation to generation are not subject to the estate tax.

T's will also left $1,000,000 outright to his daughter, D. The property, which was worth $20,000,000 when D died in 2002, was included in her estate. A tax of $10,000,000 was paid with respect to the property. Only $10,000,000 was available for distribution to D's beneficiaries.

Generation-skipping trusts were widely used by very wealthy families to provide for successive generations of descendants without subjecting the property to estate or gift taxes. Of course, once property is distributed from a trust it is subject to the estate and gift taxes in the hands of the distributee.

Troubled by the relatively widespread use of generation-skipping trusts, Congress struck back in 1976 by enacting a complex form of GSTT. The tax was intended to be substantially equivalent to the gift and estate taxes that would have been imposed had the property been transferred outright once in every generation. However, the 1976 version of the GSTT did not apply to any transfer that was subject to the estate or gift tax, but instead only applied to a taxable termination of a trust or trust equivalent or a taxable distribution from a generation-skipping trust or trust equivalent. The GSTT was imposed at the marginal estate or gift tax rate applicable to the "deemed transferor," who was most often the parent of the transferee most closely related to the grantor. Pursuing this theme, the unused portion of the deemed transferor's unified credit could be offset against the tax on transfers that took place at or after the death of the deemed transferor. The 1976 version was complex, difficult to understand, and fraught with substantial record keeping requirements.

Several significant loopholes eroded the potential effectiveness of the 1976 version of the GSTT. First, the GSTT only applied to generation-skipping trusts and trust equivalents and not to outright transfers. Thus, substantial amounts could be given outright to the members of each generation of descendants without incurring any GSTT liability. Second, the GSTT did not apply to trusts all of the beneficiaries of which belonged to the same generation. This rule encouraged the creation of separate trusts for each generational level of beneficiaries ("layered" trusts). Third, the GSTT did not apply to distributions of income. Finally, the GSTT allowed a grandchildren's exclusion of $250,000 for transfers to trusts for the children of each child of the deemed transferor.

EXAMPLE 2-23.

G's will made bequests of $1,000,000 outright to her grandchild X and to X's children, Y and Z. The outright transfers to X, Y, and Z were subject to the estate tax in G's estate, but they were not subject to the 1976 version of the GSTT. The transfers would be subject to the 1986 version of the GSTT. G also left $1,000,000 in trust to distribute the income to her niece, N, and grandniece, GN, for so long as they or the survivor of them should live. Distributions of income to GN would not have been subject to the 1976 version of the GSTT. When N died the GSTT would have applied at the marginal rate applicable to her estate.

§2.25. THE MODERN GSTT

In 1986, Congress repealed the 1976 GSTT retroactively and replaced it with a slightly less complex, more workable version. For GSTT purposes, the transferor of a generation-skipping transfer is the decedent in the case of a transfer subject to the estate tax and the donor in the case of a gift. Unlike the 1976 version, the current GSTT applies to a generation-skipping transfer in addition to the gift or estate taxes that apply to the transfer.

Each individual has a GSTT exemption that may be allocated by the individual (or his or her executor) to any transfer of which the individual is the transferor. § Sec. 2631(a). The exemption was originally set at $1 million and then was adjusted for post-1997 inflation. The 2001 Act increased the exemption to $1.5 million in 2004 and 2005. For 2006 through 2008, the GSTT exemption was $2 million, the same exemption amount applicable for purposes of the estate tax. In 2009, the GSTT exemption, like the estate tax applicable exclusion amount, increased to $3.5 million. As with the federal estate tax exclusion amount, the GSTT exemption grew to $5 million in 2010, but it is scheduled to be reduced to $1 million in 2013 thanks to the sunset provisions of the 2001 Act and the 2010 Act. As discussed at the beginning of this chapter, the lingering uncertainty as to the future application of the GSTT and its exemption amount has been most frustrating.

The modern GSTT applies to three types of generation-skipping transfers: direct skips, taxable terminations, and taxable distributions.

§2.25.1. Direct Skips and Skip Persons, §§2612(c), 2613

A direct skip is a transfer that is subject to the estate or gift tax made to a skip person. A skip person is either, (1) a natural person who is assigned to a generation which is two or more generations below the generation of the transferor, or, (2) a trust in which all interests are held by skip persons or a trust in which no person holds an interest and from which no distribution may be made to a nonskip person. §2613(a). Not surprisingly, a nonskip person is a person who is not a skip person. §2613(b). Thus, the grandchildren and more remote descendants of a transferor are skip persons, but the transferor's spouse, siblings, and children are nonskip persons. In this connection note that a transfer that skips a single generation is treated in the same way as one that skips several generations.

Skip person and other terms are defined in regulations that also contain helpful examples. Reg. §26.2612-1. Note that "an individual does not have an interest in a trust merely because a support obligation of that individual may be satisfied by a distribution that is either within the discretion of a fiduciary or pursuant to the provisions of local law substantially equivalent to the Uniform Gifts (Transfers) to Minors Act." Reg. §26.2612-1(e)(2).

Technical Advice Memorandum 200215001 concludes that transfers made at the time of a decedent's death from the decedent's revocable trust to separate trusts for the exclusive benefit of grandchildren and great-grandchildren were direct skips. Accordingly, the transfers were subject to the GSTT at the time of the decedent's death.

The disclaimer of property may result in a direct skip. For example, property that passes from a decedent's residuary estate to his or her grandchildren or to a trust for their benefit as a result of disclaimers by the decedent's surviving spouse and children is a direct skip. LR 9244012.

EXAMPLE 2-24.

T's will left gifts of $1 million to each of *T*'s child, *C*, *C*'s son, *GS*, *GS*'s daughter, *GGD*, and *GGD*'s daughter, *GGGD*. *C* is not a skip person, but *GS*, *GGD*, and *GGGD* are. Accordingly, the transfers to *GS*, *GGD*, and *GGGD* are subject to the GSTT. The transfers to *GS*, *GGD*, and *GGGD* are all taxed in the same way although the transfers skip 1, 2, and 3 generations respectively. (The method of determining generational assignments is described in § 2.34.)

The full value of a gift to a skip person for life, remainder to the transferor's child (a nonskip person), is subject to the GSTT. LR 9105006 (TAM). The transfer was treated as a deemed trust. *See* § 2.31.1.

Predeceased Parent Exception. Under a special "predeceased parent" exception a transfer to a lineal descendant of a parent of the transferor is not a direct skip if the parent who is a lineal descendant of the transferor (or the transferor's spouse or former spouse) is dead at the time of the transfer. § 2651(e). Thus, a gift to a grandchild is not a direct skip if the transferor's child who was a parent of the donee is not living at the time of the gift. Under this rule outright gifts made by a great-grandparent to great-grandchildren were treated as gifts to children where the parents and grandparents of the donees were deceased at the time of the gifts. LR 9114024. Also, the adoption of a person who otherwise qualifies for the exception will be disregarded. LR 199907015 (transfer by grandparent to grandchild whose parent was deceased, but who had been adopted by an aunt—a sibling of the grandchild's deceased parent). As explained in § 2.42.7, the scope of the exception was expanded in the 1999 Act.

EXAMPLE 2-25.

T died leaving a will that gave $1 million to her grandchild, *GC*. *T*'s daughter, *D*, the mother of *GC*, died before *T*. The transfer to *GC* is not a direct skip. A bequest by *T* to a child of *GC* would be a direct skip.

§ 2.25.2. Taxable Terminations, § 2612(a)

A taxable termination is the "termination (by death, lapse of time, release of power, or otherwise) of an interest in property held in trust" unless immediately afterwards a nonskip person has an interest in the property or at no time thereafter may a distribution be made to a skip person. § 2612(a). "Interest" is defined as a present right to receive income or corpus from the trust. § 2652(c). Also, a person, other than a charitable organization, who is a permissible distributee of income or principal has an interest in the trust.

EXAMPLE 2-26.

T left \$5 million in trust to pay the income to her son, *S*, for life. Following the death of *S* the trust is to continue for the benefit of his children and grandchildren. The life income interest of *S* is an interest in the trust that terminates upon the death of *S*, following which only skip persons hold interests in the trust. Thus, the death of *S* constitutes a taxable termination that would be subject to the GSTT except to the extent that *T*'s GSTT exemption was allocated to the trust.

The death of *S* would not constitute a taxable termination if the income of the trust had been distributable to *S* and his sister, *D*, who survived him. In that case a nonskip person, *D*, would have an interest in the property following the death of *S*. Instead, a taxable termination would take place upon the death of the survivor of *S* and *D*. For purposes of this rule a nonskip person is considered to have an interest only if the interest is significant.

§2.25.3. Taxable Distributions, §2612(b)

A taxable distribution occurs when property is distributed from a trust to a skip person, which is not "a taxable termination or a direct skip." §2612(b). Distributions of income or principal to a skip person are subject to the GSTT, but because of the quoted limitation, a distribution that also fits the definition of a taxable termination is classified as such and not as a taxable distribution. Likewise, a distribution that constitutes a direct skip is classified as such and not as a taxable distribution. Note that distributions that are "qualified transfers" under §2503(e) (*i.e.*, direct payment of tuition and medical expenses) are not generation skipping transfers. §2611(b).

EXAMPLE 2-27.

T's will established a testamentary trust that authorized the trustee to sprinkle income among T's descendants. A distribution of income to a skip person, such as one of *T*'s grandchildren, is a taxable distribution. Note that for income tax purposes distributees can deduct the GSTT imposed on distributions of income as a tax. §164(a), (b)(4). The GSTT would not apply to the direct payment of the tuition or medical expenses of *T*'s grandchildren.

§2.26. Application of GSTT; Inclusion Ratio; Applicable Fraction

The GSTT is imposed at the "applicable rate," which is determined by multiplying the maximum federal estate tax rate at the time of the transfer by the "inclusion ratio." §2641(a). In turn, the inclusion ratio is defined in §2642 as the amount by which 1 exceeds the "applicable fraction." The inclusion ratio, once determined, remains effective for the trust, subject to adjustments for such things as additions to the trust.

The numerator of the applicable fraction is the amount of the transferor's GSTT exemption allocated to the trust (or to the property transferred in a direct skip). § 2642(a)(2)(A). The denominator is the value of the transferred property less the amount of federal and state taxes recovered from the trust attributable to such property and any charitable deduction allowed for gift or estate tax purposes with respect to the property. § 2642(a)(2)(B). In Letter Ruling 200343019, in calculating the denominator of the applicable fraction, deductions were allowed for expenses that would not have been incurred but for the decedent's death and the necessity of collecting assets, paying debts and distributing other property. The deductions included attorney's fees, accountant's fees, appraiser, and expert and other professional fees. However, the expenses of maintaining the trust after the amount that passed to the trust was determined were not deductible. The time at which the fraction is determined is important because the value of the transferred property will vary over time. In general, it is best to fix the fraction as soon as possible.

EXAMPLE 2-28.

In 2011 *T* transferred $1,250,000 to her daughter, *D*, as trustee for *D*'s son, *GS*. *T* allocated $1,250,000 of her GSTT exemption to the transfer. The applicable fraction is 1 ($1,250,000 ÷ $1,250,000), the inclusion ratio is zero (1–1) and the applicable rate is zero (35% × 0). Later in 2011, *T* made an outright gift of $5,000,000 to *GS*, to which *T* allocated the $3,750,000 balance of her GSTT exemption. The applicable fraction for this transfer is 3/4 ($3,750,000/$5,000,000), the inclusion ratio is 1/4(1–3/4) and the applicable rate is 8.75% (35% × 1/4).

When determining the inclusion ratio, the manner in which the unused portion of the transferor's exemption is allocated, or is deemed to have been allocated, may affect the time the property is valued for purposes of calculating the applicable fraction. The applicable fraction may be smaller and the inclusion ratio higher if the denominator has increased in size (*i.e.*, if the value of the transferred property has increased). In particular, the time at which the allocation is made may affect the adequacy of the exemption to shield the property from application of the GSTT.

The rules prescribed by the statute are these: If the donor's exemption is allocated to a gift on a timely filed gift tax return, the value of the property determined for gift tax purposes also establishes its value for purposes of the GSTT exemption. § 2642(b)(1). If such an allocation is not made on a timely filed return, or deemed made at that time, the value of the property is determined (for purposes of the GSTT exemption) by its value at the time the allocation is filed with the Secretary. § 2642(b)(3). A delay in making the allocation can be costly.

EXAMPLE 2-29.

On December 31, 2011, *T*, a widower, made a gift of $10,000,000 to grandchild, *GC*, whose parents were both living at the time of the gift. *T* allocated his entire $5,000,000 exemption to the gift. The applicable fraction is $5,000,000 divided by $10,000,000, or 1/2. Accordingly, the inclusion ratio is 1/2 (1–1/2) and the applicable rate is 17.5% (35% × 1/2). In the case of a direct skip such as this, the amount subject to tax is the amount received by the donee. § 2623. Accordingly, a GSTT of $1,750,000 is due on the gift ($10,000,000 × 17.5%). Note that the amount of the GSTT is taken into account in calculating the gift tax on a direct skip. § 2515.

EXAMPLE 2-30.

On June 30, 2011, *W*, a widow, made a gift of $10 million to a trust in which her daughter, *D*, had a life income interest, *D'* s children were the successive life income beneficiaries, and their children were the ultimate remainder beneficiaries. *W* allocated her entire $5 million exemption to the transfer on a timely filed gift tax return. Throughout its existence the trust will have an inclusion ratio of 50 percent regardless of the growth in value of the principal. Accordingly, the tax rate applicable to each generation-skipping transfer will be half of the maximum federal estate tax rate at the time of the transfer. Note the *W'* s allocation of her exemption to the transfer fixed the value of the denominator. Because *W* allocated her exemption to the transfer in a timely filed gift tax return, the value of the denominator was fixed at the gift tax value of the property. § 2642(b)(1). If the allocation of the exemption had not been made, or been deemed made, until later, the value of the denominator (the value of the property transferred) would have been determined at the time of the allocation. Thus, an increase in the value of the property would have resulted in an increase in the inclusion ratio. § 2642(b)(3). For example, if *W'* s $5million exemption were allocated to the trust at the time of her death, when the trust property had a value of $20 million, the applicable fraction would have been 1/4 ($5million ÷ $20million) and the inclusion ratio would have been 75 percent.

A delay in allocating the exemption may be advantageous if the value of the property declines. Thus, the donor who is willing to gamble on survivorship may wish to delay allocating any part of the GSTT exemption to gifts he or she makes to an irrevocable trust that will use the funds to buy an insurance policy—which will be worth considerably less than the amount of the initial premium payments. For example, the donor may give $100,000 to the trust each year, which will be used to pay premiums on a $2 million policy on the donor's life. However, after the second premium payment the policy may have a value of only $40,000. The trust would have an inclusion ratio of zero if the donor allocated $40,000 of his or her GSTT exemption to the trust at the end of the second year, which would "save" $160,000 of the donor's GSTT exemption. In future years the donor might choose to allocate the GSTT exemption as additional funds were transferred to the trust. Of course, such a delay would be disastrous if the donor were to die prior to allocating his or her GSTT exemption to the trust. In such a case the amount of the insurance proceeds would be included in the value of the trust as a result of which the donor's GSTT exemption could shelter only one-half of the trust from the GSTT.

§2.27. GSTT Exemption

As indicated above, each individual is allowed a substantial exemption from the GSTT, which may be allocated by the individual to any property of which the individual is the transferor. §2631(a). An allocation, once made, is irrevocable. §2631(b). The amount of the GSTT exemption was $2 million in 2006 through 2008, $3.5 million in 2009. The estate tax applicable exclusion amount and the GSTT exemption amount are, and will remain, the same amount, which simplifies drafting and reduces the need to make reverse QTIP elections. *See* §§2.28 and 12.23.

As indicated above, the GSTT expired on January 1, 2010—but it is scheduled for resurrection on January 1, 2011, thanks to the 2001 Act's "sunset" provision.

Because each spouse has a GSTT exemption, the tax is of limited concern to couples whose combined estates will be substantially less than $10 million. Planning for the use of the exemption by a husband and wife with $10 million or more is easier if each of them owns one-half of their total property, which is often the case in community property states. Of course, under other circumstances the unlimited gift tax marital deduction allows a couple to equalize the sizes of their estates without tax cost. Also, the GSTT recognizes the effect of splitting gifts under §2513. §2652(1)-(2).

EXAMPLE 2-31.

In 2011, *W* made an inter vivos gift of $10million to her grandchild, *GC*, whose parent, *P*, is living. *W*'s husband, *H*, consented to be treated as donor of half of the gift for gift tax purposes. *W* and *H* may entirely insulate the gift from the GSTT by allocating their $10 million GSTT exemptions to the gift.

As explained in §2.29, the allocation of the exemption determines the rate at which the GSTT will apply to a generation-skipping transfer.

§2.28. Reverse QTIP Election, §2652(a)(3); Division of Trusts, §2654(b)

The consequence of a reverse QTIP election is that the decedent who was the creator of the QTIP trust (the first spouse to die) remains the transferor of the particular QTIP trust with respect to which the election is made. As a result, that decedent's GSTT exemption may be allocated to that QTIP trust, and the denominator of the applicable fraction is determined by reference to the value of the trust property in the gross estate of that decedent. LR 9002014.

Under § 2044, the property of a QTIP trust is includible in the gross estate of the surviving spouse. Accordingly, the surviving spouse is treated as the transferor of the property for GSTT purposes, which might cause part or all of the GSTT exemption of the first spouse to die to be wasted. Section 2652(a)(3) allows the donor (in the case of an inter vivos transfer) or the estate of the first spouse to die to elect to treat all of the property in such trust for GSTT purposes "as if the election to be treated as qualified terminable interest property had not been made." If such a "reverse QTIP election" is made, the first spouse to die is treated as the transferor of the trust for GSTT purposes. Unfortunately, § 2652(a)(3) does not permit a partial reverse election to be made. The inability to make a partial reverse QTIP election contrasts sharply with § 2056(b)(7), which allows a partial QTIP election. The ban on partial elections requires careful planning to maximize the benefit of the GSTT exemptions of both spouses.

A division of a single trust in a way that complies with the requirements of § 2642(a)(3) ("a qualified severance") allows the trusts to be treated as separate for GSTT purposes. The requirements of a qualified severance are spelled out in Reg. § 26.2642-6. Among other things, severed trusts "must provide, in the aggregate, for the same succession of interests of beneficiaries as are provided in the original trust." Reg. § 26.2642-6(b)(4). As suggested below, wills and trusts should be drafted to allow such divisions.

EXAMPLE 2-32.

W died in 1999, leaving an estate of $4 million, of which $650,000 (the estate tax exemption equivalent in 1999) passed to a credit shelter trust for the benefit of her children and their descendants. The balance of W's estate passed to a trust for the benefit of her husband, H, who survived her. The trust for H qualified for the QTIP marital deduction under § 2056(b)(7). W's' executor allocated $650,000 of W's $1 million GSTT exemption (the maximum available in 1999) to the credit shelter trust and the balance to the trust for H. W's executor also elected to claim the marital deduction with respect to the entire value of H's trust. The portion of W' s exemption that W's executor allocated to the trust for H ($350,000) was wasted because the entire value of the trust will be included in his gross estate under § 2044. For GSTT purposes the value of the property included in H's estate under § 2044 is fixed by its value in his estate.

W's executor could have made a reverse QTIP election under § 2652(a)(3). However, as a partial reverse QTIP election cannot be made, such an election would have caused W to be treated as the transferor of the entire QTIP trust. Accordingly, H could not allocate any of his GSTT exemption to the trust. A timely and effective division of the QTIP trust would have allowed H to make such an allocation.

The full benefit of the exemptions of both spouses is obtained if a separate QTIP trust is created for the surviving spouse in an amount equal to the amount of the unused portion of the GSTT exemption of the first spouse (*i.e.,* the portion that remains after the allocation of a portion of it to the credit shelter trust). Thus, the will of the first spouse to die may direct the creation of a credit shelter trust for the benefit of the surviving spouse and issue, and the creation of two QTIP trusts. The deceased spouse's executor would allocate to the credit shelter trust an amount of the decedent's GSTT exemption equal to the estate tax applicable exclusion amount, which would give it an inclusion ratio of zero. The first QTIP would be funded with an amount equal to the difference between the previously unused portion of the decedent's GSTT exemption and the amount of the GSTT exemption allocated to the credit shelter trust. The decedent's executor would make a reverse QTIP election under § 2652(a)(3) with respect to this trust. The residue of the decedent's estate would pass to the other QTIP trust. Under § 2044, the value of both QTIP trusts would be includible in the estate of the surviving spouse for estate tax purposes. However, by reason of the reverse QTIP election, for GSTT purposes the predeceased spouse would continue to be treated as the transferor of the QTIP trust with respect to which the election, was made. The surviving spouse would be treated as transferor of the other QTIP trust. The executor of the surviving spouse could allocate any unused portion of his or her GSTT exemption to that trust.

Since 2004, the estate tax applicable exclusion amount and the GSTT exemption amount have been the same amount. Accordingly, there is rarely a need for reverse QTIP elections today because the amount allocated to the credit shelter trust by the personal representative will be equal to the full GSTT exemption amount available to the decedent's estate. Such may not always be the case, however, so wills and trusts should be drafted in ways that facilitate reverse QTIP elections. For example, the fiduciary might be authorized to divide any trust into two or more trusts with identical terms. The provision should be drafted in light of the requirements of Reg. § 26.2642-6(b)(3) regarding funding. In simplest terms, the instrument should direct that the trusts be funded on a fractional basis, "such that each new trust is funded with a fraction or percentage of the entire trust," or a pecuniary amount that satisfies the requirements of Reg. § 26.2654-1(a)(1)(ii). Note also that the division of a trust may be helpful from a trust administration point of view.

A transferor's allocation of his GSTT exemption to a trust for which a QTIP election was made is void unless he also made a valid reverse QTIP election. LR 199929040. Accordingly, the amount of the transferor's remaining GSTT exemption is determined without regard to the void allocation.

A reverse QTIP election can be made on the last estate tax return filed before the due date, including extensions. LR 9552005. Importantly, an extension of time may be granted under Reg. § 301.9100-1 within which to make a reverse QTIP election. *E.g.,* LR 9608008, *See* § 12.2.4. The IRS has provided a simplified method of obtaining permission to file a late reverse QTIP election in Rev. Proc. 2004-47, 2004-2 C.B. 169. The simplified procedure is available for requests made on or after August 9, 2004.

Under Reg. § 26.2601-1(b)(1)(iii), the decedent (or donor) of a grandfathered QTIP trust is considered to have made a reverse QTIP election. LR 9635039. Accordingly, the surviving spouse is not considered to be the transferor of the trust except as to additions that were made after September 25, 1985.

Effect of Settlement of Dispute. In Letter Ruling 200026003, the IRS ruled that a decedent for whom a valid reverse QTIP election had been made would be treated as the transferor of the property distributed to the QTIP trust despite a dispute between the surviving spouse and the executor and other beneficiaries. The dispute was settled by an agreement under which the surviving spouse would sell her interest in the QTIP trust to the remaindermen for its actuarially determined value. The transfer to the QTIP trust was not a direct skip, a taxable termination, or a taxable distribution. The ruling did not deal with the gift or income tax aspects of the settlement.

§2.29. ALLOCATION OF EXEMPTION; DEEMED ALLOCATION RULES

If a transferor does not make a timely election regarding the allocation of his or her GSTT exemption, the Code prescribes how the exemption will be allocated. The unused portion of the transferor's exemption is generally allocated to lifetime direct skips to the extent necessary to reduce the inclusion ratio to zero: "If the amount of the direct skip exceeds such unused portion, the entire unused portion shall be allocated to the property transferred." § 2632(b)(1). Note, however, that an individual may specify on a timely filed gift tax return that the rule not apply to a transfer. § 2632(b)(3). That is, unlike the unified credit for gift tax purposes, GSTT permits the transferor to elect to preserve the exemption for allocation to later transfers. Reg. § 26.2632-1(b). A decedent's unused GSTT exemption can be allocated by his or her executor on a timely filed Form 706. Reg. § 26.2632-1(d). The regulations allow the exemption to be allocated on the basis of a formula. Reg. § 26.2632-1(b)(4)(i) ("e.g., the allocation may be expressed in terms of the amount necessary to produce an inclusion ratio of zero.").

A return is timely filed if it is filed on or before the date that would be the date for reporting the transfer if it were a taxable gift, including any extensions of time. Reg. § 26.2632-1(b). The regulation also provides that an automatic allocation or an election to prevent the allocation is irrevocable after the due date of the return.

Under the regulations, if more exemption is allocated to a transfer to a trust than required to result in an inclusion ratio of zero, the excess will be restored to the transferor. In particular, the regulations provide that, "Except as provided in § 26.2642-3 (relating to charitable lead annuity trusts), an allocation of GST exemption to a trust is void to the extent the amount allocated exceeds the amount necessary to obtain an inclusion ratio of zero with respect to the trust." Reg. § 26.2632-1(b)(4)(i). Curiously, the regulations adopt a rule that denies the restoration of an excess allocation of GSTT exemption to a charitable lead annuity trust. *See* Reg. § 26.2642-3, § 2.29.2.

The rules described above also generally apply to nonresident alien transferors. *See* Reg. § 26.2663-2.

In LR 9324029, the IRS ruled that an allocation of the GSTT exemption to a grandfathered trust was void. The trust created earlier by *H* was exempt from the GSTT under the grandfather rules except to the extent he added property to the trust by will. *H's* will made bequests to his grandchildren and to the trust. *H's* executor allocated part of *H's* GSTT exemption to the bequests to *H's* grandchildren and the balance to the trust. The allocation to bequests was treated as void, because the trusts were not subject to the GSTT by reason of the "Gallo" exclusion. Thus, the exemption remained available for allocation to the trust. The allocation made by the executor substantially complied with the rules regarding the allocation of the GSTT exemption, which negated the operation of the automatic allocation rules. The amount added to the trust is properly treated as a separate trust for GSTT purposes. *See also* §12.24.

Retroactive Allocation of GST Exemption. Under §2632(d), a transferor may retroactively allocate his or her GST exemption to trusts to which an allocation or deemed allocation had not previously been made. The allocation can be made upon the death of a nonskip person who was a lineal descendant of the transferor's grandparent (or of the grandparent of the transferor's spouse or former spouse), and who had an interest or future interest in a trust to which the transferor had made a transfer—typically the transferor's child. The transferor's GST exemption may be allocated on a chronological basis to any or all transfers made to the trust on a gift tax return that is timely filed for gifts made in the year of the nonskip person-descendant's death. For purposes of the allocation, the value of the transfers are determined as if the allocation had been made on timely filed gift tax returns.

Extension of Time Under Reg. §301.9100-3. The time within which to allocate the GSTT exemption to lifetime transfers may be extended under Reg. §301.9100-3. *See, e.g.,* LR 200306015. An extension under 9100-3 may be granted to allocate the exemption as of the date of the original transfer although in the meantime the taxpayer allocated the exemption on a late-filed gift tax return. LR 200407003.

§2.29.1. Certain Inter Vivos Transfers; Estate Tax Inclusion Period (ETIP)

Under §2642(f), the inclusion ratio for certain inter vivos transfers is not determined at the time of the initial transfer. Specifically, if the transferred property would be included in the transferor's gross estate (other than by reason of §2035), the GSTT exemption cannot be allocated to the property until the end of the period. (This "estate tax inclusion period" is often referred to by the acronym ETIP.) §2642(f)(3). The ETIP does not extend beyond the earlier of the date of the transferor's death or the date of a generation-skipping transfer of the property. The ETIP rule eliminates the opportunity to leverage the GSTT exemption by allocating it to a transfer in which the transferor retained an interest. Thus, the grantor of a trust in which the grantor retained a term interest cannot allocate GSTT exemption to the transfer until the end of the ETIP (*i.e.*, the date on which the transferor dies, the term of the transferor's retained interest ends, or the occurrence of a generation-skipping transfer). In the absence of a provision such as §2642(f) the transferor's GSTT exemption might be allocated to such a trust at the time it was created. If so, in calculating the applicable fraction, the denominator would be the present value of the remainder interest.

EXAMPLE 2-33.

T transferred $4 million to a trust in which he retained a term interest that was valued at $2 million under §2702. The property of the trust would be included in *T's* gross estate under §2036(a) if *T* were to die during the term of the retained interest. For purposes of determining the inclusion ratio of the trust, the value of the property will be determined at the end of the ETIP (*i.e., T's* death or the end of *T's* term interest). Without such a rule the allocation of the exemption to the trust might result in a large applicable fraction (*i.e.,* the denominator would be only the value of the remainder that *T* transferred). If *T* were to die prior to the end of the term, when the trust had a value of $8 million, the estate tax inclusion period would end and the full $8 million value of the trust would be the denominator of the applicable fraction.

Under § 2642(f)(4), except as provided in the regulations, the spouse of the transferor is treated as the transferor for purposes of the estate tax inclusion period. Under Reg. § 26.2632-1(c)(2)(ii)(A), the ETIP period (during which the exemption cannot be allocated) does not apply if the possibility of the interest being included in the estate of the transferor or the spouse of the transferor is so remote as to be negligible. The regulation continues to say that this requirement is satisfied if the actuarial probability is less than 5 percent. In addition, under Reg. § 26.2632-1(c)(2)(ii)(B), the value of property is not considered to be subject to inclusion in the gross estate of the spouse of the transferor if the withdrawal right held by the spouse is limited to a 5 or 5 power and expires not later than 60 days after the transfer to the trust. Accordingly, for GSTT purposes it can be important to limit a spouse's *Crummey* power to the 5 or 5 amount and to require that it terminate no later than 60 days after the transfer to the trust. *See* § 2.22.3.

§ 2.29.2. Charitable Lead Annuity Trusts

As explained in § 8.32, income, gift, and estate tax deductions are allowed for a gift to charity of the current interest in a trust in the form of a guaranteed annuity or unitrust interest.

A change made by the 1988 Act eliminated the possibility that the protection provided by the GSTT exemption could be leveraged by transferring property to a charitable lead annuity trust. Under § 2642(e), a special rule applies to determine the inclusion ratio for charitable lead annuity trusts created by transfers made after October 13, 1987. Previously the value of the exemption would have been leveraged to the extent the value of the property transferred to the trust increased by a rate greater than the rate used to compute the value of the charitable interest. Under § 2642(e), the amount of the numerator (the exemption allocated to the transfer) is increased by the interest rate that was applied in determining the value of the gift or estate tax charitable deduction claimed with respect to the transfer for the actual duration of the charitable lead annuity. The denominator is the value of all the property of the trust immediately after the termination of the charitable lead annuity. Thus computed the formula adjusts for the over- or under-performance of the investments of the trust—there is no leverage.

The regulations, in effect, punish the transferor for allocating more GSTT exemption to a charitable lead annuity trust than is required to result in an inclusion ratio of zero. Under Reg. § 26.2642-3(b), the amount of the excess allocated to the trust is lost to the transferor. In particular, the regulation provides that in such a case the exemption allocation originally made is not reduced. While such a rule may be administratively convenient, it is inconsistent with the general rule of Reg. § 26.2632-1(b)(4).

§2.29.3. Deemed Allocation of GSTT Exemption to Certain Lifetime Transfers

Section 2632(c), applicable to transfers made after December 31, 2000, provides for the deemed allocation of a grantor's unused GSTT exemption to a defined class of trusts called "GST trusts." As defined, the term "GST trust" means any trust that could have a generation-skipping transfer with respect to the transferor. Appropriately, seven types of trusts are excluded from the definition: (1) trusts with respect to which more than 25 percent of the corpus must be distributed to or may be withdrawn by one or more nonskip persons before attaining age 46; (2) trusts with respect to which more than 25 percent of the corpus must be distributed to or may be withdrawn by one or more nonskip persons who are living at the time of the death of another person identified in the trust instrument who is their senior by ten years or more; (3) trusts with respect to which more than 25 percent of the corpus must be distributed to the estate(s) of one or more nonskip persons if such nonskip person(s) predecease the events described in (1) or (2); (4) trusts in which any portion is includible in the estate of a nonskip person other than the transferor if he or she died immediately after the transfer; (5) charitable lead annuity trusts; (6) charitable remainder annuity trusts; and (7) charitable lead unitrusts. Under subsection (c)(5), an election against the deemed allocation may be made on a timely filed gift tax return. Consistent with other provisions, a deemed allocation under these rules will only occur at the end of the estate tax inclusion period as defined in § 2642(f)(3).

The application of the rules regarding the allocation of exemptions to inter vivos transfers is illustrated by the following example.

EXAMPLE 2-34.

On July 30, 2011, T transferred $10 million to a trust the income of which was payable to her son, S, for life and thereafter to his children for their lives. Upon the death of the last of S' s children to die, the trust principal will be distributed by right of representation to those of the issue of T who are then living. The trust is a GST trust. T did not allocate any part of her exemption to the trust. Nonetheless, T is deemed to have allocated her entire $5 million GSTT exemption to the trust, resulting in an applicable fraction of $5million ÷ $10million or 1/2. Accordingly, the inclusion ratio is 50 percent $(1-1/2)$.

§2.29.4. Default Allocation of GSTT Exemption at Death

Under § 2632(e) any portion of an individual's exemption that is not allocated on or before the date the individual's estate tax return is due is deemed to be allocated

(A) first, to property which is the subject of a direct skip occurring at such individual's death, and

(B) second, to trusts with respect to which such individual is the transferor and from which a taxable distribution or a taxable termination might occur at or after such individual's death.

Note that the "default" allocation of the exemption specified in the statute may not achieve optimal tax results. The loss of the benefit of the exemption may be particularly sharp if the exemption is allocated pro rata among trusts as provided by the default rules of § 2632(e)(2)(A).

EXAMPLE 2-35.

T's will left $5 million to a trust, the income of which could be sprinkled among *T'* s spouse, *S*, children, and grandchildren. *T* left the residue of his estate ($5 million) to a marital deduction trust, the income of which is payable to *S*. Upon the death of *S* the remainder of the marital deduction trust will be distributed to *T's* then living children and to the issue of deceased children. If *T's* exemption is not allocated by his executor it will be allocated under the default rules. Under § 2632(e)(2) the exemption would be allocated pro rata between the trusts ($2.5 million to each). Accordingly, each would have a 50 percent inclusion ratio. The entire exemption should be allocated to the discretionary trust, all of the distributions of which might be made to skip persons otherwise subject to the GSTT. In contrast, the income distributions of the marital deduction trust and distributions to children are not subject to the GSTT. The marital deduction trust is includible in the estate of *S* under § 2044. If appropriate, *S'* s $5 million GSTT exemption might be allocated to the marital deduction trust.

§ 2.30. Exclusions, §§ 2611(b); 2642(c)

Under § 2611(b)(1), the term "generation-skipping transfer" does not include "any transfer which, if made inter vivos by an individual, would not be treated as a taxable gift by reason of section 2503(e) (relating to exclusion of certain transfers for educational or medical expenses)." Accordingly, distributions from GSTT-exempt trusts for those purposes would be wasteful. Instead, the trustee of a nonexempt trust should be authorized to pay the tuition and medical care expenses of skip persons such as the transferor's grandchildren. For example, those expenses might be paid out of a nonexempt trust that the transferor created for his or her children instead of out of a separate exempt trust of which grandchildren and more remote issue were the beneficiaries.

The sting of the GSTT can also be reduced by making direct skips that qualify for gift tax exclusions, thereby giving them a zero inclusion ratio under § 2642(c)(1). For this purpose a nontaxable gift is one that is within the annual exclusion of § 2503(b) (taking into account the gift splitting possibilities of § 2513) or that is a qualified transfer under § 2503(e) (*i.e.*, a direct payment of tuition to an educational institution or of medical care expenses to a health care provider). § 2642(c)(3). Under Reg. § 25.2503-6(b)(3), the exclusion includes "amounts paid for medical insurance on behalf of any individual."

In effect, § 2642(c) allows a grandparent, each year, to transfer outright an amount equal to the gift tax annual exclusion to a grandchild free of both the gift tax and the GSTT and to make unlimited qualified transfers to a grandchild (*i.e.,* for tuition and medical care). Indeed, the exclusion of §2611(b) applies to the nonrefundable direct payment of advance tuition made by a grandparent to a private school on behalf of his two grandchildren. LR 199941013. The benefits of §2642(c) only extend, however, to a donee's interest in a trust if (1) during the life of the donee none of the income or principal could be used for the benefit of any other person, and, (2) the property will be included in the donee's estate if he or she dies before the trust terminates. §2642(c)(2).

The requirements of §2642(c)(2) were added by the 1988 Act in order to limit the extent to which property transferred to a trust could be insulated from the GSTT by giving the beneficiaries *Crummey* powers. However, the IRS has recognized that single-beneficiary *Crummey* trusts have a zero inclusion ratio. LR 8922062. A single trust can be drafted so the separate share of each grandchild will meet the requirements of §2642(c).

A §2503(c) trust for a minor meets the requirements of §2642(c)(2). Accordingly, transfers to the trust have a zero inclusion ratio to the extent annual gift tax exclusions were allowed under §2503(b) with respect to the transfers. That is, transfers to such a trust are nontaxable gifts to the extent annual gift tax exclusions were allowed.

EXAMPLE 2-36.

This year *GF* and *GM* gave $20,000 to each of their 5 grandchildren. They also paid $20,000 in tuition to the colleges the grandchildren attend. The GSTT does not apply to any of the $200,000 in gifts made by *GF* and *GM*, all of which qualify for gift splitting and the gift tax annual exclusion under §2503. Accordingly, the gifts all have zero inclusion ratios under §2642(c).

EXAMPLE 2-37.

GF and *GM* transferred $20,000 to separate trusts for each of their grandchildren. For GSTT purposes the gifts are direct skips. The beneficiary of each trust has a *Crummey* power, the noncumulative power to withdraw the property transferred to the trust within a limited time following notification of the transfer. Distributions may only be made to the beneficiary of each trust during his or her lifetime. If the beneficiary dies prior to termination of the trust the beneficiary may appoint the trust property to creditors of his or her estate. The gifts made by *GF* and *GM* to the trusts qualify for gift splitting and gift tax annual exclusions under §2503(b). The trusts also meet the requirements of §2642(c)(2). Accordingly, each trust has an inclusion ratio of zero. The exclusion offered by such a trust is particularly valuable if it invests in life insurance, the ultimate value of which may be many times the amount of the transfers to the trust.

§2.31. VALUATION OF PROPERTY

Property subject to a generation-skipping transfer is valued at the time of the transfer. §2624(a). However, in the case of a direct skip of property included in the transferor's gross estate, the value of the property will reflect the alternate valuation or special use valuation of the property under §§2032-2032A. §2624(b). Also, if a taxable termination occurs as the result of the death of an individual, an election may be made to value the property on the §2032 alternate valuation date. §2624(c). Finally, the amount of the property transferred is reduced by any consideration provided by the transferee. §2624(d).

EXAMPLE 2-38.

H, who had already used all of his GSTT exemption, left Blackacre to his grandson, *GS*. This was subject to a requirement that *GS* pay $1 million to *X*, the former wife of *GS*. *GS*, his parents, and *X* all survived *H*. Blackacre was valued at $5 million for federal estate tax purposes in *H's* estate. The devise involved a generation-skipping transfer of $4 million to *GS* (the $5 million value of Blackacre less the $1 million that *GS* was obligated to pay to *X*). The transfer of $1 million to *X* may also be treated as a generation-skipping transfer by *H*.

§2.32. TAXABLE AMOUNT OF GENERATION-SKIPPING TRANSFERS

The base on which the GSTT is computed varies depending upon the type of generation-skipping transfer. In the case of a direct skip the taxable amount is determined on a tax exclusive basis. §2623. That is, the tax is imposed only with respect to the value of the property received by the transferee. In contrast, the GSTT on taxable distributions and taxable terminations is determined on a tax inclusive basis. §§2621, 2622. In those cases, the tax base includes the amount of GSTT imposed on a taxable distribution or a taxable termination.

A general direction to pay death taxes from the residue of a decedent's estate should not suffice to shift the burden for payment of the GSTT to the decedent's estate. LR 9246009 (TAM) (based on Massachusetts statute). The Tax Court has held that the direction in the decedent's will that "all federal estate taxes, state and city inheritance or estate transfer taxes, or other death taxes attributable to the bequests . . . shall be paid from the residuum of my estate" was not sufficient under §2603(b) to shift the obligation that the GSTT be paid from the transferred property. *Estate of Louise S. Monroe*, 104 T.C. 352 (1995), *rev'd on other grounds*, 124 F.3d 699 (5th Cir. 1997).

§2.32.1. Direct Skips

The GSTT on a direct skip is determined according to the value of the property received by the transferee. For this purpose, note that the transferee may be a trust or trust equivalent. Thus, in LR 9105006 (TAM), the IRS held that the transferor had made a direct skip of the full value of property in which a life estate was given to a friend who was 40 years younger than the transferor (a skip person) and the remainder was given to the transferor's daughter (a nonskip person). By not including the amount of the GSTT in the tax base of an inter vivos direct skip the GSTT resembles the gift tax—in neither case is the amount of the tax included in the tax base. Note, however, that under §2515 the amount of any GSTT paid with respect to a direct skip is included in the gift tax base.

EXAMPLE 2-39.

In 2011, *T*, who had already used her $5 million GSTT exemption, made a gift of $1 million to *GC*, her grandchild, whose parents were both living. The transfer was subject to a GSTT of $350,000. The gift of $1,350,000 was subject to a gift tax of $472,500. Thus, the gift "cost" *T* a total of $1,822,500 ($1,350,000 + $472,500).

EXAMPLE 2-40.

T, the donor described in Example 2-394 above, died in 2011 leaving a bequest of $1 million to *GC*, whose parents both survived *T*. In order to make a net bequest of $1 million to *GC* the estate of *T* must expend $2,076,923:

Amount required	$2,076,923
Less: Estate Tax (35% rate)	726,923
Amount net of estate tax	$1,350,000
Bequest to GC	$1,000,000
GSTT on $1 million	$350,000
Total bequest & GSTT	$1,350,000

§2.32.2. Taxable Distributions

The tax base of a taxable distribution is the value of the property received by the transferee less the value of the expense incurred by the transferee with respect to the distribution. §2621(a). Under §2603(a)(1), the transferee is obligated to pay the GSTT on a taxable distribution, so the tax is computed on a tax inclusive basis: The GSTT is computed on the gross amount received by the distributee before the GSTT is paid.

EXAMPLE 2-41.

On January 1, 2011, a trust made a taxable distribution of $100,000 of income to X. The trust has an inclusion ratio of 1. The tax base is $100,000 of which X is obligated to pay a GSTT of $35,000. X is left with $65,000 after paying the GSTT. Note that for income tax purposes X is entitled to deduct the amount of the GSTT as a tax under §164. §164(b)(4).

§2.32.3. Taxable Terminations

In the case of a taxable termination the taxable amount is also determined on a tax inclusive basis. It includes the value of all property with respect to which the taxable termination has occurred including the amount of the GSTT, but is reduced by the amount of indebtedness, expenses, and taxes. §2622. The deduction is to be "similar to the deduction allowed by section 2053 (relating to expenses, indebtedness, and taxes) for amount attributable to property with respect to which the taxable termination has occurred." §2622(b).

EXAMPLE 2-42.

W, who died on October 31, 2011, left $10 million to a trust for the benefit of D, her daughter, for life after which the trust would continue for the benefit of D's issue. T's executor allocated T's $5 million exclusion to the trust. Accordingly, the trust has an inclusion ratio of 50 percent. D died survived by children and grandchildren. The trust had a value of $25 million. Thus, a taxable termination of property worth $25 million took place when D died. No deductions were allowable under §2622(b) for expenses, indebtedness, or taxes. A GSTT of $4,375,000 was payable by the trustee, which was calculated by multiplying $25 million by the maximum estate tax rate times the inclusion ratio (35% × 50%). Under §2654(a)(2) the basis of the property is "adjusted in a manner similar to the manner provided under section 1014(a); except that, if the inclusion ratio with respect to such property is less than 1, any increase or decrease shall be limited by multiplying such increase or decrease (as the case may be) by the inclusion ratio."

§2.33. IDENTIFYING AND CHANGING THE TRANSFEROR

Under the basic rule, the decedent is treated as the transferor of any property that is subject to the estate tax, §2652(a)(1)(A), and the donor is treated as the transferor of any property that is subject to the gift tax. §2652(a)(1)(B). For purposes of the GSTT, property may be transferred although "there is no transfer of property under the local law at the time the Federal estate or gift tax applies." Reg. §26.2652-1(a)(1). Under the regulations, a transfer is subject to the gift tax if a gift tax is imposed under §2501(a), Reg. §26.2652-1(a)(2), and a transfer is subject to the estate tax if the value of the property is includible in the decedent's gross estate. *Id.*

In some cases the overall transfer tax costs may be reduced if the identity of the transferor is shifted to another person whose unified credit or GST tax exemption might otherwise be unused. For example, an independent trustee might be authorized either to distribute the trust property outright to a child or other beneficiary who is a nonskip person or to amend the trust to give a general power of appointment to such a person. The distribution of the property to the beneficiary or the beneficiary's possession of the general power of appointment would cause the property to be included in the beneficiary's estate. In the later case, the beneficiary would become the transferor for GSTT purposes. In order to protect the estate plan of the original transferor the beneficiary might be given the least control possible (*e.g.*, the power to appoint the property to the creditors of his or her estate with the concurrence of a nonadverse party, §2041(b)(1)).

EXAMPLE 2-43.

T, who had fully used his GSTT exemption, left $1 million to a trust, the income of which was to be used for the benefit of *S*, his son. Following the death of *S*, the income was payable to the issue of *S*. *S* and several of his children survived *T*. Under the trust, an independent trustee had discretion to amend the trust to give *S* the testamentary power to appoint the property to the creditors of his estate. (Some transferors might prefer to allow the beneficiary's power to be exercisable only with the joinder of the trustee.) *S* owned no other property and was not indebted to any creditors. When *S*, whose gross estate would be of nominal value, became terminally ill, the trustee amended the trust to give him the testamentary power to appoint the trust property to his creditors. When he died, the trust was includible in his gross estate under §2041. Accordingly, *S* became the transferor of the trust. As a result, *S's* death did not involve a direct skip, a taxable distribution, or a taxable termination. If the trust has a value of $5 million when *S* dies in 2011, little or no estate tax would be due. Furthermore, no GSTT will be due if *S's* executor allocates *S's* full GSTT exemption to the trust.

According to the IRS, the grantor's GSTT exemption cannot be allocated to a GRAT during the estate tax inclusion period (*i.e.*, during the term of the grantor's retained interest). LR 200227022. If the grantor survives the period, distributions made outright to the grantor's children are not subject to the GSTT. Distributions to the descendants of a child who died during the ETIP period would be subject to the GSTT unless the transferor had changed. In Letter Ruling 200227022, the IRS recognized that the transferor would change to the deceased child if he or she held a testamentary general power of appointment. In such a case, distributions to the children of the deceased child would be to non-skip persons and, as a result, would not be subject to the GSTT.

The Delaware Tax Trap. An alternative technique for shifting the transferor is available in states that allow a special power of appointment to be exercised by creating a general power of appointment. As a result of such an exercise of the special power, the vesting of interests may be postponed for a period ascertainable without regard to the date of the creation of the first power. Blattmachr & Pennell, Using "Delaware Tax Trap" to Avoid Generation-Skipping Taxes, 68 J. Tax. 242 (1988). The exercise of such a post-1942 power will cause the property to be included in the estate of the holder of the special power under §2041(a)(3). For purposes of the Rule Against Perpetuities a presently exercisable general power of appointment is treated as the equivalent of outright ownership of the property.

Section 2041(a)(3) is called the "Delaware Tax Trap" because it was designed to prevent the use of Delaware law to create trusts that could indefinitely avoid imposition of the estate tax. In particular, §2041(a)(3) requires the inclusion of property subject to a post-1942 power that is exercised to postpone the vesting of an interest or to suspend the absolute power of alienation for a period that is ascertainable without reference to the date of the creation of the first power. Under the former Delaware law the period of the Rule Against Perpetuities with respect to the exercise of a special or general power of appointment ran from the date the power is exercised. Former Del. Code Ann. Tit. 25, §501(1989).

Changes Under §2653(a). The transferor is also changed if there is a generation-skipping transfer of property that remains in trust. §2653(a). For subsequent GSTT purposes the property which was subject to the transfer is treated as if "the transferor of such property were assigned to the first generation above the highest generation of any person who has an interest in such trust immediately after the transfer." *Id.* Although there is a change in the transferor the exclusion ratio of the trust remains the same. §2653(b)(1).

EXAMPLE 2-44.

T, who previously used her entire GSTT exemption, died in 2009 leaving her residuary estate in trust for the benefit of *C*, her child, for life. Following *C*'s death the income of the trust was payable to the children of *C* in equal shares. Upon the death of each child of *C* a proportionate part of the trust was distributable outright to his or her issue. *C* died in 2011 survived by three children. *C's* death constituted a taxable termination subject to GSTT. Thereafter, *C* will be treated as the transferor of the trust. When each child of *C* dies the GSTT will apply to the amount of the taxable distribution to such decedent's issue.

Under the GSTT regulations the lapse of a *Crummey* power of withdrawal may change the identity of the transferor. The point is illustrated by Example 5 of Reg. §26.2652-1(a)(5). The example provides that, "On the lapse of the withdrawal right, *C* [the holder of the *Crummey* power] becomes a transferor to the extent *C* is treated as having made a completed transfer for purposes of Chapter 12. Therefore, except to the extent that the amount with respect to which the power of withdrawal lapses exceeds the greater of $5,000 or 5 percent of the value of the trust property, *T* [the original transferor] remains the transferor of the property for purposes of Chapter 13." Note that the change in transferor only occurs to the extent the lapse of the power constituted a completed gift. Accordingly, no change would occur if the holder of the lapsed power of withdrawal also held a power of appointment over the property, such as a special testamentary power. *See* §7.38.2. The same result was reached in LR 9541029, in which the decedent continued to be treated as the transferor for GSTT purposes to the extent the beneficiaries' powers of withdrawal were limited to the greater of $5,000 or 5 percent of the property subject to the power. Within that amount the lapses were not releases that would have caused the beneficiaries to have made any taxable gifts. *See* §2.22.3. However, according to the IRS the beneficiaries would be treated as owners of the trust under §678 on a cumulative basis. *See* §7.38.10.

EXAMPLE 2-45.

Donor, *D*, transferred $40,000 to a *Crummey* trust of which child, *C*, and three grandchildren, *GC-1*, *GC-2* and *GC-3*, were the beneficiaries. Because of the *Crummey* withdrawal powers the gifts qualify for the annual gift tax exclusion. However, if the withdrawal powers lapse the grandchildren may face gift and GSTT problems if the lapse results in a completed gift to others. The transfers are not subject to the GSTT if the interests of the beneficiaries satisfy the requirements of §2642(c)(2) (*i.e.*, during the life of each beneficiary no part of the income or principal of the lapsed amount can be distributed to anyone else and the lapsed property will be included in the powerholder's estate if he dies prior to termination of the trust).

If the beneficiary does not retain a power of appointment over the lapsed interest, the lapse will result in a gift to the extent the lapse exceeds the greater of $5,000 or 5 percent of the value of the property. If the lapse causes part of the lapsed interest to be subject to the gift tax, the grandchild is treated as having received a distribution from the trust to that extent. Reg. §26.2612-1(c). The distribution is subject to the GSTT.

The problem can be avoided by limiting the rights of withdrawal to the 5 or 5 amount or crafting the skip person's interest to meet the requirements of §2642(c)(2). Giving the holder of the power of withdrawal a special testamentary power of appointment over the lapsed amount to the extent it exceeds the 5 or 5 amount avoids the gift tax problem. However, the excess is includable in the power holder's estate.

If the powerholder does not have a power of appointment over the excess, the lapse of the power will result in a gift by the powerholder. In LR 9804047, the IRS ruled that the lapse of the excess resulted in a gift by the powerholder life-income beneficiary of the full amount. According to the IRS, the powerholder's retained life estate was valued at zero under §2702(a).

The portion over which a decedent held a power of withdrawal at the time of death is includable in his or her estate under §2041. To that extent the decedent is considered to be the transferor of the property which is deemed to have been constructively added to the trust for GSTT purposes. LR 9819034.

§ 2.34. GENERATIONAL ASSIGNMENTS, § 2651

The application of the GSTT turns on the identification of skip persons; a term defined in § 2613(a) as natural persons two or more generations below the generation assignment of the transferor. A lineal descendant of a grandparent of the transferor is assigned to "that generation which results from comparing the number of generations between the grandparent and such individual with the number of generations between the grandparent and the transferor." § 2651(b)(1). Thus, the transferor and the siblings of the transferor are both two generations below their grandparents. The same rules apply in determining the generational assignment of the descendants of the grandparents of the transferor's spouse. § 2651(b)(2). Adopted persons and persons related by the halfblood are treated in the same way as full blood relations. A person who was at any time married to the transferor is assigned to the transferor's generation. § 2651(c)(1). Similarly, a person who was at any time married to a lineal descendant of a grandparent of the transferor or the transferor's spouse is assigned to the same generational level as such person. § 2651(c)(2).

EXAMPLE 2-46.

T gave $100,000 to her niece, *N*, and to *N*'s daughter, *GN*. *N* is assigned to a generation (3) only one below that of *T* (2). Thus, *N* is not a skip person. *GN* is assigned to a generation (4) that is two below that of *T*. Accordingly, *GN* is a skip person. The gift of $100,000 to *GN* is a direct skip that is subject to the GSTT.

Persons who are not descendants of the grandparents of the transferor or the transferor's spouse are assigned to generational levels based upon their dates of birth. A person born not more than $12^1/_2$ years after the date of birth of the transferor is assigned to the same generational level as the transferor. § 2651(d)(1). A person whose date of birth is more than $12^1/_2$ years, but not more than $37^1/_2$ years after the date of birth of the transferor is assigned to the first generational level below that of the transferor. § 2651(d)(2). The generational assignments of persons born more than 37 years after the transferor are made on the basis of successive 25-year generational periods. Thus, a person between $37\text{-}^1/_2$ and $62\text{-}^1/_2$ years younger than the transferor is assigned to the same generation as are the grandchildren of the transferor. *See, e.g.,* LR 9105006 (TAM).

§ 2.35. SEPARATE TRUSTS; SEPARATE SHARES, § 2654(b)

Portions of a trust attributable to transfers from different transferors are treated as separate trusts for GSTT purposes. § 2654(b)(1). In addition, substantially separate and independent shares of different beneficiaries in a trust are treated as separate trusts. § 2654(b)(2). Under the regulations, "a portion of a trust is not a separate share unless such share exists from and at all times after the creation of the trust." Reg. § 26.2654-1(a)(1). In addition, additions to or distributions from separate trusts are allocated "pro rata among the separate trusts, unless the governing instrument provides otherwise." *Id*. However, see the description, below, of the rules regarding the post-2000 division of trusts.

Trust Divisions Under the 2001 Act. An addition to §2642(a) made by the 2001 Act recognizes the effect of a post-2000 division of a trust into two or more trusts provided it meets the requirements of a "qualified severance." Importantly, the amendment allows a qualified severance to be made "at any time." §2642(a)(3)(C). A qualified severance means the division of a single trust on a fractional share basis into two or more trusts that provide, in the aggregate, for the same succession of interests of beneficiaries as in the original trust. §2642(a)(3)(B)(i). If a trust has an inclusion ratio greater than zero and less than one, a severance is a qualified severance only if it is divided into two trusts, one of which receives a fractional share of all trust assets equal to the applicable fraction of the single trust immediately before the severance. In such an allocation, the trust that receives the fractional share will have an inclusion ratio of zero and the other trust will have an inclusion ratio of one. §2642(a)(3)(B)(ii). Presumably such a qualified severance could be followed by other divisions under either §2642(a)(3)(B)(i) or §2642(a)(3)(B)(ii). The amendment is most welcome—the existing regulations only recognize the effect of divisions that were made at the inception of a trust. The generally favorable proposed regulations on qualified severances, 2004-2 C.B. 520, are discussed in Bieber & Hodgman, The Kindest Cut of All—Proposed Regs. For Making Qualified GST Severances, 32 Est. Plan. 3 (Mar. 2005).

In LR 200213014, the IRS held that the division, in accordance with state law, of two existing trusts on a fractional basis into exempt and nonexempt shares were qualified severances. The division did not affect the succession of interests or the beneficiaries. The IRS also ruled favorably with respect to gift, estate and income tax issues.

§2.36. MULTIPLE TRANSFERS, §2642(d)

If additional property is transferred to a trust, the applicable fraction for the trust is recalculated. First, the value of the property in the trust immediately before the present transfer is multiplied by the applicable fraction for the trust. The product is the "nontax portion" of the trust. §2642(d)(3). Second, the numerator of the new applicable fraction is calculated by adding the GSTT exemption allocated to the present transfer to the nontax portion of the trust. §2642(d)(2)(A). Third, the denominator of the fraction is determined by adding the value of the property transferred to the trust to the value of all property held in the trust immediately before the transfer. For this purpose the value of the property transferred to the trust is reduced by the sum of the death taxes paid from the property and the amount of the gift or estate tax charitable deductions allowed with respect to the transfer. §2642(d)(2)(B).

EXAMPLE 2-47.

In 2011, *T* transferred $5 million to a trust to which she allocated her $5 million exemption. Thus, the trust had an applicable fraction of 1 and an inclusion ratio of zero. In 2012, *T* transferred an additional $2 million to the trust. Immediately prior to the second transfer the property of the trust had a value of $6 million. The applicable fraction of the trust, recalculated as provided in § 2642(d), is 3/4 ($6 million ÷ $8 million).

§ 2.37. BASIS ADJUSTMENT, § 2654(a)

Subsection 2654(a) provides for adjustments to the bases of property similar to the adjustments that are made in the case of transfers that are subject to the gift and estate taxes. That is, property that is transferred in a taxable termination at the death of an individual is adjusted in a manner similar to the manner provided in § 1014(a) (*i.e.,* the federal estate tax value of the property becomes its basis). § 2654(a)(2). However, in the case of the GSTT adjustment, if the inclusion ratio is less than one, the increase or decrease in basis is limited by multiplying the increase or decrease by the inclusion ratio. *Id.* The following example illustrates how the basis adjustment should be computed for a taxable termination which occurs at the same time and as the result of the death of an individual.

EXAMPLE 2-48.

T died leaving $1 million in securities in trust to pay the income to *S*, his son, for life, after which the income would be paid to *S's* children for their lives. *T'* s executor allocated $500,000 of *T's* GSTT exemption to the trust. Accordingly, the trust had an inclusion ratio of 50 percent. When *S* died the securities had a basis of $1 million and a fair market value of $2 million. The basis of the securities is increased by $500,000 (the excess of the fair market value of the securities ($2 million) over their basis ($1 million) multiplied by the inclusion ratio (50%)). A GST tax of $350,000 would be paid with respect to the taxable termination resulting from *S'* s death ($2 million × (35% × 50%)).

In other cases (*i.e.,* direct skips, taxable distributions, and taxable terminations that do not result from the death of an individual), the basis of property transferred in a generation-skipping transfer is increased by an amount of the GSTT attributable to the excess of the fair market value of the property over its adjusted basis immediately before the transfer. § 2654(a)(1). The adjustment is made after any basis adjustment under § 1015, which calls for a similar adjustment to be made with respect to the gift tax attributable to the net appreciation in a post-1976 gift (*i.e.,* the amount by which the fair market value of the property exceeds the donor's basis immediately before the gift). § 1015(d)(6). Presumably the adjustment would only be made with respect to the amount of the gift (*i.e.,* the adjustment would not take into account the portion of the gift attributable to the GSTT paid with respect to the gift). While the amount of the GSTT is included in the base of the gift tax, the tax is paid in cash, for which no basis adjustment is possible. Cash has a basis equal to its face amount.

EXAMPLE 2-49.

In 2011, *T*, who had previously used his entire GSTT exemption and his applicable exclusion amount, gift of $1 million to *GD*, his granddaughter. Earlier in the year *T* made an annual exclusion gift of cash to *GD*. *T* paid a gift tax of $472,500 on the taxable gift of $1,350,000 (the amount of the gift plus the amount of the GSTT paid). The gift property had an adjusted basis of $500,000 immediately before the gift. The basis of the property would be increased by $175,000, calculated as follows: $472,500 (gift tax) x $500,000 (appreciation) ÷ $1,350,000 = $175,000. After the adjustment for the gift tax the basis of property would be $675,000. *T* also paid a GSTT of $350,000 with respect to the $1 million gift. The basis of the property would be increased by an additional $113,750 ($350,000 (GSTT) x $325,000 ÷ $1 million). Thus, the final adjusted basis of the property would be $788,750 ($675,000 + $113,750).

§2.38. RETURNS, §2662

In general, GSTT returns must be filed by the person liable under §2603(a) for the payment of the tax. §2662(a)(1). Table 2-3 indicates the persons who are required under Reg. §26.2662-1(c) to make the necessary return and pay the tax:

Table 2-3
Persons Required to File GSTT Returns

Type of Transfer	Person Responsible	Type of Return
Taxable Distribution	Skip Person Distributee	706GS(D)
Notification of Distribution from Generation-Skipping Trust	Trustee	706GS(D-1)
Taxable Termination	Trustee	706GS(T)
Inter Vivos Direct Skip	Transferor	709
Direct Skips at Death Subject to Estate Tax	Transferor's Executor	706 (Sch. R)
Direct Skip from Trust	Trustee	706 (Sched. R-1)

The IRS apparently does not issue closing letters for returns indicating a taxable termination of a GST trust (Form 706GS(T)). Where valuation is a substantial issue, this effectively forces the trustee to hold all or a portion of the trust assets in reserve pending expiration of the applicable statute of limitations.

§2.38.1. Direct Skips

Generation-skipping transfers of property that are included in the decedent's gross estate are divided between Schedules R and R-1. A direct skip that is not made from a trust is reported by the executor on Schedule R. The GSTT on such a transfer is paid by the estate. On the other hand, a direct skip from a trust is reported on Schedule R-1, which serves as a payment voucher for the trustee to remit the GSTT to the IRS. Schedule R-1 is used whether the direct skip is made to an individual or to another trust.

EXAMPLE 2-50.

S was the beneficiary of a QTIP trust for which a marital deduction was claimed by the executor of her deceased husband's will. When *S* died the trust terminated and the property was distributed outright to her adult grandchildren, whose parents were living. The trust was included in *S's* estate by reason of §2044. The distribution of the trust property to *S's* grandchildren involved direct skips. Accordingly, the transfers are reported by the trustee on Schedule R-1. *See* Reg. §26.2662-1(c)(1)(iv), (v).

§2.38.2. Trust Arrangements

In the case of property held in "trust arrangements" at the time of the transferor's death, the executor is liable for the tax and for making the return if the total value of the property involved in direct skips with respect to the same trustee is less than $250,000. Reg. §26.2662-1(c)(2)(iii). A trust arrangement is any arrangement other than an estate, which although not an explicit trust, has the same effect as an explicit trust. As indicated in the Instructions for Form 706, "[T]rust includes life estates with remainders, terms for years, and insurance and annuity contracts." The responsibility for making the return and paying the tax is illustrated in the following example from the Regulations:

> *Example (1).* On August 1, 1997, *T*, the insured under an insurance policy, died. The proceeds ($200,000) were includible in *T'* s gross estate for federal estate tax purposes. *T'* s grandchild, *GC*, was named the sole beneficiary of the policy. The insurance policy is treated as a trust under section 2652(b)(1), and the payment of the proceeds to *GC* is a transfer from a trust for purposes of Chapter 13. Therefore, the payment of the proceeds to *GC* is a direct skip. Since the proceeds from the policy ($200,000) are less than $250,000, the executor is liable for the tax imposed by Chapter 13 and is required to file Form 706. Reg. §26.2662-1(c)(2)(vi).

The regulations empower the executor to recover the tax from the trustee if the property continues to be held in trust, otherwise from the recipient of the property. Reg. §26.2662-1(c)(2)(v).

§2.38.3. Deferral of GSTT on Direct Skips of Closely-Held Business Interests, §6166(i)

Under §6166(i), the GSTT on interests in closely-held businesses that are the subject of a direct skip as a result of the decedent's death is subject to deferral. According to the House Report on the bill that became the 1986 Act, "The special rules under which estate tax attributable to interests in certain closely-held businesses

may be paid in installments also apply to direct skips occurring as a result of death."
1986-3 C.B. Vol. 2, 828.

§ 2.38.4. Redemption of Stock to Pay GSTT, § 303

If the stock of a corporation is subject to a generation-skipping transfer at the same time and as a result of the death of an individual, the redemption of the stock may qualify under § 303 as a distribution made in exchange for the stock. Again, according to the House Committee Report, "The provision permitting tax-free redemptions of stock to pay estate tax is amended to permit those redemptions to pay generation-skipping transfer tax in the case of such transfers occurring as a result of death." *Id.*

§ 2.39. RETURN DUE DATES

In the case of a direct skip other than from a trust, the GSTT return is due on or before the date on which the gift or estate tax return is required to be filed with respect to the transfer. § 2662(a)(2)(A). The return for all other generation-skipping transfers is due on or before the fifteenth day of the fourth month after the close of the taxable year of the person required to make the return. § 2662(a)(2)(B). Thus, GSTT returns by trusts are most often due on April 15 of the year following the event that triggered payment of the tax.

The IRS now recognizes that certain private delivery services satisfy the "timely mailing as timely filing/paying" rule of § 7502. *See* § 12.41.

§ 2.40. EFFECTIVE DATES; CONSTRUCTIVE ADDITIONS

The modern GSTT applies to transfers after the date of enactment (October 22, 1986), subject to the following exceptions:

1. Inter vivos transfers occurring after September 25, 1985, are subject to the modern GSTT;
2. Transfers from trusts that were irrevocable before September 26, 1985, are exempt to the extent that the transfers are not attributable to additions to the trust corpus occurring after that date;
3. Transfers pursuant to wills in existence before the date of enactment of the Act (October 22, 1986) are not subject to tax if the decedent died before January 1, 1987 [this exception was extended by the 1988 Act to transfers made before January 1, 1987 under revocable trusts executed prior October 22, 1986]; and
4. Transfers under a trust to the extent that such trusts consist of property included in the gross estate of the decedent or which are direct skips which occur by reason of the death of any decedent if the decedent was incompetent on the date of enactment of this Act (October 22, 1986) and at all times thereafter until death. General Explanation, Tax Reform Act of 1986, 1267-68.

The basic GSTT effective date rules are relatively simple: The GSTT applies to generation-skipping transfers made after October 22, 1986. However, it does not apply to generation-skipping transfers made by trusts that were irrevocable before September 26, 1985 except to the extent attributable to property added to the trust after September 25, 1985 (or made out of income attributable to property added to the trust after September 25, 1985). Under the regulations, trusts in existence on September 25, 1985 are generally considered to be irrevocable. However, a trust is not considered to be irrevocable to the extent it is includible in the grantor's gross estate under § 2038 (*i.e.,* the grantor retained a power to amend, revoke or terminate the trust). Reg. § § 26.2601-1(b)(1)(ii)(B). Similarly, a policy of life insurance that is treated as a trust under § 2652(b) is not considered to be an irrevocable trust to the extent the insured possessed any incidents of ownership that would have caused the insurance proceeds to be included in the insured's estate under § 2042. Reg. § 26.2601-1(b)(1)(ii)(C).

Estate plans should take into account the value of preserving the exemption provided by the effective date rules. Thus, assets should not be added to preexisting trusts, distribution plans should maximize the benefit of the exemption, and the exemption should be continued as long as possible. A grandfathered trust can be reformed in ways that do not affect its substantive provisions without subjecting it to the GSTT. *See* § 2.41.5.

Constructive Additions. Note that a party may be treated as having constructively added property to a trust by satisfying an obligation of the trust.

> Where a trust described in paragraph (b)(1) of this section is relieved of any liability properly payable out of the assets of such trust, the person or entity who actually satisfies the liability is considered to have made a constructive addition to the trust in an amount equal to the liability. The constructive addition takes place when the trust is relieved of liability (e.g., when the right of recovery is no longer enforceable). Reg. § 26.2601-1(b)(1)(v)(C).

Under the regulations the failure of the personal representative of a surviving spouse to exercise a right to recover the estate tax attributable to QTIP that is includible under § 2044 does not constitute a constructive addition to an exempt trust. Reg. § 26.2652-1(a)(5), Example (7) ("Because of the reverse QTIP election, for GST purposes, the trust property is not treated as includible in S's gross estate and, under those circumstances, no right of recovery exists.").

EXAMPLE 2-51.

> Prior to September 26, 1985, *T* transferred property to an irrevocable trust for the benefit of her descendants. The trustee has discretion to distribute income and principal among *T'* s children and their issue. The exempt status of the trust should be protected. In particular, no property should be added to the trust. Distributions from the trust should be coordinated with distributions from other trusts in order to maximize the benefit of the exemption. Thus, distributions from this trust might be made to *T'* s grandchildren or more remote descendants while distributions to *T'* s children and other nonskip persons are made from nonexempt trusts.

Additions to Irrevocable Trusts. The regulations illustrate how the GSTT is applied where property is added to a preexisting trust. Reg. §26.2601-1(b)(1)(iv). Following an addition the trust consists of a non-Chapter 13 portion (the preexisting portion of the trust) and a portion subject to Chapter 13 (the addition to the trust). The inclusion ratio of the non-Chapter 13 portion is zero and the inclusion ratio of the Chapter 13 portion is determined under §2642 as in other cases. When a taxable termination or a taxable distribution occurs the portion attributable to the Chapter 13 portion is determined by multiplying the amount of the termination or distribution by the "allocation fraction." The numerator of the allocation fraction is the amount of the addition to the trust and the denominator is the value of the trust immediately after the addition was made. Reg. §26.2601-1(b)(1)(iv)(C)(1).

EXAMPLE 2-52.

On January 1, 1985, *T* transferred property worth $500,000 to an irrevocable trust, the income of which was distributable to his child, *C*, for life, then to *C'* s child, *GC*, for life. When *GC* dies the trust will terminate and the trust property will be distributed to *GC'* s issue. On January 1 of this year *T* transferred an additional $500,000 to the trust. Immediately after the transfer the trust property was worth $1,500,000. The allocation fraction is 1/3 ($500,000 / $1,500,000). Accordingly, one-third of the amount of generation-skipping transfers made from the trust after January 1 of this year will be attributed to the Chapter 13 portion and will be subject to the GSTT. Of course, the inclusion ratio of the Chapter 13 portion of the trust would be zero if *T* made a timely allocation of $500,000 of his GSTT exemption to the addition to the trust.

Grandfathered Trusts. The distribution of the corpus of a grandfathered trust to the grandchildren of the grantor, or to trusts for their benefit, pursuant to a trustee's exercise of discretion does not subject the distributions to the GSTT. LR 9248010. For purposes of the ruling, the IRS treated the distributions to trusts for the benefit of the grandchildren as "equivalent to outright transfers to *A1* and *B1* [the grandchildren] because each will be the only beneficiary of his or her respective trust during his or her lifetime and the value of the assets in each trust will be includible in the beneficiary's gross estate in the event the beneficiary dies before his or her trust terminates."

Under §1433(b)(2)(C)(i) of the 1986 Act, the GSTT does not apply to a trust that is included in a decedent's estate if the decedent was incompetent on October 22, 1986, and at all times thereafter until death. *See* Reg. §26.2601-1(b)(3)(i). If the decedent had not been adjudged to be an incompetent, the exception is available only if the executor files with the estate tax return either a certification from a qualified physician that the decedent was incompetent on October 22, 1986, and at all subsequent times or other sufficient evidence to establish the decedent's condition. In the latter case the executor must also file a statement explaining why no certification was available from a physician. LR 9246022 (TAM).

§2.41. $2 MILLION EXCLUSION FOR PRE-1990 TRANSFERS, 1986 ACT §1433(b)(3)

The so-called "Gallo Amendment" allowed a GSTT exclusion of $2 million per grandchild for property transferred prior to January 1, 1990. 1986 Act §1433(b)(3). The exclusion applied to outright transfers and certain transfers in trust. In the case of a transfer in trust that met the requirements described below the exclusion also prevented application of the GSTT to either a taxable termination on the death of the grandchild or a taxable distribution to the grandchild. The transfer to a grandchild was, of course, subject to the gift tax. The exclusion encouraged very wealthy individuals to give substantial amounts of property to grandchildren at a sharply reduced transfer tax cost.

EXAMPLE 2-53.

Before January 1, 1990, *T*, who was subject to the maximum gift tax rate and had already used her $1 million GSTT exemption, made a gift of $2 million to her grandchild, *GC*. *T* paid a gift tax of $1.1 million on the gift, so her estate was reduced by $3,100,000.

If *T* instead made a testamentary gift of $3,100,000 to *GC* that did not qualify for the $2 million exclusion, *GC* would receive much less. First, the gift would be subject to an estate tax of $1,705,000, leaving $1,395,000. Second, the remainder would be subject to a GSTT of $767,250. Thus, only $627,750 would remain for distribution to *GC* ($1,395,000 − $767,250).

A comparison of the net amount received by *GC* is telling: The inter vivos transfer that qualified for the $2 million exclusion left *GC* with $2 million while the testamentary gift of $3,100,000 that did not qualify for the $2 million exclusion left *GC* with only $627,750.

Under amendments made by the 1988 Act, transfers in trust qualified for the $2 million exclusion only if the following requirements were met:

1. During the lifetime of the grandchild no portion of the corpus or income of the trust may be distributed to or for the benefit of any other person.
2. If the grandchild dies prior to termination of the trust the assets of the trust will be included in the grandchild's gross estate.
3. After the grandchild becomes 21 all of the trust income will be distributed to or for the benefit of the grandchild at least annually.

The third requirement does not apply to transfers made before June 11, 1987.

The $2 million exclusion was only allowed for transfers to grandchildren. It did not apply to transfers made to step-grandchildren. LR 9246007.

§2.42. GSTT PLANNING STRATEGIES

GSTT planning for a particular client should not be done in isolation. Instead, it must be carried out in light of the client's wishes and the constraints imposed by other relevant taxes, particularly the federal income, gift, and estate taxes. Most GSTT planning will involve the application of the basic strategies described in the following subsections.

§2.42.1. Use Each Client's GSTT Exemption

The most basic and important strategy is to make full use of each client's GSTT exemption. In the case of a couple, one of whom is wealthy and the other is not, the clients may wish to assure that the GSTT exemption of each spouse will be used. In order to guard against the possibility that the exemption of the poorer spouse might be wasted if he or she were the first to die, the wealthy spouse might make a lifetime gift to the poorer spouse or to a QTIP trust for the benefit of the poorer spouse. *See* §5.23.6.

EXAMPLE 2-54.

W, who is very wealthy, made a gift of $2 million to a QTIP trust for her relatively poor husband, *H*. Upon the death of *H* the trust will continue for the benefit of their issue. The value of the trust will be included in *H's* estate under §2044. Accordingly, *H* will be treated as the transferor of the trust for GSTT purposes. His executor may allocate *H's* GSTT exemption to the trust. Of course, if the value of the trust property is greater than $2 million at the time of *H's* death, *H's* exemption will not be sufficient to reduce the trust's inclusion ratio to zero. However, greater flexibility and optimal use of *H's* GSTT exemption may be achieved if *H* is given a special power to appoint the property to, or in trust for, their descendants

Making full use of an individual's GSTT exemption may involve creating separate exempt trusts (*i.e.*, trusts with inclusion ratios of zero) for skip persons and separate nonexempt trusts for nonskip persons.

§2.42.2. Coordinate Use of the GSTT Exemption, the Unified Credit, and the Marital Deduction

The plan for a client should take into account GSTT and estate tax considerations in order to maximize the benefit of the GSTT exemption, the unified credit, and the unlimited marital deduction. An estate plan for the wealthier spouse may involve creating three trusts: (1) a credit shelter trust for the benefit of skip persons (the trustee might also be given discretion to distribute income to the surviving spouse) to which an appropriate part of the decedent's GSTT exemption would be allocated; (2) a QTIP trust funded with an amount equal to the balance of the deceased spouse's GSTT exemption, if any, which would be allocated to this trust; (3) a residuary QTIP trust. Instead of providing explicitly for the creation of a QTIP trust in an amount equal to the unused portion of the decedent's GSTT exemption, the will of the first spouse to die might simply authorize his or her executor to divide the residuary QTIP into two or more trusts with identical provisions. *See* §2.27; LR 9002014. The deceased spouse's GSTT exemption would be allocated to the unified credit trust and the smaller QTIP trust. The full benefit of the GSTT exemption of the deceased spouse might be preserved by providing that any distributions of principal to the surviving spouse should be made from the nonexempt residuary QTIP.

Continuing, a reverse QTIP election would be made with respect to the smaller QTIP trust and the balance of the decedent's GSTT exemption would be allocated to it. As a result it would have an inclusion ratio of zero. The deceased spouse's will might also provide that the exempt trusts (unified credit and smaller QTIP trusts) would continue for the benefit of skip persons (grandchildren or great-grandchildren) following the death of the surviving spouse. In addition, the surviving spouse might be given a special power of appointment over the trusts, which would allow the survivor the greatest planning flexibility. For example, the survivor could appoint nonexempt property to nonskip persons (*e.g.,* grandchildren whose parents predeceased the survivor) and exempt property to, or in trust for, skip persons. Upon the death of the surviving spouse distributions might be made from the nonexempt trust to children or other nonskip persons.

The effects of making a reverse QTIP election and allocating the GSTT exemptions are illustrated by Rev. Rul. 92-26, 92-1 C.B. 314. The decedent *D* involved in that ruling died in 1987 leaving a will that gave *D's* residuary estate as follows: (1) $600,000 outright to *D's* child, *C*; (2) $1 million to a trust to pay income to *D's* surviving spouse, *S*, for life, the remainder of which was distributable to their grandchild, *G*; and (3) the balance to a trust (the "second trust"), the income of which was payable to *S* for life, with the remainder to *C* if *C* was then living, otherwise to *G*. The decedent's executor elected to treat the $1 million trust as QTIP, made a reverse QTIP election with respect to it, and allocated the decedent's remaining $800,000 GSTT exemption to it. The executor also elected to treat the second trust as QTIP. The decedent's child, *C*, died in 1990, and the surviving spouse *S* died in 1991. As a result the corpus of each trust was distributed to the grandchild, *G*.

The IRS ruled first that the gift of $600,000 to *C* was not a generation-skipping transfer because *C* was not a skip person. Second, by reason of the QTIP election and §2044 the property of the $1 million trust and the second trust were both includible in *S's* gross estate. However, by reason of the reverse QTIP election for GSTT purposes *D* was treated as the transferor of the $1 million trust. *S* was treated as the transferor of the second trust.

Third, the death of *S* caused a taxable termination of the $1 million trust. The distribution to *G* after the death of *S* was not a direct skip from *D* because the transferor, *D*, was not subject to an estate or gift tax at the time of the distribution. The prior allocation of the remainder of *D's* GSTT exemption sheltered a portion of the distribution from the GSTT. [Presumably, the inclusion ratio was 20 percent (1 − ($800,000 / $1,000,000)) and the applicable rate of tax was 11 percent (20% x 55%).] The predeceased parent exclusion was not applicable because the distribution was a taxable termination and not a direct skip.

Fourth, apart from the application of the predeceased parent exclusion the distribution from the second trust would have been a direct skip. As indicated in Rev. Rul. 92-26, "the general statutory framework indicates that a direct skip takes precedence over taxable terminations as well as taxable distributions." Because *C* predeceased *S* the predeceased parent exclusion operates to move *G* up a generation. According to Rev. Rul. 92-26, "the generation assignment of the grandchild is raised one generation level under section 2612(c)(2), thereby treating the grandchild as the surviving grandparent's child, [as a result of which] the distribution is not a direct skip."

To the extent the estate tax applicable exclusion amount and the GSTT exemption amount remain the same, however (as has been the case since 2004), there is less need for reverse QTIP elections. *See* § 2.28.

§ 2.42.3. Make Nontaxable Gifts, § 2642(c)

Clients should be encouraged to consider making inter vivos gifts to or for the benefit of skip persons that are treated as nontaxable for GSTT purposes. Under § 2642(c), direct skips that are nontaxable have a zero inclusion ratio. Nontaxable gifts are ones that qualify for the annual gift tax exclusion (including gifts that are split with a spouse under § 2513) and qualified transfers (*i.e.,* tuition paid directly by the donor to an educational institution and expenses of medical care paid directly by the donor to the person providing the care, § 2503(e)). *See* § 2.30. Gifts in trust qualify as nontaxable gifts if (1) distributions of income and principal can only be made for the benefit of the donee during his or her lifetime, and (2) the assets of the trust will be included in the donee's estate if he or she dies prior to receiving distribution of the trust assets. § 2642(c)(2).

A client might take advantage of this strategy by making outright annual exclusion gifts to skip persons (grandchildren or great-grandchildren) and by paying the cost of their tuition or the expenses of their medical care. As an alternative, gifts might be made to separate trusts that qualify for the annual gift tax exclusion and meet the additional requirements of § 2642(c)(2). Presumably such gifts can be made to a single trust, a separate share of which is held for each beneficiary. Maximum leverage might be obtained by making annual exclusion gifts to irrevocable life insurance trusts that meet the requirements of § 2642(c)(2).

§ 2.42.4. Make Inter Vivos Direct Skips

The cost of making generation-skipping transfers is lowest for GSTT inter vivos direct skips (*e.g.,* outright gifts to grandchildren and great-grandchildren). This is because the GSTT is determined on a tax exclusive basis. *See* § 2.32. Also, making gifts early maximizes the shelter provided by the GSTT exemption. In particular, the strategy avoids subjecting further growth in value to the GSTT.

§ 2.42.5. Preserve Status of Trusts That Are Exempt Under Effective Date Rules

Care should be taken not to jeopardize the grandfathered status of trusts that are exempt under the effective date rules. Insofar as possible, planning should be done in ways that take advantage of the existence of preexisting exempt trusts. Additional property should not be transferred to a preexisting trust that is exempt from the GSTT. Also, a preexisting trust should not be amended in any way that affects the beneficial interests in the trust. Fortunately, the exercise of a special power of appointment over a grandfathered trust does not subject the trust to the GSTT. *E.g.,* LRs 9241025; 9221037; 9235030. In LR 9330008, the IRS ruled that a decedent's exercise of a special power of appointment under a grandfathered trust did not cause the trust to become subject to the GSTT. The exercise did not postpone the vesting of the property beyond the lives of beneficiaries who were in being at the time the trust became irrevocable (1974).

EXAMPLE 2-55.

In 1984, *T* transferred $1 million to an irrevocable trust which gave the independent trustee discretion to distribute income and principal, from time to time, to those of *T's* issue who are living. Under the effective date rules the trust is exempt from application of the GSTT. *T*, who has already used his GSTT exemption, now wishes to make additional property available to his issue. Property should not be added to the 1984 trust because it is wholly exempt from the GSTT. Instead, *T* might transfer an equivalent amount to a similar trust. In order to minimize GSTT costs the trustee could make distributions from the exempt trust to skip persons and from the new trust to nonskip persons. No GSTT would be incurred on distributions from the new trust that were qualified transfers under § 2503(e).

Regulations under § 643 give general recognition to a trustee's allocation of principal to income under state laws that permit equitable adjustments to be made and ones that allow private unitrusts. *See* Chapter 10. In so far as generation-skipping trusts are concerned, the regulations provide that the administration of a trust in accordance with a state law that defines income as a unitrust amount or permits the trustee to adjust between income and principal in an impartial manner will not be considered to shift the beneficial interests in a trust. Reg. § 26.2601-1(b)(4)(i)(D)(2). Accordingly, it would not affect the grandfathered status of such a trust.

Note that under Reg. § 26.2601-1(b)(1)(v)(B), the exercise of a special power of appointment (*i.e.,* one that is not a general power under § 2041) is generally not treated as a constructive addition to a grandfathered trust. The exercise of special testamentary powers of appointment does not affect the status of a grandfathered trust. *E.g.,* LR 200206045. The regulations permit an exercise that does not postpone vesting for longer than the common law period of the Rule Against Perpetuities or the 90-year gross period that is permitted by the Uniform Rule Against Perpetuities. Reg. § 26.2601-1(b)(1)(v)(B)(2). Likewise, the release of a pre-October 22, 1942, general power of appointment and the disclaimer of interests in a trust that is exempt under the effective date rules does not jeopardize the exempt status of the trust. LR 9245011.

In contrast, the exercise, lapse or release of a general power of appointment that is a taxable transfer under Chapters 11 or 12 is treated as if the power holder had withdrawn the property and retransferred it to the trust. Reg. § 26.2601-1(b)(1)(v)(A). A divided Tax Court upheld the validity of this regulation in *Estate of Eleanor R. Gerson*, 127 T.C. 139 (2006). The regulation was amended in 2000 specifically to carve out the exception for general powers of appointment. The amendment was in response to a 1999 decision of the Eighth Circuit in which the court held that the exercise, lapse or release of a general power of appointment had no effect on the trust's grandfathered status. The estate in *Gerson* argued that the amendment was an invalid attempt by Treasury to re-write the statute and override the Eighth Circuit, but the majority agreed with the IRS that because the statute is silent on the treatment of transfers pursuant to a general power of appointment, Treasury's amendment "reasonably fills the statutory gap." Moreover, said the majority, "the regulation is consistent with the general proposition under the GST tax regime that a decedent who dies holding a general power of appointment over property is treated as the transferor of that property for purposes of GST tax." The dissenters believed the statute is not ambiguous on this point—to the extent the statute clearly applies to any transfer under a trust that was irrevocable on September 25, 1985, there is no need for Treasury to promulgate an interpretive regulation that narrows the scope of the statute in contravention of its plain meaning. On appeal, the Sixth Circuit affirmed. 507 F.3d 435 (6th Cir. 2007). It held that the statute was not clear as to whether the exercise of a power of appointment over a grandfathered trust was supposed to be protected by the grandfathering rule. Accordingly, the court held it was appropriate to rely upon the Service's regulation as a reasonable choice of two conflicting interpretations.

Pre-October 22, 1986 Instruments of Incompetents. Property that remains in trust and direct skips made under instruments executed prior to October 22, 1986 are not subject to Chapter 13 if the transferor was incompetent on that date, did not regain competency prior to his or her death, and the property is included in the transferor's gross estate. Reg. §26.2601-1(b)(3)(i). In some instances this rule can be effectively coupled with the use of disclaimers. For example, the IRS concluded that the GSTT would not apply to direct skips made to grandnephews and grandnieces as a result of disclaimers made by nephews of the right to receive the outright distribution of property under a will executed prior to October 22, 1986 where the testator was incompetent on that date and at all subsequent times. PLR 9111011.

Permissible Changes and Modifications. In general, modifications that do not affect the quality, value, or timing of any beneficiary's interests in an exempt trust will not cause it to lose its status. *E.g.*, LRs 9222042, 9324007, 9324014, 9324015, 9507016, 9528012, 9545009, and 9607011. For example, LR 9222042 permitted a change of provisions relating to selection and removal of trustees, compensation of trustees, and accounting by trustees and LR 9247020 allowed a change in provisions regarding selection of trustees. On the other hand, modifications that change the nature of the beneficiaries' interests would cause an exempt trust to lose its status and become subject to the GSTT. *E.g.*, LR 9244019.

Regulations specify the types of changes and modifications that will not jeopardize the exempt status of a grandfathered trust. Reg. §26.2601-1(b)(4)(i). Among other things, the regulations allow some types of modifications to be made without losing the grandfathered status of a trust, including: (1) certain discretionary actions regarding the distribution or retention of the principal of an exempt trust; (2) court-approved settlements of bona fide disputes regarding the administration of an exempt trust or its construction; (3) judicial construction of an ambiguity or the correction of a scrivener's error; and (4) other judicial or valid nonjudicial modifications that do not shift a beneficial interest to any beneficiary who is in a lower generation than the beneficiary who previously held the interest and does not extend the time for vesting any beneficial interest beyond the original period specified in the instrument. The regulations contain several helpful examples. The regulations regarding modification of grandfathered trusts are reviewed in Carol Harrington's paper, *Changing Grandfathered Generation-Skipping Trusts,* U. Miami, 35th Inst. Est. Plan., Ch. 10 (2001).

In LR 200305024, the IRS approved the modification of a grandfathered trust under which the trustees could distribute the greater of (1) the income of the trust, or (2) a unitrust amount of between 3 and 5 percent. According to the ruling, the change did not shift any interest to a beneficiary below the generation of those who held beneficial interests prior to the modification.

In Revenue Procedure 95-50, 1995-2 C.B. 430, the IRS stated that it would no longer issue advance rulings regarding whether a grandfathered trust would lose its exempt status if the situs of the trust is changed from the United States to a foreign situs.

Untimely Disclaimers as Additional Contributions. Untimely disclaimers of interests in a grandfathered trust are not qualified disclaimers. LR 9627010. Accordingly, the disclaimers constituted additions to the trusts by the disclaimants, which are subject to the GSTT.

Release, Lapse or Exercise of General Powers of Appointment. Under Reg. § 26.2601-1(b)(1)(v)(A) the exercise, lapse or release of a general power of appointment over a grandfathered trust that results in a taxable transfer under Chapter 11 or 12 is treated as a constructive addition to the trust. However, two Federal Courts of Appeal reached opposite conclusions regarding the application of the GSTT to grandfathered trusts where the surviving spouse held a general testamentary power of appointment. In the first case, the Second Circuit held that the GSTT applied to property with respect to which the surviving spouse allowed the power to lapse. *E. Norman Peterson Marital Trust v. Commissioner,* 78 F.3d 795 (2d Cir. 1996). In the later case the Eighth Circuit held that the GSTT did not apply to the property with respect to property over which the surviving spouse exercised a general power of appointment over a grandfathered trust, *Simpson v. United States,* 183 F.3d 812 (8th Cir. 1999), *nonacq.,* A.O.D. 2000-3.

The *Peterson* decision concluded that the property of a grandfathered marital deduction trust over which the survivor's general power of appointment lapsed as to most of the property was subject to the GSTT. At the time of the widow's death a temporary regulation provided that property which remained in a pre-1985 trust after the lapse, release, or exercise of a general power of appointment was treated as an addition to the trust. The court upheld the regulation and the policy behind it. Along the way the court stated that, "For tax purposes, a general power of appointment has for many, many years been viewed as essentially identical to outright ownership of the property."

The opinion in *Simpson v. United States,* 183 F.3d 812 (8th Cir. 1999), relies on the text of § 1433(b)(2)(A) of the act adopting the GSTT, which states that the tax would not apply to "any generation-skipping transfer under a trust which was irrevocable on September 25, 1985, but only to the extent such transfer is not made out of corpus added to the trust after September 25, 1985." The trust involved in the case was irrevocable on September 25, 1985, the power of appointment was a transfer "under" the trust, and there was no addition to the trust after that date. Interestingly, Simpson appears to be based on the same facts as LR 9630003. In it the surviving spouse's 1982 will exercised a general testamentary power of appointment over a marital trust established in 1966 by appointing the property to her eight grandchildren. The ruling treated the surviving spouse as the transferor of the property of the trust because it was includible in her estate under §2041. §2652(a)(1). The *Simpson* approach was later followed by the Ninth Circuit. *Schuler v. United States*, 281 F.3d 1078 (9th Cir. 2002). In *Bachler v. Commissioner*, 281 F.3d 1078 (9th Cir. 2002), the Ninth Circuit also agreed with the *Simpson* analysis: The exercise of a general power of appointment granted by a pre-1985 grandfathered trust did not subject the appointive property to the GSTT.

In response to the *Simpson* decision, the IRS amended Reg. §26.2601-1(b)(1)(i) to clarify the status of grandfathered trusts that are subject to general powers of appointment. The amended regulation provides:

> The provisions of chapter 13 do not apply to any generation-skipping transfer under a trust (as defined in section 2652(b)) that was irrevocable on September 25, 1985 . . . . Further, the rule in the first sentence of this paragraph (b)(1)(i) does not apply to the transfer of property pursuant to the exercise, release, or lapse of a general power of appointment that is treated as a taxable transfer under chapter 11 or chapter 12.

§2.42.6. Create and Administer Trusts in Light of Prior Use of GSTT Exemption

Trusts should be created and administered in ways that maximize the benefit of the allocation that has been made of the transferor's GSTT exemption. In particular, gifts might be made to, or separate trusts might be created for, each generation of beneficiaries (*i.e.*, the gifts might be "layered"). Making gifts to or for the exclusive benefit of children is desirable because gifts to children (or to the children of deceased children under the orphan grandchild exclusion) are not subject to the GSTT. Distributions made from nonexempt trusts to children are also not subject to the GSTT. Thus, distributions from exempt trusts should be made to skip persons and distributions from nonexempt trusts should be made to nonskip persons. Note, however, that property of a nonexempt trust could be used to pay the tuition and medical care expenses of skip persons without incurring any GSTT liability. Under §2611(b), such distributions are not generation-skipping transfers. Planning at all stages should take into account the predeceased parent exclusion. *See* §2612(c)(2).

§2.42.7. Make Use of the Predeceased Parent Exclusion, §2651(e)

Wills and trusts should be planned in ways that permit appointments and distributions to be made in light of the predeceased parent exclusion of §2651(e). If the transferor's child is deceased at the time a transfer is made, the children of the deceased child and more remote descendants move up one generation. Thus, for generation-skipping transfer tax purposes, a child of the deceased child is treated as the transferor's child.

In determining whether a transfer to, or for, the benefit of a lineal descendant of a parent of the transferor is a generation-skipping transfer, the descendant "moves up a generation" if his or her own parent is deceased. For purposes of this rule, anyone who dies within 90 days following a transfer that occurs by reason of the transferor's death, is treated as having predeceased the transferor. Reg. §26.2651-1(a)(2)(iii).

Section 2651(e), which was added by the 1997 Act, extended the predeceased parent exception in two ways; however, the exception is only available if the transferor has no living descendants. The change will benefit a relatively small class of taxpayers those with no lineal descendants, who wish to transfer property to collaterals, such as grandnieces and grandnephews, whose parents were not living at the time of the transfer.

First, if the transferor has no living descendant, the exception is extended to descendants of a parent of the transferor (or his spouse or former spouse) whose parent is deceased. Thus, the exception extends to the descendants of the transferor's nieces and nephews.

Second, according to the Conference Report, the exception is extended to apply to taxable terminations and taxable distributions, "provided that the parent of the relevant beneficiary was dead at the earliest time that the transfer (from which the beneficiary's interest in the property was established) was subject to estate or gift tax."

EXAMPLE 2-56.

W died in 1997 leaving $600,000 to a credit shelter trust, $400,000 to a QTIP trust, and her residuary estate of $2 million to another QTIP. W's $1 million GSTT exemption was allocated to the credit shelter trust and the $400,000 QTIP trust. W was survived by H, her husband, and their two children, A and B. A reverse QTIP election was made with respect to the smaller QTIP trust. Both the credit shelter and the smaller QTIP trusts have inclusion ratios of zero.

A died recently survived by his two children, GS and GD, and H. Accordingly, when H dies GS and GD will be treated as his children (i.e., nonskip persons) for GSTT purposes. W's GSTT exemption would be wasted to the extent the property of the unified credit and smaller QTIP trusts is distributed to B, a nonskip person. GS and GD are skip persons as to W, who remained the transferor of those trusts for GSTT purposes. The value of W's GSTT exemption could be fully preserved if H had a special power of appointment over the trusts. The exercise of the power should be made in light of two important GSTT considerations: (1) that B, GS, and GD are all nonskip persons as to H, and (2) that the unified credit and smaller QTIP trusts created by W are exempt from the GSTT. Accordingly, H might exercise a special power over the exempt trusts in a way that maximizes the benefit of their exempt status. Thus, H might appoint the property of those trusts to GS and GD and make compensating gifts to B or act to continue the trusts for as long as possible. H's GSTT exemption could be used to shelter outright gifts to the children of B or the establishment of trusts for their benefit.

Regulations offer rules and examples for applying the predeceased parent rule of §2651(e). Regulation §26.2651-1(a)(3) provides that an individual's interest in property or a trust is established or derived at the time the transferor is subject to federal estate or gift tax. If a transferor is subject to federal wealth transfer tax on the property transferred on more than one occasion, then the individual's interest will be considered established or derived on the earliest of those occasions. The regulation carves out an exception for remainder interests in trusts for which a QTIP election under §2056(b)(7) has been made: To the extent of the QTIP election, the remainder beneficiary's interest will be deemed to have been established or derived on the death of the transferor's spouse (the income beneficiary), rather than on the transferor's earlier death. But for this exception, a remainder beneficiary of a QTIP trust would not be eligible for the predeceased parent rule if the remainder beneficiary's parent is alive when the QTIP trust is established, but is deceased when the income beneficiary's interest terminates. The exception does not apply to any trust for which a reverse QTIP election is made under §2652(a)(3). In such cases, the grantor remains the transferor of the trust for GSTT purposes.

§2.42.8. Consider Authorizing Trustees to Make Distributions and to Amend Trust

Trusts can be drafted to allow trustees to take advantage of the unified credits and GSTT exemptions of first generation beneficiaries. In particular, trusts can permit trustees to make outright distributions to the transferor's children or other nonskip persons. As a result of the distributions the children (or other distributees) would own the property and the original transferor would no longer be connected with it for GSTT purposes. The same goal can be achieved if an independent trustee exercised a power to grant a general power of appointment to a child or another nonskip person. Granting the power would cause the property to be included in the child's estate as a result of which the child would become the transferor for GSTT purposes. The power given to the child could be the narrowest that would cause the property to be included in the child's estate and cause the child to become the transferor of the property for GSTT purposes. Thus, the child might be given the power, exercisable jointly with the trustee or another nonadverse party to appoint the property to the creditors of the child's estate. As an alternative the holder of a special power of appointment might investigate the consequences of exercising the power to create a presently exercisable general power of appointment. *See* §2041(a)(3). *See also* §2.32.

§2.42.9. GSTT and Redemption of Stock Under §303

Under §303(d), any GSTT paid by reason of a generation-skipping transfer of stock taking place at or after the death of any individual may qualify for redemption under §303. *See* §11.14. The benefit of §303, however, applies only to the extent the interest of the redeeming shareholder is reduced directly or through a binding agreement to contribute to the death and GST taxes and funeral and administrative expenses. Planning can become quite complicated where it involves the marital deduction, the GSTT exemption, and possible redemptions under §303. The benefits of the GSTT exemption and the possibility that redemptions would qualify under §303 are preserved if the obligation to pay the federal estate tax on the QTIP, to which some or all of the deceased spouse's GSTT exemption has been allocated, is imposed on stock that is not QTIP (*e.g.,* stock that is includible in the estate of the surviving other than QTIP). Beware, however, that the IRS may argue that payment of the GSTT from other property may constitute a constructive addition to the trust. *See* Budin, GST Provisions May Limit Section 303 Redemptions, 17 Estates, Gifts & Tr. J. 146 (Sept./Oct. 1992).

F. WEALTH TRANSFER TAX SYSTEM FOR NONRESIDENTS AND EXPATRIATES

§ 2.43. NONRESIDENT ALIENS

§ 2.43.1. Overview

Subject to the provisions of a treaty between the United States and another country, the regulations make it clear that the gift and estate taxes do not apply to an individual who is neither a citizen nor a resident of the United States. The gift and estate taxes do, however, apply to property that has a United States situs. First, underReg. § 20.2103-1, "in the case of a nonresident not a citizen, only that part of the entire gross estate which on the date of the decedent's death is situated in the United States is included in his taxable estate." Second, underReg. § 25.2501-1(a)(1), the gift tax applies to gifts of "all property, wherever situated, by an individual who is a citizen or resident of the United States." Finally, underReg. § 25.2501-1(a)(3)(i), "The gift tax does not apply to any transfer or gift of intangible property on or after January 1, 1967, made by a non-resident not a citizen of the United States whether or not he was engaged in business in the United States, unless the donor is an expatriate who lost his U.S. citizenship after March 8, 1967, and within the 10-years ending with the date of transfer. . . . " Given these rules, it is important for nonresident aliens not to own directly any real property located in the United States or other assets with a United States situs.

§ 2.43.2. Gift Tax

In general, the United States gift tax applies to gifts by nonresidents except ones of intangible personal property. Under § 2501(a)(2) the gift tax does not apply to "the transfer of intangible property by a nonresident not a citizen of the United States." In addition, § 2511(a) provides that "in the case of a nonresident not a citizen of the United States" the tax applies only "if the property is situated within the United States." The gift tax does not apply to contributions made to a political organization, as defined in§ 527(e)(1), for the use of the organization. IRC § 2501(a)(5); Reg. § 25.2501-1(a)(5).

Applying the foregoing principle, no gift tax is due on a gift of stock in a Canadian corporation made by a Canadian citizen who intends to move to the United States. LR 9347014. The gift will be complete in the year of the transfer although the gift is made to a trust of which the donor will be trustee and his children will be the beneficiaries. The trust will be irrevocable, and distributions will be limited by an ascertainable standard. Citing *Jennings v. Smith*, 161 F.2d 74 (2d Cir. 1947), the IRS also ruled that the trust would not be included in the donor's estate under § § 2036 or 2038 because his power to make distributions is limited by an ascertainable standard.

Income Tax Note. Under the former law the income of a grantor trust established by a nonresident alien could be taxable to the alien for his or her lifetime and not to the resident distributees. See Rev. Rul. 69-70, 1969-1 C.B. 182. The Small Business Job Protection Act of 1996 amended § 672(f) to provide that the grantor trust rules only apply to the extent they cause a portion of a trust to be treated as owned by a United States citizen, resident, or domestic corporation. *See* Reg. § 1.672(f)-1(a). The income tax consequences of gifts to trusts, including rules applicable to foreign trusts, are discussed in Chapter 10.

Charitable Deduction. Charitable gifts made by a nonresident alien are governed by the same rules as those applicable to citizens, except that they are subject to two additional restrictions: (1) Gifts made to a corporation qualify only if it is created or organized under the laws of the United States or a state or territory of the United States, and (2) gifts such as those to a trust or community chest qualify only if they must be used within the United States exclusively for religious, charitable, educational, scientific, or literary purposes, including the encouragement of art and the prevention of cruelty to children or animals. Reg. § 25.2522(b)-1.

Marital Deduction. Section 2523 allows an unlimited marital deduction for qualifying gifts made by a citizen or resident of the United States to a spouse who is a citizen of the United States. As indicated in § 2.5.8, the marital deduction for gifts made on or after July 14, 1988 is limited to gifts made to citizens of the United States. § 2523(i). However, an annual exclusion of $100,000 is allowable for gifts made to a spouse who is not a citizen of the United States. § 2523(i)(2). This exemption, adjusted for post-1997 inflation, is $136,000 in 2011.

§ 2.43.3. Estate Tax

The gross estate of a person who is neither a citizen nor a resident of the United States (a nonresident alien) includes only assets that have a situs in the United States. § 2001(a), Reg. § 20.0-1(b)(1). For this purpose, "resident" means a person who is domiciled in the United States "A person acquires a domicile in a place by living there, for even a brief period of time, with no definite present intention of later removing therefrom. Residence without the requisite intent to remain indefinitely will not suffice to constitute domicile." Reg. § 20.0-1(b)(1). A person who is present in the United States under a temporary visa may violate the terms of the visa and establish a domicile in the United States. *Estate of Jack v. United States*, 90 A.F.T.R.2d 7580 (RIA) (Ct. Cl. 2002) (cross motions for summary judgment denied).

The amount of deductions that are allowable with respect to the estate of a nonresident alien may be limited by § 2106(a). Under that section the proportion of § 2053 and 2054 items deductible under § 2106 is determined by the ratio that "the value of that part of the decedent's gross estate situated in the United States at the time of his death bears to the value of the decedent's entire gross estate wherever situated." Reg. § 20.2106-1(a)(2). *See* § § 9.9 and 12.11.

Under paragraph 1 of Article XXIX-B of the 1980 United States-Canada Tax Convention, as modified in 1995, a charitable deduction is allowable for a transfer of property subject to the United States estate tax that is made to an exempt charity located in either contracting state. The Treasury's Technical Explanation states:

A bequest by a U.S. citizen or U.S. resident (as defined for estate tax purposes under the Internal Revenue Code) to such an exempt organization generally is deductible for U.S. estate tax purposes under section 2055 of the Internal Revenue Code without regard to whether the organization is a U.S. corporation. However, if the decedent is not a U.S. citizen or U.S. resident (as defined for estate tax purposes under the Internal Revenue Code), such a bequest is deductible for U.S. estate tax purposes, under section 2106(a)(2) of the Internal Revenue Code, only if the recipient organization is a U.S. corporation.

Although the same rate schedule applies to the estates of nonresident aliens, a credit of only $13,000 (equal to the tax on a transfer of $60,000) is allowed unless otherwise required by treaty. §§ 2101-2102.

§ 2.43.4. GSTT and Transfers by Nonresident Aliens

Section 2663(2) authorizes the Secretary to issue "regulations (consistent with the principles of Chapters 11 and 12) providing for the application of this chapter in the case of transferors who are nonresidents not citizens of the United States." The estate and gift taxes, Chapters 11 and 12 respectively, only apply to transfers by nonresidents of property with a United States situs. Proposed regulations that were issued in late 1992 expanded the application of the GSTT far beyond the corresponding scope of the gift and estate taxes. The final regulations adopt a more appropriate, narrower view. Under them the GSTT only applies to the portion of property transferred by a nonresident alien that was subject to the gift or estate tax within the meaning of § 26.2654-1(a)(2). Reg. § 26.2663-2(b) and (c).

§ 2.44. Inheritance Tax on Gifts and Bequests from Expatriates

The Heroes Earnings Assistance and Relief Tax Act of 2008 imposed a new transfer tax applicable to certain wealth transfers by so-called "covered expatriates" to United States citizens or residents on or after June 17, 2008. This particular tax is noteworthy because it is imposed on the recipients of taxable transfers and not upon the donors. § 2801(b).

Under § 2801(a), a United States citizen or resident receiving a "covered gift or bequest" must pay a tax equal to the value of the covered gift or bequest times the highest marginal rate of federal estate tax (or, if greater, the highest marginal rate of federal gift tax). A "covered gift or bequest" is, generally, any gift or bequest from a "covered expatriate." § 2801(e)(1). A "covered expatriate" is an expatriate (that is, a United States citizen that has relinquished citizenship or a long-term United States resident that ceases to be a lawful permanent resident) who: (1) has an average annual net income tax liability for the five prior years of more than $124,000, as adjusted for inflation (the 2010 figure is $145,000); (2) has a net worth of $2 million or more; or (3) fails to certify under penalties of perjury compliance with all federal tax obligations for the five prior years. §§ 877A(g)(1); 2801(f).

Annual Exclusion; Reduction for Foreign Transfer Taxes Paid. The § 2801 tax is only applicable to the extent the cumulative value of all covered gifts and bequests received in a calendar year exceeds the gift tax annual exclusion amount under

§2503(b), §2801(c), and the amount of tax otherwise due under §2801 is reduced by the amount of any gift tax or estate tax paid to a foreign country with respect to such covered gift or bequest. §2801(d).

Certain Covered Gifts and Bequests Not Subject to Tax. The §2801 tax does not apply to any property reported as a taxable gift on a Form 709 filed by the covered expatriate or to any property included in the gross estate on a Form 706 filed by the estate of the covered expatriate. §2801(e)(2). The charitable and marital deductions apply here, too, so charities and spouses will not be subject to this tax. §2801(e)(3).

Covered Gifts and Bequests Made in Trust. In the case of covered gifts or bequests made to a domestic trust, the tax applies as if the trust is a United States citizen, and it is the trust that must pay the tax. §2801(e)(4)(A). Upon a covered gift or bequest to a foreign trust, the tax applies upon a distribution to a United States citizen or resident from the trust (regardless of whether the distribution consists of income or principal) that is attributable to the covered gift or bequest. §2801(e)(4)(B)(i). Thus, the recipient will pay the tax upon distribution, but he or she may claim an income tax deduction for the amount of tax paid to the extent the tax is imposed on that portion of the distribution that is included in the recipient's gross income. §2801(e)(4)(B)(ii). A foreign trust may elect to be treated as a domestic trust for this purpose, but the election cannot be revoked without the Service's consent. §2801(e)(4)(B)(iii).

G. BASIC LIFETIME ESTATE PLANNING TAX STRATEGIES

§2.45. OVERVIEW

This part describes the general strategies or approaches at the heart of most estate plans. Any of these general strategies can be achieved in a variety of ways, some of which may have different tax and nontax consequences. In some instances the use of a specific technique may serve more than one general goal. For example, the gift of an income-producing asset achieves two goals: (1) shifting future income to the donee and (2) reducing (or freezing) the size of the donor's estate for transfer tax purposes. While every client's estate plan must be based first and foremost upon the client's wishes, the methods of achieving the client's goals should be formulated in light of important tax considerations, which include the gift tax and GSTT exclusions, the unified credit, and the GSTT exemption. Where possible, the client's program should take full advantage of the gift tax annual exclusion, the exclusions for the direct payment of the tuition or medical expenses of a donee (which are also available for GSTT purposes), gift splitting between the client and the client's spouse, and the marital deduction. A substantial gift program might consume the unified credits of the client and the client's spouse.

Clients should also consider steps that will reduce current or future income tax liabilities, including contributions to regular or Roth IRAs and, perhaps, the purchasing of deferred annuities. Some clients may also wish to contribute to qualified tuition programs established by states or eligible educational institutions pursuant to §529. *See* §§2.6, 2.12. As indicated at §2.6, contributions to qualified plans are treated preferentially, as are distributions made to pay qualified higher education expenses.

Many estate planning devices were affected by the 1986 Act, which reduced and compressed the income tax rates and eliminated most of the income tax advantages of the "sophisticated" income tax shelters that proliferated in the early 1980s. Some relatively simple income tax shelters remain, such as tax-exempt municipal bonds and retirement funds. Post-mortem planning strategies are considered in detail in Chapter 12.

The following lifetime strategies are discussed in this part:

1. Shift income within the family;

2. Reduce the size of the estate;

3. Freeze the value of the estate;

4. Bypass the estates of survivors; and

5. Defer the payment of estate taxes.

As mentioned above, each of these general strategies can usually be carried out in a variety of ways. For example, several relatively simple techniques remain available by which the value of a client's estate may be frozen, such as gifts (outright or in trust), installment sales, and transfers of property in exchange for a private annuity. *See* Chapters 7 and 9. The estate planning techniques that will be recommended to a particular client will vary, of course, depending upon his or her overall circumstances. As always, the content of an estate plan should be designed to carry out the client's tax and nontax objectives.

Selecting the Property to Give. The factors that should be considered in formulating a gift plan are reviewed in Chapter 7. They include the characteristics of the property that might be given, the tax rates applicable to the donor and prospective donees and their age, experience, and physical condition. Under the general rules, the donor's basis in property carries over to the donee. However, for purposes of determining loss, the donee's basis cannot exceed the value of the property on the date of the gift. For that reason, a donor should generally not make a gift of property that has declined in value. Instead, the donor should consider giving the donee other property or selling the property, getting the tax benefit of a capital loss, and giving the proceeds to the donee.

§2.46. SHIFT INCOME WITHIN THE FAMILY

Over the past 20 years, individual income tax rates have compressed to the point that relatively little income tax advantage is produced by shifting income within the family. However, the strategy can produce some limited income tax benefits and can shift some wealth from the donor to others. Shifting income is also worth considering because of the possibility that future income tax rates may be more progressive. In brief, a family unit may enjoy an income tax benefit if investment income is divided among more family members, particularly ones with little or no other income. A shift of income from family members who are subject to the maximum rate to ones subject to lower rates results in an increase in the family's after-tax income.

EXAMPLE 2-57.

Mother, *M*, is subject to a marginal income tax rate of 31 percent. Her two children each have modest taxable incomes subject to a marginal rate of 15 percent. If *M* could deflect, say, $10,000 of taxable income to each of her children, the family's overall annual income tax liability might be cut by $3,200 ($20,000 × (31%–15%)).

Of course, under the "Kiddie Tax," the unearned income of most children under 19 (and full-time students under 24) is taxed at the maximum rate applicable to the parents. § 1(g). See § 7.9.1. Accordingly, the opportunity to shift taxable unearned income to minor children has been severely restricted. Until 2006, the Kiddie Tax only applied to the unearned income of children under 14.

A variation on the basic approach involves creating additional taxpayers (trusts and corporations) with whom the family income may be split. However, only a very small amount of the income of a trust or estate is subject to the lowest rate (15 percent).

The differences in the rates applicable to trusts and estates and to unmarried individuals are shown in Table 2-4.

Table 2-4
Income Tax Rates For 2011

Trusts and Estates		Unmarried Individuals	
Taxable Income	*Tax & Rate*	*Taxable Income*	*Tax & Rate*
		$0-$8,500	10%
$0–$2,300	15%	$8,501–$34,500	$850 + 15% on amount over $8,500
$2,301–$5,450	$345 + 25% on amount over $2,300	$34,501–$83,600	$4,750 + 25% on amount over $34,500
$5,451–$8,300	$1,132.50 + 28% on amount over $5,450	$83,601–$174,400	$17,025 + 28% on amount over $83,600
$8,301–$11,350	$1,930.50 + 33% on amount over $8,300	$174,401–$397,150	$42,449 + 33% on amount over $174,400
$11,351 and over	$2,937.50 + 35% on amount over $11,350	$397,171 and over	$110,061.50 + 35% on amount over $379,150

§ 2.46.1. Methods

Clients can select from a variety of methods by which income can be shifted within the family. However, most require the donor to give up the property permanently. They are, consequently, beyond the means of most taxpayers. An outright gift to a donee is an example of such a gift. *See* § 7.2.1. Of course, where the donee is a minor, the gift should be made in a way that avoids the necessity of a guardianship. For example, the gift might be made to a custodian under the Uniform Transfer to Minors Act (or the Uniform Gift to Minors Act) or to the trustee of a trust for the minor. *See* §§7.35-7.37. Income may also be shifted by more indirect means, such as by deflecting business or investment opportunities to a child. *See* §7.18.

The enactment of §7872 in 1986 ended the opportunity for clients with a surplus of cash to shift income by making interest-free demand loans to their children, other family members, or to trusts. Also, the decision in *Dickman v. Commissioner*, 465 U.S. 330 (1984), recognized that interest-free demand loans result in a taxable gift of the use of the transferred funds.

§2.46.2. The Assignment of Income Doctrine

> But this case is not to be decided by attenuated subtleties. It turns on the import and reasonable construction of the taxing act. There is no doubt that the statute could tax salaries to those who earned them and provide that the tax could not be escaped by anticipatory arrangements and contracts however skillfully devised to prevent the salary when paid from vesting even for a second in the man who earned it. That seems to us the import of the statute before us and we think that no distinction can be taken according to the motives leading to the arrangement by which the fruits are attributed to a different tree from that on which they grew. *Lucas v. Earl*, 281 U.S. 111, 114-115 (1930).

As indicated by a host of Supreme Court decisions, an assignment of income alone is not effective to shift the tax incidence from the assignor to the assignee. *E.g., Helvering v. Horst*, 311 U.S. 112 (1940) (father taxable on bond interest where interest coupon detached and given to son prior to payment date); *Lucas v. Earl, supra* (husband remained taxable on personal service income that he contracted to give to his wife). In general, the law distinguishes between a gift of property, which is usually effective to shift the income from the property, and a gift of the "mere" right to receive income, which is usually not effective to shift the income. That distinction is the origin of the famous fruit and tree metaphor that appears in the above quotation from *Lucas v. Earl*. However, differentiating between "property" and a "right to income" can be difficult in some cases. Because of that problem some arbitrary rules have grown up, as illustrated by the tax consequences of the assignment of the income interest in a trust.

In *Blair v. Commissioner*, 300 U.S. 5 (1937), the Supreme Court held that a life income beneficiary's gratuitous assignment of his interest in the trust income constituted a transfer of an equitable property interest sufficient to shift the income to the assignee. In a subsequent case the Court ruled that the transfer of one year's trust income was not sufficient to shift the income to the assignee. *Harrison v. Shaffner*, 312 U.S. 579 (1941). It reasoned that the donor "has parted with no substantial interest in property other than the specified payments of income which, like other gifts of income, are taxable to the donor." *Id.* at 583. Several later decisions held that assignments of trust income for ten years or more would shift the income to the assignee. *E.g., Hawaiian Trust Co. v. Kanne*, 172 F.2d 74 (9th Cir. 1949). In 1955 the IRS adopted that view, ruling that the trust income would be taxed to the assignee where it was transferred for a period of at least ten years. Rev. Rul. 55-38, 1955-1 C.B. 389.

The ruling was consistent with former § 673, under which the grantor would not be treated as owner of the trust if the reversionary interest of the grantor would not take effect for a period of ten years or more.

§ 2.47. REDUCE THE SIZE OF THE ESTATE: GIFTS AND VALUATION GAMES

> [M]any actions taken by taxpayers in positioning their investment and business assets secure significant transfer tax advantages because those acts depress the value of the property interests involved. This occurs, for example, whenever a deed of real estate splits the ownership of the asset into two or more parts. Wallace, Now You See It, Now You Don't— Valuation Conundrums in Estate Planning, U. Miami, 24th Inst. Est. Plan. ¶ 805.6 (1990).

Reducing the amount of property that is potentially includible in a client's gross estate is a primary estate planning strategy. Outright lifetime gifts are the simplest and most direct way of achieving such a reduction. Of course, as a result of the unification of the gift and estate taxes in 1976, the amount of post-1976 taxable gifts is included in the tax base at the time of the donor's death. The unification of the taxes increased the importance of reducing one's estate by making inter vivos gifts that qualify for the gift tax annual exclusion. Importantly, even deathbed gifts may be excluded from the donor's gross estate. Under § 2035, gifts made within three years of death, other than interests in life insurance, generally are not included in the donor's estate.

Taxable gifts (*i.e.*, ones in excess of the annual exclusion) can also help control the size of a client's gross estate. Although the amount of a taxable gift is includible in the donor's tax base, any subsequent appreciation in value of the transferred property is excluded. The future income from the property is also excluded from the donor's estate. Finally, any gift tax paid more than three years prior to death is not included in the donor's estate. Note that taxable gifts within the amount of the credit equivalent do not require any out of pocket tax cost.

EXAMPLE 2-58.

> In 2009, Donor, *D*, made a gift of stock worth $3,513,000 to her son, *S*. The gift did not require the payment of any gift tax—$13,000 was allowed as a gift tax annual exclusion for 2009 and the tax on the remaining $3.5 million was offset by *D's* unified credit. When *D* died in 2011, the stock *D* gave to *S* was worth $4 million (though that was not entirely typical of most stocks during that time). Because *D* made the gift of stock, *D's* transfer tax base was $487,000 smaller than it would have been without the gift. Of course, any income derived from the stock after the gift was made was also excluded from *D's* estate. By making the gift, the estate tax payable by *D's* estate was reduced by $170,450 ($487,000 × the applicable tax rate of 35 percent).

§2.47.1. Make Gifts to Qualify for Valuation Discounts

The difficulty of valuing property according to a hypothetical sale between a willing buyer and a willing seller at the time of a death or gift is referred to in the following passage from a British tax case:

> The result is that I must enter into a dim world peopled by the indeterminate spirits of fictitious or unborn sales. It is necessary to assume the prophetic vision of a prospective purchaser at the moment of death of the deceased, and firmly to reject the wisdom which might be provided by the knowledge of subsequent events. *Holt v. Inland Revenue Commissioners,* (1953) 2 All E.R. 1499, 1501.

Undivided interests in real estate and minority interests in businesses qualify for discounts that make their valuation particularly favorable—if difficult. *See* §2.14. As a result clients frequently transfer their property, including liquid assets, to limited partnerships or limited liability companies and then make gifts of interests in the partnerships or LLCs that qualify for substantial valuation discounts.

Further, gifts of interests in some types of property may result in a disproportionately large reduction in value of the donor's estate. This may occur, for example, where a gift reduces the donor's stock holding in a closely-held business from a controlling interest to a minority one. Minority interests generally qualify for a substantial discount from the liquidation value of the stock. The same interest may also be discounted for lack of marketability. Similarly, a gift of an undivided interest in real property may reduce the value of the donor's retained interest. The IRS is understandably reluctant to recognize any discount from the liquidation value of stock or real property in the case of gifts to noncharities. It is now more vigilant and vigorous in asserting the value of gifts to charities should reflect appropriate discounts. Despite IRS challenges to the valuation of non-charitable gifts, courts frequently allow substantial discounts that are supported by expert appraisals.

The possibility that a gift may result in a disproportionately large reduction in the value of the donor's retained interest exists because the value of a transfer for gift tax purposes is measured by the value of the property transferred and not the amount by which the transfer reduces the value of the donor's estate. §2512. Securing the proper discount depends upon obtaining reliable appraisals by qualified experts. As a matter of strategy some estate planners hire the appraiser or appraisers most often used by the IRS in valuing the particular type of property that is involved. The following cases illustrate the operation of the existing valuation rules:

A discount of 15 percent or more is typically allowed with respect to fractional interests in real property. *E.g., Estate of Nancy N. Mooneyham,* 60 T.C.M. 860 (1991). In *John R. Moore,* 60 T.C.M. 2650 (1991), the Tax Court allowed a discount of 35 percent for lack of marketability and minority interest with respect to partnership interests (the taxpayers had claimed a discount of 50 percent and the IRS argued for 10 percent). Note, however, that separate undivided interests that are included in a decedent's estate may be united for purposes of valuation, LR 9140002 (TAM). For purposes of estate tax valuation LR 9140002 held that the interests in real property owned by the decedent at the time of his death are appropriately combined with the interests that were includible in his estate under § 2044.

The valuation of gifts of a 25 percent undivided interest in timberlands was at issue in *Estate of Bonnie I. Barge*, 73 T.C.M. (CCH) 2615 (1997). The decedent had reported the gifts at $2,450,002, which her estate contended was appropriate using an income capitalization method. Applying a partition rationale, the IRS proposed a valuation of $12,847,252. Taking into account the cost of a partition action and the estimated four-year delay involved, the Tax Court valued the 25 percent interest at $7,404,649.

In *Stone v. United States*, 2007-1 U.S.T.C. (CCH) ¶ 60,545 (2007), *aff'd*, 2009-1 U.S.T.C. ¶ 60,572 (9th Cir. 2009), the decedent's gross estate included undivided 50-percent interests in 19 paintings. The estate valued these interests at a combined $1.42 million. The value of the 19 paintings, according to an appraisal by Sotheby's, was about $5 million, making the gross liquidation value of the decedent's 50-percent shares about $2.5 million. The estate then applied a 44 percent fractional interest discount to this amount and rounded to nearest ten thousand dollars. The IRS determined that the value of the collection was slightly higher, about $5.4 million, because Sotheby's undervalued two works by Camille Pissarro. The Service then determined that the value properly includible in the decedent's gross estate was about $2.7 million, or half the value of the entire collection. The court agreed with the Service that the Pissarro paintings were undervalued and then ruled that a fractional interest discount is not appropriate for undivided interests in works of art, finding that "a hypothetical seller who is under no compulsion to sell would not accept the 44 percent discount proposed by Plaintiffs. Both of the government's experts . . . testified that, while they were aware of sales of undivided interests in art occurring, none of these had ever occurred at a discount." The court noted that the estate's expert could not cite an example of a fractional interest discount applying to a sale of art, so the expert used fractional interest discounts in cases involving land and limited partnerships to make his calculations. The court concluded, however, that "art is simply not fungible" and that holders of undivided interests in art would likely seek to sell the entire work and split the proceeds rather than sell their undivided shares. Although the court rejected a fractional interest discount, it also held that it is appropriate to allow for some discount to reflect the costs to partition and sell the art collection. Even the government's expert conceded that a two percent discount is proper to account for the costs to sell art at auction. The court believed the estate was right to claim that the costs of a court-ordered partition should be factored into the valuation, but the court was not prepared to accept the estate's determination that such costs to partition and sell would amount to a 51 percent discount. Accordingly, it ordered the parties to reach a settlement on the appropriate valuation discount to be applied. When the parties failed to do so, the court ultimately permitted a 5 percent discount. The court's decision was upheld by the Ninth Circuit. 2009-1 U.S.T.C. ¶ 60,572 (9th Cir. 2009).

In *Estate of Paul Mitchell*, 74 T.C.M. (CCH) 872 (1997), the Tax Court allowed discounts that totaled 45 percent in valuing the decedent's 49 percent interest in a hair salon products company of which he was the cofounder and major creative force. First, the court allowed a discount of ten percent to reflect the loss of the decedent to the enterprise. It also allowed a combined discount of 35 percent for lack of marketability and minority interest. A discount of $1.5 million, or one percent, was allowed because of the possibility of a lawsuit over the compensation of the surviving founder who continued to operate the business. In effect, the Tax Court rejected the analysis of all of the experts and relied on its own analysis of the facts. The valuation by the Tax Court in *Estate of Mitchell* was vacated on an appeal by the estate and the matter was remanded to the Tax Court. 250 F.3d 696 (9th Cir. 2001). That decision was reached because the Tax Court had failed to shift the burden of proof on valuation to the Commissioner and to explain adequately its valuation of the stock.

In *Estate of Maude Furman*, 75 T.C.M. (CCH) 2206 (1998), the Tax Court allowed a combined minority and lack of marketability discount of 40 percent and a key person discount of 10 percent. As combined, the discount totaled 46 percent. The opinion was concerned in part with the failure to report a gift that resulted from a recapitalization of the corporation many years prior to the decedent's death.

EXAMPLE 2-59.

T owned 60 of the 100 outstanding shares of the common stock of *T, Inc.* In 1991 *T* gave 11 shares of *T, Inc.* stock to her child, *C*. The valuation of the 11 shares reflected the fact that they constitute a small minority interest and that they would be difficult to market. By making the gift *T* has reduced her ownership of *T, Inc.* stock to a minority interest that should later qualify for the same discounts. Discounts for minority interests were denied by the Tax Court in *Estate of Ralph E. Lenheim*, 60 T.C.M 356 (1990), and *Estate of Elizabeth B. Murphy*, 60 T.C.M. 645 (1990), where the transfers that reduced the decedent's ownership interests to minority status were made shortly prior to their deaths. From time to time legislation has been proposed that would require the undiscounted liquidation valuation of minority interests. On the other extreme, under the United Kingdom's former Capital Transfer Tax the amount of a chargeable transfer was the amount by which the transfer reduced the value of the transferor's estate. Finance Act 1975, § 20(2). The special valuation rules of Chapter 14 do not apply where, as in this example, the retained interest is of the same class as the transferred interest. *See* § 2701(a)(2)(B).

EXAMPLE 2-60.

O gave an undivided one-tenth interest in Blackacre to each of her 6 grandchildren. Each gift qualifies for the annual gift tax exclusion. In addition, each would qualify for a discount because of the undivided ownership of the property. An expert appraisal would probably sustain a discount of at least 15%. *See, e.g., Estate of Propstra*, 680 F.2d 1248 (9th Cir. 1982).

In qualifying gifts for applicable valuation discounts, it is crucial to follow the necessary formalities in conveying the gifted property. One example of a leveraged gift gone awry appears in *Senda v. Commissioner*, 88 T.C.M. 8 (2004), where a married couple formed two family limited partnerships to hold marketable securities. On the same day the partnerships were funded with marketable securities, the couple made substantial gifts of limited partnership interests in both partnerships in trust for each child. The couple claimed applicable valuation discounts on their federal gift tax returns, but the IRS argued that the transfer of the stock to the partnerships followed by the immediate gift of limited partnership interests to the children resulted in an indirect gift of the stock itself, and thus the valuation discounts should not apply. The Tax Court agreed, finding no evidence that the capital accounts of the taxpayers were ever actually increased as a result of their contributions to each entity. Failure to follow the formalities suggested that the taxpayers were more concerned with transferring interests in the stock to their children rather than transferring limited partnership interests. As the court observed:

> The informality is not surprising, inasmuch as petitioners alone, individually, or on behalf of their minor children were united in purpose and acted without restraint by any adverse interest. As a result, however, petitioners have presented no reliable evidence that they contributed the stock to the partnerships before they transferred the partnership interests to the children. At best, the transactions were integrated (as asserted by respondent) and, in effect, simultaneous.

The taxpayer in *Bianca Gross*, 96 T.C.M. 187 (2008), prevailed because of evidence that a family limited partnership created by her and her daughters was formed in July, 1998, well in advance of gift transfers of limited partnership interests to the daughters in December, 1998. The IRS had argued that the partnership was not effective until the same day as the gifts, because the partners had not executed the partnership agreement until that date. But the court held that the partnership had been created in July when the certificate of limited partnership was filed. At that time, the court concluded, the taxpayer and the daughters had agreed to the basic terms of the partnership arrangement, so the partnership was in existence as of that time. In addition, it was helpful that the gift transfers occurred 11 days after the taxpayer had completed her contributions to the partnership.

§2.47.2. Make Gifts of Life Insurance

The prospective size of a client's gross estate can often be reduced substantially by making gifts of insurance on the client's life, which may have little or no value for gift tax purposes. The assignment of term or group-term insurance can produce quite favorable results because of its low present value. *See* §6.44.1. Greater overall estate tax savings may result if the insurance is transferred, or initially acquired by, an irrevocable trust and the insurance is also insulated from inclusion in the estate of the insured's spouse. *See* §6.24.

§2.48. FREEZE THE VALUE OF THE ESTATE

Many wealthy or prospectively wealthy clients seek to prevent any further growth in value of appreciating assets by utilizing one or more devices that prevent any future growth in the value of the asset from being included in their estates. Because these devices "freeze" the value that is includible in the owner's estate they are called "estate freezes." The transfer tax advantages of estate freezes are limited by Chapter 14, § § 2701-2704. *See* Chapter 9.

Estate freeze techniques range from relatively simple approaches, such as inter vivos gifts or installment sales, to more complex ones, such as transfers of property to business entities. The uses of noncharitable gifts are reviewed in Chapter 7. The other principal methods of accomplishing an estate freeze are reviewed in Chapter 9. They include the installment sale, the private annuity, and the sale and leaseback. Of them, the installment sale is probably the least controversial and the most widely used. In an installment sale the owner exchanges an asset with significant potential for appreciation for a promissory note, the value of which is fixed. Changes made by the Installment Sales Revision Act of 1980 removed some of the income tax ploys that were formerly used. The private annuity is used less often, perhaps because of its more controversial nature and more uncertain tax consequences. A typical private annuity transaction involves the transfer by a senior family member of appreciated property to a junior family member in exchange for the latter's unsecured promise to pay the transferor a specified annual amount for life. The sale and leaseback usually involves the sale of an office or office equipment by a doctor or other professional to family members or a trust for family members, from whom the property is leased back. Although it has some estate-freezing characteristics, it is primarily intended to redistribute income within the family.

§2.49. BYPASS THE ESTATES OF SURVIVORS

Transferring property in a way that will not subject it to taxation upon the death of the transferee is one of the most fundamental strategies for limiting estate taxes. For example, the estates of married persons are often planned so the surviving spouse will receive the benefit of a portion of the deceased spouse's estate that will not be included in the survivor's estate. A qualified terminable interest property (QTIP) trust is perhaps the most popular and effective way to accomplish that result. The trust property is includible in the surviving spouse's estate only to the extent an election is made to claim the marital deduction in the estate of the first spouse to die. The balance of the property is left to a credit shelter trust which is not includible in the surviving spouse's estate. Leaving the surviving spouse a legal life estate in the property is generally a much less flexible and satisfactory way of reaching this result than using a trust.

A "credit shelter" or "bypass" trust is simply one in which the surviving spouse or other beneficiary is given substantial interests, but not ones that are sufficiently extensive to cause the trust property to be included in the beneficiary's estate. The beneficiary is commonly given a life income interest in the trust, although others are sometimes given the right to receive discretionary distributions of income or principal. (Of course, a trust that allows any distributions to others during the lifetime of the surviving spouse cannot qualify for the marital deduction.) In addition, the beneficiary may be given a 5 or 5 power to invade the trust, a power of withdrawal subject to an ascertainable standard related to the beneficiary's health, education, maintenance and support and a special testamentary power of appointment without forcing inclusion in the beneficiary's gross estate.

A bypass trust may be used to provide for the grantor's descendants. However, the tax incentive to attempt to bypass one or more generations of descendants is eroded somewhat by the GSTT. Prior to the adoption of the GSTT, wealthy individuals frequently established trusts that were designed to provide lifetime benefits to two or more generations of descendants without subjecting the trust property to taxation in the estates of the intermediate generations. Of course, the number of generations of estate tax levies that could be "skipped" by a trust is limited in most states by the Rule Against Perpetuities. Nonetheless, it is quite easy to draft a trust that skips one generation.

EXAMPLE 2-61.

Parent, *P*, created a trust to pay the income to her child, *C*, for life. Upon the death of *C* the trust property is distributable to *C's* children who survive her. The GSTT would apply to the distribution of principal to the issue of *C* when *C* dies. However, the distribution would not be taxable for GSTT purposes to the extent (1) *P* applies her GSTT exemption to the property that she transfers to the trust, or (2) the trust is included in *C's* gross estate.

So-called "dynasty trusts" for grandchildren or more remote descendants of the transferor will escape the GSTT only to the extent they are sheltered by an exclusion or exemption. Accordingly, clients should consider plans that maximize the value of their exemptions and the limited exclusions that are available. In particular, the exemption should be used in connection with trusts that would otherwise be entirely subject to the GSTT. Part of the value of the exemption is wasted if it is allocated to a QTIP trust or other trust that will make distributions to nonskip persons such as the transferor's spouse or children. Instead, the transferor might create separate trusts for the benefit of his or her children and for grandchildren or more remote descendants. The reason is simple: Distributions from trusts for the exclusive benefit of children are not subject to the GSTT. On the other hand, distributions from trusts for the exclusive benefit of grandchildren and more remote descendants are entirely subject to the GSTT.

EXAMPLE 2-62.

T wishes to transfer about $3 million in trust for the benefit of his children and grandchildren. *T* should consider establishing a $6 million discretionary trust with flexible terms for *T's* children, which allows distributions to be made to skip persons that are within the exclusion of § 2503(e), and a separate $5 million trust for *T's* grandchildren. All distributions from the trust for grandchildren will be free of the GSTT if *T's* $5 million exemption is allocated to it. In contrast, if *T* had established a single $6 million discretionary trust for children and grandchildren, the allocation of the full amount of *T's* exemption to the trust would shelter only a portion from the reach of the GSTT.

§2.50. DEFER THE PAYMENT OF ESTATE AND GST TAXES

Substantial savings can be achieved by deferring payment of estate and GST taxes. The estate tax marital deduction, which is discussed in detail in Chapter 5, is the most important deferral option. In essence it allows the payment of the estate tax on a married person's entire estate to be deferred until the death of the surviving spouse. In the interim, the funds that would have been paid in estate tax on the death of the first spouse are available for use by the surviving spouse. The estate and gift tax marital deductions can also be used to equalize the sizes of the spouses' estates and possibly reduce the overall estate tax burden because of the progressive nature of the estate tax.

EXAMPLE 2-63.

W has an estate of $12 million, but her husband, H, owns only a nominal amount of property. If W dies in 2011, leaving all of her property in a form that does not qualify for the marital deduction, her estate will have to pay estate tax of $2,450,000. Of course, in that case the property would probably not be subject to the estate tax when H dies. On the other hand, if W leaves all of her property to H in a form that qualifies for the marital deduction, such as a QTIP, no tax need be paid by her estate. Ideally, W's unified credit would be used to shelter $5 million of the property from taxation on H's death. If H died in 2012 and $5 million were effectively sheltered by use of W's unified credit, only $7 million will be subject to tax in H's estate. A tax of $700,000 would be imposed on H's estate. Thus, the combined use of the marital deduction and unified credits might reduce the overall estate tax cost of passing property from H and W to their children by about $1,750,000 (from $2,450,000 to $700,000).

A limited deferral opportunity is extended to the estates of persons who own substantial interests in closely-held businesses. Where the interest in a closely-held business comprises a large enough part of a decedent's estate, the estate tax attributable to that interest may be paid over a maximum of 15 years under §6166. *See* §§11.23-11.28. Deferral under §6166 is attractive because the tax attributable to the first $1 million in value of the business, indexed for post-1997 changes in the consumer price index, is subject to a special interest rate. *See* §12.48. The balance of the deferred amount of tax is subject to the Federal Short Term Rate plus three percentage points. *See* §6621(a)(2).

Section 6166 allows the executor to defer making any payment on the principal amount of the tax until five years after the due date of the estate tax return, after which the tax is payable in equal annual installments over a period of not more than ten years. As indicated in §2.37.3, the GSTT imposed on direct skips of closely-held business interests may be deferred under §6166. *See* §6166(h).

Lifetime planning decisions for clients who own interests in closely-held businesses should take into account the opportunity for deferral under §6166. For example, a client's gift program might be planned in a way that will leave a client's estate with a sufficient interest in the business to meet the requirements of §6166. *See*

§ 7.10 *and* Chapters 11-12. The same considerations may lead a client to transfer additional property to a corporation in order to increase the value of the client's stock holding and to reduce the nonbusiness portion of the client's estate.

BIBLIOGRAPHY

Barron, When Will the Tax Court Allow a Discount for Lack of Marketability?, 86 J. Tax. 46 (Jan. 1997)

Belcher, The Estate Planner's Pen Can Be Mightier than the IRS's Sword: Planning to Take Advantage of Valuation Discounts, U. Miami, 30th Inst. Est. Plan., Ch. 10 (1996)

Bieber & Hodgman, The Kindest Cut of All—Proposed Regs. For Making Qualified GST Severances, 32 Est. Plan. 3 (Mar. 2005)

Blattmachr & Detzel, Estate Planning Changes in the 2001 Tax Act—More Than You Can Count, 95 J. Tax. 74 (2001)

Breed & Civitella, The State Matters, Priv. Wealth 49 (Apr.-May 2008)

Bringardner, Discounting Undivided Interests in Realty, 72 J. Tax. 12 (1990)

Douglass & Smith, Generation-Skipping Planning Is Essential When Using Split-Interest Trusts, 85 J. Tax. 245 (Oct. 1996)

Frankel, Exceptions and Exclusions in Generation-Skipping: Planning Considerations, N.Y.U., 48th Inst. Fed. Tax., Ch. 15 (1990)

Grove, Taming the Tiger: Designing, Implementing and Operating an FLP to Avoid a Section 2036 Attack, U. Miami, 38th Inst. Est. Plan., Ch. 7 (2004)

Handler & Chen, Fresh Thinking About Gift-Splitting, 141 Tr. & Est. 36 (2002)

Harrington, Changing Grandfathered Generation-Skipping Trusts, U. Miami, 35th Inst. Est. Plan., Ch. 10 (2001)

Harrington, McCaffrey, Plaine & Schneider, Generation-Skipping Transfer Tax Planning After the 2001 Act, 95 J. Tax. 143 (2001)

Harrington, Old but Not Cold: Changing Grandfathered Generation-Skipping Trusts, U. Miami, 35th Inst. Est. Plan., Ch. 10 (2001)

Harrington, McCaffrey, Plaine & Schneider, Generation-Skipping Transfer Tax Planning After the 2001 Act, 95 J. Tax. 143 (2001)

Horn, J., Planning and Drafting for the Generation-Skipping Transfer Tax (1991)

Mulligan, Adequate Disclosure: Its Impact on Gift Tax Return Strategies, 28 Est. Plan. 3 (Jan. 2001)

Pennell, Valuation Discord: An Exegesis of Wealth Transfer Tax Valuation Theory and Practice, U. Miami, 30th Inst. Est. Plan., Ch. 9 (1996)

Pfefferkorn & Kirk, Calculating the Lifetime Gifts Exemption: When a Million Dollars is Not a Million Dollars, 29 Est. Plan. 426 (Aug. 2002)

Plaine, GST Tax Aspects of the United States Estate Tax Return, 136 Tr. & Est. 10 (Feb. 1997)

Plaine, Planning Beyond the $1 Million GST Exemption: To Skip or Not to Skip, That Is the Question, U. Miami, 32d Inst. Est. Plan., Ch. 4 (1998)

Peschel, J. & Spurgeon, E., Federal Taxation of Trusts, Grantors and Beneficiaries (2d ed. 1991)

Porter, Bulletproofing the Family Limited Partnership—Current Issues, U. Miami, 38th Inst. Est. Plan., Ch. 6 (2004)

Sega, Defined Value Clauses: How Much do I Love Thee? This Much—No More, No Less, U. Miami, 38th Inst. Est. Plan., Ch. 8 (2004)

Shenkman, GST Tax Planning in 2011 and 2012, 3 CCH Fin. & Est. Plan. ¶ 33,501 (2011)

Slade, Inter Vivos Generation-Skipping Transfer Tax Planning, U. Miami, 34th Inst. Est. Plan., Ch. 5 (2000)

Tiesi & London, How Family Partnerships Can Navigate the Section 2036 Minefield, 30 Est. Plan. 332 (July 2003)

Wallace, Now You See It, Now You Don't—Valuation Conundrums in Estate Planning, U. Miami, 24th Inst. Est. Plan., Ch. 8 (1990)

Weiner & Leipzig, Family Limited Partnerships Can Leverage the Annual Exclusion and Unified Credit, 82 J. Tax. 164 (Mar. 1995)

3

Concurrent Ownership and Nontestamentary Transfers

A. INTRODUCTION

§3.1. SCOPE

This chapter focuses on the three principal forms of co-ownership of legal interests in property other than the partnership or joint venture forms. They are, in order of discussion: (1) the tenancy in common, (2) the joint tenancy and the tenancy by the entirety, and (3) community property. Each part discusses the characteristics of the form, the methods by which it is created, the federal tax consequences of transactions involving its use, and its use in estate planning. Rules regarding survivorship forms of ownership for deposits in financial institutions and for United States savings bonds are considered in connection with the discussion of joint tenancies. The chapter also includes references to the use of survivorship arrangements authorized by Uniform Probate Code ("U.P.C."). §6-101 *et seq.* (2011), formerly U.P.C. §6-201 *et seq.*, and similar statutes authorizing nontestamentary transfers that are in effect in a number of states. Other forms of will substitutes, including life insurance and trusts, are discussed in later chapters.

Throughout the chapter dominant consideration is given to co-ownership of property by a husband and wife, who are more likely than others to own property together. Because of the differences in substantive and tax law treatment, an estate planner must be aware of the characteristics of the principal forms of co-ownership. Community property is discussed in some detail because of its importance to present or past residents of the ten community property states. Planners in noncommunity property states must also be aware of the basic characteristics of community property because of the migrant nature of our population. Under basic conflicts of law rules, the nature of a couple's interests in property is generally fixed at the time of acquisition and does not vary although they later move to a state with a different marital property regime.

Caution. The account forms used at some brokerage firms for various forms of multiparty and community property accounts provide that they are subject to the provisions of a "Joint Agreement" section of a master account agreement. That section in turn provides that "notwithstanding the particular form of joint ownership elected by Client on the Application . . . Client's interests in it being as a joint tenant and not as a tenant in common so that on the death of any Client the survivor(s) will be the sole owner(s) of whatever monies and Property may remain to the credit of the Joint Account." Other forms provide that on the death of one spouse, the balance of an account that stands in the name of one or both spouses as community property will belong entirely to the surviving spouse. As a result, what a client or estate planner might believe was a tenancy in common or community property account may turn out to be subject to the survivorship provisions of the agreement. If the survivorship provisions prevail, the property will not be subject to a deceased account holder's will or administration in his or her estate.

B. TENANCY IN COMMON

§3.2. SUBSTANTIVE LAW SUMMARY

Tenancy in common, like marriage, can be an unhappy relationship and the process of dissolution may be prolonged, painful and expensive. *Hegewald v. Neal*, 20 Wash. App. 517, 518, 582 P.2d 529, 530 (1978).

A tenancy in common is a form of concurrent ownership between two or more persons in which each cotenant owns an undivided fractional interest in the property. The interests are presumed to be equal unless otherwise specified in the instrument creating the tenancy. Whether or not the interests are equal, each tenant has an equal right to occupy the whole of the property.

The interest of each tenant is freely transferable and devisable. In the ordinary case there is no right of survivorship between tenants in common. However, the instrument creating the tenancy may provide for survivorship interests. Although most states follow the general rules regarding tenancies in common, there are some variations. Under Oregon law, a conveyance of real estate to two or more persons that includes a declaration of a right of survivorship creates "a tenancy in common with respect to the life estate with cross-contingent remainders in the fee simple." Or. Rev. Stat. §93.180(2) (2011); Holbrook v. Holbrook, 403 P.2d 12 (1965) ("[T]he interest created by a conveyance to co-grantees with right of survivorship could not be destroyed by severance."

A corporation, trust, or other artificial legal entity may be a tenant in common, but not a joint tenant.

The respective rights and duties of tenants in common continue to evolve. For example, a tenant in common who receives an offer from a third party to buy the property may not be obligated to inform the other tenant of the offer—not even when the offeree tenant is negotiating to buy out the other tenant. *Douglas v. Jepson*, 945 P.2d 244 (Wash. App. 1997) (the existence of a tenancy in common does not "by itself impose a duty of disclosure").

In most states, if not all, a tenant in common may petition for the partition of real property between the tenants. If a partition in kind is not possible without unduly injuring the interests of the parties, the court may order the property sold and the proceeds divided between the tenants. Note that the estimated cost of a partition action is sometimes the basis upon which a court will discount the value of a tenant's fractional interest in property.

§3.3. CREATION

A tenancy in common may be created by the express terms of a will, conveyance, or other instrument of transfer ("to X and Y as tenants in common"). However, a tenancy in common more often results from a transfer to two or more persons that does not specify the type of tenancy the transferor intended to create or the extent of each transferee's interest (*e.g.,* "to A, B, and C"). A tenancy in common also results when property passes to two or more persons under the intestate succession law. In most states, a transfer to two or more persons creates a tenancy in common and not a joint tenancy unless the instrument of transfer expressly declares an intent to create a joint tenancy. *E.g.,* Cal. Civ. Code §683 (2011); Nev. Rev. Stat. Ann. §111.060 (2011); N.Y. Est. Powers & Trusts Law §6-2.2(a) (2011); R.I. Gen. Laws §34-3-1 (2011). Those states have reversed the ancient constructional preference that favored joint tenancies. In them a conveyance "to X and Y jointly" would probably be characterized as a tenancy in common and not as a joint tenancy. More likely, the phrase "joint tenants" or "joint tenancy" would be required to indicate intent to create a joint tenancy rather than a tenancy in common. Reference to the right of survivorship inherent in joint tenancy is usually not required. In Colorado, for example, a conveyance of real property to "to X and Y as joint tenants" or "to X and Y in joint tenancy" is sufficient to create rights of survivorship. Colo. Rev. Stat. §38-31-101 (2011).

Of course, property gratuitously transferred to a husband and wife may create a tenancy by the entirety in common law states that recognize that form of ownership. N.Y. Est. Powers & Trusts Law §6-2.2(b) (2011). Property transferred to a "husband and wife" who are not married typically creates a tenancy in common. *Marriage of Smith,* 705 P.2d 197 (Or. App. 1985). However, under New York law a transfer of realty to "persons who are not legally married to one another but who are described in the disposition as husband and wife" creates a joint tenancy unless it is expressly declared to be a tenancy in common. N.Y. Est. Powers & Trusts Law §6-2.2(d) (2011). Also, except where a transfer is sufficient to create a tenancy by the entirety, under Florida law, a transfer to two or more persons creates a tenancy in common unless the instrument expressly creates a right of survivorship. Fla. Stat. Ann. §689.15 (2011).

A tenancy in common may also be created when a joint tenancy is severed, as it is when one joint tenant transfers an interest in the joint tenancy property to a third party. *E.g.,* Cal. Civ. Code §683.2 (2011).

EXAMPLE 3-1.

X devised Blackacre to his daughters, *A* and *B,* as joint tenants, which was sufficient to constitute them as joint tenants with right of survivorship.

Prior to the death of either of them, *B* conveyed her interest to her stepsister, *C*. Following the conveyance *A* and *C* own Blackacre as tenants in common (*i.e.*, the transfer from *B* to *C* severed the joint tenancy and terminated the right of survivorship). Thereafter *A* and *C* were each free to dispose of her interest in the property by deed or will.

Also, property owned by a husband and wife as joint tenants or tenants by the entirety may be converted into a tenancy in common if their marriage is dissolved and the property is not otherwise disposed of in the decree of dissolution. As pointed out in §3.4, unless otherwise provided in the decree of dissolution, former spouses generally hold as tenants in common any community property they owned at the time of divorce. *E.g.*, Wis. Stat. Ann. §766.75 (2011). Under the laws of Michigan and Ohio and U.P.C. §2-804 (2011), joint tenancies between a husband and wife are severed upon their divorce. Mich. Comp. L. §552.102 (2011); Ohio Rev. Code Ann. §5302.20(c)(5) (2011).

A joint tenancy may also be converted into a tenancy in common by an agreement of the tenants or a decree of a court that directly or indirectly terminates the right of survivorship. *E.g.*, *McDonald v. Morely*, 101 P.2d 690 (Cal. 1940) (separation agreement that terminated right of survivorship severed the joint tenancy); *Reilly v. Sageser*, 467 P.2d 358 (Wash. App. 1970) (agreement eliminating survivorship feature); *Mann v. Bradley*, 535 P.2d 213 (Colo. 1975) (divorce property settlement agreement providing for sale of premises and division of proceeds upon occurrence of certain events evidences intent no longer to hold the property in joint tenancy). As suggested by *Mann* and other cases, property settlement agreements incident to marital dissolutions should provide expressly for the disposition of all the spouses' property. A joint tenancy in a certificate of deposit issued in the names of the sole contributor and another as joint tenants with right of survivorship may be terminated in a variety of ways, including the filing, by the sole contributor, of a partition action. *See* §3.12.

Effect may be given to an agreement by two individuals that each will own an equal interest in shares of stock or other property, the legal title to which stands in one name alone. Thus, in *Estate of Davenport v. Commissioner*, 184 F.3d 1176 (10th Cir. 1999), the court gave effect to the disposition by one sister of her one-half share of stock that was registered in the name of the other sister. The decision gave effect to both a sale and a gift of shares made by one sister.

The termination of a joint tenancy that results in the property being held by the parties as tenants in common does not involve a gift. However, effectuating such a termination may, on the death of a party, reduce the amount subject to the estate tax. The reason is that the undiscounted value of the decedent's interest is includible under §2040, *See* §3.15, whereas a fractional discount would be allowable for the decedent's partial interest in a tenancy in common.

§3.4. TENANCY IN COMMON IN COMMUNITY PROPERTY STATES

Community property states allow married persons to hold title to property as tenants in common. The interests of the spouses in a deliberately created tenancy in common have sometimes been treated as separate, not community, property. However, statutes in some community property states provide that property held by husband and wife as tenants in common is presumed to be their community property. Cal. Fam. Code §2580 (2011); N.M. Stat. Ann. §40-3-8B (2011) (presumption applies to "tenants in common or as joint tenants or otherwise").

In some states property that is gratuitously transferred to a husband and wife ("to *H* and *W*") is treated as their community property. *Estate of Salvini,* 397 P.2d 811 (Wash. 1964). In Texas, property conveyed in that manner would probably be owned by the husband and wife as tenants in common. W. deFuniak & M. Vaughn, Principles of Community Property §69 (2d ed. 1971). In California, property acquired during marriage by a husband and wife in joint form (*i.e.,* as tenants in common, joint tenants, or tenants by the entirety) is presumed to be their community property upon the marriage's dissolution. Cal. Fam. Code §§2581 (2011). Some commentators believe that the courts will apply the statutory presumption at death as well.

Upon the death of a spouse, the property formerly owned as community property may be owned by the surviving spouse and the deceased spouse's successors as tenants in common. This result occurs where the community property interest of the deceased spouse is devised to a person other than the surviving spouse or where the deceased spouse dies intestate and the surviving spouse is not entitled to receive all of the deceased spouse's share in the community property under the local law. *See, e.g.,* Wis. Stat. Ann. §861.01(2) (2011); *Pritchard v. Estate of Tuttle,* 534 S.W.2d 946 (Tex. Civ. App. 1976).

EXAMPLE 3-2.

H and *W* owned Whiteacre as community property. *H*'s will devised his interest in Whiteacre to their daughter, *D*. Following *H*'s death *W* and *D* own Whiteacre as tenants in common.

Upon the dissolution of a marriage, any property that was formerly community property and is not allocated by a settlement agreement or by the court is owned by the former spouses equally as tenants in common.

If the marital relationship between a husband and wife is dissolved, the prerequisite to community property is gone. Therefore, the former community property, if not changed from its community status by a transfer while the two were married and not allocated by the court in the dissolution action, will be held by the former spouses as equal tenants in common. Cross, The Community Property Law in Washington (revised 1985), 61 Wash. L. Rev. 13, 113 (1986).

The same rule is followed in other community property states, including California, *Tarien v. Katz,* 15 P.2d 493 (Cal. 1932), and Texas, *Taylor v. Catalon,* 166 S.W.2d 102 (Tex. 1942). Under Idaho law, unless otherwise directed by the court, the divorce of a husband and wife or the annulment of their marriage severs their interests in community property with right of survivorship, which causes the property to be owned by them as tenants in common. Idaho Code §15-6-402(2) (effective July 1, 2008). All forms of existing or inchoate community property that are not allocated by decree, including employee benefits and insurance policies, are generally owned by the former spouses as tenants in common. Accordingly, it is important to provide for the disposition of all of the community property of a husband and wife upon dissolution of their marriage.

§3.5. MISCELLANEOUS

The fractional interests of tenants in common in real property may be voluntarily or involuntarily partitioned into individually owned parcels in a court proceeding. The exchange of one cotenant's undivided interest in a portion of timberland held for investment for the other cotenant's undivided interest in another portion, that was also held for investment, constitutes a like-kind exchange under §1031. LR 199926045. If a partition is not practical, a sale of part or all of the property may be required. Although the provisions vary somewhat from state to state, statutes in almost all states authorize a form of action for partition of real property. 7 R. Powell & P. Rohan, Powell on Real Property §50.07[1] (2005). Personal property may also be partitioned by voluntary or involuntary action.

§3.6. CREDITOR'S CLAIMS

The interest of a tenant in common is usually subject to creditor's claims to the same extent as other individually owned property. That is, a creditor may reach the fractional interest of the debtor-tenant, but not the interest of any other tenant. A creditor who forecloses on the debtor's interest in the tenancy becomes a tenant in common in place of the debtor.

§3.7. GIFT TAX

The creation of a tenancy in common may constitute a gift, depending upon the manner of creation and the extent of each tenant's interest in the property. A gift results when the tenants contribute unequally toward the purchase price of property which they acquire as equal tenants in common. However, such a gift would qualify for the annual gift tax exclusion. The acquisition of an asset in the names of both spouses as tenants in common would qualify for the unlimited gift tax marital deduction if the donee spouse is a United States citizen. If the donee spouse is not a United States citizen, no marital deduction is allowed. However, an annual exclusion of $100,000 (adjusted for post-1997 inflation) is available. §2523(i).

EXAMPLE 3-3.

T provided the entire purchase price of Greenacre. Title was taken in the names of *T* and *X*, who are not married. Under the local law *T* and *X* own equal undivided interests in Greenacre as tenants in common. When *T* purchased Greenacre, *T* made a gift of a one-half tenancy in common interest in the property to *X*. If *X* was a United States citizen and was married to *T*, the gift would qualify for the gift tax marital deduction under §2523.

Apart from the marital deduction, the creation of a tenancy in common between spouses is treated in the same way as the creation of the tenancy between unrelated parties.

§3.7.1. Termination

No gift occurs upon the termination of a tenancy in common if each tenant receives a share of the property or its proceeds proportional to his or her ownership interest in the tenancy. A gift does occur, however, if a tenant receives less than his or her proportionate share.

EXAMPLE 3-4.

X and *Y* each contributed one-half of the cost of acquiring Blackacre as tenants in common. They recently sold Blackacre for $100,000, of which *X* received $60,000 and *Y* received $40,000. The unequal division of the proceeds involves a gift of $10,000 from *Y* to *X* unless it was made in the ordinary course of business. *See* Reg. §25.2512-8.

§3.7.2. Conversion of Community Property into Tenancy in Common

The conversion of community property into a tenancy in common owned as separate property in equal shares by a husband and wife does not involve a taxable transfer for federal gift or estate tax purposes. *Commissioner v. Mills*, 183 F.2d 32 (9th Cir. 1950); Rev. Rul. 55-709, 1955-2 C.B. 609. In some community property states a husband and wife may hold community property in tenancy in common form. Wis. Stat. Ann. §766.60(4)(a) (2011). Also, as indicated in §3.4, upon dissolution of marriage property held by a husband and wife as tenants in common is presumed to be community property in California. Cal. Fam. Code §2581 (2011). If a conversion from community property to a tenancy in common is effective, each spouse will thereafter be free to dispose of his or her interest in the property. Although neither husband nor wife generally has the right to make gifts of community property without the consent of the other, each is free to transfer separate property without the consent of the other spouse. *See* §3.28.2. Because of the fiduciary relationship between the spouses, a conversion procured by fraud, undue influence, or other inequitable means is vulnerable to challenge by the disadvantaged spouse.

EXAMPLE 3-5.

H induced *W* to consent to the formal conversion of their community property ranch into a tenancy in common for "tax reasons." Shortly thereafter, *H* transferred all of his interest in the ranch to his nephew and instituted dissolution proceedings against *W*. The conversion would not involve any gift by *H* or *W*. However, the conversion might be subject to challenge by *W* if it was to her disadvantage.

§3.7.2

§3.7.3. Conversion of Tenancy in Common into Community Property

The conversion of separate property held by a husband and wife in a tenancy in common into a community property form of ownership should not involve a gift because the conversion does not alter the value of the interests owned by the husband and wife. Each spouse owned a one-half interest in the property before and after the transfer. *See* Rev. Rul. 77-359, 1977-2 C.B. 24. Any gift would, of course, qualify for the marital deduction if the donee spouse is a United States citizen. No gift would occur if the value of the property interests owned by each spouse does not change as a result of the transfer.

§3.8. ESTATE TAX

In general, the interest of each tenant is includible in the tenant's gross estate under §2033 in accordance with basic estate tax principles.

EXAMPLE 3-6.

T left Blackacre by will "to *A* and *B* in equal shares." Under the local law the devise was effective to constitute *A* and *B* as equal tenants in common. The interests of *A* and *B* are freely transferable. Upon the death of either *A* or *B*, the value of a one-half interest in Blackacre, discounted for its fractional character, is includible in his or her estate.

The interest of a surviving tenant in common ordinarily is not includible in a deceased tenant's estate. The potential inclusion, under §2040(a), of all interests in joint tenancy property acquired with contributions of one tenant may be avoided by converting the joint tenancies into tenancies in common. The conversion would eliminate the survivorship feature of the joint tenancy and the threat of greater inclusion. Before making such a conversion, each joint tenant should understand that his or her interest in the property would thereby become subject to disposition by will. In this connection, note that the unlimited marital deduction and the qualified joint interest rule of §2040(b) make it unnecessary for married joint tenants to attempt to avoid the application of §2040(a).

The courts and the IRS seem to agree that §2040(a) applies only to property held in joint tenancy form at the time of a decedent's death. *See, e.g., Glaser v. United States,* 306 F.2d 57 (7th Cir. 1962); Rev. Rul. 69-577, 1969-2 C.B. 173. Accordingly, the amount of property includible in a joint tenant's estate may be limited by converting a joint tenancy into a tenancy in common at any time prior to the joint tenant's death. As indicated above, such a conversion occurs if one of the tenants transfers an interest in the property to another person or the survivorship feature is eliminated by agreement or judicial action. This rule applies even when the severance is made within three years of death.

EXAMPLE 3-7.

X, who was not married to *Y*, paid the entire cost of acquiring Blackacre. Title was taken in the names of "*X* and *Y* as joint tenants with right of survivorship." The purchase of the property involved a gift from *X* to *Y* of half of the value of Blackacre. If the title remains in that form, the entire value of Blackacre is includible in *X*'s estate under § 2040(a). However, only the value of *X*'s one-half interest in Blackacre is includible in *X*'s gross estate if the joint tenancy is terminated prior to *X*'s death. The necessary termination might occur if *Y*'s interest is transferred or if the tenants agree to hold the property as tenants in common.

§ 3.9. INCOME TAX

Neither the creation nor the termination of a tenancy in common usually involves any recognition of gain or other income tax consequences. Where the sole owner of property adds another party as a tenant in common, the transferor will not recognize gain or loss if the transfer is a gift. If the addition of a co-owner represents compensation for services or payment of a debt owed to the transferee, however, the transferor will recognize gain (and, perhaps, loss).

The income from property owned as tenants in common is taxed to the tenants in accordance with their respective rights to the income under the local law. In the absence of a contrary agreement, each tenant is ordinarily entitled to a part of the income proportionate to his or her ownership interest in the property. No gain or loss is recognized on the transfer of property from one spouse to another if the transferee spouse is a United States citizen. § 1041.

Letter Ruling 9327069 recognizes that the partition of contiguous property between tenants in common is not a sale or exchange under § 1001. Accordingly, the partition does not involve a recognition of gain or loss. In this private letter ruling, the IRS followed Rev. Rul. 56-437, 1956-2 C.B. 507, which held that the severance of a joint tenancy did not involve gain or loss. The IRS declined to follow Rev. Rul. 73-476, 1973-2 C.B. 300, in which three unrelated tenants in common of three separate parcels rearranged their ownerships so that each party became the sole owner of one parcel. Applying the principles of Rev. Rul. 81-292, 1981-2 C.B. 158 (approximately equal division of marital property in a noncommunity property state was a nontaxable division), LR 9327069 concluded that following partition the owners will each have a basis equal to one-half of the former aggregate basis. Also, note that if tenancy in common property is owned for investment purposes, then one tenant's exchange of an undivided interest in a portion of jointly owned property for the other tenant's one-half interest in another portion of the property qualifies for nonrecognition as an exchange of like kind property under § 1031. LR 199926045.

§ 3.10. USE IN ESTATE PLANNING

The tenancy in common is used infrequently in planning and organizing the ownership of family wealth. However, individuals sometimes wish to convey or devise interests in real or personal property to children or other family members as tenants in common. An inter vivos transfer of undivided interests in property, of course, qualifies for a valuation discount. *See* §2.45.1. The transfer of property to multiple parties as tenants in common is often preferable to its transfer to them as joint tenants with right of survivorship. Indeed, some states bar the creation of joint tenancies and some others have abolished the incident of survivorship. *See* §3.12. In rare cases a testator may leave property to several individuals as tenants in common in order to force them to cooperate with each other—at least minimally. For example, Canadian lawyer Charles Millar left his home in Jamaica to three acquaintances "who each had an abiding dislike for one another, so naturally Millar thought it would be a good idea if they lived together." R.S. Menchin, The Last Caprice 28 (1963).

The management and operation of the property and the relations between parties are often complicated by joint ownership. Those factors may be relieved if each transferee receives a fee interest in a separate parcel of property instead of owning a larger parcel as a cotenant. It is often best to transfer the property to a trustee who can provide unified management for the benefit of multiple donees.

Marital Transfers and QPRTs. Some overall tax savings may be achieved if a partial interest in separate property owned by one spouse is transferred to the other spouse. The transfer to the donee qualifies for the gift tax marital deduction if the donee is a United States citizen. On the death of either spouse the value of the interest owned by the decedent qualifies for a fractional interest discount. If the decedent's interest is transferred to a QTIP trust for the surviving spouse, the interests will both qualify for discounts (*i.e.*, they will not be aggregated) in the estate of the surviving spouse. *Estate of Bonner v. United States*, 84 F.3d 196 (5th Cir. 1996).

Savings may also be achieved if the owner of a residence transfers an interest to his or her spouse (or another family member) prior to transferring the residence to qualified personal residence trusts (QPRTs). QPRTs are discussed at §9.44.

EXAMPLE 3-8.

H and *W* live in a residence, worth $1 million, that is owned by *H*. *H* transfers a one-half interest to *W*, who is a United States citizen. The gift, the value of which was discounted by 15% (to $425,000) qualifies for the annual gift tax exclusion and the marital deduction. *H* and *W* transfer their respective interests in the residence to QPRTs. For gift tax purposes the value of each interest transferred to the QPRTs would be similarly discounted (*i.e.*, to $425,000). This approach reduces the gift tax cost of transferring the remainder interests from what it would be if *H* were to transfer the entire, undiscounted, interest to a single QPRT. It would also eliminate the risk that the entire value of the residence would be included in *H*'s estate if he were to die prior to the end of the term of the QPRT.

An interest in the donor's residence that is transferred to a family member may allow each cotenant's interest to be discounted. However, if the donor continues to occupy the entire premises, there is a risk that the entire property will be included in his or her gross estate. *See* §7.23. The risk of inclusion is diminished if the donor and donee execute an agreement regarding use of the premises, the donor pays reasonable rental, and each party bears an appropriate portion of the taxes and the insurance and other costs associated with the property.

Limitations on Tenancies in Common. If a client contemplates transferring property to multiple parties as tenants in common, the planner should alert the client to the difficulties that can arise regarding the management and disposition of undivided interests in real property. Also, the relationship between cotenants with divergent views can be aggravated by the difficulty of extricating themselves from a tenancy in common. The cost and delay involved in obtaining a satisfactory partition or liquidation of one tenant's interest can be very frustrating. The potential for additional problems is increased if the interests of the tenants are further fractionalized upon their deaths.

Because the tenancy in common lacks a survivorship feature, it does not have the popular appeal of the joint tenancy and some of the other will substitutes. An inter vivos or testamentary trust often provides a far more flexible and intelligent method of arranging title than a tenancy in common.

Individuals sometimes choose to take title to investment property as tenants in common. Those who do should enter into an agreement regarding the management and disposition of the property if one or more tenants wish to terminate the co-ownership. Also, individuals associated in a professional practice may purchase an office building as tenants in common. For example, partners in a medical practice may acquire real property initially as tenants in common. *Perry v. United States,* 520 F.2d 235 (4th Cir. 1975), *cert. denied,* 423 U.S. 1052 (1976). However, the ownership of such a building by a limited partnership, a limited liability company, or a corporation or trust created by the parties, is more typical. *See* Chapter 11.

All in all, the creation of a tenancy in common probably results more often from the absence of effective estate planning than from an intelligently formulated plan.

C. JOINT TENANCY AND TENANCY BY THE ENTIRETY

§3.11. INTRODUCTION

The joint tenancy with right of survivorship has long been a popular form of co-ownership, particularly by husbands and wives. Hines, Real Property Joint Tenancies: Law, Fact and Fancy, 51 Iowa L. Rev. 582 (1966). The popularity of the joint tenancy is primarily attributable to the right of survivorship, which makes it a simple and effective probate avoidance device. Because of the survivorship feature, when a joint tenant dies the surviving joint tenant or tenants own the entire interest in the property by operation of law. Thus, a deceased tenant's interest is not subject to disposition by will or administration in the decedent's estate. However, under the U.P.C. joint tenancy property is included in a deceased spouse's augmented estate for purposes of the surviving spouse's right of election. U.P.C. §2-205(1) (2011).

According to the Restatement (Third), Property (Wills and Other Donative Transfers) §6.2, Comment *l* (2003), a wedding gift is implicitly conditioned on the marriage taking place. If the wedding takes place, unless otherwise specified by the donor, a wedding gift may be treated as joint tenancy property (or community property). The Comment states that the rule also applies to "couples who are planning to be united in a same-sex civil union or a same-sex commitment ceremony, except that the couple cannot take the gifts in tenancy by the entirety or as community property." The Restatement cited above, Comment *m*, also treats the gift of an engagement ring as a conditional gift. *See* §7.4.

§3.11.1. Advantages

A comprehensive article by Professor Regis Campfield, Estate Planning for Joint Tenancies, 1974 Duke L.J. 669, 671-673, identified the following commonly recognized advantages of the joint tenancy:

1. Jointly held property oftentimes enjoys preferential treatment for state death tax purposes;
2. Jointly held property is free from the claims of creditors of either spouse;
3. Joint property expresses the idea of partnership in a marriage and reinforces family security and harmony;
4. Joint property reduces administration costs;
5. Joint property avoids probate delays;
6. Joint property avoids publicity;
7. Joint property is convenient; and
8. Joint property avoids fragmentation of ownership.

In recent years some of the advantages have declined in importance and others have been eliminated. The repeal of separate state death tax systems has virtually eliminated the preferential tax treatment of joint tenancies. Similarly, under U.P.C. §6-102 (2011), a deceased cotenant's interest may be reached "to pay claims against the estate and statutory allowances to the surviving spouse and children."

§3.11.2. Disadvantages

The principal disadvantages of joint tenancies spring from their general inflexibility and the inability of tenants to dispose of the property by will except upon the death of the survivor. The potentially adverse estate tax consequences of joint ownership by spouses were largely eliminated by the adoption of the unlimited marital deduction in the 1981 Act. However, the excessive use of joint tenancies may deprive a decedent's estate of needed cash, thereby causing problems of liquidity. Their use also deprives the survivors of income-tax-splitting opportunities to the extent a decedent's estate is eliminated as a separate income-tax-paying entity. *See* §4.6. The principal vice of the joint tenancy is that the entire interest in the property passes to the surviving tenant outright—which makes it all subject to inclusion in the surviving tenant's estate.

Joint tenancies are not complete will substitutes and should not be taken as such. It is almost invariably necessary for the tenants to have wills to dispose of other assets or all of the property if the testator is the survivor, and to appoint guardians for minor children.

Some opportunities for mischief are created by the rule that a joint tenancy can be severed by the action of one joint tenant. For example, one joint tenant might secretly convey his or her interest in the joint tenancy property to a third person in trust for the transferor. The transfer might be concealed and not disclosed if the transferor survives the other original joint tenant. However, the deed might be disclosed if the transferor predeceases the other original joint tenant. Of course, the disappointed former joint tenant might be able to impose a constructive trust on the property, or achieve some other recovery, if the severance constituted a fraud or violated an ancillary agreement between the joint tenants.

In *Re v. Re,* 46 Cal. Rptr. 2d 62 (Cal. App. 1995), the court upheld a severance that took place when two of the three joint tenants (a mother and daughter) conveyed their two-thirds interest in joint tenancy real property to themselves as joint tenants. The deed excluded the other original joint tenant (a son). The court held that the conveyance by the mother and daughter to themselves as joint tenants as to their two-thirds interest severed the original joint tenancy among the three parties. As a result, following the mother's death, the daughter owned two-thirds of the property as a tenant in common with her brother.

California Civil Code § 683.2 (2011) specifies the ways in which a joint tenancy may be terminated. Execution of a will declaring a termination of a joint tenancy and disposing of an interest in the property is insufficient to work a severance under the statute. *Estate of England,* 284 Cal. Rptr. 361 (Cal. App. 1991).

Overall, the joint tenancy is neither an estate planning panacea nor a disaster. It is reasonable for some persons with small estates to hold all of their property in joint tenancies and for most persons to hold some of their property, such as checking or savings accounts, in one. "All joint tenancies are not cursed. Ordinarily, there would not seem to be any real harm in spouses holding their house as joint tenants, or maintaining their household bank account in that manner." Manning, Planning for Problems Created by Various Types of Property and Ownership, N.Y.U., 30th Inst. Fed. Tax 623, 660 (1972).

§ 3.12. FEATURES OF JOINT TENANCIES

Most states allow two or more individuals to hold real or personal property in joint tenancy, under which each tenant owns an equal, undivided interest in the property. The joint tenancy is distinguished from the tenancy in common primarily by the right of survivorship. As mentioned above, the right of survivorship operates upon the death of one tenant so that the surviving tenant (or tenants) is the exclusive owner (or owners) of the property. Because of the survivorship feature, an artificial legal entity, such as a corporation, cannot be a joint tenant. However, individual fiduciaries—trustees or personal representatives—may hold fiduciary property as joint tenants. In some states, joint tenancies between a husband and wife are severed if the spouses are divorced. *See* § 3.3.

Joint tenancies were once favored by the law; however, now they are generally disfavored by both judicial decisions and legislative enactments. 7 R. Powell & P. Rohan, Powell on Real Property § 51.01[3] (2005). The law of many states provides that a joint tenancy may only be established by a written instrument that expressly declares the interest created to be a joint tenancy. *E.g.,* Cal. Civ. Code § 683 (2011); Nev. Rev. Stat. § 111.060 (2011); N.Y. Est. Powers & Trusts Law § 6-2.2(a) (2011); Wash. Rev. Code § 64.28.010 (2011). The courts have generally required complete compliance with such statutes in order to create a valid joint tenancy. Accordingly, a conveyance "to *A* and *B* jointly" would probably not create a joint tenancy. Instead, *A* and *B* would probably hold the property as tenants in common. *See* § 3.3. Joint tenancies in land have been abolished in some states. *E.g.,* Or. Rev. Stat. §93.180 (2011). Statutes in some other states abolish survivorship as an incident of joint tenancies. *E.g.,* N.C. Gen. Stat. §41-2 (2011).

A joint tenancy may be terminated in a variety of ways, including the transfer by one tenant of his or her interest in the property. Also, in an action to foreclose federal tax liens against real property in which the debtor's former spouse held an interest, the court held that the terms of a separation agreement that gave the former spouse a life estate and remainder interest in joint tenancy property terminated the joint tenancy. *United States v. Gibbons,* 71 F.3d 1496 (10th Cir. 1995) (Colorado law). A joint tenancy in a certificate of deposit may be terminated by the action of the sole depositor in several ways. The most common are by (1) cashing in the certificate; (2) having the issuing institution make physical changes on the certificate and its books; or (3) having the issuing institution reissue the certificate in another form. *Burkholder v. Burkholder,* 48 S.W.3d 596 (Mo. 2001). In *Burkholder,* the Missouri Supreme Court held the joint tenancy in a certificate of deposit was terminated when the sole contributor, who could not obtain physical possession of the certificate, filed a partition action.

§3.12.1. Multiparty Financial Accounts

Joint accounts in financial institutions are generally subject to special statutory provisions that impose different requirements. The accounts are often called "joint tenancy accounts," but they ordinarily would not qualify under the common law definition for failure to satisfy the four unities. Unfortunately, the law in most states regarding joint accounts is confusing and unclear. The law regarding multiparty accounts is effectively rationalized and clarified by Article VI, Part II of the U.P.C. (2011). An earlier version of Part II has been widely adopted. In general, the U.P.C. recognizes that a joint account belongs to the parties in proportion to their respective net contributions to the account. U.P.C. §6-211(b) (2011). Under this approach, the interest of a party *passes* at death to the surviving account holder or holders. U.P.C. §6-212(a) (2011). It rejects the joint tenancy theory that each tenant was seized of the whole from the inception of the joint tenancy. Even apart from the U.P.C., in the case of joint accounts the courts may be more willing to treat an ambiguous account as carrying a right of survivorship. For example, in a case involving the question of whether a right or survivorship attached to an account in the name of "*A* or *B*," the Washington Court of Appeals stated that "[w]e think the modern policy favors the avoidance of probate administration by use of joint tenancy survivorship rights." *Estate of Bonness,* 535 P.2d 823, 833 (Wash. App. 1975). The laws of some states allow a husband and wife to create "a joint tenancy with right of survivorship with respect to community property deposited in a savings account." Tex. Fin. Inst. & Bus. C. §65.103 (2011). As indicated above, a joint tenancy in a certificate of deposit (or other joint account) can be terminated in a variety of ways. In some cases termination may result when one of the tenants files a partition action.

§3.12.2. Uniform TOD Security Registration Act

The 1989 revision of U.P.C. Article VI includes the Uniform Transfer on Death (TOD) Security Registration Act. U.P.C. §6-301, *et seq.* (1998). The TOD provisions authorize securities to be registered in a "beneficiary form," which indicates the owner of the security and "the intention of the owner regarding the person who will become the owner of the security upon the death of the owner." U.P.C. §6-301(1) (1998). The requisite intent is shown by registration use of the words "transfer on death," or TOD, "pay on death," or POD. *See* U.P.C. §6-305 (1998). Under U.P.C. §6-302 (1998), "[m]ultiple owners of a security registered in beneficiary form hold as joint tenants with right of survivorship, as tenants by the entireties, or as owners of community property held in survivorship form, and not as tenants in common."

§3.12.3. Simultaneous Death

Under section 4 of the 1993 revision of the Uniform Simultaneous Death Act (2001), survivorship only operates if one tenant survives the other by 120 hours or that requirement is eliminated by the terms of the governing instrument. Accordingly, if there is no clear and convincing evidence that one joint tenant survived the other by at least 120 hours, the undivided interest of each owner is distributed as if he or she had survived the other.

EXAMPLE 3-8.

A and *B*, who own Blackacre as joint tenants, die under circumstances that do not clearly establish that one tenant survived the other by at least 120 hours. The right of survivorship is inoperative. That is, one half of Blackacre will be distributed in the estate of *A* as if *A* were the surviving joint tenant and the other half will be distributed similarly in the estate of *B*.

The estate tax consequences of the simultaneous death of joint tenants are discussed in §3.17.

§3.12.4. Creditor's Rights

The creditors of a joint tenant can ordinarily reach the tenant's undivided interest in the property until the tenant's death. (If a joint tenant's interest is taken in satisfaction of a tenant's debt, the joint tenancy is severed and the holding shifts to a tenancy in common.) In contrast, the creditor of one spouse may be unable to seize property held by a husband and wife as tenants by the entirety. *Lurie v. Blackwell*, 51 P.3d 846 (Wy. 2002). However, as pointed out below, the federal tax obligation of one spouse allows a lien to be imposed on tenancy by the entirety property. *United States v. Craft*, 535 U.S. 281 (2002) (Michigan law). The common law does not allow the creditors of a deceased joint tenant to reach the property unless an action was commenced prior to the tenant's death or the property was transferred into the joint tenancy in fraud of creditors. Of course, the limitation on the reach of creditors is meaningful only if the deceased tenant's estate is insolvent or the property of the decedent's estate is otherwise exempt from the reach of creditors. *Rupp v. Kahn*, 55 Cal. Rptr. 108, 113 (Cal. App. 1966), concluded that "the entire title held by a surviving joint tenant resulting from a conveyance by an insolvent without consideration, is subject to the debts of the transferor." Thus, the alleged insulation of joint tenancy property from the claims of creditors is often illusory.

§3.12.5. Community Property in Joint Tenancy Form

Most community property states now allow spouses to acquire and hold property in joint tenancy form. Several community property states have enacted statutes under which joint tenancy property owned by a husband and wife is presumed to be their community property. Previously, the prevailing rule was that the interests of a husband in wife in joint tenancy property were separate property—not community property. Accordingly, courts in several community property states held that the joint tenancy and community property forms of ownership were mutually exclusive. In *Estate of Cooke*, 524 P.2d 176 (Idaho 1974), the court put it succinctly: "[P]roperty held in a joint tenancy between husband and wife is not community property. If a true joint tenancy exists, created according to statute, each spouse owns his or her respective interest as separate property." The same rule was formerly followed in Arizona, California, and New Mexico. *Collier v. Collier*, 242 P.2d 537 (Ariz. 1952); *King v. King*, 236 P. 912 (Cal. 1915); former N.M. Stat. Ann. §40-3-8(6) (1978).

Most community property states allow community property to be transmuted into separate forms of ownership, including joint tenancies. However, the policy favoring community property generally requires the proponent of a transmutation to prove it by clear and convincing evidence. *Estate of Bogert*, 531 P.2d 1167 (Idaho 1975).

In recent years several states have adopted statutes under which property held in joint tenancy by husbands and wives is presumed to be community property. *E.g.*, Cal. Fam. Code §2580 (2011) (with respect to dissolution and separation proceedings); N.M. Stat. Ann. 40-3-8B (2011); Wash. Rev. Code §64.28.040 (2011). Other states now allow community property to be held in survivorship form, including Nevada, Texas, and Wisconsin. Nev. Rev. Stat. §111.064 (2011); Tex. Prob. Code Ann. §451, *et seq.* (2011); Wis. Stat. Ann. §766.60(5) (2011). Revenue Ruling 87-98, 1987-2 C.B. 206, indicates that the IRS will give effect to the state law and allow the full step-up in basis with respect to community property held in joint tenancy form.

Under Tex. Prob. Code §452 (2011), spouses may create a right of survivorship in community property by a writing signed by both of them. The liberality reflected in the statutes adds desirable flexibility to estate planning. The statutes were intended to allow a survivorship feature to be attached to community property without sacrificing the full step-up in basis that is allowed with respect to community property under §1014(b)(6) on the death of either spouse.

If the interests of a husband and wife in property held by them in joint tenancy are not community property, presumably each is free to make a gratuitous transfer of his or her interest to a person outside the marital community. In contrast, some community property states do not allow a spouse to make an inter vivos gift of community property without the consent of the other spouse. *See* §3.28.2.

The New Mexico law was held in *Swink v. Fingado*, 850 P.2d 978 (N.M. 1993), to require persuasive evidence that property acquired during marriage was not community property. Merely titling the property as joint tenancy with right of survivorship did not overcome that presumption. The court held that the New Mexico statute, cited above, under which "property acquired by a husband and wife by an instrument in writing whether as tenants in common or as joint tenants or otherwise will be presumed to be held as community property unless such property is separate property within the meaning of Subsection A of this section," was meant to reaffirm this basic tenet of community property law.

§3.13. TENANCY BY THE ENTIRETY

A tenancy by the entirety is a concurrent estate between husband and wife that was traditionally viewed as "held in its entirety—without undivided shares—by the marital unit of husband and wife." 7 R. Powell & P. Rohan, Powell on Real Property §52.01[2] (2005). While the tenancy by the entirety form was once favored by the law, it has declined in importance and is now recognized by a smaller number of states than before. A tenancy by the entirety resembles a joint tenancy in that both require the four unities and carry a right of survivorship. However, unlike a joint tenancy it was classically not subject to partition between the spouses. But, like a joint tenancy it terminated upon dissolution of the marriage. Thus, in Florida, "in cases of estates by the entirety, the tenants, upon dissolution of marriage shall become tenants in common." Fla. Stat. Ann. §689.15 (2011) In addition, neither spouse may be able, unilaterally, to transfer an interest in a tenancy by the entirety. *United States v. Craft*, 535 U.S. 281 (2002) (holding that the interest of a spouse in a Michigan tenancy by the entirety was subject to a federal tax lien although neither spouse, acting alone, could transfer the property). An ordinary creditor of one spouse may be unable to seize the property of a husband and wife that is held in tenancy by the entirety form. *Lurie v. Blackwell*, 51 P.3d 846 (Wy. 2002).

The tenancy by the entirety is usually created in land, although some states permit personal property to be held in the same manner. Its characteristics vary from state to state, particularly regarding the rights of the wife. The characteristics of the tenancy, of course, have an impact on its treatment for tax purposes. Thus, under the prior North Carolina law, a gift to a husband and wife did not qualify for the annual exclusion as to the wife's interest because she had no enforceable interest in the rents, income, or profits from the property during coverture. Rev. Rul. 75-8, 1975-1 C.B. 309. The North Carolina law was later changed to assure wives an equal interest in tenancy by the entirety property. N.C. Gen. Stat. §39-13.3 (2011).

The tenancy is usually created by a conveyance of real property to a husband and wife, designated as such in the instrument of conveyance. For example, in states that recognize the tenancy, a conveyance of land "to H and W, husband and wife" is effective to create a tenancy by the entirety between them in the property. *See* Fla. Stat. §689.11 (2011). The outcome is less certain when other language is used or additional persons also receive interests under the conveyance. When an instrument is ineffective to create a tenancy by the entirety, the transferees usually hold the property as tenants in common. However, under N.Y. Est. Powers & Trusts Law §6-2.2(d) (2011) a transfer of real property to a "husband and wife" who are not married creates a joint tenancy unless expressly declared to be a tenancy in common.

None of the community property states recognize the tenancy by the entirety. It is mentioned in a Washington statute that expressly abolishes the right of survivorship as an incident of the tenancy by the entirety, Wash. Rev. Code §11.04.071 (2011), but it is not referred to in another statute that lists the permissible forms of joint ownership, Wash. Rev. Code §64.28.020 (2011). Statutes of the latter type have been construed as evidencing the unavailability of the tenancy by the entirety in the jurisdiction. *Swan v. Walden,* 103 P. 931 (Cal. 1909).

At best the common law tenancy by the entirety is an anachronistic duplication of the joint tenancy; at worst it is, or was, an unjustifiable form of discrimination against women. Its future remains uncertain. The characteristics of the tenancy favoring the husband under the former Massachusetts law were attacked in several federal court actions. *Klein v. Mayo,* 367 F. Supp. 583 (D. Mass. 1973), *aff'd mem.,* 416 U.S. 953 (1974); *D'Ercole v. D'Ercole,* 407 F. Supp. 1377 (D. Mass. 1976). Although the attacks were unsuccessful, the Massachusetts statute was subsequently amended to eliminate the discrimination against wives.

For estate planning purposes the significance of the tenancy depends upon its characteristics under the governing law. In most cases it will produce the same tax consequences as a joint tenancy, which may or may not meet the needs of a particular couple. In some cases the tenancy may also effectively shield the property from the claims of creditors of either spouse. While a tenancy by the entirety can be used to obviate the necessity of an estate administration proceeding in a state in which the client(s) owns real property or immovable personalty, it does not eliminate the need for a proceeding on the death of the surviving tenant. Overall, a revocable trust is better suited to help clients avoid ancillary estate administration proceedings.

In *Estate of Reno v. Commissioner,* 945 F.2d 733 (4th Cir. 1991), the court held that the decedent could not, under Virginia law, require a portion of the estate tax applicable to his estate to be paid from property held with his wife as tenants by the entirety. Accordingly, the full value of the tenancy by the entirety property qualified for the marital deduction. As pointed out in the dissent by five members of the en banc panel, the majority opinion in *Reno* rests upon a dubious construction of the state law. Among other things, the dissenters noted that other states have held that a decedent may, by will, direct that a portion of the estate tax should be paid from nonprobate property, including joint tenancies.

The disclaimer regulations now provide that "[A] qualified disclaimer of the survivorship interest to which the survivor succeeds by operation of law upon the death of the first joint tenant to die must be made no later than 9 months after the death of the first joint tenant to die regardless of whether such interest can be unilaterally severed under the local law . . . ." Reg. § 25.2518-2(c)(4)(i). Previously the IRS had consistently ruled that a surviving spouse could not make a qualified disclaimer of a deceased spouse's interest in a unilaterally unseverable tenancy by the entirety. *E.g.,* LR 9208003 (TAM) (Arkansas law).

§ 3.14. GIFT TAX

The gift tax consequences of creating a joint tenancy or a tenancy by the entirety depend upon whether the tenants are married to each other, their citizenship, the nature and valuation of the interests of the tenants, and the amount each tenant contributes toward the acquisition of the property. Property transferred into joint tenancy form qualifies for the unlimited gift tax marital deduction if the donee spouse is a United States citizen. § 2523. In most states one tenant acting alone can sever the joint tenancy, thereby terminating the right of survivorship and converting the holding into a tenancy in common. Accordingly, in those states each tenant is considered to have an equal interest in the joint tenancy property regardless of their respective ages. In contrast, interests must be valued actuarially where the joint tenancy is not unilaterally severable. The rule is illustrated by the following example, which is based upon LR 7946080 (Michigan law).

EXAMPLE 3-9.

X, a 78-year-old unmarried female, conveyed Blackacre into joint tenancy with right of survivorship with Y, a 45-year-old male. Under the local law (Michigan), when express words of survivorship are used a joint tenancy may be severed only with the consent of all of the joint tenants. The value of an interest dependent upon the continuation of more than one life is determined by using a special factor, which is available from the IRS upon request. Based upon the 6% sex-based tables in effect in 1978 the special factor to be used to value X's retained interest was .21388. Accordingly, the value of X's gift to Y was .78612 times the value of Blackacre.

In states that allow the unilateral severance of joint tenancies, the creation of a joint tenancy does not involve a gift if each tenant makes an equal contribution toward the acquisition of the property. For example, no gift occurs if community property is used to acquire an asset in a true joint tenancy form. However, a gift of half of the value of the property would occur where one person transfers previously owned property into a joint tenancy without any contribution by the other tenant. The same result occurs where one person provides the funds with which an asset is purchased and title is taken in the name of the donor and another as joint tenants. (There would, of course, be no gift tax liability if a joint tenancy is created between a married couple with a contribution by one of them, if the donee spouse is a United States citizen.)

EXAMPLE 3-10.

X, an unmarried man, purchased stock with his own funds, the certificates for which were issued in the names of X and Y as joint tenants with right of survivorship. X informed Y of the acquisition. The purchase of the shares involved a gift to Y of half of the fair market value of the stock. The gift tax consequences would have been the same if X had transferred the title of stock that he had already owned into the names of X and Y as joint tenants with right of survivorship.
The interest transferred to the donee qualifies for the annual gift tax exclusion. As noted above, the interest also qualifies for the marital deduction if the donor and donee are married and the donee spouse is a United States citizen. Section 2523(d) provides expressly that the survivorship interest of the donor and the right of severability do not constitute a retained interest for purposes of determining whether the interest was terminable under § 2523(b).

EXAMPLE 3-11.

W paid $50,000 of her noncommunity property for securities that were issued in the names of W and H as joint tenants with right of survivorship. The total gift to H was $25,000. The gift qualifies for the annual exclusion and, if H is a United States citizen, the marital deduction.

§3.14.1. Revocable Transfers

There is an important exception to the basic rule that a transfer of property by a donor into joint tenancy with a donee is a present gift. It treats the creation of a joint tenancy in certain types of assets as a revocable transfer that does not involve a present gift. In those cases the donor has the right to recover the entire interest in the property at any time without obligation to the donee. Within this exception are joint bank accounts; joint United States savings bonds (*i.e.,* ones acquired in the names of "donor or donee"), Reg. §25.2511-1(h)(4); and joint accounts with brokerage firms where the securities are held by the firm in "street name" (*i.e.,* the securities are registered in the name of the firm's nominee), Rev. Rul. 69-148, 1969-1 C.B. 226.

EXAMPLE 3-12.

X deposited funds in a joint account in the name of X and Y at a financial institution. Under the local law X may withdraw the entire fund without the consent of Y. X did not make a gift at the time of the deposit of the funds. However, a gift occurs at any time Y withdraws funds without any obligation to account to X.

In general, if a donor places funds in a joint tenancy that allows the donor to withdraw the full amount without obligation to the donee, no gift takes place until the donee withdraws the funds for his or her own account.

§3.14.2. Pre-1982 Transfers of Real Property to a Spouse

Prior to 1982 the creation of a joint tenancy in real property between husband and wife was not deemed a transfer for gift tax purposes regardless of the proportion of the consideration furnished by each spouse unless the donor elected to treat the transaction as a gift by filing a timely gift tax return. *See* former §2515(a), (c). If the donor spouse did not treat the creation of the joint tenancy as a gift, the donor was treated as owner of the entire property for most gift and estate tax purposes. Thus, a gift took place if the joint tenancy was later terminated and the donor spouse did not receive all of the proceeds of the termination. Former §2515(b).

EXAMPLE 3-13.

In 1979 *W* provided all of the funds used to purchase Blackacre. Title was taken in the names of *H* and *W* as joint tenants with right of survivorship. *W* did not file a gift tax return treating the purchase of Blackacre as a gift. *H* and *W* sold Blackacre in 1981 for $100,000, half of which was paid to each of them. The sale constituted a termination of the joint tenancy under former § 2515(b) and the payment of $50,000 to *H* was treated as a gift. Of course, the gift qualified for the gift tax exclusion and the pre-1982 gift tax marital deduction under § 2523.

Note that under § 2523(i)(3), if the donee spouse is not a United States citizen, the creation of a joint tenancy between a husband and wife is subject to the pre-1982 law, former §§ 2515, 2515A. However, the donor cannot elect to treat the transfer of an interest in real property as a gift. Also, according to § 2056(d)(1), "section 2040(b) shall not apply" if the surviving spouse is a noncitizen. Thus, the full amount of the property is subject to inclusion in the donor spouse's estate under § 2040(a).

The entire interest in joint tenancy property acquired by a husband and wife prior to 1977 with funds provided entirely by one spouse is includible in the donor spouse's estate. As a result, the entire interest in the property receives a stepped up basis. The point was decided in *Gallenstein v. United States*, 975 F.2d 286 (6th Cir. 1992), which held that the proportionate interest rule of § 2040(a) and not the qualified joint interest rule of § 2040(b) applied. The result follows because of the effective date provisions of the 1976 Tax Reform Act, under which the qualified joint interest rule applied only to joint tenancies created after December 31, 1976. *Gallenstein* affirmed the district court's conclusion that "since § 2040(b) does not apply to joint interests created pre-1977, the property at issue was controlled by § 2040(a), which indicates that 100% of the property should be included in Mr. Gallenstein's gross estate since he had paid the entire consideration for the purchase of the property." 975 F.2d at 289.

Gallenstein has been followed in a number of other decisions including ones from Virginia and Maryland. *Patten v. United States*, 1996-1 U.S.T.C. ¶ 60,231 (W.D.Va. 1996), *aff'd*, 116 F.3d 1029 (4th Cir. 1997); *Anderson v. United States*, 1996-2 U.S.T.C. ¶ 60,235 (D.Md. 1996); *Therese Hahn*, 110 T.C. 140 (1998), *acq.*, 2001-42 I.R.B. The acquiescence in *Therese Hahn* indicates that the IRS has finally accepted the outcome of this line of cases.

Estate tax returns should be prepared in accordance with the *Gallenstein* rule, which can result in a substantial income tax advantage. If an estate tax return has already been filed, consideration should be given to filing a supplemental return that reflects inclusion of the entire joint property in the decedent's estate.

EXAMPLE 3-14.

In 1975 *W* paid the entire $100,000 cost of acquiring Blackacre, title to which was taken in the name of "*H* and *W* as joint tenants with right of survivorship." Blackacre was worth $1 million when *H* died in 2006 survived by *W*. The entire interest in Blackacre is includible in *H*'s estate and qualifies for the marital deduction. *W*'s basis in Blackacre is $1 million.

§3.15. ESTATE TAX: GENERAL RULE, §2040(a)

Under the general rule of §2040(a) a decedent's estate includes the full value of property held with others in a joint and survivorship form except to the extent the property is traceable to contributions made by others. The rule is fleshed out in Reg. §20.2040-1(a), which requires the inclusion of:

> [P]roperty held jointly at the time of the decedent's death by the decedent and another person or persons with right of survivorship, as follows:
>
> (1) To the extent that the property was acquired by the decedent and the other joint owner or owners by gift, devise, bequest, or inheritance, the decedent's fractional share of the property is included.
> (2) In all other cases, the entire value of the property is included except such part of the entire value as is attributable to the amount of the consideration in money or money's worth furnished by the other joint owner or owners . . . .

In particular, the entire value of jointly held property is included in the estate of a deceased joint tenant "unless the executor submits facts sufficient to show that property was not acquired entirely with consideration furnished by the decedent, or was acquired by the decedent and the other joint owner or owners by gift, bequest, devise, or inheritance." Reg. §20.2040-1(a).

Amount Includible. If only a portion of joint tenancy property is includible in a decedent's estate, a proportionate part of the value is includible. According to the Tax Court no discount is allowable under §2040 for fractional interests. Specifically, in *Estate of Wayne-Chi Young,* 110 T.C. 297 (1998), the Tax Court held that §2040(b) required that real property held in joint tenancy be valued at one-half of the undiscounted total value of the property. The Tax Court concluded that under California law community property and joint tenancy forms of ownership were mutually exclusive. Although community property was used to purchase the real property, the court held that the deeds to a husband and wife as joint tenants created a rebuttable presumption that the property was held in joint tenancy and not as their community property. Accordingly, the court denied the estate a discount based upon the partial interest approach that was taken in *Propstra v. United States,* 680 F.2d 1248 (9th Cir. 1982), and similar cases with regard to a decedent's one-half interest included under §2033.

§3.15.1. Contributions by Surviving Tenant

If the survivor contributed toward the acquisition of the joint tenancy, a proportionate part of its value is excluded from the decedent's estate. This "proportionate contribution" rule applies whether or not the creation of the joint tenancy was treated as a gift. The proportionate contribution rule continues to apply to all joint tenancies *other than* qualified joint interests (*i.e.,* a tenancy by the entirety or a joint tenancy of which the decedent and his or her spouse were the only tenants, § 2040(b)). *See* § 3.16.

The application of the basic rule is illustrated in the following example.

EXAMPLE 3-15.

O and *P* each contributed half of the cost of purchasing securities. Certificates were issued in their names as joint tenants. Upon the death of either *O* or *P*, half of the value of the securities is includible in the decedent's gross estate.

However, if the decedent had given the survivor the money or other property that the survivor contributed toward the cost of acquiring the property, the entire value of the property is includible in the decedent's gross estate. The rule is the same where the property contributed by the survivor toward the acquisition increased in value between the date of the gift to the survivor and the acquisition of the joint tenancy property. Reg. § 20.2040-1(c)(4).

The contribution of the surviving joint tenant toward the cost of acquiring joint tenancy property, although derived from a gift received from the decedent, is taken into account in some cases. Specifically, any income received by the survivor on property given to him or her by the decedent and applied toward the acquisition of the joint tenancy property is counted as a contribution by the survivor. Reg. § 20.20401(c)(5). Gain received by the survivor on property given to him or her by the decedent is also taken into account. Thus, "[w]hen the transfer to the joint tenancy consists of proceeds realized by the survivor upon a sale of property acquired with monies transferred from the decedent, the sale proceeds attributable to appreciation in value during the survivor's ownership of the acquired property are considered the survivor's individual contribution to the joint tenancy for purposes of section 2040." Rev. Rul. 79-372, 1979-2 C.B. 330. *See also Estate of Marcia P. Goldsborough,* 70 T.C. 1077 (1978).

The basic proportionate contribution rule and not the special rule of § 2040(b) applies if the decedent's surviving spouse is not a United States citizen. § 2056(d)(1)(B). Thus, a decedent's estate must include the full value of a joint tenancy to which an alien surviving spouse made no contribution. However, under § 7815(d)(16) of the Omnibus Budget Reconciliation Act of 1989, an alien surviving spouse is treated as having contributed to the joint tenancy to the extent the survivor received an interest in the property by gift prior to July 18, 1988. The House Committee Report explained the provision in the following passage:

> A gift made by creating a joint tenancy in property prior to July 14, 1988 is treated as consideration belonging to the surviving spouse for purposes of determining the value of the tenancy includible in the decedent spouse's estate. Accordingly, the amount of joint tenancy property included in the spouse's estate is reduced proportionately by the amount of the gift. H.R. Rep. No. 101-247,101 Cong., 1st Sess. 1429.

The effect of the 1989 change is illustrated in the following example:

EXAMPLE 3-16.

In 1987 *W* paid $100,000 for Blackacre, title to which was taken in the name of *W* and her alien husband, *H*. The gift of a one-half interest in Blackacre was reported on a gift tax return filed by *W* for 1987. An annual gift tax exclusion of $10,000 and a marital deduction of $40,000 were claimed on the return. *W* died in 1991 when Blackacre was worth $200,000. *W* was survived by *H,* who remained an alien. For purposes of § 2040(a) *H* is treated as having contributed half of the cost of acquiring Blackacre. Accordingly, $100,000 is includible in *W'* s gross estate. A marital deduction is allowable for this amount only if *H* transfers the property to a qualified domestic trust. *See* § 2056A; § 5.25.

§ 3.15.2. Gifts to Decedent and Survivor as Joint Tenants

If an asset was gratuitously transferred to the decedent and others as joint tenants, only the decedent's pro rata share of the property is includible in his or her estate. For example, if Blackacre is devised to *A* and *B* as joint tenants, only half of the value of Blackacre would be included in the estate of the first of them to die. *See* Reg. § 20.2040-1(c), Examples 7-8. The proportionate interest includible in the gross estate of a deceased tenant is increased, however, if he or she made subsequent un-reimbursed contributions in connection with the property (*e.g.,* additions or improvements).

§ 3.16. QUALIFIED JOINT INTERESTS, § 2040(b)

In view of the unlimited marital deduction adopted by the committee bill, the taxation of jointly held property between spouses is only relevant for determining the basis of property to the survivor (under sec. 1014) and the qualification for certain provisions (such as current use valuation under sec. 2032A, deferred payment of estate taxes under secs. 6166 and 6166A, and for income taxation of redemptions to pay death taxes and administration expenses under sec. 303). Accordingly, the committee believes it appropriate to adopt an easily administered rule under which each spouse would be considered to own one-half of jointly held property regardless of which spouse furnished the original consideration. H.R. Rep. No. 97-201, 97th Cong., 1st Sess. 160 (1981).

Section 2040(b) introduced the concept of the "qualified joint interest" between husband and wife (half of which is includible in the estate of the spouse who dies first). For purposes of § 2040 a qualified joint interest is a joint tenancy (or tenancy by the entirety) in which the husband and wife are the only tenants. Note that § 2040(b) does not apply unless the surviving spouse is a United States citizen. § 2056(d)(1)(B).

Treatment as a qualified joint interest under § 2040(b) usually results in no particular advantage because the unlimited marital deduction is available to the estate of the spouse who dies first. Of course, with the exception of community property held in joint tenancy form, the application of subsection (b) results in a stepped-up basis of *only* the portion included in the decedent's estate.

EXAMPLE 3-17.

In 2004, W paid $50,000 for stock that was issued in the name of "H and W as joint tenants with right of survivorship." H was a United States citizen. The purchase of the stock resulted in a gift of $25,000 to H, which qualified for the annual gift tax exclusion and the marital deduction. When W died in 2006, survived by H, the stock was worth $200,000. Under § 2040(b), half of the value of the stock, $100,000, was included in W's gross estate, which qualified for the estate tax marital deduction. The basis of the one-half interest in the stock included in W's estate was adjusted under § 1014; H retains the unadjusted basis of $25,000 in the other half. When H dies, the full value of the stock will be includible in his estate. The results would have been the same had H predeceased W. Note that the entire basis in the stock might have been increased had it been purchased with community property funds. *See* § 3.12.5.

Essentially the same tax treatment applies to property acquired by the spouses as tenants in common where the interest of the spouse who dies first is left to the surviving spouse. In such a case the interest of the spouse first to die is included in his or her estate, but an offsetting marital deduction is allowable.

§ 3.17. ESTATE TAX: SIMULTANEOUS DEATHS

Adverse estate tax consequences may occur if joint tenants other than a husband and wife die simultaneously. Under § 3 of the prior, 1940, version of the Uniform Simultaneous Death Act, "[w]here there is no sufficient evidence that two cotenants or tenants by the entirety have died otherwise than simultaneously the property so held shall be distributed one-half as if one had survived and one-half as if the other had survived." In two Revenue Rulings the IRS asserted that under this provision, the entire value of the property is includible in the gross estate of the tenant who provided all of the consideration that was paid to acquire the property and one-half is includible in the estate of the other tenant. Rev. Rul. 66-60, 1966-1 C.B. 221; Rev. Rul. 76-303, 1976-2 C.B. 266. Presumably the IRS analysis does not apply to qualified joint interests which are subject to the special rule of § 2040(b). In other cases the adverse effect should be reduced by the availability of the previously taxed property credit under § 2013. The rule also could be avoided if the sole contributor were deemed to be the survivor.

In Rev. Rul. 66-60, 1966-1 C.B. 221, the government asserted that the full value of the property was includible under § 2040 in the gross estate of the tenant who provided the full consideration (H) and one-half was includible under § 2033 in the estate of the other tenant (W) because under the Uniform Simultaneous Death Act the survivor had the power to dispose of one-half of the property. The analysis was changed by Rev. Rul. 76-303, which held that § 2040 applies only if the other tenant survives. Accordingly, only the value of the one half of the property with respect to which *W* was considered to have survived was includible in *H*'s estate under § 2040. The full value of that half was includible because there was no evidence that *W* had furnished any consideration for the acquisition of the property. However, none of the value of the one-half interest with respect to which *H* was deemed to be the survivor was includible in *W*'s estate under § 2040 because *H* provided all of the consideration for the property.

Revenue Ruling 76-303 also held that half of the value of the property was includible in each tenant's gross estate under § 2033: "[S]ince each is considered to have survived as to one-half of the property, each is considered to have acquired an absolute, sole ownership interest in one-half of the property before death. Thus, the value of one-half of the property is includible in each of their gross estates under section 2033 of the Code." Under this approach the one-half interest included in *H*'s estate should have qualified for the marital deduction. In other instances a previously taxed property credit should be available to the survivor's estate under § 2013.

Of course, as indicated above, these rulings antedated the adoption of the qualified joint interest rule of § 2040(b). Accordingly, they only involved the proportionate contribution rule and did not indicate that any different result would occur if the joint tenants were husband and wife. In the case of the simultaneous deaths of a husband and wife after 1981, whether or not the 120 hour survivorship requirement of the new version of the Simultaneous Death Act were met, only half of the total value of the joint tenancy property would be included in each spouse's estate under § 2040(b). If each such interest is disposed of as if the decedent's spouse did not survive, then no marital deduction would be available. In such a case it would be difficult to uphold the inclusion of any additional amount of the property in either spouse's estate. On the other hand, if a marital deduction were allowed for the one-half included in one spouse's estate, then the full value of the property should be included in the other spouse's estate under § 2033.

The position taken in Rev. Rul. 76-303 might also be contested on the basis of the Tax Court's holding in *Estate of Nathalie Koussevitsky*, 5 T.C. 650 (1945), *acq.*, 1945 C.B. 4, that when § 2040 is applicable no section other than § 2035 may also be applied. The contest might be assisted by the general hostility of the courts to the operation of § 2040.

§3.18. ESTATE TAX: TERMINATION OF JOINT TENANCIES

As noted above, the application of the proportionate contribution rule of § 2040(a) is restricted if the joint tenancy is terminated, even though the termination occurs within three years of death. Section 2040 applies to property "held jointly at the time of the decedent's death by the decedent and another person or persons with right of survivorship." Reg. § 20.2040-1(a). Most important, the courts have held that § 2040 has no application to property transferred before the decedent's death. *E.g.*, *Glaser v. United States*, 306 F.2d 57 (7th Cir. 1962). If the creation of the joint tenancy is treated as a gift, a severance allows one-half of the post-gift appreciation to escape taxation on the death of the donor. Of course, this result will occur without a severance where the tenants are husband and wife and the joint tenancy is a qualified joint interest under § 2040(b). *See* § 3.16. A severance can backfire if the donee tenant predeceases the donor. In such a case the proportionate contribution rule of § 2040(a) no longer applies and the full value of the donee's interest in the property is includible in the donee's estate.

In the past some commentators complained that the treatment given terminated joint tenancies was unduly favorable and was based on an unnecessarily narrow construction of the statute. *See* C. Lowndes, R. Kramer & J. McCord, Federal Estate & Gift Taxes 284-285 (3d ed. 1974); Campfield, Estate Planning for Joint Tenancies, 1974 Duke L.J. 669, 707-708. The present treatment is undesirable in the sense that it represents a triumph of form over substance and places a premium on obtaining sophisticated estate planning advice. The law would be simpler and more straightforward if it simply required the inclusion of a proportionate interest in the property upon the death of any joint tenant.

EXAMPLE 3-18.

X paid the full $100,000 cost of acquiring Blackacre. Title was taken in the name of X and his brother, Y, as joint tenants with right of survivorship. The purchase of Blackacre resulted in a gift of $50,000 from X to Y, which qualified for the annual gift tax exclusion. The joint tenancy in Blackacre was severed a week before X died, when it had a value of $200,000. As a result, X and Y held Blackacre as tenants in common. The severance did not result in a gift, because X and Y each already owned a full one-half interest in Blackacre. *Estate of Sullivan v. Commissioner*, 175 F.2d 657 (9th Cir. 1949). X's estate includes half of the value of Blackacre at the time of his death ($100,000). The amount of the original taxable gift is probably includible in X's tax base as a post-1976 adjusted taxable gift. *See* §2001(b).

EXAMPLE 3-19.

The facts are the same as in Example 3-18, *supra*. However, instead of simply severing the joint tenancy and holding Blackacre as tenants in common, X and Y transferred their interests to a trust from which each was entitled to receive one-half of the income and to dispose of one-half of the principal. The transfer effected a severance of the tenancy. Only one-half of the trust property is includible in X's gross estate under §2036 on account of his reserved life estate. Rev. Rul. 69-577, 1969-2 C.B. 173. The same result would follow if they transferred Blackacre to other parties, reserving life estates to themselves. *United States v. Heasty*, 370 F.2d 525 (10th Cir. 1966).

§3.19. DISCLAIMERS, §§2046, 2518

Effective post-mortem planning may call for a surviving joint tenant to disclaim the right to become the sole owner of the property that was held in joint tenancy. The use of disclaimers in connection with joint tenancy interests is discussed in detail in §12.34. For example, a surviving spouse may disclaim the right to receive the decedent's interest in some joint tenancy interests that he or she would otherwise receive in order to "fine tune" the federal estate tax marital deduction. A disclaimer may also allow the survivors to salvage the benefits of a carefully constructed estate plan that would otherwise be jeopardized by the parties' unwitting transfer of too much of their property into joint tenancies. Joint tenancies and the benefits of other survivorship arrangements may also be disclaimed in order to make the decedent's fractional interest subject to his or her will. Thus, the right to receive the decedent's fractional interest in the property may be disclaimed in favor of its passage under the decedent's will to a charity or other beneficiaries or to a trust.

§3.20. INCOME TAX

The creation of a joint tenancy does not ordinarily have any immediate income tax consequences. However, the transfer of some special types of assets may generate an income tax liability. In particular, the transfer of property into joint tenancy probably constitutes at least a partial disposition of installment obligations under §453B. The creation of a joint tenancy ordinarily should not involve recapture of depreciation under §§1245 or 1250 because recapture does not take place in the case of transfers by gift. §§1245(b)(1), 1250(d)(1). No gain or loss is recognized on any transfer between spouses or incident to a divorce provided the transferee is a United States citizen. §§453B(g), 1041.

In some unusual cases the creation of a joint tenancy may be treated as a taxable event and result in the recognition of gain by one or more taxpayers. As one author indicates, "[t]axable gain may also be realized upon creation of the joint tenancy if it is created by an exchange of property owned by one of the joint tenants where the property exchanged does not constitute a like kind property within section 1031—for example, where corporate stock owned by one joint tenant is exchanged for real estate which is conveyed in joint tenancy." Young, Tax Incidents of Joint Ownership, 1959 U. III. L. Rev. 972, 977.

EXAMPLE 3-20.

F, who owned ABC stock with a basis of $100 and a fair market value of $1,000, converts that stock into a joint tenancy with *G*; in exchange *G* converts XYZ stock, which has a basis and a fair market value of $1,000, into joint tenancy with *F*. In effect *F* transfers an asset with a basis of $50 (a one-half interest in the ABC stock) in exchange for an asset worth $500 (a one-half interest in the XYZ stock). Presumably the gain is taxable to *F* at the time of the exchange. *G* has no gain or loss as a result of the transaction.

If the exchange described in Example 3-20 had involved stock in the same corporation, the transaction might not be taxable by reason of §1036. *See* Rev. Rul. 66-248, 1966-2 C.B. 303 (the conversion by a husband and wife of equal amounts of common stock in the same corporation from separate to community was nontaxable).

Although a transfer between husband and wife would not be taxable by reason of §1041, the holding of Rev. Rul. 66-248 should shield other taxpayers from any recognition of gain or loss.

§3.20.1. Income from Joint Tenancy Property

In the absence of an agreement to the contrary, each joint tenant is usually entitled under the local law to an equal share of the income from joint tenancy property. *E.g., Lipsitz v. Commissioner*, 220 F.2d 871 (4th Cir.), *cert. denied*, 350 U.S. 845 (1955) (Maryland law, tenancy by the entireties); *James A. Petrie, IV*, 70 T.C.M. (CCH) 1566 (1955) (Arizona law, joint tenancies). *But see Estate of Frances Elaine Freedman*, 93 T.C.M. 1007 (2007) (income from joint account taxed to mother who funded joint brokerage account with son, because Texas law provides that joint accounts belong to the parties in proportion to net contributions by each cotenant). The income attributable to each tenant is determined by reference to the state law—and this may or may not be according to the extent of the contributions the tenant made toward acquiring the asset. As indicated above, an unequal distribution of income may constitute a taxable gift from one tenant to the other.

§3.20.2. Income Tax Deductions

Conceptually a tenant should be entitled to deduct the taxes and interest the tenant pays only to the extent it exceeds the tenant's right to reimbursement from other tenants. However, a tenant may be entitled to deduct the amount of taxes and interest he or she actually pays on joint tenancy property where the tenants are jointly and severally liable to make the payments. Rev. Rul. 71-268, 1971-1 C.B. 58, followed such a rule in the case of a tenancy by the entirety where the husband and wife filed separate income tax returns. On the other hand, the ruling may merely evidence a more liberal policy of allowing deductions to married persons who make payments without regard to any right of reimbursement. *See* Young, Tax Incidents of Joint Ownership, 1959 U. Ill. L. Forum 972, 988. Where the joint tenants are husband and wife, the allocation of income and expenses is unnecessary if they file a joint income tax return.

§3.20.3. Basis; General Rule

The basis of the owners of joint tenancy property is determined according to the ordinary rules applicable to acquisitions by purchase, §1012, gift, §1015, and inheritance, §1014. The basis of property acquired from certain decedents dying in 2010 is determined under the modified carryover basis rules of §1022. *See* §§2.15 and 3.26.

EXAMPLE 3-21.

X provided the entire purchase price of Redacre. Title was taken in the name of X and Y as joint tenants. X has made a gift of a half interest in Redacre to Y. Y's basis in the property is one-half of X's cost basis. For the purpose of determining loss, Y's basis in Redacre would be limited to the value of the half interest at the time of the gift,—which might be reduced by a fractional interest discount.

Under § 1014(b)(9), the basis of a surviving joint tenant is determined by the federal estate tax valuation in the decedent's estate to the extent that the property is includible in the decedent's estate. Rev. Rul. 56-215, 1956-1 C.B. 324.

EXAMPLE 3-22.

F and G each paid $5,000 as the cost of acquiring Whiteacre, title to which was taken in their names as joint tenants. The property increased in value from $10,000 at the time of acquisition to $20,000 on the date of F's death. Half of the then value of Whiteacre, $10,000 (subject to a fractional interest discount) is includible in F's gross estate. G's basis in the property is $15,000, a composite of G's cost basis, $5,000, and the federal estate tax valuation of the interest included in F's estate, $10,000.

Section 2040 cannot be used by a survivor to gain an unwarranted increase in basis. That is, a survivor will not receive an increased basis in the whole of joint tenancy property merely by failing to rebut the presumption of § 2040(a) that all of the property is includible in the gross estate of the first tenant to die. *Richard v. Madden*, 52 T.C. 845 (1969), *aff'd, per curiam*, 440 F.2d 784 (7th Cir. 1971). Also, an estate cannot elect to use the alternate valuation date unless (1) the decedent's estate was required to file an estate tax return, and (2) the election decreases the value of the gross estate and the sum of the estate and generation-skipping transfer taxes. § 2032(c); Reg. § 20.2032-1(b); Rev. Rul. 56-60, 1956-1 C.B. 443.

§ 3.20.4. Special Basis Rule, § 1014(e)

Under § 1014(e), the basis of appreciated property transferred by gift to a decedent within one year prior to death is not adjusted where the property passes directly or indirectly from the donee-decedent to the donor or the donor's spouse. Thus, the rule would bar a step-up in the basis of appreciated property that a donor transfers into joint tenancy with a donee within a year prior to the donee's death. Of course, the amount included in the deceased donee's estate would be limited by § 2040(a) in any case. Note that the bar of § 1014(e) applies to property that passes directly or indirectly from the donee to the donor *or* the donor's spouse. Accordingly, there is no step-up in basis of appreciated property transferred by the donor into a joint tenancy with the donee and the donor *or* the donor's spouse. The application of this rule to community property is discussed in § 3.35.5.

A similar rule is imposed by § 1022 under the modified carryover basis rules effective for property acquired from certain decedents dying in 2010. § 1022(d)(1)(C).

§3.20.5. Depreciation Adjustment to Basis, §1014(b)(9)

Under §1014(b)(9), a survivor's basis in property acquired from a decedent prior to death *and* included in the decedent's estate is reduced to the extent the deductions were allowable to the survivor "for exhaustion, wear and tear, obsolescence, amortization, and depletion on such property before the death of the decedent." §1014(b)(9). Note that a reduction is made only with respect to the basis of an interest that is included in a decedent's gross estate. In most states, as between two joint tenants, each is entitled to half of the income and is chargeable with half of the expenses of joint tenancy property. Accordingly, the survivor's basis in the property would be reduced by half of the depreciation deductions that were allowable following the creation of the joint tenancy. Under the prior law of some states, all of the income of a tenancy by the entirety was allocable to the husband. In such a case on the death of the husband no adjustment was required under §1014(b)(9) because the survivor was not entitled to any of the income or deductions with respect to the property. *See, e.g.,* Rev. Rul. 75-142, 1975-1 C.B. 256 (tenancy by the entirety, Michigan law).

EXAMPLE 3-23.

In 2001, *X* paid $100,000 for depreciable property. Title was taken in the names of *X* and her brother, *B*, as joint tenants with right of survivorship. Depreciation deductions of $5,000 were allowable annually to *X* and *B*. *X* died in 2006, survived by *B*, when the property was worth $150,000. The full value of the property, $150,000, was included in *X*'s gross estate. *B*'s basis in the property is the federal estate tax value of the property in *X*'s estate, $150,000, *less $25,000*—the amount of depreciation allowable to *B* for the period between the creation of the joint tenancy and the death of *X*. If *X* had been entitled to all of the income under the state law, the basis of *B* would not be reduced under §1014(b)(9). Rev. Rul. 75-142, 1975-1 C.B. 256.

§3.20.6. Community Property in Joint Tenancy

If property held in a common law estate is community property under state law, it is community property for purposes of section 1014(b)(6) of the Code, regardless of the form in which title was taken. Rev. Rul. 87-98, 1987-2 C.B. 207.

As noted in §3.12.5, Wisconsin and several of the other community property states allow community property to be held in survivorship form. Others presume that property held by a husband and wife in joint tenancy or community property form is their community property. In either case, Rev. Rul. 87-98 indicates that the property would be recognized as community property entitled to a fully adjusted basis under §1014(b)(6) on the death of either spouse. The survivor's interest in community property is considered to have been acquired from the decedent and, hence, its basis is determined by reference to the federal estate tax value of the decedent's interest. When the federal estate tax value in the decedent's estate exceeds the otherwise determined basis of the survivor in the property (*e.g.*, its cost), the rule of §1014(b)(6) operates in the taxpayer's favor. In such cases the survivor's basis is increased without any tax cost whatever. A higher basis is of obvious advantage, for example, in the case of depreciable property or in the case of sale.

Because planners have focused on the use of the rule to increase the survivor's basis, it is commonly referred to as the "free step-up" of the survivor's basis.

§3.20.7. Community Property Transmuted into Separate Property Joint Tenancy

In most community property states, a husband and wife may transmute community property into any form of separate property, including a joint tenancy or tenancy in common. If community property is transmuted into a "true" joint tenancy between husband and wife, the property is equally owned by them as their separate property. (As noted above, §3.15, the law in some community property states presumes that joint tenancy acquired by a husband and wife with community property, remains their community property.) Under §2040, only half of the property is generally includible in the estate of the spouse first to die. The basis of only that one-half of the property is adjusted under §1014—the basis of the survivor's one-half interest is not adjusted. As noted above, §3.12.5, earlier decisions by courts in several community property states held that community property transferred to a validly created joint tenancy lost its character as community property. In addition, federal tax cases applying California law held that the basis of the surviving spouse is not affected by the death of a spouse in the case of community property converted to joint tenancy property, *Bordenave v. United States*, 150 F. Supp. 820 (N.D.Cal. 1957), or tenancy in common property, *Murphy v. Commissioner*, 342 F.2d 356 (9th Cir. 1965). In *Murphy*, the Ninth Circuit said "[W]e think Congress did not intend that the surviving spouse in a community property state should get a new basis for the one-half separate interest that the survivor owns in former, but converted, community property. There will, however, in such case be a new basis for the one-half interest that is in the decedent's estate, just as is true of Dr. Murphy's estate." 342 F.2d at 360.

§3.20.8. Basis Planning with Joint Tenancies

In some states, placing community property in joint tenancy form may jeopardize a tax-free increase in the basis of the survivor's share of the property. On the other hand, if it appears that the federal estate tax value of community property on the death of one spouse will be lower than its adjusted basis, a "step-down" of the survivor's basis in the property could be averted if the property is transferred into a true joint tenancy, partitioned, or otherwise converted into a tenancy in common. *See* §3.26.

§3.20.9. Termination of Joint Tenancies

The conversion of joint tenancy property into property held as tenants in common or otherwise equally owned by the tenants probably does not constitute a taxable event. Dickinson, Federal Income Tax Treatment of Divisions of Property: Marital Property Settlements, Estate and Trust Distributions, and Other Transactions, 18 U. Kan. L. Rev. 193, 229 (1970). This view is supported by Rev. Rul. 56-437, 1956-2 C.B. 507, which held that "[t]he conversion, for the purpose of eliminating a survivorship feature, of a joint tenancy in capital stock of a corporation into a tenancy in common is a nontaxable transaction for Federal income tax purposes." Also, a termination involving a transfer of the entire interest in the property to one tenant would not involve any immediate income tax consequences if it is treated as a gift under §102. Of course, a transfer between spouses or incident to divorce generally does not involve the recognition of any gain or loss. §1041. If one joint tenant murders the other, the local slayer's statute may treat the murder as having severed the joint tenancy.

§3.21. PLANNING WITH JOINT TENANCIES

Tax and nontax considerations dictate that joint tenancies should be used cautiously, if at all. The advantages of joint tenancies must be balanced against the disadvantages, including the virtually unlimited control that a joint tenant has over at least half of the joint tenancy property. Indeed, the interests of a client may best be served by holding title to property in forms that do not give anyone else any control over the property. The client's needs may be met by utilizing the multiparty bank accounts and other nontestamentary survivorship arrangements that are available under the U.P.C. and the law of many states. *See* U.P.C. §6-101 (1998).

A husband and wife may wish to hold their home and some bank accounts in joint tenancy form. However, in order to avoid bloating the survivor's estate they may not want the survivor to receive large amounts of property outright—by joint tenancy or otherwise. They may, instead, prefer to hold their property in ways that do not involve survivorship features. For example, a husband or wife may choose to leave most of his or her property to a trust for the survivor of them and, possibly, other beneficiaries. Effectuating such a plan may require rearranging the title to property including the termination of some existing joint tenancies.

On the other hand, joint tenancies and other forms of survivorship may meet the basic needs of a couple whose combined estates are likely to have a value of less than the amount sheltered by the unified credit. In any case, each spouse should have a backup will provide for the disposition of (1) any assets not held in joint tenancy in case the testator dies first, (2) the testator's share of the assets in case of simultaneous death, and (3) all of the assets in case the testator is the survivor.

There are some valid nontax reasons for a couple to hold title to the family home and some accounts at financial institutions in joint tenancy form. First, holding property in that form expresses confidence in the marriage and in the ability of the survivor to deal with the property. Second, joint tenancy bank accounts are seldom "frozen" on the death of a tenant and, thus, are fully and immediately available to the surviving spouse. Third, in some states the fees of the personal representative and the personal representative's attorney are based upon the amount of property accounted for in the estate proceeding, which does not include joint tenancy property, life insurance, and other property that passes outside of the proceeding.

Terminating a joint tenancy may reduce the amount of property that is includible in the estate of a tenant who provided more than a proportionate part of the cost of acquiring the property. *See* § 3.18. On the income tax side the position of the parties may be improved by creating or terminating a joint tenancy. As a rule of thumb the client should attempt to preserve the adjusted basis of property that has declined in value by taking steps to prevent it from being included in the client's estate. Conversely, within the limits of § 1014(e), the client may wish to take steps to cause the inclusion in the client's estate of property that has substantially appreciated in value and will qualify for the marital deduction.

EXAMPLE 3-24.

In 2004, *X* paid $500,000 for Blackacre. Title was taken in the names of *X* and her brother, *B,* as joint tenants with right of survivorship. *X* filed a gift tax return which reported a gift of a one-half interest in Blackacre, $250,000, to *B.* Early in 2006, Blackacre was appraised at $300,000 and *X* was diagnosed as being terminally ill. If title to Blackacre remains in the names of *X* and *B* as joint tenants, its entire $300,000 value will be included in *X*'s gross estate. However, if the value of *B*'s one-half interest in Blackacre were included in *X*'s gross estate, the tentative tax on *X*'s estate would be calculated without including the amount of the taxable gift that *X* made to *B* when Blackacre was acquired. § 2001(b). Under § 1014, *B*'s basis in Blackacre would be limited to $300,000. *B's* position would be improved if the joint tenancy were converted into a tenancy in common. *X* might then execute a codicil leaving her interest in Blackacre to *B.* If the joint tenancy were terminated, half of its value and the amount of the 2004 taxable gift would be included in the tax base of *X*'s estate. *B* would retain his original basis of $250,000 in his half. *B* would take an adjusted basis of $150,000 in the other one-half, which would pass to him under *X*'s will. If the joint tenancy were severed, *X*'s tax base and *B*'s basis in Blackacre would be $400,000 ($250,000 + $150,000).

D. COMMUNITY PROPERTY

§ 3.22. SCOPE

This part presents a broad overview of the community property laws in effect in ten American states,including their origins, basic characteristics, and tax consequences. The states are Alaska, Arizona, California, Idaho, Louisiana, Nevada, New Mexico,Texas, Washington, and Wisconsin. It does not present a detailed analysis of the law of any particular state. The relationship of community propertyto specific subjects is considered in later portions of the book. For example,the community property aspects of the gift and estate tax marital deductions are discussed in

Chapter 5, community property issues concerning life insurance are covered in Chapter 6, and the use of the community property widow's election is explored in Chapter 9. In general, each chapter includes a separate discussion of the relevant community property considerations.

§3.23. HISTORY

Community property concepts were introduced in this country by early settlers from France and Spain. Curiously, community property was not adopted by Florida, which was first settled by the Spanish in 1565—before any other settlement in North America. Of course, after two centuries of Spanish rule Florida became a British colony not long before the Revolutionary War. When the colonies of France and Spain were ultimately freed of foreign rule all except Florida retained the civil law marital property system. Curiously, all but Louisiana abandoned the civil law in favor of the English common law as their basic system of jurisprudence. Community property systems were adopted later in Idaho and Washington, perhaps due to the influence exerted by California.

Community property marital property systems have long been in effect in eight southern and western states: Arizona, California, Idaho, Louisiana, Nevada, New Mexico, Texas, and Washington. Short-lived community property systems were adopted in several other states in the 1940s in order to split the income of an employed spouse between husband and wife. The systems were abandoned soon after the federal income tax law was changed to permit spouses to file joint returns, which in effect provides for income splitting. Wisconsin adopted a community property system based on the Uniform Marital Property Act (1997), effective January 1, 1986. Wis. Stat. Ann. §766.01 *et seq.* (2011). The Wisconsin law refers to property acquired during marriage in which each spouse has an equal share as "marital property" rather than "community property." However, Wis. Stat. Ann. §766.001(2) (2011) states, "It is the intent of the legislature that marital property is a form of community property."

More recently Alaska has adopted an optional form of community property. Under the Alaska Community Property Act, Alaska Stat. §§34.77.010, *et seq.* (2011), spouses who are both domiciled in Alaska may classify all or any part of their property as community property. Alaska Stat. §34.77.060(a) (2011). "Whether or not both, or neither" spouse is domiciled in Alaska, a couple may classify as community property any property that is transferred to a community property trust. Alaska Stat. §34.77.060(b) (2011). A community property trust is defined in Alaska Stat. §33.77.100 (2011), as a trust at least one of the trustees of which is a "qualified person" (*i.e.,* an Alaska bank or trust company or an individual who is a permanent resident of Alaska). The trustee who is a qualified person must have the power to maintain the records of the trust and be responsible for preparing and filing the trust's income tax returns.

Despite their common origin in the marital property laws of Spain and France, the community property law of each community property state has developed into a unique body of law. Of all of the states, Louisiana adheres most closely to the original civil law rules. Elsewhere, notably California, there have been infusions of English common law principles and extensive statutory "modernization" to meet changing economic and social conditions. W. Reppy & W. de Funiak, Community Property in the United States, v (1975).

Community property states all treat a husband and wife as partners who are presumed to own equal one-half interests in property acquired during marriage. In simplest terms, a husband and wife own equal interests in property onerously acquired during marriage. Of course, the marital community ceases to exist upon the death of a spouse or dissolution of the marriage. "Each spouse has the right of testamentary disposition over his or her half of the community property." *Estate of Miramontes-Najera,* 13 Cal. Rptr. 3d 245 (Cal. App. 2004). Until relatively recent times, a husband generally had greater managerial powers over community property than his wife. Sweeping legislative changes made in the 1970s gave each spouse essentially the same powers to manage and control community property.

The community property laws of states which have assumed civil law jurisdiction over "Indians and Indian Territories" for domestic relations purposes apply to the characterization of income earned by Native Americans residing in those states. Certification from the United States Tax Court, Washington, D.C., in *Estate of Millie Cross v. Commissioner,* 126 Wash. 2d 43 (1995).

§ 3.24. Estate Planning with Community Property

Important property rights and tax consequences are affected by the characterization of property as separate or community property. Accordingly, one of an estate planner's first tasks is to determine the character of the property owned by a married person. If the character of some items is uncertain, the husband and wife may wish to enter into an agreement specifying their respective interests in those items. Of course, the lawyer should be alert to the tax consequences of interspousal agreements as well as the ethical implications of representing both spouses. The lawyer may also recommend that the status of some items be changed by agreement, conveyance, or partition. Thus, steps may be taken to assure that assets held in joint tenancy will be treated as community property in order to preserve the step-up in basis that is available for all of the community property on the death of one spouse. *See* § 3.20.6 and § 3.26. For essentially the same reason, a husband and wife moving to a community property state may wish to convert their property to community property. Conversely, in order to prevent a full step-down in the bases of assets that have declined in value the planner may recommend that they be converted into equally owned forms of separate property ownership (*e.g.,* tenancy in common or a true separate property joint tenancy).

Disregarded Entities. According to Rev. Proc. 2002-69, 2002-2 C.B. 831, a business entity that is not a corporation and is wholly owned by a husband and wife as community property under the laws of a state, foreign country, or possession of the United States may be treated by the husband and wife as either a disregarded entity or as a partnership. Thus, a limited liability company that was entirely owned by a husband and wife as their community property could be disregarded by them for federal income tax purposes. Some planners were concerned that the IRS might insist that such an entity be treated as a partnership. Under Rev. Proc. 2002-69, "If the entity is disregarded, its activities are treated in the same manner as a sole proprietorship, branch, or division of the owner." Presumably, a husband and wife could make gifts to grantor trusts of interests in a disregarded LLC without jeopardizing that status.

§3.25. PRESERVE THE COMMUNITY OR SEPARATE CHARACTER OF PROPERTY

Once the character and ownership of the items is properly arranged, the spouses should be counseled regarding the importance of maintaining the arrangement. In particular, they should be advised to keep the separate and community property completely segregated. Thus, separate and community property funds should be kept in separate bank accounts and securities registered in proper forms. The couple should also avoid changing the way in which they hold title to property.

Extra care is required in Idaho, Louisiana, Texas, and Wisconsin, which characterize the income derived from separate property as community property. In those states, the interest paid on a separate property bank account should be withdrawn at regular intervals and deposited in a community property account. Otherwise all or a substantial portion of the original account might later be treated as community property as a result of commingling the community property income with the separate property principal. Caution must also be exercised with respect to the reinvestment of the dividends on separately owned mutual funds shares. Note that in Louisiana and Wisconsin a spouse may reserve as separate property the income from his or her separate property by executing a written declaration. La. Civ. Code Ann. Art. 2339 (2011); Wis. Stat. Ann. §766.59(1) (2011).

The transfer of property to a revocable inter vivos trust is often the best way to preserve its separate or community property character. The transfer of community property to a properly drafted revocable trust should not cause any change in its character. Revocable trusts are discussed in some detail in §§10.7-10.17. The Wisconsin law expressly recognizes that the transfer of property to a trust does not by itself change the classification of the property. Wis. Stat. Ann. §766.31(5) (2011). However, in order to preserve the character of the property the trust agreement should specify that the property transferred to the trust will retain its character as community or separate property. The provisions of the trust regarding revocation, distribution of income, and other matters should, of course, be consistent with the character of the property transferred to the trust. Thus, a trust of community property ordinarily should be revocable by the joint action of husband and wife, the income should be payable to them as community property, and the property should retain its community character in the event of revocation. As an alternative, one spouse could hold, with respect to community property, a power of revocation that would be exercisable on behalf of both spouses.

Under California law, community property transferred to a revocable inter vivos trust retains its character if the trust "provides that the trust is revocable as to that property during the marriage and the power, if any, to modify the trust as to the rights and interests in that property during the marriage may be exercised only with the joinder or consent of both spouses." Cal. Fam. Code §761 (2011). *See also* Rev. Rul. 66-283, 1966-2 C.B. 297 (California law); *Katz v. United States*, 382 F.2d 723 (9th Cir. 1967) (California law). As discussed in §10.8, under California law a trust is revocable unless "expressly made irrevocable by the trust instrument." Cal. Prob. Code §15400 (2011). Also, note that the California law allows a trust to be revoked in the manner specified in the trust instrument and, unless the method specified in the trust is explicitly made the exclusive method of revocation, "by a writing (other than a will) signed by the settlor and delivered to the trustee during the lifetime of the settlor." Cal. Prob. Code §15401(a) (2011). In addition, unless otherwise specified in the trust instrument, "a power to revoke as to community property may be exercised by either spouse acting alone." Cal. Fam. Code § 761(b) (2011).

Under Idaho law, community property retains its character when it is transferred to a trust that (1) is revocable during the joint lifetimes of a husband and wife, (2) provides that the property and withdrawals from the trust will be community property and, (3) may be amended during their joint lifetimes by joint action. Idaho Code § 32-906A (2011).

§ 3.26. Preserve the Availability of Stepped-Up Basis Under § 1014(b)(6)

A major goal of estate planning in community property states is to achieve a step-up in the income tax basis of all appreciated community property under § 1014(b)(6) upon the death of either spouse. A second goal, discussed at § 3.27, is to avoid unnecessarily increasing the size of the surviving spouse's estate.

As noted above, upon the death of either spouse the bases of all of the community property are changed to their values on the federal estate tax valuation date applicable to the deceased spouse's estate. § 1014(b)(6). Accordingly, attaining this goal simply requires that the spouses establish and maintain the community property character of appreciated property. This is assisted by legislation in several community property states which creates a presumption that property held by husband and wife in joint tenancy form is community property. *E.g.*, Wash. Rev. Code § 64.28.040 (2011); Cal. Fam. Code § 2580 (2011) (by its terms the California statute only applies upon dissolution of marriage by divorce). The IRS has recognized that Wisconsin marital property is community property for federal income tax purposes. Rev. Rul. 87-13, 1987-1 C.B. 20. As indicated above, the spouses should consider taking steps to preserve the basis of property that has declined in value in order to avoid a downward adjustment of basis upon the death of either spouse. Thus, depreciated community property should be partitioned into equal separately owned interests or switched into separate property forms of ownership (*e.g.*, tenancies in common and "true" separate property joint tenancies).

From a tax perspective it is generally desirable for a husband and wife who are domiciled in a community property state to hold their property as community property. Accordingly, a husband and wife with a stable marriage who move from a common law state to a community property state may consider entering into an agreement changing their property into community property. *See* § 3.29. That step is clearly preferable to having the property characterized as quasi-community property, which is generally treated for tax purposes as the separate estate property of the spouse who acquired it. *See* § 3.38.

The 2001 Act repealed § 1014 effective January 1, 2010, and substituted a modified carryover basis regime in its place. § 1022. Subsequently, the 2010 Act limited the applicability of § 1022 to those taking property from a decedent dying in 2010, but only where the decedent's executor elected out of the application of the federal estate tax. *See* § 2.3. Under the general rule of § 1022, a recipient's basis in assets acquired from a decedent is the lesser of: (1) the decedent's adjusted basis in the asset, or (2) the fair market value of the asset on the date of the decedent's death. However, each estate may allocate an aggregate basis increase of $1.3 million among the assets included in a decedent's estate. An additional $3 million in aggregate basis may be added to the basis of assets that pass to a surviving spouse outright or to a qualified terminable interest property (similar to QTIP and QTIP trusts). Under §1022, the surviving spouse's share of community property is treated as "owned by and acquired from, the decedent if at least one-half of the whole of the community interest in such property is treated as owned by, and acquired from, the decedent without regard to this clause." §1022(d)(1)(B)(iv). This clause seemingly emulates the operation of §1014(b)(6) and result in the basis of the surviving spouse being adjusted to reflect the benefit of the full allocation of a deceased spouse's permitted aggregate adjustments to basis (*i.e.*, both the $1.3 million and the $3 million adjustments). The basis of property acquired from a decedent may not be increased above its fair market value at the time of the decedent's death. §1022(d)(2).

§3.27. AVOID UNNECESSARILY INCREASING SIZE OF SURVIVING SPOUSE'S ESTATE

The estate plan for a husband and wife in a community property state is typically drafted to avoid subjecting an unnecessarily large amount of property to taxation upon the death of the surviving spouse. Such a plan usually also seeks to preserve the benefit of each spouse's unified credit. The allowance of the marital deduction that is available for property transferred to a qualified terminable interest property (QTIP) trust has made it relatively simple to achieve this goal. In brief, QTIP property is included in a surviving spouse's estate only to the extent the marital deduction is claimed in the estate of the first spouse to die. *See* §§2044 and 2056(b)(7). *See also* §5.23. Some clients attempt to reduce the amount of property subject to tax on the surviving spouse's death and gain some other tax advantages by using a community property widow's election plan. *See* §§9.23-9.39. However, a widow's election plan is unsuitable for most clients because of its rigidity, complexity, and somewhat uncertain tax consequences. *See* §9.39.

§3.28. SEPARATE AND COMMUNITY PROPERTY

In simple terms, separate property ("individual property" under Wisconsin law) is property owned by a spouse prior to marriage and all property acquired after marriage by gift, inheritance, devise, or bequest. All other property acquired during marriage by a husband or wife is their community property. This "negative" definition of community property is simple to understand and provides the key to answering most questions regarding the characterization of property. It is important to note that marriage itself does not cause any previously owned property to become community property. Quite the contrary: Property owned prior to marriage retains its separate character unless it is changed by agreement or conduct of the parties. Thus, "Property owned at a marriage which occurs after 12:01 A.M. on January 1, 1986, is the individual property of the owning spouse . . . ." Wis. Stat. Ann. §766.31(6) (2011).

§3.28.1. Gifts of Separate Property

Each spouse is generally free to dispose of his or her separate property inter vivos or at death without restriction. However, the "quasi-community property" concept, adopted by several community property states, including California, Idaho, Washington, and Wisconsin gives the nonacquiring spouse an interest at death or dissolution of marriage in property that was acquired during marriage while the couple resided in a noncommunity property state which would have been community property had they been domiciled in the community property state. Quasi-community property is discussed further at § 3.38.

§ 3.28.2. Gifts of Community Property

Each spouse owns an equal, undivided one-half interest in all community property. *E.g.,* Wis. Stat. Ann. § 766.31(3) (2011). Consistent with that concept of ownership, each spouse has the power of testamentary disposition over only half of the community property—the other half belongs to the other spouse. California, Idaho, and Washington prohibit one spouse from making a gift of community property without the consent of the other spouse. Cal. Fam. Code § 1100 (2011); Wash. Rev. Code § 26.16.030(2) (2011); *Koenig v. Bishop,* 409 P.2d 102 (Idaho 1965). Wisconsin permits a spouse to make a gift to a third party of marital property that is subject to the donor spouse's management and control if the gifts to the donee do not exceed "$1,000 in a calendar year, or a larger amount if, when made, the gift is reasonable in amount considering the economic position of the spouses." Wis. Stat. Ann. § 766.53 (2011). The other community property states appear to permit a spouse to make reasonable gifts of community property that do not injure or defraud the other spouse. W. Reppy & W. de Funiak, Community Property in the United States 338-344 (1975); W. de Funiak & M. Vaughn, Principles of Community Property § 122 (2d ed. 1971). In order to reduce the potential for conflict, both spouses should consent in writing to any significant gifts of community property.

On the death of a spouse, the surviving spouse may recover half the value of pay-on-death accounts funded with community property that were made payable to third parties without the consent of the surviving spouse. *Estate of Miramontes-Najera,* 13 Cal. Rptr.3d (Cal. App. 2004) (recovery allowed although surviving spouse received more than half the total community property). Similarly, the surviving spouse can generally recover half the proceeds of community property life insurance that was made payable to third parties without his or her consent. *See* § § 6.16–6.16.3.

§ 3.28.3. Tracing the Character of Property

The character of property as separate or community generally persists through sales, changes in form, and reinvestments. Thus, the proceeds from the sale of an item of separate property and any property purchased with the proceeds is separate property. In all states the income derived from community property is community. Consistently, some community property states treat the income from separate property as separate. However, in Idaho, Louisiana, Texas, Wisconsin, and perhaps Arizona, the income from separate property is community property. Idaho Code § 32-906(1) (2011); La. Civ. Code Ann. art. 2339 (2011); Wis. Stat. Ann. § 766.31(4) (2011). (As noted in § 3.25, in Wisconsin, a spouse may, by written declaration, reserve the separate status of the income from separate property.) Until 1980, Texans could not overcome that rule, which caused some estate tax complications under § 2036. However, under a 1980 amendment to the Texas constitution, the income from the spouses' separate property is community property unless the spouses otherwise agree in writing. Tex. Const. art. XVI, § 15 (2011). *See* Vaughn, Texas Amends Its Constitution and Its Community Property System, 8 Community Prop. J. 59 (1981).

§ 3.28.4. Presumption Favoring Community Property

Community property states presume that property acquired during marriage, or owned at the time of dissolution of the marriage, is community property. Rebuttal of that presumption generally requires clear, cogent, and convincing evidence to the contrary. The presumption is the basis of the rule that commingled property is community in nature (*i.e.*, any separate property component is lost if it cannot be traced). "In the absence of any statutory qualification, this presumption in favor of community property is given effect regardless of whether the title to the property is taken in the name of one or the other or both of the spouses. Doctrines of the common law relative to presumptions existing when property is purchased by one spouse and taken in the name of the other or in the names of both are not entitled to recognition under a system in which the presumption is that an acquisition is community property of husband and wife." W. de Funiak & M. Vaughn, Principles of Community Property § 60 (2d ed. 1971).

§ 3.28.5. Special Problems of Characterization

Certain types of property present particularly difficult problems of characterization. Perhaps the most serious involves the characterization of the appreciation in value during marriage of a closely-held business that was owned by one spouse prior to marriage. The marital community is entitled to the fruits of the labor of the spouses during marriage. Accordingly, most community property states "first attempt to ascertain whether the community estate has been fairly compensated for the community efforts, by way of salary or otherwise. If this is the case, the entire appreciation will be awarded to the owner-spouse's separate estate." Weekley, Appreciation of a Closely-Held Business Interest Owned Prior to Marriage—Is It Separate or Community Property?, 7 Comm. Prop. J. 261, 279 (1980). If the community was not fairly compensated for the owner-spouse's efforts, some part of the appreciation will be treated as community property. In *Jensen v. Jensen*, 665 S.W.2d 107 (Texas 1984), the Supreme Court of Texas discussed two theories: the "reimbursement" theory, under which the community is entitled to be reimbursed for the reasonable value of the time and effort of both spouses, and the "community ownership" theory, under which the increase in value of separate property due to the efforts of the owner spouse is allocated to the community. In *Jensen*, which was the last of three opinions written by the Texas Supreme Court in the same case, the court adopted the reimbursement theory.

Sticky problems can also arise where mixed separate and community funds are used to acquire an asset. In community property states (with the possible exception of Louisiana), when an asset is purchased with a lump sum payment that is made up of community and separate funds, proportionate interests in the asset are held as community and separate property respectively.

EXAMPLE 3-25.

Blackacre was purchased by *H* and *W* for $10,000, of which $3,000 was community and $7,000 was *W*'s separate property. Absent a contrary agreement or evidence that *W* intended to make a gift to *H*, in most community property states *H* and *W* would own a 30% interest in Black-acre as their community property. The balance would be the separate property of *W*.

Different results may occur where a spouse contracts to buy an asset prior to marriage but some post marriage payments on the asset are made from community property. In some states the asset would be treated as separate because it was separate at the time the purchasing spouse first acquired an interest in it (this is called the "inception of title" rule). In those states the expenditure of community funds is seldom treated as a gift to the spouse who owns the separate property. Instead, the community has a right of reimbursement for the payments made from community property. *E.g., McCurdy v. McCurdy*, 372 S.W.2d 381 (Tex. Civ. App. 1963), *writ refused.* Although the community may be reimbursed, it is generally not entitled to recover any interest on the community funds that were invested in the property. *Id.* In contrast, other states apply the proportionate ownership rule to property acquired with mixed deferred payments, just as in the case of lump sum payments. *E.g., Gudelj v. Gudelj*, 259 P.2d 656 (Cal. 1953). Thus, if community funds are used to make one-third of the payments on property that was originally acquired as the separate property of one spouse, a one-third interest in the property is held as community property.

The characterization of life insurance acquired with mixed community and separate funds also varies among the states. *See* § 6.15. California and Washington generally characterize cash value life insurance according to the proportion of the premiums paid from each source, while the other states usually follow an inception of title approach under which the insurance retains its original character. However, in the latter case, the other estate would be entitled to reimbursement for premiums paid from it.

The Wisconsin law regarding the characterization of life insurance is quite different from that of the other community property states. Wis. Stat. Ann. § 766.61 (2011). Under it, interests in policies that insure the lives of married persons and the proceeds of the policies are determined in accordance with three general rules. First, a policy issued after the determination date (*i.e.,* date of marriage, date on which both spouses become domiciled in Wisconsin, or on January 1, 1986) that lists the insured spouse as owner is marital property regardless of the character of funds used to pay premiums. Wis. Stat. Ann. § 766.61(3)(a)(1) (2011). Second, a policy that lists the noninsured spouse as owner is the individual property of the noninsured spouse regardless of the character of funds used to pay premiums. Wis. Stat. Ann. § 766.61(3)(c) (2011). Third, a policy that lists a third person as owner is partially marital property if any premium is paid from marital property. "The marital property component of the ownership interest and proceeds is the amount which results from multiplying the entire ownership interest and proceeds by a fraction, the numerator of which is the period during marriage that the policy was in effect after the date on which a premium was paid from marital property and the denominator of which is the entire period the policy was in effect." Wis. Stat. Ann. §766.61(3)(d) (2011).

§3.29. AGREEMENTS REGARDING CHARACTER OF PROPERTY; DIVISION OF COMMUNITY PROPERTY

The community property states generally allow a husband and wife to enter into agreements regarding the character of their property. *See, e.g.,* Cal. Fam. Code §§721(a), 852 (2011); Nev. Rev. Stat. §123.070 (2011); Wash. Rev. Code §26.16.120 (2011). Wisconsin law also recognizes that, with certain exceptions, "a marital property agreement may vary the effect of this chapter'. Wis. Stat. Ann. §766.17(1) (2011). The restrictions formerly imposed by the Texas constitution were largely removed by a 1980 amendment of Article XVI, Section 15. *See* Vaughn, Texas Amends Its Constitution and Its Community Property System, 8 Community Prop. J. 59 (1981). Some of the states also recognize oral agreements regarding the ownership of personal property. However, in California a change in the character of property made after 1984 must be "in writing by an express declaration that is made, joined in, consented to, or accepted by the spouse whose interest in the property is adversely affected." Cal. Fam. Code §852(a) (2011).

California Family Law Code provisions, which were intended to apply primarily in a marital dissolution setting, caused unanticipated problems in the disposition of property at death. *See Estate of MacDonald,* 51 Cal. 3d 262 (1990). In response, provisions were added to the Probate Code that were intended to give greater respect to the terms of nontestamentary devices and less emphasis on the original character of the property involved. A survey of subsequent decisions indicates that "the title of marital property at the death of a spouse is playing a secondary role in the passage of that property compared to the matters of character and transmutation. Consequently, the expectations of spouses to the right to take property at death may often be frustrated, such as when the spouse learns that joint tenancy title may not in fact result in survivorship or when a duly filed beneficiary designation nevertheless fails." Oldman, *Family Law Presumptions and Passing Property at Death,* 7 Cal. Tr. & Est. Q. 28 (2001).

Spouses may use an agreement to change the character of property from separate to community or vice versa. Such changes may have important tax consequences. Of course, spouses may also partition community property into equally owned units of separate property. Perhaps most important, an agreement can be used to clarify the rights of the spouses in their property where its separate or community property character is uncertain. An agreement could be used, for example, to establish the character of commingled property or the separate or community character of property that is nominally joint tenancy. Because of the inherent conflict in the spouses' economic interests, each party to an agreement should be encouraged to obtain independent counsel. Agreements between spouses regarding the character of property should be in writing, clearly expressing the spouses' agreement, and be signed by both spouses. *See* Cal. Fam. Code §853 (2010) (to be valid a transmutation must be made by an express declaration in writing, joined in, consented to, or accepted by the spouse whose interest is adversely affected). The local law may require that an agreement be notarized if it affects the title to real property.

Non-Pro Rata Division of Community Property. Upon the death of one spouse, it is sometimes advantageous to divide the former community property between the surviving spouse and the decedent's estate on an aggregate (*i.e.,* non-pro rata) basis rather than on an item-by-item basis. The law of some states authorizes spouses to enter into written agreements that allow a non-pro rata division. For example, Wis. Stat. § 766.31(3)(b)(2) (2011) provides that a surviving spouse "and the successor in interest to the decedent's share of marital property may enter into an agreement providing that some or all of the marital property in which each has an interest will be divided based on aggregate value rather than divided item by item." In addition, Cal. Prob. Code § 100(b) (2011) provides that, "a husband and wife may agree in writing to divide their community property on the basis of a non pro rata division of the aggregate value of the community property or on the basis of a division of each individual item or asset of community property, or party on each basis." The last sentence of Cal. Prob. Code § 101(b) (2011) suggests that the law authorizes but does not require such an agreement in order to make a non-pro rata division of the community property ("Nothing in this subdivision shall be construed to require this written agreement in order to permit or recognize a non pro rata division of community property.")

Agreements to allow non-pro rata divisions are unnecessary if they are allowed by local law. For example, LR 200334030, which was not concerned with community property, held that a non-pro rata distribution of assets upon termination of a trust would not involve recognition of gain or loss because such divisions are authorized by state law. A Washington statute, Wash. Rev. Code § 11.68.090 (2011), gives a personal representative who is appointed with nonintervention the same powers that a trustee has under the trust management provisions of Wash. Rev. Code § 11.98.070 (2011), which include the power to make non-pro rata distributions of property. (Nonintervention powers are generally conferred on the personal representative of a solvent decedent's estate if the personal representative was named by the decedent in his or her will. Wash. Rev. Code § 11.68.011 (2011). The cited section also allows nonintervention powers to be conferred on personal representatives under some other circumstances.) Non-pro rata distributions are also discussed at § 12.40.

§ 3.30. Agreements Governing Disposition of Property at Death

Idaho, Texas, and Washington have statutes that expressly permit a husband and wife to enter into written agreements regarding the disposition of property at death. Idaho Code § 15-6-201 (2011); Tex. Prob. Code Ann. §§ 451-462 (2011); Wash. Rev. Code § 26.16.120 (2011). The Wisconsin law allows a marital property agreement to provide that the property of either or both of the spouses passes upon the death of either spouse "without probate to a designated person, trust or other entity by nontestamentary disposition." Wis. Stat. Ann. § 766.58(3)(f) (2011). In addition, Nevada and Wisconsin allow a right of survivorship to be attached to community property. Nev. Rev. Stat. § 111.064 (2011); Wis. Stat. Ann. § 766.60(5) (2011). *See* § 3.31. Under Wisconsin law the first deceased spouse may not dispose at death of any interest in survivorship marital property. Wis. Stat. Ann. § 766.60(5)(a) (2011). An agreement subject to the Idaho and Wisconsin laws may extend to separate and community property, but the statutes in the other states apparently apply only to community property. The Texas law provides that an agreement that satisfies the statutory requirements is effective without an adjudication. Tex. Prob. Code Ann. §458 (2011). However, it establishes a procedure by which a surviving spouse or the personal representative of a deceased spouse may apply to the court for an order "stating that the agreement satisfies the requirements of this code and is effective to create a right of survivorship in community property." Tex. Prob. Code Ann. §456(a) (2011). Use of the adjudication procedure may be required by transfer agents and others involved in the registration of title to property. Proof of death and a declaration of the facts necessary to establish the validity of the survivorship arrangement may be required in the other four states. The statutes of the states other than Texas do not provide for an estate administration proceeding or any process for adjudicating the validity of the arrangement. The Idaho statute is simply an expanded version of U.P.C. §6-101 (2011), which treats as nontestamentary a variety of arrangements that were previously often challenged as testamentary in nature. Professor Richard Effland has suggested that the amended form of U.P.C. §6-101 adopted in Arizona will sustain interspousal agreements regarding the status and disposition of property at death. Estate Planning Under the New Arizona Probate Code, 1974 Ariz. St. L.J. 1, 19. In contrast, the Texas statute was added in 1989 to implement the 1987 amendment of Article XVI, Section 15 of the Texas Constitution. Of course, Texas also adopted an amended form of the U.P.C. provision. Tex. Prob. Code Ann. §450 (2011).

A survivorship arrangement of the type under discussion is not itself a sufficient estate plan, even for a couple with a relatively small estate. The arrangement is similar to a joint tenancy between spouses; and, like a joint tenancy, it needs to be supplemented with a will to dispose of any property not subject to the agreement and to dispose of all of the property upon the death of the survivor. Also, such an arrangement is not a complete substitute. It probably cannot be used, for example, to nominate guardians for minor children, direct apportionment of taxes, exercise powers of appointment, dispose of property subject to administration in other states, etc. Finally, property subject to such an arrangement probably cannot be set apart to a surviving spouse as a family award or family allowance that is exempt from creditors. Note that a surviving spouse could disclaim the right to receive the decedent's interest in that interest subject to the agreement, which would usually subject the property to administration in the deceased spouse's estate. See §2518. See also §§12.33–12.36.

Spouses in community property states are generally free to contract regarding the content or revocability of their wills. However, contractual wills often give rise to serious tax and nontax problems. See §4.7. In most cases clients should be encouraged to use another device, such as an inter vivos trust, instead of contractual wills.

§3.31. SURVIVORSHIP COMMUNITY PROPERTY

Survivorship community property is created in Nevada when the instrument of transfer expressly declares that the husband and wife take the property as community property with right of survivorship. In Wisconsin, registration of property as "survivorship marital property" is effective to vest ownership of the property in the surviving spouse. Presumably the registration of community property as survivorship community property does not have any present tax consequences. The Alaska

Community Property Act allows the spouses to designate property as survivorship community property—which will all belong to the survivor of the couple. Alaska Stat. § 34.77.110(e) (2011). California law permits spouses to hold property as community property with right of survivorship. Cal. Civ. Code § 682.1 (2011). A similar law for real property in Idaho became effective July 1, 2008. Idaho Code § 15-6-401 (2011). The new law provides:

> An estate in community property with right of survivorship is created by a grant, transfer or devise to a husband and wife, when expressly declared in the grant, transfer or devise to be an estate in community property with right of survivorship. An estate in community property with right of survivorship may also be created by grant or transfer from a husband and wife, when holding title as community property or otherwise, to themselves or from either husband or wife to both husband and wife when expressly declared in the grant, transfer or devise to be an estate in community property with right of survivorship.

Either spouse may terminate the right of survivorship in real property by filing an affidavit in the recorder's office for the county in which the real property is located terminating right of survivorship. Idaho Code § 15-6-402(1) (2011). Unless otherwise directed by the court, the divorce of a husband and wife or the annulment of their marriage severs their interests in community property with right of survivorship, which causes the property to be owned by them as tenants in common. Idaho Code § 15-6-402(2) (2011). The goal is to allow the property to pass to the surviving spouse as simply as possible with a stepped-up basis for income tax purposes. Care should be exercised in using the new form of ownership, which should have the advantages and disadvantages of joint tenancy ownership.

The law regarding survivorship community property will probably emulate the law applicable to joint tenancies. Thus, a dissolution of the parties' marriage would terminate the survivorship feature and constitute the parties tenants in common with respect to the property. Under the Nevada statute the survivorship feature is extinguished if either spouse transfers his or her interest in the property. However, as in Wisconsin, it is doubtful that the spouse first to die could overcome the survivorship feature by a provision in his or her will. The statutes also do not deal with any rights a deceased spouse's creditors may have against the property. They do provide a shortcut to pass community property to the surviving spouse without the necessity of an estate administration proceeding, which would usually be required to pass community property to the survivor by will or under the intestate succession law. They also allow the spouses to avoid the possible income tax basis disadvantage of putting their property into joint tenancy form. *See* § 3.35.4.

§ 3.32. EMPLOYEE BENEFIT PLANS; IRAS

In most community property states, the interest of a nonemployee spouse in the employee spouse's benefit plans is recognized upon dissolution of the community upon divorce. However, although a nonemployee spouse has a community property interest in an employee spouse's qualified plan, the Employee Retirement Income Security Act (ERISA) prevents the nonemployee spouse from disposing of it except to the extent provided in a qualified domestic relations order (QDRO). *Boggs v. Boggs*, 520 U.S. 833 (1997). In *Boggs* the Court held that ERISA preempted state community property laws to the extent that recognizing them would diminish the rights of the participant. According to the Court, "The QDRO and the surviving spouse annuity provisions define the scope of a nonparticipant spouse's community property interests in pension plans consistent with ERISA." In the Court's view, the attempt by the participant's spouse to dispose of a community property interest in the pension plan by her will was "a prohibited 'assignment or alienation.'" The Court reasoned that ERISA was intended to provide benefits for participants and their designated beneficiaries. To that end it included safeguards, such as restrictions against alienation, which ensured the participants and their beneficiaries would receive the intended benefits.

> Under respondents' approach, retirees could find their retirement benefits reduced by substantial sums because they have been diverted to testamentary recipients. Retirement benefits and the income stream provided for by ERISA-regulated plans would be disrupted in the name of protecting a nonparticipant spouses' [sic] successors over plan participants and beneficiaries. 520 U.S. at 852.

The Court also recognized the rights of the participant's surviving spouse under the Retirement Equity Act (REA): "Sandra Boggs [the decedent's second wife, who survived him], as we have observed, asserts that federal law preempts and supersedes state law and requires the surviving spouse annuity to be paid to her as sole beneficiary. We agree."

Under the *Boggs* approach, the estate tax return of the deceased nonparticipant might either, (1) not report any interest in the surviving spouse's qualified plans, or (2) report half of the community property interest in the employed spouse's qualified plans. If the latter course is followed, presumably the nonemployee's estate would be entitled to claim a marital deduction of a corresponding amount. *See* § 2056(b)(7)(C). A Technical Advice Memorandum issued in 1989, LR 8943006, with respect to a Louisiana decedent is consistent with that result.

Individual Retirement Accounts (IRAs) are generally not subject to ERISA. However, the extent to which the *Boggs* rule might apply to qualified plan benefits that are rolled over into an IRA is unclear. Making such a roll over might eliminate the nonparticipant spouse's right to benefits under REA. And, doing so might also free the nonparticipant spouse to dispose of his or her interest to a person other than the employee spouse.

QDROs. The QDRO exception to the anti-alienation provisions of ERISA would appear to allow a nonparticipant spouse who predeceases the participant spouse to dispose of any interest in a qualified plan that had been awarded to him or her in a dissolution proceeding. That conclusion, of course, assumes that such an order is a QDRO. Apparently, it is not, at least not in the Ninth Circuit. In a 2-1 decision, *Branco v. UFCW-Northern California Employers Joint Pension Plan*, 279 F.3d 1154 (9th Cir. 2002), the court negated the power of the nonemployee spouse to dispose of any post-mortem interest in a qualified plan that was awarded to her in a stipulated court order in a dissolution proceeding. After quoting from the Supreme Court decision in *Boggs v. Boggs*, 520 U.S. 833 (1997), the majority wrote, "Given ERISA's concern for the living, it is consistent to conclude that the QDRO exception to ERISA's anti-alienation provision was not intended to subject significant portions of pension benefits to transfer by a predeceased spouse."

Preemption of Other State Laws. According to the United States Supreme Court, state laws which provide that for purposes of distributing nonprobate assets a former spouse is treated as having died on the date the marriage was dissolved are preempted by the provisions of ERISA insofar as employer provided benefits are concerned. In *Estate of Egelhoff,* 139 Wash.2d 557 (1999), the Washington Supreme Court held that such a state law, Wash. Rev. Code § 11.07.010 (2011), applied to the distribution of the proceeds of employer provided life insurance and pension plan benefits, both of which continued to name his former wife as beneficiary. The Washington Supreme Court, held that both should be paid to the children of his first marriage, who were the decedent's intestate successors. The court held that the life insurance was provided pursuant to a welfare benefit plan and was, accordingly, not subject to ERISA preemption. It continued to say that the state law applied to the pension plan because the state law neither referred to ERISA nor was it sufficiently connected with ERISA to justify preemption.

The decision of the Washington Supreme Court in *Egelhoff* was reversed in a 7-2 decision by the United States Supreme Court, which held that the Washington statute was pre-empted because it was "connected" to an employee benefit plan covered by ERISA. *Egelhoff v. Egelhoff,* 532 U.S. 141 (2001). The Court also concluded that the state law impermissibly "interferes with nationally uniform plan administration," which was one of the objectives of ERISA. The decision is particularly regrettable because of its broad scope.

The rigidity of the position taken by the Supreme Court in the *Boggs* and *Egelhoff* cases was confirmed in *Kennedy v. DuPont Savings and Investment Plan,* 129 S. Ct. 865 (2009), which required the plan administrator to distribute the benefits of an ERISA plan to the surviving spouse who had knowingly waived her rights in a divorce decree that was not a QDRO. The Court held that, "such a waiver is not rendered invalid by the text of the antialienation provision, but that the plan administrator properly disregarded the waiver owing to its conflict with the designation made by the former husband in accordance with plan documents." The result emphasizes again the care that must be exercised in dealing with interests in plans subject to ERISA, particularly in domestic relations disputes.

Preemption under ERISA has also been applied, albeit reluctantly, in some simultaneous death cases. For example, in *Tucker v. Shreveport Transit Management, Inc.,* 226 F.3d 394 (5th Cir. 2000), the court affirmed a decision that directed payment of a decedent's pension plan benefits to the estate of his wife, with whom he died simultaneously. The beneficiary designation made by the participant directed that if the designated primary beneficiary (the wife) died before him, he designated his brother as secondary beneficiary. According to the court, "[b]ecause ERISA governs the distribution of benefits and proceeds under the Pension Plan, we need not discuss how the proceeds would be distributed under Mr. Perkin's will or under the Louisiana Civil code articles governing commorientes [simultaneous death]." This decision is also unfortunate. It is difficult to understand why federal supremacy requires ignoring local laws of all kinds.

IRAs. IRAs are not subject to the restraints on alienation that are imposed with respect to interests in qualified plans. Accordingly, each spouse may dispose of his or her interest in an IRA that is owned as community property under the local law. In LR 8040101, the IRS ruled that the custodian of the IRA may pay one-half to the legatees under the will of a deceased spouse, which will be includible in their gross income. Where authorized by local law the IRA may be the subject of a non-pro rata distribution (for instance, the entire interest in the account might be allocated to the surviving spouse and other property allocated to the legatees of the deceased spouse). However, such an allocation might accelerate the imposition of the income tax on the community property. Otherwise, such an allocation would, presumably, support a rollover of the entire amount by the surviving spouse.

In LR 9439020, the IRS held that the partition of a community property IRA into separate equal shares owned and subject to disposition by each spouse was not a taxable event (*i.e.*, it did not constitute a distribution or transfer for purposes of § 408(d)(1)). Moreover, the partition did not result in any gift from one spouse to the other.

Laws in some community property states explicitly recognize the community property interest of a nonaccountholder spouse in a community property IRA and his or her right to dispose of that interest by will. *E.g.*, Wash. Rev. Code § 6.15.020 (2011).

Estate Planning Implications. Letter Ruling 8929046 suggests a way by which a couple might be able to avoid the restriction that *Boggs v. Boggs* places on the ability of a nonparticipant spouse to dispose of her interests in a qualified plan: The nonemployee spouse could exchange her community property interest in a qualified plan for the employee spouse's interest in other property. In LR 8929046, the IRS ruled that such an exchange involving an IRA was not taxable by reason of § 1041(b). The object is, of course, to enable the nonemployee spouse to control the disposition of the assets that were received in exchange for his or her interest in the qualified plan. Otherwise, if the nonemployee spouse dies before the employee spouse and has not effectively transferred her interest in the plan to another person, it will pass to the employee spouse—which can cause an undesirable increase in the size of the employee spouse's estate.

The estate plan for the nonemployee spouse should, of course, be prepared in light of his or her interest in his or her spouse's employee benefits. Although, under *Boggs,* the nonemployee spouse has no interest in the employee spouse's qualified plan benefits, in states other than Wisconsin the nonemployee spouse may dispose of an interest in the other spouse's IRAs and other nonqualified plans. (Under Wis. Stat. Ann. § 766.31(3) (2011) the interest of a nonemployee spouse in a deferred benefit plan terminates if he or she predeceases the employee spouse.) Of course, the disposition of the nonemployee spouse's interest may appropriately be the subject of a pre- or post-nuptial property agreement.

In LR 9439020, the IRS held that the partition of a community property IRA into separate equal shares owned and subject to disposition by each spouse was not a taxable event. It did not constitute a distribution or transfer for purposes of § 408(d)(1). Moreover, the partition did not result in any gift from one spouse to the other.

§3.33. ESTATE TAX

Community property is includible in the estate of a deceased spouse to the extent of the decedent's one-half interest. In this connection it is important to note that the characterization of property is governed by the applicable state law and not by federal rules. For example, the amount of property includible in the estate of a deceased spouse may be affected by the terms of a property agreement between the spouses if such agreements are allowed under the local law, as they generally are. Of course, an agreement between the spouses is effective to characterize their property only if the requirements of state law are satisfied. Some states demand more than others to overcome the presumption that property acquired during marriage is community property. In some states, an oral agreement may suffice, but in others more is required. For example, *Kern v. United States*, 491 F.2d 436 (9th Cir. 1974), held that under Washington law the presumption was overcome only if the evidence of separate property ownership was clear, definite, and convincing.

The estate tax regulations include some special rules regarding the inclusion of community property in the gross estate in order to preserve the equity of the estate tax. In particular, the regulations recognize that only half of the proceeds of community property life insurance is ordinarily includible in the estate of the insured spouse. Reg. §20.2042-1(b)(2). Similarly, where the noninsured spouse dies first, only half of the value of a community property policy is includible in the decedent's estate. Reg. §20.2042-1(c)(5). Although it is largely no longer of much significance because of the unlimited marital deduction, the IRS earlier recognized that only half of the value of joint tenancy property acquired with community property funds was includible in a deceased spouse's estate. Rev. Rul. 55-605, 1955-2 C.B. 382 (Nevada). Presumably, the nonemployee spouse's interest in an employee benefit plan is includible in his or her estate under §2033. However, a marital deduction is available to the extent the nonemployee spouse's interest passes to the employee spouse.

A marital deduction was allowed in *Estate of Victor W. Richman*, 68 T.C.M. (CCH) 527 (1994), with respect to Texas community property that a couple had invested in a Massachusetts Business Trust, which indicated that the trust and the rights of all parties would be determined under the law of Massachusetts. The controversy arose because the decedent's will left his share of the community property in a form that did not qualify for the marital deduction. The estate argued that the disposition of the decedent's interest in the trust was governed by the terms of their investment application, as a result of which it passed to his widow as surviving joint tenant. The application form signed by the husband and wife indicated that the investment would be as joint tenants with right of survivorship. The court held that the choice of law made in the application by the decedent and his wife would govern. As a result the interest passed to his surviving spouse and qualified for the marital deduction.

§3.33.1. Deductions

Deductions are allowable under §2053 for expenses of administration, funeral expenses, and debts, to the extent they are chargeable to the decedent's share of the community property under the local law. Thus, where only the decedent's half of the community property is subject to administration, the estate is allowed a deduction for the full amount of the administration expenses. On the other hand, if all interests in the community property are administered, the deduction is limited to one-half of the expenses of administration that are not specifically allocable to the decedent's share of the community property. Expenses that relate only to the decedent's share of the community property are *fully* deductible. Thus, the attorney's fees and other expenses incurred in connection with the determination of federal and state death taxes are fully deductible. *Lang's Estate v. Commissioner,* 97 F.2d 867 (9th Cir. 1938). Likewise, the costs of appraising the decedent's interest in the community property are fully deductible. *Ray v. United States,* 385 F. Supp. 372 (S.D. Tex. 1974), *aff'd per curiam on other issues,* 538 F.2d 1228 (5th Cir. 1976). In *Ray* the court upheld the deductibility of 95 percent of the attorney's fees.

Funeral expenses are deductible under §2053 only to the extent the decedent's estate is liable for their payment. Accordingly, half of the funeral expenses are deductible in a state that makes them a charge against the entire community property. *Lang's Estate, supra;* Rev. Rul. 70-156, 1970-1 C.B. 190. The IRS has ruled that the expenses are fully deductible in the states whose laws provide that funeral expenses are charged entirely to the decedent's share of the community property. Rev. Rul. 71-168, 1971-1 C.B. 271 (California); Rev. Rul. 69-193, 1969-1 C.B. 222 (Texas).

Deductions for losses and charitable transfers are, of course, limited to the decedent's interest in the lost or transferred property. *See* §§2054, 2055.

The redemption of a former spouse's stock may be taxable to the other former spouse if he or she is the only other shareholder. The possibility is discussed in §11.8, which reviews several cases.

§3.33.2. Marital Deduction

An unlimited marital deduction is allowable to the estates of decedents dying after December 31, 1981 regardless of the community or separate character of the decedent's property. The marital deduction allowable to the estates of decedents dying prior to 1982 was subject to qualitative and quantitative limitations. Prior to 1977, no marital deduction was allowable to an estate composed entirely of community property. Technically, the deduction was limited to 50 percent of the adjusted gross estate, which was defined as the gross estate reduced by the sum of (1) the §2053 and §2054 deductions attributable to the decedent's separate property and (2) the decedent's interest in community property. A limited marital deduction was allowed with respect to community property for decedents dying after 1977 and before 1982. In that period the marital deduction was limited to the greater of 50 percent of the adjusted gross estate or $250,000. §2056(c)(1)(A). However, the alternate $250,000 amount was reduced to the extent the community property included in the decedent's estate exceeded its pro rata share of the §2053 and §2054 deductions. §2056(c)(1)(C). Accordingly, no marital deduction was allowable if the decedent's share of the community property estate had a value of $250,000 or more, net of §2053 and §2054 deductions.

§3.33.3. Credits

The unified credit and the credits for taxes on prior transfers and foreign death taxes are allowable with respect to property included in the decedent's estate regardless of its community or separate nature.

§3.34. GIFT TAX

Taxable gifts may result from transfers of community property to third parties. In addition, transactions between spouses that affect their respective ownership interests in community property may also result in gifts between the spouses. Interspousal gifts generally qualify for the gift tax marital deduction if the donee spouse is a United States citizen. §2523. For federal and state gift tax purposes, a gift of community property to a person outside the community is treated as two gifts—one by each spouse and each for one-half of the total value of the property transferred. Accordingly, each spouse is treated as a donor of the property, whose transfer may qualify for the annual gift tax exclusion.

EXAMPLE 3-26.

In 2000 *H* and *W* gave $20,000 of community property cash to their daughter, *D*. For gift tax purposes *H* and *W* are each considered to have made a gift of $10,000 to *D*. The gifts involve present interests that qualify for the annual gift tax exclusion. Accordingly, if neither *H* nor *W* makes any other gifts to *D* in 2000, neither is required to report the gifts to *D* on a federal gift tax return.

A gift also takes place if one spouse transfers all of his or her interest in a community property asset to the other spouse, who then owns the entire interest in the asset as separate property. Such a transfer of community property qualifies for the gift tax annual exclusion and the marital deduction if the donee spouse is a United States citizen. It is unnecessary to file a gift tax return with respect to such a gift. §6019.

§3.34.1. Transfer of Separate Property into Community Property

When one spouse transfers separate property into community property, the transferor makes a gift to the other spouse of an amount equal to the value of the transferred property (*i.e.*, half the value of the property less any applicable discounts). That results because, after the transfer, each spouse owns a one-half interest in the property. When both spouses transfer separate property into community property, "a single gift will take place with respect to the conversion of the separately owned properties and the value of the single gift will be the net difference between the value of the husband's (or the wife's) separate property before its conversion into community property and the value of the husband's (or the wife's) interest in the community property resulting from the conversion." Rev. Rul. 77-359, 1977-2 C.B. 24. Such a gift should qualify for the gift tax annual exclusion and marital deduction if the donee spouse is a United States citizen.

EXAMPLE 3-27.

W transferred $100,000 of her separate property cash into a community property form of ownership with her husband, H, who is a United States citizen. The transfer involved a gift from W to H of half of the amount transferred ($100,000 × 1/2 = $50,000). Such a transfer qualifies for the gift tax annual exclusion and marital deduction. Note that if H were not a United States citizen, the gift would be sheltered from tax by the expanded annual exclusion that is available with respect to gifts to noncitizen spouses in lieu of the marital deduction ($100,000, adjusted for post-1997 inflation). If H had also transferred $50,000 of his separate property into a community property form of ownership with W, the transfers by W and H would be aggregated for purposes of determining the gift tax consequences. After the transfers were made each spouse would own a community property interest worth $75,000 (1/2 × ($100,000 + $50,000)). H would not have made a gift since he transferred property worth $50,000 and received interests worth $75,000. W would have made a gift of $25,000, since she transferred property worth $100,000 and received an interest worth only $75,000.

§3.34.2. Partition of Community Property into Separate Property

The partition of community property into equal shares of separate property does not involve a gift because each spouse continues to own an interest of equivalent value. Probably no gift occurs if each spouse receives either an equal interest in each asset or the whole interest in assets of the same total value. As indicated in §3.35.3, either type of division should not require any recognition of gain. The result should be the same regardless of the type of separate property ownership. Thus, a transfer of community property into joint tenancy or tenancy in common does not involve a gift. In 1981, Louisiana changed its laws to allow spouses voluntarily to partition community property into separate property. La. Civ. Code Ann. arts. 2336, 2341 (2011). Upon the death of a spouse only the basis in the deceased spouse's interest in the former community property is changed; the separate property interest of the surviving spouse is not affected. Rev. Rul. 68-80, 1968-1 C.B. 348 (community property in New Mexico real property traded for tenancy in common real property in Virginia).

§3.34.3. Conversion of Future Income into Separate Property

An agreement that the future income of each spouse will be his or her separate property may constitute a gift. The gift might not take place when the agreement is executed because of the impossibility of valuing the interests involved. Cf. Rev. Rul. 69-346, 1969-1 C.B. 227. Presumably gifts would occur over time as income is earned by one or both spouses. Here, again, the analysis is largely of theoretical interest since gifts to a spouse who is a United States citizen qualify for the gift tax marital deduction. As explained in § 3.35.1, the transfer of interests between spouses is not a taxable event. § 1041(a).

EXAMPLE 3-28.

H and *W* entered into an agreement, valid under the local law, that the employment income of each spouse will be the separate property of the spouse who earns it. It was impossible to determine the gift tax consequences at the time the agreement was made. In the following year *H* was unemployed and *W* received employment income of $200,000. *H* may be treated as having made a gift of $100,000 to *W* if the agreement was effective to cause the entire $200,000 to be treated as *W*'s separate property. Such a gift should qualify for the gift tax annual exclusion and marital deduction.

§ 3.35. Income Tax

In general the income tax law follows the state law characterization of income and expenditures. Thus, the income earned by a married couple in a community property state is naturally "split" between them. When the income tax rates were more progressive, the split of community property income between the spouses was of great advantage to couples who lived in community property states so long as the federal law required each spouse to file a separate income tax return. The significance of community property in that regard was largely eliminated in 1948 when Congress enacted a legislative package that sought to equalize the overall tax treatment of community and noncommunity property. Part of that package gave married persons the option to report their combined income on a single ("joint") income tax return, where it would be taxed at preferential rates.

Following the death of one spouse, one-half of the income from assets that were formerly community property is reportable by the deceased spouse's estate and the other half by the surviving spouse. *Grimm v. Commissioner*, 894 F.2d 1165 (10th Cir. 1990). As indicated in *Grimm*, one-half of the income is reportable by the surviving spouse although it is received by and administered as a part of the deceased spouse's estate.

§ 3.35.1. No Gain or Loss on Transfers Between Spouses, § 1041

The transferor of property under section 1041 recognizes no gain or loss on the transfer even if the transfer was in exchange for the release of marital rights or other consideration. This rule applies regardless of whether the transfer is of property separately owned by the transferor or is a division (equal or unequal) of community property. Reg. § 1.1041-1T(d), Q-10 and A-10.

No gain or loss is recognized on a transfer of property made after July 18, 1984 from an individual to, or in trust for the benefit of, his or her spouse. § 1041(a). Instead, the transfer is treated as a gift, with the basis of the transferor carrying over to the transferee. § 1041(b). However, the nonrecognition rule does not apply "if the spouse of the individual making the gift is a nonresident alien." § 1041(d). The same rules apply to transfers to a former spouse that are made incident to divorce.

The rules with respect to the income tax consequences for the transferee are stated in the response to Q-11 of Temp. Reg. § 1.1041-1T(d):

> The transferee of property under section 1041 recognizes no gain or loss upon receipt of the transferred property. In all cases, the basis of the transferred property in the hands of the transferee is the adjusted basis of such property in the hands of the transferor immediately before the transfer. Even if the transfer is a bona fide sale, the transferee does not acquire a basis in the transferred property equal to the transferee's cost (the fair market value). This carryover basis rule applies whether the adjusted basis of the transferred property is less than, equal to, or greater than its fair market value at the time of transfer (or the value of any consideration provided by the transferee) and applies for the purposes of determining loss as well as gain upon the subsequent disposition of the property by the transferee.

§ 3.35.2. Conversion of Separate Property into Community Property

Under § 1041, the conversion of separate property into community property is not a taxable event. Prior to the adoption of § 1041, such a conversion might have resulted in the realization of gain. However, under the prior law a conversion of the property of only one spouse was a gift by that spouse, which was not a taxable event. In contrast, a conversion by both spouses of separate property into community property might have been treated as a taxable exchange, which could have resulted in the recognition of gain. No gain was realized, however, if the separate conversions by husband and wife were determined to be gifts under § 102. LR 7821150. Most conversions probably satisfied the requirement of *Commissioner v. Duberstein*, 363 U.S. 278 (1960), that a gift in the statutory sense of § 102 must proceed from a detached and disinterested generosity out of affection, respect, admiration, charity, or like impulses. If a conversion qualifies as a gift under § 102, no gain is realized and, presumably, each spouse has a basis in the assets equal to half of the sum of the adjusted bases of the assets that were formerly held as separate property. Such a conversion could not result in a loss because of § 267, which bars the deduction of a loss on transfers between related taxpayers including spouses.

§ 3.35.3. Conversion of Community Property into Separate Property

Under § 1041, conversions of community property into separate property also do not constitute a taxable event. A conversion might involve a sale or exchange, a gift by one spouse to the other, or an equal division. Presumably the rule extends to those types of assets, such as installment obligations, the disposition of which would otherwise trigger the recognition of gain or loss. *See* § 453B. Under the prior law, the conversion of a community property asset into one that the spouses owned as equal tenants in common or as joint tenants was not taxable. *See Commissioner v. Mills*, 183 F.2d 32 (9th Cir. 1950); Rev. Rul. 56-437 1956-2 C.B. 507 (conversion of joint tenancy in stock into tenancy in common or partition and issuance of separate stock certificates is not taxable). Similarly, under the prior law, a division of community property by which each spouse received the entire interest in assets of approximately equal value was not taxable. LR 8016050. An unequal in kind division of community property was also nontaxable if the transfer of the excess property to one spouse was regarded as a gift under § 102.

Most of the prior law regarding the taxability of conversions of community property was generated by cases involving the consequences of marital dissolutions. That law is summarized in Rev. Rul. 76-83, 1976-1 C.B. 213, which held that no gain or loss resulted from the approximately equal division of the fair market value of community property. *See also Jean C. Carrieres*, 64 T.C. 959 (1975), *aff'd per curiam*, 552 F.2d 1350 (9th Cir. 1977), *acq. in result*, 1976-2 C.B. 1. The ruling involved an agreement that called for each spouse to receive community property of equal value. "However, certain community assets cannot feasibly be partitioned between the taxpayers because the nature of the assets makes them incapable of division, they are associated with a particular liability, or they are part of a business venture that can be managed by only one of the taxpayers. Under the terms of the settlement agreement, certain assets will be assigned to the husband and certain other assets of approximate equal value will be assigned to the wife. The remaining community assets will be equally partitioned between the taxpayers." *Id*. Insofar as the basis of assets is concerned, the ruling held that an asset allocated entirely to one spouse retains its community basis. It continued to say that each spouse's basis in a partitioned asset was equal to the percentage of the asset received by the spouse multiplied by the community property basis of the asset. "For example, if corporate stock that has a community basis of $15,000 is partitioned so that the husband receives 40 percent of the stock and the wife receives the remaining 60 percent of the stock, the basis of the stock received by the husband will be $6,000 (40 percent of $15,000) and the basis of the stock received by the wife will be $9,000 (60 percent of $15,000)." Presumably the same allocation of basis would be made under § 1041.

§ 3.35.4. Basis Following Death of a Spouse

The characterization of property as community or separate is also important when it comes to determining the basis of property following the death of a spouse. Under § 1014(b)(6), both shares of the community property have a basis equal to its fair market value on the valuation date applicable to the deceased spouse's estate for federal estate tax purposes (*i.e.*, either on the date of the decedent's death or on the alternate valuation date under § 2032). Thus, the survivor's share of the community property benefits from a free "step-up" in basis where the community property has appreciated in value, but suffers a decrease in basis ("step-down") if the estate tax value in the decedent's estate is below its adjusted basis at the time of the decedent's death. In contrast, the basis of the surviving spouse in his or her separate property is not changed by reason of the decedent's death. It is readily apparent, then, that the survivor's basis in a jointly owned asset depends upon whether it was held as community property or as equally owned units of separate property (*e.g.,* a separate property tenancy in common or joint tenancy). In Rev. Rul. 68-80, 1968-1 C.B. 348, the IRS ruled that the surviving spouse's basis in her undivided one-half interest in Virginia property that she held with her deceased husband as tenants in common was not affected by his death. Revenue Ruling 68-80 was concerned with a husband and wife who, "In 1965 . . . moved to Virginia and traded their community property in New Mexico for real property in Virginia to which they took title as tenants in common." The ruling treated the Virginia property as equally owned by the husband and wife as their separate property. Merely taking title to the Virginia property as tenants in common should not have resulted in a change in the character of the property from community to separate. Under basic conflicts of law principles, the Virginia property should have been characterized as community property regardless of the manner in which title was held. *See* § 3.36.

It is generally advantageous to hold an appreciated asset in community property form, which allows the basis in both halves of it to be stepped-up on the death of the first spouse to die. Presumably the step-up is available with respect to any property that is characterized as community property under the applicable state law. *See* Rev. Rul. 87-98, 1987-2 C.B. 206. *See also* § 3.20.6. As indicated in § 3.26, in some community property states all property held in joint form between husband and wife is presumed to be community property. Of course, a "full" step-up in basis is also available where the entire interest in an asset is included in a deceased spouse's estate.

EXAMPLE 3-29.

H and *W* purchased 100 shares of stock at $10 per share with their community property funds. At the same time, *H* purchased an additional 100 shares with his separate property. *H* bequeathed his interest in the 200 shares of stock to *W*, a United States citizen, who survived him. The stock had a value of $100 per share on the estate tax valuation date applicable to *H*'s estate. Insofar as the community property stock was concerned, *H*'s estate included a value of $5,000 (1/2 × $100 × 100). As a result, the basis of *H*'s half interest in the stock was increased to $5,000. *W*'s half interest in the stock was also increased to $5,000 under § 1014(b)(6). Accordingly, *W* has a basis of $10,000 in the 100 shares that were formerly owned by them as their community property and in the 100 shares that were acquired as *H*'s separate property. The inclusion of the stock in *H*'s estate is fully offset by the marital deduction allowable to his estate.

In the case of separate property, only the decedent's interest in the property is affected by § 1014. Thus, the survivor's bases in assets that stood in joint tenancy form will vary according to whether they are treated as true separate property joint tenancies or as their community property. As stated in Rev. Rul. 87-98, "If property held in a common law estate is community property under state law, it is community property for purposes of section 1014(b)(6) of the Code, regardless of the form in which title was taken." On the other hand, only the decedent's interest in a "true" (*i.e.,* separate property) joint tenancy is affected by the decedent's death. *See Murphy v. Commissioner,* 342 F.2d 356 (9th Cir. 1965); *Bordenave v. United States,* 150 F. Supp.

820 (N.D. Cal. 1957). A community property characterization might result if a presumption that joint tenancies between husband and wife are community property is not overcome, the attempt to establish the joint tenancy fails to comply with the requirements of the local law, or the joint tenancy form was used for convenience without intending to create a valid joint tenancy with right of survivorship. By way of illustration, had the 100 shares of stock acquired with community property funds in Example 3-29, *supra*, been held by *H* and *W* in a true separate property joint tenancy, *W* would have had a basis of only $5,500 in the stock following *H*'s death. That figure is the sum of *W*'s share of the original cost basis ($500) plus the basis of *H*'s one-half share determined under § 1014 ($5,000).

When the value of community property has declined below its adjusted basis, § 1014(b)(6) could cause a decrease in the basis of both halves of the property. However, that result can be avoided by partitioning the property prior to the death of a spouse. If that is done, the survivor's basis in half of the property is unaffected by the decedent's death. Only the decedent's one-half share of the property suffers a decrease in basis. The IRS has recognized this opportunity:

> There is nothing in the Internal Revenue Code or regulations that would indicate that section 1014(b)(6) of the Code relating to "community property held" was intended to include separate property that had previously been converted from community property to separate property. Accordingly, *W*'s unadjusted basis in her undivided one-half interest in the Virginia property held as tenant in common at *H*'s death is her cost. Her unadjusted basis in the undivided one-half interest she acquired by inheritance from *H* is its fair market value at the time of *H*'s death. Rev. Rul. 68-80, 1968-1 C.B. 348.

An inter vivos gift of one spouse's share in community property that has declined in value would produce essentially the same result: The donee's original interest in the property would retain its adjusted basis unaffected by the gift or the donor's death and the donee's basis in the gifted share would be limited to its fair market value on the date of the gift for the purpose of determining loss. *See* § 1015(a).

The effect of § 1014(b)(6) on a client's estate plan should be carefully considered, particularly if the client is terminally ill. An appropriate shift into or out of a community property form of ownership may leave the surviving spouse with a higher basis in the property.

§ 3.35.5. Appreciated Property Acquired from a Decedent, § 1014(e)

Section 1014(e) provides that the stepped-up basis rules of § 1014 do not apply to appreciated property acquired by the decedent by gift within a year of death that passes directly or indirectly from the donee-decedent to the original donor or the donor's spouse. The Ways and Means Committee recommended this provision because of a concern that § 1014 would otherwise encourage taxpayers to transfer appreciated property to a terminally ill person in hopes of receiving the property back upon the death of the donee, complete with a stepped-up basis. The concern was more acute because of the adoption of the unlimited marital deduction. A similar rule applies under the modified carryover basis regime in the limited cases where executors of decedents dying in 2010 elected out of the application of the federal estate tax. §1022(d)(1)(C). *See* §2.3

Trusts. It is unclear whether §1014(e) would bar a step up in the basis of property that a donee-decedent leaves in trust for his or her surviving spouse. Thus, it is uncertain whether §1014(e) would bar a step up in the basis of property that one spouse transferred to a QTIP trust in which the donor spouse held a successive life interest.

> The donor-heir might pay gift taxes on the fair market value of the gift (unless it qualified for the marital deduction or the amount of the gift is less than the donor's annual exclusion or unified credit) but will pay no income tax on the appreciation . . . .[U]pon the death of the donee-decedent, the donor-heir could receive back the property with a stepped up basis equal to its fair market value. The stepped-up basis would permanently exempt the appreciation from income tax. H.R. Rep. No. 97-201, 97th Cong., 1st Sess. 188 (1981).

It is also unclear whether §1014(e) would bar any step-up in the basis of the surviving spouse in separate property that he or she transferred into community property within a year preceding the death of the donee spouse.

EXAMPLE 3-30.

> *W* owned separate property with a basis of $50,000 and a fair market value of $500,000. Within a year preceding *H*'s death *W* transferred the property into a community property form of ownership with *H*. Thereafter *H* owned a one-half interest with a basis of $25,000 and a value of $250,000. When *H* died he left to *W* his one-half interest in the community property created by *W*'s transfer. *H*'s one-half interest ($250,000) was includible in his estate under §2033, but by reason of §1014(e) *W*'s basis in it may remain $25,000. If *W*'s basis in *H*'s half of the property is increased, presumably the basis of *W*'s one-half interest would be stepped-up under §1014(b)(6).
>
> The basis in *H*'s half of the property would have been stepped-up if *H* had left it outright to someone other than *W*. In such a case presumably *W*'s one-half interest in the property would also receive a stepped-up basis. It is unclear whether the basis of either share would be stepped-up if *H* left his one-half interest to a trust in which *W* had an interest.

Tax Basis Revocable Trusts and Joint Trusts. The basis of all of the property owned by a husband and wife who are domiciled in a noncommunity property state is generally not affected by the death of one spouse. However, counsel for the taxpayer in LR 9308002 (TAM), Paul M. Fletcher, argues that a so-called tax basis revocable trust (TBRT) can be used to step up the basis in all of their property. P.M. Fletcher, The Tax Basis Revocable Trust: New Concepts in Estate Planning (1993); Tax Basis Revocable Trusts, Tax Notes 1183 (May 30, 1994); Drafting Revocable Trusts to Facilitate a Stepped-Up Basis, 22 Est. Plan. 100 (Mar./Apr. 1995). Stated in simplest terms a TBRT gives each spouse a general power of appointment over the property contributed to the trust by the other. The suggested power is a right during lifetime to direct the trustee to pay from the trust all of the estate tax, debts, and charges enforceable against the estate of the first spouse to die. Upon the death of either spouse, all of the trust property is included in the decedent's estate. The trust is drafted so the surviving spouse's interest qualifies for the marital deduction except to the extent it is disclaimed. The planner should be alert to the conflicts of interest that exist, or may arise, in connection with the plan. A conflict exists, for example, if the plan gives each spouse a lifetime power to dispose of the entire interest in the trust. Essentially the same problem arises if the first spouse to die can dispose of the entire trust, including the share contributed by the surviving spouse. Accordingly, at the least the lawyer must explain the advantages and disadvantages to each party and obtain their written consent. *See* §1.6.7 and Model Rule 1.7(a), (b).

In LR 9308002 (TAM), the IRS held that §1014(e) barred a step up in basis in the property that the surviving spouse had transferred to the trust. According to the IRS by reading §1014(a) and (e) together, it is clear that Congress did not intend to allow a step up in basis because the deceased spouse did not have a sufficient interest in the property that the surviving spouse transferred to the trust:

> In the instant case, the surviving spouse (i.e., donor) held dominion and control over the property throughout the year prior to the decedent's death since he could revoke the trust at any time. It was only at the decedent's death that the power to revoke the trust became ineffective. Because the donor never relinquished dominion and control over the property (and the property reverted back to the donor at the spouse's death) the property was not acquired from the decedent under §1014(a) and (e), notwithstanding that it is includible in the decedent's gross estate. Taxpayer's position in this case would produce the "unintended and inappropriate" tax benefit Congress expressly eliminated in enacting §1014(e).

Letter Ruling 200101021 involves a similar approach—a revocable trust under which the spouse first-to-die is given a general testamentary power of appointment over the property contributed by the surviving spouse. The ruling concluded that under a combination of §§2038 and 2041 the entire trust was includible in the deceased spouse's gross estate. In effect, the ruling allowed the parties to take full advantage of the deceased spouse's unified credit by allocating an amount equal to the allowable exclusion to a credit shelter trust—which would not be includible in the surviving spouse's estate. However, the ruling again holds that §1014(e) precludes a step-up in the basis of the portion of the trust that the surviving spouse acquired, directly or indirectly, from the deceased spouse.

More recently, in LR 200403094, the IRS was silent as to whether §1014(e) precluded a step-up in basis of that portion of the trust assets removed from the trust by exercise of a testamentary power of appointment held by the deceased spouse, although the IRS did rule that the surviving spouse made a completed gift of such property to the deceased spouse at the time of the deceased spouse's exercise. For an argument that §1014(e) should not apply assuming the grantor spouse lives at least one year following formation of the trust, see Handler & Chen, The Estate Trust Revival: Maximizing the Full Basis Step-Up for Spouses, 140 Trusts & Estates 14 (Aug. 2001).

§3.35.5

If § 1014(e) is eliminated from consideration, a step up in basis for the property contributed to a TBRT by the surviving spouse is allowable under the literal provisions of § § 1014(a) and 1014(b)(9). Section 1014(e) bars a step up in basis for property "acquired by the decedent by gift during the one-year period ending on the date of the decedent's death" that passes from the decedent to the donor of the property. It would not be a great stretch to read "acquired by gift" to include property over which the decedent held a general power of appointment. If so, § 1014(e) bars a step up in basis of property over which the deceased spouse was given a general power of appointment within a year preceding death and which passes to (or remains) the property of the surviving spouse on the decedent's death. Presumably a step up would be allowable if the decedent survived for at least a year following receipt of a general power of appointment. Given that possibility, the IRS adopted a broader rule—that no step up is available in such a case because § 1014(e) reflects a policy that no step up should be allowed unless the decedent had "full" dominion and control over the property for a year or more prior to death. No doubt the courts will be asked to resolve the issue at an early date.

§3.36.   CONFLICT OF LAWS: BASIC RULES

> A marital property interest in a chattel, or right embodied in a document, which has been acquired by either or both of the spouses, is not affected by the mere removal of the chattel or document to a second state, whether or not this removal is accompanied by a change of domicile to the other state on the part of one or both of the spouses. The interest, however, may be affected by dealings with the chattel or document in the second state. Restatement (Second), Conflict of Laws § 259 (1971).

Under basic conflict of laws principles, the character of property acquired by a husband and wife while domiciled in one state is not changed if they move to another state. However, their rights in the property may be affected by the move, as indicated in the discussion of quasi-community property in § 3.38.

Applying the basic rule, property acquired as community property in California is recognized as community property if the couple move to a noncommunity property state such as Colorado. *People v. Bejarano*, 358 P.2d 866 (Colo. 1961). Other noncommunity property states may improperly treat imported community property as converted into a more familiar common law form of ownership, such as a tenancy in common. That approach may lead to an acceptable resolution of some tax and nontax problems if the couple's new domicile recognizes that each spouse has a one-half interest in the imported community property. However, under such an approach, only the decedent's basis in the imported community property may be increased upon the death of one spouse. *See* Rev. Rul. 68-80, 1968-1 C.B. 348, discussed in § 3.35.4. Unfortunately, the tax authorities and courts have not always recognized the ownership interest of each spouse in the imported community property. *See, e.g., Commonwealth v. Terjen*, 90 S.E.2d 801 (Va. 1956). (The court recognized that property imported from California retained its community character, but erroneously failed to recognize the wife's interest in the property because it was a "mere expectancy.")

§ 3.37. UNIFORM DISPOSITION OF COMMUNITY PROPERTY RIGHTS AT DEATH ACT

Several noncommunity property states have addressed the problem of providing for the proper disposition of community property upon the death of a spouse by adopting the Uniform Disposition of Community Property Rights at Death Act (2003). The Act, which was approved as a Uniform Act in 1971, has been adopted by an important minority of states, including Alaska, Arkansas, Colorado, Connecticut, Florida, Hawaii, Kentucky, Michigan, Montana, New York, North Carolina, Oregon, Virginia, and Wyoming. It defines the rights, at death, of a married person in community property that was acquired before the couple became domiciled in a noncommunity property state. In brief, it recognizes the right each spouse has under the community property law to dispose at death of half of the community property, the other half of which belongs to the surviving spouse. The Commissioners' Prefatory Note states that the Act was intended "to preserve the rights of each spouse in property which was community property prior to change of domicile, as well as in property substituted therefore where the spouses have not indicated an intention to sever or alter their community rights. It thus follows the typical pattern of community property which permits the deceased spouse to dispose of his half of the community property, while confirming the title of the surviving spouse in 'her half.'" Professor Stanley Johanson has argued persuasively that the Act provides an appropriate solution for the most commonly encountered problems regarding imported community property. Johanson, The Migrating Client: Estate Planning for the Couple from a Community Property State, U. Miami, 9th Inst. Est. Plan. ¶ 831 (1975).

§ 3.38. QUASI-COMMUNITY PROPERTY

When a couple moves from a noncommunity property state to a community property state, the property formerly owned by each spouse is generally characterized as his or her separate property. Thus, property acquired with the earnings of a husband while the couple was domiciled in a noncommunity property state is generally treated as his separate property following their move. This treatment works well enough in most instances. However, as a result of the move, the nonacquiring spouse usually loses any right to dower, curtesy, or an elective share that was provided by the state of their former domicile. In order to deal with that problem, California, Idaho, Washington, and Wisconsin have adopted the quasi-community property concept. Wisconsin gives a surviving spouse the right to elect to take a one-half interest in "deferred marital property" (the Wisconsin equivalent of quasi-community property) in lieu of what the surviving spouse would have otherwise received from the decedent. Wis. Stat. Ann. § 861.02 (2011).

In brief, quasi-community property is property acquired during marriage while the spouses were domiciled in a noncommunity property state that would have been community property had they been domiciled in the state of the decedent's domicile at the time of acquisition. Cal. Fam. Code § 125 (2011); Idaho Code § 15-2-201(b)

(2011); Wash. Rev. Code §§ 26.16.220-.250 (2011). Some community property states apply the same concept to the characterization of property upon dissolution of marriage. Ariz. Rev. Stat. § 25-318 (2011). Others allow the court to make a division that takes into account property acquired by the spouses while domiciled in a noncommunity property state. *E.g.,* Tex. Fam. Code Ann. § 7.002 (2011).

Upon termination of the marriage by dissolution or death of the acquiring spouse, each spouse is generally treated as having a one-half interest in the quasi-community property. Wisconsin gives the surviving spouse the right to claim an elective share in "deferred marital property," which is "property acquired while spouses are married and . . . which would have been marital property under ch. 766 if it were acquired when ch. 766 applied." Wis. Stat. Ann. § 851.055 (2011). The quasi-community property concept does not apply to dissolutions in Washington because the courts are authorized to make an equitable division of all of the community and separate property in marital dissolution actions.

Upon the death of the acquiring spouse, half of the quasi-community property is subject to the decedent's disposition and the other half belongs to the surviving spouse. Cal. Prob. Code § 101 (2011); Idaho Code § 15-2-201(a) (2011); Wash. Rev. Code § 26.16.230 (2011). In Wisconsin the surviving spouse may elect to receive not more than a one-half interest in any or all items of deferred marital property. Wis. Stat. Ann. § 861.02 (2011). The validity of the California statute in the divorce context was upheld in *Addison v. Addison,* 399 P.2d 897 (Cal. 1965). Note that neither the quasi-community property nor the Wisconsin deferred marital property approach allows the nonacquiring spouse to dispose of any portion of the property if he or she predeceases the acquiring spouse. Indeed, in *Paley v. Bank of America,* 324 P.2d 35 (Cal. App. 1958), the court held that a statute was unconstitutional which gave the nonacquiring spouse power of testamentary disposition over quasi-community property during the lifetime of the acquiring spouse.

Community property states could deal with the problem of protecting the nonacquiring immigrant spouse by giving him or her the same rights in the property that he or she would have had under the law of the place of acquisition. As pointed out by Professor Thomas Andrews, "such a borrowed law approach can be found in Arizona, New Mexico, Nevada, and Idaho, where such an approach was taken to deal with the problem of migration at divorce." Washington's New Quasi-Community Property Act: Protecting the Immigrant Spouse, 15 Comm. Prop. J. 50, 52 (1988). However, such an approach is more complicated and almost necessarily involves difficult tracing of assets. Tracing would be particularly difficult if a couple had lived in several noncommunity property states prior to their move to California, Idaho, or Washington. California earlier tried to deal with the problem by adopting a statute that converted the separate property of a married person to community property when they established a domicile in California. That approach was struck down in *Estate of Thornton,* 33 P.2d 1 (Cal. 1934), as an unconstitutional taking of the acquiring spouse's property without due process of law and as a violation of the acquiring spouse's privileges and immunities by penalizing the acquiring spouse for making a change of domicile.

For federal tax purposes quasi-community property is treated as the separate property of the acquiring spouse. Accordingly, the entire interest in quasi-community property is includible in the gross estate of the acquiring spouse. *Estate of Frank Sbicca,* 35 T.C. 96 (1960).

As provided by California law, a husband and wife should be free to agree about the manner in which quasi-community property should be divided. California specifically authorizes such an agreement: "[A] husband and wife may agree in writing to divide their quasi-community property on the basis of a non pro rata division of the aggregate value of the quasi-community property, or on the basis of a division of each individual item or asset of quasi-community property, or party on each basis." Cal. Prob. Code § 101 (2011).

§ 3.39. PROTECTING THE PROPERTY INTERESTS OF MIGRATORY SPOUSES

Preserving the character of the property owned by a husband and wife is often an important goal of estate planning, particularly when they are moving from a state with one type of marital property law to a state with another type. However, in some instances the husband and wife may wish to change the character of their property—particularly if they are moving to a community property state. In any case, a migratory couple should understand that a move from a community property state to a common law state, or from a common law state to a community property state, may affect their property interests and the manner in which their property is treated for tax purposes. First, the courts or administrative agencies of the state of the couple's new domicile may mischaracterize their property interests as the IRS appears to have done in Rev. Rul. 68-80, 1968-1 C.B. 348. Second, as indicated in § 3.38, married couples moving to some community property states are not protected by the quasi-community property concept. Instead, the property accumulated by a deceased spouse prior to moving to the community property state will probably be characterized as his or her separate property—in which the surviving spouse has no interest and limited rights to family awards and allowances. Thus, the move to a community property state may involve an exchange by the nonacquiring spouse "of a *mere* expectancy for *no* expectancy." Cantwell, Protecting Spousal Rights in a Domicile Change, 14 Comm. Prop. J. 72, 75 (Jan. 1988).

The methods by which the character of property may be preserved are discussed in § 3.25. They include the proper registration of titled assets, the transfer of assets to revocable trusts, and deposit of assets with a financial institution as agent (custodian or agency accounts). The object of the methods is simply to segregate assets of a particular character and to prevent them and their income from being intermixed with assets of a different character.

E. BENEFICIARY DEEDS (TRANSFER ON DEATH (TOD) DEEDS)

§ 3.40. GENERALLY

This part summarizes the content and effect of laws that were enacted by several states over the last decade or so which allow deeds of real property to be effective at death to transfer the title to real property (a "TOD" deed). Building on the experience with those acts, a Uniform Real Property Transfer on Death Act (URPTODA) was promulgated in 2009, which has been adopted by a few states (North Dakota, Oregon, Nevada,

Hawaii and Illinois) and is under consideration in others. Marion, Uniform Laws Update, 25 Prob. & Prop. 10 (Sept./Oct. 2011).

A beneficiary (or TOD) deed permits the owner of an interest in real property to effect the automatic conveyance of that interest upon the owner's death to one or more beneficiaries selected by the owner. Although the owner signs and records a beneficiary deed during the owner's lifetime, the transfer does not take effect until the owner's death. Accordingly, the owner usually has the right to revoke the deed prior to death. Property subject to a beneficiary deed is not part of the owner's probate estate because the transfer occurs at death by operation of applicable state law.

Through 2009 thirteen states had adopted laws authorizing the transfer of title to real property on the death of the grantor. The states are: Arizona, Arkansas, Colorado, Indiana, Kansas, Minnesota, Missouri, Montana, Nevada, New Mexico, Ohio, Oklahoma and Wisconsin. As indicated above, the Uniform Act has been adopted in a few additional states. State statutes usually specify the rights of the owners and named beneficiaries. For example, the named beneficiary usually has no legal right to or interest in the subject property during the life of the owner-grantor. The owner-grantor retains full power over the property and has no obligation to notify or obtain the consent of the beneficiary for any purpose. In addition, neither the owner-grantor nor the named beneficiary assumes the risk of exposure to the other's creditors. This makes the beneficiary deed a more attractive planning option than the traditional practice of naming the intended beneficiary as a current joint tenant or cotenant. A TOD deed may give the named grantee the benefit of crops growing on the land when the grantor dies. *Estate of Roloff*, 143 P.3d 406 (Kan. App. 2006).

To be effective, beneficiary deeds usually must be recorded before the death of the owner. If a beneficiary deed is not recorded, the owner's interest in the property will be disposed of as an asset of the owner's estate. Likewise, a beneficiary deed is invalid if it does not comply with the formalities required by the governing state statute. In *Pippin v. Pippin*, 154 S.W.3d 376 (Mo. App. 2004), Charles Pippin and his wife, Karen Pippin, executed a beneficiary deed conveying title to property owned only by Charles to "Karen Pippin for and during her natural life, and upon her death to (Charles' son) Kenneth Pippin, his heirs and assigns, forever." The deed stated that it was "not effective to convey title . . . until Grantors, Charles Pippin and Karen Pippin's death." Kenneth argued that the deed gave Karen a mere life estate in the subject property, while Karen argued that the deed was invalid so that the subject property would pass to her outright under Charles' will. An appellate court held that the deed was invalid because Karen was not an owner of the property at the time the deed was executed. Consequently, the beneficiary deed was not effective to prevent the property from passing under Charles' will.

The owner can revoke a beneficiary deed by recording a revocation of the deed or by recording another beneficiary deed executed after the revoked deed. Under Colorado law, for example, a subsequently recorded beneficiary deed revokes all prior beneficiary deeds, even if the subsequent deed does not convey the owner's entire interest in the property. Colo. Rev. Stat. § 15-15-405(2) (2011). A valid beneficiary deed trumps any contrary disposition of the property provided under the owner's will, even if the will post-dates the recording of the beneficiary deed. Colo. Rev. Stat. § 15-15-405(4) (2011).

§3.41. GIFT TAX

Because the named beneficiary usually has no legal or beneficial interest in the property until the owner's death, the execution of a beneficiary deed does not constitute a completed gift. This, too, explains the popularity of beneficiary deeds over other techniques that involve completed gifts, such as adding beneficiaries as cotenants.

§3.42. ESTATE TAX

A beneficiary deed does not convey the owner's interest in the subject real property until the owner's death as a result of which the value of the owner's interest is included in the owner's gross estate. Because the beneficiary does not possess a legal interest in the property during the grantor's life, and because the beneficiary's future interest in the property can be revoked by the owner, none of the value of the subject property is included in the beneficiary's gross estate if the beneficiary predeceases the owner.

§3.43. INCOME TAX

The owner is still liable for paying federal (and state) income tax on the income attributable to the subject real property. Likewise, the owner is still able to claim proper deductions attributable to the subject property. At the death of the owner-grantor, the property should be eligible for a stepped-up basis under § 1014 since the value of the property is included in the owner-grantor's gross estate. *See* § 1014(b)(9).

§3.44. PLANNING OPPORTUNITIES AND LIMITATIONS

The beneficiary deed is a useful alternative for clients who cannot afford a revocable living trust or who would normally seek to form a revocable living trust solely for the purpose of holding title to real estate. Certainly the costs of a beneficiary deed are much less than the costs of a revocable living trust. But the revocable living trust will still be desirable in certain situations, such as where the beneficiary is a minor, where multiple beneficiaries will own the property, and where the subject property is already owned as joint tenants with right of survivorship.

More recently, planners have used the beneficiary deed to assist in completing transfers to a revocable living trust. In one common scenario, spouses who own a parcel of real property as joint tenants with rights of survivorship execute a beneficiary deed naming their living trust as the beneficiary upon the death of the surviving spouse. This technique avoids the typical delay of formally conveying title to the trust upon the death of the surviving spouse, and it avoids complications from lenders if the property is mortgaged. Either tenant may execute the beneficiary deed, but usually the deed will have no effect unless the owner-grantor is the last surviving joint tenant. This is because most state beneficiary deed statutes will not trump the rights of survivorship held by the other joint tenants. *See, e.g.,* Colo. Rev. Stat. § 15-15-408(1) (2011).

Real property held by spouses as tenants in common or as community property can also be conveyed by a beneficiary deed. The deed could specify that the first decedent's interest in the property would pass to his or her testamentary (or inter vivos) trust upon the first decedent's death and that the balance of the property would pass to the survivor's testamentary (or inter vivos) trust upon the death of the surviving spouse.

BIBLIOGRAPHY

I. General

Committee Report, Property Owned with Spouse: Joint Tenancy, Tenancy by the Entireties and Community Property, 11 Real Prop., Prob. & Tr. J. 405 (1976)

Handler & Chen, The Estate Trust Revival: Maximizing the Full Basis Step-Up for Spouses, 140:8 Tr. & Est. 14 (Aug. 2001)

II. Joint Tenancy

Campfield, Estate Planning for Joint Tenancies, 1974 Duke L.J. 669

Danforth, Taxation of Jointly Owned Property, 823 2nd Tax. Mgmt. Port. (2004)

Fisher, Creditors of a Joint Tenant: Is There a Lien After Death?, 93 W. Va. L. Rev. 637 (1997)

Fletcher, Drafting Revocable Trusts to Facilitate a Stepped-Up Basis, 22 Est. Plan. 100 (Mar./Apr. 1995)

Fletcher, The Tax Basis Revocable Trust: New Concepts in Estate Planning (1993)

Goodman, Joint Tenancy With a Noncitizen Spouse: An Estate and Gift Tax Guide for the Perplexed, 16 Prob. & Prop. 41 (2002)

Maxfield, Some Reflections on the Taxation of Jointly Held Property, 34 Tax Law. 47 (1980)

III. Community Property

Andrews, Washington's New Quasi-Community Property Act: Protecting the Immigrant Spouse, 15 Comm. Prop. J. 50 (1988)

Bassett, Bassett on California Community Property (2011)

Cantwell, Protecting Spousal Rights in a Domicile Change, 14 Comm. Prop. J. 72 (Jan. 1988)

Crehore, Community Property—Quasi-Community Property—A Caveat for Common Law Practitioners, N.Y.U., 34th Inst. Fed. Tax. 1685 (1976)

Dionisopoulos, The Wisconsin Marital Property Law and Its Effect on Estate Planning, 13 Comm. Prop. J. 62 (July 1986)

Harms, Joint Tenancy, Transmutation and the Supremacy of the Community Property Presumption: *Swink v. Fingado,* 30 Idaho L. Rev. 893 (1994)

Hilker, Planning for the Married Couple Moving Into or Out of Community Property States, 14 Est Plan. 212 (1987)

Treacy, G., Community Property: General Considerations, 802 2nd Tax Mgmt. Port. (2005)

Kasner, Termination of the Community by Death: The California Perspective, 15 Comm. Prop. J. 64 (July 1988)

Moore, Coming Soon to Your State: Community Property, U. Miami, 34th Inst. Est. Plan., Ch. 17 (2000)

4

Wills and Related Documents

While it is increasingly popular to support the estate plan in its main parts upon inter vivos instruments, particularly the revocable living trust, the historic keystone of the arch is the will. Of all legal instruments the will is probably the most familiar; almost every person ought to have one, and every member of the bar is likely to be required, from time to time, to prepare one. Thus the estate plan may consist only of a will: for a person of modest means and "normal" family, possibly a simple will; for a person of moderate or substantial means, with or without some family member needing special attention, possibly a will with trust provisions. The estate plan may consist of several instruments, including a revocable or irrevocable trust; but there always is a will. J. Farr & J. Wright, An Estate Planner's Handbook 129 (4th ed. 1979).

A. INTRODUCTION

§4.1. OVERVIEW

This chapter opens with a review of some of the main reasons why most adults should have wills, followed by a discussion of some of the advantages of conducting an estate administration proceeding and the disadvantages of joint or contractual wills. The main portion of the chapter consists of an examination of a form of a will for a married person with a contingent trust for the testator's children. Each provision of the will is followed by comments regarding relevant tax and nontax considerations. More complex dispositive devices, such as marital deduction trusts, widow's election trusts, irrevocable life insurance trusts and charitable remainder trusts, are discussed in later chapters. The chapter concludes with a discussion of some of the other documents a client may wish to execute along with a will, including the durable power of attorney, §4.35, the so-called living will, §4.38, and the gift of bodily parts under the Uniform Anatomical Gift Act, §4.39.

As the quotation from Farr and Wright indicates, almost every adult should have a will. Even though the bulk of a client's wealth may pass under the terms of inter vivos trusts, retirement plans, life insurance policies, joint tenancies, and other will substitutes, a will is needed to provide backup protection. A will can control the disposition of assets that are not effectively disposed of by will substitutes, dispose of after-acquired assets, and perform some important functions that other instruments often cannot perform. For example, a will—and often no other instrument—may be used to:

1. Disinherit children in favor of a spouse, or otherwise deviate from the local intestate succession law;
2. Appoint guardians of the person and estate of minor children;
3. Consolidate assets in inter vivos or testamentary trusts for postmortem management;
4. Exercise testamentary powers of appointment;
5. Direct the source from which debts and death taxes should be paid;
6. Achieve income and transfer tax savings by giving survivors limited interests in testamentary trusts;
7. Dispose of the proceeds of policies of insurance on the life of the testator if the beneficiary does not survive the testator; and

8. Vary the consequences of simultaneous death or require the beneficiaries to survive the testator for a limited period.

Super Wills. Under the existing law the terms of a will generally do not affect the disposition of nonprobate property. For example, amounts payable under multiparty bank accounts, employee benefit plans, life insurance policies, and other nontestamentary devices are not subject to change by will. In some cases, however, the courts have upheld changes of beneficiary or other dispositions of nonprobate property that were made by will. *See* § 4.18.4. In the future the Uniform Probate Code (U.P.C.) may give recognition to the concept of a "super will" by which the testator could affect the disposition of some types of property that are not usually subject to estate administration. Legislation might authorize a testator, by express testamentary reference, to designate a new beneficiary of a life insurance policy or preretirement death benefit. Such authorization is probably consistent with the intention of most testators and would promote the orderly administration and disposition of property without serious hazard to insurers or financial institutions.

Legislation adopted in Washington in 1998 permits the will of a resident to control the disposition of "nonprobate assets specifically referred to in the owner's will . . . notwithstanding the rights of any beneficiary designated before the date of the will." Wash. Rev. Code § 11.11.020 (2011). The Washington law includes provisions that protect financial institutions and other third parties who deliver nonprobate assets to the designated nonprobate successors without knowledge of a testamentary disposition of the assets. It also includes provisions for the resolution of disputes regarding the assets. Under the act, a general residuary clause does not dispose of nonprobate assets. Wash. Rev. Code § 11.11.020(2) (2011). However, a disposition of all or all of a category of nonprobate assets is effective. If the owner designates a beneficiary of a nonprobate asset after the date of a will, the will does not govern disposition of the asset. Wash. Rev. Code § 11.11.020(4) (2011).

The concept of a "super will," of the type now approved in Washington, has been considered by various committees of several organizations, including the ABA. Enthusiasm for the concept was limited in the 1970s when an ABA committee considered a proposal then unfortunately titled "the blockbuster will."

§ 4.2. FEDERAL ESTATE AND GIFT TAXES IN PERSPECTIVE

As discussed in the Preface, at the time of this writing, there is substantial uncertainty as to the status of the federal estate and generation-skipping transfer (GST) taxes beyond 2012. The law currently provides that, beginning in 2013, the unified credit will shelter up to only $1 million from the federal estate and gift taxes, though many commentators expect that Congress will increase that exemption amount significantly. Even if Congress takes no action, however, the taxes are of little concern to most American families. Indeed, the data indicate that estate tax returns are filed for fewer than 2 percent of decedents. Data indicate that returns were filed with respect to 1.7 percent of the persons dying in 2002, when the estate and gift tax exemption amounts were last set at $1 million. Likewise, the GST tax exemption means that the GST tax will be of concern to a very small percentage of the United States population.

Most clients have modest wealth and relatively simple estate plans. For example, the principal goals of the estate plan of a married couple who have young children are usually (1) to transfer all of their property to the surviving parent or, if neither of them survives, to a contingent trust for their children; and (2) to appoint guardians of the person for their minor children. Their needs may be met by a "simple" will which includes a contingent trust for children (or provision for distribution to a custodian for each child under the Uniform Transfer to Minors Act), a durable power of attorney, and a living will. Those documents are explored in later parts of this chapter.

§4.3. STATUTORY WILLS

Eventually various statutory forms of wills and trusts may simplify estate planning for clients of modest means. Work on forms of statutory wills proceeded along two lines in the 1980s. The work of a committee of the Real Property, Probate, and Trust Section of the American Bar Association, chaired by John A. Perkins, culminated in the Uniform Statutory Will Act, approved by the National Conference of Commissioners on Uniform State Laws in 1984. As noted in the prefatory note to the Uniform Statutory Will Act, it is:

> A proposed statute to provide a scheme of testamentary disposition of broad utility. This Act contemplates that a testator will *adopt* the statutory *will through incorporation by reference* in a "simple will." This Act does not provide a battery of optional schemes or provisions, but it does permit modifications and additions to be made by the will which adopts the statutory will scheme generally or for some portion of the testator's estate. The statutory will may be the entire will of a testator and thus apply to all of the testator's testamentary estate, or it is adaptable to apply to a portion of the testator's estate as part of a will which includes other devises.
>
> * * *
>
> The approach of this Act is to provide attorneys a simple will embodying an estate plan workable for many clients, a will that can be prepared quickly, that can be adapted easily to special situations, and that guards against common drafting errors, all at minimum cost to the client and productive use of the lawyer's time. Although the Act is thus helpful to the legal profession, its intended and true beneficiaries are the public in terms of economical and expeditious legal services.

The Uniform Statutory Will Act has been adopted in Massachusetts, Mass. Gen. Laws ch. 191B (2011), and New Mexico, N.M. Stat. §45-2A (2011).

Another approach was taken in California, which originally authorized two complete statutory will forms. *See* former Cal. Prob. Code §§6220-6227. Beginning in 1992, California authorized a new single form of statutory will that calls for numerous blanks to be completed by the testator. Cal. Prob. Code §§6240-6243 (2011). The form includes several options regarding the disposition of the testator's personal residence, gifts of automobiles and household and personal effects, cash legacies, and residuary gifts. It also allows the testator to appoint guardians for minor children, to provide that gifts to persons under age 25 should be held until they reach that age, and to nominate executors.

An approach similar to California's has been taken in some other states, including Maine, Michigan, and Wisconsin. Me. Rev. Stat. tit. 18-A, § 2-514 (2011); Mich. Stat. Ann. § 700.2519 (2011); Wis. Stat. Ann. § § 853.50-853.62 (2011). There is some risk that individuals may misunderstand or misuse the statutory forms. The point was made by the National Commissioners in their Prefatory Note, *supra:* "Although the forms include several notices or caveats, one of which encourages the user to consult an attorney, it is believed that the forms will be used without consulting an attorney and if used that way, the forms are fraught with opportunities for misunderstanding and mistake by the unwitting." Overall, however, the statutory forms provide the public with important tools which are unquestionably superior to the printed will forms that were formerly available.

§ 4.4. Avoiding Intestacy

Although transfer taxes are not a major concern for most individuals, they do need to be concerned about providing in the most economical and efficient way for their spouses, children, and other dependents. Indeed, proper estate planning may be most important for those with the smallest estates—the persons whose dependents can least afford incurring unnecessary costs or delays.

If neither parent survives, the welfare of minor children is generally best served by consolidating all of the parents' wealth in either an inter vivos trust (through the use of a "pour-over" will) or in a testamentary trust. Through proper beneficiary designations and contractual arrangements life insurance proceeds and other nonprobate assets may also be made payable to the trustee of an inter vivos or testamentary trust. In any event, the expense, delay, and inconvenience of a guardianship of a minor's share of an estate should be avoided. These plans are discussed in more detail in connection with the residuary clause of the model will. *See* § 4.21.

Most married persons who die testate transfer all of their property at death to the surviving spouse, whether they reside in a community or a common law property state. M. Sussman, J. Cates & D. Smith, The Family and Inheritance 89-90, 143-144 (1970); Price, The Transmission of Wealth at Death in a Community Property Jurisdiction, 50 Wash. L. Rev. 277 (1975). Wills are usually needed to achieve that result because under many states' intestate succession laws a surviving spouse is not entitled to all of a deceased spouse's property. A surviving spouse is entitled to a deceased spouse's entire share of the community property in all cases under the law of some community property states—California, Idaho, Nevada, New Mexico, Washington—but not of others. For example, a surviving spouse is entitled to all of the community property under the intestate succession law of Arizona only if all of the surviving descendants are descendants of the surviving spouse. Ariz. Rev. Stat. § 14-2102 (2011). In Texas, the surviving spouse takes all of the community property only if the decedent is not survived by descendants, parents, siblings, nieces or nephews. Tex. Prob. Code § 38(b) (2011).

§4.4.1. Succession in Common Law Property States

Most common law property states limit the intestate share of the surviving spouse if the decedent was also survived by issue of any degree. *E.g.*, Fla. Stat. Ann. §732.102 (2011). Under the Florida law, the estate of an intestate decedent would be divided between a surviving spouse and the deceased spouse's children, grandchildren or other more remote descendants. In contrast, studies have repeatedly demonstrated that the overwhelming majority of married persons who die testate leave all of their property to their surviving spouses or wish to do so. *E.g.*, M. Sussman, J. Cates & D. Smith, The Family and Inheritance 133 (1970); Dunham, The Method, Process and Frequency of Wealth Transmission at Death, 30 U. Chi. L. Rev. 241 (1963); Fellows, Simon & Rau, Public Attitudes About Property Distribution at Death and Intestate Succession Laws in the United States, 1978 Am. Bar. Found. Res. J. 319. *See also* Price, The Transmission of Wealth at Death in a Community Property Jurisdiction, 50 Wash. L. Rev. 277 (1975). Perhaps believing that the studies reflect the wishes of most individuals, the U.P.C. and a growing number of states have increased the intestate shares of the surviving spouse. In a few common law property states, the surviving spouse is entitled to all of a deceased spouse's intestate property unless the decedent left issue who were not issue of the surviving spouse. *E.g.*, Iowa Code Ann. §§633.211-633.212 (2011).

Under the U.P.C., if an intestate married decedent is survived by a spouse and descendants, all of whom are also descendants of the surviving spouse, the surviving spouse is entitled to the entire estate. U.P.C. §2-102(1)(ii) (2011). (If some of the decedent's descendants are not also descendants of the surviving spouse, the surviving spouse is limited to $100,000 and half of the estate. U.P.C. §2-102(4) (2011).) Florida law provides that the surviving spouse takes the first $60,000 of the estate plus one-half of the balance if there are surviving lineal descendants of the decedent, all of whom are also lineal descendants of the surviving spouse. Fla. Stat. Ann. §732.102(2) (2011).

Under basic conflict of laws principles, when married persons move from a community property state to a common law property state the community property they bring with them should retain that character. *See* §3.36. However, courts have encountered some difficulty in properly characterizing the property. Under the Uniform Disposition of Community Property Rights at Death Act, which has been adopted by several common law property states, half of the community property brought into a common law property state is confirmed to the surviving spouse and half is subject to the deceased spouse's power of testamentary disposition. *See* §3.37.

§4.4.2. Succession in Community Property States

Under community property law, each spouse owns a one-half interest in the community property. The same is true of marital property under §4(c) of the Uniform Marital Property Act. The death of one spouse does not impair the surviving spouse's ownership of one-half of the community property. Only the deceased spouse's one-half interest in the community property and his or her separate property is subject to his or her will or to distribution under the intestate succession law. The succession law of most community property states and the alternate provisions of the U.P.C. recommended for adoption in community property states give the surviving spouse all of a deceased spouse's share of the community property. *E.g.,* Cal. Prob. Code § 6401(a) (2011); Wash. Rev. Code § 11.04.015(1)(a) (2011); Wis. Stat. Ann. § 852.01 (2011) (entire net estate); U.P.C. § 2-102A(b) (2011). In most community property states, the noncommunity property of a deceased spouse is divided between the surviving spouse and, in order of priority, the decedent's surviving descendants, parents, and issue of parents. Under the alternate provisions of the U.P.C. a surviving spouse is also entitled to all of the decedent's noncommunity property if the decedent was not survived by descendants or parents.

Again, under basic conflict of laws principles, when married persons move from a common law property state to a community property state, or vice versa, the property they owned prior to the move retains its original character in the absence of some action on their part to change it. *See* § 3.36. This typically means that in a move from a common law property state to a community property state, the imported property is treated as the separate property of the acquiring spouse—in which the nonacquiring spouse has no interest. However, in California, Idaho, and Washington the surviving spouse is entitled to a share of the quasi-community property (property acquired during marriage while residing in a noncommunity property state that would have been community property had the couple resided in a community property state at the time the property was acquired). *See* § 3.38.

§ 4.5. AN ESTATE ADMINISTRATION PROCEEDING MAY PROTECT THE SURVIVORS' ECONOMIC INTERESTS

A client may assume that it is best to "avoid probate" entirely. However, in many states the additional cost of conducting an estate proceeding is relatively slight—often more than offset by the advantages of such a course. For example, having such a proceeding makes it mandatory for the claims of creditors to be filed within a statutory period (typically four months from the first publication of notice to creditors) or they are forever barred. *See, e.g.,* Cal. Prob. Code §§ 9051, 9100 (2011); U.P.C. § 3-803 (2011). Of course, creditors will only be barred if the notice to creditors procedure meets the due process requirements of *Tulsa Professional Collection Services, Inc. v. Pope,* 485 U.S. 478 (1988).

The protection against creditors may be particularly valuable in the case of a decedent engaged in business or professional activities that might generate lingering contract or tort liabilities. In some cases a lawyer may be negligent if he or she fails to advise a client that creditors' claims may be barred by conducting an estate proceeding and publishing the requisite notice. Also, family awards and allowances that are available to a surviving spouse and minor children under the law of most states insulate a small amount of property from creditors' claims. *See* § 12.30. Finally, in recent years the cost and delay of estate administration proceedings have been reduced by the U.P.C. and other streamlined estate administration procedures.

§ 4.6. INCOME-SPLITTING BETWEEN ESTATE AND SURVIVORS

Conducting an estate administration proceeding is advantageous because a decedent's estate is treated as a separate taxable entity for income tax purposes. "Splitting" the family's income among the decedent's estate and the survivors usually produces some income tax savings. Although the compressed income tax rate structure that was adopted in 1986 limits the advantages, income-splitting retains some importance. First, an estate is entitled to a $600 deduction in lieu of a personal exemption. §642(b). Second, the income tax rates have some progressivity, at least until a taxable income of $10,050 is reached. The income tax rates applicable to estates and trusts in 2011, reflecting the adjustment for inflation, are:

Taxable Income	Tax
$0-$2,300	15% of Taxable Income
$2,301-5,450	$345 plus 25% on excess over $2,300
$5,451-8,300	$1,132.50 plus 28% on excess above $5,450
$8,301-11,350	$1,930.50 plus 33% on excess above $8,300
Over $11,350	$2,937 plus 35% on excess above $11,350

The amount of the potential savings depends largely upon the income tax position of the beneficiaries. For example, beneficiaries whose income is subject to a marginal rate of 25 percent could save as much as $290 each year ($600 (exemption) plus $2,300 (lowest bracket) times 10 percent (bracket differential)). In addition, through proper planning any excess deductions of the estate can be carried out to the beneficiaries for whom it will produce the largest income tax savings.

It is important to understand that the income tax does not "track" the estate tax in a very important respect: The income from an asset included in the gross estate is not necessarily taxed to the estate. The post-mortem income from property that passes to a survivor without estate administration is normally taxed entirely to the survivor and not to the decedent's estate. A leading text explains the point in this way:

> The property comprising the Subchapter J estate does not necessarily include all assets in which the decedent had an interest at death. Nonetheless, property subject even temporarily to administration usually is within the Subchapter J estate. Thus, many of the tax consequences . . . hinge not so much on the nature of the decedent's interests in property generating income after his death as on the degree to which the property is subject to the custody or management of the executor. C. Ferguson, J. Freeland & M. Ascher, Federal Income Taxation of Estates and Trusts §1.03 (2006).

Thus, the post-mortem income generated by property that the decedent and a survivor held as joint tenants is taxed entirely to the survivor. For most nontax purposes joint tenancy property is also not considered to pass through the decedent's estate. An asset held in joint tenancy and the income generated by it belong exclusively to the survivor by reason of the form of ownership. The same is true of property that is subject to other survivorship arrangements (*e.g.*, Totten trusts, survivorship accounts in financial institutions).

The post-mortem income from the decedent's share of the community property that is subject to an administration proceeding is taxed to the decedent's estate. The remaining half is taxed to the surviving spouse. That rule applies even if the local law subjects all of the community property to administration upon the death of one spouse.

The message is relatively short and simple—if there is no estate administration there is no separate taxable entity and no opportunity for income-splitting.

§4.7. CONTRACTUAL WILLS

A husband and wife, siblings, or other relatives often ask for wills that contain more or less reciprocal provisions. In such cases the clients need to decide the extent to which they want to restrict the survivor's right to dispose of the property inter vivos or change the dispositive provisions of his or her will. *See* Form 4-24 (Article Sixteen), §4.28. This subject should be raised, although the lawyer should conduct the discussion in a tactful way that does not promote discord between the clients or generate undue suspicions or concerns. The lawyer must also be alert to the conflict-of-interest problems that may arise if the parties wish to bind the survivor in some respect. In a word, their interests may be adverse. *See* §1.6.7.

In any case, wills that contain reciprocal provisions should generally state whether they were executed pursuant to any agreement. If so, the agreement should be set forth in the wills or in a supplemental instrument. The same practice should be followed whether the parties execute separate instruments with reciprocal provisions (mutual wills) or a single instrument (a joint will). The statement should be made even though the governing law may, like the U.P.C., make it difficult to prove will contracts. Under U.P.C. §2-514 (2011), will contracts "may be established only by (i) provisions of a will stating material provisions of the contract, (ii) an express reference in a will to a contract and extrinsic evidence proving the terms of the contract, or (iii) a writing signed by the decedent evidencing the contract. The execution of a joint will or mutual wills does not create a presumption of a contract not to revoke the will or wills." Statutes in some states are more stringent. For example, Fla. Stat. Ann. §732.701 (2011) provides that an agreement to make a will or not to revoke a will is enforceable only if "the agreement is in writing and signed by the agreeing party in the presence of two attesting witnesses." The same Florida statute provides that the execution of a joint will or mutual wills does not create a presumption of a contract to make a will or not to revoke the will or wills. Despite the best efforts of the testators to clarify their intentions, when contractual wills are executed the potential for litigation remains high.

§4.7.1. Uncertain Tax Consequences

The uncertain federal and state tax consequences of contractual wills also make them generally undesirable. For example, the interests in property that pass to a surviving spouse under a contractual will may not qualify for the marital deduction. However, in some cases the interest of the surviving spouse will qualify for the elective QTIP marital deduction under §2056(b)(7). Dobris, Do Contractual Will Arrangements Qualify for Qualified Terminable Interest Property Treatment Under ERTA?, 19 Real Prop., Prob. & Tr. J. 625 (1984). *See* §5.23. Prior to the effective date of §2056(b)(7), January 1, 1982, no deduction was allowable if the surviving spouse only received a life estate, or its equivalent, in the decedent's property with a power to consume. *Estate of Opal v. Commissioner*, 450 F.2d 1085 (2d Cir. 1971). In such a case the surviving spouse received a nondeductible interest.

Upon the death of the first spouse to die, the surviving spouse may be treated as having made a taxable gift of a future interest in his or her property to the beneficiaries named in the contractual wills. *Grimes v. Commissioner*, 851 F.2d 1005 (7th Cir. 1988); *Pyle v. United States*, 766 F.2d 1141 (7th Cir. 1985), *cert. denied*, 475 U.S. 1015 (1986). *See also* LR 7810001. Under Illinois law, applied in *Grimes* and *Pyle*, the surviving spouse is under an obligation to preserve the property and distribute what remains in accordance with the provision of the joint will. "Joint wills permit the surviving spouse to invade the corpus only for limited purposes." *Grimes*, 851 F.2d at 1007. In *Pyle*, the Seventh Circuit Court of Appeals said, "The state court's linking the word 'comfort' to the words 'health, support, and maintenance' in its construction of the will, while imposing strict limits on Grace's power to alienate her property, convinces us that the will limited her discretion by an ascertainable standard." In *Estate of Lidbury v. Commissioner*, 800 F.2d 649 (7th Cir. 1986), another Illinois case involving a joint and mutual will, the Seventh Circuit held that no gift took place upon the death of the wife because of the limited restrictions that the agreement placed upon the surviving husband's use and disposition of the property: "The contract executed by William and Rose allowed William to incur debts and alienate the property with only slight restrictions." 800 F.2d at 654. Presumably other courts would reach the same conclusion if the survivor were relatively free to use and consume the property.

The imposition of a gift tax at the time of the death of the first spouse to die is also consistent with Rev. Rul. 69-346, 1969-1 C.B. 227, which holds that in the case of a binding inter vivos widow's election, a gift of the survivor's remainder interest in the community property takes place at the time of the husband's death, when it is first possible to value the remainder interest in the property that the surviving spouse became obligated to transfer at the time she executed the election. *See* §9.24. Presumably no gift takes place if the survivor retains a power to consume or appoint his or her share of the property. *See* Reg. §25.2511-2(c). If there is a completed gift at the time of the death of the first spouse to die, §2702 may apply. If so, the retained life interest of the surviving spouse may be valued at zero, as a result of which she will be considered to have made a gift of her entire interest in the property. *See* §9.43.

The tax problems of contractual wills are illustrated by LR 9431004 (TAM). In it the surviving joint testator was held to have sufficient power over the predeceased spouse's property to require its inclusion in the decedent's estate under §2041. Under the contractual will, the survivor was given the personal property of the first to die. Upon the death of the survivor, certain shares of stock, if remaining, would pass to designated persons and other intangible personal property would pass to other beneficiaries. Under the arrangement regarding real estate, the survivor was given "full, complete, and absolute control and management of all said estate, with power to operate the same as a ranch, or to lease the same for grazing purposes." In addition, the survivor could "encumber or mortgage all or any part of said real estate" and could with respect to certain property "convey by deed of gift . . . any interest in or to the royalty in mineral production."

§4.7.2. Trusts Are Preferable

In view of the substantive law problems and uncertain tax consequences of contractual wills, an inter vivos or testamentary trust is almost invariably a better way to provide for survivors. More important, a trust may avoid the uncertainty that inheres in contractual arrangements regarding a variety of matters, including the scope of the survivor's authority to dispose of assets during his or her lifetime. Also, in the case of a trust, the legal title to the trust property is vested in the trustee, who may manage and invest the assets in accordance with the terms of the trust. A trust may also more effectively limit the control that one of the parties may exert over the property. Of course, use of a trust may avoid the necessity of establishing a guardianship should one or both of the parties become incompetent. However, in such a case the trustee must be given sufficient discretionary powers to distribute income and principal to the survivors in order to meet their needs.

§4.7.3. Conditional Wills

The effectiveness of a will, or of a provision of a will, may be made conditional on the occurrence or nonoccurrence of a specific event. Conditional wills should generally be avoided, however, because of their potential for litigation. Reflecting the presumption favoring testacy, a "condition" may be construed by a court as an indication of the reason the will was made rather than as a condition. Generally a client's needs are better met by a "regular" will, which may include conditional bequests.

B. ORGANIZATION AND CONTENT OF WILLS

§4.8. GENERAL

Professionally prepared wills are usually arranged so that the articles, or paragraphs, that deal with related subjects appear together. A will typically contains a series of articles that, successively, (1) identify the testator and the members of his or her family, revoke earlier wills, and define terms; (2) dispose of the testator's property; (3) appoint fiduciaries including guardians and trustees; (4) enumerate the powers and duties of fiduciaries and contain directions regarding the payment of debts and taxes; and (5) provide for execution by the testator and witnesses. Some lawyers prefer to locate the articles appointing fiduciaries and enumerating their powers in the fore part of the will, before the dispositive provisions, on the theory that the identity of the fiduciaries and the extent of their powers should be dealt with at the outset. In any case the substance—not the particular order of the materials—is most important.

The following sections present the provisions that might be included in a "typical" will for a married male client of modest means. After making some specific gifts, the will gives all of the client's property to his wife if she survives him, otherwise to a contingent trust for their children. Each provision is followed by a comment concerning its substantive and tax law consequences. The comments also point out why some other commonly encountered provisions should be used sparingly, if at all. The provisions are presented for the purpose of discussion and analysis and are not intended for use without the professional assistance of a competent lawyer.

Chart 4-1
Disposition of Assets
Under Will of John Q. Client

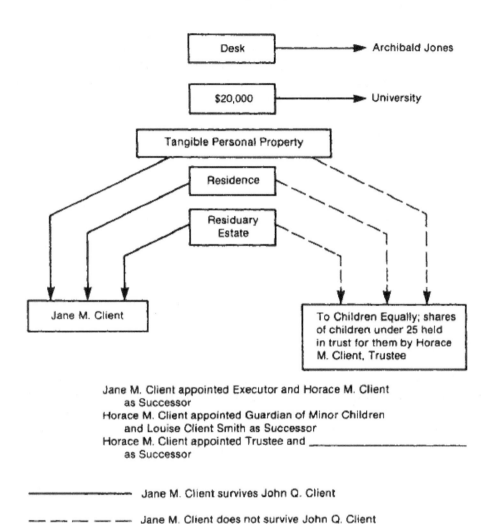

Jane M. Client appointed Executor and Horace M. Client
   as Successor
Horace M. Client appointed Guardian of Minor Children
   and Louise Client Smith as Successor
Horace M. Client appointed Trustee and _____
   as Successor

——————————— Jane M. Client survives John Q. Client

— — — — — — Jane M. Client does not survive John Q. Client

As a convenience some lawyers attach a table of contents to the wills and trusts that they prepare. A table of contents is particularly helpful to a client if it includes a brief summary of the content of each article of the will or trust. Some lawyers also attach a chart to each will or trust they prepare, which shows how various types of property will be disposed of under the client's estate plan.

A table of contents may refer to all of the provisions of the will or only to the principal dispositive provisions.

§4.8

Form 4-1
Table of Contents, John Q. Client Will

§ 4.9. Introduction to Will

Form 4-2
Introduction to Will
WILL OF JOHN Q. CLIENT

I, John Q. Client, also known as John Quincy Client, a resident of
_____(city), _____(state) declare this to be my will.

The introduction (or exordium clause) of a will indicates the name or names by which the testator is known. This may help the personal representative to identify, collect, and transfer the testator's property. The declaration may also help establish the place of the decedent's residence. Although not determinative, it is some indication of the testator's understanding and intent. The recitation may be helpful in dealing with the procedural issues, such as the jurisdiction and venue of courts. Normally the courts of the state of a decedent's domicile have jurisdiction over most estate administration matters. Within a state the venue is generally laid in the county in which the decedent was domiciled.

The determination of domicile is sometimes also significant for transfer tax purposes. In general, the state of a decedent's domicile has jurisdiction to tax all of the decedent's property except real property and tangible personal property located in other states. Most states have enacted laws that are intended to relieve the double tax burdens that might be imposed if two or more states determine that the decedent was a domiciliary. However, if at all possible the potential for conflict regarding the place of a client's domicile should be eliminated through advance planning.

Attention must also be given to the citizenship of the testator because of tax and administrative considerations. Citizenship is particularly important because the marital deduction is now generally limited to transfers to spouses who are United States citizens for deathtime gifts that are in the form of qualified domestic trusts. *See* § 5.25. Also, if a testator owns property which has a situs in another country consideration should be given to executing one will covering assets with a situs in the United States and another for each country in which assets are held.

The declaration that the instrument is the testator's will indicates that the testator is aware of the character and purpose of the instrument and evidences the requisite testamentary intent. The introduction may also include a clause revoking all prior wills, but a revocation clause is perhaps more properly the subject of a separate article. In either case the revocatory provision is equally effective.

Some lawyers favor more elaborate captions and clauses, perhaps to satisfy clients' expectations regarding the formality and quality of their wills. Thus, the caption may read "LAST WILL AND TESTAMENT OF JOHN Q. CLIENT," and the exordium may read "IN THE NAME OF GOD, AMEN, I, JOHN Q. CLIENT, also know as JOHN QUINCY CLIENT, a resident of _____, _____, being of sound mind and body and sound and disposing memory and not acting under fraud, duress, or undue influence, do make, publish, and declare the following to be my last will and testament, to wit . . . ." A recitation setting forth the soundness of the testator's mind is of little value and may even create suspicion that the testator's lawyer was uncertain about his or her testamentary capacity. Nonetheless, language of that kind still crops up in form books ... and wills.

© Mell Lazarus
By permission of Mell Lazarus and Creators Syndicate

© Mell Lazarus
By permission of Mell Lazarus and Creators Syndicate

§4.10. REVOCATION

Form 4-3
Revocation of Prior Wills

Article One: I revoke all wills and codicils previously made by me.

A complete disposition of the testator's property in a later will revokes the provisions of a former one by inconsistency. However, it is more straightforward and orderly to include an express revocation of earlier testamentary documents. There is ordinarily no virtue in leaving the issue even slightly uncertain when it can easily be nailed down.

The lawyer may wish to omit a revocation clause if the effectiveness of the will is uncertain or may be dependent upon the testator surviving for a specified period of time following execution of the will. A revocation clause might be omitted, for example, from a will that repeats a charitable bequest that was contained in an earlier will if the local law would invalidate charitable gifts unless the testator survives for a specified period following execution of the will. Otherwise, if the testator were to die prior to passage of the required length of time, the charitable bequest might be denied any effect; the bequest in the later will would be invalid under the mortmain statute and the earlier will would be ineffective because of the revocation clause. Of course, some courts might save the day by applying the doctrine of dependent relative revocation in a way that denied effect to the revocation clause, at least with respect to the charitable bequest. *In re Kaufman's Estate*, 155 P.2d 831 (Cal. 1945).

§4.11. DISPOSITION OF REMAINS

Directions regarding funeral arrangements and the disposition of remains are sometimes included in a will. The inclusion of directions ordinarily does no harm; however, they should also be included in a letter or other writing more readily accessible than the will. Perhaps the best solution is for the client to give a separate statement to the executor named in the will or to another reliable person. The statement, and perhaps the client's will, should refer to any burial plot the client owns and any funeral arrangements the client has made. As one commentator has observed, the will is perhaps the worst place to put directions regarding the disposition of the testator's remains. "Most families, when stricken by the death of a close relative, will abstain from reading the will until after the funeral. This is the result of grief, appearances, decency or ritual." T. Shaffer, The Planning and Drafting of Wills and Trusts 176 (2d ed. 1979).

If a client wishes to make a gift of part or all of his or her body for medical research or organ transplantation, the intended donee institution should be consulted regarding the acceptability of the intended gift, the form in which the gift should be made, and any other requirements the donee may impose. All states have enacted some form of the Uniform Anatomical Gift Act (1987). Section 42(b) of the Act authorizes gifts to be made by will, card, or other writing signed by the donor or by another and two witnesses in the donor's presence and at the donor's direction. *See* §4.39.

§4.12. PAYMENT OF DEBTS

Wills frequently include a direction that "my executor shall pay all of my just debts as soon as practicable after my death." Such a direction is better omitted. It is superfluous and can lead to a variety of wholly unnecessary disputes. For example, a controversy may arise concerning the necessity of exonerating requests of encumbered property or of paying debts that are barred by the statute of limitations. With respect to exoneration, U.P.C. §2-607 (2011) provides that "[a] specific devise passes subject to any mortgage interest existing at the date of death, without right of exoneration, regardless of a general directive in the will to pay debts." As indicated below, designating the source of funds that should be used to pay debts, expenses of administration, and taxes may be desirable, rather than relying on the local law regarding abatement. *See* Form 4-23, *infra*. Such a specification is permissible under U.P.C. §3-902 (2011).

§4.13. EXTENT OF TESTATOR'S PROPERTY

If a husband and wife have had some contact with a community property state during their marriage, their wills might include provisions that specify the extent to which they believe their property, or specific items of it, is community in nature. Although such a recitation is not determinative of the property's character, it is some evidence of the testator's understanding. Also, a discussion of the matter of community property, if it has not already taken place, is encouraged by such a provision. In order to fortify the effect of any other oral or written agreement between a husband and wife, it may be desirable to include a statement in their wills regarding the character of the property they own. The statement may be particularly appropriate where their property is entirely community in nature. For example, the will might state, "I declare that all of the property in which I have an interest is the community property of my wife and me." Except in cases in which there is an intent to put a surviving spouse to an election, the will might also recite, "I hereby declare that I do not intend to put my wife to any election regarding the disposition of her interest in our community property and I expressly confirm to her the one-half interest therein that belongs to her by reason of law." The community property widow's election device is explained in Chapter 9.

Uncertain language may require the surviving spouse either to elect whether to accept the benefits provided under the decedent's will and consent to the decedent's disposition of the entire community interest in a particular asset, or to reject the benefits and retain a one-half interest in all of the community property. An election may be required if, for example, the will leaves "all items of property which bear both my name and my wife's name to my wife" and "all other property to my children." In *Estate of Patton*, 494 P.2d 238 (Wash. App. 1972), the court held that such provisions required the wife to elect whether (1) to receive the entire interest in assets that stood in both their names and consent to the transfer of the entire interest in all other community property to the decedent's children, or (2) to retain her half of the community property and receive no benefits under the will. If a surviving spouse elects against the will, the local law should bar the surviving spouse from receiving an intestate share in any of the property that is undisposed of by the will as a result of the election.

In some community property states, property that is held in joint tenancy by a husband and wife is presumed to be their community property. *See* §3.12.5. The will may also confirm that the residence of the husband and wife is held by them as joint tenants and that he intends the property to belong exclusively to her if she survives him. The provision is particularly appropriate if the will leaves the testator's residuary estate to persons other than the surviving spouse—such as children by a prior marriage. The residue would be increased to the extent of half of the value of the residence if it was determined to be held by them as tenants in common or owned by them as community property. For example, under the law of some community property states, assets that are acquired in joint tenancy form with community property funds may remain the community property of the spouses.

§4.14.   Family Status and Definitions

Form 4-4
Family Status and Definitions

Article Two: I declare that I am married to Jane Martin Client ("my wife") and that I now have three children, Karen Ann Client (born August 1, 1978), Samuel Martin Client (born April 15, 1982), and John Rogers Client (born November 7, 1985). References in this will to "my children" are to them and any children later born to or adopted by me.

The term "descendants" refers to all naturally born or legally adopted descendants of all degrees of the person indicated.

Unless a definition of "children" or "descendants" is included, the testator's intention with regard to the inclusion or exclusion of adopted persons is unclear. The issue is typically resolved by resort to the intestate succession law of the state, which may apply the law in existence when the will was drawn or when a distribution must be made. In *Newman v. Wells Fargo Bank,* 926 P.2d 969 (Calif. 1996), the court concluded that the terms should be given the meaning ascribed to them by the intestate law in effect at the time the will was signed and the testator died—not according to a later change in the law. In the opinion the court stated, "We assume, as we must, that Lathrop [the testator] knew the meaning of issue and children as those terms were understood at the time she executed the will. We also assume that she knew that under form Probate Code section 257, a child adopted out of a sibling's family was not 'issue' who would inherit through his or her natural father or mother at the time." In some instances, an adult adoptee is included in the intestate definition of "child" or "descendant." *Tinney v. Tinney,* 799 A.2d 235 (R.I. 2002) (dispute between decedent's adult adopted child and natural child).

The introduction and identification of the testator's spouse and children establishes the testator's family circumstances at the time the will was executed. It also helps a reader by clarifying the relationship of the persons mentioned in the will, resolves ambiguities that might otherwise be caused by the use of terms such as "wife" and "children," and avoids the pretermission of children by naming all existing children and using a class term to include children who are later born to or adopted by the testator. The recitation also tends to establish that the testator knew "the objects of his bounty" at the time the will was executed, which is one of the elements of the traditional test of testamentary capacity. By including the dates of the children's births the client and the lawyer will be led to consider problems that might arise by reason of their minority, such as the need for guardians of their persons. The dates may also be helpful to the court, tax authorities, and others who may be called upon to deal with the instrument. The possible pretermission of descendants of a testator's deceased children under the law of some states suggests the desirability of also mentioning the testator's grandchildren by name or class (*e.g.,* descendants).

The term "descendants" is used in the instrument rather than "issue" because the former term is more understandable by lay persons. It is defined to include both naturally born and adopted persons of all degrees. A client may wish to exclude either all adopted persons or ones who are adopted after a specified age, such as 18. In some cases a restriction may be appropriate in order to prevent an adult from being adopted primarily for the purpose of qualifying to receive property under a will or trust. The definition is broad enough to include children born to unmarried parents. Under § 202 of the Uniform Parentage Act (2002) and similar laws, a child's status is recognized regardless of whether the child's parents ever intermarry. Accordingly, it may be wise expressly to include or exclude children born to unmarried parents in order to avoid their pretermission. Unless a term such as "descendants" or "issue" is adequately defined it may require construction by a court—a form of resolution that should be avoided.

In general, "heirs" is a term that should not be used in any dispositive instrument. It is inappropriate because the testator usually intends to describe a definite, more limited class of persons (*e.g.*, children or descendants). Even if the term appears to be proper, a more precise description of the intended beneficiaries is preferable. Finally, "heirs" should not be used in order to avoid any lingering possibility that the Rule in Shelley's Case or the testamentary branch of the Doctrine of Worthier Title might be applied to gifts made in the will.

Posthumously Conceived Child. Modern reproductive technology allows a child to be conceived after the death of one, or possibly both, of the individuals whose gametic material (egg or sperm) is used to create the child. Not surprisingly, the status of a postmortem child, including his or her inheritance rights, is presently unclear in most states. Several cases have been litigated concerning the right of a posthumous child to receive Social Security benefits as a dependent of a deceased father whose sperm was used to inseminate the mother. According to the Commissioner of the Social Security Administration and some courts, a posthumous child is only entitled to receive survivorship benefits if the child would be entitled to receive an intestate share of the deceased parent's estate under law of the state of the deceased parent's domicile. Applying the Commissioner's standard, some decisions have been favorable to posthumous children, e.g., Woodward v. Comm'r Soc. Sec., 760 N.E.2d 257 (Mass. 2002), Estate of Kolacy, 753 A.2d 1257 (N. J. Super. 2000), while others have not, e.g., Eng Khabbaz v. Comm'r Soc. Sec., 930 A.2d 1180 (N.H. 2007), Finley v. Astrue, 372 Ark. 103 (2008). In both the *Eng Khabbaz* and *Finley* cases the courts held that the child would not have been entitled to receive an intestate share of the deceased parent's estate under the local law.

Some courts, including the Third and Ninth Circuits, have rejected the Commissioner's standard and held that where a posthumous child is indisputably the biological offspring of a deceased wage earner and his surviving spouse the child is a child of the decedent within the meaning of the Social Security Act. *Capato v. Commissioner*, 631 F.3d 626 (3rd Cir. 2011); *Gillett-Netting v. Barnhart*, 371 F.3d 593 (9th Cir. 2004). In such a case a posthumous child qualifies for survivors' benefits if, as of the date of the deceased worker's death, "his children were dependent on or deemed dependent on him, the final requisite of the Act remaining to be satisfied." 631 F.3d at 632. The subject is discussed in Gary, Posthumously Conceived Heirs, 19 Prob. & Prop. 32 (March/April 2005) and Chester, Posthumously Conceived Heirs Under a Revised Uniform Probate Code, 38 Real Prop., Prob. & Tr. J. 727 (2004).

Professor Gary's article notes that §707 of the Uniform Parentage Act (2002) treats "a person who has provided genetic material but dies before the placement of the eggs, sperm, or embryos as a parent, only if the person consented in writing to be treated as a parent if the assisted reproduction occurred after the person's death." It also points out that written consent is required by the law of some states, including Louisiana and California, and that Florida requires that the posthumous child be provided for in the parent's will. Fla. Stat. Ann. §742.17. According to Professor Gary, the laws of Georgia and North Dakota limit inheritance to children conceived before the decedent's death.

In addition, a proposed revision of U.P.C. §2-108, described in Professor Chester's article, defines the inheritance rights of posthumously conceived children. Among the requirements are that the putative parent "donated the gametic material that resulted in the individual's birth" and that the putative parent "gave consent in a record to posthumous conception that would include the individual." Another requirement is that a complaint for determination of the individual's status be filed within three years of the putative parent's death. The latter requirement reduces somewhat the practical problems that might otherwise be faced in distributing an estate.

The provisions of Form 4-4 should be changed to comply with the requirements of the local law if a testator wishes to provide for a post-mortem child produced with the testator's genetic material. In such a case the will should at least reflect the testator's intent that a child created through the use of his or her gametic material should be treated as his or her child. In addition, the definition of "descendants" should be changed specifically to include, or exclude, descendants of persons who are conceived with the use of the testator's gametic material and are born after his or her death.

Disposition of Gametic Material. The disposition of a decedent's frozen sperm has been the subject of several cases. *Estate of Kievernagel*, 166 Cal. App.4th 1024 (2008*); Hecht v. Superior Court*, 16 Cal. App. 4th 836 (1993); *Davis v. Davis*, 842 S.W.2d 588 (Tenn. 1992). The most recent case, *Estate of Kievernagel*, recognized that an individual's gametic material was a unique type of property over which he or she has the power of disposition, including by contract:

> In this case we must decide whether a widow has the right to use her late husband's frozen sperm to attempt to conceive a child where her late husband signed an agreement with the company storing the frozen sperm providing that the frozen sperm was to be discarded upon his death. We conclude that in determining the disposition of gametic material, to which no other party has contributed and thus another party's right to procreational autonomy is not implicated, the intent of the donor must control. In this judgment roll appeal, the widow cannot challenge the probate court's finding that the decedent's intent was to have his frozen sperm discharged upon his death. Accordingly, we affirm the decision denying distribution of the frozen sperm to the widow. *Estate of Kievernagel*, 166 Cal. App.4th 1024, 1025 (2008).

If the gametic material of a client (or clients) has been preserved, the lawyer should review the terms of the contract under which the material is being stored to be sure it reflects the client's (or clients') intent. If not, the terms of the agreement should be amended. In any case, the intended disposition of the material should be specified in the client's will, or their wills.

§4.15. GIFT OF A SPECIFIC ITEM OF PERSONALTY

Form 4-5
Gift of Specific Item of Personalty

> Article Three: I give my antique mahogany desk by Samuel McIntyre to my friend Archibald Jones if he survives me. However, if the desk is not a part of my estate at the time of my death for reasons other than an inter vivos gift to Archibald Jones, I give him the sum of Five Thousand Dollars ($5,000) in place of the desk if he survives me. If Archibald Jones does not survive me no property shall pass under this Article.

A gift to an individual beneficiary should ordinarily be expressly conditioned, as here, upon the beneficiary surviving the testator. Under such a provision, if the beneficiary does not survive the testator and the gift is not "saved" by the anti-lapse statute, the property will be disposed of as a part of the testator's residuary estate. An anti-lapse statute usually does not apply if the testator indicates that it should not. For this purpose most courts accept that such an intention is evidenced if the bequest is conditioned on the beneficiary surviving the testator. W. McGovern & S. Kurtz, Wills, Trusts and Estates §8.3 (3d ed. 2004). Unfortunately, later versions of the U.P.C. adopt a contrary rule: that conditioning a bequest on survivorship is not itself sufficient evidence of an intention that the anti-lapse statute should not apply. U.P.C. §2-603(b)(3) (2011). In any case, most anti-lapse statutes only apply to gifts that are made to a relative of the testator who predeceases the testator leaving lineal descendants who survive the testator. *See, e.g.,* N.Y. Est. Powers & Trusts Law §3-3.3 (2011) (only applies to issue and siblings of the testator); Wash. Rev. Code §11.12.110 (2011). If a specific gift not conditioned on survivorship fails because the beneficiary predeceases the testator and the anti-lapse statute does not apply, the subject of the gift becomes a part of the testator's residuary estate under the common law and under the provisions of many statutes. *E.g.,* U.P.C. §2-604(a) (2011). By way of example, the Ohio Supreme Court has held that the anti-lapse statute does not apply to a gift to five named persons, "share and share alike, the same to be theirs absolutely, or to the survivor thereof." *Polen v. Baker,* 752 N.E.2d 258 (Ohio 2001). According to the court, the addition of the words "or to the survivor thereof" was enough to negate the application of the statute.

EXAMPLE 4-1.

T died leaving a will that included a bequest of "my gold watch to my uncle Harold" and gave the entire residuary estate to a charitable organization. Harold did not survive the testator, but his wife, Wilma, and two children, Adam and Claude, did. Under a typical form of anti-lapse statute, the watch would pass to Harold's children. They would, in effect, stand in the place of their parent, who was related to and predeceased *T*. If a beneficiary validly disclaims the right to receive a bequest, the beneficiary is usually treated as having predeceased the testator. *See* §12.33. Thus, if Harold survived *T*, but disclaimed the bequest of the watch, in most states it would pass to Harold's children.

In order to be consistent and avoid unnecessary problems, specific gifts of tangible personal property, such as Article Three, should be excluded from the coverage of a general gift of tangible personal property, such as made by Article Five. Form 4-8, §4.17.

§4.15.1. Ademption

Under the common law, a specific gift is adeemed and fails entirely if the property does not exist at the time of the testator's death. Thus, if the property is lost, sold, stolen, destroyed, or otherwise disposed of prior to the testator's death, the gift fails and the beneficiary is not entitled to receive any other property in its place. Where the property was insured, the right to any insurance recovery generally becomes an asset of the residuary estate. However, under some statutes the legatee of a specific gift is entitled to any proceeds unpaid at the time of the testator's death on fire or casualty insurance on the property. *E.g.*, U.P.C. §2-606(a)(3) (2011); N.Y. Est. Powers & Trusts Law §3-4.5 (2011). In all cases in which a client indicates a desire to make a specific gift, the lawyer should ask whether he or she wishes to make any alternative gift to the beneficiary if the particular property is not owned by the client at his or her death. In appropriate cases, the will should include a substitution for the gift, as in Form 4-5. The testator's intent regarding the matter should be specified in the will even if the same result might be reached under existing statutes or common law. The reasons why these should not be relied upon are obvious—the law might change or the testator might be domiciled in another jurisdiction at the time of death.

§4.15.2. Alternative Disposition

The lawyer also needs to know how the client would want the property to pass if the intended beneficiary does not survive the client. It is unwise to count on the survivorship of the intended beneficiary or the sufficiency of the local anti-lapse statute. One cannot assume that (1) the named beneficiary will survive the testator or (2) a distribution in accordance with the provisions of the local law (or the testator's intent as determined by the court) will serve the interests of the client or the client's family. A venerable Connecticut decision described the problem as follows:

It frequently happens that legatees die during the lifetime of the testator. The testatrix could have provided for such a contingency by giving it to the survivors, or to other parties. She did neither. There is, therefore some presumption that she intended that the law should settle the matter. That presumption is strengthened by the fact that she had an opportunity to change her will after one or more of the legatees had died, and failed to do so. *Bill v. Payne,* 25 A. 354 (Conn. 1892).

In short, a will should include appropriate provisions dealing with the premature death of the beneficiaries.

§4.15.3. Simultaneous Deaths

A will should also include some direction regarding the disposition of the property in the event of the simultaneous deaths of the testator and the intended beneficiary. In that way the client's intent will be clear, constructional problems will be avoided, and the lawyer will be protected against serious criticism and liability for failure to draft an unambiguous bequest.

A direction that the client's spouse should be deemed to survive the client in the event of their simultaneous deaths may be appropriate if it is important for the client's estate to qualify for the federal estate tax marital deduction. For marital deduction purposes, the estate tax regulations allow survivorship to be governed by a presumption provided by the instrument or the local law in the event of simultaneous deaths Reg. § 20.2056(e)-(2). *See* § 5.14.

§4.15.4. Survivorship for Specified Period

Many lawyers routinely recommend that testamentary gifts be conditioned upon the beneficiary surviving the testator by a specified number of days. In general the practice is a good one with the exception of a testator's spouse. The condition may be imposed with respect to an individual gift or all gifts. For example, a will might contain a provision such as in Form 4-6:

Form 4-6
General Survivorship Requirement

For the purposes of this will a beneficiary other than my wife is deemed to survive me only if he or she is living on the sixtieth day following my death.

This type of survivorship requirement prevents the same property from being subjected to the cost and delay of multiple estate administrations and possibly greater tax burdens if the beneficiary dies soon after the testator. It also prevents the property from passing in an uncontrolled manner in such cases. For example, unless the jurisdiction requires survivorship for at least 120 hours, U.P.C. § 2-702 (2011), without such a provision the antique desk left to Archibald Jones in Article Three (Form 4-5) would be distributed from Client's estate to Jones' personal representative if Jones survived the testator by any period (*e.g.,* one second). The desk would then be disposed of as an asset of Jones' estate, totally uncontrolled by John Q. Client's will. The item might pass to a person who had no appreciation of or use for it. Of course, where the deaths of the testator and beneficiary occur close together in time, a

survivorship clause might prevent a life or term interest from passing to the beneficiary, which would prevent the beneficiary's estate from claiming an otherwise allowable previously taxed property credit under §2013. The loss of the credit could be very
costly, particularly in the case of a life interest such as a QTIP that would support a
credit although no principal was includible in the beneficiary's gross estate. *See* §5.23.
Accordingly, it is generally better not to impose a survivorship provision on a spouse
unless the plan calls for equalizing the sizes of their estates.

Survivorship of more than 180 days is usually not required because (1) distributions are often made within 180 days following death and (2) a gift to a spouse may
qualify for the marital deduction if it is conditioned on the death of the surviving
spouse within six months of the testator's death and the surviving spouse survives
that period. Reg. §20.2056(b)-3(a). A lengthier survivorship period would disqualify
the gift for the marital deduction. §2056(b)(3).

Note that the U.P.C. requires survivorship of 120 hours in the case of intestate
succession, U.P.C. §2-104 (2011), and testate dispositions unless otherwise provided
in the will, U.P.C. §2-702 (2011). The requirement alleviates some of the problems of
the "almost simultaneous death," but does not deal with the problems that arise if the
beneficiary survives for more than five days. In order to negate the application of the
UPC's 120-hour survivorship requirement, the form might be expanded to say, "If
my wife survives me by any length of time, she shall be considered to have survived
me for purposes of this will."

§4.16. CASH GIFTS

Form 4-7
Cash Gift to Charity

Article Four: I give Twenty Thousand Dollars ($20,000) to the Regents of
the University of _____, to be used for such of the general
educational purposes of the University as they deem proper. However, if
the total inventory value of the property of my estate subject to administration less liens and encumbrances is less than Five Hundred Thousand
Dollars ($500,000), then the amount of this gift shall be reduced to an
amount that bears the same relation to Twenty Thousand Dollars
($20,000) as such adjusted inventory value of my estate bears to Five
Hundred Thousand Dollars ($500,000).

The aggregate amount of cash gifts can be limited in a way that protects the residuary
estate from undue diminution if the testator's estate shrinks in value after the will is
executed. Without this safeguard an unexpectedly large part of the estate might be
required to pay cash-gifts if the client's estate shrinks in value because of business
reversals, large unforeseen expenses, lifetime gifts, or any other reason. If the will
contains a number of cash bequests, the limitation can be modified to apply to all of
them. In the case of multiple cash gifts, the limitation could be expressed as a
percentage of the testator's net estate subject to administration. In such a case, it

should also provide for a pro rata reduction of each legacy if the percentage limit is exceeded.

Note that a charitable deduction is allowable for estate tax purposes only if the value of the gift is ascertainable at the time of the decedent's death. *Estate of David N. Marine,* 97 T.C. 368 (1991), *aff'd,* 990 F.2d 136 (4th Cir. 1993) (the residue of the decedent's estate was left to charity subject to reduction by an unlimited number of appointments to noncharities of up to 1 percent of the gross value of the decedent's estate). *See* §§2.16, 8.1. Accordingly, charitable gifts generally should not be made subject to reduction by post-mortem actions by others.

§4.16.1. Charitable Deduction for Tax Purposes

A gift to a charity of less than the taxpayer's entire interest in property qualifies for the estate tax charitable deduction only if the gift takes the form of an undivided portion of the property, a remainder interest in a personal residence or farm, a charitable remainder trust, a charitable income interest, or a pooled income fund. §2055(e)(2). In order to qualify for a charitable deduction, a gift of a remainder interest in trust must meet the stringent rules of §664. *See* §8.20. A gift of a life estate to a surviving spouse, remainder to charity, may qualify for the elective marital deduction under §2056(b)(7), but does not qualify for a charitable deduction in the testator's estate. The property is includible in the surviving spouse's estate under §2044 to the extent the marital deduction is claimed. The survivor's estate is entitled to an offsetting charitable deduction under §2055 for the value of the property included in her estate under §2044(a), which is considered to have passed from her for estate and GSTT tax purposes. §2044(b). LR 9043016. A gift, not in trust, of a remainder interest in a personal residence or farm does qualify for the charitable deduction. *See* §8.15.

§4.16.2. Satisfaction

A *cash gift* or other general legacy may be satisfied in whole or in part by an inter vivos gift to the legatee. Under the U.P.C., satisfaction occurs only if the will provides for the lifetime gift to be deducted, or the testator declares in a contemporaneous writing that the gift is to be deducted from the devise or is in satisfaction of the devise, or the devisee acknowledges in writing that the gift is in satisfaction. U.P.C. §2-609 (2011). If a client intends to discharge a bequest included in his or her will with an inter vivos transfer, the client should execute a new will or a codicil rather than rely on the proper application of this doctrine.

§4.16.3. Distribution in Kind

Commentators disagree about the extent to which an executor should be authorized to distribute estate assets in kind in satisfaction of pecuniary legacies. Such authority does give the executor more flexibility. However, if assets are distributed in kind in satisfaction of a pecuniary gift, the estate will realize a taxable gain in the amount by which the date of distribution value of the property exceeds its estate tax value. Reg. §1.661(a)-2(f). A distributee will take a basis in the property equal to the amount of the pecuniary claim that was discharged by the distribution. *See, e.g., Lindsay C. Howard,* 23 T.C. 962, 966 (1955), *acq.* 1955-2 C.B. 6.

If it appears that a testator's estate may not be sufficiently liquid to pay pecuniary gifts without difficulty, it may be preferable to avoid making pecuniary gifts rather than to burden the executor with the problem of deciding whether and how to make distributions in kind in satisfaction of the pecuniary gifts.

EXAMPLE 4-2.

T's will made a cash bequest of $10,000 to *B*, who survived *T*. The will gave *T*' s executor authority to satisfy cash gifts by distributing assets in kind. The executor distributed 100 shares of ABC, Inc. stock to *B* in satisfaction of the gift. The shares, which had been purchased by *T* several years before for $2,000, had a value of $8,000 on the estate tax valuation date and $10,000 on the date of distribution. The estate realized a gain of $2,000 when the shares were distributed, which is the difference between their value on the date of distribution, $10,000, and the estate's basis in the shares, $8,000. *B*'s basis in the shares following distribution will be $10,000.

§4.16.4. Forgiveness of Indebtedness

A debt owed the testator may be forgiven conditionally or unconditionally by an appropriate provision in the will. Because the forgiveness is essentially equivalent to a cash bequest, the former debtor may, depending upon the provisions of the testator's will and the local law, be obligated to contribute toward the payment of the federal estate tax. If the estate is insolvent a forgiveness directed in the will may not be effective. However, where the note or other obligation provides for forgiveness of the debt, it might be an effective nontestamentary provision. *See* U.P.C. §6-101 (2011).

The testator might, as an alternative, bequeath the note to the obligor. Keep in mind, however, that the forgiveness or other cancellation of an installment obligation triggers recognition of gain under the installment sale rules. *See* §691(a)(5); §9.6.

§4.17. TANGIBLE PERSONAL PROPERTY

Form 4-8
Gift of Tangible Personal Property

Article Five: I give all of my clothing, furniture, furnishings and effects, automobiles, and other tangible personal property of every kind except jewelry and gifts of specific items of tangible personal property made under other provisions of this will to my wife if she survives me. If my wife does not survive me, I give such tangible personal property, excluding automobiles, to those of my children who survive me, to divide among themselves as they may agree. If my children do not agree regarding the disposition of the personal property within sixty (60) days of my death, I direct my executor to divide the property among them in shares as nearly equal in value as practicable, having due regard for the personal preferences of each child. The share of any child who is a minor at the time the property is distributed may be delivered without bond to the child's guardian or to any suitable person with whom the child resides or who has custody or control of the child.

The disposition of the testator's interest in tangible personal property may pose problems if a number of beneficiaries must agree upon its distribution. If the property might pass to a minor the will should attempt to obviate the need to have a guardian of the estate appointed for the minor. For example, the will might provide that the property otherwise distributable to a minor may be delivered to the guardian of the minor's person or to other suitable persons. Where minors are involved, the client should consider excluding automobiles, boats, and airplanes from the gift. Because of jewelry's high value and its unsuitability for distribution to minors, it is excepted from this Article Five and is disposed of expressly in Article Six. *See* Form 4-9, § 4.18. Otherwise, jewelry could be included within the scope of this article.

Questions may arise regarding the extent of gifts of ill-defined scope. For example, in *Estate of Isenberg v. Berger*, 823 N.Y.S.2d 381 (App. Div. 2006), the court held that the testator's bequest to his sister of "any and all household items that she desires to take from my principal residence after my decease" extended to all paintings, figures and other art work located in the decedent's residence at the time of his death.

The executor or another responsible adult may be authorized to sell such of the items of a minor's share of the personal property as he or she believes is in the best interest of the child. In that way the insurance, storage, and other costs of retaining "white elephants" can be avoided and the proceeds invested for the minor, possibly in conjunction with a contingent testamentary trust.

The scope of Article Five may be further refined by specifically excluding money, precious metals (including coins) and unmounted gems held for investment, evidences of indebtedness, documents of title, and securities and property used in trade or business. Otherwise some beneficiaries might contend that those items are included in a bequest of "tangible personal property." Questions may arise regarding the extent of gifts of ill-defined scope. For example, in *Estate of Isenberg v. Berger*, 823 N.Y.S.2d 381 (App. Div. 2006), the court held that the testator's bequest to his sister of "any and all household items that she desires to take from my principal residence after my decease" extended to all paintings, figures and other artwork located in the decedent's residence at the time of death.

§ 4.17.1. Testamentary Gifts to Custodians for Minors

Section 5 of the Uniform Transfer to Minors Act (U.T.M.A.) and the version of the Uniform Gifts to Minors Act (U.G.M.A.) adopted in some states authorize testamentary gifts to custodians for minors. *E.g.*, Cal. Prob. Code § 3905 (2011). Under the former, all types of property may be given to a custodian for a minor. In contrast, statutes based on the U.G.M.A. usually authorize only gifts of a security, life insurance policy, annuity contract, or money to a custodian for a minor. Under both Uniform Acts each gift must be made to one minor—there cannot be multiple beneficiaries of a custodianship. The device is particularly useful in making gifts of small amounts of cash or securities to minors without requiring a full-blown trust or the appointment of a guardian for the minor.

If there is no will or the will or trust does not include a gift to a custodian for a minor the U.T.M.A. and the laws of some states allow the fiduciary to distribute property to a custodian for a minor. U.T.M.A. § 6 (2011).

§ 4.17.2. Specific Gifts and Cash Legacies

Casting gifts in the form of specific bequests or cash legacies will prevent a distribution of the property from carrying out the distributable net income of the estate to the beneficiaries. § 663(a)(1). *See* § 12.38. Such gifts may be distributed to the beneficiaries without adverse income tax consequences and without affecting the estate's income-splitting role.

Specific gifts to a surviving spouse are particularly useful to preserve income-splitting in community property states where the income from community property is naturally divided between the estate of the deceased spouse and the surviving spouse.

EXAMPLE 4-3.

H died survived by his wife, *W*, leaving a will that gave *W* a cash legacy, his interest in their tangible personal property, and the residue of his estate. Cash in satisfaction of the legacy and the personalty may be distributed to *W* without carrying out to her any of the estate's distributable net income for federal income tax purposes. In contrast, despite the separate share rule, a distribution of the residue to *W* would carry out to her some distributable net income of the estate for the year of distribution. That portion of the income would be taxed to her rather than to the estate. *See* §§ 12.37-12.38.

§ 4.17.3. Nonspecific Gifts

The estate may elect whether to report gain or loss on the distribution of property in kind in satisfaction of nonspecific gifts. § 643(e)(3). *See* § 12.39.

§ 4.18. DISPOSITION OF TANGIBLE PERSONAL PROPERTY IN ACCORDANCE WITH TESTATOR'S SUBSEQUENT DIRECTIONS

Form 4-9
Gift of Tangible Personal Property by List

Article Six: I give all of my jewelry to my wife, which I request her to dispose of as she believes would be in accordance with my wishes. I do not intend this Article in any way to obligate my wife to dispose of the jewelry to any other persons.

[*Alternative Article Six for U.P.C. states and others that allow reference to a list to be prepared in the future:* I give my jewelry to the persons and in the shares designated on a written list I intend to leave.]

The problem of drafting provisions designed to control the disposition of a large number of items of personalty to a changeable number of beneficiaries is troublesome in states that do not recognize holographic wills and do not have a specific statute, such as U.P.C. § 2-513 (2011), that authorizes reference to a list prepared later by the testator. In those states a client is generally faced with the necessity of executing codicils to effectuate changes or to transfer the property to a trust which can be more easily changed.

§ 4.18.1. Incorporation by Reference

Most jurisdictions other than New York allow a testator to incorporate in the will an extrinsic writing by reference, provided the writing is in existence at the time the will is executed, is adequately described, and is mentioned in the will with the intent to incorporate it. *E.g.,* U.P.C. § 2-510 (2011). Thus, this theory allows a will to incorporate a list or other existing writing that the testator intends to govern the distribution of property. Writings that are incorporated cannot be effectively changed after execution of the will unless the changes comply with the required testamentary formality. Uncertainties regarding the law and the risk that the incorporated document may be altered or destroyed suggest that private documents should generally not be incorporated. However, such things as statutes and regulations may be incorporated to good effect—particularly if the testator wants to "freeze" the provision in its present form.

§ 4.18.2. Facts or Acts of Independent Significance

An alternate doctrine allows a testator to control the disposition of property by appropriate reference to facts or acts of independent significance. U.P.C. § 2-512 (2011). Under this doctrine a testator could provide for a gift to a particular legatee of "all of the art objects listed on the fine arts rider to my fire and casualty insurance policy." Subsequent changes in the items listed on the rider would generally be recognized in making distribution of the testator's estate because of the independent significance of the list. Similarly, the identity of a beneficiary may be determined by independently significant facts, such as employment: "I give one hundred dollars ($100) to each person who is employed by J. Q. Client, Inc. at the time of my death."

Overall, incorporation by reference and reference to acts of independent significance are less satisfactory in dealing with the problem than the execution of a new testamentary instrument when the testator wishes to make changes in the disposition of the property. However, the preparation of a codicil or a new will may involve extended delays and additional costs. Also, codicils can cause considerable confusion where the testator leaves several—particularly if they are not entirely consistent.

§4.18.3. Bequest with Request

Some clients prefer to leave their tangible property to one person with a request that the beneficiary dispose of it as the beneficiary believes is in accordance with the testator's wishes. Under this approach the testator's wishes regarding the disposition of the property are usually expressed to the beneficiary in letters or other writings that may be changed by the testator from time to time. Although the gift does not impose a legal obligation on the person to dispose of the property in the way indicated by the testator, the approach generally works and clients are usually satisfied with it.

The state and federal transfer taxes are generally computed on the theory that the beneficiary named in the will receives outright ownership of the personalty. If the beneficiary gives some of the property to others, the beneficiary has made gifts, which may produce some gift tax liability. Consistent with that approach, the beneficiary and not the estate will be entitled to a charitable deduction for any property the beneficiary transfers to charity.

§4.18.4. Informal Lists

In states that have adopted the U.P.C. or have a similar statute, the disposition of tangible personally may be dealt with by the following direct, yet informal, method:

> Whether or not the provisions relating to holographic wills apply, a will may refer to a written statement or list to dispose of items of tangible personal property not otherwise specifically disposed of by the will, other than money. To be admissible under this section as evidence of the intended disposition, the writing must be signed by the testator and must describe the items and the devisees with reasonable certainty. The writing may be referred to as one to be in existence at the time of the testator's death; it may be prepared before or after the execution of the will; it may be altered by the testator after its preparation; and it may be a writing that has no significance apart from its effect upon the dispositions made by the will. U.P.C. §2-513 (2011).

If a client intends to utilize this procedure, the lawyer should provide the client with written instructions regarding the preparation and alteration of the list. Also, the client should be warned that the list may be ineffective if the client resides in a non-

U.P.C. state at the time of death. Coins and currency should not be disposed of under this provision because the section applies to items "other than money." If the section were construed narrowly the informal disposition of items of numismatic value might be ineffective. The client should keep any statement of this type with the will, or in a place known to the lawyer and the person named as executor. If a client wishes to change the disposition that is provided for in a list, a new one should be prepared and signed and the old one destroyed in order to avoid any uncertainties regarding the intent of the change or the identity of the person who made it.

As a precaution, items of substantial value should not be disposed of by an informal list. For example, valuable jewelry should be disposed of in the will and any changes made by codicil. If that is done, the transfer tax consequences will also be more straightforward.

If a list is executed in connection with a will that is subsequently revoked by another will, there is some risk that the list too will be considered revoked. An Idaho court held that execution of a new will revoking an old will did not also revoke the list disposing of tangible personal property that was executed in connection with the old will, because the language of the new will was broad enough to incorporate the list. *Wilkins v. Wilkins*, 48 P.3d 644 (Ida. 2002).

An informal list of gifts made pursuant to authorization in a will might look like Form 4-10.

Form 4-10
List of Gifts of Tangible Personal Property

My will states that I may leave a list that disposes of certain items of my jewelry [tangible personal property]. I make the gifts of the jewelry [tangible personal property] listed below to the persons named. The survivorship provisions of my will apply also to these gifts.

Item of Property   *Beneficiary*

_____   _____

_____   _____

_____   _____

This list was made on _____, 200_____

                                                                    _____

                                                                    Testator

The reference in the testator's will and the list should be consistent. Accordingly, consistent with the terms of Article Three (Form 4-5), the above list refers only to items of jewelry. The will and the list might instead refer to all types of tangible personal property.

A list may be effective to make a life insurance beneficiary designation. In *Burkett v. Mott*, 733 P.2d 673 (Ariz. App. 1986), the court held that the designation of the beneficiary of life insurance made in a list that was appropriately referred to in the insured's will was effective to change the beneficiary. The disposition was effective because the insurance policy was not among the types of property that were specifically excluded from the statute authorizing the disposition of property in a list. *See also* §4.20.4. Testamentary changes in life insurance beneficiary designations are generally not given effect. *See* §4.20.4.

A will may validly provide for the disposition of all of the testator's tangible personal property through a list in the testator's hand or signed by the testator. *Blodgett v. Mitchell*, 95 S.W.3d 79 (Mo. 2003). The *Blodgett* opinion also upholds the direction the testator made in a trust that "all of [decedent's] tangible personal property" be distributed to her sister. Although the inclusion in a trust of a provision for the distribution of tangible personal property that is not part of the trust is unusual, the court's decision in *Blodgett* is consistent with the intent of the statute and of the testator-grantor.

§4.19. GIFT OF CORPORATE SECURITIES

Form 4-11
Gift of Corporate Securities

> Article Seven: I give one hundred (100) shares of the common stock of ZYX, Inc., which I now own, as the same may be hereafter increased or decreased by reason of stock dividends, stock splits, mergers, consolidations, or reorganizations (but disregarding rights to purchase stock, whether exercised or not), to my brother Horace M. Client if he survives me. If I do not own a sufficient number of shares of the stock at the time of my death to satisfy this gift in full, then the gift shall be limited to the number of shares, if any, owned by me. If my brother Horace M. Client does not survive me, no property shall pass under this Article.

A gift of securities should specify whether the testator intends to give the legatee only the particular securities then owned by the testator (a specific bequest) or the specified quantity of the named securities whether or not the testator owns any at the time of his death (a general bequest). A specific gift of the type illustrated above, or as indicated by the use of the possessive pronoun "my" in describing the shares, typically carries with it any lifetime increase in the quantity of securities attributable to stock splits. If the gift were characterized as general rather than specific many courts would limit the gift to the original number of shares. The courts are divided as to whether a specific gift carries with it shares that were received as stock dividends.

The terms of this article generally parallel the provisions of U.P.C. §2-605 (2011) under which a specific gift of securities carries with it additional securities received by reason of action initiated by the issuer other than shares received as a result of the exercise of purchase options. However, even though the existing law may carry out the client's present intent without elaboration, the will should specify the effect that should be given to changes in the number of shares owned by the client. If the will contains multiple gifts of the same issue of securities the testator may wish to reduce them all proportionately if the quantity of securities owned at death is insufficient to satisfy all of the gifts in full.

Under some circumstances a gift of "all of the corporate stocks, corporate bonds, and all municipal bonds owned by me at the time of my death" is not broad enough to include mutual funds that are purchased with funds received when some of the testator's bonds matured. *Mississippi Baptist Foundation v. Estate of Matthews*, 791 So. 2d 213 (Miss. 2001). In *Estate of Matthews*, the testator's stocks and bonds were held in an investment account at a bank whose investment officer testified that the decedent wished her to invest the funds received upon maturity of the bonds in the "bank's mutual funds." Under other circumstances, a court might have found that the change from bonds to mutual funds was not a sufficient transmutation to cause the gift to be partially adeemed.

§ 4.20. Gift of Residence, Life Insurance, and Employee Benefits

Form 4-12
Gift of Residence, Life Insurance, and Employee Benefits

Article Eight: If my wife survives me, I give her all of my interest in

(a) any property we use as our principal place of residence at the time of my death that does not otherwise pass to her upon my death by right of survivorship or otherwise, together with my interest in all policies of insurance thereon including the right to receive the proceeds of all claims thereunder that are unpaid at the time of my death;

(b) all policies of insurance on her life and on the lives of our children; and

(c) all qualified and unqualified benefit plans resulting from her employment, including self-employment.

It is not strictly necessary to include a specific devise of residential real property to the surviving spouse who is also the residuary legatee. However, a specific devise may reassure the testator's spouse that he or she will receive their residential property and continue to have the right to occupy it regardless of whether title to it is held by them in a survivorship form. Such a devise may also provide some greater flexibility in making distributions to the survivor from the estate. In this connection consider the effect of § 663, discussed at § 4.17.2.

§ 4.20.1. Exoneration

The will should also specify whether an encumbrance on any specifically bequeathed or devised property should be satisfied. If so, the will should also designate the source from which the payment should be made—typically the assets of the residuary estate. Under the U.P.C. and the law of most states, an encumbrance need not be exonerated unless the testator specifically directs that the obligation be paid. U.P.C. § 2-607 (2011) provides that "[a] specific devise passes subject to any mortgage interest existing at the date of death, without right of exoneration, regardless of a general directive in the will to pay debts."

§4.20.2. Insurance on Realty and Personalty

The testator's interest in insurance on real or personal property should also be given to the beneficiaries in order to give them the benefit of insurance and to provide them with continued protection. The will should also specify whether the devisee is entitled to receive the proceeds of insurance claims that exist with respect to the property, but are unpaid at the time of the testator's death. U.P.C. §2-606(a)(3) (2011) and statutes in some states give the beneficiary the right to the unpaid insurance proceeds in such cases. *See, e.g.,* N.Y. Est. Powers & Trusts Law §3-4.5 (2011). The provision could also deal specifically with the disposition of the proceeds of any sale or condemnation of the property that remain unpaid at the time of the testator's death.

§4.20.3. Insurance on the Lives of Others

A testator's interest in policies of insurance on the lives of others should also receive special attention, particularly if the insured also owns an interest in the policies. Of course, if the noninsured spouse holds the entire interest in the policies for the purpose of keeping the proceeds out of the gross estate of the insured spouse, the noninsured spouse should leave the policies to a trust or a person other than the insured spouse. The insured generally should not serve as trustee of a trust that owns policies on the insured's life, which might cause inclusion of the proceeds of the policies in the insured's gross estate. *See* §6.28.11. Ordinarily minors should not be given an outright interest in life insurance policies or proceeds, because a guardian might have to be appointed to deal with the insurance on their behalf. If the testator's interest is given to a trustee of a trust in which the insured does not have an interest, the insured might also transfer his or her interest to the trustee in order to reduce the size of the insured's gross estate. Techniques for dealing with the life-insurance in estate planning are discussed in more detail in Chapter 6.

§4.20.4. Testamentary Changes of Beneficiary Designations; Life Insurance Policies

An attempt to change a life insurance beneficiary designation by will is generally not effective. Even if local law permits the testamentary change of beneficiaries, it is unwise to rely upon a testamentary change alone. Beneficiary designations and changes of beneficiary designations made by will have been recognized in some interpleader cases where the insurers did not object to the insured's failure to make the changes of beneficiary in the manner required by the policies. Those decisions emphasize that by recognizing the beneficiary designations the court gives effect to the insured's expressed intention. *See, e.g., Sears v. Austin,* 292 F.2d 690 (9th Cir. 1961), *cert. denied,* 368 U.S. 929 (1961) (federal employees group insurance); *Doss v. Kalas,* 383 P.2d 169 (Ariz. 1963).

The current beneficiary designations on policies in which the client has an interest must be examined. The lawyer should also advise the client to review the sufficiency of the beneficiary designations if any of the named beneficiaries dies or if the circumstances of the testator or the beneficiaries change substantially. Under the law of most states a life insurance beneficiary designation is not affected by a change in the insured's family circumstances. *See* Parotaud, Should Implied Revocation Be Applied to a Life Insurance Beneficiary Designation, 25 Fed. Ins. Couns. Q. 357 (1975). However, under the laws of some states and the U.P.C., the designation of the spouse of the insured as beneficiary is revoked if they are divorced. U.P.C. § 2-804(b) (2011); Ohio Rev. Code Ann. § 1339.63 (2011); Okla. Stat. Ann. tit. 15, § 178 (2011); Tex. Fam. Code Ann. § 9.301 (2011); Wash. Rev. Code § 11.07.010 (2011). Note that the state law regarding the effect of divorce on beneficiary designations of employer-provided insurance is preempted by ERISA. *See* § 3.32.

§ 4.20.5. Revocation by Change of Circumstances

Divorce and annulment are the only changes in family circumstances that revoke testamentary provisions under U.P.C. § 2-804 (2011). However, in most states a prenuptial will is revoked as to a surviving spouse who is not mentioned or provided for in the will or in a property settlement agreement. A will for a person who is contemplating marriage should mention or provide for the intended spouse in a way that will protect the will from revocation if the marriage takes place and the testator predeceases his or her spouse. "A reasonably prudent attorney should appreciate the consequences of a post-testamentary marriage, advise the testator of such consequences, and use good judgment to avoid them if the testator so desires." *Heyer v. Flaig,* 449 P.2d 161, 165 (Cal. 1969).

§ 4.20.6. Interest in Retirement Plans

In community property states the nonemployee spouse is generally recognized as having a transmissible interest in the employee spouse's IRAs. In contrast, the nonemployee spouse does not have a transmissible interest in plans that are subject to ERISA—qualified plans. *Boggs v. Boggs,* 520 U.S. 833 (1997); § 3.32. Some states allow the nonemployee spouse to dispose of his or her community property interest in the portion of non-ERISA retirement plans. *E.g., Farver v. Department of Retirement Systems,* 644 P.2d 1145 (Wash. 1982). In light of this possibility, the nonemployee spouse may wish to leave his or her interest to the employee spouse. Under Wisconsin law, the marital property interest of the nonemployee spouse terminates if he or she predeceases the employee spouse. Wis. Stat. Ann. § 766.3 (2011). In *Boggs v. Boggs,* the Court held that ERISA preempts state community property laws and prevents a predeceasing nonemployee spouse from transferring his or her interest in a plan subject to ERISA. *See* § 3.32. The nonemployee spouse may, however, be able to transfer his or her interest in an ERISA plan to the employee spouse.

As suggested in § 3.32, the restrictions imposed by *Boggs v. Boggs* on the disposition of the nonemployee's community property interest in a qualified plan might be avoided if, during lifetime, the nonemployee spouse transfers the interest in an employee benefit plan to the employee spouse in exchange for the employee spouse's interest in other property. After the exchange, the nonemployee spouse would be in a position to dispose of the other property without restriction.

§4.21. RESIDUARY GIFT

Form 4-13
Residuary Gift

Article Nine: I give all of my property that is not effectively disposed of by the foregoing provisions of this will, including all property over which I hold a power of appointment [excluding all property over which I only hold a power of appointment] (my "residuary estate"), as follows:

(1) If my wife survives me, I give my residuary estate to her. [If my wife survives me, but disclaims the right to receive outright any portion of my residuary estate, I give the disclaimed portion to my trustee to hold in trust for the benefit of my wife as provided in Article _____.] [*See* Form 4-16.]

(2) If my wife does not survive me, but I am survived by one or more children who are under the age of twenty-five (25) years at the time of my death, I give my residuary estate to my trustee to hold in trust for the benefit of my descendants as provided in Article Ten.

(3) If I am survived by descendants, but not by my wife or any children who are under twenty-five (25) years of age at the time of my death, I direct my executor to divide my residuary estate into as many shares of equal value as are required to carry out the following provisions:

(a) I give one (1) such share to each of my children who survives me and has attained twenty-five (25) years of age at the time of my death; and

(b) I give one (1) such share to the descendants who survive me of any child of mine who fails to survive me, such descendants to take by right of representation subject, however, to the provisions of trust for minors described in Article Eleven of this will.

(4) If I am not survived by my wife or by any of my descendants, I give one-half ($^1/_2$) of my residuary estate to the persons entitled to receive the property of my wife under the laws of the State of now in effect, as if she had died intestate at the time of my death not survived by a spouse, the shares of such persons also to be determined by said laws; and I give one-half ($^1/_2$) of my residuary estate to the persons entitled to receive my property under the laws of the State of _____ now in effect, as if I had died intestate, not survived by any spouse, the shares of such persons also to be determined by said laws now in effect.

Virtually every will should include a residuary clause, which controls not only the disposition of assets not already distributed by other provisions of the will but also the disposition of lapsed gifts and after-acquired property. Including a residuary clause will help avoid the necessity of a constructional or reformation proceeding. Importantly, a residuary clause will also prevent any property from passing by intestate succession. Some of the problems caused by failures in drafting, including the omission of a residuary clause, are illustrated in *Estate of Marie Haneberg*, 14 P.3d 1088, 1098 (Kan. 2000). That case also involved a substantial gift to the scrivener, which he was forced to disclaim. *See* § 1.6.8.

§ 4.21.1. Should the Residuary Clause Exercise All Powers of Appointment?

The residuary estate is described in Article Nine (Form 4-13) in a way that attempts to exercise any power of appointment the testator may have. If that approach is adopted some lawyers would prefer to include the word "appoint" *viz*, ("I give, devise, bequeath, and appoint..."). The bracketed alternate language should be used if the lawyer and client conclude that the attempt should not be made. Most commentators do not favor the blind exercise of powers of appointment. However, the exercise of unknown powers could be made dependent upon their nontaxability for federal estate tax purposes. A client who is given the choice may prefer to attempt the exercise in order to pass the absolute maximum amount of property to the beneficiaries he or she has designated.

There is some danger that a blind exercise may cause additional property to be included in the testator's gross estate. Property subject to a pre-October 22, 1942 general power of appointment is not includible in the donee's gross estate unless the power is exercised. § 2041(a). Of course, in some instances, a pre-October 22, 1942 power may be exercised by the donee's will although the will does not manifest any intent to exercise the power. *Stewart v. United States*, 512 F.2d 269 (5th Cir. 1975). Such results are attributable to the overly broad language of the instrument that created the power regarding the manner in which it could be exercised.

The effect of the inclusion may be ameliorated if the executor recovers the estate tax attributable to inclusion of the appointive property from the recipients of the property. *See* § 2207, § 12.43.3. However, the recovery of a proportionate amount of the estate tax will not completely offset the increase in estate taxes where the inclusion of the property drives the taxable estate into higher brackets, increasing the marginal rate and the overall effective rate of the tax.

Many lawyers oppose preparing a will that exercises powers without knowing what the tax effects of the exercise will be and what provisions the donor of the power may have included in the instrument for disposition of the property in default of exercise of the power. If a client holds an interest in a trust, the lawyer should review the terms of the trust carefully in order to ascertain the extent of the client's interest and whether or not the client holds a power of appointment over the trust property. A lawyer cannot safely rely upon a client's impression regarding the extent of his or her interest in a trust or the existence of a power of appointment.

Whatever decision is made regarding the blind exercise of powers, the will should state expressly whether the testator intends to exercise any powers. Under the majority American rule a residuary clause does not exercise a power of appointment unless the clause makes specific reference to the power or otherwise expresses an intention to exercise the power. *E.g.,* U.P.C. §2-608 (2011); Fla. Stat. Ann. §732.607 (2011). However, under New York law a testamentary power of appointment is presumably exercised by a residuary clause. *See* N.Y. Est. Powers & Trusts Law §10-6.1(a)(4) (2011). The will should eliminate any opportunity for a court to clamber into the testator's armchair in order to ascertain the testator's intent on the subject. Although the law of the testator's domicile may not recognize a residuary clause as effective to exercise a power, it may be recognized as effective by the law of the jurisdiction in which the trust is being administered. For example, in *Estate of Coffin,* 499 P.2d 223 (Wash. App. 1972), a garden variety residuary clause was recognized by the trustee of a Massachusetts trust as effective to dispose of property that was subject to a general testamentary power of appointment. At the time the Massachusetts law permitted a general power of appointment to be exercised by a residuary clause. For a general discussion of the subject, *see* French, Exercise of Powers of Appointment: Should Intent to Exercise be Inferred from a General Disposition of Property?, 1979 Duke L.J. 747.

The problems that may arise in connection with the exercise of powers of appointment and guidelines for their exercise are discussed in Bove, *Exercising Powers of Appointment—A Simple Task or Tricky Business?* 28 Est. Plan. 277 (June 2001).

§4.21.2. All to the Surviving Spouse?

Article Nine (Form 4-13) gives the entire residuary estate to the testator's wife if she survives him. Empirical studies indicate that such a disposition is in accordance with the wishes of most testators. However, it will cause all of the couple's property to be subject to disposition by the surviving spouse and may subject it to taxation upon the surviving spouse's death. If the combined estates of the spouses are large enough, or expected to be large enough, to generate any federal estate tax liability on the survivor's death, the will might allow the surviving spouse to disclaim the right to receive part or all of the residuary estate in order to make use of the deceased spouse's unified credit. The bracketed language in Form 4-13 is suitable for that purpose. Under the bracketed alternative if the testator's wife survives, any part of the residuary estate she disclaims will pass to a trust which would not necessarily be includible in her estate. The trust could take the form of either a QTIP trust, from which the surviving spouse must have the right to all of the income (*see* Form 4-16 and §5.23) or a family trust in which the trustee has discretion to distribute income to and among the surviving spouse and children. In either case the trust would not terminate prior to the death of the surviving spouse.

Under the disclaimer QTIP approach, any portion of the residuary bequest that is disclaimed by the surviving spouse would pass to a trust in which the surviving spouse would have a qualifying income interest for life. The executor would then be free to claim the QTIP marital deduction with respect to an appropriate portion of the trust. Of course, the portion of the trust with respect to which the QTIP election is made is includible in the surviving spouse's estate under §2044, but the balance of the trust (*e.g.,* an amount equal to the deceased spouse's credit equivalent) would not be included in his or her estate.

A legal life estate constitutes a qualified income interest for life for purposes of the elective marital deduction under §2056(b)(7). *See* §5.23. However, under almost all circumstances the use of a legal life estate with remainder over is a less satisfactory way of disposing of interests in real or personal property. Legal life interests create wholly avoidable problems of defining the rights of the owners *inter se* and of managing and disposing of the property. Also, the remainder beneficiaries may contest the ability of the life tenant to sell, lease, or otherwise dispose of the property and demand security and accountings. *See, e.g., Lehner v. Estate of Lehner,* 547 P.2d 365 (Kan. 1976). A trust is almost always a better choice because of its flexibility and the variety of interests that can be given to the surviving spouse.

Tax considerations aside, the maximum degree of flexibility might be achieved (and the interests of the surviving spouse protected) if the trustee were authorized to distribute the income of the trust to and among the surviving spouse and children. Of course, the marital deduction is not allowable with respect to such a trust.

Importantly, a surviving spouse may be given additional powers over the trust without jeopardizing its qualification for the marital deduction under §2056(b)(7). *See* §5.23. Specifically, a surviving spouse may be given the following powers: (1) to draw down the greater of $5,000 or 5 percent of the trust corpus annually; and (2) to invade corpus for support in his or her accustomed manner of living, for education, including college and professional education, and for medical, dental, hospital, and nursing expenses. *See* Regs. §§20.2041-1(c)(2); 25.2518-2(e)(2). The latter regulation appears to allow a surviving spouse to retain a special power to appoint property that will be includible in her gross estate (*i.e.,* the portion of the trust with respect to which a QTIP election was made). An independent trustee could also be given a discretionary power to invade trust corpus for the benefit of the surviving spouse or children without adverse impact.

Under the law of some states, the need for estate administration and attendant costs are virtually eliminated if the surviving spouse is entitled to receive all of the decedent's property. Cal. Prob. Code §13500 (2011); Tex. Prob. Code §155 (2011). Texas law provides several alternatives to formal administration of a decedent's estate, including the admission of a will to probate as a muniment of title. Tex. Prob. Code §89A (2011).

§4.21.3. A "Pot" Trust or a Separate Trust for Each Child?

The testator's will could adopt any of a variety of patterns for distributing the residuary estate to descendants if the testator's spouse does not survive. For a parent with a modest-sized estate and minor children a single "pot" trust for the children is preferable to a separate trust for each child. Article Nine places the entire residuary estate in a single trust if any of the testator's children is under 25 at the time of the testator's death. The trust will continue until the youngest living child reaches 25. Some clients will want to provide for such a trust if any child is under another age, say 30 or 35. The concept is more important than the particular age chosen.

Under the trust's distributive provisions, Article Ten, the trustee is free to use the entire income and principal of the trust flexibly to meet the needs of the testator's descendants. Form 4-15, §4.22. However, the primary emphasis is to provide for the support and education of the children who are under 21 at the time. The older children will probably be more self-sufficient and more nearly through with their formal education.

Special Needs Trust. A modified approach is often adopted if the testator has a child with special needs. In particular, a separate trust may be established for the lifetime benefit of the child. Most clients will want the trust to provide benefits to the child that are not otherwise available from public agencies. Thus, the benefits of the trust are intended to be supplemental to, and not in lieu of, public support. Accordingly, the trust should be drafted in a way that insulates the property of the trust from claims by public agencies for reimbursement for the support they provide. That can usually be achieved by giving the trustee broad discretion to provide for the beneficiary. Grassi, Estate Planning for a Special Needs Child Requires Special Attention, 34 Est. Plan. (Dec. 2007). *See also* Lombard, Planning for Disability: Durable Powers, Standby Trusts and Preserving Eligibility for Governmental Benefits, U. Miami, 20th Inst. Est. Plan. ¶ 1710 (1986). *See* Chapter 10.

Outright Shares of Residuary Estate. A testator with sufficient wealth to provide liberally for the needs of each child may prefer to divide the residuary estate into equal shares for the children at the time of the testator's death. That may also be an acceptable plan if the testator's children are older, their educational expenses have been substantially met, and they are more or less independent. Under this approach, one share could be distributed outright to each child over, say, 25, and one share held in a separate trust for each child under that age. However, in order to reduce the potential for conflict between children who would be entitled to distributions at different times, some clients prefer to provide that distributions of principal be made to all children at the same time (*e.g.*, five years after the testator's death). In any case, the lawyer should discuss the alternatives fully with the clients and counsel them regarding the choice that seems best suited to their needs. The lawyer should not routinely squeeze clients into a particular type of estate plan or a particular form of trust that the lawyer happens to favor or to have readily available.

§ 4.21.4. Consolidate the Client's Property in One Trust

Upon the death of the surviving parent, the most economical and efficient management of the property for the benefit of the children will result if the probate assets are consolidated with life insurance proceeds and other nonprobate property. Under one approach the client's will creates a testamentary trust for the benefit of minor children if the client's spouse does not survive and the policies of insurance on the client's life are made payable to "the trustee named or to be named" in the will as contingent beneficiary. State statutes typically permit such a beneficiary designation to be made without losing otherwise available exemptions of the insurance from creditors' claims and the local death tax. *E.g.*, Cal. Prob. Code § 6324 (2011); Fla. Stat. Ann. § 732.513 (2011); Wash. Rev. Code § 48.18.452 (2011).

If the local law does not expressly permit a testamentary trustee to be named as beneficiary, the desired consolidation of assets can be achieved by establishing an inter vivos trust and naming the trustee as secondary beneficiary of the life insurance policies. Such a trust is generally recognized as valid although the trust is not funded during the lifetime of the insured and the trustee merely has the right to receive the insurance proceeds upon the insured's death. *See* § 6.19.2. If such a trust is created, the testator's residuary estate should be "poured over" to the trust if the testator's spouse does not survive.

Statutes authorizing pour-overs, modeled on the Uniform Testamentary Additions to Trust Act, are in force in most states. U.P.C. § 2-511 (2011). *E.g.*, Fla. Stat. Ann.

§ 733.808 (2011). A paragraph like that in Form 4-14 might be included in the will when a pour-over plan is used.

Form 4-14
Pour-Over to Inter Vivos Trust

> (b) If my wife does not survive me and I am survived by any of my descendants, I give my residuary estate to the trustee, acting at the time of my death, of the trust created by the agreement dated January 1, 2005, between me as grantor and Horace M. Client as trustee, as the trust shall exist at the time of my death, to be added to and administered in all respects as property of the trust. I expressly direct that the trust shall not be considered to be a testamentary trust.

Other nonprobate assets, such as the balance due on notes, might also be made payable to the trustee if the testator's spouse does not survive. Such a provision for payment is treated as nontestamentary by U.P.C. § 6-101 (2011), but may be required to comply with testamentary formalities in other states.

§ 4.21.5. Discretionary Distributions

The total income tax burdens of the beneficiaries may be lighter if one trust is created and the trustee is given the power to "sprinkle" the income among them. Ordinarily a beneficiary should not serve as trustee of a discretionary trust because of the potentially adverse income, gift, and estate tax consequences. *See* § 10.27. In determining the time and amount of distributions the trustee can take into account the income tax position of the beneficiaries. The income tax bite may be smaller if most of the income is distributed to children who are over 18 (*i.e.,* not subject to the "Kiddie Tax") or are under 18 and have relatively little other unearned income. If such distributions are made the trust will be left with little taxable income. The discretionary nature of the trust also allows the trustee to distribute property in kind, which may be useful in some cases.

§ 4.21.6. Trust for Minor Descendants

Under the provisions of Article Nine (Form 4-13), if none of the testator's children is under 25, one share of the residuary estate will go to each living child and one share to the descendants of each deceased child. The share allocable to the descendants of a deceased child who are under 21 is subject to a very simple minors' trust under Article Eleven. Form 4-17, § 4.23. This approach should obviate the necessity of establishing a guardianship of the estate of a minor descendant. In states that have adopted the U.T.M.A., the will might instead provide that the share of a minor would be distributed to a custodian under the Uniform Act. "A personal representative or trustee may make an irrevocable transfer pursuant to Section 9 to a custodian for the benefit of a minor as authorized in the governing will or trust." U.T.M.A. § 5(a) (2011). The custodian may be designated in the will or trust, otherwise the personal representative or trustee may designate the custodian from those eligible to serve as such. U.T.M.A. § 5(c) (2011). Such a custodianship terminates when the beneficiary reaches age 21. U.T.M.A. § 20(1) (2011).

§ 4.21.7. Ultimate Disposition of Residue

Most wills should include a "waste-basket clause," such as Article Nine (4), that disposes of the testator's residuary estate in the event the testator's spouse, descendants, and other specifically designated beneficiaries fail to survive the testator. Form 4-13 (§ 4.21). If neither spouse nor descendants survive, a client may wish to divide the residuary estate equally between the client's surviving relations and those of the client's spouse. This article includes a form that gives half of the residue to the persons who would have been entitled to succeed to the wife's property by intestate succession had she died unmarried at the time of the testator's death, and the other half to the testator's intestate successors. Some clients will prefer to provide for some gifts to charity if none of the members of their immediate family survive.

In effect, the gift recognizes the contribution each spouse made to acquiring the property and makes a logical division of the property between the surviving relatives of each spouse. The form avoids the problems that could arise if the gift were made to the "heirs" of the client and the client's spouse: It specifies (1) the time at which the class of persons is to be ascertained, (2) the law that is to govern the identification of class members, and (3) the shares they are to take. The identification of the persons and shares should be made under the law in effect at the time the will is executed, which is known, rather than the law as it may exist at a later time, which is unknown. The testator might choose to base the distribution upon the intestate succession law of another state. *See* U.P.C. § 2-703 (2011). However, a lawyer should hesitate to draft such a provision unless he or she knows exactly what the result will be.

The disposition of half of the residuary estate to the persons who are entitled to receive the testator's noncommunity property under the intestate succession law in effect at the time the will is executed might be subject to the testamentary branch of the Doctrine of Worthier Title. However, the doctrine has been abolished in many states either legislatively or judicially and the Restatement, Property § 314(2) (1940) states that it is no longer a part of American law. In any event, the application of this branch of the doctrine would very seldom have any significance.

§ 4.22. TRUST PROVISIONS

Form 4-15
Trust for Descendants

Article Ten: The property I have given to my trustee to hold for the benefit of my descendants as provided in this Article shall be held and administered as follows:

(1) The trustee shall pay to or apply for the benefit of my children and their respective spouses and descendants so much of the net income and

principal of the trust as the trustee shall deem proper for their support, education, health, and general welfare. In making decisions regarding distributions of income or principal, or both, the trustee shall take into account other sources of funds known to the trustee to be available to them for such purposes. Further, in making decisions regarding distributions, I direct the trustee to prefer children of mine who are under twenty-one (21) years of age at the time of any payment or application of trust funds and to consider that the preservation of principal for ultimate distribution to my beneficiaries is of secondary importance. I direct the trustee to reimburse fully the guardian of the person of a child of mine for all reasonable expenses incurred by the guardian in caring for and sheltering the child. In short, I do not intend the guardian to bear any financial burden whatsoever by reason of acting as such.

The trustee may pay or apply the income and principal of the trust unequally among my children and their respective spouses and descendants and may exclude one or more of them from any payment or application of trust funds.

Any net income of the trust that is not expended pursuant to the provisions of this paragraph shall be accumulated and added to the principal of the trust at such times as the trustee determines.

(2) The trust shall terminate when there are no living children of mine under twenty-five (25) years of age ("then"). When the trust terminates I direct the trustee to divide the property of the trust into as many shares of equal value as are required to carry out the following provisions:

(a) I give one (1) such share to each of my children who is then living;

(b) I give one (1) such share to then living descendants of each of my children who is then deceased, such descendants to take by right of representation subject, however, to the provisions of Article Eleven. [A child might be given a special testamentary power to appoint to and among a limited class. *See* § 10.23 *and* Form 10-5.] Provided, however, if none of my descendants is then living, I give all such property to the persons and in the shares described in Article Nine (4), as if my wife and I had died at the time of termination of the trust.

Article Ten is designed to give the testator's children the maximum protection the testator can provide. Thus, the trustee is given very broad discretionary powers to use both the income and principal of the trust for the health, support, education and general welfare of the testator's children and their dependents. In making distributions, however, the trustee is instructed to consider particularly the needs of minor children. The trustee is also directed to consider other funds that are available to the beneficiary from any source. Finally, the trustee is directed to reimburse the guardian of the person of a child for all reasonable expenses incurred by reason of the guardianship. Some clients may wish to provide expressly that the trustee should pay the costs incurred by the guardian in acquiring furniture or enlarging, remodeling, or renovating the guardian's residence to accommodate the testator's minor children.

This article also provides that the trust will terminate when there are no living children of the testator under 25, but a client could just as well choose 30 or 35. Alternatively, the testator could provide for termination of the trust at the end of five or ten years following the testator's death. Upon termination, an equal share of the trust property will be distributed to each living child of the testator and to the living descendants of each deceased child. Under another approach, the trust might be divided into separate shares at a certain point (*e.g.,* when the youngest child reaches 25), after which portions of each trust would be distributed to its beneficiary. For example, one-third at 25, one-half of the balance at 30, and the balance at 35.

The article does not provide a share for the surviving spouses of deceased children, but some clients may wish to give each child a special testamentary power to appoint some or all of the child's share to a surviving spouse (or to and among the child's surviving spouse and children). Unfortunately, the needs of the spouses of deceased children are often overlooked in the planning process. As indicated in the bracketed material in the form, a child might be given a special power to appoint the property to and among members of a limited class if the child dies prior to termination of the trust. *See* § 10.23. If no descendants survive, the ultimate substitutional takers are the persons, determined in accordance with Article Nine (4), who would be the intestate successors of the testator and his wife as of the time of termination. Form 4-13, § 4.21.

Form 4-16
QTIP Trust

Article _____. Qualified Terminable Interest Property Trust. All property that shall pass to my trustee as a result of a disclaimer by my wife or otherwise shall be held and administered as follows:

(1) The trustee shall pay the net income of the trust to my wife in quarterly or more frequent installments.

Any income that is accrued or received but undistributed at the time of my wife's death shall be paid to her personal representative.

My wife shall have the power to compel the trustee to convert any unproductive or underproductive property and to invest it in income-producing property within a reasonable time.

(2) My executor shall have the power to elect to claim the marital deduction with respect to part or all of the trust. If a marital deduction is claimed with respect to part of the trust, I direct that the trustee hold that share as a separate marital deduction trust (the marital deduction trust) and the other share as a separate nonmarital deduction trust (the nonmarital deduction trust). All additional death taxes imposed on my

wife's estate by reason of the inclusion of the marital deduction trust in the base of such taxes shall be paid from the property of that trust unless my wife expressly provides otherwise in her will.

(3) [My wife shall have the power in each calendar year to withdraw from the principal of the marital deduction trust, an amount not to exceed the greater of $5,000 or 5 percent of the value of the principal of the trust determined as of the end of the calendar year. This power may be exercised in whole or in part each year by a written notice delivered to the trustee. The power of withdrawal is noncumulative, so that the power of withdrawal with respect to a particular calendar year can only be exercised during the calendar year.]

[In addition, my wife shall have the power to withdraw from the principal of the marital deduction trust so much as may be required to provide for her support and maintenance in health and reasonable comfort taking into account all income and property available to my wife from other sources. If the trust under this Article rule is divided into a marital deduction share and a nonmarital deduction share, I direct that no principal may be withdrawn or expended from the nonmarital deduction trust until all of the funds held in the marital deduction trust are exhausted.]

(4) Upon the death of my wife ("then") the trust or trusts under this Article shall terminate. Upon such termination I direct the trustee to divide the property of the trust or trusts into as many shares of equal value as are required to make the following distributions, which I direct the trustee to make: [As discussed below, great care must be exercised if the surviving spouse is to be given a power of appointment over a trust that was created as a result of the surviving spouse's disclaimer.]

(a) Distribute one (1) such share to each of my then living children who is 25 years of age or older;

(b) Distribute one (1) share to a separate trust under Article Ten for each then living child of mine who is under 25 years of age, provided that this share shall be added to the principal of any separate trust previously established hereunder for the benefit of such child; and

(c) Distribute one (1) such share to the then living descendants of each child of mine who is then deceased, to take by right of representation, subject however, to the provisions of Article Eleven.

(5) I intend that the trust established under this Article will qualify for the federal estate tax marital deduction to the extent my executor elects. Accordingly, I direct that all provisions of this will shall be interpreted and applied in a manner that is consistent with my intention. I authorize and direct my trustee to amend the provisions of this trust to the extent

required in order to sustain the marital deduction to the extent of my executor's election.

Form 4-16 is a simple form of QTIP trust which could be incorporated in the will and established to the extent the surviving spouse disclaims the right to receive any part of the testator's residuary estate. The first bracketed optional provision of paragraph 3 gives the surviving spouse a 5 or 5 power of withdrawal which provides some additional comfort and possibly a greater credit under § 2013 if the surviving spouse dies within ten years following the death of the testator. The IRS has recognized that giving the surviving spouse a 5 or 5 power does not prevent a trust from meeting the requirements of § 2056(b)(7). *E.g.*, LR 8943005 (TAM). The other bracketed provision in paragraph (3) gives the surviving spouse a power of withdrawal limited by an ascertainable standard related to her health, education, support or maintenance and a special testamentary power of appointment. Note that if a partial QTIP election is made, the form requires that any withdrawal of principal be made first from the marital deduction trust. These and other points are discussed in Chapter 5, which considers marital deduction planning in depth. QTIP trusts are discussed at § 5.23.

A trust can qualify for the marital deduction as a QTIP trust even where the trustee has the power to allocate receipts between income and principal, provided the trustee does so on a reasonable and equitable basis. *See* § § 5.23 and 10.46.5.

Power of Appointment. Under the regulations, a disclaimant who is a surviving spouse may not retain a power over disclaimed property unless either (1) the exercise of the power is limited by an ascertainable standard or (2) the disclaimed property will be included in the powerholder's estate. § 25.2518-2(e)(2).

§ 4.23. TRUST FOR MINORS

Form 4-17
Trust for Minor Distributees

Article Eleven: If the property of a trust or any of my residuary estate would be distributable to a person who is under the age of twenty-one (21) at such time, then I direct that, in lieu of being paid or distributed to such person, the property shall be held or retained by my trustee, in trust, as a separate trust fund for such person ("the beneficiary").

The trustee shall pay or apply so much of the income and principal of the trust for the benefit of the beneficiary as the trustee shall deem proper for the support, maintenance, health, and education of the beneficiary. In making such determinations the trustee shall take into account all other funds available for such purposes that are known to the trustee.

The trust shall terminate when the beneficiary attains the age of twenty-one (21) or sooner dies. Upon termination, the trustee shall distribute the property of the trust to the beneficiary if he or she is then living. If the beneficiary is not then living, the trustee shall distribute the trust property to the then living descendants of the beneficiary, by right of representation, but subject to this Article Eleven. If the beneficiary leaves no then living descendants, then the trust property shall be distributed to the persons and in the shares described in Article Nine (4), as if my wife and I had died at the time of termination of the trust.

Article Eleven (Form 4-17, above), establishes a simple but very flexible trust to receive and administer property that would otherwise be distributed to persons under the age of 21. As indicated in §4.21.6, some states allow the share of a minor beneficiary to be distributed to a custodian for the benefit of the minor.

In large measure this trust is intended to eliminate the need to appoint guardians of the estates of minor beneficiaries and to provide them with the benefit of a more flexible property arrangement. Article Eleven is added out of an excess of caution— its provisions will come into play very rarely. Under most circumstances the testator's estate will be distributed either to the testator's surviving spouse or to their children.

The provisions of this article do not give rise to any problem under the common law Rule Against Perpetuities. The interests will all ultimately vest when a beneficiary (whose parent was a life in being at the time of the testator's death) attains age 21 or sooner dies. If a greater age is used, the provisions may cause a violation of the Rule. Hence, a savings clause might be included in such cases. *See* § 10.48.

§4.24. PROVISIONS APPLICABLE TO ALL TRUSTS

Form 4-18
Trust Administrative Provisions

Article Twelve: (1) I appoint my brother, Horace M. Client, as trustee of each trust hereunder. If he shall fail or cease to act for any reason, I appoint _____ to serve as trustee in his place. I authorize my trustee to employ, at the expense of the trust, such attorneys, custodians, accountants, investment advisors, or other professionals as my trustee believes is in the best interest of the trust.

(2) I direct that no bond shall be required of my trustee or any successor trustee for any purpose.

(3) I expressly confirm to the trustee named herein and any successor trustee, all of the powers contained in Chapter _____ of the laws of the State of _____, as they now exist, which I incorporate by reference. In addition, I confer upon my trustee the following additional powers . . . .

(4) If more than one trust is created by this will, I authorize the trustee to hold, manage, and invest the assets of the trusts as one unit, maintaining

the separateness of the trusts by bookkeeping and not a physical segregation of assets.

(5) I authorize the trustee to invest in property of all kinds. In making investment decisions I direct the trustee to take into account the other investment, of the trust, the overall investment strategy of the trust, the duration of the trust, the needs of the beneficiaries, the tax circumstances of the trust and the beneficiaries, and the economic conditions.

(6) If the value of the principal of any trust (including the combined value of all trusts with identical terms and beneficiaries) is less than _____Thousand Dollars ($ _____), I authorize the trustee to terminate the trust and distribute the trust property to the person or persons then entitled to receive distributions from the trust. If a distributee is under the age of 21 at the time of such distribution I authorize the trustee to distribute the property to a custodian for the beneficiary under the Uniform Transfers to Minors Act [Uniform Gifts to Minors Act].

(7) I authorize the trustee to merge two or more substantially identical trusts which have the same beneficiary or beneficiaries.

(8) I authorize the trustee to divide one trust into two or more trusts with identical provisions. In particular, I encourage the trustee to do so if the trustee believes the division will maximize the benefits of the allocation of my generation-skipping transfer tax exemption. A division may be made by the trustee either on the basis of the value of each asset on the date of the division or by allocating to each trust a fractional interest in each asset.

(9) I direct that no interest of any beneficiary in the income or principal of any trust created by this will may be anticipated, assigned, or encumbered, or be subject to any creditor's claims or legal process prior to its actual distribution to the beneficiary.

§ 4.24.1. Successor Trustees

A will or trust that appoints an individual as trustee generally should appoint a successor or provide a mechanism for the selection of a successor. The first-named individual may not survive the testator or termination of the trust. Of course, the adult beneficiaries could be given the power to appoint someone other than one of themselves as successor trustee. (If taxes are not a consideration, or the trustee did not hold any "tax sensitive" powers, the beneficiaries could be given the power to appoint one of their number as successor trustee.) The appointment of a successor could involve some delay and unpleasantness unless one is named in the will. If multiple trustees are appointed, the remaining trustee or trustees could be given the power to fill any vacancy in the trusteeship. The power to replace a trustee with a person other than a beneficiary should not cause any problems.

§4.24.2. Waive Bond

Article Twelve (3) waives any requirement that a bond be required of the trustee. The provision accords with the probable intent of most testators, who prefer to save the cost of a fiduciary bond and rely upon the good faith of the trustees they have selected. State statutes commonly exempt corporate trustees from posting bonds. A client might wish to require a bond of a successor trustee if a successor is not named in the will. Again, this is a matter that should be put to the client for decision.

§4.24.3. Trustee's Powers

This will meets the problem of defining the trustee's powers by incorporating the existing state statutory provisions rather than simply restating the powers. This approach is satisfactory if the statutes confer adequate powers upon the trustees. Of course, if the local law gives a trustee adequate powers, it is not necessary to incorporate them. However, some lawyers prefer to do so in order to "freeze" the applicable law at the time and to call the powers to the attention of the trustee and others. The latter objective is, of course, better served by including a complete statement of powers in the will. If the local law does not provide the trust with adequate powers, the will may incorporate either the laws of another state or the Uniform Trustees' Powers Act which has served as a model for statutes adopted in many states. Most jurisdictions have enacted the Uniform Act or statutes based on it. Before a lawyer drafts a will that incorporates a list of powers, he or she should review the list carefully to determine whether any additions or deletions should be made based upon the circumstances of the particular client.

The trustee will often need additional powers if he or she is expected to deal with special situations or special types of property. The latter can include agricultural property, mineral interests, income-producing real property, or a business that may be continued following the testator's death. Also, it may be necessary to include special provisions regarding the allocation of receipts and disbursements between principal and income, particularly where income-producing real property is involved, and to give some specific directions to the trustee regarding depreciation and other charges. In some cases, clients will also want small stock dividends allocated to income—instead of to principal as provided in the revised (1962) version of the Uniform Principal and Income Act §6(a) and §401 of the 1997 version of the Uniform Act. *See* §10.46 *and* Gamble, If It's the 1990s It Must Be Time for Another Principal and Income Act, U. Miami, 32d Inst. Est. Plan., Ch. 8 (1998).

Special provisions may also be required in order to relieve the trustee from conflicts of interest. For example, an instrument may waive conflicts that might arise if (1) the fiduciary and the testator are partners or shareholders in a closely-held business; (2) the fiduciary and the testator are parties to a buy-sell agreement respecting stock owned by each of them; or (3) the fiduciary is a broker or other professional who might provide services to the estate.

Insofar as deletions are concerned, an informed client may wish to negate the provisions of statutes that authorize a trustee to retain all assets transferred to the trustee, including stock issued by a corporate trustee. The client also may not wish to relieve the trustee of the duty to diversify investments, Nev. Rev. Stat. §163.280

(2011). However, the client may wish to allow the trustee to invest in common trust funds and shares of regulated investment companies.

It is questionable whether a professional fiduciary should be insulated from liability for the retention of assets however they were acquired by the trust. After all, a trustee is compensated in part to provide prudent management and investment of the trust assets. Also, because of the potential conflict of interest, in most cases a corporate trustee should not be authorized to acquire or retain its own stock. If a client owns particular assets that the client desires the trustee to retain, his or her wishes should be expressed clearly in the will. In such a case the lawyer should not rely upon the general statutory authorization.

Clients may or may not wish to permit the trustee to invest in mutual funds or common trust funds. Such investments can provide broad diversification and relatively low management and transaction costs. On the other hand, some argue that such investments involve a double layer of management fees—the fee charged by the trustee *and* the one charged by the mutual fund manager. Whatever the state law may be on the point, the client should consider including an express provision in the will. Giving specific authorization removes any doubt regarding the issue and alerts the trustee to the existence of the authority. If the authority to invest in common trust funds is denied to a corporate fiduciary it may refuse to serve or charge substantially higher fees. For a discussion of trust investment provisions, *See* § § 4.24.5 and 10.44.

A client might wish to consider directing that the investments and allocation of receipts and disbursement of the trust should be governed by The Uniform Prudent Investor Act and The Uniform Principal and Income Act (1997). *See* § 10.44.1. Most clients would, most likely, want to allow the trustee to make investment decisions for total return rather than being restricted by the need to realize "income" from each asset of the trust.

§4.24.4. Unified Management of Trust Assets

Paragraph (4) of Article Twelve (Form 4-18) authorizes the trustee to hold and manage the assets of trusts under the will as a single unit. In this way the trustee may achieve some economies of scale and greater diversification of the assets of each trust. The necessary segregation of the assets of the trusts can be adequately maintained on the books of the trust. In addition, the assets of the trusts may always be physically segregated if it becomes desirable to do so.

§4.24.5. Investment Criteria

A client may wish to give the trustee broader authority and additional direction regarding the investments of the trust, allowing the trustee to pursue more promising investment strategies without liability. Article Twelve (5) is intended to permit the trustee to make individual investment decisions in light of all relevant factors, including the other assets of the trust, economic conditions, and the tax positions of the trust and its beneficiaries. This provision should free the trustee from the unreasonable application of the prudent person standard of investments.

Until the last quarter of the Twentieth Century, investment performance was usually subject to the prudent person standard that originated in an early Massachusetts decision, *Harvard College v. Amory*, 26 Mass. (9 Pick.) 446 (1830). Under it, trustees were required to "observe how men of prudence, discretion, and intelligence manage their own affairs, not in regard to speculation, but in regard to the permanent disposition of their funds, considering the probable income, as well as the probable safety of the capital to be invested." The standard, which draws an unreasonably sharp distinction between "speculation" and "safety," was traditionally applied to individual investments without regard to the other investments of the trust under consideration. The text of the standard is also premised on distinguishing between income and principal. It is unreasonable and unfair to fail to consider the role of a particular investment in a trust's overall portfolio. Modern theory and statutes allow a trustee much greater investment flexibility.

The desirability of taking other factors into account has influenced some courts and has led some states to adopt investment standards that allow other factors to be considered. For example, some statutes explicitly provide that tax consequences may be taken into account. *E.g.*, Del. Code Ann. tit. 12, § 3302(a) (2011). Legislation adopted in Washington authorizes investment decisions to be made in light of the trust's overall portfolio of assets. Wash. Rev. Code § 11.100.020 (2011). Subject to the overall investment standards, the Washington law allows the trustee to invest up to 10 percent of the value of the trust "in new, unproven, untried or other enterprises with a potential for significant growth whether producing a current return, either by investing directly therein or by investing as a limited partner in one or more commingled funds which in turn invest primarily in such enterprises." Wash. Rev. Code § 11.100.023 (2011).

Two factors frequently require trustees to consider the impact of investments upon the income and principal interests in a trust. First, under the prudent person standard the trustee must consider investments in light of their probable income as well as their safety. Second the beneficial interests in trusts are typically divided between beneficiaries who are entitled to receive the net income of the trust and ones who are entitled to the principal. The importance of the distinction is diminished if the trustee has discretion to distribute income or principal, or both, to the current beneficiaries. In those instances, the trustee is not compelled by the bifurcation of beneficial interests to make investments designed to generate income to be distributed currently to the income beneficiaries. Instead, the trustee can focus on the overall potential of the investments for growth and security. The importance of the distinction between income and principal is also largely eliminated if the current beneficiary is entitled each year to receive a unitrust amount—a fixed percentage of the principal value of the trust, determined on a specified date. For example, the current beneficiary might be entitled to receive each calendar year periodic distributions equal to 5 percent of the fair market value of the trust assets as determined on the first business day of the year.

In the case of a marital deduction trust under which the surviving spouse is entitled to receive all of the income, the effect of a unitrust can be emulated by giving the surviving spouse the noncumulative right each year to withdraw the amount by which 5 percent of the value of the principal (determined on a specified date) exceeds the net income of the trust distributed to him or her during the preceding year.

§ 4.24.5

§ 4.24.6. Authority to Terminate Uneconomical Trusts

In order to prevent the trust administration expenses from becoming too large in relation to the size of the trust, a provision might also be included that would authorize the trustee to terminate any trust if its principal value falls below a specified minimum amount, say, $50,000, at the end of any accounting period. If a trust is terminated for that reason, the trustee could be directed to distribute the fund to each person who is then entitled to receive current distributions and who is 21, otherwise to a custodian for the beneficiary under the U.T.M.A. A guardianship should be avoided because the associated expenses could easily exceed the costs of continuing the trust. California authorizes judicial modification or termination of an uneconomical trust upon petition of the trustee or any beneficiary. Cal. Prob. Code § 15408 (2011). In addition, the cited provision of the California Probate Code allows termination if the principal falls below $20,000 in value.

§ 4.24.7. Merger and Division of Trusts

In order to facilitate tax planning and to permit the more economical administration of trusts, the client may wish to authorize the trustee to merge substantially identical trusts that have the same beneficiaries. Such a provision may be sufficient alone, or with the approval of the court, to merge similar trusts, which could reduce overall trust administration expenses. California allows a trust to be merged or divided by the court upon petition of a beneficiary or trustee. Cal. Prob. Code §§ 15411-15412 (2011).

It is also desirable to authorize the trustee to divide one trust into two or more identical trusts. Giving the trustee authority to make such a division is particularly important if the executor makes a reverse QTIP election for GSTT purposes. *See* § 2.28.

Commentators often recommend that trustees be given a power to divide trusts: "Trustees must be given power to divide trusts to accomplish a variety of estate planning objectives. The drafter should provide language in the trust instrument rather than leaving the fiduciary to rely on statutory authority or to resort to court action." Suter & Repetti, Trustee Authority to Divide Trusts, 6 Prob. & Prop. (Nov./Dec. 1992) 52.

The division of a trust created at death is recognized for GSTT purposes if it is done (1) pursuant to authority granted under the governing instrument or local law, (2) prior to the due date of the transferor's estate tax return, and (3) each trust is either funded with a fractional share of the available assets or, if the governing instrument requires the division to be made on the basis of a pecuniary amount, and the amount is satisfied by a distribution in kind, the property distributed is either valued on the date of distribution or fairly reflects appreciation and depreciation in value of the property available for distribution. *See* Reg. § 26.2654-1(b).

§ 4.24.8. Spendthrift Clause

The last provision of Article Twelve (Form 4-18), makes the interest of each beneficiary inalienable to the extent permitted by local law. Most states recognize spendthrift restrictions to some extent. In some states income and principal interests can be made spendthrift, while in others only income, or some portion of income, can be protected in this way. Although the interest of a beneficiary may be inalienable because of its discretionary character, it may be desirable to make it spendthrift as well. The addition of this paragraph somewhat increases the probability that the beneficiaries will receive the intended benefits of the trust. Also, in the case of modest estates, there are usually no countervailing tax considerations that would support the omission of a spendthrift provision. The use of spendthrift clauses is reviewed in § 10.21.

§ 4.25. GUARDIAN OF MINOR CHILDREN

Form 4-19
Appointment of Guardian

Article Thirteen: If my wife does not survive me, or for any reason fails to qualify or ceases to act as guardian of the person of any of my children who are minors at the time, I appoint my brother, Horace M. Client, as guardian of the person [and estate] of each such minor child. If he fails to qualify or ceases to act as such guardian at any time during the minority of any of my children, I appoint my sister, Louise Client Smith, now of San Francisco, California, as guardian of the person [and estate] of such minor children. I direct that no bond be required of the guardian for any purpose. I expressly authorize the guardian to change the place of residence of any minor child of mine from time to time to any place within or without the state in which the child resides at the time of my death or later.

The law of many states permits a surviving parent to appoint a guardian for a minor child by will. *E.g.,* U.P.C. § 5-202 (2011); Wash. Rev. Code § 11.88.080 (2011). For obvious reasons, only individuals may serve as guardians of the person. Although a trust or custodianship is used to provide for the management of the minor's property, a guardian of the minor's estate may be appointed to deal with additional assets that are excluded from the trust or custodianship. The person serving as trustee or custodian, another individual, or a corporate fiduciary may be appointed guardian of the minor's estate. The appointment of a guardian of the person of a child is normally not required if a parent survives—the surviving parent of a minor child is the child's natural guardian, who is ordinarily entitled to the care and custody of the child.

Although the law of most states does not require a bond of the guardian of a minor's person, the imposition of a bond should be expressly waived in order to settle the matter clearly. Because of the possibility of the death of both parents as a result of a common disaster, it is wise for clients to consider appointing guardians for their minor children. Clients should, before their wills are prepared, obtain the consent of the persons they intend to name as guardians. If the prospective guardians are not family members, the clients must consider whether the provisions of the will should be disclosed to family members. A discussion might relieve problems that could arise if, for example, the family members contested the appointment made in the will. On the other hand, broaching the subject of appointing a nonfamily member could precipitate a controversy within the family.

State law often allows a minor over the age of 14 to participate in guardianship proceedings and to nominate a person to serve as his or her guardian. If the clients' children are 14 or older at the time the wills are prepared, the clients may wish to discuss the subject with them. Such a discussion can provide a valuable opportunity for the family members to examine their feelings about each other, family friends, and, importantly, about death. Some clients will readily accept this suggestion—others will reject it or merely not follow through.

Some jurisdictions allow the appointment of nonresident guardians. If the local law does not permit such an appointment, it may be difficult to meet the needs of some clients. However, a possible solution is to appoint a resident as co-guardian with the nonresident. The authorization to change the place of residence of a minor child may provide some additional flexibility, although it is given to guardians by some existing statutes. *See, e.g.,* U.P.C. § 5-208(b)(2) (2011).

§ 4.26. EXECUTORS

Form 4-20
Appointment of Executors

Article Fourteen: I appoint my wife as executor of this will. If my wife does not survive me or otherwise fails or ceases to act as executor, I appoint my brother, Horace M. Client, to serve as executor in her place. I authorize my executor to employ, at the expense of my estate, such attorneys, custodians, accountants, investment advisors, or other professionals as my executor believes are in the best interests of my estate. In addition, I authorize my executor to serve without bond and to administer and to settle my estate independently, without the participation or supervision of any court, to the maximum extent permitted by the applicable law. If an ancillary administration of my estate is required in other jurisdictions, I authorize my executor to serve in each such jurisdiction or to designate an executor to serve in each such ancillary jurisdiction.

Statutes in some states allow a personal representative to appoint a successor "pursuant to a power conferred in the will." Fla. Stat. Ann. 733.301(1)(a)(1) (2011).

The text of the article authorizes the executor to employ professionals to assist in the administration of the estate. A client who has named an individual who is not a professional as executor may wish to exonerate him or her from liability for ordinary negligence. *See* § 4.26.6. Otherwise, the fiduciary may be liable for the negligence of agents, accountants, lawyers, and other professionals. However, some state court decisions or statutes absolve a fiduciary for the negligence of agents and professionals if the fiduciary exercised reasonable care in selecting and retaining the agent or professional. *E.g., Roberts v. Roberts,* 536 S.E.2d 714 (Va. 2000).

The lawyer can help a client select an executor by explaining both the role of an executor in an estate administration and the pros and cons of having an individual executor, a corporate executor, or co-executors.

One factor to bear in mind is the cost. If a family member is appointed, either the executor will waive the right to receive a fee or the fee that is paid will remain within the family. If a nonfamily-member is appointed, a substantial fee may pass outside the family.

> Where a decedent's personal representative was compensated the cost was often substantial. However, in most cases in the sample the personal representative was a relative of the decedent who served without compensation. Sometimes a personal representative related to the decedent was paid—perhaps to minimize the aggregate estate and income taxes payable by the estate and the survivors. Even in those cases, the funds stayed within the decedent's family. Unrelated persons served as personal representatives in a small number of cases. Price, The Transmission of Wealth at Death in a Community Property Jurisdiction, 50 Wash. L. Rev. 277, 324-325 (1975); *see also* Kinsey, A Contrast of Trends in Administrative Costs in Decedents' Estates in a Uniform Probate Code State (Idaho) and a Non-Uniform Probate Code State (North Dakota), 50 N.D. L. Rev. 523, 524-527 (1974).

A fiduciary may waive the right to compensation without adverse gift or income tax consequences, provided it is done in a timely fashion. *See* § 12.8. For federal tax purposes the necessary intention to serve gratuitously is indicated if the fiduciary makes a formal waiver of any right to compensation within six months of appointment. *See* Rev. Rul 66-167, 1966-1 C.B. 20; Rev. Rul. 70-237, 1970-1 C.B. 13. Of course, when the lowest marginal estate tax rate is higher than the fiduciary's highest marginal income tax rate, some overall tax saving will result if the fiduciary is compensated.

The basic fee of a corporate fiduciary is typically determined by applying a percentage scale to some measure of the value of the property for which it must account, such as the inventory value. Current fee schedules can usually be obtained upon request by a lawyer from corporate fiduciaries. Fee schedules of corporate fiduciaries vary widely from state to state. Am. Coll. Tr. & Est. Counsel, Fees of Executors, Administrations and Testamentary Trustees. (ACTEC Study #5). A typical schedule establishes a minimum fee and rates that range from 0.6 percent or more for the first $100,000 or $200,000 to 0.35 percent on amounts in excess of $1,000,000. Some corporate fiduciaries use schedules that base their fees, in part, according to an hourly charge for the time of trust department personnel at rates comparable to those of junior lawyers.

In most jurisdictions the extent to which the lawyer for a fiduciary may disclose the misconduct of the fiduciary to the beneficiaries of the fiduciary estate or to the court is uncertain. *See* § 1.6.6 and MRPC 1.6. Accordingly, the testator may wish to condition the appointment of the executor and other fiduciaries upon their consent to the disclosure by their counsel of any breaches of trust. It is particularly appropriate to do so in the case of a corporate or other professional fiduciary. Indeed, the testator may also wish to condition the appointment of the lawyer for the fiduciary upon the lawyer's agreement to make such disclosures. However, if the fiduciary has filed the required waiver of confidentiality, the lawyer will be inclined to make the necessary disclosures in order to avoid liability for losses caused by a failure to do so. This approach is based upon a recognition that the purpose of the lawyer's services in drawing the will and representing the fiduciary is to benefit the beneficiaries designated in the will. It would be anomalous to permit the fiduciary to use the rules of professional responsibility to prevent disclosure of breaches of trust. Accordingly, the testator may wish to include a provision along the lines of Form 4-21, below.

Form 4-21
Waiver of Confidentiality by Executor

> I enjoin my executor and my trustee and counsel selected by each of them, faithfully to discharge their duties in the administration of my estate. In furtherance of my intention, I expressly condition the appointment of my executor upon [him/her] executing and filing with the court a document which permits [his/her] counsel to disclose to the court and to the beneficiaries any acts or omissions that might constitute a breach of trust by my executor or trustee, including breaches discovered through disclosures of information by my executor. I impose a similar condition upon the appointment of my trustee.

§4.26.1. Lawyer-Fiduciary

Comment [8] to Rule 1.8 states that, subject to the general conflict of interest rules of Rule 1.7, a lawyer may seek "to have the lawyer or a partner or associate of the lawyer named as executor of the client's estate or to another potentially lucrative fiduciary position" *See* §1.6.7. The Comment conflicts with E.C. 5-6, which provides that a lawyer shall not suggest directly, or indirectly that the will appoint him or her as a fiduciary. Surrogate Laurino has cautioned that, before undertaking to serve as fiduciary, a lawyer should consider the "grave legal, ethical and practical problems that he may have to overcome in order to perform his duties as a fiduciary and as an attorney." Laurino, The Duties and Responsibilities of the Attorney/Fiduciary, 19th U. Miami, Inst. Est. Plan., Ch. 16 (1985).

The lawyer should also explain to a client that the appointment of an individual as executor or trustee may require the lawyer to do more post-mortem legal work, as a result of which the lawyer's compensation might be greater than if a corporate fiduciary were appointed. On the other hand, the additional cost of legal services may be less than the cost of using a corporate fiduciary.

Although the lawyer does not serve as personal representative, some states recognize that he or she owes fiduciary duties to the beneficiaries, which may be enforced by them in appropriate cases. In *Estate of Larson*, 694 P.2d 1051 (Wash.2d 1985), the court discussed the origin of the lawyer's fiduciary duties to the beneficiaries:

> In probate, the attorney-client relationship exists between the attorney and the personal representative of the estate . . . .The personal representa-

tive stands in a fiduciary relationship to those beneficially interested in the estate. He is obligated to exercise the utmost good faith and diligence in administering the estate in the best interests of the heirs . . . .The personal representative employs an attorney to assist him in the proper administration of the estate. Thus, the fiduciary duties of the attorney run not only to the personal representative but also to the heirs. 694 P.2d at 1054.

While the rationale expressed by the Ohio Supreme Court in *Elam v. Hyatt Legal Services*, 541 N.E.2d 616 (1989), was unusual, the court concluded that the attorney for the fiduciary of an estate is liable to the beneficiary of a vested interest for damages caused by the attorney's negligence. In addition, the lawyer is obligated to act with candor toward the court. MRPC 3.3. Some courts conclude that the lawyer for the fiduciary represents the fiduciary and owes few, if any, duties to the beneficiaries. *See* § 1.36.

In most states, a lawyer who serves as fiduciary may also serve as attorney, or engage his or her firm to provide legal services. Service in both capacities is approved by the Statement of Probate Principles promulgated by the Real Property, Probate and Trust Law Section of the American Bar Association. It is permitted by some states, including New York. *Estate of Coughlin*, 633 N.Y.S.2d 610 (App. Div. 1995). However, it may be unwise for an attorney to serve as a fiduciary. In some states, a lawyer who acts in both capacities is not entitled to compensation both as executor and as lawyer for the estate.

§ 4.26.2. Corporate Fiduciary

It is impossible to generalize about the desirability of appointing a corporate fiduciary. The quality of a corporate fiduciary's performance depends in large measure on the ability and personality of the individual or individuals who are assigned to the estate or trust. The lawyer can influence the fiduciary's performance to some degree, but, after all, the lawyer is retained by the fiduciary, not vice versa. In order to enable the client to make an informed selection of fiduciaries, the lawyer should tell the client of any policy the corporate fiduciaries under consideration may have regarding the employment of lawyers who draw instruments appointing them as fiduciaries. The client should also understand that a corporate fiduciary may decline appointment, particularly if it did not review and approve of the terms of its appointment prior to the testator's death.

A corporate fiduciary is particularly appropriate where the client intends to create one or more large trusts that may continue for a substantial period of time, the services of an independent trustee are needed, or the client otherwise wishes to use a professional fiduciary. Also, when other potential appointees may be seriously affected by conflicts of interest the selection of an independent corporate fiduciary may be helpful. A client may ask the lawyer to recommend a corporate fiduciary. If so, the lawyer might suggest that the client interview trust officers at a select group of institutions and choose from among them. Of course, the client may wish to use a particular corporate fiduciary with which the client has a substantial existing relationship. With the client's approval the lawyer may inform the corporate fiduciary that it is named in the clients' will. In some instances a corporate fiduciary may be asked to review a client's will and related documents. If a corporate fiduciary has reviewed and approved the documents, it may feel obligated to serve as fiduciary. Otherwise it is not under an obligation to accept an appointment.

§4.26.3. Family Member Fiduciary

The availability, willingness, and ability of a family member to serve as executor must also be considered. After the death of a family member, the grief of a surviving spouse or other family member may be relieved by devoting some time to the details of the executor's job. In some cases the lawyer can play a valuable role by asking the survivors to do a reasonable amount of information gathering and other work. Clients often name a surviving spouse as executor, recognizing that he or she may decline to serve in favor of a child or other alternate named in the will. The lawyer should understand that a surviving spouse or other client may become emotionally attached to and overly dependent on the lawyer and his or her advice. A lawyer should be sympathetic, while at the same time discouraging the development of any undue dependence.

Some lawyers caution against the appointment of a surviving spouse as executor in blended family situations. Children of the deceased spouse may be more likely to assert claims against the surviving spouse in his or her role as a fiduciary of the estate. Suppose, for example, that a deceased spouse's will gives the surviving spouse a life interest in property with a remainder passing to the deceased spouse's children (to whom the surviving spouse is not a biological or adoptive parent). Absent a QTIP election, if one is available, the deceased spouse's estate may be liable for estate taxes on the subject property. *See* §§5.10; 5.23. But if the surviving spouse, as executor, makes a QTIP election with respect to the property, the surviving spouse's estate will have a right to recover estate taxes attributable to the property from the children of the first deceased spouse. *See* §5.23.11. If the property has appreciated substantially in value from the time of the election, the children of the first deceased spouse will be upset that they will have to pay estate taxes. As executor in this case, the surviving spouse may be fearful that any decision like whether to make a QTIP election will incite the children of the deceased spouse to cry foul.

An individual may be less reluctant to serve as a fiduciary if he or she is given express authority to retain professional advisors and assistants at the expense of the estate. In essence, the services provided by a corporate fiduciary can be approximated if an individual executor employs sufficient professional assistance. Indeed, many corporate fiduciaries have "unbundled" their fiduciary services and make individual services available to individual fiduciaries. Thus, an individual executor or trustee might retain a corporate fiduciary to provide custodial and investment management services. It is particularly appropriate to authorize the employment of professional advisors if the will names a family member as fiduciary who is unlikely to claim a fee.

§4.26.4. Co-executors

The relationship between co-executors can be a difficult one. A common cause of conflict involves the division of responsibilities and compensation. The advantages of having co-executors, including continuity in the event one dies or otherwise ceases to serve, should be balanced against the potential disadvantages, including possible disputes over fees and over the custody and management of assets. A corporate fiduciary usually wants to have custody of all of the estate's assets and to receive full compensation for its services. In some states, such as New York, each co-executor is entitled to a full statutory commission. *See* N.Y. Surr. Ct. Proc. Act, §§2313, 2307 (fiduciaries other than trustees), 2309 (trustees) (2011). Under the basic New York law if the estate (or trust) exceeds $400,000 a full commission is payable to as many as three fiduciaries. If there are more than three fiduciaries, the commission for three is divided among them. However, under N.Y. Surr. Ct. Proc. Act §2313 (2011), unless the decedent directed that greater commissions be allowed, commissions are payable to no more than two fiduciaries under instruments executed after August 31, 1993.

State law commonly requires the concurrence of both (or all) co-executors to bind the estate, which can cause some delays and require the reference of some matters to the court for instructions. Some problems are avoided if the will authorizes one executor to act during the absence or disability of the other.

§4.26.5. Alternate or Successor Executor

An alternate or successor executor should be appointed in wills that name individual executors. The first-named executor may not survive the testator, may decline to serve, or may not complete the administration of the estate. The need to name a successor is indicated by the fact that roughly 10 percent of the individual executors named in a sample of Washington wills failed to survive the testator. Price, The Transmission of Wealth at Death in a Community Property Jurisdiction, 50 Wash. L. Rev. 277, 325 n. 130 (1975). Although a corporate executor might decline to serve or later resign, it is less necessary to name a successor to a corporate fiduciary. If a successor is not named, the will should establish a procedure for the selection of one (*e.g.*, "a successor executor may be designated by a majority of my surviving adult children").

§4.26.6. Exculpatory Clause

A testator may wish to exonerate an individual personal representative from liability for official acts except in cases of willful misconduct or gross negligence. As a general proposition, corporate fiduciaries and other professionals who are fairly compensated for their services should not be relieved of liability for their acts or omissions. Of course, a lawyer may not enter into an agreement with a client that relieves the lawyer from liability for his or her acts or omissions. MRPC 1.8(h).

Form 4-22
Exculpatory Clause

Excepting acts of gross negligence or willful misconduct I relieve my Executor and my Trustee of any liability to my estate or any person interested in my estate or trusts thereunder for actions taken by either in their respective fiduciary capacities.

As pointed out by Professor Robert Whitman, the states have adopted a wide variety of rules regarding the enforceability of exoneration clauses. Whitman, Exoneration Clauses in Wills and Trust Instruments, 4 Hofstra Prop. L.J. 123 (1992). At one extreme New York bars an executor or testamentary trustee from being given immunity for failure to exercise reasonable care, diligence and prudence, or for valuation of any asset for purposes of distribution, allocation, or otherwise. N.Y. Est. Powers & Trust L. § 11-1.7 (2011). The New York courts have held, consistent with the literal language of the statute, that it does not apply to revocable trusts. At the other extreme several states, including Pennsylvania and Texas, allow the grantor of a trust to exonerate the trustee from liability for most acts.

> [I]f fiduciaries act with culpability beyond mere negligence, regardless of an underlying statute, state courts will attempt to find a way to limit the effectiveness of exoneration clauses, sometimes despite the plain language of an applicable, inflexible statute. If fiduciaries are merely negligent or have made mistakes in judgment, state courts will give effect to an exoneration clause. Courts are likely to be particularly concerned if the exoneration clause gets drafted into the will or trust through an abuse of fiduciary relationship; a clause may not be given effect based on those grounds. Whitman, *id*. at 162-163.

The inclusion of an exoneration clause should be considered in light of the lawyer's professional responsibilities. *See* § § 1.15; 10.45.

The Texas Supreme Court has given extraordinary obeisance to the Texas statute that allows a trustor to vary the duties of a trustee. Most recently, in *Texas Commerce Bank, N.A. v. Grizzle*, 96 S.W.3d 240 (2002), the Texas Supreme Court held that the Texas Trust Code allows a trustor to relieve a corporate trustee from liability for a "duty, liability, or restriction imposed by this subtitle except for those contained in sections 113.052 and 113.053." (The trust involved in the *Grizzle* case provided that, "This instrument shall always be construed in favor of the validity of any act or omission of any Trustee, and a Trustee shall not be liable for any act or omission except in the case of gross negligence, bad faith, or fraud.") The opinion continued, saying, "We disagree with the court of appeals' conclusion that public policy precludes such a limitation on liability."

§ 4.26.7. Executor's Bond

In most instances no bond is required of a personal representative under the U.P.C. *See* U.P.C. § 3-603 (2011). In some states, no bond is required except where required by the will, the nominee is a nondomiciliary, or the nominee does not possess the degree of responsibility required of a fiduciary. In many states, a bond is still routinely required of individual personal representatives unless it is waived. Cal. Prob. Code § 8480 (2011); Tex. Prob. Code § § 194, 195 (2011). However, statutes generally excuse corporate fiduciaries from the requirement of posting bond. Fiduciary bonds, which can cost $5 to $10 per $1,000 annually, are often an unnecessary expense that may deprive the surviving family members of needed funds. A client should, of course, be given the option of requiring a bond of fiduciaries but, in most cases, the additional cost should be avoided.

§4.26.8. Compensation of Executors

A will may specify the amount of compensation to be paid to a fiduciary. A fiduciary who accepts appointment of a will containing such a provision without objection is bound by it. Under some circumstances, it may be desirable to include such a provision in the will. However, the fiduciary may choose not to accept appointment or may seek to be freed of the restriction.

The states have a wide variety of arrangements for establishing the compensation of fiduciaries. For example, California and New York have statutory rate scales, while other states expect the courts to establish the "reasonable" compensation of executors and trustees.

Under Reg. § 20.2053-3(b)(2), a bequest in lieu of commissions is not deductible by the estate. However, an amount of compensation fixed in the will is deductible to the extent it does not exceed the amount allowable under the local law. A payment, but probably not a specific bequest, will be income to the executor. At some times the IRS shows greater interest in monitoring the amounts paid as commissions and challenging amounts that it considers to be unreasonable or unnecessary. *See* § 12.13.4.

§4.26.9. Authority to Settle Estate Without Court Supervision

Unsupervised administration of estates is the norm under the U.P.C. without any specific form of authorization. The expanded powers given to personal representatives under U.P.C. § 3-715 (2011), and recent changes in the laws of many states, largely eliminate the need to set forth the powers of the decedent's personal representative. Again, however, in special cases it may be desirable to give the personal representative specific powers with regard to particular assets. Some lawyers confer upon the personal representative the same powers that are given the trustee.

The powers of personal representatives in California were expanded by enactment of the Independent Administration of Estate Act, but no truly independent administration is authorized. *See* Cal. Prob. Code § 10500, *et seq.* (2011). For over a century the law of Texas has allowed a testator to provide that his or her estate be settled without any action of the court other than the probating and recording of the will and the return of an inventory, appraisement, and list of claims against the estate. Tex. Prob. Code § 145 (2011). Commentators have observed that virtually all well drafted wills prepared in Texas direct that the estate be settled by independent administration. The Washington experience with the unsupervised administration of estates has also been very good. Because of the mobility of our population and the possible enactment of similar legislation in other states, Article Fourteen authorizes the executor to settle the estate without court intervention. *See* Form 4-20.

§4.27.   DIRECTIONS REGARDING DEBTS, EXPENSES OF ADMINISTRATION, AND TAXES; CONSERVATION EASEMENT

Form 4-23
Payment of Debts, Taxes, and Expenses

Article Fifteen: (1) I direct my executor to pay all expenses of administration and all inheritance, estate, succession, and similar taxes ("death taxes") imposed upon my estate by reason of my death, other than any generation-skipping transfer tax and any estate tax attributable to property included in my gross estate by reason of I.R.C. § 2044, from the assets of my residuary estate, whether or not the expenses of administration or death taxes are attributable to property passing under this will.

(2) I authorize my executor to exercise all elections available under federal and state laws with respect to (a) the date or manner of valuation of assets, (b) the deductibility of items for state or federal income or death tax purposes, (c) the marital deduction, (d) the generation-skipping transfer tax exemption and (e) other matters of federal or state tax law, in accordance with what my executor believes to be in the best interests of my estate. I relieve my executor of any duty to make any adjustment to the shares or interest of any person who may be adversely affected by such elections and from any liability for making any such elections.

(3) I authorize my executor to create an easement that meets the requirements of a qualified conservation easement under Code § 2031(c), with respect to any real property that is included in my gross estate and to elect to claim an exclusion for such easement for federal estate tax purposes.

(4) I authorize my executor to pay the estate transmission and estate management expenses of my estate from the income or principal of my residuary estate or from the income or principal of the share of my estate to which the expenses are attributable.

A properly drawn will or trust should include a provision that identifies the fund from which expenses of administration and death taxes should be paid. It is often desirable to give the executor (and trustee) flexibility to pay the expenses of administration from principal or income, as paragraph (4) of Article Fifteen does. In this connection see the *Hubert* regulations, § § 20.2055-3; 20.2056(b)-4(d) and § 12.9. Special attention should be given to directions regarding the fund to be used to pay taxes. *See* Pennell, Tax Payment Provisions and Equitable Apportionment, U. Miami, 22d Inst. Est. Plan., Ch. 18 (1988). Rules regarding the payment of the federal estate and GST taxes are discussed in detail at § § 12.42-12.49.

Preparing a rough estimate of the amount of taxes that will be payable helps provide the lawyer and client with information that is helpful in making decisions about the allocation of tax burdens. Giving consideration to the estimates increases the probability that the client's dispositive plan will not be frustrated by the manner in which the taxes and expenses are charged. It is particularly important to include proper directions if the client's intent is not consistent with the local law that would otherwise apply (*e.g.,* if the local law calls for estate tax apportionment and the client wants all taxes paid from the residuary estate).

The tax clause generally should not undertake to pay the estate tax attributable to QTIP that is included in the testator's estate by reason of §2044. It is generally preferable for the tax on §2044 property to be recovered from the recipient as provided in §2207A. *See* §4.27.2. Similarly, the obligation to pay the GSTT generally should not be imposed on the residuary estate.

Among other things, the payment of the GSTT from other property may constitute a constructive addition to the generation-skipping property. Also, note that the apportionment acts adopted in some states may not permit a testator to direct that a portion of the estate tax be paid from nonprobate property, particularly property held by a husband and wife as tenants by the entirety. *See Estate of Reno v. Commissioner,* 945 F.2d 733 (4th Cir. 1991); §3.13.

§4.27.1. Source of Funds to Pay Federal Estate Tax

The executor is obligated to pay the federal estate tax, §2002, but the source from which the tax is paid is generally determined by state law. Many states follow the common law rule that calls for payment of the entire amount of the tax from the decedent's residuary estate. Others have adopted apportionment statutes that require the tax to be apportioned among the recipients of the decedent's taxable estate (*i.e.,* no tax is apportioned to marital or charitable bequest for which deductions are allowed). Some states have adopted apportionment rules by judicial decision. However, statutory enactment is the norm. *E.g.,* U.P.C. §3-9A-101 *et seq* (2011); Cal. Prob. Code §20100 *et seq.* (2011); N.Y. Est. Powers & Trusts Law §2-1.8 (2011). Apportionment statutes in some states also apply to the GSTT.

All states recognize that a testator may direct the tax to be satisfied from other probate property by appropriate direction in his or her will. A will provision dealing with the subject must be carefully drafted in order to prevail over the local rule. In *Estate of Lurie v. Commissioner,* 425 F.3d 1021 (7th Cir. 2005), the court held that the decedent's will sufficiently negated the default rule of apportionment by specifically referencing the decedent's revocable living trust and directing that the trust instrument govern the administration and distribution of the residue estate. Because the trust instrument expressly stated that the revocable living trust must pay the reasonable expenses of estate administration to the extent that the assets of the probate estate are insufficient, the court concluded that the decedent's will expressed the intent to negate the default rule of apportionment.

While apportionment may be the general rule, the wishes of a client with a relatively simple estate and an uncomplicated dispositive plan may best be served by providing that the death taxes are to be paid from the client's residuary estate. However, problems regarding the allocation of tax burdens arise if the residuary estate is left to charitable and noncharitable beneficiaries and the will simply directs that all death taxes be paid from the residue. In such a case the death taxes on nonresiduary gifts are deducted from the residue before it is divided between the charitable and noncharitable residuary beneficiaries. LR 9126005 (TAM). In effect, in such a case the charitable beneficiary bears a portion of the taxes attributable to the specific gifts—which, in turn, reduces the amount of the charitable deduction.

Instead, a client may wish to direct that all of the death taxes be paid from the portion of the residue allocable to the noncharitable gifts. Charging all of the death taxes to the noncharitable residuary beneficiary would preserve the size of the charitable (or marital) residuary gift but could seriously diminish or entirely eliminate the noncharitable residuary gift. An ambiguous direction that taxes be paid from a decedent's residuary estate may not require any portion to be borne by the marital deduction share where the decedent intended to minimize the taxes payable from her estate and the state law provides for equitable apportionment. *Estate of Swallen v. United States,* 98 F.3d 919 (6th Cir. 1996). *Swallen* and other cases illustrate the importance of providing carefully for the payment of taxes from the most suitable source.

Note that the estate and inheritance taxes attributable to all interests in a trust are generally payable from the principal of the trust—and not apportioned among the current and future interests. *See* Uniform Principal and Income Act § 502(a)(6) (2011) *and Malpas v. Klier,* 9 Cal.Rptr.2d 806 (Cal.App. 1992) (estate tax apportioned to life interest and remainder are both payable from the property without apportionment between the current interest and the remainder).

If a donor dies within three years of making a gift, the gift tax paid with respect to the gift is includible in the donor's estate under § 2035(b). The tax clause in a will prepared for a donor who has made, or is likely to make, gifts on which some gift tax is payable, should direct the source from which payment of any tax imposed by reason of such an inclusion should be made. Some donors may wish this part of the tax to be paid, along with other parts, from one source—typically the testator's residuary estate. However, in other cases the donors may wish to condition the gift upon the donee's agreement that the tax attributable to the "gross up" of the gift tax be paid by the donee of the inter vivos gift—or from a bequest that was left to the donee. The issue should be covered by an amendment to the estate tax apportionment statutes.

The payment of federal estate and GST taxes is also discussed in §§ 12.42-12.49.

§ 4.27.2. QTIP and § 2207A

QTIP is includible in the estate of the surviving spouse to the extent a QTIP marital deduction was claimed by the estate of the spouse first to die. § 2044. Unless otherwise provided in the surviving spouse's will, his or her executor may recover any additional estate tax attributable to the QTIP from the recipient of the property. § 2207A. The right to recover the tax is not waived by a general direction regarding the payment of death taxes. Section 2207A(a)(2) provides that the right to recover exists unless the decedent "in his will (or a revocable trust) specifically indicates an intent to waive any right of recovery under this subchapter with respect to such property."

In many cases, the surviving spouse-beneficiary does not have any control over the ultimate distribution of the property of the QTIP trust. For that reason the surviving spouse usually chooses not to direct that the estate tax on the QTIP be paid from his or her own property. Accordingly, as a general rule the will of the surviving spouse should not provide for payment of the estate tax imposed on § 2044 property. *See* § 12.43.4.

If a reverse QTIP election is made for GSTT purposes, the identity of the transferor is made without regard to the application of § § 2044, 2207A and 2519. Reg. § 26.2652-1(a)(3). Thus, the payment of estate tax by the surviving spouse's estate with respect to property for which a reverse QTIP election had been made is not a constructive addition to the trust. Reg. § 26.2652-1(a)(5) Example 6.

§ 4.27.3. § 2207B

A decedent's personal representative is entitled to recover a portion of the estate tax attributable to the inclusion of property by reason of § 2036 (relating to lifetime transfers with retained life estates). § 2207B. The amount of tax recoverable is based upon the ratio of the value of the § 2036 property to the total value of the taxable estate. Although the inclusion of the property will require the payment of tax at a higher marginal rate, the right of recovery is based upon the average rate. This distinction is less important where the estate tax is imposed at a flat rate, as is the case under current law.

The right of recovery does not exist if the decedent provides otherwise in a will or revocable trust specifically referring to § 2207B. § 2207B(a)(2). Moreover, the right to recover the tax is not waived by a general direction regarding the payment of death taxes. Specifically, the right to recover exists unless the decedent "in his will (or a revocable trust) specifically indicates an intent to waive any right of recovery under this subchapter with respect to such property." *Id.* The right of recovery provided by this section applies only to property transferred after December 31, 1987.

§ 4.27.4. Clarity

The substantial volume of litigation regarding the effect of particular tax clauses indicates the problems lawyers have had in drafting adequate provisions. For example, the term "estate" often appears in tax clauses without specifying whether it refers to the gross estate for tax purposes, the "probate" estate, or some other measure of property. Unfortunately, the cost of the litigation is almost always borne by the hapless beneficiaries and not the lawyer who drafted the inadequate provision.

If multiple dispositive instruments are involved, all of the directions for the payment of taxes should be consistent and comply with the requirements of local law. Inconsistent provisions contained in a will and a trust may cause problems in tax and substantive law that require judicial resolution. *Estate of Brenner,* 547 P.2d 938 (Colo. App. 1976). The local law may deny effect to directions regarding payment of taxes if they are not included in the will. For example, a provision of an inter vivos trust that directs the trustee to pay "any and all of the Federal Estate Tax for which no other provision for payment has been made" may not be given effect. *Hill v. Nevada National Bank,* 545 P.2d 293, 294 (Nev. 1976).

The problem of inconsistent directions in multiple instruments is addressed by a New York statute that provides that any direction in an instrument only relates to property passing thereunder unless otherwise provided. N.Y. Est. Powers & Trusts Law § 2-1.8(d) (2011). It also provides that:

(1) any such direction in a will which is later in date than a prior nontestamentary instrument which contains a contrary direction shall govern provided the later will specifically refers to the direction in such prior instrument;

(2) any such direction provided in a nontestamentary instrument which is later in date than a prior will or nontestamentary instrument and which contains a contrary direction shall govern provided the later instrument specifically refers to the direction in such prior will or instrument;

(3) any such direction provided in a nontestamentary instrument only relates to the payment of the estate tax from property passing thereunder and such direction shall not serve to exonerate such nontestamentary property from the payment of its proportionate share of the tax even if otherwise directed in the nontestamentary instrument.

In addition, this section provides that a general direction to pay taxes does not apply to the tax imposed by reason of the death of a life tenant of QTIP or the additional estate tax imposed on excess retirement accumulations.

§4.27.5. Preserving Qualification for Redemption Under §303

In drafting a provision regarding the payment of taxes it should be borne in mind that stock that is entirely relieved of the obligation to pay death taxes and funeral and administration expenses may not qualify for redemption under §303. For that reason closely-held stock that might be redeemed should not be used to satisfy a marital deduction bequest or be treated as QTIP under §2056(b)(7). In some instances, the problem can be avoided by making the closely-held stock expressly subject to a pro rata portion of taxes and expenses. Such a provision might be effective even as to stock that does not stand in the decedent's name (*e.g.,* in a joint tenancy or a trust). *See United States v. Goodson,* 253 F.2d 900 (8th Cir. 1958) (Minnesota law construed to allow will to impose obligation of contributing to the estate tax on trust beneficiaries and joint tenants).

§4.27.6. Power to Make Non-Pro Rata Distributions

In general, the executor should be authorized to make non-pro rata distributions to beneficiaries who are entitled to share equally in a pool of assets (*e.g.,* the residuary estate). The IRS has recognized that an equal, but non-pro rata, distribution to beneficiaries was not a taxable event where the decedent's will authorized such a distribution. LR 8119040. If a non-pro rata distribution is made with the consent of the beneficiaries, but without authorization by the testator or by the governing law, the beneficiaries may be treated as having made a taxable exchange. Rev. Rul. 69-486, 1969-2 C.B. 159. *See* §12.38.

EXAMPLE 4-4.

T's will give his residuary estate equally to *A* and *B* but neither his will nor local law authorized his executor to make non-pro rata distributions.

In accordance with an agreement between *A* and *B,* asset 1 was distributed entirely to *A* and asset 2 was distributed entirely to *B.* Under Revenue Ruling 69-486, *supra,* A is treated as having exchanged a one-half interest in asset 2 for *B's* one-half interest in asset 1.

The same concern regarding non-pro rata distributions applies to trusts as well. As pointed out in Chapter 5, the issue recurs in connection with distributions in satisfaction of fractional share marital deduction gifts. *See* §5.38.

§4.27.7. Tax Payments and the Marital and Charitable Deductions

Special care should also be exercised in drafting directions regarding the payment of taxes if the client is passing property that is intended to qualify for the federal estate tax marital deduction to a surviving spouse:

In the determination of the value of any property interest which passed from the decedent to his surviving spouse, there must be taken into account the effect which the Federal estate tax, or any estate, succession, legacy, or inheritance tax, has upon the net value to the surviving spouse of the property interest Reg. §20.2056(b)-4(c)(1).

The marital deduction is allowable only to the extent of the net value of property passing to the surviving spouse Reg. §20.2056(b)-4(a). The allowance of the charitable deduction is similarly limited: "Section 2055(c) in effect provides that the deduction is based on the amount actually available for charitable uses, that is, the amount of the fund remaining after the payment of all death taxes." Reg. §20.2055-3(a). The typical apportionment statute meets the problem by providing that allowances shall be made for exemptions and deductions that are available by reason of the relationship of the recipient to the decedent or by reason of the purposes for which the gift is made. *See, e.g.,* U.P.C. §3-9A-101 *et seq.* (2011).

§4.27.8. Payment of State Inheritance Tax

State inheritance taxes are usually payable by the decedent's executor but are charged against the interest of each person who receives property from the decedent. Thus, they are naturally apportioned. However, a testator may direct that the inheritance tax should be borne instead by the residuary estate or by other property. If so, the provision will probably be treated as an additional gift to the beneficiaries whose obligation to pay the inheritance tax is relieved. If the rules are adequately explained to clients they will often choose to relieve specific gifts from the burden of inheritance taxes.

§4.27.9. Statutes Relating to Payment of Federal Estate Tax

The federal laws regarding the source of payment of the federal estate tax are reviewed in §12.43 in connection with the discussion of post-mortem planning. As indicated above, the testator is generally free to choose the way in which the tax burden is allocated. In the absence of contrary direction the executor may collect a portion of the federal estate tax from insurance beneficiaries and others. *See* §§2205–2207B.

§4.27.10. Power to Make Tax Elections

The second clause of Article Fifteen (Form 4-23) is intended to alert the executor to valuable tax elections that should be considered, to authorize the executor to make the elections, and to relieve the executor from the obligation of making adjustments to interests affected by the elections. In the absence of the latter provision the executor might be required to make an equitable adjustment if alternatively deductible expenses, paid from the residuary estate, were claimed on the fiduciary income tax return rather than on the estate tax return. *See* §12.13. The authorities generally indicate that the residuary estate should be reimbursed for the additional estate tax that results from the election to claim the expenses as income tax deductions. Even so, the persons entitled to the income will receive some benefit from the election in many instances. The provision in the will merely relieves the executor from any obligation of making the adjustment, which could require a complicated accounting. It does not preclude making the adjustment.

Clauses (c) and (d) specifically authorize the executor to make elections regarding the marital deduction, such as a QTIP election under §2056(b)(7), and to allocate the testator's GSTT exemption.

§4.27.11. Qualified Conservation Easements

A provision along the lines of paragraph (3) should be included if a client wishes to authorize his or her executor to give a conservation easement to a charity in order to take advantage of the exclusion for conservation easements. Under §2031(c), an exclusion of up to 40 percent of the value of the land is allowed, reduced by 2 percent for each percentage point (or portion) by which the value of the conservation easement is less than 30 percent of the value of the land. Also, the exclusion is limited to $500,000. The easement may be established after the decedent's death by a member of the decedent's family, the executor of the decedent's estate, or the trustee of a trust the corpus of which includes the land. The easement must be created on or before the date the federal estate tax return is filed. An irrevocable election to take advantage of the deduction must be made on the decedent's federal estate tax return. Under §1014(a)(4), the basis of the property is the decedent's basis "to the extent of the applicability of the exclusion described in section 2031(c)." The benefits of §2032A may be claimed with respect to the property. In addition, §2032A was amended to provide that creating a qualified conservation easement did not constitute a disposition of the property. *See* §12.19.9.

§4.28. Wills not Pursuant to Contract

Form 4-24
Wills Not Contractual

Article Sixteen: The terms of this will and the will executed on the date hereof by my wife are essentially reciprocal in nature. That is, my wife is the principal beneficiary of this will and I am the principal beneficiary of my wife's will. However, the wills are not executed pursuant to any agreement between us. Accordingly, they may be changed or revoked at any time as each of us chooses.

The lawyer may wish to counter the uncertainty that sometimes arises regarding the revocability of reciprocal wills by including a clarifying statement in the wills. Of course, if the clients intend to have a binding agreement for the disposition of their wealth upon the death of the survivor, they should take a different course. In such a case their interests might be better served by establishing an inter vivos trust of substantially all of their property, which could become partially, or totally, irrevocable upon the death of the first spouse to die. (This approach parallels the widow's election will that is sometimes used in community property states. *See* §§9.23-9.39. In the typical widow's election will, the survivor receives the entire benefit of the property in the trust for life, with the remainder to others upon the survivor's death.) A corporate fiduciary or independent individual could assure that the survivor receives the intended benefits, yet protect the interest of the remaindermen. Even if a trust were utilized, it is difficult to provide the remaindermen with the intended degree of protection and adequately provide for the surviving spouse. However, the trustee could be given the power to invade the corpus of the trust for specified needs of the survivor. Of course, the income, gift, and estate tax consequences of such an alternative must be carefully considered.

§4.29. No Contest Clause

An "in terrorem" clause, which invalidates gifts to a beneficiary who contests the will, is routinely included by lawyers in some states. The extent to which such clauses are enforced varies from state-to-state. Courts have generally upheld such provisions, at least insofar as they prohibit contests that are not made in good faith or have no reasonable cause. *E.g., Hannam v. Brown*, 956 P.2d 794 (Nev. 1998). Under the U.P.C. such a provision is unenforceable "if probable cause exists for instituting proceedings." U.P.C. §3-905 (2011). California enforces in terrorem clauses except as to beneficiaries who contest with probable cause a provision that benefits a person who drafted or transcribed the instrument, gave directions to the drafter, or acted as a witness. Cal. Prob. Code §21307 (2011); *Estate of Peterson*, 85 Cal. Rptr. 2d 110 (Cal. App. 1999). Some states bar the enforcement of all such provisions. *E.g.,* Fla. Stat. Ann. §732.517 (2011). A contest brought by a guardian on behalf of a minor beneficiary is not subject to a no contest clause, because the minor did not voluntarily participate in the action. *Safai v. Safai*, 78 Cal. Rptr. 759 (Cal. App. 2008).

In some states, a statute or judicial decision requires no contest clauses to be strictly construed. Cal. Prob. Code § 21304 (2011); *Conte v. Conte*, 36 S.W.3d 830 (Tex. App. 2001). Under that approach an attempt to remove an executor or trustee may not fall within the terms of a broad no contest clause. *Conte v. Conte* held that a clause which invalidated any gift to "any beneficiary or remainderman under this agreement [who] in any manner, directly or indirectly, contests or challenges this trust or any of its provisions" did not extend to an action by a beneficiary to remove a fellow co-trustee. In *Preuss v. Stokes-Pruess*, 569 S.E.2d 857 (Ga. 2002), the court held that because in terrorem clauses must be strictly construed, an action to remove a co-executor was not within the scope of the clause. *See also Kershaw v. Kershaw*, 848 So. 2d 942 (Ala. 2002).

The U.P.C. and some states allow a beneficiary to contest a will or trust without risk if the contest is brought with "reasonable" or "probable" cause. However, whether a beneficiary is within that safe harbor is often unclear. For example, in *Estate of Mumby*, 982 P.2d 1219 (Wash. App. 1999), the court upheld application of a noncontest clause to a beneficiary who unsuccessfully challenged the validity of a trust on the advice of counsel to whom she had not made a full disclosure of the facts. California allows a beneficiary to bring a declaratory relief action to determine whether a proposed action is within the scope of a no contest clause. Cal. Prob. Code § 21320 (2011).

A beneficiary's interest in a will or trust is subject to forfeiture if the beneficiary violates the terms of a condition applicable to the bequest. *Marion v. Davis*, 106 S.W.3d 860 (Tex. App. 2003) (guardian-beneficiary had testator's spouse admitted to nursing home which violated the terms of the testator's conditional bequest to the beneficiaries). In some jurisdictions, conditions that are deemed to be contrary to public policy are invalid, including ones that invalidate a gift if the designated beneficiary marries a person of another religious faith. *Taylor v. Feinberg*, 891 N.E.2d 549 (Ill. App. 2008); Restatement (Third), Trusts § 29, comment *j* (2003).

In general, such a clause should not be included. The reason is simple: An in terrorem clause is unlikely to protect the integrity of the testator's actual will. Quite the contrary, such a provision may be inserted in a will by a person who does exercise undue influence over a testator and wants to discourage a contest. If a testator is concerned about the interpretation or validity of a will, some states allow the testator to seek a declaratory judgment regarding the construction or validity of the will through a proceeding in the appropriate probate court, even though the testator is still alive. One such "pre-mortem probate" process is available in Nevada. Nev. Rev. Stat. § 30.040(2) (2011).

§ 4.30. EXECUTION

Form 4-25
Execution Clause

In witness whereof, I have signed this will on _____, 200 _____, at _____.

————————

John Q. Client

————————

————————

————————

(witnesses)

The testimonium clause should indicate both the date and place of execution. Those facts, while not required, are often helpful in passing on the validity and effect of the instrument.

All states require that there be two witnesses to nonholographic wills, except Vermont, which requires three. 14 Vt. Stat. Ann. §5 (2011). However, under an amendment to Cal. Prob. C. §6110, effective January 1, 2009, a will that is not signed by two witnesses during the testator's lifetime "shall be treated as if it was executed in compliance with that paragraph [Prob. C. §6110(c)(1)] if the proponent of the will establishes by clear and convincing evidence that, at the time the testator signed the will, the testator intended the will to constitute the testator's will." Prob. C. §6110(c)(2). Estate of Stoker v. Pradia, 122 Cal. Rptr.3d 529 (Cal. App., Div. 2, 2011) (will that testator signed and declared to be his will in the presence of two witnesses was admitted to probate although the will was not signed by the witnesses). Because of the general requirement, estate planners almost invariably arrange for wills to be witnessed by at least two witnesses. Some lawyers in states other than Vermont use three witnesses, increasing the probability that at least one witness will survive the testator and be available to testify if needed. Vermont recognizes the validity of a will executed in accordance with the law of the place of execution or domicile of the testator. The U.P.C. provides a conflicts rule which recognizes the validity of wills that were executed in accordance "with the law at the time of execution of the place where the will was executed, or of the place where at the time of execution or at the time of death the testator is domiciled, has a place of abode, or is a national." U.P.C. §2-506 (2011).

Totally disinterested adults should serve as witnesses. The U.P.C. does not invalidate a gift to an interested witness. Specifically, U.P.C. §2-505(b) (2011) provides, "The signing of a will by an interested witness does not invalidate the will or any provision of it." In contrast, the law of many states deprives an interested witness of benefits under the will except to the extent the witness would receive property from the decedent if the will were not established. Of course, in any case, the credibility of a witness may be affected if the witness is also a beneficiary under the will. The lawyer who drew the will and the persons appointed as fiduciaries generally are not disqualified from acting as witnesses, but may prefer not to do so.

Form 4-26
Attestation Clause

On the date last above written John Q. Client declared to us that the foregoing instrument, consisting of _____pages including this page, was his will and requested us to act as witnesses thereto. He thereupon signed his will in our presence, all of us being present at the same time. At his request and in the presence of each other we signed our names as witnesses thereto and signed this attestation clause.

Address:_____

Address:_____

Address:_____

An attestation clause, such as Form 4-26, should be provided for signature by the witnesses if the local law does not provide for the use of self-proving affidavits, or if one is not used for some reason. The clause is not necessary for the validity of the will, but the recitation it contains of the facts required to establish due execution supports a presumption that the instrument was validly executed. The use of such a clause also makes it difficult for the witnesses later to disavow the facts of due execution recited in it.

§4.31. SELF-PROVING AFFIDAVIT

Many states now allow a will to be proved by an affidavit of the witnesses or declaration of the witnesses under penalty of perjury which shows that the requirements of the statute of wills are satisfied. *See* U.P.C. §2-504 (2011). The laws vary among the states, however, with some requiring that the witnesses sign the will as witnesses *and* complete the affidavit. The affidavit may be completed either at the time the will was executed or at a later time. Under some statutes the testator and the witnesses sign the affidavit, while under others only the witnesses sign it. Some courts have admitted a will to probate although the decedent only signed the self-providing affidavit. *E.g., Hickox v. Wilson,* 496 S.E.2d 711 (1998). Likewise, courts have admitted a will to probate where the witnesses signed only the self-proving affidavit and not the will as well, as formally required under state law. *In re Estate of Fordonski,* 678 N.W.2d 413 (Ia. 2004).

The content of the affidavit will vary according to whether the witnesses sign both the will and the affidavit or only the affidavit. Completion of the affidavit simplifies the proof of the will by recording the necessary facts in a form that is admissible as evidence. In lieu of an affidavit some states permit the use of a declaration of the witnesses made under penalty of perjury. A self-proved will may be admitted to probate without the testimony of the subscribing witnesses. The specific content of the form must comply with the applicable law, which varies somewhat.

§ 4.32. EXECUTION CEREMONY

The execution ceremony should be conducted by the lawyer in a way that meets the requirements of the law of the place of execution and the law of the most demanding state currently in effect. It should also be done in a manner that satisfies the client's expectations: What may be routine for the lawyer is, for most clients, an extremely significant event. Finally, special precautions should be taken if the lawyer believes there is a risk that the will may be contested. Extra care may be called for if an elderly, ill, or otherwise vulnerable testator is leaving a substantial portion of property to charities or to persons other than the natural objects of his or her bounty. If the lawyer believes there is such a risk, the witnesses should be carefully selected for their independence and credibility, consideration should be given to videotaping the execution ceremony, and the ceremony should be conducted in a way that clearly demonstrates the testator's capacity to the witnesses. Note in this connection that some states now authorize the use of a videotape as evidence of the proper execution of a will. Ind. Code Ann. § 29-1-5-3.2 (2011). In order to demonstrate the testator's capacity, he or she might be asked to identify his or her major property holdings, to name his or her nearest relatives, and to describe how the will disposes of his or her property.

Two or more adults who are not beneficially interested in the will should be asked to serve as witnesses and be present throughout the entire execution ceremony. In order better to establish the authenticity of the document and its integration as one document, some lawyers have the testator initial each page in the margin or at the bottom of the page and also fill in the date and place of execution in the testimonium clause. The lawyer should then ask the testator, "Do you declare this to be your will and ask the two [three] persons present with us to act as witnesses to the will and to your signature?" The testator should answer affirmatively in a voice clearly audible to all witnesses.

After the testator declares the document to be his or her will and asks the persons present to act as witnesses, the testator should sign the will in the space provided at the end of the instrument in full view of all of the witnesses. Each witness should then sign the will in the space provided immediately below the testator's signature. The testator and all of the witnesses should observe each other's signatures. However, under the U.P.C. it is not necessary for (1) the witnesses to see the testator sign the will (if the testator acknowledges the signature to them), (2) the testator to observe the witnesses sign, or (3) the witnesses observe each other sign. U.P.C. § 2-502 (2011).

If a separate attestation clause is used, the witnesses should then complete and sign it. If the local law provides for making a will self-proving by the use of an affidavit or declaration of due execution, it should be executed by the witnesses in lieu of an attestation clause. In the case of an affidavit a notary must acknowledge the witnesses' signatures and, in some cases, the testator's signature as well. The execution of affidavits such as this is facilitated if one or more persons in the lawyer's office is a notary public.

The lawyer may retain the original will for safekeeping if requested by the client to do so. If it is retained, the lawyer should give the client a receipt and make the document available to the client upon request. Some courts and bar association ethics committees have disapproved of lawyers retaining original wills. *E.g., State v. Gulban-*

kian, 196 N.W.2d 733 (Wis. 1972). Professor Johnston objects to the practice on the ground that it may unfairly advantage the lawyer who drew the will when it comes time to employ a lawyer to represent the personal representative. Johnston, An Ethical Analysis of Common Estate Planning Practice—Is Good Business Bad Ethics?, 45 Ohio St. L.J. 57 (1984). The problem could be avoided by explaining the "risk" to the client, who might nonetheless choose to leave the will with the lawyer. In any case, a decedent's personal representative is free to employ as counsel whomever the personal representative chooses. Overall, the retention of wills by lawyers is a valuable service that should be made available to clients. In this way the client's will is safeguarded, yet is readily available to the client or the executor named in the will.

In almost all circumstances, only one copy of a will should be executed by the testator and the witnesses. After the will is fully executed, it should be placed by the person having custody of it, usually the testator or the lawyer, in a safe place known to others. Multiple copies should not be executed because of the difficulty of accounting for all of them and the presumption of revocation that may arise if all of the executed copies cannot be produced. The presumption that a will was revoked by the testator with the intent to revoke may be rebutted by slight evidence when it is shown that the contestants to the will had access to it. *Dowdy v. Smith,* 818 So. 2d 1255 (Miss. App. 2002). However, at least in Oklahoma, "[t]he modern practice of executing duplicate wills . . . is to be encouraged." *Estate of Shaw,* 572 P.2d 229, 232 (Okla. 1977) (presumption of revocation of will caused by disappearance of duplicate traced to testator's possession is overcome by production of other executed copy and proof of due execution). On the other hand, it may be desirable for the testator to execute multiple copies of the durable power of attorney and of the living will (or health care directive). In that way executed copies can be provided to various persons as required.

Photocopies of the will, or conformed copies of the will with the date, place of execution, and signature blocks typed in, should be provided to the testator for reference. With the testator's approval copies could also be provided to selected persons, such as the individuals or organizations named as fiduciaries. Because of the likelihood that changes will be made in the will, clients should be wary of providing copies to all of the beneficiaries. If the testator is given the original document, he or she should be cautioned not to attempt to make changes in it or to execute a subsequent instrument intended to have testamentary effect without professional assistance. The testator should also be reminded of the necessity of reviewing the will periodically and of considering the need for changes if the testator's family or economic circumstances change substantially.

In recent years some decisions have relaxed the formal requirements of valid execution. For example, in *Truitt v. Slack,* 768 A.2d 715 (Md. App. 2001), the court held that a will was validly executed although the two neighbors who signed as witnesses did not see the testator's signature and did not know the nature of the document they were signing. Despite the relaxation, planners should be sure that documents are executed in full compliance with the applicable statutes. In *Estate of Hall,* 51 P.3d 1134 (Mont. 2002), the court upheld admission of a joint will that was signed by the testator and his wife and notarized by the scrivener, but not witnessed. The court was persuaded by evidence that the couple intended the draft to serve as a will until they executed another one.

§4.33. LETTER OF TRANSMITTAL TO CLIENT

The lawyer should send copies of the documents to the clients as soon as possible after the execution ceremony. In addition to serving as a letter of transmittal, the letter can be used to remind the clients regarding the necessity of reviewing the wills periodically, communicating with the lawyer if there are changes in circumstances, and avoiding changes of title or beneficiary designations that might adversely affect their estate plans. While practices vary, lawyers often send a statement for services separately.

Form 4-27
Letter of Transmittal

Mr. and Mrs. John Q. Client
1000 Green Street
Your City, XX, XXXXX

Dear Mr. and Mrs. Client:

Enclosed is a folder that includes photocopies of the documents you executed in my office yesterday. They are: your Wills, Directives to Physicians, and Durable Powers of Attorney. The folder also contains a roster of the names, addresses, and telephone numbers of your principal advisors including your accountants, doctors, and brokers. In accordance with your instructions, we have placed the original executed copies of the documents in our safe deposit box [office vault] for safekeeping. The documents are, of course, available to you at any time. As you requested, we have mailed one executed set of your Directive to Physicians to your principal physician, Dr. Martin A. Smith.

Periodic Review. We have now completed the active phase of our estate planning work for you. Accordingly, until we hear from you again our role will be limited to sending you periodic reminders of the desirability of reviewing your wills. As I mentioned to you, we recommend that you review your wills and basic estate plan every three to four years to be sure that they continue to meet your needs. I have made a note on my calendar to send you a reminder in three years if we don't discuss them with you before then. In the meantime, please be sure to let me know if you want to make any changes in the wills or other elements of your estate plan.

Changes in Circumstances. We also recommend that you review your wills and basic estate plan if there are any substantial changes in your personal or financial circumstances. Such a review should be made, for example, if there are any changes in your family as a result of births or deaths, marriages or divorces. A review is also indicated if you plan to move to another state or if the size or composition of your estate changes substantially. You should also be alert for any events that might affect the suitability or availability of the executors, trustees, and guardians who are named in your wills.

Forms of Property Ownership. In order for your estate plan to remain effective, you should continue the present methods of property ownership and the present beneficiary designations in your life insurance and employee benefit plans. The transfer of property into another form of ownership, such as a joint tenancy with right of survivorship (*e.g.,* John Q. and Jane M. Client, as joint tenants with right of survivorship), or a change of beneficiary designations, could affect the integrity of your estate plans and could have adverse tax consequences. Please check with me before you acquire or dispose of substantial assets, including life insurance.

Gifts. Please also let me know if you plan to make any gifts which total more than $12,000 in value to one person in any calendar year. Substantial gifts must be carefully planned in order to produce the optimum tax results. Particular attention should be given to the method by which gifts are made (*e.g.,* outright or in trust), the selection of the property to be transferred, and the time at which the gifts are made.

Please call me if you have any questions or would like to consult with me further regarding your plans.

Sincerely,

C. ADDITIONAL DOCUMENTS

§4.34. GENERAL

The lawyer should counsel clients regarding a variety of additional documents they may wish to consider. Three that have come into prominence in recent years are discussed in the following pages: a power of attorney that either becomes effective or, if presently effective, does not terminate if the principal becomes incompetent (the so-called durable power of attorney); the living will (or directive to physicians authorized by most states); and an instrument of gift under the Uniform Anatomical Gift Act.

TThe durable power of attorney, which is universally available, provides some protection against the necessity of a guardianship if the principal becomes incompetent. The 1979 Uniform Durable Power of Attorney Act has been adopted by most states and the District of Columbia. In 2006, the National Conference of Commissioners on Uniform State Laws (NCCUSL) approved the Uniform Power of Attorney Act which, so far, has only been adopted by a few states. The NCCUSL also promulgated a Statutory Form Power of Attorney Act in 1988, which includes a provision making it "durable." Executing a statutory form of power of attorney confers upon the agent the powers described in more detail in §§3-5 of the Act. Importantly, in some states the principal may give the agent authority to make health care decisions for the principal during any period of incapacity. A few states expressly authorize a durable power of attorney for health care.

Many clients are also anxious to execute a document that expresses their wishes regarding the medical care they should receive in the event they become terminally ill and are unconscious or incompetent. The scope and content of such a document depends upon the local law and should be compatible with any durable power of attorney the client may execute. Unfortunately, in some states the law does not explicitly allow one person to authorize another person to make health care decisions for him or her.

In 1989, the NCCUSL approved the Uniform Rights of the Terminally Ill Act, a form of natural death act, that has been adopted in a few states including Alaska, Arkansas, Iowa, Maine, Missouri, Montana, and Oklahoma. The Uniform Act, has a narrow scope, simply authorizes an adult to execute a declaration "instructing a physician to withhold or withdraw life-sustaining treatment in the event the person is in a terminal condition and is unable to participate in medical treatment decisions." Prefatory Note (1987).

Clients are also often interested in making gifts of their bodies or parts of their bodies for medical education, research, or transplantation. Advances in medical technology make it possible to relieve a wide range of illnesses and diseases by transplants, grafts, or other procedures. The Uniform Anatomical Gift Act provides a useful way of carrying out a client's wish to assist others.

§4.35. DURABLE POWERS OF ATTORNEY

> The National Conference included Sections 5-501 and 5-502 in the Uniform Probate Code (1969) (1975) concerning powers of attorney to assist persons interested in establishing noncourt regimes for the management of their affairs in the event of later incompetency or disability. The purpose was to recognize a form of senility insurance comparable to that available to relatively wealthy persons who use funded, revocable trusts for persons who are unwilling or unable to transfer assets as required to establish a trust. Commissioners' Prefatory Note, Uniform Durable Power of Attorney Act (1983).

All 50 states and the District of Columbia allow a person to execute a so-called "durable power of attorney," a power of attorney that will not be affected by any future physical disability or mental incapacity. Although the laws vary somewhat from state to state, they are largely traceable to the sections of the U.P.C. that provide for a durable power of attorney. *See* U.P.C. §§5-501 *et seq.* (2011). In 1979 the NCCUSL promulgated a separate act, the Uniform Durable Power of Attorney Act, which is identical to the revised provisions of the U.P.C. Slight revisions were made in the Uniform Act in 1984 and 1987. Modified forms of the Durable Power of Attorney Act have been adopted in almost all states and the District of Columbia. In 2006, the NCCUSL issued a new Uniform Power of Attorney Act. Under this Act, powers of attorney are durable by default.

Third parties may be reluctant to recognize a durable power of attorney unless the local law insulates them from liability for a good-faith reliance on the document. Legislation in many states, including Alaska, California, Florida, Illinois, Minnesota, New York, Pennsylvania, and Washington, now provides the necessary degree of protection.

Under the U.P.C., a person may specify that the power will become or remain effective in the event the maker should later become disabled. U.P.C. § 5-501 (2011). In the absence of such a statute, the usefulness of a power of attorney in estate planning is limited by the common law rule that a power of attorney is terminated by the death *or* incompetency of the principal. Fortunately, as indicated above, all states now recognize a form of durable power of attorney that makes it possible to provide for the management of the principal's property in the event the principal becomes incompetent without subjecting the property to management by a guardian or custodian. The durable power is superior to other devices because it avoids the publicity, delays, and expense that are otherwise incurred. The power also eliminates the need to account to the court and to obtain court approval for actions concerning the sale or other use of the principal's assets. A durable power is also superior to joint bank accounts and similar arrangements, which may spawn conflicting claims to the funds on deposit—even prior to the principal's death.

The death of the principal terminates a durable power just as it would an ordinary power. However, actions taken in good faith by the agent under a durable or nondurable power without knowledge of the principal's death bind the successors in interest of the principal. U.P.C. § 5-504(a) (2011). Also, "[t]he disability or incapacity of a principal who has previously executed a written power of attorney that is not a durable power does not revoke or terminate the agency as to the attorney in fact or other person, who, without actual knowledge of the disability or incapacity of the principal, acts in good faith under the power." U.P.C. § 5-504(b) (2011). Note that a dissolution of the marriage of the principal and the agent may not revoke a power of attorney—particularly one that has been recorded. *See Puget Sound National Bank v. Burt,* 786 P.2d 300 (Wash. App. 1990).

Duties of Lawyer for Attorney-in-Fact. In discussing a durable power of attorney, the lawyer and client should consider whether the client wishes to authorize the lawyer to represent the agent. The discussion should cover the possibility that the agent and client, who might be incapacitated, might disagree regarding the management of the client's property when it is no longer legally possible for the client to revoke the appointment of the agent. If the client wishes to authorize the lawyer to represent the agent, the lawyer should be given written authorization to do so. Of course, in some circumstances the lawyer would be required by Rule 1.7 to withdraw from the representation of the client, the agent, or both.

As indicated in § 1.6.11, the lawyer for a guardian may owe a duty of care to the ward. The lawyer for an attorney-in-fact may owe the same duty to the principal. In addition, a lawyer who represents the attorney-in-fact under a durable power of attorney may be treated as having an attorney-client relationship with the principal. In *Keatinge v. Biddle,* 789 A.2d 1271 (Me. 2002), the court stated that, "The mere fact that the person holding the power of attorney retains counsel does not create an attorney-client relationship between the attorney and the grantor. However . . . facts may develop in particular cases that could support a finding that such an attorney-client relationship between attorney and grantor has been created." 789 A.2d at p. 1276. *See also Albright v. Burns*, 503 A.2d 386 (N.J. Sup., App. Div. 1986).

Consent to Disclose Information. As stated in the ACTEC Commentary on MRPC 1.14, "A lawyer may properly suggest that a competent client consider executing a letter or other document that would authorize the lawyer to communicate to designated parties (e.g., family members, health care providers, a court) concerns that the lawyer might have regarding the client's capacity." ACTEC, Commentaries on the Model Rules of Professional Conduct 131 (4th ed. 2006). Such an authorization may enable the lawyer to act in the client's best interests as contemplated by MRPC 1.14 without possibly violating his or her duty of confidentiality to the client. *See* § 1.6.11. The letter or document might provide:

> If my lawyer has a reasonable doubt regarding my capacity, I give my lawyer and any person named as a fiduciary for me in an estate planning document executed by me, including a durable power of attorney, a revocable trust, or other instrument, the discretionary authority to disclose the contents of my estate planning documents to each other, to physicians or other health care providers who are attending me or have attended me, members of my family, and to a court. Further, I also waive, with respect to such fiduciaries and other persons, any privilege of confidentiality that I might have with respect to my estate planning documents and my physical and mental condition, for the purpose of authorizing them to disclose to each other and others, confidential information to the extent they reasonably believe it is in my best interests so to do.

In order more fully to protect the interests of the client, consideration should be given to the inclusion of a provision that would, in effect, require the agent to permit his or her lawyer to disclose acts or omissions that might constitute breaches of fiduciary duty. Acceptance of appointment as agent might constitute a waiver, permitting disclosures to be made to the principal, to any member of the principal's family, or to the court. *See* § 4.26 *and* Form 4-21. The provision might be expressed along these lines:

Form 4-28
Consent to Disclosure

> My agent, by accepting appointment as such, consents to the disclosure, by any lawyer who is engaged to assist [her/him] in matters relating to this durable power of attorney, to me, any member of my family, or to the court, of any act or omission of the agent that might constitute a breach of fiduciary duty, including information obtained through disclosures made to the lawyer by my agent.

State Statutory Form Powers of Attorney. A comprehensive power of attorney law in California includes provisions relating to general powers of attorney, durable powers of attorney, and statutory forms of powers of attorney. According to the comments of the Law Revision Commission parts of the law were adapted from the Uniform Durable Power of Attorney Act. The law includes very useful sections on the duties of attorneys-in-fact. *See* Cal. Prob. Code §§ 4230-4238 (2011). The Uniform Statutory Form Power of Attorney is included as Cal. Prob. Code §§ 4400-4465 (2011). According to the Law Revision Commission no substantive changes were made in the provisions regarding durable powers of attorney for health care. Cal. Prob. Code §§ 4600-4806 (2011). *See* California Law Revision Commission, 1995 Comprehensive Power of Attorney Act, 14 Cal. Est. Plan., Trust & Prob. News 26 (Winter 1994). Under Cal. Prob. Code § 4231(a) (2011), an attorney-in-fact is required to deal with the principal's property as would a prudent person dealing with the property of another. However, under subsection (b), an attorney-in-fact who is not compensated is "not liable for a loss to the principal's property unless the loss results from the attorney-in-fact's bad faith, intentional wrongdoing or gross negligence."

Almost 20 states, including Connecticut, Nebraska, North Carolina, and Texas, have enacted statutory form powers of attorney, apparently with varying levels of success. Implementation of the Uniform Power of Attorney Act might be helpful in getting more states on board. Although uniformity among the states as to the basic rules and limitations regarding durable powers of attorney is no doubt helpful, there is some concern that widespread adoption of a statutory form would increase the unauthorized practice of law, as clients and other professionals might erroneously conclude that the statutory form will protect their interests in all events.

Agent Is Subject to Fiduciary Duties. An agent under a power of attorney is a fiduciary and, as such, is subject to a strict duty of loyalty that requires the agent to act "solely for the benefit of his or her principal in all matters connected with the agency and adhere faithfully to the instructions of the principal . . . .An agent's duty is to act solely for the benefit of the principal in all matters connected with the agency, even at the expense of the agent's own interest." *Crosby v. Leuhrs,* 669 N.W.2d 635, 643-44 (Neb. 2003). In the *Crosby* case, the principal's agent transferred funds from POD accounts of which the principal's friends were beneficiaries into an account from which the agent would benefit. Although the agent may have had the power to change the registration of POD accounts, "This does not, however, authorize self-dealing absent express authority or some other compelling explanation for why the challenged transaction was in the best interest of the principal." 669 N.W.2d at 646. The court concluded that the agent engaged in impermissible self-dealing that was unjustified and not in the interest of the principal.

§ 4.35.1. Creation, Recordation, and Revocation

Some states require that a durable power be executed with the same formality as a will and that it be recorded. *E.g.,* S.C. Code Ann. § 62-5-501(C) (2011). Presumably recording is required because the agent may transfer or acquire interests in real property. In other jurisdictions a durable power need not be recorded unless the agent does enter into transactions involving real property. The possibility that the agent may engage in real estate transactions suggests the desirability that the document be acknowledged by a notary.

In order to create a durable power, the U.P.C. simply requires that the agent be designated in a writing that contains "the words 'This power of attorney shall not be affected by subsequent disability or incapacity of the principal, or lapse of time,' or

'This power of attorney shall become effective upon the disability or incapacity of the principal,' or similar words showing the intent of the principal that the authority conferred shall be exercisable notwithstanding the principal's subsequent disability or incapacity, and, unless it states a time of termination, notwithstanding the lapse of time since the execution of the instrument." U.P.C. § 5-501 (2011).

Under the U.P.C., if a conservator, guardian, or other fiduciary of the principal's estate is appointed after the execution of a durable power of attorney, the agent is required to account to the appointee. In order to avoid conflicts and unnecessary expense, the principal may nominate a guardian in the durable power—who may be the same person as the agent.

The principal may revoke a durable power at any time. In addition, a person appointed as conservator, guardian, or other fiduciary of the principal's estate has all of the powers the principal would have had to revoke, suspend, or terminate the power of attorney. U.P.C. § 5-503(a) (2011). As indicated above, the potential for conflict between the agent and the conservator or guardian is reduced if the agent is also nominated in the durable power to serve as the principal's conservator or guardian. *See* U.P.C. § 5-503(b) (2011). Such a nomination will discourage others from applying for appointment as conservator or guardian and will secure the authority of the agent against upset in the event it becomes necessary or desirable to appoint a conservator or guardian for the principal. It is often wise to designate one or more successor attorneys-in-fact lest the first-named person predecease the principal or otherwise be unable to act.

§ 4.35.2. Scope and Use

A durable power may confer on the agent as few or as many powers as the principal wishes. However, in the absence of express statutory authorization, a durable power probably cannot authorize the agent to exercise powers that are personal and nondelegable, such as the power to make a will or to exercise a power of appointment. Because a power of attorney is useful only to the extent it can be used to carry out transactions with other persons, many clients will choose to give the agent broad general powers to act with respect to their property. The acceptability of such a power of attorney is generally enhanced if it includes both a statement of the general powers that the agent may exercise and a list of the specific powers that the agent is most likely to need. A durable power of attorney may include authority to act for the principal with regard to federal income tax matters.

Regulation § 601.503(a) requires that a power of attorney for tax matters include the following:

    (1) name and mailing address of the taxpayer;
    (2) identification number of the taxpayer (i.e., social security number and/or employer identification number);
    (3) employee plan number (if applicable);
    (4) name and address of the recognized representative(s);
    (5) a description of the matter(s) for which representation is authorized which, if applicable, must include—

        (i) the type of tax involved;
        (ii) the Federal tax form number;

       (iii) the specific year(s)/period(s) involved; and

       (iv) in estate matters, decedent's date of death; and

   (6) a clear expression of the taxpayer's intention concerning the scope of authority granted to the recognized representative(s).

A properly completed Form 2848 will satisfy the foregoing requirements. However, the IRS will also recognize a power of attorney in another form provided it is submitted with a completed Form 2848.

    Under an alternative approach, the IRS will recognize a Form 2848 that is completed and signed by an agent acting under a durable power of attorney that authorizes the agent to handle federal tax matters. The agent must submit a copy of the durable power of attorney and a declaration signed under penalty of perjury that the durable power of attorney is valid under the laws of the governing state.

Form 4-29
Power to Represent Principal with Respect to Federal Tax Matters

> The agent [name and mailing address] is authorized to perform any and all acts that the principal [name, taxpayer identification number, and mailing address] can perform with respect to federal tax matters affecting principal including (1) Federal Income Tax matters, including filing and amending Form 1040, filing refund claims and representing principal in audits, conferences, and litigation, with respect to the years 2000 through 2035; (2) Federal Gift Tax matters, including filing and amending Form 709, filing refund claims and representing principal in audits, conferences, and litigation with respect to the years 2000 through 2035; and (3) Federal Generation-Skipping Transfer Tax matters, including filing and amending forms relating to the tax, filing refund claims, and representing principal in audits, conferences, and litigation.

§4.35.3. Durable Power of Attorney for Health Care

> Patients anxious to control future medical decisions should be told about durable powers of attorney. These surely do not guarantee patients that their wishes will blossom into fact, but nothing does. What matters is that powers of attorney have advantages over living wills. First, the choices that powers of attorney demand of patients are relatively few, familiar, and simple. Second, a regime of powers of attorney requires little change from current practice, in which family members ordinarily act informally for incompetent patients. Third, powers of attorney probably improve decisions for patients, since surrogates know more at the time of decision than patients can know in advance. Fourth, powers of attorney are cheap; they require only a simple form easily filled out with little advice. Fifth, powers of attorney can be supplemented by legislation (already in force in some states) akin to statutes of intestacy. These statutes specify who is to act for incompetent patients who have not specified a surrogate. In short,

durable powers of attorney are—as these things do—simple, direct, modest, straightforward, and thrifty. Fagerlin & Schneider, Enough: The Failure of the Living Will, 34 Hastings Center Report 30, 39 (no. 2 2004).

As part of the estate planning process, clients should be given the opportunity to
execute a durable power of attorney for health care (DPAHC) or broad form of
advanced health care directive (AHCD) which expresses their wishes regarding
health care matters. The Form of AHCD included in the Uniform Health-Care
Decisions Act (1993 Act), which can be modified as required to meet the needs of
individual clients, provides an excellent model. The 1993 Act has been enacted in a
small number of states, including California. Cal. Prob. Code § 4701 (2011). One
might also consider the form of DPAHC presented and discussed in Frank Collin's
comprehensive article, Planning and Drafting Durable Powers of Attorney for Health
Care, U. Miami, 22nd Inst. Est. Plan., Ch. 5 (1998), which includes extensive directions
regarding the principal's health care and the designation of a proxy to make decisions
within the parameters of those directions. *See* § 4.37.2, Uniform Rights of the Terminally Ill Act (1989).

 Cruzan v. Director, Missouri Dept. of Health, 497 U.S. 261 (1990), explicitly recognized a constitutionally protected right of a competent person to refuse medical
treatment. However, it also held that a state could impose a high standard of proof
where another person wishes to exercise that right on behalf of an incompetent
person. In particular, the Court held that a state could require clear and convincing
proof of the wishes of an incompetent where a guardian sought to discontinue
nutrition and hydration. (Note, in this connection, that the majority opinion assumed
that nutrition and hydration were properly considered to be medical treatment.)
Importantly, Justice O'Connor's concurring opinion suggests that a patient's constitutional liberty interest in refusing medical treatment may require states to enact
surrogate decision-making laws. Thus, a DPAHC or an AHCD that specifically
authorizes the agent to exercise the principal's right to refuse medical treatment
should be recognized as a legitimate exercise of the principal's constitutionally
protected rights. The opinion suggests that no one is in a position to exercise the right
to refuse medical treatment on behalf of persons who have never been competent or
who never clearly expressed their wishes.

 A DPAHC or an AHCD can be drafted to express the principal's wishes regarding medical treatment in detail or in a more general way. A general expression of
wishes with a broad delegation of authority to the agent is more flexible and
potentially more useful. In addition, a DPAHC can also include a statement of the
principal's wishes regarding other related matters, such as the principal's desire to
remain at home rather than being institutionalized. A simple version of the provision
might read along the lines suggested in Form 4-30, below.

 As indicated above, the excellent optional form of AHCD contained in § 4 of the
Uniform Health-Care Decisions Act may be used as written, or adapted to meet the
needs of specific clients.

Form 4-30
Power to Make Health Care Decisions

Principal authorizes agent [agent] to make health care decisions for Principal and to give informed consent to all forms of health care on behalf of Principal. Principal intends that agent exercise Principal's constitutionally protected right to refuse medical treatment, including nutrition and hydration. In making health care decisions for Principal, agent shall be guided by the following statement of the Principal's wishes . . . . *See* § 4.37.2 *and* the text of § 2 of the Uniform Advance Health-Care-Directive Act and § 2(c) of the Uniform Rights of the Terminally Ill Act.

Form 4-30 should be sufficient to constitute the agent as the personal representative of the principal for purposes of the Health Insurance Privacy and Accountability Act (HIPAA). *See* § 4.36.

Health Care Information. Under § 8 of the 1993 Act a person authorized to make health care decisions for a patient "has the same rights as the patient to request, receive, examine, copy, and consent to the disclosure of medical or any other health-care information." It is generally desirable to include such a provision in Durable Powers of Attorney, DPAHCs and AHCDs.

DPAHCs and AHCDs Superior to Living Wills. A DPAHC or an AHCD is superior to a living will because of its potentially greater scope and flexibility. "One major distinction between a DPAHC and a Living Will (whether statutory or otherwise) is that the DPAHC can be used for a broad range of health decisions. It need not be limited to the withholding or withdrawing of life-sustaining treatment. Quite the contrary, a DPAHC may be used to authorize maximum medical treatment under all circumstances and without regard to cost if that happens to be the desires of the principal." Collin, Planning and Drafting Durable Powers of Attorney for Health Care, U. Miami, 22nd Inst. Est. Plan. ¶ 504.3 (1988).

Mental Health Care Directives. Several states have adopted laws that expressly authorize an adult individual to authorize another person as agent to make mental health care decisions. *E.g.,* Ariz. Rev. Stat. § 36-3281, *et seq.* (2011) (the power of attorney for general health care purposes).

§ 4.35.4. Additional Powers to Deal with Property

In appropriate cases the client may wish to authorize an agent to make gifts to specified donees or classes of donees. For example, an agent might be authorized to make gifts that are within the amount of the annual gift tax exclusion and ones that qualify for exclusion under § 2503(e). Gifts that qualify for those exclusions are exempt from the GSTT. § 2642(c)(3). Such a provision might read like Form 4-31.

Form 4-31
Power to Make Gifts to Family Members

I authorize my agent (1) to make annual gifts to each descendant of the principal, which in any calendar year do not exceed the amount of the annual federal gift tax exclusion and (2) to pay directly the tuition and medical expenses of each such descendant to the extent such payments constitute qualified transfers for federal gift tax purposes.

In order to reduce the amount of death taxes that a client's estate may be obligated to pay to a state that has a death tax that does not apply to inter vivos gifts, a client may wish to authorize an agent to make other, larger gifts to a certain class of donees. *See* § 7.7. Such a provision should be carefully planned and drawn to avoid creating income and transfer tax problems for the agent.

In order to avoid creating gift and estate tax problems under § § 2514 and 2041, the power to make gifts can be drafted to prohibit the agent from making gifts to himself or herself, or to or for the benefit of any person he or she is legally obligated to support. Alternatively, the power to make gifts may be drafted to authorize a special agent to make gifts to or for the benefit of the agent and his or her dependents. If the client has created an irrevocable life insurance trust, he or she may wish to authorize the agent to continue to make annual transfers to the trust. Otherwise, there may be no practical source of funds with which to pay the premiums.

A power may enable a couple to make transfers between themselves, which may be desirable for a variety of purposes. Interspousal transfers, which are fully sheltered by the unlimited marital deduction, can be used to maximize the governmental benefits that are available and to utilize fully each spouse's unified credit and GSTT exemption.

Under the law of some states, gifts made on behalf of the principal by an agent acting under a durable power of attorney that does not expressly authorize gifts to be made are revocable. *Estate of Casey v. Commissioner*, 948 F.2d 895 (4th Cir. 1991) (Virginia); *See* § 2.4.3. *See also* the discussion in § 2.4.3 regarding the completeness of gifts made pursuant to a power of attorney.

§ 4.35.5. Power to Transfer Property to Revocable Trust

The needs of some clients are best met by a limited form of durable power that merely authorizes the agent to fund a revocable trust of which the principal and the principal's spouse are the current beneficiaries. The typical plan involves a revocable trust, a pour-over will, and a limited durable power of attorney. If the principal becomes incapable of managing property, the agent is authorized to transfer the principal's assets to the trustee for administration in accordance with the terms of the trust. Any additional assets of the principal that may be subject to testamentary disposition will be added to the trust under the terms of the principal's pour-over will. Under an alternative plan, the revocable trust only serves as a management vehicle during the principal's lifetime; upon the principal's death the trust property "pours back" to the principal's estate to be disposed of as provided in the principal's will.

There are two other common approaches to establishing a trust under a durable power of attorney. Under one, the trust agreement is presently executed and the trust is either funded with some assets or the trustee is named as beneficiary of policies of insurance on the client's life. In this case the durable power authorizes the agent to add the client's other assets to the trust. Under the other approach, a form of revocable trust agreement is attached to the durable power of attorney, which the agent is authorized to execute on behalf of the principal in the event of his or her incompetency. In such a case the durable power also authorizes the agent to transfer the principal's assets to the trustee to be held and managed as a part of the trust. Either approach should be satisfactory, although the former is, perhaps, more in accord with prior practice.

§4.35.6. Power to Modify or Revoke Trust or Other Dispositive Arrangement

An agent acting under a durable power of attorney may not have the power to revoke or change the terms of a revocable trust or other dispositive arrangement unless the durable power of attorney expressly confers the power on the agent. For example, under Cal. Prob. Code §15401(c) (2011), "A trust may not be modified or revoked by an attorney in fact under a power of attorney unless it is expressly permitted by the trust instrument." Similarly, under Wash. Rev. Code §11.94.050(1) (2011),

> [T]he attorney in fact or agent . . . shall not have the power, unless specifically provided otherwise in the document:To make, amend, alter, or revoke any of the principal's life insurance, annuity, or similar contract beneficiary designations, employee benefit plan beneficiary designations, trust agreements, registration of the principal's securities in beneficiary form, payable on death or transfer on death beneficiary designations, designation of persons as joint tenants with right of survivorship with the principal with respect to any of the principal's property, community property agreements, or any other provisions for nonprobate transfer at death contained in nontestamentary instruments described in RCW 11.02.091; to make any gifts of property owned by the principal; to make transfers of property to any trust (whether or not created by the principal) unless the trust benefits the principal alone and does not have dispositive provisions which are different from those which would have governed the property had it not been transferred into the trust, or to disclaim property.

A durable power of attorney is invalid if the principal lacked capacity to execute one at the time it was signed. Accordingly, changes to bank accounts made by an agent acting under a durable power of attorney that was signed by an incompetent principal are ineffective. *Dowdy v. Smith*, 818 So. 2d 1255 (Miss. App. 2002) ("Since we uphold the finding that the power of attorney was executed by Dowdy when she did not have the competence to do so, the changes made to bank account and certificate of deposit ownerships that were made under the authority of that instrument must be set aside.").

§4.35.7. Limitations

In some instances it is desirable to impose express limits on the power of the agent. For example, if a husband and wife execute reciprocal durable powers of attorney, the documents should limit the power of an insured spouse to deal with policies of insurance owned by the noninsured spouse. Lombard, Planning for Disability: Durable Powers, Standby Trusts and Preserving Eligibility for Governmental Benefits, U. Miami, 20th Inst. Est. Plan. ¶1705.3 (1986) and, Lombard, Planning for Disability, Health Care Issues and Developments in Assisted Suicide, U. Miami, 32nd. Inst. Est. Plan., Ch. 18 (1998). Otherwise, if the insured spouse dies first, the IRS may argue that he or she held incidents of ownership over the insurance. Also, there is always the possibility that the IRS may harden its position regarding the significance of incidents of ownership that are only exercisable in a fiduciary capacity. *See* §6.28.11.

The client may wish to allow the agent to act selectively with respect to some matters without incurring any liability for failing to act with respect to others. If so, the following text may be suitable:

Form 4-32
Authority to Act Selectively

> My agent may, in [her/his] discretion, exercise the powers given under this instrument to act in my behalf. To the extent my agent elects to act, [she/he] does so in a fiduciary capacity. However, by electing to act with respect to one or more matters my agent is not obligated to act with respect to any other matters.

§4.35.8. "Springing Powers"

The law of many states and the U.P.C. allow a durable power of attorney to become effective upon the incapacity of the principal. U.P.C. §5-501 (2011). Such a "springing power" is helpful to clients who want the protection that a durable power provides, yet are reluctant to execute a presently effective power. The problem remains of defining when the principal becomes incapacitated. That problem is typically addressed by making the power effective when the agent receives a written certification of incapacity from one or more persons designated in the instrument (*e.g.,* the principal's attending physician). A second certificate is often required, commonly from another physician, the principal's spouse, or another relative.

Unfortunately the regulations issued pursuant to the Health Insurance Portability and Accountability Act of 1996 (HIPAA) impose strict limits on the disclosure of health care information by health care professionals. Penalties may be imposed if a health care provider makes an unauthorized disclosure of an individual's protected health information (PHI). As explained at §4.36, health care providers can disclose an individual's PHI to the individual, the individual's personal representative or as specified in a valid authorization executed by the individual or the individual's personal representative. *See* 45 CFR § 164.502(g)(1) and (2). For HIPAA purposes a personal representative is a person who, under local law, has the power to make health care decisions for an individual.

The scope and effect of the Privacy Rule under HIPAA is widely misunderstood by everyone, including patients, health care providers and lawyers. Although the regulations allow health care providers to inform interested family members regarding the location, condition and care for patients, 45 CFR § 164.512, some providers refuse to make the information available. Anecdotally, one of the authors was told of a physician's receptionist that refused to allow the caller to change the time of an appointment for her husband, citing HIPAA requirements.

As explained in § 4.36, health care providers are generally prohibited from disclosing an individual's protected health information (PHI) to the others unless the individual has (1) authorized the disclosure of PHI to the other(s) in the manner specified in the regulations or (2) appointed a personal representative who has requested the PHI or authorized its disclosure to other(s). Given those restrictions physicians are, understandably, cautious about providing an individual's PHI to others, including a certification that is necessary for a springing durable power of attorney to become effective.

The privacy rule is not intended to change the law regarding health care powers of attorney. That is, whether a durable power of attorney springs depends upon the terms of the durable power of attorney and local law, not on the provisions of the HIPAA privacy rule. Nonetheless, the HIPAA rules may affect the validity of a springing durable power of attorney. For example, a durable power of attorney may not become effective if it springs only when the principal's attending physician certifies in writing that the principal is incapacitated and the physician refuses to make the necessary certification out of HIPAA concerns.

State law also affects the way one might grapple with the problems posed by springing powers. In this connection note that, although HIPAA preempts conflicting state laws, it does not preempt conflicting laws that are more stringent (*i.e.,* that go further in protecting a patient's privacy). If the state law does not restrict the time at which health care powers become effective, the surest approach to ensure that persons other than the principal will be entitled to receive PHI regarding the principal will be to give the agent the immediately effective power to make health care decisions for the principal. 45 CFR § 164.508. See the suggested addition to Form 4-33, below.

The traditional form of springing power should be effective in states that prohibit health care powers from becoming effective until a physician has determined, and recorded on an individual's medical chart, that the individual is incapable of making his or her own health care decisions. *E.g.,* N.H. Rev. Stat. Ann. § 137-J:2 III (2011) ("Under a durable power of attorney for health care, the agent's authority shall be in effect only when the principal lacks capacity to make health care decisions, as certified in writing by the principal's attending physician and filed in the principal's medical record.") Even in those states it would be helpful in dealing with health care providers if the durable power of attorney included appropriate references to HIPAA.

A court may recognize that a power which broadly defines the proof of disability that is required to spring the power was "sprung" by the principal's confinement to a hospital in another jurisdiction for dialysis treatment, the principal's inability to travel, and his inability to write. *First Colony Life Insurance Co. v. Gerdes*, 676 N.W.2d 58 (Neb. 2004). The power involved in the *Gerdes* case provided that it would become effective upon the principal's inability to handle "my own financial affairs," which "may be proved by a report of two (2) physicians, psychiatrists or psychologists who have examined me" or "by any other method of proof permitted by law."

Form 4-33
Date Power Becomes Effective

> The agent is authorized to act on behalf of principal and to exercise all powers under this Durable Power of Attorney when the agent receives written certification by two physicians that Principal is for any reason unable to manage [his/her] property, or to care for [himself/herself], or both.

Many states authorize the use of springing durable powers of attorney. The legislation typically authorizes a competent adult to designate another person to serve as his or her attorney (or agent) when a specified event or contingency occurs. Under one approach, one or more persons designated in the instrument are given the power to determine whether or not the event or contingency has occurred, which determination may be relied upon by third parties. Some commentators suggest that a determination of incapacity could be made by designated persons or by the Ethics Committee of a reputable hospital. A short or a long form can be used to designate the person or persons responsible for making a determination that the principal is incapacitated. A suggested version of the short form is simply that:

> I _____(Principal) hereby designate that _____(My Designee) shall have the power to determine conclusively that my incapacity has occurred.
> That determination shall be made by my said Designee by a written declaration under penalty of perjury. H. Spitler, A Statutory Springing Durable Power of Attorney Springs to California, 12 Est. Plan., Trust & Prob. News 1 (Summer 1992)

The long form provides that the designee shall rely upon written opinions of two physicians:

> In making a determination of my incapacity, my designee may rely upon the written opinions of these two physicians.
>
> > (a) My regular, treating physician.
> > (b) Another physician who is a specialist in whatever disease or illness [that] then afflicts me and who is acting independently of (1) my said regular, treating physician and (2) my spouse, child, parent, sibling and any other relative of mine. *Id.*

Provided, however, effective with my signature of this document, I authorize my agent to give informed consent for health care on my behalf and, as my personal representative, to authorize the use, disclosure and redisclosure of my protected health information as provided in the regulations adopted pursuant to the Health Insurance Portability and Accountability Act of 1996, 45 CFR § 164.

The addition to Form 4-33 would not achieve the desired goal in states where a durable power of attorney for health care does not become effective until a physician makes an entry on the principal's medical chart that he is incapacitated.

§4.35.9. Conclusion

Virtually every client should be given the opportunity to execute an appropriate durable power of attorney and to provide in it, or another suitable document, advance health care directions. A durable power of attorney can provide a client with important, low cost protection against the legal complications of physical or mental incapacity. Moreover, the agent can be authorized as the principal's proxy to make gifts and take other important actions to carry out the principal's wishes and minimize tax and other burdens. *Cruzan* strongly suggests that clients may express their constitutional right to refuse medical treatment in a durable power that designates a proxy to make health care decisions for them. Even before the *Cruzan* decision many commentators believed that in the absence of statutory restrictions a durable power could authorize the agent to make health care decisions for the principal. As noted above, under the provisions of some acts the principal may nominate a guardian in a durable power of attorney. The 1993 Act explicitly recognizes a DPAHC "in writing and signed by the principal," that authorizes the agent to make any health care decisions the principal could have made while competent. Presumably an authorization contained in a broader form of durable power of attorney would be recognized.

§4.36. HEALTH INSURANCE PORTABILITY AND ACCOUNTABILITY ACT OF 1996 (HIPAA)

As indicated at §4.35.8, the regulations adopted pursuant to HIPAA, which became effective April 14, 2003, create problems for some traditional estate planning practices. In particular, the new rules severely limit the ability of physicians and other health care providers to provide any information regarding the health and capacity of an individual. The new regulations, 45 CFR Parts 160 and 164, are summarized in "Summary of the HIPAA Privacy Rule" prepared by the Office of Civil Rights of the Department of Health & Human Services. Ordinary violations of the health care privacy rules are subject to civil fines. Aggravated violations are subject to criminal penalties that may result in a fine of up to $250,000 and up to one year in prison. *See* Shenkman, Estate Planning Documents Need to Address HIPAA Issues, 36 Est. Plan. 14 (Mar. 2009).

State Law Preempted. The HIPAA regulations preempt state laws. 42 U.S.C. § 1178 (2011). Presumably, however, a state law that imposes more stringent requirements on the provision of protected health information would not be preempted.

Protected Health Information; Covered Entities. The new rules define protected health information (PHI) as "individually identifiable health information" that is held or transmitted by any covered entity in any form or media. Individually identifiable health information is information that relates to an individual's present, past, or future physical or mental health or condition, the provision of health care to the individual or the present, past, or future payment for the provision of health care to an individual that identifies or can be used to identify the individual. A covered entity is any health care provider, including institutional health care providers and noninstitutional providers, such as physicians, dentists and other practitioners that electronically transmit health information. As indicated above, the rules preempt state law unless the requirements of state law are more stringent. Also, under 45 CFR § 164.502(f), the PHI continues to be protected after an individual's death.

Permitted Disclosures. The regulations permit PHI (1) to be disclosed to the individual; (2) to be used by the covered entity for its own treatment, payment and health care operations; (3) to be used or disclosed with the informed consent of the individual; (4) for disclosures in the best interests of an individual in an emergency or if an individual is incapacitated; or (5) to be used for specified national priority purposes, including pursuant to a court order or subpoena. 45 CFR § 164.502(a)(1).

Personal Representative. For the purposes of the rules, a personal representative of an individual is treated as the individual. 45 CFR § 164.502(g)(1). In turn, 45 CFR § 164.502(g)(2) provides that, "If under applicable law a person has authority to act on behalf of an individual who is an adult or an emancipated minor in making decisions related to health care, a covered entity must treat such person as a personal representative under this subchapter, with respect to protected health information relevant to such personal representation." Given these rules, an agent designated in a durable power of attorney that presently authorizes the agent to make informed health care decisions for the principal should qualify as a personal representative. Indeed, it should be enough if the durable power of attorney were currently effective only with respect to making informed health care decisions for the principal.

Draft Language for Inclusion in Durable Powers of Attorney. A provision along the lines of Form 4-34 should be sufficient to constitute the agent as the principal's personal representative under the HIPAA regulations. Form 4-30, above, should also satisfy the requirements of HIPAA. As the personal representative the agent could execute valid authorizations on behalf of the principal. *See* § 164.502(g)(1) and (2) discussed above. The effectiveness of such a provision, of course, depends upon state law, which may deny effect to health care powers until the principal is certified by a physician to be incapacitated.

Form 4-34
HIPAA Provision in Durable Power of Attorney

Authorization to make health care decisions and to authorize the use and disclosure of my protected health information under the Health Insurance Portability and Accountability Act of 1996. I authorize my

§ 4.36

agent to make informed health care decisions on my behalf and, as my personal representative, to authorize the use and disclosure of my protected health information as provided in the Health Insurance Portability and Accountability Act of 1996 and 45 CFR Part 164.

The Problem—Springing Powers of Attorney. In most, if not all, states, a durable power of attorney may "become effective upon the disability of the principal." Not surprisingly, many clients choose to take advantage of the opportunity and execute durable powers of attorney which specify that the principal will be considered to be disabled if a physician (or two, including his principal physician) certify in writing that the principal is no longer able to understand and manage his financial affairs [or make rational and reasonable health care decisions]. Unfortunately, the risk of a penalty under the HIPAA privacy rule may deter many physicians from providing the required certifications (unless, of course, the principal has independently authorized such disclosures or has a personal representative to whom PHI can safely be disclosed).

Avoiding the Problems. Rather than try to grapple directly with the problems the HIPAA privacy rule poses for springing durable powers of attorney, some clients will choose to adopt another approach. Some clients may choose to execute durable powers of attorney that are presently effective rather than effective at a future date. Others may choose to emulate the effect of a springing durable power of attorney by depositing a presently effective durable power of attorney with an escrow holder who is instructed only to deliver it to the designated agent under specified circumstances which do not require any certification by a physician. Another way of avoiding the impasse is for a client to specify that a durable power of attorney comes into effect when all, or a majority, of designated lay persons certify in writing that the principal no longer has the capacity to understand and manage his or her financial affairs (or make rational and reasonable health care decisions).

The Problem—Other Documents that May Require Determinations of Incapacity. Wills, trusts and other estate planning documents, including family limited partnerships and limited liability company agreements, have traditionally provided that an individual shall be considered to be incapacitated if a physician (or two, including his or her principal physician) certifies that the individual is unable to manage his financial affairs. Upon such a certification, the grantor may no longer have the power to revoke or amend a trust or direct the distributions that should be made from it. Similarly, such a certification may cause the managing partner of an FLP or the manager of an LLC to be automatically removed from office. Again, physicians will, naturally, be reluctant to provide the required certifications unless proper authorization or in response to a request by the individual's personal representative.

Options. The problem of having access to the information necessary to make determinations for purposes of wills, trusts and business agreements is not easily resolved. If the parties to a presently effective trust or business agreement are willing, they could each give valid authorizations for the disclosure of the necessary information upon the request of designated persons. However, under the regulations an authorization may be revoked in writing at any time. 45 CFR § 164.508(b)(5). Under another approach, the appointment of a trustee or manager of an FLP or LLC might be conditioned upon agreeing to execute the required authorization and not revoking it. If the authorization were revoked, the agreement could provide that the individual would be deemed to have resigned. Under another approach, the determination of capacity might be made by all, or a majority of, designated lay persons. In some cases, it may be enough if all, or a majority, of the beneficiaries of a trust or members of the business entity are given the power to remove and replace the individual. Care must, of course, be exercised if the trustee holds tax sensitive powers.

Valid Authorization. Under the regulations, PHI can be disclosed to the extent provided by an individual or by a personal representative in a valid authorization. Accordingly, in many estate planning situations, the solution will be to obtain the necessary authorization from the individual or from his or her "personal representative." In the case of trusts of which there is an individual trustee, one approach is to obtain a valid authorization from each individual trustee. Under another approach, a document creating a trust might condition the appointment of an individual trustee upon the individual executing a valid authorization. However, as indicated above, under 45 CFR § 164.508(b)(5), "an individual may revoke an authorization provided under this section at any time." Thus, an individual trustee could revoke an authorization that he or she was required to execute as a condition of being appointed as trustee. (Curiously, 45 CFR § 164.508(c)(2)(i)(A) requires a valid authorization to include, "The exceptions to the right to revoke and a description of how the individual may revoke the authorization.")

Electronic Copies of Authorizations. The Health & Human Services website contains helpful guidance in the form of "Frequently Asked Questions" (FAQs). For example, a covered entity can disclose PHI pursuant to a copy of a validly signed authorization including a copy that is received by facsimile or electronic transmission. FAQ 63. Also, although an earlier version required covered entities to retain original copies of authorizations, the final version of 45 CFR § 164.530(j)(1)(i) requires a covered entity to "maintain such writing *or* an electronic copy." (Emphasis added.)

State Limitations on Authorizations. Note that the law of some states imposes stricter rules regarding the validity and duration of authorizations to use or disclose PHI. For example, Washington law provides that any authorization to disclose health information expires at the end of 90 days. Wash. Rev. Code § 70.02.030(6) (2011).

Requirements for a Valid Authorization. Under 45 CFR § 164.508(c) a valid authorization must be written in plain language and contain the following "core elements" and "required statements:"

1. A description of the information to be used or disclosed that identifies the information in a specific and meaningful fashion [the description may be general and may extend to information acquired in the future, FAQ 90];

2. The name or other specific identification of the person(s), or class of persons, authorized to make the requested use or disclosure [persons who may make requests can be described in a general way—*e.g.*, by class or category, FAQ 77];

3. The name or other specific identification of the person(s), or class of persons, to whom the covered entity may make the requested use or disclosure [can also be described by class or category, FAQ 77];

4. A description of each purpose of the requested use or disclosure. The statement "at the request of the individual" is a sufficient description of the

purposes when an individual initiates the authorization and, does not, or elects not to, provide a statement of the purpose;

5. An expiration date or an expiration event that relates to the individual or the purpose of the use or disclosure [because a valid authorization can be effective following an individual's death, it may be appropriate to pro vide that the authorization continues until _____years after death];

6. A statement of the individual's right to revoke the authorization in writing and the exceptions to the right to revoke, together with a description of how the individual may revoke the authorization [however, note that in 45 CFR § 164.508(b)(5) "An individual may revoke an authorization at any time, provided that the revocation is in writing...."];

7. A statement that information used or disclosed pursuant to the authoriza-tion may be subject to redisclosure by the recipient and no longer protected by this rule;[although not a "core element" this provision is a required statement, 45 CFR § 164.508(c)(2)(iii)];

8. Signature of the individual and date; and

9. If the authorization is signed by a personal representative of the individual, a description of such representative's authority to act for the individual.

Note that an authorization need not be witnessed or notarized. FAQ 91.

Draft Form of Valid Authorization. A document intended to serve as a valid authorization for disclosure of PHI for determining the maker's capacity might be drafted along the lines of Form 4-35 (some alternative texts are shown in brackets):

Form 4-35
Authorization for Disclosure of Protected Health Information

1. I authorize all health care providers, including physicians, nurses, and all other persons (including entities) who may have provided, be providing, or in the future provide, me with any type of health care, to disclose my protected health care information [that is relevant to a determination of my capacity to understand and manage my financial affairs:]

   (a) to the agent designated in a durable power of attorney signed by me when asked by my agent to do so for the purpose of determining my capacity as defined in the power of attorney or by governing law,

   (b) to the trustee, or a designated successor trustee, of any trust of which I am a beneficiary or a trustee when asked to do so for the purpose of determining my capacity as defined in the trust,

   (c) to any partner of any partnership of which I am a member for the purpose of determining my capacity as defined in the partnership agreement,

   (d) to my lawyer, _____, for the purposes of determining my capacity to make inter vivos gifts, to execute estate planning documents, and whether, and to what extent, a guardianship or other protective proceedings for me is necessary or desirable, and

   (e) to a guardian ad litem, if one is appointed for me, for the purpose of determining whether, and to what extent, a guardianship or other protective proceedings for me is necessary or desirable.

2. This authorization is intended to provide my health care providers with the authorization necessary to allow each of them to disclose protected health care information regarding me to the persons described in (a)-(e) above for the purpose of allowing each of them to make the specified determinations regarding my capacity or the need for protective proceedings.

3. Information disclosed by a health care provider pursuant to this authorization may be subject to redisclosure and may no longer be protected by the privacy rules of CFR 11.164.

4. This authorization may be revoked by a writing signed by me or by my personal representative.

5. This authorization shall expire five years after my death unless validly revoked prior to that date.

SIGNED: _____DATED_____

§4.37. The Living Will, Advance Directives, and Natural Death Acts

The principle that a competent person has a constitutionally protected liberty interest in refusing unwanted medical treatment may be inferred from our prior decisions . . . . But for purposes of this case, we assume that the United States Constitution would grant a competent person a constitutionally protected right to refuse lifesaving hydration and nutrition. *Cruzan,* 497 U.S. at 278, 279.

Despite their grand title, living wills are very limited in scope. Two limits are critically important. First, in most states they can only be used to refuse extraordinary, life-prolonging care. Second, they are effective to refuse care only after a patient has become terminally ill—or even, in some states, when death is very near. They are not advance directives through which treatment can be refused more generally. Francis, The Evanescence of Living Wills, 24 Real Prop., Prob. & Tr. J. 141, 145 (1989).

The common statutory and nonstatutory forms of living will have limited scope and effect. Accordingly, a DPAHC or similar instrument that confers authority on another person to make health care decisions is generally preferable. Under *Cruzan,* presumably any competent adult can make an advance directive that must be recognized by the state. Thus, it may override statutes which only allow advance directives to be made by persons who are terminally ill or which limit the period during which directives are valid. Similarly, *Cruzan* casts doubt on statutes that prescribe the text of the directive to physicians that must be used. It is important to note that, consistent with *Cruzan,* statutes do not permit anyone to execute a living will on behalf of a minor or incompetent person. Thus, the statutory procedures are generally inapplicable if a patient did not execute a living will prior to incompetency. However, it may be possible for a patient's family to move the patient from a health care facility in a state with restrictive policies to a state with more liberal policies.

Section 5 of the Uniform Health-Care Decisions Act (1993) allows health care decisions to be made by a surrogate for an adult or emancipated minor if the patient's primary physician determines that the patient lacks capacity and no agent or guardian has been appointed or is not reasonably available. The surrogate is a person designated by the adult or emancipated minor. Otherwise, it is a member of the patient's family in the following order of priority:(1) spouse, unless legally separated; (2) adult child; (3) parent; or (4) adult brother or sister. In default of those persons acting, "an adult who has exhibited special care and concern for the patient, who is familiar with the patient's personal values, and who is reasonably available may act as surrogate." If more than one member of a class act as surrogates, decisions may be made by a majority of them. Under §6 of the 1993 Act, a guardian is required to follow the ward's individual instructions and may not revoke the ward's AHCD unless authorized by the appointing court. Unless otherwise provided by the court, decisions by an agent take precedence over those of a guardian. Finally, decisions made by a surrogate or guardian are effective without court approval.

Legislation adopted by Congress in 1990 requires hospitals, skilled nursing facilities, home health agencies, and hospice programs to provide information to each patient regarding an individual's right under state law to make decisions regarding health care, "including the right to accept or refuse medical or surgical treatment and the right to formulate advance directives . . . ." 42 U.S.C. § 1395cc(f)(1)(A)(i) (2011). In a later provision the term "advance directive" is defined to mean "a written instruction, such as a living will or durable power of attorney for health care . . . relating to the provision of such care when the individual is incapacitated." 42 U.S.C. § 1395cc(f)(3) (2011).

California has a comprehensive advance health care directive law. Cal. Prob. Code §§4600 *et seq.* (20109). Drafting under the law is discussed in Soskin, Drafting Advance Health Care Directives, 7 Cal. Tr. & Est. Q. 16 (2001). The law does not affect documents that were effective under the pre-existing law, but directives given after June 30, 2000, must comply with the new law. Unless prohibited by the terms of an advance directive, an agent can make donations under the Uniform Anatomical Gift Act and take other actions with respect to a decedent's remains.

§4.37.1. Immunity Against Civil or Criminal Prosecution

Natural death acts generally provide immunity against civil or criminal liability for specified persons who carry out the patient's instructions. *E.g.,* Cal. Prob. Code §4740 (2011). However, the persons to whom immunity is given and the circumstances under which it is given vary considerably. Also, some statutes prescribe penalties for the concealment, destruction, falsification, or forgery of a living will.

§4.37.2. Uniform Advance Health Care Directive Act (1993); Uniform Rights of the Terminally Ill Act (1989)

The best solution would be adoption by all states of the Uniform Rights of the Terminally Ill Act, as recently revised by the National Conference of Commissioners on Uniform State Laws. This excellent legislation covers almost every aspect in clear prose that anyone can understand and follow.

It was approved by the American Bar Association on February 13, 1990. Warnock, Living Wills: The Need for Uniform State Laws, 5 Prob. & Prop. 52 (May-June 1991).

The above statement was valid when it was made. Now, however, states should be urged to adopt the Uniform Advance Health Care Directive Act (1993), which expands the scope of the earlier Acts, adds clarification and resolves some of the problems that were not previously addressed. The original, 1985 version of the Uniform Rights of the Terminally Ill Act authorized a competent adult to execute a declaration, witnessed by two individuals, instructing a physician to withhold or withdraw life-sustaining treatment if the maker is likely to die within a reasonably short time and is no longer able to participate in medical care decisions. The 1989 Act changed the provision slightly and added subsection §2(c) that allows a competent adult to designate another person to make decisions regarding the withholding or withdrawal of life-sustaining treatment. Section 2 of the 1989 Act includes forms of declarations that may, but need not, be used. The forms, which are generally helpful, could be expanded to include reference to more specific matters.

As pointed out by Leah V. Granof, The New Health Care Decisions Law: Revision and Supplement to Existing Law, 6 Cal. Tr. & Est. Q. 25, 27 (2000), the California Act allows an individual to "create his own advance health care directive in his own writing." Importantly the Act includes a form that "may be completed or all or any part of the form be modified. The form allows an individual to make his own health care instructions with or without appointing an agent."

Form 4-36
Declarations Under the Uniform Rights of the Terminally Ill Act (1989)

[(b) A declaration directing a physician to withhold or withdraw life-sustaining treatment may, but need not, be in the following form:]

If I should have an incurable and irreversible condition that, without the administration of life-sustaining treatment will, in the opinion of my attending physician, cause my death within a relatively short time, and I am no longer able to make decisions regarding my medical treatment, I direct my attending physician, pursuant to the Uniform Rights of the Terminally Ill Act of this State, to withhold or withdraw treatment that only prolongs the process of dying and is not necessary to my comfort or to relieve pain. . . .

[(c) A declaration that designates another individual to make decisions governing the withholding or withdrawal of life-sustaining treatment may, but need not be, in the following form:]

If I should have an incurable and irreversible condition that, without the administration of life-sustaining treatment, will, in the opinion of my attending physician, cause my death within a relatively short time, and I am no longer able to make decisions regarding my medical treatment, I appoint _____or, if he or she is not reasonably available or is unwilling to serve, _____, to make decisions on my behalf regarding withholding or withdrawal of treatment that only prolongs the process of dying and is not necessary for my comfort or to alleviate pain, pursuant to the Uniform Rights of the Terminally Ill Act of this State.

Subsection 2(c) continues with the following optional language:

[If the individual(s) I have so appointed is not reasonably available or is unwilling to serve, I direct my attending physician, pursuant to the Uniform Rights of the Terminally Ill Act of this State, to withhold or withdraw treatment that only prolongs the process of dying and is not necessary for my comfort or to alleviate pain.]

§4.37.3. Conclusion

The laws and the problems addressed by the various forms of health care laws are complex and controversial. Nonetheless, most clients appreciate being advised regarding the extent to which they can control the medical care they will be given during their terminal illness if they become incompetent and the opportunity to designate an agent to make decisions on their behalf. The likelihood that health care providers will comply with an advance directive is, of course, enhanced if the directive complies with the local law. If a local form is not mandated, a client may prefer to use a form of advanced directive contained in the 1993 Act or a form of living will such as the very popular one published by the Euthanasia Educational Council, New York, N.Y. In light of *Cruzan,* a sufficiently specific form should be adequate to support discontinuance of some medical treatment, including artificial hydration and nutrition and to appoint an agent to make health care decisions.

Compliance is also enhanced if family members support the principal's directive—which suggests the importance of discussing the matter with family members. *See* Zinberg, Decisions for the Dying: An Empirical Study of Physician's Responses to Advance Directives, 13 Vt. L. Rev. 445 (1989). The advance directive should also be discussed with the principal's primary physician. Sometimes the physician's personal or religious beliefs might prevent him or her from honoring the provisions of a patient's advance directive. If the principal does not wish to change physicians, it may be advisable to include a provision in the principal's DPAHC permitting the attorney in fact to discharge the physician and hire another who will be willing and able to implement the principal's wishes as expressed in the advance directive.

The execution of an advanced directive or living will provides a valuable expression of the client's wishes that is useful even in jurisdictions which do not authorize them statutorily. They can provide the maker's family members and attending physicians with the guidance they need. As a matter of routine more than one copy should be executed. However, §12 of the 1993 Act provides that a copy shall have the same effect as an original. If more than one copy is executed, one executed copy may be given to the client, another sent to the client's regular physician, and another retained by the lawyer. If that is done, a copy of the document should be readily available in the event of illness or emergency. In addition, some members of the maker's family should also be told about the document. A copy should also be deposited with a registry if one has been established by the jurisdiction. Cal. Prob. Code § 4800 (2011). As a matter of convenience, some firms provide clients with a small (wallet-sized) laminated card that summarizes the provisions of their living wills. The cards sometimes include contact information for the attorney that prepared the documents. Other firms issue laminated cards containing only information along the lines of "I, John or Jane Doe, have executed an advanced health care directive (living will). Please contact Dr. (name and phone number) or my agent, (name and phone number)."

§ 4.38. DEATH WITH DIGNITY, CONTINUING EVOLUTION

As indicated above, the holding in *Cruzan* and the laws of most states permit competent patients to request the withdrawal or withholding of medical treatment that merely prolongs the time of death. Such withdrawal or withholding of treatment is often characterized as "passive" euthanasia, which is almost universally recognized. The justification for allowing a competent terminally ill patient to order the withdrawal or termination of such treatment is eloquently stated in the following passage from *Satz v. Perlmutter*, 362 So. 2d 160 (Fla. App. 1978), *aff'd*, 370 U.S. 2d 359 (Fla. 1980):

> It is all very convenient to insist on continuing [the patient's] life so that there can be no question of foul play, no resulting civil liability, and no possible trespass on medical ethics. However, it is quite another matter to do so at the patient's sole expense and against his competent will, thus inflicting never ending physical torture on his body until the inevitable, but artificially suspended, moment of death. Such a course of conduct invades the patient's constitutional right of privacy, removes his freedom of choice and invades his right to self-determine.

In most states, it is a crime to counsel or assist another to commit suicide, which prevents physicians and other health care professionals from prescribing life-ending medications for terminally ill patients who wish to die. However, as described below, initiatives passed in Oregon in 1994 and in Washington in 2008 permit physicians to do so in strictly limited circumstances. In addition, in 2009, the Montana Supreme Court held that a state statute under which consent is a defense to some crimes protects physicians who provide aid in dying from prosecution for homicide. *Baxter v. Montana*, 224 P.3d 1211 (Mont. 2009). Some European countries allow death with dignity: assisted suicide is permitted in Germany, and Holland permits both assisted suicide and euthanasia under strictly limited circumstances.

Strong arguments based on patient autonomy, compassion, and economics support legalization of voluntary physician assisted aid-in-dying—provided a patient is not required to request, and a physician is not required to provide, aid-in-dying. Opposition to aid-in-dying is usually based upon three broad arguments: (1) the participation by physicians in aid-in-dying is inconsistent with the Hippocratic oath and the healing objectives of the profession; (2) the nature of the medical profession and the physician-patient relationship would both be irreparably damaged if physicians were to participate in aid-in-dying; and (3) legalization of physician assisted aid-in-dying might ultimately lead to involuntary active euthanasia, as practiced in Germany in the 1930s.

In the 1990s proponents of death with dignity filed suits in federal courts that challenged the constitutionality of laws in New York and Washington that made it a crime to assist terminally ill patients to die. The Washington statute was held unconstitutional in *Compassion in Dying v. Washington,* 850 F. Supp. 1454 (W.D. Wash. 1994), on two grounds: (1) "it places an undue burden on the exercise of a protected Fourteenth Amendment liberty interest"; and (2) "it violates the right to equal protection under the Fourteenth Amendment by prohibiting physician-assisted suicide while permitting the refusal or withdrawal of life support systems for terminally ill individuals." A divided panel of the Ninth Circuit reversed that decision. 49 F.3d 586 (1995). A subsequent en banc decision of the Ninth Circuit affirmed the District Court decision. 85 F.3d 1140 (1996). The majority wrote that "a liberty interest exists in the choice of how and when one dies, and that the provisions of the Washington statute banning assisted suicide, as applied to competent, terminally ill adults who wish to hasten their deaths by obtaining medication prescribed by their doctors, violates the Due Process Clause." '

At about the same time, a three judge panel of the Second Circuit rendered a unanimous decision invalidating the prohibition that New York State law imposed on the right of competent, terminally ill persons to obtain assistance from physicians in dying. *Quill v. Vacco,* 80 F.3d 716 (1996). The District Court had earlier refused to enter an injunction in favor of the plaintiffs. *Quill v. Koppel,* 870 F. Supp. 78 (S.D.N.Y. 1994). One of the plaintiffs in that case was Dr. Timothy Quill, a physician-author who has long been an advocate for the terminally ill. See T. Quill, Death and Dignity (1993).

The Supreme Court granted certiorari in both cases and, not unexpectedly, in 1997 the Court reversed both decisions. *Vacco v. Quill,* 521 U.S. 793; *Washington v. Glucksberg,* 521 U.S. 702 (1997). In the *Glucksberg* case, the majority opinion by Chief Justice Rehnquist recast the question presented to it in the broadest terms: "The question presented in this case is whether Washington's prohibition against 'causing' or 'aiding' a suicide offends the Fourteenth Amendment to the United States Constitution." Not surprisingly, the second sentence of the opinion answered this question in the negative: "We hold that it does not." In Quill, the Court similarly broadened the question: "The question presented by this case is whether New York's prohibition on assisting suicide therefore violates the Equal Protection Clause of the Fourteenth Amendment." ' Again, the Court concluded that it did not.

Future challenges, based on state constitutional provisions, or even state statutes, may be more successful—and be relatively insulated from reversal by the Supreme Court. The potential for court actions that challenge statutes that prevent physicians from helping patients to die is illustrated by *Baxter v. Montana,* 224 P.3d 1211 (Mont. 2009). In *Baxter,* the trial court granted summary judgment for the challengers— holding that under Article II, Sections 4 and 10 of the Montana Constitution, a terminally ill patient has a right to die with dignity, which protects the physician who helps the patient die from prosecution for homicide. On appeal the Montana Supreme Court declined to pass on the constitutional issue, instead holding that under Mont. C. § 45-2-211, the consent of a terminally ill patient to a physician providing aid in dying would insulate the physician from prosecution for homicide.

Death With Dignity Initiatives. Initiatives that would have authorized voluntary active euthanasia and physician assisted suicide were narrowly defeated in Washington (1991) and California (1992). Initiative 119 in Washington was opposed by a campaign heavily financed by the Catholic Church, various right-to-life groups and the Washington State Medical Association. In November, 1994, Oregon voters passed Measure 16, which authorized physician-assisted suicide. Oregon Death With Dignity Act, Or. Rev. Stat. § 127.800 et seq. Protracted litigation instituted by opponents of the act delayed its implementation for three years. *See Lee v. Oregon,* 107 F.3d 1382 (9th Cir. 1997), *cert. denied, sub nom. Lee v. Harcleroad,* 522 U.S. 927 (1997).

Efforts led by Senator Orin Hatch and Representative Henry Hyde to prevent implementation of the Oregon act were unsuccessful. Pursuing another strategy, on November 9, 2001, the Attorney General of the United States, John Ashcroft, issued an interpretation of the Controlled Substances Act that would prevent Oregon physicians from prescribing life-ending medications for terminally ill patients. Specifically, the Attorney General issued an interpretative order that would bar physicians from prescribing drugs for the purpose of assisting terminally ill patients to die. In 2006, the Supreme Court invalidated the interpretation, holding that the Controlled Substances Act did not give the Attorney General authority to issue such an order. *Gonzales v. Oregon,* 546 U.S. 243 (2006). The majority opinion, written by Justice Kennedy, provided the following background regarding the origin of the interpretative order:

> In 2001, John Ashcroft was appointed Attorney General. Perhaps because Mr. Ashcroft had supported efforts to curtail assisted suicide while serving as a Senator, see, e.g., 143 Cong. Rec. 5589-5590 (remarks of Senator Ashcroft), Oregon Attorney General Hardy Meyers wrote him to request a meeting with Department of Justice officials should the Department decide to revisit the application of the CSA to assisted suicide. Letter of February 2, 2001, App to Brief for Patient-Respondents in Opposition 55a. Attorney General Myers received a reply letter from one of Attorney General Ashcroft's advisors, writing on his behalf, which stated:

> I am aware of no pending legislation on Congress that would prompt a review of the Department's interpretation of the CSA as it relates to physician-assisted suicide. Should such a review be commenced in the future, we would be happy to include your views in that review. Letter from Lori Sharpe (April 17, 2001), id., at 58a.

On November 9, 2001, without consulting Oregon or apparently anyone outside his Department, the Attorney General issued an Interpretative Rule announcing his intent to restrict the use of controlled substances for physician-assisted suicide. Id. at 264-254.

The Oregon law was put to a second vote in November 1997. Despite a well-financed campaign to repeal the act, and the narrow margin by which it passed the first time it was supported by almost two-thirds of the voters. In 2008, Washington voters passed an initiative, I-1000, which was virtually identical to the Oregon law. The Washington law, Washington Death With Dignity Act, Rev. Code Wash. § 70.245.010, et seq., became effective March 5, 2009.

Overview of Oregon and Washington Death With Dignity Acts. The Oregon and Washington laws allow prescriptions for life-ending medications to be given to competent adults who are residents of the state, make separate oral and written requests for the medication at least fifteen days apart and are certified by an attending physician and a consulting physician to be terminally ill. The written request must be substantially in the form included in the statutes, signed by the patient and witnessed by two persons who are neither related to the patient, the patient's attending physician, nor within certain other specified classes. The laws require the states' respective departments of health to release information concerning the utilization of the acts during the preceding year. See http://oregon.gov/DHS/ph/pas/index.shtml; http://doh.wash.gov/dwda.

Data published by Oregon and Washington indicate that relatively few patients have chosen to request prescriptions under the acts. For example, over the 12 years the act has been in effect in Oregon (1998-2009), a total of 460 patients have died from taking the medicines prescribed for them. According to the most recent report for Oregon, in 2009 prescriptions under the act were written by 55 physicians for 95 patients, of whom 53 took the medication and died (during the year another six patients with earlier prescriptions also died). The Washington report for the period the law was in effect in 2009 (March 5 through December 31) shows that prescriptions were written by 53 physicians for 63 patients of whom 36 died after ingesting the medication. In both states most patients who obtained prescriptions have been well educated, white (98%), male (53% in Oregon, 55% in Washington), between 55 and 85 years of age, covered by some form of health insurance, and choosing to die at home.

§4.39. ANATOMICAL GIFTS; UNIFORM ANATOMICAL GIFTS ACTS (1968, 1987 AND 2006)

"The [2006] revision retains the basic policy of the 1968 and 1987 anatomical gifts acts by retaining and strengthening the opt-in system that honors the free choice of an individual to donate the individual's organs (a process known in the organ transplant community as a first person consent or donor designation). This revision also preserves the right of other persons to make an anatomical gift of a decedent's organs if the decedent had not made a gift during life. And, it strengthens the right of an individual not to donate the individual's organs by signing a refusal that bars others from making a gift of the individual's organs after death." Prefatory Note, 8A U.L.A. (2008 Supp.) 30.

If the subject is raised, some clients will wish to donate part or all of their bodies to be used following their deaths to help the living and to contribute to medical education and research. Advances in medical science have made it possible to use a variety of a decedent's body parts, including corneas, kidneys, pituitary glands, and skin. Making such gifts is facilitated by the Uniform Anatomical Gift Act (UAGA), one of the versions of which has been adopted in all states and the District of Columbia..

Lifetime Gifts. Under §4 of the 2006 Act, a lifetime anatomical gift of a donor's body or part may be made for the purpose of transplantation, therapy, research, or education by a donor who is an adult, is emancipated or could apply for a driver's license under the local law, or by an agent of the donor unless the power of attorney for health care or other record prohibits the agent from making an anatomical gift. The donor's parent or guardian may make the gift if the donor is a minor. The gift may be made in a will, by a statement on a driver's license or identification card, by a simple donor's card or as otherwise specified in § 5. Sample donor cards are appended to § 5. The donor (or other authorized person) may amend or revoke a lifetime gift by, *inter alia*, a signed document. § 6. A document of gift need not be delivered during the donor's lifetime. § 13.

Importantly, an individual may refuse to make an anatomical gift, which is binding on all persons. § 7. However, if an unemancipated minor who signed a refusal dies, a parent of the minor who is reasonably available may revoke the minor's refusal. § 8(h).

Post-Mortem Gifts. Under § 9, of the 2006 Act, a gift of a decedent's body or part may be made by an expanded number of persons, including, in order of priority: an agent who at the time of the decedent's death could have made an anatomical gift immediately prior to the decedent's death; the spouse of the decedent; the children of the decedent; the parents of the decedent; adult siblings of the decedent; and so on. If there is more than one member of a class, a member may make a gift unless that person or the intended donee knows of an objection by another member of the class. A person may not make a gift if a person with higher priority is reasonably available to make or object to the making of a gift.

Conclusion. The Uniform Anatomical Gifts Act helps to relieve the need for body parts suitable for transplantation. However, there is a serious shortage of suitable anatomical gifts.

BIBLIOGRAPHY

I. WILLS

Articles:

Breyer, Dickinson & Wake, The Fine Art of Intimidating Disgruntled Beneficiaries With In Terrorem Clauses, 51 SMU L. Rev. 225 (1998)

California Will Drafting (Cal. CEB)

Chester, Posthumously Conceived Heirs Under A Revised Uniform Probate Code, 38 Real Prop., Prob. & Tr. J. 727 (2004)

Engel, The Pros and Cons of Living Trusts as Contrasted to Wills, 29 Est. Plan. 155 (April 2002)

Estate Planning for the General Practitioner (Cal. CEB)

Estate Planning Practice (2 vols., Cal. CEB)

Gamble, If It's the 1990s It Must Be Time for Another Principal and Income Act, U. Miami, 32d Inst. Est. Plan., Ch. 8 (1998)

Gary, Posthumously Conceived Heirs, 19 Prob. & Prop. 32 (March/April 2005)

Hess, The Federal Transfer Tax Consequences of Joint and Mutual Wills, 24 Real Prop., Prob. & Tr. J. 469 (1990)

Lombard, Planning for Disability, Health Care Issues and Developments in Assisted Suicide, U. Miami, 32d Inst. Est. Plan., Ch. 17 (1998)

Martin, The Draftsman Views Wills for a Young Family, 54 N.C. L. Rev. 277 (1976)

McGovern, Kurtz & Rein, Wills, Trusts and Estates (1988)

Omron, Comment, No Contest Clauses in California Wills and Trusts: How Lucky Do You Feel Playing the Wheel of Fortune?, 18 Whittier L. Rev. 613 (1997)

Pennell, Apportionment Can Make Tax Payment More Equitable, 22 Est. Plan. 3 (Jan./Feb. 1995)

Quill, Death and Dignity (1993)

Whitman, Exoneration Clauses in Wills and Trust Instruments, 4 Hofstra L. Rev. 123 (1992)

II. Powers of Attorney and Durable Powers of Attorney

Boxx, The Durable Power of Attorney's Place in the Family of Fiduciary Relationships, 36 Ga. L. Rev. 1 (2001)

Calif. Law Rev. Comm., 1995 Comprehensive Power of Attorney Law, 14 Cal. Est. Plan., Tr. & Prob. News 26 (Winter 1994)

Carrion, Estate and Gift Tax Problems of Principals and Agents Under Durable Powers of Attorney, 1995 Tax Notes 1009 (Feb. 13, 1995)

Colette, Counseling the Terminally-Ill Client, NAELA Quarterly 1 (Winter 1995)

Collin, Planning and Drafting Durable Powers of Attorney for Health Care, U. Miami, 22nd Inst. Est. Plan., Ch. 5 (1988)

Collin, F. J., Jr., Lombard, J. J., Moses, A. L., Spitler, H., Drafting the Durable Power of Attorney (1987)

Collin & Ohlandt, Gift-Giving Under Durable Powers of Attorney, 20 Est., Gifts & Tr. J. 63 (1995)

Dessin, Acting as Agent Under a Financial Durable Power of Attorney: An Unscripted Role, 75 Neb. L. Rev. 574 (1996)

Fowler, Appointing A Medical Agent, 84 Col. L. Rev. 985 (1984)

Grassi, Jr., Gifts by Terminally Ill Persons Reduce Estate Tax, 22 Est. Plan. 75 (1995)

Insel, Durable Power Can Alleviate Effects of Client's Incapacity, 22 Est. Plan. 37 (Jan./Feb. 1995)

Lombard, Planning for Disability: Durable Powers, Standby Trusts and Preserving Eligibility for Governmental Benefits, U. Miami, 20th Est. Plan. Inst., Ch. 17 (1986)

Lombard, Health Care Decisions—Right to Terminate Medical Treatment—Proxy Decision Making: Trends in the Law, 12 Prob. Notes 265 (1987)

Rhein, No One in Charge: Durable Powers of Attorney and the Failure to Protect Incapacitated Persons, 17 Elder L. J. 165 (2009)

Wentworth, Durable Powers of Attorney; Considering the Financial Institution's Perspective, 17 Prob. & Prop. 37 (Nov/Dec. 2003)

Yale, It's Right to be Left, Holding the Power of Attorney, Prob. & Prop. 54 (Jan/Feb. 2003)

III. Living Wills

Brink, A Glimpse Through the Planning Window of the Young, Terminal Client, U. Miami, 25th Inst. Est. Plan., Ch. 6 (1991)

Buckley, Videotaping Living Wills: Dying Declarations Brought to Life, 22 Val. U. L. Rev. 54 (1987)

Fagerlin & Schneider, Enough: The Failure of the Living Will, 34 Hastings Center Report 30 (No. 2 2004)

Francis, The Evanescence of Living Wills, 24 Real Prop., Prob. & Tr. J. 141 (1989)

Hughes, When Worlds Collide: The Privacy Challenge to Casual Use of Protected Medical Information in Probate Courts and Estate Planning, 24 Cal. Est. Pln. & Prob. Rptr. 133 (2003)

Kola, Indiana's Living Wills and Life Prolonging Procedures Act, 19 Ind. L. Rev. 285 (1985)

Leflar, Liberty and Death: Advance Health Care Directives and the Law of Arkansas, 39 Ark. L. Rev. 446 (1986)

Leimberg & Gibbons, Drafting an Advance Directive for Health Care: Personal Reflections, 29 Est. Plan. 422 (Aug. 2002)

Magnusson, The Sanctity of Life and the Right to Die: Social and Jurisprudential Aspects of the Euthanasia Debate in Australia and the United States, 6 Pac. Rim L. & Pol'y J. 1 (1997)

Murphy, Drafting Health-Care Proxies to Comply with the New HIPAA Regs., 30 Est. Plan. 559 (Nov. 2003)

Note, Physician-Assisted Suicide: A "Right" Reserved for Only the Competent?, 19 Vt. L. Rev. 795 (1995)

Task Force to Improve the Care of Terminally Ill Oregonians, The Final Months of Life: A Guide to Oregon Resources (1998)

The Oregon Death With Dignity Act: A Guidebook for Health Care Providers (1998)

Warnock, Living Wills: The Need for Uniform State Laws, 5 Prob. & Prop. 52 (May-June 1991)

Zartman, The Legacy of *Cruzan,* 5 Prob. & Prop. 13 (May-June 1991)

IV. ANATOMICAL GIFTS

Comment, Consent and Organ Donation, 11 Rutgers Computer & Tech. L.J. 559 (1985)

English, Gift of Life: The Lawyer's Role in Organ and Tissue Donation, 8 Prob. & Prop. 11 (1994)

Naylor, The Role of Family in Cadaveric Organ Procurement, 65 Ind. L. J. 167 (1989)

Silver, The Case for a Post-Mortem Organ Draft and a Proposed Model Organ Draft Act, 68 B.U.L. Rev. 681 (1988)

5

The Gift and Estate Tax Marital Deductions

The achievement of the purposes of the marital deduction is dependent to a great degree upon the careful drafting of wills. *Jackson v. United States,* 376 U.S. 503, 511 (1964).

We are not aware of any cases or guidelines establishing in a civil case a standard for the reasonable, diligent and competent assistance of an attorney engaged in estate planning and preparing a trust with a marital deduction provision. We merely hold that the potential tax problems of general powers of appointment in inter vivos or testamentary marital deduction trusts were within the ambit of a reasonably competent and diligent practitioner from 1961 to the present. *Bucquet v. Livingston,* 129 Cal. Rptr. 514, 521 (Cal. App. 1976).

A. INTRODUCTION

§5.1. SCOPE

The gift and estate tax marital deduction provisions are among the most important and the most complex provisions of the federal transfer tax laws. Our nomadic population and the fundamental importance of the marital deduction provisions make it necessary for lawyers in common law and community property states to know when and how to make inter vivos and deathtime gifts that qualify for the marital deduction.

The first part of this chapter reviews the history and the general contours of the marital deduction provisions. The next part examines the underlying strategies of utilizing the marital deduction, including a discussion of the general objectives of testamentary and inter vivos marital deduction gifts and the advantages and disadvantages of the principal types of formula marital deduction clauses. (A related subject, the community property widow's election, is discussed in Chapter 9 in connection with an overall review of transfers for consideration.) The closing part of the chapter considers the basic requirements of the deductions in detail, with special attention to the terminable interest rule and its most important exceptions—the life income-general power of appointment trust, the estate trust, and the qualified terminable interest property (QTIP) trust.

§5.2. THE PAST

From the inception of the estate tax in 1916 until 1942, the estate tax burdens imposed on residents of common law states and those imposed on residents of community property states were not equal. The inequality arose from the federal recognition of the natural "estate splitting" of property onerously acquired by couples who lived in the community property states. For example, if a family's material wealth was all attributable to a husband's earnings during marriage, only half of it was subject to the estate tax on his death if it had been earned in a community property state. In contrast, all of it was taxed if he had earned it during marriage in a common law state.

On the income tax side, couples who lived in community property states benefited from the natural splitting of their income: Each spouse was taxed on half of the community property income. In contrast, the income of each spouse living in a common law state was fully taxable to the recipient alone. The advantage offered by estate-splitting was enough to lead six jurisdictions to adopt community property systems between 1945 and 1947 (Hawaii, Michigan, Nebraska, Oklahoma, Oregon, and Pennsylvania). The "new" community property jurisdictions all reverted to common law systems soon after the Revenue Act of 1948 extended the principal tax benefits enjoyed by residents of community property states to residents of common law states. Equalization of advantages, the heart of the marital deduction provisions from 1948 through 1981, proved to be more acceptable and durable than equalization of the disadvantages.

§ 5.2.1. 1942 Legislation

In 1942, Congress attempted to equalize estate tax burdens of residents of community and common law states by bringing the treatment of residents of community property states more into line with that accorded residents of common law states. The estate tax amendments enacted that year required all of the community property to be included in the gross estate of the spouse first to die except to the extent it was attributable to the services or property of the survivor. This approach ordinarily required all of the community property to be included in the gross estate of the husband. If the wife died first, one-half of the community property was ordinarily includible in her gross estate because of a provision that called for the inclusion of community property over which a decedent held a power of testamentary disposition. The 1942 solution was unpopular with couples in community property states and did not improve the position of couples in common law states.

§ 5.2.2. 1948 Adoption of Marital Deduction and Joint Income Tax Returns; 1976 Liberalization

The 1948 changes affected both transfer taxes and the income tax. For estate tax purposes only the decedent's one-half interest in the community property was includible in his or her gross estate. Estate tax parity was achieved by allowing a deduction for transfers to a surviving spouse, limited ordinarily to 50 percent of the noncommunity property included in the deceased spouse's estate. Technically, the deduction was limited to half of the decedent's adjusted gross estate. (The adjusted gross estate was a concept that existed solely for the purpose of determining the maximum allowable marital deduction. *See* former § 2056(c).) The adjusted gross estate was defined as the gross estate less (1) the value of all community property included in the decedent's estate and (2) the portion of § 2053 and § 2054 deductions allocable to the noncommunity property.

EXAMPLE 5-1.

H died in 1981 leaving a gross estate of $800,000 in noncommunity property. A total of $40,000 in deductions was allowed under § 2053. *H* left $25,000 to a charity, for which a deduction was allowable under § 2055, and the balance of his estate to his wife, W. The maximum allowable marital deduction was limited to $380,000 (one-half of H's adjusted gross estate) computed as follows:

Gross estate	$800,000
Less:	
Deductions under § 2053	40,000
Adjusted gross estate	$760,000
Maximum marital deduction	$380,000

If the expenses allowable as deductions under § 2053 were not claimed on H's estate tax return, H's adjusted gross estate would have been $800,000 and the maximum allowable deduction $400,000.

In general, a deduction was allowable with respect to property transferred to a surviving spouse if the interest transferred to the survivor was sufficient to cause it to be includible in his or her gross estate. By taking advantage of these provisions, a married person could halve the amount of noncommunity property that would be subject to tax when he or she died.

The 1948 gift tax changes allowed a couple to "split" gifts made by either or both to third parties and treat the gifts as made one-half by each. They also introduced a deduction for up to 50 percent of the value of gifts of noncommunity property made to the donor's spouse. Finally, the 1948 Act allowed couples to reduce their income tax liability by filing a joint return on which their combined income was taxed at preferential rates.

The following passage recounts the purpose of the 1948 legislation:

> The 1948 tax amendments were intended to equalize the effect of the estate taxes in community property and common-law jurisdictions. Under a community property system, such as that in Texas, the spouse receives outright ownership of one-half of the community property and only the other one-half is included in the decedent's estate. To equalize the incidence of progressively scaled estate taxes and to adhere to the patterns of state law, the marital deduction permits a deceased spouse, subject to certain requirements, to transfer free of taxes one-half of his non-community property to the surviving spouse. Although applicable to separately held property in a community property state, the primary thrust of this is to extend to taxpayers in common-law States the advantages of "estate splitting" otherwise available only in community property States. The purpose, however, is only to permit a married couple's property to be taxed in two stages and not to allow a tax-exempt transfer of wealth into succeeding generations. Thus, the marital deduction is generally restricted to the transfer of property interests that will be includible in the surviving spouse's gross estate. *United States v. Stapf*, 375 U.S. 118, 128 (1963).

As the quotation indicates, the estate tax marital deduction adopted in 1948 allowed a portion of the tax otherwise payable upon the death of one spouse to be deferred until the death of the survivor. It did not allow the tax to be entirely avoided.

In 1976, Congress liberalized the marital deduction provisions in order to increase the amount of property an individual could leave to a surviving spouse free of estate tax and to allow freer interspousal lifetime transfers. The 1976 Act amended § 2056(c) to allow a minimum marital deduction of up to $250,000. Under the amendment an estate was allowed to claim a deduction of $250,000 or 50 percent of the adjusted gross estate, whichever was larger. The $250,000 minimum deduction, reduced by the amount of community property included in the gross estate, was available to estates composed entirely of community property. However, because of the reduction, the $250,000 minimum deduction was not a major factor in planning community property estates. The 1976 Act also amended § 2523 to allow a greater current deduction for post-1976 gifts to a spouse.

§ 5.3. 1981 QUANTITATIVE AND QUALITATIVE LIBERALIZATION

With relatively little fanfare the 1981 Act removed all quantitative limits on the marital deduction and relaxed the qualitative restrictions to allow two additional types of interests to qualify for the gift and estate tax deductions. The changes closely parallel two of the key recommendations made in the Treasury Department's 1969 tax reform proposals.

> It does not appear, then, that transfers of property between husband and wife are appropriate occasions for imposing tax. An especially difficult burden may be imposed by the tax when property passes to a widow, particularly if there are minor children. The present system of taxing transfers between spouses does not accord with the common understanding of most husbands and wives that the property they have accumulated is "ours." Furthermore, the distinctions drawn by existing law between transfers which qualify for the marital deduction and those which do not qualify have generated drafting complexities, artificial limitations upon dispositions, and considerable litigation.
> Under the [proposed] unified transfer tax there will be an exemption for the full amount of any property that passes to a spouse, either during the life of the transferor spouse or at his or her death. However, property received by the transferee spouse will, of course, become part of his or her taxable estate, unless consumed. U.S. Treas. Dept., Tax Reform Studies and Proposals, 91st Cong., 1st Sess., pt. 3, 358 (Comm. Print 1969).

§ 5.3.1. Quantitative Change: Unlimited Marital Deduction

The quantitative change was brought about by repealing § 2056(c) (which limited the amount of the estate tax deduction as noted above), § 2523(a)(2) (which limited the amount of the gift tax deduction), and § 2523(f) (which disallowed any gift tax deduction for gifts of community property). Accordingly, beginning in 1982, gift and estate tax marital deductions became allowable for the full value of property that passes to a spouse in a qualifying way. As a result of the repeals, the gift and estate tax marital deduction provisions no longer differentiate between community and noncommunity property. Deferral of the tax on the death of the first spouse to die is a very valuable option.

§ 5.3.2. Qualitative Changes: Additional Interests Qualify for Marital Deduction

Important qualitative changes were also made by the 1981 Act. Most important, the Act added §§ 2056(b)(7) and 2523(f), which allow elective marital deductions with respect to qualified terminable interest property (QTIP). See § 5.23. In brief, QTIP is property in which the donee spouse is given a "qualifying income interest for life." To constitute such a qualifying income interest the donee spouse must be entitled to all of the income from the property for life, payable annually or at more frequent intervals, and no person can have the power to appoint any of the property to any person other than the surviving spouse during his or her lifetime. §§ 2056(b)(7)(B)(ii), 2523(f)(2). In essence the changes allow a marital deduction for a simple life income interest, provided that no one can divert any of the property to another person during the surviving spouse's lifetime.

The lifetime and post-mortem planning opportunities created by the adoption of the QTIP changes were enhanced by the fact that the deductions are allowable on an elective basis with respect to qualifying income interests for life. In particular, the donor, or the decedent's executor, can elect whether to claim a marital deduction with respect to the property in which the donee spouse has a qualifying income interest for life. Importantly, such an election can be made with respect to all or a specific portion of the property. § 2056(b)(7)(B)(iv). The elective feature makes it possible to "fine tune" the amount of the estate tax marital deduction after the death of a spouse, when much more is known about the circumstances of the decedent's estate and of the surviving spouse. Of course, the portion of the property for which a deduction is claimed is includible in the donee spouse's estate under § 2044 unless the property is disposed of during his or her lifetime.

The 1981 Act also added provisions that allow gift and estate tax deductions for current interests in charitable remainder trusts that are transferred to a spouse. §§ 2056(b)(8), 2523(g). See § 5.24. Since the inception of the charitable remainder trust rules in 1969, gift and estate tax deductions have been allowed for the value of qualifying charitable remainder interests. See §§ 2055(e)(2), 2522(c)(2) and § 8.20. However, prior to 1982 no deductions were allowable with respect to the noncharitable current interest in such trusts. Given the shift to an unlimited marital deduction, Congress thought it was desirable to extend the deduction to this type of interest.

§ 5.4. THE FUTURE

The 2010 Act introduced the highest applicable exclusion amount ever ($5 million) but provides for a return to a $1 million applicable exclusion amount in 2013. It remains frustratingly uncertain whether Congress will further modify the applicable exclusion amount, the applicable tax rates, or both in the short term. Assuming some form of the estate tax remains on the books, it seems unlikely that the basic contours of the marital deduction would change in the near future. In particular, the unlimited marital deduction will probably remain in place. It is unlikely that the marital deduction provisions will be simplified anytime soon, but one helpful step toward simplification occurred in the early 1990s when a change in the estate tax return eliminated the necessity of checking a separate box in order to elect to claim a QTIP marital deduction. Now, if Schedule M includes property that meets the requirements of §2056(b)(7), the executor is deemed to have made the necessary election.

While some of the fine distinctions between deductible and nondeductible interests were relaxed by the 1981 Act, some of the remaining distinctions are hard to justify in terms of equity, administrative convenience, or other considerations of tax policy. The excessive technicalities of the law are particularly objectionable because of the hazards and substantial direct and indirect compliance costs they impose on taxpayers. The difficulties of complying with the technicalities are sometimes compounded by the "hidebound position taken by the Commissioner." *Estate of Smith v. Commissioner,* 565 F.2d 455, 458 (7th Cir. 1977). The principal direct costs are payments of additional fees to personal representatives and attorneys in connection with disputes spawned by the present law. The indirect costs to all taxpayers generated by the additional loads placed upon the IRS, the Department of Justice, and the courts are also substantial.

B. PLANNING FOR USE OF THE MARITAL DEDUCTION

> It is important to keep in mind the main objectives—always to chart a plan which keeps foremost the special needs and personalities and relationship of the interested parties. The practitioner does not deal with symbols *H* and *W* and estates of dollars in cash. He is concerned with particular individuals and their families and particular combinations of assets and liabilities. Much of the "buzzing, blooming confusion" about taking or not taking the marital deduction and how to do it may disappear if taxes are considered after, and not before, the main objectives are analyzed. What would the testator want to do apart from the marital deduction? How far is he led away from that by the tax law? J. Trachtman, Estate Planning 82 (rev. ed. 1968).

§5.5. Approaching the Planning Job

In formulating an estate plan, the lawyer and the client should give priority to sound planning for the welfare and security of the client and his or her family. A host of primarily nontax factors need to be considered in the process, including the age, health, ability, marital status, wealth, and feelings of the members of the client's family. For example, in some cases all of a client's estate will need to be made available to the surviving spouse for his or her support and in others it will not. The circumstances of the client and the client's family will also determine whether gifts to the surviving spouse are to be made outright or in trust and what choice of assets is made to fund the gifts. After the basic elements of a plan are agreed upon, the lawyer and client should give more direct attention to tax planning, including the use of the marital deduction, to conserve the family's property.

In order to make the necessary tax analysis, the lawyer needs to know the size and composition of the estates of both spouses and the objectives of their dispositive plans. Those factors influence to a great degree the extent to which overall tax benefits will result from the use of the marital deduction and from other dispositions of the client's property. Consideration must be given to the effect of a plan upon the amount of estate tax due upon the death of each spouse and various income tax matters, including the bases of assets. The availability of the credit for property previously taxed, § 2013, should also be taken into account.

EXAMPLE 5-2.

W's estate is worth $3 million and H's is worth less than $2 million. Under the existing law, H's unified credit is sufficient to shelter his estate from the imposition of any estate tax. Accordingly, no estate tax would be due upon H's death whether or not W survives. However, any property H leaves to W could be subject to a marginal estate tax rate of 49 45% when she dies. H's unified credit will be wasted to the extent his property passes to W in a way that will require it to be included in her estate. Of course, H and W may not be concerned about the size of the survivor's estate, particularly if all of their property will pass to charity upon the death of the survivor.

§ 5.5.1. Tax Estimates

The lawyer should provide a client with estimates of the state and federal tax consequences of the plans under consideration. Fortunately, many software programs can produce the necessary estimates, which can take into account varying assumptions about the growth in value of the spouses' estates. The planner should be sure that the estimates take into account the possibility that either spouse may die first or that they will die simultaneously. Doing so can provide a good check on the merits of a plan from the transfer tax perspective. While estimates are helpful for purposes of analysis, the lawyer and client need to remember that they are only *estimates*—informed guesses about exceedingly uncertain future events.

§ 5.5.2. Valuation of Property

Planners must also recognize that the same factors that justify discounting the value of an interest in property that passes to non-charitable beneficiaries other than a spouse may require discounting the value of a similar interest that passes to the donor's spouse or to a charity. The IRS is increasingly concerned that the value of minority or fractional interests that pass to a surviving spouse or to charity be appropriately discounted. In short, planning should be done in light of the discounts that may apply to the assets included in the client's estate *and* to the interests that pass to the surviving spouse.

The valuation of shares of stock that are included in a decedent's estate which carry with them control of the corporation will reflect a premium. *Estate of Dean Chenowith*, 88 T.C. 1577 (1987). However, the IRS may insist that a different, lower valuation apply to the distribution of a portion of the shares, which does not represent control, in satisfaction of a marital or charitable gift. For example, in LR 9403005 (TAM) the IRS placed a lower valuation on the portion of the decedent's shares that were distributed to a marital deduction trust. *See also* LR 905004 (TAM) (decedent's will divided his 100 percent interest in a closely held business between a trust for his son, 51 percent, and a trust for his widow, 49 percent) and § § 2.14 and 2.45. *See* Terry S. Jones, QTIP and Fractional Interest Discounts—Whipsaw Wonderland, 33 Idaho L. Rev. 595 (1997). The same problem exists with respect to interests in other business entities such as family limited partnerships and limited liability companies. *See* Oshins & Matz, Resolving the Mismatch of Estate Inclusion Value and Deduction Value, 35 Est. Plan, 14 (July, 2008).

The approach taken in *Estate of Dean Chenowith* was followed in *Estate of Frank M. DiSanto*, 78 T.C.M. 1220 (1999) (disclaimer by surviving spouse reduced to a minority interest the portion of a closely held business that would pass to a marital deduction trust for her benefit). In the *DiSanto* case the decedent's controlling interest was valued at $23.50 per share and the minority interest passing to the marital deduction trust was valued at $13 per share.

§ 5.6. GENERAL OBJECTIVES

Identifying and reviewing general objectives of marital deduction tax planning may be helpful in formulating and analyzing estate plans that involve use of marital deduction gifts. The tax objectives are, most commonly:

1. To equalize the sizes of the spouses' estates and to pay the least total amount of estate tax;
2. To defer the payment of any estate tax until the death of the surviving spouse; and
3. To insure that the estates of both spouses will take full advantage of the unified credit.

The objectives are not equally important and are not always entirely compatible. For example, equalizing the sizes of the spouses' estates may not minimize the amount of tax due on the death of the first spouse to die. The value of the objectives should also be kept in mind. They merely suggest general approaches that may reduce tax costs, but which must yield to the circumstances and desires of particular clients.

§ 5.7. EQUALIZING THE SPOUSES' ESTATES AND MINIMIZING OVERALL TAXES

The tax advantage that flows from equalizing the amount of property subject to tax in each spouse's estate used to be a product of the progressive tax rates in § 2001. A greater combined estate tax would be paid if one of the estates is subject to a higher marginal rate than the other. Under current law, however, the estate tax rate is a flat 35 percent, and it only applies once the taxable estate exceeds $5 million. As a result, the modern benefit of equalization is ensuring that each spouse fully utilizes the applicable exclusion amount. § 5.9. A progressive estate tax rate structure may return in 2013, when the 2001 Act and the 2010 Act sunset and the applicable exclusion amount returns to $1 million. Assuming no Congressional action before then, equalization will become more important, as estate tax rates will range from 41 percent to 55 percent. The availability of the unlimited gift and estate tax marital deductions allow the estates of a husband and wife to be equalized by making inter vivos *or* deathtime gifts.

§ 5.7.1. Equalization Clauses

The size of the gross estates of the spouses may be closely equalized as of the appropriate valuation date if the wealthier spouse dies first, leaving the surviving spouse an amount equal to the difference in value of their estates on the estate tax valuation date applicable to the decedent's estate. A proper simultaneous death clause can be combined with an equalization clause to provide the optimum tax result if the spouses die simultaneously. The necessary equalization can also be achieved through the use of a QTIP trust, which does not require an election to be made until the estate tax return is filed (*i.e.*, at least nine months after death). *See* § 5.23. Disclaimers can also be used to adjust the amount of property received by the surviving spouse, which presumably will be included in his or her estate. *See* § § 12.32-12.36.

The IRS first contended that the interest given the survivor under an equalization clause is a nondeductible terminable interest. However, the contention was rejected by the courts. *Estate of Charles W. Smith*, 66 T.C. 415, *nonacq.*, 1978-1 C.B. 3, *withdrawn and acq. substituted*, 1982-2 C.B. 1, *aff'd*, 565 F.2d 455 (1977); *Estate of Fritz L. Meeske*, 72 T.C. 73 (1979), *aff'd sub nom. Estate of Laurin v. Commissioner*, 645 F.2d 8 (6th Cir. 1981, consolidated appeal). The courts considered that the necessary interest unquestionably passed to the survivor and would be included in her gross estate. In their view only the value of the interest depended upon the subsequent valuation of assets. In early 1982 the IRS abandoned the contention and conceded that a marital deduction gift subject to an equalization clause was not a terminable interest. Rev. Rul. 82-23, 1982-1 C.B. 139.

The key clause of the will upheld in the *Smith* case read as follows:

(b) There shall then [after allocation of the Residual Portion] be allocated to the Marital Portion that percentage interest in the balance of the assets constituting the trust estate which shall when taken together with all other interests and property that qualify for the marital deduction and that pass or shall have passed to Settlor's said wife under other provisions of this trust or otherwise, obtain for Settlor's estate a marital deduction which would result in the lowest Federal estate taxes [on] Settlor's estate and Settlor's wife's estate, on the assumption Settlor's wife died after him, but on the date of his death and that her estate were valued as of the date on (and in the manner in) which Settlor's estate is valued for Federal estate tax purposes; Settlor's purpose is to equalize, insofar as possible, his estate and her estate for Federal estate tax purposes, based upon said assumptions. *Smith*, 66 T.C. at 418.

As noted above, the use of an equalization clause or a QTIP trust is particularly appropriate where both spouses are expected to die within a relatively short time period and estate taxes are imposed at progressive rates. The payment of estate tax in the estate of the first to die may support a substantial previously taxed property credit under § 2013 in the second estate, which is particularly valuable if the interest that passed to the transferee's estate is not includible in the transferee's estate (*e.g.*, a qualifying income interest for life in a QTIP trust). Note that the valuation of an interest that passes to a surviving spouse is subject to § 7520 and its corresponding regulations, but the valuation tables thereunder may not be used to value an interest if the surviving spouse is suffering from a terminal illness and is more likely than not to die within a year, or the couple die simultaneously. Reg. § 20.7520-3(b)(3)(i), (iii).

§ 5.7.2. Community Property Estates Are Already Equalized

The ownership of community property is naturally equalized by operation of state laws. Accordingly, in most cases the total estate tax burden on community property is minimized if little or no property passes to a surviving spouse in a way that will cause it to be included in the survivor's gross estate. However, many clients prefer to transfer enough of their community property to the surviving spouse to defer payment of any estate tax until the death of the survivor.

Under one of the most common plans, a client with a substantial community property estate leaves most of it to a QTIP trust (*i.e.*, one that meets the requirements of § 2056(b)(7), described in more detail in § 5.23). The interests given to the surviving spouse are not sufficient to cause the property to be included in his or her gross estate apart from the portion with respect to which the executor elects to claim the marital deduction. § 2044. Thus, the surviving spouse receives a life income interest in the trust. Importantly, the survivor may also be given: (1) the noncumulative right to draw down the greater of $5,000 or 5 percent of the value of the trust each year, § 2041(b)(2); (2) the power to invade the corpus of the trust limited by an ascertainable standard relating to the survivor's health, education, support, or maintenance, § 2041(b)(1)(A); and (3) a testamentary power to appoint the trust property to a limited class of persons, excluding herself, her creditors, her estate, and creditors of her estate, § 2041(b)(1).

Giving the surviving spouse a special power of appointment over disclaimed interests must be carefully planned. The reason is simple—unless the disclaimed interest will be included in the estate of the surviving spouse a disclaimer is not a qualified disclaimer under § 2518 if he or she retains a discretionary power over the disposition of the property. Reg. § 25.2518-2(e)(2).

In any case, a trustee other than the surviving spouse can be given the power to make discretionary distributions of corpus to the surviving spouse. Under this approach the executor can elect to claim a marital deduction for a portion of the property transferred to the trust according to the circumstances as they exist at the time the estate tax return is filed for the spouse who died first.

§5.8. MINIMIZE TAXES—DEFER PAYMENTS

The needs of a family of modest wealth may be served best by a plan that defers payment of any estate tax until the death of the surviving spouse. With the unlimited marital deduction, it is relatively easy to achieve that goal. However, such a deferral may unreasonably delay the time at which any of the property will be available to the client's children or other younger generation beneficiaries. In most cases the client will not want to "waste" the unified credit of the spouse first to die by giving all of his or her property outright to the surviving spouse. Of course, such a waste could be avoided to the extent the surviving spouse disclaims interests in the property. The goal may be more securely achieved, however, by using a QTIP trust or a marital deduction formula clause. In either case the plan preserves the maximum amount of property during the surviving spouse's lifetime. This approach can also be used to preserve, or create, fractional interest discounts in the deceased spouse's property. Also, by eliminating the need to pay any tax, the estate of the first spouse to die is relieved of the necessity to liquidate additional assets, which could require the recognition of capital gains.

If both spouses own a substantial amount of property, the total amount of transfer taxes ultimately payable by their estates may be increased by deferring the payment of any tax until the death of the surviving spouse. The tax might be greater on the surviving spouse's death because of an increase in the value of the assets or because of his or her accumulation of income. This risk is easily exaggerated—it is impossible to foresee the composition or value of the surviving spouse's estate or the rates or other provisions of the tax laws that will be in effect at the time of his or her death. In this connection recall that the substantial transfer tax changes made by the 1976, 1981, 1997, and 2001 Acts were largely unanticipated—even in the years they were adopted. Also, the amount and value of property includible in the surviving spouse's estate may be controlled by careful estate planning, including gifts, installment sales, the creation of family limited partnerships or limited liability companies, *see* Chapter 11, and other strategies. In this connection it should be noted that the unified credit allows a couple to pass $5 million free of estate, gift, and GST taxes (in 2011 and 2012).

EXAMPLE 5-3.

H died in 2011 leaving an estate of $6,000,000 to a trust in which *W* has a qualifying income interest for life. No tax will be due from *H*'s estate if his executor elects to claim a deduction with respect to $1,000,000 of the property passing to the trust (20 percent of the total trust). If *W* dies in 2012, when the applicable exclusion amount is $5 million, only 20 percent of the trust will be includible in her gross estate. Thus, if no property other than the trust is includible her estate, no estate tax will be due if the trust has a value of $25 million or less when she dies. In such a case *W*'s unified credit would be sufficient to offset the tax on her estate.

§ 5.9. TAKING ADVANTAGE OF THE UNIFIED CREDITS OF BOTH SPOUSES

In general a spouse should not provide in his or her will for a larger gift to the other spouse than is necessary to eliminate the testator's estate tax liability. That is, none of a client's unified credit should be wasted. Instead, the estate of each spouse should make maximum use of the "shelter" provided by his or her unified credit. Of course, this point generally concerns only married clients whose combined gross estates are likely to exceed the amount of the credit equivalent allowable to one person.

EXAMPLE 5-4.

H died in 2011 leaving an estate of $5 million to *W*, who owned about $3 million in property. No estate tax was due from *H*'s estate because of the unlimited marital deduction. However, the property is potentially includible in *W*'s estate. If the value of the property remains constant and *W* dies in 2012, a tax of $1,050,000 will be due from her estate if the $5 million received from H is included in her estate. No tax would have been due had *H* used his unified credit to shelter his property from taxation upon *W*'s death. For example, *H* might have left his entire estate to a QTIP trust with respect to which the shelter could have been preserved by an appropriate election by *H*'s executor.

As indicated by Example 5-4, the "shelter" provided by the unified credit may be preserved in a variety of ways. Some clients prefer to make a formula gift of an amount equal to the credit equivalent to a credit shelter trust, in which the surviving spouse may have an interest, or outright to beneficiaries other than the surviving spouse. By doing so the credit shelter amount will not be subject to inclusion in the surviving spouse's estate. Others prefer to leave substantially all of their property outright to their surviving spouses and to rely upon them to adjust the amount of the gifts through the use of disclaimers. Probably the most popular approach is based on a QTIP trust, in which the surviving spouse has a qualifying income interest for life. Its success, of course, depends upon the decedent's executor making an appropriate election under § 2056(b)(7).

If one spouse has a relatively large estate and the other spouse has an estate significantly smaller than the amount of the credit equivalent, the wealthier spouse may make inter vivos gifts to the poorer spouse in order to assure the use of the donee-spouse's full unified credit. For example, under one approach the wealthier spouse can make a gift to a trust for the benefit of the poorer spouse, for which the donor elects to take a QTIP marital deduction. As a result of the election the property of the trust will be included in the donee spouse's gross estate under § 2044. The final QTIP regulations and several letter rulings all allow the donor to retain a successive life income interest in the trust without causing the property to be included in his estate. *See* § 5.23.6. Under an alternative approach, the donor might transfer the property to a QTIP trust over which the donee spouse might be given a special power of appointment. If the donee spouse predeceases the donor, the donee could appoint the property to a QTIP trust for the benefit of the donor spouse. Presumably the property of the latter trust would be included in the estate of the donor spouse only to the extent the QTIP marital deduction was claimed by the donee's spouse's executor. However, in LR 9141027, the IRS ruled that the property of such a trust was includible in the gross estate of the donor spouse because of an implied agreement that the donee spouse would appoint the property to a trust for the benefit of the donor.

Note that the basis of property given by one spouse to the other is not increased under § 1014 if the donee spouse dies within one year of the original gift and leaves the property to the donor spouse. § 1014(e). The bar may not apply, however, if the donee spouse leaves the property to a trust for the benefit of the donor spouse. *See* § 3.35.5.

Portability Election. The 2010 Act made it easier for spouses to utilize the unified credits of both spouses through the so-called "portability" election. To the extent the first spouse to die does not utilize fully the $5 million applicable exemption amount, the first spouse's executor can, through a timely filed estate tax return, elect to allow the surviving spouse to use the remainder of the first spouse's applicable exclusion amount. To make this election, the timely filed estate tax return from the estate of the first spouse to die must compute the "deceased spousal unused exclusion amount" (DSUEA). The DSUEA is generally equal to the amount by which the basic exclusion amount of the surviving spouse's "last deceased spouse" at the time of such deceased spouse's death exceeded such deceased spouse's taxable estate. In no event, however, can the DSUEA exceed the basic exclusion amount in effect at the time of the surviving spouse's death. § 2010(c)(4). For 2011 and 2012, the basic exclusion amount is $5 million, although the 2012 amount may be adjusted upward for post-2011 inflation.

The surviving spouse can then add the DSUEA from the first spouse to die to his or her own basic exclusion amount. In Example 5-4, above, H did not use any of his $5 million basic exclusion amount, and a portability election by H's executor (likely W) would allow W to claim an applicable exclusion amount of $10 million (W's basic exclusion amount of $5 million plus the $5 million DSUEA from H's estate). *See* § 2.3.

At first blush, the portability election would appear to eliminate the need to create a credit shelter trust or to make inter vivos gifts between spouses in order to use each spouse's full applicable exclusion amount. But most estate planners continue to advise the use of credit shelter trusts, as they offer a number of comparative advantages over reliance on the portability election. First, the terms of a credit shelter trust can ensure that assets placed in the trust are not wasted by the surviving spouse, either through mismanagement or undue influence from a new lover. Second, assets placed in a credit shelter trust are usually beyond the reach of the surviving spouse's creditors, so the trust offers a degree of asset protection. Third, and perhaps most importantly, the balance of the credit shelter trust will not be included in the surviving spouse's gross estate for federal estate tax purposes, meaning that all appreciation in the value of the trust assets will not be subject to tax. If the assets are held outright by the surviving spouse, all of the appreciation would be included in the surviving spouse's gross estate and would be subject to estate tax. Finally, the credit shelter trust allows for full utilization of the first spouse to die's generational-skipping transfer tax exemption amount. *See* § 2.27. There is no "portability" election for the GSTT exemption, so if any unused GSTT exemption after the death of the first spouse is otherwise lost.

In addition, the surviving spouse's remarriage may put the DSUEA of the first spouse to die in jeopardy. The DSUEA is computed with reference to the unused applicable exclusion amount of one's "last deceased spouse." If a surviving spouse remarries a wealthier individual who also predeceases the surviving spouse, the DSUEA will likely be less because the wealthier spouse will likely use more of his or her applicable exclusion amount. That the wealthier deceased spouse's executor did not make a portability election apparently does not matter. See § 2.3. By using a credit shelter trust, planners and clients need not fret over whether the surviving spouse remarries another who is wealthier than the first spouse to die.

It is important to note that the portability election is scheduled to be repealed with the sunset of the 2010 Act. While most expect the election's availability to be extended or made permanent, planners at present cannot count on the ongoing viability of this election after 2012.

C. HOW TO QUALIFY FOR THE MARITAL DEDUCTION

§ 5.10. Estate Tax Marital Deduction; Basic Requirements

Five requirements must be met in order for a gift of an interest in property to qualify for the estate tax marital deduction. Listed in more or less ascending order of complexity and capacity for creating problems, they are as follows:

1. The decedent was a United States citizen or resident;
2. The interest in property is included in the decedent's gross estate;
3. The decedent is survived by a spouse who is a citizen of the United States;
4. The interest "passes" to the decedent's surviving spouse; and
5. The interest is a deductible one (*i.e.*, it is not a nondeductible terminable interest).

The first three requirements ordinarily do not pose any particularly difficult problems. However, if the surviving spouse is not a citizen of the United States, the marital deduction is only available for transfers to a qualified domestic trust (QDT). § 2056(d). *See* § 5.25. Sometimes disputes regarding the allowability of a marital deduction are generated by the fourth and more often the fifth requirements. In part the volume of litigation reflects the extent to which the IRS has insisted upon full compliance with some very technical provisions of the law.

The time within which a QDT or QTIP election must be made can be extended as provided in Reg. § 301.9100-1. *See* § 12.2.4.

§ 5.11. Gift Tax; Basic Requirements

Section 2523 imposes similar requirements in connection with the gift tax marital deduction. However, the 1988 Act amended § 2523(a) to eliminate the prior requirement that the donor spouse be a citizen or resident. As a result a marital deduction is available for a gift by a nonresident alien of property with a situs in the United States if the donee is a United States citizen. However, no marital deduction is allowable for a gift to a spouse who is not a United States-citizen. § 2523(i)(1). Instead, an annual exclusion of $100,000 is allowable. § 2523(i)(2). The exclusion, which was indexed for post-1997 inflation, increased to $112,000 effective January 1, 2003. Rev. Proc. 2002-70, 2002-2 C.B. 845. The annual exclusion is only available for a gift to a noncitizen spouse to the extent the gift constitutes a present interest under § 2503(b).

In order to qualify for the gift tax marital deduction the donor and the donee must be validly married at the time of the transfer. This places a premium on knowing when a gift is complete, particularly in cases that involve transfers of property pursuant to prenuptial agreements. The main differences between the gift and estate tax deductions are mentioned in the course of a detailed review of the estate tax provisions.

§ 5.12. DECEDENT WAS CITIZEN OR RESIDENT

The citizenship and residence of a client are usually clear and will not be the subject of controversy upon his or her death. The overall consequences of establishing citizenship and residence should be carefully considered when a client has ties to more than one country. In general, ambiguous relationships should be resolved one way or another before a problem arises—either by firmly establishing the relationship or by clearly severing it. The existing tax treaties do not completely eliminate the additional transfer taxes that may result if a client has ties to two or more countries. The ownership of assets in more than one jurisdiction could result in tax complications. The cautious use of trusts and corporations allows some multijurisdictional problems to be avoided. See § 10.12.

§ 5.13. INCLUSION IN GROSS ESTATE

The includibility of property in a decedent's gross estate is also usually clearly determined under other Code sections. Although an otherwise qualifying interest passes to the surviving spouse in a requisite way, no deduction is allowed unless the interest is included in the decedent's gross estate and is not otherwise deductible. For example, amounts for which a deduction is allowed under § 2053 for commissions paid to the surviving spouse as personal representative are not also deductible under § 2056. Reg. § 20.2056(a)-2(b)(2).

EXAMPLE 5-5.

W is the designated beneficiary of a policy of insurance on H's life, which is owned by W. The insurance proceeds received by W are deductible only to the extent they are included in H's gross estate. Of course, the proceeds would be includible in H's estate under § 2042(2) if he held any incident of ownership in the policy at the time of his death.

No estate tax deduction is allowed for property the decedent gave inter vivos to his or her spouse unless the property is included in the decedent's gross estate.

§ 5.14. SURVIVING SPOUSE

Neither the Code nor the Regulations define "surviving spouse." However, it is clear that the decedent and the transferee must be married at the time of the decedent's death. In that connection the IRS has ruled that "[t]he marital deduction is not allowed with respect to transferred property if the decedent was not married to the transferee at the time of death even though the decedent may have been married to the transferee at the time of the transfer." Rev. Rul. 79-354, 1979-2 C.B. 334 (gift made to spouse within three years of decedent's death, but donee predeceased donor). The same ruling allowed a marital deduction for a gift made within three years of the donor's death to a person other than the donor's surviving spouse where the donor and donee were married at the time of the donor's death.

For federal estate tax purposes the marital status of a decedent is determined under the law of the state of his or her domicile. *Estate of Goldwater v. Commissioner,* 539 F.2d 878 (2d Cir.), *cert. denied,* 429 U.S. 1023 (1976); *Estate of Spalding v. Commissioner,* 537 F.2d 666 (2d Cir. 1976); *Estate of Steffke v. Commissioner,* 538 F.2d 730 (7th Cir.), *cert. denied,* 429 U.S. 1022 (1976).

EXAMPLE 5-6.

H married *W* in 1986. *H* obtained a Mexican divorce from *W* in 1990. In 1991, *H* participated in a marriage ceremony with *R*. A court of the state in which *H* was domiciled later declared the Mexican divorce to be invalid. Thereafter *H* died, leaving his entire estate of $1 million to *R*. *W* claimed and received an elective share of $700,000 from *H*'s estate. The marital deduction is limited to the amount that passed to *W*, who was *H*'s surviving spouse under the applicable state law (*i.e.,* no marital deduction is allowable for the property left to *R*).

As the example indicates, questions of status are extremely important in resolving issues both of tax law and of substantive property law. Presumably the marital relation will be recognized for tax purposes although the spouses are living apart if their marriage has not been formally dissolved. The IRS has ruled that amounts that were paid to a person in settlement of a claim that she was the decedent's common law wife were not deductible. Although the decedent and the claimant lived together as husband and wife for 38 years, they were never married and the state in which they lived continuously did not recognize common law marriages. LR 200132004 (TAM).

If the order of death cannot be established by proof, a presumption as to survivorship provided by state law or the terms of a will or trust will be recognized. Reg. § 20.2056(c)-2(e). However, a presumption that a person who feloniously slays another has predeceased the victim for purposes of distributing the victim's property does not apply to the distribution of the estate of the slayer who committed suicide. LR 9815008. The reason is clear—the victim did not survive the slayer. Accordingly, there can be no resort to a presumption.

§ 5.15. Surviving Spouse Is United States Citizen or Property Passes to Qualified Domestic Trust (QDT)

A decedent's estate is not entitled to a marital deduction for property that passes to a surviving spouse who is not a United States citizen. However, there are two important exceptions to the general rule. First, under § 2056(d)(4) the marital deduction is allowable for an otherwise qualified gift to the surviving spouse if he or she becomes a United States citizen before the day on which the decedent's estate tax return is due and the surviving spouse was a United States resident at all times between the date of the decedent's death and the date the surviving spouse becomes a citizen. Second, a marital deduction is allowable with respect to property transferred to a qualified domestic trust (QDT or QDOT), if an election is made on the decedent's federal estate tax return. § 2056A. *See* § 5.25. A 1995 protocol amending the 1980 United States–Canada Tax Convention allows a marital credit with respect to the federal estate tax to citizens or residents of Canada.

The marital deduction is only allowable for a transfer to a trust created by the decedent if the trust is a QDT *and* meets the basic requirements of § 2056. The trust must be an estate trust, a life interest and general power of appointment trust, a QTIP trust, or a charitable remainder trust. *See* § § 2056(b)(5), 2056(b)(7), and 2056(b)(8). *See also* § § 5.22-5.25. To qualify as a QDT the trust instrument must require (1) at least one trustee of the trust be an individual citizen of the United States or a domestic corporation, and (2) that such trustee have the right to withhold the estate tax imposed by § 2056A from any distribution of principal. § 2056A(a)(1). Note that the marital deduction is allowable with respect to property that passes outright to a surviving spouse who is not a United States citizen, if he or she transfers the property to a trust that meets the requirements of a QDT described above. *See* § 20.2056A-2(b)(3); 20.2056A-4(c). In addition, the executor must elect to treat the trust as a QDT. § 2056A(a)(3). QDTs are discussed in more detail at § 5.25.

§ 5.16. Interest Must Pass to Surviving Spouse

A deduction is allowed only for interests that "pass" to the surviving spouse. The ways in which interests in property are considered to pass to a surviving spouse are listed in § 2056(c). They include interest passing by (1) bequest or devise; (2) inheritance; (3) dower or curtesy; (4) inter vivos transfer; (5) joint tenancy or right of survivorship; (6) the exercise or nonexercise of a power of appointment; and (7) policies of insurance on the decedent's life. Decedents frequently pass property to their surviving spouses in several of the ways listed in the statute.

§ 5.16.1. Spousal Elections

A controversy involving the passing requirement may arise if a surviving spouse elects against the decedent's will or, less commonly, when he or she receives (or surrenders) an interest in a decedent's estate in connection with a will contest. Any dower, statutory share, or other property a surviving spouse receives as a result of an election against the will is considered to pass from the decedent to him or her. LR 9246002 (TAM) (marital deduction allowed for commuted value of life estate in real estate that surviving spouse was entitled to receive under Indiana law as a result of her election to take against the decedent's will). However, any interest a surviving spouse is required to give up as a result of an election is not considered to pass from the decedent to him or her. Reg. § 20.2056(c)-2(c).

The value of the right of a surviving spouse to elect against the decedent's will and to receive a statutory share of the decedent's estate is not includible in the surviving spouse's gross estate if the surviving spouse dies without making the election. Rev. Rul. 74-492, 1974-2 C.B. 298. The cited ruling holds that the right is neither a property interest includible under § 2033 nor a general power of appointment includible under § 2041. Under it, "the election to take under the husband's will is treated as a disclaimer or renunciation of the alternative rights of the widow provided under state statute." *Id.* The tax consequences of a surviving spouse's election to claim (or not to claim) dower or an elective share are explored in some detail in § 12.32.

The marital deduction allowable with respect to the surviving spouse's elective share of a decedent's estate is reduced to the extent the share is liable for payment of a portion of the decedent's debts. *Estate of Doris Z. Tenenbaum,* 69 T.C.M. (CCH) 1787 (1995). The *Tenenbaum* case was reversed on the ground that state law imposed no such liability. 112 F.3d 251 (6th Cir. 1997). *See* § 9.25 for a general discussion of the so-called widow's election, including the extent to which property is subject to the election.

A distribution in satisfaction of an election against the will may carry out part or all of the estate's distributable net income to the distributee. *Brigham v. United States,* 160 F.3d 759 (1st Cir. 1998). The conclusion appears to be consistent with the separate share rule of § 663(c), *See* § 12.37.

A marital deduction is allowed for interests transferred to a surviving spouse although the surviving spouse was required to waive any right to challenge a will or trust or otherwise required to make an election in favor of accepting the interest. *See Estate of Charles Ray Tompkins,* 68 T.C. 912 (1977), *acq.,* 1982-1 C.B. 1; Rev. Rul. 82-184, 1982-2 C.B. 215; LRs 8727002, 9244020. In the cited cases, the surviving spouse had the right to accept the interest from the time of the decedent's death. Accordingly, the interest was not a terminable interest. *See also* § 5.23, p. 472.

§ 5.16.2. Will Contests

An interest is also considered to pass from the decedent to a surviving spouse if he or she receives it as a result of a bona fide recognition of enforceable rights in the estate. The necessary showing is ordinarily provided by a court decree upon the merits in an adversary proceeding following a genuine and active contest. Consistently, an interest in property is not considered to have passed to the surviving spouse to the extent he or she assigns or surrenders it in settlement of a controversy. *See* Reg. § 20.2056(c)-2(d)(2). In LR-9228004 (TAM) the IRS allowed a marital deduction for property that passed to the surviving spouse outright as a result of a family settlement and disclaimers. The ruling recognized the effectiveness under Texas law of disclaimers by decedent's children of the interests of their children.

The regulations, § 20.2056(c)-2(d)(1), (2), cited above, govern the allowance of the marital deduction with respect to property that passes to a spouse (and the denial of the deduction to the extent property passes to others) as a result of the settlement of a controversy. They apply literally only to controversies involving the decedent's will. However, two circuits have properly held that they apply more broadly to property passing as the result of the settlement of other controversies regarding the disposition of a decedent's property. *Citizens & Southern National Bank v. United States,* 451 F.2d 221 (5th Cir. 1971) (regulation applied to property settlement regarding disposition of intestate property); *United States Trust Co. v. Commissioner,* 321 F.2d 909 (2d Cir. 1963), *cert. denied,* 376 U.S. 937 (1964) (regulation applied to property passing pursuant to settlement although no will contest was involved). More recently, in *Schroeder v. United States,* 924 F.2d 1547 (10th Cir. 1991), the court held that the regulation only applied to will contests. Nonetheless, it held that the statutory passing requirement was not satisfied with respect to a settlement under which joint tenancy property that stood in the names of the decedent and the surviving spouse passed in settlement of a conflict with the decedent's surviving daughters to a trust for the benefit of the surviving spouse and the daughters. The approach taken in *Schroeder* unnecessarily restricts the scope of the regulation. Instead, in determining whether the passing requirement is satisfied, the regulation should be given an expansive reading and applied generally to the disposition of property pursuant to the settlement of any controversy regarding the disposition of property that is included in a decedent's estate. Similarly, a payment made to a charitable beneficiary in settlement of a bona fide dispute qualifies for an estate tax charitable deduction. Rev. Rul. 89-31, 1989-2 C.B. 277; LR 200128005.

§ 5.16.3. Surviving Spouse as Beneficial Owner

The regulations point out that the surviving spouse must receive the beneficial interest in the property in order to qualify for the deduction. Reg. § 20.2056(c)-2(a). Thus, no deduction is allowed for property transferred to the spouse as trustee for others. Along the same lines, the deduction is limited to the net value of the interests that pass to the spouse or to the marital deduction trust. § 2056(b)(4), *United States v. Stapf,* 375 U.S. 118 (1963); LR 8834005 (TAM). The regulations require the amount of death taxes, encumbrances, and any other obligations imposed by the decedent with respect to the passing of an interest to be deducted in computing the value of the interest received by the surviving spouse. This limitation on the amount of the deduction is discussed in *United States v. Stapf,* 375 U.S. 118 (1963). In *Stapf,* the Court properly concluded that a deduction was allowable only to the extent the value of the interests received by the decedent's widow exceeded the value of the interests she was required to transfer to others.

In LR 9113009, the IRS held that no marital deduction was allowable with respect to property passing from a decedent to the extent it could, in the event of default, be taken by a creditor in payment of loans that the decedent had guaranteed. The position taken by the IRS was sharply criticized. In LR 9409018, the IRS changed its position:

> Accordingly, in the present case, the mere presence of a loan guarantee as an encumbrance on assets passing from the taxpayer at death would not ordinarily cause the complete disallowance of the marital deduction that would otherwise be allowable for the bequest to the Estate Trust or the Marital Trust. This would be so whether the guaranteed loan had been

made to an entity owned by the taxpayer or had been made to some other borrower. Similarly, a payment made to a charitable beneficiary in settlement of a bona fide dispute qualifies for an estate tax charitable deduction. Rev. Rul. 89-31, 1989-2 C.B. 277; LR 200128005.

In LR 9546004, the IRS allowed a marital deduction with respect to a QTIP trust that was established for the benefit of the decedent's surviving spouse in settlement of a bona fide dispute between the surviving spouse and the decedent's children. The decedent's will made no provision for his surviving spouse, who petitioned the probate court to enforce the rights she had under state law to receive benefits from his estate.

A deduction was allowed in LR 9610018 with respect to property that passed to a surviving spouse in connection with the settlement of a bona fide dispute with the decedent's former spouse and children by his first marriage regarding their rights under the property settlement agreement entered into in connection with the decedent's divorce from her.

No deduction was allowed in *Estate of Carpenter v. Commissioner*, 52 F.3d 1266 (4th Cir. 1995), with respect to property left in trust by the decedent, which was equally divided by his daughter and surviving spouse pursuant to a settlement agreement. According to the court, "Property transferred pursuant to a settlement agreement—even a bona fide arm's length settlement agreement—will not qualify for the marital deduction if the surviving spouse did not, prior to the settlement, have an enforceable right under state law to an interest deductible under § 2056." The trust provided for in the decedent's will did not so qualify—under it the surviving spouse did not have a general power of appointment. The estate's belated argument that a deduction could have been claimed as QTIP property was not considered as it had not been raised before the Tax Court. Given the terms of the trust it is not entirely clear that the trust met the requirements of § 2056(b)(7).

No deduction was allowed in LR 9610004 (TAM) in which the decedent's will had been withheld from probate and his estate administered as if he had died intestate. According to the TAM the property, all of which was distributed to the surviving spouse, did not qualify for the marital deduction because it passed to her by virtue of the agreement between her and her children and not from the decedent.

Letter Ruling 9530003 denied a marital deduction for property that passed to the decedent's surviving spouse pursuant to a "settlement agreement" between his surviving spouse and children. The settlement took place prior to the surviving spouse's trial for the murder of her husband. Under the local law, persons convicted of second degree homicide, which was the charge against her, cannot receive any interest from the estate of the victim. The surviving spouse was convicted of second degree homicide. The IRS ruled that the settlement involved in this case was not the type that should be recognized for marital deduction purposes. Unlike the ordinary case, this settlement did not obviate the necessity of a court proceeding.

Nonresident Alien. The estate of a nonresident alien is only entitled to a marital deduction with respect to property that is included in the gross estate and passes to the surviving spouse. In *Estate of Hon Fing Fung*, 117 T.C. 247 (2001), *aff'd by unpub. op.*, 94 A.F.T.R.2d (RIA) 1228 (9th Cir. 2003), the decedent's will left his wife 3/8ths of his property, a large amount of which did not have a United States situs. The estate claimed a marital deduction with respect to all of the property located in the United

States on the ground that the surviving spouse had received all of it and had released her right to receive any other interest in the estate. The deduction was disallowed because the estate had not offered evidence of the value of the property located outside the United States.

§5.16.4. Family Awards and Allowances

The regulations recognize that a widow's allowance or other family award payable during the administration of an estate constitutes property that passes from a decedent to the recipient. However, as explained in §5.17, no deduction is permitted if the allowance is a nondeductible terminable interest. *See* Reg. §20.2056(b)-1(g)(8). For example, in *Jackson v. United States*, 376 U.S. 503 (1964), the Court concluded that the California widow's allowance was not a deductible interest because the widow "did not have an indefeasible interest in property at the moment of her husband's death since either her death or remarriage would defeat it." 376 U.S. at 507. Family allowances typically do not qualify for the deduction under the terminable interest rule. Note, Widow's Allowance and Marital Deductions—The Date-of-Death Rule, 63 Mich. L. Rev. 924 (1965). However, homestead allowances and awards in lieu of homestead that vest immediately at death and are not terminable do qualify for the marital deduction. *See, e.g.,* Rev. Rul. 72-153, 1972-1 C.B. 309 (Washington); Comment, Federal Estate and State Inheritance Tax Aspects of the Family Allowance, the Homestead and the In Lieu of Homestead Awards, 37 Wn. L. Rev. 435 (1962). In contrast, homestead awards that are terminable by abandonment are not deductible. *Estate of Henry H. Kyle,* 94 T.C. 829 (1990) (Texas).

The IRS has ruled that the Arizona homestead allowances of a cash sum and the exempt property allowance, which are based on the former version of U.P.C. §§2-401 and 2-402, both qualify for the marital deduction. Rev. Rul. 76-166, 1976-1 C.B. 287. Note that they qualify although the surviving spouse must survive the decedent by 120 hours and must elect to claim them. In contrast, the value of a family allowance made to a surviving spouse under U.P.C. §2-404 is a terminable interest that does not qualify for the deduction.

§5.16.5. Disclaimers

The use of disclaimers in post-mortem planning is reviewed in some detail at §§12.32-12.36. At this point it is sufficient to note that the amount passing to the surviving spouse may be increased or decreased by "qualified disclaimers." Under §§2046 and 2518, qualified disclaimers are recognized for purposes of the estate, gift, and GST taxes.

A "qualified disclaimer" is defined in §2518(b) as a written, unequivocal, and unqualified refusal to accept an interest in property (including a power with respect to property) that is received by the transferor of the interest or the transferor's legal representative not later than nine months after the day on which the transfer creating the interest was made. A disclaimer is not qualified if the disclaimant accepted the property or any benefits from it prior to making the disclaimer. As a result of the disclaimer, the interest must pass to the decedent's surviving spouse or a person other than the disclaimant. Also, the disclaimant cannot direct the transfer of the property to another person.

Qualified disclaimers can be used to prevent a surviving spouse from receiving "too much" property from the decedent's estate. In particular, disclaimers can adjust the amount of property that passes to the surviving spouse so the decedent's unified credit is not wasted and the surviving spouse's estate is not unnecessarily enlarged. They can also be used to increase the amount of property passing to the surviving spouse in ways that qualify for the marital deduction. Property that the surviving spouse receives as a result of qualified disclaimers is recognized as passing from the decedent to the surviving spouse. Reg. § 20.2056(d)-2(b).

§ 5.17. A Deductible Interest (i.e., Not a Nondeductible Terminable Interest)

[W]hile the terminable interest rule is, indeed, a thicket, the Congressional purpose of disqualifying terminable bequests was certainly not to elevate form above substance. It was, instead, to prevent the wholesale evasion of estate taxes which the skillful employment of terminable interests could have easily achieved. *Allen v. United States,* 359 F.2d 151, 153-154 (2d. Cir.), *cert. denied,* 385 U.S. 832 (1966).

The so-called terminable interest rule of § 2056(b) is intended to assure that property for which a marital deduction is allowed in the estate of the spouse first to die will be included in the gross estate of the surviving spouse, except to the extent the surviving spouse consumes or disposes of it during his or her lifetime. Accordingly, where the interest involved will be includible in the surviving spouse's estate, some courts have declared that "the Commissioner's dependence on any literal statutory language arguably contrary should not prevail, for in such an instance, form may not be elevated over substance." *Estate of Smith v. Commissioner,* 565 F.2d 455, 459 (7th Cir. 1977).

The basic terminable interest rule bars a deduction for an interest in property only where (1) the interest passing from the decedent to the surviving spouse is terminable (*i.e.,* it will terminate on the occurrence or nonoccurrence of an event or contingency), (2) the decedent also passed an interest in the same property to another person for less than adequate and full consideration in money or money's worth, *and* (3) the other person or his or her successors may possess or enjoy the property *after* the surviving spouse's interest terminates. § 2056(b)(1). The rule does not bar a deduction unless all three of the elements are present. Practically the same rule applies to inter vivos transfers. *See* § 2523(b).

Properly drafted formula marital deduction bequests and equalization clause bequests (*i.e.,* ones that give the surviving spouse interests in the deceased spouse's property sufficient to eliminate estate tax liability with respect to the deceased spouse's estate or equalize the sizes of their respective taxable estates) do not violate the terminable interest rule. In the case of the equalization clause, the interest that the surviving spouse receives is not terminable—its value is simply not determined until the survivor's estate is valued, just as the value of a formula gift is not determined until certain post-mortem valuations are made.

Obligation to Sell Assets at Discount. A deduction may not be allowed to the extent that the property passing to an otherwise qualifying marital deduction trust is subject to an option held by a person other than the surviving spouse to purchase the property at a bargain. In LR 9139001 (TAM), the IRS ruled that a trust did not meet the requirements of a QTIP where the decedent's son held an option to purchase the closely-held stock at its book value. *See* § 5.23. The IRS reasoned that the surviving spouse did not have a qualifying income interest for life because by exercising the option the decedent's son could, in effect, withdraw a portion of the trust for his benefit. In addition, according to the IRS, the surviving spouse did not have a qualifying income interest in any specific portion of the trust—as a result of which no marital deduction was allowable. Essentially the same issue also arose in LR 9147065 (TAM), in which the IRS denied the marital deduction to the extent of the closely-held stock that was subject to an option held by the decedent's children to purchase the stock at a bargain price. The IRS has ruled that the estate tax marital deduction is allowable for the value of closely held stock that passes to a QTIP trust even though the decedent's will directed that some of the decedent's closely held stock be offered for sale to an ESOP at a discounted price. FSA 200018020. "Upon review of the will and trust, it appears that the property that passed to W satisfies the requirements of section 2056(b)(7)(B)(ii) . . . .The discount sale to the ESOP does not disqualify the trust property for the marital deduction because the will directs that some of the stock be offered to the ESOP at a discount at the time of D's death, and the QTIP trust is funded after and subject to the discount sale."

§ 5.17.1. Terminable Interest

The first requirement of the terminable interest rule is satisfied only if the interest given the surviving spouse is a terminable interest. Under the regulations "[a] 'terminable interest' in property is an interest which will terminate or fail on the lapse of time or on the occurrence or failure to occur of some contingency. Life estates, terms for years, annuities, patents, and copyrights are therefore terminable interests." Reg. § 20.2056(b)-1(b). In contrast, "a bond note, or similar contractual obligation, the discharge of which would not have the effect of an annuity or a term for years, is not a terminable interest." *Id.*

EXAMPLE 5-7.

H devised Blackacre to W for life, remainder to his son, S. The life interest that H passed to W is a nondeductible terminable interest because it will terminate upon W's death and Blackacre will be owned by S or his successors, who did not pay fair and adequate consideration for the remainder interest. However, the life interest may constitute a qualifying income interest for life, for which H's executor might elect to treat as QTIP under § 2056(b)(7). *See* § 5.23.

A gift to a surviving spouse does not qualify for the marital deduction if it is subject to a requirement that the spouse "survive distribution" of the interest. *Estate of Bond*, 104 T.C. 652 (1995) (Washington law). However, a deduction was allowed in that case with respect to the decedent's real property (90 percent of his estate), which vested in the surviving spouse immediately upon the death of the decedent. Hence, it was "distributed" to her subject only to the payment of debts, when the decedent died. The court denied relief from the survivorship provision that the form of a Washington statute, Wash. Rev. Code §11.108.060, was intended to provide. Under the statute the survivorship provision of a governing instrument that contains a marital deduction gift is reduced to six months beginning with the decedent's death. Following *Estate of Heim v. Commissioner,* 914 F.2d 1322 (9th Cir. 1990), the Tax Court concluded that the statute did not operate to reform the decedent's will because "the will did not mention the marital deduction." *Id.* at 658. The reasoning of *Estate of Heim* and the present case is unnecessarily narrow—the obvious intent of the statute is to provide relief in cases such as the current one.

An outright gift of stock to one's spouse qualifies for the gift tax marital deduction although the stock is subject to a buy-sell agreement that gives the corporation and the donor a right of first refusal and certain other rights. LR 9606008. The gift is not a terminable interest because the donee's interest will not terminate or fail as he or she will receive full consideration if the option to purchase is exercised.

§5.17.2. Interest Passed to Another Person

The second requirement is met only if an interest in the same property passes for less than full and adequate consideration from the decedent to a person other than the surviving spouse. §2056(b)(1)(A). For the purposes of the terminable interest rule, "it is immaterial whether interests in the same property passed to the decedent's spouse and another person at the same time, or under the same instrument." Reg. §20.2056(b)-1(e)(1).

EXAMPLE 5-8.

H gave Blackacre to *S*, reserving the use of the property for a 20-year term. *H* died during the term and bequeathed his interest to his surviving spouse, *W*. The interest passed to *W* is a nondeductible terminable interest because *S*, who did not pay full and adequate consideration for his interest in Blackacre, will possess it after the term expires.

EXAMPLE 5-9.

H sold a remainder interest in Blackacre to his son, *S*, for full and adequate consideration, reserving a joint and survivor life estate to himself and his wife, *W*. If *W* survives *H*, the interest *W* received from *H* qualifies for the marital deduction. Although *W*'s interest is terminable and the property will be enjoyed by *S* or his successors upon her death, *S* paid full and adequate consideration for the interest he received from *H*.

EXAMPLE 5-10.

H bequeathed his entire interest in a patent to his wife, *W*. The interest given *W* will terminate upon the lapse of time. However, it is a deductible interest because no other person received any interest in the patent from *H*.

This requirement of the rule is not satisfied if the surviving spouse exercises the right to claim an absolute interest in the decedent's property, whether the elective right is conferred by the decedent's will or by state statute. In such cases the interest is not terminable and no interest in the property passes to any other person. *Estate of Neugass v. Commissioner*, 555 F.2d 322 (2d Cir. 1977) (will provision); Rev. Rul. 72-8, 1972-1 C.B. 309 (Florida award of absolute dower interests).

§ 5.17.3. Subsequent Enjoyment

The third requirement of the terminable interest rule is present only if the other person to whom an interest was transferred or that person's successors may possess or enjoy the property *after* the termination of the surviving spouse's interest. § 2056(b)(1)(B). Thus, a deduction may be allowed where the surviving spouse will possess or enjoy the property upon the termination of another interest.

EXAMPLE 5-11.

H devised Blackacre to *S* for life, remainder to his wife, *W*. *H*'s estate will be allowed a deduction for the value of the remainder interest determined in accordance with the applicable actuarial tables. The interest devised to *S* is terminable, but the interest transferred to *W* is not: No one is entitled to possess or enjoy the property *after W* as a result of *H*'s transfer.

§ 5.17.4. Executor Purchase Rule

Two subsidiary rules also restrict the allowability of a marital deduction. The first is the executor purchase rule, which prohibits a deduction for any terminable interest that "is to be acquired for the surviving spouse pursuant to the directions of the decedent, by his executor or by the trustee of a trust." § 2056(b)(1)(C). The regulations state that, "The marital deduction is not allowed even though no interest in the property subject to the terminable interest passes to another person and even though the interest would otherwise come within the exceptions described in § § 20.2056(b)-5 and 20.2056(b)-6 (relating to life estates and life insurance and annuity payments with powers of appointment)." Reg. § 20.2056(b)-1(f). Providentially, the regulation continues to provide that, "[A] general investment power, authorizing investments in both terminable interests and other property, is not a direction to invest in a terminable interest." *Id.* As indicated in the following example, the rule can be easily avoided. Given its lack of effectiveness, it is largely a trap for the unwary that should be repealed.

EXAMPLE 5-12.

H bequeathed $100,000 to his wife, *W*, subject to a direction that his executor use the funds to purchase an annuity for *W*. The bequest is a nondeductible interest. If *H* had purchased a joint and survivor annuity under which payments were to be made only to *W* after his death, the interest of *W* would be deductible. Reg. § 20.2056(b)-1(g), Example 3. There is utterly no policy justification for the difference in treatment. Note that the marital deduction would be allowed for an outright bequest to *W* that she used to purchase an annuity.

If the executor is directed to purchase a terminable interest for the surviving spouse, the last two requirements of the terminable interest rule are not satisfied. Nonetheless, because of the special rule of § 2056(b)(1)(C), no deduction is allowed.

§ 5.17.5. Unidentified Asset Rule

The other rule, often called the unidentified or "tainted" asset rule, is also intended to assure that interests for which a marital deduction is allowed will be included in the surviving spouse's gross estate. § 2056(b)(2). Under this rule a deduction is not allowed to the extent that an interest given the survivor may be satisfied with assets (or their proceeds) that are nondeductible. By way of illustration, an example in Reg. § 20.2056(b)-2(d) indicates that a bequest to a surviving spouse of one-third of the decedent's residuary estate does not qualify for the marital deduction to the extent the residuary estate includes nondeductible interests that might be assigned to the surviving spouse. A marital deduction gift can be insulated from challenge under this rule if the will or other governing instrument prohibits the fiduciary from satisfying the gift with nondeductible interests.

§ 5.17.6. Contractual Wills

As indicated in § 4.7, since the tax consequences of contractual wills are uncertain, they should be used with great caution. Accordingly, if it is important to obtain a marital deduction upon the death of the first spouse to die, the clients should adopt a plan that produces tried and true results. Because the outcome in a contractual will case depends upon the particular language used and the peculiarities of the local law, it is preferable to avoid using one. "The treatment of transfers under joint and mutual wills as gifts is an artifact of an unusual rule of common law in Illinois, and we suspect that neither the attorneys who draft these wills nor the couples who execute them understand their tax consequences." *Grimes v. Commissioner*, 851 F.2d 1005, 1010 (7th Cir. 1988). For an extensive treatment of joint and mutual wills, *see* Hess, The Federal Transfer Tax Consequences of Joint and Mutual Wills, 24 Real Prop., Prob. & Tr. J. 469 (1990).

The deductibility of an interest passing under a contractual will depends upon the nature of the interest passing to the surviving spouse and the terms of the contract. Under the pre-1982 law interests that passed to the surviving spouse under a contractual will frequently failed to qualify for the marital deduction because of the terminable interest rule. For example, in *Estate of Opal v. Commissioner*, 450 F.2d 1085

(2d Cir. 1971), no deduction was allowed for the interest that passed to the surviving spouse under a joint will because the interest was essentially a life estate with a power to consume. No marital deduction was allowed because the survivor did not have the requisite power to appoint to herself or to her estate. Of course, had the decedent died after 1981, presumably the decedent's executor could have elected to treat the property as QTIP and claimed a marital deduction under §2056(b)(7). *See* §5.23. Likewise, a marital deduction would be allowable in cases such as *Grimes* to the estate of the first spouse to die for at least a portion of the value of the life estate received by the surviving spouse. The amount of the deduction would be limited, however, to the extent the survivor was required to give up other property in exchange. *See* §2056(b)(4); *United States v. Stapf*, 375 U.S. 118 (1963). *See also* §9.33.

§5.18. EXCEPTIONS TO TERMINABLE INTEREST RULE

Several important exceptions to the terminable interest rule allow transfers to a surviving spouse to qualify for the marital deduction although all three elements of the rule are present. The exceptions apply to transfers under which:

    a. The interest of the surviving spouse will terminate if he or she dies within six months of the decedent or as a result of a common disaster, §2056(b)(3), §§5.19-5.20;

    b. The entire interest in the property will pass to the surviving spouse *or* to his or her estate (the so-called estate trust exception), §2056(b)(1) and Reg. §20.2056(e)-2(b), §5.21;

    c. The surviving spouse will receive all of the income from the property for life and will have a general power of appointment over it (the "life interest-general power of appointment" exception), §2056(b)(5), §5.22. Another subsection of the Code allows a deduction where the surviving spouse receives similar interests in the proceeds of insurance on the decedent's life, §2056(b)(6);

    d. The surviving spouse will receive all of the income from the property for life and no one, including the surviving spouse, has the power to appoint any part of the property to any person other than the surviving spouse during the surviving spouse's lifetime (*i.e.*, the property is *QTIP*). §2056(b)(7), §5.23; or

    e. The surviving spouse is the only noncharitable beneficiary of a charitable remainder annuity trust or a charitable remainder unitrust as defined in §664. §2056(b)(8), §5.24.

The exceptions permit much greater flexibility in providing for the surviving spouse than would otherwise be possible. The fourth of the listed exceptions, for QTIP, offers an appealing way of providing for the surviving spouse in a manner that allows a deduction for an elective amount. It is also appealing because the surviving spouse need not be given any control over the disposition of the property following his or her death. In any case, great care must be taken in planning and drafting marital deduction trusts to be sure that the exacting requirements of the Code and regulations are met. Much of the litigation related to the exceptions involves instruments that include either inappropriate boilerplate or otherwise appropriate provisions that have been altered in an uninformed way.

§ 5.19. LIMITED SURVIVORSHIP

Under § 2056(b)(3), a limited survivorship requirement may be imposed upon a transfer to a surviving spouse without jeopardizing the marital deduction. An interest will not be considered a terminable interest "if (1) the only condition under which it will terminate is the death of the surviving spouse within 6 months after the decedent's death, or her death as a result of a common disaster which also resulted in the decedent's death, and (2) the condition does not in fact occur." Reg. § 20.2056(b)-3(a).

The provision allows a married person to provide for an alternate disposition of property if his or her spouse survives for only a short period of time. If the spouse does not survive the specified period, the testator's will and not the will of the surviving spouse controls the disposition of the property. Such a provision can be used to avoid the additional costs that would be incurred if the same property were to pass through two successive estates. However, qualifying the surviving spouse's interest on surviving for at least six months may deprive the survivor's estate of the benefit of a substantial credit under § 2013 if it negates the creation of a trust in which the surviving spouse would have received a life interest. *See* Example 5-14, below.

EXAMPLE 5-13.

H died leaving a will that gave his residuary estate to *W* if she survived him by 6 months, otherwise to *X*. If *W* survives *H* by less than 6 months *H*'s estate will not be entitled to a marital deduction with respect to the residuary estate. However, if *W* survives *H* by 6 months, the contingent interest of *X* is extinguished and *W* is the only person to whom *H* transferred an interest in the property. In such a case, the residuary gift qualifies for the marital deduction under the exception provided for in § 2056(b)(3).

For the purposes of this rule the IRS has indicated that a month is measured from a given day in one calendar month to the corresponding numbered day in the next month. Rev. Rul. 70-400, 1970-2 C.B. 196. The ruling allowed a marital deduction for a gift to a surviving spouse which was conditioned upon survivorship for six months where the decedent died on January 1 and his widow died on July 2 (*i.e.*, the spouse survived the decedent by more than six months).

The exception also permits the use of a gift that will equalize the size of the spouses' taxable estates if they die within six months of each other. However, the objective of equalizing the sizes of the spouses' estates may be better achieved by giving the surviving spouse interests with respect to which a QTIP election can be made. Under § 2056(b)(7), the deceased spouse's executor is allowed to elect a marital deduction with respect to part or all of the interests on the estate tax return of the spouse who died first (*i.e.*, the election need not be made until nine months after his or her death). In effect, § 2056(b)(7) allows the estates to be equalized if the spouses die within nine months of each other. Of course, taking into account the credit for property previously taxed, § 2013, a considerable savings may result if the executor of the first of the spouses to die elects to pay some tax on the decedent's estate. A credit will be allowed in the surviving spouse's estate for the portion of the tax paid by the estate of the predeceased spouse with respect to the surviving spouse's life income interest although the life interest is not includible in the surviving spouse's gross estate. The credit available with respect to life income interests makes it particularly important that the interest of the surviving spouse is *not* conditioned on survivorship for any period.

EXAMPLE 5-14.

W died on June 1, 2006 leaving an estate of $3 million entirely to a trust for the benefit of H for life, remainder to their children. The trust met the requirements of § 2056(b)(7). H, who was a healthy 65-year-old at the time of W's death, survived her by only 3 months. H left his estate of $3 million to their children. W's executor may elect to claim a $1 million marital deduction with respect to the trust for H, as a result of which no federal estate tax would be payable by her estate. In that case, H's gross estate would be $4 million. Disregarding any deductions, H's estate would be subject to an estate tax of $920,000. On the other hand, if W's executor did not elect to claim the marital deduction with respect to any portion of the trust, a much better result would be achieved because of the previously taxed property credit of § 2013. In that event, W's estate would pay a tax of $450,000. However, assuming that a 6.0% rate applied under § 7520, H's life estate in the trust under W's will would have a value of .58291. Applying that factor to the net amount passing into the trust for H ($2,550,000), H's life estate would have a value of $1,486,421 (.58291 × $2,550,000). The estate tax credit allowed to H's estate for the tax paid by W's estate is determined by multiplying the amount of the tax ($450,000) by a fraction, the numerator of which is the value of the interest trans-ferred to H ($1,486,421) and the denominator of which is the net value of W's estate ($2,550,000)). The result is a credit of $262,310. The estate tax on H's estate is $450,000 against which a credit of $262,310 is allowable, requiring a payment of only $187,690. The total estate tax on both estates is $637,690. If the estates were equalized and no credit were allowable, each would pay $450,000 or a total of $900,000. As indicated above, if a marital deduction of $1 million were claimed in W's estate, H's estate would be subject to an estate tax of $920,000.

Some states have enacted statutes that are intended to reduce to six months the length of any administrative contingency that is annexed to a marital deduction gift. For example, the California statute provides as follows:

(a) If an instrument that makes a marital deduction gift includes a condition that the transferor's spouse survive the transferor by a period that exceeds or may exceed six months, other than a condition described in subsection (b), the condition shall be limited to six months as applied to the marital deduction gift. Cal. Prob. Code § 21525 (2011).

In *Estate of Heim v. Commissioner*, 914 F.2d 1322 (9th Cir. 1990), the court held that the California statute only applies to provisions that indicate the transferor's intention to make a marital deduction gift. The gift in *Heim*, which required that the decedent's wife "survive distribution," was not saved by the statute, since it was a simple outright gift that made no reference to the marital deduction. According to the court, the statute could not "operate to reform the survivorship requirement in decedent's will, since there is insufficient evidence that decedent intended the gift to qualify for a marital deduction." 914 F.2d at 1329. The decision is a harsh one. Instead, the court should have presumed the decedent intended an outright gift to his surviving spouse to qualify for the marital deduction.

§ 5.20. SIMULTANEOUS DEATH

In the event of the spouses' simultaneous deaths, the regulations provide that a presumption of survivorship provided by the local law, the decedent's will, or otherwise will be respected for marital deduction purposes.

> If the order of the deaths of the decedent and his spouse cannot be established by proof, a presumption (whether supplied by local law, the decedent's will, or otherwise) that the decedent was survived by his spouse will be recognized as satisfying paragraph (b)(1) of § 20.2056(a)-1, but only to the extent that it has the effect of giving to the spouse an interest in property includible in her gross estate under Part III of sub-chapter A of Chapter 11. Reg. § 20.2056(c)-2(e).

Under the basic rule of § 1 of the more popular (1940) version of the Uniform Simultaneous Death Act, if there is no sufficient evidence that persons have died otherwise than simultaneously and no contrary directions were given by the decedents, the property of each decedent is disposed of as if he or she survived the other.

EXAMPLE 5-15.

> *H* and *W* died under such circumstances that there was no sufficient evidence that they died other than simultaneously. In the absence of the contrary direction in the will of *H*, his property will be disposed of as if he survived *W*. Similarly, the property of *W* will be disposed of as if she survived *H*. As a result neither estate is entitled to a marital deduction. However, the IRS would respect a provision in the will of either spouse that the other spouse should be deemed to have survived the testator in the event of their simultaneous deaths.

A substantial tax savings can be achieved through the proper use of a clause that establishes a presumption of survivorship (*e.g.*, if the gross estate of one spouse is much larger than that of the other and the will of the wealthier spouse makes gifts to the poorer spouse that equalize the sizes of their taxable estates). Where the dispositive plans of a husband and wife are harmonious, the wealthier spouse should consider including a simultaneous death clause sufficient to equalize the sizes of their taxable estates in such event. The approved language for a survivorship provision is, "if she [he] shall survive me for a period of six months." *See* Rev. Rul. 70-400, 1970-2 C.B. 196.

In the case of simultaneous deaths it is unlikely that a credit will be allowed under § 2013 for the value of a life interest that was treated as having passed from one spouse to the other. For example, in *Estate of Andrew P. Carter,* 921 F.2d 63 (5th Cir. 1991), the court held that where the husband and wife died simultaneously the usufructuary interest of the one that was treated as the survivor under Louisiana law had no value. In doing so the court refused to apply the actuarial tables "to those situations in which the transferee and transferor of an indeterminate interest such as a usufruct die in a common disaster." The same result was reached in *Estate of Lion v. Commissioner,* 438 F.2d 56 (4th Cir.), *cert. denied,* 404 U.S. 870 (1971) *and Everard W. Marks, Jr.,* 94 T.C. 720 (1990). In *Marks,* which also involved Louisiana law, the Tax Court said that "it would be improper to ignore reality by placing (for tax purposes) a mythical value on the deemed surviving spouse's usufructuary interest." 94 T.C. at 729.

The regulations confirm this result. Under Reg. § 20.7520-3(b)(3)(iii) the actuarial tables, "may not be used to determine the present value of an annuity, income interest, remainder interest, or reversionary interest if the decedent, and the individual who is the measuring life, die as a result of a common accident or other occurrence." The regulations illustrate the application of this rule in the following example:

> *Example 2. Deaths resulting from common accidents, etc.* The decedent's will establishes a trust to pay income to the decedent's surviving spouse for life. The will provides that, upon the spouse's death or, if the spouse fails to survive the decedent, upon the decedent's death the trust property is to pass to the decedent's children. The decedent and the decedent's spouse die simultaneously in an accident under circumstances in which it was impossible to determine who survived the other. Even if the terms of the will and applicable state law presume that the decedent died first with the result that the property interest is considered to have passed in trust for the benefit of the surviving spouse for life, after which the remainder is to be distributed to the decedent's children, the spouse's life income interest may not be valued by the use of the mortality component described under section 7520. The result would be the same even if it was established that the spouse survived the decedent. Reg. § 20.7520-3(b)(4):

The U.P.C. and the 1991 version of the Uniform Act extend the concept of requiring survivorship for a limited period to provide that an heir, and in the absence of a contrary direction a devisee, will be deemed to have predeceased a decedent unless the heir or devisee survives the decedent by 120 hours or more. U.P.C. §§ 2-104, 2-702 (2011). The provisions of the Uniform Simultaneous Death Acts and the U.P.C. may be overridden by a contrary direction in an individual's will. Neither provision jeopardizes the allowance of a marital deduction for interests that pass to the decedent's spouse. Rev. Rul. 76-166, 1976-2 C.B. 287.

The marital deduction is not preserved under § 2056(b)(3) if the gift is contingent upon an event other than survivorship for a period of six months or less or death as the result of a common disaster. Specifically, no deduction is allowed if the gift is conditioned upon the occurrence or nonoccurrence of an administrative contingency such as admission of the decedent's will to probate or distribution of the decedent's estate.

> A decedent devised and bequeathed his residuary estate to his wife if she was living on the date of distribution of his estate. The devise and bequest is a nondeductible interest even though distribution took place within six months after the decedent's death and the surviving spouse in fact survived the date of distribution. Reg. § 20.2056(b)-3(d), Example 4.

A gift intended to qualify for the marital deduction should not require survivorship for more than six months or survivorship of the occurrence or nonoccurrence of an event.

§ 5.21. ESTATE TRUST

> Although the trustee may accumulate the income during the surviving spouse's lifetime and retain unproductive property, the bequest to the Trust nevertheless qualifies for the marital deduction because the principal and any accumulated income is to be paid to the estate of the surviving spouse upon her death. LR 9109003 (TAM).

A second and possibly unintended exception to the terminable interest rule allows a marital deduction for interests that pass entirely to the surviving spouse or to his or her estate. The basic terminable interest rule denies a marital deduction for an interest passing to a surviving spouse *only* if an interest in the same property also passed "from the decedent to any person other than such surviving spouse (or the estate of such spouse)." § 2056(b)(1). The parenthetical language has led to an interpretation of § 2056 that allows a marital deduction for the full value of an interest that passes from the decedent to the estate of a surviving spouse, although the survivor receives little, if any, lifetime benefit from the property.

> [T]here are two types of transfers that may qualify a limited interest passing to the surviving spouse, such as a life estate, for the marital deduction. The first, which is illustrated in examples (i), (ii), and (iii) of section 20.2056(e)-2(b)(1) of the regulations, is the estate trust, that is a trust that provides that the income is payable to the surviving spouse for a term of years, or for life, or is to be accumulated, with all of the undistributed trust property passing to the surviving spouse's executor or administrator at her death. In these cases the interest to the surviving spouse qualifies for the marital deduction for the reason that she does not get a nondeductible terminable interest. No one other than the surviving spouse or her estate takes any interest in the property passing from the decedent. Rev. Rul. 72-333, 1972-2 C.B. 530.

Thus, a deduction is allowed for interests transferred in trust although the lifetime benefits of the surviving spouse are limited, provided that the trust property is ultimately distributable to the surviving spouse's personal representative. The rule salvages the marital deduction where the trustee of a trust for a surviving spouse is given the discretionary power to accumulate the income of the trust or to retain unproductive assets. Rev. Rul. 68-554, 1968-2 C.B. 412.

In LR 9634020, the IRS held that a marital deduction was allowable for a residuary trust the decedent left for the benefit of his widow. The trust was to continue until the widow became 50 years of age, but in all events was required to last for ten years following the decedent's death. At the end of the term the trust would terminate and the property be distributed to the widow. The IRS concluded that the trust was an estate trust for which a marital deduction was allowable because, under state (Texas) law, the property of the trust would pass to her estate if she died prior to the termination of the trust.

The IRS disallowed the marital deduction for a trust the corpus of which was payable to the testamentary appointee of the surviving spouse, and in default of exercise thereof to his or her estate. Rev. Rul. 75-128, 1975-1 C.B. 308. According to the ruling the trust failed to qualify because the surviving spouse held a testamentary power of appointment over the property. Under Reg. § 20.2056(e)-3 the possible appointees of such a power are considered persons to whom the deceased spouse passed an interest in the property.

The operation of Rev. Rul. 75-128 might be avoided if the decedent's will were construed to pass the absolute interest in the trust property to the personal representative of the surviving spouse, subject to the general testamentary power (*i.e.,* if the power were considered to be a "power appendant"). In such event, the power should not be recognized at all. Where a person is given an absolute interest in property, any power also given to the same person is an invalid power appendant or a "lesser included interest," which may be disregarded. *See, e.g.,* V American Law of Property § 23.13 (1952); Restatement, Property § 325 (1940); Note, Appendant Powers of Appointment in the United States, 50 Harv. L. Rev. 1284 (1937). In any event, note that the deduction might be preserved in such a case if the surviving spouse disclaimed the power. There is no evident policy or revenue reason to support the unnecessarily technical position taken in Rev. Rul. 75-128.

Thus far the estate trust exception has functioned most often to "save" the marital deduction for trusts that do not qualify for the life estate-power of appointment exception because of deficient draftsmanship. *See, e.g.,* Rev. Rul. 72-333, 1972-2 C.B. 530. However, the estate trust can be very useful in some cases. As mentioned above, it allows a trustee to be directed to retain unproductive property, such as recreational real property or interests in a family business, without jeopardizing the allowance of the marital deduction. Rev. Rul. 68-554, 1968-2 C.B. 412. In contrast, no deduction is allowable where the trustee of a life interest power of appointment trust is directed to retain unproductive property, unless the surviving spouse could compel the trustee to make the property productive or to convert it within a reasonable time. Reg. § 20.2056(b)-5(f)(4) and (5).

An estate trust is also attractive because of the limitless range of provisions it allows to be made for the lifetime benefit of the surviving spouse. If the surviving spouse is expected to have a large income, some income tax savings may result from the creation of an estate trust that does not require the income to be distributed to the surviving spouse. The spouse could be adequately protected if the trustee were authorized to make discretionary distributions of income to him or her as needed to provide for care and support and to meet emergencies.

Under the earlier rules that applied to the in-kind distribution of appreciated property, the trustee of an estate trust could make distributions that resulted in a tax-free increase in the basis of property. The opportunity was eliminated by the enactment of § 643(e), under which the basis of property in the hands of a distributee is the estate's basis plus any gain recognized on the distribution at the election of the estate. Thus, an increase in the basis of the distributee is available only if the estate elects to recognize gain or loss upon all distributions made during the taxable year in the same manner as if the property had been sold to the distributees at fair market value.

For a variety of reasons the estate trust is not widely used. First, most lawyers are unaware of its existence. Second, some commentators are concerned about the validity and effect of a gift to the estate of a named person. *See* Fox, Estate: A Word to Be Used Cautiously, If at All, 81 Harv. L. Rev. 992 (1968); Huston, Transfers to the "Estate of a Named Person," 15 Syracuse L. Rev. 463 (1964); Browder, Trusts and the Doctrine of Estates, 72 Mich. L. Rev. 1507, 1517 (1975).

Third, and most important, the required distribution of the trust property to the surviving spouse's personal representative has some serious disadvantages. Most arise from the fact that the property will be subject to (1) claims creditors may have against the estate of the surviving spouse, (2) claims a subsequent spouse may have to an elective share under the law of common law property states should the surviving spouse remarry, (3) family awards, and (4) increased costs of estate settlement (particularly executor's commissions and attorney's fees). A distribution of property to the estate of the surviving spouse also involves some risk that the property will ultimately go to unintended takers (*e.g.,* the intestate successors of the surviving spouse). In addition, property distributed to the surviving spouse's estate may be subject to the state death tax although it might not be taxed under other circumstances (*e.g.,* if the surviving spouse held only a qualifying income interest for life and no power of appointment). Finally, a spouse may react negatively to a plan that does not assure him or her of all of the trust's income, but instead gives the trustee the discretionary power to make distributions.

§ 5.22.   LIFE INTEREST—GENERAL POWER OF APPOINTMENT TRUST, § 2056(b)(5)

Section 2056(b)(5) was unquestionably the most important exception to the terminable interest rule until the 1981 Act's addition of the exception for QTIP. *See* § 5.23. Under this exception a deduction is allowed for an interest that passes to a surviving spouse to the extent the surviving spouse is entitled for life to all of the income from it (or a determinable portion of it) and the surviving spouse also holds a general power of appointment over it (or a corresponding part of it). As stated in Reg. § 20.2056(b)-5(a), this exception applies only if all of the following five requirements are met:

1. The surviving spouse is entitled for life to all of the income from the entire interest, or a specific portion of the entire interest;

2. The income is payable to the surviving spouse annually or at more frequent intervals;

3. The surviving spouse is given the power to appoint the entire interest or the specific portion to himself or herself or to his or her estate;

4. The power in the surviving spouse is exercisable by him or her alone and (whether exercisable by will or during life) must be exercisable in all events; and

5. The entire interest or the specific portion is not subject to a power in any other person to appoint any part to any person other than the surviving spouse.

The exception is available whether the interests involved are legal or equitable (*i.e.*, in trust). As a matter of planning, however, the exception is used almost exclusively in connection with trusts. Under a comparable provision, a marital deduction is allowable for insurance proceeds from which installment (or interest) payments are made to the surviving spouse, who also has a general power to appoint all amounts that remain at the time of his or her death. § 2056(b)(6).

The use of this type of trust must be very carefully drafted. A failure to satisfy any one of the requirements completely will deprive the estate of the spouse first to die of the deduction, although the surviving spouse is given sufficient interests in the property to cause it to be included in his or her estate.

EXAMPLE 5-16.

H died leaving his residuary estate to a trust in which *W* had the requisite life income interest. Under the trust *W* held a power exercisable jointly with her son, *S*, to appoint the corpus of the trust to whomever she wished. The power is not exercisable by *W* alone and in all events. Accordingly, under the pre-1982 law *H*'s estate was not entitled to a marital deduction, but the corpus of the trust would be included in *W*'s gross estate under § 2041. If *S* made a qualified disclaimer of his power to join in appointing the corpus of the trust, presumably the marital deduction would be allowable. No deduction would be allowable under the post-1981 law unless the power to appoint to persons other than *W* during her lifetime was effectively disclaimed and *H*'s executor elected to treat the property as QTIP under § 2056(b)(7).

Note that a surviving spouse can convert a § 2056(b)(5) life estate-general power of appointment trust into a § 2056(b)(7) QTIP trust by disclaiming entirely the power of appointment. If that is done, the decedent's executor could make a partial election with respect to the trust.

In FSA 200119013, the IRS National Office advised that for purposes of valuation the stock owned by the decedent must be aggregated with stock held in a marital deduction trust over which she held a general power of appointment. As noted below, the FSA distinguishes this case from similar ones involving QTIP trusts over which the surviving spouse did not have a general power of appointment. This position was upheld by the Tax Court in *Estate of Aldo H. Fontana*, 118 T.C. No. 16 (2002).

§5.22.1. Right to Income

The requirement that the surviving spouse receive all of the income of a trust is met if the income is determined by a local law "that provides for a reasonable apportionment between the income and remainder beneficiaries of the total return of the trust and that meets the requirements of §1.643(b)-1." Reg. §§20.2056(b)-5(f), 25.2523(f)(1). The power to make such allocations will not be considered an impermissible power to appoint trust property to a person other than the surviving spouse. Reg. §20.2056(b)-7(d)(1).

Under the text of Reg. §1.643(b)-1:

> [A]n allocation of amounts between income and principal pursuant to applicable local law will be respected if local law provides for a reasonable apportionment between the income and remainder beneficiaries of the trust of the total return of the trust for the year, including ordinary and tax-exempt income, capital gains and appreciation. For example, a state statute providing that income is a unitrust amount of no less than 3% and no more than 5% of the fair market value of the trust assets, whether determined annually or averaged on a multiple year basis, is a reasonable apportionment of the total return of the trust. Similarly, a state statute that permits the trustee to make adjustments between income and principal to fulfill the trustee's duty of impartiality between the income and remainder beneficiaries is generally a reasonable apportionment of the total return of the trust.

The regulation continues to provide that, "A switch between methods of determining trust income authorized by state statute will not constitute a recognition event for purposes of section 1001 and will not result in a taxable gift from the trust's grantor or any of the trust's beneficiaries." In other cases, a switch may constitute a taxable event and may result in taxable gifts.

In LRs 9739015–9739018, the IRS held that the provisions of testamentary trusts which allocated, between principal and income, the payments that would be made under the terms of a partnership buy-sell agreement satisfied the requirements of either §2056(b)(5) or (b)(7).

§5.22.2. Specific Portion

If the right to income or the power of appointment or both is limited to a specific portion of the property passing from the decedent, the marital deduction is allowable only to the extent of the specific portion. Reg. §20.2056(b)-5(b). *Northeastern Pennsylvania National Bank & Trust Co. v. United States*, 387 U.S. 213 (1967), held that a specified amount of income payable annually or more frequently out of the property and its income that is not limited by the income of the property constitutes a specific portion.

However, §2056 was amended in 1992 to provide that "For purposes of paragraphs (5), (6) and (7)(b)(iv), the term 'specific portion' only includes a portion determined on a fractional or percentage basis." §2056(b)(10). A similar addition was made to §2523(e). The amendment reverses *Estate of C. S. Alexander*, 82 T.C. 39 (1984), *aff'd in unpub. opinion* (4th Cir. 1985), which allowed the marital deduction under §2056(b)(5) where the surviving spouse's power of appointment was limited to a specific dollar amount. Because of the possibility that all future appreciation in the value of the trust would be eliminated from the estate of the surviving spouse in such a case, the IRS refused to follow *Alexander.* The IRS position is made clear in Reg. §20.2056(b)-5(c)(2). Under it, no deduction is allowable under section 2056(b)(5) except to the extent the surviving spouse has the required interests in a fractional or percentile share of the property.

EXAMPLE 5-17.

> *W* left her residuary estate to a trust for *H.* Under the terms of the trust *H* was entitled to all of the income and held a testamentary general power of appointment over "one-half" of the property of the trust. For purposes of §2056(b)(5) the marital deduction would be limited to one-half of the value of the property transferred to the trust. In this connection note that if a QTIP election were made, the marital deduction would be allowable for the entire value of the trust under §2056(b)(7). If it disclaimed the power of appointment, a marital deduction would be allowable under §2056(b)(7) for the entire value of the trust.

The marital deduction is not allowed to the extent the property might be applied by a fiduciary in satisfaction of debts, taxes, or other expenses even though none of it is actually used for those purposes. *Estate of Wycoff v. Commissioner,* 506 F.2d 1144 (10th Cir. 1974), *cert. denied,* 421 U.S. 1000 (1975); Rev. Rul. 79-14, 1979-1 C.B. 309. For that reason, the governing instrument usually prohibits charging any taxes or expenses against the marital deduction gift.

The IRS has ruled that no deduction was allowable with respect to an otherwise qualifying marital deduction trust whose income was to be used to accumulate $10,000 within two years of the decedent's death to provide for the education of his grandchildren. Rev. Rul. 77-444, 1977-2 C.B. 341. "Unlike *Northeastern Pennsylvania National Bank* and [*Gelb v. Commissioner,* 298 F.2d 544 (2d Cir. 1962)], it is not possible in the instant case to determine any 'specific portion' as to which the income right of the surviving spouse relates." *Id.*

In some cases it may be advantageous and economical for a client to establish a single trust (a so-called "one lung" trust), a specific portion of which qualifies for the marital deduction under §2056(b)(5) and the remainder of which does not. Of course, this result is routinely reached by creating a QTIP trust with respect to which the decedent's executor elects to claim a partial marital deduction with only a bookkeeping segregation of the marital and nonmarital shares. If only one trust is created, savings in trustee's fees and administrative costs may result and greater diversification of investments may be possible. However, care must be exercised in funding the trust and allocating interests in it. Specifically, the surviving spouse's share should not include interests that do not qualify for the marital deduction.

§5.22.3. Frequency of Payment of Income

A trust instrument should ordinarily require income to be paid to the surviving spouse more often than annually for the convenience and protection of the beneficiary as well as to qualify for the marital deduction. For example, a trust might provide that "the trustee shall pay the net income of the trust to my surviving spouse in quarterly or more frequent installments." The marital deduction may be available although an instrument does not include any express direction regarding frequency of payment of the income to the surviving spouse. Under the regulations, "silence of a trust instrument as to the frequency of payment will not be regarded as a failure to satisfy the condition . . . that income must be payable to the surviving spouse annually or more frequently unless the applicable law permits payment to be made less frequently than annually." Reg. §20.2056(b)-5(e). The statutory requirements are satisfied if the surviving spouse is given "substantially that degree of beneficial enjoyment of the trust property during her life which the principles of the law of trusts accord to a person who is unqualifiedly designated as the life beneficiary of a trust." Reg. §20.2056(b)-5(f)(1). In some states the requirement is met by a statute that requires the income of a trust for a surviving spouse to be paid at least annually.

A marital deduction was allowed in LR 9511002 (TAM), although the trust provided that if the surviving spouse became incapacitated the trustee was required to distribute only so much of the income and principal as was necessary or advisable for the surviving spouse's health, support, and maintenance. The deduction was "saved" in this case because the surviving spouse also had the unrestricted power to amend or revoke the trust, which was not restricted should the survivor become incapacitated. In this confused instance the power served double duty under §2056(b)(5)—it assured the surviving spouse of the right to receive the income of the trust and satisfied the requirement that the survivor have a general power of appointment.

In LR 9514002 (TAM), the IRS held that the trust satisfied the requirement that the surviving spouse receive all of the income payable at least annually because the trust allowed the surviving spouse to request distribution of so much of the income as she wished to receive. Although the trust did not specifically provide that the power might be exercised for her during any period she might be incapacitated, a guardian would be able to exercise the power for her under the local (Arizona) law.

Delay in Payment. In general, the regulations require the income to be distributed currently. Reg. §20.2056(b)-5(f)(8). An interest will not satisfy this requirement to the extent that the income must be or may be accumulated. Reg. §20.2056(b)-5(f)(7). Thus, no deduction is allowed with respect to a testamentary trust that provides that, after the net income from the trust for the past year has been determined, "such income shall be quarterly paid to my wife as long as she may live . . . ." Rev. Rul. 72-283, 1972-1 C.B. 311. A deduction will not be denied, however, "merely because the spouse is not entitled to the income from the estate assets for the period before distribution of those assets by the executor, unless the executor is . . . authorized or directed to delay distribution beyond the period reasonably required for administration of the decedent's estate." Reg. §20.2056(b)-5(f)(9). Consistent with that regulation, a deduction was allowed for interests in a trust to be funded upon the settlor's death with assets from an inter vivos trust, where the trust instrument delayed funding the trust for a reasonable time until after the payment of all probate expenses and death taxes. Rev. Rul. 77-346, 1977-2 C.B. 340. In such cases, the delay in payment of the income is taken into account in valuing the interest passing to the surviving spouse. Reg. § 20.2056(b)-4(a).

Income Distribution Must be Mandatory and Not Terminable. The surviving spouse's right to income cannot be directly limited by the trustee's discretion or otherwise. However, a trustee may be given some indirect control through the exercise of administrative powers, such as ones concerning the allocation of receipts and disbursements between principal and income. Reg. § 20.2056(b)-5(f)(3). The determination of whether a particular trust meets the statutory requirement is based upon an overall consideration of the terms of the trust. A facility of payment clause that allows the trustee to pay the income to the surviving spouse or to apply it for his or her benefit is permissible. In contrast, no marital deduction is allowed if the distribution of income to the surviving spouse is discretionary in the event the survivor becomes incompetent. *See, e.g., Estate of Frank E. Tingley,* 22 T.C. 402 (1954), *aff'd sub nom. Starrett v. Commissioner,* 223 F.2d 163 (1st Cir. 1955). Similarly, no deduction is allowed if the amount of income payable to the surviving spouse may be reduced. Thus, no deduction was allowed where the surviving spouse was entitled to all of the income except such amounts as the trustee considered to be necessary to maintain the decedent's parents in their customary standard of living. Rev. Rul. 79-86, 1979-1 C.B. 311. In such a case the surviving spouse does not have an unqualified right to receive all of the income from any specified portion of the trust—an undetermined amount of the income could be diverted from the surviving spouse to the decedent's parents.

A marital deduction is not allowed if the distribution of income to the survivor will terminate or become discretionary upon the occurrence of some event such as the remarriage of the surviving spouse, his or her bankruptcy, or the attempted alienation of the beneficiary's interest in the trust. However, the deduction is not threatened merely because the instrument contains an orthodox spendthrift clause (*e.g.,* "that the right of the surviving spouse to the income shall not be subject to assignment, alienation, pledge, attachment or claims of creditors." Reg. § 20.2056(b)-5(f)(7)).

Exercise Caution in Authorizing Retention of Unproductive Assets. Care should also be exercised in drafting provisions that direct or authorize the trustee to retain the assets transferred in trust. As previously indicated, such a provision may jeopardize the deduction to the extent of the unproductive assets. *See* Reg. § 20.2056(b)-5(f)(4), (5). The deduction is allowable, however, if the instrument or the local law gives the surviving spouse power to require the trustee to "make the property productive or convert it within a reasonable time." Reg. § 20.2056(b)-5(f)(4). The deduction is not jeopardized by a provision that permits the retention of "a residence or other property for the personal use of the spouse." Reg. § 20.2056(b)-5(f)(4).

Give Spouse Power over Undistributed Income. The income that is accrued but undistributed at the time of the surviving spouse's death (the so-called "stub" income) must be subject to disposition by the surviving spouse. Reg. § 20.2056(b)-5(f)(8). That requirement is satisfied if the stub income is either distributable as the surviving spouse appoints or as an asset of the surviving spouse's estate. Again, some states have enacted statutes that give the surviving spouse a power of appointment over stub income unless otherwise provided in the trust instrument.

Under the regulations the surviving spouse need not have a right to receive or dispose of the stub income of a QTIP trust. Reg. § 20.2056(b)-7(d)(4). The position was upheld in *Estate of Howard v. Commissioner*, 910 F.2d 633 (9th Cir. 1990), *rev'g*, 91 T.C. 329 (1988). However, the Tax Court persists in holding that a trust is not QTIP unless the surviving spouse is entitled to all of the stub income. *Estate of Lucille P. Shelfer*, 103 T.C. 10 (1994), *rev'd*, 86 F.3d 1045 (11th Cir. 1996). The Federal Claims Court agrees that the surviving spouse need not receive or have the power to control the disposition of stub income in order to be treated as QTIP property. *Estate of Talman v. United States*, 97-1 U.S.T.C. ¶ 60,270 (Ct. Cl. 1997).

Under Reg. § 20.2044-1(d)(2), the surviving spouse's estate must include any undistributed income of the QTIP property. It provides, in part, that "the undistributed income is included in the decedent-spouse's gross estate under this section to the extent that the income is not so included under any other section of the Internal Revenue Code." *See* § 5.23.2.

Form 5-1
Payment of Income to Surviving Spouse (§ 2056(b)(5) Trust)

> The entire net income of the trust shall be paid in quarterly or more frequent installments to my [wife/husband]. Any income that is received or accrued in the period between the date of the last distribution to my [wife/husband] and the date of [her/his] death shall be paid to the personal representative of [her/his] estate [shall be distributed as my wife/husband shall appoint]. My [wife/husband] may require the trustee to make productive any unproductive property of the trust or to convert it to productive property.

§ 5.22.4. Power of Appointment

The surviving spouse must have a power of appointment exercisable alone (without the required joinder of any other person) and in all events (not contingent upon any event), "in favor of such surviving spouse, or of the estate of such surviving spouse, or in favor of either, whether or not in each case the power is exercisable in favor of others." *See* § 2056(b)(5); § 2523(e). A power will satisfy the requirement if it is exercisable during the lifetime of the surviving spouse (*e.g.*, an unlimited power to invade), by will, or by a combination of inter vivos and testamentary powers. The regulations recognize that the requirement may be satisfied by a combined power:

> [T]he surviving spouse may, until she attains the age of 50 years, have a power to appoint to herself and thereafter have a power to appoint to her estate. However, the condition that the spouse's power must be exercisable in all events is not satisfied unless irrespective of when the surviving spouse may die the entire interest or a specific portion of it will at the time of her death be subject to one power or the other (subject to the exception

in §20.2056(b)-3, relating to interests contingent on survival for a limited period). Reg. §20.2056(b)-5(g)(1)(iii).

A surviving spouse can convert a §2056(b)(5) life estate-general power of appointment trust into a QTIP trust by disclaiming the power of appointment. *See* §12.36.

In LR 200244002 (TAM), the IRS held that the duty of consistency required inclusion in the surviving spouse's estate of a trust over which she held a lifetime general power of appointment for which a marital deduction had been claimed in her husband's estate under §2056(b)(5). Likewise, in LR 200407018 (TAM), the IRS applied the duty of consistency to require inclusion of a painting in the surviving spouse's gross estate even though the painting should not have passed to the surviving spouse under the §2056(b)(5) trust established by the first decedent's will. Because the first decedent's estate claimed a deduction for the value of the painting on the premise that the surviving spouse held a general power of appointment over the painting, the surviving spouse's estate necessarily included the value of the painting at the surviving spouse's death.

The duty of consistency will not be applied when the inconsistency arises as a matter of law instead of a mistake of fact. In *Estate of Rose B. Posner*, 87 T.C.M. (CCH) 1288 (2004), the will of the decedent's husband created a marital trust for the decedent's benefit, and his estate claimed a marital deduction for the value of the property that passed to the trust. At the decedent's death, the estate included the value of the property in the marital trust, operating under the assumption that the spouse held a general power of appointment over the trust property. Later, the estate sued for refund, arguing that the spouse held no such power at all. The IRS fought the claim for refund, arguing that the duty of consistency required the estate to include the value of the property. The Tax Court observed that the duty does not apply "when the error is one of law arising out of a definite factual situation." Here, the inconsistency arose because of a mutual mistake between the husband's estate and the IRS as to the dispositive provisions of his will. They both determined— erroneously—that the husband's estate qualified for the marital deduction because the will gave the decedent a general power of appointment. There was thus no duty on the part of the decedent's estate to include the value of the trust property in the decedent's gross estate.

Form 5-2
Surviving Spouse's General Testamentary Power of Appointment
(§2056(b)(5) Trust)

My [wife/husband] shall have the power by [her/his] last will to appoint all of the property of the trust, including all income then accrued but not yet received and all income received but not yet distributed, to or for the benefit of such persons, including [her/his] estate and creditors of [her/his] estate, upon such terms and conditions as [she/he] chooses, either outright or upon further trust. An exercise of this power shall only be effective if it refers specifically to the power created under this instrument and expressly states my [wife's/husband's] intention to exercise it. To the extent the power is not validly exercised, the property of the trust shall be distributed to . . . .

Surviving Spouse May Hold Additional Powers of Appointment. If the surviving spouse has a power of the type required by the statute, it is immaterial that the survivor also holds other powers over the interest, such as a noncumulative power like that described in §§ 2041(b)(2) and 2514(e) to draw down the larger of $5,000 or 5 percent of the corpus each year (a "5 or 5" power). In addition, the trustee may hold powers to distribute trust principal to the surviving spouse. Additional powers should be planned with care, particularly if the trustee is also a beneficiary of the trust, whose interests may be affected by the exercise of the powers.

A 5 or 5 power to withdraw property from the trust provides the survivor with some additional independence and protection. A noncumulative 5 or 5 power given to a surviving spouse constitutes a power sufficient to support a marital deduction equal to the greater of 5 percent of the corpus of the trust or $5,000 even though the survivor is not given any other power of appointment over the trust corpus. *Estate of Jean C. Hollingshead*, 70 T.C. 578 (1978). Although the surviving spouse was entitled to all of the income of the trust for life, the deduction was limited to the amount subject to appointment under the 5 or 5 power at the time of the decedent's death because "any excess over 5 percent is not 'exercisable . . . in all events.'" 70 T.C. at 580. No marital deduction is allowable where the surviving spouse holds a 5 or 5 power and no income interest. LR 8202023.

A presently exercisable 5 or 5 power of withdrawal allows the surviving spouse to reduce the amount of property includible in his or her gross estate by withdrawing property and making annual gifts within the annual gift tax exclusion. Although all of the trust property may be included in the surviving spouse's estate in any case, the testator may wish to limit the survivor's right of withdrawal in order to assure the preservation of the trust principal and the continued source of support for the survivor. As the entire ordinary income of the trust will be taxed to the surviving spouse, the existence of a limited power of withdrawal will not be disadvantageous for income tax purposes. *See* § 678. The income tax flexibility of the trust is reduced if the surviving spouse is given an unlimited inter vivos general power of appointment. In that event the capital gains of the trust will also be taxed to him or her. *See* § 678(a)(1).

In the ordinary case, the surviving spouse is given a general testamentary power of appointment over the entire trust. Accordingly, giving the surviving spouse a 5 or 5 power does not increase the amount of the trust that is includible in his or her estate. Consistently, the existence of the power does not increase the amount of the previously taxed property credit under § 2013.

Mental Competency to Exercise Power Not Required. The mental incapacity of the surviving spouse under state law to exercise the power of appointment does not affect the allowance of the deduction under § 2056(b)(5). If the trust otherwise qualifies, "the fact that the spouse is presently incapable of exercising a power of appointment over the interest by virtue of State law regarding legal incapacity does not require disallowance of the deduction." Rev. Rul. 75-350, 1975-2 C.B. 366 (testamentary power). *See* Rev. Rul. 55-518, 1955-2 C.B. 384 (inter vivos power). The former ruling is based upon a determination that the phrase "in all events does not refer to those events that State law has determined to be sufficient to deprive a person of control of his or her property during a period of physical or mental incompetency. Otherwise, in view of the fact that any given person may become legally incompetent during his or her lifetime, no trust could ever qualify under §2056(b)(5)." 1975-2 C.B. at 368. However, if the existence of the power is restricted by the terms of the instrument, the trust would not satisfy the requirements of §2056(b)(5).

In *Fish v. United States*, 432 F.2d 1278, 1280 (1970), the Court of Appeals for the Ninth Circuit held "the matter of the decedent's competency to be immaterial." *See also Estate of Alperstein v. Commissioner*, 613 F.2d 1213 (2d Cir. 1979), *cert. denied sub. nom. Greenberg v. Commissioner*, 446 U.S. 918 (1980); *Estate of Bagley v. United States*, 443 F.2d 1266 (5th Cir. 1971); *Estate of Gilchrist v. Commissioner*, 630 F.2d 340 (5th Cir. 1980); *Pennsylvania Bank & Trust Co. v. United States*, 597 F.2d 382 (3d Cir.), *cert. denied*, 444 U.S. 980 (1979). The same conclusion has been reached in cases concerning the inclusion of property in the estate of a minor under §2041. *Estate of Rosenblatt v. Commissioner*, 633 F.2d 176 (10th Cir. 1980); Rev. Rul. 75-351, 1975-2 C.B. 368 (property includible in estate of minor who held general testamentary power of appointment even though the minor could not execute a will under local law).

§5.23. Qualified Terminable Interest Property (QTIP), §2056(b)(7)

As noted above in §5.3, the 1981 Act also created new gift and estate tax exceptions to the terminable interest rule for property in which the transferor's spouse is given a qualifying income interest for life. §§2056(b)(7), 2523(f). In simple terms this exception allows a decedent's executor to elect to claim a marital deduction for part or all of the value of property in which the transferee spouse is given a qualifying income interest for life. The deduction is allowable only if all of the income is payable to the surviving spouse annually or more frequently for life and no one has the power to appoint any of the property to a person other than the surviving spouse during his or her lifetime. A simple form of QTIP trust appears as Form 4-16 in §4.22. The QTIP election can be made with respect to a life estate in a residence. *See* Example 1 of Reg. §20.2056(b)-7(h).

The QTIP exception has two important features: (1) It can be claimed with respect to part or all of the transferred property in which the transferee spouse has the right to the income for life; (2) the surviving spouse need not be given any power of appointment over the trust. Naturally, any property for which an estate or gift tax marital deduction is claimed is includible in the estate of the transferee spouse. §2044. The basis of the property included in the donee spouse's estate under §2044 is stepped up under §1014. §1014(b)(10).

Note that inclusion in the transferee spouse's gross estate of property for which the estate tax marital deduction was claimed by the estate of the first spouse to die is required under §2044 regardless of whether the transferee spouse actually received any benefit of the qualifying income interest. In *Estate of Valeria M. Miller*, 97 T.C.M. 1602 (2009), the decedent's husband died in 2000 and his executor made a QTIP election for a trust created for the decedent's benefit. The husband's estate thus claimed a corresponding marital deduction for the value of the property transferred to the trust. The trust complied with all of the requirements for a valid QTIP election, but when the decedent died in 2003, her estate tax return did not include the value of the trust assets in her gross estate, because the decedent neither needed nor received the income from the trust. The Tax Court agreed with the IRS in holding that §2044 required inclusion in her gross estate even if she did not receive the income from the trust as required. The key is that the decedent was entitled to all of the income from the trust, not that she actually received it. The court found no evidence that the decedent ever effectively disposed of her right to the income and the fact that the income may not have been paid did not give the decedent's estate an opportunity to exclude the value of the property from her gross estate.

Overall, the QTIP exception is most similar to the one for a life interest general power of appointment trust. §2056(b)(5). *See* §5.22. However, in the case of a QTIP, the donee spouse need not be given any control over the ultimate disposition of the property. This makes the device particularly attractive to spouses who have children by previous marriages. For example, one spouse may be willing to provide a life income interest to the other spouse, provided that the property will ultimately pass to the descendants of the original owner. A surviving spouse can convert a §2056(b)(5) general power of appointment trust into a QTIP trust by disclaiming the power of appointment. *See* §12.36.

Election Can Determine Amount Passing to QTIP Trust. The regulations initially provided that the QTIP election itself could not be used to determine the interests that would pass to a trust in which the surviving spouse had a qualifying income interest for life. Thus, the IRS held that the marital deduction was not allowable if the allocation of property to such a trust was subject to the executor's election. *E.g.,* LR 9224028. The position was rejected in decisions by the Fifth, Sixth and Eighth Circuit Courts of Appeal. *Estate of Spencer v. Commissioner,* 43 F.3d 226 (6th Cir. 1995); *Estate of Robertson v. Commissioner,* 15 F.3d 779 (8th Cir. 1994). In 1997, the IRS issued temporary regulations, later made final as §20.2056(b)-7(d)(3)(i), under which "a qualifying income interest for life that is contingent upon the executor's election under section 2056(b)(7)(B)(v) will not fail to be a qualifying income interest for life because of such contingency or because the portion of the property for which the election is not made passes to or for the benefit of persons other than the surviving spouse."

As noted in §5.17, the IRS may disallow the marital deduction to the extent the property is subject to another person's option to purchase at a price other than fair market value. Accordingly, particular care must be exercised in planning marital deduction trusts if either spouse owns property that is subject to an option, including a buy-sell agreement. Consistently, no marital deduction is allowable with respect to a trust which gives a person other than the surviving spouse the right to purchase the assets of the trust at a bargain price. *Estate of Rinaldi v. U.S.,* 80 A.F.T.R.2d 5324 (Ct. Cls. 1997), *aff'd unpub. op,* 82 A.F.T.R.2d 7127 (Fed. Cir. 1998). In *Rinaldi,* the testator's will transferred closely held stock to a trust for the benefit of his wife. However, if his son gave up active management of the company, he was given the option to purchase the stock at its book value—which was substantially below its fair market value. According to the IRS and the court, granting the option precluded the trust from qualifying as QTIP. On this point the court stated that, "The trust in this case is inherently ineligible for QTIP treatment due to the provision of Rinaldi's will allowing the bargain sale of the trust's stock to a third party; the fact that the trust presently does not own the shares subject to the defective provision in question does not negate that provision's effect."

On the other hand, in LRs 9739015-9739018, the IRS held that the provisions of testamentary trusts which allocated, between principal and income, the payments that would be made under the terms of a partnership buy-sell agreement, satisfied the requirements of either § 2056(b)(5) or § 2056(b)(7).

Waiver of Right to Contest Will. The IRS has held that a requirement that the surviving spouse must waive the right to contest the taxpayer's will within six months following her death does not prevent the trust created for the benefit of the surviving spouse from being QTIP. LR 9244020. Under the terms of the will the failure to file such a waiver would cause the gift to the surviving spouse to lapse.

A requirement that the surviving spouse elects to take under a will or trust does not affect the deductibility of the interest he or she receives, as long as that interest is not terminable. LR 8727002. Similarly, Rev. Rul. 82-184, 1982-2 C.B. 215, concluded that, "[a] cash bequest in lieu of a life estate, payable unconditionally at the election of the surviving spouse within a reasonable time after the decedent's death qualifies for the estate tax marital deduction under section 2056 of the Code."

Section 2044. The donee spouse's interest in QTIP with respect to which a gift or estate tax marital deduction was previously allowed under either § 2056(b)(7) or § 2523(f) is includible in his or her gross estate under § 2044. Property that is included in the surviving spouse's gross estate under this provision is treated as passing from the surviving spouse for purposes of the estate and GST tax purposes. § 2044(c). Accordingly, the property may qualify for a charitable deduction under § 2055 or a further marital deduction under § 2056. *See* § 5.23.6. For purposes of valuation, property that is includible in a surviving spouse's estate under § 2044 will not be aggregated with property owned by the surviving spouse. *Estate of Bonner,* 84 F.3d 196 (5th Cir. 1996); *Estate of Harriet R. Mellinger,* 112 T.C. 4 (1999), *acq.,* 1999-2 C.B. 763.

Field Service Advice 200119013 accepts the outcome of *Estate of Bonner, Estate of Mellinger,* and similar cases which did not require aggregation of stock owned by the surviving stock with stock that was includible in her estate under § 2044. However, it upheld aggregation in the surviving spouse's estate of stock held in a § 2056(b)(5) trust, which is includible in the surviving spouse's estate under § 2041. The distinction was recognized by the Tax Court in *Estate of Aldo H. Fontana,* 118 T.C. 318 (2002).

Section 2519. The disposition of all or any part of a qualifying income interest in QTIP property will cause the gift tax to be imposed on the whole of the property. Under § 2519 the transferor will be treated as having transferred all interest in the QTIP property other than his or her qualifying income interest. The transferor will be treated as having transferred the qualifying income interest under § 2511. In some instances an overall tax saving may result from the imposition of the gift tax. *See* § 5.23.10. In FSA 199920016, the IRS held that the transfer of the corpus of a QTIP trust to a FLP formed by the trust and the surviving spouse's daughter and two grandchildren was not a disposition of the income interest of the trust and did not trigger the application of § 2519.

Reducing the Value of the QTIP. If permitted by local law, the trustee may take steps to reduce the estate tax value of the assets of the trust. For example, it might be possible for the trustee to transfer assets of the trust to a FLP or LLC. In FSA 199920016, the IRS held that the transfer of the corpus of a QTIP trust to a FLP formed by the trust and the surviving spouse's daughter and two grandchildren was not a disposition of the income interest of the trust and did not trigger the application of § 2519. The interests in the FLP or LLC held by the trust should be subject to a substantial discount in the estate of the surviving spouse. As a safeguard, the surviving spouse should, of course, have the power to require the trustee to convert nonincome-producing assets into income-producing ones.

In this connection, note that if the interests of the trust in the entity are too limited, or the powers of the manager of the FLP or LLC are too extensive, the IRS may argue that the trust does not meet the requirements of a QTIP. *See* the discussion of a gift tax case, *Catherine M. Hackl*, 118 T.C. 579 (2002), *aff'd*, 335 F.3d 664 (7th Cir. 2003) at § 11.31.4.

Reverse QTIP Election. A reverse QTIP election can be made for GSTT purposes, § 2652(a)(3). *See* § 2.28. However, the regulations do not allow partial reverse elections. This rule and other considerations require special planning and drafting in order to produce coordinated marital deduction and GSTT plans. In many instances wills and trusts should provide for the division of a single trust into two or more trusts in ways that comply with the requirements of § 2654 and Reg. § 26.2654-1(b).

Spendthrift Clause. The interest of the surviving spouse in a QTIP trust may be subject to a spendthrift clause under which the surviving spouse's interest is not subject to transfer or other alienation and is not subject to the claims of creditors. Reg. § 20.2056(b)-5(f)(7); LR 9548002 (TAM) (Ohio law). The terms of a trust that is intended to qualify for QTIP should not limit the circumstances under which the surviving spouse is entitled to receive the income. In LR 9548002 (TAM), the IRS held that under Ohio law the surviving spouse's express right to receive the income of the trust prevailed over the terms of a boilerplate spendthrift clause under which a beneficiary's right to receive distributions would become subject to the trustee's discretion in certain circumstances. The trust dealt with in the TAM is similar to the one before the court in *BancOhio National Bank v. United States*, 88-2 U.S.T.C. ¶ 13,776 (S.D. Ohio 1988), which reached the same conclusion.

An earlier ruling, LR 8940009 (Illinois law) held that a QTIP trust was not precluded from qualifying for the marital deduction because the trust included a spendthrift clause. In it the IRS stated that:

> Section 20.2056(b)-5(f)(7) of the Estate Tax Regulations provides that an interest passing in trust will not fail to satisfy the condition that the spouse be entitled to all the income merely because its terms provide that the right of the surviving spouse to the income shall not be subject to assignment, alienation, pledge, attachment, or claims of creditors. This principle is applicable to both section 2056(b)(5) and section 2056(b)(7) of the Code.

Effect of Settlement. If the requisite interests are created and an appropriate election is made on a decedent's Form 706, the qualification of a disposition as QTIP is made at the time of the decedent's death. Thus, in LR 200026003, the IRS ruled that a QTIP election was not affected by the subsequent settlement of a dispute between the decedent's surviving spouse and the executor of his will and other beneficiaries under which the surviving spouse sold her interest in the QTIP trust for its actuarially determined value. The ruling states that, "Since qualification for the marital deduction is determined as of the time of death, we conclude that under the facts presented, the validity of the QTIP election with respect to decedent's estate is not adversely affected by the subsequent sale of Spouse's interests in the QTIP Trust pursuant to the terms of the settlement agreement." The ruling also holds that (1) the transfer to the QTIP trust was not a direct skip, a taxable termination, or a taxable distribution, and (2) the reverse QTIP election made by decedent's executor was effective and, thus, the decedent would be treated as the transferor of the QTIP property for GSTT purposes.

§ 5.23.1. What Is QTIP?

"Qualified terminable interest property" (QTIP) is defined as property passing from the decedent in which the surviving spouse receives a qualifying income interest for life and with respect to which the decedent's executor makes an election under § 2056(b)(7). § 2056(b)(7)(B)(i). If the interest passing to the surviving spouse is a qualifying income interest for life, a deduction should be allowable—neither the passing nor the election requirement should pose any particular difficulty. Note, however, that the election "shall be made by the executor, on the return of tax imposed by Section 2001. Such an election, once made, shall be irrevocable." § 2056(b)(7)(B)(v). Although the election must be made on the return; it is not required to be made by the time fixed for filing the return (*i.e.*, normally nine months after the decedent's death). Initially QTIP elections could only be made by checking a box on the estate tax return—which was easy to overlook. Fortunately, the election is now deemed to be made by listing the property on the schedule of property for which the marital deduction is claimed, Schedule M.

For purposes of the QTIP election, the definition of the term "executor" provided in § 2203 controls. Under it, the decedent's personal representative is the executor; if none is appointed, qualified, or acting, then the executor is any person in actual or constructive possession of the decedent's property. In LR 8335033, the IRS indicated that the trustee of a funded revocable trust could make the QTIP election where no personal representative of the decedent's estate had been appointed.

§ 5.23.2. Qualifying Income Interest for Life

Under § 2056(b)(7)(B)(ii), a qualifying income interest for life must satisfy two basic requirements. The first basic requirement is that the surviving spouse must be entitled for "life to all of the income from the entire interest, or all of the income from a specific portion thereof, payable annually or at more frequent intervals." H.R. Rep. 97-201, 97th Cong., 1st Sess. 161 (1981). Income interests for a term of years or until remarriage do not satisfy this requirement. However, a legal life estate or other nontrust interest may qualify if it gives the surviving spouse "rights to income which are sufficient to satisfy the rules applicable to marital deduction trusts under present [pre-1982] law." *Id.* Consistently, Reg. § 20.2056(b)-7(d)(2) provides for the application of the principles of Reg. § 20.2056(b)-5(f) relating to whether the spouse is entitled for life to all of the income from the entire interest or a specific portion of the entire interest. *See* § 5.22. A trust meets the first requirement if the trustee is required to distribute all of the income to or for the benefit of the beneficiary-spouse. Rev. Rul. 85-35, 1985-1 C.B. 328 (marital deduction trust qualifies for the marital deduction if, under state law, the trustee has the power to distribute trust income to a relative or to a court appointed representative for the benefit of the spouse, or if the trustee may spend trust income directly for the benefit of the spouse, if the spouse becomes legally disabled); PLR 201117005 (first requirement met if the trustee is required to distribute the income of the trust to or for the benefit of the surviving spouse).

Unproductive Property as QTIP. Accordingly, care should be exercised if the trustee is authorized or directed to retain unproductive property (*e.g.,* unimproved real property, closely-held stock). In such a case the surviving spouse should be given the power to require the trustee to dispose of unproductive property or to convert it to productive property within a reasonable time. Note, however, that under Reg. §20.2056(b)-5(f)(4), "[A] power to retain a residence or other property for the personal use of the spouse will not disqualify the interest passing in trust." In connection with a surviving spouse's occupancy of a residence held in a QTIP trust, he or she may be required to pay taxes, operating costs, and the cost of minor repairs. LR 9046031. The marital deduction is allowable for a residence given to a QTIP that the surviving spouse has the exclusive right to use and occupy provided he must pay "insurance premiums, ordinary repairs, maintenance, taxes and ordinary assessments." LR 9047051. An elective QTIP marital deduction is allowable for a trust from which the surviving spouse is entitled to all of the income although the trust would be funded with shares of stock in a closely held stock on which a dividend had never been declared. LR 200339003 (TAM). The deduction was allowable because the decedent specified his intent that the trust qualify for the marital deduction and the surviving spouse had the power to require the trustee to make the trust assets productive. Real or personal property in which a surviving spouse has a life estate may qualify as QTIP if the governing law gives the surviving spouse the requisite right to all of the benefit from the property during his lifetime. Thus, a QTIP marital deduction is allowable with respect to real and personal property held in a trust that the surviving spouse had the exclusive right to use during his lifetime. LR 200222024. No deduction is allowable, however, if the life estate in a residence devised to a surviving spouse will terminate if the surviving spouse does not occupy the residence, or does not occupy it for a specified period each year. *E.g.,* LR 8742001.

A provision giving the trustee broad discretion to hold, manage, invest, and reinvest the assets without regard to the laws regarding investment of trust funds will not prevent a trust from qualifying as QTIP if the trustees are subject to the prudent person investment standard and are required to treat the beneficiaries impartially, investing for the benefit of the income and remainder beneficiaries. LR 9237009 (TAM).

Discretionary Distributions Insufficient. A surviving spouse's interest in a testamentary trust that provided for discretionary distributions of principal and income to be made to the surviving spouse to the extent required for "proper health, education, and support" did not qualify for the marital deduction. *Estate of Rapp v. Commissioner,* 140 F.3d 1211 (9th Cir. 1998). The Ninth Circuit gave no effect to an erroneous order of the probate court that reformed the trust in a manner intended to qualify for the marital deduction. The executor conceded that the order was erroneous but argued that the *Bosch* case did not allow the federal courts to consider the validity of the order, but must look only at whether the trust qualified on the date the QTIP election was made. Predictably, the court rejected the argument.

Consistently, in Technical Advice Memorandum 200505022 (TAM) the IRS held that no marital deduction was allowable with respect to a trust whose income distributions to the wife were limited to amounts the wife desires for "maintenance, education, health or support," to be determined "in consultation with the trustee."

According to the TAM, "any income distribution to be made is subject to the Trustee's approval."

S Corporation Stock Held by QTIP Trust. A QTIP election for stock in an S corporation held in trust for the benefit of the surviving spouse is possible. The trust would constitute a "qualified subchapter S trust" and thus be a permissible shareholder of the stock. Reg. § 1.1361-1(j)(4). As a result, the surviving spouse will be taxed directly on the trust's share of the S corporation's taxable income. § 1361(d). If no distributions are made from the S corporation to the trust, the trust has no "income" from the S corporation and there is, thus, nothing to pay to the surviving spouse. If, however, the corporation distributes money to pay the tax associated with the pass-through of the corporation's income to the trust, the distribution would be income for fiduciary accounting purposes (even though it would not be a taxable dividend for income tax purposes) and thus must be paid to the surviving spouse.

Termination of Qualifying Income Interest. No marital deduction is allowed with respect to a trust in which the surviving spouse's right to income may terminate if she becomes incapacitated. LR 9644001 (TAM) (trustee had right to accumulated income if the surviving spouse became incompetent. The accumulated income was distributable to the surviving spouse if she regained her competency, otherwise to her descendants).

A trust does not meet the requirements of QTIP if the surviving spouse's income interest will terminate on remarriage. *Roels v. United States,* 928 F. Supp. 812 (E.D.Wis. 1996).

No Distributions to Others. The second basic requirement for a qualifying income interest is that no one (including the transferee spouse) can have a power to appoint any part of the property subject to the qualifying income interest to any person other than the transferee spouse during his or her lifetime. As the House Ways and Means Committee pointed out, "[t]his rule will permit the existence of powers in the trustee to invade corpus for the benefit of the spouse but will insure that the value of the property not consumed by the spouse is subject to tax upon the spouse's death (or earlier disposition)." H.R. Rep. 97-201, 97th Cong., 1st Sess. 161 (1981). Powers to appoint corpus to others are permissible provided that they are "exercisable only at or after the death of the surviving spouse." § 2056(b)(7)(B)(ii). Note that the limitation restricts the time a power is exercisable and the nature of the interest subject to the power.

EXAMPLE 5-18.

W died leaving a trust from which her husband, *H,* was entitled to receive all of the income payable annually or at more frequent intervals. In addition, *H* was given the power, exercisable by deed or will, to appoint the remainder following his life income interest. The text of § 2056(b)(7)(B)(ii) and of the House Committee Report both indicate that the possible exercise of the power during the surviving spouse's lifetime would bar a deduction from being allowed for the property unless he or she effectively disclaimed the power or its lifetime exercise.

No marital deduction is allowable with respect to a trust from which any distributions can be made to others during the life of the surviving spouse. Thus, in *Estate of John D. Manscill,* 98 T.C. 413 (1992), no deduction was allowable for a trust that allowed distributions of principal to be made to the decedent's daughter with the consent of the decedent's spouse. The opinion includes the following passage from the report of the House Ways and Means Committee:

Second, there must be no power in any person (including the spouse) to appoint any part of the property subject to the qualifying income interest to any person other than the spouse during the spouse's life. *Id.* at 420.

§5.23.3. Additional Interests Surviving Spouse May Be Given in QTIP Trust

Giving the transferee spouse an unlimited power of withdrawal or other general power of appointment could negate the effect of a partial QTIP election with respect to a trust in which the surviving spouse was given a qualified income interest for life. In particular, an undisclaimed general power of appointment would require all of the property subject to the power to be included in the transferee spouse's estate under §2041. Indeed, if the transferee spouse's interest in the trust meets the requirements of both §2056(b)(5) and §2056(b)(7), it is not clear that the decedent's executor could elect to treat the property as QTIP under §2056(b)(7). Such a choice should be permitted, as there is no compelling reason to hold that the exceptions are mutually exclusive. In any event, under §2041 all property over which a decedent held a general power of appointment is includible in his or her estate. Such inclusion might result although the deceased spouse's executor claimed a marital deduction with respect to only part of the trust. §5.23.2. That is, the provisions of §2041 might override those of §2044 in such a case. Caution should be exercised in this regard until the uncertainties are clarified by regulations or otherwise.

EXAMPLE 5-19.

H died in 2006 leaving his entire $3 million estate to a trust from which *W* was entitled to receive all of the income for life. In addition, *W* was given a testamentary general power of appointment over the trust. *H*'s executor elected under §2056(b)(7) to claim a marital deduction with respect to 33 percent of the trust ($1 million). The tax on the other $2 million was offset by *H*'s unified credit. When *W* died a few years later the trust property was worth $6 million. If §2041 controls, the full $6 million is includible in *W*'s estate. On the other hand, if §2044 controls, only $2 million of the trust is includible in *W*'s estate (33% × $6 million).

Powers of Withdrawal. Giving the surviving spouse the power to withdraw funds from a QTIP trust can ensure that he or she is more adequately protected if the income of the trust is insufficient. A surviving spouse who holds a power of withdrawal will be more secure and is given a greater degree of protection against an unsympathetic and unresponsive trustee. In particular, a surviving spouse may be given nongeneral powers such as a 5 or 5 power of withdrawal over a QTIP trust. LR 8943005 (TAM) (upholding a 5 or 5 power to withdraw or to appoint the same to whomever she designates). Likewise, the deduction is not jeopardized if the surviving spouse is given a lifetime power of withdrawal limited by an ascertainable standard relating to the surviving spouse's health, education, support, or maintenance and a limited power over the ultimate disposition of the trust fund. In addition, the surviving spouse could safely be given a testamentary power to appoint the QTIP among a limited class of persons such as those of the transferor's issue who are living at the time of the transferee spouse's death. Of course, as noted above, in order to be QTIP no one can have the power to appoint it to anyone other than the transferee spouse during his or her lifetime.

Under an alternative approach a QTIP trust could be drawn to ensure that the surviving spouse would annually receive at least a specified percentage of the value of the trust property. The QTIP requirement would be met by requiring the trustee to distribute all of the income of the trust to the surviving spouse and the surviving spouse being given the noncumulative power to withdraw the amount by which say, 5 percent, of the value of the trust property on a specified annual date, exceeded the amount distributed during the year. Limiting to 5 percent the amount subject to withdrawal would cloak the power with the protection against gift and estate tax consequences provided by §§2041(b)(2) and 2514(e).

The regulations also recognize that the trustee may be given power to distribute the principal of a QTIP trust to the donee spouse. "An income interest in a trust will not fail to constitute a qualifying income interest for life solely because the trustee has a power to distribute corpus to or for the benefit of the surviving spouse." Reg. §20.2056(b)-7(c)(1). The surviving spouse may feel more secure if he or she is given the power to make withdrawals subject to an ascertainable standard permitted by §§2041(b)(1)(B) and 2514(c)(1), or limited each year to the greater of $5,000 or 5 percent of the principal value of the trust under §§2041(b)(2) and 2514(e). *See* §§10.24-10.25.

The flexibility of a QTIP trust can be increased by giving the surviving spouse the right, with the consent of an independent party, to withdraw part or all of the principal of the trust. The interests of the spouse and remaindermen would be protected by requiring the consent of the trustee or other independent party. The inclusion of such a power would, of course, require the inclusion of the trust in the surviving spouse's estate under §2041—which would jeopardize the benefit of a partial QTIP election unless the power is limited to the portion of the trust with respect to which the election was made.

A spouse who wishes to give the other spouse the full benefit of his or her property and to maximize the amount of a possible credit under §2013 should consider giving the surviving spouse the right to withdraw the property of the QTIP trust if he or she survives the decedent by 15 months or more. A 15-month period is used in order to allow the decedent's estate the maximum flexibility in determining whether to claim the QTIP deduction with respect to the property. If the surviving spouse dies within that period, the decedent's estate would not elect to claim the QTIP deduction, which would maximize the §2013 credit allowable to the surviving spouse's estate. If the surviving spouse becomes terminally ill within nine months following the decedent's death, he or she could disclaim the power. A disclaimer would limit the amount of property includible in the surviving spouse's estate. If the surviving spouse dies within the 15-month period the value of the credit would be increased by the prospective power of withdrawal even though it never became effective.

§ 5.23.4. Partial QTIP Election

If the surviving spouse has a qualifying income interest for life in the entire trust, the executor may make a partial election in order to preserve the benefit of the deceased spouse's unified credit. As indicated in § 5.23, the trust could be drafted to give the surviving spouse the income from only the elective share. The payment to the surviving spouse of the income from the nonmarital share of the trust could unnecessarily subject it to higher income taxes and increase the size of the surviving spouse's estate. Of course, the size of the surviving spouse's estate can be controlled to some extent by making annual exclusion gifts. Of course, some clients may not wish to require the payment of all of the income to the surviving spouse, or to establish a separate credit shelter trust whose income can be sprinkled among the client's surviving spouse and children by an independent trustee.

EXAMPLE 5-20.

H left his entire estate in trust, the income from which is payable to *W* for life, remainder to those of their issue who survive *W*. *H*'s executor can elect to claim a marital deduction with respect to a specific portion of the property by making a timely election under § 2056(b)(7). The trust could provide that *W* was entitled only to receive the income from the portion of the trust with respect to which *H*'s executor made a QTIP election. The income from the other share of the trust could be sprinkled among a class of beneficiaries in which the surviving spouse might be included.

If the executor makes a partial QTIP election with respect to a trust, the election must "be made with respect to a fractional or percentage share of the property so that the elective portion reflects its proportionate share of the increase or decrease in value of the entire property for purposes of applying sections 2044 or 2519." Reg. § 20.2056(b)-7(b)(2)(i). A partial election should be made by use of a formula. *See* § 12.21. If a partial election is made, the trust may be divided into separate trusts provided the fiduciary is required by the instrument or local law to make the division according to the fair market value of the assets of the trust at the time of the division. Once the division is made the trustee may direct that any distributions of principal to the surviving spouse should first be made from the marital deduction share. This approach reduces the amount includible in the surviving spouse's estate under § 2044.

§ 5.23.5. Annuity Interests; IRAs

If the surviving spouse is the only person to whom the decedent transferred an interest in an annuity, the interest qualifies for the marital deduction. *See* § 5.17.1. However, if an interest in an annuity may pass to another person upon the death of the surviving spouse, the interest of the surviving spouse may be treated as a qualified income interest under §2056(b)(7)(C). The issue may arise in connection with (1) an annuity payable the surviving spouse or (2) an annuity payable to a QTIP trust. *See* §§13.14-13.14.7.

Annuity Payable to Surviving Spouse. The 1997 Act amended §2056(b)(7)(C) to specify clearly that the marital deduction is allowable with respect to the community property interest of a nonparticipant spouse in an annuity of which the surviving spouse was the only beneficiary during his or her lifetime. The amendment responded to the concern of some commentators that a marital deduction would not be allowable for the interest of a nonparticipant spouse that was included in his or her estate under §2033. Note, however, that in LR 8943006 (TAM) (Louisiana law), the National Office held that the nonemployee spouse's estate was entitled to a marital deduction for her interest in a pension plan that passed to her husband pursuant to the terms of the plan.

Under §2056(b)(7)(C), the surviving spouse's interest in an annuity that was included in the decedent's estate under §2039 is treated as a qualifying income interest if the surviving spouse is the only person entitled to receive any payment prior to the surviving spouse's death. §2056(b)(7)(C). Thus, a QTIP marital deduction would be allowable for an annuity that was payable to the surviving spouse for life with any balance at her death payable to other beneficiaries, such as their children. Note that under §2056(b)(7)(C)(ii) the executor is treated as having made a QTIP election with respect to such an annuity unless a contrary election is made on the decedent's estate tax return. The deductible interest is "the specific portion of the property that, assuming the applicable interest rate for valuing annuities, would produce income equal to the minimum amount payable annually to the surviving spouse." Reg. §20.2056(b)-7(e)(2). Accordingly, the value of the surviving spouse's annuity, determined according to the applicable interest rate under §7520, Reg. §20.2056(b)-7(e)(4), may be more or less than the amount that is includible in the decedent's estate under §2039. The method of determining the deductible amount is illustrated by Reg. §20.2056(b)-7(h), Example (11).

For marital deduction purposes, the value of an annuity payable to the surviving spouse is determined according to the amount initially payable. The amount of the deduction is fixed by the amount of the original annuity payments and will not increase although the amount of the payments might increase. Reg. §20.2056(b)-7(e)(2). Accordingly, in *Estate of Sansone v. United States*, 87 A.F.T.R.2d (RIA) 1361 (C.D. Cal. 2001), *aff'd, unpub. op.*, 2002-2 USTC ¶60,442 (9th Cir. 2002), the court held that the amount of the deduction could not take into account prospective increases in the amount payable based upon increases in the consumer price index.

Annuity Payable to QTIP Trust. According to Rev. Rul. 2000-2, 2000-1 C.B. 305, if a decedent's executor makes a QTIP election, the marital deduction is allowable for an IRA payable to the trustee of a QTIP trust if (1) the surviving spouse has the power to "compel the trustee to withdraw from the IRA an amount equal to all the income earned on the IRA assets at least annually and to distribute that amount to the spouse" and (2) "no person has a power to appoint any part of the trust property to any person other than the spouse." The ruling simplifies the requirements and permits a surviving spouse to leave amounts in excess of the minimum required distribution in an IRA where they can generate additional tax-free income. *See also* Example (10) in Reg. §20.2056(b)-7(h) which deals with payments made from a decedent's IRA directly to the surviving spouse.

The earlier position taken by the IRS with respect to IRAs payable to QTIP trusts was stated in Rev. Rul. 89-89:

> A decedent's executor can elect under section 2056(b)(7) of the Code to treat a decedent's IRA as qualified terminable interest property if (a) the decedent elected an IRA distribution option requiring the principal balance to be distributed in annual installments to a testamentary QTIP trust and the income earned on the undistributed balance of the IRA to be paid annually to the trust and (b) the trust requires that both the income earned on the undistributed portion of the IRA which it receives from the IRA and the income earned by the trust on the distributed portion of the IRA be paid currently to the decedent's spouse for life. Rev. Rul. 89-89, 1989-2 C.B. 231.

Revenue Ruling 89-89 dealt only with a QTIP that required that all income earned by the IRA be "paid currently to the decedent's surviving spouse for life." It did not allow a QTIP marital deduction if the surviving spouse merely had the power to compel all of the income to be distributed to her. In both instances, however, the marital deduction is available with respect to the entire amount of the IRA and not merely an amount determined in accordance with Reg. § 20.2056(b)-7(e)(2). Note, however, that in order to meet the requirements of a QTIP, the payments from the IRA must be made to the surviving spouse beginning immediately after the decedent's death. Otherwise, distributions could be deferred until required by the minimum distribution rules.

Numerous private letter rulings followed the reasoning of Rev. Rul. 89-89, and allowed QTIP marital deductions for IRAs payable to QTIP trusts. *E.g.,* LR 9038015 (a QTIP marital deduction is allowable with respect to an IRA payable to a QTIP trust where the all of the income of the IRA was directed to be paid to the QTIP trust and, from the QTIP trust, to the surviving spouse); LR 9043054, (a portion of an IRA was transferred to a separate IRA trust which was required to make distributions to a QTIP trust of the greater of all of the income from the share of the IRA held in trust or the minimum amount that the IRA was required to, which the QTIP trust was required to distribute to the surviving spouse); and LRs 9245033; 9229017, 9317025, 9321035, 9321059, 9324024, 9537005, 9739034; LR 200241012 (QTIP also qualifies as QDOT). *See* §§ 13.14-13.14.7.

In LR 9544038, the IRS allowed the marital deduction with respect to an IRA that was payable to a trust that met the requirements of a QDT and QTIP. Under the terms of the trust the income was payable to the surviving spouse at least quarterly and she had the power to require the trustees to convert unproductive property into productive property. Her estate was entitled to receive any income that was accrued but undistributed at the time of her death. Under an amendment to the trust, distributions received from an IRA were allocable to principal except the portion attributable to income earned by the IRA, which was allocable to income. In addition the trustees were required to demand distributions from an IRA if not all of its income was distributed in any year. The surviving spouse was also given the right to require the trustee to make such a demand. Any income of the IRA that was accrued but undistributed at the time of the surviving spouse's death was payable to her estate. The IRS held that the arrangement complied with Rev. Rul. 89 89, 1989-2 C.B. 231, and met the requirements of both QTIP and a QDT.

§ 5.23.6. Transfer to Lifetime QTIP to Equalize Estates or to Preserve Use of Unified Credit

If one spouse is wealthier than the other, the overall gift, estate, and GST tax picture may be improved if the wealthier spouse makes a lifetime transfer to the poorer spouse, or to a QTIP trust for him or her. In particular, transfers to a QTIP can be used to equalize the sizes of their estates to enable the full use of the poorer spouse's unified credit or to make use of the poorer spouse's GSTT exemption. Notably, for purposes of valuation property that is includible in a surviving spouse's estate under § 2044 will not be aggregated with property owned by him or her. *Estate of Bonner v. U.S.*, 84 F.3d 196 (5th Cir. 1996); *Estate of Harriet R. Mellinger*, 112 T.C. 4 (1999), *acq.*, 1999-2 C.B. 763; *Estate of Ethel S. Nowell*, T.C. Memo. 1999-15 (1999); *See* § 5.23.

EXAMPLE 5-21.

W's estate is worth $3 million and her husband *H*'s only $1.2 million. *H*, who is terminally ill, intends to leave his property to their children. In order to avoid wasting part of *H*'s unified credit, *W* might transfer $800,000 to a trust in which *H* is given a qualified income interest for life, remainder to their children. If *H* were given a general power of appointment over the QTIP property, *W* might retain a successive income interest in it.

Several letter rulings have allowed a donor spouse to retain a successive life estate in an inter vivos QTIP trust that he or she established for the benefit of the donee spouse without requiring the property to be included in the donor spouse's estate unless the donee spouse or the donee spouse's estate subsequently claims a marital deduction in connection with a later transfer of the property. LRs 8944009, 9437032. The approach allows a couple to take advantage of the donee spouse's unified credit without depriving the donor of the income from the property if the donor turns out to be the survivor of them. The IRS has ruled that the favorable results are available with respect to a residence that is transferred to a trust for the benefit of a spouse for which a QTIP election is made. *E.g.*, LR 9309023. Further IRS blessing was given to the approach in the final regulations issued in 1994:

> *Treatment of interest retained by donor spouse.* (1) In general. Under § 2523(f)(5)(A), if a donor spouse retains an interest in qualified terminable interest property, any subsequent transfer by the donor spouse of the retained interest in the property is not treated as a transfer for gift tax purposes. Further, the retention of the interest until the donor spouse's death does not cause the property subject to the retained interest to be includible in the gross estate of the donor spouse. Reg. § 25.2523(f)-1(d).

The operation of the rule is illustrated by Examples (10) and (11) of Reg. § 25.2523(f)-1(e).

> *Example (10). Retention by donor spouse of income interest in property.* On October 1, 1994, *D* transfers property to an irrevocable trust under the terms of which trust income is to be paid to *S* for life, then to *D* for life, and, on *D's* death, the trust corpus is to be paid to *D's* children. *D* elects under § 2523(f) to treat the property as qualified terminable interest property. *D* dies in 1996,survived by *S*. *S* subsequently dies in 1998. Under § 25.2523(f)-1(d)(1), because *D* elected to treat the transfer as qualified terminable interest property, no part of the trust corpus is includible in *D's* gross estate because of *D's* retained interest in the trust corpus. On *S's* subsequent death in 1998, the trust corpus is includible in *S's* gross estate under § 2044.
>
> *Example (11). Retention by donor of income interest in property.* The facts are the same as in Example 10, except that *S* dies in 1996 survived by *D*, who subsequently dies in 1998. Because *D* made an election under § 2523(f) with respect to the trust, on *S's* death the trust corpus is includible in *S's* gross estate under § 2044. Accordingly, under § 2044(c), *S* is treated as the transferor of the property for estate and gift tax purposes. Upon *D's* subsequent death in 1998, because the property was subject to inclusion in *S's* gross estate under § 2044, the exclusion rule in § 25.2523(f)-1(d)(1) does not apply under § 25.2523(f)-1(d)(2). However, because *S* is treated as the transferor of the property, the property is not subject to inclusion in *D's* gross estate under §§ 2036 or 2038. If the executor of *S'* s estate made a § 2056(b)(7) election with respect to the trust, the trust is includible in *D's* gross estate under § 2044 upon *D's* later death.

Mechanics of the Inter Vivos QTIP Election.   Under § 2523(f)(4), an election to treat an inter vivos transfer as QTIP must be made "on or before the date prescribed by section 6075(b) for filing a gift tax return with respect to the transfer (determined without regard to section 6019(2)." In the past the IRS routinely denied requests for extensions of time under Reg. § 301.9100 within which to make the election. For example, LR 200314012 denied the requested extension because the taxpayer did not file a gift tax return within the time allowed, meaning the taxpayer also did not qualify for an automatic six-month extension. Some earlier rulings did not allow extensions because the provisions of Reg. § 301.9100-1 then in effect only allowed extension when the time within which the election must be made was not specified by statute. *E.g.*, LR 9641023. More recently, in LR 201025021, the IRS allowed an extension of time within which to make the election where a gift tax returned prepared by the donor's lawyer was timely filed, but mistakenly failed to make the election:

> Section 301.9100-1(c) provides that the Commissioner has discretion to grant a reasonable extension of time under the rules set forth in §§ 301.9100-2 and 301.9100-3 to make a regulatory election or a statutory election (but no more than 6 months except in the case of a taxpayer who is abroad), under all subtitles of the Internal Revenue Code except subtitles E, G, H and I.

Requests for relief under §§301.9100-2 and 301.9100-3 will be granted when the taxpayer provides evidence to establish to the satisfaction of the Commissioner that the taxpayer acted reasonably and in good faith, and that granting relief will not prejudice the interests of the government.

Section 301.9100-3(b)(1)(v) provides that a taxpayer is deemed to have acted reasonably and in good faith if the taxpayer reasonably relied on a qualified tax professional, include a tax professional employed by the taxpayer, and the tax professional failed to make, or advise the taxpayer to make, the election.

§5.23.7. QTIP with Charitable Remainder

A marital deduction is allowable under §2056(b)(7) where the surviving spouse is given a qualifying income interest for life and the remainder is given to a charity. This possibility was noted in the following footnote in the House Committee Report:

> The general rules applicable to qualifying income interests may provide similar treatment where a decedent provides an income interest in the spouse for her life and a remainder interest to charity. If the life estate is a qualifying income interest, the entire property will, pursuant to the executor's election, be considered as passing to the spouse. Therefore, the entire value of the property will be eligible for the marital deduction and no transfer tax will be imposed. Upon the spouse's death, the property will be included in the spouse's estate but, because the spouse's life estate terminates at death, any property passing outright to charity may qualify for a charitable deduction. H.R. Rep. 97-201, 97th Cong., 1st Sess., 162, n. 4 (1981).

Under §2044(c), property that is includible in the decedent's estate by reason of a QTIP election having been made is treated as having passed from the decedent for gift, estate, and GST tax purposes. Accordingly, the surviving spouse's estate should be entitled to a charitable deduction under §2055 for the value of the property included in his or her estate under §2044 that passes to a charity upon his or her death. LR 9008017, *Estate of John T. Higgins,* 91 T.C. 61 (1988) (dicta), *aff'd on other issues,* 897 F.2d 856 (6th Cir. 1990). In LR 9242006, a marital deduction was allowable for a life estate in art objects left to a surviving spouse, which would pass to a charity upon the surviving spouse's death.

Note that a QTIP election is not permissible where the surviving spouse is given an annuity interest in a charitable remainder trust. According to the regulations, "If an interest qualifies for a marital deduction under §2056(b)(8), no election may be made with respect to the property under §2056(b)(7)."

Regulation §20.2056(b)-9 makes it clear that only one deduction is allowable where a marital deduction is claimed with respect to property in which a surviving spouse is given a qualifying income interest and the remainder is given to a charity. For example, where a decedent transfers a qualifying income interest in a farm to the spouse with a remainder to charity, the entire property is, pursuant to the executor's election under section 2056(b)(7), treated as passing to the spouse. The entire value of the property qualifies for the marital deduction. No part of the value of the property qualifies for a charitable deduction under section 2055 in the decedent's estate. *Id.* Upon the death of the surviving spouse, the value of the qualified terminable interest property is includible under §2044. Under §2044(c) and Reg. §20.2044-1(b), "the property is treated as passing from the decedent for purposes of determining the availability of the charitable deduction under section 2055 . . . ." Accordingly, the inclusion of the property in the surviving spouse's estate will not result in the imposition of any estate tax.

§5.23.8. Use in Connection with Disclaimers

The opportunity to disclaim property exists independent of the §2056(b)(7) QTIP election. Thus, the surviving spouse may disclaim the right to receive property outright and cause the property to fall into a trust in which he or she has a qualifying income interest for life and with respect to which the executor can make a §2056(b)(7) election. Of course, a surviving spouse could also disclaim part or all of his or her interest in the trust. The disclaimed interest would pass according to the terms of the trust or, if there are none, according to the local law. It is essential for the surviving spouse and the executor to coordinate their planning with regard to the use of disclaimers and the §2056(b)(7) election. *See* §§12.32-12.36.

EXAMPLE 5-22.

W died in 2006 leaving her entire $3 million estate to her husband, *H*, outright, provided that any property *H* disclaimed would pass to a QTIP trust for his benefit. The trust provided that upon *H*'s death the trust would terminate and the trust property would be distributed to their then living issue by right of representation. *H* disclaimed the right to receive any of *W*'s estate outright. Accordingly, all of her property passed to the trust. *H* also disclaimed all rights in two-thirds of the trust, which had a value equal to the applicable exclusion amount ($2 million). As a result, a two-thirds interest in the trust property passed outright to the issue of *H* and *W*. The remainder of *W*'s property remained in trust for *H*. *W*'s executor elected under §2056(b)(7) to claim a marital deduction with respect to all of the property ($1 million) received by the trust. When *H* dies all of the trust property will be includible in his gross estate under §2044.

In some cases disclaimers may be used to eliminate powers or interests that otherwise prevent a trust from meeting the requirements of QTIP. For example, a trust may fail to qualify because the trustee, the surviving spouse, or others have the power, during the lifetime of the surviving spouse, to cause income or principal to be distributed to persons other than the surviving spouse. *See, e.g.,* LR 8935024 (surviving spouse disclaimed lifetime power to appoint principal to children). If a disclaimer is not made in such a case no marital deduction would be allowable with respect to the trust. *See, e.g., Estate of Roger Bowling,* 93 T.C. 286 (1989) (QTIP marital deduction not allowed where trustee had power, during the lifetime of the surviving spouse, to invade principal for the benefit of the surviving spouse and others—no disclaimer attempted). A marital deduction was allowed in LR 8443005 (TAM) where the children disclaimed the right to receive discretionary distributions of income during the surviving spouse's lifetime. As a result the surviving spouse held a qualifying income interest. A fiduciary's attempt to disclaim a power to make discretionary distributions to persons other than the surviving spouse may not be recognized for gift and estate tax purposes—at least not a disclaimer that is not authorized by local law. Rev. Rul. 90-110, 1990-2 C.B. 209. A QTIP marital deduction was allowed in LR 9247002 (TAM) where the decedent's children and grandchildren disclaimed their rights to receive discretionary distributions of income and principal.

Technical Advice Memorandum 9140004 involved a decedent's gift to his surviving spouse of the right to use and occupy the family residence so long as she continued to use it as a residence and did not remarry. If she failed to use it as a residence or remarried the property would pass to the decedent's descendants. Within nine months of the decedent's death all of his children and grandchildren executed disclaimers of any interests in the residence that might arise during the surviving spouse's lifetime. The IRS held that the disclaimers did not relate to separately created interests and, hence, were not qualified disclaimers. As a result the ruling denied the marital deduction for the determinable life tenancy in the residence given to the surviving spouse.

In LR 200801009, a surviving spouse sought to disclaim her interest in a QTIP trust, apparently sometime after the normal nine-month period for a qualified disclaimer under § 2518. The IRS ruled that the surviving spouse would be deemed to make a gift under § 2519 equal to the fair market value of the QTIP trust reduced by the value of the spouse's qualified income interest and by the amount she could recover under § 2207A(b). In addition, the transfer of the spouse's qualified income interest would be deemed to be a gift under § 2511. The relative values of these two gifts would be computed using the § 7520 valuation tables.

§ 5.23.9. Election and Authorization to Make Election

The election to claim the marital deduction with respect to part or all of the property that meets the requirements of § 2056(b)(7) is made by the decedent's executor on the federal estate tax return. Considerations regarding the use of the election and the procedure for making the election are discussed in detail in § 12.21. The regulations recognize that the amount of the election can be expressed in a formula. The use of a formula guards against the necessity of paying some estate tax, which might otherwise result if the amount of the taxable estate were increased because of a change in the valuation of assets included in the gross estate or if some deductions were disallowed. *See* § 12.21.2. For similar reasons, although the decedent's estate might not be required to pay any federal estate tax according to the federal estate tax return as filed, the decedent's executor might make a protective election. *See* § 12.21.4.

In most states a decedent's executor probably has the authority to make a QTIP election whether or not the executor is expressly given the power by the controlling instrument. However, it is desirable to eliminate any doubt by giving the executor such authority. It is also generally desirable to give the executor some guidance regarding the considerations that should govern the exercise of the power. Finally, the executor should be relieved from any liability that might otherwise result from exercise of the power. In this connection note that some states have enacted statutes that recognize the executor's right to make the election. Indeed, some statutes expressly relieve the executor from liability arising from a good faith exercise of the power. *E.g.,* Cal. Prob. Code § 21526 (20110) ("A fiduciary is not liable for a good faith decision to make any election or not to make any election, referred to in Section 2056(b)(7) or Section 2523(f) of the Internal Revenue Code.") The inclusion of a provision that expressly empowers the executor to make the election should reduce the potential for conflict among the survivors and should insulate the executor from liability resulting from an exercise of the election.

Although the decedent may direct the executor to make the election with respect to all or some part of the property, it is unwise to do so because of the possibility that the unexpected may occur. For example, the surviving spouse may die shortly after the decedent. In such a case a directed election that resulted in the payment of no estate tax by the estate of the first spouse to die would prevent the estates from minimizing the overall estate tax burden through the use of the previously taxed property credit. On balance it is preferable to authorize the executor to make the necessary election and to give the executor some guidance regarding the criteria that should be considered in making the decision. A provision directing exercise of the election gives the executor less flexibility in planning post-mortem strategy. *See* Form 5-3. For other examples, *see* Ascher, The Quandary of Executors Who Are Asked to Plan the Estates of the Dead: The Qualified Terminable Interest Election, 63 N.C. L. Rev. 1, 48 (1983); Pennell, Estate Tax Marital Deduction, 843-2nd Tax Mgmt. Port. (2006).

Form 5-3
Executor Authorized to Make Partial or Total QTIP Election

I authorize my executor, in [her/his] discretion, to elect to claim the federal estate tax marital deduction with respect to part, all, or none of the property that passes to the trust for the benefit of my [wife/husband]. My executor may make the election regardless of the impact that the election may have upon her/his interests, those of my [wife/husband], or of any other person. In particular, I exonerate my executor from liability to anyone that results from a good faith exercise of [her/his] election, which shall be binding and conclusive upon all parties. I intend my executor to be free to make the election that [she/he] believes is in the best interests of my estate and its beneficiaries. In making the election I request that my executor consider the overall estate, gift and generation-skipping transfer tax increase or decrease that the election may have upon my estate and the estate of my [wife/husband] in light of [her/his] apparent financial status, health and life expectancy. My executor may also consider the amounts of property passing to my [wife/husband] and other beneficiaries of the trust under this will and pursuant to other arrangements.

§ 5.23.10. Disposition of Qualifying Income Interest in QTIP, § 2519

Under § 2519(a), if the donee spouse transfers all or any portion of the qualifying income interest, he or she will be treated as having transferred all of the QTIP. The transfer of the qualifying income interest itself constitutes a gift, which should qualify for the annual gift tax exclusion. Any gift tax imposed on the transfer of the remainder interest may be recovered from the person who receives it. § 2207A(b). If the person who receives the QTIP in fact pays the gift tax liability of the donee spouse, such gift taxes will be included in the donee spouse's gross estate under § 2035(b) if the donee spouse does not survive for three years following the transfer of the qualifying income interest. *Estate of Anne W. Morgens,* 133 T.C. No. 17 (2009).

The donor's right to recover the gift tax paid only applies to the extent that tax is actually paid—it does not apply to any portion of the gift tax that is offset by the donor's unified credit. LR 200717016. Where some tax is recoverable by the donor, the transaction will be taxed as a net gift unless the donor waives the right to recover the tax from the donee, e.g., LRs 9736001 (TAM), 200324023, 200628007, 200801009. *See* § 7.26.

The commutation of the surviving spouse's interest in a QTIP followed by termination of the trust also invokes § 2519. Private Letter Ruling 200013015 involved a QTIP of which a charity was the remainderman. The parties proposed to terminate the trust, distribute an amount to the surviving spouse determined in accordance with the regulations under § 7520, and distribute the remainder to the charity. According to the ruling, the termination of the trust would constitute a disposition under § 2519, resulting in a gift by the surviving spouse of the value of the corpus less the amount distributed to the surviving spouse. The gift to the charity would qualify for a gift tax deduction under § 2522(a).

The problem caused by the transfer of an interest in a qualifying income interest is illustrated by the following example from Reg. § 25.2519-1(h):

EXAMPLE (1)

Under *D*'s will, a personal residence valued for estate tax purposes at $250,000 passes *S* for life and after *S*'s death to *D*'s children. *D*'s executor made a valid election to treat the property as qualified terminable interest property on the estate tax return for *D*'s estate. During 1995, when the fair market value of the property is $300,000 and the value of *S*'s life interest in the property is $100,000, *S* makes a gift of *S*'s entire interest in the property to *D*'s children. Pursuant to section 2519, *S* makes a gift in the amount of $200,000 (*i.e.,* the fair market value of the qualified terminable interest property of $300,000 less the fair market value of the *S*'s qualifying income interest in the property of $100,000). In addition, under section 2511 *S* makes a gift of $100,000 (which is the fair market value of *S*'s income interest in the property). *See* § 25.2511-2.

In order to guard against inadvertently subjecting the property to the gift tax, a trust might prohibit the surviving spouse from disposing of all or any part of the income interest without the consent of the trustee or another responsible party. The inclusion of such a spendthrift provision is permitted by the regulations in the case of life interest-general power of appointment trusts, Reg. §20.2056(b)-5(f)(7), and has been permitted in some letter rulings dealing with QTIP trusts. *E.g.*, LRs 8521155, 8532006. Spendthrift clauses are discussed in detail at §4.24.8.

Loans made to the children of the surviving spouse of part of the principal of a QTIP trust in exchange for the children's promissory notes did not constitute a disposition of the surviving spouse's interest that would trigger imposition of tax under §2519. LR 9418013. Although the interest on the notes was not payable until the death of the surviving spouse, under §2044 her estate would include both the accumulated interest and the value of the notes.

In LR 200026003, the IRS ruled that a decedent for whom a valid reverse QTIP election had been made would be treated as the transferor of the property distributed to the QTIP trust despite a dispute between the surviving spouse and the executor and other beneficiaries. The dispute was settled by an agreement under which the surviving spouse would sell her interest in the QTIP trust to the remaindermen for its actuarially determined value. The ruling held that the transfer to the QTIP trust was not a direct skip, a taxable termination, or a taxable distribution. It did not deal with the gift or income tax aspects of the settlement.

Attracting Tax Under §2519 Can Save Taxes. Transfer tax savings may result in some cases if the surviving spouse transfers his or her interest in a QTIP trust that would otherwise all be subject to tax under §2044 on a tax-inclusive basis and the surviving spouse survives the transfer by at least three years. According to LR 9434029, such an assignment does not jeopardize the allowance of the marital deduction in the predeceased spouse's estate. Under §2207A(b), the donor is entitled to recover the gift tax imposed on the disposition of an interest under §2519. Although a surviving spouse who transfers the entire life interest to a noncharity is treated as having made a gift of the entire value of a QTIP trust, he or she is only entitled to recover the gift tax on the value of the remainder interest—the portion of the gift tax attributable to the life interest is not recoverable. Reg. §25.2207A(a).

EXAMPLE 5-23.

T died in 2006 leaving $3 million to each of two QTIP trusts (Trust 1 and Trust 2) for his surviving spouse, *W*. *T*'s executor claimed marital deductions for each trust, which were allowed. In 2008, when *W*'s income interest in each trust was worth $1.5 million, *W* assigned her entire life interest in Trust 1 to her child, *C*, the remainderman of Trust 1. *W* had previously made taxable gifts that made later transfers subject to a 45-percent tax rate. Under §§2511 and 2519, *W* is treated as having transferred the entire value of the trust, $3 million. Under §2207A(b), *W* is entitled to recover the tax on a gift of the remainder, $675,000 from *C* ($1,500,000 × .45) but she is not entitled to recover the gift tax imposed on the transfer of her life interest—another $675,000. The failure to assert the right to recover the $675,000 from *C* might be treated as a further gift to *C*. *W* has no right to recover the $675,000 of gift tax paid with respect to the gift of her life interest. If *W* survives the transfer by three years, the gift tax paid by her ($675,000) will not be included in her gross estate. Thus, the transfer may ultimately save estate taxes of $303,750 or more ($675,000 × .45).

Such a transfer also freezes the value of the property subject to tax in the estate of the surviving spouse and removes further income from her estate as well.

In LR 9736001 (TAM), the IRS ruled that a nonqualified disclaimer (*i.e.,* transfer) of the life interest of a surviving spouse in a QTIP trust resulted in a net gift of the remainder. The conclusion was based on an analysis that §2207A(a) statutorily shifted the burden of the gift tax on the remainder arising under §2519 to the transferee—which supported treatment of the transfer as a net gift. The net gift treatment did not apply to the value of the life interest.

In LR 199926019, a QTIP trust was to be divided into two identical trusts (Trust A and Trust B), following which the surviving spouse would renounce (*i.e.,* make a nonqualified disclaimer of) her interest in Trust A. Following the renunciation, Trust A would be held for the benefit of her children, who would receive distributions from it, including an amount sufficient for them to pay the gift tax that resulted from her renunciation. The IRS ruled that if the surviving spouse's renunciation were conditioned on the children paying the gift tax on the transfer, the amount of the gift that resulted from the renunciation would be reduced by the gift tax paid by the children. In addition, the IRS ruled that the surviving spouse's renunciation of her interests in Trust A would not result in a gift of an interest in Trust B, and her interest in Trust B would not be valued under §2702. Overall, the arrangement prevented the gift tax from being included in the base upon which the tax is calculated, which would be the case if the trust were to remain intact until the death of the surviving spouse.

The settlement of a dispute between a surviving spouse and the deceased spouse's children can result in transfers that are, and are not, dispositions subject to §2519. For example, LR 200106029 held that a distribution to the surviving spouse of part of the principal of a marital trust was not a disposition subject to §2519. Distributions that would result from the surviving spouse's nonqualified disclaimer of any other interest in the marital trust would be treated as a disposition under §2519 of the value of her qualifying income interest in the trust, a gift of the remainder value of the trust less the value of her qualifying income interest, and a gift of the gift tax on the transfer with respect to which she waived her right of recovery under §2207A.

A distribution to a surviving spouse of delayed income from a QTIP trust is not a disposition of her qualifying income interest within the meaning of §2519. LR 199915052. The QTIP involved in the ruling initially held the stock of a closely held corporation that paid annual dividends of less than 1 percent of its inventory value. In a tax-free reorganization the stock was exchanged for stock in a publicly held company. In response to the trustees' petition for instructions the local court ruled that for purposes of the state's principal and income law the exchange was a disposition of the stock which required distribution of delayed income to the surviving spouse.

The failure to exercise the right of recovery is treated as a gift by the surviving spouse. Reg. §25.2207A-1(b). Under the regulation, a delay in exercising the right of recovery without the donee paying sufficient interest is treated as a below-market loan for purposes of §7872.

§ 5.23.11. Estate Tax on Surviving Spouse's Death

Unless otherwise directed in the surviving spouse's will, the estate tax attributable to the property included in his or her estate under § 2044 is recoverable by his or her executor from the recipients of the property. § 2207A(a). Thus, the inclusion of the property in the surviving spouse's estate ordinarily will not increase the amount of estate tax payable from the surviving spouse's property. Under § 2207A(a)(1), the surviving spouse's executor has the right to recover the entire additional amount of tax incurred by reason of the inclusion of the QTIP in the surviving spouse's gross estate. The right of recovery extends to any penalties and interest attributable to the additional taxes. § 2207(d). Where the § 2044 property is distributed to more than one person, the right of recovery may be asserted against each of them. § 2207A(c).

Under § 2207A(a)(2), the recovery provision does not apply if the decedent "in his will (or a revocable trust) specifically indicates an intent to waive any right of recover under this subchapter with respect to such property." A general direction to pay "all valid inheritance and estate taxes by reason of my death" does not relieve a QTIP trust from the obligation to reimburse the executor for a portion of the estate tax as required by § 2207A. *Firstar Trust Co. v. First National Bank of Kenosha*, 541 N.W.2d 467 (Wis. 1995). In order to shift the burden, a decedent's will must more clearly "otherwise direct." If the surviving spouse's personal representative does not exercise the right to recover the estate tax imposed on the surviving spouse's estate by reason of the inclusion of the QTIP property under § 2044, the failure does not constitute a constructive addition to the trust. Reg. § 26.2652-1(a)(5), Example 8. The position is made clear in the statutes of some states, which provide that a general direction to pay all taxes due by reason of the testator's death will not be construed to apply to the taxes imposed on QTIP property that is includible in the surviving spouse's estate under § 2044.

EXAMPLE 5-24.

H died in 2006 leaving an estate of $3 million to a QTIP trust. His executor elected to claim the marital deduction with respect to $1 million of the property. Accordingly, no estate tax was paid by *H*'s estate. When his wife, *W*, died in 2009 her taxable estate of $5 million included $1.5 million that was includible in her estate under § 2044 (one-third of the value of the trust in 2009, $4,500,000). *W*'s will did not contain any directions regarding the source of payment of the estate tax. The tax on *W*'s $3,500,000 in property was entirely offset by the applicable credit amount. *W*'s estate is subject to a tax of $675,000, all of which is recoverable by *W*'s executor from the distributees of the QTIP property.

Final Tax on estate of $5,000,000	$675,000
Less:	
Final tax payable without inclusion of QTIP property	0
Tax payable by QTIP distributees	$675,000

As noted before, a similar right of recovery applies with respect to the gift tax imposed on the inter vivos disposition of part or all of a qualifying income interest. §2207A(b). It is recoverable by the transferee spouse (the donor of the qualifying income interest) from the recipients of the property. The remainder beneficiaries of a QTIP trust can disclaim the benefit of a tax clause in a surviving spouse's will under which the estate tax resulting from the inclusion of the QTIP trust in her estate would be paid from her estate and not the trust. LR 200127007.

The doctrine of the duty of consistency was invoked in LR 9548002 (TAM) (Ohio law) as one of the grounds on which the surviving spouse's estate was obligated to include the property of a QTIP trust with respect to which a marital deduction had been claimed in the estate tax return filed with respect to the predeceased spouse's estate. According to the TAM, "The elements necessary for application of this equitable doctrine are: (1) a representation by the taxpayer; (2) the Commissioner relies on that representation; and (3) the taxpayer attempts to change its previous representation to the detriment of the Commissioner after the statute of limitations has expired for the year in which the representation was made." The estate argued that the QTIP trust should be excluded from the surviving spouse's gross estate because the boilerplate spendthrift clause that applied to all trusts under the predeceased spouse's will. Under the clause, the trust would become a discretionary trust if the beneficiary attempted to alienate, encumber, or attempt to dispose of any interest, or if the property was vulnerable to seizure by creditors. For another case in which the doctrine was invoked *see Kristine A. Cluck,* 105 T.C. 324 (1995). The duty of consistency was applied by the Tax Court in *Estate of Mildred G. Letts,* 109 T.C. 290 (1997), *aff'd without pub. op.,* 212 F.3d 600 (11th Cir. 2000), to require the surviving spouse's estate to include a trust for which her deceased husband's estate claimed a marital deduction.

In LR 9537004 (TAM) (Illinois law), the IRS ruled that the decedent's gross estate must include a trust with respect to which a QTIP election had been made by the executor of her predeceased spouse. The decedent's estate argued that the trust allowed the trustee to retain unproductive property as a result of which the trust did not meet the requirements of §2056(b)(7). According to the IRS the Illinois prudent investor rule would have required the trustee to invest and diversify the assets exercising reasonable care. The IRS also rejected the estate's contention that no QTIP election was possible because the decedent's estate was not entitled to the "stub" income (the income accrued between the date of the last payment date and the date of the decedent's death).

If a QTIP trust for the benefit of his surviving spouse is initially over-funded, the surviving spouse's estate is not required to include the excess that was later transferred to the credit shelter trust. LR 200223020 (TAM). The ruling follows Rev. Rul. 84-105, 1984-2 C.B. 197: "The ruling states that the marital deduction allowed for the decedent's estate is the amount that should have funded the trust, not the amount that was used to fund the trust." Accordingly, §2044 requires the surviving spouse's estate to include only the value of the assets held in the QTIP trust at the time of her death.

§ 5.23.12. Surviving Spouse Purchases Remainder Interest in QTIP

A commentator has suggested that the gross estate of the surviving spouse may be significantly reduced if he or she purchases the interests of the remainder beneficiaries of the QTIP trust. *See* Bettigole, Can the Olsten Scenario Save Estate Taxes?, 134 Tr. & Est. 46 (Feb. 1995) on which this summary is based. A QTIP trust is, of course, includible in the surviving spouse's gross estate to the extent a marital deduction was claimed at the time it was created. § 2044. Presumably the acquisition of the remainder interest would not increase the amount of property otherwise includible in the surviving spouse's gross estate. Logically, the property that the surviving spouse transferred in exchange for the remainder interest would likewise not be includible in his or her gross estate. The consequences under Chapter 14 are unclear. As the author of the above article noted, "Whether § 2702 applies to the within transaction is questionable. Finally, the surviving spouse, the remainderman, or both may realize gain on such a sale, depending on the value of the property involved." Section 1001(e) does not apply as the sale does not involve the transfer of a "term interest" within the meaning of that section.

In Rev. Rul. 98-8, 1998-1 C.B. 541, the IRS considered the gift tax effect of the surviving spouse's purchase of the remainder interest in a QTIP trust. The ruling holds:

> If a surviving spouse acquires the remainder interest in a trust subject to a QTIP election under § 2056(b)(7) in connection with the transfer by the surviving spouse of property or cash to the holder of the remainder interest, the surviving spouse makes a gift both under § 2519 and § § 2511 and 2512. The amount of the gift is equal to the greater of (i) the value of the remainder interest (pursuant to § 2519), or (ii) the value of the property or cash transferred to the holder of the remainder interest (pursuant to § § 2511 and 2512).

With respect to the application of § 2519, the ruling reasoned that the transaction was comparable to a commutation of the spouse's income interest in a QTIP trust, which is prohibited by the regulations, Reg. § 25.2519-1(f). *See also Estate of Helen M. Novotny*, 93 T.C. 12 (1989). "There is little distinction between the sale and commutation transactions treated as dispositions in the regulations and the transaction presented here, where S acquired the remainder interest. In both cases, after the transaction, the spouse's income interest in the trust is terminated and the spouse receives outright ownership of property having a net value equal to the value of the spouse's income interest."

On the § § 2511 and 2512 issues the ruling states that:

> [I]n the present situation, property subject to the QTIP election was intended to be subject to either gift or estate tax. S's receipt of the remainder interest does not increase the value of S's taxable estate because that property is already subject to inclusion in S's taxable estate under § 2044. Rather, S's issuance of the note results in a depletion of S's taxable estate that is not offset by S's receipt of the remainder interest. Thus, for estate and gift tax purposes, S's receipt of the remainder interest

cannot constitute adequate and full consideration under §2512 for the promissory note transferred by *S* to *C*. As was the case in *Merrill v. Fahs*, any other result would subvert the legislative intent and statutory scheme underlying §2056(b)(7). Therefore, under §2511, *S* has made a gift to *C* equal to the value of the promissory note *S* gave to *C*.

§5.24. CURRENT INTEREST IN CHARITABLE REMAINDER TRUST, §2056(b)(8)

If any individual transfers property outright to charity, no transfer taxes generally are imposed. Similarly, under the unlimited marital deduction provided in the committee bill, no tax generally will be imposed on an outright gift to the decedent's spouse. As a result, the committee finds no justification for imposing transfer taxes on a transfer split between a spouse and a qualifying charity. Accordingly, the bill provides a special rule for transfers of interest in the same property to a spouse and a qualifying charity. H.R. Rep. 97-102, 97th Cong., 1st Sess., 162 (1981).

The 1981 Act also created an exception to the terminable interest rule for the current interest in charitable remainder trusts where the surviving spouse is the only noncharitable beneficiary. §2056(b)(8). Tracking the provisions applicable to a CRT, a deduction is allowable under §2056(b)(8) for an interest payable to a surviving spouse for life or a term of 20 years or less. Reg. §20.2056(b)-8(a)(2). That provision is consistent with the text of the statute and numerous private letter rulings. A corresponding gift tax exception applies where the donor's spouse and the donor are the only noncharitable beneficiaries. §2523(g). Accordingly, a transfer to a charitable remainder unitrust qualifies for a charitable deduction under §2055 (or §2522) for the value of the charitable remainder interest and a marital deduction under §2056 (or §2523) for the value of the current (annuity or unitrust) interest. LR 9244001 (TAM). *See* Reg. §20.2056(b)-8(a)(1). Importantly, a deduction is allowable even though the transfer is conditioned on the spouse's payment of any state death taxes that might be imposed on the qualified charitable remainder trust. Reg. §20.2056(b)-8(a)(3).

A trust that meets the requirements of §2056(b)(8) may qualify as a QDT, which can permit creative planning. *See* §5.25. For example a grantor can transfer highly appreciated property to a charitable remainder trust, reserving the noncharitable interest for life and the right to revoke the successive noncharitable interest of his wife, who was not a United States citizen, with the remainder passing to charity upon the death of the survivor of the grantor and his wife. *See* §8.20.5. LR 9244013.

In the case of an inter vivos gift to a CRT, a gift tax return would not be required with respect to the marital deduction gift, but one would be required to claim the charitable deduction. Note that an inter vivos gift of this type will also qualify for an income tax charitable deduction under §170.

Unlike the QTIP, under this approach upon the death of the donee spouse nothing is includible in his or her gross estate by reason of the existence of the charitable remainder trust. Section 2044 does not apply, because no QTIP election is required to secure the marital deduction under §2056(b)(8).

A QTIP election cannot be made with respect to property that qualifies for the marital deduction under §2056(b)(8). Reg. §20.2056(b)-8(a).

§5.25. QUALIFIED DOMESTIC TRUST (QDOT), §§2056(d), 2056A

Under the general rule of §2056(d)(1), the estate tax marital deduction is not allowable for transfers to a surviving spouse for which the marital deduction would otherwise be available if the surviving spouse is not a United States citizen. The intention of this rule is to assure that the property for which the marital deduction is allowed in a decedent's estate will be subject to the gift or estate tax. The two exceptions to the rule in §2056(d)(1) are both fashioned to provide the necessary assurance. In brief, the restriction imposed by the basic rule is lifted with respect to otherwise qualifying transfers if any of the alternative requirements discussed below are satisfied. Act §501.

The first allows the deduction if the surviving spouse was a United States resident at all times following the decedent's death and becomes a citizen before the decedent's estate tax return is filed. §2056(d)(4). A failure to become a citizen before the return must be filed eliminates this option. LR 9021037. However, note the opportunity under §2056A(b)(12), discussed below, to escape from §2056A if the surviving spouse later becomes a citizen.

Under the second, the deduction is available with respect to property that passes from the decedent to a QDT. §2056(d)(2)(A). Property passing to the surviving spouse is treated as having passed to a QDT if either the property is transferred to a QDT before the decedent's tax return is filed or the property is irrevocably assigned to a QDT before the return is filed. §2056(d)(2)(B). Property that the surviving spouse receives as surviving joint tenant, beneficiary of life insurance or employee benefit plans, or by bequest may be transferred to a QDT. LRs 8952005, 9044072 (life insurance proceeds). Note, however, that the transfer of property to a QDT might subject the remainder interest to the gift tax unless the surviving spouse retains a power sufficient to make the transfer incomplete under Reg. §25.2511-2.

IRAs and QDTs. A surviving spouse may transfer to a QDT the balance of IRAs that passed to her outright upon the decedent's death. LR 9151043. A similar approach was also approved in LR 9729040.

In LR 9623063, the IRS allowed the marital deduction for a deceased spouse's share of three IRAs of which his noncitizen surviving spouse was the beneficiary. The surviving spouse rolled over the IRAs to a trusteed IRA in her name that would be the subject of an agreement that met the requirements of §2056A. Under the agreement there would be a corporate trustee that would serve as custodian of the IRAs and have the right to withhold taxes as required. The surviving spouse would be entitled to receive distributions to the extent of the trust's current income—the income earned during the calendar year. The ruling also holds that the rollover was qualified for income tax purposes.

Reformation. The determination of whether a trust is a QDT is made on the date the decedent's return is filed. §2056(d)(5)(A)(i). However, if a reformation action is filed on or before that date, the changes made to the trust in that proceeding will be taken into account. §2056(d)(5)(A)(ii). According to the IRS, a trust reformation will be recognized only if the marital deduction would have been allowable with respect to the trust but for the citizenship of the surviving spouse. LR 9043070.

Under Reg. § 20.2056A-4(a)(1), a nonjudicial reformation pursuant to the terms of the decedent's will or trust must be completed within the time for filing the estate tax return, including extensions. In the case of a judicial reformation, the regulations require that the proceeding have been commenced by the time the return is due. Reg. § 20.2056A-4(a)(2). However, prior to the time the reformation is completed the trust must be treated as a QDT. Under that regulation, "[T]he trustee is responsible for filing the Form 706-QDT, paying any § 2056A tax that is due, and filing the annual statement under Reg. § 20.2056A-2T(d)(3) if applicable."

Surviving Spouse's Funding QDT with Outright Bequests. The regulations include rules regarding the manner in which a surviving spouse may transfer to a QDT property that passed to the surviving spouse outright from the decedent. An assignment to a trust established by the surviving spouse must be in writing and comply with local law. Reg. § 20.2056A-4(b)(1). An assignment may relate to a single asset or group of assets or a fractional share of either or of a pecuniary amount. The transfer of less than an entire interest may be made by means of a formula. A copy of the instrument of transfer must be included with the decedent's estate tax return. Only assets included in the decedent's estate that passed to the surviving spouse and qualify for the marital deduction (or their proceeds) may be transferred to a QDT. In the case of a pecuniary assignment, the assignment must require either that the assets have an aggregate fair market value on the date of actual transfer amounting to no less than the amount of the pecuniary transfer or that the assets actually transferred be fairly representative of appreciation or depreciation in value of all property available for transfer to the QDT. Reg. § 20.2056A-4(b)(4). Assets irrevocably assigned before the decedent's estate tax return is filed must be actually transferred before administration of the decedent's estate is completed.

Letter Ruling 9808022 held that a marital deduction would be allowable with respect to property distributed to a surviving noncitizen spouse under the intestate succession law that she transfers to an irrevocable trust, which contains provisions that satisfy the requirements of § 2056A. If the surviving spouse becomes a citizen before the due date of the estate tax return, a marital deduction will be allowable for the property that passes to her by intestacy. If she becomes a citizen later, the trust will terminate and the trust property will be distributed to her. Because the surviving spouse would be entitled to all the income of the trust and would hold a special testamentary power of appointment over the trust, the transfer of property to the trust would not constitute a completed gift to the remaindermen.

Regulation § 20.2056A-4(b)(7) prescribes rules regarding the assignment of interests in individual retirement accounts and individual retirement annuities. Subparagraph (c) describes the procedures applicable to nonassignable annuities and other arrangements. In this connection *See* § 5.23.5.

Additional Requirements. The regulations impose detailed security arrangements: If the value of the assets passing to a QDT exceed $2 million as finally determined for estate tax purposes, the trust must require that (1) at least one trustee be a bank defined in § 581, or (2) the trustee furnish a bond equal to 65 percent of the QDT's date of death value. Reg. § 20.2056A-2(d)(1)(i). If the date of death value was $2 million or less neither requirement applies if the trust provides that no more than 35 percent of the value of the trust may be invested in real property not located in the

United States Reg. § 20.2056A-2(d)(1)(ii). The regulations allow certain letters of credit to satisfy the requirement that there be a United States bank or that a bond be furnished. Reg. § 20.2056A-2(d)(1)(i)(C). Under the regulation dealing with the bond, the governing instrument must provide that if the IRS draws on the bond, "neither the U.S. Trustee nor any other person will seek a return of any part of the remittance until April 15th of the calendar year following the year in which the bond is drawn upon." Reg. § 20.2056A-2(d)(1)(i)(B)(3). Essentially the same requirement applies to a letter of credit. The regulations deal in detail with the requirements that are applicable if the value of property fluctuates.

The regulations allow the required security provisions to be incorporated in an instrument by reference, which is a great convenience. In particular, the regulations provide: "A trust instrument that specifically states that the trust must be administered in compliance with paragraph (d)(1)(a)(A), (B), or (C) of this section is treated as meeting the requirements of paragraphs (d)(1)(i)(A), (B), or (C) for purposes of paragraphs (d)(1) and, if applicable, (d)(1)(ii) of this section." Reg. § 20.2056A-2(d)(1)(i).

Foreign Trust Rules. A QDT should be drafted in light of the rules that define domestic and foreign trusts. § 7701(a)(30), (31). Foreign trusts and their domestic beneficiaries are subject to special reporting requirements and may be subject to additional taxes. *See* § 10.53. Under § 7701(a)(30)(E) a trust is a domestic trust only if (a) a court in the United States has primary supervision over the administration of the trust, and (b) one or more United States fiduciaries control all substantial decisions of the trust. Merely appointing a foreign person (*i.e.*, a nonresident alien) as co-trustee can cause a trust to be treated as a foreign trust. In addition, the regulations indicate that a trust will be a foreign trust if a nonresident alien has the power to veto decisions, withdraw assets or remove and replace a trustee. Reg. § 301.7701-7(d)(4), Examples 2, 3 and 4. *See* Nunez, Taking the "Foreign" out of Foreign Trusts, U. Miami, 34th Inst. Est. Plan., Ch. 7 (2000).

§ 5.25.1. QDT

Under § 2056A(a), a QDT trust must require that

1. At least one trustee be an individual citizen of the United States or a domestic corporation; and

2. No distribution (other than income) be made unless the trustee who is a citizen of the United States or a domestic corporation has the right to withhold from the distribution the tax on distributions imposed by § 2056A.

In addition, the trust must meet such requirements as the Secretary may by regulation prescribe in order to assure the collection of any tax imposed by § 2056A(b). § 2056A(a)(2). In light of this requirement, the trust might authorize the trustee to amend the trust from time to time as required to comply with regulations issued pursuant to § 2056A. Finally, the decedent's executor must make an irrevocable election on the decedent's estate tax return to treat the trust as a QDT. §§ 2056A(a)(3), 2056A(d). No election can be made on a return filed more than one year after the time prescribed for filing the return, including extensions. § 2056A(d). Bear in mind that the marital deduction is only allowable if a trust created by the decedent also meets the requirements of § 2056(b) (*e.g.,* a life interest-general power of appointment trust, an estate trust, or QTIP trust). Reg. § 20.2056A-2(b)(1).

Under Reg. § 20.2056A-3(a), a QDT election must be made on the last estate tax return filed before the due date, including extensions, or, if a timely return is not filed, on the first return filed after the due date. The election must be made in the manner provided on the estate tax return, including the instructions. Reg. § 20.2056A-3(d). An election once made is irrevocable. § 20.2056A-3(a). Unfortunately, the regulations continue to provide that a partial QDT election cannot be made. Reg. § 20.2056A-3(b). However, a separate election can be made with respect to a trust that is severed in accordance with the QTIP regulations. *Id.* A protective election can be made if the executor reasonably believes that there is a bona fide issue that concerns the residency or citizenship of the decedent or of the surviving spouse, whether an asset is includible in the decedent's gross estate, or the amount or nature of the property that the surviving spouse is entitled to receive. Reg. § 20.2056A-3(c). A protective election can be "defined by means of a formula (such as the minimum amount necessary to reduce the estate tax to zero)." *Id.*

An extension of time to file the bond required for a QDT may be granted in accordance with Reg. § 301.9100-1T. LR 9803017.

§ 5.25.2. Tax on Distributions from QDT

In general any distribution from a QDT made before the death of the surviving spouse and any property remaining in a QDT at the time of the death of the surviving spouse is subject to an estate tax at the marginal rate applicable to the estate of the deceased spouse who created the trust. § 2056A(b). Upon the death of the surviving spouse, the benefits of §§ 303, 2014, 2032, 2032A, 2055, 2056, 2058, 6161, and 6166 are available. § 2056A(b)(10). Recognizing that the QDT may attract a § 2056A tax and a regular estate tax imposed on the estate of the surviving spouse, § 2056(d)(3) allows a credit under § 2013 for the § 2056A tax without regard to the date of the death of the first spouse to die. Regulation § 20.2056A-7 describes the manner in which the § 2013 credit is determined and allowed.

EXAMPLE 5-25.

H died in 2006 leaving $4 million to a QDT for his wife, *W. W* was not a United States citizen. *H* also left $2 million to a trust for his children by a prior marriage. *H*'s estate paid no estate tax. In 2007, $400,000 of principal was distributed to *W* from the QDT. The distribution was subject to a § 2056A estate tax of $180,000. In 2008, *W* died a resident of the United States and left an estate of $4 million including the QDT. *W*'s estate is entitled to a credit under § 2013 for the tax paid pursuant to § 2056A in connection with the distribution of property to her.

Distributions of Income or on Account of Hardship. The § 2056A estate tax does not apply to any distribution of income to the surviving spouse or to any distribution to the surviving spouse on account of hardship. § 2056A(b)(3). Although hardship is not defined in the statute, some guidance is provided by the regulations under

§401(k). For example, "a distribution is on account of hardship only if the distribution both is made on account of an immediate and heavy financial need of the employee and is necessary to satisfy such financial need." Reg. §1.401(k)-1(d)(2). An immediate and heavy financial need might occur in connection with the funeral expenses of a family member, but not to pay for recreational expenses such as the purchase of a boat.

Regulation §20.2056A-5(c)(1) permits a distribution of principal made on account of hardship if it was made in response to an immediate and substantial financial need relating "to the spouse's health, maintenance, education, or support, or the health, maintenance, education, or support of any person that the surviving spouse is legally obligated to support." However, a distribution in response to such need is not treated as made on account of hardship if the amount distributed could have been obtained from other sources reasonably available to the surviving spouse, such as the sale of personally owned, publicly traded stock, or the cashing in of a certificate of deposit. Although funds distributed in case of hardship are not taxable, they must be reported on a Form 706-QDT filed for the period during which the distribution was made.

Certain other types of distributions are also not subject to the estate tax, including distributions made to reimburse the surviving spouse for income taxes imposed on distributions of income. §2056A(b)(15); Reg. §20.2056A-5(c)(3)(ii). On the other hand, amounts withheld by the United States trustee to pay the estate tax on amount distributed to a surviving spouse are treated as an additional distribution to the surviving spouse in the year the tax is paid. Reg. §20.2056A-5(b)(1).

Payment Date and Liability for Payment. The §2056A tax on distributions is due on April 15 of the year following the calendar year in which the distribution was made. §2056A(b)(5)(A). The tax on the death of the surviving spouse is due nine months after the date of death. §2056A(b)(5)(B). Each trustee is personally liable for the tax. §2056A(b)(6). A lien for the §2056A tax is imposed for ten years under §6324 as if the tax were an estate tax. §2056A(b)(8).

Under Reg. §20.2056A-11(d), each trustee of a QDT (not solely the United States trustee) is personally liable for the amount of the estate tax imposed under §2056A. In the case of multiple QDTs the trustee of each is personally liable only with respect to the QDT of which he is trustee. However, the property of each trust is subject to collection of taxes imposed with respect to other of the trusts.

If the estate tax is imposed on any distribution from a QDT, the distribution is treated as a gift for purposes of §1015 and any tax paid is treated as a gift tax. Reg. §20.2056A-12. The rules of §1015 apply for the purpose of determining the basis of the property. Accordingly, the basis of the property distributed may be increased by a portion of the tax.

§5.25.3. Surviving Spouse Becomes Citizen

A trust is no longer subject to the §2056A tax if the surviving spouse becomes a citizen and the following requirements of §2056A(b)(12) are met:

1. The surviving spouse was a United States resident at all times after the date of death of the decedent and before the surviving spouse became a citizen; and

2. No §2056A tax was imposed on distributions before the surviving spouse became a citizen, *or*, the surviving spouse elects to treat any taxable distributions as taxable gifts made by her for purposes of the gift and estate taxes.

Regulation §20.2056A-10(b) explains how the election works. The surviving spouse must file a Form 706-QDT on or before April 15 of the year following the year in which he or she becomes a United States citizen (unless an extension has been granted under §6081) and attaches notification of the election required by the regulation. The election is that the surviving spouse will: (1) treat the taxable distributions that took place prior to the election as taxable gifts for United States gift and estate tax purposes, and (2) reduce the surviving spouse's unified credit by the amount of the decedent spouse's unified credit that was used to reduce the QDOT estate tax imposed on distributions prior to the year in which the surviving spouse became a United States citizen.

§5.26. WHICH FORM OF TRUST—SUMMARY

In considering the type of marital deduction gift to recommend to a client, the lawyer should bear in mind the adverse effect that an outright formula gift might have on the availability and utility of the previously taxed property credit under §2013. If the spouses die relatively close together in time, a considerable estate tax savings can result if the spouse who died first created a QTIP trust for the benefit of the surviving spouse. In such a case the overall estate tax burden can often be dramatically reduced if the estate of the predeceased spouse does not claim a QTIP marital deduction and pays some estate tax. A portion of the estate tax paid will be allowed as a credit against the estate tax otherwise payable on the death of the surviving spouse. A credit is allowable under §2013 for the portion of the tax attributable to the actuarially determined value of the income interest in the trust given to the surviving spouse although none of the trust is includible in his or her gross estate. In contrast, in the case of an outright gift, no credit is allowable against the estate tax in the survivor's estate for estate tax paid by the estate of the predeceased spouse because no estate tax was paid with respect to it. The deficiency is largely alleviated if the plan allows the surviving spouse (or his or her representative) to disclaim an outright gift into a QTIP trust.

Apart from considerations regarding the §2013 credit, the particular circumstances of the clients and their desires will determine which form of marital deduction trust, if any, should be used. Since 1981 the QTIP trust has become the dominant form of marital deduction trust, displacing almost entirely the life interest-general power of appointment trust. Both types of trust eliminate the necessity of administering the trust property upon the death of the surviving spouse. Two main factors account for the popularity of the QTIP form of trust. First, in the case of a QTIP trust the surviving spouse need not be given any power over the ultimate disposition of the property. Second, the amount of the marital deduction claimed with respect to a trust that meets the requirements of §2056(b)(7) is elective. Also, clients with large estates that may involve the GSTT may benefit from the flexibility provided by the possibility of making a reverse QTIP election for GSTT purposes under §2652(a)(3). Finally, lawyers probably feel more comfortable using a trust of the QTIP variety because it more closely resembles the traditional form of family trust.

On the other hand, the estate trust is useful in some circumstances, particularly where the surviving spouse does not need to be assured of additional lifetime income. The charitable remainder trust may be attractive to clients in special circumstances (*e.g.,* ones with no children and a strong desire to benefit one or more charities). Of course, all four types of trusts provide for the management of property during the surviving spouse's lifetime. With the exception of the estate trust the trusts also generally insulate the trust property corpus from the surviving spouse's creditors.

§5.27.   Savings Clause

The IRS and the courts give some recognition to clauses that express a decedent's intent that the provisions of an instrument be interpreted and applied so as to sustain the allowance of the marital deduction. Such a clause may save a marital deduction where a particular power, duty, or discretion of the trustee might otherwise bar the deduction. For example, Rev. Rul. 75-440, 1975-2 C.B. 372, held that a disqualifying power to invest in nonincome-producing property applied to the residuary trust but not to the marital deduction because of the decedent's intent as expressed in a savings clause. Consistently, LR 8440037 held that the marital deduction was available because a savings clause prevented the application to the marital deduction trust of a boilerplate provision that allowed the trustee to invest in or retain unproductive property. A savings clause also overrode contrary provisions of a trust in LR 199932001 (TAM). The inclusion of a clause that expresses the testator's intent that a trust qualify for the marital deduction may be enough to persuade a court to ignore a provision that would otherwise have resulted in a denial of the marital deduction. *Ellingson v. Commissioner,* 964 F.2d 959 (9th Cir. 1992) (marital deduction allowed with respect to a trust with such a clause that provided that all income be distributed to the surviving spouse and that the trustee accumulate income that was not required for the support of the surviving spouse). A savings clause helped assure the allowance of the marital deduction for a trust that was funded, in part, with stock that had never paid a dividend. LR 200339003 (TAM). Importantly, the trust also included a provision that allowed the surviving spouse to require the trustee to dispose of unproductive assets and invest in productive assets.

Savings clauses are not always sufficient to allow the marital deduction for an otherwise nonqualifying trust. For example, LR 200234017 (TAM) did not allow the marital deduction for a trust that gave the surviving spouse a lifetime special power to appoint the property of the trust to and among their issue. According to the TAM, the savings clause in the trust "purports to invalidate only executor and trustee powers that would disqualify the Marital Trust for the marital deduction. The will does not purport to invalidate dispositive provisions that might disqualify the Marital Trust for the marital deduction. Even if we were to give the savings clause any effect in determining Decedent's intent, the savings clause would be ineffective to invalidate Spouse's lifetime power of appointment."

Savings clauses are generally ineffective to overcome the effect of a disqualifying power that is clearly applicable to the trust intended to qualify for the marital deduction. The IRS and some courts have refused to recognize "condition subsequent" clauses that purport to revoke powers that apply to the trust in the event the powers are determined to prevent allowance of the marital deduction. Thus, in Rev. Rul. 65-144, 1965-1 C.B. 442, the IRS refused to give effect to a clause that attempted to revoke the powers of the trustee to the extent necessary to make the interest deductible for federal tax purposes.

Overall, it is worthwhile to include a savings clause in an instrument that is intended to generate a marital deduction. The clause provides some assurance that the instrument will be interpreted and applied in a sympathetic way. However, such a clause should not be relied upon to provide any protection against disqualifying provisions that clearly apply to the gift intended to support the marital deduction. A savings clause might be drafted along these lines:

Form 5-4
Marital Deduction Savings Clause

> I intend that the property passing from me to the trustee of the trust for the benefit of my [wife/husband] shall qualify for the federal estate tax marital deduction. Accordingly, I direct that all provisions of this will shall be interpreted and applied in a manner consistent with my intention.

D. THE GIFT TAX MARITAL DEDUCTION

§ 5.28. OVERALL CONSIDERATIONS

Two changes made by the 1981 Act sharply reduced the tax advantages of making inter vivos gifts to a spouse. They were (1) the adoption of the unlimited marital deduction, and (2) the enactment of a much larger unified credit. Together the changes significantly compressed the estate and gift tax rates. Prior to 1982, lifetime gifts to a spouse were frequently used to equalize the size of the estates of the donor and donee and to maximize the amount of property that could be passed to a spouse free of tax. Despite the 1981 changes, lifetime gifts to a spouse retain some tax advantages, particularly where the estate of one spouse is below the amount of the credit equivalent.

Of course, a decision of whether to make substantial gifts to a spouse should take various nontax factors into account, including the experience, ability and interests of the spouse and the stability of the marriage. In the nature of things few individuals make outright gifts of a substantial portion of their wealth to a spouse under any circumstances. In some cases a large gift may help to cement the relationship between the spouses by providing tangible evidence of the donor's affection for, and confidence in, the donee. The desirability of each spouse's having control over some assets and of holding others in the names of both spouses should also be recognized. However, an unanticipated dissolution proceeding may negate the "tax advantages" of gifts, including: inter vivos assignments of life insurance policies, *Moser v. Moser,* 572 P.2d 446 (Ariz. 1977); private annuities, *Stanger v. Stanger,* 571 P.2d 1126 (Idaho 1977); and other estate planning devices, *Marriage of Hadley,* 565 P.2d 790 (Wash. 1977) (agreements regarding status of assets as community or noncommunity property).

A lawyer who participates in a plan which involves substantial gifts from one spouse to the other should be alert to the conflict of interest that exists if both parties look to the lawyer for advice. Because of the conflict the prospective donor spouse should be separately represented in some cases. The same is, of course, true if the spouses wish to enter into a post-nuptial agreement regarding the ownership of, and rights to, their property.

An amendment made by the 1988 Act denies the marital deduction for gifts to noncitizen spouses. § 2523(i). However, at the same time, the annual exclusion allowed for gifts to noncitizen spouses was increased to $100,000. § 2523(i)(2). This amount is adjusted for inflation. § 2503(b)(2). The increased annual exclusion is only allowable for gifts that otherwise meet the requirements of § 2503. Thus, no annual exclusion was allowed for a gift to a trust in which the donee spouse had only a discretionary right to receive distributions of income and principal. LR 9533001 (TAM).

§ 5.29. GENERAL OBJECTIVES OF INTER VIVOS GIFTS

Some of the general objectives of making inter vivos gifts also apply in planning gifts to a spouse. First, an interspousal gift removes from the donor's estate any future appreciation in value of the property transferred. Of course, the significance of this objective is reduced by the availability of the unlimited marital deduction—tax-free gifts can be made at any time to a spouse who is a United States citizen regardless of their value. Second, such a gift may reduce the value of the non-business assets owned by the donor so the business holdings retained by the donor will constitute a large enough proportion of his estate to qualify for the special tax benefits of §§ 303, 2032A, or 6166. *See* Table 7-1. However, gifts made within three years of the donor's death are brought back into the donor's estate for purposes of §§ 303, 2032A, and 6166. § 2035(c). Third, inter vivos gifts to a spouse can also serve to create an estate for the poorer spouse in order to take advantage of the donee spouse's unified credit should he or she predecease the donor. This advantage may be secured by making a gift to a QTIP trust for the poorer spouse. As indicated above, the donor may retain a successive life estate in the trust without requiring the property to be included in the donor's estate under § 2036. *See* § 5.23.6. A gift to the poorer spouse may also preserve the use of the poorer spouse's GSTT exemption. *See* § 2.42.1.

Inter vivos gifts to a spouse of fractional interests in real estate or of noncontrol interests in business enterprises can be planned so as to qualify the interests for continuing discounts in the estate of the donee spouse. If a spouse is given the entire interest in an asset, or a controlling interest in a business, the interest will not qualify for a minority interest discount in his or her estate. A discount would be available if the donee were given, for example, a one-half interest in a parcel of real property and the donor left the other half to a QTIP trust for the benefit of the surviving spouse. *See* §§ 2.14 and 2.15.

EXAMPLE 5-26.

The residence of *H* and *W*, which is owned by *H* is worth $4 million. *H* could make a lifetime gift of a half interest to *W*. The gift of a fractional interest would be valued at a discount of 15 percent or more—as would *H*'s retained half interest. On the death of either *H* or *W*, the decedent's fractional interest will continue to qualify for the discount. If the deceased spouse's interest if left outright to the surviving spouse, the survivor will own 100 percent. No discount will be available in the survivor's estate unless he or she has made a lifetime gift of an interest.

Gifts to a spouse generally yield little, if any, income tax benefit because married persons usually benefit from filing joint income tax returns.

§5.30. EQUALIZING ESTATES BY LIFETIME GIFTS

The general importance of equalizing the sizes of the spouses' estates is reviewed in §5.7. Lifetime equalization may be undertaken to ensure that the wealthier spouse will be able to transfer some property to the ultimate donees at lower tax cost by routing it through the poorer spouse's estate, but the advantage of equalization occurs only where estate tax is imposed at varying, progressive rates instead of the flat rates applicable under current law.

If inter vivos gifts are made, the spouses' dispositive instruments should be reviewed to be sure the provisions are compatible with the gifts. For example, it may be necessary to scale down the amount of the gifts made to the donee in the donor's will to avoid unduly increasing the donee's estate. Also, the donee should plan to dispose of the gifted property in a tax-sensitive way consistent with their overall dispositive goals. For example, the donee spouse's will should be drafted so the gifted property will not return to the donor or otherwise be included in the donor's gross estate.

The unlimited marital deduction largely eliminates the gift and estate tax advantage of making lifetime equalizing gifts to a spouse. If the estates of each of the spouses exceeds the applicable exclusion amount, it is now generally just as effective to equalize by making a gift at death if the wealthier spouse dies first. However, inter vivos gifts are an effective hedge against the possibility that the opportunity to equalize will be lost by the unexpected prior death of the less wealthy spouse.

In many cases the sizes of the estates may be equalized without depriving the donor of assets of substantial current value by making gifts of life insurance. For example, the spouse with the smaller estate may be given policies of insurance on the other spouse's life or funds with which to acquire new policies. Alternatively, the insurance might be transferred to an irrevocable life insurance trust. *See* §§6.17-6.25.

§5.31. USING LIFETIME GIFTS TO TAKE ADVANTAGE OF THE POORER SPOUSE'S UNIFIED CREDIT

If the estate of one spouse substantially exceeds the amount of the credit equivalent and the estate of the other is substantially less than the credit equivalent, steps should be taken to assure that the shelter provided by the poorer spouse's credit is fully utilized.

EXAMPLE 5-27.

W's estate is worth $3 million while her husband's *H's*, estate is worth only $500,000. If *H* predeceases *W,* most of his unified credit will be wasted. *W* should consider making a substantial gift to *H,* which he could leave to a QTIP trust for the benefit of *W* if he predeceases her.

There may be some tax advantages to transferring property to a terminally ill spouse whose estate is less than the credit equivalent. However, the bases of appreciated assets given to a person within a year of the donee's death are not increased if the donee leaves them to the original donor (or his or her spouse). § 1014(e). Tact and consideration should be exercised in discussing transfers to or from terminally ill spouses because of the possibility that a discussion of tax matters may offend them and members of their family. Also, if such a gift is made, it may be necessary to change the content of the donee's will in order to take full advantage of the tax savings plan. The lawyer and client must also consider how the gifts would affect other dispositive plans and how they would be viewed by other members of the donor's family.

If assets are to be gifted to a terminally ill spouse, highly appreciated assets (*i.e.,* ones with low bases) should normally be transferred to him or her. Their bases would be increased the most by the stepped-up basis the assets would acquire under § 1014 upon the donee's death.

E. EXPRESSING A MARITAL DEDUCTION GIFT—FORMULA AND NONFORMULA GIFTS

§ 5.32. OVERVIEW

Property may pass to a surviving spouse in a variety of ways that qualify for the marital deduction. *See* § 2056(c) and § 5.16. Because property commonly passes to a surviving spouse and others under several will substitutes (*e.g.,* joint tenancies, IRAs and employee benefit plans, life insurance beneficiary designations, multiparty bank accounts), the lawyer should assist the client in reviewing, analyzing, and organizing the client's property.

Estate plans often use a formula either to define the portion of a decedent's estate that will pass to the surviving spouse in a way that qualifies for the marital deduction or to fix the amount that will pass to, or will be claimed with respect to, a trust that qualifies for the marital deduction. The formulas used for these purposes are designed to assure that no estate tax will be due from the estate of the first spouse to die and that the deceased spouse's unified credit will shelter the maximum amount from inclusion in the surviving spouse's estate. Prior to the adoption of the unlimited marital deduction the formulas were usually designed to give the surviving spouse a portion of the transferor's estate equal to the maximum allowable marital deduction.

Two basic formulas were developed in response to the problem of transferring precisely the right amount of property to the surviving spouse (or to a qualifying trust) to support the maximum marital deduction. The formulas generally sought to avoid "overfunding" the marital deduction gift. Both formulas gave the surviving spouse property equal in value to the maximum allowable marital deduction *less* the value of all other property for which the deduction was available. One formula gave the surviving spouse *an amount* of property equal to the maximum allowable marital deduction (a *pecuniary amount formula*); the other gave the survivor *a fractional interest* in a designated portion of the testator's estate (a *fractional share formula*). Both types of formula have been adapted for use in connection with the unlimited marital deduction. *See* §§ 5.33-5.40. The revised formulas are designed to preserve the testator's unified credit by limiting the amount of property passing to the surviving spouse in ways that would require the inclusion of the property in the estate of the surviving spouse.

Before turning to a consideration of the formulas it should be noted that it is unnecessary to use formula marital deduction gifts in some cases. First, it is unnecessary to use a formula when the shelter provided by the testator's unified credit will not be needed (*i.e.,* where the value of the spouse's combined estates is likely to be less than the amount of a single applicable exclusion amount ($5 million in 2011) when the surviving spouse dies). In such a case the testator may leave all of his or her estate outright to the surviving spouse—which is also simpler and gives the survivor a greater degree of control. Thus, the plan for a couple whose estates are small may provide for an outright gift of all of the testator's property to the surviving spouse with a contingent gift to a trust for their minor children. Such a plan is discussed in detail in Chapter 4. Of course, this approach involves some speculation about the value the couple's property will have and the amount of the unified credit that will be available to the surviving spouse's estate.

Second, although the spouses' estates may be large enough to generate some tax on the death of the surviving spouse, the testator may choose to rely upon the surviving spouse's use of qualified disclaimers to adjust the amount of property that passes to him or her. In its simplest form this approach merely involves an outright gift of the testator's entire estate to the surviving spouse with no special provision for the disposition of any property disclaimed by the surviving spouse. In such a case the distribution of any disclaimed property would be determined by the local law. For example, if the surviving spouse disclaims a one-half interest in the testator's residuary estate, the interest would pass to the testator's intestate successors. In order to assure that the disclaimed property will pass to others, the surviving spouse must also disclaim the right to receive any interest in the property by intestate succession. A planner should recognize that the surviving spouse may be incompetent to execute a valid disclaimer, which could jeopardize the plan unless an effective disclaimer can be made by a guardian or other personal representative. Finally, the surviving spouse may be unwilling to disclaim any property because it will pass outright to others and will not be directly available to support him or her.

Under a more sophisticated approach, the testator's will itself directs the manner in which any disclaimed property will be distributed. For example, the will might call for any disclaimed property to pass outright to designated persons or to a QTIP trust (*i.e.,* one in which the surviving spouse has a qualifying income interest for life). If the disclaimed property passes to a QTIP trust, the testator's executor can control the amount of the marital deduction through exercise of the QTIP election under § 2056(b)(7). As a further embellishment such a plan might provide that if the surviving spouse also disclaims any interest in the QTIP trust, that portion of the property will pass outright to designated persons (or to trusts for their benefit).

A formula is also unnecessary if the transferor wishes to leave most of his or her estate to a QTIP trust—thus relying upon the executor's election under § 2056(b)(7) to produce the optimum tax result. Here again, the testator could provide for the disposition of any interest in the trust that is disclaimed by the surviving spouse.

EXAMPLE 5-28.

W, who died in 2006, left her $3 million estate outright to her husband, H, if he survived her, otherwise to those of their adult children who survive her. W was survived by H and their two adult children, S and D. H disclaimed the right to receive property from W's estate that had a value equal to the applicable exclusion amount available to W's estate ($2 million). The disclaimed property passed directly to S and D. Accordingly, that portion of W's property will not be includible in H's gross estate. W's unified credit offset the amount of tax due from her estate on the disclaimed property. The $1 million remainder passed to H. Unless disposed of by H during his lifetime, it will be included in his estate.

EXAMPLE 5-29.

H died in 2006, leaving his estate of $3 million to a trust in which his wife, W, had a qualifying income interest for life. H's executor elected under § 2056(b)(7) to claim a marital deduction with respect to an interest in the trust that had a value of $1 million (a one-third interest). The election took advantage of H's unified credit by sheltering most of the trust from inclusion in W's estate (i.e., two-thirds of the trust will not be included in W's estate).

Finally, the testator may choose to approximate the effect of a formula clause by making a pecuniary nonmarital deduction (or "credit shelter") gift of an amount equal to the credit equivalent and leaving the balance of his or her estate to the surviving spouse. While this approach may not yield the optimum tax result, it is simple and easy to understand. The nonmarital pecuniary gift might be expressed along the lines suggested in Form 5-5.

Form 5-5
Nonformula Pecuniary Nonmarital Deduction Gift

If my [husband/wife] survives me, I give to A, B, & C Trust Company, in trust, subject to the terms of Article Ten [a nonmarital trust], property of my estate equal in value to my remaining applicable exclusion amount as of the date of my death.

This language takes into account the amount of the testator's adjusted taxable gifts (*i.e.,* taxable gifts made after 1976) but not necessarily other dispositions or expenses that are not deductible in computing the federal estate tax (*e.g.,* expenses of administration that are not claimed as federal estate tax deductions).

Overall, one of the most flexible plans involves creating of a QTIP trust for the surviving spouse with provision for the disposition of any interest in the trust that he or she disclaims. This disclaimed interest might pass into a family trust with respect to which the trustee would have discretion to distribute the income, and perhaps the principal, to a class consisting of the surviving spouse and the testator's descendants. Note that the surviving spouse's disclaimer would not be a qualified disclaimer if the surviving spouse held discretionary powers over the distribution of the income or principal—unless it was includible in his or her gross estate. *See* Reg. § 25.2518-2(e)(5), Example 5. *See also* § 12.33.4. The use of a QTIP trust allows the choice regarding the size of the marital deduction to be made after the testator's death when many more facts are known.

Effect of the 2001 Act. Wills and trusts that contain formula gifts should be reviewed with clients to ensure that the scheduled increases in the estate tax credit equivalent will not result in an unwanted allocation of their property. Formula gifts are usually tied to the amount of the deceased spouse's remaining unified credit. They typically take the form of either: (1) an upfront gift to the surviving spouse or to a trust for his or her benefit of the minimum amount required to reduce the estate tax to zero, or (2) an upfront gift to a credit shelter trust of the maximum amount that could pass without the imposition of any estate tax. Whichever approach is used the scheduled increases in the credit equivalent will allocate increasingly larger amounts to the nonmarital beneficiaries (*i.e.,* the credit shelter trust, the children of the deceased spouse, or others). The point is illustrated by Example 5-30.

EXAMPLE 5-30.

H's will makes a formula gift to a credit shelter trust (the beneficiaries of which are his children by his first marriage) of the maximum amount that can pass without incurring any tax liability and leaves the balance of his estate to a QTIP trust for his wife, *W*. If *H* dies in 2008, the credit shelter trust will be funded with property worth $2 million; if he dies in 2009, the trust will receive $3.5 million. The trust for *W* will receive a correlatively smaller amount.

The problem of unintentionally passing too much property to a credit shelter trust does not arise, or at least is not so intense, if the surviving spouse is also the sole or primary lifetime beneficiary of the trust. The problem also does not arise if the testator's entire estate is left to a QTIP trust, of which the surviving spouse is necessarily the only lifetime beneficiary, and with respect to which the decedent's executor could make a partial QTIP election. (The benefit of the decedent's remaining credit equivalent could be preserved by making a partial QTIP election.) Of course, even in the case of a QTIP trust the surviving spouse may need additional protection if the trustee is, or may be, hostile to her interests (possibly one or more of the decedent's children who are also the remaindermen of the trust). In such a case the surviving spouse could be given a 5 or 5 power of withdrawal, which could be limited to the amount by which 5 percent of the principal value of the trust exceeds the amount of income she received from it.

Some clients may wish to pursue another alternative if the surviving spouse or a person whose interests will not be adverse to the surviving spouse will have power to make a QTIP election. Under it the amount of property passing to a QTIP trust and to a credit shelter trust (or to others) is determined by the QTIP election itself. The surviving spouse could have an interest in the credit shelter trust and a special power of appointment over it. The regulations now allow a QTIP election to control the extent of the property in which the surviving spouse has the necessary qualifying income interest for life. Reg. §20.2056(b)-7(d)(3). The approach is akin to ones in which any interest in a QTIP trust that the surviving spouse disclaims will pass to a credit shelter trust or to others. However, in the latter case the surviving spouse cannot retain a special power of appointment over the property unless it is limited by an ascertainable standard.

In some cases, a husband or wife may wish to limit the extent to which property would pass to or for the benefit of persons other than the surviving spouse (children of the testator by a prior marriage). A client might choose to resolve the matter in a variety of ways. A testator might, for example, wish to make the children and the surviving spouse beneficiaries of fixed separate shares of the credit shelter trust. For example, the testator's children might be the beneficiaries of a fractional share of the trust. The share might be determined by a fraction, the numerator of which is $1 million (the applicable exclusion amount in 2011), and the denominator of which is the estate tax credit equivalent allowable at the time of the testator's death ($5 million in 2011, for example). The surviving spouse would be the beneficiary of the balance of the trust. Other clients might, instead, prefer to forego the full use of the credit equivalent by "capping" the amount that would pass to the children or to a credit shelter trust. A cap might also be desirable if a substantial part of the testator's estate consists of assets that fluctuate wildly in value (*e.g.*, shares of high tech, biotech, and.dot-com companies). See §4.16.

Clients may wish to adopt an approach that allows the amount of a formula gift to be determined after the death of a spouse. Three ways of accommodating that wish are for the will (or trust) of a married person to:

1. Leave substantially all of the decedent's property to a qualifying terminable interest trust (QTIP trust) for the benefit of the surviving spouse. The executor may elect the amount of the QTIP trust that will be claimed as a marital deduction by the estate of the deceased spouse. The election will determine whether any federal or state estate tax is due. All of the property will remain in the QTIP trust for the benefit of the surviving spouse.

2. Leave to a QTIP trust for the surviving spouse so much of the deceased spouse's estate as the executor elects to claim as a marital deduction and the balance to a family trust or outright to the decedent's descendants. Again, the executor's election determines whether any federal or state death tax is due. The approach is based on Reg. §20.2056(b)-7(d)(3), which allows a will or trust to provide that the "portion of the property for which the [QTIP]

election is not made passes to or for the benefit of persons other than the surviving spouse."

3. Leave substantially all of the decedent's property outright to the surviving spouse. The surviving spouse can elect to disclaim some or all of the property. Any property that is disclaimed will pass to a QTIP trust. The deceased spouse's executor can elect how much of the QTIP trust will be claimed as a marital deduction—which will determine whether any federal or state death tax is due.

States Death Tax. Marital deduction planning for residents of states that impose their own wealth transfer tax should be done in light of the nature of that tax.

§5.33. AN ASSESSMENT OF FORMULA PROVISIONS

Both the pecuniary amount and the fractional share formula clauses automatically adjust for changes in the composition and value of the testator's estate prior to death and in the amount of property that passes under will substitutes. The use of a formula clause is a reasonably effective way to ensure the proper division of property between transfers that are intended to preserve the testator's unified credit and ones to the surviving spouse that qualify for the marital deduction. Although a formula clause is capable of producing good results, it is not a universal panacea and is no substitute for careful planning and drafting. The use of a formula clause does not relieve the lawyer of the obligation to review, analyze, and organize the client's estate in a careful and deliberate way.

It is also important to appreciate the limitations of formula provisions: No mere formula clause can provide absolute protection against transferring too little or too much property to the surviving spouse. Too little may be transferred to the surviving spouse if a substantial portion of a client's estate passes to other persons under will substitutes and the probate estate is inadequate to satisfy fully the formula gift to the surviving spouse. Conversely, too much may pass to the surviving spouse if assets in excess of the amount necessary to eliminate the decedent's estate tax liability pass to the surviving spouse under will substitutes that are not subject to the limitations expressed in the formula clause. Of course, disclaimers of interests in will substitutes can be used to cure some problems of overfunding or underfunding the marital deduction. § 12.33.

Caution must also be exercised because the amount of property that passes under a formula provision may be too small to warrant the establishment of a trust. For that reason the planner should consider providing that the gift will pass to the surviving spouse outright if its value is below a certain amount. A small trust can be a nuisance, involving unnecessary expenditures of time and money preparing accountings, keeping records, and filing fiduciary income tax returns. The expense could be considerable if a trustee were appointed that required payment of a large annual fee.

To put matters further into perspective, the general disadvantages of formula provisions should be mentioned. First, by their very nature formula clauses are complicated and difficult to draft, explain, understand, and administer. Because of their complexity it is relatively easy to make a costly mistake at any step along the way. Second, the use of a formula marital deduction clause may require multiple valuations of assets and more complex accountings that can delay settlement of an estate and impose additional costs of administration. Delays could also occur because the exact amount of the gift may not be known until the valuation of property included in the gross estate is finally determined upon audit of the estate tax return. Third, the use of a formula may cause controversies between the surviving spouse and other beneficiaries regarding the proper exercise of elections by the fiduciary that affect the amount of the gifts to the surviving spouse and others. Among these elections are those regarding the use of the alternate valuation date, § 2032; the specific use valuation of assets, § 2032A; the use of the decedent's GSTT exemption; and, the return upon which alternatively deductible items are claimed for tax purposes, § 642(g). As noted in § 5.34, an election to claim an alternatively deductible item as an income tax deduction will affect the amount of a nonmarital pecuniary formula gift.

The reference in a formula gift to "adjusted gross estate," a term that was deleted from § 2056 by the 1981 Act, continues to cause unnecessary confusion. In LR 9516004 (TAM), the IRS held that under local law (Texas) the decedent did not intend in his 1987 will to refer to the meaning of the repealed term. In that form the term "adjusted gross estate" would have been determined by deducting the decedent's share of the community property from his gross estate. As his estate was entirely composed of community property no property would have passed to the surviving spouse—which was clearly not his intention. The TAM, instead, concludes that when the decedent referred in his will to the adjusted gross estate as defined on the date of his death, he must have meant the term adjusted gross estate found in § 6166—under which his share of the community property would not be excluded.

§ 5.34. FORMULA PECUNIARY AMOUNT GIFT

A formula pecuniary amount gift is generally simpler to understand and easier to administer than a formula fractional share gift. Personal observation and experience indicate that formula pecuniary gifts are used more frequently than fractional share gifts—probably because they are simpler and less expensive to administer. The IRS has agreed that a pecuniary formula can be used to express the amount of *either* the marital or nonmarital pecuniary gift that is to be satisfied according to values on the date or dates of distribution. As explained below, a pecuniary gift may be satisfied by two other forms of distribution: "fairly representative" and "minimum worth." § § 5.37.4-5.37.5.

In Rev. Rul. 90-3, 1990-1 C.B. 176, the IRS allowed a marital deduction based upon estate tax values where a pecuniary nonresiduary gift was satisfied according to date of distribution values. Because of a decline in the value of the assets of the estate, the residuary marital share actually received assets worth only $55,000 although the share had a value of $250,000 for federal estate tax purposes. Until this ruling was issued, it was not entirely clear that the IRS would accept a pecuniary nonmarital gift that could be funded according to date of distribution values. While some letter rulings had indicated that the approach was acceptable, the IRS remained free to change its mind. The question was significant primarily because, as indicated by Rev. Rul. 90-3, the amount of the pecuniary gift remains fixed although the overall value of the estate may increase or decrease. Viewed conversely, the gains or losses will all be allocated to the nonpecuniary share (usually the residuary estate). The difference is illustrated by the following simplified example:

EXAMPLE 5-31.

W's will made a formula pecuniary gift to her husband, *H*, and left the residue of her estate to a discretionary trust for *H* and their children. *W*'s estate had a federal estate tax value of $3 million, of which *H* was entitled to receive $1 million by reason of the formula gift. Under the terms of *W*'s will, the gift to *H* could be satisfied by distributing assets in kind provided they were valued for that purpose according to their values on the date of distribution. The value of the assets of the estate increased to $5 million, on the date of distribution. None of the increase is allocable to *H*'s gift. Thus, *H* received only $1 million and the residuary trust received $4 million. Note, however, that a decrease in the value of the estate's property would reduce the amount passing under the nonmarital gift (*i.e.,* the portion in the trust, sheltered by *W*'s unified credit).

It is also significant that gain or loss is realized on the transfer of appreciated property in kind in satisfaction of a pecuniary gift. *See* §5.37.1. Losses on distributions of depreciated property in satisfaction of pecuniary bequests were not deductible prior to the addition of §267(b)(13) by the 1997 Act. The planner should recognize that a larger gain may be realized where the amount that passes under a formula pecuniary gift exceeds the amount that passes under the residuary clause. Thus, for income tax purposes it may be desirable to use formula pecuniary language to describe the share (marital or non-marital) that is expected to be smaller.

Properly funding a pecuniary marital deduction gift is also important for gift tax purposes. For example, an indirect gift results if a surviving spouse allows a pecuniary marital deduction trust for his or her benefit to be underfunded. Rev. Rul. 84-105, 1984-2 C.B. 197.

§5.34.1. Credits

In computing the amount of a pecuniary marital deduction gift the formula should take into account the decedent's unified credit. In contrast, marital deduction formulas should not take into account the credits for gift taxes and foreign death taxes paid. Indeed, the formula clauses suggested by some commentators only take into account the unified credit.

An instrument should generally direct that property which qualifies for the foreign death tax credit not be distributed in satisfaction of the marital deduction gift. Such a direction will allow the estate to make the maximum use of the foreign death tax credit—the credit will not be reduced because the assets could have been used to satisfy the marital deduction. Moore, Recognition and Uses of Federal Estate Tax Credits in Estate Planning and Administration, U. Miami, 21 Inst. Est. Plan. ¶809.2 (1987).

§ 5.34.2. Charge Nonmarital Share for Principal Expenses for Which No Estate Tax Deduction Is Claimed

A marital deduction is allowable only with respect to the net amount passing to the surviving spouse. § 2056(b)(4). That rule does not cause a problem where the formula gift to the surviving spouse includes a proper adjustment for deductions charged against principal and *allowed* for federal estate tax purposes. *See* § 5.32. Administration expenses and other items that are deductible for federal estate tax purposes should not be taken into account to the extent they are claimed on the estate's income tax return. A formula that takes "allowable" expenses into account could cause some estate tax liability to arise because it required too much property to be allocated to the nonmarital share.

EXAMPLE 5-32.

H died leaving an estate of $3 million. His will contained a pecuniary formula marital deduction gift to his wife, *W,* and left the residue of his estate to a nonmarital trust. The formula provided that the amount of the marital gift should be calculated by taking into account the unified credit and all other deductions *allowed* to his estate. *H*'s estate paid a total of $100,000 in administration expenses and other items that were deductible under § 2053. However, all of the items were claimed as deductions on the estate's income tax return. The amount of the pecuniary marital deduction gift ($1 million) is equal to the difference between the gross estate ($3 million) and the amount of the credit equivalent ($2 million). Had the expenses been claimed as deductions on the estate tax return, the marital gift would have been reduced to $900,000, which represents the excess of the gross estate over the sum of the deductions allowed for estate tax purposes ($100,000) and the credit equivalent ($2 million). If the formula had provided that *allowable* deductions would be taken into account, some estate tax would have been due had the items been claimed as income tax deductions (*i.e.,* too much property would have passed to the nonmarital trust).

§ 5.35. Formula Pecuniary Marital Deduction Gift

A formula pecuniary marital deduction gift could be expressed in a variety of ways. Language such as the following reflects the points discussed above and should suffice as a preresiduary formula gift.

Form 5-6
Formula Pecuniary Marital Deduction Gift

If my [wife/husband] survives me, I give to [her/him or to a trust for her/his benefit] the smallest amount, which if allowable as a marital deduction for federal estate tax purposes in the matter of my estate will result in no federal estate tax being due from my estate, taking into account all exclusions and other deductions allowed to my estate for federal estate tax purposes and the amount of the unified credit.

A preresiduary formula pecuniary marital deduction gift is often used if the property passing under it is likely to have a lower total value than the value of the nonmarital residuary gift and the executor could satisfy the gift by distributing assets in kind, valued according to their date of distribution values. Such an approach reduces the possibility that gain will be recognized when assets are distributed in satisfaction of the formula gift. Under either the fairly representative or the minimum worth funding provision, the distribution of assets in kind would not result in the recognition of gain. Accordingly, if either such funding provision is used, no gain will be realized whether the marital or nonmarital share is defined by the formula.

§ 5.36. FORMULA PECUNIARY NONMARITAL DEDUCTION GIFT

Where the size of the marital share will exceed the nonmarital share and the gift will be funded at date of distribution values, it may be desirable to make a formula pecuniary gift of the nonmarital share. In that way the potential for the recognition of capital gain is decreased. However, if the formula nonmarital gift will be funded at date of distribution values, all of the appreciation or depreciation will be allocated to the residuary marital gift. Again, under a fairly representative or minimum worth funding provision, no gain is recognized when appreciated assets are distributed in satisfaction of the gift.

A formula nonmarital deduction gift could be expressed along these lines:

Form 5-7
Formula Pecuniary Nonmarital Deduction Gift

If my [wife/husband] survives me, I give to [the nonmarital trust or other beneficiaries] an amount equal to the excess of (1) the amount upon which the tentative tax calculated under I.R.C. § 2001(c) is equal to the unified credit over (2) the amount of post-1976 taxable gifts made by me other than gifts includible in my gross estate; the amount of property includible in my gross estate for which no charitable or marital deduction or casualty loss deduction is allowed; and the amount of administration expenses and other expenses incurred in connection with the settlement of my estate that are charged against principal and are not allowed as a deduction for federal estate tax purposes.

In this case the formula should also be fleshed out as described below by appropriate provisions regarding funding and valuation of property.

§5.37. Directions Regarding Funding a Formula Pecuniary Gift

Various options are available for specifying the manner in which a formula pecuniary gift should be satisfied. If nothing is said on the subject, local law may require the gift to be satisfied in cash. The liquidation of assets that would ordinarily be required to do so might be inconvenient and cause the estate to recognize capital gains unnecessarily. Whatever the local law may be, it is generally desirable to authorize the fiduciary to satisfy the gift by distributing assets in kind. The fiduciary needs the flexibility that such a provision provides in order to be able to select and distribute to each beneficiary the most appropriate assets, taking into account the circumstances of the estate and the beneficiaries.

Stock distributed in kind in satisfaction of a pecuniary marital deduction bequest is redeemable "only to the extent that the interest of the shareholder is reduced directly (or through a binding obligation to contribute) by any payment of" death taxes and funeral and administration expenses. §303(b)(3). The scope and operation of this limitation, applicable to the "interests of the shareholder," which would ordinarily be the decedent's executor or trustee, is uncertain. Until it is clarified the safest course is to direct that neither stock redeemed pursuant to §303 nor the proceeds of a redemption of stock that meets the requirements of §303 should be distributed in satisfaction of the marital deduction.

Properly funding a pecuniary marital deduction gift is also important for gift tax purposes. An indirect gift results if a surviving spouse allows a pecuniary marital deduction trust for his or her benefit to be underfunded. Rev. Rul. 84-105, 1984-2 C.B. 197.

§5.37.1. Valuation of Assets Distributed in Kind

A fiduciary should be given some guidance regarding the valuation of any assets that are distributed in kind in satisfaction of a formula pecuniary bequest. Of necessity some specific value must be assigned to each asset. The principal valuation methods and the income and estate tax consequences of each are described in the following sections.

Thus far the IRS has not required the income tax basis of an asset to be taken into account in valuing the asset in connection with an in kind distribution. Accordingly, neither the value of an asset nor the amount of the marital deduction has been adjusted merely because an asset will have a basis in the hands of the distributee that is less than its value for purposes of distribution. Similarly, no adjustment has been required when the assets distributed included a component of income in respect of a decedent. Thus, a marital deduction has been allowed without reduction for future income tax liability that might arise upon payment of installment notes distributed in satisfaction of the marital deduction gift. LR 7827008. Consistent with that result the Tax Court has not allowed a decedent's estate to discount the value of installment notes on account of the possible income tax payable on collections made on the notes in the future. *Estate of G. R. Robinson,* 69 T.C. 222 (1977).

At some point the IRS might require the distribution of assets that fairly reflect the overall appreciation or depreciation in value of all assets available for distribution. Beyond that, the tax consequences are probably too speculative and uncertain to take into account. Thus, future tax consequences are generally disregarded in marital dissolution planning. However, they are sometimes taken into account for other purposes. *See* Hjorth, The Effect of Federal Tax Consequences on Amount of Property Allocated to Spouses in State Court Dissolution Proceedings, 24 Fam. L.Q. 247 (1990).

§5.37.2. Value on the Date of Distribution ("True Worth")

Unless a fiduciary is directed to value the assets that are distributed in kind in some other manner, general fiduciary principles may require the fiduciary to value them at their fair market values on the date or dates of distribution. Such a requirement is imposed by some states. It is also the funding method most frequently imposed by the terms of a will or trust. In operation, a "true worth" provision assures that the value of the property distributed in satisfaction of the gift will have a total market value on the date or dates of distribution exactly equal to the amount of the marital deduction. It imposes both a ceiling and a floor on the value of assets distributed in satisfaction of a marital deduction gift. If the assets of the estate appreciate in value, the method imposes a ceiling on the value of assets that can be distributed; if they decline, it acts as a floor. A true worth provision can be used in connection with a pecuniary marital *or* nonmarital gift.

EXAMPLE 5-33.

W died leaving an estate that consisted of assets *A, B, C,* and *D.* Each of the assets was worth $800,000 on the estate tax valuation date and $1 million on the date of distribution. *W* made no taxable gifts during her lifetime and her taxable estate is $2 million. Her will made a "true worth" pecuniary formula gift to her husband, *H,* of the smallest amount that, if allowed as a marital deduction, would result in no estate tax being due from *W*'s estate. *W*'s executor determined that the formula required a marital deduction of $1.2 million. The assets distributed to *H* in satisfaction of the marital deduction formula gift must have a total value on the date or dates of distribution equal to the marital deduction of $1.2 million that was claimed by *W*'s estate. If *W*'s will instead made a pecuniary nonmarital gift, her estate would be obligated to distribute property worth $2 million on the date of distribution in satisfaction of the gift. For an estate of this size the use of a pecuniary marital deduction gift, rather than a formula nonmarital gift, limits the amount of gain that might be realized by the estate if appreciated property is distributed in satisfaction of the formula gift. A change in §267 made by the 1997 Act allows the estate to recognize a loss on the distribution of property in satisfaction of a pecuniary gift.

As noted in §5.32, if the assets of the estate appreciate substantially in value between the estate tax valuation date and the date of distribution, a true worth marital deduction gift prevents the marital gift from sharing in the appreciation. By limiting the value of property that can be distributed in satisfaction of the marital deduction gift the method helps control the size of the surviving spouse's estate. In such a case the benefit (or burden) of the appreciation passes under the other provisions of the will or trust. Of course, if the assets of the estate decline in value, the floor comes into effect and a smaller amount passes to the other beneficiaries. Thus, a pecuniary formula clause does not provide the surviving spouse with "upside" protection, but does protect against loss from a decline in the value of the estate's assets.

Revaluation and "Sale" at a Gain. Under the true worth approach assets that are distributed in satisfaction of the gift must be valued again on the date or dates of distribution. The extra valuation may be time-consuming and costly for estates that include items that are difficult to value.

A trust or estate recognizes gain if a pecuniary gift is satisfied by distributing an asset that has a date of distribution value greater than the asset's estate tax value. The gain is generally limited to the amount by which the fair market value of the property on the date of distribution exceeds its estate tax value. Note that § 1040 limits the amount of gain taxed to a trust or estate when special use property is distributed to a qualified heir in satisfaction of a pecuniary bequest. In such a case the gain is limited to the amount by which the date of distribution value of the property exceeds its estate tax value, determined without regard to § 2032A (*i.e.,* its fair market value on the estate tax valuation date). § 1040(a). The same rule applies to trust property included in a decedent's estate. § 1040(b). Where such a distribution is made, the qualified heir's basis in the property is equal to the basis of the estate or trust immediately before the distribution plus the amount of gain recognized by the estate or trust as a result of the distribution. § 1040(c).

Language of this type could be used to express a true worth valuation requirement:

Form 5-8
Date of Distribution (True Worth) Funding Clause

I authorize my executor to satisfy this gift by making distributions in cash or in kind, or part in cash and part in kind, provided that each asset that is distributed in kind shall be valued at its fair market value on the date it is distributed.

"Sale" at a Loss —§ 267. If the value of an asset is lower on the date of distribution than its basis, the fiduciary must decide whether to sell the asset to a third party or distribute it to a beneficiary in a transaction that will be treated as a sale. In either case the loss should be recognized on the fiduciary. Section 267 bars a deduction for a loss incurred in a sale or exchange directly or indirectly between related taxpayers, including a fiduciary of a trust and a beneficiary of the trust. However, it does not bar a deduction for a loss on a sale between an estate and a beneficiary of the estate. *Estate of Hanna v. Commissioner,* 320 F.2d 54 (6th Cir. 1963); Rev. Rul. 77-439, 1977-2 C.B. 85. The 1997 Act added § 267(b)(13) which prohibits a deduction for a loss on a sale or exchange between an executor and a beneficiary except for ones made "in satisfaction of a pecuniary bequest."

The true worth provision is probably used more often than any other, although it requires an additional valuation of assets and may result in recognition of gain by the fiduciary. Planners are attracted by its relative simplicity, the tax saving that may result by preventing the surviving spouse from participating in gains and protecting the surviving spouse against losses. However, as explained below, greater protection may be provided by a "minimum value" funding provision. *See* § 5.37.4.

§ 5.37.3. Estate Tax Value: Revenue Procedure 64-19

Some wills and trusts attempt to provide additional tax planning flexibility by directing that assets distributed in satisfaction of a marital deduction gift must be valued at their respective estate tax values. Under such a provision, a distribution does not result in gain or loss because each asset is deemed to have a value equal to its federal estate tax value—its basis under § 1014. However, the rule tempted fiduciaries to allocate assets that had declined in value to the marital share and assets that had increased in value to the other beneficiaries. Such an allocation was made in order to minimize the amount of property includible in the estate of the surviving spouse. (In the case of a pecuniary nonmarital gift the fiduciary would be tempted to make the reverse allocation.) The IRS responded by issuing Rev. Proc. 64-19, 1964-1 C.B. 682, which establishes the conditions under which a marital deduction will be allowed for a pecuniary gift that the fiduciary is authorized to satisfy by distributing assets in kind at their federal estate tax values.

Revenue Procedure 64-19 provides that when an instrument allows or requires a fiduciary to distribute assets in kind in satisfaction of a pecuniary marital deduction gift and specifies that the assets distributed in kind must be valued at their values as finally determined for federal estate tax purposes, a marital deduction will be allowed only if (1) the fiduciary "must distribute assets, including cash, having an aggregate fair market value at the date, or dates, of distribution amounting to no less than the amount of the pecuniary bequest or transfer, as finally determined for Federal estate tax purposes," or (2) the fiduciary "must distribute assets, including cash, fairly representative of appreciation or depreciation in the value of all property thus available for distribution in satisfaction of such pecuniary bequest or transfer." In effect, federal estate tax values can only be used if the integrity of the marital deduction is protected by the alternative requirements quoted above. Presumably the principles of Rev. Proc. 64-19 also applies where a pecuniary formula is used to express the nonmarital gift.

Revenue Procedure 64-19 also noted that the problem it addressed did not arise in some other cases. In particular, it noted that the problem was not present:

1. In a bequest or transfer in trust of a fractional share of the estate, under which each beneficiary shares proportionately in the appreciation or depreciation in the value of assets to the date, or dates, of distribution.

2. In a bequest or transfer in trust of specific assets.

3. In a pecuniary bequest or transfer in trust, whether in a stated amount or an amount computed by the use of a formula, if:

   (a) The fiduciary must satisfy the pecuniary bequest or transfer solely in cash, or

(b) The fiduciary has no discretion in the selection of assets to be distributed in kind, or

(c) Assets selected by the fiduciary to be distributed in kind in satisfaction of the bequest or transfer in trust are to be valued at their respective values on the date, or dates, of their distribution. § 4.01, Rev. Proc. 64-19, 1964-1 C.B. at 684.

However, Rev. Proc. 64-19 does not approve the use of devices in those cases that may operate to diminish the value of the interests that are transferred in satisfaction of a marital deduction gift. In particular, it does not authorize the fiduciary to select and distribute assets on a non-pro rata basis in satisfaction of a formula fractional share gift.

Under Rev. Proc. 64-19, a fiduciary may be given authority to satisfy a pecuniary marital deduction gift that requires the use of the federal estate tax value of the assets by one of two approved methods. The fiduciary may not be given a choice between them. Many commentators favor the "minimum value" method. *E.g.*, Polasky, Marital Deduction Formula Clauses in Estate Planning—Estate and Income Tax Considerations, 63 Mich. L. Rev. 809, 832 (1965) (cited hereafter as *Polasky*). The other method, which is commonly called either the "fairly representative" or "ratable sharing" provision, is more cumbersome and is less well understood by planners, courts, and the IRS.

§ 5.37.4. Estate Tax Value: Minimum Value Provisions

Under the "minimum value" method, assets distributed in kind must have an aggregate fair market value on the date or dates of distribution no lower than the amount of the pecuniary marital deduction gift. The effect of this approach is to specify a floor beneath which the value of the assets distributed in kind cannot fall (an amount equal to the pecuniary gift), but no ceiling. No gain is realized from a distribution of assets in kind in satisfaction of a minimum worth gift because such a distribution is valued at the *lower* of its basis or value at the date of distribution. Note that a minimum worth provision should not be used in connection with a pecuniary formula nonmarital gift because of the possibility that the value of a residuary marital deduction gift could be eroded by allocating "too much" to the pecuniary nonmarital gift.

EXAMPLE 5-34.

H's estate is composed of 10 assets. Each has an estate tax value of $300,000 and a date-of-distribution value of $450,000. *H*'s will makes a pecuniary formula gift to his wife, *W*, of an amount that is determined to be equal to $1 million. Under an estate tax minimum value provision, assets worth at least $1 million on the date of distribution must be transferred in satisfaction of the gift. However, assets having a date-of-distribution value of as much as $1.5 million could be distributed. On the other hand, if the assets fell to a value of $200,000 each on the date of distribution, the fiduciary would still be obligated to distribute to *W* assets with a total date-of-distribution value of at least $1 million.

A minimum worth provision can be used in conjunction with a pecuniary marital deduction gift, especially when a client wishes to permit the fiduciary to allocate some of the increase in value of assets to the marital deduction gift. However, it should not be used if a client does not want to put the fiduciary in the position of having to decide whether the marital deduction gift or other beneficiaries will benefit from an increase in the value of the estate's property. If it is used, the fiduciary should be protected against liability for a good faith exercise of the power.

Form 5-9
Minimum Worth Funding Clause

> I authorize my fiduciary to satisfy this gift by making distributions in cash or in kind or part in cash and part in kind, provided that the aggregate fair market value of the cash and other assets on the date or dates of distribution shall be no less than the amount of the gift as finally deter-mined for federal estate tax purposes.

A minimum value marital deduction gift complies with Rev. Proc. 64-19. It should also eliminate the possibility that the estate will realize gain upon the distribution of assets in kind. According to Professor Polasky, no gain or loss occurs because "the ultimate value of the bequest is not ascertainable until distribution; and the receipt of assets cannot be said to be in satisfaction of a fixed dollar amount bequest or claim." *Polasky* at 867.

§ 5.37.5. Estate Tax Value: Fairly Representative Requirement

A requirement that the assets distributed in satisfaction of the marital deduction gift fairly reflect the appreciation and depreciation in value of the estate's assets may be imposed by the local law or the instrument itself. In either case, the requirement satisfies Rev. Proc. 64-19. A fairly representative clause is safe to use in conjunction with a formula pecuniary marital or nonmarital gift. *See* Form 5-10, below.

Form 5-10
Estate Tax Value, Fairly Representative Funding Clause

> I authorize my fiduciary to satisfy this gift by distributing assets included in my gross estate (or the proceeds of their disposition), including cash, which have an aggregate fair market value fairly representative of the distributee's proportionate share of the appreciation or depreciation in value, to the date or dates of distribution, of all property then available for distribution.

A fairly representative clause assures that the marital deduction gift *and* other gifts will be treated fairly when it comes to making distributions: All will share ratably in any overall increase or decrease in the value of the assets available for distribution. However, a ratable allocation is most important where the surviving spouse will not also receive the benefit of the nonmarital share. In contrast, where the surviving spouse will receive the benefit of both shares, it is more efficient from the tax perspective to use a clause that permits the distribution to the marital deduction share of assets having as low a value as possible. By doing so the size of the surviving spouse's gross estate is minimized.

The primary disadvantage of the fairly representative approach is its difficulty of application, particularly where distributions are made at different times to multiple beneficiaries. It is administratively more complex, which increases the responsibilities of the fiduciary, which may increase the fees of the fiduciary and of the attorney.

EXAMPLE 5-35.

H's will contains a formula pecuniary marital deduction gift to his wife, *W*, that directs it to be satisfied by distributing assets at their federal estate tax values, provided they must be fairly representative of the change in value of all assets between the federal estate tax valuation date and the date or dates of distribution. *H*'s gross estate consisted of the assets that had a total federal estate tax value of $4.1 million. Expenses of administration and other costs of $100,000 will be deducted for federal estate tax purposes. If *H* made no prior taxable gifts, *H*'s estate would claim a marital deduction of $2 million. Thus, *W*'s share would be equal to half of the net amount available for distribution according to their federal estate tax values. If the assets available for distribution had an aggregate value of $4.6 million on the date of distribution, *W* would be entitled to receive assets which had a total value of $2.3 million. No gain would be realized as a result of the distribution of appreciated assets. Had the value of the assets declined to $3.6 million in value on the date of distribution, *W* would have been entitled to receive ones worth a total of $1.8 million.

§ 5.37.6. Directions Regarding Allocation of Assets to Pecuniary Formula Marital Deduction Gifts

The amount of the marital deduction is subject to reduction under the terminable interest rule if any disqualified assets (or their proceeds) could be distributed in satisfaction of the marital deduction gift. *See* § 5.17.5. Accordingly, instruments that include a formula gift typically require the fiduciary to satisfy the marital deduction portion by distributing only assets that qualify for the deduction. Without such a provision, the marital deduction would be disallowed to the extent that nondeductible interests were included in the pool of assets from which the gift could be satisfied.

Form 5-11
Distribution Limited to Assets that Qualify for the Marital Deduction

This gift shall be satisfied only by distributing assets or the proceeds of assets with respect to which a federal estate tax marital deduction is allowable.

Special directions should be included if the client owns stock that it might be desirable to redeem under §303. *See* §§5.37 and 5.39.

A will or trust might also contain a direction regarding the allocation of income in respect of a decedent (IRD). A concern arises because a distribution in satisfaction of a pecuniary bequest will trigger recognition of income by the estate. Under §691(a)(2), income must be reported if an IRD item is sold or exchanged. However, income is not triggered by the distribution of an IRD item in satisfaction of a specific bequest. Thus a planner has some flexibility in planning for the distribution of IRD items. In some cases it may be preferable to have the estate bear the tax and permit the surviving spouse to receive the income free of tax. In other cases it is preferable for the surviving spouse to be taxed on the income, which in effect reduces the size of his or her estate.

The income tax cost of IRD is ameliorated somewhat by the deduction that is available under §691(c) for the estate tax paid with respect to the IRD. Of course, if a marital deduction formula works properly the estate will pay no estate tax.

§5.38. Planning and Drafting a Formula Fractional Share Gift

The beneficiary of a fractional share gift is entitled to receive a fractional interest in each asset that is included in the pool against which the fraction is applied. The beneficiary is also entitled to receive a proportionate part of the income generated by the asset pool.

EXAMPLE 5-36.

H bequeathed half of his residuary estate to his wife, *W*. When *H*'s estate is distributed, *W* is entitled to receive an undivided one-half interest in each asset included in *H*'s residuary estate, together with half of the income derived from it. If the death taxes, costs of administration, and like items are payable from the nonmarital share of the residue, *W* may be entitled to a larger proportionate interest in each asset and a larger proportion of the income after those items are paid.

A nonformula fractional share gift (*e.g.,* "half of my residuary estate") may have a value that is more or less than the amount of the optimum marital deduction. Also, such a gift does not include any mechanism for adjusting the amount of the fraction on account of property that passes outside the will or trust. The absence of a self-adjusting mechanism makes this type of gift too unreliable for general use in marital deduction planning.

In contrast, a formula fractional share gift produces a marital deduction that is precisely equal to the amount necessary to eliminate the payment of any estate tax by the decedent's estate. Exceptions occur if either the gift is overfunded by nontestamentary transfers or the pool of assets against which the fraction is applied is too small to fund the gift fully. A formula fractional share gift also allows each beneficiary to participate in any overall change in the value of the residuary estate or other pool of assets from which the gift will be satisfied. Thus, the fraction serves two purposes.

First, it describes the proportionate share of the residuary estate that is to be qualified for the marital deduction. Necessarily this will produce an *amount*, expressed in dollars, to be claimed on the estate tax return. Second, once constituted, the fraction will be applied to allocate the aliquot shares of the described residuary estate to the marital and nonmarital trusts at the distribution date. Polasky at 841.

As the composition and value of a residuary estate will inevitably change between the estate tax valuation date and the date or dates of distribution, the value of the assets actually distributed in satisfaction of the gift may be more or less than the amount of the marital deduction.

EXAMPLE 5-37.

W died leaving a will that made a formula fractional share gift to her husband, *H*. According to the federal estate tax value of the assets of *W*'s estate, which governed for the purpose of the formula gift, *H* was entitled to receive five-ninths of *W*'s residuary estate. Accordingly, *H* was entitled to receive five-ninths fractional interest in each asset, regardless of its value on the date or dates of distribution.

A fractional share gift should be used sparingly where community property is involved. The management of the property could be complicated if it is fractionalized further by distributing part of a deceased spouse's share to a marital deduction trust for the surviving spouse and part to others or to another trust. Where community property is involved, a pecuniary formula is generally preferable.

Drafting a formula fractional share gift requires the lawyer to focus on two problems: (1) formulating the language with which to express the fraction itself, and (2) determining and describing the residue or other pool of assets against which the fraction will be applied (the multiplicand).

§ 5.38.1. Expressing the Fraction

The fraction itself may be referred to in several ways that qualify for the marital deduction. Most often, the numerator is the amount of property to be passed to the surviving spouse. Of course, a "reverse" formula could be used that would be based upon the maximum amount of property that could be passed to persons other than the surviving spouse or charities without incurring any estate tax. The denominator is the residuary estate or other pool of assets against which the fraction is applied. In order to preserve the fractional character of the gift, the denominator must also reflect the estate tax value of the assets. *See Polasky* at 842, n. 116. In drafting the gift, the lawyer must be sure that the same definition of the residue is used both for the denominator and the multiplicand. If so, the value of the gift will be the same whether the residue is constituted before the payment of cash legacies, expenses, debts, and taxes; before the payment of taxes (a "pre-tax" provision); or after the payment of all of those items (a "true residue" provision).

§ 5.38.2. Formula Fractional Share Gift

Form 5-12
Formula Fractional Share Marital Deduction Gift

If my [wife/husband] survives me, I give to [her/him or to a trust for her/his benefit] a fraction of my residuary estate, determined after payment of all pecuniary gifts, expenses of administration, debts, and death taxes that are properly chargeable against my residuary estate. The numerator of the fraction shall be the smallest amount which, if allowable as a marital deduction for federal estate tax purposes in the matter of my estate, will result in no federal estate tax being due from my estate, taking into account post-1976 taxable gifts made by me and all other deductions allowed for federal estate tax purposes, and the unified credit. The denominator of the fraction shall be the federal estate tax value of my residuary estate so determined. For the purposes of this gift, my residuary estate shall include only assets that would qualify for the federal estate tax marital deduction if they were distributed outright to my spouse.

Of course, a fractional share gift can be made outright to the surviving spouse or in trust. As explained below, most fractional share formula clauses are based on the "true residue." That is, the multiplicand and the denominator are defined as the residuary estate *after* the payment of all pecuniary gifts, expenses of administration, debts, and death taxes. The final sentence of Form 5-12 is included to prevent loss of any portion of the deduction under the unidentified (tainted) asset rule if the residue includes any terminable interests. Again, some commentators suggest using a formula that only takes into account the unified credit. Note that the value of the fractional interest distributed in satisfaction of the marital gift, and conversely, the nonmarital gift may vary depending on whether a true residue provision is used.

§ 5.38.3. Directions Regarding Allocation of Income and Capital Gains and Losses

The manner in which the income and capital gains and losses will be allocated under a formula fractional share gift is usually not clear under the local law. Accordingly, the governing instrument should contain specific directions. Without them, fiduciaries adopt different approaches regarding the allocation of income.

[A]n informal survey of corporate fiduciaries suggests varying approaches not necessarily keyed to the particular definition of the residue. Some apply the fraction produced by the formula while others allocate to the marital share only that amount of income which the average rate of return would produce on the calculated marital share. *Polasky* at 849-850.

EXAMPLE 5-38.

W left an estate that was valued at $4,150,000 for federal estate tax purposes and a will that made a formula fractional share gift of her residuary estate to her husband, *H*. Expenses of administration and debts of $150,000 were paid at the same time from the residue. *H*'s fractional share was one-half ($2 million/$4 million) under the true residue provision that was contained in *W*'s will. Income of $50,000 was earned by the estate prior to the payment of the expenses and debts. To be equitable, the nonmarital share should receive all of the income that was generated by the assets used to pay expenses, debts, and taxes. Income earned thereafter should be allocated according to the formula fraction (*i.e.*, one-half to the marital share and one-half to the other residuary beneficiaries). Of course, convenience tempts the fiduciary to allocate all of the income on the basis of a single fraction.

In an actual case the allocation is likely to be complicated by the payment of debts, expenses, and other items at various times and by the receipt of income at intervals that do not nicely coincide with those times. The same problem exists with respect to the allocation of capital gains and losses, which are frequently incurred to raise funds with which to pay expenses, debts, and taxes.

If the fiduciary is directed to allocate all income and capital gains according to the fraction determined under a true residue provision, the marital share will receive more of those items than it would under the strictly equitable approach. In operation, such a provision will inflate the survivor's gross estate to the extent of the excess. However, this approach is infinitely simpler to administer than one that calls for allocation according to the equitable approach and requires almost continuous revision. A provision that allocates income according to a formula based upon a residue constituted prior to the payment of expenses, debts, and taxes would overcompensate the nonmarital share.

§ 5.38.4. Why Use a True Residue Provision?

Use of a true residue provision is generally preferable to any other definition of the residue for purposes of the fractional share gift. In general, the use of a true residue provision increases the fiduciary's ability to select and dispose of assets in satisfaction of pecuniary legacies, expenses of administration, debts, and taxes. The increased flexibility that such a provision allows the fiduciary can be very useful. The effect of using a true residue is described in the following passage:

> Shrinking the residue to which the fraction is to be applied obviously increases the percentage interest of the marital share in the remaining available assets, since the numerator stays the same while the denominator diminishes. Further, shrinking the defined residue gives the executor an increasing power to choose assets to satisfy the general pecuniary legacy and other non-residue obligations and a concomitant power to affect the makeup, in terms of the specific assets remaining, of the pool to which the fractional share will be applied . . . . *Polasky* at 844-845.

Also, a true residue provision requires fewer adjustments to the fraction and is generally easier to administer. Finally, the need to trace assets of the estate for purposes of distribution can be eliminated if a true residue provision is used. In other cases it might be necessary to trace all of the assets that were originally included in the residuary estate in order to determine the portion of each asset that should be distributed to the marital and nonmarital shares.

The fraction will change regardless of the residuary definition if a non-pro rata distribution is made to a residuary beneficiary. For that reason, disproportionate distributions should generally be avoided when a fractional share gift is used in an instrument. If a true residue provision is used, the fraction will not have to be adjusted when pecuniary legacies, expenses of administration, debts, and taxes are paid. Adjustments are required, however, if the fraction is originally computed according to the value of the residuary estate prior to the payment of those items. In such a case the payment of each such item is in effect a distribution to the nonmarital share, which is chargeable with such payments. Accordingly, the fraction must be adjusted every time the estate pays an item that is properly chargeable to the residue.

The complexity of recomputing the fraction discourages many planners from using formula fractional share gifts. The steps involved in determining the initial and final fractions have been described as follows:

> 1. Determine the initial fraction. The numerator and denominator are based upon estate tax values as of the decedent's death if the executor does not elect the alternate valuation method. The denominator must be reduced by all administration expenses, whether or not claimed as an estate tax deduction and, if a true residuary clause is utilized, by estate taxes. If the executor elects the alternate valuation method, the assets of the residuary estate must be valued as of the appropriate alternate valuation date.
>
> 2. Divide the numerator by the denominator in order to determine the initial percentage interest of the marital share in increases and decreases of the estate until the first tax payment or distribution, whichever occurs first if a pre-tax residuary clause is utilized, or the first distribution if a true residuary clause is utilized.
>
> 3. As of the date of any tax payment or distribution, determine the fair market value of the undistributed residuary estate, including cash, and subtract therefrom any unpaid administration expenses taken into account in determining the initial denominator. Determine any net appreciation or depreciation by subtracting therefrom in the case of the first revaluation the denominator of the initial marital fraction or in the case of any revaluation other than the first, the denominator of the initial marital

fraction increased or decreased by any tax payments, distributions, increases or decreases taken into account in all prior revaluations resulting
in a change in the denominator. Allocate to the marital share its percentage interest in the difference, if any, applicable to the period during which
such appreciation or depreciation occurs.

4. Subtract from the denominator the amount of the tax payment if a pre-
tax residuary clause is utilized or, in the case of distributions, subtract
from the denominator the total amount of distributions (whether or not
made to the surviving spouse) and from the numerator only that amount
of the distribution passing to the surviving spouse.

5. After allocating the increases or decreases and subtracting the tax
payments or distributions, divide the resulting numerator by the resulting
denominator to determine the revised fractional interest of the marital
share in the undistributed assets of the residuary estate.

6. With each succeeding tax payment or distribution, apply the principles
set out in 3, 4 and 5 above. Kurtz, Allocation of Increases and Decreases to
Fractional Share Marital Deduction Bequest, 8 Real Prop., Prob. & Tr. J.
450, 460 (1973).

As indicated in the foregoing passage, the fraction must be recomputed "at each tax
payment and distribution in the case of a pre-tax residuary clause and at each
distribution in the case of a true residuary clause." *Id*. at 460.

EXAMPLE 5-39.

H died in 2006. *H* left a will that made a formula fractional share gift to his
wife, *W*, of the type described in §5.38.2. He gave the balance of his
residuary estate to a nonmarital trust. His gross estate had a value of $4
million for federal estate tax purposes, including a house held in joint
tenancy with *W* that had a total value of $400,000, survivorship bank
accounts with *W* in the amount of $25,000, and life insurance payable to
W in the amount of $75,000. In addition, *H* had made post-1976 taxable
gifts of $100,000. Debts, costs of administration, etc., payable from the
residuary estate, that will be claimed as deductions for federal estate tax
purposes amounted to $100,000. *W*'s fractional interest is four-ninths. The
fraction represents a numerator of $1.6 million ($4 million less $2.4 million
($200,000 for the qualified joint tenancy in the residence + $100,000
expenses + $25,000 in survivorship bank accounts + $75,000 of life insurance + $2 million credit equivalent)) over a denominator of $3.6 million
($4 million less $400,000 ($200,000 for the qualified joint tenancy +
$100,000 in expenses + $25,000 in the survivorship bank account and
$75,000 in life insurance)).

§5.39. Income Tax Aspects of a Formula Fractional Share Gift

A distribution in satisfaction of a fractional share gift does not cause the fiduciary to recognize any gain or loss. Reg. §§1.661(a)-2(f)(1), 1.1014-4(a)(3); *see* LR 8447003 (distribution in kind in satisfaction of gift of one-fourth of the income of a trust). This rule is generally beneficial for taxpayers and is an important reason for using a fractional share formula. Of course, its benefit depends upon the nature of the property involved and the relative income tax positions of the surviving spouse and the estate. A distribution in satisfaction of a fractional share gift does carry out the distributable net income of the estate which may increase the distributee's basis in the property. Reg. §1.661(a)-2(f)(3).

As noted in §5.37, stock may be redeemed under §303 only to the extent that the interest of the redeeming shareholder is reduced by payment of death taxes and funeral and administration expenses. The marital share, of course, is not reduced by the payment of those items. Accordingly, stock that the parties may wish to redeem under §303 should not be included in the pool of assets subject to a marital deduction formula gift.

Hybrid Clause. Under a hybrid approach the fiduciary is authorized to make nonpro rata distributions in satisfaction of fractional share interests. In such a case the value of the fractional share interest is determined on the date of distribution. Then the gift is satisfied by distributing assets in kind equal in value on the date of distribution to the amount of the gift. The approach gives the fiduciary more flexibility in selecting the assets to be distributions. Moreover, such a distribution should not be treated as a taxable exchange that would give rise to the recognition of any gain or loss. This conclusion rests in part upon the implications of Rev. Rul. 69-486, 1969-2 C.B. 159. *See* §12.40. In Rev. Rul. 69-486, the IRS concluded that the non-pro rata distribution of trust property to the two beneficiaries upon termination of the trust involved a taxable exchange between them where the trust instrument did *not* authorize the trustee to make such a distribution. According to the ruling, "Since the trustee was not authorized to make a non-pro rata distribution of property in kind but did so as a result of the mutual agreement between C and X, the non-pro rata distribution by the trustee is equivalent to a distribution to C and X of the notes and common stock pro rata by the trustee, followed by an exchange between C and X of C's pro rata share of common stock for X's pro rata share of notes." *Id.* The IRS has also held that no taxable exchange takes place when there is a non-pro rata distribution of community property as a result of which each party receives property of equal value. Rev. Rul. 76-83, 1976-1 C.B. 213. The same result was reached in LR 8016050 which involved spouses each of whom received the entire interest in assets of approximately equal value.

§5.40. Summary Choosing Between a Formula Pecuniary Gift and a Formula Fractional Share Gift

A fractional share formula has a slight edge when it comes to fairness and security against manipulation. Under a formula fractional share gift the share of each beneficiary fluctuates with changes in the composition and value of the residue, rather than being based upon a fixed amount. Of course, the actual value of the items distributed in satisfaction of a pecuniary gift depends in part upon the type of valuation clause that is used. From the income tax perspective the fractional share gift also has the advantage because the distribution of assets does not involve the realization of any gain. However, when appreciated assets are distributed in kind in satisfaction of a pecuniary gift, only the gain in value that takes place between the estate tax valuation date and the date of distribution is realized. The fractional share gift also enjoys an advantage if a portion of the income taxes attributable to sales made in order to generate funds with which to pay debts, expenses of administration, and taxes can be absorbed by the marital share without requiring any adjustment.

The formula fractional share gift has two major disadvantages. First, the fiduciary does not have as broad a power to select and allocate assets to the marital share as in the case of the pecuniary gift. This shortcoming may be alleviated if the fiduciary is given authority to make non-pro rata distributions of assets in kind. However, the tax consequences of giving the fiduciary such authority are uncertain: The IRS could argue that it converts the gift into a pecuniary one, which would require the fiduciary to recognize gain or loss upon the distribution of assets. *See* Rev. Rul. 60-87, 1960-1 C.B. 286. Second, the administration and accounting for a fractional share gift is much more complicated.

> The fraction itself is easily arrived at—initially. The problem is, that each time a non-pro rata distribution is made the fraction must be recalculated. The numerator and denominator are originally computed using federal estate tax values. The estate is then revalued at each partial distribution, reduced by all unpaid principal charges, and the fraction then recast in terms of current market values. The numerator is reduced by distributions to the spouse and the denominator is reduced by distributions to the spouse and other beneficiaries, payment of expenses (whether or not deductible), and the like. A new fraction is then arrived at which is to be used for the period until the next partial distribution. Rosen, How to Select the Proper Formula Clause to Fit Testator's Desires and Minimize Taxes, 3 Est. Plan. 20, 25 (1975).

In contrast, the administration of a formula pecuniary gift is usually very simple. Often the only complication is that the assets distributed in kind in satisfaction of the gift must be valued again at the time of distribution.

BIBLIOGRAPHY

Akers, Stirring Through the Alphabet Soup: ABCs Through XYZs of QTIPs and QDOTs, U. Miami, 28th Inst. Est. Plan., Ch. 2 (1994)

Bilter, Marital Deduction and Generation Skipping Formula Clauses: How to Get More Bang for Your Buck, U. Miami, 35th Inst. Est. Plan., Ch. 13 (2001)

Choate, Leaving Retirement Benefits to a QTIP Trust, 34 Est. Plan. 14 (Dec 2007)

Christensen, Coping With Section 2056A of the Internal Revenue Code: Making the Best of a Bad Law, N.Y.U. 50th Inst. Fed. Tax., Ch. 17 (1992)

Colburn, Englebrecht & Vollmers, Administrative Expenses and the Marital Deduction, Taxes 412 (July 1994)

Cornfeld, A Tin Cup for QTIPs—The Tenth Anniversary of the Unlimited Marital Deduction, U. Miami, 26th Inst. Est. Plan., Ch.—(1992)

Covey, R., Marital Deduction and Credit Shelter Dispositions and the Use of Formula Provisions (2d ed. 1984)

Detzel, The Heart of the Matter—Efficient Use of Formula Clauses in Estate Planning, U. Miami, 30th Inst. Est. Plan., Ch. 16 (1996)

Golden, It's Deja Vu All Over Again: Recent Developments in Marital Deduction Planning, U. Miami, 31st Inst. Est. Plan., Ch. 3 (1997) p. 101. #1

Gutierrez, Godzilla Meets Rodan: Generation-Skipping Transfer/Marital Deduction Planning, U. Miami, 23rd Inst. Est. Plan., Ch. 9 (1989)

Hilker, Skipping Through the Marital Deduction: Coordination of Marital Deduction and Generation-Skipping Planning and Drafting, U. Miami, 29th Inst. Est. Plan., Ch. 3 (1995)

Hilker, The Marital Deduction, Ch. 2 in 1 CEB Est. Plan. (1988)

Karp, Estate Planning for the Alien—The Danger of the Mixed Marriage, U. Miami, 24th Inst. Est. Plan., Ch. 9 (1990)

Kurtz, Impact of the Revenue Act of 1978 and the 1976 Tax Reform Act on Estate Tax Marital Deduction Formulas, 64 Iowa L. Rev. 739 (1979)

Llewellyn, Levin & Richmond, Computing the Optimum Marital Deduction: Is a Zero-tax Formula Appropriate?, 24 Real Prop., Prob. & Tr. J. 331 (1989)

McNair, Lifetime QTIPs Can Achieve Tax and Asset Protection Goals, 20 Est. Plan. 290 (Sept./Oct. 1993)

Newlin, QTIP Requirements Changed in New Final Regulations, 21 Est. Plan. 205 (1994)

Oshins & Matz, Resolving the Mismatch of Estate Inclusion Value and Deduction Value, 35 Est. Plan, 14 (Jul, 2008)

Pennell, Estate Tax Marital Deduction, 843-2d Tax Mgmt. Port. (2005)

Pennell, Funding Marital Deduction (and Other) Bequests, U. Miami, 35th Inst. Est. Plan., Ch. 15 (2001)

Plaine & Siegler, The Federal Gift and Estate Tax Marital Deduction for Non-United States Citizen Recipient Spouses, 25 Real Prop., Prob. & Tr. J. 385 (1990)

Polasky, Marital Deduction Formula Clauses in Estate Planning—Estate and Income Tax Considerations, 63 Mich. L. Rev. 809 (1965)

Siegel-Baum & Averill, Postnuptial Agreements Can Resolve Personal and Estate Planning Issues, 29 Est. Plan. 405 (Aug. 2002)

Siegler & Plaine, IRS Revises Security Arrangements for Payment of QDOT Tax, 84 J. Tax. 13 (1996)

Sloan, Funding Formulas Fail on Flexibility: Variations on Traditional Marital/Credit Shelter Funding Techniques, U. Miami, 38th Inst. Est. Plan., Ch. 9 (2004)

Trapp, Appreciation, Depreciation, and Basis in Drafting and Funding Marital Deduction Formula Bequests, U. Miami, 13th Inst. Est. Plan., Ch. 3 (1979)

Whitaker & Parets, My Client Married an Alien: Ten Things Everyone Should Know About International Estate Planning, 18 Prob. & Prop. 25 (2003)

6

Life Insurance

A. INTRODUCTION

§ 6.1. SCOPE

Estate planners seldom see a client whose life is not insured under at least one policy of life insurance. Indeed, for many families life insurance is the largest single investment apart from the family residence. Life insurance proceeds are commonly the largest single liquid asset that is available upon the death of the head of a family. Life insurance may also play an important role in the business context, from funding buy-sell agreements, §§ 11.6-11.12, to providing death benefits to the families of deceased employees.

Irrevocable life insurance trusts (ILITs) remain one of the most attractive opportunities for sheltering a substantial amount of property from the federal transfer taxes. See § 6.24. ILITs are sometimes recommended to provide is "wealth replacement" for the amounts the insured's estate will be required to pay in taxes: "Life insurance is a viable answer for the high net worth client faced with replacing assets lost to estate taxation. The client should get past his philosophical objections and understand that use of this product in his estate plan is an investment decision rather than a life insurance buying decision." Wilshinsky, Life Insurance: A New Dimension in Estate Planning, 130 Tr. & Est. 10 (June 1991). Because of the important role that life insurance plays in estate planning, it is important for the planner to have some familiarity with the basic substantive and tax law regarding life insurance.

A good grasp of the basic tax laws is necessary to advise clients regarding the consequences of both simple and complex insurance transactions. The existing federal tax laws offer some important opportunities for removing a very substantial amount of life insurance from the gross estate of the insured at little or no gift or income tax cost. Indeed, the tax advantages of the ILIT have made it a common element of estate plans in many circumstances. *See* § 6.24. Benefits paid under so-called death benefit only plans may also be excluded from the estate of a deceased employee. *See* § 6.79. Life insurance continues to play an important role in estate planning despite the adoption of the unlimited marital deduction and the relatively large unified credit. Indeed, the ability to defer the payment of the estate tax until the death of the second spouse to die makes it possible to provide for payment of the tax through the use of a policy that matures on the death of the second spouse to die. Such policies carry premiums much lower than would be payable on policies that matured on the death of one spouse. Second-to-die or survivorship life insurance, which is particularly attractive when used in conjunction with an ILIT, is discussed in § 6.76. Importantly, the GSTT exemption and exclusions for nontaxable gifts can be leveraged to shelter a large amount of life insurance from the GSTT. § § 2.25, 2.27.

Estate planners also need to know the basic types of life insurance policies, the advantages and disadvantages of different forms of ownership, and different types of beneficiary designations. The estate plan recommended for a client may involve the transfer, surrender, exchange, or retention of existing policies, or it may involve the acquisition of additional ones. Lawyers should recognize their own limitations, however, and should be reluctant to assume the role of insurance or investment advisor.

The increased complexity of both cash value life insurance contracts (which may be attractive because of their investment features) and the tax law make it important for clients and lawyers to obtain the advice of competent life insurance advisors. Advisors can help in choosing the most appropriate type of policy and in many other ways, including the selection of a financially sound insurer. In keeping with the practices of lawyers and accountants, many insurance advisors now charge hourly fees for their services. The recommendations regarding life insurance will depend upon a variety of factors, including the client's age, health, family circumstances, and investment and planning objectives.

This chapter includes a review of the basic types of life insurance; a consideration of the basic objectives and techniques of planning with life insurance; a discussion of the gift, estate, and income tax consequences of transactions involving life insurance; and an examination of the characteristics of some special types of life insurance and life insurance plans.

Basically, life insurance is a contractual arrangement for spreading among all members of a group the risk of suffering economic loss upon the death of any member of the group. This is accomplished by each person in the group paying a relatively small amount each year into a pool in consideration of the promise by the operator of the pool to pay a larger amount to designated persons upon the death of any group member during that year. In practice, the risk pools are operated by insurance companies subject to state laws and the supervision of state insurance commissioners.

The beneficiary designated in the insurance contract is ordinarily not subject to change by will. However, a contrary conclusion has been reached in a few cases. *E.g., Connecticut General Life Insurance Co. v. Peterson*, 442 F. Supp. 533 (W.D. Mo. 1978). *See also* § 4.18.4. In most states the right of a beneficiary to receive the proceeds of an insurance policy is not affected by a divorce of the insured and the beneficiary unless otherwise specified in the divorce decree. However, divorce generally revokes the beneficiary designation of a former spouse under U.P.C. § 2-804(b) (2011), and the laws of Michigan, Ohio, Oklahoma, Texas and Washington. *See* § 4.20.4.

§ 6.2. TERMINOLOGY; INSURABLE INTEREST

Before going further it may be helpful to review the terms that are commonly used to designate the parties to a transaction involving life insurance and to consider the requirement that the person procuring life insurance have an insurable interest in the life of the insured.

The *insurer* is the company that issues a life insurance policy. The *insured* is the person whose life is insured and upon whose death a specified sum is payable under the terms of the policy. A life insurance policy is itself property as distinct from the proceeds payable upon the death of the insured. An insured may or may not have been the *applicant* who originally applied for issuance of the policy and may or may not be the *policy owner*. Upon the death of the insured the death benefit (policy proceeds) is payable to the *beneficiary* designated in the policy or in a change of beneficiary form.

If the primary beneficiary is an individual, in most cases the owner should designate a secondary, or contingent, beneficiary to whom the proceeds will be paid if the primary beneficiary does not survive the insured. Under the terms of modern policies, the policy owner, who may or may not be the insured, has the unrestricted right to change the beneficiary unless the beneficiary has been irrevocably designated. A revocably designated beneficiary has no property interest in the policy—only a contingent interest in the proceeds. The policy owner owns and controls the policy, including the designation of the beneficiary. The irrevocable designation of a beneficiary in effect makes that person the owner of the policy. Such a designation is seldom desirable and seldom done because the substantive and tax law consequences are unclear and quite possibly adverse in many cases.

Insurable Interest. In order for a third party to acquire insurance on the life of another person, the third party must have an insurable interest in the life of the insured. The requirement is imposed in order to prevent insurance from being used for gambling purposes. The rule that limits the exclusion from income of the proceeds of life insurance paid under a policy that has been transferred for value, § 101(a)(2), is imposed for a similar reason. *See* § 6.54 and § 4.18.4. "[T]he interest commonly sought is a financial interest adversely affected if the insured dies." J. Munch, Financial and Estate Planning with Life Insurance Products ¶ 7.1.2 (1990). Individuals related by blood or law are generally presumed to have an insurable interest engendered by love and affection.

Insurable Interest; Charities. In LR 9110016, the IRS indicated that it would deny income, gift, and estate tax deductions with respect to an insurance policy that the insured-donor proposed to transfer to a charity. According to the IRS view the charity would not have an insurable interest in the life of the insured under the applicable state law, that of New York. The ruling concerned an individual who planned to (1) acquire a policy of insurance on his life, (2) assign irrevocably the policy to a charity, and (3) continue to pay premiums on the policy. The IRS concluded that the original acquisition of the insurance by the donor was intended to circumvent a state law requirement that the owner-beneficiary of a policy have an insurable interest in the life of the insured. If so, under New York law the insurer might deny liability upon the death of the insured or the insured's personal representative might recover the proceeds from the charity beneficiary. Accordingly, the IRS concluded that no income or gift tax deductions were allowable with respect to the transfer or payment of premiums, that the insurance would be includible in the insured's estate and that no charitable deduction would be allowable for estate tax purposes.

The IRS's reasoning, based on New York law, seems flawed. Once a policy is acquired by the insured, the insured should be free to transfer the policy to whomever he or she chooses. In addition, a charity should be presumed to have an insurable interest in the life of a donor. New York amended the law to eliminate the problem after which the IRS revoked LR 9110016. LR 9147040. The same issue could arise in other jurisdictions which have laws similar to former law of New York (*e.g.*, Washington, Wash. Rev. Code § 48.18.030 (2011)), but will not in other states, such as Pennsylvania, that have statutes allowing a validly issued policy to be transferred to an assignee who does not have an insurable interest in the life of the insured. "If a policy of life insurance has been issued in conformity with this section, no transfer of such policy or any interest thereunder shall be invalid by reason of a lack of insurable interest of the transferee in the life of the insured or the payment of premiums thereafter by the transferee." 40 Pa. Stat. Ann. § 512 (2011).

§6.3. DATA COLLECTION

It is important to know the current status of beneficiary designations, policy loans, and the like in order to integrate life insurance fully into the client's estate plan. Accordingly, a client should be asked to provide relevant data regarding existing policies of life insurance of any significant amount. The data could be assembled by the client, the client's insurance advisor, the lawyer, or a legal assistant. The data are necessary for current analysis and future reference. Reliable data regarding some items of information, such as the beneficiary designations, current policy values, and outstanding loan balances may only be available from the insurers. The necessary information is usually provided promptly by the insurer in response to a letter signed by the owner of the policy. The use of a standard data collection form is convenient and increases the likelihood that the necessary data will be obtained for each policy. With the approval of the client the data may be collected and submitted by the client's insurance advisor. To preserve the integrity and value of a plan, the client should be cautioned not to change beneficiary designations, to assign policies, or to take other significant action with respect to life insurance without consulting the lawyer in advance.

In appropriate cases the following information should be collected regarding each policy:

1. insurer and number of policy;
2. type of policy (term, whole life, endowment, etc.);
3. face amount;
4. amount of premium and source of payment;
5. dividend option selected;
6. accidental death benefit;
7. waiver of premium in event of disability;
8. original applicant;
9. current owner of policy;
10. successive owner of policy (if designated);

11. current beneficiary designation;

12. current cash surrender value; and

13. amount of policy loans, if any, and interest rate.

As with other property, the client should also provide information regarding the location of the policies. Other additional data may also be needed for special types of policies and ones that have been assigned to a trust.

§6.4. BASIC FUNCTIONS OF LIFE INSURANCE

Life insurance is usually purchased in order to provide funds with which to (1) pay taxes, costs, and expenses of an illiquid estate; (2) satisfy a mortgage or other substantial indebtedness; (3) fund a buy-sell agreement or other business-related transaction; or (4) support the dependents of the insured. In addition, an investment in cash value life insurance may help provide investment diversification and provide wealth replacement. See §6.1. In addition, life insurance policies and their proceeds are generally exempt from the claims of creditors. In any case, the ownership and beneficiary designations of policies can often be arranged so that none of the proceeds is includible in the insured's gross estate even though the insured paid the premiums.

Various types of cash value life insurance may be acquired as a personal investment because the earnings on the reserve attributable to a policy accumulate free of tax until withdrawal. The compounding of the tax-free accumulation of variable life policies can be particularly impressive. Finally, life insurance is often purchased in the business setting as an employee benefit. For example, an employer may provide all, or virtually all, employees with a limited amount of group-term insurance as a fringe benefit. See §6.73. Additional insurance may be provided to key employees.

Illiquid Estates. Life insurance may be needed to fund the costs of the insured's final illness and funeral, debts, death taxes, and administration expenses. In specific cases life insurance may be acquired to avoid the forced liquidation of the insured's interest in a closely-held business or other illiquid assets such as unimproved real property. Insurance may be needed although the immediate post-mortem demand for funds can be reduced through special use valuation under §2032A, redemption of stock under §303 or deferral of estate tax payment under §6166. See §§11.13-11.28, 12.19. Liquidity can, of course, be provided although the insurance is not includible in the insured's gross estate; an irrevocable life insurance trust is often used for this purpose. See §6.24.

Buy-Sell Arrangements. Life insurance is also sometimes purchased in order to provide funds with which to finance the acquisition of the decedent's interest in a partnership, closely-held corporation, or other business enterprise The amount needed for this purpose can be estimated and updated as required if the purchase price is fixed by the terms of a buy-sell agreement or is based upon a formula set forth in the agreement. Otherwise the amount may be more roughly estimated. Regardless of the form of the agreement (*e.g.*, cross-purchase or entity purchase), the ownership of the insurance and the beneficiary designations should be carefully arranged to preserve the available income and estate tax advantages. The use of buy-sell agreements is discussed in Chapter 11.

§6.5. HOW MUCH LIFE INSURANCE?

Life insurance is often purchased to support the dependents of the insured following his or her death. For this purpose some companies and advisors recommend carrying insurance equal to five or six times annual earnings or spending "at least" a specified percentage of gross or net income for cash value insurance. Unfortunately, these simple formulas are not very helpful. An individual's annual income is not necessarily a reliable indicator of the actual financial needs or circumstances of his or her dependents. Similarly, the emphasis on ordinary life insurance instead of term insurance is often misplaced.

The bias of some agents in favor of some form of cash value life insurance also contributes to the problem of some families being underinsured. In particular, the insurance needs of young families with modest resources and small children are often best met through the purchase of less expensive term insurance. Of course, in much later years term insurance may become too expensive to continue.

For the same premium, a much larger amount of term insurance can be purchased on the life of a relatively young person, which can better protect the economic security of a typical young family. By way of illustration, the annual premium cost of a $500,000 ten or twenty year renewable and convertible term policy is about $700 for a male nonsmoker aged 45, which would be about the annual premium on a cash value policy of $100,000. Also, note that the annual cost of group-term insurance is often significantly lower than individual term. In any case, it pays to shop carefully before purchasing life insurance—the price of comparable policies may vary by as much as 300 percent.

The amount of insurance needed to protect a family can be based upon a projection of the family's needs and an estimate of the resources that will be available to the family. An estimate is necessarily a rough one, because we do not know when the insured will die or what the future will bring in terms of family circumstances or general economic conditions. However, a ballpark projection can be made by preparing a family balance sheet that includes what a client's family would need to maintain its standard of living if the client were to die tomorrow and the resources, including Social Security, pension payments, interest, and dividends that the family would have available to meet those needs. Funds needed at some future time (*e.g.*, for college expenses) are discounted to current value. Various programs and online resources are also available to estimate an individual's insurance needs. Helpful, impartial information is available through consumerreports.org, some of which is free. Information regarding Social Security survivors benefits is available at www.ssa.gov.

The estate planner or another advisor can also estimate the additional amounts of life insurance coverage that may be required to meet other needs. For example, the amount of cash needed to pay estate administration expenses, debts, taxes and other death-related items can be estimated. Similarly, the amount required to fund a business buy-out can be estimated. Both estimates should be revised as circumstances change.

§6.6. Spouse Insurance

Consideration should also be given to purchasing insurance on the life of each spouse, particularly one who devotes full, or nearly full, time to childcare. Insurance can be used to meet the liquidity needs that may arise if the homemaking spouse dies first, particularly where he or she owns an estate of substantial value that produces little income. Of course, the need on the death of the first spouse to die may be reduced by the unlimited marital deduction. The proceeds from this kind of insurance protection may also be excluded from the estate of the employed spouse if the policies are owned by the trustee of an ILIT. See §6.24. They may also help offset the additional costs that may be incurred by a surviving spouse for childcare and homemaking costs. If dependent children or stepchildren live with the surviving spouse, he or she may file income tax returns at joint return rates for two years following the death of a spouse and later as a head of household.

§6.7. Basic Planning Techniques

The basic life insurance planning techniques are discussed in Part B, §§6.17-6.25. They include ownership by a person other than the insured, the cross-ownership of insurance by a husband and wife, revocable and irrevocable trusts, and business-related insurance. Particularly impressive estate tax savings can result from the use of an ILIT under which the proceeds of policies are excluded from the estates of both the insured and his or her spouse. Beneficial results are also available through plans that combine charitable remainder trusts and life insurance.

§6.8. Types of Life Insurance

At base all life insurance policies are either term insurance that provides insurance protection alone for the specified period, cash value insurance that combines insurance protection with an investment element, or a combination of the two. Term and cash value insurance are very different: Each meets the needs of some persons, but neither meets the needs of everyone. On the one hand, term insurance provides maximum current insurance protection for the premium dollar. On the other, cash value insurance provides insurance protection and a fund that is sheltered from creditors and that accumulates earnings in the hands of the insurer (the "inside" build-up) free of tax to the policy owner.

The main differences between term and cash value insurance arise from the fact that the premium on term pays only for the cost of insurance protection during the term, while the premium on cash value insurance includes an excess which is accumulated in a policy reserve that, in effect, reduces the amount at risk in later years. The reserve supports the cash surrender value or loan value of the policy, which is available to the policy owner prior to maturity of the policy. Because mortality increases with age for adults, the cost of term insurance increases with the age of the insured. What is very, very economical term insurance protection at age 30 or 40 can become very expensive at age 65 or 70.

The initial premium cost of cash value insurance is usually much greater than term, but is typically much lower in later years. However, because of the reserve fund, the premium on cash value insurance usually remains level, declines or disappears (in the case of participating policies). With favorable earnings or an increase in value within a variable life policy, the need to pay premiums on some cash value policies can disappear altogether after a few years. Another feature of the reserve fund in cash value insurance is that the amount at risk (the insurance element) decreases over time as the size of the reserve increases. In contrast, the entire amount of a term policy remains at risk throughout the term.

Life insurance agents commonly recommend that prospects buy some type of cash value life insurance—such as whole life—rather than a form of term insurance. This recommendation often reflects a sincere belief in the superior quality of cash value life insurance and on the importance of life insurance as an investment. Whole life and term are different types of insurance, but both are generally sold by the same companies, which indicates that they are both reliable. Objectively speaking, it is doubtful that (1) whole life is inherently superior or (2) cash value life insurance is a wise investment for a young family with a need for large amounts of insurance during the years the children are dependent. Also, traditional whole life has been a questionable investment, particularly during periods of high inflation. The needs of young families and some other individual life insurance purchasers might be better met if they bought much larger amounts of term insurance. The difference between the higher cost of whole life and the cost of term might be invested or used for other family purposes. Of course, some purchasers of term insurance would not save the difference, and, of those who did, some would make poor investments. In contrast, cash value life insurance involves forced savings that are readily available in case of need (or investment opportunity). It is, in effect, a form of forced saving.

Agents are also inevitably influenced to some degree by the higher commissions paid on sales of cash value life insurance. The commission on a whole life policy is a much higher percentage of the initial premium than it is for a term policy. Because the premium rate for ordinary life is often several times that of term insurance, agents have a powerful incentive to prefer sales of whole life insurance. Most states have anti-kickback laws which prohibit an agent from returning any portion of the premium. However, rebates or discounts are permitted in a few states, including California and Florida. As a result, some planners suggest that large cash value policies be purchased through agents in the states that offer discounts. As Consumer Reports suggests, lower premiums may be available through online brokers.

§6.9.   Cash Value Insurance

The following sections describe the general types of cash value policies—whole life, limited pay life, and endowment contracts. It also reviews the basic characteristics of two innovations of the late Twentieth century: Universal Life and Variable Life.

§6.9.1. Whole Life

The most common form of cash value insurance is whole life, which is also called straight life or ordinary life. Cash value policies are also sometimes called "permanent" insurance to distinguish them from term insurance that is issued for a specified term of years (*e.g.* one, five, or ten years). Of course, term insurance is typically renewable without further evidence of insurability, at increasing premiums, until the insured reaches an advanced age. Whole life policies originally provided that both the amount of insurance and the premium would remain level for the duration of the policy. However, the annual premium on policies that participated in the insurer's earnings might be partially or totally offset by those earnings.

Cash value policies are now often designed with a wide range of variations, including lower initial premiums and increasing amounts of insurance. In others the requirement of paying a premium may disappear relatively soon if there are sufficiently favorable investment results. Of course, the converse is also true—premiums may be payable much longer than projected if investment returns are inadequate. Premiums may be payable until the insured dies or the policy matures when the insured attains a very advanced age, usually 99 or 100. If the insured lives to maturity, the face amount of insurance is paid to the policy owner and the policy terminates. On the other hand, higher premiums may only be payable for a few years.

§6.9.2. Limited-Pay Life

Limited-pay life is a type of cash value policy that involves payment of premiums for a limited period—usually a fixed number of years or until the insured attains a specified age. Policies on which premiums are payable for 20 years ("twenty-pay-life") or until the insured reaches age 65 ("pay-to-sixty-five") are common examples of limited-pay policies. The premium on a limited-pay policy is higher than on an old style whole life policy in the same amount, but the cash value of the limited-pay policy usually builds up faster.

§6.9.3. Endowment Insurance

The final initial category is the endowment policy. It is essentially a whole life policy with a maturity or endowment date that occurs after a certain number of years or at a certain age, usually 65 rather than 99 or 100. The purchaser of an endowment policy should understand that when a policy matures the amount by which the amount paid out exceeds the amount of premiums paid by the insured is includible in the insured's income. Premiums are typically payable on an endowment policy until the policy endows or the insured dies. Of course, if the insured dies prior to endowment, the face amount of insurance is payable to the designated beneficiary, just as with an ordinary life policy. Because an endowment policy matures more quickly than ordinary life and its cash value also equals its face value at maturity, the premiums must be substantially higher. Traditional endowment policies issued after June 21, 1988 may have difficulty meeting the requirements of §7702. At least some may be characterized as modified endowment contracts under §7702A. *See* §6.51.

§6.9.4. Universal Life

Universal life policies allow flexible premium payments. However, the insurer requires that premiums fall within the premium payment guidelines of §7702. In general, each premium payment on a universal life policy is credited to the policy's cash value account. Deductions are made from the cash value account for an appropriate portion of the insurer's projected mortality costs (death claims) and expense charges (selling costs and commission payments). The remainder is credited with interest at a guaranteed minimum rate plus whatever higher rate may be earned and declared by the insurer. As some commentators have observed, a universal life policy resembles term insurance combined with a savings account. Of course, the internal build-up in value of the policy (the "interest" on the "savings account") is tax-free. The balance in the cash value account may be borrowed or may be withdrawn if the policy is surrendered. Expenses that are charged against the cash value account may include an initial fixed fee, a fixed dollar amount or a fixed or declining percentage of premiums, or some combination of them. As is the case with some mutual funds, some universal policies provide for a backload charge if the policy is surrendered. Backload charges typically decline each year and disappear after a specified number of years (eight, ten, or fifteen). Some policies guarantee a high rate of interest for an initial period, which may also be used for purposes of illustrations.

Universal life policies are usually available in forms that have a fixed death benefit (Option "A") or a death benefit that is composed of a fixed death benefit *plus* the balance of the cash value account (Option "B"). The cost of the latter type is naturally greater.

In comparing policy illustrations, a planner should be sure they involve the same premiums, death benefits, and interest rate assumptions. The planner should also examine the rates of interest that each company has actually credited on its universal life policies. Some illustrations indicate that the necessity of paying premiums will "vanish" after a relatively short term of years (seven or ten years are often used for illustrative purposes). However, the planner and the prospective policy owner should understand that the premiums will vanish and remain vanished only so long as the balance in the policy's cash value account is credited with amounts that equal or exceed the projected interest used in the illustration. Otherwise, the owner will be required to pay additional premiums. Policies issued by some companies tie the interest rate to an index, such as the 52-week Treasury bill rate.

Insurers frequently indicate a "target" premium that is intended to create a cash value sufficient to keep the policy in force for life. Because of the variability in the amount of charges against the account and interest credited to the account, payment of the target premiums might generate more or less than required to maintain the policy. Indeed, paying smaller premiums or skipping some premium payments might be sufficient to support the policy. Payments of larger premiums would create a larger reserve and cash value, which could remain invested or be borrowed by the policy owner.

§ 6.9.5. Variable Life

Variable life is a type of whole life that usually has a fixed premium and a guaranteed minimum amount of insurance. It is called variable insurance because an additional amount of insurance may be provided under the policy, depending upon the investment performance of the fund or funds (usually mutual funds) selected by the policy owner. In this case, the product can be viewed as term insurance combined with a mutual fund. Importantly, the yield of an equity fund may significantly exceed the amount that would otherwise be credited to the policy based upon the investment performance of the insurer's general portfolio of assets (principally bonds). Again, the key to the popularity of variable life is that the internal value of policy will increase over time and is tax-free until it is withdrawn.

The owner of a variable life policy is usually free to allocate the cash value among one or more funds that reflect different investment philosophies. However, under § 817 a fund must be diversified. In effect, this type of policy shifts the investment risk largely to the policy owner. If the arrangement is properly structured, the income, gain, or loss experienced by the fund is reportable by the insurer and not the policy owner. *E.g.,* LR 8427085. If the funds in which the cash value is invested produce a rate of return higher than the rate guaranteed in the policy, the excess may be used to purchase additional paid-up insurance. *E.g.,* LR 8349034.

Variable life plans such as the one described in Rev. Rul. 79-87, 1979-1 C.B. 73, provide for the net annual premium to be allocated to a separate account, which is invested primarily in equity securities in the discretion of the insurer. The cash surrender value, and presumably the loan value, may also increase or decrease depending upon investment experience, but with no guaranteed minimum. In the long run variable insurance can provide an attractive way to make an additional investment in equity securities and can lower cost life insurance coverage.

§ 6.10. Term Insurance

Term insurance, which may be issued either on an individual or a group basis, provides insurance protection for the period specified in the policy (usually a term of one, five, ten, or twenty years). The premium remains level for the period of the term. It is often called "pure" insurance because it does not involve any investment component and has no nonforfeiture value. Unlike cash value insurance, term insurance does not provide any loan or surrender value that can be reached in case of financial emergency. Viewed in its simplest terms, the full face amount of the insurance is at risk each term.

Term insurance is typically renewable for successive terms at increasing rates until the insured attains a certain age (e.g., 70), without further evidence of insurability. If the amount of the term insurance remains the same, the premium will increase with each renewal as the insured grows older. If the insurance is not guaranteed renewable, the insurance protection will lapse at the end of the term and a new policy will be issued only upon showing evidence of insurability. Guaranteed renewability is desirable in order to enable the insured to continue the insurance regardless of the state of the insured's health.

Term insurance is also often convertible during the term into any regularly issued form of cash value life policy issued by the insurer. In case of conversion the premium on the new policy is usually based upon the insured's attained age at the time of conversion and not the insured's age at the time the term policy was originally issued. A conversion right is also generally desirable because it can be used to continue the insurance on a permanent basis. Over the short term, renewable and convertible term insurance is usually the best buy for a relatively young person who wants to obtain the maximum amount of life insurance protection at the lowest cost. Over an extended period a whole life policy may be a better buy.

Graph 6-1
Annual Premium, Five-Year Renewable $250,000 Term Policy,
Nonsmoking Male Insured

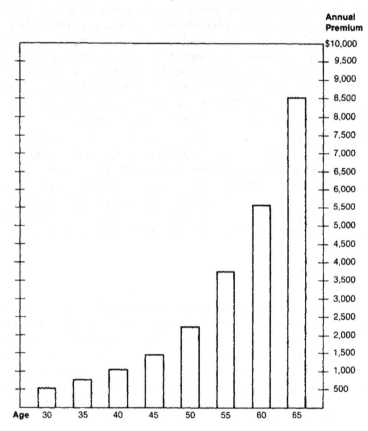

At base, the cost of term insurance is determined by the amount of death benefits the insurer expects to pay on the group of insured lives according to its mortality tables and the projected amount of other costs and expenses. Because the mortality rate for adults increases with age, the cost of a fixed amount of life insurance increases as the insured grows older. If an insurer expected two persons out of a group of one thousand aged 35 to die over a one-year period, the insurer would have to charge a premium of $20 merely to cover the cost of death benefits that would be payable under $10,000 one-year term policies issued to a group of one thousand persons of that age. Likewise, if three persons were expected to die out of a group of one thousand persons aged 40, the annual premium on a $10,000 one-year term policy would be at least $30; if four persons out of a group aged 45 were expected to die, the premium would be at least $40; if seven out of a group aged 50 were expected to die, the premium would be at least $70; if eleven out of a group aged 55 were expected to die, the premium would be at least $110; and if fifteen out of a group aged 60 were expected to die, the premium would be at least $150.

In the summer of 2006, a healthy 45 year-old male who was a nonsmoker would probably pay between $700 and $900 per year for a $500,000 policy with a twenty year term. BU, p. 13. The initial premium may be lower if the term is shorter or if the insurer reserves the right to increase the premium after a period of five or ten years. For example, if the term is ten years, the initial premium might be $660, but could be as much as $10,000 in the tenth year and almost $25,000 in the twentieth year.

§ 6.10.1. Decreasing Term

In the case of decreasing term insurance the premium remains the same over time, but the face amount of insurance decreases. Decreasing term is often used to provide for payment of the balance of a mortgage if the person who is the primary source of income in a family dies prior to its satisfaction. Terms of from five to thirty years are usually available for this purpose, depending somewhat upon the age of the insured at the time of issue. It is usually much less expensive for an individual to buy decreasing term directly than it is to buy the insurance through the mortgagor or other creditor.

§ 6.10.2. Group-Term

Very economical guaranteed renewable and convertible group-term insurance is often available through an employer, professional association, or other membership group. Many group plans do not require evidence of insurability for persons who buy a limited amount of group-term coverage when the plan is first made available or during some subsequent enrollment periods. In many cases group-term insurance fits well into an estate plan because of its low cost, its general assignability, and its slight value for gift tax purposes. However, in the case of employer provided group-term insurance, the continuation of the insurance coverage is dependent upon the continued existence of the employment relationship and the employer's continuation of the insurance plan. For example, the employer may decide to terminate a group-term plan in order to reduce expenses. Also, if the employment relationship ends, the former employee may have only the right to convert the group-term coverage to individual whole life, which could be very expensive. Moreover, a new employer may have a less generous group-term plan, or none at all.

§ 6.11. COMMON POLICY RIDERS

Insurers typically offer at least two riders that can be added to most term and cash value policies at a small increase in cost: the accidental death benefit rider and the waiver of premium rider. Each of them is discussed below. A third rider that is frequently available with respect to cash value policies allows the owner to purchase term insurance on the life of the spouse or children of the insured, or both. The need for insurance on the lives of dependents and its relative cost should be considered by the client before taking advantage of the family term insurance rider.

§6.11.1. Accidental Death

Under the accidental death benefit rider, commonly called the "double indemnity clause," an additional death benefit equal to the face amount will be paid in the event the insured dies as the result of an accidental injury. Some clauses provide for triple indemnity if the insured dies as a result of injuries suffered while riding on a bus, train, plane, or other licensed public conveyance. The cost of the rider varies, but is typically about $1 per year for each $1,000 of accidental death benefit, but it is questionable whether it is a wise purchase for most persons. In truth, a double indemnity rider does not provide insurance protection that can be relied upon to meet the needs of the survivors. Instead, it is essentially a gamble that the insured will die as the result of an accident, which is highly unlikely in any given case.

§6.11.2. Waiver of Premium

The typical waiver of premium rider provides that the insurer will waive payment of all premiums falling due under the policy while the insured is totally and permanently disabled prior to a certain age (usually 65). This type of rider also typically comes into effect only if the disability occurs prior to age 60 or 65 and lasts for six months or more. The value of the rider depends largely upon the limitations applicable to it and its cost, both of which vary substantially from policy to policy. Stripped to its essentials, the rider is a miniature disability policy. The cost of the rider varies with the age and occupation of the insured and from company to company. Some advisors consider the rider to provide useful additional protection against disability. However, the same coverage might be available at lower cost by increasing the amount of disability insurance carried by the insured instead of purchasing the waiver of premium provision.

§6.12. PARTICIPATING AND NONPARTICIPATING POLICIES

Policies upon which the insurer may pay annual dividends, usually beginning after the second or third policy year, are called participating policies. They include most cash value policies issued by mutual insurance companies and some issued by stock companies. Some term policies are also participating, but many are not. Although participating policies generally do not guarantee that any dividends will be paid, dividends that are paid can be quite substantial.

The initial premium on participating policies is generally higher than for nonparticipating policies, but the long run cost of participating policies is often much lower. In effect, the dividends represent a refund of excess premiums previously paid on a policy and part of the income derived from investing the excess. Consistent with that analysis, dividends are not taxable income until the amount recovered by the policy owner exceeds the premiums or other consideration paid for the policy. *See* §6.62. For purposes of setting the premium on nonparticipating policies, some insurers assume a low rate of return; as a result, the premium on a nonparticipating policy may actually exceed the premium on participating policies after a short time. Participating cash value policies generally give the policy owner five options regarding the use of the dividends: (1) to receive payment of the dividend in cash; (2) to apply the dividends against current premium costs; (3) to leave the dividends with the company at interest; (4) to use the dividends to purchase additional paid-up insurance; or (5) to use the dividends to purchase one-year term insurance equal to the cash value of the policy. The fifth dividend option is a key feature of some plans, such as the minimum deposit plans discussed in §6.74, and is very useful, particularly if the option can be exercised without further evidence of insurability.

It is often tempting to take dividends in cash or to apply them in reduction of the amount of the premium necessary to continue a policy. These may be poor choices. Instead, the dividends might better be used to buy additional paid-up insurance or one-year term insurance that will help maintain the real value of the insurance protection provided by the policy against the attrition of inflation. There is usually little or no reason to leave dividends at interest with the insurer at a low guaranteed rate of interest, especially since the interest is fully taxable.

§6.13. ACCELERATED DEATH BENEFITS (ADB s); VIATICAL SETTLEMENTS, §101(G)

In the late twentieth century, the ravages of AIDS, challenges of greater longevity, prosperity, and the spiraling costs of medical and health care combined to increase dramatically the desire of terminally ill insured persons to access the value of their life insurance policies and receive more than the cash surrender value specified in the policies. Responses to the interest took two forms—(1) insurers began to allow an insured to access the value through the provisions of policies or riders to policies (accelerated death benefits or ADBs) and (2) the number of viatical settlement companies, that might purchase policies purchase policies from terminally ill insureds, rapidly increased. The growth in viatical settlements generated responses from insurers, insurance commissioners, the IRS, Congress, and state legislatures. The issues regarding settlements that should be considered by clients and their advisors are discussed in Leimberg, Weinbert, Weinbert & Callahan, Life Settlements: How to Know When to Hold and When to Fold, 35 Est. Plan. 3 (Aug. 2008).

ADB Payments. Policies issued by many insurers allow insureds to withdraw part of the death benefit amount in certain emergencies. The emergencies may include one or more of the following: (1) diagnosis of a terminal illness that is expected to result in death within 6-24 months; (2) diagnosis of a specific serious medical condition, such as cancer or a stroke, that will not necessarily result in death; (3) need for long-term nursing care; and (4) confinement that is expected to be permanent in a long-term care facility. Depending upon the terms of the rider, the funds withdrawn may be paid in a single sum, in installments, or as expenses are incurred. Upon the death of the insured the balance of the death benefit would be paid to the designated beneficiaries of the policy.

The uncertain tax consequences of ADB payments discouraged reliance on them. Relief was provided in proposed regulations that the IRS issued in 1992. Prop. Regs. §§1.101-8; 1.7702-2. However, the proposed regulations did not apply to viatical settlements or other sales of policies. Congress picked up the slack in 1996 by enacting legislation that provided relief for both ADBs and viatical settlements. Specifically, under §101(g)(1), funds withdrawn from a policy by a terminally ill or chronically ill insured are treated as having been paid by reason of the death of the insured. As explained below, §101(g)(2) gives the same treatment to viatical settlements by terminally ill or chronically ill insureds. Legislatures in a majority of states have enacted some form of regulatory legislation—most often relating only to insureds who are terminally ill.

Under §101(g)(1), amounts received under a life insurance contract on the life of a "terminally ill individual" or on the life of an insured who is "chronically ill" are treated as having been paid by reason of the death of the insured. However, amounts received by chronically ill individuals are not within the statute unless the payments are for uninsured costs of providing the insured with qualified long term care services described in §7702B(c) or meet the requirements of §101(g)(3)(B), which refers to regulations and standards established, respectively, by the IRS, the National Association of Insurance Commissioners, and the states in which the policy holder resides. The same requirement applies to payments in connection with viatical settlements. §101(g)(2).

Viatical Settlements. Under §101(g)(2), the payment by a viatical insurance provider in exchange for the sale or assignment of a portion of the policy's death benefit is treated as an amount received by reason of the death of the insured. §101(g)(2)(A). For the purpose of the law, a person is terminally ill when he or she is certified "by a physician as having an illness or physical condition which can reasonably be expected to result in death in 24 months or less after the date of the certification." §101(g)(4)(A). The term "chronically ill individual" has the meaning given by §7702B(c) except it does not include a person who is terminally ill. §101(g)(4)(B).

The National Association of Insurance Commissioners has proposed model legislation and model regulations for adoption by states with respect to viatical settlements. The regulations would allow the insurance commissioners to license companies and brokers and regulate practices. Perhaps most important, the regulations would prescribe minimum amounts that must be paid based on the insured's life expectancy.

The Model Regulations issued by the National Association of Insurance Commissioners, require that viatical settlements pay persons with less than six months to live at least 80 percent of the policy's face value, while those with six to twelve months would receive 70 percent. Between 12 and 18 months the percentage is 65 percent and between 18 and 24 months it is 60 percent. For a person with a life expectancy of between two and three years, the percentage is 50 percent.

Prior to the adoption of §101(g) the IRS issued a private letter ruling that described the tax consequences of selling a policy to a viatical settlement company. LR 9443020. The ruling illustrates how the IRS would tax the sale of a life insurance policy in a transaction that is not within the shelter provided by §101(g)(2). It concluded that the insured-seller must report income in an amount equal to the consideration received from the viatical settlement company less the insured's adjusted basis in the property. For this purpose the adjusted basis is "equal to the premiums paid less the sum of (i) the cost of insurance protection provided through the date of sale and (ii) any amounts (e.g., dividends) received under the contract that have not been included in gross income." See §6.63. According to the ruling, the cost of insurance protection is approximately the difference between the premiums paid and the cash surrender value of the contract. Some commentators contend that the basis should not be reduced by the cost of the insurance protection received. *See* Adams, The New Frontier for Life Insurance Planning: Viatical Settlements, U.

Miami, 33rd Inst. Est. Plan., Ch. 18 (1999). It is unclear whether the gain on the sale should be treated as ordinary income or capital gain. The gain on the sale may be part ordinary income and part capital gain. *See* §§ 6.63, 6.64. As a transferee for value the proceeds received by the viatical settlement company are ordinary income under § 101 to the extent they exceed the total of the consideration and premiums paid. *See* § 6.54.

What viatical settlement firms thought was a sure thing became increasingly less sure: That is, the expected early demise of HIV/AIDS patients and other insureds who were seriously ill did not always occur. In particular, advances in medical therapies unexpectedly extended the lives of patients for years—thereby increasing the cost to purchasers in the viatical settlement market of maintaining policies.

§ 6.14. Life Settlements; Secondary and Tertiary Markets for Life Insurance

Life settlements are an outgrowth of the viatical settlements industry. A life settlement, much like a viatical, provides the insured the opportunity to gain financial liquidity through the sale of his life insurance policy. Instead of selling the policy for medical reasons, however, the insured seeks to sell the policy based on a change in life circumstances. Examples include divorce, death of a spouse, retirement, disability or bankruptcy. The industry targets policyholders who are 65 or older with a life expectancy between two and twelve years.

An insured engaged in a life settlement transaction typically sells his policy for a sum greater than its cash surrender value but less than the death benefit. The price offered takes into account the administrative costs of maintaining the policy—primarily continued payment of the premiums. The death benefit is ultimately paid directly to the investor, rather than to the initial insured, and the profit is computed just as in a viatical settlement. Mathews, STOLI on the Rocks: Why States Should Eliminate the Abusive Practice of Stranger Owned Life Insurance, 14 Conn. Ins. L. J. 521, 524-525 (2008).

Because of changed economic, tax or family circumstances there may be legitimate reasons why the owner of a policy insuring the life of a person who is not terminally ill may want to dispose of the policy. Until recently, virtually the only choices open to the owner were to let the policy lapse or transfer it to the insurer for its cash surrender value. Now, building on the experience gained in the viatical settlement market, an unwanted policy may be sold on an independent, essentially unregulated secondary market. The income tax consequences of a sale were illuminated in Rev. Ruls. 2009-13, 2009-1 C.B. 1029 and 2009-14, 2009-1 C.B. 1031; *see* §§ 6.63-6.65. In the secondary market, sophisticated investors seek to profit by buying existing policies on the lives of insureds, 65 or older, whose life expectancies have been shortened by illness or injury. The buyers may resell the policies separately or bundled ("securitized") with others and sold on the tertiary market.

Participating in the market is not without risk: While a sale may benefit the seller and the buyer, however, the seller may be pressured, required to provide personal health care information on a continuing basis, and may be paid less than a fair price. In short, the seller may, like the victims of mortgage frauds, be taken advantage of by an aggressive, dishonest broker or buyer. Buyers, too, must beware—to get a higher price the health care information about the seller may be tainted to indicate a seriously shortened life expectancy.

Some commentators have celebrated the development of a market in life insurance policies as a welcome financial innovation "through which companies that develop innovative actuarial analyses have been able to glean profits through their superior ability to assess mortality and other risks." Doherty & Singer, The Benefits of a Secondary Market for Life Insurance Policies, Wharton Institutions Center, 02-41, quoted in Magner, What is Life Insurance? The Evolution of Financial Products, 35 Est. Plan. 24 (Apr. 2008). Other, less sanguine, commentators point out the inherently speculative nature of the market—one that lacks any fundamental economic justification. The full-scale development of the market may be thwarted by state laws, including ones that prohibit stranger owned life insurance (STOLI) and ones requiring an insurable interest.

SPIN (Speculator-Initiated Life Insurance) Life Insurance, aka, Investor-Initiated Insurance.

> The success of the secondary market eventually led to hedge funds and institutional investors partnering with agents and brokers to solicit wealthy elderly people, usually seventy years and older, to obtain life insurance purely to make a profit by later selling the policies to speculators. These policies entered into by wealthy elderly people (with a net worth of at least $1 million) upon the inducement of investors are known as speculator-initiated life insurance, or SPIN-life insurance policies. Investors target wealthy elderly peoples that have "excess insurability"— people who have a high net worth, but who have life insurance that covers only a small percentage of that net worth (e.g., $1 million of in-force life insurance coverage when a person's net worth is $10 million). Alt, SPIN-Life Insurance Policies: A Dizzying Effect on Human Dignity and the Death of Life Insurance, 7 Ave Maria L. Rev. 605 (2009).

> Not satisfied with the relatively passive role of purchasing existing policies, investors and lenders have been busy attempting to induce affluent elders to allow life insurance policies to be written on their lives at no cost. In addition to offering cash payments, a new car or other tangible benefits, the schemes promise "'free' insurance for two years through various nonrecourse financing programs. The program is more accurately described as 'investor initiates life insurance' because both the initiative for purchasing the policy and the source of funding are from outside investors or lenders who are totally unrelated to the insured." Jones, Leimberg & Rybka, 'Free' Life Insurance: Risks and Costs of Non-recourse premium Financing, 33 Est. Plan. 3 (July 2006). As the authors point out, the promoters are motivated largely by the possibility of receiving millions in commissions by selling and reselling large amounts of insurance. Unfortunately, those who decide to participate undertake substantial

risks—some of which are not obvious. The risks include loss of privacy regarding health matters, possible unintentional failure to disclose pre-existing conditions, and possible violation of state insurance laws.

The Tertiary Life Insurance Market—Securitizing Policies. The same financial innovators whose securitization and marketing of mortgage backed securities caused a world-wide economic disaster have now transferred their expertise to buying, bundling and selling life insurance. Some believe the development is simply the outgrowth of understanding and applying modern theories and models: "Sensing an investment opportunity, investment bankers, hedge funds and international banks jumped into various aspects of the life insurance business. . . . To understand why life insurance relatively recently became attractive to institutional investors—particularly to hedge funds—an understanding of modern portfolio theory and the capital asset pricing model ('CAPM') is helpful." Magner, What is Life Insurance? The Evolution of Financial Products, 35 Est. Plan. 24, 25 (Apr. 2008). At every stage, the promoters of securitized life insurance expect to profit: Whether the insured dies earlier or later than expected, "Wall Street would profit by pocketing sizable fees for creating the bonds, reselling them and subsequently trading them." Anderson, New Exotic Investments Emerging on Wall Street, New York Times, Sept. 6, 2009, p. A-1.

The expansion of a speculative market in life insurance has been broadly criticized by some, including Steve Leimberg, who express ethical, legal and practical concerns:

> There are—or will be—serious ethical, legal, and practical economic problems—when the marketing and sale of life insurance begins and ends with no need—other than the promoters' and sellers' and investors' greed fulfilling a determination of speculators to add to their portfolio an investment in contracts on the lives of strangers. Leimberg, Investor Initiated Life Insurance: Really a "Free Lunch," or Prelude to Acid Indigestion, 41st U. Miami, Inst. Est. Plan. ¶ 403.6 (2007).

A client who is considering whether to become a participant in the stranger owner life insurance market should be counseled to exercise extreme caution. The estate planner should scrutinize the proposal with care and advise the client fully regarding the risks that participation would involved. For a helpful checklist see Jones, Leimberg & Rybka, 'Free' Life Insurance: Risks and Costs of Non-Recourse Premium Financing, 33 Est. Plan. 3 (July 2006). *See also* Leimberg, Stranger-Owned Life Insurance (STOLI): What Professionals Need to Know, ALI-ABA, 15 Est. Plan. Course Mat. J. 3 (Aug. 2009).

§6.15. FINANCIAL CONDITION OF INSURERS

> The financial soundness of an insurance company is frequently the first step in the selection process. "In my view, the consumer is not in a position to do his own financial analysis," said Joseph M. Belth, a professor of insurance at Indiana University. "What he has to do is fall back on the rating services . . . ."

> Professor Belth advises conservative insurance buyers to stay with com-
> panies that have very high ratings from at least two of the services and
> also have ratings above a minimum level from all of them. Sloan, Picking
> Life Insurers Rated as Least Risky, N.Y. Times, Dec. 19, 1992

When evaluating a life insurance plan, it is important to obtain some assurance regarding the financial responsibility of the insurers. At a minimum the planner should obtain information regarding the rating of the insurers by leading rating companies. The five leading services that rate insurers and the general categories they use are: A. M. Best Company (www.ambest.com), rankings from A+ (superior) to C, C-(fair); Fitch (formerly Duff & Phelps, Inc.) (www.fitchratings.com), rankings from AAA (highest) to D; Moody's Investor Services (www.moodys.com), rankings from Aaa (exceptional) to C (lowest); Standard and Poor's Corporation (www.standardandpoors.com), rankings from AAA (extremely strong) to D (default); and Weiss Research (weissratings.com).

Free online ratings are generally available from the rating companies and some other services (Standard and Poor's ratings are available through Insure.com and Weiss' through TheStreet.com).

Insurance advisors typically recommend that insurance only be placed with the 200-300 companies that have received an A+ or better ranking from A. M. Best, and should provide the highest degree of safety. In addition, advisors commonly recommend that a large amount of coverage be divided among two or more insurers. Diversification reduces some of the risks associated with insurance, including the possibility of poor investment performance of the insurer.

§6.16. COMMUNITY PROPERTY

If a married client lived in a community property jurisdiction at any time during marriage, the lawyer must be aware of the need to characterize the client's life insurance as separate or community property. The proper characterization is important for tax and nontax purposes. For example, under the law of most community property states the character of a policy determines the extent to which the insured spouse has the power, acting alone, to designate the beneficiary. The character of a policy may also affect the disposition of the policy in the event the marriage is dissolved. Perhaps most important, it determines the extent to which the interests in the policy, or its proceeds, are subject to state and federal gift and death taxes. In general, the state law characterization of a policy is accepted and followed for federal tax purposes. *E.g., Scott v. Commissioner*, 374 F.2d 154, 157 (9th Cir. 1967).

Happily, insurance is often characterized without difficulty: It is either entirely community or entirely separate under the rules of all community property states. By way of illustration, a policy purchased by the insured prior to marriage is entirely separate property if the insured makes all subsequent premium payments from separate property. Conversely, a policy purchased during marriage is entirely community property if all premiums are paid with community funds.

Serious problems of characterization may arise when premiums on a policy are paid partly with separate funds and partly with community funds. In those cases the community property states apply a variety of rules. The three main rules are: (1) the inception-of-title rule, (2) the apportionment rule, and (3) the risk payment doctrine. A lawyer who understands the basic features of those rules will be able to recognize and deal with most common problems of characterization—even though the law in most states is still evolving and the outcome in certain circumstances is uncertain.

§ 6.16.1. Inception-of-Title Rule

The inception-of-title rule is generally applied by Arizona, Louisiana, New Mexico, and Texas to determine the character of cash value life insurance. Under it an insurance policy and its proceeds retain the original character of the policy regardless of the source of subsequent premium payments. Thus, if a policy is acquired prior to marriage, the policy remains separate property although some later premiums are paid with community property funds. However, in such a case the community is usually entitled to reimbursement out of the insurance proceeds for premiums that were paid with community funds. *See, e.g., McCurdy v. McCurdy*, 372 S.W.2d 381 (Tex. Civ. App. 1963), *writ refused* (1964). The community's claim for reimbursement is reflected as a reduction in the amount of the insurance that is includible in the insured's gross estate. Thus, where the community paid $12,000 of the premiums on a $100,000 separate policy, $88,000 was includible in the insured's estate as insurance (§ 2042) and $6,000, representing half of the reimbursement, was includible as "owned" property (§ 2033). Rev. Rul. 80-242, 1980-2 C.B. 276. On the other hand, if the separate property funds of one spouse are used to pay premiums on a community owned policy without the intention of making a gift to the other spouse, the spouse whose funds were used is entitled to reimbursement for half of the amount of the payments.

The inception-of-title rule is criticized by some commentators as inconsistent with basic principles of community property. They favor the apportionment rule, which allocates interests in a policy according to the portion of the premiums that were paid with separate and community funds respectively.

In Rev. Rul. 94-69, 1994-2 C.B. 241 (Louisiana law), the IRS ruled that the proceeds of life insurance policies on the life of one spouse that were purchased with community property funds and transferred to the noninsured spouse were not includible in the estate of the insured under § 2042(2). Under Louisiana law, the use of community property funds to pay the premiums on a policy owned by the noninsured spouse as his or her separate property does not give the insured spouse any interest in the policy or its proceeds. As pointed out in the ruling, "In Louisiana, however, life insurance that has been purchased with community funds and is owned by one spouse is treated differently than in other community property states." Consistently, if the noninsured spouse who owns the policy has designated a third party as beneficiary, the death of the insured spouse results in the owner having made a completed gift of the entire proceeds of the policy. The ruling revoked prior rulings Rev. Rul. 48, 1953-1 C.B. 392 and Rev. Rul. 232, 1953-2 C.B. 268.

§ 6.16.2. Apportionment Rule

California apportions cash value life insurance policies. Some decisions have also apportioned term life insurance as indicated in § 6.16.3. Apportionment is usually made according to the character of the funds used to pay the premiums. *Biltoft v. Wootten*, 157 Cal. Rptr. 581 (Cal. App. 1979), following *Modern Woodman of America v. Gray*, 299 P. 754 (Cal. App. 1931). Washington apportions cash value insurance, but not term insurance. *Aetna Life Ins. Co. v. Wadsworth*, 689 P.2d 46 (Wash. 1984). The application of this rule to cash value policies is consistent with the basic principle that "where separate or community property is used to acquire other property, the latter partakes of the same nature as that of the property used for its acquisition." W. deFuniak & M. Vaughn, Principles of Community Property §79 (2d ed. 1971). It is questionable whether the same rule should apply to term policies. The payment of a premium on a term policy usually provides only insurance protection for that period—when the term ends the policy has no value in the ordinary case. Of course, the renewal right may have substantial value if the insured becomes terminally ill or is no longer insurable. Logically, at the expiration of the term there is usually no asset that is properly subject to apportionment. As explained below, the risk payment doctrine does a more satisfactory job of characterizing the proceeds of term insurance.

EXAMPLE 6-1.

> *H*, a resident of California, purchased a $25,000 nonparticipating cash value life insurance policy on which he paid five annual premiums prior to his marriage to *W*. Five subsequent premiums were paid with their community property funds. Under the apportionment rule at the end of ten years the policy is one-half the separate property of *H* and one-half the community property of *H* and *W*.

Thus far neither Idaho nor Nevada has adopted a general characterization rule. *But see Travelers Insurance Co. v. Johnson*, 544 P.2d 294 (Idaho 1975) (proceeds of employer-provided term insurance policy divided between surviving spouse and the insured's surviving former spouse who was the designated beneficiary). Often in the past Idaho courts have followed California or Washington precedents; Nevada courts have sometimes followed California law, but more often chose to follow Texas law.

§6.16.3. Risk Payment Doctrine; Term Insurance

Idaho, Washington, and the inception-of-title states (Arizona, Louisiana, New Mexico, and Texas) characterize the proceeds of term insurance under the risk payment doctrine. Under that doctrine life insurance proceeds are characterized as separate or community according to the source of the last premium payment. For example, if the last premium on a term policy was paid with community property funds, the proceeds of the policy are characterized as entirely community property. This approach recognizes that the current protection provided by term insurance depends entirely upon the last premium payment. *See Aetna Life Ins. Co. v. Wadsworth*, 689 P.2d 46 (Wash. 1984); *Phillips v. Welborn*, 552 P.2d 471 (N.M. 1976). "Premium payments in years gone by are not considered important. This is in contrast to the necessity of knowing the sources of past years' premium payments before applying the inception of title and apportionment rules." Comment, Community and Separate

Property Interests in Life Insurance Proceeds: The Risk Payment Doctrine in State
Courts and Its Federal Estate Tax Consequences, 52 Wash. L. Rev. 67, 69 (1976).
Because each premium payment only provides insurance protection for the period
and does not contribute cumulatively to the value of a term policy, it seems more
appropriate to apply the risk payment doctrine.

EXAMPLE 6-2.

W had been employed by XYZ, Inc. for five years prior to her marriage to
H. XYZ has provided W with $50,000 of group-term insurance coverage
from the time she was hired. W died five years after her marriage to H. W
had designated her mother, M, as beneficiary of the group-term insurance
without H's participation or consent. Under the risk payment doctrine the
entire proceeds are community property, of which H is entitled to half
($25,000). In contrast, under the apportionment rule, the policy was one-
half the separate property of W (attributable to five years of premium
payments by W's employer prior to W's marriage to H) and one-half
community property. Accordingly, in a state that apportions term insurance, H is entitled to claim only one-quarter of the proceeds ($12,500).

California appellate decisions are hopelessly split regarding the characterization
of group term insurance. *Biltoft v. Wootten*, 157 Cal. Rptr. 581 (1979), holds that term
insurance is subject to apportionment. In contrast, a later case holds that employment
related term insurance is not a community asset beyond the expiration of the term
acquired with community efforts regardless of the insurability of the insured spouse.
Spengler v. Spengler, 6 Cal. Rptr.2d 764 (Cal. App. 1992). Another case holds that
group-term insurance is not community property. *Lorenz v. Lorenz*, 194 Cal. Rptr. 237
(Cal. App. 1983). Yet another concludes that such a policy is a community asset with
replacement value where the insurability of the insured is lessened by age or
declining health. *Marriage of Gonzales*, 214 Cal. Rptr. 634 (Cal. App. 1985).

The risk payment doctrine was not considered by the court in *Estate of Cavenaugh
v. Commissioner*, 51 F.3d 597 (5th Cir. 1995) (Texas law), which allowed the estate of
the insured spouse to exclude one-half of the proceeds of a term life insurance policy
that were payable to his estate. The decision is based on a questionable determination
of the law of Texas and an even more doubtful reliance on *Scott v. Commissioner*, 374
F.2d 154 (9th Cir. 1967). The latter case involved California law, which characterizes
ownership according to the apportionment theory, which is inconsistent with the
basic Texas law, which relies upon the inception-of-title approach. The policy involved in *Cavenaugh* was acquired during marriage, as a result of which it was
originally community property. However, on the death of the noninsured spouse her
interest in the term policy appears to have had no value as no interest in the policy
was reported on her federal estate tax return. (The Tax Court presumed that the
policy had no value, which was equivalent to a settlement of her interest in the
policy.) The insured spouse's payment of the subsequent premiums from his separate
property should have resulted in the entire policy being his separate property. *See
also Sherman v. Roe*, 258 S.W.2d 862 (Tex. Civ. App. 1953), *rev'd in part*, 262 S.W.2d 393

(Tex. 1953), which appears to adopt the risk payment doctrine with respect to term insurance.

Moreover, in *Estate of Cavenaugh,* even if the estate of the uninsured spouse had a continuing interest in the policy, the full proceeds should have been included in the insured's estate under §2042(1). The provisions of Reg. §20.2042-1(b)(2) do not support a contrary result: "If the proceeds of an insurance policy made payable to the decedent's estate are community assets under the local community property law and, as a result, one-half of the proceeds belongs to the decedent's spouse, then only one-half of the proceeds is considered to be receivable by or for the benefit of the decedent's estate." The regulation properly refers only to instances in which the uninsured spouse survives the insured and has not consented to the designation of the insured's estate as beneficiary. If the uninsured spouse had an interest in the policy that survived her death, the continued designation of the insured's estate as beneficiary of the insurance should negate any right of the uninsured spouse's estate to the proceeds.

B. PLANNING WITH LIFE INSURANCE

§6.17. INTRODUCTION

Planning for the ownership, premium payments, and beneficiary designations of life insurance is a critical but often insufficiently considered aspect of estate planning. The overall objective is to integrate life insurance fully into the client's estate plan, which requires that it be coordinated with the client's will and other elements of the plan. As always, the federal tax considerations are important, but should not dominate the planning.

The tax attributes of life insurance make it uniquely valuable in estate planning for clients with large estates. The initial value of life insurance policies is often a very small fraction of the death benefits payable under the policies, which allows the policies to be transferred at little or no gift tax cost. *See* §6.43, *et seq.* Also, the proceeds of life insurance policies are generally not subject to the income tax. *See* §6.52, *et seq.* Through proper planning a large amount of insurance proceeds can be made available to the insured's family at little or no tax cost. Importantly, such planning generally does not require the client to give up the lifetime use of any assets of substantial present value. For example, if an ILIT is used, the proceeds of life insurance can be made available to the insured's surviving family members with little, if anything, being included in the estates of the insured or his or her surviving spouse.

The nominal value and low cost of group-term insurance generally makes it the most economical type to transfer or to acquire for a trust of a person other than the insured. Split-dollar insurance plans are also popular for essentially the same reason. *See* §6.72. Finally, the benefits payable under a death benefit only plan are generally not included in the decedent's gross estate. *See* §6.79.

Beneficiary Designation. Beneficiary designations should be carefully prepared, executed and filed. A failure to comply with all of the terms of a policy regarding beneficiary designations could lead to delays, added expense, and even payment of the proceeds to unintended recipients. Although in recent times courts have generally been inclined to recognize beneficiary designations that are made in substantial compliance with policy requirements, one should not take any unnecessary risks. A 2004 case that concerned the requirements applicable to beneficiary designations under the Federal Employees Group Life Insurance Act upheld a witnessed beneficiary designation that was undated and signed by the insured with only her first name. *Terry v. Lagrois*, 354 F.3d 527 (6th Cir. 2004).

Revocation of Beneficiary Designation by Divorce. In some states, the divorce of an insured person and his or her spouse who was named as the beneficiary of the policy revokes the beneficiary designation. The Colorado law was upheld against a constitutional challenge in *Hill v. DeWitt*, 54 P.3d 849 (Colo. 2002).

Beneficiary Designation and Slayer's Statutes. Under basic equitable principles and the provisions of the so-called Slayer's Statutes, a person who participates in the felonious murder of another may not profit from the act. The rule was first applied to a case in 1886 in which a designated beneficiary murdered the insured. *Mutual Life Insurance Co. v. Armstrong*, 117 U.S. 591 (1886). Several cases have held that the rule does not apply where the victim was the primary beneficiary designated in a policy of insurance on the life of the murderer, who killed himself after murdering his victim. *Estate of Foleno v. Estate of Foleno*, 772 N.E.2d 490 (Ind. App. 2002); *In re Estates of Covert*, 761 N.E.2d 571 (N.Y. 2001).

§ 6.18. COMBINED MARITAL ESTATES OF LESS THAN ONE CREDIT EQUIVALENT

The insurance plan for a married couple whose estates have a combined value that is unlikely to exceed the amount of the credit equivalent can be quite simple. Because no estate tax will be due on the death of either spouse it is unnecessary to attempt to eliminate the insurance proceeds, or other assets, from their gross estates. Because of the size of the GSTT exemption, the GSTT is likewise not a concern. For such clients the principal question is simply how best to settle the insurance proceeds for the benefit of the insured's dependents.

When estate taxes are not a consideration, the surviving spouse is usually named as primary beneficiary. Depending upon the ages of the insured's children they, or a trust for their benefit, are usually named as the contingent beneficiaries. The lawyer may only need to verify that the beneficiary designations are consistent with the plan. When the clients' wills include a contingent trust for children, the trustee of the trust is normally designated as the contingent beneficiary. The use of such a trust is described in § § 4.21.3-4.21.4, and the text of a trust for minors that might be appropriate appears in § 4.20.

Attention must also be given to the disposition of any interest that the noninsured spouse has in the insurance. In most cases the interest of the noninsured spouse will pass to the insured spouse by specific bequest or under the residuary clause of the noninsured spouse's will. Complications may arise if the noninsured spouse dies intestate and some interests in the policies pass to the children or parents of the noninsured spouse. Of course, where transfer taxes are a concern, the noninsured spouse should consider disposing of his or her interests in the policies in a way that will not cause them to be included in the insured's gross estate. For example, the noninsured spouse may leave his or her interests in the policies to persons other than the insured (*e.g.*, their adult children) or to a trust for their benefit.

§6.19. COMBINED MARITAL ESTATES OF LESS THAN TWO CREDIT EQUIVALENTS

When somewhat larger estates are involved, the noninsured spouse is also often named as beneficiary. However, the potential of unnecessarily subjecting property to the estate tax on the death of the surviving spouse is an important countervailing factor. In such cases the clients should consider taking steps to assure that each spouse will be able to take full advantage of the unified credit, which can shelter a substantial amount from taxation on the death of the surviving spouse.

If the proceeds are paid outright to the insured's surviving spouse, the unlimited marital deduction allows the estate tax on the proceeds to be deferred until the death of the surviving spouse. However, such an approach may unnecessarily increase the size of the surviving spouse's gross estate. Inclusion of the proceeds in the noninsured spouse's gross estate is avoided if he or she is given only a limited interest in the proceeds either under a settlement option selected by the insured or under an inter vivos or testamentary bypass trust established by the insured. When an option is selected by the insured the proceeds are not includible in the beneficiary's gross estate, but when the option is selected by the beneficiary they are includible. *See* §6.40. The cost of making the proceeds payable to the surviving spouse outright is illustrated in Example 6-3.

EXAMPLE 6-3.

H died leaving an estate of $2 million, including $500,000 in insurance, all of which passed outright to his surviving spouse, *W*. No estate tax was payable by *H*'s estate because of the unified credit available to his estate. Whatever remains of the $2 million will be includible in *W*'s estate when she dies. If *W*'s taxable estate exceeds the applicable exclusion amount, some estate tax will be due from her estate. On the other hand, no tax would be due from *W*'s estate if her taxable estate does not exceed the exclusion amount. For example, *H* could leave the proceeds to a trust for *W*'s benefit or elect a settlement option under which periodic payments would be made to her, neither of which would require the proceeds to be included in her estate.

Some clients will prefer to give the proceeds outright to the surviving spouse although it may cause the payment of some estate tax by the estate of the surviving spouse. They may choose to do so in order to give the survivor more freedom and greater control over the proceeds. After all, they reason, the surviving spouse may consume the proceeds for support or may substantially eliminate them from his or her estate by making gifts prior to death. Of course, the lawyer should discuss with the client the tax and nontax consequences of settling the proceeds in various ways consistent with the client's basic objectives.

§6.19.1. Protect Minor Children

The interests of the insured's minor children may be protected if the noninsured spouse survives the insured and the proceeds are paid outright to the survivor. If the noninsured spouse does not survive the insured, the proceeds should not be payable outright to minor children, which might necessitate the appointment of a guardian to collect and manage the proceeds. Instead, the proceeds should be made payable to the trustee of a contingent testamentary trust for the children, §4.22, or to a custodian under the Uniform Acts. A trust is generally preferable because it is more flexible and can provide greater protection for the children in the event of emergency. In some other instances the insured may also wish to leave the proceeds in trust. For example, if the noninsured spouse is not a parent of the insured's children, the insured may wish to use a trust to secure an interest in the proceeds for his or her children. Overall, the children may be best provided for if the assets are concentrated in one trust for their benefit, rather than being held in two or more trusts. *See* §4.21.3.

§6.19.2. Use Revocable Trusts

The legal fee for preparing a revocable (or irrevocable) insurance trust or a will containing a trust is usually greater than the fee for preparing a nontrust will. However, a trust may better meet the needs of the family. In addition, it may save some estate administration expenses and possibly some income, inheritance, and estate taxes.

If the plan calls for establishing a trust for the benefit of the insured's surviving spouse and children, a funded or unfunded revocable trust or a testamentary trust might suffice. For estates in the nontaxable range, the creation of an irrevocable life insurance trust is usually unnecessary. Including the insurance in the estate of the insured is not the problem—controlling the size of the surviving spouse's estate is. Also, an irrevocable trust is less flexible and may place some assets that may be needed beyond the client's control.

Before making a recommendation the lawyer needs to be sure that the local law permits the trustee of an unfunded revocable trust or a testamentary trust to be designated as beneficiary of life insurance policies. Either designation might be challenged if it is not authorized by statute or judicial decision. Fortunately, many states have adopted statutes that permit the designation of the trustee of an unfunded trust as beneficiary. *E.g.,* Ind. Code Ann. §27-1-12-16(B) (2011); N.Y. Est. Powers & Trusts Law §13-3.3(a)(1) (2011); Wash. Rev. Code §48.18.450 (2011). A larger number of states specifically authorize the designation of the trustee named or to be named in the insured's will as beneficiary. *E.g.,* Cal. Prob. Code §6321 (20110); Ind. Code Ann. §27-1-12-16(C) (2011); N.Y. Est. Powers & Trusts Law §13-3.3(a)(2) (2011); Wash. Rev. Code §48.18.452 (2011). On the other hand, the designation of the trustee of a funded revocable trust is no doubt valid in all states.

§6.19.3. Plan Based Upon a Revocable Trust

A plan based upon a revocable trust involves the preparation and execution of a trust agreement and the designation of the trustee as beneficiary of the insurance. The insurance policies may either be assigned to the trustee or be retained by the insured.

As a matter of convenience the insured often retains ownership of the policies rather than assigning them to the trust. In either case the insured is usually responsible for payment of premiums on the policies. Of course, the trust may be funded by transferring some other assets to the trust. If that is done, the trust is not vulnerable to challenge as a "dry" trust. A token fund of $10, for example, is probably sufficient for this purpose. Nonetheless, some lawyers recommend that a significant amount of assets be transferred to the trustee. Funding the trust, of course, makes dealing with the assets a bit more cumbersome. The grantor-insured will, of course, be treated as owner of the property of the trust for income tax purposes under §§ 676 and 677.

Corporate trustees commonly charge a substantial minimum annual fee to administer funded or unfunded life insurance trusts. Accordingly, it is not generally economical for clients in this estate range to utilize a corporate trustee. However, in some instances corporate trustees might not impose any substantial fees on a revocable trust with respect to which they had no significant duties until after the death of the insured. The use of a trust is attractive in part because of the extensive discretionary powers that can be given to an independent trustee without tax risk. *See* § 10.12. If the trustee is given such powers, a beneficiary of the trust cannot act as trustee without adverse tax consequences.

An inter vivos trust can be the vehicle used to consolidate the insured's assets and to provide for their unified management following his or her death. This can be accomplished by "pouring over" the client's residuary estate into the trust. The pour-over technique is validated by the Uniform Testamentary Additions to Trust Act (1991), which is incorporated in the U.P.C. as § 2-511 and is in effect in almost all states and the District of Columbia. Under a common plan the client's residence and tangible personal property are left to the surviving spouse by will and the life insurance and residuary estate pass into the trust. The plan is depicted in Chart 6-1, below. *See* § 10.10 for a more detailed discussion of pour-over provisions.

§ 6.19.4. Plan Based Upon a Testamentary Trust

When the plan is based upon a testamentary trust, the life insurance proceeds are made payable to the trustee of the trust established by the will of the insured. Such a beneficiary designation will be recognized in most, if not all, states. However, an estate planner should check to be sure that it is valid under the governing law and is not vulnerable to challenge as a testamentary transfer because the trustee cannot be ascertained and appointed until after the death of the insured.

An old Massachusetts decision, *Frost v. Frost*, 88 N.E. 446 (Mass. 1909), invalidated an attempted testamentary assignment of a policy to the trustees named in the will because it was considered to be a testamentary disposition that failed to comply with the requirements of the wills act. Although most courts would strain to uphold the designation of a testamentary trustee as beneficiary, prudence suggests adopting a more reliable approach in states that do not specifically authorize such a designation.

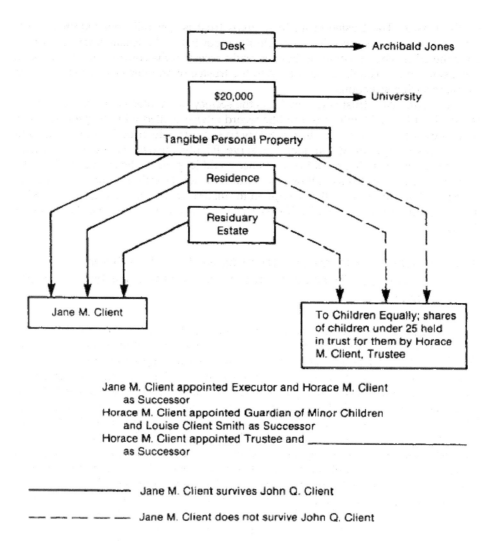

Jane M. Client appointed Executor and Horace M. Client
    as Successor
Horace M. Client appointed Guardian of Minor Children
    and Louise Client Smith as Successor
Horace M. Client appointed Trustee and _____
    as Successor

———————————— Jane M. Client survives John Q. Client

— — — — — — Jane M. Client does not survive John Q. Client

The chart for a plan based upon a testamentary trust would be practically identical to Chart 6-1. The trusts are essentially the same except for the time of creation and that a testamentary trust would be a "court" trust subject in some states to continuing supervision by the probate court.

§ 6.20. CHOOSING BETWEEN A REVOCABLE TRUST AND A TESTAMENTARY TRUST

If the local law permits the designation of the trustee of an unfunded inter vivos trust or the trustee of a testamentary trust as beneficiary of life insurance, the choice between them is a close one. In either case the surviving spouse or other beneficiary can be given substantial interests in the trust and extensive powers over the trust property without causing it to be included in his or her gross estate.

While the preparation of an inter vivos trust and a complementary will may cost more than a will with a testamentary trust, the testamentary trust may generate higher costs of administration where local law requires periodic reports and accounts by the trustee. The trustee of an inter vivos trust is generally not required to file reports and accounts with the court. On the other hand, the testamentary trust may have the edge when it comes to having ready access to the court for instructions. In some states no mechanism is available to the trustee of an inter vivos trust by which to obtain such instructions.

A testamentary trust generally lacks the secrecy of an inter vivos trust because it is contained in a will, which is a public record after it is filed with the probate court. Also, the actual operation of a testamentary trust may be deferred for some time until the trustees are appointed and qualify to serve. Finally, the designation of a testamentary trustee as a beneficiary of life insurance could jeopardize the extent to which the proceeds are exempt from creditor's claims and the local death tax. Those risks do not arise in states that preserve the exemption for insurance paid to the trustees named in a will. *Eg.*, Ind. Code Ann. § 27-1-12-16 (2011); N.Y. Est. Powers & Trusts Law § 13-3.3 (2011).

§ 6.21. COMBINED MARITAL ESTATES OF MORE THAN TWO CREDIT EQUIVALENTS: ELIMINATING THE INSURANCE FROM THE ESTATE OF THE INSURED

Estate plans for wealthier clients often attempt to insulate the proceeds of life insurance from the imposition of any estate tax on the death of the insured. The plan may be a relatively simple one which involves ownership of the insurance by a person other than the insured. The proceeds would not be included in the insured's estate if the proceeds are not paid to the insured's estate, the insured held no incidents of ownership in the insurance, and any interest the insured owned in the insurance was transferred more than three years prior to his or her death. Of course, the payment of the estate tax is deferred if the insurance is paid to or for the benefit of the surviving spouse in a way that qualifies for the marital deduction. *See* § 6.23. Note, however, the use of the marital deduction does not eliminate the insurance from the insured's estate for purposes of determining whether his or her estate satisfies the requirements of § § 303, 2032A, and 6166. For purposes of those sections, a better result may be produced if the insurance is excluded from the insured's estate. More ambitious plans may insulate the proceeds from inclusion in the estates of both spouses through the acquisition of the insurance by, or the transfer of the insurance to, an irrevocable trust. *See* § 6.24. Irrevocable insurance trusts can, of course, be created for beneficiaries other than the insured's spouse.

Planning for affluent taxpayers may include transferring the remainder interest in a qualified personal residence trust (QPRT) to the trustees of an ILIT. QPRTs are discussed at § 9.44. After the end of the retained term of the QPRT the grantors may lease the residence from the trustees at its fair market rental. If the ILIT is a grantor trust, as it almost certainly will be under § 677(a), the payment of the rental will have no income tax consequence. *See* § 9.44 and Rev. Rul. 85-13, 1985-1 C.B. 184.

§ 6.22. OWNERSHIP BY AN INDIVIDUAL OTHER THAN THE INSURED

The proceeds of insurance policies originally acquired by an individual other than the insured, or assigned by the insured more than three years prior to death, are generally not included in the insured's gross estate. However, they are includible in the estate of a beneficiary who survives the insured. In effect, the ownership of the policies by a person other than the insured allows the tax on the proceeds to be deferred until the death of the owner-beneficiary.

§6.22.1. Cross-Owned Insurance

Prior to the adoption of the unlimited marital deduction the estate plan for a husband and wife often involved "cross-ownership" of insurance (*i.e.*, each spouse owned the insurance policies on the life of the other). If the noninsured spouse were to die first, the plan usually also called for him or her to leave the insurance policy on the surviving spouse's life in a way that would not require it to be included in the estate of the insured spouse. Thus, the wife's will might leave all of her interests in insurance on the life of her husband to their children or to a trust for the benefit of their children.

A cross-ownership plan under which the noninsured spouse, who is also the policy owner, is the designated beneficiary of each policy remains very advantageous if the spouses die simultaneously. In such a case, under the version of the Uniform Simultaneous Death Act in effect in a majority of states (the 1940 Act), the beneficiary spouse is deemed to have predeceased the insured spouse. Hence only the lifetime value of the policy and not the proceeds is included in the estate of the noninsured spouse. Nothing is included in the estate of the insured. *See* §6.81. Under the 1983 version of the Uniform Simultaneous Death Act, a beneficiary who does not survive the insured by 120 hours is deemed to have predeceased the insured.

§6.22.2. Applications and Assignments

When the noninsured spouse originally applies for the insurance, the application and policy should clearly indicate that both spouses intend the applicant to own all interests in the insurance. The planner should review the application and the policy to be sure that the insured will not have any incidents of ownership in the policy. Similar precautions must be taken when the insured assigns his or her interest in the insurance to another person.

§6.22.3. Community Property

Particular attention must be given to ownership problems in community property states, where the presumption favoring community property may cause insurance acquired during marriage to be treated as community property absent clear evidence to the contrary. An oral agreement that the insurance is the separate property of the noninsured spouse may overcome the presumption in some states. *E.g., Kroloff v. United States*, 487 F.2d 334 (9th Cir. 1973) (Arizona law). Some others require the agreement to be evidenced by a writing apart from the policy. *Kern v. United States*, 491 F.2d 436 (9th Cir. 1974) (Washington law). The seriousness of this problem is reduced by the availability of the unlimited marital deduction. However, characterizing the insurance as community property is disadvantageous in some circumstances.

§6.22.4. Premium Payments

The insured makes a gift to the owner to the extent he or she pays a premium directly or indirectly on a policy owned by another person. Reg. §25.2503-3(c), Example 6; Rev. Rul. 76-490, 1976-2 C.B. 300 (employee-insured makes an indirect gift when the employer pays a premium on group-term insurance the employee had assigned to a trust). Depending upon the terms of the trust the premium payment may be a gift of a present interest that qualifies for the annual exclusion. The annual exclusion is available when the insurance is owned by another individual. Reg. §25.2503-3(c), Example 6; *see also* §6.47. The gift marital deduction may be available where the owner is the employee's spouse.

§6.22.5. Beneficiary Designations

The noninsured owner is usually designated as the primary beneficiary of the insurance. He or she may need the proceeds for support or to make the proceeds available to the insured's estate to meet taxes, debts, or expenses of administration. An individual beneficiary may choose to use the proceeds to purchase assets from the insured's estate or otherwise provide funds with which to pay the taxes and other expenses of the insured's estate. However, in some cases the beneficiary does not do so.

When the proceeds are payable to an independent trustee there is more of an assurance that the plan will be followed and the proceeds will be made available to the insured's estate. The trustee should be authorized (but not required) to loan the proceeds to the executor of the insured's estate or to use them to buy assets from his or her estate.

Gift Tax. If the owner survives the insured, the owner's acquiescence in the payment of the insurance proceeds to any other person involves a gift by the owner to the payee. *See* §6.48.

Contingent Beneficiaries. In any case, a contingent beneficiary should be designated in each policy to prevent payment of the proceeds to the estate of the insured, which might unnecessarily increase the insured's gross estate and eliminate any otherwise applicable state death tax and creditors exemptions.

§6.22.6. Successive Ownership

As noted above, the plan should also provide for disposition of the noninsured owner's interest in the insurance if the owner predeceases the insured. Generally speaking, the insurance should pass under the owner's will and not by the designation of a successive owner in the policy itself, which could be overlooked when later changes are made in the owner's estate plan.

In order to avoid subsequent inclusion of the insurance in the estate of the insured, the policy should neither be left to the insured, nor should the insured be given any incidents of ownership in it. Instead, the noninsured owner should consider bequeathing the policy to adult children or to the trustees of a trust for the benefit of minor children. If the insured is named as executor of the noninsured owner's will, his or her power over the policy should be limited in order to avoid any risk that the insurance would be included in the insured's estate should the insured die during administration of the owner's estate. Also, if a policy is left in trust, the insured should not hold any incidents of ownership in the policy in any capacity. *See* § 6.28.11. Because of the possibility that inclusion might result if the insured holds an incident of ownership in other fiduciary capacities, a policy should not be given to the insured as custodian for a minor child. For the same reason, the insured should not serve as guardian for an incompetent person who owns a policy on the life of the insured.

§ 6.23. MARITAL DEDUCTION PLANNING

The proceeds of life insurance paid to the insured's surviving spouse or to a marital deduction trust will escape taxation until the death of the surviving spouse. Such an approach has the advantage of allowing the insured to continue to own and control the policy until his or her death. Where the insurance is payable to a QTIP trust (*i.e.*, one that meets the requirements of § 2056(b)(7)), the insured's executor may elect to claim the marital deduction with respect to all or part of the insurance. *See* § 5.23. Use of the marital deduction allows the estate tax on the insurance to be deferred until the death of the surviving spouse.

§ 6.23.1. Beneficiary Designations

Under the simplest approach, the insured's spouse is designated as primary beneficiary and the insured's children as contingent beneficiaries. However, from the tax perspective the plan has greater flexibility if the insurance is payable to a trust in which the surviving spouse has an interest sufficient to support a QTIP election under § 2056(b)(7). Under a variant, the insurance may be payable to the insured's spouse or to the QTIP trust if he or she disclaims the right to receive the proceeds outright. It is less desirable to leave the proceeds on a settlement option with the insurer. When community property is involved, the one-half interest of the noninsured spouse is generally paid to him or her outright, although it could be disposed of in another way.

§ 6.23.2. Premium Payments

The insured's payment of premiums on policies owned by the insured does not involve any gift because of the insured's complete control of interests in the policy. In particular, there is no gift to the beneficiaries, whose interests are revocable. There is a gift to the insured, however, if a premium is paid by another person. There is no gift where community property funds are used to pay the premiums on a community property policy. *See* § 6.47.

§ 6.23.3. Successive Ownership

If the insured owns the entire interest in a policy there is no need to provide for disposition of the policy upon death—the policy matures at that time.

Community Property. The interest of the noninsured spouse in a community property policy should be left in a way that does not increase the insured's gross estate if the noninsured spouse dies first. As mentioned above, this usually involves leaving the noninsured spouse's interest to adult children or to the trustees of a trust for the benefit of minor children. In such a case, if the noninsured spouse dies first, the ownership interests of the insured spouse and the recipients of the noninsured spouse's interest in the policy are equal at the outset and will remain so if each contributes equally to premium payments following the death of the noninsured spouse. If one of the owners pays more than half of the subsequent premiums without intending to make a gift to the other owner, the payor's interest in the policy will increase proportionately in the states that follow the apportionment rule. *Scott v. Commissioner*, 374 F.2d 154 (9th Cir. 1967). The ownership interests probably remain equal in inception-of-title states, and the party who paid more than his or her share of the premiums will have a right of reimbursement for any excess he or she may have paid.

EXAMPLE 6-4.

H's life was insured under a $100,000 nonparticipating cash value policy that was issued 20 years ago and was owned by *H* and his wife, *W*, as their community property until *W*'s death 10 years ago. *W* bequeathed her interest in the policy to their children, *A* and *B*, who made *all* subsequent premium payments on the policy without intending to make a gift to *H*. Half of the value of the policy, determined under Reg. § 20.2031-8, was includible in *W*'s gross estate. When *H* died this year, the proceeds were paid outright to *A* and *B*. In states that follow the apportionment rule, *H*'s gross estate includes only the interest attributable to his one-half share of the premiums that were paid on the policy up to the time of *W*'s death (one-half of $50,000 or $25,000). The other $75,000 is attributable to the ownership interests that *A* and *B* received from *W* ($25,000) and to the premium payments they made after *W*'s death ($50,000). Half of the proceeds is probably includible in *H*'s estate in an inception-of-title state, subject to a claim by *A* and *B* for half of the premiums they paid following *W*'s death.

§6.24.   IRREVOCABLE LIFE INSURANCE TRUSTS

The irrevocable life insurance trust (ILIT) is one of the most significant and popular estate tax saving devices that remains available. A properly planned and drafted ILIT can:

1. Remove the life insurance proceeds from the estates of both the insured and the beneficiary of the trust, typically the noninsured spouses;
2. Incur little or no gift tax upon creation of the trust and payment of subsequent premiums;
3. Preserve the income tax exclusion for the insurance proceeds;

4. Make the proceeds available to the insured's estate for the payment of taxes, debts and expenses;

5. Preserve flexibility through the use of an independent trustee who can be given broad discretionary powers over the trust; and

6. Reduce or eliminate GSTT problems by using annual gift tax exclusions and the GSTT exemption.

§ 6.24.1. Estate Tax

The goal of excluding the proceeds of the insurance from the estates of both the insured and noninsured spouses is most easily achieved if existing insurance policies are initially acquired by the trustee of an ILIT (*i.e.*, existing policies are not transferred to the trustee). The reason is simple: If existing policies are gratuitously transferred, the insured must survive the transfer by three years or more in order to avoid inclusion under § 2035. § 2035(a)(2). If the insured is married, the trust may be drafted to reduce the tax cost of inclusion under § 2035(a)(2) if the insured dies within three years of transferring a policy to the trust. In particular, the trust may provide that if the insured dies within three years, the proceeds will be held for the benefit of the surviving spouse in a way that meets the requirements of QTIP. Alternatively, the trust may provide that any property of the trust that is includible in the insured's gross estate, which would include the proceeds of the policy if the insured dies within three years, would be paid over to the estate of the insured, where they would be distributed in a way that would qualify for a marital deduction. For an example of the latter *see* LR 9533001 (TAM).

Also, in order to avoid inclusion of the trust in the estate of the noninsured spouse under § 2036, the noninsured spouse generally should not transfer any property to the trust if he or she is a beneficiary of the trust. (The widow's election life insurance trust described in § 6.25.1 is an exception to this rule.)

Yielding to three adverse appellate decisions, the IRS will not contend that § 2035(a)(2) (formerly § 2035(d)(2)) requires inclusion in the insured's estate of insurance purchased by a trustee with funds transferred to the trustee within three years of the insured's death. A.O.D. 1991-12. *See Estate of Eddie L. Headrick v. Commissioner*, 918 F.2d 1263 (6th Cir. 1990); *Estate of Joseph Leder v. Commissioner*, 893 F.2d 237 (10th Cir. 1989); *Estate of Frank M. Perry v. Commissioner*, 927 F.2d 209 (5th Cir. 1991). The conclusion reached in the trilogy of cases is based upon a literal reading of former § 2035(d)(2). Despite AOD 91-12, cautious estate planners will continue to plan and draft ILITs with the care that was required by the pre-1981 version of § 2035. Accordingly, the trustee should be formally free to invest the funds that the grantor transfers to the trust as the trustee chooses. In addition, the transfer of funds to the trust should not be tied to the purchase of insurance on the grantor's life.

Cases arising under the broader pre-1981 version of § 2035 indicate the precautions that should be taken in order to prevent the proceeds from being included in the estate of an insured who created the trust and transferred cash to it within three years of death. Exclusion of the proceeds in such a case is likely if the trust is established in accordance with the following points:

1. An independent individual or institution is appointed as trustee of the trust.

2. The trustee is authorized to use the funds that the grantor transfers to the trust to make any type of investment. *Hope v. United States*, 691 F.2d 786 (5th Cir. 1982). That is, the trustee should not be expressly or impliedly obligated to use the funds to buy insurance on the grantor's life.

3. The grantor transfers more cash to the trustee than is required to make the anticipated initial premium payment. The client should be cautioned to avoid the mistake made by Mr. Kurihara, who gave the trustee a check in the exact amount of the insurance premium which noted that it was for payment of an insurance premium. *Estate of Tetsuo Kurihara*, 82 T.C. 51 (1984).

4. Neither the title nor terms of the trust indicate that the trustee is expected to use the funds contributed by the grantor to purchase policies of insurance on the grantor's life. Specifically, the trust should not be titled "Life Insurance Trust."

Inclusion under § 2042(1) is avoided if the trustee is not obligated to use the proceeds for the benefit of the insured's estate. Accordingly, *do not* require the trustee to make the proceeds available to the personal representative of the insured's estate or otherwise subject the proceeds to the insured's debts or taxes. The reach of § 2042(2) is avoided if the insured has no direct or indirect control over the "incidents of ownership" of the insurance and no reversionary interests in any insurance formerly owned by the insured. Accordingly, despite a more relaxed attitude on the part of the courts and the IRS, the insured should not serve as a fiduciary if that might entail any power over the incidents of ownership. The IRS has held that the proceeds of a second-to-die policy owned by the trustee of an ILIT, which the trustee had discretion to use to pay estate and inheritance taxes imposed on the estate of the surviving trustor, were not "receivable" by her estate. LR 200147039. Accordingly the proceeds were not includible in her gross estate. *See* § 6.27.

The proceeds will not be included in the estate of the noninsured spouse if he or she neither made any transfers to the trust (which avoids the reach of the transfer sections, § § 2035-2038) nor had a general power of appointment over the property of the trust.

§ 6.24.2. Gift Tax

The gift tax cost of establishing an ILIT and of making subsequent transfers to it can be minimized or eliminated entirely by including provisions that support the allowance of the annual gift tax exclusion for the transfers. When an existing policy is transferred to the trust, the value of the policy can be reduced prior to the transfer by taking out a loan against the policy. By giving each trust beneficiary a suitable *Crummey* power of withdrawal, *See* § § 7.38-7.38.12, transfers to the trust will qualify for multiple annual gift tax exclusions. Group-term insurance and split-dollar insurance plans are particularly attractive candidates for transfer to an irrevocable life insurance trust. The assignment of either type usually involves little or no gift tax liability and, thus, does not deprive the insured of the use or control of an asset with substantial current value that the insured might later need. Also, there is little current economic loss if the insured's employer or other financing party ceases making premium payments. If others were to cease making premium payments, however, the continuation of the insurance could impose a substantial burden on the insured.

When group-term insurance is assigned to the trust, the assignment should include any replacement or renewal insurance and any increase in the amount of coverage.

In planning an irrevocable life insurance trust, the lawyer and client should consider limiting the beneficiaries' rights of withdrawal by a "5 or 5" standard. By doing so, the gift and estate tax of a lapse of the power is eliminated by the provisions of §§2041(b)(2) and 2514(e). *See* LR 9748029, discussed at §7.38.2.

§6.24.3. Survivorship Policies

The diminished need for liquidity on the death of the first spouse to die that resulted from the adoption of the unlimited marital deduction has led to the development and popularity of so-called joint life or survivorship policies under which the proceeds are payable upon the death of the latter of two persons to die. *See* §6.76. Survivorship policies are also frequently acquired by the trustees of ILITs. The premiums on a joint policy are significantly lower than the premiums on a policy that insures only one life. Rates, of course, vary among insurers and the particular provisions of the policies. With proper planning the proceeds of survivorship policies can be available to meet liquidity needs when the surviving spouse dies without being included in the estate of either of the insured parties.

§6.24.4. GSTT

Life insurance and trusts holding life insurance are subject to the GSTT. Under §2652(b)(1), "The term 'trust' includes any arrangement (other than an estate) which, although not a trust, has substantially the same effect as a trust." Section 2652(b)(3) further provides that "Arrangements to which this subsection applies include arrangements involving life estates and remainders, estates for years, and insurance and annuity contracts." On the planning side it is very important to plan irrevocable life insurance trusts in light of the available exemptions from the GSTT, particularly the limited exemption under §2642(c) for transfers that qualify as nontaxable gifts and the overall GSTT exemption. §6.42.

Section 2642(c) Exclusion. The nontaxable gift exclusion of §2642(c) applies to transfers to a trust that qualify for the annual gift tax exclusion if two additional requirements are met: (1) during the lifetime of the beneficiary no portion of the corpus or income may be distributed to or for the benefit of any other person, and (2) the property of the trust is includible in the beneficiary's estate if the beneficiary dies before the trust terminates.

In order to qualify for the exclusion, a separate trust, share, or subtrust should be established for each beneficiary, of which no portion of the principal or income may be expended for any other person during the beneficiary's lifetime. Each beneficiary should also be given a power of appointment over his or her separate share sufficient to require inclusion in the beneficiary's estate under §2041. The client may choose to give the beneficiary a broad power in order to provide greater flexibility. On the other hand, the client may prefer a power that is very limited, such as a power to appoint to creditors of the beneficiary. Even so, some clients prefer to limit the power to one that is exercisable jointly with another person, who must be a nonadverse party in order to assure inclusion in the beneficiary's estate under §2041. Also, as indicated below, consideration should be given to using the grantor's GSTT exemption to the extent the transfers to the trust are not entirely sheltered by § 2642(c).

Under § 2642(c)(2), an individual for whom a separate trust, share, or subtrust is established must be the only person entitled to receive any distribution from it during his or her lifetime. Note, however, that the trustee is not required to distribute any income or principal to the beneficiary. Of course, if the beneficiary dies before termination of the trust, the entire value of the beneficiary's share is includible in his or her gross estate. If the beneficiary predeceases the insured, only a small amount may be includible, depending largely upon the type and value of the policies owned by the trustee. If the beneficiary survives the insured, a large amount may be includible in the beneficiary's estate. In such a case the beneficiary's executor may have the right under § 2207 to recover a proportionate part of the estate tax from the recipients of the property subject to the power.

GSTT Exemption. If the trust might be subject to the GSTT, the grantor should consider allocating his or her GSTT exemption to cover transfers to the trust. Specifically, the grantor could allocate a sufficient part of his or her GSTT exemption to insulate each transfer to the trust from the GSTT. If such allocations are made the trust will not be subject to the GSTT. In general the grantor's GSTT exemption should be allocated to a transfer on the gift tax return for the year in which the transfer was made. Under § 2642(b)(1) if an allocation is made on a timely filed gift tax return, the inclusion ratio for that transfer is determined according to the gift tax value of the transferred property. Thus, the inclusion ratio for a transfer of $10,000 would be zero if the grantor allocated $10,000 of his or her GSTT exemption to the transfer on a timely filed gift tax return. If the allocation were not made until after the death of the grantor-insured, the inclusion ratio would be determined according to the post-death value of the property—possibly the entire amount of the insurance proceeds. Clients should also consider establishing "layered" insurance trusts. For example, one trust might be for the exclusive benefit of the insured's spouse and children, which would not involve any generation-skipping transfers in any case (*i.e.*, it would be wholly free from the GSTT). Another trust might be for the exclusive benefit of the insured's grandchildren and more remote descendants—all distributions from which would involve generation-skipping transfers. The insured might insulate the latter trust from the GSTT by making timely allocations of his or her GSTT exemption sufficient to cover the amount of transfers made to the trust (*i.e.*, the trust would have an inclusion ratio of zero).

The value of the grantor's GSTT exemption can be highly leveraged by allocating it to cover transfers to an irrevocable life insurance trust that will involve generation-skipping transfers otherwise subject to the GSTT. The leverage results because of the small amount transferred to the trust each year to pay premiums relative to the large amount of insurance proceeds payable to the trust.

§ 6.24.5. Drafting Considerations

An ILIT should be carefully drawn to prevent the insured from holding any incident of ownership in the insurance in any capacity. This requires that all interests in preexisting policies of insurance must be completely and effectively assigned to the trustee and that the insured must not have any control over any other insurance the trustee may acquire on his or her life. The best approach is to avoid a dispute with the

IRS regarding the effect of holding incidents of ownership in a fiduciary capacity. Thus, the insured should not have any control over the insurance. Perhaps the most comprehensive protection is provided if the trust instrument prohibits the insured from acting as trustee or successor trustee. Also, to guard against inclusion in the insured's gross estate under § 2036, the trust should not permit the assets to be applied in satisfaction of the insured's obligations, including the support of dependents. Finally, the agreement should completely dispose of all interests in the insurance so the insured will not have any reversionary interests in it.

Although the following discussion focuses on an irrevocable trust created in part for the benefit of the insured's spouse, many of the points are equally applicable to trusts of which other persons are the beneficiaries.

Discretion to Provide Estate with Liquidity. The trust may safely give the trustee discretion to loan the proceeds to the insured's executor or to use them to purchase assets from the insured's estate. *See* § 6.27. A broad form of authorization is useful to allow the proceeds to be used to meet the cash requirements of the insured's estate. The provision should be carefully drafted because the proceeds are includible in the insured's estate to the extent they "are subject to an obligation, legally binding . . . to pay taxes, debts, or other charges enforceable against the estate . . . ." Reg. § 20.2042-1(b).

More aggressive planners may give an independent trustee discretion to pay such debts, expenses, taxes, and other obligations of the insured's estate as may be requested by the insured's executor. Such a use of the proceeds should not cause them to be included in the insured's gross estate. In particular, the proceeds should not be includible under § 2042(1) ("receivable by the executor"). *See* § 6.26. The power is, in effect, a special power to appoint the proceeds to the persons whose interests in the probate estate are augmented by payment of the expenses by the trust. The power might constitute a general power of appointment if it were held by a person who would benefit from its exercise. In such a case, part or all of the proceeds could be included in the gross estate of the power holder.

Marital Deduction. If the trust is structured to meet the requirements of § 2056(b)(7), the insured's executor may elect to claim a marital deduction with respect to any of the insurance that is included in the insured's estate. Such a trust is ordinarily includible in the surviving spouse's estate only to the extent a marital deduction was claimed in the estate of the deceased spouse. *See* § 2044; § 5.23. The survivor may be given the income from the trust and a special testamentary power to appoint the trust property to and among a limited class, such as his or her issue. The surviving spouse should not be given an unlimited power of withdrawal, a general power of appointment, or any other control that would cause trust assets to be included in her gross estate under § 2041. Although the surviving spouse could act as trustee, it is often preferable to have an independent trustee or at the least an independent cotrustee. One important reason for having an independent trustee is the broad range of discretionary powers that can safely be given to an independent trustee, but not to a beneficiary who is also a trustee. A cotrustee may also provide important continuity if the surviving spouse resigns or ceases to act as trustee because of death or incompetence.

Ownership and Beneficiary Designations. If existing policies are to be included in the trust, they must be assigned to the trustee. In order to eliminate any possibility that the insured retains any control over the insurance, the policies themselves should be held by the trustee. Similarly, the trustee should have possession of any policies that are subsequently acquired by or assigned to the trustee. Also, the trustee must be designated as primary beneficiary under the policies.

The trust assets are includible in the estate of the noninsured spouse under §§ 2036 or 2038 to the extent he or she is treated as a grantor of the trust and is entitled to its income or holds a power over the disposition of its income or corpus. *See* § 6.40. Accordingly, the noninsured spouse should not have any interest in the policies that are transferred to the trust. In the ideal case the policies are acquired by the trustee with funds initially contributed by a person other than the insured or the insured's spouse.

The noninsured spouse is treated as a grantor of the trust under § 2036(a)(1) to the extent he or she pays premiums on the insurance or otherwise contributes property to the trust. A noninsured spouse who pays any premiums may be treated as having transferred a proportionate part of the insurance to the trust and not merely the amount of the premiums. This problem is avoided if the premiums are paid with funds in which the noninsured spouse does not have any interest. The insured might pay the premiums from his or her own property, recognizing that the payments constitute gifts. In this connection remember that premium payments made by the insured's employer are treated as having been made by the employee. Rev. Rul. 76-490, 1976-2 C.B. 300. Of course, if the trust is funded, the premium payments may be made by the trustee. Funding requires that someone make more substantial gifts to the trust. Also, if the insured provides the funds, the income of the trust will be taxed to him or her under § 677(a) to the extent the income could be used without the consent of an adverse party to pay the cost of insurance on the insured's life or that of his or her spouse. In some cases a family member other than the noninsured spouse may pay the premiums, which involves gifts by that person but does not increase the risk that the proceeds will be included in the estate of the noninsured spouse.

Termination. Some of the rigidity of an irrevocable trust is ameliorated if the trustee or another independent party has the power to terminate the trust at any time it would be in the best interests of the beneficiary to do so. The trustee might also be specifically authorized to terminate the trust if it became uneconomical to continue it. Upon termination the trustee could be authorized to distribute the trust property to the current beneficiaries or to another irrevocable trust. For example, the trustee might be authorized to distribute the trust property to the persons currently entitled to receive distributions of income, to be divided among them in the discretion of the trustee or in some other manner (*e.g.*, by right of representation). The insured should not hold the power to terminate and distribute the trust property because that would cause the trust property to be includible in the insured's estate under §§ 2038 and 2042(2). Cautious advisors also counsel against giving such a power of termination to the spouse of the insured. Also, a potential distributee should not hold such a power because of the potential inclusion of the trust property in the power holder's estate under § 2041. Beyond those considerations, the tax effects of such a "safety valve" are not at all clear. If the safety valve is controlled by an independent party, it should not cause estate tax complications, since there would be no basis for inclusion in the estate of the insured or of the beneficiaries. However, the risk of inclusion would increase if the power holder were subservient to the insured and the insured were treated as holding the power. Finally, if the trustee is given any power to make discretionary distributions, the planner must be alert to potential GSTT problems.

Authorize Policy Ownership. As a matter of routine a trust should include a provision authorizing the trustee to receive, purchase, and maintain policies of insurance on the life of the grantor, the beneficiaries, and any person in whom the beneficiaries have an insurable interest. Such a provision will help assuage any concerns the trustee or the insurer may have regarding the propriety of the trustee's acceptance, acquisition, or continuation of life insurance policies.

The client may wish to protect the trustee against liability in connection with the retention of an existing life insurance policy or for the selection of a new policy. It is particularly appropriate to do so in the case of an individual trustee if the client has, in effect, preselected the policy or the agent from whom the policy is to be purchased. Trust provisions intended to relieve the trustee from liability relating to the selection and retention of life insurance policies must be drafted with care, particularly because the extent to which the trustee of an ILIT may be relieved of investment duties relating to life insurance policies vary from state to state. As suggested by Messrs. Flagg & Zieger in *A Shot Across the Bow*, 149 Tr. & Est. 33 (Dec. 2010), the decision in *Cochran Irrevocable Trust*, 901 N.E.2d 1128 (Ind. App. 2009), suggests that trustees of ILITs should consider delegating "investment and management functions to a prudent delegate."

A provision along the lines of Form 6-1 may be appropriately included where existing policies will be transferred to the trust:

Form 6-1
Right of Trustee to Accept and Retain Life Insurance Policies Without Liability

> The trustee may, without incurring liability to anyone interested in the trust, accept and retain any policies of insurance on the life of the grantor or any member of grantor's family or any other person in whose life the trustee has an insurable interest. The trustee shall have no duty to diversify with respect to such policies or to inquire into the suitability of any insurance policy or the financial condition of any insurer.

The client may also wish to relieve the trustee from liability in connection with the selection and purchase of new policies and for any lack of diversification that may result from investing trust funds in life insurance policies. If so, a provision along these lines should be considered:

Form 6-2
Right of Trustee to Purchase Life Insurance Without Duty to Diversify Investments

> The trustee may purchase insurance on the life of the grantor or any member of grantor's family or any other person in whose life trustee has an insurable interest. Such purchase and payment of subsequent premi-

ums may utilize all or any part of the trust assets without any duty on the part of the trustee to diversify the investments of the trust by investing in assets other than policies of life insurance. The trustee acting upon the recommendation of an experienced insurance advisor, including any Chartered Life Underwriter, may, without incurring any duty to any person interested in the trust, purchase all insurance held hereunder from one or more insurers without any duty to diversify the types of policies or to purchase the policies from more than one insurer. The trustee shall incur no liability to any person interested in the trust for any loss suffered as a result of the financial condition, including insolvency, of any insurer.

Trustee Liability. Before drafting an ILIT or other trust that may include policies of life insurance, the lawyer should discuss with a client the extent to which the client wishes the trustee to be relieved from liability with respect to the acquisition, retention, disposition or management of the policies. As indicated above, in at least some cases a client may wish to exonerate a related, or other uncompensated, individual trustee from liability. However, a client will most likely not wish to exonerate a corporate or other compensated professional trustee from liability with respect to life insurance policies. The issue is of particular concern in the states whose statutes wholly or partially exonerate the trustee of a trust that holds one or more policies of life insurance from responsibility with respect to the policies. *E.g.,* Code of Ala. § 19-3B-818 (2011); 12 Del. C. § 3302(b) (2011); Fla. Stat. § 518.112 (2011); N.D. Cent. Code § 26.1-33-44 (2011); 20 Pa. Consolidated Stat. § 7802 (2011); Wyo. Stat. § 4-10-902 (2011).

Trust Reformation. The reformation of a life insurance trust may be recognized by the IRS. Thus, in LR 9847025 the IRS gave effect to the reformation of a life insurance trust made by a court that added language preventing the grantors from appointing themselves as trustees. The ruling also concluded that the reformation was not a transfer or release of a retained interest or power that would subject the insurance to inclusion under § 2035.

§ 6.24.6. Community Property

The noninsured spouse's interest in community property insurance held in a trust is particularly vulnerable to inclusion in his or her estate under § 2036. Where the noninsured spouse has a life income interest in the trust the effect of inclusion may be ameliorated by claiming a consideration offset for the actuarial value of that interest. As in the widow's election cases (*See* § 9.31.2), the noninsured spouse may be considered to have exchanged a remainder interest in his or her community share of the proceeds for a life income interest in the other share of the proceeds. In this connection see the discussion regarding the use of the community property life insurance widow's election trust approach. § 6.25.1.

Gifts to the Insured. Some optimistic insurance advisors suggest that the possibility of inclusion in the noninsured spouse's estate under § 2036 is avoided if the noninsured spouse first makes a gift of his or her interest in the insurance to the insured. As a second step the insured would transfer the insurance policies to the trust. Unfortunately, this two-step process may not satisfy the IRS, which may argue that the noninsured spouse actually transferred his or her interest in the policy to the trust. It would argue that the noninsured spouse is the transferor and the intermediate transfer to the insured spouse served no purpose apart from attempting to avoid the estate tax upon the noninsured spouse's death. The argument is buttressed by the fact that the courts are committed to determining the tax consequences of transactions according to their substance and not their form: "The substance of a transaction rather than its form must ultimately determine the tax liabilities of individuals . . . .When one overall transaction transferring property is carried out through a series of closely related steps, courts have looked to the essential nature of the transaction rather than to each separate step to determine tax consequences of the transfer." *Johnson v. Commissioner*, 495 F.2d 1079, 1082 (6th Cir.), *cert. denied*, 419 U.S. 1040 (1974). The gift approach stands a greater chance of success if the gift and the transfer to the trust are separated in time, suggesting they are not related. Note also that the full amount of the insurance will be includible in the insured's estate under § 2035 if the insured dies within three years of transferring the entire interest in the insurance to the trust.

Sale of Policies to the Insured. There is perhaps a greater possibility of avoiding inclusion in the noninsured spouse's estate if the noninsured spouse's interest in the insurance is sold to the insured. Of course, in order to produce the desired result, the insured must make the purchase with noncommunity funds, which the insured may already have or which may be generated by partitioning some community property funds into equal units separately owned by the husband and wife. Again, there is some risk that the sale will be ignored unless the taxpayers can establish an independent (*i.e.*, nontax) purpose for it. Otherwise the IRS may argue that in substance the noninsured spouse has transferred his or her interest to the trust and reserved a life interest in the proceeds. Here also the risk of inclusion in the noninsured spouse's estate is lower where the sale and transfer are separated in time and are not directly related. Again, if the insured dies within three years of the transfer to the trust, the insurance is all includible in his or her estate. Note, however, that the trust can be structured to qualify for the marital deduction if the insurance is included in the insured's gross estate. Of course, the use of the marital deduction only defers the time at which the tax must be paid. The sale of the noninsured spouse's interest to the insured would not cause the proceeds to be included in the recipient's income. Although the transfer is made for consideration, it is within the exclusion of § 101(a)(2)(B), which exempts transfers "to the insured, to a partner of the insured, to a partnership in which the insured is a partner, or to a corporation in which the insured is a shareholder or officer."

EXAMPLE 6-5.

H purchased *W*'s one-half community property interest in a policy on his life with separate funds that resulted from the equal partition of community assets. Subsequently *H* transferred the policy to an irrevocable trust of which *W* was the life income beneficiary. If *H* dies within three years of making the transfer the entire proceeds will be included in his gross estate. However, if the trust is properly drawn, the insured's executor may elect to claim a marital deduction with respect to part or all of the proceeds. Of course, if such an election is made, a corresponding part of the trust would be included in *W*'s estate under § 2044.

If *H* lives for more than three years following the transfer of the policy to the trust in this example, none of the proceeds would be included in his gross estate and possibly none of the trust property attributable to the proceeds would be included in *W*'s estate.

Sale of Policies to the Trustee. A sale of the noninsured spouse's community property interest to the trustee is generally not feasible for two reasons. First, the trust is usually not funded with enough assets to support the purchase. Second, and more important, the sale would be a transfer of the policy for value, which could subject the proceeds to the income tax when they are paid. *See* § 6.54. Because of the transfer for value rule it is generally undesirable to sell a policy to the trustee. Of course, if the insured were treated as the owner of the trust for income tax purposes (*i.e.*, if the trust were "defective" for income tax purposes), a sale to the trust should be treated as a sale to the insured, which would not be subject to the transfer for value rule. *See* § 6.54.3.

Aggressive clients may be willing to take the risks involved in giving or selling the noninsured spouse's interest in policies to the insured spouse for addition to the trust. The decision is theirs, but the lawyer should be sure they understand the risks and appreciate the irrevocable nature of the trust. Because the trust is irrevocable its provisions cannot be changed after it is established.

§ 6.25.   OTHER TYPES OF LIFE INSURANCE TRUSTS

The inherent flexibility of the trust device challenges planners to adapt it to meet the specialized needs of particular clients. Within the limits imposed by the insurance and tax laws, there are many ways in which an insurance trust may be crafted to help a client. Some arrangements are appropriate only for clients who are willing to assume the risk of being successfully challenged by the IRS.

§ 6.25.1. Community Property Widow's Election Life Insurance Trust

If the surviving spouse will be the beneficiary of an ILIT, consideration should be given to structuring the trust in a way that minimizes the amount includible in his or her gross estate. Specifically, the amount of the insurance includible in the surviving spouse's estate may be reduced by a consideration offset under § 2043(a) if the trust is properly structured. The approach, which is more fully described in Price, The Uses and Abuses of Irrevocable Life Insurance Trusts, U. Miami, 14th Inst. Est. Plan. ¶ 1111.3 (1980), is based on a variation of the widow's election that involves community property life insurance and results in the inclusion of none of the insurance in the estate of the insured. The tax consequences of the community property widow's election are discussed in Chapter 9. The variation on the approach now before us involves the following steps:

1. Community property life insurance policies are transferred to a trust with the noninsured spouse retaining the right to revoke the trust with respect to the interest he or she contributes to it. The insured holds no interest in or

control over the trust, which is irrevocable as to the interest he or she contributes. Accordingly, none of the proceeds is includible in the insured's estate if the insured survives the creation of the trust by three years or more. Indeed, if the trust is funded with cash that is later used by the trustee to acquire policies on the life of the insured, the proceeds should escape inclusion in the estate of the insured even if the insured dies within three years. *See* § 6.33.4. Because of the noninsured spouse's retained power of revocation, the transfer of property to the trust by the noninsured spouse does not involve a gift. The transfer of the insured's interest may involve a substantial gift, depending on the value of the property transferred to the trust (cash or existing policies). Any power of withdrawal that is given to the noninsured spouse should be limited to the greater of $5,000 or 5 percent in order to avoid later inclusion of an unnecessarily large amount in the survivor's estate under § 2041. *See* § 10.24. Consideration should be given to planning the trust to take advantage of the limited exemption from the GSTT that is available for gifts in trust that qualify for the annual gift tax exclusion. *See* § 2642(c)(2); § 6.24.4.

2. Upon the death of the insured, the noninsured spouse may elect to remove from the trust the portion of the proceeds attributable to his or her contributions (*i.e.*, half of the proceeds) or leave that portion of the proceeds in the trust. In the latter case, the noninsured spouse will be entitled to receive all of the income from the trust. With the exception of that election, the trust becomes irrevocable upon the death of the insured spouse.

   The trust may use a formula to limit the value of the property that the surviving spouse must leave in the trust to the actuarially determined value of the life estate the surviving spouse will receive in the decedent's share of the proceeds. If a formula is not used, the election may involve a gift by the surviving spouse of a portion of his or her share of the proceeds. (Under the pre-Chapter 14 rules, the value of the remainder interest transferred by the surviving spouse was, for gift tax purposes, offset by the value of the life interest the survivor received in the share of the proceeds attributable to the insured spouse. *Commissioner v. Siegel*, 250 F.2d 332 (9th Cir. 1957).) In most instances § 2702 now requires that the value of the life interest retained by the surviving spouse be disregarded (unless it is a qualified interest). *See* § 9.30. In such a case, the surviving spouse will make a gift of some value unless the value of the life interest he or she receives is not less than the entire value of the property left in the trust by the noninsured spouse.

   Under an alternative plan, the surviving spouse, in exchange for leaving her share of the proceeds in the trust will receive an annuity (a qualified interest under § 2702) in that trust. the value of which will equal the difference between the total value of the property she transferred reduced by the value of the life estate she received in her husband's share of the proceeds. This approach eliminates the risk that the surviving spouse's election will result in a gift to the remainder beneficiaries of her trust.

3. If the noninsured spouse predeceases the insured, the trust would become irrevocable at that time. Because of the noninsured spouse's retained power of revocation, a portion of the value of the trust property would be includ-

ible in his or her estate (*i.e.*, half of the interpolated terminal reserve of the policies).

If the insured spouse dies first, a portion of the trust property may be included in the estate of the noninsured spouse under §2036. Under the rationale of the most recent cases, there will be no inclusion if the noninsured spouse received consideration equal to or greater than the value of the remainder in the property he or she transferred to the trust. Contrary to the IRS position, the most recent cases, including *Estate of Magnin v. Commissioner*, 184 F.3d 1074 (9th Cir. 1999), hold that the test of adequate and full consideration under §2036(a) is whether the value of the life interest in the trust created by the insured's spouse was equal to, or greater than, the value of the remainder interest in the property transferred by the surviving spouse. *See also Estate of D'Ambrosio v. Commissioner*, 101 F.3d 309 (3d Cir. 1996), *cert. denied*, 137 L.Ed.2d 1030 (1997), *and Wheeler v. United States*, 116 F.3d 749 (5th Cir. 1997).

Interestingly, after *Estate of Magnin* was remanded, the Tax Court found that the interests exchanged did not have approximately equal values. *Estate of Cyril Magnin*, 81 T.C.M. 1126 (2001). As a result, the closely held stock transferred by the decedent was includible in his estate under §2036(a).

The original IRS position was upheld in an earlier, poorly reasoned, case, *Gradow v. United States*, 1987-1 USTC ¶13,711, 11 Ct. Cl. 808 (1987), *aff'd*, 897 F.2d 516 (Fed. Cir. 1990). *See* §9.34. Of course, even the IRS would concede that no part of the trust is includible if the right of the surviving spouse to receive the income from the portion of the trust property attributable to the insured (*i.e.*, half of the proceeds) were conditioned upon the surviving spouse electing to allow proceeds of an exactly equivalent actuarial value to remain in the trust. Under the IRS *Gradow* approach, the portion of the trust attributable to the surviving spouse's transfer to the trust is includible in the estate of the surviving spouse under §2036 if the value of the one-half interest in the proceeds left in the trust by the surviving spouse exceeds the actuarial value of the life interest in the insured's share of the proceeds in the trust. In such a case the amount includible in the surviving spouse's estate is the value of the interest transferred to the trust by the surviving spouse determined on the federal estate tax valuation date applicable to the surviving spouse's estate less an offset under §2043 of the actuarial value of the life estate in the insured's share of the proceeds as determined on the federal estate tax valuation date applicable to the insured spouse's estate. This "frozen dollar" approach toward the determination of the value of the consideration received by the surviving spouse can be a serious disadvantage.

4. Neither the surviving spouse nor the trustee should realize any gain when the insured dies and the surviving spouse is considered to have transferred his or her interest in exchange for a life interest in the insured's share of the proceeds. Each of them has a basis in the proceeds equal to the amount of cash received under the insurance policies. Moreover, §1001(e) should not require any gain to be realized by the trust because the transferor's basis in the proceeds is not determined under §§1014 or 1015.

5. For income tax purposes the surviving spouse should be entitled to amortize the cost of a term interest acquired prior to July 28, 1989. *E.g., Estate of Christ v. Commissioner*, 480 F.2d 171 (9th Cir. 1971). *See* § 9.31. Under § 167(r), added by the 1989 Act, no amortization or depreciation deduction is allowable with respect to a term interest in property if the remainder is held by a related taxpayer. For interests acquired prior to July 28, 1989 the decision in *Manufacturer's Hanover Trust Co. v. Commissioner*, 431 F.2d 664 (2d Cir. 1970), indicates that the purchaser of a life income interest in a trust is allowed an amortization deduction. In that case amortization was allowed although all of the income received from the trust was tax exempt.

§ 6.25.2. Business Uses

Insurance trusts have a wide range of applications where closely-held businesses are involved. For example, the insurance proceeds paid to the trustee can be used to buy the insured's stock from the insured's executor. The terms of the trust could reflect the interests and activities of family members. For example, a child who is active in the business could be given the right to vote the shares held by an independent trustee. The insured's other children could be beneficiaries of the trust without involving them directly in the management of the company.

§ 6.25.3. Charitable Uses

An ILIT can also be used as a vehicle for making charitable contributions. Presumably the trustee of a trust established by the insured has an insurable interest in the life of the insured at least where the insured originally acquired the insurance and transferred it to the trustee. *See* § 6.2. If the trust is properly drawn, current premium payments are deductible for income and gift tax purposes. Depending on the terms of the trust the insurance proceeds might be includible in the insured's gross estate. Inclusion would result, for example, if the insured retained the right to designate the charities that would receive the proceeds. *See* § 2038. The insured's estate would be entitled to an offsetting charitable deduction. However, the inclusion of the proceeds in the insured's estate could make it more difficult for it to satisfy the percentage tests of § § 303, 2032A, 2057 and 6166.

C. ESTATE TAXATION OF LIFE INSURANCE

§ 6.26. HISTORY

Since 1918, life insurance has been subject to special estate tax rules that were substantially changed in 1942 and 1954. In brief, between 1918 and 1942 the proceeds of life insurance policies were includible in the estate of the insured if the insurance had been taken out by the insured decedent. Proceeds receivable by the executor of the insured were fully includible, but the first $40,000 receivable by others was not includible. Because of uncertainties about the criteria that should be used in determining when insurance had been taken out by the decedent, that requirement was repealed by the Revenue Act of 1942. At the same time Congress also repealed the

$40,000 exemption and changed the law regarding the inclusion of life insurance receivable by other beneficiaries to require inclusion if the insured had paid premiums on the insurance or held incidents of ownership in the policy at the time of death. Under the first ground of inclusion, called the premium payment test, insurance was includible in the insured's gross estate in the proportion that premiums paid by the insured bore to the total premiums paid on the policy.

EXAMPLE 6-6.

In 1943, X paid the first $1,000 premium on a $50,000 policy on his life and then irrevocably assigned all of his interests in it to Y. After the assignment, X paid 4 more annual premiums and Y paid 5. When X died in 1952, the $50,000 proceeds were paid to Y. Under the premium payment test, half of the proceeds were includible in X's gross estate because X had paid half of the total premiums. Under the current provisions of §2035, none of the premiums paid by X would be included in X's gross estate and none of the proceeds would be included under §2042. As noted below, the proceeds of life insurance transferred by the insured within 3 years of death are included in the insured's estate under former §2035(d)(2)—now §2035(a)(2).

The 1954 Code eliminated the premium payment test but retained the incidents of ownership rule (with one minor change). Accordingly, since 1954, insurance proceeds receivable by beneficiaries other than the insured's executor have not been includible in the insured's gross estate merely because the insured paid some of the premiums. This change created an important opportunity which allows an insured to pay the premiums on life insurance owned by a trust or other individuals without causing any of the insurance to be included in the insured's gross estate. Under most plans, the allowable annual gift tax exclusions shield the premium payments from any gift tax liability. Of course, where the premium payments are subject to the gift tax, the unification of the gift and estate tax laws in 1976 reduced the tax advantages of this approach. Under the unified tax structure the amount of any post-1976 taxable gifts, including ones that result from premium payments during the lifetime of the insured, are included in the donor's tax base at death. Also, the proceeds of policies transferred by the insured within three years of death are included under §2035. (Note that §2035 does not require the insured's estate to include insurance transferred by another person within three years preceding the death of the insured.) Premiums paid by the insured within three years of death generally are not included.

§6.27.   Life Insurance Receivable by or for the Benefit of the Estate, §2042(1)

Insurance on a decedent's life is included in his or her gross estate to the extent it is "receivable by the executor." §2042(1). However, insurance is not includible if it is payable to the estate in form and the state law requires it to be paid to the insured's surviving spouse or children. *Webster v. Commissioner*, 120 F.2d 514 (5th Cir. 1941).

Section 2042(1) requires the inclusion of insurance proceeds payable to or for the benefit of the insured's executor even though the insured neither held any incidents of ownership in a policy nor paid any premiums on it. Thus, the proceeds of a policy owned and controlled by a third party are includible to the extent they are payable to the decedent's personal representative for the benefit of the estate. *Estate of Draper v. Commissioner*, 536 F.2d 944 (1st Cir. 1976). The rule is inconsistent with the basic estate tax approach of taxing only property that was owned by the decedent at death or transferred inter vivos with some retained interest or control.

EXAMPLE 6-7.

X purchased a policy on the life of her brother, *B*, and paid all of the premiums on the policy until *B*'s death. The proceeds were paid to *B*'s personal representative in accordance with the terms of the policy. The proceeds are fully includible in *B*'s gross estate although he neither paid any premiums on the policy nor held any incidents of ownership in the policy.

Insurance is considered to be receivable by the executor if it is paid to a creditor in satisfaction of a loan or other indebtedness of the insured. *Bintliff v. United States*, 462 F.2d 403 (5th Cir. 1972); Reg. § 20.2042-1(b)(1). Thus, the proceeds of "creditor" life insurance are includible in the gross estate of the insured to the extent they are applied in satisfaction of the insured's debts.

Proceeds receivable by other beneficiaries are includible under § 2042(1) to the extent the beneficiaries are subject to a legally enforceable obligation to apply the proceeds for the benefit of the estate. Thus, although the property of a trust is not otherwise includible in the insured's gross estate, the insurance proceeds received by the trustee are includible to the extent they must be used to pay debts, taxes, and other expenses of the insured's estate Reg. § 20.2042-1(b). In such a case the proceeds are not includible if the trustee is merely authorized, or given discretion, to expend the corpus of the trust in satisfaction of the estate's obligations. *Estate of Charles Howard Wade*, 47 B.T.A. 21 (1942); *Old Colony Trust Co.*, 39 B.T.A. 871 (1939); *cf.* Rev. Rul. 73-404, 1973-2 C.B. 319 (declared obsolete by Rev. Rul. 88-85, 1988-2 C.B. 333) and *Estate of Joseph E. Salsbury*, 34 T.C.M. 1441 (1975) (both cases dealt with a comparable issue involving exclusion of qualified plan proceeds under the provisions of former § 2039(c)). Consistent with that view, the IRS has held that the proceeds of a second-to-die policy owned by the trustee of an ILIT which the trustee had discretion to use to pay estate and inheritance taxes imposed on the surviving insured's estate were not "receivable" by her estate and were not includible in her gross estate. LR 200147039. *See* § 6.24.

Insurance owned by a person other than the insured and payable to a revocable trust created by the insured is not includible in the insured's gross estate under §§ 2041 or 2042. *Margrave v. Commissioner*, 618 F.2d 34 (8th Cir. 1980); Rev. Rul. 81-166, 1981-1 C.B. 477. The cited ruling recognizes that the policy owner's revocable designation of the trustee of a trust created by the insured as beneficiary of the insurance does not constitute a gift. It also points out that the payment of the proceeds to a trust in which persons other than the policy owner have beneficial interests involves a gift by the policy owner to them. Where the policy owner is an income beneficiary of the trust, the portion of the trust corpus attributable to his or her contributions to the trust (*i.e.,* the policy proceeds) will be includible in his or her gross estate under §2036(a)(1). Rev. Rul. 81-166.

To the extent a policy was owned by a husband and wife as community property, only the half interest of the deceased insured is generally includible in his or her estate under §2042(1). Reg. §20.2042-1(b)(2). The other half of the proceeds is not includible because it always belonged to the surviving spouse. However, if the full amount of the proceeds of a community policy is paid to the insured's personal representative for the benefit of the estate, the full amount is includible in the insured's gross estate under §2042(1). This issue could arise in a variety of ways. For example, inclusion of the entire proceeds would be required if the noninsured spouse had consented to the designation of the insured's personal representative as beneficiary and the proceeds were all available for payment of debts, taxes, and expenses of the estate. In contrast, the share of the proceeds attributable to the surviving spouse's community interest in a policy is not includible in the insured's gross estate when the survivor has the right to recover it from the estate. *See* Reg. §20.2042-1(b)(2).

§6.28. INCIDENTS OF OWNERSHIP, §2042(2)

Horticultural Analogies

Congress through §2042 has given discrete statutory treatment to policies of insurance. Sections 2036, 2037, 2038, 2041, and 2042 may be consanguineous, but each has an individual personality with genetic variations. These provisions developed from a common design to tax testamentary harvests, and they reach common sorts of decedent controls. As the caselaw cross-pollinations—or pari materia interpretations—establish: Rose, the insured and the possessor of incidents of ownership, is Rose, even though garlanded by leaves of trusteeship. Each section is not identical, however. Life insurance is a specie of its own, it occupies a special place in the tax field, and we cannot simply graft terms from one provision onto another. Whether the insurance sheaves found in the decedent's hands are selected stalks from once-larger bundles, or whether they represent all that the taxpayer ever cultivated from the seed he had, the Congressional direction is to tax whatever is possessed at the end of the season. *Rose v. United States,* 511 F.2d 259, 265 (5th Cir. 1975).

We hold that estate tax liability for policies "with respect to which the decedent possessed at his death any of the incidents of ownership" depends on a general, legal power to exercise ownership, without regard to the owner's ability to exercise it at a particular moment. *Commissioner v. Estate of Noel,* 380 U.S. 678, 684 (1965).

The very phrase "incidents of ownership" connotes something partial, minor, or even fractional in its scope. It speaks more of possibility than probability. *United States v. Rhode Island Hospital Trust Co.*, 355 F.2d 7, 10 (1st Cir. 1966).

Insurance proceeds are includible in the insured's gross estate under §2042(2) if, at the time of death, the insured possessed *any* incident of ownership in the policy that was exercisable alone *or* in conjunction with any other person. Note that inclusion is required under §2042(2) if the insured *possessed* incidents of ownership. "Retention" of the incidents of ownership is not required. Inclusion does not require that the insured have ever owned the insurance and retained the incidents of ownership. *Rose v. United States*, 511 F.2d 259 (5th Cir. 1975).

The most common problems encountered under §2042(2) have been concerned with determining what constitutes an incident of ownership and under what circumstances an incident is considered to be exercisable by the insured.

§6.28.1. Policy Facts and Intent Facts

Whether an individual possesses an incident of ownership in a policy is determined in most instances according to the terms of the policy (the "policy facts") and not the intention of the parties (the "intent facts"). *Commissioner v. Estate of Noel*, 380 U.S. 678 (1965). Accordingly, if a policy permits the insured to exercise an incident of ownership, the proceeds of the policy are includible in the insured's gross estate. Some courts have recognized an exception, however, if the insurance contract does not reflect the instructions of the parties, "as where an agent, on his own initiative, inserts a reservation of right to change a beneficiary contrary to the intentions which had been expressed to him." *United States v. Rhode Island Hospital Trust Co.*, 355 F.2d 7, 13 (1st Cir. 1966). Similarly, LR 8610068 recognized that the decedent held no incidents of ownership over a policy which erroneously named him as owner instead of the corporation in which he owned a minority interest and of which he was president.

In LR 9651004 (TAM), the IRS allowed intent facts to uphold a transfer of life insurance policies more than three years prior to the death of the insured, although the actual transfer occurred within three years of his death. The evidence, including the schedule of assets transferred to the irrevocable life insurance trust, the corporate resolutions, and the conduct of the parties, prevailed over the policy facts.

§6.28.2. Incidents of Ownership

The term "incidents of ownership" is not defined in the Code, but the regulations describe the type of interests that are treated as incidents of ownership for purposes of §2042(2):

> [T]he term "incidents of ownership" is not limited in its meaning to ownership of the policy in the technical legal sense. Generally speaking, the term has reference to the right of the insured or his estate to the economic benefits of the policy. Thus, it includes the power to change the beneficiary, to surrender or cancel the policy, to assign the policy, to

revoke an assignment, to pledge the policy for a loan, or to obtain from the insurer a loan against the surrender value of the policy, etc. Reg. § 20.2042-1(c)(2).

The portion of the regulation that links incidents of ownership to the economic benefits of a policy has caused some confusion. In one view a power is not an incident of ownership unless it can be exercised for the economic benefit of the insured. A competing view is that a power can constitute an incident of ownership although it cannot be exercised in a way that economically benefits the insured or the estate of the insured. For example, the courts have divided on the question of whether the bare power to select a settlement option under an employer-provided insurance plan is an incident of ownership. In *Estate of Lumpkin v. Commissioner*, 474 F.2d 1092 (5th Cir. 1973), the proceeds of a group-term policy were included in the gross estate of the insured because he had the power to vary the time at which the benefits would be paid. The court reasoned that inclusion under § 2042 was justified by analogy to §§ 2036 and 2038 (which require the inclusion of property over which a decedent retained the power to vary the time of enjoyment). Critics hastened to point out that §§ 2036 and 2038 deal with property transferred by a decedent and that the insured in *Lumpkin* had never held or transferred any interest in the policy. Inclusion of the proceeds of the same group-term policy was rejected by the Third Circuit, which held that the insured's right "to select a settlement option with the mutual agreement of his employer and the insurer did not give him a substantial degree of control sufficient to constitute an incident of ownership." *Estate of Connelly v. United States*, 551 F.2d 545, 552 (3d Cir. 1977). The IRS will not follow the *Connelly* decision outside the Third Circuit. Rev. Rul. 81-128, 1981-1 C.B. 469.

§ 6.28.3. Power to Change Beneficiaries by Divorce, Birth, or Adoption

A change of beneficiary that results from an independently significant act of the insured does not require the insurance to be included in the insured's estate. For example, in LR 8819001 (TAM) the trust created by the insured provided that the interest of his wife would terminate if they became divorced. As the IRS concluded,

> The act of divorcing one's spouse is an act of independent significance, the incidental and collateral consequences of which is to terminate the spouse's interest in the trust. Thus, we do not believe the decedent possessed an "incident of ownership" in the insurance policy as a result of the trust provision which would terminate the interest of the decedent's spouse in the event of a divorce. *Id.*

Consistently, § 2041 does not require the inclusion in a power holder's estate of property subject to a general power of appointment that is exercisable only upon the occurrence of an independently significant event that does not occur prior to the power holder's death. *See* Reg. § 20.2041-3(b), § 10.22.

Letter Ruling 8819001 relies upon Rev. Rul. 80-255, 1980-2 C.B. 273, "which holds that a trust provision for the inclusion of after-born and after-adopted children as beneficiaries is not the equivalent of the settlor's retention of a power to change the beneficial interests of the trusts within the meaning of sections 2036(a)(2) and

2038(a)(1)." Similarly, the grantor trust rules allow after-born or after-adopted children to be added as beneficiaries of a trust without requiring the grantor to be treated as owner of the trust. *See* § 674(b)(5).

A client creating an ILIT may wish to provide for the addition or deletion of beneficiaries based upon changes in family circumstances. In some instances the grantor may wish to make the additions or deletions contingent upon other factors, such as the size of the trust, the status of the individual as beneficiary of other trusts, or the concurrence of an independent party.

§ 6.28.4. Power to Terminate Membership in Group Plans

The power to cancel employer-provided insurance by terminating employment is not an incident of ownership. *Landorf v. United States*, 408 F.2d 461 (Ct. Cl. 1969). Revenue Ruling 69-54, 1969-1 C.B. 221, indicated otherwise, but the IRS soon abandoned the position. Rev. Rul. 72-307, 1972-1 C.B. 307. The latter ruling recognized that "[a]n insured's power to cancel his insurance coverage by terminating his employment is a collateral consequence of the power that every employee has to terminate his employment." *Id.* It continued to say that "[t]he examples in section 20.2042-1(c) of the regulations, on the other hand, concern powers that directly affect the insurance policy or the payment of its proceeds without potentially costly related consequences. Where the power to cancel an insurance policy is exercisable only by terminating employment, it is not deemed to be an incident of ownership in the policy." *Id.*

In contrast, the power to terminate group life insurance by terminating membership in a voluntary organization through which the insurance was acquired might properly be viewed as an incident of ownership. The issue could arise in connection with group insurance purchased by an alumna through her university's alumnae association. The insurance would remain in effect so long as the insured remains a member of the association and pays the required premiums. In such a case the irrevocable assignment of the insurance to others more than three years prior to the insured's death might not suffice to remove the insurance from her estate. Specifically, the power to terminate the insurance by terminating membership in the alumnae organization probably would constitute an incident of ownership sufficient to require inclusion of the insurance in the insured's estate. The outcome might be different if the policy were acquired through a group in which the insured was required to retain membership in order to practice a profession (*e.g.*, membership in an integrated bar).

§ 6.28.5. Power to Convert Group Insurance to Ordinary Insurance

As noted in Rev. Rul. 72-307, discussed above, the IRS recognized that the insured's right to cancel group insurance coverage by terminating employment was not an incident of ownership. Despite that enlightened approach, the IRS later contended that an employee's right to convert group insurance to individual insurance upon the termination of employment was an incident of ownership. However, the contention was rejected by the Tax Court, which said that "[i]f quitting one's job is too high a price to pay for the right to cancel an insurance policy, it is likewise too high a price to pay for the right to convert to another policy." *Estate of James Smead*, 78

T.C. 43, 52 (1982). Ultimately, the IRS conceded that the power to convert group-term life insurance to ordinary insurance upon termination of employment was not an incident of ownership. Rev. Rul. 84-130, 1984-2 C.B. 194.

In LR 9233006, the IRS ruled that the right of a shareholder to purchase a corporate owned policy if his or her stock were either redeemed because of disability or purchased in connection with a sale or public offering, does not constitute an incident of ownership. The position taken in LR 9233006 relied upon Rev. Rul. 84-130. *See* § 6.28.6.

In LR 9141007 (TAM), the IRS held that a policy issued when a conversion right was exercised upon termination of the insured's employment was in substance the same policy as the group policy that was in effect during the period of the insured's employment. The "new" policy was issued to an irrevocable trust that had been created by the insured's children a few days earlier. According to the ruling the insured is properly treated as having transferred an incident of ownership in the insurance whether the "situation is viewed as if the decedent exercised the conversion right and then had the individual policy transferred to the trustee or whether the decedent transferred the incidents of ownership in the group policy to the trustee who then exercised the conversion right and acquired the individual policy." In either case the proceeds of the insurance, incidents of ownership in which were transferred within three years preceding the insured's death, were includible in the insured's estate under § 2035(d)(2)—now § 2035(a)(2).

§ 6.28.6. Right to Prevent Cancellation by Purchasing Employer Owned Life Insurance

In Rev. Rul. 79-46, 1979-1 C.B. 303, the IRS ruled that an employee's power to prevent cancellation of insurance coverage by purchasing the policy from his employer for its cash surrender value if the employer elected to terminate the policy was an incident of ownership. That position was rejected in *Estate of John Smith*, 73 T.C. 307 (1979), because of the contingent nature of the power: "Whatever rights Smith may have acquired under paragraph seven of his employment agreement were contingent ones dependent on an event which never occurred and over which he had no control." Of course, had Smith controlled his corporate employer through direct or indirect ownership of more than 50 percent of its stock, the incidents of ownership held by it would have been attributed to him. *See* Reg. § 20.2042-1(c)(6). *See also* § 6.29. A contingent power of the type involved in *Smith* must be distinguished from a power that is jointly exercisable by the insured and another person. *See, e.g., Commissioner v. Estate of Karagheusian*, 233 F.2d 197 (2d Cir. 1956). Inclusion *is* required under § 2042(2) if any of the incidents of ownership were exercisable by the insured "either alone or in conjunction with any other person."

§ 6.28.7. Power to Remove and Replace Trustee

In 1995, the IRS revoked Rev. Rul. 79-353, 1979-2 C.B. 325, which held that a grantor who retains the power, without cause, to remove *and* replace a corporate trustee with another corporate trustee would be treated as having reserved the powers held by the trustee. Rev. Rul. 95-58, 1995-2 C.B. 191. *See* § 10.40.1. The revocation followed two decisions that refused to follow the ruling. *Vak v. United States*, 973 F.2d 1409 (8th Cir. 1992); *Estate of Helen Wall*, 101 T.C. 300 (1993). Revenue Ruling 95-58 states that an individual who holds the power to remove and replace a trustee and appoint another individual or corporate successor who is not a related or subordinated party within the meaning of § 672(c) will not be treated as possessing the powers of the trustee. In no case should the insured have the power to become the successor trustee, for such would cause inclusion under § 2042(2).

Although Rev. Rul. 95-58 may allow the grantor to hold the power to remove and replace the trustee of a trust that includes policies of insurance on the grantor's life, to be on the safe side it is preferable not to give the grantor such a broad power. Note, however, the IRS has recognized the effect of the reformation of a trust to correct the scrivener's failure to include a provision that the grantor intended to include that would bar the trustor or a party who was related or subordinate to the trustor as defined in § 672 from serving as a successor trustee. LR 200314009. The ruling, which relies primarily on Rev. Rul. 95-58, concludes that such a reformation would remove the possibility that life insurance policies on the grantor's life would be included in her gross estate under § 2035 or § 2042(2). According to the ruling, such a reformation would not constitute a release or transfer that would result in application of § 2035.

§ 6.28.8. Negative or "Veto" Powers

A negative power, such as a power to prevent another person from changing the beneficiary, surrendering the policy, or exercising another incident of ownership, is itself an incident of ownership. *Eleanor M. Schwager*, 64 T.C. 781 (1975); Rev. Rul. 75-70, 1975-1 C.B. 301. In LR 9349002 (TAM), the IRS ruled that the insured held incidents of ownership over a policy owned by a "trustee" pursuant to a buy-sell agreement where the powers of the trustee with respect to the policy could only be exercised with the consent of the shareholders—including the insured, who owned 49.5 percent of the corporation's stock.

In *Estate of Rockwell v. Commissioner*, 779 F.2d 931 (3d Cir. 1985), the court recognized that a veto power may constitute an incident of ownership where it gives the insured control over the designation of the beneficiary. However, because of the extremely limited nature of the veto power retained by the insured, the *Rockwell* court concluded that the power was not an incident of ownership. There, the insured assigned the policies to his wife and retained the power to veto any beneficiary designation of, or assignment to, any person other than to a designated corporate trustee who did not have an insurable interest in his life. His wife later assigned the policies to a revocable trust of which she and the insured's children were the beneficiaries. The trust permitted the trustee to assign the trust property, which included the insurance policies, if the assignments were for the sole benefit of the beneficiaries. The veto power retained by the insured was redundant when he transferred the insurance policies to his wife and she transferred them to the trust. At the time the governing state law (Pennsylvania) prohibited the assignment of a life insurance policy to a person who did not have an insurable interest in the life of the insured. In passing upon the significance of the power the court, in effect, disregarded a later change in the state law which eliminated the prohibition. Moreover, when the insured's wife died in 1965 the trust became irrevocable, which effectively precluded the assignment of the insurance policies to any persons other than the beneficiaries of the trust—each of whom had an insurable interest in the life of the insured. The mere possibility that the insured's retained power might have been called into play had the trustee wished to assign the insurance policies to a person lacking an insurable interest in the insured's life in order to secure a loan, was insufficient to require the insurance to be included in the insured's estate. According to the court, "Whatever vitality, if any, the veto power may have had at one time, Clara's death and the terms of the trust agreement excluded Rockwell from any possible economic benefit. Congress' purpose in requiring the inclusion of policies in a gross estate when the decedent retains incidents of ownership is to prevent taxpayers from enjoying property without paying tax on it." *Estate of Rockwell*, 779 F.2d 931, 937 (3d Cir. 1985).

Consistently, an earlier case held that the insured's retained power to veto a sale of assets by the trustee of an irrevocable life insurance trust was not an incident of ownership. *Estate of Carlton v. Commissioner*, 298 F.2d 415 (2d Cir. 1962). In view of the trustee's fiduciary obligations and the terms of the trust, the power could not be exercised in a way that would economically benefit the insured.

In order to avoid risk of inclusion in the insured's estate, the insured should not have the power to veto any action with respect to an insurance policy, including a change of beneficiary, a surrender of the policy, or an assignment of it. If a veto power must be included in a trust, it should not extend to matters directly affecting the insurance on the power-holder's life because of the possibility that it would be considered to be an incident of ownership in policies held by the trustee.

§ 6.28.9. Incidents of Ownership Under Extraneous Contract

The insured may hold incidents of ownership in a policy owned by another person and with respect to which the insured holds no direct control. For example, in *Estate of James O. Tomerlin*, 51 T.C.M. 831 (1986), the proceeds of a policy owned by the insured's employer were included in the insured's estate because of the incidents of ownership held by the insured under a contract between the insured and his employer. Although the insured's employer (a corporation in which the insured owned 50 percent of the stock) was the owner of the policy, the insured was contractually entitled to designate the beneficiary, to veto a change of beneficiary or assignment of the policy, and to cancel and repurchase the policy at its cash surrender value. *Tomerlin* indicates the adverse tax results that may arise because of the terms of an extraneous contract, such as a split-dollar agreement. Similarly, an insured has an incident of ownership in a policy that he or she has the option to purchase from the owner. LR 9128008 (TAM). *See* § 6.39 regarding the transfer pursuant to the terms of a buy-sell agreement (or other extraneous contract) of incidents of ownership within three years of the insured's death; LR 9127007 (TAM).

§ 6.28.10. Reversionary Interests, § 2042(2)

The term "incidents of ownership" includes a reversionary interest in a policy or its proceeds, whether it arises by the express terms of the policy or other instrument or by operation of law, if the value of the reversionary interest exceeded 5 percent immediately before the death of the insured. § 2042(2). However, the insured is not considered to have an incident of ownership in a policy if the power to obtain the cash surrender value existed in some other person immediately before the insured's death and was exercisable by such other person alone and in all events Reg. § 20.2042-1(c)(3). The regulations also provide that the terms "reversionary interest" and "incidents of ownership" do not include the possibility that the decedent might receive a policy or its proceeds through the estate of another person, or as a surviving spouse under a statutory right of election or a similar right. *Id.*

Inclusion may be required if the insured retains reversionary interests in life insurance under the terms of a decree of dissolution. *E.g.*, Rev. Rul. 76-113, 1976-1 C.B. 276 (policies would revert to insured if former spouse predeceased him or remarried, the possibility of which exceeded 5 percent at time of insured's death; ruling notes the possibility of an offsetting deduction under § 2053). Effective with respect to transfers made after July 18, 1984, a deduction may be allowed under § 2043(b) to the extent the payment under the decree is in settlement of the noninsured spouse's marital or property rights or is to provide a reasonable allowance for the support of minor children of the marriage. §§ 2516 and 2043(b).

In Rev. Rul. 76-113, 1976-1 C.B. 276, the marital property settlement agreement required the insured to name his former spouse as beneficiary of several life insurance policies for so long as she lived and remained unmarried. Under its terms the policies would return to the insured or to his estate or would be subject to a power of disposition by him if his former spouse predeceased him or remarried prior to his death. When the insured died the proceeds were paid to his former spouse as beneficiary. The IRS held that the proceeds of the policies were includible in the insured's gross estate because the possibility that his former spouse would predecease him or remarry prior to his death exceeded 5 percent immediately prior to his death. The ruling recognized that in some cases an offsetting deduction is allowable under § 2053 when the proceeds are includible in the insured's estate. In the case of decedents dying after July 18, 1984, a transfer of property made pursuant to a property settlement agreement as provided in § 2516(1) is considered to be made for full consideration in money or money's worth. §§ 2043(b), 2053(e).

When a divorce decree requires the payment of a specified sum upon the insured's death to a former spouse and the insured provided for payment of the obligation by purchasing insurance, a deduction is allowable under § 2053(a)(3) as a claim against the insured's estate. Also, where the insurance proceeds that are included in the decedent's estate are paid to a former spouse in satisfaction of an indebtedness created in settlement of the decedent's marital obligations, the obligation is deductible under § 2053(a)(4). If the obligation to provide the insurance is embodied not in a divorce decree, but in a property settlement agreement, a deduction is allowed only if the agreement was contracted bona fide and for an adequate and full consideration in money or money's worth, as required by § 2053(c)(1). *Gray v. United States*, 541 F.2d 228 (9th Cir. 1976). If the divorce court lacks power to alter the terms of the settlement, the obligation is deemed to be created by the property settlement agreement and not by the divorce decree. *Id.* In this connection recall that transfers made to a spouse after July 18, 1984, are deemed to be made for adequate and full consideration to the extent they are pursuant to settlements that satisfy the requirements of § 2516.

§ 6.28.10

Revenue Ruling 78-379, 1978-2 C.B. 238, denied a deduction under §2053 for insurance proceeds that were paid to the insured decedent's minor children pursuant to a property settlement agreement and divorce decree under which the decedent's obligation to provide child support terminated at death. However, the ruling recognized that a deduction is allowable if the divorce court has power to change the property settlement agreement because it is then a judicially-imposed obligation. Similarly, a deduction should be allowed if an obligation to provide life insurance is imposed in a support decree. LR 8128005 (TAM).

In order to avoid the reach of the reversionary interest rule a trust or other instrument governing the ownership of the policy should preclude the insurance from returning to the insured or becoming subject to the insured's control. For example, a rider might be added to the policy specifying that the policy will pass to a person other than the insured if the former spouse dies or remarries prior to the death of the insured. Note, too, that a decree of divorce or a property settlement agreement may sufficiently divest the insured spouse of the incidents of ownership so that the policy proceeds will not be includible in his or her gross estate. *Estate of Theodore E. Beauregard, Jr.*, 74 T.C. 603 (1980).

According to the IRS the insured held a reversionary interest in a policy that was acquired by a "trustee" pursuant to a buy-sell agreement with funds provided by a corporation in which the insured was a 49.5 percent shareholder. LR 9349002 (TAM). The reversionary interest arose by reason of a subsequent stock redemption agreement under which the insured could, after full payment for the redeemed stock, purchase the policy for its cash surrender value (plus any unearned premium). The insured was considered to hold a reversionary interest because the trustee was held to be a mere agent for the shareholders and the policy was structured so it would have no cash surrender value until several years after the trust terminated. The TAM stretches too far in applying Reg. § 20.2042-1(c)(3) in this case. *See also* § 6.28.8.

§ 6.28.11. Incidents of Ownership Held in a Fiduciary Capacity

> [A] decedent will not be deemed to have incidents of ownership over an insurance policy on decedent's life where decedent's powers are held in a fiduciary capacity, and are not exercisable for decedent's personal benefit, where the decedent did not transfer the policy or any of the consideration for purchasing the policy to the trust from personal assets, and the devolution of the powers on decedent was not part of a prearranged plan involving the participation of decedent. Rev. Rul. 84-179, 1984-2 C.B. 195.

Prior to the issuance of Rev. Rul. 84-179, the IRS had consistently argued for a per se rule under which the insured's mere possession of incidents of ownership in a fiduciary capacity was sufficient to require inclusion in the insured's estate. Moreover, the IRS insisted that the rule should apply even in cases in which the incidents of ownership could not be exercised for the benefit of the insured-fiduciary. That position was supported by a minority of decisions, including ones by the Fifth Circuit. *See Rose v. United States*, 511 F.2d 259 (5th Cir. 1975); *Terriberry v. United States*, 517 F.2d 286 (5th Cir. 1975), *cert. denied*, 424 U.S. 977 (1976). Other courts upheld inclusion in the estate of the insured-fiduciary *only* if the powers could be exercised in a way that would benefit the insured-fiduciary. *Estate of Skifter v. Commissioner*, 468 F.2d 699 (3d Cir. 1972); *Estate of Fruehauf v. Commissioner*, 427 F.2d 80 (6th Cir. 1970); *Hunter v. United States*, 624 F.2d 833 (8th Cir. 1980); *Estate of Gesner v. United States*, 600 F.2d 1349 (Ct. Cl. 1979).

The change of position announced in Rev. Rul. 84-179 was presaged by the government's brief in *Estate of Harry Bloch, Jr.*, 78 T.C. 850 (1982), which abandoned the per se rule. The Tax Court ruled that insurance held in a trust established by the father of the insured-trustee was not includible in the insured's estate. The insurance involved was purchased by the insured-trustee after the trust was established. Inclusion was not required although the trust instrument gave the insured-trustee broad powers over the trust; according to the Tax Court the exercise of the powers was circumscribed by the insured's fiduciary duties. Interestingly, the Tax Court also concluded that the insured's breach of his fiduciary duties by pledging the insurance policies as collateral for a personal loan did not require inclusion.

In Rev. Rul. 84-179 the insured, *D*, originally acquired the insurance in 1960. However, in the same year he assigned the policy to his wife who named their child as beneficiary. In an unrelated transaction, *D*'s wife executed a will leaving her residuary estate to *D* as trustee of a trust for the benefit of their child. *D*'s wife died in 1978 and was survived by the insured. The policy of insurance on *D*'s life passed to the residuary trust. The ruling concluded that the powers that *D* held as trustee were insufficient to cause the insurance to be included in his estate: The establishment of the testamentary trust was unrelated to the assignment of the insurance to *D*'s spouse and *D* could not benefit from the exercise of any of the powers that he held as trustee. Thus, although the insured served as trustee, the insurance was not includible in his estate. The ruling was followed in LR 9111028 in which the insured served as trustee of a trust established by his wife but was barred from exercising any power with respect to insurance on his life.

Revenue Ruling 84-179 benefits taxpayers and helps to clarify the law. However, it is important to note that the ruling requires inclusion where decedent held powers in a fiduciary capacity and had transferred to the trust either the policy or any of the consideration for maintaining the policy. In addition, according to the ruling, inclusion is required if the powers could be exercised for the benefit of the insured. Although Reg. § 20.2042-1(c)(4) continues to require the inclusion of the proceeds of a policy over which the insured held an incident of ownership as trustee, whether or not the incident could be exercised for the insured's own economic benefit, Rev. Rul. 84-179 provides that the regulation will be interpreted in accordance with its provisions. Note also that it revoked an earlier ruling that took a contrary position, Rev. Rul. 76-261, 1976-2 C.B. 276.

The government might also seek inclusion in the estate of the insured under § 2042(2) if the insured held incidents of ownership over a policy as custodian for a minor whom the insured was legally obligated to support. A similar risk exists if an insured serves as guardian for an incompetent. All in all, it is safer not to appoint the insured to any fiduciary office with respect to policies on his or her life.

Insurance Acquired by Trust on Life of Former Trustee. In LR 9434028, the IRS ruled that the income beneficiary of an irrevocable trust did not possess any incidents of ownership over a policy on her life that was purchased after she resigned as a trustee of the trust. As indicated in the ruling, the outcome would be different if she resumes service as trustee and is serving as such at the time of her death or ceases to serve within three years preceding her death. In LR 9748020, the IRS held that insurance acquired by a credit shelter trust, of which the surviving spouse-insured had resigned as cotrustee, would not be included in her estate, "provided that: (1) she has not transferred any assets to Trust B; (2) the premiums on the policy are paid from the principal of Trust B; (3) she does not maintain the policy with personal assets; and (4) she is not reinstated as a trustee of Trust B." The plan described in the ruling may appeal to surviving spouses who do not need the income of the credit shelter trust and would prefer it to be invested in a life insurance policy. Making such an investment does raise issues regarding the duties of the trustee, particularly where, as in this ruling, the surviving spouse is entitled to receive all the income of the trust.

The insured should not hold any incidents of ownership in a policy as a fiduciary. Powers over a policy on the life of a trustee should be vested solely in a cofiduciary or some other party.

§ 6.29.   ATTRIBUTION OF INCIDENTS OF OWNERSHIP

Under Reg. § 20.2042-1(c)(6), incidents of ownership held by a corporation of which the decedent was the sole or controlling shareholder are attributed to the decedent to the extent the proceeds are not paid to, or applied for the benefit of, the corporation. However, the regulation provides that the power to surrender or cancel group-term life insurance as defined in § 79 will not be attributed to a decedent "through his stock ownership." An insured, who is the beneficiary of a QTIP trust will not be considered the owner of the stock held by the trust. LR 9848011.

In general, the proceeds of a policy are includible in the gross estate of a sole or controlling shareholder to the extent that they are paid to a personal beneficiary rather than to the corporation. Rev. Rul. 76-274, 1976-2 C.B. 278, situation 1. In applying § 2042(2) it makes no difference whether the decedent was the sole share-holder or the controlling shareholder, since in either case the decedent held the power to affect the disposition of the proceeds through exercise of control over the corporation. *Estate of Milton L. Levy*, 70 T.C. 873 (1978) (the full amount of proceeds paid to a personal beneficiary was included in the estate of the 80.4 percent shareholder).

EXAMPLE 6-8.

D owned a controlling interest in ABC, Inc., which owned 2 policies of insurance on *D*'s life. When *D* died the proceeds of Policy One were paid to her father, *F*, in accordance with the beneficiary designation in the policy. The proceeds of Policy Two were paid to ABC, Inc. Under Reg. § 202042-1(c)(6). the proceeds of Policy One are includible in *D*'s gross estate. The proceeds of Policy Two are not; they are taken into account in valuing *D*'s shares of ABC, Inc. stock. The proceeds of Policy Two, along with other corporate assets, are subject to any applicable discount that is applied in valuing *D*'s shares. *Estate of John L. Huntsman*, 66 T.C. 861

(1976), *acq.*, 1977-1 C.B. 1. Under the analysis of Rev. Rul. 90-21, 1990-1 C.B. 172 and LR 8906002 (TAM) if *D* had transferred Policies One and Two and the controlling interest in ABC, Inc. within 3 years of death, Policy One would be included in *D*'s estate but not Policy Two. *See* § 6.33.2.

In effect, the provisions of § 2042(2) and § 2031 are mutually exclusive—the proceeds of a policy may be includible under either but not both.

For purposes of § 2042 a decedent is the controlling shareholder only if the decedent owned stock that represented more than 50 percent of the combined total voting power of the corporation. In making that determination, a decedent is treated as owning only the stock the legal title to which was held at the time of death by (1) the decedent, or an agent or nominee of the decedent, (2) the decedent and another person jointly (but only to the extent that the decedent furnished the total considera-tion for purposes of § 2040), (3) the trustee of a voting trust to the extent of the decedent's interest, and (4) the trustee of any other trust of which the decedent was treated as the owner under §§ 671-678. Reg. § 20.2042-1(c)(6).

Where incidents of ownership are attributed to a controlling shareholder, the fiduciary duties owed by the controlling shareholder to other shareholders or credi-tors may not prevent the insurance proceeds from being included in his or her estate. *Estate of Milton L. Levy*, 70 T.C. 873 (1978). A controlling shareholder owes fiduciary duties to minority shareholders and creditors, but some incidents held by the corporation over the insurance could be exercised in a variety of significant ways without violating those duties (*e.g.*, the right to borrow against the policy). In this respect the outcome differs from the Supreme Court's decision in *United States v. Byrum*, 408 U.S. 125 (1972), in which the transferor's fiduciary duties prevented the transferor's retained right to vote stock from requiring it to be included in his estate under § 2036(a). The decision in *Byrum* led to the adoption of § 2036(b), which reversed it. *See* § 2.19.1.

§ 6.29.1. Stock Held as Community Property

When the stock of a corporation is all owned by a husband and wife as their community property, it is doubtful that either spouse will be considered to be a controlling shareholder for purposes of attributing the incidents of ownership by the corporation. In *Estate of Elizabeth Lee*, 69 T.C. 860 (1978), *nonacq.*, 1980-1 C.B. 2, *nonacq. withdrawn and acq. substituted*, 1993-1 C.B. 202, the Tax Court held that the decedent's one-half community interest in 80 percent of the stock of a closely held corporation would be valued separately as a 40 percent minority interest. In Rev. Rul. 93-12, 1993-1 C.B. 202, the IRS conceded that "in the case of a corporation with a single class of stock outstanding the family relationship of the donor, the donee, and other shareholders, the shares of the other family members will not be aggregated with the transferred shares to determine whether the transferred shares should be valued as part of a controlling interest."

A contrary result reached by a panel of the Fifth Circuit, *Estate of Bright v. Commissioner*, 619 F.2d 407 (5th Cir. 1980), was overturned when the issue was considered *en banc*, 658 F.2d 999 (5th Cir. 1981). Consistent with those decisions, *Propstra v. United States*, 680 F.2d 1248 (9th Cir. 1982), upheld the allowance of a discount in valuing the decedent's one-half community interest in real property. However, despite the foregoing decisions, the IRS may continue to raise the issue.

In the case of community property, less value may be included in a shareholder's gross estate if corporate-owned insurance is paid to the shareholder's personal beneficiaries than if it were payable to the corporation. The reason is simple: Only the insured's one-half interest in the community property shares should be taken into account in applying Reg. § 20.2042-1(c)(6). Accordingly, neither husband nor wife would be a *controlling* shareholder where all of the shares of stock are owned by them as their community property. In such a case, the proceeds of corporate-owned insurance that are paid to personal beneficiaries may escape inclusion under § 2042 or any other section of the Code. In contrast, the proceeds of corporate-owned insurance that are paid to the corporation would be taken into account under § 2031 in valuing the decedent's interest in the stock. Under the Tax Court decision in *John L. Huntsman*, 66 T.C. 861 (1976), the proceeds of insurance payable to a corporation are included along with other assets in valuing the stock, which is subject to whatever discount may apply to its valuation. In *Huntsman*, the Tax Court rejected the government's contention that the full amount of the proceeds should be added after valuing the corporation exclusive of the proceeds.

Consistent with its acquiescence in the *Lee* case, in LR 9808024 (superseding an earlier ruling) the IRS held that where a husband and wife owned 72 percent of the stock of a corporation as their community property, the estate of each would be treated as owning only half of that amount, 36 percent, for purposes of Reg. § 20.2042-1(c)(6).

The proceeds of corporate-owned insurance may be used to fund the redemption of the shares of an insured stockholder under a stock redemption agreement. *See* § 11.8. If the proceeds exceed the amount required to fund the redemption, the excess is includible in the estate of the insured under § 2038 if the insured voluntarily entered into the agreement and had control of the disposition of the excess. LR 8943082.

§ 6.29.2. Insurance Owned by a Partnership

Insurance owned by a partnership is not includible in the gross estate of a deceased partner if the proceeds are applied for the benefit of the partnership. *Estate of Frank H. Knipp*, 25 T.C. 153 (1955), *aff'd*, 244 F.2d 436 (4th Cir.), *cert. denied*, 355 U.S. 827 (1957) (appeal involved other issues); *nonacq. on insurance issue*, 1956-2 C.B. 10, *withdrawn and acq. in result substituted*, 1959-1 C.B. 4; LR 9623024. If the proceeds are instead payable to a personal beneficiary designated by the insured partner, they are includible. Rev. Rul. 83-147, 1983-2 C.B. 158. However, where more than three years prior to death a partner assigned all interests in group-term insurance that would have qualified as § 79 insurance had the partner been an employee, by analogy to Reg. § 20.2042-1(c)(6) the insured partner is not treated as having possessed any incidents of ownership in the insurance. Rev. Rul. 83-148, 1983-2 C.B. 157. The reciprocal trust doctrine, discussed in § 6.30, probably does not require inclusion of policies that are cross-owned by partners. Rev. Rul. 56-397, 1956-2 C.B. 599.

Estate of Knipp was followed in LR 200111038, in which the IRS ruled favorably with respect to §§ 101(a) and 2042(2) regarding insurance policies on the lives of partners in a limited partnership that held other assets. A caveat to the ruling states that it expresses no opinion regarding the classification of the partnership if the partnership disposes of all assets other than the insurance policies.

In LR 200214028, the IRS ruled that the proceeds of insurance policies on the life of a partner that were owned by the partnership and payable to it were not includible in the estate of the insured partner.

§ 6.30. RECIPROCAL TRUST DOCTRINE AND LIFE INSURANCE

The "reciprocal trust" or "crossed trust" doctrine was developed to determine who would be treated as the grantor of related trusts for tax purposes. Under the doctrine, where two or more trusts are created by related parties and the nominal grantor of one trust is the beneficiary of another trust, the trusts are uncrossed. That is, each person is treated as the grantor of the trust of which he or she is the beneficiary if the trusts are "interrelated, and . . . the arrangement, to the extent of mutual value, leaves the settlors in approximately the same economic position as they would have been in had they created trusts naming themselves as life beneficiaries." *United States v. Estate of Grace*, 395 U.S. 316, 324 (1969).

In *Estate of Green v. United States*, 68 F.3d 151 (6th Cir. 1995), the majority held that the reciprocal trust doctrine did not apply to trusts that the decedent and his wife had created for the benefit of their two granddaughters. The trust created by the decedent for one granddaughter named his wife as trustee and gave her discretion to reinvest and to make distributions of the income and principal of the trust. The trust created by his wife named him trustee of the trust for the other granddaughter and gave him similar discretionary powers. The two judge majority held that the reciprocal trust did not apply according to the criteria expressed in *Estate of Grace* because the powers to control investments and make distributions did not leave the decedent in approximately the same economic position he was in before the trusts were established. The well-reasoned dissent by Judge Nathaniel Jones reached a contrary conclusion, pointing out that had the decedent held the same powers over a trust he had created, the trust would have been includible in his gross estate under § 2036. *See also* § 10.30.

In LR 9643013, the IRS held that irrevocable trusts created by a husband and wife differed sufficiently that the reciprocal trust doctrine would not apply to them. The ruling does not indicate what differences the IRS considered to be determinative. However, it was notable that the wife was not a beneficiary of the trust established by her husband, although the husband was a beneficiary of the trust the wife created.

EXAMPLE 6-9.

H transferred 1,000 shares of ABC, Inc. to a trust of which W was named trustee and income beneficiary. At the same time W transferred 1,000 shares of ABC, Inc. to an identical trust of which H was the trustee and income beneficiary. The children of H and W were the remainder beneficiaries of both trusts. Upon the death of either grantor the trusts will be "uncrossed" by the reciprocal trust doctrine and H will be treated as the grantor of the trust of which he was the trustee and income beneficiary and W will be treated as the grantor of the other trust. Upon H's death the property of the trust of which he is treated as the grantor is includible in his gross estate under § 2036(a)(1).

The doctrine may be applied although the grantors do not retain any economic interest in the trusts. Thus, the doctrine was applied in *Estate of Bruno Bischoff*, 69 T.C. 32 (1977), where each nominal grantor appointed the other as trustee with discretion to distribute trust property to the beneficiaries, who were the grandchildren of the grantors.

The government has argued that the reciprocal trust doctrine applies where a husband and wife each buy and own a policy of insurance on the other's life. The doctrine was applied where a husband and wife domiciled in Texas each used community property funds to purchase substantially identical policies of insurance on each other's life and designated the uninsured spouse as the owner and benefici-ary. Rev. Rul. 67-228, 1967-2 C.B. 331. The ruling concluded that, in such circumstances,

> [T]he presumption under Texas law that the policies are community property will prevail unless it is clearly shown that the transfers were not reciprocal and that gifts were intended. Accordingly, as a community asset, one-half of the value of the property received as insurance on the life of the husband upon his death is includible in his gross estate under the provisions of section 2042 of the Code. Furthermore, one-half of the value of the policy on the life of the wife is includible in his gross estate under section 2033 of the Code as his interest in the community asset. 1967-2 C.B. at 333.

In *Estate of Dorothy C. Wilmot*, 29 T.C.M. 1055 (1970), the court refused to consider a belated argument by the government that the reciprocal trust doctrine should be applied to policies each spouse owned on the life of the other. *See also Estate of Evard W. Marks, Jr.*, 94 T.C. 720 (1990) (argument not raised; Texas law).

It is reasonable to apply the reciprocal trust doctrine where the insured and another person acquire similar policies on each other's lives and the insured in fact has the power to designate the beneficiary of the policy that is nominally owned by the other person. The doctrine should not apply where the policies are owned by business associates in connection with a buy-out agreement. Rev. Rul. 56-397, 1956-2 C.B. 599. These rules roughly parallel the ones under which the incidents of owner-ship held by a corporation or partnership are attributed to the insured. It is question-able whether the doctrine should apply merely because a husband and wife, or two other parties, each purchase a policy on the life of the other. As some commentators have pointed out, the mutual acquisition of life insurance policies by a husband and wife involves the acquisition of new wealth and not the rearrangement of existing wealth. The cross-ownership of life insurance policies should be recognized as a legitimate estate planning tool. As indicated in § 6.22.1, some incentives remain for the cross-ownership of insurance by a husband and wife. However, the most promi-nent incentive was eliminated by the adoption of the unlimited marital deduction.

The reciprocal trust doctrine is also discussed at § 7.35.2 in connection with the estate taxation of property held by custodians under the Uniform Gifts or Transfers to

Minors Act established by related donors and at § 10.30 in connection with planning the grantors' interests in irrevocable trusts.

The reciprocal trust doctrine did not apply to trusts created by the decedent and her sister where, 26 years after the trusts were created, the decedent was appointed as trustee of the trusts created by her sister. LR 9804012. From the facts, the IRS concluded that, at the time the trusts were created, it was not the intent of the grantors to create reciprocal trusts.

The reciprocal trust doctrine is reviewed in Eleanor Martin-Nelson, Taxing Reciprocal Trusts—Charting a Doctrine's Fall from Grace, 75 N.C. L. Rev. 1781 (1997).

§ 6.31. TRANSFER OF INTERESTS IN INSURANCE WITHIN THREE YEARS OF DEATH, § 2035

The case law which has been developed in respect to the applicability of section 2035 to life insurance has not been a model of clarity, at least insofar as policies taken out within 3 years of the death of the insured are concerned. *Estate of Tetsuo Kurihara,* 82 T.C. 51, 53 (1984).

Section 2035(a) itself is unchanged since 1976. Section 2035(d) is simply an added sieve through which transactions must pass before the transfer may even be tested under the 3-year rule. Although section 2035(d)(1) generally repeals the 3-year rule, perforations in the sieve are found in section 2035(d)(2) which allow the 3-year rule to be applied to a transfer of an interest in property which either (1) is included in the value of the gross estate under section 2042, or (2) would have been included under section 2042 had such an interest been retained by the decedent. *Estate of Leder,* 89 T.C. 235, 239 (1987), *aff'd,* 893 F.2d 237 (10th Cir. 1989).

§ 6.32. § 2035; PRE-1982 LAW

The 1976 Act amended § 2035 to require the inclusion of gifts made within three years of death with the exception of gifts for which the donor was not required to file a gift tax return (*i.e.,* ones within the annual gift tax exclusion). Because the exception might result in the exclusion of large amounts of life insurance, the 1978 Act amended § 2035(b) to provide that the exception did not apply "to any transfer with respect to a life insurance policy." The constitutionality of the retroactive 1978 amendment was upheld in several cases involving life insurance policies that were transferred in the post-1976 period before adoption of the 1978 amendment. *E.g., Estate of Ekins v. Commissioner,* 797 F.2d 481 (7th Cir. 1986); *Estate of Fein v. United States,* 730 F.2d 1211 (8th Cir.), *cert. denied,* 469 U.S. 858 (1984). The courts concluded that the due process clause does not bar changes in tax laws that are reasonably foreseeable and involve only fluctuations in the tax rates. Additionally, the changes were not so harsh or oppressive as to transgress the constitutional limitations.

§ 6.33. § 2035; POST-1981 LAW

Under § 2035, as amended by the 1981 Act, property transferred within three years of death is includible in the decedent's estate only if it would have been includible under § § 2036, 2037, 2038 or 2042 if the transfer had not been made. That is, §2035(a) does not apply to post-1981 transfers made within three years of the donor's death except for those described in §2035(a)(2) (formerly §2035(d)(2)).

The Tax Court and several courts of appeal have given the post-1981 law a literal reading; as a result, insurance purchased by an irrevocable trust with funds provided by the insured is not included under §2035 although the insured died within three years of the establishment of the trust. *See* §6.24.5. The IRS has stated that it will no longer litigate the issue. A.O.D. 1991-012.

The insured's estate may be required to include the proceeds of an individual insurance policy that was issued within three years of the insured's death to an irrevocable life insurance trust pursuant to an exercise of a conversion right upon the insured's termination of employment. *See* §6.28.5.

The proceeds of life insurance policies that the insured transfers to charities within three years preceding death are includible in the insured's estate under §2035(a)(2). Of course, if a policy transferred to charity is included in the insured's estate, the estate will be entitled to an offsetting charitable deduction. An inter vivos transfer of a policy would, of course, support gift and income tax charitable deductions. Presumably the income tax deduction would be limited to the lesser of the replacement value of the policy or the donor's basis. *See* §170(e).

Sometimes intentions are given legal effect: In *Estate of O'Daniel v. United States*, 6. F.3d 321 (5th Cir. 1993), the court held that the decedent's estate was not required to include the proceeds of 12 key man policies that had been owned by the decedent's former employer. *See also* LR 9651004 as described below. In June, 1979, the decedent entered into an oral agreement to buy the policies from his employer for an amount equal to their cash values. On July 8, 1979, he executed an irrevocable life insurance trust of which his wife was the trustee. On November 17, 1979, the insured requested information regarding the cash value of the policies. On May 20, 1980, the insured paid the cash value to the company into which his former employer had merged. Between May and November, 1980, the policies were transferred to the insured and from the insured to the trustee of the life insurance trust. The insured did report the transfer of the policies to the trust on a gift tax return. However, subsequent premium payments were reported. The insured died on September 18, 1982—more than three years after the insured agreed to purchase the life insurance policies and the creation of the life insurance trust, but less than three years after the actual transfer of the policies to the trustee. The court held that although the oral agreement was unenforceable, it was sufficient to transfer the incidents of ownership to the insured. On very thin evidence the court also held that "the trust agreement operated to transfer all incidences [sic] of ownership to the trust."

In LR 9323002 (TAM), the IRS ruled that the proceeds of two policies that were issued within three years of the insured's death were not included in her gross estate although she initially applied for a policy on her life. Before the first premium payment was made and the policy was issued, the insured made a supplemental application that requested the policy to be divided and issued equally to her children as owners and beneficiaries. The children paid all premiums on the policies until the insured died—which was within one year of the time the policies were issued. According to the TAM, under the law of Texas, the insurance policies did not become effective until the first premium was paid and the policies were issued and delivered to the owners. Accordingly, the policies were never issued to the insured and, hence, could not have been transferred by her.

Importantly, the 1997 Act further amended § 2035, adding § 2035(e) under which transfers from revocable trusts made within three years of death are treated as a transfer made directly by the decedent.

§ 6.33.1. Insured Transfers Owned Insurance

Under § 2035(a)(2), the proceeds of insurance policies that are transferred by an insured within three years preceding his or her death are included in the insured's estate. Such transfers are clearly within the reach of § 2035(a)(2) because the proceeds of the policies would have been included in the insured's estate under § 2042 had the policies not been transferred.

The proceeds of a policy that a former husband transferred to his former wife within three years preceding his death are includible in his estate. *Estate of Waters v. Commissioner*, 48 F.3d 838 (4th Cir. 1995). The inclusion is required because there was no bargained for exchange in connection with the transfer although it took place during the period the parties were negotiating the terms of a post-divorce property settlement.

Former § 2035(d)(2) (now § 2035(a)(2)) required the inclusion of policies that were transferred by the insured's conservator within three years preceding his death. LR 9533001 (TAM). The transfers to irrevocable trusts created by the insured's conservator constituted completed gifts for gift tax purposes.

In LR 9651004 (TAM), the IRS recognized that the intent of the parties that policies of insurance be transferred to an irrevocable trust more than three years prior to the insured's death prevailed over the fact that the policies were actually transferred to the trust within three years preceding his death. It was important that an exhibit to the trust agreement listed the policies as having been transferred to the trust. In addition, the records of the trust and of the corporation regarding a split-dollar agreement with respect to the policies indicated that the trust owned them and that the insured held no powers or rights with respect to them.

§ 6.33.2. Controlled Corporation or Other Noninsured-Owner Transfers Insurance Within Three Years of Insured's Death

Insurance policies owned by persons other than the insured that are transferred within three years of the insured's death are includible if the owner is merely the agent of the insured or if the owner's incidents of ownership are attributed to the insured. For example, Rev. Rul. 82-141, 1982-2 C.B. 209, held that the proceeds of insurance policies owned by the insured's controlled corporation were includible in the insured's estate where, within three years of the insured's death, the corporation transferred the policies to another person in a transaction that did not have a business purpose. Revenue Ruling 90-21, 1990-1 C.B. 172, amplified Rev. Rul. 82-141 to provide that inclusion under § 2035(d)(2) (now § 2035(a)(2)) is required in such a case when the insured also disposes of his or her controlling interest in the corporation within three years of death. According to LR 8906002 (TAM), inclusion under the attribution rules and former § 2035(d)(2) (now § 2035(a)(2)) is not required when, preceding the assignment of the insurance, the corporation was the designated beneficiary of the insurance. Exclusion follows in that case because Reg. § 20.2042-1(c)(6) does not provide any basis for attributing ownership to the insured when insurance owned by the insured's corporation is payable to the corporation. Consistently, LR 8509005 (TAM) required the inclusion of proceeds of a policy acquired by insured's wholly-owned corporation within three years of insured's death although the insurance was transferred by the corporation to an irrevocable trust prior to insured's death. Finally, inclusion was required under the pre-1981 form of § 2035 when the insurance, in form owned by the insured's wife, was issued at his instance within three years preceding his death and all premiums on the insurance were paid by his controlled corporation. *Estate of Levine v. United States*, 10 Cl. Ct. 135 (1986).

In other cases inclusion does not result. For example, in *Estate of Leder*, 89 T.C. 235, *aff'd*, 893 F.2d 237 (10th Cir. 1989), the insurance acquired by the insured's spouse within three years of the insured's death was not includible although the insured's wholly-owned corporation paid all of the premiums. In the view of the Tax Court, the insured did not hold any incident of ownership directly or by attribution. The manner in which the insurance was acquired and other facts distinguish *Leder* from *Levine*. In *Leder*, the Tax Court reasoned that inclusion was not proper because under the governing state law (Oklahoma) the insured never held an interest in the policy or any incident of ownership in it. Thus, former § 2035(d)(2) did not apply to lift the bar of § 2035(d)(1) and require inclusion under § 2035(a).

As noted above, the IRS has ruled that inclusion is not required where the life insurance was acquired and all premiums were paid by a corporation which the insured controlled prior to her sale of all of her stock within three years of her death. LR 8906002. Because the insurance was payable to the corporation, the incidents of ownership in the policy were not attributed to the controlling shareholder under Reg. § 20.2042-1(c)(6). "Thus, no basis exists either indirectly or directly, for including the policy proceeds in *A*' s gross estate under section 2042(2). Further, on the date of her death, *A* was not a shareholder in *X*." LR 8906002.

§ 6.33.3. Pre-1982 Law: Insured Transfers Funds Used to Purchase Insurance

Under the pre-1982 rules, the courts reached inconsistent results in cases in which an individual transferred funds within three years of death to a trustee or another person who used the funds to purchase insurance on the transferor's life. Inclusion was generally not required when the funds were transferred to an independent trustee who was free to invest the funds as the trustee saw fit. *Hope v. United States*, 691 F.2d 786 (5th Cir. 1982).

The same rule was applied where the money was given to individuals who subsequently used the funds to purchase insurance on the donor's life. "If on the other hand, decedent had given money to her children, and they, entirely on their own volition, had chosen to purchase an insurance policy on her life, it would be equally clear that only the money would have been 'transferred.'" *Estate of Inez G. Coleman*, 52 T.C. 921, 923 (1969), *acq.*, 1978-1 C.B. 1.

Inclusion was required, however, if the insured was considered, directly or indirectly, to have acquired the policy. Thus, under the pre-1982 law the insured was frequently treated as having acquired and transferred a policy that was issued to a trust at the instance of the insured within three years of the insured's death and with respect to which the insured paid the premiums directly or indirectly. *See, e.g., Estate of Tetsuo Kurihara*, 82 T.C. 51 (1984) (inclusion of insurance issued to trustee within three years of death required where insured wrote check to trustee in the amount of the insurance premium, noting that it was "premium for Life Ins. No. 10010395 Columbian Mutual Life;" in fact the trustee did not act on its own).

§ 6.33.4. Post-1981 Law: Insured Transfers Funds Used to Purchase Insurance

As discussed above, § 2035 generally does not require inclusion of transfers made within three years of the transferor's death. However, under § 2035(a)(2) a transferor's estate must include the value of interests transferred within three years of death that "would have been included in the decedent's gross estate under section 2036, 2037, 2038, or 2042 if such interest had been retained by the decedent on the date of his death." Thus, the insured's estate must include the proceeds of a life insurance policy transferred by the insured within three years of death; had the policy been retained by the insured, the proceeds would have been included in the insured's estate under § 2042.

The Tax Court and several courts of appeal have held that under the 1981 amendments, no inclusion is required unless the insured held and transferred an incident of ownership in the insurance. *Estate of Joseph Leder*, 89 T.C. 235 (1987), *aff'd*, 893 F.2d 237 (10th Cir. 1989). In particular, the decisions have not required inclusion where within three years of death the insured transferred the funds that were used to purchase the insurance but did not actually transfer the insurance itself.

> In *Estate of Joseph Leder, supra*, we held that the proceeds from the policy in that case were not includible in the gross estate of the insured where the insured did not possess at the time of his death, or at any time within the three years preceding his death, any of the incidents of ownership in the policy because (1) the conditions of section 2042 were never met; (2) the section 2035(d)(2) exception to section 2035(d)(1) is not applicable because the proceeds were not includible under section 2042 or any of the other sections cited in section 2035(d)(2); and (3) section 2035(d)(1) overrides section 2035(a). *Estate of Eddie L. Headrick*, 93 T.C. 171, 177 (1989), *aff'd*, 918 F.2d 1263 (6th Cir. 1990).

Estate of Frank M. Perry, 59 T.C.M. (CCH) 65 (1990), *aff'd*, 927 F.2d 209 (5th Cir. 1991), followed *Leder* and *Headrick*. The taxpayer in *Perry* was awarded attorney's fees of $9,206 for handling the appeal by the IRS, which the Fifth Circuit court said was not "substantially justified." 931 F.2d 1044 (5th Cir. 1991). In the court's view the IRS was continuing "to whip a dead horse in circuit after circuit . . . ." *Id.* at 1046.

In an Action on Decision issued with respect to the appellate decision in *Headrick*, the IRS has stated that it will no longer litigate the issue. After reviewing the history of § 2035(d)(2) (now § 2035(a)(2)), and the adverse opinions in *Leder, Headrick*, and *Perry*, A.O.D. 1991-012 concluded: "Although we continue to believe that substance should prevail over form and that such indirect transfers should be included in a decedent's gross estate, in light of the three adverse appellate opinions set forth above, we will no longer litigate this issue."

§ 6.33.5. Exchange of Policies Owned by Others Within Three Years of Insured's Death

An assignment of an existing life insurance policy should expressly include policies that may be issued in exchange for the existing policy and any changes in its terms and increases in the coverage. Although the IRS does not concede the validity of an anticipatory assignment, it did uphold the exclusion of the proceeds of a policy issued within three years of the insured's death in exchange for a preexisting policy that had been validly assigned by the insured more than three years prior to death. Rev. Rul. 80-289, 1980-2 C.B. 270. The IRS stated that "the [second] assignment will not be treated as a transfer under Section 2035 of the Code." *Id. See* § 6.73.10. A similar result was reached in LR 8819001 (TAM), where the original policy was assigned by the insured to irrevocable trusts more than three years prior to death. Within three years of the insured's death the trustee exchanged the original policy for one that carried a lower premium and was issued by a separate company. The insured signed the application for the new policy, acknowledging that the representations in the application were correct. Within three years of the issuance of the second policy to the trustee the insured died. "Because the decedent owned no interest in the original policy at the time of the exchange and because the decedent's signature on the policy application was not essential to the exchange, we conclude that the decedent did not make a transfer of the insurance within three years of death for purposes of section 2035 of the Code." *Id.* A contrary result was reached in *American National Bank & Trust Co. of Rockford v. United States,* 832 F.2d 1032 (7th Cir. 1987), in which the original policy was assigned to the insured's wife more than three years prior to his death. However, the assignee was required to relinquish all interests in the assigned policy in connection with the issuance of a much larger policy that was not assigned to the insured's spouse. The court viewed the second policy as a different policy that was issued by a different insurer "only on condition that they terminated the earlier policy and thereby extinguished all the rights that Mrs. Olson had under it." *Id.*

§ 6.34. INSURANCE ACQUIRED WITH JOINT OR COMMUNITY PROPERTY FUNDS

Under the regulations, half of the proceeds of community property life insurance is includible in the insured's estate. Reg. § 20.2042-1(b)(2). However, insurance acquired with community property (or jointly owned) funds more than three years prior to the insured's death may be entirely excluded if the husband and wife effectively agreed that the insurance was the separate property of the noninsured spouse. *See* § 3.29. Where money that was originally community property (or jointly owned) is used within three years of the insured's death to purchase insurance, the courts have required inclusion in some cases, but not in others. The differing outcomes are difficult to reconcile.

In *Estate of Lee J. Clay,* 86 T.C. 1266 (1986), the Tax Court upheld complete exclusion of the insurance proceeds of a policy on which the premiums were paid from a joint account of the insured and his wife. The policy was issued to the insured's wife as owner within three years of the insured's death. In *Clay* the insured contributed 73 percent of the funds in the joint account, the use of which to pay premiums on the insurance constituted a transfer from the insured to his wife. The

Tax Court rejected the tracing analysis, holding that "the mere payment of premiums with funds withdrawn from a joint account does not constitute payment by the nonwithdrawing tenant." *Id.*

Results contrary to *Clay* were reached in several cases involving community property. *Estate of Robert W. Hass*, 51 T.C.M. 453 (1986) (Nevada); *Estate of Mary Baratta-Lorton*, 49 T.C.M. 770 (1985) (California), *aff'd without opinion*, 787 F.2d 597 (9th Cir. 1986). Moreover, in *Schnack v. Commissioner*, 848 F.2d 933 (9th Cir. 1988), the court required inclusion of one-half of the proceeds of a policy issued on the insured-wife's life within three years of death. Similar policies on the lives of husband and wife were issued simultaneously and paid for with community funds that had been deposited in a joint bank account. Analogizing the facts to those of *Kurihara*, the Ninth Circuit emphasized that the insured's release of her interest in the funds was for the specific purpose of paying the premiums on the policy. That is, the funds were not available to the insured's husband to use for whatever purpose he wished.

§ 6.35. SALE OF LIFE INSURANCE BY INSURED WITHIN THREE YEARS OF DEATH, § 2035

The gross estate does not include property that is transferred within three years of death in "any bona fide sale for an adequate and full consideration in money or money's worth." § 2035(d). If adequate consideration is not received, the value of the transferred property is includible less the value of the consideration received. The consideration received should be sufficient in the ordinary case if it were equal to the value of the policy determined under Reg. § 20.2031-8(a)(2) (cost of comparable contracts or interpolated terminal reserve). However, the regulation by its terms applies to the valuation of a life insurance policy on the life of a person other than the decedent. Under the primary regulation governing valuation, "all relevant facts and elements of value as of the appropriate valuation date shall be considered." Hence, it may be necessary to consider the physical condition and insurability of the insured at the time of transfer. For example, in *Estate of James Stuart Pritchard*, 4 T.C. 204 (1944), the terminally ill insured did not receive adequate or full consideration when he sold a $50,000 policy on his life to his wife for its cash surrender value of $10,483. Note that if a policy is sold, the income tax exclusion of the proceeds may be lost. *See* § 101(a); § 6.54.

In LR 8806004 (TAM), the IRS expressed a contrary view: "Even if [the consideration received] were equal to the reserve value of the policy at the time of transfer, the consideration received is still wholly inadequate since such consideration is measured against the value at which the property is includible in the decedent's [gross]estate, or $1,000,000. Accordingly, the entire value of the policy proceeds minus the value of any consideration received by the decedent's controlled corporation is includible in her estate." It is doubtful that the position taken by the IRS in LR 8806004 would be upheld. § 6.54.

§ 6.36. Exclusion of Proportion of Proceeds to the Extent premiums Paid by Others; Silverman Rule

Part of the proceeds of a policy transferred within three years of death may be excluded from the insured's estate if some of the postassignment premiums are paid by a person other than the insured. Thus, the Tax Court has held that the insured's estate was not required to include a portion of the proceeds that bore the same relation to the total proceeds as the premium payments made by the assignee bore to the total amount of premium payments. *Estate of Morris R. Silverman*, 61 T.C. 338 (1973), *acq.*, 1978-1 C.B. 2, *other issues affirmed*, 521 F.2d 574 (2d Cir. 1975). In effect, the *Silverman* court adopted the proportional premium payment rule that the government advanced in Rev. Rul. 67-463, 1967-2 C.B. 327, and abandoned in Rev. Rul. 71-497, 1971-2 C.B. 329. *Silverman* was followed in LR 8724014, which allowed exclusion of the proportion of the proceeds that was attributable to premium payments indirectly made by assignees who reimbursed the insured for premium payments withheld by his employer.

EXAMPLE 6-10.

D irrevocably assigned a $100,000 policy on his life to his sister, *S*, within 3 years of his death. *D* paid 3 $1,000 premiums on the policy prior to the assignment and *S* paid 2 postassignment premiums of $1,000 each. Following *D*'s death the proceeds were paid to *S*. Under Silverman only 3/5ths of the total policy proceeds are includible in *D*'s gross estate. The entire proceeds would have been includible if *D* had continued to pay the premiums.

It is curious that the government acquiesced in the Tax Court's decision in *Silverman* five years after it was decided. The Second Circuit opinion does not pass upon the proration issue because the government did not appeal that portion of the Tax Court's decision. Indeed, the appellate court admitted "some uneasiness about the proper basis for holding that . . . [the assignee's] payments in the last six months of his father's life changes the result from the situation where a decedent continues to pay the premiums until death." 521 F.2d at 577. It also questioned whether the assignee's payment of a portion of the premiums justified excluding a proportionate part of the proceeds rather than the actual amount the assignee paid in premiums. Where the insured dies within three years of making a gift of insurance on his or her life, a portion of the proceeds equal to the amount of any post-gift premiums paid by the assignee should be excluded from the insured's gross estate. The exclusion of a larger amount under the *Silverman* rule is difficult to justify.

The *Silverman* rule was followed by the Tax Court in *Estate of Sidney M. Friedberg*, 63 T.C.M. (CCH) 3080 (1992), which held that the rule was not affected by the 1981 amendment of § 2035. The court properly concluded that insurance proceeds payable to an individual who also happens to be the insured's executor are not includible in the insured's estate under § 2042(1) in the absence of an obligation that the proceeds be used for the benefit of the insured's estate.

§ 6.37. INSURANCE ON THE LIFE OF A PERSON OTHER THAN THE DECEDENT, § 2035

Insurance transferred by the owner within three years of the owner's death is generally not includible in the owner's gross estate where the insurance is on the life of another person. In such a case the insurance is not subject to the rules of § 2042 that are applicable to transfers within three years of death by § 2035(a)(2). Instead, the insurance on the life of another person is subject to the same rules that apply to cash, securities, or other property transferred by a decedent within three years of death. A ruling issued prior to the 1981 Act reached a contrary conclusion, reasoning that the language of § 2035(b) did not support exclusion of the insurance in such a case. Rev. Rul. 81-14, 1981-1 C.B. 456. The ruling was questionable and appears to be over-turned by the 1981 amendment of § 2035. Insurance should be treated differently under § 2035 according to the identity of the insured. The transfer of insurance on the transferor's life, which could reduce the size of the transferor's estate by an amount much larger than the value of the insurance at the time of transfer, should be subject to a more stringent rule. The transfer of insurance on the life of another person does not pose the same risk and should, therefore, be subject to the same rules that apply to the transfer of other types of property.

§ 6.38. PREMIUMS PAID WITHIN THREE YEARS OF DEATH; PRE-1982 LAW, § 2035

Prior to amendment in 1976, § 2035 required the inclusion of premiums paid within three years of death and in contemplation of death. "[T]he value of any premiums paid by the decedent in contemplation of death within three years of death [on policies transferred more than three years prior to death] is includible in his gross estate under section 2035 of the Code." Rev. Rul. 71-497, 1971-2 C.B. 329. This rule required inclusion whether or not the premium payments were within the annual gift tax exclusion. The 1976 Act amended § 2035 to require inclusion of all transfers made within three years of death with the exception of gifts which were not required to be reported on a gift tax return (*i.e.*, gifts within the annual gift tax exclusion). Former § 2035(b). If the exception were applicable to life insurance, it might allow the exclusion of large amounts of life insurance so long as the value of the transfers was within the amount of the gift tax exclusion. Because of that concern, the 1978 Act amended the exclusion to make it inapplicable retroactively to transfers "with respect to life insurance."

Under the general rule of former § 2035(d)(1), mere premium payments made within three years of the donor's death were generally not includible in the donor's estate. That outcome reflects the general rule applicable to gifts and is simpler to understand and administer. Of course, inclusion would result if the premium payments were otherwise includible under §§ 2036, 2037, 2038, or 2042. *See* former § 2035(d)(2). *See also* § 6.32.

§ 6.39. TRANSFER OF INCIDENTS OF OWNERSHIP WITHIN THREE YEARS OF DEATH, § 2035

Section 2042(2) requires inclusion of the proceeds of policies over which the insured "possessed at his death any of the incidents of ownership." Inclusion is probably required under § 2035 if, within three years of death, the insured transferred an incident of ownership the retention of which would have required inclusion under § 2042. Section § 2035(a)(2) requires the inclusion of property transferred within three years of death if "the value of such property (or an interest therein) would have been included in the decedent's gross estate under section 2036, 2037, 2038, or 2042 if such transferred interest or relinquished power had been retained by the decedent on the date of his death."

If a policy that is owned by a trust over which the insured holds powers that constitute incidents of ownership with respect to the policy, is sold to another trust for full and adequate consideration in money or money's worth within three years preceding the insured's death, the policy will not be included in the insured's estate under § 2035 or § 2042(2). LR 9413045. Importantly, if the insured is treated as the grantor of the trust under § § 671-677, the policy will be treated as if it had been sold to the insured. Accordingly, the proceeds would be exempt from income taxation under the transfer for value rule. *See* § 6.54.3. In this connection note that in *Estate of Anders Jordhal v. Commissioner*, 65 T.C. 92 (1975), *acq.*, 1977-1 C.B. 1, the Tax Court held that the grantor's power to withdraw assets of a trust and substitute assets of equal value, one of the traditional ways of causing a trust to be treated as a grantor trust, was not an incident of ownership for purposes of § 2042(2). The position taken in *Jordhal* with respect to § 2042(2) has been followed in some private letter rulings. LRs 9843024, 9413045. In *Jordhal*, the court also held that the deceased grantor's power to withdraw the assets of a trust in exchange for assets of equal value was not a power to "alter, amend, or revoke" that would require inclusion under § 2038. *See* § 10.32.

Revenue Ruling 90-21, 1990-1 C.B. 172, holds that the insured's estate includes the proceeds of a policy transferred to an individual beneficiary within three years of insured's death by corporation controlled by the insured. The same result was reached in LR 9127007 (TAM). The TAM concluded that the insured's estate must include the proceeds of a life insurance policy that was transferred, within three years preceding the insured's death, by a corporation in which the insured was a 50 percent shareholder to an irrevocable trust established by the insured. The shares attributed to the insured were actually owned by a revocable trust that he had previously created. The policy was transferred in connection with the termination of a buy-sell agreement, which gave each shareholder the right to purchase at its cash surrender value the policy owned by the corporation that insured his or her life. According to the IRS "the decedent either exercised his right to purchase the policy from the corporation for its cash surrender value or received the policy as a distribution from the corporation with respect to his stock (*i.e.*, as either a dividend or as a return of capital under § 301 of the Code)." Regulation § 20.2042-1(c)(6) was inapplicable because the insured was not a controlling shareholder. *See also* § 6.28, which discusses incidents of ownership that are held by reason of extraneous contracts, such as the buy-sell agreement involved in LR 9127007 (TAM).

EXAMPLE 6-11.

In 2006, *T*, a widow, transferred a $100,000 whole life policy to the independent trustee of an irrevocable life insurance trust of which *T*'s children were the beneficiaries. *T* retained the power to veto any disposition of the policy. In 2007, *T* irrevocably released the veto power. *T* dies in 2009. Although *T* transferred ownership of the life insurance more than 3 years prior to death, she retained an incident of ownership over the policy which was sufficient to cause the insurance to be included in her estate under § 2042(2). Presumably the insurance would also be includible in *T*'s estate under § 2035(a)(2). One critical question would be whether such a release constituted a "transfer of an interest in property." As indicated below, the regulations and a Technical Advice Memorandum take that position.

First, regulations issued prior to the adoption of the 1981 Act state that the proceeds are includible under § 2035 if the insured transferred incidents of ownership over the policy in contemplation of death. Reg. § 20.2042-1(a)(2). The position taken by the regulation is sound and consistent with § 2035(a)(2) and other Code provisions, such as § 2038(a)(1). Second, LR 8806004 (TAM) states, "In order for [former] § 2035(d)(2) to apply the decedent must have possessed some incident of ownership in the life insurance policy at some time during the three year period before death and must have transferred this incident of ownership during the same period." As indicated by Rev. Rul. 90-21, 1990-1 C.B. 172, the rule extends to incidents of ownership that are attributed to the insured as the controlling shareholder. Indeed, Rev. Rul. 90-21 applied this rule to a situation in which the insured transferred the controlling interest in a corporation for less than full consideration within three years of death.

§ 6.40 RETAINED LIFE INTEREST, § 2036

Insurance may be included in the gross estate of a person other than the insured who directly or indirectly transfers a policy in which the transferor retains a life interest. The insurance proceeds are includible, for example, when a noninsured owner transfers a policy to the trustee of a trust in which he or she has a life interest and the insured predeceases the transferor. Inclusion also results where the insurer holds the proceeds of a policy pursuant to an election made by the beneficiary to receive the income for life and to pay the principal to others following the beneficiary's death. *Pyle v. Commissioner*, 313 F.2d 328 (3d Cir. 1963). However, the insurance proceeds are not included in the beneficiary's estate where such a settlement option was chosen by the insured and not the beneficiary. *Estate of Idamay Swift Minotto*, 9 T.C.M. 556 (1950).

EXAMPLE 6-12.

H's life was insured under 2 policies that he owned. Under Policy One the proceeds were payable outright to his wife, *W*, upon his death or according to a settlement option selected by her. After *H* died *W* elected an option under which she received the interest for life, remainder to their children. The proceeds of Policy Two were subject to the same option, which had been irrevocably selected by *H*. The proceeds of Policy One are includible in *W*'s gross estate, but not the proceeds of Policy Two. In effect, *W* transferred the proceeds of Policy One to the insurer, but she did not transfer the proceeds of Policy Two.

Two decisions have allowed insurance proceeds to be excluded from the estate of a person other than the insured who paid premiums on policies in which he or she held substantial interests. In the first, *Goodnow v. United States*, 302 F.2d 516 (Ct. Cl. 1962), the insured's wife paid premiums on policies that the insured had transferred to a revocable trust in which the wife had a life interest. The insured predeceased his wife and the proceeds of the policies were paid to the trustee. Following the wife's death the Court of Claims upheld exclusion of the proceeds from her estate. In the court's view she did not retain an interest in the same property that she transferred to the trust (*i.e.*, the premiums). Although the analysis is shallow, it was followed in *National City Bank of Cleveland v. United States*, 371 F.2d 13 (6th Cir. 1966). The insured had selected an option that called for the payment of interest to his wife for life, remainder to his children, and the insured's wife had the power during the lifetime of the insured to change the beneficiary designation and to exercise other incidents of ownership. The wife had paid most of the premiums but, the court said, "payment of [the] premiums by her did not make the insurance policies taxable as a transfer with a retained life income under §2036(a)(1)." 371 F.2d at 16.

The rationale of *Goodnow* and *City Bank of Cleveland* cannot reasonably be extended to the payment of premiums on policies held by an *irrevocable* trust in which the premium payor has a life interest. In such a case payment of the premiums is clearly a transfer with a retained life interest. Accordingly, in such cases where the insured predeceases the premium payor, the proceeds are properly includible in the gross estate of the premium payor.

Community Property. In community property states, a portion of the insurance is includible in the gross estate of the noninsured spouse when a community property policy is transferred to the trustee of an inter vivos trust in which the noninsured spouse holds a life income interest. *United States v. Gordon*, 406 F.2d 332 (5th Cir. 1969) (Texas law). In *Gordon* the court recognized that the noninsured spouse, who survived the insured, was a grantor of the trust to the extent of her community interest in the policy. Importantly, however, the court allowed her estate a consideration offset under §2043(a) that reduced the amount includible in her estate by the actuarial value of the life estate she received in the share of the insurance proceeds that the husband transferred to the trust. The court reasoned that a consideration offset was allowable here on the same theory that it is allowed in the more traditional widow's election cases—the surviving spouse exchanged a remainder interest in her share of the proceeds for a life income interest in the insured's share. *See* §9.34.

A special problem arises under the community property laws of some states. In Idaho and Louisiana the income from a spouse's separate property is characterized as community property; in Texas income from separate property is the spouses' community property unless they agree otherwise. *See* §3.29. In these states, if one spouse transfers a community property interest in a marital asset to the other spouse as the donee's separate property, the income subsequently generated by that asset is community property. The IRS had argued that the transfer of a community property interest to one's spouse under such circumstances was a transfer with a retained life estate under §2036(a)(1) because the income is still treated as community property. The Tax Court accepted this argument in several cases. *Estate of Charles J. Wyly*, 69 T.C. 227 (1977); *Estate of Winston Castleberry*, 68 T.C. 682 (1977); *Estate of Ray McKee*, 37 T.C.M. 486 (1978). It was rejected by the Fifth Circuit, which reversed both *Wyly* and *Castleberry*. The court held that §2036 does not require inclusion in such cases. *Estate of Wyly v. Commissioner*, 610 F.2d 1282 (1980). The IRS subsequently conceded the issue insofar as Texas is concerned. Rev. Rul. 81-221, 1981-2 C.B. 178.

The Fifth Circuit's reversal of *Wyly* and *Castleberry* was predicated upon two views. First, under Texas community property law, the donor's interest was not sufficient to be characterized as a "right" within the meaning of §2036(a)(1). Second, the donor's interest in the transferred property was brought about solely by operation of the Texas community property law and, thus, was not a "retention" within the meaning of §2036. The *Wyly* decision did not involve policies of life insurance, but the rationale is the same. In fact, the IRS raised, then abandoned, the application of the theory to life insurance in the *McKee* case, preferring instead to pursue an incidents of ownership argument under §2042(2). The problem for residents of Texas was also relieved by the 1980 amendment of Article XVI, Section 15 of the state constitution. 3 Tex. Const. Ann. (2011).

§6.41. State Death Taxes

Consideration must be given to the provisions of state income and death taxes in planning the disposition of life insurance. For example, state death tax laws may provide that life insurance proceeds receivable by the insured's personal representative are subject to the tax, as they are for federal purposes under §2042(1). Proceeds paid to other beneficiaries may also be subject to tax as they are under federal law or they may be partly or totally exempt. Some states that allow an exemption expressly extend it to proceeds that are paid to the trustee of an inter vivos or testamentary trust except to the extent the proceeds are used for the benefit of the estate.

In some cases a state death tax saving may result from the careful selection and designation of the insurance beneficiary. A special opportunity exists, for example, in states that allow an exemption for insurance paid to a named beneficiary and calculate the tax according to the relationship of the decedent to the transferee of property. In those states insurance proceeds should be made payable to the person who would be subject to the highest inheritance tax rates upon the client's death. Thus, insurance proceeds should be made payable to more remotely related persons and assets that are subject to the tax should be bequeathed to closer relatives.

EXAMPLE 6-13.

Client wishes to leave $50,000 to his cousin, C, and the residue of his estate to his wife and children. In states that impose an inheritance tax and allow an insurance exemption, the overall state death tax will be lower if $50,000 is paid to C as insurance proceeds rather than as a testamentary gift.

§6.42. GENERATION-SKIPPING TRANSFER TAX (GSTT)

Life insurance is generally subject to the same GSTT rules as is any other type of property. The rules apply to "arrangements involving life estates and remainders, estates for years, and insurance and annuity contracts." §2652(b)(3). Thus, the GSTT extends to the payment of life insurance proceeds to grandchildren of the insured or to other skip persons. *See* §§2612 and 2613.

EXAMPLE 6-14.

The insurance proceeds payable by reason of X's death were retained by the insurer under an option that called for the payment of interest only to the insured's nephew, N, for life and the payment of the principal sum to N's children upon N's death. The GSTT will apply when N dies.

The application of the GSTT to life insurance and annuity contracts requires that care be exercised in selecting a settlement option and the creation of trusts. The amount of GSTT may be reduced significantly or eliminated entirely by utilizing a properly created irrevocable life insurance trust. The following example illustrates the benefits of a trust that meets the requirements of §2642(c)(2).

EXAMPLE 6-15.

In January 2006, T established an irrevocable trust in which his 2 grandsons (X and Y) held completely separate interests. Under §2654(b), "substantially separate and independent shares of different beneficiaries in a trust shall be treated as separate trusts." During the lifetime of a beneficiary no distribution from a beneficiary's separate share could be made to any other person and each beneficiary held a general power of appointment over his separate share of the trust. *See* §2642(c)(2). T transferred $20,000 to the independent trustee of the trust for investment in accordance with the trustee's best judgment. Not surprisingly, the trustee purchased a $500,000 policy of insurance on T's life and paid the premium of $19,000 per year. In later years, T made similar transfers to the trust that were used to pay premiums. The withdrawal powers held by X and Y were sufficient to support the allowance of annual gift tax exclusions with respect to the gifts that T made to the trust. The gifts made by T to the trust qualified as nontaxable gifts as a result of which the inclusion ratio of each separate trust is zero (*See* §2642(c)). Following T's death in 2009, the insurance proceeds of $500,000 were received by the trustee and distributed to X and Y as directed by the trust. The insurance proceeds were neither included in T's gross estate nor subject to the GSTT.

§6.42.1. GSTT Inapplicable to Some Nontaxable Gifts

Under the original version of §2642(c)(2), transfers made to a trust that were direct skips and nontaxable by reason of the annual gift tax exclusion were exempt from the GSTT. Thus, gifts to irrevocable life insurance trusts under which the skip-person beneficiaries were given appropriate powers of withdrawal escaped both the gift tax and the GSTT. Section 2642(c) was amended effective with respect to transfers made after March 31, 1988 to limit the exclusion for transfers in trust.

Under §2642(c)(2), the exemption for nontaxable transfers made in trust is only available if:

(A) During the life of such individual, no portion of the corpus or income of the trust may be distributed to (or for the benefit of) any person other than such individual, and

(B) If such individual dies before the trust is terminated, the assets of such trust will be includible in the gross estate of such individual.

The change severely limits the utility of this exception to the GSTT for traditional forms of irrevocable life insurance trusts. However, an ILIT may be created that meets the requirements of §2642(c)(2). For example, a separate share of the trust can be set aside for each beneficiary from the inception of the trust. Under §2654(b), separate shares with different beneficiaries are treated as separate trusts. No other person would have any right to the corpus or income of that share during the beneficiary's lifetime. Upon the beneficiary's death the share would be subject to a testamentary power of appointment sufficient to require inclusion in the beneficiary's gross estate.

If transfers made to ILITs do not meet the requirements of §2642(c)(2), the grantor should consider using a portion of his or her GSTT exemption to maintain the complete exemption of the trust.

§6.42.2. GSTT Exemption

In large estates consideration should be given to applying the client's GSTT exemption against transfers to life insurance trusts of which only skip-persons are beneficiaries. The exemption is most productively applied against trusts that do not permit distributions to nonskip persons. Otherwise, part of the exemption is wasted.

Application of the exception to life insurance trusts provides significant leverage; the exemption can often be used to shelter proceeds of several million.

D. GIFT TAXATION OF LIFE INSURANCE

§6.43. GENERAL

A gift of an interest in life insurance is generally subject to the same gift tax rules as a gift of any other type of property. In particular, a gift may occur when a policy is assigned, when a premium is paid, or when the policy proceeds are settled. Reg. §§25.2511-1(h)(8), 25.2511-1(h)(9). The valuation of interests in life insurance is governed by special rules in the regulations, which have been upheld in litigation. Reg. § 25.2512-6(a). No gift occurs when the policy owner revocably designates a beneficiary. Rev. Rul. 81-166, 1981-1 C.B. 477. Under § 2702, the value of a term interest retained by the donor is usually zero for gift tax purposes unless it is a qualified interest.

An annual gift tax exclusion is generally available for an outright transfer of life insurance or the payment of a premium on a policy owned by another person, but an exclusion is generally not available when insurance is transferred to an irrevocable trust unless the beneficiary has a power of withdrawal sufficient to support the exclusion. Reg. § 25.2503-3(c), Examples 2, 6.

An outright assignment of a policy may qualify for the gift tax charitable deduction, § 2522, or marital deduction, § 2523. Similarly, the payment of a premium on a policy owned by a charity or the payor's spouse qualifies for a gift tax charitable or marital deduction. The IRS may deny a charitable deduction unless the charitable donee has an insurable interest in the life of the donor. *See* § 6.2.

§ 6.44. VALUATION OF POLICIES

For gift tax purposes the value of a life insurance policy is established by the cost of the particular policy or of comparable policies on the date of the transfer. Reg. § 25.2512-6(a). The cost of a comparable new policy better reflects value than a policy's cash surrender value. *Guggenheim v. Rasquin,* 312 U.S. 254 (1941). As explained below, the values of term insurance or a cash value policy that has been in effect for some time are determined in other ways. For purposes of § § 79, 83 and 402, the fair market value of a life insurance policy is determined as provided in Rev. Proc. 2005-25, 2005-1 C.B. 962.

EXAMPLE 6-16.

X paid $85,000 for a single-premium life insurance policy with a face amount of $250,000 and immediately assigned it to his daughter, *D*. The policy had a cash surrender value of $77,000 at the time of issue and transfer. For gift tax purposes *H* made a gift to *D* of property worth $85,000.

§ 6.44.1. Term and Group-Term Insurance

The valuation of term and group-term insurance presents a different problem. In the ordinary case the value of term insurance depends primarily upon the amount of the premium and the length of time for which the premium has been paid in advance. Of course, if the insured is terminally ill the value of renewable term insurance will approach the amount of insurance coverage.

EXAMPLE 6-17.

On January 1, X paid the annual premium of $1,000 on a $150,000 term policy on his life. X assigned the policy to Y on June 30. For gift tax purposes the term policy will probably be considered to have a value of $500, which represents the portion of the premium that is attributable to the unexpired insurance coverage. If X were terminally ill, the insurance would have a much larger value.

In the case of employer-provided group-term insurance, the value of the gift may be determined according to the Table I cost of the insurance, Reg. §1.79-3(d)(2), which is used for income tax purposes. *See* Rev. Rul. 84-147, 1984-2 C.B. 201. Revenue Ruling 84-147 holds the employer's payment of a premium on employer-provided term insurance that had been assigned to a trust is determined under Table I if the plan is nondiscriminatory or the employee is not a key employee. It continues to say that, "If the employee chooses not to use Table I for this purpose, or if the plan is discriminatory and the employee is a key employee, the employee should use the actual cost allocable to the employee's insurance by obtaining the necessary information from the employer." *Cf.* Rev. Rul. 76-490, 1976-2 C.B. 300. *See* §6.73.12.

The use of Table I is a practical solution to the problem of valuing group-term insurance when it is not possible to identify the actual premium cost attributable to the particular insurance that was assigned. However, if it is possible to identify the actual cost of the insurance, a smaller gift may occur by basing the valuation on it.

§6.44.2. Single-Premium and Paid-Up Policies

A single-premium policy or a paid-up policy that has been in effect for some time has a value equal to the current cost of a policy of the same amount on the life of a person the age of the insured. Reg. §25.2512-6(a), Example 3.

§6.44.3. Other Policies—Interpolated Terminal Reserve

The value of a policy that has been in effect for some time and on which further premium payments are to be made generally cannot be determined through the cost of comparable contracts. In such cases, the regulations provide that the value is determined by adding the interpolated terminal reserve on the date of the gift and the portion of the premium last paid that covers the period following the date of the gift. Reg. §25.2512-6(a). The application of that rule is illustrated by example 4 of that regulation:

A gift is made four months after the last premium due date of an ordinary life insurance policy issued nine years and four months prior to the gift thereof by the insured, who was 35 years of age at the date of issue. The gross annual premium is $2,811. The computation follows:

Terminal reserve at end of tenth year	$14,601.00
Terminal reserve at end of ninth year	−12,965.00
Increase	$1,636.00

One-third of such increase (the gift having been made four months following the last receding premium due date) is	$545.33
Terminal reserve at end of ninth year	+12,965.00
Interpolated terminal reserve at date of gift	$13,510.33
Two thirds of gross premium ($2,811)	+1,874.00
Value of gift	$15,384.33

§ 6.44.4. Policy Subject to a Loan

The value of a policy is reduced by the amount of any loan outstanding against the policy, including accrued interest. Accordingly, a loan may be taken out against policies in advance of a gift in order to reduce the value of the gift to an amount within the allowable annual exclusions. In this connection note that the transfer of an encumbered policy is treated as a transfer for consideration. However, in some circumstances the income tax exclusion remains available. *See* § 6.54.

§ 6.44.5. Physical Condition of Insured

For purposes of valuation, "all relevant facts and elements of value as of the time of the gift shall be considered." Reg. § 25.2512-1. In some cases this may require the physical condition and insurability of the insured to be taken into account. *See United States v. Ryerson*, 312 U.S. 260, 262 (1941), *Estate of James Stuart Pritchard*, 4 T.C. 204 (1944) (an estate tax case discussed at § 6.35).

§ 6.44.6. Form 712, Life Insurance Statement

The insurer should be asked to provide a completed copy of Form 712 for each policy that is transferred. A completed Form 712 contains detailed financial data regarding the policy that is used to value it for gift and estate tax purposes, including the interpolated terminal reserve value. The instructions for preparation of gift tax returns require that a Form 712 be attached to the gift tax return for each policy that is transferred.

§ 6.45. ANNUAL EXCLUSION

The complete, irrevocable assignment of a life insurance policy to a single donee qualifies for the annual exclusion because it gives the donee all of the interests in the policy. An exclusion is available though the principal performance under the contract, payment of the face amount of insurance, will take place at a future time (if at all). Reg. § 25.2503-3(a). As indicated by Example 6 of that regulation, the payment of a premium on a policy owned outright by another person also qualifies as a gift of a present interest. The GSTT exclusion for nontaxable transfers applies to transfers in trust that qualify for the annual exclusion and satisfy the additional criteria of § 2642(c)(2). *See* § 6.45.3.

§6.45.1. Multiple Donees

The transfer of a policy to multiple donees should qualify for the annual exclusion unless the donor has manifested an intent that the donees must act together in order to deal with the policy. *Skouras v. Commissioner*, 188 F.2d 831 (2d Cir. 1951) (no annual exclusions allowed where multiple donees must act together). Logically, an exclusion should be available if each donee has the right to transfer or otherwise deal with his or her interest in the policy independent of the other owners.

The multiple donee rule may prevent a transfer in trust from qualifying for the annual exclusion. When the policy is transferred to a trust, an annual exclusion is not available if the beneficiaries of the trust must act together in order to obtain the present use or benefit of the insurance or other assets that are transferred to the trust. *Ryerson v. United States*, 312 U.S. 405 (1941).

§6.45.2. Transfer to Trusts

The general rules regarding the availability of an annual exclusion for interests in trusts apply in the case of insurance trusts. An annual exclusion is only available if the donee receives a present interest under the trust because the beneficiaries of a trust are the donees of property transferred to a trust. *Helvering v. Hutchings*, 312 U.S. 393 (1941). In order to qualify as a present interest the beneficiary must have the unrestricted right to the use, possession, or enjoyment of the trust property or its income. Reg. §25.2503-3(b). As indicated in Reg. §25.2503-3(c), Example 2, an annual exclusion is not available if the benefits under the trust are payable only upon the death of the insured.

Although the beneficiary is given an immediate income interest in a trust, an annual exclusion is generally not available when the trust holds only life insurance policies which produce no income or where all of the income must be used to pay premiums. Rev. Rul. 69-344, 1969-1 C.B. 225; *Jesse S. Phillips*, 12 T.C. 216 (1949). However, an annual exclusion is available if the beneficiary may withdraw the principal of the trust at any time. *Harbeck Halsted*, 28 T.C. 1069 (1957), *acq.*, 1958-2 C.B. 5. An annual exclusion is also available to the extent the beneficiary holds a power of withdrawal that allows the beneficiary acting alone to withdraw property that is added to the trust within a limited period following its transfer to the trustee. *See* §§7.38-7.38.12. *E.g.*, LRs 8021058; 7935091. Note that the annual exclusion is limited to the lesser of (1) the amount that can be withdrawn under a *Crummey* power or (2) the amount of the annual exclusion allowed by §2503. Recognizing the possibility that the amount of the gift tax exclusion may be changed at some future time, the *Crummey* power may limit the amount that can be withdrawn by the beneficiary to "the lesser of (1) the value of the property transferred to the trust and (2) the amount allowable as an exclusion under IRC §2503(b) or its successor." Note that the lapse of a power to withdraw an amount that exceeds the greater of $5,000 or 5 percent of the principal value of the trust may result in the power-holder having made a taxable gift. §2514(e). Accordingly, some trusts limit the amount that can be withdrawn by the beneficiary to the "5 or 5" amount. The imposition of such a limitation bars the allowance of any annual exclusions in excess of that amount. The use of a "hanging power" may meet the needs of the donors and the power-holder by allowing withdrawal of the full amount transferred to the trust but limiting the annual lapse to the greater of $5,000 or 5 percent of the value of the trust. The use of hanging powers is discussed in more detail at §§7.38.4, 10.24.2.

The gift of a policy to a minor under the Uniform Acts, or to a §2503(c) minor's trust that authorizes the distribution of principal qualifies for an annual exclusion. Prior to recommending the transfer of life insurance to a custodian, the planner should review the local legislation to be sure that such a transfer is authorized.

§6.45.3. GSTT

Direct skips that are nontaxable gifts by reason of the annual exclusion, §2503(b), or the exclusion for the direct payment of tuition or medical expenses, §2503(e), have inclusion ratios of zero. In effect, they are exempt from the GSTT. However, §2642(c)(2) requires that transfers in trust also satisfy two other requirements. First, during the lifetime of the beneficiary none of the trust property can be distributed to anyone other than the beneficiary. Second, if the beneficiary dies prior to termination of the trust, the trust must be includible in the beneficiary's estate. As indicated in §6.42.1, trusts can be structured to qualify for this exclusion.

§6.46. TRANSFER OF A POLICY

An irrevocable assignment is generally used to transfer interests in an existing policy from the present owner to the intended donee. Insurers will generally provide assignment forms upon request; however, the forms should be examined carefully to ensure that they comply with the policy's terms and will effectively transfer all incidents of ownership in it. If an insured-owner retains any interest in the insurance, an assignment may be incomplete *and* the policy proceeds may be includible in the insured's gross estate under §2042(2). If any part of the policy is, or may be, community property, both spouses should join in the assignment. Otherwise, in some community property states the nonconsenting spouse has the power to invalidate the gift—at least in part.

§6.46.1. Irrevocable Beneficiary Designation

The irrevocable designation of a beneficiary is sometimes used instead of an assignment, but it is less satisfactory because its effects are less certain. The economic interests of an irrevocably designated beneficiary are entitled to protection against unilateral action by the designated owner of the policy in most cases. However, the extent to which such a beneficiary may exercise control over the policy is not well defined in most states. "The law of West Virginia and other jurisdictions with regard to the right of irrevocably designated beneficiaries to exercise options of a life insurance policy without the consent of the insured is unclear at best." *Morton v. United States*, 457 F.2d 750, 754 (4th Cir. 1972). The IRS may assert that an insured who is named as owner of a policy has an incident of ownership although another person is irrevocably designated as the beneficiary.

§6.46.2. Charitable and Marital Deductions; Charitable Split-Dollar

A gift tax charitable or marital deduction is available if all the interests in a policy are transferred outright to a qualified donee with an insurable interest in the donor's life. No charitable deduction is available, however, where a charity is given a split interest in a policy unless the requirements of §2522(c)(2) are met. For example, no deduction is allowed where the charity is given the cash surrender value of a policy and the donor retains the right to designate the recipient of the difference between the face amount of the policy and the cash surrender value. Rev. Rul. 76-200, 1976-1 C.B. 308.

Note also, §170(f)(10) denies charitable deductions for transfers made to a charitable organization in connection with so-called "charitable split-dollar life insurance" and subjects the charity to a special excise tax on premiums it pays on such life insurance. *See* Notice 200-24, 2000-1 C.B. 952.

A marital deduction is generally not available for a policy transferred in trust unless the donee spouse has the requisite life income interest plus the right to compel the trustee to convert the policy into income-producing property. §2523(e)-(f); Reg. §25.2523(e)-1(f)(4). Of course, a marital deduction under §2523(e) is available only if the donee spouse also has a general power of appointment. However, a deduction is available under §2523(f) on an elective basis as QTIP where the donee receives a qualifying income interest for life. No gift tax marital deduction is allowed for a transfer to a spouse who is not a United States citizen.

§6.47. PAYMENT OF PREMIUMS

The payment of a premium on a policy in which the premium payor has no interest constitutes a gift to the policy owner of an amount equal to the payment. Reg. §25.2503-3(c), Example 6. There is a gift of that amount although benefits are payable under the policy only upon the death of the donor and the donee must survive the donor in order to receive the proceeds of the policy. Reg. §25.2511-1(h)(8). The value of the gift is the amount of the premium payment, not the resulting increase in the cash surrender value of the policy. There may be no gift, however, if the insured retains an interest in the policy or some control over it. The identity of the premium payor is largely irrelevant—the payment of a premium by a person other than the policy owner generally involves a gift.

EXAMPLE 6-18.

The life of *X* is insured under a policy owned by his daughter, *D*. This year the annual premium of $5,000 was paid by *D's* brother, *B*. By paying the premium *B* made a gift of $5,000 to *D*. The gift qualifies for the annual gift tax exclusion.

No gift is involved, however, where a premium is paid in order to protect the interests of the premium payor. Thus, there is no gift where the principal beneficiary of an insurance trust pays the premiums on policies held by the trustee in order to prevent lapse or diminution in the amount of insurance coverage. *Grace B. Seligmann*, 9 T.C. 191 (1947).

The use of community property funds to pay premiums on a policy owned by one or both spouses as separate property ordinarily does not involve a gift. Under the apportionment rule, which is applied to cash value policies in California and Washington, the use of community property funds establishes a community property ownership interest in the policy in the absence of a contrary agreement. *See* § 6.16.2. This is undesirable when the objective is to exclude all of the insurance from the estate of the insured. In the inception-of-title states—Arizona, Louisiana, New Mexico, and Texas—there is no gift because the community is entitled to reimbursement for premiums on separately owned policies that were paid with community funds. *See* § 6.16.1.

EXAMPLE 6-19.

W purchased a $250,000 ordinary life insurance policy on her life when she married *H* several years ago. *W* paid the initial $2,000 premium from her premarital earnings. *W*'s mother, *M*, is the revocably designated beneficiary of the insurance. Each year since their marriage, *H* has paid the annual premium of $2,000 from his earnings. If *H* and *W* live in a noncommunity state, *H*'s payment of the annual premiums involved gifts that qualified for the gift tax exclusion. The gifts would, of course, qualify for the marital deduction, unless *W* is not a United States citizen. If *H* and *W* live in a community property state, *H*'s payment of the premiums would be treated as gifts if adequately documented. Otherwise, the payment of the premiums would not necessarily involve a gift. In the apportionment states, the premium payments made from *H*'s earnings, which were community property, could give rise to a community property interest in the insurance. In the inception-of-title states, the policy would be *W*'s separate property but the community could have an equitable claim to recover the amount of the premium payments that were made from *H*'s earnings.

A marital deduction may be allowed for the payment of premiums on a policy held in trust for the benefit of the premium payor's spouse if the trust otherwise meets the requirements of § 2523. However, no deduction is available unless the donee has the right to compel the trustee to convert the policy into income-producing property. *Estate of Charles C. Smith*, 23 T.C. 367 (1954); Reg. § 25.2523(e)-1(f)(4).

§ 6.48. PAYMENT OF PROCEEDS

When a policy is owned by a person other than the insured, a gift occurs if the proceeds are paid to a third person.

EXAMPLE 6-20.

X owned a $100,000 policy on the life of *Y* that designated *X*'s daughter, *D*, as beneficiary. Upon *Y*'s death the $100,000 policy proceeds were paid to *D*. The payment of the proceeds constituted a gift of $100,000 from *X* to *D*. The gift qualifies for the annual exclusion. The mere revocable designation of *D* as beneficiary did not involve a gift. The gift only took place when the insured died and *D*'s right to receive the proceeds became irrevocable.

The owner of a policy likewise makes a gift where the proceeds are paid to a trust for the benefit of other persons. *Goodman v. Commissioner*, 156 F.2d 218 (2d Cir. 1946); Rev. Rul. 81-166, 1981-1 C.B. 477. In that case the availability of the annual exclusion depends on the terms of the trust.

A gift may also take place when the proceeds of a community property life insurance policy are paid to a person other than the surviving spouse. This rule is stated in Reg. § 25.2511-1(h)(9):

Where property held by a husband and wife as community property is used to purchase insurance upon the husband's life and a third person is revocably designated as beneficiary and under the State law the husband's death is considered to make absolute the transfer by the wife, there is a gift by the wife at the time of the husband's death of half the amount of the proceeds of such insurance.

The regulation was applied in *Cox v. United States*, 286 F. Supp. 761 (W.D. La. 1968), which held that the surviving spouse made a gift of one-half of the proceeds of community property life insurance policies to third-party beneficiaries. The result is consistent with the item theory of community property, which recognizes that each spouse owns an undivided one-half interest in each community asset. However, the item theory approach was not applied in the later case of *Kaufman v. United States*, 462 F.2d 439 (5th Cir. 1972), where the surviving spouse received $175,000 in proceeds from community property policies on her husband's life and their daughter received $72,000 in proceeds from other community property policies. The government contended that the surviving spouse made a gift of $36,000 to the daughter by permitting the entire proceeds of $72,000 of community property policies to be paid to the daughter. The court rejected that argument and instead appeared to apply an aggregate theory of community property "since the wife received more than her share of the total community insurance proceeds, no gift can be constructively presumed." 462 F.2d at 441.

The risk that the payment of part of the proceeds of community property policies to a person other than the surviving spouse may involve a gift by the survivor is eliminated if the survivor receives at least half of the proceeds of each policy. The other portion of the proceeds is treated as a transfer by the decedent that does not involve a gift by the survivor.

EXAMPLE 6-21.

H's life was insured under two $100,000 community property policies. One of the policies designated *H*'s wife, *W*, as beneficiary and the other designated his daughter, *D*, as beneficiary. Upon *H*'s death, $100,000 in proceeds was paid to *W* and $100,000 to *D*. Under the item theory applied in *Cox* the surviving spouse made a gift of $50,000 by permitting the full amount of the proceeds of the second policy to be paid to *D*. No gift would be involved, however, under the rationale of *Kaufman*. No gift would occur under either theory if the proceeds of each policy had been paid one-half to *W* and one-half to *D*. Similarly no gift would have occurred if there had been only one $200,000 policy of which half of the proceeds would have been paid to *D* (*H*'s half) and half to *W* (*W*'s half).

The *Cox* approach is more consistent with the prevalent item theory of community property law, but the *Kaufman* approach is preferable because it is more equitable and treats similarly situated taxpayers in the same way.

E. INCOME TAXATION OF LIFE INSURANCE

§ 6.49. INTRODUCTION

Transactions involving life insurance often have important federal income tax consequences. This part discusses the income tax aspects of transactions involving life insurance, including the payment of policy proceeds, the payment of premiums, and the sale, surrender, or exchange of policies. The income tax aspects of split-dollar and group-term plans and certain other specialized arrangements are reviewed in Part F of this chapter.

§ 6.50. LIFE INSURANCE DEFINED, § 7702

In 1984, Congress adopted § 7702, which specifies the criteria which must be satisfied by contracts issued after 1984 in order to be treated as life insurance for purposes of the Code. In brief, § 7702 requires that policies issued after 1984 both qualify as life insurance under local law and meet one of two other tests: the "cash value accumulation test" or a combination test consisting of the "guideline premium" and "cash value corridor" tests.

Under the cash value accumulation test, the cash surrender value of the policy cannot at any time exceed the net single premium that would have been required to be paid in order to fund future benefits under the contract. § 7702(b)(1). For the purposes of this test the calculations are made on the basis of: (1) interest at the greater of 4 percent or the rate guaranteed in the contract, § 7702(b)(2)(A); (2) reasonable mortality charges and reasonable charges with respect to any qualified additional benefits, § 7702(b)(2)(B); and (3) current and future death benefits and qualified additional benefits, § 7702(b)(2)(C). Because of the nature of the data required to make the calculations, it is not ordinarily possible for an estate planner to determine whether or not the test has been satisfied.

The first element of the combination test is the *guideline premium test*. It is satisfied if the sum of the premiums paid under the contract does not at any time exceed the premium limitation as of such time. § 7702(c)(1). The guideline limitation is the greater of (1) the guideline single premium (*i.e.*, the amount required to fund future benefits under the contract, taking into account relevant actuarial factors) and (2) the sum of guideline level premiums to date (the level annual amount payable over a period not ending before the insured reaches age 95), § 7702(c)(4).

The second element of the combination test is the *cash corridor test*. It is satisfied if the death benefit under the contract at any time is not less than the applicable percentage of the cash surrender value as shown in Table 6-1, *infra*. For example, in order to satisfy the cash value corridor test, the death benefit on a policy with a cash surrender value of $100,000 on the life of a person aged 44 cannot be less than $215,000 (215% × $100,000).

If a contract fails to satisfy the tests specified by § 7702, it will be treated as a combination of term insurance and a currently taxable deposit fund. Accordingly, the income on the contract would be treated as ordinary income in the year paid or accrued. § 7702(g)(1)(A). For this purpose income on the contract is the sum of the increase in the cash surrender value over the year plus the cost of insurance provided for the year over the premium paid for the year. At death the excess of the amount paid by reason of the insured's death over the net cash surrender value of the contract is excluded from gross income under § 101(a). § 7702(g)(2). Thus, the beneficiary may be taxable on the remainder, except to the extent the beneficiary made an investment in the contract.

The 1986 Act amended § 7702(f)(7) to provide that a withdrawal of funds within the first 15 policy years which involves a reduction in benefits under the policy is taxable under § 72 (other than § 72(e)(5)). Accordingly, a portion of the amount withdrawn would probably be included in the recipient's income under § 72(e)(2)(B). The amount treated as income, however, may not exceed the recapture ceilings specified in the statute. After the first 15 policy years, presumably the investment made in the contract may be withdrawn first without any income tax consequences.

Table 6-1
Cash Corridor Test of § 7702(d)(2)

In the case of an insured with an attained age as of the beginning of the contract year of:		The applicable percentage decrease by a ratable portion for each full year:	
More than:	But not more than:	From:	To:
0	40	250	250
40	45	250	215
45	50	215	185
50	55	185	150
55	60	150	130
60	65	130	120
65	70	120	115
70	75	115	105
75	90	105	105
90	95	105	100

§ 6.51. Modified Endowment Contract, § 7702A

In 1988, Congress moved to limit the tax benefits of life insurance contracts with major lifetime investment characteristics. Specifically, the 1988 Act added § 7702A which defined a class of life insurance contracts as "modified endowment contracts" that would be subject to new rules under § 72 regarding the distribution of amounts other than as annuity payments. In simplest terms, most amounts received under a modified endowment contract other than as an annuity (*e.g.*, as loans or dividends) are treated as income to the extent of the income on the contract. § 72(e)(4)(A). However, for this purpose dividends retained by the insurer as a premium or other consideration paid for the contract are not includible in income. § 72(e)(4)(B). Under § 72(e)(2)(B), the income on the contract is the amount by which the cash surrender value of the contract immediately before the distribution exceeded the investment in the contract. A 10 percent additional tax is imposed on taxable distributions from modified endowment contracts, except for ones made on or after the recipient attains age 59, made as a result of the recipient's disability, or made as a part of a series of substantially equal payments made for the life of the taxpayer or of the taxpayer and a beneficiary. § 72(v).

Under § 7702A(a), a modified endowment contract is a life insurance contract entered into after June 21, 1988 (or which is received in exchange for such a contract) that fails to meet a *7-pay test*. A contract fails the 7-pay test if the accumulated amount of premiums paid (less amounts distributed other than as an annuity and not included in the recipient's income) on the contract at any time during the first seven contract years exceeds the sum of the net level premiums which would have been paid on or before such time if the contract provided for paid-up future benefits after the payment of seven level premiums. A failure to satisfy the 7-pay test affects the taxation of distributions made in all contract years beginning with distributions made within two years preceding the failure. § 7702A(d). Also, a material change in a contract causes it to be treated as a new contract subject to the 7-pay test as of the date of the material change. § 7702A(c)(3).

§ 6.52. Payment of Proceeds, § 101(a)(1)

In general, amounts received under a life insurance contract by reason of the death of the insured are not included in the recipient's gross income. § 101(a)(1). However, part or all of the proceeds may be included where the policy was transferred for value, § 101(a)(2), or the policy was held by a qualified retirement plan and paid to a beneficiary designated by the participant, § 72(m)(3)(C). Also, the proceeds exclusion applies to the proceeds of a flexible premium policy issued before January 1, 1985 only if the premiums paid and cash value accrued meet the limitations of § 101(f)(1)(A) or if the cash value accrued does not exceed the "single premium limitation" of § 101(f)(1)(B).

Subject to the requirements of § 7702, the general exclusion of § 101(a) applies to all death benefits having the characteristics of life insurance, including endowment contracts, accident and health policies, double and triple indemnity provisions, and paid-up additions. *See* Reg. § 1.101-1(a). The entire amount of the death benefit payable on a variable life insurance policy is excludable under § 101(a) although the amount of the benefit may increase or decrease (but not below a stated minimum) in accordance with the investment experience of the separate account for the policy. Rev. Rul. 79-87, 1979-1 C.B. 73. The exclusion is available whether the payment is made to the estate of the insured or to another beneficiary. Likewise, it is available whether the payment is made directly to an individual or in trust. *Id.* Importantly, the exclusion is not dependent upon the proceeds being subject to the estate tax. Thus, the proceeds are excluded from the beneficiary's gross income whether or not they are included in the gross estate of the insured.

EXAMPLE 6-22.

W's life was insured under a policy owned by her husband, *H*, which designated their child, *C*, as beneficiary. The policy provided for the payment of an additional amount equal to the face amount of the policy if the insured dies as the result of accidental injuries. *W* died in an automobile accident and *C* was paid the face amount of the policy plus the additional benefit. Although none of the insurance was included in *W*'s gross estate, the proceeds paid to *C* are excluded from *C*'s gross income.

The general exclusion extends only to the amount payable as a death benefit at the time of the insured's death. It does not apply to interest paid because of a delay in payment of the death benefit.

The exclusion is available with respect to the proceeds of a key person policy paid to a corporation on the death of a business associate who was not an employee. *M. Lucille Harrison*, 59 T.C. 578 (1973). Similarly, the exclusion applies where the proceeds are received by a creditor who is entitled to receive them regardless of the indebtedness of the insured to the creditor. *E.g., L. C. Thomsen & Sons, Inc. v. United States*, 484 F.2d 954 (7th Cir. 1973). However, the exclusion does not apply where the proceeds are payable to a creditor only to the extent of the insured's indebtedness to the creditor. *E.g., Landfield Finance Co. v. United States*, 418 F.2d 172 (7th Cir. 1972). The proceeds are not within the exclusion to the extent they are received in satisfaction of a claim by the recipient. *Tennessee Foundry & Machine Co.*, 48 T.C. 419 (1967), *aff'd*, 399 F.2d 156 (6th Cir. 1968) (insured's widow and the administrator of his estate in settlement of a state court action against his widow and his estate assigned the right to receive the proceeds of a policy on his life to the corporation from which the insured had embezzled funds).

§6.52.1. Deferred Payment of Proceeds, §§101(c), (d)

The exclusion under §101(a)(1) does not extend to additional amounts paid because of the deferred payment of the proceeds. §101(c), (d). Instead, the additional amounts are taxed as income to the recipient. The income tax treatment of the amount paid under policy options is described in §6.53.

§6.52.2. Proceeds Paid to Shareholder-Beneficiary

Insurance proceeds paid to a shareholder-beneficiary under a corporate-owned policy on which the corporation paid the premiums from its earnings and over which the corporation held the right to designate the beneficiary are taxed as a dividend to the recipient. Rev. Rul. 61-134, 1961-2 C.B. 250. The proceeds are only taxed under that rule where the recipient is a shareholder. LR 8144001 (TAM).

§6.53. SETTLEMENT OPTIONS, §§101(c), (d)

Most policies permit the insured or the beneficiary to elect to have the proceeds paid in a lump sum or under one or more settlement options. The two principal options are the interest only option and the installment option. Under the former, the beneficiary is entitled to receive only interest on the proceeds at a guaranteed rate (which, under some policies, is augmented by "excess" interest) until the principal amount is withdrawn or paid out. The installment option usually provides for payment of a fixed amount either for a specified period (*e.g.*, $2,500 per month for ten years) or for the life of the beneficiary with a certain number of payments guaranteed.

When the proceeds are held subject to an option under which only interest is paid on a current basis, the beneficiary is taxed on the interest. §101(c). For this purpose it makes no difference whether the beneficiary has the right to withdraw the principal. This rule applies to payments made of interest earned on proceeds that are held without substantial diminution of principal during the period the interest payments were made or credited. Reg. §1.101-3(a). If the payments include a substantial amount of principal, the distributions are subject to §101(d) and not §101(c). Prior to 1987, former §101(d)(a)(B) allowed the surviving spouse of an insured to exclude up to $1,000 of the interest received in connection with the deferred payment of the proceeds. This exclusion was only available with respect to payments subject to §101(d).

When payments are made under an installment option, the principal portion of each payment is not included in the beneficiary's income. §101(d). The principal component of each payment is determined by prorating the amount held by the insurer with respect to the beneficiary over the period for which payments will be made. The amount held by the insurer is usually the amount payable as a lump sum in discharge of the insurer's obligation under the policy; however, if the policy had been transferred for valuable consideration, the total amount held by the insurer cannot exceed the amount of consideration paid, plus any premiums or other amount subsequently paid by the transferee. Reg. §1.101-4(b)(3).

EXAMPLE 6-23.

The proceeds of a $100,000 policy on the life of *W* are payable to her mother, *M*, in 10 annual installments of $12,500 each. Under the basic rule of §101(d), $10,000 of each payment is excludable from *M*'s income ($100,000 ÷ 10 = $10,000). The other $2,500 of each payment is taxable as interest.

§ 6.54. Transfer For Value, § 101(a)(2)

The proceeds of a policy that is transferred for value are generally includible in the recipient's income except to the extent of the consideration paid plus premiums and other amounts subsequently paid by the recipient. § 101(a)(2). This limitation on the availability of the general exclusion was apparently intended to discourage trafficking in life insurance policies for profit. A provision with such a broad sweep is probably not necessary to achieve the desired purpose—a questionable object of the income tax law in any event. As it is, the transfer for value rule acts as a trap for the unwary and unsophisticated.

The statute only applies where there has been a transfer for value. In this connection, note that there may be circumstances in which the transfer of a policy for consideration is not treated as a transfer for value. For example, under § 1041(b) the transfer of a policy between spouses is treated as a gift. LR 200120007 (sale by trust of which the insured is treated as the owner under Subchapter J to a trust of which the insured's spouse is treated as the owner is a gift, not a sale, and is not subject to the transfer for value rule). Under Reg. § 1.101-1(b)(4), the rule only applies where there is an enforceable right in the transferee to receive all or part of the proceeds of the policy. Thus, the rule does not apply if the insured has retained the exclusive right to designate the beneficiary. Rev. Rul. 74-76, 1974-1 C.B. 30 (shareholder-employee transferred policy to employer's profit sharing plan but retained power to designate the beneficiary). Undertaking a binding obligation to designate a beneficiary may constitute a transfer of the insurance for purposes of § 101(a)(2). A transfer for consideration may take place where the shareholders of a closely-held corporation, who own insurance on each other's lives ("cross insurance"), agree to use the proceeds to buy the stock that belonged to a deceased shareholder. *Monroe v. Patterson*, 197 F. Supp. 146 (N.D. Ala. 1961); LRs 7734048; 9045004. The *Monroe v. Patterson* problem can be avoided if the shareholders are also partners in a bona fide partnership. See § 6.54.2. In such a case, the shareholder/partners might want to insulate the policies and their proceeds from inclusion in their estates, which could be done if the policies were owned by grantor trusts created by the shareholder/partners.

§ 6.54.1. Exceptions

There are two important exceptions to the transfer for value rule. First, it does not apply when the basis of the policy for the purpose of determining gain or loss is determined in whole or in part by reference to the basis of the policy in the hands of the transferor. § 101(a)(2)(A). Second, it does not apply when the transfer was made to the insured, a partner of the insured, a partnership of which the insured is a partner, or to a corporation in which the insured is a shareholder or officer. § 101(a)(2)(B).

The question of whether the transfer of a policy subject to a loan involves a transfer for consideration is unsettled. Some commentators argue that the assignment of a policy subject to a loan is not a transfer for value because a policy loan merely allows the insurer to apply the policy proceeds first to discharge the loan and does not involve any personal liability on the part of the owner. Walker, Life Insurance from the Standpoint of the Federal Corporate and Personal Income Tax, Gift Tax and Estate Tax, U. So. Cal., 18th Tax Inst. 543, 576 (1966). On the other hand, the government apparently views the transfer of an encumbered policy as a transfer for value—perhaps based upon *Crane v. Commissioner*, 331 U.S. 1 (1947). Rev. Rul. 69-187, 1969-1 C.B. 45. In this ruling the insured transferred to his wife a policy that had a cash surrender value of $85,000 but was subject to a loan of $75,000. It concluded that the proceeds were not includible in the wife's gross income. This is unsettling because it stated that the policy had been transferred in part for consideration and in part as a gift (*i.e.*, the basis was determined in part by reference to the basis of the transferor).

§6.54.2. First Exception, §101(a)(2)(A)

The transfer for value rule does not apply to a transfer in which the basis carries over to the transferee. This shelters all transfers that have a gift element; thus, a transfer that is a part gift-part sale is within the exception. Rev. Rul. 69-187, 1969-1 C.B. 45. The exception also applies where a policy is transferred from one corporation to another in a tax-free reorganization, as a result of which the transferor's basis in the policy carries over to the transferee. Reg. §1.101-1(b)(5), Example 4. Importantly, a transfer of insurance from the insured to a former spouse incident to a divorce is treated as a gift and not a transfer for value if neither spouse is a nonresident alien. §1041.

One commentator has suggested that the transfer of a policy subject to a loan in an amount greater than the owner's basis may not fall within this exception.

> In such a case, the transferor might be taxed for income tax purposes on the difference between his adjusted basis in the policy and the amount of the outstanding policy loan at the time of transfer. In addition, the IRS might conclude that the transferee's basis is not determined at least in part by the transferor's basis. Thus, the requirements of the carryover basis exception to the transfer for value rule would not be met, causing the transfer to be treated as a sale. As a sale, the death benefit proceeds received in excess of the transferee's basis would be reportable as income to the recipient. Cox, Gift of Life Insurance Policy with an Outstanding Loan Can Result in Two Taxes, 17 Est. Plan. 298, 303 (1990).

§6.54.3. Second Exception, §101(a)(2)(B)

The second exception is particularly important in planning business transactions. Under it, the transfer for value rule does not apply when the transferee is the insured, a partner of the insured, a partnership in which the insured is a partner, or a corporation in which the insured is a shareholder or officer. §101(a)(2)(B). For example, the exemption for a transfer to a partnership of which the insured is a partner applied to policies on the lives of two partners that were transferred by a corporation to the partnership in lieu of the payment of rent due to the partnership. LRs 9012063; 9347016. In LR 9701026, the IRS ruled that the transfer of a policy to a partner of the insured in connection with the creation and funding of a new buy-sell agreement was within the exception. The IRS continues to rule favorably regarding transfers of life insurance policies to partnerships in which the insured is a partner, LRs 200017051; 9725007-9725009, or to partners of the insured, LR 9727024. In LR 200111038, the IRS ruled favorably with respect to the transfer of life insurance policies from an irrevocable trust established by the insured to a limited partnership of which the insured was a limited partner. The transfers were made for consideration; however, they were made to an entity within the exemptions. As illustrated by *W. Clarke Swanson*, 33 T.C.M. (CCH) 296 (1974), *aff'd*, 518 F.2d 59 (8th Cir. 1975), the partnership exception does not apply unless it was a bona fide partnership, the existence of which would be recognized for tax purposes.

Beware, the superficial breadth of this exception is misleading—it does not protect a wide variety of fairly common transfers, among them:

1. Shareholder *A* transfers a policy insuring *A's* life to Shareholder *B* in exchange for a similar policy on *B's* life, or for other consideration, LR 7734048;
2. An employee or director of a corporation who is not a shareholder or officer transfers a policy on his or her life to the corporation in exchange for cash or other valuable consideration; and,
3. A corporation sells a policy insuring the life of an employee to the employee's spouse for a cash payment. *Estate of Rath v. United States*, 608 F.2d 254 (6th Cir. 1979).

Note that this exception does not protect transfers for value that are made to relatives of the insured. An exception for transfers to relatives would be desirable and would not conflict with the underlying purpose of § 101(a)(2).

EXAMPLE 6-24.

Father, *F*, applied for and paid the premiums on a $100,000 policy on the life of his daughter, *D*. Subsequently *F* transferred the policy to his son, *S*, in exchange for a cash payment equal to its cash surrender value of $5,000. *S* paid an additional $5,000 in premiums prior to *D's* death. *S* will probably be taxed on $90,000 of the $100,000 in proceeds he received ($100,000=$10,000). *Alcy S. Hacker*, 36 B.T.A. 659 (1937); *Bourne Bean*, 14 T.C.M. 786 (1955).

Of course, it is possible that a transfer that is not within the second exception may nonetheless fall within the scope of the first one. Thus, if any part of the transferor's basis carries over to the transferee, as it would in the case of a partial gift, the first exception would insulate the proceeds from taxation.

Transfers to Grantor Trusts. The IRS now recognizes that a life insurance policy can be transferred for consideration to a trust owned by the grantor for federal income tax purposes without triggering the transfer for value rules. In Rev. Rul. 2007-13, 2007-1 C.B. 684, the IRS held that a grantor who is treated as the owner of a trust that owns a life insurance contract on the life of the grantor is treated as the owner of the insurance contract for purposes of the transfer for value rule of § 101(a)(2). In the ruling, the grantor creates two trusts, cleverly titled TR1 and TR2. TR2 later transfers a policy on the life of the grantor to TR1 in exchange for cash. TR1 is a grantor trust, meaning the grantor is the deemed owner of the trust's assets for income tax purposes. The IRS ruled that if TR2 is also a grantor trust, there is no transfer for value, because the grantor is the deemed owner of both trusts. Consistent with the rationale of Rev. Rul. 85-13, 1985-1 C.B. 184, the IRS concluded that a transaction between two grantor trusts is disregarded, because it is, in substance, a sale of the policy by the grantor to the grantor. The IRS also ruled that if TR2 is not a grantor trust, then the transaction will not be disregarded, but the transaction will be excepted from the transfer for value rule, because it is treated as a transfer to the grantor, the insured. The ruling is consistent with *W. Clarke Swanson*, 33 T.C.M. 296 (1974), *aff'd*, 518 F.2d 59 (8th Cir. 1975) and several private letter rulings, *e.g.*, LRs 200636086, 200228019, 200247006 and 200514001. The transfer for consideration of a second-to-die policy on the lives of spouses to a trust of which one spouse is treated as the grantor is within the exception for transfers to the insured. LR 200120007.

The ruling indirectly endorses a couple of common planning techniques. If a policy sits in a grantor trust the terms of which no longer meet the needs of the insured's family, the grantor might create a new grantor trust containing more appropriate provisions, fund the new trust with cash, and have the new grantor trust purchase the policy from the old grantor trust. The ruling confirms that such a transfer would not trigger the transfer for value rule. Furthermore, if the insured currently owns the policy outright and wishes to transfer it to a trust without subjecting the transfer to the three-year rule of §2035, the owner-insured might sell the policy to a trust in which the owner-insured is the deemed owner for income tax purposes. Not only is the transfer immune from the transfer for value rule (as the ruling confirms), but because §2035(d) precludes application of the three-year rule where the owner-insured transfers the policy for its fair market value, the policy is removed from the owner-insured's gross estate even if the owner-insured dies immediately after the sale. *See* LR 9413045.

§6.55. POLICY PURCHASED BY A QUALIFIED PLAN

The proceeds of an insurance policy purchased by a qualified retirement plan on the life of an employee may not be included in the income of the plan beneficiary under §101(a) when they are distributed. However, they may be taxable under §72. If the employee paid the premiums, or the cost of the insurance was taxed to the employee under §72(m)(3)(B), the proceeds are excluded to the extent they exceed the cash surrender value of the policy immediately prior to the employee's death. §72(m)(3)(C). Beyond that, the payments are taxable under the rules of §72. On the other hand, if the employee did not pay the premiums directly and they were not taxed to the employee under §72(m)(3), no part of the proceeds paid to the plan beneficiary as a death benefit qualifies for the exclusion under §101(a). Reg. §1.72-16(c)(4). Note that, for purposes of §§79, 83 and 402, the fair market value of life insurance contracts may be valued in accordance with the safe harbors provided in Rev. Proc. 2005-25, 2005-1 C.B. 962.

The rollover of a policy on an employee's life from one qualified plan to another does not constitute a transfer for value. LR 7906051.

Life insurance advisors sometimes encourage plan participants to purchase life insurance through a qualified plan. Under the applicable rules, life insurance may be purchased by a qualified plan as long as the insurance provides only "incidental" benefits, which generally requires that the total premiums not exceed 25 percent of the employer contributions for universal and term insurance or 50 percent for cash value insurance. Rev. Rul. 74-307, 1974-2 C.B. 146; Rev. Rul. 61-164, 1961-2 C.B. 99. The value of the insurance purchased by a qualified plan, determined under Table 2001, Notice 2002-8, 2002-1 C.B. 398, is income to the participant-insured. Plans proposed by insurance advocates typically suggest that the insurance policy be sold to the participant or an irrevocable life insurance trust after the insurance has been in effect for a few years. At that time, presumably the value of the policy will be significantly less than the total of the premiums that were paid by the plan. To avoid the transfer for value trap, the trust should be a grantor trust. *See* §6.54.3. On the downside, the participant is taxed on the value of the insurance, the plan cannot invest the amount invested in the premiums, and the supposed benefits are lost if the participant dies before the policy is transferred. *See* Sanderson, *Pension Rescue,* 142 Tr. & Est. 46 (May 2003) and Choate, *Life Insurance in the Retirement Plan,* 142 Tr. & Est. 50 (May 2003).

§6.56. PREMIUM PAYMENTS

Premiums paid on personal (*i.e.,* nonbusiness) insurance are generally not deductible for income tax purposes. To begin with, premiums paid by a taxpayer on policies insuring the premium payor's life are considered to be nondeductible personal expenses. Reg. §1.262-1(b)(1). Premium payments made on policies insuring the lives of family members are also subject to that rule. In addition, premiums on policies insuring the life of another person are not deductible if the proceeds would be excluded from the premium payor's gross income under §101(a). §265(a)(1); *Jones v. Commissioner,* 231 F.2d 655 (3d Cir. 1956).

The 1997 Act amended §264 to bar all corporations from deducting any premiums paid on life insurance of which the corporation is directly or indirectly a beneficiary.

§6.56.1. Premium Payments Deductible as Alimony

A deduction is allowed under §215 for premium payments that constitute income to a spouse or former spouse of the insured under §71. In order to obtain the deduction, the policy must generally have been assigned to the former spouse in connection with a legal separation, dissolution of marriage, or decree of separate maintenance. The mere designation of the former spouse as beneficiary is not sufficient. *Henry B. Kelsey,* 27 T.C.M.(CCH) 337 (1968), *aff'd mem.,* 1969-2 U.S.T.C. ¶9619, 23 A.F.T.R.2d 69-1481 (2d Cir. 1969).

§6.56.2. Premium Payments as Charitable Contributions

Subject to the percentage limitations of §170, a charitable deduction is allowed for premiums paid on a policy that is owned by a charity or a charitable trust. *Eppa Hunton IV,* 1 T.C. 821 (1943), *acq.,* 1943 C.B. 12. When an income tax charitable deduction is sought the planner should not rely upon the mere irrevocable designation of the charity as beneficiary. *See* §6.46.1. Instead, the policy should be irrevocably assigned to the charity, which itself qualifies for the charitable deduction. In Rev. Rul. 80-132, 1980-1 C.B. 255, the IRS reached the uncertain conclusion that the gift to a private foundation of an insurance policy subject to an outstanding loan was an act of self-dealing under §4941(d)(1)(A) subject to tax under §4947(b). The rationale that the transfer of the policy relieved the donor of the obligation to repay the loan, pay interest on the loan as it accrued, or suffer continued diminution in value of the policy fails to notice the unique character of loans against life insurance policies. *See* §6.60. As indicated in §6.2, a charitable deduction is allowable only if the charity has an insurable interest in the donor's life, so it will be entitled to receive the proceeds when the donor dies.

§6.56.3. Premium Payments at a Discount

When a discount is given for premiums paid in advance, the interest earned on the advance payment or the increment in value is includible in the gross income of the premium payor in the year or years the premiums are due. Rev. Rul. 66-120, 1966-1 C.B. 14. On the other hand, an additional premium charge that is imposed when a premium is paid on a semiannual, quarterly, or monthly basis is not deductible as an interest charge under §163. Rev. Rul. 79-187, 1979-1 C.B. 95.

§6.57.   PREMIUMS PAID BY EMPLOYERS ARE DEDUCTIBLE

Under §162, an employer may deduct the premiums paid on life insurance policies on the lives of its officers and employees. The premiums are deductible business expenses if (1) the payments are in the nature of additional compensation, (2) the total amount of compensation paid to an officer or employee is not unreasonable, §162(a), and (3) the employer is not directly or indirectly the beneficiary, §264(a)(1). Rev. Rul. 56-400, 1956-2 C.B. 116. No deduction is allowed for the payment of premiums on policies insuring lives of shareholders. Such payments constitute dividend distributions rather than the payment of compensation for services. In such cases, the amount of the dividends is includible in the shareholder's income. Also, no deduction is allowed if the employer is entitled to receive any of the proceeds of a policy under a split-dollar plan or otherwise. §264(a)(1); Rev. Rul. 66-203, 1966-2 C.B. 104.

In general, the premiums paid by an employer on a policy insuring the life of an employee are includible in the employee's gross income where the proceeds are payable to the beneficiary designated by the employee. Reg. §1.61-2(d)(2)(ii)(a). Under such circumstances the premiums paid by the employer constitute additional compensation to the employee. *N. Loring Danforth*, 18 B.T.A. 1221 (1930). Special provisions of §79 allow an employee to exclude the cost of up to $50,000 of employer-provided group-term insurance. *See* §6.73.

§6.58. Cost of Insurance Protection Provided by Qualified Plans, §72(m)(3)

The cost of current life insurance protection provided an employee under a qualified retirement plan is includible in the employee's income if the proceeds are payable directly or indirectly to the participant or the participant's beneficiary. §72(m)(3); Rev. Rul. 79-202, 1979-2 C.B. 31. If the trust has a right as a named beneficiary to retain any part of the proceeds, the premiums are not taxed to the employee. Under the regulations, the proceeds are considered to be payable to the participant or the participant's beneficiary if "the trustee is required to pay over all of such proceeds to the beneficiary." Reg. §1.72-16(b)(1).

The amount of life insurance protection provided in any year is the excess of the death benefit payable over the cash surrender value of the policy. Reg. §1.72-16(b)(3). The cost of the protection is determined under the table of one-year term premiums set forth in Notice 2001-10, 2001-1 C.B. 459 (the "Table 2001 cost").

EXAMPLE 6-25.

The trustee of Employer's qualified pension plan, which provides a death benefit of $10,000, purchased a $10,000 ordinary life insurance policy on the life of Employee, who was 50 years old. The premium for the first year was $250, and at the end of that year the cash value of the policy was $0. The plan provided Employee's beneficiary with $10,000 of insurance protection. The Table 2001 cost of $1,000 insurance for a person 50 years of age is $2.30. Employee must report $23 as income for the year (10 × $2.30).

§6.59. Grantor Trusts, §677(a)(3)

The income of a trust is taxed to the grantor of a trust to the extent it may be used without the consent of an adverse party to pay premiums on policies insuring the life of the grantor or the grantor's spouse except for policies irrevocably payable for charitable purposes. §677(a)(3). See §10.4.1. This rule is intended "to prevent the avoidance of tax by the allocation of income through a trust device to the payment of life insurance premiums, which are universally recognized as a normal expense of protecting dependents but which are personal, as distinguished from business, expenses, and are therefore not deductible from gross income." *Arthur Stockstrom*, 3 T.C. 664, 668 (1944). The income of the trust is not taxed to the grantor merely because the trustee is authorized to pay premiums on policies insuring the life of the grantor or the grantor's spouse. Rather, the application of the statute depends upon the actual existence of policies upon which premiums might have been paid from trust funds. *Corning v. Commissioner*, 104 F.2d 329 (6th Cir. 1939). The grantor will be treated as the owner of a trust that acquires insurance on the grantor's life although the trust agreement specifies that the premiums of policies on the life of the grantor may be paid only from the principal of the trust.

The deductibility of interest paid by a trustee on a policy loan is discussed in §6.61.1.

§6.60. POLICY LOANS

Under most cash value life insurance policies, the owner may borrow up to the cash surrender value of the policy on the sole security of the policy. Although the payment to the owner is called a loan, there is no personal liability to repay it. The Tax Court commented on this feature of life insurance policies in *J. Simpson Dean*, 35 T.C. 1083, 1085 (1961), *nonacq.*, 1973-2 C.B. 4:

> Insurance policy loans are unique because the borrower assumes no personal liability to repay the principal or to pay interest on the amount borrowed. Such loans are based on the reserve value of the insurance policies involved. If either the principal or the interest is not repaid, it is merely deducted from the reserve value of the policy. Since the insurance company "never advances more than it already is absolutely bound for under the policy, it has no interest in creating personal liability."

In *Williams v. Union Central Life Insurance Co.*, 291 U.S. 170, 179 (1934), the Supreme Court said, "While the advance is called a 'loan' and interest is computed in settling the account, 'the item never could be sued for,' and in substance 'is a payment, not a loan.'"

The transfer of an encumbered policy may result in the realization of gain by the transferor. *See* §6.64.1.

§6.60.1. Loans on Policies Other Than Modified Endowment Contracts

A policy loan made with respect to a policy other than a modified endowment contract (defined in §7702A) is generally not treated as a distribution for income tax purposes. Accordingly, in the case of most policies, taking out a loan does not have any income tax consequences for the borrower. Under some circumstances, however, the excess of the amount borrowed on a policy over the premiums paid is includible in the borrower's gross income. The clearest case occurs when a policy is terminated for failure to pay on the loan or interest. Then the amount of the outstanding loan is an amount received under the contract for purposes of §72 and is includible in the borrower's gross income to the extent it exceeds the premiums and other amounts paid on the policy. Where the policy is not terminated or surrendered, the excess is not includible in the borrower's gross income if the transaction is treated as establishing a debtor-creditor relationship between the borrower and the insurer. In a related context the Tax Court held that a policy loan made against an employee annuity contract was not includible in the borrower-employee's income because it was not "an amount received under the contract" within the meaning of §72(e)(1)(B). *Robert W. Minnis*, 71 T.C. 1049 (1979), *nonacq.*, 1979-2 C.B. 2. The IRS has refused to follow *Minnis* and, in Rev. Rul. 81-126, 1981-1 C.B. 206, restated the position that was rejected by the Tax Court(*i.e.,* that money received by an employee as a loan against the value of an annuity contract prior to the annuity's starting date was a taxable advance).

As described in §6.61, after 1990 no income tax deduction is allowed for personal interest, such as interest paid on policy loans. §163(h). Accordingly, the owner of an insurance policy with a large outstanding loan against it may be concerned about the loan's overall cost because of the nondeductibility of interest on it. Owners who participated in insurance plans that involved substantial borrowing against policies (*e.g.*, a minimum deposit plan, §6.74) usually took steps to reduce or eliminate the relatively large nondeductible interest payments. On the other hand, owners will be less concerned where the interest is paid by further borrowing against the cash value of the policy. The following options are available to the owner of a policy with an outstanding loan:

1. Pay off the loan—which may be economically unattractive.

2. Continue making interest payments although the interest is not deductible.

3. Allow the interest to be paid by borrowing against the remaining cash value of the policy.

4. Surrender the policy, which would require the owner to report as income the excess of the amount realized (including the outstanding loan) over the owner's investment in the contract (premium payments and other consideration paid). §6.65. No deduction would be allowed if the policy owner receives less than the owner's investment in the contract. *Id.*

5. Exercise an option to convert the remaining cash value of the policy (if any) into paid-up insurance or extended term insurance. The exercise of such an option might be treated as the equivalent of receiving the remaining value of the policy and subsequently purchasing the paid-up or term insurance. *See* Rev. Rul. 68-648, 1968-2 C.B. 49 (employee's election of extended life option available under a retirement income contract that had been purchased for him by his employer, a §501(c)(3) organization, was taxable). Of course, Rev. Rul. 68-648 deals with the exchange of contracts that would not qualify for nonrecognition under §1035 in any case—an annuity contract for a life insurance contract. *See* §6.66.

6. Exchange the policy for another under the nonrecognition provisions of §1035. §6.67. An encumbered policy may be exchanged for another similarly encumbered policy of the same type, insuring the same person. *See, e.g.,* LR 8604033. The terms of the new policy may make it economically attractive to make such an exchange. However, an exchange may involve additional costs including legal fees and the loading on the new contract. In addition, the exchange will probably start a new suicide and incontestability period, at least where different insurers are involved. Finally, the new policy may carry higher interest rates on loans.

§6.60.2. Loans on Modified Endowment Contracts

A loan received with respect to a modified endowment contract is treated as a distribution. §72(e)(4)(A). The loan proceeds are includible in gross income to the extent allocable to income on the contract. §72(e)(2)(B). For this purpose the income on the contract is the excess of the cash value of the contract over the investment in the contract (*i.e.*, the sum of premiums and other consideration paid less amounts received that were excludible from gross income, §72(e)(6)).

§6.60.3. Loan Rates and Dividends

Cash value policies issued prior to 1970 generally provide that loans carry an interest rate of 5 percent or less, while policies issued later commonly specify rates of 8 percent or more or a floating rate. In order to discourage the outflow of funds when external interest rates are much higher, insurers now generally cut the dividend rate on participating policies against which there are outstanding loans at low rates unless the owners agreed to a policy amendment making a higher rate applicable to the loans. Because of the changes in dividend policy and in the income tax law, borrowing against a policy for purposes of making alternative investments is generally no longer economically attractive. However, for convenience, policy owners may borrow against their policies in order to pay policy premiums. In fact, many policies provide for an automatic loan, up to the remaining loan value of the policy, to pay any premium that is not timely paid. It is also common for an owner to borrow on a policy that the owner intends to transfer in order to reduce its value for gift tax purposes. Of course, there is some risk that the transfer of a policy subject to a loan equal to its full cash value might be treated as a transfer for value that would subject the proceeds to taxation under § 101(a)(2). *See* § 6.54.

§6.61. DEDUCTIBILITY OF INTEREST ON POLICY LOANS: GENERAL

The income tax deduction for interest paid on personal loans, such as policy loans, was completely eliminated in 1991. § 163(h)(2). In addition, no deduction is allowable with respect to interest paid on an indebtedness in excess of $50,000 related to policies purchased after June 20, 1986 that insure the life of anyone who is an officer, employee, or person who is financially interested in the taxpayer's trade or business. § 264(a)(4). However, the preexisting rules regarding the deductibility of interest on policy loans remains of some significance. For example, the old rules apply to loans of $50,000 or less with respect to business-related insurance.

§6.61.1. Who Is Entitled to Deduct Interest Paid

As stated above, a taxpayer is generally not entitled to deduct personal interest, such as the interest paid or accrued on a life insurance policy. § 163(h)(2). Also, the former owner of a policy is not entitled to deduct interest after the policy has been assigned—the owner's "obligation" to pay interest does not survive the assignment of the policy to another person. *J. Simpson Dean*, 35 T.C. 1083 (1961), *nonacq.*, 1973-2 C.B. 4. However, the assignee may not deduct interest that the assignee pays with respect to interest that accrued prior to the assignment. *Agnes I. Fox*, 43 B.T.A. 895 (1941).

When interest is deducted from the original amount of the loan, or is unpaid and is added to the principal amount of the loan, an interest deduction is allowed to a cash basis taxpayer only when the interest is actually paid. Rev. Rul. 73-482, 1973-2 C.B. 44. This point is illustrated by Example 6-26.

EXAMPLE 6-26.

In 2008, *O*, a cash basis taxpayer, borrowed $10,000 against a cash value policy on the life of an employee of *O'* s business. At the time the insurer deducted $1,000 as interest on the loan for the first year and paid *O* the $9,000 balance. None of the $1,000 interest "payment" was deductible on *O'* s income tax return for 2008. In 2009, *O* paid the insurer $10,000 in full satisfaction of the loan. *O* was entitled to claim an interest deduction in 2009 for the $1,000 in business-related interest that was paid on the loan. If the interest paid by *O* had been characterized as personal interest under § 163(h)(2) none of it would have been deductible. The same rule applies if the annual interest on a policy loan had not been paid and had, instead, been added to the principal amount of the loan: Interest is considered to have been paid when the full amount of principal and accumulated interest is paid.

If an interest deduction is otherwise allowable (*e.g.*, the interest is payable on business-related borrowings of $50,000 or less), the rule last described in Example 6-26 gives the taxpayer some flexibility in timing the interest deduction. For example, a business with little or no taxable income in one year might prefer to let the interest go unpaid and add it to principal until a later year in which an interest deduction would be more valuable for income tax purposes.

§ 6.61.2. Interest on Policy Loans: Limitations of § 264

The rules of § 264 bar a deduction for interest that would otherwise be deductible with respect to insurance-related loans. Under § 264(a)(2), no deduction is allowed for amounts paid as indebtedness incurred directly or indirectly to purchase or continue in effect a single premium life insurance, endowment, or annuity policy purchased after March 1, 1954. A contract is considered to be a single premium one if substantially all of the premiums are paid within four years from the date on which it was purchased, or if an amount is deposited after March 1, 1954 with the insurer for the payment of a substantial number of future premiums. Reg. § 1.264-2. No deduction is allowed for interest paid on a bank loan secured by a single premium annuity policy purchased after 1954. Rev. Rul. 95-53, 1995-2 C.B. 30.

Interest is also generally not deductible when paid in connection with a policy issued after August 6, 1963 under a purchase plan that contemplates the systematic direct or indirect borrowing of all or part of the increase in cash value of the policy. § 264(a)(3). Even before the interest on personal loans became nondeductible, the limitation of § 264(a)(3) reduced the attractiveness of the so-called financed life insurance or minimum deposit plan, which depended heavily upon the deductibility of interest payments made on indebtedness incurred to make premium payments. Minimum deposit plans are discussed at § 6.74.

§ 6.61.3. Exceptions to § 264(a)(3)

There are four exceptions to the general rule of § 264(a)(3). The first and most important exception, the so-called *4-in-7 exception*, applies if any four of the first seven annual premiums are paid without incurring any indebtedness in connection with the policy. §264(d)(1). For this purpose a new seven-year period starts to run if there is a substantial increase in the amount of the premium. §264(d). This exception allows the deduction of interest paid on an indebtedness incurred in connection with fewer than four of the first seven annual premiums. Also, once the 4-in-7 exception is satisfied, the deductibility of interest on policy loans is not restricted by §264(a)(3). The IRS applies the 4-in-7 rule literally—it must be satisfied within the initial 7-year period without any violation of the rule. Thus, if O borrowed against a post-August 6, 1963 policy for four of the first seven years, the exception is not available even if the full amount of the loan is repaid within the seven-year period. Rev. Rul. 72-609, 1972-3 C.B. 199.

The second exception, the *de minimis exception*, applies if the total amount paid or accrued under plans that contemplate the systematic borrowing of cash values is $100 or less. §264(d)(2). It is obviously of limited significance.

Under the third, the *unforeseen events exception*, a deduction is allowed for interest paid on indebtedness incurred because of an unforeseen substantial loss of income or an unforeseen substantial increase in financial obligations. §264(d)(3). For the purposes of this rule a loss of income or increase in financial obligations is not unforeseen if it was or could have been foreseen at the time the policy was purchased. Reg. §1.264-4(d)(3).

Lastly, the *trade or business exception* applies if the indebtedness was incurred in connection with the taxpayer's trade or business. §264(d)(4). However, the indebtedness must have been incurred to finance business obligations and not the acquisition of cash value life insurance. Specifically, borrowing to finance business life insurance, such as key person, split-dollar, or stock redemption plans is not considered to be incurred in connection with the taxpayer's business. Reg. §1.264-4(d)(4). In contrast, borrowing to finance business expansion, inventory, or capital improvements does qualify under this exception.

§6.62. DIVIDENDS

As indicated previously, dividends generally constitute a partial premium refund. *See* §6.12. In the case of policies other than modified endowment contracts, a dividend is includible in the policy owner's income only to the extent that it, together with all previous excludible payments received under the policy, exceeds the total cost of the policy (*i.e.,* premiums and other consideration). Reg. §1.72-11(b)(1). Under that rule a dividend is not includible in gross income in most cases. Of course, excludable dividends are deducted from the consideration paid or deemed paid for the purpose of computing the exclusion ratio under §72. *Id.* Also, only the net amount of premiums paid is taken into account in determining gain on amounts not received as annuities under a policy. §72(e)(1). Dividends with respect to modified endowment contracts are not includible in gross income to the extent they are retained by the insurer as a premium or other consideration paid for the contract. §72(e)(4)(B)

Interest paid or credited on dividends left with the insurer is includible in the gross income of the policy owner for the year in which the owner may withdraw it. Reg. §1.61-7(d).

The distribution under a special reserve provision of a life insurance contract (additional amounts paid with respect to the policy for the first five years, which were distributable at the end of 20 years) was a nontaxable return of premiums where it was less than the total premiums paid under the policy. *Ned W. Moseley*, 72 T.C. 183 (1979), *acq.*, 1980-1 C.B. 1. In *Moseley*, the Tax Court refused to allocate the premiums paid by the taxpayer between the special reserve and the death benefit provisions.

§6.63. BASIS AND SURRENDER, SALE OR EXCHANGE OF INSURANCE POLICIES

The IRS position regarding the income tax consequences of transactions involving life insurance policies was clarified by Rev. Ruls. 2009-13, 2009-1 C.B. 1029, and 2009-14, 2009-1 C.B. 1031. Under pre-existing authorities and those rulings, the following rules generally apply:

1. **Basis - Cash value policies.** For the purpose of determining gain or loss on the sale of a cash value policy owned by the insured or a person with an insurable or economic interest in the life of the insured, the basis of the policy is the amount of premiums and other consideration paid reduced by the cost of insurance (COI) protection provided. *But see* Rev. Rul. 70-38, 1970-1 C.B. 11 (corporation not required to report any income from sale of cash value policies it owned on the lives of its officers for their cash surrender values, which were less than total premiums paid—no reduction for COI). Unless otherwise determinable, COI of a cash value policy is presumed to be the amount by which the net premiums paid exceed the cash surrender value of the policy (including the amount of any outstanding loans). No loss is realized if the amount received is less than the net premiums and other consideration paid. The basis of a cash value policy owned by an investor who has no insurable or economic interest in the life of the insured is determined without a reduction for COI during the period the policy was owned by the investor.

2. **Basis - Term policies.** The basis of a term policy with no cash surrender value owned by the insured or a person with an insurable or economic interest in the life of the insured is the amount of net premiums paid less COI. Again, the basis of a term policy owned by an investor is determined without regard to COI for the period a policy is owned by an investor. Rev. Rul. 2009-14, 2009-1 I.R.B. 1031 (Situation 2).

3. **Surrender.** The income tax consequences of surrendering a life insurance policy are determined under §72(e). Briefly, when a life insurance policy is surrendered the amount received (other than as an annuity) is included in gross income to the extent it exceeds the investment in the contract. For this purpose, the investment in the contract is the total of premiums and other consideration paid less all amounts previously received under the contract that were not included in gross income. Rev. Rul. 2009-13, 2009-1 C.B. 1029 (Situation 1). (Presumably, the amount of any policy loans that were outstanding against the policy would be treated as part of the consideration received.) The ruling characterizes the gain as ordinary income and not capital gain, because the surrender of a policy does not constitute a "sale or

exchange." No deduction is allowed if the owner surrenders a policy and receives less than the net amount of premiums and other consideration paid.

4. **Sale.** The seller realizes gain when a life insurance policy is sold for more than its adjusted basis. Rev. Rul. 2009-13, 2009-1 C.B. 1029 (Situation 2). If a policy is sold for less than its adjusted basis, the courts have thus far not allowed a deduction. As indicated above, the adjusted basis of an insured owner or person with an insurable or economic interest in the life of the insured is the amount of premiums and other consideration paid less COI provided prior to the sale. Again, unless otherwise indicated, COI is the amount by which the net premiums paid exceed the cash surrender value of the policy. The gain is ordinary income to the extent the cash surrender value of the policy exceeds premiums and other consideration paid (the "inside build up"); any additional gain is capital gain. Again, the adjusted basis of an investor is determined without regard to COI for the period the investor owned the policy.

§6.64. SURRENDER OF POLICIES

Ordinary income is realized to the extent the proceeds received upon surrender, refund, or maturity of a policy exceed the net amount of all premiums or other consideration paid. §72(e)(5)(E); Rev. Rul. 2009-13, 2009-1 C.B. 1029. If the taxpayer, within 60 days of the day a lump sum becomes payable under a contract, exercises an option to receive an annuity in lieu of the lump sum, then no part of the lump sum is includible in gross income at the time it became payable. §72(h). That is, the gain is not taxed currently if the policyholder elects, within 60 days of the time a lump sum becomes payable under the contract, to receive an annuity in lieu of a lump sum. In the case of such an election, the annuity payments are taxed to the recipient in accordance with the basic income tax rules applicable to annuities (*i.e.*, a proportionate part of the total amount received each year is a tax-free return of capital and the balance is taxable income). §72(b).

When a policy is surrendered, any gain realized is ordinary income and not capital gain. Rev. Rul. 2009-13, 2009-1 C.B. 1029. The courts have reached that result, because the surrender, refund or maturity of a policy is not a sale or exchange. *Avery v. Commissioner*, 111 F.2d 19 (9th Cir. 1940) (maturity of endowment policy); *Bodine v. Commissioner*, 103 F.2d 982 (3d Cir.), *cert. denied*, 308 U.S. 576 (1939) (surrender of annuity policy).

When a policy is surrendered the taxpayer may receive less than the total amount of the premiums and other consideration he or she paid for it. In general, no deduction is allowed for the difference. *London Shoe Co. v. Commissioner*, 80 F.2d 230 (2d Cir. 1935), *cert. denied*, 298 U.S. 663 (1936); *Standard Brewing Co.*, 6 B.T.A. 980 (1927). Some cases disallowed a deduction because the "loss" was not incurred in a transaction that was entered into primarily for profit as required by §165(c)(2). *Industrial Trust Co. v. Broderick*, 94 F.2d 927 (1st Cir.), *cert. denied*, 304 U.S. 572 (1938) (single premium nonrefund annuity contract was purchased for reasons of security and not profit); *Arnold v. United States*, 180 F. Supp. 746 (N.D. Texas 1959) (endowment policies purchased to provide life insurance protection until maturity when they would provide secure source of income); Rev. Rul. 72-193, 1972-1 C.B. 58.

Deductions were denied in other cases because the cash surrender value was equal to the taxpayer's capital investment. *London Shoe Co., supra.* Any excess of premiums paid over cash surrender value represented the nondeductible cost of the insurance protection provided by policy. For example, in *Standard Brewing Co., supra,* the court said:

> To the extent that the premiums paid by the petitioner created in it a right to a surrender value, they constituted a capital investment. To the extent they exceeded the surrender value, they constituted a payment for earned insurance and were current expenses . . . .The surrender value of the policy was the measure of the investment and upon the surrender there was no capital lost. 6 B.T.A. at 984.

This result is consistent with the denial of a deduction for premiums paid on personal life insurance and on policies maintained on the lives of officers or employees of which the employer is a beneficiary.

§ 6.65. SALE OF POLICIES

Courts have generally considered the excess of the amount received upon the sale of a cash value policy over net premiums paid (premiums and other consideration paid less dividends received) to be ordinary income. *Gallun v. Commissioner,* 327 F.2d 809 (7th Cir. 1964). Under Rev. Ruls. 2009-13 and 2009-14 the seller's basis must be reduced by COI if the seller personally benefited from the insurance protection provided by the policy. In addition, if the proceeds exceed the policy's cash surrender value the excess may be capital gain. In dealing with the issue the courts assumed that even if the policy were a capital asset, "we are, nevertheless dealing here with the receipt as part of the purchase price—and in addition to any payment attributable to the property sold—of an amount representing income which has already been earned and which would have been ordinary income if and when received by the vendor." *Estate of Gertrude H. Crocker,* 37 T.C. 605, 612 (1962).

EXAMPLE 6-27.

X, the insured, paid premiums of $12,000 on a cash value life insurance policy, then sold it to Y for its cash surrender value, $15,000. Historically the courts have treated the $3,000 excess of the amount received over the premiums paid as ordinary income to X. Under Rev. Rul. 2009-13, the excess would be capital gain.

§ 6.65.1. Sale or Other Disposition of Encumbered Policy

The sale or other disposition of an encumbered policy may result in a gain to the transferor depending upon the manner in which the policy loan is characterized. If it is treated as an ordinary loan, some taxable gain may result if the amount of the loan exceeds the transferor's basis. Thus, the donor of an encumbered policy may be treated as having realized an amount equal to the loan balance at the time the policy is transferred. The transfer of an encumbered policy may be treated as a discharge of indebtedness. Under Reg. §1.1001-2(a)(4)(i), "[t]he sale or other disposition of property that secures a nonrecourse liability discharges the transferor from the liability."

§6.65.2. "Loss" on Sale

The excess of the net premiums paid for a policy over the amount realized upon the sale of the policy generally has not been considered to be deductible. *Century Wood Preserving Co. v. Commissioner*, 69 F.2d 967 (3d Cir. 1934). The reason is simple—the excess is considered to be attributable to the nondeductible cost of insurance protection provided over the period preceding the sale. *Keystone Consolidated Publishing Co.*, 26 B.T.A. 1210 (1932). In essence, the courts have taken the position that there is no loss.

Under the reasoning applied in Situation 2 of Rev. Rul. 2009-14, 2009-1 C.B.1032, presumably a loss would be allowed an investor, who did not have an insurable interest in the life of the insured and would suffer no economic loss on the death of the insured, who sold a policy for less than his adjusted basis in the policy (net premiums and other consideration paid). Importantly, under the ruling the investor's investment in the contract would not be reduced by the cost of insurance during the period the investor owned the policy.

§6.66. EXCHANGE OF POLICIES, §1035

Under the special nonrecognition rules of §1035, no gain or loss is recognized on certain exchanges of insurance policies where the policies exchanged relate to the same insured. Specifically, under §1035(a) no gain or loss is recognized in the following exchanges:

1. A contract of life insurance for another contract of life insurance or for an endowment or annuity contract (*e.g.*, LRs 8604033 and 8816015); or
2. A contract of endowment insurance (a) for another contract of endowment insurance which provides for regular payments beginning at a date not later than the date payments would have begun under the contract exchanged, or (b) for an annuity contract; or
3. An annuity contract for an annuity contract (*e.g.*, LR 8501012 (variable annuity issued by one company exchanged for fixed annuity issued by another company)).

Letter Ruling 200715006 held that an exchange of master account business-owned life insurance that insured the lives of active employees could be exchanged tax-free for separate business-owned policies on the lives of the employees.

An exchange of a policy which insures one person for a policy insuring the life of another person is not tax-free under §1035. *See* Rev. Rul. 90-109, 1990-2 C.B. 191.

The exchange of a joint and survivor policy with one surviving insured for a policy issued by another insurer on the life of the surviving insured is permissible under §1035. LR 9248013. The same result was reached in LR 9330040. In LR 9248013 the IRS specifically refused to express any opinion as to whether an exchange of a joint and survivor policy for a single life policy prior to the death of one of the insured parties would be within the scope of § 1035. Presumably such an exchange would not be within § 1035, which generally requires that the policies relate to the same insured.

In LR 9542037, the IRS held that the exchange of a policy insuring the life of a single person for a joint life policy covering the lives of two living persons was not permissible under § 1035. The outcome is hardly a surprise in view of the requirement of § 1035 that the policies exchanged must relate to "the same insured." Reg. § 1.1035-1(c).

Two nonparticipating flexible premium life insurance policies can be exchanged for a nonparticipating flexible premium variable deferred annuity. LR 9708016. The IRS has also ruled that § 1035 allows a life policy to be exchanged, with the payment of additional cash, for an annuity. LR 9820018.

Single premium deferred annuity contracts may also be exchanged under § 1035. LR 199905015. An annuity issued by a domestic insurer can be exchanged for an annuity issued by a foreign insurer. LR 9319024. Section 1035 is concerned with the nature and benefits of the policies involved in an exchange and not with the status of the insurer.

Not surprisingly, an investment of cash received as a distribution from one insurer in a contract issued by another does not qualify as an exchange under § 1035. LR 9346002 (TAM).

§ 6.66.1. What Constitutes an Exchange

Neither the Code nor the regulations define "exchange." The existing authorities are helpful but not entirely consistent. In planning an exchange, the owner should avoid transactions that might involve a "surrender" of the existing policy, followed by a "reinvestment" in a second one. *See* LR 9346002 (TAM) mentioned above.

§ 6.66.2. Exchange of Assignable Policies

The safest exchange transactions involve policies issued by the same insurer, with respect to which it is relatively simple to arrange an exchange. For example, in LR 8229107, a participating whole life policy with a low guaranteed interest rate was exchanged for a participating whole life policy issued by the same insurer on the life of the same insured with a higher guarantee.

When different insurers are involved it is safest to assign the existing policy to the company that will issue the new contract, being sure that there is no lapse in coverage. Rev. Rul. 72-358, 1972-2 C.B. 473. The IRS appears to accept that all such transactions qualify under § 1035. *E.g.*, LR 8604003 (TAM) (encumbered whole life policy assigned to new insurer in exchange for insurance of similarly encumbered whole life policy on same insured) and LR 8433035 (single premium retirement annuity assigned in exchange for single premium deferred annuity contract). Without an assignment a transaction involving a readily transferable annuity may be treated as a surrender and exchange of the proceeds in consideration for the second annuity. LR 8515063. In the view of the IRS such rollovers are likely not to qualify under § 1035.

§ 6.66.3. Exchange of Policies Held by Qualified Plans

Until 1990, the IRS held that annuity contracts owned by qualified plans were not assignable by reason of § 401(g). Accordingly, it was not considered possible to exchange those contracts by direct assignment. Under those circumstances the IRS generally approved arrangements under which the taxpayer entered into a binding agreement with a new issuer that required the taxpayer to surrender the existing contract and direct that the proceeds be paid directly to the new issuer as consideration for the new contract. Rev. Rul. 73-124, 1973-1 C.B. 200 (revoked as noted below). In addition, the owner would usually agree to endorse in favor of the new issuer any check that was received from the original issuer. Such arrangements were generally held to involve only a "single integrated transaction." LRs 8526038; 8424010; *contra* LRs 8343010; 8310033.

Although the IRS was generally cooperative, it sometimes concluded that a proposed transaction involved a surrender of the original annuity followed by the reinvestment of the proceeds in a new annuity. LR 8310003. Also, note that the lack of cooperation of the original issuer complicated matters in some cases and required litigation with the IRS. *See Martin I. Greene*, 85 T.C. 1024 (1985), *acq.* (result only), 1986-2 C.B. 1.

In Rev. Rul. 90-24, 1990-1 C.B. 97, the IRS revoked Rev. Rul. 73-124, holding that § 401(g) does not prevent an exchange of contracts, which is not a distribution but merely a change in the issuer or custodian of the annuity or account. So long as the funds remain subject to the same or more restrictive provisions regarding distributions, the transfer would not be treated as a distribution. Revenue Ruling 90-24 did not indicate whether a transfer of the type involved in Rev. Rul. 73-124 would continue to be nontaxable under § 1035. As pointed out in LR 9233054, the annuity contracts that are involved in the exchange cannot be "materially different." In particular, the new contract must continue to provide that it is nontransferable:

> Taxpayer received Annuity Y purchased from Company N by the trustee of Plan X representing the balance of the credit to Taxpayer after Employer C terminated Plan X. Taxpayer proposes to subsequently authorize company N to transfer all funds in Annuity Y to another insurer in exchange for a substantially similar annuity.

> Although section 1035 provides that no gain or loss shall be recognized by the exchange of an annuity contract for another annuity contract, the exchange of a qualified plan contract for a materially different contract does not come within the ambit of this section. An annuity contract that is nontaxable when distributed from a qualified plan contains certain provisions in order to comply with section 401 and to protect participants and beneficiaries. Many of these provisions must remain in effect until the last payment is received under the annuity contract. If a section 401 annuity contract is exchanged for a materially different contract, the requirements and protections of section 401 of the Code would be lost.

§6.67. Exchanges Within §1035; Permissible Exchanges; Basis

An exchange of one encumbered life insurance policy for another similarly encumbered policy issued by another insurer relating to the same insured is within the scope of §1035. LRs 8816015; 8604033. In such cases the "new" policy is considered to have been purchased on the date of the exchange—making §7702(f)(7) applicable to the policy. That is, if there is a reduction in benefits within the first 15 years as a result of which there is a cash distribution to the policyholder, the provisions of §72 other than §72(e)(5) apply to the distribution, not the "old" rules of §72 regarding the taxation of distributions.

The nonrecognition rule also applies when a life insurance endowment or fixed annuity policy is exchanged for a variable annuity policy. Rev. Rul. 68-235, 1968-1 C.B. 360. Likewise, a variable annuity contract issued by one company may be exchanged for a fixed annuity contract issued by another company. LR 8501012. Of course, for the nonrecognition rule to apply, the contracts must relate to the same insured, although they may be issued by different insurers. Rev. Rul. 72-358, 1972-2 C.B. 473.

When there is a tax-free exchange, the policy received has the same basis as the policy transferred. §1031(d). If other property is also received, the gain on the transaction must be realized by the taxpayer to the extent of the "boot" (cash or other property) received. The new contract has the same basis as the old one, adjusted as provided in §1031(d). Specifically, the basis is (1) decreased by the amount of money and the fair market value of other property received and (2) increased by the amount of gain recognized on the exchange. When a new policy and other property are received, any gain arising from the transaction is recognized but not in excess of the total value of the money and the other property received. §1031(b). In such an exchange no loss is recognized. §1031(c).

EXAMPLE 6-28.

T exchanged a life insurance policy upon which *T* had paid premiums of $40,000 for a life insurance policy that had a replacement value of $40,000 and a cash payment of $5,000. The full amount of the $5,000 payment is recognized by *T* in the year of the exchange. *T*'s basis in the new policy is $40,000 as indicated in Reg. §1.1031(d)-1(b). If *T* received no cash and the new policy were worth only $35,000, the $5,000 "loss" would not be recognized. Instead, the new policy would have a basis of $40,000.

In LR 9820018, the IRS ruled that the exchange of a life insurance policy issued by one company and cash for an annuity contract issued by another company qualifies for nonrecognition under §1035. Any administrative delays caused by the companies in processing the exchange will not prevent it from qualifying as a tax-free transaction.

§6.68. Costs of Exchanges; Exercise Care and Study the Economics

The exchange of policies may disadvantage the policy owner because of the additional costs involved in effectuating a transfer, including the loading on the new contract. Legal fees and other professional costs may also be incurred in connection with the transaction. In the case of life insurance, the exchange may also probably start a new suicide and noncontestability period, at least where different insurers are involved. Finally, the new policy may carry higher interest rates on loans.

The exchange of one insurance policy for another may cause some important tax benefits to be lost if the new policy is treated as having been acquired on the date of the exchange. For example, the benefit of a stepped up basis for some deferred annuity contracts may be lost: Under Rev. Rul. 70-143, 1970-1 C.B. 167, if the owner of a deferred variable annuity contract died prior to the annuity starting date, then the basis of the contract was stepped up under §1014. That ruling was revoked by Rev. Rul. 79-335, 1979-2 C.B. 292, as to contracts purchased prior to the date it was published, October 21, 1979 (*i.e.*, contracts that were previously acquired were "grandfathered"). In LR 9245035, the IRS ruled that the exchange, after October 21, 1979, of a deferred annuity contract for another one constituted the acquisition of a new contract that made the contract subject to the new rule expressed in Rev. Rul. 79-355. The ruling rejected the taxpayer's contention that the taxpayer should be granted relief under §7805(b). A step up in the basis of a tax deferred annuity that was acquired by the decedent in a post-1979 exchange of contracts was denied in similar circumstances in LR 9346002 (TAM).

§6.69. Exchange of Policies Not Within §1035

Exchanges not subject to §1035 are governed by the general rules regarding the recognition of gain or loss upon the sale or exchange of property. Thus, gain or loss is recognized when an endowment or annuity contract is exchanged for a life insurance contract. Gain or loss is also recognized when an annuity contract is exchanged for an endowment contract. Reg. §1.1035-1(c). Because of this rule, a taxpayer cannot avoid the taxation of earnings that have accrued on an endowment or an annuity policy by exchanging it for a life insurance policy. The accrued earnings will be taxed to the owner unless the owner dies prior to the maturity of the policy. These rules reduce the flexibility a taxpayer has in dealing with investments in endowment or annuity policies, but they are consistent with other income tax principles.

EXAMPLE 6-29.

In 2005, *T* paid $100,000 for a single premium endowment contract that would pay $140,000 to *T* in 2015 or to his beneficiary if he died before then. *T* exchanged the policy in 2010, when it had a cash value of $130,000, for a single premium paid-up life insurance policy that had a cash surrender value of $130,000. The same policy would cost $130,000 if purchased on the life of a person of *T*'s age, sex, and medical history. As a result of the exchange, *T* must recognize a gain of $30,000.

Letter Ruling 8905004 (TAM) involved the withdrawal of an amount equal to the original purchase price paid for an annuity, which was used to purchase a life insurance contract and the concurrent exchange of the taxpayer's residual interest in the original annuity contract for a new annuity. The transaction was treated as a tax-free exchange of one annuity contract for another. However, the life insurance contract was treated as taxable "boot" includible in the taxpayer's gross income.

For the purpose of determining gain, the fair market value of a single premium life insurance policy received by the taxpayer is the amount a person of the same age, sex, and condition of health as the insured would have to pay for a life policy with the same company at the date of the exchange. Here again, the measure of value is not the cash surrender value of the policy. *Charles Cutler Parsons*, 16 T.C. 256 (1951); *W. Stanley Barrett*, 42 T.C. 993 (1964), *aff'd*, 348 F.2d 916 (1st Cir. 1965) (matured endowment policies exchanged for paid-up life insurance policies); Rev. Rul. 54-264, 1954-2 C.B. 57 (exchange of single premium endowment policy for paid-up life insurance policy and cash).

§ 6.70. ALTERNATIVE MINIMUM TAX, § 56(G)(4)(B)(II)

The alternative minimum tax of a corporation for taxable years beginning after 1989 must take into account the internal build-up in value of life insurance policies as determined under § 7702(g) (*i.e.*, the increase in cash surrender value less the portion of any premium paid that is attributable to insurance coverage).

F. SPECIAL TYPES OF LIFE INSURANCE AND AGREEMENTS REGARDING LIFE INSURANCE

§ 6.71. INTRODUCTION

The most important types of special life insurance and life insurance agreements are described in this part, including split-dollar, group-term, and single premium plans. Others, such as minimum deposit plans, are mentioned although tax changes have largely eliminated their appeal. Having some knowledge of these types of life insurance policies and plans is important to planners because they are often included in executive compensation packages and insurance proposals made to clients. Each type has some special advantages and is subject to some special tax rules. Second-to-die (or survivorship) life and death benefit only plans are also reviewed although the latter is not strictly life insurance. The part concludes with a discussion of gifts of life insurance under the Uniform Transfers to Minors Act and the application of the Uniform Simultaneous Death Act to life insurance.

§ 6.72. SPLIT-DOLLAR LIFE INSURANCE PLANS: GENERAL

A split-dollar life insurance plan is most often used in the business setting to make a substantial amount of life insurance available to a key employee, or to the employee's assignee, at little or no cost to the employee. However, as described below, the approach can be adapted and used in a nonemployment setting (*e.g.,* between the trustee of an ILIT and the spouse of the insured).

In the employment setting, a split-dollar plan is a permissible form of discriminatory nonqualified employee benefit under which key employees are preferred. The concept of split-dollar is based upon a division of the interests in a cash value policy between a financing party (usually an employer) and the insured (usually the employee). Under it, the cash surrender value is usually controlled by the financing party to the extent of premiums paid by it and the risk element (*i.e.,* the excess of the face amount of the insurance over the cash surrender value of the policy) is controlled by the insured or the insured's assignee. Although split-dollar may be used in a variety of contexts, it is most commonly used to provide a substantial amount of life insurance to key employees at a relatively low cost. Actually, before a limitation was imposed on the deductibility of interest paid by a business with respect to insurance on the life of an officer or employee, § 264(a)(4), the employer frequently borrowed against its interest in life insurance in split-dollar plans. Specifically, the 1986 Act limited the deduction to the interest paid on $50,000 borrowed against policies issued after June 22, 1986 on the life of any employee. *Id.*

In a split-dollar arrangement, the financing party and the insured may split the premium cost between themselves in a variety of different ways—with the actual split affecting the income tax consequences as explained below. The financing party typically pays either the entire premium, an amount of the premium equal to the increase in cash value for the year, or the amount of the premium in excess of the employee's contribution, which is either the actual cost of the risk protection or the P.S. 58 cost (described below). In addition, if the financing party is the insured's employer, the employer may pay the insured employee a "bonus" equal to the portion of the premium paid by the employee—sometimes including the additional income tax the employee will be obligated to pay as a result of the plan. In order to prevent the risk portion from declining as the cash value increases, the dividends declared on participating policies may be applied under the fifth dividend option to buy term insurance equal to the increase in the financing party's interest in the cash value.

Under a split-dollar plan the financing party is entitled to recover some portion of the cash value of the insurance upon maturity of the policy or termination of the plan. The amount is typically: (1) the greater of the premiums paid or the cash surrender value of the policy, (2) the entire cash value regardless of the amount of premiums paid, or (3) the cash value of the policy to the extent of premiums paid.

The insured or the insured's assignee pays the portion of the premium (if any) not paid by the financing party and is entitled to name the beneficiary of the risk portion of the insurance (*i.e.,* the difference between the face amount and the cash surrender value). Although the insured may be required to pay a large part of the premium in the first year or two, the insured's share of the premium rapidly decreases. Some policies are designed to build up cash value more rapidly to avoid this problem.

The two common types of split-dollar arrangements, the endorsement system and the collateral assignment system, are described in the following excerpt from Rev. Rul. 64-328, 1964-2 C.B. 11, 12:

In the endorsement system, the employer owns the policy and is responsible for payment of the annual premiums. The employee is then required to reimburse the employer for his share, if any, of the premiums. Under the collateral assignment system, the employee in form owns the policy and pays the entire premium thereon. The employer in form makes annual loans, without interest (or below the fair rate of interest), to the employee of amounts equal to the yearly increases in the cash surrender value, but not exceeding the annual premiums. The employee executes an assignment of his policy to the employer as collateral security for the loans. The loans are generally payable at the termination of employment or the death of the employee.

The arrangements for the ownership of the policy and premium payments can, of course, be tailored to meet the needs of the parties.

§6.72.1. Income Tax Consequences

Beginning in 2001, the taxation of split-dollar insurance arrangements changed dramatically, culminating with the promulgation of final regulations in 2003. T.D. 9092. As a general rule, the final regulations make split-dollar insurance arrangements less beneficial from a tax perspective. The discussion below considers first the rules applicable to split-dollar arrangements entered into before 2002. A review of the old regime sets the stage for an analysis of the current rules applicable to split-dollar arrangements.

Historical Income Tax Treatment of Split-Dollar Arrangements. Under either the endorsement method or the collateral assignment method, the employee had gross income from the economic benefit of the insurance protection. The economic benefit to the employee was measured with reference to the so-called "P.S. 58 cost" of the insurance, as set forth in Rev. Rul. 55-747, 1955-2 C.B. 228. *See* Table 6-2. However, where the premium rates actually charged by the insurer were lower than the P.S. 58 cost, such lower rates could be used instead. Rev. Rul. 66-110, 1966-1 C.B. 12.

Table 6-2
Uniform One-Year Term Premiums for $1,000
Life Insurance Protection (P.S. 58 Cost)

Age	Premium	Age	Premium
15	$1.27	25	1.93
16	1.38	26	2.02
17	1.48	27	2.11
18	1.52	28	2.20
19	1.56	29	2.31
20	1.61	30	2.43
21	1.67	31	2.57
22	1.73	32	2.70
23	1.79	33	2.86
24	1.86	34	3.02

Age	Premium	Age	Premium
35	3.21	55	13.74
36	3.41	56	14.91
37	3.63	57	16.19
38	3.87	58	17.56
39	4.14	59	19.08
40	4.42	60	20.73
41	4.73	61	22.53
42	5.07	62	24.50
43	5.44	63	26.64
44	5.85	64	28.98
45	6.31	65	31.51
46	6.79	66	34.28
47	7.32	67	37.31
48	7.89	68	40.59
49	8.53	69	44.17
50	9.22	70	48.06
51	9.97	71	52.29
52	10.79	72	56.89
53	11.69	73	61.89
54	12.67	74	67.33

The imputed economic benefit to the employee was reduced by any contribution made by the employee.

EXAMPLE 6-30.

E, a 56 year-old employee of ABC Corp., is the insured on a life insurance policy that will pay a $1 million death benefit upon E's death. As Table 6-2 illustrates, the P.S. 58 cost of the policy for an insured age 56 is $14.91 per $1,000 of death benefit. Accordingly, the P.S. 58 cost of E's policy is $14,910. E and ABC have entered into a split-dollar arrangement whereby ABC agrees to pay a portion of the annual premium on E's policy, while E will pay the balance. If E pays $5,000 of the annual premium, E will have gross income of $9,910, the difference between the P.S. 58 cost of the policy this year and the amount E pays. If E pays $14,910 or more, E will have no gross income, because ABC is paying no portion of the imputed economic benefit of the policy. If the actual cost of the insurance protection is less than $14,910, E need only pay that lesser amount to avoid having gross income from the split-dollar arrangement. Next year, when E is age 57, the P.S. 58 cost of the policy will be $16,180, meaning E will have to pay at least that portion of the policy's annual premium (or, if less, the actual cost of the insurance protection) to avoid having gross income.

§6.72.1

A premium paid by an employer who held an interest in the cash surrender value of a policy was not deductible, because the employer was "directly or indirectly a beneficiary under such a policy" within the meaning of §264(a). Rev. Rul. 66-203, 1966-2 C.B. 104. In contrast, reasonable salary payments to employees were deductible. Accordingly, if the employer's marginal income tax rate was greater than that of the employee, the overall after-tax cost of a split-dollar plan was often lower if the employer increased the employee's salary and the employee used the increase to pay a greater part of the premium. The optimum tax result was often produced when the employee paid an amount of the premium equal to the P.S. 58 cost of the insurance provided under the plan. If the employee paid such an amount, none of the employer's premium payment was included in the employee's income. An employer could cooperate by paying the employee a "bonus" equal to the portion of the premium to be paid by the employee or a "double bonus" equal to that amount plus the income tax that the employee must pay on it.

Upon the death of the employee, the employer usually recovered the amounts it paid over the life of the policy and no more. Even though this would appear to be a below-market loan arrangement, as the employer usually charged no interest, the IRS held that there was no additional gross income to the employer or to the beneficiaries of the policy. Rev. Rul. 64-328, 1964-2 C.B. 11. Split-dollar insurance arrangements, therefore, were effectively sanctioned interest-free arrangements between employers and employees.

Notice 2002-8. On January 3, 2002, the IRS issued Notice 2002-8, 2002-1 C.B. 398, which contained comprehensive new guidance on the federal income tax aspects of split-dollar arrangements entered into after January 28, 2002, and before the effective date of final regulations. The Notice provided that split-dollar plans entered into on or before this date may still use the lower of the P.S. 58 cost or the insurer's actual premium rate to determine the imputed economic benefit to the employee. For plans entered into after January 28, 2002, and before the effective date of final regulations, however, the imputed economic benefit to the employee for periods after 2003 would be measured according to Table 2001, a revised table of insurance protection costs originally issued in Notice 2001-10, 2001-1 C.B. 459. *See* Table 6-3. The Table 2001 rates are substantially less than the P.S. 58 rates, but under Table 2001 and Notice 2002-8, there is no option to use the insurer's actual one-year term rates, which very often are lower than the Table 2001 rates. Consequently, it is important to maintain the grandfathered status of split-dollar plans entered into on or before January 28, 2002. Grandfathered plans generally should not be amended—which could affect their status.

Table 6-3
Interim Table of One-Year Term Premiums for $1,000 of
Life Insurance Protection (Table 2001 Cost)

Attained Age	Section 79 Extended and Interpolated Annual Rates	Section 79 Attained Age	Section 79 Extended and Interpolated Annual Rates	Attained Extended and Age	Interpolated Annual Rates
0	$0.70	35	$0.99	70	$20.62
1	0.41	36	1.01	71	22.72
2	0.27	37	1.04	72	25.07

Attained Age	Section 79 Extended and Interpolated Annual Rates	Section 79 Attained Age	Section 79 Extended and Interpolated Annual Rates	Attained Extended and Age	Interpolated Annual Rates
3	0.19	38	1.06	73	27.57
4	0.13	39	1.07	74	30.18
5	0.13	40	1.10	75	33.05
6	0.14	41	1.13	76	36.34
7	0.15	42	1.20	77	40.17
8	0.16	43	1.29	78	44.33
9	0.16	44	1.40	79	49.23
10	0.16	45	1.53	80	54.56
11	0.19	46	1.67	81	60.51
12	0.24	47	1.83	82	66.75
13	0.28	48	1.98	83	73.07
14	0.33	49	2.13	84	80.35
15	0.38	50	2.30	85	88.76
16	0.52	51	2.52	86	99.16
17	0.57	52	2.81	87	110.40
18	0.59	53	3.20	88	121.85
19	0.61	54	3.65	89	133.40
20	0.62	55	4.15	90	144.30
21	0.62	56	4.68	91	155.80
22	0.64	57	5.20	92	168.75
23	0.66	58	5.66	93	186.45
24	0.68	59	6.06	94	206.71
25	0.71	60	6.52	95	228.35
26	0.73	61	7.11	96	250.01
27	0.76	62	7.96	97	265.09
28	0.80	63	9.08	98	270.11
29	0.83	64	10.41	99	281.05
30	0.87	65	11.90		
31	0.90	66	13.51		
32	0.93	67	15.20		
33	0.96	68	16.92		
34	0.98	69	18.70		

Final Regulations. On September 11, 2003, Treasury and the IRS issued final regulations related to split-dollar life insurance arrangements. The regulations apply to split-dollar plans entered into after September 17, 2003, as well as preexisting plans that are materially modified after that date. The regulations provide a nonexclusive list of changes that do not constitute a material modification of a preexisting plan. Reg. § 1.61-22(j)(2)(ii). Under the final regulations, split-dollar plans in the form of an endorsement arrangement are taxed under the "economic benefit" regime, while those in the form of a collateral assignment are taxed under the "loan" regime.

Economic Benefit Regime (for Endorsement Arrangements). Under the economic benefit regime, the owner of the policy is deemed to provide economic benefits to the nonowner in an amount equal to the cost of the term protection provided by the owner. Reg. §§ 1.61-22(d)(1); 1.61-22(d)(2)(i), 1.61-22(d)(3). The cost of the term protection is the cost to obtain insurance in an amount equal to the excess of the death benefit to be paid under the policy minus all amounts payable to the owner at such time. Reg. § 1.61-22(d)(3)(i) – (ii). Presumably, such cost is determined with reference to Table 2001 and is reduced by any consideration paid by the nonowner to the owner. The exact income tax consequences of the economic benefit provided to the nonowner will depend on the relationship between the owner and the nonowner. In the traditional endorsement arrangement, where the employer is the owner and the employee is the nonowner, this economic benefit constitutes compensation.

EXAMPLE 6-31.

E, a 56 year-old employee of *ABC* Corp., is the insured on a life insurance policy that will pay a $1 million death benefit upon *E*'s death. *ABC* is the owner of the policy. *E* and *ABC* have entered into a split-dollar arrangement whereby *E* will pay $2,000 of each annual premium and *ABC* will pay the balance. As Table 6-3 illustrates, the Table 2001 cost of the policy for an insured age 56 is $4.68 per $1,000 of death benefit. Accordingly, the Table 2001 cost of *E*'s policy is $4,680. Under the split-dollar arrangement between *E* and *ABC*, *E* will have gross income of $2,680, the difference between the Table 2001 cost of the policy this year and the amount *E* pays. If *E* pays $4,680 or more of the annual premium, *E* will have no gross income. It does not matter whether the actual cost of the insurance protection is less than $4,680, for the economic benefit regime does not allow the parties to use such lower amounts in determining the economic benefit of the arrangement to *E*. Next year, when *E* is age 57, the Table 2001 cost of the policy will be $5,200, meaning *E* will have to pay at least that portion of the policy's annual premium to avoid having gross income.

In addition to the economic benefit from the current life insurance protection, the nonowner must report the economic benefit associated with any equity component of the split-dollar arrangement. Reg. § 1.61-22(d)(2)(ii) – (iii). Thus, where an employee has access to the cash surrender value of the policy (*e.g.*, through loans, withdrawals, or a partial surrender of the policy), the employee will have additional compensation income to the extent there is an increase in the amount by which the policy's cash surrender value exceeds aggregate premiums paid. Reductions in the net equity of the policy (when, for instance, the cash surrender value decreases in a given year) do not give rise to realized losses.

EXAMPLE 6-32.

Assume the same facts as Example 6-31, except that *E* is entitled to borrow amounts against the policy or otherwise access the cash surrender value of the policy. If there in an increase in the net cash surrender value of the insurance policy in any given year (the excess of the cash surrender value over the aggregate premiums paid), E will have compensation income in the amount of such increase.

In effect, then, the economic benefit regime strips the endorsement arrangement of any income tax deferral opportunities. This severely undermines one of the principal advantages of the traditional endorsement arrangement. Throwing salt into the wound, the nonowner gets no basis credit for the economic benefit reported as gross income. Reg. § 1.61-22(f)(2)(i).

Loan Regime (for Collateral Assignment Arrangements). Under the loan regime, the nonowner is treated as lending premium payments to the owner. This regime automatically governs collateral assignment split-dollar plans and also applies to any arrangement where the nonowner's premium payments are in fact loans where repayment is to be made from (or is secured by) either the policy's death benefit proceeds or its cash surrender value. Reg. § 1.7872-15(a)(2)(i).

Each payment is a separate loan. If there is no interest charged on the loan, or if the interest is charged at a rate that is less than the applicable federal rate (AFR), § 7872 applies. Under § 7872, the extent to which the interest actually charged is less than the interest that would be charged under AFR represents compensation, a dividend or a gift, as the case may be. The loan regime does not attempt to tax either the cost of life insurance protection or any equity buildup in the policy. In addition, the foregone interest that is deemed to be compensation, dividend, or a gift to the borrower is deemed to be retransferred to the lender as interest, meaning the lender will have interest income over the life of the loan. Reg. §§ 1.7872-15(e)(3)(iii)(A), 1.7872-15(e)(4)(iv). Here too, then, the income tax advantage of split-dollar arrangements is effectively lost. Interest-free split-dollar arrangements are no longer tax-favored.

The "loan" can be structured either as a demand loan or a term loan. A split-dollar loan is a demand loan if it does not have a certain term or repayment date but the lender has the right to demand repayment at any time. Reg. § 1.7872-15(b)(2). Section 7872 applies to a demand loan to the extent the interest charged by the lender is less than the short-term AFR. In the split-dollar context, the deemed transfers of foregone interest occur annually. The applicable interest rate is determined by reference to a "blended" rate published by the IRS each year that represents the average of the monthly short-term AFRs for that year. Reg. § 1.7872-15(e)(3)(ii).

EXAMPLE 6-33.

E, an employee of *ABC* Corp., is the insured on a life insurance policy that will pay a $1 million death benefit upon E's death. E is the owner of the policy, but E and *ABC* have entered into a split-dollar arrangement whereby *ABC* will pay $1,000 of the annual premium on the policy. E agrees to reimburse *ABC* for the premiums paid by *ABC* upon termination of E's employment, without interest. The split-dollar arrangement between E and *ABC* will be treated as a below-market demand loan. If the blended short-term AFR this year is 3.59 percent, then *ABC* is deemed to have transferred $35.90 on the last day of the taxable year to *E* as compensation, and *E* will be deemed to have transferred $35.90 to *ABC* as interest. *E* will have gross income of $35.90 and no deduction for the deemed interest payment. Reg. § 1.7872-15(c). *ABC* will have $35.90 of interest income and a $35.90 compensation deduction.

If the loan provides for a certain term or repayment date, it is a term loan. Reg. § 1.7872-15(b)(3). Section 7872 applies to a term loan where the amount loaned exceeds the present value of all payments due under the loan, computed using a discount rate equal to the AFR. Reg. § 1.7872-15(e)(4)(ii). In the split-dollar context, the borrower's benefit is accelerated into the first taxable year in which the loan is made and the lender has income ratably over the term of the loan. If, however, a term loan becomes payable upon the death of an individual, is conditioned on the future performance of substantial services by an individual, or is a gift, the borrower's benefit is reportable over the life of the loan and not entirely in the year of the loan. *See* Reg. § 1.7872-15(e)(5).

EXAMPLE 6-34.

E, an employee of *ABC* Corp., is the insured on a life insurance policy that will pay a $1 million death benefit upon *E*'s death. *E* is the owner of the policy. In September 2006, *E* and *ABC* entered into a split-dollar arrangement whereby *ABC* will pay $1,000 of the annual premium on the policy. *E* agrees to reimburse *ABC* for the premiums paid by *ABC*, without interest, in 2011. The split-dollar arrangement between *E* and *ABC* will be treated as a below-market term loan. The mid-term AFR in September 2006, is 5.01 percent. The present value of the $1,000 loaned in 2006 and to be repaid in five years is $783.15. Accordingly, *ABC* is deemed to have transferred $216.85 on the last day of the taxable year to *E* as compensation, and *E* will be deemed to have transferred $216.85 to *ABC* as interest. *E* will have gross income of $216.85 and no deduction for the deemed interest payment. Reg. § 1.7872-15(c). *ABC* will have $216.85 of interest income and a $216.85 compensation deduction.

Where a third party owns the policy and § 7872 applies, the transaction is treated as two loans. Thus, for example, where an employee's ILIT owns the policy and the employer is lending the premiums at a below-market rate, there is first a compensation-related loan from the employer to the employee and then a second, gift loan between the employee and the trust.

Material Modifications to Grandfathered Split-Dollar Arrangements. As explained above, the foregoing regimes apply to split-dollar life insurance arrangements entered into after September 17, 2003. For purposes of this effective date, any pre-existing arrangement that is "materially modified" after September 17, 2003, is treated as a new arrangement. Accordingly, a materially modified arrangement becomes subject to the regulations. There are two other Code provisions that are sensitive to material modifications in life insurance arrangements. First, § 101(j)(1)'s rule limiting the § 101(a)(1) exclusion in the case of employer-owned life insurance to the sum of the premiums paid only applies to insurance contracts issued after August 17, 2006, but if a pre-existing policy is "materially changed" (including a material increase in the death benefit), such policy will be subject to the reduced exclusion. Second, § 264(f)'s prohibition against deducting interest expenses allocable to "unborrowed policy cash value" only applies to life insurance policies issued after June 8, 1997, but a "material change" to a pre-existing policy will be treated as a new one subject to the rule. The IRS has announced that a material modification to a split-dollar insurance arrangement will *not* be treated as a material change to the underlying policy for purposes of §§ 101(j) and 264(f) even though such modification may trigger application of the split-dollar regulations. Notice 2008-42, 2008-15 I.R.B. 747. This is an appropriate result because a modification to a split-dollar arrangement is not a modification of the policy itself but rather a change in the relative ownership rights in the policy.

Application of §409A to Split-Dollar Arrangements. Section 409A provides that unless certain requirements are met (related to distributions, acceleration of payments, and elections), amounts deferred under a nonqualified deferred compensation plan for all taxable years beginning in or after 2005 are currently includible in gross income to the extent such amounts are not subject to a substantial risk of forfeiture and have not already been included in gross income. Many split-dollar life insurance arrangements constitute nonqualified deferred compensation under § 409A, because they allocate the cash surrender value of the policy to the insureds (employees and other service providers). In recent guidance, the IRS has indicated that if the split-dollar plan pays only death benefits to or for the benefit of the insured, the plan is not subject to § 409A. Notice 2007-34, 2007-1 C.B. 996.

If a split-dollar plan is not grandfathered under the split-dollar rules (*i.e.,* it was entered into on or before September 17, 2003) and is within the scope of § 409A, Notice 2007-34 provides that the application of § 409A depends on whether the plan is treated as loan-type arrangement or a compensation-type arrangement under the split-dollar rules. Split-dollar arrangements treated as loans "generally will not give rise to deferrals of compensation within the meaning of section 409A." But if the plan is a compensation-type arrangement under the split-dollar rules, and if "the service provider has a legally binding right . . . to economic benefits [like cash value] . . . that, pursuant to the terms of the arrangement, are payable to (or on behalf of) the service provider in a later taxable year," then § 409A applies. Specifically, "the excess of the policy cash value over the aggregate premium payments is treated as earnings."

Notice 2007-34 also provides that modifications to grandfathered split-dollar plans will not be treated as material modifications to such plans (which would cause such plans to become subject to the split-dollar rules) if: (1) § 409A applies to the plan; (2) the modification makes the agreement comply with § 409A or results in § 409A no longer being applicable; (3) the modification only changes definitions or the timing of required payments; and (4) the modification establishes a time and form of payment consistent with what would have been paid under the preexisting arrangement; and (5) the modification does not materially enhance the value of the benefits to the service provider.

§6.72.2. Gift Tax Consequences

In the typical case neither the original acquisition of employer-provided split-dollar insurance nor the payment of subsequent premiums involves a gift for federal gift tax purposes. However, if the risk element has been assigned by the employee any subsequent premium payments made by the employee do involve gifts. Rev. Rul. 78-420, 1978-2 C.B. 67 (policy owned by spouse of employee). The gift in such a case may qualify for the annual exclusion. Rev. Rul. 76-490, 1976-2 C.B. 300; *but see* Rev. Rul. 79-47, 1979-1 C.B. 312. The payment of premiums may also involve gifts where a split-dollar plan is used in a nonbusiness setting.

EXAMPLE 6-35.

Under a private split-dollar plan *M* pays a portion of the premium on an ordinary policy on the life of her daughter, *D*, equal to the increase in cash surrender value of the policy, and *D* pays the balance. As each premium is paid, *M* makes a gift to *D*. If *D* had given her interest in the policy to another person, the subsequent premium payments would involve gifts by *M* and *D* to the owner of the policy.

The transfer of a split-dollar policy that has been in effect for some time involves a gift, as does the subsequent payment of premiums on the policy. Rev. Rul. 81-198, 1981-2 C.B. 188. In Rev. Rul. 81-198, the IRS ruled that an employee-donor made a gift equal to the total value of the policy (interpolated terminal reserve plus the unearned premium) *less* the value of the employer's interest in the policy. In such a case subsequent gifts are made by the employee as the employer, the employee, or both contribute to premium payments. The gift with respect to subsequent premium payments consists of two elements: (1) the premium payment made by the employer to the extent it is treated as income to the employee and (2) the amount of the premium paid by the employee.

In LR 9604001 (TAM), the IRS ruled that the taxpayer made a gift to the irrevocable trust, which owned the policies, of the amount of the value of the one year term insurance protection provided under the split-dollar agreement plus the amount of the cash surrender increase in the value of the policy that is not recoverable by his employer.

Nonemployer (Private) Split Dollar Plans. Letter Ruling 9636033 involved a split-dollar agreement between the trustee of an irrevocable life insurance trust and the insured's spouse. The policy, owned by the trust, was collaterally assigned to the spouse. The trustee was required to pay the portion of the annual premium equal to the lower of (1) the applicable amount under the then-applicable P.S. 58 tables and (2) the cost of one-year term insurance available from the company that issued the policy. If the agreement is terminated other than by the death of the insured, the spouse was entitled to recover the cash value of the policy. On the death of the insured the spouse was entitled to receive the greater of the cash value of the policy immediately before death or the amount of premiums she had paid. In effect, the arrangement allowed the parties to pay the premiums on the policy without making gifts to the trust.

Letter Ruling 9636033 concluded that the arrangement did not involve a gift by the spouse at the time of the premium payment. Under current law, however, § 7872 would apply to this arrangement, meaning the interest-free aspect of the transaction would be treated as a gift to the trust.

Transfers to Charities. If all interests in the insurance are assigned to a qualified charity or charitable trust, presumably the assignment and the subsequent premium payments attributable to the employee qualify for the income and gift tax charitable deduction. In contrast, no deductions are allowed where the sole owner of a policy attempts to take advantage of the different interests in a policy by assigning only the cash surrender value to a charity. Thus, where the insured owned the entire interest in a policy, the irrevocable assignment of the cash surrender value does not qualify for the charitable deduction for income or gift tax purposes because only a portion of the donor's interest was transferred. The cash surrender value does not constitute an undivided interest as required in the case of split gifts of outright interests. Rev. Rul. 76-143, 1976-1 C.B. 63 (income tax); Rev. Rul. 76-200, 1976 1 C.B. 308 (gift tax). The rules applicable to charitable gifts are reviewed in detail in Chapter 8.

§ 6.72.3. Estate Tax Consequences

Upon the death of the employee, none of the proceeds paid to the employer under a split-dollar plan is usually includible in the employee's estate. However, if the insured had been the controlling shareholder of the employer corporation, the portion of the proceeds paid to the employer is included as an asset of the corporation in valuing the stock owned by the insured. Reg. § 20.2031-2(f); *see Estate of John Huntsman*, 66 T.C. 861 (1976), *acq.*, 1977 1 C.B. 1.

The proceeds attributable to the risk element of the policy are includible in the employee's estate under § 2042(1) if they were paid to the employee's estate. In other cases inclusion is required under § 2042(2) if the employee held any of the incidents of ownership at the time of death. In this connection, note that for purposes of § 2042(2) the incidents of ownership held by a corporation are attributed to the estate of the controlling shareholder. Reg. § 20.2041-1(c)(6). Accordingly, the proceeds are includible in the estate of the controlling shareholder except to the extent the proceeds are payable to the corporation or are otherwise taken into account in valuing the insured's stock. *Estate of Alfred Dimen*, 72 T.C. 198 (1979), *aff'd mem.* (unpublished opinion) 633 F.2d 203 (2d Cir. 1980); Rev. Rul. 82-145, 1982-2 C.B. 213, *modifying* Rev. Rul. 76-274, 1976-2 C.B. 278, situation 3. The proceeds of a life insurance policy payable to the insured's wholly-owned corporation that are used pursuant to a stock redemption agreement to purchase a portion of the insured's stock are not includible in the insured's estate under § 2042, but are instead reflected in the value of decedent's stock. Rev. Rul. 82-85, 1982-1 C.B. 137. In contrast, the proceeds are includible in the estate of the insured-controlling shareholder where the proceeds are paid to another corporation that uses the proceeds for its own purposes. LR 8710004 (TAM). The incidents of ownership of the controlled corporation are attributed to the insured because the proceeds of the insurance are neither payable to the corporation that owns the policy nor used for its business purposes. *Id.*

The proceeds of insurance held in an irrevocable trust are includible in the estate of an insured who retains the right to borrow against the cash surrender value of the policy. Rev. Rul. 79-129, 1979 1 C.B. 306. Specifically, the entire proceeds are includible in the estate of the insured when the insurance was assigned to an irrevocable trust but the insured retained the right to borrow against the insurance. However, the balance remaining at the time of the insured's death of the funds transferred by the insured to the trust to pay premiums is not includible in the insured's estate. Rev. Rul. 81-164, 1981 1 C.B. 458.

In LR 9709027, the IRS ruled that an S Corporation that has entered into a split-dollar agreement with an irrevocable trust does not have an incident of ownership in a second-to-die policy on the lives of the grantor of the trust and his spouse. The policy involved in the ruling was collaterally assigned to the corporation, whose rights under the split-dollar agreement were limited to the right to recover unreimbursed premiums on termination or on the death of the insured. *See also* Rev. Rul. 76-274, 1976-2 C.B. 278, *modified*, Rev. Rul. 82-142, 1982-2 C.B. 213 and LR 9651017.

§ 6.73. EMPLOYER-PROVIDED GROUP-TERM LIFE INSURANCE: GENERAL

The relatively low cost of group-term life insurance and the favorable income tax treatment it is given make it a common fringe benefit. First, the cost of employer-provided group-term insurance is generally deductible as a business expense under § 162. Of course, the premium payments are not deductible if the employer is a beneficiary under the policy. § 264(a). Second, the employee is not taxed on the cost of $50,000 of coverage. § 79(a)(1). Under Reg. § 1-79.1(d), if a group-term policy also provides permanent benefits, the fair market value of the permanent benefits, calculated as provided in Rev. Proc. 2005-25, 2005-1 C.B. 962, are included in the employee's gross income. Third, the cost of group-term insurance in excess of $50,000, determined under the Table I rate schedule set out in Table 6-4 at § 6.73.9, is includible in the gross income of an employee except to the extent the employee contributed to the cost of the coverage. The 1984 Act removed an exception that allowed an unlimited amount of group-term insurance to be provided to retired employees. Under a grandfather provision more than $50,000 of group term insurance can be provided under a plan that was in existence on or before January 1, 1984 with respect to an employee who was 55 on or before that date. Fourth, the cost of group-term insurance in excess of $50,000 is not includible when the employer or a charity is the beneficiary under the policy. § 79(b)(2). However, no charitable deduction is allowable under § 170 with respect to a policy that has been assigned or is payable to a charity. Reg. § 1.79-2(c)(3). Fifth, the cost of group-term insurance in excess of $50,000 is not includible in the gross income of a disabled former employee. § 79(b)(1). Of course, the preferential provisions of § 79 do not apply to insurance in excess of the maximum amount of group-term insurance allowable under the applicable state law. Reg. § 1.79-1(e).

The provisions of § 79(a) govern the income taxation of the cost of group-term life insurance whether or not the employee has assigned his or her interest in the insurance. Rev. Rul. 73-174, 1973-1 C.B. 43. Each time the employer pays a premium on the insurance, the employee receives additional compensation. Rev. Rul. 76-490, 1976-2 C.B. 300 (gift tax)

§6.73.1. Planning with Group-Term Insurance

The current income, gift, and estate tax rules encourage the assignment of group-term insurance to an irrevocable life insurance trust. Accordingly, group-term insurance is often included among the policies that a client assigns to an irrevocable life insurance trust. However, a client should understand that group-term insurance is not a secure source of death benefits. Group plans may be terminated by the employer and coverage terminates if the employment relationship ends. An employer's payment of premiums on group-term insurance is compensation to the employee that continues to qualify for the limited exclusion under §79 although the insurance has been assigned. Little, if any, gift tax results from the assignment of group-term insurance to an irrevocable life insurance trust. First, group-term insurance usually has a low value—typically the remaining unearned premium. Second, the beneficiaries are usually given withdrawal powers sufficient to allow annual gift tax exclusions. The assignment of group-term insurance to a properly drafted irrevocable life insurance trust may insulate the proceeds from inclusion in the estates of the insured and the insured's spouse. Of course, if the insured dies within three years of assigning the insurance, the insurance proceeds are includible in the estate of the insured. (If the insured is the controlling shareholder, the employer's incidents of ownership will be attributed to the insured under Reg. §20.2042-1(c)(6) and the insurance will be included in the estate of the insured). If the insured dies within three years of transferring the insurance to the trust, the noninsured spouse is commonly given an interest in the trust sufficient to support a QTIP marital deduction in order to allow payment of the estate tax to be deferred until the death of the insured's spouse. Otherwise no portion of the trust should be included in the estate of the noninsured surviving spouse.

§6.73.2. Insurance on Spouses and Children

In general, the cost of employer-provided group-term life insurance on the life of an employee's spouse and children is includible in the employee's gross income. Here again, the cost is calculated under the Table I rate schedule. Reg. §1.79-3(d)(2). See Table 6-4 at §6.73.9. However, the cost of up to $2,000 of group-term insurance on their lives is considered incidental and is not includible in the employee's gross income. Reg. §1.61-2(d)(2)(ii)(b). The amount of group-term insurance on the life of the employee's spouse or children is not taken into account in applying the rules of §79 since it is not insurance on the life of the employee. Reg. §1.79-3(f)(2).

§6.73.3. Nondiscrimination Rules

In the case of a discriminatory group-term life insurance plan, §79(a)(1) does not apply with respect to any key employee. §79(d)(1). For this purpose a discriminatory plan is one that discriminates regarding either eligibility to participate or as to benefits. §79(d)(2). More particularly, §79(a)(1) would not apply to a plan that either (a) discriminated in favor of key employees as to eligibility to participate or (b) discriminated in favor of key employees as to the amount and type of benefits.

§ 6.73.4. Nondiscrimination Rules as to Eligibility

Under § 79(d)(3)(A), the nondiscrimination standards regarding eligibility are satisfied if the plan meets any of the following four criteria:

1. The plan benefits 70 percent or more of the employees;
2. At least 85 percent of all employees who participate are not key employees;
3. The plan benefits employees who qualify under a classification established by the employer and found by the Secretary not to be discriminatory; or
4. In the case of a plan that is a cafeteria plan, the requirements applicable to cafeteria plans, § 125, are satisfied.

In determining whether the requirements are satisfied, § 79(d)(3)(B) allows several classes of employees to be excluded from consideration. They are: employees who have not completed three years of service; part-time or seasonal employees; employees who are included in a collective bargaining agreement, if the benefits of the plan were the subject of bargaining between the employer and the employee group; and employees who are nonresident aliens and receive no earned income from within the United States.

§ 6.73.5. Nondiscrimination Rules as to Benefits

A group-term plan must make all of the benefits that are available to key employees available to all other employees. A plan does not discriminate as to benefits if the insurance made available to nonkey employees is a multiple of total or regular compensation that is equal to or greater than the multiple that applies to key employees. Reg. § 1.79-4T, A-9.

§ 6.73.6. Basic Requirements

In order to qualify as group-term life insurance it must be part of a group-term insurance plan that meets the technical requirements set out in the regulations issued under § 79. Paraphrased, the basic requirements set forth in Reg. § 1.79-1(a) are the following:

1. The insurance provides a general death benefit that is excludable from gross income under § 101(a);
2. The insurance is provided to a group of employees;
3. The insurance is provided under a policy carried directly or indirectly by the employer;
4. The amount of insurance provided to each employee is computed under a formula that precludes individual selection (*i.e.*, the formula must be based on factors such as age, years of service, compensation, or position).

Health and accident insurance and other policies that do not provide a general death benefit do not satisfy the first requirement.

In general, the group life insurance must be provided to at least ten full-time employees in order to meet the second requirement. Reg. § 1.79-1(c)(1). However, term insurance provided to a group of less than ten employees will qualify if (1) it is provided to all full-time employees, (2) the amount of insurance is computed either as a uniform percentage of compensation or on the basis of coverage brackets established by the insurer, and (3) evidence of insurability affecting an employee's eligibility is limited to a medical questionnaire completed by the employee. Reg. § 1.79-1(c)(2). Term insurance provided to a group of less than ten employees will also qualify if (1) it is provided under a common plan of two or more unrelated employers, (2) the insurance is restricted to and mandatory for all employees who belong to or are represented by an organization (such as a union) that carries on substantial activities in addition to obtaining insurance, and (3) evidence of insurability does not affect an employee's eligibility. Reg. § 1.79-1(c)(3).

In order to prevent individual selection, each element of the formula used to determine the amount of insurance must be structured so as to apply to more than one person. *William S. Towne*, 78 T.C. 791 (1982). In *Towne*, the Tax Court upheld the disqualification of a plan that placed all employees but the president in one class, members of which were provided with life insurance coverage equal to their salary up to a maximum of $25,000, while the president was in a second class, members of which received an additional $500,000 of insurance coverage.

§ 6.73.7. Plans That Include Permanent Benefits

Under certain circumstances the regulations permit group-term coverage to be combined with other benefits, called "permanent benefits", the cost of which, determined as provided in Reg. § 1.79-1(d), less the amount paid by the employee, is included in the employee's income. Rev. Proc. 2005-25, 2005-1 C.B. 962. Prior to the revisions of the regulations in 1979 and 1983, qualifying group-term insurance and permanent benefits were more frequently provided by an employer to key employees. The revised regulations now define "permanent benefit," Reg. § 1.79-0, impose certain requirements regarding the combination of group-term and permanent benefits, Reg. § 1.79-1(b), and define the amount that an employee is required to include in income with respect to permanent benefits, Reg. § 1.79-1(d). Of course, the nondiscrimination rules make it virtually impossible to provide tax advantaged permanent benefits to key employees in conjunction with a group-term plan. An employer is more likely, instead, to increase the compensation of a key employee in order to enable him or her to acquire additional permanent insurance.

§ 6.73.8. Who Are "Employees"?

Group-term life insurance may be provided only to employees. The common law rules for determining the existence of an employer-employee relationship provide the primary guide for resolving the question of whether or not a particular individual is an employee. Regs. § § 1.79-0, 31.3401(c)-1. Clearly, a sole proprietor or partner is not an employee. A director of a corporation is also not an employee of the corporation. Reg. § 31.3401(c)-1(f), *accord, M. A. Enright*, 56 T.C. 1261 (1971). Similarly, a trustee, executor, or other fiduciary is generally not considered to be an employee. Rev. Rul. 69-657, 1969-2 C.B. 189.

§6.73.9. Determining the Amount Includible in Income

For income tax purposes the cost of any group-term life insurance provided to an employee after July 1, 1999 is determined according to the Table I rate schedule set forth in Table 6-4 below and not by the actual cost of the insurance. The table appears in Reg. §1.79-3(d)(2). Between January 1, 1989 and July 1, 1999, the cost was determined according to Table 6-5 below. For tax years beginning before 1989, the cost of group-term insurance provided to an employee over 64 was considered to be the same as the cost of insurance provided to persons in the five-year age bracket of 60 to 64. Former §79(c). For later years the cost of group-term insurance must be determined "on the basis of uniform premiums (computed on the basis of five-year age brackets) prescribed by regulations by the Secretary." §79(c). As noted above, §6.73.7, the cost of permanent benefits, less the amount paid by an employee, is included in the employee's income.

Table 6-4
Uniform Premiums for $1,000 of Group-Term Life Insurance
Protection, Effective July 1, 1999 (Table I, Reg. §1.79-3(d)(2))

5-year Age Bracket	Cost per $1,000 of protection for one month
Under 25	$0.05
25 to 29	.06
30 to 34	.08
35 to 39	.09
40 to 44	.10
45 to 49	.15
50 to 54	.23
55 to 59	.43
60 to 64	.66
65 to 69	$1.27
70 and above	$2.06

Table 6-5
Uniform Premiums for $1,000 of Group-Term Life
Insurance Protection, January 1, 1989-July 1, 1999
(Former Table I, Reg. §1.79-3(d)(2))

5-year age bracket	Cost per $1,000 of protection for one month
Under 30	.08
30 to 34	.09
35 to 39	.11
40 to 44	.17
45 to 49	.29
50 to 54	.48
55 to 59	.75
60 to 64	$1.17
65 to 69	$2.10
70 and above	$3.76

Example 6-36 illustrates how the cost of group-term insurance is calculated under Table I.

EXAMPLE 6-36.

During 2006, Employer, Inc., pays the entire cost of a $100,000 group-term life insurance on the life of its general counsel, X, who is 47 years old. X has designated her husband as beneficiary of the insurance. The amount included in X's gross income for the taxable year is calculated as follows:

Amount of group-term insurance	$100,000
Less: Tax-free amount	− 50,000
Amount of insurance subject to tax	$50,000
Table I cost of $1,000 of insurance per year as shown in Table 6-4:	$1.80
(12 × $0.15)	
Amount includible in gross income (50 × $1.80)	$90

Any amount that X contributed in 2006 toward the cost of the insurance would be deducted from $90 in determining the amount includible in her gross income. None of the cost of the insurance would be taxed to her if the policy designated her employer or a charity as beneficiary. Note that under Notice 88-82, 1982-2 C.B. 398, the amount includible in X's income is subject to FICA taxes that must be reported by Employer Inc. at least once a year.

§ 6.73.10. Assignment

The irrevocable assignment of group-term insurance is a particularly attractive estate planning tool because it permits a prospectively large item to be eliminated from the insured's gross estate at little or no gift tax cost. In general, group-term insurance is subject to the same gift and estate tax rules as other forms of life insurance. As indicated in § 6.73.11, care must be exercised to determine that the group-term insurance is assignable under the group policy and the state law.

§ 6.73.11. Estate Tax

Some of the special estate questions that arise because of the particular characteristics of group-term insurance were resolved by the IRS largely in the taxpayer's favor. First, in 1968, the IRS ruled that the proceeds of an employer-provided group policy would not be included in the employee's gross estate under § 2042 if the employee had irrevocably assigned all of his or her interests in the insurance prior to death. Rev. Rul. 68-334, 1968-1 C.B. 403, *restated and superseded*, Rev. Rul. 69-54, 1969-1 C.B. 221, *modified*, Rev. Rul. 72-307, 1972-1 C.B. 307. Following the issuance of Rev. Rul. 69-54, most states adopted statutes that expressly authorize the assignment of interests in group insurance. Unfortunately, however, some states limit the class of persons to whom such an assignment can be made. *E.g.,* Wash. Rev. Code § 48.18.375 (2011). Even when assignments are permitted by state law, they may be barred by the terms of the master group policy. Before attempting to assign group-term insurance, the planner should be sure that assignments are permitted by the master policy. Unfortunately, it is not entirely safe to rely upon the description of the insurance contained in the certificate of insurance given to the insured employee. The certificate constitutes evidence of the insurance coverage but its terms may be subordinate to those of the master policy. *Poling v. North America Life & Casualty Co.,* 593 P.2d 568 (Wyo. 1979); *contra, Fittro v. Lincoln National Life Insurance Co.,* 757 P.2d 1374 (1988) (group health coverage); *Estate of Max Gorby,* 53 T.C. 80 (1969), *acq.,* 1970-1 C.B. xvi. If the master policy prohibits assignments, the employee may ask the employer to waive the prohibition. Employers and insurers commonly cooperate promptly to remove any restrictions on assignments.

Second, although Rev. Rul. 69-54 helped clear the air regarding the effect of assignments, some nagging doubts remained regarding the effectiveness of an assignment of annually renewable term insurance under § 2035. Subsection 2035(a)(2)(and former § 2035(d)(2)) requires insurance to be included in the insured's gross estate if the insured dies within three years following a transfer of the insurance. *See* § 6.31. Planners were concerned that the IRS might treat each annual renewal as giving rise to "new" insurance each year. If so, the insurance could not be assigned more than one year prior to death and the proceeds would be includible in the estate of the insured in all cases. That concern was substantially relieved by LR 8034017 (TAM). It concluded that the proceeds of an annually renewable group-term policy were *not* includible in the insured's gross estate when the insured assigned the insurance more than three years prior to death. Further, in 1982 the IRS ruled that an employer's renewal of a group-term policy by payment of the annual premium did not give the employee any new rights in the insurance. Rev. Rul. 82-13, 1982-1 C.B. 132. Accordingly, group-term insurance was not includible in the estate of an employee who effectively assigned all interests in the insurance more than three years prior to death. The result of the ruling hinged on the nature of the policy, which provided for automatic renewal upon payment of the annual premium. Of course, the mere payment of premiums on group-term insurance by the employer within three years of the employee's death does not cause inclusion of the premiums or the insurance.

Third, a change of position by the IRS on another issue provided additional comfort to those who wished to assign group-term insurance. Initially, the IRS ruled that an insured employee could not effectively assign an interest in group insurance that was provided at the time of the employee's death under a policy that was not in effect when the assignment was made. Rev. Rul. 79-231, 1979-2 C.B. 323. The ruling involved an employee who, in 1971, assigned to his wife all of his interest in any life insurance that might be provided by his employer. The assignment was made more than three years prior to his death during a time when his group insurance was provided under a master policy issued by Company Y. In 1977 the employer terminated the master policy with Company Y and entered into a new master policy with Company Z. However, the terms of the master policies were identical in all relevant respects. Shortly after the master policy with Company Z became effective, the employee assigned all of his interest in it to his wife. Unfortunately, the employee died within three years of that assignment. Unhappily, the IRS ruled that the assignment that the employee made in 1971 was ineffective to transfer his rights in the insurance that was provided by the master policy subsequently issued by Company Z. According to the IRS, the employee could not make such an "anticipatory assignment" of insurance that was not in effect at the time. Accordingly, it held that the insurance was not assigned until 1977, as a result of which it was includible in the insured's estate under § 2035.

Revenue Ruling 79-231 was revoked by the IRS less than a year after it was issued and a contrary ruling issued. Rev. Rul. 80-289, 1980-2 C.B. 270. The later ruling held upon identical facts that "the [second] assignment will not be treated as a transfer under Section 2035 of the code." *Id*. In it the IRS "maintains the view that the anticipatory assignment was not technically effective as a present transfer of the decedent's rights in the policy issued by Company Z. Nevertheless, the IRS believes that the assignment in 1977 to *D*'s spouse, the object of the anticipatory assignment in 1971, should not cause the value of the proceeds to be includible in the gross estate of the decedent under section 2035 where the assignment was necessitated by the change of the employer's master insurance carrier and the new arrangement is identical in all relevant aspects to the previous arrangement with Company *Y*." Similar problems could arise if, subsequent to an assignment, a group policy is renewed or the amount of insurance is increased, as happens when the amount of coverage is tied to the employee's salary or position. Accordingly, an assignment of interests in existing group policies should attempt to deal with the problem by providing that the assignment covers all interests in the existing group insurance, all interests in group insurance provided by any renewal or replacement, and all changes in the amount of the insurance. Such an explicit assignment, if made more than three years prior to the assignor's death, should help insulate the proceeds of the insurance from inclusion in the insured's gross estate.

§ 6.73.12. Gift Tax

The amount of a gift resulting from the assignment of group-term insurance depends upon all of the circumstances, including the length of time for which the premiums have been paid, the extent to which the employer is obligated to make future payments, and the health of the insured. An assignment of group-term insurance may involve a gift composed of one or more of the following components:

1. An amount equivalent to the cost of a term policy for the unexpired portion of the period through which the premium on the group policy had been paid at the time of assignment (a proportionate part of the premium actually paid allocable to the cost of the unexpired period is an acceptable method of valuing this interest, Reg. § 25.2512-6(a); because that amount may be difficult or impossible to determine, it may be appropriate to use the Table I cost for this purpose);

2. The value of any right the assignment may carry with it to require the assignor or another person to make future premium payments; and

3. Any additional value the insurance may have because of the insured's poor health.

§ 6.73.12

Further gifts will occur as later premiums are paid directly or indirectly by the employer or other third party. Thus, where the insured's employer is not obligated to pay future premiums on group-term insurance that the employee has assigned, any future premium payments involve future indirect gifts by the employee to the assignee. Rev. Rul. 76-490, 1976-2 C.B. 300. On the other hand, the assignment of a group-term policy on the last day of the premium payment period does not involve a present gift where the employer is not obligated to make further premium payments. *Id.*

Without any analysis, Rev. Rul. 76-490 incorrectly concluded that the payment of future premiums on group-term insurance assigned to a trust would qualify for the annual gift tax exclusion. The conclusion is incorrect if, as indicated by the facts the beneficiary was not entitled to any current benefits in the trust. Apparently, the trustee was required to retain the insurance until the death of the insured when the proceeds would be distributed to the beneficiary. A later ruling properly holds that an annual exclusion is not available with respect to the employer's payment of premiums when the trustee of the insurance trust will retain the proceeds in trust following the death of the insured. Rev. Rul. 79-47, 1979-1 C.B. 312. The availability of the annual exclusion for a transfer of insurance to a trust turns on the extent of the beneficiary's present interests in the trust and not on whether or not the proceeds are immediately distributable by the trustee when the insured dies. When a trustee is required to retain insurance and the beneficiary is not entitled to any current benefits under the trust, the beneficiary does not have a present interest in the insurance or in subsequent premium payments. *Commissioner v. Warner*, 127 F.2d 913 (9th Cir. 1942); Reg. § 25.2503-3(c), Example 2. Of course, the original transfer to the trust and the payment of subsequent premiums may qualify for the annual exclusion if the beneficiary has a *Crummey* power to withdraw property as it is added to the trust. *See* LRs 8006109 and 8021058; *see also* § 7.37.7.

§ 6.73.13. Group-Term Life Insurance: Retired Lives Reserve (RLR)

Retired lives reserve (RLR) plans, promoted in the 1970s and early 1980s, are of interest largely for historic reasons. RLR plans were intended to allow large amounts of post-retirement life insurance coverage to be provided to key employees at no tax cost. Under an RLR plan, an employer paid the cost of providing current group-term insurance and made a contribution to a reserve fund or trust that would pay the cost of continuing the group-term insurance after an employee retired. The employer's contributions to the reserve fund, plus the tax-free income earned by the fund, were designed to be sufficient to pay the cost of providing group-term insurance to the retired employees covered by the plan. Thus, RLR plans were premised on the following assumptions: (1) that the employer's contributions to a reserve fund were currently deductible; (2) that the earnings of the reserve fund were nontaxable; (3) that disproportionately large amounts of life insurance could be provided to key employees; and (4) that none of the contributions or earnings of the plan would be included in the income of a retired employee. The 1984 Act dashed any hopes that the assumptions were justified. As matters now stand, deductions to reserve funds are limited, nondiscrimination rules apply to life insurance coverage, and the cost of group-term insurance in excess of $50,000 provided to retired employees is income to them. Group-term insurance to which § 79 applies is not subject to § 83. § 83(e)(5).

Specifically, contributions to a reserve account for post-retirement life insurance coverage is limited to the amount required to provide $50,000 of life insurance to the employee. §§ 419, 419A(c), 419A(e). In addition, § 419A(e)(1) requires life insurance plans to comply with the nondiscrimination provisions of § 505(b). The changes largely eliminated the attractiveness of RLR plans.

§ 6.74. MINIMUM-DEPOSIT LIFE INSURANCE PLANS

A minimum-deposit plan involves borrowing against the increase in cash value of a policy to pay part or all of the annual premiums. The attractiveness of minimum-deposit plans was based upon the availability of the cash value of a policy to fund substantial policy loans *and* the deductibility, for income tax purposes, of continually increasing interest payments. Of course, the amount of insurance protection was reduced by the amount borrowed against the policy. These problems plague any insurance plan that depends heavily on borrowing against policy values (the so-called "leveraged" plans). As one commentator has observed, "Some of its disadvantages (notably decreasing insurance) have been overcome by design improvements, but it still has problems. The most severe is that it does not produce policies that remain in force. At some point it becomes too cumbersome, too expensive, or both, and the insured cancels it." J. Munch, Financial and Estate Planning with Life Insurance Products, ¶ 21.2.2 (1990).

The attractiveness of minimum-deposit plans was virtually eliminated by changes in the Code that disallow a deduction for personal interest paid by individuals, § 163(h), and for interest paid by businesses on loans of more than $50,000 against a policy on the life of an employee or officer, § 264(a).

§ 6.75. SINGLE-PREMIUM WHOLE LIFE

As its name suggests, a single large premium pays the entire cost of a single-premium policy. Until the 1988 Act changed the rules, including the phased in elimination of the deduction for personal interest payments, single-premium policies were marketed aggressively because of their tax-free investment features.

A policy typically provided for a guaranteed high rate of interest to be credited on the policy for an initial period (typically the first five years), which could be borrowed by the policy owner. For example, an individual might pay a single premium of $100,000 on a policy that guaranteed a return of 10 percent. Under the old rules the owner could borrow the $10,000 increase in value each year tax-free and the interest paid with respect to the loan would be deductible. With respect to a single-premium policy issued after June 21, 1988, the owner would be required to include the loans in his or her income. In addition, the interest on most policy loans is entirely nondeductible after 1990. Perhaps of greater importance, a single-premium policy would be a modified endowment contract under § 7702A. Accordingly, loans (or other distributions) would be treated as income under § 72(e) to the extent the cash surrender value of the policy immediately before a loan exceeded the amount of the investment in the contract (*i.e.*, the single premium). See §§ 72(e)(2)(B), (3)(A), (4)(A), (10)(A).

Single-premium policies are subject to the normal gift and estate tax rules. Of course, in the case of such a policy, the gift tax value is likely to be high—except to the extent there have been loans against the policy.

§6.76. SECOND-TO-DIE OR SURVIVORSHIP WHOLE LIFE

The adoption of the unlimited marital deduction largely relieved the liquidity needs of the estate of the spouse first-to-die. However, use of the marital deduction simply defers the time for payment of the estate tax until the death of the survivor, when the effect of increases in value may require the payment of a substantially greater tax. The acquisition of a large amount of survivorship life insurance, under which the death benefit is payable on the death of the survivor of two insured persons, has become a popular way to provide liquidity upon the death of the survivor. Second-to-die policies are attractive, in part, because the annual premium is usually much lower than one for a policy insuring the life of either spouse alone.

Insurance advisors often recommend that large amounts of insurance be divided among two or more insurers. Such diversification lessens financial and investment risks and may reduce the underwriting requirements. Note, however, that serious complications can arise if the marriage of the husband and wife is dissolved. This problem is minimized if the policy or a rider allows the insurance to be split into two separate policies on the lives of the spouses. An additional charge may be made for such a rider. In the case of a split the contract or rider may require proof of insurability. The requirement is reasonable if one of the spouses was uninsurable.

Large survivorship policies are particularly attractive to couples with large estates that lack liquidity, such as estates that consist mainly of small businesses or other unique properties. In order to insulate the proceeds from the estate tax, survivorship policies are commonly acquired by or assigned to ILITs. ILITs that hold survivorship policies are usually designed so that gifts to the trust will qualify for sufficient annual exclusions to eliminate any gift tax liability. The trusts may be insulated from the GSTT by allocating the insured's GSTT exemption to the premium payments or assuring that the premium payments qualify as nontaxable transfers for purposes of §2642(c).

Because of the competitiveness of the market and the complexity of the options available with respect to the features of a survivorship policy, including the payment of premiums, the clients should consult with an expert life insurance advisor before acquiring a policy.

Under some charitable gift plans, survivorship policies are used to "replace" the economic value of property that was contributed to charity. *See* §8.20.3. For example, a client may transfer substantially appreciated property that generates relatively little current income to a charitable remainder trust. The donor will benefit from a charitable deduction for income and gift tax purposes. In addition, distributions from the trust will increase the donor's current income. The donor can use some of the income from the trust to fund premium payments on "replacement" policies owned by an irrevocable trust or by adult children.

§ 6.77. LEASED LIFE INSURANCE

In the mid-1960s some promoters touted "leased life insurance" plans under which the owner of a policy assigned it to a leasing company in exchange for its cash surrender value but retained the right to designate the beneficiary. The company then "leased" the policy back to the assignor for a level annual charge in exchange for which the company agreed to pay the annual premiums and to pay the face amount of the policy to the designated beneficiary. The annual charge represented the difference between the increase in the cash surrender value and the premium, plus the sum of the interest expense incurred by the leasing company in borrowing the cash surrender value of the policy, the cost of other expenses, and a profit. Stripped to its bare essentials the plan represented a clever attempt to allow the owner of a policy to claim an interest deduction for the excess of the annual premium over the increase in the cash surrender value. In *Murray Kay*, 44 T.C. 660 (1965), the Tax Court considered the lessor to be the agent of the lessee and allowed a deduction for the portion of the annual charge that represented interest paid to the insurer. However, an interest deduction was later held not allowable when the agreement did not establish an indebtedness on the part of the lessee. Rev. Rul. 66-298, 1966-2 C.B. 48. Aside from the absence of tax advantages, a leased life insurance plan does not adequately protect the interests of the lessee. Snyder, Leading a Tax-Sheltered Life, N.Y.U., 25th Inst. Fed. Tax. 765, 776-779 (1976). The unavailability of a deduction for personal interest also makes leased life plans unattractive.

§ 6.78. VETERANS' LIFE INSURANCE

The federal government has traditionally made a limited amount of life insurance available to members of the armed forces during active duty at little or no cost. Earlier programs allowed veterans to continue the insurance after separation from service under a variety of low cost term or cash value policies. The plan adopted by Congress in 1965 allowed members to purchase Servicemen's Group Insurance coverage of up to $15,000 from a large number of participating private insurance companies at a uniform premium cost. 38 U.S.C. § 1965-1968 (2011). However, until 1974 Servicemen's Group Insurance could only be converted into cash value policies that were available through the participating life insurance companies. 38 U.S.C. § 768(c), *repealed by* Pub. L. 93-289 § 5(a)(5), 88 Stat. 168 (1974). In 1974 Congress increased the maximum to $20,000 and authorized conversion to a new type of insurance, Veterans' Group Life Insurance. 38 U.S.C. § 1977 (2011). However, the only form of Veterans' Group Life Insurance available upon separation from service is a five-year nonparticipating and nonrenewable term policy. 38 U.S.C. § 1977(b) (2011).

The proceeds of life insurance policies issued under the World War Veterans' Act of 1924, the National Service Life Insurance Act of 1940, and the Servicemen's Indemnity Act of 1951 are includible in the estate of the deceased serviceperson or veteran. Rev. Rul. 55-622, 1955-2 C.B. 385. The proceeds of Servicemen's Group Life Insurance and Veterans' Group Life Insurance policies are also, no doubt, subject to inclusion in the gross estate of a deceased serviceperson or veteran. Inclusion of the proceeds of the latter types of policies in the gross estate of the insured under § 2042(2) is inevitable because the insured is the only person who may designate a beneficiary and neither the insurance nor any of the benefits under it may be assigned. 38 C.F.R. § 9.16, 9.20. (1990).

In *Wissner v. Wissner*, 338 U.S. 655 (1950), the Supreme Court held in a 5 to 3 decision that the spouse of a member or veteran of the armed services did not acquire an interest in a National Service Life Insurance policy under a state's community property law. It reasoned that Congress intended to provide "a uniform and comprehensive system of life insurance for members and veterans of the armed forces" and to give the insured the exclusive right to name the beneficiary. 38 U.S. at 658. From that the Court concluded that it would frustrate the intent of Congress to recognize that a member's spouse had a community property interest in a government policy. The program was held to be a constitutional exercise of the congressional power over national defense. Because the proceeds of a veteran's policy are not community property they are fully includible in his or her gross estate under § 2042(2). *Estate of Hugh C. Hutson*, 49 T.C. 495 (1968). Consistent with that rule, the proceeds of a veteran's policy were not treated as community property for purposes of calculating the pre-1982 maximum allowable marital deduction. *Hunt v. United States*, 59-2 U.S.T.C. ¶ 11, 891, 4 A.F.T.R.2d ¶ 6051 (E.D. Tex. 1959).

§ 6.79. DEATH BENEFIT ONLY PLANS

Employment contracts sometimes provide for the payment of a lump sum or an annuity to the specified surviving family members of employees who die while actively employed. Unlike many other fringe benefits, the value of such death benefit only plans is seldom included in a deceased employee's estate. That result has followed whether the plan was one of a publicly-held corporation, such as IBM, or one provided by a closely-held company. There is, of course, less risk of inclusion if the plan is one provided by a large employer to certain classes of employees (a so-called "involuntary" plan). Death benefit only plans provided by closely-held companies involve more risk. Indeed, *Estate of Stanton A. Levin*, 90 T.C. 723 (1988), indicates that inclusion will result—at least where the employee was the controlling shareholder.

The death benefit paid under such plans is analogous to the group insurance provided by some employers that is payable to beneficiaries designated by the employer and not the employee. *See* § 6.73. However, there is an important difference in the income taxation of the payments: Amounts payable under death benefit plans are taxed as income in respect of a decedent. *See* § 691(a). Accordingly, amounts paid under a death benefit plan are included in the recipient's gross income. Of course, if the payments are included in the deceased employee's gross estate, the recipient is allowed an income tax deduction under § 691(c) for the estate tax attributable to the benefits. In contrast, the proceeds of group-term insurance are generally not included in the recipient's gross income. *See* § 101(a). *See also* § 6.52.

§ 6.79.1. Estate Tax, General

The courts have rarely required pure death benefits to be included in the employee's gross estate. Inclusion is generally not required by § 2039, which only applies to contracts or agreements under which the decedent was, or might become, entitled to receive an annuity or other lifetime benefit. For the purpose of determining whether or not the decedent held such a right, consideration is given to "any combination of arrangements, understandings or plans arising by reason of the decedent's employment." Reg. §20.2039-1(b)(ii). Note, however, that §2039(a) is concerned only with post-retirement benefits. Contractual provisions for payment of a salary or disability benefits generally are not taken into account. *Estate of Schelberg v. Commissioner*, 612 F.2d 25 (2d Cir. 1979) (disability benefits); *Estate of Murray J. Siegel*, 74 T.C. 613 (1980) (disability benefits); *Estate of Firmin D. Fusz*, 46 T.C. 214 (1966), *acq.*, 1967-2 C.B. 2 (salary). More important, the IRS has ruled that benefits accruing under qualified plans are not to be considered together with rights arising under nonqualified plans (*e.g.*, death benefit only plans). Rev. Rul. 76-380, 1976-2 C.B. 270 (qualified retirement plan is not aggregated with nonqualified survivor's income benefit plan for purposes of determining includibility of the value of the survivor's benefits under §2039). Accordingly, insofar as §2039 is concerned, it is "safe" to provide an employee with a death benefit only plan and a qualified retirement plan.

§6.79.2. §2033

Courts have generally not required inclusion of pure death benefits under §2033 whether or not the benefits were subject to the unilateral control of the employer (*i.e.*, benefits were revocable). In the typical case exclusion is based on the employee's lack of any property interest in the benefits and lack of control over their disposition following his or her death. *E.g., Estate of Tully v. United States*, 528 F.2d 1401 (Ct. Cl. 1976); *Kramer v. United States*, 406 F.2d 1363 (Ct. Cl. 1969). Even when the employee has a lifetime interest in the benefits, inclusion under §2033 is precluded because the interest terminates upon the employee's death. *See Estate of Edward H. Wadewitz*, 39 T.C. 925 (1963), *aff'd on other grounds*, 339 F.2d 980 (7th Cir. 1964) (inclusion required under §2039).

§6.79.3. "Transfer" Sections, 2035-2038

Inclusion under one or more of the transfer sections, §§2035-2038, is possible if the decedent made the requisite transfer of an interest in the benefits and retained prohibited controls or interests. Several courts have found that the employee's agreement to render future services in exchange for a compensation package that included the death benefit constituted a transfer for purposes of these sections. *E.g., Estate of Tully v. United States*, 528 F.2d 1401 (Ct. Cl. 1976); *Estate of Stanton A. Levin*, 90 T.C. 723 (1988). The conclusion seems correct, but it does not itself require inclusion under any of the transfer sections. Indeed, more often than not the benefits have been excluded from the employee's estate for failure to satisfy other requirements of the transfer sections.

§6.79.4. §2035

Prior to the 1981 amendment of §2035, pure death benefits paid under contracts entered into within three years of death were potentially includible in the employee's gross estate under §2035. *See Estate of Bernard L. Porter*, 54 T.C. 1066 (1970), *aff'd*, 442

F.2d 915 (1st Cir. 1971) (death benefits paid under contracts entered into three weeks prior to decedent's death with three closely-held corporations were included under §2035). The changes made by the 1981 Act may preclude inclusion of such benefits. In the post-1981 era, transfers made within three years of death are includible only to the extent provided in §2035(a)(2). In the ordinary case, death benefits are not within the scope of §2035(a)(2). However, the risk of inclusion under §§2035 and 2038 exists for contracts entered into within three years of death when the decedent was a controlling shareholder and a member of the board of directors. *See* §6.79.7.

§6.79.5. §2036

Pure death benefits are generally not be includible in the employee's gross estate under §2036. In 1987 the IRS seemed to concede as much in a Technical Advice Memorandum that held that a death benefit payable to an irrevocable trust was not includible in the deceased employee's estate although he was the controlling shareholder and a member of the board of directors. LR 8701003 (TAM). In reaching that conclusion, the ruling pointed out that the powers held by the majority shareholder were subject to fiduciary obligations to the other shareholders, citing *United States v. Byrum*, 408 U.S. 125 (1972). In addition, §2036(a)(1) may not appropriately apply to death benefit only plans because the employee cannot possess or enjoy any of the benefits during his or her lifetime—they only arise following death. Indeed, because the covered employees cannot enjoy any of the benefits the plans are sometimes called "pure" death benefit plans. The power of the employee to affect the beneficial enjoyment of the benefits by changing the terms of the employment agreement with the employer has not generally been recognized as sufficient to require inclusion under §2036(a)(2). However, the case for inclusion is stronger where the decedent was the controlling shareholder and a member of the board of directors. *Estate of Stanton A. Levin*, 90 T.C. 723 (1988), required inclusion under §2038 in such a case. *See* §6.79.7. Even in such a case, inclusion may not be proper because §2036(a)(2) "does not include a power over the transferred property itself which does not affect the enjoyment of the income received or earned during the decedent's life." Reg. §20.2036-1(b)(3).

§6.79.6. §2037

Inclusion under §2037 is possible if the employee retains a reversionary interest in the benefits, the value of which immediately before the employee's death exceeds 5 percent of the value of the benefits. §2037(a). Thus, LR 7802002 (TAM) held that death benefits were includible in the employee's estate where the benefits were payable to the employee's estate if he was not survived by a spouse. For purposes of §2037 a reversionary interest includes a possibility that the property transferred by the decedent will return to the transferor or the transferor's estate. §2037(b)(1). However, the reach of §2037 is avoided by precluding payment of the benefits to the employee's estate. Because the right to the benefits arises after the employee's death there is no need to bar their payment *to* the employee.

§6.79.7. §2038(a)(1)

Letter Ruling 8701003 (TAM), discussed in §6.79.5, did not require the inclusion of the proceeds of a death benefit plan in the estate of the deceased majority shareholder. The benefits involved in the ruling were payable to an irrevocable life insurance trust created by the shareholder-employee. Curiously, at about the same time LR 8701003 was issued the IRS took the contrary position in a case before the Tax Court. In *Estate of Stanton A. Levin*, 90 T.C. 723 (1988), *aff'd by unpub. op.*, 891 F.2d 281 (3d Cir. 1989), the IRS successfully argued that §2038 required a pure death benefit to be included in the estate of a deceased employee because the employee held the power, exercisable alone or in conjunction with another person, to alter, amend, revoke, or terminate the enjoyment of the benefits. In *Levin* the decedent owned 80 percent of the voting stock of his employer, Marstan Industries, Inc., and was a member of its board of directors. The Tax Court held that the "decedent's ability to amend or revoke the plan in conjunction with other Marstan board members is a sufficient 'power' to compel inclusion of the value of the post mortem annuity in the decedent's estate." 90 T.C. at 730-731. Note, however, that the effect of including the value of benefits payable to the employee's surviving spouse may be offset by the availability of a marital deduction. *See* §2056(b)(7). *See also* §5.23.

For purposes of §2038 an employee's power to affect the enjoyment of the benefits by a drastic action such as divorcing a spouse, terminating employment, or renegotiating the amount of his or her salary is probably not a retained power sufficient to require inclusion. *Estate of Tully*, 528 F.2d 1401 (Ct. Cl. 1976). The position taken by the Court of Claims in *Tully* is consistent with the IRS's concession that the power to cancel employer-provided group insurance by terminating employment is not an incident of ownership for purposes of §2042(2). *See* §6.28.4. However, the retention of such powers may prevent the entry into a death benefit only plan from involving a completed gift to the designated beneficiary: In Levin the Tax Court held that the decedent did not make an inter vivos gift to his wife because the decedent "retained control over his wife's right to the post mortem annuity because he could defeat the transfer by terminating his employment with Marstan prior to his death, by divorcing his spouse, or by agreeing to terminate the plan." *Levin*, 90 T.C. at 732. The Tully court also found that the mere possibility of bilateral contract modification did not constitute a §2038(a)(1) power. *Tully*, 528 F.2d at 1405. *See also Kramer v. United States*, 406 F.2d 1363 (Ct. Cl. 1969). The Tax Court has held that an express retention by the employer and employee of the power to modify the terms of the agreement required inclusion of the death benefit under §2038(a)(1). *Estate of Murray J. Siegel*, 74 T.C. 613 (1980). The includibility of the benefit should not turn on the question of whether or not the power to modify the contract was expressly reserved by the parties—a contract may generally be modified by the parties although they have not expressly reserved the right to do so.

§6.79.8. Gift Tax

Until 1981, the IRS did not attempt to subject death benefit only plans to the gift tax. However, in declining to apply the estate tax to such benefits, some courts suggested that the contract entered into between the decedent and his or her employer involved a gift. *E.g., Tully*, 528 F.2d at 1404 ("Tully in substance, if not in form, made a gift of part of his future earnings to his wife"). Of course, the gift tax can only be imposed if the employee made a transfer of value. Moreover, the imposition of the gift tax depends upon the time at which the transfer becomes complete, the valuation of the interests transferred, and the availability of the annual exclusion. Perhaps because of its lack of success in subjecting pure death benefits to the estate tax, the IRS ruled that the employee makes a completed gift of the amount of the death benefit at the time of his or her death, when the gift first became susceptible of valuation. Rev. Rul. 81-31, 1981-1 C.B. 475, *revoked,* Rev. Rul. 92-68, 1992-2 C.B. 257. The ruling held that the gift qualifies for the annual exclusion under § 2503(b). In A.O.D. 1990-026 the IRS announced that it would acquiesce in result only in *Estate of Anthony F. DiMarco*, 87 T.C. 653 (1986) and would no longer follow Rev. Rul. 81-31 because of its inconsistency with Reg. § 25.2511-2(f).

DiMarco involved an uninsured, unfunded, noncontributory survivors benefit plan under which IBM paid three times the annual salary of a deceased employee to specified survivors in semimonthly payments of 12.5 percent of the employee's final monthly salary. The plan covered essentially all regular employees of IBM other than a small group of top executives. An employee had no control over the plan, which could be changed or terminated by IBM at any time. DiMarco became employed by IBM in 1950 and earned a salary of $5,250 per month at the time of his death in 1979. The IRS contended that at the time of his employment he made a gift that was completed at the time of his death, when it first became possible to value the gift. The Tax Court held that under Reg. § 25.2511-2(f), "transfers of property do not become complete for gift tax purposes by reason of the death of the donor." It also held that "property must be valued and the gift tax imposed at the time a completed transfer of the property occurs" regardless of the difficulty of valuation. Finally, the court held that DiMarco neither had a property interest in the plan nor took any action that could constitute a transfer. The conclusions reached by the Tax Court are entirely proper in light of the characteristics of the IBM plan.

DiMarco should not be read to insulate all death benefit plans from imposition of the gift tax on an employee's execution of an employment agreement. If the employee has a greater interest in the plan or control over the benefits payable under it, the execution of the contract may involve a transfer of value by the employee. As mentioned above, several courts have reached that conclusion in pure death benefit cases arising under the estate tax. However, the transfer may be incomplete at the time the contract is executed because of the expressly or impliedly reserved power of the employer and employee to change its terms. *See* Reg. § 25.2511-2(e).

The protection provided by the death benefit may involve a continuing indirect gift by the employee analogous to the indirect gifts made by an employee each time his or her employer pays the premium on group-term insurance that is owned by another party. *See* Rev. Rul. 76-490, 1976-2 C.B. 300. *See also* § 6.73.12. However, such indirect gifts would be difficult to value and subject to dispute in virtually every case. Although the death benefit is somewhat analogous to employer-provided term insurance, it presents a different problem as it does not involve the payment of premiums (or other amounts indicative of its value). Any continuing indirect gifts that are found to take place might qualify for the annual gift tax exclusion, depending on the terms of the employment contract and the manner in which the benefits were payable. By analogy to the group-term insurance cases, the annual exclusion may be available where the benefits are payable outright to an individual or to a trust in which an individual has a sufficient present interest.

§ 6.79.9. Income Tax

> The courts have uniformly held that post-death payments to an employee's widow are to be treated as "income in respect of a decedent" despite the fact that under the terms of the employment contract, the employee would never be entitled to actual receipt of the income. *Estate of Nilssen v. United States*, 322 F. Supp. 260, 265 (D. Minn. 1971).

The income taxation of pure death benefits is relatively simple. The payments are not includible in the income of a deceased employee who did not have the right to receive them during his or her lifetime. Instead, payments under a death benefit only plan are taxable to the recipient as income in respect of a decedent under § 691. Such a characterization is appropriate because the payments are solely attributable to the decedent's lifetime services and are not subject to any other contingencies. *See* Rev. Rul. 73-327, 1973-2 C.B. 214. Accordingly, the payments are includible in the recipient's gross.

Prior to the 1986 Act a totally voluntary payment to the members of a deceased employee's family might have constituted a nontaxable gift under § 102. Certainly a voluntary payment would have been excludable if it satisfied the test articulated in *Commissioner v. Duberstein*, 363 U.S. 278 (1960), that the gift proceed from detached and disinterested generosity or out of affection, respect, admiration, charity, or like impulses. *Id.* at 285. However, payments made to an employee's widow because of a perceived moral obligation were not gifts. *See, e.g., Margaret L. Sweeney*, 54 T.C.M. (CCH) 1003 (1987). The addition of § 102(c) to the Code by the 1986 Act probably ended the possibility that payments by an employer might be excluded as gifts: "Subsection (a) shall not exclude from gross income any amount transferred by or for an employer to, or for the benefit of, an employee." The IRS will no doubt argue that payments made to the survivors of a deceased employee were made "for the benefit of an employee."

§ 6.79.10. Installment Payment of Death Benefit Taxed as Annuity

Where a death benefit is paid in periodic installments, it is subject to the rules of § 72. The recipient is entitled to exclude a portion of each payment that bears the same relationship to the total payment as the investment in the contract, if any, bears to the total value of the benefit to be received. § 72(b).

The estate tax treatment of the death benefit does not affect the amount includible in the recipient's gross income. Whether or not the death benefit is included in the employee's gross estate, its basis is not adjusted under § 1014: "This section shall not apply to property which constitutes a right to receive an item of income in respect of a decedent under Section 691." § 1014(c). However, where the death benefit is included in the employee's gross estate, the recipient is entitled to an income tax deduction for the additional estate tax imposed because of the inclusion of the death benefit. § 691(c). In brief, the estate tax applicable to the employee's estate is computed with and without the inclusion of all items of income in respect of a decedent. The additional tax arising by reason of the inclusion of those items, for which the income tax deduction is allowed, is apportioned between them according to their respective estate tax values. Finally, a § 691(c) deduction is allowable to the recipient of an item of income in respect of a decedent proportionately as the income from the item is reported as income by the recipient.

§ 6.79.11. Reasonable and Necessary Payments Are Deductible by Employer

Death benefit payments are deductible by the employer only if they are reasonable and necessary business expenses. In some cases no deduction is allowed. *See M.S.D., Inc. v. United States*, 39 A.F.T.R.2d 1393 (N.D. Ohio 1977), *aff'd without opinion*, 611 F.2d 373 (6th Cir. 1979) (no deduction allowed for payments made by closely-held business to widow of deceased shareholder-officer, which were not necessary business expenses).

§ 6.79.12. ERISA

A properly structured death benefit only plan, which may provide benefits to the survivors of a group of key employees, should qualify for exemption from ERISA requirements on two grounds. First, the plan should be exempt as an unfunded excess benefit plan that is available only to certain employees. 29 U.S.C. § 1002(36), 1003(b)(5), 1051(7), 1081(a)(9), 1321(b)(8). Second, the plan should be exempt as an unfunded plan of deferred compensation for a select group of employees. 29 U.S.C. § 1051(2), 1081(a)(3), 1321(b)(6). Note, however, that for ERISA purposes a death benefit only plan which involves split-dollar life insurance policies on the lives of key executives may be held to be funded. *Dependhal v. Falstaff Brewing Corp.*, 491 F. Supp. 1188 (E.D. Mo. 1980), *aff'd on this issue*, 653 F.2d 1208 (1981), *cert. denied*, 454 U.S. 968 (1981). In order to avoid the result reached in *Dependhal* a death benefit only plan should not mention life insurance, the benefits payable under the plan should not be based upon the amount of insurance, and any policies owned by the employer should not be identified as having any relationship to the plan.

§ 6.80. GIFTS OF LIFE INSURANCE UNDER THE UNIFORM TRANSFERS TO MINORS ACT

Most states and the District of Columbia have adopted the Uniform Transfers to Minors Act, (1986), § 9(a)(3) of which permits custodial property to be created when a life or endowment insurance policy is held in the name of a custodian for a minor. Specifically, the Uniform Act provides that a custodianship is created when a life or endowment policy is either:

> (i) registered with the issuer in the name of the transferor, an adult other than the transferor, or a trust company, followed in substance by the words: "as custodian for (name of minor)

under the [Name of Enacting State] Uniform Transfers to Minors Act"; or

(ii) assigned in a writing delivered to an adult other than the
transferor or to a trust company whose name in the assignment
is followed in substance by the words: "as custodian for (name
of minor) under the [Name of Enacting State] Uniform Transfers to Minors Act."

A few states have retained versions of the 1966 revision of the Uniform Gifts to
Minors Act. The 1966 Act allows life insurance policies or annuity contracts on the
life of a minor or a member of the minor's family to be given to the minor by
registering them "in the name of the donor, another adult [an adult member of the
minor's family, a guardian of the minor] or a trust company, followed, in substance,
by the words: 'as custodian for (name of minor) under the [name of enacting state]
Uniform Gifts to Minors Act.'" *Id.*, § 2(a)(4).

The federal tax consequences that generally flow from the transfer of property to
a custodian for a minor also apply in the case of life insurance. *See* § 7.35. In addition,
the proceeds of a policy may be includible in the estate of the insured under § § 2038
or 2042(2) if the insured is acting as custodian at the time of his or her death. The
broad powers a custodian has to invest and reinvest the custodial property probably
constitute incidents of ownership for purposes of § 2042. Inclusion under § 2042
might occur whether or not the policy had been given to the minor by the insured-
custodian. In this connection recall the discussion of incidents of ownership held in a
fiduciary capacity at § 6.28.11. In contrast, § 2038 would apply to the insurance only if
the insured had transferred it to himself or herself as custodian for the minor.

The income from custodianship property is taxed to the minor except to the
extent it is used to discharge the legal obligation of another person to support the
minor. Of course, unearned income of a minor under 18 would be subject to the
Kiddie Tax. Presumably the income will be taxed to the minor although it is used to
pay premiums on a policy that insures the life of the donor or the donor's spouse. Of
course, if a trust were involved, the income would be taxed to the grantor to the
extent the income is or may be applied by the grantor alone, or without the consent of
an adverse party, to payment of premiums on policies of insurance on the life of the
grantor or the grantor's spouse. *See* § 677(a)(3). *See also* § 6.59.

§6.81. LIFE INSURANCE AND THE UNIFORM SIMULTANEOUS DEATH ACT

The original 1940 form of the Uniform Simultaneous Death Act ("Act") remains
in effect in a majority of states. Under the basic rule of § 1 of the Act, when devolution
depends upon the priority of death of two persons and there is no sufficient evidence
that they died otherwise than simultaneously, the property of each is disposed of as if
he or she had survived the other. Thus, if a husband and wife die simultaneously, the
husband's property is distributed as if he survived his wife and the wife's property is
distributed as if she survived her husband. The parties may prescribe a different rule
in the governing instrument that will control over the provisions of the Act. Section 3
of the 1993 version of the Uniform Simultaneous Death Act imposes a 120-hour

survivorship requirement that applies to nontestamentary transfers, including life insurance.

Section 5 of the 1940 Act provides a special rule for distribution of life or accident insurance where the insured and the beneficiary die simultaneously. Under it the proceeds of a policy are distributed as if the insured had survived the beneficiary. In such event the proceeds are paid to any contingent beneficiary or beneficiaries who survive the insured. Of course, if no beneficiary survives the insured, the proceeds will be paid in accordance with the terms of the policy, which usually call for payment either to the estate of the insured or to the owner of the policy. Payment to the estate of the insured is generally undesirable because it may unnecessarily subject the proceeds to federal and state death taxes. Payment to the insured's estate may also subject the proceeds to claims of creditors against the insured. Accordingly, insurance should generally name both primary and contingent beneficiaries.

The estate tax advantage of naming a contingent beneficiary is illustrated by the cases in which the husband's life was insured under a policy owned by his wife that named her a primary beneficiary and their children as contingent beneficiaries. *Estate of Meltzer v. Commissioner*, 439 F.2d 798 (4th Cir. 1971); *Estate of Wein v. Commissioner*, 441 F.2d 32 (5th Cir. 1971); *Old Kent Bank & Trust Co. v. United States*, 430 F.2d 392 (6th Cir. 1970); and *Estate of Chown v. Commissioner*, 428 F.2d 1395 (9th Cir. 1970). Under these decisions neither the policy nor its proceeds was includible in the gross estate of the insured. Moreover, none of the proceeds was includible in the wife's gross estate because she was deemed to have predeceased the insured. Only the interpolated terminal reserve value of the policy was includible in the wife's gross estate under §2033. As a result, the proceeds passed to the insured's children free of estate taxation except to the extent the value of the policy was included in the wife's estate.

EXAMPLE 6-37.

H's life was insured for $250,000 under a policy owned by his wife, *W*. *W* was named as primary beneficiary and their children, *D* and *S*, were named as contingent beneficiaries. *H* and *W* died simultaneously at a time when the interpolated terminal reserve value of the policy was $15,000. Under §5 of the 1940 Act and §3 of the 1993 Act, *W* (the beneficiary) is deemed to have predeceased *H* (the insured). Accordingly, only the interpolated terminal reserve ($15,000) is included in *W*'s gross estate. None of the proceeds is includible in *H*'s gross estate. Thus, the $250,000 proceeds are received by *D* and *S* at little or no estate tax cost.

Simultaneous Death: Community Property. A special problem may arise when a husband and wife die simultaneously owning a community property policy that insures the life of one of them and names the other as beneficiary. If no contingent beneficiary is named, the proceeds of the policy will be paid in accordance with the terms of the policy as if the insured had survived (*i.e.*, either in equal shares to the estates of the husband and wife as owners of the policy or entirely to the husband's estate as the insured under the policy). In California and Washington, the courts have incorrectly concluded that the presumption that the insured survived the beneficiary will persist through the distribution of the proceeds by their estates. *E.g., Estates of*

Saunders, 317 P.2d 528 (Wash. 1957); *Wedemeyer's Estate*, 240 P.2d 8 (Cal. App. 1952). Under that approach the entire proceeds may be distributed to the beneficiaries named in the insured's will or to the intestate successors of the insured. The presumption that the insured survived should only apply to the beneficiaries—not to the ultimate distribution of payments to the policy owners.

EXAMPLE 6-38.

H and his wife, W, died simultaneously owning a community property policy on H's life that named W as sole beneficiary. Both H and W died intestate. H was survived by his father, F, and W was survived by her mother, M. Under the terms of the policy the proceeds were payable to the owner of the policy if no beneficiary survived the insured. Because the insured (H) is deemed to have survived the beneficiary (W), the proceeds will be paid in equal shares to the estates of H and W. Under the California approach, W's one-half share will be distributed to H's estate because he is deemed to have survived her. For the same reason H's one-half share of the proceeds will not be distributed to W. Finally, the entire proceeds will be distributed as an asset of H's estate (*i.e.*, to F), as W did not survive H. As a result the entire proceeds of the community property policy will be paid to the relatives of the insured to the total exclusion of the relatives of the noninsured spouse. Of course, the wills of H and W could have controlled the distribution of the proceeds from their estates and could have directed that a different presumption of survivorship should govern the disposition of their estates.

This problem will not arise if the policy names a contingent beneficiary who survives the insured. It will also not arise in states, such as Wisconsin, that have adopted the substance of the amendment to §5 of the Uniform Act proposed by the Uniform Commissioners in 1953. The amendment provides that "if the policy is community property of the insured and his spouse, and there is no alternative beneficiary except the estate or personal representatives of the insured, the proceeds shall be distributed as community property under Section 4." Under §4, half of the community property is distributed as if the husband had survived and half as if the wife had survived. By way of illustration, §4 would require the proceeds of the policy described in Example 6-38 to be distributed one-half to F (H's intestate successor) and one-half to M (W's intestate successor). Consistent with that result, half of the proceeds would be included in the gross estate of each spouse. Rev. Rul. 79-303, 1979-2 C.B. 332 (Texas law).

BIBLIOGRAPHY

I. GENERAL SURVEYS OF INSURANCE AND INSURANCE LAW

Consumers Union, Life Insurance: How to Buy the Right Policy from the Right Company at the Right Price

J. Munch, Financial and Estate Planning with Life Insurance Products (1990)

Zartisky, H.M., & Leimberg, S.R., Tax Planning with Life Insurance (2d. ed. 2002)

II. GENERAL SURVEYS OF TAXATION AND INSURANCE

ABA Sec. of Real Prop. & Trust Law, Life Insurance Primer for Lawyers (1989)

Brody, Life Insurance Is Like a Box of Chocolate . . . A Perspective on Contemporary Life Insurance Products and Their Uses, U. Miami, 30th Inst. Est. Plan., Ch. 7 (1996)

Budin, Life Insurance, 826-2d Tax Mgmt. Port. (2006)

Christensen, Points to Ponder When Selecting an Insurance Carrier, 136 Tr. & Est. 54 (Dec. 1997)

Gofman & Hattenhauer, When Will IRS's Invocation of the Reciprocal Trust Doctrine Be Upheld by the Courts?, 85 J. Tax. 50 (Oct. 1996)

Jansen, Section 2042 from Soup to Nuts, U. Miami 29th Inst. Est. Plan., Ch. 14 (1995)

Jones, Uses of Life Insurance by Individual Taxpayers, N.Y.U., 45th Inst. Fed. Tax., Ch. 35 (1987)

Klein & Bahls, S Corporations and Life Insurance (2d ed. 2000)

Lee & Wilkey, Life Insurance–A Personal Guide for Evaluating Policies, 827 Tax Mgmt. Port. (2004)

Leimberg, "Policies" for Valuation of Life Insurance, 139 Tr. & Est. 46 (Mar. 2000)

Leimberg & Gibbons, Life Insurance After the 2001 Tax Act: Lease, Buy, or Replace? 29 Est. Plan. 165 (April 2002)

Leimberg & Zaritsky, Tools and Techniques of Life Insurance Planning

Mezzullo, An Estate Planner's Guide to Life Insurance (2000)

National Underwriter Law Services, Tax Facts on Life Insurance (published annually)

Ratner, Private Placement Life Products: Domestic, Offshore or Atoll: The Reality Check Please, 140 Tr. & Est. 48 (July 2001)

Schwartz, Netzorg & Bernhardt, Due Diligence in Life Insurance Selection, 11 Prob. & Prop. 39 (1994)

Slade, Some Advanced Uses of Life Insurance in Financial and Estate Planning, N.Y.U., 53rd Inst. Fed. Tax., Ch. 18 (1995)

Teitell, Charitable Gifts of Life Insurance, 139 Tr. & Est. 67 (Mar. 2000)

Weber, Understanding Life Insurance Illustrations, 133 Tr. & Est. 45 (1994)

III. SPECIFIC TOPICS

Exchanges (§ 1035)

Goldstein, Exchanging Life Insurance Policies under Section 1035, 2 ALI-ABA Est. Plan. Course Mat. J. 25 (Feb. 1996)

GSTT

Schneider, GST Planning With Irrevocable Life Insurance Trusts: Putting it All Together after the Final GST Regulations, U. Miami, 31st Inst. Est. Plan., Ch. 3 (1997)

Insurance Trusts

Blattmachr & Slade, Life Insurance Trusts: How to Avoid Estate and GST Taxes, 22 Est. Plan. 259 (1995)

Civins, Nursing the Sick ILIT, How a Trustee can Avoid Liability if an Irrevocable Life Insurance Trust Lacks Assets, 149 Tr. & Est. 16 (Dec. 2010)

Flagg & Zieger, A Shot Across the Bow, Guidance for Trustees on How Courts may Apply the Uniform Prudent Investor Act to Cases Involving ILITs, 149 Tr. & Est. 33 (Dec. 2010)

Fogel, Life Insurance and Life Insurance Trusts: Basics and Beyond, 16 Prob. & Prop. 8 (Jan./Feb. 2002)

Kingan, Combining the Benefits of a QPRT With a Life Insurance Trust, 27 Est. Plan. 486 (Dec. 2000)

Lawrence, Structuring Irrevocable Trusts in Light of Tax Changes and Proposals, N.Y.U., 44th Inst. Fed. Tax., Ch. 55 (1986)

Mirabello, Current Developments in Planning and Drafting Irrevocable Life Insurance Trusts, N.Y.U., 48th Inst. Fed. Tax., Ch. 16 (1990)

Slade, Personal Life Insurance Trusts, 807 Tax Mgmt. Port. (1999)

Smith & Denton, Life Insurance Trusts in the Estate Plan, 43 Drake L. Rev. 847 (1995)

Zaritsky, Life Insurance Trusts in the 90s—Dealing with the Newest Types of Policies, U. Miami, 28th Inst. Est. Plan., Ch. 3 (1994)

Premium-Financed Life Insurance; Investor-Initiated Life Insurance

Alt, Spin-Life Insurance Policies: A Dizzying Effect on Human Dignity and the Death of Life Insurance, 7 Ave. Maria L. Rev. 605 (2009)

Bozanic, An Investment to Die for: From Life Insurance to Death Bonds, the Evolution and Legality of the Life Settlement Industry, 113 Penn. St. L. Rev. 229 (2008)

Gallop, Benefits and Risks of Life Insurance Premium Financing, 33 Est. Plan. 2 (Nov. 2006)

Jones, Leimberg & Rybka, "Free" Life Insurance: Risks and Costs of Non-Recourse Premium Financing, 33 Est. Plan. 3 (July 2006)

Leimberg, Investor Initiated Life Insurance: Really a "Free Lunch" or Prelude to Acid Indigestion?, U. Miami, 41st Inst. Est. Plan., Ch. 4 (2007)

Leimberg, Planners Must be Aware of the Danger Signals of "Free" Life Insurance, 34 Est. Plan. 20 (Feb. 2007)

Leimberg, Stranger-Owned Life Insurance (STOLI): What Professionals Need to Know, ALI-ABA, 15 Est. Plan. Course Mat. J. 3 (Aug. 2009)

Manger, What is Life Insurance? The Evolution of Financial Products, 35 Est. Plan. 24 (Apr. 2008)

Split-Dollar Plans

Choate, Life Insurance in the Retirement Plan, 142 Tr. & Est. 50 (May 2003)

Jansen, Life Insurance Potpourri—No Employer? Try Family Split Dollar—Other Recent Developments, U. Miami, 34th Inst. Est. Plan., Ch. 5 (2000)

Jansen, Split Dollar Has Split—So How Do We Finance Premiums Now?, U. Miami, 38th Inst. Est. Plan., Ch. 12 (2004)

Rainer, Zipse and Leimberg, Planning Under the New Split-Dollar Life Insurance Prop. Regs., 29 Est. Plan. 603 (Dec. 2002)

Ratner, No Clear Picture [about split-dollar proposed regulations], 141 Tr. & Est. 12 (Aug. 2002)

Sanderson, Pension Rescue, 142 Tr. & Est. 46 (May 2003)

Simmons, Practical Guide to Use of Split-Dollar Insurance Plans, U.S.C. § 47th Tax. Inst., Ch. 26 (1995)

Winn, Split Dollar Life Insurance Book

Survivorship Life Insurance

Ford, Joint Life Insurance: It No Longer Matters Who Dies First, 3 Prob. & Prop. 42 (Nov./Dec. 1989)

Saks, Survivorship Life Insurance Policies Continuing to Attract Increasing Attention, 15 Est. Plan. 120 (1988)

Wilshinsky, Life Insurance: A New Dimension in Estate Planning, 130 Tr. & Est. 10 (June 1991)

Transfers of Life Insurance

Cornfeld, Partnerships as a Panacea for Life Insurance Problems (Penicillin or Placebo)? U. Miami, 29th Inst. Est. Plan., ch. 15 (1995)

Price, Transfers of Life Insurance: Opportunities and Pitfalls, U. Miami, 27th Inst. Est. Plan., Ch. 3 (1993)

Universal Life Insurance

Morlitz, Hamburg & Frankel, Universal Life Insurance: Where Do We Go From Here? N.Y.U., 46th Inst. Fed. Tax., Ch. 54 (1988)

Viatical Settlements and Life Settlements

Adams, The New Frontier for Life Insurance Planning: Viatical Settlements, U. Miami, 33rd Inst. Est. Plan., Ch. 18 (1999)

Frankel, Life Settlement: Sale of Life Insurance Policies on the Open Market, U. Miami, 39 Inst. Est. Plan., Ch. 9 (2005)

Leimberg, Weinbert, Weinbert & Callahan, Life Settlements: How to Know When to Hold and When to Fold, 35 Est. Plan. 3 (Aug. 2008)

7

Planning Lifetime Noncharitable Gifts

Perhaps to assuage the feelings and aid the understanding of affected taxpayers, Congress might use different symbols to describe the taxable conduct in the several statutes, calling it a "gift" in the gift tax law, a "gaft" in the income tax law, and a "geft" in the estate tax law. *Commissioner v. Beck's Estate*, 129 F.2d 243, 246 (2d Cir. 1942).

A. INTRODUCTION

§7.1. SCOPE

Lifetime gifts remain one of the most important and effective estate planning techniques. Despite the compression of the income tax brackets since 1986 and the adoption of the Kiddie Tax, some income tax savings may still be achieved by giving income-producing property to family members. Savings are possible also because of the widening gap in the rates applicable to capital gains and ordinary income. Perhaps more important than income-shifting—gifts can be used to qualify for valuation discounts—as to interests transferred and interests retained. Gifts also remove further appreciation in value from the donor's estate, to enable the donor's estate to qualify for some special tax elections, and to minimize the overall state and federal transfer tax burdens. *See* §§7.7-7.11. In particular, lifetime gifts may substantially reduce the GSTT cost of transferring property to descendants. *See* §2.42.

This chapter first reviews some of the main nontax considerations involved in counseling clients about gifts. After that it discusses the major tax objectives of gifts, the tax factors involved in selecting property to give, and the various methods of making gifts. Considerable attention is given to the various ways of making gifts to minors because of their importance and their illustrative value. Some references are made in the text to state gift tax laws that are in effect in a small minority of states, including Connecticut, Louisiana, North Carolina, and Tennessee. In recent years gift taxes were repealed by several states including Delaware and New York. Finally, this chapter considers the tax-advantaged ways of paying tuition costs and the costs of higher education via §529 plans and Coverdell Education Savings Accounts (formerly Education IRAs).

§7.2. NONTAX CONSIDERATIONS

> Ingratitude, thou marble-hearted fiend,
> More hideous when thou showest thee in a child
> Than the sea-monster! . . .
> How sharper than a serpent's tooth it is
> To have a thankless child!
> —King Lear, Act 1, scene 4

Inter vivos gifts generally do not precipitate a family tragedy as they did in King Lear's case. However, before a client adopts a gift program, careful consideration should be given to the financial, family, and emotional circumstances of the client and the prospective donee. Those factors will sometimes suggest that one or both of them might suffer if a substantial gift were made.

Despite their tax advantages, gifts should be recommended to a client only if they are consistent with the client's overall estate plan. The ultimate decision of whether to make a gift must, of course, be made by the client, but it is appropriate for the lawyer to make recommendations regarding gifts and other components of the estate plan. For example, a review of the client's affairs may lead the lawyer to recommend that the client make some noncharitable gifts as a part of the client's lifetime estate planning. Otherwise, the client's annual exclusions may go unused and the estate tax payable upon the client's death may be unnecessarily high. The lawyer must be prepared for some rejections, however. Although all of the circumstances known to the lawyer may strongly support the adoption of a gift program, the client may reject the idea because of other factual, emotional, or financial considerations. For example, a client may have philosophical convictions that are inconsistent with substantial lifetime noncharitable gifts or may be reluctant to make gifts because of memories of the Great Depression or a fear of becoming economically dependent on others.

§7.2.1. Economic Position

The economic position of the client is one of the most important factors in evaluating the desirability of a gift program. This factor involves a consideration of the client's net wealth and liquidity in view of his or her income, age, health, family obligations, and the extent to which future security is provided by employee benefit plans, medical and disability insurance, and other sources. Relatively small gifts or gifts for the support or education of a family member often have little adverse impact on the donor's economic position and are easily justifiable in many cases. For example, impressive tax reductions may result if a client consistently makes annual exclusion gifts to children and grandchildren. In this connection, note that the direct payment of tuition and medical expenses are nontaxable for gift, §2503(e), and GST, §2642(c)(3), tax purposes. Note also that a grandparent's nonrefundable prepayment of tuition expenses of grandchildren is within the exclusion. LR 199941013. The subject is reviewed at Handler, Tax-Free Gifts of Prepaid Tuition, 142 Tr. & Est. 20 (Feb. 2003).

A client may appropriately be discouraged from making substantial gifts that could jeopardize his or her economic independence or standard of living. The lawyer should be sure that a client understands the irrevocable nature of a gift, which generally means that the property cannot be counted on for the client's use or support.

§7.2.2. Age and Health

The age and health of a client are also particularly significant factors. In general, an older client is in a better position to make substantial gifts than a younger client of equivalent wealth. A younger client faces a longer time during which he or she may become disabled, suffer economic losses, or have substantial increases in family obligations. For example, an elderly widow or widower with grown, independent children is generally in a better position to make substantial gifts than a young married person of equivalent wealth who has, or may have, dependent children. On the other hand, a young parent with a modest estate may prudently make gifts within the amount of the annual gift tax exclusion to a child under the Uniform Transfers to Minors Act or its predecessor, the Uniform Gifts to Minors Act (referred to in this chapter as the "Uniform Acts"), or to a trust for the child in order to gain the benefits of income-splitting within the family and to accumulate an educational fund for the child at the lowest tax cost. Although the Kiddie Tax limits the opportunities of accumulating unearned income for children under 19 (and full-time students under 24), some possibilities still exist. The main methods of making gifts to minors are discussed at §§7.29-7.40.

Sound planning may also suggest that life insurance should be transferred to another family member or to an irrevocable life insurance trust. Doing so may involve little economic risk to the owner if the insurance has little or no current monetary value (*e.g.*, group-term insurance or the insured's interest under a split-dollar plan). Transferring life insurance can help control the size of the client's estate without giving up an asset of substantial current value. The basic plans involving life insurance are discussed at §§6.17-6.25.

In appropriate circumstances, durable powers of attorney should authorize the agent to make gifts on behalf of the principal. *See* §4.35.4. Without such authorization it may not be possible to make gifts on behalf of an incapacitated individual.

§7.2.3. Emotional and Family Circumstances

The emotional and family circumstances of the client and the client's family must also be considered in planning a gift program. The emotional attachment or identification that a client feels with respect to property that has a special significance for the client (*e.g.*, a family business, collection of art, antiques, or other unique assets) may make it difficult for the client to give it to another person without feeling some anxiety or pain. Donees may not have the same appreciation for the property, which may lead them to neglect it—or dispose of part or all of it. Similarly, a client who has built up a successful business may be reluctant to give up its management or a significant ownership interest. Giving up the challenge and the responsibility of owning and operating a business could have a morbid effect on the client, which the client may consciously or unconsciously view as a partial death. There are other circumstances in which the lawyer must be sensitive to the feelings of the client and the client's family. For example, in some circumstances tax benefits will be obtained if gifts are made by or to a dying person (*e.g.*,§§3.29, 5.7), but members of the client's family might take offense unless the topic is raised most tactfully.

The age, abilities, feelings, and financial circumstances of prospective donees and other family members must also be taken into account in formulating a gift program. For example, it may be unwise to make a substantial outright gift to a minor or a very elderly person. In either case the donee may be unable to sell or otherwise dispose of the property without the appointment of a guardian. Along with some other problems, this may be overcome by making the gift in trust rather than outright. *See* §§7.36-7.40 for a discussion of trusts for minors and Chapter 10 for a general discussion of trusts. Care should be exercised in making substantial outright gifts to persons who have little or no financial or investment experience. Also, family discord may arise if a large gift is made to one child but not to others, or if disproportionate gifts are made to children or other donees who are equally related to the client. Disproportionate gifts may be justified, however, when the needs of the donees differ and some face greater educational, medical, or other expenses than the others. If a client plans to make disproportionate gifts, the lawyer might suggest that the client discuss with the donees the reasons for doing so. Finally, a client may choose to pay some outstanding debts of a spendthrift, to whom the client may be reluctant to make a large outright gift.

Substantial gifts are most effective when they are coordinated with the donee's estate plan. In particular, a gift should generally be structured so that the gifted property will not return to the donor if the donee predeceases the donor. This problem is aggravated in the case of an outright gift to a minor or gift under the Uniform Acts because minors generally lack the capacity to make a will. This is a serious disadvantage because such gifts would be subject to distribution as intestate property if the donee dies prior to attaining his or her majority. The intestate property of an unmarried minor would usually pass to his or her surviving parent or parents. Of course, the probability that a minor will die prior to attaining majority is quite small. Also, a timely disclaimer by the parents could ameliorate that consequence. This problem is avoided entirely by making the gift to a trust under which the trust property will be distributed to persons other than the donor if the donee dies before the trust terminates. The annual exclusion is available for transfers to a trust insofar as the trust meets the requirements of §§2503(b) or (c). *See* §§7.36 and 7.37. An annual exclusion is also available to the extent the donee holds a *Crummey* power under which he or she can withdraw gifts made to the trust. *See* §7.38. If the trust contains a properly drafted *Crummey* power, the annual exclusion is available although the trust is a discretionary one (*i.e.*, the beneficiary does not have any fixed right to receive distributions of income or principal).

§7.2.4. Ethics

An estate planner must also be alert to ethical issues that might affect the lawyer's conduct and the advice given to a client. A conflict in the lawyer's duties may exist if, for example, the lawyer represents a child who might be the recipient of a gift from the client—particularly if there are other children to whom equalizing gifts are not made. In such a case, Model Rule 1.7(b) might preclude the lawyer from assisting the client in making the gift. *See* §1.6.7. Likewise, an estate planner should be conscious of the conflicts that may be involved if one spouse is pressuring the other spouse to make gifts to him or her—or to enter into a post-nuptial agreement or other arrangement for his or her benefit.

B. LOCAL PROPERTY LAW

§7.3. SIGNIFICANCE OF LOCAL LAW

In order to constitute a gift for federal gift tax purposes, a transfer must be effective under local law to pass an interest in the property to the donee. The federal law describes the types of transfers that constitute taxable gifts, but the question of whether there has been an effective gift is decided under local law. "The sole criterion, for the purpose of the gift tax, is whether the particular conveyance is effective under the local law to transfer an interest in the property to a donee." Rev. Rul. 57-315, 1957-2 C.B. 624.

A gift is not complete unless the donee is living at the time the gift is made. Thus, in *Estate of Stratton*, 674 A.2d 1281 (Vt. 1996), the court held that a trust did not arise when a father caused a certificate of deposit to be issued in his name "as trustee" for a child who he knew was deceased. It also held that the father's estate included the balance of a bank account, which he opened in his name as trustee for his daughter when she was living. Her interest in the account terminated when she predeceased him. *See* § 7.33.

Under a new Nevada statute, "The owner of an interest in real property may create a deed that conveys his interest in real property to a grantee which becomes effective upon the death of the owner. Such a conveyance is subject to liens on the property in existence on the date of the death of the owner." Nev. Rev. Stat. § 111.109(1) (2011). Under subsection (4), if the owner transfers the property to another person during his lifetime, the deed described in subsection (1) is void. Deeds executed in accordance with the section, "must not be construed to limit the recovery of benefits paid for Medicaid." Nev. Rev. Stat. § 111.109(9) (2011).

§ 7.4. INTER VIVOS GIFTS, GIFTS CAUSA MORTIS AND TRANSFER ON DEATH (TOD) DEEDS

Two general types of gifts are recognized for property law purposes: inter vivos gifts and gifts causa mortis. This chapter is concerned only with inter vivos gifts, which are usually immediately effective and irrevocable. In contrast, gifts causa mortis are made in contemplation of death and remain revocable until the death of the donor.

Most inter vivos gifts are absolute. However, some gifts are made expressly or impliedly subject to the performance of a condition. Perhaps the most common example of a conditional gift is the gift of an engagement ring, which is usually given in contemplation of marriage and on condition that the donor and donee marry. If the marriage does not take place the courts ordinarily allow the donor to recover the ring unless the donor unjustifiably terminated the engagement. *E.g., Spinnel v. Quigley*, 785 P.2d 1149 (Wash. App. 1990).

The Restatement (Third) of Property (Wills and Other Donative Transfers) § 6.2, Comment m (2003), treats the gift of an engagement ring as a gift conditioned upon marriage. Consistent with that view, the Comment states that the donor of an engagement ring "has a right to have the ring returned if the marriage is canceled, regardless of whether there was fault in terminating the engagement or who formally broke the engagement."

"If the donor of a gift of personal property was in apprehension of immediate death when making the gift, the gift is presumed to be revocable. Such a gift is referred to as a gift causa mortis. Failure to revoke within a reasonable time after the donor is no longer in apprehension of immediate death causes the donor's right of revocation to lapse." Restatement (Third) of Property (Wills and Other Donative Transfers) § 6.2, Comment zz (2003).

Gifts causa mortis are not used in estate planning because their revocable nature deprives them of any income, gift, or estate tax significance. In particular, the donor remains taxable on the income, § 676, the gift is incomplete, Reg. § 25.2511-2(c), and the property is includible in the donor's gross estate, § 2038. In addition, gifts causa mortis are generally not favored by the courts because of their similarity to oral wills, which lack the formality and evidentiary reliability of written wills.

Deeds of real property that are effective on the death of the grantor, typically called beneficiary or transfer on death (TOD) deeds, are valid in several states and are authorized by the Uniform Real Property Transfer on Death Act (URPTODA). §3.40-3.44. In general, to be effective a TOD deed must be validly executed and recorded prior to the grantor's death. A TOD deed does not affect the title of the property during the grantor's lifetime and is subject to revocation by the grantor. The real property described in a TOD deed is not subject to probate, but is subject to creditors' claims if the grantor's estate is insolvent.

§7.5. ELEMENTS OF INTER VIVOS GIFTS

For property law purposes a valid gift requires donative intent on the part of the donor, delivery to the donee or donee's agent, and some form of acceptance. In contrast, donative intent on the part of the transferor is not required in order to subject a transfer to federal gift taxation. Reg. §25.2511-1(g)(1). The local law may require a written instrument in order to transfer some interests in personal property and a deed is usually required to transfer interests in real property. Federal law governs the transfer of some types of property, such as United States Savings Bonds. *United States v. Chandler*, 410 U.S. 257 (1973).

A gift is not effective unless the donor is competent and not acting under fraud, duress, or undue influence. However, under the substitution of judgment doctrine, a guardian, conservator, or committee of an incompetent may make gifts of the ward's property. Under this doctrine the court may authorize the fiduciary to make inter vivos gifts to the ward's relatives in order to reduce the overall transfer tax burden when it is consistent with the ward's estate plan and the property will not be needed for the ward's care and support. *See, e.g., In re Morris*, 281 A.2d 156 (N.H. 1971); *In re duPont*, 194 A.2d 309 (Del. Ch. 1963). In more recent years many states have passed legislation that allows a principal to authorize an attorney-in-fact acting under a durable power of attorney to make gifts of the principal's property. *See* §4.35 for a discussion of this point and a form authorizing the attorney-in-fact to make limited gifts.

A client who intends to make a substantial inter vivos gift should make it clear whether the gift is an advancement against the interest in the client's estate that the donee would otherwise receive following the client's death. If a gift is intended to reduce the interest to be received by the donee, the client's will or trust should reflect that intention.

§7.5.1. Delivery

The type of delivery that is required in order to complete a gift depends upon the nature and location of the property involved and the circumstances of the parties. Actual physical delivery of tangible personal property or of a stock certificate or other physical evidence of a chose in action is preferred, but other forms of delivery may suffice. For example, tangible personal property contained in a locked receptacle may be delivered constructively by giving the donee the key to the receptacle. Broadly speaking, tangible or intangible personalty may also be effectively delivered if the donee is given a writing evidencing the gift (a deed of gift in the case of tangible personalty or an assignment in the case of a chose in action).

Effective delivery may also be made through a third party. In general delivery to a third party is immediately effective if the third party represents the donee, but it is not effective until ultimate delivery to the donee where the third party represents the donor. This analysis is reflected in the gift tax regulations: "If a donor delivers a properly indorsed stock certificate to the donee or the donee's agent, the gift is completed for gift tax purposes on the date of delivery. If the donor delivers the certificate to his bank or broker as his agent, or to the issuing corporation or its transfer agent, for transfer into the name of the donee, the gift is completed on the date the stock is transferred on the books of the corporation." Reg. § 25.2511-2(h).

A grantor's revocable delivery of a deed to an escrow holder other than the grantee does not satisfy the requirement of delivery. *E.g.*, *Albrecht v. Brais*, 754 N.E.2d 396 (Ill. App. 2001). In *Albrecht*, a husband and wife who jointly owned farmland executed a quitclaim deed of the property and delivered the deed to a title company which agreed to deliver the deed to the grantee after the death of the survivor of the grantors. The escrow agreement, which prohibited recording of the deed, was revocable as long as either grantor lived. The Illinois Court of Appeals held that the escrow agreement did not constitute a trust and that there was no sufficient delivery.

A deed is validly delivered if the grantor physically turns it over to a third party with instructions to deliver it to the grantee when the grantor dies. *Rothrock v. Rothrock*, 104 S.W.3d 135 (Tex. App. 2003). The *Rothrock* case concludes that the fact the grantor "could have recovered the deed from his attorney prior to his death does not constitute evidence that he did not intend to make a delivery." 104 S.W.3d at 140.

§ 7.5.2. Acceptance

Acceptance by the donee is also a necessary element of a gift. However, the significance of this requirement is diminished by a presumption of acceptance by the donee. The presumption, which applies to all donees including minors and incompetents, facilitates the completion of gifts when delivery is made to the third party.

§ 7.6. GIFTS OF COMMUNITY PROPERTY

> In Spanish law, the husband's powers of management over the community included the right to make reasonable gifts. A number of community property states have retained this principle. In such states, the issue is whether a particular gift is appropriate given its nature and the wealth of the parties. G. Blumberg, Community Property in California 423 (1987).

All of the community property states limit the power of one spouse, acting alone, to give community property to a third person. *See* § 3.28.2. Some do not allow gifts to be made without the express or implied consent of the other. Cal. Fam. Code § 1100(b) (2011) (requires written consent); Wash. Rev. Code § 26.16.030(2) (2011). The other states generally permit one spouse to make a gift of community property to a third party so long as the gift is not unfair or "constructively fraudulent." The question of whether a gift of community property to a third party is constructively fraudulent requires the court to consider a number of factors, including "the size of the gift in relation to the total size of the community estate, the adequacy of the estate remaining to support the wife in spite of the gift, and the relationship of the donor to the donee." *Horlock v. Horlock*, 533 S.W.2d 52, 55 (Tex. Civ. App. 1975). The court in *Horlock* upheld the deceased husband's gift of over 13 percent of total estate to his teenage daughters where the community estate was large and the gifts resulted in tax savings. Gifts that are capricious, excessive, and arbitrary are constructively fraudulent although the donees are the children of the donor. *Logan v. Barge*, 568 S.W.2d 863 (Tex. Civ. App. 1978).

C. TAX OBJECTIVES OF GIFTS

§7.7.   GENERAL

The main tax objectives of inter vivos gifts are discussed in this part. The objectives are largely independent, but some are inconsistent with others. For example, shifting ordinary income or capital gains from donor to donees, as described in §7.9, may not be consistent with taking steps to qualify the donor's estate for the benefits of §§303, 2032A, 2057 or 6166 (discussed in §7.10). In order to qualify for the benefits of those sections the donor might be required to make gifts that do not have the required characteristics. It is important to have the objectives in mind when it comes to helping the client choose the property to give. §§7.12-7.17. The objectives also help to identify which method should be used to make gifts to minors. §§7.29-7.40.

Inter vivos gifts may be attractive for residents of states that have a form of death tax that does not apply to deathbed gifts. The strategy may be particularly appealing to clients whose estates are large enough to otherwise require the payment of some state tax, but not so large as to require the payment of any federal estate tax. Clients who wish to assure that this option is available if they become incapacitated should consider including in their powers of attorney appropriate authorization to make gifts. §4.35.4.

Transfers that take the form of gifts, but which lack substance, will be disregarded for tax purposes. Thus, cash gifts made by a 70-year-old woman to her sons were not recognized where the exact amount of the gifts was immediately loaned back to the donor in exchange for unsecured notes that carried no interest rate and were not payable until 1995 (when the donor would be 95) or upon her earlier death. *Estate of Lulu K. Flandreau*, 63 T.C.M. (CCH) 2512 (1992), *aff'd*, 994 F.2d 91 (2d Cir. 1993) (no estate tax deduction allowed for notes given by mother to her sons in exchange for the return of funds that she allegedly had given to them). On appeal the court stated that "We have consistently rejected taxpayer attempts to use gifts to family members followed by loans back to the taxpayer to avoid federal taxes that would otherwise be imposed." *Id.* at 92.

Gifts to some donees that are, in fact, indirect gifts to other donees may be disregarded. To increase the amount of annual exclusion gifts, donors have sometimes made gifts to each of their children and to their children's' spouses—who immediately transfer their interests to the donor's children. The IRS and the courts have treated the gifts to the children's' spouses as indirect gifts to the children—for which the annual exclusions are not allowable. *E.g., Estate of Marie A. Bies*, 80 T.C.M. (CCH) 628 (2000) ("Viewed as a whole the evidence shows that the daughters-in-law were merely intermediate recipients, and that decedent intended to transfer the stock to her lineal descendants who were committed to continuing the operation of the funeral home business.").

The benefits of making an inter vivos gift are accomplished only if the gift is completed during the donor's lifetime. The general rules applicable to determining whether a gift is complete are discussed in §2.4.3. *See* §10.33 for a discussion of powers that prevent a gift in trust from being complete.

As indicated at §7.16, gifts may also be made to qualify for discounts in the valuation of the transferred and the retained property. *See also* §2.45.1. Some gift plans include a formula clause designed to discourage the IRS from challenging a valuation by providing for a gift over to charity of the value of the donative property above a specified amount. Presumably there would be little incentive for the IRS to challenge the valuation of a gift if the excess value would not be subject to the gift or estate taxes. For example, a plan might give the donor's children units in an LLC, provided that if the units are finally determined to have a value in excess of a specified amount, units equal in value to the excess will pass to a designated charity. Applying the reasoning of *Commissioner v. Procter*, 142 F.2d 824 (4th Cir. 1944), the IRS refused to give effect to such a clause. FSA 200122011. The Fifth Circuit, however, upheld the use of a formula clause to define the value of a gift of limited partnership interests in an FLP. *McCord v. Commissioner*, 461 F.3d 614 (5th Cir. 2006); *see* §10.49.

Gifts may result if a transfer for consideration is not recognized as such. For example, in *Estate of Diulio Costanza*, 81 T.C.M. (CCH) 1693 (2001), an installment sale made by a son, as trustee of his father's revocable trust, to himself was ignored as a sham. As a result, the father was treated as having made a gift to his son.

Gifts by Foreign Persons to United States Residents. United States resident donees are required to report gifts of $10,000 or more that are received from foreign donors other than charitable organizations. §6039F. The requirement applies to transfers that are treated by the donee as a gift or bequest, other than qualified transfers (*i.e.,* direct payments of tuition or medical expenses, which are within the exclusion of §2503(e)). A distribution received by a United States person from a foreign trust that is disclosed on a return filed under §6048(c) need not be disclosed by reason of this provision. *See* §10.2.

Most clients whose estates are likely to be in a taxable range (*i.e.,* more than $10 million per couple, in 2011) should consider making, or continuing to make, annual exclusion gifts. Doing so will remove the value of the gift from a donor's estate including its future growth in value and any income it generates. Annual exclusion gifts may be made in a variety of forms, most often outright or to discretionary trusts with *Crummey* withdrawal provisions. *See* §§7.38-7.38.12. Annual exclusion gifts in trust may, of course, be made to custodians for minor beneficiaries under the Uniform Transfers to Minors Act, §7.35, or to trusts for minors that meet the requirements of §2503(c), §7.37.

The same class of clients should consider funding GSTT exempt trusts with all, or the remainder, of their credit equivalent and their unused GST exemption. From the federal transfer tax perspective, the potential benefit of such trusts is enhanced if the grantor is treated as its owner for income tax purposes and, thus, remains taxable on its income. §10.31. Note in this connection that under the 2001Act, post-2009 transfers made to a trust are treated as completed gifts unless the grantor is treated as the owner of the trust for income tax purposes. Act §511, amending Code §2511(c).

The elements of a gifting plan should, of course, continue to take into account relevant nontax factors including the age, health, experience, and capacity of a client and the circumstances of the client's dependents and other intended donees or beneficiaries.

§7.8. ELIMINATE FURTHER APPRECIATION IN VALUE FROM THE DONOR'S ESTATE

One of the common reasons for making an inter vivos gift is to remove from the donor's tax base any further appreciation in the value of the donated property. In effect, a gift freezes the amount that will be taxed to the donor at the value of the property on the date of the gift less the amount of the allowable gift tax annual exclusion. An inter vivos gift also removes from the donor's estate the future income generated by the donated property. The amount of any gift tax paid is also removed from the donor's tax base if the donor survives making the gift by at least three years. §2035(b).

In considering a gift program, note that outright gifts made within three years of death are generally not includible in the donor's estate under §2035. Also, under §2035(e), added by the 1997 Tax Act, gifts made from a revocable trust (*i.e.*, a trust of which the decedent was treated by §676 as the owner), are considered to be gifts made directly by the decedent. Under the prior law a gift made via a revocable trust was potentially includible in the grantor's estate under former §2035(d)(2), now §2035(a)(2), and §2038. *See* §10.17.

§7.8.1. Annual Exclusion Gifts and Unified Credit Gifts

Inter vivos gifts are particularly attractive to the extent they qualify for the gift tax annual exclusion. Applying the rates applicable in 2011 and 2012, each annual exclusion gift of $13,000 made by an individual whose estate would otherwise be subject to tax saves $4,550 in tax (35% x $13,000). Gifts in excess of the allowable exclusions are often useful, at least when the amount of the tax is offset by the donor's unified credit. Even when some gift tax must be paid by the donor, a gift program can save a substantial amount of transfer taxes. The saving is even clearer where the property appreciates in value following the gift. As indicated above, a substantial tax saving may also result because the gift tax paid by the donor is not subject to the gift or estate tax unless the donor dies within three years and the amount of the gift tax is grossed up under §2035(b). In calculating the benefit of an inter vivos gift upon which a gift tax is paid, some consideration must be given to the effect of losing the use of the amount paid in tax. The adjusted estate tax cost of retaining the property can be compared with the adjusted gift tax cost of making a present gift of it.

§7.8.2. Carryover of Donor's Basis

In planning inter vivos gifts, one should bear in mind that the donor's basis generally carries over to the donee under §1015. However, for the purpose of determining loss, the donee's carryover basis cannot exceed the value of the gifted property on the date of the gift. §1015(a). The basis of gifted property is stepped up (or stepped down) when the donor dies only if it is included in the donor's gross estate. §1014. The carryover of basis may be a negative factor when the donee is expected to sell the property after the donor's death; it is largely irrelevant if the donee is not expected to do so. Even if the donee sells the property, the capital gains tax payable on a sale may be much less than the additional estate tax that would be payable by the donor's estate if the gift were not made. Currently, the maximum rate applicable to most capital gains is 15 percent, whereas the maximum estate tax rate is 45 percent (effective in 2007). Also, the donee's basis in the property is increased by the amount of any gift tax paid with respect to the appreciation element of the gift (the excess of the fair market value of the property at the time of the gift over the donor's adjusted basis). §1015(d)(6).

EXAMPLE 7-1.

> An unmarried donor, *D*, had made taxable gifts in prior years that absorbed the full amount of *D*'s $1 million lifetime gift tax exemption but did not require any gift tax to be paid. Earlier this year *D* gave a relative, *B*, cash in an amount equal to the annual exclusion. Before the end of the year, *D* gave *B* 100 shares of stock that had an adjusted basis of $10 per share and a current market value of $100 per share. *D* pays a gift tax of $4,100 by reason of the $10,000 gift of stock to *B*, of which 90 percent is attributable to the excess of the value of the shares over the donor's basis. *B* has a basis in the shares equal to *D*'s basis of $1,000, plus the gift tax paid by *D* with respect to the $9,000 of unrealized appreciation ($3,690, or 90% of the $4,100 gift tax paid). *B*'s basis in the stock, therefore, is $4,690. The cash and the stock will be excluded from *D*'s estate. If *D* survives making the gift by 3 years or more, the gift tax *D* paid will also be excluded from *D*'s estate.

§7.9. SHIFT INCOME FROM DONOR TO DONEE

"Income-splitting" within the family is another purpose of making inter vivos gifts. Its importance varies according to the other income of the parties and the progressivity of the income tax rate schedule. The total family income tax burden may be reduced somewhat if income-producing assets are distributed among several family members rather than being concentrated in the hands of one or both parents.

An Additional Incentive for Income Shifting: Investment Income Surtax. Shifting income to others within the family will take on added significance once the new surtax on net investment income takes effect. Introduced in the Patient Protection and Affordable Care Act of 2010, new §1411, which becomes effective in 2013, requires certain individuals to pay a 3.8-percent surtax on "net investment income." The tax only applies to individual taxpayers with a "modified adjusted gross income" (generally meaning the taxpayer's adjusted gross income plus any foreign earned income excluded under §911) in excess of the "threshold amount" ($250,000 for joint filers, $125,000 for married couples filing separately, and $200,000 for all others).

For purposes of this surtax, a taxpayer's net investment income includes interest, dividends, rents, royalties, capital gains, annuity income, and passive activity income. The statute expressly provides that net investment income does not include the income from an active trade or business, distributions from individual retirement accounts, distributions from qualified plans, gain from the sale of an active interest in a partnership or S corporation, and income taken into account in computing self-employment tax. The 3.8-percent tax is applied against the taxpayer's net investment income or the amount by which modified adjusted gross income exceeds the threshold amount, whichever is less.

§7.9.1. Kiddie Tax, §§1(g), 63(c)(5)

The potential income tax savings of transferring income-producing property to children are reduced by §§63(c)(5) and 1(g). The §1(g) "Kiddie Tax" provides that the net unearned income of a child under age 19 (or, if the child is a full-time student, under age 24) is computed at the marginal rate of the child's parent if the child has at least one parent living at the end of the year, does not file a joint return, and does not have earned income in excess of one-half of the amount of his or her support. For this purpose, net unearned income generally means unearned income in excess of an amount equal to twice the standard deduction under §63(c)(5). A parent of a child under 19 (or a full-time student under 24) may elect to report the net unearned income of the child directly on his or her return by making an election under §1(g)(7). Because of the compressed rate structure applicable to individuals, only limited income tax savings will ordinarily result in any case. In order to avoid having the unearned income of a person under 19 (or a full-time student under 24) taxed to his or her parent, the minor's property may be invested in forms that produce little or no current taxable income (*e.g.*, insurance policies) or ones that defer the recognition of income (*e.g.*, Series EE bonds). *See* §7.30. Importantly, the income of a trust is subject to the Kiddie Tax only to the extent it must be paid to the beneficiary or is distributed to him or her.

§7.9.2. Shifting Capital Gains

The capital gains tax on the sale of an appreciated asset may be reduced by transferring the property to a donee who either is in a lower income tax bracket or who can offset the gain with losses. Under former §644, which was repealed by the 1997 Tax Act, the tax on the gain was computed at the rates applicable to the donor where appreciated property was transferred to a trust that sold it within two years.

A gift is also useful when the property will be sold and the gain on a sale would be ordinary income to the donor but capital gain to the donee. The benefit will depend upon the differential between the maximum rates applicable to ordinary income and to capital gains. Of course, the gift tax consequences of the transfer must be taken into account in deciding whether to make the gift. The combined gift and capital gains taxes may be less than the income tax that the donor would pay on the gain if it were all taxed to the donor as ordinary income.

EXAMPLE 7-2.

A married donor, D, who is involved in real estate development and sales, gave his married, adult son S and S's spouse a parcel of undeveloped real property that had an adjusted D basis of $1,000 and a current value of $40,000. The entire gift to S and S's spouse is sheltered by the available annual exclusions if the gift is split between D and D's spouse. D's basis in the property ($1,000) carries over to the donees under § 1015(a), as does D's holding period. See § 1223(2) and Reg. § 1.1223-1(b). Ordinarily the real property will be a capital asset in the hands of the donees and any gain they realize will be capital gain. However, if the sale was prearranged by D, the donees may be treated as D's agents and the gain may be taxed to D as ordinary income. See *Salvatore v. Commissioner*, 434 F.2d 600 (2d Cir. 1970).

§ 7.10. REDUCE NONBUSINESS HOLDINGS OF DONOR IN ORDER TO QUALIFY FOR BENEFITS OF §§ 303, 2032A, OR 6166

Gifts of nonbusiness assets may enable the donor's estate to meet the percentage tests of § 303 (redemption of stock included in decedent's gross estate treated as payment in exchange for stock and not dividend), § 2032A (special use valuation of farm or business assets), and § 6166 (deferral and installment payment of estate tax attributable to closely-held business). However, note that transfers made within three years of death are generally brought back into the estate for purposes of determining whether an estate qualifies for the benefits of §§ 303(b), 2032A and 6166. § 2035(c)(1). The percentage requirements of those sections and their basic limits are summarized in Table 7-1. For a more detailed discussion of them, *see* Chapters 11 and 12.

The nonbusiness holdings of a client may also be reduced by transferring assets to a closely held corporation in exchange for additional stock. It may be particularly appropriate to transfer life insurance to a corporation. Importantly, the transfer of life insurance to a corporation in which the insured is a shareholder is not subject to the transfer for value rule. Accordingly, the exclusion of § 101(a) would apply to the payment of the policy proceeds to the corporation or a beneficiary designated by it. If the insured is the controlling shareholder any proceeds not paid to the corporation are includable in the insured's estate under Reg. § 20.2042-1(c)(6). Insurance proceeds paid to a closely held corporation are a nonoperating asset that is taken into account in valuing the corporation. Reg. § 20.2031-2(f). Note, however, that the stock of the deceased controlling shareholder may be discounted for lack of marketability— which, in effect, reduces the extent to which the proceeds are included in the decedent's estate. *See Estate of John Huntsman*, 66 T.C. 861 (1976), *acq.*, 1977-1 C.B. 1.

Table 7-1
Table of Statutory Benefits Under §§ 303, 2032A, and 6166

Section	Code Percentage Requirement	Nature of Benefit
303	Stock included in gross estate must exceed 35% of excess of gross estate over deductions allowable under §§ 2053 and 2054. § 303(b)(2)(A). Stock of 2 or more corporations may be aggregated if 20% or more of the value of the outstanding stock of each is included in decedent's gross estate. § 303(b)(2)(B).	Redemption of stock treated as sale and not dividend to the extent of total death taxes plus funeral and administration expenses allowable as deductions under § 2053. § 303(a).
2032A	Adjusted value of qualified real and personal property must exceed 50% of adjusted value of gross estate and adjusted value of qualified real estate must exceed 25% of adjusted value of gross estate, which must pass to qualified heirs.	Value of qualified real property for estate tax purposes may be reduced by up to $750,000 based upon its valuation for farming or closely-held business purposes. § 2032(a)(2). Tax benefit subject to recapture.
6166	Closely-held business must constitute more than 35% of gross estate, reduced by deductions allowable under §§ 2053 and 2054. § 6166(a)(1). Two or more businesses may be aggregated if 20% or more of total value of each is included in decedent's gross estate. (Same test as for § 303.)	Proportion of estate tax attributable to closely-held business may be deferred for 5 years and paid in installments over following 10 years. Interest on tax imposed on first $1 million in value of the closely held business (adjusted for inflation) is subject to 2% annual Rate. § 6601(j). Balance is subject to 45% of federal short term rate plus 3%. §§ 6601(a), 6621(a).

§7.11. Minimize State Transfer Tax Costs

Inter vivos gifts are also encouraged by the fact that only a small minority of states impose gift taxes while all states impose some form of death tax. The states imposing gift taxes include Connecticut, Louisiana, North Carolina, and Tennessee. Thus, in most states the imposition of any state transfer tax may be avoided by making inter vivos gifts. In some states, gifts made within two or three years of death are often subject to state death taxation.

A state transfer tax savings often results from inter vivos gifts even in the states that have gift tax laws. First, the laws generally allow an annual exclusion or a similar exemption, which shelters modest-sized annual gifts from the tax. Also, some allow gift-splitting, which permits a couple to transfer up to double the annual exclusion amount to each donee annually without incurring any gift tax liability. Second, the amount of state gift tax payable on a transfer is generally not included in the tax base in computing the gift tax (*i.e.,* it is not "grossed up"). Of course, the amount of the tax may be grossed up at death for state death tax purposes if the donative property is subject to the death tax and a credit is allowed for the gift tax. Third, the state transfer tax systems are not unified, which permits donors to take full advantage of the two sets of exemptions and low initial rates that are characteristic of dual transfer tax systems.

Any amount paid in state gift taxes on transfers made within three years of death is not grossed up and included in the donor's gross estate under §2035(b). That provision requires inclusion of only the federal gift tax paid by the decedent or the decedent's estate on gifts made by the decedent or his or her spouse within three years of death.

In 1981, the IRS finally conceded that a decedent's gross estate does not include the amount of a credit that was allowed for state death tax purposes in the amount of state gift tax paid during a decedent's lifetime on inter vivos gifts. Rev. Rul. 81-302, 1981-2 C.B. 170. Prior to the issuance of Rev. Rul. 81-302, the IRS contended that §2033 required inclusion of the state gift tax paid on an inter vivos gift where the property transferred was later included in the donor's inheritance tax base and a credit was allowed for the gift tax previously paid. Rev. Rul. 75-63, 1975-1 C.B. 294, *revoked by* Rev. Rul. 81-302, 1981-2 C.B. 170. In essence, the IRS viewed the gift tax in such a case as a prepayment of the donor's inheritance tax liability, which is not deductible under §2053. An earlier ruling had denied a deduction for state gift taxes unpaid at death to the extent a credit was allowable for them against the state death tax. Rev. Rul. 71-355, 1971-2 C.B. 334, *revoked by* Rev. Rul. 81-302, 1981-2 C.B. 170. However, the rulings in 1971 and 1975 did recognize that such indirect payments of state death taxes did qualify for the credit under former §2011 for state death taxes. The IRS contentions were consistently rejected by the courts. For example, in *Estate of George E. P. Gamble,* 69 T.C. 942 (1978), *acq.,* 1981-2 C.B. 1, the Tax Court pointed out, "Because the decedent's lifetime payment of his State gift tax liability resulted in nothing that was capable of passing from him at the time of his death, respondent's reliance upon section 2033 to increase the value of his gross estate is misplaced." *Id.* at 950. In *Estate of Lang v. Commissioner,* 613 F.2d 770 (9th Cir. 1980), *aff'g in part and rev'g in part,* 64 T.C. 404 (1975), *acq.,* 1981-2 C.B. 2, the court held that a state gift tax paid after death remains a gift tax and is therefore deductible under §2053. Revenue Ruling 81-302 recognizes that state gift taxes paid during the donor's lifetime on property that is later included in the donor's inheritance tax base are not assets of the estate. It also concludes that state gift taxes are deductible if they were not paid prior to death. In the latter case Rev. Rul. 81-302 concludes that the state gift taxes that were unpaid at death did not qualify for the state death tax credit under former §2011.

The transfer of property into a joint tenancy with another person can save state transfer taxes in states that treat joint tenancies favorably for tax purposes on the death of a joint tenant. In some states none of the joint tenancy property is taxed when a joint tenant dies; in others only the decedent's proportional interest is subject to tax. The overall saving will, of course, be less if the creation of the joint tenancy requires the payment of some gift tax. However, in many cases there are strong tax and nontax reasons for not transferring assets into coownership with a spouse or others. For a more complete discussion of cotenancies, *see* Chapter 3.

D. TAX FACTORS INVOLVED IN SELECTING PROPERTY TO GIVE

§7.12. GIVE APPRECIATED PROPERTY?

In making an intrafamily gift, clients generally prefer to give appreciated property rather than cash or property that has declined in value. When the donees are in lower income tax brackets than the donor, it may be advantageous to give them property with more, rather than less, built-in gain. As indicated below, a larger basis adjustment is allowable under §1015(d)(6) for gift tax paid on a gift of highly appreciated property than on a transfer of less appreciated property. The transfer of highly appreciated property is often desirable when the donees are not expected to sell the property within a short time. Also, the capital gain that may be recognized by the donor on the sale of the property retained by the donor will be smaller if the donor retains assets that have appreciated less in value. On the other hand, where the donor is very elderly or in failing health, highly appreciated property might be retained in order to take full advantage of the tax-free step-up in basis at death that is available under §1014 for property that is included in a decedent's gross estate.

EXAMPLE 7-3.

In 2009, *O* gave her daughter, *D*, 1,000 shares of XYZ, Inc. common stock, which had a basis of $10 per share and a fair market value of $200 per share. *D* made no other gifts during the year. The gift uses $187,000 of *O*'s lifetime gift tax exemption. *D* takes a basis of $10 per share in the stock. *O* dies late in 2009.

If the stock has not changed in value, *O* will have removed from her estate, free of tax, the amount of the annual gift tax exclusion ($13,000) plus any income generated by the stock. However, *D* will not have the benefit of a step up in the basis of the stock because it is not included in *O*'s gross estate.

For purposes of computing the estate tax on *O*'s estate, the taxable gift will be included in the tax base. The absence of an increase in the basis of the XYZ, Inc. stock means that *D* will have to pay a capital gain tax if she sells it. If a sale is made at $200 per share, her gain will be $190,000. At a 15 percent rate the tax will be $28,500—a considerable saving over the estate tax that would have been imposed had the stock remained in *O*'s hands.

If the stock had appreciated to $300 per share at the time of *O*'s death, the $100,000 increase in value would not have been included in her gross estate. Had *O*'s taxable estate exceeded $2 million, the stock would have been subject to a tax of 45 percent. The "savings" here is the difference between that rate and the capital gains tax rate. If the difference is 30 percent (45 percent minus 15 percent), the savings would be $90,000 (30 percent × $300,000).

If the gifts to a particular donee during the year will be large enough to require payment of some gift tax, they should be arranged to take maximum benefit of the adjustment that is available under § 1015(d)(6). Under it, the basis of the donee is increased by the portion of the gift tax that is attributable to the appreciation element. The amount of the adjustment will be higher if the donor transfers more highly appreciated property to the donee. The allocation formula under § 1015(d)(6) is:

$$\frac{\text{Net appreciation in value of gift (fair market value less adjusted basis)}}{\text{Fair market value of the gift}} \times \text{Gift tax paid} = \text{Adjustment to basis}$$

When a donor plans to give a donee both cash (or unappreciated property) and appreciated property in the same year, a larger adjustment usually results if the donor transfers the cash or unappreciated property first. The annual exclusion applies to in chronological order to the gifts made to a donee during the year, Reg. § 1.1015-5(b)(2), as a result of which any gift tax paid on gifts made to the same donee is allocable to later gifts.

EXAMPLE 7-4.

Donor, *D*, whose unified credit was used up by prior gifts, gave his son, *S*, $13,000 in cash on January 1, 2009, and 100 shares of XYZ, Inc. on December 30, 2009. The XYZ shares had an adjusted basis of $10 per share and a fair market value of $100 per share. The annual exclusion was applied to offset the gift of cash so the full amount of tax ($4,100) was imposed with respect to the gift of XYZ, Inc. stock. The donee's basis is $46.90 per share (the donor's basis of $10 per share plus the portion of the gift tax allocable to the appreciation element of each share, $36.90):

$$\frac{\$9,000}{\$10,000} \times \$4,100 = \$3,690/100 = \$36.90$$

If the XYZ stock had been transferred first and the cash second, no tax would have been payable with respect to the gift of stock and there would have been no adjustment to basis under § 1015(d). In that case the taxable gift would be limited to the amount of the cash gift. No adjustment would be allowable for two reasons. First, cash has no appreciation element. Second, cash has a carryover basis equal to its fair market value (face amount), which cannot be increased.

Married clients with a mix of high-basis assets and low-basis assets can employ a simple technique to leverage the step-up in basis. Just before death, one spouse can transfer assets with a high basis to the other spouse in exchange for an equal amount of low-basis assets. Under § 1041, neither spouse recognizes gain or loss from the exchange, and each takes the transferor's basis in the exchanged property. Accordingly, the low-basis assets will then get a step-up in basis upon the death of the first spouse, and the high-basis assets will retain their basis in the hands of the surviving spouse. If the surviving spouse is to be the recipient of the freshly stepped-up assets, § 1014(e) may foil this plan and assign the surviving spouse the same low basis that the decedent had immediately before death, but to the extent the low-basis assets will pass to persons other than the surviving spouse, this technique should work well.

§ 7.12

§7.13. DO NOT GIVE PROPERTY SUBJECT TO AN ENCUMBRANCE IN EXCESS OF ITS BASIS

In order to raise funds with which to pay the gift tax, a donor may borrow against appreciated property prior to making a gift of it. However, as explained in §7.26, the income tax consequences are neither entirely favorable nor entirely settled. A transfer of encumbered property will probably be treated as an exchange to the extent of the indebtedness, which will require the donor to realize gain if the indebtedness exceeds the donor's basis. *Johnson v. Commissioner*, 495 F.2d 1079 (6th Cir.), *cert. denied*, 419 U.S. 1040 (1974). A gift to charity of property subject to an encumbrance in excess of its basis is also treated as a sale or exchange—part gift and part sale in most instances. *See* §8.36.

A taxpayer contemplating a gift of encumbered property should consider other strategies, including a net gift of the property (*see* §7.26), a sale of it on the installment basis (*see* §§9.3-9.9), or an exchange of it for a private annuity (*see* §§9.10-9.16). A client may wish to consider the tax and nontax differences of making a complete gift, a net gift and a part-gift and part-sale. *See* §§7.25-7.28.

§7.14. DO NOT GIVE PROPERTY WITH A BASIS THAT EXCEEDS ITS CURRENT FAIR MARKET VALUE

The donor's basis in an asset generally carries over to the donee. §1015(a). However, for the purpose of determining loss the basis cannot exceed the fair market value on the date of the gift. Thus, in the case of a gift of an asset that has an adjusted basis of $10,000 and a fair market value of $5,000, the donee's basis is limited to $5,000 for the purpose of determining loss. Also, in such a case the donee's basis cannot be increased by any portion of the gift tax. None of the tax was imposed with respect to net appreciation—there wasn't any. *See* §1015(d)(6). A donor should not make a gift that involves losing the tax benefit of a loss. Instead, a donor should consider selling the depreciated property, taking advantage of the loss, and making a gift of the proceeds or of other property.

A terminally ill taxpayer may choose to sell assets that have declined in value in order to make use of the loss for income tax purposes. If depreciated assets are retained until death their bases are stepped-down and no one will be entitled to claim a loss. §1014. Of course, §267 bars a deduction for the loss on a sale to certain related taxpayers.

§7.15. DO NOT GIVE PROPERTY WITH POSITIVE TAX CHARACTERISTICS

Taxpayers who are subject to the maximum income tax rate should usually retain assets that generate tax-exempt income or that shelter other income. Thus, a donor should avoid making gifts of tax-exempt municipal bonds, depreciable assets, or other properties that are tax-exempt or generate deductions in excess of income. Instead, he or she should consider making gifts of appreciated assets that produce ordinary income.

Note, however, that a wealthy client may choose an estate plan that requires him or her to pay the income tax on income received by other family members from a trust established by the client. Such a payment is, in effect, a tax-free gift from the payor to the recipients of the income. Under the grantor trust rules the trust can be structured so the grantor will be treated as the owner of the income of the trust without causing the trust to be included in the grantor's estate. *See* § 10.31.1.

§ 7.16. VALUATION DISCOUNTS; GIVE PROPERTY THAT DIMINISHES VALUE

Inter vivos gifts of part of the donor's ownership interest in a closely-held business (a corporation, family limited partnership or limited liability company), or a parcel of real estate, will generally qualify for a discount from a proportional value of the whole. *See* §§ 2.14, 2.45. For example, if a donor who owns 60 percent of the voting stock of a closely-held corporation gives 11 percent to others, the donor has made a gift of a minority interest and retained a noncontrol minority interest—both of which will qualify for lack of marketability and minority discounts. Note, however, that in some instances the Tax Court has not allowed a minority discount, at least not when the gifts were made shortly before death. *See Estate of Elizabeth Murphy*, 60 T.C.M. 645 (1990). Of course, if the donor wants to preserve the benefits of §§ 303, 2032A, 2057 and 6166, it may be necessary to limit gifts of his or her interest in the business. *See* § 7.10.

A gift of an undivided interest in real estate will result in discounts of the value of the gifted and retained interests. Such a gift may be valued at 15 to 25 percent less than a proportionate part of the total value, at least when a discount is supported by expert testimony. *See, e.g., Propstra v. United States*, 680 F.2d 1248 (9th Cir. 1982); *Nancy N. Mooneyham*, T.C. Memo. 1991-178; Wallace, Now You See It, Now You Don't—Valuation Conundrums in Estate Planning, U. Miami, 24th Inst. Est. Plan., Ch. 8 (1990).

Until early 1993, the IRS had resisted allowing a minority discount for the transfer by one person of shares in a closely held corporation if the transferor, the transferee, and members of the transferor's family owned a controlling interest in the corporation. *See* Rev. Rul. 81-253, 1981-2 C.B. 187, *revoked, by* Rev. Rul. 93-12, 1993-1 C.B. 202. The so-called family attribution or unity of ownership theory articulated in Rev. Rul. 81-253 was abandoned in Rev. Rul. 93-12:

> [I]n the case of a corporation with a single class of stock, notwithstanding the family relationship of the donor, the donee, and other shareholders, the shares of other family members will not be aggregated with the transferred shares to determine whether the transferred shares should be valued as part of a controlling interest.

The earlier IRS position had been rejected by several courts, including the Tax Court. Indeed, in *Victor I. Minahan*, 88 T.C. 492, 500 (1987), the Tax Court held that the position of the IRS was unreasonable: "[W]e emphasize that we find respondent's position unreasonable only because, by espousing a family attribution approach, he seeks to repudiate a well-established line of cases of long and reputable ancestry, going back as far as 1940." In Rev. Rul. 93-12 the IRS cited several cases in which the courts had, in effect, held that a decedent's interest in community property was valued without regard to the other spouse's interest in the community property. *Estate of Bright v. United States*, 658 F.2d 999 (5th Cir. 1981); *Propstra v. United States*,

680 F.2d 1248 (9th Cir. 1982); and *Estate of Elizabeth Lee*, 69 T.C. 860 (1978), *nonacq.,* 1980-2 C.B. 2, *nonacq. withdrawn and acq. substituted*, 1993-1 C.B. 202.

Blockage discounts may be allowed in valuing gifts of large quantities of stock or art objects, that could not be readily absorbed by the market. However, gifts to multiple donees will not be aggregated for purposes of determining blockage discounts. Instead, blockage discounts are generally separately with respect to the interests of each beneficiary. *See Louisa J. Calder*, 85 T.C. 713 (1985) (interests of beneficiaries in a trust) and LR 9719001 (TAM). *See* §§2.14 and 2.45.

§7.17. Do Not Make Gifts That Have Adverse Income Tax Consequences for the Donor

Most property can be transferred by gift without causing the donor to realize any income. However, gain will be realized when a gift is made of some special types of assets. For example, the gift of an installment obligation constitutes a disposition of the obligation under §453B, which requires the donor to realize gain or loss measured by the difference between its basis and its fair market value at the time of transfer. *See* Reg. §1.453-9. The transfer of an installment obligation does not constitute a disposition if the transferor continues to be treated as its owner for income tax purposes. *See* Rev. Rul. 74-613, 1974-2 C.B. 153 (transfer to revocable trust is not a disposition, grantor treated as owner under §§671-677).

A gift or other disposition of investment credit property as defined in §46 may require a recapture of a portion of the credit. §50(a). Under §50(a)(4), "disposition" does not include a transfer by reason of death. Accordingly, a donor should be cautious about disposing of investment recapture property before the end of the recapture period.

Gifts of some other types of recapture property do not have the same negative tax consequences. A gift of §1245 property (depreciable personal property) or §1250 property (depreciable real property) does not trigger recapture of depreciation. §§1245(b)(1), 1250(d)(1). Instead, the potential for depreciation recapture carries over to the donee. If a taxpayer plans to sell §§1245 or 1250 property, the taxpayer should consider giving it to one or more family members who are in lower income tax brackets prior to finalizing the sale. Spreading the income among several taxpayers may reduce the capital gain tax on the sale.

Care should also be exercised in making gifts of the stock of S corporations because of the limits on the number and type of shareholders. Under §1361(b)(1)(A), an S corporation cannot have more than 100 shareholders. In addition, only certain types of trusts are permitted to be shareholders. *See* §§10.4, 11.4.

E. SPECIALIZED GIFT TECHNIQUES

"Transactions within a family group are subject to special scrutiny in order to determine if they are in economic reality what they appear to be on their face." . . . The presumption is that a transfer between closely related parties is a gift." *Estate of Pearl G. Reynolds*, 55 T.C. 172, 201 (1970).

§7.18. INTRODUCTION

Several specialized techniques of making gifts have evolved to meet the estate planning needs of wealthy clients. Among them are some arrangements that may not be treated as gifts for gift tax purposes: small below-market loans, the payment by the grantor of the income tax imposed on a grantor trust of which others are the beneficiaries, the payment by one spouse of the entire joint income or gift tax liability, and arrangements by which the donor performs services for others gratuitously or allows them the free use of property.

In addition, there are some specialized ways of favorably structuring gifts of particular types of property. They include the transfer of the donor's residence to a family member, the installment gift, the "net" gift, the gift of encumbered property, and the part-gift and part-sale.

Individuals may also provide valuable assistance to family members in other ways that are not treated as gifts but which may help them to increase their estates. For example, a wealthy parent may tell children about investment opportunities rather than acting upon them himself or herself. Similarly, a wealthy individual may assist the investment program of other family members directly or by guaranteeing loans made to them by others. In a questionable private letter ruling, LR 9113009, the IRS held that a guarantee of the obligation of another family member made without adequate consideration was a present gift. In sum, there are many ways by which one person may help another increase his or her wealth without incurring any gift tax liability. Although the IRS modified LR 9113009 with respect to issues involving the marital deduction, LR 9409018, *see* §5.16, it did not change its position with respect to the gift tax issue. In LR 200534014, however, the IRS did not find a gift where a parent took legal title to his son's stock in a corporation in which the son was the "driving force" so as to improve the creditworthiness of the company. The parent in this ruling also offered to guarantee loans to the corporation to help it obtain financing and the IRS made no mention of this as a gift to the corporation or the son. Perhaps the IRS is softening its position on this issue.

The taxation of a family's wealth can also be controlled by various types of intrafamily transfers for consideration that have donative overtones. *See* Chapter 9. Some of them, such as the sale of property on the installment method, can be used to "freeze" the value of the seller's estate. Others, such as the family annuity, seek broader tax benefits, including a reduction in the size of the seller's estate. Grantor retained annuity trusts (GRATs) are another device that is particularly attractive if the deeply discounted assets can be contributed to the trust. The qualified personal residence trust (QPRT) allows taxpayers to transfers remainder interests in personal residences at a sharply reduced gift tax cost. In some circumstances, a transfer for consideration or in which the transferor retains a term interest can provide a client with overall benefits that match the client's needs better than outright gifts.

§7.19. NONQUALIFIED STOCK OPTIONS

The tax consequences of transferring nonqualified stock options (NSOs) to family members or trusts are currently uncertain. If the outstanding issues are resolved favorably to taxpayers, gifting NSOs will offer very attractive opportunities to shift potential increases in value to lower generation family members at little or no tax cost.

Initially it seemed the IRS would respond favorably to gifts of NSOs. In LR 9349004, the IRS ruled that the transfer of stock options to a trust for the benefit of the optionee's descendants was not subject to taxation under §83 at the time of the transfer. However, §83(a) would apply at the time the options are exercised and stock is transferred to the trust.

On the transfer tax side, it seemed that gifts of NSOs would receive favorable gift tax treatment. Particularly encouraging signals were given by LR 9350016, which held that the transfer of NSOs to a trust for the optionee's descendants was a completed gift at the time of the transfer. Presumably the gift was small as the option price exceeded the current price of the stock. Importantly, it also held that §§2701 and 2703 did not apply to the transfer as the options did not represent equity in the corporation. The ruling also held that the assets of the trust would not be included in the estate of the grantor because the options will have been irrevocably transferred and the grantor will not have retained any power or control over the trust.

A later revenue ruling raised a serious obstacle to the transfer of NSOs: According to the IRS a gift of NSOs is incomplete so long as the vesting of the options is subject to the fulfillment of a condition by the donor. In Rev. Rul. 98-21, 1998-1 C.B. 975, the IRS ruled that the transfer of a compensatory NSO is completed on the later of: (1) the transfer or (2) when the donee's right to exercise the option is no longer conditioned on the performance of services by the optionee-donor. Until the donee's right to exercise the option is perfected, the donor could negate the effect of the gift by failing to perform the required services. The IRS subsequently upheld transfers of portions of options that were vested. *See* LRs 199927002; 199952012. Also, note that the valuation models that will be accepted by the IRS in valuing gifts of compensatory stock options that relate to publicly traded stock are described in Rev. Proc. 98-34, 1998-1 C.B. 983. *See* §2.14.

Although unvested NSOs may be nontransferable, if the issuer is cooperative it might be possible to achieve the desired goal in another way. For example, the corporation could issue the stock prior to fulfillment of all of the conditions of vesting, subject to a requirement that the issuer could, if the conditions are not all ultimately fulfilled, reacquire the stock for the consideration paid by the option holder. Once the stock is issued, it could be given to the intended donees. The issuance of stock subject to a condition subsequent is factually and legally distinguishable from an NSO. There is, unfortunately, no direct authority that upholds this approach.

Planning for gifts of stock options is thoughtfully discussed by Daniel H. Markstein, III in Giving Well is the Best Revenge: Planning Opportunities with Stock Options, U. Miami, 34th Inst. Est. Plan., Ch. 13 (2000).

§7.20. SMALL BELOW-MARKET LOANS

The 1984 Act added §7872, which defines the income and gift tax consequences of demand and term loans that are made at below-market rates of interest. For purposes of this section a "gift loan" is a below-market loan where the forgoing of interest is in the nature of a gift. §7872(f)(3). No gift or income tax consequences flow from gift loans between individuals that do not exceed $10,000 unless the borrower uses the proceeds to purchase or carry income-producing assets. §7872(c)(2). Thus, a gift loan of $10,000 or less between individuals is totally ignored for tax purposes unless the proceeds are directly related to the purchase or retention of income-producing property.

Below-market loans of $100,000 or less between individuals result in imputed interest paid by the borrower to the lender for income tax purposes, but only to the extent of the "net investment income" of the borrower. §7872(d)(1)(A). For this purpose the net investment income of the borrower is only taken into account if it exceeds $1,000 for the year. §7872(d)(1)(E). Interest is imputed on the full amount of the loan if one of the principal purposes of the loan is tax avoidance. §7872(d)(1)(B).

For gift tax purposes a person making a below-market loan of more than $10,000 is treated as having made a gift to the borrower. That is, the $100,000 exception does not apply for gift tax purposes. In the case of a gift loan for a term, the lender is treated as having made a gift at the time the loan was made of the excess of the amount loaned over the present value of all payments to be made under the terms of the loan. §§7872(d)(2), 7872(b)(1). In the case of a gift demand loan, the lender is treated as having made a gift of the forgone interest, calculated at the federal short-term rate, on the last day of the calendar year. §7872(a).

EXAMPLE 7-5.

On January 1, M made an interest-free demand loan of $100,000 to her daughter, D, who used the proceeds to purchase a residence. The loan remained outstanding throughout the entire year. D had no net investment income during the year. The loan has no income tax consequences. D is not considered to have paid and M is not considered to have received any interest on account of the loan. §7872(d). For gift tax purposes if the federal short-term rate were 6 percent, M would be treated as having made a gift of $6,000 to D on December 31.

In *Elizabeth B. Miller*, 71 T.C.M. (CCH) 1674 (1996), the court held that transfers of cash made by the decedent to her two sons in exchange for noninterest bearing demand notes were gifts and not bona fide loans that established a valid creditor-debtor relationship. The decedent's conduct regarding the transactions was inconsistent, including the failure to reflect cancellation of portions of the indebtedness in some of her gift tax returns. In *Estate of Musgrove v. United States*, 33 Fed. Cl. 657 (1995), the decedent's estate was required to include the value of a self-canceling note that was transferred to the decedent by his son in exchange for money that the decedent had given to his son less than a month prior to the decedent's death. Not surprisingly, the court rejected the estate's contention that the note should not have been included in the estate because of its self-canceling feature.

§7.21. PAYMENT BY ONE SPOUSE OF ENTIRE INCOME OR GIFT TAX LIABILITY

The payment by one spouse of the entire joint income tax liability for the year is not treated as a gift for gift tax purposes. Reg. §25.2511-1(d). Under that regulation, the same rule applies to the payment of the federal gift tax applicable to gifts that are split under §2513. Because of the adoption of the unlimited marital deduction, these exceptions now have little significance.

EXAMPLE 7-6.

H and *W*, who are both employed and have substantial incomes, filed a joint income tax return for the last year. *W*, the wealthier spouse, paid their entire income tax liability. In addition, *W* paid all of the gift taxes that were due on gifts she made during the year, which for gift tax purposes were split with *H* under §2513. Neither the payment of the income tax nor the gift taxes involved a gift from *W* to *H*.

§7.22. GRANTOR PAYS TAX ON INCOME OF GRANTOR TRUST

As explained in §10.31.1, an irrevocable inter vivos trust can be structured so the grantor is treated as owner of the trust for income tax purposes, but the trust will not be included in the grantor's estate. By paying the income tax on income that is actually distributed to others the grantor is able to make a tax-free gift to them. Rev. Rul. 2004-64, 2004-2 C.B. 7.

EXAMPLE 7-7.

Grantor, *G*, transferred income-producing property to a trust of which *G*'s children are the income beneficiaries. *G* retained the power, in a nonfiduciary capacity, to withdraw the principal and substitute property of equivalent value. Such a power causes *G* to be treated as the owner of the trust under §675(4)(C). *G* pays the income tax on the income of the trust although the income is actually distributed to *G*'s children. By paying the income tax *G*, in effect, makes a tax-free gift to the beneficiaries.

§7.23. FREE SERVICES AND FREE USE OF PROPERTY

[I]t is not uncommon for parents to provide their adult children with such things as the use of cars or vacation cottages, simply on the basis of the family relationship. We assume that the focus of the Internal Revenue Service is not on such traditional familial matters. When the Government levies a gift tax on routine neighborly or familial gifts, there will be time enough to deal with such a case. *Dickman v. Commissioner*, 465 U.S. 330, 341 (1984).

As yet the IRS has not sought to apply the gift tax to the free performance by one person of services for another. This position is consistent with dictum in *Commissioner v. Hogle*, 165 F.2d 352 (10th Cir. 1947), to the effect that the gratuitous performance of services does not constitute a taxable gift. It is also consistent with Rev. Rul. 66-167, 1966-1 C.B. 20, which held that a fiduciary's waiver of the right to receive statutory compensation did not constitute a gift where the fiduciary decided to serve gratuitously within a reasonable time after assuming office and the fiduciary thereafter took no action inconsistent with that position. It is consistent, further, with the Code, which purports to apply the federal gift tax only to "the transfer of property by gift." §2501. However, a gift does take place where one person (the donor) pays another person to perform services for a third person (the donee).

Allowing another person the free use of property is more vulnerable to treatment as a gift. Perhaps the IRS has not sought to impose the gift tax on those transactions because of the valuation problems and other administrative difficulties. Providing another person with the free use of property no doubt confers a benefit upon the user, but defining the rules under which an arrangement of that type would be taxed would be exceptionally difficult. The difficulty is illustrated by the complex, yet somewhat inadequate, law on "free loans" that was part of the United Kingdom's Finance Act 1976, §§115 to 117.

EXAMPLE 7-8.

F has been making annual cash gifts to his son, *S*, equal to the maximum allowable annual exclusion for gift tax purposes. This year *F* purchased a car for $30,000, which was registered in *F*'s name. *F* has allowed *S* to keep it at his apartment and drive it whenever *S* wishes. In addition, *F* has paid the $1,200 annual cost of insurance on the car. *S* agreed to make the car available to *F* when he needed one and during the periods that *S* was out of town. Under existing administrative practices, giving *S* the free use of the car and making the insurance payments are not treated as gifts to *S*.

§7.24. GIFT OF A RESIDENCE WITH CONTINUED OCCUPANCY BY DONOR— OUTRIGHT GIFTS AND QUALIFIED PERSONAL RESIDENCE TRUSTS (QPRTS)

The gift of a residence to a family member is usually intended to remove any further appreciation in its value from the donor's estate. That goal may be achieved although the donor continues to occupy it until the time of death. However, the value of achieving that goal must be balanced against the tax and nontax risks the gift involves. Often the potential saving in taxes is outweighed by the risks. A residence that a grantor continues to occupy after transferring it to an irrevocable trust is usually includible in the grantor's estate unless the grantor pays a fair market rental to the trustee. *See, e.g., Estate of Eleanor T.R. Trotter*, T.C. Memo. 2001-250.

A trust in which the grantor retains the use of a personal residence for a term of years, the QPRT described in §9.44, may be preferable because of its statutory recognition for tax purposes and better protection against the reach of creditors—at least during the term of the grantor's retained interest. The gift of an interest in a QPRT is an exception to the basic valuation rule of §2702. The gift of the remainder interest in a QPRT consists of the value of the residence less the actuarially determined value of the grantor's right to occupy the residence for the length of the reserved term. Of course, if the grantor dies during the reserved term the full value of the residence is included in the grantor's gross estate under §2036.

In *Estate of Lydia G. Maxwell*, 98 T.C. 594 (1992), the Tax Court held that a home that the decedent had nominally sold to her only child and his spouse in exchange for a promissory note and leased back from him for an amount roughly equal to the payments required under the note was includible in her gross estate:

> On this record, bearing in mind petitioner's burden of proof, we hold that, notwithstanding its form, the substance of the transaction calls for the conclusion that decedent made a transfer to her son and daughter-in-law with the understanding, at least implied, that she would continue to reside in her home until her death, that the transfer was not a bona fide sale for an adequate and full consideration in money or money's worth, and that the lease represented nothing more than an attempt to add color to the characterization of the transaction as a bona fide sale. 98 T.C. at 601.

The Second Circuit affirmed the Tax Court decision in *Maxwell*, finding a lack of substance in the alleged purchase of the residence by the decedent's son and daughter-in-law. *Estate of Maxwell v. Commissioner*, 3 F.3d 591 (2d Cir. 1993). The appellate court held that for purposes of §2036(a) the note given by the purchasers had no value at all because of the implied agreement "that the grantee would never be called upon to make any payment to the grantor." Because the transfer was made without any consideration, the court also denied any offset under §2043.

A basic problem with the transfer of a residence to family members is that the residence is includible in the donor's gross estate under §2036 if the donor dies while continuing to use or occupy it pursuant to an express or implied understanding or agreement. *Guynn v. United States*, 437 F.2d 1148 (4th Cir. 1971); Rev. Rul. 70-155, 1970-1 C.B. 189. For purposes of §2036 it is not necessary that the retained interest be expressed in an instrument of transfer or that the donor have a legally enforceable right to possession or enjoyment. *Estate of Emil Linderme, Sr.*, 52 T.C. 305 (1969). Exclusive occupancy of the residence by the donor is a very important factor in determining whether there was an understanding or agreement. *Estate of Adrian K. Rapelje*, 73 T.C. 82 (1979); *Linderme, supra*. As indicated by Rev. Rul. 78-409, 1978-2 C.B. 234, the IRS has a very expansive view of what constitutes an "understanding or agreement." On the other hand, continued co-occupancy of the residence by the donor and the donee-spouse does not of itself support an inference of an understanding or agreement regarding the retained use or enjoyment by the donor. *Estate of Allen D. Gutchess*, 46 T.C. 554 (1966). In *Estate of Eleanor T. R. Trotter*, 82 T.C.M. (CCH) 633 (2001), the Tax Court held that §2036 required the decedent's estate to include a condominium unit in which the decedent continued to reside after transferring it to an irrevocable trust of which she was not a beneficiary. Not surprisingly, the court found that there was an implied understanding or agreement that she would remain in possession of the property. However, a residence that is transferred to a trust for the benefit of the transferor's spouse for which a QTIP election is made is not includible in the transferor-spouse's estate even though he or she resides in the residence. *E.g.,* LR 9309023.

The case for exclusion of the residence from the donor's estate is improved if the gift is reported on a timely filed gift tax return and the donee pays the real estate taxes, insurance, and other costs of owning the residence. If the donor and the donee are married and both occupy the residence, it is not necessary for the donor to pay any rent for the donor's continued use of it. In other cases the donor should pay a fair rental. It is helpful if there is a written rental agreement that establishes the terms under which the donor occupies the premises.

The outright gift of a residence usually involves some other tax consequences that should also be taken into account. First, if the gift succeeds and the residence is not included in the donor's estate, the donee will take a carryover basis in the property determined under §1015 instead of an estate tax value determined under §1014. This factor is less significant if the donee does not intend to sell the residence. Second, as a result of the gift it may no longer be possible to exclude a substantial part of the gain under §121 if the residence is sold at a gain. That section allows an exclusion of up to $250,000 ($500,000 for married persons and certain surviving spouses) of the gain realized on the sale of a principal residence occupied by the seller for at least two of the five years immediately preceding the sale. (If the donor retains a term interest in a QPRT the exclusion should be available because the donor is treated as the owner of the trust property for income tax purposes.) Third, the residence may no longer qualify for the preferential property tax treatment that may be allowed under local law for residential property owned and occupied by senior citizens.

On the nontax side there is always the risk that the donee might deny the donor any use of the property. Also, in the case of an outright gift of a residence, at some point the donor may no longer be able to pay the fair rental value of the property, which could jeopardize exclusion of the property from the donor's estate if the donor were allowed to continue to occupy it. Perhaps more important, the gift makes the residence subject to disposition by the donee inter vivos and at death and reachable by the donee's creditors. Where a gift is made, the donee's will should dispose of the property in an acceptable manner should the donee predecease the donor.

Partial interests in a residence that were given by a parent to her children may not be included in her gross estate although the parent continued to reside in part of the residence. *Estate of Rebecca A. Wineman,* 79 T.C.M. (CCH) 2189 (2000).

§7.25. INSTALLMENT GIFTS: PERIODIC FORGIVENESS OF TRANSFEREE'S NOTES

> If an individual ostensibly makes a loan and, as part of a prearranged plan, intends to forgive or not collect on the note, the note will not be considered valuable consideration and the donor will have made a gift at the time of the loan to the full extent of the loan. *See* Rev. Rul. 77-299, 1977-2 C.B. 343. However, if there is no prearranged plan and the intent to forgive the debt arises at a later time, then the donor will have made a gift only at the time of the forgiveness. *See* Rev. Rul. 81-264, 1981-2 C.B. 186. Tax Litigation Bulletin 93-2 (Feb. 1993).

Various techniques are used to keep the value of a gift within the amount of the allowable annual exclusions. Thus, a donor may limit the amount of the gift made in a particular year by transferring a partial interest in an asset to the donee. However, under this approach the value of the interests retained by the donor may continue to appreciate in value. That risk can be avoided by transferring all of the donor's interests in a particular item of property in exchange for notes of the donee that have a value equal to the excess of the value of the transferred property over the amount of the allowable annual exclusions for the current year. In successive years the donor could forgive an amount of the notes equal to the annual exclusion. Of course, the forgiveness of the notes may trigger recognition of gain by the donor under the installment sales rules. *See* § 9.6. An installment sale such as this should not be subject to the special valuation rules of § 2702.

For gift tax purposes the amount of a gift is the value of the property transferred reduced by the value of notes or other consideration received in exchange by the donor. § 2512(b). "If a donor transfers by gift less than his entire interest in property, the gift tax is applicable to the interest transferred. The tax is applicable, for example, to the transfer of an undivided half interest in property, or to the transfer of a life estate when the grantor retains the remainder interest, or vice versa." Reg. § 25.2511-1(e). For income tax purposes the transfer of property in exchange for a note would be treated as a sale to the extent of the consideration received, which could be very undesirable from the donor's point of view. Of course, the taxation of the gain may be deferred unless the seller opts not to use the installment sale method of reporting. In some cases the valuation of the transferee's note is a troublesome issue. For example, the IRS has indicated that a low-interest note that is due when the borrower's home is sold has no ascertainable value. LR 8103130. Accordingly, the full amount of the loan might be treated as a gift.

A promissory note given to the transferor by the donee may not be recognized by the IRS as consideration if the note is systematically forgiven in annual increments equal to the annual gift tax exclusion. In such cases the IRS has argued that the notes should be disregarded and the transfer treated as a gift of the entire value of the property. That result must follow, according to the IRS, if the transferor intended from the outset to forgive the notes that he or she received. Rev. Rul. 77-299, 1977-2 C.B. 343. The issue has been most frequently litigated in the Tax Court, which has generally recognized valid, enforceable notes as consideration, particularly when they were secured. "This Court has held that when property is transferred in exchange for a valid, enforceable, and secured legal obligation, there is no gift for Federal tax purposes." *Estate of I. W. Kelley*, 63 T.C. 321, 324 (1974), *nonacq.*, 1977-2 C.B. 2. *See also Selsor R. Haygood*, 42 T.C. 936 (1964), *acq. in result*, 1965-1 C.B. 4, *withdrawn and nonacq. substituted*, 1977-2 C.B. 2; *Nelson Story III*, 38 T.C. 936 (1962). If no gift tax return is filed in connection with a "sale" and the transaction is later recharacterized as a gift, the vendor-donor's gift history must be adjusted. LR 199930002 (TAM).

The argument of the IRS prevailed in *Minnie E. Deal*, 29 T.C. 730 (1958), in which the Tax Court found that the notes executed by the transferee-daughters "were not intended to be enforced and were not intended as consideration for the transfer by the petitioner, and that, in substance, the transfer of the property was by gift." 29 T.C. at 736. A gift may occur where the notes have a value less than their face amounts because the interest rate provided for in the notes is less than the market rate, *Gertrude H. Blackburn,* 20 T.C. 204 (1953), or because of other factors, *e.g., Estate of Pearl Gibbons Reynolds,* 55 T.C. 172 (1970). Note that the interest rate specified in § 483 does not apply for purposes of determining whether an installment sale resulted in a gift. *See* § 9.4.

Notes can also be used to insulate transfers of cash from the gift tax. *See* § 7.20. Under the approach generally taken by the Tax Court, such notes can be written down at an annual rate equal to the allowable annual exclusions without jeopardizing their status.

Forgiveness of Intrafamily Loan. The forgiveness of a loan to a close family member that is treated as a gift will not have adverse income tax consequences for the debtor (i.e., the amount forgiven will not be included in the debtor's gross income). Rev. Rul. 2004-37, 2004-1 C.B. 583. The unqualified forgiveness of a loan should qualify for the annual gift tax exclusion. In most cases, the forgiveness of part or all of a loan that is not treated as a gift will be includible in the debtor's gross income. See § 108(a).

§ 7.26. NET GIFTS

A net gift is a gift that is conditioned upon the donee's payment of the gift tax on the transfer. It is a useful planning technique, particularly when it is desirable for the donee to sell the property in order to generate funds with which to pay the tax. For example, the donor may not have sufficient funds to pay the tax and the tax on the gain would be less if the property were sold by the donee.

In *Charles T. McCord,* 120 T.C. 358 (2003), *rev'd,* 461 F.3d 614 (5th Cir. 2006), the Tax Court held that for gift tax purposes, the amount of a gift could not be reduced by the "'mortality-adjusted present value' (mortality-adjusted present value) of the children's contingent obligation to pay the additional estate tax that would have been incurred on account of section 2035(c) . . . if that petitioner had died within 3 years of the date of the gift." As the Tax Court pointed out, "[T]he dollar amount of a potential liability to pay the 2035 tax is by no means fixed; rather, such amount depends on factors that are subject to change, including estate tax rates and exemption amount (not to mention the continued existence of the estate tax. For that reason alone, we conclude that petitioners are not entitled to treat the mortality-adjusted present value as sale proceeds (consideration received) for purposes of determining the amounts of their respective gifts at issue." The Fifth Circuit reversed, concluding that while the obligation may be contingent, it is susceptible to valuation:

> Was the limitation of three years on the Taxpayers' exposure to the additional estate taxes imposed by § 2035 (which the non-exempt donees assumed), when viewed *in pari materia* with all other relevant factors and circumstances, too speculative to be included when Mr. Frazier calculated the net taxable value of those 1996 gifts? We answer this question in the negative, because we are convinced as a matter of law that a willing buyer would insist on the willing seller's recognition that—like the possibility that the applicable tax law, tax rates, interest rates, and actuarially determined life expectancies of the Taxpayer could change or be eliminated in the ensuing three years—the effect of the three-year exposure to § 2035

estate taxes was sufficiently determinable as of the date of the gifts to be taken into account. And, after all, it is the willing buyer/willing seller test that we are bound to apply.

§7.26.1. Income Tax

A net gift generally does not have an adverse income tax consequence when the donor's basis in the property is equal to or greater than the gift tax to be paid by the donee. When the donor's basis is less than the tax, the donor realizes gain to the extent the gift tax liability assumed by the donee exceeds the donor's basis. *Diedrich v. Commissioner*, 457 U.S. 191 (1982). The gain is realized in the year the gift tax is paid, not in the year of the gift. *Estate of Weeden v. Commissioner*, 685 F.2d 1160 (9th Cir. 1982).

The holding period of the donee in net gift cases is unclear. *Citizens' National Bank of Waco v. United States*, 417 F.2d 675 (5th Cir. 1969), concluded that "tacking" of the donor's and donee's holding periods is allowable under §1223(2) because the donor's basis carried over to the donee under §1015. Thus, if a donee sells a capital asset at a gain within a year of the transfer, the donor's holding period can be taken into account in determining whether or not the gain was long term. The IRS argues that if the transfer involves a part gift-part sale, the issue is governed by Reg. §1.1015-4(a)(1). Under it the donee's basis is the greater of the amount paid for the property or the donor's adjusted basis for the property plus an adjustment under §1015(d)(6) for gift tax paid with respect to the transfer. In the case of a net gift, the donee's basis apparently includes both the amount paid by the donee (the amount of the gift tax) plus an increase in basis under §1015(b)(6) on account of the gift tax paid with respect to the appreciation element. Accordingly, the IRS will deny tacking under §1223(2) where the price paid by the donee exceeds the donor's basis. LR 7752001 (TAM).

A net gift to a trust can cause the income of the trust to be taxed to the donor to the extent it is used to pay the gift tax. Prior to the adoption of the grantor trust rules, §§671-677, the courts held that the trust income was taxable to the donor as ordinary income under the *Clifford* doctrine. *Estate of A. E Staley, Sr.*, 47 B.T.A. 260 (1942), *aff'd*, 136 F.2d 368 (5th Cir. 1943), *cert. denied*, 320 U.S. 786 (1945). Now, the income is taxed to the grantor under §677 to the extent it is, or in the discretion of a nonadverse party may be, used to pay the donor's gift tax liability. *Estate of Craig R. Shaeffer*, 37 T.C. 99 (1961), *aff'd*, 313 F.2d 738 (8th Cir.), *cert. denied*, 375 U.S. 818 (1963). Note that the income of the trust is not taxable to the grantor on that theory after the donor's obligation is discharged by payment of the tax. Thus, when the trustee borrows the funds to pay the tax, the trust's subsequent income is not taxed to the donor even when it is used to repay the loan. Repayment of the loan discharges the trust's obligation and not that of the donor. *Estate of Annette S. Morgan*, 37 T.C. 981 (1962), *aff'd*, 316 F.2d 238 (6th Cir.), *cert. denied*, 375 U.S. 825 (1963); *Victor W. Krause*, 56 T.C. 1242 (1971). In general §677 does not apply if an encumbrance is paid with funds other than trust income.

The possibility that a net gift may result in some income tax liability to the donor should not deter most clients from using it. First of all, the net gift may reduce the total amount of gift tax that the donor must pay. *See* Example 7-9. Thus, even though the donor might incur some income tax liability, the gift tax cost is reduced. Second, the recognition of gain by the donor may not result in a much larger income tax liability than if the donee were to sell the property. Where the gain will be taxed as long-term capital gain the maximum rate applicable to the donor (or the donee) will most often be lower than the rate applicable to ordinary income. Overall, the decision of whether to use a net gift should be made in light of the marginal income tax rates of the donor and the donee, the client's financial resources, and the other tax and nontax factors that are relevant to deciding whether to make a gift.

§7.26.2. Gift Tax

On the gift tax side the IRS has generally been cooperative: It recognizes that where a gift is made subject to a condition that the donee pay the gift tax, the donor receives consideration equal to the amount of the gift tax the donee is obligated to pay. Rev. Rul. 75-72, 1975-1 C.B. 310 (including formula for computation of deduction); Rev. Rul. 76-49, 1976-1 C.B. 294 (including formula for computation of deduction where donee will pay both the federal and state gift taxes). In such cases the donor makes a gift of an amount equal to the value of the property less the amount of tax payable on the transfer. The method of calculating the amount of a net gift where state gift taxes are also involved is illustrated by Example D of IRS Publication 904 (rev. May 1985), Interrelated Computations for Estate and Gift Taxes.

EXAMPLE 7-9.

Donor, D, made a gift of property worth $112,000 to his son, S, in 2008 on condition that S pay the federal gift tax on the transfer. D had made prior taxable gifts of $1 million. The deduction is $32,567 based on the formula:

$$\frac{\text{Tentative Tax}}{1 + \text{Rate of Tax}} = \text{Tax Due}$$

First, the tax is calculated without regard to the condition, which indicates a tax of $41,000 (the "tentative tax"). Next, the formula calculation is made:

$$\text{Tax Due} = \frac{\$41,000}{1 + 0.41} = \$29,078$$

Finally, the calculation is proved by using the "true tax" to calculate D's gift tax liability for the year in the ordinary way:

Gross transfer for year	$112,000
Less: Gift tax on transfer	− 29,078
Net transfer	$82,922
Less: Annual exclusion	− 12,000
Taxable gift for year	$70,922
Plus: Prior gifts by donor	+1,000,000

Total taxable gifts	$1,070,922
Tax on total gifts	$374,878
Less: Tax on prior gifts	− 345,800
Tax on gift for year	$29,078

Even in the case of a net gift, the donor's unified credit must be taken into account in computing the amount of the gift tax. Rev. Rul. 79-398, 1979-2 C.B. 338. The policy was explained in an earlier Letter Ruling as follows: "The unified credit must be used in computing the gift tax. The credit relates to the gift tax on the donor and consequently can only be used against the tax imposed upon the donor's transfers. The fact that a donee is going to satisfy the donor's primary obligation to pay the gift tax does not make the tax a tax on the donees [sic] transfers. Therefore, the unified credit to be used is the donor's credit." LR 7842068. In the view of the IRS, no consideration flows from the donee to the donor for the amount of tax equal to the donor's available unified credit. Rev. Rul. 81-223, 1981-2 C.B. 189.

The gift tax cost of a net gift may be reduced further if the donee also assumes the responsibility for paying the estate tax that §2035(b) imposes on the amount of the gift tax on the transfer if the donor dies within three years of making the gift. The concept is reviewed in Arlein & Frazier, The Net, Net Gift, 147 Tr. & Est. 24 (Aug. 2008), which helpfully describes the steps involved in valuing the donee's potential §2035(b) estate tax liability. As the article points out, although "it's not entirely clear that the IRS won't challenge a net, net gift", the concept should be considered in planning.

§7.26.3. Estate Tax

Gifts made prior to a donor's death are seldom includible in his or her estate. However, under §2035(a)(2) certain gifts, including policies of insurance on the donor's life, are included in the donor's estate if made within three years immediately preceding the donor's death. Of course, property transferred by gift is includable in the donor's estate under §§2036 and 2038 if the donor retained the use of the property or controls over its disposition.

§7.27. GIFTS OF ENCUMBERED PROPERTY

If a donor makes a gift of encumbered property, only the excess of the value of the property over the amount of the encumbrance is generally subject to the gift tax. *D. S. Jackman*, 44 B.T.A. 704 (1941), acq., 47-1 C.B. 9. This result is logical and consistent with the treatment of net gifts. *See* §7.26. However, if the donee can require the donor to satisfy the encumbrance out of other property, the value of the gift is not reduced by the amount of the encumbrance. *Estate of D. Byrd Gwinn*, 25 T.C. 31 (1955).

The income tax consequences for the donor of this type of gift should also be considered in advance. They are simple enough if the donor's basis exceeds the amount of the encumbrance—the donor does not realize any gain as a result of the gift. However, since 1971 the courts have recognized that, applying *Crane v. Commissioner*, 331 U.S. 1 (1947), the donor will realize gain if the amount of the encumbrance exceeds the donor's basis. The trend began with *Malone v. United States,* 326 F. Supp. 106 (N.D.Miss. 1971), *aff'd per curiam,* 455 F.2d 502 (5th Cir. 1972). In *Malone,* the donee, a trustee, formally assumed the donor's personal obligation for the mortgage indebtedness on the encumbered real property that was transferred to the trust. Because the indebtedness was assumed, the court readily concluded that the gift resulted in an economic benefit to the donor equal to the excess of the indebtedness over the donor's basis in the property.

The application of the *Crane* concept was significantly extended in *Johnson v. Commissioner,* 495 F.2d 1079 (6th Cir.), *cert. denied,* 419 U.S. 1040 (1974), which held that the donor received an economic benefit when encumbered stock was given to a trustee although the donor was not personally liable for the indebtedness and it was not assumed by the trustee. The taxpayer in *Johnson* borrowed $200,000 on a nonre-course basis against stock that he gave to a trustee three days later. The stock had a basis of about $11,000 and a value of $500,000 at the time of the gift. Under those circumstances the donor realized a gain of $189,000 when the gift was made. The rule established in *Johnson* is logical, fair, and consistent with Reg. § 1.1011-2(a)(3), which requires that the amount of an indebtedness be treated as an amount received for purposes of applying the bargain sale rules whether or not the transferee agrees to pay the debt.

Johnson was followed in *Estate of Aaron Levine,* 634 F.2d 12 (2d Cir. 1980), *aff'g* 72 T.C. 780 (1979), where the donor gave a trustee real property that was subject to encumbrances. The loans, which totaled far more than the donor's basis in the property, had been entered into over a long period of years. Although the timing of the loans in *Levine* did not evidence a plan to bail out the mortgage proceeds from the start, the donor nonetheless "reaped a tangible economic benefit from this transaction and such economic benefit is subject to tax under the rationale of [*Crane*]." 72 T.C. at 792.

EXAMPLE 7-10.

D owns 1,000 shares of XYZ, Inc. stock that has a basis of $1 per share and a current value of $100 per share. If *D* sells the stock for $100 per share *D* will realize a capital gain of $99 per share, or a total of $99,000. If *D* borrows $75,000 against the stock *D* will not realize any gain until *D* disposes of the stock. However, under *Johnson* and *Levine* if *D* borrows on the stock and later makes a gift of it, *D* will realize a gain at the time of the gift.

When there is a gift of encumbered property the donee's basis will reflect both the gain realized by the donor and the portion of any gift tax paid that is attributable to the appreciation element of the gift. As the court explained in *Johnson,* Congress authorized increases in a donee's basis by both the amount of gain recognized in connection with gifts to trusts and the amount of gift tax paid, although that doing so may superficially appear to be redundant.

Until the *Johnson* decision was handed down, it appears that a taxpayer could borrow against an appreciated asset, then give it away without being required to pay any income tax on the amount by which the loan exceeded his or her basis. If the transaction were carefully structured the obligation could be satisfied by the donee without any income tax liability to the donor. In the pre-*Johnson* era the grantor might be taxed on the income under § 677 in the case of a gift to a trust. Even in the case of a trust, the reach of § 677 was avoided if (1) the trustee assumed liability for the obligation, *Edwards v. Greenwald*, 217 F.2d 632 (5th Cir. 1954), or (2) the obligation was satisfied with funds other than trust income, *Estate of Annette S. Morgan*, 37 T.C. 981 (1962), *aff'd*, 316 F.2d 238 (6th Cir.), *cert. denied*, 375 U.S. 825 (1963).

§ 7.28. PART-GIFT AND PART-SALE; BARGAIN SALE

Under another approach the donor sells part of an asset to the intended donee in order to generate funds with which to pay the gift tax on a gift of the balance of the asset. The plan can be implemented in either of two ways, which have substantially different income tax consequences. Under the first, the donor gives part of the property to the donee, who uses it as security to borrow funds with which to purchase the remainder of the property. In this case the gift and the sale relate to separate interests, the separateness of which is respected for gift and income tax purposes. Under the second method, all of the property is transferred to the donee for less than adequate and full consideration in money or money's worth (*i.e.*, a bargain sale). The owner's gift tax liability is the same under both approaches. However, under the first method the gain is computed separately for the property sold, while under the second gain is determined by reference to the transferor's basis in the entire property.

EXAMPLE 7-11.

O plans to transfer 1,000 shares of XYZ, Inc. stock to his daughter, *D*, in exchange for $15,000 which *O* will use to pay the gift tax that will be due as a result of the transfer. The stock has a basis of $10 per share and a value of $50 per share. Whichever method is used, the transfer will involve a gift to *D* of property worth $35,000 for gift tax purposes.

Under the first method, *O* would give *D* 700 shares outright, which involves a gift of $35,000 ($50 × 700). The gift would not cause *O* to recognize any gain unless the shares were encumbered. *D*'s basis in those shares would be *O*'s basis ($10) plus any gift tax paid with respect to the net appreciation in value of the shares. *See* § 1015(d). Also, the time *O* held these shares could be taken into account in determining *D*'s holding period. *See* § 1223(2). If *O* sells the remaining 300 shares to *D* for $50 each, *O* would have a capital gain of $12,000 ($50 × 300-($10 × 300)). Under § 1012, *D*'s basis in those 300 shares would be their cost of $50 each, the holding period of which would begin with the date of purchase. Thus, if no gift tax were paid with respect to the gift of 700 shares, *D* would have a total basis of $22,000 in the 1,000 shares (700 × $10) + (300 × $50).

O's gain would be much smaller under the second method (*i.e.*, if *O* makes a part-gift and part-sale of the 1,000 shares to *D* for $15,000). In case of a part-gift and part-sale "the transferor has a gain to the extent that the amount realized by him exceeds his adjusted basis in the property."

Reg. § 1.1001-1(e)(1). Here the amount realized ($15,000) exceeds his basis ($10,000) by only $5,000. However, in this case *D*'s basis will be limited to the price paid ($15,000) plus the portion of the gift tax paid with respect to the net appreciation. *See* Reg. § 1.1015-4(a). Accordingly, the IRS might argue that the time *O* held the shares could not be taken into account for holding period purposes. *See* LR 7752001.

As Example 7-11 indicates, income and gift tax consequences must be taken into account in choosing which method to use in effectuating a part gift and part sale. The outcomes should also be compared with the results produced by other techniques, such as the net gift. *See* §7.26. In this connection it is important to note that bargain sales to charity are subject to different rules. *See* § 1011(b) and § 8.36.

F. GIFTS TO MINORS

§7.29. IMPORTANCE OF GIFTS TO MINORS

Income tax changes, most notably the adoption of the Kiddie Tax, the compressed income tax rate schedule, and the elimination of the income-shifting potential of short-term trusts, limit the income-shifting advantages of making gifts to minors. However, gifts to minors remain important in estate planning. By making gifts to minors, the overall income tax burdens of a family may be lightened a bit. More important, the donor's estate will include neither the property's subsequent appreciation in value nor the post-gift income from the property. Additionally, gifts to minors of undivided interests in real property or of nonmarketable minority interests in businesses may qualify for valuation discounts. Annual exclusion gifts to minors are a particularly advantageous way of reducing the donor's overall gift, estate, and GST tax burdens.

Making gifts to a trust for a minor is made more attractive by the availability of annual exclusion if the beneficiary holds a properly drafted *Crummey* power of withdrawal. *See* §7.38. In planning trusts for minors, consideration must also be given to other income tax rules, particularly the grantor trust rules.

The sections that follow discuss the principal methods of transferring property to minors, including outright gifts, Series EE or I bonds, various forms of multiparty bank accounts, gifts under the Uniform Acts and gifts in trust. The use of grantor retained annuity trusts (GRATs) is discussed in Chapter 9. The discussion illustrates the wide differences in tax and nontax consequences that flow from different methods of making gifts to or for the benefit of minors. For example, some transfers constitute completed gifts for gift tax purposes while others do not. Also, in the case of some gifts the subsequent income is taxed to the donor, while under others it is taxed to the donee, or to a trust for the donee's benefit. Finally, in some cases the property is includible in the donor's gross estate, while in others it is not.

§7.30. OUTRIGHT GIFTS

The transfer of property directly into the name of a minor is generally unwise for a number of nontax reasons. There is some risk that the minor donee might dissipate the property instead of saving it, which is usually what the donor has in mind. Importantly, in many instances it may be necessary to obtain the appointment of a guardian in order to sell, exchange, lease, or otherwise deal with property that stands in the name of a minor. Also, if the donee dies prior to attaining the age of majority, the property may return to the donor under the intestate succession law instead of passing to the donee's siblings or other relatives. Finally, even if a guardian is appointed, the donee will gain full control over the property when he or she attains the age of majority, which many clients consider to be far too soon.

If a minor owns stock, the transfer agent may require that assignments and other documents pertaining to the stock be signed by a duly appointed and acting agent. Transactions involving life insurance, real property, or other assets may also require the participation of a guardian. Local law and practice regarding the deposit and withdrawal of funds from accounts standing in the name of minors in financial institutions vary widely. Some institutions permit a minor to make small withdrawals if the minor is capable of writing his or her name and seems to understand the transaction, while others do not. As indicated below there is a simplified procedure for redemption of Series EE bonds that stand in the name of a minor.

§7.30.1. Gift Tax

The transfer of property into a minor's name is generally a gift that is subject to state and federal gift taxes. However, the annual gift tax exclusion is available with respect to bona fide transfers except when the gift consists of a future interest in property. §2503(b).

§7.30.2. Estate Tax

Property that is given to a minor is includible in the minor's gross estate under §2033 and is not generally includible in the donor's gross estate under §2035. However, the property is includible in the donor's gross estate if the donor continues to use and control the property or expends it to satisfy a legal obligation to support the donee. §§2036 and 2038.

Overall, it is generally better to make small gifts to custodians under the Uniform Acts and larger ones under a carefully planned and drafted trust. Those methods do not involve the problems of management that may arise where an outright gift is made to a minor. However, gifts made under the Uniform Acts do suffer from some of the same nontax disadvantages as outright gifts.

When an outright gift is made to a minor, a guardian may be appointed to participate in transactions affecting the property. However, a guardian cannot legitimately "undo" the gift and return the property to the donor or to a custodian under the Uniform Acts. Once an outright gift has been made to a minor, little can generally be done to relieve the situation.

§7.30.3. Income Tax

Subject to the Kiddie Tax, §1(g), the income from property that is transferred into the name of a minor is taxed to the minor if it belongs to the minor and cannot be used to satisfy the donor's legal obligation of support. *See* Rev. Rul. 58-65, 1958-1 C.B. 13. Thus, dividends paid on stock given to a minor are taxed to the minor where they are reinvested for the minor's benefit and are not borrowed or otherwise used by the donors in any way. *Sandifur v. United States,* 64-2 U.S.T.C. ¶9817, 14 A.F.T.R.2d 5082 (E.D.Wash. 1964). However, the income is taxed to the donor when he or she continues to exercise control over the property and the income it generates. *Little v. United States,* 191 F. Supp. 12 (E.D.Tex. 1960); *Henry D. Duarte,* 44 T.C. 193 (1965). In sum, the income is taxed according to the economic reality of the situation and not necessarily according to the way title is held.

§7.31. UNITED STATES SERIES EE, HH/H AND I BONDS

Series EE bonds are United States savings bonds issued after 1979 on which payment of interest is deferred until redemption. The bonds are issued in face amounts that are double their purchase price (*e.g.,* a $500 bond costs $250). No more than $30,000 in Series EE bonds may be purchased in the name of any person in any calendar year. 31 C.F.R. §351.44 (2011). In contrast Series H (now HH) bonds are ones on which interest is payable currently. However, if Series H or HH bonds were issued in exchange for matured Series E or EE bonds on which reporting of interest had been deferred, the holder may continue to defer reporting interest. The interest on Series H (HH) bonds may continued to be deferred until the bonds are cashed, stop earning interest in 20 years, or are reissued in a reportable event.

Series I bonds are ones on which the inflation linked interest accrues monthly, for up to 30 years. I bonds carry a guaranteed base rate of interest that remains the same throughout the life of the bond and a variable rate of interest that is adjusted semiannually, reflecting changes in the Consumer Price Index for all Urban Consumers. Interest on I bonds and on eligible EE bonds can be excluded so long as the proceeds are used to pay tuition and fees at a post-secondary educational institution.

Minors are often given Series EE (formerly Series E) bonds because of their security and ease of purchase. (I bonds may be given more frequently as they become better known.) The applicable federal regulations require that "[t]he registration must express the actual ownership of, and interest in, the bond. The registration is conclusive of such ownership except [to correct an error in registration]." 31 C.F.R. §315.5(a) (2011). The same rule applies to Series HH bonds. 31 C.F.R. §353.5(a) (2011). Under them, bonds owned by natural persons may be registered only in the name of one person as sole owner ("X"), two persons as coowners ("X or Y," but not "X and Y"), or two persons as owner and beneficiary ("X payable on death to Y" or "X, P.O.D., Y"). 31 C.F.R. §315.7(b) (2011). However, bonds owned by a minor may be registered in the name of the minor's guardian or in the name of a custodian under the Uniform Acts. *Id.*

Series EE bonds may be presented for redemption, if exchanged for Series HH bonds (a minimum of $500), no earlier than 12 months after purchase. 31 C.F.R. §321.8, 352.7 (2011).

For income tax purposes the unreported increase in value of a bond is ordinarily not taxed until redemption or maturity. If one person obtains payment on a bond that is registered in the names of coowners, presumably the increase is taxed to that person alone. If the ownership of a bond is changed by reissue, the prior owner is liable for the income tax on the increase in value up to the date of reissue. *See* Rev.

Rul. 54-327, 1954-2 C.B. 50. However, income is not realized where a bond is reissued at the request of the sole owner in his or her name and the name of another person as coowners. Rev. Rul. 70-428, 1970-2 C.B. 5. A change in ownership resulting from the death of an owner is also not a taxable event. Instead, the unreported increase in value to the date of death constitutes income in respect of a decedent that is subject to taxation under § 691 when received by the owner. Rev. Rul. 64-104, 1964-1 C.B. 223.

In assessing the suitability of an investment in Series EE bonds, a client must consider their rate of return compared with the yields of other secure investments. An investment in Series EE bonds for a minor under 14 is attractive because the annual increase in value of the bond is not reportable as income unless an election is made under § 454. Series EE (or I) bonds provide a safe and simple way to invest a relatively small amount on behalf of a minor. Also, they are easily purchased and redeemed. If a client intends to invest a small amount in Series EE bonds for a minor, consideration should be given to making the gift under one of the Uniform Acts. A large investment in Series EE bonds is generally not desirable.

§ 7.31.1. Minor as Sole Owner

The purchase of a bond in the name of a minor has the same tax consequences as any other outright transfer of property to a minor. As indicated in Rev. Rul. 68-269, 1968-1 C.B. 399, Situation 3, the purchase constitutes a completed gift from the purchaser to the donee regardless of when the bond is actually delivered to the minor. Accordingly, the purchase qualifies for the annual exclusion under § 2503(b). The regulations permit a minor to redeem a bond that is registered in the minor's name if the minor is sufficiently competent to sign a request for payment and understands the nature of the transaction. 31 C.F.R. § 315.62 (2011). If the minor does not meet those requirements, a bond registered in the minor's name may be redeemed by a parent with whom the minor resides or who has legal custody of him or her. 31 C.F.R. § 315.63 (2011). Otherwise, the bond may be redeemed by the person who is the primary source of support for the minor. *Id.*

If the minor dies owning the bond, it is includible in the minor's gross estate under § 2033. Under ordinary circumstances the bond is not includible in the donor's estate.

The interest on a savings bond is ordinarily reported by a cash basis taxpayer when the bond is redeemed or reaches final maturity. Under § 454(a), a taxpayer may elect to report the yearly increase in redemption value on the bond and all other appreciation-type securities. Taxpayers seldom elect to report the annual increase as it accrues because the election applies to all appreciation-type obligations and binds the taxpayer for all subsequent taxable years. Also, once the election is made, it can be changed only with the permission of the IRS.

§ 7.31.2. Minor as Coowner

Bonds purchased with the funds of a minor must be registered in the name of the minor (or in the name of a guardian for the minor) without a coowner or beneficiary. However, bonds purchased with funds not belonging to a minor may be registered in the name of the minor as owner or coowner. 31 C.F.R. § 315.6(c) (2011). Bonds purchased as a gift to a minor may also be registered in the name of a custodian under the Uniform Acts. *Id.*

The purchase of a bond in the name of the purchaser and another individual in coownership form ("*X* or *Y*") does not constitute a completed gift. A completed gift does take place if such a bond purchased by *X* is reissued in *Y*'s name alone, Rev. Rul. 55-278, 1955-1 C.B. 471, or when *Y* surrenders the bond for redemption without any duty to account to *X* for the disposition of the proceeds. Reg. § 25.2511-1(h)(4); Rev. Rul. 68-269, 1968-1 C.B. 399, situation 5. When *X* provides the entire purchase price of the bond, none of the bond is includible in *Y*'s gross estate if *Y* predeceases *X*. Of course, if *X* dies first, the bond is includible in *X*'s estate under § 2040 (*i.e.*, half of the value of the bond is included if *X* and *Y* are husband and wife, otherwise the full value is included). Generally, when either coowner dies, the bond belongs entirely to the survivor. 31 C.F.R. § 315.70(b) (2011).

While both coowners are living, either of them may redeem the bond by separate request. 31 C.F.R. § 315.37 (2011). In contrast, the bond may be reissued only upon the request of both owners. 31 C.F.R. § 315.51 (2011). A gift from one coowner to the other is effective only if the bond is reissued in the name of the donee—mere physical delivery to the intended donee is insufficient. *United States v. Chandler*, 410 U.S. 257 (1973). As the Supreme Court explained in *Chandler*, "[t]he regulations thus made the jointly issued bond nontransferable in itself and permitted a change in ownership, so long as both coowners were alive, only through reissuance at the request of both coowners." 410 U.S. at 260.

§ 7.31.3. Minor as Beneficiary

The registration of a bond in the name of "*X*, payable on death to *Y*" or "*X*, P.O.D., *Y*" has the same tax consequences as registration in the coownership form ("*X* or *Y*"). Specifically, this type of registration does not involve a gift from *X* to *Y* and the bond is fully includible in the estate of *X* if *X* predeceases *Y*. When *X* and *Y* are not husband and wife and *Y* did not contribute to the purchase of the bond, nothing is includible in *Y*'s estate if *Y* predeceases *X*. (When *X* and *Y* are husband and wife, presumably half of the value of the bond is includible under § 2040(b) in the estate of the spouse first-to-die.) Also, the annual increase in redemption value of the bond is ordinarily not taxed on a current basis for income tax purposes. Income would be realized, however, when the bond is redeemed, finally matures, or is reissued in the name of an owner other than *X* (the original purchaser). The payable-on-death form of registration is an effective will substitute insofar as Series EE and Series HH bonds are concerned.

§ 7.32. Payable-on-Death (POD) Bank Accounts

The payable-on-death (POD) form of multiparty account is recognized as nontestamentary in Part 2 of Article 6 of the U.P.C. (2011). The account is typically established in the name of a depositor, "P.O.D." to a designated party. (*E.g.*, "A, P.O.D., *X*".) A POD account belongs to the depositor during his or her lifetime. U.P.C. § 6-211 (2011). On the death of the depositor the account belongs to the designated beneficiary if he or she is then living. U.P.C. § 6-212(a) (2003). The beneficiary's interest terminates if he or she predeceases the depositor. (These rules closely resemble those applicable to Totten trusts. §7.33.)

The POD form should be used with care in non-U.P.C. states. While many non-U.P.C. states have enacted legislation validating POD accounts, some may not have. If they have not, a POD account might be treated as testamentary transfer that is invalid unless executed in the manner required of wills.

When X deposits funds in an account that stands in the name of "X payable on death to Y," the deposit does not have any significant current federal tax impact: The interest on the account is taxable to X, the deposit does not constitute a gift because the funds may be freely withdrawn by X, and the account is includible in X' s gross estate. If Y predeceases X the account is not included in Y's gross estate.

§7.33. SAVINGS ACCOUNT OR TOTTEN TRUST

The Uniform Multiple-Person Accounts Act (1989) treats "accounts in Totten trust form as POD accounts." A savings account or Totten trust is created when X opens an account in the name of "X as trustee for Y." The term "Totten trust" is derived from the name of the case, *Matter of Totten*, 71 N.E. 748 (1904), in which the arrangement was upheld as a nontestamentary transfer by the New York Court of Appeals. If X deposits funds to a Totten trust account for Y ("X as trustee for Y"), X has the right to withdraw and use funds from the account without any duty to account to Y. Y is entitled to the balance of the account if X dies first. On the other hand, the trust is terminated if Y predeceases X. *Estate of Bonness*, 535 P.2d 823 (Wash. App. 1975). At base a Totten trust is a simple form of will substitute that does not involve a present completed gift to the named beneficiary.

In *Estate of Stratton*, 674 A.2d 1281 (Vt. 1996), the court held that a trust did not arise when a father caused a certificate of deposit to be issued in his name "as trustee" for a child who he knew was deceased. It also held that the father's estate included the balance of a bank account, which he opened in his name "as trustee" for his daughter when she was living. Her interest in the account terminated when she predeceased him.

A Totten trust does not have any present income, gift, or estate tax impact. The income is taxed to the depositor-trustee because the arrangement is completely revocable. §676. For the same reason, there is not a completed gift to the donee when the trustee deposits funds in the account. Reg. §25.2511-2(c). If another party deposits funds in the account, presumably the deposit constitutes a gift to the trustee and not a gift to the trust beneficiary. Such a deposit should qualify for the annual exclusion because of the trustee's right to use the account for his or her own benefit. Any balance on hand when the trustee dies is includible in the trustee's gross estate under §§2036 and 2038 to the extent the trustee funded the account. *Estate of Sulovich v. Commissioner*, 587 F.2d 845 (6th Cir. 1978). The portion of the account funded by others is includible in the trustee's estate under §2041 if the trustee had the power to withdraw the funds and use them without restriction. Of course, if the beneficiary survives the trustee, the account becomes the beneficiary's property and is includible in the beneficiary's gross estate at death. If the beneficiary predeceases the trustee, the account is not includible in the beneficiary's estate; instead, the trust terminates and the balance of the account is owned by the trustee.

The Totten trust is generally an unsatisfactory way to hold funds for a minor. Because of its revocable nature the tax consequences are not favorable. Overall, it is preferable to make a gift to the minor under the Uniform Acts, or to a trust for the minor's benefit. Unfortunately, the personnel who handle new accounts at some financial institutions may push customers into Totten trusts because they are not sufficiently familiar with gifts to custodians under the Uniform Acts and other forms in which accounts might be opened.

A Totten trust can be revoked in the manner specified in the local law—which is usually by withdrawal of the funds or by an express direction in the depositor's will. In *Eredics v. Chase Manhattan Bank*, 790 N.E.2d 737 (N.Y. 2003), the court held that a broad waiver in a separation agreement of rights in the property of the other party did not invalidate the pre-existing beneficiary designation in a Totten trust. "[W]e conclude that a beneficiary also can waive rights in a Totten trust, so long as the waiver is explicit, voluntary and made in good faith." 790 N.E.2d at 1169.

§7.34. JOINT BANK OR SECURITIES ACCOUNTS

The deposit of funds by one person in a joint account with another ("*X* or *Y*") may give the other person a present interest in the account. If it does, the deposit constitutes a present gift to the donee and each party has a duty to account to the other for disposition of the account. On the other hand, the deposit may be a revocable gift to the other party, in which case no gift results and there is no duty to account. It is not possible to generalize about joint accounts because the state laws regarding them vary substantially. However, under U.P.C. §6-211, during lifetime a joint account belongs to the depositors in proportion to the net contribution of each to the account.

§7.34.1. Joint Bank Accounts

A joint bank account is often intended either to serve as a will substitute or to allow another person to make withdrawals as agent for the depositor. In neither case does the depositor intend that the other party will have a current beneficial interest in the account. The donor's probable intentions are recognized by U.P.C. §6-211(b), which provides that during the lifetime of all parties "an account belongs to the parties in proportion to the net contribution of each to the sums on deposit, unless there is clear and convincing evidence of a different intent." However, if the parties are married to each other, the U.P.C. presumes that each contributed an equal amount to the account. Upon the death of one of the parties, the sums on deposit "belong to the surviving party or parties." U.P.C. §6-212(a). If two or more parties survive, and one is the surviving spouse of a deceased party, the portion of the account that belonged to the decedent immediately before death belongs to the surviving spouse. Otherwise, the surviving parties to an account share equally in the portion attributable to a deceased party to the account. *Id.* Under the U.P.C. a party to an account may designate a person to act as agent for the depositor or depositors. U.P.C. §6-205. The agent does not have an ownership interest in the account.

Under the U.P.C. the deposit of funds in a joint account does not constitute a completed gift for gift tax purposes. *See* Reg. §25.2511-1(h)(4). The same result follows under other laws if the person making a deposit to a joint account has the power to withdraw all of the funds without being obligated to account to the other party. Consistently, in such a case a gift takes place when the donee withdraws funds from the account for his or her own benefit without any duty to account to the depositor. *Id*. Here again, the income from the account is taxable to the depositor.

Under the basic rule of §2040, the account is includible in the depositor's gross estate except to the extent it is traceable to funds contributed by others. Of course, if the parties are husband and wife only one-half of the account is includible, the transfer of which to the surviving spouse qualifies for the marital deduction. §§2040(b), 2056. The surviving tenant may make a qualified disclaimer of the right to receive the decedent's interest in a joint account. *See* §12.33.1.

A gift occurs at the time the deposit is made if the state law restricts the depositor's right to withdraw the funds for his or her own use.

§7.34.2. Joint Brokerage Accounts

Joint brokerage accounts with or without survivorship features may be established by complying with the requirements of local law. The transfer of property to such an account does not involve a gift unless the transfer gives the other party, or parties, an ownership interest in the account. In most circumstances transfers to joint brokerage accounts are revocable transfers that do not involve any gift to the other party. The income from the account will generally be taxed in accordance with the ownership interests of the parties. Likewise, the estate and GST tax consequences will track the ownership interests in the account.

The Uniform TOD Security Registration Act (1990) is a free-standing version of Part 3 of Article VI of the U.P.C.. Under its provisions securities may be registered in "beneficiary form" under which the securities will belong to another person upon the death of the owner or owners. Section 5 provides that "Registration in beneficiary form may be shown by the words 'transfer on death' or the abbreviation 'TOD' or by the words 'pay on death' or the abbreviation 'POD,' after the name of the registered owner and before the name of the beneficiary." Under §6, registration in beneficiary form has no effect on ownership until the owner's death. Accordingly, until the owner dies, use of this will substitute should not have any income, gift, estate or GST tax consequences.

§7.35. GIFTS TO MINORS UNDER THE UNIFORM ACTS

In order to facilitate gifts to minors all states have adopted either the Uniform Gifts to Minors Act (UGMA) in its original or revised form or the Uniform Transfers to Minors Act (UTMA). The Uniform Acts, which vary somewhat from state to state, authorize gifts of certain types of property to be made to a minor under its provisions. The basic form of UGMA permits gifts of securities, life insurance policies, annuity contracts, or money to be made under it. Some states have expanded the types of assets that may be transferred to include other types of personal property and interests in real property. UTMA allows any type of property to be transferred to a custodian. In general, a gift is made under the Uniform Acts by registering the asset, or depositing the fund, in the name of the donor, another adult, or a trust company "as custodian for (name of minor) under the (name of enacting state) Uniform Gifts to Minors Act." § 2(a)(1); § 9 UTMA. By complying with the statutory procedure the donor makes an irrevocable gift to the minor that incorporates the existing provisions of the Act. UGMA § 3(b); UTMA § 11(c). The custodian is a fiduciary whose investment and reinvestment of the property is governed by the "prudent person" standard. UGMA § 4(e); UTMA § 12(b). However, unlike property held in trust, the title to the property held by a custodian is vested in the minor and not the trustee. *Liberty National Life Ins. Co. v. First National Bank,* 151 So.2d 225, 227-228 (Ala. 1963). Although title is vested in the minor, some states permit the custodian to transfer all or a portion of the property into a § 2503(c) trust, the terms of which are described in § 7.37. *See* Wis. Stat. § 54.880(1m) (2011).

Section 4(b) of UGMA authorizes the custodian to pay over or apply any or all of the property for the support, maintenance, education, and benefit of the minor. Similarly, UTMA § 14(a) allows the custodian to pay or expend for the minor's benefit "so much of the custodial property as the custodian considers advisable for the use and benefit of the minor." In an effort to insulate the custodian from adverse tax consequences, UTMA § 14(c) provides that, "A delivery, payment, or expenditure under this section is in addition to, not in substitution for, and does not affect any obligation of a person to support the minor." Property in the hands of the custodian must be distributed to the donee when he or she reaches the age specified in the statute, which is most often 21. If the minor dies prior to attaining that age, the property must be paid to the minor's estate. UGMA § 4(d); UTMA § 20.

Section 529 Qualified Tuition Programs. Some states allow custodians under the Uniform Acts to participate in qualified tuition (§ 529) programs. For example, Cal. Educ. Code § § 69980(h) and 69986(j) (2011) allow custodians to "enter into participation agreements in accordance with regulations adopted by the board." However, the states have generally not amended the Uniform Acts to authorize custodians to invest custodial funds in § 529 plans. Presently, there is at least one major inconsistency between the interests of the minor beneficiary of a custodianship and the interests of the designated beneficiary of a § 529 account. As the "account owner" of a § 529 account, a custodian would have the power under § 529 to change the beneficiary— which cannot be done in the case of a custodianship.

Custodians should be cautious about participating in § 529 plans until the tax and nontax consequences are clarified. *See* § 7.41. Note that, as only cash can be contributed to a § 529 plan, a custodian might be required to liquidate investments to make the contribution. Information regarding § 529 plans is available from a wide range of sources—including the websites *<savingforcollege.com>* and *<collegesavings.org>*.

§ 7.35.1. Gift Tax

A gift to a custodian for a minor under the Uniform Acts constitutes a completed gift that qualifies for the annual gift tax exclusion. Rev. Rul. 59-357, 1959-2 C.B. 212. The resignation of a custodian or the termination of the custodianship does not involve a further gift. Of course, a gift by a married person may be split between the donor and the donor's spouse under § 2513. Gift-splitting does not apply to gifts of community property, which is already "split" between the spouses by reason of the form of ownership.

§7.35.2. Estate Tax

The custodial property is includible in the donor's gross estate if the donor is acting as custodian at the time of his or her death. Rev. Rul. 59-357, 1959-2 C.B. 212. In such a case the property is includible under §2038 because of the custodian's power to distribute the custodial property and, in effect, to terminate the custodial arrangement. *Stuit v. Commissioner,* 452 F.2d 190 (7th Cir. 1971). The same result follows if another person was the original custodian but the donor was acting in that capacity at the time of his or her death. Rev. Rul. 70-348, 1970-2 C.B. 193. The custodial property is not includible in the estate of the donor's spouse, although he or she elected to be treated as the donor of half of it under §2513 and was acting as custodian at the time of his or her death. Rev. Rul. 74-556, 1974-2 C.B. 300. That result is clearly correct under §§2036 and 2038—the consenting spouse did not actually own, or transfer, any part of the property of which she was acting as custodian at the time of her death. Of course, half of the property would be includible in the custodian's estate if the gift had consisted of community property. Also, if the consenting spouse has the power as custodian to apply the property to discharge a legal obligation to support the minor, there is some risk that the property would be included in the consenting spouse's estate under §2041.

The reciprocal trust doctrine applies when donors make related gifts under a Uniform Act and appoint each other as custodian. Thus, a deceased custodian's estate included the gifts nominally made by his spouse where they had made identical contemporaneous gifts to their minor children and named each other as custodian. *Exchange Bank & Trust Co. v. United States,* 694 F.2d 1261 (Fed. Cir. 1982). The doctrine is discussed at §10.29 in connection with planning the interests of grantors in irrevocable trusts.

The Uniform Acts provide an efficient and economical method of transferring limited amounts of certain types of property to minors. However, most clients are reluctant to make substantial gifts under them because the property must be paid over to the donee at an early age. Also, if the minor dies prior to attaining the age of majority, the property must be paid over to the donee's estate. Because a minor cannot make a will, the property would pass under the intestate succession law, which may be inconsistent with the donor's estate plan. Most often the donor is a parent who makes the gift to remove the property from his or her estate. Of course, a surviving parent may disclaim succession to the deceased child's intestate property, but that might further frustrate the donor's estate plan. These disadvantages are avoided, however, if the gift is made to a properly drawn trust. *See* §§7.36-7.39.

§7.35.3. Income Tax

The income from custodial property is taxed to the minor currently whether it is actually distributed or expended for his or her benefit. However, the IRS contends that to the extent the income is applied to discharge the legal support obligation of any person, the income must be taxed to that person. Rev. Rul. 56-484, 1956-2 C.B. 23, *approved in* Rev. Rul. 59-357, 1959-2 C.B. 212. Likewise, the income is taxable to the grantor to the extent it is used to satisfy the grantor's obligations. §677. For example, if the donor has assumed responsibility for paying the minor's private school tuition, the custodial income will be taxed to the donor to the extent it is used to meet that expense. *Morrill v. United States,* 228 F. Supp. 734 (D. Me. 1964) (irrevocable trust). A grantor-parent is also taxed on the income of a trust that is used to pay the private school tuition of a child if the parent is subject to that obligation under state law. *Christopher Stone,* 54 T.C.M. (CCH) 462 (1987) (California); *Frederick C. Braun, Jr.,* 48 T.C.M. (CCH) 210 (1984) (New Jersey).

The existence and extent of a parent's legal obligation to support a minor depends upon local law, which is often far from clear. *See* § 10.40.1. Although children may be emancipated at 18, some parental obligations may persist, at least in the case of incompetent or dependent children. *E.g., Frederick C. Braun, supra.* However, the income of a custodianship may be safely accumulated for the minor or expended for items of "super support" that parents are clearly not obligated to provide under the local law (*e.g.,* travel, private music or dance lessons). In one case, the IRS held that a trust beneficiary's power to appoint principal of a trust for "travel, camping trips, theater, ballet, music lessons, special schooling or instruction to enrich" the lives of the beneficiary's children was not a general power of appointment for purposes of § 2041. LR 9030005.

A custodian may not, in that capacity alone, execute a valid Subchapter S election on behalf of a minor. Rev. Rul. 66-116, 1966-1 C.B. 198, *amplified,* 68-227, 1968-1 C.B. 301. However, a guardian may do so and the IRS will recognize an election signed by a custodian if the same person is also the minor's guardian. Rev. Rul. 68-227, 1968-1 C.B. 381.

§ 7.35.4. Generation-Skipping Transfer Tax (GSTT)

A gift to a custodian for a minor skip person is subject to the GSTT. The transferor's GSTT exemption may be allocated to the transfer—if it is not, it will be deemed allocated to the transfer. Importantly, however, to the extent of the annual gift tax exclusion, the transfer to a custodian is a nontaxable transfer that is not subject to the GSTT. § 2642(c). Thus, a grandparent could make annual exclusion gifts to a custodian for a grandchild without incurring any GSTT liability.

§ 7.36. GIFTS IN TRUST

Trusts are frequently used as vehicles for making gifts to minors because of their great flexibility. In order to maximize the tax savings that result from gifts to trusts for minors, the trusts are often structured so that the transfers wills qualify for the annual gift tax exclusion. The incentive is obvious—gifts within the annual exclusion are not included in the donor's transfer tax base at any time.

A gift to a trust is a gift to the beneficiaries of the trust—not to the trustee or the trust itself. *Helvering v. Hutchings,* 312 U.S. 393 (1941). As noted in § 2.5, an annual exclusion is only allowable for donees who are born at the time of the gift. Rev. Rul. 67-384, 1967-2 C.B. 348 (no annual exclusion allowed for a gift made in December for child born in the following year). Whether a gift to a trust qualifies as a present interest depends largely on the terms of the trust. The desirability of discretionary trusts led to the development of the power of withdrawal as a means of qualifying a gift for the annual exclusion. In brief, gifts to trusts for minors can qualify for the annual exclusion is one of three ways; (1) the trust is drafted so that the beneficiary's interests meet the requirements of §2503(c) (§7.37), (2) the trust requires all of the income to be distributed to the minor currently (*i.e.*, the value of the beneficiary's income interest qualifies for the annual gift tax exclusions)(§7.39), or (3) the trust gives the beneficiary the noncumulative right to withdraw contributions to the trust (a so-called *Crummey* power, after *Crummey v. Commissioner*, 397 F.2d 82 (9th Cir. 1968)) (§7.38). Recapitulating, the right to receive the current income of a trust is a present interest, but the right to receive the income in the discretion of the trustee or the vested right to receive the principal at some future time do not.

Most clients wish to create trusts that will continue past the donee's minority and provide only for discretionary distributions to the donee. A trust with those characteristics qualifies for the annual gift tax exclusion only if the beneficiary holds a limited, noncumulative power to withdraw assets as they are added to the trust. Some trusts require the trustee to distribute the income to the minor currently, the actuarially determined value of which constitutes a present interest under §2503(b). *See* §7.39.

§7.37. Section 2503(c) Trusts

The availability of the annual gift tax exclusion for interests transferred to a minor under a §2503(c) trust encourages their use. However, as explained below, §7.38, a discretionary trust that gives the beneficiary a *Crummey* power of withdrawal may better meet the needs of most clients. Under §2503(c) a transfer for the benefit of a donee under the age of 21 is not a future interest if the following requirements are met:

1. The property and the income may be expended by or for the benefit of the donee before the donee attains 21;
2. Any portion of the property not expended for the donee's benefit will pass to the donee when the donee attains 21; and
3. The property and its income will be payable to the donee's estate or as the donee may appoint under a general power of appointment if the donee dies prior to 21.

§7.37.1. Property or Income

Section 2503(c) literally requires both the property and its income to be expended or distributed in the prescribed manner. However, the IRS has acquiesced in decisions that allow an exclusion to the extent that either the income or the principal interest meets those requirements. *Arlean I. Herr*, 35 T.C. 732 (1961), *nonacq.*, 1962-2 C.B. 6, *withdrawn and acq. substituted*, 1968-2 C.B. 2, *aff'd*, 303 F.2d 780 (3d Cir. 1962); Rev. Rul. 68-670, 1968-2 C.B. 413.

EXAMPLE 7-12.

X transferred property to *T* as trustee of a trust for the benefit of *B*, a minor. The trustee was authorized to expend income, but not principal, for the support, comfort, and general welfare of *B* until *B* reached 21 or sooner died. At that time any accumulated income was payable to *B* if *B* was then living, otherwise to *B*'s estate. After *B* attained 21 the income was payable to *B* in the discretion of the trustee. The principal of the trust and any income accumulated after *B* attained 21 was payable to *B* at age 35. An exclusion under § 2503(c) is available with respect to the actuarially determined value of the right to receive the income until *B* attains 21.

§ 7.37.2. No Substantial Restrictions

The requirement that the income or principal may be expended by or for the benefit of the donee prior to attaining 21 is met only if the trustee's discretion to expend funds is not subject to any "substantial restrictions," Reg. § 25.2503-4(b)(1). Revenue Ruling 67-270, 1967-2 C.B. 349 holds that this requirement is met if the trust property may be expended during the donee's minority "for purposes which have no objective limitations (*i.e.*, 'welfare,' 'happiness' and 'convenience') and which provisions when read as a whole approximate the scope of the term 'benefit,' as used in section 2503(c) of the Code." In contrast, no annual exclusion is allowable if the trustee's power to make distributions is limited. Thus, no exclusion is allowable where the trustee can make distributions to the donee only if "his needs are not adequately provided for by his parents and only after his separate property has been expended." Rev. Rul. 69-345, 1969-1 C.B. 226. Similarly, no annual exclusion is available if the trustee is permitted to distribute property only for educational expenses or if the beneficiary is disabled. *Illinois National Bank of Springfield v. United States*, 91-1 U.S.T.C. ¶ 60,063 (C.D. III. 1991).

A trust that provides for the discretionary use of income for a minor until 21, at which time all the accumulated income is distributable to the beneficiary and all of the income is payable to the beneficiary thereafter, qualifies under § 2503(c) only to the extent of the income interest for the beneficiary's minority. The right to receive the income after 21 is a future interest that cannot be combined with the pre-21 income interest for the purpose of the annual exclusion. The possible accumulation of the income prior to age 21 prevents the post-21 income interest from being a present interest for purposes of the annual exclusion. *Levine v. Commissioner*, 526 F.2d 717 (2d Cir. 1975).

§ 7.37.3. Payable at 21

Under the second requirement the interest must pass to the donee when he or she attains 21. In Rev. Rul. 73-287, 1973-2 C.B. 321, the IRS held that an annual exclusion was available under § 2503(c) for a transfer under a version of the UGMA that provided for distribution to the donee at age 18 instead of 21. It reasoned that § 2503(c) set the maximum age requirement that may be attached to gifts to minors: "Therefore, a provision that the custodial property be paid to the minor donee when he attains the age of 18 years will meet the requirement that the property pass to the donee at least by his attainment of age 21, and, hence, will satisfy the greater age requirement of section 2503(c) of the Code." *Id.* Accordingly, an annual exclusion should be available for a gift to a trust that requires the necessary distributions be made to the donee before he or she becomes 21.

This requirement may be satisfied although the trust does not automatically terminate when the donee reaches 21. It is sufficient if the donee has the power to compel distribution upon reaching the age of 21, whether the power is a continuing one or is exercisable only for a limited period. Rev. Rul. 74-43, 1974-1 C.B. 285. However, the failure to exercise the power may cause the donee to be treated as the transferor of any interest that others have in the trust to the extent the amount that could have been withdrawn exceeds the greater of $5,000 or five percent of the value of the property subject to the power. *See* §§ 2041 and 2514. Whether the lapse of the power constitutes a taxable gift depends upon several factors, including the extent to which the donee retains any power over disposition of the property. *See* § 7.38.2.

§ 7.37.4. Payable to Donee's Estate or as Donee Appoints

If the donee dies prior to 21, any remaining interest must be payable to the donee's estate or as the donee appoints under a general power of appointment. Apparently, this requirement was imposed "to insure inclusion of the property, which had the benefit of a gift tax exclusion, in the gross estate of the beneficiary for estate tax purposes in the event that he dies prior to reaching age 21." *Cornelius A. Ross*, 71 T.C. 897, 900 (1979), *aff'd*, 652 F.2d 1365 (9th Cir. 1981). In *Ross* no annual exclusion was allowed under § 2503(c) for a trust that provided for distribution of the property to the donee's "heirs at law" if he died prior to 21. The problem is, of course, that a distribution to the minor's "heirs at law" is not the equivalent of a distribution to the minor's estate. The requirement is satisfied if the donee is given a general testamentary power of appointment, although the donee is unable to exercise the power under the local law because of his or her minority. Reg. § 25.2503-4(b). The possession of a general power of appointment is sufficient to cause the property to be included in the gross estate of the power-holder although he or she lacks the capacity to exercise it. § 2041; Rev. Rul. 75-351, 1975-2 C.B. 368. This is consistent with the position that the IRS has taken in connection with the allowance of a marital deduction under § 2056(b)(5). *See* § 5.22.3. If the trust otherwise qualifies, a marital deduction is allowable although the surviving spouse is incapable of exercising the power of appointment because of legal incapacity. *See, e.g.,* Rev. Rul. 75-350, 1975-2 C.B. 366.

The annual exclusion is not available under § 2503(c) if the trust itself imposes any restrictions on the exercise of the power. Thus, in *Gall v. United States*, 521 F.2d 878 (5th Cir. 1975), *cert. denied*, 425 U.S. 972 (1976), the exclusion was denied where the donee was required to be 19 in order to exercise the power and state law allowed persons of 19 years of age and younger married persons to execute wills.

§ 7.37.5. Terms of § 2503(c) Trust

A § 2503(c) trust must, of course, conform to the requirements of § 2503(c). In addition, the trust ordinarily should include provisions that prohibit the trustee from exercising powers that would cause the grantor to be treated as owner of the trust under § 675. *See* § 10.37.1. The discretion the trustee must have to make distributions would require the trust to be included in the grantor's estate under § 2038 if the grantor were serving as trustee. Accordingly, the grantor should not serve as trustee. *See* § 10.36.3.

Form 7-1
Distributive Provisions of § 2503(c) Trust

Distributions Prior to 21. Until the beneficiary attains the age of 21 the trustee shall pay to, or apply for the benefit of, the beneficiary so much of the income and principal of the trust as the trustee believes is in the beneficiary's best interests.

Right of Withdrawal at Age 21. When the beneficiary attains the age of 21 the beneficiary shall have the right, by delivering written notice to the trustee, to require the trustee to distribute all of the property of the trust to the beneficiary. Such right of withdrawal shall lapse if the beneficiary does not deliver written notice of withdrawal to the trustee within 60 days after the beneficiary attains 21 years of age. The trust shall terminate to the extent the beneficiary so withdraws property from the trust.

Distributions to the Beneficiary After Attaining Age 21. After the beneficiary attains 21 years of age the trustee shall distribute all of the net income to beneficiary in quarterly or more frequent installments. In addition, the trustee may make such distributions of principal to or for the benefit of the beneficiary as the trustee believes is in the best interests of the beneficiary. All of the property of the trust shall be distributed to beneficiary when [she/he] attains 35 years of age.

General Power of Appointment. If the beneficiary dies prior to termination of the trust, the trust property shall be paid outright or upon further trust to such person or persons, including the beneficiary's estate, as the beneficiary shall appoint by [her/his] last will. In default of exercise of such power the trust property shall be distributed in shares of equal value to those of the brothers and sisters of the beneficiary as shall survive [her/him]; provided, that the share of any brother or sister for whom a trust created by the grantor on the same date as this trust, remains in existence shall be added to and become a part of the property of the trust for the benefit of such brother or sister.

§ 7.37.6. Estate Tax

The trust property is includible in the donee's gross estate if it is payable to the donee's estate, or if the donee holds a general power of appointment over it. It is also includible if the donee does not exercise a power to compel distribution of the trust property when he or she attains 21 and he or she remains a beneficiary of the trust until death. The failure to exercise the power of withdrawal constitutes a release, and the property is includible in the donee's gross estate if the release results in a disposition "of such nature that if it were a transfer of property owned by the decedent, such property would be includible in the decedent's gross estate under sections 2035 to 2038, inclusive." § 2041(a)(2). The failure to exercise the power might also involve a gift of an interest in the trust to other parties, such as contingent remainder beneficiaries who will be entitled to the property if the donee does not survive to a specified age or event.

EXAMPLE 7-13.

Parent, *P*, transferred property to a trust under which the principal and income could be expended by the trustee for the benefit of *P*'s daughter, *D*, until she reached 21. Under the trust *D* had the power to withdraw all of the trust assets by written notice delivered to the trustee within 60 days following her twenty-first birthday. The income from any property that is not withdrawn is payable to *D* annually and the principal is distributable to her when she reaches 45. If *D* dies prior to 21 the trust property is payable to her estate, but if she dies after reaching 21 and prior to 45, the trust property is payable to *P*'s then living descendants per stirpes. The trust meets the requirements of § 2503(c). Accordingly, an annual exclusion is available to *P* for property he transferred to the trust during *D*'s minority. *D*'s power to withdraw the property of the trust constitutes a general power of appointment under § 2041. If she allows the power to lapse, or otherwise releases it, she has probably made a taxable gift of the contingent remainder interest. *See* Reg. § 25.2514-3(c). However, under § 2514(e) a lapse of a general power of appointment is subject to gift tax only to the extent that the property that could have been appointed by the donee of the power exceeds the greater of (i) $5,000 or (ii) 5% of the total value of the assets out of which the exercise of the lapsed power could have been satisfied. If the lapse of the power of withdrawal results in a completed gift, the value of the gift may be determined under § 2702 without regard to the value of *D*'s retained interest. *See* § 7.38.2 and LR 9804047. If the power lapses and *D* dies prior to attaining 45, a proportion of the trust assets is includible in her estate under § 2041(a)(2). *See* Reg. § 20.2041-3(d)(3), (4).

The trust property is subject to inclusion in the donor's estate under § 2036(a)(2) or § 2038(a)(1), if the donor is serving as trustee at death, and the trustee has the power to make discretionary distributions to the beneficiary. *See Lober v. United States*, 346 U.S. 335 (1953) (donor was acting as one of the co-trustees, who together could make early distributions of principal to the beneficiary). The property might also be includible in the donor's estate under § 2036(a) if the trust provides the beneficiary with types of support that the donor is obligated to provide under the local law. On the other hand, one leading decision holds that the property is not includible in the parent-donor's estate where there is an independent trustee and none of the property was ever used for the support of the child-donee. *Estate of Jack F. Chrysler*, 44 T.C. 55 (1965), *acq.*, 1970-2 C.B. xix, *rev'd on other issues*, 361 F.2d 508 (2d Cir. 1966).

§ 7.37.7. Income Tax

The income of a § 2503(c) trust is taxed to the minor if it is distributed to the minor, or used for the minor's benefit, except to the extent the income is taxed to the grantor under § 673-677. *See* § 10.31. In other cases the income is taxed to the trust. Thus, the income from a § 2503(c) trust for the benefit of a child under 18 is not subject to the Kiddie Tax (at the marginal rate of the beneficiary's parent) unless the income is actually distributed to the minor.

The grantor may act as trustee of a § 2503(c) trust without causing the income to be taxed to him or her. In particular, under §§ 674(b)(5)-(7) any person may hold discretionary powers to distribute or accumulate income during a beneficiary's minority or to distribute corpus to the income beneficiary of a trust so long as any distribution of corpus is charged to the beneficiary's proportionate interest in the principal of the trust. This allows considerable flexibility in income tax planning.

§ 7.37.8. GSTT

The transfer of property to a § 2503(c) trust for a grandchild or other skip person should qualify for the GSTT nontaxable transfer exclusion of § 2642(c)(2). Briefly, under § 2642(c)(1) a direct skip that is a nontaxable transfer has an inclusion ratio of zero. However, in the case of transfers in trust this exclusion is only available if the trust meets the two requirements of § 2642(c)(2) (during the beneficiary's lifetime no distributions can be made to any other person and, if the trust exists when the beneficiary dies, the assets of the trust will be included in the beneficiary's gross estate). A § 2503(c) trust can satisfy those requirements.

Under § 2642(c)(3), the term "nontaxable transfer" is defined as a transfer that is not treated as a taxable gift by reason of either § 2503(b) (annual $10,000 exclusion allowed for gifts of present interests), taking into account the gift-splitting provisions of § 2513, or § 2503(e) (direct payments of tuition or of medical care are not gifts). Transfers that satisfy the requirements of § 2503(c) are not future interests for purposes of § 2503(b). Accordingly, if distributions can only be made from a § 2503(c) trust to the minor during his or her lifetime and the trust will be includible in the minor's estate if he or she dies during its existence, transfers to the trust should be within the definition of nontaxable transfers under § 2642(c).

§ 7.37.9. Conclusion

A custom-made § 2503(c) trust sometimes better meets the needs of a client who wishes to make modest gifts to a minor than a gift under the Uniform Acts. For example, the trust can be drafted to prevent the property from returning to a donor-parent if the donee dies prior to 21. That is achieved by providing for payment of the trust property to another person or to a trust for another person if the donee dies prior to 21 without validly exercising a general testamentary power of appointment. The main shortcoming of a § 2503(c) trust is the requirement that the interest pass to the donee upon attaining age 21. Of course, annual exclusions are allowable under § 2503(c) for transfers to a trust if the beneficiary is given the right to withdraw the trust property when he or she becomes 21 this requirement is satisfied and the trust can continue, whether or not the right is exercised.

Understandably, most clients would be happier if property they transfer to a trust is neither payable to the donee at 21 nor all subject to the donee's power of withdrawal at that age. Also, as indicated above, the power of withdrawal can cause gift and estate tax problems for the donee. For those reasons, if a client wants a trust to continue after the donee attains 21, it is often better to create a discretionary trust. If obtaining the annual gift tax exclusion is important, the beneficiary can be given a *Crummey* power to withdraw assets for a limited time after they are transferred to the trust. As explained in the next section, neither the property nor the income of a *Crummey* trust is required to pass to the donee when he or she attains age 21.

§7.38. DISCRETIONARY TRUST WITH POWER OF WITHDRAWAL

A trust that gives the trustee discretion to make distributions of income and principal before and after the donee attains his or her majority is an excellent way to provide for the flexible management and distribution of family wealth. Although the beneficiary does not have any fixed right to receive distributions, the annual exclusion is available for transfers to the trust if the beneficiary is given a sufficient power of withdrawal. If the trust is properly drafted, the grantor's contributions to the trust will not be includible in his or her estate. In this connection the planner should not allow the grantor to retain any rights or controls that would require inclusion in the grantor's estate under §§2036 or 2038. In addition, the grantor should not transfer any policies of insurance on his or her life to the trust that would be includible in the grantor's estate under §2035(a)(2) if the grantor were to die within three years of the transfer. The trust can be drafted to terminate when the beneficiary attains a certain age or to continue after the beneficiary's death for the benefit of the beneficiary's children or others. Importantly, a discretionary trust for a grandchild (or other skip person) can be drafted so that transfers that qualify for the annual gift tax exclusion will also qualify for the GSTT exclusion for nontaxable gifts under §2642(c).

The lawyer must be alert to the importance of nontax issues concerning *Crummey* trusts, including the possibility that the trustee has a fiduciary duty to inform the beneficiaries regarding the creation and administration of the trust. *See* §7.38.6. Also, the trustees of a *Crummey* trust are required to administer the trust in accordance with the appropriate investment standards. Accordingly, consideration should be given to the inclusion of special provisions authorizing the acquisition or retention of policies of insurance. *See* §6.24.5. Smith, Identifying *Crummey* Trust Liability Problems, 131 Tr. & Est. 36 (Dec. 1992).

The lapse of a power of withdrawal may have significant GSTT consequences. *See* Regs. §§26.2612-1(c), 26.2652-1(a)(6), Example (5), and the discussion at §2.32.

A power of withdrawal can be used in conjunction with other types of trusts. Thus, one might be included in an irrevocable life insurance trusts so cash contributions made to the trust to pay premiums qualify for gift tax annual exclusions. However, as indicated by the discussion below, the use of powers of withdrawal seriously complicates the drafting and administration of a trust. Accordingly, many lawyers encourage wealthy clients to make annual exclusion gifts outright, under the Uniform Acts, to §2503(c) trusts, or by other means and to create substantial trusts that are not encumbered by powers of withdrawal.

If a client insists on establishing a trust that includes withdrawal powers, the lawyer should educate the client about the complexities and about optional ways by which the power of withdrawal could be expressed. A simple expedient is simply to say that each beneficiary shall have the right to withdraw additions to the trust except as limited by a written notice given to the trustee at the time of the addition. There is, of course, a risk that no annual exclusion will be allowed if the beneficiary does not receive notice of a transfer. §7.38.1. Allowing withdrawals only to the extent provided in a notice is dangerous—if a donor does not accompany a gift with an appropriate specification, no annual exclusion is allowable. LR 9535001 (TAM).

Some lawyers recommend the use of "hanging" powers of withdrawal. §7.38.4. A hanging power gives the beneficiary a cumulative right to withdraw contributions to the trust that lapses each year only to the extent of the 5 or 5 shelter. Properly drawn hanging powers can help reduce or eliminate some of the complexities of discretionary trusts that are intended to qualify for the annual gift tax exclusion.

Drafting a discretionary trust with a suitable power of withdrawal can be challenging. Tracking the tax consequences of contributions to the trust, and lapses of the beneficiary's power of withdrawal is also challenging.

Note that neither the annual exclusion nor a gift tax charitable deduction is available with respect to transfers to an irrevocable trust that are subject to powers of withdrawal held by charities where the charities generally did not receive timely notice of the transfers. LR 200341002 (TAM). As pointed out in the ruling, under Reg. §25.2522(c)-3(b)(1), a charitable deduction is not allowable where the transfer to charity is dependent on the performance of an act or the happening of a precedent event unless the possibility that the charitable transfer will not become effective is so remote as to be negligible.

EXAMPLE 7-14.

On January 1, 2006, Donor, *D*, transferred $5,000 to a new trust. The terms of the trust gave the beneficiary, Child, *C*, a power of withdrawal over amounts transferred to the trust that was exercisable by giving notice to the trustee not later than 30 days after receiving notice that a gift had been made to the trust. Notice of the gift was given to *C* on January 2, 2006. *C* did not give any notice of withdrawal. *C* was entitled to receive the income of the trust for her lifetime. Upon her death the principal was distributable to her issue, per stirpes.

The lapse of the power to withdraw the initial contribution to the trust was sheltered by the 5 or 5 rule. Accordingly, it had no estate, gift or GST tax consequences. On February 15, 2006, *D* transferred an additional $5,000 to the trust as a result of which the trust had a total value of $10,000. *C* was given notice of the transfer, but did not exercise the power of withdrawal. The 5 or 5 rule does not shelter the lapse of the power to withdraw the second contribution from gift, estate and GSTT consequences.

For gift tax purposes *C* is treated as having made a gift (of a future interest) of the full amount of the second transfer—$5,000. Because of the special valuation rule of §2702, the amount of the gift is not reduced by the value of C' s retained life income interest, LR 9804047. Under the pre-§ 2702 approach, the amount of the gift would have been reduced by the value of C' s retained life interest in the fund, *See* Rev. Rul. 85-88, 1985-2 C.B. 201.

Also, for GSTT purposes C becomes the transferor of the second, lapsed, transfer, Reg. § 26.2652-1(a)(6), Example 5. The original grantor remains the transferor of the amount within the 5 or 5 limit, LR 9541029. Importantly, the amount of which each of them is considered to be the transferor will be treated as a separate trust. Because of the lapse that was not sheltered by the 5 or 5 rule, a proportionate part (one-half) of the trust is subject to inclusion in C' s estate under § 2041(a). The income of the trust may be taxed to D under the rules of § § 671-677. If it is not, C is treated as the owner of the trust for income tax purposes. § 678.

§ 7.38.1. Gift Tax

Prior to *Crummey v. Commissioner,* 397 F.2d 82 (9th Cir. 1968), the courts and IRS allowed annual gift tax exclusions for gifts to adult beneficiaries of trusts who held powers of withdrawal. The contest in *Crummey* was over whether annual exclusions were allowable with respect to transfers that were subject to powers of withdrawal held by minor beneficiaries for whom no guardian had been appointed. In *Crummey,* the IRS did not contest annual exclusions for transfers that were subject to powers held by the donors' adult children. Prior to the decision in *Crummey* the appellate courts had split on the issue of whether annual exclusions were allowable with respect to transfers in trust that were subject to powers of withdrawal held by minors. In *Crummey,* the Ninth Circuit allowed annual exclusions for the minors who held the "right" to withdraw the property. Five years later the IRS issued Rev. Rul. 73-405, 1973-2 C.B. 321, which reflected the belated acceptance by the IRS of the allowance of annual exclusions for powers of withdrawal held by minor beneficiaries.

In effect the *Crummey* court followed a 1951 appellate decision, *Kieckhefer v. Commissioner,* 189 F.2d 118 (7th Cir. 1951), in which the court concluded that the determinative issue was whether the beneficiary had the "right" to enjoy, rather than "actual" enjoyment, of the transferred property. The decision in *Kieckhefer* was soon countered by a contrary 1952 Second Circuit decision, *Stifel v. Commissioner,* 197 F.2d 107 (1952). In the latter case the court focused on the practical issue of whether a minor could make current withdrawal. Annual exclusions were denied because the minor beneficiary for whom no guardian had been appointed could not make a legally effective demand.

If a trust contains a sufficient withdrawal power, the Tax Court now allows a donor to claim an annual exclusion with respect to each donee who holds a beneficial interest in the trust and a power to withdraw contributions to the trust. Cases and IRS pronouncements accept that the age or mental competency of a power holder is immaterial. *E.g., Fish v. United States,* 432 F.2d 1278 (9th Cir. 1970); Rev. Rul. 73-405, 1973-2 C.B. 321.

The issue remains simply whether a beneficiary had the "right" to withdraw part or all of the contributed property. However, a withdrawal right is "illusory" and will be disregarded unless the power holder has a reasonable opportunity to exercise the right, which requires knowledge of the right and of the transfer of property subject to its exercise, Rev. Rul. 81-7, 1981-1 C.B. 474; LR 9532001 (TAM).

As *Crummey* powers have evolved, the IRS has elaborated and extended the requirements for the allowance of annual exclusions. The elaboration and extension complicates planning and drafting. Indeed, if the IRS positions were rigorously enforced, annual exclusions would frequently be denied. Various traps and ways to draft around them are discussed below in the course of reviewing the development of the current *Crummey* criteria.

In late 1973, the IRS issued a revenue ruling that followed the holding in the *Crummey* case. Rev. Rul. 73-405, 1973-2 C.B. 321. The ruling recognized that "it is not the actual use, possession, or enjoyment by the donee which marks the dividing line between a present and a future interest, but rather the right conferred upon the donee by the trust instrument to such use, possession, or enjoyment." Accordingly, the annual exclusion is available if a minor donee has the power to withdraw property transferred to the trust and there is no impediment under the trust or the local law to the appointment of a guardian who could exercise the power for the minor. For gift tax purposes the transfer of property to a trust that contains a properly drafted *Crummey* power is treated as if the property had been transferred outright to the holder of the power.

The content of a *Crummey* clause will vary somewhat, depending upon the other provisions of the trust and the circumstances of the parties. For example, the form may differ if (1) there are multiple rather than single beneficiaries, (2) gifts may be made to the trust by more than one donor each year, or (3) the trust principal will be distributed to the donee at some point instead of remaining in trust for the donee's lifetime. In particular, the lawyer should consider the points that are raised in the following paragraphs.

§7.38.2. Limit the Amount Subject to Withdrawal?

Under a typical *Crummey* clause, the donee is given a noncumulative power to withdraw some or all of a contribution to the trust that is exercisable within a limited period following the gift. The amount subject to withdrawal may be limited by the terms of the trust or by the terms of the transfer to the trust as described in §7.37.3. Considering the nature and purpose of the trust, it is generally undesirable to give the donee an unlimited power to make withdrawals, at least during the donee's minority. Although it is possible simply to allow each donor to define the amount subject to withdrawal, most instruments include a limit that will apply if the donor does not impose a limit in connection with an addition to the trust.

In deciding what limit to impose, consideration should be given to the tax and nontax effects of doing so. On the tax side the donor may wish to limit the amount subject to withdrawal to the amount for which an annual gift tax exclusion is allowable. The maximum annual exclusions will be allowed to the donor if the beneficiary's right of withdrawal is unlimited, or is limited to the amount of the annual exclusion (*e.g.*, the right to withdraw "$13,000 per donor or such other amount as may be allowable as an annual gift tax exclusion at the time of the transfer to the trust"). Limiting withdrawals to the amount of the annual gift tax exclusion is appropriate if the donor does not wish to use a hanging power or otherwise allow the beneficiary to withdraw any more property than necessary to support the maximum annual gift tax exclusion.

Some trusts limit the amount subject to withdrawal in order to prevent the lapse of the power from having any adverse gift or estate tax consequences for the donee. The most common limit is $5,000 or five percent of the principal value of the trust (a "5 or 5" power of withdrawal).

Other planners limit the amount subject to withdrawal to the amount of the allowable annual exclusions (*e.g.*, "not to exceed $13,000 per donor, or $26,000 per donor if the donor is married at the time the property is transferred to the trust"). Such a provision assumes that the donor's spouse will consent to split the gift. The amount that can be withdrawn should not be made to depend upon whether the gift is split—which will not be determined until after the gift is made (*i.e.*, when a gift tax return is filed). To the extent a transfer is subject to such a qualification the gift constitutes a future interest for which no annual exclusion is available. LR 8022048. Such a limit does not alone shelter the beneficiary from adverse tax consequences of a lapse. The limit can be expressed so that it would adjust with any change in the amount of the annual exclusion (*e.g.*, "the amount of the annual exclusion that is allowable for federal gift tax purposes").

If a 5 or 5 limit is imposed, the failure to exercise the power does not constitute a gift. § 2514(e); LR 8003152. Also, the lapse of such a power will not cause any of the trust to be included in the donee's gross estate. § 2041(b)(2). However, if a 5 or 5 limit is imposed, the annual exclusion is only available for that amount. Thus, the full amount of the annual exclusion would not be available to a donor who transfers $13,000 to the trust. Note, however, that the benefits of the annual exclusion and the shelter of the 5 or 5 limit of § 2041(b)(2) may be obtained if the power lapses each year only to the extent of the 5 or 5 limit. The use of such a "hanging power" is discussed in § 7.38.4.

EXAMPLE 7-15.

The grantor, *G*, established a trust for the beneficiary, *B*, who was given the noncumulative right each year to withdraw property transferred to the trust during the year. Under the terms of the trust, the amount subject to withdrawal by *B* during a calendar year could not exceed the greater of $5,000 or 5% of the value of the property held in the trust. In 2009, *G* transferred property worth $13,000 to the trust. At the time of the transfer the property held in the trust had a value of $65,000. The annual exclusion is available only with respect to $5,000 of the amount that *G* transferred to the trust. Later in 2009 another donor, *D*, transferred property worth $13,000 to the trust. No annual exclusion is available to *D* with respect to the transfer *D* made to the trust. The maximum amount subject to withdrawal by *B* had already been exhausted by *G*'s transfer to the trust.

If a client wants to preserve the annual exclusion for all transfers to the trust and is not concerned about the gift and estate tax consequences of a lapse of the power, the power can be drawn to allow the beneficiary to withdraw an unlimited amount of the property added to the trust during the year. The lapse of the right to withdraw an amount in excess of the 5 or 5 shelter may have GSTT consequences. If the lapse results in a completed gift by the powerholder, he or she will be treated as the transferor of the unsheltered amount. Reg. § 26.2652-1(a)(6), Example 5. Of course, a client should appreciate that a beneficiary might exercise an unlimited power of withdrawal—which could seriously discomfit the client.

The lapse of a power with respect to an amount in excess of the 5 or 5 shelter will not result in a completed gift if the beneficiary also holds a testamentary power of appointment over the property. *See* Reg. § 25.2511-2(b); LR 8517052; LR 8229097 (general power); LR 9030005. *See also* § 10.24.

In LR 9321050 (issue 17), the IRS ruled that the lapse of a general power of appointment did not result in a gift where the donee of the power continued to hold a special testamentary power of appointment over the property. If the powerholder does not have a power of appointment over the excess above the 5 or 5 amount, the lapse of the power will result in a gift by the powerholder. In LR 9748029, the IRS ruled that the lapse of a power of withdrawal held by the spouse of the grantor of an irrevocable life insurance trust did not cause her to be treated as the transferor of any portion of the trust because the power of withdrawal was subject to a 5 or 5 limitation. According to the ruling, the provisions of § 2514(e) shielded the lapse from adverse consequences

If the lapse does result in a completed gift, the amount of the gift will be determined under § 2702 without regard to the value of the beneficiary's interest in the trust. LR 9804047 (the lapse resulted in a gift of the amount subject to withdrawal not sheltered by the 5 or 5 limit—the powerholder's retained life income interest in the lapse amount was valued at zero under § 2702(a)). *See* § 2.31.

A transfer to a trust that is nontaxable under § 2503(b) has a zero inclusion ratio for GSTT purposes, if the beneficiary is the only person to whom distributions can be made during his or her lifetime and the property will be included in the beneficiary's estate if the beneficiary dies prior to termination of the trust. § 2642(c)(2). The lapse of a *Crummey* power to withdraw property from such a trust does not have any negative gift, estate, or GST tax consequences. For gift and estate tax purposes, the nonexercise is sheltered to the extent of 5 or 5 by the terms of § § 2041 and 2514. On the GSTT side, the lapse of such a power is not a direct skip, taxable termination, or taxable distribution. Also, to the extent the lapse does not involve a transfer that is taxable for gift or estate tax purposes the original donor remains the transferor—the lapse of the power does not cause the beneficiary to be treated as the transferor. § 2652(a); Reg. § 26.2601-1(b)(v)(A).

To the extent the lapse of the *Crummey* power is a taxable transfer for purposes of the gift or estate tax, the powerholder is treated as the transferor for tax purposes. A taxable gift of an interest in the trust would take place if the lapse resulted in a completed gift under Reg. § 25.2511-2(b). The beneficiary also becomes the transferor of the trust for GSTT purposes to the extent of the taxable gift. Of course, *Crummey* trusts are commonly drafted so the lapse of the power will not result in a taxable gift. As mentioned above, the beneficiary is typically given a testamentary power of appointment over the amount in excess of the 5 or 5 shelter in order to avoid that result. A "hanging power" of withdrawal would similarly prevent a lapse from resulting in a taxable gift. The annual lapse of a hanging power of withdrawal is limited to the amount of the 5 or 5 shelter. *See* § 7.38.4. If a beneficiary whose power has lapsed over an amount in excess of the protected 5 or 5 amount dies prior to termination of the trust a portion of the property is includible in the beneficiary's gross estate under §2041(b)(2). The inclusion would cause the deceased beneficiary to become the transferor of the trust for GSTT purposes.

§7.38.3. Allow Each Donor to Restrict the Amount That Is Subject to Withdrawal?

A trust may include a provision that permits each donor to designate whether an addition of property made by him or her shall be subject to withdrawal. *See* Keydel, Irrevocable Insurance Trusts: The Current Scene, U. Miami, 10th Inst. Est. Plan. ¶508.1 (1976). Perhaps the best approach is to provide in the trust that transfers to the trust are subject to withdrawal unless otherwise provided in an instrument of transfer. *See* Moore, Tax Consequences and Uses of *"Crummey"* Withdrawal Powers: An Update, U. Miami, 22nd Inst. Est. Plan. ¶1103 (1988); LRs 8003033; 8003152.

While a person making a gift to the trust may have the inherent right to limit the amount that would be subject to withdrawal, it is preferable to include an appropriate provision in the trust instrument. Authorizing donors to impose a limit on withdrawals should not cause any federal tax problems. In LR 8901004 (TAM), the IRS held that the power of the donor to exclude some beneficiaries from exercising a power of withdrawal over a contribution to the trust would not alone cause the donor to be treated as the grantor of the trust for income tax purposes. Of course, the annual gift tax exclusion is not allowable to the extent the donor provides that a transfer to the trust is not subject to withdrawal. Importantly, the power allows a donor to protect subsequent additions from withdrawal by the beneficiary and against the claims of his or her creditors.

A reserved power to designate whether or not additions to the trust are subject to withdrawal could be bothersome if additions to the trust may be made frequently, such as premium payments made by the insured's employer on group insurance held in the trust. Also, annual gift tax exclusions would not be allowed to the extent the donor(s) failed to indicate that the transfers were subject to withdrawal. However, that problem is eliminated if the additions are subject to withdrawal except as expressly provided in an instrument of transfer.

Form 7-2
Limitation of Withdrawal Power

Any person transferring property to the trust as a gift may, by a writing delivered to trustee at the time of the transfer, restrict or eliminate the right of a beneficiary to withdraw part or all of the transferred property.

§7.38.4. Hanging Power: A Cumulative Power of Withdrawal That Lapses at 5 or 5 Annual Rate

In some instances it may be important for a power of withdrawal to achieve two somewhat inconsistent goals: (1) allow donors to claim the annual exclusion with respect to all gifts to the trust, and (2) insulate the beneficiary from the potentially adverse tax consequences of the lapse of the power to withdraw an amount greater than $5,000 or five percent of the property subject to withdrawal. A "hanging power" is intended to support the allowance of a full annual exclusion to each donor, while limiting the lapse of the power to the 5 or 5 amount that has no adverse transfer tax consequence by reason of the provisions of §§ 2041(b)(2) and 2514(e). Thus, the power is drafted as a cumulative power of withdrawal that lapses each year at the maximum rate allowed under §§ 2041 and 2514. Of course, such a power exposes the property to withdrawal over a longer period, with all of the attendant hazards, including the possibility of subjecting the property to the claims of the powerholder's creditors, and inclusion in the power holder's estate under § 2041. Although there is no direct authority upholding the positive tax results of a hanging power, the benefits should follow, provided the power is expressed properly and not as a condition subsequent. In addition, such a power may cause the beneficiary to be treated under § 678 as the owner of a larger portion of the trust than otherwise. *See* § 7.38.10.

The 5 or 5 shelter prevents the controlled lapse of a general power of appointment, such as a hanging power, from resulting in a taxable gift.

Under § 2041(a)(2), the amount subject to a hanging power at the time of the power holder's death is includible in his or her estate. This rule naturally makes some clients and planners reluctant to use hanging powers.

EXAMPLE 7-16.

In January 2007 Donor, *D*, contributed $50,000 to a trust for the benefit of Child, *C*. *C* had a cumulative power of withdrawal over contributions to the trust that would lapse at the end of each year to the extent permitted by the 5 or 5 limit. On December 31, 2007 the trust had a value of $75,000. *C* did not exercise the power of withdrawal, which lapsed at the end of the year as to $5,000. The lapse had no gift or estate tax consequences. *C* had a continuing power to withdraw $45,000 from the trust. If *D* is not treated as owner of the trust, *C* would be treated as its owner under § 678(a).

Early in 2008 *D* contributed another $50,000 to the trust. *C* did not exercise the power of withdrawal during 2008. On December 31, 2008 the trust had a value of $200,000. On that date the power lapsed to the extent of $10,000. Again, the lapse has no gift or estate tax consequences. As § 678 is applied by the IRS, *C* continues to be treated as owner of the entire trust. After the lapse, *C* has the continuing power to withdraw $85,000. If *C* were to die at the time presumably only $85,000 would be includable in *C*'s gross estate under § 2041.

Do Not Express a Hanging Power as a Condition Subsequent. A hanging power that is dependent upon subsequent developments, such as a higher valuation of the property, may be denied effect. In LR 8901004 (TAM), the IRS refused to give effect to a hanging power that was stated as a condition subsequent: "However, the Trust provides that, if upon the termination of any power of withdrawal the person holding the power will be deemed to have made a taxable gift for federal gift tax purposes, then, such power of withdrawal will not lapse, but will continue to exist with respect to the amount that would have been a taxable gift and will terminate as soon as such termination will not result in a taxable gift." Recognition of the provision was denied on the basis of *Commissioner v. Procter*, 142 F.2d 824 (4th Cir.), *cert. denied*, 323 U.S. 756 (1944). In *Procter* the court denied effect to a provision that "in the event it should be determined by final judgment or order of a competent federal court of last resort that any part of the transfer in trust hereunder was subject to gift tax, it is agreed by all the parties hereunder that in that event the excess property hereby transferred which is decreed by such court to be subject to gift tax, shall automatically be deemed not to be included in the conveyance in trust." According to the court the provision was contrary to public policy. *See also* Rev. Rul. 86-41, 1986-1 C.B. 300, which disregarded an "adjustment" clause that would have recharacterized a transaction if the IRS determined that the gift had a value of more than $10,000, the then-applicable annual exclusion amount.

The following is an example of the form a hanging power might take:

Form 7-3
Hanging Power

> The beneficiary shall have the continuing cumulative right to exercise [his/her] power of withdrawal. Provided, however, that the right of withdrawal shall lapse on December 31 of each calendar year with respect to a portion of the amount subject to withdrawal equal to the greater of $5,000 or 5 percent of the total value of the trust property on such date (or a larger amount as a future amendment may specify in IRC Sections 2514(e) and 2041(b)(2)). Provided, however, in no case shall the beneficiary's right to withdraw transferred property lapse until 30 days after the beneficiary learns of the transfer or receives notice as provided above.

Unless the grantor is treated as owner of the trust, the holder of a hanging power will be treated as the owner under §678(a), at least to the extent the power can be exercised during the year. According to the IRS a power holder is also treated as owner of the portion of the trust attributable to portions of the trust over which the power of withdrawal had lapsed. The IRS treats the powerholder as the owner of a cumulatively increasing portion of the trust. *See* LR 9034004. In this connection note that the 5 or 5 shelter does not apply for income tax purposes. This and other discontinuities between the laws cause regrettable confusion and complexity.

§7.38.5. How Many Beneficiaries May Hold a Power of Withdrawal?

A power of withdrawal may be given to any number of beneficiaries, including incompetent persons, who have significant beneficial interests in the trust. A trust that has multiple beneficiaries usually gives each of them a power to withdraw a pro rata portion of property that is added to the trust each year—subject to whatever annual limit may be applicable to individual withdrawals. Of course, the number of annual exclusions that may be claimed is maximized if each beneficiary is given the power. As indicated by the quote below from LR 9628004 (TAM), the IRS resists allowing annual exclusions for powerholders who do have neither a current income interest in the trust nor a vested remainder.

In *Estate of Maria Cristofani*, 97 T.C. 74 (1991), the Tax Court allowed the annual exclusion for each beneficiary holding the power, including contingent remainder beneficiaries (32 grandchildren). According to the Tax Court, the critical question is whether the beneficiaries had the legal right to exercise the power of withdrawal, not whether they held vested present or future interests in the trust. The IRS acquiesced to the *Cristofani* decision, 1992-1 C.B. 1. However, in A.O.D. 1992-09 it indicated that it would continue to litigate the issue in cases that indicate a greater abuse of the *Crummey* power, particularly outside the Ninth Circuit.

A Technical Advice Memorandum, LR 9628004, states the IRS policy with respect to the allowance of annual exclusions for *Crummey* powers held by multiple beneficiaries of a trust:

> The Service generally does not contest annual gift tax exclusions for *Crummey* powers held by current income beneficiaries and persons with vested remainder interests. These individuals have current or long term economic interests in the trust and in the value of the corpus. It is understandable that in weighing these interests, they decided not to exercise their withdrawal rights. However, where nominal beneficiaries enjoy only discretionary income interests, remote contingent rights to the remainder, or no rights whatsoever in the income or remainder, their non-exercise indicates that there was some kind of prearranged understanding with the donor that these rights were not meant to be exercised or that their exercise would result in undesirable consequences or both.

The position stated in the TAM is not consistent with the position taken by the Tax Court in *Cristofani*.

A year after the TAM was issued the Tax Court allowed annual exclusions for the withdrawal powers held by contingent remainder beneficiaries. *Estate of Lieselotte Kohlsaat*, 73 T.C.M. (CCH) 2732 (1997). In *Kohlsaat* the donor transferred a building worth $155,000 to a trust of which her two children were the primary beneficiaries. The children also held special powers of appointment, in default of the exercise of which a child's share would pass to designated remainder beneficiaries (child one's share would pass to her three children and eight grandchildren; child two's share would pass to his spouse and four children).

A fight with the IRS may be avoided if the donor is willing to settle for fewer annual exclusions; giving the power to the beneficiaries who hold current or vested interests in the trust, but not to the others. The IRS has refused to recognize a power of withdrawal given to persons with no beneficial interest in the trust (a "naked" *Crummey* power). LR 8727003 (TAM). Similarly, the IRS has denied annual exclusions for *Crummey* powers held by persons with remote contingent interests. LRs 9141008 (TAM), 9045002 ("The purpose served by adding the 12 family members as beneficiaries was simply to avoid the federal gift tax through a proliferation of annual exclusions. The gifts were purportedly offered to the other 12 family members but the offers were never accepted."). Annual exclusions were allowed, however, in LR 8922062 for powers that were exercisable by beneficiaries who were only entitled to receive distributions for their support in accordance with an ascertainable standard. The IRS requirement that the power-holder have an interest in the trust apart from

§ 7.38.5

the power of withdrawal should be satisfied if each power-holder will ultimately receive, or have the power to appoint, an amount of property with a value at least equal to the total amount of the lapsed powers of withdrawal.

Reciprocal Trusts. The IRS has indicated that, based upon *United States v. Grace*, 395 U.S. 316 (1969), it will not recognize reciprocal powers of withdrawal. In particular, Rev. Rul. 85-24, 1985-1 C.B. 329, states that:

> No gift tax exclusions are allowable for the creation of reciprocal powers to withdraw corpus from a trust where two or more grantors, acting mutually, each creates a trust for the primary benefit of a child and gives each of the other grantors a corresponding power to withdraw a specified amount from the trust.

In LR 9731004 (TAM), the IRS ruled that only one annual exclusion was allowable for transfers to a trust. None were allowable with respect to *Crummey* withdrawal powers held by contingent beneficiaries. In LR 9745010 the IRS ruled that an annual exclusion was available for transfers that were subject to withdrawal by the current beneficiary if she received "immediate" notice of the transfers. However, it did not rule on whether annual exclusions were allowable for transfers subject to withdrawal by contingent beneficiaries. "Immediate" notice was also required by LRs 9809004-9809008 and 9810006.

§7.38.6. Notice to the Beneficiary

In order to qualify for the annual exclusion for property transferred to the trust, the beneficiary must have a reasonable opportunity to exercise the power of withdrawal prior to its lapse. Rev. Rul. 81-7, 1981-1 C.B. 474 (no annual exclusion for trust funded on December 29 and power lapsed on December 31). A power of withdrawal is meaningless unless the beneficiary knows of it and of transfers that are subject to it. Thus, in LR 7946007 (TAM), the IRS did not allow an annual exclusion where the adult beneficiary did not receive timely notice. Also, in LR 8006048, the IRS was unwilling to rule that the beneficiary had a present interest in the initial corpus of the trust where the trust instrument did not require the trustee to give the beneficiary notice of the power of withdrawal.

Knowledge = Notice. In several cases the IRS and the Tax Court have treated knowledge of a contribution to a trust and a power of withdrawal as equivalent to notice. Letter Ruling 8022048 states that: "In your dual capacity as donor and natural guardian, you possess actual knowledge of the legal right to withdraw trust property you have contributed." Essentially the same point is made in LR 9030005, in which the IRS stated that, "An annual exclusion is also available for *B*'s minor children where (because *B* is trustee, beneficiary, and guardian of her minor children), *B* does not give actual written notice to herself of trust distributions." Finally, in *Estate of Carolyn W. Holland*, 73 T.C.M. (CCH) 3236 (1997), the Tax Court allowed annual exclusions for transfers of which the power holders testified that they had actual knowledge although they received no formal notices.

In general, it is preferable to include a provision requiring the trustee to give the beneficiary prompt notice of additions to the trust. Even if the trust does not expressly require the trustee to give notice, the trustee of a *Crummey* trust should give prompt written notice to the beneficiary of any addition to the trust. Giving actual notice of each addition can be a nuisance, however, particularly where frequent additions are made to the trust, as may occur where the employer pays monthly premiums on group-term insurance held by the trustee. If employer-provided group-term insurance will be held in the trust, it should be possible to give a single annual notice, in advance, of premium payments that will be made during the year. Some commentators believe annual exclusions will be available if the beneficiary is given a single notice at the creation of the trust that, in effect, requires the powerholder to obtain information about such things as future transfers. Moore, Tax Consequences and Uses of *"Crummey"* Withdrawal Powers: An Update, U. Miami, 23rd Inst. Est. Plan. ¶1102.3 (1988). It is doubtful that the IRS would agree.

Some planners are reluctant to include a provision in the trust requiring the trustee to give the beneficiary written notice of the receipt of additional property. They feel it is risky to include such a provision because of the possibility that the trustee might not comply exactly with its provisions, which could jeopardize the availability of the annual exclusion if the notice is not given. In their view it is preferable to advise the trustee separately that the trustee should give the beneficiary timely notice. The availability of the annual exclusion should depend upon whether or not the beneficiary is given notice (or otherwise learns) of a transfer of property to the trust, and not whether a trust includes a provision requiring notice. On balance, it is better to require the trustee to give notice, which is more likely to satisfy the IRS, and because a direction contained in the trust puts the trustee on notice regarding the requirement. The inclusion of a notice requirement might satisfy an IRS examiner without the donor being required to prove that notice was in fact given to the beneficiary when property was added to the trust.

If a power of withdrawal is exercisable at the time of the power-holder's death, the amount subject to withdrawal is includible in the power-holder's estate, including the amount otherwise sheltered from inclusion by the 5 or 5 exclusion of §2041(b)(2). Some planners seek to avoid that result by providing that the power of withdrawal will lapse at the end of 30 days or one day prior to the death of the power-holder, whichever first occurs. LR 8922062. It is unclear whether the IRS will recognize the provision as effective to shield the 5 or 5 amount from inclusion in the power-holder's estate. The IRS might be troubled by the fact that the termination of the power caused by the death of the power-holder can only be determined retrospectively by reference to the date of his or her death. The provision is, in effect, a condition subsequent—on Day 2 the power would appear to be valid and exercisable until the time of the beneficiary's death, which would retrospectively invalidate an exercise of the power on Day 2.

Waiver. The extent to which a beneficiary can effectively waive the right to withdraw property from a trust or to receive notice of transfers to a trust without jeopardizing the allowability of annual exclusions for transfers to the trust remains uncertain. Presumably a beneficiary who receives notice of a transfer to a trust could waive the right to make a withdrawal. Such a waiver would, in effect, accelerate the time at which the power of withdrawal lapses. It might, for example, assure that the lapse occurred in the current calendar year rather than in the following one for purposes of determining whether the lapses of general powers of appointment held by the beneficiary exceeded the 5 or 5 limit. In LR 9523001 (TAM) the IRS held that the annual gift tax exclusion was not available for transfers made to a trust with respect to which the beneficiaries who held withdrawal rights had waived the right to receive any notice of future transfers to the trust. The outcome was expectable given the general insistence of the IRS that the holders of powers of withdrawal actually receive notice of transfers to the trust.

A single notice at the beginning of a calendar year given with respect to the payment of monthly premiums on life insurance policies held by the trustee (or of other regular periodic payments) may be sufficient, at least if the beneficiary waives the right to receive any additional notices for the remainder of the year. However, it is far from clear that a beneficiary could waive the right to receive all notices of future transfers without jeopardizing the allowability of annual gift tax exclusions for the transfers.

The fiduciary duties owed by a trustee to the beneficiaries of a trust ordinarily require the trustee to inform the beneficiaries of the existence of the trust and to provide them with information regarding its administration. *See* IIA A. Scott, Trusts §173 (4th ed. 1987, W. Fratcher ed.). Indeed, statutes in several states require trustees to inform beneficiaries of the existence of a trust. *E.g.*, Neb. Rev. Stat. §30-3878 (2011) (must notify beneficiary within 60 days); Tenn. Code Ann. §35-50-119(b) (2011) (must notify within 60 days). In *Karpf v. Karpf*, 481 N.W.2d 891 (Neb. 1992), the court held that the trustee's failure to inform the beneficiaries of the creation of a *Crummey* trust was a breach of the trustee's fiduciary duty to the beneficiaries. However, the uninformed holder of a *Crummey* power of withdrawal, the former spouse of one of the grantor's grandchildren, suffered no damages as a result of the breach because "it would be . . . uncertain, speculative, and conjectural to grant the wife damages in the face of her inability to swear that she would have exercised her rights." 481 N.W.2d at 897

It is unclear whether the IRS or courts would recognize "implied" waivers. One might arise if a trustee, who was a parent of a minor power holder, immediately used funds contributed to the trust to pay the initial premium on a new life insurance policy, the value of which would be considerably lower than the premium paid (and the amount subject to withdrawal). The donor-insured could argue that by paying the premium he, as trustee-parent, impliedly waived the right to withdraw the contribution, at least to the extent it exceeded the value of the policy.

§7.38.7. Must the Trust Have Liquid Assets to Satisfy a Withdrawal?

Some lawyers fear that an annual exclusion will not be available unless the trust has sufficient liquid funds to satisfy an exercise of the power of withdrawal. However, the IRS has not asserted such a requirement. Quite to the contrary, several letter rulings have allowed annual exclusions for gifts to *Crummey* trusts of term or group-term policies of insurance on the donor's life. *E.g.*, LRs 7826050; 7935091; 8006048. In fact, the IRS has indicated that when the beneficiary holds a *Crummey* power an annual exclusion is allowable for the premium payment made by an employer on a group term life insurance policy that the employee had transferred in trust. LR 8006109. Logically, the right of withdrawal should be sufficient to create a present interest in the beneficiary whether the assets transferred to the trust are cash, securities, insurance, or tangible personal property; that is, the annual exclusion should be available whether or not the trustee has liquid assets on hand during the time the power is exercisable. The power could be satisfied by the transfer of an undivided interest in whatever assets are held in the trust. Helpfully, the IRS allowed annual exclusions in LR 8445004 (TAM) although the trust held only interests in limited partnerships. It was sufficient that the trust authorized the trustee to enter into a "sale, encumbrance, loan, mortgage, or other distribution" to raise funds with which to satisfy the power of withdrawal. Nonetheless, the conservative and safer practice is to fund the trust with sufficient liquid assets to support a withdrawal by the beneficiaries equal to the amount of the annual exclusion (*i.e.*, $13,000 each). The following example illustrates the safe sequence of events to follow in making a gift to an irrevocable life insurance trust.

EXAMPLE 7-16.

On April 15, 2007, *D*, transferred $9,100 to a newly created irrevocable trust. The trust gave the beneficiary, *B*, the right to withdraw additions to the trust by a writing delivered to the trustee. If not exercised, the power would lapse 30 days following notice of an addition. A premium of $9,000 was due each year on June 15 on a life insurance policy on *D's* life. *B* was given notice of the creation of the trust, the initial transfer to the trust and of her power of withdrawal. As *B* did not exercise the power of withdrawal, the trustee used $9,000 to pay the 2007 premium. On May 1, 2008 *D* transferred $9,000 to the trustee, who deposited the funds in the trust's bank account and promptly gave notice of the addition to *B*. *B* did not exercise the power of withdrawal. On June 15 the trustee used the funds to pay the premium.

§7.38.8. How Long Should the Power Be Exercisable?

In order to qualify for the annual exclusion the beneficiary or the guardian of a minor or incompetent beneficiary must have a reasonable time within which to exercise the power of withdrawal. A power of withdrawal that is exercisable for an unreasonably short period of time will be disregarded as illusory. Trusts usually permit the beneficiary to exercise the power either (1) for a specified number of days following notice of the transfer, or (2) at any time during the calendar year in which the transfer was made, allowing a certain minimum period for withdrawals made near the end of the year. Annual exclusions were allowed in *Estate of Maria Cristofani*, 97 T.C. 74 (1991), in which the withdrawal power was only exercisable for 15 days. Private letter rulings have upheld the allowance of the annual exclusion in cases that allowed withdrawals for 30 days, LR 8004172, or 60 days, LR 7947066, following the transfer, or at any time during the calendar year, LR 7935006. A power of withdrawal that was exercisable only after six months following the transfer prevented the gift from being treated as a present interest. LR 8433024 (annual exclusion denied with respect to property transferred to trust in September, where beneficiary's power to withdraw was only exercisable in March of the following year).

Permitting a withdrawal to be made only during the calendar year in which the property is added to the trust is less desirable for two reasons. First, the IRS may deny the annual exclusion when the transfer is made late in December on the ground that the beneficiary did not have a reasonable time within which to withdraw the property. Of course, in *Crummey* an exclusion was allowed where the trust contained such a provision and the transfer was made two weeks before the end of the year. That threat can be eliminated by providing that the power may be exercised by the beneficiary during a specified minimum period in any case. For example, the beneficiary could be authorized to withdraw property at any time during the calendar year in which the property is added to the trust, or for a period of 30 days following the addition of the property, whichever is longer. Of course, the power to withdraw a gift made after December 1 in any year would lapse in the following calendar year. Such a lapse would be aggregated with any others that take place during the same calendar year for purposes of applying the 5 or 5 limits of §§ 2041 and 2514. Some planners deal with the problem by prohibiting any additions from being made to the trust after a specified date, such as November 30. *See* LR 8006048. However, that approach unduly restricts the ability of prospective donors to make qualifying gifts to the trust.

Second, the use of a clause that permits the beneficiary to withdraw the property at any time during the calendar year may increase the liquidity requirements of the trust. Also, if the power exists throughout the entire year, the beneficiary may be treated as owner of a greater portion of the trust under § 678 than if it existed only for a short time. The liquidity problem is particularly severe if the trustee must always have sufficient liquid assets on hand to satisfy all of the withdrawals that could be made at any time. Retaining that degree of liquidity should not be required in order to enable the donors to claim annual exclusions when they add property to the trust. Note also that the liquidity problem is substantially reduced if the power may be exercised only for a limited number of days following notice.

§ 7.38.9. Separate Trusts or One Trust for Multiple Donees?

In the case of multiple donees, it is usually simpler to create a separate trust for each of them than it is to create a single trust with multiple beneficiaries. Creation of separate trusts also makes it easier for transfers to the trusts to qualify as nontaxable transfers which have an inclusion ratio of zero for GSTT purposes. *See* § 2642(c); *see also* § 2.29. However, the donor is entitled to an annual exclusion for each trust beneficiary who has the right to withdraw a pro rata portion of the property that the donor transferred to the trust. Rev. Rul. 80-261, 1980-2 C.B. 279. Separate trusts can be easier to administer in some respects and are generally more beneficial from the income tax point of view because each trust is to some extent a separate taxpayer, allowing each trust a $100 exemption and separate use of the progressive rate schedule. When there are separate trusts, some economies of scale can be achieved if the assets of the trusts are managed as a unit, which can be authorized expressly in the trust instrument.

§ 7.38.10. Income Tax

A *Crummey* trust is usually subject to the same income tax rules as a § 2503(c) trust. *See* § 7.37.7. In addition, if the grantor is not treated as owner of the trust, the beneficiary is treated as the "owner" of the trust under the grantor trust rules to the extent the beneficiary holds a power to withdraw assets of the trust. § 678(a)(1). The income is taxed to the beneficiary under § 678 although the beneficiary is a minor and lacks the legal capacity to withdraw the property. "[I]t is the existence of a power rather than the capacity to exercise such a power that determines whether a person other than the grantor shall be treated as the owner of any part of the trust." Rev. Rul. 81-6, 1981-1 C.B. 385. *See also* Rev. Rul. 67-241, 1967-2 C.B. 225 (a widow who held 5 or 5 withdrawal power was treated as partial owner of trust). Accordingly, under § 678 a portion of the trust income will be taxed to the beneficiary in a year that property is added to the trust although no income is distributed to, or expended for, the benefit of the beneficiary. In LR 9034004, the IRS ruled that as each power of withdrawal lapsed the beneficiary would be treated as owner of an increasing portion of the trust. The formula to be used is:

$$\text{Increase} = \text{Amount Subject to Withdrawal} \ \times \ \frac{\text{Portion of Trust Not Already Treated as Owned by Beneficiary}}{\text{Total Value of Trust}}$$

Under § 678(b), a beneficiary who holds a power of withdrawal is not treated as owner of the trust if the grantor is treated as owner under § § 671-677. For example, the income is taxable to the grantor to the extent the grantor holds a power to control beneficial enjoyment under § 674. *See* LR 200732010 (grantor still treated as owner of trust because of retained power to add charitable beneficiaries, although beneficiaries would otherwise be treated as owners of part of the trust under § 678(a) because of the powers of withdrawal they held). *See also* LRs 200729005 through 200729016 (grantor still treated as owner of *Crummey* trust because of retained power to substitute assets of equivalent value).

§ 7.38.11. Estate Tax

The estate tax consequences of a *Crummey* trust are generally the same as those of a § 2503(c) trust. *See* § 7.37.6. Inclusion in the donee's estate is usually limited to the amount subject to withdrawal that exceeds the 5 or 5 shelter over which the donee's power of withdrawal lapsed. *See* § 2041(b)(2). Under Reg. § 20.2041-3(d)(4), the "purpose of section 2041(b)(2) is to provide a determination as of the date of the lapse of the power, of the proportion of the property over which the power lapsed which is an exempt disposition for estate tax purposes and the proportion which, if the other requirements of sections 2035 through 2039 are satisfied, will be considered a taxable disposition." The cited regulation includes the following illustration:

> For example, if the life beneficiary of a trust had a right exercisable only during one calendar year to draw down $50,000 from the corpus of a trust, which he did not exercise, and if at the end of the year the corpus was worth $800,000, the taxable portion over which the power lapsed is $10,000 (the excess of $50,000 over 5 percent of the corpus) or 1/80 of the total value. On the decedent's death, if the total value of the corpus of the trust (excluding income accumulated after the lapse of the power) on the applicable valuation date was $1,200,000, $15,000 (1/80 of $1,200,000) would be includible in the decedent's gross estate. However, if the total

value was then $600,000, only $7,500 (1/80 of $600,000) would be includible.

Insofar as the donor is concerned, none of the trust should be included in the donor's estate unless either the trust income or property is used to discharge the donor's obligations or the donor is acting as trustee at the time of his or her death.

§7.38.12. Model Power of Withdrawal

Form 7-4 below might be used to express a *Crummey* power of withdrawal for a trust with one beneficiary. The creation of a separate trust for each beneficiary is administratively simpler and can more easily be drafted to meet the requirements of the GSTT exclusion for nontaxable gifts, § 2642(c)(2). *See* LR 8922062.

Form 7-4
Model Power of Withdrawal

Withdrawal Right. The beneficiary shall have the right to withdraw from the trust an amount of the property originally transferred to the trust not to exceed $20,000 in value by giving written notice, within 30 days of [her/his] receipt of a copy of this document, to the trustee of the exercise of such right. Trustee shall deliver a copy of the trust agreement to the beneficiary, or to [her/his] guardian, on the date the property is transferred to the trust.

Notice of Additions to Trust. The trustee shall promptly give written notice to the beneficiary of the receipt of any property that is gratuitously transferred to the trust by any donor ("additions to the trust").

Right to Withdraw Additions to Trust. The beneficiary may withdraw additions to the trust by giving written request to the trustee. Such right of withdrawal shall apply only to the property added to the trust and shall lapse if it is not exercised within 30 days following receipt of the trustee's notice that property has been transferred to the trust as a gift.

Limitation of Withdrawal Right. Any person who makes a gift to the trust may, by a writing delivered to the trustee at the time of the transfer, restrict or eliminate the beneficiary's power of withdrawal with respect to part or all of the transferred property.

Guardian for Minor or Incompetent Beneficiary. If the beneficiary is a minor on the date of this instrument, or at the time of any subsequent transfer of property to the trust, or at any such time otherwise fails in legal capacity, the beneficiary's guardian may exercise on behalf of the beneficiary any right of withdrawal provided for in this article. If such right of withdrawal is exercised by the beneficiary or [her/his] guardian, the property received pursuant to such exercise shall be held for the use and benefit of the beneficiary.

§7.39. MANDATORY DISTRIBUTION OF INCOME TRUST, §2503(b)

The value of a beneficiary's interest in a mandatory distribution trust, determined in accordance with §7520, qualifies for the annual exclusion under §2503(b). In order to qualify for an annual exclusion in this way a trust for a minor may be drafted to require the income to be distributed currently to the donee, the donee's guardian, or a custodian for the donee under one of the Uniform Acts. In such cases the annual exclusion is available for the value of the income interest. However the remainder interest does not qualify for the annual exclusion, even if it is indefeasibly vested: "[A] transfer of property in trust with income required to be paid annually to a minor beneficiary and corpus to be distributed to him upon his attaining the age of 21 is a gift of a present interest with respect to the right to income but is a gift of a future interest with respect to the right to corpus." Reg. §25.2503-4(c). Of course, the value of the remainder interest can be virtually eliminated by giving the beneficiary the income interest for life, with the power to terminate the trust and obtain the principal after attaining a specified age.

EXAMPLE 7-17.

Donor, D, transferred $10,000 to an irrevocable trust of which D's 10-year-old child, C, was the income beneficiary. The income of the trust must be distributed each year to D until age 25 when the principal is distributable to C. Applying an interest rate of 7.6%, the actuarially determined value of C's right to receive the income for 15 years is $6,645. The remainder, which is a future interest, has a value of $3,355. Only the value of the term interest qualifies for the annual gift tax exclusion.

If C were entitled to receive the income for life, with the power to terminate the trust at any time after age 25, under Table S (7.6%), §20.2031-7T(d)(7), C's interest would have a value of $9,709.95. The remainder interest would have a value of only $290.05. Adopting this approach, almost all of the gift would be excluded by the annual gift tax exclusion.

§7.39.1. Nontax Considerations

From the nontax point of view a mandatory distribution trust is generally a less desirable way to provide for a minor than a discretionary trust because of the difficulty of providing for current distribution of income in a satisfactory way. Direct payment of the income to the beneficiary is generally considered to involve an unacceptable risk of waste by the beneficiary. The other methods of distribution also have some disadvantages. Requiring the appointment of a guardian to receive distributions of income involves some additional complexity in drafting and operating the trust. More important, the conduct of a guardianship proceeding is cumbersome and expensive in most states. Distribution to a custodian under the Uniform Acts is a better choice, but it has several disadvantages: (1) the custodial property must be distributed to the minor when he or she becomes 21; (2) if the minor dies prior to 21 the custodial property will be distributed as an asset of the minor's estate—quite possibly defeating a major purpose of the gifts by being distributed to the minor's parents; and (3) the plan involves additional complexity in drafting and administering the trust.

§7.39.2. Tax Considerations

The transfer of property to a mandatory distribution trust is a completed gift unless the grantor retains a power to affect the beneficial interests in the trust (which is seldom done). As indicated above, in most cases the income interest in a mandatory distribution trust qualifies for the annual gift tax exclusion. However, the IRS may challenge the availability of the annual exclusion if the trustee is obligated to retain non-income-producing property.

The grantor of a mandatory distribution trust does not usually retain any interest or control that would require the trust to be included in the grantor's estate if the grantor dies before termination of the trust. In particular, the grantor does not retain any power to control the beneficial interests in the trust or to cause its termination or revocation. If the beneficiary dies prior to termination of the trust, the trust property will not be included in the beneficiary's estate unless the beneficiary held a general power of appointment. *See* § 2041.

The income of a mandatory distribution trust is taxed to the beneficiary unless it is taxed to the grantor under the grantor trust rules of §§ 671-677. *See* § 10.4.1. In this connection, note that the income of the trust is taxable to the grantor under § 677(b) only to the extent it is actually used to discharge the grantor's legal obligation to support the beneficiary. This risk can be eliminated by providing that the trustee may not make any distributions that will satisfy the grantor's obligations, including the obligation to support any person.

A properly planned mandatory distribution trust has three relatively minor tax disadvantages. First, the remainder interest in the property transferred to the trust does not qualify for the annual exclusion. Accordingly, the grantor would be required to file a gift tax return with respect to transfers to the trust. The grantor would also be required to pay some gift tax or use a portion of his or her unified credit in order to offset the tax attributable to the value of the remainder interest. Careful drafting can reduce the value of the remainder interest. *See* Example 7-16 in § 7.38.4. Second, the income-splitting potential of the trust is limited where the distribution must be made to the minor or a custodian for him or her (income received by the custodian is taxed currently to the minor). In such a case the limited income tax saving potential of the trust is unavailable. Third, the distributions of income to or for the benefit of a child under 19 (or a full-time student under 24) are subject to the Kiddie Tax.

§7.40.   IRREVOCABLE SHORT-TERM TRUSTS

The adoption of the compressed income tax rate schedule and amendments to the grantor trust rules made by the 1986 Act virtually eliminated the income tax advantages of short-term reversionary trusts. Under §673, the grantor is treated as owner of the trust if the grantor or the grantor's spouse holds a reversionary interest in the income or principal that had a value of more than five percent of the value of the property at the time it was transferred to the trust. Prior to the 1986 Act, short-term trusts were frequently used by a taxpayer in a high income tax bracket to shift income to another family member temporarily, without permanently divesting himself or herself of all interests in the property. Importantly, the grantor could retain a reversionary interest in property transferred to the trust if the reversion would not, or was not reasonably expected to, take effect in possession or enjoyment within ten years following its transfer to the trust. Former §673(a).

G. GIFTS FOR EDUCATION

While death and taxes may be the only two certainties in life, one can certainly expect education costs to continue to spiral. This part considers two Code provisions that provide significant opportunities for clients to fund the educational pursuits of their beneficiaries. Contributions to qualified tuition programs under §529 can be treated as gifts made over five taxable years, effectively permitting a donor in 2011 to contribute up to $65,000 to a qualified tuition program without making a taxable gift. The §530 rules applicable to Education IRAs, now called Coverdell Education Savings Accounts, provide another technique for funding qualified education expenses.

§7.41. QUALIFIED TUITION PROGRAMS, §529

Because of changes in §529 made by the 2001 Act, qualified tuition programs (QTPs) now provide a more attractive way to pay the costs of higher education. Section 529, added by the 1996 Tax Act, first made it possible for states to offer tax-exempt plans in which accounts could be established to pay the costs of a designated beneficiary's tuition, books, and other expenses of higher education. The expenses permitted to be paid by distributions from a QTP are defined in §529(e)(3) as "qualified higher education expenses" (QHEEs)—which include tuition, fees, books, supplies, equipment, and room and board. Although the earnings of a plan are tax exempt, under the original version of §529 the earnings portion of distributions was taxable to the beneficiary whether made in cash or in kind.

The most important change made by the 2001 Act completely exempts distributions for QHEEs from taxation. Other changes liberalize §529 in other respects—and allow them to be established by private institutions of higher education.

Unfortunately, wide variations remain among the terms of QTPs offered by different states, which adds to complexity and makes choosing a QTP much more difficult. Clients who wish to achieve the maximum benefit from establishing a QTP will avoid brokers and instead look for states with no-load plans that have low annual management fees. Information regarding QTPs is available from a wide range of sources—including the internet. *See <savingforcollege.com>* and *<collegesavings.org>*.

Qualified Tuition Programs and Accounts. Section 529(b)(1) defines "qualified tuition program" as a "program established by a state or agency or instrumentality thereof or by 1 or more eligible educational institutions" that may be of two specified types. The first is a plan established by a state or by "1 or more educational institutions under which a person may purchase tuition credits or certificates on behalf of a designated beneficiary which entitle the beneficiary to the waiver or payment of qualified higher education expenses of the beneficiary."§ 529(b)(1)(A)(i). The second is a plan established by a state that allows a person to contribute to an account which is created for the purpose of meeting the qualified higher education expenses of a designated beneficiary. § 529(b)(1)(A)(ii). Most contributors are likely to select the second type of plan—which offers greater flexibility.

The second type of plan is also attractive because it usually does not have age restrictions. Accordingly, a contributor can establish a QTP for a fully-grown adult who will, most likely, never have qualified tuition expenses. Because the contribution to the QTP offers estate tax savings without incurring gift tax or losing control over contributed cash, as discussed below, the additional income tax on earnings from using the QTP for a purpose other than higher education (also discussed below) may well be a small price to pay.

Contributions; Investment Restrictions. QTPs must provide that contributions can be made only in cash, § 529(b)(2), and that no contributor or beneficiary can, directly or indirectly, direct investments, § 529(b)(4). QTPs also specify different minimum and maximum amounts that can be contributed to a QTP. For example, the Michigan and New York plans require a minimum contribution of at least $25 and allow contributions until an account reaches $235,000 in value. Plans must also prohibit accounts from being used as security for loans. § 529(b)(5). The cap on contributions to a QTP apparently applies on a state-by-state basis. Thus, for example, a single contributor could put up to $235,000 in a Michigan QTP and another $235,000 in a New York QTP for the same beneficiary.

Although contributors and beneficiaries cannot control investments, the proposed regulations allow the person who establishes an account to select among investment strategies offered by a QTP. Prop. Reg. § 1.529-1. A change made by the 2001 Act allows an account owner to rollover an account for the benefit of the same designated beneficiary from one qualified plan to another once every 12 months. § 529(c)(3)(C)(i). (A distribution from an account must be rolled over within two months, § 529(c)(3)(C)(iii), or it is taxable.) An account can also be moved from one plan to another if the designated beneficiary is changed to another person who is a member of the former beneficiary's family. § 529(c)(3)(C)(ii). The term "member of the family" is defined expansively in § 529(e)(2).

Account Owner. The account holder is the person designated by a QTP or in the agreement establishing the account as "entitled to select or change the designated beneficiary of an account, to designate any person other than the designated beneficiary to whom funds may be paid from the account, or to receive distributions from the account if no such other person is designated." Prop. Reg. § 1.529-1(c). A successor account owner should be designated should a replacement be required.

Trusts may invest in a QTP as a way of providing for the education of a beneficiary, provided that state's rules permit a trust to be an account owner, the trust instrument permits the trustee to delegate control over the funds to a third party, the trust instrument grants the trustee sufficiently broad investment powers to authorize the investment, and the trust instrument permits distributions of principal for the education of a beneficiary. The trust instrument should probably not require the trustee to invest in a QTP but instead give the trustee discretion to do so. After all, the beneficiary may have completed his or her education by the time the anticipated gift is to take effect.

State Variations; Investment Costs. The provisions of QTPs vary significantly from state-to-state. For example, contributions by residents of some states are deductible for state income tax purposes—in others they are not. (Contributions of up to $5,000 ($10,000 for joint returns) to a Michigan or New York QTP are deductible by residents.) The taxation of distributions for QHEEs may also vary. Importantly, a small number of states provide additional incentives for some families. Michigan, for example, adds $1 for each $3 contributed to a QTP by a resident for a resident beneficiary if the family income is $80,000 or less. Many states, including New York, allow nonresidents to establish accounts in their plans. Note that QTPs sponsored by some states may limit the institutions at which funds may be used or require that funds be held for specified periods before distributions can be made.

An article in the Wall Street Journal points out the impact that fees have on the amount of QTPs that will ultimately be available to the designated beneficiary. Asinoff, *Hefty Fees Can Crimp Your College Savings; Many Parents are Paying Big Commissions for 529 Plans that Are Available With No Load,* Wall St. J., Apr. 17, 2002 at D-2. According to the article, the QTP sponsored by New York (which is open to nonresidents), administered by TIAA-CREF, is subject to an annual management fee of only 0.65 percent of the value of an account. Assuming an annual growth rate of 7 percent, a contribution of $10,000 to a New York QTP account on the birth of a designated beneficiary would grow to be worth $30,288 at age 18. In contrast, an equal contribution to a QTP offered by Wisconsin plan, which is subject to a 2.27 percent annual fee, would grow to only $22,976 at the end of 18 years. The article also notes that QTPs managed by TIAA-CREF (including ones offered by Michigan, Minnesota, Missouri and New York) and by some other well-established fund managers are no load (*i.e.,* have no sales commission) and have very low annual fees. In contrast, plans sold by brokers are subject to up-front commissions that may be as much as 4 percent—which also seriously affects the long-term value of the investment in a QTP.

Contributions. Contributions to a QTP may be made by any person for a designated beneficiary. However, as noted above, state plans impose varying requirements regarding minimum and maximum contributions.

Changing the Designated Beneficiary. Section 529 allows the account owner to change the designated beneficiary. There is no income tax disadvantage to naming a new beneficiary, provided the new beneficiary is a member of the former beneficiary's family. § 529(c)(3)(C)(ii). Similarly, there are no gift or GST tax consequences, provided the new beneficiary does not belong to a generation below the generation of the former beneficiary. § 529(c)(5).

Gift Tax. Contributions to a QTP are treated as completed gifts of present interests and not as a qualified transfer under § 2503(e). § 529(c)(2)(A)(i). Accordingly, a contribution qualifies for the annual gift tax exclusion. Prop. Reg. § 1.529-5(b)(1). If a contribution exceeds the amount of the annual exclusion and does not exceed five times that amount, the contributor may elect to treat the contribution as having been made ratably over five years, beginning with the date of the contribution. § 529(c)(2)(B), Prop. Reg. § 1.529-5(b)(2). Under the proposed regulations, the election may be made by a husband and wife with respect to a gift that is treated as made one-half by each spouse under § 2513. Prop. Reg. § 1.529-5(b)(2)(iii). Thus, in the first year a QTP account is established for a designated beneficiary, a married couple could contribute up to $130,000 to the account in 2011 which, for gift and GST tax purposes, they could elect to treat as having been made ratably over five years.

A change of the designated beneficiary or a rollover to the account of another beneficiary is subject to the gift tax only if the new beneficiary belongs to a generation below the generation of the former beneficiary. §529(c)(5)(B). Other distributions from a QTP are not treated as taxable gifts. §529(c)(5)(A). Under the proposed regulations, if the new beneficiary belongs to a lower generation, the former beneficiary is considered to have made the transfer to the new beneficiary. Prop. Reg. §1.529-5(b)(3)(ii). In such a case, the GSTT applies if the new beneficiary belongs to a generation that is two or more below the former beneficiary's generational level. *Id.*

Some account managers allow the designated owner of a QTP account to be changed; others do not. The tax consequences of changes in the ownership of an account are uncertain. For example, although a change in ownership of an account should not be treated as a gift, there is some risk that the IRS will take that position. Similarly, some funds caution that the IRS may treat such a change as a withdrawal of the entire amount, which would be subject to a 10-percent penalty. Hopefully, the question will be resolved when final regulations are issued by the IRS, if not before.

GST Tax. The proposed regulations recognize that to the extent a contribution qualifies for the annual gift tax exclusion, it "satisfies the requirements of section 2642(c)(2) and, therefore, is also excludible for purposes of the generation-skipping transfer tax imposed under section 2601." Prop. Reg. §1.529-5(b).

Estate Tax. Under §529(c)(4)(A), "no amount shall be includible in the gross estate of any individual for purposes of Chapter 11 by reason of an interest in a qualified tuition program." However, the foregoing rule does not apply "to amounts distributed on account of the death of a beneficiary." §529(c)(4)(B). Finally, the estate of a donor who made a contribution in excess of the annual exclusion and that the donor elected to be treated as having been made over five years is required to include the "portion of such contributions properly allocable to periods after the date of the donor's death." §529(c)(4)(C).

Income Tax; Qualified Higher Education Expenses. As noted above, distributions that do not exceed the "qualified higher education expenses" (QHEEs) of the designated beneficiary are not subject to the income tax. QHEEs are defined in §529(e)(3). As before, QHEEs include "tuition, fees, books, supplies, and equipment required for" enrollment in an eligible institution of higher education, §529(e)(3)(A)(i). In addition, the term now includes the costs of special needs services, §529(e)(3)(A)(ii), and a greater portion of the costs of a student's room and board. Now the room and board costs for a beneficiary who is at least a half-time student are allowed to the extent of the greater of (1) the actual costs invoiced to a student who resides in housing owned or operated by the institution, or (2) the allowance applicable to the student for room and board included in the costs of attendance for federal financial aid programs under §472 of the Higher Education Act of 1965. §529(e)(3)(B)(ii). The earnings portion of distributions in excess of QHEEs is taxable and subject to an additional 10-percent tax. §529(c)(6).

EXAMPLE 7-18.

Mom and Dad contributed $40,000 to a QTP account for Son, S. The account has $10,000 of earnings, for a total balance of $50,000. S receives $10,000 from the account in the current year but spends only $3,000 of that amount for qualified higher education expenses. S is taxed on $1,400 (the earnings portion of the account is 20 percent of the total balance, and 20 percent of the $7,000 not used for qualified higher education expenses is $1,400). In addition, S must pay $140 of tax (the flat 10 percent tax on the amount included in gross income). Even with this surtax, the family unit likely comes out ahead because the parents were not taxed on the earnings as the account grew, and the parents were able to shift the tax bite to a child who is probably in a lower tax bracket.

Trustees and Custodians as Account Owner. Section 529 does not expressly permit trustees, custodians under the Uniform Acts, or other fiduciaries to be the account owner. However, logically, there does not appear to be any bar that would prevent them from being an account owner. Some state QTPs (like California) expressly allow trustees and custodians to be account holders—others do not. Unless local law or the trust authorize a trustee to contribute cash to an account, the appropriateness of doing so is uncertain.

Because of the inconsistent rules that govern UTMA custodial accounts and §529 accounts, custodians should be wary of "contributing" custodial funds to §529 accounts. For example, very different provisions govern the investment of funds held in custodial and §529 accounts. Under UTMA, custodians have authority to make investments while the contributor to a qualified tuition program under §529 cannot directly or indirectly control investments. §529(b)(4). Different rules also apply to the ownership of property held in custodial and §529 accounts and changes in beneficiary designations. Under UTMA, the minor designated in a custodial account is the owner of the custodial property, which cannot be changed. In contrast, the account holder can change the beneficiary designated in a §529 program. Some commentators believe that custodial funds can properly be invested in §529 programs. Pfefferkorn, *The Investment of Custodial Funds in Section 529 Qualified Tuition Programs: Tax Advantages and Fiduciary Concerns*, 30 Est. Plan. 571 (Nov. 2003).

§7.42. COVERDELL EDUCATION SAVINGS ACCOUNTS, §530

The 2001 Act increased the allowable contribution limits (from $500 to $2,000 per beneficiary) and liberalized some of the other provisions applicable to Education IRAs. §530. Education IRA accounts were renamed Coverdell Education Savings Accounts (CESAs) in memory of the late Senator Paul Coverdell. Most important, under §530(a), CESAs are exempt from federal income taxation. Aggregate cash contributions of up to $2,000 per year can be made to a CESA for a beneficiary under the age of 18. (However, contributions can be made for an older beneficiary with special needs as defined in regulations to be issued.) The contribution limit is reduced if the modified adjusted gross income of the contributor exceeds $190,000 for a couple or $95,000 for single persons or married couples filing separately. §§530(c)(1). A

CESA must be distributed to a beneficiary, other than a special needs beneficiary, within 30 days of the beneficiary's 30th birthday. §530(b)(1)(E).

Changes made by the 2001 Act allow tax-free distributions to be made from a CESA for "qualified" elementary and secondary education expenses in addition to qualified higher education expenses (as defined in §529(e)(3)). §530(d)(2). For purposes of §530, qualified elementary and secondary educational expenses include tuition, fees, tutoring, books, room and board, uniforms, transportation, and "expenses for the purchase of any computer technology or equipment (as defined in section 170(e)(6)(F)(i)) or Internet access and related services, if such technology equipment, or services are to be used by the beneficiary *and the beneficiary's family during any of the year the beneficiary is in school.*" §530(b)(4). (Emphasis added). Distributions in excess of the amount of qualified education expenses are generally includible in the beneficiary's gross income. §530(d)(2)(B). The amount of qualified education expenses is adjusted for the Hope Scholarship and Lifetime Learning Credits under §§25A. §530(d)(2)(C)(i). In addition, distributions from CESAs and §529 plans are cumulated for purposes of determining whether there has been an excess distribution. §§529(c)(3)(B)(vi), 530(d)(2)(C).

Subject to some exceptions, a 10-percent penalty applies to the amount of the tax imposed on a taxable distribution from a CESA. §530(d)(4). The penalty does not apply to amounts that are distributed to a beneficiary (or the estate of a designated beneficiary) after the death of the designated beneficiary. §530(d)(4)(B)(i).

Rollovers are not taxable provided they are made within 60 days to another CESA for the benefit of the same beneficiary or a member of the beneficiary's family (as defined in §529(e)(2)) who has not attained 30 years of age. §530(b)(5). In addition, a change in the beneficiary of a CESA is not treated as a distribution if the new beneficiary is a member of the beneficiary's family and has not attained 30 years of age. §530(d)(6). Rules similar to those of §220(f) apply to distributions made as a result of the death or divorce of the beneficiary. §530(d)(7).

Gift and GST Taxes. For gift and GST tax purposes, a contribution to a CESA is treated as a completed gift to the beneficiary that qualifies for the annual gift tax exclusion. However, such a gift is not a qualified transfer under §2503(e). §§530(d)(3), 529(c)(2). For GSTT purposes, a contribution to a CESA should be a direct skip that has an inclusion ratio of zero. §2642(c). Accordingly, grandparents can make contributions to CESAs without using their GSTT exemptions. Distributions from a CESA are not subject to the gift and GST taxes. §§530(d)(3), 529(c)(5)(A). In addition, the gift and GST taxes do not apply to the designation of a new beneficiary unless the new beneficiary belongs to a generation below that of the prior beneficiary. §§530(d)(3), 529(c)(5)(B).

Estate Tax. No amount is includible in the estate of any individual "by reason of an interest in" a CESA. §§530(d)(3), 529(c)(4)(A). However, the foregoing rule does not apply to "amounts distributed by reason of the death of a beneficiary." §§530(d)(3), 529(c)(4)(B).

CESAs are offered by many banks and brokerage firms, which charge fees that vary widely. Accordingly, clients considering CESAs should shop carefully.

BIBLIOGRAPHY

Adams, Powers of Withdrawal Held Individually or as a Fiduciary: A Pandora's Box of Tax Consequences, U. Miami, 23rd Inst. Est. Plan., Ch. 19 (1989)

Arlein & Frazier, The Net, Net Gift, 147 Tr. & Est. 24 (Aug. 2008)

Atkinson, Gifts to Minors: A Roadmap, 42 Ark. L. Rev. 567 (1989)

Budin, College Funding: New Kid on the Block (Qualified State Tuition Plan) Challenges Traditional Techniques, U. Miami, 35th Inst. Est. Plan., Ch. 8 (2001)

Caron, Taxing Opportunity, 14 Va. Tax Rev. 347 (1994)

Durham, When the Milk of Human Kindness Does Not Flow, U. Miami, 30th Inst. Est. Plan., Ch. 4 (1996)

Gingiss, The Gift of Opportunity, 41 DePaul L. Rev. 395 (1992)

Grassi, Generation Skipping Transfer Tax Aspects of Crummey Powers After the 2001 Tax Act, Part 1, 18 Prob. & Prop. (Jan./Feb. 2004); Part 2, 18 Prob. & Prop. 50 (Mar./Apr. 2004)

Handler, Tax-Free Gifts of Prepaid Tuition, 142 Tr. & Est. 20 (Feb. 2003)

Heilborn & Blattmachr, Planning with UTMA Accounts and Other Transfers to Minors, 34 Est. Plan. 3 (Dec. 2007)

Hoogendoorn, Transfers of Opportunities—An Opportunity to Avoid Transfer Tax?, 71 Taxes 892 (Dec. 1993)

Kasner, Gifts to Children and Grandchildren—With Particular Emphasis on Educational Financing, N.Y.U., 48th Inst. Fed. Tax., Ch. 22 (1990)

Linder, Helping the Kids Buy a House, U.S.C. § 47th Tax Inst., Ch. 22 (1995)

Markstein, Giving Well Is the Best Revenge: Planning Opportunities with Stock Options, U. Miami, 34th Inst. Est. Plan., Ch. 13 (2000)

Moore, Tax Consequences and Uses of *"Crummey"* Withdrawal Powers: An Update, U. Miami, 22nd Inst. Est. Plan., Ch. 11 (1988)

Muhs & Stikker, Lifetime Gifts and Transfers for Consideration, 1 Cal. CEB, Est. Plan. Prac., Ch. 6 (1988)

Narron, Non-Charitable Inter Vivos Gifts—A Plan for Tax Relief, U. Miami, 34th Inst. Est. Plan., Ch. 15 (2000)

Pfefferkorn, The Investment of Custodial Funds in Section 529 Qualified Tuition Programs: Tax Advantages and Fiduciary Concerns, 30 Est. Plan. 571 (Nov. 2003)

Price, *Crummey v. Commissioner* (1968) Revisited; Opportunities and Pitfalls of Trust Withdrawal Powers, U. Miami, 33rd Inst. Est. Plan., Ch. 8 (1999)

Price, Intrafamily Transfers: Blessed and More Blessed Ways to Give, U. Miami, 18th Inst. Est. Plan., Ch. 6 (1984)

Report, Committee on Estate Planning and Drafting, What to Give Away, 18 Real Prop., Prob. & Tr. J. 678 (1983), 19 Real Prop., Prob. & Tr. J. 806 (1984)

Shenkman, Planning Options to Help Families Fund a Child's Education, 30 Est. Plan. 24 (Jan. 2003)

Soskin, Gifts to Minors After 2001: Minor's Trusts, Qualified Tuition Programs, Education IRAs and Custodial Accounts Compared, 27 ACTEC Journal 344 (Spring 2002)

Wolff, *Dickman* Confined: The Taxation of the Gratuitous Transfers of Use, 21 Stetson L. Rev. 509 (1992)

8

Gifts to Charitable Organizations

[T]he words of such an act as the Income Tax, for example, merely dance before my eyes in a meaningless procession: cross-reference to cross-reference, exception upon exception—couched in abstract terms that offer no handle to seize hold of—leave in my mind only a confused sense of some vitally important, but successfully concealed, purport, which it is my duty to extract, but which is within my power, if at all, only after the most inordinate expenditure of time. Learned Hand, Thomas Walter Swan, 57 Yale L.J. 167, 169 (1947).

A. INTRODUCTION

§ 8.1.   Scope

Historically, Americans have generously supported charitable causes. The social value of charitable gifts is recognized in the income, gift, and estate tax laws, each of which has allowed a deduction for charitable gifts from an early time in its history. Over the years these deductions are consistently among the most important to taxpayers, both in terms of dollars involved and the number of taxpayers who claim them.

The words Judge Hand wrote about the income tax law in general apply even more forcefully to the complex provisions that apply to some gifts to charities, including gifts of appreciated property and gifts of partial interests to charitable donees ("split gifts"). Fortunately, relatively simple rules govern the deductibility of outright gifts to churches, schools, and similar charitable organizations. In those cases only the first sentence of § 170(a) is usually significant: "There shall be allowed as a deduction any charitable contribution (as defined in subsection (c)) payment of which is made within the taxable year." Pity the other donors, and their tax advisors, who must grapple with the remaining ten single-spaced pages of § 170. In spite of the need for simplification, the fiscal realities, and the perceived need to encourage charitable gifts, the deduction continues to be confusingly complex.

The charitable deduction provisions of the income tax law, § 170, the gift tax law, § 2522, and the estate tax law, § 2055, are similar in many respects. The principal differences are that the income tax law limits the amount of deductions of individuals to a percentage of the donor's adjusted taxable income (computed without regard to any net loss carryback) and requires adjustments when certain types of property are transferred, whereas the gift and estate tax laws neither impose limits nor require adjustments. There are also slight differences in the types of organizations that qualify for the deductions under the three statutes. For example, the estate and gift taxes, but not the income tax, allow deductions for gifts to foreign charities. §§ 2055(a)(2), 2522(a)(2), 170(c)(2)(A). Curiously, gifts to community chests are explicitly recognized as charitable in the income and gift tax laws, but not in the estate tax law. *Compare* §§ 170(c)(2) *and* 2522(a)(2) *with* § 2055(a)(2). It is not possible to identify any policy that is served by the differences in the language of the three statutes.

In this chapter the federal tax consequences of outright gifts to charity are discussed first. The percentage limitations on income tax deductions and the various categories of charities are developed in the context of that discussion. Gifts of partial interests, gifts in trust, and special types of transfers are explored later in the chapter.

For income tax purposes, gifts to qualifying charitable organizations are deductible by individual taxpayers who itemize. However, the deductions are subject to the percentage limitations and adjustments required by § 170. Depending upon the character of the charitable donee and the property donated, the deduction is limited to 20 percent, 30 percent, or 50 percent of the donor's adjusted gross income. From 1982 through 1986, a limited charitable contribution deduction was allowed on an experimental basis for taxpayers who did not itemize. This deduction was not extended when it expired in 1987. §§ 63(b), 170(i).

The allowance of an income tax deduction for charitable contributions has been criticized by some commentators who contend that the deduction should be replaced by a credit. They argue that a credit would be of equal value to all taxpayers whereas a deduction is of variable value, depending upon the donor's marginal income tax rate. Of course, the compression of the income tax rates that took place under the 1986 Act reduced the significance of the difference between a deduction and a credit for taxpayers who itemize. Other commentators contend that the income tax deduction should be unlimited, which would make it conform more closely to the gift and estate tax deductions.

The actual disparity in treatment of taxpayers is often increased because donors who do not itemize deductions on their income tax returns usually make cash contributions from earned income while wealthy donors frequently contribute appreciated property. Within the limits established by § 170, a deduction is usually allowed for the full value of the appreciated property without requiring the donor to recognize any gain.

EXAMPLE 8-1.

D, whose income is subject to a marginal income tax rate of 31%, wishes to give $10,000 to a public charity. *D* has owned stock for more than 12 months that has a basis of $1,000 and a fair market value of $10,000. If *D* contributes $10,000 in cash, *D*'s tax will be reduced by $3,100. If *D* instead contributes the stock, the tax savings will be the same, and the unrealized gain of $9,000 will not be taxed to *D*.

Lifetime gifts of appreciated property must be carefully planned in view of the donor's contribution base (adjusted gross income), the nature of the property, the alternative minimum tax, and the character of the donee organization. Note also that for estate tax purposes no deduction is allowed unless the value of the gift is definitely ascertainable at the time of the decedent's death. *Estate of David N. Marine*, 97 T.C. 368 (1991), *aff'd*, 990 F.2d 136 (4th Cir. 1993). *See also* §§ 2.14, 4.16. Also, an estate tax charitable deduction is allowable with respect to a payment made to a charitable beneficiary in settlement of a bona fide will contest or similar dispute. Rev. Rul. 89-31, 1989-2 CB 277; LR 200128005.

Formula Gifts Over to Charity that Are Not Intended to Take Effect. Some noncharitable gift plans include a formula clause designed to discourage the IRS from challenging a valuation by providing for a gift over to charity of the value of the donative property above a specified amount. Presumably there would be little incentive for the IRS to challenge the valuation of a gift if the excess value would not be subject to the gift or estate taxes. For example, a plan may give the donor's children units in an LLC, provided that if the units are finally determined to have a value in excess of a specified amount, units equal in value to the excess will pass to a designated charity. Applying the reasoning of *Commissioner v. Procter*, 142 F.2d 824 (4th Cir. 1944), the IRS refused to give effect to such a clause. FSA 200122011. The Tax Court sided with the IRS in *Charles T. McCord*, 120 T.C. 358 (2003), but the Fifth Circuit reversed, upholding the taxpayer's use of a formula clause in making gifts of interests in an FLP. 461 F.3d 614 (5th Cir. 2006). *See* § 10.49.

Qualified Charitable Distributions from IRAs. Individuals age 70 or older can exclude from gross income up to $100,000 in "qualified charitable distributions" from either a traditional IRA or a Roth IRA in 2006, 2007, 2008, 2009, 2010, and 2011. § 408(d)(8)(A). Such distributions are not deductible as charitable contributions, § 408(d)(8)(E), but the exclusion from gross income represents an improvement over prior law. Under prior law, the retiree had to include a minimum distribution in gross income but could donate the amount to charity and claim a deduction under § 170. The income tax deduction, was subject to the overall limitation on itemized deductions, § 68, as well as the other limitations applicable to all charitable contributions under § 170. In many cases, therefore, the income tax deduction did not offset completely the amount included in gross income even though the entire distribution was paid to charity. The new rule will appeal to those required to take minimum distributions who have sufficient funds from other sources to meet their living needs. A qualified charitable distribution is any distribution from an IRA made by the trustee directly to a public charity (i.e., one described in § 170(b)(1)(A)) to the extent such distribution would be includible in gross income if paid to the account holder.

The distribution may be made on or after the date the account holder reaches age 70^1/$_2$.

Although this opportunity is set to expire at the end of 2011, many expect that §408(d)(8)(A) may be extended into future years.

Although §408(d)(8)(A) formally provides that a qualified charitable distribution is excluded from gross income, it is worth noting that the taxpayer's satisfaction of a charitable pledge through a qualified charitable distribution will not cause the taxpayer to recognize any unrealized gain in the taxpayer's IRA. Revenue Ruling 55-410, 1955-1 C.B. 297, indicates that a charitable pledge is not a "debt" for federal income tax purposes; thus, a qualified charitable distribution pursuant to a pledge is not the satisfaction of an obligation with appreciated property.

B. FEDERAL TAX CONSEQUENCES OF OUTRIGHT GIFTS

§8.2. QUALIFIED CHARITIES, §170(c)

For income tax purposes a charitable deduction is allowable only for gifts made "to or for the use of" an organization listed in §170(c). In the case of contributions by individuals the list includes:

1. A state or federal governmental unit, if the gift is made for exclusively public purposes (including an Indian tribal government, §7871(a));
2. A domestic corporation, trust, community chest, fund, or foundation that is created or organized in the United States or any possession of the United States and is organized and operated exclusively for religious, charitable, scientific, literary, or educational purposes, to foster national or international sports competition or for the prevention of cruelty to children or animals;
3. A post or other organization of war veterans organized in the United States or any possession of the United States;
4. A domestic fraternal organization, operating under the lodge system, but only if the gift is exclusively for religious, charitable, scientific, literary, or educational purposes, or for the prevention of cruelty to children or animals; and
5. A nonprofit cemetery company.

Gifts to or for the use of organizations listed in items 1, 2, and 3, and gifts to organizations listed in item 4 usually qualify for gift and estate tax deductions. *See* §§2055(a), 2522(a). Also, note that gifts to or for the use of a fraternal organization qualify for the estate and gift tax deductions. §§2055(a)(3); 2522(a)(3). A gift to a cemetery company (item 5) does not qualify for a gift or an estate tax deduction. *See Mellon Bank v. United States*, 762 F.2d 283 (3rd Cir. 1985), *cert. denied*, 475 U.S. 1032 (1986).

When a nonqualified entity collecting charitable contributions is simply acting as an agent for a qualified charity, the payment is treated as if it were made directly to the qualified charity. Rev. Rul. 85-184, 1985-2 C.B. 85. On the other hand, if a qualified domestic charity is collecting funds which will be used by a foreign charity (a nonqualified charity) and the domestic charity has control and discretion over the funds, and the funds are used in furtherance of specific purposes approved by the domestic charity, contributions are treated as made to the domestic charity. Rev. Rul.

66-79, 1966-1 C.B. 48. Also, "the statute does not preclude the deductibility of contributions to a domestic charitable corporation which uses its funds for a charitable purpose in a foreign country." Rev. Rul. 69-80, 1969-1 C.B. 65.

An estate tax deduction is allowable only with respect to property that is included in a decedent's gross estate. §2055; Reg. §20.2055-1(a). Accordingly, the estate of a nonresident alien is not entitled to an estate tax charitable deduction for a gift of works of art left to qualified charities to the extent they are not included in the decedent's gross estate. LR 9040003. An estate tax deduction is allowable with respect to property to be distributed to qualified charities selected by a personal representative or trustee. Thus, an estate tax charitable deduction is allowable for property of a revocable trust that is distributable by the trustee among religious charities selected by the trustee. LR 9634025. Under the governing state law (New York) the courts would require the trustee to transfer the assets to the intended charitable beneficiaries that would be restricted to ones within the definition of §2055(a). Such a gift should generally require that the charities be limited to ones that satisfy the requirements of §§170(c), 2055, and 2522.

Qualified charities are themselves divided into two classes: (1) the so-called "public charities" described in §170(b)(1)(A) (also called 509(a)(1), (2) or (3) organizations), §8.3; and (2) all others ("nonpublic charities"), §8.4. Churches, hospitals, and schools are common examples of public charities. Gifts to public charities qualify for the maximum allowable income tax deduction, which is either 30 percent or 50 percent of the donor's contribution base depending upon the nature of the property transferred. The term "contribution base" is defined as adjusted gross income, computed without regard to any net operating loss carryback under §172. §170(b)(1)(F). A ceiling of 30 percent applies to gifts made to other charities described in §170(c) such as cemetery companies, posts or organizations of war veterans, fraternal lodges, and private nonoperating foundations. It also applies to gifts made *for the use of* public charities.

§8.2.1. Foreign Charities

Contributions made directly to foreign charities are not deductible for income tax purposes except for certain Canadian charities under the tax treaty between the United States and Canada. The deduction is also limited to the amount that would be allowed under Canadian law as if the taxpayer's Canadian source income were aggregate income. *See* Rev. Proc. 59-31, 1959-2 C.B. 949; Convention Between the United States of America and Canada with Respect to Taxes on Income and Capital, Article XXI, par. 5.

A gifting program that will benefit foreign charities can be configured so that contributions will be deductible. For example, contributions to a qualified §501(c)(3) United States foundation for the benefit of a university or school located in a foreign country are deductible. LR 9651031. The contributions qualified because the United States charity was not a mere conduit, but exercised discretion and control over contributions. The foundation approved a request by the university that it assist with a major capital campaign to raise funds for the university. Similarly, contributions made by an S Corporation to a charitable foundation are deductible by the shareholders of the corporation although some of the contributions are used by the foundation for charitable purposes outside the United States. LR 9703028.

An estate tax charitable deduction is allowable for property that passes to a foreign government or charity exclusively for charitable purposes. Rev. Rul., 74-523, 1974-2 C.B. 304; LR 200019011, 200024016. An estate tax charitable deduction is not allowed for an unrestricted bequest to a foreign government. LR 8748001 (TAM). The necessary restriction must be imposed by the transferor. It is not enough if the donee state attempts to create the required restriction by a unilateral declaration. *Estate of Leona Engelman,* 121 T.C. 54 (2003). Similarly, an income tax deduction is not allowable under § 642(c) for distributions made by a trust to a political subdivision of a foreign government.

§ 8.2.2. Cumulative List of Charitable Organizations; Requests for Rulings

A list of organizations that meet the requirements of § 170(c) is available online at *<http://apps.irs.gov/app/pub78>*. In addition, the list is published annually by the IRS. Cumulative List of Organizations Described in Section 170(c) of the Internal Revenue Code of 1986, I.R.S. Pub. No. 78. Additions, deletions, and changes are published in quarterly supplements. The Cumulative List is available on a subscription basis from:
Superintendent of Documents
U.S. Government Printing Office
Washington, D.C. 20402
A donor has some assurance that a deduction will be allowed for a gift made to an organization named in the Cumulative List. If the IRS subsequently revokes a letter ruling or determination letter previously issued to the organization, a deduction will generally be allowed for gifts made prior to publication in the Internal Revenue Bulletin of an announcement that gifts to the organization are no longer deductible. Rev. Proc. 82-39, 1982-1 C.B. 759. Accordingly, an estate tax charitable deduction was allowed for a gift to a charity that was listed in the Cumulative List at the time the decedent transferred a remainder in her personal residence to the charity and at the time of her death—the later revocation of the organization's exempt status did not bar the allowance of the deduction. LR 9005001 (TAM).

Requests for rulings must include a completed checklist of the type published in the currently applicable Revenue Procedures—which are published in the first issue of the Internal Revenue Bulletin each calendar year. The request must indicate that the applicant has read and complied with the procedures published that year, including the issues on which the IRS will not rule. Rulings should be requested with respect to unusual or complex nonfactual issues regarding the gift, estate, and generation-skipping transfer tax (GSTT) consequences of transfers involving charitable gifts.

§ 8.3. PUBLIC CHARITIES, § 170(b)(1)(A)

As indicated above, a larger income tax deduction is allowable for gifts made to a certain group of preferred charities, loosely called "public charities." In contrast, the estate and gift tax laws do not distinguish between the character of qualified charities.

In 1969, the maximum deduction was increased to 50 percent for a wide range of public charities described in § 170(b)(1)(A)(i)-(viii). The charities that qualify include churches; schools with a regular faculty, curriculum, and student body; organizations that provide medical or hospital care or perform medical research or education; organizations that receive a substantial part of their support from federal and state sources and from the general public and use their funds for educational organizations owned or operated by a state or a state agency; and state or federal governmental units to the extent gifts are made exclusively for public purposes. § 170(b)(1)(A)(i)-(v). Trusts, funds, or foundations described in § 170(c)(2), such as publicly or governmentally supported museums, libraries, community centers, United Funds, and the American Red Cross, also qualify provided they receive a substantial amount of their support from a state or federal governmental unit or from the general public, § 170(b)(1)(A)(vi) (commonly called "509(a)(1)" organizations). Three types of private foundations described in § 170(b)(1)(E) also qualify for the 50 percent limitation. They are:

1. A private operating foundation described in § 4942(j)(3), Reg. § § 53.4942(b)-1 and 53.4942(b)-2;

2. A private nonoperating foundation that distributes all of the contributions it receives to public charities or makes certain other qualifying distributions within two and one-half months following the close of its taxable year (Reg. § 1.170A-9(g)); and

3. A private foundation that pools contributions in a common fund and allows contributors (or their spouses) to designate the public charities that will receive the annual income and the portion of the fund attributable to their gifts. *See* Reg. § 1.170A-9(h).

Finally, organizations described in § 509(a)(2) or (3) are also treated as public charities for purposes of the 50 percent limit. § 170(b)(1)(A)(viii). Importantly, organizations that qualify under § 509(a)(1), (2) or (3) are not private foundations and are relieved from complying with the private foundation excise tax provisions of § § 4940-4948. Section 509(a)(2) describes certain types of organizations that have broad public support, normally receive more than one-third of their support from gifts, grants, contributions, or membership fees, and do not receive more than one-third of their support from gross investment income. *See* Reg. § 1.509(a)-3. A § 509(a)(3) organization (a "supporting organization") is one that is organized and operated exclusively to support one or more specified public charities; operated, supervised, or controlled by or in connection with one or more public charities; and not controlled directly or indirectly by the donor or "disqualified" persons. *See* Reg. § 1.509(a)-4. The use of supporting organizations as a vehicle for charitable gifts is popular because they are treated as public charities for income tax purposes and they are not subject to the private foundation rules.

§8.4. NONPUBLIC CHARITIES

The deduction for gifts to private foundations and other charities not described in § 170(b)(1)(A) is limited to the lesser of (1) 30 percent of the donor's contribution base for the year, or (2) the excess of 50 percent of the donor's contribution base over the amount of the donor's gifts to public charities. § 170(b)(1)(B). As indicated above, gifts "for the use of" all charities are subject to a 30 percent limit.

EXAMPLE 8-2.

During a year in which *D* had a contribution base of $25,000 *D* made cash gifts that totaled $10,000 to churches and schools described in §170(b)(1)(A). *D* also gave $5,000 in cash to the local post of the war veterans. The gift of $10,000 to public charities is fully deductible as it does not exceed 50% of *D*'s contribution base. Only $2,500 of the gift made to the war veterans' organization, a nonpublic charity, is deductible. The gift does not exceed 30% of *D*'s contribution base, but it does exceed the difference between 50% of his contribution base ($12,500) and the amount of his gifts to public charities ($10,000). The portion of a gift that is not deductible currently because of the percentage limitations can be carried over and deducted in the following five years. *See* §§170(b)(1)(B), 170(d)(1). *See also* §8.5.

§8.4.1. Gifts for the Use of a Charitable Organization

For the purposes of §170 a gift of an income interest is considered to be a gift "for the use of" the charity, whether or not the gift is made in trust. In contrast, a gift of a remainder interest is a gift "to" the charity unless the remainder will be held in trust after the termination of the preceding interests, in which case it is a gift "for the use of" the donee. Reg. §1.170A-8(a)(2).

EXAMPLE 8-3.

D transferred Blackacre to the trustee of a charitable remainder annuity trust that meets the requirements of §664(d)(1). The trust provides that an annuity of 5% of the initial fair market value of the property transferred to the trust will be paid to *D* and, upon the death of *D*, Blackacre will be distributed to the H Hospital, a public charity that meets the requirements of §170(b)(1)(A). *D* made a gift of the charitable remainder interest "to" the H Hospital.

§8.4.2. Gifts of Services and the Use of Property

No deduction is allowed for the value of services performed for a charity. Thus, an attorney was not allowed a deduction for the fair market value of services performed for a charity free of charge. *W. W. Grant*, 84 T.C. 809 (1985), *aff'd*, 800 F.2d 260 (4th Cir. 1986); Reg. §1.170A-1(g). However, a deduction is allowable for un-reimbursed expenses incurred incident to rendering gratuitous services to a charitable organization. Such contributions are considered made "to" rather than "for the use of" the organization. Rev. Rul. 84-61, 1984-1 C.B. 39; *Rockefeller v. Commissioner*, 676 F.2d 35 (2d Cir. 1982).

A limited deduction is allowed for costs incurred to maintain a student in the donor's home under an organized program. The costs are treated as payments "for the use of" the organization. § 170(g).

Unreimbursed out-of-pocket expenses incurred in activities for qualified charities may also be deductible, including mileage on passenger automobiles at a rate of 14 cents per mile. § 170(i). For years prior to 1998 the rate was 12 cents per mile.

In *Davis v. United States*, 495 U.S. 472 (1990), the Supreme Court resolved a split in the circuits regarding the deductibility, as contributions to a church, of travel and living expenses paid by the taxpayer on behalf of a child who was serving as a church missionary. The Court affirmed the Ninth Circuit decision in *Davis* denying a deduction for the expenses. 861 F.2d 558 (1988). According to the Court, such payments were not contributions "to" or "for the benefit of" the church. Moreover, the regulations allow taxpayers to claim deductions *only* for expenditures made in connection with their own contribution of services. Reg. § 1.170A-1(g). Decisions allowing deductions had been rendered in the Fifth and Tenth Circuits. *Brinley v. Commissioner*, 782 F.2d 1326 (5th Cir. 1986); *White v. United States*, 725 F.2d 1269 (10th Cir. 1984).

Travel expenses, whether paid directly or reimbursed, are not deductible if there is a significant element of personal pleasure, recreation, or vacation. § 170(k).

The contribution of the use of a vacation home for a week to a charity auction does not qualify for a charitable contribution deduction. Rev. Rul. 89-51, 1989-1 C.B. 89. In the same ruling the IRS concluded that the individual who purchased the use of vacation home at an auction for the benefit of the charity was not entitled to a deduction: "A payment to a charity is not a contribution to the extent that valuable consideration is received in return." Finally, for purposes of determining the right of the owner to deduct expenses associated with the vacation home, the week contributed to charity is counted as a week of personal use by the owner. See § 280A.

§ 8.4.3. No Charitable Deduction Allowed for Gifts to Charitable Organizations for the Benefit of Designated Individuals

As indicated in the *Davis* case, *supra*, no deduction is allowed for contributions that are made for the use or benefit of specific individuals. The underlying test is whether the charity has control over the disposition of the funds. If it does not, the donor is not allowed a charitable deduction for the contribution. The IRS pointed to this restriction in Notice 94-87, 1994-2 C.B. 559, which dealt generally with the provision of emergency assistance to victims of floods in the Southeast. The notice stated that, "the tax law does not allow taxpayers to deduct contributions earmarked for relief of any *particular* individual or family."

§ 8.4.4. No Part of Tuition Payments to Charities Deductible

No deduction is allowed for any part of a payment made to a religious organization as tuition for a child. *Sklar v. Commissioner*, 282 F.3d 610 (9th Cir. 2002). In *Sklar*, the court rejected the taxpayers' argument that the issue was no longer controlled by *Hernandez v. Commissioner*, 490 U.S. 680 (1989), which barred the deductibility of payments made to the Church of Scientology by members for "auditing" and "training."

In effect, the Sklars claimed that each tuition payment made by them was of a dual nature—part was, in fact, a tuition payment and part was a charitable contribution. However, applying *United States v. American Bar Endowment*, 477 U.S. 05 (1988), the court held that the Sklars had failed to establish that the tuition payments exceeded the value of the secular education received by their children. The Sklars had argued that because 55 percent of the school time was devoted to religious subjects, a corresponding portion of their tuition payments was a contribution made in consideration of solely intangible religious benefits. According to the court, the Sklars "have not shown that any dual tuition payments they may have made exceeded the market value of the secular education their children received . . . .The market value is the cost of a comparable secular education offered by private schools." A second attempt at a deduction by the same taxpayers was again rejected by the Ninth Circuit. *Sklar v. Commissioner*, 549 F.3d 1252 (9th Cir., 2008).

§8.5. CHARITABLE CONTRIBUTIONS CARRYOVER, §170(d)(1)

In general, contributions may be carried over for the next five taxable years to the extent they exceed the applicable percentage limit for the current year (20 percent, 30 percent, or 50 percent). §§170(b)(1)(A), (B), 170(b)(1)(C)(ii), 170(b)(1)(D)(ii), 170(d)(1).

EXAMPLE 8-4.

H and *W*, who file joint returns, have a contribution base of $50,000 in Year 1 and $40,000 in Year 2. In Year 1 they made cash gifts of $30,000 to a public charity and $2,000 to a nonpublic charity. In Year 2 they gave $18,000 in cash to a public charity. Under §170(b)(1) they are entitled to a deduction of $25,000 for Year 1 (50% of their contribution base), which leaves a carryover under §170(d)(1) of $5,000 to Year 2. No deduction is allowed with respect to the $2,000 contribution to the nonpublic charity because of the 30% limit, but the contribution may be carried over. §170(b)(1)(B). *H* and *W* are entitled to a deduction of $20,000 for Year 2 with respect to public charities ($18,000 plus $2,000 of the $5,000 carryover from Year 1). Their carryover to Year 3 will be $3,000 with respect to public charities, §170(d)(1), and $2,000 with respect to nonpublic charities, §170(b)(1)(B).

§8.6. WHEN IS A GIFT COMPLETED? REG. §1.170A-1(b)

The time at which a gift is considered to be made can be of vital importance to the donor. It affects both the year in which a gift may be deducted and the total amount of gifts made in a particular year.

> Ordinarily a contribution is made at the time delivery is effected. The unconditional delivery or mailing of a check which subsequently clears in due course will constitute an effective contribution on the date of delivery or mailing. If a taxpayer unconditionally delivers or mails a properly endorsed stock certificate to a charitable donee or the donee's agent, the gift is completed on the date of delivery or, if such certificate is received in the ordinary course of the mails, on the date of mailing. If the donor delivers the stock certificate to his bank or broker as the donor's agent, or to the issuing corporation or its agent, for transfer into the name of the donee, the gift is completed on the date the stock is transferred on the books of the corporation. Reg. § 1.170A-1(b).

A note given to a charity by its maker is a mere promise to pay, which is not deductible until it is paid. Rev. Rul. 68-174, 1968-1 C.B. 81. Similarly, a pledge made to a charity is deductible when it is paid, not at the time it is made. *Mann v. Commissioner*, 35 F.2d 873 (D.C. Cir. 1929); *cf.*, Rev. Rul. 78-129, 1978-1 C.B. 67. In contrast, a gift made to a charity by charging an amount against the donor's bank credit card is deductible in the year the charge is made even though the bank is not paid until the following year. Rev. Rul. 78-38, 1978-1 C.B. 67. For estate tax purposes a gift to a charity by check relates back to the date of delivery and is considered paid on that date if the payee promptly presents the check and it is duly paid by the bank. *Estate of Belcher*, 83 T.C. 227 (1984*), see also Estate of Elizabeth C. Dillingham*, 88 T.C. 1569 (1987), *aff'd*, 903 F.2d 760 (10th Cir. 1990).

The delivery of a stock certificate to a broker does not constitute delivery to the intended charitable donee unless the broker is acting as agent for the donee. If the broker is not, the donor may be taxed on the gain realized from a sale or merger that had "ripened from an interest in a viable corporation to a fixed right to receive cash" before the gift was complete. *Ferguson v. Commissioner*, 174 F.3d 997 (9th Cir. 1999) ("anticipatory assignment of income").

Conrad Teitell has provided a useful summary of the rules by which the IRS determines the completion of gifts to charity. Taxwise Giving 8-9 (Nov. 2001). The summary notes that gifts by check are completed when deposited in the United States mail or hand-delivered to the charity. Gifts by credit card are treated as complete on the date the charge is authorized. The same general rules apply to the delivery of properly endorsed stock certificates. Delivery to the corporate issuer or to the donor's agent is not complete until a new certificate is issued in the name of the charity.

Donor's Ownership of Contributed Property. A donor must legally own the contributed property to claim that a completed charitable gift has occurred. This means that the taxpayer must affect a valid gift under applicable state law. *Leslie Stephen Jones*, 129 T.C. 146 (2007). In *Jones*, the taxpayer was lead defense counsel for Timothy McVeigh, the man convicted of the 1995 Oklahoma City bombing. During the course of his work, the taxpayer received copies of documents, photos, and other materials prepared or compiled by government agents in investigating and prosecuting McVeigh. The documents included witness statements, medical exam reports, and copies of correspondence written by McVeigh to family and friends. The taxpayer shared these items with McVeigh as requested by his client but retained possession of them following the proceedings. The taxpayer then donated these items to the University of Texas in December of 1997 and claimed a charitable contribution deduction for the appraised value of the materials. The IRS disallowed the deduction on the grounds that the taxpayer did not personally own the materials provided to him for purposes of preparing McVeigh's defense. The Tax Court agreed, holding that in order to make a valid gift for income tax purposes, a transfer must at least be a valid gift under the applicable state law. Applicable state law in *Jones* (Oklahoma law) provides that a valid gift has three elements: donative intent, actual delivery, and the donor's relinquishment of all ownership and dominion. This last element requires that the donor own the property at issue. Oklahoma law did not directly address the ownership of materials related to a representation in a lawyer's possession, so the court looked to other aspects of Oklahoma law as well as the precedent in other states. While possession of property is normally prima facie evidence of ownership, the court held that the taxpayer here did not own the materials because of the "unique fiduciary relationship between an attorney and his client." The taxpayer held the materials as McVeigh's agent and did not have any beneficial title to them. The court observed that even in those jurisdictions where attorneys and clients have ownership rights in case files, the lawyer's right is usually limited to work product produced by the attorney and not to documents or materials prepared by others.

§8.7. APPRAISALS, SUBSTANTIATION, AND VALUATION OF GIFTS, REG. §§1.170A-13(c), 1.170A-13(b)(2)-(4); §6662

In order to qualify for the charitable deduction the donor must satisfy the appraisal and substantiation requirements that were added by the 1984 Act. Under the regulations individuals, closely-held corporations, personal service corporations, partnerships, and S corporations must file an appraisal summary (Form 8283, Noncash Charitable Contributions Summary) with respect to gifts of property, other than money or traded securities, that have a claimed value of over $5,000. Reg. §1.170A-13(c). In addition, the taxpayer must obtain a qualified written appraisal of the property from a qualified appraiser, who must execute the certification of appraiser which is included on Form 8283. In the case of a charitable gift of nonpublicly traded stock, the value of which is not more than $10,000, Form 8283 must be filed but an appraisal is not required. In connection with the new requirements note that the value of similar property contributed to one or more charitable donees during the taxable year is aggregated. In addition, when similar items of property are contributed to more than one charitable organization, a separate Form 8283 must be filed with respect to each donee.

The reporting and substantiation requirements for charitable contributions of property were made more rigorous in 2004 with the enactment of §170(f)(11)-(12). Generally, for any contribution of property for which a deduction of more than $500 is claimed, some form of substantiation is required unless the property is readily traded or unless the taxpayer was unable to meet the required substantiation for good cause. The level of substantiation required varies according to the claimed amount of the deduction:

Contribution level	*Required substantiation*
More than $500	Taxpayer must attach to the return a description of the property

More than $5,000	Taxpayer must obtain a qualified appraisal of the property and attach to the return such information as the IRS may require
More than $500,000	Taxpayer must attach to the return a qualified appraisal of the property

With respect to contributions of used vehicles, moreover, the taxpayer must substantiate any claimed contribution in excess of $500 by a "contemporaneous written acknowledgment" from the charity. A copy of the acknowledgment must be furnished to the IRS. Finally, if the charity sells the donated vehicle without any significant intervening use or material improvement to the vehicle, the amount of the deduction cannot exceed the charity's gross proceeds from the sale.

As illustrated by *John T. Hewitt*, 109 T.C. 258 (1997), *aff'd without pub. op.*, 166 F.3d 332 (4th Cir. 1998), the charitable deduction for contributions of nonpublicly traded stock is limited to the donor's basis in the stock. In *Hewitt* the taxpayers did not obtain qualified appraisals of the stock prior to filing the returns and did not attach a summary to the returns. Although the amount claimed by taxpayers represented the actual fair market value of the contributed stock, the deduction was limited to its basis. Conrad Teitell has pointed out that a deduction should have been allowed to each taxpayer for $5,000, which is the maximum allowable without a qualified appraisal for gifts of property other than publicly traded securities. C. Teitell, Lack of Qualified Appraisal Fatal to Deduction, 137 Tr. & Est. 65 (Feb. 1998). The taxpayers unsuccessfully argued that they had substantially complied with the requirements of the Reg. §1.170A-13.

The abuses that the substantiation rules are intended to prevent are illustrated by *Peter J. Lio*, 85 T.C. 56 (1985), *aff'd as to other parties sub nom. Orth v. Commissioner*, 813 F.2d 837 (7th Cir. 1987). Dr. Lio purchased 150 unframed lithographs by an artist (Nelson) from the artist's sole publisher and distributor for $50 each. The agreement specified that "at the time of delivery, AAA will supply Dr. Lio with two 'independent appraisals' stating that the fair market value of each lithograph is not less than $150." It also provided that, "within 1 year after the investment portfolios are delivered to Dr. Lio, AAA shall, upon request, supply at no additional charge a list of charitable organizations which will accept a donation of the lithographs and two independent appraisals setting forth their then current fair market value." 85 T.C. at 59. After Dr. Lio had owned the lithographs for more than nine months, he contributed them, unframed, to a museum. In the same year two other individuals made similar gifts of 200 lithographs by the same artist to the museum. "The museum has not accessioned the Nelson lithographs to its permanent collection or displayed them, nor does it have a present intention to do so. The museum does not insure the lithographs." 85 T.C. at 59.

Dr. Lio claimed a charitable deduction of $24,688 for the 150 Nelson lithographs based upon a value of slightly over $164 each, which was the average of the appraisals he received from AAA. During the same year AAA sold 12,225 Nelson lithographs, "97% of which were sold for $50 or less." None of the lithographs from the five Nelson editions purchased by Dr. Lio was sold for more than $50. The Tax Court found that the relevant market for the lithographs was the market maintained by AAA and that the sale to Dr. Lio was, in effect, a sale to the ultimate consumer and the best evidence of the value of the lithographs. The appraisals submitted by Dr. Lio were not persuasive. There was no evidence that Dr. Lio received any special discount or that the lithographs had appreciated in value in the period following their purchase. Accordingly, the charitable deduction was limited to $50.

EXAMPLE 8-5.

During the same taxable year, *D* gave original prints valued at $20,000 to the M Museum and original prints worth $35,000 to the Art Department of the U University. *D* must obtain a qualified appraisal of the prints from a qualified appraiser. The appraiser must be a person who must hold himself out to the public as an appraiser and cannot be the donor, the donee, a party to the gift, employed by, or related to, any of the parties, or a person whose relationship to the parties would cause a reasonable person to question his independence. A separate Form 8283 must be completed with respect to each gift, acknowledged by an appropriate official of the donees, and the certification must be signed by the appraiser.

If a contribution is made in property other than money, the amount of the contribution is the fair market value of property at the time of the gift. Reg. § 1.170A-1(c)(2), *Robert C. Chiu*, 84 T.C. 722, 730 (1985). For real property, fair market value is generally based on its highest and best use. Reproduction cost is a relevant measure of value where the property is unique, its market limited, and there are no comparable sales. *Estate of Palmer v. Commissioner*, 839 F.2d 420, 424 (8th Cir. 1988). Because the valuation of art objects is often difficult, since the 1960s a panel of art experts has advised the IRS regarding valuation of art valued at $20,000 or more. Of course, where the property has a value in excess of its basis, the amount of the gift that is deductible for income tax purposes must be reduced in some cases. Reg. § 1.170A-1(c). *See* §§ 8.9-8.12.

A gift of encumbered property qualifies for the charitable deduction only to the extent the fair market value of the property exceeds the amount of the encumbrances. *Winston F.C. Guest*, 77 T.C. 9 (1981).

Qualified Appraisals. As previously discussed, some contributions must be substantiated through a qualified appraisal, which § 170(f)(11)(E) generally defines as one performed by a "qualified appraiser" in accordance with generally accepted appraisal standards. A qualified appraiser is one who regularly performs appraisals for a fee and who possesses either an appraisal designation from a recognized professional appraiser organization or minimum education and experience requirements.

Presumably, a report complying with "generally accepted appraisal standards" would follow the Uniform Standards of Professional Appraisal Practice as issued by the Appraisal Standards Board. However, the Tax Court has indicated that "a noncompliant valuation report is not per se unreliable. Full compliance with professional standards is not the sole measure of an expert's reliability." *Whitehouse Hotel Limited Partnership*, 131 T.C. 112 (2008), *rev'd on other grounds*, 2010-2 U.S.T.C. ¶ 50,564 (5th Cir. 2010).

Regulations proposed in 2008 offer an extensive and helpful list of the contents of a qualified appraisal. Prop. Reg. § 1.170A-17(a)(3). They also define a "qualified appraiser" as an individual with "verifiable education and experience in valuing the relevant type of property for which the appraisal is performed." Prop. Reg. § 1.170A-17(b)(1). Guidance for meeting these requirements is also set forth in the proposed regulations.

§ 8.7.1. Substantiation Rules

Detailed rules govern the substantiation of deductions. For taxable years beginning after August 17, 2006, taxpayers claiming deductions for charitable contributions of money must maintain a bank record or some written communication from the donee indicating the donee's name, the date of the contribution, and the amount of the contribution. No deduction is allowed for charitable contributions of money for which the required records are not kept. § 170(f)(17).

For property donations, the donor is generally required to maintain a receipt from the donee which shows, among other things, the date, location, donee and the description of the property. Reg. § 1.170A-13(b)(1). In addition, if the deduction for a contribution of property exceeds $500, the donor's written records must show the manner of acquisition and the cost or basis of the property. Reg. § 1.170A-13(b)(3). For property other than money or publicly traded securities, no deduction is allowable unless the donor obtains a qualified appraisal and attaches an appraisal summary (IRS Form 8283) to the tax return. Reg. § 1.170A-13(c). A partially completed appraisal summary form suffices in certain cases, including gifts of nonpublicly traded stock worth between $5,000 and $10,000. Reg. § 1.170A-13(c)(2)(i)(B).

Extensive substantiation requirements were adopted by Congress, effective January 1, 1994. The requirements are elaborated, with examples, in Regs. § § 1.170A-1(h) and 1.170A-13(f). Under them, no charitable deduction is allowed for contributions of $250 or more unless the contribution is supported by a contemporaneous written acknowledgement of the contribution by the donee. § 170(f)(8)(A). The acknowledgement must include information regarding the amount of cash contributed; a description (but not the value) of other property; whether the donee organization provided any goods or services in consideration of the contribution; and a good faith estimate of the value of goods or services given in exchange. § 170(f)(8)(B)(i)-(iii); Reg. § 1.170A-13(f)(2). The acknowledgement must also disclose any goods or services received by the donor other than ones that consist solely of intangible religious benefits, provided exclusively by an organization organized exclusively for religious purposes. Under § 170(f)(8)(D), substantiation is not required if the donee organization files a return which, in accordance with regulations issued by the IRS, includes the information called for by § 170(f)(8)(B). A charitable deduction may not be allowed unless the donor receives a contemporaneous written acknowledgement by the earlier of the date the return is filed or the due date, including extensions. § 170(f)(8)(C). Under the regulations a written acknowledgement is contemporaneous if it is obtained by the donor before the earlier of (1) the date the donor files the tax return for the year in which the contribution was made, or (2) the due date for filing the donor's original tax return for the year. Reg. § 1.170A-13(f)(3).

Under § 6115, a charity that receives a "quid pro quo" contribution of more than $75 must provide the donor with a statement that provides the donor with a good faith estimate of the value of goods or services received by the donor and states the amount of the contribution that is deductible for federal income tax purposes is limited to the amount by which the contribution exceeds the value of goods or services provided by the organization. (For this purpose IRS Publication 1771 states, "Separate payments of $75 or less made at different times of the year for separate fundraising events will not be aggregated for purposes of the $75 threshold.") A quid pro quo contribution is defined in § 6115(b) as "a payment made partly as a contribution and partly in consideration for goods or services provided to the payor by the donee organization." However, a quid pro quo contribution does not include "any payment made to an organization, organized exclusively for religious purposes, in return for which the taxpayer receives solely an intangible religious benefit that generally is not sold in a commercial transaction outside the donative context." A special rule, discussed in the next paragraph, applies to the deductibility of amount paid to a tax exempt educational institution in exchange for the right to purchase tickets to athletic events.

Right to Purchase Tickets to Athletic Events. Section 170(l) provides that 80 percent of the amount paid to an exempt educational institution in exchange for the right to purchase tickets for athletic events is allowable as a charitable deduction. In contrast, § 274(l)(2) disallows a business expense deduction for the amount by which the cost of a leased sky-box or other luxury box exceeds the cost of non-luxury box seats in such a box. The IRS has ruled that the amount deductible under § 170 is not limited by § 274. LR 200004001.

Pre-2005 Gifts of Vehicles. Revenue Ruling 2002-67, 2002-2 C.B. 873, clarified some of the issues regarding the allowance of a charitable deduction for the gift of an automobile to an agent for a charitable organization. The ruling concludes that the transfer of a vehicle to an authorized agent for the charity is properly treated as a transfer to the charity. It also held that the agent may give the contemporaneous acknowledgement that is required by § 170(f)(8)(A) to substantiate gifts of $250 or more. Finally, the ruling holds that a donor may use an established vehicle pricing guide to determine the value of a vehicle contributed to charity.

In 2003, the IRS advised taxpayers to use caution in donating vehicles to charity. "The IRS advises that taxpayers contemplating such donations should ask many questions and carefully consider just how much of the proceeds from the car will go to their intended charity." IR-2003-139. The IRS cautioned that a donor may deduct only the fair market value of the vehicle at the time of donation—which "may be significantly different from the 'Blue Book' value." The IRS also referred to a GAO study that found that in some instances contributions made through fund raising organizations produced very little benefit to charities. "In one donation reviewed by the General Accounting Office (GAO), a taxpayer donated a 1983 vehicle valued at $2,400, but after the fundraiser sold the vehicle at auction and deducted administrative and advertising costs, the charity received $31.50."

The GAO study, Benefits to Charities and Donors, but Limited Program Oversight, GAO-04-73, concluded that, the proceeds received by charities that participated in vehicle donation programs were often small. "In addition, for two-thirds of the 54 specific vehicles donations GAO examined, charities received 5 percent of the value donors claimed as deductions on their tax returns. Differences in proceeds received by the charity and value claimed by a taxpayer were due in part, to vehicles being sold at auctions at wholesale prices, and proceeds being reduced by vehicle processing and fundraising costs."

§ 8.7.1

Post-2004 Gifts of Vehicles, Boats and Planes. The 2004 Act added §170(f)(12) that limits the deduction for the gift of a vehicle, boat or plane, the value of which is claimed to exceed $500, to the amount of the gross proceeds received by the charity. In addition, strict new substantiation rules apply, including a requirement that the donor file a detailed acknowledgment by the charity of the gift and sale price. Notice 2005-44, 2005-1 C.B. 1287.

§8.7.2. Penalty for Underpayment of Tax

Under §6662, a penalty applies where there is any underpayment of $5,000 or more in income tax due to a substantial valuation overstatement. For this purpose a substantial valuation overstatement occurs if the value claimed is 150 percent or more of the correct valuation. §6662(e)(1). If the overstatement is 400 percent or more, the penalty is 40 percent. §6662(h)(1), (2). In order to avoid imposition of a penalty the taxpayer should obtain the required appraisals and make an independent inquiry into the value of the property. Under Reg. §1.6664-4(a), no penalty will be imposed under §6662 with respect to any portion of an underpayment for which there was reasonable cause. "Reliance on an information return, professional advice, or other facts, however, constitutes reasonable cause and good faith if, under all the circumstances, such reliance was reasonable and the taxpayer acted in good faith." Reg. §1.6664-4(b).

§8.7.3. Report of Disposition of Property by Charity

If a charitable donee sells or otherwise disposes of donated property for which the donor claimed a deduction of over $5,000 (including similar property contributed by the donor to other charitable donees), the charity must file an information return (Form 8282) with the IRS (with a copy to the donor) identifying the donor and providing information regarding the sale. §6050L. Form 8282 must be filed by a donee charity if the contributed property is disposed of within three years of the contribution. The form must include the donor's name, address, and taxpayer identification number, a description of the property, the date of the contribution, the amount received of the disposition of the property, and the date of the disposition. §6050L(a).

As indicated, the reporting requirement applies when the value of the contributed property, other than cash and publicly traded securities, exceeds $5,000. Penalties apply under §6721 for failure to file the required report. The IRS does not have any discretion in imposing a penalty if a donee charity fails to include the donor's taxpayer identification number or other required information on a Form 8282. Instead, once a penalty notice is sent, the charity may request that it be waived. LR 200101031.

§8.7.4. Fraud Penalties

Under §6663(a), a penalty of 75 percent may be imposed with respect to the part of any underpayment of tax that is due to fraud. If the IRS establishes that any portion of an underpayment was due to fraud, the entire underpayment is treated as attributable to fraud except to the extent the taxpayer establishes by a preponderance of the evidence that the underpayment was not due to fraud. §6663(b). Thus, a fraud penalty may be imposed for underpayments of tax due to the fraudulent overstatement of charitable gifts. *Murray F. Hardesty*, 65 T.C. M. (CCH) 2743 (1993) (fraud penalties imposed regarding a variety of matters on a tax lawyer who also taught estate planning and wrote several articles on taxation; matters included the deduction of the total amount he paid to charities at auctions, unreduced by value of goods and services received in exchange). (Subsequently Mr. Hardesty pleaded guilty to three counts of an 11 count indictment that charged him with embezzlement of $2.1 million from trusts of which he was trustee, mail fraud and money laundering. *United States v. Hardesty*, 105 F.3d 558 (10th Cir. 1997).)

§8.7.5. Charitable Split-Dollar Insurance Plans

The IRS and Congress have curbed the promotion of charitable split dollar arrangements that were heavily promoted in the late 1990s. A ban on deductions for transfers in connection with charitable split-dollar insurance plans was added by the Tax Relief Extension Act of 1999, §170(f)(10). *See* §6.72.

Notice 99-38, 1999-2 C.B. 138 described the typical arrangement as follows:

> In general, a charitable split-dollar insurance transaction involves a transfer of funds by a taxpayer to a charity, with the understanding that the charity will use the transferred funds to pay premiums on a cash value life insurance policy that benefits both the charity and the taxpayer's family. Typically, as part of this transaction, the charity or an irrevocable life insurance trust formed by the taxpayer (or a related person) purchases the cash value life insurance policy. The designated beneficiaries of the insurance policy include both the charity and the trust. Members of the taxpayer's family (and, perhaps, the taxpayer) are beneficiaries of the trust.
>
> In a related transaction, the charity enters into a split-dollar agreement with the trust. The split-dollar agreement specifies what portion of the insurance policy premiums is to be paid by the trust and what portion is to be paid by the charity. . . .Although the terms of these agreements vary, the common feature is that, over the life of the split-dollar agreement, the trust has access to a disproportionately high percentage of the cash-surrender value and death benefits under the policy, compared to the percentage of premiums paid by the trust.
>
> As part of the charitable split-dollar insurance transaction, the taxpayer (or a related person) transfers funds to the charity. Although there may be no legally binding obligation expressly requiring the taxpayer to transfer funds to the charity to assist in making premium payments, or expressly requiring the charity to assist in making premium payments, or expressly requiring the charity to use the funds transferred by the taxpayer for premium payments in accordance with the split-dollar agreement, both parties understand this will occur.

Notice 99-38 concluded by warning that the IRS might challenge, on the basis of private inurement, or impermissible private benefit, the tax-exempt status of a charity that participates in charitable split-dollar arrangements. In addition, the IRS indicated that it might assess taxes under §§ 4958 or 4941 against any disqualified person who benefits from such a transaction. Tax liability might also be asserted under § 4945 against a private foundation and its managers. In addition, a charity that provides written substantiation of a charitable contribution in connection with a charitable split-dollar insurance transaction may be subject to penalties for aiding and abetting the understatement of tax liability under § 6701. The Service will also consider whether to require charities to report participation in charitable split-dollar insurance transactions in their annual information returns. The Notice also warned that the IRS may impose penalties on participants in charitable split-dollar transactions, including accuracy related and return preparer penalties, a promoter penalty under § 6700 and a penalty under § 6701 for aiding and abetting.

In *Charles H. Addis*, 118 T.C. 528 (2002), the Tax Court held that no charitable deduction was allowable for contributions made to a charity that were expected to be used, and were used, to pay premiums on a policy of insurance on the life of one of the donors pursuant to a split-dollar arrangement. The court held that (1) the charity provided consideration in exchange for the contributions, and (2) the receipts provided by the charity did not meet the substantiation requirements of § 170(f)(8) because it "incorrectly stated in the receipts that petitioners received no consideration for their payments." On appeal, the Ninth Circuit affirmed the Tax Court. 374 F.3d 881 (9th Cir. 2004). The same result was reached in *Gary L. Weiner*, T.C. Memo. 2002-153.

Under § 170(f)(10)(A), no charitable deduction is allowed for contributions to charities that are used, "directly or indirectly," or are expected to be used, to pay premiums on a life insurance, annuity, or endowment contract. In addition, a charity that makes such payments is subject to a penalty equal to the total amount of premiums paid by it. § 170(f)(10)(F).

§8.8.   GIFTS OF DEPRECIATED PROPERTY

As a general rule, property with a basis in excess of its fair market value (depreciated property) should not be given to charity. The reason is simple: Property given to charity is valued at its fair market value for purposes of the charitable deduction. Reg. § 1.170A-1(c). Also, no loss deduction is allowable under § 165 where depreciated property is given to a charity. *Lavar Withers*, 69 T.C. 900 (1978).

Two rules prevent taking a loss deduction when depreciated property is given to charity. First, noncasualty losses of an individual are deductible only if they are incurred in a trade or business or in a transaction entered into for profit although not connected with a trade or business. § 165(c)(1), (2). Charitable gifts are not made in either of those contexts. Second, a deduction is allowed only when a loss is "sustained," which requires that the loss be recognized for income tax purposes. Although a loss may be "realized" as a result of a gift to charity, no loss is "recognized." As *Withers* points out, a gift to charity constitutes a "sale or other disposition" that may cause a loss to be realized but does not constitute the "sale or exchange" necessary for a loss to be "recognized." *See also* § 1001(a), (c); Reg. § 1.1001-1(a).

§8.9. Gifts of Ordinary Income Property, §170(e)(1)(A)

A special rule applies to gifts of "ordinary income property" (*i.e.,* property that would not generate long-term capital gain if it were sold for its fair market value on the date of the transfer). Thus, it includes capital assets held for one year or less, property held for sale in the ordinary course of business, works of art and manuscripts created by the donor, depreciable tangible personal property or real property, §306 stock, and in some cases, partnership interests. *See* Reg. §1.170A-4(b)(1). When ordinary income property is given to a charity, the amount of the contribution is reduced to the extent the gain would not have been long-term capital gain had the property been sold by the donor at its fair market value on the date of the gift. *See* Rev. Rul. 80-33, 1980-1 C.B. 69 (contribution of §306 stock).

In effect, this rule puts the donor in the same position he or she would have been in had the property been sold for its fair market value and the proceeds contributed to charity.

EXAMPLE 8-6.

D gave a charity ordinary income property that had a basis of $3,000 and a fair market value of $10,000. The contribution is reduced by $7,000, the amount of the gain that would not have been capital gain had *D* sold the property. Thus, *D* is treated as having made a gift of $3,000. The outcome would be the same if *D* had sold the property for $10,000 and given the proceeds to charity. In that case *D*'s income would have been $7,000 greater, but the amount of *D*'s contribution would be $10,000, unreduced under §170(e)(1)(A). Of course, in the latter case, *D* might not be entitled to deduct the full amount of the gift, depending upon the particular character of the donee and the size of the donor's contribution base.

Under §170(e), the deduction allowed to an artist who contributes to charity a work the artist created is limited to his or her basis in the work—the cost of materials. *Maniscalco v. Commissioner*, 632 F.2d 6 (6th Cir. 1980).

In some cases, property that gives rise to ordinary income can be ideal for a charitable gift. For example, income in respect of a decedent is income that has accrued as of the date of death, but has not been paid. It is not includible in the decedent's final income tax return, but is taxable income to the estate or beneficiaries when received. It is also includible in the gross estate. Thus, when a charitable bequest is satisfied by a transfer of the right to receive income in respect of a decedent, both the estate tax and subsequent income tax will be avoided. Presumably the same rule applies where an installment sales obligation is distributed in satisfaction of a nonpecuniary charitable gift.

§8.10. Gifts of Capital Gain Property: General, §§170(b)(1)(C), (D); 170(e)

Special rules also apply to a gift of property that would have produced long-term capital gain had it been sold for its fair market value on the date of the gift, including property used in a trade or business as defined in §1231(b). §170(b)(1)(C)(iv). In general, the charitable deduction for a gift of such "capital gain property" cannot exceed 30 percent of the donor's contribution base for public charities and 20 percent of the contribution base for nonpublic charities. Thus, a donor's gift of capital gain property to a public charity is generally subject to an overall 30 percent limit instead of the basic 50 percent limit.

EXAMPLE 8-7.

Last year, when *D* had a contribution base of $20,000, *D* made gifts of $10,000 in cash and $6,000 in capital gain property to public charities. *D*'s charitable deduction for the year is limited to $10,000 (50% × $20,000). *D* is entitled to carry over the $6,000 gift of capital gain property to the next year. If the entire $16,000 in contributions were 30% capital gain property, *D* could deduct $6,000 for last year and carry over the balance for the following 5 years. §170(d)(1) and Reg. §1.170A-10(c)(1)(ii).

A 50 percent limit applies if the donor elects to reduce the amount of the gift by the capital gain that would have been realized had the property been sold. *See* §8.11. Gifts of capital gain property to nonpublic charities remain subject to a 20 percent limit. In addition, the deduction for gifts of capital gain property to nonpublic charities is generally reduced to their adjusted bases by §170(e)(1). However, this limitation does not apply where publicly traded stock is and the total amount contributed by the donor and members of the donor's family as defined in §267(c)(4) does not exceed 10 percent in value of all of the outstanding stock of the corporation. §170(e)(5)(C). The deduction was made permanent by the 1998 Act, which eliminated the limit on the period during which deductible contributions could be made to a private nonoperating foundation.

A contribution of 30 percent property is taken into account *after* gifts of other property, except that a contribution of 20 percent property is taken into account *after* gifts of 30 percent property. §§170(b)(1)(C)(i), 170(d)(1)(D)(i).

Qualified Appreciated Stock. The charitable deduction allowable for stock that is given to a private foundation is reduced by the portion that would have been long term capital gain unless the stock is "qualified appreciated stock." §170(e)(1). Under §170(e)(5)(B), the term qualified appreciated stock only applies to stock that is capital gain property and for which market quotations are readily available. Accordingly, stock in a publicly traded corporation that is subject to restriction under SEC Rule 144, for which quotations are not available, is not qualified appreciated stock. LR 9247018, LR 9320016. However, a deduction is allowable if Rule 144 stock that is contributed to the foundation may be sold by the foundation without restriction. The particular concern is whether the stock would be subject to the volume and resale limitations. LR 9734034 suggests a way of dealing with the problem. In that ruling, the donor and the donee foundation agreed that the donor would not make sales of the stock that would result in restricting sales by the donee foundation. The terms of the agreement satisfied the requirements of §170 and the relevant regulations. The IRS has ruled that unlisted Class B stock that is convertible into listed Class A stock does not satisfy the statutory requirement that market quotations be readily available.

LR 199915053. While the ruling follows the literal language of § 170(e)(5), it seems unnecessarily narrow and restrictive. The IRS has ruled that mutual fund shares for which quotations are readily available constitute qualified appreciated stock. LR 199925029.

A carryover charitable deduction is allowable with respect to qualified appreciated stock that was contributed at a time during which a deduction for contributions of such stock was allowable. LR 9437031. Analogizing to the holding in Rev. Rul. 90-111, 1990-2 C.B. 30, the IRS ruled that "in determining the tax character for carryovers, the focus is on the tax character of the property when the contribution is made. Thus, so long as Taxpayer's contribution qualifies for 'qualified appreciated stock treatment' at the time that it is made, the excess carryover will be given the same treatment. § 170(e)(5)."

An individual who receives stock in his or her employer upon termination of a qualified plan should consider contributing the stock to a charitable remainder trust. The elements, and advantages, of doing so are described below at § 8.20.6.

Stock that has been traded only a few times in the past decade is not qualified appreciated stock. Thus, in *John C. Todd,* 118 T.C. 354 (2002), the charitable deduction for closely held stock that was contributed to a private foundation was limited to the donor's basis ($33,338) not the amount the foundation received a week later ($553,847) when the stock was purchased in connection with a merger.

Alternative Minimum Tax. The alternative minimum tax (AMT) was adopted to impart greater fairness to the tax system by requiring a tax payment from those individuals and entities (estates, trusts, and corporations) that otherwise might pay no federal income tax. Between 1986 and 1993 the appreciation element in charitable gifts of appreciated capital gain property was an item of tax preference that was taken into account in computing the AMT. See former § 57(a)(6). During that period contributions of substantially appreciated capital gain property could have given rise to an AMT liability.

§ 8.11. Gifts of Capital Gain Property: Election to Reduce Amount of Gift, §§ 170(b)(1)(C)(iii), 170(e)

A donor may elect to have the 50 percent limit apply to all gifts of capital gain property made to public charities during the year. § 170(b)(1)(C)(iii). However, if the donor so elects, the amount of the gifts is reduced by the gain the donor would have realized had the property been sold. § 170(e)(1). The election can be used to increase the amount of the current deduction when the 30-percent ceiling would otherwise apply, but at the expense of losing the deduction for the appreciation element. In some cases the election may be used to increase the amount deductible in the current year and the amount deductible during the carryover period. That may occur where the gifts during the year far exceed the amount that could be deducted in that year and during the carryover period. The election does not apply to gifts of capital gain property to nonpublic charities.

EXAMPLE 8-8.

D expects to have an adjusted gross income of about $25,000 in this year and each of the following 5 years. Earlier this year *D* gave a parcel of real property that *D* had held for more than a year to a public charity. The property had a basis of $100,000 and a fair market value of $200,000. Without the election *D*'s deduction is limited to $7,500 per year (30%x $25,000) or a total of $45,000 over the 6-year period during which the deductions could be claimed. If *D* elects to reduce the amount of the gift by the gain component, *D*'s contribution deduction will be subject to the 50% limitation. By reducing the amount of the gift by $100,000, *D* could deduct $5,000 more each year. The deduction would be $12,500, which is 50% of *D*'s contribution base. Thus, by making the election, *D* could deduct a total of $75,000 instead of only $45,000.

It may also be useful to elect under §170(b)(1)(C)(iii) when a gift to a public charity exceeds 30 percent of the donor's contribution base, but the gain component is relatively small. Here again, if the donor reduces the amount of the gift by the gain, the limit on the amount of the deduction is increased from 30 percent to 50 percent.

EXAMPLE 8-9.

D had a contribution base of $50,000 in a year during which she made a gift of securities worth $25,000 to a public charity. The securities, which *D* had held for more than a year, had a basis of $24,500. Unless the election is made *D* could only deduct $15,000 for the year of the gift (30%x $50,000). The remaining $10,000 would be carried over to the next year. If *D* elects to reduce the amount of her gift by $500, she could deduct $24,500 this year, but would have no carryover to next year. The return earned on the tax saved by the additional $9,500 deduction this year could more than offset the $500 reduction in the amount of the contribution.

If *D* does not want to make the election under §170(b)(1)(C)(iii) because of charitable deduction carryovers to the current year or some other reason, a similar result can be reached by selling the securities during the tax year and contributing the cash proceeds. In this case, *D* would realize a gain of $500 from the sale. However, she would be entitled to deduct the $25,000 cash contribution in full. Of course, the additional taxable income may affect her tax return in other ways, for example, by limiting her other itemized deductions. The additional income also raises her contribution base.

Finally, an election under §170(b)(1)(C)(iii) may be used to increase the amount of the deduction that can be taken on a decedent's final income tax return or by a terminally ill donor. The election may produce a saving because a decedent's excess charitable contributions cannot be carried over to his or her successors. Some other deductions can be carried over to the decedent's estate. See §691(b). Of course, the unused portion of an excess contribution that is attributable to the surviving spouse may be carried over and used by the surviving spouse in a later year. *See* Reg. §1.170A-10(d)(4)(iii).

If the donor elects to have §170(b)(1)(C)(iii) apply to gifts of capital gain property, the amount of the gift is reduced for all purposes. Thus the amount of the gift is reduced for the purpose of determining the amount of any carryover deductions. Also, when an election is made for a year subsequent to the gift (*i.e.*, a carryover year), the amount of the carryover must be recomputed. In some cases an election totally eliminates the carryover.

EXAMPLE 8-10.

D gave a public charity stock he had owned for more than a year, which had a fair market value of $90,000 and a basis of $70,000. In the following year D gave the charity an additional $75,000 of stock he had also owned for more than a year and that had a basis of $65,000. In each year D had a contribution base of $200,000 and made no other charitable gifts. Ordinarily, D would be entitled to deduct $60,000 each year (30%x $200,000). If D elects to subject the first gift to §170(e)(1), the charitable deduction for the first year would be increased to $70,000, but there would be no carryover. Specifically, under §170(e)(1) the $90,000 gift would be reduced by the $20,000 gain. If D instead makes the election only in the second year, the amount of the first year's gift would be recomputed under §170(e)(1) to determine whether there would be any carryover to the second year. In this case there would be a carryover of $10,000 since the basis of the gift ($70,000) exceeded the deduction claimed in the first year ($60,000). An election in both years would produce deductions of $70,000 and $65,000 respectively for Year 1 and 2 and no carryovers. Thus, D could choose between the various options on the basis of whether and the extent to which carryovers could be used in future years. If D chose to elect in Year 1, Year 2's results might be improved by a sale of the asset and contribution of the proceeds since the Year 1 carryover would be fully preserved.

If a gift of capital gain property is planned or made, the planner should be alert to the consequences of making an election under §170(b)(1)(C)(iii). Once the election is made, it cannot be revoked after the original due date of the income tax return. *Jack J. Grynberg v. Commissioner*, 83 T.C. 255 (1984).

§8.12. GIFTS OF CAPITAL GAIN PROPERTY: TANGIBLE PERSONAL PROPERTY, §§170(e)(1)(B)(i)(I); 170(e)(7)

The deduction for a gift of tangible personal property is not reduced when the donee's use of the property is *related* to its exempt functions. However, the amount of a gift of tangible personal property must be reduced by the gain component where the donee's use of the property is unrelated to the purpose for which its tax exemption was granted under §501(c). This rule applies independently of the overall 30-percent and 50-percent limitations on the amount of a donor's charitable deduction. The application of the rule is illustrated in the following passage: "For example, if a painting contributed to an educational institution is used by that organization for educational purposes by being placed in its library for display and study by art students, the use is not an unrelated use; but if the painting is sold and the proceeds used by the organization for educational purposes, the use of the property is an unrelated use." Reg. § 1.170A-4(b)(3). *See also* LR 8143029. Applying this rule, the amount of the contribution was reduced where the donor gave an antique automobile to a college and could not show that the automobile would not be put to an unrelated use. LR 8009027.

Note that if the donee of a charitable gift of tangible personal property sells, exchanges or disposes of the property within three years following the date of the gift, the gain component of the gift is recaptured (i.e., the gain component is included in the donor's income for the taxable year in which the disposition occurs). § 170(e)(7). Woe unto the donor who contributes a highly appreciated bottle of wine to a charity auction! Under § 170(e)(7)(D) the gain component is not recaptured if an officer of the donee organization certifies, under penalty of perjury, that (1) the use of the property was related to the donee's purpose or function and describes how the property was used and how such use furthered the organization's purpose or function and (2) states the intended use of the property by the donee at the time of the contribution and certifies that such use has become impossible or infeasible to implement. Presumably the gain component is not recaptured if the donor dies prior to the calendar year in which the charity disposes of the property.

A gift or estate tax deduction is available for the value of tangible personal property that is transferred outright to a charity. While gifts of less than the donor's entire interest generally do not qualify for a deduction (*see* Part C *infra*), a gift of a work of art to a charity whose use of the property is related to its exempt purpose is subject to a special rule added by the 1981 Act. *See* § § 2055(e)(4), 2522(c)(3); Reg. § § 20.2055-2(e)(1)(ii), 25.2522(c)-(3)(c)(1)(ii). Under the special rule, the work of art and the copyright on the work of art are treated as separate properties. Thus, a charitable contribution deduction is allowable for the value of a work of art although the donor retains the copyright or transfers it to a noncharity (and vice versa). As noted in § 8.16, a deduction is available for a charitable timeshare. The gift to a charitable donee of the possession and control of the property for a specified portion of each year qualifies as a gift of an undivided interest in property. Reg. § 1.170A-7(b)(1)(i). See § 8.16.1.

§ 8.13. Gifts of Future Interests in Tangible Personal Property, § 170(a)(3), Reg. § 1.170A-5

A present charitable deduction is usually not allowed for the transfer of a future interest in tangible personal property. Under § 170(a)(3), a gift of a future interest in tangible personal property is treated as made only when all intervening interests in the property (1) have expired or (2) are held by persons other than the taxpayer or those standing in a relationship to the taxpayer described in § § 267(b) or 707(b).

EXAMPLE 8-11.

Last year *D* transferred a painting to a museum by deed of gift, reserving a life (or term) interest in it. For purposes of §170 the gift was not complete at the time of the transfer. For purposes of §170, a gift of the painting will take place if *D* relinquishes all interest in the painting and transfers present possession of it to the museum. A charitable deduction for a portion of the value of the painting would be available if *D* gave the museum the exclusive right to the possession and use of the painting for a specified period of each year. *See* §8.16.

As noted above, the deduction for a contribution of appreciated tangible personal property must be reduced where the donee's use of the property is unrelated to the purpose or function for which its exemption was granted under §501(c).

No gift or estate tax deduction is usually allowable for gifts of future interests in tangible personal property unless the interest is a remainder interest in a charitable remainder annuity trust or a charitable remainder unitrust. *See* §§8.19-8.35. However, a marital deduction could be claimed with respect to the full value of tangible personal property in which the donor's spouse is given a qualifying income interest for life. *See* §2056(b)(7). Of course, in such a case the property would be includible in the donee spouse's estate under §2044. If the property passes to charitable remainder beneficiaries on the death of the donee spouse, his or her estate can claim a charitable deduction under §2055 for the value of the property passing to charities.

EXAMPLE 8-12.

D transferred a collection of antique dolls to a local museum by deed of gift, but retained the possession of them for life. The transfer does not qualify for an income tax deduction until *D*'s interest terminates. The transfer of a future interest in the dolls constituted a completed gift for gift tax purposes. Most important, no gift tax charitable deduction was allowable. §2522(c)(2). The value of the dolls is includible in *D*'s estate if *D* retains possession of them until his death. §2036. If so, *D*'s estate would be entitled to an equivalent deduction as an outright gift to the qualified charity. §2055(a). Double taxation is avoided by excluding from the estate tax base any taxable gifts that are included in a decedent's estate. §2001(b).

A deduction may be allowed for a portion of the donor's basis in tangible personal property that is contributed to a charitable remainder trust and sold by the trustee. Thus, in Letter Ruling 9452026, the IRS ruled that if the trustee sold a musical instrument in a sale that had not been pre-arranged by the donor, the donor would be allowed to deduct "that portion of Taxpayer's basis which is allocable to the remainder interest in the musical instrument under section 170(e)(1)(B)(i) of the Code." The ruling also held that, provided the sale of the instrument was not pre-arranged, the sale would not result in any gain to the donor. As pointed out in the ruling, if the charitable remainder beneficiary is, or may be, a private foundation other than a foundation described in §170(b)(1)(E), the amount of the contribution deduction is reduced by the gain that would have been long-term capital gain had the property been sold. In addition, in such a case, the amount of the charitable contribution deduction is limited to 20 percent of the donor's contribution base. § 170(b)(1)(D).

C. GIFTS OF PARTIAL INTERESTS

§ 8.14. GENERAL

The 1969 Act strictly limited the availability of income, gift, and estate tax deductions for gifts of partial interests to charities. In general, charitable gifts of less than the donor's entire interest in property do not qualify for an income, estate or gift tax charitable deduction unless they are in the form of a charitable remainder trust (CRT), a pooled income fund, or a charitable lead trust (CLT). *See* Part D, *infra;* § § 8.19-8.35. Two major exceptions to this rule allow deductions for gifts, not in trust, of (1) a remainder interest in a personal residence or a farm, or (2) an undivided portion of the donor's entire interest in property, including a qualified conservation contribution. *See* § § 8.15-8.16. A deduction is also allowable for a gift of the donor's entire interest in property, even though it is a partial interest in the property. § 8.17. However, no deduction is allowable for an interest that may be defeated by the occurrence of an act or event unless the possibility that the act or event will occur is so remote as to be negligible. § 8.18.

§ 8.15. REMAINDER INTEREST IN PERSONAL RESIDENCE OR FARM

A gift of a remainder interest in a personal residence or farm qualifies for the income, gift, and estate tax deductions. § § 170(f)(3)(B)(i), 2055(e)(2), 2522(c)(2). The donor may retain a life estate or may transfer a life estate to another or others. (The gift of a life estate to others would, of course, be subject to the gift tax.) Unfortunately, the IRS has restricted the deductions to *nontrust* gifts of remainder interests, although the availability of the deductions is not so limited by the statutes. Reg. § § 1.170A-7(b)(3), (4); 20.2055-2(e)(2)(ii), (iii); 25.2522(c)-3(c)(2)(ii), (iii); *Ellis First National Bank of Bradenton v. United States*, 550 F.2d 9 (Ct.Cl. 1977); *Estate of Sara C. Cassidy*, 49 T.C.M. (CCH) 580 (1985); Rev. Rul. 76-357, 1976-2 C.B. 285. The restriction is unwise because the interests of a remainder beneficiary are better protected when a trust is used. The rule is also undesirable because it discourages the use of a trust to make a residence or farm available to an improvident or incompetent individual for life. The gift of a legal life interest to such a person might necessitate the appointment of a guardian, which is frequently cumbersome and expensive. So long as the IRS adheres to its present view, charitable gifts of remainder interests in personal residences and farms should not be made in trust.

For purposes of the deductions, "personal residence" means any property used by the donor as a personal residence, even though it is not the donor's principal residence. Thus, a vacation home qualifies as a personal residence. The donor's stock in a cooperative housing corporation also qualifies as a personal residence if the donor used the unit as a personal residence. Reg. § § 1.170A-7(b)(3); 20.2055-2(e)(2)(ii), 25.2522(c)-3(c)(2)(ii). Similarly, a condominium used by the donor as a personal residence qualifies under this exception. "Farm" is defined as "any land used by the taxpayer or his tenant for the production of crops, fruits, or other agricultural products or for the sustenance of livestock." Reg. §§ 1.170A-7(b)(4), 20.2055-2(e)(2)(iii), 25.2522(c)-3(c)(2)(iii). Buildings such as a house, barn, or other improvements located on a farm are included in the term.

Factors for the valuation of remainders in personal residences and farms after May 1, 1999 appear in IRS Pub. No. 1459, Actuarial Values, Gelph Volume (1999). The volume may be purchased from the Superintendent of Documents, U.S. Government Printing Office, Washington, D.C., 20402. It is available online at <*www.irs.gov*>. The factors are also included in some charitable planning and federal tax software programs.

§ 8.15.1. Life Estate Transferred to Spouse or Others

The transfer of a presently possessory life estate to an individual donee qualifies for the annual gift tax exclusion. In contrast, a successive life estate is a future interest for which no annual exclusion is available. No gift tax would be imposed if a donor gave a life estate in a farm or residence to his or her spouse, remainder to a charity, provided the spouse was a United States citizen. A QTIP gift tax marital deduction is allowable with respect to the gift of a life estate to a citizen spouse. § 2523(f). Note, however, that a successive life estate does not qualify for a QTIP marital deduction because the donee spouse's interest is not a qualified income interest (*i.e.*, the donee spouse is not entitled to all of the income (use of) the property for life). As suggested by Conrad Teitell, the donor may wish to retain a power to revoke the successive life estate in order for it to be an incomplete gift. Teitell, Charitable Gifts of Property— Tangible and Intangible, Real and Unreal, U. Miami, 20th Inst. Est. Plan., ¶ 918.3 (1986). If the donor exercises the power to revoke the successor life estate, the donor should be entitled to income and gift tax charitable deductions for the value of the life estate that was terminated in favor of the charitable remainder beneficiary.

§ 8.15.2. Charitable Gift of Remainder in Part of Farm or Residence

The exception for the gift of a remainder interest applies when the charity will receive the donor's entire interest in the personal residence or in a part of a farm upon termination of the preceding life or term interest. The exception applies even if state law requires the charity to dispose of the farm within ten years of acquisition. Rev. Rul. 84-97, 1984-2 C.B. 196. A gift of a remainder interest in a personal residence to a charitable organization (10 percent) and an individual (90 percent) as tenants in common qualifies for the charitable deduction. Rev. Rul. 87-37, 1987-1 C.B. 295, *revoking* Rev. Rul. 76-544, 1976-2 C.B. 285.

Discount Applies to Partial Interest. As indicated in Rev. Rul. 87-37, "the value of the charitable interest must be reduced to reflect the appropriate valuation discount for the cotenancy arrangement." The amount of the discount would depend largely upon expert testimony, particularly as to comparable sales of partial interests. In an estate tax case involving the valuation of the decedent's one-half interest in real property, the Tax Court allowed a discount of 12.5 percent. *Estate of George W. Youle*, T.C. Memo. 1989-138.

A gift of a remainder in a specified portion of the donor's farm acreage also qualifies for the deduction. Rev. Rul. 78-303, 1978-2 C.B. 122. That result follows because "farm" is defined in the Regulations as "any land" used for agricultural purposes. Accordingly, a gift of any portion that is so used meets the requirements of this exception.

§8.15.3. Sale Required upon Termination of Life Estate

The IRS has contended that no deduction is available when, under the terms of the gift, the personal residence or farm is to be sold upon the termination of the life estate. Rev. Rul. 77-169, 1977-1 C.B. 286. However, that position was rejected by the Tax Court in a case in which the state law gave the charitable remainder beneficiary the right to take the real property rather than the proceeds of sale. *Estate of Eliza W. Blackford*, 77 T.C. 1246 (1981), *acq. in result*, 1983-2 C.B. 1. *See also* Rev. Rul. 83-158, 1983-2 C.B. 159; LR 8141037(TAM). In some cases if a residence is transferred to a trust, the remainder of which will pass to charity on the death of a decedent's spouse, the trust can be reformed to qualify the remainder interest for an estate tax deduction under §2055. LR 8912027.

§8.15.4. Depreciation and Depletion

For income tax purposes, the value of a remainder interest in real property must take into account depreciation and depletion of the property. 170(f)(4)§170(f)(4). Under Reg. §1.170A-12(a)(1), depreciation is calculated on the straight-line method and depletion is determined by the cost recovery method. When a remainder consists of both depreciable and nondepreciable property, the depreciation or depletion is based only upon the fair market value of the depreciable or depletable interests. Thus, the fair market value of a residence must be allocated between the improvements, which are depreciable, and the land, which is not. The expected value of the property at the end of its life is also considered to be nondepreciable for this purpose. Reg. §1.170A-12(a)(2). The regulations provide the formulas that are used to calculate the value of remainder interests following a single life, Reg. §1.170A-12(b), a term of years, Reg. §1.170A-12(c), and more than one life or a term of years concurrent with one or more lives, Reg. §1.170A-12(e). The method of valuation is illustrated by Example 8-13.

EXAMPLE 8-13.

W, a 60-year-old widow, gave the remainder interest in her residence to a public charity. At that time, the residence was worth $75,000, of which $25,000 was allocable to the land and $50,000 to the improvements. The improvements have a useful life of 45 years at the end of which they will be worth $5,000. For purposes of §170 the gift consists of $45,000 in depreciable property (the value of the house ($50,000) less the expected value of its improvements at the end of 45 years ($5,000)) and $30,000 in nondepreciable property (the value of the land ($25,000) plus the expected value of the improvements at the end of 45 years ($5,000)).

The value of the remainder interest in the nondepreciable property is discounted to present value by applying the appropriate factor to determine the value of a remainder interest following the life of a 60-year-old donor to the nondepreciable property.

The value of the remainder interest in the depreciable property is calculated in the same manner, but first the remainder factor must be reduced by a factor determined in the manner described in Reg. § 1.170A-12(b)(2). The adjustment involves dividing (1) the difference between the R-factor for a donor aged 60 from column 2 of Table C of Reg. § 1.170A-12 less the R-factor for the donor's terminal age (either 110 or the sum of the age of the life tenant and the estimated useful life of the depreciable property) by (2) the product of multiplying (a) the useful life of the property by (b) the D-factor for a donor aged 60 from column 3 of Table C. The R-factors for ages 60 and 105 are 718.0316 and .00543664 respectively and the D-factor is 261.1947.

$$\frac{718.0316 - .00543664}{45 \times 261.1947} = 0.6109$$

The value of the interest in the depreciable property is $8,730 ($45,000 × (.25509 − .06109)). The total charitable deduction is $16,383 ($7,653 + $8,730).

§8.16. UNDIVIDED PORTION OF DONOR'S ENTIRE INTEREST

An exception to the partial interest rule is also made for a gift of an undivided portion of the donor's entire interest in property. §§ 170(f)(3)(B)(ii), 2055(e)(2), 2522(c)(2). According to the IRS, a gift of an undivided interest made in trust does not fall within the exception although the statutes do not expressly impose that limitation. Reg. §§ 1.170A-7(b)(1), 20.2055-2(e)(2)(i), 25.2522(c)-3(c)(2)(i). The IRS position is illustrated by a ruling that denied an estate tax deduction where the decedent gave his residuary estate to a trust under which the income was payable in equal shares to his surviving spouse and a charity for the spouse's lifetime and, upon her death, the principal was distributable one-half to the charity and one-half to the decedent's heirs. Rev. Rul. 77-97, 1977-1 C.B. 285. The ruling noted that a deduction would have been allowed if the decedent had created two separate trusts: one for charitable purposes and one for private purposes. The IRS could just as easily have recognized that the charity's right to a specified share of the income and principal was a sufficiently distinct portion to justify treatment as a separate trust. Interestingly, Reg. § 20.2056(b)-5(c) recognizes that a fractional or percentage share of a trust is sufficiently separate to qualify for the marital deduction. See § 5.22.1.

In order to qualify under this exception, the regulations require that an undivided interest consist of a fraction or percentage of every substantial interest or right that the donor owns in the property, which must extend over the entire term of the donor's interest. Reg. § 1.170A-7(b)(1)(i). Thus, if an individual owns a remainder interest in a trust that was created by another person, the remainder beneficiary's gift to charity of a fractional interest in the remainder qualifies as an undivided interest.

If the donor makes a charitable gift of an undivided interest in property in one year and later makes another charitable gift of an undivided interest in the same property, special valuation rules come into play. For example, if a donor contributes a

20 percent interest in a $100,000 painting to a local museum in one year, the donor may claim a charitable contribution deduction of $20,000 assuming the rules described in § 8.16.1 are met. If the donor makes another gift of a 20 percent interest in the same painting to the same museum in the next year, and the value of the painting has increased to $125,000, the donor's deduction is limited to $20,000, because the deduction for additional contributions of tangible personal property in which the donor had made a previous contribution of an undivided fractional interest is equal to the lesser of the value of the property used to determine the deduction for the initial contribution or the value of the property at the time of the additional contribution. § 170(o)(2). On the other hand, if the donor makes a gift of another 20 percent undivided interest in the same painting to the same museum in the following year, but the value of the painting has slipped to $75,000, the charitable contribution is $15,000 (20 percent of the lower fair market value at the time of the gift). Similar rules are provided for purposes of the estate and gift tax charitable deductions, §§ 2055(g)(1) and 2522(e)(2), and the rules apply to contributions, bequests, and gifts made after August 17, 2006.

§8.16.1. Gift of Property for Specific Period Each Year

Importantly, Reg. § 1.170A-7(b)(1)(I) treats a gift of the possession and control of property for a specified portion of each year as a gift of an undivided interest. Accordingly, a contribution of an undivided interest in an art collection to a museum is deductible when the collection remains in the donor's home if the museum has the right to possession and use during an appropriate portion of the year. *See* § 8.10. *James L. Winokur*, 90 T.C. 733 (1988); LR 8333019.

§8.16.2. Qualified Conservation Contribution, §§ 170(f)(3)(B) and 170(h)

Charitable deductions are allowed for the value of certain partial interests in real property given to qualified charitable organizations. §§ 170(f)(3)(B)(iii) and (h), 2055(f), and 2522(d). For income tax purposes, the contribution must be exclusively for conservation purposes as defined in § 170(h)(4)(A), discussed below, § 170(h)(1). But the 1986 Act relaxed the purpose requirement for estate and gift tax purposes. The rationale for the relaxation was stated in the Senate Finance Committee Report on the 1986 Act:

> The committee is concerned that applying the same conservation purpose standards for income, estate and gift tax deductions may cause undesirable results in some cases. If a conservation contribution is made and it later is established that the conservation purpose requirement for the contribution to be deductible is not satisfied, the donor loses his or her income tax deduction, and may also be subject to gift or estate tax. This is true notwithstanding the fact that a charitable organization owns the property interest and the donor may not have other property or funds with which to pay the gift or estate tax. S. Rep. No. 99-313, 99th Cong., 2d Sess. 284 (1986).

The amount of the gift of such an interest is equal to the amount by which it reduces the value of the property retained by the donor. *See* Rev. Rul. 76-376, 1976-2 C.B. 53; *Michael G. Hillborn,* 85 T.C. 677 (1985). It does not take into account any reduction in the value of the donor's contiguous property that results from the gift. *Leo A. Drey v. United States,* 535 F. Supp. 287 (E.D.Mo. 1982), *aff'd,* 705 F.2d 965 (8th Cir.), *cert. denied,* 464 U.S. 827 (1983). However, if the gift enhances the value of other property owned by the donor or related persons, the deduction is reduced by the increased value of the other property. Reg. § 1.170A-14(h)(3)(i). Such a gift may generate a substantial income tax deduction and reduce the value of the donor's retained interests for real property tax purposes without interfering with the donor's use of the property. However, gifts for conservation purposes should be carefully planned in light of the provisions of § 170(h).

Prior law treated contributions of qualified conservation real property to public charities the same as any other contribution to public charities: to the extent the property was capital gain property in the hands of the donor, the most that could be deducted in any one year was 30 percent of the taxpayer's contribution base (generally, adjusted gross income) with a carryover of up to five years. Since 2006, however, such contributions are allowed up to 50 percent of the taxpayer's contribution base and with a carryover of 15 years. § 170(b)(1)(E). Moreover, the 50 percent limitation is increased to 100 percent in the case of "qualified farmers and ranchers" (those whose gross income from farming or ranching business exceeds 50 percent of their total gross incomes), provided the property is restricted to remain generally available for agriculture or livestock production. The IRS has provided guidance on the applicable percentage limitations for qualified conservation contributions in Notice 2007-50, 2007-1 C.B. 1430. Note that these expanded limitations expired at the end of 2009. Unless extended, the limitations will revert back to the pre-2006 figures (a 30 percent limitation and a five-year carryover).

Serious consideration should be given to the deleterious effect that perpetual restrictions could have on the property retained by the donor *and* on the broader community. The value of preservation easements placed on historic property is discussed in McCall, Are There Added Preservatives in Section 170(h) of the Tax Code?: The Role of Easements in Historic Preservation, 39 Real Prop., Prob. & Tr. J. 807 (2005).

The partial interests for which a deduction may be claimed are defined in § 170(h)(2) to include:

1. The entire interest of the donor other than his or her interest in subsurface oil, gas, or other minerals and the right of access to such minerals;

2. A remainder interest; and

3. A restriction (granted in perpetuity) on the use which may be made of the real property.

The last category covers easements and other interests in real property that have similar attributes under local law (*e.g.,* restrictive covenants).

In order to satisfy the requirements of § 170(h), it is only necessary to meet one of four objectives listed under § 170(h)(4)(A). They are limited to the following:

1. The preservation of land for outdoor recreation by, or for the education of, the general public;

2. The protection of a relatively natural habitat of fish, wildlife, or plants or similar ecosystem;

3. The preservation of open space (including farmland and forest land) where the preservation is for the scenic enjoyment of the general public or, is pursuant to a clearly defined Federal, State, or local governmental conservation policy and will yield a significant public benefit; or

4. The preservation of an historically important land area or a certified historic structure. *See also* Reg. § 1.170A-14(d).

The qualified organizations to which contributions may be made are limited to governmental units and publicly supported charitable organizations. § 170(h)(3); Reg. § 1.170A-14(c). The IRS has determined that some taxpayers are making inappropriate use of the qualified easement contribution deduction in connection with the purchase of real property. Accordingly, the IRS will subject such transactions to increased scrutiny. Notice 2004-41, 2004-2 C.B. 31.

Qualified conservation contributions of encumbered property may not qualify for the income tax charitable contribution deduction. In *Gordon and Lorna Kaufman*, 134 T.C. No. 9 (2010), the taxpayers granted a façade easement restricting the use of a single-family rowhouse located in a historic preservation district in Boston to the National Architectural Trust (NAT), but the property was subject to a mortgage. The Service disallowed the claimed deduction for the decline in the value of the subject property and the Tax Court, in a reviewed opinion, granted the Service's motion for summary judgment on the issue. As the court explained, "Petitioners concede that . . . the bank retained a 'prior claim' to all proceeds of condemnation and to all insurance proceeds as a result of any casualty, hazard, or accident occurring to or about the property. Moreover, petitioners do not dispute that the bank was entitled to those proceeds 'in preference' to NAT until the mortgage was satisfied and discharged. The right of NAT to its proportionate share of future proceeds was thus not guaranteed."

§ 8.16.3. Qualified Conservation Easement, § 2031(c)

The 1997 Act amended § 2031 to allow an executor to elect to reduce the value of land made subject to a qualified conservation easement granted after 1997 and within the period during which the estate tax return must be filed. The value may be reduced by a portion of its value, not to exceed 40 percent, up to a maximum of $500,000. The exclusion is not coordinated with § 2032A and is allowable, under certain circumstances, with respect to a decedent's interest in land held by partnerships, corporations, and trusts. The provision only applies to property situated in the United States and held for three years preceding death. The exclusion is allowable with respect to easements created by the decedent, a member of the decedent's family, the executor of the decedent's estate or the trustee of a trust, the corpus of which includes the land subject to the easement. § 2031(c)(8).

Conservation easements may be granted by entities as well as individuals. Charitable contributions by a partnership, or limited liability company, are treated as pro rata gifts by each partner or member. Reg. § 1.702-1(a)(4). Accordingly, each partner is entitled to deduct a portion of the value of a conservation easement granted by the partnership. LR 200208019. With regard to the amount deductible, the cited ruling points out that, "As a general rule, the amount allowed as a deduction for a conservation easement is the difference between the value of the burdened property before and after the donation. *See Symington v. Commissioner*, 87 T.C. 891 (1984). It is possible that the value of Taxpayer's retained property may increase as a result of the easement."

Some states allow a tax credit for the value of conservation easements. The IRS has ruled that the allowance of the credit does not diminish the amount of the state tax deduction allowable to the donors under § 164. CCA 200126005 (Technical Assistance Memorandum for Area Counsel) (Colorado law).

The IRS has ruled that § 642(c) does not allow a trust to deduct the value of a qualified conservation easement that is contributed from the principal of the trust. Deductions under § 642(c) are only allowed to a trust for contributions that are paid from the trust's gross income. Rev. Rul. 2003-123, 2003-2 C.B. 1200.

§ 8.17. Donor's Entire Interest in Property

A deduction is allowed for a gift of the donor's entire interest in property, although it is only a partial interest. "Thus, if securities are given to *A* for life, with the remainder over to *B*, and *B* makes a charitable contribution of his remainder interest to an organization described in section 170(c), a deduction is allowed under section 170 for the present value of *B*'s remainder interest in the securities." Reg. § 1.170A-7(a)(2)(i); Rev. Rul. 79-295, 1979-2 C.B. 349 (gift tax deduction allowable). But when a bequest of corporate stock is made to charity and the income during the period of administration of the estate is paid to a private donee, a split-interest gift is made and no deduction is allowable. Rev. Rul. 83-45, 1983-1 C.B. 780. Similarly, a deduction is not allowed when the partial interest results from a division of the property that was made by the donor in order to avoid the restrictions imposed by § 170(f)(3)(A). Rev. Rul. 79-295, 1979-2 C.B. 349. Thus, no deduction is allowed when the donor transfers a remainder interest in property to a private donee and immediately thereafter transfers the reserved life estate to a qualified charity. *Id.* A deduction is allowed, however, where the donor contributes all of the interests in a property to charities. Reg. § 1.170A-7(a)(2)(ii). For example, a deduction for the full value of the property is allowed where the donor gives an income interest in property to one charity and at the same time gives the remainder to another charity.

§ 8.18. Transfers Subject to a Condition or Power

A deduction is not allowed for a gift to a charity that may be defeated by the subsequent performance of some act or the happening of some event, unless the possibility of occurrence of the act or event is so remote as to be negligible. Reg. §§ 1.170A-1(e), 1.170A-7(a)(3). Thus, a deduction is allowable for a gift of land to a qualified charity for so long as it is used for park purposes only if the possibility that the land would be used for other purposes appears on the date of the gift to be so remote as to be negligible. Reg. § 1.170A-1(e). However, because the test is essentially a factual one that may be questioned by the IRS, it is generally not desirable to give a defeasible fee interest to a charity. A gift of a defeasible fee is also undesirable because it may restrict the use of the property for generations, involve subsequent litigation, and require a substantial expenditure to trace the donor's successors. In this connection, see the discussion of *Brown v. Independent Baptist Church of Woburn*, 91 N.E.2d 922 (Mass. 1950) in W. Leach & J. Logan, Future Interests and Estate Planning 44 (1961).

In LR 9443004 (TAM), the IRS held that a charitable bequest that is subject to a possibility of reverter, which is only valid for 30 years under the local (Maryland) law, is deductible under §2055(c) if the possibility that the charity will be divested of the property is so remote as to be negligible.

A deduction is allowable for a contribution of land when mineral or timber rights are retained by the donor and exercise of the rights is unlikely or is subject to approval by the donee which is unlikely to be granted. Rev. Rul. 75-66, 1975-1 C.B. 85; Rev. Rul. 77-148, 1977-1 C.B. 63, *Nelda C. Stark*, 86 T.C. 243 (1986). But when the rights are exercisable solely by the donor, or when payments under an existing timber lease are retained by the donor, a deduction is not allowable. Rev. Rul. 76-331, 1976-2 C.B. 52. Also, no contribution deduction is allowable where voting shares are contributed if the donor retains the voting rights. Rev. Rul. 81-282, 1981-2 C.B. 78.

D. GIFTS IN TRUST

§8.19.   General Limitations

For federal income, gift and estate tax purposes, charitable deductions are generally allowed for a post-1969 gift of a remainder interest in split interest trust only if the trust is a charitable remainder annuity trust (CRAT), a charitable remainder unitrust (CRUT), or a pooled income fund. *See* §170(f)(2)(A). Note that the GSTT may apply to the noncharitable interests in any form of split interest trust. Of course, the GSTT is more likely to be a concern in the case of charitable lead trusts (CLTs), which involve noncharitable remainder beneficiaries, than in the case of other types of split interest trusts.

Charitable remainder trusts (CRTs) and pooled income funds are discussed in §§8.20-8.30. Estate and gift tax charitable deductions are allowed for a gift to a charity of the current interest in a split interest trust only if the charitable interest is in the form of a guaranteed annuity or a unitrust interest. No income tax deduction is allowed to the donor for a gift of such an income interest unless the donor is treated as the owner of the trust under the grantor trust rules. *See* §170(f)(2)(B). Otherwise, the transfer of property to a trust of which there is a charitable income beneficiary and private remainder beneficiaries does not qualify for any present charitable deduction. However, as explained in §8.33, it is possible to structure the trust so that a transfer to it does not constitute a completed gift and that deductions will be available for income and gift tax purposes for the annual income distributions to charity.

The transfer of a legal life estate to a spouse with remainder to a charity qualifies for the gift and estate tax marital deductions. §§2056(b)(7), 2523(f). On the death of the donee spouse the property is includible in his or her estate under §2044 and an offsetting charitable deduction is allowable under §2055. *See* §5.23.7.

The IRS has ruled that, where a possibility exists that federal estate or state death taxes may be paid out of the assets of a CRT, no deduction is allowable. Rev. Rul.

82-128, 1982-2 C.B. 71. This ruling requires that trust instruments be drafted to preclude liability of the trust for death taxes in order to protect the charitable deduction. The ruling could be extended to apply to pooled income funds, CLTs, and charitable remainders in personal residences and farms. However, it may not apply to a CRT where the only noncharitable beneficiary is the grantor's surviving spouse. §§ 2056(b)(8), 2523(g). Such a CRT, if it is otherwise qualified, will be considered qualified for purposes of the marital deduction. Thus, no federal estate or gift-tax would be apportioned to the income interest in the trust. However, state taxes could still cause disqualification under the ruling.

A CRT must function as such from the time of its creation. Reg. § 1.664-1(a)(4). Under that regulation, "the trust will be deemed to be created at the earliest time that neither the grantor nor any other person is treated as the owner of the entire trust under [§§ 671-678.]" In LR 9015049, the IRS held that if mortgaged property is transferred to a trust that will be responsible for making payments on the mortgage, the grantor will be treated as owner of the trust under § 677. Applying the rule of Reg. § 1.664-1(a)(4), the trust would not be a CRT. Accordingly, no deduction would be allowed for the transfer to the trust. Also, the transfer of mortgaged property to a CRT would be prohibited by the self-dealing rules unless the mortgage was placed on the property more than ten years prior to the transfer to the trust. § 4941(d)(2)(A).

In LR 9419021, the IRS recognized that a limited partnership could be the donor and the permissible noncharitable distributee of a CRUT.

No charitable deduction is allowable with respect to a split-interest trust that is not a CRAT, CRUT, pooled income fund, or CLT. However, in some instances a defect can be cured. For example, the noncharitable beneficiaries may disclaim their interests, as a result of which a charitable deduction would be allowed as only charities would be beneficiaries. See § 12.35. In other cases, the trust may be reformed to comply with the requirements that must be met by a split-interest trust. See § 8.35. Finally, in some cases the trust may be divided with the result that there is an exclusively noncharitable trust and an exclusively charitable trust. See LR 9526027 described in § 8.35. In other cases the split-interest trust cannot be divided or reformed in a way that would sustain a charitable deduction. See LR 9531003 (TAM).

Software programs are available that calculate the value of the private and charitable interests in charitable remainder and CLTs. Extensive calculations can be made by many such programs. For those who do not have access to a suitable program, most values for transfers after April 30, 1999 can be calculated by using the formulas and factors included in Actuarial Values, Book Aleph, IRS Pub. No. 1457 (1999) and Actuarial Values, Book Beth, IRS Pub. No. 1458 (1999). Some of the relevant actuarial tables appear in the regulations under §§ 664 and 2031.

§ 8.20. CHARITABLE REMAINDER TRUSTS (CRTS) IN GENERAL, § 664(d)

A trust qualifies as a CRT only if it satisfies the requirements of a CRAT, § 664(d)(1), or a CRUT, § 664(d)(2). The 1997 Act added a requirement that, effective July 29, 1997, the charitable remainder interest must have a value, determined under § 7520, that is at least 10 percent of the fair market value of all property transferred to the trust. §§ 664(d)(1)(D), (d)(2)(D). A CRT may be created inter vivos or at death. Importantly, a CRT can be created by the exercise of a power of appointment. Thus, a valid CRUT is created when the holder of a power of appointment over a private trust appoints the property of the trust to a CRUT with the noncharitable interest payable to the private trust for a term of 20 years. LR 9821029. The grantor can serve as trustee of a CRT, providing valuation of unmarketable assets is performed, as described below, by an independent trustee or based on a current qualified appraisal. Overall, it is often preferable for the charitable remainder beneficiary or an independent party to act as trustee. A grantor may, of course, serve as trustee of a CRT. *E.g.,* LR 200245058.

The requirements imposed by § 664 are designed to assure that the charitable remainder beneficiaries will receive the full benefit of the remainder interest. The requirements, which are elaborated in the regulations, severely restrict the nature and extent of the permissible noncharitable interests.

Prior to liberalizing amendments made in 1984, the IRS disqualified trusts on picayune grounds. For example, it disallowed deductions for trusts that included "in terrorem" clauses (*i.e.,* one that would terminate the interest of any beneficiary who contested the validity of the will), LR 7942073, and ones that included a provision under which payments to an individual would terminate on remarriage, Rev. Rul. 76-291, 1976-2 C.B. 284. However, such provisions are allowable under § 664(f), which was added by the 1984 Act, effective for transfers made after 1978.

Contribution of Tangible Personal Property to CRT. A deduction may be allowed for a portion of the donor's basis in tangible personal property that is contributed to a charitable remainder trust and sold by the trustee. Thus, in LR 9452026, the IRS ruled that if the trustee sold a musical instrument in a sale that had not been pre-arranged by the donor, the donor would be allowed to deduct "that portion of Taxpayer's basis which is allocable to the remainder interest in the musical instrument under section 170(e)(1)(B)(i) of the Code." The ruling also held that, provided the sale of the instrument was not pre-arranged, the sale would not result in any gain to the donor. As pointed out in the ruling, if the charitable remainder beneficiary is, or may be, a private foundation other than a foundation described in § 170(b)(1)(E), the amount of the contribution deduction is reduced by the gain that would have been long-term capital gain had the property been sold. In addition, in such a case, the amount of the charitable contribution deduction is limited to 20 percent of the donor's contribution base. § 170(b)(1)(D).

Operation of CRT Must Comply With Requirements. In *Estate of Melvine Atkinson,* 115 T.C. 26 (2000), the Tax Court held that no charitable deduction was allowable with respect to a CRAT from which no annuity payments were made to the decedent during her lifetime. The Tax Court stated that, "[b]ecause the trust value was undiminished and no transfer of funds occurred, operationally the trust did not meet the express 5-percent requirement of the statute and cannot qualify for treatment as a charitable remainder trust." The Tax Court decision was affirmed by the Eleventh Circuit, which concluded that, "It is not sufficient to establish a trust under the CRAT rules, then completely ignore the rules during the trust's administration, thereby defeating the policy interests advanced by Congress in enacting the rules themselves." *Estate of Atkinson v. Commissioner,* 309 F.3d 1290, 1296 (11th Cir. 2002). The decision illustrates the necessity of complying with all of the requirements applicable to CRTs. *See* Teitell, Imperfectly Operated CRAT Disqualified, 140 Tr. & Est. 68 (2001).

Minimum Value of Charitable Interests. Transfers in trust made after July 28, 1997 must meet a minimum remainder valuation. The requirement does not apply to preexisting trusts. For trusts established after July 28, 1997, the value of the charitable interest must be at least 10 percent of the initial fair market value of the property (or in the case of additions to a unitrust, the value must be at least 10 percent of the value of the property at the time of the addition).

Additions to an existing CRT are treated separately and will not operate to disqualify a trust that previously met all the requirements. Planners might consider including a provision in CRTs that allows the trustee to reduce the amount or duration of the payout to the noncharitable beneficiary in order to meet the minimum value requirement. Clients who propose to make additions to existing CRUTs should be alerted to the minimum value requirement.

In LR 200245058, the IRS ruled favorably regarding a wide range of issues involving a CRUT, including one concerning the application of the 10-percent rule. In particular, the ruling approved a provision which required that an addition to a trust be treated as a separate trust and that the percentage distributable to the noncharitable beneficiaries of the separate trust be reduced to the extent necessary to satisfy the 10-percent rule, but not below the required minimum of 5 percent.

Qualified Contingencies. Under § 664(f), the deductibility of the charitable interest in a trust is not jeopardized by the inclusion of a "qualified contingency." A qualified contingency is a provision under which the happening of a contingency would cause the noncharitable interest to expire no later than it would otherwise expire. § 664(f)(3). The inclusion of a qualified contingency does not increase the amount of the charitable deduction—the valuation of the charitable contribution is made without regard to the qualified contingency. § 664(f)(2). Consistent with the provisions of § 664(f), the IRS has ruled that the early termination of the life interest of the noncharitable beneficiary of a charitable remainder trust is a permissible qualified contingency. LR 9322031. Note that the qualified contingency rules apply only to trusts, they do not apply to pooled income funds.

Trust as Noncharitable Beneficiary of a CRT. A CRT may provide that distributions of the required amount be made to another trust provided that latter trust is maintained for the exclusive benefit of an incompetent individual. Rev. Rul. 76-270, 1976-2 C.B. 194; LR 9232019. Private letter rulings that approved such a dual trust arrangement for the benefit of competent beneficiaries, LRs 9619042, 9619043, and 9619044, were subsequently withdrawn by rulings that added, but not retroactively, a requirement that the individual beneficiary of the second trust be incompetent. LRs 9710008, 9710009, 9710010 (revoked by LR 9718030). The foregoing rules are traceable to the regulations under which only an individual or a charity described in § 170(c) can be the beneficiary of a CRT created for the life of an individual. Regs. § 1.664-2(a)(5); § 1.664-3(a)(5).

The IRS has ruled that a trust for the benefit of a financially disabled individual may be the beneficiary of a CRT for the life of the individual. Rev. Rul. 2002-20, 2002-1 C.B. 794. The holding states that,

> A trust may qualify as a charitable remainder unitrust under § 664 if the unitrust amounts will be paid for the life of a financially disabled individual to a separate trust that will administer those payments on behalf of that individual and, upon the individual's death, will distribute the remaining assets either to the individual's estate or, after reimbursing the state for any Medicaid benefits provided to the individual, subject to the individual's general power of appointment.

As Conrad Teitell has pointed out, under §6511(h)(2)(B), a person is not "financially disabled" during any period that a spouse or other person is authorized to act on his behalf in financial matters. Teitell, Not Your Father's CRT, 141 Tr. & Est. 13 (Dec. 2002). However, later information received by Conrad Teitell indicates that for purposes of determining whether a person is financially disabled the IRS appears willing to disregard whether another person is authorized to act for him or her. Teitell, Taxwise Giving 7 (Jan. 2003). That position is consistent with Rev. Rul. 2002-20, which only referred to §6511(h)(2)(A), under which a person who is "unable to manage his own financial affairs by reason of a medically determinable physical or mental impairment that (1) can be expected to result in death or (2) has lasted or can be expected to last for a continuous period of not less than 12 months."

Despite the rulings referred to above, the IRS recognizes that payments for a fixed term of 20 years or less can be made to any person, including a trust, corporation, or other entity. LRs 8749052 (the CRT provided that payments be made to the grantor for 20 years and, if he died during the term, to a separate trust to provide support for the education of 15 named individuals); 9340043 (approving a CRT with a 20-year term of which a subchapter S corporation was the beneficiary).

Unmarketable Assets. Effective with respect to trusts created on or after December 10, 1998, if unmarketable assets are transferred to a trust, the trust will not qualify as a CRT unless, whenever the trust is required to value the assets, the valuation is either (1) performed exclusively by an independent trustee or (2) determined by a current qualified appraisal by a qualified appraiser. Reg. §§1.664-1(a)(7)(i), 1.664-1(f)(4). Unmarketable assets are defined as assets that are not cash or cash equivalents or assets that can be readily sold or exchanged for cash or cash equivalents. Examples include, real property, closely held stock and unregistered securities for which there is no exemption allowing a public sale. An independent trustee is "a person who is not the grantor of the trust, a noncharitable beneficiary, or a related or subordinate party to the grantor, the grantor's spouse, or a noncharitable beneficiary (within the meaning of section 672(c) and the applicable regulations)." Reg. §1.664-1(a)(7)(iii). A trust created prior to December 10, 1998 that requires an independent trustee to value unmarketable assets can be amended or reformed to permit the use of an approved valuation method. Reg. §1.664-1(f)(4). "Current qualified appraisal" and "qualified appraiser" are defined in Reg. §§1.170A-13(c)(3) and 1.170A-13(c)(5), respectively.

Changes in Noncharitable Beneficial Interests. The IRS has ruled that a proposed change in the order in which the noncharitable beneficiaries will receive payments from a charitable remainder trust would disqualify the trust as a charitable remainder trust. LR 9143030. The letter ruling particularly relied upon Reg. §1.664-3(a)(4), which states, in part, that "The trust may not be subject to a power to invade, alter, amend, or revoke for the beneficial use of a person other than an organization described in section 170(c)."

As indicated by LR 9517020, a CRT may allow the grantor to retain the power to revoke or terminate the interest of any noncharitable recipient. By retaining such a power the gift of any successive interest to a noncharity is incomplete, which defers the potential application of the gift tax. (Retention of such a power might be particularly important if the donor's spouse is not a United States citizen. *See* §8.20.5.) The grantor may, of course, also reserve the right to change the charitable remainder beneficiaries of the trust.

Changes in Charitable Beneficial Interests. The grantors may retain the right to change the identity of the charitable beneficiaries and the shares in which they will participate in the remainder. LR 9504012.

Acceleration of Charitable Interests. The noncharitable beneficiary of a CRT may accelerate the time for distribution of all or a portion of the charitable remainder by transferring part or all the noncharitable interest to the remainder beneficiary. For example, in LR 8221078, the IRS approved a plan under which the noncharitable beneficiary would transfer a portion of his interest in each charitable trust to charitable remainder beneficiaries. "The proposed transfer to the charitable remainder beneficiaries, in the case of each trust, of an undivided portion of the right to the entire unitrust payments, would result in a merger of the income and remainder interest of the undivided entire portion, allowing payment of that interest to the charitable remainder beneficiaries, pursuant to the terms of the trust." The IRS ruled that a charitable deduction would be allowed to the transferor for income tax purposes in the amount of the fair market value of the property in the unitrust less the value of the remainder interest on the date of the contribution. *See also* Rev. Rul. 86-60, 1986-1 C.B. 302 (transfer to charitable remainder beneficiaries of annuity interest in CRAT); LRs 9409017; 9550026 (transfer of 20 percent of grantor's unitrust interest to a university, which was the charitable remainder beneficiary); LR 9712031 (approving accelerated distribution of part or all the assets of the unitrust to charities during the term of the trust but such distribution must be made on the last day of the taxable year of the trust, with redetermination of unitrust amount on the first day of the next taxable year) LR 200207026 (donor transferred an undivided fractional share of her unitrust interest to the charitable remainder beneficiary). In this connection, note that the regulations require that a trust provide that if an amount other than the unitrust amount is paid to a charity in the case of distributions in-kind, the adjusted basis of the property distributed must be fairly representative of the adjusted basis of the property available for distribution on the date of the payments. Reg. § 1.664-3(a)(4). A trust should provide that the payment of a unitrust or annuity trust amount to a noncharity in-kind should meet the same requirement. General Counsel Memorandum 37776 states that the requirement should apply to both types of in-kind distributions. For a general discussion of the subject, *see* Conrad Teitell's article, Gift of Donors' Life Income Interest in CRT, 137 Tr. & Est. 74 (April 1998).

The IRS has allowed limited acceleration of charitable interests in some other instances. For example, in LR 200052035 the trustees of a charitable remainder annuity trust were permitted to amend the trust to allow them to distribute excess amounts to charities selected by the trustees. The proposed amendment is summarized in the following passage from the ruling:

> The trustees of the CRAT propose to modify Trust to authorize the trustees to make distributions of principal and income from time to time during A's lifetime to any one or more Qualified Charities selected by the trustees, but only to the extent that the fair market value of the assets of the CRAT exceed × at the time of such distributions. The trustees shall make no distribution of principal or income from the CRAT to the extent that such distribution would endanger the ability of the CRAT to pay the required fixed 5 percent annuity to A for the duration of A's lifetime.

Division of CRT and Acceleration of Charitable Interest in One of the Divided Trusts. It is possible to divide a CRT into separate trusts without adverse results. In Rev. Rul. 2008-41, 2008-2 C.B. 170, for example, a CRT had two individual beneficiaries entitled to receive an equal portion of the lead amount annually for life. Upon the death of the first beneficiary, the survivor will receive the deceased recipient's lead amount for the balance of the survivor's life; when the survivor dies, the designated charities will take the remainder. A state court approved a pro rata division of the trust into separate and equal CRTs. Each asset of the original trust was to be divided equally among the separate new trusts. The lead beneficiaries would pay the costs of the trust division, including legal, court, and administrative fees. Further, each separate trust would have the same governing provisions as the original trust except that: (1) each new trust would have only one lead beneficiary; (2) each new trust would be administered and invested independently by its trustee; (3) upon the lead beneficiary's death, each asset of the new trust would be transferred to the surviving lead beneficiary's separate trust (if the trusts are annuity trusts, the annuity amount payable to the lead recipient would be increased by an equal share of the deceased recipient's annuity amount, and, if the trusts are unitrusts, the unitrust amount of the survivor's trust would likewise be increased); and (4) upon the last surviving lead beneficiary's death, the remaining assets would be distributed to the charities. On these facts, the IRS ruled that the division of the original CRT: (i) does not cause the original trust or any of the new trusts to fail to qualify as CRTs; (ii) is not a sale, exchange, or other disposition producing gain or loss and the basis of each new trust's share of each asset is the same share of the basis of that asset in the hands of the original trust just before the division (complete with a tacked holding period from the original trust); and (iii) does not constitute an act of self-dealing.

In LR 200140027, the IRS allowed the trustees of a CRUT to divide it, on a fractional basis, into two identical trusts—one consisting of 85 percent of its assets and the other consisting of 15 percent. After the division, the noncharitable beneficiary, who had reserved the right to change the charitable remainder beneficiary, would (1) irrevocably designate the charitable remainder beneficiary of the smaller CRUT, and (2) assign his interest in the smaller trust to the designated charity. Under the local law, the current and remainder interests in the trust would merge and the charity would be entitled to receive all of the assets of the trust. The IRS properly concluded that the noncharitable beneficiary's assignment of his interest would qualify for the gift and income tax charitable deductions and would not jeopardize the status of the other trust.

Grantor's Interest in CRT Reachable by Trustee in Bankruptcy. The Bankruptcy Court for the District of Minnesota has ruled that the interests of a bankrupt in a self-settled CRT are assets of the bankrupt estate. According to the court, neither federal nor Minnesota law prevent the trustee in bankruptcy from reaching the interests, including the right to appoint and remove trustees of the CRT and to amend it to preserve its tax status. *Jeffrey Charles Mack,* 89 A.F.T.R.2d (RIA) 1227 (2001).

CRTs are Tax Exempt; UBTI. Charitable remainder trusts are generally exempt from the federal income tax. However, a CRT with unrelated business taxable income for any taxable year is subject to an excise tax equal to 100 percent of the CRT's unrelated business taxable income. §664(c); Reg. §1.664-1(c). *See Leila G. Newhall Unitrust v. Commissioner,* 105 F.3d 482 (9th Cir. 1997) (income of partnership in which the CRT owned partnership units was UBTI because it resulted from activities that would have been unrelated had they been carried on directly by the trust). *See also* § 8.24.

Division of CRUT on Dissolution of Marriage. In LR 200035014 the IRS held that the division of a CRUT into two separate CRUTs made pursuant to court order upon the dissolution of the marriage of a husband and wife who were its noncharitable beneficiaries, "did not cause the Trust, the two new separate unitrusts, or the trustees to realize income or gain for federal income tax purposes under section 61(a)(3) or section 1001." The IRS also allowed a CRUT to be divided on divorce without adverse tax consequences in LR 200120016. In this ruling, the IRS stated that there would be no income tax consequences to either spouse by reason of § 1041. In addition, the division would not result in any gift tax liability because, under § 2516, it was considered to have been made for full and adequate consideration.

The ruling reaches the following generally favorable conclusions: (1) The termination is a sale by the noncharitable beneficiary's interest to the charitable remainder beneficiary. (2) The amount realized by the beneficiary is the fair market value of cash and other property he or she receives. (3) The beneficiary's basis in his or her term interest is determined in the manner specified in § 1015. Accordingly, § 1001(e) requires that the beneficiary's basis be disregarded for the purpose of determining gain or loss. (4) The sale of an income interest in a trust is the sale of a capital asset that is short- or long-term according to the date the taxpayer first held the interest. (5) A distribution to a noncharitable beneficiary upon termination of a CRUT is not subject to the characterization rules of § 664(b) that apply to distributions of the required unitrust amount. The distribution is, instead, subject to the rules of § 1001. (6) The distribution does not constitute an act of self-dealing under § 4941. The ruling was conditioned on the termination being permitted by state law, pursuant to a court order in a proceeding to which the state attorney general is a party, that the amount distributed is determined in accordance with § 7520, and that any distribution of assets in kind is made in a pro rata manner.

Distribution to Noncharitable Beneficiary on Termination of Trust. Several private letter rulings deal with the excise and income tax consequences of prematurely terminating a CRT and distributing its assets to the charitable and noncharitable beneficiaries. LRs 200727013, 200252092, 2127023, and 8948023. The rulings conclude that an early termination of a CRT and the distribution of its assets is not an act of self-dealing. They further hold that a distribution made in accordance with the actuarial values of the respective interests results in a sale of a term interest by the noncharitable beneficiary that is subject to the rules of § 1001(e). Accordingly, the entire amount received by the noncharitable beneficiary will be capital gain. LR 200727013. Private Letter Ruling 200252092 approved determining the actuarial values of the interests in a CRT according to the interest rate in effect under § 7520 on the date of termination and using the methodology described in Reg. § 1.664-4. Accordingly, the value received by the noncharitable beneficiary is all treated as gain from the disposition of a capital asset. The assumptions stated in LR 20012723 are instructive:

> The above conclusions are based on the assumptions that the proposed termination of Trust is not prohibited by state law; that the proposed termination will be made pursuant to a court order resulting from a proceeding to which the state attorney general is a party; and that the

amounts distributed to A are determined and distributed pursuant to the valuation rules set forth in section 7520. This ruling is also contingent on the fact that any distribution of assets in kind is made in a pro rata manner.

The involvement of a state's attorney general is generally required in proceedings that involve charitable trusts.

Private Letter Ruling 200127023 only deals with the income tax consequences of the termination of a CRT. Presumably such a termination of a CRT would prevent the inclusion in the noncharitable beneficiary's estate of any amount other than the property received upon termination. In this connection, note that Rev. Rul. 82-105, 1982-1 C.B. 133, held that a portion of the property held in the CRT was includible in the estate of the deceased grantor-annuitant under § 2036. "[T]he portion of the value of a charitable remainder annuity trust that is includible in D's gross estate at death is the amount necessary, at the rate of 6 percent as specified under section 20.2031-10 of the regulations, to yield the guaranteed annual payment." The position taken in Rev. Rul. 82-105 is consistent with regulations issued in 2008 that require inclusion in the gross estate of "that portion of the trust corpus necessary to provide the decedent's retained use or retained annuity, unitrust, or other payment (without reducing or invading principal)." Prop. Reg. § 20.2036-1(c)(2)(i). *See* § 9.43.5.

Transfer of Noncharitable Interest in CRUT to Charitable Remainder Beneficiary in Exchange for Annuity. Letter Ruling 200152018 deals with a generally favorable technique by which the corpus of a CRT can be made immediately available to the charitable remainder beneficiary. In that case, an educational institution that was the remainder beneficiary of a CRUT "was in need of funds to be used for the construction of an academic building." The noncharitable beneficiary ("taxpayer") was willing to transfer his interest to the remainder beneficiary in exchange for a life annuity to be paid from the charity's general funds. The ruling holds that the excess of the value of the transferred interest over the value of the annuity can be deducted by taxpayer for income and gift tax purposes—subject to the 30-percent limit. In addition, following *McAllister v. Commissioner*, 157 F.2d 235 (3d Cir. 1946), *cert. denied*, 330 U.S. 826 (1947), the ruling concludes that the unitrust interest transferred by the taxpayer is a capital asset, the sale of which would result in long-term capital gain. Accordingly, the amount of income tax charitable deduction is not reduced under § 170(e)(1). However, by reason of § 1001(e), the taxpayer has a zero basis in the unitrust interest. Accordingly, the taxpayer "will have long-term capital gain in the amount of the value of the annuity, reported as provided in example (8) of 1.1011-2(c) of the regulations."

Surviving Spouse's Elective Share Right. In most noncommunity property states the law allows a surviving spouse to elect to receive a statutory share of a deceased spouse's augmented estate. The IRS has been concerned that in some states the property of a CRT would be included in a deceased spouse's augmented estate and would be subject to a surviving spouse's right of election. ("The assets of the CRAT or CRUT may be included in the augmented estate and, therefore, may be used to determine and satisfy the elective share amount.") A trust would not qualify as a CRT if any of its property other than the required annuity or unitrust payments could be made to anyone other than a charity. Specifically, under § § 664(d)(1)(B) and (d)(2)(B) no amount other than the prescribed annuity or unitrust payments may be made from a CRT to any person other than a designated charity.

Sales of All Interests in CRTs. Some types of coordinated sales by the grantor and the charitable remainder beneficiaries of their respective interests in a CRT are "transactions of interest" that must be reported to the IRS. Reg. § 1.6011-4(b)(6); Notice 2008-99, 2008-2 C.B. 1194. The IRS is sensitive to situations where, for instance, the trustee sells appreciated property contributed by the grantor to diversify the trust's investments, and then the grantor and the charity with the remainder interest sell their respective interests to a third party for an amount equal to the value of the assets the trustee just purchased. Apparently, some grantors claim a deduction for the value of the remainder interest (itself a fraction of the value of the original property contributed) while simultaneously computing the gain from the sale by taking into account the portion of uniform basis allocable to the grantor's term interest, said uniform basis to be computed from the basis of the new assets purchased by the trustee (i.e., the fair market value) and not the basis of the contributed property. All of this means the gain on the sale of the contributed property is never taxed. The IRS considers this strategy to be "the manipulation of the uniform basis rules to avoid tax on gain from the sale or other disposition of appreciated assets." Accordingly, reporting is required for transactions like this entered into on or after October 31, 2008.

Safe Harbor; Waivers. Rev. Proc. 2005-24, 2005-1 C.B. 909, creates a safe harbor under which the existence of a surviving spouse's right of election will be disregarded if the surviving spouse irrevocably waives "the right of election with regard to the assets of the CRAT or CRUT to ensure that no part of the trust will be used to satisfy the elective share." No waiver is required if the governing law does not give the surviving spouse a right of election with respect to the assets of the CRT.

A CRT created before June 28, 2005 with respect to which the surviving spouse has a right of election will not be treated as a CRT if the surviving spouse (1) does not waive the right of election and (2) exercises the right of election. As pointed out in the Revenue Procedure, a waiver of the surviving spouse's right of election will "provide certainty that the right of election will not cause the trust to fail to qualify under § 664(d) continuously since its creation."

A trust created on or after June 28, 2005 with respect to which a surviving spouse would have a right of election will not qualify as a CRT unless the required waiver is made on or before the date that is six months after the due date (excluding extensions) of Form 5227, *Split-Interest Information Return*, for the year in which (1) the trust is created, (2) the trustor's marriage takes place, (3) the trustor becomes a resident of, or domiciled in, a state that provides a right of election that could be exercised with respect to the assets of the trust or, (4) a state law creating a right of election becomes effective.

§ 8.20.1. Double Deductions

A client who is charitably inclined may be influenced to make an inter vivos gift to a CRT because it produces multiple charitable deductions—for income *and* gift tax purposes. In contrast, a testamentary gift to a qualified charity supports only an estate tax charitable deduction. While the income tax deduction that is allowed for the value of the remainder interest may be only 10 percent, it is an important consideration for some taxpayers. An inter vivos gift may also be more satisfying to the donor because of the recognition that can result and knowing that it may also encourage gifts by others. In addition, as indicated in § 8.20.2, a CRT may appeal to some taxpayers because the trustee can sell appreciated assets and diversity investments without incurring any capital gains tax.

Note also that a testamentary gift to a surviving spouse can produce multiple tax benefits. Notably, greater tax benefits than a bequest directly to a charity. First, the marital deduction insulates the property given to a spouse from the estate tax. Second, a subsequent gift to charity by the surviving spouse qualifies for both income and gift tax returns.

§ 8.20.2. Diversification of Investments

Charitable remainder trusts are exempt from the federal income tax, which allows the trustee to sell appreciated property without incurring any tax liability. Accordingly, CRTs are frequently used as a vehicle to diversify the grantor's investments and increase the grantor's current cash flow: The taxpayer gets a current income tax deduction *and* the trustee sells appreciated assets and invests the proceeds in higher yielding forms of investment. Thus, a taxpayer who holds highly appreciated assets that generate a low rate of return may transfer them to a CRT. Indeed, the tax-free status of CRTs leads some taxpayers to transfer property to trusts that are designed to produce the maximum allowable benefit to the taxpayer and gives a minimum 10 percent interest to charity. Under this approach, the trustee, who might be the grantor, sells the appreciated assets and invests the entire proceeds in assets that provide the liquidity and security to support the required distributions to the grantor.

§ 8.20.3. Wealth Replacement Plans

A grantor may use part of the increased cash flow from a CRT to "replace" the value of the principal that will pass to charity on the death of the grantor instead of being distributed to individual beneficiaries. The grantor may, for example, contribute part of the cash flow to an irrevocable trust to be invested in growth assets or used to make premium payments on life insurance on the grantor's life. Under a simple alternative, the grantor makes annual gifts of a portion of his or her current income to his or her children. The children, in turn, use the funds to buy policies in insurance on the donor's life. In either case, the plan is designed to allow the insurance proceeds or other property to pass to the beneficiaries tax free (*i.e.*, the proceeds or other property is not included in the grantor's estate).

§ 8.20.4. Substitute for Tax-Exempt Retirement Plan

A CRT can be used as a substitute for, or a supplement to, a retirement plan. In the simplest case a client transfers highly appreciated property to a CRT, reserving substantial payments for life, or for the lives of the client and his or her spouse. Clements, Maximizing Capital Asset Returns Through Charitable Remainder Trusts, 3 J. Tax. Est. & Tr. 18 (1991). The plan may be economically attractive because of three factors: the gain on the trust's sale of the appreciated property is not taxed and the value of the charitable remainder will generate some income tax savings.

Under another approach, a client makes gifts to a CRUT over time, the gains of which will accumulate free of tax. A unitrust is used because additional contributions cannot be made to a CRAT. The unitrust would be a NIMCRUT (*i.e.*, a "net-income-with-makeup" unitrust—that provides for the annual distribution of the lesser of the actual income or a specified percentage of the value of the assets. Reg. §1.664-3(a)(1)(b)). If current income is less than the specified percentage, the trust would require the deficiency to be made up during periods when the current income exceeds the specified unitrust percentage. The growth in value of such a trust is sheltered from taxation until distributions are made to the grantor or other noncharitable beneficiary. Thus, a donor might contribute highly appreciated property to a NIMCRUT that would later be sold and reinvested in assets that produced substantial income—to support makeup distributions. The transfer to the trust would, of course, have to satisfy the 10 percent charitable remainder requirement. The key is for the trustee to reinvest in assets that produce little, if any, income until after the donor retires and has a greater need for income. In the interim, the value of the trust assets would continue to increase, reflecting an investment strategy that was designed to defer the receipt of income and maximize growth. Greater income would be generated after the donor's retirement, as the trustee receives the delayed income on zero coupon bonds and other carefully selected investment. At that point, the trustee would change the investments of the trust in order to generate more current income to support current and make-up distributions to the grantor.

§8.20.5. Marital Deductions

The gift and estate tax marital deductions are generally available where the grantor's spouse is the only noncharitable beneficiary of a CRT. §§2056(b)(8), 2523(g). The marital deduction is not available if the grantor's spouse is not a current beneficiary, or is not a United States citizen. §2523(i). However, an annual exclusion of $100,000 indexed by the Taxpayer Relief Act of 1997 is allowed for gifts to noncitizen spouses. In either case, the grantor can avoid the imposition of a gift tax by reserving the right by will to terminate the noncharitable interest of his or her spouse. *See* §8.21. If the trust is properly planned, an estate tax marital deduction will be available to the grantor's estate if the grantor dies survived by a spouse and without having revoked the surviving spouse's successive noncharitable interest. Of course, if the surviving spouse is not a United States citizen, the trust must meet the requirements of a qualified domestic trust under §2056A. *See* §5.25. The estate tax imposed by §2056A does not apply to distributions of income, such as distributions from an income-only unitrust. However, an annual exclusion of $100,000 indexed by the Taxpayer Relief Act of 1997 is allowed for gifts to noncitizen spouses.

The analysis described in the preceding paragraph was applied in LR 9244013. In that ruling the taxpayer proposed to create a charitable remainder unitrust of which the unitrust amount would be payable to himself for life, then to his wife, a non-United States citizen, if she survived him. The grantor proposed to retain the right to change the charitable remainder beneficiaries of the trust and to revoke his spouse's right to receive the unitrust amount if she survived him. The IRS ruled that the trust met the requirements of a charitable remainder unitrust, that the gift to the surviving spouse was incomplete because of the grantor's retained right of revocation, that upon the grantor's death a marital deduction would be allowable under §§2056(b)(8) and 2056A if his spouse survived him, and that in computing the additional estate tax under §2056A upon the death of the surviving spouse a charitable deduction would be allowable under §2055.

§8.20.6. Employer's Stock Distributed by Qualified Plan Contributed to CRT

The creation of a CRT may also be attractive to an employee who receives shares of stock in a corporate employer at retirement. The overall tax results are relatively attractive if the shares are contributed to a CRT instead of rolling them over to an IRA. First, the employee is only required to include the cost basis of the shares in his income. The net unrealized appreciation in the stock will not be taxed to the retiree or the CRT. Second, under §170 the charitable contribution deduction will be computed on the basis of the fair market value of the stock at the time of its contribution to the extent the gain would have been long-term gain (which is the entire gain to the date the stock is distributed). Third, no tax will be due when the stock is sold by the CRT. Fourth, the gain on the sale by the CRT will be long-term capital gain, which will be taken into account under §664 in characterizing the nature of distributions from the CRT. Finally, if the remainder beneficiary is a private foundation, the amount of the charitable deduction is not reduced if the stock is qualified appreciated stock, §170(e)(5). *See* §8.10.

In two letter rulings, the IRS has approved plans that follow the scenario described above. That is, they involved a retiring employee contributing to a CRT some of the shares of stock in his former employer that were distributed to him upon termination of his employment. LRs 200038050, 199919039. Upon distribution the distributee is only taxed on the cost basis of the shares—which is often a small fraction of the value of the shares. Under §402(e)(4)(B) the net unrealized appreciation (NUA) in shares of an employer corporation that are distributed to an employee is excluded from the employee's gross income. For this purpose the NUA is the difference between the cost basis of the stock and its fair market value at the time of distribution. Thus, if a qualified plan had paid $25,000 for shares of stock in the employer corporation that were worth $250,000 at the time of distribution, the NUA would be $225,000 ($250,000–$25,000). Any taxable gain realized from the subsequent disposition of the stock is treated as long-term capital gain. After the stock is contributed to a CRT the gain will not be subject to tax, but it will affect the character of the distributions made from the CRT as provided in §664.

§8.21. CHARITABLE REMAINDER ANNUITY TRUST (CRAT)

Charitable remainder trusts must make specified annual distributions to one or more beneficiaries, of whom at least one is a noncharity. However, the grantor may retain a power exercisable only by will to revoke or terminate the interest of any noncharitable beneficiary. Reg. §1.664-2(a)(4). The retention of such a power can be used to prevent the transfer of property to a CRAT from involving a gift to the holder of a successor noncharitable interest. Although a charity must have an irrevocable remainder interest in the trust, the grantor may reserve the right to change the charitable remainder beneficiary. The amount of the annual distributions to noncharitable beneficiaries is strictly limited by the Code and the regulations. A CRAT must provide for an annual payout of a fixed sum that must be at least 5 percent, and not more than 50 percent, of the initial net fair market value of the trust property. § 664(d)(1)(A). The amount may be expressed either as a specified dollar amount or as a percentage or fraction of the initial fair market value of the trust assets. In the latter case the trust must provide for appropriate adjustments to be made if the initial value of the trust is incorrectly determined. Reg. § 1.664-2(a)(1)(iii). Because the amount of the payments is fixed at the outset, the payout may not vary from year to year and no additional property may be transferred to the trust.

In the case of a CRAT, the specified amount must be paid, not less often than annually, to one or more beneficiaries at least one of whom is not a charitable organization. Only an individual or a charitable organization may receive distributions for the life of an individual (*i.e.*, payments may not be made to noncharitable organizations). In any case, the period of the payments cannot extend beyond either the life or lives of named individuals who are living at the time of creation of the trust or a term of years not to exceed 20 years. § 664(d)(1)(A); Reg. § 1.664-2(a)(5)(i). Specifically, the period for which the amount must be paid "begins with the first year of the CRT and continues either for the life or lives of a named individual or individuals or for a term of years not to exceed 20 years." Reg. § 1.664-2(a)(5). No amounts other than the required distribution may be paid to or for the use of any person other than the charitable remainder beneficiary. Thus, a trust may not allow invasions of principal to meet emergency needs of the individual beneficiaries. This limitation deters many prospective donors from establishing a CRAT.

Regulation § 1.664-2(a)(5)(ii) indicates that the following are appropriate periods for payments to be made under a CRAT:

1. To *A* and *B* for their joint lives and then to the survivor for life;

2. To *A* for life or for a term of years not longer than 20 years, whichever is longer (or shorter);

3. To *A* for a term of years not longer than 20 years and then to *B* for life (provided *B* was living at the time the trust was created);

4. An amount to *A* for life and concurrently an amount to *B* for life (with amount distributable to each to terminate at death), provided that the amount paid to each is at least 5 percent of the initial fair market value of the property of the trust; or

5. An amount to *A* for life and concurrently an amount to *B* for life, and at the death of the first to die, the trust to distribute one-half of the then value of its assets to a charitable organization, if the total of the amounts given to *A* and *B* is not less than 5 percent of the initial fair market value of the property of the trust.

As noted later in this section, no charitable deduction is allowed if the distributions to the noncharitable beneficiary of a CRAT are so large that there is a greater than 5 percent, and not more than 50 percent, probability that they will entirely exhaust the assets of the trust, leaving nothing for the charitable remainder beneficiary. § 664(d)(2)(A). *See* Rev. Rul. 77-374, 1977-2 C.B. 329.

EXAMPLE 8-14.

D transferred securities worth $200,000 to a trust from which *D* is entitled to an annual payment of $10,000 for life. The trust provides for the minimum 5% annual annuity payment required by § 664(d)(1). So long as the value of the charitable remainder had a value of 10% or more of the original transfer, the trust could have called for a larger annual payment to *D*, but not a smaller one.

The charitable interest for a CRAT created after April 30, 1999 is valued according to the actuarial tables printed in Actuarial Values, Book Aleph, IRS Pub. No. 1457 (1999). Publication 1457 is available from the Superintendent of Documents at the address shown in § 8.15 and online at *<www.irs.gov>*.

§ 8.22.   CHARITABLE REMAINDER UNITRUST (CRUT)

In general, a CRUT must satisfy requirements similar to the ones that apply to a CRAT, except it must provide for a different type of payout. In particular, it must require a payout each year to the noncharitable beneficiaries of a fixed percentage of at least 5 percent, and not more than 50 percent, of the annually determined net fair market value of its assets. § 664(d)(2)(A). Thus, the amount of the annual payment made from a unitrust will vary from year to year according to the value of the trust corpus. Unlike a CRAT, property may be added to a CRUT if the trust instrument contains provisions that require appropriate adjustments in the amount of the payout. *See* Reg. § 1.664-3(b).

NICRUTs and NIMCRUTs. An exception made by § 664(d)(3) recognizes a type of unitrust that provides for distributions based upon the net income of the trust. To qualify under this exception, the unitrust may be either: (1) an "income-only" unitrust, which provides for payment to the noncharitable beneficiary of only the net income of the trust in the years that it does not exceed a specified unitrust percentage of at least 5 percent (NICRUT), or, (2) an "income-with-make-up" unitrust, which provides for payment to the noncharitable beneficiary of only the income in years it does not exceed a specified percentage and such amount *plus* a make-up payment out of the net income for the current year above the unitrust percentage, to the extent that the payments for prior years were less than the specified unitrust amount for those years (NIMCRUT).

A NIMCRUT may be particularly attractive to a person who does not currently need additional income and would like the corpus of the trust to continue to grow on a tax-free basis. The donor's goals would be furthered by investments that generate little, if any, income in the early years—later shifting to assets that produce more income (or capital gains that are treated as income by the trustee, as explained below).

EXAMPLE 8-15.

A NIMCRUT provided for distribution of the net income of the trust to the extent it did not exceed 5% of the value of the trust and so much of the net income for the current year in excess of 5% as may be required to make up for the deficiencies in distributions for prior years. The net income of the trust for the first year was $4,000 and the unitrust amount was $5,000. Accordingly, the trustee was required to distribute $4,000. The income of the trust for the second year was $6,000 and, the principal having the same value, the unitrust amount was $5,000. For the second year the trustee was required to distribute the full $6,000 in order to make up for the $1,000 deficiency in the first year.

Capital Gain on Property Contributed to NIMCRUT. Effective for sales or exchanges made after April 18, 1997, Reg. § 1.664-3(b)(4) requires that proceeds from the sale or exchange of assets contributed by the donor "must be allocated to principal and not to trust income at least to the extent of the fair market value of those assets on the date of contribution."

Crackdown on Abusive NIMCRUTs. In 1998, the regulations under § 2702 were amended to prevent the use of NIMCRUTs to shift distributions from the grantor to a successor noncharitable beneficiary. As Treasury explained when issuing the regulations in proposed form, Reg. 209823-96:

> For example, a donor establishes a NIMCRUT to pay the lesser of trust income or a fixed percentage to the donor for a term of 15 years or his life, whichever is shorter, and then to the donor's daughter for life. If the tables under section 7520 are used to value the donor's retained interest and the donor's gift to the daughter, the amount of the donor's gift to the daughter is relatively small compared to the amount the daughter may actually receive. To illustrate, the trustee may invest in assets that produce little or no income while the donor retains the unitrust interest, creating a substantial makeup amount. At the end of the donor's interest, the trustee alters the NIMCRUT's investments to generate significant amounts of trust income. The trustee then uses the income to pay to the donor's daughter the current fixed percentage amount and the makeup amount, which includes the makeup amount accumulated while the donor was the unitrust recipient.

To prevent taxpayers from taking advantage of this opportunity, Reg. § 25.2702-1(c)(3) was amended to provide that the special valuation rules of § 2702 apply to the valuation of interests in NIMCRUTs unless the "either there are only two consecutive noncharitable beneficial interests and the transferor holds the second of the two interests, or the only permissible recipients of the unitrust amount are the transferor, the transferor's United States citizen spouse, or both the transferor and the transferor's U.S. citizen spouse."

Fixing the Unitrust Percentage. Setting the percentage at an amount below the anticipated income of the unitrust may result in greater overall distributions to the private beneficiaries. For example, assuming a 10-percent rate of return, the distributions from a 10-percent unitrust would remain the same. In contrast, because of the effect of compounding, distributions from an 8-percent unitrust would exceed the distributions from the 10-percent unitrust beginning in the 13th year. Over an extended period the total distributions from the 8-percent unitrust would be much larger than distributions from the 10-percent unitrust. The differences would naturally be even greater in the case of unitrusts with even lower distribution rates. Note, too, that the charitable remainder will be worth more if the unitrust payment is lower than the annual rate of return.

An income-based unitrust may be appropriate where the current beneficiary will not need a stable flow of funds for support and the property contributed to the trust may generate little, or no, income in some years, particularly the early ones. It has been used by some planners, for example, in connection with gifts of appreciated real property that generate little, if any, current income. As indicated above, it may also be appropriate to delay distributions of income where the unitrust is part of the donor's retirement plan. The trustee could select growth-oriented investments during the donor's working years, and higher yielding investments after retirement. This would allow for larger make-up payments during the early retirement years.

Actuarial tables for valuing CRUTs are printed in Actuarial Values, Beta Volume, IRS Pub. No. 1458 (1999) at the address shown in § 8.15 and online at *<www.irs.gov>*.

§ 8.22.1. Treating Capital Gain as Income of NIMCRUTs

In LR 9442017, the IRS approved a NIMCRUT that included a provision under which the trustee could "make a reasonable allocation of capital gains to income, rather than corpus, upon the sale of assets." The issue arose under Nebraska law, which allows a grantor to "make provision in the creating instrument for the manner of ascertainment of income and principal." The approach is attractive because it allows the trustee to pursue investment policies that maximize overall appreciation while allowing a reasonable portion of capital gains to be treated as income. Additionally, the tax imposed on capital gains that are distributed to a beneficiary is usually substantially lower than the income tax that would be imposed on distributions of ordinary income.

In LR 9511007, the IRS approved a net income with makeup, 10 percent unitrust that provided that the trustee allocate all capital gains to income. In determining the required payment the trustee was directed to take into account the amount of the cumulative income shortfall that the trustee might be required to make up in future years. The ruling observed that it was necessary to include the latter provision in order to prevent the trustee from manipulating the trust to the detriment of the charitable remainder beneficiaries. According to this ruling, in determining the fair market value of the assets on the annual valuation date, the governing instrument must require the trustee to treat as a liability the amount of any deficiency for prior years computed under section 664(d)(3)(B). The amount treated as a liability need not exceed the trust's unrealized appreciation that would be trust income under the terms of the governing instrument and applicable local law if the trustee sold all the assets in the trust on the valuation date. This trust provision will ensure that the timing of the realization of the gain by the trustee cannot be manipulated to the detriment of the charitable remainder interest. Note that the requirement was not included in the regulations later adopted by the IRS.

In LR 9609009, the IRS recognized a similar type of NIMCRUT as a valid CRT. The same result was reached in LR 9711013 ("[B]ecause the Trust provision allocating certain post-contribution gains to Trust income is coupled with a provision treating a specific amount of any unitrust deficiency as a liability in valuing the trust's assets, these provisions comply with the requirements of a charitable remainder unitrust described in sections 664(d)(2) and (d)(3) of the regulations thereunder.").

Several rulings approve NIMCRUTs that grant the trustee a power, consistent with state law, to allocate a reasonable portion of the post-contribution capital gains to income. *E.g.,* LR 199907013. An earlier ruling recognized the addition of such a power pursuant to court order where the power was inadvertently omitted by reason of a scrivener's error. LR 9833008.

As noted below, 1.664-3(a)(1)(i)(b)(4) requires that proceeds from the sale or exchange of any assets contributed to the trust by the donor must be allocated to principal and not to trust income, at least to the extent of the fair market value of those assets on the date of contribution.

Regulations under § 643(b) permit income to be determined by state law. The regulations recognize state laws that allow the use of private unitrusts and that permit adjustments by trustees to treat a portion of capital gains as income. The final form of the regulations under § 643(b) is summarized at § 10.4.3.

§ 8.22.2. Flip NIMCRUTs

A unitrust can be designed to provide initially for the pay out of a specified percentage, limited to its net income, but switch at a later point to a percentage payout that is not limited to its net income. The approach is useful if the trust is initially funded with illiquid assets that do not produce a significant amount of income. Out of a concern that such an approach could be used abusively the regulations were amended to provide that the switch can be made only in certain circumstances. Reg. §§ 1.664-3(c)-1.664-3(d). Under subsection (c), the switch can be triggered on a specific date or by a single event, "whose occurrence is not discretionary with, or within the control of, the trustee or any other persons" or at the beginning of the taxable year next following such a specific event. Subsection (d) provides that the sale of unmarketable assets, or the "marriage, divorce, death, or birth of a child with respect to any individual will not be considered discretionary with, or within the control of, the trustee or any other person."

§ 8.22.3. Short-Term High-Payout CRUTs

Notice 94-78, 1994-2 C.B. 555, attempts to prevent avoidance of taxes through the transfer of highly appreciated assets to a short term unitrust with a high payout rate. In pertinent part the notice reads as follows:

> The Internal Revenue Service is aware of proposed transactions that attempt to use a § 664 charitable remainder unitrust to convert appreciated assets into cash while avoiding a substantial portion of the tax on the gain.

> In these transactions, appreciated assets are transferred to a short-term charitable remainder unitrust that has a high percentage unitrust amount. For example, assume that capital assets with a value of $1 million and a zero basis are contributed to the trust on January 1. Assume further that the assets pay no income and that the term of the trust is two years. The

unitrust amount is set at 80 percent of the fair market value of the trust assets valued annually.

The unitrust amount required to be paid for the first year is $800,000, but during the first year no actual distributions are made from the trust to the donor as the recipient of the unitrust amount. At the beginning of the second year, all the assets are sold for $1 million, and the unitrust amount for the first year is distributed to the donor between January 1 and April 15 of the second year. The unitrust amount for the second year is $160,000 (80 percent times the $200,000 net fair market value of the trust assets). At the end of the second year the trust terminates, and $40,000 is paid to the charitable organization.

Proponents of this transaction contend that the tax treatment of this example would be as follows. Because no assets are actually sold or distributed to the donor during the first year, the entire $800,000 unitrust amount is characterized as a distribution of trust corpus under § 664(b)(4) of the Internal Revenue Code. The $160,000 unitrust amount for the second year is characterized as capital gain, on which the donor pays tax of $44,800 ($160,000 times the 28 percent tax rate for capital gains). The donor is left with net cash of $915,200 ($800,000 from the first year and $115,200 net from the second year). If the donor had sold the assets directly, the donor would have paid tax of $280,000 on the $1 million capital gain, and would have net cash of only $720,000.

Depending on the particular facts of each case the Service will challenge transactions of this type based on one or more legal doctrines. A mechanical and literal application of the regulations that would yield a result inconsistent with the purposes of the charitable remainder trust provisions may not be respected. The tax consequences to the donor vary with the legal doctrine that is applied.

Notice 94-78 continued to say that the Service may not respect the form of the transaction, that gain on the sale by the trustee may constitute gross income to the donor and not to the trust, that the qualification of the trust as a charitable remainder trust may be challenged and that the Service may apply appropriate legal doctrines to recast the entire transaction for tax purposes. In addition, the Service may seek to impose the tax on self-dealing under § 4941 and may seek to impose penalties on the participants.

Final regulations, effective for taxable years ending after April 18, 1997 impose requirements that are designed to bar the abusive use of short term CRTs of all types. Reg. §§ 1.664-2(a)(1)(i), 1.664-3(g)-(l). The regulations permit payment of the annuity amount to be made within a reasonable time after the close of the taxable year with respect to most CRUTs. The explanation of the regulations state that,

> [F]or CRATs and fixed percentage CRUTs, the annuity or unitrust amount may be paid within a reasonable time after the close of the year for which it is due if (a) the character of the annuity or unitrust amount in the recipient's hands is income under section 664(b)(1), (2), or (3); and/or (b) the trust distributes property (other than cash) that it owned as of the close of the taxable year to pay the annuity or unitrust amount and the

trustee elects of Form 5227, "Split-Interest Trust Information Return," to treat any income generated by the distribution as occurring on the last day of the taxable year for which the amount is due. In addition, for CRATs and fixed percentage CRUTs that were created before December 10, 1998, the annuity or unitrust amount may be paid within a reasonable time after the close of the taxable year for which it is due if the percentage used to calculate the annuity or unitrust amount is 15 percent or less.

§8.23. SAMPLE DECLARATIONS OF TRUST

In 2003, the IRS published a new set of sample inter vivos and testamentary CRAT forms. Rev. Procs. 2003-53 through 2003-60, 2003-2 C.B. 230-274. The forms are reviewed by Conrad Teitell in, An IRS Assist on CRATs, Tr. & Est. 74 (Oct. 2003). In the article, Teitell emphasizes the necessity of reading the "fine print":

> But don't just look at the specimens; also be careful to examine the footnotes (the annotations and alternative provisions)—they provide invaluable assistance in customizing a CRAT. Someone once said that a footnote is equivalent to going downstairs on one's wedding night to answer the doorbell. When it comes to the footnotes to the IRS specimens, you ignore the doorbell at your peril, because some of the alternative clauses should be in the vast majority of CRATs.

Treasury has also issued new sample CRUT forms. Each of the eight new sample forms meets the requirements of a valid CRUT, and the IRS has announced that trust instruments that are "substantially similar" to the samples will be recognized as a valid CRUT. The first form is an inter vivos CRUT for one measuring life, Rev. Proc. 2005-52, 2005-2 C.B. 326. The second form is an inter vivos CRUT for a term of years, Rev. Proc. 2005-53, 2005-2 C.B. 339. The third form is an inter vivos CRUT with consecutive lead interests for two measuring lives, Rev. Proc. 2005-54, 2005-2 C.B. 353. The fourth form is an inter vivos CRUT using concurrent and consecutive lead interests for two measuring lives, Rev. Proc. 2005-55, 2005-2 C.B. 367. The fifth form is a testamentary CRUT for one measuring life, Rev. Proc. 2005-56, 2005-2 C.B. 383. The sixth form is a testamentary CRUT for a term of years, Rev. Proc. 2005-57, 2005-2 C.B. 392. The seventh form is a testamentary CRUT with consecutive lead interests for two measuring lives, Rev. Proc. 2005-58, 2005-2 C.B. 402. The eighth form is a testamentary CRUT using concurrent and consecutive lead interests for two measuring lives, Rev. Proc. 2005-59, 2005-2 C.B. 412. Each form includes a number of annotations and alternative provisions that can be used to customize the form to a client's specific situation.

A trust that omits any of the provisions or includes additional substantive provisions is not assured of qualification under the Revenue Procedures. However, the IRS has pointed out that sample declarations "are not intended to preclude other permissible provisions in the governing instrument." LR 9436035 (in the context of older sample CRT forms issued from 1988-1990). Because of the complexity of the requirements and the potential that the IRS will take hypertechnical positions as it has in the past, CRTs that deviate from the sample forms should be drafted very carefully—preferably with the participation of an expert.

The sample forms should not be taken as complete and sufficient in all respects. For example, the use of the specimen forms will involve a gift to the holder of a successive noncharitable interest. The completion of a gift can be avoided, however, by making the successive interest subject to termination by provision in the grantor's will.

As Conrad Teitell has suggested, every charitable trust should include a provision authorizing the trustee to amend the trust for the purpose of complying with the relevant provisions of the Code and Regulations. Teitell, Philanthropy & Estate Planning Column, 128 Tr. & Est. 56 (1989). In particular, he recommends the use of the following type of form:

> The trustee shall have the power, acting alone to amend the trust for the sole purpose of complying with the requirements of the code [insert section] and regulations [insert section] governing [insert type of split interest trust]. *Id.* at 57.

§8.24.   INCOME TAXATION OF CRTs

The income taxation of CRTs and their beneficiaries is governed by §664. To begin with, the trusts themselves are ordinarily exempt from taxation. §664(c)(1). Note, however, that CLTs are not tax exempt. Amounts distributed by a CRT to the beneficiaries are characterized as ordinary income to the extent of the trust's ordinary income for the current year plus any undistributed ordinary income for prior years. §664(b)(1). Next, the distributions are considered to be composed of capital gain to the extent the trust has capital gain for the year and undistributed gain for prior years. §664(b)(2). Finally, distributions are constituted of other income (*e.g.*, tax-exempt income) to the extent the trust has any for the current year and undistributed other income for prior years. §664(b)(3). Any remaining amount of a current distribution is considered to be composed of principal. §664(b)(4). Note that a trust with acquisition indebtedness, which may arise if mortgaged property is transferred to a CRT, loses its tax exemption. §514(c)(2)(A).

Under regulations finalized in 2005, capital gains of CRTs that were received before January 1, 2003, but were not distributed before 2003 will be treated as subject to the new maximum capital gains tax rate of 15 percent. Similarly, capital gains from sales made before the effective date of the new rates, May 6, 2003, will be subject to the new maximum rate if they are not distributed in 2003. Gains from sales made on or after May 6, 2003, are subject to the new rates. Reg. §1.664-1(d)(1)(vi). *See* Teitell, Last-Minute Gift from the Feds, 143 Tr. & Est. 64 (Apr. 2004), and Fox, New Prop. Regs. on Distributions from CRTs Provide Opportunity, 31 Est. Plan. 172 (Apr. 2004).

Appreciated corporate stock that the parties anticipate may be redeemed by the corporation may be transferred to a charitable remainder trust without causing the grantor to be taxed on the gain. LR 9452020. *See also* §8.38.

The grantors of a charitable remainder trust are not treated as the owners of the trust for income tax purposes merely because they retained the right to "change the identity of the charitable organizations that will receive the remainder and to change the proportion of the remainder that will pass to any particular charitable organization." LR 9504012.

If there is depreciable property in the trust, depreciation deductions are allowed. The deductions are normally apportioned between the trustee and the beneficiaries on the basis of the trust income allocable to each. However, if the trust instrument provides otherwise, they may be allocated in another manner. LRs 8610067; 8535048.

The transfer of property to a CRT does not usually involve the realization of any gain or loss. Accordingly, a donor may increase the current yield generated by assets or achieve a degree of tax-free diversification by transferring appreciated assets to a CRT that sells them and invests the proceeds in other assets.

Trust distributions to the noncharitable beneficiaries must be limited to the specified annuity or unitrust amounts. §§ 664(d)(1)(B), (2)(B). Thus, a trust will not qualify as a CRT if it permits any other use or application of trust assets for the benefit of noncharities. The inability to distribute additional amounts in case of accident, illness, or other emergency is a major drawback that deters some individuals from establishing CRTs.

Under Reg. § 1.664-1(a)(3), a CRT cannot "include a provision which restricts the trustee from investing the trust assets in a manner which would result in the annual realization of a reasonable amount of income or gain from the sale or disposition of trust assets." Accordingly, a trust generally should not direct the trustee to retain any particular asset or assets or impose any limits on the trustee's power to sell or dispose of trust assets.

Charitable remainder trusts may invest in tax-exempt securities, but pooled income funds may not. *See* § 8.30. However, if there were an understanding or agreement that the trustee would sell the property transferred to a CRT and invest in tax-exempt securities, the donor might be taxed on the gain. *See* Rev. Rul. 60-370, 1960-2 C.B. 203, dealing with the so-called Pomona College Plan.

A CRT that has unrelated business taxable income for any taxable year must pay an excise tax equal to 100 percent of its unrelated business taxable income. § 664(c)(2). Under § 513(a) the term "unrelated trade or business" is defined as "any trade or business the conduct of which is not substantially related (aside from the need of such organization for funds or the use it makes of the profits derived) to the exercise or performance by such organization of its charitable, educational, or other purpose or purpose constituting the basis of its exemption. . . ." Passive income, such as dividends, rents, and royalties are generally exempt from the tax. § 512(b). Accordingly, a CRT faces liability for the 100 percent excise tax for any year in which it regularly engages in a trade or business that is unrelated to the activities that otherwise justified its exemption. For example, if a farm is transferred to a CRT, presumably the trustee could lease the farm to a tenant without becoming subject to the tax. On the other hand, if the farm were operated by the trustee, and farming was not related to the exempt purpose of the beneficiary of the charitable remainder, presumably the income from the activity would be subject to the excise tax. In *Leila G. Newhall Unitrust*, 104 T.C. 236 (1995), *aff'd*, 105 F.3d 482 (9th Cir. 1997), the courts held that the trust had unrelated business taxable income from interests in partnerships acquired prior to the amendment of § 512(c), as a result of which the trust's entire income was subject to taxation. *See* § 8.20.

§8.25. Valuing Charitable Remainders

For the decade between May 1, 1989 and May 1, 1999, the fair market value of a remainder interest in a CRAT following one life, two lives, or a term of years was determined under the unisex actuarial tables printed in Actuarial Values, Alpha Volume, IRS Pub. No. 1457 (1989). Now it is determined under revised tables, printed in the 1999 Book Aleph. The valuation is based upon 120 percent of the Federal Midterm rate that was in effect during the month the gift was made or either of the preceding two months. *See* §7520. Between December 1, 1983 and May 1, 1989, the determinations were made according to the unisex 10 percent tables of Reg. §20.2031-7. Earlier transfers were valued according to gender-based actuarial tables based on a 6 percent return. Reg. §20.2031-10. These tables were held to be constitutional in *Manufacturers Hanover Trust Co. v. United States*, 775 F.2d 459 (2d Cir. 1985), *cert. denied*, 475 U.S. 1095 (1986).

EXAMPLE 8-16.

On her fiftieth birthday, *D* contributed $200,000 to a CRAT that provides that an annual payment of $10,000 be made to *D*. (If the payments were made more frequently the payout rate would be adjusted by a factor from Table K of Aleph. Volume.) Under §7520(a), *D* could choose to value the gift according to the interest rate for the month during which the gift was made or for either of the 2 preceding months. *D* chose to value the gift based upon a 9% rate. The factor for the value of an annuity for a person aged 50 is 9.56 computed under Table S of the Aleph Volume. Thus, the charitable gift is $104,400 ($200,000 – ($10,000 × 9.56)).

For the period May 1, 1989 to May 1, 1999, the value of the remainder interest in a CRUT after one life, two lives, or a term of years was calculated according to the actuarial tables printed in the Beta Volume, IRS Pub. No. 1458 (1989). Now it is based on the 1999 Book Beth. The IRS will, upon request, furnish a factor for the value of remainder interests in a CRUT that cannot be calculated from the tables.

EXAMPLE 8-17.

(Based on Reg. §1.664-4T(e)(4) Example). On January 1, *D*, age 44 years and 11 months, transferred securities worth $100,000 to a CRUT. The trust called for the payment to *D* semiannually (on June 30 and December 31) 9% of the fair market value of the trust as determined at the beginning of each tax year of the trust. The §7520 rate for January is 9.6%. Under Table F (9.6), the appropriate adjustment factor is .933805 for semiannual payments payable at the end of the semiannual periods. The adjusted payout rate is 8.404 (9% × .933805). Based on the remainder factors in Table U(1), the present value of the remainder interest is $10,109, computed as follows:

Factor for donor aged 45, 8.4% payout	.10117
Factor for donor aged 45, 8.6% payout	.09715
Difference	.00402

Interpolation adjustment:

$$\frac{8.408 - 8.4\%}{8.6 - 8.4\%} = \frac{X}{.00402}$$

$$X = .00016$$

Factor for donor aged 45, 8.4% payout	.10117
Less interpolation adjustment	.00016
Interpolated factor	.10101

Present value of remainder in $100,000:

$$(\$100,000 \times .10101) = \$10,101$$

When the grantor of a CRAT contributes the retained interest to a charitable beneficiary, the contribution generally qualifies for income and gift tax deductions. Rev. Rul. 86-60, 1986-1 C.B. 302.

No charitable deduction is allowed where the probability exceeds 5 percent that the noncharitable beneficiary of a CRAT will survive the exhaustion of a fund in which a charity has the remainder interest. Rev. Rul. 77-374, 1977-2 C.B. 329. The determination of whether the fund of an annuity trust will be exhausted prior to the life beneficiary's death is based upon the use of the appropriate actuarial tables. In Rev. Rul. 77-374, using the old gender-based tables and a 6 percent rate of return (applicable to decedents dying after November 30, 1983)the computations indicated that the annual payments of $40,000 per year for life from a fund of $400,000 to a 61-year-old female would completely exhaust the fund in less than 16 years was greater than 63 percent, therefore no charitable contribution was allowed. Applying an assumed 10 percent rate of return would change this result since the fund would never be exhausted: the annual income and payout would be equal.

The Tax Court rejected the IRS's mechanical application of these tests in *Estate of George H. Moore*, 43 T.C.M. 1530 (1982). In it the Tax Court concluded that the chance the charitable remainder in two trusts would be exhausted was negligible where the probable return on assets was in excess of the assumed rate used in the Regulations, and using the rates in the Regulations, the chances of exhaustion were 7.63 percent and 7.09 percent, respectively.

§8.26. CHARITABLE TRUSTS AND THE PRIVATE FOUNDATION RULES

Charitable remainder trusts are "split interest" trusts, the governing instruments of which must comply with the requirements of §508(e). §4947(a)(2). Accordingly, the instruments must prohibit the trustee from self-dealing, §4941(d), and making taxable expenditures, §4945(d). In addition, the instruments must ban any jeopardy investments, §4944, and excess business holdings, §4943, during any period that any annuity or unitrust amount is payable to a charity. *See* §§508(e), 4947(b)(3)(B); Reg.

§ 53.4947-2(b)(1). Most states have adopted legislation under which charitable trusts are deemed to include the required provisions. However, it is prudent to include the prohibitions in the trust instruments themselves, if only to alert the trustees to their existence. Private foundations are discussed generally in § 8.42.

Self-Dealing. The retention of an undivided interest in real property of which another undivided interest was transferred to a charitable remainder trust may violate the self-dealing rules that apply to charitable remainder trusts and private foundations. The concern is based on Reg. § 53.4941(d)-2(f)(1) under which the use by a disqualified person of the assets of a private foundation (or charitable remainder trust) is an act of self-dealing. The mere co-ownership of property as tenants in common by a private foundation and a disqualified person does not necessarily constitute self-dealing. *See* G.C.M. 39770.

Although mere co-ownership of property does not constitute an act of self-dealing, the steps leading up to the issuance of LR 9114025 suggest that it may. Apparently the taxpayers who applied for the ruling initially proposed that they transfer an undivided interest in real property to a CRT and retain the remaining undivided interest. The IRS indicated that the co-ownership of the property would involve an act of self-dealing. Ultimately the IRS blessed an alternate plan proposed by the taxpayers that involved transferring the real estate to a partnership in exchange for partnership units, some of which were subsequently transferred by the donors to a CRT. The shift to a partnership was, in the view of the IRS, sufficient to avoid any self-dealing.

Some commentators suggest that the transfer to a CRT of an undivided interest in real property may be structured in a way that eliminates the risk of self-dealing. In particular, they propose that the client be merely a co-owner, without any right to use the property or participate in its management or sale. Of course, the value of the undivided interest transferred to the charitable remainder trust would be subject to a fractional interest discount. *See* § § 2.13; 5.5. On the other hand, the discount should be smaller if the trustee is given the exclusive right to manage and sell the property.

EXAMPLE 8-18.

T had a basis of $100,000 in her personal residence, the fair market value of which was $1,000,000. *T* transferred an undivided one-half interest in the residence to a CRT in connection with which *T* surrendered the right to occupy any of the residence and gave the trustee the exclusive right to manage and sell the property. The mere coownership of the residence should not involve a prohibited act of self-dealing. The trustee should be free to sell the property, the trust's interest in which should not be subject to any capital gains tax. If *T* otherwise qualified, presumably under § 121 she could exclude $250,000 of the gain attributable to the sale of her portion of the property. Importantly, the trust fund, from which *T* was entitled to receive distributions, would remain intact, undiminished by any capital gains taxes. If *T* wished to engage in a wealth replacement plan, *see* § 8.20.3, she could use a portion of the funds distributed to her each year to make gifts to an irrevocable life insurance trust.

§8.27. REQUESTS FOR RULINGS

Having issued sample forms, the IRS will not ordinarily issue rulings with respect to whether an inter vivos remainder trust for one or two measuring lives meets the requirements of §§664, 2055, or 2522. However, a planner should consider applying for a ruling if the provisions of a CRT will be unusual or vary substantially from the standard forms. Requests should be prepared in accordance with the procedural rules that are published in a Revenue Procedure that is included in the first Internal Revenue Bulletin published each year. A companion Revenue Procedure lists the subjects on which rulings will not be issued. Instructions for requesting a ruling are set forth in the Revenue Procedure.

§8.28. ADVANTAGES OF CRTS

A lifetime gift to a CRT or pooled income fund is attractive mainly because it supports current income and gift tax charitable deductions though the charity will not have the beneficial use of the property until the expiration of the private interests. In the meantime the donor, or other noncharitable beneficiaries, may receive payments from the trust. Also, in the case of NIMCRUTs, distributions to the noncharitable beneficiaries can be deferred. As pointed out above, because CRTs are not subject to taxation, §664(c)(1), the trustee can sell the property that is transferred to it without incurring any income tax on the gain. Thus, the transfer of property to a CRT may facilitate its sale, diversification of investments, and, in effect, the receipt of a higher net yield by the donor. The investment advantages of diversification through a CRT are discussed in Willis, Using the Charitable Remainder Trust as an Investment Tool, 30 Est. Plan. 509 (Oct. 2003).

EXAMPLE 8-19.

D, age 55, is a successful executive with an adjusted gross income of $200,000. Two years ago, he invested $100,000 in a startup electronics company, and the stock, which is now publicly traded, is worth $500,000 although it pays no dividends. D expects to retire in 3 years, and would like to convert his investment to a more stable, income-producing asset (*e.g.*, bonds yielding 7 percent). D would also like to make a substantial contribution to the state university.

If D sells the electronics stock for $500,000, the capital gain will result in a tax of $60,000 (assuming the applicable tax rate is 15 percent), leaving $440,000 to invest. At 7 percent interest the fund will provide annual income to D of $30,800.

If D, instead, contributes the electronics stock to a CRAT, which sells it and invests the proceeds in bonds yielding 7 percent, D would receive $35,000 per year—or $4,200 per year more. As indicated above, the trustee can sell the electronics stock and reinvest the proceeds without subjecting taxation. In addition, D will be entitled to a charitable deduction, which would result in an income tax savings.

Additionally, a CRT could be useful when the donor wishes to provide support for another person who is in a lower income tax bracket. Because the income (annuity or unitrust payment) is taxable to the beneficiary and not the donor, the overall income tax burden may be reduced. In addition, the donor benefits from a current income tax deduction for the charitable contribution, subject to the applicable percentage limits of § 170.

§ 8.29.   COMPARISON OF CRATS AND CRUTS

CRATs and CRUTs are similar in many respects; however, there are some important distinctions. Often a client's choice between them is based upon the client's judgment regarding the desirability of a trust that has a fixed payout or one that depends upon the annual value of the trust assets. The payout of a CRAT is fixed—it neither increases if the value of the trust assets increases in an inflationary period, nor decreases if the value of the assets falls during an economic downturn. A CRUT is generally considered to protect the beneficiary better against the inroads of inflation—assuming the assets of the trust increase in value, which is not always the case.

The grantor may serve as trustee of a CRAT or CRUT provided that the trustee has no discretion regarding distributions to the noncharitable beneficiaries. Of course, as noted above, § 8.20, special provisions must be included if unmarketable assets are transferred to the trust. Although the grantor can serve as trustee, the use of an independent trustee is generally preferable. A CRAT or CRUT may give the grantor or another person the power to designate the charitable remainder beneficiaries or to substitute one qualified charitable organization for another. Rev. Rul. 76-8, 1976-1 C.B. 179 (power reserved by grantor); Rev. Rul. 76-7, 1976-1 C.B. 179 (power given income beneficiary). The IRS has also recognized that the power may be held by the donor and the charitable beneficiaries. LR 9445010. (The donor and three beneficiaries may retain the power to designate alternate charitable remainder beneficiaries of a CRUT.)

The annual valuation of assets, which is required for a CRUT, may also be difficult and involve additional costs. However, the fact that a CRUT may provide for the subsequent addition of assets, but a CRAT cannot, is important to some clients. A CRAT may support a higher charitable deduction where the payout rate is less than the assumed rate of return. In such a case the excess of the assumed rate of return over the payout rate is attributed to the remainder that will pass to charity. However, in the case of a CRUT, the payout is assumed to increase each year by the specified percentage of the annual increase in principal (the excess of the assumed rate of return over the payout rate).

§ 8.30.   POOLED INCOME FUND, § 642(c)(5)

Income, gift, and estate tax deductions are also available for the charitable remainder interest in property that is transferred to a pooled income fund, which is defined as a trust:

(A) to which each donor transfers property, contributing an irrevocable remainder interest in such property to or for the use of [a public charity], and retaining an income interest for the life of one or more beneficiaries (living at the time of the transfer);

(B) in which the property transferred by each donor is commingled with property transferred by other donors who have made or make similar transfers;

(C) which cannot have investments in securities which are exempt from the taxes imposed by this subtitle

(D) which include only amounts received from transfers that meet the requirements of this paragraph;

(E) which is maintained by the organization to which the remainder interest is contributed and of which no donor or beneficiary of an income interest is a trustee; and

(F) from which each beneficiary of an income interest receives income, for each year for which he is entitled to receive the income interest referred to in subparagraph (A), determined by the rate of return earned by the trust for such a year. § 642(c)(5).

When property is transferred to a pooled income fund, participation units in the fund are allocated to the holder of the life interest. As in the case of a common trust fund, the number of units depends upon the value of the property transferred to the fund and the value of the fund's other assets. The Regulations contain detailed rules for the valuation of assets of the fund and allocation of units. *See* Reg. § § 1.642(c)-5, 1.642(c)-6. The IRS has ruled that an exempt organization, as trustee, may commingle assets of pooled income funds with those of CRTs. LR 8903019.

Under Reg. § 1.642(c)-6(e)(3), the rate of return on a pooled income fund created after April 30, 1989, that has been in existence for less than three years preceding the taxable year in which the gift is made, is determined as follows:

> If a pooled income fund has been in existence for less than 3 taxable years immediately preceding the taxable year in which the transfer is made to the fund and the transfer to the fund is made after April 30, 1989, the highest rate of return is deemed to be the interest rate (rounded to the nearest two-tenths of 1 percent) that is 1 percent less than the highest annual average of the monthly section 7520 rates for the 3 calendar years immediately preceding the calendar year in which the transfer to the pooled income fund is made. The deemed rate of return for transfers to new pooled income funds is recomputed each calendar year using the monthly section 7520 rates for the 3-year period immediately preceding the calendar year in which each transfer to the fund is made until the fund has been in existence for 3 taxable years and can compute its highest rate of return for the 3 taxable years immediately preceding the taxable year in which the transfer of property to the fund is made in accordance with the rules set forth in the first sentence of paragraph (e)(2)(ii) of this section.

The deemed rate of return for newly created pooled income funds during 2011 was 2.8 percent. Rev. Rul. 2011-2, 2011-2 I.R.B. 256.

A pooled income fund is taxable under § 641. As such the trust is entitled to a distribution deduction for amounts paid to noncharitable beneficiaries. In addition, it is entitled to a charitable deduction under Reg. § 1.642(c)-3 for net long-term capital gain that is permanently set aside for charitable purposes. A pooled income fund is taxed on any short-term capital gain that is not distributed to the noncharitable beneficiaries. If distributions to noncharitable beneficiaries were made on the basis of a unitrust amount or an equitable adjustment, no deduction would be allowed for net long-term capital gains. Prop. Reg. § 1.642(c)-2(c).

Sample Forms. The IRS has published sample forms of pooled income fund trust and instruments of transfer. *See* Rev. Proc. 88-53, 1988-2 C.B. 712, discussed below. Earlier the IRS published sample provisions for inclusion in the governing instruments of pooled income funds. Rev. Rul. 82-38, 1982-1 C.B. 96, as *amplified by* Rev. Rul. 85-57, 1985-1 C.B. 182. Because of the complexity of the rules regarding pooled income funds, a donor should be hesitant to transfer property to a fund unless either (1) the pooled income fund and instruments of transfer are substantially in the form of the samples issued by the IRS, or (2) the charity has obtained a ruling from the IRS verifying that the fund meets the requirements of § 642(c)(5).

A trust does not satisfy the requirements of § 642(c)(5)(A) if the trustee is permitted to invest in depreciable property unless the governing instrument or the state law requires the trustee to establish a depreciation reserve with respect to depreciable property. Rev. Rul. 90-103, 1990-2 C.B. 159. Accordingly, a trust should either prohibit the trustee from holding depreciable property or require the trustee to establish a depreciation reserve. Revenue Ruling 90-103 amplifies Rev. Rul. 82-38 to approve the following sample provisions:

> If the trustee accepts or invests in depreciable or depletable property, it shall establish a depreciation or depletion reserve in accordance with Generally Accepted Accounting Principles (GAAP).
>
> The trustee shall not accept or invest in any depreciable or depletable assets.

The amount of the charitable deduction for property transferred to a pooled income fund depends upon the age of the income beneficiaries and the rate of return earned by the fund over the preceding three years. Under § 642(c)(5), the life income interests are valued according to the highest rate of return earned by the fund in the preceding three years. Funds in existence before May 1, 1989 with less than three years of experience were deemed to have 9 percent rate of return (6 percent for transfers before December 1, 1983). Reg. § 1.642(c)-6(b)(2). "[T]he first taxable year of a pooled income fund is the taxable year in which [it] first receives assets." Rev. Rul. 85-20, 1985-1 C.B. 183. Under Notice 89-60, 1989-1 C.B. 700,

The donor may retain a testamentary power to revoke or terminate the income interest of any designated beneficiary other than the public charity. Reg. § 1.642(c)-5(b)(2). However, the retention of such a power does not affect the valuation of the charitable remainder.

The present value of a remainder interest dependent upon the termination of one life or two lives is determined according to actuarial Table R(1) and R(2), respectively, of Aleph Volume, IRS Pub. No. 1457 (1999). When a life income interest terminates, the corresponding charitable remainder interest must be severed from the fund and paid over to, or retained for the benefit of, the designated public charity. Reg. § 1.642(c)-5(b)(8).

No gain or loss is incurred by the donor when property is transferred to a qualified pooled income fund. However, gain may be recognized if the donor either receives any property from the fund in addition to the income interest or transfers encumbered property to the fund. Reg. § 1.642(c)-5(a)(3). The fund and the beneficiaries are generally taxed according to the rules applicable to a noncharitable trust, except that the grantor trust rules do not apply. Reg. § 1.642(c)-5(a)(2).

Overall, a pooled income fund offers an attractive way for a donor to make a charitable gift that would not justify the expense of establishing and operating a separate CRT. The opportunity to achieve tax-free diversification of investments is an important advantage of a fund. However, unlike CRTs, a fund cannot invest in tax exempt securities, § 642(c)(5)(C), Reg. § 1.642(c)-5(b)(4). Accordingly, none of the income received from a pooled fund is tax-exempt. Also, the statute bars a donor or beneficiary from serving as a trustee of the fund. § 642(c)(5)(E). However, "[t]he fact that a donor of property to the fund, or a beneficiary of the fund is a trustee, officer, director or other officer of the public charity to or for the use of which the remainder interest is contributed ordinarily will not prevent the fund from meeting the requirements of section 642(c)(5) and this paragraph." Reg. § 1.642(c)-5(b)(6).

A transfer to a pooled income fund could involve the GSTT if the donor's grandchildren or others in their generation are income beneficiaries of the fund.

The IRS has recognized that a national charity that carries out its activities through local affiliates with which it has an identity of purposes can create and maintain a single pooled income fund that benefits itself and its local affiliates that consent to participate in the fund. Rev. Rul. 92-107, 1992-2 C.B. 120; LR 9345007. The ruling involved a governing instrument that allowed a donor to designate that the remainder be transferred either to the national organization or to one of the participating affiliates. It also provided that a designated local charity could not sever its interest prior to the death of the beneficiary and if a designated local organization was no long affiliated with the national organization when the remainder interest was to be transferred, the remainder would be distributed to the national organization or a local affiliate designated by the national organization.

A companion ruling held that a community trust could create and maintain a single pooled income fund to which various donors could make contributions if the donors permit the community trust to designate how, and by whom, the remainder interest would be used for charitable purposes. Rev. Rul. 92-108, 1992-2 C.B. 121. The same ruling held that a single fund could not be created by a community trust if the donors retained the power to designate the specific charitable organization for whose benefit the community trust would use the remainder interest.

In Rev. Proc. 88-54, 1988-2 C.B. 715, the IRS announced that it would no longer issue rulings as to whether a pooled income fund qualified under § 642(c)(5) or whether the contributions to the fund were deductible. However, in Rev. Proc. 88-53, 1988-2 C.B. 712, the IRS announced that donors who transfer property to a pooled income fund that substantially complies with the model instruments are assured that the charitable remainder interests are deductible without obtaining a ruling. By issuing these procedures the IRS strongly encourages the use of the sample instruments.

§ 8.31. Gifts to Charitable Lead Trusts, §§ 170(f)(2)(B), 2055(e)(2)(B), 2522(c)(2)(B)

Charitable deductions are also allowed for a gift to charity of a current interest in a trust that is in the form of a guaranteed annuity or unitrust interest. *See* § 8.32. A trust that provides for such current payments to charity is usually called a "charitable lead trust" (CLT). A gift of a guaranteed annuity or unitrust interest is deductible for income tax purposes only if the income of the CLT will be taxed to the donor under the grantor trust rules. § 170(f)(2)(B). If the income is not taxed to the donor, any accumulated income including capital gains will be taxed to the trust. The IRS has ruled that a CLT may provide that income in excess of the amount needed to make the required payments to charity may be accumulated for distribution to noncharities upon termination of the trust. Rev. Rul. 88-82, 1988-2 C.B. 336. No charitable deduction is available if the trust provides for current distribution of excess income to noncharitable beneficiaries. Contributions to a typical CLT qualify for the gift tax charitable deduction; the grantor is not taxed on the income of the trust and, under § 642(c), the trust may deduct distributions of income to the charitable beneficiaries. LR 20021020.

The IRS has issued sample trust forms for both intervivos charitable lead annuity trusts (CLATs), Rev. Proc. 2007-45, 2007-2 C.B. 89, and testamentary CLATs, Rev. Proc. 2007-46, 2007-2 C.B. 102. The guidance for intervivos CLATs contains two forms. One form creates an intervivos CLAT designed to last for a term of years and to be treated as a separate taxpayer. The other form creates an intervivos CLAT for a term of years intended to function as a grantor trust. The forms contain alternate provisions for basing annuities on the life of an individual, leaving apportionment of the annuity amount in the trustee's discretion, phrasing the annuity in the form of a specific dollar amount, naming alternate charitable beneficiaries, and, in the case of the grantor trust, restricting the charitable beneficiary to a public charity. The sample testamentary CLAT instrument in Rev. Proc. 2007-46 contains a lead interest for a term of years, together with alternate provisions for basing annuities on the life of an individual, leaving apportionment of the annuity amount in the trustee's discretion, phrasing the annuity in the form of a specific dollar amount, and naming alternate charitable beneficiaries. For an analysis of the forms, *see* Fox, A Guide to the IRS Sample Lead Trust Forms-Part 1, 36 Est. Plan. 7 (Apr. 2009), and Fox, A Guide to the IRS Sample Lead Trust Forms-Part 2, 36 Est. Plan. 13 (May 2009).

The IRS has also issued sample trust forms for intervivos charitable lead unitrusts (CLUTs), Rev. Proc. 2008-45, 2008-2 C.B. 224, and testamentary CLUTs, Rev. Proc. 2008-46, 2008-2 C.B. 238. There are two sample forms for intervivos CLUTs, one that structures the CLUT as a separate taxable entity and another that causes the CLUT to qualify as a grantor trust. Both forms create the lead interest for a term of years followed by distributions to one or more individuals that are United States citizens or residents. The form for a testamentary CLUT likewise uses a term of years for the charitable lead interest. All of these forms include a number of annotations and alternative provisions that can be used to customize the form to a client's specific situation.

Subject to the other limitations imposed by § 170, including the 30 percent limit for gifts "for the use of" a qualified charity, Reg. § 1.170A-8(a)(2), a donor is entitled to a present income tax deduction for the full value of a guaranteed annuity or unitrust interest given during the year to a qualified charity if the donor is treated as the owner of the trust for income tax purposes. A gift of a guaranteed annuity or unitrust amount also qualifies for a gift tax deduction, LR 8338108, and a bequest of an income interest similarly qualifies for an estate tax deduction.

A CLT may also be an attractive method for transferring appreciating property to private beneficiaries. The contribution to a trust can be structured to provide a charitable deduction for part or all of the assets contributed. The gift tax on the transfer to beneficiaries is based on the total asset value less the charitable contribution. Later, the appreciated remainder is distributed to designated beneficiaries free from the gift or estate tax.

A CLT may appeal to a client whose future income will be in lower tax brackets, since the gift accelerates the deduction for the future payments to the charity, while the income to fund those payments is taxed later when received. The rules prevent a donor from taking a large deduction at the outset and avoiding taxation on the trust income in later years by relinquishing the interests or controls that caused the donor to be treated as its owner under the grantor trust rules: If the donor ceases being treated as owner of the trust, he or she must recapture part of the deduction as current income. The amount recaptured is the excess of the deduction received for the gift, over the discounted value of the income that was taxed to the donor under the grantor trust rules. § 170(f)(2)(B). The amount must be included in the donor's final income tax return if the donor ceases to be treated as owner of the trust by reason of death. Reg. § 1.170A-6(c)(5), Example 3.

A CLT is not tax-exempt. Accordingly, the trust instrument may direct that distributions to charity consist of ordinary income to the extent available, otherwise from capital gain (distributions of which would qualify for the § 642(c) charitable deduction). *See* Rev. Rul. 83-75, 1983-1 C.B. 114; LRs 8026032; 8030054.

For income tax purposes a CLT is entitled to deduct the amount of the annuity payable to the charitable beneficiary. § 642(c). However, under § 642(c)(1), no deduction is allowable for amounts payable to the charitable beneficiary in excess of the amount of the annuity unless made "pursuant to the terms of the instrument." In *Rebecca K. Crown Income Charitable Fund*, 98 T.C. 327 (1992), no deduction was allowed under § 642(c) or 661 for amounts paid to the charitable beneficiary in excess of the annuity amount where the trust instrument under certain circumstances allowed additional amounts to be paid "in commutation of future amounts payable hereunder" and no such commutation was made. In the course of the opinion the Tax Court emphasized, "however, that we express no opinion here as to whether the payment of a charitable lead annuity may be accelerated consistent with the requirement of section 2522(c)(2)(B) that the charitable interest be in the form of a guaranteed annuity." 98 T.C. at 336.

The IRS has ruled that no charitable deduction is allowable with respect to a CLT that gives the trustee the power to commute and prepay the charitable beneficiary the value of the future annuity payments which it is entitled to receive. Rev. Rul. 88-27, 1988-1 C.B. 331. The ruling reached that conclusion based on the provisions of Reg. § 25.2522(c)-3(c)(2)(vi)(a), which define a "guaranteed annuity" as requiring the payment of a determinable amount for a specified term. The right of the trustee to commute and prepay the annuity deprives the charitable beneficiary of the right to receive payments of a fixed amount over a specified term. Accordingly, the trust failed to qualify for a charitable deduction.

Interestingly, a private letter ruling concluded that the termination of a CLT pursuant to a court decision which authorized commuting and prepaying the charitable beneficiary would not violate any of the private foundation rules. LR 8808031. The ruling did not consider whether or not the commutation and prepayment would jeopardize the charitable deductions that were allowed to the grantor 11 years before.

The rules regarding the determination of the GSTT inclusion ratio for CLATs prevent the ratio from being determined at the time the trust was created, which would have given the transferor the benefit of considerable leverage. *See* § 2642(e). Specifically, for transfers taking place after October 13, 1987, the GSTT inclusion ratio of a CLAT requires use of the "adjusted GSTT exemption" and the value of the property of the trust "immediately after the termination of the charitable lead annuity." Under § 2642(e) the adjusted GSTT exemption (the amount of the transferor's GSTT exemption that was allocated to the trust adjusted by the interest rate that was applied to determine the amount of the charitable deduction purposes of § 2055 (estate tax) or § 2522 (gift tax)) is the numerator and the value of all of the property in the trust immediately after termination of the charitable lead annuity is the denominator.

Measuring Lives. Regulations restrict the persons whose lives may be used to measure the duration of the lead interest in a CLT to an individual who, with respect to all noncharitable beneficiaries, is either a lineal ancestor or the spouse of a lineal ancestor of the noncharitable beneficiaries. § § 1.170A-6(c)(2)(i)(A), 1.170A-6(c)(2)(ii)(A); 20.2055-2(e)(2)(vi)(a). The requirements will be met if there is less than a 15 percent chance that individuals who are not lineal descendants of the current beneficiaries will receive any corpus of the trust. The probability is determined on the date assets are transferred to the CLAT, taking into consideration the interests of all persons who are living at that time.

The restriction was adopted because of schemes that have been marketed based on limiting the duration of the charitable lead interest to the life of an unrelated individual who is seriously ill, but not terminally ill as defined in the regulations. According to the IRS,

> These charitable lead trusts are being marketed in a package which includes the name of a seriously ill individual and access to the individual's medical records. A token payment is made to the ill individual who is serving as a measuring life. Sometimes the individual is led to believe that a charitable organization interested in the individual's particular illness will receive some benefit of the transaction. In the words of one author, "[t]his technique (which is not strictly wealth transfer planning for the terminally ill, but rather wealth transfer planning using the terminally ill) falls somewhere between ghoulish and grotesque." Marketing schemes that exploit the misfortune of some for the benefit of others are contrary to public policy. Notice of Proposed Rulemaking, Background, 65 F.R. 17835.

CLT Payments to Private Foundation. A private non-operating charitable foundation may be funded with the right to receive distributions from a CLT. The approach can be used where the donor wishes to combine the benefits of a CLT with a distributive mechanism that allows the corpus of the foundation to grow substantially over time. Contrary to the position taken by the IRS in the regulations, the private foundation distributable amount does not include the income portion of the distributions received from the CLT. *Ann Jackson Family Foundation,* 97 T.C. 534 (1991), *aff'd,* 15 F.3d 917 (9th Cir. 1994). *See* Wood, Ninth Circuit Validates Private Foundation/Charitable Lead Trust Planning, 80 J. Tax. 290 (1994).

The transfer of property by an S corporation to a charitable lead trust is treated as a gift by the shareholders, which qualifies for the charitable gift tax deduction to the extent of the charitable interest. LR 9512002.

If the duration of the charitable lead interest is measured by the donor's life, the actuarial life expectancy of the donor will not be used if the donor is terminally ill. In LR 9504004 (TAM) the IRS held that where the donor was known to be terminally ill and died 19 days after the transfer, the value of the annuities and the remainders were to be valued according to the donor's actual life expectancy on the date of the transfer.

A CLT qualifies for a gift tax charitable deduction under §2522 although the trustees are given the power to apportion the charitable annuity among qualified charitable beneficiaries. LR 9748009. The deduction is allowable although the donor's child serves as a cotrustee of the trust. The ruling also held that no portion of the trust was includible in the donor's gross estate. The same result was reached in LR 9801013.

The donor of a CLT should not retain the right to change the charitable beneficiary. In LR 200328030, the IRS ruled that a gift to a CLT that was subject to such a power was not a completed gift and, accordingly, no charitable deduction was allowable with respect to the gift. In addition, the ruling held that if the donor died during the term of the CLT, the value of the trust's assets would be includible in the donor's estate under §2038(a)(1).

If the charitable interest in a CLAT is payable to a family foundation, the assets of the CLAT are excluded from the donor's estate if the donor did not retain any control over either the CLAT or the distributions made to the foundation. *E.g.,* LRs 9725012, 199908002, and 200043039. If the donor retains control over the distribution of funds by the foundation, the assets are potentially includible in the donor's estate under §§2036 and 2038. A gift to a CLAT, the charitable interest of which is payable to a private foundation, is complete and the property is not included in the donor's estate although the donor is an officer or trustee of the foundation, if the foundation's governing documents provide that payments from the CLAT must be segregated and the donor cannot participate in any decision regarding them. *See* LRs 200108032 and 200138018, which include the text of the provisions governing the foundation that were acceptable to the IRS.

Early Termination of CLATs. The IRS has ruled favorably on the early termination of a CLAT that would result from a present court-approved payment of the full, undiscounted, amount of all future payments that would be due to the charitable beneficiary over the balance of the term of the CLAT. LR 200225045. The circumstances involved in the ruling are described in this passage:

> Due to the appreciation in the Partnership's investment portfolio, X [the CLAT] is able to meet its charitable obligations to C [a private foundation] earlier than originally anticipated. A prepayment of X's obligations would increase C's resources as well as enable C to increase its charitable

commitments over time. Accordingly, X now wishes to pay C, in one lump sum payment, the remaining amount due to C under the Trust document in the form of case and/or publicly traded stock, without discount.

The ruling reasoned that the payment does not constitute a termination under § 507(a) because, "The decision by all parties to make the charitable payments prior to the end of the term of the trust does not render the payment any less mandatory, nor is it deemed discretionary with the trustee, merely because all parties agree to make the charitable payment earlier than required by the trust document." In addition, the ruling held that the prepayment to the charity without discount would not be an act of self-dealing under § 4941 and would not be a taxable expenditure under § 4945. The ruling did not deal with the income tax consequences of a prepayment, such as might arise from the distribution of appreciated assets to the charity.

§ 8.32. GUARANTEED ANNUITY INTERESTS AND UNITRUST INTERESTS

Income, gift, and estate tax deductions are allowed for gifts of guaranteed annuity interests to charity. For this purpose a guaranteed annuity interest is an irrevocable right, pursuant to the trust, to receive an amount each year that is determinable on the date of the gift for a fixed term or for the life or lives of individuals who are living on the date of the gift. Reg. § 1.170A-6(c)(2)(i)(A). An interest does not qualify unless it is a guaranteed annuity interest in all respects. Thus, the right to receive payments under an income-only unitrust (the lesser of a fixed amount or the actual income of the trust) does not qualify. Rev. Rul. 77-300, 1977-2 C.B. 352 (gift tax). Similarly, according to the regulations, an interest does not qualify if a payment may be made from the trust for a private purpose prior to the expiration of the charitable annuity interest unless the payments must be made from assets that are devoted exclusively to private purposes. Reg. § § 20.2055-2(e)(2)(vi)(e), (vii)(e). However, the Tax Court held the regulations invalid when a unitrust income interest is payable to charity following the death of one private beneficiary and prior to the distribution of the remainder interest on the death of the other private income beneficiaries. *Estate of Minnie L. Boeshore*, 78 T.C. 523 (1982), *acq.*, 1987-2 C.B. 5. Any income in excess of the annuity amount may also be payable to a charity, but it will not increase the amount of the allowable deduction for the year in which the income interest was gifted. Consistent with the government's acquiescence in the *Boeshore* case, regulations remove the rule barring a private annuity interest that precedes the charitable interest in a CLAT. Reg. § § 1.170A-6(c)(2)(i)(E); 20.2055-2(e)(vi)(e); 20.2055-2(e)(vi)(f); 20.2055-2(e)(2)(vii)(e); 25.2522(c)-3(c)(2)(vi)(f); and 25.2522-3(c)(2)(vii)(e).

A charitable deduction is allowable for gift tax purposes when the CLAT accumulates any income that is not required to make annuity payments, and adds it to corpus. Rev. Rul. 88-82, 1988-2 C.B. 336. In Situation 2, Rev. Rul. 88-82 points out that if the excess income may be paid to a noncharitable beneficiary, the charitable interest is not a guaranteed annuity and no deduction is available. Finally, as noted in § 8.31, the charitable beneficiary's right to receive annuity payments is not a guaranteed annuity if it can be commuted and prepaid.

A unitrust interest is an irrevocable right to receive payment each year of a fixed percentage of the net fair market value of the trust assets, determined annually. The value may be determined either on one date each year or by taking the average value on more than one date, provided that the same method is used each year. Reg. § 1.170A 6(c)(2)(ii)(A). In general, the other rules applicable to a guaranteed annuity also apply to a unitrust interest.

EXAMPLE 8-20.

D transferred $100,000 in trust to pay $5,000 a year for the first 5 years and $7,500 for the next 5 years to a qualified charity, *C*. At the end of the 10-year period the trust property will be distributed to *D*'s then living issue, per stirpes. The interest given to *C* is a guaranteed annuity, Reg. § 1.170A-6(c)(2)(i)(B), but it is not deductible by *D* for income tax purposes unless *D* is treated as the owner of the trust under the grantor trust rules. Gift and estate tax deductions are available for the gift to *C* in any case. The interest would qualify as a unitrust interest if it were expressed as a fixed percentage (*e.g.*, 8%) of the fair market value of the trust assets determined on a specified date each year (*e.g.*, January 15). No annual exclusions are allowable with respect to the remainder interests in the trust.

§8.33. GIFTS OF INCOME INTERESTS

An ordinary income interest in a trust does not qualify for the income, gift, or estate tax charitable deductions. However, the disallowance of the income tax deduction may be circumvented to some extent if the income is not taxed to the donor under the grantor trust rules.

EXAMPLE 8-21.

D created a trust this year that provided for the net income to be paid to a qualified charity, *C*, for 10 years at the end of which the trust property will be distributed to *D*'s then living issue. The transfer to the trust does not qualify for an income tax deduction under § 170. However, the income of the trust will not be taxed to *D* unless *D* is treated as the owner of the trust under the grantor trust rules. Importantly, the trust is entitled to a deduction for the amount distributed to charity each year. § 642(c). Note that the transfer does not qualify for the gift tax charitable deduction because it is not in the form of a guaranteed annuity or fixed percentage of the fair market value of the property distributed annually. § 2522(c)(2)(B). As explained below, the gift tax disadvantage would be eliminated if the gift of the income were incomplete when the trust was created. The gift would be incomplete if, for example, *D* retained the power each year to appoint the accumulated income to and among a class of charities. *See, e.g.*, LR 8338095.

A less satisfactory result follows where the donor is treated as the owner of the trust under the grantor trust rules, §§ 671-677. A donor who is required to report the income of the trust should be entitled to a deduction for the amount paid to charity, subject to the limits and other provisions of § 170. However, the transfer to the trust would not qualify for the gift tax deduction.

The gift tax detriment of transferring property to a trust of which the income is payable to charity is avoided if the gift to the charity is not completed until the income is ready for distribution to the charity. *See, e.g.*, LR 8017058. For example, the gift is incomplete at the time of the initial transfer if the donor retains the right to designate the charity that will receive the net income earned by the trust during each year. *See* Rev. Rul. 77-275, 1977-2 C.B. 346. The grantor is not taxed on the income of a trust under the grantor trust rules merely because the grantor retains the power to allocate income or principal among charities. § 674(b)(4); *see* § 10.37.1. Importantly, the retention of such a power renders the gift incomplete until the power is exercised. Reg. § 25.2511-2(c). When the donor designates the charity to receive the accumulated income, the gift is completed. The gift consists of the entire interest in the trust's accumulated income, which is not a split interest and for which an offsetting gift tax deduction is allowable under § 2522(a). LR 8144051. Note that a gift tax deduction is not allowable where the donor designates the charity in advance of the receipt of the income. Rev. Rul. 77-275, *supra*. In such a case the designation gives the charity an income interest that does not qualify for the gift tax deduction: "No deduction is allowable under section 2522 of the Code with respect to such a completed gift due to [the donor's] retained right to reversion of the trust property upon termination and because the income right is not in the form prescribed by section 2522(c)(2)." The grantor of such a trust should instead retain the power to choose the charities to receive the net income for each year after the income is in hand. The payment to the charities in such a case is deductible under § 642(c)(1) for income tax purposes even thought it is paid after the close of the trust's taxable year. LR 8152078. Under that section, "[I]f a charitable contribution is paid after the close of [the] taxable year and on or before the last day of the year following the close of such taxable year, then the trustee or administrator may elect to treat such contribution as paid during such taxable year."

The slight differences between the charities described in § 170(c), and those described in §§ 2055(a) and 2522(a), can also cause tax problems for the donor. For example, a gift tax deduction is not allowable where a trust permits the grantor, or another person, to designate the charitable recipient from among charitable organizations described in § 170(c). In order to assure that a gift tax charitable deduction is also available, the selection must be limited to charities that are described in § 2522(a). The point is elaborated in LR 8017058 with respect to an irrevocable short term trust. In most instances the authority to make distributions of trust property to undesignated charities should be limited to ones that meet the requirements of §§ 170(c), 2055(a) and 2522(a).

§8.34. Payments to Charity from a Trust Upon Death of Grantor

For a variety of purposes it is important to distinguish between gifts made "in trust" and "not in trust." The distinction should be drawn in projecting the tax consequences that flow from the transfer of property to a trust from which payments will be made to charity following the grantor's death. The transfer of property to a revocable trust does not generally have any significant present tax consequences because of its revocable character. The grantor may safely provide for a distribution to be made to charity upon the grantor's death. By way of illustration, Rev. Rul. 75-414, 1975-2 C.B. 371, pointed out that a trust may be used as a conduit to make outright distributions of a specified percentage of the trust corpus to a charity upon the grantor's death. The ruling allowed an estate tax deduction for a specified percentage of the trust property, augmented by a pour-over from the grantor's estate, which was payable to charity upon the grantor's death. A deduction was allowed because the gift constituted an outright transfer of an undivided interest in the trust property. An estate tax deduction is also allowable where a trust provides for payment of a specified sum to charity upon the grantor's death. In that case the gift would constitute the grantor's entire interest in that particular sum. Of course, a charitable deduction is allowable only to the extent that the property given to charity is included in the decedent's gross estates. § 2055(d).

The transfer of property to an irrevocable trust that provides for a later distribution to charity may have very different consequences. For example, the transfer usually constitutes a completed gift for gift tax purposes. However, a charitable gift tax deduction is not allowed unless the charitable interest is in the form of a CRAT, a CRUT, or a guaranteed annuity or unitrust amount. Thus, some gift tax liability could be incurred at the time the charitable interest is created. The transfer to the trust also would not qualify for an income tax deduction unless it took one of those forms. Presumably the grantor's estate would be entitled to an estate tax charitable deduction for the value of the payment made from the trust at the time of the grantor's death. Recall that the marital deduction is available on an elective basis with respect to the full value of the property transferred to a trust in which the surviving spouse has a qualifying income interest for life. § § 2056(b)(7), 2523(f). The value of such property is includible in the donee-spouse's estate under § 2044. As noted above, if the remainder passes to charity upon the donee-spouse's death, the donee-spouse's estate will be entitled to an offsetting charitable deduction under § 2055.

Alternatively, if the donor desires to make a substantial irrevocable transfer that will later be distributed to charity, it may be appropriate to create a private foundation to receive the contribution. This would facilitate income, gift, and estate tax deductions for the transfer without the use of a qualifying charitable remainder or lead trust. Private foundations are subject to the rules of § § 4940-4948 as well as reporting requirements.

§8.35. Salvaging Charitable Deductions for Nonqualifying Interests

Gifts to charitable trusts sometimes fail to qualify for the intended income, gift, and estate tax deductions because of noncompliance with technical rules. There are, fortunately, two major methods by which the deductions may be salvaged. The first is the use of disclaimers to eliminate interests or powers that prevent a gift from qualifying.

EXAMPLE 8-22.

T died leaving a will that gave her residuary estate to an individual, *X*, as trustee of a trust that was intended to qualify as a CRAT. However, the trust authorized *X* to distribute principal to or for the benefit of *T*'s husband, *H*, as required to maintain his standard of living. On the twentieth anniversary of *T*'s death the trust corpus is to be paid over to the *C* Church. The gift does not qualify for a charitable deduction under § 2055 because of *X*'s power to distribute principal to or for the benefit of *H*. If *H* effectively disclaims the right to receive distributions of principal, the value of *C* Church's remainder interest will be deductible.

The 1984 Act added provisions that allow the reformation of charitable trusts, pooled income funds, and gifts of remainder interests in personal residences or farms, for purposes of the income, gift, and estate tax laws. Detailed rules regarding reformations are contained in § 2055(e)(3), to which references are made in §§ 170(f)(7) and 2522(c)(4). The rules recognize the effect of "qualified reformation" of "reformable interests." Also, note that a trust that does not meet the minimum 10 percent remainder interest requirement can be reformed. § 2055(e)(3)(J).

An overview of the provisions of § 2055(e)(3) is provided by IRS News Release IR-84-101:

In the case of a charitable interest created under a will executed or a trust created after December 31, 1978, the interest will generally qualify as a "reformable interest" only if all payment to noncharitable beneficiaries are expressed either in specified dollar amounts or in a fixed percentage of the fair market value of the property. If this requirement is not met, the interest may nevertheless qualify as a "reformable interest" if judicial proceedings are commenced on or before the later of (i) the 90th day after the last date for filing the estate tax return (including extensions); (ii) if no estate tax return is required to be filed, the 90th day after the last date for filing the first income tax return of the split-interest trust (including extensions); or (iii) on or before October 16, 1984.

In general, a trust can be reformed if it would have qualified for the charitable deduction apart from the requirement that it be in the form of a CRAT, a CRUT, or a guaranteed annuity or unitrust interest (*i.e.*, under the pre-1969 rules). § 2055(e)(3)(C)(i). In the case of post-1978 instruments, an interest is not reformable unless the noncharitable interests are specified in terms of a fixed dollar amount or a fixed percentage and a judicial reformation proceeding is initiated before the expiration of the estate tax limitations period. However, those requirements do not apply if the judicial proceedings are begun not later than the 90th day after the last date for filing the estate tax return (or, if no return is required, the 90th day after the last date for filing the income tax return for the first year of the trust). § 2055(e)(3)(C)(iii).

In order to constitute a qualified reformation, it must be retroactive to the date of death (or creation of the trust). § 2055(e)(3)(B)(iii). In addition, the reformation may not result in a change of more than 5 percent in the value of the reformable interest. § 2055(e)(3)(B)(i). Also, the reformation cannot change the duration of the charitable and noncharitable interests—except for reducing the term of the noncharitable interest of more than 20 years to a term of 20 years. § 2055(e)(3)(B). A CRUT to which an addition was made, that had four successive individual beneficiaries, could be reformed to meet the 10 percent requirement. LR 20002214. The addition was severed and divided into four separate CRUTs, each of which had a single noncharitable beneficiary and met the 10 percent requirement.

Reformation was recognized in LR 9611019 in which the decedent's will created a trust from which an individual was entitled to receive the income for life and a qualified charity would receive the remainder.

Reformation of a trust was also upheld in LR 9610005 in which the noncharitable beneficiaries disclaimed their rights to receive distributions of principal from the trust. The right to receive distributions of principal was treated as separate from the right to receive distributions of unitrust amounts, although they might be payable from principal.

In LR 9549016, the IRS ruled that the charitable interest in a nonqualifying split-interest trust was not reformable as no charitable deduction would have been allowed under the pre-1970 law because the value of the charitable remainder was not determinable. The value of the charitable remainder was not determinable because the individual beneficiary was entitled to receive distributions of principal in the sole discretion of the trustee. The problem would have been eliminated had the individual beneficiary executed a qualified disclaimer of the right to receive distributions of principal.

No reformation is possible if the split-interest trust gives the trustee discretion to distribute principal to the noncharitable beneficiary. LR 9549016. Similarly, where the amounts of income and principal distributable to the charitable and noncharitable beneficiaries is not determinable.

In LR 9526027, the IRS recognized the effect of dividing a nonqualifying split-interest trust as a result of which one trust was exclusively devoted to charitable purposes. The original trust required the trustee to care for the seven dogs and cats owned by the decedent at the time of his death and to use the balance of the residue for charitable activities related to medical procedures "of spaying and neutering cats and dogs." According to the ruling the amount required to provide for the animals was restricted by a fixed standard (the amount necessary to care for the animals) and was readily ascertainable. The IRS concluded that if the trust were divided by the court into two separate trusts, a charitable deduction would be allowable with respect to the trust to provide medical procedures for cats and dogs.

In some cases the trustee may be able to make distributions, disclaim a power, or take other action that preserves or increases the amount of the charitable deduction. For example, in LR 9532026, the charitable deduction was, in effect, increased when the trustee exercised its discretion to distribute principal to the surviving spouse who, in turn, gave a portion of the principal to the charities that were the ultimate intended beneficiaries of part of the trust. As drafted the QTIP trust provided that on the death of the surviving spouse the trustee was to determine the portion of the principal that was then to be distributed to the charities, and the balance was to be held in charitable remainder unitrusts of which his two sons were the life benefi-ciaries. Thus, the charitable deduction that would have been allowable to the estate of the surviving spouse for the portion of the trust includible in her estate under § 2044 would have been limited to the minimum amount that would pass to the charities—the value of the remainder following the deaths of the decedent's two sons.

In LR 9526031, the CRUT only provided for the distribution of 3 percent to the decedent's siblings with the remainder passing to charity. The IRS held that the trust was reformable and that it would recognize a reformation that gave the charity a 2 percent unitrust interest, as a result of which the trust would provide for the required minimum 5 percent payout.

In *Estate of Anthony J. Tamulis*, 92 T.C.M. (CCH) 189 (2006), the decedent, a Catholic priest, bequeathed his entire estate to his revocable living trust. The trust provided for specific bequests followed by annual payments of specific amounts to various relatives provided certain conditions were met, with the remainder of the trust's net income to be shared equally between two of the decedent's grandnieces. After ten years (or, if longer, after the deaths of two trust beneficiaries) the trust will terminate and the remainder will be payable to the church. The estate claimed a § 2055 deduction of nearly $1.5 million for the value of the church's remainder interest, but the IRS disallowed the deduction and asserted a deficiency, because the terms of the trust did not qualify as a charitable remainder trust a gift to which would be eligible for the deduction. The estate argued that the church's remainder interest was a "reformable interest" under § 2055(e)(3). The Tax Court held that "where the payout to the noncharitable beneficiaries has been 'basically expressed as an annuity interest or a unitrust interest'—that is, as specified dollar amount or as a fixed percentage of the fair market value of the trust property, in accordance with section 2055(e)(3)(C)(ii)—then a reformation may be effected even after an audit has com-menced." The problem here, said the court, is that some of the amounts payable to the noncharitable beneficiaries were not expressed in the form of an annuity or a unitrust amount. One bequest, for example, provided for the payment of real prop-erty taxes on a residence owned by the decedent. In addition, the payment to the grandnieces of all remaining net income was neither an annuity or unitrust amount. The fact that total annual distributions to the noncharitable beneficiaries always totaled 5 percent of the fair market value of the trust's assets (*i.e.*, that it was effectively managed as if it were a charitable remainder unitrust) did not matter to the court. An appellate court affirmed this decision. 509 F.3d 343 (7th Cir. 2007). The estate asked the Seventh Circuit's mercy, arguing that the bequest was in "substantial compliance" with the requirements for the charitable deduction, but the court held that the substantial compliance doctrine should be limited to cases where the tax-payer has a good excuse for failing to comply with either an unimportant require-ment or a requirement that is unclearly stated in the statute or regulations. The estate did not meet this standard because there was no good excuse for failing to qualify the church's remainder as a reformable interest. If it was enough that the estate and the decedent acted in good faith, said the court, the statute would not set forth the requirements in absolute terms.

No recognition is given to the reformation of an otherwise nonqualifying split-interest trust that is made solely for tax purposes. *Estate of Eugene E. La Meres*, 98 T.C. 294 (1992).

In LR 9327006 (TAM), the IRS ruled that a revocable trust that did not satisfy requirements of § 2055(a) at time of decedent's death could not be reformed pursuant to § 2055(e)(3) to meet the requirements. Under the terms of the trust, the trustee had discretion to distribute the trust property to organizations that were exempt from Indiana's inheritance tax (and any organization defined in § 170(c) that was exempt under § 501(c)(3)). The Indiana law exempts transfers to cemetery associations, contributions to which do not qualify for a deduction under § 2055(a). Accordingly, because the trustees had discretion to transfer property to organizations that do not qualify under § 2055, the estate was not entitled to any charitable deduction. No deduction is allowable where the trustee could distribute property to a beneficiary that is not within the scope of § 2055.

In LR 9326056, the IRS recognized for estate tax purposes the reformation, following the death of *D*, of a revocable trust created by *D* under which the remainder was given to charity, *C*, subject to a requirement that *C* pay $250 per month to *J* for life and $2,000 to *B* for life. The balance of the trust income would be used by *C* for educational purposes. The amounts payable to *J* and *B* were less than 5 percent of the value of the trust property (*i.e.*, the remainder was substantially greater than 20 times the total of annual annuities). The decedent's representative petitioned to reform the trusts to create a trust of $60,000 for *J* (from which 5 percent or $3,000 per year would be payable to *J*) and $480,000 for *B* (from which 5 percent or $24,000 per year would be payable to *B*), with qualifying charitable remainders to *C*. The balance of the property of the trust (*i.e.*, the amount in excess of $540,000) would be distributed outright to *C*. The ruling concluded that the interests were reformable because they would have qualified for deduction except for the requirement of § 2055(e)(2)(A) that a charitable remainder interest must be in the form of annuity trust, unitrust, or pooled income fund. The trust was not a CRAT under § 664(d)(1)(A) because the annual payout was too small. Under that section, a trust is not a CRAT unless the annual pay out to noncharities is at least 5 percent of the initial fair market value of the trust (*i.e.*, the initial fair market value of the trust cannot be greater than 20 times annual annuity amount). In this case, the requirement will be met after reformation.

E. SPECIAL TYPES OF TRANSFERS

§ 8.36. Bargain Sales to Charity, § 1011(b)

A "bargain sale" (or "part gift and part sale") occurs when property is sold to a charity for less than its fair market value. It may be an appropriate technique for a donor who wants to recover part or all of his or her investment in an asset. For example, a client who does not want to make an outright gift of property to a charity may be willing to transfer it to the charity for an amount equal to its cost. The excess of the fair market value of the property over the consideration received by the donor (the "gift" portion) usually qualifies as a charitable contribution subject to the provisions of § 170. *E.g.*, PLR 8433061.

Under § 1011(b), a portion of the seller's adjusted basis is disregarded for the purpose of determining gain on the sale:

If a deduction is allowable under section 170 (relating to a charitable contribution) by reason of a sale, then the adjusted basis for determining the gain from such sale shall be that portion of the adjusted basis which bears the same ratio to the adjusted basis as the amount realized bears to the fair market value of the property. *Id.*

Thus, the following formula should be used to calculate the donor's adjusted basis under § 1011(b):

$$\frac{\text{Amount realized}}{\text{Fair market value of property transferred}} \times \text{Adjusted basis} = \text{Adjusted basis to compute gain}$$

In the case of a bargain sale, the donor recognizes the same amount of gain as if the donor sold a separate portion of the property for its full value and made a gift of the remainder to the charity. In this way, a bargain sale to charity is different from a part gift and part sale of property to another person. Where the buyer is not a charity, the seller can recover his or her full basis before recognizing gain; only charitable bargain sales requires the apportionment of basis. Reg. § 1.1001-1(e).

Where the elective reduction of § 170(e)(1) is applied, and the reduction on the *whole* property sold exceeds the amount of gift, the regulations allow no § 170 deduction, and allocate the whole of the basis to the portion of the property sold. Reg. §§ 1.170A-4(c)(2)(ii), 1.1011-2(a)(1). The Tax Court held these regulations invalid in *Estate of Bullard*, 87 T.C. 261 (1986) and instead allocated basis to the sale and gift portions of a bargain sale transaction on a pro rata basis under the general principles of § 1011(b).

EXAMPLE 8-23.

For more than a year, *D* has owned closely-held stock that cost $50,000 and has a fair market value of $150,000. *D* sold the stock to *C* Church for $60,000. The charitable contribution is $90,000, but since *D*'s contribution base is only $20,000 each year, *D* could only deduct $6,000 currently (30% x $20,000). Accordingly, *D* would probably not be able to make full use of the available deduction even with the benefit of the allowable five-year carryover. *D* might therefore elect to reduce the contribution by the capital gain element in accordance with § 170(b)(1)(C)(iii) to take advantage of the 50% limitation and increase the annual deduction to $10,000. Under Reg. § 1.1011-2(a)(1), the contribution is reduced by the capital gain portion as if the whole property had been sold to determine if there is an allowable deduction under § 170:

Total contribution	$90,000
Capital gain portion	−100,000
Allowable deduction	0

Reg. § 1.170A-4(c)(2)(ii) therefore allocates all of the basis to the sale part of the property, and none to the gift part, thus eliminating the gift deduction:

Total sale	$60,000
Basis	−50,000
Recognized gain on sale	$10,000
Gift	$90,000
Basis of gift	0
Capital gain element	$90,000
Gift reduced by capital gain element, to arrive at § 170 deduction	0

Under the Tax Court holding in *Estate of Bullard*, 87 T.C. 261 (1986), the basis would be ratably allocated between the gifted and sold portions of the property, resulting in a $40,000 capital gain ($60,000 − $20,000 basis) and a charitable contribution deduction of $90,000.

Section 1011(b) is applicable to the transfer to charity of encumbered capital gain property although the donor had already made capital gain contributions to charity that exceeded the amount deductible for the current taxable year. *Warner W. Hodgdon*, 98 T.C. 424 (1992). In *Hodgdon* the Tax Court upheld Reg. § 1.1011-2(a)(2), which provides that the bargain sale rules apply where the transfer gives rise to a charitable contribution that is carried over to a subsequent tax year. As the court noted, "Congress did not provide any 'first-in, first-out' rule or any other rule under which one contribution of capital gain property could be considered made before another contribution of the same type of property made in the same taxable year." 98 T.C. at 431-432.

A bargain sale can be made in exchange for an installment note which can be crafted to spread payments over the desired period. If the donor dies prior to the end of the installment period, the remaining payments could be made to designated others or the obligation of the charity to make additional payments could be terminated. By using an installment note, the recognition of the capital gain element can be spread over the term of the note.

Under the pre-1970 law, if property were sold to a charity in a bargain sale, the proceeds were not taxable to the extent of the seller's entire adjusted basis in the property. In addition, the seller was entitled to a charitable deduction for the excess of the fair market value of the property over the sale price.

In the case of an outright transfer in connection with a bargain sale, the donor is entitled to a gift tax deduction in the amount of the gift portion. Similarly, the donor's estate is entitled to an estate tax charitable deduction if the property is included in the donor's gross estate. Where the donor makes a bargain sale of a partial interest in property, such as a remainder interest, a deduction is not allowed unless the interest falls within one of the exceptions to the split-interest rules. *See* §§ 8.14-8.18.

Encumbered Property. For purposes of § 1011(b), if property is transferred subject to an indebtedness, the amount of the indebtedness is treated as an amount realized by the seller even though the transferee does not agree to assume or pay the indebtedness. Reg. § 1.1011-2(a)(3). The principles of *Crane v. Commissioner*, 331 U.S. 1 (1947), apply in such a case, with the result that the donor may realize income as a consequence of making the gift. *Winston F. C. Guest*, 77 T.C. 9 (1981); *Ebben v.*

Commissioner, 783 F.2d 906 (9th Cir. 1986). In *Ebben* the court stated, "we hold that every contribution of mortgaged property to a charity is a 'sale' and basis is computed under § 1011(b)." 783 F.2d at 911. The income tax consequences of a bargain sale of encumbered property are also illustrated in Rev. Rul. 81-163, 1981-1 C.B. 433.

§ 8.37. CHARITABLE GIFT ANNUITIES

Charitable deductions are also allowable when property is transferred to a charity in exchange for an annuity. The rate of the annuity is usually established in accordance with the recommendations of the Committee on Gift Annuities. A gift tax charitable deduction is allowed for the excess of the value of the property transferred over the value of the annuity. Rev. Rul. 80-281, 1980-2 C.B. 282. An estate tax charitable deduction may be allowed for a testamentary gift to a charity that is conditioned upon the payment of an annuity to a designated person. The IRS has ruled that an estate tax charitable deduction is allowable for the excess of the value of an IRA that is payable to a charity provided the charity pays an annuity to a designated person. LR 200230018. Gift and estate tax deductions should be available because, as explained in Rev. Rul. 80-281 with respect to the gift tax, such a gift does not create charitable and noncharitable interests in the same property.

On May 12, 2003, the following rates were approved by the American Council on Gift Annuities, effective July 1, 2001, for singles' lives at the ages indicated. The complete tables are available at www.acga-web.org.

Age	*Rate of Annual Income*
60	6.4%
65	6.7%
70	7.2%
75	7.9%
80	8.9%
85	10.4%
90 and over	12.0%

The new rates for two annuitants of the same age are:

Ages	*Rate of*
60 and 60	5.4%
60 and 61+	5.5%
65 and 65	5.6%
65 and 66-70	5.7%
65 and 71+	5.8%
70 and 70-71	5.9%
70 and 72-74	6.0%
70 and 75-77	6.1%
70 and 78-82	6.2%
70 and 83+	6.3%

75 and 75	6.3%
75 and 76-77	6.4%
75 and 78-79	6.5%
75 and 80-82	6.6%
85 and 85	7.9%
85 and 86	8.0%
85 and 87	8.1%
90 and 90	9.3%

An action filed in 1994 claimed that the use by charities of gift annuity tables promulgated by the American Council on Gift Annuities violated antitrust and securities laws. Later the action was certified as a class action against a broad group of charities. In 1995 Congress responded by enacting the Charitable Gift Annuity Antitrust Relief Act of 1995, P.L. 104-63, which exempts charities from the threat of liability under federal and state antitrust laws. Later Congress passed the Philanthropy Protection Act of 1995, which limits the extent to which charities are subject to the federal securities laws. In particular, it exempts charities from liability for the "collective investment and reinvestment" of pooled income funds, CRTs, CLTs, and charitable gift annuities. A section of the latter Act requires charities to provide each donor with "written information describing the material terms of the operation of such fund" at the time of a contribution. Unfortunately, the Act did not describe the type of information that must be provided to donors. However, a disclosure statement of the type used previously by many charities should satisfy the requirement. Organizations that issue charitable gift annuities remain subject to some state regulations.

A donor who makes a transfer to a charity in exchange for an annuity is treated as having made a charitable gift of the amount by which the value of the transferred property exceeds the value of the annuity contract. For this purpose the annuity is valued according to the tables in Aleph Vol., IRS Pub. No. 1457. For transfers prior to May 1, 1999 the tables set forth in the Alpha volume apply. Pre-May 1, 1989 transfers are valued under the tables published in Reg. §§20.2031-7(f) and 25.2512-5(f). *See* Rev. Rul. 84-162, 1984-2 C.B. 200.

Gift annuities that provide for current payments are generally of most interest to older clients. Some younger clients may be interested in deferred gift annuities—ones that provide for annuity payments to begin in the future. The donor of a deferred gift annuity is entitled to present federal income and gift tax deductions for the value of the interest given to charity (*i.e.*, the value of the property transferred less the present value of the annuity payments). The potential advantage of a deferred gift annuity is that, due to tax-free compounding during the deferral period, payments will be substantially larger when they begin than if payments had begun at the outset.

EXAMPLE 8-24.

D, a 72-year-old, transferred securities with a basis of $20,000 and a current value of $100,000 to a public charity, C, in exchange for its nonassignable promise to pay D $5,000 each year in monthly installments for life. Considering the §7520 interest rates for the current and immediate past 2 months, the donor chose to use an 9.6 percent rate for purposes of valuing the charitable interest. The value of the right to receive payments of $5,000 per year for the life of a 72-year-old is $33,451. That figure is determined by multiplying the amount of the annual payment ($5,000) by the factor for a 72-year-old from Table S of Aleph Volume. (1999) as increased by a factor from Table K of 1.0433 for monthly payments. *D* made a gift to *C* of the $66,549, the amount by which the value of the property transferred ($100,000) exceeded the value of the annuity ($35,131). *D* realized gain on the transfer, which is determined under the bargain sale rules and is usually reported over the life expectancy of the annuitant in the manner described below.

EXAMPLE 8-25.

A couple aged 50, *H* and *W*, transferred property worth $100,000 to a public charity in exchange for annuity payments to begin at age 65. The payments would be $13,200 (13.2%). In addition, *H* and *W* would be entitled to an income tax deduction of $73,623. At a 31 percent rate the deduction would result in an income tax saving of $22,823. Of course, if *H* and *W* transferred appreciated property to the charity, the transaction will involve the realization of some gain.

The bargain sale rules apply to charitable gift annuity transactions that give rise to a charitable deduction under §170. Reg. §1.1011-2; LR 8117045. Accordingly, a donor will realize some gain when appreciated property is transferred to a charity in exchange for an annuity. In this respect a gift annuity has less favorable income tax consequences than a gift to a CRT or a pooled income fund. However, if the annuity contract is not assignable and the donor is one of the annuitants, the gain is not reported immediately. Instead, a portion of each payment is reported as gain over the period of the annuitant's life expectancy. Reg. §1.1011-2(a)(4). The portion treated as gain is determined by dividing the gain by the annuitant's life expectancy according to Table I or Table V of Reg. §1.72-9 depending on when the transfer to the charity took place. However, the gain is reported only from the portion of the annual payment that represents the return on the donor's investment in the contract as determined under §72. Otherwise, even if the annuitant lives longer than expected, none of the portion attributable to the annuitant's investment in the contract is taxed. The application of these rules is illustrated by Example 8-26, which is a slightly changed and updated version of Reg. §1.1011-2(c), Example 8.

EXAMPLE 8-26.

A donor aged 72, *D*, transferred securities after May 1, 1999 which were worth $100,000 and had a basis of $20,000 to a public charity, *C*, in exchange for its nonassignable promise to pay *D* $5,000 per year in monthly installments for life. The present value of the annuity, calculated as described above is $33,451. Thus, *D* made a gift to *C* of $66,549. Under the bargain sale rules, *D*'s adjusted basis in the securities was $6,690:

$$\frac{\$33,451}{\$100,000} \times \$20,000 = \$6,690$$

Accordingly, *D* realized a gain on the transfer of $26,761 ($33,451-$6,690), which will be reported over the 20 year period the payments are expected to be made according to Table V of Reg. § 1.72-9. *D* must report a gain of $1,338 each year out of the portion of the payment attributable to the investment in the contract. The portion of each payment that is attributable to *D*'s investment in the contract is determined by dividing the investment ($33,451) by the expected return on the contract ($100,000). The expected return is simply the amount of the annual payment ($5,000) multiplied by *D*'s life expectancy of 20 years determined under Table V of Reg. § 1.72-9. *D*'s investment in the contract is $33,451, the present value of the annuity, or 33.451 percent of the expected return ($100,000). The annual payment of $5,000 is multiplied by the exclusion ratio (33.451%) to determine the amount that is excludible each year from *D*'s income ($1,673). However, the gain of $1,405 must be reported out of that portion of each payment until the full gain ($26,761) has been taxed. Thereafter, the full $1,673 is received tax free. The gain is the excess of *D*'s investment in the contract ($33,451) over the adjusted basis in the sale portion ($6,690). Each year *D* must report as ordinary income the amount ($3,327) by which the annuity payment ($5,000) exceeds the exclusion portion ($1,673).

A gift tax charitable deduction is allowable under § 2522 for the excess of the value of the property transferred to the charity over the value of the annuity. Transfers made prior to May 1, 1989 were valued according to the former 10 percent unisex actuarial tables of Reg. §§ 20.2031-7 and 25.2512-5. Rev. Rul. 84-162, 1984-2 C.B. 200. The deduction is allowable although the gift does not take the form of a CRT or pooled income fund because the donor did not retain an interest in the same property that was transferred to the charity. Rev. Rul. 80-281, 1980-2 C.B. 282. As is the case with other annuities, nothing is ordinarily includible in the donor-annuitant's gross estate at death. Some value would be included under § 2039 if the annuity is payable to another person following the donor's death.

State Regulation. In many states charitable gift annuities are subject to insurance regulations. A few, such as Washington, exempt charities from regulation.

§ 8.38. GIFT AND REDEMPTION OF APPRECIATED STOCK

An outright gift of closely-held stock to a charity, followed by a redemption of the stock, can be an effective way of making a charitable gift that may not reduce the donor-shareholder's after-tax income. The redemption would prevent the shares from being transferred by the charity to outsiders. Also, a redemption may operate to increase the proportionate interests of the other shareholders without the imposition of a gift tax. In most cases, the valuation of the shares for income and gift tax purposes will require an appraisal by an expert. Of course, the amount paid in redemption of the shares is some evidence of their value. In order to avoid problems with the IRS or ethical problems, the amount claimed as a charitable deduction should not exceed the amount for which the stock is redeemed.

The redemption of the shares is not taxed to the donor if the gift placed the shares beyond the donor's control and the donee was not legally obligated to surrender the shares for redemption, *Carrington v. Commissioner*, 476 F.2d 705 (5th Cir. 1973); *Palmer v. Commissioner*, 62 T.C. 684 (1974), *aff'd on another issue*, 523 F.2d 1308 (8th Cir. 1975); Rev. Rul. 78-197, 1978-1 C.B. 83. Such a redemption is not taxed even if the donor and donee discussed the redemption prior to the gift. The IRS continues to stand by the principles of Rev. Rul. 78-197, under which a contribution of stock to charity with a subsequent redemption will not cause income from redemption to be attributed to the donor if the charity was not legally obligated to sell or redeem the shares. *E.g.*, LRs 9825031, 9611047, 9523016-017, 9427009. Letter Ruling 200321010 dealt with the consequences of a retired executive's transfer to a CRUT of corporate stock that was subject to a restrictive agreement under which the corporation had the right, for a period of 60 days, to purchase shares that any shareholder proposes to sell, transfer or encumber. The ruling properly concludes that if the shares are transferred to the CRUT, the donor will not realize any income if the shares are subsequently redeemed by the corporation. The conclusion assumes that there is "no prearranged sale contract whereby the CRUT is legally bound to sell the stock on the contribution."

Dicta in *Blake v. Commissioner*, 697 F.2d 473 (2d Cir. 1982), expressed concern that Rev. Rul. 78-197 as reading too much into the *Carrington* and *Palmer* decisions. *Blake* held that a mere understanding that a redemption of shares would take place and that a subsequent purchase of another asset from the donor would follow was a "step transaction" requiring the donor to realize income on the redemption of shares. Further, when the redemption price is set well below fair market value, so that the effect of the charitable contribution and subsequent redemption is a shift of ownership and control between shareholders, the transaction might be viewed by the IRS as a redemption of the donor's shares, and a gift of the proceeds. LR 8552009.

In LR 9652009, the IRS allowed a CRT to become a party to a pre-existing shareholders' agreement and for the closely held corporation to redeem the shares contributed to it without triggering gain on the part of the donor.

The donors may be required to recognize gain on the sale of stock by charities made pursuant to a tender offer and merger agreement. *Michael Ferguson*, 108 T.C. 244 (1997), *aff'd*, 174 F.3d 997 (9th Cir. 1999). In *Ferguson*, at the time of the contributions, the possibility that tendered stock might be withdrawn and the purchase not proceed was disregarded. Instead, the Tax Court concluded:

> The reality and substance of events surrounding the merger agreement, the tender offer, and the gifts to the Charities indicate that the stock of AHC was converted from an interest in a viable corporation to a fixed right to receive cash prior to the date of the gifts. Therefore, petitioners are taxable on the gain in the stock transferred to the Charities under the anticipatory assignment of income doctrine.

Gift of Other Types of Appreciated Property. The transfer of other types of appreciated property, such as warrants to purchase stock at a favorable price, is also potentially subject to being treated as an anticipatory assignment of income. For example, in *Gerald A. Rauenhorst*, 119 T.C. 157 (2002), the IRS argued that the taxpayers' gifts to charities of warrants to purchase stock that were subsequently sold by the charities were properly treated as sales by the taxpayers. The Tax Court concluded otherwise based on Rev. Rul. 78-197, 1978-1 C.B. 83, which, the court stated, the IRS could not disavow in the litigation. Under Rev. Rul. 78-197, a transfer and redemption such as the one involved in *Palmer v Commissioner* is treated as an anticipatory assignment of income "only if the donee is legally bound, or can be compelled by the corporation to surrender the shares for redemption." 119 T.C. at 165. Neither of the conditions specified in Rev. Rul. 78-197 existed in the present case. The Tax Court opinion emphasized that the IRS could not disregard its own publicly issued guidance: "The Commissioner's revenue ruling has been in existence for nearly 25 years, and has not been revoked or modified. No doubt, taxpayers have referred to that ruling in planning their charitable contributions and, indeed, petitioners submit that they relied upon that ruling in planning the charitable contributions at issue. Under the circumstances of this case, we treated the Commissioner's position in Rev. Rul. 78-197, 1978-1 C.B. 83, as a concession." 119 T.C. at 173.

EXAMPLE 8-27.

X owns a majority interest in Zero, Inc., and *X*'s 2 children have minority interests. Zero, Inc. has excess cash, and *X* would like to make a charitable contribution of $100,000. Any dividends paid to *X* would be subject to an income tax rate of 15%. But, a $100,000 increase in dividends would be offset by the charitable contribution, allowing the dividend and contribution to take place without any tax to *X*. However, this would also require a dividend to other shareholders, the 2 children. *X* would prefer to increase the children's ownership, and avoid cash distributions to them. Therefore, *X* contributes stock worth $100,000 to the charity, and Zero, Inc. later redeems the stock. The gift has the effect of completing a $100,000 cash transfer to the charity but does not require payments to the other shareholders as a dividend payment would. The proportionate shareholdings of *X* and his children have been changed as well, since the number of shares owned by *X* has been reduced while the 2 children still own the same number of shares. There is an added bonus for *X* in that the charitable contribution deduction results in an income tax saving for *X* equal to the marginal income tax rate applicable to *X* times the amount that would have been distributed in dividends ($100,000).

This transaction could be compared to a salary increase, or a bonus to *X* of $100,000, which would be deductible to Zero, Inc. and would have the same tax result to *X* as a dividend, but would not require distributions to the other shareholders. There may be difficulty in justifying an additional $100,000 in compensation, however, and a challenge by the IRS could result in the additional compensation being classified as a dividend.

§8.38

§8.39. Gift of Life Insurance

A person acquiring insurance on the life of another person is generally required to have an insurable interest in the life of the insured. *See* §6.2. In the case of close relatives, the requirement is fulfilled by love and affection; in the case of others, such as employers or creditors, it is fulfilled by the existence of a financial interest.

In LR 9110016, the IRS concluded that under New York law a charity did not have an insurable interest in the life of a donor which might either allow the insurer to avoid payment of the policy proceeds or allow the insured's personal representative to recover the proceeds from the charity. Accordingly, the IRS ruled that no charitable income, gift, or estate tax deductions were available. Moreover, the insurance proceeds were includible in the estate of the insured under either §2035 or §2042(1). *See* Christensen, IRS Letter Ruling 9110016, Part of Controversy, Zeroes in on Policies Which Benefit Charities, 130 Tr. & Est. 73 (June 1991), which reports that "the Insurance Department of the State of New York has taken the position that the IRS has misconstrued New York Insurance Law Sec. 3205, which was the basis of the holding in Letter Ruling 9110016." The IRS revoked LR 9110011 following an amendment of the New York law. As noted in §6.2, the law of some states clearly allows the assignment of insurance that was originally issued to a person who had an insurable interest in the life of the insured to another person, such as a charity. 40 Pa. Stat. Ann. §512 (2011).

§8.40. Charitable Pledges

A charitable pledge generally does not involve a present transfer. Accordingly, it has no current income or gift tax consequences. However, deductions may be allowed when a pledge is fulfilled. For estate tax purposes a deduction is allowable under §2053(c) for an enforceable charitable pledge to the extent (1) the pledge was contracted bona fide for full consideration, or, (2) a deduction would have been allowed for the pledge under §2055 had it been a bequest. Reg. §20.2053-5. Clients who wish to make charitable contributions at death and qualify their estates for the benefits of §§303 and 6166 may benefit by making charitable pledges rather than bequests. A charitable pledge may be advantageous because qualification for the benefits of §§303 and 6166 depend upon the stock (or business interest) constituting more than 35 percent of the decedent's gross estate less deductions allowable under §§2053 and 2054. This point is elaborated at §11.17.

§8.41. Gifts of Income in Respect of a Decedent, §691

In choosing the property to give to a charity at death, consideration should be given to making gifts of items that constitute income in respect of a decedent (IRD). By doing so, an overall tax saving may be achieved since the gift will qualify for an estate tax charitable deduction and will not result in the recognition of income by the estate or its beneficiaries. (The income ultimately received by the charitable beneficiary is not subject to any tax.)

Income in respect of a decedent inheres in IRAs and qualified plans. An overall tax saving may result if interests in them are given to charities. However, they should not be used to satisfy pecuniary bequests, which will cause the estate to recognize income equal to the amount that was paid in satisfaction of the gift. *See* Mezzullo, Using an IRA for Charitable Giving, 9 Prob. & Prop. 41 (1995); Shumaker & Riley, Charitable Planning with Retirement Benefits, 9 Prob. & Prop. 56 (1995).

In LR 9537011, the IRS held that the decedent's estate did not recognize any IRD when it made a non-pro rata allocation of Series E and Series HH bonds with unreported interest to a charity, which was one of the decedent's residuary legatees. According to the IRS the non-pro rata distribution was authorized by the state law and the decedent's will. Accordingly, the allocation was not treated as a pro rata distribution to the residuary legatees followed by an exchange among them. *See also* §§ 4.27.6 and 12.39. In contrast, income is realized by a trust established by the decedent during his lifetime that uses Series E bonds to satisfy a pecuniary gift to charity. LR 9507008. The payment of a pecuniary bequest constitutes a sale or exchange that requires the trust to recognize the unreported increment in value of the bonds.

An IRA can be used to fund a CRT created by the participant's will. Also, in LR 9818009, the IRS ruled that the proceeds of IRAs and qualified plans that are left to a private foundation will qualify for the estate tax charitable deduction and will be IRD to the foundation when distributed and not IRD to the estate or the beneficiaries of the decedent's estate. A transfer to a trust that is not in satisfaction of a pecuniary gift does not trigger recognition of gain. LR 9237020. Moreover, no tax will be due from the trust, which is tax exempt.

If done properly, IRAs and qualified plan benefits can be made payable to the participant's estate, which may use them to satisfy charitable bequests without incurring any income tax liability. For example, annuities made payable to an estate which could satisfy bequests by making non-pro rata distributions in cash or in kind could use annuities or portions of annuities to satisfy percentage bequests to charity without realizing any income. LR 200234019. The ruling states that, "the assignment of the Retirement Accounts in satisfaction of their percentage shares of the Estate will not cause either the Estate or any of the individual beneficiaries to have taxable income, nor will the assignment cause any amounts to be taken into account in the computation of the Estate's DNI for the taxable year of the assignment. The charities will realize income in respect of a decedent by reason of the distributions to them from the Retirement Accounts distributed to them, to the extent of the value of the Retirement Accounts as of D1, but such income will not be taxable by reason of the charities' exempt status under section 501(c)(3)."

§ 8.42. PRIVATE FOUNDATIONS

A private family foundation is often the charitable vehicle of choice for individuals who want to ensure that their charitable goals are realized. Private foundations are particularly attractive because they allow the donor and members of the donor's family to be involved in their management and administration. The features of private foundations that make them popular with many donors are reviewed in this section. After a general overview of private foundations, the following pages review their advantages, entity structures, types, special rules and tax deductions as well as planning and funding considerations, including the use of life insurance.

The administrative burdens that are involved in the creation, management and operation of a private foundation lead some clients to pursue an alternate course. Transferring assets to a donor advised fund operated by a public charity is a popular alternative. The concept is a simple one: The donor makes a contribution to a public charity which manages the fund and receives and considers recommendations made by the donor regarding distributions from the fund. Making a gift to a donor advised fund can support higher current income tax deductions for contributions of cash (50 percent of adjusted gross income as opposed to 30 percent for most foundations) and of appreciated assets (30 percent of adjusted gross income as opposed to 20 percent). Most important, by adopting the donor advised fund approach the donor is relieved of administrative burdens, including the preparation and filing of tax and informational returns. A donor advised fund is subject to an annual fee, which can be negotiated, but is typically between 1 and 2 percent of the net value of the assets held in the fund. Some charities that operate donor advised funds are affiliated with commercial organizations, such as the Fidelity Fund and the National Philanthropic Foundation. Donor advised funds may also be created within and operated by community foundations, such as the Seattle Foundation.

Most community foundations accept contributions to donor advised funds if the contributions are of sufficient value and consist of cash or other suitable property. The foundations may charge separate fees for investment management of the fund and for administration—which may total as much as 2 percent or more. Community foundations can be located through the Council on Foundations (Tel. (202) 466-6512; e-mail www.cflocate.org).

Donor advised funds can also be established at an increasing number of financial organizations. The fees and the minimum amount required initially to create a fund and to make additions to it vary among the organizations. Most require an initial contribution of $10,000 or more and charge annual fees that range between 65 and 300 basis points (0.65–3.0 percent).

§ 8.42.1. Overview of Private Foundations

The term "private foundation" describes a trust or corporation created for exclusively charitable purposes that qualifies as a tax-favored § 501(c)(3) charitable organization. A private foundation is managed by a board of directors if it is a corporation, or by trustees if it is a trust. The directors, or trustees, including the donor and members of the donor's family, can be paid reasonable compensation for their services. Otherwise, the donor and members of the donor's family cannot receive benefits from the foundation. The opportunity to exercise continuing control over the activities of a foundation is an important factor for many individuals with philanthropic interests.

The most common type of private foundation is one that receives and manages property and makes grants to charities and individuals. In contrast, private operating foundations, which are seldom created, are required to spend their revenue directly on their charitable programs (*i.e.*, they do not make grants). An example is the Williamsburg Foundation which owns and operates most of Historic Williamsburg. The least common type of private foundation is the conduit foundation, which is required to distribute all contributions received in a year within two and a half months of the end of its taxable year. Contributions to private operating foundations and conduit foundations qualify for the higher charitable deduction limits (50 percent for cash and 30 percent for appreciated assets). Private foundations of all categories are generally subject to the same restrictions imposed by the excise tax rules. *See* §§ 8.26, 8.42.6.

As previously noted, contributions to a private foundation qualify for gift tax deductions, estate tax deductions, and income tax deductions. However, as noted in § 8.4, income tax deductions for contributions to private nonoperating foundations, which are classified as "nonpublic" charities, are more limited than are deductions for contributions to "public" charities. Many donors, nevertheless, feel the control they can exercise over a private foundation more than offsets the less favorable tax treatment a foundation receives.

A § 501(c)(3) charitable organization is treated as a private foundation unless it falls within one of the exceptions to the rule, which seldom occurs.

§ 8.42.2. Tax Deductions

Contributions to qualified charities, including private foundations, qualify for unlimited gift and estate tax deductions. §§ 2055(a), 2522(a). Importantly, property that is transferred to a private foundation during the donor's lifetime eliminates the property and its income from the donor's gift and estate tax base.

Subject to the generally applicable percentage limitations on deductions, the donor is generally allowed an income tax charitable deduction based on the value of the property contributed to a private foundation. The excess of the value of a contribution over the amount that is deductible in the current year can be carried forward and deducted over the following five years.

The percentage limits that apply to charitable deductions for contributions to private foundations depend on the nature of the private foundation and the character of the contributed property. The following limits apply to gifts to most common types of private foundations: Gifts of cash are deductible up to 30 percent of the donor's adjusted gross income. Gifts of "qualified appreciated stock," that is, stock that capital gain property and is traded on an established stock exchange are subject to a 20 percent limit. *See* § 8.10. Gifts of other types of appreciated property are generally deductible only to the extent of their cost basis. Lifetime gifts of cash or appreciated property in excess of the amount currently deductible can be carried over and deducted over five years following the gift. As noted earlier, deductions for contributions to public charities and private operating foundations are subject to higher limits.

§ 8.42.3. Continuing Control Over Distributions

Within relatively broad limits the creator of a private foundation can control the distribution of the foundation's assets to charities in a manner consistent with the donor's charitable goals. In addition, future distributions will be governed by the terms of the document creating the foundation.

§8.42.4. Compensation for Services

A private foundation can pay reasonable compensation to the donor and members of the donor's family who serve as directors or trustees. Being able to compensate younger family members while they "learn the ropes" as directors or trustees is particularly attractive to some donors, who count on the younger family members to carry out their charitable wishes in the future.

§8.42.5. Corporate or Trust Form?

A private foundation may be structured as either a corporation or a trust. Each type of entity has advantages and disadvantages.

Corporations. Creating a private foundation as a corporation is generally considered to provide greater flexibility. The flexibility generally allows a foundation that is organized as a corporation to adjust better to changing circumstances. This flexibility stems from two major attributes of corporations. First, the board of directors and officers can readily be elected or replaced. Second, within limits, the corporation bylaws and rules can be changed. Where the donor desires flexibility, the corporation is the entity of choice.

Trusts. While a trust is generally much easier to create than a corporation, a trust is less flexible because of its irrevocable nature. In some instances it is possible to change the terms of a trust by court order, it is not always possible. Also, obtaining a court order can be a costly and prolonged process. On the other hand, creating and administering a trust involves less paperwork than forming and operating a corporation. Where the donor wishes to ensure continuation of the foundation's goals, a trust is the entity of choice.

Liability Issues. In choosing between using a trust or a corporation, some consideration should be given to the relative levels of liability of the entity's managers. Trustees are generally subject to a higher standard of care than are the directors of a corporation. Unless exonerated, trustees are generally held to a negligence standard of care. In contrast, corporate directors are subject to the more liberal "business judgment rule," which generally reduces their liability, except for acts or omissions of gross negligence or willful misconduct. However, a trust can be drafted to indemnify the trustees—but perhaps not for acts of gross negligence or willful misconduct. Similarly, corporate documents can be prepared to insulate directors and officers against liability.

§8.42.6. Excise Tax Rules Applicable to Private Foundations, §§4940-4945

Some special rules apply to private foundations in order to deter abuses that were common prior to 1969. Failure to comply with the rules can result in the imposition of taxes and penalties against the foundation and the manager of the foundation. The rules are summarized below:

Net Investment Income. A private foundation is subject to a 2 percent excise tax on its net investment income (gross net investment income plus net capital gains and less specified deductions). §4940(a), (b). The excise tax rate can be reduced to 1 percent if the foundation distributes an amount equal to the value of its assets multiplied by average percentage payout rate for the base period plus 1 percent of the foundation's net investment income for the current year. §4940(e). For this purpose the base period is the five preceding taxable years. If the foundation has been in existence for less than five years, then the base period consists of the taxable years during which it has been in existence.

Self Dealing. Strict rules prohibit donors and other disqualified persons from engaging in any self-dealing with the foundation. Section 4941(d) provides that self-dealing includes the following:

1. selling, exchanging or leasing property;
2. lending money or providing credit;
3. furnishing goods or services;
4. paying compensation or reimbursing expenses (except for a nonexcessive amount which is reasonable and necessary);
5. transferring foundation income or assets to or for the use of a "disqualified person"; or
6. furnishing foundation money or property to a government official.

A tax is imposed on a disqualified person who engages in an act of self dealing and on a foundation manager who participates in such an act. §4941(a). The "disqualified person" is subject to an initial tax of 5 percent which can be followed by a 200 percent additional tax if the self dealing is not remedied in a timely manner. §4941(b). Foundation managers who knowingly engage in acts of self-dealing are subject to a tax of 2 percent which can be followed by an additional tax of 50 percent if they do not correct the act (limited to $ 10,000). §4941(a), (b). Under the personal services exception of §4941(d)(2)(E), payments to a disqualified person for personal services that are reasonable and necessary to carrying out the exempt purposes of a private foundation do not violate the self-dealing rules. In LR 200315031 the IRS held that payments by a private foundation to an LLC that was owned and managed by disqualified persons for "a range of professional and managerial financial and real estate investment services which are comparable to the broker, lawyer, and investment management examples in the regulations" was within the personal services exception.

Required Distributions. In broad terms, §4942 requires a private foundation to distribute each year at least 5 percent of the value of its assets (other than the value of ones used directly in performing its exempt purposes). The amount by which the required distribution exceeds the amount actually distributed, is subject to a tax of 15 percent. §4942(a), (c), (d), (e). A tax of 100 percent applies to the undistributed amount if the private foundation fails to distribute the required amount by the date the tax is assessed or by the date the IRS issues a notice of deficiency.

Excess Business Holdings. A private foundation and disqualified persons cannot own more than a 20 percent interest in a corporation or partnership (unless the private foundation's interest does not exceed 2 percent of the stock and value of the corporation). §4943. The ownership of a greater interest is an excess business holding. A tax equal to 5 percent is imposed on the value of an excess holding. §4943(a). The tax can increase to 200 percent if the situation is not remedied. §4943(b). Some other exceptions apply, depending upon the percentage of voting stock owned by the foundation and by disqualified persons.

Jeopardy Investments. A private foundation that invests its income and funds in a way that jeopardizes the charitable purpose of that foundation is subject to an excise tax of 5 percent of the amount so invested. §4944(a). If the jeopardized investments are not disposed of by the end of the taxable period, a tax of 25 percent is imposed on the jeopardized amount. §4944(b). A foundation manager who knowingly made such investment is subject to a penalty, not to exceed $5,000 per investment. §4944(d). However, a penalty of $10,000 may also be imposed with respect to the same investment if the manager refuses to removal of all or part of the investment from jeopardy. §4944(b), (d).

Taxable Expenditures—Legislative Activities. A private foundation is prohibited from applying funds for legislative activities or political propaganda. §§4945(a), (d). A violation is subject to an excise tax of 10 percent. In addition, the foundation manager can be liable for an additional 2 percent. An additional tax of 100 percent can be imposed on the foundation and up 50 percent (up to a maximum total of $15,000) on the manager if the expenditure is not corrected.

§8.42.7. Adding Property from a Charitable Remainder Trust

As noted above, property held by a CRT can be added to a private foundation when the CRT terminates-typically upon the death of the donor and the donor's spouse. CRTs are commonly created during a donor's lifetime in order to allow a highly appreciated asset to be converted to an income producing one at no tax cost. The CRT can sell appreciated property without subjecting the gain to tax. Thus, by contributing appreciated property to a CRT a donor can receive a higher income stream, qualify for a charitable income tax deduction, and reduce the size of his or her estate. A portion of the increased income can be used by the donor to pay the cost of premiums on "wealth replacement" life insurance for the donor's family. At the end of the term of the CRT, its property could be distributed to a private foundation.

§8.42.8. Form 1023

After a private foundation is created, the IRS must be notified that it is filing for recognition as a tax exempt entity. In particular, Form 1023 must be filed within 15 months of the end of the month when the private foundation (trust or corporation) was formed.

§8.42.9. Terminating Private Foundations

There are four ways to terminate private foundation status. The first two (in order below) are subject to a termination tax. The last two are tax-free terminations.

Voluntary Termination. A private foundation may terminate its private foundation status by notifying the IRS of its intention and paying a termination tax. The termination tax equals the lower of the aggregate tax benefit which was obtained by the private foundation as a tax exempt organization or the fair market value of its net assets.

Involuntary Termination. A private foundation can be subject to an involuntary termination if the IRS finds that the private foundation engaged in willful, repeated violations or a willful and flagrant violation of the rules. The termination tax equals the lower of the aggregate tax benefit which was obtained by the private foundation as a tax-exempt organization or the fair market value of its net assets.

Transfer of Assets to a Charity. A private foundation will lose its status by distributing its net assets to a public charity or charities that have been in existence for at least five years. The public charity or charities must be public charities as described in IRC Sec. 170(b)(1)(a)(i)-(vi) and the private foundation cannot be in violation of any of the requirements of Chapter 42.

Operation as a Public Charity. The status of a private foundation will also change if it operates as a public charity for 60 months.

§ 8.42.10. Summary

Creating and funding a private foundation offers very attractive benefits. Before doing so, an individual should give careful consideration to the pros and cons as well as to possible alternatives. Individuals with long term charitable objectives should give careful consideration to the creation of a private foundation, particularly if he or she wishes to exert control over the charitable activity to fulfill a very specific intent and is willing to accept greater limits on income tax deductions and stringent limitations on the operation of the foundation.

BIBLIOGRAPHY

Abbin, No More "Gravy Train": 1997 Law Revisions Dramatically Affect the Economics of CRTs—Only Those With True Charitable Motivation Should Create Them, U. Miami, 34th Inst. Est. Plan., Ch. 14 (2000)

Barwick & Watson, Retirement Planning: A New Wrinkle on Charitable Remainder Trusts, 5 Prob. & Prop. 31 (Mar.-Apr. 1991)

Clark, I Get a Kick Out of Unitrusts (And Flip Over NIMCRUTs), U. Miami, 32d Inst. Est. Plan., Ch. 16 (1998)

Comeau & Popovich, Giving and Loaning Art to Charity, 147 Tr. & Est. 38 (May 2008)

Daniels & Leibell, Planning for the Closely Held Business Owner: The Charitable Options, U. Miami, 40th Inst. Est. Plan., Ch. 14 (2006)

Douglass & Smith, Generation-Skipping Planning Is Essential when Using Split-Interest Trusts, 85 J. Tax. 245 (Oct. 1996)

Eiseman, Value Added: Donor-Advised Funds at Community Foundations, 136 Tr. & Est. 17 (Mar. 1997)

Fox, A Guide to the IRS Sample Lead Trust Forms-Part 1, 36 Est. Plan. 7 (Apr. 2009)

Fox, A Guide to the IRS Sample Lead Trust Forms-Part 2, 36 Est. Plan. 13 (May 2009)

Fox, New Prop. Regs. on Distributions from CRTs Provide Opportunity, 31 Est. Plan. 172 (Apr. 2004)

Gopman & Mielnicki, Planning with Testamentary Charitable Lead Annuity Trusts, 138 Tr. & Est. 46 (June 1999, July 1999)

Henry & Hays, How to Avoid Costly Mistakes in Charitable Planning, 30 Est. Plan. 78 (Feb. 2003)

Hodgman, Beiber & Huft, IRS Rulings Provide Guidance on Early Termination of CRUTs, 30 Est. Plan. 1 (Jan. 2003)

Katzenstein, Counseling the Client on Charitable Remainder Trusts and Pooled
Income Funds, 2 ALI-ABA Est. Plan. Course Mat. J. 5 (Feb. 1996)

Knight & Knight, Obtaining Deductions for Contributions of Qualified Conservation
Property, 4 J. Tax. Invest. 336 (1987)

Lerner, Works of Art and Other Items of Tangible Personal Property: Valuation – Tax
Planning, U. Miami, 37th Inst. Est. Plan., Ch. 4 (2003)

Lerner, Picasso, Warhol, Koons: What Do I Do With My Stuff, U. Miami, 42nd Inst.
Est. Plan., Ch. 6 (2008)

Levin, Soled & Arnell, Refining the Estate Planning Potential of the Near-Zero CRUT
Technique, 85 J. Tax. 355 (June 1996)

Madsen, Funding a CLAT With a Note Can Accelerate the Transfer of Wealth to
Heirs, 30 Est. Plan. 495 (Oct. 2003)

McCoy, Don't Forget the "T" in CRT, U. Miami, 30th Inst. Est. Plan., Ch. 14 (1996)

Mezzullo, Using an IRA for Charitable Giving, 9 Prob. & Prop. 41 (1995)

McCall, Are There Added Preservatives in Section 170(h) of the Tax Code?: The Role
of Easements in Historic Preservation, 39 Real Prop., Prob. & Tr. J. 807 (2005)

Miree, The Family Foundation: An Owner's Manual, U. Miami, 35th Inst. Est. Plan.,
Ch. 16 (2001)

Note, Taxation of Charitable Gift Annuities: Valuation and Policy Considerations, 67
Va. L. Rev. 1523 (1981)

Osteen, More than You Ever Wanted to Know About Private Foundations and Public
Charities, U. Miami, 30th Inst. Est. Plan., Ch. 13 (1996)

Peebles, Here There Be Dragons: Navigating the Waters of Cross-Border
Philanthropy, U. Miami, 31st Inst. Est. Plan., Ch. 7 (1997)

Scheid, Charitable Contributions of Real Property to Conservation Organizations, 71
Taxes 702 (1993)

Schlesinger & Goodman, Back to Basics: A Primer for Charitable Remainder Trusts,
35 Est. Plan. 9 (Mar. 2005)

Shapiro, The "Temporary Private Foundation," 141 Tr. & Est. 16 (Dec. 2002)

Sherman and Patel, Pointers in Selecting Assets to Fund Charitable Trusts, 29 Est.
Plan. 181 (April 2002)

Shumaker & Riley, Charitable Planning With Retirement Benefits, 9 Prob. & Prop. 56
(1995)

Teitell, Charitable Gifts of Property—Tangible and Intangible, Real and Unreal, U.
Miami, 20th Inst. Est. Plan., Ch. 9 (1986)

Teitell, Charitable Lead Trusts (1991)

Teitell, Charitable Giving Strategies: Windfalls and Pitfalls, U. Miami, 27th Inst. Est.
Plan., Ch. 11 (1993)

Teitell, Deferred Giving (2 vols.)

Teitell, Gift of Donors' Life Income Interest in CRT, 137 Tr. & Est. 74 (April 1998)

Teitell, Maximizing Carryovers from Charitable Deductions, 136 Tr. & Est. 56 (Dec.
1997)

Teitell, Not Your Father's CRT, 141 Tr. & Est. 13 (Dec. 2002)

Teitell, Outright Charitable Gifts

Teitell, Planned Giving

Teitell, Sample CLATs, 146 Tr. & Est. 74 (Oct. 2007)

Teitell, Taxwise Giving (Nov. 2001)

Willis, Using the Charitable Remainder Trust as an Investment Tool, 30 Est. Plan. 509 (Oct. 2003)

9

Limiting Estate Size Through Intrafamily Transactions

First, inquiries into subjective intent, especially in intrafamily transfers, are particularly perilous. The present case illustrates that it is, practically speaking, impossible to determine after the death of the parties what they had in mind in creating trusts over 30 years earlier. Second, there is a high probability that such a trust arrangement was indeed created for tax-avoidance purposes. And, even if there was no estate-tax-avoidance motive, the settlor in a very real and objective sense did retain an economic interest while purporting to give away his property. Finally, it is unrealistic to assume that the settlors of the trusts, usually members of one family unit, will have created their trusts as a bargained for exchange for the other trust. "Consideration," in the traditional legal sense, simply does not normally enter into such intrafamily transfers. *United States v. Estate of Grace*, 395 U.S. 316, 323-324 (1969).

A. INTRODUCTION

§9.1. Overview

This chapter covers a variety of techniques that are sometimes used as alternatives to gifts and simpler estate planning devices. Most are designed to limit or diminish the size of the estate of a senior family member. The techniques are generically referred to as "estate freezes" although some may reduce rather than freeze the value of property. Of course, outright gifts often produce the best overall tax results, particularly gifts within the allowable annual gift tax exclusions. Taxable gifts within the amount of the donor's unified credit and taxable gifts made more than three years prior to death are also very effective tax-saving devices.

Several of the techniques reviewed in this chapter are, perhaps, most easily understood by analogizing them to commercial annuities: In them, the client transfers property in exchange for an obligation that will expire on, or before, the client's date of death. If the transaction is properly planned no gift tax liability is incurred, none of the transferred property is includible in the transferor's estate, and the income tax costs are acceptable. Such a transfer involves shifting the risk of appreciation or loss to the "purchaser" in exchange for a fixed obligation—often one that expires on the transferor's death. Sales of remainders and joint purchases are simply variations on this theme. However, their use by related taxpayers has been made less attractive by the valuation rules of §2702, which usually increases dramatically the gift tax cost of the transaction.

Despite contrary decisions by three circuits, the IRS may continue to assert that the transferred property is includible in the estate of the transferor under §2036 unless he or she received consideration equal to the full value of the property at the time of the transfer. The IRS position was upheld in *Gradow v. United States*, 11 Cl. Ct. 808 (1987), *aff'd*, 897 F.2d 516 (Fed. Cir. 1990), which was followed by two lower court decisions, including the Tax Court in *Estate of Cyril Magnin*, T.C. Memo. 1996-25, *rev'd*, 184 F.3d 1074 (9th Cir. 1999). More important, the IRS was rebuffed by three successive appellate decisions. *Estate of Cyril Magnin v. United States*, 184 F.3d 1074 (9th Cir. 1999); *Wheeler v. United States*, 116 F.3d 749 (5th Cir. 1997); *Estate of Rose D'Ambrosio*, 101 F.3d 309 (3rd Cir. 1996). If there were inclusion, the senior family member's estate would be entitled to a consideration offset under §2043 limited to the value of the consideration received, valued at the time of the original transfer. *See* §9.34. Interestingly, on remand the Tax Court found that the interests exchanged in *Estate of Magnin* were not of approximately equal values. *Estate of Cyril Magnin*, T.C. Memo. 2001-31. As a result the closely held stock transferred by the decedent was includible in his estate under §2036(a).

Some techniques, including the installment sale, the family annuity, and some grantor retained interest trusts may result in significant tax savings if the transferred property appreciates substantially in value and it is not drawn back into the transferor's estate. Indeed, any transfer that removes an asset from the transferor's estate (*i.e.*, the transfer results in a "freeze") may result in a substantial tax saving if the asset greatly appreciates in value.

In LR 9436006, the IRS ruled that the sale of publicly traded stock and closely held partnership units to a trust in which the grantor was not a beneficiary or trustee was not subject to §§2701 or 2703. According to the ruling, "Debt is not an interest that is subject to the provisions of § 2701." The same result was reached in LR 9535026 with respect to the inapplicability of §§ 2701 and 2702 to a beneficiary's sale of stock to an irrevocable trust in exchange for a note. The note provides for the payment of interest for 20 years at a rate that satisfies the requirements of § 7872, after which a balloon payment of principal will be due. According to the ruling,

> In this case, B, C, and D will sell Stock to their RST [respective separate trust], and immediately afterwards, will hold debt. A debt instrument is not an applicable retained interest that is subject to the provisions of § 2701. Therefore, we conclude that § 2701 does not apply to these transactions.
>
> In this case, B, C, and D will sell Stock to their RST. In exchange they will receive debt. Under the facts presented here, the debt instrument involved is not a "term interest" within the meaning of § 2702(c)(3) and the applicable regulations. Therefore, we conclude that the valuation rules provided in § 2702 do not apply to these transactions.

Installment Sale. The installment sale is, perhaps, the best established and most widely used of the devices. However, changes in the income tax rules have limited its use. The private annuity has some advantages, but its tax and nontax disadvantages impair its attractiveness to clients. It is, however, free from some of the limitations that apply to installment sales, including the restrictions on resale by family members.

Joint Purchases. Prior to the adoption of § 2702 planners gave some attention to the potential benefits of the so-called "joint purchase," which typically involves the purchase of an asset by a senior generation family member *and* a junior family member. *See* § 9.42. Under such an approach, the senior member typically contributes an amount toward the purchase equal to the actuarially determined value of a life interest in the property and the junior member contributes the balance. The senior receives a life estate in the property and the junior receives a vested remainder. The arrangement can work very well if the interests are valued actuarially applying the tables issued under § 7520 and the purchasers are not members of the same family.

Regulations governing the use of actuarial tables were adopted effective December 13, 1995. Under the regulations the tables may not be used to value an annuity, interests for life or for a term of years, or a remainder or reversionary interest of a person who is known to be terminally ill and there is at least a 50 percent probability that the individual will die within one year. Reg. § 20.7520-3(b)(3). *See* § 2.5.2. The same regulations were promulgated under the income tax and the gift tax laws. Pursuant to the requirements of § 7520, new actuarial tables apply to transfers made after April 30, 1999. *See* Reg. § 20.2031-7T.

The special valuation rules of § 2702 apply if the purchasers of the term and remainder interests are members of the same family as defined in § 2704(c)(2). If they are, the holder of the term interest is deemed to have purchased the entire property and transferred the remainder to the remainder beneficiary in exchange for the consideration contributed by the remainder beneficiary. That is, the senior family member is treated as transferring the entire property to the remainder beneficiary in exchange for the consideration contributed by the remainder beneficiary. The senior member's life interest is treated as having no value whatsoever. In this connection, see the examples in Reg. § 25.2702-4(d). Importantly nieces, nephews, cousins, aunts, and uncles are *not* considered to be members of the family. As indicated above, if the parties to a joint purchase are not family members and the transaction is properly structured, the acquisition of the property will not involve any gift and nothing will be includible in the estate of the purchaser of the life estate. In such a case, the technique produces better tax results than an outright gift to the donee of an equivalent amount.

Grantor Retained Interest Trusts. An irrevocable trust in which the grantor retains an interest can take the form of a simple grantor retained interest trust, in which the grantor reserves an income interest for a term, a grantor retained annuity trust (GRAT), a grantor retained unitrust (GRUT) or a qualified personal residence trust (QPRT). GRATs, GRUTs and QPRTs exist primarily because they are exempt from the special gift tax valuation rules of § 2702. The approach embodied in each involves the transfer of property to a trust in which the transferor retains an interest for a term of years and transfers the remainder to others. The special valuation rules of § 2702 apply to trusts in which the grantor retains an interest, other than QPRTs, if the holder of the term interest and the remainder beneficiaries are members of the same family. If the parties are family members, the general rule treats the term interest retained by the senior family member as having no value. However, the actuarially determined value of the transferor's retained term interest is recognized if it is in the form of a qualified interest. § 2702(a)(2)(B). For this purpose, a qualified interest is the right to receive annually or more frequently either a fixed amount or an amount that is a fixed percentage of the value of the trust determined annually. § 2702(b), § 9.43.2.

QPRTs. Under another important exception, the gift tax valuation rules of § 2702 do not apply to the transfer in trust "all the property in which consists of a residence to be used as a personal residence by persons holding term interests in such trust." § 2702(a)(3)(A)(ii). In turn, the regulations recognize a form of trust that satisfy those requirements—the QPRT. *See* § 9.44. If the grantor survives the term of the retained interest, none of the trust property is includible in his or her estate.

Sale and Leaseback; Widow's Election. The gift (or sale) and leaseback and the widow's election each involves significant drawbacks. However, each is thoroughly explored because of its own significance and illustrative value. In some instances, one or the other produces better overall tax results than an outright gift. *E.g., Hudspeth v. Commissioner,* 509 F.2d 1224 (9th Cir. 1975) (sale and leaseback of agricultural land recognized for tax purposes).

Each of the techniques discussed in this chapter has attributes that make it more suitable for use in some cases than in others. Of the ones discussed here, the installment sale and the private annuity resemble each other the most. They are both designed to "cap" a client's estate by transferring appreciating property to a younger family member at little or no gift tax cost. If the transfer is properly planned and executed, the property is not includible in the transferor's estate. Joint purchases and retained interest trusts of various kinds are also intended to produce substantial gift and estate tax savings. However, the potential savings are reduced by § 2702 unless the transferor and the donee of the remainder interest are not family members within the meaning of § 2704(c)(2). The QPRT, § 9.44, and some retained qualified interest trusts can produce attractive tax results. A gift (or sale) and leaseback may limit further growth in the donor-lessee's estate and produce limited income tax benefits.

However, the advantage of shifting income from the donor-lessee to the donee-lessor is limited by the compressed income tax rate structure. Also, income-shifting does not place if the grantor or the grantor's spouse retains a reversionary interest in a trust worth more than five percent at the time of the transfer. *See* § 673. *See also* § 10.36.1. The widow's election is primarily a testamentary device, which distinguishes it from the others. While it is usually intended to produce gift and estate tax savings, in some cases it can also generate some income tax savings.

§ 9.2. PROFESSIONAL RESPONSIBILITY

A lawyer should be sensitive to the conflict of interest problems that are inherent in advising both parties to an intrafamily transfer. In some respects the conflicts are worse in a family setting, where one or both parties to a transaction may be less alert than in dealing with an unrelated party. In many instances it is appropriate for the same lawyer to represent multiple parties regarding estate planning matters, including parents and children. *See* DR 5-105; E.C. 5-14 through E.C. 5-18; and Model Rule 1.7 (conflict of interest). However, in all such cases the lawyer should carefully consider whether acting for more than one party is appropriate under the rules. If so, the lawyer should be sure the clients understand the consequences of the multiple representation and consent to the lawyer functioning in that capacity. In particular, they need to understand and agree that information regarding the common representation will be shared with all clients (*i.e.,* as between clients there will be no secrets regarding the subject of the common representation).

The parties and the lawyer should appreciate the potential for conflict and disagreement—particularly if the transaction under consideration does not produce the anticipated benefits. For example, in a private annuity transaction the transferee may complain if the annuitant "lives too long" and the transferee winds up paying more for the property than if it had been purchased in an installment sale, or by another method. On the other hand, the transferor may complain if the transferee is unable to make annuity payments and the transferor has no security interest in the property. Likewise, if the transferor dies "early," other members of the transferor's family may complain that the transferee did not pay enough for the property. At a minimum, the lawyer should point out the existence of the conflicts and the lawyer's inability to represent all parties with equal zeal. Everyone, including the lawyer, is better off if each party is represented separately by a competent lawyer.

B. THE INSTALLMENT SALE

[T]he term "installment method," means a method under which the income recognized for any taxable year from a disposition is that proportion of the payments received in that year which the gross profit (realized or to be realized when payment is completed) bears to the total contract price. § 453(c).

§9.3. GENERAL

The installment sale is a very useful device that allows owners of appreciated property to achieve a variety of planning goals. On the nontax side, an installment sale may help retain a unique asset within the family. The seller realizes some cash flow from the asset without subjecting the entire gain to taxation at the time of the sale. The responsibility for the property, and its future appreciation, are shifted to other (usually younger and more active) family members. The gain on an installment sale is deferred and taxed ratably as payments are received (or as the purchaser's notes are cancelled) unless the seller elects not to use the installment method of reporting. *See* §453(d); LR 8501014. An election may be made at any time up to the due date, including extensions, for filing the income tax return for the year of sale. A later election may be made with the permission of the IRS, which may be granted in case of a tax return preparer's unintended failure to make the election. Rev. Rul. 90-46, 1990-1 C.B. 107. In Rev. Rul. 90-46, the IRS indicated that it would not allow late elections which the taxpayer wished to make because of a change in the law or because of a change of mind.

Recognition of gain by the seller is accelerated in some cases if a related purchaser resells the property or an installment obligation is cancelled or otherwise terminated. §453(e). *See* §§9.6-9.8.

When property is sold for full and adequate consideration, only the value of the installment obligation is included in the seller's estate—any further appreciation in value of the property is excluded. Thus, an installment sale can effectively freeze the value of a portion of the seller's estate. Although the same goals may be achieved through use of a private annuity (*See* Part C) the installment sale is superior in several respects. The most important differences between the two devices are:

1. The overall cost of the property and the duration of payments are known in the case of an installment sale, but not where the property is exchanged for a private annuity.

2. Without jeopardizing the income tax consequences the seller may retain a security interest in the property in the case of an installment sale. In contrast, the retention of a security interest will cause a private annuity to be taxed as a closed transaction (*i.e.,* all of the gain will be taxed at the time of sale).

3. Subject to the rule banning deductions for personal interest, §163(h), the purchaser may deduct interest payments made in connection with an installment sale, but no part of the payments made under a private annuity is deductible. Under §163(h), the interest deduction is allowed for interest on the purchase of a qualified residence, investment interest (to the extent of investment income), and for purchases allocable to a trade or business.

It is unclear whether the rules of §2702 apply to installment sales or private annuities. Arguably, they should not because the transferor has not retained an interest in the property transferred. Moreover, if the rules do apply, perhaps the payments due the transferor will be treated as qualified interests. *See* §9.43.2.

The terms of §453 are broad enough to support taxing a private annuity transaction as an installment sale: "For purposes of this section—(1) In general. The term 'installment sale' means a disposition of property where at least 1 payment is to be received after the close of the taxable year in which the disposition occurs."

§ 453(b). Also, the scope of the installment sales rules was expanded to include sales where the sales price or the payment period is indefinite. § 453(j)(2). However, private annuities may continue to be treated differently. The House Ways and Means Committee Report on the Installment Sales Revision Act of 1980 noted that private annuities were also used to make intrafamily sales of appreciated property. It continued to say that "[t]he bill does not deal directly with this type of arrangement." H.R. Rep. No. 1042, 96th Cong., 2d Sess., n. 12 (1980). The possible extension of the installment sales rules to private annuities appears to have been left to the IRS. According to G.C.M. 39503, "In our view this [the above quoted] language does not mean that private annuities are not installment sales; rather, it was meant to leave room for the Service to determine what constitutes an installment sale and what constitutes a private annuity. In other words, the Committee meant that the Act does not deal with private annuities as such, but does effectively deal with them to the extent that they are determined to be installment sales."

The tax consequences of an installment sale should also be compared with those of an inter vivos gift or a disposition at the owner's death. In general, the best tax results flow from inter vivos gifts that qualify for the annual gift tax exclusion or are within the amount of the donor's unified credit. Of course, not all clients are able to make substantial inter vivos gifts that deprive them of all current use of the property—particularly if the gifts will require payment of gift taxes as well. The gift tax cost of transferring an asset is not necessarily reduced by making the gifts over a number of years. The reason is simple: The interests retained by the donor may continue to increase in value until they are finally disposed of or the donor dies.

EXAMPLE 9-1.

An unmarried taxpayer, *T*, owns property worth $100,000, which is appreciating at an annual rate of 10%. An outright gift of the entire interest to a single donee in 2009 would result in a taxable gift of $87,000. Instead, *T* could transfer undivided 20% interests to the donee each year for 5 years. Assuming that no discount would be available for a gift of a fractional interest, the taxable gift in the first year would be $7,000 ($20,000 − $13,000). However, the 80% retained by *T* would be worth $88,000 at the end of the year (80% × $110,000). The next gift would have a value of $22,000 (20% × $110,000) and so on.

The installment sale allows the seller to transfer the property while retaining an interest and continuing to realize cash flow (interest and principal) from the property. Indeed, the terms may provide for interest only to be paid for a specific term, with a balloon payment at the end. But it does not precipitate a gift tax if the sale is for full value. Thus, a donor can freeze the value of the property by an installment sale, with the possibility of making later annual exclusion gifts, which, in effect, offset part, or all of the installment obligation.

Also, in the case of a gift, the donee usually takes only a carryover basis in the property. In contrast, a person who acquires property in an installment purchase has a basis equal to the purchase price, and a person who acquires property from a decedent will have a stepped-up basis determined under § 1014. When the property is retained by the owner until death, the unrealized appreciation in its value will never be taxed for income tax purposes. In general, the gain on an installment sale *will* be taxed at some point. Gain will be taxed upon virtually any lifetime disposition of the obligation, whether or not any consideration is received by the seller. The inter vivos cancellation of an installment obligation and the bequest of an obligation to the obligor are both taxable dispositions. *See* §§453B(f) and 691(a)(5). *See also* §§9.6.3-9.6.4. The gain is also taxed if the obligation otherwise becomes unenforceable, as it might if the seller allows the statute of limitations to run with respect to its payment. In that case the seller would also have made a gift. *See* §9.4.

§9.4. Gift Tax Consequences

> [S]ection 1274, like section 483, has nothing to do with gift tax valuation. The rationale behind sections 483 and 1274 is to prevent the use of below-market loans to avoid Federal income taxes in seller financed transactions. *Edwin H. Frazee*, 98 T.C. 554 (1992).

> Intrafamily transactions are subject to rigid scrutiny, and transfers between family members are presumed to be gifts. A sale of property from a parent to a child in exchange for an installment obligation will not be "bona fide" absent an affirmative showing that there existed at the time of the transaction a "real indebtedness." *Estate of Diulio Costanza*, 81 T.C.M. (CCH) 1693 (2001).

If property is transferred for less than adequate and full consideration, the amount by which the value of the property exceeds the value of the consideration is a gift, except when the transfer is made in the ordinary course of business. §2512(b); Reg. §25.2512-8. Accordingly, when the valuation of the property is subject to dispute, the sale price should be based upon a competent appraisal in order to reduce the risk that the transaction involves a gift. If an obligation with a fixed term carries a below-market rate of interest, it is worth less than its face value. Prior to the adoption of §483 the Tax Court held that for gift tax purposes an installment obligation with a fixed payment schedule is worth less than its face value if it carries a below-market rate of interest. *Gertrude H. Blackburn*, 20 T.C. 204 (1953) (gift tax case involving sale of real property to children for notes carrying 2 1/4 percent interest when market rate on similar notes was 4 percent). A demand note is probably worth its face amount regardless of the rate of interest it bears. Under §453(f)(4) a demand note is treated as a payment received in the year of sale, which would require the gain to be recognized at that time.

The effect of the "safe harbor" provisions of §483 was considered in *Ballard v. Commissioner*, 854 F.2d 185 (7th Cir. 1988), which held that the safe harbor rate of six percent applied for income *and* gift tax purposes. Accordingly, the court held that the installment obligation could not be discounted for gift tax purposes. Although §483 provides that it applies "for purposes of this title," the IRS and some courts agree that its safe harbor only applies for income tax purposes. *Lester H. Krabbenhoft*, 94 T.C. 887

(1990), *aff'd*, 939 F.2d 529 (8th Cir. 1991). Congress should resolve the conflict by making a clarifying amendment to § 483.

In *Edwin H. Frazee*, 98 T.C. 554 (1992), the Tax Court held that for gift tax purposes a note given in connection with the installment sale of property in a part gift-part sale transaction would be valued under § 7872 and not § 483 or § 1274. Accordingly, the value of the note should be determined by applying the applicable federal rate current at the time of the transaction. In this connection § 7872(f)(8) provides that, "[t]his section shall not apply to any loan to which section 483 or 1274 applies." Presumably the enactment of § 7520, which provides for term interests, etc. to be valued at 120 percent of the applicable federal rate, would not apply for purposes of valuing a note given in a part gift-part sale transaction. The Tenth Circuit agreed with *Krabbenhoft*, which intensifies the conflict between the circuits. *Schusterman v. United States*, 63 F.3d 986 (10th Cir. 1995). The *Schusterman* case holds that "§ 483 does not determine the interest rate at which the IRS must value an installment sales contract for gift tax purposes under § 2512." 63 F.3d at 993. According to the court, "The safe harbor interest rate only prevents the IRS from using § 483(a) to manipulate the ratio of principal to interest in each contract payment. Thus, we agree with the Eighth Circuit that 'section [483] merely characterizes payments as principal or interest, while gift tax valuation is concerned with the value of all payments, whether of principal or interest.'" 63 F.3d at 993.

A transfer nominally structured as a sale may be disregarded by the IRS and treated as a gift where it lacks substance. The IRS has frequently asserted that an intrafamily transfer of property in exchange for notes of the transferee is taxable as a gift where the transferor does not intend to enforce the notes. *E.g.*, Rev. Rul. 77-299, 1977-2 C.B. 343. *See* § 7.24. It is questionable whether the gift tax outcome should turn upon a subjective matter such as the transferor's intent to forgive the notes in the future. The courts have generally disregarded the transferor's intent and characterized the transfer as a sale where valid, enforceable, interest-bearing notes are given in exchange for property. *See, e.g., Estate of J. W. Kelley*, 63 T.C. 321 (1974), *nonacq.*, 1977-2 C.B. 2; *Selsor R. Haygood*, 42 T.C. 936 (1964), *acq. in result*, 1965-1 C.B. 4, *acq. withdrawn and nonacq. substituted*, 1977-2 C.B. 2. The initial transfer of a remainder interest in unimproved, non-income-producing real property was held to be a gift where the transferor took back noninterest-bearing, unsecured demand notes that she subsequently forgave at the rate of $3,000 per year. *Minnie E. Deal*, 29 T.C. 730 (1958). Aside from the *Deal* case the IRS has generally been unsuccessful in the courts. In *Estate of Diulio Costanza*, T.C. Memo. 2001-128, *rev'd*, 320 F.3d 595 (6th Cir. 2003), the Tax Court disregarded the self-canceling installment note (SCIN) that a son gave in exchange for property held in his father's revocable trust—of which the son was the trustee. The Tax Court concluded that, "decedent's transfer to Michael [the son] was a gift to the extent that it exceeded the consideration actually paid." On appeal, the Sixth Circuit reversed the Tax Court's holding that the transaction was not bona fide. It remanded the case back to the Tax Court for more analysis as to the value of the SCIN at issue.

A gift also occurs if the transferor gratuitously transfers the obligation or cancels or forgives it. For this purpose allowing the statute of limitations to run is treated as a forgiveness. *Estate of Lang v. Commissioner*, 613 F.2d 770 (9th Cir. 1980). Of course, any such disposition of an installment obligation would also trigger recognition of gain by the transferor. *See* § 9.6.2. Cancellation of accrued interest alone involves a gift of the interest. *Republic Petroleum Corp. v. United States*, 397 F. Supp. 900, 917 (E.D.La. 1975), *mod. on other issues*, 613 F.2d 518 (5th Cir. 1980).

§9.5. ESTATE TAX CONSEQUENCES

If an installment sale is made for full and adequate consideration in money or money's worth, the property that was transferred is not includible in the transferor's estate. Instead, under §2033 the proceeds that were received are included in the transferor's estate (*i.e.*, the fair market value of the installment obligation). For estate tax purposes the value of the obligation may be discounted if it carries a below-market rate of interest. *Estate of G. R. Robinson*, 69 T.C. 222 (1977) (the $1,120,000 unpaid balance of note for installment sale of stock that carried 4 percent interest was discounted by stipulation to yield 8 1/2 percent, or $930,100); *see also* Reg. §20.2031-4.

Transferee's Estate. If the transferee's estate is liable for the indebtedness, his or her estate is entitled to a deduction under §2053 for the amount of the obligation, including interest accrued to the date of death. Reg. §20.2053-7. However, where only a portion of the property is included in the transferee-decedent's estate, only a corresponding portion of the obligation is usually deductible. *Estate of Horace K. Fawcett*, 64 T.C. 889 (1975), *acq.*, 1978-2 C.B. 2. In most cases the full value of the property is includible in the transferee's gross estate and a deduction is allowable for the unpaid balance of the obligation.

If the transferee's estate is not liable for the indebtedness, only the value of the property less the amount of the indebtedness is includible in his or her estate. Reg. §20.2053-7. Thus, only the net value of the property is includible in the transferee's estate where the purchase was financed with a nonrecourse note.

EXAMPLE 9-2.

D purchased Blackacre from *X* for $100,000, of which *D* paid $10,000 down and gave a note for $90,000. *D* and *D*'s estate were personally liable on the note. When *D* died, Blackacre was worth $150,000 and the note had been paid down to $40,000. Under Reg. §20.2053-7, if the full value of Blackacre is included in *D*'s estate, it is entitled to claim a deduction for $40,000. If *D*'s estate were not liable on the note, only the value of Blackacre net of the note would be reported on Schedule A of *D*'s estate tax return and no deduction would be allowed. The latter rule should be taken into account when arranging for the purchase of an asset with a situs in the United States by a nonresident alien. In the case of a nonre-course loan only the net value of the property is includible in the nonresident alien's estate. Otherwise, the full value of the property is includible and only a portion of the indebtedness is allowable as a deduction. *See* §9.9.

§9.6. INCOME TAX CONSEQUENCES

The tax deferral brought about by the income tax rules applicable to installment sales was significantly curtailed by the 1986 Act. For a discussion of the changes, *see* Roche, Installment Reporting After the Tax Reform Act of 1986, 66 J. Tax. 80 (1987). The most significant estate planning features of the installment sales rules are discussed below. Note that these restrictions do not apply to private annuities, which may make them more attractive to some clients. The income tax rules applicable to installment sales are intended to allow the gain on the sale of real property or a casual sale of personal property to be reported as payments are received. Gain on an installment sale is reported on the installment method unless the transferor makes a timely election not to use that method. §453(d). Further, an installment sale of depreciable real or personal property will result in recapture of depreciation in the year of sale, with other gain reported under the installment method. §453(i). A taxpayer might elect not to use the method where he or she has current losses that would offset the gain on the sale. The method does not affect the character of gain as capital gain or ordinary income. It also does not affect the way in which losses are reported—the installment method is totally inapplicable to losses.

In general, the installment method applies to any disposition of property where one or more payments will be received in future years. §453(b)(1). It is unavailable with respect to sales of stock or securities that are traded on an established securities market. §453(k)(2). Also, installment sales treatment does not apply to a sale of depreciable property between the taxpayer and a controlled (more than 50-percent owned) entity, or two controlled entities. §453(g)(1); §1239(b). By reason of §1239 the gain recognized on a sale of depreciable property to a controlled corporation is ordinary income. Similarly, the gain on the sale of a noncapital asset to a controlled partnership is treated as ordinary income. §707(b)(2).

Under the installment method, the gain recognized for a tax year is "that proportion of the payments received in that year which the gross profit (realized or to be realized when payment is completed) bears to the total contract price." §453(c). Sometimes that proportion is called the gross profit ratio, which can also be expressed as a percentage. For purposes of the ratio, gross profit is calculated by reducing the gross selling price by the transferor's adjusted basis and the expenses of sale. For example, if property having a basis of $10,000 is sold for $50,000, the transferor's gross profit is $40,000. The total contract price is the amount the transferor will ultimately receive as a result of the sale, including cash, notes, and other property received, but not encumbrances on the property except to the extent they exceed the transferor's adjusted basis. Except where the property is sold subject to an encumbrance, the total contract price is essentially the sale price of the property. Reg. §15A.453-1(b)(2)(iii). The selling price does not include interest, whether stated or unstated, or original issue discount. Reg. §15A.453-1(b)(2)(ii).

EXAMPLE 9-3.

T sold property to *X* that had a basis of $50,000, subject to a $20,000 mortgage. The purchase price was $100,000, of which $10,000 was paid in the year of sale and the balance of $70,000 was due in equal annual installments with a reasonable rate of interest over the following 7 years. *X* gave *T* a nonnegotiable promissory note for the balance. For purposes of the installment sale rules, *T*'s gross profit was $50,000 (the $100,000 selling price less *T*'s basis of $50,000). The total contract price is $80,000, which is the total amount *T* will receive disregarding the mortgage that is within the amount of *T*'s basis. Accordingly, 62.5% of each payment ($50,000 ÷ $80,000) must be recognized as gain. In addition, *T* must report the interest element of each payment. A purchaser such as *X* is ordinarily not entitled to deduct any portion of the payments made to the seller. Unless the property falls within one of the exceptions to §163(h) the interest payments by *X* will be personal interest expense, which is nondeductible.

§9.6.1. Payments Received

In general, gain is recognized only as payments are received by the seller, or when the obligation is sold, exchanged, or otherwise disposed of by him or her. For the purposes of the installment sale rules, the word "payment" has a broad and somewhat undefined meaning. The planner must be alert to the circumstances under which the seller may be treated as having received payment without having actually received any cash or other property.

The receipt of an evidence of indebtedness of the purchaser is not ordinarily treated as payment. §453(f)(3). However, the receipt of an obligation that is payable on demand does constitute payment. §453(f)(4)(A). The receipt of a readily traceable obligation issued by a corporation or government or political subdivision thereof is also treated as payment. §453(f)(4)(B). Assignment of the installment obligation as collateral security on a loan substantially equal to the amount of the installment obligation is also a disposition. Rev. Rul. 65-185, 1965-2 C.B. 153; *Bogatin v. United States,* 78-2 U.S.T.C. ¶9733 (W.D.Tenn. 1978); *but see* LR 8711002 (TAM). The following paragraph reviews some other situations that have been found to involve the receipt of payment by the seller.

Security Interests and Escrow Accounts. The transferor's retention of a security interest in the property does not constitute a payment or otherwise jeopardize the application of the installment sale method. However, funds deposited in an escrow account for future distribution to the transferor are considered to be a payment unless there is a substantial restriction, other than the passage of time, upon the transferor's right to receive the sale proceeds. Rev. Rul. 73-451, 1973-2 C.B. 158. Thus, "the substitution of the escrow deposit for the deed of trust as collateral for the installment sale obligation represents payment of the remaining unpaid balance of the installment obligation." Rev. Rul. 77-294, 1977-2 C.B. 173, 174, *amplified by* Rev. Rul. 79-91, 1979-1 C.B. 179. In order to qualify as a substantial restriction upon the transferor's right to the proceeds, the provision "must serve a bona fide purpose of the purchaser, that is, a real and definite restriction placed on the seller or a specific economic benefit conferred on the purchaser." In *Rebecca J. Murray,* 28 B.T.A. 624 (1933), *acq.,* XII-2 C.B. 10 (1933), for example, receipt of the payments from the escrow account was contingent on the "sellers refraining from entering a competing business for a period of five years." Rev. Rul. 79-91, 1979-1 C.B. 179.

Property Subject to Encumbrance. Where an existing mortgage is assumed by the purchaser, the mortgage is treated as a payment received only to the extent it exceeds the transferor's basis after adjustment for selling expenses. Reg. § 15A.453-1(b)(3)(i). That treatment is consistent with the recognition of gain when the owner makes a gift of property that is subject to encumbrances in excess of its basis. *See* § 7.13. Along the same line, the IRS earlier ruled that in the case of a casual sale of personal property, the buyer's assumption and payment of secured and general unsecured liabilities is not considered to be a payment received by the seller if the liabilities were incurred in the ordinary course of business and not to avoid the pre-1980 Act requirement that the initial payment not exceed 30 percent of the selling price. Rev. Rul. 73-555, 1973-2 C.B. 159.

§ 9.6.2. Inter Vivos Disposition of Obligation

Gain or loss is usually recognized whenever the seller sells, exchanges, or otherwise disposes of the installment obligation. § 453B. However, transfers to spouses are excepted from this rule. § § 453B(g), 1041. Also, the IRS concedes that the transfer of an obligation to the trustee of a trust is not a disposition if the income of the trust is taxable to the transferor under the grantor trust rules. Rev. Rul. 74-613, 1974-2 C.B. 153. Thus, there is not a § 453B disposition where the grantor of the trust is considered the owner of the corpus under § 677(a)(2) and therefore is taxable on the principal payments on the installment obligation, even if another taxpayer is the income beneficiary and is taxed on other income of the trust. LR 8450031. Accordingly, the installment sale rules should not deter the holder of an installment obligation from creating a revocable trust. *See* § 10.32.3.

A change of underlying security, interest rate, and of the term of the note are not sufficient to be treated as a disposition. LR 8545010. Similarly, pledging installment receivables as security for a line of credit is not a disposition. LR 8711002.

For estate planning purposes perhaps the most important rule is one that treats the cancellation of an installment obligation as a taxable disposition. § 453B(f). When a note is cancelled or otherwise becomes unenforceable, the seller is treated as having received the full face amount of the obligation where the obligor is a related person. § 453B(f)(2). The term "related person" is discussed in the next section. § 9.7.1. In effect, § 453B(f) reverses the questionable conclusion of *Miller v. Usry*, 160 F. Supp. 368 (W.D.La. 1958), that a father's forgiveness of his son's installment note did not constitute a disposition of the note for income tax purposes. If the obligor is not a related party, gain or loss is limited to the difference between the seller's basis and the fair market value of the obligation. § 453B(a), (f)(1).

EXAMPLE 9-4.

T sold Blackacre, which had a basis of $10,000, to *X* for $100,000, represented by an interest-bearing note on which no principal payments were due until 5 years following the sale. *T* gave the note to *X* before any principal payments had been made. If *X* is a related party, *T* will recognize a gain of $90,000 in the year the note becomes unenforceable by reason of the gift. If *X* is not a related party, *T* will recognize gain in an amount equal to the excess of the fair market value of the note over his or her basis in it.

§9.6.3. Disposition at Death

In general, the rules regarding the inter vivos disposition of an installment obligation do not apply to the transmission of an installment obligation at death. §453B(c). Instead, the unreported gain attributable to an installment obligation is treated as an item of income in respect of a decedent. §691(a)(4). As such, the gain component is barred by §1014(c) from acquiring a new basis by reason of the holder's death. For that reason the person who receives an installment obligation from a decedent is taxed on payments in the same manner the decedent would have been. §691(a)(1)(B). However, for income tax purposes, the seller's successor is allowed a deduction for the portion of the federal and state death taxes paid by the seller's estate with respect to the unreported gain. §691(c). Where an installment obligation is transferred by a trust to a remainder beneficiary by reason of the life tenant's death, the transfer is a disposition, which triggers gain to the distributing trust. LR 8317050.

EXAMPLE 9-5.

T bequeathed an installment note of an unrelated party to a child, *C*. The note had a value in *T*'s estate equal to its face amount, $20,000, of which $10,000 was attributable to the unreported long-term capital gain. *T*'s estate paid $4,000 in estate tax with respect to the unreported gain. If *C* receives payment of the entire amount due on the note in one year, $20,000, *C* must include the full $10,000 gain in gross income. However, *C* is entitled to a $4,000 deduction for the estate tax paid with respect to the gain. Thus, only $6,000 of the gain is ultimately subject to tax.

The rules cannot be avoided by bequeathing the obligation to the obligor or providing in the seller's will for cancellation of the obligation. Under the 1980 Act, any cancellation of the obligation or its transmission to the obligor triggers the recognition of gain "by the estate of the decedent (or, if held by a person other than the decedent before the death of the decedent, by such person)." §691(a)(5); LR 9108027 (testamentary forgiveness of balance of installment note causes recognition of income by decedent's estate). Although a self-canceling installment note may work for estate tax purposes (*i.e.*, nothing is included in the seller's gross estate: *See* §9.8.1), the cancellation triggers recognition of the unrealized gain. Rev. Rul. 86-72, 1986-1 C.B. 253.

In *Estate of Robert Frane*, 98 T.C. 341 (1992), *rev'd*, 988 F.2d567 (8th Cir. 1993), the Tax Court held that for purposes of §453B the death of the obligee of a self-canceling installment note was a cancellation that constituted a taxable disposition by the decedent. As a result, because the decedent and the obligors were related, "gain was recognized equal in amount to the excess of the face amount of the obligations over basis 'at the time of' the transaction—the date of the decedent's death." 98 T.C. at 353. Because the gain was properly reportable by the decedent, under §691(a)(1) it was not income in respect of a decedent reportable by his estate. Interestingly, "[o]n its federal estate tax return, the estate disclosed the promissory notes in question, but did not include any balance due in respect thereof in decedent's gross estate. Respondent audited the estate tax return and issued a closing letter without making any adjustments to decedent's gross estate with respect to any balance due under the promissory notes." 98 T.C. at 345. On appeal, the Eighth Circuit held that under §691(a)(5)(A)(iii) the gain was recognizable by the estate and not the decedent. *Estate of Frane v. Commissioner*, 998 F.2d 567 (8th Cir. 1993).

EXAMPLE 9-6.

T sold capital gain property to a related party, *P*, in exchange for *P'* s note that was payable at the end of 10 years. *T* died prior to the payment of the note, which *T* bequeathed to *P*. Under §691(a), the bequest of the note to *P*, a related obligor, requires *T*'s estate to recognize all of the unreported gain on the sale. The same result would follow if the obligation were cancelled by *T*'s will. Of course, no gain would be recognized by *T*'s estate if the note were bequeathed to a person other than the obligor.

Because of this rule it is particularly important to plan carefully for the transmission of the installment obligation of family members. For example, the obligation might be bequeathed to the obligor's children or to a trust for their benefit instead of being left to the obligor. Even where the obligations will pass to the obligors, the tax cost can be reduced by canceling or distributing them during a year in which the estate either has capital losses or other deductions to offset the gain or has little or no other income. The transfer of an installment obligation in satisfaction of a pecuniary marital deduction constitutes a disposition triggering gain. LR 9123036.

§9.6.4. Imputed Interest or Original Issue Discount

Intrafamily installment sale transactions must be planned in light of the imputed interest rules of §483 and the original issue discount (OID) rules of §§1272-1275. In general, these rules are designed to prevent the parties from converting into a capital gain the portion of deferred payments that would otherwise constitute interest by increasing the purchase price and reducing or eliminating any provision for payment of interest. Thus, a seller cannot treat the full amount of deferred payments as the proceeds of sale and none of it as interest, and a seller usually cannot defer interest if the OID rules apply.

Section 1274 defines debt instruments to which the OID rules apply. These include, generally, debt instruments that are not publicly traded that are issued in exchange for property where there are payments due more than six months after the date of sale or exchange and there is unstated or deferred interest. Unstated interest occurs when the stated interest rate falls below the "test rate" (the "applicable federal rate" or AFR) at or about the time of the contract for sale. Imputed interest is considered paid when payments are made on the contract for cash basis taxpayers, and accrues when payments are due for accrual basis taxpayers. LR 8545003 (TAM).

Exempt Intrafamily Transactions. Fortunately, the complex rules of §§ 1272-1275 do not apply to many common intrafamily transactions. The following transfers are specifically exempted by § 1274(c)(3) and are, therefore, subject to § 483: (1) sales of farms for $1 million or less by individuals, estates, testamentary trusts, and certain corporations and partnerships, (2) sales of a principal residence by an individual, (3) sales involving $250,000 or less in total payments (principal and interest), (4) sales of patents for a royalty, and (5) qualified sales of land to a family member as defined in § 483(e).

Exception for Qualified Debt Instruments. Under § 1274A, the test and imputation rate to be applied to qualified debt instruments for purposes of §§ 483 and 1274 is the lesser of the AFR or 9 percent compounded semiannually. A qualified debt instrument is one given in exchange for the sale of property other than new § 38 property, the principal amount of which does not exceed $2.8 million (adjusted for inflation since 1989). § 1274A(b). For sales at prices in excess of $2.8 million and all sales of § 38 property the test rate is equal to the AFR. Table 9-1 shows the AFR for debt instruments of varying durations. § 1274(d).

Section 483 only applies to payments that are due more than six months after a sale or exchange of property, one or more of which is due more than one year after the transaction. § 483(c)(1)(A). Accordingly, no interest is imputed if all payments are due within one year of the sale. Reg. § 1.483-1(b). The interest may be imputed on deferred payments when a sale results in a loss just as it would in the case of a sale at a gain.

Table 9-1
Applicable Federal Rates

Duration of Debt Obligation	Applicable Federal Rate
Not over 3 years	Short-term rate
Between 3 and 9 years	Mid-term rate
Over 9 years	Long-term rate

For both the imputed interest and OID rules, the AFR is used to test deferred payments made with respect to sales, exchanges, and contracts entered into after June 30, 1985. These rates are determined monthly under § 1274(d) based on the market rates on U.S. obligations. Table 9-2 shows the semiannual compounded rates for October 2011. Rev. Rul. 2011-22, 2011 I.R.B. LEXIS 551.

Table 9-2
Applicable Federal Rates for October 2011

Term	Rate
Short-term—up to 3 years	0.16%
Mid-term—more than 3 years, up to 9 years	1.19%
Long-term—over 9 years	2.95%

§ 9.6.5. Sale of Land to Family Member

Under a special provision, imputed interest on $500,000 of sale proceeds for sales or exchanges of land by an individual to a member of his or her family is limited to six percent compounded semiannually. §483(e). For this purpose the term "family" has the same meaning as it does in §267(c)(4) (*i.e.,* siblings, spouse, ancestors, and lineal descendants). However, the interest rate limit only applies to the extent the sales price for such sale (or sales) between the same individuals does not exceed $500,000 for the calendar year. The interest rate limit also does not apply if any party to the sale or exchange is a nonresident alien individual.

§9.7. RESALE BY RELATED PERSON, §453(e)

Prior to the enactment of the Installment Sales Revision Act of 1980 the installment sale was often used to transfer appreciated property to a family member or to the trustee of a trust established by the transferor, who would promptly sell the property for its full market value. In most cases, neither the original transferor nor the related buyer was required to recognize any gain at the time of the resale. *See, e.g., Rushing v. Commissioner,* 441 F.2d 593 (5th Cir. 1971); *William D. Pityo,* 70 T.C. 225 (1978). If the resale did not involve a payment to the original seller, the resale usually did not require him or her to recognize any gain. The related seller usually had no gain on the resale because his or her basis in the property was fixed by the installment sale. In effect, the installment sale technique allowed a family group to realize the gain without subjecting it to current taxation. Again, the restrictions imposed on installment sales do not apply to private annuities.

Changes made by the 1980 Act do not directly prohibit the use of the installment method of reporting gain on sales to related parties. Instead, §453(e) provides that the disposition of the property by a related purchaser triggers recognition of gain by the original transferor. In general, recognition is not triggered if the resale of property other than marketable securities occurs more than two years after the installment sale. (As noted below, after the 1986 Act marketable securities could not be sold on the installment method.) Where the resale rule applies, gain is recognized by the original transferor only to the extent the amount realized on the resale exceeds the total payments made on the original transaction. To that extent the gain flows through and is taxed to the original transferor as if the original transferor received the proceeds of the resale. If the original transferor is required to recognize gain because of a resale, any later payments received by him or her are not taxed until they equal the amount realized from the resale that triggered the acceleration of gain. §453(e)(5).

§9.7.1. Related Person

For purposes of §453, the term "related person" means one whose stock would be attributed to the original transferor under §318(a), excluding paragraph (4), or a person who bears a relationship described in §267(b) to the person disposing of the property. §453(f)(1). Accordingly, the term extends to spouses, brothers and sisters, ancestors and lineal descendants, as well as many trusts, partnerships, and corporations in which the transferor has a direct or indirect interest. For example, the trustee of a trust would be treated as a related party if any of the enumerated relatives of the original transferor is a beneficiary.

§9.7.2. What Dispositions Constitute Resales?

In general, the resale rule applies to voluntary dispositions made by the related party unless it is established to the satisfaction of the IRS that none of the dispositions had the avoidance of federal income tax as one of its principal purposes. §453(e)(7). Thus, the recognition of gain by the original transferor normally will be accelerated if the resale violates the basic rules. However, an exception insulates a corporation's sale of stock that it had purchased in an installment sale. §453(e)(6)(A). Also, a disposition following the death of the original transferor or the related party is not treated as a resale. §453(e)(6)(C). In this connection the Senate Report states that the death exception applies "after the death of either spouse when the spouses hold their interest in the installment obligation or the purchased property as community property or as equal undivided joint interests." S. Rep. No. 1000, 96th Cong., 2d Sess. 16 (1980).

In *James M. Shelton*, 105 T.C. 114 (1995), the Tax Court held that a resale by a related party had taken place within the proscribed two-year period. The taxpayer owned all of the stock of JMS Liquidating Corp. (JMS), which, as a part of a plan of liquidation, made an installment sale of its 97 percent stock holding in El Paso Sand Products, Inc. (EPSP) to Wallington Co. (W), a corporation owned by the taxpayer's son and trusts that his son had established for his two minor daughters. The installment note issued by W in payment for the stock of EPSP was distributed to the taxpayer in 1981 when JMS liquidated. On March 31, 1983, W and EPSP adopted plans of liquidation pursuant to §337. On the same day, EPSP sold all of its operating assets to another corporation for $35 million in cash and the assumption of $4 million of its liabilities. On about March 15, 1984, EPSP and W liquidated. The IRS successfully contended that the liquidation of EPSP in March 1983 was a second disposition by W, which was a related party under the applicable attribution rules. According to the Tax Court, "In the instant case, cash and other property flowed into the related group when the assets of EPSP were sold and the stock of EPSP was liquidated. This is a situation at which section 453(e) is aimed, to prevent the related group from cashing out the appreciation in the stock on a current basis while deferring recognition of the gain." 105 T.C. at 122-123. The court also found that the running of the two-year period was tolled by the sale of assets by EPSP on March 31, 1983, which substantially diminished the risk of loss with respect to the stock. See §453(e)(2)(B).

EXAMPLE 9-7.

T sold land with a basis of $20,000 and a fair market value of $100,000 to his son, *S*, in exchange for a $100,000 nonnegotiable promissory note that provided for 6% interest, compounded semiannually. Under the note, no principal payments were due for 10 years. *S* sold the land for $100,000 cash immediately after he received it from *T*. Under the resale rule *T* must recognize the full $80,000 gain in the year in which *S*, a related party, sold the land. *S* realized no gain on the sale because his cost basis in the land was $100,000. Any subsequent payments received by *T* are tax-free since all of the gain has been taxed to him already under the resale rule. If the second sale had occurred more than 2 years after the original transfer, *T* would not have been required to recognize any gain on the resale.

§9.7.3. Involuntary Transfers

Section 453(e)(6)(B) exempts gain arising from an involuntary conversion if the original transfer occurred before the threat or imminence of the conversion. The House Report also indicates that other involuntary conversions will fall within the nonavoidance exception, including foreclosure by a creditor of the related party and bankruptcy of the related party.

§9.7.4. Marketable Securities

For sales in tax years beginning after 1986, the installment method does not apply to sales of marketable securities. §453(k)(2). Under §453(f)(2), "the term 'marketable securities' means any security for which, as of the date of the disposition, there was a market on an established securities market or otherwise."

§9.8. Self-Canceling Installment Notes (SCINs)

It is possible that neither the value of the transferred property nor the value of the unpaid balance of the purchaser's obligation will be included in the seller's estate if the obligation terminates on the death of the seller. At least two cases have reached that result where the sale was bona fide and for full and adequate consideration and the provision for cancellation was bargained for by the parties. *Estate of John A. Moss*, 74 T.C. 1239 (1980), *acq.*, 1981-1 C.B. 2 (note given in connection with redemption of decedent's stock by corporation, the other stock in which was owned by unrelated employees of the corporation); *Ruby Louise Cain*, 37 T.C. 185 (1961) (note given in connection with redemption of decedent's stock by corporation, the other stock in which was owned by decedent's son and daughter-in-law). In *Estate of Musgrove v. United States*, 33 Fed. Cl. 657 (1995), the decedent's estate was required to include the value of a self-canceling note that was issued to the decedent by his son in exchange for money that the decedent had given to the son within a month prior to the decedent's death.

In order to be recognized as a SCIN it is important that the terms of the note reflect the fact that the self-canceling feature was bargained for. In particular, the total purchase price should be higher than it otherwise would be. As noted in §9.6.4, in *Estate of Robert Frane*, 98 T.C. 341 (1992), *aff'd*, 998 F.2d 567 (8th Cir. 1993), the audit of the decedent's estate tax return was closed without proposing that any amount be included in the decedent's estate by reason of the unpaid balance of the SCINs of which the decedent's children were the obligors and the decedent was the obligee. If the purported SCIN transaction constitutes a gift rather than a sale, the gift tax will apply. *Estate of Diulio Costanza*, 320 F.3d 595 (6th Cir. 2003).

General Counsel Memorandum 39503 (1986) states the following basic rules for determining whether a sale for deferred payments is an annuity or an installment sale:

Where the conveyor of property receives a right to periodic payments for the remainder of his life, with no monetary limit . . . the payments represent an annuity and should be governed by section 72.

When the terms of a property transaction are structured so that there is a stated maximum payout that will be achieved in a period less than the life expectancy of the transferor (as determined at the time of the transaction in accordance with Table I, Treas. Reg. §1.72-9), then the transaction will be characterized as an installment sale with a contingent sale price, and will be treated in accordance with the installment sale rules.

As a corollary of the second rule, when a sale under which a maximum sale price is to be paid over a period that extends beyond the seller's life expectancy, determined under the appropriate IRS table, the transaction will be characterized as an annuity. Thus, G.C.M. 39503 characterized the following transaction as an annuity: "*A* transfers property to *B* in return for *B*'s agreement to make annual payments of $10,000x to *A* until $100,000x is paid, or until *A*'s death, whichever occurs first. *A*'s actuarial life expectancy at the time of the agreement . . . is 9.1 years."

§9.8.1. Estate Tax

The use of SCINs received a boost in G.C.M. 39503 (1986), which states that SCINs and private annuities should be treated in the same way for federal estate tax purposes:

We conclude that in the case of an installment sale, when a death-extinguishing provision is expressly included in the sales agreement and any attendant installment notes, the notes will not be included in the transferor's gross estate for Federal estate tax purposes.

A private annuity also should not be included in the transferor's gross estate for Federal estate tax purposes. Thus, the estate tax consequences of a private annuity and an installment obligation with a death terminating provision are identical in our opinion.

If the transferor receives less than full and adequate consideration, there is some risk that the value of the property at the time of the transferor's death will be included in the transferor's estate under §§ 2035-2038. Because of the possibility that the consideration may not equal the value of the property, the transferor should not retain any interests or controls that could cause inclusion under those sections. Thus, an individual should not make sales to trusts over which he or she retains discretionary powers of distribution. However, in such a case the amount includible is limited to the excess of the value of the property on the appropriate estate tax valuation date over the consideration received by the transferor. § 2043(a).

EXAMPLE 9-8.

T sold Blackacre, which was worth $125,000, to a relative, *X*, for a total consideration of $125,000, of which $25,000 was paid at the time of transfer and $100,000 was represented by a note on which a reasonable rate of interest and $10,000 of principal was payable annually. *T* had a life expectancy of 30 years at the time of the sale. The note provided that if *T* died before it was fully paid, no further payments would be due. Under G.C.M. 39503 the note is a SCIN. Accordingly, if *T* dies before all payments are made on the note, under G.C.M. 39503 that note is not includible in *T*'s estate. However, for income tax purposes the cancellation of the note of a relative is treated as a disposition of the note at its fair market value, which cannot be less than its face amount.

§9.8.2. Gift Tax

The transfer of property in exchange for a self-canceling installment note of equal value does not involve a gift. If property is exchanged for a note of lesser value the transaction is a bargain sale, which involves a gift to the transferee of the property. Thus, although the sale for self-canceling note is bona fide, it may trigger gift tax as a bargain sale. *Estate of Dulio Costanza v. Commissioner*, 320 F.3d 595 (6th Cir. 2003). In *Costanza*, the decedent sold two parcels of real estate to his son in late December 1992 for the appraised value of the property in exchange for a note, payable over 11 years, which was secured by a mortgage on the real estate. The note provided that it would be cancelled if the father died prior to full payment of the note. The son made payments for January, February, and March 1993 by back-dated checks that were delivered on March 8, 1993. The father, who had suffered from heart disease for 15 years, died on May 12, 1993, due to complications from a heart bypass operation. Medical experts testified that he had a life expectancy of between 5 and 13.9 years at the time of the operation. The SCIN was reported at no value on the father's federal estate tax return. Predictably, the IRS issued a deficiency, contending that the sale was not bona fide or was a bargain sale. The estate challenged the deficiency in the Tax Court, which concluded that the sale was not bona fide. On appeal, the Sixth Circuit reversed, finding that the son had successfully rebutted the presumption against enforceability of a family SCIN by showing that there was an expectation of repayment and an intent to enforce the note. The case was remanded to the Tax Court to determine whether there was a bargain sale subject to the gift tax.

§9.8.3. Income Tax

In some respects, a SCIN resembles a private annuity. However, unlike an annuity, the termination of the obligation would probably cause the seller's estate or the seller-decedent to be taxed on the unreported portion of the gain. *See* §9.6.3. That position was taken in G.C.M. 39503, *supra*: "Thus, the cancellation of the obligation would trigger recognition of gain under section 453B(f)." In connection with consideration of the *Moss* and *Cain* cases, note that the redemption of the stock might be treated as a distribution in the nature of a dividend unless it qualifies under one of the exceptions of §302(b). *See* §11.24.

For purposes of §453B, the death of the decedent-obligee of a SCIN results in a cancellation of the indebtedness that is reportable in the decedent's final income tax return. *Estate of Robert Frane*, 98 T.C. 341 (1992), *aff'd*, 998 F.2d 567 (8th Cir. 1993). On appeal, the Eighth Circuit held that the gain was recognizable by the decedent's estate and not the decedent. *Estate of Frane* is discussed in more detail at § 9.6.3.

§ 9.9. INSTALLMENT SALES TO NONRESIDENT ALIENS

For estate tax purposes the extent to which the installment indebtedness can be enforced against the transferee's estate is important, particularly in the case of nonresidents who are not citizens of the United States. If the loan is without recourse and can be collected only from the property and not from the debtor's estate as a whole, the estate may claim the full amount of the indebtedness as a deduction. *Estate of Harcourt Johnstone*, 19 T.C. 44 (1952), *acq.*, 1953-1 C.B. 3. Otherwise, the estate may deduct only that proportion of the indebtedness (and other § § 2053 and 2054 items) "which the value of that part of the decedent's gross estate situated in the United States at the time of his death bears to the value of the decedent's entire gross estate wherever situated." Reg. § 20.2106-2(a)(2). In *Estate of Hon Hing Fung*, 117 T.C. 247 (2001), the Tax Court followed *Johnstone* and upheld Reg. § 20.2053-7, which requires inclusion of the full value of property that is subject to a mortgage, and not its net value, if the estate is liable for the mortgage. If the indebtedness is without recourse, only the net value is includible in the decedent's estate. The allowable deduction would be limited by § 2106(a) and the regulations to a portion of the mortgage indebtedness.

C. THE PRIVATE ANNUITY

A private annuity is generally an arrangement whereby an individual transfers property, usually real estate, to a transferee who promises to make periodic payments to the transferor for the remaining life of the transferor. A private annuity may also include a transaction whereby the transferee agrees to make periodic payments until a specific monetary amount is reached or until the transferor's death, whichever occurs first. Private annuity arrangements are often used for intra-family transfers whereby an older family member transfers appreciated property to a younger family member in order to gain tax advantages, *e.g.*, removal of the property from the transferor's gross estate . . . .Neither the statute nor the regulations prescribe any special or different rules where an annuitant uses property to purchase an annuity instead of using cash. G.C.M. 39503 (1986).

§ 9.10. GENERAL

As indicated in G.C.M. 39503 (1986), a private annuity is usually entered into between family members in order to achieve gift and estate tax savings. It may be used instead of the installment sale to lower the potential gift and estate tax costs of retaining a unique asset within the family. However, the tax and nontax risks of using a private annuity are formidable enough to deter most planners and clients.

In its simplest terms a private annuity involves the transfer of property from one person to another in return for a promise to pay the transferor a specified periodic sum for an agreed period. *Samuel v. Commissioner,* 306 F.2d 682 (1st Cir. 1962). Usually, appreciated property is transferred by an older to a younger family member. If the transaction is properly structured, the initial transfer does not give rise to any current income or gift tax liabilities and no part of the property is includible in the transferor's estate. Achieving a favorable gift tax result may hinge on whether or not the valuation rules of § 2702 apply to private annuities and, if so, how the rules are applied. *See* § 9.40. Unfortunately, the income tax rules applicable to such a transfer are also not entirely clear.

The tax effects of a private annuity may be disregarded if the parties do not carry out its terms. Thus, in LR 9513001 (TAM), the decedent's estate was required to include the properties that he exchanged for annuities, on which payments were not made. In addition, the decedent was in extremely poor health at the time the annuity transactions took place and died 13 months later.

§ 9.10.1. Transfer to Trust in Exchange for Annuity

Where the transfer is made to the trustee of a trust created by the transferor, the transaction may be attacked by the IRS as a transfer with a retained income interest. A transfer in trust may be preferable to a transfer to an individual obligor, whose creditors may reach the property. If the transaction is treated as a retained interest trust, the income is taxable to the grantor under § 677(a), *Weigl v. Commissioner,* 84 T.C. 1192 (1985); the transfer of the remainder in the trust is taxable as a gift, *Lazarus v. Commissioner,* 513 F.2d 824 (9th Cir. 1975); and the trust principal is includible in the grantor's estate, § 2036(a). The degree of control the annuitant retains over the assets transferred was considered the most significant factor by the court in *Weigl,* while the use of the transferred property as the source of annuity payments was apparently considered the most significant factor in *Lazarus.* The Tax Court has rejected annuity treatment where the form of the transaction is disregarded by the annuitant to such an extent as to constitute a sham transaction. *Arthur W. Horstmier,* 46 T.C.M. 738 (1983). As described below, the Ninth Circuit Court of Appeals has overturned several decisions of the Tax Court that treated transactions with trusts as retained interest transfers rather than annuities.

Private annuity transactions have been upheld against IRS attack where the annuitant transferred appreciated stock to a foreign trust in exchange for an annuity of equal value. *Stern v. Commissioner,* 747 F.2d 555 (9th Cir. 1984); *Syufy v. United States,* 818 F.2d 1457 (9th Cir. 1987). Key factors in these decisions were: (1) the limited control exercised by the annuitant over the assets transferred to the trust; and (2) the fact that the trusts were not mere conduits for the income from the assets, but rather, assumed a risk that all of the assets would be consumed in paying the annuity. It is interesting to note that while control by the grantor over the trust was limited, there still was some evidence of control (*e.g.,* changing trustees, changing trust situs, selecting of new investment counselor, and loans to the grantors). In *Stern,* the Ninth Circuit observed, in note 13, that, "[W]here there is no tie between the trust income and an annuity, the transaction should not be recharacterized as a transfer in trust unless the circumstances indicate that the taxpayers retain control or beneficial enjoyment of the trust assets."

§ 9.10.2. Planning Considerations

A private annuity is not subject to the limitations that apply to installment sales. Thus, the transferee (obligor) may promptly resell the property free of the resale rules that apply to installment sales. In addition, private annuities are not subject to the interest and OID rules. In structuring private annuities, favorable outcomes depend upon the proper valuation of the property transferred, and of the annuity. Accordingly, property that does not have a ready market value should be valued by an expert. If an annuity is properly structured, the interest of the annuitant (valued according to the actuarial factors prescribed by the IRS) should have a value exactly equal to the transferred property. Although these income tax consequences are favorable, proposed regulations described below will, if finalized, pose adverse income tax consequences that might outweigh these advantages. *See* § 9.12.

A private annuity transaction should not involve a gift element, particularly where a trust is the transferee-obligor. Where the property is transferred to a trust in exchange for an annuity, the amount of the annuity should be fixed and not related to the income of the trust and the annuitant should not retain control over the trustee or of investments of the trust. Importantly, the typical annuitant's interest, the right to receive specific amounts at least annually, should be a qualified interest for purposes of § 2702.

A private annuity for a term of years may fit the circumstances of some clients better than an ordinary private annuity, installment sale, or SCIN. A private annuity for a term could provide the annuitant with larger annual payments and limit the maximum number of payments the obligor is required to make. GRATs, § § 9.43-9.43.2, which are similar, involve a gift element.

A private annuity for a term of years calls for payments to be made to the annuitant for a period of years that exceeds the annuitant's normal life expectancy. Such an arrangement gives the transferee-obligor the assurance that the number of payments will not exceed the stated maximum. This type of annuity is almost indistinguishable from a SCIN, the main difference being a term in excess of the annuitant's life expectancy, while a SCIN has a term shorter than the transferor's life expectancy. *See* G.C.M. 39503 (1986). Presumably life expectancy would be determined according to the Life Table 90CM. *See* Actuarial Values, Book Aleph, IRS Pub. No. 1457 (1999).

§ 9.10.3. Sale to Intentionally Defective Grantor Trust

Some of the risks of the traditional form of a private annuity transaction and of the grantor retained annuity trust (GRAT) should be reduced or eliminated if the transaction takes the form of a sale to an intentionally defective grantor trust in exchange for an annuity for a fixed term. The approach is more fully described in Price, Estate Planning With GRATs and Near GRATs—Opportunities, Pitfalls and a Promising Alternative, U. Miami, 38th Inst. Est. Plan., Ch. 11 (2003). Structuring the transaction in this way should avoid the risk that the property transferred to the trust would be included in the transferor's estate under § 2036. As a precaution, the annuity should meet the requirements of a qualified annuity under § 2702. Doing so should eliminate some valuation risks, including ones concerning the creditworthiness of the trust. Gift tax consequences are minimized or eliminated if, as in *Aubrey J. Walton,* 115 T.C. 589 (2000), the annuity payments for the entire term must be made to the grantor, or if the grantor dies during the term, to his or her estate.

The approach involves the following steps:

1. Client creates an intentionally defective grantor trust, from which discretionary distributions may be made to the client's children and grandchildren. (Grantor trust tax status can be achieved in a variety of ways, one of the most popular of which is to allow a third party to add a charity as a beneficiary. *See* § 674(a), *Bernard Madorin,* 84 T.C. 667 (1985), LR 199936021, and § 10.32.)

2. Client transfers a significant amount of property, say $100,000 or more, to the IDIT. Client's GSTT exemption is allocated to the transfer, so the IDIT will be completely GSTT exempt.

3. Client transfers assets to the trust that qualify for a substantial valuation discount (*e.g.,* closely held stock or units of an LLC or family limited partnership (FLP) in exchange for an annuity for a fixed term. If the grantor dies before the end of the term, the remaining payments are to be made to the grantor's estate. Funds with which to make payments could be borrowed, or the FLP or LLC could be liquidated. As indicated above, the agreement should be drafted to meet the requirements of § 2702. As in *Stern v. Commissioner,* 747 F.2d 555 (9th Cir. 1984), the agreement should not impose on the trustee any personal liability for making payments.

Income Tax Consequences. Under Rev. Rul. 85-13, 1985-1 C.B. 184, transfers between a grantor trust and the grantor of the trust have no income tax consequences. Accordingly, neither the transfer of property to the trust in exchange for the annuity nor the annuity payments would have any income tax consequence. Eliminating the income tax consequences of the annuity removes one of the serious disadvantages of the traditional form of private annuity transactions. Because the income tax consequences are governed by the principles of Rev. Rul. 85-13, whether the transaction constitutes an annuity or an installment sale under the criteria set forth in GCM 39503 is irrelevant.

Gift Tax Consequences. By following the *Walton* approach, the annuity transaction can be zeroed-out, so there is no gift element. The gift tax consequences should be assured if the annuity meets the requirements of a qualified annuity under § 2702. As in the case of GRATs, it should be possible to provide that the amount of the annuity would increase by 20 percent each year. Reg. § 25.2702-3(c)(1)(ii).

Estate Tax Consequences. If the annuitant survives the term, nothing is includible in the annuitant's estate. If the annuitant dies during the term, the discounted value of the remaining payments is includible in his estate under § 2033. In *Stern v. Commissioner,* 747 F.2d 555 (1984), and *LaFargue v. Commissioner,* 689 F.2d 845 (1982), the Ninth Circuit recognized that a transfer made in exchange for an annuity that is treated by the parties as an annuity and the amount of which is not tied to the income of the transferred property, will be treated as a private annuity and not a gratuitous transfer that is subject to the grantor trust rules. The approach was later applied to determine the outcome of private annuity cases that involved the application of

§ 2036. *Ray v. United States,* 762 F.2d 1361 (9th Cir. 1985) (property includible because transaction was not structured or operated as an annuity) and *Estate of Mollie Fabric,* 83 T.C. 932 (1984) (no inclusion under § 2036). The favorable results in the *Stern, LaFargue,* and *Fabric* cases were reached primarily because the establishment of the trust and the subsequent purchase of a private annuity from the trustee were treated as separate transactions that were entitled to respect although they were planned and entered into for tax reasons.

The decision in *Estate of Mollie Fabric* is particularly relevant. It held that the annuitant's estate was not required by § 2036 to include any of the property held by an irrevocable trust to which she had transferred a substantial amount of property in exchange for a private annuity. The Tax Court felt bound to apply the principles established by the *Stern* and *LaFargue* cases although they were concerned with income tax issues. Ms. Fabric first entered into a trust agreement with Cayman National Bank for the benefit of her children and their descendants to which she transferred $750. Second, almost coincident with the creation of the trust, Ms. Fabric proposed to transfer $1,150,000 to the trustee in exchange for a private annuity. The trustee accepted the proposal, the property was transferred to the trustee, and most payments were made to Ms. Fabric as provided in the annuity agreement.

None of the property of the trust is includible under § 2039, which requires inclusion of "the value of an annuity or other payment receivable by any beneficiary by reason of surviving the decedent." The private annuity agreement does not result in any amount being "receivable by anyone by reason of surviving the decedent." Instead, the obligations under the annuity agreement terminate at the end of the term. Whatever remains in the trust is to be administered and distributed in accordance with its terms—not those of the annuity agreement.

With proper planning, if the grantor dies during the term of the annuity, the amount includible in the grantor's estate under § 2033 will qualify for the marital deduction. For example, the private annuity can provide that if the grantor dies during the term the amount payable to the grantor's estate shall be the greater of the annuity amount or the income generated by the property transferred to the trust in exchange for the annuity. In turn, the grantor's will would provide that the amount received under the annuity agreement would be payable to the grantor's surviving spouse or to her estate if she dies before the last payment is made.

Generation-Skipping Transfer Tax Consequences. The initial funding of the trust would have GSTT consequences unless the grantor's exemption is allocated to the transfer. If it is, there should be no further GSTT consequences. The transfer of property to the trust in exchange for the annuity will have no consequences if the value of the property transferred does not exceed the value of the annuity. A sale for full and adequate consideration is not subject to the GSTT.

§ 9.11. NONTAX CONSIDERATIONS

As mentioned above, a private annuity may help preserve a farm, business enterprise, or other unique asset within the family and free the transferor from the burdens and risks of management. A forced sale of the property to an outsider may be avoided if the family member-transferee can afford to make the necessary payments. However, the overall tax savings may be diminished if the transferee must sell the property in order to make payments or to meet other expenses.

The uncertain duration of the payments of an ordinary annuity may be a source of financial problems as well as family discord. When a parent and a child are parties to a private annuity, the arrangements may cause some resentment on the part of other children—particularly if the parent does not survive as long as expected according to the actuarial tables that were used to calculate the amount of the annuity payments. In that case, the child-purchaser enjoys a windfall of sorts. On the other hand, the child-purchaser may become resentful if the annuitant "lives too long." These concerns may suggest the desirability of exploring the use of a private annuity for a fixed term of years.

Before entering into a private annuity, the parties should consider very carefully the financial, emotional, and domestic relations aspects of the transaction.

First, some risk is involved because of the requirement that the transferee's promise be unsecured in order to defer the taxation of the gain element. However, the risk caused by the unsecured nature of the obligation is reduced if a trust is the transferee-obligor. Second, the property may be entirely expended during the annuitant's lifetime, and the transferee will be unable to make later annuity payments. The transferee might also be unable to make the required payments because of unrelated tort claims, business reverses, or other events. Third, continuation of the payments could be threatened if the transferee predeceases the annuitant. The obligation to continue the payments could deplete the transferee's estate, particularly if the annuitant lives longer than expected. However, these problems can be relieved to some degree by insuring the transferee's life. Fourth, the planned retention of the property within the family could be jeopardized by dissolution of the transferee's marriage. For example, a decree of dissolution may allocate the property between the transferee and the transferee's spouse. *See, e.g., Stanger v. Stanger,* 571 P.2d 1126 (Idaho 1977) (ranch received by husband in exchange for annuity is community property).

Substantial legal costs and other expenses may be incurred in connection with a private annuity. Because of the complex and evolving nature of the tax rules, it is almost always necessary for the planner to do some legal research. Additional time is also required to project the tax consequences and to prepare the necessary documents. The uncertainty of the tax rules and the overall complexity of the transaction may cause the fees to be significantly greater for a private annuity than for an inter vivos trust or an installment sale. As noted above, independent representation of the transferor and transferee is desirable because of the inherent conflict in their economic interests. It is usually necessary to obtain a professional appraisal of any property for which there is not a ready market.

§9.12. INCOME TAX CONSEQUENCES OF TRANSFER

Under current law, no gain or loss arises at the time of the initial transaction (*i.e.,* when the property is transferred for an unsecured private annuity). According to the courts the transferee's obligation cannot be valued: "Where both the annuitant's life span and the obligor's ability to pay are uncertain no fair market value should be ascribed to the contract or obligation." *Commissioner v. Kann's Estate,* 174 F.2d 357, 359 (3d Cir. 1949). Ordinarily, gain or loss in a private annuity transaction is reported by the annuitant as annuity payments are received. *See* §9.13.

The same rules apply in the case of an annuity issued by a corporation that writes annuity contracts infrequently. *See 212 Corp.*, 70 T.C. 788, 799 (1978). In contrast, gain is recognized immediately by the transferor where appreciated property is transferred to a corporation, trust, or other organization that, from time to time, issues annuity contracts. Rev. Rul. 62-136, 1962-2 C.B. 12. In *Dix v. Commissioner*, 392 F.2d 313 (4th Cir. 1968), the court held that the ruling only applied to corporations that wrote enough annuity contracts to get a good spread of the actuarial risk.

In two cases a bare majority of the Tax Court held that the gain on a private annuity must be reported in the year of the transfer if the annuity is adequately secured. *212 Corp.*, 70 T.C. at 802-803; *Estate of Lloyd G. Bell*, 60 T.C. 469 (1973). According to those cases, if appreciated property is transferred for an annuity that has an actuarially determinable value in excess of the transferor's basis, "the exchange represents a 'closed transaction' and the resulting gain is taxable in the year of exchange." *212 Corp.*, 70 T.C. at 803. Presumably this approach would also apply where the transfer results in a loss. That is, where property with a fair market value below its adjusted basis is transferred in exchange for a secured annuity, the loss would be deductible in the year of the exchange, subject to the other provisions of the Code, particularly § 267. In the long run it seems likely that the Tax Court approach will be rejected in favor of one that allows the annuitant to report a pro rata part of each payment as gain. That approach was suggested by the dissenting judges in *Bell* and *212 Corp.*, who pointed out that the Regulations provide for proration where appreciated property is transferred to a charitable organization in exchange for an annuity. *See* § 8.37. The mere fact that the annuity is secured should not cause such a radically different tax result.

If an annuity is secured, it is unclear whether the transferor could invoke the revised installment sales rules to avoid reporting all of the gain in the year of transfer. As mentioned above, Congress apparently did not intend that private annuity transactions should be subject to the installment sales rules. *See* § 9.3.

Proposed Regulations. Regulations proposed in 2006 would effectively end the deferral of the capital gain from sales in the form of a private annuity. Prop. Reg. § 1.72-6. Under the proposed regulations, the transferor will recognize gain or loss at the time of the exchange, regardless of the transferor's accounting method, and such gain or loss will factor into the computation of the transferor's "investment in the contract" for purposes of computing the exclusion ratio to be applied to future payments, as discussed more fully in § 9.13. Treasury intends that the proposed regulations leave transferors in the same situation regardless whether they enter into a private annuity contract with their transferees or simply sell the property for cash and use the proceeds to purchase an ordinary annuity contract. The proposed regulations are intended to apply to any property exchanges entered into on or after October 18, 2006, with a delayed effective date of April 18, 2007, for transactions involving an unsecured sale to an individual of property not subsequently disposed of by the individual within two years.

§ 9.13. INCOME TAXATION OF ANNUITANT

The tax treatment of annuity payments is simple enough where no gain results from the transfer of property in exchange for an annuity. That will occur, for example, when cash or property with a basis equal to its fair market value is transferred in exchange for an annuity. Since no gain results from the transfer, each annuity payment will consist of only two elements—a nontaxable recovery of capital, and a fully taxable annuity element. The amount allocated to each element depends upon the exclusion ratio, which is simply the investment in the contract divided by the expected return. In these "no gain" cases, the investment in the contract is the amount of cash or the value of the property transferred. The expected return is the amount of the annual payment multiplied by the life expectancy of the annuitant.

The proper income tax treatment of annuity payments is less clear where appreciated property is transferred to a noncharity in exchange for an unsecured annuity. In this case the annuitant is also entitled to exclude a portion of each payment based upon the exclusion ratio. However, the IRS has ruled that the investment in the contract is limited to the transferor's adjusted basis in the property transferred in exchange for the annuity and not its fair market value. Rev. Rul. 69-74, 1969-1 C.B. 43. It reasoned that "[s]ince the amount of the gain is not taxed in full at the time of the transaction, such amount does not represent a part of the 'premiums or other consideration' paid for the annuity contract." *Id*. Logically, then, if the proposed regulations described in §9.12 are finalized, any gain recognized by the transferor at the time the transferor exchanges property for the annuity will be added to the transferor's "investment in the contract" for purposes of computing the exclusion ratio, effectively meaning that the transferor's investment in the contract would be the fair market value of the property transferred (its adjusted basis plus recognized gain).

According to the IRS, each payment is initially composed of three elements: a tax-free return of capital, a capital gain element, and a fully taxable ordinary income element. The tax-free element is determined by dividing the investment in the contract (the adjusted basis in the property transferred) by the expected return. The capital gain element is calculated by dividing the gain (the value of the annuity determined by applying the appropriate factor from Table S of IRS Pub. No. 1457, less the adjusted basis in the property) by the life expectancy of the annuitant according to Table V, Reg. §1.72-9. All of the gain is taxed if the annuitant survives as long as expected under the mortality table. According to Rev. Rul. 69-74, the capital gain element of any payments after expiration of life expectancy per the tables is taxed as ordinary income. Finally, the remainder of each payment is taxed as ordinary income (total payment-(return of capital + capital gain)). For annuities with starting dates after 1986, once the period of life expectancy originally projected has expired, all payments will be taxed as ordinary income as the full amount of invested capital and capital gain will have been recovered. §72(b).

Revenue Ruling 69-74 conflicts with the 1939 Code rules as set forth in Rev. Rul. 239, 1953-2 C.B. 53. It also conflicts with the pre-1987 methods of taxing payments received under a gift annuity issued by a charitable organization. Reg. §1.1011-2(c), Example 8. *See* §8.29 for a discussion of the gift annuity rules.

The exclusion ratio for charitable gift annuities is based on a "top down" approach. The fair market value of the property contributed, rather than its basis, is used to calculate the exclusion ratio, and the capital gain element is a portion of the exclusion. Reg. §1.1011-2(c), Example 8. *See* §8.37.

Under Rev. Rul. 69-74, the exclusion ratio is computed according to the transferor's basis in the property, and the capital gain element is computed separately and in addition to the exclusion ratio. The significance of this difference is that under the pre-1987 provisions of § 72(b) the exclusion ratio was nontaxable after the amount of the capital gain was recognized. Thus, an annuity resulting from a transfer to a charitable organization resulted in a larger total exclusion for transferors who survived beyond their normal life expectancy. Since the 1986 Act revised § 72, the exclusion ratio applies only until the full amount of investment is recovered. This reconciles the differences between the above approaches to calculating the exclusion ratio. The change to § 72 applies to annuities with starting dates after December 31, 1986.

A further difference between a charitable gift annuity and a private annuity results from the basis allocation rules of § 1011(b). In a charitable gift annuity, the basis is allocated between the gift and the annuity elements. In other annuities, the basis is apparently allocated first to the annuity purchase, and then to the gift. This difference is demonstrated by Rev. Rul. 69-74 and Reg. § 1.1011-2(c), Example 8.

A transfer of appreciated property involves a gift from the transferor to the transferee-obligor where the value of the property transferred exceeds the value of the annuity. Unless such an exchange is an ordinary business transaction, Rev. Rul. 69-74 requires the excess to be disregarded in determining the income tax consequences to the transferor. The gift portion is significant when it comes to determining the transferee's basis for purposes of determining gain or loss or computing depreciation. *See* Rev. Rul. 55-119, 1955-1 C.B. 352. *See also* § 9.14.

Finally, it might be possible to use a private annuity to circumvent the resale rule of § 453(e) that applies to installment sales. G.C.M. 39503 (1986). For example, if the family unit wishes to dispose of an asset, the gain on sale can still be recognized over a period of years if the asset is exchanged for an annuity and subsequently sold by the transferee. This could even be applied to marketable securities, which are not eligible for installment sale treatment. *See* § 9.7.4.

§ 9.14. INCOME TAXATION OF TRANSFEREE

A transferee has not been allowed any income tax deduction for payments made to the annuitant even though the annuitant must report part of each payment as income. That rule prevailed prior to the amendment of § 163(h), which prohibits deductions for personal interest. "Most courts hold that the entire amount of each annuity payment constitutes a payment of the purchase price of the assets received in exchange for the promise to pay the annuity. Thus the payments constitute capital expenditures, no part of which is excludible [deductible] as 'interest on indebtedness.'" *Dix v. Commissioner*, 392 F.2d 313, 318 (4th Cir. 1968). The denial of a deduction is consistent with the method for determining the transferee's basis in the assets, which takes into account the total amount of payments made by the transferee. *See, e.g., Perkins v. United States*, 701 F.2d 771 (9th Cir. 1983). Without a specific statutory basis for a deduction, it is unlikely that a deduction for any part of the payments made by the transferee will be allowed. In contrast, in the case of an installment sale the actual or imputed interest paid by the purchaser is interest that is deductible to the extent it is not personal interest. *See* § 163(h).

The general rules for calculating depreciation and gain or loss are set out in Rev. Rul. 55-119, 1955-1 C.B. 352, which was issued under the 1939 Code. Its rules applied to transactions arising under the 1954 Code. Rev. Rul. 72-81, 1972-1 C.B. 98. Presumably, they will also apply under the 1986 Code.

§9.14.1. Depreciation

The allowance for depreciation of the property in the hands of the obligor is initially based upon the value of the annuity contract determined under Table S of IRS Pub. No. 1457. Annuity payments in excess of that value are added to the basis of the property for the purpose of determining future depreciation. Once the annuitant dies, the depreciation allowance is fixed by the total amount of annuity payments made reduced by the amount of depreciation deductions previously allowed.

§9.14.2. Gain or Loss

If the property is disposed of by the obligor after the annuitant's death, its basis, for purposes of determining gain or loss is the total of the payments made under the contract, less the total amount of depreciation that was allowed.

The computation of gain or loss is more complicated if the transferee disposes of the property prior to the annuitant's death. For the purpose of determining gain the transferee's basis is the total of payments made under the contract (reduced by the total amount of allowable depreciation) plus the value of future payments due under the contract. *See, e.g.,* LR 8102029. When it comes to calculating the amount of a loss, the basis is limited to the total amount of payments made to the time of sale reduced by the total amount of depreciation allowable. Additional gain or loss may be recognized by the transferee depending upon how many future payments are made by the time of the annuitant's death. For example, further gain is recognized if the annuitant dies before the transferee has made payments equal to the amount of the basis used for purposes of computing gain. In the case of a disposition that gives rise to a recognized loss, any subsequent payments made to the annuitant give rise to losses in the year or years made. Section 267 does not prevent the obligor from deducting a loss that results from the sale of the property to an unrelated third party. 1998 FSA LEXIS 423.

§9.15. Gift Tax Consequences

For purposes of §2702, the transferor's interest in a typical private annuity should meet the requirements of a qualified interest (*i.e.,* the right to receive fixed amounts payable annually or more frequently). In such cases the gift tax consequences will be determined in the traditional way. That is, whether the transaction involves a gift will be determined by comparing the value of the property transferred with the actuarially determined value of the annuity. If the value of the property exceeds the value of the annuity, the transfer involves a gift unless it is an ordinary business transaction. Rev. Rul. 69-74, 1969-1 C.B. 43; *LaFargue v. Commissioner*, 800 F.2d 936 (9th Cir. 1986).

In the case of an outright transfer to an individual obligor, any gift should qualify for the annual exclusion. *See* §2503(b). On the other hand, the gift tax exclusion may not be available with respect to a transaction between an individual and a trustee. Of course, the transferor makes a gift to the annuitant when the annuity is payable to a person other than the transferor. Such a gift qualifies for the annual exclusion where the commencement of the annuity payments is not deferred.

See Reg. § 25.2503-3(b). Conversely, the obligor will have made a gift to the annuitant if the value of the annuity exceeds the value of the property transferred. Here again, the annual exclusion should be available if the annuity is payable currently.

Private annuity transactions are usually planned to avoid any gift element and to avoid inclusion in the transferor's estate. Avoiding a gift should be possible if the value of the annuity is taken into account—(*i.e.* if the annuity constitutes a qualified interest under § 2702(b)). In any case, the property to be transferred should be valued carefully. The amount of the annuity should be planned in light of the proper interest rate under § 7520 (120 percent of the federal midterm rate for the month in which the transfer is made) and the appropriate factor from Table S. Before entering into a private annuity the parties should also consider the economic realities of the transaction, including the impact of income taxes on the transferor and transferee.

The final regulations issued under § 7520 provide that the actuarial tables may not be used in valuing interests if there is more than a 50-percent chance that the party will die within one year. *See* § 2.13. Not surprisingly, wholly apart from the proposed regulations, in LR 9504004 (TAM) the IRS held that the actuarial tables could not be used to value the annuity interest of a critically ill cancer patient who died 19 days after the transfer. Under the extreme facts involved, the TAM stated that "we can only conclude that it was obvious to everyone that the donor was not likely to survive more than a year from May 31, 1990 [the date of the transaction]."

§ 9.16. ESTATE TAX CONSEQUENCES

Significant estate tax problems are likely to arise in two situations: (1) where the value of the property transferred exceeds the value of the annuity, and (2) where the annuity is payable to another person after the death of the transferor. As noted above, the property may be includible in the transferor's estate when the annuity is issued by a trust, particularly when there is a tie-in between the amount of the trust income and the amount of annuity payments and the annuitant retains some control. Also, if the transferor retains use of the property for life through an implied agreement or understanding, the transferred property is includible in the gross estate under § 2036. *Estate of Maria Bianchi*, T.C. Memo. 1982-389. In other situations the threat of inclusion in the transferor's estate is virtually eliminated because of the full adequacy of the consideration received in exchange for the property transferred (*i.e.,* the value of the annuity equals or exceeds the value of the property transferred). In this connection note that the valuation rules of § 2702 only apply for gift tax purposes. If the value of the property transferred exceeds the value of the annuity, the amount includible in the transferor's estate is reduced by the value of the annuity at the time of transfer. § 2043(a).

If the annuity is payable to another person after the transferor's death, the amount includible in the transferor's estate is determined under § 2039. The annuity is first valued under Table S. Next, the portion of the annuity value includible in the decedent's estate is determined by the proportion of the purchase price that he or she contributed. § 2039(b). Thus, if the decedent had paid half of the cost of the annuity, only half of its value would be included in his or her gross estate. A marital deduction should be allowable where the successor annuitant is the decedent's surviving spouse who is a U.S. citizen. *See* § 2056(b)(7)(C).

The property transferred to the obligor is includible in the obligor's estate. Of course, if the obligor predeceases the annuitant, the obligor's estate is entitled to a deduction for the actuarial value of the payments it is required to make to the annuitants. *Estate of Charles H. Hart*, 1 T.C. 989 (1943). However, if the annuitant dies prior to the time the obligor's estate tax return is filed, the deduction may be limited to the amount of the payments actually made. *Estate of Chesterton v. United States*, 551 F.2d 278 (Ct.Cl.), *cert. denied*, 434 U.S. 835 (1977).

Sham Transactions. Assets sold through a private annuity may be included in the decedent's gross estate if the annuity transaction is a sham. In *Estate of Thelma G,. Hurford*, 97 T.C.M. (CCH) 422 (2008), the court held that a private annuity transaction was "a sham—nothing more than a substitute for a will leaving [the decedent's] estate in equal shares to her children." The transaction at issue involved a sale of interests in two family limited partnerships to two of the decedent's three children. The third child was not included in the transaction in part because of concerns over that child's creditors. Accordingly, the two purchasing children agreed to share the wealth with their sibling after the decedent's death. The court was clearly troubled by this promise and by the fact that the purchasing children made no annuity payments from their own assets (and not even from the income of the partnership's assets); instead, they simply transferred back to the decedent "bits and pieces" of the assets contributed to the partnerships. According to the court, "this makes the private annuity look much more like a testamentary substitute than a bona fide sale." The court ultimately held that the decedent's gross estate included the value of the assets contributed to the partnerships, as there was also evidence that the decedent continued to enjoy the benefit of those assets after contribution to the partnership. *See* §2.19.1.

D. THE GIFT OR SALE AND LEASEBACK

§9.17. GENERAL

The relatively compressed income tax rate structure adopted in 1986 largely eliminated the attractiveness of a gift or sale and leaseback. Prior to the 1986 Act, many high income individuals used the transfer and leaseback of business property to shift income to family members or trusts that would be subject to lower income tax rates. The tax advantages previously enjoyed by taxpayers who entered into such transactions are no longer available. First, the income tax advantage of shifting income to another family member is severely limited by the compressed income tax rate structure. Second, the 1986 Act destroyed the income tax advantage of creating short-term irrevocable trusts. Under §673 the grantor is treated as the owner of a trust if at the inception of the trust the reversionary interest of the grantor (or the grantor's spouse) has a value of five percent or more. The inability to retain a reversionary interest that will take effect after a relatively short period (formerly ten years) killed the interest of many taxpayers in the use of trusts—at least those who would be reluctant to give or sell the property to other family members, or to trusts for the benefit of others. The attractiveness of the device was also limited by other changes, including the adoption of the Kiddie Tax. *See* §7.9.1.

Prior to the 1986 Act, a typical plan involved the transfer of property used in the transferor's business to the trustee of a short-term trust who leased the property back to the transferor. At the end of ten years (the minimum period required under the pre-1986 version of § 673), the property would revert to the grantor. In the interim the grantor would deduct the lease payments made to the trustee, who would claim depreciation deductions on the income tax returns of the trust. With the change in § 673 noted above, the income tax goals can be achieved only by making more permanent transfers. In earlier years the main problem with transfer-leasebacks, particularly in the case of short-term reversionary trusts, was the IRS challenge to the deductibility of rental payments by the transferor-lessee.

The chance that the IRS and the courts will allow the transferor's rental payments to be deducted is vastly greater if the lessee does not serve as trustee and does not retain any interest in the property. For example, in one case the IRS denied a deduction for rental payments made while the lessee held a reversionary interest in the property, but allowed a deduction for rental payments made after the lessee relinquished his reversionary interest. *C. James Mathews*, 61 T.C. 12, 15 (1973), *rev'd*, 520 F.2d 323 (5th Cir. 1975), *cert. denied*, 424 U.S. 967 (1976). In some instances the IRS had challenged the deduction although there was an independent trustee and the transferor did not retain a reversionary interest. *E.g., Skemp v. Commissioner*, 168 F.2d 598 (7th Cir. 1948).

Deductions were also challenged, but allowed, in one case where the transferees were minors and the transferor acted as their guardian. *Brooke v. United States*, 468 F.2d 1155 (9th Cir. 1972). The probability that deductions will not be allowed is also greater where the property is sold to a trust or another family member. Of course, the gift tax cost of an outright transfer and the economic effects of not retaining an interest in the property must also be considered.

Some circuit courts disallowed rental deductions with respect to pre-March 2, 1986 transfers to short-term trusts, while five or more of the circuit courts and the Tax Court allowed deductions when certain requirements are met. Kiley, The Evolving Gift-Leaseback Analysis in Light of *May* and *Rosenfeld*, 59 Notre Dame L. Rev. 921, 922 (1984). The IRS has announced that it will not litigate three-party gift-leasebacks (*e.g.*, where property is gifted from one family member to another, and leased to a family-owned corporation). A.O.D. 1984-038.

An installment sale and leaseback is a variation on the theme that involves little or no gift tax cost. However, a sale and leaseback transaction is ordinarily more complicated than a gift and leaseback and could require the transferor to report a gain. The gain would be taxable as ordinary income to the extent it involved depreciation recapture under §§ 1245 and 1250. An installment sale and leaseback transaction may also involve annual forgiveness of the installment notes, as in *Hudspeth v. Commissioner*, 509 F.2d 1224 (9th Cir. 1975). In *Hudspeth*, the parents avoided the 160-acre limit on the quantity of federally irrigated land that may be owned by one person (320 acres by a husband and wife), by making installment sales of the excess acreage to their children. The children in turn leased the purchased property to their parents. Installment payments were made by the children in part with rental payments from the parents and the balance with cash gifts from the parents. The Tax Court held that the original transfers to the children were not bona fide sales and, therefore, constituted gifts of the entire interest in the property. On appeal the Ninth Circuit reversed, holding that the transfers were sales and not gifts.

"The parents were under no obligation to continue to make annual gifts to the children although they expected to do it. The children's obligation to make the annual payments continued regardless of whether the parents made these gifts." 509 F.2d at 1227.

On the negative side, an outright gift or sale of the property involves some of the same nontax risks as a private annuity. For example, the property is subject to disposition by the transferee and to the claims of the transferee's creditors. However, in the case of a sale the transferor could retain a security interest without significantly jeopardizing the outcome. The seller's interests might also be protected to some degree by the terms of the lease.

§9.18. OVERALL CONSEQUENCES

Some current income tax savings may result from a gift and leaseback transaction if the transferee is subject to a lower income tax rate than the transferor. The Kiddie Tax and the relatively steep income tax rates applicable to trusts sharply reduces or eliminates the differential in most cases. Viewed most simply, the transaction will increase the income tax deductions available to the transferor by the excess of the annual rental cost over the otherwise allowable depreciation deduction. The taxes and interest paid by the transferor may also be deductible where he or she retains an interest in the property and is personally liable for them. *Walther v. Commissioner*, 316 F.2d 708 (7th Cir. 1963) (Indiana law; grantor is liable for and may deduct mortgage interest payments on property transferred to short-term trust).

The depreciation deduction for property held in trust is generally allocated between the beneficiaries and the trustee on the basis of the trust income allocable to each. §167(d). Where the income must be computed and distributed without regard to depreciation, the entire amount of the deduction is allowed to the beneficiary. In contrast, where local law or the instrument requires the establishment of a depreciation reserve, the deduction is allowed to the trustee and not to the beneficiary. Reg. §1.167(h)-1(b). The beneficiaries' cash flow position is enhanced if the deduction is available to them. A trust instrument should contain an appropriate provision dealing with this issue. The original Uniform Principal and Income Act, 7B U.L.A. 183 (1985), does not authorize a depreciation reserve. However, §13(a)(2) of the Revised Uniform Principal and Income Act, 7B U.L.A. 176 (1985), generally requires that a charge be made against income for depreciation where it is called for by generally accepted accounting principles. Section 503 of the 1997 Principal and Income Act, 7B U.L.A. 38 (2000 Supp.), generally allows a trustee to establish a depreciation reserve.

In the case of a transfer in exchange for an annuity, or in a bargain sale for an annuity, the gift and estate tax consequences should be considered. In a bargain sale, gift tax may apply. If there is a reversionary interest, it is includible in the transferor's gross estate, and therefore, one cannot assume that an annuity transaction will reduce the size of the transferor's gross estate. *See* §9.22.

If the transaction takes the form of a sale, the savings are reduced to the extent the transferor must pay taxes on the gain. However, a sale does increase the basis against which the transferee may compute depreciation. A sale for the full market value of the property eliminates any taxable gift and prevents the property from being included in the transferor's gross estate if the rental is fair and the transaction is properly planned. *See* § 9.22.2.

In evaluating the transaction, the lawyer and client must also consider the professional fees and other costs of carrying out the transaction. When those costs are aggregated with the offsetting tax considerations, the potential savings may be slight. The evaluation is incomplete unless the client also takes into account the nontax consequences of the transaction. For some, the loss of the ability to deal directly with the property is significant. Aggressive clients may savor the opportunity to duel with the IRS, while more cautious ones would prefer to increasing the risk of an audit and confrontation with the IRS.

§ 9.19. INCOME TAX CONSEQUENCES OF TRANSFER

A gift of business property to a trust or other beneficiary does not ordinarily require the transferor or the transferee to report any income. In the case of a gift, the transferor's basis in the property carries over to the transferee as provided in § § 1015 and 1041 for purposes of depreciation and otherwise.

Where the transfer is made by sale, gain may be recognized by the transferor, which can be reported on the installment basis in appropriate cases. *See* Part B. Installment obligations arising in the sale-leaseback context are subject to more stringent interest rate rules under § 1274. The minimum interest rate is 110 percent of the AFR (§ 1274(e)); the maximum "lower discount rate" of nine percent under § 1274A(a) does not apply. *See* § 9.6.5.

A sale at the market price of the property would avoid the imposition of any gift tax on the transaction and should avoid any threat of inclusion in the transferor's estate. However, a sale may involve depreciation recapture where § 1245 (personal) property or § 1250 (real) property is transferred. The rules of those sections apply to sale and leaseback transactions. Reg. § 1.1245-1(a)(3).

EXAMPLE 9-9.

Last year *T* sold equipment to an irrevocable trust for $8,000. *T* had paid $10,000 for the equipment and had taken depreciation deductions of $4,000 during the time *T* owned it. *T*'s gain on the sale was $2,000—the difference between the $8,000 sale price of the equipment and its $6,000 adjusted basis. The entire amount of the gain is ordinary income under § 1245(a) and not gain realized from the sale of § 1231 property. *See* Reg. § 1.1245-1(b).

The gain would also be ordinary income if the sale is made by (1) an individual and an entity controlled, such as a corporation, controlled by the individual, (2) an individual and a trust of which the individual or his or her spouse is a beneficiary, or (3) an executor and a beneficiary in satisfaction of a pecuniary bequest. § 1239. Of course, under § 267 losses on transfers to related taxpayers are generally not deductible.

§9.20. INCOME TAX CONSEQUENCES OF RENTAL PAYMENTS

If the transaction is properly structured the rental payments should be deductible. However, the IRS has taken a very narrow view of the circumstances in which rental payments are properly deductible in leaseback cases. Section 162(a) allows a deduction as an ordinary and necessary business expense for,

> (3) rentals or other payments required to be made as a condition to the continued use or possession, for purposes of the trade or business, of property to which the taxpayer has not taken or is not taking title or in which he has no equity.

If there is a prearranged plan of transfer and leaseback, the IRS has argued that no deduction is allowable because the overall transaction lacks any valid business purpose. Thus, the rental payments made by the lessee are not ordinary and necessary expenses for which a deduction is allowable. Where the lessee retains a reversionary interest the IRS has sometimes also denied the deduction because the taxpayer had an equity interest in the property. *See* § 162(a)(3).

The Tax Court and most appellate courts have rejected the IRS position, concluding instead that it is sufficient if the lease itself serves a valid business purpose. As the court observed in *Quinlivan v. Commissioner*, 599 F.2d 269, 273 (8th Cir.), *cert. denied*, 444 U.S. 996 (1979), "Congress had specified that the business purpose test is concerned with the continued use or possession' of the property. There is no justification for adding an inquiry into the origin of the lessor's title in applying this requirement." *See also Rosenfeld v. Commissioner*, 706 F.2d 1277 (2d Cir. 1983); *Brown v. Commissioner*, 180 F.2d 926 (3d Cir.), *cert. denied*, 340 U.S. 814 (1950); *Skemp v. Commissioner*, 168 F.2d 598 (7th Cir. 1948). On the other hand, the Fourth Circuit will not bifurcate the transfer and leaseback—it insists that the overall transaction have a valid business purpose. *Perry v. United States*, 520 F.2d 235 (4th Cir. 1975), *cert. denied*, 423 U.S. 1052 (1976).

§9.20.1. Economic Reality

The Fifth Circuit once championed the business purpose test. *Van Zandt v. Commissioner*, 341 F.2d 440 (5th Cir.), *cert. denied*, 382 U.S. 814 (1965). However, that court later stated that it was not enough to "conjure up some reason why a businessman would enter into this sort of arrangement." *Mathews v. Commissioner*, 520 F.2d 323, 325 (5th Cir. 1975), *cert. denied*, 424 U.S. 967 (1976). In *Mathews* the court focused on the substance of the overall transaction and held that no deduction is allowable unless it has some economic reality. Although "economic reality" is a term not infrequently used in appellate opinions, *e.g.*, *May v. Commissioner*, 723 F.2d 1434 (9th Cir. 1984), its meaning is by no means clear. The *Mathews* opinion does state that economic reality is not present where there is a prearranged agreement to lease the property back to the transferor. According to the court, the prearrangement assures that the transferor will continue to have control over the property regardless of the independence of the trustee. The economic reality test could be very difficult to satisfy, particularly if the taxpayer must establish the absence of an express or implied prearrangement in the context of a family transaction. An analogous problem arises where a transferor continues to occupy a residence given to another family member. *See* §7.23.

§9.20.2. No Equity Interest

Rental payments are only deductible as rent if the taxpayer has no equity in the rental property. §162(a)(3). In several cases the IRS has argued that the statute bars a deduction where the lessee holds a reversionary interest in the property. The argument was rejected by most courts. However, it was accepted in at least two cases. *Chace v. United States*, 303 F. Supp. 513 (M.D.Fla. 1969), *aff'd per curiam*, 422 F.2d 292 (5th Cir. 1970), and *Hall v. United States*, 208 F. Supp. 584 (N.D.N.Y. 1962). The pertinent part of §162(a)(3) is ambiguous, but most courts agree that the requirement is intended to prevent taxpayers from converting a capital expenditure (purchase of asset) into a currently deductible expense (rent). For example, in *C. James Mathews*, 61 T.C. 12, 23 (1973), *rev'd on other grounds*, 520 F.2d 323 (5th Cir. 1975), *cert. denied*, 424 U.S. 967 (1976), the Tax Court said, "section 162(a)(3) should not be read to cause rental payments to become nondeductible merely by virtue of a lessee's property rights in an asset, which rights are not derived from the lessor or under the lease, and which will become possessory only after the lease expires." *See also Quinlivan v. Commissioner*, 599 F.2d 269 (8th Cir.), *cert. denied*, 444 U.S. 996 (1979). This ban on deductions should not pose any problem for most gift and leaseback transactions.

§9.20.3. Tax Court Requirements

The Tax Court has established specific requirements that must be met in order to sustain the deductibility of rental payments in leaseback cases. *See Hobart A. Lerner, M.D., P.C.*, 71 T.C. 290 (1978); *C. James Mathews, supra*, 61 T.C. at 18-19; and *Richard R. Quinlivan*, T.C. Memo. 1978-70, *aff'd*, 599 F.2d 269 (8th Cir.), *cert. denied*, 444 U.S. 996 (1979). The requirements were also adopted by the Eighth Circuit in the appellate opinion in *Quinlivan*, 599 F.2d at 273, and by the Second Circuit in *Rosenfeld*, 706 F.2d at 1280:

1. The grantor must not retain "substantially the same control over the property that the grantor had before" the gift;
2. The leaseback should normally be in writing and must require the payment of a reasonable rental;
3. The leaseback (as distinguished from the gift) must have a bona fide business purpose; and
4. The taxpayer must not possess a disqualifying equity interest in the property.

The first requirement implies the necessity of having an independent trustee, which has been stated explicitly in some cases. *E.g., Brooke v. United States*, 468 F.2d 1155 (9th Cir. 1972) (involving a guardianship and not a trust); *Alden B. Oakes*, 44 T.C. 524, 529-(1965). In *Lewis H. V. May*, 76 T.C. 7 (1981), *aff'd*, 723 F.2d 1434 (9th Cir. 1984), the Tax Court left open the question of whether there must be an independent trustee in all cases. Although some courts are willing to treat the lessee's lawyer or accountant as an independent party for this purpose, it is safer to use a corporate trustee.

§9.20.4. Suggested Approach

A leaseback from a family member or a trustee is subject to challenge by the IRS unless it is a three-party transaction covered by A.O.D. 1984-038. A deduction for rental payments will be upheld by most courts if the transaction has these characteristics:

1. The trustee is independent (preferably a corporate trustee);
2. The lease is written and enforceable under the local law;
3. The lease terms, including its duration and rental, are negotiated after the initial transfer;
4. The rental is reasonable—neither inadequate nor excessive;
5. The lease of the property serves a legitimate business purpose of the lessee; and
6. The lessor and lessee respect and enforce the terms of the lease.

The taxpayer's cause is helped immeasurably if there are valid nontax business purposes for the overall transaction. It is often relatively easy to identify some plausible nontax motives where the initial transfer involves an outright gift or sale. For example, in *Brooke v. United States*, 468 F.2d 1155 (9th Cir. 1972), the nontax motives for a gift to minor children and leaseback from their guardian were found to be "abundant and grounded in economic reality." They included a desire to provide for the health and education of the minors, to avoid friction with medical partners, to withdraw assets from the threat of malpractice suits, and to diminish the ethical conflict arising from ownership of a medical practice and an adjoining pharmacy.

§9.20.5. Grantor Trust Rules

The benefit of the deduction is lost if the income of the trust is taxable to the transferor under §§671-677. For example, the income from transfers to a short-term trust is taxable to the transferor under §677(a) when an independent trustee has discretion to accumulate trust income for distribution to the transferor upon termination of the trust. *Duffy v. United States*, 487 F.2d 282 (6th Cir. 1973), *cert. denied*, 416 U.S. 938 (1974). The same applies to the income from any post March 1, 1986 transfers in trust where the value of the grantor's reversionary interest exceeds five percent of the value of the transferred property. §673(a). From the income tax point of view, treatment as a grantor trust generally eliminates the consequences of transactions between the grantor and the trustee. Rev. Rul. 85-13, 1985-1 C.B. 184. Of course, such a taxpayer suffers some overall loss because of the costs incurred in creating the trust and the imposition of a gift tax on the transfer to the trust. The grantor trust rules are examined in detail in Part D of Chapter 10, §§10.30-10.41.

§9.21. GIFT TAX CONSEQUENCES

The initial transfer of property to a trust involves a gift to the extent the value of the transferred property exceeds the sum of the value of the interests retained by the grantor (to the extent allowed by §2702) and the consideration received by the grantor. Of course, in most cases the grantor no longer retains any interest in the trust. The interests retained by the transferor and the consideration received by the transferor. For this purpose an interest retained by the transferor would ordinarily be disregarded under § 2702 (*i.e.,* unless the retained interest is a qualified interest as defined in § 2702(b).

A trust is usually planned so that transfers to it will qualify for the maximum allowable number of gift tax annual exclusions. In this connection, recall that where a trust is involved annual gift tax exclusions are available only if, (1) the beneficiaries are entitled to current distributions of income, (2) the trust satisfies the requirements of § 2503(c), or (3) the beneficiaries are given sufficient powers of withdrawal to be a present interest under § 2503(b). *See* § § 7.35-7.38. In appropriate cases the transfer could be structured to qualify for the marital or charitable gift and estate tax deductions. For example, the initial transfer might be made outright to a charity or to a charitable remainder trust or charitable lead trust. Great caution is required in planning a transfer to a charitable trust because of the complexity of the tax rules. *See* § § 8.19-8.35.

If the special valuation rules of § 2702 do not apply, the donees' interests are valued under the usual gift tax rules. Accordingly, term or other limited interests are valued by reference to the actuarial tables pursuant to § 7520. However, when the rental is fixed at the time of the initial transfer, the value of the gift is "measured by the present worth of the right to receive the net rentals from the property during the term of the trust, provided the right to such rentals is under the terms of the transfer and applicable State law fixed or vested." Rev. Rul. 57-315, 1957-2 C.B. 624. The Ruling also points out that the gift of the rentals is complete at the time of transfer although the rentals are not deductible by the lessee for income tax purposes.

When the gift is valued by reference to the actuarial tables, the transaction may result in either a partially nontaxable transfer or the imposition of an unnecessary gift tax (*i.e.,* where the rental payments are less than the actuarially determined value of the gift). The latter will occur if the reasonable rental payments under the lease are lower than the amount of income projected by applying the appropriate factor under § 7520.

§ 9.22. ESTATE TAX CONSEQUENCES

If the special valuation rules of § 2702 do not apply, a gift to a trust may improve the donor's transfer tax position, at least if the trust is not includible in his or her estate. On the other hand, no improvement is likely if the donor retains a reversionary interest in the property. In the latter case the gift tax applies to the actuarially determined value of the beneficial interests in the trust that were given to others. Moreover, if the grantor dies during the term of the trust the value of the grantor's reversionary interest is includible in his or her estate under § 2033. The full value of the property may be included in the transferor's estate under § 2036(a) if the lease was prearranged or the rental is not adequate. *Estate of William du Pont, Jr.,* 63 T.C. 746 (1975) (inclusion where property transferred outright and leased back at inadequate rental); *Estate of Roy D. Barlow,* 55 T.C. 666 (1971), *acq.,* 1972-2 C.B. 1, 3 (no inclusion where property transferred outright more than three years prior to death and decedent paid fair rental under written leases). If the grantor survives termination of the trust, the trust property will be distributed to the grantor.

§9.22.1. Outright Gift and Leaseback

If the transfer is made by an outright gift, all of the property may escape inclusion in the donor's estate if the donor leases the property back at a reasonable rental. The available annual gift tax exclusions and the unified credit may reduce or eliminate the out-of-pocket gift tax cost of transferring the property. If the gift and leaseback are beyond the reach of §2036, the property may be entirely excluded from the donor's gross estate. The gift and estate tax consequences of adopting this approach are illustrated by the following example:

EXAMPLE 9-10.

In 2009, *O* transferred a new office building worth $700,000 to the independent trustee of an irrevocable trust of which *O*'s 5 children were the life income beneficiaries and their issue were the remainder beneficiaries. *O* did not retain any interest in the property and held no control over the trust. After the transfer, *O* leased the building from the trustee on reasonable terms. At the time of the transfer to the trust, *O* made gifts of the entire value of the property. Assuming that 5 $13,000 annual exclusions were available, and no discount applied, the transfer resulted in a taxable gift of $635,000. If *O* had not previously made any taxable gifts, the gift tax on the transfer would be offset by *O*'s unified credit. Only the amount of the taxable gifts ($635,000) would be taken into account in later determining the tentative tax on *O*'s estate. However, the full value of the property is includible in *O*'s estate if *O* in effect retained the use of the property by paying an unreasonably low rental or if the transaction otherwise ran afoul of §§2036 to 2038. Note that the trust is subject to the GSTT. Accordingly, *O* might choose to allocate part or all of his GSTT exemption to the transfer to the trust. §2631(a). Finally, note that the gift tax cost could be further reduced if *O*'s grandchildren were also given powers of withdrawal sufficient to qualify for the annual gift tax exclusions.

§9.22.2. Sale and Leaseback

If the initial transfer takes the form of a bona fide sale for the full value of the property, the property is not includible in the seller's estate. In this case the consideration received by the seller is includible in lieu of the property itself. The value of an installment note or other obligation received as consideration would depend upon a variety of factors, including the interest rate, security, and collectibility. *See* Reg. §20.2031-4. In this connection recall that more stringent interest rate rules apply to installment obligations in a sale-leaseback arrangement. *See* §9.19. If the sale price is inadequate the property may be included in the seller's estate under §§2035 to 2038. However, in such a case the estate would be entitled to an offset under §2043(a) for the consideration received.

E. THE WIDOW'S ELECTION IN COMMUNITY PROPERTY AND COMMON LAW STATES

§9.23. INTRODUCTION

Life or other limited interests in property are transferred for consideration in a wide variety of settings. Several of the most important litigated tax cases have involved the community property widow's election, which serves as the primary focus of this part. The tax consequences of the transfers are determined according to more or less universal rules that apply regardless of slight variations in the settings or relationships of the parties. For example, the purchaser of a life or other term interest in a trust acquired after July 27, 1989 is not entitled to amortize the cost of the purchase for any period during which the remainder is held directly or indirectly by a related party. §167(e). Previously purchased life or other term interests may be amortized whether they were purchased from a decedent's estate in connection with a widow's election, *Estate of Christ v. Commissioner*, 480 F.2d 171 (9th Cir. 1973), or from the settlor of the trust, *Manufacturer's Hanover Trust Co. v. Commissioner*, 431 F.2d 664 (2d Cir. 1970). The same estate tax rules also apply whether the interest is acquired in the context of a will contest, *United States v. Righter*, 400 F.2d 344 (8th Cir. 1968), or a widow's election, *Estate of Vardell v. Commissioner*, 307 F.2d 688 (5th Cir. 1962). It is important to have a basic grasp of the tax rules and to be alert for circumstances in which they may apply—the rules can also be very helpful in planning other types of transactions. It is also important to be alert to the potential application of §2702 and of the GSTT.

The planning device under discussion was labeled the "widow's election" long ago. While it is equally applicable to spouses of either sex, wives more often survive their husbands. Consequently, this part generally refers to the first spouse to die as the "husband" and to the surviving spouse as the "widow." No suggestion of marital or sexual inequality is intended by this choice of language. The convention is adopted in the interest of brevity and consistency.

In community property states, the term "widow's election" originally referred to the choice that a widow was forced to make when her deceased husband's will provided for the disposition of all of their community property. Such a will caused a problem because neither spouse has the right to dispose of the entire community interest. When confronted with this issue the courts could have limited the effect of the husband's will to his half of the community property. Instead, they concluded that such a will required the widow to elect whether to, (1) accept the provisions of the will and allow her share of the property.

The widow's election was often used to establish a trust of all of the community property for the lifetime of the widow. Such a disposition was attractive because it resulted in the unified management of the community property, made the entire community property available for the support of the surviving spouse, and provided for the distribution of the property when she died. Typically the surviving spouse could not alter the disposition of the property upon her death.

§9.24. Testamentary Elections

A transfer for consideration may result from a testamentary election that is expressly or impliedly required by a decedent's will. For example, a testamentary gift may be conditioned upon the beneficiary transferring an asset he or she owns to another person. In other cases the necessity of making an election is implied rather than expressed directly in the will. Thus, *T* may make a gift to *X* and purport to give *Y* an item of property that is actually owned by *X*. In such a case *X* may elect either, (1) to accept the gift from *T* and transfer the item of his or her property to *Y*, or (2) to reject the gift from *T* and not transfer any of his or her own property to *Y*. An election may also be required where the testator and the beneficiary of a testamentary gift are joint tenants in other property that the testator's will gives to a third party. *E.g., Estate of Waters*, 100 Cal.Rptr. 775, 778 (Cal.App. 1972).

EXAMPLE 9-11.

T owned the entire interest in Blackacre, which *T*'s will devised to *X*. Although *T* and *X* owned Whiteacre as joint tenants with right of survivorship, *T*'s will purported to devise Whiteacre to *Y*. The devise of Blackacre to *X* may be construed by a court as being conditioned upon *X* transferring Whiteacre to *Y*.

§9.25. Widow's Election Described

The term "widow's election" has quite different meanings in common law and community property states. In common law property states, the term usually refers to the statutory right of a surviving spouse to elect to receive a specified share of the deceased spouse's estate (a so-called nonbarrable share) in lieu of taking under the decedent's will. The concept is an important one that may have significant tax consequences in some instances, such as cases involving the marital deduction.

Under the U.P.C. and other laws of many states, a married decedent's "augmented estate" is subject to the surviving spouse's election to take a specified share of the property in lieu of the provision made by the decedent for the survivor. In other states, the election relates only to the property subject to estate administration. *See* §5.16 for a discussion of the consequences of an election on the marital deduction and the extent to which a marital deduction is allowable with respect to property the surviving spouse receives as a result of electing against the provisions of the deceased spouse's will.

A surviving spouse's elective share constitutes a separate share for income tax purposes regardless of whether it is entitled to income or depreciation and appreciation following the date of death. §663(c); Reg. §1.663(c)-4. Previously, some courts had held that a distribution in satisfaction of an election in a common law state carried out the estate's distributable net income. *Brigham v. United States*, 160 F.3d 759 (1st Cir. 1998). *See* §§5.16 and 12.29.

In community property states the term usually refers to a plan under which the widow is given an interest in the deceased husband's share of the community property, conditioned upon her making a specified disposition of her share of the community property. The widow is forced to make an election because neither spouse can unilaterally dispose of more than one-half of the community property. *See* § 3.28.2. As explained below, if the widow elects to take under the husband's will the tax cases generally treat her as having purchased the proffered interest in the husband's share of the community property by making the required transfer of her share of the community property.

The basic concept of the community property widow's election can be adapted for use in common law property states. For example, if each spouse owns a substantial amount of separate property, the husband's will can make a gift of an appropriate part of his property to a trust of which his wife is the life income beneficiary, conditioned upon the transfer by her of a specified amount of her property to the trust, or to a similar, separate trust. Some commentators have suggested that a modified form of widow's election could be used where the wife does not have a substantial estate. They suggest that the husband's will could create a life estate-general power of appointment marital deduction trust and a residuary credit shelter trust. Then, the wife could be given the power to draw down the principal of the marital deduction trust and exchange part of it for a life income interest in the residuary trust. If she makes the exchange, she might be treated as a purchaser of the income interest in the residuary trust. As such, she might be entitled to the same tax benefits as the widow-beneficiary of a community property widow's election trust. However, the tax consequences of this approach are not established. In addition, the technique is subject to the same uncertainty as the community property widow's election regarding the application of § 1001(e) to the sale by the residuary trust of a life interest to the widow. *See* § 9.31.

The substantive law regarding the community property widow's election has evolved largely from cases that arose prior to the advent of significant income, gift, or estate taxes. *E.g., In re Estate of Smith,* 40 P. 1037 (Cal. 1895). The cases usually involved a husband's will that attempted to dispose of all of the community property, yet made some provision for his widow. Although a will is generally presumed to dispose of only the testator's property, if it was clear that he had attempted to dispose of all of the community property, the courts held that the widow was required to elect whether to accept the provisions of the will and allow her share of the community property to pass under the will or to reject the will and retain her share of the community property. *E.g., Herrick v. Miller,* 125 P. 974 (Wash. 1912). Litigation was frequently required in order to determine whether an election was required and whether the widow had made an election by accepting benefits under the will or by acquiescing in the distribution of some property in accordance with the terms of the will.

The uncertainties inherent in the original form of the widow's election device are generally avoided in modern wills, which usually require the election to be made in a particular way, within a specified time following the testator's death. Modern wills also generally make a conditional gift to the widow of an interest in a trust funded with the husband's share of the property rather than attempting also to dispose directly of her interest in community property. However, some commentators still write of the election as if the husband were disposing directly of the entire interest in the community property.

§9.26. Typical Widow's Election Plan

Under a typical widow's election plan, the husband's will leaves his share of the community property to a trust, all of the income of which is distributable to his widow if she also transfers her share of the community property to the same trust, or to a separate trust that has essentially the same terms. Their children are usually the remainder beneficiaries of the trust or trusts. The widow will receive no benefit from the trust of the husband's share of the community property unless she transfers her share to the trust. In any event the widow is usually entitled to receive specific bequests and a family allowance from the husband's estate. An election to accept the benefits of the deceased husband's will may result in a gift by the widow and may cause some or all of her share of the property to be included in her gross estate. The gift tax result will generally implicate §2702, and the estate tax consequences will be shaped by recent cases favorable to the taxpayer, particularly *Estate of Cyril Magnin*, 184 F.3d 1074 (9th Cir. 1999). As indicated in §9.1, when *Estate of Magnin* was remanded, the Tax Court found that the decedent had not received adequate and full consideration. *Estate of Cyril Magnin*, T.C. Memo. 2001-31. Accordingly, the decedent's estate was required to include the closely held stock the decedent had transferred.

The application of §2702 may deter the use of widow's elections or cause widow's election wills to be drawn differently—at least if the widow and the remainder beneficiaries are members of the same family. The §2702 gift tax problem can be avoided in at least two ways. First, no gift occurs and none of the value of the trust will be included in the widow's gross estate if the total value of the property transferred by the widow does not exceed the actuarially determined value of the life interest she receives in the trust established by her deceased husband. From an economic standpoint such an election may not produce a particularly helpful overall result—unless the amount of income generated by the trust established by the husband is very limited. Second, no gift occurs, and there will be no inclusion in the widow's estate under §2036, if the interest retained by the widow is a qualified interest for purposes of §2702 and its value, together with the actuarially determined value of the life estate she receives in the trust established by her husband exceeds the value of the property she transfers to the trust.

The widow's election can be adapted for use in connection with an inter vivos trust, or in connection with gifts to persons other than a spouse. *See, e.g., United States v. Righter*, 400 F.2d 344 (8th Cir. 1968) (estate tax approach of widow's election cases applied to trust created by decedent and others in settlement of will contest). However, this part generally focuses on testamentary widow's election plans involving married persons. The nontax considerations are discussed first, after which the tax consequences are developed in some detail. The tax concepts are discussed at some length because they may be applied in other contexts in community and common law states.

The husband and wife are each transferors for GSTT purposes, which requires some special planning. In particular, careful consideration should be given to the allocation of the GSTT exemption and the use of multiple trusts. In some cases, there is a possibility that the widow's contributions to the trust may escape the GSTT. *See* §9.35.

§ 9.27. INTER VIVOS OR POST-MORTEM ELECTION?

The testator's spouse may agree during the testator's lifetime to accept the benefit of the plan and be bound by the terms of the will. *E.g., In re Estate of Wyss,* 297 P. 100 (Cal. App. 1931); Rev. Rul. 69-346, 1969-1 C.B. 227. Use of a binding inter vivos election is generally unwise because it deprives the widow of the opportunity to evaluate the suitability of the plan after her husband's death. One of the attractive features of the traditional, post mortem, widow's election is the "second look" it gives the widow.

If a plan involves an inter vivos election, the lawyer should seriously consider suggesting that each spouse be advised by independent counsel:

> There may be many cases where a single attorney is consulted and no question exists about the fairness or reasonableness of the agreement to both parties. The presence of advice from independent counsel is a desirable cautionary step, however, where there is a possibility that the fairness or reasonableness of the agreement will be subject to later attack. *Whitney v. Seattle-First National Bank,* 579 P.2d 937, 940 (Wash. 1978).

The surviving spouse should also be advised by independent counsel with respect to an election made following the testator's death. In that way the lawyer who drafted the deceased spouse's will, who also generally serves as counsel to the executor, will avoid an otherwise difficult conflict of interest.

When the plan contemplates a post-mortem election, the husband's will should specify the period during which the widow may elect under the will. It is important that the widow be given ample time to consider the tax and nontax effects of an election before it must be made. For example, a widow might be permitted to elect at any time prior to final distribution of the testator's estate. The will should also specify whether the election may be made on the widow's behalf by her guardian (or her personal representative if she survives her husband, but dies before making an election). Even apart from such a provision, some states permit the widow's personal representative to make the election. *Estate of Murphy,* 544 P.2d 956 (Cal. 1976). In contrast, the U.P.C. and some states do not permit an election to take a nonbarrable share to be made by the survivor's personal representative. U.P.C. § 2-212 (2011); Mich. L. Ann. § 700.2202 (2011).

§ 9.28. "VOLUNTARY" WIDOW'S ELECTION

Some couples reject the use of a "forced" election of the type described above in favor of a non-coercive plan that permits the widow to add some or all of her property to the trust created under her husband's will. Under this plan the widow is not required to transfer any of her property to the trust in order to receive the income from her husband's share of the property. Instead, any property the widow transfers to the trust is typically held in a separate fund, which may be withdrawn by her at any time. Such a plan facilitates unified management of the community property, yet provides the surviving spouse with a high degree of flexibility. The husband's share of the community property is usually left to a trust that meets the requirements of a qualified terminable interest property trust under § 2056(b)(7). Of course, the property of the trust is includible in the widow's estate under § 2044 to the extent the husband's executor claims a marital deduction with respect to the trust. However, the plan does not produce any of the tax advantages that are typically sought through the use of the forced widow's election. In particular, the amount included in her estate will not be reduced by a consideration offset under § 2043(a). *See* § 9.30.2. Also, even apart from § 167(e), the surviving spouse would not be entitled to an amortization deduction.

§ 9.29. NONTAX CONSEQUENCES OF A FORCED ELECTION

A widow's election plan may be attractive to some clients because of its nontax features. For example, the plan offers unified management of community assets, which is particularly helpful in the case of closely-held business interests. There may also be an advantage to having the entire community property managed by a trustee if the widow does not have any business experience or does not want to manage the property. The plan also assures that the community property, or at least the husband's share, will pass to the remainder beneficiaries named in his will. Furthermore, the property held in trust is not subject to an estate administration upon the widow's death. Of course, some of the advantages are available under the other plans, such as a voluntary widow's election.

A forced election plan is more complex than one under a simple will that transfers the community property to the surviving spouse or to a trust for her benefit. As a result it may be more difficult for clients to understand, and more costly to implement. In addition, there is always a risk that some of the tax advantages sought by the parties will be challenged. Overall, the forced widow's election is not suitable for most clients. A widow's election plan should be used only if it is understood by the husband and wife and is completely acceptable to them. Otherwise, there is too great a risk that the widow will resent the plan and feel that she was not treated fairly by her husband and his planner. In short, the plan should be consensual and not imposed on a spouse who does not understand it, or objects to it.

§ 9.30. GIFT TAX CONSEQUENCES, § 2702

Prior to the adoption of § 2702, the gift tax consequences of a typical widow's election were determined simply by comparing the values of the remainder interest the widow is considered to have transferred in her share of the property with the value of the life interest she receives in the decedent's share. *Commissioner v. Siegel*, 250 F.2d 339 (9th Cir. 1957); *Zillah Mae Turman*, 35 T.C. 1123 (1961), *acq.*, 1964-2 C.B. 7. Under this approach the widow does not make a gift if the actuarially determined value of the life interest she receives is equal to, or greater than, the value of the remainder in the property she transfers. The same analysis will continue to apply if the remainder beneficiaries are not members of the widow's family. For this purpose family members include lineal ascendants, lineal descendants, brothers and sisters, and their spouses. It does not include aunts, uncles, nephews, nieces, cousins and their spouses. § 2704(c)(2).

If the remainder beneficiaries are family members, the special valuation rules of § 2702 apply to the transaction. Accordingly, the value of the interest the widow retains in the share of the property she transfers will be disregarded unless it is a qualified interest (*i.e.,* either a guaranteed annuity interest or a guaranteed unitrust interest payable at least annually). A widow's election trust could be structured to make payments that are qualified interests.

EXAMPLE 9-12.

H's executor transferred his net share of the community property, worth $500,000, to a typical widow's election trust, the *H* trust, from which his widow would receive the income if she elected to take under the will and transfer her share of the community property to a similar trust, the *W* trust. At a time when an 8% interest rate applied, the decedent's 75-year-old widow, *W*, elected to transfer her share of the community property, worth $600,000, to the *W* trust. By reason of the election *W* was entitled to receive the net income of the *H* trust for life. According to Table S, based on Life table 90CM, the life interest in the *H* trust had a value of $257,630 (.51526 x $500,000). Under the terms of *H*'s will, *W* was entitled to receive a guaranteed annual annuity payment from the *W* trust. The amount of the payment was required to be an amount that would cause the annuity to have a total value equal to the excess of the value of the property she transfers to the trust ($600,000 in this case) less the value of the life interest she received in *H*'s trust ($257,630). The annual annuity payable to *W* would be $53,157.27 ($600,000—$257,630) divided by 6.4407 (the applicable annuity factor under Table S). The annuity would have a value of $342,370—exactly equal to the net value of the property *W* transferred to the *W* trust (*i.e.,* $600,000 less the value of the life estate she received in the *H* trust, $257,630). Accordingly, *W*'s election and her transfer of property to the W trust, would not result in a gift. Likewise, applying the rationale of *Estate of Cyril Magnin*, 184 F.3d 1074 (9th Cir. 1999), *W* received full and adequate consideration for the transfer of her property to the *W* trust. Consequently, none of the *W* trust would be includible in her gross estate.

§9.30.1. Powers of Appointment

An election to take under the husband's will does not result in a gift if the transfer is incomplete because the widow retained a power of appointment over the property she transferred to the trust. Reg. § 25.2511-2(b). Thus, in LR 7746044 (TAM), the IRS recognized that the widow's gift was not complete at the time of her election because she retained a special power of appointment over the property she transferred to the trust. However, the ruling concluded that under *Estate of Sanford v. Commissioner*, 308 U.S. 39 (1939), the gift became complete when she subsequently released the power of appointment. At that time she made a gift of the entire remainder value of the trust attributable to the property she transferred to the trust. The widow's gift in LR 7746044 (TAM) was not reduced by the value of the lifeinterest in her husband's share of the property which she had already received and was not affected by her release. The gift was larger because it took place later, which increased the value of the remainder interest, and because the widow received no consideration for the transfer. The analysis of LR 7746044 (TAM) was followed by the Tax Court in *Myra B. Robinson*, 75 T.C. 346 (1980), *aff'd*, 675 F.2d 774 (5th Cir.), *cert. denied*, 459 U.S. 970 (1982).

The widow's retention of any power of appointment over the property she transfers threatens the treatment of the election as a transfer for value. As Professor Stanley Johanson has pointed out, where a power is retained the transaction more closely resembles a gratuitous transfer than a transfer for value. Johanson, Revocable Trusts, Widow's Election Wills, and Community Property: The Tax Problems, 47 Tex. L. Rev. 1247, 1309-1311 (1969). That is a serious problem because the tax advantages of the widow's election are lost if the transaction is not characterized as a transfer for value. In particular, the widow's estate will be unable to claim a consideration offset under § 2043(a) for the value of the life estate she receives. The Tax Court has held that the widow's estate is not entitled to a consideration offset where the widow held a general power of appointment over the property. *Estate of Bluma Steinman*, 69 T.C. 804 (1978). Given the uncertainty regarding this issue, either the widow should not retain any power, or the power should be limited to a testamentary special power to appoint the corpus to and among their descendants, or some other limited class.

§ 9.30.2. Voluntary Election

If a widow's election is a voluntary one, the widow receives no consideration in exchange for her transfer. Accordingly, the amount of her gift is not reduced by the value of the interest she receives in her deceased husband's estate. The amount of her gift will depend upon whether any reduction is allowable under § 2702 for the interest she retained in the property she transferred. If no reduction is allowable, she has made a gift of the full value of the property. A reduction is allowable if the remainder beneficiaries are not family members or if the retained interest is a qualified interest as defined in § 2702. However, no completed gift occurs where she retains a general or special power of appointment over the property she transfers.

If the widow retains a general or special power of appointment over the property she transferred, the full value of the property is includible in the widow's estate, and the amount of the taxable gift that she made at the time of the election is excluded in computing the estate tax on her estate. In effect, the widow can hold a general or special power of appointment without additional tax cost—the full value of the property is includible in her estate in any case. A power of appointment can add important flexibility to the estate plan. Of course, the widow's estate is not entitled to a consideration offset under § 2043(a).

§ 9.31. Income Tax Consequences

Amounts paid as interest to the holder of a life or other term interest acquired by gift, bequest, or inheritance cannot be reduced by a deduction on account of shrinkage in value of the interest due to the passage of time. § 273. On the other hand, a life interest in a testamentary trust is treated as a capital asset for purposes of characterizing the gain realized on a sale or exchange of the interest. *McAllister v. Commissioner*, 157 F.2d 235 (2d Cir. 1946), *cert. denied*, 330 U.S. 826 (1947); *Rev. Rul.*

72-243, 1972-1 C.B. 233. Under § 167(e) no depreciation or amortization deduction is allowable with respect to a term interest acquired after July 27, 1989 for any period during which the remainder is held by a related person as defined in § § 267(b) or (e). For purposes of § 267(b), family includes only "brothers and sisters (whether by the whole or half blood), spouse, ancestors, and lineal descendants." § 267(c)(4). In the case of transfers made prior to July 28, 1989, the purchaser of a life or other term interest is allowed to amortize its cost over its life, thereby reducing or eliminating the tax on income received from it. *Commissioner v. Fry,* 283 F.2d 869 (6th Cir. 1960), *aff'g,* 31 T.C. 522 (1958); *Bell v. Harrison,* 212 F.2d 253 (7th Cir. 1954); Rev. Rul. 62-132, 1962-2 C.B. 73. That rule would apply to later transfers if the remainder beneficiaries are not related within the meaning of § § 267(b) and (e) (*e.g.,* in-laws, uncles, aunts, nieces, nephews, and cousins).

Prior to the 1969 Act, where a life estate or other term interest was sold, the seller's basis was determined by multiplying his or her entire basis by a factor to value the life estate. Rev. Rul. 72-243, 1972-1 C.B. 233. Under this rule, the seller seldom realized any gain on the sale. Moreover, under the *McAllister* line of authority any gain would be capital gain and not ordinary income.

The 1969 Act added § 1001(e), under which the seller's basis is disregarded to the extent it arises under § § 1014, 1015, or 1041. As a result of this change, the full amount received by the seller of a term interest acquired by gift or bequest is gain where the sale takes place after October 9, 1969. The legislation only disadvantages the seller of a life or other term interest—it does not prevent the purchaser from amortizing the cost of the life interest.

EXAMPLE 9-13.

T died in 2006 leaving $100,000 in trust to pay the income to the beneficiary, *B*, for life. Upon *B*'s death the corpus is distributable to *X*. The income of the trust is taxable to *B*, who is barred by § 273 from claiming any amortization deduction. *B*'s interest constitutes a capital asset for purposes of characterizing the gain realized on any sale or other disposition. If *B* sold his interest *B*'s basis would be zero pursuant to § 1001(e).

The legislative history of § 1001(e) does not indicate whether Congress considered the possibility of applying the provision in the widow's election context. In the early 1970s it was rumored that the IRS would issue a ruling to the effect that § 1001(e) would not apply to a widow's election unless a distribution from the estate was made in satisfaction of the widow's right to receive a specific dollar amount or a specific item of property. Committee Report, Estate Planning Through Family Bargaining, 8 Real Prop., Prob. & Tr. J. 223, 265 (1973). However, the ruling was never issued. The possibility that § 1001(e) will apply to the widow's election deters some planners from recommending that a client use a forced widow's election plan. Neither the Code nor any identifiable considerations of tax policy prevent the application of § 1001(e).

§ 9.31.1. The Trustee

In a situation involving a widow's election where the taxpayer exchanges the remainder interest in her community property for a life interest in her husband's community property, what actually occurs can be characterized as part gratuitous disposition part sale or exchange. Where the wife receives property worth more than the value of the property she transfers, the property received in excess should be viewed as a "bequest" from the husband which is not amortizable. But where the wife transfers property worth more than the value of that which she receives, she purchases property equivalent to the value of the "received" property and is deemed to have made a gift to the beneficiaries of the estate of [sic], and should pay a gift tax on, the excess. *Kuhn v. United States,* 392 F. Supp. 1229, 1239-1240 (S.D.Tex. 1975).

In a forced widow's situation, the widow's election may cause the husband's estate or the trustee of his trust to realize a substantial gain. The gain will occur if § 1001(e) applies to the transaction and the estate's basis in the life interest transferred to the widow is disregarded to the extent it is determined under § 1014. In such a case, the full amount realized by the estate (or trust) would probably constitute gain—albeit capital gain. The amount realized would be equal to the actuarially determined value of the remainder interest the widow transfers to the trust. (The rules of § 2702, which only apply for gift tax purposes, will not affect the treatment of the transaction for income tax purposes.) However, if the value of the remainder interest exceeds the actuarially determined value of the life interest transferred to the widow, the amount realized by the estate (or trust) is probably limited to the value of the latter—the life interest received by the widow. Lane, The Widow's Election as a Private Annuity: Boon or Bane for Estate Planners, 44 S. Cal. L. Rev. 74, 93 (1971). In determining the amount realized, this analysis properly ignores the gift element of the transaction. Such an approach is consistent with the cases that imposed a similar limit on the amount amortizable by the widow for income tax purposes in the case of transfers made prior to July 28, 1989. *Estate of Christ v. Commissioner,* 480 F.2d 171 (9th Cir. 1973).

EXAMPLE 9-14.

H's executor transferred property worth $500,000 to a typical widow's election trust, the *H* trust, of which the children of *H* were the remainder beneficiaries. At the time the applicable interest rate was 8.2%. *H*'s 80-year-old widow, *W*, transferred property worth $600,000 to an identical trust, the *W* trust, as required by *H*'s will. Under § 2702, if *W* retained only the right to receive the income from the *W* trust, the transfer involved a gift of $381,625 ($600,000 less $218,375, the value of the life estate she received in the *H* trust). In particular, § 2702 would require the gift tax result to be determined without regard to the value of *W*'s retained life interest in the trust of her share of the property. However, for income tax purposes the amount realized by *H*'s trust is probably limited to $218,375, the value of the life estate *W* received in the exchange. In the case of a transfer prior to July 28, 1989, *W*'s amortization would probably be limited to the same amount. No amortization would be allowed for later transfers.

The gift by *W* would be smaller if the remainder beneficiaries were not members of *W*'s family or if §2702 otherwise did not apply in determining the gift tax consequences. Thus, if the remainder beneficiaries were *W*'s nephews, nieces, or cousins the gift would only be $131,025, which is the value of the remainder in the *W* trust, $337,950 ($600,000 × .56325), less the life estate she received in the *H* trust, $218,375 ($500,000 × .43675). The amount realized by the *H* trust and subject to amortization by *W* would probably be based on $218,375, the value of the amount she received in the exchange and not the full value of the remainder interest transferred by *W*. The excess constituted a gift from *W* to the remainder beneficiaries of the *W* trust.

If §1001(e) does not apply to a widow's election, the trust's basis will be determined under §1014. Accordingly, the trust will usually have little or no gain to report. Assuming that the amount realized by the trust is limited in the manner described above, the trust will seldom realize an amount greater than the trust's basis in the interest transferred. Under Reg. §1.1014-5, the trust's basis in the life interest transferred to the widow is determined by multiplying the adjusted basis of the decedent's share of the property by the factor for the widow's life estate. The widow's life interest will have an equivalent value if the assets held in the trust are valued for federal estate tax purposes on the date of the husband's death and the widow's election is effective on that date. Because of fluctuations in the value of the assets held by the trust, the life interest will have a different value if the valuation date and the date of the election are not the same.

The trust does not realize gain in the case of a voluntary widow's election because the widow's transfer of property to the trust is entirely gratuitous and does not involve any exchange or transfer for consideration.

Any gain realized by the trust will probably be characterized as capital gain rather than ordinary income. Some commentators have suggested that the transaction might be treated as an assignment of income by the trust, in which case the gain would be ordinary income. *See* Freeland, Lind & Stephens, What Are the Income Tax Effects of an Estate's Sale of a Life Interest?, 34 J. Tax. 376 (1971); Lane, Widow's Election as a Private Annuity: Boon or Bane for Estate Planners, 44 So. Cal. L. Rev. 74, 93-95 (1971). However, the existing appellate court decisions support treating the gain as capital gain. They include a closely analogous case that involved the sale of a legal life estate that the seller carved out of a fee interest that he owned, *Estate of Johnson N. Camden*, 47 B.T.A. 926 (1942), *nonacq.*, 1943 C.B. 28, *aff'd per curiam*, 139 F.2d 697 (6th Cir. 1944), *nonacq.*, 1944 C.B. 34. Capital gain status was also recognized where the taxpayer sold a remainder interest in her ranch and retained a life estate. *Eileen M. Hunter*, 44 T.C. 109 (1965). Of course, if an amortization deduction is allowable to the widow under §167(e), any tax cost incurred as a result of the sale may be more than offset by the amortization deduction. *See* §9.32.

§ 9.31.2. The Widow

[W]here the value of the rights surrendered [by the widow] exceeds the value of the rights received, only a portion of what is surrendered is allocated to the "purchase price," of the rights received and the rest is presumed to be a gift to the remainder beneficiaries. *Estate of Christ v. Commissioner*, 480 F.2d 171, 172 (9th Cir. 1973).

The widow may also realize a gain if she elects to transfer her share of the community property to the trust. In broad terms the widow is viewed as exchanging a remainder interest in her share of the community property for a life interest in her deceased husband's net share of the property. As a result of the exchange, she realizes an amount that cannot exceed the actuarially determined value of the life interest she receives. If the value of the life interest the widow receives exceeds the value of the remainder she transfers, the amount realized is probably limited to the value of the remainder. In such a case the amount by which the value of the life estate exceeds the value of the remainder is properly characterized as a bequest to the widow.

The amount of the widow's gain, if any, depends upon her basis in the property she transferred, which can only be determined after identifying the nature of the interest she transferred. Based upon the approach taken in the amortization cases (reflected in the quotation above), the widow will be treated as having transferred a remainder interest in her share of the community property, but only to the extent its value does not exceed the value of the life interest she received. Both of those values are determined by reference to the fair market value of the underlying assets and not their bases. She is considered to have made a gift to the remainder beneficiaries to the extent the remainder may have a greater value than the life interest.

Under § 1014(b)(6), the widow is considered to have acquired her share of the community property from her deceased husband. Accordingly, the federal estate tax value of her husband's interest in the community property becomes the basis of her interest. When she transfers her share of the community property to the trust, the total basis should be allocated between her life estate and the remainder according to the respective actuarial factor for each. Such a method is applied to determine the bases of life estates and remainder interest in property acquired from a decedent. Reg. § 1.1014-5. "Neither the Code nor the regulations prescribe a method for allocating a lump-sum basis when the owner of a fee simple interest conveys, inter vivos, a less-than-fee estate." *Eileen M. Hunter*, 44 T.C. 109, 115 (1965). Although *Hunter* involved a slightly different method of allocation, the Tax Court seemed to approve the approach taken in Reg. § 1.1014-5, which had also been applied in an earlier case, *Estate of Johnson N. Camden*, 47 B.T.A. 926 (1942), *nonacq.*, 1943 C.B. 28, *aff'd per curiam*, 139 F.2d 697 (6th Cir. 1944), *nonacq.*, 1944 C.B. 34.

EXAMPLE 9-15.

H's executor transferred property worth $650,000 to a typical widow's election trust, the *H* trust. His 65-year-old widow, *W*, transferred property with a basis and a value of $800,000 to an identical trust, the *W* trust, as required by *H*'s will. The interest rate used in valuing interests transferred was 9%. Under Table S, using Life Table 90CM, the factor for *W*'s life estate is .70070 and the factor for the remainder is .29930. Thus, the life estate in *H*'s share of the property was worth $455,455 ($650,000 × .70070) and the value (and basis of) the remainder in *W*'s trust is $234,960 ($800,000 × .29370). *W* should not recognize a gain on the transaction. Although the value of the life estate she received in the *H* trust exceeded the basis of the remainder in the property she transferred to the *W* trust, the excess constituted a bequest from *H* to *W*. *W* might have a gain, however, if *H*'s executor elected to use the alternate valuation date when the property had a lower value than on the date of distribution. Thus, *W* would have a gain in this example if her share of the community property had a value of $800,000 on the date it became subject to the trust and a basis of $700,000 (its value on the alternate valuation date). The value of the remainder transferred by *W*, which would limit the amount realized by her, would remain $234,960 but the basis allocable to the remainder would be reduced to $208,110. Presumably the $26,850 difference would constitute gain to *W*.

Any gain realized by the widow should be capital gain, just as it would be if realized by the trust. *See* § 9.31.1.

§ 9.32. INCOME TAX CONSEQUENCES OF TRUST DISTRIBUTIONS

For income tax purposes the trust is recognized as a separate taxpaying entity. Under the basic income tax rules applicable to trusts, the trust acts as a conduit of the income that is distributed to the beneficiaries: That portion of the income is taxed to them and not to the trust. The remainder of the income is taxed to it. *See* § 10.4. However, capital gains are taxed to the trust and not to the beneficiaries to the extent the gains are allocated to corpus and are not paid, credited, or required to be distributed during the taxable year. *See* § 643(a)(3); Reg. § 1.643(a)-3(a). Presumably distributions to the widow are taxed in accordance with those rules, even though she is treated as a purchaser of the life interest in the decedent's share of the trust property.

An amortization deduction is barred by § 167(e) unless either, (1) the transfer was made prior to July 28, 1989, or (2) the remainder beneficiaries are not related to the widow—the holder of the term interest. If an amortization deduction is allowable, it is based on the cost of the life interest she purchased in her deceased husband's share of the trust. *Estate of Daisy F. Christ*, 54 T.C. 493 (1970), *aff'd*, 480 F.2d 171 (9th Cir. 1973); *Gist v. United States*, 296 F. Supp. 526 (S.D.Cal. 1968), *aff'd*, 423 F.2d 1118 (9th Cir. 1970); *Kuhn v. United States*, 392 F. Supp. 1229 (S.D.Tex. 1975). As yet no court has accepted the IRS's counterargument that the widow's life interest was acquired gratuitously and, hence, no deduction was allowable because of § 273. "Interpreting § 273 to prohibit amortization in a case such as this one could only occur by permitting form to conquer substance. The instant taxpayer does not receive income from the subject life estate as a result of a 'gift, bequest or inheritance.' She has acquired the life estate after exchanging valuable property, the right to which was undisputedly hers at the time of the exchange. She therefore will be permitted to amortize the cost basis of life estate payments received and reduce her taxable income by ratable annual deductions, pursuant to 26 U.S.C. § 167(h)." *Kuhn*, 392 F. Supp. at 1240.

No amortization deduction is allowable to a widow who accepts the income interest in a trust established by her husband's will in lieu of a statutory share of his property. *Helvering v. Butterworth*, 290 U.S. 365 (1933). In that case the Court reasoned that by electing to accept the provisions of his will the widow waived her statutory rights instead of exchanging them for a life interest in the trust. The courts have thus far refused to follow the *Butterworth* approach in cases involving community property.

If an amortization deduction is allowable, it is determined by dividing the cost of the life interest the widow acquired by her life expectancy according to Table V, Reg. § 1.72-9. *Gist v. United States, supra.* For this purpose the cost is the lesser of the actuarially determined values of, (1) the remainder interest she transferred, or (2) the life estate she received.

EXAMPLE 9-16.

> *H*'s executor transferred property worth $200,000 to a typical widow's election trust established under *H*'s will, the *H* trust, the remainder beneficiaries of whom were not related to *W*. At a time when 9% interest rates applied, *H*'s 70-year-old widow, *W*, transferred property worth $300,000 to an identical trust, the *W* trust, as required by *H*'s will. *W*'s life estate in the *H* trust is worth $125,698 and the remainder she transferred in the *W* trust is worth $111,453. Under Table V, Reg. § 1.72-9, *W*'s life expectancy is 16 years. *W* may deduct $6,246 each year ($99,933 ÷ 16).

An amortization deduction not otherwise barred by § 167(e) is allowable although7 the term interest that was purchased generates tax-exempt income. Section 265 denies deductions that are otherwise allowable under § 212 for expenses of producing tax-exempt income. It does not affect amortization deductions, which are allowable under § 167. *Manufacturer's Hanover Trust Co. v. Commissioner*, 431 F.2d 664 (2d Cir. 1970). Accordingly, a widow may be entitled to amortize the full cost of the life interest although it generates tax-exempt income.

No amortization deduction is allowable in the case of a voluntary election. The deduction is allowable only where the life interest was acquired for consideration.

The termination of a widow's election trust and distribution of all of its assets to the surviving spouse under a court order does not give rise to income to the surviving spouse where the trust instrument allowed the trustee to invade corpus for the surviving spouse's needs. LR 8335032.

§ 9.33. Estate Tax: The Husband's Estate

The use of a forced widow's election does not affect the amount of property included in the husband's gross estate on his death. Only his share of the community property is includible whether or not his widow elects to transfer her property in accordance with his plan. If the widow elects to accept an interest in the testamentary trust created by his will and to transfer her share of the community property to the trust, it does not augment his estate in any way. Instead, the widow's share passes directly from her to the trustee and does not become part of his estate. *Coffman-Dobson Bank & Trust Co.,* 20 B.T.A. 890 (1930), *acq.,* X-1 C.B. 13 (1931). The same rule applies where the transfer is made pursuant to an inter vivos election. *Pacific National Bank,* 40 B.T.A. 128 (1939), *acq.,* 1939-2 C.B. 28. If the widow elects to take under the husband's will, she receives a life income interest in the trust. The life interest in the husband's trust may constitute a qualifying income interest for life for which a marital deduction would be available under § 2056(b)(7). Presumably, the amount of the deduction would be reduced by the value of the remainder interest that the surviving spouse was required to give up in her share of the property. *See* § 2056(b)(4); *United States v. Stapf,* 375 U.S. 118 (1963). As indicated by Reg. § 20.2056(b)-4(b), "if an obligation is imposed upon the surviving spouse by the decedent in connection with the passing of a property interest, the value of the property interest is to be reduced by the amount of the . . . obligation." Determining the amount allowable as a marital deduction in the husband's estate should not be affected by § 2702.

§ 9.34. ESTATE TAX: THE WIDOW'S ESTATE

The widow should not hold any power over the property her husband transferred to the trust that might cause it to be included in her estate under § 2041. Of course, any portion of the trust with respect to which a marital deduction was allowed to the husband's estate under § 2056(b)(7) is includible in the widow's estate under § 2044. Apart from those concerns, the main issue is the extent to which the property the widow transferred to the trust is includible in her estate under § 2036(a)(1). Nothing is includible if the widow received full and adequate consideration in exchange for the property she transferred to the trust.

According to the IRS and the decision in *Gradow v. United States,* 897 F.2d 516 (Fed. Cir. 1990), inclusion is required unless the consideration received by the widow has a value at least equal to the full value of the property she transferred, not just a remainder in it. *See* § 9.26. From the economic point of view the consideration should be sufficient if it equals the actuarially determined value of the remainder interest transferred by the widow.

> [F]or the purpose of evaluating whether [plaintiffs] election constituted full and adequate consideration within the meaning of § 2036(a), the consideration flowing from [plaintiff] consists of the property which would otherwise have been included in her gross estate by virtue of her retention of a life estate—*i.e.,* her half of the community property. *Gradow,* 11 Cl. Ct. at 816, *quoted with approval in aff'g decision,* 897 F.2d 516, 518 (Fed. Cir. 1990).

Subsequent appellate decisions involving comparable issues reject the IRS approach which improperly ignore the value of the life estate the widow retained in her share of the property. Under the proper application of § 2036, whether the widow received adequate consideration requires a comparison of the value of the remainder interest she gave up in the property she transferred and the value of the life interest she received in the trust established by her deceased husband.

The proper analysis was employed in three later cases that were not widow's election cases, but involve the same issue: In *Estate of D'Ambrosio v. Commissioner*, 101 F.3d 309 (3d Cir. 1996), *cert. denied*, 520 U.S. 1230 (1997), the Court held that a decedent's estate properly excluded property that the decedent transferred, retaining an income interest for life, in exchange for other property, the fair market value of which equaled the value of the remainder interest the decedent transferred. The Court found this result to be consistent with a proper reading of §2036 and the regulations and with economic reality. "Even looking at this case in policy terms, it is difficult to fathom either the tax court's or the Commissioner's concerns about the 'abusiveness' of this transaction." The *D'Ambrosio* decision was followed by the Fifth Circuit in *Wheeler v. United States*, 116 F.3d 749 (5th Cir. 1997), and by the Ninth Circuit in *Estate of Magnin v. Commissioner*, 184 F.3d 1074 (9th Cir. 1999).

In *Wheeler*, the court held that a decedent's estate properly excluded a ranch that the decedent had sold to his two sons when he was 60 years of age, subject to a retained life interest, for interest-bearing notes, the face amounts of which was equal to the actuarially determined value of the remainder interest. The notes were paid off by the sons more than three years prior to their father's death, which took place almost seven years after the sale. The court found that the sale was bona fide and that it was made for adequate and full consideration. The court emphasized that "we take no position as to how section 2702 would affect this particular transaction had it been entered into after October 8, 1990 (transfers prior thereto being excluded from section 2702 . . .)."

In *Estate of Magnin* the decedent (Cyril) and his father (Joseph) had entered into an agreement under which "Joseph had to bequeath his JM and Specialty stock to Cyril as sole trustee for Cyril's life, during which time Cyril would have the sole right to vote the stock. Cyril had to will in trust all of his JM and Specialty stock to a bank trustee for the benefit of his three children." Joseph and Cyril complied with the terms of the agreement. On Cyril's death the IRS included the shares owned by Cyril in his gross estate under §2036(a), less the value of the consideration received, valued at the time of Joseph's death. According to the IRS and the Tax Court, the adequacy of the consideration received by Cyril was determined by comparing the full value of the shares owned by Cyril with the value of the life interest Cyril received in the shares owned by Joseph. The Ninth Circuit reversed, stating that, "we hold that 'adequate and full consideration' is measured against the actuarial value of the remainder interest rather than the fee-simple value of the property transferred to the trust." 184 F.3d at 1080.

EXAMPLE 9-17.

The community property estate of *H* and his wife, *W*, had a total value of $1,200,000 when *H* died in 1990. Under *H*'s will, his net share of the property, $450,000, passed to the trustee of a widow's election trust, the *H* trust. All of the net income of the *H* trust was payable to *W* for life if she survived him and transferred her share of the community property to an identical trust, the *W* trust. Upon *W*'s death, the remainder interests in both trusts were distributable to their children. If *W* did not transfer her share of the community property to the *W* trust, she would have received no benefit from the *H* trust. *W* was 77 when she elected to transfer her share of the community property, $550,000, to the *W* trust. At the time an 11.2% rate applied for purposes of valuing the interest. Under the tables then in effect the factor for the life estate of a 77-year-old was .55830 and the factor for the remainder was .44170. Thus, *W*'s life interest in *H*'s share of the property was worth $251,235 and the remainder was worth $198,765. *W*'s life interest in her share of the property was worth $307,065 and the remainder was worth $242,935.

Under the *Gradow* IRS approach, *W* received a life estate in *H*'s property, worth $251,235, in exchange for the full value of her share of the property, $550,000. This approach ignores the value of the life interest *W* retained in her share of the property, which, at 11.2%, should yield her income with a present value of $307,065 over her lifetime. The IRS would require *W*'s estate to include the value of the *W* trust on the estate tax valuation date applicable to her estate less the consideration she received, valued in accordance with §2043(a) at the time of her election. This "frozen dollar" approach limits the consideration offset to $251,235 regardless of any increase in the size of the trust corpus. *See United States v. Past*, 347 F.2d 7 (9th Cir. 1965).Under the proper approach, exemplified by the *D'Ambrosio, Wheeler* and *Magnin* cases, the widow received full and adequate consideration—*W* transferred an interest worth $242,935 for which she received an interest worth slightly more, $251,235.

The "frozen dollar" approach of §2043(a) is used to value the consideration received by the widow. This value is limited to its actuarial value on the date of her election. *United States v. Past*, 347 F.2d 7 (9th Cir. 1965). The consideration offset is not based on the actual amount of income she received (*i.e.*, the consideration offset is a fixed dollar amount and not a proportional part of the trust). Also, the value of the offset is determined by the actuarial tables in effect on the date of the election that were used to determine the gift tax consequences of the transfer, and not on subsequently adopted tables that assume a higher yield. *Estate of Elfrida G. Simmie, 69* T.C. 890 (1978), *aff'd*, 632 F.2d 93 (9th Cir. 1980).

No offset is allowable in the case of a voluntary election because the widow does not receive any additional interests by reason of the election and transfer.

§9.35. GSTT

Given the arcane nature of the widow's election and its infrequent use, it is hardly surprising that the GSTT was adopted without any consideration of its potential application to widow's election trusts. Without any guidance other than the GSTT itself, the manner in which it will apply to widow's election trusts is far from clear. However, the probable results are suggested by matching the established estate and gift tax treatment of widow's election trusts with the provisions of the GSTT. The analysis should be equally applicable to transfers that do not involve community property.

First, in the case of a typical widow's election the husband may be treated as the transferor of the portions attributable to the remainder interests in both the trust to which his property was transferred and the trust to which his widow transferred property. In effect, the husband would have made a gratuitous transfer of the remainder in his trust and would be, indirectly, the settlor of the widow's trust. As explained above, if the widow received adequate and full consideration for that transfer of her property she is not a transferor for GSTT purposes. That analysis comports with the transfer for consideration analysis that applies for gift and estate tax purposes.

If the husband were treated as the transferor of both remainder interests, presumably the executor of his will could allocate any of the husband's remaining GSTT exemption to one or both trusts. If the widow were considered to be the transferor of the portion of the two trusts attributable to the her life income interests, presumably she could make a contemporaneous allocation of her GSTT exemption (*i.e.,* there is no estate tax inclusion period (ETIP)).

Alternatively, the husband might be treated as the transferor of the property that passes from his estate to the trust and the widow will be treated as the transferor of the property she transfers in trust. If so, the widow should be able to make a contemporaneous, lifetime allocation of her GSTT exemption. Again, if she received adequate and full consideration for the transfer of the remainder in her trust there is no estate tax inclusion period (ETIP) that would prevent a current allocation.

Because of the special valuation rules of §2702, widow's election trusts are likely to be drafted in a way that allows the widow to retain a qualified interest (*i.e.,* annuity) in the property she transfers, the value of which will equal the excess of the total value of the property she transfers over the actuarially determined value of the life estate she receives in the trust established by her deceased husband.

EXAMPLE 9-18.

H died leaving Blackacre, worth $1 million, to his widow, *W*, on condition that she transfer Whiteacre, worth $600,000, to their granddaughter, *D*. If *W* accepts the gift, *H* will be treated as having given $400,000 to *W* and $600,000 to *D*. *H*'s gift of $600,000 to *D* is a direct skip that is subject to the GSTT. *W* neither made a gift for gift tax purposes nor a transfer for GSTT purposes.

EXAMPLE 9-19.

H transferred Blackacre, worth $1 million, to a widow's election trust on condition that *W* transfer Whiteacre, worth $600,000, to a similar trust. The value of the life estate *W* received in the trust created by *H* was greater than $600,000. Their granddaughter, *D*, is a contingent remainder beneficiary of the trust. For GSTT purposes, if *W* accepts the condition, *H* will probably be treated as the transferor of $600,000 to one trust and $400,000 to the other trust. *W*'s election did not result in a gift and none of the trust created by *W* is includible in her estate. Accordingly, *W* should not be treated as the transferor of any part of the trusts.

Second, the foregoing analysis is supported by the separate share rule of §2654(b). Under it, the portion of a trust transferred by each spouse would be treated as a separate trust. Specifically, §2654(b) provides that, "the portions of a trust attributable to transfers from different transferors shall be treated as separate trusts."

Third, as indicated above, presumably the amount contributed by each spouse will be determined in light of the consideration analysis that is applied for gift and estate tax purposes. That result should apply although §2624(d) provides that a consideration reduction is expressly allowed only for "the amount of any consideration provided by the transferee." §2624(d).

EXAMPLE 9-20.

H died in 2006 leaving a typical widow's election will. *W* elected to accept a life estate worth $500,000 in a $1 million testamentary trust provided for in *H*'s will. Their grandchildren are the remainder beneficiaries of the trust. As required by the husband's will *W* transferred property worth $750,000 to a trust in which she retained a life estate worth $375,000. Presumably *H*'s executor could elect to claim a QTIP marital deduction for up to $625,000—the difference between $1 million value of the property transferred to the trust and the $375,000 value of the remainder in *W*'s property that she was required to give up. For gift tax purposes §2702 requires that the value of *W*'s retained income interest be disregarded because it is not a qualified interest. Accordingly, *W* made a gift of $250,000 (the $750,000 value of the property she transferred, less the $500,000 value of the life estate she received). The transfer would not have involved a taxable gift if the total value of the property she transferred did not exceed the value of the life estate she received in her husband's trust. Presumably *W* could allocate her GSTT exemption to the transfer. (There is no ETIP for purposes of §2642(f) because *W* received full and adequate consideration for the value of the remainder she transferred.) *See* §2.28.1. *W* died and was survived by her son, *S*, and *S*'s daughter, *D*. When *W* died the property of her trust, worth $1 million, passed outright to *D*.

Under the *Gradow* IRS approach, *W* did not receive adequate consideration in the exchange (*i.e.,* the total value of the property *W* transferred exceeded the value of the life estate she received in the trust under *H*'s will). Accordingly, the value of the widow's trust would be includible in her estate less the value of the consideration she received. Under the proper approach, exemplified by the *D'Ambrosio, Wheeler* and *Magnin* cases, *W* received adequate consideration (*i.e.,* the value of the life estate she received in *H*'s trust, $500,000, exceeded the value of the remainder in the property she transferred, $375,000). Of course, if *H*'s executor elected to claim a QTIP marital deduction, a portion of *H*'s trust would be includible in *W*'s estate under §2044. To that extent (and unless a reverse QTIP election had been made), *W* would become the transferor of *H*'s trust for GSTT purposes. The distribution of its corpus to D would be subject to the GSTT. In addition, the distribution of the $1 million corpus of W's trust to D would be a taxable termination subject to the GSTT. If not previously allocated, W's executor could allocate W's GSTT exemption to the transfer. The distribution to D of the corpus of H's trust is also a taxable termination subject to the GSTT.

Section 2642(f) prevents a transferor from allocating his or her GSTT exemption to the transfer if the property transferred would be includible in the transferor's estate if the transferor were to die immediately after the transfer. In such a case the allocation can only be made at the end of the estate tax inclusion period. *See* § 2.28.1. If the transferor received adequate and full consideration for the transfer, the transfer would not result in a gift and the property would not be includible in the transferor's gross estate. If the transfer neither results in a gift nor inclusion of the property in the widow's estate, there is no transferor. Accordingly, the transfer cannot result in a generation-skipping transfer. Otherwise, perhaps the widow could file a gift tax return for the year in which the election was made and attempt to allocate some part of her GSTT exemption to the transfer. If so, the valuation of property for purposes of determining the inclusion ratio is its gift tax value. § 2642(b)(1). The widow would argue that the value of the gift is its net value—determined after offsetting it by the value of the life estate received by the widow—zero. The value is the denominator of the applicable fraction. The amount of the GSTT exemption allocated to the transfer is the numerator. Thus, if she allocates $0 to the transfer the applicable fraction is 1. Accordingly, the inclusion ratio—one minus the applicable fraction—is zero. In response the IRS could be expected to argue that the value of the gift referred to in § 2642(b)(1) is the value of the property transferred without regard to a consideration offset, even one that is allowed for gift tax purposes.

EXAMPLE 9-21.

The facts are the same as in Example 9-20, except H's will only required W to transfer an amount of property equal in value to the actuarially determined value of her life estate in H's trust. H's will allocated $1 million to the trust, in which W's life estate was worth $500,000. Electing to take under the will, W transferred property worth $500,000 to a trust in which her retained life estate was worth $250,000. H's executor may claim a QTIP marital deduction of up to $750,000 ($1,000,000 less the $250,000 value of the remainder interest of W in the property that W was required to transfer to the trust). *See* § 2056(b)(4). Under § 2702, the value of W's retained life interest is disregarded for gift tax purposes. Even so, W has made no gift because the value of the property she transferred, $500,000, does not exceed the value of the life estate she received. For GSTT purposes if W allocates $0 of her GSTT exemption to the transfer the inclusion ratio of the trust may be zero. As a protective matter she should file a gift tax return reporting the transfer to the trust, reflecting the offset for the consideration received, and electing to allocate $0 of her GSTT exemption to the trust. When W dies none of the property she transferred to the trust is includible in her gross estate. Of course, if *H*'s executor elected to claim a QTIP marital deduction with respect to *H*'s trust, a portion of it will be included in *W*'s estate under §2044. Unless *H*'s executor had made a reverse QTIP election, *W* would also be treated as the transferor of that portion of the trust. *W*'s executor could allocate her GSTT exemption to the portion of the trust that is included in her estate under §2044.

§9.36. WIDOW'S ELECTION VARIATIONS

Because of §2702 the traditional widow's election technique is likely to result in a taxable gift by the widow—if the remainder beneficiaries of the trust she funds are members of her family. If the remainder beneficiaries are family members a gift would occur if the total value of the property the widow transferred was greater than the value of the life estate she received in her deceased husband's property. However, under the rationale of the *D'Ambrosio, Wheeler* and *Magnin* cases nothing would be includible in the widow's estate if the value of the remainder in the property she transferred was not greater than the value of the life estate she received. Incurring a gift tax would, in effect, freeze the amount includible in the widow's estate.

The traditional plan can be varied to create scenarios in which the widow will incur neither gift nor estate taxes with respect to part or all of her share of the property. First, the widow might only be required to transfer property to the extent of the value of the life interest she would receive in her deceased husband's property. In that case no gift or estate tax would be payable with respect to the property she transferred. Perhaps the GSTT would not be applicable as she was not the transferor as defined in §2652(a) and Reg. §26.2652-1(a)(2). Second, no gift or estate tax would be incurred if the value of the remainder interest transferred by the widow did not exceed the combined value of the life estate she receives in her husband's property and the value of a qualified interest she retains in the property transferred by her. Of course, under §2044 her estate would include any portion of the husband's trust for which his executor had claimed a marital deduction.

The modified plans should involve the same income tax consequences as the traditional election. Thus, the husband's estate or trust may realize a substantial gain under §1001(e). The widow might also realize a small gain. Again, the widow would only be entitled to amortize the cost of the life interest if the remainder beneficiaries are not closely related to her.

EXAMPLE 9-22.

H left his residuary estate to the trustee of a testamentary trust who was authorized to sell a life interest in the trust to *W* in exchange for the transfer by *W* of property with a total value equal to the actuarial value of the life interest to the trustee of a separate trust for the benefit of their adult children. Under *H*'s will, the life estate was required to be valued by multiplying the fair market value of the trust assets by the appropriate life interest factor based upon *W*'s age. For example, if *H* transferred property worth $500,000 to the trust, W was 65, and the interest rate used for valuation was 9.2%, W's life estate in H's trust would have a value of $353,320. Thus, W would be required to transfer property worth $353,320 to the trust in order to receive a life estate in H's share of the property. The transfer by W would not involve a gift of any interest in the remainder. More important, even the IRS would concede that for estate tax purposes W would receive full consideration in money or money's worth in exchange for the property she transferred to the trust.

Because of § 1001(e) the trustee of H's trust might realize a gain of the full amount, $353,320, as a result of the exchange. Section 167(e) would prevent W from claiming an amortization deduction. W might also realize a gain on the transaction, but it would probably be quite small because the basis in the property she transferred is adjusted to its estate tax value in H's estate under § 1014.

§ 9.37. WIDOW'S ELECTION INSURANCE TRUST

In the insurance trust approach, described in more detail at § 6.24, the insured spouse transfers his community property interest in an insurance policy to an irrevocable insurance trust. The interest of the noninsured spouse is also transferred to the trust. However, her interest is revocable until she elects, following the death of the insured, either to withdraw her half of the insurance proceeds, or to permit them to become a part of the irrevocable trust. In the latter case the surviving spouse will be entitled to receive the income from the husband's share of the trust and an annuity from her share.

The insured spouse may control the incidence of gift tax on the initial transfer by borrowing against the life insurance policies, or by granting withdrawal powers to the beneficiaries other than the noninsured spouse. The surviving uninsured spouse may make a gift to the remainder beneficiaries upon the death of the insured spouse, but her gift is reduced by the value of the life interest she receives in the insured's portion of the trust. The amount of the gift would also be offset by the value of the annuity she retained in her share of the trust (the amount of the annuity would be determined by a formula). Under the formula approach, none of the trust property should be includible in her gross estate. In essence the approach follows one of the variations described in § 9.36, which eliminate any gift and any inclusion of the proceeds in the noninsured spouse's gross estate.

Section 1001(e) should not prove to be a problem to the trustee who sells an interest to the uninsured spouse, since the basis in the trust assets is not determined under §§ 1014, 1015, or 1041. For a further discussion of this type of trust, *see* Price, The Uses and Abuses of Irrevocable Life Insurance Trusts, U. Miami, 14th Est. Plan., ¶ 1111.3 (1980). *See also* § 6.24.

§ 9.38. STATE TAX CONSEQUENCES

The state income and transfer tax consequences of a widow's election should not be ignored at any stage. A widow's election plan may have an important impact on the state death tax when the husband dies. For example, the election may be taxed as if the deceased husband transferred his share of the community property to the remainder beneficiaries of the widow's election trust. *In re Estate of Brubaker*, 98 Cal.Rptr. 762 (Cal.App. 1971) (former California inheritance tax law). The transfer may also result in a taxable gift from the widow to the remainder beneficiaries. Finally, when the widow dies, some of the property she transferred to the trust will probably be subject to the death tax. Some states that impose inheritance taxes may not allow the widow's share of the property to be reduced by any consideration she received from her husband. *E.g., In re Estate of Patten*, 419 P.2d 157 (Wash. 1966) (former Washington inheritance tax law). Such states reason that a consideration analysis is inappropriate where the state tax is based upon the value of the property received by the transferee and not upon the value of the property to the decedent or to his or her estate.

§ 9.39. WIDOW'S ELECTION PLANNING

The forced widow's election is not suitable for most clients. Although the widow can be given the benefit of a second look at the plan after her husband's death, her options are very limited. In order for the election to qualify as a bargained for exchange, the plan must be relatively inflexible and the widow must, in effect, be disinherited if she elects against the will. The overall tax consequences can be at least moderately favorable, except for the possibility that § 1001(e) will require the husband's estate or trust to realize a large gain if the widow elects to take under the will. That consideration alone is sufficient to deter some planners from recommending a forced widow's election plan. Some tax advantages remain, however, if the widow is only required to transfer an amount in trust equal to the actuarially determined value of the life estate she receives in the husband's trust. As discussed above, such a transfer does not generate any gift or estate tax liability and may escape the GSTT as well. *See* § 9.35.

A voluntary widow's election plan is consistent with the overall planning goals of many clients. The attractiveness of a voluntary plan is enhanced by the availability of the unlimited marital deduction for QTIP trusts. In particular, the estate tax on the deceased spouse's share of the community property may be deferred if the surviving spouse receives a qualifying income interest for life. § 2056(b)(7). Unfortunately, however, such a trust cannot allow any distributions to be made to any other person during the widow's lifetime. Flexibility can be added to the plan if the husband transfers an amount equal to the amount sheltered by the unified credit to a discretionary trust from which distributions could be made to the widow and other family members. In addition, the widow could be given a special testamentary power to appoint the assets of one or both trusts. Prior to the adoption of the unlimited marital deduction some commentators encouraged the use of a voluntary widow's election instead of a forced one. *See, e.g.*, Kahn & Gallo, The Widow's Election: A Return to Fundamentals, 24 Stan. L. Rev. 531 (1972).

F. DIVIDING INTERESTS: SALES OF REMAINDERS, JOINT PURCHASES, GRITS, GRATS, GRUTS AND QUALIFIED PERSONAL RESIDENCE TRUSTS (QPRTS)

§ 9.40. INTRODUCTION

Clients have attempted to transfer property at substantially reduced gift and estate tax cost through a variety of approaches that are based on the limited application of the estate tax to life interests in property and on the valuation of temporally divided interests in property according to assumed rates of return and mortality tables. Several key features of the law encouraged those approaches. First, upon the death of the owner of a life interest in property the value of the underlying property is ordinarily not includible in the decedent's estate. Second, with the exception of inter vivos transfers subject to § 2702, annuities, life interests, term interests and remainders are all valued according to actuarial tables based upon 120 percent of the applicable federal rate. The tables cannot be used if the values relate to the lifetime of a person for whom there is less than a 50 percent chance of living for a year or more. Reg. § 20.7520-3(b)(3). During periods when the current interest rates are high, the actuarial tables place a correspondingly high value on life interests and term interests whether or not the income paid to the life or term tenant actually reaches the actuarially determined level.

The more-or-less mechanical application of the valuation rules enhanced the appeal of some unusual estate planning techniques, particularly the sale of remainder interests, the joint purchase of property, and the transfer of property to trusts in which the grantor retains an interest for a term that is likely to end before his or her death. However, the gift tax rules of § 2702 restrict the ability to benefit from sales of remainders, joint purchases, and the use of most other devices that depend upon the retention of term interests. Some attractive opportunities remain—notably the creation of trusts in which the grantor retains an annuity for a term that is expected to end prior to his or her death and ones which the grantor retains a term interest in a personal residence. Qualified personal residence trusts (QPRTs) are discussed below at § 9.44.

The general approach of § 2702 is reflected in the following passages from Reg. § 25.2702-1:

> (a) Scope of section 2702. Section 2702 provides special rules to determine the amount of the gift when an individual makes a transfer in trust to (or for the benefit of) a member of the individual's family and the individual or an applicable family member retains an interest in the trust . . . .
>
> (b) Effect of section 2702. If section 2702 applies to a transfer, the value of any interest retained by the transferor or any applicable family member is determined under § 25.2702-2(b). The amount of the gift, if any, is then determined by subtracting the value of the interests retained by the transferor or any applicable family member from the value of the transferred property. If the retained interest is not a qualified interest . . . the retained interest is generally valued at zero, and the amount of the gift is the entire value of the property.

Note that § 2702 only applies when the transferor *retains* an interest in the transferred property. This point is illustrated by the following example from Reg. § 25.2702-2(d):

EXAMPLE 3

D transfers property to an irrevocable trust under which the income is payable to *D*'s spouse for life. Upon the death of *D*'s spouse, the trust is to terminate and the trust corpus is to be paid to *D*'s child. *D* retains no interest in the trust. Although the spouse is an applicable family member of *D* under section 2702, the spouse has not retained an interest in the trust because the spouse did not hold the interest both before and after the transfer. Section 2702 does not apply because neither the transferor nor an applicable family member has retained an interest in the trust. The result is the same whether or not *D* elects to treat the transfer as a transfer of qualified terminable interest property under § 2056(b)(7).

This interpretation of § 2702 creates a loophole of sorts that is analogous to the spousal remainder trusts that were used to shift the income of a short-term trust until § 672(e) was amended in 1986 to treat the grantor as holding any interest that was transferred to his or her spouse. While the transferor will be treated as having transferred the full value of the property in Example 3 of Reg. § 25.2702-2(d), the transferor and the donee may use the property for the donee's lifetime. Of course, if a QTIP marital deduction is claimed in connection with the original transfer of the property, it will be included in the estate of the donee spouse. Otherwise, it will not be included in the donee's estate, who received only a life interest in the property. Under this approach, the use of the property may be retained for the donee's lifetime without taxing any appreciation in value that takes place over the donee spouse's lifetime.

The value of an annuity, term interest, remainder or reversionary interest in a trust that is not subject to the special valuation rules of § 2702, is usually valued according to the applicable actuarial tables. However, Reg. § 20.7520-3(b)(3) provides that the tables may not be used "if an individual who is a measuring life is terminally ill." The regulation continues to state that "an individual who is known to have an incurable illness or other deteriorating physical condition is considered terminally ill if there is at least a 50 percent probability that the individual will die within 1 year."

§ 9.41. SALE OF REMAINDER INTEREST

In the sale of a remainder interest, a senior family member who owns an asset sells a remainder interest in the property to a junior family member for its actuarially determined value. Such a sale made to a family member prior to October 8, 1990, the effective date of § 2702, did not involve a gift. Of course, if the property had appreciated in value during the time it was owned by the senior family member, some gain might result from the sale of the remainder interest. Some private letter rulings suggested that such a transfer of a remainder interest removed the asset from the owner's estate, which is a logical result. If the actuarial tables function properly the value of the consideration received in exchange for the remainder interest will grow to equal the value of the entire property at the expiration of the retained life estate. For example, LR 8145012 (TAM) concluded that,

> [O]n these facts we have determined that the sale of the remainder interest in the X Ranch, as described, would not result in the inclusion of any part of the value of the property in decedent's gross estate by reason of section 2036 of the Code. Of course, the proceeds of such a transfer, owned by the decedent at her date of death, would be includible in her gross estate under section 2033 of the Code.

That result is consistent with the holdings in the *D'Ambrosio, Wheeler* and *Magnin* cases described in §9.34, above. Under them, the sale of a remainder interest in property removes the property from the seller's estate if he or she received consideration in money or money's worth equal to the actuarially determined value of the remainder interest. Accordingly, the sale of a remainder for its actuarially determined value would remove the property from the seller's estate.

If a client decides to sell a remainder interest in property with the object of removing the asset from his or her estate, the planning requires a reliable determination of the fair market value of the property. In the case of publicly traded securities and some other properties, quotations are readily available. In other cases an expert appraisal should be obtained. The reason is simple: If the transferor receives less than the full fair market value of the property, the sale may involve a gift and the property may be included in the transferor's estate.

Gift to Spouse for Life and Sale of Remainder. Aggressive clients looking to utilize their $5 million applicable exemption may wish to consider combining the gift of a life interest to a spouse with the sale of the remainder interest for its fair market value. The gift tax marital deduction is available although the donee spouse's interest is a terminable interest. The terminable interest rule of §2523(b) does not apply to such a disposition if the donor spouse receives full and adequate consideration in exchange for the transfer of remainder interest.

§9.41.1. Gift Tax Consequences

> *Sale of remainder interest and joint purchase of interests in property.* Under the bill, the retention of a term interest (including a life estate) in property is treated like the retention of an interest in trust. Moreover, a joint purchase of property is treated as an acquisition of the entire property by the holder of the term interest, followed by a transfer of the remainder interest. Thus, for purposes of determining the amount of the gift, the bill effectively treats the purchaser of a new life estate pursuant to a joint purchase as making a transfer of the entire property less the consideration paid by the remainder beneficiaries. Senate Finance Committee Report, S. Rep. No. 3209, 101st Cong., 2d Sess., 136 Cong. Rec. §15629, 15629 (1990).

Pre-§2702 Rules. Under traditional analysis, the sale of a remainder interest results in a gift from the owner to the remainder beneficiary *only* if the remainder beneficiary pays too little for the remainder interest. Similarly, the transaction involves a gift from the remainder beneficiary to the seller if the remainder beneficiary pays too much for the remainder interest. Prior to October 9, 1990 the possibility of either party making a gift was avoided if the remainder beneficiary paid the actuarially proper amount for the remainder. Of course, if the seller were terminally ill at the time, the valuation of the remainder interest according to the actuarial tables would be inappropriate. *See Estate of James Stuart Pritchard,* 4 T.C. 204 (1944) (sale of insurance policy by terminally ill insured for cash surrender value was not made for full and adequate consideration). Reliance upon the actuarial tables in such a case might result in the seller making a gift the remainder beneficiary. As noted above in §9.40, the actuarial tables cannot be used to value life interests, remainders and the like if the person who serves as a measuring life has less than a 50 percent chance of surviving for a year or more.

The valuation rules of §2702 apply to the sale of a remainder interest to a family member after October 8, 1990 (the effective date of §2702). The seller is treated as having transferred the entire property in exchange for the consideration paid by the remainder beneficiary. The resulting gift does not qualify for the annual gift tax exclusion. Note, however, that under §2702(c)(4) the fair market value of a retained term interest in nondepreciable tangible property is taken into account in determining the amount of the gift. Such an approach also applies to a joint purchase of such property by members of the same family. §2702(c)(2). *See* §9.42. Of course, the preexisting rules would continue to apply to the sale of remainder interests to persons who are not within the definition of family members in §2704(c)(2). Note also that the new rules do not apply to transfers of property that the transferor uses as a personal residence. *See* §9.44.

EXAMPLE 9-23.

Seller, *S,* sold a remainder interest in a commercial building to her cousin, *C,* for cash equal to its actuarially determined value. A cousin is not considered to be a family member for purposes of §2702. *See* §2704(c)(2). Accordingly, the valuation rules of §2702 do not apply to the sale. As the transfer was made for an amount equal to its actuarially determined value, the transfer did not involve a gift. Also, because *S* received adequate and full consideration under the *D'Ambrosio, Wheeler* and *Magnin* cases, §9.34, the transferred property is not includible in *S's* gross estate.

Section 2702 would have applied to *S* in Example 9-23 if the sale had been made to a spouse, ancestor, lineal descendant, or brother or sister, or the spouse of any of them. If so, *S* would have been treated as having transferred the entire value of the property in exchange for only the value of the remainder interest. According to the Senate Committee Report the special rule of §2702(c)(4) does not apply to depletable or, presumably, depreciable, property. Finally, §2702 would not apply to the sale of a remainder interest in a personal residence used by the seller.

§9.41.1

§ 9.41.2. Estate Tax Consequences

No rational person would ever purchase a remainder interest for the price of the full fee-simple interest in the same property. If such a transaction were to occur, the purchaser would likely incur gift tax, which in these situations is calculated by comparing the consideration received to the value of the remainder interest in the property . . . .*Estate of Cyril Magnin v. Commissioner*, 184 F.3d 1074, 1078 (9th Cir. 1999).

The most significant estate tax issue involved in the sale of a remainder interest is whether the decedent received full and adequate consideration in exchange for the transferred property. Under § 2036(a), property transferred during lifetime in which the transferor retained a life interest is includible in the transferor's estate unless the transferor received "adequate and full consideration" in connection with the transfer. As discussed in § 9.34, the IRS and the rationale of the *Gradow* case require that the consideration received be equal to the full value of the transferred property. Such a requirement is not required by the text of § 2036(a). It requires the inclusion of "all property to the extent of any interest therein of which the decedent has at any time made a transfer (except in the case of a bona fide sale for an adequate and full consideration in money or money's worth)." Under the actuarial tables the a transferor who is entitled to receive payments, the present value of which is equal to the present value of the remainder interest (the right to the outright ownership of the property upon the transferor's death), has received adequate and full consideration.

A simple economic assumption underlies the valuation of life and term interests: The value of the right to receive property upon the death of a person of a certain age is the present value of that property, discounted by an appropriate interest rate. Stated in a different way: The present value of a remainder interest (*i.e.*, the right to receive the property at the end of a fixed period—the end of the life expectancy of the life tenant) is equal to the amount that, invested at the assumed rate, at the end of the fixed period would equal the present value of the property. The following example indicates the shortcomings of the IRS *Gradow* approach.

EXAMPLE 9-24.

T owns Blackacre, which is worth $100,000. Based upon *T*'s age and the applicable interest rate, *T*'s life estate in Blackacre is worth $70,000 and the remainder is worth $30,000. The figures assume that if $30,000 were invested at the applicable interest rate for *T*'s lifetime, the fund would equal $100,000 at the time of *T*'s death. Under *Gradow* a sale of the remainder interest in Blackacre would not have been for adequate and full consideration unless *T* received an amount equal to its full fair market value, $100,000. If that were the appropriate approach, what must *T* receive in order to avoid the reach of § 2036(a) if *T* later sells her retained life estate? Another $100,000, or, would $70,000 suffice?

Under the economically sound approach approved in the *D'Ambrosio* line of cases, the seller of a remainder interest receives adequate and full consideration if he or she receives an amount equal to the actuarially determined value of the remainder interest. As indicated above, that value is determined according to the transferor's age and the interest rate that applies to the valuation of term interests, life estates, remainders, and annuities for the month in which the transfer takes place.

§9.41.3. Income Tax Consequences

The sale of a remainder interest in appreciated property will result in a gain to the seller. The gain is determined according to the difference between the consideration received and the portion of the seller's basis attributable to the remainder interest. If the property is encumbered in an amount that exceeds that portion of the seller's basis, the seller will realize an additional amount of gain. Note that a loss in a sale to a related person would not be deductible by the seller. § 267(a).

The seller, as life tenant, should be entitled to continue to claim depreciation with respect to the underlying property. Under the basic rule of § 167(d) the life tenant is entitled to claim depreciation on the property. § 167(d). The life tenant will not be able to amortize the remaining basis in the property as a cost of acquisition. § 167(e).

The life tenant should be able to claim any losses that are generated by the property. Gain or loss on a sale of the underlying property is apportioned between the life tenant and remainder beneficiary. Rev. Rul. 71-122, 1971-1 C.B. 224 (gain on condemnation of inherited life estate and remainders in real property taxed to life tenant and remainder beneficiaries). However, a life tenant with power of sale who is required to hold and reinvest the proceeds of sale for the ultimate benefit of the remainder beneficiaries may be treated as a trustee and required to file a Form 1041 with respect to the gain or loss. Rev. Rul. 61-102, 1961-1 C.B. 245.

§9.42. Joint Purchases

The acquisition of divided interests in property not previously owned by the purchasers is involved in a joint purchase. In a joint purchase the senior family member contributes an amount toward the purchase price that is equal to the actuarially determined value of the life estate or other term interest that he or she will receive in the property. The junior family member contributes the balance of the purchase price. Presumably, nothing is includible in the senior's estate if the funds used by the junior to purchase the remainder did not originate with the senior. A joint purchase has a better chance than the sale of a remainder interest of preventing the property from being included in the senior purchaser's estate.

One commentator has suggested that split interest purchases made through QPRTs and GRATs or GRUTs are within an exception to the special valuation rules of § 2702. Blattmachr, Split Purchases and Other Ways to Live with Section 2702, U. Miami, 29th Inst. Est. Plan., Ch. 10 (1995). Moreover, if the holder of the term interest does not survive the term of a QPRT, the argument goes, nothing should be includible in his or her gross estate. In the case of GRATs and GRUTs, if a term holder dies before the end of the term, the IRS is likely to assert that a portion of the trust property is includible in his or her estate under § 2039. *See* LR 9412036 (parents and children transferred property to trust from which parents were entitled to receive successive life unitrust distributions).

The IRS largely validated Blattmachr's argument in a letter ruling which held that if the grantor dies prior to the end of the reserved term, none of the value of a residence is includible in the grantor's estate under §§ 2033 or 2039 if the residence was acquired by a QPRT in a "split purchase" to which the grantor contributed the actuarially appropriate amount. LR 200112023. Unfortunately, the IRS declined to rule on the "applicability of section 2036 to the transaction." As indicated in § 9.42.2, none of the residence should be includible under § 2036.

§ 9.42.1. Gift Tax Consequences

Prior to the adoption of § 2702 a joint purchase by family members did not involve a gift if the interests were properly valued and each contributed an amount equal to the actuarially determined value of the interest acquired. This "old rule" will continue to apply with respect to joint purchases by persons who are not family members within the definition contained in § 2704(c)(2). Effective after October 8, 1990, a joint purchase by family members (as defined in § 2704(c)(2)) will almost certainly involve a gift from the senior to the junior. Under § 2702(c)(2), if a joint purchase is made by family members, the holder of the term is treated as having acquired the entire interest in the property and having transferred the remainder in exchange for the consideration contributed by the remainder beneficiary. For purposes of § 2702, the term "family member" does not include nieces, nephews, cousins, and more remotely related persons and their spouses.

EXAMPLE 9-25.

During a month when a 9.8% interest rate applied under § 7520, Aunt, *A*, aged 71, and Nephew, *N*, purchased commercial real property for $200,000. *A* and *N* are not treated as family members under § 2704(c)(2). Under Table S (9.8), *A*'s life estate had a value of .63702 and *N*'s remainder a value of .36298. Accordingly, *A* contributed $127,404 to the purchase price and *N* contributed $72,596. The joint purchase did not involve a gift by *A* or *N*; each contributed the required amount to the joint purchase.

EXAMPLE 9-26.

The facts are the same as in Example 9-25, except the parties are family members—Mother, *M*, aged 71, and Son, *S*. For gift tax purposes § 2702(c)(2) requires that *M* be treated as having transferred the entire property, worth $200,000, in exchange for a consideration of $72,596. Thus, *M* is considered to have made a gift to *S* of $127,404. Presumably the gift does not qualify for the annual exclusion. Perhaps *M* would not be treated as having made a gift if the property acquired were a personal residence to be used by *M*. *See* § 2702(a)(3). In the latter case *M* and *S* should enter into an ancillary agreement containing the provisions required for the arrangement to be treated as a qualified personal residence trust.

Section 2702(a)(3) should allow the joint purchase of a personal residence by family members. In order to satisfy the requirements of the Regulations, Reg. § 25.2702-5, the acquisition should be made with funds contributed to a QPRT. In LR 9841017, the IRS ruled favorably on all issues except § 2036 with respect to the purchase of a personal residence by the trustee of a QPRT with a contribution by a husband and wife of funds equal to the actuarial value of their life interest, and by the wife's son, from his independent means, of funds equal to the value of the remainder. The § 2036 issue should be resolved in favor of the taxpayer in light of the *D'Ambrosio* line of cases.

Under an alternative, the parties to the joint purchase of a personal residence might enter into an agreement containing the provisions required in the case of qualified personal residence trusts. In particular, the parties would have to enter into an agreement that included certain mandatory provisions. Thus, in Example 9-26 *M* and *S* might enter into an agreement ancillary to the purchase of the personal residence for *M* which contained the required terms. In order to reduce the risk that the residence would be included in *M*'s estate under § 2036 she might purchase a term of years rather than a life interest in the property.

Term Interests in Tangible Property. Under § 2702(c)(4), a special rule applies to the valuation of a term interest in tangible property, the use of which does not have a substantial effect upon the valuation of the underlying property. As explained in the following excerpt from the Senate Finance Committee Report, such a term interest is valued according to its market value.

> A special rule applies to a term interest in tangible property where the non-exercise of the term-holder's rights does not substantially affect the value of the property passing to the remainder beneficiary. In that case, the value of the term interest is the amount for which the taxpayer establishes that the term interest could be sold to an unrelated third party. Such amount is not determined under the Treasury tables, but by reference to market norms, taking into account the illiquidity of such interests.
>
> For example, the rule could apply to the joint purchase of a painting or undeveloped real estate (the value of which primarily reflects future development potential). On the other hand, the rule would not apply to a joint purchase of depletable property. Treasury regulations would provide for the proper treatment of improvements or other changes in property governed by this special rule. S. Rep. No. 3209, 101st Cong., 2d Sess. 136 Cong. Rec. S15629, 15683-15684 (1991).

Presumably this section would apply to the transfer of a piece of jewelry or an art object that was transferred subject to the transferor's right to the exclusive use of the item for a fixed period. Of course, establishing the fair market value of the right to use a $2.5 million diamond necklace for ten years may be difficult. The application of this provision is illustrated by Reg. § 25.2702-2(d), Examples 8-10.

EXAMPLE 9-27.

A and his child, *B*, purchased a painting for $1 million. *A* acquired a 10-year term interest and *B* the remainder. According to the actuarial valuation of their interests pursuant to § 7520, *A* paid $501,056 of the purchase price and *B* paid the balance. The painting is a type of property covered by § 2702(c)(4). *A* established that an unrelated party would pay $100,000 for a 10-year term interest in the painting. *A* is treated as having made a gift of $401,056, the difference between his contribution to the purchase of the painting and the fair market value of the term interest.

§ 9.42.2. Estate Tax Consequences

The goal of excluding the property from the senior family member's estate should be achieved if, (1) the property is acquired from a third party, (2) the property is properly valued, and (3) the senior and junior family members each contribute the actuarially appropriate amount toward the purchase price. If each party contributes the actuarially appropriate amount toward the purchase of the property from a third party, under the rationale of the *D'Ambrosio, Wheeler* and *Magnin* cases none of the underlying property should be included in the senior's estate. Note that inclusion would not be required under § 2035 if the purchase were made within three years preceding the life tenant's death.

If the funds contributed to a joint purchase by the remainder beneficiary are traceable to gifts received from the life tenant, the life tenant may be treated as having purchased the entire property and donated the remainder to the remainder beneficiary. If so, § 2036(a) would require the entire property to be included in the senior's estate. This result is indicated by a TAM in which the funds contributed by the remainder beneficiary were indirectly contributed by the senior family member in a joint purchase. LR 9206006 (TAM). In this TAM, the decedent and her daughter and the daughter's husband purchased a condominium unit for $320,000. The decedent, aged 82, acquired the life interest, actuarially valued at .40295, and the daughter and her husband acquired the remainder. The daughter and her husband paid $9,000 of the $15,000 down payment. Their remaining contribution toward the purchase price, $183,000, was borrowed from the decedent's revocable trust of which the daughter was the trustee. Citing several cases including *Gradow*, the IRS ruled that the entire condominium was includable in the decedent's estate except for the portion attributable to the $9,000 contribution made by the daughter and her husband (2.81 percent). The ruling emphasized the control retained by the decedent, "because the Decedent had power to revoke the trust, the Decedent also had full power and control over the trust assets and over the official actions of the trustee (who was the Decedent's daughter)."

Note that the rules of § 2702 regarding the treatment of joint purchases only apply for gift tax purposes and *not* for estate tax purposes. In particular, § 2702(a)(1) provides that, "[s]olely for purposes of determining whether a transfer of an interest in trust to (or for the benefit of) a member of the transferor's family is a gift (and the value of such transfer), the value of any interest in such trust retained by the transferor or any applicable family member (as defined in section 2701(e)(2)) shall be determined as provided in paragraph (2)."

§9.42.3. Income Tax Consequences

A joint purchase may involve significant income tax consequences that vary depending upon whether the joint purchase was made on or before July 27, 1989. To begin with, the initial purchase from a third party should not have any immediate income tax consequences. In addition, under the basic rules the senior family member is entitled to amortize the cost of acquiring the term interest. However, in the case of interests created after July 27, 1989, no amortization deduction is allowable "for any period during which the remainder interest in such property is held (directly or indirectly) by a related person." § 167(e)(1). Although no amortization deductions are allowed, the senior's basis is reduced and the remainder beneficiary's basis in the remainder is increased by the amount of the disallowed amortization deductions. § 167(e)(3).

§9.43. GRANTOR RETAINED INTEREST TRUSTS (GRITs, GRATs AND GRUTs)

GRITs were used, beginning in the 1980s, to reduce the gift and estate tax costs of transferring property within the family. Under a typical plan, a senior family member transfers securities or other valuable property to an irrevocable trust from which the grantor is entitled to receive the income for a term of years with remainder to his or her children or other beneficiaries. At the end of the term the property would pass outright to the designated remainder beneficiaries. The gift of the remainder interest is a future interest that did not qualify for the annual gift tax exclusion. However, prior to the adoption of §2702, the gift tax cost of making the gift was reduced by the actuarially determined value of the term interest retained by the grantor. Of course, if the grantor died during the term of the trust it would be includible in the grantor's estate under §2036(a).

The enactment of §2702 dramatically changed the gift tax rules. Under it, retained interests other than "qualified interests" are valued at zero in determining the gift tax consequences of most transfers. For this purpose a qualified interest is, (1) the right to receive a fixed annual payment (a grantor retained annuity trust, or GRAT); (2) the right to receive each year a fixed percentage of the value of the principal determined annually (a grantor retained unitrust, or GRUT); or (3) a noncontingent remainder interest following a GRAT or GRUT. Importantly, the rules of §2702 do not apply if, (1) the remainder beneficiaries are not members of the grantor's family, or (2) the only property transferred to the trust is a personal residence used by the grantor. As explained in §9.42.1, a special valuation rule applies to term interests in tangible property. The rules regarding qualified interests are spelled out in Reg. §25.2702-3, which imposes some mandatory requirements. The regulation permits the dollar amount or fractional or percentage amount payable in any year to be 120 percent of the amount payable in the immediate preceding year. Reg. §25.2702-3(b)(1), (c)(1).

In order to allow the grantor some flexibility in meeting the tax problems that would arise if he or she died before the end of the term, grantors often retained a reversionary interest or a power of appointment in such a case. In particular, trusts usually provide that if the grantor dies before the end of the term, the trust property would be distributed either, (1) to the grantor's estate (*i.e.*, the grantor retained a reversionary interest) or (2) as the grantor appointed under a general power of appointment. In such a case married grantors typically dispose of the interest in a way that qualifies for the marital deduction—which defers the time for payment of the estate tax. In the case of a transfer creating a qualified interest, the retention of a reversion or a general power of appointment apparently would not be assigned any value (*i.e.*, neither the reversion nor the power of appointment is not a qualified interest). Reg. §25.2702-3(e), Example 1. Thus, the retention of such a power would not reduce the amount of the gift to the remainder beneficiaries. However, as noted above, in order to hedge against the possibility that the grantor might die during the term, it is often best for the grantor to retain a reversion or general power of appointment. Although the retained interest has no value for purposes of §2702, it will allow the grantor to make the most effective disposition of the property.

Regulations limiting the use of actuarial tables in some cases were adopted effective December 13, 1995. Under the regulations, the tables may not be used to value an annuity, interests for life or for a term of years, or a remainder or reversionary interest of a person who is known to be terminally ill and there is at least a 50 percent probability that the individual will die within one year. Reg. §20.7520-3(b)(3). *See* §2.5.2. The same regulations were promulgated under the income tax and the gift tax laws.

While the retained term income interest in a traditional form of retained interest trust with a family member as remainder beneficiary is usually valued at zero, under §2702, such a trust may be attractive to some clients who are interested in retaining some interest in the property while removing further appreciation in value from their estates. The arrangement, of course, will result in the inclusion of the property in the transferor's estate if the transferor dies during the term of the retained interest. Again, however, the risk of inclusion is eliminated if the term interest is transferred to the donor's spouse.

EXAMPLE 9-28.

Donor, *D*, owns all of the stock of *D, Inc.*, which has a value of $5 million. *D* is unwilling to make an outright gift of a substantial portion of the stock, but is willing to transfer 20% of the stock to a trust in which *D* will hold an income interest for a 10-year term, at the end of which the trust will terminate and the property will be distributed to *D*'s children. Under §2702, *D*'s retained interest would be valued at zero for gift tax purposes. Recognizing discounts for lack of marketability and minority interest, the transferred stock might be valued at only $600,000-700,000. *D*'s unified credit will offset the gift tax on the transfer. If the value of *D, Inc.* were to grow at an annual rate of 7% compounded quarterly, the trust's proportionate interest would more than double in value in 10 years. The transfer may be particularly attractive if *D, Inc.* is likely to be acquired by another company or to go public and *D* is interested in an increased income stream. Of course, if *D* dies during the 10-year term the trust is all included in *D*'s estate.

The grantor in Example 9-28 might better choose to transfer the 20 percent minority interest to a GRAT, which would substantially reduce the gift tax cost of the transfer. The return that the stock would have to generate in order to satisfy the GRAT payments is, in effect, reduced by the discount that applies to the valuation of the stock. Also, it is important to note that the IRS has ruled that GRAT payments can be made by distributing to the grantor the assets that were initially transferred to the trust. Because the grantor is treated as the owner of the trust for income tax purposes, no gain or loss would be recognized if the trust distributes the stock to the grantor in satisfaction of the annuity.

It is important to stress that the valuation rules in §2702 apply only for purposes of determining the amount of a gift when an individual makes a transfer in trust and not in other situations. For example, some practitioners recommend that a child create a trust with a retained interest that is not a "qualified interest" and then sell the remainder interest in the trust to the child's parents. In determining the fair market value of the remainder interest to be sold to the parents, these practitioners claim that the valuation rules of §2702 must apply. Thus, if the retained annuity interest is valued at zero under §2702, the fair market value of the remainder interest must be equal to the entire value of the assets contributed to the trust by the child. This interpretation allows the parents to transfer to the child the same amount the child used to fund the trust without incurring a taxable gift. Moreover, there would be no gift on the payments made to the child pursuant to the child's retained interest.

This technique should not work because §2702 does not govern the determination of the value of the remainder interest for purposes of a sale. Section 2702 was intended to assure that an individual who transfers property to an irrevocable trust actually receives the benefits equal to the value that was claimed for gift tax purposes of the interest(s) the grantor retained. It was not enacted, and does not prescribe the manner of determining, the value of remainder interests in such a trust that are transferred by the remainder beneficiaries to the grantor. Consistently, the value of the remainder purchased by the parents in the proposed transaction should be determined without regard to the rules of §2702. The difference is suggested by the text of §2702, which applies to "a transfer of an interest in trust" and the corresponding regulations (the rules apply "to determine the amount of the gift when an individual makes a transfer in trust to (or for the benefit of) a member of the individual's family . . . ."). There is no indication that the rules of §2702 should apply to an outright sale of the remainder interest in a trust.

§9.43.1. Gift Tax Consequences

The gift tax consequences of transferring property depend upon the time at which the trust was created, the relationship between the grantor and the remainder beneficiaries, the terms of the trust and the type of property involved. The strict valuation rules of §2702 generally apply to transfers made after October 8, 1990 in which the grantor retains a term interest and the remainder is transferred to a member of the grantor's family. As indicated above, the term members of the family include the grantor's spouse, ancestors, lineal descendants, brothers and sisters, and the spouses of any of them. §2704(c)(2). In such cases the retained interest is generally treated as having a value of zero unless it is a qualified interest as defined in §2702(b).

In LR 9707001, the IRS analyzed the gift tax consequences of creating a five-year GRAT that provided that if the grantor died prior to the end of the term the remaining payments would be made to his spouse for so long as she lived (if he had not revoked her right to receive the payments), otherwise, the payments were to be made to his estate. Relying primarily on Examples (1), (5), and (6) of Reg. §25.2702-2(e), the ruling concluded that "the right to receive the balance of the annuity payments to be made, if the Donor dies during the annuity term, to the Spouse or the Donor's estate are not qualified interests." The same result was reached in LR 9741001, which analyzed the differences between Example (6) and (7) of Reg. §25.2702-2(e).

For gift tax purposes if the rules of §2702 were applied without mitigation the same interest may be taxed more than once. For example, a retained term interest might be valued at zero under §2702 in connection with the transfer of a remainder interest in property, but be valued at fair market value when it is later transferred. In light of this possibility, the regulations provide for a reduction in the total amount of an individual's taxable gifts if he or she transfers an interest other than a qualified interest that was previously valued under §2702. Reg. §25.2702-6. The amount of the reduction is the lesser of (1) the increase in the individual's taxable gifts resulting from the interest being initially valued under §2702 and (2) the increase in the individual's taxable gifts (or taxable estate) resulting from the subsequent transfer of the interest. Reg. §25.2702-6(b)(1). In determining the increase in taxable gifts resulting from the subsequent transfer of the interest, the transferor's annual exclusion is considered to apply first to transfers other than the transfer of the interest previously valued under §2702. *Id.*

§9.43.2. Qualified Interests (GRATs and GRUTs)

The value of a qualified interest retained by the transferor is taken into account in determining gift tax consequences under §2702. For purposes of §2702 a qualified interest is an annuity interest, a unitrust interest, or a noncontingent remainder following an annuity or unitrust interest. In particular, under §2702(b) a qualified interest is:

1. Any interest which consists of the right to receive fixed amounts payable not less frequently than annually,

2. Any interest which consists of the right to receive amounts which are payable not less frequently than annually and are a fixed percentage of the fair market value of the property in the trust (determined annually),

3. Any noncontingent remainder interest if all of the other interests in the trust consist of interests described in paragraph (1) or (2).

The annuity or unitrust amount may be payable based on either the anniversary date of the creation of the trust or the taxable year of the trust. Regs. §§25.2702-3(b)(3), (c)(3). Amounts payable on the anniversary date of an annuity or unitrust must be paid by the anniversary date. Regs. §§25.2702-3(b)(4), (c)(4).

The value of the grantor's retained annuity or unitrust interest is determined in accordance with § 7520 (*i.e.,* according to the actuarial tables, based upon 120 percent of the applicable federal midterm rate for the month in which the transfer was made). The regulations allow the amount of the annuity or unitrust payments to increase by 20 percent per year. Reg. § 25.2702-3(b)(1), (c)(1).

EXAMPLE 9-29.

> Grantor, G, aged 50, transferred property worth $200,000 to a trust in which she retained the right to receive a payment of $20,000 each year for 15 years, at the end of which the trust property would be distributed to her son, S. An assumed interest rate of 9.2% applied to the valuation of interests in the trust. According to Table B, the right to receive $1 each year for 15 years is worth 7.9664. Accordingly, G's retained interest had a total value of $159,328. G made a gift of only $40,672. The transfer may be attractive to G, particularly if the property generates enough income to make the annual payments and may appreciate to be worth more than $200,000 at the end of the 15-year term.

The amount distributable under a GRUT will vary from year to year according to the value of the trust. As the examples indicate, a GRUT will also produce a smaller remainder interest than a GRAT with initial payout rate. Accordingly, the amount of gift in a GRUT will be smaller. Distributions from a GRUT may keep up with inflation. However, that advantage is offset by the additional difficulty of having to value the trust property annually.

The regulations define the criteria that must be met in order for a term interest to be treated as a qualified interest. Reg. § 25.2702-3. Some of the requirements track those of charitable remainder trusts. The requirements include mandatory and optional provisions. Those applicable to qualified annuity interests are described in Reg. § 25.2702-3(b); those applicable to qualified unitrust interests are described in Reg. § 25.2702-3(c); and those applicable to both types of trusts are described in Reg. § 25.2702-3(d). Among the requirements: an annuity trust must prohibit additions to the trust and all types of trusts must prohibit commutation of the interest of the transferor or applicable family member.

Note that effective September 20, 1999 GRATs and GRUTs must both prohibit the trustee from using notes, other debt instruments, options, or similar financial arrangements to satisfy the annuity or unitrust payment obligation. Reg. § 25.2702-3(d)(5). Also, under the cited regulation trusts created prior to September 20, 1999 must not use such modes of payment. The regulation reflects the position the IRS took in LR 9717008 (TAM). In order to make payments due under a GRAT or GRUT a trustee may borrow funds from an unrelated third party. According to the introduction to the final form of the regulations, "[T]he step transaction doctrine will be applied where a series of transactions is used to achieve a result that is inconsistent with the regulations." Treas. Dec. 8899, 65 Fed. Reg. 53587 (Sept. 5, 2000).

Satisfying Annuity by Distributing Trust Assets. In several rulings the IRS has held that if the grantor is treated as the owner of all of the property of the trust, the trustee may, in satisfaction of the required annuity payments, return to the grantor the very assets that were initially transferred to the trust. *E.g.,* LRs 9352017, 9449012. In LR 9352017, the IRS stated,

> In accordance with the principle set forth in Rev. Rul. 85-13, we conclude that neither the trust grantor nor the trust will recognize any gain or loss as a result of the grantor's transfer of shares of Company A or Company B, to fund the trust, or as the result of the transfer from a trust to a grantor in payment of an annuity, or as a result of the substitution by the grantor of cash or other property for shares of stock.

By distributing assets of the trust in kind in satisfaction of the annuity, it is not required to liquidate any of the shares, the gains of which would be subject to taxation. (Of course, the trustee might be able to borrow funds with which to make the annuity payments—which would also avoid the necessity of a sale.) If the grantor were not treated as the owner of the trust, presumably the trust would realize capital gains when appreciated assets, such as the stock originally contributed by the grantor, were distributed in satisfaction of a required fixed payment.

S corporation stock may be held in a GRAT or GRUT if the grantor is treated as the owner of the trust under the grantor trust rules. *E.g.,* LRs 9248016, 9519029. A trust of which a nongrantor is treated as the owner under §678 may also hold S corporation stock, LR 9810006, as may a qualified subchapter S trust (QSST), LR 9724010. The trust could also hold S corporation stock if the trust is an electing small business trust. §1361(e). *See* §11.4.

§9.43.3. The Zeroed-Out GRAT

Depending on the selected annuity or unitrust payment, the length of the grantor's retained interest, and the §7520 rate in effect at the formation of the trust, the value of the grantor's retained interest may be equal to the fair market value of the property transferred in trust. In such a case, the value of the remainder interest (and, thus, the amount of the taxable gift) would be zero. In a former regulation, Reg. §25.2702-3(e)(3), Example (5), the IRS took the position that the formation of a trust with a qualified interest could never result in a gift of zero. According to the IRS, the risk that the grantor might not survive the entire term of the trust had to be reflected in valuing the grantor's retained interest. Such a risk, of course, would lower the value of the retained interest, meaning the remainder interest had to have at least *some* value.

The famous "Example (5)" limitation on the valuation of a grantor's retained interest in a GRAT was rejected by the Tax Court in *Audrey J. Walton,* 115 T.C. 589 (2000) *acq.,* Notice 2003-72, 2003-2 C.B. 964. The Tax Court instead upheld the donor's argument that the Code and Reg. §25.2702-3(d)(3) both recognize that a retained interest could be (1) for the life of the term holder, (2) for a specified term of years, or (3) for the shorter of those periods. Accordingly, the retained interest in *Walton* was valued as an annuity payable for a fixed period of two years. According to the Tax Court, if an annuity is to be paid to the grantor for a specified number of years, and to the grantor's estate if the grantor dies during the term, the retained interest is valued as an annuity for a fixed term—without any reduction on account of the possibility the grantor might die during the term. The Tax Court held that Example

(5) of Reg. §25.2702-3(e)(3) was invalid to the extent it required that the value of the retained interest reflect the possibility that the donor would die within the term. The decision in *Walton*, which was not appealed, makes it possible for grantors to "zero-out" the value of a transfer to a GRAT.

In 2005, Treasury finalized a revision to Example (5) of Reg. §25.2702-3(e) to conform to *Walton*. Under the example as revised, a unitrust amount payable for a specified term of years to the grantor, or to the grantor's estate if the grantor dies prior to the expiration of the term, is a qualified interest for the specified term. The revised example applies to trusts created on or after July 26, 2004.

Planning GRATs in Light of Walton. The planning approach taken in *Walton* in effect increases the value of the donor's interests in a GRAT, which makes it easier to reduce—or eliminate—the gift tax cost of establishing a GRAT. However, it is also necessary to plan for the possibility that the grantor might die during the term of the GRAT. Accordingly, if the grantor is married the immediate estate tax cost is eliminated if all interests in the GRAT pass to the surviving spouse in a manner that qualifies for the marital deduction. The amount payable to the grantor's estate should be the greater of the annuity amount or the income of the trust, which is permissible under Reg. §25.2702-3(d)(5). The GRAT should provide that if the grantor dies during the term any other interest that is includible in the grantor's estate should be distributed to the surviving spouse, or to a marital deduction trust for her benefit.

The estate tax consequences of dying during the term of a GRAT are also eliminated by providing that if the grantor dies during the term of the GRAT, the trust property will be distributed to the grantor's estate from which it will pass in a way that qualifies for the marital deduction. However, according to the IRS the benefit achieved in the *Walton* case is not allowable in such a case. In particular, an example that was not challenged in the *Walton* case provides that the value of the grantor's retained interest does not include the value of a "contingent reversion" in the corpus of the GRAT. Reg. §25.2702-3(e), Example 1. Thus, if the grantor retains an annuity for 10 years, at the end of which the trust corpus is distributable to the grantor's child, and, if the grantor dies during the term, the trust property is distributable to the grantor's estate—the grantor's retained interest is limited to the actuarially determined value of the right to receive the annuity for 10 years or until the grantor's earlier death. According to the example, "The contingent reversion is valued at zero." If the grantor dies during the term of a GRAT, the GRAT may provide that the grantor will have a general testamentary power of appointment over the trust. *See* LR 200227022. The grantor could exercise the power by appointing the property to a QTIP trust for his spouse or in another way that would reduce the estate tax applicable to his estate.

The use of a variation on the private annuity as a promising alternative to a GRAT is described at §9.10.3. The approach should produce the benefits of a zeroed-out GRAT, while avoiding the risk that the transferred property would be includible in the grantor's estate under §§2036 and 2039 if the grantor died during the term of the annuity.

Under the alternative strategy described at §9.10.3, if the grantor dies during the term of the annuity, only the amount payable to the grantor's estate is includible in the grantor's estate. The marital deduction will be available with respect to that amount if the private annuity provides that the greater of the annuity amount or the amount of income attributable to the property transferred in exchange for the annuity will be payable to the grantor's estate. The grantor's will would, of course, provide that the amount received by reason of the annuity would be payable to the grantor's surviving spouse or to her estate.

§ 9.43.4. Successive Term Interests

Under Reg. § 25.2702-3(d)(3), the term of a qualified interest "must be for the life of the term holder, for a specified term of years, or for the shorter (but not the longer) of those periods. Successive term interests for the benefit of the same individual are treated as the same term interest." For this purpose a grantor's retained power to revoke a spouse's qualified interest is treated as a qualified interest retained by the grantor. Reg. § 25.2702-2(a)(5). Under these rules the grantor of a GRAT that provides for the payment of the annuity to the grantor for ten years, then to the grantor's spouse for ten years—subject to the grantor's retained power to revoke—is considered to have retained the annuity for 20 years. Reg. § 25.2702-2(d)(3) Example (7). In contrast, the grantor is not treated as having retained the successive revocable term interest of a spouse if the grantor's initial interest will terminate at the end of a specified term or the grantor's earlier death. *William A. Cook,* 115 T.C. 15 (2000). In such a case the interest of the surviving spouse will extend for a term of years (or another life) beyond the life of the grantor. Compare Examples (6) and (7) of Reg. § 25.2702-3(d)(3).

§ 9.43.5. Grantor's Death During Term

If the grantor dies during the term of a GRAT or GRUT, the full value of the trust may not be includible in the grantor's gross estate. Under regulations effective July 11, 2008, the amount included in the gross estate is "that portion of the trust corpus necessary to provide the decedent's retained use or retained annuity, unitrust, or other payment (without reducing or invading principal)." Reg. § 20.2036-1(c)(2)(i). In an example from the regulations, the decedent transferred $100,000 to a GRAT that paid $12,000 each year (in $1,000 monthly installments) to the decedent for a term of ten years or until the decedent's death, whichever occurred first. At the decedent's death, prior to the end of the term, the trust had $300,000 in assets and the § 7520 rate was six percent. The example states that the amount included in the decedent's gross estate is determined by dividing the annual annuity amount (as adjusted for monthly payments) by the § 7520 rate. Here, the annual annuity amount is $12,000 and the Table K adjustment factor for monthly annuity payments is 1.0272. The product of the annual annuity amount and the adjustment factor is $12,326.40. This product is then divided by the six percent § 7520 rate in effect at the decedent's death, resulting in $205,440, the amount of principal required to yield the annual annuity. Accordingly, $205,440 of the $300,000 principal is required to be included in the decedent's gross estate. Reg. § 20.2036-1(c)(2)(iii), Example 2.

The regulations resolved conflicting rulings that applied different Code provisions to reach different results on the question. In Rev. Rul. 76-273, 1976-2 C.B. 268, the IRS ruled that because the grantor-lead beneficiary of a CRUT retained a unitrust interest worth more than the value of the right to all of the income from the trust, the entire value of the trust principal must be included in the grantor-lead beneficiary's gross estate under § 2036. Later, in Rev. Rul. 82-105, 1982-1 C.B. 133, the IRS held that only a portion of the property held in a CRAT was includible in the estate of the deceased grantor-annuitant under § 2036. "[T]he portion of the value of a charitable remainder annuity trust that is includible in D's gross estate at death is the amount necessary, at the rate of 6 percent as specified under section 20.2031-10 of the regulations, to yield the guaranteed annual payment." The ruling specifically did not consider whether any additional portion of the trust would be included in the grantor-annuitant's gross estate under other provisions of the Code.

That left the door open for the IRS to consider the application of § 2039 in LR 200210009 (TAM). The TAM involved a grantor who died in the sixth year of a ten-year GRAT which provided that if the grantor died during the term, the remaining payments were to be made to his estate. The remainder was distributable to his daughter if she survived the ten-year term, otherwise to his wife if she survived the term. The TAM, consistent with the rulings described above, concluded that if the grantor dies during the term of a GRAT, § 2036 requires a portion of the value of the corpus of the GRAT to be included in the grantor's estate. The portion is the amount necessary to generate the amount of the annual GRAT payment at the assumed rate of interest equal to the § 7520 rate on the date of the decedent's death. The TAM then concluded, however, that the entire corpus of the GRAT is includible in the grantor's estate under § 2039(a). The IRS reasoned that § 2039(a) requires full inclusion of the GRAT principal because:

> the annuity payable to the Decedent, and the payments to be made after Decedent's death, are all payable under the terms of a trust instrument, which constitutes a contract or agreement, as required under § 2039(a). Further, the annuity was paid to Decedent for a period that did not in fact end before his death. Finally, under the terms of the GRAT, the annuity and other payments receivable by the estate (and, thus, the estate beneficiaries) and the remainder beneficiaries of the GRAT, are receivable by reason of surviving the Decedent.

The TAM is consistent with LR 9345035, where the IRS held that if the grantor died during the term of the trust the entire trust corpus would be included in his gross estate under § 2039.

The final regulations provide that only § 2036 applies in these cases and not § 2039. Reg. § 20.2039-1(e)(1). As Treasury stated in the preamble to the regulations when they were proposed in 2007, "section 2039 appears to have been intended to address annuities purchased by or on behalf of the decedent and annuities provided by the decedent's employer." It apparently is not intended to apply to the interests retained by grantors in GRATs, CRTs, and similar trusts.

Although the final regulations come as welcome news to planners because Treasury chose the lesser of two evils (inclusion of a portion under § 2036 beats inclusion of all under § 2039), there is an argument that inclusion under § 2036 is likewise inappropriate. In LR 7835002, a ruling involving the grantor-annuitant of a CRAT, the IRS stated that:

> The 1971 transfer in consideration of the charity's promise to pay a self and survivor annuity to the decedent and his wife is not includible in the

decedent's gross estate under section 2036 of the Code. The survivor annuity, however, is includible under section 2039.

The reasoning was explained at an earlier point in the ruling:

> The risk that a purchased private annuity will be considered as a transfer with a retained life estate arises primarily where the transferor retains some security interest in the transferred property. Lowndes, Kramer and McCord, Federal Estate and Gift Taxes (3rd ed. 1974) at 237. Ordinarily, if the property is exchanged solely for the transferee's promise to pay the annuity with no reservation of an interest in the property transferred, the transaction will be treated as a purchased annuity and not as a transfer with a reserved life estate. Estate of Bergan v. Commissioner, 1 T.C. 5643 (1943); Estate of Becklenberg v. Commissioner, 273 F.3d 297 (7th Cir. 1959). See also Fidelity-Philadelphia Trust Company v. Smith, 356 U.S. 874 (1958), 1958-1 C.B. 557.

To the extent inclusion under § 2036 is inconsistent with the authorities cited in this ruling, one could argue that inclusion under § 2036 is questionable. The fact remains, however, that the grantor of a GRAT who dies before the end of the term retained a right to income, possession, or enjoyment of a portion of the trust property for a period that did not in fact end before the grantor's death. A strict construction of § 2036(a) supports the conclusion reached by the regulations.

§ 9.43.6. Contingent Annuity or Unitrust Interests

An annuity or unitrust interest that is contingent is not a qualified interest because it is not for a fixed term. Reg. § 25.2702-3(d)(3). However, the grantor's retention of the power to revoke a qualified interest given to his or her spouse is treated as the retention of a qualified interest. Reg. § 25.2702-2(a)(5). Also, the term of an annuity or unitrust interest must be for the life of the term holder, for a specified number of years, or for the shorter of those periods. By way of illustration, a revocable annuity interest that is payable to the grantor's spouse only if she survives the grantor and is married to the grantor at the time of his death is not a qualified interest. *Cook v. Commissioner,* 269 F.3d 854 (7th Cir. 2001). The decision in *Cook* is correct because the interest of the donor's spouse is contingent upon her remaining married to the grantor.

In *Patricia A. Schott & Stephen C. Schott,* T.C. Memo. 2001-110, *rev'd,* 319 F.3d 1203 (9th Cir. 2003), the Tax Court held that the revocable interest of a grantor's spouse that was not contingent on remaining married was not a qualified interest. (The outcome was questionable based on the text of Example 7 of Reg. § 25.2702-2(d)(1).) The GRATs involved in the *Schott* cases provided for payments of 11.54 percent of the initial value of the trust to be made to the grantor for 15 years or until the earlier death of the grantor. If the grantor died before the end of the 15-year term, payments for the remainder of the term were to be made to the grantor's spouse if he was living and the grantor had not revoked the interest. On February 18, 2003, the Ninth Circuit reversed the Tax Court decision in *Schott,* in an opinion that relies heavily upon Example 7 of Reg. § 25.2702-2(d)(1). Here is the text of the example:

EXAMPLE (7)

The facts are the same as in Example (6), except that both the term interest retained by A and the interest transferred to A's spouse (subject to A's right of revocation) are qualified annuity or unitrust interests. [In Example (6), "A transfers property to an irrevocable trust, retaining the right to receive the income for 10 years. Upon expiration of 10 years, the income for the trust is payable to A's spouse for 10 years if living. Upon expiration of the spouse's interest, the trust terminates and the trust corpus is payable to A's children. A retains the right to revoke the spouse's interest."] The amount of the gift is the fair market value of the property transferred to the trust reduced by the value of both A's qualified interest and the value of the qualified interest transferred to A's spouse (subject to revocation).

In the *Schott* opinion, the Tax Court agreed with the IRS that the "'[I]f living' language in Example 6 [which is incorporated in Example 7] . . . should be interpreted to read that, if the spouse is living at the end of the grantor's 10-year term, annuity payments shall be payable to the spouse, but, if the spouse is not living at the end of the grantor's 10-year term, the spouse's 10-year term interest is payable to the estate of the spouse." Actually there is no language in Example 7 that justifies such an interpretation. On appeal, the Ninth Circuit rejected the Tax Court interpretation, concluding, "The annuity created by each Schott trust for the lives of the grantor and spouse or fifteen years is as qualified as the annuity in Example 7 paying a fixed amount for ten years to the grantor, then to the spouse if living. As the Tax Court pointed out, 'the principal objective of section 2702 was to prevent undervaluation of gifted interests.' A two-life annuity, based on the lives of the grantor and spouse with a limit of fifteen years, falls 'within the class of easily valued rights' that Congress meant to qualify." 319 F.3d at 1207.

Treasury has defended its position in *Schott* as follows:

In *Example 7*, beginning at the expiration of a 10-year term, the spouse's annuity is payable to the spouse for 10 years or until the spouse's prior death. Thus, the spouse's annuity in the example meets the requirements of § 25.2702-3(d)(3), that the term of the annuity must be for either the life of the holder (the spouse), for a specified term of years, or for the shorter but not the longer of these two periods and, assuming the spouse survives until the commencement of his or her interest, the spouse will receive that interest in all events (subject to the transferor's retained right of revocation). In contrast, in *Schott*, the spouse's annuity does not meet the requirements of § 25.2702-3(d)(3) because the spousal annuity is payable, if at all, only if the grantor dies prior to the termination of the term of the trust and, if payable at all, is payable for a period that depends on the length of the unexpired portion of the trust's term when the grantor dies. 69 FR 44476 (2004).

Accordingly, Treasury in 2005 finalized a revision to Reg. § 25.2702-2(a)(6), clarifying that the revocable spousal interest exception applies only if the spouse's interest, standing by itself, would constitute a qualified interest that meets the requirements of § 25.2702-3(d)(3), but for the grantor's revocation power.

§ 9.44. PERSONAL RESIDENCE TRUSTS; QUALIFIED PERSONAL RESIDENCE TRUSTS (QPRTS)

The valuation rules of § 2702 do not apply if the only property transferred is a "residence to be used as a personal residence by persons holding term interests in such trust." § 2702(a)(3)(iii). Under the regulations, the exception applies to a trust "the governing instrument of which prohibits the trust from holding for the original duration of the term interest, any asset other than one residence to be used or held for use as a personal residence by the term holder." Reg. § 25.2705-2(b)(1).

Personal Residence. A personal residence is defined as either the principal residence of the term holder as determined under § 1034 or one other residence which would be treated as the term holder's dwelling under § 280A(d)(1), without regard to § 280A(d)(2), or an undivided fractional interest in either. Reg. § 25.2702-5(b)(2).

Under § 280A(d)(1), a dwelling unit is treated as the taxpayer's residence if the taxpayer uses it more than the greater of 14 days or 10 percent of the number of days it was rented during the taxable year. A residence may be rented for a portion of the year so long as the requirements of § 280A are met. Reg. § 25.2702-5(d), Example 2. The personal residence may include appurtenant structures used by the term holder for residential purposes and adjacent land that is reasonably appropriate for residential purposes. Reg. § 25.2702-5(b)(2)(ii). A personal residence may be subject to a mortgage, but may not include any personal property. Regulation § 25.2702-5(b)(1) authorizes expenses, whether or not attributable to principal, to be paid directly by the term holder. Spouses may transfer their interests in the residence to the same personal residence trust, provided that the governing instrument prohibits anyone other than a spouse from holding a term interest in the residence concurrently with the other spouse. Reg. § 25.2702-5(b). Thus, if one spouse dies the interest of the deceased spouse should not pass for the unexpired balance of his or her term interest to any person other than the surviving spouse. Beyond these requirements the regulations give relatively little guidance regarding a personal residence trust. Importantly, the regulations create a safe harbor for trusts that meet the requirements of a "qualified personal residence trust" and, therefore, are treated as personal residence trusts. Reg. § 25.2702-5(a).

Payment of Taxes, Insurance and Other Items. If the grantor is treated as the owner of the trust property under § 677, the grantor is entitled to deductions for taxes, mortgage interest, and other deductions attributable to a co-op apartment and allocable to income. LR 9249014. Also, as the person entitled to occupy the premises, the grantor may appropriately pay recurring taxes, insurance, and other items that are properly chargeable to the term tenant under the principal and income law.

Encumbered Residence. A residence that is subject to a mortgage or other encumbrance does not affect its status as a personal residence. Reg. § 25.2702-5(b)(2)(ii). The existence of an encumbrance on a residence would, of course, affect the size of the gift that is made at the time a personal residence trust is established (*i.e.*, the gift would be smaller than if the residence were not encumbered). Each subsequent payment of principal would involve a further gift to the remainder beneficiaries, which requires additional gift tax returns to be filed. Some donors attempt to avoid this outcome by having the grantor enter into an agreement with the trustee of the personal residence trust under which the grantor is obligated to make all future mortgage payments.

§9.44.1. Two Personal Residence Limit

Under Reg. §25.2702-5(a), a trust of which the term holder is the grantor is not a personal residence trust (or a qualified personal residence trust) if, at the time of the transfer, the term holder of the trust already holds term interests in two trusts that are personal residence trusts (or qualified personal residence trusts) of which the term holder was the grantor. Accordingly, it appears that a husband and wife could participate in a maximum of three personal residence trusts: (1) one which is their principal residence (whether or not it is hers, his, or theirs); (2) one which is the wife's separate property; and, (3) one which is the husband's separate property.

§9.44.2. Qualified Personal Residence Trust (QPRTs)

A qualified personal residence trust must meet the requirements of Reg. §25.2702-5(c). In brief, the term personal residence is defined in the same way as above. Similarly, a QPRT may include appurtenant structures, but no personal property such as furniture and furnishings. More important, the regulations require the inclusion of certain terms and allow the inclusion of others. Most clients will probably prefer a trust that includes some of the optional terms—particularly ones that allow the proceeds of a sale, involuntary conversion, or destruction of a residence to be reinvested in a replacement residence or converted into a qualified annuity interest for the remainder of the term holder's interest.

In order to meet the requirements of a QPRT, a trust *must:*

1. Require that any income of the trust be distributed to the term holder not less frequently than annually;
2. Prohibit the distribution of corpus to any beneficiary other than the grantor prior to the termination of the term interest;
3. Prohibit the trust from holding, for the entire term of the trust, any asset other than one residence. However, the trust may permit additions of cash to a separate account of the trust in amounts that do not exceed the costs of trust expenses for six months and improvements to be paid within six months. In addition, the trust may permit contributions to be made to finance the purchase of the initial residence within three months if the trustee has previously entered into a contract to purchase the residence. Similarly, additions may be made for the purchase of a residence to replace another residence within three months of the addition, provided that the trustee has already entered into a contract to purchase the residence;
4. Require, if the trust permits the addition of cash to the trust, the trustee to determine, not less often than quarterly, the amounts held by the trust for payment of expenses in excess of the amounts permitted. Any excess must be immediately distributed to the term holder;

5. Require, upon termination of the term holder's interest, the trustee to distribute outright to the term holder within 30 days of termination, any excess of additions to the trust not required to pay trust expenses due and payable on the date of termination;

6. Provide that the trust ceases to be a qualified personal residence trust if the residence ceases to be used or held for use as a personal residence by the term holder;

7. Provide that the trust ceases to be a qualified personal residence trust upon sale of the property if the trust does not permit the trust to hold the proceeds of sale in a separate account. A trust that allows the proceeds to be retained must provide that the trust ceases to be a personal residence trust with respect to the proceeds of sale (or the proceeds of involuntary conversion or insurance payments caused by damage or destruction of the residence) not later than the earlier of the date (a) two years after the sale; (b) the termination of the term holder's interest in the trust; and (c) the date on which a new residence is acquired by the trust;

8. Provide that no later than 30 days after the trust ceases to be a personal residence trust with respect to certain assets (*e.g.*, the proceeds of sale that are not used to purchase a replacement residence within two years), the assets must either be distributed outright to the term holder or be converted into a qualified annuity interest held in a separate share of the trust for the balance of the term holder's interest. Alternatively, the trustee may be given the sole discretion to make either such a distribution to the term holder or such a conversion to a qualified annuity interest;

9. The governing instrument must prohibit "the trust from selling or transferring the residence, directly or indirectly, to the grantor, the grantor's spouse, or an entity controlled by the grantor or the grantor's spouse during the original term interest of the trust, or at any time after the original term." § 25.2702-5(c)(9). This last requirement is effective with respect to trusts created after May 16, 1996.

In June 2003, the IRS issued a sample QPRT with alternate provisions. Rev. Proc. 2003-42, 2003-1 C.B. 993.

Joint Purchase. The acquisition of a residence by a QPRT with funds contributed in actuarially appropriate amounts by the grantors and their children can avoid gift and estate tax consequences. LR 20012023. Of course, the funds contributed by the children cannot themselves have been given to them by the grantors. In LR 20012023, the IRS ruled that "no gift from the life interest beneficiaries to the remainder beneficiary results from the creation of the trust, the assignment of the contract to purchase Property to the trust and the purchase by the trustee of Property with funds delivered in trust by Taxpayers and son after the assignment has taken place." The ruling continues to hold that the residence is not includible in the grantors' estates under § § 2033 or 2039. Unfortunately, the IRS declined to rule on the possibility of inclusion under § 2036. *See* § 9.42.

Reformation. Regulation § 25.2702-5(a)(2) provides that a trust that does not comply with its requirements will be treated as satisfying the requirements of a reformation action is commenced within 90 days after the due date for filing the gift tax return (including extensions) reporting the transfer of the residence. The new requirement was incorporated in the terms of a QPRT that was approved in LR 9639064.

Involuntary Conversion. Under the regulations, part or all of the proceeds of a sale, involuntary conversion or of the insurance proceeds resulting from damage or destruction of the residence may be used within two years of the sale, involuntary conversion, or damage or destruction of the residence, to acquire another residence for the term holder. Any excess cash must be distributed to the term holder or converted to a qualified annuity interest and held as a separate share of the trust. Reg. § 25.2702-5(c)(8). The requirements for a qualified annuity interest are set out in Reg. § 25.2702-5(c)(8)(C)(ii).

Grantor Trust. If the grantor is treated as owner of the trust for income tax purposes, the benefits of § § 121 and 1033 should be available if the residence is sold or involuntarily converted. *See* § 9.44.4. Until banned by an amendment to the regulations, the holding of Rev. Rul. 85-13, 1985-1 C.B. 184, would have allowed the tax free sale of the residence to the grantor—which could be particularly attractive toward the end of the term of the trust. As indicated above, a grantor who is treated as owner of the trust is also entitled to deductions for mortgage interest, taxes, and other expenses paid by the grantor that are appropriately chargeable to the term tenant under the principal and income law. § 163(h).

Consideration should be given to the benefits of having the trust continue as a grantor trust following the end of the grantor's reserved term. Doing so would, of course, allow the grantor to require the trustee to rent the residence to the grantor for a fair market rent. In addition, doing so may provide some important income tax benefits. *See* § § 10.4.1, 10.32-10.32.7.

Rental of Residence After End of Term. The IRS has consistently ruled that a QPRT may allow a grantor who survives the trust term to lease the residence at a fair market rental. LRs 9249014 (coop apartment); 9433016, 9626041; 9714025; 9735011, 9735012. The right of the grantor to lease the residence after the end of the term is recognized in the "Background" section of the Treasury Decision that adopts the final regulations on QPRTs. It notes that the rental of the property for its fair market value will not require the property to be included in the grantor's estate. It notes, however, that "if the residence is leased from a trust that is a grantor trust with respect to the grantor, the IRS under some circumstances may contend that the grantor has retained the economic benefit of the property."

Appurtenant Structures and Adjacent Land. Under Reg. § 25.2702-5(c)(2)(C)(ii), a QPRT may include "appurtenant structures used by the term holder for residential purposes and adjacent land not in excess of that which is reasonably appropriate for residential purposes (taking into account the residence's size and location)." This has allowed a QPRT to hold a large house and an adjacent guest house where the use of the guest house by family members and friends would be at the sufferance of the grantors. LR 9328040. In another case the IRS has allowed ten acres that are regarded as a single parcel for tax purposes to be treated as a single residence although they constituted three lots on a development plat. LR 9442019. *See also,* LR 9529035 (three parcels that are shown as one lot on the tax assessor's map allowed). Similarly, in LR 9503025 the IRS treated as a single residence a vacation home purchased in 1949 and two vacant lots across the street opposite the home. The lots had been used for various family activities, protected the view of the water from the home, and allowed the family aces to the water for boat launching. A residence, including outbuildings and surrounding land comparable to other properties in the locale, may be transferred to a QPRT. LR 200241039. The ruling involved land that was subject to a perpetual conservation easement.

A QPRT may include all of the property of a family's vacation complex, including main residence, separate guest facilities, caretaker's house, and appurtenant structures. LR 9718007. The occupancy of part of the premises by caretakers and temporary house guests is consistent with the requirements of a QPRT.

An historic manor house and adjacent property that the grantor uses as a vacation home qualify as a personal residence for purposes of §2702. LR 9533025. They qualify although they are subject to a pre-existing perpetual historic easement that requires the grantor and his successors to maintain the property in essentially its present condition to preserve its historic, aesthetic, and cultural character and appearance.

Sale of Residence and Conversion to Annuity. As mentioned above, the sale of a highly appreciated residence and the conversion of the proceeds into a qualified annuity interest might prevent the residence's appreciation in value from being included in the term holder's estate if he or she died during the balance of the term.

If the original residence appreciates in value and is sold, a portion of the proceeds may be invested in a replacement residence and the balance converted to an annuity. LR 200220014. The ruling concludes that a conversion made in accordance with the regulations does not result in an additional gift.

Once a QPRT has converted to a qualified annuity interest, the trustee may loan cash to the grantor or the grantor's spouse, although there may be income tax consequences with respect to interest payments made by the borrower if the trust no longer qualifies as a grantor trust. Although Reg. §25.2702-3(d)(6) prohibits the grantor from loaning money to a trust in connection with the payment of the annuity, there is no prohibition against loans from the trustee to the grantor or the grantor's spouse. To be cost effective, however, the borrower will need to pay interest at a rate at least equal to the appreciation in value of the trust's assets; otherwise, the loan transaction inhibits the amount of wealth that can pass tax-free to the beneficiaries if the grantor survives the trust term.

Grantor as Trustee. The regulations do not prohibit the grantor from serving as trustee. Nonetheless, an independent trustee, who may be given broader discretion, is preferable. Put simply, if an independent party serves as trustee the trust is less likely to arouse suspicion by the IRS, and more likely to accomplish its purposes unchallenged.

Continuation of Trust After Term Ends. Following the death of the term holder a QPRT may be drawn to continue as a trust for the benefit of the remainder beneficiaries. As noted above, after the end of the term the trustee may lease the residence to the grantor for fair market value. In most cases the owner of a residence should not enter into a QPRT if it is critical that he or she have the use of the residence following the expiration of the term.

If the trust will continue after the end of the term, consideration should be given to assuring that the trust will continue to be effective for income tax purposes. Doing so will avoid the imposition of any income tax on rental payment made by the grantor to the trustee and will preserve for the grantor the benefit of deductions associated with the property. In addition, it will preserve the potential benefits of §§121 and 1033.

Retained Reversionary Interest. Several considerations may persuade a grantor to retain a partial or total reversionary interest in a personal residence trust, to take effect if he or she dies prior to the expiration of his or her term interest. First, the retention of such an interest will increase the value of the interests he or she retains in the trust and, correlatively, diminish the amount of the gift to the remainder beneficiaries. Second, in most cases it will also assure that the benefits of §§ 121 and 1033 will be available (*i.e.,* the grantor will be treated as owner of the trust income and principal under § 673). Third, the retention of a reversionary interest may enable the grantor better to address the estate tax problems that will arise if he or she dies during the term of the trust. In particular, if the grantor dies during the term without having retained a reversionary interest, the trust will be included in the grantor's estate, but he or she will have no power of disposition over the property. Thus, the trust might create a substantial estate tax liability without providing the grantor's estate with any resources with which to pay the tax. On the other hand, if the grantor retains a reversionary interest he or she would have the power to dispose of the property of the trust in a way that qualifies for the marital or charitable deduction. Alternatively, the grantor might choose to use the assets received as a result of the reversion to pay the expenses of his or her estate, including any estate tax liability that might arise on account of the personal residence trust.

Some clients prefer to take a different approach to making gifts of interests in vacation homes or other residences. For example, some prefer to give fractional interests to donees over a period of years. The fractional interest given away and the one retained are both valued at a discount. *See* § 2.43.1. Others prefer to transfer the residence to a family limited partnership after which the limited partnership interests are transferred at heavily discounted values to children or other donees. *See* § 11.34.

Using Two QPRTs to Reduce the Value of the Gift. Where the grantor holds an absolute interest in only one residence, a common technique is for the grantor to create two QPRTs, each to hold a one-half interest in the residence. By transferring a one-half interest to each trust, the gifts quality for a valuation discount applicable to fractional interests. Some practitioners go so far as to have the two trusts, now co-tenants in the residence, waive their rights to partition the property, which presumably would reduce further the value of the gift to the trust.

Reverse QPRTs. In a series of private rulings, the IRS has approved a technique whereby, following the termination of a QPRT established by a grantor, the remainder beneficiaries transfer the residence to a new QPRT of their own, this one giving the original grantor another occupancy right for a term of years. Following the term of years, the second QPRT terminates and the house is distributed back to the remainder beneficiaries in equal shares as tenants in common. In the rulings, the IRS concluded that these "reverse" QPRTs qualify for the exception to the zero-value in § 2702(a) assuming the trusts comply with all of the statutory and regulatory requirements for a traditional QPRT. LRs 200848003, 200848007, 200848008, 200901019, 200935004, 201006012, 201014044, 201019006, 201019007, 201019012, 201024012.. The IRS expressly refused to opine as to whether the residence would be included in the original grantor's gross estate under § 2036 if the original grantor dies during the term of the reverse QPRT. To the extent the transfer to the reverse QPRT is a gift from the remainder beneficiaries to the original grantor, it would seem that the residence should not be included in the original grantor's gross estate, for the original grantor's retained interest in the original gift transfer has already expired.

§9.44.3. Estate Tax Consequences

If the grantor dies during the term of a trust in which the grantor has retained the benefit of the property, the trust is fully includible in the grantor's estate under §2036(a). *See* Reg. §20.2036-1(c)(2)(iii), Example 5. Accordingly, if the grantor dies during the term of a QPRT, the grantor's estate must include the portion of the trust attributable to his or her contributions. However, in the case of a GRAT (or a QPRT that has converted to an annuity) the grantor's estate only includes so much of the trust property as is required to generate the specified annuity amount, using the appropriate assumed interest rate under §7520. *Marvin L. Pardee*, 49 T.C. 140 (1967), *acq.*, 1973-2 C.B. 3; Rev. Rul. 82-105, 1982-1 C.B. 133 (charitable remainder annuity trust); Reg. §§20.2036-1(c); 20.2039-1(e) (limiting inclusion of GRAT assets in grantor's gross estate to "that portion of the trust corpus necessary to yield the decedent's retained use or retained annuity, unitrust, or other income payment"). This possibility suggests that a QPRT should include an optional provision that allows it to convert to a qualified annuity trust if the personal residence is sold during the term. Such a sale and conversion could be very advantageous if the grantor were likely to die before the end of the term and the residence had appreciated greatly in value.

Under Rev. Rul. 82-105, 1982-1 C.B. 133, in the case of a lifetime annuity the amount includible in the grantor's estate is determined according to the following formula:

$$\frac{\text{Annuity Payable}}{\text{7520 Interest Rate}} = \text{Amount Includible}$$

This same formula is used by regulations effective July 11, 2008. Reg. §§20.2036-1(c); 20.2039-1(e).

Revenue Ruling 76-273, 1976-2 C.B. 268, adopts a similar approach in the case of charitable remainder unitrusts, which should also apply to GRUTs. First, the equivalent income interest rate is calculated by dividing the unitrust adjusted payout rate by 1 minus that rate. If the equivalent income interest rate is equal to, or greater than, the adjusted payout rate, the full amount of the trust is includible in the grantor's estate. If the adjusted income interest rate is less than the adjusted payout rate, "then a correspondingly reduced proportion of the trust assets would be includible in the gross estate under §2036(a)(1)." The includible portion would be determined by dividing the equivalent income interest rate by the §7520 rate. Of course, if the grantor dies during the term of a GRIT, GRAT, or GRUT, any unified credit claimed by the grantor when the trust was established will be restored. In addition, the grantor will be allowed a credit for any gift tax paid with respect to the transfer of property to the trust. On the other hand, if the grantor survives the term of the retained interest, none of the property of the trust is includible in his or her estate.

As described in §9.44.2, the grantor may choose to retain a reversionary interest that will take effect if he or she dies during the term of the trust. By doing so, the grantor may be able to ameliorate the tax effects of the trust being included in his or her estate. For example, the trust might provide that if the grantor were to die during the term the grantor's proportionate interest would pass to the grantor's surviving spouse, or in another way that would potentially qualify for the federal estate tax marital deduction. Inclusion of a reversion may also cause the grantor to be treated as the owner of the corpus, which can be beneficial for income tax purposes.

None of the value of a residence is includible in the grantor's estate under §§ 2033 or 2039 if the residence was acquired by a QPRT in a "split purchase" to which the grantor contributed the actuarially appropriate amount. LR 200112023. Unfortunately, the IRS declined to rule on the "applicability of section 2036 to the transaction."

§ 9.44.4. Income Tax Consequences

The transfer of property to a QPRT does not have any immediate income tax consequences. For income tax purposes the grantor will be treated as the owner of the income of a QPRT under § 677(a). The grantor will be treated as owner of the income and the corpus if the grantor retains a reversionary interest the value of which exceeds 5 percent of the value of the trust property. In such a case, the income and capital gains would be taxed to the grantor. LRs 9447036, 9402011. Being taxed on the capital gains is important in order to assure that the benefits of §§ 121 and 1033 will be available. LR 199912026. Also, during the term of the grantor's interest the trust may hold the stock of an S corporation. § 1361(c)(2)(A)(i).

§ 9.45. Conclusion

The adoption of § 2702 sharply reduced the potential tax benefits of the sales of remainder interests and joint purchases. However, the favorable outcomes of *Estate of D'Ambrosio v. Commissioner*, 101 F.3d 309 (3d Cir. 1996), *Wheeler v. United States*, 116 F.3d 749 (5th Cir. 1997), and *Estate of Magnin v. Commissioner*, 184 F.3d 1074 (9th Cir. 1999), support expanded opportunities for joint purchases and other mixed transactions. *See* § 9.26. While § 2702 also limits the tax benefits of some, but not all grantor retained interest trusts, valuable opportunities remain. In particular, benefits remain if either the holders of the term and remainder interests are not "family members," the retained interest is in the form of a qualified interest, or the only property involved is a residence used by the holder of the term interest. QPRTs offer particularly advantageous tax saving opportunities.

BIBLIOGRAPHY

ALI-ABA, Study Materials, Estate Planning under Chapter 14 and the Proposed Regulations (1991)

Adams & Herpe, The 1990 Tax Act: Reading Between the Lines, 130 Tr. & Est. 20 (1991)

Aucutt, Fourteen Tips and Traps in Dealing with Chapter 14, 20 Est. Plan. 259 (Sept./ Oct. 1993)

Blattmachr, Split Purchases and Other Ways to Live with Section 2702, U. Miami, 29th Est. Plan. Inst., Ch. 10 (1995)

Committee on Tax and Estate Planning, Report: Predeath Estate Planning Through Family Bargaining, 8 Real Prop., Prob. & Tr. J. 223 (1973)

Emory & Hjorth, An Analysis of the Changes Made by the Installment Sales Revision Act of 1980, 54 J. Tax. 66, 130 (1981)

Freeland, Lind & Stephens, What Are the Income Tax Consequences of an Estate's Sale of a Life Interest?, 34 J. Tax. 376 (1971)

Goldsbury, If *Walton* is Correct, Every GRAT Should be Zeroed-Out, 29 Est. Plan. 174 (April 2002)

Handler & Oshins, The GRAT Remainder Sale, 141 Tr. & Est. 33 (Dec. 2002)

Harris, GRITs, GRATs & Grantor Trusts: Be Graciously Greedy While the Grass is Green, Before It Gradually Grows Grisly & Grim, U. Miami, 29th Inst. Est. Plan., Ch. 9 (1995)

Hesch & Manning, Beyond the Basic Freeze: Further Uses of Deferred Payment Sales, U. Miami, 34th Inst. Est. Plan., Ch. 16 (2000)

Hesch & Manning, Family Deferred Payment Sales: Installment Sales, SCINs, Private Annuity Sales, OID and Other Enigmas, U. Miami, 26th Inst. Est. Plan., Ch. 3 (1992)

Howard, The Benefits of Installment Sales Involving Nongrantor Trusts, 35 Est. Plan. 24 (Mar. 2005)

Johanson, Revocable Trusts, Widow's Election Wills and Community Property: The Tax Problem, 47 Tex. L. Rev. 1247 (1969)

Katzenstein, Running the Numbers—An Economic Analysis of GRATs and QPRTs, U. Miami, 32d Inst. Est. Plan., Ch. 14 (1998)

Kess, Westlin & Whitman, Model Qualified Personal Residence Trust, vol. 2, Financial and Estate Planning (CCH) ¶ 5895

Lane, Widow's Election as a Private Annuity: Boon or Bane for Estate Planners, 44 S. Cal. L. Rev. 74 (1971)

Malloy & Bufkin, Critical Tax and Financial Factors that Must Be Considered When Planning a Private Annuity, 3 Est. Plan. 2 (1975)

McCaffrey, Asset Freezes—New Rules, U. Miami, 25th Inst. Est. Plan., Ch. 8 (1991)

McCaffrey & Schneider, Planning for GRATs and QPRTs, U.S.C. § 47th Tax Inst., Ch. 27 (1995)

Melcher & Graziano, Getting a Grip on GRITs, 72 Taxes 235 (1994)

Moore, Grantor Retained Income Trusts—Fish or Fowl? 130 Tr. & Est. 18 (1991)

Mulligan, New Tax Law Restricts GRITs and Related Planning Tools But Opportunities Remain, 18 Est. Plan. 66 (1991)

Neumann, Estate Freeze Techniques Outside of Chapter 14, N.Y.U., 53rd Inst. Fed. Tax., Ch. 21 (1995)

O'Sullivan, The Private Annuity: A New Look at an Old Estate Planning Tool, 17 Washburn L.J. 466 (1978)

Painter, Chapter 14 Split Interests: Splits and Splats, N.Y.U., 53rd Inst. Fed. Tax., Ch. 19 (1995)

Price, Estate Planning With GRATs and Near GRATs—Opportunities, Pitfalls and a Promising Alternative, U. Miami, 38th Inst. Est. Plan., Ch. 11 (2003)

Rivlin, Section 2702 of the Internal Revenue Code: Overview and Planning, N.Y.U. 50th Inst. Fed. Tax., Ch. 18 (1992)

Scanlan, GRITs, GRATs & GRUTs: A Phoenix Rises from the Ashes of Section 2036(c), U. Miami, 27th Inst. Est. Plan., Ch. 14 (1993)

Teitell, Charitable Contribution Tax Strategies: Avoiding Near-Death Tax Experiences and Bad Heir Days, U. Miami, 42nd Inst. Est. Plan. Ch. 18 (2008)

Tiesi, Qualified Personal Residence Trusts—Give Your Home Away and Live in It Too, 72 Taxes 82 (1994)

10

Trusts

The purposes for which we can create trusts are as unlimited as our imagination. There are no technical rules restricting their creation. The trust can be and has been used to accomplish many different purposes. One of the most important is and has always been to provide for the creator's family, over time. Through the trust it is possible to separate the benefits of ownership from the burdens of ownership. The responsibility for managing the property is exclusively that of the trustee. Trusts enable us to create successive interests that would be difficult, if not impossible, to create with successive legal interests. It is possible to make the extent of beneficiaries' interests dependent upon the trustee's discretion. It is possible as well, at least to a certain extent, to protect the beneficiaries' enjoyment of their interests by making them inalienable and putting them beyond the reach of creditors. Scott, Fratcher & Ascher, 1 Scott and Ascher on Trusts § 1.1 at 4 (5th ed. 2006).

A. INTRODUCTION

§ 10.1. SCOPE

This chapter surveys the most important and most common types of trusts, including the revocable trust, § 10.7-10.17; the beneficiary's interests in irrevocable trusts, § 10.18-10.29; and, the grantor's interests in irrevocable trusts, § 10.30-10.41.

The opening sections of this chapter, § 10.4 – 10.6, summarize the basic income, gift, and estate tax consequences of establishing trusts. Some consideration is also given to GSTT planning, although it is considered primarily in Chapter 2, § 2.24-2.42, and in connection with other topics, such as *Crummey* powers of withdrawal, § 7.38, and life insurance trusts, § 6.24. This part also includes a review of the basic income tax rules applicable to trusts. Because the trust is widely used as a probate avoidance device, some comparisons are drawn between the tax treatment given trusts on the one hand and estates on the other. Some of the same tax points recur at later places in the chapter, particularly in the review of the grantor trust rules in § 10.32-10.32.8.

Part B takes a long look at the revocable trust, which is probably the most common form of trust. It includes a review of some of the substantive law regarding the use of the trust, a discussion of its advantages and disadvantages, and a summary of the principal tax consequences applicable to the revocable trust.

Planning the powers and interests of a beneficiary in an irrevocable trust is the subject of Part C, which extends from a consideration of the use of multiple trusts through the nature and transferability of the beneficiary's interest, to the conferral of powers of appointment and the appointment of the beneficiary as fiduciary. Part D is a companion piece that is concerned with planning the grantor's interests in an irrevocable trust. Those parts also include a consideration of the grantor trust rules, § 671-677. These rules define the circumstances under which the grantor will be treated as the owner of the trust (and, consequently, of the trust's income) for income tax purposes.

Part E, briefly discusses the choice of trustee and the selection of property to transfer to the trustee. Although this book does not give detailed attention to trust administration (itself a substantial and complicated subject), Part E does discuss two matters about which additional directions should often be given: the investment of trust funds and the allocation of receipts and disbursements between income and principal. A planner must be concerned about a host of other matters regarding administration of the trust, of which these two serve as good illustrations. The part concludes with a discussion of the Rule Against Perpetuities and the use of perpetuities savings clauses.

Finally, Part F considers several of the specialized types of trusts often employed by planners. While many of these trusts are discussed more thoroughly in other chapters, Part F also considers trusts formed for creditor protection purposes, trusts for the care of pets, and foreign trusts.

§ 10.2. ENCOURAGE FLEXIBILITY

A carefully planned and drafted trust is a valuable estate planning tool. Particular care is required in the case of an irrevocable trust because the permanency of the arrangement may seriously limit its ability to meet the beneficiaries' long-term needs. In general, the planner is challenged to make a trust sufficiently flexible without giving up any of the potential tax savings or falling into any of the potential tax traps. The dual objectives of flexibility and tax savings can be attained if the client is willing to have any discretionary powers over distributions exercised by an independent trustee (or by a "special trustee"). Such discretionary powers are "tax-sensitive" and cannot be safely retained by the grantor or given to a beneficiary. In general, only nondiscretionary powers can safely be retained by the grantor or held by a beneficiary. However, beneficiaries can generally be given special powers of appointment over the trust property without adverse tax effects. The ultimate balance between flexibility and tax savings should be struck by the client after receiving an adequate explanation from the planner. A client should not be permitted to create a trust unless he or she understands its terms and effect. Above all, a client must understand the extent to which a trust is irrevocable.

§10.3.   Avoid Sham Trusts and Trusts With no Economic Substance

The planner and client should be wary of tax-saving trust plans that lack economic reality or substance; the tax savings are often illusory. For example, no interest deduction is available to the grantor for interest paid to the trustee in a transaction involving a circular flow of funds that appears designed only to generate a tax deduction for the grantor. Rev. Rul. 86-106, 1986-2 C.B. 28 (when parent-grantor transferred $50,000 to trustee of trust for children with oral agreement that trustee would subsequently loan the same amount to grantor, no interest deduction allowed for annual payment of $7,500 to trust); *Guaranty Trust Co. v. Commissioner*, 98 F.2d 62 (2d Cir. 1938); Rev. Rul. 87-69, 1987-2 C.B. 46 (gift to child, no trust involved); LR 8709001. Evading gift taxes through the transfer of assets to intermediaries who retransfer the donative property to relatives of the donors (*i.e.*, sham gifts) may also attract fraud penalties. *Heyen v. United States*, 945 F.2d 359 (10th Cir. 1991). *See* § 2.5.

In the 1970s and 1980s many gullible taxpayers, often medical professionals and others with large personal service incomes, bought expensive trust packages that were intended to insulate their income from taxation. Often those trust schemes did not work. Instead, the taxpayers were denied any deduction under § 212 for the cost of the trust package, Rev. Rul. 79-324, 1979-2 C.B. 119, taxed on the income of the trust, and held liable for a percent penalty for "negligence or intentional disregard of rules and regulations." *E.g., Richard L. Wesenberg*, 69 T.C. 1005 (1978) (physician); *Louis Markosian*, 73 T.C. 1235 (1980) (dentist). In *Estate of Floyd G. Paxton*, 86 T.C. 785 (1986), the Tax Court recounted the income tax treatment of "so-called family trusts" and held that the assets of such trusts were includible in the grantor's gross estate:

> In such cases, the trusts have been denied income tax effect on the grounds that the trusts were shams, *Holman v. United States*, 728 F.2d 462, 465 (10th Cir. 1984); *cf. Zmuda v. Commissioner*, 731 F.2d 1417, 1421 (9th Cir. 1984), *aff'g* 79 T.C. 714 (1982); were grantor trusts under secs. 671 to 677, *Vnuk v. Commissioner*, 621 F.2d 1318, 1321 (8th Cir. 1980), *aff'g* a Memorandum Opinion of this Court; or involved assignments of income, *Vnuk v. Commissioner*, 621 F.2d at 1320; *Hanson v. Commissioner*, 696 F.2d 1232, 1234 (9th Cir. 1983). In *United States v. Buttorff*, 761 F.2d 1056 (5th Cir. 1985), a promoter was enjoined from selling pure equity or family trust packages. The PFO trust involved in the instant case was held to be a grantor trust under secs. 676 and 677 in *Paxton v. Commissioner*, 520 F.2d 923 (9th Cir. 1975), *aff'g* 57 T.C. 627 (1972). *Paxton*, 86 T.C. at 801, n. 7.

Trusts of the type involved in the *Wesenberg* and *Markosian* cases have been marketed under a variety of names. The arrangements typically call for the taxpayer to transfer all of his or her property and future services to a trust in which the taxpayer retains substantial interests and over which the taxpayer and other nonadverse parties hold significant controls. By some miraculous alchemy the income received by the trust is supposed to escape taxation. Quite to the contrary, because of the taxpayer's retained interests and controls, the income of the trust is taxed to the grantor under § 671-677. Rev. Rul. 75-257, 1975-2 C.B. 251. *See also Paul G. Dubois*, 51 T.C.M. 895 (1986). For the same reason, the transfer of property to the trust is not a completed gift, Rev. Rul. 75-260, 1975-2 C.B. 376, and the property transferred to the trust is fully includible in the transferor's estate. *Estate of Floyd G. Paxton, supra*; Rev.

Rul. 75-259, 1975-2 C.B. 361. Evading gift taxes through the transfer of assets to intermediaries who retransfer the donative property to relatives of the donors (*i.e.,* sham gifts) may also attract fraud penalties. *Heyen v. United States,* 945 F.2d 359 (10th Cir. 1991). *See* § 2.5.

Another expensive but ineffective package involves the transfer of property to a "foreign tax haven double trust." Rev. Rul. 80-74, 1980-1 C.B. 137. The promoter of the "double trust" involved in Rev. Rul. 80-74 represented that the trust would radically reduce or eliminate the taxpayer's income tax liability, avoid probate, eliminate estate and gift tax liabilities, and avoid state and local taxes. The plan involves the creation of a trust in a foreign country by an agent of the promoter, to which the taxpayer transfers income-producing property. The income of the trust is distributed to a second foreign trust that, in turn, makes distributions to the taxpayer and his or her family as directed by the taxpayer as trustee. Not surprisingly, Rev. Rul. 80-74 concluded that the creation of the trusts is a sham that will not be recognized for tax purposes. Instead, all of the income will be taxed to the grantor, who is not entitled to a deduction under § 212 for the expenses incurred in connection with the establishment of the "double trust." *See, e.g., George V. Zmuda,* 79 T.C. 714 (1982), *aff'd,* 731 F.2d 1417 (9th Cir. 1984); *Professional Services,* 79 T.C. 888 (1982).

In Notice 97-24, 1997-1 C.B. 409, the IRS alerted "taxpayers about certain trust arrangements that purport to reduce or eliminate federal taxes in ways that are not permitted by federal tax law." (The Notice refers to such arrangements as "abusive trust arrangements.") The Notice described five examples of abusive trust arrangements (The Business Trust; The Equipment or Service Trust; The Family Residence Trust; The Charitable Trust; and The Final Trust). The Notice mentioned that the IRS has undertaken a national coordinated enforcement initiative to deal with abusive trust schemes and notes that participants in such schemes may be subject to civil and criminal penalties. The Notice received extensive coverage in academic journals and treatises, but to date it appears the IRS has not engaged in a full-scale assault against abusive trust arrangements.

Courts have not been as reticent as the IRS. In *Homer L. Richardson,* T.C. Memo. 2006-69, Judge Wherry summarized the approach used by the Tax Court:

> In ascertaining whether a trust has no economic substance apart from tax considerations, the Court has identified four pertinent factors: (1) Whether the taxpayer's relationship, as grantor, to the property ostensibly transferred to the trust differed materially before and after the trust's formation; (2) whether the trust had a bona fide independent trustee; (3) whether an economic interest in the trust passed to other beneficiaries; and (4) whether the taxpayer felt bound by any restrictions imposed by the trust itself or the law of trusts. *Markosian v. Commissioner,* 73 T.C. 1235, 1243-1244 (1980); *Gouveia v. Commissioner,* T.C. Memo. 2004-256; *Norton v. Commissioner,* T.C. Memo. 2002-137; *Castro v. Commissioner,* T.C. Memo. 2001-115; *Muhich v. Commissioner,* T.C. Memo. 1999-192 (addressing the Heritage/Aegis multitrust system), *aff'd,* 238 F.3d 860 (7th Cir. 2001); *Buckmaster v. Commissioner,* T.C. Memo. 1997-236; *Hanson v. Commissioner,* T.C. Memo. 1981-675, *aff'd,* 696 F.2d 1232 (9th Cir. 1983).

Applying these factors, Judge Wherry disregarded the trusts at issue in the *Richardson* case. As a result, the income reported by the trusts was taxable to the grantors.

§10.4. INCOME TAX SUMMARY

For federal income tax purposes, a trust other than one that is treated as owned by its grantor under §§671-677 or by a non-grantor under §678 is generally recognized as a separate taxable entity. Perhaps most important, a trust acts as a conduit with respect to amounts that are distributed to beneficiaries during the taxable year. In particular, a trust is allowed to deduct, and the beneficiaries are required to report, amounts that were properly distributed, or were required to be distributed, to beneficiaries. Otherwise, trusts are generally subject to the same basic tax rules that apply to individuals. Thus, a trust reports the same items of income and is usually entitled to the same types of deductions and credits as individuals.

However, the 2 percent floor on the deductibility of miscellaneous itemized deductions does not apply to "the deductions for costs which are paid or incurred in connection with the administration of the estate or trust and which would not have been incurred if the property were not held in such trust or estate." §67(e)(1). *See* §10.4.7. A complex trust is also allowed a deduction for amounts of gross income paid to a charity. §642(c)(1). In addition, estates and trusts created prior to October 9, 1969 are allowed deductions for amounts permanently set aside for charitable purposes. §642(c)(2). Charitable deductions are allowed under §642(c) only for amounts that are paid pursuant to the terms of the governing instrument. Thus, no deduction is allowed for unauthorized distributions made to a charity in excess of the specified amount of a charitable lead annuity. *Rebecca K. Crown Income Charitable Fund,* 98 T.C. 327 (1992), *aff'd,* 8 F.3d 571 (7th Cir. 1993).

The optimum income tax results may be attained if a trustee is given discretion to sprinkle income among a class of beneficiaries, or accumulate it for later distribution. *See* §10.20.2. Flexibility is increased if the trustee is also given authority to distribute trust principal to the beneficiaries. However, such powers should not be held by the grantor or a potential distributee because of the adverse income, gift, and estate tax consequences. An adroit sprinkling of income among beneficiaries may help reduce the overall income tax cost of trust distributions.

The relatively compressed income tax rate structure limits the tax savings that can be achieved by splitting income among multiple taxpayers. However, it is possible, and may be profitable, to split income between one or two discretionary trusts and a beneficiary. In such a case the trustees can optimize the allocation of income among the taxpayers by accumulating or distributing the income of the trusts. The trusts could, for example, authorize the trustees to make income distributions to a minor beneficiary or to a custodian for the minor under the Uniform Transfers to Minors Act or the Uniform Gifts to Minors Act. Such a distribution would enable an adult to retain control over the funds although they are treated as having been distributed to the minor. In any event, the income accumulated during the beneficiary's minority will be taxed to the trust. It will often be desirable to make distributions to beneficiaries and to take other steps in order to reduce the taxable income of trusts and estates. Of course, the planner and the trustees must take into account the effect of the Kiddie Tax on distributions. Under § 1(g), unearned income of a child under 19 (or a full-time student under 24) in excess of $1,900 (the amount for 2011) is taxed at the marginal rate applicable to the child's parent. Specifically, the first $950 of such unearned income is not taxed at all, while the next $950 of unearned income is taxed at the normal tax rate applicable to the child. Unearned income in excess of $1,900 is taxed at the parent's marginal tax rate, which could be as high as 35 percent.

Where the grantor or another person is treated as the owner of the entire trust under § 671-678, a fiduciary income tax return (Form 1041) should not be filed for the trust. "Instead, all items of income, deductions, and credit from the trust should be reported on the individual's Form 1040 in accordance with its instructions." Reg. § 1.671-4(b). In other cases, the income, deductions, and credits attributable to the part of a trust of which the grantor or another person is treated as the owner are not reported by the trust on its Form 1041, but should be shown on a separate statement attached to that form. Reg. § 1.671-4(a).

State Income Tax Issues. Planners should be sensitive to the impact of state income taxes on trusts. Some states claim jurisdiction to tax the income from any trust governed by their laws, even if none of the trustees or the beneficiaries is a resident of that state and even if none of the assets are situated within that state. For some states, it is sufficient that the grantor was a resident of the state either at the time of formation (in the case of an inter vivos trust) or at death (in the case of a testamentary trust). For a helpful discussion of state income tax issues, see Richard W. Nenno, Planning to Minimize or Avoid State Income Tax on Trusts, 34 ACTEC J. 131 (2008).

Under Reg. § 1.671-4(b), if the same individual is both grantor and trustee (or cotrustee) and that individual is treated as owner of the trust under § 676 (a revocable trust), a Form 1041 should not be filed. "Instead, all items of income, deduction, and credit from the trust should be reported on the individual's Form 1040 in accordance with its instructions." Essentially the same rule applies where a husband and wife are the sole grantors, one or both of them are trustees or cotrustees, and they are treated as the owners by reason of § 676. Reg. § 1.671-4.

§ 10.4.1. Grantor Trust Rules, § § 671-678

The separate existence of a trust is largely disregarded to the extent the grantor or any other person is treated as owner of the trust under § 671-678. The rules of those sections establish the exclusive means by which the income of a trust is includible in the income of a grantor or other person solely by reason of his or her dominion and control over the trust. Reg. § 1.671-1(c). However, the rules do not govern the outcome of cases involving the assignment of income, whether or not the assignment is to a trust: "[F]or example, a person who assigns his right to future income under an employment contract may be taxed on that income even though the assignment is to a trust over which the assignor has retained none of the controls specified in sections 671 through 677." Id. Under § § 671-677, the grantor is treated as the owner of a trust to the extent he or she retains any of the interests or controls proscribed by § § 673-677, (e.g., has a reversionary interest in a portion of a trust that is worth more than 5 percent of that portion, § 673; holds controls over the beneficial enjoyment of the trust, § 674; possesses extensive administrative controls, § 675; or, holds a power to revoke the trust, § 676). See § § 10.30-10.41. So long as the grantor (or, in some cases, a third party) holds the power, the grantor is taxed on the trust's income. If the grantor (or third party) relinquishes the power, grantor trust status may terminate. In this way, grantors may have some ability to "toggle" the trust's status between being a separate taxable entity and being a grantor trust.

The Tax Management Portfolio on grantor trusts by Howard Zaritsky, 858-2d Grantor Trusts: Section 671-679 (2001), is a valuable guide to tax issues relating to §§ 671-679. *See also* Donaldson, Understanding Grantor Trusts, U. Miami, 40th Inst. Est. Plan., Ch. 2 (2006). The income tax reporting requirements that apply to grantor trusts are summarized in Blattmachr & Crawford, Grantor Trusts and Income Tax Reporting Requirements: A Primer, 16 Prob. & Prop. 18 (Mar./Apr. 2002).

§ 10.4.2. Non-Grantor Treated as Owner, § 678

A person other than the grantor of a trust is treated as its owner to the extent he or she has the power, acting alone, to vest the corpus or income of the trust in himself or herself. § 678(a). *See* § 10.20.6. However, with respect to a beneficiary's power to vest income in himself or herself, the beneficiary is not treated as the owner of any part of the trust of which the grantor is treated as the owner under §§ 671-677 (*i.e.,* these provisions prevail over those of § 678). § 678(b). Thus, if the grantor of a *Crummey* trust is treated as owner of the trust under §§ 673-677, the grantor and not the power-holder will be taxed on the trust's income provided the *Crummey* power is exercisable against trust income. § 7.38.1; I.R. 200732010. If the grantor is not treated as the owner, the holder of the power of withdrawal is treated as owner over the portion of the trust with respect to which the power has lapsed. *See* Price, *Crummey v. Commissioner* (1968) Revisited; Opportunities and Pitfalls of Trust Withdrawal Powers, U. Miami, 34th Inst. Est. Plan., ¶ 803 (1999).

§ 10.4.3. Definition of "Income," § 643(b)

For purposes of subchapter J (the federal income taxation of trusts and estates), "income" means fiduciary accounting income as determined under the terms of the trust instrument and applicable state law. Accordingly, one must refer to both the trust instrument and to the applicable state's principal and income act to arrive at fiduciary accounting income. Late in 2003, Treasury finalized regulations that modify the definition of income under § 643(b) to give effect to "changes in the definition of trust accounting income under state laws," T.D. 9102, namely allowing trustees to pursue a total return investment strategy and to facilitate the creation of unitrusts. *See* § 10.46.5.

The regulations disregard the effect of "provisions that depart fundamentally from traditional concepts of income and principal . . .. For example, if a trust instrument directs that all the trust income shall be paid to the income beneficiary but defines ordinary dividends and interest as principal," the trust's attempted allocation of such items to principal will be ignored. Reg. § 1.643(b)-1. However, state laws that permit trustees reasonably to apportion the total return of a trust between the income and principal beneficiaries will be recognized. For this purpose, the regulations provide that an allocation to income of between 3 and 5 percent of the annual fair market value of the assets is reasonable. *Id.* The allocation of capital gains to income will be respected if the allocation is pursuant to either: (1) the terms of the trust instrument and applicable state law; or (2) the trustee's reasonable and impartial exercise of discretion pursuant to either the trust instrument or applicable state law. Reg. § 1.643(a)-3(b). Such allocations will be recognized for marital deduction purposes. Reg. § § 20.2056(b)-5(f)(1), 20.2056(b)-(7)(d)(1), 20.2056A-5(c)(2), 25.2523(e)-1(f)(1).

In addition, for GSTT purposes the administration of a trust in accordance with a state law that defines income as a unitrust amount or permits the trustee to adjust between income and principal in an impartial manner will not be considered to shift the beneficial interests in a trust. Reg. § 26.2601-1(b)(4)(i)(D)(2). Accordingly, such allocations will not affect the grandfathered status of such a trust. These regulations are generally effective with respect to taxable years that begin on or after January 2, 2004.

§ 10.4.4. Distributable Net Income, § 643(a)

The term "distributable net income" (DNI) is significant only in connection with the income taxation of estates and trusts and their beneficiaries. DNI is a concept that limits the deductions allowable to estates and trusts for amounts paid, credited, or required to be distributed to beneficiaries. It is also used to determine how much of an amount paid, credited, or required to be distributed to a beneficiary is includible in the beneficiary's gross income. Finally, it is also used to determine the character of distributions to the beneficiaries. DNI, for any taxable year means the taxable income of the estate or trust as modified by § 643(a)(1) – (7).

The taxable income of the trust, therefore, is the starting point from which DNI is computed. No deductions are taken into account for the distributions to beneficiaries or for the personal exemption otherwise allowable under § 642(b). § 643(a)(1), (2). Capital gains are excluded unless they are, (1) allocated to income, or (2) paid, credited, or required to be distributed to a beneficiary during the taxable year. However, capital gains are taken into account to the extent a charitable deduction under § 642(c) was allowed with respect to the gains. § 643(a)(3); Reg. § 1.643(a)-3(a)(3). An exercise of discretion by a trustee, allocating capital gains to income and distributing them to the beneficiaries, will be recognized for income tax purposes. *See, e.g.,* LR 8728001. Losses from the sale or exchange of capital assets are excluded from DNI except to the extent they enter into the determination of any capital gains that are paid, credited, or required to be distributed to any beneficiary during the year. The treatment of capital gains and losses accords with normal trust accounting rules under which they do not enter into the determination of net income. Because of the compressed income tax rates the overall tax burden may be lessened if capital gains are distributed—at least in part. Gains and losses are taken into account in computing the DNI of a trust in some circumstances, such as the year in which the trust terminates or makes partial distributions. *See* Reg. § 1.643(a)-3(d), Examples 4, 5.

Under § 643(a)(4), extraordinary dividends and taxable stock dividends received by a simple trust are excluded to the extent the trustee in good faith allocates them to corpus and does not pay or credit them to any beneficiary. Conversely, extraordinary dividends and stock dividends are included in computing DNI in the case of a complex trust, or where the dividends are not allocated to corpus for trust accounting purposes. Here again, the distinction parallels normal trust accounting rules.

The amount of tax-exempt interest received by the trust is included in computing DNI, reduced by the expenses attributable to it that are not deductible by reason of §265 (which bars the deduction of expenses under §212 to the extent they are incurred in connection with the production of tax-exempt income). §643(a)(5). The amount included in DNI is also reduced by a portion of the tax-exempt interest that is deductible under §642(c). §643(a), flush. The latter reduction is required because the full amount of the charitable deduction is allowed under §642(c). The computation of DNI under §643 is illustrated by the following example from Reg. §1.643(d)-2(a):

> Under the terms of the trust instrument, the income of a trust is required to be currently distributed to W during her life. Capital gains are allocable to corpus and all expenses are charged against corpus. During the taxable year the trust has the following items of income and expenses:
>
> | | |
> |---|---:|
> | Dividends from domestic corporations | $30,000 |
> | Extraordinary dividends allocated to corpus by the trustee in good faith | 20,000 |
> | Taxable interest | 10,000 |
> | Tax-exempt interest | 10,000 |
> | Long-term capital gains | 10,000 |
> | Trustee's commissions and miscellaneous expenses allocable to corpus | 5,000 |
>
> (2) The "income" of the trust determined under §643(b) which is currently distributable to W is $50,000, consisting of dividends of $30,000, taxable interest of $10,000 and tax-exempt interest of $10,000. The trustee's commissions and miscellaneous expenses allocable to tax-exempt interest amount to $1,000 (10,000/50,000 × $5,000).
>
> (3) The "distributable net income" determined under section 643(a) amounts to $45,000 computed as follows:
>
> | | | |
> |---|---:|---:|
> | Dividends from domestic corporations | | $30,000 |
> | Taxable interest | $10,000 | |
> | Nontaxable interest | $10,000 | |
> | Less: Expenses allocable thereto | 1,000 | 9,000 |
> | Total | | $49,000 |
> | Less: Expenses ($5,000 less $1,000 allocable to tax-exempt interest) | | 4,000 |
> | Distributable net income | | $45,000 |
>
> In determining the distributable net income of $45,000, the taxable income of the trust is computed with the following modifications: No deductions are allowed for distributions to W and for personal exemption of the trust (section 643(a)(1) and (2)); capital gains allocable to corpus are excluded . . . (section 643(a)(3)); the extraordinary dividends allocated to corpus by the trustee in good faith are excluded (section 643(a)(4)); and the tax-exempt interest (as adjusted for expenses) and the dividend exclusion . . . are included (section 643(a)(5) and (7)) . . . .

§10.4.5. Income Tax Consequences of Distributions, §§651, 652, 661-663

Trusts and estates are allowed deductions, not subject to the 2 percent floor, for amounts paid, credited, or required to be distributed to beneficiaries during the year. §§651(a), 661(a). In order to be "properly . . . credited" to a beneficiary for purposes of §661, the income must be allocated to the beneficiary beyond recall. *Commissioner v. Stearns*, 65 F.2d 371 (2d Cir.), *cert. denied*, 290 U.S. 670 (1933). A mere allocation to the beneficiary of the income on the books of the accountant, or the fiduciary, is not sufficient. *Estate of Keith W. Johnson*, 88 T.C. 225, *aff'd*, 838 F.2d 1202 (2d Cir. 1987). The deduction for distributions is limited, however, to the DNI of the trust. As explained above, DNI is the taxable income of the trust adjusted as provided in §643(a). The beneficiaries who receive distributions from a trust are required to report in their returns an amount equal to the total distribution deduction claimed by the trust. §652(a), 662(a). However, tracking the provisions of §102, a trust is not allowed to deduct, and the beneficiaries are not required to report, a distribution made in satisfaction of a specific gift of money or other property that is payable all at once or in not more than three installments. §663(a). Not surprisingly, no distribution deduction is allowed to a noncharitable trust for the cost of providing care to specific animals. Rev. Rul. 76-486, 1976-2 C.B. 192. Also for purposes of the GSTT the interests of animals are also disregarded—a dog is not a person. LR 9036043.

Reflecting the conduit principle, a distribution has the same character in the hands of a beneficiary as it had in the hands of the trustee. §652(b), 662(b). Specifically, a distribution is considered to consist of the same proportion of each class of items entering into the computation of the trust's DNI as the total of each class bears to the total DNI of the trust, unless the trust instrument or local law specifically allocates different classes of income to different beneficiaries. Trusts generally do not attempt to allocate specific classes of income to particular beneficiaries. However, some trusts do, particularly where there is a wide disparity in the income tax rates applicable to the beneficiaries or where there is a charitable beneficiary. Examples of provisions the IRS will recognize as specific allocations of income to different beneficiaries are set forth in Reg. §1.652(b)-2(b). The general allocation principles are described in Reg. §1.652(b)-1, 1.662(b)-1, 1.662(b)-2.

The separate share rule of §663 applies to distributions made by trusts and estates. *See* §10.4.9.

§10.4.6. No Standard Deduction; Personal Exemptions

A trust is not entitled to a standard deduction and is not subject to the tax on self-employment income. §63(c)(6). Limited personal exemptions are allowed to trusts: a trust that must distribute all of its income currently, has no charitable beneficiaries, and makes no distributions of principal during the year (a "simple" trust) is entitled to a $300 exemption; all other trusts ("complex" trusts) are entitled to $100 exemptions. §642(b). Estates are generally subject to the rules applicable to complex trusts, but are entitled to a $600 personal exemption. §642(b).

§10.4.7. Two-Percent Floor on Miscellaneous Itemized Deductions, §67

Under §67, no deduction is allowed for miscellaneous itemized deductions to the extent of 2 percent of adjusted gross income (AGI). Most trusts are unlikely to pay much, if any, additional tax because of §67, for three reasons. First, and most important, in computing AGI for trusts and estates, deductions are fully allowable for distributions to beneficiaries under §651 and 661, personal exemptions under §642(b), and administration expenses "which would not have been incurred if the property were not held in such trust or estate." §67(e)(1). Because these deductions are available in full, a trust's AGI will tend to be lower, which in turn reduces the impact of the 2-percent limitation. The 2-percent floor will generally be of concern only to trusts (and beneficiaries of trusts) with large AGIs (*e.g.,* trusts with substantial, undistributed capital gains).

Second, §67(e)(1) generally provides that deductions paid or incurred by estates and trusts in connection with the administration of the estate or trust which would not be incurred if the related property were not held by such estate or trust are treated as "above-the-line" deductions solely for purposes of avoiding the 2-percent limitation. §67(a). This provision allows a full deduction for many trust expenses, including the fees of the trustee and the lawyer for the trustee. Likewise, the fees of accountants required to prepare annual accountings and tax returns for the trust would be deductible in full.

The key to the application of §67(e)(1) is determining whether a particular expense is one that individuals would not commonly incur. *Knight v. Commissioner,* 128 S. Ct. 782, 169 L. Ed. 2d 652 (2008), resolved a conflict regarding whether investment advisory fees paid by a trust are subject to the 2-percent floor. *O'Neill v. Commissioner,* 994 F.2d 302 (6th Cir. 1993), held that an investment advisor's fee is not subject to the 2-percent floor, while *Scott v. United States,* 338 F.3d 132 (4th Cir. 2003), *Mellon Bank v. United States,* 265 F.3d 1275 (Fed. Cir. 2001), and *William L. Rudkin Trust v. Commissioner,* 467 F.3d 149 (2d Cir. 2006), held that the fees of investment advisors were subject to the 2-percent floor. Put simply, *Knight* holds that "§67(e)(1) excepts from the 2% floor only costs that it would be *un* common (or unusual, or unlikely)" for an individual to incur (emphasis supplied). In reaching that conclusion the Court rejected two competing arguments: First, the Court rejected the "more exacting test" that the Second Circuit had imposed in its decision in *Knight*—that the costs are subject to the floor unless they "could not have" been incurred by an individual property owner. (The "could not have" test, which was included in the proposed regulations issued in 2007, Prop. Reg. §1.67-4, will not be included in the permanent version of the regulations.) Second, the Court rejected the trustee's contention that investment advisory fees are deductible because they are "caused by the trustee's obligation 'to obtain advice on investing trust assets in compliance with the Trustees' particular fiduciary duties.'" In the Court's view, the trustee's argument was circular: "trust investment advice fees are caused by the fact the property is held in trust . . . . Adding the modifier 'trust' to costs that otherwise would be incurred by an individual surely cannot be enough to escape the 2% floor."

Although the *Knight* Court held that the fees that a trust (or estate) pays to an investment advisor are subject to the 2-percent floor of §67(e) unless it would have been uncommon, unusual or unlikely for an individual to incur a similar cost, the Court acknowledged that in some circumstances "the incremental cost of expert advice beyond what would normally be required for the ordinary taxpayer would not be subject to the 2% floor." For instance, if the trust has "an unusual investment objective" or mandates "a specialized balancing of the interests of various parties, such that a reasonable comparison with individual investors would be improper," the cost of additional expert advice would be spared from the 2-percent floor.

Finally, the personal exemption ($300 for simple trusts, $100 for complex trusts, and $600 for estates) is available to absorb the 2 percent of miscellaneous itemized deductions that are not deductible in computing AGI. For example, in the case of a simple trust the $300 personal exemption offsets the disallowance of 2 percent of miscellaneous itemized deductions of $15,000. An estate's exemption of $600 offsets 2 percent of $30,000 and the $100 exemption of a complex trust absorbs 2 percent of $5,000.

§ 10.4.8. Passive Activity Losses (PALs)

Simply stated, the interrelationship of the passive-activity loss limitation rules of Section 469 with Subchapter J, which establishes rules for taxation of fiduciaries and beneficiaries, is an unmitigated nightmare. Abbin, To Be [Active] or Not To Be [Passive]: That Is the Question Confronting Fiduciaries and Beneficiaries Trying to Apply the Passive Activity Loss (PAL) Rules, U. Miami, 23rd Inst. Est. Plan., Ch. 3 (1989). Generally, individuals, trusts and estates, personal service corporations, and closely-held subchapter C corporations may not deduct the net amount of losses incurred in connection with passive business activities. § 469(a). For purposes of applying § 469 the income and losses from passive activities are netted for each year. More particularly, as defined in § 469(d)(1) the term "passive activity loss" means the amount by which aggregate losses from all passive activities for the year exceed the aggregate income from passive activities for the year. Passive activities are ones that involve the conduct of a trade or business in which the taxpayer does not materially participate, § 469(c)(1), including any rental activity, § 469(c)(2), but not the ownership of oil and gas working interests, § 469(c)(3). In order to constitute material participation the taxpayer must be involved in the operations of an activity on a basis which is "regular, continuous, and substantial." § 469(h)(1). In the case of trusts and estates, presumably it is the fiduciary who must materially participate in the trade or business, and not the beneficiaries. Except as otherwise provided by regulation, no limited partner is considered to have materially participated in the activities of a limited partnership. § 469(h)(2).

Net losses are carried over from year to year and may be offset against the net income from passive activities in later years. § 469(b). The disposition of a passive activity property is subject to special rules. First, a disposition by gift results in an increase in the basis of the property by the amount of the PALs allocable to it; however, the resulting basis cannot exceed the fair market value of the property at the time of the gift. Second, under § 469(g)(1) accumulated losses in a passive activity are fully deductible if the taxpayer's entire interest is disposed of in a fully taxable transaction to a person other than a related taxpayer described in § 267(b) or § 707(b)(1). Third, an installment sale of a passive activity allows a portion of the accumulated PALs allocable to the activity to be deducted. § 469(g)(3). The deductible portion bears the same ratio to "all such losses as the gain recognized on such sale during such taxable year bears to the gross profit from such sale (realized or to be realized when payment is completed)." *Id.* Fourth, when a passive activity is transferred at death, the accumulated losses are deductible, but only to the extent they exceed the amount of the increase of the basis in the property that took place upon the taxpayer's death. §469(g)(2). Fifth, it appears that distributions from trusts or estates do not carry out PALs to beneficiaries. Instead, under §469(j)(12) the basis of the property distributed is increased by the amount of PALs allocable to it. Such PALs are not allowable as a deduction for any taxable year.

Individual taxpayers are allowed to deduct up to $25,000 in PALs attributable to rental real estate activities in which they actively participate. However, the amount of this offset is reduced by 50 percent of the amount by which the taxpayer's adjusted gross income exceeds $100,000. §469(i). Also, under §469(i)(4) the estate of a taxpayer who was actively engaged in rental activities remains entitled to the $25,000 offset for two years following the taxpayer's death. The amount allowable to the estate is reduced to the extent the decedent's surviving spouse makes use of the offset.

§10.4.9. Rules Applicable to Simple Trusts, §§651, 652

A trust that requires the distribution of all of its income currently, does not provide for payment of any charitable gifts, and does not make any distribution other than of current income is a "simple" trust. §651; Reg. §1.651(a)-1. Income for this purpose has reference to its income as determined for trust accounting purposes. All other trusts are "complex" trusts. The classification, which affects the computation of DNI, the personal tax exemptions, and other tax matters, is made each year. Accordingly, a trust that requires all income to be distributed currently and authorizes the trustee to make discretionary distributions of principal is a simple trust except for years during which it distributes principal. On the other hand, a trust that authorizes the trustee to accumulate income is necessarily a complex trust. Note that a trust is a complex trust in its final year and in the year in which it makes any partial distributions of corpus. Estates are subject to most of the rules applicable to complex trusts.

Under §651(a), a simple trust is entitled to deduct the amount it is required to distribute currently. However, the amount of the deduction cannot exceed the trust's DNI, reduced by the amount of items reflected in DNI, but not included in the trust's income (*e.g.,* life insurance excludable under §101(a) and municipal bond interest exempt under §103). §651(b). It is necessary to make the reduction so the trust will not benefit doubly from the items—once because they are excluded from income and again as the result of a distribution deduction. The application of the rule is illustrated in this example from Reg. §1.651(b)-1:

> Assume that the distributable net income of a trust as computed under §643(a) amounts to $99,000 but includes nontaxable income of $9,000. Then distributable net income for the purpose of determining the deduction allowable under section 651 is $90,000 ($99,000 less $9,000 nontaxable income).

The beneficiary of a simple trust includes in his or her income the amount of income required to be distributed currently for such year, regardless of whether it was actually distributed. §652(a); Reg. §1.652(a)-1. However, the amount includible in the beneficiary's income cannot exceed the trust's DNI for the year. When the amount required to be distributed exceeds DNI, each beneficiary includes in his or her income an amount equivalent to his or her proportionate share of DNI. Each item distributed to a beneficiary has the same character in his or her hands that it had in the hands of the trust. "For example, to the extent that the amounts specified in § 1.652(a)-1 consist of income exempt from tax under section 103, such amounts are not included in the beneficiary's gross income." Reg. § 1.652(b)-1. This exclusion is consistent with the disallowance of a distribution deduction for items excluded from the trust's income as noted above.

Amounts included in a beneficiary's gross income are treated as consisting of the same proportion of each class of items entering into DNI as the total of each class bears to DNI. A different result follows if the terms of the trust specifically allocate different classes of income to different beneficiaries. This point is illustrated by the following example from Reg. § 1.652(b)-2(a):

> Assume that under the terms of the governing instrument beneficiary *A* is to receive currently one-half of the trust income and beneficiaries *B* and *C* are each to receive currently one-quarter, and the distributable net income of the trust (after allocation of expenses) consists of dividends of $10,000, taxable interest of $10,000, and tax-exempt interest of $4,000. *A* will be deemed to have received $5,000 of dividends, $5,000 of taxable interest, and $2,000 of tax-exempt interest; *B* and *C* will each be deemed to have received $2,500 of dividends, $2,500 of taxable interest, and $1,000 of tax-exempt interest. However, if the terms of the trust specifically allocate different classes of income to different beneficiaries, entirely or in part, or if local law requires such an allocation, each beneficiary will be deemed to have received those items of income specifically allocated to him.

Allocation of Deductions. In determining the nature of amounts distributed to the beneficiaries and included in their incomes, it is necessary to allocate the deductions of a trust that enter into the computation of DNI. The rules under which the allocations are made are described in Reg. § 1.652(b)-3. First, all deductible items directly attributable to one class of income are allocated to it (with the exception of excludable dividends and interest). Examples include expenses incurred in carrying on a trade or business and expenses incurred in connection with the rental of property. Second, deductions not directly attributable to a specific class of income may be allocated to any class of income, including capital gains, that is taken into account in computing DNI. Examples of expenses that are not directly attributable to a specific class of income include trustee's commissions, safe deposit box rental, and state income and personal property taxes. Reg. § 1.652(b)-3(c).

EXAMPLE 10-1.

> The trust had income of $40,000, consisting of $10,000 of business income, $10,000 of rental income, $10,000 of taxable interest, and $10,000 of tax-exempt income. The trustee's commissions, not subject to the 2-percent floor, were $4,000. One-fourth of the commissions must be allocated to the nontaxable income. The trustee may allocate the balance of the deductions

in his or her discretion among items included in DNI (*e.g.,* business income or rental income). The balance of $3,000 must be used to reduce the amount includible in the beneficiaries' income even though the governing instrument or local law treats a portion of the commissions as attributable to corpus because they relate to capital gains or other items not included in income for trust accounting purposes. Reg. § 1.652(b)-3. In effect, charging a portion of the commissions to corpus increases the amount of income received tax-free by the beneficiary. The increase, of course, comes at the expense of corpus, which bears the expense.

Third, if any deductions directly attributable to one class of income exceed that class of income, they may be allocated to another class of income. However, excess deductions attributable to nontaxable income may not be allocated to any other class of income. In general the same rules apply to complex trusts. Reg. § 1.662(b)-1, 1.662(b)-2.

§ 10.4.10. Rules Applicable to Complex Trusts and Estates, § § 661-663

In computing the taxable income of a complex trust, the trust is allowed a deduction under § 661(a) of an amount equal to the sum of two classes (or *tiers*) of distributions. The first tier consists of the amount of income the trust is required to distribute currently, including the amount of an annuity or other item required to be paid currently out of income or corpus to the extent it is paid out of income for the current year. This amount corresponds to the deduction allowable to simple trusts. The second tier consists of any other amounts properly paid or credited or required to be distributed during the taxable year. It includes, for example, an annuity to the extent it is not payable out of current income, distributions of property in kind, and discretionary distributions of corpus. Of course, the distribution deduction cannot exceed the trust's DNI, reduced as in the case of a simple trust, by the amount of nontaxable items included in DNI (*e.g.,* life insurance proceeds excludable under § 101(a) and municipal bond interest that is tax-exempt under § 103).

The character of the amounts deducted by the trust and includible in the beneficiaries' income is determined in essentially the same manner as in the case of a simple trust. Thus, the character of each distribution consists of a proportionate amount of each class of income. § 661(b), 662(b). However, adjustments may be required, depending upon the amount of the distributions, the tiers to which they belong, and the amount of the trust's DNI. In brief, first tier distributions are taken from DNI first in determining the consequences of the distributions. Thus, if the first tier distributions absorb the full amount of the trust's DNI, no income is carried out to the second tier beneficiaries. In such a case, each first tier beneficiary is taxed on a proportionate amount of the distribution.

EXAMPLE 10-2.

The trust provides for distribution of all current income in equal shares to *A, B,* and *C.* In addition, the trustee, *T,* is authorized to make discretionary distributions of principal to the income beneficiaries, their spouses, or their children. Last year the trust income was $30,000 and its DNI was $27,000. *T* distributed $10,000 to each of *A, B,* and *C. T* also made a discretionary distribution of $5,000 of principal to *B.* The trust has a distribution deduction of $27,000 (the amount of its DNI for the year), equal portions of which are reportable as income by *A, B,* and *C.* Under the tier system, *A, B,* and *C* each report $9,000 of income. The second tier distribution of $5,000 to *B* is neither deductible by the trust nor includible in *B'*s gross income.

When the distributions to the first tier beneficiaries are less than the trust's DNI, a proportionate amount of the excess is included in the income of the second tier beneficiaries who receive distributions. For example, had the DNI of the trust in Example 10-2 been $32,000, each first tier beneficiary would have included $10,000 in his or her income and the second tier beneficiary, *B,* would have included the remaining $2,000 in his income. As pointed out by Arthur Michaelson and Jonathan Blattmachr, "The rationale of the tier system is that first-tier distributions are more realistically distributions of income than are other distributions by the trust, and hence should be the first to be taxed as income and thus to absorb distributable net income." Blattmachr & Michaelson, Income Taxation of Estates & Trusts 2-24 (14th ed. 2005).

Separate Share Rule, §663(c). The separate share rule of §663(c) applies to complex trusts that have more than one beneficiary with substantially separate and independent shares for the sole purpose of determining the amounts of DNI allocable to each beneficiary under §661 and 662. The rule also applies to estates that have more than one beneficiary who have substantially separate and independent shares. The application of the rule is significant when income is accumulated for one beneficiary and a distribution is made to another beneficiary in excess of his or her proportionate share of income.

Under the regulations:

> Ordinarily, a separate share exists if the economic interests of the benefici-ary or class of beneficiaries neither affect nor are affected by the economic interests accruing to another beneficiary or class of beneficiaries. Separate shares include, for example, the income on bequeathed property if the recipient of the specific bequest is entitled to such income and a surviving spouse's elective share that under local law is entitled to income and appreciation or depreciation. Reg. § 1.663(c)-4(a).

A pecuniary formula bequest that is not entitled to share in income or appreciation and depreciation qualifies as a separate share if the governing instrument does not provide that it is to be paid or credited in more than three installments. Reg. § 1.663(c)-4(b).

Under Reg. § 1.663(c)-(3)(b), separate share treatment does not apply to a trust or portion of a trust that is subject to a power to:

(1) Distribute, apportion, or accumulate income, or

(2) Distribute corpus

to or for one or more beneficiaries within a group or class of beneficiaries unless payment of income, accumulated income, or corpus of a share of one beneficiary cannot affect the proportionate share of income, accumulated income, or corpus of any of the other beneficiaries, or unless substantially proper adjustment must be thereafter be made (under the governing instrument) so that substantially and independent shares exist.

Accordingly, separate shares do not exist when there are multiple beneficiaries of a trust (or residuary estate) unless the distributions made to each beneficiary are charged against his or her separate share.

EXAMPLE 10-3.

T's will directs that his residuary estate be divided into two shares, one for the benefit of *A* and the other for *B*. The trustee has discretion, with respect to each share, to distribute income and principal to the beneficiary. The shares constitute separate shares under § 663(c). They would not constitute separate shares if the trustee had authority to distribute principal of one share to the beneficiary of the other share unless the possibility of such a distribution was so remote as to be negligible. Reg. § 1.663(c)-3(a), (b), (d).

The separate share rules does not permit the separate shares to be treated as separate for any other purpose. Thus, the rule does not affect the filing of returns, the personal exemptions available, or the allocation of excess deductions on termination of the trust. The separate share treatment is mandatory, not elective. Reg. § 1.663(c)-1(d).

§ 10.4.11. Recognition of Loss, § 267

Section 267 bars a deduction for a loss arising from a sale or exchange of property between certain related parties. Insofar as trusts are involved, no deduction is allowed where property is sold by the fiduciary of a trust, (1) to a beneficiary of the trust, § 267(b)(6); (2) to the fiduciary of another trust created by the same grantor, § 267(b)(5); or (3) to the beneficiary of another trust created by the same grantor, § 267(b)(7). However, loss that is not allowable to the transferor under § 267 may be utilized by the purchaser-transferee for purposes of computing gain on a subsequent disposition of the property. § 267(d). (Note that the benefit of this rule is only available to the original purchaser-transferee and not to subsequent assignees. Reg. § 1.267(d)-1(a)(3).)

EXAMPLE 10-4.

A trustee, *T*, sold stock with a basis of $1,500 to a beneficiary, *X*, of the trust for $1,000. *T* is not allowed to deduct the $500 "loss" on the sale to *X*. If *X* later sells the stock for $2,000, *X* realizes a gain of $1,000, but is required to recognize only $500, which is the excess of the realized gain ($1,000) over the loss ($500) not allowed to *T*. If *X* had given the stock to another person, *P*, *P* could not make use of *T*'s disallowed loss to offset any gain realized by *P* on a subsequent sale or exchange.

As for estates, no deduction is allowed for losses realized on the sale or exchange of property between the executor and a beneficiary of the estate. § 267(b)(13). Losses realized by the estate upon a sale or exchange in satisfaction of a pecuniary bequest, however, are deductible by the estate. *Id.*

§ 10.4.12. Losses on Small Business Stock, § 1244

A limited ordinary loss deduction is allowed under § 1244 for loss of up to $50,000 ($100,000 in the case of a husband and wife filing a joint return) on the sale or exchange of the stock in a qualifying small business corporation. However, the loss is only allowed to an individual or partner who held the stock continuously from the time of its original issue. In particular, "[a] corporation, trust, or estate is not entitled to ordinary loss treatment under section 1244 regardless of how the stock was acquired." Reg. § 1.1244(a)-1(b). Thus, the transfer of otherwise qualifying stock to a trust appears to cut off any possibility of obtaining an ordinary loss deduction under § 1244. However, the deduction should be available if the grantor is treated as owner of the trust under the grantor trust rules, because the income tax rules see the grantor and the trust as the same taxpayer. *See* Rev. Rul. 74-613, 1974-2 C.B. 153 (transfer of an installment obligation to a trust is not a disposition of the obligation where the grantor is treated as the owner of the trust).

§ 10.4.13. S Corporation Stock

Only certain types of trusts may hold stock in an S corporation. If another type of trust acquires S corporation stock, the corporation's S election is terminated, meaning the corporation reverts to the status of a C corporation. It is therefore critical for the planner to recognize the types of trusts eligible to hold S corporation stock. The six types of eligible trusts are: (1) grantor trusts; (2) § 678 trusts; (3) voting trusts; (4) testamentary trusts; (5) qualified subchapter S trusts; and (6) electing small business trusts. Estates may also generally hold S corporation stock.

Grantor Trusts. If the grantor is treated as the owner of a trust, the trust is an eligible S corporation shareholder provided the grantor is a citizen or resident of the United States. § 1361(c)(2)(A)(i). An eligible grantor trust will continue to be an eligible S corporation shareholder for two years following the grantor's death. § 1361(c)(2)(A)(ii). For purposes of applying the 100-shareholder limitation, among other limitations, the grantor is treated as the shareholder. § 1361(c)(2)(B)(i) – (ii). Consequently, stock held by a grantor trust will be counted as held by only one shareholder regardless of the number of trust beneficiaries.

§ 678 Trusts. As with grantor trusts, trusts that are treated as owned by an individual other than the grantor under § 678 may hold stock in an S corporation. § 1361(c)(2)(A)(i). A § 678 trust may continue as an S corporation shareholder for two years following the deemed owner's death. § 1361(c)(2)(A)(ii).

Voting Trusts and Testamentary Trusts. A trust created primarily for the purpose of exercising the voting power of stock transferred to it is an eligible S corporation shareholder. § 1361(c)(2)(A)(iv). Similarly, a testamentary trust may hold stock in an S corporation, but only for two years from the date of transfer. § 1361(c)(2)(A)(iii).

Qualified Subchapter S Trust (QSST). The individual beneficiary of a "qualified subchapter S trust" (QSST) may elect to be a shareholder. § 1361(d). Briefly, a QSST is one under which all of the income is payable currently to an individual who is a United States citizen or resident. In addition, the terms of the trust must provide that: (1) during the life of the current income beneficiary there shall only be one income beneficiary, § 1361(d)(3)(A)(i); (2) any corpus distributed during the lifetime of the current income beneficiary must be distributed to him or her, § 1361(d)(3)(A)(ii); (3) the income interest of the income beneficiary shall terminate on the earlier of the death of the beneficiary or termination of the trust, § 1361(d)(3)(A)(iii); and (4) upon termination during the life of the current income beneficiary, the trust shall distribute all of its assets to such beneficiary, § 1361(d)(3)(A)(iv).

A trust that will terminate and distribute its assets to persons other than the income beneficiary if the trust ceases to hold shares of an S corporation is not a QSST. Rev. Rul. 89-55, 1989-1 C.B. 268. Likewise, a trust is not a QSST if it provides that a portion of the corpus must be used to fund a separate trust for any grandchildren who are born after the creation of the trust. Rev. Rul. 89-45, 1989-1 C.B. 267. *See* § 11.4.

A trust is not precluded from being a QSST "merely because the terms of the trust permit accumulation of income when the trust no longer holds stock of an S corporation." Rev. Rul. 92-20, 1992-1 C.B. 301. In contrast, a trust that qualifies as a charitable remainder trust cannot be a QSST. Rev. Rul. 92-48, 1992-1 C.B. 301. In particular, Rev. Rul. 92-48 noted the income tax rules applicable to QSSTs and charitable remainder trusts were incompatible:

> To the extent that a QSST's assets consist of S corporation stock, the QSST's beneficiary is treated as the owner of a grantor trust under subpart E. This tax result is incompatible with the rule that a charitable remainder trust function exclusively under section 664 of the Code.

Consistently, Rev. Rul. 92-73, 1992-2 C.B. 224, held that an individual retirement account under § 408(a) cannot be a QSST; the requirements applicable to IRAs and QSSTs are incompatible. Note, however, the suggestion contained in both Rev. Rul. 92-48 and Rev. Rul. 92-73 that relief may be requested under § 1362 if a shareholder inadvertently causes termination of S corporation status by transferring stock to a charitable remainder trust or an IRA.

Initially it appeared that the beneficiary of a QSST who is treated as its owner must report any gain or loss arising from the sale of stock by the QSST whether or not the gain or loss is properly allocable to corpus. Rev. Rul. 92-84, 1992-2 C.B. 216. This result followed because the beneficiary of a QSST is treated as the owner of that portion of the trust that consists of stock in an S corporation with respect to which an S corporation election was made. *See* § 1361(d)(1)(A) – (B). The outcome of Rev. Rul. 92-84 was reversed by regulations. Under Reg. § 1.1361-1(j)(8), an income beneficiary who is deemed to be the owner of the trust "only by reason of section 1361(d)(1) will not be treated as the owner of the S corporation stock in determining and attributing the federal income tax consequences of a disposition of stock by the QSST."

The regulations make it clear that the beneficiary of a testamentary QTIP may make a QSST election if the requirements of Reg. § 1.1361-1(j)(1)(i) and (ii) are met. Reg. § 1.1361-1(j)(4). The same regulation points out that the income beneficiary of an inter vivos QTIP cannot make a QSST election because the grantor is treated as the owner of the income portion of the trust by reason of § 677. *Id.* On the other hand, the grantor can make the election if the grantor is treated as the owner of the entire trust under § 671-677. *Id.*

A QSST trust will be disqualified if a trust distribution satisfies the grantor's legal obligation to support the beneficiary. Reg. § 1.1361-1(j)(2)(ii)(B).

Electing Small Business Trust (ESBT). Section 1361(e) permits an ESBT to be a shareholder in an S Corporation. The definition of ESBT is deceptively simple—it is a trust that does not have a beneficiary other than an individual, an estate, or a charitable organization described in any of § 170(c)(2) – (5). In addition, no interest in the trust may have been acquired by purchase. The term does not include a QSST or any trust that is exempt from the income tax. ESBTs are discussed further at § 11.4.

Estates. The estate of a deceased shareholder is an eligible shareholder for so long as required to complete the administration of the estate. *See* § 12.4. The IRS earlier recognized that an estate may remain an eligible shareholder during the period that payment of the estate tax is deferred under a prior version of § 6166. Rev. Rul. 76-23, 1976-1 C.B. 264.

§ 10.4.14. Redemptions Under § 303

Section 303 applies to distributions in redemption of stock included in a decedent's estate and held by any person at the time of redemption, including the trustee of a trust created by the decedent. Reg. § 1.303-2(f). When the value of the stock included in the decedent's estate constitutes more than 35 percent of the decedent's adjusted gross estate, a redemption distribution is treated as full payment in exchange for the redeemed stock. However, the amount that may be so treated is limited to the sum of the death taxes imposed on the decedent's estate and the amount of funeral and administration expenses that are deductible under § 2053. § 303(b)(2)(A). For this purpose the GSTT on a generation-skipping transfer that occurs at the time of the decedent's death is treated as a death tax. § 303(d).

Note that § 303 applies only to the extent that the interest of a redeeming shareholder is liable for payment of the taxes and administration expenses. § 303(b)(3). Thus, stock that the parties might wish to redeem under § 303 should not be transferred to a beneficiary or a trust that is not liable for payment of death taxes and expenses of administration. For a more complete discussion of redemptions under § 303, *see* § 11.13-11.22. The preferential tax rate that applies to qualified dividend income will generally not make it less necessary to bring redemptions within the safe harbor rules of § 302 or the exception of § 303. Under § 1(h)(11) qualified dividend income is subject to the same rates as apply to net capital gains (*i.e.*, a maximum rate of 15 percent). However, a distribution that does not meet the requirements of § 302 or § 303 would be entirely taxable as a dividend—not just the gain element. Accordingly, a significant difference remains.

§10.4.15. Taxable Year of the Trust

Trusts other than tax-exempt trusts are generally required to report income on the basis of a calendar year. §644. There are, however, two exceptions to the rule. First, under a rule that is of benefit primarily to corporations that establish grantor trusts for charitable or other reasons, a trust that is treated as owned by the grantor for income tax purposes is not required to adopt a calendar year. Rev. Rul. 90-55, 1990-2 C.B. 161. The existence of grantor trusts is largely ignored for federal income tax purposes, so this result is logical. Second, following the death of the grantor of a revocable trust, the trustee and the decedent's executor may elect to treat the trust as part of the estate for income tax purposes. §645. As explained in §10.15, a decedent's executor and the trustee of a revocable trust that was treated as owned by the decedent under §676 may elect to treat and tax the trust as if it were part of the decedent's estate. §645. The elective treatment is available for taxable years of the estate that begin after the date of a decedent's death and end (1) before two years after the date of the decedent's death if no estate tax return was required to be filed or (2) before six months after the date on which the estate tax liability of the decedent's estate is finally determined.

The designation of a fiscal year in a charitable remainder trust (CRT) may still allow some deferral in the taxation of distributions to noncharitable beneficiaries. Specifically, if a CRT and its noncharitable beneficiaries have different tax years, the amount the beneficiary is required to report as income in a particular year is based on the income and distributions made by the trust for the year (or years) that end within the beneficiary's taxable year. Reg. §1.664-1(d)(4)(i). The last cited Regulation provides, in part, that:

> If a recipient has a different taxable year (as defined in section 441 or 442) from the taxable year of the trust, the amount he is required to include in gross income to the extent required by this paragraph shall be included in his taxable year in which or with which ends the taxable year of the trust in which such amount is required to be distributed. Reg. §1.664-1(d)(4)(i).

Under §664(b), distributions of charitable remainder trusts are deemed successively to have the following character: ordinary income, capital gains, other income, and corpus. Thus, the selection of the taxable year for a charitable remainder trust may result in some delay in the payment of income tax on distributions to the noncharitable beneficiaries.

EXAMPLE 10-5.

A charitable remainder trust was established on July 1, 2007, the first day of its taxable year. The noncharitable beneficiaries are cash basis taxpayers who file calendar year returns. The amount of distributions reported by the beneficiaries in their returns for calendar 2008 are determined by the trust's return (Form 5227) for the year beginning on July 1, 2007, and ending on June 30, 2008. The same rule applies where the first year of the trust is a short one (*e.g.,* if the charitable trust were established on December 1, 2007).

The fiduciary of a trust (or estate) may elect under § 663(b) to treat any amount that is properly paid or credited to a beneficiary within the first 65 days following the close of the taxable year as an amount properly paid or distributed on the last day of such taxable year. This 65-day rule allows trustees to avoid the unintentional accumulation of income, which might otherwise be subject to the throwback rules of § 665-668. The election, of course, has an impact on the distribution deduction of the trust and the amounts reportable as income by the beneficiaries.

§ 10.4.16. Estimated Income Tax Payments

Insofar as quarterly estimated tax payments are concerned, estates still enjoy an advantage. Under § 6654(l), most trusts must make quarterly estimated payments of their income tax. In contrast, that requirement does not apply to estates with respect to any taxable year ending before the date two years after the date of the decedent's death. § 6654(l)(2). (The same exemption applies to trusts of which the decedent was treated as the owner under the grantor trust rules and to which the residue of the decedent's estate will pass by will.) Relief from the requirement to make estimated tax payments is another reason to consider the § 645 election. *See* § 10.15.

Any required estimated tax payments must be at least the lesser of 100 percent of the prior year's tax liability (110 percent if the trust's adjusted gross income for the prior year exceeds $150,000), or 90 percent of the current taxable year liability. § 6654(d)(1)(B). To the extent the estimated tax payments of the trust exceed its liability the trustee may allocate estimated tax payments to the beneficiaries. The allocation is made on the tax return for the trust. The tax credited to a beneficiary is considered to be a distribution and to have been paid as a part of the beneficiary's January 15 estimated tax payment.

§ 10.4.17. Who Reports the Income, § 671

The grantor of a revocable trust usually reports all the income, credits, and deductions of the trust on his or her income tax return. The trustee does not file a Form 1041 for the trust. Instead, the trustee should provide the grantor or other person who is treated as owner of the trust with a statement of the income, deductions, and credits of the trust. As stated in the instructions for Form 1041: "The income taxable to the grantor or another person under sections 671 through 678 and the deductions and the credits applied to the income must be reported by that person on his or her own income tax return." Three optional filing methods are also described in the instructions.

§ 10.5. GIFT TAX SUMMARY

The transfer of property to a trust constitutes a gift only to the extent of the value of the interests that pass from the grantor's control. Reg. § 25.2511-2(a), (b). Accordingly, the grantor's transfer of property to a revocable trust does not constitute a completed gift because the disposition of all interests in the property transferred to the trust remains subject to the grantor's control. Regulations issued under the gift tax are helpful in determining what powers are sufficient to prevent a transfer from constituting a completed gift. Reg. §25.2511-2; §10.33. A gift is likewise incomplete if the grantor retains the power to change the beneficiaries. Reg. §25.2511-2(f).

Although there is no completed gift if the grantor retains a power of revocation, the regulations require the grantor to file a gift tax return in such a case, specifying the reasons he or she believes the transfer is not taxable. Reg. §25.2511-2(j), 25.6019-3(a). However, in practice, gift tax returns are seldom filed with respect to the transfer of property to a revocable trust.

Subject to the rules of §2702, a gift to an irrevocable trust does not include the value of interests retained by the grantor.

Annual Gift Tax Exclusion. The annual gift tax exclusion has no significance with respect to transfers to revocable trusts, which do not involve completed gifts. An annual gift tax exclusion is available insofar as a trust beneficiary is entitled to the unrestricted right to "the immediate use, possession, or enjoyment of property or the income from property . . . ." Reg. §25.2503-3(b). *See* §2.5.2. In general, no exclusion is available with respect to the beneficiary's interests in a discretionary trust. However, transfers to a trust qualify for the annual exclusion to the extent the beneficiary has a *Crummey* power that allows him or her to withdraw the transferred property for his or her own use. *See* §7.38.1.

For gift tax purposes the dispositions provided for in a revocable trust become complete if the power to affect the beneficial enjoyment of the property is released or otherwise terminates during the grantor's lifetime. *Estate of Sanford v. Commissioner,* 308 U.S. 39 (1939), Reg. §25.2511-2(f). However, the gifts do not become complete merely because the grantor loses competency and may no longer exercise the retained power.

EXAMPLE 10-6.

T transferred Blackacre to *X* as trustee of an irrevocable trust. Under the terms of the trust the income of the trust is payable in the trustee's discretion to *T*'s siblings, *A*, *B*, and *C*. Upon the death of the survivor of *A*, *B*, and *C*, the trust assets are distributable to their then living issue. The transfer of Blackacre to the trust constituted a completed gift with respect to which no annual exclusions are available. The interests of *A*, *B*, and *C* in the income are not definite enough to support annual exclusions and the gift of the remainder is a future interest for which no annual gift tax exclusion is allowed. Annual exclusions would be available to the extent the beneficiaries were given *Crummey* powers of withdrawal. §7.38.1. Note that the gifts would be incomplete to the extent *T* retains a special power of appointment over the trust. *See* Reg. §25.2511-2(b).

§10.6. ESTATE TAX SUMMARY

The value of assets held in a trust may be included in the grantor's estate under any of the provisions of §2035 to 2038. *See* §2.18 – 2.19. In some cases a decedent's estate may be required to include part or all of a trust under §2039, 2041, or 2042. Problems of inclusion most commonly arise under §2036 or 2038 with respect to powers the grantor retained with respect to the disposition of trust property. Under §2036 and 2038, the trust is includible in the grantor's estate if a proscribed power is exercisable by the grantor alone *or* in conjunction with any other person. Note also that those sections make no exception for powers held by the decedent in a fiduciary capacity (*i.e.*, as trustee). A trust is, of course, includible in the grantor's estate under §2036(a)(1) to the extent he or she has directly or indirectly retained the use or benefit of the property.

§10.6.1. Right to Vote Stock of Controlled Corporation, §2036(b)

Shares of stock in a controlled corporation are includible in the grantor's estate if he or she retained the right to vote the shares. §2036(b). For this purpose a corporation is a controlled corporation if the decedent owned or had voting control of 20 percent or more of its stock within three years of decedent's death after giving effect to the attribution rules of §318. §2036(b)(2). Thus, stock in a controlled corporation that is transferred to a trust of which the transferor is the trustee and holds the power to vote the stock is includible in the transferor-trustee's gross estate. The application of §2036(b) is explored more fully in §§2.19.4, 11.5.1.

§10.6.2. Retirement Benefits and IRAs

Interests in an employee benefit plan or an individual retirement arrangement are sometimes made payable to the trustee of an inter vivos or testamentary trust in order to consolidate the employee's assets in one trust for purposes of management and administration. However, doing so may sharply reduce the period over which interests in the plan or IRA must be paid out. *See* §§13.12.1, 13.13.1. The payout should not be made to a bypass trust unless there is otherwise insufficient property to fund the trust. This accords with the general rule that items of IRD should not be passed to a credit shelter trust.

In general, estate taxation of interests in plans is governed by §2039. In brief, §2039(a) requires the inclusion of the value of annuities or other payments receivable by any beneficiary by reason of having survived the decedent (other than insurance on the life of the decedent) if the annuity was payable to the decedent or if the decedent had the right to receive payments under it. However, the inclusion of qualified plan benefits in a deceased employee's estate may not be particularly hurtful.

The availability of the marital deduction with respect to employee benefits payable to a trust is discussed at §5.23.5. Additionally, if the employee's surviving spouse is the only person entitled to receive annuity payments before the death of the surviving spouse, the marital deduction is available. *See* §2056(b)(7)(C). Of course, the marital deduction is not available to the extent it is subject to a legally binding obligation to pay estate expenses. *See* §2056(b)(4).

The marital deduction is not available with respect to plan benefits if the surviving spouse is not a United States citizen unless the benefits are settled in a manner that meets the requirements of qualified domestic trust under §2056A. If the decedent's spouse is not a citizen, the decedent's employer might cooperate by modifying the plan to meet those requirements, or the surviving spouse might roll over the benefits into an IRA that does meet those requirements. Otherwise, withdrawing the funds and transferring them to a qualified domestic trust will subject them to income taxation, which generally should be avoided. The elections available with respect to the income and estate tax treatment of lump sum distributions are discussed at § 12.26.

§ 10.6.3. General Power of Appointment, § 2041

Property transferred by another person to a trust that is revocable by the grantor is includible in the grantor's estate under § 2041(a)(2) (with the increasingly minor exception of property subject to an unexercised power created before October 22, 1942). Of course, under § 2041 the property of a trust is includible in the estate of a person other than the grantor who holds a power to withdraw the property. Similarly, the property is includible in the estate of a non-grantor who holds a power to appoint the property to himself, his creditors, his estate, or creditors of his estate.

§ 10.6.4. Life Insurance Proceeds, § 2042

The proceeds of a life insurance policy owned by a trust are included in the insured-grantor's gross estate under § 2042(2) if he or she held any incidents of ownership in the policy. Under Reg. § 20.2041-1(c)(4), the power to change the beneficial ownership of an insurance policy or its proceeds is an incident of ownership. Thus, policies of insurance on the life of the grantor of a revocable trust are includible in the grantor's estate even where the trust is named the legal owner of the policy.

The proceeds of policies owned by other parties are also includible in the insured's estate to the extent the proceeds are "receivable by the executor" although the insured had no incidents of ownership in the insurance. § 2042(1). *See* § 6.27. For that reason life insurance proceeds that are otherwise not includible in the insured's estate should not be made subject to a legally binding obligation to pay debts, taxes, and other expenses of the insured's estate. However, if insurance proceeds are payable to a trust, the trustee may be given the discretionary power to use the proceeds to buy estate assets or make loans to the estate. Under the existing authorities, the trustee may also be given the discretionary power to use the proceeds to satisfy obligations of the estate. *See* § 6.27.

§ 10.6.5. Alternate Valuation Date

Property held in a trust qualifies for the alternate valuation date election just as do other assets that are included in the decedent's gross estate. *See* § 12.15. However, property that is distributed, sold, exchanged, or otherwise disposed of within six months after the decedent's death is valued on the date of its distribution, sale, exchange, or other disposition. The distributive provisions of a revocable trust should thus be drafted with an eye toward § 2032 in order to preserve the full benefit of the alternate valuation date election for the trust assets. *See* § 12.15.

§ 10.6.6. Deduction of Expenses, § 2053

Section 2053(a) allows a deduction for administration expenses incurred with respect to property subject to an estate administration proceeding. Section 2053(b) offers a comparable deduction for expenses of administration incurred with respect to property includible in the decedent's gross estate (*e.g.*, property held in a revocable trust) but not subject to the claims of the decedent's creditors. The deduction is allowable to the extent that the costs are paid before expiration of the period of limitations for assessments under § 6501 (*i.e.*, within three years following the date upon which the estate tax return is due). Deductions are limited to expenses "occasioned by the decedent's death and incurred in settling the decedent's interest in the property or vesting good title to the property in the beneficiaries. Expenses not coming within [this] description . . . but incurred on behalf of the transferees are not deductible." Reg. § 20.2053-8(b).

§ 10.6.7. Deferral of Estate Tax, § 6166

The estate tax attributable to a closely-held business interest that is includible in the decedent's estate may be deferred under § 6166. *See* § 11.23-11.28 and 12.48. Deferral is available whether the business interest is held outright or in a trust. Where the business constitutes more than 35 percent of the decedent's adjusted gross estate, § 6166 allows the tax to be paid in installments over a ten-year period, the first of which is due five years after the estate tax return is filed.

§ 10.6.8. Discharge of Executor and Other Fiduciaries from Personal Liability for Estate Tax

Federal law provides that an executor or other fiduciary is personally liable for debts due the United States, including federal tax liabilities, to the extent the fiduciary disposes of the decedent's property without paying the debts due the United States. 31 U.S.C. § 3713. *See* § 12.50. An executor may apply for discharge from personal liability for the estate tax under § 2204(a), in which case the government must notify the executor of the amount of the tax within nine months of the time the estate tax return must be filed. § 12.50.1. The executor is discharged from personal liability upon payment of the amount found to be due and upon furnishing bond for any amount the payment of which has been deferred under § 6161, 6163, or 6166. Section 2204 was amended in 1970 to extend essentially the same opportunity to fiduciaries other than executors. § 2204(b). *See* Price, Recent Tax Legislation—The Excise, Estate and Gift Tax Adjustment Act of 1970, 47 Wn. L. Rev. 237, 273-279 (1972). Accordingly, the trustee of a revocable trust to obtain a discharge from personal liability for the decedent's estate tax. The prior inability to obtain such a discharge was a matter of some concern to trustees. The change removed one of the obstacles to the use of a revocable trust as the principal dispositive instrument in an estate plan.

B. THE REVOCABLE TRUST

§10.7. SCOPE

This part is concerned with the tax and nontax aspects of the revocable trust, which is one of the most important and flexible devices available to the estate planner. Although a revocable trust has no current tax impact—it is "tax neutral"—its flexibility and substantial nontax advantages make it a favorite of many planners and their clients. The advantages of revocable trusts have been extolled for decades by leading academics and other proponents. *See, e.g.,* Casner, Estate Planning—Avoidance of Probate, 60 Colum. L. Rev. 108 (1960); H. Abts, The Living Trust (1989); N. Dacey, How to Avoid Probate (1965). The advantages and disadvantages of revocable trusts are reviewed in Engel, *The Pros and Cons of Living Wills as Compared to Wills,* 29 Est. Plan. 155 (Apr. 2002). Unfortunately many individuals have been victimized by unprofessional promoters who often charge excessive fees for "canned" forms of revocable trusts that frequently do not meet the individuals' needs. Often, although the trusts are signed, they are never funded. Attorneys general in some states have obtained injunctions against promoters who have engaged in deception and fraud.

For income tax purposes, the grantor of a trust that is revocable by the grantor or a nonadverse party is treated as the owner of the trust. §676(a). The transfer of property to a trust that is revocable by the grantor alone or with the consent of a nonadverse party is not a completed gift. Reg. §25.2511-2(e); LR 8911028. Finally, the property of a trust that is revocable by the grantor alone or in conjunction with any other party is includible in the grantor's gross estate.

The opening sections of this part discuss some important matters of substantive law. They are followed by ones that review the basic advantages and disadvantages of revocable trusts. The concluding sections summarize the principal income, gift, and estate tax consequences of using a revocable trust in an estate plan.

A revocable trust may be funded or unfunded, but the funded variety receives most of the attention in this part. The revocable life insurance trust, discussed at §6.19.3, is one of the most common forms of the unfunded revocable trust.

Funded Revocable Trust. Perhaps most often a funded revocable trust is established to provide lifetime management of the grantor's property and to serve as a will substitute. The latter quality, which may enable the grantor's estate to "avoid probate," is a major selling point of revocable trusts—particularly in states that have statutory fee schedules for personal representatives and their counsel. When a revocable trust has a single grantor, it usually becomes completely irrevocable upon his or her death. The trust may include any of a wide variety of plans for the administration and distribution of the property following the grantor's death. A particular client's choice will depend upon the age, experience, and needs of his or her dependents and other intended beneficiaries. Thus, the assets of the trust may be distributed soon after the grantor's death, or held in trust for a substantial period, such as the lifetime of one or more beneficiaries. A revocable trust that will continue following the grantor's death should be planned in view of the general considerations applicable to irrevocable trusts (*see* Parts C and D, below).

Backup Will and Pour Over. A client may intend to transfer all of his or her property to the trust in order to avoid probate completely. Even in such a case the client should have a backup will to dispose of any property or claims that may not be included in the trust at the time of the client's death. A backup will usually provides for a gift of the grantor's residuary estate to the trustee of the revocable trust. The residuary estate is "poured over" to the trust and is not held in a separate trust under the will. The validity of the pour-over will is discussed at § 10.10. Life insurance proceeds, employee benefits, and other property may also be made payable to the trustee. Such a program is attractive because it facilitates the unified management and administration of the grantor's property and the distribution of the property according to a single plan.

Pour Back or Reverse Pour Over. A grantor's assets are most frequently unified by a pour over of the type discussed above. However, in some cases the assets of a revocable trust are "poured back" and added to the probate estate for purposes of disposition. A pour back is less common because it reduces or eliminates some of the basic advantages of a revocable trust (*e.g.,* reducing probate costs, preserving se-crecy). It also eliminates any uncertainty regarding the validity of the disposition, which might affect a pour over in some jurisdictions. The use of a pour back also allows the grantor to control the ultimate disposition of the property simply by changing the terms of his or her will, which is ambulatory and can be changed unilaterally. The trustee is not required to concur in such a change and need not know the terms of the grantor's will as it exists from time to time.

Joint Trust or Tax Basis Revocable Trust. The IRS has resisted efforts designed to allow spouses in noncommunity property states to obtain the full step-up in basis that is allowed by § 1014(b)(6) with respect to community property on the death of the first spouse to die. The efforts have generally involved establishing a revocable trust to which the spouses transfer all of their liquid assets, over which the spouse-first-to-die holds a general testamentary power of appointment. The IRS has ruled that the entire trust is includible in the estate of the deceased spouse, which can help make full use of the deceased spouse's unified credit. LR 200101021. However, in the same ruling the IRS held that § 1014(e) bars a step-up in basis with respect to the surviving spouse's share of the property. *See* § 3.35.5.

§ 10.8. RESERVING THE POWER TO REVOKE

Under the law of most states, a written trust is irrevocable unless the power to amend or revoke is expressly or impliedly reserved in the trust instrument. *Holmes v. Holmes,* 118 P. 733 (Wash. 1911); Restatement (Second) Trusts § 330 (1959). However, the modern trend is to provide that a voluntary trust is revocable unless the instrument that creates the trust expressly provides that it is irrevocable. Cal. Prob. Code § 15400 (2011); Okla. Stat. § 175.41 (2011); Tex. Prop. Code § 112.051 (2011). *See also* Uniform Trust Code § 602(a) (2000). Note that the California rule, Cal. Prob. Code § 15400, only applies "where the settlor is domiciled in this state when the trust is created, where the trust instrument is executed in this state, or where the trust instrument provides that the law of this state governs the trust." The provision regarding applicability of the California rule could cause unintended complications with respect to a California settlor who creates a trust that does not contain a revocability clause in a jurisdiction in which trusts are irrevocable unless otherwise provided. Complications could also arise if a settlor not domiciled in California executes a trust that does not contain a revocability clause that states that it shall be governed by California law.

Whatever the local law may be, a trust instrument should specify whether it is amendable or revocable. Otherwise, there is some risk that the character of the trust might not be properly established or understood by the grantor. It is important to eliminate as many uncertainties as possible in order to avoid disputes with the client, the client's successors, and the tax authorities. For example, the failure of a Texas trust to provide that the trust was irrevocable caused the corpus of the trust to be included in the grantor's gross estate under § 2038. *Estate of Alvin Hill*, 64 T.C. 867 (1975), *acq.*, 1976-2 C.B. 2, *aff'd by order*, 568 F.2d 1365 (5th Cir. 1978).

A reservation of the power to revoke the trust should include a suitable provision specifying the manner in which the power may be exercised and how the property will be disposed of upon revocation. The same paragraph often governs amendments of the trust. In Form 10-1, below, optional alternative sentences appear in brackets. One of them should be included regarding the exercise of the power by a representative of the grantor.

Form 10-1
Reserved Power to Amend or Revoke

The grantor reserves the power to amend or revoke this trust in whole or in part by an instrument in writing delivered to the trustee during the grantor's lifetime. However, without the trustee's consent an amendment, other than a revocation of the trust or withdrawal of assets of the trust, may not substantially increase the duties or liabilities of the trustee or change the compensation of the trustee. If the trust is completely revoked, the trustee shall promptly deliver all of the trust fund to the grantor or as the grantor may designate. [This power is personal to the grantor and may not be exercised on the grantor's behalf by a guardian, custodian, or other representative.][This power may be exercised by an attorney-in-fact for the grantor acting under a durable power of attorney or by a guardian of the grantor's estate.]

In most states, the exercise of the power of revocation is effective only if it complies with the terms of the trust. For example, under the provisions of Form 10-1, neither an oral revocation nor a written revocation that was not delivered to the trustee during the grantor's lifetime would be valid. Note, however, that under California law trusts are also revocable "by a writing (other than a will) signed by the settlor and delivered to the trustee during the lifetime of the settler" unless the trust instrument explicitly provides that the method specified in the trust instrument is the exclusive method of revocation. *Masry v. Masry*, 82 Cal. Rptr. 3d 915 (Cal. App. 2008). A written revocation that is not delivered to the trustee during the grantor's lifetime, or otherwise does not comply with the terms of the trust, would also be ineffective. *See, e.g., In re Estate of Button*, 490 P.2d 731 (Wash. 1971); Restatement (Third) of Trusts § 63, comment i (2003); Uniform Trust Code § 602(c) (2000). A revocable trust is not revoked by a subsequent will that neither refers to the trust nor makes any statement regarding it. *Estate of Ellen M. Sanders*, 929 P.2d 153 (Kan. 1996) (trustor reserved power to revoke or terminate by writing delivered to trustee, "which shall specify the term of such amendment or revocation").

Community Property. Among the reasons for establishing a revocable trust, a husband and wife may wish to preserve the character of their respective interests in the property transferred to the trust. This reason is particularly important if they are moving to a state that has a different marital property regime. *See* § 3.25, 3.39. For example, a husband and wife who are moving from a community to a noncommunity property state may wish to transfer their community property to such a trust. The community property character of assets transferred to the trust is preserved if the trust satisfies the requirements of the local law. *See* § 3.25; Rev. Rul. 66-283, 1966-2 C.B. 297 (decedent's estate includes only his one-half community property interest in the trust; step-up in basis under § 1014(b)(6) also allowed for the survivor's interest in the trust) (California). *See also Katz v. United States*, 382 F.2d 723 (9th Cir. 1967).

Manner of Revocation. An attempt to revoke a revocable trust generally fails unless the act is performed in the manner specified in the trust. As a corollary to the nontestamentary nature of revocable trusts, unless otherwise provided in a revocable trust, the trust is generally not subject to revocation by the grantor's will. *Will of Tamplin*, 48 P.3d 471 (Alaska 2002), *but see* Alaska Stat. § 13.36.340 (passed after the decedent executed her will; requires that a revocation be made by a signed writing other than a will).

§ 10.9. Nontestamentary Nature of Revocable Trusts

Historically, the validity of revocable trusts was sometimes challenged for failure to comply with the formal requirements of the Statute of Wills. Challengers argued that the grantor's retention of a life interest in the trust and an unrestricted power of revocation made the trust testamentary. To them, a revocable trust was comparable to a testamentary disposition that became operative only upon the death of the maker and did not affect the maker's title until that time. Most courts resolved the issue according to whether the establishment of the trust gave another person an interest in the property transferred to the trust. If an interest were created in another person, the trust was held to be nontestamentary even though the grantor reserved a life interest and retained the power to revoke the trust. Restatement (Second) Trusts § 57 (1959). The influential decision in *National Shawmut Bank v. Joy*, 53 N.E.2d 113 (Mass. 1944), put it this way: "The reservation by the settlor, in addition to an interest for life, of a power to revoke the trust, did not make incomplete or testamentary the gift over to the statutory next of kin." 53 N.E.2d at 124. Cases involving declarations of trust provided by mutual fund companies generally reach the same result. *E.g., Farkas v. Williams*, 125 N.E.2d 600 (Ill. 1955). For the purpose of determining the validity of the trust, the interest of the beneficiary other than the grantor suffices if it is a contingent equitable remainder (*i.e.*, the beneficiary's interest is contingent upon surviving the grantor).

§10.10. VALIDITY OF POUR-OVER TO REVOCABLE TRUST

Until the widespread adoption in the 1960s of the Uniform Testamentary Additions to Trust Act, most recently modified in 1992, the validity and effect of a testamentary addition to a revocable trust was uncertain. The most recent version of the Uniform Act, which validates pour-overs to pre-existing trusts as well as trusts yet to be established, is included in the Uniform Probate Code as §2-511 (2011). In one form or another, the Uniform Act has been adopted by almost all states and the District of Columbia. Because of slight local variations in the statute, the governing form of the statute should be examined carefully before drafting a testamentary pour over or an amendment of a trust with respect to which a pour-over will has already been executed. Note that the Act authorizes a pour over to a trust created by the will of a person who predeceased the testator, but does not authorize a pour over to a trust provided for in the will of a living person. Also, remember that incorporation by reference or the doctrine of independent significance may be used in some cases to uphold a particular disposition. That is, the Act should not be considered the exclusive method by which the assets of a probate estate can be made subject to the terms of a previously written trust.

Under U.P.C. §2-511, property poured over to a pre-existing trust will be administered in accordance with the provisions of the trust including any amendments made before or after the death of the testator. However, some states limit the pour-over to the trust as it existed when the will was executed (*i.e.*, insofar as the pour over is concerned, no effect is given to subsequent amendments). Under the Uniform Act the testator's will may provide that the pour-over shall also be subject to amendments to the trust made after the testator's death.

The Act provides that the pour-over may be made to "a funded or unfunded life insurance trust, although the trustor has reserved any or all rights of ownership of the insurance contracts." §6.19.3. On the other hand, it does not affect the validity of designating the trustee of a revocable trust as beneficiary of life insurance or pension benefits. Many states have statutes that expressly validate such designations.

A pour-over will and trust should contain coherent and coordinated directions regarding the tax issues, including the source from which death taxes should be paid. *See* §§4.27 and 12.41-12.49.3. Litigation may be required if there are inadequate or ambiguous provisions regarding taxes. *E.g.*, *Estate of Wathen*, 64 Cal. Rptr. 2d 805 (Cal. App. 1997) (the court admitted extrinsic evidence, including testimony of scrivener, in case of ambiguity); *Estate of Meyer*, 702 N.E.2d 1078 (Ind. App. 1998) (in case of conflict, directions in later instrument controls).

Form 10-2
Residuary Clause for Pour-Over Will

I give all of my property that is not effectively disposed of by the foregoing provisions of this will, excluding all property over which I hold a power of appointment (my "residuary estate"), to _____, trustee of the John Q. Client Revocable Trust dated _____as the terms of the trust exist at the time of my death, to be held and administered as a part of such trust. If for any reason the foregoing gift to [name of the trustee] is ineffective, I incorporate by reference the John Q. Client Revocable Trust, dated _____, as the same shall exist on the date of this will and I give my residuary estate to First Bank as trustee to be held and administered as part of such incorporated trust.

§10.11. CLAIMS OF CREDITORS AGAINST GRANTOR

The grantor's creditors can generally reach any beneficial interest the grantor retains in a revocable (or irrevocable) trust. This rule applies although the trust includes a spendthrift clause that purports to restrict the voluntary or involuntary transfer of the grantor's interests. Restatement (Third) of Trusts § 58 (2003); Uniform Trust Code § 505(a)(2) (2000). As indicted below, courts in several states have allowed creditors to reach the assets of revocable self-settled trusts after the grantor's death.

Power of Revocation. In the absence of a statute, most courts have concluded that the grantor's creditors cannot reach the assets of a revocable trust that was established for the benefit of others at a time when the grantor was solvent. *E.g., Guthrie v. Canty,* 53 N.E.2d 1009 (Mass. 1944); *Van Stewart v. Townsend,* 28 P.2d 999 (Wash. 1934). Of course, the creditors can reach the assets if the grantor revokes the trust and takes possession of them. Many states have statutes that allow the grantor's creditors to reach the assets of a revocable trust, including, Indiana and Kansas. Ind. Code Ann. § 30-1-9-14 (2011); Kan. Stat. Ann. § 58-2414 (2011).

Bankruptcy. Under § 70(a)(3) of the former Bankruptcy Act, the trustee in bankruptcy could exercise any power that the bankrupt could have exercised for his own benefit. The language of the Revised Bankruptcy Act (the "Bankruptcy Code"), adopted in 1978 and codified in Title 11, U.S.C. is less explicit on the point, but presumably the rule continues to apply. This conclusion is supported by a negative implication drawn from § 541(b)(1) of the Bankruptcy Code: "Property of the [debtor's] estate does not include any power that the debtor may only exercise solely for the benefit of an entity other than the debtor." 11 U.S.C. § 541(b)(1) (2000). Also, the leading treatise states that "[t]he same result would apply under the [Bankruptcy] Code." 5-541 Collier on Bankruptcy ¶ 541.19 (15th ed. rev. 2006).

General Power of Appointment. In some states creditors are allowed to reach property of a trust over which the grantor retained a general power of appointment. Others limit their reach to trusts in which the grantor also reserved a life interest. Where the grantor retained an inter vivos power that is exercisable in his or her own favor, the grantor's creditors should be able to reach the assets of the trust as the trustee in bankruptcy is permitted under the Bankruptcy Code.

It is uncertain whether creditors can reach the assets of a trust that was not created by the debtor but over which the debtor possesses a general power of appointment. One technique that might be helpful in circumventing the ability of creditors to reach trust assets was described in LR 200403094. In the ruling, Wife transfers title in all assets to Husband, who in turn conveys the assets to a revocable living trust. Wife is given a testamentary general power of appointment over trust assets should she predecease Husband. This power is exercisable to the extent of Wife's remaining exemption amount after factoring in lifetime taxable gifts and any other assets included in Wife's taxable estate. The ruling confirmed that the trust assets subject to Wife's general power of appointment are included in her gross estate and that Husband is deemed to make a gift to Wife equal to that portion of the trust assets subject to Wife's exercise of the power of appointment (though such gift qualifies for the unlimited marital deduction for federal gift tax purposes). Because Wife is not the grantor of the revocable trust, it is uncertain whether Wife's creditors could reach the assets remaining in the trust after Wife's exercise of the general power of appointment. The ruling does not address the asset protection issues associated with this arrangement, though asset protection might well explain why Husband and Wife entered into this complicated arrangement. As for the income tax basis issues associated with this arrangement, see §3.35.5.

Spouse's Elective Share. The extent to which the property of a revocable trust is subject to a surviving spouse's elective share varies according to the terms of the local law. Under U.P.C. §2-205(1)(i), property over which the decedent held a presently exercisable general power of revocation is included in the decedent's augmented estate. The New York law is to the same effect. N.Y. Est. Powers & Trusts Law §5-1.1(b)(1)(E) (2011) (applies to powers of revocation held by the decedent and any other person). In the absence of statute, the outcome may turn on whether the court determines that a particular transfer in trust is "illusory" or a "fraud on the surviving spouse." Some courts have held that the surviving spouse's elective right does not extend to property that the deceased spouse had transferred to an inter vivos revocable trust. *E.g., Soltis v. First of America Bank-Muskegon,* 513 N.W.2d 148 (Mich. App. 1994).

Other Creditors of a Deceased Grantor. The extent to which the grantor's creditors can reach the assets of a revocable trust following the grantor's death is uncertain in most jurisdictions. However, if the grantor retained a beneficial interest in the trust the creditors may be able to reach the assets.

> [W]here a person places property in trust and reserves the right to amend and revoke, or to direct disposition of principal and income, the settlor's creditors may, following the death of the settlor, reach in satisfaction of the settlor's debts to them, to the extent not satisfied by the settlor's estate, those assets owned by the trust over which the settlor had such control at the time of his death as would have enabled the settlor to use the trust assets for his own benefit. *State Street Bank & Trust Co. v. Reiser,* 389 N.E.2d 768,771 (Mass. App. 1979).

Under a common form of statute, a self-settled trust is void as to existing and future creditors of the grantor. For example, in *Johnson v. Commercial Bank,* 588 P.2d 1096 (Or. 1978), the court held that such a statute allowed a creditor to reach the assets of a trust in which the grantor retained a life income interest and a power of revocation. The Oregon statute applied in the *Johnson* case provided that,

> All deeds of gift, all conveyances and all verbal or written transfers of goods, chattels or things in action made in trust for the person making the same, are void as against the creditors, existing or subsequent of such person. 588 P.2d at 1098.

Creditors of the deceased grantor are allowed to reach the assets of a revocable trust in some cases. *E.g., Ackers v. First National Bank of Topeka,* 387 P.2d 840 (Kan. 1963), *on reh'g,* 389 P.2d 1 (1964), *and In re Matter of Granwell,* 228 N.E.2d 779 (N.Y.

1967) (creditors of the deceased grantor allowed to reach the assets of the grantor's revocable trust). The latter decision was based on New York law, under which the grantor of a revocable trust is considered to have retained ownership of the trust assets until death insofar as creditors are concerned.

The possibility that the assets of a revocable trust cannot be reached by the grantor's creditors following the grantor's death is cited by some planners as an additional advantage of establishing a revocable trust. The interposition of a trust between creditors and the grantor's property no doubt makes it more difficult for the creditors. However, a revocable trust generally does not completely insulate the property from the claims of creditors. Instead, the "advantage" may prove to be more costly if the trustee is required to engage in litigation after the grantor's death.

Federal tax liens against the settlor-trustee of trusts may be enforced to the extent he or she had the power to eliminate the other beneficiaries of the trust and treat the property of the trusts as his or her own. *Markham v. Fay,* 74 F.3d 1347 (1st Cir. 1996) (Massachusetts law). Relying on *State Street Bank & Trust Co. v. Reiser,* 389 N.E.2d 768 (Mass. App. Ct. 1979), and similar cases, the court reasoned that the property of a revocable trust was vulnerable to the claims of the settlor's creditors, including federal tax obligations.

The procedures that a deceased grantor's creditors must follow in pursuing a claim vary from state to state. In some states, a creditor must pursue a claim in an estate administration proceeding before attempting to recover from the trust. Some states allow a trustee to publish a notice to creditors, which may have the effect of shortening the otherwise applicable limitations period.

§ 10.12. PRINCIPAL ADVANTAGES OF REVOCABLE TRUSTS

Revocable trusts offer a number of nontax advantages both during the grantor's lifetime and thereafter. The principal lifetime advantages arise from the trustee's management of, or availability to manage, the trust property. Although the grantor may start out as trustee, a successor trustee can assume the responsibility for managing the trust property if the grantor resigns or becomes unable or unwilling to act as trustee. The trust can also serve as an important probate avoidance device for assets such as real estate located in states other than the state of the grantor's domicile.

Inexperienced or Absent Grantor. A revocable trust may be suitable to provide for the management of property that belongs to a client who lacks investment experience or confidence. In such a case, the grantor's responsibility for investment of the trust fund can be increased as he or she gains experience. A revocable trust may be a suitable vehicle for the management of assets to be received by an individual when he or she reaches the age for distribution of a custodianship or trust. The trustee's professional management of the trust property may also appeal to a client whose work, studies, or other activities will take him or her out of the country or otherwise make him or her unavailable for protracted periods.

Avoiding Guardianships. The establishment of a revocable trust is often especially attractive to older clients because the existence of the trust may obviate the necessity of having a guardian appointed if the grantor becomes incompetent or is otherwise unable or unwilling to manage property. By creating a trust the client can avoid the expense, complications, delays, and publicity of a guardianship proceeding. Also, the grantor is free to choose the trustee and successor trustees who will manage the property and make disbursements for his or her benefit in the event of disability or incompetency. Helping a client minimize the adverse effects of possibly becoming incompetent is an important function of estate planning. § 1.6.11.

The trust instrument should authorize the trustee to disburse funds to or for the benefit of the grantor at any time, including payment of the cost of providing for the grantor's care and support during any period he or she is disabled or incompetent. The trust may bar any amendment or revocation of the trust while the grantor is incompetent, or may allow certain changes to be made by his or her attorney-in-fact under a durable power of attorney. For this purpose the trust should define incompetency in a way that coordinates with the terms of any durable power of appointment executed by the grantor (*e.g.*, certification by two physicians, one of whom must be the grantor's attending physician, that the grantor is unable to understand and manage financial affairs unassisted).

A durable power of attorney (*see* § 4.35) may also obviate the necessity of a guardianship if the power is broad enough and a designated attorney-in-fact remains available to act for the principal. A trust offers more comprehensive protection and greater flexibility than a durable power of attorney. The devices can be coupled, however, to provide for the creation of a revocable trust if the principal becomes incompetent. Specifically, a durable power can authorize the attorney-in-fact to transfer the principal's property to the trustee of a revocable trust in the event of the principal's incapacity. Perhaps the surest method is to attach the form of the trust to be used to the durable power of attorney. *See* § 4.35.

Maintaining Ownership Characteristics of Grantors' Property. As indicated above, a revocable trust may be used to preserve the character of the property owned by a husband and wife, which is particularly important if they are moving between states with different marital property regimes. For example, for residents moving to a community property state, it may be important to prevent the inadvertent commingling of assets and loss of their separate identity. § 3.25. It may also be important to maintain the separate character and identity of property where the husband or wife, or both, have children by prior marriages.

A "Trial Run." A revocable trust allows the grantor to observe the operation of the trust and the conduct of the trustee during the grantor's lifetime. The trust can be left in place if the grantor is satisfied. In many instances a revocable trust serves as the grantor's principal estate planning instrument. If it is, the grantor's insurance is made payable to the trustee, and the grantor's other assets can be poured over into the trust. § 6.19.3. If the grantor is not satisfied with the operation of the trust or the conduct of the trustee, the grantor can amend or revoke the trust or change the trustee.

Avoiding Delays; Providing Continuity. When an individual dies, there is usually some unavoidable delay in the appointment of a personal representative and the management of his or her "owned" property. That property is subject to an estate administration proceeding, which in some states involves detailed court supervision, delays, and additional expenses. In contrast, property held in a revocable trust is not subject to administration. Accordingly, the assets of the trust may not be included in the base on which statutory fees are determined in the states whose laws provide for statutory fees for the grantor's personal representative or for the personal representative, or both.

The trustee may continue to invest and manage trust property without interruption following the death of the grantor. Thus, distributions of income and principal can continue to be made to the grantor's family. Subject to the liabilities of the trust for taxes, debts, expenses of administration, and the like, the trustee may also promptly distribute the assets of the trust. Of course, a trustee might be reluctant to make any large distributions soon after the grantor's death—the distribution of property would fix the alternate valuation date of any assets distributed and could subject the trustee to personal liability for the decedent's unpaid taxes. *See* § 12.15 and 12.49. The delays are minimized and the continuity is best if a person other than the grantor is serving as trustee at the time of the grantor's death.

In order to avoid unnecessary delays in filling the office of trustee, the trust should name at least one successor trustee. It is particularly important to do so where an individual is named as the initial trustee. Trusts frequently authorize the individual trustee or the adult beneficiaries of the trust to name a further successor trustee. Of course, if the trustee has discretion to make distributions, a beneficiary generally should not have the power to become successor trustee because of the potentially adverse income and estate tax consequences. *See* § 10.20.6.

Secrecy. A revocable trust may also appeal to a person who does not want the disposition of his or her property to be a matter of public record. A relatively high degree of secrecy can be maintained with respect to the content of an inter vivos trust. However, in some jurisdictions the public has access to the state death tax file for an individual decedent, which may include a copy of any revocable trusts created by the decedent. Also, the trustee may be asked to provide a copy of the trust to a stockbroker or transfer agent in order to transfer securities held in the trust. However, such a request may be satisfied without providing a copy of the trust if the lawyer provides the stockbroker with a letter stating that the trust was validly created and is revocable by the grantor.

Wills and other documents involved in the administration of an estate are matters of public record. The wills of prominent individuals may be reported by the press or made the subject of subsequent books. Some publications have routinely featured the "wills of the month."

Avoiding Ancillary Estate Administration Proceedings. In general, an estate administration proceeding must be conducted in each state in which a decedent owned real property. The necessity of conducting multiple proceedings can be avoided by transferring the properties to a revocable trust. Thus, a resident of California might transfer his or her condominium in Hawaii to a revocable trust. In order to facilitate disposition of the property the trustee should be given the power to sell or lease the property of the trust without court hearing or notice.

By using a trust, the grantor has some latitude in choosing the law that will apply to the construction and administration of the trust. The choice of law could have an important effect on the rights of creditors and the extent of a surviving spouse's right to claim an elective share of the grantor's property. *See* § 9.25.

Avoiding Court Supervision. In some states, testamentary trusts are subject to continuing court supervision, which may involve burdensome and expensive requirements to file annual reports and accounts with the court. A revocable trust is a noncourt trust that is generally not subject to those requirements either during or after the grantor's lifetime. In some circumstances it is beneficial for a trust to be treated as a "court trust" with prompt access to the court for instructions and settlement of disputes. However, the advantage of court trusts in this regard is slight. The court's jurisdiction over the parties concerned with a noncourt trust can usually be invoked by an action brought under the appropriate state's general declaratory judgments act, by another civil action, or by a judicial accounting proceeding.

Increased FDIC Insurance Coverage. According to the Federal Deposit Insurance Corporation, the insurance coverage available to revocable trusts is based upon the number of beneficiaries. According to information available on the FDIC website (www.myfdicinsurance.gov), neither a trust nor the trustee is treated as a beneficiary. For purposes of determining coverage, "The beneficiaries are the people or entities entitled to an interest in the trust when the last owner dies. Contingent or alternative trust beneficiaries are not considered to have an interest in the trust deposits and other assets as long as the primary or initial beneficiaries are still living, with the exception of revocable living trusts with a life estate interest." Thus, if a revocable trust created by a single grantor names three remainder beneficiaries, a total of $1 million will be covered ($250,000 for the grantor and each of the three remainder beneficiaries); the coverage is doubled if the trust were created by a husband and wife.

Not all of the advantages apply in every case. Nonetheless, a revocable trust often provides a client with the most satisfactory way of organizing and managing his or her property.

§10.13. Principal Disadvantages of Revocable Trusts

As a general rule the legal costs of preparing a revocable trust and a suitable pour-over will are somewhat higher than those for preparing a will that includes a comparable trust. The difference is traceable in part to the greater complexity of the revocable trust. It may also be due, at least in part, to the past tendency to draft wills and related documents as "loss leaders." The trustee's fees can also be a substantial additional cost, at least where there is a professional trustee. Subject to the 2 percent floor applicable to miscellaneous itemized deductions, the cost of establishing the trust is often deductible. More important, the costs of administering a trust that would not have been incurred if the property were not held in trust are deductible in computing the adjusted gross income of the trust (*i.e.*, the 2 percent floor does not apply to them). On the other hand, the cost of preparing a will is generally a nondeductible personal expense.

Two additional problems may arise if real property is transferred to a trust. First, title insurance coverage may be lost unless an endorsement is obtained from the insurer that extends coverage to the trustee. Second, if the property is subject to an encumbrance, the transfer may trigger a "due on sale" clause—which could require payment of the full amount of the indebtedness.

Returns and Recordkeeping. As described above, §10.4, an employer identification number is not required if the grantor is serving as trustee or cotrustee of a revocable trust. In such a case under Reg. §1.671-4(b) a Form 1041 is not filed. Instead, all items of income, deduction, and credit are reported on the grantor's individual income tax return.

In other cases, the trustee must obtain a taxpayer identification number for the trust. § 6109. Also, the trustee will be required to prepare a statement of the income, deductions, and credits of the trust although the income is all taxable to the grantor.

The assets of the trust should be transferred into the name of the trustee of the particular trust (*i.e.*, "*X*, as trustee under trust agreement dated March 1, 2000"). In order to handle receipts and disbursements of the trust, and to deal efficiently with the trust assets, it is generally necessary to open bank and brokerage accounts in the name of the trustee.

The trustee's fiduciary duties also require the assets of the trust to be segregated from other property and accounted for carefully. Accordingly, the trustee must keep accurate records of transactions affecting the trust. The overall accounting and bookkeeping requirements can be burdensome if performed by a family member as trustee, and an unexpected cost if performed by someone hired by the family member. Again, however, the costs are generally deductible under § 212. *See* § 1.24.

Miscellaneous. The transfer of property to a trust may also involve some other income tax disadvantages. The transfer of § 1244 stock to a trust may prevent a subsequent loss in the stock from qualifying as an ordinary deduction. Also, § 267 bars a deduction for a loss on a sale of trust property to a beneficiary. However, the transfer of property to a revocable trust will not trigger recapture of depreciation under § 1245 or 1250 or the recognition of gain on an installment sale under § 453B.

§ 10.14. Summary of Tax Consequences

A revocable living trust is generally created for other than tax reasons. The creation of the trust has almost no immediate tax consequences, and is generally neutral as to taxes for the long run. The income is taxed to the grantor so long as the grantor holds the power to revoke. On the estate tax side, the transfer of assets to the trust does not remove them from the grantor's gross estate. The power to revoke and also the retained life estate require this result. Transfers to a revocable trust do not involve a taxable gift because of the grantor's retained power of revocation. On the grantor's death such a trust can split into marital deduction and family trusts in order to minimize overall estate tax costs. However, such a function could be accomplished as well by a testamentary trust. In short, revocable living trusts do not enjoy any particular tax advantage over other methods of disposition.

§ 10.15. Income Tax

In general, the creation of a revocable trust has no significant income tax consequences during the grantor's lifetime. Because the trust is revocable, its income is fully taxed to the grantor under the grantor trust rules regardless of whether it is distributed or accumulated. *See* § 676. The transfer of property to a revocable trust generally does not constitute a taxable event or otherwise trigger the realization of gain. For example, the IRS has recognized that the transfer of an installment obligation to a revocable trust is not a "disposition" under § 453B. Rev. Rul. 74-613, 1974-2 C.B. 153 (applying the pre-1980 rules of former § 453(d)). In contrast, the transfer of an installment obligation to an irrevocable trust of which the grantor is not treated as the "owner" under §671 to 677 is a disposition that triggers recognition of gain. Rev. Rul. 76-530, 1976-2 C.B. 132.

Subject to the 2 percent floor of §67, the legal and accounting costs of establishing a revocable trust are usually deductible by the grantor under §212(2). Of course, the cost of operating the trust is deductible by the trust without regard to the 2 percent floor. *See* §10.4.7. The costs are not deductible to the extent they are attributable to tax-exempt income. §265.

On the negative side, if the trust holds all of the grantor's property, the grantor's estate is lost as a separate taxpayer. *See* §4.6.

The transfer of stock to a revocable trust does not impair the ability to redeem the stock under §303. Such a trust is an eligible stockholder of an S corporation during the grantor's lifetime and for two years following death. §10.4.14.

The transfer of stock to a revocable trust may cause it to lose its character as §1244 stock. §1244(d)(4). Accordingly, any loss subsequently realized on the stock may not be deductible as an ordinary loss.

Revocable trusts should be drawn to assure the availability of a step-up in basis for the entire community property upon the death of one spouse. §3.25, 3.26. In particular, revocable trusts that are intended to preserve the character of community property that is transferred to them should include provisions designed to support that result. Even without specific language, community property that is transferred to a revocable trust should retain its character. Statutes in some community property states are helpful in that regard. For example, Cal. Prob. Code §104.5 provides that, "Transfer of community and quasi-community property to a revocable trust shall be presumed to be an agreement, pursuant to Sections 100 and 101, that those assets retain their character in the aggregate for purposes of any division provided by the trust."

Election to Treat Revocable Trust as Part of Deceased Grantor's Estate, §645. The trustee of a decedent's "qualified revocable trust" and the decedent's personal representative may elect under §645, for the taxable years ending after the decedent's death and before the "applicable date," to treat the trust as part of the estate.

For purposes of §645, a qualified revocable trust (QRT) is one that the decedent is treated as owning under §676. §645(b)(1). This includes trusts that are treated as revocable by the decedent under §676 by reason of a power that was jointly exercisable by the decedent and a nonadverse party or by the decedent and his or her spouse. However, a trust that was treated as owned by the decedent under §676 solely by reason of a power held either by a nonadverse party or the decedent's spouse cannot qualify. Reg. §1.645-1(b)(1). Importantly, foreign trusts may qualify. However, information reporting under §6048 will continue to apply to foreign trusts.

The applicable date is a date two years after the decedent's death if no federal estate tax return is filed, otherwise a date six months after the date on which the decedent's final estate tax liability is determined. §645(b)(2). The election must be made not later than the time prescribed for filing the income tax return for the first taxable year of the estate, including extensions. §645(c). The requirements of an election are set forth in Reg. §1.645-1(c).

If an executor has been appointed for a decedent's estate, the executor and the trustee of the decedent's QRT must join in filing the Form 8855 (Election to Treat a Qualified Revocable Trust as Part of an Estate). If no executor has been appointed, the election is made by the trustee of each QRT that wishes to join in it. Reg.

§ 1.645-1(c)(2). Although a QRT and the grantor's estate may file a joint 1041, the trustee and the executor remain subject to separate responsibilities for filing the return and paying their respective share of the tax. The tax burden must be allocated between the trust and the estate in a manner that reasonably reflects its proportionate share of the tax. In addition, "Under the separate share rules of section 663(c), the electing trust and related estate are treated as separate shares for purposes of computing distributable net income (DNI) and in applying the distribution provisions of sections 661 and 662." Reg. § 1.645-1(e)(2)(iii).

The election period begins on the date of the decedent's death and ends on the "earlier of the day on which both the electing trust and related estate, if any, have distributed all of their assets, or the day before the applicable date." Reg. § 1.645-1(f)(1). For this purpose, the term "applicable date" depends upon whether a federal estate tax return is required to be filed. If no return is required, the applicable date is two years after the date of the decedent's death. If a return was required, "the applicable date is the later of the day that is two years after the date of the decedent's death, or the day that is 6 months after the date of final determination of liability for the estate tax." Reg. § 1.645-1(f)(2)(ii). In turn, the date of final determination of liability is the earliest of (1) the date that is six months after the issuance of a closing letter, (2) the date of final disposition of a claim for refund, unless suit is instituted within six months after a final disposition of the claim, (3) the date of execution of a settlement agreement with the IRS; (4) the date of issuance of a final judgment by a court determining the liability for the estate tax, and (5) the date of expiration of the period of limitations for assessment of the estate tax. Reg. § 1.645-1(f)(2).

Under Reg. § 1.663(c)-4(a), "a qualified revocable trust for which an election is made under section 645 is always a separate share of the estate and may itself contain two or more separate shares. Conversely, a gift or bequest of a specific sum of money or of property as defined in section 663(a)(1) is not a separate share."

§ 10.16. GIFT TAX

The transfer of property by the grantor to a revocable trust does not have any immediate gift tax consequences. Any gift provided for in the trust is incomplete at the time of transfer. Under Reg. § 25.2511-2(c), "A gift is incomplete in every instance in which a donor reserves the power to revest the beneficial title to the property in himself." A gift is also incomplete if the power of revocation is exercisable in conjunction with a person whose interests are not substantially adverse. Reg. § 25.2511-2(e). As noted above, the regulations require a gift tax return to be filed specifying the reasons the grantor of a trust believes the transfer is not taxable. Reg. § 25.2511-2(j), 25.6019-3(a). Filing a gift tax return to report an incomplete gift is not effective to commence the running of the period within which the IRS may assess gift tax with respect to such gift. Instead, the assessment period commences once the gift is complete. Reg. § 301.6501-1(f)(5).

The gifts provided for in a revocable trust become complete if the power to affect the beneficial enjoyment of the property is released or otherwise terminates during the grantor's lifetime. *Estate of Sanford v. Commissioner*, 308 U.S. 39 (1939); Reg. § 25.2511-2(f). However, the gifts probably do not become complete merely because the grantor becomes incompetent and may no longer validly exercise the power. In analogous cases, the tax consequences of a power are generally determined without reference to the legal capacity of its holder. *See* § 5.22.3. *See also* Rev. Rul. 75-350, 1975-2 C.B. 366. A gift, of course, takes place when trust property is distributed to a person other than the grantor.

EXAMPLE 10-7.

T transferred Blackacre to the trustee of a revocable trust under which the income is payable to T for life. Upon T's death the corpus is distributable to T's children, A, B, and C. The transfer of Blackacre to the trust did not constitute a completed gift. However, any distribution of property from the trust to any person other than T during T's lifetime would constitute a completed gift. Also, the gift of the remainder interest to A, B, and C will become complete if T releases the power of revocation and does not retain any other power to affect the beneficial enjoyment of the trust.

§ 10.17. ESTATE TAX

The transfer of property to a revocable trust is largely unimportant insofar as the grantor's estate tax liability is concerned. The property of the trust is includible in the grantor's gross estate under § 2036(a)(2) and 2038(a)(1). Note that under both sections the property of the trust is includible in the grantor's estate if the power to revoke is exercisable by the grantor alone or in conjunction with any other person. The alternate valuation date election is available with respect to property held in a revocable trust. *See* § 2032. For alternate valuation date purposes, the division of the assets of a formerly revocable trust into separate trusts upon the death of the grantor constitutes a distribution. *See* Rev. Rul. 73-97, 1973-1 C.B. 404. *See also* § 12.15.

Prior to 1997, the IRS had ruled that a decedent's gross estate included any transfers made from revocable trusts within three years of the grantor's death. This position was based upon its literal reading of former § 2035(d)(2). That provision required the inclusion of property "which is included in the value of the gross estate under section 2036, 2037, 2038, or 2042 or would have been included under any of those sections if such interest had been retained by the decedent." Because of the retained power to revoke, the IRS concluded that the property of a revocable trust is includible in the grantor's gross estate under § 2036 or 2038. LRs 8609005 (TAM), 9117003 (TAM), and 9139002 (TAM). Today, § 2035(e) makes it clear, both for purposes of § 2035's three-year rule and for purposes of § 2038 generally, that transfers made from a revocable trust (*i.e.,* one of which the decedent was treated as the owner under § 676) are treated as transfers "made directly by the decedent." This assumption effectively eliminates the potential inclusion of transfers made from revocable trusts within three years of the grantor's death.

Deductions are allowable for funeral expenses, debts, claims, and administration expenses actually paid from the property of the trust before the expiration of the period of limitation for assessment provided in § 6501 (three years after the estate tax return is filed). § 2053(b). Also, deductions are allowable for qualifying charitable transfers, § 2055, and transfers to a surviving spouse, § 2056.

C. PLANNING THE BENEFICIARY'S INTERESTS IN AN IRREVOCABLE TRUST

§10.18. SCOPE

This part is concerned with planning and drafting the powers and interests of a beneficiary of an irrevocable trust. The material is generally applicable to irrevocable trusts, including testamentary trusts and trusts that begin life as revocable trusts. Issues regarding the grantor's powers and interests in irrevocable trusts are discussed in more detail in Part D. While some nontax considerations are mentioned, this part is primarily concerned with the federal tax consequences of giving the beneficiary certain important interests or powers. The coverage ranges from sections concerning multiple trusts and the mandatory or discretionary distribution of income to ones concerning the consequences of giving the beneficiary general or special powers of appointment and the appointment of the beneficiary as trustee.

Incentive or Discretionary Trusts? On the nontax side, careful consideration should be given to the directions given regarding distributions to the beneficiaries. Limiting the amount and purpose of distributions can prevent a trust from providing the beneficiaries with the assistance they need. The risk is particularly high with "incentive trusts" of some types. Published reports indicate that some individuals have established trusts that limit distributions to certain benchmarks such as the amount of the beneficiary's annual earnings, the amount by which a beneficiary's income increases over a prior year, or the amount of the beneficiary's charitable contributions are unwise. Limits of that type may inappropriately discourage, or penalize, a beneficiary who is a school teacher, a public service employee, or in another occupation with relatively low pay scales. The trustor's goals might better be achieved if the trustee of such a trust were also given broad discretion to encourage and assist the beneficiary in achieving broadly worthwhile goals.

A trust can, in effect, give an independent trustee the same broad power to make distributions that the trustor enjoys with respect to his or her own property. A trust, for example, might give the trustee discretion to distribute so much of the income and principal as the trustee believes reasonable and appropriate to enable and encourage the beneficiary to (a) continue, formally and informally, his or her education, (b) become financially independent, (c) participate in activities of charitable organizations and make contributions to them, (d) develop and maintain contacts with other family members, and (e) be a responsible citizen and participate in civic life. A trust might also direct the trustee to provide the beneficiary with the financial assistance the trustee believes is appropriate to permit the beneficiary to purchase a residence, form or acquire and interest in a business venture, or to engage in other activities that the trustee reasonably believes will assist the beneficiary in living a full, meaningful life. Some issues relating to the use of incentives are reviewed in Hodgman & Stetter, *Can Incentive Trusts Encourage Children to Behave Responsibly?*, 27 Est. Plan. 459 (Dec. 2000).

Beneficiaries Must be Real. A deceased person cannot be the beneficiary of a trust. An attempt to create a trust for a deceased person fails. In *Estate of Stratton*, 674 A.2d 1281 (Vt. 1996), the court held that a trust was not created when a father opened a bank account in his name as trustee for a daughter, who he knew was then deceased. The court held that the father's estate included that account and a similar one that was created during his daughter's lifetime. The daughter's interest in the latter account terminated on her death.

§ 10.19. MULTIPLE TRUSTS

The steeply progressive income tax rates applicable to estates and trusts have seriously diminished the income tax advantage of creating multiple trusts. The repeal of the throwback rules, § 665-667, as to most domestic trusts and the repeal of § 644, do not offset that disadvantage.

In earlier days multiple accumulation trusts were frequently used to decrease a family's overall income tax liability by proliferating the number of separate taxpayers among whom income could be divided for tax purposes. Prior to 1969 the utility of accumulation trusts was based in large measure on rather broad exceptions to the throwback rules. For example, the rules did not apply to capital gains, to income accumulated more than five years prior to the current distribution, or where there had not been an addition to the trust for more than nine years. The advantage of using multiple trusts, of course, depended on recognition of the trusts as separate taxpayers. As noted above in § 10.4, trusts that are administered separately have a good chance of being recognized by the courts as separate for income tax purposes.

§ 10.20. UNITRUST, MANDATORY, OR DISCRETIONARY DISTRIBUTIONS?

The distributive provisions of each trust must be planned in light of the grantor's goals, the purposes of the trust, the circumstances of the beneficiaries and the provisions of the governing law. Traditionally most trusts have directed either the mandatory distribution of income to the beneficiary (which is, of course, required in order to qualify for the marital deduction under § 2056(b)) or the discretionary distribution of income. In either case flexibility was sometimes added by giving the beneficiary a limited power to withdraw principal and giving the trustee the discretionary power to distribute principal. Often, however, the distributive provisions of trusts were far too rigid—permitting only distributions of net income to the current beneficiary and not giving the trustee discretion to make any additional distributions.

One of the most important decisions is the extent to which the trustee should be given discretionary authority to distribute income and principal. In the past trusts were too often entirely rigid—typically allowing only the net annual income to be distributed to the current beneficiary. It is generally preferable to give the trustee discretion to accumulate income or to "sprinkle" income among several beneficiaries and to distribute principal among them.

In some cases a trust that simply provides for the distribution of current income alone may meet the needs of the income beneficiaries and remaindermen. Often such a trust is too inflexible to meet the beneficiaries' overall, long-range tax and nontax needs. In particular, the mandatory distribution of all of the income to one income beneficiary may provide the beneficiary with too little or too much income. The danger of receiving too little in the way of income is most serious.

Mandatory distributions of income may also swell the beneficiary's estate, which could cause the imposition of an otherwise avoidable estate tax bite. If there are multiple current beneficiaries, the flexibility of a trust is enhanced and some income tax savings may be possible if the trustee is given discretion to distribute income among several beneficiaries and to accumulate undistributed income and add it to principal.

A trust that gives the trustee broad discretion to distribute income and principal among the beneficiaries will often best provide for the beneficiaries. Of course, a trust that can accumulate income does not qualify for the marital deduction unless it is in the form of an estate trust. §5.21. It may be prudent to allow the trustee to make distributions for the benefit of skip persons (*e.g.*, the transferor's grandchildren) that are not treated as generation-skipping transfers. §2.42.3. A trust's direct payment of tuition and medical costs is not a generation-skipping transfer. §2611(b)(1).

A discretionary trust is generally also the preferred way to provide supplemental benefits for a beneficiary who is, or may become, the recipient of publicly provided care or benefits. Such a trust is intended to enable the beneficiary to receive public welfare benefits without disqualifying the beneficiary and without subjecting the trust assets to reimbursing the public entity.

From the beneficiary's point of view a trust in which distributions are subject to the exercise of discretion by another person is less satisfactory than one that provides for mandatory distributions. However, the potential for conflict between the beneficiary and trustee is reduced if the trustee communicates frequently and effectively with the beneficiary regarding the needs of the beneficiary, the status of the trust, and the trustee's plans for making distributions. The security of the beneficiary is also enhanced if he or she holds a limited power to withdraw trust assets, such as a "5 or 5" power of withdrawal (*i.e.*, the noncumulative power to withdraw each year the greater of $5,000 or 5 percent of the value of the trust property). *See* §10.24.

The indefiniteness of the beneficiary's interest in a discretionary trust generally prevents the beneficiary from transferring his or her interest. The indefiniteness of the interest also precludes the allowance of a previously taxed property credit to the beneficiary's estate for the estate tax paid in the grantor's estate. *See* §2013. As stated in Rev. Rul. 67-53, 1967-1 C.B. 265:

> Where a trustee possesses the power, in his or her absolute and uncontrolled discretion, to pay out net income to the income beneficiary of a trust or to accumulate such income, the beneficiary's interest cannot be valued according to recognized valuation principles as of the date of the transferor's death. Therefore, notwithstanding the fact that such income was actually paid to the decedent-transferee, the credit for tax on prior transfers under section 2013 of the Code is not allowable with respect to such an interest.

In contrast, a noncumulative power to withdraw the greater of $5,000 or 5 percent of the value of the trust property qualifies as property for purposes of the credit for tax on prior transfers to the extent of the value of the power on the date of the first decedent's death. Rev. Rul. 79-211, 1979-2 C.B. 319.

§ 10.20.4. Powers Limited by an Ascertainable Standard, § 674(d)

A trustee, other than the grantor or a spouse living with the grantor, can hold a power to "distribute, apportion, or accumulate income for a beneficiary or beneficiaries or to, for, or within a class of beneficiaries" without making the grantor the deemed owner of the trust for income tax purposes if the power is limited by a reasonably definite external standard set forth in the trust instrument. § 674(d). Under § 674(d), a power is within the exception whether or not the conditions of § 674(b)(6) or (7) are satisfied. Thus, the power over income may be exercised by the trustee without regard to the age or competency of the beneficiaries or the ultimate disposition of the income or corpus. The powers permitted by this exception are very helpful where one seeks to avoid grantor trust treatment but the requirements of § 674(c) cannot be met (*e.g.*, the trustee is not independent), or the grantor does not wish to give the trustee broader discretion. The power is particularly appropriate where the trust will last beyond the minority of multiple beneficiaries, some of whom may need more income than others to provide for education, support, medical care, or emergency expenses. Reg. § 1.674(b)-1(b)(5) describes powers that are limited by reasonably definite external standards in the following passage:

> It is not required that the standard consist of the needs and circumstances of the beneficiary. A clearly measurable standard under which the holder of a power is legally accountable is deemed a reasonably definite standard for this purpose. For instance, a power to distribute [income] for the education, support, maintenance, or health of the beneficiary; for his reasonable support and comfort; or to enable him to maintain his accustomed standard of living; or to meet an emergency, would be limited by an ascertainable standard. However, a power to distribute [income] for the pleasure, desire, or happiness of a beneficiary is not limited by a reasonably definite standard.

As in the case of § 674(c), the exception in § 674(a) does not apply if any person has a power to add beneficiaries, except where the power is limited to providing for after-born or after-adopted children.

Unless the grantor wishes to be treated as the owner of a trust, it should not include a provision that might prevent judicial review of the trustee's actions regarding distributions made in accordance with an ascertainable standard. Such a provision may cause the grantor to be treated as the owner of the trust. Under the regulations a power is not limited by an ascertainable standard if the "trust instrument provides that the determination of the trustee shall be conclusive with respect to the exercise or nonexercise of a power." Reg. § 1.674(b)-1(b)(5); Reg. § 1.674(d)-1.

The retention of a power to make distributions of trust property limited by an ascertainable standard does not cause the property to be included in the grantor's gross estate. *See* § 10.34.1.

§ 10.20.5. "Absolute" or "Uncontrolled" Discretion

A trust may provide that the trustee's discretion shall be "absolute," "unlimited," or "uncontrolled." Whether it should is another matter. Such a provision generally does not insulate the trustee's conduct from all court review, but it severely limits the court's supervisory role. According to the Restatement, in such a case the court will not consider whether the trustee acted beyond the bounds of reasonable judgment. Rather, the court will only consider whether the trustee acted in a state of mind contemplated by the trustor. Restatement (Third) of Trusts § 50, comment c (2003). Thus, a court's inquiry might be limited to determining whether the trustee acted arbitrarily or dishonestly. Because of the restricted review and reduced protection for the beneficiaries, it is generally undesirable to give the trustee such broad and unfettered discretion. In addition, the inclusion of such a provision may negate the effect of an ascertainable standard and cause the grantor to be treated as owner of the trust. *See* § 10.20.4.

§ 10.20.6. Standards to Guide the Exercise of Discretion

It is helpful to the trustee and beneficiaries if the trust provides some guidance regarding the manner in which discretion should be exercised in making distributions. *See* Halbach, Problems of Discretion in Discretionary Trusts, 61 Colum. L. Rev. 1425 (1961). A trust might include, for example, a statement of the primary and secondary purposes of the trust. In addition, the trust could indicate whether priority should be given to one or another of the beneficiaries. For example, when it comes to making distributions of principal, the trustee is helped by an indication that the grantor was primarily (or secondarily) concerned with the needs of the current beneficiaries as opposed to the preservation of principal for the remaindermen. A client might also wish to authorize the trustee to make distributions that would allow a beneficiary to buy a residence, finance the acquisition of a business or equipment, or facilitate or encourage particular activities by the beneficiary.

The trust should also indicate the extent to which the resources or income of the beneficiaries should be taken into account in making a decision regarding distributions. A provision may require the trustee to consider the beneficiary's resources (or income), authorize the trustee to consider them, or direct the trustee to disregard them. In most instances it is appropriate to provide that the trustee should consider them to the extent known to him or her.

§ 10.20.7. Transferability of the Beneficiary's Interest in a Discretionary Trust

In the case of a discretionary trust other than a self settled trust, a transferee or creditor of the beneficiary cannot force the trustee to make any payments of income or principal. Restatement (Third) of Trusts § 60, comment e (2003). *See also* Uniform Trust Code § 502(c). However, this rule only applies where the trustee has uncontrolled discretion to pay the income or principal of the trust to the beneficiary. Neither a transferee nor a creditor can require the discretion to be exercised in favor of making a payment. A transferee or creditor is generally entitled to the benefit of any payment the trustee decides to make unless the trust includes a valid restraint on alienation. *Id.* Thus, "[a] trustee who knows of an assignment and nevertheless distributes trust funds to the original beneficiary is personally liable to the transferee in the absence of a valid spendthrift . . . or complete forfeiture . . . provision." *Id.* at comment b.

The same general rule applies to the interest of a beneficiary in a trust that gives the trustee the discretion to make payments to a group of beneficiaries. Neither a beneficiary nor a transferee, or creditor of a beneficiary, can force the trustee to make any payment. However, the trustee may be liable if a payment is made to a beneficiary after the trustee receives notice that the interest of the beneficiary has been assigned. *Id.* at comment d.

§10.20.8. Discretionary Distribution Form

A provision authorizing discretionary distributions could be expressed in a variety of ways. The following represents one possible approach to the challenge of drafting the basic provision. The provision could be expanded to cover related matters, such as the extent to which unequal distributions of principal or income are to be taken into account upon a final distribution of the trust.

Form 10-3
Discretionary Distributions

Distributions. The trustee shall distribute so much of the income and principal of the trust to or for the benefit of my surviving spouse and issue as the trustee believes is desirable to provide for the comfortable support, maintenance, education, health, and general welfare of each of them. The trustee is authorized to make distributions to one or more of them in unequal amounts and to exclude one or more of the others of them from such distributions. In making decisions regarding distributions, the trustee shall give: (1) primary consideration to the needs of my surviving spouse and secondary consideration to the needs of all others, and (2) such consideration as the trustee deems appropriate to the resources and income that are reasonably available to each beneficiary apart from the beneficiary's interest in this trust.

§10.21. Spendthrift Clauses—Restricting the Transfer of a Beneficiary's Interests

In the absence of a restriction imposed by the trust, the equitable interests of a beneficiary in the income and principal of an ordinary trust are freely alienable and may be reached by the beneficiary's creditors. Most states, however, recognize "spendthrift clauses" that restrict the right of a beneficiary to transfer an interest in the income or principal of a trust. Restatement (Third) of Trusts §58 (2003), Uniform Trust Code §502(c), 504(b) (2000). For example, Cal. Prob. Code §15300 (2011) provides, with some exceptions, that "if the trust instrument provides that a beneficiary's interest in income is not subject to voluntary or involuntary transfer, the beneficiary's interest in income under the trust may not be transferred and is not subject to enforcement of a money judgment until paid to the beneficiary." Spendthrift clauses are not recognized in England and in a small minority of American states. Scott, Fratcher & Ascher, 2 Scott and Ascher on Trusts § 9.3.11 at 515 (5th ed. 2006).

A spendthrift trust is one in which the beneficiary is expressly unable, whether by the trust instrument or applicable law, to transfer the right to future payments of income or capital and whose creditors are unable to subject the beneficiary's interest to the payment of their claims. Such a trust does not involve any restraint on alienability or creditor's rights with respect to property after it is received by the beneficiary from the trustee, but rather merely a restraint with regard to his rights to future payments under the trust.

The planner should advise a prospective grantor regarding the effect of including or excluding a spendthrift clause. The inclusion of a spendthrift clause is effective in most states to prevent the beneficiary from making any gift or sale of an interest in income or principal. For example, such a clause might prevent an immature beneficiary from transferring an interest to a religious cult, making an unwise sale of the interest, or otherwise dissipating the trust fund. A spendthrift clause is also usually effective to insulate the trust assets from the claims of most creditors, although many states allow the beneficiary's interests to be reached by certain preferred creditors including: (1) a former spouse or dependents for support in accordance with a court order, (2) creditors who provide the beneficiary with the necessities of life, and (3) the United States, with respect to tax liens and other claims arising by statute. *See* Restatement (Third) of Trusts § 59 (2003), Uniform Trust Code § 503(b) (2000).

A majority of courts do not allow tort judgment creditors of a spendthrift trust's beneficiary to obtain any recovery from a spendthrift trust that was not established by the beneficiary himself or herself. For example, in *Duvall v. McGee*, 826 A.2d 416 (Md. App. 2003), the court affirmed summary judgment that had been granted to the trustee of a spendthrift trust, which had been established by the beneficiary's mother. The beneficiary had been convicted of the felony murder of the victim, whose estate was the principal claimant. According to the court, the victim's estate was simply another judgment creditor, to whom the trustee owed no special duties. The opinion in *Duvall* does acknowledge that a minority of states allow recovery against spendthrift trusts on behalf of victims of intentional or gross negligence torts, citing, inter alia, *Sligh v. First National Bank*, 704 So. 2d 1020 (Miss. 1997).

The inclusion of a spendthrift clause reduces the beneficiary's flexibility in dealing with interests in a trust. Thus, the clause prevents an income beneficiary from assigning his or her income interest to another person. Such a restriction could prevent the family from making a beneficial reallocation of the income within the family in order to reduce the overall income tax burden. However, a spendthrift clause generally does not prevent a beneficiary from disclaiming an interest in the trust. Many disclaimer statutes specifically provide that a beneficiary may disclaim an interest whether or not it is subject to a spendthrift provision or similar restriction. *E.g.*, U.P.C. § 2-1105(a); Cal. Prob. Code § 286 (2011); Wash. Rev. Code § 11.86.061 (2011).

§ 10.21.1. Form of Spendthrift Clause

A short form of spendthrift clause of the following type is adequate for most purposes:

Form 10-4
Spendthrift Clause

No interest of a beneficiary in the principal or income of this trust may be anticipated, assigned or encumbered, or subjected to any creditor's claim or legal process prior to its actual distribution to the beneficiary.

A more detailed clause may require the trustee to pay the income or principal directly to or for the benefit of the beneficiary and not upon any written or oral direction or assignment by the beneficiary. Even if the trust prohibits the beneficiary from transferring the interest, the beneficiary may validly direct the trustee to distribute the interest in the trust to another person. In such case the beneficiary's direction is recognized as a revocable authorization to pay. Restatement (Third) of Trusts, § 58, comment d(1) (2003). *See also* Uniform Trust Code § 502, Comment (2000).

Planners should be aware of the extent to which the governing law exempts interests in trusts from the claims of creditors and the extent to which grantors can further restrict the voluntary or involuntary alienation of a beneficiary's interest. Many clients believe that a beneficiary's interest in a trust should be insulated from the beneficiary's own inexperience or imprudence. Their trusts should include provisions that prevent any voluntary or involuntary transfers of the beneficiary's interests in the trust.

§ 10.21.2. Self-Settled Trusts

An owner of property generally cannot insulate it from the reach of existing or subsequent creditors by transferring it to a trust of which the owner is a beneficiary. *See In re Brooks,* 217 Bank. Rptr. 98 (D. Conn. 1998) (trust is subject to this rule where property transferred through settlor's spouse to trusts subject to the laws of Bermuda and The Channel Islands). On the contrary, the beneficial interest of the owner in such a trust generally is transferable and reachable by the owner's creditors. Restatement (Third) of Trusts § 58(2) (2003); Uniform Trust Code § 505(a)(2) (2000); Scott, Fratcher & Ascher, 2 Scott and Ascher on Trusts § 12.3 at 705 (5th ed. 2006). Indeed, many states have statutes under which transfers in trust for the use of the transferor are void as to existing or future creditors. No gift occurs if the property of the trust can be reached by the grantor's creditors. *Commissioner v. Vander Weele,* 254 F.2d 895 (6th Cir. 1958).

There is some concern that giving the beneficiary of a spendthrift trust a *Crummey* power (*see* § 7.38) might convert the trust into a self-settled trust because of the beneficiary's power to access trust principal. In response to this concern, some states have adopted statutes providing that a beneficiary of a spendthrift trust is not considered a grantor of the trust simply by possessing a *Crummey* power. The Texas statute, for example, states that "[a] beneficiary of the trust may not be considered a settlor merely because of a lapse, waiver, or release of the beneficiary's right to withdraw a part of the trust property if the value of the property that could have been withdrawn by exercising the right of withdrawal in any calendar year does not exceed at the time of the lapse, waiver, or release the greater of the amount specified in (1) Section 2041(b)(2) or 2514(e), Internal Revenue Code of 1986; or (2) Section 2503(b), Internal Revenue Code of 1986." Tex. Prop. Code § 112.035(e) (2011).

The identity of the grantor and the extent of the grantor's interests are also important for federal gift and estate tax purposes. The reciprocal trust doctrine is sometimes applied to determine the true identity of the grantor of trusts established at the same time by related taxpayers for the benefit of each other. The doctrine is explained at § 6.29. By applying the doctrine, the trusts are "uncrossed" with the result that the beneficiary of each trust is treated as its grantor. Accordingly, the trust assets may be fully includible in the beneficiary's estate under § 2036 or 2038.

The transfer of property to an irrevocable trust nominally for the benefit of others is an incomplete gift if the assets of the trust are subject to the claims of the grantor's creditors whenever the claims arise. In Rev. Rul. 76-103, 1976-1 C.B. 293, state law provided that the property of a trust with respect to which the trustee had the absolute discretion to distribute income and principal to the grantor was subject to the claims of the grantor's creditors. Accordingly, the transfer to the trust was incomplete for gift tax purposes and the trust property was includible in the grantor's estate because of the grantor's "retained power to, in effect, terminate the trust by relegating the grantor's creditors to the entire property of the trust." The same result was reached in LR 199917001 (California law).

§ 10.22. GENERAL POWERS OF APPOINTMENT

"The term 'general power of appointment' means a power which is exercisable in favor of the decedent, his estate, his creditors, or the creditors of his estate . . . ." § 2041(b)(1). A general power of appointment is the antithesis of a spendthrift restraint. Powers that might be characterized as general powers of appointment under § 2041 and 2514 should seldom be conferred, except as required to qualify for a specific tax benefit such as the marital deduction under § 2056(b)(5) or causing the power-holder to become the transferor of the subject property for GSTT purposes.

General powers of appointment are usually avoided because of their potentially adverse income, gift, and estate tax consequences for the holder: The income from property subject to a presently exercisable general power is taxable to the holder under § 678 unless the grantor is treated as owner of the trust; the exercise or lapse of a general power often results in a taxable gift under § 2514; and property subject to a general power is includible in the power-holder's estate under § 2041. Also, the grantor may not want to confer such a broad power of disposition on another person—a special power of appointment may provide sufficient flexibility.

The statutory definition of a general power of appointment is broad and encompasses "all powers which are in substance and effect powers of appointment regardless of the nomenclature used in creating the power and regardless of local property law connotations." Reg. § 20.2041-1(b)(1). Importantly, the definition extends to powers held in a fiduciary capacity, and to joint powers, with the exception of joint powers held with either the creator of the power or a party whose interest that would be adversely affected by an exercise of the power, § 2041(b)(1)(C)(i), (ii). *See* § 10.26.

A power of invasion that is not measured by an ascertainable standard relating to the health, education, maintenance, or support of the power holder is a general power of appointment. Thus, a power holder's estate is required to include property subject to a power of invasion unless the power is limited by such an ascertainable standard. As noted above, inclusion is required even though the power is jointly held by the decedent and a non-adverse party. In *Estate of Vissering v. United States*, 990 F.2d 578 (10th Cir. 1993), the Tenth Circuit held that under Florida law a joint power to invade principal "for the continued comfort, support, maintenance, or education" of the power holder was not a general power of appointment. According to the court the standard imposed was indistinguishable from the examples in the regulations that were deemed to be subject to ascertainable standards. *See* Reg. § 20.2041-1(c)(2).

A trustee's power to distribute income among the members of a class that includes the trustee is a general power of appointment over the income. Also, the property of a trust is includible in the beneficiary's estate where the beneficiary and two other persons hold the power, as trustees, to terminate the trust and distribute the trust property to the beneficiary. *Maytag v. United States*, 493 F.2d 995 (10th Cir. 1974). If the trustee has discretion to make distributions to the beneficiary, the beneficiary should not have the power to remove the trustee and become successor trustee, unless the beneficiary is barred from participating in the exercise of the discretionary powers. A person who has the power to become trustee is treated as having all of the powers of the trustee. Reg. § 20.2041-1(b)(1).

State Limits on Trustee's Exercise of Power. The IRS will recognize the effect of a state statute that bars a trustee from exercising a discretionary power to distribute income or principal to himself or herself. *E.g.,* LR 200014002 (TAM) (Missouri law). The TAM is based on Rev. Rul. 54-153, 1954-1 C.B. 185, which gave effect to a New York state law that provided, "A power, vested in a person in his capacity as trustee of an express trust, to distribute principal to himself cannot be exercised by him; if the power is vested in two or more trustees it may be exercised by the trustee or trustees who are not so disqualified; if there is no trustee qualified to execute the power, its execution devolves on the supreme court . . . ."

In some cases the conferral of a general power of appointment carries tax benefits that outweigh the potential disadvantages. Thus, the beneficiaries of a permanent irrevocable trust may be given *Crummey* withdrawal powers so the gift tax annual exclusion will be available with respect to property transferred to the trust. *See* § 7.38. Giving a beneficiary a power that will require the trust to be included in his or her estate is sometimes done in order to support an increase in the basis of the assets of the trust under § 1014. Thus, the power-holder and a nonadverse party might be given the power to terminate the trust and distribute the trust assets to the power-holder. Allowing the trustee to grant a general power of appointment to a beneficiary can be used in order to change the transferor of the trust for GSTT purposes to the holder of the power. *See* § 2.32, 2.41.8.

Property subject to a general power of appointment that is exercisable at the time of the power-holder's death is includible under § 2041(a)(2). However, as stated in Reg. § 20.2041-3(b), "a power which by its terms is exercisable only upon the occurrence during the decedent's lifetime of an event or contingency which did not in fact take place during such time is not a power in existence at the time of the decedent's death." Accordingly, in LR 9141027 the IRS ruled that a general power that was exercisable only in the event the grantor and the power-holder divorced or legally separated would not require inclusion if they were not divorced or separated at the time of the power-holder's death. *See also* Rev. Rul. 80-255, 1980-2 C.B. 272; § 6.28.3.

Unauthorized distributions made from a trust over which the deceased beneficiary held a general power of appointment are includible in the beneficiary's gross estate under § 2041. LR 9337001 (Oregon law). The decedent was the sole beneficiary of the trust for her lifetime, during which the trustee was authorized, after consultation with her, to distribute principal to her, for her "care, support, maintenance, and comforts." After consultation with her the trustee made distributions that did not exceed the amount of the allowable gift tax exclusions to members of her family and to trusts for their benefit.

In LR 9805025, the IRS recognized the effect of a local court order that reformed a testamentary power of appointment over a credit shelter trust that the decedent's will gave to his surviving spouse. The IRS accepted the court's finding deleting a power to appoint to a class that included "the estate of his surviving spouse" which was included due to a scrivener's error. Similarly, in LR 9743033 the IRS held that it would recognize a state court reformation which would correct a scrivener's error. As executed, the instrument gave the beneficiary a power to appoint to "persons other than the grantor, the grantor's estate, creditors of the grantor or the grantor's estate." According to the evidence, the scrivener was directed to draft the instrument to preclude the beneficiary from making such appointments. Other rulings similarly recognize the effect of court orders that reduce the scope of a general power of appointment that was erroneously created due to a typographical or scrivener's error. *E.g.,* LR 199936029.

Precatory Language. The beneficiary of a testamentary trust created by her aunt did not hold a general power of appointment over the trust by reason of a clause in the will which stated that the testator would have preferred leaving the property outright to her niece, "but in view of potential benefits to her and to her estate and beneficiaries, I leave the matter on a discretionary basis with the trustee, but I am desirous that the same [corpus] be paid and distributed to her in accord with her wishes." LR 9722001 (TAM) (Indiana law). In light of the Indiana law, the statement was considered to be precatory and not binding on the trustee.

§ 10.23. SPECIAL POWERS OF APPOINTMENT

A client's plan can be made more flexible by giving the current beneficiary of the trust a special testamentary power of appointment over the income or principal. For example, a surviving spouse may be given a testamentary special power to appoint the trust assets to and among the trustor's descendants rather than requiring a fixed method of distribution. In such a case the exercise of the power would not cause the trust to be included in the surviving spouse's estate. In order to avoid inclusion of the trust property in the beneficiary's estate, the power should expressly prohibit an appointment in favor of the beneficiary, "his estate, his creditors, or the creditors of his estate." § 2041(b)(1). A trust beneficiary's powers to withdraw an amount of property from a trust that is necessary to provide for his "health and maintenance in reasonable comfort" and to appoint the trust corpus among his wife's descendants are not general powers of appointment. LR 200130030. In addition, the ruling held that for estate tax purposes the power-holder was not treated as having transferred any property to the trust, although for gift tax purposes, he was treated as transferor of half of the property by reason of split-gift elections he made with respect to gifts his wife made to the trust.

The exercise of a special power of appointment over a GSTT-exempt trust is not subject to the estate tax or the GSTT. LR 200219034.

A power is more flexible if it is exercisable during the beneficiary's lifetime. However, it is more common to create powers that are only exercisable upon the beneficiary's death (*i.e.*, a testamentary power). Such a limitation helps preserve the trust property during the beneficiary's lifetime and insulates the beneficiary from pressure by permissible appointees to exercise the power currently in their favor. Limiting the power to an exercise at death also eliminates the risk that the power might be characterized as a general power where it is exercisable in favor of persons for whom the power-holder has a lifetime legal obligation to support. *See* Reg. § 20.2041-1(c). On the other hand, giving the beneficiary a currently exercisable power allows greater flexibility in meeting the economic and estate planning objectives of the family group. Thus, the holder may appoint trust property to family members in lieu of transferring "owned" property to the appointee. The appointment of trust corpus pursuant to a special power of appointment does not constitute a gift of the corpus. § 2514(b), (c).

Appointment Can Result in Gift. If the power-holder is entitled to receive the income of the trust for life, a lifetime appointment of any portion of the trust corpus to another person may constitute a gift of a proportionate part of the holder's income interest. Reg. § 25.2514-1(b)(2); Rev. Rul. 79-327, 1979-2 C.B. 342; *Estate of Ruth B. Regester*, 83 T.C. 1 (1984); *contra, Self v. United States*, 142 F. Supp. 939 (Ct.Cl. 1956).

From a future interest perspective, an income beneficiary's special power may be an invalid power appendant to the extent it applies to his or her right to the income from the trust. He or she holds that right apart from the purported power. Presumably no gift would occur in case of the exercise of a special power over the corpus if the power-holder were only entitled to receive distributions of income in the discretion of another person.

Under § 678, the exercise of a power of appointment in favor of persons the power-holder is obligated to support is taxable to the power-holder only to the extent the distribution satisfies that obligation. On the other hand, that result is avoided if the trust requires the beneficiary to appoint an independent party to exercise such a power. Such an "add-a-trustee" approach was upheld in LR 9036048. Also, a beneficiary could safely be authorized to make distributions to his or her dependents for "super support"—items such as private lessons that the beneficiary is not obligated to provide to his or her dependents. LR 9030005.

The provision creating a power should indicate when and how the power is exercisable, whether the property may be appointed on a further trust, in whose favor it may be exercised, and whether the property may be appointed unequally or to the complete exclusion of some permissible appointees. In addition, the power should specify what will become of the trust property to the extent the power is not validly exercised. Form 10-5 is a sample of a testamentary special power of appointment.

Form 10-5
Special Testamentary Power of Appointment

Upon the death of the beneficiary, the trustee shall distribute the trust property, including the net income then in the hands of the trustee and all income then accrued but uncollected, to and among such of the beneficiary's spouse and issue as the beneficiary shall appoint by a will executed after the date this trust is created. An exercise of this power shall only be effective if it refers to the instrument by date and states expressly the beneficiary's intention to exercise the power. The beneficiary may appoint the trust property in such shares or interests and upon such terms and conditions as [she/he] chooses, either outright or upon a further trust. In exercising this power the beneficiary is authorized to appoint the trust property to or for the benefit of one or more of the possible appointees to the total exclusion of the other or others of them. However, in no event may this power be exercised in favor of the beneficiary, [her/his] creditors, [her/his] estate, or the creditors of [her/his] estate.

To the extent the beneficiary does not validly exercise this power, the trustee shall distribute the trust property to those of [her/his] issue who survive [her/him], such issue to take by right of representation and not per capita. If none of the beneficiary's issue survive [her/him], the trustee shall distribute the trust property to _____.

In the case of an inter vivos power, the instrument should also specify how the power could be exercised inter vivos or upon the death of the holder of the power.

Include Charities as Objects? The overall flexibility of a special power can be increased if it includes charitable organizations as potential appointees. The tax cost of passing property intergenerationally may be reduced if a surviving spouse's special power to appoint a QTIP trusts includes charities. For example, the surviving spouse might appoint some or all of the property to a charitable lead trust, §8.31 or a charitable remainder trust, §8.20-8.22. The IRS has recognized that a person who holds a power of appointment over a private trust may appoint the property to charitable remainder trust. LR 9821029.

§10.24. $5,000 OR 5 PERCENT POWER OF WITHDRAWAL

For estate and gift tax purposes, the lapse of a post-1942 general power of appointment is treated as a release of that power; in turn, the release of such a power is treated as a transfer of the property subject to the power. §2041(a)(2); 2514(b). However, a major exception to that rule allows a beneficiary to hold, without any adverse gift or estate tax consequences, a noncumulative, inter vivos power to withdraw an amount each year that does not exceed the greater of $5,000 or 5 percent of the value of the property subject to the power. Practitioners often use the term "5 or 5 power" to describe such a withdrawal power.

The lapse of general powers of appointment during a calendar year is significant for gift and estate tax purposes only to the extent that the total amount that could have been appointed exceeds the amount that could be appointed under a 5 or 5 power. §2041(b)(2) (estate tax) and 2514(e) (gift tax). However, property subject to an unlapsed power of withdrawal at the time of the power-holder's death is includible in his or her estate even if such power is limited by the "5 or 5" standard. §2041(b)(2). For GSTT purposes, the decedent is considered to be the transferor of the portion includible in his or her estate. LR 9809049. Thus, a portion of the otherwise grandfathered trusts involved in that ruling was treated as constructively added by the decedent.

Powers of withdrawal, including *Crummey* powers, *see* §7.38, are often tailored so the total amount subject to withdrawal (or lapse) each year by a beneficiary does not exceed the 5 or 5 limit. In this connection note that the amount sheltered by this exception is limited to a total of $5,000 or 5 percent annually for all powers held by a single individual. Rev. Rul. 85-88, 1985-2 C.B. 202. Thus, the planner must proceed with caution where the power-holder is, or may be, the beneficiary of more than one trust. However, the lapse of a power to withdraw an amount in excess of the 5 or 5 limit does not have any adverse gift tax consequences if the power-holder also has a general or special power of appointment over the lapsed portion. In such a case Reg. §25.2511-2(b) indicates that the lapse would result in an incomplete gift: "[I]f a donor transfers property to another in trust to pay the income to the donor or accumulate it in the discretion of the trustee, and the donor retains a testamentary power to appoint the remainder among his descendants, no portion of the transfer is a completed gift." *See* LRs 8229097; 8517052; 9030005.

Because of the favorable gift and estate tax treatment of 5 or 5 powers, it is common to give one to the surviving spouse or other life income beneficiary of an irrevocable trust. Giving the power obviously increases the flexibility of the trust and reduces the beneficiary's dependence on the trustee. It also increases the beneficiary's "comfort level," which can be important if the beneficiary and the trustee are to establish and maintain a good relationship. Some beneficiaries enjoy having the power to withdraw some amount each year as "mad money" to use as they wish.

If lapses of post-1942 general powers in any calendar year exceed the 5 or 5 limit, the excess is ultimately treated as a transfer by the power-holder, which may involve a taxable gift. The amount of the gift is subject to the special valuation rules of §2702 if the remaindermen are family members. §7.38, LR 9804047. Also, the excess is includible in the power-holder's estate if the lapse is "of such a nature that if it were a transfer of property owned by the decedent, such property would be includible in the decedent's gross estate under sections 2035 to 2038, inclusive." §2041(a)(2). Thus, the property in excess of the 5 or 5 limit over which a power had lapsed is includible in the power-holder's estate if he or she may receive the income from that property after the lapse.

EXAMPLE 10-9.

B, the life income beneficiary of a trust, had the power to withdraw $50,000 of principal in a specified calendar year. *B* did not exercise the power, as a result of which it lapsed. The principal of the trust was worth $800,000 at the end of that calendar year. *B* is treated as having transferred property worth $10,000 to the trust. That figure represents the excess of amount *B* could have withdrawn ($50,000) over the greater of $5,000 or 5 percent of the value of the property subject to the power (5% × $800,000 = $40,000). Accordingly, for estate tax purposes, *B* is treated as the grantor of the trust principal ($10,000/$800,000). Reg. §20.2041-3(d)(4). Thus, if the trust has a value of $1,200,000 at the time of *B*'s death $15,000 would be includible in *B*'s gross estate. Note that if the lapse of the power results in a completed gift, the value of *B*'s retained life interest may be disregarded for purposes of § 2702. LR 9804047.

A 5 or 5 power is often given to a surviving spouse who is the beneficiary of a testamentary trust. It is permissible to do so even in the case of marital deduction trusts, including ones that meet the requirements of a QTIP trust under § 2056(b)(7). As noted above, the power provides desirable flexibility to the trust and security to the surviving spouse.

Form 10-6
5 or 5 Power of Withdrawal

Beneficiary shall have the power in each calendar year to withdraw from the principal of the trust an amount not to exceed the greater of $5,000 or five percent of the value of the principal of the trust determined as of the end of the calendar year. This power may be exercised in whole or in part each year by a written notice delivered to Trustee. The power of withdrawal is noncumulative, so that the power of withdrawal with respect to a particular calendar year can only be exercised during the calendar year.

Modify Form to Limit Potential Inclusion. The potential that the interest subject to withdrawal will be included in the estate of the power-holder can be minimized by restricting the period during each calendar year during which the power can be exercised. Thus, the power might provide that the power can be exercised by the beneficiary only if he or she is living on the last day of the calendar year (or during the last 15 days, or another relatively short period).

Conditions Precedent. Under Reg. § 20.2041-3(b), property subject to a power of withdrawal is includible in the power holder's estate although the exercise of the power is subject "to the precedent of giving notice, or even though the exercise of the power takes effect only on the expiration of a stated period after its exercise, whether or not on or before the decedent's death notice has been given or the power has been exercised." Continuing, the next sentence tells us that "a power which by its terms is exercisable only upon the occurrence during the decedent's lifetime of an event or contingency which did not in fact take place or occur during such time is not a power in existence on the date of the decedent's death." Thus, if a power is exercisable only if the power holder reached a certain age is disregarded if he or she dies prior to that age.

In *Estate of Kurz v. Commissioner*, 68 F.3d 1027 (7th Cir. 1995), the court required inclusion of property subject to a 5 or 5 power of withdrawal over the assets of one trust (the "Family Trust") that was exercisable only if the assets of another trust (the "Marital Trust") were exhausted because the decedent held an unlimited power to withdraw assets of the latter trust. In an entertaining opinion Judge Frank Easterbrook pointed out that the decedent had the power, at any time, to satisfy the condition precedent to the exercise of the 5 or 5 power:

Suppose, for example, that the Family Trust could not have been touched until Ethel Kurz said "Boo!" Her power to utter the magic word would have been no different from her power, under the Marital Trust, to send written instructions to the trustee. 68 F.3d at 1028.

In *Estate v. Kurz,* the IRS had argued that a condition on the exercise of a general power of appointment should be disregarded unless it was beyond the decedent's control. The IRS position was reiterated in LR 9535047, which states that:

> The lapse of this noncumulative demand power is treated as a partial release or other modification for purposes of section 678(a)(2). The trust corpus and income continue to be accumulated for future distribution to the beneficiary; if possessed by a grantor, this control over trust property would subject the grantor to treatment as the owner of the trust under section 677(a)(2). Therefore, the beneficiary is treated as the owner under section 678(a)(2) of the portion of the trust subject to the beneficiary's control after the 60-day period has expired.

§10.24.1. Income Tax

Under §678(a)(1), the holder of a power of withdrawal exercisable by the power-holder alone is treated as owner of the portion of the trust subject to withdrawal. *See* §10.27.1. The rule only applies if the grantor is not treated as the owner of the trust under §673-677. §678(b). Of course, the rule is of no consequence if the power-holder is taxable on all of the income in any case.

The existence of such a power may cause the power-holder to be taxed on a portion of the income of a trust that is distributable to other beneficiaries. Rev. Rul. 67-241, 1967-2 C.B. 225 (surviving spouse with 5 or 5 power is taxable on proportionate part of income payable to decedent's two children). According to the IRS, "until the power is exercised, released or allowed to lapse, [the power-holder] will be treated as the owner for each year of that portion of [the trust] that is subject to the power of withdrawal." LR 9034004.

The power-holder may release a power of withdrawal which subjects the power-holder to taxation under §678(a). *E.g.,* LR 9535047. Of course, the release of such a power may have estate and gift tax consequences. Under §678(a)(2), a person who releases or otherwise modifies a power remains treated as owner of the trust if the power-holder retained "such control as would, within the principles of sections 671 to 677, inclusive, subject a grantor of a trust to treatment as the owner thereof." *See, e.g.,* LR 200022035. Thus, a beneficiary who had released an unlimited power of withdrawal would remain taxable on all of the income of the trust if, for example, a nonadverse trustee could make discretionary distributions of income to the beneficiary. A grantor to whom discretionary distributions could be made by a nonadverse party would be treated as owner of the trust under §677(a). On the other hand, a person who releases an unlimited power of withdrawal would not be treated as owner of the trust following release of the power if he or she retains no interest in the trust.

The question of whether the lapse of a power of withdrawal should be treated as a "release or modification" under §678(a)(2) has not been answered by the courts. Not surprisingly, the IRS equates the lapse of a power of withdrawal with a release. Accordingly, in a long series of private letter rulings the IRS has ruled that a person who permits a noncumulative annual power of withdrawal to lapse is properly treated as the owner of a proportionate part of the trust under the principles of §671 to 677. E.g., LRs 200022035, 9812006, 9535047, 9034004; 8545076; 8308033; 8142061. In effect the rulings treat the person whose power of withdrawal has lapsed as the grantor of that portion of the trust.

A person other than the grantor, whose power of withdrawal has lapsed in more than one year and who retained "such control as would, within the principles of sections 671 to 677, inclusive, subject a grantor of a trust to treatment as the owner thereof," §678(a)(2), will be treated as the owner of an increasing portion of the trust. E.g., LR 200022035. The portion is determined in the manner indicated in LR 9034004:

> During each succeeding year in which A fails to exercise her power, A will be treated as the owner of an increasing portion of the corpus of T [the trust]. For purposes of determining the increase in her deemed ownership her current withdrawal power for any particular year will cause an increase in the amount of corpus which she is treated as owning equal to the product of the amount which she could withdraw multiplied by a fraction the numerator of which is the portion of trust corpus which she is not already treated as owning and the denominator of which is the total of trust corpus from which the withdrawal could be made. Discretionary distributions made by the trustee from corpus will be treated as coming from both the portion of corpus which the beneficiary is treated as owning and from the portion which she is not treated as owning in the same ratio as the fraction mentioned above.

EXAMPLE 10-10.

X is beneficiary of an inter vivos trust established 2 years ago by her uncle, U. Income of the trust is payable to X in the discretion of an independent trustee. Also, X has the annual noncumulative right to withdraw the greater of $5,000 or 5 percent of the value of the trust property determined on the last business day of the year. In the first year X's power to withdraw a maximum of $10,000 lapsed. X's power to withdraw $10,000 in the second year also lapsed. At the end of the second year the trust had a total value of $200,000. Under the IRS approach, X is treated as owning a $19,500/$200,000 interest in the trust, meaning X will be taxed on that fraction of the trust's income. The numerator of the fraction is the sum of the $10,000 that could have been withdrawn by X in the first year and the portion ($9,500) of the $10,000 that could have been withdrawn in the second year from the part of the trust that she was not already treated as owning. The latter amount is determined as follows:

$$\$10,000 \times \frac{\$190,000}{\$200,000} = \$9,500$$

§10.24.2. "Hanging Power"

As indicated above, no adverse gift, estate or GSTT consequences result from the annual lapse of powers of withdrawal that do not, in the aggregate, exceed the 5 or 5 amount. *See* §7.38.4. A hanging power is designed to achieve two goals: (1) to support the donor's qualification for a full annual gift tax exclusion by giving the beneficiary the power to withdraw the full annual exclusion amount; and (2) to prevent the beneficiary from experiencing any adverse gift or estate tax consequences by limiting the extent to which the power of withdrawal lapses each year to the sheltered 5 or 5 amount. Of course, the full amount of property subject to withdrawal at the time of the power-holder's death is subject to inclusion in the power-holder's gross estate. Thus, the use of a hanging power contemplates that the power-holder will live sufficiently long after the last gift to the trust to permit the power of withdrawal to lapse in full. A Technical Advice Memorandum, LR 8901004, held that the relatively simple form of hanging power there involved was an ineffective condition subsequent, which would be disregarded. Without express discussion of the nature of the power, the IRS allowed annual exclusions with respect to contributions to a trust that were subject to a hanging power. LR 200130030.

The inclusion of a hanging power is particularly appropriate if the trust is likely to continue beyond the lifetime of the power-holder, as a result of which the portion of the trust attributable to lapses in excess of the 5 or 5 amounts would be includible in the power-holder's gross estate. Its use is less significant if the power-holder is most likely to survive termination of the trust and receive distribution of the trust property. In such a case, all of the trust property will be included in the power-holder's estate in any case.

Hanging powers are discussed in more detail in §7.38.4, which includes a sample form, Form 7-3.

EXAMPLE 10-11.

T transferred $10,000 each year for 5 years to an irrevocable trust of which T's adult child, C, was the beneficiary. T made no more transfers to the trust. Under the terms of the trust C had a hanging power of withdrawal that lapsed at the end of each year in an amount equal to the greater of $5,000 or 5 percent of the value of the trust. In the first year C had a power to withdraw $10,000, of which the power to withdraw $5,000 lapsed at the end of the year. The power to withdraw the other $5,000 carried over to the next year. In the second year C had the right to withdraw a total of $15,000, composed of the $5,000 carryover and the $10,000 transferred to the trust by T. If values remain constant and C makes no withdrawals, at the end of 5 years of $10,000 gifts to the trust the trust corpus will consist of $50,000, of which *C* has the power to withdraw $25,000. In subsequent years the power of withdrawal would lapse to the extent of $5,000 each year. If *C* dies before the power of withdrawal lapsed entirely, the amount that remained subject to withdrawal at the time of *C*'s death would be included in *C*'s gross estate.

§10.25. POWER TO WITHDRAW TRUST ASSETS LIMITED BY AN ASCERTAINABLE STANDARD, §2041(b)(1)(A), 2514(c)(1)

The flexibility of the trust can also be increased somewhat without significant adverse gift or estate tax consequences by giving the beneficiary a power to withdraw trust property, "which is limited by an ascertainable standard relating to the health, education, support, or maintenance" of the power-holder. §2041(b)(1)(A), 2514(c)(1). Note that the standard must be ascertainable and must relate to the power-holder's health, education, support, or maintenance to qualify under this exception. Such a power is often most important because of the increased sense of security it gives to the power-holder.

Whether holding such a power will cause the beneficiary to be treated as owner of the trust under §678 is not entirely clear. The existing authorities are split. *See U.S. v. DeBonchamps*, 278 F.2d 127 (9th Cir. 1960) (although §678 is applicable to a life tenant with power to consume principal for specified purposes, the power is not "equivalent of a power to vest in themselves the corpus of the estate or the capital gains in question"); *Smither v. United States*, 108 F. Supp. 772 (S.D. Texas 1952), *aff'd*, 205 F.2d 518 (5th Cir. 1953) (income subject to withdrawal limited by an ascertainable standard may be taxed to non-grantor holder of the power to the extent the power is exercisable).

A power only falls within the scope of this exception if it is subject to an ascertainable (*i.e.*, objective) standard and not an indefinite (*i.e.*, subjective) standard. State law determines the nature and extent of a right of withdrawal conferred by a trust. However, the Regulations contain helpful examples of provisions that are acceptable. They include powers that are exercisable for the holder's "support," "support in reasonable comfort," "maintenance in health and reasonable comfort," "support in his or her accustomed manner of living," "education, including college and professional education," "health," and "medical, dental, hospital and nursing expenses and expenses of invalidism." Reg. §20.2041-1(c)(2). The same regulation points out that "[a] power to use property for the comfort, welfare, or happiness of the holder of the power is not limited by the requisite standard." Thus, in *Estate of John Russell Little*, 87 T.C. 599 (1986), the Tax Court held that a power to invade for purposes including "general happiness" was a general power of appointment. The decedent's power to invade the corpus of a testamentary trust created by his mother for his "care and comfort, considering his standard of living as of the date of my death" was held not to require inclusion in his gross estate. *Estate of Victor J. Strauss*, T.C. Memo. 1995-248 (Illinois law). *See also* §10.20.4.

A power of withdrawal that is limited by an ascertainable standard should clearly indicate the extent, if any, to which the other income or resources available to the beneficiary should be taken in account.

A power that is intended to escape treatment as a general power because of this exception must be carefully drawn. The safest course is to couch the power in exactly the language of one of the examples set forth in the regulation. Any deviation from the approved language creates a risk the IRS will treat the power as a general power of appointment. Thus, the IRS has argued that a power to invade corpus "in case of emergency or illness" was a general power, although a sympathetic appellate court rejected the Service's position. *Estate of Ida Maude Sowell,* 74 T.C. 1001, *rev'd,* 708 F.2d 1564 (10th Cir. 1983). In another case, an uncontrolled right, power, and authority to use and devote such of the corpus of the trust from time to time as the beneficiary in her judgment believed necessary for her maintenance, comfort, and happiness was held to be limited by an ascertainable standard under Massachusetts law. *Estate of Brantingham v. United States,* 631 F.2d 542 (7th Cir. 1980). The IRS believes that the *Brantingham* case was incorrectly decided and has stated that it will not follow the holding. Rev. Rul. 82-63, 1982-1 C.B. 135.

Form 10-7
Power of Withdrawal Limited by an Ascertainable Standard

> Beneficiary shall have the right, from time-to-time, to withdraw as much of the principal of the trust as may be required to provide for [her/his] maintenance, education, support and health in [her/his] accustomed manner of living ["determined in light of other income and resources reasonably available to Beneficiary," or "without regard to other income or resources that may be reasonably available to Beneficiary"].

§10.26. OTHER NONGENERAL POWERS OF APPOINTMENT

The other two types of post-1942 powers of withdrawal that are not treated as general powers are of little use for planning purposes in typical circumstances. *See* §2041(b)(1), 2514(c). The first exception is for a power only exercisable in conjunction with the creator of the power. §2041(b)(1)(C)(i), 2514(c)(3)(A). Such a power is generally not used because the property subject to powers of distribution jointly exercisable by the grantor and another is includible in the grantor's gross estate under §2038(a)(1). *Lober v. United States,* 346 U.S. 335 (1953); LR 9016079. The exception is also unsuitable for planning purposes if it may only be exercised during the lifetime of the creator of the power.

If it were possible for an independent party to be treated as the creator of a joint power for purposes of §2041(b), the first exception could allow additional flexibility to trusts. It is extremely doubtful that such a plan would work. For example, if *T* transferred *T's* residuary estate in trust for the benefit of his daughter, *D,* an independent party, *I,* could be given the power to amend the trust to provide that *D* could, with the concurrence of *I,* withdraw an unlimited amount of the trust corpus. If *I* made such an amendment of the trust, a court is likely to conclude that *D's* possession of the joint power would cause the full value of the trust to be included in *D's* estate under §2041. It would reason that "creator" as used in §2041 means the grantor of the trust and that a post-transfer amendment of the trust would be treated under orthodox power of appointment analysis as relating back to the initial creation of the trust. Any other interpretation would expand the exception beyond the apparent intention of Congress.

The second exception is for a power that is only exercisable in conjunction with a person having a substantial interest in the property adverse to an exercise of the power by the beneficiary. § 2041(b)(1)(C)(ii), 2514(c)(3)(B). This exception is also of little or no use in estate planning because it is highly unlikely that such a power would ever be exercised, as the power-holder must hope for the cooperation of a person whose interest will be diminished if the power is exercised. In LR 9030032, the surviving spouse and a child held a jointly-exercisable power to distribute corpus to the surviving spouse. The power was not limited by an ascertainable standard relating to the health, education, support and maintenance of the surviving spouse. However, because the child was entitled to an aliquot portion of the trust upon the death of the surviving spouse, the power was not a general power of appointment as to the surviving spouse, meaning the trust was not includible in the surviving spouse's gross estate. The child, as remaindermen, held an adverse interest in the trust.

§ 10.27. REMOVAL AND REPLACEMENT OF TRUSTEE

Giving a beneficiary the power to remove a trustee and replace the trustee with a person other than a beneficiary provides the beneficiary with valuable protection against an indolent or unresponsive trustee. In Rev. Rul. 95-58, 1995-2 C.B. 191, the IRS ruled that an individual who holds the power to remove a trustee and appoint as trustee another individual or corporate successor who is not related or subordinate to the power-holder within the meaning of § 672(c) will not be treated as possessing the powers of the trustee. § 10.20.3. *See also* LR 200551020 (no inclusion results from power to remove cotrustees and appoint parties who are not related or subordinate). Consistently, the IRS has ruled that the power of an individual who is the beneficiary and cotrustee of a testamentary trust to remove an independent trustee and appoint a successor who is not a related or a subordinate party within the meaning of § 672(c) will not require the trust to be included in her estate. LR 9746007.

A person who has the unlimited power to remove the trustee and appoint himself or herself as successor trustee, however, is treated as holding all of the powers of the trustee. *See* Reg. § 20.2041-1(b)(1). But in such a case the beneficiary's power to remove and replace the trustee will not require the trust property to be included in the beneficiary's estate unless the powers held by the trustee would require inclusion in the beneficiary's estate under § 2041 if they were held by the beneficiary. *See* LR 8922062. Accordingly, the IRS will argue that the assets of a trust are includible in the estate of a beneficiary who holds an unrestricted power to remove and replace a trustee who has discretion to make distributions to or for the benefit of the beneficiary or persons the beneficiary is obligated to support.

Care should be exercised if a client wishes to: (1) give the trustee tax-sensitive powers such as the power to make discretionary distributions to the beneficiaries; and (2) authorize someone to remove and replace the trustee who holds tax-sensitive powers. The possibility of including a removal and replacement power should be thoroughly explored with the client. In many cases it is sufficient if the beneficiaries cannot appoint themselves to succeed trustees who hold tax-sensitive powers. Because of the potentially adverse estate and income tax consequences, it is often desirable either to limit the powers that might be held by a beneficiary-trustee or to prohibit a beneficiary from becoming successor trustee.

§ 10.28. PLANNING SUMMARY

Adverse income and estate tax results are avoided if a non-grantor does not hold powers that are within the scope of § 678 or 2041. The reach of § 678 is avoided if the beneficiary does not hold "a power exercisable solely by himself to vest the corpus or the income therefrom in himself." For example, a beneficiary who holds the power to distribute income to members of a class that includes the beneficiary would be taxed on the income of the trust. However, that result is avoided if the power is exercisable only with the consent of another person (including a spouse) who does not need to have an adverse interest. Because of the reach of § 2041 a beneficiary should not hold a power to use or apply the income or corpus of the trust for his or her own benefit, except to the extent the power is protected by one of the exceptions: (1) a power limited by an ascertainable standard relating to the beneficiary's health, education, maintenance or support; (2) a noncumulative annual power limited to the greater of $5,000 or 5 percent of the value of the trust; or (3) a power exercisable only with the consent of its creator or an adverse party. In order to avoid a potential conflict with the IRS a beneficiary should neither hold any power with respect to insurance on his or her life nor have the right to become a successor trustee of such a trust.

D. PLANNING THE GRANTOR'S INTERESTS IN AN IRREVOCABLE TRUST

> Technical considerations, niceties of the law of trusts or conveyances, or the legal paraphernalia which inventive genius may construct as a refuge from surtaxes should not obscure the basic issue. That issue is whether the grantor after the trust has been established may still be treated as owner of the corpus . . . . And where the grantor is the trustee and the beneficiaries are members of his family group, special scrutiny of the arrangement is necessary lest what is in reality but one economic unit be multiplied into two or more by devices which, though valid under state law, are not conclusive so far as § 22(a) [now § 61(a)] is concerned. *Helvering v. Clifford,* 309 U.S. 331, 334-335 (1940).

§ 10.29. SCOPE

The income, gift, and estate tax consequences that flow from the grantor's retention of a power to revoke the trust are considered in Part B, § 10.7 – 10.17. The following sections examine the tax consequences that occur where the grantor retains other common interests or powers over the trust. Unfortunately, the criteria for determining the consequences of the retention of interests or powers are not the same for income, gift, and estate tax purposes. In fact, while the lack of coordination between the tax laws creates serious traps, they also create opportunities that taxpayers can sometimes exploit to their advantage.

The reciprocal trust doctrine, §6.30, may be applied in determining who is to be treated as the grantor of a trust for federal tax purposes. *See also* §7.35.2. Under the doctrine if trusts are established by related parties for the benefit of each other, the beneficiary of each trust may be treated as its grantor. Thus, if *A* transfers property to a trust for the benefit of *B*, and *B* transfers property to a similar trust for the benefit of *A*, *A* may be treated as the grantor of the trust for his benefit and *B* may be treated as the grantor of the trust for her benefit. As indicated in §7.35.2 the doctrine may be applied to custodianships or other arrangements. The IRS has asserted that it should apply to the acquisition by a husband and wife of cross-owned life insurance policies. *See* §6.40. The doctrine may be applied where trusts that are established by a parent for the benefit of his children, each of whom serves as trustee of a trust for the other, with discretion to make distributions of principal for the other. LR 9235025 (New York law).

Annual exclusions are not allowed for equivalent gifts of stock made by each parent-sibling and his wife to trusts for their children and for the children of other parent-siblings. The transfers were related and resulted in each transferor being in an essentially unchanged position. *Sather v. Commissioner*, 251 F.3d 1168 (8th Cir. 2001) (reciprocal trust doctrine applied). *See* §§7.35.2 (gifts to custodians) and 2.5.

As described in §10.31, grantors of trusts sometimes wish to be treated as the owner of the trust for income tax purposes. For example, foreign grantor trusts enjoyed a special tax advantage: a nonresident alien would be treated as the owner of a grantor trust that did not include assets located in the United States. Accordingly, the IRS ruled that the income of a grantor trust created by a nonresident alien was attributed to the grantor although it was not subject to tax as a result of which the income of the trust could be distributed tax-free to beneficiaries who were residents of the United States. That advantage was eliminated in 1996 when the law was changed to provide generally that the grantor trust rules would only be applied to the extent they cause an amount to be taken into account in determining the income of a citizen or resident of the United States or a domestic corporation. §672(f).

An irrevocable trust that is treated as a grantor trust under Subchapter J may be included in the grantor's gross estate to the extent the trustee is required to reimburse the grantor for the income taxes attributable to income of the trust that is includible in the grantor's income. According to Rev. Rul. 2004-64, 2004-2 C.B. 7, a trust is fully includible in the grantor's estate under §2036(a)(1) if the trustee is required to reimburse the grantor for the income tax payable on income of the trust that is treated as owned by the grantor, or where the trustee has the discretion to pay such reimbursements and the trustee's pattern of making such payments suggests an implicit arrangement between the grantor and the trustee that such payments will nearly always be made.

Post-2009 Gifts to Trusts. Section 2511(c) provides that gifts in trust after 2009 are completed gifts unless the grantor is treated as the owner of the entire trust for income tax purposes. If this rule becomes effective, clients should generally avoid making taxable gifts beyond the amount of the gift tax credit equivalent. The grantor can be made the deemed owner of the trust for income tax purposes in a variety of ways. *See* §10.31. For flexibility, a power that causes the gift to a trust to be incomplete under this rule should be subject to termination by an independent party.

§10.30. BASIC INCOME TAX RULES

The grantor trust rules of §671-677 are applied to determine whether or not the income of a trust is taxed to the grantor. Viewed differently, the rules specify the requirements that must be met in order to cause the income to be taxed to the trust or its beneficiaries and not to the grantor. Reg. §1.671-1(a) contains this concise statement of the circumstances under which the grantor will be treated as owner and taxed on the income:

(1) If the grantor has retained a reversionary interest in the trust, within specified time limits, §673;

(2) If the grantor or a nonadverse party has certain powers over the beneficial interests under the trust, §674;

(3) If certain administrative powers over the trust exist under which the grantor can or does benefit, §675;

(4) If the grantor or a nonadverse party has a power to revoke the trust or return the corpus to the grantor, §676; or

(5) If the grantor or a nonadverse party has the power to distribute income to or for the benefit of the grantor or the grantor's spouse, §677.

The income of a trust is not taxed to the grantor to the extent it is taxable to the grantor's spouse under §71 (alimony and separate maintenance) or §682 (income of estate or trust payable to spouse in case of divorce or separate maintenance).

Under §678, if the grantor is not treated as the owner of the trust, the income is taxed to a non-grantor who has the sole power to vest corpus or income in himself or herself. This provision can cause a person who holds a *Crummey* power to withdraw contributions to the trust to be treated as the owner of all or a portion of the trust. §7.38.

To the extent the grantor is treated as owner of the trust, he or she must report the items of income, deduction, and credit attributable to the trust. In such cases, the grantor's income is not limited to the distributable net income of the trust. Under Reg. §1.671-4, the trust does not report the income, deductions, and credits on its fiduciary income tax return (Form 1041). Instead they are shown on a separate statement attached to the trust's return. The trust must obtain a tax identification number although it is not required to file fiduciary income tax returns. *See* Reg. §1.671-4(b).

Prior to the Tax Reform Act of 1986, the rules of §671-677 usually involved irrevocable trusts in which the grantor's reversionary interest would take effect at the end of ten years or more. During this time, short-term irrevocable *"Clifford"* or "ten-year" trusts were popular, principally because they could be used to shift income from grantors subject to high income tax rates to beneficiaries in substantially lower brackets. At that time, income-shifting was possible although the grantor retained a reversionary interest that would take effect at the end of a ten-year term. The compressed income tax rates established by the 1986 Act reduced the attractiveness of such trusts. More importantly, the 1986 Act amended §673 to require the grantor to be treated as owner of any portion of a trust in which he or she held a reversionary interest, if at the inception of the trust, the value of the reversionary interest exceeded 5 percent of the value of such portion. Accordingly, it is no longer possible to shift the income to the beneficiaries of ten-year trusts.

Another change made by the 1986 Act required the grantor to be treated as holding any interest or power held by his spouse. § 672(e). That change eliminated the attractiveness of short-term irrevocable spousal remainder trusts, which some individuals created in order to shift the income for periods of less than ten years. A spousal remainder trust usually gave the income to children for a short term, say two years, and the remainder to the grantor's spouse. The gift tax exposure was limited because of the short duration of the trust and the unlimited marital deduction, which sheltered the remainder from the gift tax.

Under the preexisting law, the short-term irrevocable trust was a valuable estate planning tool, because of its ability to shift income within the family without requiring the grantor to surrender all of his or her interests in the property. If the trust was properly prepared and administered, the income from the property was taxed to the beneficiary and not to the grantor. Also, the actual amount of the trust's income was not included in the grantor's estate. For example, a short-term trust could shift the income from a parent to a child who was in a lower tax bracket. The short-term trust lost some of its luster because of the unification of the gift and estate tax laws that took place in 1976. However, it remained for the 1986 Act to eliminate its principal advantage—the grantor's retention of a reversionary interest that would become possessory in a relatively short time.

§ 10.30.1. Adverse Party

For purposes of § 671-677, the term "adverse party" is defined as "any person having a substantial beneficial interest in the trust which would be adversely affected by the exercise or nonexercise of the power which he possesses respecting the trust. A person having a general power of appointment over the trust property shall be deemed to have a beneficial interest in the trust." § 672(a). A trustee is not an adverse party merely because of his or her interest as trustee. Reg. § 1.672(a)-1(a). Powers over the trust are often sanitized for income tax purposes by making their exercise subject to the consent of an adverse party.

A beneficiary is ordinarily an adverse party to a power-holder. However, if the beneficiary only has the right to share in part of the income or corpus, the beneficiary may be an adverse party only as to that part. Reg. § 1.672(a)-1(b). In addition, a person who is an adverse party with respect to the income interest in a trust may or may not be adverse with respect to the exercise of a power over corpus. In determining whether a person is an adverse party, the critical question involves the effect of the exercise or nonexercise of the power on the power-holder's beneficial interests in the trust—not the effect on the grantor's interests. The last point is illustrated by Reg. § 1.672(a)-1(d):

> [I]f the grantor creates a trust which provides for income to be distributed to A for 10 years and then for the corpus to go to X if he is then living, a power exercisable by X to revest the corpus in the grantor is a power exercisable by an adverse party; however, a power exercisable by X to distribute part or all of the ordinary income to the grantor may be a

power exercisable by a nonadverse party (which would cause the ordinary income to be taxed to the grantor).

The proper identification of adverse parties is important because an adverse party is allowed to hold broad powers over a trust without causing the grantor to be treated as its owner. In particular, an adverse party may hold powers that: (1) affect the beneficial enjoyment of the trust, § 674; (2) cause a revocation of the trust and the return of the trust property to the grantor, § 676; or (3) permit the income of the trust to be accumulated or distributed to or for the benefit of the grantor or the grantor's spouse, § 677(a). The existence of such a power does not ordinarily cause any income, gift, or estate tax problems for the grantor. However, the mere existence of the power can have negative tax consequences for the power-holder. Specifically, if the grantor is not treated as owner of a trust, any other person who holds the power "to vest the corpus or the income therefrom in himself" is treated as the owner of the trust under § 678(a). In addition, the exercise or nonexercise of a power held by an adverse party may involve a gift to the other persons who are beneficially interested in the trust. *See* Reg. § 25.2514-1(b)(2).

§ 10.30.2. Jointly Exercisable Powers

An adverse party who holds a power that is jointly exercisable with the grantor or another person generally escapes harsh income, gift, or estate tax treatment. *See* § 678(a), 2041(b)(1)(C), and 2514(c)(3). Specifically, the holder of a joint power is not treated as the owner of a trust under § 678(a), for that subsection only applies to powers that are exercisable solely by a person other than the grantor. For gift and estate tax purposes a joint power exercisable by the adverse party and the grantor is not a general power of appointment. *See* § 2041(b)(1)(C)(iv), 2514(c)(3)(A). Accordingly, the exercise or nonexercise of such a joint power should not ordinarily involve a gift of the entire interest by the adverse party. However, the grantor's retention of a joint power would cause the trust property to be included in the grantor's gross estate under § 2036 and 2038.

§ 10.31. Grantor Treated as Owner of Trust Under Subchapter J

The lack of coordination between the income and the gift and estate tax laws create opportunities as well as traps. A client usually wishes to avoid being treated as the owner of a trust under the grantor trust rules that would require the client to report the income, deductions, and credits attributable to the trust. However, in some circumstances a careful consideration of the client's objectives and the rules applicable to grantor trusts may suggest that the client should seek to be treated as owner of a trust. In this connection, note that the beneficiary of a trust created by a foreign person is treated as grantor of the trust to the extent the beneficiary has transferred property directly or indirectly by gift to such foreign person. § 672(f). Also, as noted above, § 672(f)(1) provides that the grantor trust rules are generally inapplicable unless they result in an amount being taxed to a citizen or resident or a domestic corporation.

Trusts that are designed to qualify as grantor trusts under §671-677 are often called "intentionally defective trusts," a reference to the fact that grantor trust status historically is undesirable. The "defect" used in order to cause the grantor to be treated as the owner of the trust must be carefully planned so that it will not require the trust to be included in the grantor's estate. Thus, the trust should not be revocable nor should the grantor have discretion to make distributions to the beneficiaries, which would cause inclusion under §2036 and 2038. Ideally the trust should be planned so that the "defect" can be eliminated and the grantor status of the trust terminated without additional tax cost. Two popular "safe" powers are: (1) a power "to reacquire the trust corpus by substituting other property of equivalent value" exercisable by any person in a nonfiduciary capacity without the approval or consent of a person in a fiduciary capacity, §675(4)(C), *e.g.,* LR 199922007, and (2) a power held by a person other than the grantor or the grantor's agent to add charitable beneficiaries, §674(c), LR 199936031. *See* §10.36. The release of either such power should not have any adverse income, gift, estate or GST tax consequences for anyone.

Grantor trust status is generally desirable given the very thin tax brackets applicable to trusts taxed as separate entities. *See* §1(e). In most cases, less total income tax will be paid if the trust's income is taxed directly to the grantor. There are situations, however, where grantor trust status can be disadvantageous, although these situations are relatively rare. For example, if the grantor resides in a state that imposes a significant income tax, planners often try to locate the trust in a jurisdiction that imposes less (or no) income tax. If the tax is a grantor trust, however, such planning may be for naught, as all of the trust's income will likely be imputed to the grantor for state tax purposes as well. In addition, where the trust is insolvent but the grantor solvent, the cancelation of debt owed by the trust will give rise to taxable income since the trust is ignored for income tax purposes. In this situation, the trust would be unable to employ the exclusion in §108(a)(1)(B).

The IRS no longer issues rulings regarding whether the grantor will be treated as the owner of a trust with respect to which the grantor has retained a nonfiduciary power to reacquire the property of the trust by substituting property of equivalent value. The IRS justifies its position by asserting that whether the power is held in a nonfiduciary capacity is a question of fact, which cannot be determined in advance. *See, e.g.,* LR 200434012.

In *Estate of Anders Jordhal,* 65 T.C. 92 (1975), *acq.,* 1977-1 C.B. 1, the Tax Court held that a deceased grantor's power to substitute the assets of a trust with assets of equal value was not a power to "alter, amend, or revoke" that would require inclusion under §2038. In addition, the Tax Court held that such a power to substitute assets of equal value for life insurance policies held by the trust was not an incident of ownership for purposes of §2042(2). As noted in LR 9413045, in *Jordahl* the court held that "in the case of an insurance policy the only asset that should be of equal value would be another insurance policy with 'equal cash surrender and face value, comparable premiums, and a similar form of policy.'" The position taken in *Jordhal* with respect to §2042(2) has been followed in some private letter rulings. *See, e.g.,* LRs 9843024, 9413045.

Under §677, the grantor is, of course, taxable on the income of a trust where the income may be accumulated for the grantor or his spouse without the approval or consent of an adverse party. LR 9535008 (TAM). Such a power may require the trust to be included in the grantor's gross estate under §2038.

Sale to Intentionally Defective Trusts. Neither the grantor nor a trust of which the grantor is treated as the owner will recognize gain or loss on the sale or exchange of assets between them. Rev. Rul. 83-15, 1983-1 CB. 184. The opportunity to sell assets to an intentionally defective trust at deeply discounted prices without making a gift or recognizing any gain or loss is at the heart of a variety of highly touted planning techniques. *See* § 10.31.7.

Power to Add Beneficiaries. If a nonadverse party is given the power to add beneficiaries, even charitable organizations, the grantor is treated as the trust's owner under § 674(a). *Bernard Madorin,* 85 T.C. 667 (1985) (power to add charitable beneficiaries). The IRS reached the same result in several private letter rulings. *See* LRs 199936021, 200030018, 200030019. The cited letter rulings also hold that the existence of such a power will not cause the trust to be included in the grantor's estate unless the power-holder is treated as an agent of the grantor. Accordingly, it should be relatively safe to confer the power upon an independent party. A degree of protection against unwanted tax consequences is added if the trust expressly provides that the power-holder may disclaim or release the power.

§ 10.31.1. Grantor Makes Free Gift of Income Tax on Trust

A grantor who is treated as owner of the trust under Subchapter J must pay the income tax on the income of the trust. As pointed out by Professor Halbach,

> [A] settlor sometimes wishes to be taxable on trust income that is nevertheless payable to an adult child whose tax bracket is comparable to that of the settlor. By paying the income tax that would otherwise be charged to the child, the settlor makes what amounts to an additional transfer to the child each year without having an additional taxable gift. Halbach, Tax-Sensitive Trusteeships, 63 Or. L. Rev. 381, 384 n. 11 (1984).

Making such "free" gifts of the annual income tax imposed on the trust is clearly attractive to wealthy grantors who wish to make additional gifts without incurring any gift or GST tax.

Revenue Ruling 2004-64, 2004-2 C.B. 7, confirms that no gift results when the grantor, who is treated as the owner of a trust under § § 671-677, pays the income tax imposed on the income of the trust: "When the grantor of a trust, who is treated as the owner of the trust under subpart E, pays the income tax attributable to the inclusion of the trust's income in the grantor's taxable income, the grantor is not treated as making a gift of the amount of the tax to the trust beneficiaries." The ruling also holds that the beneficiaries of a grantor trust do not make a gift to the grantor if, pursuant to the requirements of the trust or a discretionary power exercised by an independent trustee, the trust reimburses the grantor for the income tax paid by the grantor with respect to the income of the trust.

With respect to the estate tax, Rev. Rul. 2004-64 reached two important conclusions. First, "[i]f, pursuant to the trust's governing instrument or applicable local law, the grantor must be reimbursed by the trust for the income tax payable by the grantor that is attributable to the trust's income, the full value of the trust's assets is includible in the grantor's gross estate under § 2036(a)(1)." According to the ruling, the IRS will not apply this holding to trusts that were created before October 4, 2004.

Second, inclusion of the trust in the grantor's estate is not required if the instrument or the governing law merely gives the trustee the discretion to reimburse the grantor, whether or not the power is exercised. However, the second holding is subject to: (1) there being no understanding or agreement between the grantor and the trustee regarding the exercise of discretion by the trustee; (2) the grantor not having the power to remove the trustee and appoint himself or herself as trustee; (3) the retained discretionary power does not subject the principal of the trust to the claims of creditors. (With respect to the last point, *see* § 10.39.3.) This holding is generally consistent with LR 200120021, in which the IRS ruled that the discretionary power of an independent trustee or trust protector (*i.e.*, one who is neither related nor subordinate as defined in § 672) to pay the income tax liability of the grantor with respect to the income of the trust would not cause the trust to be included in the grantor's estate under § 2036. The IRS may seek inclusion under § 2036(a)(1) if, under the governing law, the principal of the trust is subject to the claims of the grantor's creditors.

In light of Rev. Rul. 2004-64, planners may seek to add discretionary tax reimbursement clauses to the grantor trusts they draft for clients. For existing trusts, planners may consider reforming the trust to include such a provision. This can be done without adverse tax consequences. *See* LR 200822008 (reformation of grantor trust to include discretionary reimbursement clause will not, by itself, cause trust assets to be included in grantor's gross estate).

§ 10.31.2. Trust Holds S Corporation Stock

A trust of which the grantor (or another citizen or resident of the United States) is treated as the owner is a permissible shareholder in an S corporation. § 1361(c)(2)(A)(i). Private Letter Ruling 199936021, among many others, recognized that because the grantor was treated as owner of the trust, the trust could hold S corporation stock. If the stock of an S corporation continues in trust after the death of the grantor-owner, the trust could be designed to continue to qualify as a qualified Subchapter S trust. *See* § 1361(d).

§ 10.31.3. Trust Holds Installment Obligations

The transfer of an installment obligation to an irrevocable trust of which the grantor is not treated as the owner ordinarily triggers the recognition of gain by the grantor. Rev. Rul. 67-167, 1967-1 C.B. 107; Rev. Rul. 76-530, 1976-2 C.B. 132, both applying former § 453(d). However, a transfer to a grantor trust is not a disposition that triggers acceleration of the tax on an installment sale. Instead, the income from the installment obligation remains taxable to the grantor.

§ 10.31.4. Capital Gains of Grantor Trust Offset by Grantor's Losses

If the grantor is treated as the owner of a trust, the grantor's losses can be used to offset the gains of the trust. The gain on a sale of appreciated property by a grantor trust is taxed to the grantor. Depreciated property should not be transferred to a standard, non-grantor trust because the possibility that the grantor might recognize a loss on the disposition of the property would be lost as a result of the transfer: recall in this connection that under § 1015(a) the basis of property for loss purposes in the hands of the donee (here, the trust) cannot exceed its fair market value at the time of the gift.

§ 10.31.5. Exclusion of Some Gain on Sale of Grantor's Principal Residence, § 121

An individual who is treated as owner of a trust for income tax purposes is entitled to the benefit of the exclusion of up to $250,000 (individual) or $500,000 (married persons and certain surviving spouses) on the sale of a principal residence that is allowable under § 121. LR 199912026. This is consistent with an earlier ruling that the provisions of former § 121 were available with respect to a personal residence that is transferred to a personal residence trust, provided that the requirements of § 121 were satisfied. Rev. Rul. 85-45, 1985-1 C.B. 183. *See* § 9.44.2.

§ 10.31.6. Nonrecognition of Gain on Certain Dispositions

If the grantor is treated as the owner of the trust, the nonrecognition provisions of § 1033 (condemnation and replacement of property) are also available. Rev. Rul. 70-376, 1970-2 C.B. 164. Nonrecognition is permitted where property owned by the grantor was condemned and replacement property was acquired by a trust of which the grantor was treated as the owner. Rev. Rul. 88-103, 1988-2 C.B. 304. Revenue Ruling 88-103 treats the grantor as the taxpayer who acquired the property.

§ 10.31.7. No Gain on Sale of Property Between Trust and Grantor; Intentionally Defective Trusts

According to the IRS, the sale of property from a grantor to a grantor trust, or a sale by the grantor trust to the grantor, is not a transaction that gives rise to gain or loss. Rev. Rul. 85-13, 1985-1 C.B. 184 (involving a grantor who had triggered grantor trust status under § 675(3) by borrowing the corpus of the trust). In the view of the IRS, a grantor trust is not regarded as a taxpayer capable of engaging in a sales transaction with the grantor. Note that the Second Circuit Court of Appeal rejected the IRS position in *Rothstein v. United States*, 735 F.2d 704 (2d Cir. 1984). The holding in *Rothstein* has been criticized by some commentators. Ascher, When to Ignore Grantor Trusts: The Precedents, a Proposal, and a Prediction, 41 Tax L. Rev. 253 (1986). This point is also discussed in § 10.37.1.

Neither the grantor nor the intentionally defective trust recognizes gain or loss on the sale or exchange of assets between them. The opportunity to sell assets to an intentionally defective trust at deeply discounted prices without recognition of gain or loss lies at the heart of a variety of highly touted estate planning arrangements. *See* Mulligan, Sale to an Intentionally Defective Irrevocable Trust for a Balloon Note—An End Run Around Chapter 14?, U. Miami, 32nd Inst. Est. Plan., Ch. 15 (1998), *and* Oshins, King & McDowell, Sale to a Defective Trust: A Life Insurance Technique, 139 Tr. & Est. 35 (Apr. 1998). The following example illustrates the potential benefits from its use:

EXAMPLE 10-12.

Grantor, G, forms a family limited partnership (FLP) of which G is general partner and G's child, C, is the limited partner. G transfers $20 million in financial assets to the FLP in exchange for 1 general partner unit and 98 limited partner units, while C transfers $200,000 to the partnership in exchange for 1 limited partner unit.

G then transfers $1 million of cash to an intentionally defective trust of which G's three children and their children are the beneficiaries. G allocates G's $1 million GSTT exemption to the transfer. The independent trustee of the intentionally defective trust, T, buys all 98 of G's limited partner units at their fair market value (appraised at a 50-percent discount), $9,800,000 ($19,600,000 × .50), paying for them with a balloon installment note on which interest only is paid for several years. No gain is recognized on the sale or as interest payments are made to G. Under the grantor trust rules, G will continue to be taxed on the income of the trust—which many perceive to be an important additional advantage. T uses excess income received on the FLP units to buy $5 million in life insurance on G's life. If the approach succeeds, G's estate will only include the value of the note (or the proceeds received when it is paid). The FLP units transferred to the trust, including further appreciation, and the life insurance will be excluded from his estate.

In contrast, if the grantor of a GRAT dies during the period the annuity is payable, at least some portion of the trust itself is includible in his or her gross estate. *See* § 9.43.5.

§ 10.31.8. Grantor Trust May Sell Stock to ESOP

For purposes of § 1042 a sale of qualified securities by a grantor trust to an employee stock ownership plan (ESOP) is treated as a sale by the grantor. LR 9041027. Accordingly, the grantor is the appropriate party to make the election not to recognize gain on the sale to the ESOP and the acquisition, by the trust, of qualified replacement securities.

§ 10.32. Basic Gift Tax Rules

The transfer of property to a trust constitutes a gift of the value of the property transferred, less the value of the donor's retained interest. Rev. Rul. 58-242, 1958-1 C.B. 251. In this connection note that a term interest, other than a "qualified interest," retained by the grantor is generally valued at zero under § 2702 if the remaindermen are family members. *See* § 9.40, 9.43. Otherwise, retained interests are valued in the manner prescribed by § 7520. The rules generally apply in valuing life and other term interests, remainders and annuities. However, the actuarial tables prescribed by the IRS are not applicable if the beneficiary does not have a "standard" interest. Thus, the right to receive the income of a trust funded with unproductive property that the beneficiary cannot compel the trustee to make productive, is not valued according to the generally applicable tables. Reg. § 20.7520-3(b), (b)(2)(v), Example 1.

The limitation on the use of the actuarial tables imposed by the regulations under §7520 accords with prior law under which the actuarial tables were not applicable if their use would "violate reason and fact." Rev. Rul. 77-195, 1977-1 C.B. 295 (tables used to value income interest in stock the trustee was required to retain although it had historically yielded only a 3 percent return). Thus, the IRS had ruled that it is inappropriate to use the tables where the trustee has the power to retain common stock (or other property) that has historically produced little or no income. LR 8642028 (TAM).

In LR 200014004 (TAM), the IRS ruled that the taxpayer's acquiescence in the payment of excessive trustee's fees to the trustees, her children, involved taxable gifts to them. Similarly, gifts resulted from the grantors' failure to require the trustee to replace unproductive assets of trusts in which they held income interests for a term. In LRs 8801008 and 8806082, the grantors retained the power to replace unproductive assets of the trusts of which they were income beneficiaries for specified terms of years. The IRS ruled that the failure of the grantor of each trust to require the trustee to make the trust property productive resulted in a gift each year of the difference between the right to receive income of 10 percent of the value of the trust corpus and the amount of income actually received from the trust. This approach was adopted by the IRS to combat the attempt to use grantor retained interest trusts (GRITs) to take advantage of the actuarial tables to shift wealth to the remaindermen at little or no transfer tax cost. The valuation loophole that made GRITs attractive has largely been closed by §2702. §9.43.

The entire value of the transferred property may be treated as a gift where the income is payable to persons other than the grantor and the trustee is empowered to distribute the trust principal as income, Rev. Rul. 76-275, 1976-2 C.B. 299, or allocated capital gains to income and capital losses to principal. Rev. Rul. 77-99, 1977-1 C.B. 295. The gift includes the amount of any appreciation in the property at the time of the transfer where the trustee may sell the property and distribute the gain to the income beneficiary. Accordingly, a trust ordinarily should not allow distribution of capital gains to the beneficiary even though the grantor is taxed currently under §677(a)(1) on gains that are accumulated for later distribution to the grantor.

A gift also occurs if the period during which others are entitled to the income of the trust is extended by the grantor. Of course, the right to receive the income for an additional period is a future interest for which no annual exclusion is allowed. Rev. Rul. 76-179, 1976-1 C.B. 290.

The IRS has ruled that the payment by the grantor of a grantor trust of the income tax attributable to the inclusion of the trust's income in the grantor's taxable income does not constitute a gift by the grantor. Rev. Rul. 2004-64, 2004-2 C.B. 7.

§10.32.1. Annual Exclusion

A transfer to a trust qualifies for the annual gift tax exclusion under §2503(b) to the extent the beneficiary's interest is a "present interest." Rev. Rul. 58-242, 1958-1 C.B. 251; *see* §2.5.2-2.5.4. The beneficiary's income interest in a trust qualifies for the annual exclusion if income is distributable currently to the beneficiary, to a custodian for a minor beneficiary under the Uniform Transfers to Minors Act or the Uniform Gifts to Minors Act, or to a guardian for the minor beneficiary. *Jacob Konner*, 35 T.C. 727 (1961), *nonacq.*, 1963-2 C.B. 6, *withdrawn and acq. sub.*, 1968-2 C.B. 2 (§2503(c) trust); *see also Carl E. Weller*, 38 T.C. 790 (1962), *acq.*, 1963-1 C.B. 4, *withdrawn and nonacq. sub.*, 1963-2 C.B. 6, *withdrawn and acq. sub.*, 1968-2 C.B. 3.

When the income is currently distributable to a class of beneficiaries, such as the grantor's children, the gifts to the members of the class living at the time of the transfer are present interests. However, exclusions are allowable only to the extent the grantor can show that the present interests have present value. This burden is relieved a little by Rev. Rul. 55-678, 1955-2 C.B. 389, which states that "[i]n such cases it is not necessary that the exact value of the gift of the present interest in property be determinable on the basis of recognized actuarial principles." *See also* Rev. Rul. 55-679, 1955-2 C.B. 390. Nonetheless, in order to qualify for the annual exclusion, a trust with multiple beneficiaries should give each beneficiary a discrete interest in the income.

In any case, the value of the income interest in the trust should qualify for the annual exclusion if the beneficiary at the time the trust is created has the power to elect to receive the net income of the trust each year. *See* Price, Intrafamily Transfers: Blessed and More Blessed Ways to Give, U. Miami, 18th Inst. Est. Plan., Ch. 6 (1984). Under a variation, the beneficiary might be given the noncumulative power to withdraw an amount each year equal to the trust's net income for the year. Both approaches are based on the *Crummey* power to withdraw trust assets, that is recognized as conferring a present interest on the beneficiary to the extent the power is presently exercisable. *Crummey v. Commissioner*, 397 F.2d 82 (9th Cir. 1968); Rev. Rul. 73-405, 1973-2 C.B. 321; *see also* §7.38.

Where non-income-producing property is transferred to the trust, the IRS may contend that the income interest has no value. *See* Rev. Rul. 69-344, 1969-1 C.B. 225 (trustee authorized to invest in life insurance policies that are not considered to be income-producing property). The problem is most likely to arise if the trustee has no power to dispose of non-income-producing assets and invest in income-producing property. *Berzon v. Commissioner*, 534 F.2d 528 (2d Cir. 1976). However, some courts have denied an annual exclusion for the beneficiary's income interest even though the trustee had the power to dispose of the property and invest the proceeds in income-producing property. *Fischer v. Commissioner*, 288 F.2d 574 (3d Cir. 1961); *Stark v. United States*, 477 F.2d 131 (8th Cir.), *cert. denied*, 414 U.S. 975 (1973); *Van Den Wymelenberg v. United States*, 397 F.2d 443 (7th Cir.), *cert. denied*, 393 U.S. 953 (1968); *contra, Rosen v. Commissioner*, 397 F.2d 245 (4th Cir. 1968). The transfer of nonincome-producing property to a trust invites a challenge by the IRS—particularly if the trustee lacks the power to sell the property.

§10.32.2. Charitable Deduction

Caution must be exercised in making a charitable gift of an interest in a trust: Ordinarily, a gift tax charitable deduction is not allowable for the transfer of a simple income or remainder interest to charity. *See* §2522(c)(2). As explained in Chapter 8, the deduction is only available for a split interest given to charity when the interest is in the form of a "guaranteed annuity or . . . a fixed percentage distributed yearly of the fair market value of the property (to be distributed yearly)." §2522(c)(2)(B). However, this trap is avoided if the grantor retains the right to select the annual charitable recipient of the income until after it is received, which renders the initial gift incomplete. *See* §8.33 for a more complete description of the device. Of course, the grantor is only entitled to an income tax deduction for an "income" interest to the extent the grantor is treated as the owner of the trust under §671. §170(f)(2)(B). In essence, a present income tax deduction is available at the cost of being taxed on the future income of the trust.

§10.33. POWERS THAT RESULT IN TRANSFERS BEING INCOMPLETE

In some circumstances, a client may wish to transfer property to an irrevocable trust in a way that does not constitute a completed gift. For example, a client in declining health may wish to establish an irrevocable trust that places the property beyond his or her direct control, but does not require the payment of any gift tax that would deplete the amount available for his or her support. The client's retained interests would, of course, require the trust to be included in his or her estate. *See* §§2036 and 2038. The retention of powers that are exercisable jointly with another individual who does not have an adverse interest is often a satisfactory way to make the gift incomplete.

A client may wish to make a transfer to a trust incomplete for other reasons. For example, in connection with the establishment of a charitable remainder trust, the grantor may wish the transfer of a successive noncharitable interest in the trust to be incomplete until the grantor's death.

A transfer to an irrevocable trust is not complete if the grantor retains a lifetime or testamentary power to change the beneficiaries. PLR 9535008 (TAM). *See* §2.4.3, 10.37.1. Such a gift becomes complete when the power is exercised, released, or terminated.

§10.33.1. Joint Power to Make Discretionary Distributions

The grantor's retention of a power to make discretionary distributions that is only exercisable jointly with a nonadverse party is treated in the same way as the grantor's retention of a sole power over distributions. Such a power causes the transfer of property to the trust to be incomplete for gift tax purposes. Rev. Rul. 75-260, 1975-2 C.B. 376; Reg. §25.2511-2(c). However, gifts become complete when property of the trust is distributed to others.

> A donor is considered as himself having a power if it is exercisable by him in conjunction with any person not having a substantial adverse interest in the disposition of the transferred property . . . . A trustee, as such, is not a person having an adverse interest in the disposition of the trust property or its income. Reg. §25.2511-2(e).

The retention of a joint power to make distributions may be adequate to insulate the property from improvident transfers by the grantor. It may also provide some protection against creditors. In contrast, the IRS contends that the transfer of property to an independent trustee who has complete discretionary power to make distributions to the grantor is a completed gift. Rev. Rul. 77-378, 1977-2 C.B. 347. Of course, the grantor would be treated as owner of the trust for income tax purposes and it would be included in the grantor's estate. Note also that gifts made from the trust within three years of the grantor's death pursuant to the joint action of the grantor and another party would almost certainly be includible in the grantor's estate under §2035(a)(2).

§10.33.2. Joint Power to Terminate Trust

The power, exercisable jointly with a nonadverse party, to terminate an otherwise irrevocable trust would also make the transfers to the trust incomplete. LR 8940008 (citing Reg. §25.2511-2(c), (e)). In LR 8940008, the grantor retained power to amend, modify, revoke, or terminate in whole or in part with approval of an independent trustee. The IRS properly concluded that the transfer was incomplete for gift tax purposes.

§10.33.3. Retained Testamentary Power to Appoint Remainder

The grantor's retention of a testamentary special power to appoint the remainder interest is sufficient to make the transfer of property to the trust incomplete for gift tax purposes. Reg. §25.2511-2(c), (e). In LR 9021017, the grantor retained the power to change the interests of the remainder beneficiaries. According to LR 9021017, "The retention of this power is sufficient, in and of itself, to render the transfer to the trust wholly incomplete for federal gift tax purposes." Thus, a retained power to appoint the remainder to and among lineal descendants or charitable organizations is sufficient to make a transfer incomplete.

§10.33.4. Retained Testamentary Power to Revoke Successive Noncharitable Interest

A client may wish to make a present transfer to a charitable remainder trust in which the client and the client's spouse or other relative is given a successive interest. In order to avoid the imposition of the gift tax, or for a variety of nontax reasons, the client may wish to make the successive interest terminable. If the donor retains the right by will to revoke the successive interest, the gift of the successive interest is incomplete, but the gift of the charitable remainder is complete. This device might also be of use where the donee of the successive interest is a noncitizen with respect to whom no gift tax marital deduction would be allowable. Indeed, it might be possible to structure the trust as an income-only unitrust, which could qualify on the client's death for the marital deduction under §2056(b)(8) and 2056A if the client's spouse survives. *See* §5.24. Of course, distributions from a qualified domestic trust, other than distributions of income or in cases of hardship, are subject to the §2056A tax. Presumably, the IRS would treat distributions made from an income-only unitrust as distributions of income.

§10.34. BASIC ESTATE TAX RULES

If the grantor dies prior to termination of the trust, the value of any reversionary interest retained by the grantor is includible in the grantor's estate under §2033. Such a reversionary interest is valued in accordance with the valuation tables issued pursuant to §7520. The calculation is based in part on the interest rate, announced monthly in the Internal Revenue Bulletin, based on 120 percent of the federal midterm rate, compounded annually (rounded to the nearest two-tenths of 1 percent). The actuarial tables effective May 1, 1999 are published in IRS Pub. No. 1457, Book Aleph, (Remainder, Income and Annuity Factors for One Life, Two Lives and Terms Certain; Interests Rates from 2.2 Percent to 22.0 Percent) (1999); and IRS Pub. No. 1458, Book Beth (Unitrust Remainder Factors for One Life, Two Lives, and Terms Certain; Adjusted Payout Rates from 2.2 Percent to 22.0 Percent) (1999). If the tables are not available, the value of some interests can be calculated easily. As pointed out in Notice 89-24, 1989-1 C.B. 660, the applicable formula for calculating the value of a remainder interest following a term is:

$$\text{Remainder Factor} = \frac{1}{(1+j)t}$$

In this formula, "i" equals 120 percent of the applicable federal midterm interest rate and the exponent "t" equals the number of years in the term. The income factor is simply 1.0 less the value of the remainder factor calculated according to the foregoing formula.

An unintended reversionary interest may arise under the Doctrine of Worthier Title where the grantor attempts to create a remainder in his or her own heirs. *See* § 10.35.3. Fortunately, however, the Doctrine has been abolished in most states.

Of course, if the grantor survives termination of a trust, the property formerly held in the trust is includible in his or her estate. As explained below, inclusion may result under other sections, particularly § 2036 and 2038.

EXAMPLE 10-13.

G transferred property worth $100,000 to a trust the income of which was payable to G's sister, S, for 15 years, at the end of which the corpus would return to G. The transfer involved a gift to S of the actuarially determined value of the right to receive the income for 15 years. G died 7 years after the trust was established, at a time when the trust property had a value of $150,000 and the applicable interest rate was 8.8 percent. Under Table B of Book Aleph, Pub. 1457 (1999), the value of the right to receive $150,000 at the end of 8 years, assuming an interest rate of 8.8 percent is $76,394 (factor of .509294 × $150,000). Accordingly, $76,394 is includible in G's gross estate.

If the income and corpus of a trust can be reached by the grantor's creditors, the trust property is includible in the grantor's estate under § 2036(a)(1) and 2038. LR 199917001 (TAM) (California law). That TAM concluded that the gifts of property to the irrevocable trusts were incomplete because the trust property could be subject to the grantor's creditors—which also subjected the trusts to inclusion in his estate.

§ 10.34.1. Retained Enjoyment or Powers Over Trust Property, § 2036

Inclusion under § 2036 could occur, for example, where the income of the trust is used to discharge the grantor's legal obligation to support a minor child or to make principal payments on a mortgage. Reg. § 20.2036-1(b)(2); LR 9032002 (TAM) (dicta regarding inclusion because a trust discharged the grantor's support obligation). Of course, § 2036(a)(2) mandates inclusion if the grantor retained the power to control beneficial enjoyment of the property (*e.g.*, to designate which of two beneficiaries will receive the income). Inclusion may also result if the decedent is identified as the grantor under the reciprocal trust doctrine and the grantor holds powers sufficient to cause inclusion under § 2036(a)(2) or 2038. *See Estate of Bruno Bischoff,* 69 T.C. 32 (1977). *See also* § 6.30. Inclusion is also required if the property of the trust is subject to the claims of the grantor's creditors. LR 199917001 (California law; trustees could make discretionary distributions of income and principal to the grantor with the consent of his wife).

The retention of a power over transferred property that is limited by an ascertainable standard does not require the property to be included in the transferor's estate under § 2036 or 2038. *Estate of Wilson v. Commissioner,* 13 T.C. 869 (1949), *aff'd,* 187 F.2d 145 (3d Cir. 1951), *Estate of Robert W. Wier,* 17 T.C. 409 (1951), *acq.,* 1952-1 C.B. 4, *acq. partially withdrawn,* 1966-2 C.B. 8.

EXAMPLE 10-14.

T transferred securities worth $100,000 to a trust of which *T*'s sister, *S*, was the trustee and *S*'s children were the beneficiaries. The trust instrument gave *S* as trustee discretion to sprinkle the income among the beneficiaries and to make distributions of principal to them for their comfort, welfare and happiness. *S* transferred $100,000 in securities to *T* as trustee of a similar trust for the benefit of *T*'s children. Under the reciprocal trust doctrine *T* will be treated as the grantor of the trust for the benefit of *T*'s children and *S* will be treated as the grantor of the trust for the benefit of *S*'s children. The principal of each "uncrossed" trust is includible in the gross estate of its grantor under § § 2036 and 2038.

§ 10.34.2. Reversionary Interests, § 2037

If the grantor retains a reversionary interest contingent on surviving the income beneficiary that is worth more than 5 percent of the value of the property immediately before the grantor's death, the entire value of the property is includible in the grantor's estate under § 2037. *E.g.,* Rev. Rul. 76-178, 1976-1 C.B. 273 (real property transferred in trust to pay the income to the trust beneficiary for life, after which the property would return to the grantor if living, otherwise to the grantor's children). The threat of inclusion under § 2037 can be avoided by drafting the trust to exclude the retention of any reversionary interest by the grantor.

§ 10.34.3. Retained Power to Alter, Amend, Revoke or Terminate, § 2038

The trust corpus is includible in the grantor's estate under § 2038(a) if the grantor at death holds a power to alter, amend, revoke, or terminate the trust, exercisable alone or in conjunction with any other person. Inclusion is also required where such a power is "relinquished during the three-year period ending on the date of the decedent's death." § 2038(a)(1). As mentioned above in connection with § 2036, inclusion is required if the property of the trust was subject to the claims of the grantor-decedent's creditors, which is primarily an issue of state law. LR 199917001 (TAM).

EXAMPLE 10-15.

T transferred income-producing property worth $100,000 to an irrevocable trust. The trustee has discretion to distribute the income each year to and among *T*'s children, *A*, *B*, and *C*. The trust prohibits the trustee from making distributions to *A*, *B*, or *C* that would relieve *T* of any legal obligation. At the end of 10 years the trust property will be distributed to *T*'s brother, *X*. The transfer involves gifts to *A*, *B*, *C*, and *X*, none of which qualifies for an annual gift tax exclusion. None of the trust property is includible in *T*'s gross estate. Note, however, that the full value of the trust property would be included in *T*'s gross estate if *T* retained the power to remove or discharge the trustee and appoint himself or herself as trustee. Reg. § 20.2036-1(b)(2).

§ 10.35.   RETAINED REVERSIONARY INTEREST

The retention of a reversionary interest often has undesirable income and estate tax consequences. First, the grantor will be taxed on the income of the trust under § 673, which requires the grantor to be treated as the owner of "any portion of a trust in which he has a reversionary interest in either the corpus or the income therefrom, if, as of the inception of that portion of the trust, the value of such interest exceeds five percent of the value of such portion." Second, the reversionary interest is includible in the grantor's estate under § 2033. It may also be includible under § 2037 or 2042.

§ 10.35.1. Income Tax Consequences

The utmost care must be exercised in planning the grantor's interest in any trust that is intended to shift the income liability to others. An exception to the general retained interest rule of § 673 applies to a reversionary interest that might take effect upon the death of a beneficiary who is a lineal descendant of the grantor before such beneficiary attains age 21. § 673(b).

The postponement of the date for reacquisition of the possession or enjoyment of the reversionary interest is treated as a new transfer commencing with the date on which the postponement is effective. § 673(d). However, the grantor is not treated as the owner of the trust by reason of such a postponement where the grantor would not have been treated as owner apart from the postponement. § 673(d).

§ 10.35.2. Gift Tax Consequences

The transfer of an income interest constitutes a gift to the extent of its actuarially determined value. The income interest qualifies for the annual gift tax exclusion if the income is payable currently to the income beneficiary or to a guardian or custodian for the beneficiary. Reg. § 25.2503-3(b). A technique for maximizing the value of the beneficiary's income interest is illustrated by Example 7-17 at § 7.39. Unless the trust is a § 2503(c) trust, no annual exclusion is available if the trustee may withhold payments of income from the beneficiary. Reg. § 25.2503-3(c), Example 1.

§ 10.35.3. Estate Tax Consequences

The actuarially determined value of a reversionary interest is includible in the grantor's estate under § 2033. Inclusion is required whether the reversion was expressly retained or is deemed to have been retained under the Doctrine of Worthier Title. *See Beach v. Busey,* 156 F.2d 496 (6th Cir. 1946), *cert. denied,* 329 U.S. 802 (1947). Where the Doctrine has not been abolished judicially or legislatively, it exists as a rule of construction that may prevent a transferor from creating a remainder in his or her own heirs. For a judicial repudiation of the Doctrine, *see Hatch v. Riggs National Bank,* 361 F.2d 559 (D.C. Cir. 1966). Under the Doctrine the grantor is considered to have retained a reversion where property is transferred in trust with a life estate in the grantor (or others) and a remainder to the heirs of the grantor. *See* Johanson, Reversions, Remainders and the Doctrine of Worthier Title, 45 Tex. L. Rev. 1 (1966).

As noted in § 10.34.2, property in which the grantor retains a reversionary interest may be included in his or her estate under § 2037. However, that section only applies where the possession or enjoyment of the property can, through the ownership of the transferred interest, be obtained only by surviving the grantor and the grantor retained a reversionary interest in the property that had a value immediately before the transferor's death in excess of 5 percent of the value of the property. It is unusual to create a trust that involves a reversionary interest that would subject it to § 2037. Also, under § 2042(2) a decedent is considered to have an incident of ownership in insurance with respect to which the decedent held a reversionary interest that had a value greater than 5 percent of the value of the policy immediately before the decedent's death. Because of this rule an insured person should not retain any interest in insurance policies that are owned by others. To be safe a policy rider should prevent the insured from acquiring any ownership interest in the policy.

§ 10.36. RETAINED CONTROL OF BENEFICIAL ENJOYMENT

Adverse income and estate tax consequences may occur if the grantor retains control over the beneficial interests in a trust. First, under § 674 the grantor may be treated as owner of the trust for income tax purposes. Second, the retention of a power over the beneficial interests of a trust may prevent a transfer to the trust from being a completed gift. Reg. §25.2511-2(c). Third, the trust may be included in the grantor's estate under §§2036 or 2038.

§10.36.1. Income Tax Consequences

Under §674(a), the grantor is treated as the owner of a trust if the beneficial enjoyment of the corpus or income is subject to the control of the grantor (or the grantor's spouse), a nonadverse party, or both, without the consent of an adverse party. Accordingly, the grantor is taxed on the income of a trust if the grantor or a nonadverse party holds the right to add or delete beneficiaries, to increase or decrease the shares of the beneficiaries in income or principal, or to determine when distributions will be made. However, the rigor of §674(a) is relaxed by important exceptions for: (1) certain powers held by anyone including the grantor, §674(b); (2) powers held by an independent trustee, §674(c); and (3) powers held by a trustee or trustees, none of whom is the grantor or the grantor's spouse, that are limited by an ascertainable standard set forth in the trust instrument, §674(d). The exception for powers of distribution held by an independent trustee is discussed at §10.20.3. In general, the scope of each exception varies directly with the degree of the power-holder's independence (*i.e.,* the narrowest exception applies to the grantor or a nonadverse party and the broadest to a totally independent party).

The exceptions carved out by §674(b) allow the grantor or any other person to hold a variety of powers over income and corpus without making the grantor the deemed owner of the trust for federal income tax purposes. Accordingly, the trust may permit some degree of flexibility over distributions. For example, the exceptions are broad enough to permit the grantor to act as trustee of a §2503(c) trust of which a dependent child is a beneficiary (the grantor would only be taxed on the income actually applied to discharge the grantor's obligation to support the child). Section 2503(c) trusts are discussed in more detail at §7.37.

The exceptions of §674(b)(1) – (4) are of limited general significance in planning irrevocable trusts. Briefly, they provide that grantor trust status does not exist where the grantor or a nonadverse party holds powers:

1. To apply income to the support of a dependent of the grantor to the extent the grantor would not be taxed under §677(b) (*i.e.,* the grantor is taxable only to the extent the income is actually applied to satisfy his or her legally enforceable obligation to provide support), §674(b)(1);

2. To control the beneficial enjoyment of the trust only after the occurrence of an event such that the grantor would not be treated as the owner under §673 if the power were a reversionary interest, §674(b)(2);

3. To appoint the principal or income of the trust by will, other than income accumulated in the discretion of the grantor or a nonadverse party, or both, §674(b)(3); or

4. To allocate the principal or income among charitable beneficiaries. §674(b)(4).

The exception of §674(b)(1) does allow the grantor or a nonadverse party to hold the power to allocate income to the grantor's dependents without triggering grantor trust status except to the extent the power is actually exercised.

The exception of § 674(b)(4) allows the creation of a specialized form of charitable income trust in which the grantor retains the power to designate each year the recipient of the income earned by the trust. *See* § 8.33. In operation, the use of such a trust permits the grantor to make an unlimited charitable deduction: The grantor is not taxed on the income of the trust, which the trust is entitled to deduct in full for income tax purposes. Moreover, the creation of such a trust does not involve a completed gift because of the grantor's retained power to allocate the income among charitable organizations. Of course, the retention of such a power would require the trust property to be included in the grantor's gross estate under § 2036(a).

The remaining exceptions to grantor trust treatment, set forth in § 674(b)(5) – (8), are of greater significance in estate planning. The § 674(b)(5) exception permits the grantor to hold the power to distribute corpus to or for the benefit of any current income beneficiary if the distribution will be charged against the distributee's proportionate share of the trust fund as if the corpus constituted a separate trust. In addition, this subsection permits the grantor to distribute corpus to any beneficiary or a class of beneficiaries provided that the power is limited by a reasonably definite standard set forth in the trust instrument (*e.g.*, to defray costs of education or medical care).

Section 674(b)(6) allows the grantor to distribute or withhold income temporarily from a beneficiary without invoking grantor trust status if any accumulated income must be either: (1) ultimately paid to the beneficiary, to his or her estate, or to his or her appointees; or (2) distributed on termination of the trust to the current beneficiaries of the trust in shares irrevocably specified in the trust instrument. This exception provides a degree of flexibility that encourages creating trusts with separate shares.

Under § 674(b)(7), the grantor may withhold income from a beneficiary during his or her incompetency or minority without creating a grantor trust. To qualify under this exception it is not necessary that the accumulated income be payable to the beneficiary from whom it was withheld or to his or her estate or appointees. Reg. § 1.674(b)-1(b)(7). Thus, income accumulated during the minority of a beneficiary may be added to corpus and ultimately distributed to others. Of course, provision for distribution to others could prevent the income interest from qualifying for the annual exclusion under § 2503(c).

Finally, § 674(b)(8) excepts a power to allocate receipts and disbursements between principal and income, even though expressed in broad language. This exception permits a desirable degree of flexibility regarding principal and income allocations without triggering grantor trust status.

§ 10.36.2. Gift Tax Consequences

The retention of powers that are within the exceptions of § 674(b) may have adverse gift tax consequences for the grantor. For example, although the grantor retains the power to withhold income from the beneficiary, the gift will be complete for gift tax purposes. Reg. § 25.2511-2(d). However, the income interest generally will not qualify for the annual gift tax exclusion unless the trust satisfies the requirements of a minor's trust under § 2503(c). *See* § 7.37.2. The retention of other powers could also prevent the trust from meeting the requirements of § 2503(c). Under Reg. § 25.2511-2(e), the donor is treated as holding a power if it is exercisable by the donor and a person not having a substantial adverse interest in the trust. For this purpose "[a] trustee, as such, is not a person having an adverse interest in the disposition of the trust property or its income." *Id.*

§ 10.36.3. Estate Tax Consequences

Perhaps more important, the retention of a power, alone or in conjunction with any other party, to distribute or withhold income or corpus will often cause the trust to be included in the grantor's gross estate under § 2036 and 2038. *See Lober v. United States*, 346 U.S. 335 (1953). For this reason the grantor should not act as a trustee of a § 2503(c) trust. *See* § 7.37.6. Also, recall that for estate tax purposes inclusion in the gross estate is required if a proscribed power is exercisable by the grantor alone or in conjunction with any other person. In other words, there is no exception for powers that are jointly exercisable with a person who has an adverse interest in the trust. § 2036(a)(2), 2038(a)(1).

The retention of a power, exercisable in conjunction with other persons, over the termination of a trust or disposition of the trust property requires inclusion of the transferred property under § 2038. In this connection, note that under § 2035(a) the transferor's gross estate includes interests over which she held such powers that were transferred within three years immediately preceding her death. LR 9502005 (Illinois land trust). In *Commissioner v. Estate of Bowgren*, 105 F.3d 1156 (7th Cir. 1997), *rev'g*, 70 T.C.M. (CCH) 748 (1995), the court held that the decedent's retained power over units in an Illinois land trust required their inclusion in her gross estate under § 2038.

§ 10.37. ADMINISTRATIVE POWERS

The grantor's retention of routine powers of administration do not have adverse tax consequences, at least where they are exercisable in a fiduciary capacity. However, a grantor who retains unusually broad powers of administration may be the deemed owner of the trust for income tax purposes and may also suffer adverse estate tax consequences. Indeed, under § 675, grantor trust status may result if certain administrative powers are exercisable by nonadverse parties or persons not acting in fiduciary capacities.

§ 10.37.1. Income Tax Consequences

The grantor is taxed on the income of a trust under § 675 if certain powers of administration are held by the grantor or a nonadverse party. In general the powers are ones that indicate the trust may be operated substantially for the benefit of the grantor instead of the beneficiaries. A power may be present either because of the terms of the trust instrument or because of the manner in which the trust is operated. Reg. § 1.675-1(a). The powers described in § 675 are:

> (1) *Power to deal for less than adequate and full consideration.* A power exercisable by the grantor or a nonadverse party, or both, without the approval or consent of any adverse party that enables the grantor or any other person to purchase, exchange, or otherwise deal with or dispose of

the corpus or the income therefrom for less than an adequate consideration in money or money's worth. § 675(1).

(2) *Power to borrow without adequate interest or security.* A power exercisable
by the grantor or a nonadverse party, or both, that enables the grantor to
borrow the corpus or income, directly or indirectly, without adequate
interest or without adequate security except where a trustee (other than
the grantor) is authorized under a general lending power to make loans to
any person without regard to interest or security. § 675(2).

(3) *Borrowing of the trust funds.* The grantor has directly or indirectly
borrowed the corpus or income and has not completely repaid the loan,
including any interest, before the beginning of the taxable year. The
preceding sentence shall not apply to a loan which provides for adequate
interest and adequate security, if such loan is made by a trustee other than
the grantor and other than a related or subordinate trustee subservient to
the grantor. § 675(3).

In addition, under § 675(4) the grantor is treated as the owner of any part of the
trust in respect of which any person in a nonfiduciary capacity has, without the
consent of any person in a fiduciary capacity:

(A) a power to vote or direct the voting of stock or other securities of a
corporation in which the holdings of the grantor are significant from the
viewpoint of voting control;

(B) a power to control the investment of the trust funds either by directing
investments or reinvestments, or by vetoing proposed investments or
reinvestments, to the extent that the trust funds consist of stocks or
securities in corporations in which the holdings of the grantor and the
trust are significant from the viewpoint of voting control; or

(C) a power to reacquire the trust corpus by substituting other property of
an equivalent value.

Note that the tests under § 675(1) and (2) are whether "the grantor or a nonadverse party, or both" have certain powers over the trust property (or income). The
grantor is treated as owner of any portion of the trust over which such a power exists.
In contrast, § 675(3) focuses on whether the grantor has in fact borrowed the corpus
or income of the trust. The grantor may be treated as owner of the entire trust if such
a borrowing takes place. *See Larry W. Benson,* 76 T.C. 1040 (1981) (grantor borrowed
entire income of trusts).

As noted in § 10.31.7, in *Rothstein v. United States,* 735 F.2d 704 (2d Cir. 1984), the
court treated the grantor as owner of a trust from which he purchased stock in
exchange for an unsecured promissory note that carried interest at 5 percent. The sale
made by a subservient trustee on credit without adequate security was, in effect, a
loan for purposes of § 675(3). However, the trust was recognized as a separate
taxpayer for purposes of determining the effect of the sale—the grantor obtaining a
basis in the stock equal to the value of his note. In Rev. Rul. 85-13, 1985-1 C.B. 184, the
IRS concluded that in such a case (where the grantor is treated as owner of the trust),
the "sale" of the stock to the grantor should not be recognized because, for income
tax purposes, the same person is the seller and the buyer. Revenue Ruling 86-82,
1986-1 C.B. 253, held that under § 675(3) the grantor-trustee is properly treated as the

owner of a trust from which he borrowed the entire corpus at the market rate and with adequate security although the loan was repaid during the same year. The effect of borrowing only a portion of the corpus of the trust is not clear. Presumably the grantor-borrower would be treated as owner of only a proportionate part of the trust. *See O'Neil Bennett*, 79 T.C. 470 (1982) (borrowing of part of trust income by partnerships of which grantors were members was treated as indirect borrowing by grantors).

None of the powers proscribed by § 675 are necessary for the legitimate administration of most trusts. In fact, the exercise of most of the powers described in § 675 would constitute a breach of the trustee's fiduciary duties with respect to investments unless expressly authorized. Accordingly, § 675 should not cause accidental treatment as a grantor trust in the ordinary case. The simplest and most effective way to guard against an inadvertent triggering of grantor trust status under § 675 is to provide expressly in the trust instrument that the trustee may not exercise any of the powers described in the section.

§ 10.37.2. Gift Tax Consequences

The retention of purely administrative powers does not render a gift incomplete, although doing so necessarily has some impact on the beneficial enjoyment of interests in the trust. Thus, a gift is not incomplete merely because the grantor retains the power, exercisable in a fiduciary capacity, to control the investment of trust assets or to allocate receipts and disbursements between income and principal. A transfer is incomplete, however, if the grantor retains the power to change beneficial interests in the trust unless the power is a "fiduciary power limited by a fixed or ascertainable standard." Reg. § 25.2511-2(c).

§ 10.37.3. Estate Tax Consequences

> We hold that no aggregation of purely administrative powers [retained by the grantor] can meet the government's amorphous test of "sufficient dominion and control" so as to be equated with ownership. *Old Colony Trust Co. v. United States*, 423 F.2d 601, 603 (1st Cir. 1970).

The rule set forth in the *Old Colony Trust Co.* case is consistent with the treatment of administrative powers in other contexts under the estate tax law. For example, administrative powers held in a fiduciary capacity do not constitute a general power of appointment for purposes of § 2041. *See* Reg. § 20.2041-1(b)(1).

Power to Substitute Assets of Equivalent Value ("Swap Power"). One common method to create a grantor trust that avoids estate tax inclusion is to give the grantor or other nonadverse party a power, exercisable in a nonfiduciary capacity, to take possession of trust assets by substituting property of equivalent value under § 675(4)(C) (a "swap power"). For many years the consensus among practitioners was that a swap power could not provide for inclusion of trust assets in the grantor's gross estate because the right to substitute assets does not allow the grantor to make additional wealth transfers or to diminish the value of the trust's holdings. In *Estate of*

Jordahl v. Commissioner, 65 T.C. 92 (1975), *acq.* 1977-1 C.B. 1, the Tax Court held that a swap power was not a power to alter beneficial enjoyment under § 2036(a) or § 2038(a). The court also held that there was no incident of ownership of life insurance by virtue of the swap power, thus negating inclusion under § 2042 where the trust owned a policy of insurance on the grantor's life. *See* LR 9227013. Still, skeptics cautioned that the swap power in *Jordahl* was arguably exercisable only in a fiduciary capacity and thus not effective to confer grantor trust status for income tax purposes. Moreover, some commentators worried that a power to replace income-producing property with non-income-producing property of equivalent value was, in effect, a power to alter or amend beneficial enjoyment of the trust's income and principal. If that was correct, inclusion of the trust principal in the grantor's gross estate would be required by § 2036 or § 2038. So while planners still used swap powers to create grantor trusts, they did so at least to some extent on faith.

The Service eased much of this anxiety with Rev. Rul. 2008-22, 2008-1 C.B. 796, in which the Service concludes a swap power held by the grantor will not, by itself, cause inclusion of the trust assets in the grantor's gross estate "provided the trustee has a fiduciary obligation (under local law or the trust instrument) to ensure the grantor's compliance with the terms of this power by satisfying itself that the properties acquired and substituted by the grantor are in fact of equivalent value, and further provided that the substitution power cannot be exercised in a manner that can shift benefits among the trust beneficiaries." Accordingly, planners seeking assurance should make sure that any swap power satisfies these two conditions.

The ruling's first condition that the trustee must have a duty to ensure that swapped assets have equivalent value, on its face, appears easy to meet. Very likely, applicable state law imposes such a duty anyway, for accepting property with the value less than the value of the property to be surrendered would be a breach of the trustee's fiduciary duties. To be clear, the trust instrument could specifically impose this duty on the trustee, but planners must use extreme caution here: if the power is construed such that the grantor needs the trustee's permission to exercise the swap power, the power would not be sufficient to confer grantor trust status for income tax purposes. A swap power must be exercisable without the consent of anyone acting in a fiduciary capacity if it is to create a grantor trust under § 675(4)(C).

The second condition, that the power cannot be exercised so as to shift benefits, would appear more problematic. For example, if an irrevocable grantor trust pays income to one beneficiary for his or her life followed by a distribution of the principal to another beneficiary upon the death of the income beneficiary, the grantor's exercise of a swap power to reacquire income-producing property in exchange for non-income-producing property would presumably affect the income beneficiary's interest adversely while possibly enhancing the value of the remainder beneficiary's interest. Rev. Rul. 2008-22 implies that the grantor would face inclusion of the trust assets in his or her gross estate because of the grantor's retained power to control the scope of the interests held by the income beneficiary and the remainder beneficiary. Fortunately, the IRS offered some relief on this point, stating that the second condition will be met if *either* "the trustee has both the power (under local law or the trust instrument) to reinvest the trust corpus and a duty of impartiality with respect to the trust beneficiaries," *or* "the nature of the trust's investments or the level of income produced by any or all of the trust's investments does not impact the respective interests of the beneficiaries, such as when the trust is administered as a unitrust (under local law or the trust instrument) or when distributions from the trust are limited to discretionary distributions of principal and income." To the extent many, perhaps most, trusts are drafted so as to provide only for discretionary distributions of income and principal during the term of the trust, satisfaction of the second condition will likely not be a significant issue. Accordingly, the risk of gross estate inclusion from a swap power will usually be very low.

Right to Vote Stock. The right to vote publicly traded stock transferred to a trust is usually an unobjectionable administrative power. However, the situation is different where the grantor retains the right to vote stock in a corporation in which the grantor and related persons own or have the right to vote 20 percent or more of the voting stock. In 1967 the IRS ruled that the retention of voting control of a corporation, combined with restrictions on the disposition of the transferred stock, was equivalent to retaining the right to control the enjoyment of the income of the trust. *See* Rev. Rul. 67-54, 1967-1 C.B. 269, *revoked,* Rev. Rul. 81-15, 1981-1 C.B. 457 (noting the control may have an effect on the value of the stock). However, when the issue was litigated, the Supreme Court rejected the IRS position. *United States v. Byrum,* 408 U.S. 125 (1972). In *Byrum* the Court held that the grantor's retained power "to affect, but not control" trust income was insufficient to cause the trust property to be included in his gross estate under § 2036. In the Court's view the grantor's power to vote a majority of the stock was so constrained by the fiduciary duties applicable to majority shareholders and directors that it did not warrant inclusion of the stock in his estate.

Congress responded to the *Byrum* decision by enacting § 2036(b) in 1976, which was modified in 1978. Under the so-called Anti-*Byrum* amendment, stock in a "controlled corporation" is included in the grantor's estate if the grantor retained the right to vote the stock. For this purpose, a "controlled corporation" is one in which the grantor owned or had the right to vote at least 20 percent of the voting stock at some time after the transfer of the stock and within three years of the grantor's death. The constructive ownership rules of § 318 are applied in determining the ownership of stock in the corporation. § 2036(b)(2). Section 2036(b) is thoroughly reviewed in McCord, The 1978 Anti-*Byrum* Amendment: A Cruel Hoax, U. Miami, 14th Inst. Est. Plan., Ch. 12 (1980).

The donor's retention of the power to vote the stock of a controlled corporation requires inclusion of the stock under § 2036(b), regardless of the capacity inwhich the power was retained. Thus, inclusion would be required if a parent were to transfer stock in a controlled corporation to himself or herself as custodian for a minor child under the Uniform Transfers (Gifts) to Minors Act. The same result would follow if the stock were transferred to a trust of which the donor was the trustee. The IRS has ruled that inclusion is required if the transfer were to a partnership of which the transferor were a general partner who had the right to vote the stock. LR 199938005 (TAM). *See* § 11.5.1.

It is less certain whether a retained swap power over a trust holding stock in a controlled corporation would cause inclusion of the stock in the grantor's gross estate under § 2036(b). Revenue Ruling 2008-22, discussed above, makes no mention of § 2036(b), and its analysis of § 2036 is confined to § 2036(a). The IRS, therefore, would not be precluded from arguing that a retained power to reacquire controlled corporation stock is effectively a retained power to vote that stock. The argument, however, would be inconsistent with its position in the ruling that a swap power is not really a retained power over the trust assets where the power cannot effectively shift benefits among the trust beneficiaries. Moreover, until the swap power is exercised, the grantor is unable to vote the shares held by the trust. That the grantor could conceivably one day reacquire the right to vote the shares is not the same as an expressly retained right to vote the shares currently.

§ 10.38. POWER TO REVEST TITLE IN GRANTOR

The grantor is treated as the owner of property held by a trust that can be revoked by the grantor. Thus, the income of a revocable trust is taxed to the grantor, transfers to the trust are not completed gifts, and the trust is includible in the grantor's estate. In order to remove any question regarding the revocability of a trust, the trust instrument should specify that the trust is irrevocable. This is particularly necessary if the trust might be subject to the laws of the small minority of states in which a trust is generally revocable unless otherwise specified in the trust instrument. *See* § 10.8.

§ 10.38.1. Income Tax Consequences

Under § 676(a), the grantor is treated as the owner of any portion of a trust "where at any time the power to revest in the grantor title to such portion is exercisable by the grantor or a nonadverse party, or both." Thus, the grantor will be taxed on the income of the trust that is revocable by the grantor, a nonadverse party, or both the grantor and a nonadverse party. Apparently the grantor will not be treated as the owner of a trust where the power to revoke is held by an adverse party or may be exercised only with the consent of an adverse party. Thus, the existence of a power to revoke may be shielded by the involvement of an adverse party. However, a distribution to the grantor under such a power would probably involve a gift by the adverse party.

The general rule of § 676(a) does not extend to powers that can only affect enjoyment of the income for a period commencing after the end of a period of sufficient duration that the grantor would not be treated as owner under § 673 if the power were a reversionary interest. § 676(b).

§ 10.38.2. Gift Tax Consequences

A gift is, of course, incomplete to the extent it is revocable by the grantor. For this purpose, a grantor is considered to have a power that is exercisable jointly with any person who does not have a substantial adverse interest in the property. Reg. § 25.2511-2(e). The fact that a nonadverse party has the sole power to revest title in the grantor does not make the transfer incomplete.

§ 10.38.3. Estate Tax Consequences

Under § 2038, property transferred to a trust is includible in the grantor's estate if the grantor retained the power, alone or in conjunction with any other person, to amend, revoke, or terminate the trust. The rule of § 2038(a)(1) extends to powers held at death or relinquished within three years immediately preceding death. *See also* § 2035(a)(2). The grantor's estate does not include the property of a trust merely because another person holds a power to amend, revoke, or terminate the trust. Understandably, where "the decedent had the unrestricted power to remove or discharge a trustee at any time and appoint himself trustee, the decedent is considered as having the powers of the trustee." Reg. § 20.2038-1(a)(3). Here again, some caution must be exercised in creating the power to remove and replace the trustee. *See* § 10.41.8.

The IRS may argue that an insured who holds a power of substitution with respect to a policy owned by the trustee of an irrevocable trust holds an incident of ownership over the policy. The possibility is suggested by LR 9128008, in which the IRS held that insurance owned by another party was includible in the estate of the insured who had an option to purchase the insurance from the owner. Accordingly, in appropriate cases the grantor's power of substitution should exclude policies of insurance on his or her life. *See* §§ 6.28.9, 10.31.

§ 10.39. RETAINED INCOME INTEREST

A grantor may choose to retain an income interest in a trust for valid nontax reasons—there are virtually no tax reasons for doing so. For example, a grantor may transfer property to such a trust in order to protect himself or herself against unwise expenditures or waste of property. Of course, creditors can reach the interest of the grantor in such a self-settled trust. *See* §§ 10.11, 10.21.2. For income and estate tax purposes such a transfer is largely ignored: The ordinary income of the trust is taxed to the grantor whether or not it is distributed; in addition, the entire value of the trust is includible in the grantor's estate under § 2036(a).

§ 10.39.1. Income Tax Consequences

The basic income tax rule is a broad one: The grantor is treated as the owner of a trust if, without the consent of an adverse party, the income is or may be: (1) distributed to the grantor or the grantor's spouse; (2) held or accumulated for later distribution to the grantor or the grantor's spouse; or (3) used to pay premiums on policies of insurance on the life of the grantor or of the grantor's spouse. § 677(a). The latter rule is not avoided by including a provision in the trust that prohibits use of trust income to pay premiums on policies insuring the life of the grantor. LR 8839008.

Under § 677(a), the grantor is taxed on the ordinary income of the trust if the grantor or any nonadverse party, such as an independent trustee, has discretion to accumulate the income for later distribution to the grantor. *Duffy v. United States*, 487 F.2d 282 (6th Cir. 1973), *cert. denied*, 416 U.S. 938 (1974). Likewise, the grantor is taxed currently on capital gains that are allocable to corpus and will be distributed to the grantor or the grantor's spouse at the end of the trust term. Rev. Rul. 66-161, 1966-1 C.B. 164; Rev. Rul. 75-267, 1975-2 C.B. 254. However, capital gains are not taxed to the grantor where they are allocated to corpus and will not be distributed to the grantor or the grantor's spouse. Reg. § 1.677(a)-1(g), Example 1.

Section 677(a) also extends to the use of trust income to satisfy legal obligations of the grantor or of the grantor's spouse, such as contractual payments due from the grantor (*e.g.,* mortgage installments). Income that may be used to discharge the grantor's obligation to support a beneficiary other than the grantor's spouse is taxed to the grantor only to the extent it is actually used for that purpose. § 674(b)(1), 677(b). Income that is used to pay private school tuition of the grantor's minor child is taxed to the grantor if the grantor is expressly or impliedly obligated to make the payments. *Morrill v. United States,* 228 F. Supp. 734 (D. Me. 1964). However, in another case the Court of Claims held that where the local law did not require the grantor to send his children to a private day school, the income of the trust used to pay their tuition is not taxable to him. *Wyche v. United States,* 36 A.F.T.R.2d 75-5816 (Ct.Cl. Trial Judge's opinion, 1974) (South Carolina law). Later cases from several states indicate that parents may be obligated to provide their children with private school educations and, hence, taxed on the income of trusts used to pay private school tuition. *E.g., Frederick C. Braun, Jr.,* T.C. Memo. 1984-285 (New Jersey law), and *Christopher Stone,* T.C. Memo. 1987-454 (California).

Income that might be used to pay premiums of policies insuring the life of the grantor or the life of the grantor's spouse is taxed to the grantor only if policies actually exist during the tax year, "upon which it would have been physically possible for the trustees to pay premiums." *Genevieve F. Moore,* 39 B.T.A. 808, 812-813 (1939), *acq.,* 1939-2 C.B. 25. *See* § 6.40. "There were no existing policies upon which premiums might be paid, and no part of the trust income was used for that purpose. In this situation we have held that no part of the income of the trust estate is taxable to the grantor." *Corning v. Commissioner,* 104 F.2d 329, 333 (6th Cir. 1939). Where policies do exist, the reach of the statute is not defeated by a nominal requirement that income be distributed to an individual beneficiary or to another trust.

EXAMPLE 10-16.

W transferred income-producing property to Trust A, the income of which was payable in equal shares to W's children. At the same time W transferred policies of insurance on her life to Trust B, in which the children will each have a one-third interest. W will be taxed on the income of Trust A if it is paid to Trust B pursuant to the consent of the children who are beneficiaries of Trust A. Rev. Rul. 66-313, 1966-2 C.B. 245. *See also L. B. Foster,* 8 T.C. 197 (1947), *acq.,* 1947-1 C.B. 2.

Under § 677(b), the income of a trust that may "in the discretion of another person, the trustee, or the grantor acting as trustee or cotrustee" be applied "for the support or maintenance of a beneficiary (other than the grantor's spouse) whom the grantor is legally obligated to support or maintain," is taxed to the grantor only "to the extent that such income is so applied or distributed." This provision prescribes the exclusive rule for the taxation of such support payments. Accordingly, the grantor is not treated as having a reversionary interest, within the meaning of § 673, in a trust from which an independent trustee has discretion to make distributions for the support of his or her dependent children. Rev. Rul. 61-223, 1961-2 C.B. 125.

By reason of § 674(b)(1) and 677(b) the income of a trust such as a § 2503(c) minor's trust is not taxed to the grantor merely because the income could be used to satisfy his or her legally enforceable obligation to support the beneficiary. Instead, the income is taxed to the grantor only to the extent it is actually used to discharge his or her support obligations. For this purpose, the extent of the grantor's obligation is measured by the applicable local law. *Brooke v. United States,* 468 F.2d 1155 (9th Cir. 1972); Rev. Rul. 56-484, 1956-2 C.B. 23. For example, the *Brooke* court did not require the parent-guardian to report the income that was used to pay for "private school tuition, musical instruments, music, swimming and public speaking lessons," the cost of an automobile for his oldest child, or the payment of travel expenses to New Mexico for an asthmatic child. The uncertain status of a parent's support obligation in most states, and the consequent tax uncertainty, would be relieved if a federal standard were adopted. As indicated by the cases discussed above, the law of some states obligates parents to provide "extras" for their children that are consistent with the family's standard of living.

In most states, the grantor is not taxed on the income of trusts that provide the grantor's children with items of "super" support, such as private school tuition, music lessons, or the "luxuries"—which the grantor would otherwise pay out of his or her own after-tax dollars. However, the grantor is taxable to the extent the trustee pays expenses that the grantor is obligated to pay. Thus, the grantor is taxable to the extent the trustee pays for private school tuition that the grantor is contractually obligated to pay. As a protective measure trusts for the super support of children should prohibit the trustee from using the funds to provide any item of support the local law required the grantor to furnish. Of course, it is generally preferable to give a trustee broad discretion to make distributions to beneficiaries.

§10.39.2. Gift Tax Consequences

For gift tax purposes, the transfer of property to a trust involves a gift of the actuarially determined value of any interest the grantor does not retain. In this connection recall the valuation rules of §2702. Of course, the gift of a remainder is incomplete and not presently taxable if the grantor retains the power to change the disposition of the remainder interest. *See* Reg. §25.2511-2(c). A gift of the remainder is a gift of a future interest that does not qualify for the annual gift tax exclusion. §2503(b).

There is some uncertainty regarding the gift tax consequences of the grantor's retention of the discretionary right to receive income. The regulations suggest that the grantor has made a gift of the income interest. Reg. §25.2511-2(b). In Rev. Rul. 77-378, 1977-2 C.B. 347, the IRS ruled that where the grantor's creditors could not reach any interest in the trust property, the grantor made a completed gift of the entire value of the property. However, where the income interest can be reached by the grantor's creditors, the transfer is not considered to involve a completed gift of the income interest. *Mary M. Outwin,* 76 T.C. 153 (1981); *Alice Spaulding Paolozzi,* 23 T.C. 182 (1954), *acq.,* 1962-2 C.B. 5; Rev. Rul. 76-103, 1976-1 C.B. 293.

§10.39.3. Estate Tax Consequences

A retained discretionary interest in income does not alone require the trust property to be included in the grantor's estate under §2036(a)(1). However, the property of such a trust is includible in the grantor's estate where the income is regularly distributed to the grantor, apparently by prearrangement. *Estate of Skinner v. United States,* 316 F.2d 517 (3d Cir. 1963). Property transferred outright more than three years prior to the transferor's death is likewise includible if the transferor continued to receive the income from the property by prearrangement. *Estate of McNichol v. Commissioner,* 265 F.2d 667 (3d Cir.), *cert. denied,* 361 U.S. 829 (1959). A prearrangement is not implied if the income is not regularly paid to the grantor. *Estate of Uhl v. Commissioner,* 241 F.2d 867 (7th Cir. 1957).

The property of trusts over which the trustees had power to make discretionary distributions to the grantor are includible in the grantor's gross estate under § 2036(a) because, under state law, the property held by the trustees was subject to the claims of creditors. LR 199917001 (TAM).

§ 10.40. POWER TO APPOINT SUCCESSOR TRUSTEES

Trusts generally should provide a method for the selection of successor trustees. Indeed, it is often desirable to provide a mechanism for the removal and replacement of trustees. However, provisions dealing with the removal and replacement of trustees should be drafted with care. If the trustee does not hold any tax-sensitive powers, such as the discretion to make distributions, and the trust does not include policies of insurance on the grantor's life, the grantor or a beneficiary can hold an unrestricted power to remove and replace the trustee. However, such an unrestricted power poses potential problems if the trustee holds any tax-sensitive powers, including the power to deal with policies of insurance on the life of the person holding such a power.

§ 10.40.1. Power to Remove Trustee and Appoint Another

In Rev. Rul. 79-353, 1979-2 C.B. 325, the IRS stated that the "reservation by the settlor of the power to remove the trustee at will and appoint another trustee is equivalent to reservation of the trustee's powers." The ruling was rejected by the Tax Court in *Estate of Helen S. Wall,* 101 T.C. 300 (1993) and was subsequently revoked by the IRS. Under Rev. Rul. 95-58, 1995-2 C.B. 191, an individual who holds the power to remove a trustee and appoint a replacement who is not a related or subordinate party within the meaning of § 672(c) will not be treated as possessing the powers of the trustee. Clients often wish to allow themselves and, later, the beneficiaries, the power to remove and replace the trustee—at least to the extent allowed by Rev. Rul. 95-58.

§ 10.40.2. Power to Remove Trustee and Appoint Self

A grantor or other person who holds the power to remove the trustee and appoint himself or herself (or a related or subordinate party) as successor trustee is properly treated as holding the powers of the trustee. Reg. § 20.2036-1(b)(3) (grantor); Reg. § 20.2038-1(a)(3) (grantor); Reg. § 20.2041-1(b)(1) (non-grantor). Indeed, the grantor may be treated as holding the powers of the trustee if the grantor has a *contingent* power to appoint himself or herself as trustee if the original trustee resigns, is removed, or becomes unable to act. For example, in Rev. Rul. 73-21, 1973-1 C.B. 405, inclusion was required under § 2036 where grantor held contingent power to appoint a successor trustee, including himself, and the trustee had power to vary distributions. It is interesting to note that G.C.M. 34730 indicated that the IRS was not confident that Rev. Rul. 73-21 would be upheld by the courts:

> Although we agree that the proposed revenue ruling [73-21] currently reflects the law, we believe that the position taken in the revenue ruling will be a hazardous one to defend in litigation.

§10.40.3. Factors in Planning Power to Appoint Successor Trustees

Drafting a power to appoint successor trustees must be done in light of the other provisions of the trust. The extent to which a power of removal and replacement should be held by the grantor or a beneficiary depends largely upon the extent to which the trustee has discretion to make distributions to or for the benefit of the grantor or the beneficiaries. If the trustee has only the nondiscretionary power to make distributions, the grantor or a beneficiary can safely serve as trustee—or hold the power to remove and replace the trustee with anyone.

Overall, the following tax-related factors should be considered: (1) the choice of trustee (tax-sensitive powers can more safely be given to an independent trustee or cotrustee); (2) the extent to which the trustee is authorized to make discretionary distributions or distributions that satisfy the legal obligation of the grantor or a beneficiary; (3) the circumstances under which the grantor or beneficiary has the power to remove and replace a trustee; (4) the limits, if any, on the appointment of the grantor or beneficiary as trustee; and (5) the extent to which the grantor or beneficiary is prohibited from taking any action affecting any life insurance on his or her life that may be held in the trust, including the appointment of a trustee of the trust.

§10.40.4. Independent Trustee or Cotrustee

An independent trustee, cotrustee, or special trustee may have discretion to make distributions without causing the property to be included in the estate of the grantor or a beneficiary. Although an independent trustee may not be needed at the outset, the trust may provide that one should be added in order to avoid an otherwise adverse tax result. Thus, at some point—say, the birth of children—an independent trustee (or special trustee) might be added to the trust to make decisions regarding discretionary distributions. Under a variation of this approach, a beneficiary-trustee might be given the power to appoint a special trustee to exercise the power to make distributions to persons the beneficiary is legally obligated to support. LR 9036048 (trust not included in the beneficiary's estate under §2041 where the beneficiary was authorized to appoint, but not to remove, a special trustee who would have authority to make distributions to the beneficiary's minor children). In short, an independent trustee with tax-sensitive powers should not be subject to unrestricted removal and replacement by the grantor or a beneficiary.

Tax-sensitive powers should be exercisable only by an independent trustee—not jointly by such a trustee and the grantor or beneficiary. A grantor who holds discretionary powers to make distributions would be treated as the owner of the trust for income tax purposes unless the powers were within the exceptions of §674(b). More important, for estate tax purposes the grantor should not hold a joint power to make discretionary distributions. In LR 8916032 the IRS stated, "For purposes of sections 2036 and 2038, it is immaterial whether a power is exercisable by the decedent alone or in conjunction with persons having an adverse interest." *See Lober v. United States*, 346 U.S. 335 (1953) and §10.36.3.

Similarly, a beneficiary's joint power to distribute to himself causes inclusion under §2041 unless the coholder of the power is the creator of the power or an adverse party. §2041(b)(1)(C)(ii). In practical terms the exception for such powers has limited utility, as explained in §10.40.9.

§10.40.5. Extent of Trustee's Discretionary Powers or Authority to Make Distributions that Satisfy Legal Obligations

The grantor or a beneficiary can safely serve as trustee if the trustee has no discretion to make distributions or exercise other tax-sensitive powers. However, in order to increase the flexibility of trusts it is often desirable to allow the trustee, or an independent party serving as special trustee, some discretion in making distributions. As indicated above, tax-sensitive powers should generally be entrusted only to an independent trustee or third party who is not a beneficiary. In addition, if the trustee holds any tax sensitive powers, the trust should generally prohibit the grantor or a beneficiary from becoming a successor trustee. Note that §2041 only deals with instances in which a donee may have power to remove or discharge the trustee and appoint himself or herself as successor trustee:

> A power in a donee to remove or discharge a trustee and appoint himself may be a power of appointment. For example, if under the terms of a trust instrument, the trustee or his successor has the power to appoint the principal of the trust for the benefit of individuals including himself, and the decedent has the unrestricted power to remove or discharge the trustee at any time and appoint any other person including himself, the decedent is considered as having a power of appointment. Reg. §20.2041-1(b)(1).

On the other hand, a trust is not includible in the grantor's gross estate merely because the grantor holds nondiscretionary powers to vary distributions to persons whom the grantor is not obligated to support. Rev. Rul. 73-143, 1973-1 C.B. 407. The IRS has ruled that a trust is not includible under §2041 in the estate of a beneficiary who holds a joint power to remove and replace the trustee where the trustee's power to make distributions to the beneficiary is limited by an ascertainable standard relating to maintenance, education, support or health. LR 9043052. According to LR 8916032, which may have been superseded by Rev. Rul. 95-58, 1995-2 C.B. 191, a beneficiary who held the power to remove and replace an independent trustee who was authorized to make distributions to persons the beneficiary was obligated to support would face gross estate inclusion. *See also* Rev. Rul. 79-154, 1979-1 C.B. 301 (life insurance fund subject to withdrawal by surviving spouse to support adult children was not includible in her estate, but would have been includible if it could have been used to discharge surviving spouse's legal obligation to support dependent children).

§10.40.6. Prohibit Distributions that Satisfy Legal Obligations

Another important safeguard is to prohibit the trustee from making any distribution that satisfies a legal obligation of the trustee. Such a provision may avert an inclusion that would otherwise be required by §2036 or 2041. Without such a limitation, inclusion might be required under §2036 if the grantor held such a power. Reg. §20.2036-1(b)(2). In this connection consider the text of Reg. §20.2041-1(c)(1):

> A power of appointment exercisable for the purpose of discharging a legal obligation of the decedent or for his pecuniary benefit is considered a power of appointment exercisable in favor of the decedent or his creditors.

Dicta in Rev. Rul. 79-154, 1979-1 C.B. 301, states that a decedent who holds the power to make appointments from an insurance fund that would meet her obligation to support her minor children would be treated as holding a general power of appointment over the fund. In such a case the threat of inclusion arises because the power is limited by a standard relating not to the power-holder herself, but to a person the power-holder is legally obligated to support. Inclusion in the power-holder's estate would not have been required under §2041 if the power had been limited by an ascertainable standard relating to her own maintenance, education, support, or health. Inclusion under this theory is blocked by including in the trust a provision that prohibits the trustee from making distributions that would satisfy any legal obligation of the trustee, including the duty to support a distributee. Of course, the statutes in some states prohibit a trustee from expending funds to meet the trustee's obligation to support a beneficiary.

§10.40.7. Income Tax Consequences of Distributions for Support

The power of the trustee to make distributions that satisfy the grantor's obligation to support a dependent is not generally taken into account for income tax purposes. Thus, under §677(b), only the amount actually distributed by a trustee in ways that satisfy the grantor's legal obligation of support is taxable to the grantor under §677(b). Similarly, under §678(c), the power of a non-grantor to make distributions of income that satisfy the power-holder's obligations of support and maintenance require him or her to be treated as owner of the trust only to the extent the income is so applied. Here again, allowing the power-holder to make distributions to his or her dependents subject to an ascertainable standard probably would not prevent inclusion in the power-holder's income to the extent the distributions satisfy his or her obligation of support.

§ 10.40.8. Drafting Power of Grantor or Beneficiary to Remove and Replace Trustee with Tax-Sensitive Powers

If a grantor wishes to create a discretionary trust and retain the power to remove and replace the trustee, the trust should ordinarily prohibit the grantor from appointing himself or herself. Alternatively, the trust might provide that if the grantor becomes a successor trustee an independent cotrustee or "special trustee" must make all tax-sensitive decisions. Otherwise, the trust might provide that the successor trustee only make nondiscretionary distributions. In the latter case, the removal and replacement of the trustee would cause the trust to shift from a discretionary one to a nondiscretionary one. The grantor should, of course, not hold any power with respect to incidents of ownership in life insurance on his or her life. Insurance over which the insured holds any incident of ownership is includible in the insured's gross estate although the power was held in a fiduciary capacity. § 2042(2).

§ 10.40.9. Prohibit Self-Appointment by Grantor or Beneficiary

> [T]he course that best combines flexibility with simplicity and safety is to exclude the settlor from the role of trustee. Halbach, Tax-Sensitive Trusteeships, 63 Or. L. Rev. 381, 397 (1984).

Tax problems are most likely to arise if the grantor serves as trustee or retains the power to appoint himself or herself as successor trustee. The regulations treat the grantor as holding the powers of the trustee if the grantor has the power to remove the trustee and appoint himself or herself. In addition, the IRS has treated a grantor as holding the powers of the trustee where the grantor held a contingent power to become successor trustee upon the death, resignation or removal of the original trustee. Rev. Rul. 73-21, 1973-1 C.B. 405. Accordingly, if the trustee holds any discretionary powers of distribution, the trust generally should not permit the grantor to become successor under any circumstances. As suggested above, if a trustee holds any discretionary powers to make distributions the beneficiaries should also be prohibited from serving as trustee.

At least one court has applied the theory of Rev. Rul. 73-21 where the grantor had a contingent power to appoint himself as successor trustee. In *First National Bank of South Carolina v. United States,* 81-2 U.S.T.C. ¶ 13,422 (D.S.C. 1981), the grantor held the power to appoint himself as successor trustee upon the resignation of the corporate trustee. A comparable problem arises under § 2041 if a beneficiary has the power to remove the trustee and to appoint himself as successor trustee and the trustee has power to make discretionary distributions to the beneficiary or ones that satisfy the legal obligations of the beneficiary. Note that the regulations limit inclusion to cases in which the power exists at the time of the decedent's death:

> [I]f under the terms of a trust instrument, the trustee or his successor has the power to appoint the principal of the trust for the benefit of individuals including himself, and the decedent has the unrestricted power to remove or discharge the trustee at any time and appoint any other person

including himself, the decedent is considered as having a power of appointment. However, the decedent is not considered to have a power of appointment if he only had the power to appoint a successor, including himself, under limited conditions which did not exist at the time of his death, without an accompanying unrestricted power of removal. Reg. §20.2041-1(b)(1).

In *First National Bank of Denver v. United States*, 648 F.2d 1286 (10th Cir. 1981), the court refused to include the trust under §2041 in the estate of a beneficiary who had the power to remove the trustee and appoint a successor other than himself.

Reformation of a trust that mistakenly allows the grantor to appoint himself or herself as trustee may eliminate the risk that a trust would be included in the grantor's estate. *See* §10.40.12.

§10.40.10. Disclaimers

The adverse tax effects of holding a power to remove and replace a trustee may be avoided if the holder disclaims the power. LR 8122075. However, in order for the disclaimer to be a qualified disclaimer, the disclaimant must give up all discretionary powers to control the disposition of any property affected by the power. Specifically,

> [A] disclaimer of a power of appointment with respect to property is a qualified disclaimer only if any right to direct the beneficial enjoyment of the property which is retained by the disclaimant is limited by an ascertainable standard. Reg. §25.2518-3(a)(1)(iii).

See also Reg. §25.2518-3(d), Example 9. Finally, note that the IRS will not recognize an attempted disclaimer by a fiduciary of a power to invade corpus for a specific beneficiary if the disclaimer is not effective for state law purposes. Rev. Rul. 90-110, 1990-2 C.B. 209.

§10.40.11. Releases

The threat of inclusion in the grantor's estate may be reduced if the offending power is released. Of course, inclusion would be required if the grantor dies within three years after releasing a tax-sensitive power. §2035(a)(2), 2038(a)(1). It is more difficult for a beneficiary to eliminate the threat of inclusion by releasing a power. Under §2041(a)(2), the property is includible if the

> [D]ecedent has at any time exercised or released such a power of appointment by a disposition which is of such nature that if it were a transfer of property owned by the decedent, such property would be includible in the decedent's gross estate under sections 2035 to 2038, inclusive.

Thus, for example, a beneficiary's release of a power of appointment would not insulate the property from inclusion in his or her estate if he or she retained an income interest in the trust. Inclusion would be required because the retention by a transferor of an income interest in a trust would require the trust to be included in his or her estate under § 2036.

§ 10.40.12. Eliminating Powers by Court Order

A favorable outcome may also result if the power of the grantor or beneficiary is terminated by a court decree during his lifetime. The IRS recognized the effectiveness of a court order terminating the grantor's power to appoint himself as trustee although the decree was inconsistent with existing state law:

> A lower state court construed the trust instrument to mean that the decedent had reserved the right to remove and appoint a trustee only once, that this power did not include the right to appoint himself; and that once having exercised that power, decedent would have exhausted his reserved powers. Rev. Rul. 73-142, 1973-1 C.B. 405.

Subsequent to the decree the decedent removed the trustee and appointed a successor other than himself. As a result, according to the court decree, which was binding on the decedent, the decedent no longer held the power to remove and replace the trustee. After the decree became final the decedent's power was, according to the IRS, "effectively extinguished."

The IRS has recognized the reformation of a trust to correct the scrivener's failure to include a provision that barred the trustor or a party who was related or subordinate to the trustor as defined in § 672 from serving as a successor trustee. Thus, LR 200314009 concludes that such a reformation would remove the possibility that life insurance policies on the grantor's life would be included in the grantor's gross estate under § 2035 or § 2042(2). The ruling relied upon Rev. Rul. 95-58, 1995-2 C.B. 191. According to the ruling, such a reformation would not constitute a release or transfer that would result in application of § 2035.

E. ADDITIONAL ISSUES

§ 10.41. INTRODUCTION

This part is concerned with several additional matters that the planner and the client should consider in planning trusts. They include: the selection of trustees, § 10.42; the selection of property to transfer to the trust, § 10.43; provisions regarding investment of trust funds, § 10.44; directions regarding the allocation of receipts and disbursements between principal and income, § 10.46; and the use of a perpetuities savings clause, § 10.48. The topics discussed do not exhaust the matters that should receive the serious attention of the planner and client. They are, however, fairly illustrative of the breadth of concerns that must be considered from the tax and the nontax points of view.

A trustee is a fiduciary with respect to the beneficiaries of the trust, to whom the trustee owes the highest duties of loyalty, integrity, and honesty. In managing the trust estate, a trustee is required to avoid conflicts of interest and to act for the best interests of the beneficiaries. As explained below, a trustee is required to exercise care in investing trust funds, and a trustee with greater skill is required to exercise it on behalf of the trust. §§ 10.44, 10.44.1. Indeed, a corporate trustee may be liable to a grantor's intended beneficiaries if it does not warn a grantor that additional steps must be taken to amend a trust to carry out the grantor's intention. *Wisconsin Academy of Sciences, Arts & Letters v. First Wisconsin National Bank*, 419 N.W.2d 301 (Wis. 1987).

§ 10.42. SELECTION OF TRUSTEE

Except as limited by law, any individual, association, partnership, or corporation that has the capacity to take and hold property may act as a trustee. Restatement (Third) of Trusts § 32, 33 (2003). Practically speaking, the choice is generally between an individual, such as the grantor or a beneficiary, and a corporate trustee. The choice may be dictated, however, by economic or family circumstances: in the case of a small trust, the appointment of a corporate trustee may be uneconomical. On the other hand, there may be no suitable family member or other individual available to serve as trustee. Some jurisdictions, including provinces of Canada, provide a public trustee who may be appointed in such cases. However, the concept has not caught on in the United States. The needs of some clients are best met by using multiple trustees (*e.g.,* an individual and a corporate trustee, or two or more individual trustees). The practice of appointing co-fiduciaries may be too expensive—at least in jurisdictions such as New York, that allow a full statutory fee to each fiduciary. For a discussion of the criteria for selecting an individual trustee, *see* Street, Growls or Gratitude? Practical Guidelines for Selection of Individual Trustees and Design of Trustee Succession Plans, U. Miami, 40th Inst. Est. Plan. Ch. 3 (2006). Consideration should also be given to the appointment of special trustees, whose only task might be to exercise certain tax-sensitive powers. Doing so involves little if any tax risk. *See* J. Kasner, The Special Trustee—An Idea Whose Time Has Come, 62 Tax Notes 750 (1994).

A lawyer and a client who intends to create a trust should discuss the role of the trustee in some detail before the client chooses a trustee. The client's choice should be made in light of all relevant factors including the purposes of the trust, the extent of the duties imposed on the trustee, the complexity and probable duration of the trust, and the reliability and experience of the beneficiaries and other family members. The lawyer can usually help the client make an appropriate choice by pointing out the advantages and disadvantages of the alternatives. The availability of a convenient local office of a corporate trustee, for instance, is important to some clients.

Duties of Fiduciaries. A trustee, like any fiduciary, is generally not required to review a document to determine its effectiveness in achieving a purported tax benefit. *Hatleberg v. Norwest Bank Wisconsin*, 700 N.W.2d 15 (Wis. 2005) (court declined "to impose a general duty to review a trust document drafted by another and draw legal conclusions as to its effectiveness"). However, a trustee that negligently encouraged a grantor to continue making gifts to a trust that did not qualify for annual gift tax exclusions is liable for the additional estate taxes on the grantor's estate. *Id.*

§10.42.1. Corporate Fiduciary

A corporate fiduciary may be chosen as trustee or cotrustee because of its financial responsibility, its continuity of life, and its overall administrative capabilities. Those considerations are particularly important in the case of large trusts, which usually require more attention to administrative details, investment decisions, and accounting matters. However, an individual trustee can be authorized to retain accountants, investment advisors, attorneys, and others who may provide the trust with essentially the same services that are available from a corporate fiduciary. Indeed, some corporate fiduciaries will provide some administrative support services to individual trustees on a contract basis. In choosing a corporate fiduciary, the client should interview at least one of the representatives of the ones under consideration and review their investment performance and investment philosophy. Corporate fiduciaries will typically wish to have authority to invest the assets of all but the largest trusts in common trust funds, of which they typically offer a variety designed to serve varying investment objectives. Thus, a corporate fiduciary typically offer common trust funds designed to maximize income, to generate a balance of income and growth, or to produce maximum growth.

A trust that is likely to endure for a long period usually requires either the appointment of a corporate trustee or the establishment of a suitable mechanism for the selection of successor individual trustees. Where a corporate trustee is appointed trustee of a long-term trust, it is often desirable to provide some mechanism for the removal and replacement of the trustee. Because of the generally disadvantageous tax consequences a beneficiary generally should not be empowered to remove the trustee and appoint himself or herself as successor trustee. *See* §10.40.9. In the case of individual trustees, the trust might name several successor individual trustees or cotrustees and authorize the survivor of them (or other responsible persons) to appoint further successors.

The quality of services provided by a corporate fiduciary varies according to the ability and interest of the personnel assigned to a particular trust. If a client wishes, a trust may express the grantor's desire that a designated trust officer work on, or supervise, the account and provide that the trust should follow the trust officer if he or she later moves to a different corporate trustee. Of course, such a provision introduces a degree of instability and could result in the imposition of additional trustees' fees if the designated trust officer changes employment.

§10.42.2. Lawyer as Trustee

The appointment of the scrivener as fiduciary is discussed at §1.6.7. Although a lawyer may serve as trustee, it is unwise unless the lawyer has the necessary expertise and is willing to take the time to apply it for the benefit of the trust. In general, a lawyer should not serve as trustee unless there is no qualified corporate or individual trustee available. The lawyer should be aware of the ethical issues involved in accepting an appointment as fiduciary, the most serious of which are conflicts of interest and the appearance of impropriety. Concerns that accepting such an appointment involves offensive solicitation of business have largely abated.

Ethical Consideration 5-6 is concerned with appointment of the draftsman as fiduciary:

A lawyer should not consciously influence a client to name him as executor, trustee, or lawyer in an instrument. In those cases where a client wishes to name his lawyer as such, care should be taken by the lawyer to avoid even the appearance of impropriety.

Model Rule 1.8 does not expressly prohibit such an appointment. However, the appointment would be subject to the general conflict of interest provision Model Rule 1.7 and the specific requirements of Model Rule 1.8. *See* Wash. Informal Op. 86-1 (1986).

In order to eliminate most questions regarding the efficacy of the appointment, a client who wishes to appoint his or her lawyer as fiduciary should obtain legal advice from an independent lawyer. The independent lawyer should draw the trust instrument, or at least the part designating the trustees. Some states bar lawyers from drafting instruments in which they are appointed as fiduciaries (a practice frequently condemned by courts in other states). *E.g., In re Estate of Shaughnessy*, 702 P.2d 132 (Wash. 1985).

If a client is considering the appointment of his or her lawyer as fiduciary, the lawyer should discuss the relevant factors with the client. Specifically, the lawyer should point out that the trustee will usually require legal representation, which is not included in the fee for the trustee's services. In short, the appointment of the lawyer as trustee may not save any fees.

Law firms or their affiliates have traditionally served as trustees in some locales, notably Boston and Philadelphia. An increasing number of firms are interested in serving as fiduciaries—which could be a potentially profitable service to clients.

§ 10.42.3. Grantor as Trustee

It is common for the grantor to serve as trustee or cotrustee of a revocable trust, which generally does not involve any tax disadvantages. *See* §§ 10.15-10.17. In such a case the trust should designate a successor to serve following the grantor's death or disability. For example, another person might be named to serve as cotrustee with the grantor and as sole trustee following the grantor's death or disability. Under another approach the surviving trustee is given the power to appoint a person to fill the vacancy and serve as cotrustee. A corporate fiduciary may be reluctant to serve following an individual trustee unless its potential liability for acts of its predecessor is eliminated by the terms of the trust, an accounting, or agreement of the beneficiaries.

In the case of an irrevocable trust, the grantor can serve as trustee without tax disadvantage if the grantor's powers are appropriately circumscribed. *See* §§ 10.30 – 10.37. Serious tax disadvantages may arise, however, if the grantor retains the power, alone or in conjunction with any other person, to make discretionary distributions. *See* § 2036(a)(2), 2038(a)(1). The grantor may be willing to take that risk where the trust is relatively small and will probably terminate during the grantor's lifetime. For example, a grantor might decide to serve as trustee of a § 2503(c) trust although doing so would cause the trust to be included in the grantor's estate if he or she were to die prior to distribution of the trust. A similar issue exists with respect to a discretionary trust that will terminate when the beneficiary attains a relatively young age. Along the same lines, the grantor may choose to serve as custodian of a gift under the Uniform Transfers to Minors Act or the Uniform Gifts to Minors Act. § 7.35-7.35.4.

Because of the generally adverse income and estate tax consequences, great care must be exercised if the grantor will have any discretion to make distributions. To begin with, the possession of the power to make discretionary distributions of income or principal may cause the income to be taxed to the grantor under § 674. *See* § 10.36.1. As mentioned above, the grantor is taxable on the trust's income if a discretionary power of distribution is held by a nonadverse party other than an independent trustee within the exception of § 674(c). Finally, where the grantor is trustee, it is likely that any discretionary powers of distribution held by the grantor-trustee will cause the trust to be included in the grantor's estate under § 2036 and 2038. Thus, in *United States v. O'Malley*, 383 U.S. 627 (1966), the irrevocable trusts that the decedent established for his wife and daughters were included in his estate because of his power, as cotrustee, to pay out or accumulate the income of the trusts. Moreover, under § 2038 the trust is includible in the grantor's estate where the grantor holds the power, as trustee, to accelerate the distribution of the trust property to the beneficiary. *Lober v. United States*, 346 U.S. 335 (1953).

§ 10.42.4. Beneficiary as Trustee

> [F]iduciary powers in the hands of the wrong persons may constitute dangerous powers for tax purposes either under the grantor rules of the income and estate tax laws or, in the case of a beneficiary serving as trustee, under various rules (especially those relating to general powers of appointment) of the estate, gift and income tax laws. Halbach, Discretionary Trusts and Income Tax Avoidance After the 1976 Tax Reform Act, U. Miami, 12th Inst. Est. Plan. ¶ 308 (1978).

The suitability of appointing a beneficiary as trustee or cotrustee depends primarily on family planning and tax considerations. Insofar as the trust law is concerned, the appointment of a beneficiary as trustee does not impair the validity of the trust so long as the trust has either another trustee or another beneficiary. Put somewhat differently: The sole beneficiary of a trust cannot be the sole trustee. Uniform Trust Code § 402(a)(5) (2000). As the Restatement (Third) of Trusts § 32, comment b (2003) explains, "[a] person who receives both the sole legal title to property and the entire beneficial interest in that property, whether by will or by inter vivos transfer, takes the property free of trust because of the doctrine of merger." The Restatement (Second) of Trusts was even more explicit:

> (1) One of several beneficiaries of a trust can be one of several trustees of the trust.

> (2) One of several beneficiaries of a trust can be the sole trustee of the trust.

> (3) The sole beneficiary of a trust can be one of several trustees of the trust.

(4) If there are several beneficiaries of a trust, the beneficiaries may be the trustees.

(5) The sole beneficiary of a trust cannot be the sole trustee of the plan.

Restatement (Second) Trusts § 99 (1959).

The planner must recognize and attempt to deal with the potential conflict between the economic interests of the beneficiary and the duties of a beneficiary as trustee. One approach is to attempt to eliminate the sources of potential conflicts through the use of special trustees and the imposition of limits on the powers of the beneficiary-trustee. However, such an approach can cause the trust to be complicated and potentially confusing. (A special trustee is one who holds only limited powers over the trust—usually in order to insulate a beneficiary-trustee from adverse tax consequences that would result if such powers were held by the beneficiary-trustee.) Another, perhaps more common, approach is to refer to the existence of potential conflicts in the trust and to authorize the trustee to act with regard to those matters regardless of his or her personal interest.

The income, gift, and estate tax ramifications of appointing a beneficiary as trustee are considered in the following paragraphs. Giving the beneficiary power to remove the trustee and appoint a successor is reviewed in § 10.27.

Income Tax. The appointment of a beneficiary as trustee of an inter vivos trust may cause the income to be taxed to the grantor under the grantor trust rules unless the beneficiary-trustee is an adverse party as defined in § 672 (*i.e.*, the holder of a substantial interest that would be adversely affected by the exercise or nonexercise of the power). The risk that the income will be taxed to the grantor arises primarily under § 674, under which the grantor is generally treated as the owner of a trust to the extent the grantor or a nonadverse party has the power to control the beneficial enjoyment of the income or principal of the trust. However, as noted below, the exceptions of § 674(b) permit the grantor or a nonadverse party to hold some limited, but important, powers regarding distributions. *See* § 10.36.1.

If the grantor is not treated as owner of the trust, the appointment of a beneficiary as trustee may cause the income of the trust to be taxed to the beneficiary under § 678. In general, § 678(a) treats a person other than the grantor as owner of a trust if the person has a power, acting alone, to acquire the corpus or income. The rule does not apply to income that is taxable to the grantor under § 671-677. § 678(b). Note that the risk of inclusion is eliminated if a distribution to the beneficiary requires the consent of another person, who does not need to have an adverse interest.

EXAMPLE 10-17.

O transferred property to a trust that is revocable by the joint action of *O* and *O's* sister, *S.* The trustee of the trust is *O's* brother, *B,* who has the power to distribute income each year to one or more members of a class that includes *B.* The power held by *B* is not within any of the exceptions created by § 674(b). However, the income is not taxed to *O* under § 674 because *B* is an adverse party as to the power over income. Instead, *O* is treated as the owner of the entire trust under § 676 because of the power of revocation held jointly with *S*, a nonadverse party. Following the death of *O*, the income of the trust will be taxed to *B* under § 678.

If the grantor of a trust is not treated as its owner for income tax purposes, the income of the trust is taxable to a person who holds the power, acting alone, to use the income or corpus of the trust to satisfy his or her own legal obligations. Reg. § 1.678(a)-1(b). However, a trustee is not taxed on the income of a trust merely because the trustee holds the power to apply the income to the support or maintenance of a person the trustee is legally obligated to support except to the extent the income is so used. § 678(c). The latter rule is analogous to the one applicable to grantors under § 677(b).

If a trustee-beneficiary's power to distribute income or corpus to himself or herself is limited by an ascertainable standard so as to avoid inclusion of the trust assets in the trustee-beneficiary's gross estate, it is uncertain whether the trust income is taxed to the trustee-beneficiary under § 678. On the one hand, § 678(a) requires only two things: First, that the trustee-beneficiary hold a power exercisable solely by himself or herself; and, second, that pursuant to that power, the trustee-beneficiary may receive distributions of income or principal. Any limitations on the exercise of that power are seemingly permissible as long as they do not interfere with these two requirements. The IRS seems to interpret the statute in this manner. See LR 8211057 (trustee-beneficiary taxed on trust income under § 678(a) even though trustee-beneficiary's power to access principal and income is limited by an ascertainable standard).

On the other hand, the two requirements of § 678(a) could be read to mean that the trustee-beneficiary's power must be absolute. In *United States v. DeBonchamps*, 278 F.2d 127 (9th Cir. 1960), the court held that § 678 did not apply where the trustee-beneficiary lacked "the unlimited power to take the corpus of the estate to herself" because of an ascertainable standard for trust distributions. The *DeBonchamps* court was also troubled by the fact that the trustee-beneficiary did not hold a testamentary general power of appointment over the subject property. Accordingly, *DeBonchamps* supports the more stringent interpretation of § 678(a).

Gift Tax. A taxable gift may occur if a beneficiary-trustee distributes any of the income or principal of a trust to another person. For example, a gift takes place if the beneficiary-trustee appoints to another person income to which he or she is otherwise entitled to receive. Reg. § 25.2514-3(e), example 1. In such a case, the beneficiary, in effect, exercises a general power of appointment in favor of the other person. The appointment of principal to others may also involve a taxable exercise of a general or special power of appointment under § 2514. A gift would occur, for example, where the beneficiary-trustee distributes to others principal that he or she was free to distribute to himself or herself. The distribution of principal to others under a special power of appointment may involve a gift where the holder of the power is entitled to receive income distributions from the trust that will be diminished by the appointment. Reg. § 25.2514-1(b)(2); Rev. Rul. 79-327, 1979-2 C.B. 342. *See* § 10.23. A gift occurs when the holder of a general power of appointment over the corpus of one trust allows a recapitalization of the stock held by the trust, as a result of which a portion of the value of the stock is shifted to another trust with respect to which the power-holder does not have any power or interest. Rev. Rul. 86-39, 1986-1 C.B. 301. If the power-holder is an income beneficiary of the second trust, the property transferred to the other trust is includible in the power-holder's estate under § 2036 (transfer with retained life interest).

Estate Tax. The property of who holds a power, exercisable alone or in conjunction with others, to apply the principal of the trust for his or her own benefit. § 2041(a)(2). However, as explained in § 10.25, the rule does not apply to powers that are limited by certain ascertainable standards and to certain joint powers. Laws enacted in several states are designed to prevent a trustee from being inadvertently given a power that would constitute a general power of appointment. Unless otherwise expressly provided in the trust, the laws typically prohibit a trustee from exercising a discretionary power for his or her own benefit except to the extent the power is limited by an ascertainable standard. *See, e.g.,* Fla. Stat. Ann. § 737.402(4) (2011); Ohio Rev. Code § 1340.22(A) (2011); and Wash. Rev. Code § 11.98.200 (2011). In several letter rulings and a revenue procedure, the IRS has indicated that it will recognize the effect of such statutes. *See* LRs 9510065 (Florida), 9516051 (North Carolina), and 9323028 (Ohio); Rev. Proc. 94-44, 1994-2 C.B. 683 (Florida). In LR 9852031, the IRS ruled that the adoption of such a retroactive protective statute in California, Cal. Prob. Code § 16081, did not result in any gift, estate or GST tax liability.

No inclusion is required merely because a beneficiary holds routine administrative powers. Reg. § 20.2041-1(b)(1). Also, a surviving spouse may hold the power to veto the sale or disposition of the assets of the trust. LR 9042048.

In order to avoid a contest with the IRS, a person should not be authorized to use principal for the support of persons the power-holder is obligated to support (*e.g.,* minor or disabled children). The risk of confrontation arises because of Reg. § 20.2041-1(c)(1), which provides, "A power of appointment exercisable for the purpose of discharging a legal obligation of the decedent or for his pecuniary benefit is considered a power of appointment exercisable in favor of the decedent or his creditors." In this connection, note that the exception for powers limited by an ascertainable standard only applies to standards "relating to the health, education, support or maintenance *of the decedent.*" Reg. § 20.2041-1(c)(2) (emphasis added). In particular, the exception does not apply to a power, limited by an ascertainable standard, to make distributions to the dependents of the power-holder. § 2041(b)(1)(A). *See* § 10.25.

An individual beneficiary, such as the primary income beneficiary, can serve as trustee. The appointment of a beneficiary is logical because of the beneficiary's obvious interest, but it is generally unwise unless the beneficiary is reliable, has reasonably good judgment, and has a modicum of financial or business experience. The planner should be alert to the possibility that the appointment of one beneficiary as trustee may cause concern on the part of other beneficiaries. On the tax side, care must be exercised not to give the beneficiary any powers that would cause adverse income, gift, or estate tax consequences. *See* § 10.20. The planner should be particularly careful not to give the beneficiary-trustee a power that might be construed as a general power of appointment under § 2041, such as an unlimited power to invade trust principal for the beneficiary's own benefit. For gift and estate tax purposes, a beneficiary-trustee could, however, be given powers to invade the trust principal that are, (a) "limited by an ascertainable standard relating to [his or her] health, education, support or maintenance," § 2041(b)(1)(A), or (b) limited to a noncumulative power to withdraw the greater of $5,000 or 5 percent of the value of the trust corpus, §2041(b)(2). *See* §10.24-10.25.

Under §678(a) and (b), unless the grantor is treated as the owner of the trust, a beneficiary-trustee is taxable on the income of the trust to the extent the beneficiary has the power, acting alone, to acquire the principal or income. *See* §10.24.1. Thus, all of the income of a trust is taxed to a beneficiary-trustee who holds the power to distribute all of the income or principal to himself or herself. On the estate tax side, a trust over which a beneficiary-trustee holds a discretionary power to make distributions to himself or herself is to that extent includible in his or her estate under §2041. In contrast, a beneficiary can safely hold purely administrative powers. Reg. §20.2041-1(b).

If a beneficiary's power to withdraw is limited by an ascertainable standard, the beneficiary should not be treated as the owner of the trust under §678. *United States v. DeBonchamps*, 278 F.2d 127 (9th Cir. 1960) (the life tenants' power to expand corpus that was limited by an ascertainable standard did not cause them to be taxed on capital gains).

§10.42.5. Cotrustees

If the grantor or a beneficiary is a trustee, the appointment of a cotrustee may help avert unwanted tax consequences. For example, the appointment of a trustee with an adverse interest may prevent the grantor from being treated as the owner of a trust for income tax purposes. Similarly, the appointment of a cotrustee may prevent a non-grantor from being treated as owner of the trust under §678.

The appointment of a cotrustee is often most important for a variety of nontax reasons. For example, a corporate fiduciary might be appointed as a cotrustee because of its superior administrative capacity and immortality. On the other hand, an individual might be appointed because of his or her familiarity with the beneficiaries and the grantor's wishes. In order to reduce the risk of conflict and avoid the threat of a deadlock, each cotrustee could be given exclusive authority over specific activities of the trust. For example, one of the cotrustees might be given exclusive power to make certain decisions (*e.g.*, discretion to make distributions) or to act with respect to certain property. Doing so may avoid the adverse tax consequences that would follow if the power were shared with the other trustee. *See* §6.28.11. Before appointing cotrustees, some thought should also be given to the manner of their compensation. Depending on the circumstances, each trustee may receive a full fee, a single fee may be divided between them, or the individual trustee may forego receiving any compensation. However, it is generally unwise to set forth a rigid compensation schedule in the trust instrument because of the difficulty in anticipating the services that may be required of the trustee and the difficulty of obtaining approval of any change in such a schedule.

§10.42.6. Removal of Trustees

In most states it is difficult, if not impossible, to obtain the judicial removal of a trustee unless the trustee has engaged in an egregious breach of trust. Accordingly, the grantor may wish to give a responsible person the power to remove and replace a trustee. The power is particularly valuable in the case of a corporate trustee, which otherwise might serve indefinitely. Again, a beneficiary ordinarily should not have the power to appoint himself or herself, unless the beneficiary could have acted from the outset without adverse tax consequences. Care must be exercised in planning and drafting a power to remove and replace a trustee. *See* §§ 10.40.3, 10.40.8.

§ 10.43. SELECTION OF PROPERTY TO TRANSFER IN TRUST

The choice of property to transfer to the trustee is very important, especially in the case of an irrevocable inter vivos trust. In general the same factors that must be considered in selecting property to transfer by way of inter vivos gift, § 7.12-7.17, must be taken into account when it comes to selecting property to transfer in trust. In brief, the grantor should avoid transferring property that will cause the recognition of income (*e.g.,* an installment obligation), or will have other adverse income tax consequences. A grantor who creates an irrevocable trust for the benefit of others might fund it with appreciated stock rather than municipal bonds that produce tax-exempt income. The trustee must also exercise care in selling property transferred to the trust. The grantor should also avoid disposing of any business interests that might prevent his or her estate from qualifying for the benefits of § 303, 2032A, and 6166. *See* § 7.10. The grantor should also be aware that the potential availability of some income tax advantages may be lost if stock in a small business corporation is transferred to a trust. In particular, the ordinary loss deduction that is allowed under § 1244 for a loss suffered on small business stock is allowed only to the original shareholder—not to a trust or other successor shareholder. *See* Reg. § 1.1244(a)-1(b). Also, a trust generally cannot be a shareholder in a Subchapter S corporation unless: (1) the grantor is treated as its owner, § 671-677; (2) the trust is a qualified subchapter S trust, § 1361(c)(2), (d); or (3) the trust is an electing small business trust, § 1361(e). *See* §§ 10.4.13, 11.4.

The selection of property to transfer to a revocable trust is usually much less significant because the grantor is generally treated as the owner of the property for tax purposes. For example, the transfer of an installment obligation to such a trust is not treated as a disposition that triggers recognition of gain. *See* § 9.6.3. Similarly, property held in the trust is included in the grantor's gross estate. Hence it may be used to fund a marital gift, and is counted for purposes of meeting the percentage requirement of §§ 303, 2032A, and 6166.

§ 10.44. PROVISIONS REGARDING TRUST INVESTMENTS

In most instances a trust should not restrict the types of property in which the trustee may invest. Indeed, many lawyers prefer to include in the trust instrument a list of the types of property in which the trustee is authorized to invest, although the same types are permitted by a local statute. Some lawyers believe that including the list will cause the trustee to keep them in mind. In addition, either a statutory list may change in the future or the situs of the trust may be changed to another jurisdiction. Overall, imposing a limit on permissible investments can unduly restrict the trustee's ability to respond to changing economic circumstances, and can impair the value of the trust. In most jurisdictions a court may authorize the trustee to deviate from an investment restriction where there has been an unanticipated change in circumstances and adherence to the restriction would result in substantial losses to the trust and frustrate accomplishment of trust purposes. *See, e.g., In re Trusteeship Under Agreement with Mayo,* 105 N.W.2d 900 (Minn. 1960); Restatement (Third) of Trusts § 66 (2003); Uniform Trust Code § 412 (2000). Drafters must also take into account the impact of the Uniform Prudent Investor Act and the Revised Uniform Principal and Income Act. *See* Cline, Trustee Investments, 861 Tax Mgmt Port. (2008) and Cline, The Uniform Prudent Investor and Principal and Income Acts: Changing the Trust Landscape, 42 Real Prop., Prob. & Tr. J. 611 (2008). *See also* Nenno, The Power to Adjust and Total-Return Unitrust Statutes: State Developments and Tax Considerations, 42 Real Prop., Prob. & Tr. J 657 (2008); Medlin, Limitations on the Trustee's Power to Adjust, 42 Real Prop., Prob. & Tr. J. 755 (2008).

Where the trust is intended to qualify for the marital deduction, the trustee should not be prevented, directly or indirectly, from investing in income-producing property. In fact, because of the requirements of § 2056(b)(5), (b)(7), and 2523(f), the decedent's (or donor's) spouse should be given the power to compel the trustee to invest in income-producing property. Along the same lines, a charitable remainder trust should not restrict the trustee from making investments that would produce a reasonable amount of income or gain. *See* Reg. § 1.664-1(a)(3). *See also* § 8.24.

A corporate trustee that fails to diversify the assets of a trust may not be protected from surcharge by an indemnity agreement signed by the beneficiaries. *Estate of John P. Saxton,* 712 N.Y.S.2d 225 (App. Div., 3d Dept., 2000) (trust contained no specific directions regarding investments). The testamentary trust in *Saxton* was funded entirely with IBM stock in 1958—none of which was sold before the termination of the trust in 1993 despite requests by the beneficiaries that sales be made. In July 1987 the trust corpus had a value of $7,000,000. When it terminated in 1993 its value was $2,987,617.50. Responding to the trustee's contention that the agreement "insulated it from liability," the court stated: "Where a beneficiary has requested or consented to what essentially amounts to mismanagement by a fiduciary, equitable rather than contractual principles must govern . . . Hence, petitioner, as the fiduciary, must demonstrate, if the IDA [investment direction agreement] is to be enforced as a contract, that the beneficiaries had the intent to form a contract and so formed it with actual and full knowledge of all legal rights." *Id.* at 231.

A grantor may relieve the trustee of liability for the good faith retention of assets and consequent failure to diversify the assets of the trust. *Americans for the Arts v. Ruth Lilly Charitable Remainder Annuity Trust,* 855 N.E.2d 592 (Ind. App. 2006).

*"The little match girl realized too late what her mistake
had been. She had failed to diversify."*

Drawing by Handelsman; © 1987
The New Yorker Magazine, Inc.

§ 10.44.1. Investment Standards

The grantor has a free hand in specifying the criteria that will govern the
investment duties of the trustees—including the factors that should be considered in
making investments, the types of property in which to invest, the degree of risk to be
undertaken, and the extent to which the investments of the trust should be diversified. If a trust is silent, the local law will supply the standards that the trustee should
apply, and by which the trustee's performance will be evaluated.

A trustee is generally required to make the trust property productive within a
reasonable time. Restatement (Third) of Trusts § 227, comment a (1992). Under Cal.
Prob. Code § 16007 (2011), "The trustee has a duty to make the trust property
productive under the circumstances and in furtherance of the purposes of the trust."
In making investments, however, trustees may not prefer the interests of one beneficiary over another (*i.e.*, the trustee must be impartial as between beneficiaries or classes
of beneficiaries). *E.g.*, Cal. Prob. Code § 16003 (2011); Restatement (Third) of Trusts
§ 232 (1992).

In this connection note that the interests of the current beneficiaries and the
remaindermen are more likely to conflict if one beneficiary or class of beneficiaries is
only entitled to receive distributions of income, and the corpus of the trust is reserved
for the remaindermen. Conversely, conflict is less likely to occur where the distinc-

tion between income and principal is reduced or eliminated. (Diminishing or elimi- nating the differences also generally frees the trustee to pursue potentially more advantageous investment policies.) The distinction can be largely eliminated if the trustee is given discretion to distribute income or principal to the current benefi- ciaries. A trustee who is given such discretion should, as a corollary, be authorized to make investments without regard to the income producing capacity of the assets— and focus on maximizing the overall return of the trust. The differentiation between income and principal is also largely eliminated if the current beneficiary is entitled to receive a fixed amount each year (an annuity) or a fixed percentage of the current value of the trust property (a unitrust amount). Relating distributions to annuity or unitrust amounts makes the amount of income generated by the trust largely irrele- vant, at least from the perspective of the beneficiary receiving the annuity or unitrust amount.

If the current beneficiaries are only entitled to receive the current income of the trust, the trustee must invest with a view toward the production of income. In the case of the discretionary trust, an annuity trust, or a unitrust, the trustee can be relieved of the burden of investing only in assets that produce a reasonable level of current income. Instead, with proper authorization, the trustee can safely invest with a view to increasing the overall value of the trust. Of course, in any case the investments must be consistent with the terms and purposes of the trust. As indi- cated above, the types of permissible investments may be defined in the trust.

Traditional Prudent Person Rule. The traditional prudent person rule remains in effect in many states. Under it the trustee is permitted to make any investment that a prudent person "would make of his own property having in view the preservation of the estate and the amount and regularity of the income to be derived." Restatement (Second) of Trusts §227(a) (1959). From its origins in *Harvard College v. Amory,* 26 Mass. (9 Pick.) 446 (1830), the prudent person rule has evolved in a way that focuses on the propriety—principally the safety—of each investment. It has emphasized the necessity of avoiding the risk of loss as to each investment rather than considering its place in the trust's portfolio and its role in fulfilling the overall investment strategy of the trust. Thus, a trustee who makes an investment that itself does not meet the prudent person standard could be surcharged for any loss that resulted.

Restatement (Third)'s Prudent Investor Rule. In contrast, the Prudent Investor Rule that is included in the Restatement (Third) of Trusts (1992), and the law of a growing number of states provides that the appropriateness of an investment should be determined in light of the purposes of the trust, its overall portfolio, and other relevant factors. The Prudent Investor Rule, Restatement (Third) of Trusts §227 (1992), states that:

> The trustee is under a duty to the beneficiaries to invest and manage the funds of the trust as a prudent investor would, in light of the purposes, terms, distribution requirements, and other circumstances of the trust.
>
> (a) This standard requires the exercise of reasonable care, skill, and caution, and is to be applied to investments not in isolation but in the context of the trust portfolio and as a part of an overall investment strategy, which should incorporate risk and return objectives reasonably suitable to the trust.

§10.44.1

(b) In making and implementing investment decisions, the trustee has a duty to diversify the investments of the trust unless, under the circumstances, it is prudent not to do so.

(c) In addition, the trustee must:

    (1) Conform to fundamental fiduciary duties of loyalty (§ 170) and impartiality (§ 183);

    (2) act with prudence in deciding whether and how to delegate authority and in the selection and supervision of agents (§ 171); and

    (3) incur only costs that are reasonable in amount and appropriate to the investment responsibilities of the trusteeship (§ 188).

(d) The trustee's duties under this Section are subject to the rule of § 228, dealing primarily with contrary investment provisions of a trust or statute.

Uniform Prudent Investor Act. The Uniform Prudent Investor Act (1994), 7B U.L.A. 57 (1999 Supp.), that has been enacted by all but a handful of states, includes a list of factors to be considered by the trustee in making investment. Section 2 of the Uniform Prudent Investor Act provides that:

(a) A trustee shall invest and manage trust assets as a prudent investor would, by considering the purposes, terms, distribution requirements, and other circumstances of the trust. In satisfying this standard, the trustee shall exercise reasonable care, skill, and caution.

(b) A trustee's investment and management decisions respecting individual assets and courses of action must be evaluated not in isolation, but in the context of the trust portfolio as a whole and as a part of an overall investment strategy having risk and return objectives reasonably suited to the trust.

(c) Among circumstances that are appropriate to consider in investing and managing trust assets are the following to the extent that they are relevant to the trust or its beneficiaries:

    (1) general economic conditions;

    (2) the possible effect of inflation or deflation;

    (3) the expected tax consequences of investment decisions or strategies;

    (4) the role that each investment or course of action plays within the overall trust portfolio, [which may include financial assets, interests in closely held enterprises, tangible and intangible personal property, and real property];

    (5) the expected total return from income and appreciation of capital;

    (6) other resources of the beneficiaries;

(7) needs for liquidity, regularity of income, and preservation or appreciation of capital;

(8) an asset's special relationship or special value, if any, to the purposes of the trust or to one or more of the beneficiaries.

(d) A trustee shall make a reasonable effort to ascertain facts relevant to the investment and management of trust assets.

(e) A trustee may invest in any kind of property or type of investment consistent with the standards of this Act.

(f) A trustee who has special skills or expertise, or is named trustee in reliance upon the trustee's representation that the trustee has special skills or expertise, has a duty to use those special skills or expertise.

The provisions of this section of the Act are generally beneficial and suitable to govern the investments of most trusts. It would certainly be appropriate and desirable to include such provisions in a trust to be created in a jurisdiction in which the traditional prudent person rule remains in effect. It might be useful to do so even in jurisdictions that have adopted the Act in order better to assure that the trustee is aware of the applicable standards. In some cases the lawyer might choose to incorporate the provisions of the statute by reference.

Diversification. The prudent person rule was generally recognized as requiring a trustee to diversify the investments of a trust. Restatement (Second) Trusts §228 (1959). Diversification is expressly required by the Restatement (Third)'s prudent investor rule, §227(b) above, unless it is prudent not to do so. *See also* Cal. Prob. Code §16048 (2011). However, under the prudent person standard, the courts did not uniformly impose a duty to diversify the assets of a trust. It is logical to require diversification—modern portfolio theory emphasizes the need to diversify in order to spread the risk of loss.

In most circumstances a trustee should not concentrate trust investments in a single type of investment (*e.g.*, real estate, common stocks, bonds). Similarly, investments in common stocks should not generally be limited to the stock of a single company or industry. As an approach a trustee might invest as broadly as possible, which would avoid risks associated with most eventualities—oil shortages, recessions, labor problems, tax changes, inflation, and so forth. Overall a trust might best be protected by investing in a broad range of assets, including ones that, if viewed in isolation, would traditionally be viewed as too risky (speculative). Inclusion of such investments are now perceived to add to portfolio stability. Some have suggested that the best refuge is in stock index funds—against which the performance of a trustee might be measured.

Uniform Principal and Income Act (UPIA). The significance of the distinction between income and principal is diminished to some extent by the 1997 version of the Uniform Principal and Income Act (UPIA). Under UPIA, a trustee who has managed the assets of a trust as a prudent investor may make appropriate adjustments between principal and income. UPIA §104(a) (2000). The provisions of UPIA are reviewed in more detail at §10.46.

In *Matter of Janes*, 681 N.E.2d 332 (N.Y. 1997), the court held that if a fiduciary fails to diversify the holdings of a trust, "[t]he inquiry is simply, whether under all the facts and circumstances of the particular case, the fiduciary violated the prudent person standard in maintaining a concentration of a particular stock in the estate's portfolio of investments." 681 N.E.2d at 337. In that case the corporate fiduciary was subjected to a multi-million dollar surcharge for having failed to diversify its holding of Kodak stock, which constituted 71 percent of the initial corpus of the trust.

§ 10.44.2. Trustees with Greater Skill

The Uniform Prudent Investor Act and statutes in many states require that a trustee who has special skills or expertise will exercise those skills or expertise in managing the trust. States in which the prudent person rule remains in effect also often recognize that the standard represents a minimum that is increased for professional trustees and others with special skills or expertise. *See, e.g.,* Wash. Rev. Code § 11.100.020(1) (2011) ("if the fiduciary has special skills or is named trustee on the basis of representations of special skills or expertise, the fiduciary is under a duty to use those skills"); U.P.C. § 7-302, 8 U.L.A. 507 (1999); Restatement (Third) of Trusts § 227, comment d (1992); Uniform Trust Code § 806 (2000). *See also Estate of Beach v. Carter,* 542 P.2d 994 (Cal. 1975), *cert. denied,* 434 U.S. 1046 (1978); *In re Estate of Killey,* 326 A.2d 372 (Pa. 1974).

The terms of a trust may, of course, vary the duties of the trustee, including the duties regarding the investment of trust property. Of course, the trust may authorize (or direct) the trustee to retain specific assets and attempt to relieve the trustee from any liability that would otherwise attach for failure to dispose of the assets. A direction naturally provides a higher degree of protection to a trustee that retains assets. Regardless of the terms of such a provision, the trustee cannot be completely relieved of all responsibility for trust investments. Despite a direction to retain particular assets, at some point it may be necessary for the trustee to take steps to dispose of them or face the possibility of a surcharge.

The grantor may authorize or direct the trustee to make otherwise improper investments, or may prohibit the trustee from making otherwise lawful investments. Thus, a grantor who does not want a corporate trustee to invest in a common trust fund may prohibit it from doing so. Along the same lines, a grantor may prohibit an individual trustee from investing in mutual funds (which, naturally, pay a management fee to their investment advisor). However, most grantors recognize that it makes little sense to prevent a trustee from making investments that are broadly diversified—and best protect the trust against loss. In addition, from a practical point of view, restrictive or unusual investment directions may discourage a trustee from accepting a trusteeship or may result in the imposition of higher annual fees than normal. If an individual is appointed as trustee, it may be desirable to authorize him or her to obtain investment advice at the expense of the trust, and to rely upon the advice without any duty to inquire regarding the reliability of the advice provided by the investment advisor.

§ 10.44.3. Additional Directions Regarding Specific Assets

The nature of the trust property, the relationship of the parties, or other factors, sometimes make it desirable to give the trustee more specific directions or authorization. It is particularly appropriate to do so if the trust will hold interests in a closely-held enterprise. The trustee needs, and deserves, some specific direction (and authority) regarding the retention of the investment and the operation of the business. In such cases it is often appropriate to exonerate the trustee from liability for retaining the stock. The planner should also attempt to deal with the conflicts of interest that might arise between the trustee, the beneficiaries, nonbeneficiary shareholders, or partners and other persons who are interested in the business. It may also be necessary to give the trustee some specific directions regarding the allocation of receipts and disbursements between income and principal. *See* § 10.48.

Conflicts regarding investments can arise where trust and the trustee personally are interested in the same business or other property. Likewise, the interests of a trustee-beneficiary may conflict with the interests of other beneficiaries, including remaindermen. The planner must be alert to potential conflicts and should discuss any that can be identified with the grantor and, when possible, with the intended trustee. An instrument can identify a particular conflict and authorize the trustee to act with respect to the matter without liability. The problem might arise, for example, where the real property transferred to the trust is leased to the intended trustee or a business in which he or she is interested. In such a case the trust might specifically authorize the trustee to lease the property from the trust upon the same terms and conditions (or upon such other terms and conditions as the trustee deems appropriate). In the case of a corporate trustee, the trust may authorize it to retain and vote any of its own stock that is originally transferred to the trust. It is generally undesirable to authorize a corporate trustee to acquire more of its shares for the account of the trust.

§ 10.44.4. Investment Advisors

A grantor who has particular confidence in the skill of a particular investment advisor, may direct that the trustee follow the investment directions given by the advisor. Such directions must be carefully drafted and clearly define the duties of the advisor and the trustee with respect to investments. Diamond & Todd, *The Trustee's Role in Directed Trusts, Share the Responsibility With an Advisor for Discretionary and Ministerial Decisions,* 149 Tr. & Est. 24 (Dec. 2010). Where the trust instrument contains such directions, the trustee would normally be required to follow the advisor's directions. *See* Restatement (Third) of Trusts § 75 (2003). Presumably a trustee subject to such directions is substantially relieved of investment responsibilities and liabilities.

A person who has authority to direct or control the investments of the trust may be treated as a fiduciary. Under a fairly common approach, such a person is "deemed to be a fiduciary and shall be liable to the beneficiaries of the trust and to the designated trustee to the same extent as if he or she were a designated trustee in relation to the exercise or nonexercise of such a power or authority." Wash. Rev. Code § 11.100.130 (2011). Some investment advisors are, understandably, unwilling to act in such a capacity and assume the responsibilities of a trustee. Yet they may not have much of a choice if state law follows the Uniform Prudent Investor Act and provides that advisors can be held accountable in the court of local jurisdiction for failure to follow established investment policy. *See* Uniform Prudent Investor Act § 9 (1995).

§ 10.45.   EXCULPATORY CLAUSES

The grantor may wish to exonerate an individual trustee from liability for loss to the trust except for intentional misconduct or gross negligence, particularly if the trustee is a family member serving without compensation. *See* § 4.26.6 (exculpatory clause for executors). In this connection, note that the trustee is likely to be held to the same standard of performance whether or not the trustee is compensated. With regard to exculpation, the Restatement (Second) Trusts explained, "[I]f by the terms of the trust it is provided that the trustee shall not be liable 'except for his willful default or gross negligence,' although he is not liable for mere negligence, he is liable if he intentionally does or omits to do an act which he knows to be a breach of trust or if he acts or omits to act with reckless indifference as to the interest of the beneficiary." Restatement (Second) Trusts, § 222, comment a. The Restatement (Third) of Trusts presently contemplates that an exculpatory clause would be disregarded "to the extent it purports to relieve the trustee altogether from accountability and the duty to provide information to beneficiaries . . . or to relieve the trustee from liability even for dishonest or reckless acts." Restatement (Third) of Trusts § 29, comment m (2003). Similarly, the Uniform Trust Code provides that an exculpatory clause "is unenforceable to the extent that it: (1) relieves the trustee of liability for breach of trust committed in bad faith or with reckless indifference to the purposes of the trust or the interests of the beneficiaries; or (2) was inserted as the result of an abuse by the trustee of a fiduciary or confidential relationship to the settlor." Uniform Trust Code § 1008(a) (2000).

Exculpatory clauses should be used sparingly and only in exceptional circumstances in the case of professional fiduciaries, of whom a higher standard of performance is reasonably required. It is also generally inappropriate for an exculpatory clause to be included in an instrument that appoints the scrivener as fiduciary.

As noted in § 4.26.6, some states limit the extent to which executors or testamentary trustees can be absolved from liability for breaches of duty. Others, including Pennsylvania and Texas, allow a trustor to exonerate a trustee from liability for most acts. The Texas Supreme Court has accorded extraordinary breadth to the statute that allows a trustor to vary the duties of a trustee. Most recently, in *Texas Commerce Bank, N.A. v. Grizzle*, 96 S.W.3d 240 (Tex. 2002), the Texas Supreme Court held that the Texas Trust Code allows a trustor to relieve a corporate trustee from liability for a "'duty, liability, or restriction imposed by this subtitle' except for those contained in sections 113.052 and 113.053." (The trust involved in the *Grizzle* case provided that, "This instrument shall always be construed in favor of the validity of any act or omission of any Trustee, and a Trustee shall not be liable for any act or omission except in the case of gross negligence, bad faith, or fraud.") The opinion continued, saying that, "We disagree with the court of appeals' conclusion that public policy precludes such a limitation on liability."

§ 10.46.   POWER TO ALLOCATE BETWEEN PRINCIPAL AND INCOME

The trustee generally should be given discretion to allocate receipts and disbursements between principal and income. An allocation is necessary because of the bifurcated nature of the beneficial interests in most trusts—the income and principal beneficiaries generally are not the same. The income of the trust is usually payable to one beneficiary (or group of beneficiaries), upon whose death the principal is distributable to another beneficiary (or group of beneficiaries). Most states responded to the allocation problem by adopting either the Uniform Principal and Income Act (1931) (the "Original Act"), or the Revised (1962) Uniform Principal and Income Act (the "Revised Act"). As of 2011, 42 states and the District of Columbia have enacted the most recent version of the Uniform Act, originally published in 1997 and amended in 2000 ("UPIA"). Some important non-adopters to date include Georgia, Illinois, and Minnesota.

The rules prescribed by the Original and Revised Acts were generally fair and workable. However, they did not deal with some issues and did not satisfactorily resolve others. The current version of UPIA breaks new ground in many respects. Importantly, it allows a trustee freedom to adjust "between principal and income to the extent the trustee considers necessary if the trustee invests and manages trust assets as a prudent investor, the terms of the trust describe the amount that may or must be distributed to a beneficiary by referring to the trust's income, and the trustee determines, after applying the rules in Section 103(a), that the trustee is unable to comply with Section 103(b)." UPIA § 104(a). In deciding whether to make an adjustment UPIA § 104(b) requires the trustee to consider all factors relevant to the trust and its beneficiaries, including an enumerated list of factors. Under UPIA § 104(c) trustees are prohibited from making certain adjustments that would have adverse tax consequences. Paragraphs (7) and (8) bar a trustee from making an adjustment if the trustee is a beneficiary or would otherwise, directly or indirectly, benefit from the adjustment.

UPIA § 103(a) provides that the trustee shall make allocations between principal and income in accordance with the terms of the will or trust; may exercise a discretionary power in a manner not consistent with the act; and shall make allocations as provided in the act unless otherwise provided in the will or trust or unless the trust gives the trustee a discretionary power to make such allocations. Furthermore, the trustee shall allocate all items not otherwise allocated under UPIA to principal. UPIA § 103(a)(4).

Under UPIA § 103(b), a trustee is required to "administer a trust impartially, based on what is fair and reasonable to all of the beneficiaries, except to the extent that the terms of the trust or the will clearly manifest an intention that the trustee shall or may favor one or more of the beneficiaries." A determination in accordance with UPIA is presumed to be fair and reasonable to all the beneficiaries. *Id.*

Planners often meet the allocation problem by giving the trustee discretion to allocate receipts and disbursements between income and principal as the trustee believes is reasonable and equitable under the circumstances. Such a power is recognized by UPIA, as it was by the Original and Revised Acts. A trustee with such power has more flexibility in dealing with the complex problems of principal and income allocations while carrying out the terms of the trust and meeting the needs of the beneficiaries. Doing so, of course, provides the trustee with little or no guidance and, in effect, deprives the beneficiaries of some protection.

Under § 2 of the Original and Revised Acts, if a trustee is given discretion to make allocations of principal and income, "no inference of imprudence or partiality arises from the fact that the trustee has made an allocation contrary to a provision of this Act." §2(b), 7B U.L.A. 151 (1999). Essentially the same provision is contained in UPIA §103(a)(2).

Importantly, a discretionary power to allocate receipts and disbursement between principal and income that is exercisable in a fiduciary capacity is not treated as a general power of appointment for federal estate tax purposes: "The mere power of management, investment, custody of assets, or the power to allocate receipts and disbursements as between income and principal, exercisable in a fiduciary capacity, whereby the holder has no power to enlarge or shift any of the beneficial interests therein except as an incidental consequence of the discharge of such fiduciary duties is not a power of appointment." Reg. §20.2041-1(b)(1). Similarly, the existence of such a power does not jeopardize the allowance of the marital deduction for an otherwise qualifying interest in a trust. *See* Reg. §20.2056(b)-7(d)(2).

It is often desirable to give the trustee some specific directions (or additional authorization) regarding certain allocation matters. The directions in a particular case may run counter to the basic provisions of the acts. The following paragraphs discuss some of the matters about which trusts often provide additional guidance. They include the treatment of stock splits and stock dividends, the amortization of bond premium, and the accumulation of discount, the handling of depreciation, and the treatment of unproductive or underproductive property.

§10.46.1. Stock Splits and Stock Dividends

The lawyer may find it necessary or desirable to specify a rule regarding allocation of stock splits and stock dividends contrary to the basic rule of UPIA. Under §5 of the Original Act and §6 of the Revised Act, all stock splits and stock dividends of the issuing corporation were entirely allocated to principal. Similarly, UPIA §401(c)(1) characterizes non-cash distributions from an entity as principal.

The rule expressed in all three acts prejudices current income beneficiaries where the trust includes stock in corporations that regularly issue small stock dividends in lieu of cash dividends, or in addition to small cash dividends. The power given trustees by UPIA to make adjustments is not universally available to relieve this problem. This shortcoming can be relieved by providing that the trustee may allocate stock dividends to income in accordance with a formula such as the New York statutory formula. Under N.Y. Est. Powers & Trusts Law §11-2.1(e)(2) (2011), stock distributions of 6 percent or less are allocated to income whether the distribution is called a stock split or a stock dividend. Such a rule may fairly meet the needs of the beneficiaries and those of the trustee.

§10.46.2. Amortization of Bond Premium and Accumulation of Discount

Corporate and municipal bonds usually carry a fixed rate of interest that is payable semiannually until redemption at face value upon maturity. Because the market rate of interest fluctuates, the current market price of a bond typically depends on two factors: (1) the length of time until the maturity of the bond, and (2) the difference between the current market rate of interest and the rate specified in the bond. Thus, a bond that carries a rate of interest above the going rate will sell at a price in excess of its redemption value (*i.e.*, it will sell at a premium). If a bond is purchased at a premium and held until maturity, the principal account will be depleted unless an amount equal to the premium is recovered from income. The problem can be met by allocating a portion of each income payment to principal (*i.e.*, the premium is amortized over the life of the bond). However, the Revised Act prohibited amortization unless the instrument provides otherwise or the trustee was empowered to make discretionary allocations between principal and income. The Original Act also did not provide for amortization or accumulation of discount.

EXAMPLE 10-18.

At a time when the going rate of interest was 8%, Trustee paid $5,500 for a $5,000 bond that carried a 12-percent rate. Under § 7(a) of the Revised Act, the full amount of each semiannual interest payment would be allocated to income. 7B U.L.A. 165 (1985). If the bond were held until maturity the proceeds of $5,000 would be allocated to principal, resulting in a "loss" of $500.

Section 7(a) of the Revised Act also prevented accumulation of discount when a bond is purchased for less than its redemption value. 7B U.L.A. 165 (1985). That is, when the trustee purchases a bond for less than its redemption value and holds it until maturity, none of the appreciation received is allocable to income. In this case the income account is disadvantaged by the purchase of a bond that carried an interest rate below the market rate at the time of purchase.

UPIA § 406 follows suit, disallowing the amortization of both bond premiums and discounts. These rules appear unduly restrictive. They may discourage the trustee from making otherwise attractive investments or result in unfairness to one class of beneficiaries. However, because interest rates and bond prices fluctuate over time, it may be equally undesirable to require the amortization of premium or the accumulation of discount. Instead, the trust may be drafted to give the trustee discretion to deal with the bonds as required to avoid unfairness to the income beneficiaries or the remaindermen according to overall circumstances.

§ 10.46.3. Depreciation

The Original Act did not contain any provision regarding depreciation. Under § 13(a)(2) of the Revised Act, the trustee was required to make a reasonable charge against income for depreciation where it is appropriate to do so under generally accepted accounting principles. However, no charge for depreciation is required for the "portion of any real property used by a beneficiary as a residence or for . . . any property held by the trustee on the effective date of this Act for which the trustee is not then making an allowance for depreciation." 7B U.L.A. 175 (1999). Of course, if depreciation is charged, a smaller amount of income will be available for distribution to the income beneficiaries.

UPIA maintains this general rule, treating depreciation as a reduction of income and an increase to principal. UPIA § 503(b).

For income tax purposes, the depreciation deduction is allocated between the trustee and the beneficiaries on the basis of the income allocable to each. § 167(d);

Reg. §1.167(h)-1(b). However, the depreciation deduction is first allocated to the trustee to the extent the income is set aside for a depreciation reserve. Reg. §1.167(h)-1(b). Overall, it is preferable to give the trustee discretion regarding the establishment of a depreciation reserve.

§10.46.4. Unproductive and Underproductive Property

Unless it is otherwise provided by the terms of the trust, if property held in trust to pay the income to a beneficiary for a designated period and thereafter to pay the principal to another beneficiary produces no income or an income substantially less than the current rate of return on trust investments, and is likely to continue being unproductive or underproductive, the trustee is under a duty to the income beneficiary "to make the trust estate reasonably productive." Restatement (Third) of Trusts, §227, comment i (1992). Whether this duty requires the trustee to sell or dispose of an underproductive asset hinges on whether "an appropriate overall balance is not otherwise reasonably and prudently achieved." *Id.*

The Original and Revised Acts addressed the problem by allocating a portion of the net proceeds received upon the sale of underproductive property to the income beneficiaries. Section 11 of the Original Act and §12 of the Revised Act provided a similar remedy as to trust property that has not produced an average net income of at least 1 percent per year. Under the Original Act upon sale of the property the amount allocated to principal had to equal the amount which, "had it been placed at simple interest at the rate of five per centum per annum for the period during which the change was delayed, would have produced the net proceeds at the time of change." The Revised Act provided for the allocation to principal to be based upon a 4 percent rate.

EXAMPLE 10-19.

ich the Revised Act is in effect, an unproductive
was acquired by the trust on January 1, 1995. The
$130,000 on January 1, 2000. Expenses and taxes of
ring the time the property was owned by the trust.
ct $100,000 of the net proceeds will be allocated to
alance ($20,000) to income. The amounts are deter-
the following formula:

$$ \text{Principal} = \frac{\$130{,}000 - \$10{,}000}{1 + (5)(4\%)} $$

UPIA §413(b) eliminates the requirement that the income beneficiary be allocated some portion of the proceeds from the sale of underproductive property. Instead, such proceeds "are principal without regard to the amount of income the asset produces during an accounting period." UPIA §413(b). This makes UPIA consistent with the Uniform Prudent Investor Act, an acronymically similar act that better tolerates underproductive assets provided the entire portfolio, on balance, is productive. *See* § 10.44.1.

EXAMPLE 10-20.

Assume the same facts as Example 10-19, above, except that the jurisdiction has enacted UPIA. The entire $120,000 in net proceeds will be allocated to principal.

§ 10.46.5. Unitrust or "Total Return Trust"

Except where compelled by transfer tax consideration, the drafters of private trusts should immediately stop the practice of defining the interests of the current beneficiary in terms of a right to receive all accounting income. The traditional formula is almost certain to result in second-rate and ill-suited investment performance and a steady decline in the market value of the trust property when adjusted for inflation. There are vastly superior trust architectures. Hosington, Modern Trust Design: New Paradigms for the 21st Century, U. Miami, 31st Inst. Est. Plan., Ch. 6 (1997).

Articles by several commentators in the late 1990s rekindled interest in the so-called total return trust. The articles include the chapter by Hosington cited above, Horn, Prudent Investor Rule, Modern Portfolio Theory, and PrivateTrusts: Drafting and Administration Including the "Give me Five" Unitrust, 33 Real Prop., Prob. & Tr. J. 1 (1998), and Wolf, Total Return Trusts—Can Your Clients Afford Anything Less, 33 Real Prop., Prob. & Tr. J. 131 (1998). The tax ramifications of a noncharitable unitrust were explored in 1968 in a lengthy three-part article by Professors DelCotto and Joyce:

Under a unitrust instrument, all income would be combined with principal in a single fund and there would be no distinction between income and principal. All items received, whether they be dividends, rents or splits, would be termed "receipts" and all items paid out would be termed "payouts." The payout would be direction in fractions or in specific dollar amounts—for example, five percent of the market value of the total fund as of the first day of the fiscal year, but no more (or less) than a specific dollar amount—and no one interested in the trust would have merely an interest in income or principal.

The unitrust thus removes any conflict of interest between the parties beneficially interested in the trust. Many advantages result. There is no longer any need to allocate receipts and expenditures between principal and income since these separate funds are irrelevant to any purpose or need of the trust or its beneficiaries. Accounting requirements are simplified and time and money saved. More important, any requirement that the trustee must invest for yield is eliminated: the trustee is no longer required to produce a reasonable income. DelCotto & Joyce, Taxation of a Unitrust, 23 Tax L. Rev. 229, 260 (1968).

The necessity of differentiating between income and principal is largely eliminated if the interests of the current trust beneficiaries are discretionary or are defined as a specified amount payable annually (an annuity), or as a percentage of the value of the trust determined annually. One can expect more private annuity trusts or unitrusts to be created in the future because of the valuation rules of § 2702, which do not disregard the value of a retained interest in the form of a qualified annuity trust or a qualified unitrust. *See* § 9.43.2. In the past some commentators have suggested that a private unitrust could be used to avoid problems of allocating between principal and income. *E.g.,* Lovell, The Unitrust: A New Concept to Meet an Old Problem, 105 Tr. & Est. 215 (1966).

A unitrust also substantially eliminates the clash of interests between current beneficiaries and remainder beneficiaries regarding investments: their interests are not affected by the characterization of a receipt or disbursement as income or principal. Instead, the total annual amount of distributions to the current beneficiaries of a unitrust would be based on a specified percentage of the annually determined value of the trust assets. Thus, the unitrust would not require any allocation between income and principal and the interests of both the current and ultimate beneficiaries would be served by a growth-oriented investment policy. By way of illustration, a unitrust might provide for the payment to the current beneficiary of an amount each year equal to 5 percent of the total value of the trust assets on the last business day of the preceding calendar year.

A trust that incorporates the unitrust concept should include some specific directions regarding investments. Unless the governing law includes the Uniform Prudent Investor Act, or its equivalent, the trust might expressly authorize the trustee to make investments without regard to the amount of income they generate (the "probable income" to be derived from an asset is one element of the generally applicable prudent person investment standard). Put positively, the trustee might be authorized to invest for the overall return produced by the trust without regard to the income produced by the assets.

The total portfolio approach of the Uniform Prudent Investor Act and the adjustment power included in the Uniform Principal and Income Act may ultimately eliminate the problem of differentiating between income and principal. Even so, some grantors may wish to specify that the current beneficiary of a trust is entitled to receive annual distributions of a specified amount or specified percentage of the trust's value. Such an approach is not inconsistent with either the Uniform Prudent Investor Act or the 1997 version of the Uniform Principal and Income Act.

All but a handful of states have enacted some form of total return trust legislation. The majority of states have enacted new principal and income laws that permit the trustee to make adjustments between principal and income. In addition, many states, including several that permit the trustee to make adjustments, have enacted laws that allow a trust to be converted to a unitrust with a fixed payout rate. Indeed, the Delaware law allows the trustee to choose a payout rate of between 3 and 5 percent. 12 Del. Code §3527(f) (2011). The changes should result in much broader use of trusts that give trustees discretion to make equitable adjustments between principal and income and in the increased creation of total return unitrusts.

Regulations Under §643(b) Encourage Total Return Trusts and UPIA. Late in 2003, Treasury finalized regulations proposed in 2001 that facilitate and encourage the adoption of statutes that recognize total return unitrusts and ones that permit trustees to allocate income and principal in an impartial and equitable manner. The regulations are discussed at §10.4.3 above.

§10.47. PROVIDING BENEFICIARIES WITH NOTICE AND INFORMATION

In most states, the extent of a trustee's duty to inform beneficiaries regarding the existence and terms of a trust and the details of its administration is ill-defined and uncertain. Berry, *The Whether, Why, Whom, What, and When of the Trustee's Duty to Notify Beneficiaries*, U. Miami, 45th Inst. Est. Plan. Ch. 14 (2011). Despite the uncertainty regarding its scope, a trustee is almost certainly subject to a duty to disclose, which a grantor cannot totally eliminate. While grantors not infrequently want to prevent beneficiaries from learning of the existence of a trust, a trustee who fails to inform beneficiaries of its existence and details sufficient to allow them to protect their interests runs a serious risk. O'Brien, The Trustee's Duty to Provide Information to Beneficiaries: When Can the Settlor Say, "Don't Ask, Won't Tell?", 40 U. Miami, Inst. Est. Plan., Ch. 5 (2006); Fitzsimmons, Navigating the Trustee's Duty to Disclose, 23 Prob. & Prop. 40 (Jan/Feb 2009).

Section 813 of the Uniform Trust Code (UTC), which in varying forms has been adopted by almost half the states, subjects trustees to a mandatory duty to inform and report to the beneficiaries of a trust. Under §813(d) a beneficiary may waive the right to receive information as required by the section and may withdraw a waiver previously given. Under a controversial provision of the UTC that adopting states frequently change or omit, the terms of a trust may not relieve a trustee of the duty to notify "qualified beneficiaries" of an irrevocable trust who are 25 years of age or older of the existence of the trust, the identity of the trustee, and their right to receive reports. In addition, a qualified beneficiary of an irrevocable trust is entitled to receive trustee's reports and other information regarding the administration of the trust.

§10.48. RULE AGAINST PERPETUITIES; PERPETUITIES SAVINGS CLAUSE

The lawyer should also be alert to the problems that might arise under the applicable form of the Rule Against Perpetuities. The Rule varies somewhat from state to state in terms of both its basic provisions and the availability of remedial devices. For example, the common law rule tests the validity of interests at the time of creation while the Uniform Statutory Rule Against Perpetuities (1990) waits for 90 years. The Uniform Act was adopted in several important jurisdictions, including Connecticut, Florida, Michigan, Minnesota, Montana, Nebraska, Nevada, Oregon and South Carolina. Indeed, the Uniform Rule combines a 90-year wait and see period with a judicial reformation of interests that are determined to be invalid under the common law rule as applied at the end of the 90-year period. Because of the uncertainty regarding the rule that might apply, modern trusts typically include a perpetuities savings clause appropriate to the jurisdiction. It is desirable to include a savings clause in most trusts although the rigors of the Rule have been relaxed significantly in a number of states by judicial decisions and statutory modifications of the common law Rule.

Beginning in the 1990s, legislatures in several states have enacted laws that, in effect, abolish the Rule Against Perpetuities. More recently several other states have substantially modified the Rule Against Perpetuities, greatly extended the period during which interests must vest, or abolished it entirely. They include: Alaska (abolished entirely, with a 1,000-year limitation on powers of appointment), Arizona (abolished entirely), Delaware (abolished for personal property but not real property), Florida (360 years), Idaho (abolished for personal property but not entirely for real property), Illinois (abolished entirely), Nevada (365 years), New Jersey (abolished entirely), Ohio (if document provides, trust is perpetual), Rhode Island (abolished entirely), South Dakota (abolished entirely), Utah (1,000 years), Washington (150 years), Wisconsin (abolished as long as trustee retains power to allocate corpus) and Wyoming (1,000 years). Because of the changes, lawyers must check the applicable law before drafting documents that may be affected by the Rule. A helpful collection of each state's position on the Rule Against Perpetuities may be found at Sitkoff and Schanzenbach, Jurisdictional Competition for Trust Funds: An Empirical Analysis of Perpetuities and Taxes, 115 Yale L.J. 356, 430-33 (2005).

Such legislation was promoted, at least in part, in order to give local corporate trustees a competitive advantage in the affluent client market. Various commentators, some of whom are closely identified with corporate trustees doing business in those states, have written enthusiastically about the advantages of creating dynasty trusts. It remains to be seen whether abolishing the Rule Against Perpetuities will prove to be wise or a socially undesirable instance of the tax tail wagging the dog.

Savings Clauses. A common savings clause simply provides for the vesting of any interest in the trust that has not vested within the period allowable under the local law (most often 21 years after the death of the survivor of a reasonable number of designated individuals who are alive when the period of the rule begins to run). This approach vests any interests that are not vested according to the terms of the trust at the end of the common law period. Accordingly, at the time the trust is created it can be said with certainty that all unvested interests will fail or vest within the period of the Rule. Of course, the savings clause should provide expressly for the disposition of the interests involved to the extent they do not vest within the allowable period. The alternative dispositive plan must describe interests that vest at the end of 21 years after the death of the named individuals referred to in the savings clause. A savings clause might take the following form:

Form 10-8
Perpetuities Savings Clause

This trust shall terminate not later than 21 years after the death of the survivor of my issue living on my death and the trust property shall be distributed outright to my issue then living, by representation [or, in equal shares to the beneficiaries then entitled to receive current distributions from the trust].

As suggested by the form, the persons who are designated to take the property on termination of the trust could be specified in a variety of ways. Another approach, suggested by Professors Leach and Logan, involves giving a corporate fiduciary authority to reform an interest that offends the Rule in a manner that carries out the grantor's intent. *See* Leach & Logan, Perpetuities: A Standard Saving Clause to Avoid Violations of the Rule, 74 Harv. L. Rev. 1141 (1961). The approach taken by Leach and Logan gives a corporate trustee a cy pres power similar to ones that have been given to the courts by some statutes in recent years and ones that have been exercised by some courts on their own. *E.g., Estate of Chun Quan Yee Hop*, 469 P.2d 183 (Hawaii 1970) (reducing a 30-year contingency to 21 years).

In drafting a savings clause of the first type of described above, the planner must recognize the difference in the effective dates of a will and an irrevocable trust. A will is effective and the period of the Rule begins to run only upon the testator's death, but an irrevocable trust is effective and the period of the Rule begins to run from the date the trust is created. Because a revocable trust is subject to change or revocation until the time of the grantor's death, it is treated in the same way as a will. Thus, a savings clause that provides for termination of a trust 21 years after the death of a survivor of a class of persons living at the time of the grantor's death is suitable for inclusion in a will, but is not suitable in the case of an irrevocable inter vivos trust. Instead, the clause used in an irrevocable trust should provide for termination of the trust 21 years after the death of the last survivor of designated persons or a class of persons living at the time the trust was created or who are designated by name. It is easy to overlook the difference in the effective dates and to include an improper clause in an irrevocable trust.

In jurisdictions that retain a Rule Against Perpetuities of some kind, it is important to understand it and to prepare instruments with a view toward its provisions. Such preventive drafting is desirable although a savings clause, statute, or judicial doctrine might "save" an offending interest. Overall, preventive drafting is clearly the best approach. In particular, in jurisdictions that have not abolished the Rule, a planner should view with suspicion any gift that is contingent upon the attainment of an age greater than 21 and avoid making gifts when an event in the administration of an estate or trust takes place (*e.g.,* when all debts are paid off or the estate is distributed). Note in this connections that gifts subject to an administrative contingency may fail to qualify for the marital deduction.

§10.49. Formula Clauses

Grantors often intend to fund trusts with a specific amount of property. For instance, a grantor may intend to give that amount of assets that will generate a taxable gift exactly large enough to fully utilize (but not exceed) the grantor's applicable exclusion amount. Likewise, where the grantor's grandchildren will be beneficiaries of the trust, the grantor may intend to give exactly that amount that would fully utilize (but not exceed) the grantor's remaining GSTT exemption. Making such precise gifts is tricky business, especially where the gifted property consists of interests eligible for valuation discounts. If the grantor applies valuation discounts in excess of what the IRS or courts subsequently permit, the grantor may have accidentally made a gift to the trust that would trigger liability for gift tax or GST tax.

To hedge against the risk of valuation error, some gift plans include a formula clause designed to discourage the IRS from challenging a valuation by providing for a gift over to charity of the value of the donative property above a specified amount. Presumably there would be little incentive for the IRS to challenge the valuation of a gift if the excess value would not be subject to the gift or estate taxes. For example, a plan may give the donor's children units in an LLC, provided that if the units are finally determined to have a value in excess of a specified amount, units equal in value to the excess will pass to a designated charity.

In *Commissioner v. Procter*, 142 F.2d 824 (4th Cir. 1944), the court refused to enforce a formula clause on grounds of public policy. The trust instrument at issue provided that if any portion of the grantor's transfer to the trust gave rise to gift tax liability, that portion would revert to the grantor. The court held that the formula clause imposed a condition subsequent on the transfer, which would make enforcement by the IRS fruitless by definition—if the formula clause was enforceable and the IRS argued that the property was undervalued, no additional tax liability would result.

Subsequently, the Tax Court held a similar formula clause to be unenforceable, similarly concerned that no one would ever challenge valuation because such challenge would always be for naught if the formula clause was upheld. *Charles W. Ward*, 87 T.C. 78 (1986). *See also Estate of McClendon v. Commissioner*, T.C. Memo. 1993-459, *rev'd on other grounds*, 77 F.3d 447 (5th Cir. 1995) (ignoring formula clause and refusing to spend "precious judicial resources to resolve the question of whether a gift resulted from the . . . transaction only to render that issue moot").

But in *King v. United States*, 545 F.2d 700 (10th Cir. 1976), a formula clause that increased the sale price of stock to fair market value as determined by the IRS was viewed by the court as evidence that the seller intended a sale at arms-length.

Relying on *Procter* and its progeny, the IRS announced that it would not give effect to formula clauses. FSA 200122011. The transfer at issue in the FSA involved a gift transfer of a limited partnership interest to a trust where the amount in excess of a stated dollar amount would pass to charity. Consistent with this announcement, the IRS in LR 200245053 (TAM) disregarded a formula clause in the context of a purchase and sale agreement for a limited partnership interest. *See also* LR 200337012 (TAM) (IRS refused to recognize a gift of "that fraction of Assignor's Limited Partnership Interest in Partnership which has a fair market value on the date hereof of $*a*" as violating public policy even though the donor retained no reversion in the transferred property).

A formula clause was also denied effect in *Charles T. McCord*, 120 T.C. 358 (2003), *rev'd*, 461 F.3d 614 (5th Cir. 2006). Here, the donors conveyed limited partnership interests to three groups of beneficiaries: their children, certain trusts, and two charities. The assignment agreement signed by the donors stated that the amounts passing to the children and the trusts would be roughly $6.9 million, with any extra value passing to the charities. Following the assignment, the beneficiaries all executed a "confirmation agreement" that reflected the exact percentage amounts of the gifted interests received by each beneficiary. The Tax Court refused to apply the formula clause in the assignment agreement because the formula was based on fair market value and not "fair market value as finally determined for Federal gift tax purposes." Instead, it gave effect to the allocations set forth in the confirmation agreement, ultimately causing more to pass to the children and the trusts than the donors likely intended.

On appeal, the Fifth Circuit reversed the Tax Court. As the court stated, the "core flaw in the [Tax Court's] inventive methodology was its violation of the long-prohibited practice of relying on post-gift events. Specifically, the [Tax Court] used the after-the-fact Confirmation Agreement to mutate the Assignment Agreement's dollar-value gifts into percentage interests in [the partnership]. It is clear beyond cavil that the [Tax Court] should have stopped with the Assignment Agreement's plain wording." The court continued that fair market value is determined on the day the donor completes the gift, so the Tax Court's reference to value as of the time of the Confirmation Agreement was erroneous. The Fifth Circuit thus respected the tax-payer's formula clause and rejected the valuations of the Tax Court and the IRS. While the court stopped short of proclaiming that formula clauses will always be respected, the case is a clear sign that at least one appellate court is willing to enforce them.

Despite its position in *McCord*, the IRS specifically sanctions the use of formula clauses in certain specified situations. These include formula bequests qualifying for the marital deduction, Rev. Proc. 64-19, 1964-1 C.B. 682; using a formula to define the annuity amount payable under a GRAT, Reg. § 25.2702-3(b)(1)(ii)(B); formula clauses in charitable remainder trusts, Rev. Rul. 82-128, 1982-2 C.B. 71; and formula disclaimers, Reg. § 25.2518-3(c), 25.2518-3(d), Example (20).

F. SPECIALIZED TYPES OF TRUSTS

§ 10.50. SCOPE

This part considers some of the more specialized types of trusts that estate planners may have occasion to suggest to clients. This part does not consider all of the many forms of trust arrangements. Some features of specialized types of trusts are reviewed in other chapters (*e.g.*, marital deduction trusts are discussed in Chapter 5, insurance trusts in Chapter 6, trusts for minors in Chapter 7, charitable remainder trusts in Chapter 8, and grantor retained interest trusts including grantor retained annuity trusts (GRATs), grantor retained unitrusts (GRUTs) and qualified personal residence trusts (QPRTs) and widow's election trusts in Chapter 9). Rather, this part discusses those trust arrangements not addressed in detail elsewhere.

It should go without saying, but this chapter does not advocate the use, or suitability, of any particular type of trust. The propriety of any trust arrangement, as with any estate planning technique, depends upon several fact-intensive considerations, including the client's objectives, the client's tolerance for risk, the nature of the assets to be held in trust, the interests and characteristics of the beneficiaries, and the anticipated time horizon.

§10.51. DOMESTIC ASSET PROTECTION TRUSTS

For decades, offshore asset protection trusts have been formed in jurisdictions like the Cook Islands and various countries in the Caribbean to give grantors spendthrift protection from current and future creditors. In recent years, some states have enacted laws that authorize the creation of so-called Domestic Asset Protection Trusts (DAPTs). Designed principally to minimize claims from creditors and often to avoid wealth transfer taxes as well, a DAPT is an irrevocable trust that appoints an independent trustee (not the grantor) who may, in the independent trustee's absolute discretion, distribute trust income and principal to a pre-defined class of beneficiaries that includes the grantor. The state statutes authorizing the DAPT provide that creditors of the grantor generally may not reach assets held in the trust.

As of 2009, the states with DAPT statutes are Alaska, Delaware, Missouri, Nevada, Oklahoma, Rhode Island, South Dakota, Tennessee, Utah, and Wyoming. Farr, Nenno, Rothschild, Terill & Sullivan, Planning and Defending Asset Protection Trusts 34 (2009). By requiring DAPTs to use resident trustees and, in some cases, house trust assets within their borders, these states are willing to confer enhanced protection from creditors in exchange for increased investment activities. Some states, like Delaware and Nevada, permit the addition of a nonresident cotrustee if the grantor wishes. An excellent survey of the various state DAPT statutes can be found at Nenno, Planning with Asset-Protection Trusts: Part II, 40 Real Prop. Prob. & Tr. J. 477 (2005).

§10.51.1. Income Tax Aspects

If the grantor retains the right to income from a DAPT, or if the grantor has the right to demand distributions of all or a portion of the trust principal, the DAPT will be treated as a grantor trust under §§671–677. Accordingly, the grantor would be taxed on all of the income from the DAPT. If the grantor's right to income and principal is exercisable only with the consent of an independent trustee, however, the DAPT should be a separate taxpayer. LR 200247013.

DAPTs are preferable to offshore asset protection trusts in that the ownership of assets by a foreign trust can result in a deemed sale of the trust assets for federal income tax purposes at the time the trust no longer qualifies as a grantor trust, whether at formation or upon the death of the grantor. See §684, §10.53. No such deemed sale occurs with respect to a DAPT.

§10.51.2. Gift Tax Aspects

The transfer of assets to a DAPT would constitute a completed gift unless, for example, the grantor retained a limited power of appointment over trust assets. *See* LR 200148028. Although retention of a power of appointment would render the transfer an incomplete gift for federal gift tax purposes until actual distributions are made to beneficiaries other than the grantor, it would cause the trust assets to be included in the grantor's gross estate.

§10.51.3. Estate Tax Aspects

Because the grantor of a DAPT typically relinquishes the power to reclaim assets transferred to the trust, none of the trust assets should be included in the decedent's gross estate under §2036 or §2038. Some statutes permit the grantor to retain the right to income from the trust assets. *See* 12 Del. C. §3570(9). A retained right to income, of course, triggers inclusion of the trust assets in the grantor's gross estate, so this option should not be exercised when the grantor seeks to minimize exposure to wealth transfer taxes.

While a pattern of regular distributions to the grantor risks inclusion in the grantor's gross estate because it would appear that the grantor has retained control over the trust assets, a discretionary power given to the independent trustee to reimburse the grantor for any federal income tax liability associated with the DAPT probably does not give rise to gross estate inclusion. *See* Rev. Rul. 2004-64, 2004-2 C.B. 7.

§10.51.4. Creditor Protection Aspects

Although the DAPT is designed to place trust assets beyond the reach of creditors, most statutes permit some creditors to pierce the veil of protection. For example, Delaware law permits creditors who commence an action within four years of the transfer to the DAPT (or, in the case of pre-existing creditors, within one year of learning of the transfer to the DAPT, if later) to reach trust assets if they can prove by clear and convincing evidence that the transfer was fraudulent as to the creditor. Creditors with alimony and child support claims can also access DAPT assets formed under the Delaware statute without regard to the four-year window and without the need to demonstrate fraud by clear and convincing evidence, as can a pre-existing creditor with a claim for personal injury or property damage for which the grantor is liable. 12 Del. C. §3572(a), 3570(2), 3573(1).

Proving that the grantor of a DAPT made a fraudulent transfer with respect to a particular creditor is usually made with reference to the fraudulent conveyance provisions under both the federal Bankruptcy Code and state law. Under these rules, a creditor can prove that transfer is fraudulent if the grantor made the transfer either with the intent to defraud the creditor or without receiving reasonably equivalent value in exchange for the transfer. Various factors can prove intent to defraud, including the presence or threat of a lawsuit at the time of transfer, retention of control over trust assets by the grantor, a transfer of substantially all of the grantor's assets to the DAPT, and a transfer shortly before or after the grantor incurs a substantial debt. The central inquiry, in effect, is whether the grantor reasonably anticipated the creditor's claim upon funding the DAPT.

Because the grantor is often a permissible beneficiary of income or principal distributions from a DAPT, there is some risk that a pattern of distributions to the grantor might enable a creditor to establish that the grantor has substantial control over at least a portion of the trust assets.

The DAPT is not without controversy. Many commentators suggest that the promised protection from creditors is far from certain, especially given the relatively short history of these state statutes. Whether the state DAPT statutes violate the full faith and credit clause or the supremacy clause of the Constitution, and whether the statutes violate fundamental notions of the conflict of laws or fraudulent conveyance laws is still open to debate. For various viewpoints, *see* Robert T. Danforth, "Rethinking the Law of Creditors' Rights in Trusts," 53 Hastings L. J. 287 (2002); Karen E. Boxx, "Gray's Ghost—A Conversation About the Onshore Trust," 85 Iowa L. Rev. 1195 (2000).

More importantly, recent changes to the Bankruptcy Code substantially undermine the ability of DAPT grantors to obtain protection from creditors. Enacted as part of the Bankruptcy Abuse Prevention and Consumer Protection Act of 2005, § 548(e)(1) of the Bankruptcy Code, 11 U.S.C. § 548(e)(1), provides:

> (e)(1) In addition to any transfer that the trustee may otherwise avoid, the trustee may avoid any transfer of an interest of the debtor in property that was made on or within 10 years before the date of the filing of the petition if—
>
> (A) such transfer was made to a self-settled trust or similar device;
>
> (B) such transfer was by the debtor;
>
> (C) the debtor is a beneficiary of such trust or similar device; and
>
> (D) the debtor made such transfer with actual intent to hinder, delay, or defraud any entity to which the debtor was or became, on or after the date that such transfer was made, indebted.

The typical DAPT falls squarely within this rule. A DAPT is nearly always a self-settled trust in which the grantor is a beneficiary, and transfers of assets to the DAPT are often made with the intent to hinder or delay, if not defraud, creditors. Section 548(e)(1) of the Bankruptcy Code permits the bankruptcy trustee to set aside all qualifying transfers made to a DAPT within the ten-year period ending on the date the bankruptcy petition is filed. As a result, creditors in bankruptcy will have access to assets transferred to a DAPT during this ten-year look-back period, effectively stripping the DAPT of its asset-protection features. The ten-year look-back period is extreme, given that the ordinary bankruptcy look-back period is two years, 11 U.S.C. § 548(a), and most state laws impose a four-year look-back period for challenging fraudulent transfers.

Note, too, that § 548(e)(1) of the Bankruptcy Code protects not only those creditors existing at the time assets are transferred to the DAPT but also those who become creditors after the transfer but before the bankruptcy petition is filed. Clients and their advisors should thus be skeptical of claims that there is no risk of fraudulent transfers if there are no current creditors on the scene.

Practitioners must exercise extreme caution in advising clients with respect to DAPTs. Assisting clients in removing assets from the reach of current and potential creditors presents ethical issues and, in some cases, may expose a lawyer to civil and criminal sanctions. Practitioners should receive assurances as to a client's financial situation and risk for legal liability. They should advise clients not to transfer substantially all of their assets to a DAPT, for such substantial transfers invite heightened scrutiny. Even where the client intends to transfer only some assets to a DAPT, the practitioner should advise the client of the ten-year look-back rule and other limitations on the ability to secret assets from creditors. The message is clear: proceed at your own risk.

§10.52. Trusts for Pets

A noncharitable trust must generally have one or more individual beneficiaries who are identified or will be identified within the period of the Rule Against Perpetuities, if any. Trust law has never embraced the concept of a trust for the care and support of animals. *See* Restatement (Third) of Trusts §28, comment 1 (2003). Courts have, however, sometimes given effect to a testator's intent to create a noncharitable trust for specific purposes although the trust did not have any human beneficiaries. In some cases the courts, in effect, upheld the testator's intent by holding that the intended trustee would be allowed to accept the property and apply it to the intended specific purpose, such as the support of a designated animal, but could not be required to do so. Enforcement of the intended trust would be ensured by the individuals who would otherwise be entitled to the property—those who would be motivated to "look over the trustee's shoulder." A trust created for the benefit of an unidentified group of animals is a charitable trust, enforceable by the Attorney General, which does not present a problem.

Until recently, the safest approach in using a trust to provide for the needs of an animal was to name a caretaker as the beneficiary of the trust who would receive distributions provided the animal was still alive and receiving adequate care. The trustee would then supervise the caretaker's handling of the animal. The trustee was usually given the power to take possession of the animal and deliver it to a new caretaker-beneficiary if the trustee reasonably believed the prior caretaker was not providing adequate care. Because such a trust has human beneficiaries, it would be enforceable in all jurisdictions.

More recently, legislation permits the creation of trusts that name animals as beneficiaries. Some states take an indirect approach. Wisconsin, for example, permits an "honorary trust," one formed for a specific *purpose* rather than for the benefit of human beneficiaries. Wis. Stat. Ann. §701.11 (2011). The honorary trust would be suitable for the care of pets. The trustee may use the trust funds for the care of named pets, but is not required to so. Should the trustee stop using the trust funds for that purpose (*e.g.,* because the pets have died), a "resulting trust" is formed and the funds pass to those who would have received them had no trust been created.

Other statutes tackle the issue more directly. The Uniform Probate Code permits trusts for the care of a designated animal. U.P.C. §2-907(b). A version of the U.P.C. section has been enacted in the majority of states. In addition, §408(a) of the Uniform Trust Code (2000) permits trusts "created to provide for the care of an animal alive during the settlor's lifetime." The Uniform Trust Code also provides that the trust may be enforced by a designated person or one appointed by the court. Uniform Trust Code §408(b) (2000).

Enabling legislation solves only part of the problem with trusts for pets. The common law form of the Rule Against Perpetuities can also be an obstacle to the creation of trusts for specific animals that might survive the creation of the trust by more than 21 years. However, courts are sometimes willing to get around the Rule in one way or another. In some cases the courts upheld the intended trust for the shorter of 21 years or the life of the animal. The general subject is discussed in Breyer, Estate Planning for Pets, 15 Prob. & Prop. 6 (July/Aug. 2001). The U.P.C. simply provides that a trust for pets terminates when no loving animal is covered by the trust. U.P.C. §2-907(b).

§10.53. Foreign Trusts

The Internal Revenue Code classifies all trusts as either domestic trusts or foreign trusts. To this point, this chapter has considered rules applicable to both domestic and foreign trusts. While there are no special rules unique to domestic trusts, foreign trusts raise additional federal income tax and reporting issues. Under §7701(a)(30)(E), a trust is a domestic trust only if: (a) a court within the United States has primary supervision over the administration of the trust, and (b) one or more United States fiduciaries control all substantial decisions of the trust. The regulations give some examples of the "substantial decisions" related to a trust that a fiduciary may have. Reg. §301.7701-7(d)(1)(ii). These include, among others: (1) whether and when to make distributions of income and principal; (2) the amount of distributions; (3) whether a receipt is allocated to income or principal; (4) the selection of a beneficiary; and (5) whether to appoint a successor trustee to succeed another trustee that is unable or willing to serve or continue to serve.

Under these rules it is easy for a domestic trust to accidentally become a foreign trust. A trust with a domestic trustee might name a foreign person as successor trustee, for instance. When the domestic trustee dies or resigns, the foreign person would become trustee and, very likely, the trust would become a foreign trust. The regulations solve for this problem by stating that if the "death, incapacity, resignation, change in residency or other change with respect to a person that has a power to make a substantial decision of the trust" would cause the trust to become a foreign trust and if the appointment of a foreign person as successor trustee was not intended to cause the trust to become a foreign trust, the trust has 12 months to "cure" the problem by appointing a domestic trustee (or by having the foreign trustee become a United States person). Reg. §301.7701-7(d)(2)(i).

§10.53.1. Income Tax Rules Applicable to Foreign Trusts

There are two important income tax consequences attached to foreign trust status. First, under §679, where a United States grantor (one who is either a citizen or resident of the United States) gratuitously makes an inter vivos transfer of property to a foreign trust that has one or more United States beneficiaries, the United States grantor is the deemed owner as to his or her portion of the trust. This result occurs even if the United States grantor does not have any of the powers under §671-677 that would have triggered grantor trust status if the trust were a domestic trust. Reg. §1.679-1(b). Grantor trust status under §679 also overrides §678, so a beneficiary's power to withdraw principal from a §679 trust will not cause the beneficiary to be the deemed owner of the trust. *Id.*

Section 679 takes aim at grantors who would form foreign non-grantor trusts to hold foreign-source investment assets. The income earned by these trusts would not be subject to United States taxation until distributions were made to a United States beneficiary. Indeed, such trusts would often be formed in tax havens such that the trusts paid absolutely no tax to any jurisdiction. Congress thought that foreign trusts should not be entitled to defer United States taxation to the detriment of domestic trusts. By enacting §679 to make a United States grantor the deemed owner of the trust, the United States grantor can no longer achieve deferral through use of a foreign trust.

Because only gratuitous transfers by a United States grantor to a foreign trust with one or more United States beneficiaries trigger § 679, United States grantors have an incentive to structure their transfers so that they appear not to be gratuitous. The regulations contain anti-avoidance rules in this regard. Indirect transfers through an intermediary are viewed as made by the United States grantor directly where the beneficiary is related to the United States grantor and the transfer has a tax-avoidance purpose. Reg. § 1.679-3(c)(2). Likewise, constructive transfers to the foreign trust (*e.g.*, the United States grantor's payment or assumption of the foreign trust's debt) will be treated as gratuitous transfers by the United States grantor. Reg. § 1.679-3(d)(1). Furthermore, certain loans by United States persons to foreign trusts with United States beneficiaries are viewed as gratuitous transfers. § 679(a)(3). The regulations treat any loan to a foreign trust from a related United States person (the United States grantor, a United States beneficiary, or any United States person related to the United States grantor or a United States beneficiary) that is not a "qualified obligation" (a written loan denominated in United States dollars with a term of not more than five years and with a yield to maturity not less than the § 1274(d) rate on the date of issuance) as giving rise to a gratuitous transfer. Reg. § 1.679-4(c), 1.679-4(d).

The second important income tax consequence of foreign trust status is that the gratuitous transfer of appreciated property by a United States person to a foreign trust may cause the transferor to recognize gain in the year of the transfer. § 684(a). This rule does not apply if the foreign trust is a grantor trust as to any person. § 684(b), Reg. § 1.684-3(a). This means that the United States grantor will not be taxed on the transfer of property to the foreign trust if the United States grantor will be the deemed owner of the trust under § 679. It also means that no other United States transferor will recognize gain from the gratuitous transfer of property to a foreign trust provided the United States grantor is still alive and is still the deemed owner of the trust under § 679. Section 684(a) will therefore generally apply in two situations: (1) where the foreign trust becomes a non-grantor trust (*i.e.*, where § 679 ceases to apply); and (2) a domestic trust becomes a foreign trust.

If a § 679 trust ceases to be a § 679 trust during the United States grantor's lifetime (*e.g.*, because the foreign trust lost its last United States beneficiary and the foreign trust is not otherwise a grantor trust under § 671-677), the foreign trust is deemed to have sold all of its appreciated property the United States grantor was deemed to own immediately before the cessation of § 679 status. Reg. § 1.684-2(e)(1), 1.684-4(a). More likely, however, cessation of § 679 status will be a result of the United States grantor's death. Here, the deemed sale of the foreign trust's assets immediately before death will give rise to gain under § 684(a) only to the extent such assets do not receive a step-up in basis under § 1014(a). Reg. § 1.684-3(c). This could happen, for example, where the foreign trust assets are not included in the United States grantor's gross estate and the gift transfers to the foreign trust were complete.

Section 684(a) is much more likely to apply where a domestic trust becomes a foreign trust. § 684(c). The deemed sale of the assets occurs on the same date the domestic trust coverts to a foreign trust, but immediately before the conversion. Reg. § 1.684-4(b). As discussed above, one can correct for the inadvertent conversion of a domestic trust into a foreign trust. Absent such corrective action, gain will likely be recognized. If conversion to foreign trust status occurs while the United States grantor is still alive, however, §684(a) will not apply because the trust will be treated as a grantor trust under §679. §684(b).

Although §684(a) itself is not limited to gratuitous transfers, the regulations provide that §684(a) does not apply to transfers for fair market value provided the trust is not a "related foreign trust." Reg. §1.684-3(d). A transferor is "related" to the foreign trust if the transferor is: (1) the deemed owner of the trust for federal income tax purposes; (2) a beneficiary of the trust; or (3) related to any grantor, deemed owner, or beneficiary of the trust. *Id.* If a United States person sells appreciated property to a related foreign trust that is not a grantor trust, §684(a) would apply, effectively precluding the transferor from using the installment method or claiming the benefit of a nonrecognition provision. *See* Preamble to Proposed Regulations, 2000-2 C.B. 187.

For helpful explanations of these rules, *see* Moore, Don't Even Go There-Federal Income Tax Aspects of Transfers to Foreign Trusts, ALI-ABA International Trust and Estate Planning (2005). *See also* Nunez, Taking the "Foreign" out of Foreign Trusts, U. Miami, 34th Inst. Est. Plan., Ch. 7 (2000). Planning for the beneficiaries of foreign trusts is important. *See* Robinson, U.S. Trusts with Foreign Beneficiaries: Issues and Observations, 35 Est. Plan. 25 (Aug. 2008). *See also* Harrington, Planning for U.S. Beneficiaries of Foreign Trusts Under Recent Regulations, 28 Est. Plan. 258 (June 2001); Lawrence, Trust Classification Times Four, U. Miami, 38th Inst. Est. Plan., Ch. 14 (2004).

§10.53.2. Compliance Requirements for Foreign Trusts

United States citizens and residents are required to report the direct or indirect transfer of cash or property to a foreign trust. §6048(a). This rule applies regardless of whether the foreign trust is a §679 trust. The death of the deemed owner of a §679 trust is considered a "transfer" that must be reported under this rule. §6048(a)(3)(A)(iii). Transfers are reported on a Form 3520 and are filed with the transferor's federal income return for the year of the transfer. Failure to file the Form 3520 can lead to a penalty equal to 35 percent of the amount of the transfer. §6677(b). An additional penalty of $10,000 per month may be added if the transferor fails to comply with the reporting requirement after receiving notice from the IRS. §6677(a).

A foreign trust that is a grantor trust under any of §671–679 must file an annual information return, the Form 3520-A. §6048(b)(1)(A). Portions of the information return must be copied and sent to the United States grantor and to United States beneficiaries that received distributions. The Form 3520-A must be filed by the fifteenth day of the third month following the end of the trust's taxable year (generally, March 15). The penalty for failure to file the Form 3520-A is 5 percent of the gross value of the foreign trust's assets. §6677(a).

United States beneficiaries in receipt of a distribution from a foreign trust must report the receipt on a Form 3520 in the year of distribution. §6048(c)(1). The Form 3520 is filed with the beneficiary's federal income tax return. Reporting is required regardless of whether the foreign trust is a §679 trust.

For more on compliance requirements, *see* Armstrong, Foreign Trust and Gift Compliance Rules: Border Crossing Becomes Dangerous, 18 CEB, Estate Planning & California Probate Reporter 129 (Apr. 1997).

BIBLIOGRAPHY

Abbin, B., Carlson, D. & Vorsatz, M., Income Taxation of Fiduciaries and Beneficiaries (1997)

Acker, Electing to Treat Certain Trusts as Part of Estate, 2 Est. Tax Plan. Advisor 1 (Mar. 2003)

Akers, But I Just Wanted a Few Strings Over the Trust Assets for Me and My Family, U. Miami, 38th Inst. Est. Plan., Ch. 3 (2004)

Armstrong, Foreign Trust and Gift Compliance Rules: Border Crossing Becomes Dangerous, 18 CEB, Estate Planning & California Probate Reporter 129 (Apr. 1997)

Aucutt, Old But Not Cold—Restructuring, Refocusing and Retiring Irrevocable Trusts, U. Miami, 38th Inst. Est. Plan., Ch. 5 (2004)

Baskies, Recent Ruling Affects Powers to Remove & Replace Trustees, 135 Tr. & Est. 62 (1996)

Becker, David M., Perpetuities and Estate Planning (1993)

Berry, The Whether, Why, Whom, What, and When of the Trustee's Duty to Notify Beneficiaries, U. Miami, 45th Inst. Est. Plan. Ch. 14 (2011)

Breyer, Estate Planning for Pets, 15 Prob. & Prop. 6 (July/Aug. 2001)

Bogert, G., Trusts and Trustees (2d ed. Rev. 1979)

Casner, A. J., Estate Planning (5th ed. 1986) (Pennell Supp.)

Casner, A. J. & Pennell, J.N., Estate Planning (6th ed.)

Calif. CEB, Drafting California Irrevocable Living Trusts (3d ed. 1997)

Calif. CEB, Drafting California Revocable Living Trusts (3d ed. 1994)

Cline, Trustee Investments, 861 Tax Mgmt Port. (2008)

Cline, The Uniform Prudent Investor and Principal and Income Acts: Changing the Trust Landscape, 42 Real Prop., Prob. & Tr. J. 611 (2008)

Cline & Jory, The Uniform Prudent Investor Act: Trust Drafting and Administration, 26 Est. Plan. 4 (1999)

Coleman, The Grantor Trust: Yesterday's Disaster, Today's Delight, Tomorrow's? U. Miami, 30th Inst. Est. Plan., Ch. 8 (1996)

Denby, Creative Approaches to Get the Most out of Your Trusts, 135 Tr. & Est. 41 (1996)

Diamond & Todd, The Trustee's Role in Directed Trusts, 149 Tr. & Est. 24 (Dec. 2010)

Donaldson, Understanding Grantor Trusts, U. Miami, 40th Inst. Est. Plan., Ch. 2 (2006)

Dorsett, "Having Your Cake and Eating it Too"—Parental Control over Irrevocable Trusts for Children, 16 Prob. & Prop. 58 (Nov./Dec. 2002)

Engel, The Pros and Cons of Living Trusts as Compared to Wills, 29 Est. Plan. 155 (Apr. 2002)

Ferguson, M.C., Freeland, J.J., & Ascher, M.L., Federal Income Taxation of Estates, Trusts and Beneficiaries (3d ed. 1999)

Fitzsimmons, Navigating the Trustee's Duty to Disclose, 23 Prob. & Prop. 40 (Jan/Feb 2009)

Fletcher, Paul M., The Tax Basis Revocable Trust: New Concepts in Estate Planning (1993)

Fletcher, Tax Basis Revocable Trusts, Tax Notes 1183 (May 30, 1994)

Friedman, Right to Remove Trustee and Other Problem Powers of Grantors, Beneficiaries and Trustees, U. So. Cal., 33rd Tax Inst., Ch. 16 (1981)

Gallo, Drafting and Exercising Powers of Appointment, 120 Tr. & Est. 41 (1981)

Gamble, If It's the 1990s, It Must Be Time for Another Principal and Income Act, U. Miami, 32d Inst. Est. Plan., Ch. 8 (1998)

Halbach, Problems of Discretion in Discretionary Trusts, 61 Colum. L. Rev. 1425 (1961)

Halbach, Trust Investment Law in the Third Restatement, 77 Iowa L. Rev. 1151 (1992)

Halbach, Powers of Distribution, Invasion and Appointment, U. So. Cal., 32nd Tax Inst., Ch. 14 (1980)

Halbach, Tax-Sensitive Trusteeships, 63 Or. L. Rev. 381 (1984)

Handler & Lothes, The Case for Principle Trusts and Against Incentive Trusts, 147 Tr. & Est. 30 (Oct. 2008)

Harrington, Planning for U.S. Beneficiaries of Foreign Trusts Under Recent Regulations, 28 Est. Plan. 258 (June 2001)

Harrison, Structuring Trusts to Permit the Donor to Act as Trustee, 22 Est. Plan. 331 (1995)

Haskel, The Prudent Person Rule for Trustee Investment and Modern Portfolio Theory, 69 N.C. L. Rev. 87 (1990)

Hayes, Protecting the Fiduciary by Drafting in Anticipation of Administration, U. Miami, 24th Inst. Est. Plan., Ch. 15 (1990)

Hodgman & Collins, The "Double Skip" Trust: A Valuable GST Tax Planning Tool, 22 Est. Plan. 273 (1995)

Hodgman & Stetter, Can Incentive Trusts Encourage Children to Behave Responsibly?, 27 Est. Plan. 459 (Dec. 2000)

Horn, Whom do You Trust: Planning, Drafting and Administering Self and Beneficiary-Trusteed Trusts, U. Miami, 20th Inst. Est. Plan., Ch. 5 (1986)

Hosington, Modern Trust Design: New Paradigms for the 21st Century, U. Miami, 31st Inst. Est. Plan., Ch. 6 (1997)

Janes & Kelly, When Using a Power of Substitution—Take Nothing for Granted, 34:8 Est. Plan. 3 (2007)

Keydel, Trustee Selection, Succession, and Removal: Ways to Blend Expertise With Family Control, U. Miami, 23rd Inst. Est. Plan., Ch. 4 (1989)

Lawrence, Trust Classification Times Four, U. Miami, 38th Inst. Est. Plan., Ch. 14 (2004)

McBryde & Keydel, Building Flexibility in Estate Planning Documents, 135 Tr. & Est. 56 (1996)

Medlin, Limitations on the Trustee's Power to Adjust, 42 Real Prop., Prob. & Tr. J. 755 (2008)

Michaelson, A. & Blattmachr, J., Income Taxation of Trusts (13th ed. 1989)

Moore, Don't Even Go There-Federal Income Tax Aspects of Transfers to Foreign Trusts, ALI-ABA International Trust and Estate Planning (2005)

Moore, New Horizons in the Grant and Exercise of Discretionary Powers, U. Miami, 15th Inst. Est. Plan., Ch. 6 (1981)

Myers & Samp, South Dakota Trust Amendments and Economic Development: The Tort of "Negligent Trust Situs" at its Incipient Stage, 44 S.D. L. Rev. 662 (1999)

Nagel, Income and Estate Tax Consequences of Removal and Replacement of Corporate Fiduciaries, N.Y.U., 39th Inst. Fed. Tax., Ch. 52 (1981)

Nenno, Planning to Minimize or Avoid State Income Tax on Trusts, 34 ACTEC J. 131 (2008)

Nenno, Planning with Asset-Protection Trusts: Part II, 40 Real Prop. Prob. & Tr. J. 477 (2005)

Nenno, The Power to Adjust and Total-Return Unitrust Statutes: State Developments and Tax Considerations, 42 Real Prop., Prob. & Tr. J 657 (2008)

Nunez, Taking the "Foreign" out of Foreign Trusts, U. Miami, 34th Inst. Est. Plan., Ch. 7 (2000)

O'Brien, The Trustee's Duty to Provide Information to Beneficiaries: When Can the Settlor Say, "Don't Ask, Won't Tell?", 40 U. Miami, Inst. Est. Plan., Ch. 5 (2006)

O'Brien, An Analysis of the Deductibility of Maintenance Expenses for Residential Property Owned by a Trust and Occupied by a Trust Beneficiary, 7 B.U. J. Tax L. 37 (1989)

Osborne, New Age Estate Planning: Offshore Trusts, U. Miami, 27th Inst. Est. Plan., Ch. 17 (1993)

Peschel, J. & Spurgeon, E., Federal Taxation of Trusts, Grantors and Beneficiaries (2d ed. 1990)

Price, Powers to the Right People: Flexibility Without Taxability, U. Miami, 25th Inst. Est. Plan., Ch. 7 (1991)

Randall & Megaard, Defective Grantor Trusts Can Be Effective Education Funding Vehicles After RRA '93, 78 J. Tax. 150 (1993)

Robinson, U.S. Trusts with Foreign Beneficiaries: Issues and Observations, 35 Est. Plan. 25 (Aug. 2008)

Rothschild, Protecting the Estate from In-Laws and Other Predators, U. Miami, 35th Inst. Est. Plan., Ch. 17 (2001)

Schindel, How to Modify or Terminate an Irrevocable Trust, 22 Est. Plan. 323 (1995)

Schlesinger, Income Taxation of Trusts and Estates Under RRA '93, N.Y.U., 53rd Inst. Fed. Tax., Ch. 31 (1995)

Schwab, How Special Are Special Powers of Appointment? U. Miami, 32d Inst. Est. Plan., Ch. 7 (1998)

Scott, A., Trusts (4th ed., Fratcher ed. 1987)

Strauss, Drafting Trustee Substitution Clauses to Avoid the Adverse Impact of Rev. Rul. 79-353, 53 J. Tax. 66 (1980)

Strauss & Thornburgh, IRS Rationale on Trustee Substitution May Spread to Powers of Appointment, 55 J. Tax. 224 (1981)

Street, Growls or Gratitude? Practical Guidelines for Selection of Individual Trustees and Design of Trustee Succession Plans, U. Miami, 40th Inst. Est. Plan. Ch. 3 (2006)

Suter & Repetti, Trustee Authority to Divide Trust, 6 Prob. & Prop. (Nov./Dec. 1992) 54

Taylor, Pour-Over Wills: Drafting for Testamentary Additions to Trusts, 15 Prob. & Prop. 15 (Jan./Feb. 2001)

Turner, G., Irrevocable Trusts (3d ed. 1996)

Uniform Prudent Investor Act (1994 Act), 7B U.L.A. 97 (1999 Supp.)

Wade, The New California Prudent Investor Rule: A Statutory Interpretive Analysis, 20 Real Prop., Prob. & Tr. J. 1 (1985)

Waggoner, The Uniform Statutory Rule Against Perpetuities, 21 Real Prop., Prob. & Tr. J. 569 (1986)

Weinstock, Nontaxable Grantor and Beneficiary Powers, N.Y.U., 43d Inst. Fed. Tax., Ch. 51 (1985)

Wiensch & Beetz, The Liberation of Total Return, 143 Tr. & Est. 44 (Apr. 2004)

Wolf & Leimberg, Total Return Trusts Approved by New Regs., but State Law is Crucial, 31 Est. Plan. 179 (Apr. 2004)

Wolf, Drafting the Duty to Disappoint Equally—The Total Return Trust, 23 ACTEC Notes 46 (1997)

Wolven & Zaluda, Practical Strategies for Managing a Trustee's Liability Exposure, 33 Est. Plan. 31 (Sept. 2006)

Zaritsky, Grantor Trusts: Sections 671-679, 858-2d Tax Mgmt. Port. (2001)

11

Closely-Held Business Interests

A. INTRODUCTION

§ 11.1. OVERVIEW

Planning for the formation, management and disposition of a client's interests in a family business is a vital element in consideration and formulation of the client's estate plan. Whatever the existing form of a business, the owner should develop an appropriate succession plan. Development of the plan requires the consideration of the client's objectives, and the circumstances of the client's family. Numerous factors, including the age, health, interests, experience, and capacities of younger generation family members may dictate whether it is feasible for the business to be continued within the family after the client's death. Consideration must also be given to the valuation and liquidity problems that may arise when substantial gifts are made or the owner dies. A succession plan is an essential requirement for a business whether it is a sole proprietorship, a partnership, a C corporation, an S corporation, or a limited liability company (LLC). Indeed, the client may decide upon a plan that involves shifting the business from one type of entity to another.

Even clients without a closely-held business can avail themselves of the strategies described in this chapter by creating one. Planners often recommend the formation of a family entity to manage, operate, or control various investment assets and activities. Doing so offers significant nontax advantages like centralized management, investment diversification, efficient transfers of ownership and limited liability. It also offers important tax benefits, chiefly the application of the various valuation discounts applicable to closely-held businesses. Most commonly, the family entity takes the form of a so-called "family limited partnership" (FLP), but they can be (and many times are) in the form of any limited liability entity, including the LLC and the S corporation.

Planning for the creation and disposition of a business entity should take info account the potential that the per unit value of a controlling interest in a business will almost certainly be valued at a higher amount than the per unit value of a minority interest that passes to a decedent's surviving spouse or a charity. The issue is discussed at §5.5.2. *See also* Oshins & Matz, Reolving the Mismatch of Estate Inclusion Value and Deduction Value, 35 Est. Plan. 14 (July 2008).

§11.1.1. Growth of S Corporations, FLPs and LLCs

In the 1980s family business enterprises increasingly took the form of S corporations and FLPs. Legislation in all the states and the District of Columbia in the 1980s and 1990s authorized the creation of LLCs. Unfortunately, the legislation, much of which antedates the promulgation of the Uniform Limited Liability Company Act (1996), varies somewhat from state-to-state.

Propelled by tax and nontax considerations and considerable hype, the LLC has become the vehicle of choice. Indeed, some commentators believe that LLCs enjoy such an advantage over S corporations and partnerships of all kinds, that LLCs will emerge as the nontaxable entity of choice. W. Bagley & P. Whynott, The Limited Liability Company §1.30 (1999).

While both FLPs and LLCs file informational income tax returns, neither pays any income tax—their income, credits and deductions flow through to their owners. As described below, within broad limits, both can provide for differences in the participation in profit, gains and losses. Perhaps most important, the limited partners of an FLP and the members of an LLC both enjoy limited liability, which is, of course, the most important nontax attribute of a corporation. Partnerships generally require at least two partners, but corporations and, in most states, LLCs, may have a single shareholder or member.

§11.1.2. Valuation Discounts

Noncontrolling interests in business entities that are not publicly traded are generally valued at substantial discounts for lack of marketability and lack of control (minority interests). An expert appraisal is required to determine the appropriate amount of the discount(s), and to sustain the discount(s) if challenged by the IRS. The discounts applicable to the transfer of noncontrolling interests in corporations, FLPs, and LLCs often range from 30 to 60 percent—and sometimes more. For example, in *Estate of Anthony J. Frank, Sr.*, 69 T.C.M. (CCH) 2255 (1995), the Tax Court upheld a lack of marketability discount of 30 percent and a minority interest discount of 20 percent. *See* § 2.43.1. The availability of large valuation discounts has encouraged families to transfer businesses and financial assets (*e.g.*, stocks, bonds and cash) to FLPs or LLCs. Planners can generally identify sufficient legitimate business purposes of the transfers to defend the transactions before the IRS.

Interests in FLPs and LLCs are discounted, in part, because of the difference between the value of a transferor's interest, which includes both economic interests and membership interests (possible participation in management, entitlement to greater information and greater protection), and of the "assignee" interest received by the transferee. Keatinge, Transfer of Partnership and LLC Interests—Assignees, Transferees, Creditors, Heirs, Donees and Other Successors, U. Miami 32nd Inst. Est. Plan., Ch. 5 (1998). Mr. Keatinge's paper points out that, "the statutes governing partnership law (and limited liability company statutes, which are based on similar considerations) provide that while an owner's economic rights may be transferred, no transferee shall be admitted as a substitute partner or member without the consent of the other partners or members." *Id.* at ¶ 501.1. Thus, to the "willing buyer" of an ownership interest in such an entity, the value of the interest is certainly worth less than its liquidation value (the interest's proportionate share of the entity's net equity).

As explained below, the enactment in 1990 of Chapter 14, § 2701-2704, severely restricted the valuation advantages previously enjoyed with respect to the transfer of interests in a multiclass business. Prior to that time multiclass corporations and partnerships were commonly created to allow the senior generation owners to transfer the rights to all future appreciation to junior generation family members at little or no gift tax cost. Section 2701 now generally bars that approach. However, the special valuation rules of § 2701 do not apply to some transfers, including ones that involve only one class of equity. In addition, § 2701 only applies to transfers to a relatively narrow class of family members as defined in § 2704.

Sales Shortly After Death. The valuation of an asset at the time of the owner's death may be affected by subsequent events. For example, in *Estate of Alice Kaufman v. Commissioner*, 243 F.3d 1145 (9th Cir. 2001), the court reversed a Tax Court valuation of the decedent's 19.86 percent interest in a closely held company. The appellate court held that the value of the shares at death was controlled by the sale of two smaller blocks of the company's stock made two months after the decedent's death at a price determined by an appraisal made by a securities firm. Courts have generally not recognized the effect of post-death events on the value of contingent claims or liabilities. *See* § 12.11.

§ 11.1.3. Income Tax Considerations—Qualifying as a Flow-Through Entity; "Check-the-Box" Regulations

Until the late 1990s the treatment of an entity as a partnership (flow-through) or corporation (taxable, other than S Corporations) for income tax purposes depended upon whether the entity possessed associates, the objective of engaging in business for profit, and a majority of four other characteristics inherent in corporations: (1) continuity of life; (2) centralized management; (3) limited liability; and (4) free transferability of interests. FLPs, LLCs and corporations, of course, all possess associates and the requisite profit motive. Thus the key to preserving partnership status was ensuring that the entity had no more than two of the other characteristics. This was possible—but caused unreasonable and unjustifiable limitations on their use and effectiveness.

In the early 1990s, the IRS took a more liberal approach in applying the characterization rules. The evolution culminated in the adoption in December, 1996 of the so-called "Check-the-Box" regulations that allow a business broad freedom to choose whether to be taxed as a partnership or a corporation. Reg. § 301.7701-3. Under them, a separate entity that is not otherwise classified as a corporation or trust is allowed to choose between being taxed as a corporation or a partnership. Regulation § 301.7701-3(a) provides that, "An eligible entity with at least two members can elect to be classified as either an association (and thus a corporation under Reg. § 301.7701-2(b)(2)) or a partnership, and an eligible entity with a single owner can elect to be classified as an association or to be disregarded as an entity separate from its owner."

A check-the-box election is made by filing Form 8832 to the tax return for the year in which the election is made. Reg. § 301.7701-3(c)(1)(ii). The form must be signed by each owner of the electing entity or by an authorized officer, manager or director. Reg. § 301.7701-3(c)(2)(i). Typically, FLPs and LLCs do not need affirmatively to elect to be taxed as a partnership because eligible entities with at least two members will, by default, be taxed as partnerships. Similarly, an LLC with a single member will, by default, be disregarded (*i.e.*, taxed as a sole proprietorship).

Liability Issues for Disregarded Entities. While most state statutes very clearly intend that single-member LLCs offer the same protection from creditors as that offered by a single-shareholder corporation, there is some uncertainty whether a single-member LLC offers the same level of limited liability. In one case, the bankruptcy trustee was allowed to liquidate a single-member LLC after the court saw no reason to limit a creditor to a charging order where the debtor was the only owner of the LLC. *In re Ashley Albright*, 291 B.R. 538 (Bankr. D. Col. 2003).

Disregarded Entities Owned by Married Couples. According to Rev. Proc. 2002-69, 2002-2 C.B. 831, a business entity that is not a corporation and is wholly owned by a husband and wife as community property under the laws of a state, foreign country, or possession of the United States, may be treated by the husband and wife as either a disregarded entity or a partnership. Until the issuance of this revenue procedure, it was unclear whether the IRS would insist that such an entity be treated as a partnership. Some planners were concerned that the IRS might insist that such an entity be treated as a partnership. Under Rev. Proc. 2002-69, "If the entity is disregarded, its activities are treated in the same manner as a sole proprietorship, branch, or division of the owner." Presumably, a husband and wife could make gifts to grantor trusts of interests in a disregarded LLC without jeopardizing that status.

In addition, married couples in all states may elect to be treated as "qualified joint venturers" instead of partners, provided the only members of the business are a husband and wife and provided both materially participate in the business. § 761(f). If they make this election, each will be required to account for his or her share of the income and deductions of the business as if he or she were a sole proprietor. Electing couples will now ensure that both get credit for paying Social Security and Medicare taxes.

§11.1.4. Management and Control

The creator of an FLP or LLC can preserve a high degree of control without transfer tax disadvantage, so long as his or her conduct is subject to the ordinarily applicable fiduciary duties. See §11.5.1. If all interests have the same distribution rights the FLP or LLC will be treated as having only one class of equity ownership— that is, the interest that also carries management power is not treated as a second class of equity for purposes of §2701. *See* Reg. §25.2701-1(c)(3). In this respect an FLP or LLC is preferable to a trust—the assets of which would be includible in the estate of a transferor who retained control over them. *See* §§2036(a), 2038(a). Also, an FLP or LLC may own life insurance on the lives of members without risking inclusion of the entire proceeds in the estate of an insured member.

§11.1.5. Buy-Sell Agreements

Tax and nontax considerations usually support the preparation and execution of a buy-sell agreement covering the owners' interests in a corporation, FLP, or LLC. *See* §11.6-11.12; Cornfeld, Non-Tax Considerations in Preparing Buy-Sell Agreements, U. Miami, 28th Inst. Est. Plan., Ch. 10 (1994). On the tax side, an agreement that survives the tests imposed by §2703 may establish the value of the decedent's interest in the business.

Without an effective buy-sell agreement, the valuation of an interest in an entity that is not publicly traded may be the subject of intense controversy with the IRS— and with the other owners. The difficulty of valuing private business interests under the "willing buyer-willing seller" test is legendary. The difficulty of attempting such a valuation are indicated by an English jurist's plaint:

> The result is that I must enter into a dim world peopled by the indetermi- nate spirits of fictitious or unborn sales. It is necessary to assume the prophetic vision of a prospective purchaser at the moment of the death of the deceased, and firmly to reject the wisdom which might be provided by the knowledge of subsequent events. *Holt v. Inland Revenue Commis- sioners,*[1953] All E.R. 1499, 1501.

As indicated above, even without a binding buy-sell agreement, a minority interest in an FLP, LLC, or corporation may qualify for substantial valuation dis- counts—often 30 to 60 percent or more.

§11.1.6. Gifts and Other Transfer Strategies

Estate plans for owners of closely held businesses often involve the client making inter vivos gifts of his or her business interests to family members, trusts, or charities. In some cases a client will choose more sophisticated plans, such as ones involving charitable lead trusts, charitable remainder trusts, installment sales or family annuities. Other approaches involve transferring business interests to grantor retained annuity trusts (GRATs). *See* §9.43. Outright gifts remain one of the simplest and most effective lifetime estate planning techniques.

Transfers of business interests should be planned carefully because the transfer of some types of ownership interests may have negative tax consequences, such as the loss of qualification of corporate stock under §1244. Under that section, only the original owner is entitled an ordinary loss deduction for a loss incurred with respect to stock in a small business—successive owners are not. In contrast, if a loss is characterized as a capital loss, it can only be used to offset capital gains plus up to $3,000 in any single year. §1211. Gifts may also jeopardize the ability of the donor's estate to meet the requirements of §§303 and 6166.

The following example illustrates the transfer tax savings that may result from lifetime gifts of stock—or other equity interests. Gifts may, of course, be subject to the special valuation rules of §2701. However, the rules do not apply to outright gifts of interests that are "of the same class as the retained interest." §2701(a)(2) (*e.g.* stock in a corporation that has issued only one class of stock).

EXAMPLE 11-1.

W, who has not previously made any taxable gifts, owned 100% of the common stock of W, Inc., which was worth a total of $5,000,000. In 2006, *W* transferred 15% of the stock to each of her 2 children, *D* and *S*. Discounting each gift for lack of marketability and lack of control, the stock given to each child had a value of $512,000. *W*'s annual gift tax exclusions reduced the gifts to $500,000 each. The gift tax imposed on the gifts was completely offset by *W*'s gift tax exemption amount. The gifts effectively removed 30% of the value of W, Inc. from *W*'s estate ($1,500,000) at no out-of-pocket tax cost. Of course, any increase in the value of the transferred stock will also be excluded from *W*'s estate. Note, too, that the gifts also removed from her estate any income that the gifted stock might generate in the future. On the negative side, *W*'s basis in the stock carries over to *D* and *S*—it will not be stepped up when *W* dies.

§11.1.7. Sections 303 and 6166

Although the C corporation may be of declining popularity—it remains useful in many contexts. *See* Aucutt, Using C Corporations in Estate Planning, U. Miami, 33d Inst. Est. Plan., Ch. 10 (1999). Because it remains important to plan for the disposition of a client's interest in a closely-held corporation, this chapter includes a discussion of the post-mortem redemption of stock under §303. §11.13-11.22. It also includes a lengthy consideration of the deferral of estate and GST taxes under §6166, which is important for all types of entities.

The preferential tax rate that applies to qualified dividend income under current law will not make it less desirable to attempt to bring redemptions within the safe harbor rules of §302 or the exception of §303. Under §1(h)(11), qualified dividend income is subject to the same rates as apply to net capital gains (*i.e.*, a maximum rate of 15 percent). However, the entire amount of the distribution in redemption that is not within the scope of §§302 or 303 will be subject to tax as a dividend—not just the gain element.

§11.1.8. Recapitalizations

The recapitalization of a corporation or partnership may be desirable in order to create separate classes of ownership, gifts of some of which will meet the differing needs and interests of family members. For example, following a recapitalization, common stock or its equivalent might be distributed to family members who are active in the business and preferred stock or its equivalent to those who are inactive. On the down side, transfers of interests in an entity with more than one class of equity are subject to the special valuation rules of §2701. Note also that FLPs and LLCs have an advantage here over S corporations, which can only have one class of stock. However, under §1361(c)(4) and Reg. §1.1361-1(l)(1), "a corporation is treated as having only one class of stock if all outstanding shares of stock of the corporation confer identical rights to distribution and liquidation proceeds." Differences in voting rights are disregarded.

Special care should be exercised in a recapitalization to be sure that the arrangement meets the present, and anticipated future, needs of the parties. Depriving some interests of control may create tax advantages, but it can also can create ugly future problems—which may return to haunt the lawyer. Accordingly, the lawyer should be particularly conscious of conflicts problems that may be present, or inhere, in the situation.

§11.1.9. Sale to an ESOP, §1042

The benefits of making a tax free sale of business interests to an employee stock ownership plan (ESOP) under §1042 is only available with respect to the stock of a C or S corporation that is not publicly traded. §1042(c)(1)(A). Accordingly, a client who wishes to take advantage of the benefits of §1042 may be required to incorporate a sole proprietorship. A sale is tax free under §1042 only if it is made to an ESOP or an eligible worker-owned cooperative that must, immediately after the sale, own at least 30 percent of the shares of each class of stock, §1042(b)(1)-(2), and the selling taxpayer invests in qualified replacement property within the replacement period, §1042(a).

§11.1.10. Ethics—Conflicts of Interest; Confidentiality; Engagement Letters

> [E]ach of the shareholders and the corporate entity have conflicting interests in the negotiation and drafting of a buy-sell agreement even though they have a common enemy in the Internal Revenue Service. While theoretically each party should have his or her or its separate and independent counsel, the parties will most often want to have only one lawyer involved, primarily for obvious economic reasons.
>
> For self-protection, the lawyer must advise the parties of potential conflicts and offer them the opportunity to retain (and pay for) separate counsel. If they elect not to seize such opportunity, their decision and consent to the joint representation should be memorialized in an engage-

ment letter or in the agreement itself. Cornfeld, U. Miami, 28th Inst. Est. Plan., ¶ 1005.1 (1994).

A lawyer who is asked to assist in the formation of a business entity must recognize the ethical questions that may arise—particularly ones involving conflicts of interest and problems of confidentiality. Model Rules 1.7 and 2.2 (the latter deleted by the ABA from the Model Rules in 2002) are particularly relevant to the consideration of conflict issues. *See* §§ 1.6.7 *and* 11.11. The problem extends both to the formation of business entities and the representation of the entities themselves—each phase of which can involve particularly daunting conflicts questions. The representation may also involve the application of Model Rule § 1.13, which deals with the representation of clients that are entities.

An engagement letter should be used to identify the person or persons the lawyer will represent, to clarify the scope of the representation, to explain the basis upon which the lawyer's fee will be determined and, in the case of multiple representations, to specify the extent to which the lawyer will (or may) disclose the confidences of one client to the other or others. If multiple clients are involved, the letter should also explain conflict issues and how they will be handled. For a sample engagement letter, *see* Form 1-1, § 1.6.2.

Courts have reached very different conclusions regarding the extent to which the lawyer who represents a partnership owes duties to the partners, particularly the limited partners. The same analysis will most likely be applied to LLCs. For example, in *Arpadi v. First MSP Corp.*, 628 N.E.2d 1335 (Ohio 1994), the court held that a lawyer who represents a partnership has duties to individual partners. In contrast, in *Griva v. Davison*, 637 A.2d 830 (D.C. App. 1994), the court held that the representation of partnership is representation of an entity and not of partners.

If an engagement letter does not satisfactorily deal with conflict issues, the lawyer may later be required to make extremely difficult decisions regarding disclosures. Potential problems involve the extent to which information received from one investor or family member must be shared, or withheld, from another. *See* Model Rule 1.6, discussed in § 1.6.6.

§ 11.2. PRINCIPAL FEATURES OF CORPORATIONS, FLPS, AND LLCS

Several important nontax features of the corporate form made it the a popular choice for business and estate planners—most of which are now available to FLPs and LLCs. Corporate shares are almost always nonassessable, which means that the shareholder is liable only for the initial cost of shares purchased from the corporation. The limited liability of the shareholders of a corporation was, historically, a prime reason for conducting a business in the corporate form. The limited liability of the corporate form contrasts with the unlimited liability of a general partner or sole proprietor. Now, of course, limited partners and members of LLCs also enjoy limited liability.

The free transferability of interests in a corporation is another important feature of corporations that is often a critical element of an estate plan. Of course, the transfer of shares in a closely-held corporation is often restricted by the terms of its articles, bylaws, or a buy-sell agreement or other arrangement. Free transferability of interests in FLPs and LLCs is now also available—without jeopardizing treatment as a flow through entity. As described above, the Check-the-Box regulations that govern the classification of entities as corporations or partnerships for income tax purposes now leave the choice primarily to the entity.

The theoretical free transferability of shares or interests may be of very little value in the case of a minority shareholder. From a practical point of view unless the minority shareholder and his or her successors are protected by the terms of a buy-sell agreement they are largely at the mercy of the majority. Finally, a corporation has a potentially indefinite existence, unrelated to the life of any shareholder. Thus, a corporation can continue to function without interruption following the death of a shareholder.

Comparison of Basic Characteristic. The following table summarizes many of the important characteristics of C corporations, S Corporations, FLPs and LLCs.

Table 11-1
Characteristics of Various Business Entities

Characteristic	C Corp.	S Corp.	FLP	LLC
Limited Liability	Yes	Yes	Yes (Except gen'l partner)	Yes
Continuity of Existence	Yes	Yes	Varies	Yes
Number of Members	Unlimited	1-100	Unlimited	Unlimited
Character of Members	Unlimited	Limited	Unlimited	Unlimited
More than One Class of Interest (Note, § 2701 Not Applicable if Only One Class of Equity)	O.K.	No (but voting and nonvoting stock O.K.)	O.K.	O.K.
Interests Can Be Transferred— Subject to Local Law, Articles and Agreements	O.K.	O.K.	O.K.	O.K.
Variable Interests in Profits and Losses	No	No	Possible	Possible
Can Members Participate in Management	Yes	Yes	No (Limited Partners can't participate)	Yes
Single Member	O.K.	O.K.	No	Varies
Tax-Free Formation	Available	Available	Available	Available

Characteristic	C Corp.	S Corp.	FLP	LLC
Entity Taxable	Yes	No	No	No
Deferral Under §6166	Available	Available	Available	Available
Buy-Sell Agmt	Useful	Useful	Useful	Useful
Discount Value Of Noncontrol Interests	Yes	Yes	Yes	Yes
Liquidation or Redemption Nontaxable	Receipts taxed, unless Nondividend, §§302, 303	Varies	Varies	Varies

§11.3. INCOME TAXATION OF SUBCHAPTER C CORPORATIONS

Currently the maximum income tax rate generally applicable to individuals (35 percent) slightly exceeds the maximum income tax rate generally applicable to C corporations (34 percent). However, as described below, the potential application of the income tax at both the corporate and shareholder levels remains a serious disadvantage. In earlier times it was more attractive to incorporate for the purpose of accumulating income within the corporation in order to shelter the income from higher individual income tax rates.

For federal income tax purposes C corporations are taxed as separate entities at rates which increase from 15 percent on the first $50,000 to 38 percent on taxable income between $15,000,000 and $18,333,333. An additional tax of five percent is imposed on taxable income from $100,000-$335,000. Corporations with a taxable income between $335,000 and $10,000,000 pay an effective income tax rate of 34 percent. A C corporation is not allowed a deduction for dividends distributed to shareholders. Thus, the income of profitable C corporations may be subject to a form of double taxation: The income of a C corporation that is distributed to shareholders is subject to income taxation at both the corporate and the individual levels. As noted above, however, a maximum rate of 15 percent now applies to dividends, regardless of the amount of dividends received or the amount of other income received by the taxpayer. Thus, while the C corporation's income is still subject to a double tax, the combined bite is substantially less.

EXAMPLE 11-2.

The income of X Corp. last year was subject to an effective federal income tax rate of 34%. Thus, X Corp. paid $34 on every $100 of taxable income. Later X Corp. paid a cash dividend of $66 to its shareholders. A maximum rate of 15 percent applies to qualified dividend income. Accordingly, a dividend of $66 received by Shareholder A would be subject to a maximum tax of $9.90. The aggregate tax paid by A and X Corp. is $43.90, an effective tax rate of 43.9%.

The double tax still arises if *X* Corp. retains its earnings because the increase in value will result in a capital gain when *A* sells the shares of *X* Corp. Of course, if *A* holds the shares until death, the basis in the shares will be stepped up to their federal estate tax value without the imposition of any income or gains tax.

In contrast to the nondeductibility of dividend distributions, a corporation is entitled to a deduction for interest paid on indebtedness. Not surprisingly, the IRS and taxpayers frequently clash over whether a particular arrangement is debt or a species of stock.

The amount taxed to a C corporation is reduced to the extent salaries are paid to employees. The deductibility of the salaries to employee-shareholders eliminates the double tax bite that might take place if a profitable corporation made a distribution to its shareholders. The income tax liability of a profitable corporation is also reduced by the wide range of fringe benefits that are deductible by the corporation, but are not currently taxable to the employees. They range from contributions to qualified retirement plans (which is generally the most important benefit) to payment of the cost of health, group life insurance coverage, §79, and club dues and membership fees. In contrast, fringe benefits for shareholders of S corporations are generally not deductible by the corporation. §1372. When all is said and done, the present income tax law does not encourage family businesses to use the C corporation format.

The use of a C corporation entity has little tax disadvantage so long as it is not profitable. However, it is important to understand that once it becomes profitable it is practically impossible to withdraw its earnings for the benefit of the shareholders without attracting income tax liabilities (*i.e.*, virtually any distribution is taxable as a dividend to the extent the corporation has accumulated earnings and profits). This is, of course, not a problem for newly formed C corporations, which will have no accumulated income. While most assets can be transferred to a corporation tax-free under §351, distributions from a C corporation to the shareholders are usually treated as dividends, subject to taxation as ordinary income. Under the *General Utilities* doctrine, which was repealed by the 1986 Act, a corporation generally did not recognize gain or loss when appreciated property was distributed to shareholders in a partial or total liquidation. *See General Utilities & Operating Co. v. Helvering*, 296 U.S. 200 (1935). Now, under §311(b), a corporation recognizes gain when appreciated property is distributed to a shareholder. Paraphrasing a popular epigram: Incorporate in haste; repent at leisure.

§11.4. Income Taxation of S Corporations

Although LLCs have become the vehicle of choice, family businesses are often organized as corporations that elect to be taxed under subchapter S, §§1361-1379. Under subchapter S a domestic corporation with only one class of stock and 100 or fewer shareholders is not taxed as a corporation. In effect, an S corporation is treated as a conduit, much like a partnership, through which the income and losses flow to the shareholders on a current basis. Under §1366(b), the character of income, loss, deduction, or credit is passed through to the shareholder. More complicated rules apply to corporations that shift from a regular C corporation to S corporation status.

At base, an S corporation combines the attributes of a partnership with the limited liability and greater legal certainty of the corporate legal form. Under § 1372, an S corporation is treated like a partnership for purposes of the income tax treatment of employee fringe benefits. Thus, an owner of two percent or more of the stock of an S corporation cannot exclude from income the corporation's payment of life, accident, and health insurance and employer-provided meals and lodging. There are, however, important differences between S corporations and partnerships and LLCs. Among them are the limited character and number of shareholders an S corporation may have and the requirement that it have only one class of stock. In contrast, a partnership or LLC can have an unlimited number of members of varying types (*e.g.*, estates, trusts, and other corporations). In addition, partners and members can have differing interests in income and capital.

§11.4.1. Shareholder Limitations

For purposes of determining the number of shareholders, a "husband and wife (and their estates) shall be treated as 1 shareholder." § 1361(c)(1)(A)(i). This rule is similar to the ones applicable for purposes of determining qualification under § 303 and 6166. In general, § 1361(b) bars an S corporation from having any nonresident alien or institutional shareholders. However, an estate may be a shareholder during the period required for administration of the estate, § 1361(b)(1)(B), including the period the estate tax is deferred under § 6166. Rev. Rul. 76-23, 1976-1 C.B. 264 (involving the predecessor of § 6166). Revenue Ruling 76-23 was followed in LR 9247035, which held that the estate was an eligible S corporation shareholder during the period the estate was kept open to make payments due under § 6166.

Voting trusts, grantor trusts, qualified subchapter S trusts (QSSTs) and electing small business trusts (ESBTs) may also be shareholders. §§ 1361(c)(2), (d), (e). *See* § 10.4.14. As explained in § 10.32-10.32.2, a trust may purposefully be made "defective" under the grantor trust rules in order to cause the grantor to be treated as the owner, and taxed on all of the income of the trust. Such a grantor trust is allowed to be a shareholder in an S corporation although the trust does not meet the requirements of a QSST. For example, so long as the trust is treated as a grantor trust it may have multiple beneficiaries. Of course, if the trust ceases to be a grantor trust, the S election will terminate after a period of time, § 1361(c)(2)(A)(ii), (iii), unless the trust becomes a QSST or an ESBT. Under the existing rules, a GRAT that is treated as a grantor trust, can hold S corporation stock. *E.g.,* LRs 9519029, 9448018, 944403 (modified by LR 9543049). *See also* § 9.43.2. A trust of which a beneficiary is treated as owner under § 678 may also be a shareholder of an S corporation. LRs 9810006, 8724010.

QSSTs. Under § 1361(d)(3), a QSST is a trust which requires that: (1) A single income beneficiary be the only beneficiary for his or her lifetime, (2) any principal that is distributed during the lifetime of the income beneficiary may only be distributed to him or her, (3) the income interest terminates when the income beneficiary dies or the trust earlier terminates, (4) if the trust terminates during the lifetime of the income beneficiary, all of the trust assets must be distributed to the beneficiary, and (5) all income be distributed currently to a single beneficiary that is a United States citizen or resident. Note that the requirements of a QTIP trust and a QSST are consistent. That is, a QTIP trust can be drafted to meet the requirements of a QSST.

Thus, an active spouse may leave stock in an S corporation to a QTIP trust for the benefit of the surviving spouse who is inactive in the business. Final regulations regarding QSST elections by testamentary trusts were adopted in 2003. Reg. § 1.1361-1.

An election to treat a QSST as a trust described in § 1361(c)(2)(A)(i), and thus a permitted shareholder, must be made and filed by the income beneficiary of the QSST in the manner described in Reg. § 1.1361-1(j)(6). (The beneficiary of a QSST is treated as the shareholder, not the QSST.) Consistently, if a person is the beneficiary of more than one QSST that holds S corporation stock in the same corporation, the person is treated as one shareholder. *E.g.*, LR 9526021.The QSST election must be made within two months and 15 days following the transfer of S corporation stock to the trust. § 1361(d)(2)(D), Reg. § 1361-1(j)(6)(iii).

If voting stock is transferred to a QSST, § 2036(b) dictates that the transferor should not serve as trustee. For a discussion of the application of § 2036(b), *see* § 2.18.1 and 11.38.1.

In Rev. Rul. 92-20, 1992-1 C.B. 301, the IRS ruled that a trust may qualify as a QSST although the trust instrument includes a provision that allows the trustee to accumulate income during any period the trust does not hold any shares of an S corporation.

A trust that qualifies as a charitable remainder trust cannot be a QSST. Rev. Rul. 92-48, 1992-1 C.B. 301. According to this ruling a corporation's election to be treated as an S corporation is terminated if a charitable remainder trust becomes a share-holder. QSSTs are also discussed at § 10.4.14.

Electing Small Business Trusts. Section 1361(e) allows an electing small business trust (ESBT) to be a shareholder of an S corporation. The basic purpose of Congress in allowing ESBTs to be shareholders of S corporations was to permit trusts of which there were multiple beneficiaries to hold S corporation stock. The income of an ESBT from an S Corporation (other than capital gains) is taxed to the trust at the highest rate applicable to trusts and estates (currently 35 percent). In contrast, a QSST's income from an S Corporation is taxed to the beneficiaries at their regular rates. In computing an ESBT's income from an S corporation, the only items taken into account are: (1) the trust's shares of the S corporation's item of income, gain, loss, deduction, and credit; (2) gain or loss from the trust's sale of the S corporation stock; (3) state or local income taxes and administrative expenses allocable to the S corpora-tion stock; and (4) interest paid or accrued on debt used to acquire stock in the S corporation. § 641(c)(2)(C).

Under § 1361(e)(1) an ESBT is a trust in which no interest was acquired by purchase and its only beneficiaries are, "(I) an individual, (II) an estate, or (III) an organization described in paragraph (2), (3), (4) or (5) of section 170(c)." In determin-ing whether this requirement is met, any person with a present, remainder, or reversionary interest in the trust is considered a beneficiary of the trust. Reg. § 1.1361-1(m)(1)(ii)(A). In applying the 100-shareholder limitation applicable to S corporations, each potential current beneficiary (*i.e.*, one entitled to or eligible to receive distributions of trust income or principal) is treated as a shareholder. Reg. § 1.361-1(m)(4)(i). Possible appointees under a power of appointment are treated as beneficiaries for purposes of this rule. Reg. § 1.1361-1(m)(4)(vi)(A). The temporary waiver or release of a power of appointment will not be recognized, but a permanent relinquishment of a power of appointment that is effective under local law will be recognized. Reg. § 1.1361-1(m)(4)(vi)(B).

The election to be treated as an ESBT is made by the trustee. Reg. § 1.1361-1(m)(2)(i). Regulations specify the required contents of an ESBT election. Reg. § 1.1361-1(m)(2)(ii).

Converting From an ESBT to a QSST and From a QSST to an ESBT. In Rev. Proc. 98-23, 1998-1 C.B. 662, the IRS provides guidance regarding the manner in which a QSST could be converted to an ESBT and, conversely, how an ESBT could be converted to a QSST.

§ 11.4.2. One Class of Stock

Although an S corporation can have only one class of stock, it is not "treated as having more than 1 class of stock solely because there are differences in voting rights among the shares of common stock." § 1361(c)(4). This rule allows an S corporation to be structured in a way that permits a parent to retain voting control while giving a majority of the common stock to family members or charities. The retention of voting stock does not subject the transferred nonvoting stock to inclusion in the transferor's estate under § 2036(b). Likewise, bona fide stock purchase or redemption agreements are generally disregarded. Reg. § 1.1361-1(l)(2)(iii). For example, an agreement that provides for the redemption of the shares of one shareholder of an S corporation does not constitute a second class of stock. LR 9808024. Also, note that the valuation rules of § 2701 do not apply if the retained and the transferred interests are of the same class of equity. § 2701(a)(2)(B).

Straight Debt. Shareholders or others may make loans to an S corporation without the indebtedness being treated as a second class of stock if the debt qualifies as "straight debt" under § 1361(c)(5). Straight debt is defined as an unconditional written promise to pay a fixed amount on demand or on a specified date which is not convertible into stock, the interest rate is not contingent on profits, the borrower's discretion, or similar factors and the creditor is "an individual (other than a nonresident alien), an estate, or a trust" that is a permissible S corporation shareholder.

Split-Dollar Life Insurance Agreement.—A split-dollar agreement between a trust and an S corporation, under which a second to die policy is collaterally assigned by the trust to the corporation, does not give rise to a second class of stock where the only right of the corporation is to recover the amount of unreimbursed premiums. LR 9709027. *See also* LRs 9248019, 9331009, 9318007, and 9309046.

§ 11.4.3. Election to Be S Corporation

All of a corporation's shareholders must consent to make a Subchapter S election. § 1362(a). An election is effective for the following taxable year, except that an election made in the first two and a half months of a taxable year is effective on the first day of the taxable year. § 1362(b). Once an election is effective, the income, losses, deductions, and credits of the corporation flow through to the shareholders automatically. § 1366(b).

§11.4.4. Termination of S Corporation Status

An S election may be terminated in three ways. First, a majority of the taxpayers may elect to revoke the status. §1362(d)(1). Second, S corporation status terminates automatically if the corporation ceases to qualify (*e.g.*, it issues a second class of stock or has more than 100 shareholders or an alien, nonqualified trust, or corporation becomes a shareholder). §1362(d)(2). Finally, termination will result if an S corporation has subchapter C earnings and profits for three successive years and has gross receipts in each of those years, more than 25 percent of which constituted passive investment income. §1362(d)(3). A buy-sell agreement may include provisions that prohibit actions that would result in termination of the election. Thus, an agreement might bar the issuance of a second class of stock, the addition of too many shareholders to an S corporation, or the addition of nonqualifying shareholders (*e.g.*, a trust that is not eligible to be a shareholder).

Relief From Inadvertent Termination. Section 1362(f) grants the IRS discretion to treat a corporation as an S corporation where its election was inadvertently invalid or its status as an S corporation was inadvertently terminated. The IRS regularly exercises this discretion where the shareholders take prompt corrective action and provide a reasonable explanation for the inadvertent termination or invalid election. In LR 9527018, the IRS gave relief from an inadvertent termination of S corporation status that was due to the failure of the trustee of trusts created by the deceased spouse's will to elect to treat the trusts as QSSTs. The two trusts, a QTIP trust and a credit shelter trust, both met the requirements of a QSST.

S Corporation Stock Distributed from ESOP Rolled Over to IRA. An S corporation election will not terminate if an ESOP distributes the S corporation stock to one or more participants who make a direct rollover of the stock to an IRA, from which the stock is immediately redeemed. LR 200122034. In reaching this practical conclusion the ruling stated that, "[i]n the case of a direct rollover of stock, the momentary designation of the custodian of the IRA as owner of the stock under the particular facts described above will not cause Company's S election to terminate."

§11.4.5. Income, Distributions, and Basis

Under §1366(a), a shareholder of an S corporation is treated as having received a proportionate share of an S corporation's income for the taxable year regardless of whether it was actually distributed. Accordingly, a shareholder may be taxed on income he or she did not actually receive. In particular, under §1367(a)(1) a shareholder's basis in the stock of an S corporation is increased by the amount of income that is taxed to the shareholder under §1366. Consistently, a shareholder's basis is reduced, but not below zero, by the amount of distributions. §1367(a)(2)(A). However, under §1368(b)(2) a distribution in excess of basis is treated "as gain from the sale or exchange of property."

EXAMPLE 11-3.

Y contributed $10,000 to *Y* Corp., in exchange for which *Y* received all of its stock. *Y* Corp. made a timely election to be treated as an S corporation, to which *Y* consented as required by § 1362(a). In its first year of operation *Y* Corp. had earnings of $1,000 which were not distributed to *Y*. *Y* was required to report the earnings of *Y* Corp. as income. However, as the earnings were not distributed, *Y*' s basis in the *Y* Corp. stock was increased by an equal amount, to $11,000.

Limitation on Deductions and Losses. As indicated above, losses and deductions also pass through to shareholders on a current basis. The amount of losses and deductions which flow through to a shareholder reduce the basis in the S corporation stock. However, a shareholder's basis cannot be reduced below zero, so losses and deductions in excess of a shareholder's basis are suspended until a later year when the shareholder has sufficient basis against which to apply the suspended losses and deductions. § 1366(d).

EXAMPLE 11-4.

The facts are the same as in Example 11-3. In its second year of operation *Y* Corp. had deductions of $2,000, but no earnings, and made no distributions to *Y*. The deductions were passed through and reported by *Y*. The deductions reduce *Y*'s stock basis by $2,000 to $9,000.

Special Rule for Charitable Contributions. A special rule applicable for 2006, 2007, 2008, and 2009 provides that an S corporation's charitable contribution will only cause a shareholder's stock basis to be reduced by the shareholder's pro rata share of the adjusted basis of the contributed property. § 1367(a)(2). Thus, for example, if an S corporation with two equal shareholders donated to charity real property worth $100,000 in which the corporation's basis was $40,000, each shareholder could be eligible to claim a $50,000 charitable contribution (half of the $100,000 value) while only reducing stock basis by $20,000 (half of the $40,000 basis). This special rule confers a tremendous benefit to S corporation shareholders, especially where the contributed property would have triggered liability for tax under § 1374, a corporate-level tax imposed upon some dispositions of assets containing built-in gain on the day the corporation's S election became effective. Charitable contributions of such property do not trigger the § 1374 tax, because there is no recognized gain from a charitable contribution. Under this special rule, the contributions may also give a fair market value deduction to the shareholders at a cost equal only to the basis of the contributed property.

Distributions of Appreciated Property. Except as otherwise provided, the rules of subchapter C apply to S corporations and their shareholders. § 1371(a). Applying the rules of subchapter C, an S corporation's distributions of appreciated property are treated as sales or exchanges by the corporation. Accordingly, the sales generate gain that flows through to the shareholders of the S corporation. *See* § 311(b). Accordingly, the shareholders must report the gain as income. The distribution has no effect on the basis of the shareholder—while the shareholder's basis is increased in the amount of the gain, it is reduced an equivalent amount on account of the distribution. § 1367(a).

§ 11.4.5

EXAMPLE 11-5.

The facts are the same as in Example 11-3. In its third year of operation Y Corp. distributed property to Y which had a basis of $2,000 and a fair market value of $3,000. Y Corp. has a gain of $1,000 as a result of the distribution, which is passed through to Y. Accordingly, Y is taxed on the $1,000 gain. Y's basis is in the S corporation stock is reduced by a net of $2,000 on account of the distribution. (While Y's basis is increased by $1,000 on account as a result of Y being taxed on the gain, Y's basis is reduced by $3,000 because of the distribution.)

§11.4.6. Relationship of Income Tax Rates to S Corporation Planning

If the income tax rates applicable to corporations are lower than the rates applicable to the individual shareholders, is may be desirable to elect S corporation status for the early years of a corporation's existence—if it has losses. By doing so the shareholders may be able to take advantage of its losses on their income tax returns depending on whether the passive loss or at risk rules apply. If the corporation later becomes profitable, the shareholders could terminate the S corporation election. Under the rules applicable to C corporations the profit of the corporation would be taxed to it and not the shareholders. Of course, income that is sheltered within a C corporation cannot be extracted without tax cost.

§11.4.7. Valuation

In valuing S corporation stock under the discounted future cash flow approach, the Tax Court and, by a divided court, the Sixth Circuit have held that it is not proper to deduct hypothetical corporate income taxes. *Gross v. Commissioner*, 272 F.3d 333 (6th Cir. 2001). Discounts for built in capital gains have been applied in valuing stock in C corporations. *See* §2.13.

§11.5. INCOME TAXATION OF PARTNERSHIPS AND LLCS

Beginning in the 1980s, FLPs and, later, LLCs became the entity of choice to operate family-owned businesses or manage the family's capital. In gross terms the tax treatment of an FLP or LLC is essentially the same given an S corporation. However, in some respects an FLP or LLC is preferred. In particular, an FLP or LLC can have more than 100 partners, and can include partners or members who are not permitted to be shareholders in an S corporation (*e.g.,* nonresident aliens and trusts of various types). As pointed out below, FLPs and LLCs can generally be formed tax free and appreciated assets can generally be contributed to FLPs and LLCs without incurring any tax liability. §721. Importantly, the capital interests of the partners and their rights to receive income can vary (*i.e.,* there can be more than one type of partnership equity interest—but having more than one type may cause valuation problems under §2701). The rights of members of LLCs can also vary according to the provisions of the articles of organization, or the terms of the operating agreement.

The contribution of property to an FLP or LLC in exchange for a partnership interest is generally not a taxable event. §721. Instead, the partner or member has a basis in the interest equal to the amount of money and the basis of other property that he or she contributed to the partnership. §722. Consistently, the entity takes a carryover basis in the contributed property. §723. The distinction between one's basis in his or her interest (the outside basis) and the FLPs or LLCs basis in the property it owns (the inside basis) is particularly important in postmortem planning. Upon an owner's death, the value of his or her interest is adjusted under §1014, but the basis of the partnership property is unaffected unless a timely election is made under §754. See §12.5. The general rule that contributions of property to an FLP or LLC are not taxable does not apply if the FLP or LLC is an "investment partnership" for federal income tax purposes. Generally, if more than 80 percent of the entity is composed of securities and cash, it will be considered an investment partnership, contributions to which will trigger gain recognition where the contributions of the founding partners result in the diversification of their respective investments. See Donaldson, Income Tax Aspects of Family Limited Partnerships, U. Miami 39th Inst. Est. Plan., Ch. 14 (2005).

Caveat. The tax-free contribution of appreciated property to a FLP or LLC may not be possible if the FLP or LLC is classified as an investment company. Specifically, §721(b) provides that the nonrecognition rule of §721(a) does not apply "to gain realized on a transfer of property to a partnership which would be treated as an investment company (within the meaning of section 351) if the partnership were incorporated." In simplest terms: There is a risk of recognition if the FLP or LLC is more than 80 percent funded with marketable securities.

Happily, partnerships and LLCs are also not subject to the special taxes on personal holding company income, §§541-547, the tax on unreasonable accumulation of earnings, §§531-537, and the taint that attaches to some corporate stock by reason of §305 and 306. Also, appreciated property can be distributed by an FLP or LLC without the entity or distributees incurring any tax liability.

§11.5.1. Management

An FLP is managed by the general partner—limited partners who participate in management may lose their insulation from liability. In contrast, members of an LLC can participate in management without jeopardizing their limited liability. Management may be shared by the members of an LLC—typically in proportion to the extent of their interests. Often, however, the management of an LLC is assigned to one or more managers—often the senior generation members who founded the LLC.

Management responsibilities of the general partner of an FLP or the manager of an LLC should be exercisable only in a fiduciary capacity. Under *United States v. Byrum*, 408 U.S. 125 (1972), there is little risk that any junior interests that are transferred by a managing partner or member will be included in the transferor's estate under §2036(a). LRs 9415007, 9131006 (TAM). However, as explained below, a different result may follow if the manager is given too much discretionary control over economic matters, without accountability.

Beware of Transferor Having Right to Vote Controlled Stock The anti-*Byrum* rule of §2036(b) requires that particular care be taken in transferring stock in a controlled corporation to a partnership so as to avoid giving the donor having the right to vote the stock directly or indirectly. The stock may be included in the donor's estate under § 2036(b) if the donor, as general partner, holds the right to vote the stock. *See* LR 199938005. The Joint Committee Explanation of The Tax Reform Act of 1976 stated that "For purposes of the provision [§ 2036(b)], the capacity in which the decedent could exercise voting rights is immaterial." Committee Explanation at 588. *See* § 2.18.1.

One way of avoiding the problem is to designate another person as general partner with the right to vote the stock. The Senate Committee Report on P.L. 95-600 indicates that the voting rights would not be considered retained by the donor if the donor could not vote the stock. "For example, where a decedent transfers stock in a controlled corporation to his son and does not have the power to vote the stock at any time during the three-year period prior to his death, the rule does not apply even where the decedent owned, or could vote, a majority of the stock." Another way would be to divide the stock of the corporation into voting and nonvoting stock of which the donor would only transfer nonvoting stock to the partnership. Again, as indicated in the Senate Committee Report, "Similarly, where the decedent owned both voting and nonvoting stock and transferred the nonvoting stock to another person, the rule does not apply to the nonvoting stock simply because of the decedent's ownership of the voting stock." The scope and application of § 2036(b) is also discussed in § 2.17.

Transfer Tax Impact. In addition, as indicated in § 2.5.7, for transfer tax purposes limited partnership interests typically qualify for multiple valuation discounts. Of critical importance to some clients, the donor may be a (or the) general partner or manager of the LLC without jeopardizing the favorable transfer tax results. The transfer of limited partnership interests in an ordinary FLP to the donees constitutes completed gifts although the donor holds full powers of management over the partnership including the discretion to control the timing of distributions. As indicated in LR 9415007, the general partner's powers must be exercised in a fiduciary capacity. Also, the powers held by the general partner of an ordinary FLP do not require the transferred interests to be included in the general partner's gross estate under § 2036. LRs 9131006 (TAM); 9415007.

§ 11.5.2. Participation in Profits, Losses

Subject to the limits imposed by § 704, the participation in items of income, loss, credit, and deduction may be allocated among the partners of an FLP, or the members of an LLC, however they agree. These elements should be planned in light of the requirements of Reg. § 1.704-1(e) applicable to family partnerships. Thus, an FLP or LLC may consist of two classes of interests: a preferred ("senior") interest, and an ordinary ("junior") interest. The senior interest is typically entitled to a specified annual payment, the right to participate in income above a certain annual level, and a fixed preference upon liquidation. The junior interest is usually entitled to a participation in income after the senior preference is satisfied and to the remainder of the assets upon liquidation.

Importantly, if the distribution rights of limited and general partnership interests are the same, they will be treated as a single class for purposes of § 2701. § 2701(a)(2)(B), Reg. § 25.2701-1(c)(3). The same rule should apply to interests in an LLC.

§11.5.3. Multiclass Entities; §2701

Under the special valuation rules of Chapter 14, the transfer of interests in a multiclass FLP or LLC will often result in a substantial gift. (Of course, the same is generally true of multiclass corporations.) In particular, under §2701 retained interests will generally be valued at zero for gift tax purposes and under §2704 lapsing voting or liquidation rights may be disregarded. A sale of interests to a trust in exchange for a note is not subject to §2701. In LR 9535026, the IRS ruled that the sale of stock by beneficiaries to a trust they established is a disposition in exchange for note and is not subject to §2701 or 2702 so long as the notes are debt and not equity. This seemingly opens the door to sales of interests in multiclass entities to intentionally defective grantor trusts.

As noted above, §2701 does not apply to gifts of interests that are of the same class as the retained interest. §2701(a)(2). In this connection note that the IRS has ruled that the shares of two classes of stock that were "substantially identical" would be treated as a single class of stock for purposes of §2701. LR 9451051. Accordingly, the special valuation rules of §2701 did not apply to the donor's contribution of capital to the corporation in exchange for the issuance of Class A preferred stock.

Under Reg. §25.2701-1(c)(4), a gift of equity interests to family members is not subject to §2701 to the extent the transfer results in a proportionate reduction of each class of equity held by the transferor and all applicable family members. For this purpose applicable family members are the transferor, the transferor's spouse, any ancestor of the transferor or the transferor's spouse and the spouse of any such ancestor. §2701(e)(2). Accordingly, the transfer by a husband and wife to their son and daughter of proportionate amounts of all classes of equity held by them in a corporation is not subject to §2701. LR 9248026. Section 2701 was also held inapplicable to a reorganization or other capital changes "if each family member holds substantially the same interest after the transaction as the individual held before the transaction." LR 9511028.

A senior family member who creates a multiclass FLP or LLC and transfers the junior interests may be subject to a substantial gift tax. The result may be ameliorated or eliminated by various strategies. For example, a multiclass partnership might initially be created in which future appreciation is largely allocated to the holders of the junior partnership interests. Likewise, an existing partnership that generated substantial earnings might be recapitalized with the senior family members receiving interests that carried fixed rights to periodic payments that met the requirements of qualified payments, the value of which would be taken into account under §2701. An example of the latter approach is described in the next paragraph.

In LR 9808010, the IRS ruled that the transfer of real property to a limited partnership by a couple who had given almost all their limited partnership interests to their children in 1994 constituted completed gifts under §2511. The post-formation transfer of real property to the partnership, the value of which was credited to the partners' capital accounts, involved gifts to the other partners that would be valued under the subtraction method of §2701. The amount of the gifts would be offset, however, by the requirement that the partnership make payments to them of an amount that constituted a guaranteed annuity (*i.e.,* a qualified interest). The IRS refused to rule on whether the terms of the proposed redemption agreement would be exempt from the application of §2703(a). Note also that §2701 does not apply to the pro rata addition of property to the partnership by its members. LR 9427023.

§11.5.4. Family Partnership Rules, §704(e)

The family partnership rules of §704(e) must be borne in mind in structuring an FLP or LLC. The basic rules are relatively simple, but some uncertainties remain regarding their application.

Since 1951, the income tax law has provided for the recognition of family partnerships in which capital is a material income-producing factor. §704(e)(1). Prior to that time the law was quite confused and family partnerships were often disregarded as mere assignments of income. If capital is not a material income-producing factor, the partnership may be disregarded and the income "taxed to the person who earns it through his own labor and skill and the utilization of his own capital." Reg. §1.704-1(e)(1)(i).

EXAMPLE 11-6.

X, who receives substantial fees for lecturing on inner peace and self-fulfillment, formed a partnership with his 2 minor children, A and B. X contributed a nominal amount of capital to the partnership on behalf of A and B. In exchange A, B, and X each received an equal one-third interest in the partnership. The interests of A and B are held by an independent guardian. The partnership assumed the responsibility of booking X's lectures, received the lecture fees, paid X a fixed amount (usually one-half of the total fee), and divided the balance of the income equally between A, B, and X. Under the circumstances capital is not a material income-producing factor for the partnership. Accordingly, the partnership would be disregarded under §704(e)(1) and all of the income would be taxed to X, whose personal services generated the income.

Capital as a Material Income-Producing Factor. Under the Regulations, capital constitutes a material income-producing factor if,

[A] substantial portion of the gross income of the business is attributable to the employment of capital in the business conducted by the partnership. In general, capital is not a material income-producing factor where the income of the business consists principally of fees, commissions, or other compensation for personal services performed by members or employees of the partnership. Reg. §1.704-1(e)(1)(iv).

Of course, even where capital is a material income-producing factor, a family member is not recognized as a partner, "unless such interest is acquired in a bona fide transaction, not a mere sham for tax avoidance or evasion purposes, and the donee or purchaser is the real owner of such interest." Reg. §1.704-1(e)(1)(iii). The reality of a donee's ownership is determined from all of the circumstances, beginning with the execution of legally sufficient deeds or other instruments of gift. However, the actual conduct of the parties is an important factor. Some of the other most important factors are considered in the following subsections. *See also* Reg. § 1.704-1(e)(2).

Trustees and Minors as Partners A trustee who is unrelated to and independent of the grantor is usually recognized as legal owner of the partnership interests that are held in trust. Reg. § 1.704-1(e)(2)(vii). Presumably the IRS or a court would look to the grantor trust rules of § 672 for the purpose of determining who is unrelated and independent. Where the grantor is trustee or the trustee is amenable to the will of the grantor, all of the circumstances will be taken into account in determining whether to recognize the trustee as legal owner of the interest. In such a case the trustee will be recognized as a partner only if the trustee actively represents the interests of the beneficiaries in accordance with the obligations of a fiduciary and does not subordinate their interests to those of the grantor. Overall, it is very desirable to have an independent trustee, such as a bank or trust company, where the trust will hold FLP or LLC interests.

A minor child who is competent to manage his or her own property will be recognized as a partner. Under the regulations, a minor is competent if he or she has "sufficient maturity and experience to be treated by disinterested persons as competent to enter business dealings and otherwise to conduct his [or her] affairs on a basis of equality with adult persons, notwithstanding legal disabilities of the minor under State law." Reg. § 1.704-1(e)(2)(viii). If the minor does not satisfy that test, he or she generally will not be recognized as a partner unless the partnership interest is controlled by another person as fiduciary for the sole benefit of the minor, subject to judicial supervision. An independent guardian would suffice for this purpose. Presumably a custodian under the Uniform Gifts to Minors Act or the Uniform Transfers to Minors Act would also suffice. *Joseph A. Garcia*, 48 T.C.M. 425 (1984). All things considered, a trust is preferable to a guardianship or custodianship.

Allocation of Income The allocation of income made in the partnership agreement generally controls for income tax purposes. However, where a partnership interest is acquired by gift, the allocation is respected only when, (1) the donor partner is allocated reasonable compensation for services he or she renders to the partnership, and (2) the share of the income allocated to the donated capital of the donee is not proportionately greater than the share of the income allocated to the donor's capital. § 704(e)(2). For purposes of this rule, an interest purchased from a family member is treated as having been acquired by gift. § 704(e)(3). An individual's family includes "his spouse, ancestors, and lineal descendants, and any trusts for the primary benefit of such persons." *Id.* Thus, the income allocation cannot initially be structured in a way that unduly favors a partner who is a family member. However, the regulations permit the allocation to take into account the fact that "a general partner, unlike a limited partner risks his credit in the partnership business." Reg. § 1.704-1(e)(3)(ii)(c). In light of the recognition of the differences in their interests, presumably the income share of the donee general partners can be allowed to grow if the partnership prospers without any increase in the share of the senior limited partner. Note also that the income tax rules of § 704(e) do not bar the allocation of future appreciation in value of the partnership property to a donee partner. Such an allocation is, of course, the *raison d'etre* of the partnership freeze.

Retained Control by Donor. The income tax rules allow the donor to retain controls over the business that are "common in ordinary business relationships" provided the donee "is free to liquidate his interest at his discretion without financial detriment." Reg. § 1.704-1(e)(2)(ii)(d). Accordingly, the terms of a buy-sell agreement must avoid terms that would diminish the economic value of a donee's interest. A right of first refusal should not be objectionable. In any case, however, the donee should not be obligated to transfer his or her interest to another party at less than its fair market value. Although a donor is permitted to retain ordinary controls, the donor may not retain undue control over the distribution of income. In addition, the donor may not retain control over assets that are essential to the business. Thus, the donor may not personally retain assets that are required for the conduct of the business and lease them to the partnership. The regulations also point out that consideration will be given to the existence of controls that may be exercised indirectly through a separate business organization, estate, trust, individual, or other partnership. Reg. § 1.704-1(e)(2)(iii). Estate tax problems may arise under §§ 2036(a)(2) and 2038 if the donor retains too many controls over an FLP or LLC. *See* LR 9751003.

B. BUY-SELL AGREEMENTS

§ 11.6.   Overview

This part reviews the basic tax and nontax considerations involved in drafting buy-sell agreements that either obligate the entity to purchase a deceased or retiring owner's stock or partnership interest (an "entity-purchase" agreement) or obligate the other owners to purchase his or her interest (a "cross-purchase" agreement). The pros and cons of the two types of agreements are reviewed in § 11.8. Either form of agreement can serve important nontax needs of the owners of a closely-held business. In addition, a properly drafted agreement can establish the value of a decedent's stock or partnership interest, which may limit the liability for the payment of state and federal death taxes. The worst case occurs if an agreement fixes a relatively low value on a decedent's interest for purposes of the agreement and a much higher value is placed on the interest for federal estate tax purposes.

Note that the IRS may argue that the redemption of the taxpayer's shares should be considered a gift to the other shareholders—whose proportionate ownership interests increase as a result of the redemption. A redemption, of course, results in a gift if the redeeming shareholder accepts less than the fair market value of the redeemed shares. *Estate of Mary D. Maggos,* 79 TCM (CCH) 1861 (2000) (the decedent made a taxable gift when she allowed shares worth $4,900,000 to be redeemed for $3,000,000).

§ 11.6.1. The Continuing Effect of Pre-§ 2703 Rules

Prior to the October 9, 1990 effective date of § 2703, the extent to which a buy-sell agreement would fix the value of an interest in a closely-held business for estate tax purposes was determined under Reg. § 20.2031-2(h):

> Another person may hold an option or a contract to purchase securities owned by a decedent at the time of his death. The effect, if any, that is given to the option or contract price in determining the value of the

securities for estate tax purposes depends upon the circumstances of the particular case. Little weight will be accorded a price contained in an option or contract under which the decedent is free to dispose of the underlying securities at any price he chooses during his lifetime. Such is the effect, for example, of an agreement on the part of a shareholder to purchase whatever shares of stock the decedent may own at the time of his death. Even if the decedent is not free to dispose of the underlying securities at other than the option or contract price, such price will be disregarded in determining the value of the securities unless it is determined under the circumstances of the particular case that the agreement represents a bona fide business arrangement and not a device to pass the decedent's shares to the natural objects of his bounty for less than an adequate and full consideration in money or money's worth.

Broken down into its constituent elements, the Regulation provides that the value of a decedent's interest established by an option or agreement will be recognized if the option or agreement:

1. Fixed the price of the shares directly or by way of a formula;
2. Restricted the decedent's power to dispose of the interest during his or her lifetime;
3. Obligated the decedent's successors to sell the shares for that price following his or her death;
4. Was a bona fide business arrangement; and
5. Was not merely a device for passing the interest to the natural objects of the decedent's bounty for less than an adequate and full consideration.

Whether the first three requirements are satisfied can be determined from the face of an option or agreement. In contrast, the latter two elements require the consideration of other factors.

Regulation § 20. 2031-2(h) builds on a prior published ruling that an agreement was effective to fix the value of the shares if, (1) it was a bona fide business arrangement, and (2) either required the corporation or the other shareholders to purchase the decedent's shares, or gave the corporation or the other shareholders the option to purchase the shares. Rev. Rul. 157, 1953-2 C.B. 255.

No doubt Reg. § 20.2031-2(h) will continue to apply to agreements entered into prior to October 9, 1990 and to agreements that are not subject to § 2703. Presumably it will also apply to restrictions subject to § 2703 except to the extent it was affected by § 2703. Thus, the regulation and related authorities provide valuable guidance regarding the effect that will be given to future agreements. The legislative history indicates that § 2703 was otherwise not intended to change the requirements for giving recognition to a buy-sell agreement. *See* S. Rep. No. 3209, 101st Cong., 2d Sess. (1990), *reprinted in* 136 Cong. Rec. S15629, S15683 (1990). For example, it leaves intact present rules requiring that an agreement have lifetime restrictions in order to be binding on death. *E.g.,* LR 8634004 (agreement which did not specify price at which decedent would be allowed to sell stock to new employees is not binding for federal estate tax purposes). On the positive side, the IRS and courts should continue to recognize that various purposes, including continued family control of a corporation, are bona fide business purposes for having a buy-sell agreement.

The IRS will not recognize a price fixed by an agreement that does not have a bona fide business purpose. LR 8710004 (TAM) (redemption agreements between uncle and two nephews to whom he had given shares of stock in two corporations were not devices for transferring interests in the corporations to his nephews for less than adequate and full consideration and were not bona fide business arrangements). *See also St. Louis County Bank v. United States,* 674 F.2d 1207 (8th Cir.) (agreement must be bona fide business arrangement and not a device for transferring value to family members for less than full consideration).

In LR 9419001 (TAM), the IRS ruled that the stated liquidation value of the decedent's preferred stock in a closely held company did not fix the maximum value of the shares for federal estate tax purposes. The decedent owned 99.86 percent of the voting shares, the others of which were 25 shares of voting common stock that were owned by her children. Valuing the stock at its liquidation value was not required as it appeared that the business would be continued and the decedent and her successors, with absolute voting control, could have prevented liquidation.

§ 11.6.2. Section 2703

Options, agreements, and other restrictions affecting the valuation or disposition of property that are entered into or substantially modified after October 8, 1990 are subject to the provisions of § 2703. Under § 2703 options, agreements to acquire property or ones restricting the right to sell or use property (the "provision") will be recognized for estate, gift, and generation-skipping transfer tax purposes only if they satisfy the tripartite test of § 2703(b):

1. It is a bona fide business arrangement;
2. It is not a device to transfer property to members of the decedent's family for less than full and adequate consideration; and
3. Its terms are comparable to similar arrangements entered into by persons in an arms' length transaction.

The first two requirements are essentially restatements of the substantive requirements of Reg. § 20.2031-2(h). They should be construed and applied in light of the regulation and related authorities. They adopt the reasoning of *St. Louis County Bank, supra,* which requires that an agreement be a bona fide business arrangement and not be a device to transfer wealth.

The third requirement of § 2703 is a new one. The rigor of the requirement is relaxed to some extent by the report of the Conference Committee on the 1990 Act, which states that,

> The conferees do not intend the provision governing buy-sell agreements to disregard such an agreement merely because its terms differ from those used by another similarly situated company. The conferees recognize that general business practice may recognize more than one valuation methodology, even within the same industry. In such situations, one of several generally accepted methodologies may satisfy the standard contained in the conference agreement. H. Conf. Rep. No. 101-964, 101 Cong.2d Sess. 1137 (1990).

Reflecting that intention, the regulations provide that "A right or restriction is treated as comparable to similar arrangements entered into by persons in an arms' length transaction if the right or restriction is one that *could have been obtained in a fair bargain among unrelated parties in the same business dealing with each other at arm's length*." Reg. § 25.2703-1(b)(4)(i) (emphasis added). In making the latter determination, consideration will be given to factors including "the expected term of the agreement, the current fair market value of the property, anticipated changes in value during the term of the arrangement, and the adequacy of any consideration given in exchange for the rights granted." *Id*.

In LR 9550002, the IRS ruled that the closely held stock owned by the decedent and held in a QTIP trust of which she was a beneficiary must be valued without regard to the right of a beneficiary to "buy back the shares on a contract over five years with interest at the prime rate" because the right is disregarded under § 2703— it is not a bona fide business arrangement, may be a device to transfer property to family members at a reduced value, and is not comparable to similar arrangements entered into by persons in arms' length transactions.

§ 11.6.3. Substantial Modifications

Changes in the terms of rights or restrictions established under options, articles, buy-sell agreements, and other arrangements entered into prior to October 9, 1990, should be made in light of the provisions of § 2703. A substantial modification of a preexisting right or restriction will subject it to the terms of § 2703. Under the regulations, a right or restriction is substantially modified if there is a discretionary modification of the right or restriction other than a *de minimis* one. Reg. § 25.2703-1(c)(1). A mandatory change in value is not treated as a subsequent modification. Reg. § 25.2703-1(c)(2)(i).

The addition of any family member as a party to a right or restriction is considered a substantial modification unless the addition is mandatory or the added family member is assigned to a generation no lower than the lowest generation of the persons who are already parties to the right or restriction. Reg. § 25.2703-1(c)(1). Under the regulation, a gift of an interest to a child (a discretionary transfer) as a result of which the child must become a party to a buy-sell agreement may be a substantial modification—at least to the extent of the interests affected by the child's joinder. On the other hand, the gift of an interest to the donor's spouse—a person in the same generational level—is not "a substantial modification of the right or restriction. Reg. § 25.2703-1(d), Example 2.

Under the foregoing rules, a transfer of shares to children and the release of the transferred shares from the restrictions of a shareholders' agreement is a substantial modification that causes the agreement to lose its grandfathered status. LR 9620017. Accordingly, the transferred shares would be valued for gift tax purposes without regard to the terms of the agreement. Consistently, in LR 9324018, the IRS ruled that a gift of common stock to children and addition of them as parties to pre-existing buy-sell agreement would be a substantial modification of the agreement, as a result of which the agreement would be subject to § 2703.

§11.6.4. Insubstantial Modifications

Under Reg. §25.2703-1(c)(2), the following are not substantial modifications:

    (i) A modification required by the terms of a right or restriction;

    (ii) A discretionary modification of an agreement conferring a right or restriction if the modification does not change the right or restriction;

    (iii) A modification of a capitalization rate used with respect to a right or restriction if the rate is modified in a manner that bears a fixed relationship to a specified market interest rate; and

    (iv) A modification that results in an option price that more closely approximates fair market value.

Applying these criteria, a change in the interest rate applicable to the deferred payment of the cost of acquiring a deceased partner's interest in a general partnership from five percent to the greater of five percent or the federal long term rate applicable under §1274, compounded annually, was not substantial. LR 200015012. Rather, the change will result in a price that more closely approximated fair market value.

The redemption of the shares of a shareholder that does not change the terms of the agreement applicable to other shareholders is not a substantial modification. *E.g.,* LR 200010015. The same ruling concluded that the adoption of an option and stock appreciation plan for the benefit of key employees, none of whom are parties to the agreement, would not constitute a substantial modification. Likewise, the issuance of shares to employees, not related to the parties to the agreement, in recognition of their services and the repurchase of those shares upon termination of employment is not a substantial modification. LR 9620017.

A substitution of investors for previous debt holders as parties to a shareholders agreement does not involve a material modification. LR 9248026. Similarly, the addition of family member-donees of corporate stock (the children of the donors) as parties to the shareholders agreement does not constitute a material modification if their addition is mandatory under the terms of the agreement and they are not assigned to a generation lower than the lower generation occupied by individuals who were already parties to the agreement as determined under §2651. Reg. §25.2703-1(c)(1), (2); LR 9248026.

The reorganization of a company into a holding company and the execution of a shareholders' agreement that is virtually identical to the pre-existing one results in only minor changes that do not amount to a substantial modification of the agreement. LR 9711017.

The amendment of a shareholders' agreement to provide for the redemption, on the death of a parent-shareholder, of the stock owned by a child of the decedent will not cause the shares to be included in the deceased parent's estate under §2035(d)(2). LR 9509027. *See* §2.43.1.

§11.6.5. Scope and Effect of §2704

The conference agreement provides that the lapse of a voting or liquidation right in a family-controlled corporation or partnership results in a transfer by gift or an inclusion in the gross estate. The amount of the transfer is the value of all interests in the entity held by the transferor immediately before the lapse (assuming the right was nonlapsing) over the value of the interests immediately after the lapse. The conference agreement grants the Secretary of the Treasury regulatory authority to apply these rules to rights similar to voting and liquidation rights. H.R. Conf. Rep. 101-964, 101st Cong., 2d Sess. 1137 (1990).

Section 2704 prescribes two independent rules. First, under §2704(a) the lapse of voting or liquidation rights in a family-controlled business is treated as a transfer of value for gift and estate tax purposes. *See* Reg. §25.2704-1. Thus, any reduction in value that results from the lapse of voting or liquidation rights in a family-controlled business will be subject to the gift or estate tax. The use of voting or liquidation rights that lapse upon the death of the owner of an interest in a business is sometimes appropriate for nontax reasons. Section 2704 is designed to prevent such a lapse from depressing the value of the owner's interest for gift or estate tax purposes. *See* Reg. §25.2701-1(d).

A voting right or a liquidation right may be conferred by, or lapse by reason of, state law, a corporate charter or bylaws, an agreement, or any other means. Reg. §25.2704-1(a)(4). In general, "a transfer of an interest that results in the lapse of a liquidation right is not subject to this section if the rights with respect to the transferred interest are not restricted or eliminated." Reg. §25.2704-1(c).

Second, under §2704(b), the value of an interest in a family-controlled business that is transferred to a member of the transferor's family is determined without regard to certain restrictions on liquidation ("applicable restrictions"). The rule of §2704(b) applies to restrictions that prevent the transferee from liquidating business. §2704(b)(2). In effect, the transferred interest is to be valued as if the business did not impose any restrictions on the transferee's right to liquidate. Both the statute and the regulations indicate that the rules do not apply to a commercially reasonable restriction on liquidation imposed by an unrelated person providing financing to the entity for trade or business operations. §2704(b)(3); Reg. §25.2704-2(b). They also do not apply to any restriction imposed by state or federal law. *Id.* Also, note that according to the Conference Committee Report, "These rules do not affect minority discounts or other discounts available under present law." H.R. Conf. Rep. 91-964, 101st Cong., 2d Sess. 1137 (1990). Thus, lack of marketability and minority discounts will continue to be available in valuing interests in closely-held businesses.

According to the Conference Committee Report, §2704 was adopted in order to overturn *Estate of Daniel J. Harrison,* 52 T.C.M. 1306 (1987), which permitted the lapse of a liquidation right at the death of the decedent to diminish substantially the value of the interest included in the decedent's estate. *Id.* The lapse of the decedent's liquidation right reduced the value of his interest from almost $60 million to $33 million—costing the federal fisc about $16 million.

Under §2704, limitations on the ability to liquidate that are more restrictive than generally applicable state law are disregarded in valuing the interests. If the state law requires that limited partnerships be created for a specified minimum number of years, presumably the effect of a partner not being able to withdraw during that period would be recognized and further depress the value of a partner's interest.

In LR 9804001 (TAM), the IRS ruled that a decedent general partner's voting and liquidation rights, which lapsed on his death, were subject to §2704. The decedent had a right as a general partner in the family limited partnership to withdraw funds from the partnership. No limited partner held such a right. Under state law the interest of a withdrawing partner is automatically redeemed for its fair market value. The TAM holds that the decedent's estate must include, under §2704, the difference between the value of the decedent's interests immediately prior to death (*i.e.*, before the voting and liquidation rights lapsed) and the value of the interests immediately after his death.

The operation of §2704 is illustrated by Examples 11-7, 11-8, and 11-9, which are adapted from the Conference Committee Report.

EXAMPLE 11-7.

X and her child, *C*, control a corporation. The voting rights associated with *X*'s stock will terminate on her death. Under §2704(a), the federal estate tax value of *X*'s stock is determined without regard to the lapse of her voting right. *See* Reg. §25.2704-1(a).

EXAMPLE 11-8.

X owns a general interest in a partnership and her daughter, *D*, owns a limited interest. Under the terms of the partnership agreement the general partner has the right to liquidate the partnership, which expires after 10 years. When the liquidation right of the general partnership interest lapses, *X* is treated as having made a gift to *D*. The gift is equal to the excess of (1) the value of the general partnership interest before the lapse over (2) the value of the general partnership interest after the lapse.

EXAMPLE 11-9.

X and her daughter, *D*, are the only partners of a general partnership. The partnership agreement provides that the partnership cannot be terminated by one partner alone. *X* left her partnership interest to her son, *S. D* and *S* acting together could remove the restriction on termination of the partnership. The federal estate tax value of *X*'s partnership interest is determined without regard to the restriction on termination. However, the interest might qualify for a fractional interest discount.

Under the regulations, the transfer of an interest does not result in the restriction or elimination of a right if the voting right of the transferred interest itself is not restricted or eliminated. Specifically, Reg. §25.2704-1(c) provides that, "Except as otherwise provided, a transfer of an interest that results in the lapse of a liquidation right is not subject to this section if the rights with respect to the transferred interest are not restricted or eliminated." The point is made clear in Example 7, Reg. § 25.2704-1(f):

> D owns all the stock of Corp. X, consisting of 100 shares of non-voting preferred stock and 100 shares of voting common stock. Under the by-laws, Corp. X can only be liquidated with the consent of at least 80 percent of the voting shares. D transfers 30 shares of common stock to D's child. The transfer is not a lapse of a liquidation right with respect to the common stock because the voting rights that enabled D to liquidate prior to the transfer are not restricted or eliminated . . . .

Example 4 of the regulation deals with the same point and is, perhaps, even clearer.

Applicable Restrictions. Under § 2704(b), restrictions on liquidation are taken into account in valuing a transferred interest unless the interest is an "applicable restriction." In turn, Reg. § 25.2704-2(b) provides that, "An applicable restriction is a limitation on the ability to liquidate the entity (in whole or in part) that is more restrictive than the limitations that would apply under the state law generally applicable to the entity in the absence of the restriction." Accordingly, § 2704(b) does not prohibit consideration of the effect of provisions that track the governing state law.

§ 11.7. NONTAX CONSIDERATIONS

The interests of all owners are protected by an agreement that provides a fair method of valuing the interests of a deceased, disabled, or terminated party. Without such an agreement a disabled or terminated owner, or the family of a deceased minority owner, may lack the bargaining power necessary to negotiate a satisfactory agreement with the business or the remaining owners for the disposition of the decedent's interest. Of course, an agreement also provides important protection for the remaining owners. Thus, an agreement can prevent the transfer of interests to unwanted or hostile outsiders.

Restrictions on transfers are particularly important in the case of an S corporation in order to prevent the corporation from exceeding the permissible number of shareholders (100), and from adding ineligible shareholders such as corporations, nonresident aliens, or unqualified trusts. In addition, an agreement might also be used to obligate the shareholders to continue the S election. The IRS long ago recognized that entry into a restrictive agreement does not constitute a second class of stock that would terminate an S election. Rev. Rul. 73-611, 1973-2 C.B. 312. Finally, under Reg. § 1.1361-1(*l*)(2)(iii), a bona fide buy-sell agreement is generally disregarded in determining whether there is more than one class of stock.

The preparation of an agreement is also beneficial because it requires the parties to consider the long-term plans for the business and the need to generate funds with which to purchase the interest of a deceased shareholder. As indicated below, funds are typically provided either by insurance on the lives of owners or by earnings of the business that are accumulated in another form. Of course, the liquidity crunch is eased somewhat if the agreement permits an installment purchase of a deceased owner's interest.

§11.8. ENTITY PURCHASE OR CROSS-PURCHASE?

The type of agreement to be used in any given case depends upon the preference of the parties and a number of tax and nontax factors. Particular care must be exercised in choosing the type of agreement where the ownership and control of the entity is balanced between two or more groups. In such a case a redemption of a decedent's interest might disrupt the balance more than would a pro rata purchase of the decedent's shares by the remaining stockholders. Of course, a preexisting balance may also be upset if the surviving shareholders purchase pro rata interests in the decedent's shares. Note that the IRS would probably not accept a valuation made under an agreement that provided for the sale of shares only to a decedent's nuclear family to the exclusion of other shareholders. Such an agreement would be vulnerable to attack as an effort to shift the stock to the natural objects of the decedent's bounty at a bargain price, in violation of §2703(b). From the tax viewpoint, perhaps the greatest flexibility is provided if the entity and the other owners successively have the right to purchase the interest of a deceased owner.

A buy-sell agreement is also useful to close a partnership's tax year. In the absence of an agreement the tax year does not terminate on the death of a partner. §706(c)(1). Closing the tax year at the time of a partner's death, which ends the decedent's final income tax year, can be helpful for income tax purposes. The tax year terminates as to a deceased partner "when such partner's interest (held by his estate or other successor) is liquidated or sold or exchanged . . . ." Reg. §1.706-1(c)(2).

§11.8.1. Entity Purchase

Some planners prefer an entity-purchase agreement because a purchase by the business (redemption of the stock or liquidation of a partner's interest) is simpler and more easily accomplished than the purchase of the decedent's interest by a number of other owners under a cross-purchase agreement. Also, purchase of insurance or other provision for funding by an entity (the business) may be surer and more easily arranged and maintained than purchases by several owners. However, for C corporations life insurance has significant alternative minimum tax (AMT) implications. First, the annual internal build-up in value of life insurance is taken into account in determining adjusted current earnings. §56(g)(4)(B)(ii). Second, the excess of death benefits over the basis in the policy is also included in adjusted current earnings. Reg. §1.56(g)-1(c)(5)(v). The AMT does not apply to S corporations.

From the surviving shareholder's perspective, a redemption of the stock of a deceased shareholder may be less attractive. A redemption does not increase the bases of the interests of the surviving owners. The increase in basis resulting from a cross purchase can be an important factor if the surviving owners intend to sell their interests. In addition, insurance proceeds paid to a business may be depleted by claims of creditors and other business obligations. On the other hand, it may be more economical for a business to purchase a single policy of insurance on the life of each owner than it would be for each owner to purchase a pro rata amount of insurance on the life of each other owner. Recall in this connection that neither the corporation nor the shareholders is able to deduct the premiums on the insurance for income tax purposes. *See* § 6.57.

Insurance proceeds received by the business are not generally includible in the estate of the insured shareholder or partner. However, the proceeds may be includible in unusual circumstances. For example, LR 8943082 held that insurance proceeds in excess of the amount required to purchase the decedent's stock were includible because they were payable to a beneficiary designated by the insured, to his spouse, or to his estate. In LR 8943082, the IRS reasoned that the "excess" proceeds were includible under § 2038 because the decedent, by executing the buy-sell agreement, had made a transfer of an interest in the insurance but retained the right to control the disposition of the "excess" proceeds. For income tax purposes, LR 8943082 held that the excess proceeds were taxable as an employee benefit under § 101(b) except to the extent of $5,000 (the exclusion from income of $5,000 was subsequently repealed). Note that life insurance proceeds payable to a decedent's estate pursuant to a buy-sell agreement are income in respect of a decedent to the extent they represent compensation for "cases or work in progress." *Estate of Cartwright v. Commissioner*, 183 F.3d 1034 (9th Cir. 1999).

Unless life insurance is used as a funding mechanism, there is often a risk that when an owner dies the business will lack sufficient surplus or other funds that the local corporate law allows to be used to redeem stock. However, if financing is required, it may be less expensive for the business, rather than the surviving shareholders, to obtain the financing necessary to purchase a decedent's interest.

§ 11.8.2. Tax Aspects of Entity Purchases

Redemptions by C Corporations. A redemption by a C corporation is taxed as a dividend to the distributee except to the extent the redemption is treated as a sale or exchange under § 303, or is within one of the exceptions of § 302(b). *See* § 11.13-11.22. If the redemption is treated as a sale or exchange, the distributee usually recognizes little gain, if any, because the decedent's death caused the basis of the shares to be adjusted under § 1014 (*i.e.*, the basis of the shares is changed to their federal estate tax value in the decedent's estate). Of course, in any case a distribution is not a dividend if the corporation has no earnings and profits. § 316(a). However, if appreciated property is distributed, the corporation will recognize gain under § 311(b), which will increase its earnings and profits. A distribution that is treated as a dividend reduces the corporation's earnings and profits. § 312(a). On the other hand, a redemption treated as an exchange reduces earnings and profits only to the extent of a ratable share of the corporation's earnings and profits. § 312(n)(7).

EXAMPLE 11-10.

When *X* died in 2006 she owned 3,000 shares of *X* Corp. common stock that were worth $3,000,000 for federal estate tax purposes. *X* Corp. is a C corporation with substantial accumulated earnings and profits. Her shares of *X* Corp. qualified for redemption under § 303 to the extent of $500,000 (the sum of death taxes imposed by reason of her death and funeral and administration expenses for which deductions were allowable under §2053). X Corp. redeemed 500 shares of X Corp. stock from X's estate in exchange for a payment of $1,000 each, a total of $500,000. Under §303 the payment by X Corp. is treated as a distribution in exchange for the stock and not as a dividend. Accordingly, X's estate received no income and realized no capital gain as a result of the redemption. A redemption of the remainder of X's shares would be treated as a distribution in the nature of a dividend unless it qualified for one of the exceptions of §302. In some cases the distribution might be within the exception of §302(b)(3) as a complete termination of the shareholder's interest in X Corp.

Redemptions by S Corporations. In determining the income tax consequences that result from redeeming a deceased shareholder's stock in an S corporation, the redemption is first classified under the C corporation rules as either a sale or exchange (under §302 or §303) or a distribution in the nature of a dividend. If the redemption is treated as a sale or exchange, the gain or loss of the redeeming shareholder is determined in the same way as in the case of a redemption by a C corporation: The gain or loss is determined according to the difference between the amount of the redemption proceeds and the redeeming shareholder's basis in the redeemed stock. Although such a redemption does not require the distributee to report any dividend income, it results in a proportionate reduction in the S corporation's accumulated adjustment account, §1368(e)(1)(B), and earnings and profits, if any, §1371(c)(2). If the corporation has earnings and profits, such a redemption benefits the remaining shareholders by reducing the corporation's earnings and profits, which will reduce the amount ultimately taxable to them.

The tax consequences of a redemption by an S corporation that does not qualify as a sale or exchange are determined under §1368. Under §1368(b), if the corporation has no earnings and profits the distribution is not included in the distributee's gross income to the extent of the distributee's adjusted basis in the stock (*i.e.*, basis is recovered first, tax-free). In this connection bear in mind that the basis in the stock will have been stepped up (or down) to its federal estate tax value by reason of the decedent's death. Any excess is treated as gain from the sale or exchange of property. If the corporation has accumulated earnings and profits, the redemption distribution is treated as a tax-free return of basis to the extent of the corporation's accumulated adjustments account, then as a dividend to the extent of the accumulated earnings and profits of the corporation, and finally, as a sale or exchange as to the remainder. §1368(c).

A redemption distribution made by an S corporation does not give rise to any gain unless appreciated property is distributed. The distribution of appreciated property causes the corporation to realize gain under §311(b). Under the conduit rules applicable to S corporations, the gain flows through to *all* shareholders, including the redeeming shareholder. However, the flow through of the gain is of limited significance to the redeeming shareholder, whose basis was stepped up by, (1) the federal estate tax value in the decedent's estate, and (2) the portion of the gain that flowed through as a result of the distribution of appreciated property. In effect, the gain that flows through to the redeeming shareholder is offset by the loss which results from the receipt of a redemption distribution worth less than the redeeming shareholder's basis.

EXAMPLE 11-11.

T owned half of the shares of S Corp. They had an estate tax value of $500,000. In redemption of T's stock S Corp. distributed an asset which had a basis of $100,000 and a fair market value of $500,000. The distribution resulted in a gain of $400,000 to S Corp. Half of that gain ($200,000) flowed through to each of the shareholders. The unredeemed shareholder has a gain of $200,000. The flow through of the gain increased the basis of T's estate in the stock to $700,000. The distribution of property worth $500,000 to T's estate in redemption of the stock resulted in a loss of $200,000 ($700,000—$500,000). The loss offset the gain of an equal amount that flowed through to the estate as a result of the distribution.

Under § 1377(a)(2), if the interest of a shareholder is terminated during the taxable year, the remaining shareholders may elect to end the taxable year of the terminating shareholder on the date of the termination of his interest.

Partnership Payments. Payments in liquidation of a retiring or deceased partner's interest (or interest in an LLC) are treated as distributions that are categorized for income tax purposes according to § 736. Such payments are generally nontaxable to the extent of the partner (or member's) basis and the balance is capital gain. As explained in W. McKee, W. Nelson & R. Whitmire, Federal Taxation of Partnerships and Partners § 22.01[4][b] (3d ed. 1997), "All payments that are not § 736(b) payments are § 736(a) payments." Under § 736(b), distributions made in exchange for the retired or deceased partner's interest in partnership property, other than unrealized receivables and goodwill, result in capital gain or loss. *See* Reg. § 1.736-1(b). A reasonable payment made with respect to a partner's share of goodwill is within the scope of § 736(b) to the extent provided in an agreement. Reg. § 1.736-1(b)(3).

In contrast, distributions of partnership income or guaranteed payments are ordinary income as provided in § 736(a). *See* Reg. § 1.736-1(a)(4). The latter types of payments either reduce the taxable income attributable to the remaining partners or are deductible by the partnership under § 162(a). *Id.* The remaining partners generally benefit to the extent distributions are subject to § 736(a).

§ 11.8.3. Cross-Purchase

If a decedent's interest in a corporation, FLP, or LLC is sold to the remaining owners, the transaction is treated as a sale or exchange. A sale may result in gain or loss to the estate based upon the difference between the selling price and the estate's basis in the stock or interest. However, little, if any, gain or loss usually results from such a sale if the price fixed in the buy-sell agreement is effective determine the value (and basis) of the interest in the decedent's estate and for purposes of the sale. The gain, if any, on the sale of a decedent's interest is ordinarily capital gain. However, in the case of a partnership, any gain attributable to unrealized receivables and inventory of a partnership is not classified as capital gain. § § 741, 751(a). The remaining partners usually benefit if a substantial portion of the sale price is allocated to unrealized receivables and inventory, which reduces their future ordinary income.

The cost of a partnership interest purchased from a decedent's estate is its purchase price. Reg. § 1.742-1. The basis of an interest acquired gratuitously from a decedent's estate is its fair market value on the federal estate tax valuation date. The cross-purchase of a decedent's interest in a corporation or partnership is generally attractive because it increases the overall bases of the purchasers. In the case of an S corporation the increased bases will shelter more distributions from taxation under § 1368, decrease the amount of gain that would be realized on a sale of the stock, and enhance the shareholder's ability to deduct his or her share of the S corporation's losses under § 1366. In contrast, an entity purchase (redemption) does not increase the bases of the surviving shareholders.

In the case of a C corporation the cost of cross-owned insurance may be lower if the funds necessary to support the agreement are made available to the shareholders as salaries, which are deductible by the corporation. Salaries, which are only subject to taxation at the shareholder level, are preferable to dividends, which are diluted by income taxes at the corporate and shareholder levels. In some cases life insurance that is provided to shareholder-employees as additional compensation under a split-dollar agreement produces the same overall result as a salary increase. *See* § 6.72 for a discussion of split-dollar life insurance arrangements.

§ 11.8.4. Shifting from an Entity to a Cross-Purchase Agreement

Motivated in part by changes in the tax rules, including the inclusion of insurance proceeds in the adjusted current earnings of a C corporation for AMT purposes, some corporations shifted from an entity to a cross-purchase form of agreement. The potential application of the transfer for value rule to the shift, which would cause the insurance proceeds to be included in the income of the recipient(s), § 101(a)(2), is a serious concern if the corporation assigns existing policies to the shareholders. *Monroe v. Patterson*, 197 F. Supp. 146 (N.D.Ala. 1961). The transfer for value rule is discussed in detail at § 6.54. Note, however, that the transfer for value rule does not apply to transfers that are made to the insured, to a partner of the insured, to a partnership in which the insured is a partner, or to a corporation in which the insured is a shareholder or officer. § 101(a)(2)(B). Thus, the transfer for value rule does not apply to policies that are distributed by a corporation to its shareholders who are partners in a bona fide partnership. *E.g.*, LRs 9727024, 9045004, 9012063. The distribution of an existing policy to the insured shareholder is exempt from the transfer for value rule. While LR 8906034 held that the transfer for value rule would not apply if the policy were subsequently transferred by gift to another shareholder, § 101(a)(2)(A), it noted that the outcome depended upon the transfer being treated as a gift, which was a question of fact on which the ruling expressed no opinion. Letter Ruling 8906034 offers little comfort because determination that the insured's subsequent transfer of the policy was the outcome hinges on a factual determination that the IRS would probably contest. Under the approach taken in *Monroe v. Patterson*, a court might conclude that the subsequent transfer was a transfer for value and not a gift which involved a carryover of the donor's basis.

§11.8.5. Redemption Required by Agreement or Divorce Decree

An entity redemption may, in some cases, be treated as a cross purchase. *Arnes v. United States*, 981 F.2d 456 (9th Cir. 1992). In *Arnes* the redemption of one spouse's community property interest in the stock of a closely held corporation pursuant to a decree of divorce was treated as a transfer between the spouses. In *Arnes* a panel of the Ninth Circuit held that §1041 applied to the redemption as a result of which the redeeming shareholder recognized no gain: "We hold that Joann's transfer to Moriah [the corporation] did relieve John of an obligation, and therefore constituted a benefit to John. Joann's transfer of stock should be treated as a constructive transfer to John, who then transferred the stock to Moriah." The Ninth Circuit decision in *Arnes* has been followed in some other cases. *E.g., Craven v. United States*, 70 F. Supp.2d 1323 (N.D.Ga. 1999); *Carol M. Read*, 114 T.C. No. 2 (2000).

The court's broad reading of §1041 is consistent with Temp. Reg. §1.1041-1T(c), Q & A 9:

> There are three situations in which a transfer of property to a third party on behalf of a spouse (or former spouse) will qualify under section 1041, provided all other requirements of the section are satisfied. The first situation is where the transfer to the third party is required by a divorce or separation agreement. The second situation is where the transfer to the third party is pursuant to the written request of the other spouse (or former spouse). The third situation is where the transferor receives from the other spouse (or former spouse) a written consent or ratification of the transfer to the third party . . . .In the three situations described above, the transfer of property will be treated as made directly to the nontransferring spouse (or former spouse) and the nontransferring spouse will be treated as immediately transferring the property to the third party. The deemed transfer from the nontransferring souse (or former spouse) to the third party is not a transaction that qualifies for nonrecognition of gain under section 1041.

Following the *Arnes* saga, in *John A. Arnes*, 102 T.C. 522 (1994) ("Arnes II"), the husband escaped taxation on the redemption of the stock. According to the Tax Court, the husband did not receive a constructive dividend when the stock was redeemed because he was not primarily and unconditionally obligated to purchase the stock received (and submitted for redemption) by his former wife. According to the Tax Court, a constructive dividend occurs only "where the obligation of the remaining shareholder is both primary and unconditional." 102 T.C. at 527. The Tax Court also distinguished and refused to follow *Arnes* in *Gloria T. Blatt*, 102 T.C. 77 (1994), in which capital gains taxes were imposed on the redemption of stock by transferee wife. In LR 9427009 (involving community property), the IRS ruled that no constructive dividend results where the remaining shareholder was not obligated to buy or facilitate the redemption of the other former spouse's stock.

In *Mary Ann Hayes*, 101 T.C. 593 (1993), the Tax Court held that the former husband did receive a constructive dividend when the corporation redeemed stock that had been owned by the former wife—which discharged the former husband's primary and unconditional obligation to purchase the stock. That element was not present in the *Arnes* or *Blatt* cases.

Treasury issued regulations to clarify the income taxation of redemptions made pursuant to divorce. Under Reg. §1.1041-2, if the redemption of shares owned by a spouse pursuant to a divorce is treated as a constructive distribution to the other spouse under corporate tax principles, then the transaction will be treated as if it occurred in two steps. First, the redeemed spouse transferred his or her shares to the other spouse (a transfer which qualifies the redeemed spouse for nonrecognition under §1041). Second, the other spouse has the shares redeemed by the corporation for the cash used to pay the redeemed spouse (a dividend includible in the other spouse's gross income, assuming sufficient earnings and profits). If, on the other hand, the redemption is not a constructive distribution to the other spouse, then § 1041 does not apply to the redemption and the redeemed spouse will be taxed on any resulting gain.

A stock redemption is treated as a constructive distribution to the other spouse where the other spouse has the primary and unconditional obligation to buy the redeemed spouse's shares. So if the divorce agreement imposes an obligation on the other spouse to purchase the redeemed spouse's shares, the corporation's satisfaction of the other spouse's obligation via the redemption is a constructive distribution to him or her. If the divorce agreement states only that the redeemed spouse shall sell his or her shares to the corporation, then the redemption is not a constructive distribution to the other spouse because he or she is not primarily and unconditionally obligated to purchase the shares. The regulations, however, specifically permit the spouses to agree to treat a corporate redemption as though there had been a transfer first to the other spouse followed by a corporate redemption. The regulations also permit the spouses to agree in writing that the redemption will be taxable to the redeemed spouse notwithstanding that the redemption might otherwise result in a constructive distribution to the other spouse. Treasury acquiesced to this request. In other words, the parties can determine who should bear the tax bite and structure the divorce agreement accordingly. This offers tremendous flexibility in planning the income tax consequences of stock redemptions in the divorce context.

§11.9. Valuation

For tax and nontax reasons careful consideration must be given to the selection of a method for fixing the value of the shares that are subject to the agreement. Of course, under §2703 the agreement cannot be a device for transferring the property to the natural objects of a stockholder's bounty (*i.e.*, the shareholder's intestate successors under the local law) for less than full and adequate consideration. Fixing the purchase price at some current dollar value of the shares without provision for future adjustment is usually inappropriate because changes in value will inevitably take place before a sale occurs. When the need to purchase the shares arises, the price set forth in the agreement may be either too high or too low. Thus, an agreement that establishes a current price should provide for periodic adjustments of the price and include a backup method of valuation should the parties fail to agree upon an adjustment in the future.

An agreement may provide for the value of the shares to be fixed by reference to a single factor, such as their book value or the capitalized earnings of the corporation. However, the use of a single factor is also inappropriate because it can distort the value of the shares. For example, in *St. Louis County Bank v. United States,* 674 F.2d 1207 (8th Cir. 1982), a formula based solely on a multiple of net earnings was fair at the time the agreement was entered into. However, the moving and transfer business was sold and the proceeds invested in rental real estate. Application of the formula to the new business produced a value of $0 for the decedent's interest, although it had a $200,000 book value.

Some parties are content to leave the valuation to one or more appraisers named in the agreement, or later to be designated by the parties. In any case, the agreement can provide for arbitration if a dispute arises. Often the best choice is to provide for valuation of the shares under a multifactor formula that takes into account factors such as the corporation's book value, its average earnings for the most recent three- to five-year period, and the price-earnings ratio of publicly traded corporations in the same line of business.

A requirement that the corporation or other shareholders purchase all of the shares of a deceased shareholder shortly after death should be used with caution. Such a provision is particularly dangerous because the sale or other disposition of all of a decedent's shares will prevent the decedent's estate from deferring the time for payment of any portion of the estate tax under § 6166. It will also accelerate the time for payment of any estate tax that had been deferred under § 6166. *See* Part D, *infra.* Because of that problem, it may be desirable to limit the number of shares that must be sold at the outset. The limit might be based upon the maximum number of shares that could be disposed of without triggering an acceleration under § 6166, or exceeding the amount redeemable under § 303.

Where appropriate, an agreement might give the corporation or the other share-holders an option to purchase the remainder of the shares. A contract for the sale of the shares might be drawn in a way that attempts to fix the price of the shares to be sold without having the contract treated as a disposition of the shares for purposes of § 6166. Such a contract should provide for transfer of the stock certificates at the specified future times, prior to which the seller would be entitled to vote the stock, receive the dividends, and so forth. Alternatively, the number of shares to be redeemed by a corporation with earnings or profits might be limited in order to avoid the risk that the redemption of all of a decedent's stock would cause part of the distribution to be taxed as a dividend. Thus, the agreement might limit the mandatory purchase to a number of shares that have a value equal to the maximum amount redeemable under § 303 (*i.e.,* equal to the sum of the state and federal wealth transfer taxes, and the funeral and administration expenses that are deductible under § 2053). *See* § 11.14. As explained below, the redemption of some shares is treated as a sale or exchange where the stock comprises more than 35 percent of the excess of the value of the decedent's gross estate over the amounts allowable as deductions under § 2053 and 2054. *See* §§ 11.15-11.16.

Any excess distribution made in redemption of the stock will be taxed as a dividend under § 301 unless it qualifies under one or more of the three exceptions created by § 302(b). It may be difficult to fit within one of the exceptions where a family corporation is involved because of the application of the stock attribution rules of § 318. The exceptions are discussed further in § 11.22.1.

Buy-sell agreements that apply only upon the death or retirement of a party have generally not been effective to fix the value of the shares for gift tax purposes. Although the price fixed in an agreement may establish the price for the shares for nontax purposes, it will not be binding for gift tax purposes unless it gives the other parties the right to purchase the gifted shares. *See Commissioner v. McCann*, 146 F.2d 385 (2d Cir. 1944) (restrictive provision in by-laws); *Krauss v. United States*, 140 F.2d 510 (5th Cir. 1944) (restrictive provision in charter).

§11.10. FUNDING THE PURCHASE

Insurance on the lives of shareholders is often used to fund a buy-sell agreement because of its positive characteristics: liquidity, reliability, and general availability. Unfortunately, however, the exact amount required to fund a purchase may not be known until a shareholder dies and it becomes possible to value his or her shares under the agreement. The problem is more difficult if one or more of the shareholders is, or becomes, uninsurable—or is much older than the others. In some cases the corporation may establish a reserve for the purpose of funding the agreement, which could be invested in liquid assets other than cash value insurance. Of course, the AMT problem described in §11.8 discourages the use of insurance owned by a C corporation. Earnings accumulated in the year of a shareholder's death or thereafter are exempt from the accumulated earnings tax to the extent needed to redeem the decedent's stock, but not in excess of the maximum amount redeemable under §303. §537(a)(2), (b)(1). Note that §537 does not insulate earnings retained in prior years from the reach of the accumulated earnings tax.

While it is common to use life insurance to fund buy-sell agreements, the planner must be alert to the possible application of the transfer for value rule of §101(a)(2). In particular, the IRS may argue that the transfer for value rule applies to a shareholders' agreement that obligates them to use the proceeds of cross-owned insurance to purchase the stock of a deceased shareholder. *Monroe v. Patterson*, 197 F.Supp. 146 (N.D. 1961); LRs 7734048, 9045004. See §6.54. Maintaining the necessary number of insurance policies is usually simple enough when an entity purchase agreement is involved and the policies are owned by the corporation or partnership. In such a case, the business ordinarily acquires and owns one policy on the life of each shareholder. Under §264(a), the business is not allowed a deduction for premiums paid on such policies. The insurance proceeds received by the business are generally not subject to the income tax. §101(a).

The value of the insurance on a shareholder's life that is payable to the corporation is not directly includible in his or her gross estate. Under Reg. §20.2042-1(c)(6), if the proceeds are paid to the corporation, the corporation's incidents of ownership are not attributed to the sole or controlling shareholder. *See* Rev. Rul. 82-85, 1982-1 C.B. 137. *See also* §6.29. Instead, the proceeds received by the corporation may be reflected in the value of the decedent's interest in the corporation. However, the value of the decedent's interest should be controlled by the agreement, which is not necessarily related to the amount of the insurance proceeds. If the insurance is taken into account in valuing the stock in the corporation, the decedent's shares may be worth more, thereby increasing the amount to be received by the decedent's successors. Also, the value of the decedent's shares, including a proportionate share of the insurance proceeds, may be discounted because of a lack of marketability.

Where a cross-purchase agreement is involved, each owner must own a policy on the life of each other owner. An almost unmanageable number of policies is required if there are more than three or four owners. For example, 30 policies of insurance are required if there are six owners (each owner must own policies on the lives of the other five). The problem is exacerbated if the owners own unequal interests in the business, which requires them to own policies of varying amounts. Complications may also arise in disposing of policies held by a deceased owner on the lives of the survivors. A sale of policies to the surviving partners would fall within an exception to the transfer for value rule. § 101(a)(2)(B). While there is no exception to the transfer for value rule for the inter-shareholder transfer of policies, such a transfer may be within an exception such as the exception for transfers to a partner of the insured. Accordingly, the proceeds of the policies paid to a fellow shareholder may be subject to taxation under § 101(a)(2). *See* § 6.54. In general, an owner should avoid purchasing a policy on his or her own life, which would subject the entire proceeds to the estate tax. The payment of premiums on individually-owned policies on the lives of other owners is not deductible for income tax purposes. If a corporation pays the premiums on policies owned by the shareholders, they will be considered to have received a constructive dividend unless they are employees and the premium payments are treated as additional compensation.

Insurance Owned by a Partnership or LLC. The proceeds of insurance owned by and payable to a partnership or LLC should not be directly or indirectly included in the estate of a deceased insured partner or member. In order to achieve this result the individual partners should not hold any incidents of ownership over the policies which might require inclusion under § 2042. *See* § 6.29.1. The receipt of the proceeds will not affect the valuation of the decedent's interest in the partnership if its value is effectively fixed in a binding buy-sell agreement. Again, the proceeds should not be included in the income of the partnership. § 101(a).

§ 11.10.1. Installment Payments

A deceased shareholder's stock may be redeemed on the installment basis. *See, e.g.,* LR 8043030. The immediate cash requirements of a redemption are reduced if the agreement provides for payment of the purchase price in installments or if a deceased shareholder's successors are willing to sell the decedent's stock on that basis. *See* LR 7941037. The installment payment of the purchase price could also reduce the tax cost to the redeeming shareholder, which could be very important if the redemption does not qualify as a sale or exchange of the stock (*i.e.,* if the proceeds were taxed as dividends). The circumstances in which an installment sale is feasible depend upon the financial stability of the company and the shareholders, the relationships between the shareholders, and the needs of the decedent's successors. In some cases the sellers may feel it is necessary to obtain some further assurance that payments will be made when due, such as a guarantee by individual shareholders or others. An installment sale must also be planned carefully in light of the tax circumstances of the decedent's estate. Consideration must be given to the fact that an installment sale would ordinarily involve a disposition of the decedent's stock that could accelerate the time for payment of any estate tax deferred under § 6166. *See* § 11.27. Finally, interest will be imputed on the unpaid balance unless the purchaser pays at least the rate required by § 483 or the original issue discount rules of § § 1271-1275. *See* § 9.6.5.

§11.10.2. Medium of Payment

In some cases the parties do not take any steps to provide that the required funds will be available upon the death of a shareholder. Instead, they are content to rely upon the availability of borrowed funds or the distribution of appreciated assets in exchange for the shares. However, neither of those methods is sufficiently reliable in most cases. It may be impossible or very expensive to borrow the necessary funds under the circumstances that exist at the time of a shareholder's death. The distribution of appreciated property in redemption of a decedent's stock is generally not attractive because it requires the corporation to recognize gain. §311(b).

§11.10.3. Accumulated Earnings Tax, §§531-537

The retention of earnings by a C corporation for the purpose of funding an entity purchase agreement may be subject to the tax on unreasonable accumulated earnings. *See* §§531-537. The risk exists whether or not the earnings are invested in insurance on the lives of the shareholders. The tax is imposed at a flat rate of 35 percent of accumulated taxable income. §531. However, an operating company may accumulate $250,000 ($150,000 in the case of professional service corporations) without being subject to the tax. §535(c)(2). Importantly, the tax only applies if the accumulation was made to avoid the income tax with respect to the shareholders. §532(a). An S corporation (the income of which flows through to its shareholders) is normally not concerned with the accumulated earnings tax. However, the tax might come into play if a C corporation with unreasonable accumulated earnings elected to be treated as an S corporation.

A corporation may accumulate earnings for the purpose of redeeming a decedent's shares under §303, provided the accumulations take place in the year of the shareholder's death or later. §537(a)(2). Accumulations made prior to the shareholder's death may be subject to the tax. In most cases the tax should not apply, however, because an accumulation of earnings for the purpose of funding a buy-sell agreement is within the reasonable needs of the corporation. Also, such accumulations are not generally made in order to permit the shareholders to avoid income taxation.

§11.11.   Ethical Considerations

A lawyer who advises more than one of the owners of a business regarding the preparation of a buy-sell agreement must recognize the potential for conflicts of interest between them. The discussion should also deal with issues of confidentiality and the basis upon which the lawyer's fees will be determined. Because of the potential for conflicts, the lawyer should explain to them at the outset the desirability of having independent counsel and the difficulty of representing any of them adequately to the extent their interests may actually conflict. *See* §§1.6.7 *and* 11.1.10. Independent counsel should also be recommended in connection with a corporate recapitalization or the formation or restructuring of a partnership or LLC. A lawyer can represent more than one party if they all consent to the multiple representation after full disclosure and it is clear that the lawyer can represent them without adversely affecting their interests.

§11.12. COMMUNITY PROPERTY ASPECTS

Additional factors must be taken into account where the interests are community property, including the events which will trigger a sale or redemption. For example, the parties may wish to provide for the sale of all of the interest belonging to a husband and wife upon the death of the spouse who is active in the business. A sale or redemption will serve the tax and nontax interests of the other owners and of the surviving spouse. The other owners often prefer to eliminate the surviving spouse as an owner—who probably prefers to be cashed out rather than "locked in." An agreement that meets the requirements of §2703 will fix the estate tax value of the interest, which can be critically important to all parties. Of course, the immediate estate tax concerns are ameliorated if the decedent's interest passes in a way that qualifies for the marital deduction.

A husband and wife and the other owners might not want to require the sale of the interest upon the death of a spouse who is not active in the business. Such a sale could deprive the surviving active spouse of important control and equity interests in the business.

The estate tax valuation of an interest is not fixed by a buy-sell agreement unless the interest is subject to a binding obligation to sell. As noted above, a husband and wife will usually want the marital deduction to be available upon the death of either in order to defer the payment of estate tax until the death of the surviving spouse. Accordingly, they may wish to provide for a QTIP trust, which allows the executor to elect the extent to which the marital deduction will be claimed. See §5.23. In any case they will want to preserve the value of a deceased spouse's unified credit. If it is consistent with the couple's overall plans, the will of the inactive spouse should dispose of his or her interest in the stock in a way that will not inadvertently subject it to estate taxation again upon the death of the active spouse. Such a disposition is most important where their interest taken together represents control of a corporation. For example, the interest of an inactive spouse in the stock may be left to a credit shelter trust (or other nonmarital deduction trust) of which the active spouse may be a beneficiary, and over which the active spouse has some degree of control—but not enough to cause the stock to be included in the survivor's estate. They should also take into account the benefits available under §§303 and 6166 if a deceased spouse's estate pays some tax. In particular, the redemption of stock within the limits of §303 is unlikely to cause any income tax liability because it is treated as a sale or exchange and not as a dividend. §§11.13-11.22. In addition, payment of the estate tax attributable to interests in a small trade or business may be deferred under §6166. §§11.23-11.28.

C. REDEMPTIONS UNDER §303

§11.13. OVERVIEW

Congress has been sensitive to the problem of generating sufficient funds to pay estate settlement costs where an interest in a closely-held trade or business is a major asset of an estate. The present relief provisions are embodied in §§303 and 6166.

Under §303, the redemption of stock included in a decedent's estate is treated as a sale or exchange if the stock was worth more than 35 percent of the decedent's gross estate less allowable deductions under §§2053 and 2054. The estate tax attributable to a closely-held business interest may be deferred and paid in installments over 15 years under §6166 if the value of the business interest exceeds 35 percent of the value of the decedent's adjusted gross estate. For this purpose, a closely-held business includes a proprietorship and certain partnership and corporate interests.

The provisions of §§303 and 6166 were liberalized and coordinated in 1981. At that time the percentage tests of §§303 and 6166 were reduced to 35 percent of the decedent's gross estate less deductions allowable under §§2053 and 2054. §6166(a). In addition, both §§303 and 6166 were amended to allow the decedent's stock in two or more corporations to be aggregated for the purpose of satisfying the percentage test if the decedent's estate includes 20 percent or more of the value of each corporation. *See* §11.16. Finally, the 1981 Act liberalized several of the acceleration provisions of §6166(g). Most important was the increase from one-third to one-half in the amount of stock that could be disposed of, or the amount that could be withdrawn from the business, without accelerating the time for payment of the tax. *See* §11.27.

In planning a redemption program the parties must consider at least two important nontax questions. First, will the redemption result in an undesirable shift of corporate control? Second, will the distribution of funds in redemption of the stock unduly hamper corporate operations or growth? If the answer to either question is "yes," the parties should consider redeeming fewer shares or adopting an alternative plan for raising funds.

§11.14. INTRODUCTION TO §303

Section 303 largely eliminates the income tax cost of withdrawing enough funds from a closely-held business to pay the death taxes and administration expenses incurred by a deceased shareholder's estate. If the value of the stock exceeds 35 percent of the decedent's gross estate less deductions allowable under §§2053 and 2054, the redemption of a limited amount of stock is treated as a sale or exchange the proceeds of which qualify for capital gains treatment. Little, if any, gain is usually realized upon a redemption because the stock will have acquired a basis equal to its estate tax value in the decedent's estate. §1014(a). Treatment as a sale or exchange extends to all qualifying redemptions—it does not depend upon the cash position of the estate. Thus, a redemption may be made with respect to qualifying stock although the decedent's estate is awash with cash and does not need the proceeds of redemptions to pay the taxes and expenses. Without the benefit of §303 the redemption of a decedent's stock would be treated as a dividend unless it fell within one of the exceptions of § 302(b). Of course, the fact that qualified dividend income is taxed at the same rate as net capital gain under current law lessens the severity of dividend treatment. Estates will still want to qualify under § 303, however, to the extent the stepped-up basis of the stock allows withdrawals under § 303 to be entirely tax-free.

The provisions of § 303 extend to the redemption of "new" stock, the basis of which is determined by reference to "old" stock that was included in the decedent's estate. § 303(c); Reg. § 1.303-2(d). Thus, nonvoting common stock or preferred stock received in connection with a reorganization under § 368, a tax-free exchange under § 1036 or a distribution under § 305(a), can be redeemed under § 303. The opportunity to redeem "new" stock can be of particular value where the shareholders wish to maintain the pre-mortem balance of voting stock among the families of shareholders. *E.g.,* Rev. Rul. 87-132, 1987-2 C.B. 82 (distribution of nonvoting common to decedent's estate and surviving shareholder was nontaxable under § 305(a), the carryover of basis provisions of § 307(a) apply to the distribution, and the distributed stock is redeemable by the estate under § 303).

Amount Redeemable. The amount redeemable under § 303 is limited to the sum of the state and federal death taxes, including penalties and interest and the funeral and administration expenses that are deductible under § 2053. § 303(a). For purposes of § 303 generation-skipping transfer taxes (GSTT) imposed at the same time as a decedent's death by reason of the decedent's death are treated as death taxes. § 303(d). Also, a redemption *only* qualifies to the extent "the interest of the shareholder is reduced directly (or through a binding obligation to contribute) by any payment" of death taxes and funeral and administration expenses. § 303(b)(3). Accordingly, shares specifically bequeathed to one party may not be redeemed under § 303 where the obligation to pay death taxes and funeral and administration expenses is imposed on another party. Because of the marital deduction, shares that pass to a surviving spouse are not normally subject to a charge for a portion of the death taxes and expense. If the shares passing to a surviving spouse were subject to an agreement to contribute, the marital deduction would be reduced by a similar amount. *See* § 2056(b)(4).

Transfers Within Three Years of Death, §2035(c). For purposes of determining whether the 35 percent requirement is satisfied, a decedent's estate is treated as including all property transferred within three years of death. § 2035(c). Thus, the inclusion of property transferred within three years of death may qualify or disqualify an estate for the benefit of § 303. In particular, stock transferred within three years of death is taken into account for purposes of the percentage requirement of § 303(b), although it is not included in the decedent's estate. However, stock not actually included in the decedent's gross estate cannot be redeemed under § 303. Rev. Rul. 84-76, 1984-1 C.B. 91. In order to be redeemed under § 303 the stock *must* be included in the decedent's estate. § 303(a). In short, the ability of an estate to meet the percentage requirement of § 303 cannot be enhanced by deathbed transfers.

EXAMPLE 11-12.

In 2006 *T* transferred stock in ABC, Inc. worth $1,000,000 to a child, *C. T* died in 2008 leaving an estate of $4,000,000 of which $1,000,000 was stock in ABC, Inc. Deductions allowable under §§ 2053 and 2054 amounted to

$500,000. For purposes of the percentage requirement of §303(b), *T*'s estate is treated as also including the stock transferred to *C* in 2006. Thus, *T*'s estate is treated as having an overall value of $5,000,000, including ABC, Inc. stock worth $2,000,000. The value of the stock ($2,000,000) is greater than 35% of the value of *T*'s gross estate ($5,000,000) less allowable deductions ($500,000). The ABC, Inc. stock actually included in *T*'s estate may be redeemed under §303 up to an amount equal to the total of all death taxes and allowable funeral and administration expenses. *See* Rev. Rul. 84-76, 1984-1 C.B. 91.

EXAMPLE 11-13.

In 2006 *T* transferred Blackacre, worth $600,000, to his children. *T* died in 2008 leaving an estate of $2,000,000, of which $800,000 was stock in XYZ, Inc. Deductions allowable under §§2053 and 2054 amounted to $200,000. *T*'s estate would meet the 35% requirement of §303(b) if the gift of Blackacre were not considered:

$$\frac{\$800,000}{\$2,000,000 - \$200,000} = 44.44\%$$

However, including Blackacre as required by §2035(c), the XYZ, Inc. stock does not constitute a large enough percentage of *T*'s estate:

$$\frac{\$800,000}{\$2,600,000 - \$200,000} = 33.33\%$$

Transfers made within three years of death are also included for purposes of §2032A, §2035(c)(1)(B); §6166, §2035(c)(2); and the lien provisions of subchapter C of Chapter 64; §2035(c)1)(C).

Redemptions More Than Four Years After Death. The use of the proceeds of a redemption made within four years of the decedent's death is not restricted. §303(b)(1). Later redemptions qualify under §303 only to the extent of the lesser of, (1) the amount of death taxes and funeral and administration expenses that were unpaid immediately before the distribution, and (2) the amount that is applied within one year following the distribution toward payment of the death taxes and funeral and administration expenses. §303(b)(4). Redemptions made more than four years after the decedent's death must be carefully coordinated with payment of the estate tax installments under §6166.

Redemptions of Stock Subject to GSTT. Stock subject to the GSTT by reason of a generation-skipping transfer occurring at and as a result of the death of an individual may also be redeemed under §303. §303(d). For purposes of applying §303 the stock is considered to be included in the gross estate of the individual; the relationship of the stock to the decedent's estate is measured by reference to the amount of the generation-skipping transfer; the GSTT and similar taxes are treated as an estate tax imposed by reason of the individual's death; and the period within which distribution may be made in redemption of the stock is measured from the date of the generation-skipping transfer.

§11.15. THIRTY-FIVE PERCENT REQUIREMENT, §303(b)(2)(A)

Stock included in a decedent's gross estate qualifies for redemption under §303 only if its federal estate tax value exceeds 35 percent of the decedent's gross estate less the amount of deductions allowable under §§2053 and 2054. §303(b)(2)(A). For purposes of this computation the amounts deducted under §§2053 and 2054 (*i.e.*, debts, funeral and administration expenses, and casualty losses) are taken into account whether or not they are claimed as deductions for federal estate tax purposes. §303(b)(2)(a)(ii). *See* Rev. Rul. 56-449, 1956-2 C.B. 180 (declared obsolete by Rev. Rul. 80-367, 1980-2 C.B. 386). Note that the amount of the charitable and marital deductions do not figure into the computation.

EXAMPLE 11-14.

T's gross estate was $2,200,000 including stock in X Corp. that had an estate tax value of $950,000. The deductions allowable to *T*'s estate under §§2053 and 2054 amounted to $200,000. The 35% requirement is met in this case because the value of the stock included in *T*'s gross estate ($950,000) comprised more of *T*'s estate than required by §303(b)(2)(A):

$$\frac{\$95,000}{\$2,200,000 - \$200,000} = 47.5\%$$

Special planning may be called for if a client wishes to make a gift to charity at death and qualify for the benefits of §303 (or §6166). A charitable bequest does not reduce the amount of the gross estate for purposes of determining whether the 35 percent requirement is met. However, a deduction is allowable under §2053 for an enforceable charitable pledge to the extent it was contracted bona fide and would have been deductible if it had been a bequest. Reg. §20.2053-5. Accordingly, allowance of the pledge as a deduction under §2053 reduces the amount of the 35 percent threshold.

EXAMPLE 11-15.

X died leaving a gross estate of $5,000,000, which included stock in X Corp. worth $1,400,000. *X*'s will left $1,000,000 to a tax-exempt charity. Deductions allowable under §§2053 and 2054 amounted to $100,000. *X*'s estate could not redeem any stock under §303 because the value of *X*'s stock in X Corp. ($1,400,000) is only 28.57% of *X*'s gross estate less deductions allowable under §§2053 and 2054 ($5,000,000—$100,000).

X's stock in X Corp. would have exceeded the 35% threshold had *X* made an enforceable pledge of $1,000,000 to the charity instead of making a bequest to it. In planning the administration of the estate the personal representative must recognize that the valuation of the stock and other assets may determine whether or not the 35 % test is satisfied.

§11.16.   STOCK IN TWO OR MORE CORPORATIONS, §303(b)(2)(B)

Stock of two or more corporations may be combined for purposes of satisfying the 35 percent requirement if at least 20 percent in value of the outstanding stock of each corporation is included in the decedent's gross estate. §303(b)(2)(B). In order to qualify for aggregation, the decedent's estate must include at least 20 percent of the total value of all issues of each corporation's stock. That is, the test does not require that the decedent's estate include 20 percent of each issue of stock. Thus, the stock in corporations *A* and *B* is considered to be the stock of a single corporation for purposes of the 35 percent requirement if the decedent's estate includes common or preferred stock of each corporation that has a value of more than 20 percent of all of its stock. In this connection remember that the value of a minority block of closely-held stock is usually subject to valuation discounts.

EXAMPLE 11-16.

T's gross estate had a federal estate tax value of $3,000,000, including 30% of the outstanding stock of *A* Corp. and 25% of the outstanding stock of *B* Corp. A total of $200,000 was allowable to *T*'s estate as deductions under §§2053 and 2054. *T*'s stock in *A* Corp. was worth $800,000 of its total value of $3,800,000, and *T*'s stock in *B* Corp. was worth $400,000 of its total value of $1,800,000. Thus, more than 20% in value of the stock of both corporations was included in *T*'s gross estate. The total value of the stock in the two corporations included in *T*'s estate ($1,200,000) exceeds 35% of the value of *T*'s gross estate reduced by deductions allowable under §§2053 and 2054 ($3,000,000 - $200,000). Accordingly, the 35% requirement of §303(b)(2) is satisfied.

For purposes of the 20 percent test, the surviving spouse's interest in stock held by the decedent and the surviving spouse as community property, joint tenants, tenants by the entirety, or as tenants in common is considered to be included in the decedent's gross estate. §303(b)(2)(B); *cf.,* Rev. Rul. 61-91, 1961-1 C.B. 714 (comparable issue under former §6166A). However, the surviving spouse's interest in such stock is not included in the decedent's estate. In particular, the value of the surviving spouse's stock cannot be counted for purposes of satisfying the basic 35 percent test.

§11.17.   MAXIMUM AMOUNT REDEEMABLE, §303(a)

Under §303(a), the maximum amount that can be received in redemption of qualifying stock is the sum of the death taxes imposed by reason of the decedent's death and the amount of funeral and administration expenses deductible under §2053. For this purpose the GSTT imposed by reason and as a result of the decedent's

death is treated as a death tax. § 303(d). As indicated above, the funeral and administration expenses are included in the computation whether they are taken as estate tax
or as income tax deductions. Note, however, that debts and casualty losses are not
included in determining the ceiling.

Care must be exercised in planning the sequence of distributions in redemption
of a decedent's stock. Where more than one distribution takes place, the distributions
are applied against the total amount that is redeemable under § 303 in the order in
which the distributions are made. Reg. § 1.303-2(g)(1). Redemption distributions in
excess of the amount redeemable under § 303 are taxable as dividends unless they fall
within one of the exceptions to § 302. *See* § 11.22. Rev. Rul. 71-261, 1971-1 C.B. 108.

EXAMPLE 11-17.

A maximum of $500,000 of stock was redeemable under § 303 from *T*'s
estate by *X* Corp. On January 15 of this year, *X* Corp. distributed $400,000
to *T*'s son, *S*, in redemption of shares *T* had transferred to a trust and that
were included in *T*'s estate under § 2036. In February, *X* Corp. redeemed
$200,000 shares held by the executor of *T*'s will. Under the local estate tax
apportionment law all of the shares of X Corp. were required to contribute
proportionately to payments of estate tax. The first $500,000 received in
redemption of the estate's shares qualifies under § 303. Half of the distribution received by *T*'s executor ($100,000) does not qualify under § 303.

§ 11.18. TIME LIMIT ON REDEMPTIONS, § 303(b)(1), (4)

Under the basic limitation of § 303(b)(1) a redemption must take place within
three years and 90 days after the date the federal estate tax return is filed.
§ 303(b)(1)(A). The proceeds of a redemption made within that period may be used
for any purpose. If a petition for redetermination of estate tax by the Tax Court is
timely filed, a redemption may be made at any time within 60 days after the Tax
Court decision becomes final. § 303(b)(1)(B). Also, where the payment of the estate tax
is deferred under § 6166, a redemption may be made within the time determined
under that section for payment of the estate tax in installments. § 303(b)(1)(C).

A redemption made more than four years after the decedent's death qualifies
only to the extent it does not exceed the lesser of, (1) the amount of death taxes and
funeral and administration expenses that remained unpaid immediately before the
distribution, and (2) the amount paid toward those expenses within one year following the date of the distribution. § 303(b)(4). Of necessity the latter amount is always
the lesser. In planning a redemption program the parties should consider the restrictions imposed on the use of the proceeds of redemptions made more than four years
after the decedent's death. It is particularly important to do so where payment of the
estate tax has been deferred under § 6166 because of the acceleration provision of that
section. *See* § 11.27.

§11.19.   What May be Distributed

Cash is ordinarily distributed in a redemption under §303. Until amended in 1986 the provisions of §311 allowed appreciated property to be distributed by a corporation in redemption of stock without recognition of gain. In addition, the taxpayer did not recognize any gain on the distribution. Effective January 1, 1987 a corporation recognizes gain if appreciated property is distributed in a stock redemption. In addition, the property that is distributed must be selected carefully to avoid distributions that have other adverse tax consequences. For example, the distribution of §1245 or §1250 property triggers depreciation recapture by corporations other than S corporations.

§11.20.   Inter Vivos Planning for Redemptions Under §303

The shareholder and the corporation should ordinarily both do some careful advance planning where a shareholder's stock holdings may meet the requirements of §303. To begin with, the shareholder should avoid making any inter vivos gifts or other dispositions of the stock that might reduce the value of his or her holdings below the required 35 percent. (Of course, reducing a shareholder's stock holdings to a minority block that qualify for a minority discount might be best in overall tax terms.) If the stock might be below the 35 percent threshold, steps might be taken to increase the value of the stock relative to the value of the shareholder's other assets. For example, assets that the shareholder owns outright might be transferred to the corporation, tax free, in exchange for additional shares of stock. Such a transfer does double duty by reducing the value of assets outside the business and increasing the amount of stock the shareholder holds.

A change in the beneficiary designation of corporate-owned life insurance may also boost the value of the shareholder's stock. Where the shareholder has control of a majority of the corporation's stock, its incidents of ownership are attributed to the shareholder and the proceeds are includible in the shareholder's estate under §2042 if the proceeds are payable to a beneficiary other than the corporation. *See* Reg. §20.2042-1(c)(6). In contrast, the proceeds are taken into account in valuing the shareholder's stock where the proceeds are payable to the corporation. Rev. Rul. 82-85, 1982-1 C.B. 137.

Special care must be exercised when the shareholder owns stock in several corporations, the holdings in none of which is by itself sufficient to satisfy the 35 percent test. Of course, the stock of two or more corporations can be aggregated for this purpose where more than 20 percent in value of each corporation is included in the shareholder's estate. §303(b)(2)(B). *See* §11.16. More sophisticated planning may be called for where the client's stock holdings in any one corporation are not large enough to satisfy the 35 percent requirement and aggregation is prevented because the shareholder owns less than 20 percent of the stock of each corporation. The effect of aggregation could be approximated, however, if the corporations in which the shareholder-owned stock are merged or consolidated prior to the shareholder's death. As a result, the value of the stock in the surviving corporation might be more than adequate to satisfy the 35 percent test. Stock in two or more corporations could, of course, be transferred to a holding company in exchange for some of its stock. Such a step might also allow the estate to defer payment of the estate tax under §6166(b)(8), which is slightly less advantageous than deferral under the basic provisions of §6166. *See* §11.24.5.

The planner should also consider whether it is necessary or desirable to obtain a commitment from the corporation to redeem the stock through an entity purchase agreement or similar arrangement. *See* §11.6-11.12. The potential for future problems may be reduced if all shareholders are informed of the plans and approve of them. Some consideration must also be given to the availability of liquid assets to the corporation for the purpose of financing the redemption. A redemption may be adequately financed if, for example, retained earnings are used to purchase insurance on the shareholder's life or to invest in some other relatively liquid form. In any case, the corporation should avoid the imposition of the accumulated earnings tax under §§531-537. As noted above, §537 permits a corporation to accumulate funds in the year of a shareholder's death or later, for the purpose of funding a redemption under §303. For purposes of §537 the accumulation of earnings in years prior to the stockholder's death for the purpose of funding a redemption may not be considered a reasonable business need.

The planner should also inquire into any restrictions that may be imposed on redemptions by the local law or by the corporation's financing arrangements. Some states restrict redemptions to the amount of the corporation's earned surplus. However, a redemption may be made under §6.40 of the Model Business Corporation Act so long as the corporation is not insolvent, and the net assets of the corporation are not reduced below the amount payable to the shareholders who would have prior or equal rights to the assets of the corporation if it were liquidated.

As mentioned in §11.14, the stock to be redeemed should only be given to a person whose interest in the stock will be chargeable for death taxes and funeral and administration expenses allowable under §2053. The stock qualifies under §303 only if the interest of the shareholder is reduced by payment of the death taxes and other expenses. §303(b)(3).

§11.21. WORKSHEET FOR §303

In the planning process it is important to determine whether a particular shareholder's stock meets the requirements of §303 and, if so, how much might be redeemed. It is safer and more efficient if the planner uses computer software or a worksheet of the following type to make the necessary calculations:

Section 303 worksheet

Part I. Qualifications
1. Adjusted Gross Estate (estimate or enter from Form 706, page 1, line 1; including property transferred within 3 years of death per §2035(c)(1)) $_____

    Less: Deductions allowable under §§2053 and 2054   −_____

    Adjusted Gross Estate (item 1)   _____
2. Value of decedent's stock in corporation, including stock transferred within 3 years of death (the value of 2 or more businesses may be aggregated under §303(b)(2)) (item 2)   _____

3. Divide item 2 by item 1. (If the closely held business, item 2, has a value of more than 35% of the adjusted gross estate, item 1, the requirements of § 303 are met.)   _____

Part II. Amount Redeemable

4. Death taxes, including GSTT and interest and penalties, paid by reason of decedent's death, § 303(a)(1), (d):   _____

    a. Net estate tax (estimate or enter from Form 706, page 1, line 21)   _____

    b. State death tax   +_____

    Total (item 4)   _____

5. Funeral and administrative expenses allowable as deductions under § 2053, whether or not claimed   +_____

    on Form 706 (§ 303(a)(2)) (item 5) $_____

6. Total amount redeemable (item 4 plus item 5) $_____

Caveat; *See* § 303(b)(1) regarding the time within which the redemptions must be accomplished.

§11.22. Redemptions That do Not Qualify Under §303

A redemption is also treated as a sale or exchange and not a dividend if the effect of the redemption is essentially the same as a sale to an unrelated party. Stated conversely, a redemption that does not qualify under § 303 will be treated as a distribution in the nature of a dividend unless it qualifies under one of the exceptions of § 302(b). The exceptions apply to redemptions that, (1) are not essentially equivalent to a dividend, § 302(b)(1); (2) are substantially disproportionate, § 302(b)(2); or (3) result in a complete termination of the shareholder's interest, § 302(b)(3). A redemption that effects a partial liquidation of the corporation also qualifies for sale treatment under § 302(b)(4). The discussion below does not consider partial liquidations as they are encountered substantially less frequently by estate planners.

§11.22.1. Redemption Not Essentially Equivalent to a Dividend, §302(b)(1)

The first exception establishes a subjective test under which a redemption is treated as a sale or exchange if it is "not essentially equivalent to a dividend" in light of all of the facts and circumstances. § 302(b)(1). Unfortunately, the scope of the exception is unclear, which makes it of little use in planning. Court decisions, the regulations, revenue rulings, and private letter rulings provide some guidance, albeit somewhat conflicting.

In the leading case, *United States v. Davis,* 397 U.S. 301 (1970), the Supreme Court held that the exception does not apply unless the redemption results in a meaningful reduction in the shareholder's proportionate interest in the corporation. In *Davis* the corporation needed to increase its capital by $25,000 in order to qualify for a loan from the Reconstruction Finance Corporation. The taxpayer transferred $25,000 to the corporation in exchange for 1,000 shares of $25 par preferred stock with the understanding that the preferred stock would be redeemed after the loan was repaid. Later, when the preferred stock was redeemed the taxpayer and members of his family owned all of the corporation's stock. Under the family attribution rules of §318(a)(1), the taxpayer was considered to own all of the corporation's common stock before and after the redemption of the preferred stock. The redemption was treated as a dividend although there had been a valid business purpose for the original issuance of the preferred stock.

What constitutes a meaningful reduction in the shareholder's proportionate interest in the corporation is not clear. In Rev. Rul. 75-502, 1975-2 C.B. 111, the IRS listed three interests of a shareholder that are relevant for purposes of the meaningful reduction test: "(1) the right to vote and thereby exercise control; (2) the right to participate in current earnings and accumulated surplus; and (3) the right to share in net assets on liquidation." Nonetheless, the authorities are difficult to reconcile. For example, Rev. Rul. 78-401, 1978-2 C.B. 127, holds that a reduction from 90 percent to 60 percent was not meaningful because no action was contemplated which required a two-thirds affirmative vote. On the other hand, in *Henry T. Patterson Trust v. United States*, 729 F.2d 1089 (6th Cir. 1984), the court held that a reduction from 80 percent to 60 percent was meaningful. Indeed, under the unique facts of the case the court stated that a decrease in stock ownership from 97 percent to 93 percent was a "meaningful reduction."

Not surprisingly, the regulations are consistent with the meaningful reduction test articulated in *Davis*. In particular, Reg. §1.302-2(b) indicates that a pro rata redemption does not qualify where only one class of stock is outstanding. ("All distributions in pro rata redemptions of a part of the stock of a corporation will be treated as distributions under section 301 if the corporation has only one class of stock outstanding.") However, a pro rata redemption might qualify as a partial liquidation under §302(b)(4). The regulations also provide that a redemption of all of one class of the stock of a corporation is generally not within the exception of §302(b)(1) if all classes of stock are held in the same proportions. Reg. §1.302-2(b). As illustrated by *Davis*, the family attribution rules make it difficult for a family-owned corporation to meet the requirements of §302(b)(1).

EXAMPLE 11-18.

When Magma, Inc. was incorporated, its 15,000 shares of common stock were issued equally to H (7,500) and W (7,500). Subsequently H and W each sold 2,500 shares to a key employee, C, who was unrelated to them. When H died, Magma redeemed H's remaining 5,000 shares from his estate in accordance with the terms of a buy-sell agreement that bound all of the shareholders regarding the disposition of their shares. The redemption reduced the estate's actual ownership of Magma stock from one-third to zero and its constructive ownership of stock from two-thirds to one-half. The IRS has ruled that such a redemption is not essentially equivalent to a dividend. LR 8044034. The redemption would not fall within the terms of this exception if C were a beneficiary of H's estate because the estate would be treated as the constructive owner of C's shares as well. *See* §318(a)(3); Reg. §1.318-3(a).

Attribution Rules. Whether a redemption qualifies under the exceptions of §302(b) often depends upon an application of the attribution rules. Without thoroughly exploring the complexity and subtlety of the rules, some features should be noted. First, family attribution under §318(a)(1) is limited to an individual's spouse, children, grandchildren, and parents. Thus, there is no attribution between siblings. Also, while there is attribution from grandchild to grandparent, there is no attribution from grandparent to grandchild. Importantly, the operating rules of §318(a)(5)(B) bar double attribution under the family attribution rules. For example, stock owned by a parent cannot be attributed to a child and then attributed from the child to the child's spouse.

EXAMPLE 11-19.

All of the stock of *X* Corp. is owned by *X* (50%) and *X*'s children, *D* (25%) and *E* (25%). If *X* Corp. redeems all of *X*'s stock the family attribution rules will prevent the redemption from reducing *X*'s interest in *X* Corp. Specifically, *X* will be treated as owning the stock of both of his children. Accordingly, the redemption would not result in a meaningful reduction in *X*'s interest. However, the redemption would qualify as a complete termination of *X*'s interest under §302(b)(3) if the family attribution rules can be waived under §302(c)(2).

Second, under the entity attribution rules the stock owned by an estate, trust, partnership or corporation may be attributed pro rata to its beneficiaries, partners or shareholders. Third, stock owned by a beneficiary, partner, or shareholder may be attributed to the entity. Again, the operating rules of §318(a)(5)(C) prevent the double attribution of stock through an entity. That is, stock attributed to an entity may not be reattributed to its beneficiaries, partners or shareholders. Fourth, a person who holds an option to acquire stock is treated as owning the stock. §318(a)(4). In this connection note that stock which may be considered as owned by an individual under the family attribution rules of §318(a)(1) or the option rule of §318(a)(4) will be considered as owning the stock under the option rule. §318(a)(5)(D).

Hostility between family members does not prevent application of the attribution rules. *David Metzger Trust v. Commissioner,* 76 T.C. 42 (1981), *aff'd,* 693 F.2d 459 (5th Cir.), *cert. denied,* 463 U.S. 1207 (1982); *Michael N. Cerone,* 87 T.C. 1 (1986) ("Family hostility does not prevent application of the attribution rules.")

§11.22.2. Substantially Disproportionate Redemption, §302(b)(2)

The second exception applies if the redemption is "substantially disproportionate with respect to the shareholder." §302(b)(2). In order to qualify under this exception the redemption must satisfy three mathematical tests. Again, satisfying the tests is made difficult by the application of the stock attribution rules. §§302(c)(1), 318. In brief, the tests require that immediately after the redemption the shareholder must own less than:

1. 50 percent of the combined voting power of all classes of stock;

2. 80 percent of the voting stock that the shareholder owned immediately before the redemption; and

3. 80 percent of the common stock (whether voting or nonvoting) that the shareholder owned immediately before the redemption.

Because of the second of the tests, "Section 302(b)(2) only applies to a redemption of voting stock or to a redemption of both voting stock and other stock. Section 302(b)(2) does not apply to the redemption solely of nonvoting stock (common or preferred)." Reg. § 1.302-3(a). Where a redemption is one of a series, the applicability of this exception is determined by the aggregate effect of the redemptions and not the effect of the one redemption alone. A redemption is not disproportionate if all of the stock of one class is redeemed or if the same percentage of each shareholder's stock is redeemed. It is also significant that § 302(b)(2) does not impose any percentage test with respect to nonvoting preferred stock.

EXAMPLE 11-20.

W, X, Y, and *Z* each owned 100 shares of the 400 outstanding shares of the common stock of Comet Corp. In addition, *X* and *Y* each owned 100 shares of the outstanding 200 shares of Comet's nonvoting preferred stock. The shareholders were not related parties within the meaning of the attribution rules of § 318(a). Comet Corp. redeemed 60 shares of common stock from *W,* 25 shares from *X,* and 15 shares from *Y.* In order to qualify under § 302(b)(2), after the redemption a shareholder must own less than 20% (80% times 25%) of the 300 shares of common stock that remain outstanding. No test is imposed with respect to the nonvoting preferred stock, none of which was redeemed. After the redemption *W* owned 40 shares (13.33%), *X* owned 75 shares (25%); and *Y* owned 85 shares (28.33%). Accordingly, the redemption is disproportionate only with respect to *W. See* the example in Reg. § 1.302-3(b).

§ 11.22.3. Complete Termination of Interest, § 302(b)(3)

Finally, § 302(b)(3) treats a redemption of the entire interest of a shareholder as an exchange. This exception is superficially easy to satisfy, but it is complicated by the application of the attribution rules. However, the family attribution rules of § 318(a)(1) can be waived for purposes of § 302(b)(3) if the requirements of § 302(c)(2) are met. Waiver is allowed under § 302(c)(2) if the following requirements are satisfied: (1) after the redemption the former shareholder has no interest in the corporation (including an interest as officer, director, or employee) other than as a creditor; (2) the former shareholder acquires no interest in the corporation for a period of ten years other than by bequest or inheritance; and (3) the former shareholder agrees to inform the Treasury of the acquisition of any interest in the corporation within that period. § 302(c)(2)(A). In addition, attribution may not be waived if, within the preceding ten years, the former shareholder either acquired any of the redeemed stock from a person whose stock would be attributed to the former shareholder under § 318(a) or transferred any stock in the corporation to a person whose stock is attributable to the former shareholder under § 318(a). However, the forgoing additional rules do not apply if the avoidance of the federal income tax was not one of the principal purposes of the acquisition or transfer of the shares.

Under a change made by the 1982 Act, the family attribution rules of § 318(a)(1) may be waived by an entity such as a trust or estate if some additional requirements are met. § 302(c)(2)(C). In particular, all of the persons through whom stock might be attributed to the entity must meet the requirements of § 302(c)(2)(A)(i), (ii) and (iii) and agree to be jointly and severally liable for any deficiency that may result from the acquisition of an interest within ten years (other than by bequest or inheritance). The IRS had previously taken the view that where shares were redeemed from a trust or estate (or other entity), the family attribution rules could not be waived by the entity. Under the IRS approach it was much more difficult to qualify under this exception where closely-held stock was to be redeemed from a trust or estate.

EXAMPLE 11-21.

H and his daughter, *D*, were the only shareholders in Alpha Corp. *H* died survived by *D*, his widow, *W*, who was the sole beneficiary under his will. *H*'s interest in Alpha Corp. did not constitute a sufficient portion of his estate to qualify for the redemption under § 303. A redemption of the shares formerly owned by *H* will qualify as an exchange only if the redemption of the estate's stock will qualify under one of the exceptions to the basic rule of § 302. A complete termination of the estate's interest, § 302(b)(3), is possible if *D*'s shares are not attributed to *W* and from *W* to *H*'s estate. Section 302(c)(2)(C) would allow *H*'s estate to waive family attribution of *D*'s shares to *W* under § 318(a)(1) so that there would be no shares to attribute from *W* to the estate.

Under another approach, *H*'s shares of Alpha Corp. might be distributed by his estate to *W*. A redemption of all of the shares owned by *W* would qualify as a complete termination under § 302(b)(3) if the family attribution from *D* to *W* could be waived under § 302(c)(2). Even prior to the 1982 Act the IRS treated such a redemption as a complete termination of *W*'s interest. Rev. Rul. 79-67, 1979-1 C.B. 128.

§ 11.22.4. No Waiver of Entity Attribution

Attribution to or from an entity under § 318(a)(2) and (3) cannot be waived. Thus, a trust, estate, partnership, or corporation will be treated as owning all of the stock held by its beneficiaries, partners or stockholders. § 318(a)(3). Conversely, beneficiaries, partners, or stockholders will be considered to own a pro rata interest in the trust, estate, partnership, or corporation. Under the operating rules of § 318(a)(5) stock that is attributed to an entity is not considered as owned by it for purposes of attributing ownership to a beneficiary, partner or shareholder. Thus, an interest of a beneficiary that is attributed to a trust cannot be reattributed to another beneficiary. Of course, the stock owned by one beneficiary may be attributed to another beneficiary under the family attribution rules of § 318(a)(1).

EXAMPLE 11-22.

A brother and sister, *X* and *Y*, each own 20% of the stock of ABC, Inc. The other 60% is owned by the XYZ Partnership in which *X*, *Y*, and *Z* are equal partners. Under the family attribution rules stock owned by one sibling is not attributed to another. While the stock owned by one sibling may be attributed to a parent under the family attribution rules, the operating rules of § 318(a)(5)(B) prevent the stock from being reattributed to the other sibling (or any other family member). Stock owned by *X* and *Y* is attributed to the XYZ Partnership under the attribution-to-entity rule of § 318(a)(3). Again, the operating rules of § 318(a)(5)(C) prevent the stock attributed to the Partnership from being reattributed to individual partners. However, the stock actually owned by the XYZ Partnership is attributed equally to *X*, *Y*, and *Z*. Thus, *X* and *Y* are each considered to own 40% of the stock of ABC, Inc.

Prior to the 1982 Act, the IRS and the Tax Court had concluded that entity attribution could not be waived. *David Metzger Trust*, 76 T.C. 42 (1981), *aff'd*, 693 F.2d 459 (5th Cir. 1982), *cert. denied*, 463 U.S. 1207 (1983). However, the Fifth Circuit allowed entity waiver in an earlier, poorly reasoned, and much maligned opinion, *Rickey v. United States*, 592 F.2d 1251 (5th Cir. 1979). While *Rickey* created some uncertainty regarding this issue, the Conference Report that accompanied the 1982 Act made it clear that entity attribution could not be waived.

D. DEFERRAL OF ESTATE TAX UNDER § 6166

§ 11.23. OVERVIEW

Payment of the portion of the estate tax attributable to a closely-held business interest may be deferred under § 6166 if the value of the closely-held interest exceeds 35 percent of the decedent's adjusted gross estate. An interest in a partnership, LLC or corporation must either, (1) constitute 20 percent or more of the capital interest in the partnership or 20 percent or more of the voting stock of the corporation, or (2) the partnership, LLC or corporation must have 45 or fewer owners (partners, members or shareholders). For purposes of the 35-percent requirement, the term "adjusted gross estate" means the gross estate reduced by the deductions allowable under §§ 2053 and 2054 (funeral and administration expenses, debts, and losses). § 6166(b)(6). The amount of those items is taken into account whether or not they are claimed as deductions on the federal estate tax return. The percentage test is, of course, the same as is imposed under § 303. As noted above in connection with § 303, a legally enforceable charitable pledge is deductible under § 2053, which reduces the size of the decedent's gross estate and the amount of the 35 percent threshold. *See* § 11.15. In Rev. Rul. 93-48, 1993-2 C.B. 270, the IRS ruled that the post-death interest on deferred estate tax payable with respect to testamentary transfers does not ordinarily reduce the date-of-death value of charitable bequests.

The GSTT imposed on a direct skip that takes place at, and by reason of, the decedent's death, is treated as additional estate taxes imposed by § 2001. § 6166(g). Accordingly, that portion of the GSTT may be extended under § 6166. The possibility of deferred payment of the GSTT does not apply to other generation skipping transfers such as a taxable termination. LR 9314050.

The estate's ability to meet the 35 percent requirement is affected by the inclusion of assets in the estate and the estate tax valuation of assets. § 6166(b)(4). Accordingly, the executor must carefully consider decisions that affect the valuation of assets, including the use of the alternate valuation and special use valuation methods. The latter method allows the value of "qualified real property" to be reduced by as much as $750,000, adjusted for post 1997 inflation. *See* § 12.19. In general an election may be made to value qualified real property under § 2032A where the real and personal property used in the business constitute 50 percent or more of the adjusted value of the gross estate and the qualified real property constitutes 25 percent or more of the adjusted value of the gross estate. Because of the requirements of § 6166, an executor should not make an election under § 2032A without first determining whether it will prevent the estate from satisfying the 35 percent test.

Interests held by the decedent in two or more businesses may be aggregated if 20 percent or more in value of each is included in his or her gross estate. § 6166(c). Presumably the decedent's interests in a partnership and a corporation could be combined under this rule. *See* LR 9015009 (decedent's interests in partnership and corporation could not be combined where partnership was not engaged in an active trade or business). Also, for purposes of § 6166(c), the surviving spouse's interest in property held by a husband and wife as community property, joint tenants, tenants by the entirety, or as tenants in common is treated as included in the decedent's gross estate.

EXAMPLE 11-23.

H's gross estate had a value of $4,000,000, including his interest in the stock of Corporations One and Two. The funeral and administration expenses, debts, and other deductions allowable under § § 2053 and 2054 amounted to $200,000. *H* and *W* held stock in Corporation One as joint tenants, which represented 20% ($1,600,000) of its voting stock. *H* and *W* also owned 30% in value ($1,400,000) of the voting stock of Corporation Two as tenants in common. *H*'s estate includes only 10% in value of the stock of Corporation One. (The stock constitutes a qualified joint interest under § 2040(b), as a result of which only one-half is includible in *H*'s gross estate.) *H*'s estate also includes only half of the Corporation Two stock owned by *H* and *W*, 15% in value. The total percentage interests of *H* and *W* in the stock of both corporations are considered to be owned by *H* for purposes of satisfying the 20% threshold necessary to allow them to be treated as one corporation. As a result, the value of *H*'s interests in Corporation One ($800,000) and Corporation Two ($700,000) may be aggregated for purposes of the 35% test. Because their total value ($1,500,000) exceeds 35% of *H*'s adjusted gross estate ($3,800,000), the tax attributable to *H*'s interest in the two corporations may be deferred under § 6166. Note that the value of the stock owned by *H* and *W* cannot be combined in order to satisfy the 35% requirement. As noted above, effective with respect to decedents dying after 2001, the 2001 Act increased the number of permissible owners from 15 to 45.

§11.24. CLOSELY-HELD BUSINESS

Various ownership interests in a trade or business qualify for the benefits of §6166 including the interest of a sole proprietor. §6166(b)(1)(A). As noted in §11.24.2, a decedent's interest in a trust that is engaged in a trade or business may qualify for deferral under §6166. As indicated above, an interest in a partnership also qualifies if 20 percent or more of the capital interest in the partnership is included in the decedent's gross estate or the partnership had 45 or fewer partners. §6166(b)(1)(B). Similarly, stock in a corporation engaged in a trade or business qualifies if 20 percent or more of the voting interest in the corporation is included in the decedent's gross estate or there are 45 or fewer shareholders. §6166(b)(1)(C). The determination of whether an estate satisfies the requirements of the section is made as of the time immediately before the decedent's death. The limits should be borne in mind in planning the capital structure of a new enterprise or making changes in existing ones (*e.g.*, mergers, recapitalizations, and the restructuring of partnerships).

§11.24.1. Who Is Counted as a Partner, Member, or Shareholder

Importantly, for purposes of determining whether the decedent's interest qualified as a closely-held business, the stock, partnership, or LLC interests held by a husband and wife as community property or as cotenants (joint tenants, tenants in common, or tenants by the entirety) are considered to be owned by one person. §6166(b)(2)(B). As noted above, the same rule applies in determining whether interests in two or more closely-held businesses can be treated as one under §6166(c). Thus, the community property or joint tenancy interests of a decedent and his or her spouse in two or more active businesses could be combined and treated as owned entirely by the decedent. However, while the community property and cotenancy interests of both spouses are taken into account for purposes of §6166(b), only the value of the interests actually included in the decedent's estate is considered for purposes of the 35 percent requirement of §6166(a).

EXAMPLE 11-24.

W died owning 25% in value of the voting stock of ABC, Inc. In addition, *W* and her spouse, *H*, owned 30% in value of the voting stock of XYZ, Inc. as joint tenants. Neither *W*'s 25% interest in ABC, Inc. nor her 15% interest in XYZ, Inc. has a value in excess of 35% of her adjusted gross estate. However, the combined value of her interests in the two corporations exceeds the 35% requirement. Under §6166(c) *W* is treated as owning 20% or more of the value of both corporations which are treated as "an interest in a single closely-held business." Accordingly, her interests in them, 25% and 15% respectively, can be combined for purposes of the 35% requirement of §6166(a).

Family Attribution. A broader attribution rule provides that, "All stock and all partnership interests held by the decedent or by any member of his family (within the meaning of section 267(c)(4)) shall be treated as owned by the decedent." §6166(b)(2)(D). For purposes of determining the number of partners or shareholders, a decedent is treated as owning all of the partnership interests or stock held by the decedent's spouse, siblings, ancestors, or descendants. *Id.* (The decedent is not treated as holding the interests of family members for purposes of the percentage ownership tests of §6166(b)(2)(B) and (C). *See* §11.24.4.)

Indirect Ownership. Under §6166(b)(2)(C), each person who holds an interest in a corporation, partnership, trust, or estate is considered to own a proportionate interest in the property it owns. Thus, the number of partners or shareholders is not reduced by transferring interests to a trust or other entity. According to the staff report, this provision was included to prevent avoidance of the shareholder and partner limits by the use of partnerships, trusts, and tiers of corporations. General Explanation of the 1976 Act 548.

EXAMPLE 11-25.

W and her husband, *H*, hold stock in XYZ, Inc. as joint tenants. There are 43 other unrelated individual shareholders. In addition, shares of XYZ, Inc. are owned by a trust of which there are 5 current income beneficiaries. For purposes of §6166, *H* and *W* are considered to be one shareholder. Accordingly, other than the trust there are 44 actual shareholders. However, under the indirect ownership rule of §6166(b)(2)(C) each of the beneficiaries of the trust is considered to be a shareholder. Thus, XYZ, Inc. has 49 shareholders.

Various holdings of a trust may be aggregated to satisfy the requirements of §6166. For example, aggregation was applied to the stock of an operating company in which the decedent was actively involved and land and buildings used by the company, all of which was held in a trust that was included in the decedent's estate. LR 200006034. The cited ruling allowed the assets held by the trust to be combined for purposes of §6166: "Although the core of the business was the Corporation, the individually owned land and buildings constituted a fundamental part of the overall operation of the wholesale automotive supply business. Thus, the Decedent was carrying on his wholesale automotive supply business as a corporation and as a proprietor of a proprietorship."

§11.24.2. Trade or Business

Section 6166 was enacted to permit the deferral of the payment of the federal estate tax where, in order to pay the tax at one time, it would be necessary to sell assets used in a going business and, thereby disrupt or destroy the business enterprise. This section was not intended to protect continued management of income producing property or to permit deferral of tax merely because the payment of tax might make necessary the sale of income-producing, except where they formed a part of an active enterprise producing business income, rather than income solely from the ownership of property ownership. Section 6166 was intended to apply only with respect to a business such as a manufacturing, mercantile, or service enterprise, as distinguished from management of investment assets. LR 9832009.

Deferral is available only for interests of a proprietor, partner, or stockholder in a "trade or business." § 6166(b)(1). The term is not defined in the Code. However, several revenue rulings that were issued under former § 6166A during the time it was designated as § 6166 indicate that the trade or business must be an active one in order to qualify for deferral. Additional guidance is provided by some private letter rulings and TAMs.

Under the published rulings, a farming, manufacturing, or service enterprise is a trade or business, but a collection of investment assets is not. "[S]ection 6166 was intended to apply only with regard to a business such as a manufacturing, mercantile, or service enterprise, as distinguished from management of investment assets." Rev. Rul. 75-365, 1975-2 C.B. 471.

Real Estate Operations Classified as Trade or Business. Farm real estate constitutes a trade or business where it is operated by tenant farmers under rental agreements whereby the decedent receives a portion of the rental and bears a portion of the expenses and participates in management decisions. Rev. Rul. 75-366, 1975-2 C.B. 472. Real estate development and sales also qualify as a trade or business. Rev. Rul. 75-367, 1975-2 C.B. 472. *See also* Rev. Rul. 61-55, 1961-1 C.B. 713 (ownership, exploration, development, and operation of oil and gas properties was a trade or business, but mere ownership of royalty interests was not).

In LR 9602017, the IRS recognized that the decedent's interests in five corporations in each of which was the sole shareholder could be combined under § 6166. The active management of the real estate owned by the corporations qualified their operation to be considered to be an active trade or business. The same was true with respect to one real estate partnership in which the decedent held a 50 percent interest. Private Letter Ruling 199929025 holds that more than 30 parcels of real estate and the stock of a corporation that managed the real estate constituted a trade or business. The ruling noted that the activities of agents and employees are taken into account in determining the decedent's level of activity in the business. In contrast, the activities of independent contractors and lessees are disregarded.

Private Letter Ruling 200340012 allowed eight parcels of real estate in which the decedent owned at least a one-half interest to be aggregated and treated as a single closely held business for purposes of § 6166. Decedent was the sole owner and operator of 109 rental units on six parcels of real estate (multifamily residences owned with his son, as tenants in common). In addition, he owned a one-half interest in an LLC that operated another multifamily residence. The ruling treats the decedent as a partner in the tenancy in common with his son and in the LLC. Decedent and his son, assisted by eight part-time employees, provided all services in connection with the maintenance and operation of the properties. Another ruling allowed the aggregation of real property owned by two S corporations, all of the stock of which was owned by the decedent's revocable trust. LR 200339043. The decedent actively participated in the management and operations of the properties, assisted by employees of the two corporations.

Real Estate Operations Not Considered a Trade or Business. The rental of real estate to children in exchange for their agreement to pay taxes and other expenses of the property does not qualify as a trade or business. LR 8020101. Similarly, The

National Office has ruled that leasing ranchland to a corporation did not constitute a trade or business. LR 9403004 (TAM).

Trusts. In some cases a decedent's interest in a trade or business that is held in a trust will qualify as an active trade or business. For example, in LR 9015003, deferral was allowed with respect to a grantor's one-third interest in timber property that was held in trust. The trustee who directly managed the timber property was considered to be an agent for the three grantors, all of whom participated "in the decision process in running the timber business." In LR 9801009, the IRS held that real estate interests that the decedent transferred to a revocable trust two weeks prior to his death constituted a trade or business for purposes of §6166. Under §6166(b)(2)(C), the property owned by the trust was considered to be owned proportionately by the beneficiaries. In this instance the IRS considered the decedent's level of activity in managing the assets to be sufficient because they were more than those of a mere owner managing investment assets for the rent they would normally produce. §101(a).

§11.24.3. Passive Assets, §611(b)(9); Farmhouses, §6166(b)(3)

The value of passive assets owned by a business is not taken into account in determining whether the 35 percent requirement of §6166(a)(1) has been satisfied. §6166(b)(9). For this purpose a passive asset is any asset other than one used in the trade or business. §6166(b)(9)(B)(i). By way of example, the IRS has treated the proceeds of a policy that insured the life of a sole proprietor and that was used from time to time as security for business loans as a passive asset. LR 8848002 (TAM). On the other hand, the proceeds received by a real estate corporation in eminent domain were not passive assets if reinvested within three years. LR 8829013. If the eminent domain proceeds were not reinvested, they would be treated as a disposition as of the first day of the replacement period.

Stock in Other Corporations. Stock in any other corporation is generally treated as a passive asset. §6166(b)(9)(B)(ii). However, stock in another corporation does not constitute a passive asset in two cases. The first applies where a §6166(b)(8) holding company election is involved; the other where the other corporation is closely held and 80 percent or more of the value of both corporations is involved in an active trade or business.

As discussed in §11.24.5, if the requirements of §6166(b)(8) are met, an executor may elect to treat stock in a business company that is owned directly or indirectly by a holding company as owned by the shareholders of the holding company. Such stock is not a passive asset. §6166(b)(9)(B)(ii)(I). For this purpose only non-readily tradeable stock is taken into account. §6166(b)(8)(B). Also, an estate that elects under §6166(b)(8) is treated as having elected not to defer the time for payment of the first installment of principal and the favorable two percent interest rate is not applicable to the deferred tax.

The second exception applies if a corporation owns 20 percent or more of the value of the voting stock of another corporation or the other corporation has 45 or fewer shareholders and 80 percent or more of the value of the assets of each corporation is attributable to assets used in a trade or business. In such a case the corporations are treated as one for purposes of §6166(b)(9)(B)(iii). Accordingly, there is no "stock in another corporation" for purposes of applying the passive asset rule.

For purposes of the 35 percent requirement of §6166(a) a closely-held business that is engaged in farming "includes an interest in residential buildings and related improvements on the farm which are occupied on a regular basis by the owner or lessee of the farm or by persons employed by such owner or lessee for purposes of operating or maintaining the farm." §6166(b)(3).

Qualifying Lending and Finance Businesses. The 2001 Act added a special provision that allows the estate tax attributable to interests in qualifying lending and finance businesses to be paid in five equal installments. §6166(b)(10). This rule, which narrowly defines the businesses to which it applies, allows any asset used in such a business to be treated as an asset used in a trade or business for pur–poses of §6166. Deferral is not available with respect to any interest in an entity if the stock or debt of the entity or a group of which the entity was a member was readily tradeable on an established securities or secondary market. §6166(b)(10)(B)(iii).

§11.24.4. Partnerships and Stock That Is Not Readily Tradeable, §6166(b)(7)

Deferral on less favorable terms may be available for the estates of decedents which include interests in partnerships or stock that is not readily tradeable, but do not qualify for deferral under the basic provisions of §6166. In particular, a form of deferral may be available although a decedent's interest does not qualify as a closely-held business under §6166(b)(2)(B) or (C). Deferral is available under §6166(b)(7) if the decedent is treated as having owned 20 percent or more of the value of the partnership or corporation after the application of the entity ownership and family attribution rules of §6166(b)(2).

If an executor elects to claim the benefits of §6166(b)(7), he or she is treated as having elected to make the first payment on the date the federal estate tax return is due. That is, the executor may not elect to defer making the first installment payment, which otherwise could be deferred for five years. In addition, the favorable two percent rate of interest, that otherwise applies to some or all of the tax attributable to the closely-held business does not apply. §6166(b)(7)(A)(ii), (iii).

Under §6166(b)(7)(B), stock qualifies as not readily tradeable if there was no market for the stock on an exchange or in an over-the-counter market at the time of the decedent's death.

EXAMPLE 11-26.

When *T* died she owned 10% in value of the voting stock of TNT, Inc., which had 50 shareholders. Thus *T*'s estate could not satisfy the alternate requirements of §6166(b)(1)(C). *T*'s sister, *S*, owned an additional 10% in value of the voting stock of TNT, Inc. There was no market for stock in TNT, Inc. on any exchange or on the over-the-counter market. *T*'s gross estate had a total value of $4,200,000, of which the stock in TNT, Inc. comprised $2,000,000. Items allowable as deductions under §§2053 and 2054 amounted to $200,000. *T*'s interest in TNT, Inc. does not meet the requirements of §6166(b)(1)(C). However, *T* is treated as owning the 10% of the stock held by *S*. If *T*'s executor elects to take advantage of §6166(b)(7), *T* will be treated as owning 20% in value of the stock of TNT,

Inc., which satisfies the requirement of §6166(b)(2)(C). In addition, the TNT, Inc. stock owned by *T* and included in her estate more than satisfies the percentage requirement of §6166(a)(2)—the value of her stock represents 50% of her adjusted gross estate ($2,000,000) ($4,200,000 — $200,000)). Thus, half of the estate tax due from *T*'s estate may be paid in installments. §6166(a)(2). The first installment is due on the date provided for payment of the federal estate tax and the special 2% rate of interest does not apply to any portion of the deferred tax.

§11.24.5. Holding Companies, §6166(b)(8)

The 1984 Act added §6166(b)(8) which clarified the extent to which deferral is allowable under §6166 with respect to a decedent's interest in a holding company. Previously it was unclear whether the ownership of shares in a holding company could constitute the conduct of an active trade or business required by §6166. For purposes of §6166(b)(8), "the term 'holding company' means any corporation holding stock in another corporation," and "the term 'business company' means any corporation carrying on a trade or business." §6166(b)(8)(D). Note, however, that stock is only taken into account if it is not readily marketable, §61661(b)(8)(B) (*i.e.*, there is no market for it on a stock exchange or in an over-the-counter market), §6166(b)(7)(B). If an election is made under §6166(b)(8), the estate is treated as having elected not to defer the time for payment of the first installment of principal and the favorable two percent interest rate is unavailable with respect to the deferred tax. §6166(b)(8)(A)(ii), (iii).

Under §6166(b)(8), a decedent's executor may elect to treat "the portion of the stock of any holding company which represents direct ownership (or indirect ownership through 1 or more other holding companies) by such company in a business company" as stock in such business company. In effect, if an election is made under §6166(b)(8), a decedent who owned shares in a holding company is treated as owning a proportional interest in each business in which the holding company held an interest.

Deferral under the special provisions of §6166(b)(8) is only available if the stock which the decedent is deemed to have owned in the business company meets the percentage requirements of §6166(b)(1)(C). For this purpose §6166(b)(8)(C) provides that the stock the decedent is deemed to have owned is "treated as voting stock to the extent that . . . the holding company owns directly (or through the stock of 1 or more other holding companies) voting stock in the business company."

§11.25.   QUALIFICATION UNDER §6166

The election must be made no later than the time the estate tax return is required to be filed, taking into account any extensions of time that are granted for filing the return. §6166(d).

If it is made at the time the estate tax return is filed, the election is applicable both to the tax originally determined to be due and to certain deficiencies. If no election is made when the estate tax return is filed, up to the full amount of certain later deficiencies (but not any tax originally determined to be due) may be paid in installments. Reg. § 20.6166-1(a).

An election must contain the following:

1. the decedent's name and taxpayer identification number;
2. the amount of tax to be paid in installments;
3. the date for payment of the first installment;
4. the number of installments in which the tax is to be paid;
5. the properties shown on the estate tax return that constitute the closely-held business; and
6. the facts that form the basis of the executor's conclusion that the estate qualifies for payment of the tax in installments. Reg. § 20.6166-1(b).

§ 11.25.1. Protective Election

Although an estate does not appear to satisfy the requirements of § 6166 when the return is filed, the executor may make a protective election to defer payment of any portion of the tax remaining unpaid at the time values are finally determined and any deficiencies that are attributable to the closely-held business. "A protective election is made by filing a notice of election with a timely filed estate tax return stating that the election is being made." Reg. § 20.6166-1(d).

§ 11.25.2. Acceptance or Rejection of Election

The District Director is responsible for determining whether an election meets the requirements of § 6166. Rev. Proc. 79-55, 1979-2 C.B. 539. Under Revenue Procedure 79-55, if the District Director determines that an election satisfies the requirements of § 6166 no notice will be given to the executor. If the District Director determines that an election is not proper, the executor will be notified. Upon request the determination can be reviewed at an appellate conference. The IRS will communicate the decision on appeal to the executor. Also, under Revenue Procedure 79-55, "An executor, etc., may request that the issue of whether the election under section 6166 . . . is proper be referred to the National Office for technical advice on the grounds that a lack of uniformity exists as to the disposition of the issue, or that the issue is so unusual or complex as to warrant consideration by the National Office."

The Tax Court does not have jurisdiction over a § 6166 determination made by the IRS. *Estate of Floyd Sherrod*, 82 T.C. 523 (1984), *rev'd on other grounds*, 774 F.2d 1057 (11th Cir.), *cert. denied*, 479 U.S. 814 (1986). However, the Tax Court does have jurisdiction to determine the deductibility of interest payments as expenses of administration, which may have an effect on the qualification of the estate for deferral under § 6166. *Estate of Dorothy H. Meyer*, 84 T.C. 560 (1985).

The IRS cannot insist upon a bond or a special lien on certain assets under § 6324A before accepting an otherwise valid and timely election under § 6166. *Estate of Edward P. Roski*, 128 T.C. 113 (2007). In *Estate of Roski*, the IRS required the estate seeking § 6166 relief either to post a bond equal to twice the amount of tax deferred or elect to provide a special lien under § 6324A. The estate immediately replied to the IRS, asking the IRS not to require the posting of a bond or the imposition of a special lien. Its letter listed several reasons for the request, including the fact that no bonding company was willing to underwrite such a large amount for the duration of the payment period, that the nature of the family business and the acumen of its manager mitigated the risk of default, and that a special lien would hurt the estate's ability to carry on the business (directly contrary to the policy of §6166). The IRS replied with a notice of determination that the estate could not make a §6166 election.

When the estate challenged this determination in a Tax Court petition, the IRS moved to dismiss for lack of jurisdiction. It argued that the requirement of a bond or special lien is not within the scope of the court's review jurisdiction under §7479, the special rule added in 1997 that gives the court power to review disputes involving §6166 elections. According to the IRS, §7479 gives the Tax Court jurisdiction to review only whether an estate is eligible to make a §6166 election. The *Estate of Roski* court rejected this interpretation, concluding it had jurisdiction in this matter. "Ironically, respondent argues that we have jurisdiction over only the eligibility requirements for the section 6166 election while simultaneously taking the position that the provision of a bond or a special lien is required for any estate to be eligible for the election." The Service's interpretation of §7479, said the court, "would frustrate the legislative purpose behind both sections 6166 and 7479. Congress enacted section 7479 because '[it] believed that taxpayers should have access to the courts to resolve disputes over an estate's eligibility for the section 6166 election, without requiring potential liquidation of the assets that the installment provisions of sections 6166 are designed to protect.'" Furthermore, the court held that the IRS has no authority to require a bond or a special lien in every case. By doing so, the IRS is effectively adding requirements to the statute, and that is for Congress to do. The bond obligation was intended to be discretionary, not mandatory. "Implicit in this grant of discretion is a statutory obligation to exercise discretion." The court did not go so far as to hold that the estate should not be required to post a bond or grant a special lien; instead it held only that the IRS could not summarily require a bond or a lien in every §6166 election.

In response to *Estate of Roski*, the IRS has announced that it will propose regulations establishing standards to be applied on a case-by-case basis for determining when a bond or lien will be required. Notice 2007-90, 2007-2 C.B. 1003. In the meantime, the IRS will consider three factors in determining on a case-by-case basis whether there is a sufficient credit risk to warrant a bond or special lien: (1) the duration and stability of the business (including the nature of the business, market factors, and managerial experience); (2) the ability to pay the installments of tax and interest in a timely manner; and (3) the business's compliance history with respect to all federal tax payment and filing requirements. The IRS indicated this approach will be used for all §6166 elections made after November 12, 2007, and for all estates under audit as of April 12, 2007.

§11.25.3. Overpayments

The overpayment of an installment will be applied against future installments. An estate may not obtain a refund of an excess payment and enjoy the privilege of deferred payment of the balance of the estate tax. *Estate of Laura V. Bell*, 92 T.C. 714, *aff'd*, 928 F.2d 901 (9th Cir. 1991).

§ 11.25.4. Deficiencies

If an estate tax deficiency is asserted, the estate qualifies for deferral, and the executor has made no prior election, the executor may elect to defer the deficiency under § 6166(a). § 6166(h)(1). However, deferral is not available with respect to deficiencies due to negligence, intentional disregard of rules, or fraud with intent to evade taxes. The election must be made not later than 60 days after the IRS issues a notice of deficiency. § 6166(h)(2).

If an election is made to defer payment of a deficiency, the deficiency is prorated to the installments which would have been due had the election been timely made when the estate tax return was filed. § 6166(h)(3). The portion of the deficiency prorated to installments which would already have been due must be paid at the time the election is made. *Id.*

§ 11.26. INSTALLMENT PAYMENTS UNDER § 6166

Under § 6166(a)(2), the maximum amount of the estate tax (reduced by credits against the tax) that can be paid in installments is determined by the ratio of the value of the closely-held business to the adjusted gross estate. Thus, the formula is:

$$\frac{\text{Value of Closely-Held Business}}{\text{Adjusted Gross Estate}} \times \text{Net Estate Tax} = \text{Amount Subject to Deferral}$$

Again, for purposes of § 6166 the term "adjusted gross estate" means the gross estate reduced by the amount of deductions allowable under §§ 2053 and 2054, whether or not actually claimed as deductions. § 6166(b)(6). The tax may be paid in two to ten equal annual installments, the first of which is due not more than five years after the date on which the federal estate tax was due to be paid. § 6166(a)(3). (The first payment of principal attributable to an interest that is not readily marketable, § 6166(b)(7), or to a holding company, § 6166(b)(8), is due with the return.) Each succeeding installment is due on or before a date one year after the due date for the preceding payment.

Interest Payments. If the executor elects to take advantage of the maximum deferral, usually only interest is paid for a maximum of four years following the date on which the estate tax was due to be paid. § 6166(f)(1). Interest and principal payments are due in each of the following years until all of the installment payments have been made.

Estates of Decedents Dying Before 1998. The estates of decedents who died prior to 1998 pay a preferential interest rate of four percent on the greater of, (1) $345,800 less the amount of the unified credit applicable to the decedent's estate (a maximum of $192,800) and (2) the amount of the estate tax that is deferred under § 6166. § 6601(j). Thus, the four percent rate usually applied to $153,000, which is equal to the estate tax on the first $1 million of the closely-held business included in the decedent's estate less the allowable unified credit. The balance is subject to a rate equal to the variable short-term federal rate plus three percent. § 6621(a)(2).

Under § 6601(j)(3), each principal payment of tax reduces proportionally the amounts that are subject to the four percent and the variable interest rates. Specifically, each principal payment reduces the portion of the tax that is subject to the four percent rate by an amount that bears the same ratio to the amount of the principal payment as the original amount of the four percent portion bears to the total amount of tax deferred under §6166. A formula puts it more concisely:

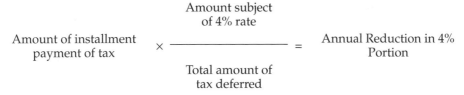

$$\text{Amount of installment payment of tax} \times \frac{\text{Amount subject of 4\% rate}}{\text{Total amount of tax deferred}} = \text{Annual Reduction in 4\% Portion}$$

Deduction for Interest Payments. The estates of persons dying prior to 1998 may deduct the annual payments of interest on the deferred tax as administration expenses under §2053(a)(2). Rev. Rul. 78-125, 1978-1 C.B. 292. However, the deduction is only allowed for interest actually paid—not for estimated future payments. *Estate of Pierre L. Bailly,* 81 T.C. 246 (1983), *on reconsideration,* 81 T.C. 949 (1983). The allowance of additional deductions for interest payments of course reduces the amount of estate tax, including the amount of future installments. As each interest payment is made the estate should file a supplemental Form 706, captioned "Supplemental Information." Rev. Proc. 81-27, 1981-2 C.B. 548. According to the IRS the supplemental 706 can be filed with the annual installment payment or later.

Estates of Decedents Dying After 1997. The 1997 Act amended §6601(j) to increase the amount of estate tax that is subject to the lower, preferential, interest rate and to reduce the rates of interest imposed on the entire amount of the deferred estate tax. As a tradeoff, the Act also amended §§163 and 2053 to eliminate, for estates subject to the new rates, any income and estate tax deductions for interest paid on the deferred estate tax.

An interest rate of two percent applies to so much of the deferred tax as does not exceed the tentative tax that would be imposed on the sum of a taxable estate of $1 million adjusted for inflation plus the amount of the applicable exclusion amount applicable under §2010(c). This tentative tax is then reduced by the applicable credit amount. The resulting amount is the maximum amount of deferred tax eligible for the two-percent rate. The maximum amount is adjusted, in case of the estates of decedents dying after 1998, in $10,000 increments for increases in the inflation rate after 1997. The two-percent rate does not apply with respect to interests in holding companies and nonreadily tradable business interests. They are, instead, be subject to the higher rate.

Under the 1997 Act, interest on the amount of the deferred estate tax above the amount that is subject to the two-percent ceiling is imposed at a variable rate equal to 45 percent of the federal short-term rate plus three percent. Apparently the latter rate is loosely based on the difference between the net cost of paying the full amount of the interest rate that previously applied (*i.e.,* the short-term rate plus three percent) and the maximum estate tax benefit of a deduction of that amount at that time (*i.e.,* 100%—55% = 45%). The trade-off is that no deduction for interest payments is allowed for income or estate tax purposes.

Deduction for Additional Administration Expenses. In recomputing the amount of the estate tax, deductions may be allowed for additional attorney's and accountant's fees incurred in the administration of the estate. LR 9246005. The ruling states that if the IRS does not allow a deduction for the additional administration expenses after the final installment payment is made the estate may file a claim for refund.

§11.27. ACCELERATION UNDER §6166(g)

The deferral election is terminated and the date for payment of the tax is accelerated under a variety of circumstances enumerated in §6166(g). Acceleration occurs if one-half or more in value of the decedent's interest in the business is redeemed, sold, exchanged, or otherwise disposed of. Thus, the sale of a decedent's interest in a closely-held business pursuant to a buy-sell agreement would accelerate the time for payment of the tax. However, acceleration does not occur as a result of certain dispositions. Corporate reorganizations and tax-free exchanges are exempted by §6166(g)(1)(C). A liquidation under §331 after which the same business is continued by a partnership, in which the estate and other parties will have the same proportionate interest as before, does not constitute a disposition or withdrawal of assets. LR 8103066. Similarly, a liquidation under §331 and distribution of the corporation's assets to a family trust was not treated as a disposition or withdrawal of assets for purposes of §6166(g). LR 8829013.

The sale of a portion of the assets of a business, such as a farm, in order to pay mortgages on the property is treated as a transaction in the ordinary course of business that does not constitute a disposition that would trigger acceleration. LR 8441029. In contrast, the sale by one beneficiary to another of real property used in the farming business is a disposition. LR 8730006.

Coordinating §§303 and 6166. Redemptions made under §303 can be coordinated with the provisions of §6166(g)(1)(B) so there is no acceleration. For example, in LR 9202020 the IRS ruled that there would be no acceleration under a buy-sell agreement that provided for redemption of as much stock as would qualify for treatment as a sale or exchange under §303 on a schedule that was coordinated with the extended payment of the estate tax under §6166. The agreement also provided for an increase of the redemption price for redemptions made more than three years after the death of a shareholder.

In LR 9427029, the IRS held that a recapitalization did not involve a disposition of the decedent's stock for purposes of §6166(g) (the operating company in which the decedent held stock was to be merged into a newly created subsidiary of a holding company). The ruling continued to say that the recapitalization would not subject the decedent's stock to the provisions of §6166(b)(8) or (9). Those provisions only apply to the decedent's interest at the time of death.

§11.27.1. Distribution Under Will, §6166(g)(1)(D)

Acceleration is not triggered by a distribution of an interest in a decedent's business to a person entitled to receive it by reason of the decedent's will, the law of intestate succession, or a trust created by the decedent. §6166(g)(1)(D). *See, e.g.,* LR 8339023 (the division of a farm into two parcels by the decedent's heirs does not trigger acceleration, but discontinuance of the use of the property as a farm would accelerate). Likewise, a transfer by reason of the subsequent death of a person who received the property from the decedent (or a transferee of such person) is also exempt, provided that each transferee is a family member (within the meaning of §267(c)(4)) of the transferor. §6166(g)(1)(D).

Under §6166(g)(1)(D), no acceleration takes place when there is a transfer by the decedent "to a person entitled by reason of the decedent's death to receive the property under the decedent's will, the applicable law of descent and distribution, or a trust created by the decedent." In LR 9149015, the IRS held that there was no acceleration when an estate distributed stock to a trust. However, there was acceleration when an individual exercised an option to buy the stock from the trust.

The transfer by a distributee of an interest in the decedent's business to a grantor trust is not a disposition that will trigger acceleration. LR 8326023. The result reached in LR 8326023 is consistent with that reached in other contexts. For example, the transfer of an installment obligation to a grantor trust is not treated as a disposition under §453B. *See* §9.6.3.

§11.27.2. Withdrawals of Money or Other Property, §6166(g)(1)

The time for payment of the tax is accelerated if half or more of the value of interests in the business are distributed, sold, withdrawn from the business. §6166(g)(1)(A). However, a redemption that qualifies under §303 is not counted for purposes of the one-half withdrawal rule if an amount equal to the redemption distribution is paid on the remaining balance of the estate tax within one year of the distribution. §6166(g)(1)(B). Instead, under this exception the amount of the redemption reduces the base against which the one-half is calculated. *Id.*

EXAMPLE 11-27.

D's adjusted gross estate had a value of $4,100,000 upon which a net estate tax of $1,000,000 was due after giving effect to all allowable credits. *D*'s interest in a closely-held corporation was worth $3,100,000 or about 75.6% of *D*'s adjusted gross estate. Pursuant to an election made by *D*'s executor, the time for payment of $756,000 of the tax was deferred under §6166. Under §6166(g)(1)(A) the time for payment of the tax would be accelerated if one-half or more in value of the estate's stock were redeemed, sold, exchanged, or otherwise disposed of. Thus, acceleration would take place if the estate redeemed or disposed of a total of $1,550,000 or more of *D*'s stock unless some payments were made on the estate tax liability. However, under §6166(g)(1)(B) amounts received in a distribution that met the requirements of §303 are not counted if they are applied in payment of the tax. Thus, if $300,000 of *D*'s stock were redeemed under §303 and the proceeds were applied in payment of the tax, the amount of the redemption would not be counted toward the one-half limit. Instead, the base for computing the one-half limit would be reduced from $3,100,000 to $2,800,000. In effect, the withdrawal and application of funds in payment of the principal amount of the tax only causes a one-half reduction in the amount that can be withdrawn without restriction as to its use.

Until 1986, it was unclear whether the exception of §6166(g)(1)(B) would be applied on a "redemption-by-redemption" basis, a "cumulative" basis, or both. The redemption-by-redemption approach requires the estate to pay the amount or a §303 redemption toward the estate tax and interest within one year following the receipt of the redemption distribution. An estate might experience difficulty in satisfying this test—funds received in a §303 redemption could be required for other purposes, such as the payment of debts or expenses of administration. Under the cumulative approach the total of all §303 redemptions may not exceed the total of all estate tax and interest payments made within one year following the redemption distribution. The application of the funds received in a particular redemption is disregarded. Happily, in Rev. Rul. 86-54, 1986-1 C.B. 356, the IRS ruled that it will "permit the cumulative approach and the redemption-by-redemption approach to be used interchangeably. Estates, therefore, may qualify for the exclusion under section 6166(g)(1)(B) if a section 303 redemption (or each of a series of redemptions) qualifies under either approach."

§11.27.3. Estate Has Undistributed Income, §6166(g)(2)

If an estate has undistributed net income for a taxable year ending on or after the date for payment of the first installment, the estate must pay an amount equal to the undistributed income toward the tax on or before the date the income tax return must be filed for the year. §6166(g)(2).

§11.27.4. Failure to Pay Income and Principal on Time, §6166(g)(3)

If any payment of principal or interest is not made on time, the unpaid portion of the tax must be paid upon notice and demand from the Secretary. §6166(g)(3). However, if the delinquent amount is paid within six months of the time it was due, acceleration does not occur. Instead, the preferential interest rate does not apply to the payment and a penalty of five percent of the amount of the payment is imposed for each month the payment was late. §6166(g)(3)(B).

§11.28. WORKSHEET FOR MAKING §6166 INTEREST AND TAX PAYMENT ESTIMATES

Software programs allow projections and calculations involving §6166 to be made. They should differentiate between the estates of persons dying before 1998 and after 1997. A program for the former should make the interrelated computations that are required in order to take into account the deductibility of the interest paid by the estate on the amount of the tax deferral. If a program is not readily available the following form can be used to make an estimate.

Section 6166 Worksheet (Fifteen-year deferral)

Part I. Qualifications

1. Gross estate (estimate or enter from Form 706, page 1, line 1, including the value of property transferred within 3 years of death per §2035(a)) (item 1) $_____

2. *Less:* Deductions allowable under § 2053 and 2054, whether or not claimed on Form 706:

   a. Debts, funeral, and administrative expenses (allowable under § 2053)   _____

   b. Casualty losses (allowable under § 2054)   +_____

   Total (item 2)   −_____

3. Adjusted gross estate (item 1 less item 2) (item 3) $_____

4. Value of closely-held business (a proprietorship, partnership, or corporation carrying on a trade or business in which decedent was one of 45 or fewer owners or in which decedent owned 20% or more of the capital interest. § 6166(b). Two or more businesses may be aggregated if at least 20% of the total value of each business is included in the decedent's estate. § 6166(c)) (item 4) $_____

5. Divide item 4 by item 3. (If the closely-held business represents more than 35% of the adjusted gross estate, item 3, the requirements of § 6166 are met.) (item 5)   _____

Part II. Amount to be deferred

6. Net federal estate tax (estimate or enter from Form 706, line 21) (item 6)   _____

   Plus: GSTT on direct skips   +_____

   Total § 2001 taxes $_____

7. Enter percentage from item 5 above (item 7)   _____

8. Maximum deferrable amount (item 6 × item 7) (item 8) $_____

9. Years over which payments to be made (2-10) (item 9)   _____

(The executor may elect to pay part or all of the amount of tax shown at item 8 in 2-10 equal installments, the first of which is due no more than 5 years after the date prescribed for payment of the tax (9 months after death). Under § 2056(b)(7) and (b)(8) the first payment of principal of the tax on holding company stock and on nonreadily tradable interests is due with Form 706. Each succeeding installment is due one year after the preceding installment. § 6166(a)(3).)

10. Amount of annual principal installments (divide item 8 by item 9) (item 10)   _____

Part III. Interest rates

A. Estates of Decedents Dying After 1997

11. Amount of tax deferred (item 8 above) (item 11)   _____

12. Amount subject to special 2% interest rate

   a. Applicable exclusion amount   _____

   b. $1,000,000   + $1,000,000

   c. Sum (item 12(a) plus item 12(b))   _____

   d. Estate tax credit available at decedent's death (item 12)   _____

13. Initial amount subject to variable rate, item 11 less (item 12) (item 13) $_____

B. Estates of Decedents Dying Before 1998

14. Amount of tax deferred (item 8 above) (item 14) _____

15. Amount subject to special 4% interest rate _____

   a. $345,800 _____

   b. Estate tax credit available at decedent's death _____

   c. Difference (item 15(a) less item 15(b)) _____

   d. Lesser of item 15(c) or item 14 (item 15). _____

16. amount subject to variable rate (item 14 less item 15) (item 16) _____

Part IV. Amount of payments years 1-4) for Decedent Dying After 1997 (Estimated)

17. Estimated annual interest payments, years 1-4: Item 12 × 2% _____

   Plus: Item 13 × estimated variable rate +_____

   Total payment, years 1-4 (item 17) _____

18. Estimated total payments years 1-4 (item 17 × 4) _____

Part V. Payments in years 5-14 (Estimated)

The amounts payable will vary if any amount of the deferred tax is subject to the variable rate or if payments are accelerated voluntarily or involuntarily. Also, the amount payable by the estates of persons dying before 1998 is generally smaller in each successive year because the amount of interest paid is deductible under § 2053. Because the IRS will not allow the deduction until the interest has actually been paid, the amount of the federal estate tax must be recalculated after each payment. *See* § 12.13. Each principal payment reduces the amount subject to each interest rate by a proportionate amount. *See* § 6601(j)(3).

E. FAMILY LIMITED PARTNERSHIPS AND LLCS

§ 11.29. OVERVIEW

By forming a business entity a client can add some arrows to the estate planner's quiver. As shown above, estates can utilize the benefit of § 303 to minimize the income tax consequences of paying estate tax and other administrative expenses. Planners can also use § 6166 in many cases to defer the payment of estate tax over a substantial period. Perhaps the most significant benefit of the business interest is the application of valuation discounts, chiefly the discounts for lack of marketability and minority interests. These two discounts conceivably apply to any minority interest that is not readily marketable, but they are most commonly applied to business interests. Accordingly, it has become an accepted practice for clients with substantial investment assets to transfer them to a newly formed entity like a limited partnership or LLC, converting their holdings from investment assets to business interests in an FLP. This facilitates discounted gifting and better utilizes a client's applicable exclusion amount with respect to interests still held by the client at death. Although these FLPs would not normally qualify for § 303 or § 6166 because the entities usually do not engage in an active trade or business, they can still qualify for valuation discounts.

The IRS has never approved of this technique, although most of its attempts to defeat the use of FLPs and LLCs to discount the value of investment assets have failed. This part considers many of the attacks launched by the IRS against the FLP technique. The analysis separates the unsuccessful arguments from the successful ones. Discussion of the successful arguments includes, where appropriate, suggestions for planning around these attacks.

§11.30. FAILED IRS ATTACKS

The IRS cannot be accused of permitting the FLP technique to go unchallenged. A number of IRS arguments against the use of FLPs and LLCs have been rejected by courts, leading the IRS on some occasions to withdraw the arguments in pending cases.

§11.30.1. Gift on Formation

The IRS has argued that a taxpayer makes a gift to other partners to the extent the FLP interest received in exchange for contributed assets is less than the value of the contributed assets. *See, e.g.,* LR 9842003 (TAM). Thus, for example, if a taxpayer contributes $1,000,000 in assets to the FLP in exchange for general and limited partner interests worth, after applicable discounts, only $700,000, the IRS argues the taxpayer has made a $300,000 gift to the other partners. This argument has some force if the other partners have made no contributions of their own to the FLP, but to date no court has agreed with the IRS that a gift on formation occurs even where all the partners make pro rata contributions. In *Church v. United States*, 85 AFTR2d (RIA) 804 (W.D.Tex. 2000), for example, the court concluded that no gift on formation occurs where the partners make proportionate property contributions.

> Implicit in the Government's argument is the notion that since the value of Mrs. Church's Partnership interest was less than the assets she contributed, someone must have received a gratuitous transfer of the difference. This was not the case, and never could be in the formation of a business entity in which each investor's interest is proportional to the capital contributed.

See also Estate of Albert Strangi, 115 T.C. 478 (2000), *aff'd* on this issue, *Gulig v. Commissioner*, 293 F.3d 279 (5th Cir. 2002) (gift on formation argument rejected); *Estate of Theodore R. Thompson*, T.C. Memo. 2002-246, *aff'd*, 382 F.3d 367 (3d Cir. 2004) (transfers did not shift wealth to other partners but "simply caused them to lose value").

Where the founders of the FLP are married, there is even less concern, as any gift on formation would be eligible for the marital deduction.

Additional Contributions as Gifts to Other Partners. Although the gift at formation argument is dead, a related argument is very much alive. Where a partner makes an additional contribution to the FLP's capital without a corresponding increase in the contributing partner's capital account, there is effectively a gift to the other partners. *See* §2.5.7. This is akin to the rule that additional contributions to the capital of a corporation are indirect gifts to the other shareholders. Reg.

§ 25.2511-1(h)(1). In the FLP context, the IRS takes the position that the amount of the gift is equal to the undiscounted value of the property contributed to the FLP. LR 200212006 (TAM) (contribution of municipal bonds ruled to be indirect gifts of bonds with no discount allowed in determining the value of the gifts). The letter ruling went one step further, concluding that the same result applies even if the contributing partner's capital account is credited with the value of the contributed property. This last step is questionable—as long as the contributing partner's capital account reflects the value of the contributed property, there can hardly be a gift to the other partners since the contributing partner's increased capital account effectively preserves the partner's ability to get the added value back at liquidation.

Certainly the position of the IRS has merit where the added value from an additional contribution is reflected in the capital accounts of the noncontributing partners. Thus, in *J.C. Shepherd*, 115 T.C. 376 (2000), *aff'd* 283 F.3d 1258 (11th Cir. 2002), a father made gifts to his two sons when he contributed land and stock to the FLP in which his sons each held 25-percent interests because the transfers were allocated proportionately to each partner's capital account rather than to the father's capital account only. The concurring and dissenting opinion of Judge Beghe in *Shepherd* added humor and analysis: "With all the woofing these days about using family partnerships to generate big discounts, the majority opinion provides salutary reminders that the 'gift' is measured by the value of the property passing from the donor, rather than by the property received by the donee or upon the measure of enrichment of the donee . . . This is the 'estate depletion' theory of the gift tax, given its most cogent expression by the Supreme Court in *Commissioner v. Wemyss*, 324 U.S. 303 (1945)."

There is authority that indirect gifts to the other partners from additional contributions will qualify for the gift tax annual exclusion. *Wooley v. United States*, 736 F.Supp. 1506 (S.D. Ind. 1990).

Where partners make additional contributions to an FLP, detailed records of the contributions and their effects on the partners' capital accounts should be maintained and preserved. Lack of documentation to support the taxpayer's claims that contributions to the FLP increased their own capital accounts prior to making gifts of FLP interests to beneficiaries doomed the taxpayers in *Mark and Michele Senda*, T.C. Memo. 2004-160, *aff'd*, 433 F.3d 1044 (2006). As the court concluded, the taxpayers "presented no reliable evidence that they contributed the stock to the partnerships before they transferred the partnership interests to the children. At best, the transactions were integrated (as asserted by respondent) and, in effect, simultaneous."

Gifts at Formation as Indirect Gifts of Property Contributed to FLP. The IRS has also argued that when partners form an FLP and give a significant percentage of their limited partnership interests to their beneficiaries shortly after formation, there is effectively an indirect gift of a proportionate share of the assets. This is a variation of the common law step transaction doctrine, for the IRS claims that the transfers to the partnership and the transfers of the limited partner interests are interdependent and thus should be viewed as equivalent to the contributing partners gifting shares of the underlying assets and not (discounted) FLP interests.

The argument did not work in *Thomas H. Holman, Jr.*, 130 T.C. 170 (2008), *aff'd*, 601 F.3d 763 (8th Cir. 2010). In that case, the taxpayers (a father and mother) formed an FLP by transferring a large block of stock in Dell Computer Corp. for general and limited partnership interests. Six days later, the taxpayers gifted a total 84.32 percent limited partnership interest for the benefit of their children. The IRS argued that the gift represented an indirect gift of 84.32 percent of the Dell stock and not direct gifts of limited partner interests. The Tax Court rejected this argument, finding that the six-day delay between the funding and gift transfers was meaningful in that the taxpayer and his spouse had a genuine economic risk of a change in the net asset value of the partnership during that time. Thus, where there is some meaningful period of time between formation of the FLP and gift transfers of limited partnership interests, there is little worry about the IRS's indirect gift argument.

§11.30.2. Economic Substance Doctrine

One of the first attacks launched by the IRS in the 1990s was the argument that an FLP or LLC should be disregarded for transfer tax purposes if it lacks economic substance or a business purpose. At its core the argument urges that an FLP or LLC be ignored if the entity is a sham, formed only to generate valuation discounts. The IRS advanced this argument in court proceedings and administrative rulings. *See, e.g.,* LR 9842003 (TAM); *Ina F. Knight*, 115 T.C. 506 (2000). The Tax Court in *Knight* rejected this argument, finding it sufficient that both the partnership and the transfer restrictions imposed on partnership interests in the partnership agreement were enforceable under state law.

The IRS routinely lost the economic substance argument. *See, e.g., Estate of W.W. Jones II*, 116 T.C. 121 (2001) (court refused to disregard partnerships even though court determined partnerships were created to generate discounts); *Estate of Theodore R. Thompson*, T.C. Memo. 2002-246, *aff'd*, 382 F.3d 367 (3d Cir. 2004) (because potential buyers of assets would not disregard the partnerships, they had "sufficient substance to be recognized for Federal estate and gift tax purposes").

The IRS acknowledged defeat in *Estate of Elma Dailey*, T.C. Memo. 2002-301, when the court awarded attorney fees to the estate with respect to the issue of economic substance. The IRS conceded it was not substantially justified in arguing the partnership at issue lacked economic substance. Since *Dailey*, the IRS has essentially abandoned the economic substance argument.

§11.30.3. §2703

Section 2703(a)(2) states that the value of property is to be determined without regard to any restriction on the right to sell or use the property. The IRS has argued that the FLP itself is a restriction on the right to sell or use the assets transferred to the FLP by the contributing partners. *See, e.g.,* LR 9719006 (TAM). To reach this result, the IRS treats the initial contributions to the FLP and the subsequent transfers of limited partner interests as a single, integrated transaction. Because the partnership agreement imposes restrictions on a contributing partner's right to sell or use the assets once they are titled in the name of the FLP, says the IRS, the partnership itself is a restriction that should be ignored, meaning the transfer of FLP interests is really an undiscounted transfer of a proportionate share of each of the FLP's assets. Furthermore, since the transaction is not a bona fide arrangement but instead a device to gift property to members of the transferor's family, argues the IRS, the §2703(b) exception does not apply.

Courts have rejected this argument. In *Church v. United States*, 85 AFTR2d (RIA) 804 (W.D. Tex. 2000), the court rejected the government's contentions that under § 2703, (1) the value of the "property" to be determined is the value of the property transferred to the FLP and not the value of the decedent's interest in the FLP, and (2) the "agreement" that may be disregarded is the FLP agreement itself. According to the court, "It [the government] first suggests that the term 'property' refers to the assets Mrs. Church contributed to the Partnership prior to death, rather than her partnership interest. There is no statutory basis for this contention. Mrs. Church did not own the assets she contributed to the Partnership on the date of her death; she owned a Partnership interest." The court also stated that "The Government alternatively contends that if I.R.C. § 2703 does require taxation of Mrs. Church's Partnership interest, it may nonetheless disregard the term restriction and restrictions on sale in the Partnership Agreement that serve to reduce its market value. No case supports the Government's position, and nothing in the legislative history or the regulations adopted by the IRS itself, convince this court to read into Section 2703 something that is not there."

In *Estate of Albert Strangi*, 115 T.C. 478 (2000), *aff'd sub. nom. Gulig v. Commissioner*, 293 F.3d 279 (5th Cir. 2002), the court concluded that the "property" referred to in § 2703(a)(2) meant the FLP interests and not the entity's inside assets. This was because the decedent transferred FLP interests in a bona fide entity, not proportionate shares of the assets held by the FLP. Because there were no restrictions on the decedent's ability to transfer the FLP interests, the court held § 2703(a) inapplicable. Shortly after this and other cases, the IRS began dropping this argument in pending cases.

Restrictions on the transfer of FLP interests, however, can be disregarded if § 2703(b) does not apply. In *Smith v. Commissioner*, 94 AFTR2d (RIA) 5627 (W.D.Pa. 2004), the FLP agreement set the price and terms of purchase that would apply if the FLP exercised its right of first refusal upon the transfer of an interest in the FLP. The court held that these terms were restrictions that should be ignored in valuing the gifted interests under § 2703(a). *Smith* illustrates that restrictions on the transfer of FLP interests are subject to being disregarded under § 2703(a), but it appears well settled that § 2703(a) cannot be used to disregard the entire FLP arrangement.

A variation on the IRS's § 2703 argument, however, was successful in *Thomas H. Holman, Jr.*, 130 T.C. 170 (2008), *aff'd*, 601 F.3d 763 (8th Cir. 2010). In this case, the founding partners of an FLP made annual exclusion gifts of limited partnership interests and claimed applicable marketability and minority interest discounts. Part of the marketability discount was justified by a provision in the partnership agreement that prohibited transfers of limited partnership interests without the consent of the general partners. If a limited partner transferred his or her interest without such consent, the partnership had a right to redeem the transferred interest for its fair market value. Because the fair market value of a limited partnership is (thanks to applicable discounts) less than its share of the partnership's net asset value, the Tax Court agreed with the IRS that this redemption right was effectively a device by which the general partners (the parents) could enhance the value of the remaining limited partnership interests held for the benefit of their children. The court also agreed with the IRS that there was no business purpose for this transfer restriction in the partnership agreement because the FLP did little other than hold Dell stock. Thus, the § 2703(b) exception did not apply and the transfer restriction would be disregarded under § 2703(a)(2). The court's logic in *Holman* is twisted. It is true that the redemption of one limited partner's interest at fair market value will add to the liquidation value of the surviving partners' interests, but that does not mean the redemption right is a method by which the founding partners can make gifts to their other children. Further, and perhaps more important, the fact that this FLP was a holding company and not an active business enterprise has nothing to do with whether the redemption right itself is a bona fide business arrangement for purposes of the § 2703(b) exception. It is sufficient that such a provision would appear in any arm's length partnership agreement negotiated between unrelated partners, and that would easily be the case with the redemption right at issue in *Holman*. That the partnership itself does not engage in an active trade or business is irrelevant to the determination of whether the redemption right is a commercially reasonable provision that unrelated partners would accept.

On appeal to the Eighth Circuit, the taxpayers in *Holman* maintained that the Tax Court's decision improperly imposed an operating business requirement into § 2703(b). They claimed the "bona fide business arrangement" prong should be applied by looking only at a taxpayer's stated intentions and not the actual context or underlying assets. The appellate court concluded, however, that the Tax Court properly assessed the personal and testamentary nature of the partnership's transfer restrictions. The court agreed that the transfer restrictions were mainly intended for estate planning, tax reduction, wealth transference, protection against dissipation by the children, and education of the children. In reaching this decision, the court noted several facts that were not helpful to the taxpayers. First, the partnership was not engaged in any business activity at all. Second, it held only a small fraction of the stock in a highly liquid and easily valued company. Finally, the taxpayers expressed no intentions as to the partnership's investment strategies, including whether the partnership would hold or sell the stock.

§ 11.30.4. § 2704

The IRS has hinted that FLP interests may be subject to § 2704. FSA 200049003. The Field Service Advice does not indicate whether an attack using § 2704 would focus on § 2704(a) or § 2704(b) (or both). Under § 2704(a), the lapse of a taxpayer's voting or liquidation right with respect to an entity is treated as a transfer for wealth transfer tax purposes if the taxpayer and "members of the family" control the entity before and after the lapse. The amount of the transfer is the excess of the value of all interests held by the taxpayer immediately before the lapse over the value of such interests after the lapse. The regulations provide an example where a decedent owned a general partner interest and partnership agreement allowed any general partner to liquidate the partnership. The decedent's death caused the decedent to lose this power, and this was treated as a transfer at death. Reg. § 25.2704-1(f), Example (5). Supposedly, the IRS could argue that where an FLP continues after the death of a general partner who held the power to liquidate the entity, § 2704(a) applies. This is easily avoided by making sure no partner ever has the unilateral right to force liquidation of the partnership, or by making sure no individual serves as general partner. This might explain why the IRS has not attacked an FLP using § 2704(a) in any case decided by a court.

Under § 2704(b), where a taxpayer transfers to a family member an interest in an FLP controlled by the taxpayer and members of the family, any liquidation restrictions that lapse upon the transfer or which can be removed by the taxpayer or any family member must be disregarded in valuing the transferred interest. Legislative history indicates that § 2704(b) is not intended to supplant minority or fractional interest discounts that otherwise apply to FLP interests. *See* § 11.6.5. Furthermore, § 2704(b) applies only where the restrictions are more restrictive than applicable state law. Accordingly, if state law provides that the transferred interest would carry no right to liquidation anyway, § 2704(b) will not apply.

The IRS rightly lost one case where it tried to apply § 2704(b) to defeat an FLP arrangement. In *Blain P. Kerr*, 113 T.C. 449 (1999) (Texas law), the Tax Court granted summary judgment to the taxpayer because the restriction at issue (that the partnership could only be liquidated before the date specified in the agreement with the consent of all the partners) did not satisfy the requirement that the restriction must be removable by the "transferor or any member of the transferor's family either alone or collectively" as provided in § 2704(b)(2)(B). This requirement was not met because the restriction could only be removed with the consent of the University of Texas, to which a partnership interest had been assigned.

§ 11.31. SUCCESSFUL IRS ATTACKS

The IRS has occasionally defeated the application of valuation discounts to FLP interests. Until more recently, the IRS's success was limited to cases involving rather extreme facts. Once the IRS earned a victory using § 2036(a), however, planners took more notice.

§ 11.31.1. § 2036(a)

Assets transferred to an FLP or an LLC may be includible in the transferor's estate under the "reinclusion" provisions of the Code, §§ 2035-2038. The most common and most serious issues generally arise under § 2036. As explained at § 2.19, the transfer of assets to an FLP or LLC in exchange for interests in the entity does not necessarily fall within the parenthetical exception for transfers made in connection with "a bona fide sale for an adequate and full consideration in money or money's worth." § 2036(a). Accordingly, assets that are otherwise subject to inclusion by reason of a retained interest, § 2036(a)(1), or retained control, § 2036(a)(2), may not be excludible by reason of the exception.

Whether assets transferred to an FLP or LLC are includible in a decedent's estate under § 2036(a)(1) is a highly fact-specific issue. The outcome sometimes turns upon whether the decedent was entitled to the use or possession of the property in accordance with an informal understanding or agreement. *See* § 2.19.1. Of course, in some cases, inclusion is required because the transferor continued to use the property that had been transferred to the partnership as if it were his own. *E.g., Estate of Charles L. Reichardt*, 114 T.C. 144 (2000).

Avoiding Inclusion under § 2036(a). Inclusion can be avoided if (1) attention is given to legitimate business purposes of an FLP or LLC (*e.g.*, centralization of management of assets, limited liability, continuing of management), (2) the entity is properly formed and respected—including the formal transfer of assets to it, (3) the fiduciary obligations of the manager are expressed in the FLP or LLC agreement and are not diminished, (4) proper business procedures are followed, (5) all members receive current information regarding FLP or LLC matters and participate in appropriate ways, (6) distributions are made pro rata and are not subject to the transferor's discretion (it helps if distributions are subject to an ascertainable standard), and (7) neither the transferor's residence nor substantially all of his or her liquid assets was transferred to the FLP or LLC. As explained at § 2.19.2, the reach of § § 2036(a)(2) and 2038 may be blunted if the transferor is automatically removed as manager if he or she becomes incapable of understanding and managing business affairs (or if the transferor does not serve as manager).

The continued personal use of assets that were nominally transferred to an FLP or LLC strongly supports the inclusion of the assets in the transferor's estate. *E.g., Estate of Lea K. Hillgren*, T.C. Memo. 2004-46 ("In this case, neither decedent's interest in the properties that were transferred to the partnership nor legal title changed once the partnership was established.").

§ 11.31.2. Failure to Respect Business Form

The creation, existence and characteristics of a business entity will be given effect for tax purposes only if the existence of the entity is respected by its owners. The creation of an FLP and transfer of its units will not be recognized for estate tax purposes if the creator continues to operate as before—with no regard to limitations imposed by the formation of the entity. For example, in *Estate of Charles E. Reichardt*, 114 T.C. 144 (2000), the assets that had been transferred to an FLP were included in the decedent's estate under § 2036(a) and his gifts of 30.4 percent interests to his two children were disregarded. According to the court, "Decedent did not curtail his enjoyment of the transferred property after he formed the partnership. Nothing changed except legal title . . . .Decedent commingled partnership and personal funds. He deposited some partnership income in his personal account." *See also Estate of Dorothy M. Schauerhamer*, T.C. Memo. 1997-242.

In *Estate of Morton Harper*, T.C. Memo. 2002-121, the Tax Court relied on *Reichardt* and *Schauerhamer* in concluding that property transferred by the decedent's trust to a limited partnership were includible in his estate under § 2036(a). The conclusion was reached primarily because of the "egregious" disregard of the partnership form, including the deposit of partnership income in the trust's bank account. According to the Tax Court, although the partnership was created prior to the decedent's death and there was "some change in the formal relationship of those involved in the assets, we are satisfied that any practical effect during the decedent's life was minimal. Rather, the partnership served primarily as an alternate vehicle through which decedent would provide for his children at his death." Importantly, the court rejected the estate's contention that the transfer had been made to the partnership in a bona fide sale for full and adequate consideration. First, there was no bona fide sale— the decedent stood on both sides of the transaction. Second, the transfer was not made in exchange for consideration. "In actuality, all decedent did was to change the form in which he held his beneficial interest in the contributed property. We see little practical difference in whether the Trust held the property directly or as a 99-percent partner (and entitled to a commensurate 99-percent share of profits) in a partnership holding the property." In the court's view the transfer to the partnership simply involved a circuitous "recycling" of value.

In *Estate of Edna Korby*, 89 T.C.M. (CCH) 1143 (2005), the decedent and her husband transferred nearly $2 million in investment assets (mostly stocks and bonds) to an FLP in exchange for partnership interests. They then gifted their 98-percent limited interests to trusts for their children. Following these transfers, the partnership continued to pay a number of the personal expenses of the decedent and her husband by making disproportionate distributions to the general partner, the living trust established by the decedent and her husband. The decedent's estate tax return included her remaining interest in the partnership, but the IRS determined that all of the partnership's assets were includible in her gross estate under §§ 2036 and 2038. The Tax Court agreed with the IRS, finding an implied agreement between the founding partners that they would receive as much income and principal from the partnership as they would need. It did not help that both the decedent and her husband had major health problems when they committed virtually all of their investment assets to the partnership, leaving their living trust with substantially less resources than it would need to cover their medical expenses. The estate argued that the payments made by the partnership were management fees, but the court rejected the claim, noting that not all of the living trust's co-trustees received distributions and that payments were made on demand and not as part of some fixed compensatory schedule. In deciding that the bona fide sale exception to § 2036 did not apply, the court recited several facts that suggested the formation of the partnership was not a bona fide transaction, including the founding partners' dependence on the distributions, the commingling of partnership and personal assets, and even a failure to formally transfer some of the assets to the partnership.

On appeal, the Eighth Circuit affirmed. 471 F.3d 848 (8th Cir. 2006). The court rejected the estate's argument that the payments were management fees, because there was no management agreement between the partnership, the decedent, and her husband. There were no records to support the amount of time either the decedent or her husband spent on partnership affairs, and the decedent's husband failed to report the payments as self-employment income. The court agreed with the Tax Court and the IRS that the partnership was formed not for substantial business purpose but instead with the intent to make a testamentary transfer at a discounted value.

§ 11.31.3. Deathbed Formations and Transfers

In "extreme" cases the courts may value closely held business interests without regard to gifts made shortly before death. *Estate of Elizabeth B. Murphy,* 60 TCM (CCH) 645 (1990). In *Murphy* the court stated: "Briefly, control was kept in and exercised continuously by the Murphy family, including decedent, followed by her children. Decedent implemented a plan 18 days before her death with the sole and explicit purpose to obtain a minority discount. We are aware of no case where a court has allowed a minority discount in this situation." Importantly, Mrs. Murphy had suffered from lung cancer and obstructive pulmonary disease for more than a year prior to the transfers. In contrast, the creation and transfer of interests in a business entity shortly before death will be respected if the actions had legitimate purposes apart from reducing taxes—at least when the transferor did not have a terminal illness. *E.g., Church v. United States,* cited above.

§11.31.4. No Annual Exclusions

In the ordinary course, gifts of FLP interests qualify for the federal gift tax annual exclusion because they represent gifts of present interests. This is because the donees of FLP interests can usually sell or assign the gifted interests, perhaps subject only to a right of first refusal. *See, e.g.,* LR 9415007; LR 9131006 (TAM). In the late 1990s, the IRS took the position that where FLP interests are subject to stricter transfer restrictions than what is normally the case under state law, gifts of such interests may no longer be present interests eligible for the annual exclusion. LR 9751003 (TAM). The partnership agreement involved in the letter ruling gave the general complete discretion with respect to the timing and composition of distributions, and it prohibited limited partners from assigning any portion of their interest. As a result, the limited partner interests gifted to the beneficiaries "lacked the tangible and immediate economic benefit required . . . for a present interest in property."

Annual exclusions are allowable if the donor does not retain exceptional controls. LR 9131006 (TAM). In this ruling, neither the income component nor the partnership interests themselves qualified as present interests. Under the partnership agreement the income was distributable to the limited partners "in the complete discretion of the general partner." Also, the general partner was empowered to retain income "for any reason whatsoever." According to the IRS, "The provision effectively obviates the fiduciary duty ordinarily imposed upon a general partner, and clothes the general partner with the authority to withhold income for reasons unrelated to the conduct of the partnership." As to the partnership interests themselves, "the donees could not transfer or assign the gifted interests; nor could they withdraw from the partnership or receive a return of capital contributions until the year 2022."

The IRS's position was bolstered by *Christine Hackl*, 118 T.C. 279 (2002), *aff'd*, 335 F.3d 664 (7th Cir. 2003). The donor had formed an LLC to own a tree farming business. In 1996, the donor made annual exclusion gifts of membership interests to 41 different beneficiaries. The IRS disallowed the claimed annual exclusions on the grounds that the gifts were not present interests in property. The LLC's operating agreement provided that no member could withdraw from the LLC or exercise his or her right to partition the LLC's property. Members could not sell their interests in the LLC without the consent of the LLC's manager, the donor. The non-managing members had no power to compel distributions or liquidation of the entity. On top of that, it was apparent the company would not be generating any net income for at least the next six years. The Tax Court upheld the IRS's determination that the gifted membership interests lacked any substantial present economic benefit to the donees. The Seventh Circuit affirmed, noting that the "operating agreement clearly foreclosed the donee's ability to realize any substantial present economic benefit . . . .[The] restrictions on the transferability of the shares meant that they were essentially without immediate value to the donees."

The opinions in *Hackl* suggest measures that FLP and LLC owners can take to ensure that gifts of entity interests qualify for the annual exclusion. First, the general partners or managers could expressly be made subject to fiduciary duties with respect to distributions, ensuring donees that there would be some access to entity income. Donees might also be given a right to sell their interests subject to a right of first refusal exercisable by the entity. Some planners give donees a temporary right to put their interests to the entity at fair market value, effectively giving the donees a right akin to a *Crummey* power. Finally, donors could give cash to their donees that would enable them to purchase interests in the entity directly.

A similar result occurred in *Walter M. Price*, 99 T.C.M. 1005 (2010). In 1997, the taxpayers created a family limited partnership and funded it with stock in a closely-held equipment distribution corporation and three parcels of commercial land leased to the corporation and another company. Over the course of six years, the taxpayers made gifts of limited partnership interests to their three adult children. On their federal gift tax returns, the taxpayers claimed annual exclusions for each of the gifts, together with "substantial discounts for lack of control and lack of marketability of the transferred partnership interests." The Service issued deficiency notices for each of the years in question on the grounds that the gifts were of future interests and thus ineligible for the annual exclusion under *Hackl*. The Service observed that the partnership agreement barred transfers of limited partnership interests to third parties and limited partners had no power to compel distributions (the agreement did not even provide for mandatory distributions to cover taxes). In attempting to distinguish *Hackl*, the taxpayers argued that the interests were freely transferrable between partners or to the general partner. But the Tax Court held that:

> contingencies stand between the donees and their receipt of economic value for the transferred partnership interests so as to negate finding that the donees have the immediate use, possession, or enjoyment of the transferred property. Pursuant to . . . the partnership agreement, unless all partners consented the donees could transfer their partnership interests only to another partner or to a partner's trust. In addition, any such purchase would be subject to the option-to-purchase provisions . . . of the partnership agreement, which gives the partnership itself or any of the other partners a right to purchase the property according to a complicated valuation process but without providing any time limit for exercising the purchase option with respect to a voluntary transfer.

Accordingly, the taxpayers lost out on the ability to claim an annual exclusion, because they could not show that the gifts of partnership interests gave the recipient an "unrestricted and noncontingent right to immediately use, possess, or enjoy either the property itself or income from the property."

On similar facts, a district court agreed. In *Fisher v. United States*, 2010-1 U.S.T.C. ¶ 60,588 (S.D. Ind. 2010), the taxpayers transferred a parcel of Michigan lakefront property to an LLC. Over the course of three years, the taxpayers gave small interests in the LLC to each of their seven children. They claimed the annual exclusion for each of these gift transfers, but the Service assessed gift tax deficiencies on the grounds that the LLC interests were not gifts of "present interests." As in *Price*, the LLC's operating agreement provides that the timing and amount of all distributions is to be determined by the entity's general manager, no other member can compel a distribution for any reason, and no distributions are required. The taxpayers argued that the children had present interests, because each had "the unrestricted right to receive distributions," but the court reasoned that this right did not mean much given that all discretion with regard to distributions lay with the general manager. The taxpayers then argued that the children had present interests, because they had the right to use the lakefront property. The court could not find this right in the operating agreement, but it concluded that even if the children had this right as members of the LLC, "the right to possess, use, and enjoy property, without more, is not a right to a 'substantial present economic benefit.'" Accordingly, none of the gifts qualified for the annual exclusion.

Planners should be hesitant to challenge *Hackl, Price* and *Fisher*. While the decisions undermine the use of the annual exclusion when making gifts of FLP interests, they do so on the grounds that the transferred interests lack "any substantial present economic benefit." Interests that lack such benefit would certainly be less appealing to a hypothetical willing buyer. Indeed this trilogy of cases can be read to validate the significant minority interest and marketability discounts applied to FLP interests.

§11.31.5. Arguments to Limit Discounts

Where the IRS cannot defeat the FLP technique, it often turns to an attack on the specific discounts applied to interests in an FLP or LLC. Courts have not shied from conducting their own fact-intensive inquiries to determine the fair market value of gifted or bequeathed FLP interests. In a famous case involving Paul Mitchell, the famous hair styling guru, the issue before the Tax Court was the valuation of a corporation founded by Mitchell and his partner. In 1987, an unrelated buyer offered $100 million for the company, and the shareholders countered at $125 million. The counter-offer was refused. In 1988, however, the buyer offered $125 million. The shareholders again refused, claiming they had an offer from Gillette for $150 million. Mitchell was then diagnosed with cancer, and he died in 1989. In valuing the decedent's shares, the Tax Court rejected the appraisals from the estate and the IRS, instead performing its own analysis. The court started with the $150 million figure that was offered from Gillette, and then discounted that amount by ten percent to reflect the decedent's death (a key person discount). The court then applied a 35-percent aggregate discount for lack of marketability and a minority interest, together with another $1.5 million discount for possible litigation. *Estate of Paul Mitchell*, T.C. Memo. 1997-461. The estate appealed, and the Ninth Circuit remanded the case back to the Tax Court. 250 F.3d 696 (9th Cir. 2001). The Ninth Circuit determined that the Tax Court's analysis was inadequately explained. On remand, the Tax Court stuck to its guns and affirmed the original valuation, this time elaborating further into the step-by-step calculation and the rationale for each step. T.C. Memo. 2002-98. On its second appeal, the Ninth Circuit accepted the extended explanation and affirmed the decision of the Tax Court. *Fujieki v. Commissioner*, 83 Fed. Appx. 987 (9th Cir. 2003).

In this connection note that the testimony of an overly partisan expert may be disregarded. Thus, in *Ina F. Knight*, 115 T.C. 506 (2000), the Tax Court rejected the testimony of the taxpayer's expert in support of a 44 percent discount and applied a combined minority and lack of marketability discount of only 15 percent.

It is difficult to generalize the attacks the IRS might make against any particular FLP or LLC, as every case is unique to its facts. The IRS has stated that discounts in the case of entities to which financial assets have been transferred can be limited by arguing that for valuation and transfer tax purposes FLPs and LLCs are analogous to irrevocable trusts. FSA 200049003. To the extent the role and fiduciary duties of a general partner and a trustee are similar, one should expect smaller discounts as the risk to limited partners is not as great as in the case of an active trade or business.

The Field Service Advise also mentions that interests in an FLP or LLC should be valued by analogy to the valuation of closed-end mutual funds. The FSA acknowledges that there is a valuation discount of 4 to 12 percent for closed-end funds, in addition to which the interest would be subject to discount for lack of marketability. The IRS also believes that in applying the willing buyer-willing seller test for fair market value, one should consider that the founders of the entity are not likely to sell the interests they received at deep discounts.

F. RECAPITALIZATIONS

§ 11.32. OVERVIEW

Until the advent of Chapter 14, preferred stock recapitalizations were commonly made in order to attempt to shift all future growth in the value of a business to younger generation family members at little or no gift tax cost. In brief, senior generation family members who owned all of the stock of an existing corporation (or partnership) would enter into a tax free reorganization. The reorganization would involve the exchange of their present interests for two types of interests—senior interests roughly equal to the total present value of the corporation, and junior equity interests which had little or no present value. Subsequently the owners would gift the junior equity interests, which had little, if any, value to younger members of their families.

The degree of success of a recapitalization depended upon substantially all of the value of the corporation being absorbed by the preferred stock which was retained by the donor-parents. In order to create preferred stock of sufficiently high value the preferred stock had to carry high dividend rates. Taxpayers often tried to squeak by with noncumulative preferred, but the cumulative feature was typically required in order to support a sufficiently high valuation of the preferred stock. As a practical matter, preferred stock recapitalizations were out of reach for most closely-held corporations simply because they could not afford to pay high annual dividends on preferred stock. The payment of preferred stock dividends was costly because the payments were not deductible by the corporation for income tax purposes although they were includible in the recipients' income.

The concern of the IRS that the preferred stock retained by the donors be properly valued led to the publication of Rev. Rul. 83-119, 1983-2 C.B. 57, and Rev. Rul. 83-120, 1983-2 C.B. 170. In particular, Rev. Rul. 83-120 emphasized that the valuation of preferred stock was primarily dependent upon its dividend rate and preference, the capacity of the corporation to pay the dividends, and the extent of the liquidation protection and preference. It also pointed out the extent to which the preferred stock had voting rights might increase its value. Finally, Rev. Rul. 83-120 noted that the common stock would have a substantial value if all future appreciation in value was allocated to the common stock.

The Limited Life of §2036(c). Continuing concerns about abusive valuations used in recapitalizations and similar wealth-shifting techniques led to the enactment of former §2036(c) in 1987. Section 2036(c) was an extraordinarily complex attempt to control the use of estate freezes through the estate tax. In simplest terms, §2036(c) required the inclusion in a decedent's estate of interests in an enterprise that were transferred during lifetime if, (1) they were entitled to a disproportionate share in the appreciation of the enterprise, and (2) the transferor retained an interest in the income or rights in the enterprise. The uncertainty generated by the statute led to the eventual publication of an explanatory notice (Notice 89-99, 1989-2 C.B. 422) of unusual complexity and difficulty.

Special Valuation Rules Added in 1990. In 1990, Congress repealed §2036(c) retrospectively and substituted an approach that relies upon the objectively supportable valuation of retained interests. The provisions of particular relevance to the valuation of interests arising in recapitalization freezes are found in §§2701 and 2704, which are designed to eliminate the potential for abusive valuations. Section 2703, which is concerned with the effect of options, buy-sell agreements, and other rights to acquire property at less than its fair market value, and §2704, which deals with lapsing rights, are reviewed in Part B, above.

A corporation that is recapitalized will have two or more classes of stock and would, accordingly, no longer qualify as an S corporation. The loss of S corporation status is one of the factors that a client must consider in deciding whether or not to recapitalize. Because of the tax advantages of FLPs and LLCs and the advent of the new valuation rules of §2701, the use of corporate recapitalizations will probably continue to decline.

§11.33. Recapitalizations Not Subject to §2701

Recapitalizations and transfers that are not subject to §2701 (*i.e.,* recapitalizations in which the transferees are not members of the transferor's family as defined by §2701(e)(1)), remain attractive in some circumstances. For purposes of §2701, members of the family include the transferor's spouse; lineal descendants of the transferor and the transferor's spouse; and the spouses of such descendants. Thus, the term does not include siblings, nieces and nephews, cousins, and ascendant relatives.

EXAMPLE 11-28.

Cosmos, Inc. had 1,000 shares of voting common stock outstanding all of which were owned by X. X wished to turn over more management responsibilities to his nieces all of whom were employed by Cosmos. In order to encourage their continued participation in the business of Cosmos, the capital structure was reorganized so his nieces would be the primary beneficiaries of any future growth. Specifically, X exchanged his 1,000 shares of common stock for 10,000 shares of voting $100 par value 10% cumulative preferred stock and 5,000 shares of common stock. This should qualify as a tax-free recapitalization under §368(a)(1)(E). X gave the common stock to his nieces.

The gifts of common stock are not subject to §2701 because the transferees are not members of X's family. Accordingly, the common stock gifted by X is valued according to its fair market value. The value was traditionally fixed at the amount by which the value of the preferred stock received by X, determined according to its fair market value, was less than the value of the common stock that X exchanged for it. If the gifts had been made to children or other family members, the amount of X's gifts would be determined under §2701 according to a similar sub-traction method. That is, the gift would be equal to the total value of Cosmos reduced by the value of the "distribution rights" retained by X. *See* Reg. §25.2701-1(a)(2). However, the value of any distribution right in a controlled corporation is zero unless it is a qualified payment right. Under §2701(c)(3), a fixed cumulative dividend is a qualified payment right. Accordingly, the value of the preferred stock retained by X would be taken into account in determining the amount of X's gift. In any case, however, the common stock would have a value equal to 10% of the total value of all equity interests in Cosmos. §2701(a)(4)(A).

The proper valuation of the business and the senior interests are, obviously, critical to the tax success of a recapitalization effort. The valuation of a closely-held business is difficult enough without adding the difficulty of placing a value on senior interests issued in a recapitalization. Additionally, the valuation of the interest is a factual matter upon which the IRS will not issue an advance ruling. As indicated above, rulings are not generally issued concerning the recapitalization of closely-held corporations. In general, recapitalizations should be planned with the advice of a valuation expert, who will be available to testify if the taxpayer's valuations are challenged.

Although a recapitalization qualifies under §368(a)(1)(E), the exchange of stock may have gift, income, or estate tax consequences under other sections of the Code. For example, where the value of the preferred stock received by a shareholder is less than the value of the common stock surrendered by the shareholder, the recapitaliza-tion will involve a gift to the other shareholders, or the payment of additional compensation to them. Where the other shareholders are unrelated, the transaction may be treated as a bona fide business transaction that does not give rise to any gift tax liability. *See* Reg. §25.2512-8. If the exchanging shareholder is related to the other shareholders, the IRS will be tempted to charge that the recapitalization involved a gift to the others. The opposite result occurs where the value of the preferred stock received by a shareholder exceeds the value of the common stock he or she surren-dered: Either the other shareholders made a gift to the exchanging shareholder or additional compensation was paid to him or her. The IRS has stated that it would apply that analysis to recapitalizations:

> However, if *A* receives shares of preferred stock having a fair market value in excess of the fair market value of the common stock surrendered, or surrenders shares of common stock having a fair market value in excess of the fair market value of the preferred stock received, the amount representing such excess will be treated as having been used to make gifts, pay compensation, satisfy obligations of any kind, or for whatever purpose the facts indicate. Rev. Rul. 74-269, 1974-1 C.B. 87.

If a post-1981 exchange involves an outright gift, presumably none of the value of the common stock is includible in the exchanging shareholder's estate although he or she dies within three years of the exchange. Of course, any common stock included in the shareholder's estate under §2035, §2036(b), or another provision of the Code will be valued on the estate tax valuation date applicable to the shareholder's estate.

However, the shareholder's estate should be entitled to an offset under §2043 for the value of the stock that the decedent received in exchange.

EXAMPLE 11-29.

X, the controlling shareholder of Titan, Inc., exchanged 1,000 of the outstanding 1,500 shares of Titan common stock for 10,000 shares of 8% noncumulative voting preferred stock that had a par value of $100. The recapitalization assumed that X's common stock and the preferred stock he received were each worth $1,000,000, which was roughly two-thirds of the total value of Titan ($1,500,000). The exchange qualified as a tax-free recapitalization under §368(a)(1)(E). The other common shareholders in Titan at the time of the exchange were related to X but were not members of his family within the meaning of §2701(e)(1). The exchange would involve a gift by X to the extent the value of the common stock that he surrendered exceeded the value of the preferred stock he received. In such a case, presumably only the value of the preferred stock would be included in X's estate.

Other Tax Considerations. A recapitalization will deprive the parties of two tax advantages otherwise available to small business corporations. Their significance will depend in part on the profitability of the corporation under consideration. First, a corporation is not eligible for Subchapter S treatment if it has more than one class of stock. §1361(b)(1)(D). Thus, a recapitalization into common and preferred shares will prevent the corporation from electing subchapter S treatment and will terminate an existing election. When income tax rates are lower for individuals than for corporations, S corporations are more attractive than C corporations. Second, an ordinary loss deduction is available under §1244 only with respect to common stock. §1244(c)(1). Accordingly, a loss suffered on the sale or exchange of preferred stock cannot be claimed as an ordinary loss under §1244 even though the common stock originally qualified under that section. Of course, the disqualification is of limited significance for profitable corporations.

The preferred stock issued in connection with a recapitalization typically carries the right to a large cumulative dividend. It may be impractical or undesirable for a corporation to undertake such a substantial cash drain. Before proceeding with a recapitalization the parties should also understand that the preferred stock dividends are ordinary income to the recipient but are not deductible by the corporation. This consideration often deters clients from adopting recapitalization plans.

Recapitalization Strategies. A carefully planned recapitalization remains a valuable estate planning tool—particularly for nontax purposes. For example, recapitalization can be used in order to allocate a fixed interest (preferred stock) to family members who are not active in the business, and equity interests (common stock) to the family members who play an active part in the business. In the latter case, often only the common stock would carry the right to vote. In any case, the terms of a recapitalization should be based upon valuations made by a qualified expert. In some cases the income tax advantages will make it desirable to use an S corporation.

Although an S corporation may only have one class of stock, it may be divided into voting and nonvoting shares.

In some circumstances, a recapitalization may have an attractive estate freezing potential, particularly if § 2701 does not apply. For example, transfers made to donees who are not family members are not subject to the cumbersome and disadvantageous rules of § 2701. In addition, a preferred stock recapitalization may result in significant overall tax savings where the corporation has a cash flow sufficient to support substantial preferred stock dividends and it is likely to grow in value. Planners should not ignore the simple expedient of making gifts of interests in a corporation or partnership without undergoing a recapitalization. The gift approach typically qualifies for valuation discounts (*e.g.*, lack of marketability and minority interest), is simpler, involves fewer costs, and is easier to understand. A client's particular circumstances may indicate that a more exotic approach—such as a "reverse freeze,"—should be considered. In a reverse freeze, a preferred interest is transferred to a younger generation family member while the donor retains a junior equity interest. A reverse freeze could have beneficial estate tax results if the business grows slowly or declines in value.

§ 11.34. FAMILY PARTNERSHIP FREEZES

Family partnerships with more than one type of capital interest (multiclass partnerships), such as limited partnerships, have been used for a wide variety of tax and nontax purposes. When individual income tax rates were steeply progressive family partnerships were used as income-shifting devices. However, the compaction of income tax rates and the adoption of the Kiddie Tax reduce the incentive to shift income within the family. See § 7.9.1. Through the 1980s multiclass partnerships were sometimes used instead of multiclass corporations to achieve an estate freeze. Partnership freezes and multiclass corporations were usually intended to cap the value of the senior family member's estate, to assure him or her of a steady flow of income, and to shift some of the income from the business to other family members. The senior family member may be entitled to a fixed basic payment and a participation in additional profits, which provides some protection against inflation.

A partnership freeze, like a preferred stock recapitalization, may involve a substantial gift to donees who receive the junior equity interests. The enactment of § 2701 seriously dampened the interest in multitiered partnerships. Although the gift and estate tax dynamics have changed, family partnerships and LLCs continue to have income tax advantages over C corporations and the nontax advantage of incredible flexibility.

As mentioned previously, the anti-*Byrum* rule of § 2036(b) requires that particular care be taken in transferring stock in a controlled corporation to a partnership so as to be sure that the donor does not have the right to vote the stock directly or indirectly. The stock would be includible in the donor's estate under § 2036(b) if the donor, as general partner, held the right to vote the stock. A Technical Advice Memorandum, LR 199938005, held that § 2036(b) would require a general partner's estate to include the stock of a controlled corporation that was transferred to a family partnership of which the decedent was one of the general partners who were entitled to vote the stock. The memorandum relied upon the text of § 2036(b) which requires inclusion if the decedent retained "the right to vote (directly or indirectly)" shares of stock of a controlled corporation. The problem is, of course, avoided if someone other than the transferor holds the right to vote the stock in a controlled corporation.

FLPs and LLCs are of particular interest to the IRS because of their potential for abuse. The concern is reflected in the Regulations, TAMs, and the litigation posture taken by the government. For example, the income tax regulations provide that,

> A donee or purchaser of a capital interest in a partnership is not recognized as a partner under the principles of section 704(e)(1) unless such interest is acquired in a bona fide transaction, not a mere sham for tax avoidance or evasion purposes, and the donee or purchaser is the real owner of such interest. To be recognized, a transfer must vest dominion and control of the partnership interest in the transferee. The existence of such dominion and control in the donee is to be determined from all the facts and circumstances. A transfer is not recognized if the transferor retains such incidents of ownership that the transferee has not acquired full and complete ownership of the partnership interest. *Transactions between members of a family will be closely scrutinized, and the circumstances, not only at the time of the purported transfer but also during the periods preceding and following it, will be taken into consideration in determining the bona fides or lack of bona fides of the purported gift or sale.* Reg. § 1.704-1(e)(1)(iii). (Emphasis added.)

§ 11.35. CONCLUSION

Effective planning for family businesses can produce important tax and nontax advantages. The flexibility offered by FLPs and LLCs is particularly attractive, especially when combined with the deep discounts that usually apply to transferred noncontrol interests. An expert appraisal is required in order to determine, and sustain, the amount of a valuation discount. Planning should, of course, take into account the tax saving opportunities offered by estate tax deferral under § 6166. However, tax planning must take a back seat to informed, enlightened and effective planning for the needs of the client and the client's family. The lodestar should be planning based on the client's circumstances and wishes. Finally, planners must give particular attention to ethical issues that attend transactions that involve multiple parties.

BIBLIOGRAPHY

I. GENERAL DISCUSSIONS OF PLANNING FOR CLOSELY-HELD BUSINESSES

August, Artificial Valuation of Closely Held Interests: Sec. 2704, 22 Est. Plan. 339 (1995)

Bagley, W. & Whynott, P., The Limited Liability Company (6 vols. 1999)

Bittker, B. & Eustice, J., Federal Income Taxation of Corporations and Shareholders

Eustice, J and Kuntz, J., Federal Income Taxation of S Corporations (3d ed. 1992)

Frankel, Planning for the Family Business Under New IRC Sec. 2701, N.Y.U. 50th Inst. Fed. Tax., Ch. 16 (1992)

Grant, I. & Christian, W., Subchapter S Taxation (1990)

Hesch, J., Partnerships; Overview, Conceptual Aspects and Formation, 710 Tax. Mgmt. Port. (1996)

Howell, Fewer Trusts May Qualify as ESBTs Under New Final Regs., 29 Est. Plan. 618 (Dec. 2002)

Lay, Estate Planning for the S Corporation Shareholder, N.Y.U., 48th Inst. Fed. Tax., Ch. 10 (1990)

Markstein, Giving Well is the Best Revenge: Planning Opportunities With Stock Options, U. Miami, 34th Inst. Est. Plan., Ch. 13 (2000)

McMahan, What, Me Worry?—Limited Liability for the Operation of Family Business Without Extra Tax Costs—A Comparison of Limited Liability Companies, Family Partnerships, and Corporations, U. Miami, 28th Inst. Est. Plan., Ch. 12 (1994)

Mulligan, Metamorphic Estate Planning: The Results When a Transfer Changes Value, 27 Est. Plan. 291 (Aug./Sept. 2000)

Robinson, S Corporations: The Best of Entities and the Worst of Entities, U. Miami, 28th Inst. Est. Plan., Ch. 11 (1994)

Russo, Hodges, Ellis, Edwards & Coghill, Estate Planning and Closely Held Stock Transactions and S Corporations, 242-3rd Tax Mgmt. Port. (1986)

Sederbaum, Lapse of Voting and Liquidation Rights in the Family Business: IRC § 2704, N.Y.U. 50th Inst. Fed. Tax., Ch. 15 (1992)

Smith, Gifts of Family Corporate Stock, 135 Tr. & Est. 16 (1996)

Starr, S. and Crnkovich, R., Limited Liability Companies, 725 Tax. Mgmt. Port. (1995)

Starr, S., S Corporations: Formation and Termination, 730 Tax. Mgmt. Port. (1992)

Stoneman, C., and Miller, W., Estate Planning for Owners of Closely Held Business Interests, 809 Tax. Mgmt. Port. (1994)

Streng, W., Choice of Entity, 700-2d Tax Mgmt. Port. (1999)

Testa, A., Chapter 14, 835 Tax Mgmt. Port. (1999)

W. McKee, W. Nelson & R. Whitmire, Federal Taxation of Partnerships and Partners (3d ed. 1997)

II. Buy-Sell Agreements

Bonn, Buy-Sell Agreements, N.Y.U., 48th Inst. Fed. Tax., Ch. 24 (1990)

Cornfeld, Non-Tax Considerations in Preparing Buy-Sell Agreements, U. Miami, 28th Inst. Est. Plan., Ch. 10 (1994)

Fife, Structuring Buy-Sell Agreements to Fix Estate Tax Value, 22 Est. Plan. 67 (1995)

Gamble, Buy-Sell Agreements, Transfer Restrictions and Section 2703: Have Buy-Sells Gone Bye-Bye, N.Y.U. 50th Inst. Fed. Tax., Ch. 19 (1992)

Harrison, Coordinating Buy-Outs and Installment Payment of Estate Tax, 22 Est. Plan. 139 (1995)

Jacobowitz, Structuring and Funding a Buy-Sell Agreement for the Closely Held Corporation, N.Y.U., 49th Inst. Fed. Tax., Ch. 3 (1991)

Johnson & Greenstein, Using Buy-Sell Agreements to Establish the Value of a Closely Held Business, 81 J. Tax. 362 (1994)

Zuckerman & Grall, Corporate Buy-Sell Agreements as Estate and Business Planning Tools, 28 Est. Plan. 599 (Dec. 2001)

III. Redemptions Under § 303 and Estate Tax Deferral Under

Blum, Estate Tax Payment and Liabilities, 219-3rd Tax Mgmt. Port. (1986)

Blum & Trier, Planning for Maximum Benefits of 303 Redemptions with Estate Tax Deferral, 53 J. Tax. 236 (1980)

Budin, GST Provisions May Limit Section 303 Redemptions, 17 Est., Gifts & Tr. J. 1346 (Sept./Oct. 1992)

Knickerbocker, Corporate Stock Redemption—Section 303, BNA 91-5th Tax Mgmt. Port. (1986)

IV. Planning with Partnerships Limited Liability Companies and S and C Corporations

Aucutt, Using C Corporations in Estate Planning, U. Miami, 33d Inst. Est. Plan., Ch. 10 (1999)

Belcher, Drafting Agreements to Take Advantage of Valuation Discounts, U. Miami, 30th Inst. Est. Plan., Ch. 10 (1996)

Blatt, The Effect of Sec. 2701 on Preferred Interest Freezes, 130 Tr. & Est. 8 (1991)

Brown, Maximizing Minority Discounts for Limited Partnerships in An Integrated Estate Plan, 93 J. Tax. 306 (Nov. 2000)

Daniels & Leibell, Planning for the Closely Held Business Owner: The Charitable Options, U. Miami, 40th Inst. Est. Plan., Ch. 14 (2006)

DeBruyn, Choice of Entity and Structuring Limited Liability Entities for the Best of Both Worlds, U. Miami, 31st Inst. Est. Plan., Ch. 9 (1997)

Dees, Using a Partnership to Freeze the Value of Pre-IPO Shares, U. Miami, 33d Inst. Est. Plan., Ch. 11 (1999)

Donald, Corporate Buy-Out Agreements, 106-5th Tax Mgmt. Port. (1990)

Donaldson, Income Tax Aspects of Family Limited Partnerships, U. Miami 39th Inst. Est. Plan., Ch. 14 (2005)

Eastland & Christian, Proposed Valuation Regulations Provide Harsh Results Under Adjustment and Lapse Rules, 75 J. Tax. 364 (1991)

Fiore, Dual Capital Partnerships as an Estate Planning Device, N.Y.U., 39th Inst. Fed. Tax., Ch. 54 (1981)

Fiore & Prokey, The 2036 Threat: Safeguard FLP and LLC Valuation Discounts, 142 Tr. & Est. 40 (Mar. 2003)

Gardner, Estate Freezes in 1990 and Beyond: The Story of the Repeal of Section 2036(c) and the Valuation Rules That Took Its Place, 64 Taxes 3 (1991)

Grove, Taming the Tiger: Designing, Implementing an FLP to Avoid a Section 2036 Attack, U. Miami, 38th Inst. Est. Plan., Ch. 7 (2004)

Harris, Family Tax Planning Using Partnerships, N.Y.U., 49th Inst. Fed. Tax., Ch. 14 (1991)

Kasner, Planning with Family Limited Partnerships, N.Y.U., 53d Inst. Fed. Tax., Ch. 22 (1995)

Keating, Transfers of Partnership and LLC Interests—Assignees, Transferees, Creditors, Heirs, Donees, and Other Successors, U. Miami, 32d Inst. Est. Plan., Ch. 5

Klein & Gardner, Sales and Liquidations of S Corporations, N.Y.U., 47th Inst. Fed. Tax., Ch. 9 (1989)

Kuntz, S Corporation Operating Problems, N.Y.U., 47th Inst. Fed. Tax., Ch. 10 (1989)

Lipton, IRS Improves Partnership Anti-Abuse Regs., But Major Problems Remain, 82 J. Tax. 132 (Mar. 1995)

Manning, Nontax Aspects of Planning for a Family Business, 22 Est. Plan. 345 (1995)

Mezzullo, An Estate Planner's Guide to Buy-Sell Agreements for the Closely Held Business (2002)

Mezzullo, An Estate Planner's Guide to Family Business Entities: Family Limited Partnerships, Limited Liability Companies, and More (3d ed. 2010)

Mezzullo, Choice of Family Business Entity for Estate Planning Purposes, U. Miami, 34th Inst. Est. Plan., Ch. 9 (2000)

Mezzullo, Family Limited Partnerships and Limited Liability Companies, 812 Tax Mgmt. Port. (1999)

Mezzullo, Estate Planning with Limited Partnerships and Limited Liability Companies, N.Y.U., 53rd Inst. Fed. Tax., Ch. 8 (1995)

Mulligan & Brady, Family Limited Partnerships Can Create Discounts, 21 Est. Plan. 195 (July/Aug. 1994)

Porter, Bulletproofing the Family Limited Partnership—Current Issues, U. Miami, 38th Inst. Est. Plan., Ch. 6 (2004)

Renn & Angkatavanich, The Resurrection: How *Holman* Revived Section 2703 Arguments – Long Thought to be Dead and Buried—to Defeat a Family Limited Partnership, 147 Tr. & Est. 20 (Oct. 2008)

Robinson, Making Sure Your Transfer Tax Planning Doesn't Create Income Tax Nightmares When You Sell the Family Business, U. Miami, 34th Inst. Est. Plan., Ch. 10 (2000)

Robinson, S. Corporations: Grumpy Old Entities or Ugly Ducklings, U. Miami, 31st Inst. Est. Plan., Ch. 10 (1997)

Saccarcio, Planning Issues and Opportunities Impacting Entrepreneurs, U. Miami, 35th Inst. Est. Plan., Ch. 7 (2001)

Smith & Olsen, Fractionalized Equity Planning: Preservation of Post-Mortem Valuation Discounts, U. Miami, 34th Inst. Est. Plan., Ch. 11 (2000)

Tiesi & London, How Family Partnerships Can Navigate the Section 2036 Minefield, 30 Est. Plan. 332 (July 2003)

12

Post-Mortem Planning

A. INTRODUCTION

§ 12.1. SCOPE

Death is only the beginning! Post-mortem estate planning provides important opportunities to minimize the overall tax costs and to preserve the maximum amount of property for a decedent's intended beneficiaries. The estate plan adopted during an individual's lifetime fixes the basic pattern for the disposition of property at death. However, the post mortem consequences of the plan can vary substantially depending upon the elections made, and other actions taken, by the decedent's fiduciaries and beneficiaries. The personal representative is frequently referred to as the "executor" throughout this chapter. The executor may make elections regarding matters that range from the treatment of medical expense deductions on the decedent's final income tax return to the payment or deferral of the federal estate tax. Importantly, beneficiaries may rearrange the distribution of property to some degree through the use of disclaimers and applications for family awards and allowances. A comprehensive checklist of post-mortem matters is included at the end of this chapter in § 12.50.

This chapter first reviews the opportunities that arise by reason of the executor's obligation to file a final income tax return for the decedent, § § 12.3-12.8. Where the decedent leaves a surviving spouse, one of the most important matters to consider is whether the decedent's final income tax return should be a joint one with the surviving spouse. Other income tax elections concern the use of medical expense deductions and the accrual of interest income. The decisions made regarding the decedent's final income tax return also have an impact on the income tax planning for his or her estate. That planning includes decisions that are very important to the estate and the beneficiaries, especially the choice of the estate's taxable year and the elections regarding expenses that may be claimed as deductions on the estate's income tax return, the estate tax return, or on both, § § 12.9-12.14.

Decisions that directly affect the value of property includible in the estate are discussed in Part D, including the use of the alternate valuation method, § 12.15, the special use valuation of real property used in a farm or closely-held business, § 12.19, and the qualified conservation easement exclusion, § 12.20. That part also covers a number of other elections, including ones that are available with respect to the treatment of qualified plan benefits, § 12.26, and the effect of life insurance settlement options, § 12.28.

Part E deals with devices by which the distribution of property may be reordered and reviews the use of family awards and allowances and the so-called widow's election, § § 12.30-12.31. It concludes with a discussion of the law regarding disclaimers, including a section on planning for the use of disclaimers, § § 12.32-12.36.

The planning and income tax consequences of estate distributions are reviewed in Part F, § § 12.37-12.41. Estates are generally subject to the same income tax rules that apply to complex trusts. See § § 10.4, 10.4.3-10.4.18. As noted below, distributions by an estate have important tax consequences. If the distributions from an estate are carefully planned they may minimize the overall income tax burdens of the estate and the beneficiaries. Part F includes a discussion of the consequences of making distributions, which can be used to spread the estate's income among several taxpayers. Under the basic rule applicable to distributions, the distributable net income of the estate is carried out to the extent of the lesser of the basis of the property or its fair market value at the time of distribution. Applying it, the basis of the estate in the distributed property carries over to the distributee. However, under § 643(e) the executor may elect to treat an in kind distribution as a taxable event resulting in recognition of gain or loss as if the property had been sold to the distributee. If the election is made, the basis of the distributee is increased to the fair market value of the property. The consequences of non-pro rata distributions of community property are also discussed in this part.

The final part is concerned with the payment of the federal estate and GST taxes, including the general rules regarding the allocation of the obligation to pay the tax.

The various opportunities for deferring the tax are reviewed in §§ 12.46-12.48. The chapter concludes with sections that deal with the release of personal representatives from liability for federal taxes, § 12.49, and the checklist of post-mortem matters, § 12.50.

§ 12.2. INITIAL STEPS

From the outset the lawyer who represents the executor should strive to establish a good rapport with the personal representative and persons who are beneficially interested in the estate. The lawyer's relationship with them is likely to be better if the lawyer provides them with an adequate explanation of the steps that will be involved in settling the estate, and communicates with them regularly throughout the administration of the estate. As previously noted, the lawyer for the personal representative should inform the beneficiaries of the lawyer's role in the proceedings—particularly that the lawyer does not represent them as clients. Some lawyers routinely advise beneficiaries that they should consider retaining independent counsel to advise them.

§ 12.2.1. Letter or Memorandum for the Personal Representative; Locating and Protecting Decedent's Property

At the outset the lawyer should give the personal representative a letter, or memorandum, that outlines his or her duties, reviews the important steps in the estate proceeding, and estimates the state and federal death taxes that will be due. In appropriate cases the lawyer should mention the possible use of disclaimers by the beneficiaries of the estate. It should also outline the legal services that will be performed and repeat the terms of their agreement regarding the amount and payment of the lawyer's compensation. (Under Model Rule 1.5 the lawyer should provide the client with a written explanation of the basis upon which the lawyer's fee will be determined.) It may also be useful and appropriate for the lawyer to communicate directly with the beneficiaries. However, the lawyer should make it clear to the beneficiaries that the lawyer does not represent them directly.

The lawyer should also advise the personal representative regarding the duty to locate and protect the decedent's property. Locating a decedent's investment accounts may require a review of the decedent's income tax returns and other records, interviews of family members, searching real property records, and sending letters of inquiry to financial institutions. Various services can assist in locating particular types of property. For example, a service for locating life insurance policies is offered by MIB Solutions, Inc., at a reasonable cost. The duty to protect the decedent's property requires a personal representative to be sure that adequate insurance coverage is in place to protect the decedent's real and personal property.

The lawyer for an individual personal representative to whom fees were paid during a calendar year might provide him or her with a Form 1099 covering the payments. Although an estate is not required to provide Forms 1099, it may be helpful to the personal representative.

§12.2.2. Cash Needs

At an early stage the lawyer should prepare and provide the personal representative with a projection of the estate's cash needs and the time at which funds will be required for payment of taxes, administration expenses, legacies, and other purposes. The amount of some items such as cash legacies will be known, but others, such as the amount of taxes, can only be estimated. If the decedent had an accountant or other financial advisor, the information and the help he or she can provide should not be overlooked. In many cases it is helpful if the personal representative retains the same person to keep the books for the estate and to prepare, or assist in preparing, the estate's fiduciary income tax returns and the estate tax return. An accountant's help is useful even when the lawyer's office will keep the books and use its computer to produce the necessary cash projections and accountings.

The personal representative, the lawyer and any other professionals who are involved in the estate settlement should clearly establish the allocation of responsibilities among them. The lawyer should assure that tax notices and returns are prepared and filed within the time allowed. Otherwise, penalties may be imposed and the estate may be unable to make advantageous elections. The lawyer should also review the work performed by other professionals, such as tax returns prepared by accountants or trust officers.

Once the cash projection is prepared, the personal representative, the accountant, and the lawyer must consider the steps that should be taken to raise the necessary funds. In that connection they must take into account the tax and nontax impact that each step will have on the estate and the beneficiaries. For example, the respective income tax brackets of the estate and the beneficiaries should be taken into account in planning the tax year the estate will use, how long the estate will remain open, and the policies that should be adopted regarding sales and distributions. The projection provides the factual base upon which many decisions can be made. It is most useful if it is prepared with care and updated as circumstances require. The parties should all recognize that it is only a projection, which is only as reliable as the assumptions upon which it is based (*e.g.*, estimates of the amount of taxes, value of assets).

§12.2.3. Federal Tax Notices

The lawyer should also counsel the personal representative regarding the filing of Form 56, Notice Concerning Fiduciary Relationship, which also serves as notice of qualification of executor. *See* §§6036 *and* 6903. Under the regulations the notice required by §6036 is satisfied by filing the estate tax return as required by §6018. Reg. §20.6036-2. If a notice is filed under §6903, the IRS must communicate directly with the fiduciary regarding the tax liabilities of the decedent. In contrast, if the notice is not filed, the fiduciary may not receive direct notice of a deficiency assessed against the decedent and mailed by the IRS to his or her last known address. Some lawyers advise against filing the notice because it may trigger an audit of the decedent's income and gift tax returns, and no penalty is imposed if the notice is not filed. Nevertheless, it is generally advisable to file the notice if the personal representative and the lawyer are not too familiar with the decedent's business affairs.

§ 12.2.4. Extensions of Time, Reg. § 301.9100

Under Reg. § 301.9100-1(a), the Commissioner may for good cause shown grant extensions of time within which to make an election in respect of any tax under all subtitles of the Code except E, G, H and I. An extension may be granted if the time for making the election is not specified in a statute, the request is filed with the Commissioner within a reasonable time, and granting the extension will not jeopardize the interests of the government. Thus, an extension may be granted in order to make a partnership election under § 754, § 12.5.1, to file an alternate valuation date election, LRs 199911030, 9602014, to make a QTIP election under § 2056(b)(7), § 12.21, to make a QDT election and to make an irrevocable assignment of property to a QDT, § 12.22, to allocate a GSTT exemption, § 12.24, or make a reverse QTIP election under § 2652(a)(3), § 12.23. *See, e.g.,* LRs 199926041, 9813013, 9724012, 9608008 and 9611011. But an extension for making an election to defer payment of estate tax under § 6166 is not allowed, because the requirement to make an election no later than the due date for the estate tax return is expressly required by the statute. LR 200721006. The standards applicable to granting extensions are set forth in Rev. Proc. 92-85, 1992-2 C.B. 490, *as modified by* Rev. Proc. 93-28, 1993-2 C.B. 344. Recently, the IRS adopted a policy of denying extension requests in cases involving transfers of property at a discount if the statute of limitations for challenging the valuation has expired. If the statute of limitations has not expired, the IRS appears willing to grant an extension, but the return may be sent for audit on the valuation issue.

An automatic 12-month extension is allowed by Reg. § 301.9100-2 for specified elections provided the taxpayer takes corrective action within that period. What constitutes corrective action is described in Reg. § 301.9100-2(c). The estate-related matters for which extensions are permitted under this subsection include, (1) a § 754 partnership election, § 12.5; (2) a special use valuation election under § 2032A, if an examination of the return has not yet begun, § 12.19; (3) a gift tax election to treat a qualified payment right as other than a qualified payment under § 2701(c)(3)(C); and (4) a gift tax election to treat any distribution right as a qualified payment under § 2701(c)(3)(C)(ii). Reg. § 301.9100-2(a)(2)(vi)-(ix).

An automatic six-month extension from the due date of a return is allowed "to make regulatory or statutory elections whose due dates are the due date of the return or the due date of the return including extension provided the taxpayer timely filed its return for the year the election should have been made" if the taxpayer takes corrective action within the period of the extension.

Extensions are allowed in other cases if the taxpayer's request for relief establishes that the taxpayer acted reasonably and in good faith and the grant of relief will not prejudice the interests of the government. Reg. § 301.9100-3(a). Applying this regulation, the IRS, in LR 200118037, allowed a reverse QTIP election to be made several years following the decedent's death.

The time within which to allocate the GSTT exemption to lifetime transfers may be extended under Reg. § 301.9100-3. *E.g.,* LR 200306015.

B. INCOME TAX

§ 12.3. THE DECEDENT'S FINAL INCOME TAX RETURN: GENERAL

A final personal income tax return must be filed for the period beginning with the first day of the decedent's taxable year and ending on the day of his or her death. § 443(a)(2). The same rates and personal exemption apply although the final year is a short one (*i.e.*, less than 12 full months). The return for the final year must be made by the decedent's "executor, administrator, or other person charged with the property of such decedent." § 6012(b)(1). The due date for the final return is the same as if the decedent had lived through the entire taxable year. § 6072(a); Reg. § 1.6072-1(b). Thus, the final return for a calendar year decedent is April 15 of the year following death. In the unlikely event of a decedent who filed on the basis of a fiscal year, the decedent's final return is due on the fifteenth day of the fourth month following the close of the decedent's regular taxable year. Reg. § 1.6072-1(b). The final return of a resident decedent is filed with the district director, or the service center, for the district in which the personal representative resides or has his or her principal place of business. § 6091(b)(1)(A); Reg. § 1.6091-2(a)(1).

Note that if a decedent dies early in the year, it may be necessary for the personal representative to file an income tax return for the preceding calendar year.

EXAMPLE 12-1.

X died on February 20, prior to filing an income tax return for the preceding calendar year. The return for that year must be filed by *X*'s personal representative on or before April 15. The return for *X*'s final, short taxable year (January 1—February 20) must be filed on or before April 15 of the following year.

The tax due with respect to a decedent's income tax return must be paid when the return is due. However, the time for payment of the tax may be extended for up to six months. § 6161(a)(1). Under Reg. § 1.6161-1(b), an extension will be granted only upon a satisfactory showing that payment on the due date will result in "undue hardship." For taxable years beginning before January 1, 1987, former § 6152(b)(1) allowed a personal representative to elect to pay the income tax due with respect to an estate's return in four equal quarterly installments instead of a single payment without the imposition of any penalty or interest.

Estimated Tax; Installment Payments. An estate, or a trust that was treated as owned by a decedent, is not required to file a declaration and make estimated tax payments for the taxable years ending before the date two years after the decedent's death. § 6654(l)(2). *See* § 12.6. A declaration and estimated tax payment is required for subsequent periods.

§ 12.3.1. Election to File a Joint Return

Under § 6013(a)(2), a joint return may be filed for the decedent and his or her surviving spouse if the surviving spouse does not remarry before the end of the year and the length of the tax year of either has not been shortened by reason of a change of accounting period under § 443(a)(1). A joint return for a decedent and his or her surviving spouse includes the income of the decedent through the date of death and the income of the surviving spouse for the entire taxable year. Where a personal representative is appointed prior to the last day for filing the return, the joint return must be made by both the surviving spouse and the personal representative. § 6013(a)(3). If no return has been filed for the decedent and no personal representative has been appointed, the surviving spouse may file a joint return. However, if the surviving spouse files such a joint return, a later appointed personal representative for the decedent may disaffirm it within one year of the last day for filing the surviving spouse's return. *Id*.

§ 12.3.2. Advantages of Filing a Joint Return

The principal tax advantage of filing a joint return is traceable to the generally more favorable "split" rates that apply to joint returns. Of course, a surviving spouse who files a separate return may take advantage of the same rates for two years following the decedent's death if the surviving spouse is supporting a dependent child or stepchild. § § 1(a), 2(a).

Filing a joint income tax return often results in a lower overall income tax liability than if separate returns were filed. That result will follow where, for example, an individual received a large amount of income in his or her final taxable year and the surviving spouse will have little or no income for the taxable year. A similar tax saving is available in the converse case (*i.e.*, where the decedent had little or no income but the survivor will receive a large amount of income during the year).

A joint return often allows the parties to make better use of the income tax deductions attributable to a decedent's final taxable year. In some cases the deductions, which cannot be carried over to the decedent's estate, would be wasted if a joint return were not filed. For example, an individual may have made charitable contributions prior to death which exceed the amount that is deductible when measured by the decedent's contribution base alone. If a joint return were filed, a larger charitable deduction would be allowable because the percentage limitations would be applied to a contribution base that includes the combined income of the decedent and the surviving spouse. If a joint return were not filed, the portion of the charitable contribution in excess of the amount allowable as a deduction on the decedent's final return would be wasted: in such a case the excess cannot be carried over and used by the deceased donor's estate. *See* Reg. § 1.170A-10(d)(4)(iii). A like advantage of filing a joint return exists where the decedent realized a net capital loss in his or her final taxable year and the surviving spouse had a net capital gain during the year. A net capital loss is deductible only to the extent of $3,000 ($1,500 in the case of married taxpayers filing separately). § 1211(b)(1). More importantly, a decedent's excess capital loss cannot be carried over and claimed on the returns filed by the decedent's personal representatives. However, if a joint return were filed, the decedent's net loss could offset any capital gains realized by the surviving spouse during the taxable year, before or after the decedent's death. *Cf.* Rev. Rul. 74-175, 1974-1 C.B. 52 (capital and net operating losses sustained by a decedent during the decedent's final taxable year are deductible only on the decedent's final return). If the surviving spouse's income would not otherwise be sufficient to absorb the full amount of the deductions, the surviving spouse's income might be increased by making distributions to the surviving spouse from the decedent's estate. Such distributions would carry out some of the estate's distributable net income to the surviving spouse. Of course, the distributions would be of assistance in this regard only if the estate's taxable year ended within the taxable year of the surviving spouse for which the joint return is being filed.

EXAMPLE 12-2.

H died on January 31 of this year survived by his wife, *W*. Earlier in January *H* suffered a long-term capital loss of $50,000. Apart from the capital loss deduction, *H*'s adjusted gross income for his short final tax year would be $10,000. *W* expects to have an income of about $50,000 this year aside from any income she may receive from *H*'s estate. *W* has owned some publicly traded securities for more than a year that have a current value of $40,000 over their bases. *H*'s personal representative and *W* should consider filing a joint income tax return for the year. If they do, *H*'s capital loss could be used to offset the full $40,000 of capital gain that *W* would realize if she sold the publicly traded securities that she owns. Otherwise, the tax benefit of *H*'s capital loss would be wasted except for the $3,000 deduction that could be claimed on his final return.

§12.3.3. Disadvantages of Filing a Joint Return

The principal disadvantage of filing a joint return is the joint and several liability that attaches to the estate and the surviving spouse for the amount of taxes, interest, and penalties. §6013(d)(3). Thus, if a joint return is filed, the assets of the estate may be liable for deficiencies and penalties attributable to the survivor's negligence or misconduct. This disadvantage is, of course, not present where the surviving spouse is the personal representative and the principal beneficiary of the decedent's estate.

Under the "innocent spouse" provisions of §6015, an estate may not be liable where the personal representative did not know and had no reason to know that the joint return substantially understated the income of the surviving spouse attributable to grossly erroneous treatment of items of income, deductions, credits, or bases.

§12.3.4. Deduction of Medical Expenses, §213

Under §213(a), individuals are allowed a deduction for income tax purposes of uncompensated medical expenses paid during the taxable year to the extent that the expenses exceed 7.5 percent of the taxpayer's adjusted gross income. Legislation in 2009 increased the threshold to 10 percent, except the rate remains 7.5 percent for the years 2013 through 2016 if the taxpayer or the taxpayer's spouse has reached age 65 before the end of the taxable year. § 213(a), (f). A remedial provision added in 1958 permits medical expenses that are paid within one year following the decedent's death to be treated as if they had been paid when they were incurred. § 213(c)(1). As a result, expenses paid within that period may be deducted on the decedent's income tax return for the appropriate taxable year or years. So long as there is no duplication of the deductions claimed, a portion of the medical expenses may be claimed for estate tax purposes and the remainder for income tax purposes. In order to be entitled to claim the expenses as income tax deductions, the estate must file both a statement that the "amount paid" has not been allowed as a deduction for estate tax purposes under § 2053 and a waiver of any right to claim it as a deduction under § 2053. § 213(c)(2). In any case, no refund or credit will be allowed for any taxable year for which the statutory period for filing a claim has expired. Reg. § 1.213-1(d)(1). A decedent's estate realizes income in respect of a decedent to the extent it is reimbursed by insurance for amounts deducted on the decedent's final return. Rev. Rul. 78-292, 1978-2 C.B. 233.

According to the IRS, where the expenses are claimed as deductions for income tax purposes, the amount within the nondeductible threshold (*i.e.,* 7.5 percent of the decedent's adjusted gross income under current law, and 10 percent of adjusted gross income as of 2013) is not deductible for income or estate tax purposes. Specifically, in 1977 the IRS ruled that the statement and waiver must recite that the "amount paid" has not been nor will it be at any time allowed as a deduction under § 2053. Rev. Rul. 77-357, 1977-2 C.B. 328. This contrasts with the treatment of some other types of expenses for which no income tax deduction is allowed, but which are deductible for estate tax purposes. For example, in Rev. Rul. 59-32, 1959-1 C.B. 245, the IRS ruled that the portion of expenses attributable to tax-exempt income, which is not deductible for income tax purposes, may be deducted on the estate tax return.

EXAMPLE 12-3.

T died last December 2011, after a 3-month illness during which medical expenses of $20,000 were incurred. The expenses were paid by *T*'s executor in January of this year. In order to reduce the potential estate tax liability of *T*'s estate to zero, *T*'s executor claimed an estate tax deduction for $5,000 of the expenses under § 2053. The necessary statement and waiver were filed with regard to the other $15,000 of expenses that were claimed on the decedent's final income tax return, which showed an adjusted gross income of $100,000. Under these circumstances, an estate tax deduction of $5,000 is allowable together with an income tax deduction of $7,500. The latter amount represents the excess of the expenses claimed for income tax purposes ($15,000) over 7.5% of the decedent's adjusted gross income for the period ($7,500). According to the IRS, no income or estate tax deduction is allowable for the other $7,500, which is within the 7.5% floor.

§12.3.5. Passive Activity Losses, §469

When passive activity property is transferred at death, the accumulated passive activity loss allocable to the property is deductible on a decedent's final income tax return as a loss not from a passive activity. The deduction is limited to the amount by which the total loss exceeds the excess of the basis of the property in the hands of the transferee (its stepped-up basis) over the adjusted basis of the property in the hands of the decedent immediately prior to death. §469(g)(2). As noted in §10.4.7, other dispositions are subject to different rules. For example, if passive activity property is disposed of in a fully taxable transaction, the accumulated passive losses are deductible in full. §469(g)(1).

§12.3.6. Miscellaneous Itemized Deductions, §67

The 1986 Act amended§67(a) to provide that miscellaneous itemized deductions are allowable to individual taxpayers only to the extent that they exceed two percent of the taxpayer's adjusted gross income. Section 67(b) defines "miscellaneous itemized deductions" negatively by enumerating twelve deductions that are not "miscellaneous." Among the nonmiscellaneous deductions are ones for interest, taxes, charitable gifts, and medical expenses. Estates and trusts are subject to the same rules except that they are allowed deductions (1) that are allowable under §§642(b), 651, and 661 and (2) "for costs which are paid or incurred in connection with the administration of the estate or trust and which would not have been incurred if the property were not held in such trust or estate" §67(e). In 2008 the Supreme Court held that the deductibility of an expense under §67(e) depended on whether the cost was "commonly" or "customarily" incurred when similar property was owned by an individual. Knight v. Commissioner, 128 S. Ct. 782, 169 L. Ed. 2d 652 (2008). The test adopted by the Court was inconsistent with the one contained in Prop. Reg. §1.67-4. As a consequence the proposed regulation was withdrawn and a different one proposed in 76 FR 55322 (September 7, 2011).

The 2011 version of the proposed regulation track the Supreme Court opinion and only except from the 2-percent floor costs that it would be uncommon, unusual or unlikely for an individual to incur. Prop. Reg. §1.67-4. In particular, investment advisory fees are subject to the 2 percent floor except for costs of investment advice beyond the amount that would be charged to an individual investor. In addition, a single fee paid to a fiduciary includes both costs for services subject to the 2 percent floor and ones that are not (a "bundled" fee), the bundled fee must be allocated in a reasonable way between costs that are subject to the 2-percent floor and ones that are not. See §§10.4.7; 12.13.1.

The joint return strategy with respect to miscellaneous deductions is the same as with medical deductions: A joint return is appropriate where the decedent's deductions will exceed his or her income and the deductions can be used to shelter from taxation some of the income of the surviving spouse.

§12.3.7. Election to Report Accrued Interest as Income, §454

The periodic increase in value of a Series EE United States Savings Bond, or similar obligation, does not constitute income to a cash basis taxpayer. However, a cash basis taxpayer may elect to report the increase in redemption value as income for the period in which it accrues. §454(a). If the election is made, the taxpayer must report all of the accrued increase in value of all such bonds (*e.g.*, Series EE, H, and HH United States Bonds) in the electing taxpayer's income tax return for the year in which the election is made. Thereafter an electing taxpayer must report the amount that accrues each year as income, unless the Secretary permits the taxpayer, under whatever conditions the Secretary deems necessary, to change the method of reporting such items. *Id.*

In the case of obligations owned by a decedent, the accrued interest may be reported on, (1) the decedent's final return, (2) a return filed for the estate, or (3) on a return filed by the distributee of the bonds. The IRS recognizes that the person who is obligated to file the decedent's final income tax return may elect to report all of the accrued increase in value as income on that return. Rev. Rul. 68-145, 1968-1 C.B. 203. If such an election is made with respect to the decedent's final return, it does not bind any other taxpayer (*e.g.*, the decedent's estate or the ultimate recipient of the bonds). If the election is made, it may increase the income tax due on the decedent's final return, which is deductible for estate tax purposes. *See* Reg. §20.2053-6(f). In such a case there will be no income in respect of a decedent attributable to the accrued interest and no deduction will be allowable under §691(c).

The IRS has allowed a decedent's executor to make an election under §454(a) although the decedent had transferred the bonds to a revocable trust. Rev. Rul. 79-409, 1979-2 C.B. 208. The IRS reasoned that because the grantor could have made the election regarding bonds in the trust (the interest on which was taxable to him under §676), the fiduciary required to file the deceased grantor's final income tax return "assumed the powers and duties of [the decedent] for this purpose, including the right to make an election under section 454(a) of the Code." *Id.*

If the election is not made, the unreported increment in value reflected in the redemption value of the bonds as of the date of the decedent's death constitutes income in respect of a decedent. Rev. Rul. 64-104, 1964-1 C.B. 223. As such, the taxpayer who must ultimately include the income in his or her income is entitled to a deduction under §691(c) for the state and federal death taxes that are attributable to it. In this connection note that the §691(c) deduction is not a miscellaneous itemized deduction that is subject to the two percent floor discussed above. §67(b)(7).

The decedent's personal representative, or the distributee of the bonds, may elect under §454(a) to report as income the amount that accrued during the decedent's lifetime. If the election is made, the taxpayer must report as current income the increment in value that accrues in each subsequent year. If no election is made the entire amount of accrued interest is reported in the year in which the bonds are disposed of, redeemed, or reach final maturity. Rev. Rul. 64-104, 1964-1 C.B. 223.

The election is typically made when it will cause the accrued interest to be reported on a return that has relatively little, or no other, income. Depending upon the circumstances, that return might be the decedent's final return, the estate's first or last return, a return for a testamentary trust, or a return for an individual distributee.

The key is to be aware of the options and to make the necessary decisions in a timely fashion.

The full value of bonds, including accrued interest, is includible in the decedent's gross estate whether or not an election is made under § 454.

§ 12.3.8. Election to Treat Qualified Revocable Trust as Part of Decedent's Estate for Income Tax Purposes

The 1997 Act added § 645, which allows an executor and the trustee of a qualified revocable trust to treat the trust as part of the estate. The election is discussed at § 10.15.

§ 12.3.9. Income from Assets That Were Formerly Community Property

Following the death of one spouse, one-half of the income from assets that were formerly the couple's community property is reportable by the estate and the other half by the surviving spouse. *Grimm v. Commissioner*, 894 F.2d 1165 (10th Cir. 1990). As indicated in *Grimm*, one-half of the income is reportable by the surviving spouse although it is received by and administered as a part of the deceased spouse's estate.

§ 12.4. S CORPORATION ELECTION, § 1362

At an early point the lawyer should determine whether or not an election has been made under § 1362 with respect to the estate's stock in S corporations. Under §§ 1361-1368, certain domestic small business corporations are permitted to elect that their income should be taxed directly to their shareholders rather than to the corporation. In general, an electing corporation may not have more than one class of stock, § 1361(b)(1)(D), or more than 100 shareholders, § 1361(b)(1)(A), all of whom must be individuals, estates, or trusts described in § 1361(c)(2). *See* §§ 11.4.-11.4.4.

An estate may be a shareholder of an electing corporation whether the election is made before or after the decedent's death. Where the election is made after the decedent's death, the estate and all other shareholders must give their consent. § 1362(a)(2); Reg. §§ 1.1362-1(a), 1.1362-6(b)(2)(ii).

The death of a shareholder does not affect an election that was previously made. In contrast, under prior law the decedent's personal representative was allowed to terminate an election by "affirmatively refusing to consent" to the election. Former § 1372(e)(1)(A). A personal representative no longer has such a power: Now an election may be terminated by the action of "more than one-half of the shares." § 1362(d)(1)(B).

An estate may continue as a shareholder of a Subchapter S corporation for the entire period the estate is under administration. The IRS has recognized, for example, that an estate may remain a shareholder during the period that payment of the estate tax is deferred under the predecessor of § 6166. Rev. Rul. 76-23, 1976-1 C.B. 264. Certain trusts may also be shareholders during and following the grantor's death. *See* § 10.4.14.

§12.5. PARTNERSHIP ELECTIONS, §§754, 732(d)(4)

A deceased partner's interest in a partnership is includible in his or her gross estate. The basis of the partnership interest in the hands of the decedent's estate or successors is equal to its federal estate tax value under §1014, increased by the successors' share of partnership liabilities and decreased to the extent that the value of the interest is attributable to items of income in respect of a decedent. §742; Reg. §1.742-1. The basis in the decedent's partnership interest (the so-called outside basis) is used to determine the income tax consequences of transactions involving the decedent's partnership interest (*e.g.*, sales or liquidations).

A partnership may elect under §754 that the basis of partnership property will be adjusted upon the transfer of an interest in the partnership by sale or exchange, upon the death of a partner, or upon the distribution of partnership property. Under Reg. §1.754-1(b), the election must be made in a written statement filed with the partnership return for the taxable year in which the partnership interest is transferred (*i.e.*, the year of the partner's death). If such an election is in effect, on the death of a partner the interest of the partner's estate or successors in each item of partnership property is increased or decreased in order to reflect the federal estate tax value of the deceased partner's interest in the partnership. Importantly, the adjustment also extends to a surviving spouse's interest in a community property partnership interest. Rev. Rul. 79-124, 1979-1 C.B. 225. The election must be made in a timely-filed return. However, tardy elections are commonly allowed under the provisions of Reg. §301.9100-1.

The regulations make it clear that the adjustment is only made with respect to the interests of the estate or successors of a deceased partner: "The amount of the increase or decrease constitutes an adjustment affecting the basis of partnership property with respect to the transferee [or deceased] partner only. Thus, for purposes of depreciation, depletion, gain or loss, and distributions, the transferee partner will have a special basis for those partnership properties which are adjusted under section 743(b) . . . ." Reg. §1.743-1(b).

As noted above, in the absence of an election under §754, the death of a partner does not affect the basis of the assets held by the partnership (the so-called inside basis). In such cases, a deceased partner's estate or successors will have a stepped-up basis in the decedent's partnership interest, but the bases of the partnership assets will be unchanged. Thus, the sale of an appreciated partnership asset may require the partnership and, derivatively, the surviving partners and the deceased partner's estate or successors, to recognize gain on the sale. Unless an effective election is made under §754, the outside basis is generally disregarded in determining the income tax consequences of transactions involving partnership assets. On the other hand, if an election under §754 is in effect, the inside basis is adjusted up or down with respect to the interest of the decedent partner's estate or his successors. Accordingly, if the partnership property has appreciated in value, such an election and adjustment may increase the depreciation deduction or reduce the gain allocated to the estate or the successors.

The inside-outside basis distinction is, in effect, extinguished if a decedent's partnership interest is completely liquidated. In the case of such a liquidation, the decedent's estate or successors take a basis in the distributed assets equal to their basis in the partnership, reduced by the amount of any cash received. §732(b).

The estate or the successors of a deceased partner are most likely to benefit from a §754 election where the partnership interest will not be liquidated and the fair market value of the partnership assets exceed their bases. Unless an election is made under §754, the income tax rules do not provide any current tax advantages where a deceased partner's estate or successors remain in the partnership. In particular, their bases in the partnership assets are not adjusted for purposes of computing gain or loss, depreciation or depletion, and so forth. §743(a).

EXAMPLE 12-4.

X's one-third interest in the XYZ partnership was valued at $100,000 in X's estate. The partnership owned 3 parcels of real property, each of which had a basis of $10,000 and a fair market value of $100,000. If no election is made under §754, the sale of Parcel One for $100,000 would result in a gain of $30,000 to each partner. On the other hand, if the partnership makes a timely election under §754, the basis of X's estate or successors in Parcel One would be increased to $33,333. Accordingly, the estate (or successors) would realize no gain as a result of its sale.

§12.5.1. Extensions to Make Election, Reg. §301.9100

Regulation 301.9100-2(a) allows an automatic 12-month extension to make a §754 election provided corrective action is taken within that period. §12.2.4. If a taxpayer establishes good cause for failure to make an income tax election within the period of time required by a regulation, the Commissioner may grant an extension under Reg. §301.9100-1. Reg. §1.754-1(b). The election must relate to the income, gift, estate, or generation-skipping transfer (GST) tax, the time for making the original election must be specified in the regulations, the request must be filed within a reasonable time, and the Commissioner must be satisfied that granting the extension will not prejudice the government's interests. Originally, extensions were limited to income tax elections. However, Reg. §301.9100 now applies to gift, estate and GST taxes as well. The standards applicable to extensions are stated in Rev. Proc. 92-85, 1992-2 C.B. 390, *as modified by* 93-28, 1993-2 C.B. 344.

§12.5.2. Section 732 Election

If a partnership does not make an election under §754, some relief may be provided by §732(d) to the extent property other than cash is distributed to the estate or to other successors within two years of the deceased partner's death. The estate or other successor must make an election under §732 for the year of the distribution if the distribution includes any property subject to depreciation, depletion, or amortization. Otherwise, the election must be made for the first taxable year of the transferee partner in which the basis of any distributed property is pertinent in determining his or her income tax. An election under §732 should be considered if an election under §754 would have been valuable but was not made by the partnership. Also, if the sale of an appreciated partnership asset occurs within two years of the deceased partner's death and no §754 election is in effect, the successors of the deceased partner are allowed to elect to have their share in the sale proceeds given the basis it would have taken had a §754 election by the partnership been in effect. §732(d); Reg. §1.732-1(d).

§12.5.3. Partnership Agreements

A properly drawn partnership agreement should specify whether the partnership is obligated to make a §754 election if a partnership interest is sold or exchanged or a partner dies. Some partnership agreements require the partnership to make the election at the request of the personal representative of a deceased partner. The failure to make a §754 election can subject the estate of a deceased partner to the imposition of substantial income tax liabilities that might otherwise be deferred or avoided. *See Estate of Ernest D. Skaggs,* 75 T.C. 191 (1980), *aff'd per curiam,* 672 F.2d 756 (9th Cir.), *cert. denied,* 459 U.S. 1037 (1982). (Large income tax deficiencies upheld against widow and deceased husband's estate on income from farming partnership. No §754 election was made; widow and estate improperly assigned stepped-up basis to crops sold and depreciable assets of partnership.)

A partnership may be reluctant to make a §754 election because of the permanency of the election, which at some future time might prove to be disadvantageous. (An election may only be revoked with the approval of the IRS.) An election might, for example, require a downward adjustment in the value of partnership property that had declined in value. An election also imposes additional administrative burdens on the partnership, which must keep separate records with respect to the interests of each affected partner—transferees and future admittees.

§12.6. DECLARATION AND PAYMENT OF ESTIMATED TAX

As noted above, estates are required to make estimated tax payments with respect to taxable years beginning after December 31, 1986 and ending two years or more after the date of the decedent's death. §6654(l). Trusts are also required to make estimated tax payments. Prior to 1987 neither an estate nor a trust was required to file a declaration of estimated tax or make any estimated tax payment. Former §6015(h) (repealed 1986).

The application of §6654 to an estate is illustrated by Example 12-5.

EXAMPLE 12-5.

D died on January 31, 2010. The personal representative of *D*'s estate elected to report the estate's income on the basis of a fiscal year ending June 30. No estimated tax payment is due with respect to the estate's initial short taxable year (January 31, 2010–June 30, 2010) or its second full taxable year (July 1, 2010–June 30, 2011). Estimated tax payments would be due, however, with respect to the estate's third taxable year, beginning July 1, 2011, unless the estate is closed and its final taxable year ends prior to January 31, 2012.

An addition to tax is imposed in the case of the underpayment of an installment of estimated tax. The addition to tax is calculated by multiplying the amount of the underpayment by the underpayment rate established by § 6621(a)(2) for the period of the underpayment. No addition to tax is imposed where, (1) the tax liability, less the credit allowable under § 31, is less than $1,000 for the current year, or (2) the preceding tax year was a full 12 months, the taxpayer had no tax liability for the year, and the taxpayer was a citizen or resident of the United States for the preceding tax year. § 6654(e)(1), (2).

No payment of estimated tax need be made with respect to an individual after the date of his or her death. However, a surviving spouse remains liable for the payments shown on a joint declaration of estimated tax unless he or she files an amended declaration. Where payments of estimated tax were made on a joint declaration, the surviving spouse and the decedent's personal representative are free to allocate the payments between the surviving spouse and the decedent. If they cannot agree on an allocation, the surviving spouse is allocated an amount that bears the same relation to the total payments as the amount of income tax that would be due on the surviving spouse's separate income tax return bears to the total amount of income tax due on the surviving spouse's separate return and the final return of the decedent. Reg. § 1.6015(b)-1(c)(2). If a sufficient amount of the payment is allocated to the surviving spouse and the surviving spouse files an amended declaration, it may be unnecessary for the surviving spouse to make any further payments of estimated tax for the year.

A trust making estimated tax payments may elect on a return filed within 65 days of the close of its taxable year to assign any amount of its quarterly payments to one or more of the beneficiaries of the trust. § 643(g). The amount subject to the election is treated as a distribution that carries out distributable net income to the beneficiaries on the last day of the taxable year of the trust. Accordingly, the trust is eligible for a § 661 deduction if it makes a valid election under § 643(g).

§ 12.7. SELECTION OF A TAXABLE YEAR FOR AN ESTATE OR TRUST, § 441

The estate of a decedent is treated as a separate taxpayer for federal income tax purposes. An income tax return must be filed for each taxable year in which the estate has gross income of $600 or more. § 6012(a)(3).

As a new taxpayer, the personal representative may choose a taxable year for the estate. The estate's income may be reported on a calendar year basis or on the basis of a fiscal year ending on the last day of any month within 12 months of the decedent's death. § 441(b).

An estate's fiduciary income tax return (Form 1041) must be filed on or before the fifteenth day of the fourth month following the close of the taxable year. § 6072(a). The election of a taxable year is made by timely filing a return for the taxable year on the basis of which the return was prepared. For example, if the decedent died on May 15, the personal representative could elect to report the estate's income on the basis of a calendar year or on the basis of a fiscal year ending on the last day of any month from May through April. The personal representative could elect to use the calendar year by filing a return on or before the following April 15, reporting the income of the estate for the period from April 15 through December 31. The first taxable year of the estate will ordinarily be a short one. *See* §443(a)(2). However, succeeding taxable years must consist of 12 months, except for the last taxable year of the estate, which ends on the day the administration of the estate is completed. Reg. §1.441-1T(b)(1)(i)(B); §443(a)(2). The selection of a taxable year for the estate should be based upon the overall circumstances of the estate and its beneficiaries. In particular, the personal representative should project the receipt of income by the estate, the length of time the estate will remain open, the amount of deductions that may be claimed for income tax purposes, and the time at which distributions will be made. The planning should also take into account the circumstances and tax brackets of the beneficiaries, which will affect policy decisions that are made regarding such things as distributions and deduction of expenses.

It appears that some auditors have (mistakenly) argued that a Form 1128, Application to Adopt, Change, or Retain a Tax Year, must be filed in order for an estate to elect a fiscal year. The regulations, however, provide that the "taxable year of a new taxpayer is adopted by filing its first Federal income tax return using that taxable year." Reg. §1.441-1(c)(1). The Form 1128 would be used only in the case of an estate that has already filed its first return and seeks to change its taxable year.

In selecting a taxable year for the estate, the overall objective of minimizing the tax costs to the estate and its beneficiaries often calls for the adoption of a taxable year that will result in the division of the estate's income into as many taxable years as possible. Such an approach provides the estate with the maximum number of $600 exemptions, one of which is allowed for each taxable year the estate is in existence. §642(b). It may also help prevent bunching of too much income in the estate's initial taxable year and equalize the amount of income that is taxable to the estate in each taxable year.

EXAMPLE 12-6.

T died on February 20 and the executor received a large payment on March 15 that constituted income in respect of a decedent. The estate is expected to remain open for 18 months. If no distributions of income-producing property are made, the gross income of *T*'s estate is expected to remain relatively constant over the period the estate is open. The executor should consider adopting a tax year that ends soon after receiving the March 15 payment in order to minimize the other income that the estate will report for the period. Thus, the executor might adopt a fiscal year ending on March 31. Such an election would spread the estate's income over 3 taxable years instead of 2, such as would occur if the executor adopted a calendar year. Based upon a fiscal year ending March 31, the 3 taxable years would be:

    Year One: Date of death through March 31.
    Year Two: April 1 through March 31.
    Year Three: April 1 through August 20.

In selecting the taxable year and planning distributions, the executor may also seek to defer the income taxation of income that is carried out to the beneficiaries as a result of making distributions to them. The opportunity to defer exists if the selection of a taxable year and distributions are carefully planned. The governing rule requires a beneficiary to report income that is carried out by an estate distribution in the year that includes the end of the estate's taxable year during which the distribution was made, § 662(c). The rule sounds complicated, but it is really rather simple, as indicated by the following example:

EXAMPLE 12-7.

T died on January 10, 2010. *T*'s personal representative elected to file income tax returns for the estate on the basis of a fiscal year ending on February 28. Any income that was carried out by distributions made to a beneficiary during the estate's first taxable year (January 10—February 28, 2010) would be included in the income of the beneficiary for that year. Income carried out by distributions made during the remainder of that calendar year (March 1–December 31, 2010) would not be included in the beneficiary's 2007 return. Instead, those distributions would be reflected on the estate's return for the period March 1, 2010—February 28, 2011 and reported in the beneficiary's 20110 return. Thus, a calendar year beneficiary who received a distribution on March 15, 2010 would report income arising from the distribution in the beneficiary's return for 2011 unless the estate terminated prior to January 1, 2011. If the estate did not terminate during 2010, its taxable year for the period during which the distribution was made would end on February 28, 2011. In that case the tax on the distribution would not have to be paid until April 15, 2012, more than 2 years after the distribution was made.

Short Final Tax Year. The personal representative may plan for a short final taxable year for the estate in which a large portion of the estate administration expenses will be paid, which will maximize the amount of the estate's nonbusiness deductions that can be carried out to the beneficiaries under § 642(h). *See* § 12.13.5. The excess deductions are carried out to the "beneficiaries succeeding to the property of the estate or trust," § 642(h), who are usually the residuary beneficiaries. Reg. § § 1.642(h)-3(c), (d). Distributions of the estate may be planned, together with the selection of a tax year and payment of estate expenses, in a way that maximizes the tax benefit of the excess deductions.

The deductions carried out to a beneficiary will largely be miscellaneous itemized deductions for purposes of § 67. They, together with other miscellaneous itemized deductions, will be deductible by the beneficiary only to the extent they exceed two percent of the individual beneficiary's adjusted gross income. The overall tax burden may be lower if a deduction for these items is claimed on the federal estate tax return where they are not subject to any floor.

Estates and trusts are generally taxed as individuals. However, as noted in § 12.6, estates are not required to make estimated tax payments with respect to taxable years that end within two years after the date of the decedent's death. The income taxation of trusts is summarized at § 10.4.

§ 12.8. WAIVER OF FEES

If a family member or other beneficiary is serving as personal representative, he or she may wish to consider waiving the right to be compensated. Accordingly, at an early point the lawyer should discuss the question with the personal representative. Family members who serve as personal representative often waive the right to receive a fee either to avoid conflict with other beneficiaries or, possibly, to improve the overall tax results. A personal representative with a modest income might choose to accept payment of a fee each year that would support an equivalent deductible annual contribution to an IRA. The right to receive compensation may be waived without risk of adverse gift or income tax consequences provided the waiver is made at a sufficiently early stage.

Amounts received for serving as a personal representative are earned income and are generally deductible by the estate for either income or estate tax purposes. *See* § 12.13. The tax impact of accepting compensation for serving as personal representative can be ameliorated if the fee is paid in installments over two or more tax years. Of course, if no fees are paid, the personal representative is usually not required to report any amount as compensation and the estate is not entitled to any deduction. Under Rev. Rul. 56-472, 1956-2 C.B. 21, a fiduciary may waive all or a portion of the fees he or she is entitled to receive. A waiver should be executed promptly if the personal representative decides to forego receiving his or her fee. Otherwise, the personal representative could face a costly tax conflict with the IRS. Importantly, the compensation received by a nonprofessional fiduciary is generally not considered to be income from a trade or business. Rev. Rul. 58-5, 1958-1 C.B. 322. Accordingly, it is not subject to the self-employment tax.

The crucial test of whether the executor of an estate or any other fiduciary in a similar situation may waive his right to receive statutory commissions without thereby incurring any income or gift tax liability is whether the waiver involved will at least primarily constitute evidence of an intent to render a gratuitous service. If the timing, purpose, and effect of the waiver make it serve any other important objective, it may then be proper to conclude that the fiduciary has thereby enjoyed a realization of income by means of controlling the disposition thereof, and at the same time, has also effected a taxable gift by means of any resulting transfer to a third party of his contingent beneficial interest in a part of the assets under his fiduciary control. Rev. Rul. 66-167, 1966-1 C.B. 20.

Revenue Ruling 66-167 concludes that the requisite intent to serve gratuitously will be deemed to have been established if the fiduciary, within six months of his or her initial appointment, delivers a formal waiver of the right to any compensation to one or more of the estate's primary beneficiaries The ruling also indicates that an intent to serve gratuitously may be implied where the fiduciary fails to claim fees or commissions at the time of filing the tax returns and accounts and if all of the other facts and circumstances evidence a fixed and continuing intent to serve gratuitously. For this purpose the claiming of fees as a deduction on one or more of the estate's tax returns is considered to be inconsistent with a fixed and definite intent to serve without compensation.

In *George M. Breidert*, 50 T.C. 844 (1968), *acq.*, 1969-2 C.B. xxiv, the Tax Court refused to follow the test set out in Rev. Rul. 66-167 and held that the taxpayer had not realized any income despite an ineffective waiver of executor's fees and an actual award of fees by the probate court. The taxpayer did not, in fact, receive the fees and the court found sufficient intent to waive the fees so as to avoid subjecting them to tax.

EXAMPLE 12-8.

D died in 2011, leaving all of his property in equal shares to his unmarried, retired nephew, *N,* and his cousin, *C. N* is the executor of *D*'s will for which he is entitled to receive a fee this year of $50,000. *D*'s taxable estate, apart from any executor's fee paid to *N,* will be $5,500,000. *N* expects to have a taxable income of $100,000 this year excluding any fee he receives from *D*'s estate. If *N* does not waive the right to receive the fee, he will have $50,000 more of income, subject to the federal income tax at a 28% rate ($14,000). On the other hand, *D*'s taxable estate will be reduced by $50,000, which would otherwise be subject to tax at a 35% rate ($17,500). Thus, the total amount of federal taxes paid by *D*'s estate and *N* will be $3,500 lower if the fee is paid.. In an actual case, the parties must also consider the potential impact of state income taxes. Also, note that the fees of a nonprofessional individual fiduciary are treated as earned income, which may support a contribution to an IRA, but are not subject to self-employment taxes. As indicated above, a timely waiver of the fee would not involve any gift from *N* to the other beneficiary.

C. ESTATE TAX AND INCOME TAX DEDUCTIONS

§ 12.9. GENERAL

This part is concerned with the deductibility of various costs, expenses, and losses for estate tax and income tax purposes and the effect that the deductions may have on charitable and marital deductions. One class of deductions, called "deductions in respect of a decedent," can be claimed for both estate and income tax purposes. § 12.10. From the planning perspective, perhaps the most important items are those that may be deducted on either return, but not both. § 12.13. Such alternatively deductible items give the planner an opportunity to affect the amount of the marital and charitable deductions, to defer the payment of some taxes, and to achieve overall tax savings by carefully allocating the deductions among the estate's tax returns. The planner should recognize that the elections open to the personal representative sometimes involve serious conflicts of interest—ones that may invite court intervention and litigation. It may be necessary to make an equitable adjustment of accounts between beneficiaries when the deductions are claimed for income tax purposes and, perhaps, in other cases. *See* § 12.14. An equitable adjustment of the classic type relieves the residuary beneficiaries of the burden of the increase in the federal estate tax that results from claiming alternatively deductible expenses that are paid from the residue as income tax, rather than estate tax deductions. Of course, such elective use of the deductions will be relatively rare when the income tax rate applicable to an estate is below the estate's marginal estate tax rate.

Planning for the decedent's final return also involves consideration of the income tax consequences for the decedent's estate and its beneficiaries. The income tax rules applicable to complex trusts reviewed in § 10.4 generally apply to estates. As in the case of trusts, the concept of distributable net income (DNI) limits the tax consequences of distributions by an estate to its beneficiaries. *See* § § 10.4.3, 12.37.2. Complex trusts and estates are entitled to deduct the amounts paid, credited, or required to be distributed to beneficiaries during the year. § § 10.4.4, 12.37.1. The distribution deduction is limited, however, to the amount of the estate's DNI. For their part, the beneficiaries who receive distributions must report an amount equal to the distribution deduction allowed to the trust. Note that an executor may elect to treat a distribution of gross income by an estate in a taxable year as having been made in the preceding taxable year of the estate. § 642(c)(1).

The allocation among beneficiaries is refined by the application of the separate share rule, § § 10.4.9, 12.37, and the tier system under which distributions carrying out DNI are first allocated to beneficiaries who are entitled to receive the income required to be distributed currently. *See* § § 10.4.9, 12.37.3. If any DNI remains, it is allocated to the other beneficiaries (the second tier). Distributions to beneficiaries have the same character in the hands of the beneficiaries as they did in the hands of the estate. Planning for distributions is reviewed in § § 12.37-12.41. An estate is entitled to an exemption of $600. *See* § 10.4.5. Once income is taxed to an estate it is not taken into account in determining the income tax consequences of making distributions to beneficiaries.

The amount of charitable and marital deductions may be affected if expenses of administration are paid from the charitable or marital bequest or from its income. A series of court decisions on the point culminated in *Estate of Hubert v. Commissioner,* 117 S.Ct. 1124 (1997), which held that the regulations then in effect did not require the value of a charitable or marital bequest to be reduced by the amount of income used to pay expenses of administration unless the amount was quantitatively material.

The regulations issued in December 1999 in response to *Estate of Hubert* require the marital deduction to be reduced by the amount of estate expenses paid from the principal of the property interest or from the income it produced that would not have been incurred had the decedent not died. Reg. § 20.2056(b)-4(d). Estate transmission expenses include "executor commissions and attorneys fees (except to the extent of commissions or fees specifically related to investment, preservation, or maintenance of the assets), probate fees, expenses incurred in construction proceedings and defending against will contests, and appraisal fees." Reg. § 20.2056(b)-4(d). On the other hand, the amount is not reduced by estate management expenses, which include "investment advisory fees, stock brokerage commissions, custodial fees, and interest." Reg. § 20.2056(b)-4(d). However, to prevent a double deduction, the amount of a marital or charitable deduction must be reduced to the extent its share of interest or principal is used to pay management expenses deducted under § 2053. § 2056(b)(9); Reg. § 20.2056(b)-4(d)(3). In this connection, note that management expenses may be paid from the marital or charitable share and deducted for income tax purposes without affecting the amount of the marital or charitable deduction. Reg. § 20.2056(b)-4(d)(5), Example 4. Under Reg. § 20.2055-3 the same general rules apply in valuing transfers to charity.

The portion of the costs and expenses allocable to production of tax-exempt income received by an estate is not deductible for income tax purposes. § 265(a). However, that portion may be claimed as a deduction for estate tax purposes. *See* Reg. § 1.642(g)-2.

§ 12.10. DEDUCTIONS IN RESPECT OF A DECEDENT

Both income and estate tax deductions are allowed for taxes, interest, business expenses, and some other items for which the decedent was liable, but which were not properly allowable as deductions on the decedent's final income tax return. The dual deductibility of deductions in respect of a decedent is recognized in Reg. § 1.642(g)-2, which provides that "deductions for taxes, interest, business expenses, and other items accrued at the date of a decedent's death so that they are allowable as a deduction under section 2053(a)(3) for estate tax purposes as claims against the estate, and are also allowable under section 691(b) as deductions in respect of a decedent for income tax purposes. However, section 642(g) [denial of double deductions] is applicable to deductions for interest, business expenses, and other items not accrued at the date of the decedent's death so that they are allowable as deductions for estate tax purposes only as administration expenses under section 2053(a)(2)." Of course, the deductions for interest and taxes are allowable only to the extent the respective requirements of § § 163 and 164 are satisfied.

Income tax deductions are allowed for miscellaneous itemized deductions only to the extent they exceed 2 percent of the taxpayer's adjusted gross income. § 67. For purposes of § 67, miscellaneous itemized deductions includes all itemized deductions other than ones allowed under 12 Code sections enumerated in § 67(b) including § 163 (interest), § 164 (taxes), § 165(a) (losses), § 170 (charitable contributions), and § 642(c) (amounts paid or permanently set aside for a charitable purpose). The overall tax burden may be lessened by claiming any administration expenses that might be subject to the two percent floor as deductions on the federal estate tax return. That approach makes full use of the deductions and may simultaneously reduce the amount of the marital deduction that must be claimed on the decedent's return in order to eliminate the necessity of paying any estate tax. Of course, a reduction in the amount of the marital deduction also reduces the amount that is potentially includible in the surviving spouse's estate.

The estate is usually the taxpayer entitled to claim deductions in respect of a decedent. § 691(b)(1)(A). However, if the estate is not liable to discharge an obligation, the deduction is allowed to the person who succeeds to the decedent's property subject to the obligation. § 691(b)(1)(B).

The IRS has allowed a decedent's estate both income and estate tax deductions for periodic payments made by the estate to the decedent's former spouse under a divorce decree. The estate tax deduction for the commuted value of the payments was allowable under § 2053(a)(3) as a claim against the estate. Payments to the former spouse are deductible under § 661 as distributions for income tax purposes. *See* Rev. Rul. 67-304, 1967-2 C.B. 224.

§12.11. Deductions Allowed Only for Estate Tax Purposes

Some expenses are deductible under §2053 for estate tax purposes but not for income tax purposes. This category includes funeral expenses, gift taxes, federal income taxes due in connection with the decedent's final return, or any prior return, and the debts and obligations of the decedent. Also, because of the limitation imposed by §265, administration expenses attributable to tax-exempt income are not deductible for income tax purposes. Rev. Rul. 59-32, 1959-1 C.B. 245. However, such expenses are deductible for estate tax purposes. The costs incurred in selling the decedent's residence are deductible administration expenses under §2053(a) to the extent the expenses were incurred in order to pay the decedent's debts and expenses of settling the estate. LR 9342002 (TAM).

Regulations finalized in 2009 require that debts and expenses be bona fide in order to be deductible. Toward that end, the regulations describe the extent to which events that occur after a decedent's death may be taken into account in determining whether, and to what extent, deductions are allowable under §2053 for claims and expenses. Reg. §20.2053-1(b)(2). Claims and expenses that satisfy all of the applicable requirements, but have not been paid, are deductible if "the amount to be paid is ascertainable with reasonable certainty and will be paid." Reg. §20.2053-1(d)(4)(i). Of course, no deduction is allowable for a claim or expense that is essentially donative in nature. Reg. §20.2053-1(b)(2)(i). Contingent, unmatured and contested claims are generally not deductible, but may become deductible to the extent they become enforceable. Reg. §20.2053-4(d)(1), (2). In order to preserve the deductibility of such an item if it is later paid, an estate may file a claim for refund; if it is not paid within the period of limitation for the filing of a claim for refund, the estate may file a protective claim for refund. Id. An item is deductible on the estate tax return only to the extent the requirements of §2053 are satisfied. In general, an expense must be: (1) actually paid, (2) reasonable in amount, and (3) properly allowable under the local law. The last requirement is one that sometimes causes a deduction to be denied. Section 2106 limits the proportion of §§2053 and 2054 items that are deductible by the estate of a nonresident alien. Under §2106(a), the portion that is deductible is limited to the same proportion that the value of the assets with a United States situs at the time of the decedent's death bears to the total value of his gross estate, wherever located. *See* §9.9.

Funeral Expenses. The requirement that an expense be allowable under local law bars the deductibility of part or all of the funeral expenses in some states. In particular, no deduction is allowable for funeral expenses imposed on and paid by the surviving spouse in accordance with local law. Rev. Rul. 76-369, 1976-2 C.B. 281. Similarly, only half of the amount of the funeral expenses is deductible in community property states that impose the liability for payment of the expenses upon the entire community. *Estate of Lang v. Commissioner,* 97 F.2d 867 (9th Cir. 1938) (Washington law); Rev. Rul. 70-156, 1970-1 C.B. 190 (pre-June 17, 1970 California law). Because of that rule, several states, including Texas, California, and New Mexico amended their laws to relieve the surviving spouse from any obligation to pay the funeral expenses of a deceased spouse, making an estate tax deduction allowable for the full amount. Rev. Rul. 71-168, 1971-1 C.B. 271 (California); Rev. Rul. 69-193, 1969-1 C.B. 222 (Texas); N.M. Stat. Ann. §45-2-805 (2011). Under Idaho law the decedent's funeral expenses are also fully deductible. *Estate of W. S. Lee,* 11 T.C. 141 (1948), *acq.,* 1948-2

C.B. 3. Because of the availability of the unlimited marital deduction since 1981, the issue has decreased in importance.

Charitable Pledges. Note that an enforceable charitable pledge may be deductible under §2053(c), which may be of more advantage to the estate than a charitable deduction under §2055. Reg. §20.2053-5. In particular, such a deduction may assist the estate in qualifying for the benefits of §§303, 2057, and 6166. *See* Parts C and D of Chapter 11. Decisions confirm that, charitable pledges are only deductible to the extent they are enforceable under local law. *Estate of Jack H. Levin,* T.C. Memo. 1995-81 (Florida law). Also, in LR 9718031 the IRS ruled that the decedent's estate was entitled to deduct the full amount of the estate's payment to a university in fulfillment of the decedent's charitable pledge to a building campaign that was enforceable under local law.

Obligations to Family Members. Claims and expenses involving family members are subject to special scrutiny. Reg. §20.2053-1(b)(2)(ii). In one case, however, a deduction was allowed for amounts the decedent's estate paid to his children pursuant to an agreement with a former spouse in consideration of her forgoing the right to seek higher support payments. *Estate of Kosow v. Commissioner,* 45 F.3d 1524 (11th Cir. 1995). In another, *Estate of Waters v. Commissioner,* 48 F.3d 838 (4th Cir. 1995), a deduction was allowed for amounts paid pursuant to a postmarital settlement agreement equitably dividing their property. A deduction was also allowed in LR 9527007 (TAM) for the value of the interests of the decedent's former spouse in a trust that was created pursuant to a property settlement agreement between them. Interestingly, as a result of the deduction the value of the surviving spouse's interest may not be taxed in either of their estates.

§12.12. DEDUCTIONS ALLOWED ONLY FOR INCOME TAX PURPOSES

Some expenses incurred after death are deductible for income tax purposes, but not for estate tax purposes. They include state income taxes on the estate's post-mortem income, real estate taxes that accrue after death, and interest that accrues after death to the extent it is not allowable as an expense of administration under local law. Note, however, that interest accrued after death may be deductible as an expense of administration under §2053(a)(2). *See* §12.13.

The IRS has generally resisted allowing a deduction for postmortem interest on loans outstanding at the time of the decedent's death. *See* Rev. Rul. 77-461, 1977-2 C.B. 324. However, the Tax Court has allowed a deduction in such instances where the interest was paid to extend debts incurred by the decedent. *Estate of William M. Wheless,* 72 T.C. 470 (1979), *nonacq.,* 1982-1 C.B. 1; *Estate of Jane deP. Webster,* 65 T.C. 968 (1976), *acq. and nonacq.,* 1977-2 C.B. 2. According to the Tax Court in the *Wheless* case, "the expenses sought to be deducted as administration expenses must be actually and necessarily incurred in the administration of the estate and they must be allowable administration expenses under local law." 72 T.C. at 479. The estates of persons dying before 1998 were allowed to deduct interest actually paid with respect to the amount of estate tax that was deferred under §6166 or under former §6166A. Rev. Rul. 78-125, 1978-1 C.B. 292; Rev. Rul. 80-250, 1980-2 C.B. 278 (deduction under §2053(a)(2) disallowed for estimated future tax expense under §6166A); Rev. Proc. 81-27, 1981-2 C.B. 547. For decedents dying after 1997, the 1997 Act lowered the interest rate payable on the portion of the estate tax that is deferred under § 6166 and amended § § 163 and 2053 to bar the any deduction for interest payments with respect to the deferred portion. *See* § 11.28. Post-mortem interest on income tax deficiencies accrued while contesting decedent's income tax liabilities is also deductible. Rev. Rul. 69-402, 1969-2 C.B. 176.

Estates are generally bound by the same rules on business and capital losses as individuals. Capital gains and losses retain their distinct character, separate from ordinary income, and capital losses are first netted against capital gains. A capital asset be held for 12 months or more for gain or loss on sale or exchange to be characterized as long-term.

The 1986 Act introduced a new category of loss: the passive activity loss. § 469. *See* § § 12.3.5, 10.4.7. An activity is characterized as passive where the taxpayer is involved in a trade or business in which the taxpayer does not materially participate, including any rental activity whether or not the taxpayer materially participates. An activity is characterized as passive whether it is conducted by an individual, estate, trust, pass-through entity, or closely-held Subchapter C corporation. Passive activity losses are generally only allowable against passive activity income. However, losses from real estate rental activity are allowed to offset up to $25,000 of ordinary income for any "natural person." § 469(i). The offset available to natural persons is phased out for those with adjusted gross incomes exceeding $100,000. Importantly, this offset is not allowed to estates or trusts.

§ 12.13. Deductions Allowable for Either Income or Estate Tax Purposes

Administration expenses and casualty losses are deductible either for income tax or estate tax purposes, but not both. Administration expenses include the fees of the personal representative and the lawyer, which together often account for the bulk of an estate's deductions. For that reason, the personal representative's election regarding the use of the deductions can be very important. As noted below, where all of the community property is subject to administration upon the death of a spouse, only a portion of the expenses of administration are deductible. Under § 642(g), an income tax deduction is allowable only if a statement is filed in duplicate to the effect that the items have not been allowed as deductions from the gross estate of the decedent under § § 2053 or 2054 and that all rights to claim the items as deductions under those sections are waived. Reg. § 1.642(g)-1. That regulation permits the statement to be filed at any time before the expiration of the limitations period for the taxable year for which the deduction is sought. However, an income tax deduction is not allowable if an estate tax deduction has been finally allowed. *Id*. Filing the statement prevents the executor from changing the plan and claiming the items instead as estate tax deductions. Accordingly, some commentators suggest that the statement and waiver should not be filed because it limits the executor's future flexibility. They reason that the executor can file the statement at any time until the expiration of the limitations period, after which the IRS could not disallow the deductions in any case.

The regulations permit alternatively deductible items to be claimed wholly on either return or partly on one return and partly on the other. "One deduction or portion of a deduction may be allowed for income tax purposes if the appropriate statement is filed, while another deduction or portion is allowed for estate tax purposes." Reg. § 1.642(g)-2. Of course, a cash basis taxpayer may only deduct the expenses for income tax purposes on the return for the year in which they were paid. As noted in § 12.9, the portion of costs and expenses attributable to tax-exempt income is not deductible for income tax purposes. § 265(a).

Fees of Personal Representatives and Trustees. To be deductible as an expense of administration under § 2053, the expense must meet the requirements of local and federal law. *Estate of Grant v. Commissioner*, 294 F.3d 352 (2d Cir. 2002). *Estate of Grant* holds that the deduction for the personal representative's fee is limited to the amount "necessary" for the administration of the estate. Accordingly, it is limited to the portion, properly allowable under state law, of the value of the estate subject to administration ($11,253). The opinion states, "By choosing to convey the bulk of her assets through a trust, Grant limited the amount of her property that was transferred in her estate and consequently limited the estate's tax deduction for administration expenses."

Interest on Deferred Estate Tax. The estates of persons dying before 1998 were allowed to claim an estate tax deduction for the interest on deferred estate taxes. The 1997 Act lowered the interest rate payable on the amount of any deferred estate tax and barred the deduction of interest under§ § 163 and 2053. § § 163(k), 2053(c)(1)(D).

Expenses of Maintaining Property. In an *en banc* decision, *Estate of Millikin*, 125 F.2d 339 (6th Cir. 1997), the court held that a deduction is allowed for an expense only if it is both an administration expense as the Regulations define the phrase and it is allowable in the jurisdiction in which the estate is administered. *Estate of Millikin* vacated an earlier decision by a panel of the court, *Estate of Millikin*, 106 F.3d 1263 (6th Cir. 1997), and overruled an earlier contrary decision, *Estate of Park v. Commissioner*, 475 F.2d 673 (6th Cir. 1973). On remand the Tax Court disallowed deductions for maintaining an extensive estate and for its sale. 76 T.C.M. (CCH) 1076 (1998).

The expenses of operating a cattle ranch, which was nonprobate asset, was deductible under § 2053(b) because they were necessary to protect and preserve the value of the estate. *Estate of Edna P. Lockett*, 75 T.C.M. (CCH) 1731 (1998).

In *Estate of Rinaldi v. United States*, 80 A.F.T.R.2d 5234 (Ct. Cl. 1997) the court upheld casualty loss deductions based upon the diminution in the value of separate citrus groves as a result of a freeze in 1989. It rejected the government's argument that the loss must be limited to the diminution in value of each tree: "Under the facts of this case, the freeze damage inflicted on the entire grove must be considered in determining plaintiff's allowable deduction for casualty losses."

§ 12.13.1. Miscellaneous Itemized Deductions, § 67

The 2-percent floor for miscellaneous itemized deductions,§ 67, does not limit the deductibility of administration expenses of trusts and estates that would not otherwise have been incurred. See § 10.4.7. In particular, under § 67(e) for purposes of computing the adjusted gross income of an estate or trust, deductions are allowable "for costs which are paid or incurred in connection with the administration of the estate or trust and which would not have been incurred if the property were not held in such trust or estate." Guidance regarding the application of this rule was provided by the Supreme Court in Knight v. Commissioner, 128 S. Ct. 782, 169 L. Ed. 2d 652 (2008). In addition, in computing adjusted gross income, § 67(e) allows the deductions described in § 642(b) (personal exemption), § § 651 and 661 (distribution deductions).

As indicated above, the overall tax burdens may be lightened if miscellaneous itemized deductions that would be within the 2-percent floor are claimed on the estate tax return.

In September 2011, the version of regulations under § 67(e) that were proposed in 2007 were withdrawn and a new ones were issued that follow the Knight decision. Under the proposed regulations costs are subject to the 2-percent floor costs except for ones that it would be uncommon, unusual or unlikely for an individual to incur. Prop. Reg. § 1.67-4(b). In addition, investment advisory fees are subject to the 2 percent floor except for costs of investment advice that exceed the amount that would be charged to an individual investor. Importantly, a single fee paid to a fiduciary includes both costs for services subject to the 2 percent floor and ones that are not (a "bundled" fee), the bundled fee must be allocated in a reasonable way between costs that are subject to the 2-percent floor and ones that are not. See § § 10.4.7.

§ 12.13.2. Expenses of Sale: Capital Gain Offset or Estate Tax Deduction, § 642(g)

The expense of selling an item is deductible under § 2053 if the sale is necessary in order to "pay the decedent's debts, expenses of administration, or taxes, to preserve the estate, or to effect distribution." A deduction is not allowed for the costs of a sale that was not required for those purposes. *Estate of Millikin*, 76 T.C.M. (CCH) 1076 (1998), described above.

Under § 642(g), an item may not be used to offset the sales price for income tax purposes if it is deducted for estate tax purposes. (Prior to 1977, the expenses of making a necessary sale of the property of an estate were allowable both as an offset against the selling price for the purpose of determining gain or loss and as a deductible expense of administration for estate tax purposes. Rev. Rul. 71-173, 1971-1 C.B. 204 (declared obsolete by Rev. Rul. 89-75, 1989-1 C.B. 319, as to tax years ending after October 4, 1976).) Accordingly, an executor must choose whether to claim the item as an offset to the capital gain or as an estate tax deduction. Where the estate will pay any estate tax, it is generally preferable to claim it as an estate tax deduction.

§ 12.13.3. Planning Considerations

The planner should make a decision regarding the return on which the administration expenses and casualty losses will be taken as deductions only after considering carefully the impact on the estate and the beneficiaries. In particular, the planner should note that casualty losses claimed on the estate's income tax return are subject to § 67 (the 2-percent floor for miscellaneous itemized deductions). As noted above, § 67(e) exempts costs incurred for estate administration which would not otherwise have been incurred. Thus, the estate should be allowed to deduct fully executor's and attorney's fees. However, in some instances the IRS has required confirmation that the accounting and legal services were actually provided to, and paid for by, the estate. *See* § 10.7.4.

§12.13.4. IRS Access to Attorney's Time Records

The IRS may subpoena an attorney's time records and other documents that relate to the attorney's fees for which an estate tax deduction is claimed, *United States v. White*, 853 F.2d 107 (2d Cir. 1988), *cert. dismissed as improvidently granted*, 493 U.S. 5 (1989). According to *White* the subpoena must be issued if the IRS meets the requirements of *United States v. Powell*, 379 U.S. 48 (1964). They are: "(1) the investigation will be conducted pursuant to a legitimate purpose; (2) the inquiry may be relevant to that purpose; (3) the information sought is not already within the Commissioner's possession; and (4) the administrative steps required by the Code have been followed."

§12.13.5. Comparative Tax Benefits of Deductions

In order to determine the return upon which deductions will be claimed, the planner should compare the marginal estate tax and income tax rates that will apply. Of course, under the existing rate structures the marginal federal estate tax rate is invariably higher than the marginal federal income tax rate. Accordingly, alternatively deductible items are most often claimed as deductions on the estate tax return. Where the overall tax costs are essentially the same the benefit of the deductions may be maximized by splitting them between the two returns. In other cases, it may be beneficial to claim the deductions all on one of the returns. Consideration must also be given to other impacts of claiming the deductions on one return or the other. They include the applicability of state income taxes, the effect on the marital deduction and other gifts, and the effect on the beneficiaries of the estate.

The planning should also take into account the possibility of carrying out to the estate's beneficiaries the estate's excess income tax deductions in its final taxable year. *See* §642(h). *See also* §12.7 (selection of tax year); §12.37.5 (distributions). The benefit of the carryover of the deductions is usually maximized if the estate's final taxable year is a short one, during which it has little income. As noted above, expenses are deductible by the estate for income tax purposes only in the year they are paid. Here, again, the planner should be alert to the possible impact of §67, the 2-percent floor of which may apply to deductions carried out by §642(h)—even where it would not apply to the same deduction were it claimed by the estate.

In some cases the combined income tax liability of the estate and the beneficiaries will be reduced if excess deductions arise in the estate's final taxable year and are carried out to the estate's beneficiaries. §642(h). Excess deductions may arise where, for example, substantially all of the lawyer's and executor's fees are paid in the estate's final, short taxable year. In order to plan most effectively for the payment of the fees and closure of the estate, the lawyer must be aware of the income tax position of the beneficiaries. Where it will assist the beneficiaries, the lawyer may agree to defer payment of his or her fee until the estate's final taxable year. The deferral, of course, conflicts with the lawyer's interest in being paid currently. A lawyer may be willing to defer payment of a fee where it produces a significant tax saving. However, the possibility that payment of the fee might be deferred should be discussed with the executor at the outset along with other matters relating to the lawyer's compensation. They might agree, for example, that interest should be paid by the estate on any portion of the fee that is unpaid for more than a specified period after it is earned and billed. However, it may be inappropriate to do so, particularly where the local law prescribes a statutory fee which is customarily not paid until termination of the estate. Charging interest may also be questionable unless the lawyer charges interest on the unpaid balance of fees owed by other clients. In any case, the lawyer should be cautious in dealing with the matter because of conflict-of-interest concerns. Whether or not there is a technical conflict of interest, the beneficiaries are interested parties whose interests and concerns should be taken into account. Overall, it seems doubtful that a lawyer would be required to forego payment of the fee for a protracted period in order to confer a tax advantage on the beneficiaries of an estate.

§ 12.13.6. Community Property Administration Expenses

Where only the decedent's half interest in the community property is subject to administration, the full amount of the expenses of administration relating to that property is deductible under § 2053. *Estate of William G. Helis,* 26 T.C. 143 (1956), *acq.,* 1956-2 C.B. 6. In contrast, where all of the community property is subject to administration upon the death of a spouse, only the expenses of administration attributable to the deceased spouse's share of the community property are deductible. The IRS has recognized that, "expenses which can be specifically allocated to the decedent's share of the community property, such as attorney's fees incurred in the determination or litigation of estate and inheritance taxes in connection with his share of the property, are fully deductible." The leading case on the subject allowed the estate to deduct half of the ordinary expenses of administration and the full amount of attorney's fees and expenses incurred in connection with the settlement and adjustment of death taxes. *Estate of Lang v. Commissioner,* 97 F.2d 867 (9th Cir. 1938) (Washington law). In *Ray v. United States,* 385 F. Supp. 372 (S.D.Tex. 1974), *aff'd on other issues,* 538 F.2d 1228 (5th Cir. 1976), the court allowed the estate to deduct, (1) attorney's fees incurred in connection with determining state and federal death taxes and income taxes and those incurred in performing ordinary probate services for the decedent's estate, which together amounted to 95 percent of the attorney's fees, and (2) administration expenses that would not otherwise have been incurred, including appraisal fees and costs of selling the decedent's interest in property.

§ 12.14. EQUITABLE ADJUSTMENTS

An equitable adjustment is a reallocation of assets from the account of one beneficiary, or from some other person beneficially interested in a trust or estate, to the account of another to compensate for disproportionate sharing of a tax burden. Generally, reallocations are made when tax elections by trustees, executors, administrators, and other fiduciaries otherwise would have disparate impacts on beneficiaries.

Equitable adjustment is a form of equitable apportionment, a doctrine that requires fiduciaries, in order to deal with beneficiaries fairly, to reallocate or reapportion benefits or burdens received in an initially unfair form under standard accounting rules. Dobris, Equitable Adjustments in Post-mortem Income Tax Planning: An Unremitting Diet of *Warms,* 65 Iowa L. Rev. 103, 148 (1979).

In some cases, an election made by an executor gives some beneficiaries an economic benefit while it causes others to suffer an economic loss. Where the election involves claiming administration expenses as an income tax deduction, some states require an equitable adjustment to be made in the absence of contrary direction in the will. As pointed out in a comprehensive article by Carrico and Bondurant cited above, there is no uniformity among the states regarding equitable adjustments: Several states require certain adjustments and others restrict the availability of some adjustments. Carrico & Bondurant, Equitable Adjustments: A Survey and Analysis of Precedents and Practice, 38 Tax L. Rev. 545 (1983).

Thus far courts have been reluctant to recognize claims for adjustment based on losses allegedly suffered as a result of an executor's election regarding the use of the alternative valuation date or the distribution of property in kind in satisfaction of bequests.

In making tax elections the fiduciary is often subject to conflicting duties, among which are the duties to be impartial to the beneficiaries and to minimize taxes. A will or trust should give the fiduciary some guidance in making the elections. Instead, many wills and trusts attempt to relieve the executor from the necessity of making any adjustments by waiving any obligation that the executor do so, or by giving the executor discretion to make an appropriate adjustment. Provisions that give a fiduciary discretion regarding elections must be carefully drafted, particularly if an exercise of discretion could involve a serious conflict of interest (*e.g.,* when an executor is also a beneficiary). In some cases a fiduciary should consider asking the court for guidance, particularly where the fiduciary is in a conflict-of-interest position.

Most of the reported cases have involved an executor's election to claim administration expenses as a deduction on the estate's income tax return instead of on the estate tax return. Such a use of the deductions is proper where it will result in an overall tax saving (*i.e.,* where the income tax liability will be reduced by a larger amount than the resulting increase in the estate tax liability). The claim for an adjustment arises where the beneficiaries whose share of the estate bears the cost of the administration expenses *and* the additional estate tax that results from claiming the expenses on the income tax return do not benefit from the income tax saving. Essentially the same problem is presented where an estate distribution carries out distributable net income of the estate, but is characterized as principal for trust accounting purposes (a "trapping" distribution). An adjustment is appropriate in the case of a trapping distribution because the income tax on the distribution is borne by principal, but benefits the income beneficiaries of the estate. *See* § 12.41.

EXAMPLE 12-9.

X died leaving a will that gave income-producing securities to his widow, *W*, and gave the residue of his estate to his child, *C*. Under the local law *W* was entitled to the income from the securities, reduced only by the income taxes and other expenses directly attributable to them. The local law also requires the administration expenses and the estate tax to be paid out of the residuary estate. If the executor elects to claim administration expenses as deductions on the estate's income tax return, *W*'s income tax liability will decrease and *C*'s estate tax liability will increase. Depending on the terms of *X*'s will and the local law, *C* may have a claim for an equitable adjustment (to the extent the estate tax is increased by deducting the administration expenses on the estate's income tax return in a way that only benefits *W*).

In cases similar to the foregoing example, the courts have typically required that the residuary beneficiaries be reimbursed from estate income in an amount equal to the increase in the estate tax that resulted from claiming the expenses as income tax deductions. The leading cases are *Estate of Bixby*, 295 P.2d 68 (Cal. App. 1956), and *Estate of Warms*, 140 N.Y.S.2d 169 (Surr. Ct. 1955). Statutes in some states require a similar adjustment. *See, e.g.,* N.Y. Est. Powers & Trusts Law § 11-1.2(A) (2011). Under such an approach, the income beneficiaries do enjoy the net saving in taxes.

It is not necessary to make any adjustment where the administration expenses are claimed as a deduction on the estate tax return. In that case the deduction ordinarily benefits the beneficiaries whose share of the estate bore the expenses that generated the deduction. Of course, the executor may be subject to criticism if a greater overall tax saving would result if the expenses had been claimed as a deduction on the estate's income tax return.

D. ELECTIONS AFFECTING ESTATE AND GST TAXES

§ 12.15. ALTERNATE VALUATION METHOD, § 2032

Until 1935, the gross estate was valued on the date of death and the federal estate tax was due one year later. As a result of the steep decline in property values that took place during the Great Depression of the 1930s the tax often amounted to a disproportionately large portion of the value of the estate on the payment date. The alternate valuation method was added to the Code in 1935 in order to prevent the virtual confiscation of estates when there was a large decline in market values. Revenue Act of 1935, § 202, 49 Stat. 1022. Under it, the assets of the estate could be valued on the date of death, or as of a date one year after death. In order to permit an estate to take full advantage of the alternate valuation date, the date for payment of the tax was extended from one year after death to 15 months after death. S. Rep. No. 1240, 74th Cong., 1st Sess. (1935), *reprinted at* 1939-1 C.B. 651. Effective January 1, 1971, the alternate valuation date and the date for payment of the tax were both advanced by six months as a part of a plan to accelerate tax collections. *See* Price, Recent Tax Legislation—The Excise, Estate and Gift Tax Adjustment Act of 1970, 47 Wash. L. Rev. 237 (1972).

Under § 2032, property included in the gross estate is valued as of the time of the decedent's death unless the executor makes a timely election on the estate tax return to value the gross estate according to the alternate valuation method. An election is not effective, however, unless the decedent's gross estate is sufficiently large to require a federal estate tax return to be filed. Reg. § 20.2032-1(b)(1).

If the alternate valuation method is elected, all items are valued as follows:

1. Property distributed, sold, exchanged, or otherwise disposed of within six months of the decedent's death is valued as of the date of distribution, sale, exchange, or other disposition.

2. Property not distributed, sold, exchanged, or otherwise disposed of within six months after the decedent's death is valued as of the date six months after the decedent's death.

3. Items that are affected by the mere lapse of time are included at their values as of the date of death (instead of the later date), adjusted for any differences in value that are not due to the mere lapse of time. *See* § 2032(a).

The choice of valuation date affects the valuation of assets for estate tax purposes, which directly affects the size of the gross estate. Derivatively, the election affects the amount of the federal estate tax itself. It may also determine whether the estate meets the percentage requirement of § 303 (*see* § § 11.13-11.23), § 2032A (*see* § 12.19), or § 6166 (*see* § § 11.25-11.30).

The estate tax valuation of assets also establishes their bases for income tax purposes. § 1014(a). Thus, the use of the alternate valuation date will have an impact on the income tax liability of estates and distributees. The gain or loss realized on the sale of property acquired from the decedent is long-term by reason of § 1223(11). Under that provision, a person to whom property passes from a decedent within the meaning of § 1014 is considered to have held the property for more than one year.

Where assets in the gross estate have declined significantly in value since the date of the decedent's death, a distribution of the property to beneficiaries before the date that is six months after the decedent's death can lock in the lower value for federal estate tax purposes. Some practitioners employed this strategy late in 2008 when the value of most publicly-traded securities nosedived over a period of very few days. Where the beneficiaries are confident that the assets will regain value in the near term, this strategy is especially useful.

The value of the decedent's right to receive annual lottery payments for 20 years is treated as an annuity. LR 9637006. Under the alternate valuation date method, it is appropriately valued using the applicable federal rate on the alternate valuation date.

In LR 200203031, the IRS allowed a § 301.9100-1(c) extension of time to elect the alternate valuation date. Relief was granted although the application for an extension was made after a closing letter was issued. The tax return preparer, an attorney, failed to advise the personal representative to make the election although it would have been beneficial to do so. The ruling concludes that the taxpayer met the requirements of § 301.9100-3 that "the taxpayer acted reasonably and in good faith and granting relief will not prejudice the interests of the government." The result reached in LR 200203031 would be barred by the provisions of Reg. § 20.2032-1(b)(3), discussed below.

Regulation § 20.2032-1(b)(3) provides that, "A request for an extension of time to make the election pursuant to § § 301.9100-1 and 301.9100-3 of this chapter will not be granted unless the return of tax imposed by section 2001 is filed no later than 1 year after the due date of the return (including extensions of time actually granted)." The limitation is imposed because of the statutory requirement that an alternate valuation date election be made no later than one year after the due date, including extensions. § 2032(d)(2).

§12.15.1. Limits on Use of Alternate Method

The alternate valuation date may be elected only if the election will decrease **both** the value of the gross estate and the sum of the estate and the GST taxes. §2032(c). Thus, the executor may not elect to use the alternate method if it will cause an overall increase in the value of the decedent's gross estate. *E.g.,* LR 9001001 (TAM). This limitation is consistent with the original purpose of the alternate valuation date—to offer estates some protection against precipitous declines in value. It was enacted largely to prevent use of the alternate valuation date to increase the income tax basis of assets in estates that would pay no estate tax because of the unlimited marital deduction.

Proposed regulations provide that the election to use the alternate valuation date is available to estates that, according to the Preamble accompanying the proposed regulations,"experience a reduction in the value of the gross estate following the date of the decedent's death due to market conditions, but not due to other post-death events." Prop. Reg. §20.2032-1(f). The proposed regulations define "market conditions" as "events outside of the control of the decedent (or the decedent's executor or trustee) or other person whose property is being valued that affect the fair market value of the property being valued." They define "post-death events" to include "a reorganization of an entity (for example, corporation, partnership, or limited liability company) in which the estate holds an interest, a distribution of cash or other property to the estate from such entity, or one or more distributions by the estate of a fractional interest in such entity." These proposed regulations are almost certainly in response to *Herbert V. Kohler*, 92 T.C.M. 48 (2006), *nonacq.* 2008-9 I.R.B. ii, in which the Tax Court held that the reorganization of a corporation was not a disposition of pre-reorganization shares. *Kohler* was a stinging defeat for the IRS because it valued the pre-organization stock at over $144 million while the estate's expert appraised the decedent's post-reorganization stock at over $47 million (the reorganization cashed out a substantial number of small shareholders and thus drained a large amount of cash from the company's reserves). Once finalized, the proposed regulations will apply to estates of decedents dying after April 24, 2008.

Protective Alternate Valuation Election. A protective alternate valuation election can be made in certain circumstances. For example, in *Estate of Kenneth Mapes*, 99 T.C. 511 (1992), the Tax Court recognized an election that was to be effective only if special use valuation was denied. In LR 9846002 (TAM), the IRS allowed an election that was to be effective only if either, (1) the support trust did not qualify for the marital deduction, or (2) the surviving spouse exercised her right to elect against the will and receive a specified share of his estate. Neither condition had been fulfilled when the return was filed. The surviving spouse later elected against the will and the executor filed supplemental information recalculating the tax based on the alternate valuation date method. The regulations permit a protective election to be made to use the alternate valuation method if it is later determined that use of the alternate method would result in a reduction in both the gross estate and the estate's tax liability. Reg. §20.2032-1(b)(2). The regulation provides that, "The protective election is irrevocable as of the due date of the return (including extensions of time actually granted)."

In some cases, post-mortem elections can be made that will allow an estate to make the alternate valuation date election, as a result of which the amount of the credit shelter gift can be increased substantially. The opportunity arises where there is a pecuniary marital formula gift and the value of the property has declined. By disclaiming or making a partial QTIP election some amount of estate tax will be due using date-of-death values—which will decrease if alternate valuation date values are used. As a result, the estate could elect to use the alternate valuation date—which would increase the portion passing to the noncharitable residuary beneficiaries. The approach is discussed in Dawkins, *Another Bite at the Apple: Using the Alternate Valuation Election to Restore a Credit Shelter Trust*, 16 Prob. & Prop. 28 (Jan./Feb. 2002).

§12.15.2. Income Tax Impact of Using Alternate Method

If the alternate valuation method is used, all assets that are sold, exchanged, distributed, or otherwise disposed of within six months immediately following the decedent's death are valued at their respective values on the date or dates of their disposition. Thus, where the alternate valuation method is elected, the estate will not recognize any gain or loss on sales or exchanges that are made within six months following death. Where the election is made, all assets that are not sold or otherwise disposed of during the six months immediately following death are valued according to their respective fair market values at the end of that period.

EXAMPLE 12-10.

T died last year leaving a gross estate that consisted of the following items, each of which is followed by its date of death and alternate date values:

Asset	Date of Death Value	Alternate Date Value
Cash	$ 250,000	$ 250,000
Life insurance	500,000	500,000
Residence	1,000,000	1,000,000
Blackacre	500,000	400,000
ABC Co. stock	2,000,000	1,800,000
XYZ, Inc. stock	1,500,000	1,400,000
Municipal bonds	2,000,000	1,900,000
Total	$7,750,000	$7,350,000

Within 6 months of *T*'s death the ABC stock was sold for $,800,000 and the residence was distributed at a time when it was worth $1,100,000. If the date of death values are used in valuing the estate, the estate will realize a loss of $200,000 on the sale of the stock. No gain or loss would be realized on the distribution of the residence unless it was distributed in satisfaction of a pecuniary bequest. Instead, the estate tax valuation would generally carry over and become the basis of the devisee in the residence.

If the alternate valuation date is elected, the gross estate will be $7,350,000. In such a case, the estate will realize neither any loss on the sale of stock, nor any gain on the distribution of the residence. In addition, the devisee would take a $1,100,000 basis in the residence.

§ 12.15.3. Property Affected by Alternate Method

Property that forms a part of the decedent's gross estate at the time of death is "included property," which is subject to alternate valuation under § 2032. Such property remains included even though it may change form during the alternate valuation period. On the other hand, property earned or accrued after the date of death is generally "excluded property," which is not taken into account for purposes of § 2032. Thus, interest or rent accrued *prior* to death is *included* property, but interest or rent accrued *after* death is *excluded* property. Likewise, dividends declared and payable to stockholders of record prior to the decedent's death are included property, but dividends declared to shareholders of record after the decedent's death are excluded property. In either case the item would constitute income to the recipient. However, an included item might constitute income in respect of a decedent for which the recipient would be entitled to a deduction under § 691(c) for the estate tax attributable to it.

The statute and the regulations provide some guidance regarding the alternate valuation of items whose value changes merely due to the lapse of time. An item, such as a patent, life estate, remainder or term of years, is included in the decedent's gross estate at its value on his or her date of death, adjusted as required for any difference in value not due to the mere lapse of time. § 2032(a)(3). The nature of the adjustment is illustrated by Example 12-11, which is based on Reg. § 20.2032-1(f)(1).

EXAMPLE 12-11.

D owned a life estate and *S* a vested remainder in Blackacre. *S* died survived by *D*, who was then 40 years old. When *S* died Blackacre was worth $1,000,000. On the alternate valuation date applicable to his estate Blackacre was worth $500,000. The vested remainder is includible in *S*'s gross estate under § 2033. Its date of death value is determined by multiplying the date of death value of Blackacre ($1,000,000) by the factor for valuation of a remainder interest following the life interest of a person aged 40. The value of the vested remainder on the alternate valuation date is determined by multiplying the value of Blackacre on the alternate valuation date ($500,000) by the same factor. The approach takes into account the change in value of the underlying asset, but no change is made in the factor for the life estate, remainder, or other limited interest.

If the executor elects to use the alternate valuation method a mortgage or similar obligation included in the decedent's estate is returned at its value on the alternate valuation date. However, in such a case the estate must also include any principal payments received between the date of death and the alternate valuation date. Rev. Rul. 58-576, 1958-2 C.B. 625. Special rules apply in the case of other assets. Rev. Rul. 58-436, 1958-2 C.B. 366, *modified,* Rev. Rul. 64-289, 1964-2 C.B. 173 (livestock and crops); Rev. Rul. 71-317, 1971-2 C.B. 328 (mineral interests). The value of the decedent's right to receive annual lottery payments for 20 years is treated as an annuity.

LR 9637006 (TAM). Under the alternate valuation date method, the right is appropriately valued using the applicable federal rate on the alternate valuation date.

§ 12.15.4. Effect on Special Use Valuation

An estate may elect to use both the alternate valuation method and special use valuation, discussed at § 12.19. Rev. Rul. 88-89, 1988-2 C.B. 333. If an estate makes both elections, the special use calculations must be based on values on the alternate valuation date. *Id.*

The 1984 Act amended § 2032(d) to provide that the alternate valuation election could be made on a return, whether filed timely or late, so long as the return was filed no more than one year after the due date, including extensions. *See* § 12.15. The 1986 change provided that the election could only be made if it would result in a reduction in both the value of the gross estate and in the total estate and GST tax liability of the estate.

§ 12.15.5. Alternate Valuation Election

Under § 2032(d) and Reg. § 20.2032-1(b)(2), an election to use the alternate valuation date must be made on the estate tax return. An election is allowed only if it is made on a return filed within one year after the time prescribed (including extensions) for filing. § 2032(d)(2). An election once made is irrevocable. § 2032(d)(1). Relief may be granted and a belated election can be made upon application under § 301.9100. *See* § 12.5.1.

§ 12.15.6. Distributed, Sold, Exchanged, or Otherwise Disposed of

In general, the phrase "distributed, sold, exchanged, or otherwise disposed of" describes all possible ways by which property ceases to form a part of a decedent's gross estate. Reg. § 20.2032-1(c). However, the term does not extend to transactions that are mere changes in form. Thus, it does not apply to a tax-free exchange of stock in a corporation for stock in the same corporation, or in another corporation such as in a merger, reorganization, or other transaction described in § § 355 or 368(a), with respect to which no gain or loss is recognized for income tax purposes under § § 354 or 355. *Id. See also Herbert V. Kohler*, 92 T.C.M. 48 (2006), *nonacq.* 2008-9 I.R.B. ii (reorganization of corporation is not a disposition of pre-reorganization shares). The existing authorities have evolved a test that turns on whether the assets have been placed beyond the dominion and control of the fiduciary or surviving cotenant, or have been the subject of a decree that shifts the economic benefit of the property to a successor. *See Hertsche v. United States*, 244 F. Supp. 347 (D. Or. 1965), *aff'd per curiam*, 366 F.2d 93 (9th Cir. 1966).

The economic benefit analysis of *Hertsche* was followed in Rev. Rul. 78-378, 1978-2 C.B. 229, which was concerned with whether the passage of property by operation of law to a decedent's devisee constituted a distribution of the property where it remained subject to claims against the estate until a final court order. Under the ruling,

> The delivery of property to the distributee that is subject to a subsequent court decree is not a delivery within the meaning of section 20.2032-1(c)(2)(iii) of the regulations. Under these circumstances, there is not a shifting of economic benefits until the court decree.

For purposes of § 2032 property may be sold, exchanged, or otherwise disposed of by the executor, a trustee, or other donee to whom the decedent transferred the property inter vivos, an heir or devisee to whom the property passes directly under local law, a surviving joint tenant, or any other person. Reg. § 20.2032-1(c)(3). Entering into a binding contract for the sale, exchange, or other disposition of property constitutes a sale, exchange, or other disposition of the property on the effective date of the contract where the contract is subsequently carried out substantially in accordance with its terms. For example, property that is sold by a trustee or surviving joint tenant within six months of the decedent's death will be valued on the date of sale if the executor elects to use the alternate valuation date. On the other hand, the transfer of property by a surviving joint tenant to a revocable trust is not considered to be a sale, exchange, or other disposition because for tax purposes the surviving joint tenant is not considered to have relinquished any authority or power of ownership over the property. Rev. Rul. 59-213, 1959-1 C.B. 244.

The IRS has ruled that the division of the corpus of a revocable trust into two equal parts upon the grantor's death in order to facilitate the payment of income to two income beneficiaries did not constitute a distribution. Rev. Rul. 57-495, 1957-2 C.B. 616. A contrary result was reached in Rev. Rul. 73-97, 1973-1 C.B. 404, where the corpus of the original trust was divided into two separate trusts upon the grantor's death. Under the latter ruling, "when the trustee divided the corpus of the original trust into separate trusts, he effectuated a 'distribution' within the meaning of section 2032 of the Code." Revenue Ruling 73-97 indicates that the difference in the outcome of the two rulings resulted because the original trust involved in Rev. Rul. 57-495 continued after the division of the corpus into shares whereas the trust involved in Rev. Rul. 73-97 ceased to exist when its corpus was divided and transferred to the trustee of the successor trusts. The distinction is consistent with an earlier ruling that held that the bookkeeping division of estate assets into separate accounts, one for each of the three separate trusts created by the decedent's will, did not constitute a distribution within the meaning of § 2032 where the executor retained control over the property held in the accounts. Rev. Rul. 71-396, 1971-2 C.B. 328. Under Rev. Rul. 78-431, 1978-2 C.B. 230, a division of community property into two shares, followed by the transfer of the surviving spouse's share into a separate trust, does not constitute a distribution for purposes of § 2032. That result is reached because the share of the community property that was included in the decedent's estate remained in the original trust, subject to the control of the original trustee.

The valuation of minerals or oil and gas produced during the alternate valuation period can be controversial. In *Estate of Holl v. Commissioner*, 54 F.3d 648 (10th Cir. 1995), the court again directed that the value of oil and gas produced during the alternate valuation period be valued by determining its "in-place" value at the times of severance. For the second time the appellate court rejected the approach of the Tax Court, which adopted the method of valuation proposed by the government's expert, which was based on the discounted sale price of the oil and gas less a reasonable adjustment for uncertainty.

§ 12.15.7. Alternate Method and GSTT

For GSTT purposes, the value of property that is included in the transferor's gross estate and passes as a direct skip is the same as its value for purposes of the estate tax. § 2624(b). If one or more taxable terminations occur at the same time as, and as a result of the death of an individual, an election may be made to value all property included in such termination in accordance with § 2032. § 2624(c). Where two or more members of the same generation have present interests in the same trust, a taxable termination does not occur until the last of the interests terminates. § 2612(a)(1). In that case the alternate valuation date may be used to value all of the trust assets when the final interest terminates.

EXAMPLE 12-12.

T's will transferred property to a trust that provided for the income to be distributed among *T*'s children *A*, *B*, and *C*. Upon the death of the last survivor of *A*, *B*, and *C*, the trust property is to be distributed to *T*'s then living grandchildren. Under § 2612(a)(1), a taxable termination will take place upon the death of the survivor of *A*, *B*, and *C*. At that time the trustee may elect to value all of the trust property according to the alternate valuation method.

§ 12.16. PENALTIES FOR INCORRECT VALUATION OF ASSETS ON RETURNS DUE PRIOR TO JANUARY 1, 1990

Former § 6660 imposed an addition to tax where an estate or gift tax was underpaid by $1,000 or more because of an undervaluation of property. For this purpose, there was a valuation understatement if the value of any property reported on the return was 66 percent or less of its correct value. The addition to tax was a variable percentage of the underpayment the amount of which depended upon the extent of the undervaluation.

The addition to tax could be waived by the IRS if the taxpayer showed that there was a reasonable basis for the valuation claimed on the return and that the claim was made in good faith. Former § 6660(e). Basing the claim upon a valuation by a qualified expert probably constitutes a reasonable basis for a valuation by the executor.

Former § 6659 imposed a penalty in the form of an addition to tax where the overvaluation of property by an individual, a closely-held corporation, or a personal service corporation results in the underpayment of income tax by $1,000 or more in any taxable year. No penalty applied, however, unless the valuation was 150 percent or more of its correct valuation. Under former § 6659(b), the addition to tax was an increasing percentage of the underpayment caused by an overvaluation, depending upon the extent of the overvaluation.

The addition to tax was a flat 30 percent where property contributed to charity was overvalued. The IRS could waive the underpayment penalty for overvaluation of property contributed to charity only if (1) the claimed value of the property was based on a qualified appraisal made by a qualified appraiser, and (2) the taxpayer made a good faith investigation of the value of the property. Former § 6659(f)(2).

In *Estate of Berg v. Commissioner*, 976 F.2d 1163 (8th Cir. 1992), the court held that the imposition of a § 6660 penalty involved an abuse of discretion where the taxpayer's valuation was based upon a valuation by a qualified expert. A penalty under § 6660 was imposed with respect to one bank account, the balance of which was underreported in the federal estate tax return without reasonable cause, but not with respect to another. *Estate of Jack Brown Owen*, 104 T.C. 498 (1995). *See also Estate of Louise S. Monroe*, 104 T.C. 352 (1995), discussed at § 12.33. An underpayment penalty was also upheld in *Estate of Sylvia P. Goldman*, T.C. Memo. 1996-29 (New York law), for excluding the amounts of checks written by the decedent's daughter acting pursuant to a power of attorney that did not authorize gifts to be made. *See* § 4.35.4. Fraud penalties were imposed in *Estate of Nathalie N. Fox*, T.C. Memo. 1995-30, *aff'd unpub. op.* (2d Cir. 1996), for underpayment of estate tax on items improperly excluded from the estate.

§ 12.17. INCORRECT VALUATION OF ASSETS ON ESTATE OR GIFT TAX RETURNS DUE AFTER 1989, § 6662

The penalties for underpayment of tax due to inaccurate valuations are contained in § 6662. In case of an underpayment of tax described in § 6662, an amount equal to 20 percent of the underpayment is imposed as an addition to tax. § 6662(a). In the case of gross valuation misstatements the addition to tax is 40 percent. § 6662(h). Underpayments subject to § 6662 include ones due to negligent disregard of rules or regulations, substantial understatements of income tax, and any substantial estate or gift tax understatement. § 6662(b)(1), (2), (5).

No addition to tax is made if the underpayment of estate or gift tax due to a substantial valuation understatement of $5,000 or less. § 6662(g)(2). For this purpose there is a substantial valuation understatement if the property is valued at 65 percent or less of its correct value. § 6662(g)(1). However, a gross valuation misstatement is made if the property is valued at 40 percent or less of its correct value. § 6662(h)(2)(C).

An addition to tax for underpayment of income tax may be imposed if the amount of the understatement exceeds the greater of ten percent of the tax or $5,000. § 6662(d). The amount of an understatement is reduced by the portion attributable to a position for which there is substantial authority or with respect to which the facts were adequately disclosed. § 6662(d)(2)(B).

An addition to tax may be made under § 6662(e) if the income tax is underpaid by more than $5,000 due to an overstatement of the value of property. For this purpose there is an overstatement if the property is valued at 200 percent or more of its correct value. There is a gross valuation misstatement, subject to a 40 percent addition to tax, if the property was valued at 400 percent or more of its correct value. § 6662(h).

Under § 6664, no penalty may be imposed with respect to any portion of an underpayment that is shown to be attributable to reasonable cause if the taxpayer acted in good faith.

§12.18. Avoid Incurring Valuation Penalties

Where the valuation of a substantial estate asset is uncertain, the executor should obtain a written appraisal by a qualified expert. A good faith valuation made in accordance with an appraisal by an expert should protect the estate from the imposition of an addition to tax under §6662 if the property is later found to have been incorrectly valued. §6664; *see* Reg. §1.6664-4(b).

§12.19. Special Use Valuation, §2032A

The Act provides that, if certain conditions are met, the executor may elect to value real property included in the decedent's estate which is devoted to farming or closely held business use on the basis of that property's value as a farm or in the closely held business, rather than its fair market value determined on the basis of its highest and best use. General Explanation of the 1976 Act, 537.

In 1976, Congress enacted a complex provision, §2032A, which permits an executor to elect to value real property that was used as a farm or in connection with a closely-held business ("qualified real property") according to its actual use rather than its highest and best use. The maximum allowable reduction under §2032A is $750,000, as adjusted for inflation.

The value of property included in the gross estate is usually based upon its fair market value, which takes into account the highest and best use to which the property can be put. Congress was concerned that valuation of real property used for farming or other closely-held business purposes at its fair market value could result in unreasonably high estate taxes and make "continuation of farming, or the closely held business activities, not feasible because the income potential from these activities is insufficient to service extended tax payments or loans obtained to pay the taxes. Thus, the heirs may be forced to sell the land for development purposes." General Explanation of the 1976 Act, at 537.

A special use election may be made only if the decedent was a United States citizen or resident at the time of his or her death. §2032A(a)(1)(A). In addition, the election is available only with respect to qualified real property, which means "real property located in the United States which was acquired from or passed from the decedent to a qualified heir of the decedent and which, on the date of the decedent's death, was being used for a qualified use by the decedent or a member of the decedent's family." §2032A(b)(1). The election is also conditioned on satisfying two percentage tests. First, the adjusted value of real or personal property used for qualified purposes on the date of the decedent's death must constitute 50 percent or more of the adjusted value of the gross estate (the gross estate less the amount of unpaid mortgages and indebtedness in respect of property). §2032A(b)(1)(A). Second, 25 percent or more of the adjusted value of the gross estate must consist of the adjusted value of real property that, for a period of at least five of the eight years immediately preceding the decedent's death, was owned and used by the decedent or a family member who materially participated in the operation of the farm or other trade or business. For purposes of the percentage tests, apparently the entire value of qualified real property that is held as community property is taken into account. *See*

§2032A(e)(10). If so, it would only be logical to include the full value of all community property to determine if the tests were satisfied.

If the executor has substantially complied with the requirements necessary to make an election under §2032A then he or she is allowed up to 90 days after notification of a failure to provide the information or agreements necessary to constitute a valid election. §2032A(d)(3). According to *Estate of Hudgins v. Commissioner,* 57 F.3d 1393 (5th Cir. 1995), the intent of Congress was to "allow correction for only such hypertechnical glitches as the signing of the Recapture Agreement for a minor by a parent when a guardian ad litem was required." 57 F.3d at 1401. In *Estate of Hudgins,* after reviewing federal court decisions regarding the requirements of substantial compliance, the court wrote: "We follow constant jurisprudence, as reflected by the decisions of every court that has directly addressed the issue, in holding that there can be no substantial compliance with the requirements of Code §2032A without, inter alia, the contemporaneous filing of a Recapture Agreement or its equivalent." 57 F.3d at 1406. *Hudgins* was followed in a thoughtful decision by the Eleventh Circuit. *Estate of Lucas v. United States,* 97 F.3d 1401 (11th Cir. 1996), *cert. denied,* 117 S.Ct. 1469 (1997).

The 1997 Act also expanded the opportunities for achieving special use valuation although the requirements of the section were not fully met at the outset. In particular, if the executor makes an election under §2032A and files the agreement, but the notice of election does not contain all the required information or the signatures of one or more persons are not included on the agreement, the executor has a reasonable time, not to exceed 90 days, after notification of the failure, to provide the information or the signatures. §2032A(d)(3).

§12.19.1. Election

An election to value qualified real property under the special use method must be made on the decedent's estate tax return. §2032A(d). In addition, the executor must file an agreement to the election signed by all parties having an interest in the property that is binding under the local law. Originally the election could only be made on a timely filed estate tax return. However, an amendment made by the 1981 Act allows the election to be made on a late return, if it is the first estate tax return filed by the executor. Once made, an election is irrevocable.

Under §2032A(d)(3), the IRS is required to establish procedures that allow an executor a reasonable period of time (not exceeding 90 days) to perfect an election that was timely filed and substantially complied with the regulations. This opportunity exists where, (1) the notice of election does not contain all required information, or (2) the agreement consenting to application of the recapture tax is missing some signatures or the agreement does not contain some required information such as social security numbers and addresses of the qualified heirs and copies of written appraisals of the property.

In *Gettysburg National Bank v. United States,* 92-2 U.S.T.C. ¶60,108 (M.D.Pa. 1992), the decedent's estate was allowed to perfect a special use election where the agreement was missing the signatures of two persons, whose interests represented a minority of the property involved. The estate was likewise permitted to perfect the election in *Estate of McAlpine v. Commissioner,* 968 F.2d 459 (5th Cir. 1992), where the agreement was initially signed by the trustee to which the decedent left the qualified real property but not by the beneficiaries, who were 22, 20, and 9 years of age at the time of the decedent's death. Within 90 days of notification of the defect the estate filed an amended notice of election and an amended recapture agreement signed by the beneficiaries except for the youngest beneficiary, whose mother signed as her guardian ad litem. In *Estate of McAlpine* the court stated that, "substantial compliance is achieved where the regulatory requirement at issue is unclear and a reasonable taxpayer acting in good faith and exercising due diligence nevertheless fails to meet it." 968 F.2d at 462.

An extension of time to make an election under § 2032A may be granted under Reg. § 301.9100. *See, e.g.,* LR 199911030. Extensions of time under Reg. § 301.9100 are discussed at § 12.2.4.

§ 12.19.2. Protective Election

An executor may make a protective election for special use valuation. Reg. § 20.2032A-8(b). The election is made by a notice of election filed with a timely-filed estate tax return. The regulation provides that the notice must include the decedent's name and the estate's taxpayer identification number, a statement of the relevant qualified use and the items of real and personal property on the return that are used in a qualified use and pass to qualified heirs. If it is later determined that the estate qualifies for special use valuation, an additional notice of election must be filed within 60 days of that determination. *Id.*

§ 12.19.3. Maximum Reduction in Value of Property

The maximum reduction in the value of qualified real property allowable as a result of the special use valuation method is $750,000, indexed for post-1997 inflation (($1,020,000 in 2011, Rev. Proc. 2010-40, 2010-2 C.B. 663). In the case of community property, the limit applies to the decedent's share of the property regardless of the ownership interest of the surviving spouse. Rev. Rul. 83-96, 1983-2 C.B. 156; § 2032A(e)(10). *See also* LRs 8301008 (TAM) and 8229009 (TAM). The special use value establishes the basis of the qualified real property for income tax purposes. However, if a recapture tax is imposed because of disposition of the qualified real property or cessation of the qualified use, the basis of the qualified real property may be increased to its fair market value on the estate tax valuation date applicable to the decedent's estate. § 1016(c). If the qualified heir elects this basis adjustment, interest must be paid at the floating rate of § 6621 on the amount of the recapture tax from a date nine months after the decedent's death until the due date of the recapture tax. § 1016(c)(5)(B).

In determining the maximum reduction allowable under the ceiling of § 2032A(a)(2), consideration must be given to the effect of any discounts that are properly applicable in valuing the decedent's interest in qualified real property. Thus, the majority opinion in *Estate of Hoover v. Commissioner*, 69 F.3d 1044 (10th Cir. 1995), recognized the propriety of first allowing a discount in valuing the decedent's 26 percent interest in a cattle ranch:

> Proper application of § 2032A(a)(2) must involve an accurate determina-
> tion of fair market value, which necessarily incorporates the minority

discount. The $750,000 maximum reduction from fair market value under §2032A(a)(2) is a reduction from the value that would otherwise be reported if no §2032A election were made. Clearly, if no §2032A election is made, the value of the property includable in the gross estate would incorporate a minority interest discount. *See* I.R.C. §2031; Treas. Reg. §20.2031-2(f). Without applying the minority interest discount, the "value" of the decedents 26% interest is not its fair market value at all. 69 F.3d at 1047.

§12.19.4. Basic Requirements

The valuation requirements of §2032A are relatively simple. Real property used in a farm or other business qualifies for special use valuation if the adjusted value of the real or personal property used in connection with the farm or business accounts for at least 50 percent of the value of the adjusted value of the gross estate. In addition, the adjusted value of the real property must amount to at least 25 percent of the value of the adjusted gross estate. §2032A(b)(1)(B). (The election to value property under the special use method may be made with respect to a portion of the decedent's real property "but sufficient property to satisfy the [25 percent] threshold requirements of section 2032A(b)(1)(B) must be specially valued under the election." Reg. §20.2032A-8(a)(2)). The IRS takes the position that §2035(d)(3)(B) allows the decedent's estate to use property transferred within three years of death to meet the 50 percent requirement of §2031(b)(1) if it remained qualified property until the time of death, as long as other property in the estate meets that section's 25 percent requirement. Rev. Rul. 87-122, 1987-2 C.B. 221.

Some other relatively simple requirements are also imposed by §2032A. As indicated above, the decedent must have been a citizen or resident of the United States, §2032A(a)(1)(A), and the real property must be located in the United States, §2032A(b)(1). Also, the real property must pass to a "qualified heir" which is defined as a member of the decedent's family, including the decedent's ancestors (*e.g.*, parents and grandparents) or spouse; lineal descendants of the decedent or of the decedent's spouse or parents (*e.g.*, nieces or nephews); or the spouse of any lineal descendant of the decedent, the decedent's spouse, or the decedent's parents. §2032A(e)(1), (2).

§12.19.5. De Minimis Interests Passing to Nonqualified Heirs

Under the regulations, all interests must pass to qualified heirs. Reg. §20.2032A-8(a)(2). However, the courts have rejected the IRS position that the passage of a remote de minimis interest to a nonqualified heir disqualifies the property from §2032A valuation. For example, in *Estate of Davis*, 86 T.C. 1156 (1986), the Tax Court held that the gift over of the real property to charities (*i.e.*, entities that were not qualified heirs) if the decedent's children were to die not leaving descendants was so remote as not to preclude an election under §2032A. A Federal District Court reached a similar result regarding a *de minimis* remote interest that passed to persons who were not qualified heirs. *Smoot v. Commissioner*, 1988-1 U.S.T.C. ¶13,748 (D.C. Ill. 1987). In *Smoot* the court also held that the special use election could be made although the decedent's surviving spouse held a special testamentary power of appointment that could be exercised in favor of persons who were not qualified heirs.

§12.19.6. Ownership, Use, and Material Participation

More complex requirements relate to the ownership, use, and material participation in the management of the property. Unfortunately the liberalizing amendments made by the 1981 Act added to the already staggering complexity of §2032A. The complexity has not been relieved by subsequent acts. On the date of the decedent's death the real property must have been in use by the decedent or a family member as a farm or for other business purposes. In addition, for at least five of the last eight years preceding the decedent's death, the decedent or family member must have, (1) owned the real property, and (2) used the real property for farming or other business purposes. §2032A(b)(1)(C). The decedent or a family member must also have materially participated in the operation of the farm or other business for at least five of the last eight years preceding the decedent's date of death, disability, or commencement of social security retirement benefits. §2032A(b)(1)(C), (b)(4). Importantly, real property owned indirectly through the ownership of an interest in a partnership, corporation, or trust qualifies for special use valuation to the extent the requirements of the regulations are satisfied. §2032A(g); Reg. §20.2032A-3(f).

§12.19.7. Cropshare Leases

Both the decedent's and the qualified heirs' use and material participation in the management of farm property may be satisfied although the property is subject to a cropshare lease, which may relieve the owner of much of the labor required to conduct farming operations on the property. Under the regulations, "physical work and participation in management decisions are the principal factors to be considered" in determining whether material participation is present. Reg. §20.2032A-3(e)(2). The regulation continues, pointing out that, "[a]s a minimum, the decedent and/or a family member must regularly advise or consult with the other managing party on the operation of the business." For a case involving a crop lease with respect to which the lessor's conservator was sufficiently involved in the farming operation to constitute material participation, *see Mangles v. United States*, 828 F.2d 1324 (8th Cir. 1987). *See also* §12.19.9.

§12.19.8. Special Use Valuation Methods

Section 2032A provides three methods for valuing farm property for farming purposes. Where comparable land is located in the same locality, from which the average gross cash rental can be calculated, the executor may value the real property by dividing, (1) the excess of the average annual gross cash rental for comparable land over the average annual state and local taxes by, (2) the average annual effective interest rate for all new Federal Land Bank loans. §2032A(e)(7)(A). If there is no comparable land from which the average cash rentals may be calculated, the value may be based on the average net share rentals received by the lessors of comparable land in the same locality. §2032A(e)(7)(B). Finally, if there is no comparable land in the same locality from which the average cash or net share rentals can be calculated, the real property will be valued according to a multifactor formula. § 2032A(e)(8). It is based upon the following factors:

1. Capitalization of income;
2. Capitalization of fair rental value for special use purposes;
3. Assessed land values in states that provide a differential or use value assessment law;
4. Comparable sales of other farm or closely-held business property in the same area; and
5. Any other factor that fairly values the farm or closely-held business use of the property.

§ 12.19.9. Recapture

The tax benefit of the special use valuation is recaptured if the qualified heir disposes of the real property or ceases to use it for the qualified use within ten years following the decedent's death and before the death of the qualified heir. § 2032A(c)(1). The recapture period was originally fifteen years, with a declining percentage subject to recapture in the final five years. No disqualification results if the qualified heir commences to use the qualified real property within two years following the decedent's death. § 2032A(c)(7)(A).

Cessation of the qualified use may occur if the qualified heir and members of his or her family fail to participate materially in the management of the real property for an aggregate of more than three years of any eight-year period ending after the date of the decedent's death. § 2032A(c)(6). The qualified heirs' one-year cash lease of qualified farm property to a nonrelative constituted a cessation of the qualified use that triggered recapture of the tax. *Martin v. Commissioner*, 783 F.2d 81 (7th Cir. 1986). In such a case the heirs become passive investors for the duration of the lease, without any stake in the productivity of the farm or in the prices for which its produce were sold. However, the *Martin* court noted that the government had conceded that "if the lease had been on a sharecropping basis so that part of the risk of the farming remained on the heirs rather than being totally shifted to the lessee, the case would be different." As explained above, if a qualified heir leases farm property to others under a cropshare lease, the heir's participation may still suffice to avoid the recapture penalty. The 1988 Act added a sentence to § 2032A(c)(7)(E) under which the decedent's "surviving spouse . . . shall not be treated as failing to use qualified real property in a qualified use solely because such spouse . . . rents such property to a member of the family of such spouse . . . on a net cash basis."

The sale of a conservation easement is a disposition that triggers recapture of the estate tax. *Estate of Gibbs v. United States*, 151 F.2d 242 (8th Cir. 1998). The cash lease of a farm by the qualified heir to his nephew constituted a shift to a passive use of the farm and cessation of a qualified use that triggered recapture. *Williamson v. Commissioner*, 974 F.2d 1525 (9th Cir. 1992). In *Williamson* the court also held that by entering into a crop lease the taxpayer had not made a disposition of the property to a member of his family that under § 2032A(e)(1) would cause the transferee to become the qualified heir with respect to the property. The transfer of an interest in qualified real property in exchange for an interest in qualified exchange property (real property that is to be used for the same qualified use in which the exchanged real property originally qualified for special use valuation) is not a disposition for purposes of § 2032A(i). PLR 9503015 (undivided interests in ranches and farms exchanged for undivided interests in others in order to consolidate ownership to secure mortgage financing).

In some instances, a cash lease of farm land does not preclude special use valuation under § 2032A. *Estate of Gavin v. United States*, 113 F.3d 802 (8th Cir. May 8, 1997); *Minter v. United States*, 19 F.3d 426 (8th Cir. 1994) (cash lease by qualified heirs to corporation stock of which was held by trust of which they were the beneficiaries). In *Gavin* the court, referred to the House Committee Report and stated that "the identity of the farmer is relevant to determining whether a Decedent's heirs were 'mere landlords collecting a fixed rent,' or qualified heirs engaging in a qualified use." *Estate of Gavin*, 113 F.3d at 807. While cash rental to a nonfamily member is not a qualified use, cash rental to family members may be—particularly where the rental paid is related to production.

A change made by the 1997 Act provides that the cash lease of special use property by a lineal descendant of the decedent to a member of his or her family who operates the property does not trigger recapture. This change clarifies the law with respect to a point that has divided the courts and encouraged controversy. Under another change, the creation of a qualified conservation easement under § 2031(c) does not constitute a disposition of special use property.

§ 12.19.10. Additional Tax

The amount subject to recapture is the lesser of, (a) the excess of the amount realized upon disposition of the interest (or, in the absence of a bona fide sale or exchange, the fair market value of the interest) over the special use value of the interest, and (b) the excess of the estate tax liability that would have been incurred had the special use valuation method not been used over the estate tax liability based upon special use valuation. This amount is called the "additional tax." § 2032A(c)(2).

§ 12.19.11. Involuntary Conversions and Like Kind Exchanges

An involuntary conversion of the qualified real property during the recapture period does not trigger recapture of the tax if the proceeds are completely reinvested in qualified replacement property. § 2032A(h). In general, the replacement property must meet the requirements of § 1033(a) (*i.e.*, qualify for special use valuation). § 2032A(h)(3)(B). The recapture period is extended by any period beyond the two-year period referred to in § 1033(a)(2)(B)(1) during which the qualified heir was permitted to replace the converted property. § 2032A(h)(2)(A).

Like kind exchanges of qualified real property also do not trigger the recapture tax except to the extent that property is received in the exchange other than real property that is used for the same qualified use as the original property. § 2032A(i). An exchange of special use valuation farm property for other farm property of like kind does not trigger recapture if the qualified heir continues to use the property received for the same qualified use. LR 9604018.

§ 12.19.12. Personal Liability

A qualified heir is personally liable for the amount of the tax that is subject to recapture with respect to his or her interest in the property. § 2032A(c)(5). The personal liability terminates, (1) when the qualified heir dies, (2) when the recapture period passes, or (3) if he or she provides a bond in an amount equal to the maximum amount attributable to his or her interest that might be recaptured. *See* § 2032A(e)(11). A qualified heir may request that the IRS advise him or her of the maximum amount of additional tax attributable to his or her interest. The IRS must notify the heir of that amount within one year of the request. In determining the maximum amount the IRS may not consider any interest on the amount for which the heir might be personally liable.

§ 12.19.13. Special Lien

If special use valuation is employed, § 6324B imposes a lien on the special use property in the amount of the maximum additional tax.

§ 12.19.14. Practical Concerns

The special use valuation provides some estate tax relief for estates that include sufficient amounts of qualified real property. However, many planners are reluctant to advise a client to elect to use the method because of its complexity, the potential for recapture, the personal liability of the qualified heir, and the special lien. Where there are multiple qualified heirs there is also the risk that they may disagree regarding the use or disposition of the property.

§ 12.19.15. Planning for Special Use Valuation and Marital Deduction

Careful consideration must be given to the interrelationship between special use valuation and the unlimited marital deduction. The planner must bear in mind that the surviving spouse will be treated as the transferor of property for which the marital deduction is claimed in the estate of the deceased spouse. Accordingly, special use valuation will not be available if the property passes on the death of the surviving spouse to beneficiaries who are not members of the surviving spouse's family (*e.g.*, where the surviving spouse is the beneficiaries' step parent).

An election to claim alternate use valuation reduces the estate tax value of the estate and, by extension, the amount of a formula marital deduction gift. Such an election, which may correspondingly increase the amount that passes to the residuary beneficiaries of an estate, does not involve a taxable gift by the surviving spouse if she is serving as executor. LR 8934004.

In some instances the interested parties will not elect to make use of special use valuation (with the consequent limitation on basis) where the real property passes to a surviving spouse in a way that qualifies for the unlimited marital deduction. On the negative side, however, if the estate does not use special use valuation, a much larger marital deduction must be claimed in order to eliminate the estate tax liability of the estate. That amount is subject to inclusion in the estate of the surviving spouse. Thus, not taking advantage of special use valuation may unnecessarily increase the amount of property subject to inclusion in the gross estate of the surviving spouse.

EXAMPLE 12-13.

> *H* died in 2011 survived by his wife, *W. H*'s will leaves an estate which has a value of $6,000,000, of which $3,000,000 consists of real property that could be valued at $2,000,000 under §2032A. *H*'s will makes a formula gift to a trust for *W* of an amount sufficient to reduce to zero the estate tax liability of his estate. If special use valuation is elected, *H*'s gross estate will have a value of $5,000,000—all of which is sheltered by *H*'s unified credit—nothing is required to be transferred to the marital deduction trust for W. If special use is not elected, $1,000,000 must be transferred to the trust in order to zero out the tax liability of *H*'s estate—which will be included in W's estate under §2044.

Transferring appreciated qualified real property in satisfaction of a pecuniary marital deduction gift may result in the realization of gain by the estate. However, under §1040(a) the amount is limited to the excess of the fair market value of the property on the date of distribution over the federal estate tax value of the property, not taking into account its special use valuation.

§12.19.16. Impact of Special Use Valuation on Other Provisions

Note that an election to use the special use valuation method may affect the ability of the estate to qualify for benefits available under other provisions of the Code. For example, special use valuation may disable the estate from meeting the requirements for stock redemptions under §303, or the 15-year deferral of estate taxes under §6166. *See* §12.48.

§12.20. Qualified Conservation Easement Exclusion, §2031(c)

The 1997 Act added an exclusion for the value, subject to some limitations, of conservation easements created after the death of the decedent. Under §2031(c), an exclusion of up to 40 percent of the value of the land is allowed, reduced by 2 percent for each percentage point (or portion) by which the value of the conservation easement is less than 30 percent of the value of the land. Also, the ceiling of the exclusion is $500,000. In order to qualify, the land must have been owned for three years preceding death. The easement may be established after the decedent's death by a member of the decedent's family, the executor of the decedent's estate, or the trustee of a trust the corpus of which includes the land. The easement must be created on or before the date the federal estate tax return is filed. An irrevocable election to take advantage of the deduction must be made on the decedent's federal estate tax return. The 1997 Act also amended §1014(a)(4) to provide that the basis of the property is the decedent's basis to the extent the exclusion applies.

The benefits of §2032A may also be claimed with respect to the property. In addition, §2032A was amended to provide that creating a qualified conservation easement did not constitute a disposition of the property. *See* §12.19.9. Form 4-23, §4.27, includes a provision that authorizes the decedent's executor to create a qualified conservation easement and claim the estate tax exclusion.

No Income Tax Deduction under §642(c). The IRS has ruled that §642(c) does not allow a trust to deduct the value of a qualified conservation easement that is contributed from the principal of the trust. Deductions under §642(c) are only allowed to a trust for contributions that are paid from the trust's gross income. Rev. Rul. 2003-123, 2003-2 C.B. 1200.

§12.21. MARITAL DEDUCTION QTIP ELECTION, §2056(b)(7)

The 1981 Act added §2056(b)(7), which makes the marital deduction available on an elective basis for the value of property in which a surviving spouse receives a "qualifying income interest for life." *See* §5.23. A qualifying income interest for life is defined as one in which, (1) the surviving spouse is entitled to all of the income for life, payable at least annually, and (2) no person has a power to appoint any of the property to a person other than the surviving spouse so long as he or she lives. §2056(b)(7)(B)(ii). The House Report notes that, "income interests granted for a term of years or life estates subject to termination upon remarriage or the occurrence of a specified event will not qualify under the committee bill. The bill does not limit qualifying income interests to those placed in trust. However, a qualifying life income interest in any other property must provide the spouse with rights to income that are sufficient to satisfy the rules applicable to marital deduction trusts under present law. (Treas. Reg. §20.2056(b)-(f))." H.R. 4242, 97th Cong., 1st Sess. 161 (1981). The regulations recognize that a legal life estate constitutes a qualified life income interest if the surviving spouse is entitled to the exclusive and unrestricted use of the property. Reg. §20.2056(b)-7(h), Example (1). Installment distributions from an IRA to a QTIP trust may qualify for the marital deduction. *See* §5.23.5.

Note that a QTIP election once made, is irrevocable. Reg. §20.2056-7(b)(4)(ii). Accordingly, an estate which filed an estate tax return that mistakenly elected QTIP treatment for both the credit shelter and marital deduction trusts cannot later change the election. LR 9848041. An extension of time within which to make a QTIP election can be obtained under Reg. §301.9100. *See* §12.2.4.

Relief from Unnecessary Election. In Rev. Proc. 2001-38, 2001-2 C.B. 124, the IRS held that it would disregard QTIP elections made by the estate of a predeceased spouse where the election "was not necessary to reduce the estate tax liability to zero." The procedure mentions as examples instances in which (1) a QTIP election was made although the deceased spouse's taxable estate was less than the applicable exclusion amount, or (2) QTIP elections were made with respect to a credit shelter trust and a QTIP trust when the election for the credit shelter trust was unnecessary to reduce the estate's tax liability to zero. The relief provided by the Revenue Procedure is not available for instances in which the executor made an excessive partial QTIP election, made a protective election, or made a formula election.

An estate was granted relief under Rev. Proc. 2001-38 for an unnecessary election to treat the property of a credit shelter trust as QTIP. The IRS treated the election as void because no estate tax would have been due had the election not been made. LR

200226020. As a result, the property of the credit shelter trust would not be included in the surviving spouse's estate and a transfer of interests in the trust would not be subject to §2519. In addition, the surviving spouse would not be treated as the transferor for GSTT purposes.

In LR 200219003, the IRS denied relief that was requested under §301.9100 to modify a QTIP election that was made with respect to the entire marital trust. Relief was denied because a QTIP election is irrevocable. According to the ruling, relief was not allowable under Rev. Proc. 2001-38 because, 'The revenue procedure does not apply in situations in where a partial QTIP election was required with respect to a trust to reduce the estate tax liability and the executor made the election with respect to more trust property than was necessary to reduce the estate tax liability to zero.

Consequences of Overfunding a QTIP Trust. If a QTIP trust was overfunded, the surviving spouse's estate is not required to include the excess that was erroneously transferred to the QTIP. Thus, if a QTIP trust was initially overfunded, the surviving spouse's estate is not required to include the excess that was later transferred to the credit shelter trust. LR 200223020 (TAM). The letter ruling follows Rev. Rul. 84-105, 1984-2 C.B. 197, which it said, "states that the marital deduction allowed for the decedent's estate is the amount that should have funded the trust, not the amount that was used to fund the trust." Accordingly, §2044 requires the surviving spouse's estate to include only the value of the assets held in the QTIP trust at the time of her death.

§12.21.1. Partial QTIP Election

A QTIP election can be made with respect to all or part of any separate property (including a trust) in which the surviving spouse has a qualifying income interest for life. Under Reg. §20.2056(b)-7(d)(3), "a qualifying income interest for life that is contingent upon the executor's election under section 2056(b)(7)(B)(v) will not fail to be a qualifying income interest for life because of such contingency or because the portion of the property for which the election is not made passes to or for the benefit of persons other than the surviving spouse." Thus, the existence of the spouse's qualifying income interest can depend upon the election.

The final regulations provide guidance regarding the extent to which a partial election can be made. In particular, Reg. §20.2056(b)-7(b)(2) provides,

> The election may relate to all or any part of property that meets the requirements of §2056(b)(7)(B)(i), provided that any partial election must be made with respect to a fractional or percentage share of the property so that the elective portion reflects its proportionate share of the increase or decrease in value of the entire property for purposes of applying sections 2044 or 2519. The fraction or percentage may be defined by formula.

Thus, an election can be made with respect to a percentage or fraction of an entire trust (*e.g.*, 50 percent of the trust or three-quarters of the trust). As indicated in Reg. §20.2056(b)-7(h), Example (9), an executor may be authorized to divide a trust into separate shares to reflect the effect of a partial QTIP election. Under Reg. §20.2056(b)-7(b)(2)(ii), "any such division must be accomplished no later than the end of the period of estate administration. If, at the time of the filing of the estate tax return, the trust has not yet been divided, the intent to divide the trust must be unequivocally signified on the estate tax return." In LR 9505007, the estate was allowed, under Reg. § 301.9100-1(a), to amend the estate tax return to indicate that the trust would be divided into separate QDT and QTIP trusts. Note that a decedent's executor may be authorized to divide a trust that otherwise qualifies as QTIP into a share for which the marital deduction was claimed and another share, and to charge any payments of principal to the surviving spouse. Reg. § 20.2056(b)-7(h), Example (9).

§ 12.21.2. Formula QTIP Election

The fraction or percentage of a QTIP deduction may be defined by a formula, which is a useful approach because it automatically adjusts for changes in the value of assets and the allowance, or disallowance, of deductions for federal estate tax purposes.

EXAMPLE 12-14.

W died survived by her husband, *H*. *W* left the residue of her estate to a trust, all of the income of which was payable quarterly or more frequently to *H*. None of the trust property could be distributed to anyone other than *H* during his lifetime. *W'* s executor may elect to claim a marital deduction with respect to a fractional share of the residuary estate by using language along the following lines: "The election specifies that the numerator of the fraction is the amount of deduction necessary to reduce the Federal estate taxes to zero (taking into account final estate tax values) and the denominator of the fraction is the final estate tax value of the residuary estate (taking into account any specific bequests or liabilities of the estate paid out of the residuary estate)." Reg. § 20.2056(b)-7(h), Example (7). *See also* Reg. § 20.2056(b)-7(h), Example (8).

In this connection it is important to note that the opportunity to disclaim property exists in addition to the election allowed by § 2056(b)(7). *See* § 12.29 *et seq.*

If a partial election is made with respect to a trust, the trust may be divided into separate shares to which assets are allocated in accordance with the election. As noted above, the regulations require a partial election to be made with respect to a fraction or percentage of the whole trust. However, once the election is made, it should be possible to allocate entire assets to each of the separate shares in accordance with their respective fair market values at the time. *See* Reg. § 20.2056(b)-(7)(h), Example (14).

If a formula election is made, the estate tax return need not indicate the assets or portions of assets that will be allocated to the marital deduction share. PLR 9116003 (TAM).

The text of the formula QTIP election in Form 12-1 is based on the model form of pecuniary marital deduction gift discussed at § 5.35. It is consistent with the example in the Regulations discussed above.

Form 12-1
Formula QTIP Election

Executor elects the QTIP marital deduction with respect to the smallest amount of the trust, which if allowable as a marital deduction for Federal Estate Tax purposes, will result in no Federal Estate Tax being due from decedent's estate taking into account all other deductions allowed decedent's estate for Federal Estate Tax purposes and the amount of the unified credit and other credits allowable to decedent's estate, and the amount of gift tax payable with respect to decedent's post-1976 taxable gifts.

A QTIP formula election can be expressed in the form of a percentage or fraction of the trust. Reg. § 20.2056(b)-7(h), Example (7):

The election specifies that the numerator of the fraction is the amount of deduction necessary to reduce the federal estate tax to zero (taking into account final estate tax values) and the denominator of the fraction is the final estate tax value of the residuary estate (taking into account any specific bequests or liabilities of the estate paid out of the residuary estate). The formula election is of a fractional share. The value of the share qualifies for the marital deduction even though the executor's determinations to claim administration expenses as estate or income tax deductions and the final estate tax values will affect the size of the fractional share.

A fractional formula may be expressed in other ways. Thus, the following language from Example (8) of the same regulation is treated as a valid fractional share election: "I elect to treat as qualified terminable interest property that portion of the residuary trust, up to 100 percent, necessary to reduce the Federal estate tax to zero, after taking into account the available unified credit, final estate tax values, and any liabilities and specific bequests paid from the residuary estate."

Technical Advice Memorandum 9327005 illustrates the problems that can arise if a QTIP election is made in a fixed amount. The election was made for "$67,542 of the amount transferred to the trust (10.35 percent) for the marital deduction." On audit, the value of closely held stock was increased, which increased value of the decedent's gross estate. In this case, the value of the stock was determined without regard to the terms of a stock redemption agreement. The TAM rejected the taxpayer's argument that the estate had made a percentage or fractional election and held that the election with respect to a specified portion of the trust could not be adjusted. If a formula election had been made, the IRS would have allowed the marital deduction to be adjusted. The TAM also pointed out that although the IRS may value the stock without regard to the buy-sell agreement, the estate is still obligated to sell the stock at the agreed price. Accordingly, the increased amount would not pass to the trust in any case.

Under the QTIP regulations, a trust can be funded "on a fractional or percentage basis to reflect the partial election. However, the separate trusts do not have to be funded with a pro rata portion of each asset held by the undivided trust." Reg. § 20.2056(b)-7(b)(2)(ii)(B). *See* § 5.23.4.

§ 12.21.3. Making the QTIP Election

Under § 2056(b)(7)(B)(v), a QTIP election is made by the executor on Schedule M of the federal estate tax return. According to the instructions for Form 706, the election is made by listing the QTIP on Schedule M and deducting its value. Some prior 706 forms required the executor to check a box on line 2 of Schedule M and list the QTIP in part 2 of the schedule. Note that the election is made by the decedent's executor, not the decedent's surviving spouse. The election must be made on "the last estate tax return filed by such executor on or before the due date of the return, including extensions or, if a timely return is not filed, the first estate tax return filed by the executor after the due date." Reg. § 20.2056(b)-7(b)(4)(i). An election, once made, is irrevocable. § 2056(b)(7)(b)(4)(ii). The decedent may authorize or direct the executor to exercise the election in a particular way. *See* Reg. § 20.2056(b)-7(h), Example (9)

As a general rule, an executor should plan the election in a manner that preserves the full benefit of the decedent's unified credit. An "over election" will cause an unnecessarily large portion of the property to be included in the surviving spouse's estate. Thus, where the decedent's surviving spouse receives a qualifying income interest for life in the decedent's entire estate, the executor should usually not elect to claim a deduction with respect to all of the property. Instead, the executor's decision should preserve the benefit of the decedent's unified credit. The executor should, of course, take into account all relevant considerations including the size of the surviving spouse's estate, the age and health of the surviving spouse, and the advantages of equalizing the sizes of the spouses' taxable estates. If a decedent's surviving spouse is expected to die relatively soon, an overall tax saving can result from not claiming the QTIP deduction and paying some estate tax in the decedent's estate for which a credit will be allowed under § 2013. *See* § § 5.19-5.26.

EXAMPLE 12-15.

H died in leaving his entire $8,000,000 estate to a trust that satisfies the requirements of § 2056(b)(7). In the year of *H*'s death the applicable exclusion amount was $5,000,000. *W, H*'s widow, is in good health, and has an estate of similar size. *H*'s executor should not elect more than $3,000,000 as QTIP. In that way the portion of the trust that is sheltered by *H*'s unified credit ($3,000,000/$8,000,000) will not be included in *W*'s estate under § 2044. *W* would, of course, be treated as the transferor of the remainder of the trust. On a related point, keep in mind that *H*'s executor may elect under § 2652(a)(3) that *H* be treated as the transferor of the trust for GSTT purposes and to allocate *H*'s GSTT exemption to the trust. *See* § § 12.23-12.24.

§12.21.4. Protective Election

The executor may choose to make a protective QTIP election in order to protect against the imposition of an estate tax if the size of the gross estate increases, or if the amount of allowable deductions decreases. Because of inherent uncertainties a protective election should be in the form of a formula. A protective formula QTIP election may be expressed in the language of Form 12-1, *supra,* which is consistent with the examples in the Regulations. *See* Example 12-14, *supra;* Reg. §2056(b)-7(h), Examples (7)-(8).

Regulation §20.2056(b)-7(c)(1) expresses a narrow view regarding the availability of a protective election. It provides that:

> A protective election may be made to treat property as qualified terminable interest property only if, at the time the federal estate tax return is filed, the executor of the decedent's estate reasonably believes that there is a bona fide issue that concerns whether an asset is includible in the decedent's gross estate, or the amount or nature of the property the surviving spouse is entitled to receive, *i.e.,* whether property that is includible is eligible for the qualified terminable property election. The protective election must identify either the specific asset, group of assets, or trust to which the election applies and the specific basis for the protective election.

The regulation continues to provide that a protection election, once made on a filed estate tax return is irrevocable. Reg. §20.2056(b)-7(c)(2).

§12.21.5. Professional Responsibility

An executor is subject to a general duty to preserve estate assets and to minimize taxes. *See, e.g., Estate of Bixby,* 295 P.2d 68 (Cal. App. 1956) (alternative deduction of administration expenses, application of equitable adjustment); Ascher, The Fiduciary Duty to Minimize Taxes, 20 Real Prop., Prob. & Tr. J. 663 (1985). The election to claim a QTIP marital deduction with respect to eligible interests may reduce overall current tax liabilities. However, a greater estate tax may be due later—which may be payable out of the interests of beneficiaries who did not benefit from the deferral of the tax. Put bluntly, an election may have an adverse effect on the interests of some beneficiaries. In such a case the executor is in a difficult position—the executor's duty to minimize taxes conflicts with the duty of impartiality among beneficiaries. *See* Ascher, The Quandary of Executors Who Are Asked to Plan the Estates of the Dead: The Qualified Terminable Interest Property Election, 63 N.C. L. Rev. 1 (1984). This dilemma is relieved to some extent if the decedent authorized or directed the executor to make a QTIP election. *See* §5.23. In some cases, identifying the best course to follow with respect to the election is clouded because of the uncertain future of the federal transfer taxes. Given this existing uncertainty, deferring the tax may be best.

The ethical duties of the lawyer for a personal representative are discussed in Chapter 1.

§12.22. Marital Deduction QDT Election, §2056A

The 1988 Act amended §2056 to provide that no marital deduction is allowable if the surviving spouse of the decedent is not a United States citizen. §2056(d). However, the bar does not extend to "property passing to the surviving spouse in a qualified domestic trust." §2056(d)(2). Qualified domestic trusts are described at length in §5.25. Note that under the terms of §2056(d) the effect of the exception is simply to remove the disqualification imposed by the general rule of §2056(d). That is, in order to qualify for the marital deduction for a transfer to a QDT the trust must meet other requirements of §2056. Accordingly, in order to sustain the allowance of the marital deduction, a transfer to a QDT must satisfy one of the exceptions to the terminable interest rule (*e.g.,* it may be a QTIP trust or a life income-general power of appointment trust) or the property must pass outright to the surviving spouse and be transferred by her to a trust that satisfies the QDT requirements. As described below the marital deduction is allowable with respect to a QDT only if the executor so elects on a decedent's estate tax return.

Under §2056A, a QDT must meet the following requirements:

1. The trust instrument requires that at least one trustee be an individual citizen of the United States or a domestic corporation, and provide that no distribution other than income may be made from the trust unless such trustee has the right to withhold from such distribution the tax imposed by §2056A on such distribution.
2. The trust meets the requirements prescribed by the Secretary in order to ensure payment of the estate tax imposed upon the trust. According to the Conference Committee Report, "it is expected that the Treasury regulations will require that sufficient trust assets be subject to U.S. jurisdiction so as to ensure collection of estate tax with respect to the trust. The regulations might, for example, require that a portion of trust property to be [sic] situated in the United States or that the trustee be an institution with substantial U.S. assets."
3. The executor makes an irrevocable election with respect to the trust on the estate tax return.

In effect, the election defers payment of the tax on the QDT until, (1) the property is distributed to the surviving spouse, or (2) the death of the surviving spouse. In contrast to other types of marital deduction transfers, the tax on the property of a QDT is imposed at the marginal rate applicable to the estate of the deceased spouse. Such a method of determining the tax may be advantageous in some circumstances.

EXAMPLE 12-16.

H died in 2011 and was survived by his wife *W*, who was not a United States citizen. At the time of *H's* death his estate consisted of property worth $6,000,000. *H's* will established a credit shelter trust of $5,000,000 and a trust for *W* that met the requirements of a QDT to which he left the residue of his estate ($1,000,000). *H's* executor elected to treat the trust for *W* as a QDT. When *W* dies the property of the QDT will be subject to the estate tax rate applicable to *H's* estate (35%).

Section 2056A(b) imposes an estate tax on, (1) any distribution from a QDT before the death of the surviving spouse, and (2) the value of the property remaining in the trust on the date of the death of the surviving spouse. *See* §5.25.2. The tax does not apply to a distribution of income to the surviving spouse or a distribution made to the surviving spouse on account of hardship. §2056A(b)(3). Each trustee is personally liable for payment of the tax. §2056A(b)(6). The tax is due on the 15th day of the fourth month following the end of the calendar year in which the taxable event occurs (*i.e.*, April 15). The benefits of §§303, 2032, 2032A, 2055, 2056, 6161(a)(2) and 6166 are available with respect to property of a QDT that is includible in the surviving spouse's estate. §2056A(b)(10). In addition, any tax that is imposed under §2056A on a distribution during the surviving spouse's lifetime is treated as a gift tax that may result in an adjustment to basis under §1015. §2056A(b)(13). From 2004 forward, the estate tax credit equivalent and the GSTT exemption will be at the same level, which will simplify drafting and reduce the need to make reverse QTIP elections. *See* §2.27.

§12.23. REVERSE QTIP ELECTION FOR GSTT PURPOSES, §2652(a)(3)

As explained in §2.26, if a reverse QTIP election is made, the decedent who created the QTIP trust continues to be treated as transferor of the trust for GSTT purposes although the trust is includible in the estate of the surviving spouse under §2044. *See, e.g.,* LR 9002014. Unfortunately, §2652(a)(3) does not permit a partial reverse election to be made—the election must relate to the entire trust with respect to which it is made. However, in order to facilitate a reverse QTIP election a trust may be divided. Reg. §26.2654-1(b). Since 2004, however, the estate tax credit equivalent and the GSTT exemption have been at the same level, which simplifies drafting and reduces the need to make reverse QTIP elections. *See* §2.27.

Under the GSTT rules, the transferor of property is the person who was the donor of the property for gift tax purposes or in whose estate the property was included for estate tax purposes. §2652(a)(3). In the case of QTIP the deceased spouse is treated as the transferor until the property is treated as having been transferred by the surviving spouse for gift or estate tax purposes. Upon the death of the surviving spouse the QTIP is includible in the surviving spouse's estate under §2044. Accordingly, in the ordinary case the surviving spouse becomes the transferor of QTIP for GSTT purposes. Such a shift in the identity of the transferor may, in effect, waste the GSTT exemption of the spouse first-to-die. That result can be avoided by making an election under §2652(a)(3) to treat the property as if the QTIP election had not been made for GSTT purposes. Regulation §26.2652-2(c) provides that the election, which is irrevocable, is made on the return on which the QTIP election is made. The instructions for Form 706 state that the election is made by listing qualifying property on part 1, line 9 of Schedule R.

Extension of Time to Make Election. If the executor fails to make a timely reverse QTIP election an extension of time within which to make the election may be requested under Reg. §301.9100-1. *See* §§12.2.4, 12.5.1. Extensions of time relating the QITP trusts continue to be granted under Reg. §301.9100. *E.g.*, LRs 199926041, 9813013, 9724012, and 9608008.

Division of Trusts. Under Reg. § 26.2654-1(b), the division of a trust is recognized for GSTT purposes if the division is directed in the governing instrument or is authorized either by the instrument or local law **and** the terms of the new trusts provide for the same succession of interests and beneficiaries and the division (or a reformation proceeding is commenced) before the date for filing the federal estate tax return, including extensions. However, a division is recognized only if, (1) the trust is divided on a fractional basis, or (2) the governing instrument requires the division to be made on the basis of a pecuniary amount, appropriate interest must be paid and either the amount is paid on the basis of date of distribution values or assets are allocated on the basis that fairly reflects appreciation and depreciation in the values of the available assets. Importantly, if a division is made on a fractional share basis, the regulation allows the trusts "to be funded on a non pro rata basis provided funding is based on either the fair market value of the assets on the date of funding or in a manner that fairly reflects the net appreciation or depreciation in the value of the assets." *See* § § 2.26 *and* 4.24.7. A reverse QTIP election can be made on the last estate tax return filed before the due date, including extensions. LR 9552005. Applying Reg. § 301.9100-3, in LR 20018037, the IRS allowed a reverse QTIP election to be made several years after the decedent's death. *See* § 12.2.4. The IRS has provided a simplified method of obtaining permission to file a late reverse QTIP election in Rev. Proc. 2004-47, 2004-2 C.B. 169. The simplified procedure is available for requests made on or after August 9, 2004.

§ 12.24. ALLOCATION OF GSTT EXEMPTION, § 2631(a)

The executor may allocate any unused portion of a decedent-transferor's GSTT exemption. § 2631(a). The allocation must be made within the time allowed to file the federal estate tax return, including extensions, regardless of whether such a return is required to be filed. § 2632(a). The allocation is made on Schedule R of the federal estate tax return. An allocation, once made, is irrevocable. § 2631(b). However, an election that the deemed allocation rules of § 2632(b) *not* apply to lifetime transfers may be revoked. Thus, the executor might choose to allocate a portion of the decedent's exemption to a lifetime transfer. In the absence of a direction from the transferor regarding allocation of the exemption the executor may have to balance conflicting duties to treat beneficiaries impartially and to minimize overall tax burdens. In 2011 and 2012, the GSTT exemption is $5,000,000, adjusted for increase in the cost of living beginning in 2012. If the adjustment is not a multiple of $10,000, the amount will be rounded off to the nearest multiple of $10,000.

EXAMPLE 12-17.

T died in 2011 survived by her daughter, *D,* who is 30 and in good health, and her son, *S,* who is 40, unemployed, and an alcoholic. *D* and *S* each have 2 children. *T* had not used any part of her $5,000,000 GSTT exemption during her lifetime. *T*'s will left $5,000,000 to a trust to pay the income to *D* until she becomes 35, when the trust will terminate and the trust property will be distributed to her. If *D* dies before becoming 35 the trust will continue for the benefit of her issue. *T* also left $5,000,000 to a trust to pay the income to *S* for life. When *S* dies the property of the trust is distributable by right of representation to those of his issue who survive him. *D* will probably survive to age 35 when the property of her trust will be distributed to her. A distribution to *D* would not be a generation-skipping transfer as she is not a skip person. On the other hand, if *D* does not survive termination of the trust, her death will likely be a taxable termination for GSTT purposes. (A generation-skipping transfer would not take place on her death if she was not survived by issue and the property of her trust was added to the trust for *S*.) When *S* dies, a generation-skipping transfer of his trust is likely to take place.

Pursuing strict impartiality *T*'s executor might allocate *T*'s $5,000,000 exemption one-half to the trust for *D* and one-half to the trust for *S*. However, it is likely that any of the exemption that is allocated to the trust for *D* will be wasted (*i.e.*, *D* will survive to age 35 and receive distribution of the trust property). More taxes are likely to be saved if *T*'s exemption is allocated entirely to the trust for *S*, as a result of which it would have an inclusion ratio of zero. The termination of the trust for *S* will almost certainly involve a generation-skipping transfer.

The parties might reach an agreement that maximizes the value of *T*'s exemption and protects the interests of *D*. For example, they might agree that, (1) *T*'s entire exemption be allocated to the trust for *S*, and (2) the trustee of the trust for *S* would reimburse *D*'s trust for one-half of the amount of any GSTT that is imposed on it if *D* dies prior to termination of the trust. (The trustee might acquire term insurance on *D*'s life to insure against any loss.)

Deemed Allocations Under §2632(c). Any portion of a decedent-transferor's GSTT exemption that is not allocated within the time allowed is deemed allocated in accordance with the provisions of §2632(c). *See* §2.28. Under them the exemption is deemed allocated first, proportionally among direct skips occurring at the decedent's death and, second, proportionally among trusts of which the decedent is the transferor and from which a taxable distribution or a taxable termination might occur after the decedent's death. Deemed allocations may not make the most effective use of the exemption. Accordingly, the executor must give careful consideration to the preparation of Schedule R.

EXAMPLE 12-18.

Under the facts of Example 12-17, above, if *T*'s executor does not allocate *T*'s exemption, it will be allocated proportionately to the 2 trusts under the rules of §2632(c). Thus, *T*'s exemption would be equally divided between the 2 trusts, giving each an inclusion ratio of 50%. As *D* is in good health and will most likely survive another 5 years, the portion of *T*'s exemption allocated to *D*'s trust will probably be wasted. As suggested in Example 12-17, the parties might agree to an allocation that maximizes the benefit provided by the exemption, yet protects *D*'s trust against loss by reason of *T*'s exemption being entirely allocated to the trust for *S*.

§12.25. Consent to Split Gifts, §2513

Under §6019, the donor's executor is responsible for reporting taxable gifts for which no return has been filed. If both spouses give their written consent, under §2513 all gifts made by them to others during the calendar year are considered to be made one-half by each of them, provided both are United States citizens or residents at the time of the gifts. §2.7. Note in this connection that the effect of splitting gifts is recognized for purposes of the GSTT. §2652(a)(2). ("If, under section 2513, one-half of a gift is treated as made by an individual and one-half of such gift is treated as made by the spouse of such individual, such gift shall be so treated for purposes of this chapter.") Following the death of a spouse, the surviving spouse and the decedent's personal representative may elect under §2513 to split gifts made during the decedent's lifetime. Reg. §25.2513-2(c). The election can only apply to gifts that were completed prior to the decedent's death. Rev. Rul. 55-506, 1955-2 C.B. 609 (1939 Code). The surviving spouse may execute the consent on behalf of the decedent when the decedent did not leave an estate subject to administration and no personal representative was appointed. When the gifts are split the surviving spouse and the decedent's estate are jointly liable for the tax. §2513(d).

§12.25.1. Time of Consent

A consent to split gifts may be signified at any time following the close of the year in which the gift was made. However, a consent may not be given after either spouse has filed a gift tax return for the same year. Consent may be given after April 15 if neither spouse has filed a gift tax return for the year. Consent may not be given after either spouse has received a notice of deficiency with respect to the gift tax for the year. A Technical Advice Memorandum, LR 8843005, held that gifts could not be split where the initial returns filed on behalf of the husband and wife did not report a large gift that resulted from a noninterest-bearing loan to their son. It distinguished *Alex Frieder*, 28 T.C. 1256 (1957), *acq.*, 1958-2 C.B. 5, which concerned gifts made by the wife prior to marriage and by the husband after marriage. Briefly, the Tax Court held that a gift tax return reporting only the wife's gift, which was filed by an agent on her behalf, did not bar the husband and wife from filing subsequent "spouse" returns that split the gifts. The Tax Court also pointed out that the wife ratified the return filed by her son as agent after the gift tax returns were filed by her and her husband that split the gifts.

§12.25.2. Revocation of Consent

A consent may be revoked by filing duplicate signed statements of revocation before April 15th of the year following the year in which the gift was made. §2513(c); Reg. §25.2513-3(a). The statement must be filed with the internal revenue officer with whom the return is required to be filed. Reg. §25.2513-3(b). There is no right to revoke a consent that is filed after April 15 of the year following the year in which the gift was made. §2513(c)(2).

§12.25.3. Deceased Spouse Was Donor

Subject to the rules described above, the surviving spouse may consent to split gifts made by the decedent prior to his or her death. The question of whether or not consent should be given requires consideration of a number of factors, such as, (1) the includibility of the gift(s) in the decedent's estate, (2) the relative sizes of the spouses' estates, and (3) the availability of annual gift tax exclusions and unified credits.

§12.25.4. Gifts Not Included in Decedent's Gross Estate

A lifetime gift may not be includible in the donor's gross estate. However, if the amount of the gift exceeds the allowable annual exclusion the executor is required to file a gift tax return reporting the gift. If a return is required, the executor and the surviving spouse must consider whether or not gifts made by the decedent and the surviving spouse should be split. In this connection note that under §2035(b) the decedent's gross estate is increased by the amount of any gift tax paid by the decedent or the decedent's estate on any post-1976 gift made by the decedent or the decedent's spouse during the three-year period ending on the date of the decedent's death. However, an offsetting deduction is available under §2053 for the amount of gift tax payable by the decedent's estate.

In *Brown v. United States*, 329 F.3d 664 (9th Cir. 2003), the court held that, applying the step transaction doctrine, §2035(b) requires a donor's estate to include the funds that were used by his wife to pay the gift tax on gifts indirectly made by him. The opinion in *Brown* emphasized that the wife merely acted as a conduit for the gift and the funds that were used to pay the tax and noted: "Where a party acts as a mere 'conduit' of funds—a fleeting stop in a predetermined voyage toward a particular result—we have readily ignored the role of the intermediary in order appropriately to characterize the transaction." 329 F.3d at 672.

If a gift is not included in the decedent's gross estate, splitting the gift may reduce the estate tax payable by the decedent's estate and increase the amount of property available for distribution to the beneficiaries of the decedent's estate. In effect, part of the tax burden is shifted to the surviving spouse. If the surviving spouse does consent to be treated as donor of half of the decedent's gifts, the surviving spouse may assume the responsibility for payment of the transfer tax attributable to one-half the amount of the decedent's gifts. That result follows because a splitting of the gifts would reduce the amount of the decedent's adjusted taxable gifts otherwise includible in the decedent's tax base under §2001(b) in computing the estate tax on the decedent's estate. Of course, the tax attributable to such a gift is not shifted to the surviving spouse if the gift is entirely drawn back into the decedent's estate under §2035. However, outright gifts of property other than life insurance made within three years of the donor's death are seldom includible in the donor's estate.

When the surviving spouse is treated as the donor of half of the decedent's gifts, the decedent's estate is given the benefit of any gift tax the surviving spouse paid with respect to gifts that are included in the decedent's estate. *See* §2001(b)(2). Under the statute, the total amount of the gift taxes paid by both spouses with respect to such gifts is deducted from the tentative tax in determining the amount of estate tax on the donor's estate.

EXAMPLE 12-19.

T made outright gifts of $312,000 to each of his 3 children shortly before his death (a total of $513,000). Previously neither *T* nor his wife, *W,* had made any taxable gifts. Apart from the gifts, *T's* taxable estate is $1,539,000. If the gifts are not split with *W,* the tentative tax on *T's* estate would be based on the total amount of adjusted taxable gifts ($1,500,000) plus the amount of any gift tax paid by *T* with respect to the gifts ($0) and the amount of *T's* taxable estate ($4,200,000). The estate tax on *T's* estate would be $245,000 ($700,000 x 35%). On the other hand, if *W* consented to split the gifts, she would be treated as having made gifts of $730,500 in the years of his death (($1,539,000/2) - $39,000). In such a case, the amount of *T's* estate subject to the estate tax would be reduced by one half the gifts ($769,500) or $4,930,500. Of course, by making the election *W* would be treated as having made taxable gifts of $730,500 in the year of *T's* death. Doing so would reduce the amount of *W's* unified credit that would be available to shelter later gifts and the amount of her estate.

Upon the death of the consenting spouse, an adjustment is made where the entire amount of a split gift is included in the donor's estate by reason of § 2035. In particular, under § 2001(e) the amount of such a gift is not included as an adjusted taxable gift in computing the tentative tax on the consenting spouse's estate. Unfortunately, none of the unified credit used by the surviving spouse is restored to him or her in such a case. Also, the amount of gift tax treated as payable by the consenting spouse is not allowed under § 2001(b)(2) as an offset in calculating the estate tax on his or her estate. The amount of gift tax paid by the consenting spouse is includible in the gross estate of a consenting spouse who dies within three years of the date of the gifts. § 2035(c).

By splitting gifts, a surviving spouse may increase the amount of property that passes to the beneficiaries of the deceased donor's estate where the splitting requires the surviving spouse to pay some gift tax. This occurs because the tax paid by the survivor in effect reduces the amount of estate tax payable by the donor's estate. As a result, the amount that passes to the donor's beneficiaries is increased. Here, again, the survivor's payment of the tax on the split gift does not appear to constitute a gift. *See* Reg. § 25.2511-1(d).

§ 12.25.5. Surviving Spouse Was the Donor

The deceased spouse's executor may consent to split gifts that were made by the surviving spouse prior to the decedent's death. Reg. § 25.2513-2(c). However, the estate of a deceased spouse may not consent to split gifts after a gift tax return was filed by the donor spouse for the year in which the gifts were made. That rule applies although the return filed by the donor spouse did not report the gift at issue. LR 8843005 (TAM). In some cases, an overall tax saving will result if a decedent's executor consents to split the gifts. Such a consent makes the decedent's annual gift tax exclusions and unified credit available with respect to the gifts. On the other hand, the decedent's share of any taxable gifts will increase the tax base on which the tentative tax payable by his or her estate is computed. If the consent results in the imposition of a gift tax liability on the decedent's estate, an offsetting deduction may not be allowed under § 2053.

EXAMPLE 12-20.

> *T* made a gift of $1,000,000 to his daughter, *D*. Shortly thereafter *T*'s wife, *W*, died. *W*, who had not made any taxable gifts during her lifetime, left her entire gross estate of $4,000,000 to *D*. *W*'s personal representative may consent to split the gift made by *T*. If the consent is given, *W* will be treated as the donor of half of the gift ($500,000), but the estate tax applicable to her estate will still be well within the amount of her unified credit. Most important, the personal representative's consent to split the gift would preserve some of *T*'s unified credit, which could be used later.

A tax saving may also result where the consent would increase the estate tax payable by the decedent's estate by a smaller amount than the corresponding decrease in the gift tax payable by the donor. However, the personal representative should be reluctant to subject the decedent's estate to a greater transfer tax liability unless the donor is also the person who bears the burden of the increase in the estate tax. Needless to say, a serious conflict of interest arises where the donor spouse serves as the deceased spouse's personal representative and the estate tax burden is borne by others.

§ 12.26. QUALIFIED PLAN BENEFITS

Until the early 1980s, the value of benefits payable to survivors under qualified plans was not includible in a decedent's estate. Former § 2039(c). The exclusion was reduced by the 1982 Act and eliminated entirely by the 1984 Act for persons dying after 1984.

Under the basic rules of § 2039, an annuity or other payment under a qualified plan is included in the decedent's estate to the extent it is receivable by any beneficiary by reason of surviving the decedent and the decedent had a right to payment under the annuity contract or agreement. § 2039(a). Any part of the annuity attributable to either the employee's or the employer's contributions is deemed to be contributed by the employee and taxed under this section. § 2039(b).

The community property interest of a deceased nonemployee spouse in an employee benefit plan is includible in the decedent's estate under § 2033 if the nonemployee spouse dies first. *See* § 3.32. Of course, a corresponding marital deduction is allowable if the interest passes to the employee spouse—which is required by ERISA. *Id.* The Department of Labor has ruled that the plan administrator is not required to follow a probate court order directing the disposition of the nonemployee spouse's community property interest in the plan. *See* Dept. of Labor AO 90-46A (1990); Dept. of Labor AO 90-47A (1990). *See also* § 4.20.6.

§12.26.1. Special Exceptions

Under the 1984 Act, the unlimited exclusion is available with respect to a person dying after 1982 who had irrevocably elected the form of benefit payable under the plan (including survivor's benefits) before 1983 and whose plan was in pay status on December 31, 1982. Similarly, the unlimited exclusion remains available to a plan participant who dies after 1984 to the extent that he or she had irrevocably elected the form of benefits payable under the plan (including survivor's benefits) before July 18, 1984 and the decedent's interest was in pay status on December 31, 1984. *See* Temp. Reg. §20.2039-1T. Under the 1986 Act the unlimited exclusion was restored for the qualified plan benefits of decedents who separated from service before 1982 and do not change the form of benefits prior to death. In addition, a $100,000 exclusion is available with respect to decedents who separated from service before 1985 and do not change the form of benefits prior to death.

The marital deduction may be allowable with respect to distributions made to QTIP trusts from IRAs and qualified plans. *See* §5.23.5.

§12.26.2. Distributions to Surviving Spouse

A surviving spouse who receives a distribution from a qualified plan may elect to defer income taxation of the distribution by rolling it over within 60 days to an IRA under §402(c)(9). Otherwise the distribution is subject to taxation presently. Note also that §408(d)(3)(C), in effect, permits surviving spouse to rollover part or all of a distribution received from a deceased spouse's IRA. Letter Ruling 8911006 permitted such a rollover where the IRA was payable to the estate of the decedent husband and his widow was the sole beneficiary under his will.

In order to defer the income taxation of the distribution, the rollover to an IRA must be made within 60 days following receipt of the distribution. In making the decision the surviving spouse should take into account the fact that the income of an IRA accumulates free of income tax until it is distributed. It is also significant that a contributor may retain investment direction over property held in an IRA. Note that an individually directed account is generally barred from investing in "collectibles" which included works of art, rugs, antiques, metals, gems, stamps, coins, and alcoholic beverages. §408(m). However, §408(m) permits individually directed investments in certain coins and bullion made of silver, gold or platinum.

The proceeds of a qualified plan that are distributed to a surviving spouse may be rolled over by the surviving spouse to an IRA provided the rollover is made within 60 days following receipt. In LR 9247026, the rollover was allowed although the proceeds passed to the surviving spouse by reason of disclaimers executed by her and other beneficiaries of their interests in a trust which the decedent had designated as beneficiary of the IRA. The same result was reached in LR 9609052 in which an IRA payable to his estate would have passed to a credit shelter trust for the benefit of his surviving spouse for life, the remainder to his issue. As a result of disclaimers executed by the decedent's surviving spouse and issue of their interests in the trust, the IRA passed to the surviving spouse under the residuary clause of the decedent's will. The ruling holds that the surviving spouse will be entitled to roll over the IRA and treat it as her own.

§12.26.3. Income Taxation of Lump Sum Distributions

Special tax treatment of lump sum distributions that are the subject of a tax free roll over was repealed by the 1996 Act with respect to tax years beginning after 1999. However, under a transitional rule taxpayers born before 1936 are allowed to continue to make certain elections (ten year averaging and the application of a 20 percent flat rate to the portion attributable to pre-1974 contributions). Five year averaging was repealed for tax years beginning after 1999.

A lump sum distribution from a qualified plan will consist of one or more of the following three parts: (1) a part attributable to the employee's previously taxed contributions, which is not taxable, (2) a part attributable to the employer's pre-1974 contributions, which is taxed as ordinary income unless the distributee elects to treat it as capital gain, and (3) a part attributable to the employer's post-1973 contributions, which is taxed as ordinary income.

A taxpayer may, of course, elect to treat the taxable portion of a lump sum distribution as ordinary income. For tax years beginning after 1999 two other options are available with respect to taxpayers born before 1936. First, the taxpayer may elect the ten year averaging method, in which the tax is based on one-tenth of the taxable amount of the distribution, which is then multiplied by ten. Second, the pre-1974 amount may be based on a flat 20 percent tax rate.

§12.27. FORMER §4980A; TAX ON EXCESS DISTRIBUTIONS AND EXCESS ACCUMULATIONS OF QUALIFIED PLANS

Former §4980A (originally designated as §4981A), added in 1986, imposed a 15 percent tax on excess distributions from and, at death, the excess accumulations of, qualified retirement plans. The tax on excess distributions is imposed in addition to the income tax that otherwise applies. The complex and unpopular tax was repealed by the 1997 Act effective with respect to distributions received after 1996 and to accumulations of decedents dying after 1996.

§12.28. LIFE INSURANCE PROCEEDS

The beneficiary of a life insurance policy may accept the benefits under the policy or disclaim the right to receive them. Also, a beneficiary is usually free to receive the proceeds outright or to leave them with the insurer under a settlement option. A beneficiary who elects a settlement option is treated as having received the proceeds outright and having transferred them back to the insurer in exchange for its commitment to make payments under the option. The estate and income tax consequences of electing an optional settlement mode are described at §§6.40 and 6.53.

EXAMPLE 12-21.

H's life was insured under a policy that designated his wife, W, as the beneficiary. Following H's death W elected to receive the policy proceeds in monthly installment payments over a 20-year period. If W dies prior to the end of the 20-year period, the commuted value of any remaining payments would be paid to her surviving children. *W*'s election was not a disclaimer. Instead, *W* will be treated as if she had received the proceeds outright and transferred them to the insurer in exchange for its commitment to make payments to her for a 20-year period. The interest element of each payment will be taxed to *W*. If *W* dies prior to the end of the 20-year period, the amount that will be paid to her children is includible in her gross estate under § 2036. *See* § 6.40.

The settlement options are usually based upon a low guaranteed rate of interest. Some options do provide for the interest payments to be augmented at the election of the insurer. A beneficiary may receive a higher, equally secure, net return by taking the proceeds outright and investing them in higher yielding, relatively liquid investments (*e.g.,* certificates of deposit, corporate or municipal bonds). The election to leave the funds with the insurer may be attractive to a beneficiary, assuming the insurer is financially sound, because it will not require any further supervision or any payment of fees or commissions.

E. REORDERING THE DISTRIBUTION OF PROPERTY

§ 12.29. GENERAL

This part deals with several important devices by which the distribution of property can be reordered after a decedent's death. The family awards and allowances available to a surviving spouse or to minor children are discussed first. The awards and allowances are usually quite limited in amount, but can provide important economic protection for the survivors. Next, the focus shifts to the option that most states give a surviving spouse to receive a statutory share of the decedent's property in lieu of the benefits provided for in the decedent's will. The concluding sections review the law regarding disclaimers and the circumstances in which they may be used to advantage.

§ 12.30. FAMILY AWARDS AND ALLOWANCES

The share of a decedent's estate that passes to the decedent's surviving spouse or minor children may be increased if they take advantage of the family awards and allowances that are allowed by local law. The family awards generally include a limited probate homestead allowance and a limited allocation of exempt property. *See* U.P.C. § § 2-402, 2-403 (2011). Importantly, they usually prevail over any contrary testamentary disposition made by the decedent. However, a surviving spouse may be barred from claiming the awards if he or she waived the right to them in connection with a property settlement agreement. The awards are often of special value because they are usually exempt from creditors' claims against the decedent *and* against the decedent's surviving spouse or dependent children. The marital deduction may be allowable with respect to awards and allowances received by a surviving spouse. *See* § 5.16.1.

Most states permit a surviving spouse or minor or dependent children to claim a homestead or award in lieu of homestead and an allocation of exempt property. However, the awards are usually limited to very small amounts. In addition, state laws often allow a surviving spouse and children to claim a "reasonable" allowance in money out of the estate for their support during the period of administration. *E.g.,* U.P.C. §2-404 (2011). Some states limit the duration or amount, or both the duration and amount, of family allowance payments. A family allowance is typically payable to the surviving spouse for his or her support and the support of the minor or dependent children. If the decedent did not leave a surviving spouse, it is payable to the children or to the persons who have the care and custody of them. The family allowance is also generally exempt from all claims of the decedent's creditors. If a decedent leaves a small estate the protection from creditors can be very important to the family.

The awards and allowances are generally allowable in addition to any property the survivors are entitled to receive by will, intestate succession, or otherwise. However, a testamentary gift to a survivor may be conditioned upon the survivor not claiming a family award or allowance. If so, the beneficiary may not be entitled to receive the gift if he or she makes such a claim. Also, a surviving spouse might be barred from claiming an award or allowance by reason of the provisions of a prenuptial or post-nuptial agreement with the decedent.

§12.30.1. Estate Tax

Homestead and exempt property awards of the type provided for in the U.P.C. vest in the survivors upon the decedent's death and qualify as deductible interests for purposes of the estate tax marital deduction. *See* §5.16. Accordingly, use of the awards could play a role in deferring some of the taxes that would otherwise be payable by reason of the decedent's death. In contrast, the family support allowances are usually terminable interests that do not qualify for the marital deduction.

§12.30.2. Income Tax

A homestead or exempt property award should be treated as an inheritance that is not subject to taxation by reason of §102(a) and does not constitute a distribution for purposes of §§661 and 662. By reason of the latter feature, such an award does not entitle the estate to a deduction or require the recipient to report any income. A different rule applies in the case of family support allowances. Under Reg. §1.661(a)-2(e), the estate is entitled to a deduction for family allowance payments made from income or principal. A recipient is, of course, required to report family allowance payments as income to the extent of the recipient's share of the estate's distributable net income. Reg. §1.662(a)-2(c). The income tax consequences of family allowance payments must be taken into account in, for example, selecting the estate's tax year or making distributions. The lawyer should explain the income tax impact of the payments to the surviving spouse in order to facilitate planning for any income tax liability that may result from them.

Under the separate share rule, a distribution in satisfaction of an election against the decedent's will carries out part of the estate's distributable net income. *See*

§ 663(c) and § 10.4.9. Courts were previously split on the issue, with *Brigham v. United States*, 160 F.3d 759 (1st Cir. 1998), holding that a distribution to the electing spouse could carry out all of the estate's DNI. *See* § § 5.26, 9.25.

§ 12.31. WIDOW'S ELECTION

Under the law of most noncommunity property states, a surviving spouse may elect to receive a specified share of the decedent's property outright in lieu of the property he or she is entitled to receive under the decedent's will. *See also* § 9.25. The size of the elective share, the property from which it is payable, and the election procedure, vary from state to state. Perhaps the U.P.C. provides the surviving spouse with the most extensive protection. In particular, the U.P.C. greatly expands the property base that is used to compute the surviving spouse's elective share. Under U.P.C. § 2-202 (2011), the surviving spouse is entitled to claim a portion of the "augmented estate," which includes the surviving spouse's net estate *and* the decedent's probate estate and reclaimable estate. The elective share of the surviving spouse increases with the length of the marriage to a maximum of 50 percent after 15 years. U.P.C. § 2-202 (2011). However, the share the survivor is entitled to receive is reduced by the value of property received from the decedent during lifetime or at death. The augmented estate concept serves both to prevent a person from transferring property to others in a way that would defeat a spouse's right to a share in the property, and to prevent a surviving spouse from claiming a share in the probate estate where he or she had already received a substantial amount of property from the decedent.

The interests in a decedent's property that a surviving spouse receives pursuant to an election against the decedent's will are considered to pass to the surviving spouse from the decedent for marital deduction purposes. Reg. § 20.2056(e)-2(c). When the surviving spouse receives outright interests in property as a result of the election, the interests normally qualify for the marital deduction. According to the Regulations, if the surviving spouse does not elect against the will, "then the dower or other property interest relinquished by her is not considered as having passed from the decedent to his surviving spouse." Reg. § 20.2056(e)-2(c). Prior to 1982, an uncommuted common law dower interest in property was treated as a nondeductible terminable interest. In the case of decedents dying after 1982, the surviving spouse might have a qualifying income interest for life in the property subject to his or her dower interest. If so, the value of the property would be deductible under § 2056(b)(7) at the executor's election. *See* § § 5.23, 12.21. The commuted value of a survivor's dower interest, if requested and paid in accordance with state law, is a deductible nonterminable interest. Rev. Rul. 72-7, 1972-1 C.B. 308. Thus, a marital deduction is allowable for a dower interest that is an absolute interest that vests at death under state law. Rev. Rul. 72-8, 1972-1 C.B. 309 (Florida law). Also, the commuted value of a surviving spouse's dower interest that is paid under a negotiated, bona fide settlement of the interest is also deductible under § 2056 if the amount is no more than would have been received in a court proceeding; a court decree is not needed. Rev. Rul. 83-107, 1983-2 C.B. 159. (The portion of a decedent's estate that passes to his or her surviving spouse in settlement of a bona fide dispute qualifies for the marital deduction. § 5.16.) From the estate planning perspective, a decision regarding the exercise of the spouse's election should only be made after projecting the overall tax and nontax consequences. In some cases the election may help salvage the estate from the ravages of an unwise or ineffective estate plan.

§12.32. DISCLAIMERS: GENERAL

A disclaimer (or "renunciation," as it is sometimes called) is an unequivocal refusal to accept an interest in, or a power over, property to which the disclaimant is otherwise entitled by lifetime or deathtime transfer or operation of law. Disclaimers were part of the common law of many states. However, most states have adopted more or less comprehensive statutes on the subject. A disclaimed interest in property generally passes as if the disclaimant had predeceased the attempt to transfer the property to him or her. Because a disclaimed interest usually passes along to another person, a disclaimer can be used to decrease the amount of property passing to a named beneficiary and to increase the amount passing to others (*e.g.*, the disclaimant's children, the decedent's surviving spouse, a charity). The opportunity to reorder the distribution of property free of tax is one of the most important tools available to the estate planner.

A small number of states have adopted the comprehensive Uniform Disclaimer of Property Interests Act (1978), or its more limited companions, the Uniform Disclaimer of Transfers by Will, Intestacy or Appointment Act (1978) and the Uniform Disclaimer of Transfers Under Nontestamentary Instruments Act (1978). Other forms of disclaimer statutes have been enacted by a number of other states.

State laws generally require a disclaimer to be made without consideration and within a reasonable time of the original transfer. The acceptance of any benefit from a transfer generally precludes a valid disclaimer. The underlying theory is that an individual should be relatively free to accept or reject an interest that others attempt to transfer to him or her. However, in order to protect creditors, some states prohibit insolvent persons from disclaiming interests in property.

The federal gift and estate tax consequences of a disclaimer are determined by federal law. It was clarified considerably by the adoption of §2518 in 1976, which introduced the concept of a qualified disclaimer (*i.e.*, one that satisfies federal requirements for a disclaimer). The 1981 Act went further and, in effect, established a national standard for disclaimers that was largely independent of state law. *See* §2518(c)(3). Prior to 1977, the tax consequences of disclaimers were determined according to a scattered and uncoordinated group of statutes and regulations, augmented by a few judicial decisions. In general, a disclaimer was considered to be effective if it was valid under the governing state law and was made within a reasonable time after the disclaimant learned of the attempted transfer to him or her. Because of the wide differences in state law, identical refusals to accept property made in different states sometimes had different federal gift and estate tax consequences.

A disclaimer must be distinguished from a release, which involves the relinquishment of a power or interest that had been accepted. The difference in concept is recognized by Reg. §20.2041-3(d)(6)(i):

> A disclaimer or renunciation of a general power of appointment created . . . after December 31, 1976 is not considered to be a release of the power if the disclaimer or renunciation is a qualified disclaimer as de-

scribed in section 2518 and the corresponding regulations . . . .If the disclaimer or renunciation is not a qualified disclaimer, it is considered a release of the power by the disclaimant.

Although a disclaimed power ordinarily does not pass to another person, most powers can be validly disclaimed under § 2518.

Before recommending that a client execute a disclaimer the lawyer must learn of the client's family circumstances and be aware of the impact of all of the relevant state laws. For example, in *Webb v. Webb*, 301 S.E.2d 570 (W.Va. 1983), a son's disclaimer of an intestate interest did not cause the disclaimed property to pass to his mother as intended. Instead, the property passed to the disclaimant's infant daughter, of whose existence he neglected to inform his counsel. Under the intestate succession law of West Virginia the disclaimed intestate share passed to the infant daughter, who lived with the son's former wife. The court refused to set aside the disclaimer, which was executed because of the negligence of the son and his counsel: "We are of the opinion that counsel's mistake, like that of the appellant, arises from a lack of diligence. We believe that, in the circumstances presented, counsel had a duty to inquire of the appellant whether he had any children before advising him to execute the disclaimer." 301 S.E.2d at 576. As indicated in Example 12-22, below, a state's anti-lapse statute may similarly cause a disclaimed bequest to pass to the issue of the disclaimant. Finally, "a disclaimer that is wholly void or that is voided by the disclaimant's creditors cannot be a qualified disclaimer." Reg. § 25.2518-1(c)(2). However, the mere fact that a disclaimer is *voidable* by the disclaimant's creditors has no effect on the determination of whether or not it is a qualified disclaimer. Also, where the transferor did not direct the disposition of the property in the event of disclaimer, the consequences of a disclaimer may be affected by the local anti-lapse statute.

EXAMPLE 12-22.

T died leaving a will which bequeathed the residue of his estate to his 2 daughters. The daughters wished to make the funds available to their mother, *T*'s widow, for her support. The daughters disclaimed their right to receive the residue with the intent that it pass to their mother under the local intestate succession law. Instead, the residuary estate passed to the daughter's minor children by reason of the local anti-lapse statute. Under the local law, in the absence of contrary direction by the decedent, a bequest to a beneficiary who was related to the testator passes to the beneficiary's descendants by right of representation if the beneficiary predeceases the testator. LR 7833008 (TAM). *See also* LR 8926001 (TAM).

Reversing the Tax Court, a marital deduction was allowed with respect to property that the decedent's son disclaimed, which the appellate court determined then passed to the decedent's surviving spouse. *DePaoli v. Commissioner*, 62 F.3d 1259 (10th Cir. 1995). The Tax Court had disallowed the martial deduction on the ground that the disclaimed property passed at the direction of the son and not from the decedent. In its view the disclaimed property would have passed under the New Mexico anti-lapse statute to his two illegitimate children. The Court of Appeals disagreed, concluding the decedent's son had not recognized his illegitimate children in a manner sufficient to allow them to take under the anti-lapse statute. Accordingly, the decedent's property did pass to his surviving spouse as a result of the disclaimer.

§12.33. Qualified Disclaimers, §2518

> [T]he disclaimer of all or an undivided portion of any separate interest in property may be a qualified disclaimer even if the disclaimant has another interest in the same property. In general, each interest in property that is separately created by the transferor is treated as a separate interest. For example, if an income interest in securities is bequeathed to *A* for life, then to *B* for life, with the remainder interest in such securities bequeathed to *A*'s estate . . . *A* could make a qualified disclaimer of either the income interest or the remainder, or an undivided portion of either. *A* could not, however, make a qualified disclaimer of the income interest for a certain number of years. Reg. §25.2518-3(a)(1).

Section 2518 added the term "qualified disclaimer" to the estate planner's vocabulary. In brief, a disclaimer that meets the requirements of §2518(b) is a "qualified disclaimer" that will be recognized as effective for gift and estate tax purposes. Under §2518(a), if a person makes a qualified disclaimer with respect to an interest in property, the gift and estate tax laws apply as if the interest had never been transferred to the disclaimant. The provisions of §2518 apply to taxable transfers made after December 31, 1976 that create an interest in the party attempting to disclaim the interest. Reg. §25.2518-1(a). Interests created by pre-1977 transfers are subject to the prior law.

Disclaimers made for consideration do not constitute qualified disclaimers. Reg. §25.2518-2(d)(1). By extension, the Tax Court concluded that no marital deduction was allowable with respect to property that passed as a result of disclaimers made by 29 legatees in order to allow the property to pass to the decedent's surviving spouse, where the disclaimants "expected" that they would receive the amounts of the disclaimed legacies in the form of a gift or legacy from the decedent's surviving spouse. *Estate of Louise S. Monroe,* 104 T.C. 352 (1995) (penalty under §6662 upheld for underpayment of tax). Alas, however, *Estate of Monroe* was reversed on appeal by the Fifth Circuit, 127 F.3d 699 (1997). On appeal the court parsed the statute and the regulations, concluding that disclaimers are valid unless revocable or qualified in some way. "None of the written disclaimers challenged by the Commissioner can be attacked as being subject to revocation or subject to some condition; the documents executed by the disclaimants are irrevocable and unqualified on their face." The opinion flatly rejected the Tax Court's conclusion that a disclaimer is not qualified if it rests on "an 'implied promise' that the disclaimant will be better off executing the disclaimer than not doing so."

The sale by a decedent's personal representative of some items of the decedent's property does not preclude some of the decedent's intestate successors from disclaiming the right to receive any interest in those items. LR 9509003 (TAM) (Illinois law). Finally, recitation in a disclaimer of the disclaimant's understanding and intention regarding the disposition of the disclaimed property is precatory and will be disregarded. *Id.*

§ 12.33.1. Powers

A power with respect to property is generally treated as an interest in that property, and may therefore be disclaimed. § 2518(c)(2). A power, such as a general power of appointment, that is disclaimed normally terminates. However, as in the case of other interests, a power may be partially disclaimed. *See* Reg. § 25.2518-3(d), Example 21 (qualified disclaimer of testamentary power to appoint one-half of the trust corpus). As noted in the Regulations, "a disclaimer of a power of appointment with respect to property is a qualified disclaimer *only* if the right to direct the beneficial enjoyment of the property which is retained by the disclaimant is limited by an ascertainable standard" (emphasis added). In contrast, a disclaimer is ineffective if the disclaimant retains a discretionary power to allocate the property among the beneficiaries. *See* Reg. § 25.2518-2(d)(2); Reg. § 25.2518-3(a)(1)(iii). Example 7 of Reg. § 25.2518-2(e)(5) suggests that an otherwise valid disclaimer is not disqualified by reason of the disclaimant's retention of a 5 or 5 power of withdrawal (*i.e.*, the power to withdraw the greater of $5,000 or five percent of the value of the trust). In some cases a disclaimed power may pass to another party—which is acceptable so long as the disclaimant cannot direct the transfer of the power. Reg. § 25.2518-2(e).

A trustee may not unilaterally make a qualified disclaimer of a power to invade trust corpus for the benefit of a specified beneficiary unless authorized to do so by the trust or state law. Rev. Rul. 90-110, 1990-2 C.B. 209. Consistently, in LR 9818005 (TAM) the IRS held that an attempt by a testamentary trustee to disclaim the right to make distributions of principal and income was ineffective, and the trust could not qualify for the marital deduction, because neither the local law nor the governing instrument permitted the trustee to make such a disclaimer. In contrast, LR 9818008 recognized the effect of a disclaimer by a surviving spouse of the power to amend or revoke a credit shelter trust created by the deceased spouse. In order to save the marital deduction a surviving spouse may disclaim the lifetime power to appoint the principal of a trust to and among her children. LR 8935024.

§ 12.33.2. Disclaimer of Benefit of Tax Clause

The right to have estate taxes on property passing outside of the probate estate paid out of the residuary estate in accordance with the provisions of the tax clause of a will may be disclaimed. *Estate of Boyd*, 819 F.2d 170 (7th Cir. 1987). That outcome is consistent with the general rule that treats "each interest in property that is separately created by the transferor" as a separate interest subject to disclaimer. Reg. § 25.2518-3(a)(1)(i). Similarly, the remainder beneficiaries of a QTIP trust can disclaim the benefit of a tax clause in a surviving spouse's will under which the estate tax resulting from the inclusion of the QTIP trust in her estate was to be paid from her estate and not the trust. LR 200127007 (applying Pennsylvania disclaimer law).

Disclaimer After Attaining Majority. In LR 200047027, the IRS confirmed that the beneficiary of an irrevocable trust created in 1955 could, within nine months of reaching majority under the local law, disclaim a contingent remainder in the trust. The ruling, which dealt with a pre-1977 trust, is, of course, consistent with the requirements of § 2518 and of Reg. § 25.2518-2(a)(3), that apply to post-1976 trusts. LR 200333023 (which involved a child's disclaimer of intestate interest in a parent's estate within nine months of the child becoming 21 years of age).

§ 12.33.3. Pre-1977 Transfers

The disclaimer of an interest created under a pre-1977 transfer will be recognized for gift and estate tax purposes if, (1) it is unequivocal and effective under state law, and (2) it is made within a reasonable time after knowledge of the transfer. Reg. § 25.2511-1(c)(2). The "transfer" referred to in the Regulations occurs when the interest is created and not later when it vests or becomes possessory. *Jewett v. Commissioner*, 455 U.S. 305 (1982).

§ 12.33.4. Statutory Requirements for Qualified Disclaimers

In order to constitute a qualified disclaimer under § 2518, Reg. § 25.2518-2(a) requires that:

(1) The disclaimer be irrevocable and unqualified;

(2) The disclaimer be in writing;

(3) The writing be received by [the transferor or his legal representative] not later than the date that is 9 months after the later of—

  (i) The date on which the transfer creating the interest in the disclaimant is made, or

  (ii) The day on which the disclaimant attains age 21;

(4) The disclaimant has not accepted the interest disclaimed or any of its benefits; and

(5) The interest disclaimed passes either to the spouse of the decedent or to a person other than the disclaimant without any direction on the part of the person making the disclaimer.

Each of the requirements is considered briefly in the following paragraphs. In order to satisfy the statutory requirements a disclaimer must be in writing, irrevocable and be valid under state law. LR 9640005 (TAM). The cited TAM holds that substantial compliance with the requirements is insufficient—the requirements must be strictly followed. In *Estate of Delaune v. United States*, 96-1 U.S.T.C. ¶ 60,221 (M.D. La. 1996), the court held that an intended disclaimer that was not executed prior to the decedent's death was ineffective. Unlike most states, Louisiana does not allow a disclaimer to be made by the personal representative of a decedent.

Estate of Delaune was reversed on appeal, 143 F.3d 995 (5th Cir. 1998), in an opinion that began: "This case will demonstrate how, under the Louisiana Law Civil, the past is not dead, that the past will not die, and how, indeed, the past is not even past." The appellate court concluded that, based upon the history of the Code Napoleon and its enactment in Louisiana, the Louisiana law did allow for the renunciation of a legacy by the heirs of an heir. Accordingly, the attempted renunciation constituted a qualified disclaimer under § 2518. *See* § 12.36.

No qualified disclaimer occurred in LR 200437032 (TAM), where the decedent's will left a bequest to his sister, a nun who had taken a vow of poverty. Under applicable Cannon Law, the sister's property acquired after taking the vow "belongs to the [church], in accordance with the [church's] own law." Interestingly, the decedent's will provided that if the sister did not survive to claim the bequest, the gift was to pass to the same church. The estate's position in the ruling was that because of the sister's vow of poverty and the operation of Cannon Law, the sister made a qualified disclaimer of the gift. And since the property passes to the church under the terms of the decedent's will, the bequest should qualify for a charitable deduction. The IRS concluded that there was no effective disclaimer under state and federal law. Because the language of the xCannon Law and the sister's vow did not comport with the requirements of § 2518 (the vow did not designate the particular property and the property was not in fact transferred to the church within nine months of decedent's death), the disclaimer could not be respected. Consequently, the estate could not claim a charitable contribution deduction.

Irrevocable and Unqualified. The requirement that the disclaimer be irrevocable and unqualified usually does not pose any problem for the planner. In order to avoid any question on this point, a disclaimer should state that it is irrevocable and is not subject to any qualifications or conditions.

In Writing. The requirement that the disclaimer be in writing is also unlikely to cause any problem. However, the planner should be sure that the disclaimer also satisfies the local law regarding formalities of execution. For example, some state laws require that disclaimers be acknowledged, witnessed, or recorded.

Received Within Nine Months. Under § 2518(b)(2), the disclaimer must be received by the transferor within nine months after the date on which the original transfer was made. Under the regulations, a timely mailing will be treated as a timely delivery if the mailing requirements of Reg. §§ 301.7502-1(c)(1), (c)(2), and (d) are met. Reg. § 25.2518-2(c)(2). A disclaimer can be drafted to provide evidence of the date on which it was received by the transferor. *See* Form 12-2, below. Section 2518(b)(2) requires a disclaimer to be received by the transferor within nine months after the day on which the transfer was made. An extension of time within which to file the federal estate tax return does not extend the time within which the disclaimer must be received. *Fitzgerald v. United States*, 94-1 U.S.T.C. ¶ 60,152 (W.D.La. 1993), *aff'd*, 35 F.3d 562 (5th Cir. 1994). *See* Reg. § 25.2518-2(c) A disclaimer could include a form of receipt to be signed by the transferor such as in Form 12-2.

Form 12-2
Acknowledgment for Receipt of Disclaimer

Receipt of this disclaimer on _____, 200 ____ is acknowledged.

_____

[Transferor]
In the case of a death time transfer, the transferor is the decedent's personal representative.

Under the regulations, the time limit is generally computed separately with respect to each taxable transfer. Reg. § 25.2518-2(c)(3). In general, a taxable transfer occurs when there is a completed transfer for federal gift or estate tax purposes. However, a disclaimer that is executed within nine months of a taxable transfer will not be effective if the disclaimant previously accepted an interest in the property.

In most situations, the time period within which disclaimer must occur starts at the time of the original transfer. For example, if the remainder beneficiaries of a QTIP trust wish to disclaim, they must do so within nine months of the creation of the trust, not nine months after the corpus of the trust is subject to taxation under § 2044 or § 2519. *See* Reg. § 25.2518-2(c)(3). Similarly, a "person who receives an interest in property as the result of a qualified disclaimer of the interest must disclaim the previously disclaimed interest no later than 9 months after the date of the transfer creating the interest in the preceding disclaimant." *Id.* In contrast, those who take through the exercise or lapse of a general power of appointment may disclaim within nine months of its exercise or lapse. Of course, the holder of that power must disclaim within nine months of the creation of the power. *Id.*

No Acceptance of Benefits. A qualified disclaimer cannot be made if the disclaimant accepted the interest or any of its benefits, expressly or impliedly, prior to making the disclaimer. As the Regulations state, "Acts indicative of acceptance include using the property or the interest in the property; accepting dividends, interest or rents from the property; and directing others to act with respect to the property or interest in the property. However, merely taking delivery of an instrument of title, without more, does not constitute acceptance." Reg. § 25.2518-2(d)(1). For purposes of this rule, a disclaimant is treated as having accepted a benefit from the property if the disclaimant receives any consideration in exchange for the disclaimer, including the agreement of another party to dispose of the property in a way specified by the disclaimant. Reg. § 25.2518-2(d)(1). However, actions taken by the disclaimant in a fiduciary capacity to preserve or protect the property do not constitute an acceptance of benefits. For example, an executor may direct the harvesting of a crop or the general maintenance of a building. Reg. § 25.2518-2(d)(2). A disclaimant is not treated as having accepted property merely because the title to the property vests in the disclaimant under the local law immediately upon the owner's death. The exercise to any extent of a power of appointment by the donee of the power is an acceptance of its benefits. *Id.*

Exercise of Power of Appointment. The exercise of a power of appointment by a nontestamentary instrument may constitute an acceptance of an interest in the property subject to the power. The issue arose in *Estate of Leona Engelman*, 121 T.C. 54 (2003), which concerned the includibility in the estate of a widow who survived her husband by only three months of the assets of a revocable trust previously established by the husband and wife. Applying California law, the Tax Court held that the surviving spouse's execution of a power of appointment that would control the disposition of a portion of a trust upon her death was an acceptance of an interest in the trust that precluded the administrator of her estate from disclaiming any interest in the property that was subject to the exercise of the power. In addition, no charitable deduction was allowed for the value of the residue of the trust that passed to the State of Israel, because the use of the property was not limited by the transferor to a charitable use. *See* § 8.2.1 and Supp. § 8.2.1. The *Engelman* decision relied upon the Ninth Circuit's opinion in a bankruptcy case, *Cassel v. Kolb*, 321 F.3d 868, *modified*, 326 F.3d 1030 (9th Cir. 2003), which held that under Cal. Prob. Code § 285(b)(3), a contingent beneficiary was unable to disclaim his contingent remainder interest in a trust that he had declared on numerous loan applications was owned by him.

The acceptance of a distribution from a gift or bequest is treated as an acceptance of a proportionate part of the income earned by the bequest or gift. Accordingly, the acceptance of partial distribution may not bar a subsequent disclaimer of a pecuniary amount of the gift or bequest. The principle is illustrated by Reg. §25.2518-3(c) and Reg. §25.2518-3(d), Example 17. Thus, the receipt of a distribution of a portion of a brokerage account only bars the recipient from disclaiming that proportion of the account. *Id.*

Pass to Surviving Spouse or Others Without Direction. The requirement that the property pass to the decedent's surviving spouse or to a person other than the disclaimant without any direction on the disclaimant's part can be troublesome, particularly where trusts are involved. A disclaimant may have to disclaim the right to receive a particular interest by more than one method in order to satisfy this requirement. For example, the disclaimer by a residuary beneficiary (other than a surviving spouse) of the right to receive a decedent's estate would not be a qualified disclaimer if the disclaimant were entitled to receive the residuary estate under the intestate succession law. Reg. §25.2518-2(e)(5), Example (3).

A similar problem arose in *Estate of Helen Christiansen*, 130 T.C. 1 (2008), *aff'd*, 586 F.3d 1061 (8th Cir. 2009). In this case, the decedent's will left her entire estate to her daughter. The decedent's will provided that any amounts her daughter disclaimed would pass 25 percent to a charitable foundation and 75 percent to a charitable lead trust that would pay an annuity to the foundation for 20 years with the remainder to pass to the daughter if she was then living. The daughter disclaimed a portion of her outright bequest, but did not disclaim the contingent remainder interest in the charitable lead trust. The IRS disallowed a charitable deduction for the amount passing directly to the foundation and for the present value of the foundation's lead interest in the charitable lead trust because the daughter failed to disclaim the contingent remainder interest in the lead trust. By retaining her contingent remainder interest, concluded the IRS, the daughter effectively disclaimed the interest to herself. Reg. §25.2518-2(e)(3) provides that "if a disclaimant who is not a surviving spouse receives a specific bequest of a fee simple interest in property and as a result of the disclaimer of the entire interest, the property passes to a trust in which the disclaimant has a remainder interest, then the disclaimer will not be a qualified disclaimer unless the remainder interest in the property is also disclaimed." Before the Tax Court, the estate acknowledged that the regulation was valid but argued that the contingent remainder interest was either "severable property" or "an undivided portion of the property." The Tax Court, in a divided (12-2) opinion, rejected these arguments. The contingent remainder was not severable property because it could not be divided into separate parts that would maintain complete and independent existences. The court observed, for example, that a block of stock can be severed into individual shares, but an intangible right cannot be severed into present and remainder interests because each such interest has very different rights and characteristics. Furthermore, the contingent remainder was not an "undivided portion" of the property disclaimed because it was not a "fraction or percentage of each and every substantial interest or right owned by disclaimant." So while the daughter could have disclaimed 40 percent of the total bequest, she could not disclaim only the lead interest and retain a remainder interest.

A disclaimer by a surviving spouse is not a qualified one if he or she retains the right to direct the future beneficial enjoyment of the property in a transfer that will not be subject to the federal gift or estate tax. (A power that is limited by an ascertainable standard is not within this rule.) A surviving spouse can validly disclaim an outright bequest if the property will pass to a trust over which the spouse holds no power of appointment. Such a disclaimer would not be a qualified one if the spouse were to retain a special power of appointment over the trust that was not limited by an ascertainable standard. Reg. §25.2518-2(e)(5), Example (5). In such a case, the surviving spouse must also disclaim the power.

§12.33.5. Disclaimers Not Recognized by Local Law

Changes made by the 1981 Act effective with respect to interests created after 1981, provide that a written transfer which does not qualify as a disclaimer under local law will be recognized as a qualified disclaimer if it meets the requirements of §§2518(b)(2) and (3) and the transferred property passes to the persons who would have received the property had the transferor made a qualified disclaimer. Under §§2518(b)(2) and (3), the attempted disclaimer must be timely (*i.e.*, made within nine months after the transfer to the present transferor), §2518(b)(2), and the present transferor must not have accepted the interest or any of its benefits, §2518(b)(3).

Finally, partial disclaimers are allowed under the federal law but the interests that may be partially disclaimed are limited. *See* §12.35.

§12.34. DISCLAIMER OF JOINT TENANCY INTERESTS

The tax position of the survivors is often improved if a joint tenancy interest is validly disclaimed. Unfortunately, the state laws are often unclear regarding the ability of a surviving joint tenant to disclaim an interest in the joint tenancy property. The common law generally did not permit joint tenancy interests to be disclaimed because the survivor's title was acquired by operation of law and not by transfer from the decedent at his death. However, the Uniform Disclaimer of Property Interests Act (1978), 8A U.L.A. 86 (1983), and some state disclaimer statutes expressly allow survivorship interest to be disclaimed. Even where a joint tenancy interest cannot be disclaimed under local law, a surviving joint tenant may be able to execute a qualified disclaimer if the requirements of §2518(c)(3) are met.

The regulations provide some guidance regarding the disclaimer of interests in joint tenancies. The general rule of Reg. §25.2518-2(c)(4) provides that a qualified disclaimer of an interest that arises upon creation of a joint tenancy must be made within nine months of creation. In contrast, a qualified disclaimer of the survivorship interest must be made within nine months following the other tenant's death. The regulations helpfully recognize that, "[i]n the case of residential property, held in joint tenancy by some or all of the residents, a joint tenant will not be considered to have accepted the joint interest merely because the tenant resided on the property prior to disclaiming his interest in the property." Reg. §25.2518-2(d)(1). As explained below, in the case of a "revocable" joint tenancy the nine-month period during which a disclaimer must be made runs from the time of death of one of the tenants. Reg. §25.2518-2(c)(4)(iii); *Dancy v. Commissioner*, 872 F.2d 84 (4th Cir. 1989).

In LR 200503024 the IRS allowed a surviving joint tenant to disclaim the right to receive the deceased tenant's share of a brokerage account. Because each tenant's contributions to the account were subject to withdrawal prior to a tenant's death, the transfer of the deceased tenant's interest did not take place until his death. The disclaimer was allowed although the survivor had transferred all of the assets into an account in her name and, before disclaiming, had made some withdrawals from the account, and had directed that certain securities be sold and others purchased. Under Reg. §25.2518-2(d)(1) the transfer of the account into the survivor's name did not constitute the acceptance of a benefit in the account. The survivor's withdrawal of cash from the account and the sale of some securities in the account were considered to have been made from her severable share of the assets in the account. Accordingly, the survivor was free to disclaim the survivorship interest in the assets attributable to the decedent's share of the account.

§12.34.1. Revocable Transfers

A disclaimer need not be made within nine months of the original transfer of property into a joint tenancy that is revocable by the transferor. Typical forms of revocable joint tenancies include joint bank accounts and joint brokerage accounts. A joint bank account is revocable if the governing law allows a party who transfers funds into a joint bank account to withdraw his or her contributions without a duty to account to the other tenant(s). Reg. §§25.2518-2(c)(4(iii); 25.2518-2(c)(5), Example (12). This outcome is consistent with the recognition that the creation of a joint tenancy bank account does not constitute a taxable transfer for gift tax purposes. *See* §3.14.1. Note that a surviving joint tenant cannot disclaim any part of a joint account that is attributable to consideration furnished by him or her. Reg. §25.2518-2(c)(4)(iii). This is consistent with LR 8824033 which held that a survivor could not disclaim any interest in a joint brokerage account to which he had made all of the contributions.

EXAMPLE 12-23.

H and *W* both signed a joint and survivor signature card in connection with the establishment of a savings account in a financial institution. *H* deposited $10,000 in the account. Six months prior to *H*'s death he received a distribution of $10,000 from the estate of his father, *F*, which he also deposited in the account. *W* could make a qualified disclaimer of part or all of the interests in the account within 9 months following *H*'s death. If *H* had survived *W*, he could not make a qualified disclaimer of any interest in the account.

Under the circumstances of Example 12-23, the survivor has the right to disclaim the entire $20,000 unless she had accepted some benefit from the account. The disclaimer of the original amount in the account, or of an undivided portion or a pecuniary amount out of the account, should be possible if the requirements of Reg. §25.2518-3 are met.

§12.34.2. Property Subject to Partition

Several courts have held that the transfer of property to a joint tenancy that is subject to partition by the tenants should be treated the same way as revocable transfers are. In such instances a surviving joint tenant could disclaim his or her survivorship interest at any time within nine months following the death of the first tenant to die.

The regulations do not discuss the effects of a power to partition. Yet the prospect of partition means that only the one-half undivided interest has been transferred irrevocably; the survivorship interest may be withdrawn at will, just as funds in a joint account may be. *Kennedy v. Commissioner*, 804 F.2d 1332, 1335 (7th Cir. 1986).

There is no principled distinction between a joint tenancy with right of survivorship that is subject to partition by either cotenant and a joint bank account with right of survivorship that can be depleted through withdrawals by either cotenant. In both instances it is impossible to ascertain whether a cotenant has any right of survivorship until the other cotenant dies. *Dancy v. Commissioner*, 872 F.2d 84, 88 (4th Cir. 1989).

The Eighth Circuit reached a similar result in *McDonald v. Commissioner*, 853 F.2d 1494 (8th Cir. 1988), *cert. denied,* 490 U.S. 1005 (1989), as did the Fourth Circuit in *Dancy v. Commissioner, supra*.

§12.35. DISCLAIMER OF PARTIAL INTERESTS

Special care must also be exercised in disclaiming partial interests in property, particularly where a trust is involved. The Code, §2518(c)(1), permits the disclaimer of an "undivided portion" of an interest. *See also* Reg. §§25.2518-3(a) and (b). The position taken by the IRS on this issue has important implications for marital planning, including the use of the election under §2056(b)(7) to claim a deduction with respect to part of the property in which the surviving spouse has the requisite life interest. *See* §5.23.

Separate Interests. The regulations recognize that a separate interest in property can be validly disclaimed even though the disclaimant has another interest in the same property. For example, where an income interest in property is bequeathed to *A* for life, then to *B* for life, remainder to *A*'s estate, *A* may disclaim either the income interest, or the remainder interest, or an undivided portion of either. Reg. §25.2518-3(a)(1)(i) However, a disclaimer cannot be used to create separate interests in property. Thus, if property is bequeathed to *A* outright, *A* cannot disclaim it, yet reserve a life interest or a remainder. Reg. §25.2518-3(b) The regulations permit the disclaimer of severable property, such as the disclaimer of some of the shares of stock bequeathed to the disclaimant. Reg. §25.2518-3(a)(1)(ii) For this purpose severable property is defined as that "which can be divided into separate parts each of which, after severance, maintains a complete and independent existence." *Id.*

In *Walshire v. United States*, 288 F.3d 342 (8th Cir. 2002), the court upheld Reg. §25.2518-3(b) which generally does not allow the disclaimer of a remainder interest to be treated as a qualified disclaimer if the disclaimant retains an income interest in the property. The case involved a beneficiary who disclaimed the remainder interest in the one-fourth interest he was entitled to receive in the residuary estate of his brother. Such a "horizontal" disclaimer did not meet the requirements of the regulation, which the court held was a valid implementation of the statute.

In *Boyd v. Commissioner*, 819 F.2d 170 (7th Cir. 1987) (*see* §12.33.2), the court recognized the effectiveness of a disclaimer of the benefits of a tax apportionment clause made by the sole beneficiary under the decedent's will. The court analogized the benefits of such a tax clause as equivalent to a direct pecuniary bequest of an equivalent amount.

Pecuniary Amount. A specific pecuniary amount can be disclaimed out of a pecuniary or nonpecuniary bequest or gift, provided that the disclaimant receives no income or other benefit from the disclaimed amount before or after the disclaimer. Reg. § 25.2518-3(c) The final form of the disclaimer regulations allow the disclaimer of a pecuniary amount of a residuary gift. Reg. § 25.2518-3(d) Examples (18) and (19). As indicated below, a pecuniary amount determined by a formula can be disclaimed.

Interests in Trusts. More complex rules apply where a trust is involved. A beneficiary may disclaim his or her entire interest in a trust, whether that interest is in the income, corpus, or both. Alternatively, a beneficiary may disclaim an undivided portion of his or her interest. Reg. § 25.2518-3(a)(2) For example, an income beneficiary of a trust who also holds a general testamentary power of appointment over the corpus of the trust may disclaim the power to appoint one-half of the trust corpus.Reg. § 25.2518-3(d), Example (21). The beneficiaries' disclaimers of the right to receive distributions of principal from a nonqualifying charitable trust were permitted in conjunction with a reformation proceeding as a result of which they would hold unitrust interests. LR 9610005. The disclaimers were allowed although the unitrust amounts might be payable, in part, from principal.

In general, the beneficiary of a trust cannot disclaim the income interest or the income and remainder interests in a particular trust asset *and* retain the right to receive income from the trust unless the disclaimer results in the removal of the asset from the trust. Reg. § 25.2518-3(a)(2) According to the cited regulation, a disclaimer of interests in specific trust assets is only effective if "as a result of such disclaimer, such assets are removed from the trust and pass, without any direction on the part of the disclaimant, to persons other than the disclaimant or to the spouse of the decedent." Where property is transferred to the trust at different times, a qualified disclaimer can be made with respect to each transfer.

Undivided Interests. The regulations also permit the disclaimer of undivided portions of the disclaimant's separate interests in property (including powers). However, in such a case the disclaimer must extend to a fraction or percentage of *all* interests the disclaimant holds in the property. Reg. § 25.2518-3(b) In addition, the disclaimer must cover the entire term of the disclaimant's interest in the property. *Id.* Thus, the beneficiary of a life income interest could not validly disclaim the right to receive the income for a period of years. Reg. § 25.2518-3(a).

EXAMPLE 12-24.

T devised Whiteacre and Blackacre in trust to pay the income to *X* for life remainder to *Y*. *X* may disclaim all or a fractional or percentage portion of the income interest in the trust. *X* may also disclaim the right to receive the income from Whiteacre (or Blackacre), provided that Whiteacre is removed from the trust and distributed without any direction by *X*. *Y* could disclaim all or part of the interests in the remainder of the trust.

Disclaimer by Formula. The regulations and letter rulings recognize the validity of disclaimers of fractional shares or pecuniary amounts determined by formula. For example, Reg. § 25.2518-3(d), Example (20), recognizes the effectiveness of a disclaimer of a fractional share of a decedent's residuary estate. *See also* LR 8514095 (disclaimer by decedent's child of portion of fractional share of her intestate interest in the decedent's estate). Disclaimers of pecuniary amounts determined by formula are also effective, as indicated by LR 8502084 (disclaimer by surviving spouse of an amount equal to the credit equivalent). A pecuniary formula disclaimer was also upheld in LR 9513011.

§ 12.36. DISCLAIMER PLANNING

A disclaimer can be used effectively in a wide variety of circumstances. Some common opportunities that involve federal tax benefits include:

1. Skipping a Generation. A financially secure child may disclaim the right to receive an outright bequest, to allow the property will pass to the disclaimant's children outright or to a trust for their benefit. Of course, such a disclaimer would subject the bequest to the GSTT (*i.e.,* the transfer to the disclaimant's child would be a direct skip). *See* LR 9815046 (several of decedent's children disclaimed portions of their bequests; the disclaimed property passed to decedent's grandchildren; and decedent's GSTT exemption applied to the gifts, resulting in a zero inclusion ratio).

2. Decreasing (or Increasing) Gifts to a Surviving Spouse. A surviving spouse may disclaim the right to receive property that would be sheltered from federal taxation by the decedent's unified credit. A disclaimer in such a case will help control (*i.e.,* limit) the size of the surviving spouse's gross estate Reg. § 20.2056(d)-1(a). *See* LRs 8429085 and 8443005 (TAM) (which involve disclaimers by children in order to qualify trusts for the marital deduction). A disclaimer by the guardian of minor grandchildren was recognized in LR 8701001 (TAM) which supported a larger marital deduction. In *Estate of Robert W. Gorre Jr.,* T.C. Memo. 1994-331, the Tax Court upheld a marital deduction resulting from partial disclaimer of intestate property made with Probate Court approval, by surviving spouse as guardian of the decedent's minor children. Consistently, in LR 9329025, the marital deduction was allowed after the surviving spouse disclaimed several interests, including a special lifetime power of appointment that otherwise would have prevented the marital deduction from being allowed with respect to one of the trusts.

By disclaiming a general power of appointment, a surviving spouse may convert a § 2056(b)(5) trust into a § 2056(b)(7) QTIP trust, which would allow an election to be made to claim a partial marital deduction. *See* § 5.22. The IRS has also recognized disclaimers executed by personal representatives on behalf of deceased spouses and others. *E.g.,* LR 200003011.

3. Perfecting or Increasing Charitable Gifts. A wealthy beneficiary may disclaim a life interest in a trust, that would accelerate the charitable remainder in a way that would qualify for the charitable deduction under § 2055. Of course, outright gifts may also be disclaimed in favor of charitable alternate takers. A disclaimer of a dollar amount of a QTIP trust is a qualified disclaimer where the disclaimed interest will pass to a charitable foundation established by the disclaimant and will be allocated to a separate fund over which the disclaimant will have no discretionary powers. LR

9823043. If a beneficiary disclaims the right to receive distributions of principal, a qualified reformation of a trust may be possible. LR 200302029 (approving a reformation that will create a 6.6-percent noncharitable unitrust interest).

4. *Eliminating a Generation-Skipping Transfer.* A grandchild or more remote descendant may disclaim a bequest in a way that will prevent a generation-skipping transfer from taking place. Moreover, the GSTT does not apply to direct skips made under wills executed prior to the effective date of the GSTT if the testator was incompetent on that date and did not regain competency prior to death. Thus, the GSTT does not extend to bequests under such a will that pass outright to grandnephews and grandnieces (*i.e.,* direct skips) as a result of qualified disclaimers by the testator's nephews. LR 9111011.

5. *Eliminating Nonqualified Heirs.* Where an estate qualifies for special use valuation under §2032A but for the interests passing to nonqualified heirs, the nonqualified heirs may disclaim their interests.

6. *Avoiding Multiple Administrations and Unnecessary Taxation.* If a beneficiary dies within nine months of the decedent, the beneficiary's personal representative may disclaim the right to receive property from the decedent's estate in order to avoid multiple administrations and multiple taxation of the same property (the previously taxed property credit, §2013, may provide protection against multiple taxation).

7. *Disclaimer by Surviving Spouse.* The personal representative of a surviving spouse may disclaim the right to receive property from a predeceased spouse's estate. LR 200030011. The disclaimer in this ruling probably resulted in the allowance of a previously taxed property credit under §2013—the disclaimed residuary property passed to a credit shelter trust from which the surviving spouse was entitled to receive the income for life.

In some circumstances a surviving spouse's disclaimer can produce adverse tax consequences. *See* also §5.5.2. For example, the estate tax obligation of a deceased spouse's estate can soar if the estate includes the controlling interest in a closely held business and the surviving spouse or a marital deduction trust receives only a minority interest because of a disclaimer. In *Estate of Frank M. DiSanto,* 78 T.C.M. 1220 (1999), the decedent's controlling interest was valued at $23.50 per share and the minority interest that passed to the marital deduction trust was valued at $13 per share.

8. *Terminating a Trust.* A disclaimer by the life income beneficiary may cause the remainder to accelerate, resulting in distribution of the trust corpus and termination of the trust. In some cases a disclaimer by the remainder beneficiaries may result in termination of the trust. Termination would also usually result if all beneficiaries disclaim their interests.

9. *Medicaid Planning.* A person who receives a gift or bequest may lose his or her qualification to receive Medicaid benefits. State law may allow either the recipient or his or her guardian or conservator to disclaim the interest. Note, however, that some states now treat disclaimers as a transfer of resources for Medicaid purposes.

10. *IRA Rollover.* If persons other than the decedent's surviving spouse are designated as beneficiaries of an IRA they may disclaim their interests in order to allow the surviving spouse to receive and roll over the IRA as provided in §408(d)(3). *See* §13.9.1. LR 9615043 (disclaimers resulted in termination of trust to which IRA was payable as a result of which the surviving spouse was entitled to receive IRA under intestate succession law). LR 9615043 (disclaimers by decedent's descendants of interests in IRAs under trusts and as intestate successors caused IRA to pass to surviving spouse as intestate successor). LRs 9626049, 9623064.

A planner can provide valuable help to clients by alerting them to the possibilities offered by disclaimers. Indeed, the failure to advise beneficiaries of the availability and consequences of a disclaimer by the surviving spouse may constitute actionable professional malpractice under the local law. *Linck v. Barokas & Martin*, 667 P.2d 171 (Alaska 1983). Advice to clients should, of course, include appropriate caveats regarding the uncertainties and limitations regarding the use of disclaimers. Finally, the planner should also be sensitive to the conflicts of interest that may arise in advising parties regarding disclaimers. For example, a lawyer should exercise great care in undertaking to advise grandchildren regarding the use of disclaimers if the lawyer represents their parents, who will receive any property the grandchildren disclaim.

A faulty charitable remainder trust may be reformed if the noncharitable beneficiaries disclaim disqualifying interests in the trust, such as a power to invade principal for support, health, or maintenance. LR 9347013. *See* J. Kasner, Using Disclaimers to Reform a Defective Charitable Remainder Trust, Tax Notes 749 (Feb. 7, 1994).

Estate planners should also watch for situations in which it may be advantageous to use a disclaimer even though doing so will not produce any federal tax benefits. For example, differences between the state and federal transfer tax laws may cause a disclaimer to result in a state tax saving although there is no federal tax saving. Finally, it may be desirable to use a disclaimer to help rearrange property ownership even where it will not save any taxes. For example, a disclaimer could be made by a guardian ad litem to deflect property from a beneficiary to a trust for the disclaimant's benefit where an outright transfer would subject the property to an expensive and cumbersome guardianship. Of course, such a disclaimer can be made only where authorized by local law, and often only with court approval.

F. PLANNING ESTATE DISTRIBUTIONS

The 1954 Code policy adverted to can be both a serious trap for the unwary and an important post-mortem tax planning tool in the hands of the sophisticated fiduciary; a tax trap in that the unwary estate practitioner familiar only with fiduciary accounting principles may suddenly find that the distribution of a family automobile results in income to the recipient. On the other hand, the sophisticated use of distributions in creating multiple entities such as testamentary trusts, has significant tax saving possibilities . . . .*Estate of Holloway*, 327 N.Y.S.2d 865, 866 (Surr. Ct. 1972).

§12.37. General; Separate Share Rule

Estate distributions have important estate and income tax consequences. For estate tax purposes distributions have a particularly important impact on the alternative valuation of assets. *See* §12.15. The income tax consequences of distributions remain significant despite the compressed rate structure. Overall, the proper planning of estate distributions is at the very heart of post-mortem income tax planning. Distribution planning must be considered in connection with the selection of the estate's tax year, *see* §12.7, and the payment of estate expenses, *see* §12.13.

The proper treatment of some payments by an estate or trust is not always clear. For example, the payment of the costs of maintenance of a personal residence used by a beneficiary may be treated as an expense of the estate incurred in order to maintain a capital asset rather than a distribution. *See Henry Bradley Plant,* 30 B.T.A. 133 (1934), *acq.,* 1976-1 C.B. 1, *aff'd,* 76 F.2d 8 (2d Cir. 1935); LR 8341005 (TAM).

Separate Share Rule for Estates. The 1997 Act amended §663(c) to provide that the income tax rules would treat "separate and independent shares of different beneficiaries in an estate having more than 1 beneficiary as separate estates." *See* §10.4.9. Accordingly, if the share of a beneficiary is a separate share, distributions to the beneficiary would only carry out the distributable net income (DNI) of the estate attributable to that share. Conversely, DNI attributable to one beneficiary's share would not be carried out to others if distributions were made to them. *See* Newlin, Coping with the Complexity of Separate Shares Under the Final Regs., 27 Est. Plan. 243 (July 2000).

Sixty Five Day Rule Applies to Estates. The 1997 Act also amended §663(b) to allow an executor to elect to treat distributions made in the first 65 days of a taxable year as having been made in the preceding tax year.

The rules added by the 1997 Act will allow personal representatives to control better the tax effects of distributions. Perhaps most importantly, executors can treat distributions made in the first 65 days of a taxable year as having been made in the preceding year. Also, distributions to the beneficiary of a separate share will now only carry out the DNI attributable to his or her share.

The opportunities for creative post-mortem income tax planning arise in large part because an estate is recognized as a separate entity for income tax purposes. Subject to the separate share rules, an estate generally acts as a conduit for estate income. In brief, an estate is taxed on any income that is neither currently distributed nor required to be distributed to its beneficiaries. As a result, all of the income received by an estate during a taxable year net of deductions is taxed to the estate to the extent it does not make any nonspecific distributions during the year. Generally speaking, once an item of income is taxed to an estate its origin as an item of income has no significance in determining the income tax consequences of future distributions to the beneficiaries.

EXAMPLE 12-25.

The estate of *T* had a taxable income of $25,000 in its second taxable year, during which it made no distributions. The estate closed early in the following taxable year, at which time it distributed all of its assets, and during which it received no income. The distribution of the estate's assets, including the $25,000 of accumulated income, is not taxed to the distributees. Under § 642(h), the estate's beneficiaries are entitled to the benefit of the estate's deductions for its final taxable year in excess of its gross income, and of the estate's net operating loss and capital loss carryovers. However, under § 67 miscellaneous itemized deductions are generally subject to the 2-percent floor in the hands of the beneficiaries.

§ 12.37.1. Basic Rule

An estate is allowed deductions for income required to be distributed currently and "other amounts" properly paid, credited, or required to be distributed during the taxable year. § 661(a). Rounding out the picture, the amounts that are deductible by the estate must be reported as income by the beneficiaries. § 662(a). Each item distributed retains its particular character in the hands of the beneficiaries (*e.g.*, dividends and tax-exempt interest). In general, each distribution is considered to consist of a proportionate part of each item. § 662(b); Reg. § 1.662(b)-1.

§ 12.37.2. Distributable Net Income (DNI)

The amount deductible by the estate and reportable by the beneficiaries is limited to the DNI of the estate, a concept that is significant mainly for that purpose. DNI is basically the taxable income of the estate, computed without regard to the distribution deduction and adjusted for capital gains that are added to principal and for certain other items. *See* § 643. *See also* § 10.4.3.

§ 12.37.3. Tier System

Under the so-called tier system, DNI is allocated first to beneficiaries who are entitled as a matter of right to receive distributions of income. § 662(a)(1). It is allocated to the first tier beneficiaries in the same proportion that the income required to be distributed currently to each bears to the total amount required to be distributed currently to all beneficiaries. *See* Reg. § 1.662(a)-2(b) Where DNI exceeds the amount distributable currently to first tier beneficiaries the excess is allocated to the second tier beneficiaries in proportion to the distribution each of them receives. *See* § 10.4.9. Under this method of allocation, a distribution of principal may require the distributee to report a portion of the estate's income, depending upon whether DNI is completely absorbed by first tier distributions. (The separate share rule, also described at § § 10.4.9 and 12.37, is important for planning purposes.)

EXAMPLE 12-26.

X and *Y* are each entitled to receive $10,000 of current income from the estate each year. *X* and another beneficiary, *Z*, are entitled to receive equal shares of the corpus of the estate. During a year in which the estate's DNI was $20,000, the executor distributed $20,000 to X, $10,000 to Y, and $10,000 to Z. X and Y are each taxable on $10,000. Apart from the statute the income might be taxed in proportion to the value of each distribution (i.e., 50% to X, 25% to Y, and 25% to Z). As it is, the $10,000 of the amount distributed to X and the $10,000 distributed to Z are not taken into account because the estate's DNI was exhausted by the distributions of income that were required to be made to the first tier beneficiaries, X and Y. Had the estate's DNI been $30,000, then X would be taxed on a total of $15,000, Y on $10,000, and Z on $5,000. In that event, the additional $10,000 of DNI would be taxed to the second tier beneficiaries, X and Z, in proportion to the amount of corpus distributed to each of them.

§12.37.4. Specific Gifts

Distributions in satisfaction of gifts of specific sums of money or of specific items of property that are paid all at once, or in three or fewer installments, are neither deductible by the estate nor includible in the distributee's income. *See* §663(a). *See also* §12.38. In order to qualify under this provision, the amount of money or the identity of specific property must be ascertainable under the terms of the will on the date of the testator's death. Reg. §1.663(a)-1(b) As pointed out in the Explanation of Provisions accompanying the final separate share regulations under §663, the separate share rules do not apply to specific gifts under §663(a): "Bequests described in section 663(a)(1) are not subject to the distribution provisions and are therefore not separate shares."

EXAMPLE 12-27.

T's will left $10,000 to X, 1,000 shares of ABC stock to Y, and the residue of his estate to Z. The estate had income of $25,000 during the year, which was accumulated and added to corpus for estate accounting purposes. During the year the executor distributed $10,000 to X, 1,000 shares of ABC stock to Y, and nothing to Z. The distributions to X and Y are neither deductible by the estate nor includible in the income of X or Y. However, any distribution of residue made to Z during the year would have carried out the estate's DNI to Z to the extent of the distribution.

The regulations characterize a formula pecuniary gift as a separate share. Distributions in satisfaction of a formula pecuniary gift carry out DNI unless the amount of the gift was specifically ascertainable on the date of death. Reg. §1.663(a)-1(b) Because of uncertainties about the amounts that will be claimed for various deductions, the amount that will be distributable to a credit shelter trust or under a pecuniary marital deduction formula clause may not be ascertainable at the time of the decedent's death.

§ 12.37.5. Timing of Distributions

The extension of the separate share rule to estates has made planning more complex. However, combined with the opportunity to select a fiscal year for the estate and the election regarding the use of the alternate valuation date, carefully planned distributions can help to minimize the overall income tax burden of the estate and the beneficiaries. The timing of distributions has an important impact on the taxation of the estate and the beneficiaries. For example, nonspecific distributions can often be accelerated or deferred to generate the most desirable tax results for the estate and the beneficiaries (*e.g.*, distributions that will carry out DNI might be made during a year in which the estate will have little or no income to carry out to the distributees). Of course, in some circumstances it is desirable to make distributions that carry out income (*e.g.*, when the beneficiaries have excess deductions available to offset the income carried out to them by reason of the distributions). A determination of whether or not an amount is properly paid or credited for purposes of § § 661 and 662 depends upon the terms of the governing instrument and the state law. *See Bohan v. United States*, 456 F.2d 851 (8th Cir. 1972), which the IRS announced it will not follow, Rev. Rul. 72-396, 1972-2 C.B. 312.

Distributions can be planned and made in ways that maximize the benefit of deductions for estate administration expenses and other items. Careful planning can, for example, often allow excess deductions to be carried out to the distributee who will benefit the most from them. A distribution should be adequately documented (with a court order, if required by state law). *See, e.g., Bohan, supra.* In particular a distribution supported only by informal workpapers prepared in the ordinary course of business is insufficient to evidence "a commitment to set aside funds beyond the recall of petitioner, its creditors, and its other beneficiaries," which is the relevant test. *Estate of Keith W. Johnson*, 88 T.C. 225, 236, *aff'd*, 838 F.2d 1202 (2d Cir. 1987).

EXAMPLE 12-28.

T's will left his residuary estate in equal shares to 4 charities and an individual, *X*. No estate tax is due from *T*'s estate, which has relatively little income, but will pay substantial expenses of administration. Each of the residuary beneficiaries will probably be treated as the beneficiary of a separate share. *See* Reg. § 1.663(c)(4) The executor might plan to pay the estate's expenses of administration in a final, short tax year, as a result of which most could be carried out to the residuary distributees. The amount of the expenses carried out to *X* will be maximized if the distributions in satisfaction of the charitable bequests are made in a preceding tax year— optimally the estate's last full tax year. By doing so, *X* will be the only residuary beneficiary to whom distributions are made in the estate's taxable year and to whom excess deductions will be carried out. Making the distributions to the charities earlier than the distribution to *X* may superficially violate the executor's duty of impartiality. However, by so arranging the distributions the executor has also preferred *X*. If asked, *X* would, no doubt, consent to the plan.

§ 12.37.6. Distributions to Trusts

The composition and timing of distributions to trusts are also important, particularly when a distribution can be used to carry out DNI to a trust, where it will be "trapped" and not taxed to the trust beneficiaries. (The use of trapping distributions is discussed in § 12.41.)

§ 12.37.7. In Kind Distributions

In some cases it is helpful to the beneficiaries to make in kind distributions. However, consideration must be given to the tax consequences. The planner should recall that in kind distributions cannot be used to effect a tax-free increase in the basis of the property. § 643(e). However, § 643(e) allows an executor to elect to recognize gain or loss on the distribution as if the property distributed had been sold to the distributee at its fair market value. In such a case, the distributee takes a basis equal to the fair market value of the property. The election should be made with respect to the distribution of appreciated property if the estate has losses on other sales which would offset any gain resulting from the distribution. In addition, the distributee would receive an increased basis in the property.

In planning distributions it is important to bear in mind that in kind distributions to residuary beneficiaries that are non-pro rata can involve a taxable exchange between the distributees. *See* § 12.40. However, they may involve a tax-free exchange of property under § 1031. *See* LR 8404099. In kind distributions require the estate to recognize gain where appreciated property is distributed in satisfaction of a pecuniary gift. § 12.39. An estate, but not a trust, may deduct a loss that is incurred as a result of satisfying a pecuniary bequest with property that has a fair market value lower than its basis. § 267(b)(13).

§ 12.37.8. Lump Sum IRA Distributions

Some or all of the amount distributed by a decedent's IRA in a lump sum to the beneficiaries is income in respect of a decedent. Under Rev. Rul. 92-47, 1992-1 C.B. 198, the portion that equals the balance in the IRA at the time of the decedent's death, including unrealized appreciation and income accrued to that date, less the total amount of the decedent's nondeductible contributions, is income under § 408(d)(1), and income in respect of a decedent under § 691(a)(1). Accordingly, it is includible in the gross income of the beneficiary for the taxable year in which it is received. Of course, the beneficiary is entitled to a deduction under § 691(c) for the estate tax attributable to the amount of income in respect of a decedent that is included in gross income. Finally, amounts distributed that reflect appreciation and income accruing after the decedent's date of death are taxable to the beneficiary under §§ 408(d) and 72.

§ 12.38. Distributions That Do Not Carry Out DNI, § 663(a)(1)

Distributions can be made in satisfaction of most specific gifts without affecting the income taxation of the estate or of the distributees. Specifically, under § 663(a)(1), a distribution in satisfaction of a gift of a specific sum of money or of specific property does not carry out the estate's DNI if it is paid or credited all at once or in not more than three installments. This exclusion is traceable to the basic rule of §102 that gross income does not include gifts, bequests, and inheritances. In order to come within the ambit of this rule, the specific sum of money or the specific property must be ascertainable under the terms of the decedent's will at the date of death. Reg. §1.663(a)-1(b)(1) Thus, gifts of $10,000 or of 100 shares of XYZ, Inc. stock both qualify as specific gifts, but a gift of one-half of the residue of the estate does not. A bequest of assets in cash or in kind equal to a specific dollar amount is a bequest of a sum of money for purposes of §663. Rev. Rul. 86-105, 1986-2 C.B. 82.

As pointed out above, pecuniary formula marital deduction gifts are not treated as specific bequests for purposes of §663 because the amount of the gifts depends upon the exercise of the executor's discretion regarding a number of matters including the valuation of estate assets and the return upon which administration expenses would be claimed. *See* Reg. §1.663(a)-1(b)(1) Any distribution made in satisfaction of such a pecuniary gift is subject to the ordinary distribution rules of §§661 and 662 (*i.e.*, it would carry out some part of the estate's DNI to the distributee). In this connection, note that the separate share rules may apply to formula pecuniary gifts. Reg. §1.663(c)-4(b).

§12.38.1. Annuities and Similar Payments from Income

The regulations also provide that the specific gift rule does not apply to annuities or other amounts that are payable only from the income of an estate. Reg. §1.663(a)-1(b)(2) The regulations illustrate the application of this rule to a trust in the following example:

> *Example (3)* Under the terms of a trust instrument, income is to be accumulated during the minority of A. Upon A's reaching the age of 21, $10,000 is to be distributed to B out of income or corpus. Also, at that time, $10,000 is to be distributed to C out of the accumulated income and the remainder of the accumulations are to be paid to A. A is then to receive all the income until he is 25, when the trust is to terminate. Only the distribution to B would qualify for the exclusion under section 663(a)(1). Reg. §1.663(a)-1(b)(3).

In this example the distribution to B qualifies for the exclusion because it could be satisfied out of income or principal. In contrast, no exclusion is available for the distribution to C, which was payable solely out of accumulated income.

§12.38.2. Specifically Devised Real Property

Specifically devised real property that passes directly to the devisee under local law is not taken into account for purposes of applying the rules of §§661 and 662. Regs. §§1.661(a)-2(e), 1.663(a)1(c)(1)(ii). In such a case the real property does not form a part of the Subchapter J estate and is not paid, credited, or required to be distributed by the estate. Accordingly, the devisee and not the estate is required to report the income, deductions, and credits attributable to the real property from the time of the decedent's death. Presumably the same rule applies to any property that passes directly from the decedent to another person under local law. *See* Rev. Rul. 68-49, 1968-1 C.B. 304.

The rules of §663(a)(1) should be borne carefully in mind at all stages. Proper drafting in light of an estate's distribution options can give the estate plan valuable additional flexibility. Also, the income tax consequences of various types of distributions must be taken into account in planning and making distributions from the estate.

§12.39. DISTRIBUTIONS IN KIND

Under §643, a person to whom an estate asset is distributed takes a basis equal to the property's adjusted basis in the estate prior to distribution, adjusted for any gain or loss recognized by the estate on the distribution. Where a distribution in kind is made, the amount of the distribution, for purposes of §§661 and 662, is generally deemed to be the lesser of the basis in the hands of the distributee, or the fair market value of the property. However, §643(e)(3)(A)(ii) allows the estate to elect to recognize gain or loss upon such distributions, "in the same manner as if such property had been sold to the distributee at its fair market value." If the election is made, the fair market value of the property is taken into account for purposes of §§661 and 662. Under §643(e)(3)(B), the election, which is made on the income tax return of the trust or estate, applies to all distributions made during the year. Finally, §643(e) does not apply to any distribution described in §663(a) (gifts or bequests of specific property or specific amounts of money). §643(e)(4).

An estate which had incurred losses for the year might distribute appreciated property in order to benefit from making an election under §643(e). In such a case the losses could be used to offset the gains that the estate would recognize as a result of the distributions. In addition, the basis of the distributee would be increased as a result of the election. Note that §267 may bar a trust from recognizing losses arising from distributions. Also, recall that under §663(a) a distribution in kind made in satisfaction of a right to receive the specific property distributed does not carry out DNI to the distributee. §12.38.

EXAMPLE 12-29.

This year *T*'s estate has DNI of $20,000. *T*'s executor plans to distribute property worth $10,000 to the residuary beneficiary, *B*. The distribution will give *B* some needed cash and will carry out half of the estate's income to *B*. Such a distribution would effectively split the estate's income between the estate and *B*. The executor might distribute cash of $10,000 or 1,000 shares of XYZ, Inc., which have an estate tax value of $5,000 and a present value of $10,000. In the latter case the executor must decide whether to make an election under §643(e). If the election is not made, *B* will take the estate's basis in the XYZ, Inc. stock ($5,000), which is the amount that will be taken into account for purposes of §§661 and 662. On the other hand, if the election is made, the estate will realize a gain of

$5,000 on the distribution, *B* will have a basis of $10,000 in the shares, and $10,000 is the amount taken into account for purposes of §§ 661 and 662.

As indicated in Example 12-29, the basis of the distributee is affected by whether the estate makes an election under § 643(e). In this connection note that the distributee's basis is determined without regard to the estate's DNI. While the extent of the estate's DNI determines the amount of the estate's distribution deduction under § 661, and the amount taken into the beneficiary's income under § 662, it does not affect the beneficiary's basis in the property. In brief, the estate's DNI is irrelevant to the calculation of the distributee's basis under § 643(e).

EXAMPLE 12-30.

T's will made a bequest of $10,000 to a friend, *F. T*'s will authorized his executor to satisfy cash gifts by making distributions in kind, with distributions valued at their fair market value at the time of the distributions. The executor plans to satisfy the gift to *F* by distributing property that has an estate tax value of $5,000 and a current fair market value of $10,000. Presumably such a distribution is not subject to § 643(e) by reason of the exception described in § 643(e)(4). The prior rules probably continue to apply—the estate will recognize a gain of $5,000 if the appreciated property is distributed to *F* in satisfaction of the gift. Of course, under § 1223(11) the gain on the sale would be long term. *F* would have a basis of $10,000 in the property.

The cancellation of an installment obligation upon the death of the payee accelerates the recognition of gain by the payee's estate. Rev. Rul. 86-72, 1986-1 C.B. 253. *See* § 9.6.3. Similarly, the transfer of an installment obligation to the obligor is treated as a transfer that triggers the recognition of gain. § 691(a). *See* § 9.6.3.

IRAs and IRD. Gifts of IRAs to charities qualify for the estate tax charitable deduction and do not require the decedent or the decedent's estate to recognize any income. *E.g.,* LR 199939039. The distribution of items that constitute income in respect of a decedent in satisfaction of charitable bequests may result in significant income tax savings. The distribution of an IRD item to a specific or residuary charitable legatee does not require the estate to realize any income. In contrast, the distribution of an IRD item in satisfaction of a pecuniary bequest would ordinarily require the estate to realize income

§ 12.40. Non-Pro Rata Distributions

A personal representative should be cautious about making non-pro rata distributions to the residuary beneficiaries unless such distributions are authorized either by the decedent's will or by the governing state law. In the absence of such authorization a non-pro rata distribution may involve a taxable exchange between the residuary beneficiaries and possibly a violation of the personal representative's fiduciary duty of impartiality. In a letter ruling the IRS has held that an equal but non-pro rata distribution to three estate beneficiaries did not result in any gain where the decedent's will authorized such a distribution. LR 8119040.

A non-pro rata distribution may be treated as a taxable exchange when it is made pursuant to an agreement among the residuary beneficiaries and not by reason of the executor's authority. The problem arises because each residuary beneficiary is generally entitled to a proportionate interest in each asset of the residuary estate. The nature of the problem is illustrated in Example 12-32.

EXAMPLE 12-31.

T's will gave his residuary estate "in equal shares to those of my children who survive me." *T* was survived by 2 children, *D* and *S*. *T*'s residuary estate consists of $10,000 and 100 shares of XYZ, Inc. stock, which was worth $5,000 on the estate tax valuation date and $10,000 on the date of distribution. Under the local law *D* and *S* are each entitled to receive $5,000 and 50 shares of XYZ, Inc. stock. If the executor distributes $10,000 to *S* and 100 shares of stock to *D* pursuant to their agreement, the distribution may be taxed as if *S* sold "his" 50 shares of stock to *D* for "her" $5,000. If so, *S* would be required to report a gain of $2,500 on the transaction ($5,000 sale proceeds, less $2,500 basis under § 1014). The gain would be long-term under § 1223(11). As purchaser, *D* would have a basis of $5,000 in the 50 shares she purchased from *S* and a basis of $2,500 in the other 50 shares. (The result is different if such a distribution is authorized by *D*'s will or by state law.) No loss could result from an exchange between related taxpayers because of the provisions of § 267.

In Rev. Rul. 69-486, 1969-2 C.B. 159, the IRS held that a non-pro rata in kind distribution to the two beneficiaries of a trust involved a taxable exchange between the beneficiaries where the distribution was made pursuant to their agreement and was not authorized by the trust.

Since the trustee was not authorized to make a non-pro rata distribution of property in kind but did so as a result of the mutual agreement between *C* and *X*, the non-pro rata distribution by the trustee to *C* and *X* is equivalent to a distribution to *C* and *X* of the notes and common stock pro rata by the trustee, followed by an exchange between *C* and *X* of *C*'s pro rata share of common stock for *X*'s pro rata shares of notes. *Id.*

Consistently, in PLR 9429012 the IRS held that a non-pro rata division of trust assets was a taxable exchange where the division was not authorized by the instrument or state law. Presumably there would not have been a taxable exchange if the trust or the local law had authorized the trustee to make a non-pro rata in kind distribution. The IRS validated that proposition in LR 200334030 which held that a non-pro rata distribution of assets upon termination of a trust will not involve recognition of gain or loss because such divisions are authorized by state law. Non-pro rata distributions are also discussed at § 3.30.

§ 12.40

§12.40.1. Fiduciary Duty of Impartiality

An unauthorized non-pro rata distribution may violate the fiduciary's duty of impartiality toward the beneficiaries. Without the consent of the beneficiaries, or authorization in the instrument or by the governing law, the in kind non-pro rata distribution of assets to the two beneficiaries of an estate is a questionable practice even though the assets received by each are of equal value on the date of distribution. Distributing all of asset *A* to one beneficiary, and all of asset *B* to another beneficiary, without their consent invites criticism by one or both beneficiaries because of inherent differences in the properties and their income tax bases. A violation would certainly occur if the persons who were entitled to an equal share of the bequest did not receive assets of equal value on the date of distribution. The extent to which a fiduciary may be required to take the income tax bases of the assets into account in making a distribution is not settled in most states. Some courts have refused to take the income tax bases of assets into account in the context of a marital dissolution. A careful fiduciary should take the bases of assets into account in planning sales and distributions.

§12.40.2. Community Property

Following the death of a spouse, the surviving spouse generally continues to own a one-half interest in the assets previously owned by them as community property. In general, a husband or wife may only dispose by will of his or her interest in the community property. An attempt to dispose of a greater interest in the property may involve the rules applicable to widow's election arrangements. *See* §§ 9.23-9.39.

Under the item theory of community property, each spouse owns, and is entitled to dispose by will of, an equal interest in each community property asset. *See Estate of Patton*, 494 P.2d 238 (Wash.App. 1972). Where the item theory applies, the surviving spouse and other persons who are beneficiaries under the will of the deceased spouse will hold the former community property as tenants in common. However, in some states, a personal representative or trustee is authorized to make non-pro rata distribution of property. See § 3.29. Unless authorized by local law a non-pro rata distribution of the former community property to the surviving spouse and the beneficiaries under the will of the deceased spouse might be treated as a taxable exchange under Rev. Rul. 69-486, discussed above. Recognition of a loss arising from such a distribution-exchange is barred by § 267. It is doubtful that such a non-pro rata division would be treated as a nonrecognition transfer "from an individual to (or in trust for the benefit of)—(1) a spouse . . . ." § 1041(a). Section 1041 was adopted in order to make the tax laws less intrusive with respect to transfers between spouses or former spouses. There is no indication that it was intended to apply after the death of one or both of the spouses.

EXAMPLE 12-32.

H and *W* owned Blackacre and Whiteacre as their community property. When *H* died, he devised his one-half interests in Blackacre and Whiteacre to their daughter, *D*, and left the residue of his estate to *W*. *W*, of course, would continue to own a one-half interest in each parcel. After the death of *H*, Blackacre and Whiteacre would be owned by *D* and *W* as tenants in common. Unless authorized by local law, a taxable exchange might take place if, pursuant to an agreement between *D* and *W*, a fee interest in Blackacre were distributed to *D*, and the fee interest in Whiteacre were distributed to *W* (or vice versa).

In several private letter rulings, the IRS has indicated that a taxable exchange does not occur if the surviving spouse and the successors of the deceased spouse receive non-pro rata distributions of assets equal in value. LRs 8037124, 8016050, LR 9422052. If the letter rulings are followed, no gain would result from the distribution described in the foregoing example. The rulings are based largely upon Rev. Rul. 76-83, 1976-1 C.B. 213, which held that an equal division of the fair market value of community property between spouses made in the context of a separation or divorce was not a taxable event. *See also, Jean G. Carrieres*, 64 T.C. 959 (1975), *aff'd per curiam*, 552 F.2d 1350 (9th Cir. 1977).

The extension of the holding of Rev. Rul. 76-83 to dispositions at death is desirable because of the flexibility it gives the parties, its fairness, and its simplicity of administration. The case for not taxing such a distribution is strengthened if the executor of a deceased spouse has the power to administer all of the community property, and is given authority to make non-pro rata distributions of community property assets. If local law does not allow non-pro rata distributions to be made, the spouses might consider entering into an inter vivos agreement under which the executor of the first spouse to die has the power to make non-pro rata distributions of the entire interest in community property in satisfaction of residuary bequests. However, such an agreement might cause the estate of a deceased spouse to lose its claim to a discount in the value of the decedent's one-half community property share in closely-held stock if the agreement required the decedent's interest to be valued at one-half of the entire community property interest. That is, the agreement might overcome the favorable holdings of *Estate of Bright*, 658 F.2d 999 (5th Cir. 1981), and *Estate of Elizabeth Lee*, 69 T.C. 860 (1978), *nonacq.*, 1980-1 C.B. 2. *See* § 2.13.

A non-pro rata distribution in which the surviving spouse and the successors of the deceased spouse each receive assets of equal value would not involve a taxable exchange if the aggregate theory of community property is followed. Under it, the spouses do not each have a fixed and equal interest in each community property asset. Instead, each of them is merely entitled to receive assets that have a value equal to one-half of the total value of all of the community property. For an application of this theory in the gift tax context, *see Kaufman v. United States*, 462 F.2d 439 (5th Cir. 1972), discussed at § 6.48.

§ 12.41. TRAPPING DISTRIBUTIONS

A trapping distribution is a distribution from an estate to a trust that carries out DNI to the trust, where the income is "trapped" and taxed to the trust. Cornfeld, Trapping Distributions, U. Miami, 14th Inst. Est. Plan., Ch. 14 (1980); Income Tax Opportunities and Pitfalls in Estate Distributions, 13 Real Prop., Prob. & Tr. J. 835, 868-871 (1978). The typical case involves a distribution of property that is characterized as principal under the local law. As principal the property is not distributable by the trustee to the income beneficiaries of the trust. The income carried out in a trapping distribution is taxed to the trust permanently, or temporarily, depending on the provisions of the trust regarding distributions. Carefully planned trapping distributions permit an estate's income to be split among the maximum number of taxpayers: the estate, individual distributees of the estate, the trust, and the beneficiaries of the trust. The compressed income tax rates adopted in 1986 severely restrict the utility of planned trapping distributions. Because the rates applicable to trusts and estates escalate rapidly, there is little opportunity to trap income at a favorable rate in an estate or trust.

The ultimate tax consequences of a trapping distribution depend to a large extent on whether the distributee trust is a simple trust or a complex trust. *See* Cohan & Frimmer, Trapping Distributions—The Trap That Pays, 112 Tr. & Est. 766 (1973). A trapping distribution is generally effective to trap the distributed income permanently in a simple trust.

The technique of making trapping distributions is of some limited value in minimizing the impact of income taxes. Where it is desirable to do so, some estate income can be deflected to the trust, or trusts, each year by making appropriate distributions that would be characterized as principal under local law. Of course, income-splitting can be extended to the trust's beneficiaries where the distribution it receives from the estate includes items that are properly characterized as income of the trust that can be distributed to the beneficiaries of the trust.

When a trapping distribution is made the income tax liability imposed on the trust should be charged to the trust account to which the distribution is allocated under the local law. Thus, the income tax is appropriately paid from the principal account where the trapping distribution is characterized as principal. Conversely, it is chargeable to income where the distribution is characterized as income. In the latter case, it may be necessary to make an equitable adjustment to the principal and income accounts where the tax liability is initially paid from principal. *Estate of Holloway*, 327 N.Y.S.2d 865 (Surr. Ct. 1972), *mod'g*, 323 N.Y.S.2d 534 (Surr. Ct. 1971).

G. PAYMENT OF ESTATE AND GST TAXES

§12.42. INTRODUCTION

The next section reviews the rules that govern the allocation of the estate tax burden. Succeeding sections examine the options that are available to the executor in making payment of the federal estate tax, most of which involve deferral of payment of the estate tax. Payment of the tax or a deficiency in the estate tax may be deferred under §6161 for reasonable cause. In addition, portions of the tax may be deferred under §6163 (remainder and reversionary interests) and §6166 (closely-held business interests). The last section (§12.50) is a checklist of post-mortem matters. The rules governing the payment of the GSTT are discussed in §§2.22-2.40.

Between September 1 and March 1 of each year the IRS publishes a list of private delivery services that would be recognized for purposes of the "timely filing/paying" rule of §7502. They currently include Airborne Express, DHL, Worldwide Express, Federal Express, and United Parcel Service.

§ 12.43. SOURCE OF PAYMENT OF ESTATE TAX

The federal estate tax must be paid by a decedent's executor. § 2002. The term "executor" is defined in § 2203 as the decedent's executor or administrator or, if none, any person in actual or constructive possession of the decedent's property. The executor in turn must be sure that the proper parties bear the burden of the tax. A person is generally free to designate in his or her will or trust the source of funds that should be used to pay the tax. When no source is designated, the state law determines how the tax should be paid. Many states have a form of apportionment law that allocates the burden among the beneficiaries according to the value of the property each of them receives from the decedent. *See* Uniform Estate Tax Apportionment Act (2003) that is Part 9A of U.P.C. Article III and Uniform Estate Tax Apportionment Act (1964) and (1958), that is former U.P.C. § 3-916. *See also* § 4.27. The common law of other states generally requires the tax to be paid from the residuary estate in the absence of contrary direction by the decedent. However, courts in a few states have required equitable apportionment of the federal estate tax.

Tax apportionment clauses are discussed at § 4.27. The law of some states may not allow a decedent's will to direct that a portion of the estate tax be paid from nonprobate property, in particular property that was held by a husband and wife as tenants by the entirety. *See Estate of Reno v. Commissioner*, 945 F.2d 733 (4th Cir. 1991); § § 3.13, 4.27. Likewise, some state laws may not permit estate tax liability to be apportioned to lifetime gifts by the decedent. *See In re Metzler*, 176 A.D. 2d 15 (N.Y. App. Div. 1992). On the other hand, the executor in *Necaise v. Seay*, 915 So.2d 449 (2005) was permitted to apportion a portion of the estate's liability for estate taxes to closely-held stock given to the decedent's son during the decedent's life. Mississippi's statute apportions estate tax among "all persons interested in the estate." According to the court, the decedent's son was one such person even though he received his share of the decedent's estate during the decedent's life.

The provisions of the New Hampshire estate tax apportionment statute were overcome by the express provisions of a decedent's will, although the provisions conflicted to some degree with the terms of an inter vivos trust. *Estate of Lillian J. Lewis*, 69 T.C.M. (CCH) 2396 (1995). The right to have estate taxes paid from the residue might have been disclaimed by the decedent's children, who were the other beneficiaries of her will and trust. *See* § 12.31.2.

A general direction that death taxes should be paid from a designated source is insufficient to shift the obligation under § 2603(b) to pay the GSTT from the transferred property. *Estate of Louise S. Monroe*, 104 T.C. 352 (1995). *See also* § § 2.30-2.31.3.

If a donor dies within three years of making a taxable gift, the gift tax paid with respect to the gift is includible in the donor's estate under § 2035(b). Neither the Estate Tax Apportionment Act nor the terms of most tax clauses will identify the source for payment of the estate tax imposed by reason of the inclusion. Logically, the tax that results from the "gross up" of the tax should be paid from the donative property.

Five Code sections deal with the question of where the federal estate tax burden will fall in the absence of contrary direction by the decedent. As explained in § 12.33.2, the parties who would benefit by the payment of the estate tax as provided in those sections may disclaim that benefit. Those sections and the apportionment acts adopted by many states both recognize that directions by the decedent prevail over their provisions. In some instances if the provisions of the federal and local law conflict, the federal law prevails. In this connection, *see* the discussion in *McAleer v. Jernigan*, 804 F.2d 1231 (11th Cir. 1986). *McAleer* allowed the decedent's personal representative acting under §2206 to recover a portion of the federal estate tax from the recipient of proceeds of life insurance that were includible in the decedent's gross estate. The personal representative's right to do so prevailed over a state statute that directed all estate taxes to be paid from the residuary estate and relieved the personal representative from recovering any portion of the tax from the recipients of any other property including life insurance.

§12.43.1. Recovery of Estate Tax from Estate or Beneficiaries, §2205

Under the first section, §2205, if a person other than the executor pays any portion of the tax, that person may be entitled to reimbursement from the estate or contribution from the other beneficiaries of the estate. The provision is intended primarily to assure the tax is paid from the appropriate source, whether payment occurs prior or subsequent to distribution of the estate. The section recognizes rights to reimbursement, but it does not attempt to establish a particular rule of contribution by the beneficiaries.

§12.43.2. Recovery of Estate Tax from Insurance Beneficiaries, §2206

In the absence of a contrary direction in the decedent's will, the second section, §2206, allows the executor to collect a proportionate part of the estate tax from the beneficiary of life insurance proceeds that were included in the gross estate. If there is more than one beneficiary, the amount recoverable from each is calculated according to the following formula:

Proceeds of Policy × Total Tax = Amount Recoverable Taxable Estate

However, the section does not allow a recovery from a surviving spouse to the extent that a marital deduction is claimed and allowed with respect to the property. As indicated in *McAleer*, discussed above, the right to recover a portion of the tax from the payee of a life insurance policy on the decedent's life may prevail despite a contrary state statute.

§12.43.3. Recovery of Estate Tax from Property Subject to General Power, §2207

The third section, §2207, similarly allows an executor to recover a proportionate part of the estate tax from persons who receive property that was included in the decedent's estate under §2041 by reason of the exercise, nonexercise, or release of a power of appointment. Under it, the executor has the right to recover from the recipients "unless the decedent directs otherwise in his will." As in the case of §2206, however, it is inapplicable to the extent the property qualifies for the marital deduction.

§12.43.4. Recovery of Tax on QTIP, §2207A

Under the fourth section, §2207A, the executor has the right to recover from the recipients of qualified terminable interest property any additional estate tax imposed because the property was included in the decedent's estate under §2044. The provision also extends to penalties and interest attributable to the additional estate tax incurred by reason of the inclusion of the property. §2207A(d). Thus, the surviving spouse (the "decedent" under §2207A) can assume the responsibility for payment of any additional tax. For that reason care must be exercised regarding the type of tax clause included in the surviving spouse's will. Thus, §2207A now eliminates the possibility that a boilerplate tax clause directing the payment of "all death taxes from the residue of my estate" might overcome the executor's right of recovery under §2207A.

The executor's failure to exercise the right of recovery available under §2207A constitutes a constructive addition to the trust for GSTT purposes. *See* Reg. §26.2601-1(b)(1)(v)(C) An express direction by the surviving spouse to pay the tax imposed by §2044 would, presumably, also result in a constructive addition to the trust for purposes of the GSTT. *Id*. If so, the surviving spouse would be treated as the transferor of the addition.

As amended by the 1997 Act, §2207A(a)(2), the executor's right to recover exists unless the decedent "in his will (or a revocable trust) specifically indicates an intent to waive any right of recovery under this subchapter with respect to such property."

§12.43.5. Recovery of Tax on §2036 Property, §2207B

Finally, under §2207B, if property is included in the decedent's gross estate under §2036, the decedent's estate is entitled to recover a proportionate amount of the tax from the person receiving the property. A contrary direction in the decedent's will (or revocable trust) prevails over the general rule only if it specifically refers to §2207B. §2207B(a)(2). The decedent's estate has no right of recovery against a charitable remainder trust. §2207B(d). Again, the 1997 Act amended §2207B to eliminate the risk that a boilerplate provision might negate the effect of the statute. Subsection 2207B(a)(2) now provides that the right to recover exists unless the decedent "in his will (or a revocable trust) specifically indicates an intent to waive any right of recovery under this subchapter with respect to such property."

By relieving the charitable remainder of any obligation to contribute to payment of the estate tax, §2207B(e) avoids the problem of determining which interest should be charged with the estate tax attributable to the nondeductible current interest. A problem can arise because of the conflict between two general rules. Under the first, where income and remainder interests are involved, the estate tax is entirely chargeable to the remainder interest. *See, e.g., Estate of Williamson*, 229 P.2d 312 (Wash. 1951). State apportionment acts typically exempt temporary interests from being charged with any part of the estate tax. Of course, payment of the tax from principal operates to reduce the amount of the income that is distributable.

The second general rule exempts charitable interests from any obligation to contribute to payment of the estate tax in the absence of contrary direction by the decedent. In *Estate of Anne B. Leach*, 82 T.C. 952 (1984), *aff'd per curiam*, 782 F.2d 179 (11th Cir. 1986), the Tax Court held that the estate tax on a charitable remainder annuity trust was entirely recoverable from the charitable remainder. *Leach* involved the Florida Apportionment Act, which did not specify how the tax is to be charged when an annuity interest is involved.

§ 12.43.6. Transferee Liability

Note that the foregoing sections do not restrict the government's right to collect the tax from any person who received property from the decedent. For example, § 6324 allows the government to recover from the beneficiary of a life insurance policy that was included in a decedent's estate any unpaid estate tax up to the total amount of the proceeds received by the beneficiary. *Richard Baptiste v. Commissioner*, 29 F.3d 1533 (11th Cir. 1994). That case allowed the government also to recover interest on the amount of property received by the beneficiary. In a case involving the same decedent, *Gabriel J. Baptiste, Jr.*, 63 T.C.M. 2649 (1992), *aff'd in part, rev'd in part*, 29 F.3d 433 (8th Cir. 1994), *cert. denied*, 513 U.S. 1190 (1995), the government was allowed to recover the full amount of the insurance received by the beneficiary, but no interest. *See also United States v. Geniviva*, 16 F.3d 522 (3d Cir. 1994).

§ 12.44. Extension of Time to File Estate Tax or GSTT Return, § 6081

Under § 6081, an executor may apply for an extension of time to file an estate tax or GSTT return by filing Form 4768 (Application for Extension of Time to File U.S. Estate Tax Return and/or Pay Estate Tax). That form may also be used to request an extension of time within which to pay the estate tax or GSTT. Both requests may be made on a single form. An extension under § 6081 is limited to six months unless the executor is out of the country. The regulations provide that the application for extension "should be made before the expiration of the time within which the return otherwise must be filed and failure to do so may indicate negligence and constitute sufficient cause for denial." Reg. § 20.6081-1(b) Form 4768 should be filed with the internal revenue officer with whom the federal estate tax return is required to be filed. *Id*. Regulations automatically allow a six-month extension of the time to file the return.Reg. § § 20.6075-1, 20.6081-1(a), (b), (f). An automatic extension is available to estates that file a completed Form 4768 on or before the date the Form 706 was originally due.

An extension of time within which to file an estate tax or GSTT return does not extend the time for payment of the tax. Accordingly, unless the executor also requests an extension of time within which to pay the tax, Form 4768 should be accompanied by payment of the estimated amount of tax due.

§ 12.45. Extension of Time to Pay Estate Tax, § 6161

The 1976 Act substituted a "reasonable cause" standard for the "undue hardship" standard that previously applied for purposes of the discretionary ten-year extension of time to pay the estate tax. § 6161(a)(2). Under that provision an extension may also be granted with respect to the payment of any installment of tax deferred under § 6166. The explanation prepared by the staff of the Joint Committee of Taxation stated that, "for this purpose, the term 'reasonable cause' is to have the same meaning as the term is used for granting discretionary extensions of up to twelve months (regs. § 20.6161-1(a))." General Explanation of the Tax Reform Act of 1976, 546 (1976). The regulation referred to in the quotation provides that an extension may be granted if an examination of all the facts and circumstances shows that there is reasonable cause. Reg. § 20.6161-1(a) The regulation also presents several helpful examples of situations that are recognized as constituting reasonable cause for this purpose.

An extension may be applied for by submitting a request that includes a statement of the period of the extension requested and a declaration that the statement is made under penalties of perjury. The request should be made on Form 4768 and filed with the Internal Revenue officer with whom the estate tax return must be filed. Reg. § 20.6161-1(b).

If an extension is granted, the district director may require the executor to furnish bond for payment of the deferred amount of the tax. Reg. § 20.6165-1(a) However, the bond may not exceed double the amount of the deferred tax. Interest is charged at the annually adjusted rate under § 6621 on the amount of the unpaid tax.

§ 12.46. Deferral of Estate Tax on Reversions and Remainders, § 6163

Where a reversionary or remainder interest in property ("the future interest") is included in the decedent's gross estate, the executor may elect to defer payment of the estate tax attributable to the future interest until six months after all of the precedent interests terminate. § 6163(a). Under the regulations the election is made by filing a notice with the district director before the date prescribed for payment of the tax. Reg. § 20.6163-1(b) The notice may be in the form of a letter to the district director accompanied by a certified copy of the will or other instrument under which the future interest was created. Where the duration of the precedent interest is dependent upon the life of any person, the notice must also show the date of birth of that person. Again, interest is charged at the annually adjusted rate on the amount of tax that is deferred.

Regulations issued under § 6165 require payment of the tax and accrued interest to be secured by a bond equal to double the amount of the tax and accrued interest for the estimated duration of the precedent interest. Reg. § 20.6165-1(b) If the duration of the precedent interest is indefinite, the bond must be conditioned upon the principal or surety promptly notifying the district director when the precedent interest terminates and upon his or her notifying the district director in September of each year as to the continuance of the precedent interest.

When the decedent's estate includes both a future interest and other property, the amount of tax that can be deferred is determined by the following formula, described in Reg. § 20.6163-1(c):

$$\frac{\text{Adjusted value of future interest}}{\text{Adjusted value of Gross estate}} \times \text{Estate tax} = \text{Tax that may be deferred}$$

For purposes of the calculation, the value of the future interest is reduced by, (1) the amount of outstanding liens on the interest, (2) losses deductible under § 2054 with respect to the interest, (3) amounts deductible in respect of the interest as charitable transfers under § 2055, and (4) amounts deductible in respect of the interest as a marital deduction under §2056. Similar reductions are made in the value of the gross estate.

§12.47. DEFERRAL OF ESTATE AND GST TAX UNDER §6166

Section 6166 allows the estate tax attributable to a closely-held business interest to be paid in ten installments, the first of which is due five years after the federal estate tax return is due. Deferral under §6166 is allowed if the value of the closely-held business interest exceeds 35 percent of the decedent's gross estate less the amount of deductions allowable under §§2053 and 2054. (The percentage requirement was 65 percent for decedents who died between 1976 and 1982.) Again, recall that a deduction is allowable under §2053 and not §2055 for enforceable charitable pledges. *See* §11.17. For purposes of §6166, the decedent's interests in two or more businesses may be aggregated if 20 percent or more of the value of each of them is included in the decedent's estate. In essence, the 1981 Act made the more impressive benefits of §6166 available to estates that met the less onerous percentage requirement of the former §6166A. For a more detailed discussion of §6166, *see* §§11.25-11.30. Under §6166(i), the GSTT on direct skips of closely-held businesses is treated as an additional estate tax imposed under §2001.

Pre-1998 Rules. Interest is due each year on the unpaid amount of the tax. For estates of persons dying before 1998, the tax on the first $1 million in value of the business interest is subject to interest at only four percent. §6601(j). The amount subject to this special rate was the lesser of, (1) $153,000 ($345,800, the amount of the estate tax on $1 million, minus $192,800, the amount of the unified credit allowable under §2010(a)), assuming it remains available, or (2) the amount of the tax extended under §6166. The remainder of the tax is subject to the quarterly adjusted rate. Deferral of more than the four percent amount was not particularly attractive when the floating rate was high.

For estates of persons dying before 1998, the interest paid on the unpaid portion of the estate tax is deductible as an expense of administration under §2053(a)(2). *See* §12.13. However, the deduction is only allowed as the interest is paid—an anticipatory deduction is not allowed. Accordingly, as additional interest is paid a Form 706 with the supplemental information should be filed as provided in Rev. Proc. 81-27, 1981-2 C.B. 547. *See* §11.28. A similar procedure should be followed in order to claim a credit under §2011 for deferred payment of state death taxes. Also, note that the entire amount of interest might be deductible if the executor borrowed the funds with which to pay the tax and the interest were paid in advance (*i.e.*, if the interest were deducted from the loan at the outset).

Post-1997 Rules. The 1997 Act amended §6166 effective with respect to decedents dying after 1997. The amendment reduced the 4 percent rate to 2 percent and expanded the amount subject to the lower rate to the amount of the estate tax on the first $1 million attributed to the qualified interests above the amount of the unified credit for the year. Specifically, the lower rate applies to the lesser of, (1) the tentative tax calculated with respect to the sum of $1 million plus the applicable exclusion amount less the amount of the applicable credit (the unified credit allowable for the year), and (2) the amount of the tax that is extended under §§6166. The rate applicable to the balance of the extended tax was changed to 45 percent of the rate established under § 6601(a), which is the federal short term rate plus three percent. Also, §§ 162 and 2053 were amended to provide that no deduction is allowable for any interest on the extended portion of the tax. A worksheet that can be used to estimate the amount of estate tax that can be deferred, and the amount of annual payments is located at § 11.30.

§ 12.48. FEDERAL TAX LIEN; RELEASE FROM LIABILITY FOR TAXES

A representative of a person or estate is liable for the payment of claims of the government, including taxes. The liability is based upon 31 U.S.C. § 3713, which codified the provisions of §§ 3466 and 3467 of the Revised Statutes. Subsection 3713(a) provides that "claim of the United States Government shall be paid first when— . . . (B) the estate of a deceased debtor, in the custody of the executor or administrator, is not enough to pay all debts of the debtor." Under subsection 3713(b) "A representative of a person or estate . . . paying any part of a debt of the person or estate before paying a claim of the Government is liable to the extent of the payment for unpaid claims of the Government." An estate's administration expenses have a priority over the federal tax lien. *Estate of Capato v. United States,* 70 A.F.T.R.2d ¶ 6291 (D.Or. 1992) (court followed definition of administration expenses in Reg. § 20.2053-3(a)) In *David Shawn Beckwith,* T.C. Memo. 1995-20, the court upheld the petitioner's personal liability for an estate tax deficiency both as executor and as a beneficiary-transferee of estate assets.

Potential liability under § 3713 is of concern to fiduciaries because federal tax liabilities are considered to be debts due the United States, and the distribution of property to a beneficiary is treated as the payment of a debt. Reg. § 20.2002-1Funeral expenses, costs of administration, a family allowance, and a limited number of other items are not considered to be debts. *See, e.g., United States v. Weisburn,* 48 F. Supp. 393 (E.D.Pa. 1943), *and Malcolm D. Champlin,* 6 T.C. 280 (1946) (estate administration expenses). Accordingly, those items may be paid without risk. On the other hand, expenses of the decedent's last illness are considered to be debts. The risk of personal liability naturally discourages fiduciaries from distributing estate property before a decedent's tax liabilities are settled.

The problem of the fiduciary's potential liability is relieved somewhat by § 2204, which permits the executor or other fiduciary to apply for prompt determination of the estate tax liability. Also, § 6905 establishes a procedure under which the executor can obtain a discharge from personal liability for the decedent's income and gift taxes.

The Federal Tax Lien Act of 1966, which provides that a federal tax lien "shall not be valid" against judgment lien creditors until a prescribed notice has been given, prevails over § 3713(a), which requires that a government lien "be paid first." *United States v. Estate of Romani,* 523 U.S. 517 (1998) (private party perfected lien prior to the time the government filed notice of its tax lien; death of insolvent debtor did not give the government lien priority).

§12.48.1. Request for Prompt Determination of Estate Tax, §2204

Section 2204 allows an executor or other fiduciary to apply for prompt determination of estate tax liability and discharge from personal liability for the tax. The request should be made in a letter that is filed with the estate tax return when it is filed. In the case of an executor, the IRS is generally required to notify the executor of the amount of the tax within nine months of the time the estate tax return was required to be filed. The executor is discharged from personal liability upon payment of the amount that the IRS advises is due from the estate (other than any amount the time for payment of which is extended under §6161, 6163 or 6166) and upon furnishing any bond that may be required for any amount, the payment of which has been extended. If not timely notified, the executor is discharged from personal liability for any deficiency thereafter found as to the executor's personal assets. Reg. §20.2204-1(a) A fiduciary other than an executor can obtain a release from personal liability for estate tax on essentially the same terms. §2204(b). An agreement that meets the requirements of §6324A (relating to the special lien for estate tax deferred under §6166) is treated as the furnishing of a bond for purposes of §2204.

By filing an application for prompt determination of estate tax, the estate tax liability of the estate must be fixed within 18 months following a decedent's death. Many executors and other fiduciaries file requests under §2204 in order to facilitate the early distribution of assets from estates and trusts. However, some planners are reluctant to file a request under §2204 because they believe that doing so increases the probability the decedent's estate tax return will be audited.

§12.48.2. Request for Discharge from Personal Liability for Income and Gift Taxes, §6905

An executor can also apply under §6905 for discharge from personal liability for a decedent's income and gift tax liabilities. Such a request is filed with the same office as the decedent's federal estate tax return, if one is filed, otherwise where the decedent's final income tax return was required to be filed. Reg. §301.6905-1(a) If such a request is filed, the executor is released from personal liability if he or she is not notified of the amount due within nine months of the receipt of the executor's request. Otherwise, the executor is released upon payment of the amount that the IRS advises is due.

§12.48.3. Request for Prompt Assessment of Income and Gift Taxes, §6501(d)

In general, an executor may limit the assessment of "any tax (other than the tax imposed by chapter 11 of subtitle B, relating to estate taxes) for which a return is required in the case of a decedent," §6501(d), by filing a request for prompt assessment. Presumably, a request can be filed with respect to the GSTT.

The provisions of §6501(d) require that the tax liabilities of a decedent be assessed within 18 months after receipt of a request for prompt assessment, which must be filed after the return of such tax is made. In the ordinary case, if the 18 months pass without an assessment being made, the executor cannot be held personally liable for the taxes unless he or she had personal knowledge of the liability, or had such knowledge as would put a reasonably prudent person on inquiry. Again, the filing of such a request may trigger an audit of the decedent's income or gift tax returns. Assessment of a tax due to substantial omission of items, or false, fraudulent, or no return, is not barred by proceeding under § 6501(d).

§ 12.49. CHECKLIST OF POST-MORTEM MATTERS

I. Income Tax

  A. Decedent's final income tax return

    1. Joint return with surviving spouse, §§ 6013(a)(2), (3), § 12.3.1
    2. Medical expenses paid within 1 year of death, § 213(c)(1), § 2053, § 12.3.4
    3. Miscellaneous itemized deductions, § 67, § 12.3.6
    4. Accrued interest on Series EE bonds and similar obligations, § 454, § 12.3.7
    5. Election to reduce amount of gift of capital gain property, §§ 170(b)(1)(C)(iii), 170(e), § 8.11

  B. Estate's income tax return

    6. Election of tax year, § 441(b), § 12.7
    7. Election to treat qualified revocable trust as part of estate, § 645, § 10.15, § 12.3.8.
    8. Estate administration expenses, § 642(g), § 12.13
    9. Estate selling expenses, § 642(g), § 12.13.2
    10. Distributions of estate assets and excess deductions in final year, § 642(h), §§ 12.37.-.12.41
    11. Election to recognize gain on distribution of appreciated assets in kind, § 643(e), § 12.37.7
    12. Distribute income in respect of a decedent in satisfaction of marital or charitable gifts, § 12.37
    13. Election to deduct, in prior taxable year, the distribution of income to charitable organizations. § 642(c)(1), § 12.9.
    14. Distribution of installment obligation to obligor, § 691(a)(5), § 9.6
    15. Redemption of stock under § 303, §§ 11.13-11.23

  C. Other income tax elections

    16. S corporation election, § 1362(d)(1), § 12.4
    17. Partnership election to increase basis in assets in which decedent had proportionate interest, § 754, (if election not made in time, apply for extension under Reg. § 301.9100-1), § 12.5
    18. If an election is not made under § 754 and property other than cash is distributed within 2 years following the death of a partner, consider election under § 732(d). § 12.5.2.
    19. Waiver of the personal representative's fees, Rev. Rul. 66-167, 1966-1 C.B. 20; § 12.8
    20. Rollover of lump sum payments to surviving spouse, §§ 402(a)(7), § 13.2(1)(d)

II. Estate Tax

    21. Alternate valuation, § 2032, § 12.15

22. Special use valuation, § 2032A, § 12.19
23. Marital deduction, qualified terminable interest property § 2056(b)(7), § 12.21
24. Marital deduction, qualified domestic trust election, § 2056A, § 12.22
25. Estate administration expenses and expenses of selling estate assets, § 642(g), items 8 and 9 above
26. Election to claim qualified conservation easement exclusion. § 2031(c); § 12.20
27. Application for extension of time to file Estate Tax Return (Form 4768), § 12.44
28. Application for extension of time to pay estate tax (Form 4768), § 12.45
29. Deferral of estate tax on reversions and remainders, § 6163, § 12.46
30. Reformation of charitable interests, to qualify for deductions, § 2055(e)(3), § 8.35
31. Election for deferred payment of tax, § 6166, § 12.48

III. Generation-Skipping Transfer Tax

32. Alternate valuation on taxable termination at death, § 2624(c), § 12.15.7
33. Application for extension of time to file GSTT return, § 6081, § 12.44
34. Application for extension of time to pay GSTT, § 6081, § 12.44
35. Allocation of GSTT exemption, § 2631(a), § 12.24
36. Reverse QTIP election, § 2652(a)(3), § 12.23
37. Election to defer payment of GSTT on direct skips of closely-held business, § 6166(i), § 12.48
38. Extension of time to allocate GSTT exemption, § 12.2.4

IV. Other Tax Notices and Elections

39. Application for employer identification number (Form SS-4), § 6109
40. Notice concerning fiduciary relationship (Form 56) also serves as notice of qualification of executor under § 6036. Announcement 86-78, 1986-26 I.R.B. 35, § 12.2.3
41. Request for prompt assessment of gift, income, and GST taxes, § 6501(d), § 12.49.3
42. Application for discharge for personal liability of estate tax, § 2204, § 12.49
43. Consent to split gifts of decedent or surviving spouse, § 2513, § 12.25 and § 2.7
44. Notice of termination of fiduciary relationship (Form 56 may be used for this purpose), § 6903, Announcement 86-78, 1986-26 I.R.B. 35, § 12.2.3

V. Reordering Distribution of Property

45. Disclaimers, § 2518, § § 12.32-12.36
46. Surviving spouse's election against will, § 12.31
47. Family awards and allowances, § 12.30
48. Optional settlement of life insurance proceeds. § § 6.36, 12.28

VI. Extension of Time for Returns, Payment and Most Tax Elections

49. Application for extension of time to file estate tax return. § 6651. § 12.44
50. Application for extension of time to pay estate tax. § § 6161, § 12.45

51. Election to extend time for payment of estate tax on reversionary or remainder interest. § 6163, § 12.46.
52. Election to defer payment of estate tax on closely held business. § 6166, § 12.48
53. Extension of time to make elections. Reg. § 301.9100 § 12.2.4

VII. Reformations

54. Institute reformation proceedings as required to perfect charitable and marital gifts, § § 2055(e)(3), 2056(d)(5), § § 5.25, 8.35.

BIBLIOGRAPHY

I. GENERAL

Akers, After the Fact, But It's Still Not too Late—An Overview of Post-Mortem Tax Planning Strategies, U. Miami, 34th Inst. Est. Plan., Ch. 12 (2000)

Brackney, Post-Mortem Tax Planning for Estates, 15 Wake Forest L. Rev. 581 (1979)

Cornfeld, Fiduciary Elections, U. Miami, 18th Inst. Est. Plan., Ch. 10 (1984)

Dawkins, Another Bite at the Apple: Using the Alternate Valuation Election to Restore a Credit Shelter Trust, 16 Prob. & Prop. 28 (Jan./Feb. 2002)

Ferguson, C., Freeland, J. & Ascher, M., Federal Income Taxation of Estates, Trusts, and Beneficiaries (3d ed. 1999)

J. Kasner, Post Mortem Tax Planning (1988)

Martin, 2032A Special Valuation—Often Overlooked Opportunities, U. Miami, 29th Est. Plan. Inst., Ch. 19 (1995)

Mariani, Executors' Elections, vol. 12, No. 2 ALI-ABA Course Materials J. 59 (1987)

McPherson, Yussman & Filcik, Postmortem Strategies that Enhance a Client's Estate Plan, 22 Est. Plan. 91 (1995)

Moore, Post-Mortem Planning and Administration for Unlimited Marital Deduction Estates, U. Miami, 20th Inst. Est. Plan., Ch. 12 (1986)

Randal, Gardner & Stewart, Distributions of Property from Estates and Trusts: Avoiding Income Tax Traps, 27 Est. Plan. 312 (Aug./Sept. 2000)

Watenmaker & Yardley, Death of a Spouse: "Now What Do I Do . . . ?" Selected Tax Issues for the Surviving Spouse, U.S.C. § 47th Tax Inst., Ch. 25 (1995)

II. DISCLAIMERS

Coleman, Disclaimers—New Developments, Opportunities and Unsettled Areas, U. Miami, 33d Inst. Est. Plan., Ch. 15 (1999)

Frimmer, A Decade Later: Final Disclaimer Regulations Issued Under Section 518, U. Miami, 21st Inst. Est. Plan., Ch. 6 (1987)

Hirsch, The Uniform Disclaimer of Property Interests Act: Opportunities and Pitfalls, 28 Est. Plan. 571 (Dec. 2001)

Moore, The Ever-Expanding Use of Disclaimers in Estate Planning: An Update, U. Miami, 24th Inst. Est. Plan., Ch. 17 (1989)

Thompson, When it is Better to Disclaim Than to Receive, U. Miami, 39th Inst. Est. Plan. Ch. 13 (2005)

III. Estate Distributions

Barnett, The Taxation of Distributions In Kind—What Hath the President and Congress Designed? U. Miami, 20th Inst. Est. Plan., Ch. 15 (1986)

Freeland, Maxfield & Sawyer, Estate and Trust Distribution of Property In Kind After the Tax Reform Act of 1984, 38 Tax L. Rev. 449 (1985)

Randal, Gardner & Stewart, Distributions of Property from Estates and Trusts: Avoiding Income Tax Traps, 27 Est. Plan. 312 (Aug./Sept. 2000)

IV. Estate Tax Payment and Apportionment

Gerzog, Equitable Apportionment: Recent Cases and Continuing Trends, 41 Real Prop., Prob. & Tr. J. 671 (2007)

Hirschson & Bochner, § 6166 and All That, U. Miami, 25th Inst. Est. Plan., Ch. 16 (1991)

Kahn, Revised Uniform Estate Tax Apportionment Act, 38 Real Prop, Prob. & Tr. J 613 (2004)

Pennell, Apportionment Can Make Tax Payment More Equitable, 22 Est. Plan. 3 (Jan./Feb. 1995)

V. Miscellaneous

Akers, Administration Expenses: Those "Ho-Hum" Expenses Can Really Add Up, U. Miami, 31st Inst. Est. Plan., Ch. 18 (1997)

Bryant & Warchuck, Steps to Take to Preserve Deductions for Beneficiaries at the Termination of a Trust or Estate, 86 J. Tax. 51 (Jan. 1997)

Budin, GST Provisions May Limit Section 303 Redemptions, 17 Est., Gifts & Tr. J. 146 (Sept./Oct. 1992)

Carrico & Bondurant, Equitable Adjustments: A Survey and Analysis of Precedents and Practice, 63 Tax L. 545 (1983)

Dobris, Limits on the Doctrine of Equitable Adjustment in Sophisticated Postmortem Tax Planning, 66 Iowa L. Rev. 273 (1981)

Kasner, The "Optimum" Marital Deduction—Pay Now or Pay Later?, N.Y.U., 43d Inst. Fed. Tax., Ch. 54 (1985)

Moore, Recognition and Uses of Federal Estate Tax Credits in Estate Planning and Administration, U. Miami, 21st Inst. Est. Plan., Ch. 8 (1987)

Pennell, Minimizing the Surviving Spouse's Elective Share, 32d U. Miami, Inst. Est. Plan., Ch. 9 (1998)

Report, Current Problems in Administration and Distribution of Tangible, Collectible Property in the Estate of a Decedent, 16 Real Prop., Prob. & Tr. J. 320 (1981)

Siegler, When Bad Things Happen to Good People: Relief for Missed Tax Elections, U. Miami, 32d Inst. Est. Plan., Ch. 12 (1998)

Strategies for Using Conservation Easements in Tax and Estate Planning, 16 Prob. & Prop. 15 (Nov./Dec. 2002)

Zaritsky, Attack of the Surviving Spouse: The Evolving Problems of the Elective Share, U. Miami, 23rd Inst. Est. Plan., Ch. 4 (1989)

13

Estate Planning for Retirement Plans and IRAs

BY: GAIR BENNETT PETRIE J.D., LL.M.

RANDALL | DANSKIN
1500 Bank of America Financial Center
Spokane, Washington 99201-0653
(509) 747-2052
gbp@randalldanskin.com

GAIR B. PETRIE is a shareholder in the law firm of Randall | Danskin, P.S. in Spokane, Washington. He graduated from Gonzaga School of Law and received an LL.M. in federal taxation from the University of Florida. His primary areas of practice include estate planning, qualified and non-qualified retirement plans and compensation related matters. Mr. Petrie is a frequent lecturer at continuing legal education programs for Idaho, Washington and Oregon Lawyers and Certified Public Accountants. In addition, he has published several articles in national publications dealing with estate planning and qualified retirement plan issues. He taught estate planning as an adjunct professor of law at Gonzaga School of Law for over 20 years. Mr. Petrie is a Fellow in the American College of Trust and Estate Counsel ("ACTEC").

Date Revised:
October 2011

Gair Bennett Petrie
Summary

The author expresses no legal, tax, or other opinions herein or with regard to the forms appearing as appendices (or any other forms attached to this Article). Also, the author takes no responsibility for misstatements or errors that may appear herein as these materials cannot be relied upon as research materials. The following should only be used upon a thorough review of the client's facts and applicable law. Moreover, the reproduction of Reg. 1.401(a)(9)-9 appearing at Appendix I is for illustrative purposes only and, due to possible updates and computer glitches, only the actual regulation from a service publishing the same should be used to make a calculation

§13.1 SCOPE AND COVERAGE

This chapter will analyze the complicated interplay between various federal and Washington state laws that the planner must take into consideration in planning with a client's tax-qualified retirement plan or IRA. Throughout this chapter, references to the Internal Revenue Code, Title 26 U.S.C., will be indicated as I.R.C., and references to Treasury Regulations, Title 26 C.F.R., will be indicated as Treas. Reg.

§13.2 INCOME TAX FACTORS

This section discusses the principal income tax factors that should be considered when selecting the beneficiary of the working spouse's account.

(1) Minimum distribution rules

Assets held by a qualified retirement plan or individual retirement account (IRA) are allowed to grow without being subject to the income tax until distributed to the participant or the participant's beneficiary. I.R.C. §501(a). Thus, clients who do not need current distributions to provide for their support will generally choose to defer receiving distributions as long as possible. Because the primary purpose of exempting the accounts from the federal income tax was to allow taxpayers to accumulate the funds needed for support in retirement, the law includes a complex set of rules that are intended to assure that funds in a retirement account are used for that purpose. I.R.C. 401(a)(9). Clients will most often wish to preserve the option of allowing the funds in an account to grow for the longest possible period. Income tax deferral, of course, is subject to the minimum distribution rules of I.R.C. 401(a)(9) and final Treasury Regulations issued thereunder. The minimum distribution rules establish when distributions must begin and the methodology by which minimum required distributions are calculated both before and after the account holder's death.

- RMD Holiday for 2009. The Pension Act of 2008 added IRC §401(a)(9)(H) under which no RMD is required for the 2009 calendar year from tax-qualified retirement plans under IRC §401(a), 403(b) plans, 457(b) plans of governmental entities (but not 457(b) plans of tax-exempt organizations) and IRAs.

  The holiday is for RMDs required *for calendar year 2009*. This can lead to interesting results:

  ○ Example 1. Sam attains age 70$^1/_2$ in 2008 but decides to defer his first RMD (that required for 2008) until April 1, 2009. Under the holiday provisions, Sam must still take the 2008 RMD by April 1, 2009. Sam's second RMD which would have otherwise been required by December 31, 2009, is no longer required.

  ○ Example 2. Sam attains age 70$^1/_2$ in 2009. The holiday excuses Sam's first RMD (for calendar year 2009). However, Sam's 2010 RMD must be made by December 31, 2010.

  For an account holder who had an RMD requirement in 2009, the 2009 distribution is simply missed and the account holder commences again in

2010 based on the account holder's age in 2010 under the Uniform Lifetime Table.

The RMD holiday also applies to inherited IRAs so that an IRA beneficiary who would otherwise have an RMD requirement for the 2009 calendar year, does not have to take the 2009 RMD. Although there would be no RMD in 2009, the divisor for the 2010 RMD and each year's RMD thereafter is still calculated as though the 2009 RMD occurred. In other words, the divisor is still reduced by one (1) for 2009.

If an inherited IRA is subject to the five (5) year payout rule, calendar year 2009 will be disregarded effectively extending the five-year rule by one year.

(a) Required beginning date

Under I.R.C. § 401(a)(9), distribution must begin not later than the "required beginning date." Generally, the required beginning date is April 1 of the calendar year following the calendar year in which the participant attains the age of 70 1/2 without regard to the actual date of retirement. However, an individual, other than a five-percent owner (defined at I.R.C. § 416), may defer commencement of distribution from a retirement plan (but not an IRA) until April 1 of the calendar year following the calendar year during which the individual terminates employment. I.R.C. § 401(a)(9)(C). An individual is a five-percent owner if he owns, with application of the attribution rules of I.R.C. § 318, more than five percent of the employer. Moreover, a different required beginning date may apply if an old "§ 242(b)(2) election" is in place. Treas. Reg. 1.401(a)(9)-8, Q-13, A-13.

For the purpose of *determining* the required beginning date, an employee attains the age of 70 1/2 on the date that is six months after the 70th anniversary of that employee's birth. Treas. Reg. 1.401(a)(9)-2, Q-3, A-3.

Generally, the participant's first "distribution calendar year" is the year the participant attains the age of 70 1/2. Treas. Reg. § 1.401(a)(9)-5, Q-1, A-1(b). Thus, if a participant attains the age of 70 1/2 in *2005*, and under the required beginning date rules defers the initial distribution until 2006, two minimum distributions must occur in 2006. The minimum distribution for 2005 must occur by April 1, 2006, and the minimum distribution for 2006 must occur before December 31, 2006.

Distributions pursuant to a valid TAX EQUITY AND FISCAL RESPONSIBILITY ACT (TEFRA) § 242(b)(2) election do not have to comply with the required beginning date rule. Treas. Reg. § 1.401(a)(9)-8, Q-13, A-13. A TEFRA § 242(b)(2) election was a transitional election that could only be made on or by December 31, 2003. The election, if properly made and if not revoked, could permit an account holder who is a more than five percent owner of an employer to defer the required beginning date under the employer's retirement plan until the calendar year following the calendar year of retirement.

(b) Distributions while the participant is living

When the account holder is alive on his required beginning date, minimum distributions are made with reference to the Uniform Lifetime Table of Treas. Reg. § 1.401(a)(9)-9. This table is as follows:

Uniform Lifetime Table

Age of Account Holder	Distribution Period
70	27.4
71	26.5
72	25.6
73	24.7
74	23.8
75	22.9
76	22.0
77	21.2
78	20.3
79	19.5
80	18.7
81	17.9
82	17.1
83	16.3
84	15.5
85	14.8
86	14.1
87	13.4
88	12.7
89	12.0
90	11.4
91	10.8
92	10.2
93	9.6
94	9.1
95	8.6
96	8.1
97	7.6
98	7.1
99	6.7
100	6.3

To properly apply the Uniform Lifetime Table, the attained age of the account holder in the year in question is used. For example, if the account holder was born in the first half of the year, then he or she will have only attained age 70 in the year he or she reaches age 70 1/2. The first minimum distribution would be 1/27.4. If, by contrast, the account holder's birthday was in the second half of the calendar year, then he or she would have attained age 71 in the first distribution calendar year and the first minimum distribution would be 1/26.5.

The applicable divisor under the Uniform Lifetime Table is applied to the account balance as of the last valuation date in the calendar year immediately preceding the distribution calendar year. For example, if the account holder attains age 70 1/2 in 2010 but defers the first minimum distribution until April 1, 2011, assuming a calendar year plan (or an IRA), the valuation date for the first minimum distribution would be December 31, 2009 (for the 2010 minimum distribution deferred to the required beginning date) and December 31, 2010 (for the 2011 minimum distribution required by December 31, 2011). Treas. Reg. § 1.401(a)(9)-5, Q-3, A-3(a). It should be noted that, in the case of a qualified plan on a fiscal year, adjustments may be made for contributions or distributions following the valuation date during the calendar year containing the valuation date. *Id.* However, in the case of an IRA maintaining its records on the calendar year, contributions or adjustments following the December 31 date will not affect the account balance to be used in determining the appropriate minimum distribution for that calendar year. Thus, if one were calculating the minimum distribution for the 2010 calendar year with respect to an IRA, contributions after December 31, 2009 would be disregarded in determining the account balance. Of course, distributions in 2010 would be applied against any further required minimum distribution.

The identity of the account holder's designated beneficiary on the required beginning date is irrelevant with one exception. If the spouse is the sole beneficiary of an account (or when the spouse is the sole beneficiary of a separate account under Treas. Reg. § 1.401(a)(9)-8, Q-2, A-2), and the spouse is more than ten years younger than the account holder, the actual joint life expectancy of the participant and spouse under Treas. Reg. § 1.401(a)(9)-9, Q-3, A-3, recalculated annually (only during the couple's lifetime), may be used. Treas. Reg. § 1.401(a)(9)-5, Q-4, A-4(b). The regulations specify that marital status is determined on January 1 of each year. Treas. Reg. § 1.401(a)(9)-5, Q-4, A-4(b)(2). Thus, if the exception is being used and the spouse dies (or the couple divorces) during the calendar year, the account holder would, in the succeeding calendar year, switch to the Uniform Lifetime Table.

To illustrate the effect on the minimum distribution calculations of tying the required beginning date to age 70 1/2, consider the following: If an account holder's date of birth is June 30, 1936, the 70th anniversary of the account holder's birth is June 30, 2006. The account holder attains the age of 70 1/2 on December 30, 2006. In such case, the account holder's first minimum distribution would be due not later than April 1, 2007, and would be the account balance on December 31, 2005, divided by 27.4. If, instead, the account holder's date of birth was July 1, 1936, he or she would be age 70 1/2 on January 1, 2007. This would push the required beginning date off to April 1, 2008; and, because the account holder attained age 71 in the year he or she reached age 70 1/2, the first minimum distribution would be the December 31, 2006, account balance divided by 26.5.

(c) Distributions after death

Under Treas. Reg. § 1.401(a)(9)-5, Q-4, A-4, minimum distributions essentially accrue on January 1 of each calendar year. Thus, in the year the account holder dies, the minimum distribution for that year will be calculated under the Uniform Lifetime Table and distributed no later than December 31 of the year of death. Depending on the language of the applicable plan or IRA document, this distribution belongs to the designated beneficiaries and is taxed to those beneficiaries. As discussed below, postdeath distributions commence in the calendar year following the calendar year of death. In sum, if an account holder dies after his or her required beginning date, there is still a minimum distribution for the year of death in addition to the minimum distribution required for the year after death and each year thereafter. As discussed below, Rev. Rul. 2005-36 permits a beneficiary to receive the decedent's final RMD without such receipt disqualifying a later disclaimer.

The regulations under § 401(a)(9) unify, with a few exceptions, the rules applicable to the account of a participant who dies either before or after the required beginning date. The key issue is the identity of the beneficiary whose life expectancy, determined under Treas. Reg. § 1.401(a)(9)-9, Q-1, A-1, will be used to calculate minimum distributions following the death of the account holder. The beneficiary may be identified in the beneficiary designation of the account holder or pursuant to the terms of the custodial account agreement or the plan (i.e., default provisions). Treas. Reg. § 1.401(a)(9)-4, Q-1, A-1. Beneficiaries may be designated by class (i.e., children) as long as the class member with the shortest life expectancy at the time of the account holder's death is identifiable. *Id.*

There are really only two differences between death before versus death after the required beginning date: (i) if the account holder dies before the required beginning date and there is no designated beneficiary as described below (or if there is a beneficiary and the plan or IRA so mandates), the entire account must be distributed within five years under Treas. Reg. § 1.401(a)(9)-3, Q-2, A-2 (known as the "Five Year Rule"), and (ii) if the designated beneficiary is the surviving spouse, he or she may defer commencement of minimum distributions until the account holder would have reached age 70 1/2 under Treas. Reg. § 1.401(a)(9)-3, Q-5, A-5. Otherwise, the post-death distribution rules are essentially unified regardless of whether death occurred before or after the required beginning date. It should be noted that the terms of the plan or the IRA custodial agreement may elect or require the Five Year Rule in the case of the account holder dying before his or her required beginning date, although such language is becoming rare. Moreover, sometimes the plan language permits the beneficiary of an account holder who dies before his or her required beginning date to elect the Five Year Rule in accordance with the terms of the plan or IRA document.

In private letter ruling 200811028, an IRA owner died before his required beginning date with a child as his designated beneficiary. The IRA stated that, if the account holder died before his required beginning date, RMDs will be computed over the designated beneficiary's life expectancy with the first such distribution to occur by December 31 of the calendar year following the calendar year of the account holder's death all in accordance with the regulations. The IRA document went on to say that the beneficiary may elect distributions in accordance with the five-year rule wherein the entire IRA must be distributed by the end of the fifth calendar year following the calendar year of death. In this case, the beneficiary missed the RMD for the first two calendar years after the calendar year of the account holder's death. However, when the beneficiary realized the mistake, makeup RMDs were immediately taken and the 4974(a) 50% penalty paid. The issue was whether the beneficiary may compute RMDs over the beneficiary's life expectancy or whether failure to take RMDs in the first couple of years when they were required constituted an election of the five-year rule.

> The IRS focused on the language of the IRA. The default rule under the
> IRA was the life expectancy rule with the five-year rule being elective.

The IRS concluded that the beneficiary had done nothing to affirmatively elect the five-year rule and therefore permitted the life expectancy RMD calculation.

The regulations impose a key date of September 30 of the calendar year following the calendar year of death. If a beneficiary receives payment of his or her portion of the account before the September 30 date, the beneficiary will be disregarded. Treas. Reg. § 1.401(a)(9)-4, Q-4, A-4(a). If the beneficiary named as of the account holder's death disclaims in favor of a successor beneficiary, the successor beneficiary's life expectancy will control. *Id.* Interestingly, the regulations specify that if a named beneficiary dies between the account holder's death and the September 30 date, the successors to the deceased beneficiary will use the deceased beneficiary's life expectancy to determine minimum distributions. Treas. Reg. § 1.401(a)(9)-4, Q-4, A-4(c). It does not make sense that a child could disclaim in favor of a grandchild whose significantly longer life expectancy would then be used, whereas if the child were to die before the September 30 date, the grandchild would be stuck with the child's life expectancy. Of course, one might consider having the estate of the deceased child disclaim on behalf of the child. The regulations, however, require disclaimer by the named beneficiary before death. *Id.*

The regulations make clear that one cannot go beyond the beneficiary designation in the applicable document (i.e., plan or IRA document) to determine the beneficiary. *Id.* Thus, an individual who is entitled to a portion of the account under a will *"or otherwise under applicable state law"* is not a designated beneficiary. For example, if the designated beneficiary (either by terms of the beneficiary designation or the applicable plan or IRA document) is the estate of the account holder, an individual entitled to all or a portion of the estate by reason of a will or intestacy laws will not be considered the beneficiary for purposes of calculating minimum distributions. Rather, the estate will be considered the beneficiary. As described below, this may have serious ramifications.

If an account holder dies before his/her required beginning date, the first distribution calendar year is the year in which the initial distribution is required to be made to the designated beneficiary (December 31 of the calendar year following the calendar year of death, unless the surviving spouse is the sole beneficiary, in which case distribution may be deferred until December 31 of the calendar year in which the participant would have attained age 70 1/2). Treas. Reg. § 1.401(a)(9)-5, Q-5, A-5(a).

With the above rules in mind, let's examine the applicable distribution period for certain beneficiaries.

(d) Spouse

If the spouse is the designated beneficiary, that spouse may always roll over his or her interest in the plan or account into an IRA in his or her name, in which case the minimum distribution rules apply to the spouse as the account holder. If a spouse will *not* complete a rollover, there are several different rules that may applicable.

If the account holder passed away before his or her required beginning date and the spouse is the sole beneficiary of the account, the spouse may defer commencement of distribution until the end of the calendar year in which the participant would have reached 70 1/2. Treas. Reg. § 1.401(a)(9)-3, Q-3, A-3(b). This rule only applies when the spouse is the sole beneficiary of the account. However, if under Treas. Reg. §1.401(a)(9)-8, Q-2, A-2 the spouse is one of several beneficiaries and his or her interest in the account is segregated during the calendar year following the year of the participant's death, the spouse will be deemed as sole beneficiary of a separate account and this special deferral rule should apply.

Under Treas. Reg. §1.401(a)(9)-4, Q-4, A-4(b), if the account holder dies before his or her required beginning date, and the spouse does not rollover to an account of his or her own and the spouse dies before the end of the year the account holder would have attained age 70 1/2, then the beneficiaries of *the spouse* will be treated as beneficiaries for RMD purposes. This is an unusual rule but does have a practical application in at least one setting. Assume the surviving spouse is under 59 1/2 and does not wish to complete a rollover so that he or she may take distributions from the decedent's account free from the 10% penalty of IRC §72(t). In this case, should the young surviving spouse die before the end of the calendar year the deceased account holder would have been age 70 1/2, the spouse's beneficiaries will be treated as beneficiaries for RMD purposes.

If the account holder dies after the required beginning date with the spouse as the sole beneficiary of the account, and the spouse does not complete a rollover, the applicable period for the distribution will be the spouse's life expectancy, recalculated annually; but, after the spouse's death, that life expectancy will revert to the remaining unrecalculated life expectancy of the spouse. Treas. Reg. §1.401(a)(9)-5, Q-5, A-5(c)(2). If the spouse is one of several beneficiaries of the IRA, this special treatment will only apply if the separate account rule of Treas. Reg. §1.401(a)(9)-8, Q-2, A-2 applies.

To the extent the surviving spouse is the beneficiary of the working spouse's account, he or she may roll over all or any portion of the death distribution to an IRA in his or her name. I.R.C. §408(d)(3)(C). If the surviving spouse is the sole beneficiary of the participant's IRA and has the unlimited right to withdraw amounts from that IRA, the spouse may elect to treat the IRA as his or her own for minimum distribution purposes. This election may be made at any time after the minimum distribution (if the participant was beyond his or her required beginning date) for the calendar year of death has been made. Treas. Reg. §1.408-8, Q-5, A-5. The election may be made by the surviving spouse redesignating the account into his or her name, by missing a minimum distribution applicable to a surviving spouse beneficiary under the regulations, or by making contributions to the account. It is interesting to note that the above cited regulations pertaining to the election will not apply when a trust is the beneficiary of the IRA, even if the surviving spouse is the sole beneficiary of the trust. A series of Private Letter Rulings, issued prior to the regulations, permitted allocation of an IRA from a trust or estate to the surviving spouse to facilitate a rollover because, in those rulings, the spouse had the unilateral right to withdraw the IRA from the trust or estate. Recently issued Letter Rulings confirm the rollover through an estate or trust in certain circumstances. *See* discussion later in my outline. Further, the rollover may occur even though prior installments may have been paid to the working spouse during his or her lifetime.

Moreover, in Private Letter Ruling 95-24-020 (Mar. 21, 1995), a surviving spouse in a non-community property state exercised her right to a "forced share" of the estate and thereafter exercised her power to choose assets included in the forced share in order to allocate the retirement benefit to herself. The ruling allowed her to roll over the account to an IRA in her name.

Private Letter Ruling 200634065 contained a statement by the IRS broadly interpreting the ability of the surviving spouse to complete a rollover through a trust or an estate. In this case, the decedent's IRA was payable to his estate. The decedent's wife was the sole beneficiary and personal representative of the estate. The wife's plan was to have the custodian distribute the IRA to the estate and from the estate to the spouse and, finally, from the spouse to a rollover IRA within 60 days of the initial distribution. The IRS noted the distinction between an inherited IRA (not eligible for a rollover) and the exception to the inherited IRA for payment to a surviving spouse under IRC § 408(d)(3)(C)(ii). The IRS then dealt with the statement in the final § 401(a)(9) regulations pertaining to the surviving spouse's ability to elect to treat the decedent's IRA as his or her own. The IRS noted that this type of election is only available if the surviving spouse is the sole beneficiary of the IRA with an unlimited right to make a withdrawal. In addition, the IRS noted the statement in the regulations that the surviving spouse will not be able to elect to treat the decedent's IRA as his or her own if the beneficiary of the IRA is a trust (even if the surviving spouse is the sole beneficiary of the trust). The IRS went on to differentiate this language from the situation where the surviving spouse actually receives the distributed IRA funds through an estate or trust and concluded as follows:

> [A] surviving spouse who actually receives a distribution from an IRA is permitted to roll that distribution over into his/her own IRA even if the spouse is not the sole beneficiary of the deceased's IRA as long as the rollover is accomplished within the requisite 60-day period. A rollover may be accomplished even if IRA assets *pass through either a trust and/or an estate*. (Emphasis added.)

In LR 200915063, an IRA was payable to a revocable living trust where the decedent died prior to his required beginning date. The surviving spouse was the sole trustee of the living trust. The IRA custodian advised the surviving spouse to pay the IRA to a *taxable* trust account. Less than sixty days later, the surviving spouse, in her capacity as trustee, requested that the custodian reverse the distribution back to the decedent's IRA. The custodian declined. In this private letter ruling, the IRS permitted (i) allocation of the IRA distribution to the revocable portion of the revocable living trust, (ii) extension of the rollover period under IRC § 408(d)(3); and (iii) rollover by the surviving spouse into an IRA in her name.

See the discussion of additional private letter rulings in this area at Section 1.3(2), below.

(e) Nonspouse individual beneficiary

If the employee dies after the required beginning date and an individual who is not the account holder's spouse is the designated beneficiary, the maximum distribution period will be the designated beneficiary's life expectancy (determined with reference to the beneficiary's birthday in the calendar year following the calendar year of the account holder's death) and using the tables under Treas. Reg. § 1.401(a)(9)-9, Q-1, A-1. The applicable distribution period will be reduced by one for each calendar year elapsing after the calendar year following the account holder's death. Treas. Reg. § 1.401(a)(9)-5, Q-5, A-5(c).

For example, assume the surviving spouse passes away naming the couple's only child as beneficiary and that the child's attained age in the year following the surviving spouse's death is 45. Under the single life table of Treas. Reg. 1.401(a)(9)-9, Q-1, A1, the divisor will start at 38.8 to be reduced by one year for each calendar year elapsing after the calendar year following the surviving spouse's death. This is known as a "stretch-out" IRA because the minimum distributions are so small.

(f) Non-individual (or no) designated beneficiary

Under the regulations, only individuals and certain trusts may be designated beneficiaries for the purposes of creating a distribution period. Treas. Reg. § 1.401(a)(9)-4, Q-3, A-3. This rule can cause problems when the participant's estate is the beneficiary. If the participant died before his or her required beginning date, the estate as beneficiary will trigger application of the five-year rule, under which distribution must be complete by the calendar year containing the fifth anniversary of the participant's death. (Note: The 2009 calendar year does not count due to the RMD Holiday of § 408(a)(g)(H). This could extend the five year period another year.) Treas. Reg. § 1.401(a)(9)-3A(b), Q-2, A-2. If, by contrast, the participant died after the required beginning date and the estate was the designated beneficiary, distribution may be made over the remaining life expectancy of the account holder without recalculation. Treas. Reg. § 1.401(a)(9)-5, Q-5, A-5(c)(3). The above rules would also apply when a charity or a trust that is not a "qualified trust" is designated beneficiary.

In Private Letter Ruling 2003-43-030 (July 31, 2003), the decedent (who died after his required beginning date) died without designating a beneficiary of his IRA. Under the IRA custodial account agreement, the decedent's estate was the beneficiary. The decedent's three children were equal residual beneficiaries of the estate. A daughter asked the I.R.S. to approve the segregation of her one-third share of the IRA and a subsequent IRA-to-IRA transfer to a new IRA custodian. The I.R.S. permitted the segregation and the IRA-to-IRA transfer; provided, however, that this process did not result in a "stretch-out". Rather, the daughter was required to take minimum distributions over the decedent father's remaining life expectancy. The same result was reached in Private Letter Ruling 201128036.

See the discussion of LR200846028 under the "Reformation" heading under Trusts as beneficiaries, below.

(g) Multiple beneficiaries

If, on the last day of the calendar year following the participant's death, there are several beneficiaries of the account and the account has not been separated as described below, the beneficiary (as of September 30th of that year) with the shortest (or no) life expectancy will be used to determine minimum distributions. Thus, if several children were beneficiaries of the account, then, absent the separate account treatment, the life expectancy of the oldest child, unrecalculated, would be used to determine distributions from the account. If a charity or estate were one of several beneficiaries, absent corrective action (i.e., division into separate accounts before the end of the calendar year following the calendar year of death), the account holder could be deemed to have died without a designated beneficiary. Treas. Reg. § 1.401(a)(9)-5, Q-7, A-7.

As mentioned above, the rules that focus on the beneficiary with the shortest (or no) life expectancy may be significantly mitigated in most events through timely compliance with the separate account rule of Treas. Reg. § 1.401(a)(9)-8, Q-2, A-2.

(h) Separate accounts/quasi-separate accounts

The regulations permit a single account to be divided into separate accounts, each having different minimum distribution rules, as long as separate accounting, including allocating investment gains and losses, is established. Treas. Reg. § 1.401(a)(9)-8, Q-2, A-2(a). If there are separate IRAs (or separate accounts as per the regulations), different minimum distribution rules may apply with respect to each such account. The segregation must occur no later than the end of the calendar year following the calendar year of death. *Id.*

Practice Tip:

> If after the participant's required beginning date a spouse (or trust for a spouse) who is more than ten years younger than the participant and other beneficiaries will be named, the separate account for that beneficiary should be established prior to the calendar year for which separate account treatment is sought.

The importance of separate IRAs (or accounts) cannot be overstated. From a minimum distribution standpoint, each individual beneficiary will, after the participant's death, have a maximum deferral period equal to his or her own unrecalculated life expectancy. Moreover, each beneficiary will have the right to use that deferral or take earlier distributions as each he or she chooses. Each beneficiary will have the right to make his or her own investments. Finally, each beneficiary could select his or her own custodian of the decedent's IRA, through an IRA-to-IRA transfer. *See* Priv. Ltr. Rul. 2000-08-044 (Dec. 3, 1999). Note: The IRA account is still "owned" by the decedent, for the benefit of the beneficiary; only a spouse as beneficiary can transfer the decedent's IRA to the spouse's own IRA.

The regulations make clear that the separate account treatment is not available to beneficiaries of a trust. Treas. Reg. § 1.401(a)(9)-4, Q-5, A-5(c). Thus, if a qualified trust is a beneficiary and that trust divides into equal shares for the deceased account holder's children, the life expectancy of the oldest child will determine minimum distributions, even if the IRA is segregated into separate IRAs for each separate trust fund. The planner could likely avoid this rule by including, in the IRA beneficiary designation itself, a direction to divide the IRA into separate and equal IRAs for each trust fund.

In Private Letter Rulings 2003-17-041 through 2003-17-044 (Dec. 19, 2002), the I.R.S. took a very harsh approach with regard to separate share treatment for separate trust funds. In those rulings, one trust was designated as beneficiary of the IRA.

However, both the beneficiary designation language and the trust language allowed for division into separate trusts for each of the decedent's three children. Essentially, the I.R.S. stated in the ruling that because the separate trusts and shares were not automatically established at death, separate share treatment was not available and each trust's maximum distribution period would be measured with respect to the oldest child. The IRS followed this approach in LRS 200634068, 200634069 and 200634070. The only way to avoid the result of this ruling would be to direct the trustee (in the trust document) to establish the three separate trusts effective at death *and*, in the beneficiary designation, set forth a required division of the IRA into separate IRAs for each of the trusts. In other words, all fiduciary discretion should be taken out of the equation. Even if this occurs, it is not clear from these rulings that separate share treatment would apply. The I.R.S. might still argue that because the separate trusts were not technically in existence at death, separate share treatment is not available.

It should be noted that an IRA beneficiary designation giving multiple beneficiaries fractional interests in the account may take advantage of the separate account rules, as most states require fractional gifts to receive a pro rata share of income, appreciation, depreciation and the like. However, the practitioner should take care using pecuniary formulas in an IRA beneficiary designation. If the practitioner wishes to set up separate account treatment, the language of the IRA beneficiary designation must state that the pecuniary gift will receive its share of appreciation, depreciation, income, and the like.

There is now a concept that practitioners are referring to as the "quasi-separate account." This situation usually occurs when an estate or trust has been designated as beneficiary and the fiduciary later directs the IRA custodian to divide the IRA into separate accounts, each payable to a separate beneficiary or trust fund. If dealing with a trust in which both the trust document and beneficiary designation require division of the IRA into separate IRAs (one payable to each separate trust fund), true separate account status will be achieved, because, assuming each separate trust adequately deals with the qualified trust rules and contingent beneficiary issue, the beneficiary of each trust will be used for minimum distribution purposes. If, however, the segregation into separate IRAs is at the direction of the trustee (without a requirement in the beneficiary designation itself), then true separate account status is not achieved. In such a case, the oldest trust beneficiary's life expectancy will control minimum distribution calculations for all of the trusts after segregation. Priv. Ltr. Ruls. 2003-17-041 through 2003-17-044 (Dec. 19, 2002), 2004-10-020 (Dec. 9, 2003), & 2004-44-033 (Aug. 3, 2004) (trustee directed segregation of an IRA into separate IRAs; one for each individual beneficiary of the trust.). When the estate is designated as beneficiary and the personal representative directs division of the IRA into separate shares for each of the estate's beneficiaries, the I.R.S. will approve the division, but true separate share status is not achieved. Rather, minimum distributions will be calculated with reference to the decedent's remaining life expectancy (if the decedent died after his required beginning date) or under the five-year rule.

(i)   Trusts as beneficiary (multiple beneficiaries and the "conduit trust")

The practitioner should be aware that successfully using a trust as a beneficiary of a retirement plan or IRA is a tricky proposition. The qualified trust rules described above must be complied with and the practitioner must take care to avoid any problems with multiple beneficiaries as described above. Moreover, there is a true economic concern. A spousal trust (i.e., credit shelter or QTIP trust) should be compared with naming the surviving spouse as outright beneficiary. When the surviving spouse is outright beneficiary, both the participant and, after rollover, the participant's spouse will each independently be able to use the liberal Uniform Lifetime Table. After both husband and wife have died, assuming separate accounts, each child will have his or her own unrecalculated life expectancy for distributions. This method provides a very long "stretch-out." In contrast, when a trust is the designated beneficiary, the participant will be able to use the Uniform Lifetime Table while living, but after his or her death, the life expectancy of the spouse will be all that is available.

There are other income tax concerns as well. If the trust is a "simple trust" under income tax rules (i.e., the trust is required to distribute all of its income at least annually), the interplay between the minimum distribution rules and the required income distribution is important. The trust will only be required to distribute fiduciary accounting income. If the minimum distribution is greater than the fiduciary accounting income, the trust must treat the entire minimum as income in respect of a decedent, hence distributable net income. However, if the trust only distributes the fiduciary accounting income portion of the minimum distribution, it may only deduct that distribution and the balance of the minimum distribution will be taxed at the trust's rates.

Qualified Trust Rules. Under the RMD rules, there are two key issues the planner must contend with; (i) the "qualified trust rules" and (ii) properly drafting the trust so as to segregate a trust beneficiary whose life expectancy will be used determine RMDs to the trust. If a trust is the beneficiary, the underlying beneficiaries of the trust may be considered designated beneficiaries if the qualified trust rules of Treas. Reg. § 1.401(a)(9)-4, Q-5, A-5(b), and A-6 are met on a timely basis. To be timely, compliance must occur as follows:

- Assuming distributions will be made with reference to the Uniform Lifetime Table during the participant's lifetime, the qualified trust rules do not need to be complied with until *October 31* of the calendar year following the calendar year of the participant's death. Treas. Reg. § 1.401(a)(9)-(4), Q-6, A-6(b).

- If the participant's spouse is more than ten years younger than the participant, and the participant wishes to name a trust as beneficiary yet look through the trust to treat the spouse as beneficiary in order to use the actual joint life expectancy of the participant and the spouse, the qualified trust rules must be met, presumably before the due date of any minimum distribution to be so calculated. Treas. Reg. § 1.401(a)(9)-4, Q-6, A-6(b).

The qualified trust requirements are fairly straightforward:

- The trust is a valid trust under state law, or would be but for the fact that there is no corpus.

- The trust is irrevocable or will, by its terms, become irrevocable upon the death of the participant.

- The beneficiaries of the trust who could be treated as designated beneficiaries under the rules discussed below, are identifiable from the trust instrument.

- The documentation required by Treas. Reg. § 1.401(a)(9)-4, Q-6, A-6(a) or (b) has been provided to the plan administrator (or IRA custodian) on a timely basis.

To meet the documentation requirement, the account holder (or after death, the trustee) must provide a copy of the trust instrument and agree to provide any trust amendment within a reasonable time in the future. In the alternative, the following may be provided: (i) a list of the beneficiaries (including remainder beneficiaries and the conditions of their entitlement), (ii) a certification that the list is complete and correct, (iii) an agreement that, if the trust is amended, corrected information will be provided, and (iv) an agreement to provide a copy of the trust instrument upon demand.

The problem is this: if an individual has a general power of appointment over the portion of the trust estate containing retirement assets, it could be argued that the trust lacks identifiable beneficiaries and so the trust would not qualify. For example, a general power of appointment may be exercised in favor of an estate or a charity (neither of which has a life expectancy for I.R.C. § 401(a)(9) purposes). A special power of appointment would likely not cause a problem provided that, at the time of death, the individual within the class with the shortest life expectancy is identifiable. Would the mere fact that a much older individual could be adopted into the class create a problem? Of course, these issues may be avoided by including a limitation that the power holder may only exercise the power in favor of individuals younger than the power holder.

In Private Letter Rulings 2002-35-038 through 2002-35-041 (June 4, 2002), separate trusts were set up for each child of the decedent. Each child had a testamentary general power of appointment over the balance of his or her trust remaining at death. However, the trust did not permit the child to appoint to a non-individual beneficiary or an individual who would have a shorter life expectancy than the decedent's oldest child. This arrangement satisfied the qualified trust rules. According to one commentator, the exclusion was added after the death of the account holder by way of court reformation. *Commentary No. 136, PLRs 200235838 through 200235041 – Minimum Distribution and Trusts*, STEVE LEIMBERG'S EMPLOYEE BENEFIT AND RETIREMENT PLANNING NEWSLETTER (Leimberg Info. Serv.), Sept, 23, 2002 (hereinafter Commentary 136). Compare this Private Letter Ruling 201021038 (described below) wherein the IRS refused to give effect to a trust reformation for RMD purposes.

Which Trust Beneficiary is the RMD Beneficiary? Satisfying the qualified trust rules is really a threshold requirement. Once these rules are satisfied one "looks through" the trust to its underlying beneficiaries in order to apply the RMD rules. Recall that the rules applicable to multiple beneficiaries state that the beneficiary with the shortest (or no life expectancy) will control to determine RMDs to all multiple beneficiaries (unless separate accounts are established). Therefore, in the context of a trust as beneficiary, look through treatment causes the beneficiaries of the trust to be multiple beneficiaries. Therefore, a key question is which trust beneficiaries (i.e., current and remainder) will be considered in the group or "basket" of multiple beneficiaries for this test. Sadly, the regulations are not clear on this point:

A person will not be considered a beneficiary for purposes of determining who is the beneficiary with the shortest life expectancy . . . or whether a person who is not an individual is a beneficiary merely because the person could become the successor to the interest of one of the employee's beneficiaries after that beneficiary's death. *However, the preceding sentence does not apply to a person who has any right (including a contingent right) to an employee's benefit beyond being a mere potential successor to the interest of one of the employee's beneficiaries upon the beneficiary's death.* (Emphasis added.)

Treas. Reg. § 1.401(a)(9)-5, Q-7, A-7(c)(1).

As a result, the regulations create a key issue: Which of the current and remainder beneficiaries will be the multiple beneficiaries so as to pluck out the beneficiary with the shortest or no life expectancy to be used to determine RMDs to the trust?

<u>Conduit Trust Safe Harbor.</u> The key safe harbor approach is commonly known as the "conduit trust" although that term is not used anywhere in IRC § 401(a)(9) or the regulations. Rather, the conduit trust appears as an example under Reg. 1.401(a)(9)-5, QA7(c)(3) (Ex.2). This example tells us that a trust beneficiary will be treated as the sole beneficiary for RMD purposes (hence, his or her life expectancy will be used to determine RMDs to the trust) if during the lifetime of said beneficiary, any and all distributions or withdrawals from the account are required, by the terms of the trust, to be distributed to said beneficiary. In other words, the trustee does not have the opportunity to accumulate any amounts withdrawn or distributed from the IRA. Here are some tips concerning this valuable safe harbor:

- The conduit trust permits the trustee to leave the IRA intact, investing and reinvesting its assets. The RMDs from the IRA will be determined with reference to the conduit beneficiary's life expectancy as though the conduit beneficiary were the sole individual beneficiary of the account. In other words, the only required distributions from the account to the conduit beneficiary will be each year's RMD. Amounts in excess of the RMD may be withdrawn by the trustee and distributed to the conduit beneficiary in accordance with the terms of the trust (e.g., for health, maintenance, education, support).

- Conduits trusts are an excellent choice with regard to trusts for minor children. Although there is no authority on point, there is absolutely no reason why distributions made by the trustee to a guardian of a minor child would not be treated as made to that child for conduit trust purposes.

- The conduit trust may also be used for a "pot trust" for minor children wherein the trustee has the discretion to sprinkle distributions among the decedent's minor children. So long as the trust requires the trustee to distribute any and all withdrawals from the IRA or retirement plan to any one or more of the children, the life expectancy of the oldest child should govern for RMD purposes.

- Although not expressly stated in the regulations, use of IRA funds to pay trustee expenses should not disqualify the trust as a conduit trust. In LR 200620026, a trust was deemed to be a conduit trust even though IRA funds were used to pay asset management fees of the trustee.

- Of course, a conduit trust is not a good option for a "special needs trust" for a disabled beneficiary. This is because the required distributions would likely disqualify the disabled beneficiary from needs based assistance.

- The conduit trust approach is not a good option for a Q-Tip or credit shelter trust for a surviving spouse. In a Q-Tip trust, if the surviving spouse lives long enough, the RMDs will grow and the surviving spouse will receive outright distributions of an increasing larger portion of the IRA, hence defeating the purpose of the Q-Tip trust in the first place. In the case of a credit shelter trust, as the surviving spouse ages and RMDs grow, assets will shift to the surviving spouse, hence increasing his or her gross estate.

- The identity of the remainder beneficiaries is irrelevant to a conduit trust. Therefore, the conduit trust beneficiary may be given an unlimited general power of appointment over trust assets exercisable by Will. Or, remainder beneficiaries could include charities or charitable trusts.

<u>Immediate Outright Remainder Safe Harbor (Sort Of)</u>. In Treas. Reg. 1.401(a)(9)-5, Q-7, A-7(c)(3) (Ex. 1) the trust in question allowed principal to be distributed to a surviving spouse based on a standard set forth in the trust instrument. Upon the surviving spouse's death, the trust would terminate and be distributed to the children of the account holder. The regulation concludes that the beneficiaries of such trust for RMD purposes will be the surviving spouse and the children. In other words, the regulation did not speculate as to who would be default beneficiaries in the event none of the children survived the account holder's spouse. Instead, the regulation focused on who would take the trust assets outright immediately following the death of the surviving spouse. This approach was also taken by the IRS in Rev. Rul. 2006-26, discussed below. In addition, the Service has taken this position in private letter rulings such as LR 200610027 and 200843042, discussed below.

This approach is a form of "accumulation trust" for RMD purposes as the trustee can accumulate or distribute the IRA with distribution according to the standards in the trust.

This immediate outright remainder approach can be simple or complicated. For example, a trust that provides for the account holder's sister for life and remainder outright to the account holder's children would result in those of the account holder's sister and children living on the account holder's death being treated as beneficiaries for RMD purposes. Presumably, the sister would be the oldest as among them. Therefor, her life expectancy would be used to determine RMDs to the trust.

Here is another example: Discretionary trust for the account holder's child until he reaches 45 years of age at which time the trust will be terminated; provided, that if the child dies before reaching age 45, the trust will be distributed outright to the heirs at law of the child. Assume that, on the date of the account holder's death, the child survives the account holder and that, should the child die immediately following the account holder, the child's uncle would be his oldest "heir at law". In this case, the life expectancy of the uncle would be used to determine RMDs to the trust.

The immediate outright remainder approach is likely the best alternative for a special needs trust for a disabled beneficiary. As described above, a conduit trust is not a viable alternative in this case. However, you could design the trust so that, following the account holder's death, special needs distributions only are permitted to the disabled child and, upon his or her death, the trust assets are distributed immediately and outright to the disabled child's siblings. In this case, the child and his or her siblings living on the date of the account holder's death will be the RMD beneficiaries of the trust. The life expectancy of the oldest of such group will be used to determine RMDs to the trust.

The immediate outright remainder approach must be used with caution because there is always the possibility that one or more of the remainder beneficiaries may predecease the account holder thereby changing the analysis of who is the oldest beneficiary. This issue may be addressed through "fire wall language" described below.

Finally, and as mentioned above, the immediate remainder approach allows the trust to accumulate distributions from the IRA, so it really is a form of what is often referred to as a "accumulation trust". Thus, the planner should include proper firewall language described below.

There are a couple of interesting private letter rulings dealing with the immediate outright remainder approach:

- In LR 200610027 an IRA was payable to a trust for the benefit of a minor grandchild. Discretionary distributions were permitted until the grandchild reached age 25 at which time the trust would terminate and be distributed to the grandchild. If the grandchild died before reaching 25, the assets would pass to the grandchild's heirs at law. At the time of the account holder's death, the oldest of the grandchild's heirs at law who would be entitled to the trust in the event the grandchild died before reaching age 25 was the grandchild's father. Therefore, the Service concluded that the father's life expectancy would be used to determine RMDs to the trust. Of course, this result could have been avoided through a conduit trust.

- In LR 200843042 the decedent's son was the beneficiary of a trust that would continue until the son reached age 40. If the son were to die before reaching age 40, the trust was to be distributed to the son's children; or if none, his heirs at law. At the time of the account holder's death, the son had no children. Moreover, the oldest heir at law of the son's was his mother and so her life expectancy was used to determine RMDs to the trust. Once again, this result could have been avoided through the use of a conduit trust.

Accumulation Trust. If the trust is not a "conduit trust" then, for the RMD analysis, the trust is an "accumulation trust" as the trustee has the power to accumulate all or a portion of distributions taken from the retirement plan or IRA. As described above, the immediate outright remainder approach may, if properly structured, sufficiently zero in on the trust beneficiary to be used for RMD purposes. However, the drafter should give consideration to "firewall language" in any accumulation trust that, for example, (i) precludes the exercise of powers of appointment relative to a retirement plan or IRA assets (or limits the appointees to individuals no older than the other beneficiaries of the trust), (ii) prevents an adopted individual from becoming a trust beneficiary relative to IRA or retirement plan assets when that adopted individual might be older than the stated beneficiaries of the trust, and (iii) precludes the use of IRA or retirement plan assets for the payment of estate and other expenses.

A tough question with accumulation trusts is whether the trustee may have the ability to use IRA or retirement plan assets to pay the deceased account holder's debts, expenses and estate taxes (or similar expenses of the trust beneficiary). Of course, the fear is that such power will cause the "estate" to be within the group or basket of beneficiaries; and, because the estate has no life expectancy, the Five Year Rule would apply if the account holder died before his required beginning date (or distribution would be made over the balance of the account holder's unrecalculated life expectancy if the account holder died after his required beginning date). If one is drafting an accumulation trust, this should be easy enough to plan for assuming the accumulation trust will have other assets to pay these types of expenses. The planner can simply state that the IRA/retirement plan assets will not participate in payment of these expenses. What happens if this issue was not addressed in the planning stage (i.e., crops up after death):

- As an initial matter, the IRS has never formally (or informally through a private letter ruling), disqualified a trust based on its ability to pay these expenses of the decedent's estate.
- There are multiple private letter rulings which take the position that, so long as the IRA is protected from claims of creditors, the estate could not be considered a beneficiary of the trust because the trustee could not be forced by the personal representative to participate in payment of expenses. *See* LRs 200209057, 2004440031 and 200750019.
- In the estate administration process, the estate could be removed as a potential beneficiary simply by having its participation in these types of expenses completed or released by the September 30th date.
- PLRs 200432027, 029 and 031 did not disqualify a trust simply because the retirement benefits remained subject to payment of estate taxes after the September 30th date.

Allocation to Subtrusts. What if the beneficiary of the account is a trust which, pursuant to the terms of said trust is to be divided among subtrusts? Reg. 1.401(a)(9)-4QA5(d) tells us that the qualified trust requirements as well as the basket of beneficiaries issue must be analyzed with respect to each subtrust to which benefits may be allocated. What if the trust contains language stating that it is the decedent's intent that, to the extent possible, retirement benefits be allocated to one particular subtrust over another? (LR 199903050 still required all possible recipient trusts to be analyzed whereas LR 200620026 required only the favored trust to be so analyzed.)

As described above, Reg. 1.401(a)(9)-4QA5(c) makes clear that separate account treatment is not available for beneficiaries of a trust. This is an important rule for the planner to pay attention to:

- If the account is payable to a living trust and a living trust is ultimately distributed outright to the decedent's children, the analysis is as follows: First, the trust will need to be a qualified trust. Second, the basket of beneficiaries will be the decedent's children (assuming no other beneficiaries of the revocable trust). Thus, at the conclusion of trust administration, the trustee can direct the IRA custodian to create separate inherited IRAs from the decedent's IRA; one for each of the decedent's children. However, RMDs for each of these inherited IRAs will be determined with reference to the life expectancy of the oldest child. (*See* LRs 200634068, 200750019).

  Of course, this result could be avoided by naming the decedent's children as outright beneficiaries of the IRA, in which case, they could divide the IRA after death to obtain separate account treatment under which each of their respective life expectancies would be used for their respective inherited IRAs.

- What if the revocable living trust breaks into separate trusts for the decedent's children following the decedent's death? As described above, if the revocable living trust is the designated beneficiary, both the revocable living trust and each child's subtrust must be analyzed under the above trust rules for RMD purposes. However, because the revocable living trust itself is named, even if the children are deemed to be the sole beneficiaries, true separate account treatment will not be obtained. The trustee will be able to cause creation of separate inherited IRAs; one for each subtrust. However, RMDs with respect to each said IRA will be determined with reference to the life expectancy of the oldest child of the decedent.

  The way to create pure separate account treatment under the above scenario would be more specificity in the beneficiary designation. If the beneficiary designation requires the account be divided into separate accounts in accordance with the separate account rules; one for each of the trusts under the revocable living trust, then RMDs from each inherited IRA will be calculated with reference to the life expectancy of the child beneficiary of the trust to which it is payable (assuming, with respect to each said trust, the child is the RMD beneficiary under the rules described in this outline, above).

- Remember, an estate is a bad beneficiary. For example, if the decedent names an estate as beneficiary and the Will provides that the estate is to be divided into separate trusts for the decedent's children, the results would be as follows: The personal representative of the estate could cause the custodian to divide the IRA into separate inherited IRAs; one for each trust. However, RMDs for each trust will be calculated as though the estate is the beneficiary (Five Year Rule if the account holder died before his or her required beginning date; remaining unrecalculated life expectancy of the account holder if the account holder died after such date).

  A better result could be obtained as follows: The beneficiary designation would require that the IRA be divided into separate accounts; each payable to the trust established for the child under the decedent's Will. Assuming each said trust complies with all the trust rules described above, and that the accounts are divided as required for separate account treatment, RMDs from each separate inherited IRA will be calculated with reference to the child beneficiary of the trust.

- What if the decedent wants there to be multiple trusts for each child (e.g., GSTT exempt/GSTT non-exempt)? Here is how to plan for this scenario: The Will or revocable living trust could pass the trust balance (or estate residue) to a single trust which will be divided between the GSTT exempt and GSTT non-exempt portion. Thereafter, each child will have a GSTT exempt and non-exempt trust. If this overall trust is named as beneficiary, and the trust rules described above are complied with for the overall and each underlying trust, the oldest child of the decedent will be treated as the RMD beneficiary for each and every GSTT exempt and non-exempt trust so created. Although this may not be the optimal result for RMD purposes, it does provide significant flexibility by adding the retirement benefits to the "pot" for division between a GSTT exempt and non-exempt share.

- **Reformation.**

Three Private Letter Rulings (LRs 200616039, 200616040 and 200616041) involved a fact pattern under which the husband had an IRA of which he had designated his wife as primary beneficiary and his daughters as contingent beneficiaries. The husband rolled the IRA to a new custodian and directed the custodian to complete the beneficiary designations as with the previous IRA.

The husband died after his required beginning date and the wife died soon afterward. Shortly thereafter, the wife's estate disclaimed the wife's interest as primary beneficiary of the husband's IRA.

Because the second IRA custodian had not followed the husband's instructions, his daughters were not named contingent beneficiaries. Therefore, after the disclaimer, the State Court reformed the beneficiary designation to include the daughters as contingent beneficiaries. The reformation was based, in part, on an affidavit from the second IRA custodian stating that the husband's instructions that the second IRA be set up exactly like the first IRA had not been followed.

Thereafter, the IRA custodian created two new f/b/o IRAs; one for each daughter.

The IRA approved (i) the disclaimer, (ii) the establishment of the two f/b/o IRAs by way of IRA-to-IRA transfer and (iii) each daughter's ability to compute RMDs over the life expectancy of the oldest daughter.

Of course, it is very beneficial that the IRS recognized the reformation of the beneficiary designation.

However, there are a couple of observations about these Letter Rulings:

- These rulings may be incorrect with regard to the use of the oldest daughter's life expectancy for RMD purposes. The LR cites the language in the §401(a)(9) regulations that states that a person's disclaimer between the date of death and the September 30th date, eliminates the disclaimant as an RMD beneficiary. What the reviewer may have missed, however, is additional language in the regulations that states that a person who dies after the account holder but before the September 30th date without disclaiming, continues to be treated as the beneficiary as of the September 30 date without regard to the identity of the successor beneficiary. Reg. 1.401(a)(9)-4Q-4A-4(c). In other words, the correct answer was that the separate accounts could be established, but RMDs would be required over the deceased wife's life expectancy.

- Another interesting point is as follows: Even if the IRS were correct with regard to its conclusion that the disclaimer by the wife's estate changed the beneficiaries to the daughters, it was incorrect in the conclusion that the life expectancy of the oldest daughter should be used. It appears that separate IRAs were created so that use of each daughter's life expectancies would have been permitted.

PLR 200707158 was a nasty situation. The account holder had two cousins (Cousin A and Cousin B). The account holder designated cousin A's three children as beneficiaries of an IRA. After the account holder's death, separate fbo or inherited IRAs were set up for each of Cousin A's children. Cousin B sued Cousin A and his children arguing undue influence. After conducting discovery and proceeding towards trial, a settlement was reached and court approved. A judgment reformed the IRA beneficiary designation effective the date before the account holder's death so that Cousin B would be the beneficiary of the IRA. In the private letter ruling, the IRS confirmed that (i) the settlement did not constitute a taxable gift by Cousin A's children to Cousin B, (ii) the transfer of the three inherited IRAs of Cousin A's children to an inherited IRA for Cousin B pursuant to the settlement agreement, was not taxable and (iii) Cousin B would be taxed on distributions from his IRA in the future.

In PLR 200742026, the account holder maintained an IRA with a beneficiary designation naming his wife as primary beneficiary and daughter as secondary beneficiary. On a subsequent beneficiary designation, the account holder again named his wife as primary beneficiary but, in spite of a reminder from the IRA custodian, neglected to complete the secondary beneficiary. The account holder died before signing the new form. There were two other very bad facts: (i) the account holder's spouse predeceased him and (ii) the custodial account agreement provided that, absent a designated beneficiary, the estate became the beneficiary.

> The account holder's daughter was the sole beneficiary of the account holder's estate. In the process of the probate, the account holder's daughter obtained a court order amending the IRA beneficiary designation to name the daughter as beneficiary of the IRA.
>
> The IRS cited Reg. 1.401(a)(9)-4, QA-1 which states that:
>
> A designated beneficiary is an individual designated as a beneficiary under the terms of the IRA or by an affirmative election of the IRA owner. Moreover, the fact that an IRA owner's interest passes to a certain individual under a Will or under *otherwise applicable state law*, does not make the individual a designated beneficiary . . .

The IRS concluded that, because there was no designated individual beneficiary under the above rules and the account holder died after the required beginning date, the RMDs will be computed with reference to the account holder's life expectancy. In other words, the court reformation was ignored.

- LR 200846028. The account holder of an IRA died before his required beginning date. The account holder's beneficiary designation stated that the beneficiary was: *as stated in Wills*.

  The account holder's estate plan was designed around a revocable living trust. Thus, the account holder had a pour-over Will.

  Under the revocable living trust, specific bequests of real estate were made to certain beneficiaries and the balance of the trust was to be divided and distributed among eight individuals.

  The trustee pursued and received a state court order interpreting the beneficiary designation as a designation of the eight individual beneficiaries of the revocable living trust. In short, the court order had the effect of moving the beneficiaries of the revocable living trust into the IRA beneficiary designation as though they were direct beneficiaries under the IRA beneficiary designation.

  Of course, the stakes of this private letter ruling were high. If the state court order was recognized by the IRS, the eight beneficiaries could each have separate IRAs and take RMDs over the life expectancy of the oldest such beneficiary. If, on the other hand, the language of the beneficiary designation was interpreted to specify the estate as beneficiary, the entire IRA must be distributed within five years of the date of the decedent's death.

The IRS relied heavily on Reg. 1.401(a)(9)-4QA1 which states as follows:

The fact that an account passes to individuals under a will or otherwise under applicable state law does not make that individual a designated beneficiary unless the individual is designated as a beneficiary under the plan.

Relying on the above, the IRS said that the court order was meaningless for RMD purposes. Therefore, the estate would be treated as beneficiary and the five-year rule applies.

- PLR 201021038. Bad news for estate planners – IRS refuses to recognize trust reformation for RMD purposes. The key facts involved in this private letter ruling were as follows: Husband was the IRA account holder. Wife had predeceased husband. At wife's death, a bypass trust was created for husband with wife's assets. The bypass trust provided that, upon husband's death, the trust would be divided into two equal trusts; one for each of the couple's children ("children's trusts"). The children's trusts were lifetime trusts under which the child/trustee could make distributions of income and principal based on MESH and an independent trustee could make distributions to the child's descendants. Each child had a lifetime and testamentary special power of appointment ("SPOA") under which permissible distributes included charities. The children's trusts were not structured as conduit trusts. Nor was there any appropriate "firewall language" necessary for accumulation trusts under the RMD rules.

  However, there was an odd statement of intent under which the trustor clearly desired "stretch out" treatment under which RMDs from the IRA to the trusts would be computed over as long a period as permissible. The problem with this language, however, is that it was not specific as to whose life expectancy should be used nor was the trustee given any authority to amend the trust.

  Husband died with the bypass trust named as beneficiary of the IRA. He died after his required beginning date. After the husband's death, the trustees filed for and obtained a retroactive court-ordered trust amendment which essentially did two things: First, the children's trusts were converted to "conduit trusts" under which IRA distributions to the trusts could not be accumulated. Rather, any distributions from the IRA would have to be distributed to the child/beneficiary. Second, "firewall" language was added so as to (i) remove charities from the appointees under the SPOAs, (ii) prohibit use of IRA funds to pay debts and administration expenses, etc., and (iii) prohibit distribution of IRA funds to descendants older than the oldest child.

  It is interesting to note that had either approach been taken prior to death, such approach would have worked. In other words, the approach taken in the reformation was a bit of "belt and suspenders".

The IRS took a hard line. Citing case law authority for the proposition that a reformation of a trust is not effective to change the tax consequences of a completed transaction, the IRS refused to recognize the trust reformation. As a result, it concluded that, without the reformation:

- Amounts distributed from the IRA to the children's trusts could be accumulated; and,

- To these accumulations, charitable organizations are clearly authorized as possible beneficiaries.

As a result of the above, the IRS concluded that, for RMD purposes, there was no designated beneficiary which would mean that the RMDs to the trusts must be distributed over the period of the husband's remaining life expectancy. This all points to a troubling trend.

For a while, the IRS seemed relatively willing to allow post-mortem corrections to RMD situations. In PLRs 200616039 through 41, the IRS approved a reformation which actually designated a contingent beneficiary. More recently, however, the IRS refused to recognize a contingent beneficiary created by reformation. PLR 200742026. In PLR 200846028, the IRS refused to recognize a reformation of somewhat ambiguous language in a beneficiary designation and, instead, treated the decedent's estate as beneficiary.

Previous private letter rulings have allowed trust reformations for RMD purposes. See Commentary Number 136, PLRs 200235038 through 200235041 – minimum distributions and trusts, Steve Leimberg's employee benefit and retirement planning newsletter, September 23, 2002. It now appears that, at least the rulings department is taking a harder line with regard to reformations. This position may be at odds with the September 30th "shake out" date concept. If a beneficiary can be eliminated for RMD purposes between death and the shake out date, why can't a trust reformation occur which effectively eliminates charities, decedent's estates and beneficiaries over a certain age?

In light of this private letter ruling, the best advice to practitioners is as follows:

- Take great care in drafting a trust that will be the beneficiary of an IRA or retirement plan account. You must make certain that you qualify the trust as a "qualified trust" under the regulations and incorporate either the conduit trust approach or appropriate firewall language. (This is really nothing new, but due to the IRS's antagonism towards post-death reformations, it is even more important.)

- If one of these scenarios lands in your lap post-death, you need to advise the client that the conservative approach would be that the situation cannot be fixed through a post-death reformation. However, bear in mind that a private letter ruling such as that discussed above is not necessarily the outcome if the matter were to be litigated. A more aggressive client might decide to reform the trust but not submit for a private letter ruling. If this is the case, you need to advise such client of the 50% penalty under IRC § 4974 for failure to take the full RMD in any particular year.

- PLR 201008049. In this case, the designated IRA beneficiary lost the right to his benefits under a states slayer statute. Apparently, there was not a contingent beneficiary so the court ordered that, pursuant to the decedent's will, a "rightful beneficiary" was the taker.

Even though the slayer statute treats the slayer as having predeceased the decedent, the decedent did not actually predecease for RMD purposes, the slayer's life expectancy will be used for RMD purposes. However, the 50% penalty for failure of the rightful beneficiary to take RMDs (as she did not control the IRA through the course of the estate's litigation) and the negligence penalty were waived as well.

(j) Beneficiary's right to name a beneficiary/transfer account

Assume that both husband and wife have died and a child is the beneficiary of a "stretch-out" IRA. As discussed above, minimum distributions will be computed with reference to the child's life expectancy. If the plan or IRA document so provides, the beneficiary may designate who will receive the undistributed account following the beneficiary's death. The recipient would be subject to the same minimum distribution rules as the deceased beneficiary. Treas. Reg. § 1.401(a)(9)-5, Q-7, A-7(c)(2).

Moreover, even though the surviving spouse is the only beneficiary who may roll over an IRA (and therefore restart the minimum distribution rules), a nonspouse individual beneficiary may transfer the decedent's IRA from one custodian to another in a direct IRA-to-IRA transfer as long as the account remains in the decedent's name "f/b/o" the beneficiary, and the minimum distribution rules applicable to that account do not change. *See* Priv. Ltr. Rul. 2000-2408-044 (Dec. 3, 1999). As well, a formally unsegregated IRA may be segregated by the beneficiaries, and custodian-to-custodian transfers may thereafter occur with respect to the segregated IRAs. *Id.* The ability to transfer from one IRA custodian to another can be quite valuable. If one institution will not work efficiently with the family (i.e., permitting a beneficiary to designate a death beneficiary, etc.), the account may be moved in a trustee-to-trustee transfer. It is interesting that there is no code section permitting the trustee-to-trustee transfer, for this power comes solely from the regulations. Treas. Reg. 1.408-8, A-8. Again, the key to the trustee-to-trustee transfer is that the funds may not be distributed to the IRA beneficiary.

In Private Letter Ruling 2003-43-030 (July 31, 2003), the decedent (who died after his required beginning date) died without designating a beneficiary of his IRA. Under the IRA custodial account agreement, the decedent's estate was the beneficiary. The decedent's three children were equal residual beneficiaries of the estate. A daughter asked the I.R.S. to approve the segregation of her one-third share of the IRA and a subsequent IRA-to-IRA transfer to a new IRA custodian. The I.R.S. permitted the segregation and the IRA-to-IRA transfer, provided, however, that this process did not result in a "stretch-out." Rather, the daughter was required to take minimum distributions over the decedent father's remaining life expectancy.

In another ruling, a son was named as beneficiary of his deceased mother's IRA. Mistakenly, following his mother's death, the IRA was distributed to the son and a Form 1099-R (Distributions From Pensions, Annuities, Retirement or Profit-Sharing Plans, IRAs, Insurance Contracts, etc.) was issued to the son. Immediately the son transferred the funds to an IRA at another financial institution in the name of the mother, deceased account holder for the benefit of the son. The I.R.S. ruled that even though the financial institutions involved later agreed to treat the entire transaction as an IRA-to-IRA transfer, the son would be taxed on the IRA. Priv. Ltr. Rul.

2002-28-023 (Apr. 15, 2002). This error stresses the importance of a nonspouse beneficiary never touching IRA funds when the IRA is moved from one institution to another.

In yet another ruling, a taxpayer instructed the administrators of his retirement plan to liquidate his account and directly transfer the proceeds to an IRA in the taxpayer's name. All of the paperwork necessary to complete this transaction was submitted to the Plan Administrator. Before liquidation of the assets and the transfer could occur, however, the taxpayer died. The taxpayer's nonspouse beneficiaries requested a ruling that would permit the direct rollover to occur because all the paperwork had been concluded before the taxpayer's death. The I.R.S. ruled that the rollover could not occur. In short, the Service concluded that for the rollover to be valid, all of the steps, including the actual transfer of assets, would have to have taken place while the taxpayer is alive. Priv. Ltr. Rul. 2002-04-038 (Oct. 30, 2001).

In one case, the account holder of an IRA removed the funds from his IRA and transferred them into a nonqualified annuity through American Express Life Insurance Company. Of course, the following year he received an I.R.S. Form 1099-R reporting the amount as income. The taxpayer did not report the income on his return. After the I.R.S. contacted the taxpayer, the financial institution prepared a corrected Form 1099-R and moved the annuity funds into a qualified IRA annuity. The Tax Court had no sympathy for the taxpayer and held that the corrective action was not sufficient, thus requiring the taxpayer to include the amount in his income in the year of withdrawal. *Crow v. Comm'r*, 84 T.C.M. (CCH) 91 (2002).

Note that the above disallowed IRA rollovers (except possibly the *Crow* case) would not likely be treated more favorably by a "kinder and gentler" I.R.S., which now has the authority to grant "waivers" for failure to meet the 60-day deadline for reasons of "hardship," as described in Revenue Procedure 2003-16, 2003-1 C.B. 359. *E.g.*, Priv. Ltr. Rul. 2004-07-023 (Nov. 7, 2003); Priv. Ltr. Rul. 2004-07-025 (Nov. 17, 2003); Priv. Ltr. Rul. 2004-04-056 (Oct. 27, 2003). The "waiver" rulings deal with fact patterns where the recipient could make the rollover, but did not do so correctly or in a timely manner. Nonspouse death beneficiaries cannot do a rollover in the first place.

(k) Non-Spouse "Rollover"

Prior to the Pension Protection Act of 2006, a surviving spouse beneficiary of a qualified retirement plan could roll the decedent's account into an IRA in the surviving spouse's name. However, only the surviving spouse was permitted this opportunity. The new law permits a "rollover" by non-spouse beneficiary of a retirement plan account to an "f/b/o IRA." The f/b/o IRA will then be subject to the RMD rules applicable to non-spouse beneficiaries. If a trust is the beneficiary of the retirement plan, the trust may complete such a rollover. The trust must be a "Qualified Trust" under the § 401(a)(9) regulations to do so.

Under IRC § 402(f)(2)(A), beginning in 2010, retirement plans are required to offer the non-spouse rollover.

- The IRS issued Notice 2007-7 to provide some additional detail concerning non-spouse rollovers. According to the Notice:

- The retirement plan does not have to offer the non-spouse rollover option. This is surprising (and perhaps wrong) in light of the wording of the new statute. IRC § 402(c)(11)(A) which was amended by the 2008 Pension Act requires tax-qualified retirement plans to offer the non-spouse rollover for plan years beginning after December 31, 2009. Until then, offering the non-spouse rollover is up to the sponsoring employer.

- The recipient IRA must be established in a manner that identifies the deceased individual and the beneficiary (i.e., "Tom Smith as beneficiary of John Smith").

- If a trust is the beneficiary and wishes to complete the non-spouse rollover, the Notice states that said trust must meet the requirements of a qualified trust of 1.401(a)(9)-4Q&A-5.

- Unfortunately, the Notice takes the position that the RMD rules applicable to the non-spouse beneficiary under the retirement plan will likewise apply with regard to the IRA. This will not make a difference if the decedent dies after his or her RBD (note, however, that many plans postpone the RBD to actual retirement for employees who are not 5% owners).

  If the decedent dies before the RBD, and the terms of the plan have elected the five-year RMD rule, according to the Notice, the beneficiary cannot get out of the five-year rule by completing the non-spouse rollover. For example, the plan might state that, following death, the beneficiary must take a lump sum distribution sometime before the end of the fifth calendar year following death. This would be viewed as an election of the five-year rule by the plan which apparently could not be changed by the non-spouse rollover.

  In IRS employee plan news issued on February 13, 2007, there was a softening of the foregoing point. If, under the plan, the five-year rule applies for determining RMDs because the account holder died before his or her required beginning date and the plan in question has elected the five-year rule, the non-spouse beneficiary may escape the five-year rule if (i) the plan allows the non-spouse rollover and (ii) the rollover is completed before the end of the calendar year following the calendar year of the participant's death.

In PLR 200717022, the IRS stated that, for the non-spouse rollover rules to apply, a plan need only be amended in time to permit the rollover. In other words, having the language in the plan at the time of the account holder's death should not be required.

(l) Excess distributions

If amounts are distributed in any calendar year in excess of the minimum required distribution, no credit will be given in subsequent years for that distribution. Treas. Reg. § 1.401(a)(9)-5, Q-2, A-2. However, when a distribution is actually made to the participant during the first distribution calendar year (rather than on the succeeding April 1), amounts so distributed will be credited toward the required distribution to be made on or before the participant's required beginning date.

(m) Penalties for failure to meet MDIB

There are penalties for failing to meet the minimum required distribution under both the minimum distribution incidental benefit (MDIB) and the minimum distribution rules. The 1986 Act amended § 4974 to impose on the payee, effective in 1989, a 50 percent tax on the amount by which the retirement plan fails to satisfy the minimum distribution rule or the MDIB. The penalty may be waived if the shortfall was due to reasonable error. Treas. Reg. § 54.4974-2, Q-7, A-7.

Under prior instructions to IRS Form 5329, the 50% penalty of IRC § 4974(a) for failure to timely withdraw an RMD could be waived for reasonable cause (defined in the regulations), but only if the failure was reported on IRS Form 5329 and accompanied by payment of the penalty amount. In other words, the IRS got the money first and the reasonable cause waiver was really in the form of a request for a refund. Under the revised instructions issued for the 2007 5329, a waiver request may be made on Form 5329 without payment of the penalty amount.

(n) Liquidity planning

From the tax and investment perspectives, it is generally desirable to take full advantage of the I.R.C. § 401(a)(9) rules in order to maximize the income-tax-deferred growth of the account. A prudent plan gives the working spouse, nonworking spouse, and the couple's children the flexibility to take minimum distributions over the maximum time period allowed under I.R.C. § 401(a)(9). The rules of § 401(a)(9), however, allow income, but not estate tax, deferral. With proper planning, described below, the estate tax marital deduction will be allowable with respect to the account. Thus, no estate tax will be due on an account until the death of the surviving spouse.

Upon the death of the surviving spouse, the rules of I.R.C. § 401(a)(9) may allow the beneficiaries to defer distributions for a significant additional period. However, the beneficiaries may be required to withdraw a substantial portion of the account if there is no other source of funds available to pay the estate taxes. Withdrawals are, of course, subject to the imposition of income taxes. Accordingly, clients often wish to provide another source of liquid assets with which to pay estate taxes on the death of the surviving spouse. A common source is an irrevocable life insurance trust that holds second-to-die policies of insurance on the lives of the spouses.

(2) Income in respect of a decedent (IRD)

Both the right to a lump sum distribution and the right to an installment or annuity payout are treated as income in respect of a decedent (IRD) under I.R.C. § 691. M. Carr Ferguson et al., FED. INCOME TAX'N OF ESTATES, TRUSTS AND BENEFICIARIES (3d ed. 1998 & Supp. 2005). As a general rule, IRD is taxed to the recipient in the year of receipt. I.R.C. § 691(a)(1). However, the imposition of the income tax is accelerated if an IRD item is transferred within the meaning of I.R.C. § 691(a)(2). The rule constitutes a serious trap that the planner must take into account. The transfer of an item of IRD in satisfaction of a pecuniary bequest, including a formula marital deduction bequest, may subject the item to the income tax.

A recipient who includes a retirement PLAN distribution in gross income is allowed an income tax deduction to the extent the distribution gave rise to an estate tax. I.R.C. § 691(c). However, if the death distribution is a lump sum distribution, the deduction reduces the amount subject to special income tax averaging. I.R.C. § 691(c)(5).

(3) Early distribution penalty, I.R.C. § 72(t)

Distributions made before the working spouse attains the age of 59 1/2 are generally subject to a 10 percent penalty under I.R.C. § 72(t). However, distributions made to the participant's death beneficiary are not subject to the penalty. I.R.C. § 72(t)(2)(A)(ii). This is true even if distributions are made to the beneficiary in installments from the deceased participant's account. Priv. Ltr. Rul. 90-04 -042 (Nov. 6, 1989). This is also true even when the surviving spouse transfers the deceased's interest to an IRA in the deceased's name and commences distributions as beneficiary (rather than owner) of the IRA. Priv. Ltr. Rul. 94-18-034 (Feb. 10, 1994). In Private Letter Ruling 2001-10-033 (Dec. 13, 2000), the I.R.S. permitted a surviving spouse to roll over the decedent's IRA more than two years after the decedent's death and after the surviving spouse had taken distributions from the decedent's IRA under the exemption from the 10 percent penalty. *See also Charlotte and Charles T. Gee*, 127 T.C. 2006. *However*, if a surviving spouse under 59 1/2 years of age is the death beneficiary and rolls the funds into an IRA in his or her name, subsequent distributions from the IRA are subject to the 10 percent penalty tax. The penalty may be avoided, however, with proper planning under the equal payment exception of I.R.C. § 72(t)(2)(A)(iv). Under that provision the penalty tax does not apply to a distribution that is made as part of a series of substantially equal periodic distributions, made annually or more frequently, for the life or the life expectancy of the participant or for the joint lives or joint life expectancies of the participant and his or her designated beneficiary. What constitutes a series of substantially equal periodic payments is defined in I.R.S. Notice 89-25, 1989-1 C.B. 662.

(4) Roth IRAs/§ 401(k) Accounts

A detailed discussion of Roth Accounts is beyond the scope of this chapter. However, Roth Accounts differ greatly from regular IRAs and § 401(k) Accounts in three key respects: (1) contributions to Roth Accounts are made on an after-tax basis; (2) qualified distributions from Roth Accounts are income tax-free; and (3) no minimum distributions from a Roth IRA are required during the joint lifetime of the account holder and the account holder's spouse, if the surviving spouse effectuates a rollover, so that minimum distributions only begin after the death of the Roth IRA account holder and spouse. I.R.C. § 408A(a); I.R.C. § 408A(e); I.R.C. § 408(A)(d)(3)(E)(ii). In sum, an individual can, within the Roth IRA rules of § 408A and Roth § 401(k) rules, establish a Roth Account with after-tax contributions, allow those contributions to grow on an income-tax-free basis, defer distributions until the death of the individual and his or her spouse and, when minimum distributions commence to the couple's children, they will be income tax free so that the growth on the Roth Account is never subject to income tax.

A key element of Roth planning is the ability to convert a regular IRA to a Roth IRA. Under the Roth IRA rules, an individual with a regular IRA who meets the income limitation described below may cause all or any portion of the IRA to be distributed from the regular IRA and thereafter contributed to a Roth IRA. There is no limit on the amount that may be so converted. The conversion, of course, triggers income tax on the regular IRA distribution. Roth IRA conversions are not subject to the 10 percent penalty of I.R.C. §72(t). I.R.C. §408A(d)(3)(A)(ii). However, as a condition for escaping the 10 percent penalty, the taxpayer may not take distributions from the Roth IRA for a period of five years. I.R.C. §408A(d)(3)(F). The key requirement for the Roth conversion is that the taxpayer's adjusted gross income for the taxable year of conversion may not exceed the limit of I.R.C. §408A(c)(3)(B). Required minimum distributions will be disregarded in computing this limit. I.R.C. § 408A(c)(3)(C)(i)(II). Moreover, after 2009, the income ceiling for Roth conversions is repealed so that any taxpayer may make a Roth conversion. Also, for conversions occurring in 2010, the income caused by the conversion will be taxed one-half in 2011 and one-half in 2012.

The most attractive element of a Roth conversion is the fact that the legislation allows the income tax resulting from a conversion to be paid with funds other than the converted IRA. In a sense, through the Roth IRA conversion process, Congress is allowing the taxpayer to contribute to the Roth IRA the income tax liability associated with the regular IRA. Stated another way, the entire converted IRA, as opposed to the converted IRA net of income tax, is allowed to pick up the Roth IRA benefits (e.g., no minimum distributions and no income tax on distributions). For this reason alone, individuals with significant wealth inside and outside a regular IRA and who have the ability to keep their adjusted gross income within the required conversion limits should consider a Roth conversion.

The Roth conversion may be an excellent planning tool in many circumstances. In the case of an individual who has significant wealth both inside and outside the IRA and who has not yet reached his required beginning date, a Roth conversion may be attractive. By capturing the income tax liability on the IRA at an early date, deferring minimum distributions until the death of the second spouse, and allowing all tax-free buildup to escape income taxation altogether in the hands of the children, the conversion may create the greatest economic benefit to the family.

Under rules pertaining to §401(k) plans, if the §401(k) plan so permits, the participant may designate that all or any portion of his or her §401(k) salary reduction contribution be treated as a Roth contribution. Unlike Roth IRA conversions which have an income ceiling through 2009, there is no income ceiling with regard to Roth §401(k) contributions. A Roth §401(k) account is treated the same as a Roth IRA with the exception that RMDs are required during the account holder's lifetime. Of course, the RMDs could be escaped by taking a distribution from the Roth §401(k) and rolling it into a Roth IRA. Moreover, under the Pension Protection Act of 2006, an individual may complete a Roth conversion by directing a rollover from a regular qualified retirement plan account (including a §401(k), §403(b) or §457(f) plan) directly into a Roth IRA. This applies for tax years after December 31, 2007 and, for 2007 through 2009, will be subject to the income ceiling described above.

As mentioned above, effective in 2010, the rules for converting a regular IRA to a Roth IRA have been liberalized. Under current law, a regular IRA can be converted to a Roth IRA or a non-spouse beneficiary of a retirement plan may roll into a Roth IRA. The conversion of an IRA (or non-spouse rollover) will trigger income in the year of conversion in the amount of the converted account. Prior to 2010, taxpayers with adjusted gross income in excess of $100,000 could not make a Roth conversion or non-spouse rollover. Effective in 2010, the income ceiling is repealed. Moreover, for IRA conversions occurring in 2010, the income caused by the conversion will be taxed one-half in 2011 and one-half in 2012 (or, at the taxpayer's election, be included as 2010 income). If the taxpayer is under $59^1/2$ years of age, the income from the conversion will not be subject to the 10% penalty of IRC §72(t), so long as the tax on conversion is paid with funds outside the IRA. Under current law, an inherited IRA may not be converted to a Roth IRA, although this will likely be changed. Post-conversion, only "qualified distributions" may be taken from the Roth account on a tax favored basis. Qualified distributions are those made after the taxpayer is $59^1/2$, distributions made to a death beneficiary, distributions attributable to the taxpayer's disability or distributions that qualify for certain special purposes (e.g., first time home buyer). IRC §408A(d)(2)(A). However, any distributions within five years of a contribution to a Roth IRA or conversion of a Roth IRA will not be qualified distributions. See 408A(d)(2)(B) for the calculations of this five (5) year period. Amazingly, the Roth IRA rules do not create an exception to this five-year rule in the case of death. A non-qualified distribution is one that either fails to satisfy the five-year rule or the triggering event requirement. If non-qualified distributions are made, there is no tax until the total amount initially contributed by the taxpayer has been returned to the taxpayer. However, under §408A(d)(3)(F) there may be a 10% penalty on amounts withdrawn within five (5) years of a conversion by a taxpayer who is under $59^1/2$.

A taxpayer who converts a regular to a Roth IRA may later change his mind and "undo" the conversion. If the taxpayer changes his mind about the conversion (i.e., the value of the IRA declines post-conversion), generally, the deadline for a Roth IRA conversion to be recharacterized to a regular IRA is the due date, including extension of the taxpayer's 1040 (or, October 15 of the year following the conversion). The law does not permit "cherry picking" recharacterization within a single IRA. Thus, a smart Roth strategy is to segregate different investments into different traditional IRAs by way of IRA-to-IRA transfers before the conversion occurs. Thereafter, each separate IRA holding separate types of investment funds or investments will be converted. Under current law, each separate IRA may be left converted or recharacterized on a "pick and choose" basis by the October 15th deadline giving the taxpayer significant flexibility. Remember, if a taxpayer is over $70^1/2$ and beyond his/her required beginning date, the RMD for the calendar year in question may not be converted to a Roth IRA. Rather, it must be distributed before the conversion.

Of course, the decision to convert a regular IRA to a Roth IRA is tricky. Of course, the longer the Roth account remains undisturbed, the more likely there will be a benefit to the conversion. Therefore, conversions while husband and wife are both alive and with a joint life expectancy of at least 15 years, can make a lot of sense; provided they will not have a need for the funds. Conversion in years where a taxpayer will be in a low income tax bracket or has business or other ordinary losses also makes sense, so long as there is no near term need for the funds. Conversion should also be considered in years where a taxpayer might make large charitable contributions. One might even consider conversion close to death if the converted

IRA will be left to a generation-skipping trust for grandchildren which is a "qualified trust". By doing this, the income tax will be removed from the estate and, if the trust is properly structured, RMDs from the account will be measured based on the grandchild's life expectancy.

There is a misconception that estate planning with Roth IRAs is easier than with regular IRAs. These guidelines should be considered:

- Of course, Roth accounts should be left to a surviving spouse so as to permit the rollover and avoid any lifetime RMDs.

- Roth accounts left to a credit shelter trust or a Q-Tip trust are a bit of a waste as the tax-free growth will be shut down fairly rapidly (i.e., based on the life expectancy of the surviving spouse). In short, no stretch out will be available under this scenario.

- As with traditional IRAs, it should be possible with proper planning, to use a non-pro rata division of the community property to have the Roth pass to the surviving spouse in exchange for other assets passing to a credit shelter trust.

- Roth accounts left to children will be subject to the same RMD rules as regular IRAs. That is, smart planning suggests creation of separate accounts post-death and stretch out RMDs keyed to each beneficiary's life expectancy under Treasury regulations.

- Trusts which are beneficiaries of Roth accounts need to be structured as "conduit trusts" or accumulation trusts with appropriate firewall language so that RMDs will be computed with reference to the trust beneficiary's life expectancy. In other words, all of the RMD complexities of trusts as IRA beneficiaries apply to Roth IRAs in the same way as regular IRAs. Remember, even though qualified distributions to a trust from a Roth IRA will not be income for tax purposes, a portion will be income for fiduciary accounting purposes.

- An estate should not be the designated beneficiary of a Roth account. This is because the post-death RMDs will be calculated with reference to the deceased account holder's remaining life expectancy.

- Unlike traditional IRAs, Roths should not be left to charity because the income tax has already been paid.

§13.3 ESTATE TAX

On the death of the working spouse, his or her community property interest in the account is includible in his or her gross estate under I.R.C. § 2039. However, if his or her interest passes to the surviving spouse, it may qualify for a marital deduction under I.R.C. § 2056. The key planning question is how the included amounts will be coordinated with the client's estate plan. Generally, the surviving spouse will roll over the account to an IRA. This will defer the estate taxes on the funds until the surviving spouse's death.

At the current time, the status of our estate tax laws is in a state of flux. For the years 2011 and 2012, the death tax exemption under IRC § 2010 is $5 million. Thereafter, it is anyone's guess as to the future of the estate tax.

- The high death tax credit means it is more likely that clients wishing to fully fund the credit shelter trust of the first spouse to die may need to involve their retirement plans or IRAs.
- To preserve flexibility, it is likely that planners will rely heavily on disclaimers.
- Under IRC § 2010(c)(2) the unused death tax exemption of the first spouse to die may be transferred to the surviving spouse for use in his or her estate provided that an election is made in the estate of the first spouse to die. Under current law, this only applies if the first spouse dies in 2011 or 2012. This provision might be helpful for couples with large retirement accounts as the account could pass to the surviving spouse (instead of a credit shelter trust) without loss of the federal death tax exemption of the first spouse to die. Of course, this is not available for Washington state estate tax purposes.

Over the years, practitioners have questioned the inclusion of IRAs and retirement plan benefits in estate plans without some discount or adjustment for the income tax associated with those accounts on distribution following death. In Tech. Adv. Mem. 2002-47-002 (July 16, 2002), the I.R.S. explicitly rejected any such discount, even if the estate needed withdrawals to meet cash needs. Tech. Adv. Mem. 2004-44-021 (June 21, 2004). *See also Smith v. United States*, 391 F.3d 621 (5thCir. 2004) and *Estate of Davis Kahn,* (2005) 125 T.C. No. 11..

If the nonworking spouse is not a citizen of the United States, it is very difficult to obtain the income tax benefits of the rollover and the estate tax benefits of the estate tax marital deduction. First, the surviving spouse must be the beneficiary of an account to be able to roll it over into an IRA in her name. Second, to qualify for the marital deduction the arrangement must meet the requirements of I.R.C. § 2056A. In Private Letter Ruling 96-23-063 (Mar. 13, 1996), the surviving spouse, who was not a U.S. citizen, rolled over the decedent's account to an IRA in her name and entered into an agreement with the IRA custodian to comply with the I.R.C. § 2056A qualified domestic trust rules. The I.R.S. allowed the marital deduction. The qualified domestic trust (QDT) regulations contain specific rules concerning qualification of an IRA or retirement plan for QDT treatment. *E.g.,* Treas. Reg. 20.20 26A-4(b)(7)(iii).

(1) Disclaimer

Estate plans are often designed so that a qualified disclaimer under I.R.C. § 2518 may be used to modify a plan after the death of the transferor. For example, a client may wish to allow flexibility as to how much and exactly what assets will be used to fund a credit shelter trust. A client who wishes to leave this decision to his or her surviving spouse can leave everything outright to the surviving spouse and provide that any property that the surviving spouse disclaims will pass to a credit shelter trust. However, note that the surviving spouse can only disclaim the working spouse's share of an account — the surviving spouse cannot disclaim his or her own interest in it. The regulations specifically address the impact of disclaimer. Treas. Reg. § 1.401(a)(9)-4, Q-4, A-4(a) permits a change of beneficiary for minimum distribution purposes by reason of disclaimer.

Note that if the surviving spouse disclaims in favor of one or more of the couple's children, the minimum distributions will be driven by the beneficiaries resulting from the disclaimer. If the entire account is disclaimed in favor of the children, then the children are the only designated beneficiaries. If, by December 31 of the calendar year following death, the account is divided as per Treas. Reg. § 1.401(a)(9)-8, Q-2, A-2(a), the children will each have their own life expectancy to compute minimum distribution. The account could be so divided by the December 31 date to facilitate separate distribution periods and the spouse could rollover his or her portion of the account.

Qualified disclaimers of retirement plan benefits and IRAs require careful pre-death planning. In the context of an IRA, the practitioner should review the custodial account agreement itself to make sure a disclaimer will be recognized. Retirement plans involve issues of plan language as well as spousal rights under ERISA. The beneficiary designation should contemplate disclaimer or death of the surviving spouse. Thus, for example, the primary beneficiary could be the spouse, with the instruction that any portion disclaimed by the spouse would pass to the credit shelter trust, and the secondary beneficiary (to take in the event the spouse is deceased) would be the couple's children.

A question of key concern with respect to postmortem estate planning has been the interplay between the required minimum distribution (RMD) of a deceased account holder who had lived beyond his or her required beginning date and the concept of "acceptance" under the disclaimer regulations. For example, assume a widow, age 75, named her child as primary beneficiary of an IRA with a trust for a grandchild named as secondary beneficiary. Also assume that, in the calendar year of death, the widow had not taken her RMD. Now the child is contemplating disclaiming all or a part of his or her interest in favor of the trust for the grandchild. Under the disclaimer rules, absent an "acceptance," the child will be able to make the disclaimer decision as late as nine months after the widow's death. However, assume the widow died in December so that the RMD for the year of death must occur by the end of the year (long before the disclaimer decision must be made). The question is whether the RMD could be paid to the child without the child being deemed to have "accepted" the IRA, thus cutting off the disclaimer opportunity. According to Revenue Ruling 2005-36, 2005-26 I.R.B. 1368, the primary beneficiary may take the RMD without being deemed to have accepted the IRA. The ruling notes that the primary beneficiary should take both the RMD and postdeath earnings on the RMD amount.

Even after this Revenue Ruling, the planner should take care to avoid an "acceptance" in the processing of the RMD. Quite often, an IRA custodian will insist that, as a precedent to taking the RMD, the primary beneficiary must go through the process of changing the account from the decedent's name into a "beneficiary" or "f/b/o" account in the name of the primary beneficiary. Under the logic of the Revenue Ruling, this should not be a problem. However, this type of reregistration process should be avoided if possible.

If the IRA is later to be segregated into separate IRAs under the separate account rules, there does not need to be a reconciliation with regard to the RMD. In other words, the primary beneficiary may, in the I.R.S.'s eyes, retain the full RMD amount.

Although not explicit in the ruling, there is the possibility that a distribution taken by the primary beneficiary other than an RMD could be treated likewise. For example, under the logic of this ruling, the primary beneficiary could take a withdrawal from the IRA and be treated as having accepted that amount without accepting the entire IRA. Of course, to avoid a problem, the practitioner would clearly document with the custodian that only the distribution is being accepted.

The Revenue Ruling's results are not contingent upon whether a disclaimer is structured as a pecuniary or a fractional disclaimer. Either way, the primary beneficiary may retain the RMD (and postdeath earnings), yet disclaim a pecuniary amount or fraction of the underlying IRA.

Although not addressed in the ruling, the planner should give careful consideration to how the separate IRAs will be "funded" after disclaimer. For example, if there is a pecuniary disclaimer, the safest course of action may be a liquidation of the assets of the IRA so that the separate IRAs may be funded with actual dollar amounts. In the case of a fractional disclaimer, it may be safest to have the holdings of the IRA divided according to the fractions established through the disclaimer. Otherwise, the disclaimant might be viewed as having exercised control over the disclaimed assets following the disclaimer.

(2) Funding the credit trust; non-pro rata distribution planning

Under IRC § 2010(c)(2) the unused death tax exemption of the first spouse to die may be transferred to the surviving spouse for use in his or her estate provided that an election is made in the estate of the first spouse to die. Under current law, this only applies if the first spouse dies in 2011 or 2012 (and we do not know the future of this provision after 2012). This provision might be helpful for couples with large retirement accounts as the account could pass to the surviving spouse (instead of a credit shelter trust) without loss of the federal death tax exemption of the first spouse to die. Of course, this is not available for Washington state estate tax purposes.

Example: Assume Jim and Sally have $8 million of community property comprised of Jim's $6 million IRA and $2 million of other assets. Assume Jim's Will leaves his share of the probate community assets to a credit shelter trust for Sally's benefit and his IRA beneficiary designation names Sally as outright beneficiary. At Jim's death, Sally rolls the IRA into her name and Jim's $1 million interest in the other assets passes into a credit shelter trust for Sally's benefit. Also assume that an estate tax release is filed for Jim's estate transferring the unused exemption to Sally. When Sally dies, her estate will be $7 million comprised of her interest in the other assets ($1 million) plus the $6 million IRA. She will have her $5 million federal death tax exemption and, assuming Jim's estate made the proper election, she will have the balance of Jim's unused exemption ($4 million) for total exemptions of $9 million. Therefore, no federal estate tax will be owing. How this will all work after 2012 is yet to be determined.

Of course, another alternative to utilizing the death tax exemption of the first spouse to die yet, at the same time, allowing the retirement assets to pass to the surviving spouse is the non-pro rata funding technique described below.

Two Private Letter Rulings issued in 1999 provide excellent guidance for funding the credit shelter trust in a community property situation. Assume that the couple has a net worth which will subject the family to estate tax on the death of the second spouse (or, alternatively, that full use of the credit shelter amount of the first spouse to die will be necessary to prevent estate tax on the death of the second spouse). Also assume that a significant portion of the couple's net worth is in a rollover IRA. Upon the death of the account holder, the best tax outcome would result if all of the IRA were allocated to the surviving spouse for rollover and stretch out planning, and other assets of the community were used to fund the credit shelter trust. In a sense, the estate exchanges with the spouse a portion of the decedent's community interest in the IRA for the surviving spouse's interest in non-IRA community assets of an equivalent value.

In Private Letter Ruling 1999-25-033 (Mar. 25, 1999), an IRA was payable to a revocable living trust. The surviving spouse, as trustee of the revocable living trust, proposed to allocate the former community property so that non-IRA assets would pass to the irrevocable portion of the trust (representing the decedent's community property) and the IRA would pass to the revocable portion of the trust (representing the survivor's community property), with the IRA later distributed directly to the surviving spouse. The I.R.S. approved this non-pro rata division and rollover and specifically stated that acceleration of IRD would not result. Following this ruling, a practitioner could structure the situation so that the decedent's half of the IRA is payable to the estate, and the surviving spouse, as sole personal representative of the estate, is given the power (preferably under the language of the will) to allocate the decedent's half interest to himself or herself in a non-pro rata division in exchange for other assets that will pass according to the credit shelter trust and marital share terms of the will.

In Private Letter Ruling 1999-12-040 (Dec. 29, 1998), an IRA was payable to a revocable living trust that provided that on the death of the account holder spouse, the trust would be divided into a credit shelter trust and a "survivor's trust." The surviving spouse was given complete access to the assets of the survivor's trust. The account holder designated the revocable trust as beneficiary of the IRA. After the account holder's death, the surviving spouse requested a ruling from the I.R.S. that the non-pro rata allocation of the IRA to the survivor's trust (for distribution to her and rollover by her) in exchange for other trust assets to fund the credit shelter trust would not cause income to be recognized on the IRA. The I.R.S. stated that because both local law and the trust document permitted non-pro rata distribution powers, income would not be accelerated, and the rollover was permitted. From a planning standpoint, the rationale of this ruling should apply whether a revocable living trust or a will is involved. If a will is used, the terms could state that the residue will pass to a trust to be divided, on a fractional basis, between a marital share and a credit shelter trust. The will should also provide flexibility for non-pro rata distributions and the direction that, to the extent possible, in the non-pro rata distribution process, the IRA should be allocated to the marital share to be distributed to the surviving spouse for rollover.

In Private Letter Ruling 2000-32-044 (May 15, 2000), the estate was the designated beneficiary of an IRA and a § 403(b) annuity. The surviving spouse was the sole personal representative of the estate and a one-third residuary beneficiary. The I.R.S. allowed the surviving spouse to allocate the IRA and the § 403(b) annuity to the surviving spouse in a "non-pro rata distribution" in satisfaction of her one-third residuary beneficiary interest. The I.R.S. also sanctioned the surviving spouse's rollover of these benefits.

In Private Letter Ruling 2000-52-041 (Oct. 22, 2000), an IRA was payable to a revocable living trust and the spouse had the right to remove the IRA. The service ruled that, following removal, a rollover would be permitted. Although this Private

Letter Ruling involved the pre-2001 proposed minimum distribution regulations, it was issued after the 2001 proposed regulations. In another set of facts reviewed by the I.R.S., the husband passed away without naming a beneficiary of his IRA. The husband had died intestate. Under the laws of the state of domicile, the wife was the sole beneficiary of an intestate estate. The wife was appointed personal representative of the decedent husband's estate. Under the IRA custodial account, failure to designate a beneficiary resulted in the IRA proceeds being paid to the decedent's estate. The wife proposed to use her powers as personal representative to allocate the IRA proceeds to herself for rollover. In Private Letter Ruling 2001-29-036 (Apr. 23, 2001), the I.R.S. approved the rollover. Unfortunately, at the end of the Private Letter Ruling the Service noted that because the decedent passed away before the new minimum distribution regulations (issued in 2001), the ruling did not address "any issues that may arise under the proposed regulations."

In Private Letter Ruling 2002-34-019 (May 13, 2002), the I.R.S. ruled that a non-pro rata allocation of various IRAs to charities that were residual beneficiaries of an estate did not accelerate income under I.R.C. § 691. This is a further indication that the I.R.S. does not view assignment or transfer of interests in IRAs in the estate process in satisfaction of a fractional interest as an income tax event.

There are two regulations that raise questions concerning the non-pro rata technique:

1) The fact that an employee's interest under the plan passes to a certain individual under a will or otherwise under applicable state law does not make that individual a designated beneficiary unless the individual is designated as a beneficiary under the plan. Treas. Reg. § 1.401(a)(9)-4, Q-1, A-1.

2) [For the surviving spouse to elect to treat the decedent account holder's IRA as his or her own and thereby avoid an actual distribution and rollover], "the spouse must be the sole beneficiary of the IRA and have an unlimited right to withdraw amounts from the IRA. If a trust is named as beneficiary of the IRA, this requirement is not satisfied even if the spouse is the sole beneficiary of the trust. Treas. Reg. § 1.408-8, Q-5, A-5(a).

Did the Treasury intend these statements to halt the practice of running all or a portion of an IRA through an estate, revocable living trust, or credit shelter trust, and then through a non-pro rata distribution, and then back out to the surviving spouse for a rollover?

In Private Letter Ruling 2003-46-025 (Aug. 21, 2003), the I.R.S. again ruled that the surviving spouse may roll over an IRA when a living trust was the beneficiary and the spouse had the unilateral power to allocate the IRA to herself. This ruling apparently confirmed that the final regulations have not eliminated the indirect rollover technique.

It should be noted that Marjorie Hoffman, the primary drafter of the final regulations, has indicated that although the final regulations do not expressly so state, a spousal rollover will be available under the following set of facts: 1) the IRA is payable to a trust in which the spouse is the beneficiary, and 2) the trustee of the trust directs that all or a portion of the IRA be paid directly to the surviving spouse. The surviving spouse could then take the payment so received and roll it into an IRA. Be aware that this is merely a statement that Marjorie Hoffman has made (although one could read the preamble to the final regulations as authorizing such a rollover).

Private Letter Ruling 200634065 contained a statement by the IRS broadly interpreting the ability of the surviving spouse to complete a rollover through a trust or an estate. In this case, the decedent's IRA was payable to his estate. The decedent's wife was the sole beneficiary and personal representative of the estate. The wife's plan was to have the custodian distribute the IRA to the estate and from the estate to the spouse and, finally, from the spouse to a rollover IRA within 60 days of the initial distribution. The IRS noted the distinction between an inherited IRA (not eligible for a rollover) and the exception to the inherited IRA for payment to a surviving spouse under IRC §408(d)(3)(C)(ii). The IRS then dealt with the statement in the final §401(a)(9) regulations pertaining to the surviving spouse's ability to elect to treat the decedent's IRA as his or her own. The IRS noted that this type of election is only available if the surviving spouse is the sole beneficiary of the IRA with an unlimited right to make a withdrawal. In addition, the IRS noted the statement in the regulations that the surviving spouse will not be able to elect to treat the decedent's IRA as his or her own if the beneficiary of the IRA is a trust (even if the surviving spouse is the sole beneficiary of the trust). The IRS went on to differentiate this language from the situation where the surviving spouse actually receives the distributed IRA funds through an estate or trust and concluded as follows:

[A] surviving spouse who actually receives a distribution from an IRA is permitted to roll that distribution over into his/her own IRA even if the spouse is not the sole beneficiary of the deceased 's IRA as long as the rollover is accomplished within the requisite 60-day period. A rollover may be accomplished even if IRA assets *pass through either a trust and/or an estate*. (Emphasis added.)There has been much discussion about the best method to take advantage of the above Private Letter Rulings. Of course, in a perfect world where the complexities and costs of a revocable living trust would be of no consequence, it would be easy to follow the Private Letter Rulings by naming the surviving spouse as sole trustee of the revocable living trust and giving the spouse, as trustee, full non-pro rata division and distribution powers. The revocable living trust could be directly named as primary beneficiary, in which case all of the issues concerning trusts as beneficiaries would need to be addressed. As an alternate approach, the revocable living trust could be the beneficiary in the event the surviving spouse disclaims. Private Letter Ruling 97-07-008 (Nov. 12, 1996) permits a surviving spouse to exercise his or her non-pro rata distribution (and presumably non-pro rata division) powers over assets disclaimed by the spouse.

Another approach is for the couple to use wills for their estate plan. If the estate is named as beneficiary, then presumably the surviving spouse, as sole personal representative of the estate, could allocate the IRA to him or herself in a non-pro rata division of the former community property. Another approach would be to name the surviving spouse as beneficiary with the right to disclaim in favor of the estate. Following the disclaimer, the disclaimed portion of the IRA would be involved in the non-pro rata division of the former community property. The problem with this approach is that there is not absolute certainty about the impact on the minimum distribution rules of the estate being a disclaimer beneficiary on the account holder's required beginning date. Yet another approach is to name the surviving spouse as sole personal representative of the estate and sole trustee of the credit shelter trust and give the surviving spouse, as trustee and personal representative, full and complete authority to engage in a non-pro rata division of the former community property involving all of the couple's assets following death. If the credit shelter trust is in the disclaimer position, then, following actual disclaimer, the surviving spouse (individually, as trustee and personal representative) would complete the non-pro rata division of the former community property. This technique should fall within the protection of Revenue Ruling 76-83, 1976-1 C.B. 213, which is the support for the two community property Private Letter Rulings discussed above

Here are examples of the many Private Letter Rulings involving a rollover by a surviving spouse where a trust (or estate) was named as beneficiary were issued:

- LR 200603032. In this private letter ruling, a trust was the beneficiary of an
  IRA. The surviving spouse was sole trustee of the trust. The trust instrument gave the trustee the power to withdraw the IRA and pay it to the surviving spouse. As trustee, the surviving spouse proposed taking distribution of the IRA in the name of the trust then paying the distribution over to the surviving spouse. Thereafter, the surviving spouse, in her personal capacity, proposed rolling the amounts she received into an IRA.

  The IRS stated that, although the regulations generally preclude a rollover if the IRA is paid to the trust then to the surviving spouse (even if the spouse is the sole beneficiary of the trust), the rollover will be permitted under the facts of the ruling because the surviving spouse was the sole trustee of the trust in addition to being the sole beneficiary of the trust. This private letter ruling is a clear indication that previous letter rulings issued by the IRS allowing "indirect rollovers" have not been revoked.

- LR 200603036. This private letter ruling involved a retirement plan payable to
  a trust for a surviving spouse. Under the terms of the trust, the surviving spouse was entitled to all of the income and trust principal for her health, maintenance, education and support. The surviving spouse was sole trustee of the trust and represented to the IRS that, as trustee, she had the power to direct payment of the total amount of the retirement plan directly from the retirement plan to herself. The surviving spouse proposed to the IRS that she be allowed to rollover this distribution. Following the logic of the preamble (and citing Reg. 1.402(c)-2) the IRS stated that, even though the spouse was not the beneficiary of the retirement plan, payment directly to the surviving spouse at the direction of the trustee was enough to permit the surviving spouse to complete the rollover.

- LR 200605019. This letter ruling involved several IRAs, several problems and
  overall a nasty situation. Nonetheless, the IRS permitted an indirect rollover of some IRA funds (i.e., distribution to the trust then to the surviving spouse followed by a rollover) and distribution of other IRA funds directly from the IRAs to the spouse at the spouse's direction as trustee of the trust. All were approved for rollover.

- LRs 200644028, 200644031 and 200705032. All of these rulings deal with
  indirect rollovers by a surviving spouse:

- In LR 200644028, the decedent died after his RBD with an IRA. A trust was
  beneficiary. The wife was the sole trustee and she proposed directing the custodian to do an IRA-to-IRA transfer into an IRA in wife's name. The IRS

permitted this under a narrow reading of Reg. 1.408-8, Q-5A-5(a). The IRS interprets this regulation as preventing a spouse from electing to treat the decedent's IRA as her own (but not preventing the spouse from a rollover or IRA-to-IRA transfer).

- In LR 200644031, the decedent died after his RBD naming an estate as beneficiary of his IRA. The surviving spouse was the sole personal representative and, after specific bequests, the entire estate passed to the surviving spouse. Moreover, the IRS noted that the surviving spouse had the right to make *non-pro rata distributions* in settling the estate.

  The surviving spouse proposed to allocate the IRA to the spouse in a non-pro rata distribution and direct the custodian of the IRA to complete a direct IRA-to-IRA transfer into an IRA in the surviving spouse's name.

  The IRS noted that the surviving spouse could not, in these circumstances, elect to treat the IRA as her own. However, if the surviving spouse actually receives the distribution, she may roll it over, even if she is not the designated beneficiary. In this case, the IRS treated the IRA-to-IRA transfer as such a rollover.

- In LR 200705032, the decedent died naming his revocable living trust as beneficiary of several IRAs. The revocable living trust provided for a marital deduction trust which was funded with a pecuniary formula. Under the terms of the marital deduction trust, the spouse had an absolute right to withdrawal principal. The spouse proposed to the IRS that the IRAs be distributed to the trust and, thereafter, immediately distributed to the spouse for rollover. Again, the IRS narrowly read Reg. 1.408-8QA5 so as to prevent a spouse from electing to treat an IRA payable to a trust for the benefit of the spouse as his or her own. Rather, the IRS stated as follows:

  A surviving spouse who actually receives a distribution from an IRA is permitted to roll that distribution over into his/her own IRA even if the spouse is not the sole beneficiary of the deceased's IRA as long as the rollover is accomplished within the requisite 60-day period. A rollover may be accomplished even if IRA assets pass through either a trust and/ or an estate.

  This ruling is also interesting from the standpoint that no mention was made of the possibility of IRD acceleration by virtue of the allocation of the IRAs to the marital trust in satisfaction of the pecuniary marital gift. Nonetheless, this is not a position the planner should get him or herself into. If there is the possibility of allocating an IRA to a marital bequest, the marital bequest should be structured as a fractional gift.

PLR 200704033 involved the reformation of a trust to permit a spouse the right to allocate an IRA to herself without anyone's consent. Based on this, the spouse was permitted to complete a rollover. (Also, in this ruling, there was a problem with the 60-day rollover period which the IRS waived.)

PLR 200703047 also involved a reformation allowing two IRAs to be paid to the surviving spouse. Also, the 60-day rollover deadline was botched in this private letter ruling and the IRS permitted an extension.

In PLR 200703035 an estate was beneficiary, but the spouse was the sole personal representative and had the right to allocate the IRA to herself. The rollover occurred by a distribution from the account holder's IRA to a non-IRA account of the spouse. The non-IRA account of the spouse was to be rolled into an IRA in the spouse's name within 60 days. However, the 60-day time frame was missed. Again, the IRS approved the rollover and waived the 60-day rollover deadline.

In PLR 200705032, the question was an independent trustee's allocation of an IRA to a trust over which the spouse had a right of withdrawal. The IRS noted that this allocation was consistent with the co-trustees' fiduciary obligations and permitted the spouse to rollover the IRA following its allocation to said trust.

As a result of the above, the prudent course of action following death of the account holder spouse and a disclaimer by the surviving spouse, may be to have the surviving spouse in his or her individual capacity and as personal representative and trustee, to request an actual distribution of the deceased spouse's IRA to the surviving spouse. The surviving spouse would then rollover within the 60-day rollover period. In the non-pro rata settlement of the former community property, non-IRA assets would be allocated to the credit shelter trust in exchange for the portion of the IRA disclaimed by the surviving spouse. This may allow the practitioner to be within the 1999 private letter rulings as well as make use of the theory that a spouse may rollover a distribution made directly to him or herself at the direction of a trustee. The added advantage to this approach is that the 1099 will be issued by the IRA custodian directly to the surviving spouse which, of course, helps to prevent attracting unnecessary scrutiny from the IRS. It should be noted that these 2006 letter rulings follow similar logic of a letter ruling issued late in 2005 (LR 20054901).

In PLR 200938042, an IRA was payable to a testamentary trust for the surviving spouse created under the decedent's will. The surviving spouse disclaimed her interest under the trust. Apparently, under the IRA beneficiary designation and custodial account, this caused the beneficiary designation to "fail" so that, under the custodial account, the estate became beneficiary. The surviving spouse thereafter sought to allocate the IRA from the estate to herself as part of her outright bequest from the estate and requested the IRS to sanction the rollover. The IRS ruled that because the residue of the estate passes outright to the surviving spouse and, as a result of the disclaimer, the residue of the estate included the IRA, the spouse essentially became the sole beneficiary of the IRA. The IRS noted that the surviving spouse may not elect to treat the IRA as her own, but may, by an actual distribution, rollover the IRA into an IRA in her name.

In PLR 200944059, the IRS showed that there is a limit to its approval of indirect rollovers. In this case, the IRA was payable to a trust for a surviving spouse. She was the sole trustee and income beneficiary of the trust. Distributions to the trust were permitted based on health, maintenance, education and support. Nonetheless, she obtained a state court order allowing her to cause the IRA to be distributed to the trust and then distributed to her. She asked the IRS for a ruling allowing her to roll the funds into an IRA in her name.

The IRS stated that because she did not have unrestricted access to the IRA she could not be treated as the IRA beneficiary for rollover purposes. Moreover, the IRS noted that distribution of the IRA to the spouse would have constituted a gift from the remainder beneficiaries.

(3) QTIP trust

As discussed previously, tremendous tax advantages can result if the nonworking spouse is the outright beneficiary of an account. A client should forego these benefits only if significant countervailing nontax reasons exist. For example, the working spouse may wish to prevent the nonworking spouse from having direct control over the working spouse's assets. In such a case, the client may wish to create a credit shelter trust to be funded with the credit shelter amount and a QTIP trust to be funded with the remainder of the working spouse's estate. Because of the income tax liability associated with the account, the planner will most likely want to name a QTIP trust as beneficiary. Of course, a lump sum payment to the QTIP trust could easily qualify for the estate tax marital deduction. Priv. Ltr. Rul. 97-29-015 (Apr. 16, 1997). Dribbling out the account to the QTIP trust, however, is a tricky task.

Any distribution from the retirement plan or IRA must comply with I.R.C. §401(a)(9). In short, a minimum distribution must be made each year and the period of distribution must comply with the rules of §401(a)(9). It is important to note that the I.R.C. §401(a)(9) minimum distribution is not tied to the actual income earned by the account. In the early years of a "dribble-out" distribution, it is typical for the minimum distribution required by §401(a)(9) to be quite less than the actual income earned by the account. As discussed above, a trust should only be designated as a beneficiary with great care.

Property qualifies for the marital deduction under the QTIP rules of I.R.C. §2056(b)(7) only if (a) the *surviving* spouse is entitled to all of the income payable at least annually during his or her lifetime, (b) the surviving spouse is the only one to whom any distributions can be made during his or her lifetime, (c) the surviving spouse has the right to require the trustee promptly to convert unproductive property to productive property, and (d) a proper election is made on I.R.S. Form 706 (United States Estate (and Generation-Skipping Transfer) Tax Return.

Revenue Ruling 2000-2, 2000-3 I.R.B. 305, replaced and superseded Revenue Ruling 89-89, 1989-2 C.B. 231, with regard to qualification of an IRA as QTIP property when the IRA is payable to a QTIP trust. Under the facts of the ruling, the decedent died before his required beginning date and a testamentary QTIP trust was named as beneficiary of the decedent's IRA. The decedent's wife was the income beneficiary of the QTIP trust and the decedent's children were the sole remainder beneficiaries of the trust. The testamentary QTIP trust fully complied with the requirements of I.R.C. §2056(b)(7). In addition, language in the QTIP trust gave the surviving spouse the power to demand that, in any year, the income of the IRA be withdrawn from the IRA, passed through the QTIP trust, and distributed to the spouse. In the Revenue Ruling, the I.R.S. noted that the QTIP trust was a "qualified trust" for determining minimum distributions after the decedent's death. The I.R.S. also stated that the beneficiaries taken into account to determine minimum distributions were the surviving spouse and the decedent's children. This is consistent with Treas. Reg. §1.401(a)(9)-5, Q-7, A-7(c)(3)(Ex. 2). Because the surviving spouse had the shortest life expectancy, minimum distributions to the trust would be computed with reference to the life expectancy of that surviving spouse and were required to begin on December 31 of the calendar year following the calendar year of the decedent's death.

In *structuring* distributions to a QTIP trust, the requirements of the income and estate tax rules must be satisfied. The I.R.S. provided important guidance in Revenue

Ruling 2000-2..To satisfy the rules, the lawyer must study the distribution provisions of the applicable retirement plan or IRA. Many IRAs permit virtually any type of distribution method and allow the account holder or beneficiaries to make withdrawals of any amounts at any time, provided the § 401(a)(9) rules are satisfied. Some qualified retirement plans allow the death beneficiary the option of accelerating and withdrawing the account at any time after the working spouse's death. If the planner is dealing with a document where such flexibility exists, meeting the requirements of Revenue Ruling 2000-2 may be fairly easy. However, if the plan document is restrictive with regard to distributions, it may be virtually impossible for the planner to structure the beneficiary designation and QTIP trust language to satisfy the requirements of Revenue Ruling 2000-2.

The IRS released Revenue Ruling 2006-26 which deals with the concept of "Q-Tipping" an IRA. The Revenue Ruling builds upon Revenue Ruling 2000-2 by including an extensive discussion of the interplay between various income and principal laws and the requirement that all income be distributed to (or be subject to withdrawal by) the surviving spouse. Essentially, situation 1 and situation 2 described in this new Revenue Ruling sanction Q-Tip treatment where the trustee has the right to convert principal to income or to convert the trust to a 4% unitrust as provided by RCW 11.104A.020 and RCW 11.104A.040. However, in regard to the power to convert principal to income, the Revenue Ruling dealt with the Uniform Principal and Income Act ("UPIA") version of the law which states that only 10% of any distribution (i.e., an RMD) will be considered income. In this regard, the IRS notes that the 10% figure will not satisfy the income requirements for Q-Tip treatment. Therefore, the trustee must, under said UPIA provision, exercise the authority to convert additional amounts to income. In response to Revenue Ruling 2006-26, the Uniform Law Commission amended the revised Uniform Principal and Income Act to provide the "trust within a trust concept" under which internally generated income of the IRA (determined as if it were a separate trust) would be treated as income in the case of a Q-Tip trust.

RCW 11.104A.180 was recently amended to provide the trust within a trust approach (RCW 11.104A.180(b)). However, if the IRA does not generate or calculate income in such fashion, four percent (4%) of the total value of the IRA will be treated as income. RCW 11.104A.180.

The Revenue Ruling also addresses which beneficiaries of the Q-Tip trust are taken into account to determine the beneficiary with the shortest life expectancy. The IRS specifies that, unless the Q-Tip trust is a "conduit trust" (which makes little sense in the context of a Q-Tip trust) the beneficiaries will be the surviving spouse and the remainder beneficiaries.

Finally, as stated above, Q-Tipping an IRA has a tremendous income tax cost as distributions, both during and after the surviving spouse's life will be computed with reference to the surviving spouse's life expectancy. In short, the possibility to stretch out the IRA is lost. Moreover, any portion of the RMDs accumulated by the trustee may be subject to tax at very high trust income tax rates.

(4) Charity as beneficiary

If the account holder is charitably inclined, the best overall tax results may be achieved if he or she leaves a retirement plan or IRA to a tax-exempt charity. Of course, this does not apply to a Roth account because income taxes have already been paid. As charitable organizations are exempt from income taxes, no income taxes will ever be imposed on the deferred income represented by the account. However, the client will have to balance the benefits of making the gift to charity against the significant additional economic growth that the client's family might enjoy over an extended distribution period if the account were left to them. In other words, from a practical standpoint, naming the charity as beneficiary amounts to a gift of both the date of death value of the account as well as the substantial future economic growth that is possible under I.R.C. § 401(a)(9). The planner should, of course, verify the exact name of the charity and confirm that it is an exempt organization. Based on the author's calculations, there are scenarios in which the account holder's children (or GSTT trusts for grandchildren) would be better off receiving IRA or retirement plan benefits, rather than cash or securities, because the power of continued income tax-deferred growth is quite significant. Generally, this is the case when there are sufficient nonretirement plan or IRA assets to pay estate taxes on the IRA or retirement plan and the children will have the economic ability to take only minimum distributions for some period of time.

Care should be taken in naming a charity as beneficiary of part of the account. A charity is not a "qualified trust" for purposes of I.R.C. § 401(a)(9). Naming the charity as a sole beneficiary of an account does not create any particular problems with the minimum distribution rules, because after the required beginning date the participant will be entitled to use the Minimum Distribution Table to determine distributions during his or her lifetime. The same treatment would be available after the required beginning date even if the charity and individual beneficiaries were named beneficiaries of a particular account. However, when beneficiaries include both individuals and a charity, separate accounts under Treas. Reg. § 1.401(a)(9)-8, Q-2, A-2(a) or separate IRA accounts should be considered, to ensure that following the participant's death, the individual beneficiaries will have the right to take distributions over their respective lifetimes.

It should be noted that during the participant's lifetime, a distribution directly to the charity will be treated as a distribution to the participant followed by a contribution to the charity. Any such distribution is subject to regular income tax and the I.R.C. § 72(t) penalty for premature distribution. Under the Pension Protection Act of 2006, special rules apply to Qualified Charitable Distributions ("QCDs") for 2006-2009 (extended for 2010, 2011 and 2012). Under these rules, a taxpayer may exclude from income QCDs of up to $100,000 per year. There are several requirements for a QCD:

- The QCD must be made directly from the IRA to the charity (the account holder cannot receive the funds him or herself).
- The QCD must be made after the date the IRA owner has attained age 70$\frac{1}{2}$.
- The IRA may be a regular or Roth IRA but may not be a SEP or Simple.
- The charity must be one described in I.R.C. § 408(d)(8)(F) which excludes donor advised funds and certain supporting organizations under I.R.C. § 509(a)(3).

These changes were made by way of amendments to I.R.C. §408(d)(8)(F). Interestingly, a taxpayer's QCD will be considered as part of the taxpayer's RMD for the calendar year.

- With respect to the charitable rollover provisions of §408(d)(8), the following clarifications are made in the Notice 2007-7:
- The limit is $100,000, regardless of how many IRAs the owner has and regardless of whether the taxpayer is married filing a joint return. If both a husband and wife each have IRAs, they each have a $100,000 limit.
- The rollover must be directly to a charity described at §170(b)(1)(A) and may not be to a supporting organization described at §509(a)(3) or a donor advised fund described at §4966(d)(2).
- Although a direct rollover may not occur from a simple IRA or a SEPP IRA, the Notice permits the direct rollover from such an arrangement if it is not an "ongoing Simple or SEPP." An ongoing Simple or SEPP is one for which an employer made a contribution for the plan year ending with or within the account holder's taxable year in which the charitable contribution will be made.
- The Notice expands the charitable rollover to an f/b/o IRA. If the beneficiary of the f/b/o IRA is over $70^1/_2$ years of age, such beneficiary may complete a charitable rollover.
- The charitable rollover is not subject to withholding and the custodian may rely upon "reasonable representations" made by the IRA owner.
- The charitable rollover may be made by a check payable from the IRA custodian to the charitable organization even though the check is delivered by the IRA owner.
- The charitable rollover will not be considered a prohibited transaction under IRC §4975 because, for prohibited transaction purposes, the distribution is treated as having been received by the account holder. Thus, it appears that a charitable pledge may be satisfied through the charitable rollover.
- Under the 2010 Tax Relief Act, there is a special rule for QCDs made in January of 2011. These QCDs may be treated as if made on December 31, 2010 (so as to count towards a 2010 $100,000 limitation) and so as to satisfy the taxpayer's RMD for 2010.

Charitable Trusts. Charitable trusts are arrangements under which tax-exempt organizations ("Charities") and individual heirs share the economic benefits of a trust in successive fashion. A Charitable Remainder Trust ("CRT") is a trust under which the individual beneficiary or beneficiaries receive payments for some specified time period; and, at the end of the specified period, the remaining trust principal is distributed to Charities. For example, a CRT may be designed to provide benefits for a spouse during his or her lifetime; and, upon his or her death, pass to Charities. There are two types of CRTs:

- A charitable remainder annuity trust or "CRAT" is an arrangement in which a fixed dollar amount is distributed from the trust to the individual beneficiary each year.
- A charitable remainder unitrust or "CRUT" is a trust which pays the individual beneficiary a fixed percentage (at least 5% but no more than 50%) of each

year's opening value of the trust. This type of distribution is a "unitrust distribution". Because CRUTs tend to be more flexible and provide some inflationary protection to the individual beneficiaries, they are more common than CRATs.

CRTs must comply with rigorous rules under IRC § 664 CRTs, if so qualified, are exempt from income tax. Thus, IRA distributions to a CRT may be exempt from income tax. However, as will be discussed below, what is known as the unrelated business taxable income or "UBTI" rules apply to CRTs.

The second type of charitable trust is known as a charitable lead trust or "CLT". Under this arrangement, the charity is provided with an annuity or unitrust distribution for a period of time; and, at the end of such period, the balance of the trust is distributed to or in trust for individual beneficiaries. Unlike CRTs, however, CLTs are not exempt from income taxes. Thus, a CLT would have to pay income tax on amounts it receives from an IRA. Because of this, creating a CLT as beneficiary of your IRA will likely not be advantageous. Therefore, the balance of this discussion will focus on CRTs.

Here is how the RMD rules work with a CRT:

- RMDs While Account Holder is Alive. While the account holder is living, RMDs will be computed under the "Uniform Lifetime" table of the regulations.

  The key planning move that would change the RMD calculation would be the conversion of all or a part of the IRA to a Roth IRA. After 2009, a taxpayer will be able to convert all or any portion of an IRA to a Roth IRA as there will no longer be a prohibition on individuals with adjusted gross income of more than $100,000 making such a conversion. The portion of the IRA converted to a Roth IRA will no longer be subject to RMD rules while the account holder is living. Moreover, if the spouse is beneficiary of the Roth IRA, there will be no RMDs during his or her lifetime as well. Any portion of an IRA which is converted to a Roth would likely be better left to the account holder's spouse and ultimately to children as opposed to a CRT.

- RMDs Following Death. Following the account holder's death, RMDs to the CRT will be computed as follows: The first RMD will be determined using a divisor equal to the account holder's life expectancy under Treasury tables based on his/her actual age at death. For example, if the account holder passed away at age 77, the initial divisor would be 12.1. Each year thereafter, the divisor would be reduced by 1. This creates a relatively fast distribution from the IRA to the CRT. If the account holder dies before the required beginning date, the CRT must take distribution under the five (5) year rule.

  However, if the CRT is tax-exempt, the CRT does not pay income tax on these distributions. Moreover, the CRT may reinvest these proceeds. Earnings on the reinvestments, likewise, are tax-free to the CRT assuming it is tax-exempt.

  Although the CRT itself may be tax-exempt, distributions from the CRT to the individual beneficiary are not. Instead, distributions to the individual beneficiary are classified as income to the individual beneficiary according to what is known as the "four-tier system". Essentially, as amounts are received by the CRT tax-free, the CRT must, nonetheless, keep a running total of the amount of different types of income it has received (i.e., ordinary income, capital gain, tax exempt income or principal). Funds received by a CRT from a decedent's IRA are allocated to the ordinary income running total.

When the individual beneficiary of the CRT receives his or her annual distribution from the CRT, the taxation of such distribution is determined according to a priority in the four-tier system. Not surprisingly, until the CRT's ordinary income tier is completely distributed by way of annual distributions to the individual beneficiary, such distributions are ordinary income to the individual beneficiary. For example, if an account holder creates a CRT and designated it as beneficiary of all or part of the IRA and such CRT is structured so that his or her spouse is the individual beneficiary, (i) distributions from the IRA to the CRT may be exempt from income tax and (ii) distributions to the spouse from the CRT will be taxed to his/her as ordinary income.

A CRT in which the spouse is the sole individual beneficiary will qualify for the estate tax marital deduction and the Charity's interest in the CRT will qualify for the charitable estate tax deduction. Thus, if the CRT is structured this way, there will be no estate tax on the CRT. Under the Internal Revenue Code, the foregoing treatment is only permitted if the spouse is the sole individual beneficiary of the CRT.

As mentioned at the beginning of this discussion, CRTs are subject to the Tax Code's UBTI rules. Under Prop. Reg. 1.664-1, a CRT with UBTI no longer loses its tax exempt status, but an excise tax is imposed and is equal to the full amount of the UBTI. This, of course, would cause a loss of a key benefit of naming a CRT as beneficiary of the IRA. Although most commentators believe that IRA distributions to a CRT should not be treated as UBTI, this issue has not been conclusively resolved. In PLR 200230018, the IRS ruled that a payment from an IRA directly to a charity did not constitute UBTI. If an account holder were to proceed with a CRT to be beneficiary of all or a portion of an IRA, it may be wise to get a private letter ruling from the Internal Revenue Service concerning this key issue.

If a charity is a beneficiary of an IRA or retirement then as long as the charity is a qualified recipient under I.R.C. § 2055, the estate will be entitled to a charitable deduction.

On a couple of occasions, the IRS has allowed the personal representative of an estate to allocate IRAs in non-pro rata distributions to charitable beneficiaries. In other words, the estate was designated as beneficiary of the IRA and there were charitable gifts under the decedent's Will. The Service permitted allocation of the IRAs to the charitable beneficiaries without causing income to the estate under IRC § 691. LR 20052004, LR 200633009 and 200826028.

- LR 200644020 illustrates the importance of form over substance when it comes to gifts to charities of an IRA. In this ruling, a revocable living trust was designated beneficiary of the decedent's IRA. The dispositive provisions of the trust called for a $100,000 distribution "in cash or in kind" to charities. The residue of the trust was to be distributed to the decedent's children. *There was no specific direction that IRA proceeds payable to the trust be used to satisfy this pecuniary charitable bequest.*

The trustee directed the IRA custodian to create f/b/o IRAs for each of the charities to satisfy the $100,000 charitable bequest.

Here is how the IRS analyzed this situation:

- The IRA was IRD under IRC §691 and its allocation to the charities was not specifically required by the trust, therefore, the allocation to the charities constitutes a sale, exchange or other disposition under IRC §691(a)(2).

- As a result, the trust has income of $100,000. However, because the trust did not require that its income be set aside for charitable purposes, no *income tax charitable deduction* is available under IRC §642(c)(1).

The foregoing result is premised on the old *Kenan v. Comm'r*, 25 AFTR 607 (2d Circ. 1940) case. Stated another way, this result is premised on the fact that the charitable bequest under the trust was *pecuniary* and not *fractional*.

One could argue that the IRS reads IRC §691(a)(2) too narrowly and that the trustee's general power to make distributions in cash, in kind or both would put the charities in a position of an entity acquiring the IRA pursuant to said entity's right to receive such amount. This is a dangerous precipice to stand on. There are ways to avoid the results of this ruling:

- The easiest (and best) way to avoid the result of the ruling is to directly designate the charity as beneficiary of a fraction of the IRA. If the decedent has a dollar amount in mind, say $100,000, the safest approach in the IRA beneficiary designation would be as follows: "That portion of my IRA determined with reference to a fraction, the numerator of which is $100,000 and the denominator of which is the date of death value of my IRA". This method will also satisfy the requirements for separate IRA treatment with regard to the non-charitable portion of the IRA.

- If the planner wishes to have the IRA payable to a living trust (or estate) and thereafter divided among charitable and non-charitable beneficiaries, care should be taken to either set up the charitable bequest as a fractional gift or make it a pecuniary gift with the direction that it be satisfied first with IRAs. *See* LR 200608032. Even if the planner takes one of these alternate approaches, running the IRA through a trust or estate involves additional issues with regard to DNI, the trust's treatment as a qualified trust and identification of beneficiaries for RMD purposes.

- If the charity had been a residual beneficiary, then, under IRC §691, there would be no acceleration when the f/b/o IRA is allocated to it. LR 200652028.

The foregoing discussing concerning charitable gifts applies to any form of pecuniary gift that might be satisfied with an IRA. However, it is interesting to note that LR 200705032 allowed an IRA to be allocated to a surviving spouse to satisfy a pecuniary marital bequest and, thereafter, the surviving spouse completed an "indirect rollover."

- LR 201013033. In this case, the decedent did not name a beneficiary of the IRA. Under the custodial account, the decedent's estate became the beneficiary. The decedent's estate was to "pour over" to a living trust. The living trust provided that a charity receive a percentage of the trust. The estate proposed transferring the IRA to the trust followed by a transfer of the IRA by the trust to the charity in satisfaction of its fractional gift. The IRS concluded that this transfer did not accelerate or cause taxation of the IRA income to the trust because the charity was a specific residuary legatee within the meaning of Reg. 1.691(a)-4(b)(2).

- LR 200845029. Under this private letter ruling, a defined benefit plan was payable to an estate. A charity was a residual beneficiary of the estate. The estate proposed to assign its right to the defined benefit plan to the charity.

  The IRS ruled that under 691(a)(2) an item of IRD may be transferred without accelerating income tax to the person entitled to such item. The charity's position as residual beneficiary entitled it to the item of IRD so that the transfer by the estate did not accelerate income tax.

(5) Estate Tax Allocation Issue

Let's assume the decedent had a § 401(k) plan account and an IRA. Also assume that under the decedent's estate plan, he did the following: (i) by beneficiary designations, left the retirement plan and IRA ("Retirement Benefits") to Child A and (ii) by Will and/or other dispositive documents, all other assets to Child B. Let's also assume that decedent's Will either says nothing about estate tax apportionment or invokes RCW 83.110A. Let's assume that Child B is the personal representative of the estate and Child A has no assets other than the inherited Retirement Benefits.

As an initial matter, there is no federal estate tax apportionment with respect to Retirement Benefits. In fact, the federal estate tax apportionment applicable to life insurance proceeds does not apply to annuities.

Under RCW 83.110A.030, the estate taxes attributable to the IRA are apportioned to Child A. Assuming Child A is a deadbeat, RCW 6.15.020 prevents attachment of the IRA and IRC § 401(a)(13) (and its ERISA counterpart) prevent attachment of the § 401(k) plan account.

This means that Child B, as personal representative, would be required to pay the taxes him or herself as required by RCW 83.110A.080 and, based on this payment, have a right of reimbursement under RCW 83.110A.090. I suppose this would allow Child B to attach RMDs and other distributions as taken by Child A.

Let's assume that, instead of the Retirement Benefits being paid to Child A in our example, the Retirement Benefits are, instead, payable to a trust of which Child A is the beneficiary. In this case, RCW 83.110A.030 does require some apportionment to the principal of the trust. However, the "person" responsible to pay the taxes so apportioned would be the trust itself and the trustee could assert the protection of ERISA and RCW 6.15.020. In short, I think the result would be the same.

It should be noted that IRC and ERISA protection for the § 401(k) plan is subject to a federal tax levy. Thus, it is possible with the Retirement Benefits that, if the taxes were not paid, Child B could face transferee liability and a levy could be imposed upon the § 401(k) plan account and, perhaps, under some notion of federal preemption, the IRA. I am not sure if this would actually happen as Washington's estate tax apportionment provisions seem to require that Child B pay the tax and seek reimbursement from Child A.

§13.4 GIFT TAX

When completing a beneficiary designation or electing a form of payout on behalf of the working spouse, the planner must also consider the federal gift tax implications. Prior to the 1986 Act, I.R.C. §2517(a) provided that the exercise or nonexercise by an employee of an election or option whereby plan benefits would become payable to any beneficiary after the employee's death would not be considered a gift. Former I.R.C. §2517(c) provided that a transfer of retirement benefits to a designated beneficiary would not be treated as a gift of the nonworking spouse's community one-half interest by the nonworking spouse. The 1986 Act repealed I.R.C. §2517. If the nonworking spouse waives, before the death of the participant, any survivor benefit or right to such survivor benefit under I.R.C. §401(a)(11) or I.R.C. §417, the waiver is not to be treated as a transfer of property by gift. Under I.R.C. §2523(f)(6), the acceptance of a qualified joint and survivor annuity form of payment by the nonworking spouse will be treated as a gift from the working spouse. That gift will qualify for a marital deduction unless the working spouse elects otherwise.

§13.5 SPOUSAL PROTECTION UNDER ERISA

I.R.C. §§401(a)(11) & 417 and ERISA provide safeguards for the nonworking spouse's interest in the working spouse's qualified retirement plan benefits. Generally, distributions from a qualified plan that begin during a participant's life must be in the form of a single life annuity with respect to a single participant, or a qualified joint and survivor annuity with respect to a married participant. I.R.C. §401(a)(11)(A)(i). A qualified joint and survivor annuity is an annuity payable over the joint lives of the working and nonworking spouse with payments to the nonworking spouse being equal to one-half of those made to the working spouse. I.R.C. §417(b)(1). For example, if the working spouse's lifetime payments were $300 per month, the nonworking spouse's monthly payments must be $150 after the death of the working spouse.

If a married participant dies before distributions from a retirement plan have begun, the participant's spouse is entitled to a preretirement survivor annuity. I.R.C. §401(a)(11)(A)(ii). In the defined benefit plan context, a preretirement survivor annuity equals what the surviving spouse's benefits would have been under the survivor portion of a qualified joint and survivor annuity. I.R.C. §417(c)(1). Under a defined contribution plan, the surviving spouse is entitled to an annuity payable over the nonworking spouse's lifetime from one-half of the deceased participant's account balance. I.R.C. §417(c)(1).

Profit sharing plans (i.e., §401(k) plans) receive a limited exemption from the annuity requirements. This exemption is available only if the plan provides that upon his or her death, the participant's benefit is payable in full to the participant's surviving spouse, and the participant does not elect payment of benefits in the form of a life annuity. I.R.C. §401(a)(11)(B)(iii). The annuity requirements, however, attach to any profit sharing account that represents benefits formerly held by a plan that were subject to the annuity requirements. *Id.* Importantly, the annuity requirements do not apply to IRAs.

In short, there are valuable federal property rights for the spouse of a participant. In the case of a typical money purchase pension plan or other plan fully subject to the annuity rules, the spousal protection applies to any distributions made during the participant's lifetime and at the participant's death. In the case of a plan not subject to the annuity requirements (i.e., a profit sharing or § 401(k) plan), the surviving spouse must be the sole beneficiary of the participant's account, unless the spouse consents otherwise. Essentially, under the annuity requirements, the spouse is given a one-half interest in the plan. Under the profit sharing plan exception, the spouse has no rights during the participant's lifetime (other than those provided under community property laws) but is entitled to be the sole beneficiary at the participant's death. A plan subject to the spousal annuity rules may require the participant and spouse to be married one year before the spousal annuity rules apply to the participant's account. These rights may only be waived in accordance with the terms of the applicable plan document.

Of course, the spousal rights of the Retirement Equity Act of 1984 (REA), Pub. L. 98-397, 98 Stat. 1426 (1984), can create problems in the area of prenuptial agreements. In this context, the practitioner must differentiate between the divorce and the death setting. In *Critchell v. Critchell*, 746 A.2d 282 (D.C. 2000), the court held that a future spouse's waiver of claims against a retirement plan benefit may be upheld in a divorce setting but will not be valid at the participant's death. *See also Hurwitz v. Sher*, 982 F.2d 778 (2d Cir. 1992), *cert. denied*, 508 U.S. 912 (1993); Treas. Reg. § 1.401(a)-20, Q-28, A-28. In the case of *Ford Motor Co. v. Ross*, 129 F. Supp. 1070 (2001), the issue was a prenuptial agreement under which the future spouse waived all interest in retirement benefits. After marriage, the spouse never signed the proper consents and waivers required by REA. The participant died and the spouse claimed her ERISA protected benefits. Citing *Boggs v. Boggs*, 520 U.S. 833, 117 S. Ct. 1754, 138 L. Ed. 2d 45 (1996), the court held that ERISA preempted the prenuptial agreement. Moreover, the court rejected an attempt by the decedent's children to impose a constructive trust on the benefits, as such a constructive trust would frustrate the ERISA spousal annuity rights. The Fourth Circuit Court of Appeals confirmed that a prenuptial agreement does not satisfy the requirements of REA. *Hagwood v. Newton*, 282 F.3d 285 (2002). In that case, the spouse had executed a prenuptial agreement but not the required REA waivers. Thus, on the death of the working spouse, the nonworking spouse was entitled to the benefits purportedly waived by the prenuptial agreement. Interestingly, the court, in dicta, stated that while the working spouse was still alive, he possibly could have compelled execution of the REA waivers as required by the prenuptial agreement. *See also Manning v. Hayes*, 212 F.3d 866, 870 (5th Cir. 2000), *cert. denied*, 532 U.S. 941 (2001).

In *Hamilton v. Washington State Plumbing & Pipefitting Industry Pension Plan* (2006, CA 9) 2006 WL 44305, the participant divorced his first wife, Linda, in 1996. The dissolution decree required that the participant name his children as beneficiaries of his pension. After the divorce, the participant married his second wife, Mary. The participant died in 2002. Under the terms of the plan, Mary was to receive the entire benefit in the event of death before retirement. She asserted this right under the terms of the plan. The children asserted that the 1996 marital dissolution order was a QDRO and that they should receive the benefits. The Ninth Circuit determined that the prior order was a QDRO. However, the Ninth Circuit also found that the plan spousal rights were based on ERISA § 205(a)(2) and superseded the QDRO.

In the context of a prenuptial agreement in Washington state, the practitioner may wish to consider (i) delineating what benefits will be considered community versus separate, (ii) including a waiver by the future spouse of the participant's separate property retirement benefits in the context of a divorce, and (iii) requiring the future spouse to sign appropriate REA documents to waive spousal death benefit rights and tying the waivers to some type of economic sanction. Of course, the participant should be counseled that the provision in the agreement requiring the future spouse to execute REA waivers may not be enforceable, and perhaps the penalty for failure to waive the REA rights may likewise be unenforceable.

Private Letter Ruling 2002-15-061 (Jan. 16, 2002) permitted a postnuptial agreement setting out the division of an IRA in the event of divorce. Importantly, there was no division or distribution pursuant to the agreement unless and until divorce.

> DAVENPORT V. DAVENPORT, 146 F. Supp. 2d 770 (M.D.N.C. 2001). In *Davenport*, the participant and his spouse had been married seven years. The participant had a sizeable account balance under a profit sharing plan. Prior to the participant's death, the couple separated and began the dissolution process. During this time, the participant executed a new will, leaving his entire estate to his four children. The participant did not change the beneficiary designation on his profit sharing plan. As noted above, ERISA would have required the spouse to consent to such a change. The participant committed suicide, the surviving spouse applied to the plan administrator for benefits, and the plan administrator brought an action in equity to have the benefits paid to the participant's estate. The Unites States District Court held that because the participant's spouse was the designated beneficiary and the participant had not named another beneficiary (nor had the spouse consented to designation of another beneficiary), she was entitled to the plan benefits.

Owens v. Automotive Machinists Pension Trust 2007 U.S. Dist. LEXIS 7797 (W.D. Wash. 2007). This is a fascinating case arising in Washington State. Under evolving case law in Washington State, non-spouse cohabitants can accrue community-like property which can be divided in divorce and handled at death in the same manner as community property. This case involved a couple who lived together for over 30 years and had two children together. The court found that the pension was "community-like property" and issued a qualified domestic relations order or "QDRO" requiring payment of a portion of the pension to the other cohabitant. The trustees of the plan refused to recognize the Order on the basis that the couple were never legally married and that to be a QDRO, the Order must relate to child support, alimony or marital property rights. Also, the trustees objected on the basis that the alternate payee was not a spouse, former spouse or child of the participant. The court held that the community-like property was a "marital property right" under ERISA and could, therefore, be subject to a QDRO.

A 2007 Court of Appeals case dealt with a spousal waiver to a retirement plan account contained in a prenuptial agreement. In this case, the account holder spouse committed suicide after marriage, but before he had completed a beneficiary designation and obtained his new wife's waiver of ERISA's spousal protection. The prenuptial agreement clearly provided that the wife had waived any rights under the plan. Both the United States District Court and Court of Appeals found that (i) the waiver contained in the prenuptial agreement was not worth the paper it was written on as it did not satisfy ERISA's spousal consent requirements (most notably that the consent be obtained after marriage in the form provided by the plan) and (ii) the wife was not in breach of the agreement as she had not been asked to sign a waiver and consent while the husband was living. *Greenbaum Dahl & McDonald PLLC v. Sandler*, 2007 U.S. App. LEXIS 28823 (6th Cir. 2007).

- Carmona v. Carmona, (September 17, 2008 U.S.C.A. 9). This is a fascinating case. Mr. Carmona retired and commenced taking a joint and survivor annuity from a pension plan. The annuity provided for a payment of a certain amount to Mr. Carmona during his lifetime with payments to continue to his then wife ("wife one") following Mr. Carmona's death.

    Mr. Carmona and wife one divorced. The divorce decree awarded Mr. Carmona his entire interest in the defined benefit plan.

    Mr. Carmona later remarried ("wife two"). When he attempted to convince the pension plan administrator to change the survivor beneficiary to wife two, the plan administrator refused.

    The United States Court of Appeals held that wife one will continue as the survivor beneficiary of the pension plan payment. The Court reasoned that she never waived her right to survivorship benefits at the time payment began. The state divorce court's later order is therefore preempted by ERISA.

The Ninth Circuit Court of Appeals recently ruled that the spousal protection of ERISA does not transfer from a §401(k) plan to an IRA. In this case, the decedent took distribution of a §401(k) plan and rolled it into an IRA. The decedent designated his four adult children as the IRA's beneficiaries. Following the decedent's death, the surviving spouse asserted that ERISA's protections should apply to the IRA because it emanated from a §401(k) plan. The lower court granted summary judgment in favor of the decedent's children and this was upheld by the Court of Appeals. This decision is correct because ERISA does not provide the surviving spouse death benefit protection until the death of the spouse. At that time, the plan in question must be an ERISA plan for the protection to apply. *Charles Schwab & Co. v. Chandler*, 105 AFTR 2d, 2010-690.

§13.6 COMMUNITY PROPERTY

Retirement plan benefits are generally considered to accrue from day to day and year to year until they finally ripen into vested and matured interests. In community property states the benefits that accrue during marriage are community property. The courts treat such benefits as if the benefits had been purchased by the employee out of earnings. Thus, such property is owned in separate and community proportions according to the character of the hypothetical earnings used to make the "payments." Harry M. Cross, *The Community Property Law in Washington* (rev. 1985), 61 WASH. L. REV. 13, 29 (1986)

Although IRAs may be classified as community property for state law purposes, I.R.C. §408(g) requires that the income tax rules governing IRA distributions be applied without regard to community property law. This requirement can create traps for the unwary. In *Bunney v. Commissioner*, 114 T.C. No. 17 (2000), the husband, in the process of a divorce, had a portion of his IRA distributed to the wife. The I.R.S.

asserted that the sole means to divide an IRA in a divorce is through I.R.C. § 408(d), which requires a direct transfer from one spouse's IRA to the divorcing spouse's IRA. Moreover, the I.R.S. asserted that because the husband was the account holder, the husband was liable for income tax and a 10 percent penalty under I.R.C. § 72 relative to the IRA distribution to his ex-wife. The husband argued that the wife should be considered the distributee for income tax purposes because she was receiving her community property interest in the IRA. The Tax Court agreed with the I.R.S. and taxed the husband.

In *Morris v. Commissioner*, 83 T.C.M. (CCH) 1104 (2002), the Tax Court again ignored community property laws by refusing to allow the I.R.S. to proceed against the non-account-holder spouse with an income tax deficiency resulting from the account holder spouse's withdrawals from a community property IRA.

Tax-qualified retirement plan benefits may be awarded to a former spouse or children pursuant to a qualified domestic relations order under I.R.C. § 414(p). I.R.C. § 402 specifically provides that the income tax associated with a distribution to the ex-spouse under such an order is allocated to the ex-spouse. What catches practitioners by surprise, however, is that distributions pursuant to a qualified domestic relations order to anyone *other than* the ex-spouse (i.e., children of the couple or death beneficiary of the ex-spouse) are fully taxable to the participant.

As discussed below, the community property interest of the decedent nonworking spouse in a tax-qualified retirement plan essentially disappears in the event that the nonworking spouse predeceases the working spouse.

There have been other clashes between ERISA and state laws. The Washington Supreme Court held that a statute revoking beneficiary designations upon divorce (RCW 11.07.010) would apply to a § 401(k) plan beneficiary designation. *In re Estate of Egelhoff*, 139 Wn.2d 557 (1998). However, the United States Supreme Court reversed this decision, stating that the Washington statute is preempted by ERISA in the case of a § 401(k) plan. *Egelhoff v. Egelhoff*, 532 U.S. 141, 121 S. Ct. 1322, 149 L. Ed. 2d 264 (2001). The United States Supreme Court reversal calls into question another Washington case. In *In re Estate of Gardner*, 103 Wn. App. 557, 13 P.3d 655 (2000), the court reviewed a divorce decree under which the spouses divided their property and waived all claims against each other. The husband died before changing the beneficiary designation on his TIAA-CREF plan. To complicate matters, the husband had remarried prior to his death. The plan administrator took the position that the second spouse was entitled to her 50 percent interest under ERISA and the remaining 50 percent should pass to the first spouse as per the beneficiary designation. The Washington Court of Appeals, citing *Egelhoff* and RCW 11.07.010(2)(a), held that divorce revoked the beneficiary designation and held that the second spouse was to receive all of the benefits (50 percent under ERISA and 50 percent in recognition of her community property).

The Texas Supreme Court has also not agreed with the *Egelhoff* result. In *Keen v. Weaver*, 121 S.W.3d 721 (Tex.), *cert. denied*, 488 U.S. 1006 (2003), the plan participant and wife were divorced, but the participant died without changing the beneficiary designation for plan benefits, leaving his former wife as the primary beneficiary and his mother as the contingent beneficiary. Texas had a "redesignation" statute similar to that at issue in the *Egelhoff* decision. The Texas Supreme Court stated that although ERISA preempts the Texas redesignation statute, federal common law principles would recognize the former spouse's voluntary and knowing waiver of the plan's benefits. Not surprisingly, this was a five/four decision with the dissenters believing that the former spouse should receive the benefits.

In yet another case indicating a strong trend in favor of ERISA preemption, the Fifth Circuit Court of Appeals stated that in a simultaneous death setting, payment of benefits is governed by ERISA, the plain meaning of the plan language, and beneficiary designation. *Tucker v. Shreveport Transit Mgmt, Inc.*, 226 F.3d 394 (5th Cir. 2000). In this case, the court refused to take into consideration a "simultaneous death" provision in the decedent's will as well as Louisiana's statute concerning presumed survivorship.

In a postnuptial agreement, husband and wife agreed to disposition of husband's IRA in the event of a divorce. The IRA was not currently segregated or divided in any way. The I.R.S. concluded that this arrangement did not cause any form of deemed distribution or a prohibited transaction within the meaning of I.R.C. § 4975(c). Priv. Ltr. Rul. 2002-15-061 (Jan. 16, 2002).

If the nonworking spouse has a community property interest in the working spouse's accounts, consideration must be given to planning for the disposition of his or her interest. Unfortunately, the extent to which the nonworking spouse may control the disposition of the interest is unclear. Most community property states regard the nonworking spouse as having a community property interest in the working spouse's retirement plans to the extent the benefits accrued during marriage. The same is true of IRAs. The community property states that have addressed the issue allow the nonworking spouse to dispose of that interest by will if he or she predeceases the working spouse. *In re Estate of Mundell*, 124 Idaho 152, 857 P.2d 631 (1993); *In re Estate of MacDonald*, 51 Cal. 3d 262, 794 P.2d 911 (1990); *Allard v. Frech*, 754 S.W.2d 111 (Tex. 1988), *cert. denied*, 488 U.S. 1006 (1989); *Farver v. Dep't of Retirement Sys.*, 97 Wn.2d 344, 644 P.2d 1149 (1982).

Although the state courts have generally recognized that the nonworking spouse has a community property interest in the portion of a qualified plan that accrues during marriage, the United States Supreme Court has held that the anti-alienation provisions of ERISA prevent the nonworking spouse from disposing of his or her interest with respect to qualified plans. In *Boggs v. Boggs*, 520 U.S. 833, 117 S. Ct. 1754, 138 L. Ed. 2d 45 (1996), the Supreme Court essentially followed the logic of and came to the same conclusion as the Ninth Circuit Court of Appeals in *Ablamis v. Roper*, 937 F.2d 1450 (9th Cir. 1991). Thus, although the nonworking spouse may have a community property interest in a retirement plan during his or her nonworking spouse's lifetime, that interest is inaccessible following his or her death. Like the *Ablamis* decision, the *Boggs* decision significantly impacts planning in a community property jurisdiction. For example, if the couple wishes to have the entire community property of the first spouse to die pass into trusts for the benefit of the surviving spouse, that wish could be carried out relative to the retirement plan if the working spouse dies first. However, if the nonworking spouse dies first, the working spouse could assert the *Boggs* decision to prevent the deceased nonworking spouse's interest from being awarded to a trust under the deceased nonworking spouse's will. In such a case, could the estate of the nonworking spouse obtain some sort of "charging order" against the surviving working spouse's interest in the couple's community property? Or, would such a charging order likewise be preempted by ERISA and the *Boggs* decision?

A charging order would likely be unobtainable. The *Boggs* decision denied both access to the retirement plan benefits and an "accounting" from other assets. Moreover, the United States Supreme Court, in *Yiatchos v. Yiatchos,* 376 U.S. 306, 84 S. Ct. 742, 11 L. Ed. 2d 724 (1964), held that relative to United States Savings Bonds, federal law prevails over inconsistent state law. In *Yiatchos,* the heirs attempted to preclude a surviving joint tenant from taking United States Savings Bonds and, in the alternative, argued for a charging order against other assets. The Supreme Court made quick work of both arguments and stated that awarding the joint tenancy assets to the co-owner but requiring the co-owner to account for one-half of the value of those assets would render the federal law and award of title meaningless.

The *Boggs* decision could prevent the nonworking spouse from making full use of his or her unified credit. In particular, the rule may prevent a nonworking spouse who owns few assets (other than a retirement plan account) from sheltering enough other assets from inclusion in the estate of the working spouse. As a result, the estate of the surviving spouse may be required to pay a larger estate tax than otherwise. A planning approach might be an agreement prior to death for a division of the former community property on an "aggregate" approach. The same result could be obtained after death in states permitting non-pro rata divisions of the former community property. Query: Would the I.R.S. use the *Boggs* rule to assert that such a division results in a gift by the surviving working spouse?

Existing law appears to recognize that the nonworking spouse has much more control over the disposition of his or her community property interest in an IRA. *See* RCW 6.15.020. This statute states that the nonworking spouse's community property interest in the working spouse's IRA may pass under the nonworking spouse's will. How the interest would actually be disposed of to someone other than the working spouse is a difficult question.

In Private Letter Ruling 94-39-020 (July 7, 1994), the I.R.S. held that an IRA can be partitioned (within one IRA account) into equally owned units without adverse tax effects. It held that the partition of a community property IRA into separate equal shares owned and subject to disposition by each spouse (but held within the working spouse's IRA) was not a taxable event and did not constitute a transfer or distribution for purposes of I.R.C. § 408(d)(1). In such a case the nonworking spouse could dispose of his or her interest in the IRA in a way that shelters it from inclusion in the working spouse's estate. This possibility should be explored in connection with planning for large estates. The Service also held that such a partition did not involve any gift by either spouse. It should be noted that an actual transfer of one spouse's IRA into an IRA in the name of the other spouse is, absent a divorce, a taxable distribution to the account holder spouse. *See Rodoni v. Commissioner,* 105 T.C. 29 (1995).

In an earlier Private Letter Ruling, the I.R.S. held that a predeceasing spouse may dispose of his or her community property interest in an IRA. Priv. Ltr. Rul. 80-40-101 (July 15, 1980). In this ruling the I.R.S. allowed the nonworking spouse's community property interest in the working spouse's rollover IRA to be distributed pursuant to the will of the nonworking spouse. It further determined that the distribution would not be taxed to the surviving working spouse. Rather, the benefits were taxable to the individuals who received them. The I.R.S. also concluded that the custodian of the IRA could recognize the probate court's order to distribute to the beneficiaries of the nonworking spouse's will. The above result may no longer be valid after the Tax Court's decisions in *Bunney* and *Morris*.

In light of Private Letter Rulings 1999 -25-033 (June 25, 1999) and 1999-12-040 (Dec. 29, 1998), the disclaimer approach may be the best option for "funding" the credit shelter trust upon the death of the nonworking spouse. Preparation for such funding would be as follows: (1) the surviving spouse should be named as sole personal representative of the will and given broad non-pro rata division and distribution powers, (2) the will should specifically provide that the deceased spouse's interest in the surviving spouse's IRA will pass to the surviving spouse, but if the surviving spouse disclaims, the disclaimed interest will pass to the estate, and (3) the will should provide that, to the extent possible, the decedent's interest in the surviving spouse's IRA will be allocated to the surviving spouse in any non-pro rata distribution. After death, the amount necessary to fully fund the credit shelter trust could be disclaimed and then allocated back to the surviving spouse in a non-pro rata distribution in exchange for the surviving spouse's community interest in non-IRA assets. If the I.R.S. does not change the approach it took under the above Private Letter Rulings, it is likely that the non-pro rata distribution will not accelerate income. Moreover, it appears that the I.R.S. does not take issue with the non-pro rata distribution by the surviving spouse in his or her capacity as personal representative following a disclaimer by the surviving spouse in his or her capacity as an heir of the estate. *See* Priv. Ltr. Rul. 97-07-008 (Nov. 12, 1996).

§13.7 CREDITORS' CLAIMS

Both retirement plan assets and IRAs enjoy creditor protection for citizens of Washington state. Retirement plans are protected by federal law. *Patterson v. Schumate,* 504 U.S. 753, 112 S. Ct. 932, 117 L. Ed. 2d 104 (1992); *Barkley v. Conner (In re Conner),* 73 F.3d 258 (9th Cir.), *cert. denied,* 519 U.S. 817 (1996). IRAs enjoy creditor protection only as provided by state law. *See* RCW 6.15.020. Recently, the Sixth Circuit ruled that a Michigan statute similar to RCW 6.15.020, which purported to protect IRAs from creditors' claims, was preempted by ERISA. The court reasoned that because ERISA did not extend creditor protection to IRAs, a state's attempt to do so would be preempted. This is an odd and troubling case. *Lampkins v. Golden,* 28 Fed. Appx. 409 (2002). It should be noted that the *Lampkins* case involved a simplified employee pension plan (SEP IRA). Also, bankruptcy was not an issue. It should also be noted that in a bankruptcy case after *Lampkins,* Michigan's IRA exemption was upheld even though the trustee in bankruptcy argued that *Lampkins* should apply. *In re Tomlin,* 315 B.R. 439 (Bankr. E.D. Mich. 2004); *accord In re Rayl,* 299 B.R. 465 (Bankr. S.D. Ohio 2003); *In re Mitchell,* No. 02-13713, 2002 WL 31443051 (Bankr. N.D. Ohio 2002). The author believes that the *Lampkins* case is somewhat of an aberration and that state statutes exempting IRAs from creditors' claims should be upheld. *See also In re Moses,* 167 F.3d 470 (9th Cir. 1999).

It should be noted that ERISA protection does not apply if the retirement plan is sponsored by an employer and the only participants in the plan are the husband and wife who own the employer. *Gill v. Stern (In re Stern),* 345 F.3d 1036 (9th Cir. 2003), *cert. denied,* 541 U.S. 936 (2004). In other words, the plan must have a participant other than the husband and wife who own the business. The time of this participation is measured at the time the creditor asserts the claim. *Id.* Interestingly, it appears that a debtor could transfer from a nonexempt retirement plan to a fully exempt retirement plan without the transaction being considered a fraudulent conveyance under the bankruptcy rules. *Id.* Thus, for example, an owner of a business who is facing severe creditor trouble could either (i) hire an employee who immediately participates in the plan or (ii) the owner himself could take a job with another employer that has participant employees and transfer his benefits to that employer's plan.

> IN RE HAGEMAN, 260 B.R. 852 (Bankr. S.D. Ohio 2001). In *Hageman*, a spouse was awarded an interest in the participant's retirement plan. Before the interest was distributed, the spouse filed bankruptcy. The bankruptcy court held that the creditors' protection of ERISA (*see Patterson v. Shumate*, 504 U.S. 753, 112 S. Ct. 2242 119 L. Ed. 2d 519 (1992)) was inapplicable to rights segregated for a spouse under a qualified domestic relations order (QDRO). Moreover, the court held that the protection for benefits under Ohio state law likewise did not apply to the spouse's interest.

The BANKRUPTCY ABUSE PREVENTION AND CONSUMER PROTECTION ACT OF 2005, Pub. L. 109-8, 119 Stat. 23 (2005), was signed into law on April 20, 2005. There are key changes made to a debtor's ability to exempt IRAs and certain tax-qualified retirement plans in bankruptcy.

To understand the changes, it is helpful to review the prior bankruptcy scheme. The ability of a debtor to exempt assets from creditors' claims in a bankruptcy proceeding is governed by 11 U.S.C. § 522. For ease of reference, we will refer to this statute in its pre-amendment form as the "prior law". Under the prior law, the debtor was permitted to elect either a list of federal exemptions or the exemptions provided by applicable state law. The debtor could not pick and choose from the two groups of exemptions. Of course, either way, qualified retirement plans governed by ERISA were exempt by virtue of ERISA. *Patterson v. Schumate*, 504 U.S. 753. However, as discussed above, it is possible for a qualified retirement plan to lack ERISA protection. With respect to a debtor's IRA (and a qualified plan not covered by ERISA), the decision to elect federal or state exemptions was critical. A debtor who elected the Washington state exemptions would rely on RCW 6.15.020, which exempts IRAs and many non-ERISA plans from creditors' claims. RCW 6.15.020. This exemption is unlimited. If federal exemptions were elected, the prior law stated as follows:

> A payment under a stock bonus, pension, profit sharing, annuity or similar plan or contract on account of illness, disability, death, age, or length of service, *to the extent reasonably necessary for the support of the debtor* and any dependent of the debtor . . . (Emphasis added.)

Former 11 U.S.C. § 522(d).

Under the prior law, there was a question as to whether the federal exemption applied to IRAs at all. This issue was settled by the Supreme Court in *Rousey v. Jacoway*, ___ U.S. ___, 125 S. Ct. 1561, 161 L. Ed. 2d 563, 73 U.S.L.W. 4277 (2005) In the *Rousey* case, the debtor elected the federal exemptions. The Court held that the above quoted section of the prior law applies to IRAs, but only permitted the debtors to exempt that which was reasonably necessary for their support. Had the *Rousey* bankruptcy occurred in the state of Washington and the state exemptions been elected, the debtor's entire IRA would have been exempt.

Section 224 of Pub. L. 109-8 substantially changes 11 U.S.C. § 522 with respect to its treatment of IRAs and qualified plans not covered by ERISA. This "new law" includes the following provisions:

- If the debtor elects state exemptions, IRAs and qualified plans not covered by ERISA have exempt status unless applicable state law specifically states otherwise. Therefore, for a Washington resident electing the state exemptions, RCW 6.15.020 along with the new law will exempt the IRA subject only to a dollar limit that has a very narrow application, discussed below.

- If the debtor elects the federal list of exemptions under the new law, there is now a specific exemption for IRA and tax-qualified non-ERISA plans. This exemption is not subject to the "reasonably necessary for support" test of the prior law. 11 U.S.C.A. 522(d)(12). This exemption is also subject to a very narrowly worded limit, described below.

- The new law includes a limit for the dollar amount of an IRA that may be exempt. 11 U.S.C.A. 522(n). This dollar limit applies whether the debtor elects state or federal exemptions. Thus, this dollar limit theoretically could limit application of RCW 6.15.020 when a Washington resident has elected state exemptions. The limit is $1 million; however,

  1) Amounts in an IRA attributable to a rollover from a qualified plan are *not* taken into account in the $1 million limit. This means that the $1 million limit really only applies to traditional annual IRA contributions and earnings thereon.

  2) The $1 million exemption limit does not apply to a SEP (simplified employee pension) account or a SIMPLE retirement account. This makes sense as these are employer-sponsored IRAs similar to 401(k) plans.

Comment:

The new law is good news for debtors. It is now clear that IRAs may be protected under both the federal and applicable state exemptions. Because the $1 million limit does not apply to rollover contributions, it is advisable to keep rollover IRAs separate from an IRA funded by annual contributions. The new law really does not affect the treatment of accounts in a tax-qualified retirement plan that is fully covered by ERISA. As mentioned above, ERISA provides the exemption for these accounts. However, the new law improves the protection for an account in a tax-qualified plan that is not covered by ERISA, such as the §401(k) plan in the *In Re Stern* case described above. Under the prior law, such an account was only protected if the debtor elected state exemptions and the state exemptions provided protection for such an account. Under the new law, as long as the arrangement is tax-qualified, the federal exemptions provide protection.

In the context of a bankrupt individual with an interest in a qualified retirement plan, the creditors may have the incentive to look for problems with plan language or administration leading to plan disqualification. The IRS has a program to retroactively correct qualification defects as "EPCRS" under Rev. Proc. 2008-50. A bankruptcy court should honor such a retroactive correction.

Another area of concern involves IRAs. Under IRC §408(e)(2), an IRA will lose its tax qualified status in the year a prohibited transaction under IRC §4975 occurs with respect to the IRA. In *In Re Ernst W. Willis*, 104 AFTR. 2d 2009-5195, the creditors asserted the existence of prohibited transactions with regard to the debtor's IRA in order to defeat creditor protection and obtain access to the IRA. There is no IRS correction program for IRA prohibited transactions. See the discussion below concerning inherited IRAs and creditor protection.

§13.8 INHERITED IRA

- **What is an inherited IRA?**

An inherited IRA is an IRA received by a beneficiary of a deceased account holder. As discussed below, the decedent may have left an IRA to said beneficiary or a retirement plan account to said beneficiary which retirement plan account is transferred to the inherited IRA by way of a "non-spouse rollover" under IRC §402(c)(11).

If the decedent's surviving spouse is the beneficiary of the decedent's IRA; then, until the surviving spouse completes a spousal rollover into an IRA in the name of the surviving spouse, the decedent's IRA is technically an inherited IRA with regard to the surviving spouse. However, once the surviving spouse rolls the decedent's IRA into an IRA in the surviving spouse's name, the surviving spouse becomes the account holder with respect to said IRA and said rollover IRA is not an inherited IRA.

- **How are inherited IRAs created?**

An inherited IRA may emanate from a decedent's IRA as follows: The account holder of an IRA dies designating a beneficiary of his or her IRA. Assuming the beneficiary is not the surviving spouse (so that there will be no spousal rollover), the IRA will now be registered in the decedent's name for the benefit of ("f/b/o") the non-spouse beneficiary. If the deceased account holder named several beneficiaries, the IRA may be divided in compliance with required minimum distribution ("RMD") rules into separate f/b/o accounts; each in the name of the decedent f/b/o a specified beneficiary.

Example:

Sally Smith dies in 2007 at age 72 with her three children designated as beneficiaries of her IRA. Sally's three children make sure that her 2007 RMD is taken before December 31, 2007. Sally's children thereafter direct the custodian of the IRA to divide Sally's IRA by way of direct IRA-to-IRA transfers into three new IRAs; each in the name of Sally, deceased f/b/o a specific child. Each of these three IRAs are inherited IRAs which will be treated as separate IRAs for RMD purposes under Reg. 1.401(a)(9)-8, QA2.

Example:

Fred dies designating his wife, Sue, as beneficiary of his IRA. Sue is only 55 years of age and fears she may need distributions from Fred's IRA to live on. Sue is advised that distributions taken from an inherited IRA are exempt from the 10% penalty of Section 72(t) so she leaves the IRA registered in Fred's name f/b/o Sue. While the IRA is so registered, it is an inherited IRA with regard to Sue. After attaining age 59^1/$_2$ (when Sue would no longer be subject to the premature distribution penalty of IRC §72(t)), Sue rolls Fred's IRA into an IRA in Sue's name. Sue's rollover IRA is not an inherited IRA. It is a rollover IRA of which Sue is the account holder having all rights of an account holder (e.g., Sue can delay commencing RMDs until April 1 of the calendar year following the calendar year Sue attains age 70^1/$_2$, Sue may convert the IRA to a Roth IRA, Sue may designate beneficiaries whose life expectancies will be utilized for a stretch out distribution following Sue's death under the RMD rules).

The second way that an inherited IRA may be created is by way of a "non-spouse rollover" under IRC §402(c)(11). Under this new Code section, if the retirement plan so allows, a non-spouse beneficiary may direct the administrator of the decedent's retirement plan to transfer the decedent's account to an inherited IRA. This is different than the spousal rollover option. If an account holder in a retirement plan dies designating the spouse as beneficiary, the spouse has the right to take distribution of the decedent's account and roll it into an IRA in the spouse's name. Again, the spousal rollover IRA is not an inherited IRA. Rather, the spouse will be the account holder with respect to the IRA. Section 402(c)(11) allows a non-spouse beneficiary to have the decedent's account in a retirement plan transferred to an inherited IRA.

Example:

Bill dies in 2007 designating his daughter, Kate, as beneficiary of a §401(k) plan account. The plan in question permits a non-spouse rollover. Kate may direct the plan to make a direct plan-to-IRA transfer of Bill's account to an IRA in Bill's name, deceased f/b/o Kate (an inherited IRA). This direct transfer may occur in one of two ways. The funds could be directly transferred from the §401(k) plan account to the inherited IRA account. Or, a check in the name of the IRA custodian may be issued to Kate which Kate takes to the IRA custodian. However, the §401(k) plan may not issue the check in Kate's name. Section 402(c)(11)(A).

- **How are RMDs calculated from an inherited IRA?**

A discussion of the RMD rules can be found at Section 1.2(1), above. However, for purposes of this section, let's assume that there is one individual beneficiary or that the separate account rules of Reg. 1.401(a)(9)-8 have been complied with so that, for RMD purposes, each beneficiary would be treated separately. Finally, because special rules apply to a surviving spouse (a spousal rollover opportunity and the ability to delay RMDs) the following assume an individual non-spouse beneficiary. Initially, if the decedent was already beyond his or her required beginning date, the beneficiaries must make certain that the decedent's RMD for the year of death is made. Reg. 1.401(a)(9)-5, QA4. Unless the "five-year rule" (described below) applies, a non-spouse recipient of an inherited IRA must begin RMDs no later than the end of the calendar year following the account holder's death.

Example:

Betty dies in 2007 at age 75 after taking her 2007 RMD naming her daughter, Shirley, as beneficiary. Shirley's first RMD is due December 31, 2008 and will be computed with reference to the December 31, 2007 IRA account balance. For her 2008 RMD, Shirley will divide said account balance by her life expectancy under the single life table ("SLT") of Reg. 1.401(a)(9)-9, QA1 based on Shirley's attained age in 2008. This process repeats each calendar year by reducing Shirley's initial divisor by one. In short, the table is only consulted in the first year (2008) as the divisor, once established in 2008, reduces by one for each year thereafter. This method is known as a "stretch out".

If the account holder dies before his or her required beginning date, there is the possibility that the five-year rule may apply. This rule requires that the account be completely distributed by the end of the calendar year containing the fifth anniversary of the participant's death. Reg. 1.401(a)(9)-3A(b), QA2. Generally speaking, the five-year rule is not a concern where the decedent's account was in an IRA. However, it is not uncommon for retirement plans to employ the five-year rule. For example, a §401(k) plan might require that a non-spouse beneficiary receive complete distribution within five years of the decedent's death. The beneficiary may nonetheless escape the five-year rule, if (i) the plan permits a non-spouse rollover and (ii) the beneficiary completes the non-spouse rollover before the end of the calendar year following the calendar year of the participant's death. Notice 2007-7, QA17(c)(2) and IRS clarification by newsletter dated February 13, 2007.

Example:

Fred dies at age 60 leaving his §401(k) plan account to his daughter, Pebbles. The §401(k) plan permits non-spouse rollovers but also states that non-spouse beneficiaries must complete distribution within five years of death. If Pebbles completes a non-spouse rollover before the end of the year following Fred's death, the five-year rule will not apply to her inherited IRA. Instead, Pebbles will obtain the "stretch out" described above. Note, if Pebbles completes the non-spouse rollover in the year after Fred's death, her RMD for such year may not be transferred to the inherited IRA.

- **What about trusts as beneficiaries?**

If a decedent dies naming a trust as beneficiary of an IRA, complicated rules apply in determining RMDs applicable to the trust (see §13.2(1)(i), above. Said IRA will be an inherited IRA in the name of the decedent f/b/o the trust. Moreover, if the decedent of a retirement plan account dies naming a trust as beneficiary, the trustee could direct the retirement plan to transfer the account directly to an inherited IRA if (i) the plan so allows and (ii) the trust is a qualified trust under the RMD rules. Notice 2007-7.

- **What key rights does a beneficiary of an inherited IRA have?**

  - The beneficiary may take as little as the required RMD each year or additional amounts as permitted by the applicable IRA custodial account agreement.
  - If the beneficiary wishes to move the IRA from one custodian to another, he or she may do so by way of a direct IRA-to-IRA transfer. Section 402(c)(11).
  - As part of his or her estate plan, the beneficiary may designate who will receive the balance of the inherited IRA upon the beneficiary's death. This beneficiary designation does not affect the calculation of RMDs following

the beneficiary's death. Thus, for example, if the beneficiary of an inherited IRA dies naming a trust as his or her successor, the trustee will be required to continue the RMD calculation as was formerly utilized by the beneficiary.

- The beneficiary of an inherited IRA may take distributions before he or she attains age $59^1/_2$ free of the 10% penalty of IRC §72(t).
- The beneficiary of an inherited IRA may deduct from his or her income tax liability associated with IRA withdrawals the estate tax attributable to such IRA under IRC §691(c).
- In the process of a non-spouse rollover from a qualified plan, the beneficiary can convert the account to a Roth under the rules described at Section 1.2(4), above.

- **What rights does a beneficiary of an inherited IRA not have?**

  - The beneficiary of an inherited IRA may not consolidate said IRA with an IRA of which the beneficiary is an account holder.
  - The beneficiary of an inherited IRA may not make pre-tax or after tax contributions to the inherited IRA.
  - A non-spouse beneficiary may not receive a distribution in the beneficiary's name and then roll the distribution to another IRA. This could be accomplished, however, by way of an IRA-to-IRA direct transfer.
  - The beneficiary may not roll an inherited IRA into a retirement plan account in the beneficiary's name.
  - Under current law, an inherited IRA cannot be converted to a Roth IRA.

As mentioned above, if a surviving spouse is the beneficiary of an IRA, until such IRA is rolled over into an IRA in the spouse's name, the IRA is an inherited IRA in the hands of the surviving spouse. Under IRC §408 and §402, a surviving spouse may take a distribution of the IRA and roll it into an IRA in his or her name. Thereafter, the rollover IRA is no longer an inherited IRA but an IRA of which the spouse is the account holder for all purposes.

- **Creditor protection of an inherited IRA.**

Whether an inherited IRA is entitled to creditor protection is an issue "in process". For debtors asserting the federal bankruptcy exemptions, there are two conflicting rulings. In the case of *In re Chilton*, (Bankr. Ct, TX 35 2010), the Bankruptcy Court found that inherited IRAs are not entitled to federal bankruptcy protection. However, a United States Bankruptcy Court in the District of Minnesota came to the opposite conclusion. *In re Nessa*, (Bankr. Ct. Minn. 2010). As to the application of state protective statutes (where the state exemptions are elected in the bankruptcy), there have been several cases (Alabama, California, Illinois, Oklahoma, Texas and Wisconsin) where protection has been denied. For a discussion of these cases, *see* "Are Inherited IRAs Protected Under a State Exemption Statute?" Steve Leimberg's Employee Benefits and Retirement Planning Email Newsletter – Archive Message No. 427. In *In re McClelland*, 2008 W.L. 89901 (Bankr. D. Idaho), the court allowed protection for an inherited IRA under Idaho's statute. Here in Washington state, RCW 6.15.020 is very broadly written (and very similar to the Idaho statute) so that absent a "result oriented decision" the correct answer should favor exemption of an inherited IRA under said statute. As a result of all of this, if the account holder is very worried about creditor protection for his beneficiaries, a trust as beneficiary (as opposed to the beneficiaries outright) should be considered.

Appendices

The author expresses no legal, tax, or other opinions herein or with regard to the forms appearing as appendices (or any other forms attached to this Article). Also, the author takes no responsibility for misstatements or errors that may appear herein as these materials cannot be relied upon as research materials. The following should only be used upon a thorough review of the client's facts and applicable law. Moreover, the reproduction of Reg. 1.401(a)(9)-9 appearing at Appendix I is for illustrative purposes only and, due to possible updates and computer glitches, only the actual regulation from a service publishing the same should be used to make a calculation

§ 13.22. Appendix A Beneficiary Designation Agreement—Surviving Spouse Naming Multiple Children

IRA BENEFICIARY DESIGNATION AGREEMENT

The undersigned "IRA Custodian" (_____) and the under-signed "Participant" (_____) do hereby agree as follows with respect to the IRA Custodial ("Account") maintained by the IRA Custodian on behalf of the Participant:

1. <u>Primary Beneficiaries</u>. The Primary Beneficiaries of the Participant's Account and their respective shares for purposes of Section 2 herein, shall be as follows:

¶

Beneficiary	Social Security Number	Percentage
		%
		%
		%
		%

2. Separate IRAs. The Participant's Account shall be divided into separate IRAs for the Primary Beneficiaries with each said Primary Beneficiary's IRA to have allocated to it the percentage of the Participant's Account designated above. If a Primary Beneficiary fails to survive the Participant but leaves at least one lineal descendant who survives the Participant, said Primary Beneficiary's IRA shall be further divided, per stirpes, into separate IRAs for said deceased Primary Beneficiary's lineal descendants who survive the Participant (who shall be considered Primary Beneficiaries hereunder); or, if the deceased Primary Beneficiary leaves no lineal descendant surviving the Participant, the percentage of the Participant's Account as designated under Section 1 for the deceased Primary Beneficiary shall be added, pro rata, to the other separate IRAs created hereunder. The identity of the Primary Beneficiaries under this Beneficiary Designation and the shares used to establish each of their separate IRAs under this Section 2, shall be provided to the Custodian by the Personal Representative of the Participant's estate as soon as practicable following the Participant's death and the Custodian shall have no liability whatsoever with regard to said division. Said division shall occur as soon as practicable following the death of the Participant and shall be effective upon the death of the Participant.

3. Separate IRAs. Each Primary Beneficiary's separate IRA under Section 2 shall be and remain a separate IRA in the name of the deceased Participant (F/B/O the Primary Beneficiary). Each separate IRA shall thereafter be paid to its respective Primary Beneficiary in annual payments equal to the required minimum distribution under IRC §401(a)(9) to be initiated and calculated by the Primary Beneficiary; provided, however, that at any time or times requested by the Primary Beneficiary, the Custodian shall distribute to said Primary Beneficiary, from his or her separate IRA, such amount as said Primary Beneficiary may request in writing. Upon written request by the Primary Beneficiary of a separate IRA hereunder, the Custodian shall transfer said Primary Beneficiary's separate IRA to such other trust or custodial account specified by said Primary Beneficiary; provided that the transferee account is an IRA under IRC §408. Each Primary Beneficiary shall have the power to determine the investment of his or her separate IRA. In the event a Primary Beneficiary of a separate IRA dies before his or her IRA has been distributed to said deceased Primary Beneficiary, the remaining assets in said IRA of said deceased Primary Beneficiary shall be divided into separate IRAs for the beneficiary or beneficiaries designated by said deceased Primary Beneficiary on a form reasonably acceptable to the Custodian; or, to the extent a beneficiary has not been so designated, the deceased Primary Beneficiary's IRA shall be divided, per stirpes, into separate IRAs for the lineal descendants of the deceased Primary Beneficiary who survive said Primary Beneficiary or, if none, per stirpes for the then living lineal descendants of the Participant, the identity of whom and shares of which the Personal Representative of the deceased Primary Beneficiary's estate shall provide to the Custodian. Distributions from an

IRA created for a beneficiary of a deceased Primary Beneficiary shall occur as required by IRC § 401(a)(9) and shall be calculated and initiated by said beneficiary. Moreover, said beneficiary shall, with respect to his or her IRA, have all rights of a Primary Beneficiary described above relative to additional withdrawals, transfer and investment control.

4. Miscellaneous. By entering into this Beneficiary Designation Agreement, the IRA Custodian does hereby acknowledge and agree that:

(a) No Required Distributions Other than Minimum Distributions. Other than the minimum distributions required by law, neither the Participant nor any beneficiary shall be required to take any distribution at any time.

(b) Responsibility for Minimum Distributions. Any minimum distribution shall be initiated and calculated by the Participant while living and, after the Participant's death, the beneficiary with respect to his or her separate IRA. The Custodian shall be under no obligation to initiate or calculate any minimum distribution.

(c) Modification of IRA Trust. By its acceptance of this Beneficiary Designation Agreement, the Custodian agrees that its printed IRA Agreement is amended so that the provisions of this Beneficiary Designation Agreement shall control in the event of any difference or conflict between this Beneficiary Designation Agreement and the terms of the printed IRA Agreement. Accordingly, this Beneficiary Designation Agreement amends the printed IRA Agreement to include provisions not otherwise in the printed IRA Agreement and to supersede and replace any provisions otherwise inconsistent with the provisions of this Beneficiary Designation Agreement; provided, however, that nothing herein that would be contrary to the requirements of IRC § 408 or § 401(a)(9) relative to an individual retirement account and distributions therefrom shall be effective.

(d) Agreement Revocable. This Beneficiary Designation Agreement may be altered, changed or revoked during the Participant's lifetime. Upon the Participant's death, this Beneficiary Designation Agreement shall become irrevocable.

DATED this ___ day of _____, 20___.

Participant: _____

_____

IRA Custodian: _____

By: _____

Its: _____

§13.23. Appendix A-1 Primary Beneficiary: Surviving Spouse— Secondary Beneficiary: Children

BENEFICIARY DESIGNATION

The undersigned "IRA Custodian" (_____) and the undersigned "Participant" _____ do hereby agree as follows with respect to the IRA Custodial ("Account") maintained by the IRA Custodian on behalf of the Participant:

1. Primary Beneficiary. If _____ (spouse) survives the Participant, the beneficiary of the Account shall be _____. _____ may roll over all or any portion of the Account payable to her hereunder into an IRA in _____'s name, whether or not the custodian or trustee of the recipient IRA is the IRA Custodian hereunder. The IRA Custodian shall fully cooperate with _____ with regard to such a rollover.

2. Contingent Beneficiaries. In the event _____ does not survive the Participant, the Secondary Beneficiaries of the Participant's Account and their respective shares for purposes of Section 2.a herein, shall be as follows:

Beneficiary_____ Percentage

_____ ___%

_____ ___%

a. Separate IRAs. The Participant's Account shall be divided into separate IRAs for the Secondary Beneficiaries with each said Secondary Beneficiary's IRA to have allocated to it the percentage of the Participant's Account designated above. If a Secondary Beneficiary fails to survive the Participant but leaves at least one lineal descendant who survives the Participant, said Secondary Beneficiary's IRA shall be further divided, per stirpes, into separate IRAs for said deceased Secondary Beneficiary's lineal descendants who survive the Participant (who shall be considered Secondary Beneficiaries hereunder); or, if the deceased Secondary Beneficiary leaves no lineal descendant surviving the Participant, the percentage of the Participant's Account as designated under this section for the deceased Secondary Beneficiary shall be added, pro rata, to the other separate IRAs created hereunder. The identity of the Secondary Beneficiaries under this Beneficiary Designation and the shares used to establish each of their separate IRAs under this section shall be provided to the Custodian by the Personal Representative of the Participant's estate as soon as practicable following the Participant's death and the Custodian shall have no liability whatsoever with regard to said division. Said division shall occur as soon as practicable following the death of the Participant and shall be effective upon the death of the Participant.

b. <u>Separate IRAs.</u> Each Secondary Beneficiary's separate IRA under this section shall be and remain a separate IRA in the name of the deceased Participant (F/B/O the Secondary Beneficiary). Each separate IRA shall thereafter be paid to its respective Secondary Beneficiary in annual payments equal to the required minimum distribution under IRC § 401(a)(9) to be initiated and calculated by the Secondary Beneficiary; provided, however, that at any time or times requested by the Secondary Beneficiary, the Custodian shall distribute to said Secondary Beneficiary, from his or her separate IRA, such amount as said Secondary Beneficiary may request in writing. Upon written request by the Secondary Beneficiary of a separate IRA hereunder, the Custodian shall transfer said Secondary Beneficiary's separate IRA to such other trust or custodial account specified by said Secondary Beneficiary; provided that the transferee account is an IRA under IRC § 408. Each Secondary Beneficiary shall have the power to determine the investment of his or her separate IRA. In the event a Secondary Beneficiary of a separate IRA dies before his or her IRA has been distributed to said deceased Secondary Beneficiary, the remaining assets in said IRA of said deceased Secondary Beneficiary shall be divided into separate IRAs for the beneficiary or beneficiaries designated by said deceased Secondary Beneficiary on a form reasonably acceptable to the Custodian; or, to the extent a beneficiary has not been so designated, the deceased Secondary Beneficiary's IRA shall be divided, per stirpes, into separate IRAs for the lineal descendants of the deceased Secondary Beneficiary who survive said Secondary Beneficiary or, if none, per stirpes for the then living lineal descendants of the Participant, the identity of whom and shares of which the Personal Representative of the deceased Secondary Beneficiary's estate shall provide to the Custodian. Distributions from an IRA created for a beneficiary of a deceased Secondary Beneficiary shall occur as required by IRC § 401(a)(9) and shall be calculated and initiated by said beneficiary. Moreover, said beneficiary shall, with respect to his or her IRA, have all rights of a Secondary Beneficiary described above relative to additional withdrawals, transfer and investment control.

3. <u>Miscellaneous.</u> By entering into this Beneficiary Designation Agreement, the IRA Custodian does hereby acknowledge and agree that:

a. <u>No Required Distributions Other than Minimum Distributions.</u> Other than the minimum distributions required by law, neither the Participant nor any beneficiary shall be required to take any distribution at any time.

b. <u>Responsibility for Minimum Distributions.</u> Any minimum distribution shall be initiated and calculated by the Participant while living and, after the Participant's death, the beneficiary with respect to his or her separate IRA. The Custodian shall be under no obligation to initiate or calculate any minimum distribution.

c. <u>Modification of IRA Trust.</u> By its acceptance of this Beneficiary Designation Agreement, the Custodian agrees that its printed IRA Agreement is amended so that the provisions of this Beneficiary Designation Agreement shall control in the event of any difference or conflict between this Beneficiary Designation Agreement and the terms of the printed IRA Agreement. Accordingly, this Beneficiary Designation Agreement amends the printed IRA Agreement to include provisions not otherwise in the printed IRA Agreement and to supersede and replace any provisions otherwise inconsistent with the provisions of this Beneficiary Designation Agreement; provided, however, that nothing herein that would be contrary to the requirements of IRC § 408 or § 401(a)(9) relative to an individual retirement account and distributions therefrom shall be effective.

    d. <u>Agreement Revocable</u>. This Beneficiary Designation Agreement may be altered, changed or revoked during the Participant's lifetime. Upon the Participant's death, this Beneficiary Designation Agreement shall become irrevocable.

Dated this _____ day of _____, 20___.

          Participant: _____

              Spouse: _____

    IRA Custodian: _____

                 By: _____

                 Its: _____

§ 13.23. Appendix A-2—Short Form Designations

<u>BENEFICIARY DESIGNATION</u>

- <u>Primary Beneficiary</u>. [Spouse]; provided, however, that any portion of the account disclaimed by [spouse] shall pass to the [spouse] Trust under Article V of the Last Will of _____.

- <u>Secondary Beneficiary</u>. If [spouse] does not survive the account holder, the account shall be divided into separate accounts; one for each child of the account holder's who survives the account holder and one for each deceased child of the account holder's who leaves at least one lineal descendant surviving the account holder. The separate accounts with respect to a deceased child of the account holder's who leaves a lineal descendant surviving the account holder shall be further divided, per stirpes, into separate accounts for the descendants of the deceased child who survive the account holder. The separate account of any descendant of a deceased child of the account holder's who is then under thirty (30) years of age shall be payable to said descendant's trust under Article VI.B of the Last Will of _____.

§13.24. Appendix B—Revocable Living Trust Provisions (Non-Pro Rata Powers)

Division of Trust Property Upon Death of First Grantor. As soon as practicable after the death of the first of the Grantors to die, the Trustee shall divide this Trust into two (2) separate shares, one separate trust share to be designated the "Surviving Grantor's Trust", and the other separate trust share to be designated the "Family Trust". The Surviving Grantor's Trust shall consist of the surviving Grantor's community property and separate property interests held by (or, as a result of the death of the deceased Grantor distributed to), this Trust and the surviving Grantor's separate property interest held by this Trust. The Family Trust shall consist of the deceased Grantor's community property and separate property interests held by (or, as a result of the death of the deceased Grantor distributed to), this Trust.

Non-Pro Rata Division/Retirement Benefits. The Trustee (and the deceased Grantors' Personal Representative) are fully and completely authorized to agree with the surviving Grantor to make an approximately equal non-pro rata division of the Grantors' former community property (both probate and non-probate); provided, however, that property shall be exchanged as its exchange date value. In making said non-pro rata division, the Grantors intend, to the maximum extent possible, that any right to "Retirement Benefits" (individual retirement account, annuity, bond or SEPP under IRC § 408, a tax deferred annuity under IRC § 403, or a retirement plan under IRC § 401) shall be allocated to the Surviving Grantor's Trust. Notwithstanding any other provision of this Trust to the contrary, the Surviving Grantor shall have the unilateral right to withdraw, at any time, any right to a Retirement Benefit allocated to the Surviving Grantor's Trust under the sentence immediately preceding. In the event that, notwithstanding the preceding, a right to a Retirement Benefit is allocated to the Family Trust, then, it is the Grantor's intent, that, to the maximum extent possible, the same be allocated to the portion of said Family Trust for which a federal estate tax marital deduction is elected; provided, however, immediately after said allocation, said right shall be distributed to the Surviving Grantor, outright.

Retirement Benefits. Notwithstanding any other provision of this Trust, the Trustee may not distribute to or for the benefit of either Grantor's estate, any charity or any other non-individual beneficiary any Retirement Benefits. It is the Grantor's intent that all Retirement Benefits be distributed to or held for only individual beneficiaries, within the meaning of Section 401(a)(9) and applicable regulations. Moreover, notwithstanding any other provision of this Trust or state law, a person's "lineal descendants" for purposes of this instrument shall not include any individual who is a lineal descendant by virtue of legal adoption if such individual (i) was adopted after the Grantor's death and (ii) is older than the oldest beneficiary of this Trust who is living on said date. Any power of appointment under a Trust hereunder shall not be exercisable with respect to Retirement Benefits, to the extent the existence or exercise of said power would result in the Trust failing to have "identifiable beneficiaries" for purposes of the qualified Trust Rules of Treasury Regulation 1.401(a)(9)-4QA5 or to the extent the existence or exercise of said power would result in the Trust being considered to have a beneficiary older than the oldest beneficiary of this Trust who is living on the date specified above. [As an alternative, this provision could specify that, to the extent a Trust becomes a beneficiary of a Retirement Benefit, any withdrawals or distributions from the Plan or IRA will be distributed to the income beneficiary. *See* Reg. § 1.401(a)(9)-5QA7(c)(3)(Ex.2).]

§ 13.25. Appendix C—Beneficiary Designation

Designation of Surviving Spouse (With Disclaimer Opportunity) and Contingent Beneficiary "Safe Harbor" Trust for Children

The undersigned "IRA Custodian" (_____) and the undersigned "Participant" (_____) do hereby agree as follows with respect to the IRA Custodial ("Account") maintained by the IRA Custodian on behalf of the Participant:

1. Primary Beneficiary. If _____ survives the Participant, the beneficiary of the Account shall be _____; provided, however, that any portion of the account disclaimed by her shall pass to the _____ Family Trust.

2. Contingent Beneficiary. In the event _____ does not survive the Participant, the Account shall be divided into equal accounts: one account for each child of the Participant's who survives the Participant and one account for each child of the Participant's who fails to survive the Participant but who leaves at least one lineal descendant of his or hers surviving the Participant. The account of a surviving child of the Participant's shall be payable to said child as provided herein. The account of a deceased child of the Participant's who leaves at least one lineal descendant surviving the Participant, shall be divided, per stirpes, into separate accounts, for the descendants of said deceased child who survive the Participant and said separate accounts shall be payable to the respective beneficiaries thereof as provided herein.

3. Additional Provisions. By entering into this Beneficiary Designation Agreement, the IRA Custodian does hereby acknowledge and agree that:

   a. No Required Distributions Other than Minimum Distributions. Other than the minimum distributions described herein (or required by law) neither the Participant nor any beneficiary shall be required to take any distribution at any time.

   b. Computation of Minimum Distributions. If _____ predeceases the Participant, then the shares under Section 2 shall be divided into separate IRAs under Reg. 1.401(a)(9)-8QA2; and minimum distributions to each beneficiary of a separate account shall be determined with reference to said beneficiary's life expectancy.

   c. Special Rules for Contingent Beneficiaries. The identity of the beneficiaries under this Section 2, and their respective accounts, shall be provided to the IRA Custodian by the personal representative of the Participant's estate as soon as practicable following Participant's death. Each such separate account shall thereafter be paid to its respective beneficiary in annual payments equal to the required minimum distribution under IRC § 401(a)(9) to be initiated and calculated by the beneficiary; provided, however, that at any time or times requested by the beneficiary of said separate account, the IRA Custodian shall distribute to said beneficiary, from his or her separate account, such amount as said beneficiary may request in writing. Upon written request by the beneficiary of a separate account hereunder, the IRA Custodian shall transfer said beneficiary's separate account to such other trust or custodial account specified by said beneficiary; provided that the transferee account is an IRA under IRC § 408. After the death of the Participant, the beneficiary shall have the power to determine the investment of his or her Account. *The foregoing provisions of this Section 3(c) notwithstanding, however, during any period in which a child of the Participant for whom a separate account is established hereunder is under _____ (___) years of age (or a descendant of a deceased child of the Participants' for whom a separate account is established hereunder is under _____ (___) years of age), the Trustee of said beneficiary's separate trust fund under the _____ Family Trust shall have the sole and exclusive right to exercise the powers enumerated in this Section 3(c) on behalf of said beneficiary; provided, however, that any distribution (but not IRA to IRA transfer) from said beneficiary's account shall be made to said beneficiary.* [The foregoing sentence is an example of a "Conduit Trust" format.]

d. <u>Spousal Rollover</u>. If _____ survives the Participant, the Account

payable to her under Section 1 herein, may be rolled over into an IRA in _____'s name, whether or not the custodian or trustee of the recipient IRA is the IRA Custodian. The IRA Custodian will fully cooperate with _____ with regard to such a rollover.

e. <u>Responsibility for Minimum Distributions</u>. Any minimum distribution shall

be initiated and calculated by the Participant while living and, after the Participant's death, the beneficiary. The Custodian shall be under no obligation to initiate or calculate any minimum distribution.

f. <u>Modification of IRA Trust</u>. By its acceptance of this beneficiary Designation

Agreement, the IRA Custodian agrees that its printed IRA Trust document is amended so that the provisions of this Beneficiary Designation Agreement shall control in the event of any difference or conflict between this Beneficiary Designation Agreement and the terms of the printed IRA Trust document. Accordingly, this Beneficiary Designation Agreement amends the printed IRA Trust document to include provisions not otherwise in the printed IRA Trust document and to supersede and replace any provisions otherwise inconsistent with the provisions of this Beneficiary Designation Agreement; provided, however, that nothing herein that would be contrary to the requirements of IRC § 408 or § 401(a)(9) relative to an individual retirement account and distributions therefrom shall be effective.

g. <u>Agreement Revocable</u>. This Beneficiary Designation Agreement may be al-

tered, changed or revoked during the Participant's lifetime. Upon the Participant's death, this Beneficiary Designation Agreement shall become irrevocable.

Dated this _____ day of _____, 20___.

Participant: _____

Spouse of Participant: _____

IRA Custodian: _____

By: _____

Its: _____

§13.26. Appendix D—Will Provisions (Non-Pro Rata Powers)

Allocation of Retirement Benefits in Non-Pro Rata Division. In the furtherance of the settlement of my estate and all Trusts created under this Will, I fully and completely authorize my Personal Representative and the Trustee of any Trust created by this Will to agree with my wife to make an approximate equal division of our former community property (both probate and non-probate). Therefore, my Personal Representative and Trustee may exchange with my wife any interest I may have in community property for my wife's community property. The property shall be exchanged at its exchange date value. It is my intent that, to the extent possible, in the process of any non-pro rata division of community property, any interest in an IRA under IRC §408, a tax deferred annuity under IRC §403 or a retirement plan under IRC §401 be allocated to my wife. Moreover, it is my intent that, in any non-pro rata distribution of assets under Article _____, above, to the extent possible, any such benefits be allocated to that portion of the Trust that would be included in my wife's estate if she died immediately before such division; *provided, however, that immediately after such allocation, the right to such assets shall be distributed, outright, to my wife.*

§13.27. Appendix E—Sample QTIP Beneficiary Designation Agreement

The undersigned _____ ("Account Holder") and the undersigned SEI Investments ("Custodian") do hereby agree as follows with respect to the Account Holder's IRA maintained by Custodian, account number _____ ("Account").

1. *Primary Beneficiaries*. If _____ ("_____") survives the Account Holder, the Beneficiary of the Account shall be the Trust under Section 5.2 of the Account Holder's Will (the "Marital Trust"). Said IRA shall be known as the "Marital Trust IRA" and shall be payable as follows:

   (a) *Distributions*. At least annually, the Custodian shall distribute from the Marital Trust IRA to the Marital Trust the greater of (A) all of the net income of the Account or (B) the required minimum distribution ("RMD") under Section 401(a)(9) of the Internal Revenue Code of 1986 (IRC) required for such year. In addition, the Custodian shall distribute to the Marital Trust from the Marital Trust IRA so much of said IRA as the Trustee of the Marital Trust may, from time to time, request in writing. Under the terms of the Marital Trust, the Trustee of the Marital Trust shall distribute to _____, no less frequently than annually, that amount of the foregoing as equals the net income of the Marital Trust IRA. For the purposes of this paragraph, "net income" shall be determined by the Trustee of the Marital Trust in accordance with Washington State law and the Marital Trust and the Custodian shall have no liability for such determination. Moreover, for the purposes of the foregoing, it is the Account Holder's intent that the Marital Trust shall be considered a "qualified trust" under Reg. 1.401(a)(9)-5 and RMDs from the Marital Trust IRA shall be computed with reference to the life expectancy of _____ under Reg. 1.401(a)(9)-5QA5(c)(1).

(b) *Account Holder's Intent.* The Account Holder intends that the Marital Trust IRA and the Marital Trust qualify for the marital deduction allowable in determining the federal estate tax upon the Account Holder's estate. No provision contained in this Beneficiary Designation Agreement or the IRA plan which would prevent the Marital Trust IRA from so qualifying shall apply to the Marital Trust IRA and it is the Account Holder's intent that any court having jurisdiction over this Beneficiary Designation, the IRA Plan and the Marital Trust construe said documents accordingly.

2. *Contingent Beneficiaries.* In the event _____ does not survive the Account Holder, the contingent beneficiaries and their shares shall be as follows:

3. *Miscellaneous.*

(a) *Transfers.* Upon written request by the Trustee of the Marital Trust, the Custodian shall transfer said trust's IRA to another institution specified by the trustee provided that (i) the transferee account is an IRA under §408 and (ii) prior to said transfer, the transferee agrees, in writing, to be bound by all terms and provisions of this Beneficiary Designation Agreement.

(b) *Limitations.* Nothing herein that would be contrary to the requirements of IRC §408 or §401(a)(9) relative to an individual retirement account and RMDs therefrom shall be effective.

(c) *Agreement Revocable.* This Beneficiary Designation Agreement may be altered, changed or revoked by the Account Holder during his lifetime and shall become irrevocable on his death.

DATED this ___ day of _____, 20__.
Participant: _____
Spouse of Participant: _____
Custodian: _____
By _____
_____, Its _____

§13.28. Appendix F—Sample IRA QTIP Trust Provisions

MARITAL IRA TRUST

IRAs Payable to The Marital Trust of _____. The following shall apply with respect to any and all IRAs of which the Marital Trust of _____ has been designated as beneficiary (and the following shall supersede any contrary provision of this Will):

a. *Withdrawals From IRA.* I contemplate that I may designate the _____ Trust as beneficiary of a portion of one or more individual retirement accounts ("IRA") in my name. To the extent an IRA is payable to the said Trust, such IRA shall be referred to herein as the "Account." The Trustee shall withdraw from the Account and distribute to my wife, during her lifetime, in annual or more frequent installments, all of the "Net Income" of the Account (to be determined in the manner set forth at Section 5.1(e)(b), below). If, during any calendar year, the withdrawal of "Net Income" does not satisfy the required minimum distribution ("RMD") for such calendar year under Section 401(a)(9) ("RMD"), the Trustee shall withdraw from the Account and deposit to the Trust that amount required to satisfy the RMD requirement for such calendar year.

b. *Definition of Net Income.* The Trustee shall, in accordance with the Washington State Principal and Income Act of 2002 (RCW 11.104A et seq.) or its successor and in a manner necessary for both the Account and this Trust to qualify for "Q-Tip" treatment under Rev. Rul. 2006-26: (i) determine all questions as to what is income and what is principal of the Account and the Marital Trust and (ii) to credit or charge to income or principal or to apportion between them any receipt or gain and any charge, disbursement or loss. The power to either (i) convert principal to income under RCW 11.104.020 or (ii) exercise the powers given by RCW 11.104.040 with respect to creation, modification or elimination of a "uni-trust" interest shall be available to and exercisable by the Trustee in accordance with the terms of said statutes. For the purposes of determining the Net Income required to be distributed to my wife hereunder, the Net Income of the Account shall be determined under the foregoing principles as though the assets of the Account are held directly by this Trust.

c. *Account Q-Tip and Minimum Distributions.* With regard to the Account, the Trustee (and/or my Personal Representative) shall (i): take any and all action so that the Account qualifies as qualified terminable interest property under Section 2056 of the Code; and (ii) is authorized, in the Personal Representative's sole and absolute discretion, to elect that any part or all of the Account be treated as qualified terminable interest property for the purpose of qualifying for the marital deduction allowable in determining the federal estate tax and/or Washington State estate tax upon my estate. Further, the Trustee of the Trust shall: (i) at my wife's request, direct the Custodian of the Account to promptly convert unproductive or under productive assets of the Account to productive assets; and (ii) take all other actions and do all things as may be necessary so that the Account and the Trust be treated as qualified terminable interest property for the purpose of qualifying for the marital deduction allowable in determining the federal estate tax and/or Washington State estate tax upon my estate. I hereby direct that no provision contained herein which would prevent the Account or this Trust from so qualifying shall apply to the Account or this Trust. It is my intention that any court having jurisdiction over this Trust construe it accordingly.

d. *RMD Calculation.* I intend that RMDs from the Account be calculated with reference to my wife's life expectancy. Therefore, it is my intent that the Trust be a Qualified Trust within the meaning of Reg. 1.401(a)(9)-4QA5 and that my wife be considered the oldest beneficiary of the Trust for RMD purposes (without application of the "conduit trust" rules of Reg. 1.401(a)(9)-5QA7(c)(3) (Ex. 2). To that end, the following shall apply: (i) during my wife's lifetime, the Trustee shall not make any distributions from the Trust (or cause distributions from the Account) to anyone other than my wife as set forth in this Section 5, (ii) the Trustee may not distribute any portion of the Account to or for the benefit of my estate or use the Account for payment of my debts, taxes, expenses of administration, claims against my estate or payment of taxes due on account of my death, (iii) following my wife's death, no portion of the Account may be distributed to any individual beneficiary older than my wife or, subject to contrary and superseding federal or state law, a non-individual; and, (iv) where used in this trust, the terms children, lineal descendants or words of similar import shall exclude anyone older than my wife.

e. *Division of Account and Transfers Following my Wife's Death.* To facilitate the division and distribution set forth at Section 5.3 of this Will following my wife's death, the Trustee shall establish separate IRAs from the Account for each beneficiary under said Section 5.3. Each such separate IRA will receive said beneficiary's percentage portion of the Account as determined under Section 5.3. Each such IRA shall be in my name (deceased) for the benefit of ("f/b/o") the beneficiary for whom the IRA is established. The actual division shall occur by way of a direct transfer from the Account to each of the separate IRAs in accordance with IRC §402(c)(11). With respect to a separate IRA payable to a trust under Section 5.3(4) of this Will, any amount withdrawn from said IRA by the Trustee shall be paid to the beneficiary of the trust as it is my intent that said trust qualify as a conduit trust within the meaning of Reg. 1.401(a)(9)-5QA7(c)(3) (Ex. 2).

§ 13.29. Appendix G—Specific Bequest of Non-Working Spouse's Community Interest

IRAs/Retirement Plans of Wife. If my wife survives me, I hereby give, devise and bequeath to her any community property interest I may have in any of the following held in my wife's name or for her benefit: An individual retirement account, annuity or bond under IRC § 408, a tax deferred annuity under IRC § 403 or a retirement plan under IRC § 401. To the extent my wife should disclaim any interest hereunder, said disclaimed amount shall pass as part of the residue of my estate.

§ 13.30. Appendix H—Will Provisions—Miscellaneous Retirement Plan IRA Matters

Retirement Benefits.

1. Retirement Benefits Defined. For the purposes of this Article ___, the term "Retirement Benefits" shall mean and refer to any plan or account which is subject to the minimum distribution rules of IRC § 401(a)(9).

2. Non-Pro Rata Division. The Trustee of the [spousal trust] shall have the full and complete power to agree with [my spouse] to an equal division, on a non-pro rata basis, of our former community property. In this regard, it is my intent that, to the extent practicable and advisable under federal tax law, any Retirement Benefits be allocated to [my spouse] as her share of our former community property.

3. Retirement Benefits Allocated to [spousal trust]. To the extent Retirement Benefits remain payable to the [spousal trust] after any non-pro rata division of our former community property, it is my intent that required minimum distributions ("RMD") be calculated with reference to the life expectancy of [spouse]. Therefore it is my intent that this Trust be a Qualified Trust within the meaning of Reg. 1.401(a)(9)-4QA5 and that my [husband/wife] be considered the oldest beneficiary of the Trust for RMD purposes (without application of the "conduit trust" rules of Reg. 1.401(a)(9)-5QA7(c)(3) (Ex. 2). To that end, the following shall apply: (i) during my [husband/wife]'s lifetime, the Trustee shall not make any distributions from the Trust (or cause distributions from a Retirement Benefit) to anyone other than my [husband/wife] as set forth by Article V, above, (ii) the Trustee may not distribute any portion of a Retirement Benefit to or for the benefit of my [husband/wife]'s estate or use a Retirement Benefit for payment of my debts, taxes, expenses of administration, claims against my estate or payment of taxes due on account of my death, (iii) no portion of a Retirement Benefit may be distributed to any individual beneficiary older than my [husband/wife], or, subject to contrary and superseding federal or state law, a non-individual; and, (iv) where used in this Trust, the terms descendants, lineal descendants or words of similar import shall exclude anyone older than my [husband/wife].

4. Retirement Benefits Payable to Trust for Descendant under Thirty (30) Years of Age. To the extent any Retirement Benefits are payable to a trust for a descendant of mine under Article ____, above, by virtue of said trust being designated beneficiary thereof, any and all RMDs, as well as any and all other withdrawals or distributions taken by the Trustee, shall be distributed to the beneficiary for whom the Trust is established as it is my intent that said Trust qualify as a "conduit trust" under Reg.

1.401(a)(9)-5A7(c)(3) (ex. 2). Any provision of this Will which would prevent said Trust from being considered a conduit trust under said regulation shall not apply to this Trust with respect to the Retirement Benefit and provision needed for said qualification which has been omitted from this Will shall be added under Washington state's Trust and Estate Dispute Resolution Act.

5. Qualified Trust. If a Retirement Benefit is payable to any Trust under this Will, it is my intent that said Trust be considered a "qualified trust" under Reg. 1.401(a)(9). Any provision of this Will which would result in said Trust failing to so comply, shall not apply and any provision needed for said qualification which has been omitted from this Will, shall be added under Washington state's Trust and Dispute Resolution Act.

6. Copy of Will to Custodian/Administrator. My Personal Representative and/or Trustee shall provide a copy of this Will to the plan administrator or custodian of the Retirement Benefits payable to a Trust under this Will within the time period required under Reg. 1.401(a)(9) which, as of the time of this Will is no later than October 31 of the calendar year following the year of my death.

7. Power to Deal with Plan Administrator/Custodian. My Personal Representative and Trustees shall each have full power and authority to request information from and provide information to the custodian or plan administrator of any Retirement Benefit.

8. RMD for Year of Death. If, as of my death, I have not taken the full RMD for the calendar year of my death, (i) said RMD shall be taken no later than the December 31st of the calendar year of my death, (ii) my Personal Representative shall have the power to cause such RMD, and (iii) said RMD shall be the property of the beneficiary of the Retirement Benefit (subject to the conduit trust rules of Section 4, above).

9. Division of Retirement Benefits/Transfers. If a Trust created by this Will is later divided into separate shares for additional trusts and/or individuals, the Retirement Benefits of which said Trust is a beneficiary shall be divided into separate accounts, pro rata, according to the respective shares to be so created. Each such account shall be in my name, deceased for the benefit of ("f/b/o") the individual or Trust for whom the separate account is established. Said division shall occur by way of a direct transfer from the Retirement Benefit as it existed before the division to each of the separate accounts. In the case of an IRA, the separate account shall be established as separate f/b/o IRAs in the manner described above. With respect to these successor accounts and IRAs, RMDs shall continue to be calculated in the manner as was initially commenced following my death. Upon the attainment of an age by a child of mine for whom a separate trust was established which age entitled said child to a portion of his or her Trust outright, a corresponding portion of the Retirement Benefit as then so constituted shall be directly transferred in an f/b/o account (or in the case of an IRA, a separate f/b/o IRA) in the name of my child.

10. Non-Spouse Rollover. If the Retirement Benefit is a retirement plan (as opposed to an IRA) and said retirement plan permits a non-spouse rollover pursuant to IRC § 402(c)(11), I direct my Trustee to complete the non-spouse rollover from said retirement plan to an IRA. Said transferee IRA shall be fully subject to all of the foregoing provisions of this Section ____. Under current IRS guidelines, if I should die before reaching my "required beginning date" with respect to a retirement plan, the non-spouse rollover must be completed by the end of the calendar year following

the calendar year of my death so as to obtain with regard to the transferee IRA the RMD calculation described at this Article ____.

§ 13.31. Appendix I—Life Expectancy and Distribution Period Tables

Reg. 1.401(a)(9)-9

Reg § 1.401(a)(9)-9. Life expectancy and distribution period tables.

Caution: Reg. § 1.401(a)(9)-9, following, is effective 1/1/2003.

Q-1. What is the life expectancy for an individual for purposes of determining required minimum distributions under section 401(a)(9)?

A-1. The following table, referred to as the Single Life Table, is used for determining the life expectancy of an individual:

Single Life Table

Age	Life Expectancy	Age	Life Expectancy	Age	Life Expectancy	Age	Life Expectancy
0	82.4	29	54.3	58	27.0	87	6.7
1	81.6	30	53.3	59	26.1	88	6.3
2	80.6	31	52.4	60	25.2	89	5.9
3	79.7	32	51.4	61	24.4	90	5.5
4	78.7	33	50.4	62	23.5	91	5.2
5	77.7	34	49.4	63	22.7	92	4.9
6	76.7	35	48.5	64	21.8	93	4.6
7	75.8	36	47.5	65	21.0	94	4.3
8	74.8	37	46.5	66	20.2	95	4.1
9	73.8	38	45.6	67	19.4	96	3.8
10	72.8	39	44.6	68	18.6	97	3.6
11	71.8	40	43.6	69	17.8	98	3.4
12	70.8	41	42.7	70	17.0	99	3.1
13	69.9	42	41.7	71	16.3	100	2.9
14	68.9	43	40.7	72	15.5	101	2.7
15	67.9	44	39.8	73	14.8	102	2.5
16	66.9	45	38.8	74	14.1	103	2.3
17	66.0	46	37.9	75	13.4	104	2.1
18	65.0	47	37.0	76	12.7	105	1.9
19	64.0	48	36.0	77	12.1	106	1.7
20	63.0	49	35.1	78	11.4	107	1.5
21	62.1	50	34.2	79	10.8	108	1.4
22	61.1	51	33.3	80	10.2	109	1.2
23	60.1	52	32.3	81	9.7	110	1.1
24	59.1	53	31.4	82	9.1	111+	1.0
25	58.2	54	30.5	83	8.6		
26	57.2	55	29.6	84	8.1		

Age Expectancy	Life	Age Expectancy	Life	Age Expectancy	Life	Age Expectancy	Life
27	56.2	56	28.7	85	7.6		
28	55.3	57	27.9	86	7.1		

Q-2. What is the applicable distribution period for an individual account for purposes of determining required minimum distributions during an employee's lifetime under section 401(a)(9)?

A-2. Table for determining distribution period. The following table, referred to as the Uniform Lifetime Table, is used for determining the distribution period for lifetime distributions to an employee in situations in which the employee's spouse is either not the sole designated beneficiary or is the sole designated beneficiary but is not more than 10 years younger than the employee.

Uniform Lifetime Table

Age of employee	Distribution period	Age of employee	Distribution period
70	27.4	92	10.2
71	26.5	93	9.6
72	25.6	94	9.1
73	24.7	95	8.6
74	23.8	96	8.1
75	22.9	97	7.6
76	22.0	98	7.1
77	21.2	99	6.7
78	20.3	100	6.3
79	19.5	101	5.9
80	18.7	102	5.5
81	17.9	103	5.2
82	17.1	104	4.9
83	16.3	105	4.5
84	15.5	106	4.2
85	14.8	107	3.9
86	14.1	108	3.7
87	13.4	109	3.4
88	12.7	110	3.1
89	12.0	111	2.9
90	11.4	112	2.6
91	10.8	113	2.4
92	10.2	114	2.1
93	9.6	115+	1.9

Q-3. What is the joint life and last survivor expectancy of an individual and beneficiary for purposes of determining required minimum distributions under section 401(a)(9)?

A-3. The following table, referred to as the Joint and Last Survivor Table, is used for determining the joint and last survivor life expectancy of two individuals:

Joint and Last Survivor Table

AGES	0	1	2	3	4	5	6	7	8	9
0	90.0	89.5	89.0	88.6	88.2	87.8	87.4	87.1	86.8	86.5
1	89.5	89.0	88.5	88.1	87.6	87.2	86.8	86.5	86.1	85.8
2	89.0	88.5	88.0	87.5	87.1	86.6	86.2	85.8	85.5	85.1
3	88.6	88.1	87.5	87.0	86.5	86.1	85.6	85.2	84.8	84.5
4	88.2	87.6	87.1	86.5	86.0	85.5	85.1	84.6	84.2	83.8
5	87.8	87.2	86.6	86.1	85.5	85.0	84.5	84.1	83.6	83.2
6	87.4	86.8	86.2	85.6	85.1	84.5	84.0	83.5	83.1	82.6
7	87.1	86.5	85.8	85.2	84.6	84.1	83.5	83.0	82.5	82.1
8	86.8	86.1	85.5	84.8	84.2	83.6	83.1	82.5	82.0	81.6
9	86.5	85.8	85.1	84.5	83.8	83.2	82.6	82.1	81.6	81.0
10	86.2	85.5	84.8	84.1	83.5	82.8	82.2	81.6	81.1	80.6
11	85.9	85.2	84.5	83.8	83.1	82.5	81.8	81.2	80.7	80.1
12	85.7	84.9	84.2	83.5	82.8	82.1	81.5	80.8	80.2	79.7
13	85.4	84.7	84.0	83.2	82.5	81.8	81.1	80.5	79.9	79.2
14	85.2	84.5	83.7	83.0	82.2	81.5	80.8	80.1	79.5	78.9
15	85.0	84.3	83.5	82.7	82.0	81.2	80.5	79.8	79.1	78.5
16	84.9	84.1	83.3	82.5	81.7	81.0	80.2	79.5	78.8	78.1
17	84.7	83.9	83.1	82.3	81.5	80.7	80.0	79.2	78.5	77.8
18	84.5	83.7	82.9	82.1	81.3	80.5	79.7	79.0	78.2	77.5
19	84.4	83.6	82.7	81.9	81.1	80.3	79.5	78.7	78.0	77.3
20	84.3	83.4	82.6	81.8	80.9	80.1	79.3	78.5	77.7	77.0
21	84.1	83.3	82.4	81.6	80.8	79.9	79.1	78.3	77.5	76.8
22	84.0	83.2	82.3	81.5	80.6	79.8	78.9	78.1	77.3	76.5
23	83.9	83.1	82.2	81.3	80.5	79.6	78.8	77.9	77.1	76.3
24	83.8	83.0	82.1	81.2	80.3	79.5	78.6	77.8	76.9	76.1
25	83.7	82.9	82.0	81.1	80.2	79.3	78.5	77.6	76.8	75.9
26	83.6	82.8	81.9	81.0	80.1	79.2	78.3	77.5	76.6	75.8
27	83.6	82.7	81.8	80.9	80.0	79.1	78.2	77.4	76.5	75.6
28	83.5	82.6	81.7	80.8	79.9	79.0	78.1	77.2	76.4	75.5
29	83.4	82.6	81.6	80.7	79.8	78.9	78.0	77.1	76.2	75.4
30	83.4	82.5	81.6	80.7	79.7	78.8	77.9	77.0	76.1	75.2
31	83.3	82.4	81.5	80.6	79.7	78.8	77.8	76.9	76.0	75.1
32	83.3	82.4	81.5	80.5	79.6	78.7	77.8	76.8	75.9	75.0
33	83.2	82.3	81.4	80.5	79.5	78.6	77.7	76.8	75.9	74.9
34	83.2	82.3	81.3	80.4	79.5	78.5	77.6	76.7	75.8	74.9
35	83.1	82.2	81.3	80.4	79.4	78.5	77.6	76.6	75.7	74.8
36	83.1	82.2	81.3	80.3	79.4	78.4	77.5	76.6	75.6	74.7
37	83.0	82.2	81.2	80.3	79.3	78.4	77.4	76.5	75.6	74.6
38	83.0	82.1	81.2	80.2	79.3	78.3	77.4	76.4	75.5	74.6

AGES	0	1	2	3	4	5	6	7	8	9
39	83.0	82.1	81.1	80.2	79.2	78.3	77.3	76.4	75.5	74.5
40	82.9	82.1	81.1	80.2	79.2	78.3	77.3	76.4	75.4	74.5
41	82.9	82.0	81.1	80.1	79.2	78.2	77.3	76.3	75.4	74.4
42	82.9	82.0	81.1	80.1	79.1	78.2	77.2	76.3	75.3	74.4
43	82.9	82.0	81.0	80.1	79.1	78.2	77.2	76.2	75.3	74.3
44	82.8	81.9	81.0	80.0	79.1	78.1	77.2	76.2	75.2	74.3
45	82.8	81.9	81.0	80.0	79.1	78.1	77.1	76.2	75.2	74.3
46	82.8	81.9	81.0	80.0	79.0	78.1	77.1	76.1	75.2	74.2
47	82.8	81.9	80.9	80.0	79.0	78.0	77.1	76.1	75.2	74.2
48	82.8	81.9	80.9	80.0	79.0	78.0	77.1	76.1	75.1	74.2
49	82.7	81.8	80.9	79.9	79.0	78.0	77.0	76.1	75.1	74.1
50	82.7	81.8	80.9	79.9	79.0	78.0	77.0	76.0	75.1	74.1
51	82.7	81.8	80.9	79.9	78.9	78.0	77.0	76.0	75.1	74.1
52	82.7	81.8	80.9	79.9	78.9	78.0	77.0	76.0	75.0	74.1
53	82.7	81.8	80.8	79.9	78.9	77.9	77.0	76.0	75.0	74.0
54	82.7	81.8	80.8	79.9	78.9	77.9	76.9	76.0	75.0	74.0
55	82.6	81.8	80.8	79.8	78.9	77.9	76.9	76.0	75.0	74.0
56	82.6	81.7	80.8	79.8	78.9	77.9	76.9	75.9	75.0	74.0
57	82.6	81.7	80.8	79.8	78.9	77.9	76.9	75.9	75.0	74.0
58	82.6	81.7	80.8	79.8	78.8	77.9	76.9	75.9	74.9	74.0
59	82.6	81.7	80.8	79.8	78.8	77.9	76.9	75.9	74.9	74.0
60	82.6	81.7	80.8	79.8	78.8	77.8	76.9	75.9	74.9	73.9
61	82.6	81.7	80.8	79.8	78.8	77.8	76.9	75.9	74.9	73.9
62	82.6	81.7	80.7	79.8	78.8	77.8	76.9	75.9	74.9	73.9
63	82.6	81.7	80.7	79.8	78.8	77.8	76.8	75.9	74.9	73.9
64	82.5	81.7	80.7	79.8	78.8	77.8	76.8	75.9	74.9	73.9
65	82.5	81.7	80.7	79.8	78.8	77.8	76.8	75.8	74.9	73.9
66	82.5	81.7	80.7	79.7	78.8	77.8	76.8	75.8	74.9	73.9
67	82.5	81.7	80.7	79.7	78.8	77.8	76.8	75.8	74.9	73.9
68	82.5	81.6	80.7	79.7	78.8	77.8	76.8	75.8	74.8	73.9
69	82.5	81.6	80.7	79.7	78.8	77.8	76.8	75.8	74.8	73.9
70	82.5	81.6	80.7	79.7	78.8	77.8	76.8	75.8	74.8	73.9
71	82.5	81.6	80.7	79.7	78.7	77.8	76.8	75.8	74.8	73.8
72	82.5	81.6	80.7	79.7	78.7	77.8	76.8	75.8	74.8	73.8
73	82.5	81.6	80.7	79.7	78.7	77.8	76.8	75.8	74.8	73.8
74	82.5	81.6	80.7	79.7	78.7	77.8	76.8	75.8	74.8	73.8
75	82.5	81.6	80.7	79.7	78.7	77.8	76.8	75.8	74.8	73.8
76	82.5	81.6	80.7	79.7	78.7	77.8	76.8	75.8	74.8	73.8
77	82.5	81.6	80.7	79.7	78.7	77.7	76.8	75.8	74.8	73.8
78	82.5	81.6	80.7	79.7	78.7	77.7	76.8	75.8	74.8	73.8
79	82.5	81.6	80.7	79.7	78.7	77.7	76.8	75.8	74.8	73.8

AGES	0	1	2	3	4	5	6	7	8	9
80	82.5	81.6	80.7	79.7	78.7	77.7	76.8	75.8	74.8	73.8
81	82.4	81.6	80.7	79.7	78.7	77.7	76.8	75.8	74.8	73.8
82	82.4	81.6	80.7	79.7	78.7	77.7	76.8	75.8	74.8	73.8
83	82.4	81.6	80.7	79.7	78.7	77.7	76.8	75.8	74.8	73.8
84	82.4	81.6	80.7	79.7	78.7	77.7	76.8	75.8	74.8	73.8
85	82.4	81.6	80.6	79.7	78.7	77.7	76.8	75.8	74.8	73.8
86	82.4	81.6	80.6	79.7	78.7	77.7	76.7	75.8	74.8	73.8
87	82.4	81.6	80.6	79.7	78.7	77.7	76.7	75.8	74.8	73.8
88	82.4	81.6	80.6	79.7	78.7	77.7	76.7	75.8	74.8	73.8
89	82.4	81.6	80.6	79.7	78.7	77.7	76.7	75.8	74.8	73.8
90	82.4	81.6	80.6	79.7	78.7	77.7	76.7	75.8	74.8	73.8
91	82.4	81.6	80.6	79.7	78.7	77.7	76.7	75.8	74.8	73.8
92	82.4	81.6	80.6	79.7	78.7	77.7	76.7	75.8	74.8	73.8
93	82.4	81.6	80.6	79.7	78.7	77.7	76.7	75.8	74.8	73.8
94	82.4	81.6	80.6	79.7	78.7	77.7	76.7	75.8	74.8	73.8
95	82.4	81.6	80.6	79.7	78.7	77.7	76.7	75.8	74.8	73.8
96	82.4	81.6	80.6	79.7	78.7	77.7	76.7	75.8	74.8	73.8
97	82.4	81.6	80.6	79.7	78.7	77.7	76.7	75.8	74.8	73.8
98	82.4	81.6	80.6	79.7	78.7	77.7	76.7	75.8	74.8	73.8
99	82.4	81.6	80.6	79.7	78.7	77.7	76.7	75.8	74.8	73.8
100	82.4	81.6	80.6	79.7	78.7	77.7	76.7	75.8	74.8	73.8
101	82.4	81.6	80.6	79.7	78.7	77.7	76.7	75.8	74.8	73.8
102	82.4	81.6	80.6	79.7	78.7	77.7	76.7	75.8	74.8	73.8
103	82.4	81.6	80.6	79.7	78.7	77.7	76.7	75.8	74.8	73.8
104	82.4	81.6	80.6	79.7	78.7	77.7	76.7	75.8	74.8	73.8
105	82.4	81.6	80.6	79.7	78.7	77.7	76.7	75.8	74.8	73.8
106	82.4	81.6	80.6	79.7	78.7	77.7	76.7	75.8	74.8	73.8
107	82.4	81.6	80.6	79.7	78.7	77.7	76.7	75.8	74.8	73.8
108	82.4	81.6	80.6	79.7	78.7	77.7	76.7	75.8	74.8	73.8
109	82.4	81.6	80.6	79.7	78.7	77.7	76.7	75.8	74.8	73.8
110	82.4	81.6	80.6	79.7	78.7	77.7	76.7	75.8	74.8	73.8
111	82.4	81.6	80.6	79.7	78.7	77.7	76.7	75.8	74.8	73.8
112	82.4	81.6	80.6	79.7	78.7	77.7	76.7	75.8	74.8	73.8
113	82.4	81.6	80.6	79.7	78.7	77.7	76.7	75.8	74.8	73.8
114	82.4	81.6	80.6	79.7	78.7	77.7	76.7	75.8	74.8	73.8
115+	82.4	81.6	80.6	79.7	78.7	77.7	76.7	75.8	74.8	73.8

AGES	10	11	12	13	14	15	16	17	18	19
10	80.0	79.6	79.1	78.7	78.2	77.9	77.5	77.2	76.8	76.5
11	79.6	79.0	78.6	78.1	77.7	77.3	76.9	76.5	76.2	75.8
12	79.1	78.6	78.1	77.6	77.1	76.7	76.3	75.9	75.5	75.2
13	78.7	78.1	77.6	77.1	76.6	76.1	75.7	75.3	74.9	74.5

AGES	10	11	12	13	14	15	16	17	18	19
14	78.2	77.7	77.1	76.6	76.1	75.6	75.1	74.7	74.3	73.9
15	77.9	77.3	76.7	76.1	75.6	75.1	74.6	74.1	73.7	73.3
16	77.5	76.9	76.3	75.7	75.1	74.6	74.1	73.6	73.1	72.7
17	77.2	76.5	75.9	75.3	74.7	74.1	73.6	73.1	72.6	72.1
18	76.8	76.2	75.5	74.9	74.3	73.7	73.1	72.6	72.1	71.6
19	76.5	75.8	75.2	74.5	73.9	73.3	72.7	72.1	71.6	71.1
20	76.3	75.5	74.8	74.2	73.5	72.9	72.3	71.7	71.1	70.6
21	76.0	75.3	74.5	73.8	73.2	72.5	71.9	71.3	70.7	70.1
22	75.8	75.0	74.3	73.5	72.9	72.2	71.5	70.9	70.3	69.7
23	75.5	74.8	74.0	73.3	72.6	71.9	71.2	70.5	69.9	69.3
24	75.3	74.5	73.8	73.0	72.3	71.6	70.9	70.2	69.5	68.9
25	75.1	74.3	73.5	72.8	72.0	71.3	70.6	69.9	69.2	68.5
26	75.0	74.1	73.3	72.5	71.8	71.0	70.3	69.6	68.9	68.2
27	74.8	74.0	73.1	72.3	71.6	70.8	70.0	69.3	68.6	67.9
28	74.6	73.8	73.0	72.2	71.3	70.6	69.8	69.0	68.3	67.6
29	74.5	73.6	72.8	72.0	71.2	70.4	69.6	68.8	68.0	67.3
30	74.4	73.5	72.7	71.8	71.0	70.2	69.4	68.6	67.8	67.1
31	74.3	73.4	72.5	71.7	70.8	70.0	69.2	68.4	67.6	66.8
32	74.1	73.3	72.4	71.5	70.7	69.8	69.0	68.2	67.4	66.6
33	74.0	73.2	72.3	71.4	70.5	69.7	68.8	68.0	67.2	66.4
34	73.9	73.0	72.2	71.3	70.4	69.5	68.7	67.8	67.0	66.2
35	73.9	73.0	72.1	71.2	70.3	69.4	68.5	67.7	66.8	66.0
36	73.8	72.9	72.0	71.1	70.2	69.3	68.4	67.6	66.7	65.9
37	73.7	72.8	71.9	71.0	70.1	69.2	68.3	67.4	66.6	65.7
38	73.6	72.7	71.8	70.9	70.0	69.1	68.2	67.3	66.4	65.6
39	73.6	72.7	71.7	70.8	69.9	69.0	68.1	67.2	66.3	65.4
40	73.5	72.6	71.7	70.7	69.8	68.9	68.0	67.1	66.2	65.3
41	73.5	72.5	71.6	70.7	69.7	68.8	67.9	67.0	66.1	65.2
42	73.4	72.5	71.5	70.6	69.7	68.8	67.8	66.9	66.0	65.1
43	73.4	72.4	71.5	70.6	69.6	68.7	67.8	66.8	65.9	65.0
44	73.3	72.4	71.4	70.5	69.6	68.6	67.7	66.8	65.9	64.9
45	73.3	72.3	71.4	70.5	69.5	68.6	67.6	66.7	65.8	64.9
46	73.3	72.3	71.4	70.4	69.5	68.5	67.6	66.6	65.7	64.8
47	73.2	72.3	71.3	70.4	69.4	68.5	67.5	66.6	65.7	64.7
48	73.2	72.2	71.3	70.3	69.4	68.4	67.5	66.5	65.6	64.7
49	73.2	72.2	71.2	70.3	69.3	68.4	67.4	66.5	65.6	64.6
50	73.1	72.2	71.2	70.3	69.3	68.4	67.4	66.5	65.5	64.6
51	73.1	72.2	71.2	70.2	69.3	68.3	67.4	66.4	65.5	64.5
52	73.1	72.1	71.2	70.2	69.2	68.3	67.3	66.4	65.4	64.5
53	73.1	72.1	71.1	70.2	69.2	68.3	67.3	66.3	65.4	64.4
54	73.1	72.1	71.1	70.2	69.2	68.2	67.3	66.3	65.4	64.4

AGES	10	11	12	13	14	15	16	17	18	19
55	73.0	72.1	71.1	70.1	69.2	68.2	67.2	66.3	65.3	64.4
56	73.0	72.1	71.1	70.1	69.1	68.2	67.2	66.3	65.3	64.3
57	73.0	72.0	71.1	70.1	69.1	68.2	67.2	66.2	65.3	64.3
58	73.0	72.0	71.0	70.1	69.1	68.1	67.2	66.2	65.2	64.3
59	73.0	72.0	71.0	70.1	69.1	68.1	67.2	66.2	65.2	64.3
60	73.0	72.0	71.0	70.0	69.1	68.1	67.1	66.2	65.2	64.2
61	73.0	72.0	71.0	70.0	69.1	68.1	67.1	66.2	65.2	64.2
62	72.9	72.0	71.0	70.0	69.0	68.1	67.1	66.1	65.2	64.2
63	72.9	72.0	71.0	70.0	69.0	68.1	67.1	66.1	65.2	64.2
64	72.9	71.9	71.0	70.0	69.0	68.0	67.1	66.1	65.1	64.2
65	72.9	71.9	71.0	70.0	69.0	68.0	67.1	66.1	65.1	64.2
66	72.9	71.9	70.9	70.0	69.0	68.0	67.1	66.1	65.1	64.1
67	72.9	71.9	70.9	70.0	69.0	68.0	67.0	66.1	65.1	64.1
68	72.9	71.9	70.9	70.0	69.0	68.0	67.0	66.1	65.1	64.1
69	72.9	71.9	70.9	69.9	69.0	68.0	67.0	66.1	65.1	64.1
70	72.9	71.9	70.9	69.9	69.0	68.0	67.0	66.0	65.1	64.1
71	72.9	71.9	70.9	69.9	69.0	68.0	67.0	66.0	65.1	64.1
72	72.9	71.9	70.9	69.9	69.0	68.0	67.0	66.0	65.1	64.1
73	72.9	71.9	70.9	69.9	68.9	68.0	67.0	66.0	65.0	64.1
74	72.9	71.9	70.9	69.9	68.9	68.0	67.0	66.0	65.0	64.1
75	72.8	71.9	70.9	69.9	68.9	68.0	67.0	66.0	65.0	64.1
76	72.8	71.9	70.9	69.9	68.9	68.0	67.0	66.0	65.0	64.1
77	72.8	71.9	70.9	69.9	68.9	68.0	67.0	66.0	65.0	64.1
78	72.8	71.9	70.9	69.9	68.9	67.9	67.0	66.0	65.0	64.0
79	72.8	71.9	70.9	69.9	68.9	67.9	67.0	66.0	65.0	64.0
80	72.8	71.9	70.9	69.9	68.9	67.9	67.0	66.0	65.0	64.0
81	72.8	71.8	70.9	69.9	68.9	67.9	67.0	66.0	65.0	64.0
82	72.8	71.8	70.9	69.9	68.9	67.9	67.0	66.0	65.0	64.0
83	72.8	71.8	70.9	69.9	68.9	67.9	67.0	66.0	65.0	64.0
84	72.8	71.8	70.9	69.9	68.9	67.9	67.0	66.0	65.0	64.0
85	72.8	71.8	70.9	69.9	68.9	67.9	66.9	66.0	65.0	64.0
86	72.8	71.8	70.9	69.9	68.9	67.9	66.9	66.0	65.0	64.0
87	72.8	71.8	70.9	69.9	68.9	67.9	66.9	66.0	65.0	64.0
88	72.8	71.8	70.9	69.9	68.9	67.9	66.9	66.0	65.0	64.0
89	72.8	71.8	70.9	69.9	68.9	67.9	66.9	66.0	65.0	64.0
90	72.8	71.8	70.9	69.9	68.9	67.9	66.9	66.0	65.0	64.0
91	72.8	71.8	70.9	69.9	68.9	67.9	66.9	66.0	65.0	64.0
92	72.8	71.8	70.9	69.9	68.9	67.9	66.9	66.0	65.0	64.0
93	72.8	71.8	70.9	69.9	68.9	67.9	66.9	66.0	65.0	64.0
94	72.8	71.8	70.8	69.9	68.9	67.9	66.9	66.0	65.0	64.0
95	72.8	71.8	70.8	69.9	68.9	67.9	66.9	66.0	65.0	64.0

AGES	10	11	12	13	14	15	16	17	18	19
96	72.8	71.8	70.8	69.9	68.9	67.9	66.9	66.0	65.0	64.0
97	72.8	71.8	70.8	69.9	68.9	67.9	66.9	66.0	65.0	64.0
98	72.8	71.8	70.8	69.9	68.9	67.9	66.9	66.0	65.0	64.0
99	72.8	71.8	70.8	69.9	68.9	67.9	66.9	66.0	65.0	64.0
100	72.8	71.8	70.8	69.9	68.9	67.9	66.9	66.0	65.0	64.0
101	72.8	71.8	70.8	69.9	68.9	67.9	66.9	66.0	65.0	64.0
102	72.8	71.8	70.8	69.9	68.9	67.9	66.9	66.0	65.0	64.0
103	72.8	71.8	70.8	69.9	68.9	67.9	66.9	66.0	65.0	64.0
104	72.8	71.8	70.8	69.9	68.9	67.9	66.9	66.0	65.0	64.0
105	72.8	71.8	70.8	69.9	68.9	67.9	66.9	66.0	65.0	64.0
106	72.8	71.8	70.8	69.9	68.9	67.9	66.9	66.0	65.0	64.0
107	72.8	71.8	70.8	69.9	68.9	67.9	66.9	66.0	65.0	64.0
108	72.8	71.8	70.8	69.9	68.9	67.9	66.9	66.0	65.0	64.0
109	72.8	71.8	70.8	69.9	68.9	67.9	66.9	66.0	65.0	64.0
110	72.8	71.8	70.8	69.9	68.9	67.9	66.9	66.0	65.0	64.0
111	72.8	71.8	70.8	69.9	68.9	67.9	66.9	66.0	65.0	64.0
112	72.8	71.8	70.8	69.9	68.9	67.9	66.9	66.0	65.0	64.0
113	72.8	71.8	70.8	69.9	68.9	67.9	66.9	66.0	65.0	64.0
114	72.8	71.8	70.8	69.9	68.9	67.9	66.9	66.0	65.0	64.0
115+	72.8	71.8	70.8	69.9	68.9	67.9	66.9	66.0	65.0	64.0

AGES	20	21	22	23	24	25	26	27	28	29
20	70.1	69.6	69.1	68.7	68.3	67.9	67.5	67.2	66.9	66.6
21	69.6	69.1	68.6	68.2	67.7	67.3	66.9	66.6	66.2	65.9
22	69.1	68.6	68.1	67.6	67.2	66.7	66.3	65.9	65.6	65.2
23	68.7	68.2	67.6	67.1	66.6	66.2	65.7	65.3	64.9	64.6
24	68.3	67.7	67.2	66.6	66.1	65.6	65.2	64.7	64.3	63.9
25	67.9	67.3	66.7	66.2	65.6	65.1	64.6	64.2	63.7	63.3
26	67.5	66.9	66.3	65.7	65.2	64.6	64.1	63.6	63.2	62.8
27	67.2	66.6	65.9	65.3	64.7	64.2	63.6	63.1	62.7	62.2
28	66.9	66.2	65.6	64.9	64.3	63.7	63.2	62.7	62.1	61.7
29	66.6	65.9	65.2	64.6	63.9	63.3	62.8	62.2	61.7	61.2
30	66.3	65.6	64.9	64.2	63.6	62.9	62.3	61.8	61.2	60.7
31	66.1	65.3	64.6	63.9	63.2	62.6	62.0	61.4	60.8	60.2
32	65.8	65.1	64.3	63.6	62.9	62.2	61.6	61.0	60.4	59.8
33	65.6	64.8	64.1	63.3	62.6	61.9	61.3	60.6	60.0	59.4
34	65.4	64.6	63.8	63.1	62.3	61.6	60.9	60.3	59.6	59.0
35	65.2	64.4	63.6	62.8	62.1	61.4	60.6	59.9	59.3	58.6
36	65.0	64.2	63.4	62.6	61.9	61.1	60.4	59.6	59.0	58.3
37	64.9	64.0	63.2	62.4	61.6	60.9	60.1	59.4	58.7	58.0
38	64.7	63.9	63.0	62.2	61.4	60.6	59.9	59.1	58.4	57.7
39	64.6	63.7	62.9	62.1	61.2	60.4	59.6	58.9	58.1	57.4

AGES	20	21	22	23	24	25	26	27	28	29
40	64.4	63.6	62.7	61.9	61.1	60.2	59.4	58.7	57.9	57.1
41	64.3	63.5	62.6	61.7	60.9	60.1	59.3	58.5	57.7	56.9
42	64.2	63.3	62.5	61.6	60.8	59.9	59.1	58.3	57.5	56.7
43	64.1	63.2	62.4	61.5	60.6	59.8	58.9	58.1	57.3	56.5
44	64.0	63.1	62.2	61.4	60.5	59.6	58.8	57.9	57.1	56.3
45	64.0	63.0	62.2	61.3	60.4	59.5	58.6	57.8	56.9	56.1
46	63.9	63.0	62.1	61.2	60.3	59.4	58.5	57.7	56.8	56.0
47	63.8	62.9	62.0	61.1	60.2	59.3	58.4	57.5	56.7	55.8
48	63.7	62.8	61.9	61.0	60.1	59.2	58.3	57.4	56.5	55.7
49	63.7	62.8	61.8	60.9	60.0	59.1	58.2	57.3	56.4	55.6
50	63.6	62.7	61.8	60.8	59.9	59.0	58.1	57.2	56.3	55.4
51	63.6	62.6	61.7	60.8	59.9	58.9	58.0	57.1	56.2	55.3
52	63.5	62.6	61.7	60.7	59.8	58.9	58.0	57.1	56.1	55.2
53	63.5	62.5	61.6	60.7	59.7	58.8	57.9	57.0	56.1	55.2
54	63.5	62.5	61.6	60.6	59.7	58.8	57.8	56.9	56.0	55.1
55	63.4	62.5	61.5	60.6	59.6	58.7	57.8	56.8	55.9	55.0
56	63.4	62.4	61.5	60.5	59.6	58.7	57.7	56.8	55.9	54.9
57	63.4	62.4	61.5	60.5	59.6	58.6	57.7	56.7	55.8	54.9
58	63.3	62.4	61.4	60.5	59.5	58.6	57.6	56.7	55.8	54.8
59	63.3	62.3	61.4	60.4	59.5	58.5	57.6	56.7	55.7	54.8
60	63.3	62.3	61.4	60.4	59.5	58.5	57.6	56.6	55.7	54.7
61	63.3	62.3	61.3	60.4	59.4	58.5	57.5	56.6	55.6	54.7
62	63.2	62.3	61.3	60.4	59.4	58.4	57.5	56.5	55.6	54.7
63	63.2	62.3	61.3	60.3	59.4	58.4	57.5	56.5	55.6	54.6
64	63.2	62.2	61.3	60.3	59.4	58.4	57.4	56.5	55.5	54.6
65	63.2	62.2	61.3	60.3	59.3	58.4	57.4	56.5	55.5	54.6
66	63.2	62.2	61.2	60.3	59.3	58.4	57.4	56.4	55.5	54.5
67	63.2	62.2	61.2	60.3	59.3	58.3	57.4	56.4	55.5	54.5
68	63.1	62.2	61.2	60.2	59.3	58.3	57.4	56.4	55.4	54.5
69	63.1	62.2	61.2	60.2	59.3	58.3	57.3	56.4	55.4	54.5
70	63.1	62.2	61.2	60.2	59.3	58.3	57.3	56.4	55.4	54.4
71	63.1	62.1	61.2	60.2	59.2	58.3	57.3	56.4	55.4	54.4
72	63.1	62.1	61.2	60.2	59.2	58.3	57.3	56.3	55.4	54.4
73	63.1	62.1	61.2	60.2	59.2	58.3	57.3	56.3	55.4	54.4
74	63.1	62.1	61.2	60.2	59.2	58.2	57.3	56.3	55.4	54.4
75	63.1	62.1	61.1	60.2	59.2	58.2	57.3	56.3	55.3	54.4
76	63.1	62.1	61.1	60.2	59.2	58.2	57.3	56.3	55.3	54.4
77	63.1	62.1	61.1	60.2	59.2	58.2	57.3	56.3	55.3	54.4
78	63.1	62.1	61.1	60.2	59.2	58.2	57.3	56.3	55.3	54.4
79	63.1	62.1	61.1	60.2	59.2	58.2	57.2	56.3	55.3	54.3
80	63.1	62.1	61.1	60.1	59.2	58.2	57.2	56.3	55.3	54.3

AGES	20	21	22	23	24	25	26	27	28	29
81	63.1	62.1	61.1	60.1	59.2	58.2	57.2	56.3	55.3	54.3
82	63.1	62.1	61.1	60.1	59.2	58.2	57.2	56.3	55.3	54.3
83	63.1	62.1	61.1	60.1	59.2	58.2	57.2	56.3	55.3	54.3
84	63.0	62.1	61.1	60.1	59.2	58.2	57.2	56.3	55.3	54.3
85	63.0	62.1	61.1	60.1	59.2	58.2	57.2	56.3	55.3	54.3
86	63.0	62.1	61.1	60.1	59.2	58.2	57.2	56.2	55.3	54.3
87	63.0	62.1	61.1	60.1	59.2	58.2	57.2	56.2	55.3	54.3
88	63.0	62.1	61.1	60.1	59.2	58.2	57.2	56.2	55.3	54.3
89	63.0	62.1	61.1	60.1	59.1	58.2	57.2	56.2	55.3	54.3
90	63.0	62.1	61.1	60.1	59.1	58.2	57.2	56.2	55.3	54.3
91	63.0	62.1	61.1	60.1	59.1	58.2	57.2	56.2	55.3	54.3
92	63.0	62.1	61.1	60.1	59.1	58.2	57.2	56.2	55.3	54.3
93	63.0	62.1	61.1	60.1	59.1	58.2	57.2	56.2	55.3	54.3
94	63.0	62.1	61.1	60.1	59.1	58.2	57.2	56.2	55.3	54.3
95	63.0	62.1	61.1	60.1	59.1	58.2	57.2	56.2	55.3	54.3
96	63.0	62.1	61.1	60.1	59.1	58.2	57.2	56.2	55.3	54.3
97	63.0	62.1	61.1	60.1	59.1	58.2	57.2	56.2	55.3	54.3
98	63.0	62.1	61.1	60.1	59.1	58.2	57.2	56.2	55.3	54.3
99	63.0	62.1	61.1	60.1	59.1	58.2	57.2	56.2	55.3	54.3
100	63.0	62.1	61.1	60.1	59.1	58.2	57.2	56.2	55.3	54.3
101	63.0	62.1	61.1	60.1	59.1	58.2	57.2	56.2	55.3	54.3
102	63.0	62.1	61.1	60.1	59.1	58.2	57.2	56.2	55.3	54.3
103	63.0	62.1	61.1	60.1	59.1	58.2	57.2	56.2	55.3	54.3
104	63.0	62.1	61.1	60.1	59.1	58.2	57.2	56.2	55.3	54.3
105	63.0	62.1	61.1	60.1	59.1	58.2	57.2	56.2	55.3	54.3
106	63.0	62.1	61.1	60.1	59.1	58.2	57.2	56.2	55.3	54.3
107	63.0	62.1	61.1	60.1	59.1	58.2	57.2	56.2	55.3	54.3
108	63.0	62.1	61.1	60.1	59.1	58.2	57.2	56.2	55.3	54.3
109	63.0	62.1	61.1	60.1	59.1	58.2	57.2	56.2	55.3	54.3
110	63.0	62.1	61.1	60.1	59.1	58.2	57.2	56.2	55.3	54.3
111	63.0	62.1	61.1	60.1	59.1	58.2	57.2	56.2	55.3	54.3
112	63.0	62.1	61.1	60.1	59.1	58.2	57.2	56.2	55.3	54.3
113	63.0	62.1	61.1	60.1	59.1	58.2	57.2	56.2	55.3	54.3
114	63.0	62.1	61.1	60.1	59.1	58.2	57.2	56.2	55.3	54.3
115+	63.0	62.1	61.1	60.1	59.1	58.2	57.2	56.2	55.3	54.3
AGES	30	31	32	33	34	35	36	37	38	39
30	60.2	59.7	59.2	58.8	58.4	58.0	57.6	57.3	57.0	56.7
31	59.7	59.2	58.7	58.2	57.8	57.4	57.0	56.6	56.3	56.0
32	59.2	58.7	58.2	57.7	57.2	56.8	56.4	56.0	55.6	55.3
33	58.8	58.2	57.7	57.2	56.7	56.2	55.8	55.4	55.0	54.7
34	58.4	57.8	57.2	56.7	56.2	55.7	55.3	54.8	54.4	54.0

AGES	30	31	32	33	34	35	36	37	38	39
35	58.0	57.4	56.8	56.2	55.7	55.2	54.7	54.3	53.8	53.4
36	57.6	57.0	56.4	55.8	55.3	54.7	54.2	53.7	53.3	52.8
37	57.3	56.6	56.0	55.4	54.8	54.3	53.7	53.2	52.7	52.3
38	57.0	56.3	55.6	55.0	54.4	53.8	53.3	52.7	52.2	51.7
39	56.7	56.0	55.3	54.7	54.0	53.4	52.8	52.3	51.7	51.2
40	56.4	55.7	55.0	54.3	53.7	53.0	52.4	51.8	51.3	50.8
41	56.1	55.4	54.7	54.0	53.3	52.7	52.0	51.4	50.9	50.3
42	55.9	55.2	54.4	53.7	53.0	52.3	51.7	51.1	50.4	49.9
43	55.7	54.9	54.2	53.4	52.7	52.0	51.3	50.7	50.1	49.5
44	55.5	54.7	53.9	53.2	52.4	51.7	51.0	50.4	49.7	49.1
45	55.3	54.5	53.7	52.9	52.2	51.5	50.7	50.0	49.4	48.7
46	55.1	54.3	53.5	52.7	52.0	51.2	50.5	49.8	49.1	48.4
47	55.0	54.1	53.3	52.5	51.7	51.0	50.2	49.5	48.8	48.1
48	54.8	54.0	53.2	52.3	51.5	50.8	50.0	49.2	48.5	47.8
49	54.7	53.8	53.0	52.2	51.4	50.6	49.8	49.0	48.2	47.5
50	54.6	53.7	52.9	52.0	51.2	50.4	49.6	48.8	48.0	47.3
51	54.5	53.6	52.7	51.9	51.0	50.2	49.4	48.6	47.8	47.0
52	54.4	53.5	52.6	51.7	50.9	50.0	49.2	48.4	47.6	46.8
53	54.3	53.4	52.5	51.6	50.8	49.9	49.1	48.2	47.4	46.6
54	54.2	53.3	52.4	51.5	50.6	49.8	48.9	48.1	47.2	46.4
55	54.1	53.2	52.3	51.4	50.5	49.7	48.8	47.9	47.1	46.3
56	54.0	53.1	52.2	51.3	50.4	49.5	48.7	47.8	47.0	46.1
57	54.0	53.0	52.1	51.2	50.3	49.4	48.6	47.7	46.8	46.0
58	53.9	53.0	52.1	51.2	50.3	49.4	48.5	47.6	46.7	45.8
59	53.8	52.9	52.0	51.1	50.2	49.3	48.4	47.5	46.6	45.7
60	53.8	52.9	51.9	51.0	50.1	49.2	48.3	47.4	46.5	45.6
61	53.8	52.8	51.9	51.0	50.0	49.1	48.2	47.3	46.4	45.5
62	53.7	52.8	51.8	50.9	50.0	49.1	48.1	47.2	46.3	45.4
63	53.7	52.7	51.8	50.9	49.9	49.0	48.1	47.2	46.3	45.3
64	53.6	52.7	51.8	50.8	49.9	48.9	48.0	47.1	46.2	45.3
65	53.6	52.7	51.7	50.8	49.8	48.9	48.0	47.0	46.1	45.2
66	53.6	52.6	51.7	50.7	49.8	48.9	47.9	47.0	46.1	45.1
67	53.6	52.6	51.7	50.7	49.8	48.8	47.9	46.9	46.0	45.1
68	53.5	52.6	51.6	50.7	49.7	48.8	47.8	46.9	46.0	45.0
69	53.5	52.6	51.6	50.6	49.7	48.7	47.8	46.9	45.9	45.0
70	53.5	52.5	51.6	50.6	49.7	48.7	47.8	46.8	45.9	44.9
71	53.5	52.5	51.6	50.6	49.6	48.7	47.7	46.8	45.9	44.9
72	53.5	52.5	51.5	50.6	49.6	48.7	47.7	46.8	45.8	44.9
73	53.4	52.5	51.5	50.6	49.6	48.6	47.7	46.7	45.8	44.8
74	53.4	52.5	51.5	50.5	49.6	48.6	47.7	46.7	45.8	44.8
75	53.4	52.5	51.5	50.5	49.6	48.6	47.7	46.7	45.7	44.8

§13.31

AGES	30	31	32	33	34	35	36	37	38	39
76	53.4	52.4	51.5	50.5	49.6	48.6	47.6	46.7	45.7	44.8
77	53.4	52.4	51.5	50.5	49.5	48.6	47.6	46.7	45.7	44.8
78	53.4	52.4	51.5	50.5	49.5	48.6	47.6	46.6	45.7	44.7
79	53.4	52.4	51.5	50.5	49.5	48.6	47.6	46.6	45.7	44.7
80	53.4	52.4	51.4	50.5	49.5	48.5	47.6	46.6	45.7	44.7
81	53.4	52.4	51.4	50.5	49.5	48.5	47.6	46.6	45.7	44.7
82	53.4	52.4	51.4	50.5	49.5	48.5	47.6	46.6	45.6	44.7
83	53.4	52.4	51.4	50.5	49.5	48.5	47.6	46.6	45.6	44.7
84	53.4	52.4	51.4	50.5	49.5	48.5	47.6	46.6	45.6	44.7
85	53.3	52.4	51.4	50.4	49.5	48.5	47.5	46.6	45.6	44.7
86	53.3	52.4	51.4	50.4	49.5	48.5	47.5	46.6	45.6	44.6
87	53.3	52.4	51.4	50.4	49.5	48.5	47.5	46.6	45.6	44.6
88	53.3	52.4	51.4	50.4	49.5	48.5	47.5	46.6	45.6	44.6
89	53.3	52.4	51.4	50.4	49.5	48.5	47.5	46.6	45.6	44.6
90	53.3	52.4	51.4	50.4	49.5	48.5	47.5	46.6	45.6	44.6
91	53.3	52.4	51.4	50.4	49.5	48.5	47.5	46.6	45.6	44.6
92	53.3	52.4	51.4	50.4	49.5	48.5	47.5	46.6	45.6	44.6
93	53.3	52.4	51.4	50.4	49.5	48.5	47.5	46.6	45.6	44.6
94	53.3	52.4	51.4	50.4	49.5	48.5	47.5	46.6	45.6	44.6
95	53.3	52.4	51.4	50.4	49.5	48.5	47.5	46.5	45.6	44.6
96	53.3	52.4	51.4	50.4	49.5	48.5	47.5	46.5	45.6	44.6
97	53.3	52.4	51.4	50.4	49.5	48.5	47.5	46.5	45.6	44.6
98	53.3	52.4	51.4	50.4	49.5	48.5	47.5	46.5	45.6	44.6
99	53.3	52.4	51.4	50.4	49.5	48.5	47.5	46.5	45.6	44.6
100	53.3	52.4	51.4	50.4	49.5	48.5	47.5	46.5	45.6	44.6
101	53.3	52.4	51.4	50.4	49.5	48.5	47.5	46.5	45.6	44.6
102	53.3	52.4	51.4	50.4	49.5	48.5	47.5	46.5	45.6	44.6
103	53.3	52.4	51.4	50.4	49.5	48.5	47.5	46.5	45.6	44.6
104	53.3	52.4	51.4	50.4	49.5	48.5	47.5	46.5	45.6	44.6
105	53.3	52.4	51.4	50.4	49.4	48.5	47.5	46.5	45.6	44.6
106	53.3	52.4	51.4	50.4	49.4	48.5	47.5	46.5	45.6	44.6
107	53.3	52.4	51.4	50.4	49.4	48.5	47.5	46.5	45.6	44.6
108	53.3	52.4	51.4	50.4	49.4	48.5	47.5	46.5	45.6	44.6
109	53.3	52.4	51.4	50.4	49.4	48.5	47.5	46.5	45.6	44.6
110	53.3	52.4	51.4	50.4	49.4	48.5	47.5	46.5	45.6	44.6
111	53.3	52.4	51.4	50.4	49.4	48.5	47.5	46.5	45.6	44.6
112	53.3	52.4	51.4	50.4	49.4	48.5	47.5	46.5	45.6	44.6
113	53.3	52.4	51.4	50.4	49.4	48.5	47.5	46.5	45.6	44.6
114	53.3	52.4	51.4	50.4	49.4	48.5	47.5	46.5	45.6	44.6
115+	53.3	52.4	51.4	50.4	49.4	48.5	47.5	46.5	45.6	44.6

AGES	40	41	42	43	44	45	46	47	48	49
40	50.2	49.8	49.3	48.9	48.5	48.1	47.7	47.4	47.1	46.8
41	49.8	49.3	48.8	48.3	47.9	47.5	47.1	46.7	46.4	46.1
42	49.3	48.8	48.3	47.8	47.3	46.9	46.5	46.1	45.8	45.4
43	48.9	48.3	47.8	47.3	46.8	46.3	45.9	45.5	45.1	44.8
44	48.5	47.9	47.3	46.8	46.3	45.8	45.4	44.9	44.5	44.2
45	48.1	47.5	46.9	46.3	45.8	45.3	44.8	44.4	44.0	43.6
46	47.7	47.1	46.5	45.9	45.4	44.8	44.3	43.9	43.4	43.0
47	47.4	46.7	46.1	45.5	44.9	44.4	43.9	43.4	42.9	42.4
48	47.1	46.4	45.8	45.1	44.5	44.0	43.4	42.9	42.4	41.9
49	46.8	46.1	45.4	44.8	44.2	43.6	43.0	42.4	41.9	41.4
50	46.5	45.8	45.1	44.4	43.8	43.2	42.6	42.0	41.5	40.9
51	46.3	45.5	44.8	44.1	43.5	42.8	42.2	41.6	41.0	40.5
52	46.0	45.3	44.6	43.8	43.2	42.5	41.8	41.2	40.6	40.1
53	45.8	45.1	44.3	43.6	42.9	42.2	41.5	40.9	40.3	39.7
54	45.6	44.8	44.1	43.3	42.6	41.9	41.2	40.5	39.9	39.3
55	45.5	44.7	43.9	43.1	42.4	41.6	40.9	40.2	39.6	38.9
56	45.3	44.5	43.7	42.9	42.1	41.4	40.7	40.0	39.3	38.6
57	45.1	44.3	43.5	42.7	41.9	41.2	40.4	39.7	39.0	38.3
58	45.0	44.2	43.3	42.5	41.7	40.9	40.2	39.4	38.7	38.0
59	44.9	44.0	43.2	42.4	41.5	40.7	40.0	39.2	38.5	37.8
60	44.7	43.9	43.0	42.2	41.4	40.6	39.8	39.0	38.2	37.5
61	44.6	43.8	42.9	42.1	41.2	40.4	39.6	38.8	38.0	37.3
62	44.5	43.7	42.8	41.9	41.1	40.3	39.4	38.6	37.8	37.1
63	44.5	43.6	42.7	41.8	41.0	40.1	39.3	38.5	37.7	36.9
64	44.4	43.5	42.6	41.7	40.8	40.0	39.2	38.3	37.5	36.7
65	44.3	43.4	42.5	41.6	40.7	39.9	39.0	38.2	37.4	36.6
66	44.2	43.3	42.4	41.5	40.6	39.8	38.9	38.1	37.2	36.4
67	44.2	43.3	42.3	41.4	40.6	39.7	38.8	38.0	37.1	36.3
68	44.1	43.2	42.3	41.4	40.5	39.6	38.7	37.9	37.0	36.2
69	44.1	43.1	42.2	41.3	40.4	39.5	38.6	37.8	36.9	36.0
70	44.0	43.1	42.2	41.3	40.3	39.4	38.6	37.7	36.8	35.9
71	44.0	43.0	42.1	41.2	40.3	39.4	38.5	37.6	36.7	35.9
72	43.9	43.0	42.1	41.1	40.2	39.3	38.4	37.5	36.6	35.8
73	43.9	43.0	42.0	41.1	40.2	39.3	38.4	37.5	36.6	35.7
74	43.9	42.9	42.0	41.1	40.1	39.2	38.3	37.4	36.5	35.6
75	43.8	42.9	42.0	41.0	40.1	39.2	38.3	37.4	36.5	35.6
76	43.8	42.9	41.9	41.0	40.1	39.1	38.2	37.3	36.4	35.5
77	43.8	42.9	41.9	41.0	40.0	39.1	38.2	37.3	36.4	35.5
78	43.8	42.8	41.9	40.9	40.0	39.1	38.2	37.2	36.3	35.4
79	43.8	42.8	41.9	40.9	40.0	39.1	38.1	37.2	36.3	35.4
80	43.7	42.8	41.8	40.9	40.0	39.0	38.1	37.2	36.3	35.4

AGES	40	41	42	43	44	45	46	47	48	49
81	43.7	42.8	41.8	40.9	39.9	39.0	38.1	37.2	36.2	35.3
82	43.7	42.8	41.8	40.9	39.9	39.0	38.1	37.1	36.2	35.3
83	43.7	42.8	41.8	40.9	39.9	39.0	38.0	37.1	36.2	35.3
84	43.7	42.7	41.8	40.8	39.9	39.0	38.0	37.1	36.2	35.3
85	43.7	42.7	41.8	40.8	39.9	38.9	38.0	37.1	36.2	35.2
86	43.7	42.7	41.8	40.8	39.9	38.9	38.0	37.1	36.1	35.2
87	43.7	42.7	41.8	40.8	39.9	38.9	38.0	37.0	36.1	35.2
88	43.7	42.7	41.8	40.8	39.9	38.9	38.0	37.0	36.1	35.2
89	43.7	42.7	41.7	40.8	39.8	38.9	38.0	37.0	36.1	35.2
90	43.7	42.7	41.7	40.8	39.8	38.9	38.0	37.0	36.1	35.2
91	43.7	42.7	41.7	40.8	39.8	38.9	37.9	37.0	36.1	35.2
92	43.7	42.7	41.7	40.8	39.8	38.9	37.9	37.0	36.1	35.1
93	43.7	42.7	41.7	40.8	39.8	38.9	37.9	37.0	36.1	35.1
94	43.7	42.7	41.7	40.8	39.8	38.9	37.9	37.0	36.1	35.1
95	43.6	42.7	41.7	40.8	39.8	38.9	37.9	37.0	36.1	35.1
96	43.6	42.7	41.7	40.8	39.8	38.9	37.9	37.0	36.1	35.1
97	43.6	42.7	41.7	40.8	39.8	38.9	37.9	37.0	36.1	35.1
98	43.6	42.7	41.7	40.8	39.8	38.9	37.9	37.0	36.0	35.1
99	43.6	42.7	41.7	40.8	39.8	38.9	37.9	37.0	36.0	35.1
100	43.6	42.7	41.7	40.8	39.8	38.9	37.9	37.0	36.0	35.1
101	43.6	42.7	41.7	40.8	39.8	38.9	37.9	37.0	36.0	35.1
102	43.6	42.7	41.7	40.8	39.8	38.9	37.9	37.0	36.0	35.1
103	43.6	42.7	41.7	40.8	39.8	38.9	37.9	37.0	36.0	35.1
104	43.6	42.7	41.7	40.8	39.8	38.8	37.9	37.0	36.0	35.1
105	43.6	42.7	41.7	40.8	39.8	38.8	37.9	37.0	36.0	35.1
106	43.6	42.7	41.7	40.8	39.8	38.8	37.9	37.0	36.0	35.1
107	43.6	42.7	41.7	40.8	39.8	38.8	37.9	37.0	36.0	35.1
108	43.6	42.7	41.7	40.8	39.8	38.8	37.9	37.0	36.0	35.1
109	43.6	42.7	41.7	40.7	39.8	38.8	37.9	37.0	36.0	35.1
110	43.6	42.7	41.7	40.7	39.8	38.8	37.9	37.0	36.0	35.1
111	43.6	42.7	41.7	40.7	39.8	38.8	37.9	37.0	36.0	35.1
112	43.6	42.7	41.7	40.7	39.8	38.8	37.9	37.0	36.0	35.1
113	43.6	42.7	41.7	40.7	39.8	38.8	37.9	37.0	36.0	35.1
114	43.6	42.7	41.7	40.7	39.8	38.8	37.9	37.0	36.0	35.1
115+	43.6	42.7	41.7	40.7	39.8	38.8	37.9	37.0	36.0	35.1

AGES	50	51	52	53	54	55	56	57	58	59
50	40.4	40.0	39.5	39.1	38.7	38.3	38.0	37.6	37.3	37.1
51	40.0	39.5	39.0	38.5	38.1	37.7	37.4	37.0	36.7	36.4
52	39.5	39.0	38.5	38.0	37.6	37.2	36.8	36.4	36.0	35.7
53	39.1	38.5	38.0	37.5	37.1	36.6	36.2	35.8	35.4	35.1
54	38.7	38.1	37.6	37.1	36.6	36.1	35.7	35.2	34.8	34.5

AGES	50	51	52	53	54	55	56	57	58	59
55	38.3	37.7	37.2	36.6	36.1	35.6	35.1	34.7	34.3	33.9
56	38.0	37.4	36.8	36.2	35.7	35.1	34.7	34.2	33.7	33.3
57	37.6	37.0	36.4	35.8	35.2	34.7	34.2	33.7	33.2	32.8
58	37.3	36.7	36.0	35.4	34.8	34.3	33.7	33.2	32.8	32.3
59	37.1	36.4	35.7	35.1	34.5	33.9	33.3	32.8	32.3	31.8
60	36.8	36.1	35.4	34.8	34.1	33.5	32.9	32.4	31.9	31.3
61	36.6	35.8	35.1	34.5	33.8	33.2	32.6	32.0	31.4	30.9
62	36.3	35.6	34.9	34.2	33.5	32.9	32.2	31.6	31.1	30.5
63	36.1	35.4	34.6	33.9	33.2	32.6	31.9	31.3	30.7	30.1
64	35.9	35.2	34.4	33.7	33.0	32.3	31.6	31.0	30.4	29.8
65	35.8	35.0	34.2	33.5	32.7	32.0	31.4	30.7	30.0	29.4
66	35.6	34.8	34.0	33.3	32.5	31.8	31.1	30.4	29.8	29.1
67	35.5	34.7	33.9	33.1	32.3	31.6	30.9	30.2	29.5	28.8
68	35.3	34.5	33.7	32.9	32.1	31.4	30.7	29.9	29.2	28.6
69	35.2	34.4	33.6	32.8	32.0	31.2	30.5	29.7	29.0	28.3
70	35.1	34.3	33.4	32.6	31.8	31.1	30.3	29.5	28.8	28.1
71	35.0	34.2	33.3	32.5	31.7	30.9	30.1	29.4	28.6	27.9
72	34.9	34.1	33.2	32.4	31.6	30.8	30.0	29.2	28.4	27.7
73	34.8	34.0	33.1	32.3	31.5	30.6	29.8	29.1	28.3	27.5
74	34.8	33.9	33.0	32.2	31.4	30.5	29.7	28.9	28.1	27.4
75	34.7	33.8	33.0	32.1	31.3	30.4	29.6	28.8	28.0	27.2
76	34.6	33.8	32.9	32.0	31.2	30.3	29.5	28.7	27.9	27.1
77	34.6	33.7	32.8	32.0	31.1	30.3	29.4	28.6	27.8	27.0
78	34.5	33.6	32.8	31.9	31.0	30.2	29.3	28.5	27.7	26.9
79	34.5	33.6	32.7	31.8	31.0	30.1	29.3	28.4	27.6	26.8
80	34.5	33.6	32.7	31.8	30.9	30.1	29.2	28.4	27.5	26.7
81	34.4	33.5	32.6	31.8	30.9	30.0	29.2	28.3	27.5	26.6
82	34.4	33.5	32.6	31.7	30.8	30.0	29.1	28.3	27.4	26.6
83	34.4	33.5	32.6	31.7	30.8	29.9	29.1	28.2	27.4	26.5
84	34.3	33.4	32.5	31.7	30.8	29.9	29.0	28.2	27.3	26.5
85	34.3	33.4	32.5	31.6	30.7	29.9	29.0	28.1	27.3	26.4
86	34.3	33.4	32.5	31.6	30.7	29.8	29.0	28.1	27.2	26.4
87	34.3	33.4	32.5	31.6	30.7	29.8	28.9	28.1	27.2	26.4
88	34.3	33.4	32.5	31.6	30.7	29.8	28.9	28.0	27.2	26.3
89	34.3	33.3	32.4	31.5	30.7	29.8	28.9	28.0	27.2	26.3
90	34.2	33.3	32.4	31.5	30.6	29.8	28.9	28.0	27.1	26.3
91	34.2	33.3	32.4	31.5	30.6	29.7	28.9	28.0	27.1	26.3
92	34.2	33.3	32.4	31.5	30.6	29.7	28.8	28.0	27.1	26.2
93	34.2	33.3	32.4	31.5	30.6	29.7	28.8	28.0	27.1	26.2
94	34.2	33.3	32.4	31.5	30.6	29.7	28.8	27.9	27.1	26.2
95	34.2	33.3	32.4	31.5	30.6	29.7	28.8	27.9	27.1	26.2

AGES	50	51	52	53	54	55	56	57	58	59
96	34.2	33.3	32.4	31.5	30.6	29.7	28.8	27.9	27.0	26.2
97	34.2	33.3	32.4	31.5	30.6	29.7	28.8	27.9	27.0	26.2
98	34.2	33.3	32.4	31.5	30.6	29.7	28.8	27.9	27.0	26.2
99	34.2	33.3	32.4	31.5	30.6	29.7	28.8	27.9	27.0	26.2
100	34.2	33.3	32.4	31.5	30.6	29.7	28.8	27.9	27.0	26.1
101	34.2	33.3	32.4	31.5	30.6	29.7	28.8	27.9	27.0	26.1
102	34.2	33.3	32.4	31.4	30.5	29.7	28.8	27.9	27.0	26.1
103	34.2	33.3	32.4	31.4	30.5	29.7	28.8	27.9	27.0	26.1
104	34.2	33.3	32.4	31.4	30.5	29.6	28.8	27.9	27.0	26.1
105	34.2	33.3	32.3	31.4	30.5	29.6	28.8	27.9	27.0	26.1
106	34.2	33.3	32.3	31.4	30.5	29.6	28.8	27.9	27.0	26.1
107	34.2	33.3	32.3	31.4	30.5	29.6	28.8	27.9	27.0	26.1
108	34.2	33.3	32.3	31.4	30.5	29.6	28.8	27.9	27.0	26.1
109	34.2	33.3	32.3	31.4	30.5	29.6	28.7	27.9	27.0	26.1
110	34.2	33.3	32.3	31.4	30.5	29.6	28.7	27.9	27.0	26.1
111	34.2	33.3	32.3	31.4	30.5	29.6	28.7	27.9	27.0	26.1
112	34.2	33.3	32.3	31.4	30.5	29.6	28.7	27.9	27.0	26.1
113	34.2	33.3	32.3	31.4	30.5	29.6	28.7	27.9	27.0	26.1
114	34.2	33.3	32.3	31.4	30.5	29.6	28.7	27.9	27.0	26.1
115+	34.2	33.3	32.3	31.4	30.5	29.6	28.7	27.9	27.0	26.1

AGES	60	61	62	63	64	65	66	67	68	69
60	30.9	30.4	30.0	29.6	29.2	28.8	28.5	28.2	27.9	27.6
61	30.4	29.9	29.5	29.0	28.6	28.3	27.9	27.6	27.3	27.0
62	30.0	29.5	29.0	28.5	28.1	27.7	27.3	27.0	26.7	26.4
63	29.6	29.0	28.5	28.1	27.6	27.2	26.8	26.4	26.1	25.7
64	29.2	28.6	28.1	27.6	27.1	26.7	26.3	25.9	25.5	25.2
65	28.8	28.3	27.7	27.2	26.7	26.2	25.8	25.4	25.0	24.6
66	28.5	27.9	27.3	26.8	26.3	25.8	25.3	24.9	24.5	24.1
67	28.2	27.6	27.0	26.4	25.9	25.4	24.9	24.4	24.0	23.6
68	27.9	27.3	26.7	26.1	25.5	25.0	24.5	24.0	23.5	23.1
69	27.6	27.0	26.4	25.7	25.2	24.6	24.1	23.6	23.1	22.6
70	27.4	26.7	26.1	25.4	24.8	24.3	23.7	23.2	22.7	22.2
71	27.2	26.5	25.8	25.2	24.5	23.9	23.4	22.8	22.3	21.8
72	27.0	26.3	25.6	24.9	24.3	23.7	23.1	22.5	22.0	21.4
73	26.8	26.1	25.4	24.7	24.0	23.4	22.8	22.2	21.6	21.1
74	26.6	25.9	25.2	24.5	23.8	23.1	22.5	21.9	21.3	20.8
75	26.5	25.7	25.0	24.3	23.6	22.9	22.3	21.6	21.0	20.5
76	26.3	25.6	24.8	24.1	23.4	22.7	22.0	21.4	20.8	20.2
77	26.2	25.4	24.7	23.9	23.2	22.5	21.8	21.2	20.6	19.9
78	26.1	25.3	24.6	23.8	23.1	22.4	21.7	21.0	20.3	19.7
79	26.0	25.2	24.4	23.7	22.9	22.2	21.5	20.8	20.1	19.5

AGES	60	61	62	63	64	65	66	67	68	69
80	25.9	25.1	24.3	23.6	22.8	22.1	21.3	20.6	20.0	19.3
81	25.8	25.0	24.2	23.4	22.7	21.9	21.2	20.5	19.8	19.1
82	25.8	24.9	24.1	23.4	22.6	21.8	21.1	20.4	19.7	19.0
83	25.7	24.9	24.1	23.3	22.5	21.7	21.0	20.2	19.5	18.8
84	25.6	24.8	24.0	23.2	22.4	21.6	20.9	20.1	19.4	18.7
85	25.6	24.8	23.9	23.1	22.3	21.6	20.8	20.1	19.3	18.6
86	25.5	24.7	23.9	23.1	22.3	21.5	20.7	20.0	19.2	18.5
87	25.5	24.7	23.8	23.0	22.2	21.4	20.7	19.9	19.2	18.4
88	25.5	24.6	23.8	23.0	22.2	21.4	20.6	19.8	19.1	18.3
89	25.4	24.6	23.8	22.9	22.1	21.3	20.5	19.8	19.0	18.3
90	25.4	24.6	23.7	22.9	22.1	21.3	20.5	19.7	19.0	18.2
91	25.4	24.5	23.7	22.9	22.1	21.3	20.5	19.7	18.9	18.2
92	25.4	24.5	23.7	22.9	22.0	21.2	20.4	19.6	18.9	18.1
93	25.4	24.5	23.7	22.8	22.0	21.2	20.4	19.6	18.8	18.1
94	25.3	24.5	23.6	22.8	22.0	21.2	20.4	19.6	18.8	18.0
95	25.3	24.5	23.6	22.8	22.0	21.1	20.3	19.6	18.8	18.0
96	25.3	24.5	23.6	22.8	21.9	21.1	20.3	19.5	18.8	18.0
97	25.3	24.5	23.6	22.8	21.9	21.1	20.3	19.5	18.7	18.0
98	25.3	24.4	23.6	22.8	21.9	21.1	20.3	19.5	18.7	17.9
99	25.3	24.4	23.6	22.7	21.9	21.1	20.3	19.5	18.7	17.9
100	25.3	24.4	23.6	22.7	21.9	21.1	20.3	19.5	18.7	17.9
101	25.3	24.4	23.6	22.7	21.9	21.1	20.2	19.4	18.7	17.9
102	25.3	24.4	23.6	22.7	21.9	21.1	20.2	19.4	18.6	17.9
103	25.3	24.4	23.6	22.7	21.9	21.0	20.2	19.4	18.6	17.9
104	25.3	24.4	23.5	22.7	21.9	21.0	20.2	19.4	18.6	17.8
105	25.3	24.4	23.5	22.7	21.9	21.0	20.2	19.4	18.6	17.8
106	25.3	24.4	23.5	22.7	21.9	21.0	20.2	19.4	18.6	17.8
107	25.2	24.4	23.5	22.7	21.8	21.0	20.2	19.4	18.6	17.8
108	25.2	24.4	23.5	22.7	21.8	21.0	20.2	19.4	18.6	17.8
109	25.2	24.4	23.5	22.7	21.8	21.0	20.2	19.4	18.6	17.8
110	25.2	24.4	23.5	22.7	21.8	21.0	20.2	19.4	18.6	17.8
111	25.2	24.4	23.5	22.7	21.8	21.0	20.2	19.4	18.6	17.8
112	25.2	24.4	23.5	22.7	21.8	21.0	20.2	19.4	18.6	17.8
113	25.2	24.4	23.5	22.7	21.8	21.0	20.2	19.4	18.6	17.8
114	25.2	24.4	23.5	22.7	21.8	21.0	20.2	19.4	18.6	17.8
115+	25.2	24.4	23.5	22.7	21.8	21.0	20.2	19.4	18.6	17.8
AGES	70	71	72	73	74	75	76	77	78	79
70	21.8	21.3	20.9	20.6	20.2	19.9	19.6	19.4	19.1	18.9
71	21.3	20.9	20.5	20.1	19.7	19.4	19.1	18.8	18.5	18.3
72	20.9	20.5	20.0	19.6	19.3	18.9	18.6	18.3	18.0	17.7
73	20.6	20.1	19.6	19.2	18.8	18.4	18.1	17.8	17.5	17.2

AGES	70	71	72	73	74	75	76	77	78	79
74	20.2	19.7	19.3	18.8	18.4	18.0	17.6	17.3	17.0	16.7
75	19.9	19.4	18.9	18.4	18.0	17.6	17.2	16.8	16.5	16.2
76	19.6	19.1	18.6	18.1	17.6	17.2	16.8	16.4	16.0	15.7
77	19.4	18.8	18.3	17.8	17.3	16.8	16.4	16.0	15.6	15.3
78	19.1	18.5	18.0	17.5	17.0	16.5	16.0	15.6	15.2	14.9
79	18.9	18.3	17.7	17.2	16.7	16.2	15.7	15.3	14.9	14.5
80	18.7	18.1	17.5	16.9	16.4	15.9	15.4	15.0	14.5	14.1
81	18.5	17.9	17.3	16.7	16.2	15.6	15.1	14.7	14.2	13.8
82	18.3	17.7	17.1	16.5	15.9	15.4	14.9	14.4	13.9	13.5
83	18.2	17.5	16.9	16.3	15.7	15.2	14.7	14.2	13.7	13.2
84	18.0	17.4	16.7	16.1	15.5	15.0	14.4	13.9	13.4	13.0
85	17.9	17.3	16.6	16.0	15.4	14.8	14.3	13.7	13.2	12.8
86	17.8	17.1	16.5	15.8	15.2	14.6	14.1	13.5	13.0	12.5
87	17.7	17.0	16.4	15.7	15.1	14.5	13.9	13.4	12.9	12.4
88	17.6	16.9	16.3	15.6	15.0	14.4	13.8	13.2	12.7	12.2
89	17.6	16.9	16.2	15.5	14.9	14.3	13.7	13.1	12.6	12.0
90	17.5	16.8	16.1	15.4	14.8	14.2	13.6	13.0	12.4	11.9
91	17.4	16.7	16.0	15.4	14.7	14.1	13.5	12.9	12.3	11.8
92	17.4	16.7	16.0	15.3	14.6	14.0	13.4	12.8	12.2	11.7
93	17.3	16.6	15.9	15.2	14.6	13.9	13.3	12.7	12.1	11.6
94	17.3	16.6	15.9	15.2	14.5	13.9	13.2	12.6	12.0	11.5
95	17.3	16.5	15.8	15.1	14.5	13.8	13.2	12.6	12.0	11.4
96	17.2	16.5	15.8	15.1	14.4	13.8	13.1	12.5	11.9	11.3
97	17.2	16.5	15.8	15.1	14.4	13.7	13.1	12.5	11.9	11.3
98	17.2	16.4	15.7	15.0	14.3	13.7	13.0	12.4	11.8	11.2
99	17.2	16.4	15.7	15.0	14.3	13.6	13.0	12.4	11.8	11.2
100	17.1	16.4	15.7	15.0	14.3	13.6	12.9	12.3	11.7	11.1
101	17.1	16.4	15.6	14.9	14.2	13.6	12.9	12.3	11.7	11.1
102	17.1	16.4	15.6	14.9	14.2	13.5	12.9	12.2	11.6	11.0
103	17.1	16.3	15.6	14.9	14.2	13.5	12.9	12.2	11.6	11.0
104	17.1	16.3	15.6	14.9	14.2	13.5	12.8	12.2	11.6	11.0
105	17.1	16.3	15.6	14.9	14.2	13.5	12.8	12.2	11.5	10.9
106	17.1	16.3	15.6	14.8	14.1	13.5	12.8	12.2	11.5	10.9
107	17.0	16.3	15.6	14.8	14.1	13.4	12.8	12.1	11.5	10.9
108	17.0	16.3	15.5	14.8	14.1	13.4	12.8	12.1	11.5	10.9
109	17.0	16.3	15.5	14.8	14.1	13.4	12.8	12.1	11.5	10.9
110	17.0	16.3	15.5	14.8	14.1	13.4	12.7	12.1	11.5	10.9
111	17.0	16.3	15.5	14.8	14.1	13.4	12.7	12.1	11.5	10.8
112	17.0	16.3	15.5	14.8	14.1	13.4	12.7	12.1	11.5	10.8
113	17.0	16.3	15.5	14.8	14.1	13.4	12.7	12.1	11.4	10.8

AGES	70	71	72	73	74	75	76	77	78	79
114	17.0	16.3	15.5	14.8	14.1	13.4	12.7	12.1	11.4	10.8
115+	17.0	16.3	15.5	14.8	14.1	13.4	12.7	12.1	11.4	10.8

AGES	80	81	82	83	84	85	86	87	88	89
80	13.8	13.4	13.1	12.8	12.6	12.3	12.1	11.9	11.7	11.5
81	13.4	13.1	12.7	12.4	12.2	11.9	11.7	11.4	11.3	11.1
82	13.1	12.7	12.4	12.1	11.8	11.5	11.3	11.0	10.8	10.6
83	12.8	12.4	12.1	11.7	11.4	11.1	10.9	10.6	10.4	10.2
84	12.6	12.2	11.8	11.4	11.1	10.8	10.5	10.3	10.1	9.9
85	12.3	11.9	11.5	11.1	10.8	10.5	10.2	9.9	9.7	9.5
86	12.1	11.7	11.3	10.9	10.5	10.2	9.9	9.6	9.4	9.2
87	11.9	11.4	11.0	10.6	10.3	9.9	9.6	9.4	9.1	8.9
88	11.7	11.3	10.8	10.4	10.1	9.7	9.4	9.1	8.8	8.6
89	11.5	11.1	10.6	10.2	9.9	9.5	9.2	8.9	8.6	8.3
90	11.4	10.9	10.5	10.1	9.7	9.3	9.0	8.6	8.3	8.1
91	11.3	10.8	10.3	9.9	9.5	9.1	8.8	8.4	8.1	7.9
92	11.2	10.7	10.2	9.8	9.3	9.0	8.6	8.3	8.0	7.7
93	11.1	10.6	10.1	9.6	9.2	8.8	8.5	8.1	7.8	7.5
94	11.0	10.5	10.0	9.5	9.1	8.7	8.3	8.0	7.6	7.3
95	10.9	10.4	9.9	9.4	9.0	8.6	8.2	7.8	7.5	7.2
96	10.8	10.3	9.8	9.3	8.9	8.5	8.1	7.7	7.4	7.1
97	10.7	10.2	9.7	9.2	8.8	8.4	8.0	7.6	7.3	6.9
98	10.7	10.1	9.6	9.2	8.7	8.3	7.9	7.5	7.1	6.8
99	10.6	10.1	9.6	9.1	8.6	8.2	7.8	7.4	7.0	6.7
100	10.6	10.0	9.5	9.0	8.5	8.1	7.7	7.3	6.9	6.6
101	10.5	10.0	9.4	9.0	8.5	8.0	7.6	7.2	6.9	6.5
102	10.5	9.9	9.4	8.9	8.4	8.0	7.5	7.1	6.8	6.4
103	10.4	9.9	9.4	8.8	8.4	7.9	7.5	7.1	6.7	6.3
104	10.4	9.8	9.3	8.8	8.3	7.9	7.4	7.0	6.6	6.3
105	10.4	9.8	9.3	8.8	8.3	7.8	7.4	7.0	6.6	6.2
106	10.3	9.8	9.2	8.7	8.2	7.8	7.3	6.9	6.5	6.2
107	10.3	9.8	9.2	8.7	8.2	7.7	7.3	6.9	6.5	6.1
108	10.3	9.7	9.2	8.7	8.2	7.7	7.3	6.8	6.4	6.1
109	10.3	9.7	9.2	8.7	8.2	7.7	7.2	6.8	6.4	6.0
110	10.3	9.7	9.2	8.6	8.1	7.7	7.2	6.8	6.4	6.0
111	10.3	9.7	9.1	8.6	8.1	7.6	7.2	6.8	6.3	6.0
112	10.2	9.7	9.1	8.6	8.1	7.6	7.2	6.7	6.3	5.9
113	10.2	9.7	9.1	8.6	8.1	7.6	7.2	6.7	6.3	5.9
114	10.2	9.7	9.1	8.6	8.1	7.6	7.1	6.7	6.3	5.9
115+	10.2	9.7	9.1	8.6	8.1	7.6	7.1	6.7	6.3	5.9

AGES	90	91	92	93	94	95	96	97	98	99
90	7.8	7.6	7.4	7.2	7.1	6.9	6.8	6.6	6.5	6.4
91	7.6	7.4	7.2	7.0	6.8	6.7	6.5	6.4	6.3	6.1
92	7.4	7.2	7.0	6.8	6.6	6.4	6.3	6.1	6.0	5.9
93	7.2	7.0	6.8	6.6	6.4	6.2	6.1	5.9	5.8	5.6
94	7.1	6.8	6.6	6.4	6.2	6.0	5.9	5.7	5.6	5.4
95	6.9	6.7	6.4	6.2	6.0	5.8	5.7	5.5	5.4	5.2
96	6.8	6.5	6.3	6.1	5.9	5.7	5.5	5.3	5.2	5.0
97	6.6	6.4	6.1	5.9	5.7	5.5	5.3	5.2	5.0	4.9
98	6.5	6.3	6.0	5.8	5.6	5.4	5.2	5.0	4.8	4.7
99	6.4	6.1	5.9	5.6	5.4	5.2	5.0	4.9	4.7	4.5
100	6.3	6.0	5.8	5.5	5.3	5.1	4.9	4.7	4.5	4.4
101	6.2	5.9	5.6	5.4	5.2	5.0	4.8	4.6	4.4	4.2
102	6.1	5.8	5.5	5.3	5.1	4.8	4.6	4.4	4.3	4.1
103	6.0	5.7	5.4	5.2	5.0	4.7	4.5	4.3	4.1	4.0
104	5.9	5.6	5.4	5.1	4.9	4.6	4.4	4.2	4.0	3.8
105	5.9	5.6	5.3	5.0	4.8	4.5	4.3	4.1	3.9	3.7
106	5.8	5.5	5.2	4.9	4.7	4.5	4.2	4.0	3.8	3.6
107	5.8	5.4	5.1	4.9	4.6	4.4	4.2	3.9	3.7	3.5
108	5.7	5.4	5.1	4.8	4.6	4.3	4.1	3.9	3.7	3.5
109	5.7	5.3	5.0	4.8	4.5	4.3	4.0	3.8	3.6	3.4
110	5.6	5.3	5.0	4.7	4.5	4.2	4.0	3.8	3.5	3.3
111	5.6	5.3	5.0	4.7	4.4	4.2	3.9	3.7	3.5	3.3
112	5.6	5.3	4.9	4.7	4.4	4.1	3.9	3.7	3.5	3.2
113	5.6	5.2	4.9	4.6	4.4	4.1	3.9	3.6	3.4	3.2
114	5.6	5.2	4.9	4.6	4.3	4.1	3.9	3.6	3.4	3.2
115+	5.5	5.2	4.9	4.6	4.3	4.1	3.8	3.6	3.4	3.1
AGES	100	101	102	103	104	105	106	107	108	109
100	4.2	4.1	3.9	3.8	3.7	3.5	3.4	3.3	3.3	3.2
101	4.1	3.9	3.7	3.6	3.5	3.4	3.2	3.1	3.1	3.0
102	3.9	3.7	3.6	3.4	3.3	3.2	3.1	3.0	2.9	2.8
103	3.8	3.6	3.4	3.3	3.2	3.0	2.9	2.8	2.7	2.6
104	3.7	3.5	3.3	3.2	3.0	2.9	2.7	2.6	2.5	2.4
105	3.5	3.4	3.2	3.0	2.9	2.7	2.6	2.5	2.4	2.3
106	3.4	3.2	3.1	2.9	2.7	2.6	2.4	2.3	2.2	2.1
107	3.3	3.1	3.0	2.8	2.6	2.5	2.3	2.2	2.1	2.0
108	3.3	3.1	2.9	2.7	2.5	2.4	2.2	2.1	1.9	1.8
109	3.2	3.0	2.8	2.6	2.4	2.3	2.1	2.0	1.8	1.7
110	3.1	2.9	2.7	2.5	2.3	2.2	2.0	1.9	1.7	1.6
111	3.1	2.9	2.7	2.5	2.3	2.1	1.9	1.8	1.6	1.5
112	3.0	2.8	2.6	2.4	2.2	2.0	1.9	1.7	1.5	1.4
113	3.0	2.8	2.6	2.4	2.2	2.0	1.8	1.6	1.5	1.3

AGES	100	101	102	103	104	105	106	107	108	109
114	3.0	2.7	2.5	2.3	2.1	1.9	1.8	1.6	1.4	1.3
115+	2.9	2.7	2.5	2.3	2.1	1.9	1.7	1.5	1.4	1.2

AGES '	110	111	112	113	114	115+
110	1.5	1.4	1.3	1.2	1.1	1.1
111	1.4	1.2	1.1	1.1	1.0	1.0
112	1.3	1.1	1.0	1.0	1.0	1.0
113	1.2	1.1	1.0	1.0	1.0	1.0
114	1.1	1.0	1.0	1.0	1.0	1.0
115+	1.1	1.0	1.0	1.0	1.0	1.0

Q-4. May the tables under this section be changed?

A-4. The Single Life Table, Uniform Lifetime Table and Joint and Last Survivor Table provided in A-1 through A-3 of this section may be changed by the Commissioner in revenue rulings, notices, and other guidance published in the Internal Revenue Bulletin. See § 601.601(d)(2)(ii)(b) of this chapter.

Glossary

2% Floor. Under § 67, miscellaneous itemized deductions are not allowable to the extent of 2 percent of the taxpayer's adjusted gross income.

2503(c) trust. A trust created for the sole benefit of a beneficiary who is under 21 that meets the requirements of § 2503(c), transfers to which are not treated as future interests for purposes of the annual gift tax exclusion.

303 Redemption. If the stock included in a decedent's estate was worth more than 35 percent of the decedent's gross estate less deductions under § § 2053 and 2054, the redemption of an amount not to exceed the sum of the state and federal death taxes and funeral and administrative expenses, is treated as a sale or exchange of the stock and not a dividend.

5 or 5 power. A power to withdraw the greater of $5,000 or 5 percent of the total value of property subject to withdrawal. The lapse or release of such a power is not a gift and does not require inclusion in the power-holder's estate of the property with respect to which the power has lapsed. Giving a trust beneficiary such a power increases the flexibility of the trust. § § 2041(b)(2), 2514(e).

Abatement. The appropriation of assets disposed of by will to satisfy the testator's debts. In the absence of testamentary direction the usual order of abatement is, (1) intestate property, (2) residuary estate, (3) general bequests, and (4) specific bequests. *See* U.P.C. § 3-902.

Active management. For special use valuation purposes under § 2032A, active management means the making of management decisions of a business other than daily operating decisions. § 2032A(e)(12).

Ademption. A common law doctrine under which a specific gift fails if the specifically bequeathed property is not owned by the testator at the time of his or her death. *See* U.P.C. § 2-606; § 4.15.1.

Advance directives. A document in which a competent adult may give directives regarding health care. Directives are authorized by Natural Death Acts and similar legislation.

Advancement. An inter vivos gift made to an heir apparent as an advance on the amount the donee may be entitled to receive as an intestate share of the donor's estate. *See* U.P.C. § 2-109.

Alternate valuation date. A date, six months after death, on which a decedent's executor can elect to value the assets of the decedent's estate. If the election is made, assets sold or otherwise disposed of within six months of death are made on the date or dates of sale or distribution. Under § 2032(c) the election can only be made if it will result in a reduction of the value of the gross estate and the sum of the estate and GST taxes applicable to assets included in the decedent's gross estate.

Alternative minimum tax (AMT). A tax that is tentatively calculated at a rate of 26 or 28 percent on the amount of a taxpayer's alternative minimum taxable income (AMTI) in excess of the applicable exemption. The AMT for a taxpayer is the tentative tax less the amount of regular income tax paid for the year.

Alternatively deductible expenses. Expenses paid by a decedent's estate that are deductible either for income or estate tax purposes.

Anatomical gifts. Gifts of a decedent's body or body parts for transplantation or medical research. Usually made pursuant to the Uniform Anatomical Gifts Act.

Ancillary administration. The administration of a decedent's estate carried out in a jurisdiction other than the one in which the decedent was domiciled at the time of his or her death.

Annual gift tax exclusion. Under §2503(b) an annual gift tax exclusion of $13,000 is allowed with respect to transfers of present interests to each donee.

Annuity. A fixed amount payable to the annuitant for life or for a fixed period. A private annuity, defined below, is an example.

Ante-nuptial agreement. *See* Pre-nuptial agreement

Anti-*Byrum* rule. Congress enacted §2036(b) to overturn *United States v. Byrum*, 408 U.S. 125 (1972). Under §2036(b) a deceased transferor's estate includes stock in a controlled corporation over which the decedent retained the right to vote in any capacity.

Anti-lapse statutes. Statutes under which the interest of a beneficiary who predeceases the testator is distributed to the beneficiary's lineal descendants unless otherwise directed in the will. Anti-lapse statutes typically apply only to testamentary gifts made to relatives of the testator other than the testator's spouse. *See* U.P.C. §2-603.

Applicable credit amount. The amount of the credit allowed by §2010(c) for the year in question with respect to specified applicable exclusion amounts. The amount for 2009 is $1,455,800, the tax on a transfer of $2,000,000. *See* Unified credit.

Applicable exclusion amount. The amount by reference to which the applicable credit amount is determined under §2010(c) for a specified year. For 2009, the applicable exclusion amount is $3,500,000.

Applicable family member. Defined in §2701(e)(2) as the transferor's spouse, an ancestor of the transferor or the transferor's spouse, or the spouse of any such ancestor. *See* Family members.

Applicable federal rate. Under §1274(d) the applicable federal rate for debt instruments of various terms is fixed by the average market yield for marketable obligations with various terms of the United States. Annuities, term interests, remainders, and reversions are valued by applying a rate equal to 120 percent of the federal mid-term rate (*i.e.*, for United States obligations with terms of between three and nine years). §7520(a).

Applicable fraction. For GSTT purposes, a fraction used in determining the inclusion ratio. The numerator of the fraction is the amount of the transferor's GSTT exemption allocated to the trust or other disposition; the denominator is the value of the property transferred less the death taxes recovered from such property and any charitable deduction allowed with respect to it. §2642(a).

Applicable rate. For GSTT purposes, the product of multiplying the maximum federal estate tax rate by the inclusion ratio. § 2641(a).

Applicable restriction. A restriction, described in § 2704(b)(2), on the right of a partnership or corporation to liquidate that either lapses after a transfer or may be removed by the transferor and members of his or her family. Applicable restrictions are disregarded under certain circumstances in determining the value of a transferred interest in a corporation or partnership controlled by the transferor and members of his or her family.

Applicable retained interest. Either (1) an interest in a partnership or corporation with respect to which there is a liquidation, put, call, or conversion right or (2) an interest with respect to which there is a distribution right in a corporation or partnership controlled by the transferor and applicable family members. § 2701(b).

Apportionment. This term usually refers to one of the methods by which the burden of the federal estate tax is allocated. *See* Equitable apportionment *and* Estate tax apportionment.

Ascertainable standard. A limitation applicable to the exercise of a power to invade, consume, or use property or the income from property. For purposes of § 2041, "a power is limited by such a standard if the extent of the holder's duty to exercise and not to exercise the power is reasonably measurable. . . . " Reg. § 20.2041-1(c)(2). Property subject to a power to consume that is limited by an ascertainable standard relating to the decedent's health, education, support, or maintenance is not includible in his or her estate under § 2041.

Asset protection trust. A self-settled irrevocable trust created in one of the states (or foreign jurisdictions) that protects self-settled trusts against most types of claims that might be brought against the grantor. The extent of protection provided varies substantially according to the law of the jurisdiction and generally does not protect property that was transferred in fraud of creditors.

Attorney-in-fact. A person designated in a power of attorney to act as agent for the principal.

Attribution rules. Rules under § 318 and similar provisions by which the ownership of stock is attributed from one person or entity to another person or entity. Attribution is required to determine, *inter alia,* whether a decedent had control of a corporation for purposes of § 2036(b).

Bargain sale. The sale of property for less than its fair market value. In the case of a bargain sale to charity, for purposes of determining gain the adjusted basis of the property is reduced as provided in § 1011(b).

Basis. For income tax purposes the basis of property is generally its cost. § 1012. The donor's basis in property generally carries over to the donee under § 1015. The basis of property acquired from a decedent is fixed by its federal estate tax value in the decedent's estate. § 1014. As provided in § 1016, the basis of property is adjusted for post-acquisition improvements, depreciation, and other items.

Below-market loan. A loan made at a below-market interest rate on which interest may be imputed for income and gift tax purposes under the rules of § 7872.

Beneficiary Deed. Also known as a transfer on death (or TOD) deed, it permits the owner of an interest in real property to effect the automatic conveyance of that interest upon the owner's death to one or more beneficiaries selected by the owner. Although the owner signs and records a beneficiary deed during the owner's lifetime, the transfer does not take effect until the owner's death. Accordingly, the owner usually has the right to revoke the deed prior to death. Property subject to a beneficiary deed is not part of the owner's probate estate, because the transfer occurs at death by operation of applicable state law.

Blockage. A theory upon which a discount is allowed in valuing a large holding of marketable securities or art objects, the sale of which would depress the market.

Buy-sell agreement. An agreement under which interests in a partnership or corporation will be purchased by the other owners or by the entity when an owner dies or another triggering event occurs. The agreement may be a cross-purchase agreement (*i.e.*, one that calls for the other owners to purchase the interest of a deceased party) or an entity-purchase agreement (*i.e.*, one that calls for the corporation or partnership to purchase the decedent's interest).

Bypass trust. A trust that will not be includible in the estate of the decedent's surviving spouse (or of the other initial beneficiary). The amount placed in the trust is often fixed by formula at the amount of the decedent's credit equivalent. *See also* Credit shelter trust and Unified credit.

Byrum, United States v.See Anti-Byrum rule.

C corporation. A C corporation is a corporation that, for federal income tax purposes, is not an S corporation. § 1361(a)(2). A C corporation is a separate taxable entity that pays tax on its taxable income under the table set forth in § 11. When a C corporation distributes after-tax earnings and profits to a shareholder, the shareholder must pay tax on the dividend received. § § 61; 316. The earnings of a C corporation are thus said to face a "double tax," once at the corporate level and then again at the shareholder level.

Capital asset. Formally, any asset not described in any of § § 1221(a)(1)–(8). Generally, the term refers to assets held for investment or personal use as opposed to business use.

Capital gains (losses). The difference between the amount realized upon the sale or exchange of a capital asset and its adjusted basis. Gains and losses are short term if the asset was held for one year or less prior to sale and long term if it was held for more than one year. § 1222.

Carryover basis. For purposes of determining gain or loss, the donor's basis in property generally carries over to the donee, adjusted as provided in § 1015.

Charitable contribution carryover. Charitable contributions that exceed the maximum amount deductible in the current tax year for income tax purposes may generally be carried over for the next five years.

Charitable lead trust (CLT). A split-interest trust in which a charity holds the right to receive current distributions of a guaranteed annuity or unitrust amount for a designated term. A guaranteed annuity is a determinable amount, payable at least annually for a fixed term or for the life or lives of designated persons who are living at the time of the transfer. Reg. § 1.170A-6(c)(2)(i)(A). A unitrust is a fixed percentage of the fair market value of the property determined annually, and payable for the same period as a guaranteed annuity.

Charitable remainder annuity trust (CRAT). A split-interest trust that provides for the annual distribution to a noncharitable beneficiary or beneficiaries of a fixed amount, not less than 5 percent of the initial value of the trust property for the life or lives of living persons or for a term of not more than 20 years. The remainder must pass to a qualified charity. § 664.

Charitable remainder trust. A split-interest trust in which a current interest meeting the requirements of § 664 is held by a noncharity and the remainder is held by a charity. Income, gift, and estate tax deductions are allowed for interests in charitable remainder trusts that are either a charitable remainder annuity trust or a charitable remainder unitrust as defined in § 664.

Charitable remainder unitrust (CRUT). A split-interest trust that must provide for the payout each year to a noncharitable beneficiary of a fixed percentage (at least 5 percent) of the annually determined net fair market value of its assets. The remainder must pass to a qualified charity. § 664.

Check-the-box regulation. A regulation adopted in December 1996, Reg. § 301.7701-3, that allows an unincorporated business entity broad freedom to choose whether to be taxed as a corporation or a partnership.

Clifford **trust.** A short-term irrevocable trust of which the grantor was treated as owner under *Helvering v. Clifford*, 309 U.S. 331 (1940). Sections 671-677, adopted in 1954, now govern the income tax treatment of grantor trusts. *See* Short-term trust.

Closely-held corporation. A corporation, the stock of which is held by a small number of shareholders—often members of a single family. The shares of a closely-held corporation are not publicly traded, as a result of which they may be valued by applying a discount for lack of marketability.

Code. The Internal Revenue Code of 1986.

Common trust fund. A trust fund maintained by a financial institution exclusively for the collective investment of funds held by it in a fiduciary capacity (i.e., as personal representative, trustee, custodian under the Uniform Gifts to Minors Act or the Uniform Transfers to Minors Act). An institution typically maintains several funds, each with a different investment objective.

Community property. A marital property regime followed by eight western and southwestern states and Wisconsin under which a husband and wife own equal interests in property acquired during marriage. In 1997 Alaska adopted an optional form of community property.

Community property agreement. An agreement between husband and wife regarding the disposition of community property upon the death of either or both of them. Such agreements are generally recognized as valid in community property states.

Community property joint tenancy. Statutes in several community property states provide that property held in a joint tenancy by a husband and wife is presumed to be their community property.

Complex trust. For income tax purposes, a trust that either is not required to distribute all of its income currently, provides for the payment of charitable gifts or distributes amounts other than income. § 661.

Controlled corporation. A corporation in which an individual or entity is treated as having control over the requisite interest in the stock after applying one or another form of the attribution rules. § 318. For purposes of § 2036(b) a corporation is controlled if the decedent had the right to vote 20 percent or more of its stock while § 2701(b)(2)(A) defines control as 50 percent or more.

Credit equivalent. The taxable amount ($3,500,000 in 2009) that can be transferred by a donor or decedent without the payment of any federal estate tax by reason of the unified credit. *See* Applicable credit amount *and* Applicable exclusion amount. § 2010.

Credit shelter trust. A trust funded with a portion of the decedent's estate equal to the remaining credit equivalent available at death. The trust is usually drafted to avoid any portion being included in the estate of the decedent's surviving spouse. § 2.46.

Cross-owned life insurance. A husband and wife may each own policies of insurance on the life of the other. Such cross-ownership of life insurance can result in substantial estate tax savings if the husband and wife die simultaneously. § 6.21.1.

Cross-purchase agreement. A buy-sell agreement which obligates the other shareholders or partners to buy the interest of a deceased or withdrawing owner. Subject to § 2703 the agreement may fix the value of the interest of the deceased or withdrawing owner.

***Crummey* power (*Crummey* trust).** A beneficiary's noncumulative power to withdraw property transferred to a discretionary trust that enables the donor to claim the annual gift tax exclusion with respect to the transfer. Such a power is named after *Crummey v. Commissioner*, 397 F.2d 82 (9th Cir. 1972), which allowed an annual gift tax exclusion for assets transferred to a discretionary trust for a minor.

Custodian. Under the Uniform Gifts to Minors Act and the Uniform Transfers to Minors Act, the custodian is the person in whose name property may be registered in order to make an irrevocable gift to a minor. The custodian is a fiduciary having broad powers to manage and distribute the property for the benefit of the minor.

Date of distribution value. Assets that are distributed in kind in satisfaction of a pecuniary gift are ordinarily valued on the date or dates they are distributed. This method of valuation, also called "true worth," may be used in satisfying a pecuniary marital deduction gift.

Death benefit only (DBO) plan. An arrangement under which an employer makes a payment upon the death of an employee to designated members of the employee's family. Benefits paid under a DBO plan are generally not includible in the employee's gross estate.

Decedent's final return. A decedent's income tax return for the income tax year in which he or she died. The return may be filed jointly with the decedent's surviving spouse.

Defective grantor trust (intentionally defective income trust or IDIT). A trust that is deliberately drafted in a way that causes the grantor to be treated as owner of the trust for income tax purposes but without causing the property to be included in the grantor's estate.

Direct skip. For GSTT purposes a direct skip is a transfer to a skip person (including a trust all of the interests of which are held by skip persons). §§ 2612(c), 2613(a).

Directive to physicians. A document authorized by statutes in most states by which a competent adult gives some directions regarding the health care he or she wishes to receive. *See* Living will *and* Durable power of attorney for health care.

Disclaimer (or renunciation). *See* Qualified disclaimer. A refusal by a donee to accept a gift, bequest, or other attempted transfer. Disclaimers must be contrasted with assignments and releases, which are premised on acceptance by the donee: Once accepted, the property received may be assigned or a power released.

Discounts. Discounts are generally allowed in valuing fractional interests in real estate (*see* Fractional interest discount), large holdings of marketable securities or art objects (*see* Blockage), and noncontrol interests in partnerships and limited liability companies (*see* Minority interest discount and Lack of marketability discount).

Discretionary trust. A trust with respect to which the trustee has discretion to distribute income (or principal) to one or more beneficiaries. The annual gift tax exclusion is not allowed for transfers to such a trust unless the beneficiary holds a sufficient (*i.e., Crummey*) power of withdrawal.

Distributable net income (DNI). For income tax purposes DNI limits the amount deductible by estates and trusts for amounts paid, credited, or distributed to beneficiaries. § 643(a). It also fixes the character of the distributions to the beneficiaries and limits the amount reportable by the beneficiaries as income.

Distribution deduction. The amount, limited to the distributable net income of a trust or estate, that it is allowed to deduct with respect to amounts required to be distributed currently to beneficiaries and other amounts properly paid, credited, or required to be distributed to beneficiaries. The beneficiaries are required to include the same amount in their incomes. §§ 651, 652, 661, 662.

Diversification. A principle, generally considered to be a part of the prudent person rule, that investments of a trust should be diversified.

Domestic asset protection trust. An irrevocable trust formed under the laws of one of the roughly ten jurisdiction that appoints an independent trustee (not the grantor) who may, in the independent trustee's absolute discretion, distribute trust income and principal to a pre-defined class of beneficiaries that includes the grantor. *See* Asset protection trust.

Durable power of attorney (DPA). A power of attorney that remains effective although the principal becomes incompetent. A DPA may be presently effective or become effective only upon the incompetency of the principal.

Durable power of attorney for health care (DPAHC). A durable power of attorney that authorizes the agent to make health care decisions for the principal if he or she becomes incompetent.

Duty of consistency. Where the discounted value of an asset included in the decedent's gross estate for federal estate tax purposes is accepted by the IRS, this common law doctrine prevents the estate or the beneficiaries from claiming a higher, undiscounted value in the property as its basis for federal income tax purposes.

Dynasty trust. A trust established for the benefit of grandchildren and more remote descendants, often structured so as to exist as long as permitted under the Rule Against Perpetuities. Dynasty trusts are often established in jurisdictions that have abolished the Rule so that there is no legal limit on the trust's duration.

Electing small business trust (ESBT). An electing small business trust may be a shareholder in an S corporation. An ESBT is a trust that does not have a beneficiary other than an individual, an estate, or a charitable organization defined in §§ 170(c)(2)–(5), no interest in which was acquired by purchase. § 1361(e).

Equalization clause. A marital deduction formula clause under which the surviving spouse is given a portion of the decedent's estate sufficient to equalize the sizes of their estates for federal estate tax purposes. Such a clause normally directs that the surviving spouse be presumed to have died immediately after the decedent and that the estate of the surviving spouse be valued as of the same date and in the same manner as the decedent's estate.

Equitable adjustment. An adjustment between the principal and income accounts of an estate or trust that is equitably required by reason of an election made by a fiduciary. The adjustment originated in order to compensate the principal account for the loss suffered when administration expenses paid by principal were claimed as income tax deductions rather than estate tax deductions.

Equitable apportionment. A principle under which courts in jurisdictions that have not enacted an estate tax apportionment law allocate the estate tax burden among a decedent's beneficiaries according to the amounts they receive of the decedent's estate for which no estate tax deductions were allowed. The principle does not apply to the estate of a decedent who has directed the source from which the estate tax should be paid.

ESBT. *See* Electing small business trust.

Estate freeze techniques. Devices, such as installment sales, by which assets that may increase in value are converted into ones with fixed values.

Estate tax inclusion period (ETIP). Under § 2642(f) the transferor's GSTT exemption cannot be allocated to an inter vivos transfer until the end of the ETIP. The ETIP is the period during which the transferred property would be included in the transferor's gross estate (other than by reason of § 2035) if the transferor were to die. The ETIP ends when the transferor dies or there is a GST of the property.

Estate tax value. The value of an asset for estate tax purposes. It equals the fair market value of an asset on the date of its owner's death or on the alternate valuation date if it is elected by the owner's executor.

Estate trust. A type of marital deduction trust under which all of the income and principal will pass to the estate of the surviving spouse upon her death. § 2056(b)(1); § 5.21.

ETIP. *See* Estate tax inclusion period.

Excess accumulation tax. An additional estate tax that was imposed by § 4980A on the amount by which the value of a decedent's interest in qualified retirement plans exceeds the present value of a single life annuity of specified amounts. The excess accumulation tax was repealed in 1997.

Excess distribution tax. An additional tax that was imposed by §4980A on the amount of retirement distributions during any year that exceeded specified amounts. The excess distribution tax was repealed in 1997.

Exculpatory clause. A provision, often narrowly construed by the courts, that exonerates a fiduciary from liability.

Exemption equivalent. *See* Credit equivalent.

Exoneration. The right of the devisee of real property to have an encumbrance discharged by the estate.

Fair market value. Defined as "the price at which the property would change hands between a willing buyer and a willing seller, neither being under any compulsion to buy or sell and both having reasonable knowledge of relevant facts." Reg. §20.2031-1(b).

Family limited partnership (FLP). A limited partnership created to hold a business or investment assets, the limited interests in which usually qualify for substantial valuation discounts. An FLP is usually funded largely by senior generation family members who are the general partners. Limited partnership units are subsequently transferred to junior generation family members.

Family members. For gift and estate tax purposes family members are persons who are related in certain ways by blood or marriage to a donor or decedent. *E.g.*, §§2032A(e)(2), 2704(c)(2).

Flower bonds. Certain issues of United States Treasury bonds issued before 1971 that were redeemable at par in payment of the federal estate tax. The bonds were called flower bonds because they "blossomed" (*i.e.*, were redeemable at par) upon death. The last bonds that qualified for redemption matured on November 15, 1998.

FLP. *See* Family limited partnership.

Formula clauses. Clauses of a will or trust that express the extent of a beneficiary's interest by reference to a formula. The interest passing to a surviving spouse or to a marital deduction trust for the benefit of a surviving spouse is commonly determined by reference to a pecuniary formula clause or a fractional share formula clause. Elections, such as a QTIP election, may also be made by reference to a formula.

Fractional interest discount. A discount in the valuation of property for federal transfer tax purposes that is allowed because two or more persons hold interests in the same asset.

Fractional share formula. A fractional share formula clause is used in marital deduction planning to fix the percentage in a pool of assets, typically the testator's residuary estate, that must pass to the surviving spouse in order to reduce to zero the amount of federal estate tax payable by the decedent's estate.

Free step-up (or down) in basis. *See* Stepped-up basis.

Future interest. Property interests that have not immediately vested. Gifts of future interests do not qualify for the annual exclusion from federal gift taxes. The term "includes reversions, remainders, and other interests or estates, whether vested or contingent, and whether or not supported by a particular interest or estate, which are limited to commence in use, possession or enjoyment at some future date or time." Reg. § 25.2503-3(a).

General power of appointment. A power that may be exercised in favor of the "decedent, his estate, his creditors, or the creditors of his estate." §§ 2041(b)(1), 2514(c).

General Utilities **doctrine.** A doctrine traceable to *General Utilities & Operating Co. v. Helvering*, 296 U.S. 200 (1935), under which a corporation did not recognize gain or loss on a distribution of assets to shareholders in partial or total liquidation. The 1986 Act repealed the doctrine, as a result of which gain or loss is generally recognized by a corporation when it makes a liquidating distribution or sale of assets. *See* § 311(b).

Generation assignment. For GSTT purposes, the generational assignment of a person is determined by his or her relationship to the transferor or by his or her age relative to the age of the transferor. § 2651.

Gift-splitting. Under § 2513 a husband and wife who are both United States citizens may elect to report gifts made by them during the calendar year as made one-half by each.

Grantor retained annuity trust (GRAT). A trust in which the grantor retains for life or for a term of years the right to receive a fixed amount payable not less frequently than annually. § 2702(b)(1). The value of the grantor's retained interest in GRAT is taken into account for gift tax purposes.

Grantor retained income trust (GRIT). A trust in which the grantor retains an income interest for life or for a term of years. For gift tax purposes the value of the grantor's retained interest is determined according to § 2702 if the remainder beneficiaries are members of the grantor's family. § 2702.

Grantor retained unitrust (GRUT). A trust in which the grantor retains the right for life or for a term of years to receive amounts that are payable not less frequently than annually and are a fixed percentage of the fair market value of the property in the trust (determined annually). § 2702(b)(2). The value of grantor's retained interest in a GRUT is taken into account for gift tax purposes.

Grantor trust. A trust of which the grantor is treated as owner for income tax purposes. §§ 671-677. *See* Short-term trust.

Group life insurance. Life insurance that is made available to members of a particular group, such as the members of a particular voluntary association.

Group-term life insurance. Group-term life insurance that is made available to employees by their employer under a non-discriminatory plan that meets the requirements of § 79. Employers are not taxed on the first $50,000 of group-term life insurance.

GST. A generation-skipping transfer, such as an outright gift or bequest to a grandchild or other skip person or a taxable distribution or taxable termination.

GSTT. The generation-skipping transfer tax, which is imposed by Chapter 13 of the Code, §§ 2601-2663.

GSTT exemption. For purposes of determining the inclusion ratio, each transferor is allowed an exemption of $3,500,000 (for 2009) that may be allocated to any property with respect to which the individual is the transferor. § 2631.

GST Trust. Any trust that could have a generation-skipping transfer with respect to the transferor.

Hanging power. A cumulative power of withdrawal that lapses each year at the maximum rate allowed without potentially adverse gift and estate tax consequences to the power-holder (*i.e.*, the power lapses with respect to the greater of $5,000 or 5 percent of the value of the property subject to withdrawal).

Health care directive. Statutes in most states allow a competent adult to direct that medical treatments of certain types be withheld or withdrawn under certain circumstances. *See* Living will.

Heirs. The persons who are the intestate successors of a decedent.

HIPAA. The Health Insurance Portability and Accountability Act of 1996, and the regulations issued thereunder, impose strict limitations on the disclosure of health care information by heathcare providers. § 4.36.

IDIT. *See* Defective grantor trust.

ILIT. *See* Irrevocable life insurance trust.

Imputed interest. Interest that is imputed to the seller in an installment sale if the installment obligation does not carry the interest rate required by § § 483 or 1274. Also applies to below-market loans under § 7872.

In terrorem clause. A provision in a will that invalidates gifts to a beneficiary who contests the will. The extent to which such clauses are enforced varies from state-to-state. Courts generally uphold such provisions, at least insofar as they prohibit contests that are not made in good faith or have no reasonable cause.

Inception of title rule. In some community property states, an asset is treated as separate property because it was separate at the time the purchasing spouse first acquired an interest in it.

Incidents of ownership. Interests in, or controls over, the economic benefits of life insurance that will cause it to be included in the insured's gross estate. § 2042(2).

Inclusion ratio. For GSTT purposes, the excess of 1 over the applicable fraction. § 2642(a).

Income in respect of a decedent (IRD). Income a decedent was entitled to receive at the time of his or her death. There is no step-up (or step-down) in basis for property that is IRD. IRD is taxed to the decedent's estate or to the other persons receiving payment; they are entitled to deduct the portion of the federal and state death taxes paid by the decedent's estate with respect to the IRD. § 691.

Individual property. Wisconsin's term for separate property. *See* Separate property.

Individual retirement account (IRA). A tax-exempt trust created in the United States exclusively for an individual or his or her beneficiaries. § 408.

Installment gift. The sale of property followed by the staged forgiveness of the purchaser's obligation. The amount forgiven each year is often equal to the amount of the annual gift tax exclusion.

Installment sale method. An income tax rule under which the gain on a sale of property in which the purchase price is received in more than one taxable year of the seller is reported ratably as payments are received. A seller may elect against application of the rule and report all of the gain in the year of sale. The installment sale is a classic form of estate freeze (*i.e.*, the seller's estate will include only the proceeds of the sale—not any further appreciation in value of the property). A self-canceling installment note (SCIN) is sometime used in connection with an installment sale. *See* Self-canceling installment note. § 453.

Intentionally defective income trust. *See* Defective grantor trust.

Inter vivos trust. *See* Irrevocable trust. A trust created during the grantor's lifetime; frequently a revocable inter vivos trust used as a will substitute. An irrevocable trust is largely neutral for income, gift, estate, and GST tax purposes.

Insurable interest. An insurance contract is valid only if the owner has an economic interest in the life of the insured. Close family members are presumed to have the requisite interest.

Irrevocable life insurance trust (ILIT). A popular type of irrevocable trust that receives, or acquires, insurance on the grantor's life that is intended to be excluded from the grantor-insured's gross estate.

Irrevocable trust. A type of inter vivos trust that cannot be revoked or terminated by the grantor. Irrevocable trusts are frequently created for the benefit of persons other than the grantor in order to remove the property from the grantor's gross estate. §§ 10.18-10.29.

Joint account. A multiparty account in a financial institution that may be with or without right of survivorship. *See* U.P.C. § 6-201.

Joint or survivorship life. A policy of insurance insuring the life of the later of two persons to die, usually a husband and wife. Joint life policies can have favorable premiums. They are often acquired by irrevocable life insurance trusts.

Joint purchase. A technique by which a senior family member and a junior family member join in the purchase of an asset. The senior receives a life estate for which he or she pays the portion of the purchase price equal to the actuarially determined value of the life estate. The younger family member contributes the balance of the cost. Joint purchases are subject to the valuation rules of § 2702.

Joint return. An income tax return filed by a husband and wife on which all of their income is reported. A joint return may be filed by the surviving spouse and the personal representative of a deceased spouse.

Joint tenancy with right of survivorship. A form of coownership under which two or more individuals own undivided interests in real or personal property. Upon the death of a tenant the surviving tenant or tenants become the exclusive owners of the property.

Junior equity interest. Under § 2701(a)(4)(B) a junior equity interest is an interest in a corporation or partnership whose rights to income and capital are junior to all other classes of equity.

Kiddie tax. Under § 1(g) unearned income in excess of $1,900 (for 2010, the threshold is adjusted annually for inflation) of a child under 19 years of age (or a full-time student under age 24) is taxed at the highest marginal rate applicable to his or her parent.

Lapse. The termination of a power of withdrawal such as a *Crummey* power for failure to exercise the power within the time allowed. Also, the failure of a testamentary gift due to the death of the beneficiary before the death of the testator. The lapse of a voting or liquidation right held by an individual in a corporation or partnership controlled by the transferor and members of his family is treated as a transfer of an amount equal to the difference in value of the transferor's interest before and after the lapse. § 2704(a).

Life income-general power of appointment trust. A type of marital deduction trust that meets the requirements of § 2056(b)(5).

Limited liability company (LLC). A business entity often created by senior generation family members to hold business interests or investment assets. LLCs are taxed as partnerships unless the members elect to have the entity taxed as a corporation. The members of an LLC enjoy limited liability from the debts and obligations of the entity.

Living will. A document in which an individual expresses his or her wishes regarding the use or nonuse of medical treatments that prolongs vital bodily functions if he or she is terminally ill and incompetent. Living wills are statutorily authorized by most states; in some of which they are called "directives to physicians" or "health care directives." *See* Durable power of attorney for health care.

LLC. *See* Limited liability company.

Lock-in effect. The impetus to retain appreciated property that is created by the combined effect of the capital gains tax and the free step-up in basis that occurs at death.

Lump sum distribution. A distribution of a participant's interest in a qualified plan in a single payment. Lump sum distributions qualify for some special income tax benefits, including a tax-free rollover by a surviving spouse into an IRA under § 401(a)(9).

Marital deduction. A gift tax deduction is allowed for outright transfers and interests in certain types of trusts given to a spouse who is a U.S. citizen. *See* § 2523. A similar deduction is allowed for estate tax purposes. § 2056. The estate tax marital deduction is also allowable for such transfers to a surviving spouse. If a decedent's surviving spouse is not U.S. citizen, the deduction is allowable only if the transfers are made to a qualified domestic trust (QDT). § 2056A.

Marital property. The Wisconsin equivalent of community property. *See* Community property.

Marketability discount. A discount that reflects the fact that the subject property cannot readily be sold, either because the number of potential buyers is limited or because of contractual or legal restrictions on the transfer of the property.

Marketable retained interest. A right with respect to an applicable retained interest for which market quotations are available on an established exchange. § 2701(a)(2).

Minority interest discount. A discount typically allowed in the valuation of minority interests in closely-held entities including corporations, partnerships, and limited liability companies.

Miscellaneous itemized deductions. Under § 67 an individual may only deduct miscellaneous itemized deductions to the extent they exceed 2 percent of his or her adjusted gross income.

National service life insurance (NSLI). *See* Veteran's life insurance.

Natural Death Act. *See* Advance directive.

Net gift. A gift with respect to which the donee assumes the obligation of paying the portion of the donor's gift tax attributable to the gift. The amount of the gift is reduced to the extent of that obligation. The obligation is also considered to be an amount realized by the donor for capital gains purposes.

No-interest loan. *See* Below-market loan.

Nonpublic charities. Charitable organizations other than public charities, contributions to which qualify for smaller maximum income tax deductions.

Nonskip person. A person who is not a skip person. *See* Skip person. § 2613(b).

Nontaxable gifts. For GSTT purposes, a transfer that is not treated as a taxable gift by reason of the annual gift tax exclusion or the exclusion for qualified transfers under §§ 2503(e), 2642(c).

Nontestamentary transfers. Transfers effective at death that are not required to comply with the requirements of the Statute of Wills. *See* U.P.C. § 6-101.

One-lung trust. A single trust in which there are separate shares, one of which is usually intended to qualify for the marital deduction.

Option. A right to acquire specified property upon terms fixed in the option. Under § 2703 an option or similar right to acquire property for less than its fair market value may be disregarded.

Part gift-part sale. *See* Bargain sale. A transfer of property in exchange for less than full consideration.

Partnership election. An election by a partnership that the basis of partnership property will be adjusted upon the transfer of an interest in the partnership by sale or exchange, upon the death of a partner, or upon the distribution of the partnership property. § 754.

Partnership freeze. A type of estate freeze involving the creation of a partnership, equity interests in which are typically transferred to younger generation members of the donor's family. The valuation rules of § 2701 severely restrict the opportunities to utilize partnership freezes.

Passive activity losses (PAL). The amount by which the aggregate passive activity losses for the year exceed the aggregate income from passive activities. As defined in § 469(c), a passive activity is any activity involving the conduct of a trade or business in which the taxpayer does not materially participate. No deductions are allowed for PALs incurred by individuals, trusts and estates, personal service corporations, and closely-held C corporations. § 469.

Perpetuities savings clause. *See* Savings clause.

Personal interest. Interest for which no deduction is allowed to taxpayers other than corporations by reason of § 163(h); specifically, interest other than investment interest, interest with respect to a trade or business, interest taken into account for purposes of § 469, and qualified personal residence interest.

Personal representative. Another term for the executor of an estate.

Personal residence trust. Under § 2702(a)(3), for gift tax purposes a trust "all of the property of which consists of a residence to be used as a personal residence by persons holding term interests in such trust." *See* Qualified personal residence trust.

Pooled income fund. A type of split-interest trust maintained by a charity, in which property contributed by individual donors is commingled. Donors are entitled to retain a proportionate part of the income for the life of one or more beneficiaries and the remainder is held by the charity. A pooled income fund is similar to a common trust fund in which the property transferred by donors is commingled. § 642(c)(5).

Pour-over will. A will that bequeaths the entire probate estate to the trustee of a trust with the instruction that the assets be held, administered and distributed according to the terms of the trust instrument.

Power of appointment. A power that allows the power-holder to designate, in the manner and within the limits prescribed, who is to receive the property subject to the power. *See* General power of appointment *and* Special power of appointment.

Predeceased parent exclusion. In determining whether a transfer is a direct skip for GSTT purposes, a grandchild of the transferor (or of the transferor's spouse) is treated as a child of the transferor if the grandchild's parent who is a child of the transferor (or of the transferor's spouse) is deceased at the time of the transfer. § 2612(c). The exception was expanded in 1997 to apply to descendants of a parent of the transferor (or of his spouse or former spouse) if the transferor has no living descendants. The exception also applies to taxable terminations and taxable distributions if the parent of the relevant beneficiary was dead at the earliest time the transfer was subject to the gift or estate tax.

Pre-nuptial agreement. An agreement entered into between a man and a woman in contemplation of marriage. Such an agreement usually attempts to fix the character of the property acquired by them or either of them during marriage and the rights each of them will have in such property. Representing both parties to a pre-nuptial agreement usually involves a serious conflict of interest.

Preferred stock recapitalization (freeze). A type of estate tax freeze involving the recapitalization of a closely-held corporation which results in the corporation having both common and preferred stock. Under the plan a senior generation family member exchanges his or her common stock for preferred stock of roughly equivalent value and new common stock having presumably little, if any, value. The common stock, which represents the entire equity interest in the company, is given to younger generation family members. The valuation rules of § 2701 severely restrict the use of this type of estate freeze.

Pretermitted child. A child who is not mentioned or provided for in the will of a parent. Such a child may be entitled to receive an intestate share of the deceased parent's estate. In some states the right is limited to children born after the execution of the parent's will.

Private annuity. A transaction, usually between family members, in which property is transferred from one person to another in exchange for the other's promise to pay a fixed amount each year for a term of years or for the life of the annuitant. The tax and nontax consequences of private annuities are complex and not entirely favorable.

Private foundation. A trust or corporation created for exclusively charitable purposes that qualifies as a tax-favored § 501(c)(3) charitable organization. A private foundation is managed by a board of directors if it is a corporation or by trustees if it is a trust. The directors or trustees, including the donor and members of the donor's family, can be paid reasonable compensation for their services. Otherwise, the donor and members of the donor's family cannot receive benefits from the foundation.

Private letter ruling (PLR). A written statement issued by the IRS at the request of a taxpayer that interprets and applies the tax laws to a specific set of facts. Reg. § 301.6110-2(d). A PLR is not authority and may not be cited. § 6110(k)(3). The first Revenue Procedure issued by the IRS each year describes the procedure to follow in requesting rulings and defines the areas in which rulings will and will not be issued.

Protective elections. Tax elections that are contingent upon one or more factors, such as the size of a decedent's estate. For example, an executor may make a contingent election to defer the payment of a portion of the estate tax under § 6166 if the estate meets the necessary requirements.

Prudent investor rule. A rule embodied in Restatement (Third) Trusts § 227, under which the appropriateness of the investments of a trust is determined by reference to the purposes of the trust, its overall portfolio and other relevant factors. The Uniform Prudent Investor Act includes a list of factors to be considered in making investments.

Prudent person rule. The standard by which the investments of trustees have traditionally been measured. Under it, each investment made by a trustee must satisfy the standard or the trustee may be liable for any loss incurred by the trust.

Public charities. Charitable organizations described in § 170(b)(a)(1)(A). Contributions to them qualify for the maximum allowable income tax deductions.

Qualified appreciated stock. Under § 170(e)(5) an income tax deduction is allowable for the fair market value of publicly traded stock that is given to a private foundation.

Qualified charitable contributions. Individuals age $70^1/_2$ or older can exclude from gross income up to $100,000 in direct transfer from either a traditional IRA or a Roth IRA to a public charity in 2006 and 2007. § 408(d)(8)(A). Such distributions are not deductible as charitable contributions. § 408(d)(8)(E).

Qualified conservation easement. Section 2031(c) allows a limited elective exclusion from the gross estate for easements created by a decedent, a member of the decedent's family, the executor of the decedent's estate, or the trustee of a trust created by the decedent that meet the requirements of § 170(h).

Qualified contingency. A provision of a charitable remainder trust under which the occurrence of an event would cause the noncharitable interest to terminate not later than it was scheduled to expire. § 664(f).

Qualified decedent. A decedent who is either, (1) a citizen or resident of the United States who dies while on active service in a combat zone or as a result of wounds, injuries, or disease suffered in the line of duty while serving in a combat zone, or (2) a person (other than a participant or conspirator) who dies as a result of wounds or injuries suffered in the Oklahoma City terrorist attack of April 19, 1995 or the terrorist attacks of September 11, 2001 or who dies as a result of an anthrax attack occurring on or after September 11, 2001 and before January 1, 2002. Under § 2201(a), the executor of a qualified decedent may elect to determine the decedent's estate tax liability according to the rates set forth in § 2201(c) rather than those of § 2001(c).

Qualified disclaimer. A disclaimer that meets the requirements of § 2518. The person making a qualified disclaimer is not treated as having transferred the property with respect to which it was made. § 2518.

Qualified domestic trust (QDT or QDOT). Property that is transferred to a surviving spouse who is not a United States citizen only qualifies for the marital deduction it passes to a QDT. § 2056A.

Qualified heir. For purposes of special use valuation under § 2032A, a qualified heir is a member of the decedent's family who acquired the property from the decedent. § 2032A(e)(1).

Qualified higher education expenses (QHEE). Generally, "tuition, fees, books, supplies, and equipment required for" enrollment in an eligible institution of higher education. § 529(e)(3)(A)(i). Distributions from a qualified tuition program under § 529 are tax-free to the extent they are used for QHEEs.

Qualified interest. Under § 2702(b), for gift tax purposes, a qualified interest is a right to receive a fixed amount payable annually (a qualified annuity interest) or the right to receive a fixed percentage of the fair market value of the property determined annually (a qualified unitrust interest), or a noncontingent remainder.

Qualified joint interest. A tenancy by the entirety or a joint tenancy with right of survivorship in which a husband and wife are the only joint tenants. § 2040(b).

Qualified joint venturers. Married couples in all states may elect to be treated as qualified joint venturers instead of partners, provided the only members of the business are a husband and wife and provided both materially participate in the business. § 761(f).

Qualified payment. Amounts payable on a periodic basis at a fixed rate, such as ones payable with respect to cumulative preferred stock or an equivalent interest in a partnership. § 2701(c)(3).

Qualified personal residence trust (QPRT). A trust of a personal residence that meets the requirements of Reg. § 25.2702-5(e). The actuarially determined value of a retained interest in a qualified personal residence trust is taken into account for gift tax purposes. § 2702(a)(3).

Qualified plan. Employer-created trust formed as a part of a stock bonus, pension, or profitsharing plan for the exclusive benefit of employees that meets the minimum participation, nondiscrimination, and other requirements.

Qualified real property. For purposes of special use valuation under § 2032A qualified real property is real property located in the United States that passed from the decedent to a qualified heir and was being used for a qualified use. In addition, the percentage requirements of § 2032A(b)(1) must be satisfied.

Qualified revocable trust. A trust that the decedent is treated as owning under § 676. § 645(b)(1). The trustee of a decedent's "qualified revocable trust" and the decedent's personal representative may elect under § 645 to treat the trust as part of the estate.

Qualified severance. A division of a single trust in a way that complies with the requirements of § 2642(a)(3) allows the trusts to be treated as separate for GSTT purposes. The requirements of a qualified severance are spelled out in Reg. § 26.2642-6. Among other things, severed trusts "must provide, in the aggregate, for the same succession of interests of beneficiaries as are provided in the original trust." Reg. § 26.2642-6(b)(4).

Qualified subchapter S trust (QSST). A type of trust, defined in § 1361(d), that may be a shareholder in an S Corporation. The income of a QSST is taxed to its beneficiary.

Qualified terminable interest property (QTIP). Property in which the surviving spouse has a qualifying income interest for life (*i.e.*, he or she is entitled to all of the income for life, payable annually or more frequently and with respect to which no person has a power to appoint any part of the property to any other person during the surviving spouse's lifetime). The marital deduction is allowed with respect to QTIP to the extent the decedent's executor elects to claim the marital deduction. § 2056(b)(7).

Qualified transfer. For gift tax purposes amounts paid directly as tuition to an educational institution or directly to any person providing medical care to the donee. § 2503(e).

Qualified tuition program (QTP). Also known as a "§ 529 plan," a "program established by a state or agency or instrumentality thereof or by 1 or more eligible educational institutions" that may be of two specified types. § 529(b). The first is a plan established by a state or by "1 or more educational institutions under which a person may purchase tuition credits or certificates on behalf of a designated beneficiary which entitle the beneficiary to the waiver or payment of qualified higher education expenses of the beneficiary." § 529(b)(1)(A)(i). The second is a plan established by a state that allows a person to contribute to an account which is created for the purpose of meeting the qualified higher education expenses of a designated beneficiary. § 529(b)(1)(A)(ii).

Qualified use. For special use valuation under § 2032A, qualified use is the use of property as a farm or for farming purposes or use in a trade or business other than farming. § 2032A(b)(2).

Qualifying income interest for life. *See* qualified terminable interest property (QTIP).

Quasi-community property. Property acquired during the marriage of a husband and wife while domiciled in another state that would have been community property had they been domiciled in California, Idaho, or Washington at the time of acquisition.

Reciprocal trust doctrine. Where two or more trusts are created by related parties and the nominal grantor of one trust is the beneficiary of another, for federal transfer tax purposes the trusts are "uncrossed." As a result, each person is treated as grantor of the trust of which he or she is the beneficiary.

Renunciation. *See* Disclaimer.

Retained interests. *See* Applicable retained interests. Interests retained by a transferor. Under § 2702, for gift tax purposes, term interests retained by the grantor of a trust are valued at zero unless they are qualified interests.

Revenue Procedure 64-19. An important pronouncement of the IRS with regard to the circumstances under which the marital deduction is allowable with respect to formulas that provide for property distributed in kind to be valued at its federal estate tax value.

Revenue Ruling. A statement published by the IRS with respect to the treatment that will be given to a particular transaction for federal tax purposes. Rulings are published weekly in the Internal Revenue Bulletin and semiannually in collected form in the Cumulative Bulletin.

Reverse QTIP election. For GSTT purposes an election that the deceased spouse be treated as the transferor of a QTIP trust. § 2652(a)(3). If such an election is not made, the surviving spouse will be treated as the transferor of the QTIP.

Reverse split-dollar insurance plan. A split-dollar insurance plan in which the employee is the financing party and the employer controls the disposition of the risk portion of the insurance.

Rule against perpetuities. A rule that requires an interest to vest or fail within a specified period. The common law rule required interests to vest or fail within 21 years following lives in being at the time the interest was created. *See* Savings clause.

S Corporation. A small business corporation of 100 or fewer shareholders with a single class of stock that elects not to be taxed as a C corporation. Nonresidents and business entities may not be shareholders in an S corporation. The income of an S corporation flows through and is taxed to its shareholders regardless of whether it is actually distributed. §§ 1361-1379.

Sale of remainder. The sale, by the owner of property, of a remainder interest in the property for its actuarially determined value for the purpose of excluding the property from his or her estate at death. The sale of a remainder interest to a family member is subject to § 2702.

Savings clause. A direction in a will or trust that it be construed in accordance with the maker's intention that it meet the requirements of a specified provision of the tax laws. For example, it is common for such a provision to be included with regard to a marital deduction trust. § 5.27. A perpetuities savings clause may be included in a will or trust.

Self-proving affidavit (or will). An affidavit, or declaration under penalty of perjury, of the witnesses to a will, establishing its due execution. Many states authorize its use in lieu of personal appearance of the witnesses.

Separate property. In community property states the property owned by a husband or wife that is not community property (*e.g.*, property owned prior to marriage or acquired thereafter by gift or inheritance).

Separate share rule. An income tax rule applicable to trusts and estates which determines (*i.e.*, limits) the amount of distributable net income that is carried out by distributions made to the beneficiaries of substantially separate shares.

Separate trusts. For GSTT purposes the portions of a trust attributable to different transferors and the portions of a trust that are held for beneficiaries and are substantially separate and distinct from other portions of the trust, are treated as separate trusts. § 2654(b). For purposes of determining distributable net income, substantially separate and distinct shares of a trust or estate that are held for different beneficiaries are treated as separate trusts. *See* Separate share rule. § 663(c).

Short-term trust. An irrevocable trust in which the grantor retains a reversionary interest that becomes possessory at the end of ten years or more. Under § 673, for income tax purposes the grantor is treated as the owner of such a trust.

Simple trust. A trust that is required to distribute all of its income currently, has no charitable beneficiaries, and makes no principal distributions during the year. Reg. § 1.651(a)-1.

Sixty-five day rule. The fiduciaries of trusts and estates may elect to treat distributions that are made within the first 65 days of a taxable year as having been made in the preceding taxable year. § 663(b).

Skip person. For GSTT purposes a skip person is, (1) a person assigned to a generation that is two or more below the transferor's generation, (2) a trust in which all interests are held by skip persons, or (3) a trust if there are no persons holding an interest in it or at no time may a distribution be made from the trust to a nonskip person. § 2613(a). All other persons are nonskip persons. For example, a transferor's grandchild is a skip person if his or her parent is a child of the transferor and is living at the time of the transfer.

Special needs trust. A trust intended to be supplemental to, and not in lieu of, public support. A special needs trust should be drafted in a way that insulates the property of the trust from claims by public agencies for reimbursement for the support they provide. That can usually be achieved by giving the trustee broad discretion to provide for the beneficiary.

Special power of appointment. A power of appointment other than a general power of appointment. Property that is subject to a nongeneral power of appointment is not includible in the power-holder's estate under § 2041. *See* General power of appointment *and* Ascertainable standard.

Special trustee. A trustee who holds a specific power or powers that for tax reasons cannot be safely held by a beneficiary-trustee. For example, a special trustee may be designated to deal with policies of insurance on the life of the trustee.

Special use valuation. A valuation method by which the executor can elect to value real property used as a farm or in connection with a closely-held business for estate tax purposes according to its actual use rather than its highest and best use. § 2032A.

Spendthrift clause. A provision that prevents a beneficiary from transferring his or her interests in a trust and prevents the beneficiary's creditors from reaching them.

Spilt-dollar insurance plan. A plan under which the interests in a cash value insurance policy are divided between a financing party (usually the insured's employer) and the insured (usually the employee). The insured pays a portion of the premium attributable to the cost of the insurance proceeds controlled by him or her.

Status agreement. An agreement between a husband and wife regarding the separate or community property status of the property owned by them or either of them.

Stepped-up (or down) basis. In general, property acquired from a decedent takes a basis equal to its value on the date of the decedent's death or on the alternate valuation date applicable to the decedent's estate. § 1014. The tax-free increase in basis at death should be contrasted with the carryover of basis that applies to gifts.

Straight debt. Nonconvertible debt held by an individual (other than a nonresident alien), an estate, or certain trusts, that has a fixed maturity date, a fixed interest rate, and fixed payment dates. Straight debt does not constitute a second class of stock for S corporation purposes. § 1361(c)(5).

Stub income. Income that is accrued but undistributed at the time of the surviving spouse's death.

Substituted judgment doctrine. A doctrine under which a guardian or conservator is permitted to make gifts of the property of a ward.

Supporting organization. One that is organized and operated exclusively to support one or more specified public charities; operated, supervised, or controlled by or in connection with one or more public charities; and not controlled directly or indirectly by the donor or certain disqualified persons. *See* Reg. § 1.509(a)-4.

Survivorship community property. A husband and wife may create survivorship community property in Nevada and survivorship marital property in Wisconsin. Upon the death of either spouse property so held belongs entirely to the surviving spouse.

Survivorship insurance policy. See joint or survivorship life.

Tainted asset rule. A deduction is not allowed to the extent that an interest given the survivor may be satisfied with assets (or their proceeds) that are nondeductible. § 2056(b)(2).

Taxable distribution. For GSTT purposes, any distribution from a trust to a skip person, other than a taxable termination or direct skip. § 2612(b).

Taxable termination. The termination by death, lapse, time, or otherwise of an interest in property held in a trust unless either (1) immediately after the termination, a nonskip person has an interest in such property or (2) at no time after the termination may any distribution to a skip person be made. §2612(a)(1).

Technical Advice Memorandum (TAM). A TAM is a written statement issued by the National Office to a district director with respect to the examination of a taxpayer's return or a consideration of a taxpayer's claim for refund or credit. Reg. §301.6110-2(f). TAMs are published with private letter rulings each week in pamphlet form.

Tenancy by the entirety. Form of joint ownership with right of survivorship by husband and wife in noncommunity property states.

Tenancy in common. A form of coownership without right of survivorship in which each tenant owns an undivided interest in the subject property.

Tentative tax. The tax determined by applying the unified rate schedule to the sum of the post-1976 taxable gifts and the taxable estate. §2001(c). Applicable credits, including the applicable credit amount, are then applied to determine the final estate tax liability.

Term interest. For gift tax purposes a term interest is defined in §2702(c)(3) as a life interest in property or an interest in property for a term of years. For purposes of determining gain or loss on the disposition of a term interest, an income interest in a trust is also included.

Terminable interests. Sections 2056(b) and 2523(b) impose strict limits on the types of interests that qualify for the marital deduction if the interest of the decedent's or the donor's spouse will terminate or fail upon the lapse of time or the occurrence (or nonoccurrence) of an event or contingency. The term also refers to the rule under which the interest of a nonemployee spouse in an employee benefit plan terminates upon his or her death.

Testamentary power of appointment. A power of appointment that is exercisable only by the will of the power-holder.

Throwback rules. Income tax rules, no longer generally applicable to domestic trusts, under which a distribution made by a trust that has undistributed income is taxed to the distributee as if it had been received by the distributee over the accumulation period. §§665-667.

Tier system. For income tax purposes amounts distributed are divided into classes (or "tiers") of distributions. The first consists of amounts of income the trust is required to distribute currently. The second consists of all other amounts properly paid, credited, or required to be distributed. Distributions to first tier beneficiaries are deducted from DNI. If distributions to first tier beneficiaries exhaust the DNI of the trust, no income is carried out to second tier beneficiaries. Otherwise, distributions to second tier beneficiaries will carry out the balance of the DNI.

Toggling. The ability to control the income tax status of a trust, usually through the exercise or release of a power with respect to trust assets or trust administration. A trust treated as a separate entity for income tax purposes may be converted to a grantor trust where, for example, the grantor borrows the trust assets on an unsecured basis and the loan remains outstanding on the first day of the taxable year at issue. A grantor who engages in such a transaction is said to have "toggled" grantor trust status.

Transfer on death (TOD) deed. *See* Beneficiary deed.

Transferor. For GSTT purposes the transferor is the decedent in the case of a transfer subject to the estate tax and the donor in the case of a transfer subject to the gift tax. § 2652(a)(1).

Trapping distribution. A distribution from an estate or trust to a trust that carried out DNI, where the income is "trapped" and taxed to the trust.

Underproductive or unproductive property. For principal and income purposes, property that has not yielded the required average rate of return during the time it was held in trust. A trust that is required to retain such property may not qualify for the marital deduction.

Unified credit. Each citizen or resident is allowed a credit against the estate tax imposed on his or her estate, § 2010, of an amount equal to the tax on the applicable exclusion amount. The credit for 2009 is $1,455,800, the amount of tax imposed on a transfer of $3,500,000. For gift tax purposes, there is a separate credit amount of $345,800, the amount of tax imposed on a transfer of $1,000,000. *See* Applicable credit.

Uniform Anatomical Gift Act (UAGA). Establishes the procedure by which individuals or certain agents can make inter vivos or post mortem gifts of the donor's body or body parts for transplantation, education or research. § 4.39.

Uniform Gifts to Minors Act (UGMA). Provisions under which irrevocable gifts to minors can be made by transferring property into the name of a custodian for the minor. *See* Uniform Transfers to Minors Act.

Uniform Probate Code (UPC). A comprehensive code governing wills, trusts, intestate succession, and related subjects.

Uniform Simultaneous Death Act. An act containing rules that apply where the title to property or its disposition depends upon the priority of death and there is no sufficient evidence that the persons have died otherwise than simultaneously.

Uniform Transfer on Death (TOD) Security Registration Act. An act permitting transfer on death registration of securities.

Uniform Transfers to Minors Act (UTMA). An act, similar to the UGMA, under which a broader range of property may be transferred to a custodian for a minor.

Unrelated business taxable income (UBTI). The gross income of an exempt organization derived from any trade or business the conduct of which is not substantially related to the organization's conduct of its exempt function.

Veteran's life insurance. Life insurance made available in limited amounts upon very favorable terms to persons who have served in the United States armed forces.

Widow's election. In noncommunity property states the right of a surviving spouse to elect to receive a statutory share of a deceased spouse's estate in lieu of the benefits provided by the decedent's will. In community property states the right of a surviving spouse to retain his or her share of the community property rather than disposing of it in accordance with the will of his or her deceased spouse.

Table of Cases

[References are to sections.]

Table of Internal Revenue Code Sections

Table of Treasury Regulations

References are to sections.

Table of Revenue Rulings, Procedures, Notices, and Letter Rulings

References are to sections.

72-307, 1972-1 C.B. 307	6.28.4, 6.28.5, 6.73.11	75-259, 1975-2 C.B. 361	10.3
		75-260, 1975-2 C.B. 376	10.3, 10.33.1
72-333, 1972-2 C.B. 530	5.21	75-267, 1975-2 C.B. 254	10.39.1
72-358, 1972-2 C.B. 473	6.66.2, 6.67	75-350, 1975-2 C.B. 366	5.22.4, 7.37.4, 10.16
72-396, 1972-2 C.B. 312	12.37.5		
72-545, 1972-2 C.B. 179	1.6.5	75-351, 1975-2 C.B. 368	5.22.4, 7.37.4
72-609, 1972-3 C.B. 199	6.61.3		
73-21, 1973-1 C.B. 405	10.40.2, 10.40.9	75-365, 1975-2 C.B. 471	11.24.2
		75-366, 1975-2 C.B. 472	11.24.2
73-97, 1973-1 C.B. 404	10.17, 12.15.6	75-367, 1975-2 C.B. 472	11.24.2
		75-414, 1975-2 C.B. 371	8.34
73-124, 1973-1 C.B. 200	6.66.3	75-440, 1975-2 C.B. 372	5.27
73-142, 1973-1 C.B. 405	10.40.12	75-502, 1975-2 C.B. 111	11.22.1
73-143, 1973-1 C.B. 407	10.40.5	76-7, 1976-1 C.B. 179	8.29
73-174, 1973-1 C.B. 43	6.73	76-8, 1976-1 C.B. 179	8.29
73-287, 1973-2 C.B. 321	7.37.3	76-23, 1976-1 C.B. 264	10.4.13, 11.4.1, 12.4
73-327, 1973-2 C.B. 214	6.79.9		
73-404, 1973-2 C.B. 319	6.27		
73-405, 1973-2 C.B. 321	7.38.1, 10.32.1	76-49, 1976-1 C.B. 294	7.26.2
		76-83, 1976-1 C.B. 213	3.35.3, 5.39, 12.40.2, 13.3(2)
73-451, 1973-2 C.B. 158	9.6.1		
73-476, 1973-2 C.B. 300	3.9		
73-482, 1973-2 C.B. 44	6.61.1		
73-555, 1973-2 C.B. 159	9.6.1	76-103, 1976-1 C.B. 293	10.21.2, 10.39.2
73-611, 1973-2 C.B. 312	11.7	76-113, 1976-1 C.B. 276	6.28.10
74-43, 1974-1 C.B. 285	7.37.3	76-143, 1976-1 C.B. 63	6.72.2
74-76, 1974-1 C.B. 30	6.54	76-166, 1976-2 C.B. 287	5.16.4, 5.20
74-175, 1974-1 C.B. 52	12.3.2		
74-269, 1974-1 C.B. 87	11.33		
74-307, 1974-2 C.B. 146	6.55	76-178, 1976-1 C.B. 273	10.34.2
74-492, 1974-2 C.B. 298	5.16.1	76-179, 1976-1 C.B. 290	10.32
74-523, 1974-2 C.B. 304	8.2.1	76-200, 1976-1 C.B. 308	6.46.2, 6.71.2
74-556, 1974-2 C.B. 300	2.7, 7.35.2		
74-613, 1974-2 C.B. 153	7.17, 9.6.2, 10.4.12, 10.15	76-261, 1976-2 C.B. 276	6.28.11
		76-270, 1976-2 C.B. 194	8.20
		76-273, 1976-2 C.B. 268	9.43.5, 9.44.3
75-8, 1975-1 C.B. 309	3.13	76-274, 1976-2 C.B. 278	6.29, 6.72.3
75-63, 1975-1 C.B. 294	7.11		
75-66, 1975-1 C.B. 85	8.18	76-275, 1976-2 C.B. 299	10.32
75-70, 1975-1 C.B. 301	6.28.8	76-291, 1976-2 C.B. 284	8.20
75-72, 1975-1 C.B. 310	7.26.2	76-303, 1976-2 C.B. 266	3.17
75-128, 1975-1 C.B. 308	5.21	76-331, 1976-2 C.B. 52	8.18
75-142, 1975-1 C.B. 256	3.20.5	76-357, 1976-2 C.B. 285	8.15
75-257, 1975-2 C.B. 251	10.3	76-369, 1976-2 C.B. 281	12.11

9111028	6.28.11	9235030	2.42.5
9113009	5.16.3,	9237009 (TAM)	5.23.2
	7.18	9237020	8.41
9114023	2.5.6	9241025	2.42.5
9114024	2.25.1	9242006	5.23.7
9114025	8.26	9244001 (TAM)	5.24
9116003 (TAM)	12.21.2	9244004 (TAM)	2.10.2
9117003 (TAM)	10.17	9244012	2.25.1
9123036	9.6.3	9244013	5.24,
9126005 (TAM)	4.27.1		8.20.5
9127007 (TAM)	6.28.9,	9244019	2.42.5
	6.39	9244020	5.16.1,
9128008	10.38.3		5.23
9128008 (TAM)	6.28.9	9245011	2.22.4,
9131006 (TAM)	2.5.7,		2.42.5
	2.19.2,	9245033	5.23.5
	11.5.1,	9245035	6.68
	11.31.4	9246002 (TAM)	5.16.1
9139001 (TAM)	5.17	9246005	11.26
9139002 (TAM)	10.17	9246009 (TAM)	2.32
9140002 (TAM)	2.46.1	9246022 (TAM)	2.40
9140004 (TAM)	5.23.8	9247002 (TAM)	5.23.8
9141007 (TAM)	6.28.5	9247018	8.10
9141008 (TAM)	7.38.5	9247020	2.42.5
9141027	5.9, 10.22	9247026	12.26.2
9143030	8.20	9247035	11.4.1
9147040	6.2	9248010	2.40
9147065 (TAM)	5.17	9248013	6.66
9149015	11.27.1	9248016	9.43.2
9151043	5.25	9248019	11.4.2
9152005 (TAM)	2.14.2	9248026	11.5.3,
9202020	11.27		11.6.4
9206006 (TAM)	9.42.2	9249014	9.44,
9207004 (TAM)	2.14.2		9.44.2
9208003 (TAM)	3.13	9250004	2.4.2
9214027	2.18	9308002 (TAM)	3.35.5
9221037	2.42.5	9309023	5.23.6,
9222042	2.42.5		7.24
9224028	5.23	9309046	11.4.2
9227013	10.37.3	9314050	11.23
9228004 (TAM)	5.16.2	9317025	5.23.5
9229017	5.23.5	9318007	11.4.2
9232019	8.20	9319024	6.66
9233006	6.28.5	9320016	8.10
9233054	6.66.3	9321035	5.23.5
9235025	10.29	9321050	7.38.2

9511007	8.22.1	9543050	2.19.4
9511028	11.5.3	9544038	5.23.5
9512002	8.31	9545009	2.42.5
9513001 (TAM)	4.35.4,	9546004	5.16.3
	9.10	9548002 (TAM)	5.23,
9514002 (TAM)	5.22.3		5.23.11
9515003 (TAM)	2.19.4	9549016	8.35
9516004 (TAM)	5.33	9550002	11.6.2
9516051	10.42.4	9550026	8.20
9517020	8.20	9552005	2.28,
9518002 (TAM)	2.19.4		12.23
9519029	9.43.2,	9601002 (TAM)	4.35.4
	11.4.1	9602014	12.2.4
9523001 (TAM)	7.38.6	9602017	11.24.2
9523016	8.38	9604001 (TAM)	6.72.2,
9523017	8.38		6.72.3
9524020	13.2	9604018	12.19.11
9526021	11.4.1	9606008	5.17.1
9526027	8.19, 8.35	9607011	2.42.5
9526031	8.35	9608008	2.28,
9527007 (TAM)	12.11		12.2.4
9527018	11.4.4	9609009	8.22.1
9527025	2.4, 2.19.4	9609052	12.26.2
9528012	2.42.5	9610004 (TAM)	5.16.3
9529035	9.44.2	9610005	8.35,
9530003	5.16.3		12.35
9531003 (TAM)	8.19	9610018	5.16.3
9532001 (TAM)	7.38.1	9611011	12.2.4
9532026	8.35	9611019	8.35
9533001 (TAM)	5.28,	9611047	8.38
	6.24.1,	9615043	12.36
	6.33.1	9619042	8.20
9533025	9.44.2	9619043	8.20
9535001 (TAM)	7.38	9619044	8.20
9535008 (TAM)	2.4.3,	9620017	11.6.3,
	10.31,		11.6.4
	10.33	9623024	6.29.2
9535026	9.1, 11.5.3	9623063	5.25
9535047	10.24,	9623064	12.36
	10.24.1	9626041	9.44.2
9537004 (TAM)	5.23.11	9626049	12.36
9537005	5.23.5	9627010	2.42.5
9537011	8.41	9628004 (TAM)	7.38.5
9541029	2.33, 7.38	9630003	2.42.5
9542037	6.66	9634020	5.21
9543049	11.4.1	9634025	8.2

9813013	12.2.4	199912040	13.3(2),
9815008	5.14		13.6
9815023	2.19.1	199915052	5.23.10
9815046	12.36	199915053	8.10
9818005 (TAM)	12.33.1	199917001 (TAM)	10.21.2,
9818008	12.33.1		10.34,
9818009	8.41		10.34.1,
9818042	2.5		10.34.3,
9819034	2.33		10.39.3
9820018	6.66, 6.67	199917001	10.22
9821029	8.20,	199919039	8.20.6
	10.23	199920016 (FSA)	5.23
9823043	12.36	199922007	10.31
9825031	8.38	199925029	8.10
9832009	11.24.2	199925033	13.3(2),
9833008	8.22.1		13.6
9841017	9.42.1	199926019	5.23.10
9842003 (TAM)	11.30.1,	199926041	12.2.4
	11.30.2	199926045	3.5, 3.9
9843024	6.39,	199927002	2.4.3, 7.19
	10.31	199929025	11.24.2
9846002 (TAM)	12.15.1	199929040	2.28
9847025	6.24.5	199930002 (TAM)	7.25
9848011	6.29	199932001 (TAM)	5.27
9848041	12.21	199936021	9.10.3,
9852031	10.42.4		10.20.3,
20002214	8.35		10.31,
20011901 (FSA)	2.14.3		10.31.2
20012023	9.44.2	199936029	10.22
20012723	8.20	199936031	10.31
20018037	12.23	199938005	2.19.4
20021020	8.31	199938005 (TAM)	2.19.4,
20052004	13.3(4)		10.37.3,
83200007 (TAM)	2.5.2,		11.5.1,
	2.5.4		11.34
89403010	2.5.6	199939039	12.39
199903025	2.19.4	199941013	2.30, 7.2.1
199903050	13.2.1(i)	199941013 (TAM)	2.6, 7.2.1
199905015	6.66	199943003 (TAM)	2.14.1
199907013	8.22.1	199952012	7.19
199907015	2.25.1	200003011	12.36
199908002	8.31	200004001	8.7.1
199911030	12.2.4,	200006034	11.24.1
	12.19.1	200008044	13.2(1)(h),
199912026	9.44.4,		13.2(1)(j)
	10.31.5	200010015	11.6.4
		200013015	5.23.10

200014002 (TAM)	10.22	200127007	5.23.11, 12.33.2
200014004 (TAM)	10.32	200127023	8.20
200015012	11.6.4	200128005	5.16.2, 5.16.3, 8.1
200017051	6.54.3	200129036	13.3(2)
200018020 (FSA)	5.17	200130030	10.23, 10.24.2
200019011	8.2.1	200132004 (TAM)	5.14
200020011	12.13	200138018	8.31
200022035	10.24.1	200140027	8.20
200024016	8.2.1	200147039	6.24.1, 6.27
200026003	2.28, 5.23, 5.23.10	200148028	10.50.2
200030011	12.36	200152018	8.20
200030018	10.20.3, 10.31	200203031	12.15
200030019	10.20.3, 10.31	200204038	13.2(1)(j)
200032044	13.3(2)	200206045	2.42.5
200035014	8.20	200207026	8.20
200038050	8.20.6	200208019	2.5.7, 8.16.3
200043039	8.31	200209057	13.2(1)(i)
200047027	12.33.4	200210009 (TAM)	9.43.5
200049003 (FSA)	11.30.4, 11.31.5	200212006 (TAM)	2.5.7, 11.30.1
200052035	8.20	200213014	2.35
200052041	13.3(2)	200214028	6.29.2
200101021	3.35.5, 10.7	200215001 (TAM)	2.25.1
200101031	8.7.3	200215061	13.5, 13.6
200106029	5.23.10	200219003	12.21
200108032	8.31	200219034	10.23
200110033	13.2(3)	200220014	9.44.2
200111038	6.29.2, 6.54.3	200221010	2.10.3
200112023	9.42, 9.44.3	200222024	5.23.2
200119013 (FSA)	5.22, 5.23	200223020 (TAM)	5.23.11, 12.21
200118037	12.2.4	200225045	8.31
200120007	6.54, 6.54.3	200226015	13.2(1)(i)
200120016	8.20	200226020	12.21
200120021	10.31.1	200227022	2.33, 9.43.2
200122011 (FSA)	2.14.3, 7.7, 8.1, 10.49	200228019	6.54.3
		200228023	13.2(1)(j)
200122034	11.4.4	200230018	8.37, 13.3(4)
200126005 (TAM)	8.16.3	200234017	5.27

200234019	8.41, 13.3(2)	200343019	2.26
200235038	13.2(1)(i), 13.2(1)(i)	200343030	13.2(1)(f), 13.2(1)(j)
200235039	13.2(1)(i), 13.2(1)(i)	200346025	13.3(2)
		200403094	3.35.5, 10.11
200235040	13.2(1)(i), 13.2(1)(i)	200404056	13.2(1)(j)
200235041	13.2(1)(i), 13.2(1)(i)	200407003	2.29
		200407018 (TAM)	5.22.4
200241012	5.23.5	200407023	13.2(1)(j)
200241039	9.44.2	200407025	13.2(1)(j)
200244002	5.22.4	200410020	13.2(1)(h), 13.2(1)(i)
200245053 (TAM)	2.14.3, 10.49	200432016 (TAM)	2.18
200245058	8.20	200432027	13.2, 13.2.1(i)
200247001 (TAM)	2.14.2	200432029	13.2.1(i)
200247002 (TAM)	13.3	200432031	13.2.1(i)
200247006	6.54.3	200434012	10.31
200247013	10.50.1	200437032 (TAM)	12.33.4
200252092	8.20	200438044	13.2(1)(i)
200302029	12.36	200440031	13.2(1)(i)
200303010 (TAM)	2.14.1	200444021	13.3
200305024	2.42.5	200444033	13.2(1)(h)
200306015	2.29, 12.2.4	200503024	12.34
		200505022	5.23.2
200314009	6.28.7, 10.40.12	200514001	6.54.3
		200522012	13.2(1)(i)
200315031	8.42.6	200534014	7.18
200317041	13.2(1)(h)	200549017	13.3(2)
200317042	13.2(1)(h)	200551020	10.27
200317043	13.2(1)(h)	200603032	13.3(2)
200317044	13.2(1)(h)	200603036	13.3(2)
200321010	8.38	200605019	13.3(2)
200324023	5.23.10	200608032	13.2(1)(i), 13.3(4)
200328030	8.31		
200333023	12.33.2	200610027	13.2(1)(i)
200334030	3.29, 12.40	200616039	13.2(1)(i)
		200616040	13.2(1)(i)
200337012 (TAM)	2.14.3, 10.49	200616041	13.2(1)(i)
		200620025	13.2(1)(i)
200339003 (TAM)	5.23.2, 5.27	200620026	13.2(1)(i)
		200628007	5.23.10
200339043	11.24.2	200633009	13.3(4)
200340012	11.24.2	200634065	13.2(1)(d), 13.3(2)
200341002 (TAM)	2.5.1, 7.38		

Table of Miscellaneous Federal Citations

References are to sections.

Table of Statutes

References are to sections.

Index

References are to sections.

A

Accelerated death benefits (ADB), 6.13
Accidental death benefit rider, 6.11.1
Accrual of interest income, 12.37
Accumulated earnings tax, 11.10.3
ACTEC Commentaries, 1.2.4
ADB payments, 6.13
Ademption, 4.15.1
Administrative expense deduction, 10.6.6
Advanced health care directive (AHCD), 4.35.3, 4.37
Adverse party, 10.30.1
AHCD, 4.35.3, 4.37
AICPA guidelines, 1.1
Alternate valuation method, 12.15
Ambiguous documents, 1.6.1
Anatomical gifts
. action by others, 4.39.5
. conclusion, 4.39.8
. donees, 4.39.2
. donor card, 4.39.7
. generally, 4.39
. planning, 4.39.6
. revocation/amendment, 4.39.4
. U.A.G.A., 4.39, 4.39.1
. ways of making gift, 4.39.3
Annual gift tax exclusion, 2.5, 11.31.4
Annuity
. charitable gifts, 8.37
. estate distributions, 12.38.1
. private. *See* Private annuity
. single life, 8.37
Anti-Byrum rule, 11.34
Applicable exclusion amount, scheduled increases, 2.3
Applicable fraction, 2.26
Apportionment rule, 6.16.2

Appreciated stock, 8.38
Attorney-client privilege, 1.6.6
Attorney-in-fact gifts, 2.4.3
Attorneys. *See* Professional responsibility/ conduct
Attribution rules, 11.22.1, 11.22.4, 11.24.1

B

Bankruptcy Abuse Prevention and Consumer Protection Act of 2005, 13.7
Bargain sale, 7.28, 8.36
Basis
. community property, 3.26
. estate tax, 2.15
. gift tax, 2.4.5
. joint tenancy, 3.20.3-3.20.5
Below-market loans, 7.20
Beneficiary deeds, 3.40-3.44
Bequests from expatriates, 2.43
Blockage discounts, 2.14.1, 7.16
Bona fide sales, 2.19.1, 2.19.3
Buy-sell agreements
. accumulated earnings tax, 11.10.3
. community property, 11.12
. cross-purchase, 11.8.3, 11.8.4
. entity purchase, 11.8.1, 11.8.2
. ethical considerations, 11.11
. funding, 11.10
. installment payments, 11.10.1
. insubstantial modifications, 11.6.4
. medium of payment, 11.10.2
. nontax considerations, 11.7
. overview, 11.1.5, 11.6
. partnership payments, 11.8.2
. pre-section 2703 rules, 11.6.1
. redemption by C corporation, 11.8.2
. redemption by S corporation, 11.8.2
. redemption pursuant to agreement/divorce, 11.8.5
. section 2703, 11.6.2
. section 2704, 11.6.5